FEATURES AND BENEFITS
Algebra 1 ©2005

See page(s):

Curriculum and Instructional Design	... presents a coherent curriculum that effectively organizes and integrates important mathematical ideas.	
	• Chapters are grouped by units to bring depth to algebra concepts.	iii
	• Lessons are divided into two related objectives to allow teachers flexibility in presenting the lesson.	120
Student Support	... is provided throughout the text to help all students succeed in algebra.	
	• Foldables™ Study Organizers help students actively organize key concepts and create their own review materials.	255
	• Key Concept and Concept Summary boxes help students identify main concepts.	256, 258
	• Study Tips in the margins help students understand new material.	120, 121
	• Homework Help in the margin of the exercise sets links homework exercises to corresponding examples within the lesson.	138
Reading / Writing In Mathematics	... strategies and activities are essential for student success in mathematics.	
	• Reading Math Study Tips help clarify mathematical terms.	121, 129
	• Reading Mathematics pages help students learn to read effectively in mathematics and make connections to everyday meanings of terms.	165, 393
	• Practice in vocabulary usage in each lesson and at the end of each chapter builds reading and writing skills.	179, 246
	• Writing in Math exercises require students to summarize what they have learned in the lesson.	164
Daily Intervention	... opportunities are provided throughout the program.	
	• Prerequisite Skills at the beginning of each chapter and in each lesson assess student readiness.	191, 415
	• The Student Handbook contains review and practice of prerequisite skills.	797–819
	• Daily Intervention features provide suggestions for addressing various learning styles and helping students who are having difficulty.	13, 33
	• A variety of Online Study Tools are readily accessible to students.	1
Test Preparation and Assessment	... provides targeted practice for local, state, and national tests.	
	• Standardized Test Practice questions appear in each lesson.	55
	• Standardized Test Practice Examples help students learn how to approach test questions.	39
	• Two pages of Standardized Test Practice at the end of each chapter include multiple-choice, short-response/grid-in, and extended-response questions.	64–65 116–117
	• Preparing for Standardized Tests includes examples and practice to help students become better test takers.	867–884
	• Interactive Standardized Test Practice is available in the Online Study Tools.	1
Staff Development	... features are available to assist new teachers and those teaching outside of their primary subject area.	
	• Mathematical Connections and Background provides an overview of the mathematics in the chapter and links to prior knowledge and future topics.	4C, 4D
	• Building on Prior Knowledge links what students have previously learned to the content of the current lesson.	43
	• Tips for New Teachers provide helpful suggestions for classroom management, teaching techniques, and assessment.	27, 36
Education Partnership	... strengthens the relevance of applications and projects.	
	• USA TODAY Snapshots® provide current topics and data in graphs, charts, and tables and enhance the unit WebQuest pr	3, 258

"Sticky Notes" in Chapter 1 provide a "walk-through" of key features. pp. 4–65

D1377922

GLENCOE MATHEMATICS

Algebra 1

Teacher Handbook

Holliday

Cuevas

Moore-Harris

Carter

Marks

Casey

Day

Hayek

Glencoe McGraw-Hill

New York, New York
Columbus, Ohio
Chicago, Illinois
Peoria, Illinois
Woodland Hills, California

 **Glencoe**

The *McGraw·Hill* Companies

Send all inquiries to:
Glencoe/McGraw-Hill
8787 Orion Place
Columbus, OH 43240

ISBN: 0-07-865113-1 (Student Edition)

ISBN: 0-07-865114-X (Teacher Edition)

4 5 6 7 8 9 10   055/071   12 11 10 09 08 07 06

Michigan
Edition

Algebra 1

Teacher Wraparound Edition

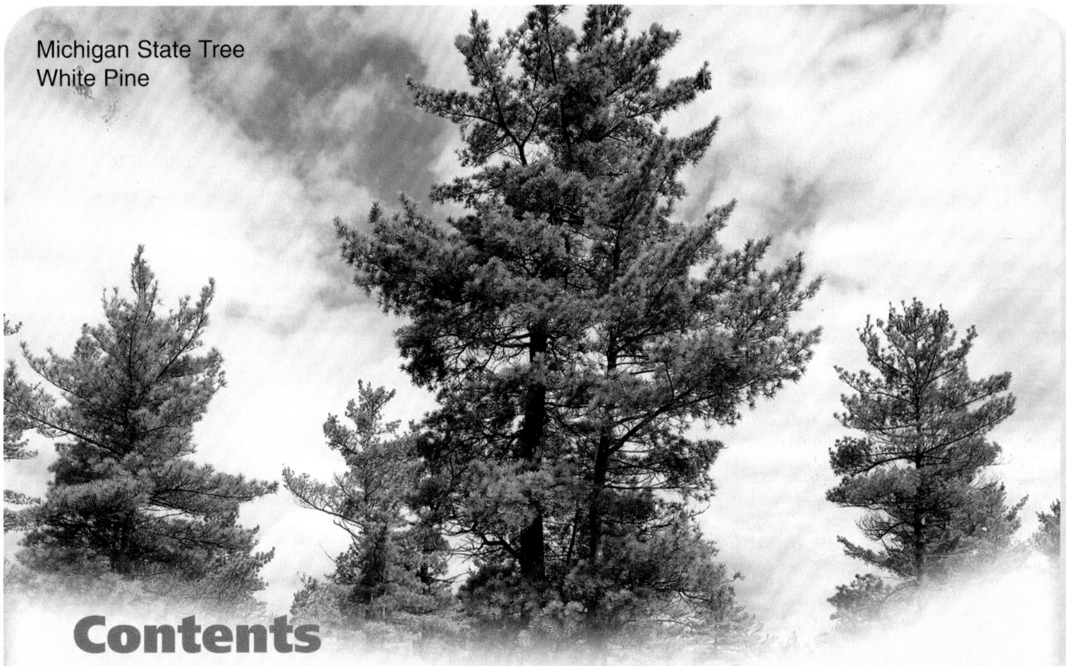

Michigan State Tree
White Pine

Contents

Glencoe

ISBN: 0-07-869681-X *(Michigan Student Edition)*   0-07-869683-6 *(Michigan Teacher Wraparound Edition)*
3 4 5 6 7 8 9 10   055/127   12 11 10 09 08 07 06

Just for Michigan!

Algebra 1

Features of the Michigan Teacher Wraparound Editions

Exclusively from Glencoe

Additional Michigan Resources

Preparing for the Michigan Tests CD-ROM Includes questions that can help your students prepare for success on Michigan tests.

Exclusively from Glencoe

Michigan TeacherWorks™ An all-in-one lesson planner and resource center that helps you customize lesson plans and reproduce classroom resources quickly and easily.

Michigan StudentWorks™ This backpack solution CD-ROM allows students instant access to the Student Edition, lesson worksheet pages, and web resources.

Michigan Algebra 1 & 2 Guide to Daily Intervention A lesson-by-lesson guide to available resources to reach students in need of intervention/remediation.

Exam*View*® Pro A customizable testmaker with built-in Michigan curriculum correlations.

Michigan Teacher Reviewers

James Leo Oliver, Reviewer Teacher of the Emotionally Impaired, Lakeview Junior High School, Battle Creek

Richard P. Strausz, Reviewer Math and Technology Coordinator, Farmington Schools, Farmington

For more information, visit: www.mi.algebra1.com

Michigan Teacher Advisory Board

Photo Credits: MI i Peter Griffith/Masterfile,
MI ii Jeffrey Foltice/Travel Michigan

Grand Rapids Skyline

Michigan Grade Level Content Expectations, Grade 8, Correlated to *Glencoe Algebra 1*

Grade Level Content Expectation		Student Edition Lesson(s)
STRAND N NUMBER AND OPERATIONS		
N.ME.08.01	Understand the meaning of a square root of a number and its connection to the square whose area is the number; understand the meaning of a cube root and its connection to the volume of a cube.	**2-7**, 8-1, **9-6, 11-1,** 11-4
N.ME.08.02	Understand meanings for zero and negative integer exponents.	**8-2**
N.ME.08.03	Understand that in decimal form, rational numbers either terminate or eventually repeat, and that calculators truncate or round repeating decimals; locate rational numbers on the number line; know fraction forms of common repeating decimals, e.g., $0.\overline{1} = \frac{1}{9}$; $0.\overline{3} = \frac{1}{3}$.	**2-1**, PS4
N.ME.08.04	Understand that irrational numbers are those that cannot be expressed as the quotient of two integers, and cannot be represented by terminating or repeating decimals; approximate the position of familiar irrational numbers, e.g., $\sqrt{2}$, $\sqrt{3}$, π on the number line.	**2-7**, 10-4
N.FL.08.05	Estimate and solve problems with square roots and cube roots using calculators.	**2-7, 9-6, 10-3,** 11-2, **11-3**
N.FL.08.06	Find square roots of perfect squares and approximate the square roots of nonperfect squares by locating between consecutive integers, e.g., $\sqrt{130}$ is between 11 and 12.	**2-7, 9-6, 10-3,** 11-2, 11-3
N.MR.08.07	Understand percent increase and percent decrease in both sum and product form, e.g., 3% increase of a quantity x is $x + .03x = 1.03x$.	**3-7**
N.MR.08.08	Solve problems involving percent increases and decreases.	**3-7**
N.FL.08.09	Solve problems involving compounded interest or multiple discounts.	**10-6**
N.MR.08.10	Calculate weighted averages such as course grades, consumer price indices, and sports ratings.	**3-9**

P = Preview Lesson, F = Follow-Up Lesson, PS = Prerequisite Skill Lessons (pages 798–819)

Grade Level Content Expectation		Student Edition Lesson(s)
N.MR.08.11	Solve problems involving ratio units such as miles per hour, dollars per pound, or persons per square mile.	3-6, PS3
STRAND A ALGEBRA		
A.RP.08.01	Identify and represent linear functions, quadratic functions, and other simple functions including inverse functions $\left(y = \dfrac{k}{x}\right)$, cubics $(y = ax^3)$ roots, $(y = \sqrt{x})$, and exponentials $(y = a^x, a > 0)$, using tables, graphs, and equations.	**1-8, 4-6, 10-1, 10-2, 10-4, 10-5**
A.PA.08.02	For basic functions, e.g., simple quadratics, direct and indirect variation, and population growth, describe how changes in one variable affect the others.	**5-2, 12-1**
A.PA.08.03	Recognize basic functions in problem context, e.g., area of a circle is πr^2, volume of a sphere is $\dfrac{4}{3}\pi r^3$, and represent them using tables, graphs, and formulas.	1-1, **1-2, 3-1,** 3-4, 8-1, 8-2, **8-6, 8-7, 9-3,** 9-4, 11-1, 11-2, PS9, PS10
A.RP.08.04	Use the vertical line test to determine if a graph represents a function in one variable.	**4-6**
A.RP.08.05	Relate quadratic functions in factored form and vertex form to their graphs and vice versa; in particular, note that solutions of a quadratic equation are the x-intercepts of the corresponding quadratic function.	**10-1, 10-2, 10-4**
A.RP.08.06	Graph factorable quadratic functions, finding where the graph intersects the x axis and the coordinates of the vertex; use words "parabola" and "roots"; include functions in vertex form those with leading coefficient -1, e.g., $y = x^2 - 36$, $y = (x - 2)^2 - 9$; $y = -x^2$; $y = -(x - 3)^2$.	**10-1, 10-2, 10-4**
A.FO.08.07	Recognize and apply the common formulas: $(a + b)^2 = a^2 + 2ab + b^2$ $(a - b)^2 = a^2 - 2ab + b^2$ $(a + b)(a - b) = a^2 - b^2$; represent geometrically.	**9-5, 9-6**
A.FO.08.08	Factor simple quadratic expressions with integer coefficients, e.g., $x^2 + 6x + 9$, $x^2 + 2x - 3$ and $x^2 - 4$; solve simple quadratic equations, e.g., $x^2 = 16$ or $x^2 = 5$ (by taking square roots); $x^2 - x - 6 = 0$, $x^2 - 2x = 15$ (by factoring); verify solutions by evaluation.	**9-2, 9-3, 9-4, 9-5, 9-6, 10-3, 10-4,** 12-9
A.FO.08.09	Solve applied problems involving simple quadratic equations.	**9-3, 9-4, 9-5, 9-6, 10-3, 10-4**

P = Preview Lesson, F = Follow-Up Lesson, PS = Prerequisite Skill Lessons (pages 798–819)

Grade Level Content Expectation		Student Edition Lesson(s)
A.FO.08.10	Understand that to solve the equation $f(x) = g(x)$ means to find all values of x for which the equation is true, e.g., determine whether a given value, or values from a given set, is a solution of an equation (0 is a solution of $3x^2 + 2 = 4x + 2$, but 1 is not a solution).	**1-3, 7-1**
A.FO.08.11	Solve simultaneous linear equations in two variables by graphing, by substitution, and by linear combination; estimate solutions using graphs; include examples with no solutions and infinitely many solutions.	**7-1, 7-2, 7-3, 7-4**
A.FO.08.12	Solve linear inequalities in one and two variables, and graph the solution sets.	**7-5**
A.FO.08.13	Set up and solve applied problems involving simultaneous linear equations and linear inequalities.	**7-1, 7-2, 7-3, 7-4, 7-5**
STRAND G GEOMETRY		
G.GS.08.01	Understand at least one proof of the Pythagorean Theorem; use the Pythagorean Theorem and its converse to solve applied problems including perimeter, area, and volume problems.	**11-4**
G.LO.08.02	Find the distance between two points on the coordinate plane using the distance formula; recognize that the distance formula is an application of the Pythagorean Theorem.	**11-5**
G.SR.08.03	Understand the definition of a circle; know and use the formulas for circumference and area of a circle to solve problems.	1-1, 3-8, 5-2, 8-2, 9-6, 11-3, **PS10**
G.SR.08.04	Find area and perimeter of complex figures by sub-dividing them into basic shapes (quadrilaterals, triangles, circles).	3-4, 8-2, **8-6,** 8-8, **9-2,** 9-4
G.SR.08.05	Solve applied problems involving areas of triangles, quadrilaterals, and circles.	1-1, 3-8, 6-2, 8-1, 8-2, 8-6, 8-7, 8-8, 9-1, 9-3, 9-4, 11-1, 11-2, 11-3, 11-4, **PS9, PS10**
G.SR.08.06	Know the volume formulas for generalized cylinders ((area of base) $\times$ height), generalized cones and pyramids $\left(\frac{1}{3}\,(\text{area of base}) \times \text{height}\right)$ and spheres $\left(\frac{4}{3}\pi(\text{radius})^3\right)$ and apply them to solve problems.	**3-1,** 8-1, 8-2, 8-4, 8-7
G.SR.08.07	Understand the concept of surface area, and find the surface area of prisms, cones, spheres, pyramids, and cylinders.	1-1, **3-1, 8-1F**

P = Preview Lesson, F = Follow-Up Lesson, PS = Prerequisite Skill Lessons (pages 798–819)

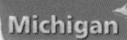
	Grade Level Content Expectation	Student Edition Lesson(s)
G.SR.08.08	Sketch a variety of two-dimensional representations of three-dimensional solids including orthogonal views (top, front, and side), picture views (projective or isometric), and nets, use such two-dimensional representations to help solve problems.	**8-1F**
G.TR.08.09	Understand the definition of a dilation from a point in the plane, and relate it to the definition of similar polygons.	**4-2**
G.TR.08.10	Understand and use reflective and rotational symmetries of two-dimensional shapes, and relate them to transformations to solve problems.	**4-2**
STRAND D DATA AND PROBABILITY		
D.AN.08.01	Determine which measure of central tendency (mean, median, mode) best represents a data set, e.g., salaries, home prices for answering certain questions; justify the choice made.	**2-5, PS12**
D.AN.08.02	Recognize practices of collecting and displaying data that may bias the presentation or analysis.	**1-9, 13-1,** 13-3, 13-5
D.PR.08.03	Compute relative frequencies from a table of experimental results for a repeated event, and be able to answer questions about the result, using relationship of probability to relative frequency.	**14-5**
D.PR.08.04	Apply the Basic Counting Principle to find total number of outcomes possible for independent and dependent events, and calculate the probabilities using organized lists or tree diagrams.	**14-1,** 14-2, 14-3
D.PR.08.05	Understand the relationship of probability to relative frequency.	**14-5**
D.PR.08.06	Understand the difference between independent and dependent events, and recognize common misconceptions involving probability, e.g., Alice rolls a 6 on a die three times in a row; she is just as likely to roll a 6 on the fourth roll as she was on any previous roll.	**14-3**
D.AN.08.07	Compute relative frequencies from a table of experimental results for a repeated event; understand the relationship of experimental probability to relative frequency; answer questions regarding the results.	**14-5**

P = Preview Lesson, F = Follow-Up Lesson, PS = Prerequisite Skill Lessons (pages 798–819)

Michigan Content Standards and Working Draft Benchmarks for High School Correlated to Glencoe's *Algebra 1, Geometry,* and *Algebra 2*

Lessons in which the benchmark is a primary focus are indicated in **bold**.

Standard and Working Draft Benchmarks		Student Edition Lesson(s)		
		Algebra 1	**Geometry**	**Algebra 2**
Strand I PATTERNS, RELATIONSHIPS, AND FUNCTIONS				
Content Standard 1: *Students recognize similarities and generalize patterns, use patterns to create models and make predictions, describe the nature of patterns and relationships, and construct representations of mathematical relationships. (Patterns)*				
I.1.1	Analyze and generalize mathematical patterns including sequences, series and recursive patterns.	4-7P, 4-7, 10-7	6-1F	11-1, 11-2, 11-3, 11-4, 11-5, 11-6
I.1.2	Analyze, interpret and translate among representations of patterns including tables, charts, graphs, matrices and vectors.	1-8, 1-8F, 4-3P, 4-3, 4-5, 4-5F, **4-7**, 4-8, 10-1	PS8	1-2F, 2-1, 2-2, 2-4, 4-1, 11-1, 11-2, 11-3, 11-4, 11-5, 11-6
I.1.3	Study and employ mathematical models of patterns to make inferences, predictions and decisions.	4-5, 4-5F, **4-7**, 4-8, 5-7, **11-3**		1-2F, 11-1, 11-2, 11-3, 11-4, 11-5, 11-6
I.1.4	Explore patterns (graphic, numeric, etc.) characteristic of families of functions; explore structural patterns within systems of objects, operations or relations.	**4-7**, 4-8, 5-1, 5-2, **5-3P, 5-3, 5-3F,** 5-4, 5-5, 5-6, **10-1F**		2-6, 6-6P, 6-6, 7-1, 7-2, 7-8, 7-9, 9-3, 9-3F, 9-5, 10-1P, 10-1, 10-2, 14-1, 14-2
I.1.5	Use patterns and reasoning to solve problems and explore new content.	4-7		1-2F, 11-1, 11-2, 11-3, 11-4, 11-5, 11-6P, 11-6
Content Standard 2: *Students describe the relationships among variables, predict what will happen to one variable as another variable is changed, analyze natural variation and sources of variability, and compare patterns of change. (Variability and Change)*				
I.2.1	Identify and describe the nature of change and begin to use the more formal language such as rate of change, continuity, limit, distribution and deviation.	5-1, 5-2, 5-3P, 5-3, 5-4, 5-5, 5-6, 10-7F	3-3	2-3, 11-4P
I.2.2	Develop a mathematical concept of function and recognize that functions display characteristic patterns of change (e.g., linear, quadratic, exponential).	1-8, 4-3P, 4-3, 4-5, 4-5F, **4-6**	PS8	2-1, 2-2, 2-4, 2-5, 2-6, 6-1, 7-1, 7-2, 7-9, 9-3, 9-5, 10-1P, 10-1, 10-6

P = Preview Lesson, F = Follow-Up Lesson, PS = Prerequisite Skill Lessons (pages 798–819),
RM = Reading Math Lesson

Standard and Working Draft Benchmarks		Student Edition Lesson(s)		
		Algebra 1	Geometry	Algebra 2
I.2.3	Expand their understanding of function to include non-linear functions, composition of functions, inverses of functions, and piecewise- and recursively defined functions.	10-1, 10-1F, 10-2, 10-3F, 10-5		2-2, 2-6, 6-1, 6-6, 7-1, 7-2, 7-7, 7-8, 7-9, 9-3, 9-5, 10-6, 13-3, 13-6, 13-7, 14-1
I.2.4	Represent functions using symbolism such as matrices, vectors and functional representation ($f(x)$).	4-6		2-1, 2-2, 2-6, 6-1, 7-1, 9-3, 9-5
I.2.5	Differentiate and analyze classes of functions including linear, power, quadratic, exponential, circular and trigonometric functions, and realize that many different situations can be modeled by a particular type of function.	4-5, 10-1, 10-1F, 10-2, 10-3F, 10-5		2-2, 2-6, 6-1, 7-1, 7-2, 9-3, 9-3F, 9-5, 10-1P, 10-1, 10-2, 10-6, 13-3, 13-6, 13-7
I.2.6	Increase their use of functions and mathematical models to solve problems in context.	1-8F, 4-6, 10-2, 10-3, 10-3F, 10-4, 10-5, 10-6, RM10		2-5, 2-6, 6-1, 7-1, 7-2, 9-5, 10-1, 10-2, 10-6

Strand II GEOMETRY AND MEASUREMENT

Content Standard 1: *Students develop spatial sense, use shape as an analytic and descriptive tool, identify characteristics and define shapes, identify properties and describe relationships among shapes. (Shape and Shape Relationships)*

		Algebra 1	Geometry	Algebra 2
II.1.1	Use shape to identify plane and solid figures, graphs, loci, functions and data distributions.	RM6, PS7, PS8	1-6, 4-1, 8-2, 8-4, 8-5, 8-6, RM8, 10-1, 12-1, 12-2	8-2, 8-3, 8-4P, 8-4, 8-5, 8-6P, 8-6
II.1.2	Determine necessary and sufficient conditions for the existence of a particular shape and apply those conditions to analyze shapes.	11-4	1-1, RM1, 1-6, 4-1, 4-2, 4-3, 4-4, 4-5, 4-6, RM4, 5-1, RM5, 5-2, 5-4, 8-2, 8-3, 8-4, 8-5, 8-6, RM8, 10-1, 10-2, 10-3	8-2, 8-3, 8-4P, 8-4, 8-5, 8-6P, 8-6
II.1.3	Use transformational, coordinate or synthetic methods to verify (prove) the generalizations they have made about properties of classes of shapes.		2-1, 2-2, 2-3, RM2, 2-4, 2-4F, 2-5, 2-7, 2-8, 3-5, 4-4, 4-5, 4-5F, 4-7, 5-3, 8-7	
II.1.4	Draw and construct shapes in two and three dimensions and analyze and justify the steps of their constructions.		3-1, 4-1, 4-4, 4-5, 4-5F, 4-6, 5-1P, 6-6, 6-6F, 8-2, 8-4, 8-5, 8-5F, 12-1, 12-2	8-2, 8-3, 8-4P, 8-4, 8-5, 8-6, 8-6F

P = Preview Lesson, F = Follow-Up Lesson, PS = Prerequisite Skill Lessons (pages 798–819),
RM = Reading Math Lesson

Standard and Working Draft Benchmarks		Student Edition Lesson(s)		
		Algebra 1	Geometry	Algebra 2
II.1.5	Study transformations of shapes using isometries, size transformations and coordinate mappings.	4-2	9-1P, 9-1, 9-2, 9-3, 9-4, 9-4F, 9-5, 9-7	4-4, 8-2, 8-3, 8-4P, 8-4, 8-5, 8-6, 8-6F
II.1.6	Compare and analyze shapes and formally establish the relationships among them, including congruence, similarity, parallelism, perpendicularity and incidence.	5-6, 11-6	1-5F, 3-1, 3-2, 3-5, 3-6, 4-3, 4-4, 4-5, 4-6, 4-7, 5-5, 6-2, 6-3, 6-4, 6-5, 6-6P, 6-6, 13-4	PS3
II.1.7	Use shape, shape properties and shape relationships to describe the physical world and to solve problems.	11-4	This objective is addressed throughout the text.	8-2, 8-3, 8-4, 8-5, 8-6

Content Standard 2: *Students identify locations of objects, identify location relative to other objects, and describe the effects of transformations (e.g., sliding, flipping, turning, enlarging, reducing) on an object. (Position)*

II.2.1	Locate and describe objects in terms of their position, including polar coordinates, three dimensional Cartesian coordinates, vectors and limits.	4-1, 11-5	1-3, 4-7, 9-6, 9-7, 13-5	3-5P, 8-1, 8-1F, 8-2, 8-3, 8-4P, 8-4, 8-6F
II.2.2	Locate and describe objects in terms of their orientation and relative position, including displacement (vectors), phase shift, maxima, minima and inflection points; give precise mathematical descriptions of symmetries.	11-5	9-6	8-2, 8-3, 8-4, 8-5, 8-6, 8-6F, 13-6, 14-1, 14-2
II.2.3	Give precise mathematical descriptions of transformations and describe the effects of transformations on size, shape, position and orientation.	4-2	9-1P, 9-1, 9-2, 9-3, 9-4, 9-4F, 9-5, 9-6, 9-7	4-4, 8-2, 8-3, 8-4P, 8-4, 8-5, 8-6, 8-6F, 14-2
II.2.4	Describe the locus of a point by a rule or mathematical expression; trace the locus of a moving point.		10-8, 12-7F	8-2, 8-3, 8-4P, 8-4, 8-5, 8-6, 8-6F
II.2.5	Use concepts of position, direction and orientation to describe the physical world and to solve problems.	4-1, 11-5	1-3, 4-7, 9-1, 9-2, 9-3, 9-4, 9-5, 9-6, 9-7, 13-5	8-1, 8-1F, 8-2, 8-3, 8-4P, 8-4, 8-5, 8-6, 8-6F

Content Standard 3: *Students compare attributes of two objects, or of one object with a standard (unit), and analyze situations to determine what measurement(s) should be made and to what level of precision. (Measurement)*

II.3.1	Select and use appropriate tools; make accurate measurements using both metric and common units, and measure angles in degrees and radians.		1-2, 1-4, 1-6F	13-2, 13-2F

P = Preview Lesson, F = Follow-Up Lesson, PS = Prerequisite Skill Lessons (pages 798–819),
RM = Reading Math Lesson

Standard and Working Draft Benchmarks		Student Edition Lesson(s)		
		Algebra 1	Geometry	Algebra 2
II.3.2	Continue to make and apply measurements of length, mass (weight), time, temperature, area, volume, angle; classify objects according to their dimensions.	8-1F, PS9, PS10, PS11	1-2, 1-4, 1-5, 1-6F, 2-7, 2-8, 3-1, 3-2, 4-2P, 4-2, 8-1, 8-1F, 10-1, 10-2, 10-3, 10-4, 10-5, 10-6, 10-7, 11-1, 11-2, 11-3, 11-4, 11-5, 12-3, 12-4, 12-5, 12-6, 12-7, 13-1, 13-2, 13-3, PS3	13-2, 13-2F
II.3.3	Estimate measures with a specified degree of accuracy and evaluate measurements for accuracy, precision and tolerance.		1-2, 1-4	13-2, 13-2F, PS5
II.3.4	Interpret measurements and explain how changes in one measure may affect other measures.	8-1F	1-5, 2-7, 2-8, 4-2, 13-1F	13-1P
II.3.5	Use proportional reasoning and indirect measurements, including applications of trigonometric ratios, to measure inaccessible distances and to determine derived measures such as density.	11-6, 11-7P, 11-7	7-1, 7-2P, 7-3, 7-4, 7-5, 7-6, 7-7	13-1P, 13-1, 13-4, 13-5, 14-3, 14-4, 14-5, 14-6, PS4
II.3.6	Apply measurement to describe the real world and to solve problems.		1-5, 3-6, 7-2P, 7-2, 7-5, 7-6, 7-7, 11-1, 11-2, 11-3, 11-4, 12-3, 12-4, 12-5, 12-6, 12-7, 13-1, 13-2, 13-3	13-2, 13-2F, 13-4, 13-5, 14-4, 14-5, 14-6, PS4

Strand III DATA ANALYSIS AND STATISTICS

Content Standard 1: *Students collect and explore data, organize data into a useful form, and develop skill in representing and reading data displayed in different formats. (Collection, Organization and Presentation of Data)*

III.1.1	Collect and explore data through observation, measurement, surveys, sampling techniques and simulations.	RM2, 13-1, RM13		12-8F, 12-9
III.1.2	Organize data using tables, charts, graphs, spreadsheets and data bases.	1-8F, 2-5, 13-5, PS5, PS6		2-5, 4-1, 4-1F
III.1.3	Present data using the most appropriate representation and give a rationale for their choice; show how certain representations may skew the data or bias the presentation.	1-9, 1-9F, 2-5, 13-5, RM13, PS5, PS6		PS6
III.1.4	Identify what data are needed to answer a particular question or solve a given problem and design and implement strategies to obtain, organize and present those data.	13-1, RM13		12-8F, 12-9

P = Preview Lesson, F = Follow-Up Lesson, PS = Prerequisite Skill Lessons (pages 798–819),
RM = Reading Math Lesson

Standard and Working Draft Benchmarks		Student Edition Lesson(s)		
		Algebra 1	Geometry	Algebra 2
Content Standard 2: *Students examine data and describe characteristics of a distribution, relate data to the situation from which they arose, and use data to answer questions convincingly and persuasively. (Description and Interpretation)*				
III.2.1	Critically read data from tables, charts or graphs and explain the source of the data and what the data represent.	1-9, 2-5, RM2, 13-3, 13-5, 13-5F		2-5, PS6, PS7, PS8
III.2.2	Describe the shape of a data distribution and determine measures of central tendency, variability and correlation.	RM2, 13-3, 13-4, 14-4, PS12		12-6, 12-7, 12-8
III.2.3	Use the data and their characteristics to draw and support conclusions.	1-9, 2-5, RM2, 13-3		12-8
III.2.4	Critically question the sources of data; the techniques used to collect, organize and present data; the inferences drawn from the data; and the sources of bias and measures taken to eliminate such bias.	1-9, RM2, 13-1, RM13		12-9
III.2.5	Formulate questions and problems and gather and interpret data to answer those questions.	RM2, 13-1, RM13		12-8F
Content Standard 3: *Students draw defensible inferences about unknown outcomes, make predictions, and identify the degree of confidence they have in their predictions. (Inference and Prediction)*				
III.3.1	Make and test hypotheses.			12-8, 12-8F, 12-9F
III.3.2	Design investigations to model and solve problems; also employ confidence intervals and curve fitting in analyzing the data.	13-3F		6-2F, 7-2F, 12-9F, 10-2F
III.3.3	Formulate and communicate arguments and conclusions based on data and evaluate their arguments and those of others.	1-7, 13-3		2-5, 2-5F
III.3.4	Make predictions and decisions based on data, including interpolations and extrapolations.	5-7, 5-7F, 13-3, 13-3F		2-5, 2-5F, 6-2F, 7-2F, 10-2F
III.3.5	Employ investigations, mathematical models, and simulations to make inferences and predictions to answer questions and solve problems.	RM13		12-8F
Strand IV NUMBER SENSE AND NUMERATION				
Content Standard 1: *Students experience counting and measuring activities to develop intuitive sense about numbers, develop understanding about properties of numbers, understand the need for and existence of different sets of numbers, and investigate properties of special numbers. (Concepts and Properties of Numbers)*				
IV.1.1	Develop an understanding of irrational, real and complex numbers.	2-7		1-2, 5-9

P = Preview Lesson, F = Follow-Up Lesson, PS = Prerequisite Skill Lessons (pages 798–819),
RM = Reading Math Lesson

Standard and Working Draft Benchmarks		Student Edition Lesson(s)		
		Algebra 1	Geometry	Algebra 2
IV.1.2	Use the $(a + bi)$ and polar forms of complex numbers.			5-9
IV.1.3	Develop an understanding of the properties of the real and complex number systems and of the properties of special numbers including π, i, e, and conjugates.	1-4, 1-5, 1-6, 2-1, 2-7		1-2, 5-9
IV.1.4	Apply their understanding of number systems to model, and solve mathematical and applied problems.	2-1, 2-7		1-2

Content Standard 2: *Students recognize that numbers are used in different ways such as counting, measuring, ordering and estimating, understand and produce multiple representations of a number, and translate among equivalent representations. (Representation and Uses of Numbers)*

IV.2.1	Give decimal representations of rational and irrational numbers and coordinate and vector representations of complex numbers.	2-1, 2-7, 8-3		5-5, 11-5
IV.2.2	Develop an understanding of more complex representations of numbers, including exponential and logarithmic expressions, and select an appropriate representation to facilitate problem solving.	8-1, 8-2		5-6, 5-7, 10-3, 10-4, 10-5
IV.2.3	Determine when to use rational approximations and the exact values of numbers such as e, π, and the irrational.	2-7		5-5, 10-5, 11-5
IV.2.4	Apply estimation in increasingly complex situations.			5-5, 6-2
IV.2.5	Select appropriate representations for numbers, including representations of rational and irrational numbers and coordinate and vector representations of complex numbers, in order to simplify and solve problems.	2-1, 8-3		5-7

Content Standard 3: *Students investigate relationships such as equality, inequality, inverses, factors and multiples, and represent and compare very large and very small numbers. (Number Relationships)*

IV.3.1	Compare and order real numbers and compare rational approximations to exact values.	2-1		PS1
IV.3.2	Express numerical comparisons as ratios and rates.	3-6	6-1, 6-1F, 7-3, 7-4	13-1, 13-3
IV.3.3	Extend the relationships of primes, factors, multiples and divisibility in an algebraic setting.	8-1, 8-2, 9-1		5-4
IV.3.4	Express number relationships using positive and negative rational exponents, logarithms and radicals.	2-7, 11-1, 11-2		5-1, 5-6, 10-3, 10-4, 10-5
IV.3.5	Apply their understanding of number relationships in solving problems.	2-1, 2-7, 3-7, RM3	6-1	5-1, 5-6, 10-6, 13-1, 13-3, 13-4, 13-5

P = Preview Lesson, F = Follow-Up Lesson, PS = Prerequisite Skill Lessons (pages 798–819),
RM = Reading Math Lesson

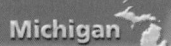

Standard and Working Draft Benchmarks	Student Edition Lesson(s)		
	Algebra 1	Geometry	Algebra 2

Strand V   NUMERICAL AND ALGEBRAIC OPERATIONS AND ANALYTICAL THINKING

Content Standard 1: *Students understand and use various types of operations (e.g., addition, subtraction, multiplication, division) to solve problems. (Operations and their Properties)*

		Algebra 1	Geometry	Algebra 2
V.1.1	Present and explain geometric and symbolic models for operations with real and complex numbers and algebraic expressions.	**1-1, RM1, 8-4P, 8-5P, 8-6, 8-7P, 9-2P, 9-3P, RM12**	**1-3F, 7-1**	**5-4, 6-4**
V.1.2	Compute with real numbers, complex numbers, algebraic expressions, matrices and vectors using technology and, for simple instances, with paper-and-pencil algorithms.	**1-1, 1-2, 2-2, 2-3, 2-4, 2-7, 3-7, 8-3, 8-4, 8-5P, 8-5, 8-6, 8-7P, 8-7, 8-8, 9-2, 9-3, 9-4, 9-5, 9-6, 11-1, 12-2, 12-3, 12-4, 12-5, 12-6, 12-7, 12-8, 13-2, PS1, PS2**	**6-1, PS4, PS5, PS10, PS11, PS12, PS13, PS14**	**1-1, 4-2, 4-3, 4-5, 4-7, 5-1, 5-2, 5-3, 5-4, 5-5, 5-6, 5-7, 7-4, 7-7, 9-1, 9-2, 10-3, 10-4, 10-5, PS2**
V.1.3	Describe the properties of operations with numbers, algebraic expressions, vectors and matrices, and make generalizations about the properties of given mathematical systems.	**1-1, RM1, 1-2, 1-4, 1-5, 1-6**		**1-2, 4-2, 4-3, 4-5, 4-7**
V.1.4	Efficiently and accurately apply operations with real numbers, complex numbers, algebraic expressions, matrices and vectors in solving problems.	**1-2, 1-4, 1-5, 2-2, 2-3, 2-4, 2-7, 3-7, RM3, 8-3, 8-4, 8-5P, 8-5, 8-6, 8-7P, 8-7, 8-8, 9-2, 9-3, 9-4, 9-5, 9-6, 11-1, 11-2, 12-2, 12-3, 12-4, 12-5, 12-6, 12-7, 12-8, 13-2, PS1, PS2**	**6-1, PS4, PS5, PS10, PS11, PS12, PS13, PS14**	**4-2, 4-3, 4-5, 4-7, 5-1, 5-2, 5-3, 5-4, 5-5, 5-6, 5-7, 7-4, 7-7, 9-1, 9-2, 10-3, 10-4, PS2**

Content Standard 2: *Students analyze problems to determine an appropriate process for solution, and use algebraic notations to model or represent problems. (Algebraic and Analytic Thinking)*

		Algebra 1	Geometry	Algebra 2
V.2.1	Identify important variables in a context, symbolize them and express their relationships algebraically.	**1-1, RM1, 3-1, 3-8, 3-9, 3-9F**		**1-1**
V.2.2	Represent algebraic concepts and relationships with matrices, spreadsheets, diagrams, graphs, tables, physical models, vectors, equations and inequalities; and translate among the various representations.	**3-1, 3-2, 3-3, 3-4, 3-5, RM3, 3-8, 3-9, 3-9F, 4-8, 6-1, 6-2, 6-3, 6-4**	**3-4, PS8**	**1-1, 1-3, 1-4, 1-5, 1-6, 4-1**

P = Preview Lesson, F = Follow-Up Lesson, PS = Prerequisite Skill Lessons (pages 798–819),
RM = Reading Math Lesson

Standard and Working Draft Benchmarks		Student Edition Lesson(s)		
		Algebra 1	Geometry	Algebra 2
V.2.3	Solve linear equations and inequalities algebraically and non-linear equations using graphing, symbol-manipulating or spreadsheet technology; and solve linear and non-linear systems using appropriate methods.	1-3, 3-2P, 3-2, 3-3, 3-4P, 3-4, 3-5, 3-8, 4-4, 6-1, 6-2P, 6-2, 6-3, 6-4, 6-5, 6-6, 7-1P, 7-1, 7-1F, 7-2, 7-3, 7-4, RM7, 7-5, 10-2, 10-3, 10-4, 10-4F, 11-3, 12-9	PS6, PS7, PS9	1-3, 1-4, 1-5, 1-6, 2-7, 3-1, 3-2, 3-3, 3-3F, 3-4, 3-5P, 3-5, 4-1, 4-6, 4-8, 4-8F, 5-8, 5-9, 6-2, 6-2F, 6-3, 6-4, 6-5, 6-7, 7-3, 7-5, 7-6, 8-7
V.2.4	Analyze problems that can be modeled by functions, determine strategies for solving the problems and evaluate the adequacy of the solutions in the context of the problems.	4-5, 4-5F, 4-7	3-4	3-4, 6-2, 6-3, 6-4, 6-5, 6-7
V.2.5	Explore problems that reflect the contemporary uses of mathematics in significant contexts and use the power of technology and algebraic and analytic reasoning to experience the ways mathematics is used in society.	1-9, 1-9F, RM3, 3-9, 3-9F, RM4	1-6F, 3-6F, 7-6F, 8-1F	3-3F, 3-4, 5-9, 6-2F

Strand VI PROBABILITY AND DISCRETE MATHEMATICS

Content Standard 1: *Students develop an understanding of the notion of certainty and of probability as a measure of the degree of likelihood that can be assigned to a given event based on the knowledge available, and make critical judgments about claims that are made in probabilistic situations. (Probability)*

		Algebra 1	Geometry	Algebra 2
VI.1.1	Develop an understanding of randomness and chance variation and describe chance and certainty in the language of probability.	2-6, 14-1, 14-3	1-2F, 11-5	12-1, 12-3, 12-4
VI.1.2	Give a mathematical definition of probability and determine the probabilities of more complex events, and generate and interpret probability distributions.	2-6F, 14-3	1-2F, 11-5	12-1, 12-3, 12-4
VI.1.3	Analyze events to determine their dependence or independence and calculate probabilities of compound events.	14-3		12-1, 12-3, 12-4
VI.1.4	Use sampling and simulations to determine empirical probabilities and, when appropriate, compare them to the corresponding theoretical probabilities; understand and apply the law of large numbers.	14-5		12-8, 12-8F
VI.1.5	Conduct probability experiments and simulations, to model and solve problems, including compound events.	14-5	11-5	12-8, 12-8F

P = Preview Lesson, F = Follow-Up Lesson, PS = Prerequisite Skill Lessons (pages 798–819),
RM = Reading Math Lesson

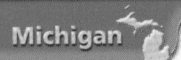

Standard and Working Draft Benchmarks		Student Edition Lesson(s)		
		Algebra 1	Geometry	Algebra 2
Content Standard 2: *Students investigate practical situations such as scheduling, routing, sequencing, networking, organizing and classifying, and analyze ideas like recurrence relations, induction, iteration, and algorithm design. (Discrete Mathematics)*				
VI.2.1	Derive and use formulas for calculating permutations and combinations.	14-2, RM14		12-2
VI.2.2	Use sets and set relationships to represent algebraic and geometric concepts.	2-1	8-5	1-2, 5-9
VI.2.3	Use vertex-edge graphs to solve network problems such as finding circuits, critical paths, minimum spanning trees and adjacency matrices.	14-1F	beyond the scope of this course	beyond the scope of this course
VI.2.4	Analyze and use discrete ideas, such as induction, iteration and recurrence relations.		6-6P, 6-6	11-6, 11-6F
VI.2.5	Describe and analyze efficient algorithms to accomplish a task or solve a problem in a variety of contexts, including practical, mathematical and computer related situations.		6-6P, 6-6	
VI.2.6	Use discrete mathematics concepts as described above to model situations and solve problems; and look for whether or not there is a solution (existence problems), determine how many solutions there are (counting problems) and decide upon a best solution (optimization problems).	14-1	1-1	12-1, 12-8

P = Preview Lesson, F = Follow-Up Lesson, PS = Prerequisite Skill Lessons (pages 798–819),
RM = Reading Math Lesson

Algebra 1 Pacing Chart

Bold indicates the benchmark(s) most directly addressed by the lesson.
Pacing is given in school calendar days.

Lesson	Grade 8 GLCE	Grades 9–12 Curriculum Framework	Michigan Pacing Regular Schedule	Block Schedule
1-1	A.PA.08.03, G.SR.08.03, G.SR.08.05, G.SR.08.07	V.1.1, V.1.2, V.1.3, **V.2.1**	1	0.5
RM1		V.1.1, V.1.3, **V.2.1**	0	0
1-2	A.PA.08.03	V.1.2, V.1.3, **V.1.4**	1	0.5
1-3	A.FO.08.10	**V.2.3**	2	1
1-4		IV.1.3, **V.1.3**, V.1.4	1	0.5
1-5		IV.1.3, **V.1.3**, V.1.4	1	0.5
1-6		IV.1.3, **V.1.3**	1	0.5
1-7		**III.3.3**	1	0.5
1-8	A.RP.08.01	**I.1.2**, I.2.2	1	0.5
1-8F		I.1.2, I.2.6, **III.1.2**	0	0
1-9	D.AN.08.02	III.1.3, **III.2.1**, III.2.3, III.2.4, V.2.5	1	0.5
1-9F		**III.1.3**, V.2.5	0	0
Chapter 1 Review & Testing			2	1
2-1	N.ME.08.03	IV.1.3, IV.1.4, **IV.2.1**, IV.2.5, IV.3.1, IV.3.5, VI.2.2	1	0.5
2-2		**V.1.2**, V.1.4	2	1
2-3		**V.1.2**, V.1.4	1	0.5
2-4		**V.1.2**, V.1.4	1	0.5
2-5	D.AN.08.01	**III.1.2**, III.1.3, III.2.1, III.2.3	1	0.5
RM2		III.1.1, III.2.1, III.2.2, III.2.3, III.2.4, **III.2.5**	0	0
2-6		**VI.1.1**	1	0.5
2-6F		**VI.1.2**	0	0
2-7	N.ME.08.01, N.ME.08.04, N.FL.08.05, N.FL.08.06	**IV.1.1**, IV.1.3, IV.1.4, IV.2.1, IV.2.3, IV.3.4, IV.3.5, V.1.2, V.1.4	1	0.5
Chapter 2 Review & Testing			2	1
Content Standards Practice	In addition to the lessons assigned in the next 5 days, complete the problems on page MI 7.			
3-1	A.PA.08.03, G.SR.08.06, G.SR.08.07	V.2.1, **V.2.2**	1	0.5
3-2P		**V.2.3**	0	0
3-2		V.2.2, **V.2.3**	2	1
3-3		V.2.2, **V.2.3**	1	0.5
3-4P		**V.2.3**	0	0
3-4	A.PA.08.03, G.SR.08.04	V.2.2, **V.2.3**	2	0.5
3-5		V.2.2, **V.2.3**	1	0.5
3-6	N.MR.08.11	**IV.3.2**	1	0.5
3-7	N.MR.08.07, N.MR.08.08	IV.3.5, V.1.2, **V.1.4**	1	0.5
Content Standards Practice	In addition to the lessons assigned in the next 5 days, complete the problems on page MI 8.			
RM3		IV.3.5, V.1.4, **V.2.2**, V.2.5	0	0

Lesson	Grade 8 GLCE	Grades 9–12 Curriculum Framework	Michigan Pacing	
			Regular Schedule	Block Schedule
3-8	G.SR.08.03, G.SR.08.05	V.2.1, V.2.2, **V.2.3**	2	1
3-9	N.MR.08.10	V.2.1, V.2.2, **V.2.5**	2	1
3-9F		V.2.1, V.2.2, **V.2.5**	0	0
Chapter 3 Review & Testing			2	1
4-1		**II.2.1**, II.2.5	1	0.5
4-2	G.TR.08.09, G.TR.08.10	II.1.5, **II.2.3**	2	1
4-3P		**I.1.2**	0	0
4-3		**I.1.2**	2	1
4-4		**V.2.3**	1	0.5
4-5		**I.1.2**, I.1.3	2	1
4-5F		**I.1.2**, I.1.3	0	0
4-6	A.RP.08.01, A.RP.08.04	**I.2.2**, I.2.4, I.2.6	1	0.5
4-7P		**I.1.1**	0	0
Content Standards Practice		In addition to the lessons assigned in the next 5 days, complete the problems on page MI 9.		
4-7		I.1.2, I.1.3, I.1.4, I.1.5, **V.2.4**	2	1
RM4		**V.2.5**	0	0
4-8		I.1.2, I.1.3, I.1.4, **V.2.2**	1	0.5
Chapter 4 Review & Testing			2	1
5-1		I.1.4, **I.2.1**	1	0.5
RM5			0	0
5-2	A.PA.08.02, G.SR.08.03	I.1.4, **I.2.1**	1	0.5
5-3P		**I.1.4**, I.2.1	0	0
5-3		**I.1.4**, I.2.1	2	1
5-3F		**I.1.4**	0	0
5-4		**I.1.4**, I.2.1	2	1
5-5		**I.1.4**, I.2.1	2	1
5-6		I.1.4, I.2.1, **II.1.6**	2	1
5-7		I.1.3, **III.3.4**	2	1
5-7F		**III.3.4**	0	0
Chapter 5 Review & Testing			2	1
6-1		V.2.2, **V.2.3**	1	0.5
6-2P		**V.2.3**	0.5	0.5
6-2	G.SR.08.05	V.2.2, **V.2.3**	1.5	0.5
6-3		V.2.2, **V.2.3**	1	0.5
RM6		**II.1.1**	0	0
6-4		V.2.2, **V.2.3**	2	1
Content Standards Practice		In addition to the lessons assigned in the next 5 days, complete the problems on page MI 10.		
6-5		**V.2.3**	2	1
6-6		**V.2.3**	2	1
6-6F			0	0
Chapter 6 Review & Testing			2	1
7-1P		**V.2.3**	0	0
7-1	A.FO.08.10, A.FO.08.11, A.FO.08.13	**V.2.3**	2	1
7-1F		**V.2.3**	0	0

Lesson	Grade 8 GLCE	Grades 9–12 Curriculum Framework	Michigan Pacing	
			Regular Schedule	Block Schedule
7-2	A.FO.08.11, A.FO.08.13	**V.2.3**	2	1
7-3	A.FO.08.11, A.FO.08.13	**V.2.3**	2	1
7-4	A.FO.08.11, A.FO.08.13	**V.2.3**	2	1
RM7		V.2.3	0	0
7-5	A.FO.08.12, A.FO.08.13	**V.2.3**	1	1
Chapter 7 Review & Testing			2	1
8-1	N.ME.08.01, A.PA.08.03, G.SR.08.05, G.SR.08.06	**IV.2.2**, IV.3.3	1	0.5
8-1F	G.SR.08.07, G.SR.08.08	**II.3.2**, II.3.4	0	0
8-2	N.ME.08.02, A.PA.08.03, G.SR.08.03, G.SR.08.04, G.SR.08.05, G.SR.08.06	IV.2.2, **IV.3.3**	2	1
RM8			0	0
8-3		**IV.2.1**, IV.2.5, V.1.2, V.1.4	1	0.5
8-4P		**V.1.1**	0	0
8-4	G.SR.08.06	**V.1.2**, V.1.4	2	1
8-5P		V.1.1, V.1.2, **V.1.4**	0	0
8-5		V.1.2, **V.1.4**	2	1
8-6	A.PA.08.03, G.SR.08.04, G.SR.08.05	V.1.1, V.1.2, **V.1.4**	2	1
8-7P		V.1.1, V.1.2, **V.1.4**	0	0
8-7	A.PA.08.03, G.SR.08.05, G.SR.08.06	V.1.2, **V.1.4**	1	0.5
8-8	G.SR.08.04, G.SR.08.05	V.1.2, **V.1.4**	1	0.5
Chapter 8 Review & Testing			2	1
Content Standards Practice	In addition to the lessons assigned in the next 5 days, complete the problems on page MI 11.			
9-1	G.SR.08.05	**IV.3.3**	1	0.5
9-2P		**V.1.1**	0	0
9-2	A.FO.08.08, G.SR.08.04	V.1.2, **V.1.4**	1	0.5
9-3P		**V.1.1**	0	0
9-3	A.PA.08.03, A.FO.08.08, A.FO.08.09, G.SR.08.05	V.1.2, **V.1.4**	2	1
9-4	A.PA.08.03, A.FO.08.08, A.FO.08.09, G.SR.08.04, G.SR.08.05	V.1.2, **V.1.4**	2	1
9-5	A.FO.08.07, A.FO.08.08, A.FO.08.09	V.1.2, **V.1.4**	2	1
RM9			0	0
9-6	N.ME.08.01, N.FL.08.05, N.FL.08.06, A.FO.08.07, A.FO.08.08, A.FO.08.09, G.SR.08.03	V.1.2, **V.1.4**	2	1
Chapter 9 Review & Testing			2	1
Content Standards Practice	In addition to the lessons assigned in the next 5 days, complete the problems on page MI 12.			
10-1	A.RP.08.01, A.RP.08.05, A.RP.08.06	I.1.2, I.2.3, **I.2.5**	2	1
10-1F		I.1.4, I.2.3, **I.2.5**	0	0

Lesson	Grade 8 GLCE	Grades 9–12 Curriculum Framework	Michigan Pacing	
			Regular Schedule	Block Schedule
10-2	A.RP.08.01, A.RP.08.05, A.RP.08.06	I.2.3, I.2.5, **I.2.6**, V.2.3	1	0.5
10-3	N.FL.08.05, N.FL.08.06, A.FO.08.08, A.FO.08.09	I.2.6, **V.2.3**	2	1
10-3F		I.2.3, **I.2.5**, I.2.6	0	0
10-4	N.ME.08.04, A.RP.08.01, A.RP.08.05, A.RP.08.06, A.FO.08.08, A.FO.08.09	I.2.6, **V.2.3**	2	1
10-4F		**V.2.3**	0	0
10-5	A.RP.08.01	I.2.3, **I.2.5**, I.2.6	2	1
10-6	N.FL.08.09	**I.2.6**	2	1
RM10		**I.2.6**	0	0
10-7		**I.1.1**	1	0.5
10-7F		**I.2.1**	0	0
Chapter 10 Review & Testing			2	1
Content Standards Practice	In addition to the lessons assigned in the next 5 days, complete the problems on page MI 13.			
11-1	N.ME.08.01, A.PA.08.03, G.SR.08.05	**IV.3.4**, V.1.2, V.1.4	2	1
11-2	N.FL.08.05, N.FL.08.06, A.PA.08.03, G.SR.08.05	IV.3.4, **V.1.4**	2	1
11-3	N.FL.08.05, N.FL.08.06, G.SR.08.03, G.SR.08.05	I.1.3, **V.2.3**	1	0.5
11-3F			0	0
11-4	N.ME.08.01, G.GS.08.01, G.SR.08.05	**II.1.2**, II.1.7	1	0.5
11-5	G.LO.08.02	**II.2.1**, II.2.2, II.2.5	1	0.5
11-6		**II.1.6**, II.3.5	1	0.5
11-7P		**II.3.5**	0	0
11-7		**II.3.5**	2	1
RM11			0	0
Chapter 11 Review & Testing			2	1
12-1	A.PA.08.02		0	0
12-2		**V.1.2**, V.1.4	1	0.5
12-2F			0	0
12-3		**V.1.2**, V.1.4	2	1
12-4		**V.1.2**, V.1.4	1	0.5
RM12		**V.1.1**	0	0
Content Standards Practice	In addition to the lessons assigned in the next 5 days, complete the problems on page MI 14.			
12-5		**V.1.2**, V.1.4	1	0.5
12-6		**V.1.2**, V.1.4	1	0.5
12-7		**V.1.2**, V.1.4	2	1
12-8		**V.1.2**, V.1.4	2	1
12-9	A.FO.08.08	**V.2.3**	2	1
Chapter 12 Review & Testing			2	1
13-1	D.AN.08.02	III.1.1, III.1.4, **III.2.4**, III.2.5	1	0.5
RM13		III.1.1, III.1.3, III.1.4, **III.2.4**, III.2.5, III.3.5	0	0

Lesson	Grade 8 GLCE	Grades 9–12 Curriculum Framework	Michigan Pacing	
			Regular Schedule	Block Schedule
13-2		V.1.2, **V.1.4**	1	0.5
13-3	D.AN.08.02	**III.2.1**, III.2.2, III.2.3, III.3.3, III.3.4	2	1
13-3F		**III.3.2**, III.3.4	0	0
13-4		**III.2.2**	2	1
13-5	D.AN.08.02	**III.1.2**, III.1.3, III.2.1	2	1
13-5F		**III.2.1**	0	0
Chapter 13 Review & Testing			2	1
Content Standards Practice	In addition to the lessons assigned in the next 5 days, complete the problems on page MI 15.			
14-1	D.PR.08.04	VI.1.1, **VI.2.6**	1	0.5
14-1F		**VI.2.3**	0	0
14-2	D.PR.08.04	**VI.2.1**	2	1
RM14		**VI.2.1**	0	0
14-3	D.PR.08.04, D.PR.08.06	VI.1.1, **VI.1.2**, VI.1.3	2	1
Content Standards Practice	In addition to the lessons assigned in the next 5 days, complete the problems on page MI 16.			
14-4		**III.2.2**	2	1
14-5	D.PR.08.03, D.PR.08.05, D.AN.08.07	**VI.1.4**, VI.1.5	1	0.5
Chapter 14 Review & Testing			2	1
PS1		**V.1.2**, V.1.4	0	0
PS2		**V.1.2**, V.1.4	0	0
PS3	N.MR.08.11		0	0
PS4	N.ME.08.03		0	0
PS5		**III.1.2**, III.1.3	0	0
PS6		**III.1.2**	0	0
PS7		**II.1.1**	0	0
PS8		**II.1.1**	0	0
PS9	A.PA.08.03, G.SR.08.05	**II.3.2**	0	0
PS10	A.PA.08.03, G.SR.08.03, G.SR.08.05	**II.3.2**	0	0
PS11		**II.3.2**	0	0
PS12	D.AN.08.01	**III.2.2**	0	0
Total Days of Instruction			174	87

How To...

Master the Michigan Content Standards

Content Standards Practice

Pages MI7–MI16 of this text include a section called **Content Standards Practice**. These questions assess the mathematics concepts and skills from the Michigan Content Standards and Working Benchmarks for High School. A list of these standards and benchmarks can be found on pages MI3–MI5 of this textbook.

Content Standards Practice
You should plan to complete one practice set each week to help you master the mathematics content standards.

One-a-Day
Plan to spend a few minutes each day working on the problem(s) for that day unless your teacher asks you to do otherwise.

Variety
Each practice set contains problems that are similar to those on high school tests.
• Monday, constructed response
• Tuesday through Friday, selected response (multiple-choice)

Reviewing Skills
If you have difficulty with any problem, you can refer to the lesson that is referenced in parentheses after the problem.

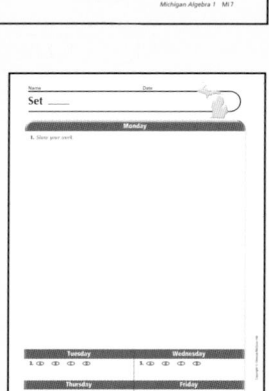

Record Answers
Your teacher can provide you with an answer sheet to record your work and your answers for each week. A printable answer sheet is also available at mi.algebra1.com. At the end of the week, your teacher may want you to turn in the answer sheet.

Pacing

The questions in the Content Standards Practice are sequentially aligned with the sequence of the Student Edition so students may integrate this test practice as they progress through the text.

To best align the Content Standards Practice with the Student Edition content, you may wish to delay coverage of the Standards Practice until the third or fourth week of your school calendar.

Set 1

Monday

1. Mr. Diaz made this stem-and-leaf plot to record the chapter test scores of the students in his fourth-period class. *(Lesson 2-5) (III.1.2, III.2.2)* **A–C. See margin.**

Stem	Leaf
9	8 6 6 4 1
8	9 7 7 5 2
7	6 4 2 0 0
6	9 5 5 5
5	6 2 0
4	8 6 2 4|8 = 48

A. Find the mean, median, and mode for the test scores. Show your work.
B. Which of these three measures of central tendency is easiest to find? Which is most difficult to find? Explain the reasons for your choices.
C. Which of these three measures of central tendency would be most useful to Mr. Diaz in evaluating how well his students have learned the material in this chapter? Which would be the least useful? Explain your reasoning.

Tuesday

2. Lakita rented a car at a rate of $28 per day plus $0.23 per mile. If she kept the car for d days and drove it m miles, which expression represents the amount in dollars that she paid for the rental, not including taxes? *(Lesson 1-2) (V.2.1)* **C**
   - Ⓐ $28d + 23m$
   - Ⓑ $0.28d + 0.23d$
   - Ⓒ $28d + 0.23m$
   - Ⓓ $0.23d + 28m$

Wednesday

3. The equation $t = \sqrt{\dfrac{d}{16}}$ gives the time t, in seconds, that it takes an object dropped from a height of d feet to reach the ground. The Marriott Renaissance Center Tower in Detroit is the tallest building in Michigan and the tallest hotel in the United States, with a height of 726 feet. About how long would it take a ball dropped from the top of this building to hit the ground? *(Lesson 2-7) (I.2.3, IV.2.1)* **A**
   - Ⓐ 7 sec
   - Ⓑ 23 sec
   - Ⓒ 27 sec
   - Ⓓ 46 sec

Thursday

4. Which type of graph would be **MOST** effective for displaying the relative amounts of a family's budget that go towards various expenses? *(Lesson 1-9) (III.1.3)* **B**
   - Ⓐ line graph
   - Ⓑ circle graph
   - Ⓒ bar graph
   - Ⓓ scatter plot

Friday

5. What are **ALL** the properties used to rewrite $18(5 + 23)$ as $5(18) + 23(18)$? *(Lessons 1-5, 1-6)* *(IV.1.3, V.1.3)* **D**
   - Ⓐ Distributive Property
   - Ⓑ Associative Property of Multiplication
   - Ⓒ Distributive Property and Commutative Property of Addition
   - Ⓓ Distributive Property and Commutative Property of Multiplication

Michigan Algebra 1   MI7

Content Standards Practice

This set also addresses the following Michigan Grade Level Content Expectations

Question 1	D.AN.08.01
	D.RE.07.01
Question 2	N.FL.07.07
Question 3	N.FL.08.06
Question 4	D.RE.07.01
Question 5	A.PA.07.11

1A. mean = 73, median = 72, mode = 65

1B. Sample answer: The mode is the easiest to find because you just have to look for the number that appears the most often on the list. The median is also pretty easy because the numbers are arranged in increasing order on the stem-and-leaf plot, and I just have to count to find the middle score, which is the 13th score from the top or bottom. The mean is most difficult because you have to add up all 25 scores and divide by 25.

1C. Sample answer: The mean and median, which are almost the same for these data, both give good measures of the "average" performance of the students. The mode is not useful. It is not important that three students happened to get the same score, 65. This tells nothing about how the class did as a whole.

Content
Standards
Practice

Content
Standards Practice

Set 2

Monday

1. If the radius of a circle is known, its circumference can be found by using the formula $C = 2\pi r$, and its area can be found by using the formula $A = \pi r^2$. *(Lesson 3-8) (II.3.2, II.3.4, V.2.1)* **A–B. See margin.**
   A. Solve both of these formulas for r. Show your work.
   B. Melissa wants to increase the size of a circular flower garden in her backyard. How should she change the radius of the garden in order to double its circumference? How should she change the radius if she wants to double its area? Show your work.

This set also addresses the following Michigan Grade Level Content Expectations

Question 1   A.PA.08.03
             G.SR.08.03

Question 2   N.MR.07.06

Question 3   N.MR.08.08

Question 5   N.ME.08.04

1A. Circumference:
$r = \dfrac{C}{2\pi}$; Area: $r = \sqrt{\dfrac{A}{\pi}}$
1B. Sample answer:
To double the circumference, she should double the radius. To double the area, she should multiply the radius by $\sqrt{2}$, which is about 1.4.

Tuesday

2. Which of the following does **NOT** describe the number $-\sqrt{49}$? *(Lesson 2-7) (IV.1.1)* **B**
   (A) real number
   (B) whole number
   (C) integer
   (D) rational

Wednesday

3. A coat is on sale for 30% off the original price. If the original price was $72, what is the sale price? *(Lesson 3-7) (Prerequisite Skill)* **A**
   (A) $50.40
   (B) $48.00
   (C) $42.00
   (D) $21.60

Thursday

4. Look at the graph of Mrs. Meyer's trip to the mall and back by car. What most likely was happening between 3:00 P.M. and 5:00 P.M.? *(Lesson 1-8) (II.2.1)* **C**

   Distance Traveled (vertical axis)
   Time of Day (P.M.) (horizontal axis) 1 2 3 4 5

   (A) Mrs. Meyer got tired and went home.
   (B) Mrs. Meyer was driving the speed limit.
   (C) Mrs. Meyer was at the mall shopping.
   (D) Mrs. Meyer was looking for a parking space.

Friday

5. What is the correct order of the following real numbers from least to greatest? *(Lesson 2-7) (IV.3.1)* **C**
   $$5.8, \sqrt{29}, \frac{32}{5}, 5.\overline{8}$$

   (A) $\frac{32}{5}, 5.\overline{8}, 5.8, \sqrt{29}$
   (B) $5.\overline{8}, \sqrt{29}, 5.8, \frac{32}{5}$
   (C) $\sqrt{29}, 5.8, 5.\overline{8}, \frac{32}{5}$
   (D) $5.8, 5.\overline{8}, \frac{32}{5}, \sqrt{29}$

Set 3

Monday

1. The tables show several selected ordered pairs that belong to two relations, S and T. *(Lessons 4-3, 4-6) (I.2.2, I.2.3, V.2.2)*
   A. Assume that each relation is made up of an infinite number of ordered pairs and that there is a rule for each relation that describes the connection between the x values and the y values. Write a rule in the form "$y =$" for each relation.
   B. Sketch the graph of each relation.
   C. Are relations S and T functions? Explain how you can tell from the two tables and how you can tell from the two graphs. **A–C. See margin.**

Relation S	
x	y
-2	7
-1	4
0	3
1	4
2	7

Relation T	
x	y
0	0
4	2
9	3
4	-2
9	-3

Tuesday

2. Under which transformation is Triangle I the image of Triangle II? *(Lesson 4-2) (II.1.5)* **C**

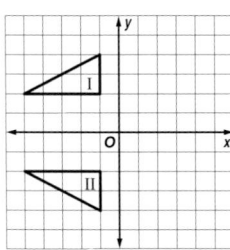

   (A) translation upward 4 units
   (B) rotation 90° about the origin
   (C) reflection over the x-axis
   (D) reflection over the y-axis

Wednesday

3. Which of these equations is linear? *(Lesson 4-5) (I.2.5)* **A**
   I. $3x - 7y = 2x + 8$
   II. $2x - 8 = y^2$
   (A) I only
   (B) II only
   (C) Both are linear.
   (D) Neither are linear.

Thursday

4. For the data table, what is the rule when $x = n$? *(Lesson 4-8) (I.1.1, I.1.2)* **D**

x	1	2	3	4
y	-1	3	7	11

   (A) $5n + 4$
   (B) $5n - 4$
   (C) $4n + 5$
   (D) $4n - 5$

Friday

5. According to the U.S. Census, the population of Michigan was 9,295,287 in 1990 and 9,938,444 in 2000. What is the approximate annual rate of change in the population of Michigan over this 10-year period? *(Lesson 5-1) (I.2.1, IV.3.2)* **B**
   (A) 59,500 per year
   (B) 64,300 per year
   (C) 70,000 per year
   (D) 99,700 per year

This set also addresses the following Michigan Grade Level Content Expectations

Question 1   A.RP.08.01
             A.RP.08.04
             A.RP.07.02

Question 2   G.TR.08.10

Question 3   A.PA.07.01

Question 5   A.PA.07.06

1A. Relation S:
$y = x^2 + 3$; relation T:
$y = \pm\sqrt{x}$

1B. Relation S

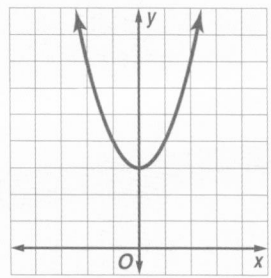

Relation T

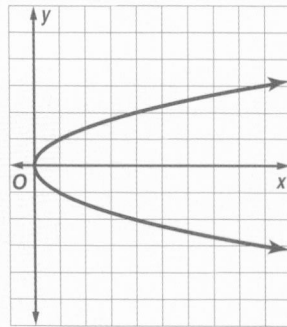

1C. Relation S is a function, but relation T is not. The tables show that S is a function because it has no repeated x values, while T is not a function because it contains repeated x values. For example, the x value of 4 is paired with two different y values, 2 and -2. From the graphs, I can see that S is a function because no vertical line intersects the graph more than once, while T is not a function because there are many vertical lines that I can draw that will intersect the graph in two different points.

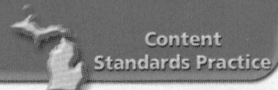

Set 4

Monday

1. Liam is a furniture salesman. He is paid a base salary of $400 a week, plus a commission of 5% on all of his sales. *(Lessons 4-6, 6-3) (I.2.4, 1.2.6, V.2.3, V.2.4)*
   A. Let s = the value of Liam's weekly sales and E = Liam's weekly earnings. Using function notation, write an equation that describes the relationship between these two variables as a function. $E(s) = 400 + 0.05s$
   B. Liam wants to make an average of at least $850 a week. What is the average total value of the furniture he must sell each week in order to make his goal? Write an inequality, show all your work to solve it, and answer the question with a complete sentence. **See margin.**

This set also addresses the following Michigan Grade Level Content Expectations

Question 1   A.FO.08.12

Question 2   A.PA.07.04
             N.FL.07.05

Question 4   A.FO.08.12

Question 5   A.PA.07.01

1B.

$400 + 0.05s \geq 850$

$s \geq 9000$

Liam must sell an average of $9000 worth of furniture per week to make his goal.

Tuesday

2. Ava's pay varies directly with the number of hours she works. If she earns $126 for 21 hours of work, how much will she earn if she works 49 hours? *(Lesson 5-2) (I.2.6)* **A**
   Ⓐ $294
   Ⓑ $252
   Ⓒ $245
   Ⓓ $45

Wednesday

3. Kenny is in a bowling league. Over the past month his bowling scores have ranged from 126 to 133. If x represents his bowling scores, which inequality represents all of Kenny's possible scores over the past month? *(Lesson 6-5) (V.2.2)* **C**
   Ⓐ $x \leq 133$
   Ⓑ $|x - 129| \leq 4$
   Ⓒ $|x - 129.5| \leq 3.5$
   Ⓓ $|x - 129.5| \geq 3.5$

Thursday

4. Three times a number is less than or equal to 10 more than four times twice the number. Which graph shows all possible values for this number? *(Lesson 6-3) (V.2.2, V.2.3)* **D**

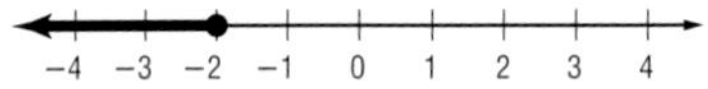

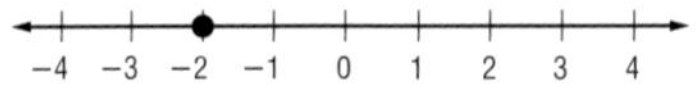

   Ⓐ number line from -4 to 4, closed dot at 2, arrow left
   Ⓑ number line from -4 to 4, closed dot at -2, arrow left
   Ⓒ number line from -4 to 4, closed dot at -2, arrow right
   Ⓓ number line from -4 to 4, closed dot at -2, arrow right

Friday

5. On a car trip to Muskegon, Tyron kept a record of his gas mileage. What is an equation that describes this relationship shown in the table? *(Lesson 4-8) (I.1.5)* **B**

Gasoline x (gallons)	1	2	3	4	5
Distance y (miles)	31	62	93	124	155

   Ⓐ $y = x + 31$
   Ⓑ $y = 31x$
   Ⓒ $x = y + 31$
   Ⓓ $x = 31y$

Monday

1. Study the pattern below. *(Lesson 4-6)* **(I.1.3, I.1.4)** A–C. See margin.

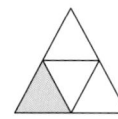 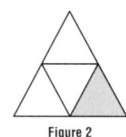 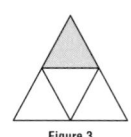 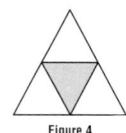 

Figure 1   Figure 2   Figure 3   Figure 4   Figure 5

   A. Draw the next three figures in the pattern. Describe how you planned how to draw each figure based on the previous figure.
   B. Write a rule that you can use to find any specific figure in the pattern if you know the figure number.
   C. Draw the 38th figure in the pattern. Explain how you applied your rule from Part B.

Tuesday	Wednesday

2. Which expression represents the volume of the rectangular prism? *(Lesson 8-1)*

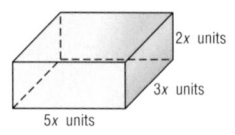

2x units
3x units
5x units

   Ⓐ $62x^2$ units³   *(II.3.2, V.1.4)* **B**
   Ⓑ $30x^3$ units³
   Ⓒ $15x^2$ units³
   Ⓓ $10x$ units³

3. On a day in August, the Detroit Tigers were in fifth place in the American League Central Division. At this point in the season, the team had played a total of 106 games, of which exactly half were played at home in Comerica Park. Of these home games, the Tigers won one more game than they lost. How many home games had the Tigers won by this day in August? *(Lessons 7-2, 7-3)* **(V.2.3) B**
   Ⓐ 53
   Ⓑ 27
   Ⓒ 26
   Ⓓ 23

Thursday	Friday

4. The thickness of a single red blood cell is 2.4×10^{-6} meters. What is the thickness of 12,000 red blood cells stacked on top of each other, if they could be placed so that there is no space between them? *(Lesson 8-3)*
   Ⓐ 2.88 m   *(II.3.2, II.3.6, V.1.4)* **B**
   Ⓑ 2.88 cm
   Ⓒ 2.4 cm
   Ⓓ 2.88×10^{-24} m

5. What is the greatest common factor of $45a^3b$ and $60ab^2$? *(Lesson 9-1)* **(IV.3.3) C**
   Ⓐ $3ab$
   Ⓑ $5ab$
   Ⓒ $15ab$
   Ⓓ $180a^3b^2$

This set also addresses the following Michigan Grade Level Content Expectations

Question 2	A.FO.07.12
Question 3	A.FO.08.13
Question 4	N.ME.08.02

1A.

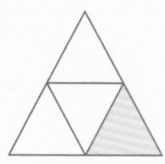
Figure 6

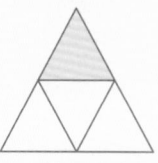
Figure 7

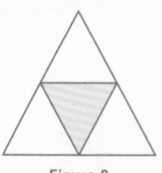
Figure 8

Sample answer: I continued the pattern of shading first the lower left triangle, then the lower right triangle, then the upper triangle, and then the center triangle.

1B. Sample answer: To figure out which of the smaller triangles to shade, divide the figure number by 4 and look at the remainder. If the remainder is 1, shade the lower left triangle. If it is 2, shade the lower right triangle. If it is 3, shade the upper triangle. If it is 0, shade the center triangle.

1C. Sample answer: When I divided 38 by 4, I got 9 with a remainder of 2, so I knew that I needed to shade the lower right triangle.

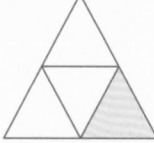
Figure 38

Set 6

Monday

1. A furniture store sells office chairs in two models. The Model A chair sells for $50 and the Model B chair sells for $65. *(Lessons 7-2, 7-4) (V.2.2, V.2.3)* **A–B. See margin.**
   A. In one week, the store sold a total of 40 office chairs for a total of $2120. How many chairs of each model were sold? Show your work and answer the question with a complete sentence.
   B. The following week the store sold twice as many Model B chairs as the first week, but only half as many Model A chairs as the first week. Was the store's revenue from selling office chairs greater the first week or the second week? How much greater? Show your work and write a complete sentence to answer both questions.

Tuesday

2. Most companies have fixed costs, like electricity, and variable costs, like raw materials, that depend on the number of units produced. The graph shows the **TOTAL** cost C for two different companies to produce x skateboards.

   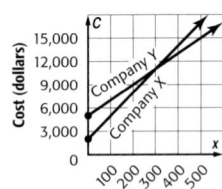

   Production Cost

   Which statement is **TRUE**? *(Lesson 7-1) (V.2.3)*
   Ⓐ Company Y has lower fixed costs.   **D**
   Ⓑ Both companies have the same variable cost.
   Ⓒ The total cost to produce a certain number of skateboards is always greater for Company X than for Company Y.
   Ⓓ Company X has a greater variable cost than Company Y.

Wednesday

3. The track and soccer field at a high school is enclosed by a fence. Which expression represents the total area contained by the fence, including the two semicircular ends? *(Lesson 8-4) (II.3.2, V.1.2)* **B**

   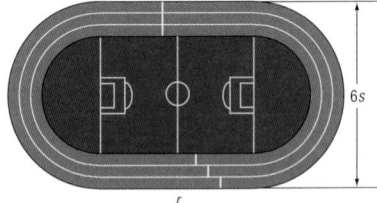

   Ⓐ $6\pi rs + 2$
   Ⓑ $6rs + 9\pi s^2$
   Ⓒ $8rs + 9\pi rs^2$
   Ⓓ $6rs + 9\pi s^2$

Thursday

4. Which binomial is a factor of $x^2 - 9x - 36$? *(Lesson 9-3) (IV.3.3)* **C**
   Ⓐ $x + 12$ Ⓑ $x - 3$
   Ⓒ $x + 3$ Ⓓ $x - 4$

Friday

5. The area of a circle is $(x^2 - 10x + 25)\pi$ square centimeters. What is the diameter of the circle? *(Lesson 9-6) (II.3.2, V.1.4)* **A**
   Ⓐ $(2x - 10)$ cm   Ⓑ $(2x + 10)$ cm
   Ⓒ $(x - 5)$ cm   Ⓓ $(x - 10)$ cm

This set also addresses the following Michigan Grade Level Content Expectations

Question 1	A.FO.08.10
	A.FO.08.13
	A.FO.07.13
Question 2	A.FO.08.13
Question 3	G.SR.08.03
	G.SR.08.04
Question 4	A.FO.08.08
Question 5	A.FO.08.08
	G.SR.08.03

1A. The store sold 32 Model A chairs and 8 Model B chairs.

1B. The revenue for the first week was $280 greater than the revenue from the second week.

Set 7

Monday

1. Mr. and Mrs. Cortez want to put a fence around a rectangular portion of their backyard for their dog. They have purchased 48 feet of fencing. The area will be directly behind the house, so no fencing is needed along the side of the house. *(Lesson 10-1)* **(I.2.4, I.2.6, V.2.3)**

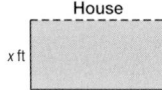

House

x ft

A. Let A be the area fenced in and x be the width. Write an equation in function form that gives the area as a function of its width. **$A(x) = x(48 - 2x)$**
B. Find the dimensions of the portion that Mr. and Mrs. Cortez should fence in for their dog to have the maximum possible area. Show your work. **24 ft by 12 ft**
C. What would be the maximum area of this space? Show your work. **288 ft²**

Tuesday	Wednesday

2. The graph represents the function $y = f(x)$.

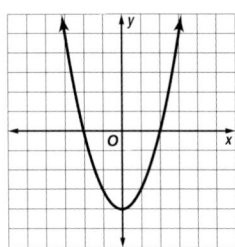

What appears to be **ALL** solutions of the equation $f(x) = 0$? *(Lesson 10-2)* **(V.2.2, V.2.3) D**
- Ⓐ -4
- Ⓑ 0
- Ⓒ $0, 2$
- Ⓓ $-2, 2$

3. The perimeter of each inscribed square is 70% of the perimeter of the next larger square. Approximately what is the perimeter of the smallest square? *(Lesson 10-7)* **(I.1.5) C**

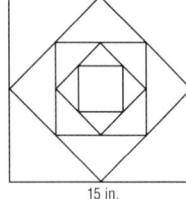

15 in.

- Ⓐ 8.9 in.
- Ⓑ 10.1 in.
- Ⓒ 14.4 in.
- Ⓓ 20.6 in.

Thursday	Friday

4. Cheng-Yu rented an apartment for $600 a month. Each year, when he renewed his lease, his landlord raised the rent by 5% and rounded to the nearest dollar. What is Pedro's monthly rent during the fifth year in his apartment? *(Lesson 10-7)* **(I.1.1) B**
- Ⓐ $720
- Ⓑ $730
- Ⓒ $750
- Ⓓ $766

5. What is the simplified form of $\frac{\sqrt{4}\sqrt{8}}{\sqrt{2}}$? *(Lesson 11-1)* **(IV.2.5) B**
- Ⓐ $2\sqrt{2}$
- Ⓑ 4
- Ⓒ $8\sqrt{2}$
- Ⓓ 16

This set also addresses the following Michigan Grade Level Content Expectations

Question 1   A.FO.08.09

Question 2   A.RP.08.05

Question 3   G.SR.08.04

Question 4   N.MR.08.08

Set 8

Monday

1. Triangle PQR has vertices $P(-3, -1)$, $Q(0, 5)$, and $R(6, 2)$. *(Lesson 11-5)* **(II.1.3)** A–B. See margin.
   A. Draw $\triangle PQR$ on a coordinate plane. Make a conjecture about $\triangle PQR$ that describes the triangle as specifically as possible.
   B. Using the coordinates of $\triangle PQR$, prove that your conjecture is correct. Identify by name all formulas that you use.

This set also addresses the following Michigan Grade Level Content Expectations

Question 1   G.LO.08.02

Question 2   N.MR.08.11
             A.PA.07.05
             A.PA.07.06

Question 5   N.MR.08.11

1A.

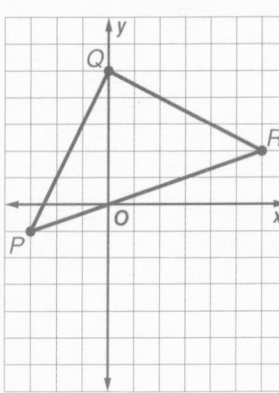

Conjecture: $\triangle PQR$ is an isosceles right triangle.

Tuesday

2. It took Mia exactly 4 hours to drive from Grand Rapids to Mackinaw City at an average speed of 55 miles per hour. On the return trip, there was road construction on part of the route, so her average speed was only 40 miles per hour. How long did it take Mia to drive back from Mackinaw City to Grand Rapids? *(Lesson 12-1)* **(I.2.6)** D
   - Ⓐ 2 hr 55 min
   - Ⓑ 4 hr 24 min
   - Ⓒ 5 hr
   - Ⓓ 5 hr 30 min

Wednesday

3. From a point on the ground 20 feet from the base of a tree, the angle of elevation to the top of the trunk is 60°.

60°
20 ft

Which is the height of the trunk to the nearest tenth of a foot? *(Lesson 11-7)* **(II.3.5)** C
   - Ⓐ 11.5 ft
   - Ⓑ 17.3 ft
   - Ⓒ 34.6 ft
   - Ⓓ 40.0 ft

Thursday

4. A flu epidemic in a town began slowly and then increased exponentially. After several weeks, the number of new flu cases increasingly declined. What graph **BEST** shows the relationship between time and the number of flu cases? *(Lesson 10-5)* **(I.2.5)** C

Ⓐ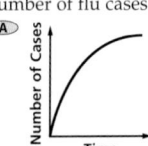

Ⓑ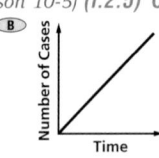

Ⓒ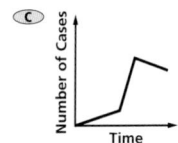

Ⓓ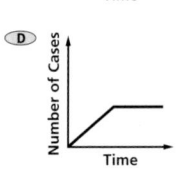

Friday

5. The density of a substance is its mass per unit volume. Which of the four substances listed in the table has the **GREATEST** density? *(Lesson 12-5)* **(II.3.5)** B

Substance	Mass (g)	Volume (cm³)
aluminum	27.0	10.0
gold	96.5	5.0
iron	117.0	15.0
lead	226.0	20.0

   - Ⓐ aluminum
   - Ⓑ gold
   - Ⓒ iron
   - Ⓓ lead

1B. Sample answer: Use the Distance Formula to find the length of each side of the triangle.

$$PQ = \sqrt{[0 - (-3)]^2 + [5 - (-1)]^2} = \sqrt{(3)^2 + 6^2} = \sqrt{9 + 36} = \sqrt{45}$$
$$QR = \sqrt{(0 - 6)^2 + (5 - 2)^2} = \sqrt{(-6)^2 + 3^2} = \sqrt{36 + 9} = \sqrt{45}$$
$$PR = \sqrt{[6 - (-3)]^2 + [2 - (-1)]^2} = \sqrt{9^2 + 3^2} = \sqrt{81 + 9} = \sqrt{90}$$

Because $PQ = PR$, $\triangle PQR$ is isosceles by the definition of an isosceles triangle. Because $(PQ)^2 + (QR)^2 = 45 + 45 = 90 = (PR)^2$, $\triangle PQR$ is a right triangle by the Pythagorean Theorem. Therefore, $\triangle PQR$ is an isosceles right triangle.

Set 9

Monday

1. A club has 20 members, of whom 12 are women and 8 are men. A committee of 4 club members needs to be selected to run a fund-raising event. *(Lesson 14-2) (VI.1.2, VI.2.1)* A–C. See margin.
   A. Does selecting the committee members involve a permutation or a combination? Explain your reasoning.
   B. How many different 4-member committees are possible? Show your work, including any formulas that you use.
   C. What is the probability that a randomly selected 4-member committee will include 2 women and 2 men? Show your work, including any formulas that you use.

Tuesday

2. Carmen is organizing a pizza sale to raise money for new band uniforms. She wants to estimate how many pizzas the band members are likely to sell. To do this, she plans to conduct a survey of selected students. Which method of selecting her survey sample would be least biased? *(Lesson 13-1) (III.1.1, III.1.4)* A
   Ⓐ Ask every 20th student who enters the school on a particular day.
   Ⓑ Ask every member of the band.
   Ⓒ Ask her friends.
   Ⓓ Ask every 10th student attending a school football game.

Wednesday

3. Nita is playing a board game in which each player must roll one die and toss one penny at the beginning of each turn. What is the probability that she will get an even number on the die and heads on the penny? *(Lesson 14-3) (VI.1.3)* B
   Ⓐ $\frac{1}{6}$
   Ⓑ $\frac{1}{4}$
   Ⓒ $\frac{1}{2}$
   Ⓓ 1

Thursday

4. For a set of standardized test scores, which of the following statements must **ALWAYS** be true? *(Lesson 13-4) (III.2.2)* D
   Ⓐ The lower quartile is less than or equal to the mean.
   Ⓑ The upper quartile is greater than or equal to the mode.
   Ⓒ The median is less than or equal to the mean.
   Ⓓ The lower quartile is less than or equal to the median.

Friday

5. In order to use a certain Web site, a user must choose a password made up of two letters followed by four numerals. Letters and numerals may be repeated. How many possible passwords are there for this Web site? *(Lesson 14-1) (Prerequisite Skill)* A
   Ⓐ 6,760,000
   Ⓑ 3,276,000
   Ⓒ 10,676
   Ⓓ 92

Michigan Algebra 1 MI 15

This set also addresses the following Michigan Grade Level Content Expectations

Question 2   D.AN.08.02
Question 3   D.PR.08.06
Question 4   D.AN.07.04
Question 5   D.PR.08.04

1A. Combination; Sample answer: The selection is a combination because the order in which the committee members are selected does not matter.

1B. 4845 different committees are possible.

1C. $\frac{1848}{4845}$ or $\frac{616}{1615}$

Content
Standards
Practice

Content
Standards Practice

Set 10

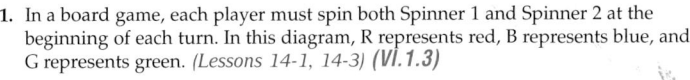

**This set also addresses
the following Michigan
Grade Level Content
Expectations**

Question 1   D.PR.08.04

Question 2   D.PR.08.06

Question 4   D.RE.07.01

Monday

1. In a board game, each player must spin both Spinner 1 and Spinner 2 at the beginning of each turn. In this diagram, R represents red, B represents blue, and G represents green. *(Lessons 14-1, 14-3)* **(VI.1.3)**

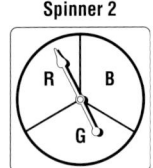

Spinner 1   Spinner 2

   A. Make a tree diagram to show all possible results from spinning the first spinner and then the second. What are the probabilities of each result? **See margin.**
   B. What is the probability that **AT LEAST** one of the spinners will land on red? Show your work. $\frac{2}{3}$

Tuesday

2. A bag contains 3 red marbles, 4 blue marbles, and 5 yellow marbles. If one marble is drawn from the bag and not replaced, and then a second marble is drawn, what is the probability that both marbles will be blue? *(Lesson 14-3)* **(VI.1.3) C**

   Ⓐ $\frac{20}{33}$ Ⓑ $\frac{1}{9}$

   Ⓒ $\frac{1}{11}$ Ⓓ $\frac{2}{33}$

Wednesday

3. Based on the 2000 Census, Michigan now has 15 congressional districts, each with approximately the same population. If two Michigan residents are chosen at random, what is the probability that they will live in the same district? *(Lesson 14-3)* **(VI.1.2, VI.1.3) D**

   Ⓐ $\frac{14}{15}$ Ⓑ $\frac{1}{15}$

   Ⓒ $\frac{1}{210}$ Ⓓ $\frac{1}{225}$

Thursday

4. The box-and-whisker plot shows the ages in years of the first 9 people to ride the Tilt-a-Whirl on opening day at the Michigan State Fair. What is the range? *(Lesson 13-5)* **(III.2.1, III.2.3) A**

   14 16 18 20 22 24 26 28 30 32 34

   Ⓐ 18
   Ⓑ 16
   Ⓒ 10
   Ⓓ 8

Friday

5. The chart shows the possible sums when the two dice are rolled. What is the probability that a sum is greater than 8? *(Lesson 14-5)* **(VI.1.1) C**

+	1	2	3	4	5	6
1	2	3	4	5	6	7
2	3	4	5	6	7	8
3	4	5	6	7	8	9
4	5	6	7	8	9	10
5	6	7	8	9	10	11
6	7	8	9	10	11	12

   Ⓐ $\frac{5}{36}$ Ⓑ $\frac{2}{9}$

   Ⓒ $\frac{5}{18}$ Ⓓ $\frac{5}{12}$

1A.

Spinner 1	Spinner 2	Result	Probability
R	R	RR	$\frac{1}{6}$
	B	RB	$\frac{1}{6}$
	G	RG	$\frac{1}{6}$
B	R	BR	$\frac{1}{12}$
	B	BB	$\frac{1}{12}$
	G	BG	$\frac{1}{12}$
G	R	GR	$\frac{1}{12}$
	B	GB	$\frac{1}{12}$
	G	GG	$\frac{1}{12}$

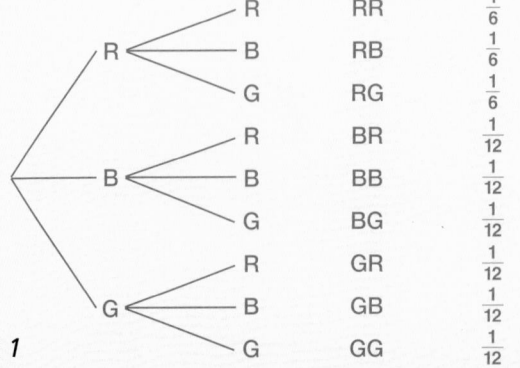

Contents in Brief

Authors

Berchie Holliday, Ed.D.
Former Mathematics
    Teacher
Northwest Local School
    District
Cincinnati, OH

Gilbert J. Cuevas, Ph.D.
Professor of Mathematics
    Education
University of Miami
Miami, FL

Beatrice Moore-Harris
Educational Specialist
Bureau of Education
    and Research
League City, TX

John A. Carter, Ph.D.
Director of Mathematics
Adlai E. Stevenson High
    School
Lincolnshire, IL

Consulting Author

Carol Malloy, Ph.D
Associate Professor, Curriculum Instruction,
    Secondary Mathematics
The University of North Carolina at Chapel Hill
Chapel Hill, NC

Authors

Daniel Marks, Ed.D.
Associate Professor of
   Mathematics
Auburn University at
   Montgomery
Montgomery, AL

Ruth M. Casey
Mathematics Teacher
   Department Chair
Anderson County High
   School
Lawrenceburg, KY

Roger Day, Ph.D.
Associate Professor of
   Mathematics
Illinois State University
Normal, IL

Linda M. Hayek
Mathematics Teacher
Ralston Public Schools
Omaha, NE

Contributing Authors

USA TODAY
The USA TODAY Snapshots®, created by
USA TODAY®, help students make the connection
between real life and mathematics.

Dinah Zike
Educational Consultant
Dinah-Might Activities, Inc.
San Antonio, TX

Content Consultants

Each of the Content Consultants reviewed every chapter and gave suggestions for improving the effectiveness of the mathematics instruction.

Mathematics Consultants

Gunnar E. Carlsson, Ph.D.
Consulting Author
Professor of Mathematics
Stanford University
Stanford, CA

Ralph L. Cohen, Ph.D.
Consulting Author
Professor of Mathematics
Stanford University
Stanford, CA

Alan G. Foster
Former Mathematics Teacher & Department Chairperson
Addison Trail High School
Addison, IL

Les Winters
Instructor
California State University, Northridge
Northridge, CA

William Collins
Director, The Sisyphus Math Learning Center
East Side Union High School District
San Jose, CA

Dora Swart
Mathematics Teacher
W.F. West High School
Chehalis, WA

David S. Daniels
Former Mathematics Chair
Longmeadow High School
Longmeadow, MA

Mary C. Enderson, Ph.D.
Associate Professor of Mathematics
Middle Tennessee State University
Murfreesboro, TN

Gerald A. Haber
Consultant, Mathematics Standards and Professional Development
New York, NY

Angiline Powell Mikle
Assistant Professor Mathematics Education
Texas Christian University
Fort Worth, TX

C. Vincent Pané, Ed.D.
Associate Professor of Education/ Coordinator of Secondary & Special Subjects Education
Molloy College
Rockville Centre, NY

Reading Consultant

Lynn T. Havens
Director
Project CRISS
Kalispell, MT

ELL Consultant

Idania Dorta
Mathematics Educational Specialist
Miami-Dade County Public Schools
Miami, FL

Teacher Reviewers

Each Teacher Reviewer reviewed at least two chapters of the Student Edition, giving feedback and suggestions for improving the effectiveness of the mathematics instruction.

Susan J. Barr
Department Chair/Teacher
Dublin Coffman High School
Dublin, OH

Diana L. Boyle
Mathematics Teacher, 6–8
Judson Middle School
Salem, OR

Judy Buchholtz
Math Department Chair/Teacher
Dublin Scioto High School
Dublin, OH

Holly A. Budzinski
Mathematics Department Chairperson
Green Hope High School
Morrisville, NC

Rusty Campbell
Mathematics Instructor/Chairperson
North Marion High School
Farmington, WV

Nancy M. Chilton
Mathematics Teacher
Louis Pizitz Middle School
Birmingham, AL

Teacher Reviewers

Lisa Cook
Mathematics Teacher
Kaysville Junior High School
Kaysville, UT

Bonnie Daigh
Mathematics Teacher
Eudora High School
Eudora, KS

Carol Seay Ferguson
Mathematics Teacher
Forestview High School
Gastonia, NC

Carrie Ferguson
Teacher
West Monroe High School
West Monroe, LA

Melissa R. Fetzer
Teacher/Math Chairperson
Hollidaysburg Area Junior High
  School
Hollidaysburg, PA

Diana Flick
Mathematics Teacher
Harrisonburg High School
Harrisonburg, VA

Kathryn Foland
Teacher/Subject Area Leader
Ben Hill Middle School
Tampa, FL

Celia Foster
Assistant Principal Mathematics
Grover Cleveland High School
Ridgewood, NY

Patricia R. Franzer
Secondary Math Instructor
Celina City Schools
Celina, OH

Candace Frewin
Teacher on Special Assignment
Pinellas County Schools
Largo, FL

Larry T. Gathers
Mathematics Teacher
Springfield South High School
Springfield, OH

Maureen M. Grant
Mathematics Teacher/Department
  Chair
North Central High School
Indianapolis, IN

Marie Green
Mathematics Teacher
Anthony Middle School
Manhattan, KS

Vicky S. Hamen
High School Math Teacher
Celina High School
Celina, OH

Kimberly A. Hepler
Mathematics Teacher
S. Gordon Stewart Middle School
Fort Defiance, VA

Deborah L. Hewitt
Mathematics Teacher
Chester High School
Chester, NY

Marilyn S. Hughes
Mathematics Department
  Chairperson
Belleville West High School
Belleville, IL

Larry Hummel
Mathematics Department
  Chairperson
Central City High School
Central City, NE

William Leschensky
Former Mathematics Teacher
Glenbard South High School
College of DuPage
Glen Ellyn, IL

Sharon Linamen
Mathematics Teacher
Lake Brantley High School
Altamonte Springs, FL

Patricia Lund
Mathematics Teacher
Divide County High School
Crosby, ND

Marilyn Martau
Mathematics Teacher (Retired)
Lakewood High School
Lakewood, OH

Kathy Massengill
Mathematics Teacher
Midlothian High School
Midlothian, VA

Marie Mastandrea
District Mathematics Coordinator
Amity Regional School District #5
Woodbridge, CT

Laurie Newton
Teacher
Crossler Middle School
Salem, OR

James Leo Oliver
Teacher of the Emotionally Impaired
Lakeview Junior High School
Battle Creek, MI

Shannon Collins Pan
Department of Mathematics
Waverly High School
Waverly, NY

Cindy Plunkett
Math Educator
E.M. Pease Middle School
San Antonio, TX

Ann C. Raymond
Teacher
Oak Ave. Intermediate School
Temple City, CA

Sandy Schoff
Math Curriculum Coordinator K–12
Anchorage School District
Anchorage, AK

Susan E. Sladowski
Assistant Principal–Mathematics
Bayside High School
Bayside, NY

Paul E. Smith
Teacher/Consultant
Plaza Park Middle School
Evansville, IN

Dr. James Henry Snider
Teacher–Math Dept. Chair/Curriculum
  & Technology Coordinator
Nashville School of the Arts
Nashville, TN

Diane Stilwell
Mathematics Teacher/Technology
  Coordinator
South Middle School
Morgantown, WV

Richard P. Strausz
Math and Technology Coordinator
Farmington Schools
Farmington, MI

Patricia Taepke
Mathematics Teacher and BTSA
  Trainer
South Hills High School
West Covina, CA

C. Arthur Torell
Mathematics Teacher and Supervisor
Summit High School
Summit, NJ

Lou Jane Tynan
Mathematics Department Chair
Sacred Heart Model School
Louisville, KY

Julia Dobbins Warren
Mathematics Teacher
Mountain Brook Junior High School
Birmingham, AL

Jo Amy Wynn
Mathematics Teacher
Captain Shreve High School
Shreveport, LA

Rosalyn Zeid
Mathematics Supervisor
Union Township School District
Union, NJ

Teacher Advisory Board

Glencoe/McGraw-Hill wishes to thank the following teachers for their feedback on Glencoe *Algebra*. They were instrumental in providing valuable input toward the development of this program.

Field Test Schools

Glencoe/McGraw-Hill wishes to thank the following schools that field-tested pre-publication manuscript during the 2001–2002 school year. They were instrumental in providing feedback and verifying the effectiveness of this program.

Teacher Handbook

Table of Contents

Designed to be in more

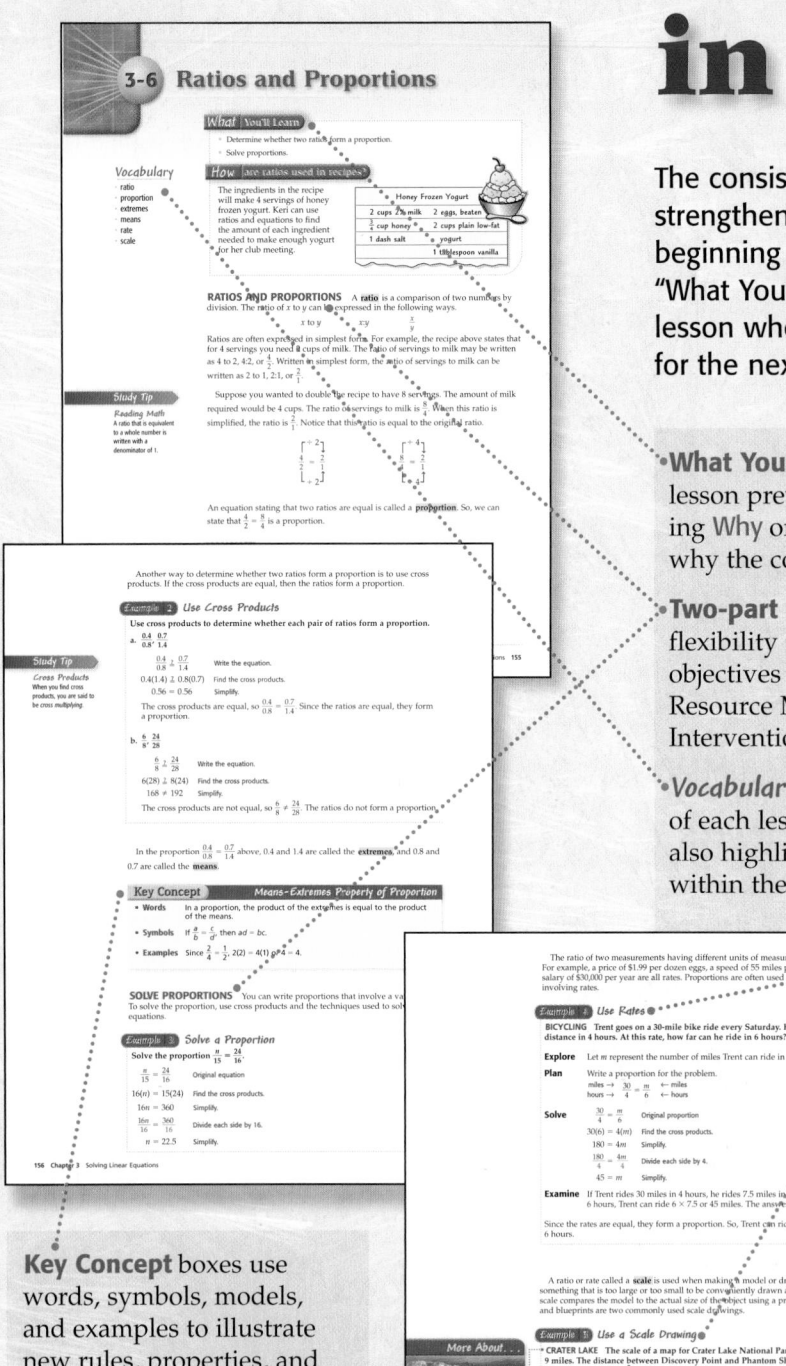

The consistent instructional design of the lessons strengthens student learning–from the very beginning of each lesson where students see "What You'll Learn," to the very end of each lesson where they have a chance to prepare for the next lesson.

• **What You'll Learn** at the beginning of each lesson previews the topics to come, and engaging Why or How questions help students see why the concepts are relevant.

• **Two-part lesson structure** gives you the flexibility to teach the two related lesson objectives together or separately. The Chapter Resource Masters contain a Study Guide and Intervention Master for each objective.

• **Vocabulary** terms are listed at the beginning of each lesson for easy reference, and they're also highlighted in yellow as they appear within the lesson.

Completely worked-out examples with clear explanations are paralleled by the Guided Practice and Practice and Apply exercises that follow. Examples often include strategies for problem-solving and mastering standardized test questions.

Key Concept boxes use words, symbols, models, and examples to illustrate new rules, properties, and definitions, so students can build their reading skills as they build their math skills. **Concept Summary** boxes provide a concise overview of key topics.

effective,
ways than one.

Check for Understanding

You can use this portion of exercises in class to ensure that all students understand the concepts.

- *Concept Check* exercises give students opportunities to define, describe, and explain the mathematical concepts they've just learned.

- *Guided Practice* presents a representative sample of the exercises in the Practice and Apply section. A key is provided in the **Teacher Wraparound Edition** that correlates the exercises with appropriate examples.

- *Application* problems give students the opportunity to use the skills they have learned in a real-world setting.

Practice and Apply

- **Skill Exercises** correspond to the Guided Practice exercises and are structured so that students practice the same concepts whether they are assigned odd- or even-numbered problems. Homework Help is provided so students can refer to examples in the lesson as they complete the exercises.

- **Applications** give students frequent opportunities to apply concepts to both real-life and mathematical situations.

- **CRITICAL THINKING** exercises in each lesson require students to explain, make conjectures, and prove mathematical relationships.

- *Standardized Test Practice* Ⓐ Ⓑ Ⓒ Ⓓ questions provide students with ongoing opportunities to sharpen their test-taking skills.

Maintain Your Skills

- *Mixed Review* includes spiraled, cumulative exercises from the two previous lessons as well as earlier lessons.

- *Getting Ready for the Next Lesson* exercises give students the chance to preview prerequisite skills for the coming lesson. A reference is provided should students need additional help.

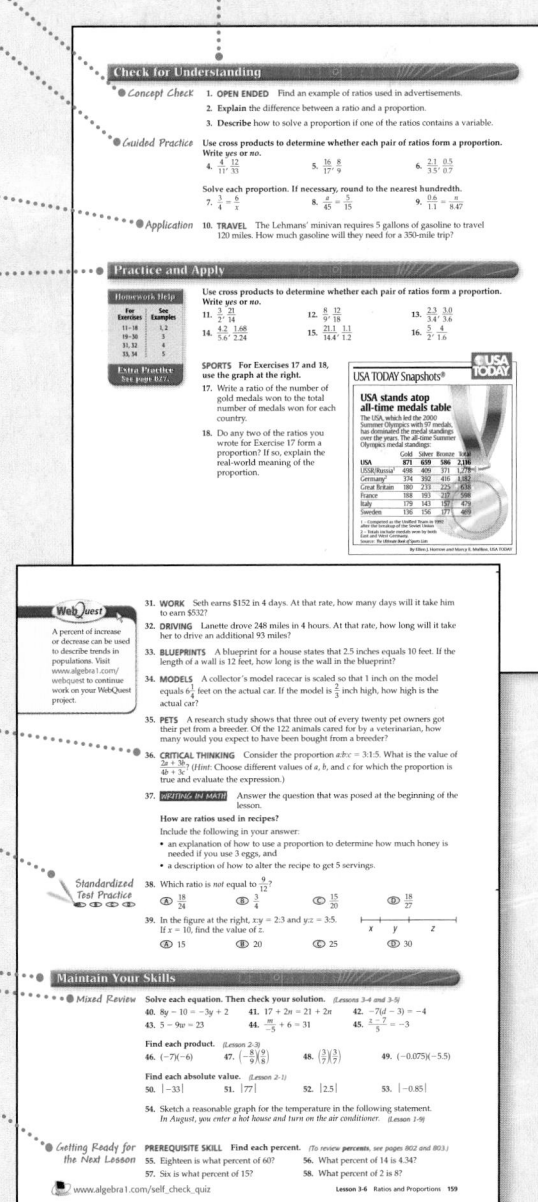

Accomplish more

Glencoe Algebra 1 provides so many resources for lesson planning and teaching that you can create a complete, customized course in Algebra 1 quickly...and easily.

This is where you start.

The **Teacher Wraparound Edition** is your key to all of the teaching resources in *Glencoe Algebra 1*. In addition to teaching suggestions, additional examples, and answers, the Teacher Wraparound Edition provides a guide for all of the print and software materials available for each lesson.

FAST FILE Chapter Resource Masters contain all of the core supplements you'll need to begin teaching a chapter of *Glencoe Algebra 1*. Each chapter booklet features convenient tabs for easy filing.

FAST FILE

- **Vocabulary Builder** helps students locate and define key vocabulary words from the chapter.
- **Study Guide and Intervention** for each objective summarizes key concepts and provides practice.
- **Skills Practice** provides ample exercises to help students develop basic computational skills, lesson by lesson.
- **Practice** mimics the computational and verbal problems in each lesson at an average level.
- **Reading to Learn Mathematics** provides students with various reading strategies to master the mathematics presented in each lesson.
- **Enrichment** activities extend students' knowledge and widen their appreciation of how mathematics relates to the world around them.
- **Assessment** options for each chapter include six forms of chapter tests, assessment tasks, quizzes, mid-chapter test, cumulative review, and standardized test practice.

Reading and Writing

WebQuest and Project Resources include teacher notes and answers for the Internet WebQuest projects, as well as other long-term projects that can be used with *Glencoe Algebra 1*.

Reading and Writing in the Mathematics Classroom features suggestions and activities for including reading as an integral part of the mathematics curriculum, as well as differentiated approaches to teaching mathematics that promote English learning and inclusion.

Teaching Mathematics with Foldables™ offers guidelines for using Foldables interactive study organizers in your class. The booklet was written by Foldables creator Dinah Zike.

More information on options for reading and writing in Glencoe Algebra 1 is available on pages T6-T7.

Applications

Science and Mathematics Lab Manual includes lab activity masters and teaching suggestions for integrating science into the mathematics classroom.

School-to-Career Masters feature activities that show how mathematics relates to various careers.

Graphing Calculator and Spreadsheet Masters include activities to incorporate the TI-83 Plus calculator and spreadsheets into your Algebra 1 course.

Real-World Transparencies and Masters feature colorful transparencies with accompanying student worksheets to show how mathematics relates to real-world topics.

than you'd ever imagine
in less time than you'd ever believe

Assessment and Intervention

5-Minute Check Transparencies with Standardized Test Practice include a transparency for each lesson that evaluates what students have learned in the previous lesson. Each transparency also includes a standardized test practice question.

Closing the Gap for Absent Students provides an easy-to-use summary of all the materials you have covered in the chapter in a format that can be posted or distributed to students who have missed class.

DAILY INTERVENTION Guide to Daily Intervention offers suggestions for daily assessment and tips on how to help students succeed.

Prerequisite Skills Workbook: Remediation and Intervention includes worksheets to review the arithmetic skills needed in Algebra 1.

Staff Development

Answer Key Transparencies provide answers to Student Edition exercises.

Lesson Planning Guide features a daily resource guide for planning your curriculum, as well as pacing for block scheduling.

Solutions Manual includes completely worked-out solutions for all exercises in the Student Edition.

Using the Internet in the Mathematics Classroom provides guidelines for using the Internet, as well as a guide to additional mathematics resources available on the Internet.

Teaching Algebra with Manipulatives features activities and teaching suggestions to help you present algebraic concepts with manipulatives and hands-on materials.

Technology Support for Teachers

Glencoe offers many timesaving software products to help you develop creative classroom presentations...fast.

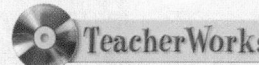 **TeacherWorks All-in-One Lesson Planner and Resource Center** CD-ROM includes a lesson planner and interactive Teacher Edition, so you can customize lesson plans and reproduce classroom resources quickly and easily, from just about anywhere.

Answer Key Maker software allows you to customize answer keys for your assignments from the Student Edition exercises.

Interactive Chalkboard CD-ROM includes fully worked-out examples, the 5-Minute Check Transparencies, and Your Turn problems in a customizable Microsoft® PowerPoint® format.

And more... Additional technology products and Internet resources for students, teachers, and parents are discussed on pages T6-T13 and T17.

HELP your students become fluent

Glencoe Algebra 1 makes it easy for you to incorporate constructive reading and writing strategies into every class you teach.

Reading Mathematics

Translating from English to Algebra

You learned in Lesson 1-1 that it is often necessary to translate words into algebraic expressions. Generally, there are "clue" words such as *more than, times, less than,* and so on, which indicate the operation to use. These words also help to connect numerical data. The table shows a few examples.

Words	Algebraic Expression
four times *x* plus *y*	$4x + y$
four times the sum of *x* and *y*	$4(x + y)$
four times the quantity *x* plus *y*	$4(x + y)$

Notice that all three expressions are worded differently, but the first expression is the only one that is different algebraically. In the second expression, parentheses indicate that the *sum, x + y,* is multiplied by four. In algebraic expressions, terms grouped by parentheses are treated as one quantity. So, $4(x + y)$ can also be read as *four times the quantity x plus y.*

Words that may indicate parentheses are *sum, difference, product,* and *quantity.*

Reading to Learn

Read each verbal expression aloud. Then match it with the correct algebraic expression.

1. nine divided by 2 plus *n*
2. four divided by the difference of *n* and six
3. *n* plus five squared
4. three times the quantity eight plus *n*
5. nine divided by the quantity 2 plus *n*
6. three times eight plus *n*
7. the quantity *n* plus five squared
8. four divided by *n* minus six

a. $(n + 5)^2$
b. $4 \div (n - 6)$
c. $9 \div 2 + n$
d. $3(8) + n$
e. $4 \div n - 6$
f. $n + 5^2$
g. $9 \div (2 + n)$
h. $3(8 + n)$

Write each algebraic expression in words.

9. $5x + 1$
10. $5(x + 1)$
11. $3 + 7x$
12. $(3 + x) \cdot 7$
13. $(6 + b) \div y$
14. $6 + (b \div y)$

10 Chapter 1 The Language of Algebra

Reading Mathematics activities help students master new mathematics vocabulary words and develop technical reading skills so they can understand and apply the language of math in their daily lives.

Student Edition

Foldables™ Study Organizers at the beginning of each chapter provide students with tools for organizing what they are reading and studying.

Reading Math Study Tips appear throughout each chapter, to help students learn and use the language of algebra.

Writing in Math questions in every lesson require students to use critical thinking skills to develop their answers.

Vocabulary terms are listed at the beginning of each lesson and highlighted when defined. The **Vocabulary and Concept Check** in each Study Guide and Review checks students' understanding of the key concepts of the chapter.

Key Concepts are illustrated using Words, Symbols, Models, and Examples, as appropriate. This approach improves reading comprehension by using multiple representations.

WebQuest Internet Projects are long-term projects that use problem-based learning to give students the opportunity to develop their research and creative writing skills.

in the Language of MATHEMATICS

Teacher Wraparound Edition

Study Notebook suggestions provide motivational ideas to help students create study notebooks that are thorough and effective.

Concept Check questions require students to describe, write, and explain the mathematical concepts they have learned in each lesson.

Modeling, Speaking, and **Writing** in every lesson require students to summarize what they have learned by responding to open-ended prompts.

ELL Resources highlight features and activities that help English-Language Learners grasp content.

Differentiated Instruction features help students at all points on the learning spectrum develop their reading, writing, and comprehension skills.

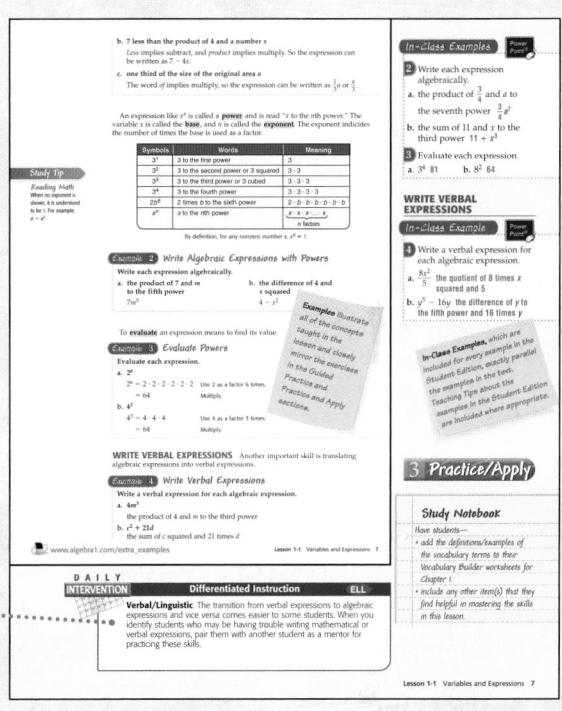

Technology Support

StudentWorks™ Glencoe's backpack solution, includes the entire Student Edition, formatted like the hardbound book, so students can study from just about anywhere—no book required. Students can also print their own lesson worksheet pages and get instant access to interactive web resources.

www.algebra1.com/vocabulary_review is a Glencoe site that provides online study tools for reviewing the vocabulary of each chapter.

Vocabulary PuzzleMaker software creates crossword, jumble, and word search puzzles using vocabulary lists that you can customize.

Multimedia Applications: Virtual Activities CD-ROM provides in-depth interactive activities that help students explore the main concepts of each chapter in a real-world setting.

Additional Resources

Chapter Resource Masters
- Vocabulary Builder
- Reading to Learn Mathematics

Teaching Mathematics with Foldables™

Reading and Writing in the Mathematics Classroom

WebQuest and Project Resources

For more information on these products, see pp. T4-T5.

Quick Review Math Handbook: Hot Words, Hot Topics is Glencoe's mathematical handbook for students. The Hot Words section includes a glossary of terms while the Hot Topics section consists of an explanation of key mathematical concepts. An exercise set is also included.

With these TOOLS,
you'll always know

Whether you need daily intervention resources integrated right into the program, or supplemental materials for after school and summer school programs, *Glencoe Algebra 1* puts it all right at your fingertips!

Diagnosis

Glencoe's **Diagnostic and Placement Tests** help you identify the key mathematical objectives that students are struggling with so you can make course placement decisions more effectively. A list of intervention resources is provided for each Glencoe program prior to and including *Glencoe Algebra 1*.

Prerequisite Skills

Students often struggle in algebra because they have not mastered the prerequisite skills needed to be successful. *Glencoe Algebra 1* provides several opportunities to check student skills and determine which students need additional review and practice.

- The **Prerequisite Skills** at the beginning of every chapter help students identify and practice the skills they'll need for each new concept.

- Additional **prerequisite skills practice** is provided at the end of each lesson and includes page references to help students get extra review whenever they need it. More prerequisite skill practice appears in the Student Handbook section at the back of the Student Edition.

- The **Prerequisite Skills Workbook** provides extra practice on the basic skills needed for success in Algebra 1.

Daily Intervention Opportunities

Guide to Daily Intervention offers suggestions for using Glencoe materials to intercept students who are having difficulties and prescribe a system of reinforcement to promote student success.

The **Chapter Resource Masters** include several types of worksheets that can be used for daily intervention in each lesson. For a description of each worksheet, see page T4.

- **Study Guide and Intervention***
- **Skills Practice***
- **Practice***
- **Reading to Learn Mathematics**

  * *Each of these types of worksheets is available as a **consumable workbook** in both English and Spanish.*

The **Student Edition** contains additional problems to help students master each lesson before completing the chapter assessment.

- **Extra Practice**, located in the back of the Student Edition, provides additional, immediate practice with the concepts from each lesson.

- **Mixed Problem Solving**, also in the back of the Student Edition, includes numerous verbal problems to help students reinforce their problem-solving skills.

who needs
EXTRA HELP.
And you'll be able to *DELIVER* it.

Technology Resources for Intervention

In addition to print resources, Glencoe offers a variety of timesaving technology tools to help students build their math skills more effectively.

AlgePASS: Tutorial Plus CD-ROM provides an interactive, self-paced tutorial for a complete Algebra 1 curriculum. The 35 lessons are correlated directly to *Glencoe Algebra 1*. Each lesson, or concept, includes a pretest, tutorial, guided practice, and posttest. Students' answers to the pretests automatically determine whether they need the tutorial for each concept, so students can take responsibility for their own learning — without taking teacher time for grading.

Online Study Tools include comprehensive review and intervention tools that are available anytime, anyplace simply by logging on to

www.algebra1.com.

Additional Teacher Resources

The following materials are available to help you determine which students need intervention and allow you to develop strategies for giving students the help they need. For a description of each feature, see page T5.

- **5-Minute Check Transparencies with Standardized Test Practice**
- **Daily Intervention** features in the Teacher Wraparound Edition
- **Closing the Gap for Absent Students**

Self-check quizzes are available for every lesson, and immediate feedback helps students check their progress and find specific pages and examples in the Student Edition whenever they need extra review. These Online Study Tools also include extra examples, chapter tests, standardized test practice, and vocabulary review.

ALEKS® is an online, intuitive, individualized tutor that students can take anywhere. This artificial intelligence-based system analyzes student answers and targets what the student is prepared to learn next. ALEKS is available by subscription only on the Internet.

Give ASSESSMENT

Glencoe Algebra 1 gives you all the tools you need to prepare students for success—including Standardized Test Practice in each lesson and the powerful ExamView® Pro.

Student Edition

Every lesson contains two Standardized Test Practice questions, and every chapter contains a completely worked-out standardized test example as well as two full pages of Standardized Test Practice with Test-Taking Tips.

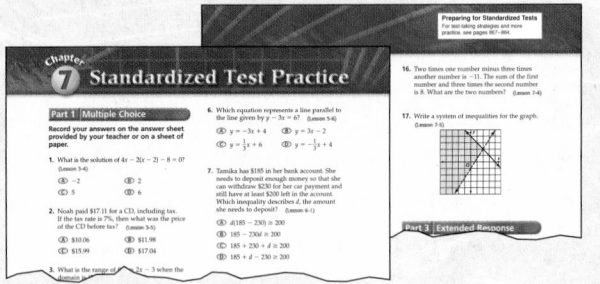

Preparing for Standardized Tests is designed to help your students become better test-takers. Included are examples and practice for the types of questions and concepts commonly seen on standardized tests.

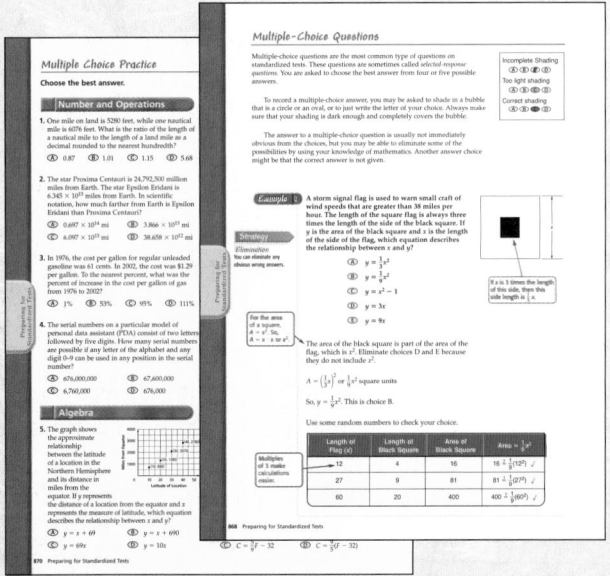

Chapter Study Guide and Review provides Vocabulary and Concept review—a Glencoe exclusive—and Lesson-by-Lesson Review, all at the point of use for students.

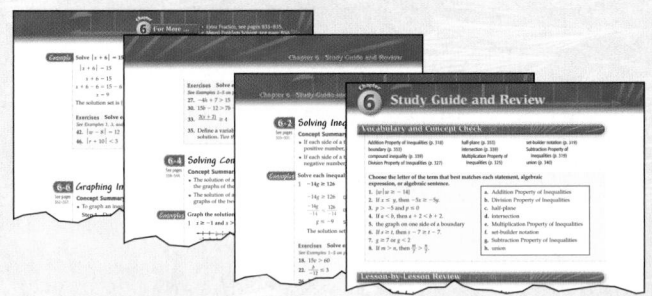

Practice Quizzes (2 per chapter) and a **Practice Test** for each chapter provide the variety of practice questions students need to succeed on tests.

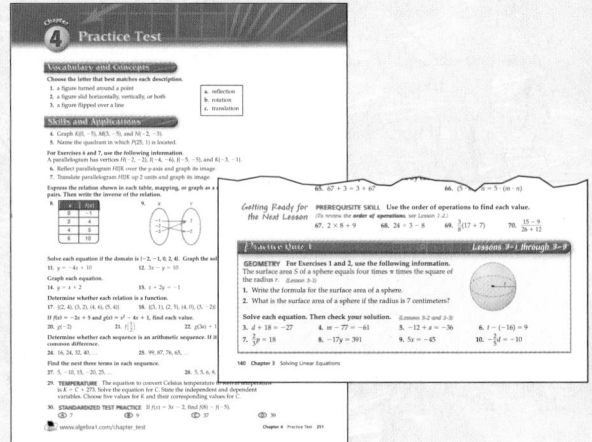

Teacher Wraparound Edition

An **Open-Ended Assessment** activity is provided in each lesson in the margin of the Teacher Wraparound Edition.

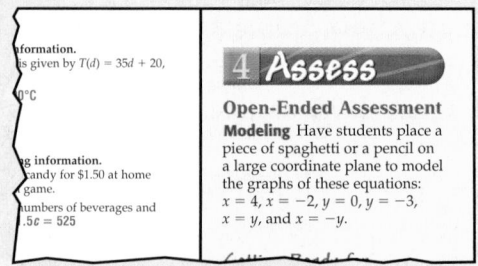

the extra attention it deserves, without the extra prep time.

Teacher Classroom Resources

5-Minute Check Transparencies with Standardized Test Practice provide full-size transparencies with questions covering the previous lesson or chapter. Standardized Test Practice Questions are also included.

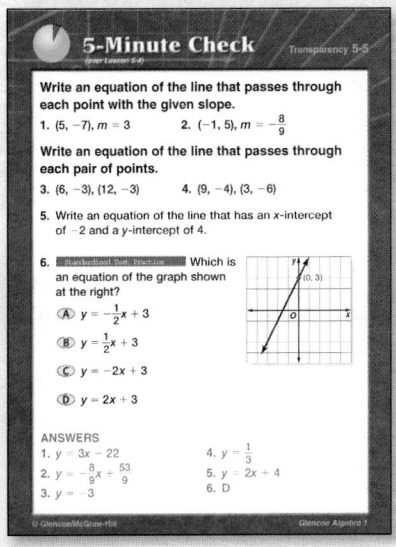

Assessment Options in the Chapter Resource Masters

These assessment resources are available for each chapter in *Glencoe Algebra 1*.

- 6 Chapter Tests
- Open-Ended Assessment with Scoring Rubric
- Vocabulary Test and Review **Glencoe Exclusive!**
- 4 Quizzes
- Mid-Chapter Test
- Cumulative Review
- 2-page Standardized Test Practice

Unit Tests, Semester Tests, and a **Final Test** are also available at point of use in the Chapter Resource Masters.

Technology Support

Use the networkable **ExamView® Pro** to:

- Create **multiple versions** of tests.
- Create **modified** tests for *Inclusion* students.
- **Edit** existing questions and **add** your own questions.
- Use built-in **state curriculum correlations** to create tests aligned with state standards.
- Change **English** tests to **Spanish** and vice versa.

MindJogger Videoquizzes present chapter-by-chapter review sessions in a game show format to make review more interesting and active to students…especially great for reluctant readers. Available on VHS or on DVD with Real-Life Math Videos.

Online Study Tools

- Self-Check Quizzes
- Chapter Test Practice
- Vocabulary Review
- Standardized Test Practice

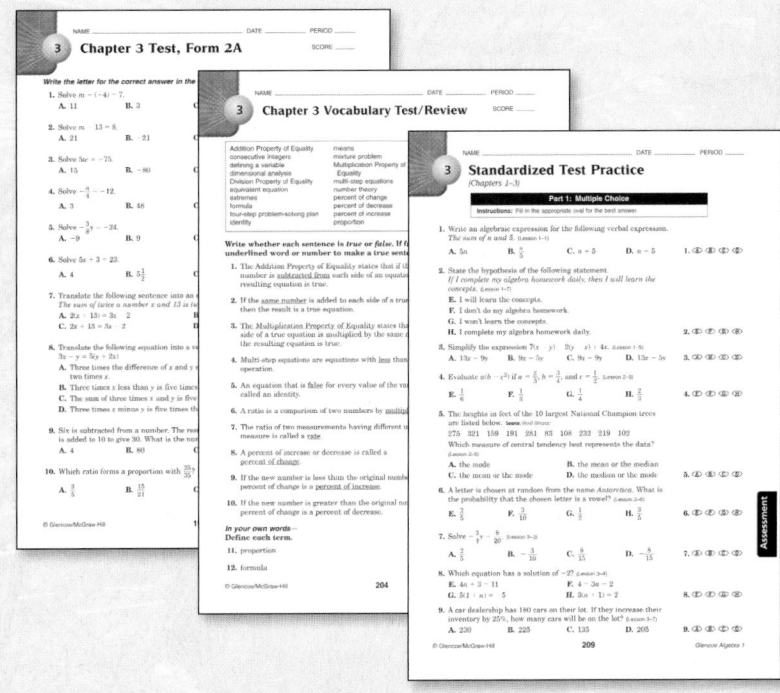

Introducing our new partner

USA TODAY® Education

USA TODAY Snapshots®

This is the same up-to-date data you know so well. But now, in an exclusive partnership with Glencoe/McGraw-Hill, USA TODAY® Education has brought its powerful, one-of-a-kind perspective and dynamic content to the pages of *Glencoe Algebra 1*. USA TODAY Snapshots® explode off the page to make algebra come alive with current, relevant data.

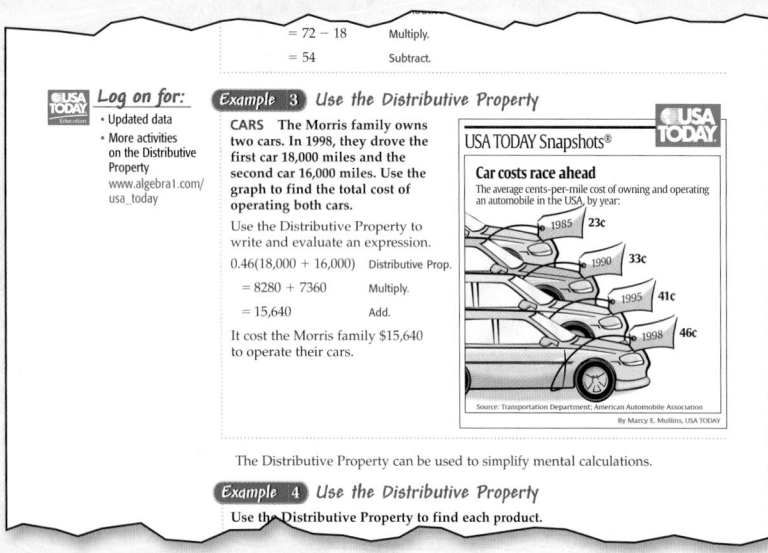

- www.algebra1.com/usa_today provides additional activities related to the topics presented in the USA TODAY Snapshots®.

- www.education.usatoday.com, USA TODAY® K-12 Education's Web site offers resources and interactive features connected to each day's newspaper. *Experience Today*, USA TODAY®'s daily lesson plan, is available on the site and delivered daily to subscribers. This plan provides instruction for integrating USA TODAY® graphics and key editorial features into your mathematics classroom.

Stay current with additional charts and graphs with USA TODAY®. Log on to www.education.usatoday.com, or call USA TODAY® at (800) 757-TEACH.

WebQuest: Online Projects

www.algebra1.com/webquest gives students the chance to work through a long-term project to enable them to develop their research, creative writing, and presentation skills.

- WebQuests often utilize USA TODAY Snapshots® or USA TODAY® articles.

- Special features in the Student Edition prompt students to complete each stage of their WebQuest.

- Parents can use the guided instruction to help students become familiar with the Internet in a safe, productive manner.

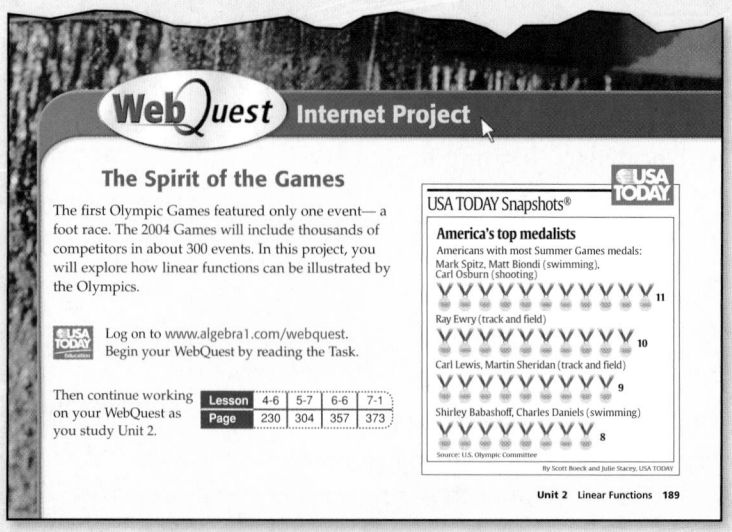

The INTERNET: One TOOL. Endless possibilities.

Many of your students may already be familiar with the Internet, but may not have discovered the full potential of this powerful research tool. With *Glencoe Algebra 1*, your students can use the Internet to build their algebra skills. And you can access a wide variety of resources to help you plan classes, extend lessons, even meet professional development requirements.

For Students

Online Study Tools, referenced on the Student Edition pages are keyed specifically to *Glencoe Algebra 1*.

- www.algebra1.com/extra_examples features additional fully worked-out examples.
- www.algebra1.com/self_check_quiz allows students to check their progress in each lesson.
- www.algebra1.com/vocabulary_review lets students check their vocabulary comprehension.
- www.algebra1.com/chapter_test provides additional practice in test taking.
- www.algebra1.com/standardized_test simulates questions that appear on standardized and proficiency tests.

Other Online Resources

- www.algebra1.com/webquest offers an online research project.
- www.algebra1.com/usa_today provides additional activities related to the topics presented in the USA TODAY Snapshots®.
- www.algebra1.com/data_update features links to updated statistical data presented in exercises.
- www.algebra1.com/careers offers information about career opportunities.
- www.algebra1.com/other_calculator_keystrokes provides keystroke instructions for various calculators to accompany graphing calculator activities and exercises in the Student Edition.

For Teachers
Powerful tools to make your job easier
- Classroom Games
- Key Concepts: Mathematical Background and Teaching Notes www.algebra1.com/key_concepts
- Problem of the Week Activities
- USA TODAY® K-12 Education daily lesson plans
- Sharing Ideas with Other Teachers
- Cool Math Links
- State and National Resources

Staff Development Sites
- NCTM links
- Teaching Today link
- McGraw-Hill Learning Network link
- Cooperative learning suggestions
- Using the Internet in the Mathematics Classroom

For Parents
Help parents get involved with their child's learning
- Parent and Student Study Guide www.algebra1.com/parent_student
- Involving Parents and Community in the Mathematics Classroom

DISCOVER how a **simple sheet of paper** can CHANGE the way your students THINK about math... forever.

Students love Foldables™ because they're fun. Teachers love them because they're effective.

Foldables are easy-to-make, three-dimensional interactive graphic organizers that students create out of simple sheets of paper. These unique hands-on tools for learning and reviewing were created exclusively for *Glencoe Algebra 1* by teaching specialist Dinah Zike.

Building Prereading Skills

At the beginning of each chapter, students construct one of a variety of Foldables. Each Foldable helps students create an interactive strategy for organizing what they read and observe. As they work through each chapter, students add more detail to their Foldable until they have created a comprehensive, interactive snapshot of the key concepts and vocabulary of the chapter.

Reading and Writing

Each Foldable helps students practice basic reading and writing skills, find and report main ideas, organize information, review key vocabulary terms, and more.

Review and Reinforcement

The completed Foldable is a comprehensive overview of the chapter concepts — perfect for preparing for chapter, unit, and even end-of-course tests.

Assessment

Foldables present an ideal opportunity to probe the depth of your students' understanding of chapter concepts. You'll get detailed feedback on what your students know and what misconceptions they may have.

Staff Development

Teaching Mathematics with Foldables™ equips teachers to extend the use of Foldables in their classrooms by exploring the different Foldable formats and providing suggestions for using them throughout the mathematics curriculum.

Give students control,

so that they leave your classroom with *knowledge and power* over their *own learning.*

Study Skill

Project CRISS(SM) (**CR**eating **I**ndependence Through **S**tudent-Owned **S**trategies) is a research-based staff development program created to help students better organize, understand, and retain course information. In short, students receiving the CRISS method of instruction will "LEARN HOW TO LEARN".

CRISS strategies are designed to develop thoughtful and independent readers and learners.

To enhance student learning, CRISS employs several concepts drawn from cognitive psychology.

- Students must be able to integrate new information with prior knowledge.
- Students need to be actively involved in their own learning by discussing, writing, and organizing information.
- Students must self-monitor to identify which strategies are the most effective for their own learning.

These behaviors need to be taught by content teachers to maximize student learning.

CReating **I**ndependence Through **S**tudent-Owned **S**trategies

Reading and Writing in Mathematics

Glencoe Algebra 1 provides numerous opportunities to incorporate reading and writing into the mathematics classroom.

Student Edition
- Foldables Study Organizer, p. 67
- Concept Check questions require students to verbalize and write about what they have learned in the lesson. (pp. 70, 76, 81, 86, 91, 98, 107)
- Reading Mathematics, p. 95
- Writing in Math questions in every lesson, pp. 68, 72, 78, 82, 87, 94, 100, 109
- Reading Study Tip, pp. 69, 96, 97, 103
- WebQuest, p. 100

Teacher Wraparound Edition
- Foldables Study Organizer, p. 67, 110
- Study Notebook suggestions, pp. 70, 76, 81, 85, 91, 95, 99, 102, 107
- Modeling activities, pp. 72, 109
- Speaking activities, pp. 78, 94
- Writing activities, pp. 83, 86, 101
- Differentiated Instruction, (Verbal/Linguistic), p. 72
- ELL Resources, pp. 66, 72, 71, 77, 82, 87, 93, 95, 100, 108, 110

For more information on Reading and Writing in Mathematics, see pp. T6–T7.

Additional Resources
- Vocabulary Builder worksheets require students to define and give examples for key vocabulary terms as they progress through the chapter. (Chapter 2 Resource Masters, pp. vii–viii)
- Reading to Learn Mathematics master for each lesson (Chapter 2 Resource Masters, pp. 79, 85, 91, 97, 103, 109, 115)
- Vocabulary PuzzleMaker software creates crossword, jumble, and word search puzzles using vocabulary lists that you can customize.
- Teaching Mathematics with Foldables provides suggestions for promoting cognition and language.
- Reading and Writing in the Mathematics Classroom
- WebQuest and Project Resources

Study Skill

A comparison map can help students understand the differences in two or more similar concepts. Show students the sample map at the right that compares line plots and stem-and-leaf plots in Lesson 2-5.

While studying Chapter 2, have students work in small cooperative groups to design comparison maps showing how to add, subtract, multiply, and divide rational numbers.

CReating **I**ndependence Through **S**tudent-Owned **S**trategies

Chapter 2 Real Numbers 66F

Implementing CRISS Strategies

Project CRISS Study Skills were developed with leaders from Project CRISS to facilitate the teaching of each chapter of *Glencoe Algebra 1*. These strategies appear in the interleaf of the Teacher Wraparound Edition.

For more information on project CRISS(SM), visit www.projectcriss.com

Reading and Writing in Mathematics

Glencoe Algebra 1 provides numerous opportunities to incorporate reading and writing into the mathematics classroom.

Student Edition
- Foldables Study Organizer, p. 191
- Concept Check questions require students to verbalize and write about what they have learned in the lesson. (pp. 194, 200, 208, 214, 221, 228, 236, 243)
- Reading Mathematics, p. 239
- Writing in Math questions in every lesson, pp. 196, 203, 210, 216, 222, 231, 238, 245
- Reading Study Tip, pp. 198, 199, 227, 230, 233, 234
- WebQuest, p. 230

Teacher Wraparound Edition
- Foldables Study Organizer, pp. 191, 246
- Study Notebook suggestions, pp. 194, 200, 208, 215, 221, 229, 232, 236, 239, 243
- Modeling activities, pp. 196, 203, 238, 245
- Speaking activities, pp. 217, 231
- Writing activities, pp. 211, 223
- Differentiated Instruction, (Verbal/Linguistic), pp. 196, 213
- ELL Resources, pp. 190, 195, 196, 201, 209, 213, 216, 222, 230, 237, 239, 244, 246

For more information on Reading and Writing in Mathematics, see pp. T6–T7.

Additional Resources
- Vocabulary Builder worksheets require students to define and give examples for key vocabulary terms as they progress through the chapter. (Chapter 4 Resource Masters, pp. vii–viii)
- Reading to Learn Mathematics master for each lesson (Chapter 4 Resource Masters, pp. 217, 223, 229, 235, 241, 247, 253, 259)
- Vocabulary PuzzleMaker software creates crossword, jumble, and word search puzzles using vocabulary lists that you can customize.
- Teaching Mathematics with Foldables provides suggestions for promoting cognition and language.
- Reading and Writing in the Mathematics Classroom
- WebQuest and Project Resources

ENGLISH LANGUAGE LEARNERS

Lesson 4-3 Language Experience Approach to Illustrations

Have groups create, compare, and contrast graphic organizers of the four transformations in the lesson on a sheet of paper. Students should make the organizer with four columns showing how they are alike, how they are different, an example of each transformation, similarities and differences among the four, and a conclusion.

Lesson 4-6 Higher-Level Thinking

Give students in groups several index cards with relations in different forms. Have them find the domain and range of each relation. Then have them determine whether each relation represents a function and explain their reasoning.

Lesson 4-8 Peer Tutoring

Have students work in pairs to translate sequences into equations. If possible, pair English-Language Learners with a bilingual student. Help students to see the connection between the domain and range, and the linear relationship. Have the students write the difference between x and y values on the table or graph.

Chapter 4 Graphing Relations and Functions 190F

ENGLISH LANGUAGE LEARNERS

English Language Learners may need specialized help in overcoming a language barrier to learn mathematics. Hands-on activities, modeling, working in flexible groups, and vocabulary building activities are particularly helpful to ELL students. Suggested strategies appear in the interleaf of the Teacher Wraparound Edition.

It's Staff Development,

As professional development continues to take on greater importance for educators across the country, teachers are constantly looking for easy-to-use tools to help them stay abreast of current trends and issues. At Glencoe, we know how valuable your time is, so we've developed a variety of staff development tools to help you meet your district's requirements.

Teacher Wraparound Edition

Mathematical Connections and Background found at the beginning of each chapter gives you an overview of the mathematics skills required in each lesson. Information about prior knowledge as well as future connections lets you see the continuity of instruction.

Building on Prior Knowledge provides you with information that links what students have previously learned to the content of the lesson.

Tips for New Teachers offers helpful suggestions for such things as classroom management, assessment, teaching techniques, and more.

Teaching Tips can be found not only in the margins but also on the reduced student pages at point of use.

Teacher Classroom Resources

Glencoe Mathematics Staff Development Series is a series of publications that allows you to stay current with issues that affect your teaching effectiveness. The series is intended to help you implement new mathematics strategies and enhance your classroom performance.

Available in print

* *Using the Internet in the Mathematics Classroom*
* *Reading and Writing in the Mathematics Classroom*
* *Teaching Mathematics with Foldables™*
* *Teaching Algebra with Manipulatives*

Available online at
www.math.glencoe.com

* *Graphing Calculators in the Mathematics Classroom*
* *Cooperative Learning in the Mathematics Classroom*
* *Alternative Assessment in the Mathematics Classroom*
* *Involving Parents and the Community in the Mathematics Classroom*

made convenient.

Technology Support

At www.math.glencoe.com, you'll find:

- a Staff Development site that addresses current issues in education.
- a Teacher Forum that allows teachers to discuss issues and ideas with colleagues.
- a State and National Resources site that links to math and math education resources, nationally and by state.

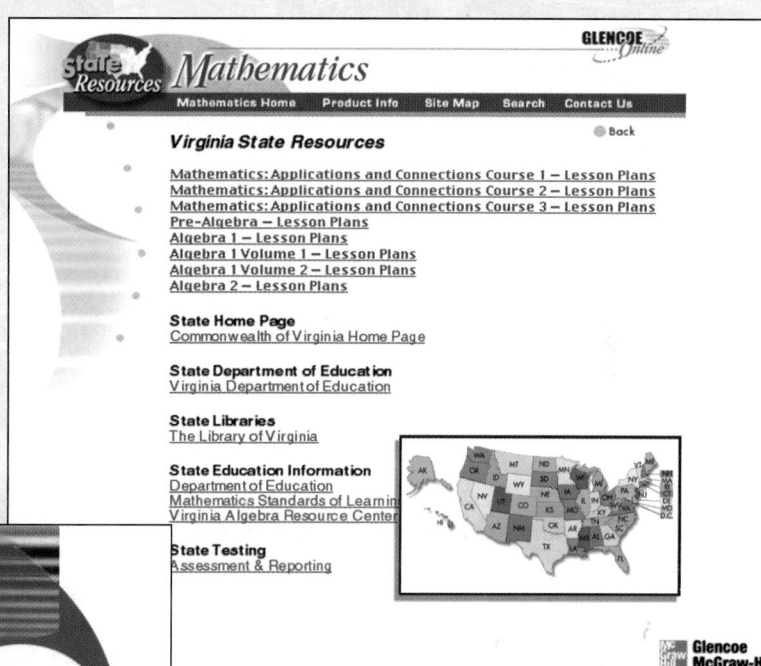

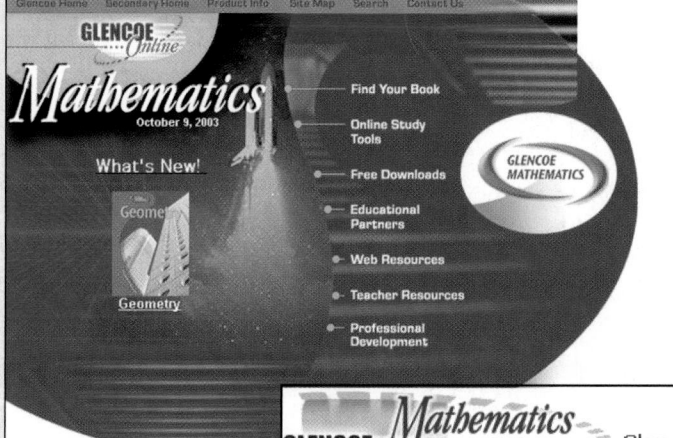

Glencoe Mathematics Programs—
Research-
Based and

Glencoe's mathematics programs are the product of ongoing classroom and educational research activities involving students, teachers, curriculum supervisors, administrators, parents, and college-level mathematics educators, mathematicians, and researchers.

SOUND

Prior to the publication of any Glencoe mathematics program, the following initial research is completed.

- Monitoring of national and state changes and information such as state graduation requirements, standardized test exams, the latest NCTM and NAEP reports, as well as NCLB (No Child Left Behind) mandates.

- Incorporating the most current and applicable educational research in which reported results show significant improvement on student learning and achievement.

- Reviewing all comments and correspondence on appropriate prior editions in terms of specific lessons. This helps Glencoe to build in staff development support, which makes the programs easy to implement from the first day of use.

- Analyzing returns from independently contracted mailing and telephone surveys.

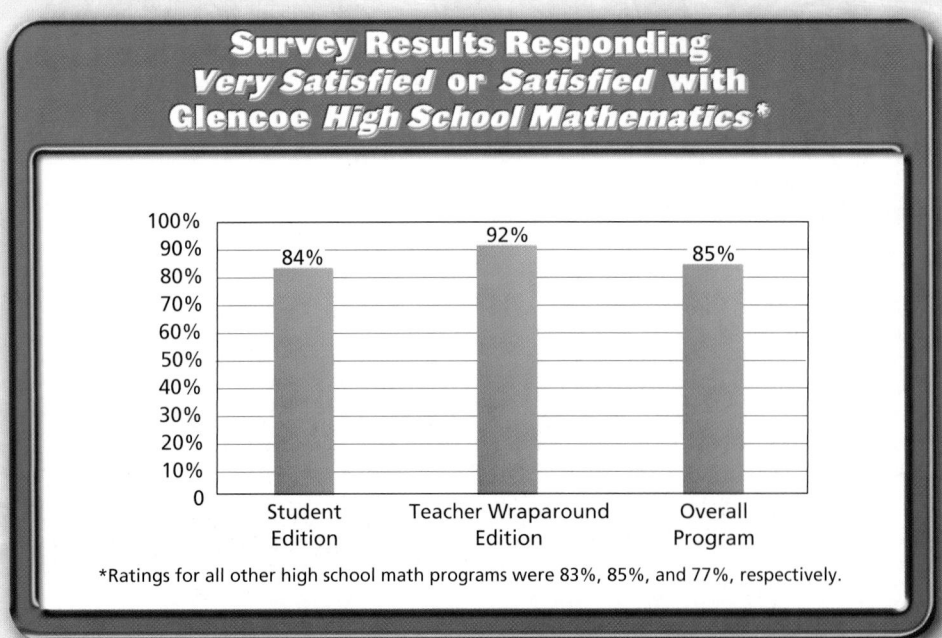

Survey Results Responding Very Satisfied or Satisfied with Glencoe High School Mathematics*

*Ratings for all other high school math programs were 83%, 85%, and 77%, respectively.

Source: High School Mathematics Longitudinal Survey, 2003

tested to ensure success.

PROVEN

Prior to the publication of *Glencoe Algebra 1*, extensive research was conducted using manuscript and pre-publication versions of the program.

- Nationwide discussion groups were conducted, which involved mathematics teachers, department chairpersons, supervisors, and educational learning specialists.
- Face-to-face interviews were carried out with mathematics teachers.
- Reviewers and consultants reviewed *Glencoe Algebra 1* manuscripts for accuracy, content development, and thoroughness.
- Before the design of the Student Edition was completed, an independent research company was contracted to organize and conduct blind focus groups with algebra teachers in various cities. The teachers' reactions and comments were recorded and used for improvements.
- Follow-up interviews, observations, and surveys of users of Glencoe mathematics programs are continuously conducted and monitored.
- Glencoe conducts Learner Verification Research in which students and teachers use pre-publication manuscript in the classroom. The results, compiled by an independent contractor, for *Glencoe Algebra 1* are summarized below.

Top-Line Results

- The research indicates that test scores significantly increased among students using *Glencoe Algebra 1*.
- Roughly eight out of ten students earned higher scores after using the Glencoe program.
- The program was equally effective with boys and girls, and with minority and non-minority students
- Overall, the gap between the average pre-test score and a perfect score closed by 36%. Stated differently, on average, scores increased 23% after students used *Glencoe Algebra 1*.

EFFECTIVE

What do teachers say? Here are some testimonials from Learner Verification Research teachers.

- *easy to understand step-by-step examples*
- *great variety of problems in each section for different learning levels*
- *abundance of outstanding resource materials*
- *allows for independent use by a student*
- *plentiful activities and real-world connections*

For more details of Glencoe's research, please contact us at www.math.glencoe.com.

Planning *Your*

Glencoe Algebra 1 and the accompanying support materials allow you to create a first-year algebra course that meets the needs of each class of students. The charts below and at the top of the facing page offer suggestions for pacing for average and advanced levels with standard class periods and block schedule class periods.

Average Pacing is for those students who have a fairly good mathematical preparation for algebra. You may want to use one of the chapter tests in the *Chapter Resource Masters* as a pretest to determine how well your students are prepared for each chapter. If you find that they are well prepared, consider using the Study Guide and Review at the end of the chapter as a one-day lesson and proceed to the next chapter.

Advanced Pacing is for students with a strong preparation for algebra. These students may have successfully completed a pre-algebra course in the previous grade or block semester. In advanced pacing, Unit 1 (Chapters 1-3) may be considered as a review. You can use the Study Guide and Review at the end of each chapter to refresh students' memories of these topics and identify those with which they are less familiar. One of the six chapter tests provided in the *Chapter Resource Masters* can also be used as a pretest for each chapter.

Year-Long Schedule
45–50 minute periods

Grading Period	Average		Advanced	
	Chapter	Days	Chapter	Days
1	1	14	Review of 1, 2, and 3	12
	2	11	4	14
	3	16	5	13
			Lessons 6-1 and 6-2	2
2	4	14	Lessons 6-3 to 6-6	11
	5	14	7	12
	6	14	8	19
3	7	10	9	13
	8	16	10	15
	9	13	11	13
4	10	14	12	18
	11	12	13	13
	12	13	14	10
optional	13	0		
	14	0		
	Total	161	Total	165

The total number of days in each level of pacing is less than the typical 180-day school year and 90-day semester to allow for flexibility in planning due to testing, school cancellation, or shortened class periods. *A more detailed Suggested Pacing chart for one-year courses appears in the interleaf page A preceding each chapter in the Teacher Wraparound Edition.*

Modifying Average Pacing for Basic Students

For those students who are less prepared for Algebra 1, spend more time on Units 1 and 2 (Chapters 1-7). Chapters 12-14 may be omitted.

Algebra Course

Block Schedule Pacing for average and advanced courses is given in the chart below. The pacing is designed for classes that meet once each day for one semester or every other day for one year.

Block Schedule
90-minute periods

Chapter	1	2	3	4	5	6	7	8	9	10	11	12	13	14	Total
Days (Average)	6.5	6	8	7	7	6	5	8	7	7	6	6.5	0	0	80
Days (Advanced)		4		6.5	7	7	6	10	7	8	7	9	6	5.5	83

Two-Year Pacing is for those students who want to take algebra, but find the abstract concepts difficult to grasp. This pacing allows students to cover the same material and work the same problems as students using the average or advanced pacing. Students will be able to spend more time on each concept and will have more time to complete hands-on labs and activities that help develop and internalize the abstract concepts presented in this course.

In year one, students cover the first seven chapters of the book. In year two, students begin by reviewing the first seven chapters and then continue with Chapters 8 through 12. If less time is needed for review of Chapters 1 through 7, more time will be available for covering the more difficult concepts and activities in the last five chapters of the book.

Year 1 Schedule | Year 2 Schedule

Chapter	Days	Chapter	Days
1	26	Review 1–7*	42
2	20	8	28
3	28	9	24
4	26	10	24
5	25	11	21
6	20	12	24
7	18		
Total	163 Days	Total	163 Days

* Six days are allotted for each chapter in the review.

Implementing the NCTM Principles and Standards

In 1989, the National Council of Teachers of Mathematics (NCTM) published their *Curriculum and Evaluation Standards for School Mathematics*, which gave mathematics teachers their first set of goals toward a national mathematics curriculum. Teachers and supervisors have embraced these Standards and developed state standards based on this framework. In 2000, the National Council of Teachers of Mathematics published a revision of these guidelines entitled *NCTM Principles and Standards for School Mathematics*.

NCTM Principles for School Mathematics	Glencoe Algebra 1
Equity *Excellence in mathematics education requires equity—high expectations and strong support for all students.*	Glencoe's product line encourages high achievement at every level. Numerous teacher support materials provide activities for **differentiated instruction,** promotion of **reading and writing, pacing** for individual levels of achievement, and **daily intervention.**
Curriculum *A curriculum is more than a collection of activities: it must be coherent, focused on important mathematics, and well articulated across the grades.*	Glencoe authors developed a philosophy and scope and sequence to ensure a continuum of mathematical learning that builds on **prior knowledge** and extends concepts toward more **advanced mathematical thinking.**
Teaching *Effective mathematics teaching requires understanding what students know and need to learn and then challenging and supporting them to learn it well.*	Glencoe offers a plethora of teacher support materials. A comprehensive *Teacher Wraparound Edition* provides **mathematical background,** teaching tips, resource management guidelines, and **tips for new teachers.**
Learning *Students must learn mathematics with understanding, actively building new knowledge from experience and prior knowledge.*	The *Teacher Wraparound Edition* includes instruction on building from prior knowledge with materials in each interleaf and in **Building On Prior Knowledge** features. **Find the Error** and **Unlocking Misconception** teaching tips help to evaluate how students are thinking and learning.
Assessment *Assessment should support the learning of important mathematics and furnish useful information to both teachers and students.*	The **Practice Quizzes** and the **Chapter Practice Test** provide ways for students to check their own progress. Online Study Tools, such as **Self-Check Quizzes,** offer a unique way for students with Internet access to monitor their progress. The assessment tools in the *Chapter Resource Masters* contain different levels and formats for tests, as well as intermediate opportunities for assessment.
Technology *Technology is essential in teaching and learning mathematics; it influences the mathematics that is taught and enhances students' learning.*	The *Student Edition* includes opportunities to utilize graphing calculators and spreadsheets in the exploration of algebra concepts. The *Teacher Wraparound Edition* offers teaching tips on using technology. *Graphing Calculator and Spreadsheet Masters* has additional activities. Glencoe's Web site is constantly updated to meet the needs of students and teachers in excelling in mathematics education.

NCTM Standards for School Mathematics

The Standards portion of the *NCTM Principles and Standards for School Mathematics* center upon ten areas of mathematics curriculum development. The number assigned to each standard is for easy reference and is not part of each standard's official title.

Instructional programs from prekindergarten through grade 12 should enable all students to:

1 Numbers and Operations

- Understand numbers, ways of representing numbers, relationships among numbers, and number systems
- Understand the meaning of operations and how they relate to each other
- Compute fluently and make reasonable estimates

Pages: 6-36, 43-56, 68-109, 120-178, 232-245, 368, 425-430, 474-479, 567-573, 586-597, 605-622, 642-653, 655-695, 708-728, 731-744, 754-758, 760-788

2 Algebra

- Understand patterns, relations, and functions
- Represent and analyze mathematical situations and structures using algebraic symbols
- Use mathematical models to represent and understand quantitative relationships
- Analyze change in various contexts

Pages: 6-36, 43-48, 120-178, 192-203, 205-245, 256-307, 318-358, 369-398, 410-423, 431-463, 474-514, 524-573, 586-592, 598-621, 642-695

3 Geometry

- Analyze characteristics and properties of two- and three-dimensional geometric shapes and develop mathematical arguments about geometric relationships
- Specify locations and describe spatial relationships using coordinate geometry and other representational systems
- Apply transformations and use symmetry to analyze mathematical situations
- Use visualization, spatial reasoning, and geometric modeling to solve problems

Pages: 6-9, 155-159, 192-231, 240-245, 256-262, 271-277, 292-297, 416, 501-506, 567-572, 605-630, 759

4 Measurement

- Understand measurable attributes of objects and the units, systems, and processes of measurement
- Apply appropriate techniques, tools, and formulas to determine measurements

Pages: 256-277, 339-351

5 Data Analysis and Probability

- Formulate questions that can be addressed with data and collect, organize, and display relevant data to answer them
- Select and use appropriate statistical methods to analyze data
- Develop and evaluate inferences and predictions that are based on data
- Understand and apply basic concepts of probability

Pages: 6-55, 68-109, 120-126, 128-140, 142-178, 192-203, 205-223, 226-245, 256-262, 272-305, 318-358, 368-398, 410-430, 432-436, 439-449, 452-463, 474-514, 524-573, 586-621, 623-630, 642-653, 655-695, 708-744, 754-788

6 Problem Solving

- Build new mathematical knowledge through problem solving
- Solve problems that arise in mathematics and in other contexts
- Apply and adapt a variety of appropriate strategies to solve problems
- Monitor and reflect on the process of mathematical problem solving

Pages: 37-42, 96-102, 256-262, 278-279, 292-307, 416, 531-532, 545, 622, 759

7 Reasoning and Proof

- Recognize reasoning and proof as fundamental aspects of mathematics
- Make and investigate mathematical conjectures
- Develop and evaluate mathematical arguments and proofs
- Select and use various types of reasoning and methods of proof

Pages: 6-56, 68-109, 120-126, 128-140, 142-177, 192-223, 226-231, 233-245, 256-307, 318-358, 369-374, 376-398, 410-415, 417-430, 432-436, 439-449, 452-463, 474-514, 524-552, 554-573, 586-621, 623-630, 642-695, 708-742, 754-788

8 Communication

- Organize and consolidate their mathematical thinking through communication
- Communicate their mathematical thinking coherently and clearly to peers, teachers, and others
- Analyze and evaluate the mathematical thinking and strategies of others
- Use the language of mathematics to express mathematical ideas precisely

Pages: 6-56, 68-109, 120-126, 128-140, 142-178, 192-203, 205-223, 226-231, 233-245, 256-277, 280-307, 318-358, 368-374, 376-398, 410-415, 417-430, 432-436, 439-449, 452-463, 474-479, 481-486, 489-514, 524-530, 533-544, 546-552, 554-573, 586-603, 605-621, 623-630, 642-653, 655-695, 708-744, 754-788

9 Connections

- Recognize and use connections among mathematical ideas
- Understand how mathematical ideas build on one another to produce a coherent whole
- Recognize and apply mathematics in contexts outside of mathematics

Pages: 6-56, 68-109, 120-126, 128-140, 142-178, 192-203, 205-223, 226-231, 233-245, 256-277, 280-307, 318-358, 368-374, 376-398, 410-415, 417-430, 432-436, 439-449, 452-463, 474-479, 481-486, 489-514, 524-530, 533-544, 546-552, 554-573, 586-603, 605-621, 623-630, 642-653, 655-695, 708-744, 754-788

10 Representation

- Create and use representations to organize, record, and communicate mathematical ideas
- Select, apply, and translate among mathematical representations to solve problems
- Use representations to model and interpret physical, social, and mathematical phenomena

Pages: 6-56, 68-109, 120-177, 192-203, 205-231, 233-245, 256-307, 318-358, 368-398, 410-415, 417-463, 474-514, 524-530, 533-544, 546-552, 554-573, 586-603, 605-621, 623-630, 642-653, 655-695, 715-728, 731-744, 754-788

UNIT 1

Expressions and Equations 2

WebQuest Internet Project

- Introduction 3
- Follow-Ups 55, 100, 159
- Culmination 177

Lesson 1-7, p. 41

Table of Contents

Prerequisite Skills
- Getting Started 5
- Getting Ready for the Next Lesson 9, 15, 20, 25, 31, 36, 48

FOLDABLES Study Organizer 5

Reading and Writing Mathematics
- Translating from English to Algebra 10
- Reading Math Tips 18, 37
- Writing in Math 9, 15, 20, 25, 31, 35, 42, 48, 55

Standardized Test Practice
- Multiple Choice 9, 15, 20, 25, 31, 36, 39, 40, 42, 48, 55, 63, 64
- Short Response/Grid In 42, 65
- Extended Response 65

 USA TODAY. Snapshots 3, 27, 50, 53

Chapter ❷ Real Numbers 66

Lesson 2-4, p. 87

Prerequisite Skills
- Getting Started **67**
- Getting Ready for the Next Lesson **72, 78, 83, 87, 94, 101**

 Study Organizer 67

Reading and Writing Mathematics
- Interpreting Statistics **95**
- Reading Math Tips **97, 103**
- Writing in Math **72, 78, 82, 87, 94, 100, 109**

Standardized Test Practice
- Multiple Choice **72, 78, 83, 87, 94, 101, 106, 107, 109, 115, 116**
- Short Response/Grid In **117**
- Extended Response **117**

USA TODAY Snapshots 78, 80

Chapter ③   **Solving Linear Equations**   **118**

Lesson 3-4, p. 142

Prerequisite Skills

- Getting Started 119
- Getting Ready for the Next Lesson
  126, 134, 140, 148, 154, 159,
  164, 170

FOLDABLES™

Study Organizer 119

Reading and Writing Mathematics

- Sentence Method and Proportion Method 165
- Reading Math Tips 121, 129, 155
- Writing in Math 126, 134, 140, 147, 154, 159, 164, 170, 177

Standardized Test Practice

- Multiple Choice 126, 134, 140, 147, 151, 152, 154, 159, 164, 170, 177, 185, 186
- Short Response/Grid In 187
- Extended Response 187

USA TODAY. Snapshots 133, 158

Linear Functions

Chapter ❹   Graphing Relations and Functions

190

WebQuest Internet Project

- Introduction **189**
- Follow-Ups **230, 304, 357, 373**
- Culmination **398**

Lesson 4-5, p. 222

Prerequisite Skills
- Getting Started **191**
- Getting Ready for the Next Lesson **196, 203, 211, 217, 223, 231, 238**

FOLDABLES Study Organizer **191**

Reading and Writing Mathematics
- Reasoning Skills **239**
- Reading Math Tips **192, 198, 233, 234**
- Writing in Math **196, 203, 210, 216, 222, 231, 238, 245**

Standardized Test Practice
- Multiple Choice **196, 203, 210, 216, 223, 228, 229, 231, 238, 245, 251, 252**
- Short Response/Grid In **210, 253**
- Extended Response **253**

 Snapshots 189, 210

Chapter 5   Analyzing Linear Equations   254

Lesson 5-2, p. 266

Chapter 6 — Solving Linear Inequalities 316

Lesson 6-1, p. 322

Chapter 7 Solving Systems of Linear Equations and Inequalities 366

Lesson 7-2, p. 380

Prerequisite Skills
- Getting Started 367
- Getting Ready for the Next Lesson 374, 381, 386, 392

FOLDABLES™ Study Organizer 367

Reading and Writing Mathematics
- Making Concept Maps 393
- Writing in Math 374, 381, 386, 392, 398

Standardized Test Practice
- Multiple Choice 374, 381, 384, 385, 386, 392, 398, 403, 404
- Short Response/Grid In 405
- Extended Response 405

 Snapshots 386

xv

Polynomials and Nonlinear Functions

406

WebQuest Internet Project

- Introduction **407**
- Follow-Ups **429, 479, 537**
- Culmination **572**

Lesson 8-2, p. 422

Prerequisite Skills
- Getting Started **409**
- Getting Ready for the Next Lesson **415, 423, 430, 436, 443, 449, 457**

 **Study Organizer 409**

Reading and Writing Mathematics
- Mathematical Prefixes and Everyday Prefixes **424**
- Reading Tips **410, 425**
- Writing in Math **415, 423, 430, 436, 443, 448, 457, 463**

Standardized Test Practice
- Multiple Choice **415, 420, 421, 423, 430, 436, 443, 448, 457, 463, 469, 470**
- Short Response/Grid In **471**
- Extended Response **471**

 Snapshots 407, 427

Chapter 9   Factoring   472

Prerequisite Skills

- Getting Started 473
- Getting Ready for the Next Lesson 479, 486, 494, 500, 506

FOLDABLES™

Study Organizer 473

Reading and Writing Mathematics

- The Language of Mathematics 507
- Reading Tips 489, 511
- Writing in Math 479, 485, 494, 500, 506, 514

Standardized Test Practice

- Multiple Choice 479, 486, 494, 500, 503, 505, 506, 514, 519, 520
- Short Response/Grid In 494, 506, 521
- Extended Response 521

USA TODAY. Snapshots 494

Lesson 9-5, p. 505

Chapter **10** **Quadratic and Exponential Functions** **522**

Lesson 10-4, p. 551

Prerequisite Skills
- Getting Started **523**
- Getting Ready for the Next Lesson **530, 538, 544, 552, 560, 565**

 **Study Organizer 523**

Reading and Writing Mathematics
- Growth and Decay Formulas **566**
- Reading Tips **525**
- Writing in Math **530, 537, 543, 552, 560, 565, 572**

Standardized Test Practice
- Multiple Choice **527, 528, 530, 538, 543, 552, 560, 565, 572, 579, 580**
- Short Response/Grid In **572, 581**
- Extended Response **581**

 Snapshots 561, 563, 564

Chapter 11 Radical Expressions and Triangles

584

 **Internet Project**

- Introduction 583
- Follow-Ups 590, 652
- Culmination 695

Prerequisite Skills

- Getting Started 585
- Getting Ready for the Next Lesson 592, 597, 603, 610, 615, 621

FOLDABLES

Study Organizer 585

Reading and Writing Mathematics

- The Language of Mathematics 631
- Reading Tips 586, 611, 616, 623
- Writing in Math 591, 597, 602, 610, 614, 620, 630

Standardized Test Practice

- Multiple Choice 591, 597, 602, 606, 608, 610, 615, 620, 630, 637, 638
- Short Response/Grid In 639
- Extended Response 639

 Snapshots 583, 615

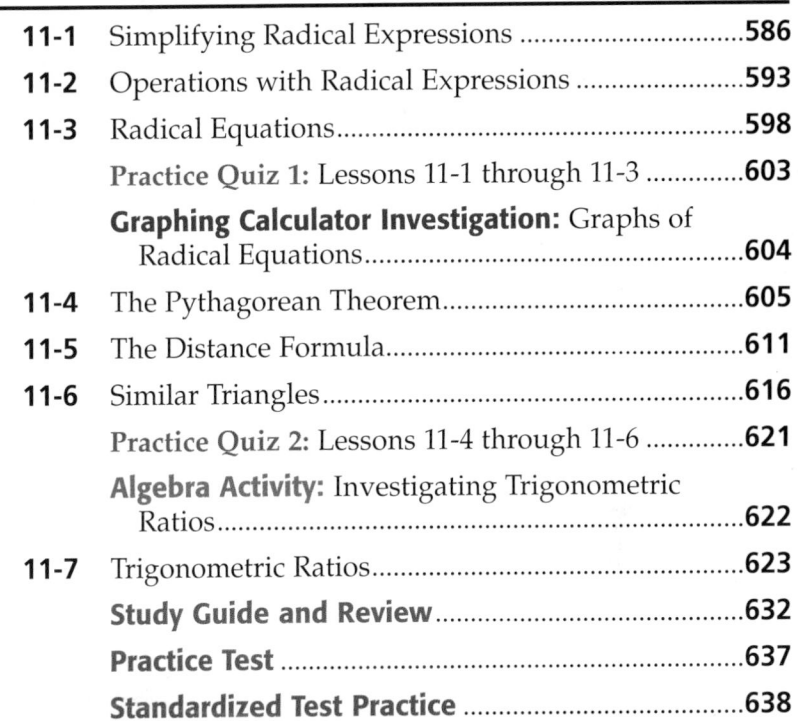

Lesson 11-2, p. 596

Chapter 12

Rational Expressions and Equations 640

Lesson 12-5, p. 670

Chapter ⑬ Statistics

706

 **Internet Project**

• Introduction **705**
• Follow-Ups **742, 766**
• Culmination **788**

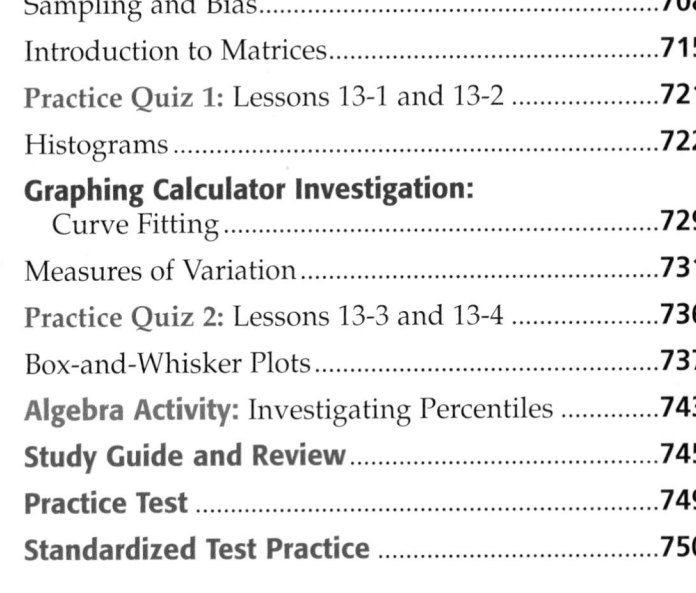

Lesson 13-5, p. 738

Prerequisite Skills
• Getting Started **707**
• Getting Ready for the Next Lesson **713, 721, 728, 736**

 **Study Organizer 705**

Reading and Writing Mathematics
• Survey Questions **714**
• Reading Tips **732, 737**
• Writing in Math **713, 720, 728, 736, 742**

Standardized Test Practice
• Multiple Choice **713, 720, 723, 724, 726, 728, 736,**
742, 749, 750
• Short Response/Grid In **751**
• Extended Response **751**

USA TODAY. Snapshots 705, 730

Chapter ⑭ Probability 752

Student Handbook

Skills

Reference

Lesson 14-1, p. 756

Prerequisite Skills
- Getting Started 753
- Getting Ready for the Next Lesson
  758, 767, 776, 781

FOLDABLES™

Study Organizer 753

Reading and Writing Mathematics
- Mathematical Words and Related Words 768
- Reading Tips 771, 777
- Writing in Math 758, 766, 776, 780, 787

Standardized Test Practice
- Multiple Choice 758, 762, 764, 766, 776, 780, 787, 793, 794
- Short Response/Grid In 795
- Extended Response 795

USA TODAY Snapshots 780

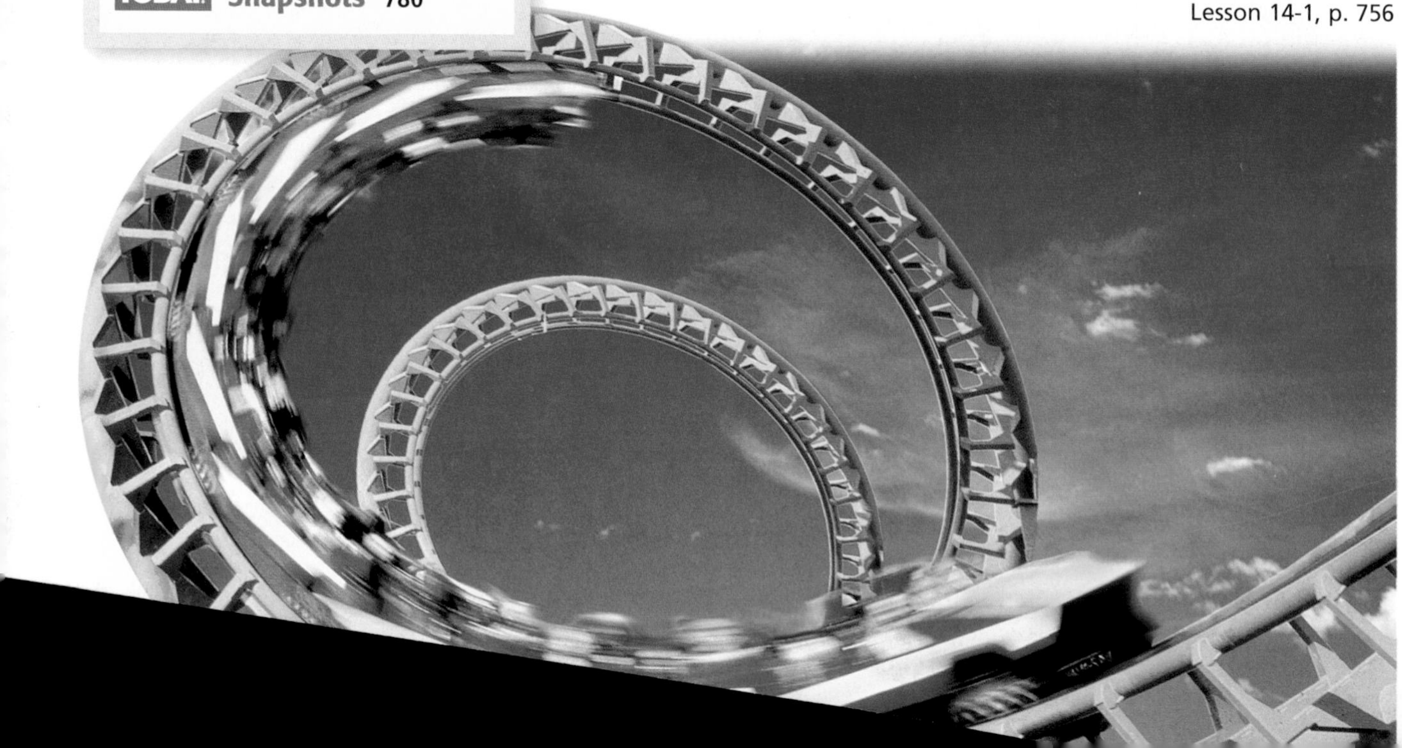

Need extra help or information? Log on to math.glencoe.com or any of the Web addresses below to learn more.

Online Study Tools

- www.algebra1.com/extra_examples shows you additional worked-out examples that mimic the ones in your book.
- www.algebra1.com/self_check_quiz provides you with a practice quiz for each lesson that grades itself.
- www.algebra1.com/vocabulary_review lets you check your understanding of the terms and definitions used in each chapter.
- www.algebra1.com/chapter_test allows you to take a self-checking test before the actual test.
- www.algebra1.com/standardized_test is another way to brush up on your standardized test-taking skills.

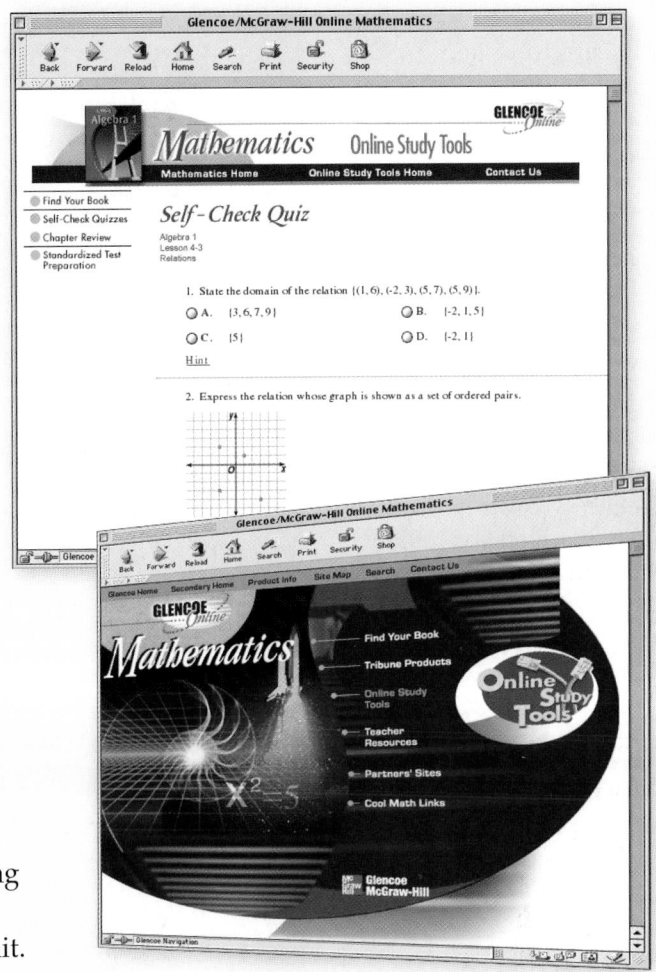

Research Options

- www.algebra1.com/webquest walks you step-by-step through a long-term project using the Web. One WebQuest for each unit is explored using the mathematics from that unit.
- www.algebra1.com/usa_today provides activities related to the concept of the lesson as well as up-to-date Snapshot data.
- www.algebra1.com/careers links you to additional information about interesting careers.
- www.algebra1.com/data_update links you to the most current data available for subjects such as basketball and family.

Calculator Help

- www.algebra1.com/other_calculator_keystrokes provides you with keystrokes other than the TI-83 Plus used in your textbook.

Get Started!

- To help you learn how to use your math book, use the Scavenger Hunt at www.algebra1.com.

UNIT
1

Expressions and Equations

Introduction

In this unit, students will explore using variables to represent data. They will learn to write, evaluate, and simplify variable expressions. They will build on this to write and solve linear equations.

Students will perform operations with real numbers. They will display and analyze statistical data and find probabilities of simple events.

You can use algebraic expressions and equations to model and analyze real-world situations. In this unit, you will learn about expressions, equations, and graphs.

Assessment Options

 Unit 1 Test Pages 211–212 of the *Chapter 3 Resource Masters* may be used as a test or review for Unit 1. This assessment contains both multiple-choice and short answer items.

ExamView® Pro

This CD-ROM can be used to create additional unit tests and review worksheets.

Yearly Progress Pro

An online, research-based, instructional, assessment, and intervention tool that provides specific feedback on student mastery of state and national standards, instant remediation, and a data management system to track performance. For more information, contact mhdigitallearning.com.

Chapter 1
The Language of Algebra

Chapter 2
Real Numbers

Chapter 3
Solving Linear Equations

Real-Life Math Videos

What's Math Got to Do With It? Real-Life Math Videos engage students by showing them how math is used in everyday situations. Use Video 1 with this unit.

WebQuest Internet Project

Can You Fit 100 Candles on a Cake?

Source: *USA TODAY,* January, 2001

"The mystique of living to be 100 will be lost by the year 2020 as 100th birthdays become commonplace, predicts Mike Parker, assistant professor of social work, University of Alabama, Tuscaloosa, and a gerontologist specializing in successful aging. He says that, in the 21st century, the fastest growing age group in the country will be centenarians—those who live 100 years or longer." In this project, you will explore how equations, functions, and graphs can help represent aging and population growth.

 Log on to www.algebra1.com/webquest. Begin your WebQuest by reading the Task.

Then continue working on your WebQuest as you study Unit 1.

Lesson	1-9	2-6	3-6
Page	55	100	159

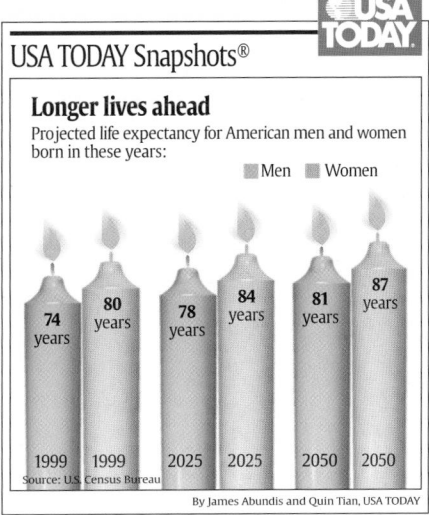

USA TODAY Snapshots®

Longer lives ahead
Projected life expectancy for American men and women born in these years:

■ Men ■ Women

74 years (1999) • 80 years (1999) • 78 years (2025) • 84 years (2025) • 81 years (2050) • 87 years (2050)

Source: U.S. Census Bureau

By James Abundis and Quin Tian, USA TODAY

The Language of Algebra
Chapter Overview and Pacing

Year-long and two-year pacing: pages T20–T21.

LESSON OBJECTIVES

LESSON OBJECTIVES	PACING (days)			
	Regular		Block	
	Basic/ Average	Advanced	Basic/ Average	Advanced
1-1 Variables and Expressions *(pp. 6–9)* • Write mathematical expressions for verbal expressions. • Write verbal expressions for mathematical expressions.	1	optional	0.5	optional
1-2 Order of Operations *(pp. 11–15)* • Evaluate numerical expressions by using the order of operations. • Evaluate algebraic expressions by using the order of operations.	1	optional	0.5	optional
1-3 Open Sentences *(pp. 16–20)* • Solve open sentence equations. • Solve open sentence inequalities.	2	optional	0.5	optional
1-4 Identity and Equality Properties *(pp. 21–25)* • Recognize the properties of identity and equality. • Use the properties of identity and equality.	1	optional	0.5	optional
1-5 The Distributive Property *(pp. 26–31)* • Use the Distributive Property to evaluate expressions. • Use the Distributive Property to simplify expressions.	1	optional	0.5	optional
1-6 Commutative and Associative Properties *(pp. 32–36)* • Recognize the Commutative and Associative Properties. • Use the Commutative and Associative Properties to simplify expressions.	1	optional	0.5	optional
1-7 Logical Reasoning *(pp. 37–42)* • Identify the hypothesis and conclusion in a conditional statement. • Use a counterexample to show that an assertion is false.	1	optional	0.5	optional
1-8 Graphs and Functions *(pp. 43–49)* • Interpret graphs of functions. • Draw graphs of functions. *Follow-Up:* Use grid paper to investigate real-world functions.	2 (with 1-8 Follow-Up)	optional	0.5	optional
1-9 Statistics: Analyzing Data by Using Tables and Graphs *(pp. 50–56)* • Analyze data given in tables and graphs (bar, line, and circle). • Determine whether graphs are misleading. *Follow-Up:* Use a computer spreadsheet to display data in different ways.	2 (with 1-9 Follow-Up)	optional	1 (with 1-8 Follow-Up)	optional
Study Guide and **Practice Test** *(pp. 57–63)* **Standardized Test Practice** *(pp. 64–65)*	1	3	1	1
Chapter Assessment	1	1	0.5	0
TOTAL	14	4	6.5	1

*An electronic version of this chapter is available on **StudentWorks**™. This backpack solution CD-ROM allows students instant access to the Student Edition, lesson worksheet pages, and web resources.*

Chapter Resource Manager

CHAPTER 1 RESOURCE MASTERS

Study Guide and Intervention	Practice (Skills and Average)	Reading to Learn Mathematics	Enrichment	Assessment	Prerequisite Skills Workbook	Applications *	Parent and Student Study Guide Workbook	5-Minute Check Transparencies	Interactive Chalkboard	AlgePASS: Tutorial Plus (lessons)	Materials
1–2	3–4	5	6		9–10		1	1-1	1-1		
7–8	9–10	11	12		5–12, 21–24	GCS 23, SC 1	2	1-2	1-2	1	
13–14	15–16	17	18	69	1–2, 5–12, 25–26, 47–50, 55–58, 61–62	GCS 24, SM 29–32	3	1-3	1-3		
19–20	21–22	23	24		5–8, 11–12, 21–22, 25–26, 55–56		4	1-4	1-4		
25–26	27–28	29	30	69, 71	49–50, 55–56, 77–78		5	1-5	1-5		algebra tiles, product mat
31–32	33–34	35	36		49–50, 77–78		6	1-6	1-6	2	
37–38	39–40	41	42	70			7	1-7	1-7		
43–44	45–46	47	48		95–96		8	1-8	1-8		grid paper
49–50	51–52	53	54	70		SC 2	9	1-9	1-9		grid paper
				55–68, 72–74			10				

Key to Abbreviations: GCS = Graphing Calculator and Spreadsheet Masters,
      SC = School-to-Career Masters,
      SM = Science and Mathematics Lab Manual

ELL Study Guide and Intervention, Skills Practice, Practice, and Parent and Student Study Guide Workbooks are also available in Spanish.

Mathematical Connections and Background

Continuity of Instruction

Prior Knowledge

In previous courses, students simplified algebraic expressions involving one operation, such as addition, subtraction, multiplication, or division. Students have intuitively translated verbal expressions to algebraic expressions each time they have solved a simple word problem. Students have interpreted graphs and charts in previous courses and in real-life.

This Chapter

Students discover the relationship between algebraic expressions and verbal expressions. They apply their knowledge of basic operations to expressions that include variables. They use the order of operations to solve open sentence equations and inequalities containing a variable. Students learn to recognize and use the properties of identity and equality, and the Distributive, Commutative, and Associative Properties. They use these properties to simplify expressions and evaluate equations. Students use tables and coordinates to draw graphs of functions. They analyze the shapes of graphs to interpret what is happening.

Future Connections

Writing algebraic expressions for verbal expressions shows students how math is used in everyday life. Using the order of operations and algebraic properties is essential to solving equations and formulas throughout all mathematics from algebra on.

1-1 Variables and Expressions

Expressions and equations containing variables are the basis of algebra. Algebraic expressions consisting of one or more numbers and variables along with one or more arithmetic operations can also be written as verbal expressions, and vice versa. Algebraic expressions may contain powers. To evaluate a power, you multiply the base the number of times indicated by the exponent.

1-2 Order of Operations

The order of operations is a rule that specifies which operation to perform first in an expression. First, perform the operation inside any grouping symbols. Next, evaluate all powers. Then do all multiplication and division from left to right followed by all addition and subtraction from left to right. If there are multiple operations within grouping symbols, use the order of operations to simplify that expression. Grouping symbols include parentheses, brackets, and fraction bars. If an expression needs a grouping symbol around terms that are already inside parentheses, brackets are used to help eliminate confusion.

1-3 Open Sentences

An open sentence is an algebraic statement that contains at least one variable and an equality or inequality symbol. Find the value of the variable in an open sentence through a process called solving the open sentence. Algebraic expressions do not contain equality or inequality symbols. Therefore, the value of the variable cannot be determined. However, the value of the variable can be determined in equations since equations do contain equal signs. It is also possible to find the solution set, the set of numbers that make an open sentence true, for an inequality, since an inequality sign is in the place of an equal sign.

1-4 Identity and Equality Properties

There are two Identity Properties. The Additive Identity states that adding 0 to any number or expression does not change its value. The Multiplicative Identity states that multiplying a number or expression by 1 does not change its value. Properties of equality, such as the Reflexive, Symmetric, Transitive, and Substitution Properties, preserve equality between the two sides of an equation. These properties can be used to solve equations.

1-5 The Distributive Property

In the Distributive Property, a term outside the parentheses is distributed by multiplication to each term inside the parentheses. Apply the Distributive Property when simplifying expressions and solving equations.

Like terms have the same variable or variables with the same powers. When there are like terms in an expression, combine the coefficients in front of the variables, resulting in a new equivalent expression. Writing expressions in simplest form first makes evaluating equations easier.

1-6 Commutative and Associative Properties

The Commutative Property and the Associative Property can only be applied to expressions containing addition or multiplication. The order in which numbers are added or multiplied does not change their sum or product. The order in which numbers are subtracted or divided changes their difference or quotient. Therefore, these properties cannot be applied to subtraction or division. When using these properties, look for ways to make mental calculations easier. Finding amounts that add or multiply to a product of 10 make other operations easier.

1-7 Logical Reasoning

Conditional statements are named such because one certain condition must be present before another condition occurs. Many conditional statements are not actually written in if-then form, but they can be rewritten in that format and retain the same meaning. The part of the statement inferred by "if" is the hypotheses. The part inferred by "then" is the conclusion. Deductive reasoning is used many times everyday in real-world contexts. Any time a decision is made on facts or rules, this concept has been applied.

1-8 Graphs and Functions

The coordinate system can be used to interpret data in a table and help determine the relationship between the data. First, determine which data is the independent variable and which is dependent. Then graph the ordered pairs from the table onto a coordinate plane. By analyzing the graphs, you can determine any trends in the data and make predictions.

1-9 Statistics: Analyzing data by Using Tables and Graphs

Three graphs that can be used to display data are bar graphs, circle graphs, and line graphs. Each is used to make different types of comparisons. Bar graphs are generally used to compare different categories of numerical information. Circle graphs represent data that compare parts of a whole set. To show change over time, line graphs are the most useful.

Using different methods to distort the appearance of data, such as extra small or large scales or other irregularities can form misleading graphs.

Quick Review Math Handbook

Hot Words includes a glossary of terms while Hot Topics consists of explanations of key mathematical concepts with exercises to test comprehension. This valuable resource can be used as a reference in the classroom or for home study.

Lesson	Hot Topics Section	Lesson	Hot Topics Section
GS1	1.5, 2.4, 2.6, 7.4	1-6	1.2, 6.3
1-1	6.1, 6.3	1-7	2.8, 5.1, 5.2
1-2	1.3, 6.2	1-8	4.2, 6.7
1-3	2.4, 6.4, 6.6	1-8F	6.7
1-4	1.2, 6.3	1-9	4.2, 4.3
1-5	1.2, 7.5	1-9F	4.2, 9.4

GS = Getting Started, F = Follow-Up

 Additional mathematical information and teaching notes are available at www.algebra1.com/key_concepts.

Chapter 1

DAILY
INTERVENTION and Assessment

Key to Abbreviations:
TWE = Teacher Wraparound Edition; CRM = Chapter Resource Masters

Type	Student Edition	Teacher Resources	Technology/Internet
INTERVENTION			
Ongoing	Prerequisite Skills, pp. 5, 9, 15, 20, 25, 31, 36, 42, 48 Practice Quiz 1, p. 20 Practice Quiz 2, p. 36	5-Minute Check Transparencies *Prerequisite Skills Workbook,* pp. 1–2, 5–12, 21–26, 47–50, 55–58, 61–62, 77–78, 95–96 Quizzes, *CRM* pp. 69–70 Mid-Chapter Test, *CRM* p. 71 Study Guide and Intervention, *CRM* pp. 1–2, 7–8, 13–14, 19–20, 25–26, 31–32, 37–38, 43–44, 49–50	AlgePASS: Tutorial Plus, Lessons 1 and 2 www.algebra1.com/self_check_quiz www.algebra1.com/extra_examples
Mixed Review	pp. 15, 20, 25, 31, 36, 42, 48, 55	Cumulative Review, *CRM* p. 72	
Error Analysis	Find the Error, pp. 13, 29 Common Misconceptions, p. 38	Find the Error, *TWE* pp. 13, 29 Unlocking Misconceptions, *TWE* pp. 13, 51 Tips for New Teachers, *TWE* p. 27	
Standardized Test Practice	pp. 9, 15, 20, 25, 31, 36, 39, 40, 42, 48, 55, 64–65	*TWE* pp. 64–65 Standardized Test Practice, *CRM* pp. 73–74	Standardized Test Practice CD-ROM www.algebra1.com/standardized_test
ASSESSMENT			
Open-Ended Assessment	Writing in Math, pp. 9, 15, 20, 25, 31, 35, 42, 48, 55 Open Ended, pp. 8, 13, 18, 23, 29, 34, 39, 46, 53 Standardized Test, p. 65	Modeling: *TWE* pp. 36, 48 Speaking: *TWE* pp. 15, 25, 55 Writing: *TWE* pp. 9, 20, 31, 42 Open-Ended Assessment, *CRM* p. 67	
Chapter Assessment	Study Guide, pp. 57–62 Practice Test, p. 63	Multiple-Choice Tests (Forms 1, 2A, 2B), *CRM* pp. 55–60 Free-Response Tests (Forms 2C, 2D, 3), *CRM* pp. 61–66 Vocabulary Test/Review, *CRM* p. 68	ExamView® Pro (see below) MindJogger Videoquizzes www.algebra1.com/vocabulary_review www.algebra1.com/chapter_test

For more information on Yearly ProgressPro, see p. 2.

Algebra Lesson	Yearly ProgressPro Skill Lesson(s)
1-1	Variables and Expressions
1-2	Order of Operations with Numbers Substitution of Numbers for Variables
1-3	Open Sentences
1-4	Identity and Equality Properties
1-5	Distributive Property: Algebra
1-6	Commutative and Associative Properties
1-7	Logical Reasoning
1-8	Graphs and Functions
1-9	Analyze Data by Using Tables and Graphs

ExamView® Pro

Use the networkable **ExamView® Pro** to:
- Create **multiple versions** of tests.
- Create **modified** tests for *Inclusion* students.
- **Edit** existing questions and **add** your own questions.
- Use built-in **state curriculum correlations** to create tests aligned with state standards.
- Change **English** tests to **Spanish** and vice versa.

For more information on Intervention and Assessment, see pp. T8–T11.

Reading and Writing in Mathematics

Glencoe Algebra 1 provides numerous opportunities to incorporate reading and writing into the mathematics classroom.

Student Edition

- Foldables Study Organizer, p. 5
- Concept Check questions require students to verbalize and write about what they have learned in the lesson. (pp. 8, 13, 18, 23, 29, 34, 39, 46, 53)
- Reading Mathematics, p. 10
- Writing in Math questions in every lesson, pp. 9, 15, 20, 25, 31, 35, 42, 48, 55
- Reading Study Tip, pp. 7, 17, 18, 28, 37, 43, 51
- WebQuest, p. 55

Teacher Wraparound Edition

- Foldables Study Organizer, pp. 5, 57
- Study Notebook suggestions, pp. 7, 10, 13, 18, 23, 29, 34, 39, 46, 49, 53, 56
- Modeling activities, pp. 36, 48
- Speaking activities, pp. 15, 25, 55
- Writing activities, pp. 9, 20, 31, 42
- Differentiated Instruction, (Verbal/Linguistic), p. 7
-  Resources, pp. 4, 5, 7, 8, 10, 14, 19, 24, 30, 35, 40, 47, 54, 57

Additional Resources

- Vocabulary Builder worksheets require students to define and give examples for key vocabulary terms as they progress through the chapter. (*Chapter 1 Resource Masters,* pp. vii-viii)
- Reading to Learn Mathematics master for each lesson (*Chapter 1 Resource Masters,* pp. 5, 11, 17, 23, 29, 35, 41, 47, 53)
- *Vocabulary PuzzleMaker* software creates crossword, jumble, and word search puzzles using vocabulary lists that you can customize.
- *Teaching Mathematics with Foldables* provides suggestions for promoting cognition and language.
- *Reading and Writing in the Mathematics Classroom*
- *WebQuest and Project Resources*

For more information on Reading and Writing in Mathematics, see pp. T6–T7.

ELL ENGLISH LANGUAGE LEARNERS

Lesson 1-2
Using Multisensory Activities

Give half of the class an index card with an expression. Give the other half an index card with the corresponding answer. Have students solve their expressions using order of operations and seek out the student with the correct answer. Pairs will verify the correct answer and share how to solve their expressions with the class.

Lesson 1-4
Flexible Groups

Give groups of students a set of index cards with several examples of the properties mentioned. Students can come to consensus and write the name of the property on the back of each card. Then students can add their own mathematical or real-world examples of the properties and explain them in their own words.

Lesson 1-7
Peer Tutoring

Ask English Language Learners to sit with an English-speaking or bilingual student and read the math problems. When identifying hypotheses and conclusions, have students read the problem and then ask what is being asked.

What You'll Learn

Have students read over the list of objectives and make a list of any words with which they are not familiar.

Why It's Important

Point out to students that this is only one of many reasons why each objective is important. Others are provided in the introduction to each lesson.

The chart below correlates the objectives for each lesson to the NCTM Standards 2000. There is also space for you to reference your state and/or local objectives.

Lesson	NCTM Standards	Local Objectives
1-1	1, 2, 3, 6, 8, 9, 10	
1-2	1, 2, 6, 8, 9, 10	
1-3	1, 2, 6, 8, 9, 10	
1-4	1, 2, 6, 8, 9, 10	
1-5	1, 2, 6, 8, 9, 10	
1-6	1, 2, 6, 8, 9, 10	
1-7	6, 7, 8, 9, 10	
1-8	1, 2, 6, 8, 9, 10	
1-8 Follow-Up	1, 6, 8, 9, 10	
1-9	1, 5, 6, 8, 9, 10	
1-9 Follow-Up	1, 5, 8, 9, 10	

Key to NCTM Standards:

1=Number & Operations, 2=Algebra,
3=Geometry, 4=Measurement,
5=Data Analysis & Probability, 6=Problem
Solving, 7=Reasoning & Proof,
8=Communication, 9=Connections,
10=Representation

Chapter 1 The Language of Algebra

What You'll Learn

- **Lesson 1-1**   Write algebraic expressions.
- **Lessons 1-2 and 1-3**   Evaluate expressions and solve open sentences.
- **Lessons 1-4 through 1-6**   Use algebraic properties of identity and equality.
- **Lesson 1-7**   Use conditional statements and counterexamples.
- **Lessons 1-8 and 1-9**   Interpret graphs of functions and analyze data in statistical graphs.

Key Vocabulary

- variable (p. 6)
- order of operations (p. 11)
- identity (p. 21)
- like terms (p. 28)
- counterexample (p. 38)

Why It's Important

In every state and in every country, you find unique and inspiring architecture. Architects can use algebraic expressions to describe the volume of the structures they design. A few of the shapes these buildings can resemble are a rectangle, a pentagon, or even a pyramid. *You will find the amount of space occupied by a pyramid in Lesson 1-2.*

Vocabulary Builder   ELL

The Key Vocabulary list introduces students to some of the main vocabulary terms included in this chapter. For a more thorough vocabulary list with pronunciations of new words, give students the Vocabulary Builder worksheets found on pages vii and viii of the *Chapter 1 Resource Masters*. Encourage them to complete the definition of each term as they progress through the chapter. You may suggest that they add these sheets to their study notebooks for future reference when studying for the Chapter 1 test.

▶ **Prerequisite Skills** To be successful in this chapter, you'll need to master these skills and be able to apply them in problem-solving situations. Review these skills before beginning Chapter 1.

For Lessons 1-1, 1-2, and 1-3   Multiply and Divide Whole Numbers

Find each product or quotient.

1. $8 \cdot 8$ **64**   **2.** $4 \cdot 16$ **64**   **3.** $18 \cdot 9$ **162**   **4.** $23 \cdot 6$ **138**

5. $57 \div 3$ **19**   **6.** $68 \div 4$ **17**   **7.** $\frac{72}{3}$ **24**   **8.** $\frac{90}{6}$ **15**

For Lessons 1-1, 1-2, 1-5, and 1-6   **Find Perimeter**

Find the perimeter of each figure. *(For review, see pages 813 and 814.)*

9.   **16.6 m**
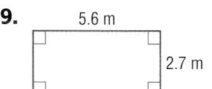
5.6 m / 2.7 m

10.   **19.1 cm**
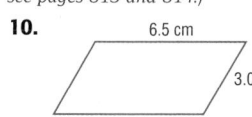
6.5 cm / 3.05 cm

11. $5\frac{1}{2}$ **ft**
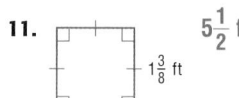
$1\frac{3}{8}$ ft

12. $135\frac{3}{4}$ **ft**
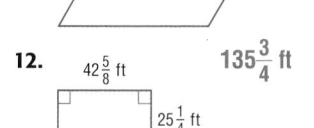
$42\frac{5}{8}$ ft / $25\frac{1}{4}$ ft

For Lessons 1-5 and 1-6   Multiply and Divide Decimals and Fractions

Find each product or quotient. *(For review, see pages 800 and 801.)*

13. $6 \cdot 1.2$ **7.2**   **14.** $0.5 \cdot 3.9$ **1.95**   **15.** $3.24 \div 1.8$ **1.8**   **16.** $10.64 \div 1.4$ **7.6**

17. $\frac{3}{4} \cdot 12$ **9**   **18.** $1\frac{2}{3} \cdot \frac{3}{4}$ $1\frac{1}{4}$ **19.** $\frac{5}{16} \div \frac{9}{12}$ $\frac{5}{12}$ **20.** $\frac{5}{6} \div \frac{2}{3}$ $\frac{5}{4}$ **or** $1\frac{1}{4}$

FOLDABLES™ Study Organizer

Algebraic Properties Make this Foldable to help you organize your notes. Begin with a sheet of notebook paper.

Step 1   **Fold**

Fold lengthwise to the holes.

Step 2   **Cut**

Cut along the top line and then cut 9 tabs.

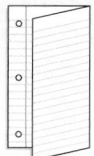

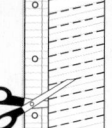

Step 3   **Label**

Label the tabs using the lesson numbers and concepts.

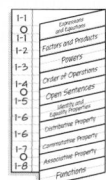

Reading and Writing Store the Foldable in a 3-ring binder. As you read and study the chapter, write notes and examples under the tabs.

This section provides a review of the basic concepts needed before beginning Chapter 1. Page references are included for additional student help.

Additional review is provided in the *Prerequisite Skills Workbook*, pp. 1–2, 5–12, 21–26, 47–50, 55–58, 61–62, 77–78, 95–96.

Prerequisite Skills in the Getting Ready for the Next Lesson section at the end of each exercise set review a skill needed in the next lesson.

For Lesson	Prerequisite Skill
1-2	Operations with Decimals and Fractions (p. 9)
1-3	Operations with Decimals and Fractions (p. 15)
1-4	Multiplying Fractions (p. 20)
1-5	Order of Operations (p. 25)
1-6	Finding Area (p. 31)
1-7	Evaluating Expressions (p. 36)
1-8	Percents (p. 42)
1-9	Making Bar Graphs (p. 48)

Each chapter opens with Prerequisite Skills practice for lessons in the chapter. More Prerequisite Skill practice can be found at the end of each lesson.

FOLDABLES™ Study Organizer

For more information about Foldables, see *Teaching Mathematics with Foldables.*

ELL **Vocabulary and Writing Definitions** Use this Foldable to help students better understand the language of algebra, to organize information they learn about algebraic properties, and to give them practice writing concise definitions in their own words. On each cut tab, have students write a word or concept on the front and its definition on the back. Under the tabs, ask students to include an example of each concept.

Foldables™ are a unique way to enhance students' study skills. Encourage students to add to their Foldable as they work through the chapter, and use it to review for their chapter test.

1 Focus

5-Minute Check Transparency 1-1 Use as a quiz or a review of the previous course materials.

Mathematical Background notes are available for this lesson on p. 4C.

What expression can be used to find the perimeter of a baseball diamond?

Ask students:

• How do you find the perimeter of a square? **Add the lengths of each side. Since the side lengths are the same in a square, multiply a side length by 4.**

• What do you suppose the expression 4s stands for? **four times s**

2 Teach

WRITE MATHEMATICAL EXPRESSIONS

In-Class Example | Power Point®

1 Write an algebraic expression for each verbal expression.

a. five less than a number c
  $c - 5$

b. 9 plus the product of 2 and the number d $9 + 2d$

c. two thirds of the original volume v $\dfrac{2}{3}v$

What You'll Learn

• Write mathematical expressions for verbal expressions.
• Write verbal expressions for mathematical expressions.

Vocabulary
• variables
• algebraic expression
• factors
• product
• power
• base
• exponent
• evaluate

What expression can be used to find the perimeter of a baseball diamond?

A baseball infield is a square with a base at each corner. Each base lies the same distance from the next one. Suppose *s* represents the length of each side of the square. Since the infield is a square, you can use the expression 4 times *s*, or 4*s* to find the perimeter of the square.

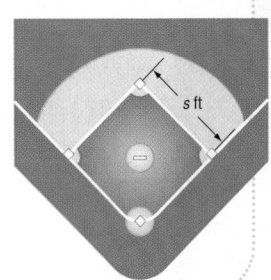
s ft

Lessons open with a question that is designed to engage students in the mathematics of the lesson. These opening problems should also help to answer the question "When am I ever going to use this?"

WRITE MATHEMATICAL EXPRESSIONS In the algebraic expression 4*s*, the letter *s* is called a variable. In algebra, **variables** are symbols used to represent unspecified numbers or values. Any letter may be used as a variable. *The letter s was used above because it is the first letter of the word side.*

An **algebraic expression** consists of one or more numbers and variables along with one or more arithmetic operations. Here are some examples of algebraic expressions.

$$5x \qquad 3x - 7 \qquad 4 + \frac{p}{q} \qquad m \times 5n \qquad 3ab \div 5cd$$

In algebraic expressions, a raised dot or parentheses are often used to indicate multiplication as the symbol × can be easily mistaken for the letter *x*. Here are several ways to represent the product of *x* and *y*.

$$xy \qquad x \cdot y \qquad x(y) \qquad (x)y \qquad (x)(y)$$

In each expression, the quantities being multiplied are called **factors**, and the result is called the **product**.

It is often necessary to translate verbal expressions into algebraic expressions.

Example 1 *Write Algebraic Expressions*

Write an algebraic expression for each verbal expression.

a. eight more than a number *n*

The words *more than* suggest addition.

$$\underset{8}{\underbrace{\text{eight}}} \quad \underset{+}{\underbrace{\text{more than}}} \quad \underset{n}{\underbrace{\text{a number } n}}$$

Thus, the algebraic expression is $8 + n$.

Resource Manager

📁 Workbook and Reproducible Masters

Chapter 1 Resource Masters
• Study Guide and Intervention, pp. 1–2
• Skills Practice, p. 3
• Practice, p. 4
• Reading to Learn Mathematics, p. 5
• Enrichment, p. 6

Parent and Student Study Guide Workbook, p. 1
Prerequisite Skills Workbook, pp. 9–10

📺 Transparencies
5-Minute Check Transparency 1-1
Answer Key Transparencies

💿 Technology
Interactive Chalkboard

b. 7 less the product of 4 and a number x

Less implies subtract, and *product* implies multiply. So the expression can be written as $7 - 4x$.

c. one third of the size of the original area a

The word *of* implies multiply, so the expression can be written as $\frac{1}{3}a$ or $\frac{a}{3}$.

An expression like x^n is called a **power** and is read "x to the nth power." The variable x is called the **base**, and n is called the **exponent**. The exponent indicates the number of times the base is used as a factor.

Symbols	Words	Meaning
3^1	3 to the first power	3
3^2	3 to the second power or 3 squared	$3 \cdot 3$
3^3	3 to the third power or 3 cubed	$3 \cdot 3 \cdot 3$
3^4	3 to the fourth power	$3 \cdot 3 \cdot 3 \cdot 3$
$2b^6$	2 times b to the sixth power	$2 \cdot b \cdot b \cdot b \cdot b \cdot b \cdot b$
x^n	x to the nth power	$\underbrace{x \cdot x \cdot x \cdot \ldots \cdot x}_{n \text{ factors}}$

By definition, for any nonzero number x, $x^0 = 1$.

Study Tip

Reading Math
When no exponent is shown, it is understood to be 1. For example, $a = a^1$.

Example 2 Write Algebraic Expressions with Powers

Write each expression algebraically.

a. the product of 7 and m to the fifth power

$7m^5$

b. the difference of 4 and x squared

$4 - x^2$

To **evaluate** an expression means to find its value.

Example 3 Evaluate Powers

Evaluate each expression.

a. 2^6

$2^6 = 2 \cdot 2 \cdot 2 \cdot 2 \cdot 2 \cdot 2$ — Use 2 as a factor 6 times.

$ = 64$ — Multiply.

b. 4^3

$4^3 = 4 \cdot 4 \cdot 4$ — Use 4 as a factor 3 times.

$ = 64$ — Multiply.

Examples illustrate all of the concepts taught in the lesson and closely mirror the exercises in the Guided Practice and Practice and Apply sections.

WRITE VERBAL EXPRESSIONS Another important skill is translating algebraic expressions into verbal expressions.

Example 4 Write Verbal Expressions

Write a verbal expression for each algebraic expression.

a. $4m^3$

the product of 4 and m to the third power

b. $c^2 + 21d$

the sum of c squared and 21 times d

 www.algebra1.com/extra_examples

Lesson 1-1 Variables and Expressions **7**

In-Class Examples Power Point®

2 Write each expression algebraically.

a. the product of $\frac{3}{4}$ and a to the seventh power $\frac{3}{4}a^7$

b. the sum of 11 and x to the third power $11 + x^3$

3 Evaluate each expression.

a. 3^4 81   **b.** 8^2 64

WRITE VERBAL EXPRESSIONS

In-Class Example Power Point®

4 Write a verbal expression for each algebraic expression.

a. $\frac{8x^2}{5}$ the quotient of 8 times x squared and 5

b. $y^5 - 16y$ the difference of y to the fifth power and 16 times y

In-Class Examples, which are included for every example in the Student Edition, exactly parallel the examples in the text. Teaching Tips about the examples in the Student Edition are included where appropriate.

3 Practice/Apply

Study Notebook

Have students—
• add the definitions/examples of the vocabulary terms to their Vocabulary Builder worksheets for Chapter 1.
• include any other item(s) that they find helpful in mastering the skills in this lesson.

DAILY INTERVENTION   **Differentiated Instruction**   **ELL**

Verbal/Linguistic The transition from verbal expressions to algebraic expressions and vice versa comes easier to some students. When you identify students who may be having trouble writing mathematical or verbal expressions, pair them with another student as a mentor for practicing these skills.

Write Mathematical Expressions In the algebraic expression, ℓw, the letters ℓ and w are called **variables**. In algebra, a variable is used to represent unspecified numbers or values. Any letter can be used as a variable. The letters ℓ and w are used above because they are the first letters of the words *length* and *width*. In the expression ℓw, ℓ and w are called **factors**, and the result is called the **product**.

Example 1 Write an algebraic expression for each verbal expression.

a. four more than a number n
The words *more than* imply addition.
four more than a number n
$4 + n$
The algebraic expression is $4 + n$.

b. the difference of a number squared and 8
The expression *difference of* implies subtraction.
the difference of a number squared and 8
$n^2 - 8$
The algebraic expression is $n^2 - 8$.

Example 2 Evaluate each expression.

a. 3^4
$3^4 = 3 \cdot 3 \cdot 3 \cdot 3$ Use 3 as a factor 4 times.
$= 81$ Multiply

b. five cubed
Cubed means raised to the third power.
$5^3 = 5 \cdot 5 \cdot 5$ Use 5 as a factor 3 times.
$= 125$ Multiply

Exercises

Write an algebraic expression for each verbal expression.

1. a number decreased by 8 $b - 8$
2. a number divided by 8 $\frac{h}{8}$
3. a number squared n^2
4. four times a number $4n$
5. a number divided by 6 $\frac{n}{6}$
6. a number multiplied by 37 $37n$
7. the sum of 9 and a number $9 + n$
8. 3 less than 5 times a number $5n - 3$
9. twice the sum of 15 and a number $2(15 + n)$
10. one-half the square of b $\frac{1}{2}b^2$
11. 7 more than the product of 6 and a number $6n + 7$
12. 30 increased by 3 times the square of a number $30 + 3n^2$

Evaluate each expression.

13. 5^2 25
14. 3^3 27
15. 10^4 10,000
16. 12^2 144
17. 8^3 512
18. 2^8 256

Write an algebraic expression for each verbal expression.

1. the difference of 10 and u
$10 - u$
2. the sum of 18 and a number
$18 + x$
3. the product of 33 and j
$33j$
4. 74 increased by 3 times y
$74 + 3y$
5. 15 decreased by twice a number
$15 - 2x$
6. 91 more than the square of a number
$x^2 + 91$
7. three fourths the square of b
$\frac{3}{4}b^2$
8. two fifths the cube of a number
$\frac{2}{5}x^3$

Evaluate each expression.

9. 11^2 121
10. 8^3 512
11. 5^4 625
12. 4^5 1024
13. 9^3 729
14. 6^4 1296
15. 10^5 100,000
16. 12^3 1728
17. 100^4 100,000,000

Write a verbal expression for each algebraic expression. 18–25. Sample answers are given.
18. $23f$
the product of 23 and f
19. 7^3
seven cubed
20. $5m^2 + 2$
2 more than 5 times m squared
21. $4d^3 - 10$
4 times d cubed minus 10
22. $x^3 \cdot y^4$ x cubed times y to the fourth power
23. $b^2 - 3c^3$ b squared minus 3 times c cubed
24. $\frac{k^5}{6}$ one sixth of the fifth power of k
25. $\frac{4n^2}{7}$ one seventh of 4 times n squared

26. **BOOKS** A used bookstore sells paperback fiction books in excellent condition for $2.50 and in fair condition for $0.50. Write an expression for the cost of buying e excellent-condition paperbacks and f fair-condition paperbacks. $2.50e + 0.50f$

27. **GEOMETRY** The surface area of the side of a right cylinder can be found by multiplying twice the number π by the radius times the height. If a circular cylinder has radius r and height h, write an expression that represents the surface area of its side. $2\pi rh$

ELL

Pre-Activity What expression can be used to find the perimeter of a baseball diamond?
Read the introduction to Lesson 1-1 at the top of page 6 in your textbook. Then complete the description of the expression $4s$.
In the expression $4s$, 4 represents the ___number___ of sides and s represents the ___length___ of each side.

Reading the Lesson

1. Why is the symbol $\times$ avoided in algebra?
It is easily confused with the variable x.

2. What are the factors in the algebraic expression $3xy$?
$3, x, y$

3. In the expression x^6, what is the base? What is the exponent?
$x; n$

4. Write the Roman numeral of the algebraic expression that best matches each phrase.
a. three more than a number n ___IV___   I. $5(x - 4)$
b. five times the difference of x and 4 ___I___   II. x^4
c. one half the number r ___III___   III. $\frac{1}{2}r$
d. the product of x and y divided by 2 ___V___   IV. $n + 3$
e. x to the fourth power ___II___   V. $\frac{xy}{2}$

Helping You Remember

5. Multiplying 5 times 3 is not the same as raising 5 to the third power. How does the way you write "5 times 3" and "5 to the third power" in symbols help you remember that they give different results?
Sample answer: "5 times 3" is written with the numbers 5 and 3 on the same level, as in $5 \cdot 3$ or $5(3)$. "5 to the third power" is written as 5^3, with the exponent 3 on a higher level than the number 5.

---

c. 5^3
five to the third power or five cubed

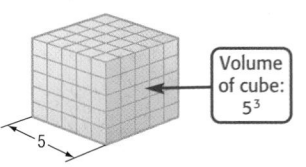
5
Volume of cube: 5^3

Check for Understanding

Concept Check
1. See margin.

1. **Explain** the difference between an algebraic expression and a verbal expression.
2. **Write** an expression that represents the perimeter of the rectangle. **Sample answer:** $2\ell + 2w$
3. **OPEN ENDED** Give an example of a variable to the fifth power. **Sample answer:** a^5

4–5. Sample answers are given.

Guided Practice Write an algebraic expression for each verbal expression.

GUIDED PRACTICE KEY	
Exercises	Examples
4, 5	1, 2
6, 7	3
8, 9	4
10	2

4. the sum of j and 13 $j + 13$
5. 24 less than three times a number
$3x - 24$

Evaluate each expression.

6. 9^2 **81**
7. 4^4 **256**

Write a verbal expression for each algebraic expression.

8. $4m^4$ the product of 4 and m to the fourth power
9. $\frac{1}{2}n^3$ one half of n cubed

Application
10. **MONEY** Lorenzo bought several pounds of chocolate-covered peanuts and gave the cashier a $20 bill. Write an expression for the amount of change he will receive if p represents the cost of the peanuts. $20 - p$

★ indicates increased difficulty

Practice and Apply

Homework Help	
For Exercises	See Examples
11–18	1, 2
21–28	3
31–42	4

Extra Practice
See page 820.

Write an algebraic expression for each verbal expression. 15. $49 + 2x$ 17. $\frac{2}{3}x^2$

11. the sum of 35 and z $35 + z$
12. the sum of a number and 7 $x + 7$
13. the product of 16 and p $16p$
14. the product of 5 and a number $5y$
15. 49 increased by twice a number
16. 18 and three times d $18 + 3d$
★ 17. two-thirds the square of a number
★ 18. one-half the cube of n $\frac{1}{2}n^3$
11–18. Sample answers are given.

19. **SAVINGS** Kendra is saving to buy a new computer. Write an expression to represent the amount of money she will have if she has s dollars saved and she adds d dollars per week for the next 12 weeks. $s + 12d$

20. **GEOMETRY** The area of a circle can be found by multiplying the number π by the square of the radius. If the radius of a circle is r, write an expression that represents the area of the circle. πr^2

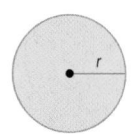
r

Evaluate each expression.

21. 6^2 **36**
22. 8^2 **64**
23. 3^4 **81**
24. 6^3 **216**
25. 3^5 **243**
26. 15^3 **3375**
27. 10^6 **1,000,000**
28. 100^3 **1,000,000**

29. $8.5b + 3.99d$

29. **FOOD** A bakery sells a dozen bagels for $8.50 and a dozen donuts for $3.99. Write an expression for the cost of buying b dozen bagels and d dozen donuts.

Enrichment, p. 6

The Tower of Hanoi

The diagram at the right shows the Tower of Hanoi puzzle. Notice that there are three pegs, with a stack of disks on peg a. The object is to move all of the disks to another peg. You may move only one disk at a time and a larger disk may never be put on top of a smaller disk.

As you solve the puzzle, record each move in the table shown. The first two moves are recorded.

Peg a   Peg b   Peg c

	Peg a	Peg b	Peg c
1			
2			
3			

Solve.

1. Complete the table to solve the Tower of Hanoi puzzle for three disks.

2. Another way to record each move is to use letters. For example, the first two moves in the table can be recorded as 1c, 2b. This shows that disk 1 is moved to peg c, and then disk 2 is moved to peg b. Record your solution

	Peg a	Peg b	Peg c
2			
3		1	

There is a Study Guide and Intervention, Skills Practice, Practice, Reading to Learn Mathematics, and Enrichment Master for every lesson in the Student Edition. These masters can be found in the Chapter Resource Masters.

35. three times x squared plus four

36. 2 times n cubed plus 12

37. a to the fourth power times b squared

38. n cubed times p to the fifth power

More About...

Recycling •··············•

In 2002, about 30% of all waste was recycled.

Source: U.S. Environmental Protection Agency

39. Sample answer: one-fifth 12 times z squared

40. Sample answer: one-fourth 8 times g cubed

41. 3 times x squared minus 2 times x

42. 4 times f to the fifth power minus 9 times k cubed

Standardized Test Practice
(A) (B) (C) (D)

30. TRAVEL Before starting her vacation, Sari's car had 23,500 miles on the odometer. She drives an average of m miles each day for two weeks. Write an expression that represents the mileage on Sari's odometer after her trip. **$23,500 + 14m$**

Write a verbal expression for each algebraic expression. **34. five to the fourth power**

31. $7p$ **7 times p**   **32.** $15r$ **15 times r**   **33.** 3^3 **three cubed**   **34.** 5^4

35. $3x^2 + 4$ **36.** $2n^3 + 12$ **37.** $a^4 \cdot b^2$ **38.** $n^3 \cdot p^5$

★ **39.** $\frac{12z^2}{5}$ ★ **40.** $\frac{8g^3}{4}$ ★ **41.** $3x^2 - 2x$ ★ **42.** $4f^5 - 9k^3$

43. PHYSICAL SCIENCE When water freezes, its volume increases. The volume of ice equals the sum of the volume of the water and the product of one-eleventh and the volume of the water. If x cubic centimeters of water is frozen, write an expression for the volume of the ice that is formed. **$x + \frac{1}{11}x$**

★ **44. GEOMETRY** The surface area of a rectangular prism is the sum of: **$2\ell w + 2\ell h + 2wh$**
- the product of twice the length ℓ and the width w,
- the product of twice the length and the height h, and
- the product of twice the width and the height.

Write an expression that represents the surface area of a prism.

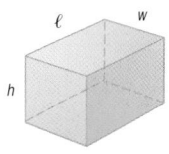

45. RECYCLING Each person in the United States produces approximately 3.5 pounds of trash each day. Write an expression representing the pounds of trash produced in a day by a family that has m members. **Source:** *Vitality* **$3.5m$**

46. CRITICAL THINKING In the square, the variable a represents a positive whole number. Find the value of a such that the area and the perimeter of the square are the same. **4**

47. **WRITING IN MATH** Answer the question that was posed at the beginning of the lesson. **See margin.**

What expression can be used to find the perimeter of a baseball diamond?

Include the following in your answer:
- two different verbal expressions that you can use to describe the perimeter of a square, and
- an algebraic expression other than $4s$ that you can use to represent the perimeter of a square.

48. What is 6 more than 2 times a certain number x? **D**
(A) $2x - 6$ (B) $2x$ (C) $6x - 2$ (D) $2x + 6$

49. Write $4 \cdot 4 \cdot 4 \cdot c \cdot c \cdot c \cdot c$ using exponents. **B**
(A) $3^4 4^c$ (B) $4^3 c^4$ (C) $(4c)^7$ (D) $4c$

Maintain Your Skills

Getting Ready for the Next Lesson

PREREQUISITE SKILL Evaluate each expression.
*(To review **operations with fractions**, see pages 798–801.)*

50. $14.3 + 1.8$ **16.1**   **51.** $10 - 3.24$ **6.76**   **52.** 1.04×4.3 **4.472**   **53.** $15.36 \div 4.8$ **3.2**

54. $\frac{1}{3} + \frac{2}{5}$ **$\frac{11}{15}$**   **55.** $\frac{3}{4} - \frac{1}{6}$ **$\frac{7}{12}$**   **56.** $\frac{3}{8} \times \frac{4}{9}$ **$\frac{1}{6}$**   **57.** $\frac{7}{10} \div \frac{3}{5}$ **$\frac{7}{6}$ or $1\frac{1}{6}$**

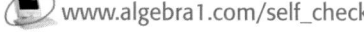 www.algebra1.com/self_check_quiz

Answers

1. Algebraic expressions include variables and numbers, while verbal expressions contain words.

47. You can use the expression $4s$ to find the perimeter of a baseball diamond. Answers should include the following.
- four times the length of the sides and the sum of the four sides
- $s + s + s + s$

About the Exercises...

Organization by Objective
- **Write Mathematical Expressions:** 11–20, 29–30, 43–45
- **Write Verbal Expressions:** 31–42

Odd/Even Assignments
Exercises 11–42 are structured so that students practice the same concepts whether they are assigned odd or even problems.

Assignment Guide
Basic: 11–15 odd, 19–37 odd, 43, 45, 46–57
Average: 11–45 odd, 46–57
Advanced: 12–44 even, 46–49 (optional: 50–57)

The Assignment Guides provide suggestions for exercises that are appropriate for basic, average, or advanced students. Many of the homework exercises are paired, so that students can do the odds one day and the evens the next day.

4 Assess

Open-Ended Assessment

Writing Challenge students to write an algebraic expression that they think will be very hard to change into a verbal expression. Then have students exchange expressions and translate into verbal expressions.

Getting Ready for Lesson 1-2

PREREQUISITE SKILL Students will learn about order of operations in Lesson 1-2. The expressions that they evaluate following the order of operations involve decimals and fractions. Use Exercises 50–57 to determine your students' familiarity with operations with decimals and fractions.

Translating from English to Algebra

You learned in Lesson 1-1 that it is often necessary to translate words into algebraic expressions. Generally, there are "clue" words such as *more than, times, less than,* and so on, which indicate the operation to use. These words also help to connect numerical data. The table shows a few examples.

Words	Algebraic Expression
four times x plus y	$4x + y$
four times the sum of x and y	$4(x + y)$
four times the quantity x plus y	$4(x + y)$

Notice that all three expressions are worded differently, but the first expression is the only one that is different algebraically. In the second expression, parentheses indicate that the *sum*, $x + y$, is multiplied by four. In algebraic expressions, terms grouped by parentheses are treated as one quantity. So, $4(x + y)$ can also be read as *four times the quantity x plus y*.

Words that may indicate parentheses are *sum, difference, product,* and *quantity*.

Reading Mathematics features help students learn and use the language of mathematics.

Reading to Learn

Read each verbal expression aloud. Then match it with the correct algebraic expression.

1. nine divided by 2 plus n **c**
2. four divided by the difference of n and six **b**
3. n plus five squared **f**
4. three times the quantity eight plus n **h**
5. nine divided by the quantity 2 plus n **g**
6. three times eight plus n **d**
7. the quantity n plus five squared **a**
8. four divided by n minus six **e**

a. $(n + 5)^2$
b. $4 \div (n - 6)$
c. $9 \div 2 + n$
d. $3(8) + n$
e. $4 \div n - 6$
f. $n + 5^2$
g. $9 \div (2 + n)$
h. $3(8 + n)$

9–14. Sample answers are given.

9. one more than five times x
10. five times the quantity x plus one
11. three plus the product of seven and x
12. the sum of three and x multiplied by seven
13. the sum of six and b divided by y
14. six plus the quotient of b and y

Write each algebraic expression in words.

9. $5x + 1$
10. $5(x + 1)$
11. $3 + 7x$
12. $(3 + x) \cdot 7$
13. $(6 + b) \div y$
14. $6 + (b \div y)$

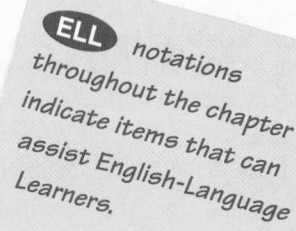

ELL notations throughout the chapter indicate items that can assist English-Language Learners.

What You'll Learn

* Evaluate numerical expressions by using the order of operations.
* Evaluate algebraic expressions by using the order of operations.

Vocabulary
* order of operations

How is the monthly cost of internet service determined?

Nicole is signing up with a new internet service provider. The service costs $4.95 a month, which includes 100 hours of access. If she is online for more than 100 hours, she must pay an additional $0.99 per hour. Suppose Nicole is online for 117 hours the first month. The expression $4.95 + 0.99(117 - 100)$ represents what Nicole must pay for the month.

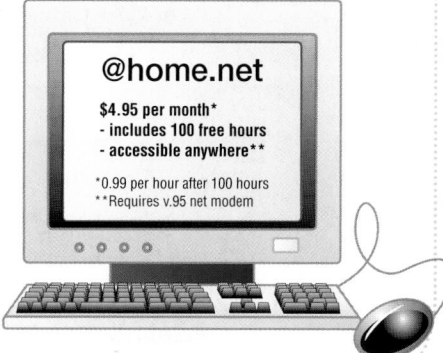

@home.net

$4.95 per month*
- includes 100 free hours
- accessible anywhere**

*0.99 per hour after 100 hours
**Requires v.95 net modem

EVALUATE RATIONAL EXPRESSIONS Numerical expressions often contain more than one operation. A rule is needed to let you know which operation to perform first. This rule is called the **order of operations**.

TEACHING TIP
Students may find a memory device helpful. The first letters of "Please Excuse My Dear Aunt Sally" represent parentheses, exponents, multiplication, division, addition, subtraction.

Key Concept — Order of Operations

Step 1 Evaluate expressions inside grouping symbols.
Step 2 Evaluate all powers.
Step 3 Do all multiplications and/or divisions from left to right.
Step 4 Do all additions and/or subtractions from left to right.

Example 1 Evaluate Expressions

Evaluate each expression.

a. $3 + 2 \cdot 3 + 5$

$$3 + 2 \cdot 3 + 5 = 3 + 6 + 5 \quad \text{Multiply 2 and 3.}$$
$$= 9 + 5 \quad \text{Add 3 and 6.}$$
$$= 14 \quad \text{Add 9 and 5.}$$

b. $15 \div 3 \cdot 5 - 4^2$

$$15 \div 3 \cdot 5 - 4^2 = 15 \div 3 \cdot 5 - 16 \quad \text{Evaluate powers.}$$
$$= 5 \cdot 5 - 16 \quad \text{Divide 15 by 3.}$$
$$= 25 - 16 \quad \text{Multiply 5 by 5.}$$
$$= 9 \quad \text{Subtract 16 from 25.}$$

Lesson 1-2 Order of Operations **11**

EVALUATE RATIONAL EXPRESSIONS

In-Class Examples

1 Evaluate each expression.

a. $6 + 4 - 2 \cdot 3$ **4**

b. $48 \div 2^3 \cdot 3 + 5$ **23**

2 Evaluate each expression.

a. $(8 - 3) \cdot 3(3 + 2)$ **75**

b. $4[12 \div (6 - 2)]^2$ **36**

3 Evaluate $\dfrac{2^5 - 6 \cdot 2}{3^3 - 5 \cdot 3 - 2}$. **2**

EVALUATE ALGEBRAIC EXPRESSIONS

In-Class Examples

4 Evaluate $2(x^2 - y) + z^2$ if $x = 4$, $y = 3$, and $z = 2$. **30**

5 **ARCHITECTURE** Each of the four sides of the Great Pyramid at Giza, Egypt, is a triangle. The base of each triangle originally measured 230 meters. The height of each triangle originally measured 187 meters. The area of any triangle is one-half the product of the length of the base b and the height h.

a. Write an expression that represents the area of one side of the Great Pyramid.
$\dfrac{1}{2}(bh)$

b. Find the area of one side of the Great Pyramid. **21,505 m²**

Interactive Chalkboard CD-ROM offers a dynamic alternative to traditional classroom presentations,

---

Grouping symbols such as parentheses ( ), brackets [ ], and braces { } are used to clarify or change the order of operations. They indicate that the expression within the grouping symbol is to be evaluated first.

Example 2 Grouping Symbols

Evaluate each expression.

a. $2(5) + 3(4 + 3)$

$\begin{aligned}
2(5) + 3(4 + 3) &= 2(5) + 3(7) & \text{Evaluate inside grouping symbols.} \\
&= 10 + 21 & \text{Multiply expressions left to right.} \\
&= 31 & \text{Add 10 and 21.}
\end{aligned}$

b. $2[5 + (30 \div 6)^2]$

$\begin{aligned}
2[5 + (30 \div 6)^2] &= 2[5 + (5)^2] & \text{Evaluate innermost expression first.} \\
&= 2[5 + 25] & \text{Evaluate power inside grouping symbol.} \\
&= 2[30] & \text{Evaluate expression in grouping symbol.} \\
&= 60 & \text{Multiply.}
\end{aligned}$

A fraction bar is another type of grouping symbol. It indicates that the numerator and denominator should each be treated as a single value.

Example 3 Fraction Bar

Evaluate $\dfrac{6 + 4^2}{3^2 \cdot 4}$.

$\dfrac{6 + 4^2}{3^2 \cdot 4}$ means $(6 + 4^2) \div (3^2 \cdot 4)$.

$\begin{aligned}
\dfrac{6 + 4^2}{3^2 \cdot 4} &= \dfrac{6 + 16}{3^2 \cdot 4} & \text{Evaluate the power in the numerator.} \\
&= \dfrac{22}{3^2 \cdot 4} & \text{Add 6 and 16 in the numerator.} \\
&= \dfrac{22}{9 \cdot 4} & \text{Evaluate the power in the denominator.} \\
&= \dfrac{22}{36} \text{ or } \dfrac{11}{18} & \text{Multiply 9 and 4 in the denominator. Then simplify.}
\end{aligned}$

EVALUATE ALGEBRAIC EXPRESSIONS Like numerical expressions, algebraic expressions often contain more than one operation. Algebraic expressions can be evaluated when the values of the variables are known. First, replace the variables with their values. Then, find the value of the numerical expression using the order of operations.

Example 4 Evaluate an Algebraic Expression

Evaluate $a^2 - (b^3 - 4c)$ if $a = 7$, $b = 3$, and $c = 5$.

$\begin{aligned}
a^2 - (b^3 - 4c) &= 7^2 - (3^3 - 4 \cdot 5) & \text{Replace } a \text{ with 7, } b \text{ with 3, and } c \text{ with 5.} \\
&= 7^2 - (27 - 4 \cdot 5) & \text{Evaluate } 3^3. \\
&= 7^2 - (27 - 20) & \text{Multiply 4 and 5.} \\
&= 7^2 - 7 & \text{Subtract 20 from 27.} \\
&= 49 - 7 & \text{Evaluate } 7^2. \\
&= 42 & \text{Subtract.}
\end{aligned}$

Interactive Chalkboard
PowerPoint® Presentations

This CD-ROM is a customizable Microsoft® PowerPoint® presentation that includes:

- Step-by-step, dynamic solutions of each In-Class Example from the Teacher Wraparound Edition
- Additional, Your Turn exercises for each example
- The 5-Minute Check Transparencies
- Hot links to Glencoe Online Study Tools

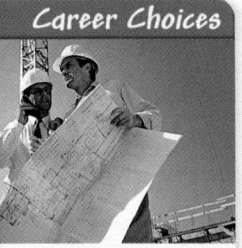
Example 5 *Use Algebraic Expressions*

•• **ARCHITECTURE** The Pyramid Arena in Memphis, Tennessee, is the third largest pyramid in the world. The area of its base is 360,000 square feet, and it is 321 feet high. The volume of any pyramid is one third of the product of the area of the base B and its height h.

a. Write an expression that represents the volume of a pyramid.

$$\underbrace{\text{one third}}_{\frac{1}{3}} \quad \underbrace{\text{of}}_{\times} \quad \underbrace{\substack{\text{the product of area} \\ \text{of base and height}}}_{(B \cdot h)} \quad \text{or } \frac{1}{3}Bh$$

b. Find the volume of the Pyramid Arena.

Evaluate $\frac{1}{3}(Bh)$ for $B = 360{,}000$ and $h = 321$.

$$\frac{1}{3}(Bh) = \frac{1}{3}(360{,}000 \cdot 321) \quad B = 360{,}000 \text{ and } h = 321$$

$$= \frac{1}{3}(115{,}560{,}000) \quad \text{Multiply } 360{,}000 \text{ by } 321.$$

$$= \frac{115{,}560{,}000}{3} \quad \text{Multiply } \frac{1}{3} \text{ by } 115{,}560{,}000.$$

$$= 38{,}520{,}000 \quad \text{Divide } 115{,}560{,}000 \text{ by } 3.$$

The volume of the Pyramid Arena is 38,520,000 cubic feet.

Check for Understanding

Concept Check

1. Sample answer: First add the numbers in parentheses, $(2 + 5)$. Next square 6. Then multiply 7 by 3. Subtract inside the brackets. Multiply that by 8. Divide, then add 3.

1. Describe how to evaluate $8[6^2 - 3(2 + 5)] \div 8 + 3$.

2. OPEN ENDED Write an expression involving division in which the first step in evaluating the expression is addition. **Sample answer: $(2 + 4) \div 3$**

3. FIND THE ERROR Laurie and Chase are evaluating $3[4 + (27 \div 3)]^2$.

Laurie	Chase
$3[4 + (27 \div 3)]^2 = 3(4 + 9^2)$	$3[4 + (27 \div 3)]^2 = 3(4 + 9)^2$
$= 3(4 + 81)$	$= 3(13)^2$
$= 3(85)$	$= 3(169)$
$= 255$	$= 507$

Who is correct? Explain your reasoning. **Chase; Laurie raised the incorrect quantity to the second power.**

Guided Practice

Evaluate each expression.

4. $(4 + 6)7$ **70**

5. $50 - (15 + 9)$ **26**

6. $29 - 3(9 - 4)$ **14**

7. $[7(2) - 4] + [9 + 8(4)]$ **51**

8. $\frac{(4 \cdot 3)^2 \cdot 5}{9 + 3}$ **60**

9. $\frac{3 + 2^3}{5^2(4)}$ **$\frac{11}{100}$**

Evaluate each expression if $g = 4$, $h = 6$, $j = 8$, and $k = 12$.

10. $hk - gj$ **40**

11. $2k + gh^2 - j$ **160**

12. $\frac{2g(h - g)}{gh - j}$ **1**

Application

13. $20.00 + 2 \times 9.95$

SHOPPING For Exercises 13 and 14, use the following information.
A computer store has certain software on sale at 3 for $20.00, with a limit of 3 at the sale price. Additional software is available at the regular price of $9.95 each.

13. Write an expression you could use to find the cost of 5 software packages.

14. How much would 5 software packages cost? **$39.90**

 www.algebra1.com/extra_examples

Lesson 1-2 Order of Operations **13**

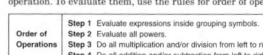

Study Guide and Intervention, p. 7 (shown) and p. 8

Evaluate Rational Expressions Numerical expressions often contain more than one operation. To evaluate them, use the rules for order of operations shown below.

Order of Operations	Step 1 Evaluate expressions inside grouping symbols.
	Step 2 Evaluate all powers.
	Step 3 Do all multiplication and/or division from left to right.
	Step 4 Do all addition and/or subtraction from left to right.

Example 1 Evaluate each expression.

a. $7 + 2 \cdot 4 - 4$
$7 + 2 \cdot 4 - 4 = 7 + 8 - 4$ Multiply 2 and 4.
$= 15 - 4$ Add 7 and 8.
$= 11$ Subtract 4 from 15.

b. $3(2) + 4(2 + 6)$
$3(2) + 4(2 + 6) = 3(2) + 4(8)$ Add 2 and 6.
$= 6 + 32$ Multiply left to right.
$= 38$ Add 6 and 32.

Example 2 Evaluate each expression.

a. $3[2 + (12 \div 3)^2]$
$3[2 + (12 \div 3)^2] = 3(2 + 4^2)$ Divide 12 by 3.
$= 3(2 + 16)$ Find 4 squared.
$= 3(18)$ Add 2 and 16.
$= 54$ Multiply 3 and 18.

b. $\dfrac{3 + 2^3}{4^2 \cdot 3}$
$\dfrac{3 + 2^3}{4^2 \cdot 3} = \dfrac{3 + 8}{4^2 \cdot 3}$ Evaluate power in numerator.
$= \dfrac{11}{4^2 \cdot 3}$ Add 3 and 8 in the numerator.
$= \dfrac{11}{16 \cdot 3}$ Evaluate power in denominator.
$= \dfrac{11}{48}$ Multiply.

Exercises

Evaluate each expression.

1. $(8 - 4) \cdot 2$ **8**
2. $(12 + 4) \cdot 6$ **96**
3. $10 + 2 \cdot 3$ **16**
4. $10 + 8 \cdot 1$ **18**
5. $15 - 12 \div 4$ **12**
6. $\dfrac{15 + 60}{30 - 5}$ **3**
7. $12(20 - 17) - 3 \cdot 6$ **18**
8. $24 \div 3 \cdot 2 - 3^2$ **7**
9. $8^2 \div (2 \cdot 8) + 2$ **6**
10. $3^2 \div 3 + 2^2 \cdot 7 - 20 \div 5$ **27**
11. $\dfrac{4 + 3^2}{12 + 1}$ **1**
12. $\dfrac{8(2) - 4}{8 + 4}$ **6**
13. $250 - [5(3 \cdot 7 + 4)]$ **2**
14. $\dfrac{2 \cdot 4^2 - 8 \div 2}{(5 + 2) \cdot 2}$ **2**
15. $\dfrac{4 \cdot 3^2 - 3 \cdot 2}{3 \cdot 5}$ **2**
16. $\dfrac{4(5^2) - 4 \cdot 3}{4(4 \cdot 5 + 2)}$ **1**
17. $\dfrac{5^2 - 3}{20(3) + 2(3)}$ **$\frac{1}{3}$**
18. $\dfrac{8^2 - 2^2}{(2 \cdot 8) + 4}$ **3**

Skills Practice, p. 9 and Practice, p. 10 (shown)

Evaluate each expression.

1. $(15 - 5) \cdot 2$ **20**
2. $9 \cdot (3 + 4)$ **63**
3. $5 + 7 \cdot 4$ **33**
4. $12 + 5 - 6 \cdot 2$ **5**
5. $7 \cdot 9 - 4(6 + 7)$ **11**
6. $8 + (2 + 2) \cdot 7$ **14**
7. $4(3 + 5) - 5 \cdot 4$ **12**
8. $22 + 11 - 9 \div 3^2$ **9**
9. $6^2 + 3 \cdot 7 - 9$ **48**
10. $3[10 - (27 \div 9)]$ **21**
11. $2[5^2 + (36 \div 6)]$ **62**
12. $162 + [6(7 - 4)^2]$ **3**
13. $\dfrac{5^2 \cdot 4 - 5 \cdot 4^2}{5(4)}$ **1**
14. $\dfrac{(2 \cdot 5)^2 + 4}{3^2 - 5}$ **26**
15. $\dfrac{7 + 3^2}{4^2 \cdot 2}$ **$\frac{1}{2}$**

Evaluate each expression if $a = 12$, $b = 9$, and $c = 4$.

16. $a^2 + b - c^2$ **137**
17. $b^2 + 2a - c^2$ **89**
18. $2c(a + b)$ **168**
19. $4a + 2b - c^2$ **50**
20. $(a^2 + 4b) + c$ **8**
21. $c^2 \cdot (2b - a)$ **96**
22. $\dfrac{bc^2 + a}{c}$ **39**
23. $\dfrac{2c^3 - ab}{4}$ **5**
24. $\dfrac{2(a - b)^2}{5c}$ **$\frac{9}{10}$**
25. $\dfrac{b^2 - 2c^2}{a + c - b}$ **7**

CAR RENTAL For Exercises 26 and 27, use the following information.
Ann Carlyle is planning a business trip for which she needs to rent a car. The car rental company charges $36 per day plus $0.50 per mile over 100 miles. Suppose Ms. Carlyle rents the car for 5 days and drives 180 miles.

26. Write an expression for how much it will cost Ms. Carlyle to rent the car.
$5(36) + 0.5(180 - 100)$

27. Evaluate the expression to determine how much Ms. Carlyle must pay the car rental company. **$220.00**

GEOMETRY For Exercises 28 and 29, use the following information.
The length of a rectangle is $3n + 2$ and its width is $n - 1$. The perimeter of the rectangle is twice the sum of its length and its width.

28. Write an expression that represents the perimeter of the rectangle.
$2[(3n + 2) + (n - 1)]$

29. Find the perimeter of the rectangle when $n = 4$ inches. **34 in.**

Reading to Learn Mathematics, p. 11   ELL

Pre-Activity   **How is the monthly cost of internet service determined?**
Read the introduction to Lesson 1-2 at the top of page 11 in your textbook.
In the expression $4.95 + 0.99(117 - 100)$, ___4.95___ represents the regular monthly cost of internet service, ___0.99___ represents the cost of each additional hour after 100 hours, and ___(117 - 100)___ represents the number of hours over 100 used by Nicole in a given month.

Reading the Lesson

1. The first step in evaluating an expression is to evaluate inside grouping symbols. List four types of grouping symbols found in algebraic expressions.
parentheses, brackets, braces, and fraction bars

2. What does *evaluate powers* mean? Use an example to explain.
Sample answer: To evaluate a power means to find the value of the power. To evaluate 4^3, find the value of $4 \times 4 \times 4$.

3. Read the order of operations on page 11 in your textbook. For each of the following expressions, write *addition, subtraction, multiplication, division,* or *evaluate powers* to tell what operation to use first when evaluating the expression.
   a. $400 - 5[12 + 9]$ **addition**
   b. $26 - 8 + 14$ **subtraction**
   c. $17 + 3 \cdot 6$ **multiplication**
   d. $69 + 57 \div 3 + 16 \cdot 4$ **division**
   e. $\dfrac{19 + 3 \cdot 4}{6 \div 2}$ **multiplication**
   f. $\dfrac{51 + 729}{9^2}$ **evaluate powers**

Helping You Remember

4. The sentence *Please Excuse My Dear Aunt Sally* (PEMDAS) is often used to remember the order of operations. The letter P represents parentheses and other grouping symbols. Write what each of the other letters in PEMDAS means when using the order of operations.
E—exponents (powers), M—multiply, D—divide, A—add, S—subtract

---

★ indicates increased difficulty

Practice and Apply

Homework Help

For Exercises	See Examples
15–28	1–3
29–31	5
32–39	4, 5

Extra Practice
See page 820.

27. $\dfrac{87}{2}$ or $43\frac{1}{2}$

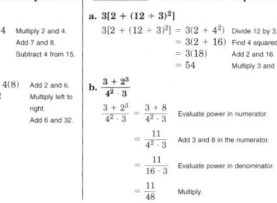

Homework Help charts show students which examples to refer to if they need additional practice. Extra Practice for every lesson is provided on pages 820–852.

Evaluate each expression.

15. $(12 - 6) \cdot 2$ **12**
16. $(16 - 3) \cdot 4$ **52**
17. $15 + 3 \cdot 2$ **21**
18. $22 + 3 \cdot 7$ **43**
19. $4(11 + 7) - 9 \cdot 8$ **0**
20. $12(9 + 5) - 6 \cdot 3$ **150**
21. $12 \div 3 \cdot 5 - 4^2$ **4**
22. $15 \div 3 \cdot 5 - 4^2$ **9**
23. $288 \div [3(9 + 3)]$ **8**

Evaluate each expression.

24. $390 \div [5(7 + 6)]$ **6**
25. $\dfrac{2 \cdot 8^2 - 2^2 \cdot 8}{2 \cdot 8}$ **6**
26. $\dfrac{4 \cdot 6^2 - 4^2 \cdot 6}{4 \cdot 6}$ **2**
★27. $\dfrac{[(8 + 5)(6 - 2)^2] - (4 \cdot 17 \div 2)}{[(24 \div 2) \div 3]}$
★28. $6 - \left[\dfrac{2 + 7}{3} - (2 \cdot 3 - 5)\right]$ **4**

29. **GEOMETRY** Find the area of the rectangle when $n = 4$ centimeters. **44 cm²**

$2n + 3$

ENTERTAINMENT   For Exercises 30 and 31, use the following information.
Derrick and Samantha are selling tickets for their school musical. Floor seats cost $7.50 and balcony seats cost $5.00. Samantha sells 60 floor seats and 70 balcony seats, Derrick sells 50 floor seats and 90 balcony seats.

30. Write an expression to show how much money Samantha and Derrick have collected for tickets. $60(7.5) + 70(5) + 50(7.5) + 90(5)$

31. Evaluate the expression to determine how much they collected. **$1625**

Evaluate each expression if $x = 12$, $y = 8$, and $z = 3$.

32. $x + y^2 + z^2$ **85**
33. $x^3 + y + z^3$ **1763**
34. $3xy - z$ **285**
35. $4x - yz$ **24**
36. $\dfrac{2xy - z^3}{z}$ **55**
37. $\dfrac{xy^2 - 3z}{3}$ **253**
★38. $\left(\dfrac{x}{y}\right)^2 - \dfrac{3y - z}{(x - y)^2}$ **$\frac{15}{16}$**
★39. $\dfrac{x - z^2}{y \div x} + \dfrac{2y - x}{y^2 \div 2}$ **$\frac{37}{8}$ or $4\frac{5}{8}$**

40. **BIOLOGY** A certain type of bacteria can double its numbers every 20 minutes. Suppose 100 of these cells are in one culture dish and 250 of the cells are in another culture dish. Write and evaluate an expression that shows the total number of bacteria cells in both dishes after 20 minutes.
$100 \cdot 2 + 250 \cdot 2$; **700 bacteria cells**

BUSINESS   For Exercises 41–43, use the following information.
Mr. Martinez is a sales representative for an agricultural supply company. He receives a salary and monthly commission. He also receives a bonus each time he reaches a sales goal.

41. Write a verbal expression that describes how much Mr. Martinez earns in a year if he receives four equal bonuses.
41. the sum of salary, commission, and 4 bonuses

42. Let e represent earnings, s represent his salary, c represent his commission, and b represent his bonus. Write an algebraic expression to represent his earnings if he receives four equal bonuses. $e = s + c + 4b$

43. Suppose Mr. Martinez's annual salary is $42,000 and his average commission is $825 each month. If he receives four bonuses of $750 each, how much does he earn in a year? **$54,900**

Enrichment, p. 12

The Four Digits Problem

One well-known mathematic problem is to write expressions for consecutive numbers beginning with 1. On this page, you will use the digits 1, 2, 3, and 4. Each digit is used only once. You may use addition, subtraction, multiplication (not division), exponents, and parentheses in any way you wish. Also, you can use two digits to make one number, such as 12 or 34.

Answers will vary. Sample answers are given.

Express each number as a combination of the digits 1, 2, 3, and 4.

$1 = (3 \times 1) - (4 - 2)$	$18 = $ ___$(2 \times 3) \times (4 - 1)$___	$35 = 2^{(4+1)} + 3$	
$2 = $ ___$(4 - 3) + (2 - 1)$___	$19 = 3(2 \times 4) + 1$	$36 = $ ___$34 + (2 \times 1)$___	
$3 = $ ___$(4 - 3) + (2 \times 1)$___	$20 = $ ___$21 - (4 - 3)$___	$37 = $ ___$31 + 2 + 4$___	
$4 = $ ___$(4 - 2) + (3 - 1)$___	$21 = $ ___$(4 + 3) \times (2 + 1)$___	$38 = $ ___$42 - (3 + 1)$___	
$5 = $ ___$(4 - 2) + (3 \times 1)$___	$22 = $ ___$21 + (4 - 3)$___	$39 = $ ___$42 - (3 \times 1)$___	

44. CRITICAL THINKING Choose three numbers from 1 to 6. Write as many expressions as possible that have different results when they are evaluated. You must use all three numbers in each expression, and each can only be used once. Sample answer: Using 1, 2, 3: $1 + 2 + 3 = 6$; $1 + 2 \cdot 3 = 7$; $1 \cdot 2 + 3 = 5$; $3 - 2 \cdot 1 = 1$; $(2 - 1) \cdot 3 = 3$

45. WRITING IN MATH Answer the question that was posed at the beginning of the lesson. **See margin.**

How is the monthly cost of internet service determined?

Include the following in your answer:
- an expression for the cost of service if Nicole has a coupon for $25 off her base rate for her first six months, and
- an explanation of the advantage of using an algebraic expression over making a table of possible monthly charges.

Standardized Test Practice
(A)(B)(C)(D)

46. Find the perimeter of the triangle using the formula $P = a + b + c$ if $a = 10$, $b = 12$, and $c = 17$. **A**
  (A) 39 mm   (B) 19.5 mm
  (C) 60 mm   (D) 78 mm

47. Evaluate $(5 - 1)^3 + (11 - 2)^2 + (7 - 4)^3$. **B**
  (A) 586   (B) 172   (C) 106   (D) 39

Graphing Calculator **EVALUATING EXPRESSIONS** Use a calculator to evaluate each expression.

48. $\dfrac{0.25x^2}{7x^3}$ if $x = 0.75$ **0.0476190476**

49. $\dfrac{2x^2}{x^2 - x}$ if $x = 27.89$ **2.074377092**

50. $\dfrac{x^3 + x^2}{x^3 - x^2}$ if $x = 12.75$ **1.170212766**

Maintain Your Skills

Mixed Review Write an algebraic expression for each verbal expression. *(Lesson 1-1)*

51. the product of the third power of a and the fourth power of b $a^3 \cdot b^4$

52. six less than three times the square of y $3y^2 - 6$

53. the sum of a and b increased by the quotient of b and a $a + b + \dfrac{b}{a}$

54. $4(r + s) + 2(r - s)$ **54.** four times the sum of r and s increased by twice the difference of r and s

55. triple the difference of 55 and the cube of w $3(55 - w^3)$

Evaluate each expression. *(Lesson 1-1)*

56. 2^4 **16**   **57.** 12^1 **12**   **58.** 8^2 **64**   **59.** 4^4 **256**

Write a verbal expression for each algebraic expression. *(Lesson 1-1)*

60–63. See margin.

60. $5n + \dfrac{n}{2}$ **61.** $q^2 - 12$ **62.** $\dfrac{(x + 3)}{(x - 2)^2}$ **63.** $\dfrac{x^3}{9}$

64. 0.4925 **65.** 7.212 **66.** 2.884 **67.** 14.7775

Getting Ready for the Next Lesson **PREREQUISITE SKILL** Find the value of each expression.
(To review operations with decimals and fractions, see pages 798–801.)

64. $0.5 - 0.0075$ **65.** $5.6 + 1.612$ **66.** $14.9968 \div 5.2$ **67.** $2.3(6.425)$

68. $4\dfrac{1}{8} - 1\dfrac{1}{2}$ $2\dfrac{5}{8}$ **69.** $\dfrac{3}{5} + 2\dfrac{5}{7}$ $3\dfrac{11}{35}$ **70.** $\dfrac{5}{6} \cdot \dfrac{4}{5}$ $\dfrac{2}{3}$ **71.** $8 \div \dfrac{2}{9}$ **36**

Open-Ended Assessment
Speaking Write an algebraic or numerical expression with grouping symbols on the chalkboard. Have student volunteers explain how to evaluate the expression using the order of operations.

Getting Ready for Lesson 1-3
PREREQUISITE SKILL Students will learn how to solve open sentences in Lesson 1-3. Many of the expressions they must simplify in this process involve decimals and fractions. Use Exercises 64–71 to determine your students' familiarity with operations with decimals and fractions.

Answers

45. Use the order of operations to determine how many extra hours were used then how much the extra hours cost. Then find the total cost. Answers should include the following.
- $6[4.95 + 0.99(n)] - 25.00$
- You can use an expression to calculate a specific value without calculating all possible values.

60. five times n plus n divided by 2

61. 12 less than q squared

62. the sum of x and three divided by the square of the quantity x minus two

63. x cubed divided by nine

DAILY INTERVENTION   **Differentiated Instruction**

Logical/Mathematical Some students may be particularly fond of solving puzzles that depend on logic. Write on the board order of operations puzzles such as the following: Evaluate $15 + \left[\dfrac{2c(a + b - 18)}{c \div 3}\right]$ if a = number of days in a week, b = number of months in a year, and c = number of hours in a day. **21**

1 *Focus*

5-Minute Check Transparency 1-3 Use as a quiz or a review of Lesson 1-2.

Mathematical Background notes are available for this lesson on p. 4C.

How can you use open sentences to stay within a budget?

Ask students:

* What does the symbol ≤ mean? **The symbol ≤ means less than or equal to.**

* How would you translate the sentence $15.50 + 5n \leq 135$? **15.50 plus five times *n* is less than or equal to 135**

* What does the variable *n* represent in the sentence? ***n* represents the number of garage sale kits purchased**

* Why is *n* multiplied by 5? **the additional garage sale kits cost $5 each**

Vocabulary words are listed at the beginning of the lesson and are highlighted in yellow at point of use.

The Resource Manager lists all of the resources available for the lesson, including workbooks, blackline masters, transparencies, and technology.

1-3 Open Sentences

What You'll Learn

* Solve open sentence equations.
* Solve open sentence inequalities.

Vocabulary

* open sentence
* solving an open sentence
* solution
* equation
* replacement set
* set
* element
* solution set
* inequality

How can you use open sentences to stay within a budget?

The Daily News sells garage sale kits. The Spring Creek Homeowners Association is planning a community garage sale, and their budget for advertising is $135. The expression $15.50 + 5n$ can be used to represent the cost of purchasing $n + 1$ kits. The open sentence $15.50 + 5n \leq 135$ can be used to ensure that the budget is met.

Garage sale kit includes:
* Weekend ad
* Signs
* Announcements
* Balloons
* Price stickers
* Sales sheet

COMPLETE PACKAGE
$15.50

Additional kits available for $5.00 each

SOLVE EQUATIONS A mathematical statement with one or more variables is called an **open sentence**. An open sentence is neither true nor false until the variables have been replaced by specific values. The process of finding a value for a variable that results in a true sentence is called **solving the open sentence**. This replacement value is called a **solution** of the open sentence. A sentence that contains an equals sign, =, is called an **equation**.

A set of numbers from which replacements for a variable may be chosen is called a **replacement set**. A **set** is a collection of objects or numbers. It is often shown using braces, { }, and is usually named by a capital letter. Each object or number in the set is called an **element**, or member. The **solution set** of an open sentence is the set of elements from the replacement set that make an open sentence true.

Example 1 *Use a Replacement Set to Solve an Equation*

Find the solution set for each equation if the replacement set is {3, 4, 5, 6, 7}.

a. $6n + 7 = 37$

Replace *n* in $6n + 7 = 37$ with each value in the replacement set.

n	$6n + 7 = 37$	True or False?
3	$6(3) + 7 \stackrel{?}{=} 37 \rightarrow 25 \neq 37$	false
4	$6(4) + 7 \stackrel{?}{=} 37 \rightarrow 31 \neq 37$	false
5	$6(5) + 7 \stackrel{?}{=} 37 \rightarrow 37 = 37$	true ✓
6	$6(6) + 7 \stackrel{?}{=} 37 \rightarrow 43 \neq 37$	false
7	$6(7) + 7 \stackrel{?}{=} 37 \rightarrow 49 \neq 37$	false

Since $n = 5$ makes the equation true, the solution of $6n + 7 = 37$ is 5. The solution set is {5}.

Resource Manager

📁 **Workbook and Reproducible Masters**

Chapter 1 Resource Masters
* Study Guide and Intervention, pp. 13–14
* Skills Practice, p. 15
* Practice, p. 16
* Reading to Learn Mathematics, p. 17
* Enrichment, p. 18
* Assessment, p. 69

Graphing Calculator and Spreadsheet Masters, p. 24
Parent and Student Study Guide Workbook, p. 3
Prerequisite Skills Workbook, pp. 1–2, 5–12, 25–26, 47–50, 55–58, 61–62
Science and Mathematics Lab Manual, pp. 29–32

 Transparencies
5-Minute Check Transparency 1-3
Answer Key Transparencies

 Technology
Interactive Chalkboard

b. $5(x + 2) = 40$

Replace x in $5(x + 2) = 40$ with each value in the replacement set.

x	$5(x + 2) = 40$	True or False?
3	$5(3 + 2) \stackrel{?}{=} 40 \rightarrow 25 \neq 40$	false
4	$5(4 + 2) \stackrel{?}{=} 40 \rightarrow 30 \neq 40$	false
5	$5(5 + 2) \stackrel{?}{=} 40 \rightarrow 35 \neq 40$	false
6	$5(6 + 2) \stackrel{?}{=} 40 \rightarrow 40 = 40$	true ✓
7	$5(7 + 2) \stackrel{?}{=} 40 \rightarrow 45 \neq 40$	false

The solution of $5(x + 2) = 40$ is 6. The solution set is {6}.

You can often solve an equation by applying the order of operations.

Example 2 *Use Order of Operations to Solve an Equation*

Solve $\dfrac{13 + 2(4)}{3(5 - 4)} = q$.

$\dfrac{13 + 2(4)}{3(5 - 4)} = q$ Original equation

$\dfrac{13 + 8}{3(1)} = q$ Multiply 2 and 4 in the numerator.
Subtract 4 from 5 in the denominator.

$\dfrac{21}{3} = q$ Simplify.

$7 = q$ Divide.   The solution is 7.

Study Tip

Reading Math
Inequality symbols are read as follows.
$<$ *is less than*
$\leq$ *is less than or equal to*
$>$ *is greater than*
$\geq$ *is greater than or equal to*

SOLVE INEQUALITIES   An open sentence that contains the symbol $<$, $\leq$, $>$, or $\geq$ is called an **inequality**. Inequalities can be solved in the same way as equations.

Example 3 *Find the Solution Set of an Inequality*

Find the solution set for $18 - y < 10$ if the replacement set is {7, 8, 9, 10, 11, 12}.

Replace y in $18 - y < 10$ with each value in the replacement set.

y	$18 - y < 10$	True or False?
7	$18 - 7 \stackrel{?}{<} 10 \rightarrow 11 \not< 10$	false
8	$18 - 8 \stackrel{?}{<} 10 \rightarrow 10 \not< 10$	false
9	$18 - 9 \stackrel{?}{<} 10 \rightarrow 9 < 10$	true ✓
10	$18 - 10 \stackrel{?}{<} 10 \rightarrow 8 < 10$	true ✓
11	$18 - 11 \stackrel{?}{<} 10 \rightarrow 7 < 10$	true ✓
12	$18 - 12 \stackrel{?}{<} 10 \rightarrow 6 < 10$	true ✓

The solution set for $18 - y < 10$ is {9, 10, 11, 12}.

Example 4 *Solve an Inequality*

FUND-RAISING   Refer to the application at the beginning of the lesson. How many garage sale kits can the association buy and stay within their budget?

Explore   The association can spend no more than $135. So the situation can be represented by the inequality $15.50 + 5n \leq 135$.

(continued on the next page)

www.algebra1.com/extra_examples

---

2 Teach

SOLVE EQUATIONS

In-Class Examples   Power Point®

1 Find the solution set for each equation if the replacement set is {2, 3, 4, 5, 6}.

a. $4a + 7 = 23$ {4}

b. $3(8 - b) = 6$ {6}

2 Solve $\dfrac{5(8 + 2)}{18 - (5 - 3)^3} = k$. 5

SOLVE INEQUALITIES

In-Class Example   Power Point®

Reading Tip Remind students to pay close attention to the inequality sign when finding solutions for inequalities. For example, if students mistake a less than or equal sign ($\leq$) for the less than sign in Example 3, then they might mistakenly include 8 in the solution set.

3 Find the solution set for $z + 11 \geq 32$, if the replacement set is {20, 21, 22, 23, 24}. **{21, 22, 23, 24}**

4 **OUTDOORS** A four-wheel-drive tour of Canyon de Chelly National Monument in Arizona costs $45 for the first vehicle and $15 for each additional vehicle. How many vehicles can the Velo family take on the tour if they want to spend no more than $100? **They can take up to 4 vehicles.**

Daily Intervention notes help you help students when they need it most. Differentiated Instruction suggestions are keyed to eight commonly-accepted learning styles.

DAILY
INTERVENTION   **Differentiated Instruction**

Naturalist Challenge students to write open sentences about a plant or animal they are interested in. For example, the gestation period of armadillos can be described using the sentence
60 days $\leq$ gestation period $\leq$ 120 days.

Study Notebook

Have students—
- add the definitions/examples of the vocabulary terms to their Vocabulary Builder worksheets for Chapter 1.
- copy the Reading Math Study Tip from page 17.
- include any other item(s) that they find helpful in mastering the skills in this lesson.

Study Notebook tips offer suggestions for helping your students keep notes they can use to study this chapter.

Study Tips offer students helpful information about the topics they are studying.

Study Tip

Reading Math
In {1, 2, 3, 4, ...}, the three dots are an *ellipsis*. In math, an ellipsis is used to indicate that numbers continue in the same pattern.

About the Exercises...

Organization by Objective
- Solve Equations: 14–25, 29–36, 45–46
- Solve Inequalities: 26–28, 37–44, 47–48

Odd/Even Assignments
Exercises 14–25 and 29–44 are structured so that students practice the same concepts whether they are assigned odd or even problems.

Assignment Guide

Basic: 15–25 odd, 26–28, 29–33 odd, 45–46, 49–67

Average: 15–25 odd, 26–28, 29–43 odd, 45–46, 49–67

Advanced: 14–24 even, 30–44 even, 45–59 (optional: 60–67)

All: Practice Quiz 1 (1–10)

Plan Since no replacement set is given, estimate to find reasonable values for the replacement set.

Solve Start by letting $n = 10$ and then adjust values up or down as needed.

$$15.50 + 5n \le 135 \quad \text{Original inequality}$$
$$15.50 + 5(10) \le 135 \quad n = 10$$
$$15.50 + 50 \le 135 \quad \text{Multiply 5 and 10.}$$
$$65.50 \le 135 \quad \text{Add 15.50 and 50.}$$

The estimate is too low. Increase the value of n.

n	$15.50 + 5n \le 135$	Reasonable?
20	$15.50 + 5(20) \overset{?}{\le} 135 \rightarrow 115.50 \le 135$	too low
25	$15.50 + 5(25) \overset{?}{\le} 135 \rightarrow 140.50 \not\le 135$	too high
23	$15.50 + 5(23) \overset{?}{\le} 135 \rightarrow 130.50 \le 135$	almost
24	$15.50 + 5(24) \overset{?}{\le} 135 \rightarrow 135.50 \le 135$	too high

Examine The solution set is {0, 1, 2, 3, ..., 21, 22, 23}. In addition to the first kit, the association can buy as many as 23 additional kits. So, the association can buy as many as $1 + 23$ or 24 garage sale kits and stay within their budget.

Check for Understanding

Concept Check   1–3. See margin.

1. **Describe** the difference between an expression and an open sentence.
2. **OPEN ENDED** Write an inequality that has a solution set of {8, 9, 10, 11, ...}.
3. **Explain** why an open sentence always has at least one variable.

Guided Practice

GUIDED PRACTICE KEY	
Exercises	Examples
4–7	1
8, 9	2
10, 11	3
12, 13	4

Find the solution of each equation if the replacement set is {10, 11, 12, 13, 14, 15}.

4. $3x - 7 = 29$ **12**

5. $12(x - 8) = 84$ **15**

Find the solution of each equation using the given replacement set.

6. $x + \frac{2}{5} = 1\frac{3}{20}; \left\{ \frac{1}{4}, \frac{1}{2}, \frac{3}{4}, 1, 1\frac{1}{4} \right\}$ $\frac{3}{4}$

7. $7.2(x + 2) = 25.92; \{1.2, 1.4, 1.6, 1.8\}$ **1.6**

Solve each equation.

8. $4(6) + 3 = x$ **27**

9. $w = \frac{14 - 8}{2}$ **3**

Find the solution set for each inequality using the given replacement set.

10. $24 - 2x \ge 13; \{0, 1, 2, 3, 4, 5, 6\}$
    {0, 1, 2, 3, 4, 5}

11. $3(12 - x) - 2 \le 28; \{1.5, 2, 2.5, 3\}$
    {2, 2.5, 3}

Application **NUTRITION** For Exercises 12 and 13, use the following information.
A person must burn 3500 Calories to lose one pound of weight.

12. Write an equation that represents the number of Calories a person would have to burn a day to lose four pounds in two weeks. $C = \frac{3500 \cdot 4}{14}$

13. How many Calories would the person have to burn each day? **1000 Calories**

Answers

1. Sample answer: An open sentence contains an equals sign or inequality sign.

2. Sample answer: $x > 7$

3. Sample answer: An open sentence has at least one variable because it is neither true nor false until specific values are used for the variable.

★ indicates increased difficulty

Practice and Apply

Homework Help

For Exercises	See Examples
14–25	1
26–28	4
29–36	2
37–44	3

Extra Practice
See page 820.

Find the solution of each equation if the replacement sets are $a = \{0, 3, 5, 8, 10\}$ and $b = \{12, 17, 18, 21, 25\}$.

14. $b - 12 = 9$ **21**

15. $34 - b = 22$ **12**

16. $3a + 7 = 31$ **8**

17. $4a + 5 = 17$ **3**

18. $\frac{40}{a} - 4 = 0$ **10**

19. $\frac{b}{3} - 2 = 4$ **18**

Find the solution of each equation using the given replacement set.

20. $x + \frac{7}{4} = \frac{17}{8}; \left\{\frac{1}{8}, \frac{3}{8}, \frac{5}{8}, \frac{7}{8}\right\}$ **$\frac{3}{8}$**

21. $x + \frac{7}{12} = \frac{25}{12}; \left\{\frac{1}{2}, 1, 1\frac{1}{2}, 2\right\}$ **$1\frac{1}{2}$**

22. $\frac{2}{5}(x + 1) = \frac{8}{15}; \left\{\frac{1}{6}, \frac{1}{3}, \frac{1}{2}, \frac{2}{3}\right\}$ **$\frac{1}{3}$**

23. $2.7(x + 5) = 17.28; \{1.2, 1.3, 1.4, 1.5\}$ **1.4**

24. $16(x + 2) = 70.4; \{2.2, 2.4, 2.6, 2.8\}$ **2.4**

25. $21(x + 5) = 216.3; \{3.1, 4.2, 5.3, 6.4\}$ **5.3**

MOVIES For Exercises 26–28, use the table and the following information.
The Conkle family is planning to see a movie. There are two adults, a daughter in high school, and two sons in middle school. They do not want to spend more than $30.

26. The movie theater charges the same price for high school and middle school students. Write an inequality to show the cost for the family to go to the movies. **$2a + 3s \le 30$**

27. How much will it cost for the family to see a matinee? **$22.50**

28. How much will it cost to see an evening show? **$28.50**

Admission Prices		
	Evening	**Matinee**
Adult	$7.50	
Student	$4.50	**All Seats**
Child	$4.50	**$4.50**
Senior	$3.50	

Solve each equation.

29. $14.8 - 3.75 = t$ **11.05**

30. $a = 32.4 - 18.95$ **13.45**

31. $y = \frac{12 \cdot 5}{15 - 3}$ **5**

32. $g = \frac{15 \cdot 6}{16 - 7}$ **10**

33. $d = \frac{7(3) + 3}{4(3 - 1)} + 6$ **9**

34. $a = \frac{4(14 - 1)}{3(6) - 5} + 7$ **11**

★ **35.** $p = \frac{1}{4}[7(2^3) + 4(5^2) - 6(2)]$ **36**

★ **36.** $n = \frac{1}{8}[6(3^2) + 2(4^3) - 2(7)]$ **21**

Find the solution set for each inequality using the given replacement set.

37. $a - 2 < 6; \{6, 7, 8, 9, 10, 11\}$ **{6, 7}**

38. $a + 7 < 22; \{13, 14, 15, 16, 17\}$ **{13, 14}**

39. $\frac{a}{5} \ge 2; \{5, 10, 15, 20, 25\}$ **{10, 15, 20, 25}**

40. $\frac{2a}{4} \le 8; \{12, 14, 16, 18, 20, 22\}$ **{12, 14, 16}**

41. $4a - 3 \ge 10.6; \{3.2, 3.4, 3.6, 3.8, 4\}$

42. $6a - 5 \ge 23.8; \{4.2, 4.5, 4.8, 5.1, 5.4\}$

43. $3a \le 4; \left\{0, \frac{1}{3}, \frac{2}{3}, 1, 1\frac{1}{3}\right\}$ **$\left\{0, \frac{1}{3}, \frac{2}{3}, 1, 1\frac{1}{3}\right\}$**

44. $2b < 5; \left\{1, 1\frac{1}{2}, 2, 2\frac{1}{2}, 3\right\}$ **$\left\{1, 1\frac{1}{2}, 2\right\}$**

41. {3.4, 3.6, 3.8, 4}

42. {4.8, 5.1, 5.4}

 **FOOD** For Exercises 45 and 46, use the information about food at the left.

45. Write an equation to find the total number of glasses of milk, juice, and soda the average American drinks in a lifetime. **$g = 15{,}579 + 6220 + 18{,}995$**

46. How much milk, juice, and soda does the average American drink in a lifetime? **40,794 glasses**

MAIL ORDER For Exercises 47 and 48, use the following information.
Suppose you want to order several sweaters that cost $39.00 each from an online catalog. There is a $10.95 charge for shipping. You have $102.50 to spend.

47. Write an inequality you could use to determine the maximum number of sweaters you can purchase. **$39n + 10.95 \le 102.50$**

48. What is the maximum number of sweaters you can buy? **2**

More About. . .

Food •

During a lifetime, the average American drinks 15,579 glasses of milk, 6220 glasses of juice, and 18,995 glasses of soda.

Source: USA TODAY

www.algebra1.com/self_check_quiz

Study Guide and Intervention, p. 13 (shown) and p. 14

Solve Equations A mathematical sentence with one or more variables is called an **open sentence**. Open sentences are **solved** by finding replacements for the variables that result in true sentences. The set of numbers from which replacements for a variable may be chosen is called the **replacement set**. The set of all replacements for the variable that result in true statements is called the **solution set** for the variable. A sentence that contains an equal sign, =, is called an **equation**.

Example 1 Find the solution set of $3a + 12 = 39$ if the replacement set is $\{6, 7, 8, 9, 10\}$.

Replace a in $3a + 12 = 39$ with each value in the replacement set.

$3(6) + 12 \stackrel{?}{=} 39 \rightarrow 30 \ne 39$	false
$3(7) + 12 \stackrel{?}{=} 39 \rightarrow 33 \ne 39$	false
$3(8) + 12 \stackrel{?}{=} 39 \rightarrow 36 \ne 39$	false
$3(9) + 12 \stackrel{?}{=} 39 \rightarrow 39 = 39$	true
$3(10) + 12 \stackrel{?}{=} 39 \rightarrow 42 \ne 39$	false

Since $a = 9$ makes the equation $3a + 12 = 39$ true, the solution is 9. The solution set is $\{9\}$.

Example 2 Solve $\frac{2(3 + 1)}{3(7 - 4)} = b$.

$\frac{2(3 + 1)}{3(7 - 4)} = b$ Original equation

$\frac{2(4)}{3(3)} = b$ Add in the numerator; subtract in the denominator.

$\frac{8}{9} = b$ Simplify.

The solution is $\frac{8}{9}$.

Exercises

Find the solution of each equation if the replacement sets are $X = \left\{\frac{1}{4}, \frac{1}{2}, 1, 2, 3\right\}$ and $Y = \{2, 4, 6, 8\}$.

1. $x + \frac{1}{2} = \frac{5}{2}$ {2}

2. $x + 8 = 11$ {3}

3. $y - 2 = 6$ {8}

4. $x^2 - 1 = 8$ {3}

5. $y^2 = 34$ {6}

6. $x^2 + 5 = 5\frac{1}{16}$ $\left\{\frac{1}{4}\right\}$

7. $2(x + 3) = 7$ $\left\{\frac{1}{2}\right\}$

8. $\frac{1}{4}(y + 1)^2 = \frac{9}{4}$ {2}

9. $y^2 + y = 20$ {4}

Solve each equation.

10. $a = 2^3 - 1$ 7

11. $n = 6^2 - 4^2$ 20

12. $w = 6^2 \cdot 3^2$ 324

13. $\frac{1}{4} + \frac{5}{8} = k$ $\frac{7}{8}$

14. $\frac{18 - 3}{2 + 3} = p$ 3

15. $x = \frac{15 - 6}{27 - 24}$ 3

16. $18.4 - 3.2 = m$ 15.2

17. $k = 9.8 + 5.7$ 15.5

18. $c = 3\frac{1}{2} + 2\frac{1}{4}$ $5\frac{3}{4}$

Skills Practice, p. 15 and Practice, p. 16 (shown)

Find the solution of each equation if the replacement sets are $A = \left\{0, \frac{1}{2}, 1, \frac{3}{2}, 2\right\}$ and $B = \{3, 3.5, 4, 4.5, 5\}$.

1. $a + \frac{1}{2} = 1$ $1\frac{1}{2}$

2. $4b - 8 = 6$ 3.5

3. $6a + 18 = 27$ $\frac{3}{2}$

4. $7b - 8 = 16.5$ 3.5

5. $120 - 28a = 78$ $\frac{3}{2}$

6. $\frac{28}{b} + 9 = 16$ 4

Find the solution of each equation using the given replacement set.

7. $\frac{7}{8} + x = \frac{17}{12}; \left\{\frac{1}{2}, \frac{13}{24}, \frac{7}{12}, \frac{5}{8}, \frac{2}{3}\right\}$ $\frac{13}{24}$

8. $\frac{3}{4}(x + 2) = \frac{27}{8}; \left\{\frac{1}{2}, 1, 1\frac{1}{2}, 2, 2\frac{1}{2}\right\}$ $2\frac{1}{2}$

9. $1.4(x + 3) = 5.32; \{0.4, 0.6, 0.8, 1.0, 1.2\}$ 0.8

10. $12(x + 4) = 76.8; \{2, 2.4, 2.8, 3.2, 3.6\}$ 2.4

Solve each equation.

11. $x = 18.3 - 4.8$ 13.5

12. $w = 20.2 - 8.95$ 11.25

13. $\frac{37 - 9}{18 - 11} = d$ 4

14. $\frac{97 - 25}{41 - 23} = k$ 4

15. $y = \frac{4(22 - 4)}{3(6) + 6}$ 3

16. $\frac{5(2^3) + 4(3)}{4(2^3) - 4^2} = p$ 2

Find the solution set for each inequality using the given replacement set.

17. $a + 7 < 10; \{2, 3, 4, 5, 6, 7\}$ {2}

18. $3y \le 42; \{10, 12, 14, 16, 18\}$ {14, 16, 18}

19. $4x - 2 < 5; \{0.5, 1, 1.5, 2, 2.5\}$ {0.5, 1, 1.5}

20. $4b - 4 > 3; \{1.2, 1.4, 1.6, 1.8, 2.0\}$ {1.8, 2.0}

21. $\frac{3y}{5} \le 2; \{0, 2, 4, 6, 8, 10\}$ {0, 2}

22. $4a \ge 3; \left\{\frac{1}{8}, \frac{1}{4}, \frac{3}{8}, \frac{1}{2}, \frac{5}{8}, \frac{3}{4}\right\}$ $\left\{\frac{3}{4}\right\}$

23. TEACHING A teacher has 15 weeks in which to teach six chapters. Write and then solve an equation that represents the number of lessons the teacher must teach per week if there is an average of 8.5 lessons per chapter. $n = \frac{6(8.5)}{15}$; 3.4

LONG DISTANCE For Exercises 24 and 25, use the following information.
Gabriel talks an average of 20 minutes per long-distance call. During one month, he makes eight in-state long-distance calls averaging $2.00 each. A 20-minute state-to-state call costs Gabriel $1.50. His average budget for the month is $20.

24. Write an inequality that represents the number of 20 minute state-to-state calls Gabriel can make this month. $8(2) + 1.5s \le 20$

25. What is the maximum number of 20-minute state-to-state calls that Gabriel can make this month? 2

Reading to Learn Mathematics, p. 17   **ELL**

Pre-Activity How can you use open sentences to stay within a budget?
Read the introduction to Lesson 1-3 at the top of page 16 in your textbook.

How is the open sentence different from the expression $15.50 + 5n$? The open sentence has two expressions joined by the $\ge$ symbol.

Reading the Lesson

1. How can you tell whether a mathematical sentence is or is not an open sentence? An open sentence must contain one or more variables.

2. How would you read each inequality symbol in words?

Inequality Symbol	Words
<	is less than
>	is greater than
≤	is less than or equal to
≥	is greater than or equal to

3. Consider the equation $3n + 6 = 15$ and the inequality $3n + 6 \le 15$. Suppose the replacement set is {0, 1, 2, 3, 4, 5}.

a. Describe how you would find the solutions of the equation. Replace n with each member of the replacement set. The members of the replacement set that make the equation true are the solutions.

b. Describe how you would find the solutions of the inequality. Replace n with each member of the replacement set. The members of the replacement set that make the equation true are the solutions.

c. Explain how the solution set for the equation is different from the solution set for the inequality. The solution set for the equation contains only one number, 3. The solution set for the inequality contains the four numbers 0, 1, 2, and 3.

Helping You Remember

4. Look up the word *solution* in a dictionary. What is one meaning that relates to the way we use the word in algebra? Sample answer: answer to a problem

Enrichment, p. 18

Solution Sets

Consider the following open sentence.

It is the name of a month between March and July.

You know that a replacement for the variable *It* must be found in order to determine if the sentence is true or false. If *It* is replaced by either April, May, or June, the sentence is true. The set {April, May, June} is called the solution set of the open sentence given above. This set includes all replacements for the variable that make the sentence true.

Write the solution set for each open sentence.

1. It is the name of a state beginning with the letter A. {Alabama, Alaska, Arizona, Arkansas}

2. It is a primary color. {red, yellow, blue}

3. Its capital is Harrisburg. {Pennsylvania}

Open-Ended Assessment

Writing Write a solution set on the chalkboard or overhead projector. Have students write open sentences that match the solution set.

Each lesson ends with Open-Ended Assessment strategies for closing the lesson. These include writing, modeling, and speaking.

Getting Ready for Lesson 1-4

PREREQUISITE SKILL Students will learn about the identity and equality properties in Lesson 1-4. The Multiplicative Inverse Property requires finding the product of two fractions. Use Exercises 60–67 to determine your students' familiarity with multiplying fractions.

Assessment Options

Practice Quiz 1 The quiz provides students with a brief review of the concepts and skills in Lessons 1-1 through 1-3. Lesson numbers are given to the right of exercises or instruction lines so students can review concepts not yet mastered.

Quiz (Lessons 1-1 through 1-3) is available on p. 69 of the *Chapter 1 Resource Masters*.

Answers

50. You can use equations to determine how much money you have to spend and how you can spend your money. Answers should include the following.
    • Sample answers: calculating gasoline required for a trip, cooking time

---

49. The solution set includes all numbers less than or equal to $\frac{1}{3}$.

49. **CRITICAL THINKING** Describe the solution set for x if $3x \le 1$.

50. **WRITING IN MATH** Answer the question that was posed at the beginning of the lesson. **See margin.**

How can you use open sentences to stay within a budget?

Include the following in your answer:
• an explanation of how to use open sentences to stay within a budget, and
• examples of real-world situations in which you would use an inequality and examples where you would use an equation.

Standardized Test Practice
Ⓐ Ⓑ Ⓒ Ⓓ

51. Find the solution set for $\frac{(5 \cdot n)^2 + 5}{(9 \cdot 3^2) - n} < 28$ if the replacement set is {5, 7, 9, 11, 13}. **B**
    Ⓐ {5}   Ⓑ {5, 7}   Ⓒ {7}   Ⓓ {7, 9}

52. Which expression has a value of 17? **C**
    Ⓐ $(9 \times 3) - 63 \div 7$ Ⓑ $6(3 + 2) \div (9 - 7)$
    Ⓒ $27 \div 3 + (12 - 4)$ Ⓓ $2[2(6 - 3)] - 5$

Maintain Your Skills

Mixed Review Write an algebraic expression for each verbal expression. Then evaluate each expression if $r = 2$, $s = 5$, and $t = \frac{1}{2}$. *(Lesson 1-2)*

53. r squared increased by 3 times s $r^2 + 3s$; **19**
54. t times the sum of four times s and r $t(4s + r)$; **11**
55. the sum of r and s times the square of t $(r + s)t^2$; $\frac{7}{4}$
56. r to the fifth power decreased by t $r^5 - t$; $31\frac{1}{2}$

Evaluate each expression. *(Lesson 1-2)*
57. $5^3 + 3(4^2)$ **173**
58. $\frac{38 - 12}{2 \cdot 13}$ **1**
59. $[5(2 + 1)]^4 + 3$ **50,628**

Getting Ready for the Next Lesson **PREREQUISITE SKILL** Find each product. Express in simplest form. *(To review **multiplying fractions**, see pages 800 and 801.)*

60. $\frac{1}{6} \cdot \frac{2}{5}$ $\frac{1}{15}$
61. $\frac{4}{9} \cdot \frac{3}{7}$ $\frac{4}{21}$
62. $\frac{5}{6} \cdot \frac{15}{16}$ $\frac{25}{32}$
63. $\frac{6}{14} \cdot \frac{12}{18}$ $\frac{2}{7}$
64. $\frac{8}{13} \cdot \frac{2}{11}$ $\frac{16}{143}$
65. $\frac{4}{7} \cdot \frac{4}{9}$ $\frac{16}{63}$
66. $\frac{3}{11} \cdot \frac{7}{16}$ $\frac{21}{176}$
67. $\frac{2}{9} \cdot \frac{24}{25}$ $\frac{16}{75}$

Practice Quiz 1
Lessons 1-1 through 1-3

Write a verbal expression for each algebraic expression. *(Lesson 1-1)* **1–4. See margin.**
1. $x - 20$ 2. $5n + 2$ 3. a^3 4. $n^4 - 1$

Evaluate each expression. *(Lesson 1-2)*
5. $6(9) - 2(8 + 5)$ **28**
6. $4[2 + (18 \div 9)^3]$ **40**
7. $9(3) - 4^2 + 6^2 \div 2$ **29**
8. $\frac{(5 - 2)^2}{3(4 \cdot 2 - 7)}$ **3**

9. Evaluate $\frac{5a^2 + c - 2}{6 + b}$ if $a = 4$, $b = 5$, and $c = 10$. *(Lesson 1-2)* **8**

10. Find the solution set for $2n^2 + 3 \le 75$ if the replacement set is {4, 5, 6, 7, 8, 9}. *(Lesson 1-3)* {4, 5, 6}

1. twenty less than x
2. five times n plus two
3. a cubed
4. n to the fourth power minus one

What You'll Learn

- Recognize the properties of identity and equality.
- Use the properties of identity and equality.

Vocabulary
- additive identity
- multiplicative identity
- multiplicative inverses
- reciprocal

How are identity and equality properties used to compare data?

During the college football season, teams are ranked weekly. The table shows the last three rankings of the top five teams for the 2000 football season. The open sentence below represents the change in rank of Oregon State from December 11 to the final rank.

	Dec. 4	Dec. 11	Final Rank
University of Oklahoma	1	1	1
University of Miami	2	2	2
University of Washington	4	3	3
Oregon State University	5	4	4
Florida State University	3	5	5

Rank on December 11, 2000	plus	increase in rank	equals	final rank for 2000 season.
4	+	r	=	4

The solution of this equation is 0. Oregon State's rank changed by 0 from December 11 to the final rank. In other words, $4 + 0 = 4$.

IDENTITY AND EQUALITY PROPERTIES The sum of any number and 0 is equal to the number. Thus, 0 is called the **additive identity**.

Key Concept — Additive Identity

- **Words**   For any number a, the sum of a and 0 is a.
- **Symbols** $a + 0 = 0 + a = a$
- **Examples** $5 + 0 = 5,\ 0 + 5 = 5$

There are also special properties associated with multiplication. Consider the following equations.

$$7 \cdot n = 7$$

The solution of the equation is 1. Since the product of any number and 1 is equal to the number, 1 is called the **multiplicative identity**.

$$9 \cdot m = 0$$

The solution of the equation is 0. The product of any number and 0 is equal to 0. This is called the **Multiplicative Property of Zero**.

$$\frac{1}{3} \cdot 3 = 1$$

Two numbers whose product is 1 are called **multiplicative inverses** or **reciprocals**. Zero has no reciprocal because any number times 0 is 0.

Lesson 1-4 Identity and Equality Properties **21**

5-Minute Check Transparency 1-4 Use as a quiz or a review of Lesson 1-3.

Mathematical Background notes are available for this lesson on p. 4C.

How are identity and equality properties used to compare data?

Ask students:
- Did any of the teams change in rank between December 11 to the final ranking? **no**
- By how many positions did the University of Washington and Oregon State University change between December 4 and December 11? **They each changed by one position.**
- By how many positions did Florida State University change between December 4 and December 11? **They changed by two positions.**
- How would you represent Florida State's change in position in an equation? **Sample answer: $3 + r = 5$**

Resource Manager

Workbook and Reproducible Masters

Chapter 1 Resource Masters
- Study Guide and Intervention, pp. 19–20
- Skills Practice, p. 21
- Practice, p. 22
- Reading to Learn Mathematics, p. 23
- Enrichment, p. 24

Parent and Student Study Guide Workbook, p. 4
Prerequisite Skills Workbook, pp. 5–8, 11–12, 21–22, 25–26, 55–56

 Transparencies
5-Minute Check Transparency 1-4
Answer Key Transparencies

 **Technology**
Interactive Chalkboard

2 Teach

IDENTITY AND EQUALITY PROPERTIES

In-Class Example Power Point®

1 Name the property used in each equation. Then find the value of n.

a. $n \cdot 12 = 0$ Multiplicative Property of Zero; $n = 0$

b. $n \cdot \frac{1}{5} = 1$ Multiplicative Inverse Property; $n = 5$

c. $0 + n = 8$ Additive Identity Property; $n = 8$

USE IDENTITY AND EQUALITY PROPERTIES

In-Class Example Power Point®

2 Evaluate $\frac{1}{4}(12 - 8) + 3(15 \div 5 - 2)$. Name the property used in each step.

$\frac{1}{4}(12 - 8) + 3(15 \div 5 - 2)$

$= \frac{1}{4}(4) + 3(15 \div 5 - 2)$
  Substitution; $12 - 8 = 4$

$= \frac{1}{4}(4) + 3(3 - 2)$
  Substitution; $15 \div 5 = 3$

$= \frac{1}{4}(4) + 3(1)$ Substitution;
  $3 - 2 = 1$

$= \frac{1}{4}(4) + 3$ Multiplicative
  Identity; $3 \cdot 1 = 3$

$= 1 + 3$ Multiplicative
  Inverse; $\frac{1}{4} \cdot 4 = 1$

$= 4$ Substitution; $1 + 3 = 4$

Key Concept — Multiplication Properties

Property	Words	Symbols	Examples
Multiplicative Identity	For any number a, the product of a and 1 is a.	$a \cdot 1 = 1 \cdot a = a$	$12 \cdot 1 = 12,$ $1 \cdot 12 = 12$
Multiplicative Property of Zero	For any number a, the product of a and 0 is 0.	$a \cdot 0 = 0 \cdot a = 0$	$8 \cdot 0 = 0,$ $0 \cdot 8 = 0$
Multiplicative Inverse	For every number $\frac{a}{b}$, where $a, b \neq 0$, there is exactly one number $\frac{b}{a}$ such that the product of $\frac{a}{b}$ and $\frac{b}{a}$ is 1.	$\frac{a}{b} \cdot \frac{b}{a} = \frac{b}{a} \cdot \frac{a}{b} = 1$	$\frac{2}{3} \cdot \frac{3}{2} = \frac{6}{6} = 1,$ $\frac{3}{2} \cdot \frac{2}{3} = \frac{6}{6} = 1$

Example 1 Identify Properties

Name the property used in each equation. Then find the value of n.

a. $42 \cdot n = 42$

Multiplicative Identity Property

$n = 1$, since $42 \cdot 1 = 42$.

b. $n + 0 = 15$

Additive Identity Property

$n = 15$, since $15 + 0 = 15$.

c. $n \cdot 9 = 1$

Multiplicative Inverse Property

$n = \frac{1}{9}$, since $\frac{1}{9} \cdot 9 = 1$.

There are several properties of equality that apply to addition and multiplication. These are summarized below.

Key Concept — Properties of Equality

Property	Words	Symbols	Examples
Reflexive	Any quantity is equal to itself.	For any number a, $a = a$.	$7 = 7,$ $2 + 3 = 2 + 3$
Symmetric	If one quantity equals a second quantity, then the second quantity equals the first.	For any numbers a and b, if $a = b$, then $b = a$.	If $9 = 6 + 3$, then $6 + 3 = 9$.
Transitive	If one quantity equals a second quantity and the second quantity equals a third quantity, then the first quantity equals the third quantity.	For any numbers a, b, and c, if $a = b$ and $b = c$, then $a = c$.	If $5 + 7 = 8 + 4$ and $8 + 4 = 12$, then $5 + 7 = 12$.
Substitution	A quantity may be substituted for its equal in any expression.	If $a = b$, then a may be replaced by b in any expression.	If $n = 15$, then $3n = 3 \cdot 15$.

D A I L Y
INTERVENTION   **Differentiated Instruction**

Intrapersonal If students have difficulty remembering the names of the properties that they learned in this lesson, remind them that they probably already know how to use the properties. Encourage students to think of word associations that will help them build on what they already know to remember the correct names of the properties.

USE IDENTITY AND EQUALITY PROPERTIES The properties of identity and equality can be used to justify each step when evaluating an expression.

Example 2 *Evaluate Using Properties*

Evaluate $2(3 \cdot 2 - 5) + 3 \cdot \frac{1}{3}$. Name the property used in each step.

$$2(3 \cdot 2 - 5) + 3 \cdot \frac{1}{3} = 2(6 - 5) + 3 \cdot \frac{1}{3} \quad \text{Substitution; } 3 \cdot 2 = 6$$

$$= 2(1) + 3 \cdot \frac{1}{3} \quad \text{Substitution; } 6 - 5 = 1$$

$$= 2 + 3 \cdot \frac{1}{3} \quad \text{Multiplicative Identity; } 2 \cdot 1 = 2$$

$$= 2 + 1 \quad \text{Multiplicative Inverse; } 3 \cdot \frac{1}{3} = 1$$

$$= 3 \quad \text{Substitution; } 2 + 1 = 3$$

Check for Understanding exercises are intended to be completed in class. Concept Check exercises ensure that students understand the concepts in the lesson. The other exercises are representative of the exercises used for homework.

Study Notebook

Have students—
- add the definitions/examples of the vocabulary terms to their Vocabulary Builder worksheets for Chapter 1.
- list all properties and examples of each.
- include any other item(s) that they find helpful in mastering the skills in this lesson.

Check for Understanding

Concept Check
2–3. See margin.

1. **Explain** whether 1 can be an additive identity. no; $3 + 1 \neq 3$

2. **OPEN ENDED** Write two equations demonstrating the Transitive Property of Equality.

3. **Explain** why 0 has no multiplicative inverse.

Guided Practice

Name the property used in each equation. Then find the value of *n*.

GUIDED PRACTICE KEY	
Exercises	Examples
4–6	1
7, 8	2
9–11	1, 2

4. $13n = 0$ Mult. Prop. of Zero; 0   5. $17 + 0 = n$ Add. Identity; 17   6. $\frac{1}{6}n = 1$ Mult. Inverse; 6

7. Evaluate $6(12 - 48 \div 4)$. Name the property used in each step.

8. Evaluate $\left(15 \cdot \frac{1}{15} + 8 \cdot 0\right) \cdot 12$. Name the property used in each step.

7–8. See margin.

Application

HISTORY For Exercises 9–11, use the following information.
On November 19, 1863, Abraham Lincoln delivered the famous Gettysburg Address. The speech began "Four score and seven years ago, . . ." 9. $4(20) + 7$

9. Write an expression to represent four score and seven. (*Hint*: A score is 20.)

10. Evaluate the expression. Name the property used in each step. See margin.

11. How many years is four score and seven? 87 yr

★ indicates increased difficulty

Practice and Apply

Homework Help	
For Exercises	See Examples
12–19	1
20–23	1, 2
24–29	2
30–35	1, 2

Extra Practice
See page 821.

Name the property used in each equation. Then find the value of *n*.

12. $12n = 12$ 13. $n \cdot 1 = 5$ 14. $8 \cdot n = 8 \cdot 5$

15. $0.25 + 1.5 = n + 1.5$ 16. $8 = n + 8$ 17. $n + 0 = \frac{1}{3}$

18. $1 = 2n$ 19. $4 \cdot \frac{1}{4} = n$ 20. $(9 - 7)(5) = 2(n)$

21. $3 + (2 + 8) = n + 10$ ★ 22. $n\left(5^2 \cdot \frac{1}{25}\right) = 3$ ★ 23. $6\left(\frac{1}{2} \cdot n\right) = 6$

12–29. See pp. 65A–65B.

Evaluate each expression. Name the property used in each step.

24. $\frac{3}{4}[4 \div (7 - 4)]$ 25. $\frac{2}{3}[3 \div (2 \cdot 1)]$ 26. $2(3 \cdot 2 - 5) + 3 \cdot \frac{1}{3}$

27. $6 \cdot \frac{1}{6} + 5(12 \div 4 - 3)$ 28. $3 + 5(4 - 2^2) - 1$ 29. $7 - 8(9 - 3^2)$

www.algebra1.com/extra_examples

About the Exercises...
Organization by Objective
- Identity and Equality Properties: 12–23, 37–40
- Use Identity and Equality Properties: 24–29, 31, 36

Odd/Even Assignments
Exercises 12–29 are structured so that students practice the same concepts whether they are assigned odd or even problems.

Alert! Exercise 36 involves research on the Internet or other reference materials.

Assignment Guide
Basic: 13–21 odd, 25–29 odd, 30–33, 37–40, 44–62
Average: 13–29 odd, 30–33, 37–40, 44–62 (optional: 41–43)
Advanced: 12–28 even, 34–56 (optional: 57–62)

Answers

2. Sample answer: $5 = 3 + 2$, and $3 + 2 = 4 + 1$, so $5 = 4 + 1$; $5 + 7 = 8 + 4$, and $8 + 4 = 12$, so $5 + 7 = 12$

3. Sample answer: You cannot divide by zero.

7. $6(12 - 48 \div 4) = 6(12 - 12)$ Substitution
   $= 6(0)$ Substitution
   $= 0$ Mult. Prop. of Zero

8. $\left(15 \cdot \frac{1}{15} + 8 \cdot 0\right) \cdot 12 = (1 + 8 \cdot 0) \cdot 12$ Mult. Inv.
   $= (1 + 0) \cdot 12$ Mult. Prop. of Zero
   $= 1 \cdot 12$ Additive Identity
   $= 12$ Mult. Identity

10. $4(20) + 7$
    $= 80 + 7$ Substitution
    $= 87$ Substitution

Identity and Equality Properties The identity and equality properties in the chart below can help you solve algebraic equations and evaluate mathematical expressions.

Additive Identity	For any number a, $a + 0 = a$.
Multiplicative Identity	For any number a, $a \cdot 1 = a$.
Multiplicative Property of 0	For any number a, $a \cdot 0 = 0$.
Multiplicative Inverse Property	For every number $\frac{a}{b}$, $a, b \neq 0$, there is exactly one number $\frac{b}{a}$ such that $\frac{a}{b} \cdot \frac{b}{a} = 1$.
Reflexive Property	For any number a, $a = a$.
Symmetric Property	For any numbers a and b, if $a = b$, then $b = a$.
Transitive Property	For any numbers a, b, and c, if $a = b$ and $b = c$, then $a = c$.
Substitution Property	If $a = b$, then a may be replaced by b in any expression.

Example 1 Name the property used in each equation. Then find the value of n.

a. $8n = 8$
Multiplicative Identity Property
$n = 1$, since $8 \cdot 1 = 8$

b. $n \cdot 3 = 1$
Multiplicative Inverse Property
$n = \frac{1}{3}$, since $\frac{1}{3} \cdot 3 = 1$

Example 2 Name the property used to justify each statement.

a. $5 + 4 = 5 + 4$
Reflexive Property

b. If $n = 12$, then $4n = 4 \cdot 12$.
Substitution Property

Exercises

Name the property used in each equation. Then find the value of n.

1. $6n = 6$
Mult. Identity; 1

2. $n \cdot 1 = 8$
Mult. Identity; 8

3. $6 \cdot n = 6 \cdot 9$
Substitution Property; 9

4. $9 = n + 9$
Add. Identity; 0

5. $n + 0 = \frac{3}{8}$
Add. Identity; $\frac{3}{8}$

6. $\frac{3}{4} \cdot n = 1$
Mult. Inverse; $\frac{4}{3}$

Name the property used in each equation.

7. If $4 + 5 = 9$, then $9 = 4 + 5$.
Symmetric Property

8. $0 + 21 = 21$
Add. Identity

9. $0(15) = 0$ Mult. Prop. of Zero

10. $(1)94 = 94$ Mult. Identity

11. If $3 + 3 = 6$ and $6 = 3 \cdot 2$, then $3 + 3 = 3 \cdot 2$. Transitive Property

12. $4 + 3 = 4 + 3$
Reflexive Property

13. $(14 - 6) + 3 = 8 + 3$
Substitution Property

Name the property used in each equation. Then find the value of n.

1. $n + 9 = 9$
Additive Identity; 0

2. $(8 + 7X4) = n(4)$
Substitution Prop.; 15

3. $5n = 1$
Multiplicative Inverse; $\frac{1}{5}$

4. $n \cdot 0.5 = 0.1 \cdot 0.5$
Reflexive Prop.; 0.1

5. $49n = 0$
Multiplicative Prop. of Zero; 0

6. $12 = 12 \cdot n$
Multiplicative Identity; 1

Evaluate each expression. Name the property used in each step.

7. $2 + 6(9 - 3^2) - 2$

$= 2 + 6(9 - 9) - 2$ Substitution
$= 2 + 6(0) - 2$ Substitution
$= 2 + 0 - 2$ Mult. Prop. of Zero
$= 2 - 2$ Additive Identity
$= 0$ Substitution

8. $5(14 - 39 \div 3) + 4 \cdot \frac{1}{4}$

$= 5(14 - 13) + 4 \cdot \frac{1}{4}$ Substitution
$= 5(1) + 4 \cdot \frac{1}{4}$ Substitution
$= 5 + 4 \cdot \frac{1}{4}$ Multiplicative Identity
$= 5 + 1$ Multiplicative Inverse
$= 6$ Substitution

SALES For Exercises 9 and 10, use the following information.
Althea paid $5.00 each for two bracelets and later sold each for $15.00. She paid $8.00 each for three bracelets and sold each of them for $9.00.

9. Write an expression that represents the profit Althea made. $2(15 - 5) + 3(9 - 8)$

10. Evaluate the expression. Name the property used in each step.
$2(15 - 5) + 3(9 - 8) = 2(10) + 3(1)$ Substitution
$= 20 + 3(1)$ Substitution
$= 20 + 3$ Multiplicative Identity
$= 23$ Substitution

GARDENING For Exercises 11 and 12, use the following information.
Mr. Katz harvested 15 tomatoes from each of four plants. Two other plants produced four tomatoes each, but Mr. Katz only harvested one fourth of the tomatoes from each of these.

11. Write an expression for the total number of tomatoes harvested. $4(15) + 2\left(4 \cdot \frac{1}{4}\right)$

12. Evaluate the expression. Name the property used in each step.
$4(15) + 2\left(4 \cdot \frac{1}{4}\right) = 60 + 2\left(4 \cdot \frac{1}{4}\right)$ Substitution
$= 60 + 2(1)$ Multiplicative Inverse
$= 60 + 2$ Multiplicative Identity
$= 62$ Substitution

Pre-Activity How are identity and equality properties used to compare data?

Read the introduction to Lesson 1-4 at the top of page 21 in your textbook.

Write an open sentence to represent the change in rank r of the University of Miami from December 11 to the final rank. Explain why the solution is the same as the solution in the introduction.
$2 + r = 2$; Sample answer: The rank did not change for either team from the date given to the final rank.

Reading the Lesson

1. Write the Roman numeral of the sentence that best matches each term.

a. additive identity ___V___

b. multiplicative identity ___III___

c. Multiplicative Property of Zero ___VIII___

d. Multiplicative Inverse Property ___I___

e. Reflexive Property ___II___

f. Symmetric Property ___IV___

g. Transitive Property ___VI___

h. Substitution Property ___VII___

I. $\frac{5}{7} \cdot \frac{7}{5} = 1$

II. $18 = 18$

III. $3 \cdot 1 = 3$

IV. If $12 = 8 + 4$, then $8 + 4 = 12$.

V. $6 + 0 = 6$

VI. If $2 + 4 = 5 + 1$ and $5 + 1 = 6$, then $2 + 4 = 6$.

VII. If $n = 2$, then $5n = 5 \cdot 2$.

VIII. $4 \cdot 0 = 0$

Helping You Remember

2. The prefix *trans-* means "across" or "through." Explain how this can help you remember the meaning of the Transitive Property of Equality.
Sample answer: The Transitive Property of Equality tells you that when $a = b$ and $b = c$, you can go from a through b to get to c.

FUND-RAISING For Exercises 30 and 31, use the following information.
The spirit club at Marshall High School is selling items to raise money. The profit the club earns on each item is the difference between what an item sells for and what it costs the club to buy.

School Spirit Items		
Item	Cost	Selling Price
Pennant	$3.00	$5.00
Button	$1.00	$2.50
Cap	$6.00	$10.00

30–31. See pp. 65A–65B.

30. Write an expression that represents the profit for 25 pennants, 80 buttons, and 40 caps.

31. Evaluate the expression, indicating the property used in each step.

MILITARY PAY For Exercises 32 and 33, use the table below.

Enlisted Personnel Monthly Pay Rates, Effective July 1, 2001								
	Years of Service							
Grade	< 2	> 2	> 3	> 4	> 6	> 8	> 10	> 12
E-5	1381.80	1549.20	1623.90	1701.00	1779.30	1888.50	1962.90	2040.30
E-4	1288.80	1423.80	1500.60	1576.20	1653.00	1653.00	1653.00	1653.00
E-3	1214.70	1307.10	1383.60	1385.40	1385.40	1385.40	1385.40	1385.40
E-2	1169.10	1169.10	1169.10	1169.10	1169.10	1169.10	1169.10	1169.10
E-1	1042.80	1042.80	1042.80	1042.80	1042.80	1042.80	1042.80	1042.80

Source: U.S. Department of Defense

32. $1169.10 + y = 1169.10$, where $y = 0$

33. $1653y = 1653$, where $y = 1$

34. $350,000 + 50,000 = 350,000 + 50,000$

32. Write an equation using addition that shows the change in pay for an enlisted member at grade E-2 from 3 years of service to 12 years.

33. Write an equation using multiplication that shows the change in pay for someone at grade E-4 from 6 years of service to 10 years.

FOOTBALL For Exercises 34–36, use the table of base salaries and bonus plans.

34. Suppose a player rushed for 12 touchdowns in 2002 and another player scored 76 points that same year. Write an equation that compares the two salaries and bonuses.

35. Write an expression that could be used to determine the base salaries and bonuses in 2004 for the following: **See margin.**

- eight players who keep their weight under 240 pounds and are involved in at least 35% of the offensive plays,

- three players who score 12 rushing touchdowns and score 76 points, and

- four players who gain 1601 yards of total offense and average 4.5 yards per carry.

36. Evaluate the expression you wrote in Exercise 35. Name the property used in each step. **See margin.**

More About. . .

Football

Nationally organized football began in 1920 and originally included five teams. In 2004, there were 32 teams.

Source: www.infoplease.com

NFL Salaries and Bonuses	
Year	Base Salary
2002	$350,000
2003	375,000
2004	400,000
2005	400,000

Goal	Bonus
Involved in 35% of offensive plays	$50,000
Average 4.5 yards per carry	50,000
12 rushing touchdowns	50,000
12 receiving touchdowns	50,000
76 points scored	50,000
1601 yards of total offense	50,000
Keep weight below 240 lb	100,000

Goal—Rushing Yards	Bonus
1600 yards	$1 million
1800 yards	1.5 million
2000 yards	2 million
2100 yards	2.5 million

Source: ESPN Sports Almanac

Online Research Data Update Find the most recent statistics for a professional football player. What were his base salary and bonuses? Visit www.algebra1.com/data_update to learn more.

Closure

A *binary operation* matches two numbers in a set to just one number. Addition is a binary operation on the set of whole numbers. It matches two numbers such as 4 and 5 to a single number, their sum.

If the result of a binary operation is always a member of the original set, the set is said to be *closed* under the operation. For example, the set of whole numbers is closed under addition because $4 + 5$ is a whole number. The set of whole numbers is not closed under subtraction because $4 - 5$ is not a whole number.

Tell whether each operation is binary. Write *yes* or *no*.

1. the operation ⌐|, where a ⌐| b means to choose the lesser number from a and b **yes**

2. the operation ©, where a © b means to cube the sum of a and b **yes**

3. the operation *sq*, where *sq*(a) means to square the number a **no**

37. sometimes;
Sample answer: true:
$x = 2$, $y = 1$, $z = 4$,
$w = 3$; $2 \cdot 4 > 1 \cdot 3$;
false: $x = 1$, $y = -1$,
$z = -2$, $w = -3$;
$1(-2) < (-1)(-3)$

37. CRITICAL THINKING The Transitive Property of Inequality states that if $a < b$ and $b < c$, then $a < c$. Use this property to determine whether the following statement is *sometimes*, *always*, or *never* true.

$$\text{If } x > y \text{ and } z > w, \text{ then } xz > yw.$$

Give examples to support your answer.

38. WRITING IN MATH   Answer the question that was posed at the beginning of the lesson. **See margin.**

How are identity and equality properties used to compare data?

Include the following in your answer:
- a description of how you could use the Reflexive or Symmetric Property to compare a team's rank for any two time periods, and
- a demonstration of the Transitive Property using one of the team's three rankings as an example.

Standardized Test Practice
Ⓐ Ⓑ Ⓒ Ⓓ

39. Which equation illustrates the Symmetric Property of Equality? **A**
- Ⓐ If $a = b$, then $b = a$.
- Ⓑ If $a = b$, $b = c$, then $a = c$.
- Ⓒ If $a = b$, then $b = c$.
- Ⓓ If $a = a$, then $a + 0 = a$.

40. The equation $(10 - 8)(5) = (2)(5)$ is an example of which property of equality? **B**
- Ⓐ Reflexive
- Ⓑ Substitution
- Ⓒ Symmetric
- Ⓓ Transitive

Extending the Lesson
The sum of any two whole numbers is always a whole number. So, the set of whole numbers $\{0, 1, 2, 3, \ldots\}$ is said to be closed under addition. This is an example of the **Closure Property**. State whether each of the following statements is *true* or *false*. If false, justify your reasoning.

41, 43. See margin.

41. The set of whole numbers is closed under subtraction.

42. The set of whole numbers is closed under multiplication. **true**

43. The set of whole numbers is closed under division.

Maintain Your Skills

Mixed Review
Find the solution set for each inequality using the given replacement set.
(Lesson 1-3)

45. {11, 12, 13}
46. {6, 6.1, 6.2, 6.3}
47. {3, 3.25, 3.5, 3.75, 4}

44. $10 - x > 6$; $\{3, 5, 6, 8\}$ **{3}**

45. $4x + 2 < 58$; $\{11, 12, 13, 14, 15\}$

46. $\frac{x}{2} \geq 3$; $\{5.8, 5.9, 6, 6.1, 6.2, 6.3\}$

47. $8x \leq 32$; $\{3, 3.25, 3.5, 3.75, 4\}$

48. $\frac{7}{10} - 2x < \frac{3}{10}$; $\left\{\frac{1}{2}, \frac{1}{3}, \frac{1}{4}, \frac{1}{5}, \frac{1}{6}\right\}$ $\left\{\frac{1}{2}, \frac{1}{3}, \frac{1}{4}\right\}$

49. $2x - 1 \leq 2$; $\left\{1\frac{1}{4}, 2, 3, 3\frac{1}{2}\right\}$ $\left\{1\frac{1}{4}\right\}$

Evaluate each expression. *(Lesson 1-2)*

50. $(3 + 6) \div 3^2$ **1**

51. $6(12 - 7.5) - 7$ **20**

52. $20 \div 4 \cdot 8 \div 10$ **4**

53. $\frac{(6 + 2)^2}{16} + 3(9)$ **31**

54. $[6^2 - (2 + 4)2]3$ **72**

55. $9(3) - 4^2 + 6^2 \div 2$ **29**

56. Write an algebraic expression for the sum of twice a number squared and 7. *(Lesson 1-1)* $2x^2 + 7$

Getting Ready for the Next Lesson
PREREQUISITE SKILL   Evaluate each expression.
*(To review **order of operations**, see Lesson 1-2.)*

57. $10(6) + 10(2)$ **80**

58. $(15 - 6) \cdot 8$ **72**

59. $12(4) - 5(4)$ **28**

60. $3(4 + 2)$ **18**

61. $5(6 - 4)$ **10**

62. $8(14 + 2)$ **128**

Teaching Tip The Closure Property is difficult for students to comprehend. Sometimes they will understand the concept better if shown counterexamples. For example, $\{0,1\}$ is closed under multiplication because $0(0)$, $0(1)$, and $1(1)$ all belong to the set. However, the same set is not closed under addition because $1 + 1$ is not a member of the set.

4 Assess

Open-Ended Assessment
Speaking Name one of the multiplicative or additive properties that students learned in this lesson. Have students describe the meaning of the property, and give examples of how the property is used in evaluating expressions or solving equations.

Getting Ready for Lesson 1-5
PREREQUISITE SKILL Students will learn about evaluating expressions using the Distributive Property in Lesson 1-5. Use Exercises 57–62 to determine your students' familiarity with evaluating expressions without using the Distributive Property.

Answers

35. $8(100,000 + 50,000 + 400,000) + 3(50,000 + 50,000 + 400,000) + 4(50,000 + 50,000 + 400,000)$

36. $8(100,000 + 50,000 + 400,000) + 3(50,000 + 50,000 + 400,000) + 4(50,000 + 50,000 + 400,000)$

$= 8(550,000) + 3(500,000) + 4(500,000)$ **Substitution**

$= 4,400,000 + 1,500,000 + 2,000,000$ **Substitution**

$= 7,900,000$ **Substitution**

38. You can use the identity and equality properties to see if data is the same. Answers should include the following.
- Reflexive: $r = r$, or Symmetric: $a = b$, so $b = a$
- Oklahoma, week 1 $= a$, week 2 $= b$, week 3 $= c$. $a = b$ and $b = c$ so $a = c$.

41. False; $4 - 5 = -1$, which is not a whole number.

43. False; $1 \div 2 = \frac{1}{2}$, which is not a whole number.

1 Focus

5-Minute Check Transparency 1-5 Use as a quiz or a review of Lesson 1-4.

Mathematical Background notes are available for this lesson on p. 4D.

Questions are provided at the beginning of each lesson to help you use the problem provided there to engage and inform students.

How can the Distributive **Property** be used to calculate quickly?

Ask students:

- How can you represent the price of a bargain game and a new release as one quantity? **(14.95 + 34.95)**

- Since 8 customers bought a bargain game and a new release, by what would you need to multiply the quantity in parentheses to find the total amount of money taken in? **multiply by 8**

- How can you represent the price of a bargain game and a new release, multiplied by 8, as one quantity? **8(14.95 + 34.95)**

What You'll Learn

- Use the Distributive Property to evaluate expressions.
- Use the Distributive Property to simplify expressions.

Vocabulary
- term
- like terms
- equivalent expressions
- simplest form
- coefficient

How can the Distributive Property be used to calculate quickly?

Instant Replay Video Games sells new and used games. During a Saturday morning sale, the first 8 customers each bought a bargain game and a new release. To calculate the total sales for these customers, you can use the Distributive Property.

Sale Prices	
Used Games	$9.95
Bargain Games	$14.95
Regular Games	$24.95
New Releases	$34.95

EVALUATE EXPRESSIONS There are two methods you could use to calculate the video game sales.

Method 1			Method 2		
sales of bargain games	plus	sales of new releases	number of customers	times	each customer's purchase price
8(14.95)	+	8(34.95)	8	×	(14.95 + 34.95)

$= 119.60 + 279.60$ $= 8(49.90)$

$= 399.20$ $= 399.20$

Either method gives total sales of $399.20 because the following is true.

$$8(14.95) + 8(34.95) = 8(14.95 + 34.95)$$

This is an example of the **Distributive Property**.

Key Concept	Distributive Property

- **Symbols**   For any numbers a, b, and c,
  $a(b + c) = ab + ac$ and $(b + c)a = ba + ca$ and
  $a(b - c) = ab - ac$ and $(b - c)a = ba - ca$.

- **Examples** $3(2 + 5) = 3 \cdot 2 + 3 \cdot 5$ $4(9 - 7) = 4 \cdot 9 - 4 \cdot 7$
                 $3(7) = 6 + 15$ $4(2) = 36 - 28$
                 $21 = 21$ ✓ $8 = 8$ ✓

Notice that it does not matter whether a is placed on the right or the left of the expression in the parentheses.

The Symmetric Property of Equality allows the Distributive Property to be written as follows.

     If $a(b + c) = ab + ac$, then $ab + ac = a(b + c)$.

Resource Manager

 Workbook and Reproducible Masters

Chapter 1 Resource Masters
- Study Guide and Intervention, pp. 25–26
- Skills Practice, p. 27
- Practice, p. 28
- Reading to Learn Mathematics, p. 29
- Enrichment, p. 30
- Assessment, pp. 69, 71

Parent and Student Study Guide Workbook, p. 5
Prerequisite Skills Workbook, pp. 49–50, 55–56, 77–78
Teach Algebra With Manipulatives Masters, pp. 10–11, 17, 33

Transparencies
5-Minute Check Transparency 1-5
Answer Key Transparencies

 **Technology**
Interactive Chalkboard

Example 1 Distribute Over Addition

Rewrite $8(10 + 4)$ using the Distributive Property. Then evaluate.

$$
\begin{aligned}
8(10 + 4) &= 8(10) + 8(4) &&\text{Distributive Property} \\
&= 80 + 32 &&\text{Multiply.} \\
&= 112 &&\text{Add.}
\end{aligned}
$$

Example 2 Distribute Over Subtraction

Rewrite $(12 - 3)6$ using the Distributive Property. Then evaluate.

$$
\begin{aligned}
(12 - 3)6 &= 12 \cdot 6 - 3 \cdot 6 &&\text{Distributive Property} \\
&= 72 - 18 &&\text{Multiply.} \\
&= 54 &&\text{Subtract.}
\end{aligned}
$$

Log on for:
- Updated data
- More activities on the Distributive Property
  www.algebra1.com/ usa_today

Example 3 Use the Distributive Property

CARS The Morris family owns two cars. In 1998, they drove the first car 18,000 miles and the second car 16,000 miles. Use the graph to find the total cost of operating both cars.

Use the Distributive Property to write and evaluate an expression.

$$
\begin{aligned}
0.46(18{,}000 + 16{,}000) &\quad\text{Distributive Prop.} \\
= 8280 + 7360 &\quad\text{Multiply.} \\
= 15{,}640 &\quad\text{Add.}
\end{aligned}
$$

It cost the Morris family $15,640 to operate their cars.

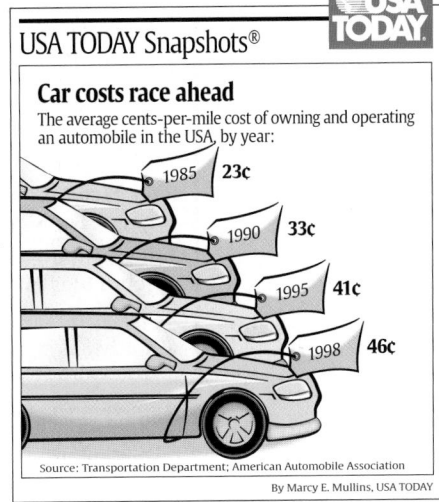

USA TODAY Snapshots®

Car costs race ahead

The average cents-per-mile cost of owning and operating an automobile in the USA, by year:

1985 23¢
1990 33¢
1995 41¢
1998 46¢

Source: Transportation Department; American Automobile Association

By Marcy E. Mullins, USA TODAY

The Distributive Property can be used to simplify mental calculations.

Example 4 Use the Distributive Property

Use the Distributive Property to find each product.

a. $15 \cdot 99$

$$
\begin{aligned}
15 \cdot 99 &= 15(100 - 1) &&\text{Think: } 99 = 100 - 1 \\
&= 15(100) - 15(1) &&\text{Distributive Property} \\
&= 1500 - 15 &&\text{Multiply.} \\
&= 1485 &&\text{Subtract.}
\end{aligned}
$$

b. $35\left(2\frac{1}{5}\right)$

$$
\begin{aligned}
35\left(2\frac{1}{5}\right) &= 35\left(2 + \frac{1}{5}\right) &&\text{Think: } 2\frac{1}{5} = 2 + \frac{1}{5} \\
&= 35(2) + 35\left(\frac{1}{5}\right) &&\text{Distributive Property} \\
&= 70 + 7 &&\text{Multiply.} \\
&= 77 &&\text{Add.}
\end{aligned}
$$

www.algebra1.com/extra_examples

---

2 Teach

EVALUATE EXPRESSIONS

In-Class Examples Power Point®

1 Rewrite $5(7 + 2)$ using the Distributive Property. Then evaluate.

$$
\begin{aligned}
5(7 + 2) &= 5(7) + 5(2) \\
&\qquad\text{Distributive Property} \\
&= 35 + 10 \text{ Multiply.} \\
&= 45 \text{ Add.}
\end{aligned}
$$

2 Rewrite $(16 - 7)3$ using the Distributive Property. Then evaluate.

$$
\begin{aligned}
(16 - 7)3 &= 16 \cdot 3 - 7 \cdot 3 \\
&\qquad\text{Distributive Property} \\
&= 48 - 21 \text{ Multiply.} \\
&= 27 \text{ Subtract.}
\end{aligned}
$$

3 **CARS** Find what the total cost of the Morris family operating two cars would have been in 1985, if they drove the same number of miles. **It would have cost them $7,820. Some students may have noticed that the cost per mile in 1985 was half that in 1998, so the total cost was half also.**

4 Use the Distributive Property to find each product.
a. $12 \cdot 82$ **984**
b. $27\left(3\frac{2}{3}\right)$ **99**

 **Tips for New Teachers**

Intervention In Example 4, students learn how to use the Distributive Property to simplify mental calculations. Consider having students complete additional practice of this skill. Mental calculations with the Distributive Property also prepares students for multiplying algebraic expressions in later chapters of this text.

SIMPLIFY EXPRESSIONS

  Power Point®

5 Rewrite each product using the Distributive Property. Then simplify.

a. $12(y + 3)$
$12(y + 3) = 12 \cdot y + 12 \cdot 3$
        Distributive Property
        $= 12y + 36$ Multiply.

b. $4(y^2 + 8y + 2)$
$4(y^2 + 8y + 2)$
     $= 4(y^2) + 4(8y) + 4(2)$
        Distributive Property
     $= 4y^2 + 32y + 8$ Simplify.

6 Simplify each expression.

a. $17a + 21a$ $38a$

b. $12b^2 - 8b^2 + 6b$ $4b^2 + 6b$

Teaching Tip Remind students that since y^2 is in the numerator of $\dfrac{3y^2}{4}$, the expression can be rewritten as $\dfrac{3}{4}y^2$. The latter form makes identifying the coefficient much easier. Write the following on the board for clarification.
$$\frac{3}{4} \cdot y^2 = \frac{3}{4} \cdot \frac{y^2}{1} = \frac{3y^2}{4}$$

Answers

4.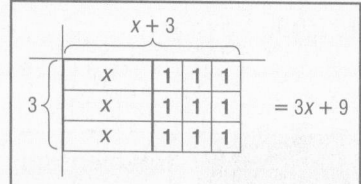

5.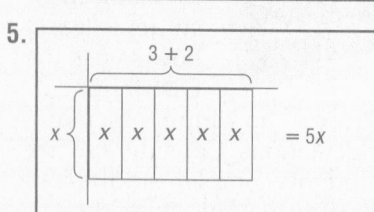

6. Rachel; Sample answer:
$3(x + 4) = 3(x) + 3(4) =$
$3x + 12.$

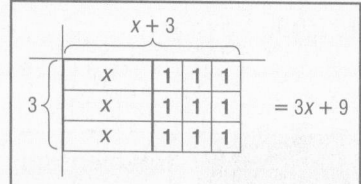

Algebra Activities use manipulatives and models to help students learn key concepts. There are teacher notes for every Algebra Activity in the Student Edition.

SIMPLIFY EXPRESSIONS You can use algebra tiles to investigate how the Distributive Property relates to algebraic expressions.

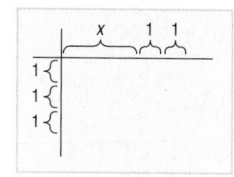

Algebra Activity

The Distributive Property

Consider the product $3(x + 2)$. Use a product mat and algebra tiles to model $3(x + 2)$ as the area of a rectangle whose dimensions are 3 and $(x + 2)$.

Step 1 Use algebra tiles to mark the dimensions of the rectangle on a product mat.

Step 2 Using the marks as a guide, make the rectangle with the algebra tiles. The rectangle has 3 x-tiles and 6 1-tiles. The area of the rectangle is
$x + 1 + 1 + x + 1 + 1 + x + 1 + 1$ or
$3x + 6$. Therefore, $3(x + 2) = 3x + 6$.

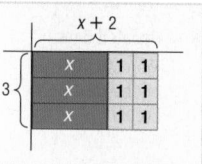

Model and Analyze

Find each product by using algebra tiles.

1. $2(x + 1)$ $2x + 2$ **2.** $5(x + 2)$ $5x + 10$ **3.** $2(2x + 1)$ $4x + 2$

Tell whether each statement is *true* or *false*. Justify your answer with algebra tiles and a drawing. 4–5. See margin for drawings.

4. $3(x + 3) = 3x + 3$ **5.** $x(3 + 2) = 3x + 2x$

6. Rachel says that $3(x + 4) = 3x + 12$, but José says that $3(x + 4) = 3x + 4$. Use words and models to explain who is correct and why. **See margin.**

4. false;
   $3(x + 3) = 3x + 9$
5. true

You can apply the Distributive Property to algebraic expressions.

Example 5 **Algebraic Expressions**

Rewrite each product using the Distributive Property. Then simplify.

a. $5(g - 9)$
    $5(g - 9) = 5 \cdot g - 5 \cdot 9$ Distributive Property
             $= 5g - 45$ Multiply.

b. $3(2x^2 + 4x - 1)$
    $3(2x^2 + 4x - 1) = (3)(2x^2) + (3)(4x) - 3(1)$ Distributive Property
                   $= 6x^2 + 12x - 3$ Simplify.

> **Study Tip**
>
> *Reading Math*
> The expression $5(g - 9)$ is read *5 times the quantity g minus 9* or *5 times the difference of g and 9.*

A **term** is a number, a variable, or a product or quotient of numbers and variables. For example, y, p^3, $4a$, and $5g^2h$ are all terms. **Like terms** are terms that contain the same variables, with corresponding variables having the same power.

$$2x^2 + 6x + 5$$
three terms

$$3a^2 + 5a^2 + 2a$$
like terms   unlike terms

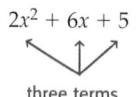

Algebra Activity

Materials: algebra tiles, product mat

- To save time and algebra tile sets, consider having students work in groups.
- Remind students that with algebra tiles, one of the quantities being multiplied goes on the left side and the other quantity goes on the top.

The Distributive Property and the properties of equality can be used to show that $5n + 7n = 12n$. In this expression, $5n$ and $7n$ are like terms.

$$5n + 7n = (5 + 7)n \quad \text{Distributive Property}$$
$$= 12n \quad \text{Substitution}$$

The expressions $5n + 7n$ and $12n$ are called **equivalent expressions** because they denote the same number. An expression is in **simplest form** when it is replaced by an equivalent expression having no like terms or parentheses.

Example 6 Combine Like Terms

Simplify each expression.

a. $15x + 18x$

$$15x + 18x = (15 + 18)x \quad \text{Distributive Property}$$
$$= 33x \quad \text{Substitution}$$

b. $10n + 3n^2 + 9n^2$

$$10n + 3n^2 + 9n^2 = 10n + (3 + 9)n^2 \quad \text{Distributive Property}$$
$$= 10n + 12n^2 \quad \text{Substitution}$$

The **coefficient** of a term is the numerical factor. For example, in $17xy$, the coefficient is 17, and in $\frac{3y^2}{4}$, the coefficient is $\frac{3}{4}$. In the term m, the coefficient is 1 since $1 \cdot m = m$ by the Multiplicative Identity Property.

Study Tip

Like Terms
Like terms may be defined as terms that are the same or vary only by the coefficient.

Find the Error exercises (like Exercise 3 below) help students identify and address common errors before they occur.

Check for Understanding

Concept Check

1. **Explain** why the Distributive Property is sometimes called The Distributive Property of Multiplication Over Addition. **See pp. 65A–65B.**

2. **OPEN ENDED** Write an expression that has five terms, three of which are like terms and one term with a coefficient of 1.

3. **FIND THE ERROR** Courtney and Ben are simplifying $4w^4 + w^4 + 3w^2 - 2w^2$.

Courtney	Ben
$4w^4 + w^4 + 3w^2 - 2w^2$	$4w^4 + w^4 + 3w^2 - 2w^2$
$= (4 + 1)w^4 + (3 - 2)w^2$	$= (4)w^4 + (3 - 2)w^2$
$= 5w^4 + 1w^2$	$= 4w^4 + 1w^2$
$= 5w^4 + w^2$	$= 4w^4 + w^2$

2. Sample answer:
$4ab + 3b + a + 2ab + 7ab$

Who is correct? Explain your reasoning.
Courtney; Ben forgot that w^4 is really $1 \cdot w^4$.

Guided Practice Rewrite each expression using the Distributive Property. Then simplify.

GUIDED PRACTICE KEY	
Exercises	Examples
4	2
5, 6	5
7, 8	4
9–12	6
13, 14	3

4. $6(12 - 2)$ **60**   5. $2(4 + t)$ **$8 + 2t$**   6. $(g - 9)5$ **$5g - 45$**

Use the Distributive Property to find each product.

7. $16(102)$ **1632**   8. $\left(3\frac{1}{17}\right)(17)$ **52**

Simplify each expression. If not possible, write *simplified*.

9. $13m + m$ **$14m$**   10. $3(x + 2x)$ **$9x$**

11. $14a^2 + 13b^2 + 27$ **simplified**   12. $4(3g + 2)$ **$12g + 8$**

3 Practice/Apply

Study Notebook

Have students—
• add the definitions/examples of the vocabulary terms to their Vocabulary Builder worksheets for Chapter 1.
• list several terms and identify the coefficient of each.
• include any other item(s) that they find helpful in mastering the skills in this lesson.

DAILY
INTERVENTION **FIND THE ERROR**
Remind students that when they simplify expressions, they must first identify like terms. Tell students to look at the first step in Courtney's and Ben's simplification to make sure they identified all like terms.

About the Exercises...
Organization by Objective
• **Evaluate Expressions:** 15–18, 29–41
• **Simplify Expressions:** 19–28, 42–53

Odd/Even Assignments
Exercises 15–28, 31–36, and 42–53 are structured so that students practice the same concepts whether they are assigned odd or even problems.

Assignment Guide
Basic: 15–25 odd, 29–30, 31–35 odd, 43–51 odd, 54–72
Average: 15–27 odd, 29–30, 31–35 odd, 37–38, 43–53 odd, 54–72
Advanced: 16–28 even, 32–36 even, 37–41, 42–52 even, 54–69 (optional: 70–72)

DAILY
INTERVENTION **Differentiated Instruction**

Kinesthetic With masking tape, mark a set of parentheses on the classroom floor that are large enough for three students to stand in. Then call on five volunteers. Distribute x tiles, x^2 tiles, and one tiles to the students, making sure to give two or three of the students the same kind of tiles. Ask students to identify "like terms" by comparing the tiles that they have. To model the Distributive Property, have students with "like" tiles give them to you and then stand in the parentheses.

Application   **COSMETOLOGY**   For Exercises 13 and 14, use the following information.
Ms. Curry owns a hair salon. One day, she gave 12 haircuts. She earned $19.95 for each and received an average tip of $2 for each haircut.

13. Write an expression to determine the total amount she earned. $12(19.95 + 2)$
14. How much did Ms. Curry earn? $263.40

★ indicates increased difficulty

Practice and Apply

Homework Help

For Exercises	See Examples
15–18	1, 2
19–28	5
29, 30, 37–41	3
31–36	4
42–53	6

Extra Practice
See page 821.

Rewrite each expression using the Distributive Property. Then simplify.

15. $8(5 + 7)$ 96
16. $7(13 + 12)$ 175
17. $12(9 - 5)$ 48
18. $13(10 - 7)$ 39
19. $3(2x + 6)$ $6x + 18$
20. $8(3m + 4)$ $24m + 32$
21. $(4 + x)2$ $8 + 2x$
22. $(5 + n)3$ $15 + 3n$
23. $28\left(y - \frac{1}{7}\right)$ $28y - 4$
24. $27\left(2b - \frac{1}{3}\right)$ $54b - 9$
25. $a(b - 6)$ $ab - 6a$
26. $x(z + 3)$ $xz + 3x$
★ 27. $2(a - 3b + 2c)$ $2a - 6b + 4c$
★ 28. $4(8p + 4q - 7r)$ $32p + 16q - 28r$

OLYMPICS   For Exercises 29 and 30, use the following information.
At the 2000 Summer Olympics in Australia, about 110,000 people attended events at Olympic Stadium each day while another 17,500 fans were at the aquatics center.

29. Write an expression you could use to determine the total number of people at Olympic Stadium and the Aquatic Center over 4 days. $4(110,000 + 17,500)$
30. What was the attendance for the 4-day period? 510,000

Use the Distributive Property to find each product.

31. $5 \cdot 97$ 485
32. $8 \cdot 990$ 7920
33. $17 \cdot 6$ 102
34. $24 \cdot 7$ 168
35. $18\left(2\frac{1}{9}\right)$ 38
36. $48\left(3\frac{1}{6}\right)$ 152

COMMUNICATIONS   For Exercises 37 and 38, use the following information.
A public relations consultant keeps a log of all contacts made by e-mail, telephone, and in person. In a typical week, she averages 5 hours using e-mail, 12 hours of meeting in person, and 18 hours on the telephone.

37. Write an expression that could be used to predict how many hours she will spend on these activities over the next 12 weeks. $12(5 + 12 + 18)$
38. How many hours should she plan for contacting people for the next 12 weeks? 420

INSURANCE   For Exercises 39–41, use the table that shows the monthly cost of a company health plan.

Available Insurance Plans—Monthly Charge			
Coverage	Medical	Dental	Vision
Employee	$78	$20	$12
Family (additional coverage)	$50	$15	$7

39. Write an expression that could be used to calculate the cost of medical, dental, and vision insurance for an employee for 6 months. $6(78 + 20 + 12)$
40. How much does it cost an employee to get all three types of insurance for 6 months? $660
41. How much would an employee expect to pay for individual and family medical and dental coverage per year? $1956

Enrichment, p. 30

Tangram Puzzles

The seven geometric figures shown below are called **tans**. They are used in a very old Chinese puzzle called **tangrams**.

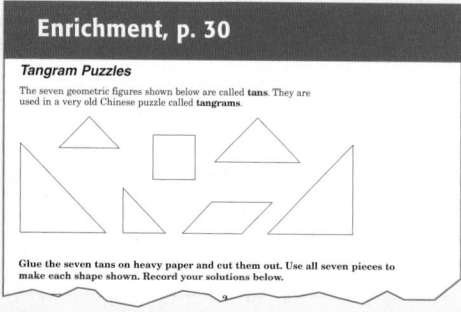

Glue the seven tans on heavy paper and cut them out. Use all seven pieces to make each shape shown. Record your solutions below.

Simplify each expression. If not possible, write *simplified.* **50.** $30a + 6b$

42. $2x + 9x$ $11x$ **43.** $4b + 5b$ $9b$ **44.** $5n^2 + 7n$ simplified

45. $3a^2 + 14a^2$ $17a^2$ **46.** $12(3c + 4)$ $36c + 48$ **47.** $15(3x - 5)$ $45x - 75$

48. $6x^2 + 14x - 9x$ $6x^2 + 5x$ **49.** $4y^3 + 3y^3 + y^4$ $7y^3 + y^4$ **50.** $6(5a + 3b - 2b)$

51. $5(6m + 4n - 3n)$ ★ **52.** $x^2 + \frac{7}{8}x - \frac{x}{8}x^2 + \frac{3}{4}x$ ★ **53.** $a + \frac{a}{5} + \frac{2}{5}a$ $\frac{8}{5}a$
$30m + 5n$

54. CRITICAL THINKING   The expression $2(\ell + w)$ may be used to find the perimeter of a rectangle. What are the length and width of a rectangle if the area is $13\frac{1}{2}$ square units and the length of one side is $\frac{1}{5}$ the measure of the perimeter? $\ell = 4\frac{1}{2}$ **units,** $w = 3$ **units**

55. **WRITING IN MATH**   Answer the question that was posed at the beginning of the lesson. **See margin.**

How can the Distributive Property be used to calculate quickly?

Include the following in your answer:
• a comparison of the two methods of finding the total video game sales.

Standardized Test Practice
Ⓐ Ⓑ Ⓒ Ⓓ

56. Simplify $3(x + y) + 2(x + y) - 4x$. **D**

Ⓐ $5x + y$ Ⓑ $9x + 5y$ Ⓒ $5x + 9y$ Ⓓ $x + 5y$

57. If $a = 2.8$ and $b = 4.2$, find the value of c in the equation $c = 7(2a + 3b)$. **C**

Ⓐ 18.2 Ⓑ 238.0 Ⓒ 127.4 Ⓓ 51.8

Maintain Your Skills

Mixed Review   **Name the property illustrated by each statement or equation.**   *(Lesson 1-4)*

58. If $7 \cdot 2 = 14$, then $14 = 7 \cdot 2$. **Symm.**   **59.** $8 + (3 + 9) = 8 + 12$ **Subst.**

60. $mnp = 1mnp$ **Mult. Identity**   **61.** $3\left(5^2 \cdot \frac{1}{25}\right) = 3 \cdot 1$ **Mult. Inverse**

62. $\left(\frac{3}{4}\right)\left(\frac{4}{3}\right) = 1$ **Mult. Inverse**   **63.** $32 + 21 = 32 + 21$ **Reflexive**

PHYSICAL SCIENCE   For Exercises 64 and 65, use the following information.
Sound travels 1129 feet per second through air.   *(Lesson 1-3)*

64. Write an equation that represents how many feet sound can travel in 2 seconds when it is traveling through air. $d = 1129(2)$

65. How far can sound travel in 2 seconds when traveling through air? **2258 ft**

Evaluate each expression if $a = 4$, $b = 6$, **and** $c = 3$.   *(Lesson 1-2)*

66. $3ab - c^2$ **63**   **67.** $8(a - c)^2 + 3$ **11** **68.** $\frac{6ab}{c(a + 2)}$ **8**   **69.** $(a + c)\left(\frac{a + b}{2}\right)$ **35**

Getting Ready for the Next Lesson   **PREREQUISITE SKILL**   **Find the area of each figure.**
*(To review **finding area**, see pages 813 and 814.)*

70. 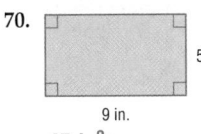 5 in. 9 in. **45 in²**

71. 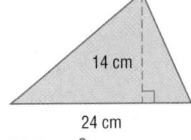 14 cm 24 cm **168 cm²**

72. 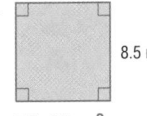 8.5 m **72.25 m²**

Answer

55. You can use the Distributive Property to calculate quickly by expressing any number as a sum or difference of more convenient numbers. Answers should include the following.

• Both methods result in the correct method. In one method you multiply then add, and in the other you add then multiply.

Open-Ended Assessment

Writing Have students look up the verb *distribute* in the dictionary and then write a paragraph or two comparing the definition to how the Distributive Property is used to simplify or evaluate expressions.

Getting Ready for Lesson 1-6

PREREQUISITE SKILL Students will learn about the Commutative and Associative Properties in Lesson 1-6. One application of the Commutative Property of Multiplication is for students to realize that the expression $\ell \cdot w$ for area is the same as $w \cdot \ell$. Use Exercises 70–72 to determine your students' familiarity with finding area.

Assessment Options

Quiz (Lessons 1-4 and 1-5) is available on p. 69 of the *Chapter 1 Resource Masters*.

Mid-Chapter Test (Lessons 1-1 through 1-5) is available on p. 71 of the *Chapter 1 Resource Masters*.

Assessment Options lists the quizzes and tests that are available in the Chapter Resource Masters.

By having your students complete the Getting Ready exercises, you can target specific skills they will need for the next lesson.

1-6 Commutative and Associative Properties

1 Focus

5-Minute Check Transparency 1-6 Use as a quiz or a review of Lesson 1-5.

Mathematical Background notes are available for this lesson on p. 4D.

How can properties help you determine distances?

Ask students:

- Evaluate 0.4 + 1.5. **1.9**
- Evaluate 1.5 + 0.4. **1.9**
- Because 0.4 + 1.5 and 1.5 + 0.4 have the same sum, what can you say about the order in which you add two numbers? **The order in which the two numbers are added does not matter, the result is the same.**
- Does the order in which numbers are subtracted matter? Explain. **Sample answer: Yes; for example, 0.4 − 1.5 = −1.1 but 1.5 − 0.4 = 1.1.**

Key Concept boxes highlight definitions, formulas, and other important ideas. Multiple representations—words, symbols, examples, models—reach students of all learning styles

What You'll Learn

- Recognize the Commutative and Associative Properties.
- Use the Commutative and Associative Properties to simplify expressions.

How can properties help you determine distances?

The South Line of the Atlanta subway leaves Five Points and heads for Garnett, 0.4 mile away. From Garnett, West End is 1.5 miles. The distance from Five Points to West End can be found by evaluating the expression 0.4 + 1.5. Likewise, the distance from West End to Five Points can be found by evaluating the expression 1.5 + 0.4.

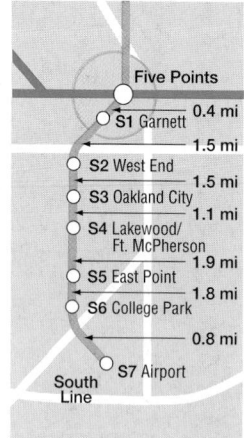

Five Points
S1 Garnett — 0.4 mi
— 1.5 mi
S2 West End
— 1.5 mi
S3 Oakland City
— 1.1 mi
S4 Lakewood/ Ft. McPherson
— 1.9 mi
S5 East Point
— 1.8 mi
S6 College Park
— 0.8 mi
S7 Airport
South Line

COMMUTATIVE AND ASSOCIATIVE PROPERTIES In the situation above, the distance from Five Points to West End is the same as the distance from West End to Five Points. This distance can be represented by the following equation.

The distance from Five Points to West End $\underbrace{0.4 + 1.5}$ | equals = | the distance from West End to Five Points. $\underbrace{1.5 + 0.4}$

This is an example of the **Commutative Property**.

Key Concept — *Commutative Property*

- **Words** The order in which you add or multiply numbers does not change their sum or product.
- **Symbols** For any numbers a and b, $a + b = b + a$ and $a \cdot b = b \cdot a$.
- **Examples** $5 + 6 = 6 + 5$, $3 \cdot 2 = 2 \cdot 3$

An easy way to find the sum or product of numbers is to group, or associate, the numbers using the **Associative Property**.

Key Concept — *Associative Property*

- **Words** The way you group three or more numbers when adding or multiplying does not change their sum or product.
- **Symbols** For any numbers a, b, and c, $(a + b) + c = a + (b + c)$ and $(ab)c = a(bc)$.
- **Examples** $(2 + 4) + 6 = 2 + (4 + 6)$, $(3 \cdot 5) \cdot 4 = 3 \cdot (5 \cdot 4)$

Resource Manager

 Workbook and Reproducible Masters

Chapter 1 Resource Masters
- Study Guide and Intervention, pp. 31–32
- Skills Practice, p. 33
- Practice, p. 34
- Reading to Learn Mathematics, p. 35
- Enrichment, p. 36

Parent and Student Study Guide Workbook, p. 6
Prerequisite Skills Workbook, pp. 49–50, 77–78

 Transparencies

5-Minute Check Transparency 1-6
Answer Key Transparencies

Technology

AlgePASS: Tutorial Plus, Lesson 2
Interactive Chalkboard

Example 1 Multiplication Properties

Evaluate 8 · 2 · 3 · 5.

You can rearrange and group the factors to make mental calculations easier.

$$8 \cdot 2 \cdot 3 \cdot 5 = 8 \cdot 3 \cdot 2 \cdot 5 \qquad \text{Commutative } (\times)$$
$$= (8 \cdot 3) \cdot (2 \cdot 5) \qquad \text{Associative } (\times)$$
$$= 24 \cdot 10 \qquad \text{Multiply.}$$
$$= 240 \qquad \text{Multiply.}$$

Example 2 Use Addition Properties

TRANSPORTATION Refer to the application at the beginning of the lesson. Find the distance between Five Points and Lakewood/Ft. McPherson.

Five Points to Garnett		Garnett to West End		West End to Oakland City		Oakland City to Lakewood/Ft. McPherson
0.4	+	1.5	+	1.5	+	1.1

$$0.4 + 1.5 + 1.5 + 1.1 = 0.4 + 1.1 + 1.5 + 1.5 \qquad \text{Commutative } (+)$$
$$= (0.4 + 1.1) + (1.5 + 1.5) \qquad \text{Associative } (+)$$
$$= 1.5 + 3.0 \qquad \text{Add.}$$
$$= 4.5 \qquad \text{Add.}$$

Lakewood/Ft. McPherson is 4.5 miles from Five Points.

SIMPLIFY EXPRESSIONS The Commutative and Associative Properties can be used with other properties when evaluating and simplifying expressions.

More About. . .

Transportation
New York City has the most extensive subway system, covering 842 miles of track and serving about 4.3 million passengers per day.

Source: *The Guinness Book of Records*

Concept Summary — Properties of Numbers

The following properties are true for any numbers a, b, and c.

Properties	Addition	Multiplication
Commutative	$a + b = b + a$	$ab = ba$
Associative	$(a + b) + c = a + (b + c)$	$(ab)c = a(bc)$
Identity	0 is the identity. $a + 0 = 0 + a = a$	1 is the identity. $a \cdot 1 = 1 \cdot a = a$
Zero	——	$a \cdot 0 = 0 \cdot a = 0$
Distributive	$a(b + c) = ab + ac$ and $(b + c)a = ba + ca$	
Substitution	If $a = b$, then a may be substituted for b.	

Example 3 Simplify an Expression

Simplify $3c + 5(2 + c)$.

$$3c + 5(2 + c) = 3c + 5(2) + 5(c) \qquad \text{Distributive Property}$$
$$= 3c + 10 + 5c \qquad \text{Multiply.}$$
$$= 3c + 5c + 10 \qquad \text{Commutative } (+)$$
$$= (3c + 5c) + 10 \qquad \text{Associative } (+)$$
$$= (3 + 5)c + 10 \qquad \text{Distributive Property}$$
$$= 8c + 10 \qquad \text{Substitution}$$

www.algebra1.com/extra_examples

---

2 Teach

COMMUTATIVE AND ASSOCIATIVE PROPERTIES

In-Class Examples Power Point®

1 Evaluate $2 \cdot 8 \cdot 5 \cdot 7$.
$$2 \cdot 8 \cdot 5 \cdot 7$$
$$= 2 \cdot 5 \cdot 8 \cdot 7$$
$$= (2 \cdot 5) \cdot (8 \cdot 7)$$
$$= 10 \cdot 56$$
$$= 560$$

Teaching Tip Remind students that when adding several numbers they should look for pairs that combine to form numbers ending in 5 or 0.

2 **TRANSPORTATION** Refer to Example 2 in the Student Edition. Find the distance between Lakewood/Ft. McPherson and Five Points. Explain how the Commutative Property makes calculating the answer unnecessary.
The distance is 4.5 miles. Calculating the answer is unnecessary because the route is the opposite of the one in Example 2. The Commutative Property states that the order in which numbers are added does not matter.

SIMPLIFY EXPRESSIONS

In-Class Example Power Point®

3 Simplify $8(2b + 4) + 7b$.
$23b + 32$

DAILY INTERVENTION

Differentiated Instruction

Visual/Spatial If students have difficulty with the concepts of the Commutative and Associative Properties, consider using manipulatives to reinforce the concepts. Express each property using objects that visually verify the property. For example, a big bucket of water and a small bucket of water is the same as a small bucket of water and a big bucket of water.

4 Use the expression *three times the sum of 3x and 2y added to five times the sum of x and 4y.*

a. Write an algebraic expression for the verbal expression.
$3(3x + 2y) + 5(x + 4y)$

b. Simplify the expression and indicate the properties used.
$3(3x + 2y) + 5(x + 4y)$
$= 3(3x) + 3(2y) + 5(x) + 5(4y)$
       Distributive Property
$= 9x + 5x + 6y + 20y$
       Multiply.
$= (9x + 5x) + (6y + 20y)$
       Associative (+)
$= (9 + 5)x + (6 + 20)y$
       Distributive Property
$= 14x + 26y$ **Substitution**

---

3 Practice/Apply

Study Notebook

Have students—

• add the definitions/examples of the vocabulary terms to their Vocabulary Builder worksheets for Chapter 1.

• copy the Concept Summary from p. 33.

• include any other item(s) that they find helpful in mastering the skills in this lesson.

Example 4 **Write and Simplify an Expression**

Use the expression *four times the sum of a and b increased by twice the sum of a and 2b.*

a. Write an algebraic expression for the verbal expression.

four times the sum of *a* and *b*	increased by	twice the sum of *a* and 2*b*
$4(a + b)$	$+$	$2(a + 2b)$

b. Simplify the expression and indicate the properties used.

$4(a + b) + 2(a + 2b) = 4(a) + 4(b) + 2(a) + 2(2b)$ Distributive Property
$= 4a + 4b + 2a + 4b$ Multiply.
$= 4a + 2a + 4b + 4b$ Commutative (+)
$= (4a + 2a) + (4b + 4b)$ Associative (+)
$= (4 + 2)a + (4 + 4)b$ Distributive Property
$= 6a + 8b$ Substitution

Check for Understanding

Concept Check
1. **Define** the Associative Property in your own words. **See margin.**

2. **Write** a short explanation as to whether there is a Commutative Property of Division. **Division is not commutative. For example, $10 \div 2 \neq 2 \div 10$.**

3. **OPEN ENDED** Write examples of the Commutative Property of Addition and the Associative Property of Multiplication using 1, 5, and 8 in each.
Sample answer: $1 + 5 + 8 = 8 + 1 + 5$; $(1 \cdot 5)8 = 1(5 \cdot 8)$

Guided Practice Evaluate each expression.

GUIDED PRACTICE KEY	
Exercises	Examples
4–7	1, 2
8–13	3
14	4
15	2

4. $14 + 18 + 26$ **58** 5. $3\frac{1}{2} + 4 + 2\frac{1}{2}$ **10** 6. $5 \cdot 3 \cdot 6 \cdot 4$ **360** 7. $\frac{5}{6} \cdot 16 \cdot 9\frac{3}{4}$ **130**

Simplify each expression.

8. $4x + 5y + 6x$ **$10x + 5y$** 9. $5a + 3b + 2a + 7b$ 10. $\frac{1}{4}q + 2q + 2\frac{3}{4}q$ **$5q$**
                                    $7a + 10b$
11. $3(4x + 2) + 2x$ **$14x + 6$** 12. $7(ac + 2b) + 2ac$ 13. $3(x + 2y) + 4(3x + y)$
                                    $9ac + 14b$ **$15x + 10y$**
14. Write an algebraic expression for *half the sum of p and 2q increased by three-fourths q.* Then simplify, indicating the properties used. **See margin.**

Application 15. **GEOMETRY** Find the area of the large triangle if each smaller triangle has a base measuring 5.2 centimeters and a height of 4.5 centimeters. **46.8 cm²**

★ indicates increased difficulty

Practice and Apply

Evaluate each expression. **19. 20.5**

16. $17 + 6 + 13 + 24$ **60** 17. $8 + 14 + 22 + 9$ **53** 18. $4.25 + 3.50 + 8.25$ **16**

19. $6.2 + 4.2 + 4.3 + 5.8$ 20. $6\frac{1}{2} + 3 + \frac{1}{2} + 2$ **12** 21. $2\frac{3}{8} + 4 + 3\frac{3}{8}$ **$9\frac{3}{4}$**

22. $5 \cdot 11 \cdot 4 \cdot 2$ **440** 23. $3 \cdot 10 \cdot 6 \cdot 3$ **540** 24. $0.5 \cdot 2.4 \cdot 4$ **4.8**

25. $8 \cdot 1.6 \cdot 2.5$ **32** 26. $3\frac{3}{7} \cdot 14 \cdot 1\frac{1}{4}$ **60** 27. $2\frac{5}{8} \cdot 24 \cdot 6\frac{2}{3}$ **420**

Answers

1. Sample answer: The Associative Property says that the way you group numbers together when adding or multiplying does not change the result.

14. $\frac{1}{2}(p + 2q) + \frac{3}{4}q = \frac{1}{2}p + \frac{1}{2}(2q) + \frac{3}{4}q$ **Distributive Property**

$= \frac{1}{2}p + q + \frac{3}{4}q$ **Multiply.**

$= \frac{1}{2}p + 1\frac{3}{4}q$ **Substitution**

Homework Help

For Exercises	See Examples
16–29	1, 2
30, 31	2
32–42	3
44–47	4

Extra Practice
See page 821.

TRAVEL For Exercises 28 and 29, use the following information.
Hotels often have different rates for weeknights and weekends. The rates of one hotel are listed in the table.

28. If a traveler checks into the hotel on Friday and checks out the following Tuesday morning, what is the total cost of the room? **$270**

Hotel Rates	
Weeknights (M–F)	$72
Weekends	$63
Weekly (5 weeknights)	$325

29. Suppose there is a sales tax of $5.40 for weeknights and $5.10 for weekends. What is the total cost of the room including tax? **$291**

ENTERTAINMENT For Exercises 30 and 31, use the following information.
A video store rents new release videos for $4.49, older videos for $2.99, and DVDs for $3.99. The store also sells its used videos for $9.99.

30. Write two expressions to represent the total sales of a clerk after renting 2 DVDs, 3 new releases, 2 older videos, and selling 5 used videos.

30. **Sample answer:**
$2(3.99) + 3(4.49) + 2(2.99) + 5(9.99);$
$2(3.99 + 2.99) + 3(4.49) + 5(9.99)$

31. What are the total sales of the clerk? **$77.38**

Simplify each expression. 39. $9.5x + 5.5y$

32. $4a + 2b + a$ **$5a + 2b$**

33. $2y + 2x + 8y$ **$2x + 10y$**

34. $x^2 + 3x + 2x + 5x^2$ **$6x^2 + 5x$**

35. $4a^3 + 6a + 3a^3 + 8a$ **$7a^3 + 14a$**

36. $6x + 2(2x + 7)$ **$10x + 14$**

37. $5n + 4(3n + 9)$ **$17n + 36$**

38. $3(x + 2y) + 4(3x + y)$ **$15x + 10y$**

39. $3.2(x + y) + 2.3(x + y) + 4x$

40. $3(4m + n) + 2m$ **$14m + 3n$**

41. $6(0.4f + 0.2g) + 0.5f$ **$2.9f + 1.2g$**

★ 42. $\frac{3}{4} + \frac{2}{3}(s + 2t) + s$ **$\frac{3}{4} + \frac{5}{3}s + \frac{4}{3}t$**

★ 43. $2p + \frac{3}{5}(\frac{1}{2}p + 2q) + \frac{2}{3}$ **$\frac{2}{3} + \frac{23}{10}p + \frac{6}{5}q$**

Write an algebraic expression for each verbal expression. Then simplify, indicating the properties used. 44–47. See pp. 65A–65B.

44. twice the sum of s and t decreased by s

45. five times the product of x and y increased by $3xy$

46. the product of six and the square of z, increased by the sum of seven, z^2, and 6

★ 47. six times the sum of x and y squared decreased by three times the sum of x and half of y squared

48. **Sometimes;**
sample answer:
$4 - 3 \neq 3 - 4$, but
$4 - 4 = 4 - 4$.

48. **CRITICAL THINKING** Tell whether the Commutative Property *always*, *sometimes*, or *never* holds for subtraction. Explain your reasoning.

49. **WRITING IN MATH** Answer the question that was posed at the beginning of the lesson. See pp. 65A–65B.

How can properties help you determine distances?

Include the following in your answer:
• an expression using the Commutative and Associative Properties to determine the distance from the airport to Five Points, and
• an explanation of how the Commutative and Associative Properties are useful in performing calculations.

Stop	Distance from Previous Stop
Five Points	0
Garnett	0.4
West End	1.5
Oakland City	1.5
Lakewood/ Ft. McPherson	1.1
East Point	1.9
College Park	1.8
Airport	0.8

 www.algebra1.com/self_check_quiz

Lesson 1-6 Commutative and Associative Properties **35**

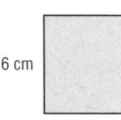
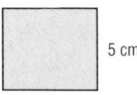

About the Exercises...

About the Exercises...

Organization by Objective
- **Commutative and Associative Properties:** 44–47
- **Simplify Expressions:** 16–43

Odd/Even Assignments
Exercises 16–27 and 32–47 are structured so that students practice the same concepts whether they are assigned odd or even problems.

Assignment Guide

Basic: 17–27 odd, 28–29, 33–41 odd, 45, 47, 48–66

Average: 17–27 odd, 28–29, 33–47 odd, 48–66

Advanced: 16–26 even, 30–31, 32–46 even, 48–61 (optional: 62–66)

All: Practice Quiz 2 (1–10)

4 Assess

Open-Ended Assessment

Modeling Have students use beans, coins, or other manipulatives to model and explain the Commutative and Associative Properties, using simple equations such as 2 + 3 = 5.

Getting Ready for Lesson 1-7

PREREQUISITE SKILL In Lesson 1-7, students will learn the terminology of simple logic. One skill needed is the ability to interpret if/then statements. Use Exercises 62–66 to determine your students' familiarity with evaluating expressions presented in an if-then form.

Assessment Options

Practice Quiz 2 The quiz provides students with a brief review of the concepts and skills in Lessons 1-4 through 1-6. Lesson numbers are given to the right of exercises or instruction lines so students can review concepts not yet mastered.

Standardized Test Practice Ⓐ Ⓑ Ⓒ Ⓓ

50. Simplify $6(ac + 2b) + 2ac$. **C**

Ⓐ $10ab + 2ac$ Ⓑ $12ac + 20b$ Ⓒ $8ac + 12b$ Ⓓ $12abc + 2ac$

51. Which property can be used to show that the areas of the two rectangles are equal? **B**

Ⓐ Associative
Ⓑ Commutative
Ⓒ Distributive
Ⓓ Reflexive

6 cm · 5 cm   5 cm · 6 cm

Maintain Your Skills

Mixed Review   Simplify each expression. *(Lesson 1-5)*

52. $5(2 + x) + 7x$ **$12x + 10$**   **53.** $3(5 + 2p)$ **$15 + 6p$**   **54.** $3(a + 2b) - 3a$ **$6b$**

55. $7m + 6(n + m)$ **$13m + 6n$**   **56.** $(d + 5)f + 2f$ **$df + 7f$**   **57.** $t^2 + 2t^2 + 4t$ **$3t^2 + 4t$**

58. Name the property used in each step. *(Lesson 1-4)*

$$3(10 - 5 \cdot 2) + 21 \div 7 = 3(10 - 10) + 21 \div 7 \quad \textbf{Subst.}$$
$$= 3(0) + 21 \div 7 \quad \textbf{Subst.}$$
$$= 0 + 21 \div 7 \quad \textbf{Mult. Prop. of Zero}$$
$$= 0 + 3 \quad \textbf{Subst.}$$
$$= 3 \quad \textbf{Add. Identity}$$

Evaluate each expression. *(Lesson 1-2)*

59. $12(5) - 6(4)$ **36**   **60.** $7(0.2 + 0.5) - 0.6$ **4.3**   **61.** $8[6^2 - 3(2 + 5)] \div 8 + 3$ **18**

Getting Ready for the Next Lesson   **PREREQUISITE SKILL** Evaluate each expression for the given value of the variable.
*(To review **evaluating expressions**, see Lesson 1-2.)*

62. If $x = 4$, then $2x + 7 = \underline{\;?\;}$. **15**   **63.** If $x = 8$, then $6x + 12 = \underline{\;?\;}$. **60**

64. If $n = 6$, then $5n - 14 = \underline{\;?\;}$. **16**   **65.** If $n = 7$, then $3n - 8 = \underline{\;?\;}$. **13**

66. If $a = 2$, and $b = 5$, then $4a + 3b = \underline{\;?\;}$. **23**

Practice Quiz 2   Lessons 1-4 through 1-6

Write the letters of the properties given in the right-hand column that match the examples in the left-hand column.

1. $28 + 0 = 28$ **j**
2. $(18 - 7)6 = 11(6)$ **c**
3. $24 + 15 = 15 + 24$ **i**
4. $8 \cdot 5 = 8 \cdot 5$ **f**
5. $(9 + 3) + 8 = 9 + (3 + 8)$ **g**
6. $1(57) = 57$ **d**
7. $14 \cdot 0 = 0$ **b**
8. $3(13 + 10) = 3(13) + 3(10)$ **a**
9. If $12 + 4 = 16$, then $16 = 12 + 4$. **h**
10. $\frac{2}{5} \cdot \frac{5}{2} = 1$ **e**

a. Distributive Property
b. Multiplicative Property of 0
c. Substitution Property of Equality
d. Multiplicative Identity Property
e. Multiplicative Inverse Property
f. Reflexive Property of Equality
g. Associative Property
h. Symmetric Property of Equality
i. Commutative Property
j. Additive Identity Property

Tips for New Teachers

Assessment
Lessons 1-7 through 1-9 may be considered optional material. However, much of what is covered in these lessons are concepts presented on standardized tests.

Two Quizzes in each chapter review skills and concepts presented in previous lessons.

Logical Reasoning

What You'll Learn

- Identify the hypothesis and conclusion in a conditional statement.
- Use a counterexample to show that an assertion is false.

Vocabulary

- conditional statement
- if-then statement
- hypothesis
- conclusion
- deductive reasoning
- counterexample

How is logical reasoning helpful in cooking?

Popcorn is a popular snack with 16 billion quarts consumed in the United States each year. The directions at the right can help you make perfect popcorn. If the popcorn burns, then the heat was too high or the kernels heated unevenly.

Stovetop Popping
To pop popcorn on a stovetop, you need:
- A 3- to 4-quart pan with a loose lid that allows steam to escape
- Enough popcorn to cover the bottom of the pan, one kernel deep
- 1/4 cup of oil for every cup of kernels (Don't use butter!)

Heat the oil to 400–460 degrees Fahrenheit (if the oil smokes, it is too hot). Test the oil on a couple of kernels. When they pop, add the rest of the popcorn, cover the pan, and shake to spread the oil. When the popping begins to slow, remove the pan from the stovetop. The heated oil will pop the remaining kernels.
Source: Popcorn Board

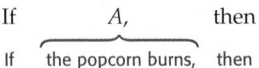

Study Tip

Reading Math
Note that "if" is not part of the hypothesis and "then" is not part of the conclusion.

CONDITIONAL STATEMENTS   The statement *If the popcorn burns, then the heat was too high or the kernels heated unevenly* is called a conditional statement. **Conditional statements** can be written in the form *If A, then B*. Statements in this form are called **if-then statements**.

If   *A,*   then   *B.*

If   the popcorn burns,   then   the heat was too high or the kernels heated unevenly.

The part of the statement immediately following the word *if* is called the **hypothesis**.

The part of the statement immediately following the word *then* is called the **conclusion**.

Example 1 Identify Hypothesis and Conclusion

Identify the hypothesis and conclusion of each statement.

a. If it is Friday, then Madison and Miguel are going to the movies.

Recall that the hypothesis is the part of the conditional following the word *if* and the conclusion is the part of the conditional following the word *then*.

Hypothesis: it is Friday

Conclusion: Madison and Miguel are going to the movies

b. If $4x + 3 > 27$, then $x > 6$.

Hypothesis: $4x + 3 > 27$

Conclusion: $x > 6$

TEACHING TIP

The words *hypothesis* and *hypothetical* have the same root. Ask students how this can help them remember the definition of hypothesis.

1 Focus

 5-Minute Check Transparency 1-7 Use as a quiz or a review of Lesson 1-6.

Mathematical Background notes are available for this lesson on p. 4D.

How is logical reasoning helpful in cooking?

Ask students:

- What is the purpose of the following sentence? *If the popcorn burns, then the heat was too high or the kernels heated unevenly.* **The sentence gives two reasons why the popcorn might have burned.**

- Does this sentence mean that the popcorn will burn? Explain. **No. The sentence begins with the word *if*.**

- Suppose you are cooking popcorn and the heat is too high. What does the sentence tell you about your situation? **Because the heat is too high, the popcorn will likely burn.**

Resource Manager

Workbook and Reproducible Masters

Chapter 1 Resource Masters
- Study Guide and Intervention, pp. 37–38
- Skills Practice, p. 39
- Practice, p. 40
- Reading to Learn Mathematics, p. 41
- Enrichment, p. 42
- Assessment, p. 70

Parent and Student Study Guide Workbook, p. 7

 Transparencies
5-Minute Check Transparency 1-7
Answer Key Transparencies

 Technology
Interactive Chalkboard

CONDITIONAL STATEMENTS

In-Class Examples Power Point®

1 Identify the hypothesis and conclusion of each statement.

a. If it is raining, then Beau and Chloe will not play softball.
Hypothesis: it is raining
Conclusion: Beau and Chloe will not play softball.

b. If $7y + 5 \leq 26$, then $y \leq 3$.
Hypothesis: $7y + 5 \leq 26$
Conclusion: $y \leq 3$

2 Identify the hypothesis and conclusion of each statement. Then write each statement in if-then form.

a. I eat light meals.
Hypothesis: I eat a meal;
Conclusion: it is light; If I eat a meal, then it is light.

b. For a number a such that $8 + 5a = 43$, $a = 7$.
Hypothesis: $8 + 5a = 43$
Conclusion: $a = 7$
If $8 + 5a = 43$, then $a = 7$.

DEDUCTIVE REASONING AND COUNTEREXAMPLES

In-Class Example Power Point®

3 Determine a valid conclusion that follows from the statement, "If one number is odd and another number is even, then their sum is odd" for the given conditions. If a valid conclusion does not follow, write *no valid conclusion* and explain why.

a. The two numbers are 5 and 12.
5 is odd and 12 is even, and 5 + 12 = 17.
Conclusion: The sum of 5 and 12 is odd.

b. The two numbers are 8 and 26.
8 and 26 are even so the hypothesis is false.
No valid conclusion.

Sometimes a conditional statement is written without using the words *if* and *then*. But a conditional statement can always be rewritten as an if-then statement. For example, the statement *When it is not raining, I ride my bike* can be written as *If it is not raining, then I ride my bike.*

Example 2 *Write a Conditional in If-Then Form*

Identify the hypothesis and conclusion of each statement. Then write each statement in if-then form.

a. **I will go to the ball game with you on Saturday.**
Hypothesis: it is Saturday
Conclusion: I will go to the ball game with you
If it is Saturday, then I will go to the ball game with you.

b. **For a number x such that $6x - 8 = 16$, $x = 4$.**
Hypothesis: $6x - 8 = 16$
Conclusion: $x = 4$
If $6x - 8 = 16$, then $x = 4$.

DEDUCTIVE REASONING AND COUNTEREXAMPLES

Deductive reasoning is the process of using facts, rules, definitions, or properties to reach a valid conclusion. Suppose you have a true conditional and you know that the hypothesis is true for a given case. Deductive reasoning allows you to say that the conclusion is true for that case.

Example 3 *Deductive Reasoning*

Determine a valid conclusion that follows from the statement "If two numbers are odd, then their sum is even" for the given conditions. If a valid conclusion does not follow, write *no valid conclusion* and explain why.

a. **The two numbers are 7 and 3.**
7 and 3 are odd, so the hypothesis is true.
Conclusion: The sum of 7 and 3 is even.
CHECK $7 + 3 = 10$ ✓ The sum, 10, is even.

b. **The sum of two numbers is 14.**
The conclusion is true. If the numbers are 11 and 3, the hypothesis is true also. However, if the numbers are 8 and 6, the hypothesis is false. There is no way to determine the two numbers. Therefore, there is no valid conclusion.

Not all if-then statements are always true or always false. Consider the statement "If Luke is listening to CDs, then he is using his portable CD player." Luke may be using his portable CD player. However, he could also be using a computer, a car CD player, or a home CD player.

To show that a conditional is false, we can use a counterexample. A **counterexample** is a specific case in which a statement is false. It takes only one counterexample to show that a statement is false.

Study Tip

Common Misconception
Suppose the conclusion of a conditional is true. This does not mean that the hypothesis is true. Consider the conditional "If it rains, Annie will stay home." If Annie stays home, it does not necessarily mean that it is raining.

DAILY INTERVENTION

Differentiated Instruction

Interpersonal Logic is a branch of mathematics that is not familiar to students. Encourage students to work together discussing examples in this lesson. You may also want them to complete some exercises cooperatively.

Example 4 Find Counterexamples

Find a counterexample for each conditional statement.

a. If you are using the Internet, then you own a computer.

You could be using the Internet on a computer at a library.

b. If the Commutative Property holds for multiplication, then it holds for division.

$$2 \div 1 \overset{?}{=} 1 \div 2$$
$$2 \neq 0.5$$

Example 5 Find a Counterexample

Multiple-Choice Test Item

> Which numbers are counterexamples for the statement below?
>
> *If $x \div y = 1$, then x and y are whole numbers.*
>
> (A) $x = 2, y = 2$ (B) $x = 0.25, y = 0.25$
> (C) $x = 1.2, y = 0.6$ (D) $x = 6, y = 3$

Read the Test Item

Find the values of x and y that make the statement false.

Test-Taking Tip

Since choice B is the correct answer, you can check your result by testing the other values.

Solve the Test Item

Replace x and y in the equation $x \div y = 1$ with the given values.

(A) $x = 2, y = 2$
$2 \div 2 \overset{?}{=} 1$
$1 = 1$ ✓

The hypothesis is true and both values are whole numbers. The statement is true.

(B) $x = 0.25, y = 0.25$
$0.25 \div 0.25 \overset{?}{=} 1$
$1 = 1$ ✓

The hypothesis is true, but 0.25 is not a whole number. Thus, the statement is false.

(C) $x = 1.2, y = 0.6$
$1.2 \div 0.6 \overset{?}{=} 1$
$2 \neq 1$

The hypothesis is false, and the conclusion is false. However, this is not a counterexample. A counterexample is a case where the hypothesis is true and the conclusion is false.

(D) $x = 6, y = 3$
$6 \div 3 \overset{?}{=} 1$
$2 \neq 1$

The hypothesis is false. Therefore, this is not a counterexample.

The only values that prove the statement false are $x = 0.25$ and $y = 0.25$. So these numbers are counterexamples. The answer is B.

Check for Understanding

Concept Check

1. **OPEN ENDED** Write a conditional statement and label its hypothesis and conclusion.

2. **Explain** why counterexamples are used.

3. **Explain** how deductive reasoning is used to show that a conditional is true or false.

 www.algebra1.com/extra_examples

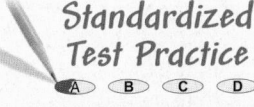
Example 5 Point out that x and y must not only fit the equation but also be whole numbers. Therefore, students could skip testing the values in choice B as these cannot be correct solutions.

Each chapter contains an example that gives students practice in solving problems on standardized tests. Standardized Test Practice suggestions give students additional methods for achieving success on standardized tests.

---

4 Provide a counterexample for each conditional statement.

a. If Joe did not eat lunch, then he must not feel well.
Perhaps Joe was not hungry.

b. If the traffic light is red, then the cars must be stopped.
A driver could run the red light.

5 Which numbers are counterexamples for the statement below? **B**
$x - y \neq y - x$
A $x = 2, y = 3$
B $x = 4, y = 4$
C $x = 0, y = 1$
D $x = 7, y = -7$

3 Practice/Apply

Study Notebook

Have students—
* *add the definitions/examples of the vocabulary terms to their Vocabulary Builder worksheets for Chapter 1.*
* *include any other item(s) that they find helpful in mastering the skills in this lesson.*

Answers

1. Sample answer:
   If it rains, then you get wet.
   H: it rains
   C: you get wet

2. Sample answer: Counterexamples are used to disprove a statement.

3. Sample answer: You can use deductive reasoning to determine whether a hypothesis and its conclusion are both true or whether one or both are false.

Identify the hypothesis and conclusion of each statement.

4. If it is January, then it might snow. **H: it is January; C: it might snow**

5. If you play tennis, then you run fast. **H: you play tennis; C: you run fast**

6. If $34 - 3x = 16$, then $x = 6$. **H: $34 - 3x = 16$; C: $x = 6$**

Identify the hypothesis and conclusion of each statement. Then write the statement in if-then form. 7–9. See margin.

7. Lance watches television when he does not have homework.

8. A number that is divisible by 10 is also divisible by 5.

9. A rectangle is a quadrilateral with four right angles.

Determine a valid conclusion that follows from the statement *If the last digit of a number is 2, then the number is divisible by 2* **for the given conditions. If a valid conclusion does not follow, write** *no valid conclusion* **and explain why.**

10. The number is 10,452. **The number is divisible by 2.**

11. The number is divisible by 2. **11. No valid conclusion; the last digit could be any even number.**

12. The number is 946. **No valid conclusion; the last digit is a 6.**

Find a counterexample for each statement. 13–14. See margin.

13. If Anna is in school, then she has a science class.

14. If you can read 8 pages in 30 minutes, then you can read any book in a day.

15. If a number x is squared, then $x^2 > x$. **$x = 1$**

16. If $3x + 7 \ge 52$, then $x > 15$. **$x = 15$**

 **Standardized Test Practice**

17. Which number is a counterexample for the statement $x^2 > x$? **A**
    Ⓐ 1   Ⓑ 4   Ⓒ 5   Ⓓ 8

★ indicates increased difficulty

Practice and Apply

Identify the hypothesis and conclusion of each statement.

18. If both parents have red hair, then their children have red hair.

19. If you are in Hawaii, then you are in the tropics.

20. If $2n - 7 > 25$, then $n > 16$. **H: $2n - 7 > 25$; C: $n > 16$**

21. If $4(b + 9) \le 68$, then $b \le 8$. **H: $4(b + 9) \le 68$; C: $b \le 8$**

22. If $a = b$, then $b = a$. **H: $a = b$; C: $b = a$**

23. If $a = b$ and $b = c$, then $a = c$. **H: $a = b$ and $b = c$; C: $a = c$**

Identify the hypothesis and conclusion of each statement. Then write the statement in if-then form. 24–29. See margin.

24. The trash is picked up on Monday.

25. Greg will call after school.

26. A triangle with all sides congruent is an equilateral triangle.

27. The sum of the digits of a number is a multiple of 9 when the number is divisible by 9.

28. For $x = 8$, $x^2 - 3x = 40$.

29. $4s + 6 > 42$ when $s > 9$.

Answers

7. **H: Lance does not have homework; C: he watches television; If Lance does not have homework, then he watches television.**

8. **H: a number is divisible by 10; C: it is divisible by 5; If a number is divisible by 10, then it is divisible by 5.**

Determine whether a valid conclusion follows from the statement *If a VCR costs less than $150, then Ian will buy one* for the given condition. If a valid conclusion does not follow, write *no valid conclusion* and explain why.

30. A VCR costs $139. **Ian will buy a VCR.** **31.** A VCR costs $99. **Ian will buy a VCR.**

32. Ian will not buy a VCR. **33.** The price of a VCR is $199.

34. A DVD player costs $229. **35.** Ian bought 2 VCRs.

32. The VCR cost $150 or more.
33–35. See margin.

Find a counterexample for each statement. **36–39. See margin.**

36. If you were born in Texas, then you live in Texas.

37. If you are a professional basketball player, then you play in the United States.

38. If a baby is wearing blue clothes, then the baby is a boy.

39. If a person is left-handed, then each member of that person's family is left-handed.

40. If the product of two numbers is even, then both numbers must be even. $2 \cdot 3 = 6$

41. If a whole number is greater than 7, then two times the number is greater than 16. $2(8) = 16$

42. If $4n - 8 \geq 52$, then $n > 15$. $4(15) - 8 = 52$

43. If $x \cdot y = 1$, then x or y must equal 1. $\frac{6}{3} \cdot \frac{1}{2} = 1$

44–45. See margin.
GEOMETRY For Exercises 44 and 45, use the following information.
If points P, Q, and R lie on the same line, then Q is between P and R.

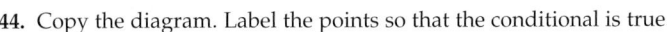

44. Copy the diagram. Label the points so that the conditional is true.

45. Copy the diagram. Provide a counterexample for the conditional.

46. RESEARCH On Groundhog Day (February 2) of each year, some people say that if a groundhog comes out of its hole and sees its shadow, then there will be six more weeks of winter weather. However, if it does not see its shadow, then there will be an early spring. Use the Internet or another resource to research the weather on Groundhog Day for your city for the past 10 years. Summarize your data as examples or counterexamples for this belief. **See students' work; there will probably be both examples and counterexamples.**

NUMBER THEORY For Exercises 47–49, use the following information.
Copy the Venn diagram and place the numbers 1 to 25 in the appropriate places on the diagram.

★ **47.** What conclusions can you make about the numbers and where they appear on the diagram?

★ **48.** What conclusions can you form about numbers that are divisible by 2 and 3?

★ **49.** Find a counterexample for your conclusions, if possible. **no counterexamples**

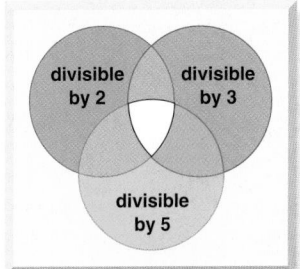

Lesson 1-7 Logical Reasoning **41**

---

47. Numbers that end in 0, 2, 4, 6, or 8 are in the "divisible by 2" circle. Numbers whose digits have a sum divisible by 3 are in the "divisible by 3" circle. Numbers that end in 0 or 5 are in the "divisible by 5" circle.

48. Sample answer: If a number is divisible by 2 and 3, then it must be a multiple of 6.

Answers

27. H: a number is divisible by 9; C: the sum of its digits is a multiple of 9; If a number is divisible by 9, then the sum of its digits is a multiple of 9.

28. H: $x = 8$; C: $x^2 - 3x = 40$; If $x = 8$, then $x^2 - 3x = 40$

29. H: $s > 9$; C: $4s + 6 > 42$; If $s > 9$, then $4s + 6 > 42$.

33. No valid conclusion; the hypothesis does not say Ian won't buy a VCR if it costs $150 or more.

34. No valid conclusion; the conditional statement does not mention DVD players.

35. No valid conclusion; the conditional does not mention Ian buying 2 VCRs.

36. People move to other states

37. There is a professional team in Canada.

38. Girls can wear blue clothes.

39. Left-handed people can have right-handed parents.

44. Sample answer:

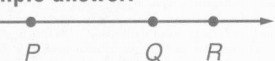

45. Sample answer:

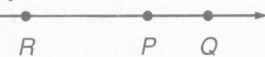

Answers

9. H: a quadrilateral has four right angles; C: it is a rectangle; If a quadrilateral has four right angles, then it is a rectangle.

13. Anna could have a schedule without science class.

14. A book that has more than 384 pages.

24. H: it is Monday; C: the trash is picked up;

If it is Monday, then the trash is picked up.

25. H: it is after school; C: Greg will call; If it is after school, then Greg will call.

26. H: a triangle has all sides congruent; C: it is an equilateral triangle; If a triangle has all sides congruent, then it is an equilateral triangle.

Open-Ended Assessment

Writing Have students write five conditional statements on a piece of paper. Tell them to write some statements that are always true, and some that may or may not be true. Then ask students to exchange papers and determine whether the conditional statements are true or false. If the conditional statements are false, students should provide a counterexample.

Getting Ready for Lesson 1-8

PREREQUISITE SKILL Students will learn about graphs and functions in Lesson 1-8. One of the examples includes a graph of percents. Use Exercises 73–78 to determine your students' familiarity with calculating percents.

Assessment Options

Quiz (Lessons 1-6 and 1-7) is available on p. 70 of the *Chapter 1 Resource Masters*.

Answer

51. You can use if-then statements to help determine when food is finished cooking. Answers should include the following.
  • Hypothesis: you have small, underpopped kernels
    Conclusion: you have not used enough oil in your pan
  • If the gelatin is firm and rubbery, then it is ready to eat. If the water is boiling, lower the temperature.

---

50. **CRITICAL THINKING** Determine whether the following statement is always true. If it is not, provide a counterexample.

*If the mathematical operation * is defined for all numbers a and b as a * b = a + 2b, then the operation * is commutative.* **No; sample answer: Let $a = 1$ and $b = 2$; then 1 * 2 = 1 + 2(2) or 5 and 2 * 1 = 2 + 2(1) or 4.**

51. **WRITING IN MATH** Answer the question that was posed at the beginning of the lesson. **See margin.**

   How is logical reasoning helpful in cooking?

   Include the following in your answer:
   • the hypothesis and conclusion of the statement *If you have small, underpopped kernels, then you have not used enough oil in your pan*, and
   • examples of conditional statements used in cooking food other than popcorn.

Standardized Test Practice Ⓐ Ⓑ Ⓒ Ⓓ

52. **GRID IN** What value of n makes the following statement true?
   If $14n - 12 \geq 100$, then $n \geq$ __?__ . **8**

53. If # is defined as $\#x = \dfrac{x^3}{2}$, what is the value of #4? **C**

   Ⓐ 8   Ⓑ 16   Ⓒ 32   Ⓓ 64

Maintain Your Skills

Mixed Review **Simplify each expression.** *(Lesson 1-6)*

54. $2x + 5y + 9x$ **$11x + 5y$**   55. $a + 9b + 6b$ **$a + 15b$**   56. $\dfrac{3}{4}g + \dfrac{2}{5}f + \dfrac{5}{8}g$ **$1\dfrac{3}{8}g + \dfrac{2}{5}f$**

57. $4(5mn + 6) + 3mn$ **$23mn + 24$**   58. $2(3a + b) + 3b + 4$ **$6a + 5b + 4$**   59. $6x^2 + 5x + 3(2x^2) + 7x$ **$12x^2 + 12x$**

60. **ENVIRONMENT** According to the U.S. Environmental Protection Agency, a typical family of four uses 100 gallons of water flushing the toilet each day, 80 gallons of water showering and bathing, and 8 gallons of water using the bathroom sink. Write two expressions that represent the amount of water a typical family of four uses for these purposes in d days. *(Lesson 1-5)*
$100d + 80d + 8d$, $(100 + 80 + 8)d$

Name the property used in each expression. Then find the value of n. *(Lesson 1-4)*

61. $1(n) = 64$ **Mult. Identity; 64**   62. $12 + 7 = 12 + n$ **Reflexive; 7**   63. $(9 - 7)5 = 2n$ **Subs.; 5**

64. $\dfrac{1}{4}n = 1$ **Mult. Inverse; 4**   65. $n + 18 = 18$ **Add. Identity; 0**   66. $36n = 0$ **Mult. Prop. of Zero; 0**

Solve each equation. *(Lesson 1-3)*

67. $5(7) + 6 = x$ **41**   68. $7(4^2) - 6^2 = m$ **76**   69. $p = \dfrac{22 - (13 - 5)}{28 \div 2^2}$ **2**

Write an algebraic expression for each verbal expression. *(Lesson 1-1)*

70. the product of 8 and a number x raised to the fourth power **$8x^4$**

71. three times a number n decreased by 10 **$3n - 10$**

72. twelve more than the quotient of a number a and 5 **$12 + (a \div 5)$**

Getting Ready for the Next Lesson **PREREQUISITE SKILL** **Evaluate each expression. Round to the nearest tenth.**
*(To review **percents**, see pages 802 and 803.)*

73. 40% of 90 **36**   74. 23% of 2500 **575**   75. 18% of 950 **171**

76. 38% of 345 **131.1**   77. 42.7% of 528 **225.5**   78. 67.4% of 388 **261.5**

Graphs and Functions

What You'll Learn

- Interpret graphs of functions.
- Draw graphs of functions.

Vocabulary

- function
- coordinate system
- *x*-axis
- *y*-axis
- origin
- ordered pair
- *x*-coordinate
- *y*-coordinate
- independent variable
- dependent variable
- relation
- domain
- range

How can real-world situations be modeled using graphs and functions?

The graph shows the relationship between blood flow to the brain and the number of days after the concussion. The graph shows that as the number of days increases, the percent of blood flow increases.

The return of normal blood flow to the brain is said to be a function of the number of days since the concussion.

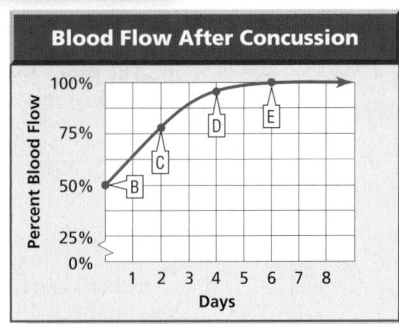

Blood Flow After Concussion

Source: Scientific American

INTERPRET GRAPHS   A **function** is a relationship between input and output. In a function, the output depends on the input. There is exactly one output for each input.

A function is graphed using a **coordinate system**. It is formed by the intersection of two number lines, the *horizontal axis* and the *vertical axis*.

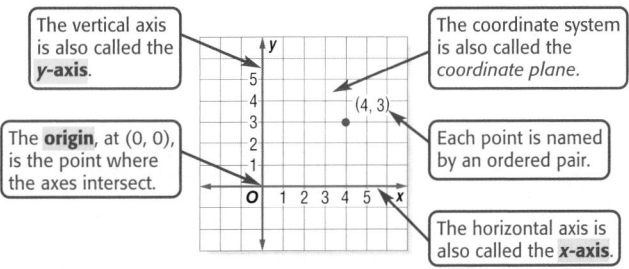

The vertical axis is also called the **y-axis**.

The coordinate system is also called the *coordinate plane*.

The **origin**, at (0, 0), is the point where the axes intersect.

Each point is named by an ordered pair.

The horizontal axis is also called the **x-axis**.

Study Tip

Reading Math
The *x*-coordinate is called the *abscissa*. The *y*-coordinate is called the *ordinate*.

Each input *x* and its corresponding output *y* can be represented on a graph using ordered pairs. An **ordered pair** is a set of numbers, or *coordinates*, written in the form (*x*, *y*). The *x* value, called the **x-coordinate**, corresponds to the *x*-axis and the *y* value, or **y-coordinate**, corresponds to the *y*-axis.

Example 1 Identify Coordinates

MEDICINE   Refer to the application above. Name the ordered pair at point *C* and explain what it represents.

Point *C* is at 2 along the *x*-axis and about 80 along the *y*-axis. So, its ordered pair is (2, 80). This represents 80% normal blood flow 2 days after the injury.

---

1 *Focus*

 5-Minute Check Transparency 1-8 Use as a quiz or a review of Lesson 1-7.

Mathematical Background notes are available for this lesson on p. 4D.

Building on Prior Knowledge

Many of the graphing terms in this lesson may already be familiar to your students. If this is the case, consider covering only Examples 2 and 3.

How can real-world situations be modeled using graphs and functions?

Ask students:

- What does point B on the graph represent? **The blood flow to the brain the day of the injury.**
- About what percent of normal blood flow occurs two days after the injury? **about 80%**
- Does the blood flow to the brain increase evenly from the day of the injury to day 6? Explain your answer. **No. The blood flow seems to increase evenly between day 0 and day 2, but then the increase is lower between day 2 and day 4, and lower still between day 4 and day 6.**
- What feature of the graph shows the rate of increase in blood flow? **the slope of the line**

Resource Manager

Workbook and Reproducible Masters

Chapter 1 Resource Masters
- Study Guide and Intervention, pp. 43–44
- Skills Practice, p. 45
- Practice, p. 46
- Reading to Learn Mathematics, p. 47
- Enrichment, p. 48

Parent and Student Study Guide Workbook, p. 8
Prerequisite Skills Workbook, pp. 95–96

 Transparencies
5-Minute Check Transparency 1-8
Real-World Transparency 1
Answer Key Transparencies

Technology
Interactive Chalkboard
Multimedia Applications

INTERPRET GRAPHS

1 **SPORTS MEDICINE** Refer to the graph on page 43 of the Student Edition. Name the ordered pair at point *E* and explain what it represents. **(6, 100). This represents about 100% normal blood flow 6 days after the injury.**

2 **ENERGY** In warm climates, the average amount of electricity used in homes each month rises as the daily average temperature increases, and falls as the daily average temperature decreases. Identify the independent and dependent variables in this function of temperature and electricity usage. **Temperature is the independent variable. The amount of electricity used is the dependent variable.**

3 The graph represents the temperature in Ms. Ling's classroom on a winter school day. Describe what is happening in the graph.

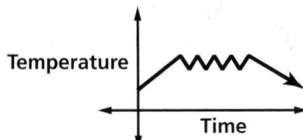

Sample answer: The temperature is low until the heat is turned on. Then the temperature fluctuates up and down because of the thermostat. Finally, the temperature drops when the heat is turned off.

In Example 1, the percent of normal blood flow depends on the number of days from the injury. Therefore, the number of days from the injury is called the **independent variable** or *quantity*, and the percent of normal blood flow is called the **dependent variable** or *quantity*. Usually the independent variable is graphed on the horizontal axis and the dependent variable is graphed on the vertical axis.

Example 2 Independent and Dependent Variables

Identify the independent and dependent variables for each function.

a. **In general, the average price of gasoline slowly and steadily increases throughout the year.**

Time is the independent variable as it is unaffected by the price of gasoline, and the price is the dependent quantity as it is affected by time.

b. **The profit that a business makes generally increases as the price of their product increases.**

In this case, price is the independent quantity. Profit is the dependent quantity as it is affected by the price.

Functions can be graphed without using a scale on either axis to show the general shape of the graph that represents a function.

Example 3 Analyze Graphs

a. **The graph at the right represents the speed of a school bus traveling along its morning route. Describe what is happening in the graph.**

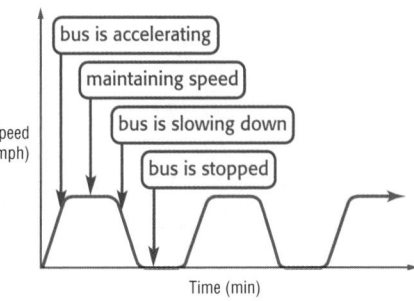

At the origin, the bus is stopped. It accelerates and maintains a constant speed. Then it begins to slow down, eventually stopping. After being stopped for a short time, the bus accelerates again. The starting and stopping process repeats continually.

b. **Identify the graph that represents the altitude of a space shuttle above Earth, from the moment it is launched until the moment it lands.**

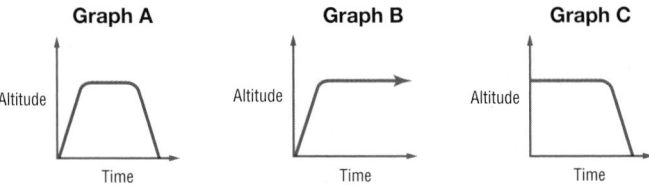

Before it takes off, the space shuttle is on the ground. It blasts off, gaining altitude until it reaches space where it orbits Earth at a constant height until it comes back to Earth. Graph A shows this situation.

TEACHING TIP

Graphing problems such as Example 3 help students develop an understanding of rate of change that will be developed in later physics and calculus courses.

Teacher to Teacher features contain teaching suggestions from teachers who are creatively teaching Algebra in their classrooms.

Teacher to Teacher

Larry Hummel   Central City H.S., Central City, NE

"I like to introduce the CBL or CBR with a graphing calculator with Example 3. I give students a graph and see if they can duplicate it by moving back and forth in front of the range finder. It really makes them think about what the graph represents."

DRAW GRAPHS Graphs can be used to represent many real-world situations.

Example 4 Draw Graphs

An electronics store is having a special sale. For every two DVDs you buy at the regular price of $29 each, you get a third DVD free.

a. **Make a table showing the cost of buying 1 to 5 DVDs.**

Number of DVDs	1	2	3	4	5
Total Cost ($)	29	58	58	87	116

b. **Write the data as a set of ordered pairs.**

The ordered pairs can be determined from the table. The number of DVDs is the independent variable, and the total cost is the dependent variable. So, the ordered pairs are (1, 29), (2, 58), (3, 58), (4, 87), and (5, 116).

c. **Draw a graph that shows the relationship between the number of DVDs and the total cost.**

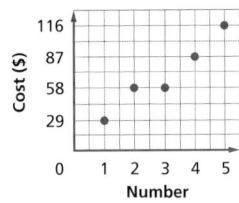

A set of ordered pairs, like those in Example 4, is called a **relation**. The set of the first numbers of the ordered pairs is the **domain**. The domain contains all values of the independent variable. The set of second numbers of the ordered pairs is the **range** of the relation. The range contains all values of the dependent variable.

Example 5 Domain and Range

JOBS Rasha earns $6.75 per hour working up to 4 hours each day after school. Her weekly earnings are a function of the number of hours she works.

a. **Identify a reasonable domain and range for this situation.**

The domain contains the number of hours Rasha works each week. Since she works up to 4 hours each weekday, she works up to 5 × 4 or 20 hours a week. Therefore, a reasonable domain would be values from 0 to 20 hours. The range contains her weekly earnings from $0 to 20 × $6.75 or $135. Thus, a reasonable range is $0 to $135.

b. **Draw a graph that shows the relationship between the number of hours Rasha works and the amount she earns each week.**

Graph the ordered pairs (0, 0) and (20, 135). Since she can work any amount of time up to 20 hours, connect the two points with a line to include those points.

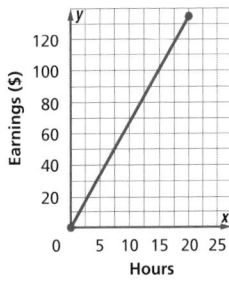

Lesson 1-8 Graphs and Functions **45**

Study Tip

Different Representations
Example 4 illustrates several of the ways data can be represented—tables, ordered pairs, and graphs.

In-Class Examples   Power Point®

4 There are three lunch periods at a school cafeteria. During the first period, 352 students eat lunch. During the second period, 304 students eat lunch. During the third period, 391 students eat lunch.

a. Make a table showing the number of students for each of the 3 lunch periods.

Period	1	2	3
Number of Students	352	304	391

b. Write the data as a set of ordered pairs. **(1, 352), (2, 304), (3, 391)**

c. Draw a graph that shows the relationship between the lunch period and the number of students.

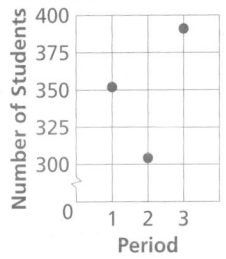

5 **ENTERTAINMENT** Mr. Mar is taking his biology classes to the zoo. The admission price is $4 per student, and at most, 120 students will go.

a. Identify a reasonable domain and range for this situation. **Domain: 0–120; Range: $0 to $480**

b. Draw a graph that shows the relationship between the number of students who go to the zoo, and the total price of admission.

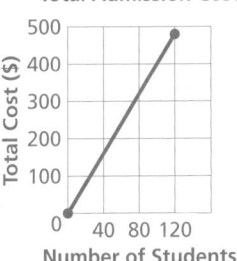

Study Notebook

Have students—
- add the definitions/examples of the vocabulary terms to their Vocabulary Builder worksheets for Chapter 1.
- include any other item(s) that they find helpful in mastering the skills in this lesson.

About the Exercises...

Organization by Objective
- **Interpret Graphs:** 10–13, 24
- **Draw Graphs:** 15, 18, 21–22

Odd/Even Assignments
Exercises 10–21 are structured so that students practice the same concepts whether they are assigned odd or even problems.

Assignment Guide

Basic: 11, 13–16, 21–32
Average: 11, 13–16, 21–32
Advanced: 10, 12, 17–20, 22–31 (optional: 32)

Answers

1. The numbers represent different values. The first number represents the number on the horizontal axis and the second represents the number on the vertical axis.

2. Sample answer: A dependent variable is determined by the independent variable for a given function.

8.
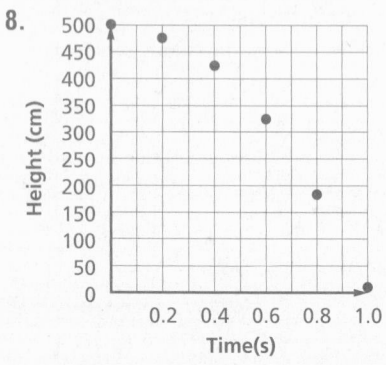

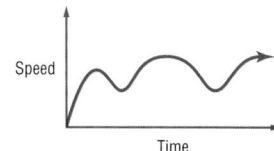

Concept Check

1–2. See margin.
3. See students' work.

1. **Explain** why the order of the numbers in an ordered pair is important.
2. **Describe** the difference between dependent and independent variables.
3. **OPEN ENDED** Give an example of a relation. Identify the domain and range.

Guided Practice

GUIDED PRACTICE KEY	
Exercises	Examples
4, 5	2, 3
6–9	4, 5

4. The graph at the right represents Alexi's speed as he rides his bike. Give a description of what is happening in the graph. **Sample answer: Alexi's speed decreases as he rides uphill, then increases as he rides downhill.**

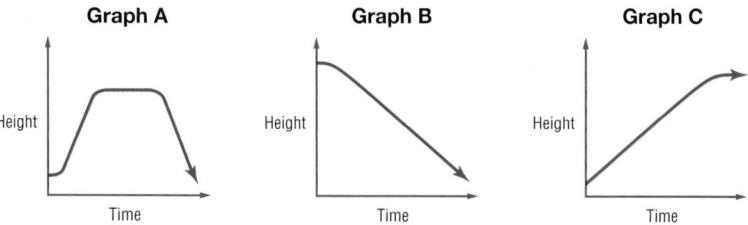

5. Identify the graph that represents the height of a skydiver just before she jumps from a plane until she lands. **Graph B**

Graph A   **Graph B**   **Graph C**

Applications

PHYSICAL SCIENCE For Exercises 6–8, use the table and the information.
During an experiment, the students of Ms. Roswell's class recorded the height of an object above the ground at several intervals after it was dropped from a height of 5 meters. Their results are in the table below.

Time (s)	0	0.2	0.4	0.6	0.8	1
Height (cm)	500	480	422	324	186	10

6. Time is the independent variable, and height is the dependent variable.

7. (0, 500), (0.2, 480), (0.4, 422), (0.6, 324), (0.8, 186), (1, 10)

6. Identify the independent and dependent variables.
7. Write a set of ordered pairs representing the data in the table.
8. Draw a graph showing the relationship between the height of the falling object and time. **See margin.**

9. **BASEBALL** Paul is a pitcher for his school baseball team. Draw a reasonable graph that shows the height of the baseball from the ground from the time he releases the ball until the time the catcher catches the ball. Let the horizontal axis show the time and the vertical axis show the height of the ball. **See margin.**

Homework Help	
For Exercises	**See Examples**
10, 11	2
12, 13	3
14–21	4, 5

Extra Practice
See page 822.

10–11. See margin.

10. The graph below represents Michelle's temperature when she was sick. Describe what is happening in the graph.

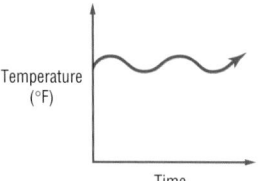

11. The graph below represents the balance in Rashaad's checking account. Describe what is happening in the graph.

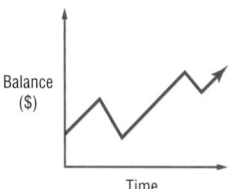

9.
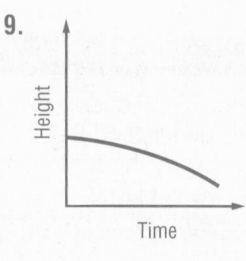

10. Michelle gets a fever and takes some medicine. After a while her temperature comes down, then slowly begins to go up again.

11. Rashaad's account is increasing as he makes deposits and earns interest. Then he pays some bills. He then makes some deposits and earns interest, and so on.

12. TOYS Identify the graph that displays the speed of a radio-controlled car as it moves along and then hits a wall. **Graph C**

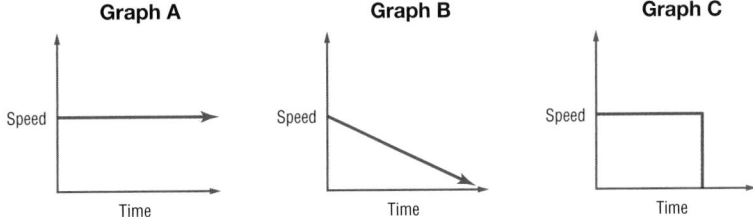

Graph A Graph B Graph C

13. INCOME In general, as a person gets older, their income increases until they retire. Which of the graphs below represents this? **Graph B**

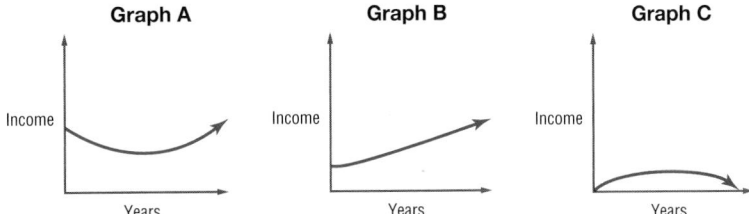

Graph A Graph B Graph C

TRAVEL For Exercises 14–16, use the table that shows the charges for short-term parking at an airport. **14–15. See pp. 65A–65B.**

Time (h)	0–1:59	2–3:59	4–5:59	6–11:59	12–24
Cost ($)	1	2	4	5	30

After 24 hours: An additional $15 per day or portion thereof

14. Write the ordered pairs with whole-number coordinates that represent the cost of parking for up to 36 hours.

15. Draw a graph to show the cost of parking for up to 36 hours.

16. What is the cost of parking if you arrive on Monday at 7:00 A.M. and depart on Tuesday at 9:00 P.M.? **$45**

GEOMETRY For Exercises 17–19, use the table that shows the relationships between the sum of the measures of the interior angles of convex polygons and the number of sides of the polygons.

Polygon	triangle	quadrilateral	pentagon	hexagon	heptagon
Sides	3	4	5	6	7
Interior Angle Sum	180	360	540	720	900

17. Identify the independent and dependent variables. **17–18. See pp. 65A–65B.**

18. Draw a graph of the data.

19. Use the data to predict the sum of the measures of the interior angles for an octagon, nonagon, and decagon. **1080, 1260, 1440**

20. CARS A car was purchased new in 1970. The owner has taken excellent care of the car, and it has relatively low mileage. Draw a reasonable graph to show the value of the car from the time it was purchased to the present. **See pp. 65A–65B.**

21. CHEMISTRY When ice is exposed to temperatures above 32°F, it begins to melt. Draw a reasonable graph showing the relationship between the temperature of a block of ice as it is removed from a freezer and placed on a counter at room temperature. (*Hint:* The temperature of the water will not exceed the temperature of its surroundings.) **See pp. 65A–65B.**

More About . . .

Cars ·············

Most new cars lose 15 to 30 percent of their value in the first year. After about 12 years, more popular cars tend to increase in value.

Source: *Consumer Guide*

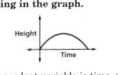
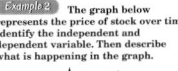
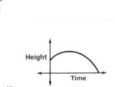
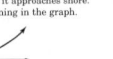
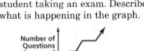
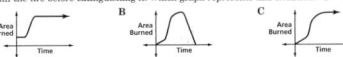
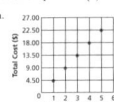
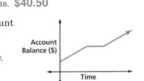
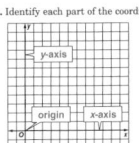

Open-Ended Assessment

Modeling Have students use the position of their hands to show the height of water in a tub as the tub is filled, the water is turned off, a person gets into the tub, then gets out, and drains the tub. Have students sketch a graph that shows the relationship you described.

Getting Ready for Lesson 1-9

PREREQUISITE SKILL Students will learn about analyzing data by using tables and graphs in Lesson 1-9. Many of the data are expressed as bar graphs. Use Exercise 32 to determine your students' familiarity with constructing bar graphs.

Answers

22a.

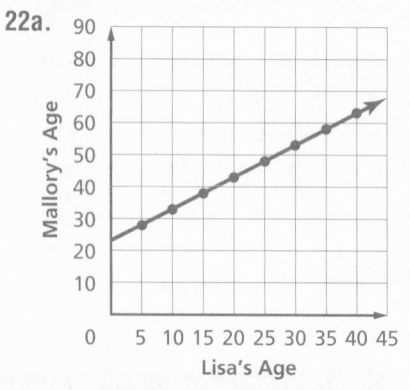

22b. (23, 46)

23. Real-world data can be recorded and visualized in a graph and by expressing an event as a function of another event. Answers should include the following.

- A graph gives you a visual representation of the situation which is easier to analyze and evaluate.

- During the first 24 hours, blood flow to the brain decreases to 50% at the moment of the injury and gradually increases to about 60%.

- Significant improvement occurs during the first two days.

---

22. **CRITICAL THINKING**   Mallory is 23 years older than Lisa. **a–b. See margin.**
    a. Draw a graph showing Mallory's age as a function of Lisa's age for the first 40 years of Lisa's life.
    b. Find the point on the graph when Mallory is twice as old as Lisa.

23. **WRITING IN MATH**   Answer the question that was posed at the beginning of the lesson. **See margin.**

    How can real-world situations be modeled using graphs and functions?

    Include the following in your answer:
    - an explanation of how the graph helps you analyze the situation,
    - a summary of what happens during the first 24 hours from the time of a concussion, and
    - an explanation of the time in which significant improvement occurs.

Standardized Test Practice
Ⓐ Ⓑ Ⓒ Ⓓ

24. The graph shows the height of a model rocket shot straight up. How many seconds did it take for the rocket to reach its maximum height? **B**

    Ⓐ 3   Ⓑ 4   Ⓒ 5   Ⓓ 6

25. Andre owns a computer backup service. He charges his customers $2.50 for each backup CD. His expenses include $875 for the CD recording equipment and $0.35 for each blank CD. Which equation could Andre use to calculate his profit p for the recording of n CDs? **A**

    Ⓐ $p = 2.15n - 875$ Ⓑ $p = 2.85 + 875$
    Ⓒ $p = 2.50 - 875.65$ Ⓓ $p = 875 - 2.15n$

Maintain Your Skills

Mixed Review

Identify the hypothesis and conclusion of each statement.   *(Lesson 1-7)*

26. You can send e-mail with a computer.

27. The express lane is for shoppers who have 9 or fewer items.

28. Name the property used in each step.   *(Lesson 1-6)*

$ab(a + b) = (ab)a + (ab)b$	Distr. Prop.
$= a(ab) + (ab)b$	Comm. ($\times$)
$= (a \cdot a)b + a(b \cdot b)$	Assoc. ($\times$)
$= a^2b + ab^2$	Subst.

Name the property used in each statement. Then find the value of n.   *(Lesson 1-4)*

29. $(12 - 9)(4) = n(4)$ 30. $7(n) = 0$ 31. $n(87) = 87$
    Subst.; 3   Mult. Prop. of Zero; 0   Mult. Identity; 1

Getting Ready for the Next Lesson

32. **PREREQUISITE SKILL**   Use the information in the table to construct a bar graph.
    *(To review **making bar graphs**, see pages 806 and 807.)* **See pp. 65A–65B.**

U.S. Commercial Radio Stations by Format, 2000					
Format	country	adult contemporary	news/talk	oldies	rock
Number	2249	1557	1426	1135	827

Source: *The World Almanac*

26. H: you use a computer; C: you can send e-mail

27. H: a shopper has 9 or fewer items; C: the shopper can use the express lane

---

Answers (page 49)

3. Sample answer: Average the enrollment numbers for 1900 and 1920 and then for 1970 and 1980.

4. Sample answer: If the U.S. population does not increase as quickly as in the past, then the number of students may be too high.

Algebra Activity

A Follow-Up of Lesson 1-8

Algebra Activity

Investigating Real-World Functions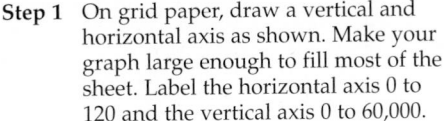

The table shows the number of students enrolled in elementary and secondary schools in the United States for the given years.

Year	Enrollment (thousands)	Year	Enrollment (thousands)
1900	15,503	1970	45,550
1920	21,578	1980	41,651
1940	25,434	1990	40,543
1960	36,807	1998	46,327

Source: *The World Almanac*

Step 1 On grid paper, draw a vertical and horizontal axis as shown. Make your graph large enough to fill most of the sheet. Label the horizontal axis 0 to 120 and the vertical axis 0 to 60,000.

Step 2 To make graphing easier, let x represent the number of years since 1900. Write the eight ordered pairs using this method. The first will be (0, 15,503).

Step 3 Graph the ordered pairs on your grid paper.

Analyze

1. Use your graph to estimate the number of students in elementary and secondary school in 1910 and in 1975. **Sample answers: 18,540,000 in 1910; 43,600,000 in 1975**

2. Use your graph to estimate the number of students in elementary and secondary school in 2020. **Sample answer: 54,390,000**

Make a Conjecture 3–4. See margin. 5. See pp. 65A–65B

3. Describe the methods you used to make your estimates for Exercises 1 and 2.

4. Do you think your prediction for 2020 will be accurate? Explain your reasoning.

5. Graph this set of data, which shows the number of students per computer in U.S. schools. Predict the number of students per computer in 2010. Explain how you made your prediction.

Year	Students per Computer	Year	Students per Computer	Year	Students per Computer	Year	Students per Computer
1984	125	1988	32	1992	18	1996	10
1985	75	1989	25	1993	16	1997	7.8
1986	50	1990	22	1994	14	1998	6.1
1987	37	1991	20	1995	10.5	1999	5.7

Source: *The World Almanac*

Getting Started

Objective Create a graph to represent the data in a data table.

Materials
grid paper

Teach

- Explain to students that the enrollment numbers in the data table represent the number of students in thousands. That means that each number is multiplied by 1000 to represent the actual number of students enrolled. So the number 15,503 actually represents 15,503,000 students.

- While representing the year 1900 as 0, 1920 as 20, etc. makes the graphing easier, it also makes the graph harder to interpret. Suggest that students also write the actual year on their graph below the scale.

Assess

Exercise 3 Students should realize that in order to predict the number of students in 2020, they need to extend the x-axis of their graph beyond the year 1998. This method assumes that the increase in the number of students will remain steady through 2020.

Resource Manager

📁 Teaching Algebra with Manipulatives

- p. 1 (master for grid paper)
- p. 35 (student recording sheet)

Study Notebook

You may wish to have students summarize this activity and what they learned from it.

1 Focus

 5-Minute Check Transparency 1-9 Use as a quiz or review of Lesson 1-8.

Mathematical Background notes are available for this lesson on p. 4D.

Why are graphs and tables used to display data?

Ask students:

• Why do you think graphs are used to display data? **Sample answer: Graphs make it easy to compare data.**

• Why do you think tables are used to display data? **Sample answer: Tables are a good way to organize data.**

• What does the graph of the Florida election results help to demonstrate about the number of votes for Bush and Gore? **Because it is virtually impossible to tell the difference in height between the Bush and Gore columns on the graph, the graph helps to demonstrate the closeness of the election.**

What You'll Learn

• Analyze data given in tables and graphs (bar, line, and circle).

• Determine whether graphs are misleading.

Vocabulary
• bar graph
• data
• circle graph
• line graph

TEACHING TIP
You may wish to point out to students that in the Snapshot, the measures in feet and inches vary due to rounding.

Why are graphs and tables used to display data?

For several weeks after Election Day in 2000, data regarding the presidential vote counts changed on a daily basis.

The bar graph at the right illustrates just how close the election was at one point. The graph allows you to compare the data visually.

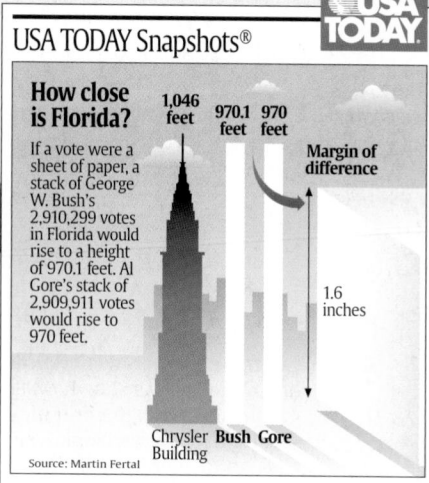

USA TODAY Snapshots®

How close is Florida?
If a vote were a sheet of paper, a stack of George W. Bush's 2,910,299 votes in Florida would rise to a height of 970.1 feet. Al Gore's stack of 2,909,911 votes would rise to 970 feet.

1,046 feet / 970.1 feet / 970 feet

Margin of difference 1.6 inches

Chrysler Building Bush Gore

Source: Martin Fertal

By Frank Pompa, USA TODAY

ANALYZE DATA A **bar graph** compares different categories of numerical information, or **data**, by showing each category as a bar whose length is related to the frequency. Bar graphs can also be used to display multiple sets of data in different categories at the same time. Graphs with multiple sets of data always have a key to denote which bars represent each set of data.

Example 1 *Analyze a Bar Graph*

The table shows the number of men and women participating in NCAA championship sports programs from 1995 to 1999.

NCAA Championship Sports Participation 1997–2001				
Year	'97–'98	'98–'99	'99–'00	'00–'01
Men	200,031	207,592	208,481	206,573
Women	133,376	145,832	146,617	149,115

Source: NCAA

Study Tip

Graphs and Tables
Graphs are useful for visualizing data and for estimations. Tables are used when you need precise data for computation.

These same data are displayed in a bar graph.

a. **Describe the general trend shown in the graph.**

The graph shows that the number of men has remained fairly constant while the number of women has been increasing.

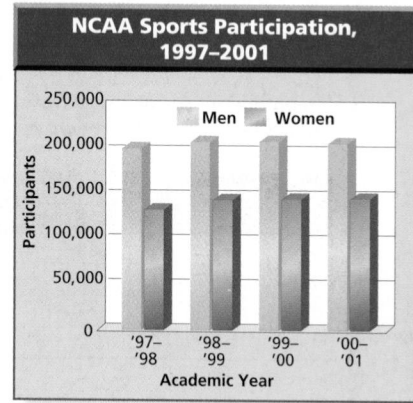

NCAA Sports Participation, 1997–2001

Men Women

Participants: 250,000 / 200,000 / 150,000 / 100,000 / 50,000 / 0

Academic Year: '97–'98 '98–'99 '99–'00 '00–'01

Resource Manager

 Workbook and Reproducible Masters

Chapter 1 Resource Masters
• Study Guide and Intervention, pp. 49–50
• Skills Practice, p. 51
• Practice, p. 52
• Reading to Learn Mathematics, p. 53
• Enrichment, p. 54
• Assessment, p. 70

Parent and Student Study Guide Workbook, p. 9
School-to-Career Masters, p. 2

Transparencies
5-Minute Check Transparency 1-9
Answer Key Transparencies

Technology
Interactive Chalkboard

b. Approximately how many more men than women participated in sports during the 1997–1998 school year?

The bar for the number of men shows about 200,000 and the bar for the women shows about 130,000. So, there were approximately 200,000–130,000 or 70,000 more men than women participating in the 1997–1998 school year.

c. What was the total participation among men and women in the 2000–2001 academic year?

Since the table shows the exact numbers, use the data in it.

Number of men	plus	number of women	equals	total participation.
206,573	+	149,115	=	355,688

There was a total of 355,688 men and women participating in sports in the 2000–2001 academic year.

Another type of graph used to display data is a circle graph. A **circle graph** compares parts of a set of data as a percent of the whole set. The percents in a circle graph should always have a sum of 100%.

Example 2 Analyze a Circle Graph

A recent survey asked drivers in several cities across the United States if traffic in their area had gotten better, worse, or had not changed in the past five years. The results of the survey are displayed in the circle graph.

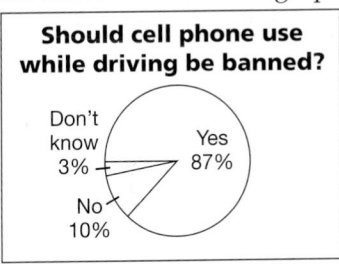

National Traffic Survey

3% Not Sure
26% Same
63% Worse
8% Better

Source: *USA TODAY*

a. If 4500 people were surveyed, how many felt that traffic had improved in their area?

The section of the graph representing people who said traffic is better is 8% of the circle, so find 8% of 4500.

8%	of	4500	equals	360.
0.08	×	4500	=	360

360 people said that traffic was better.

b. If a city with a population of 647,000 is representative of those surveyed, how many people could be expected to think that traffic conditions are worse?

63% of those surveyed said that traffic is worse, so find 63% of 647,000.

$0.63 \times 647,000 = 407,610$

Thus, 407,610 people in the city could be expected to say that traffic conditions are worse.

A third type of graph used to display data is a line graph. **Line graphs** are useful when showing how a set of data changes over time. They can also be helpful when making predictions.

www.algebra1.com/extra_examples

Lesson 1-9 Statistics: Analyzing Data by Using Tables and Graphs   **51**

In-Class Example

Power Point®

3 Refer to the graph in Example 3 to answer these questions.

a. How would the change in enrollment between 1997 and 1999 compare to the change in enrollment between 1995 and 1999? **Since enrollment changed little between 1995 and 1997, the two changes in enrollment would be about the same.**

b. Why can't you simply extend the line on the graph beyond 1999 to predict the number of students enrolled in 2005? **The graph is not large enough. The line would extend beyond the edge of the graph.**

MISLEADING GRAPHS

In-Class Example

Power Point®

4 Joel used the graph below to show his algebra grade for the first four reporting periods of the year. Does the graph misrepresent the data? Explain.

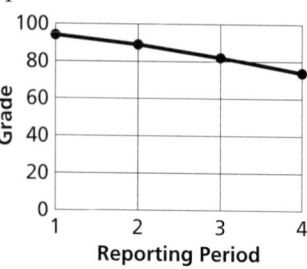

Yes; the scale on the _x_-axis is too large, and minimizes the amount that Joel's grade dropped.

Career Choices

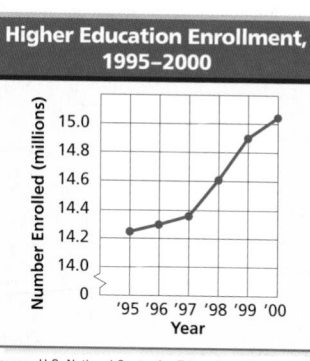

Professor

A college professor may teach by lecturing to several hundred students at a time or by supervising students in small groups in a laboratory. Often they also do their own research to expand knowledge in their field.

Online Research
For information about a career as a professor, visit:
www.algebra1.com/careers

Concept Summary boxes are great for review because they summarize several related topics and illustrate the similarities and differences among them.

Example 3 Analyze a Line Graph

• **EDUCATION** Refer to the line graph below.

a. Estimate the change in enrollment between 1995 and 1999.

The enrollment for 1995 is about 14.25 million, and the enrollment for 1999 is about 14.9 million. So, the change in enrollment is $14.9 - 14.25$ or 0.65 million.

b. If the rate of growth between 1998 and 1999 continues, predict the number of people who will be enrolled in higher education in the year 2005.

Based on the graph, the increase in enrollment from 1998 to 1999 is 0.3 million. So, the enrollment should increase by 0.3 million per year.

$14.9 + 0.3(6) = 14.9 + 1.8$ Multiply the annual increase, 0.3, by the number of years, 6.
$= 16.7$ Enrollment in 2005 should be about 16.7 million.

Higher Education Enrollment, 1995–2000

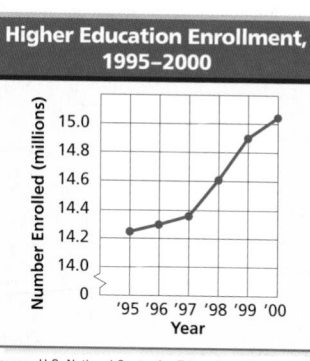

Source: U.S. National Center for Educational Statistics

Concept Summary   *Statistical Graphs*

Type of Graph	bar graph	circle graph	line graph
When to Use	to compare different categories of data	to show data as parts of a whole set of data	to show the change in data over time

MISLEADING GRAPHS Graphs are very useful for displaying data. However, graphs that have been constructed incorrectly can be confusing and can lead to false assumptions. Many times these types of graphs are mislabeled, incorrect data is compared, or the graphs are constructed to make one set of data appear greater than another set. Here are some common ways that a graph may be misleading.

- Numbers are omitted on an axis, but no break is shown.
- The tick marks on an axis are not the same distance apart or do not have the same-sized intervals.
- The percents on a circle graph do not have a sum of 100.

Example 4 Misleading Graphs

AUTOMOBILES The graph shows the number of sport-utility vehicle (SUV) sales in the United States from 1990 to 1999. Explain how the graph misrepresents the data.

The vertical axis scale begins at 1 million. This causes the appearance of no vehicles sold in 1990 and 1991, and very few vehicles sold through 1994.

Sport-Utility Vehicle Sales, 1990–1999

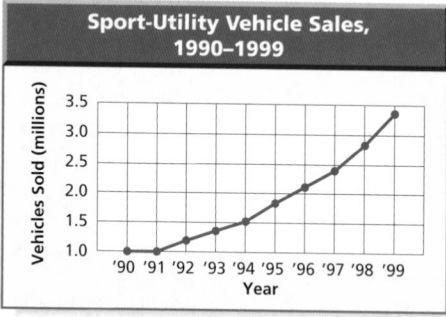

Source: *The World Almanac*

DAILY INTERVENTION

Differentiated Instruction

Visual/Spatial If students have difficulty understanding how graphs can be misleading, have them redraw the graph in Example 4 with the scale on the _y_-axis starting at zero. Ask them to compare their new graph to the original one and explain the differences.

Concept Check

1. **Explain** the appropriate use of each type of graph.
   - circle graph **Compare parts to the whole.**
   - bar graph **Compare different categories of data.**
   - line graph **Show changes in data over time.**

2. **OPEN ENDED** Find a real-world example of a graph in a newspaper or magazine. Write a description of what the graph displays. **See students' work.**

3. **Describe** ways in which a circle graph could be drawn so that it is misleading. **Sample answer: The percentages of the data do not total 100.**

Guided Practice

SPORTS For Exercises 4 and 5, use the following information. There are 321 NCAA Division I schools. The graph at the right shows the sports that are offered at the most Division I schools.

GUIDED PRACTICE KEY	
Exercises	Examples
4, 5	1
6, 7	1, 2
8, 9	3, 4

4. How many more schools participate in basketball than in golf? **38**

5. What sport is offered at the fewest schools? **tennis**

USA TODAY Snapshots®

Men's basketball leads college offerings

There are 321 NCAA Division I schools, all of which sponsor men's basketball. Sports that are offered at the most NCAA Division I schools:

Basketball	321
Cross country	300
Baseball	285
Golf	283
Tennis	276

Source: NCAA

By Ellen J. Horrow and Marcy E. Mullins, USA TODAY

EDUCATION For Exercises 6–9, use the table that shows the number of foreign students as a percent of the total college enrollment in the United States.

Country of Origin	Total Student Enrollment (%)
Australia	0.02
Canada	0.15
France	0.04
Germany	0.06
Italy	0.22
Spain	0.03
United Kingdom	0.05

Source: *Statistical Abstract of the United States*

8. No; the data do not represent a whole set.

9. Bar graph; a bar graph is used to compare similar data in the same category.

6. There were about 14.9 million students enrolled in colleges in 1999. How many of these students were from Germany? **8940**

7. How many more students were from Canada than from the United Kingdom in 1999? **14,900**

8. Would it be appropriate to display this data in a circle graph? Explain.

9. Would a bar or a line graph be more appropriate to display these data? Explain.

3 Practice/Apply

Study Notebook

Have students—
- complete the definitions/examples for the remaining terms on their Vocabulary Builder worksheets for Chapter 1.
- Include any other item(s) that they find helpful in mastering the skills in this lesson.

About the Exercises...

Organization by Objective
- **Analyze Data:** 12–15, 18
- **Misleading Graphs:** 16, 17

Assignment Guide

Basic: 12, 13, 17–28

Average: 12–15, 17–28

Advanced: 14–16, 18–28

Online Lesson Plans

USA TODAY Education's Online site offers resources and interactive features connected to each day's newspaper. *Experience TODAY*, USA TODAY's daily lesson plan, is available on the site and delivered daily to subscribers. This plan provides instruction for integrating USA TODAY graphics and key editorial features into your mathematics classroom. Log on to **www.education.usatoday.com**.

Glencoe's exclusive partnership with USA TODAY provides actual USA TODAY Snapshots® that illustrate mathematical concepts.

Study Guide and Intervention, p. 49 (shown) and p. 50

Analyze Data Graphs or tables can be used to display data. A **bar graph** compares different categories of data, while a **circle graph** compares parts of a set of data as a percent of the whole set. A **line graph** is useful to show how a data set changes over time.

Example The circle graph at the right shows the number of international visitors to the United States in 2000, by country.

a. If there were a total of 50,891,000 visitors, how many were from Mexico?
50,891,000 × 20% = 10,178,200

b. If the percentage of visitors from each country remains the same each year, how many visitors from Canada would you expect in the year 2003 if the total is 59,000,000 visitors?
59,000,000 × 29% = 17,110,000

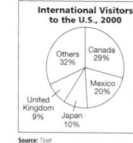
International Visitors to the U.S., 2000
Others 32%, Canada 29%, Mexico 20%, Japan 10%, United Kingdom 9%
Source: Tinet

Exercises

1. The graph shows the use of imported steel by U.S. companies over a 10-year period.

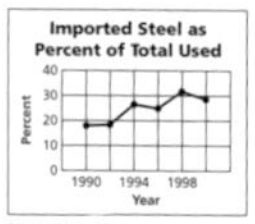

   a. Describe the general trend in the graph. The general trend is an increase in the use of imported steel over the 10-year period, with slight decreases in 1996 and 2000.

   b. What would be a reasonable prediction for the percentage of imported steel used in 2002? about 30%

   Imported Steel as Percent of Total Used
   Source: Chicago Tribune

2. The table shows the percentage of change in worker productivity at the beginning of each year for a 5-year period.

   a. Which year shows the greatest percentage increase in productivity? 1998

   b. What does the negative percent in the first quarter of 2001 indicate? Worker productivity decreased in this period, as compared to the productivity one year earlier.

Worker Productivity Index	
Year (1st Qtr.)	% of Change
1997	+1
1998	+4.6
1999	+2
2000	+2.1
2001	−1.2
   Source: Chicago Tribune

Skills Practice, p. 51 and Practice, p. 52 (shown)

MINERAL IDENTIFICATION For Exercises 1–4, use the following information.

The table shows *Moh's hardness scale*, used as a guide to help identify minerals. If mineral A scratches mineral B, then A's hardness number is greater than B's. If B cannot scratch A, then B's hardness number is less than or equal to A's.

1. Which mineral(s) will fluorite scratch? talc, gypsum, calcite

2. A fingernail has a hardness of 2.5. Which mineral(s) will it scratch? talc, gypsum

3. Suppose quartz will not scratch an unknown mineral. What is the hardness of the unknown mineral? at least 7

4. If an unknown mineral scratches all the minerals in the scale up to 7, and corundum scratches the unknown, what is the hardness of the unknown? between 7 and 9

Mineral	Hardness
Talc	1
Gypsum	2
Calcite	3
Fluorite	4
Apatite	5
Orthoclase	6
Quartz	7
Topaz	8
Corundum	9
Diamond	10

SALES For Exercises 5 and 6, use the line graph that shows CD sales at Berry's Music for the years 1998–2002.

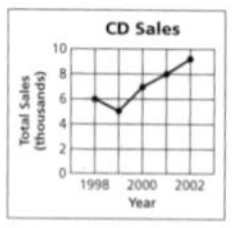

5. Which one-year period shows the greatest growth in sales? from 1999 to 2000

6. Describe the sales trend. Sales started off at about 6000 in 1998, then dipped in 1999, showed a sharp increase in 2000, then a steady increase to 2002.

   CD Sales

MOVIE PREFERENCES For Exercises 7–9, use the circle graph that shows the percent of people who prefer certain types of movies.

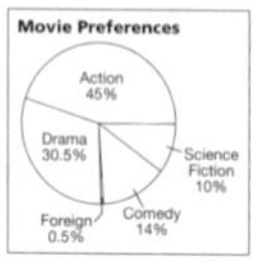

7. If 400 people were surveyed, how many chose action movies as their favorite? 180

8. Of 1000 people at a movie theater on a weekend, how many would you expect to prefer drama? 305

9. What percent of people chose a category other than action or drama? 24.5%

   Movie Preferences
   Action 45%, Drama 30.5%, Science Fiction 10%, Comedy 14%, Foreign 0.5%

TICKET SALES For Exercises 10 and 11, use the bar graph that compares annual sports ticket sales at Mars High.

10. Describe why the graph is misleading. Beginning the vertical axis at 20 instead of 0 makes the relative sales for volleyball and track and field seem low.

11. What could be done to make the graph more accurate? Start the vertical axis at 0.

    Ticket Sales
    Basketball, Football, Track & Field, Volleyball

Reading to Learn Mathematics, p. 53 [ELL]

Pre-Activity Why are graphs and tables used to display data?

Read the introduction to Lesson 1-9 at the top of page 50 in your textbook.

Compare your reaction to the statement, *A stack containing George Bush's votes from Florida would be 970.1 feet tall, while a stack of Al Gore's votes would be 970 feet tall* with your reaction to the graph shown in the introduction. Write a brief description of which presentation works best for you. See students' work.

Reading the Lesson

1. Choose from the following types of graphs as you complete each statement.

   bar graph   circle graph   line graph

   a. A __circle graph__ compares parts of a set of data as a percent of the whole set.

   b. __Line graphs__ are useful when showing how a set of data changes over time.

   c. __Line graphs__ are helpful when making predictions.

   d. __Bar graphs__ can be used to display multiple sets of data in different categories at the same time.

   e. The percents in a __circle graph__ should always have a sum of 100%.

   f. A __bar graph__ compares different categories of numerical information, or data.

2. Explain how the graph is misleading. Sample answer: The first interval is from 0-200 and all other intervals are in units of 25, so the price rise appears steeper than it is.

   Stock Price

Helping You Remember

3. Describe something in your daily routine that you can connect with bar graphs and circle graphs to help you remember their special purpose. Sample answer: circle graphs—parts of a pizza; bar graphs—number of slices left in a loaf of bread

---

HOME ENTERTAINMENT For Exercises 10 and 11, refer to the graph.

10. Describe why the graph is misleading.

    10. Sample answer: The vertical axis shows only partial intervals.

11. What should be done so that the graph displays the data more accurately?
    The vertical axis needs to begin at 0.

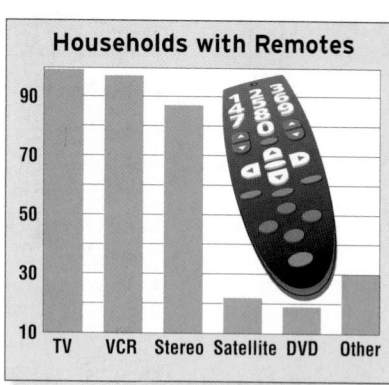
Households with Remotes
TV, VCR, Stereo, Satellite, DVD, Other

Practice and Apply

Homework Help

For Exercises	See Examples
12, 13	1
14, 15	2
16	3, 4
17	2–4

Extra Practice
See page 822.

VIDEOGRAPHY For Exercises 12 and 13, use the table that shows the average cost of preparing one hour of 35-millimeter film versus one hour of digital video.

12. What is the total cost of using 35-millimeter film? **$4864.60**

13. Estimate how many times as great the cost of using 35-millimeter film is as using digital video. Sample answer: about 250 times as great

35 mm, editing video	
Film stock	$3110.40
Processing	621.00
Prep for telecine	60.00
Telecine	1000.00
Tape stock	73.20
Digital, editing on video	
Tape stock (original)	$10.00
Tape stock (back up)	10.00

BOOKS For Exercises 14 and 15, use the graph that shows the time of year people prefer to buy books.

14. Suppose the total number of books purchased for the year was 25 million. Estimate the number of books purchased in the spring.

    14. Sample answer: about 5 million

15. Suppose the manager of a bookstore has determined that she sells about 15,000 books a year. Approximately how many books should she expect to sell during the summer?
    Sample answer: about 2250

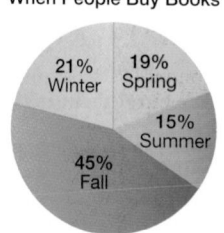
When People Buy Books
19% Spring, 15% Summer, 45% Fall, 21% Winter
Source: USA TODAY

16. **ENTERTAINMENT** The line graph shows the number of cable television systems in the United States from 1995 to 2000. Explain how the graph misrepresents the data. The vertical axis is extended and does not begin at 0. It gives the impression that the number of cable television systems is decreasing rapidly.

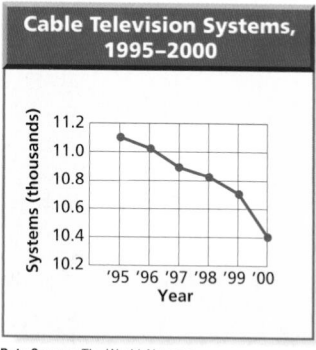
Cable Television Systems, 1995–2000
Data Source: The World Almanac

Enrichment, p. 54

Percentiles

The table at the right shows test scores and their frequencies. The frequency is the number of people who had a particular score. The cumulative frequency is the total frequency up to that point, starting at the lowest score and adding up.

Example 1 What score is at the 16th percentile?

A score at the 16th percentile means the score just above the lowest 16% of the scores.

16% of the 50 scores is 8 scores.

The 8th score is 55.

The score just above this is 56.

So, the score at the 16th percentile is 56.

Notice that no one had a score of 56 points.

Score	Frequency	Cumulative Frequency
95	1	50
90	2	49
85	5	47
80	6	42
75	7	36
70	8	29
65	7	21
60	6	14
55	4	8
50	3	4
45	1	1

17. FOOD Oatmeal can be found in 80% of the homes in the United States. The circle graph shows favorite oatmeal toppings. Is the graph misleading? If so, explain why and tell how the graph can be fixed so that it is not misleading. **Yes, the graph is misleading because the sum of the percentages is not 100. To fix the graph, each section must be drawn accurately and another section that represents "other" toppings should be added.**

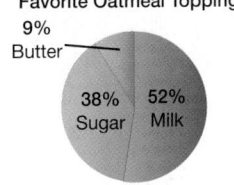

Favorite Oatmeal Topping

9% Butter
38% Sugar
52% Milk

Data Source: NPD Group for Quaker Oats

Web Quest

A graph of the number of people over 65 in the U.S. for the years since 1900 will help you predict trends. Visit www.algebra1.com/webquest to continue work on your WebQuest project.

18. CRITICAL THINKING The table shows the percent of United States households owning a color television for the years 1980 to 2000. **a–c. See margin.**

a. Display the data in a line graph that shows little increase in ownership.

b. Draw a line graph that shows a rapid increase in the number of households owning a color television.

c. Are either of your graphs misleading? Explain.

Households with Color Televisions	
Year	Percent
1980	83
1985	91
1990	98
1995	99
2000	99

Source: The World Almanac

19. WRITING IN MATH Answer the question that was posed at the beginning of the lesson. **See margin.**

Why are graphs and tables used to display data?

Include the following in your answer:

- a description of how to use graphs to make predictions, and
- an explanation of how to analyze a graph to determine whether the graph is misleading.

Standardized Test Practice
Ⓐ Ⓑ Ⓒ Ⓓ

20. According to the graph, the greatest increase in temperature occurred between which two days? **C**

Ⓐ 1 and 2   Ⓑ 6 and 7
Ⓒ 2 and 3   Ⓓ 5 and 6

21. A graph that is primarily used to show the change in data over time is called a **C**

Ⓐ circle graph.   Ⓑ bar graph.
Ⓒ line graph.   Ⓓ data graph.

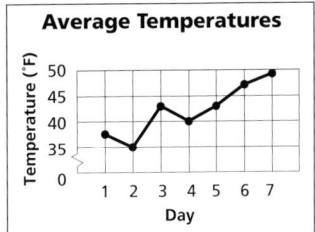

Average Temperatures

Maintain Your Skills

Mixed Review

22. PHYSICAL FITNESS Pedro likes to exercise regularly. On Mondays, he walks two miles, runs three miles, sprints one-half of a mile, and then walks for another mile. Sketch a graph that represents Mitchell's heart rate during his Monday workouts. *(Lesson 1-8)* **See margin.**

23-24. Sample answers are given.
Find a counterexample for each statement. *(Lesson 1-7)*

23. If $x \le 12$, then $4x - 5 \le 42$. **$x = 12$**   **24.** If $x > 1$, then $x < \frac{1}{x}$. **$x = \frac{3}{2}$**

25. If the perimeter of a rectangle is 16 inches, then each side is 4 inches long.
$6 + 6 + 2 + 2 = 16$

Simplify each expression. *(Lesson 1-6)*

26. $7a + 5b + 3b + 3a$ **27.** $4x^2 + 9x + 2x^2 + x$ **28.** $\frac{1}{2}n + \frac{2}{3}m + \frac{1}{2}m + \frac{1}{3}n$

26. $10a + 8b$
27. $6x^2 + 10x$
28. $\frac{5}{6}n + 1\frac{1}{6}m$

 www.algebra1.com/self_check_quiz   **Lesson 1-9** Statistics: Analyzing Data by Using Tables and Graphs **55**

4 *Assess*

Open-Ended Assessment

Speaking Have students explain which type of graph they think is the easiest to interpret, a bar graph, a circle graph, or a line graph. Then ask students to discuss whether different types of graphs might be better for different types of data.

Assessment Options

Quiz (Lessons 1-8 and 1-9) is available on p. 70 of the *Chapter 1 Resource Masters*.

Answers

18a.
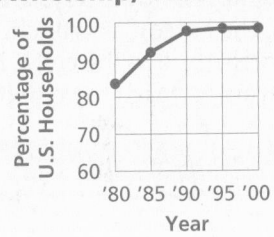

Color Television Ownership, 1980–2000

18b.
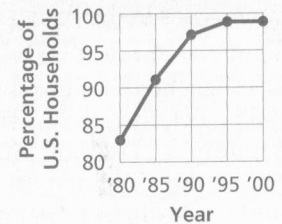

Color Television Ownership, 1980–2000

18c. See students' graphs and explanations.

22.
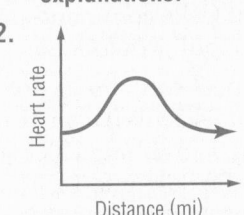

Answer

19. Tables and graphs provide an organized and quick way to examine data. Answers should include the following.

- Examine the existing pattern and use it to continue a graph to the future.
- Make sure the scale begins at zero and is consistent. Circle graphs should have all percents total to 100%. The right kind of graph should be used for the given data.

Getting Started

Objective Graph data in a table using a computer spreadsheet.

Materials
computer
spreadsheet software

Maneuvering within a Spreadsheet Explain that there are several ways to navigate between cells in a spreadsheet. Hitting the Enter or Return keys usually moves the cursor to the next cell down. The Tab key usually moves the cursor one cell to the right. The arrow keys will also move the cursor, as will clicking the mouse above the cell where you want to place the cursor.

Teach

- Suggest that students work in pairs, with the pairs taking turns reading aloud the data while the partner types in the data.

- Students may find that when they enter the data into the spreadsheet, the alignment of the numbers may look different from the alignment of the sample spreadsheet The alignment of text or numbers in cells can be accomplished with the Format Cells command in the Format pull-down menu.

- If spreadsheet software is not available, this activity can also be done on a graphing calculator. Enter the data into LISTS and use the connected mode.

Assess

In **Exercises 1 and 2**, students should discover that creating a graph from spreadsheet data usually involves several steps, including choosing the type of graph they want.

Statistical Graphs

You can use a computer spreadsheet program to display data in different ways. The data is entered into a table and then displayed in your chosen type of graph.

Example
Use a spreadsheet to make a line graph of the data on sports equipment sales.

In-line Skating and Wheel Sports Equipment Sales								
Year	1990	1992	1993	1994	1995	1996	1997	1998
Sales (million $)	150	268	377	545	646	590	562	515

Source: National Sporting Goods Association

Step 1 Enter the data in a spreadsheet. Use Column A for the years and Column B for the sales.

Step 2 Select the data to be included in your graph. Then use the graph tool to create the graph.

The spreadsheet will allow you to change the appearance of the graph by adding titles and axis labels, adjusting the scales on the axes, changing colors, and so on.

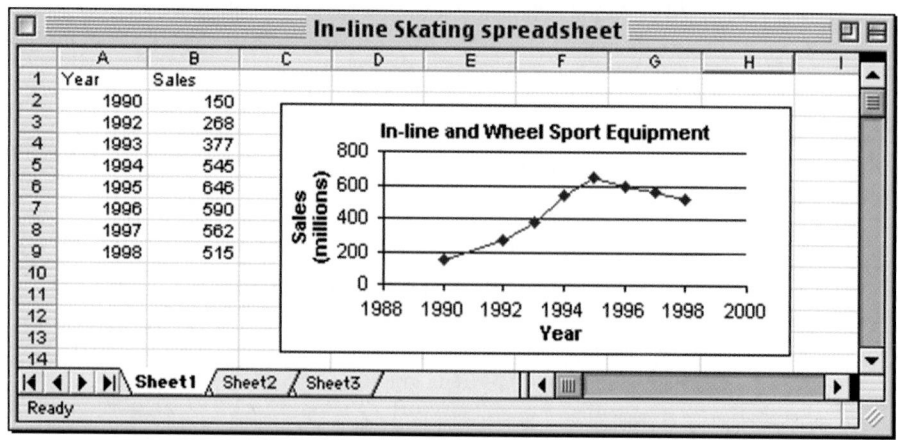

Exercises 1–2. See pp. 65A–65B.

For Exercises 1–3, use the data on snowmobile sales in the table below.

Snowmobile Sales								
Year	1990	1992	1993	1994	1995	1996	1997	1998
Sales (million $)	322	391	515	715	910	974	975	957

Source: National Sporting Goods Association

1. Use a spreadsheet program to create a line graph of the data.
2. Use a spreadsheet program to create a bar graph of the data.
3. Adjust the scales on each of the graphs that you created. Is it possible to create a misleading graph using a spreadsheet program? Explain.

3. Yes; you can change the scales to begin at values other than zero, or change the intervals on the scale to be misleading.

Study Notebook

You may wish to have students summarize this activity and what they learned from it.

Graphing Calculator and Spreadsheet Investigations empower students to use technology tools to solve problems.

Chapter 1 Study Guide and Review

Vocabulary and Concept Check

additive identity (p. 21)
algebraic expression (p. 6)
Associative Property (p. 32)
bar graph (p. 50)
base (p. 7)
circle graph (p. 51)
Closure Property (p. 25)
coefficient (p. 29)
Commutative Property (p. 32)
conclusion (p. 37)
conditional statement (p. 37)
coordinate system (p. 43)
coordinates (p. 43)
counterexample (p. 38)
data (p. 50)
deductive reasoning (p. 38)
dependent quantity (p. 44)
dependent variable (p. 44)
Distributive Property (p. 26)
domain (p. 45)
element (p. 16)
equation (p. 16)
equivalent expressions (p. 29)
exponent (p. 7)
factors (p. 6)
function (p. 43)
horizontal axis (p. 43)
hypothesis (p. 37)
if-then statement (p. 37)
independent quantity (p. 44)
independent variable (p. 44)
inequality (p. 17)
like terms (p. 28)
line graph (p. 51)
multiplicative identity (p. 21)
Multiplicative Inverse Property (p. 22)
multiplicative inverses (p. 21)
Multiplicative Property of Zero (p. 21)
open sentence (p. 16)
order of operations (p. 11)
ordered pair (p. 43)
origin (p. 43)
power (p. 7)
product (p. 6)
range (p. 45)
reciprocal (p. 21)
Reflexive Property of Equality (p. 22)
relation (p. 45)
replacement set (p. 16)
set (p. 16)
simplest form (p. 29)
solution (p. 16)
solution set (p. 16)
solving an open sentence (p. 16)
Substitution Property of Equality (p. 22)
Symmetric Property of Equality (p. 22)
term (p. 28)
Transitive Property of Equality (p. 22)
variables (p. 6)
vertical axis (p. 43)
x-axis (p. 43)
x-coordinate (p. 43)
y-axis (p. 43)
y-coordinate (p. 43)

Choose the letter of the property that best matches each statement.

1. For any number a, $a + 0 = 0 + a = a$. a
2. For any number a, $a \cdot 1 = 1 \cdot a = a$. e
3. For any number, a, $a \cdot 0 = 0 \cdot a = 0$. g
4. For any nonzero number a, there is exactly one number $\frac{1}{a}$ such that $\frac{1}{a} \cdot a = a \cdot \frac{1}{a} = 1$. f
5. For any number a, $a = a$. h
6. For any numbers a and b, if $a = b$, then $b = a$. j
7. For any numbers a and b, if $a = b$, then a may be replaced by b in any expression. i
8. For any numbers a, b, and c, if $a = b$ and $b = c$, then $a = c$. k
9. For any numbers a, b, and c, $a(b + c) = ab + ac$. b
10. For any numbers a, b, and c, $a + (b + c) = (a + b) + c$. d

a. Additive Identity Property
b. Distributive Property
c. Commutative Property
d. Associative Property
e. Multiplicative Identity Property
f. Multiplicative Inverse Property
g. Multiplicative Property of Zero
h. Reflexive Property
i. Substitution Property
j. Symmetric Property
k. Transitive Property

Lesson-by-Lesson Review

1-1 Variables and Expressions

See pages 6–9.

Concept Summary

- Variables are used to represent unspecified numbers or values.
- An algebraic expression contains letters and variables with an arithmetic operation.

www.algebra1.com/vocabulary_review

FOLDABLES™ Study Organizer

For more information about Foldables, see *Teaching Mathematics with Foldables.*

Have students look through the chapter to make sure they have included notes and examples in their Foldables for each lesson of Chapter 1.

Encourage students to refer to their Foldables while completing the Study Guide and Review and to use them in preparing for the Chapter Test.

Chapter 1 Study Guide and Review

Vocabulary and Concept Check

- This alphabetical list of vocabulary terms in Chapter 1 includes a page reference where each term was introduced.
- **Assessment** A vocabulary test/review for Chapter 1 is available on p. 68 of the *Chapter 1 Resource Masters.*

Lesson-by-Lesson Review

For each lesson,

- the main ideas are summarized,
- additional examples review concepts, and
- practice exercises are provided.

Vocabulary PuzzleMaker

ELL The Vocabulary PuzzleMaker software improves students' mathematics vocabulary using four puzzle formats—crossword, scramble, word search using a word list, and word search using clues. Students can work on a computer screen or from a printed handout.

MindJogger Videoquizzes

ELL MindJogger Videoquizzes provide an alternative review of concepts presented in this chapter. Students work in teams in a game show format to gain points for correct answers. The questions are presented in three rounds.

Round 1 Concepts (5 questions)
Round 2 Skills (4 questions)
Round 3 Problem Solving (4 questions)

Answers

18. the product of two and a number *p* squared

19. the product of three and a number *m* to the fifth power

20. the sum of one half and 2

Key concepts from the lesson, one or two examples, and several practice problems are included in the Lesson-by-Lesson Review.

Examples

1 Write an algebraic expression for *the sum of twice a number x and fifteen.*

twice a number x, sum of fifteen
$2x$ $+$ 15 The algebraic expression is $2x + 15$.

2 Write a verbal expression for $4x^2 - 13$.

Four times a number x squared minus thirteen.

Exercises Write an algebraic expression for each verbal expression.
See Examples 1 and 2 on pages 6 and 7.

11. a number x to the fifth power x^5 **12.** five times a number x squared $5x^2$

13. the sum of a number x and twenty-one $x + 21$

14. the difference of twice a number x and 8 $2x - 8$

Evaluate each expression. *See Example 3 on page 7.*

15. 3^3 **27** **16.** 2^5 **32** **17.** 5^4 **625**

Write a verbal expression for each algebraic expression. *See Example 4 on page 7.*

18. $2p^2$ **19.** $3m^5$ **20.** $\frac{1}{2} + 2$

18–20. See margin.

1-2 Order of Operations

See pages 11–15.

Concept Summary

- Expressions must be simplified using the order of operations.

  Step 1 Evaluate expressions inside grouping symbols.

  Step 2 Evaluate all powers.

  Step 3 Do all multiplications and/or divisions from left to right.

  Step 4 Do all additions and/or subtractions from left to right.

Example Evaluate $x^2 - (y + 2)$ if $x = 4$ and $y = 3$.

$$x^2 - (y + 2) = 4^2 - (3 + 2) \quad \text{Replace } x \text{ with 4 and } y \text{ with 3.}$$
$$= 4^2 - 5 \quad \text{Add 3 and 2.}$$
$$= 16 - 5 \quad \text{Evaluate power.}$$
$$= 11 \quad \text{Subtract 5 from 16.}$$

Exercises Evaluate each expression. *See Examples 1–3 on pages 11 and 12.*

21. $3 + 2 \cdot 4$ **11** **22.** $\frac{(10 - 6)}{8}$ **$\frac{1}{2}$** **23.** $18 - 4^2 + 7$ **9**

24. $8(2 + 5) - 6$ **50** **25.** $4(11 + 7) - 9 \cdot 8$ **0** **26.** $288 \div [3(9 + 3)]$ **8**

27. $16 \div 2 \cdot 5 \cdot 3 \div 6$ **20** **28.** $6(4^3 + 2^2)$ **408** **29.** $(3 \cdot 1)^3 - \frac{(4 + 6)}{(5 \cdot 2)}$ **26**

Evaluate each expression if $x = 3$, $t = 4$, and $y = 2$. *See Example 4 on page 12.*

30. $t^2 + 3y$ **22** **31.** xty^3 **96** **32.** $\frac{ty}{x}$ **$\frac{8}{3}$ or $2\frac{2}{3}$**

33. $x + t^2 + y^2$ **23** **34.** $3ty - x^2$ **15** **35.** $8(x - y)^2 + 2t$ **16**

1-3 Open Sentences

See pages 16–20.

Concept Summary

- Open sentences are solved by replacing the variables in an equation with numerical values.
- Inequalities like $x + 2 \geq 7$ are solved the same way that equations are solved.

Example Solve $5^2 - 3 = y$.

$5^2 - 3 = y$ Original equation

$25 - 3 = y$ Evaluate the power.

$22 = y$ Subtract 3 from 25.

The solution is 22.

Exercises Solve each equation.   *See Example 2 on page 17.*

36. $x = 22 - 13$ **9**

37. $y = 4 + 3^2$ **13**

38. $m = \dfrac{64 + 4}{17}$ **4**

39. $x = \dfrac{21 - 3}{12 - 3}$ **2**

40. $a = \dfrac{14 + 28}{4 + 3}$ **6**

41. $n = \dfrac{96 \div 6}{8 \div 2}$ **4**

42. $b = \dfrac{7(4 \cdot 3)}{18 \div 3}$ **14**

43. $\dfrac{6(7) - 2(3)}{4^2 - 6(2)}$ **9**

44. $y = 5[2(4) - 1^3]$ **35**

Find the solution set for each inequality if the replacement set is {4, 5, 6, 7, 8}.
See Example 3 on page 17.

45. $x + 2 > 7$ **{6, 7, 8}**

46. $10 - x < 7$ **{4, 5, 6, 7, 8}**

47. $2x + 5 \geq 15$ **{5, 6, 7, 8}**

1-4 Identity and Equality Properties

See pages 21–25.

Concept Summary

- Adding zero to a quantity or multiplying a quantity by one does not change the quantity.
- Using the Reflexive, Symmetric, Transitive, and Substitution Properties along with the order of operations helps in simplifying expressions.

Example Evaluate $36 + 7 \cdot 1 + 5 (2 - 2)$. Name the property used in each step.

$36 + 7 \cdot 1 + 5(2 - 2) = 36 + 7 \cdot 1 + 5(0)$ Substitution

$ = 36 + 7 + 5(0)$ Multiplicative Identity

$ = 36 + 7$ Multiplicative Prop. of Zero

$ = 43$ Substitution

Exercises Evaluate each expression. Name the property used in each step.
See Example 2 on page 23. **48–53. See margin.**

48. $2[3 \div (19 - 4^2)]$

49. $\dfrac{1}{2} \cdot 2 + 2[2 \cdot 3 - 1]$

50. $4^2 - 2^2 - (4 - 2)$

51. $1.2 - 0.05 + 2^3$

52. $(7 - 2)(5) - 5^2$

53. $3(4 \div 4)^2 - \dfrac{1}{4}(8)$

Answers

48. $2[3 \div (19 - 4^2)]$

$= 2[3 \div (19 - 16)]$ Subst.

$= 2[3 \div 3]$ Substitution

$= 2 \cdot 1$ Substitution

$= 2$ Multiplicative Identity

49. $\dfrac{1}{2} \cdot 2 + 2[2 \cdot 3 - 1]$

$= \dfrac{1}{2} \cdot 2 + 2[6 - 1]$ Subst.

$= \dfrac{1}{2} \cdot 2 + 2 \cdot 5$ Substitution

$= 1 + 2 \cdot 5$ Mult. Inverse

$= 1 + 10$ Substitution

$= 11$ Substitution

50. $4^2 - 2^2 - (4 - 2)$

$= 4^2 - 2^2 - (2)$ Substitution

$= 16 - 2^2 - 2$ Substitution

$= 16 - 4 - 2$ Substitution

$= 12 - 2$ Substitution

$= 10$ Substitution

51. $1.2 - 0.05 + 2^3$

$= 1.2 - 0.05 + 8$ Subst.

$= 1.15 + 8$ Substitution

$= 9.15$ Substitution

52. $(7 - 2)(5) - 5^2$

$= 5(5) - 25$ Substitution

$= 5(5) - 25$ Substitution

$= 25 - 25$ Substitution

$= 0$ Substitution

53. $3(4 \div 4)^2 - \dfrac{1}{4}(8)$

$= 3(1)^2 - \dfrac{1}{4}(8)$ Substitution

$= 3 \cdot 1 - \dfrac{1}{4}(8)$ Substitution

$= 3 - \dfrac{1}{4}(8)$ Mult. Identity

$= 3 - 2$ Substitution

$= 1$ Substitution

Answers

72. $5(x + y) - 2x$
$= 5(x) + 5(y) - 2x$ Distr. Prop.
$= 5x - 2x + 5y$ Comm. Prop.
$= 3x + 5y$ Substitution

73. $2pq + pq$
$= (2 + 1)pq$ Distr. Prop.
$= 3pq$ Substitution

74. $6a + (8b + 2a)$
$= 6a + (2a + 8b)$ Comm. Prop.
$= (6a + 2a) + 8b$ Assoc. Prop.
$= 8a + 8b$ Substitution

75. $3x^2 + (x^2 + 7x)$
$= (3x^2 + x^2) + 7x$ Assoc. Prop.
$= 4x^2 + 7x$ Substitution

1-5 **The Distributive Property**

See pages 26–31.

Concept Summary

- For any numbers a, b, and c, $a(b + c) = ab + ac$ and $(b + c)a = ba + ca$.
- For any numbers a, b, and c, $a(b - c) = ab - ac$ and $(b - c)a = ba - ca$.

Examples **1** Rewrite $5(t + 3)$ using the Distributive Property. Then simplify.

$5(t + 3) = 5(t) + 5(3)$ Distributive Property
$\quad\quad\quad = 5t + 15$ Multiply.

2 Simplify $2x^2 + 4x^2 + 7x$.

$2x^2 + 4x^2 + 7x = (2 + 4)x^2 + 7x$ Distributive Property
$\quad\quad\quad\quad\quad\quad = 6x^2 + 7x$ Substitution

Exercises Rewrite each product using the Distributive Property. Then simplify.
See Examples 1 and 2 on page 27.

54. $2(4 + 7)$ **22**
55. $8(15 - 6)$ **72**
56. $4(x + 1)$ **$4x + 4$**
57. $3\left(\frac{1}{3} - p\right)$ **$1 - 3p$**
58. $6(a + b)$ **$6a + 6b$**
59. $8(3x - 7y)$ **$24x - 56y$**

Simplify each expression. If not possible, write *simplified*. *See Example 6 on page 29.*

60. $4a + 9a$ **$13a$**
61. $4np + 7mp$ **simplified**
62. $3w - w + 4v - 3v$ **$2w + v$**
63. $3m + 5m + 12n - 4n$ **$8m + 8n$**
64. $2p(1 + 16r)$ **$2p + 32pr$**
65. $9y + 3y - 5x$ **$12y - 5x$**

1-6 **Commutative and Associative Properties**

See pages 32–36.

Concept Summary

- For any numbers a and b, $a + b = b + a$ and $a \cdot b = b \cdot a$.
- For any numbers a, b and c, $(a + b) + c = a + (b + c)$ and $(ab)c = a(bc)$.

Example Simplify $3x + 7xy + 9x$.

$3x + 7xy + 9x = 3x + 9x + 7xy$ Commutative (+)
$\quad\quad\quad\quad\quad = (3 + 9)x + 7xy$ Distributive Property
$\quad\quad\quad\quad\quad = 12x + 7xy$ Substitution

Exercises Simplify each expression. *See Example 3 on page 33.*

66. $3x + 4y + 2x$ **$5x + 4y$**
67. $7w^2 + w + 2w^2$ **$9w^2 + w$**
68. $3\frac{1}{2}m + \frac{1}{2}m + n$ **$4m + n$**
69. $6a + 5b + 2c + 8b$ **$6a + 13b + 2c$**
70. $3(2 + 3x) + 21x$ **$30x + 6$**
71. $6(2n - 4) + 5n$ **$17n - 24$**

Write an algebraic expression for each verbal expression. Then simplify, indicating the properties used. *See Example 4 on page 34.* **72–75. See margin.**

72. five times the sum of x and y decreased by $2x$
73. twice the product of p and q increased by the product of p and q
74. six times a plus the sum of eight times b and twice a
75. three times the square of x plus the sum of x squared and seven times x

1-7 Logical Reasoning

See pages 37–42.

Concept Summary

- Conditional statements can be written in the form *If A, then B*, where *A* is the hypothesis and *B* is the conclusion.
- One counterexample can be used to show that a statement is false.

Example Identify the hypothesis and conclusion of the statement *The trumpet player must audition to be in the band*. Then write the statement in if-then form.

Hypothesis: a person is a trumpet player

Conclusion: the person must audition to be in the band

If a person is a trumpet player, then the person must audition to be in the band.

Exercises Identify the hypothesis and conclusion of each statement. Then, write each statement in if-then form. *See Example 2 on page 38.* **76–77. See margin.**

76. School begins at 7:30 A.M.   77. Triangles have three sides.

Find a counterexample for each statement. *See Example 4 on page 39.*

78. If $x > y$, then $2x > 3y$.   79. If $a > b$ and $a > c$, then $b > c$.
    $x = 13, y = 12$ $a = 15, b = 1, c = 12$

1-8 Graphs and Functions

See pages 43–48.

Concept Summary

- Graphs can be used to represent a function and to visualize data.

Example A computer printer can print 12 pages of text per minute.

a. Make a table showing the number of pages printed in 1 to 5 minutes.

Time (min)	1	2	3	4	5
Pages	12	24	36	48	60

b. Sketch a graph that shows the relationship between time and the number of pages printed.

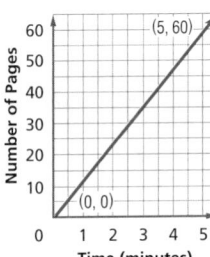

Exercises

80. Identify the graph that represents the altitude of an airplane taking off, flying for a while, then landing. *See Example 3 on page 44.* **Graph C**

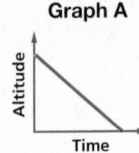

Graph A

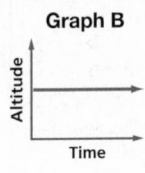

Graph B

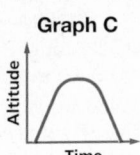

Graph C

Chapter 1 For More ... • Extra Practice, see pages 820–822.
• Mixed Problem Solving, see page 853.

Answers

81.

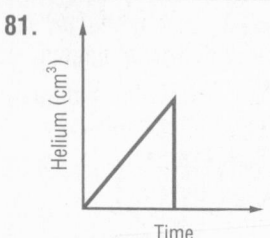

82.

Earth Years	Mars Years
5	2.7
10	5.4
15	8.1
20	10.8
25	13.5

83.

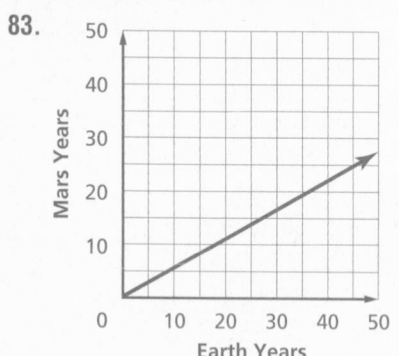

Answers (page 63)

14–15. See below right.

19. Running for 15 minutes does not mean you can run for a few hours.

21.

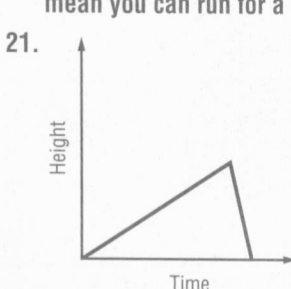

22.

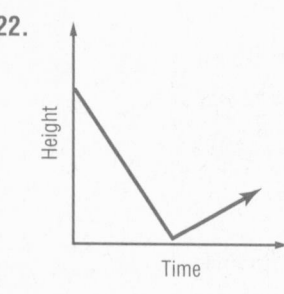

---

81. Sketch a reasonable graph that represents the amount of helium in a balloon if it is filled until it bursts. *See Examples 3–5 on pages 44 and 45.* **See margin.**

For Exercises 82 and 83, use the following information.
The planet Mars takes longer to orbit the sun than does Earth. One year on Earth is about 0.54 year on Mars. *See Examples 4 and 5 on page 45.*

82. Construct a table showing the relationship between years on Earth and years on Mars. **See margin for sample answer.**

83. Draw a graph showing the relationship between Earth years and Mars years. **See margin.**

1-9 Statistics: Analyzing Data by Using Tables and Graphs

See pages 50–55.

Concept Summary

• Bar graphs are used to compare different categories of data.
• Circle graphs are used to show data as parts of a whole set of data.
• Line graphs are used to show the change in data over time.

Example The bar graph shows ways people communicate with their friends.

a. **About what percent of those surveyed chose e-mail as their favorite way to talk to friends?**

The bar for e-mail is about halfway between 30% and 40%. Thus, about 35% favor e-mail.

b. **What is the difference in the percent of people favoring letters and those favoring the telephone?**

The bar for those favoring the telephone is at 60%, and the bar for letters is about 20%. So, the difference is 60 − 20 or 40%.

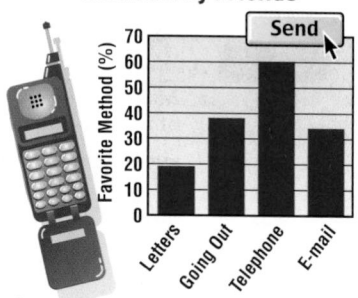

Favorite Method of Contacting Friends

Source: *USA TODAY*

Exercises

CLASS TRIP For Exercises 84 and 85, use the circle graph and the following information.
A survey of the ninth grade class asked members to indicate their choice of locations for their class trip. The results of the survey are displayed in the circle graph. *See Example 2 on page 51.*

84. If 120 students were surveyed, how many chose the amusement park? **54**

85. If 180 students were surveyed, how many more chose the amusement park than the water park? **36**

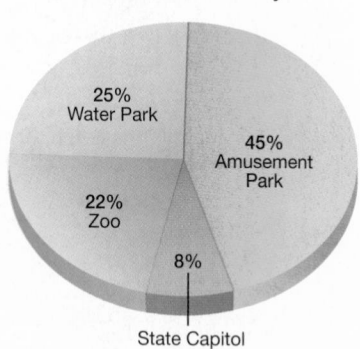

9th Grade Class Survey

---

14. $3^2 - 2 + (2 - 2)$
$= 3^2 - 2 + 0$ Substitution
$= 9 - 2 + 0$ Substitution
$= 7 + 0$ Substitution
$= 7$ Additive Identity

15. $(2 \cdot 2 - 3) + 2^2 + 3^2$
$= (4 - 3) + 2^2 + 3^2$ Substitution
$= 1 + 2^2 + 3^2$ Substitution
$= 1 + 4 + 3^2$ Substitution
$= 1 + 4 + 9$ Substitution
$= 5 + 9$ Substitution
$= 14$ Substitution

Vocabulary and Concepts

Choose the letter of the property that best matches each statement.

1. For any number a, $a = a$. **d**

2. For any numbers a and b, if $a = b$, then b may be replaced by a in any expression or equation. **a**

3. For any numbers a, b, and c, if $a = b$ and $b = c$, then $a = c$. **c**

a. Substitution Property of Equality
b. Symmetric Property of Equality
c. Transitive Property of Equality
d. Reflexive Property of Equality

Skills and Applications

Write an algebraic expression for each verbal expression.

4. the sum of a number x and 13 $x + 13$

5. the difference of 7 and a number x squared $7 - x^2$

Simplify each expression.

6. $5(9 + 3) - 3 \cdot 4$ **48**

7. $12 \cdot 6 \div 3 \cdot 2 \div 8$ **6**

Evaluate each expression if $a = 2$, $b = 5$, $c = 3$, and $d = 1$.

8. $a^2b + c$ **23**

9. $(cd)^3$ **27**

10. $(a + d)c$ **9**

Solve each equation.

11. $y = (4.5 + 0.8) - 3.2$ **2.1**

12. $4^2 - 3(4 - 2) = x$ **10**

13. $\dfrac{2^3 - 1^3}{2 + 1} = n$ $\dfrac{7}{3}$ or $2\dfrac{1}{3}$

Evaluate each expression. Name the property used in each step. 14–15. See margin.

14. $3^2 - 2 + (2 - 2)$

15. $(2 \cdot 2 - 3) + 2^2 + 3^2$

Rewrite each expression in simplest form.

16. $2m + 3m$ **5m**

17. $4x + 2y - 2x + y$ **2x + 3y**

18. $3(2a + b) - 5a + 4b$ **a + 7b**

Find a counterexample for each conditional statement.

19. If you run fifteen minutes today, then you will be able to run a marathon tomorrow. **See margin.**

20. If $x \le 6$, then $2x - 3 < 9$. $x = 6$

Sketch a reasonable graph for each situation. 21–22. See margin.

21. A basketball is shot from the free throw line and falls through the net.

22. A nickel is dropped on a stack of pennies and bounces off.

ICE CREAM For Exercises 23 and 24, use the following information.
A school survey at West High School determined the favorite flavors of ice cream are chocolate, vanilla, butter pecan, and bubble gum. The results of the survey are displayed in the circle graph.

23. If 200 students were surveyed, how many more chose chocolate than vanilla? **60**

24. What was the total percent of students who chose either chocolate or vanilla? **94%**

25. **STANDARDIZED TEST PRACTICE** Which number is a counterexample for the statement below? **D**

If a is a prime number, then a is odd.

Ⓐ 5   Ⓑ 4   Ⓒ 3   Ⓓ 2

Favorite Ice Cream

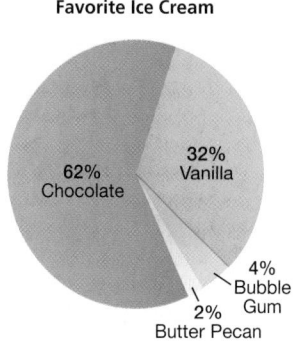

62% Chocolate
32% Vanilla
4% Bubble Gum
2% Butter Pecan

Assessment Options

Vocabulary Test A vocabulary test/review for Chapter 1 can be found on p. 68 of the *Chapter 1 Resource Masters.*

Chapter Tests There are six Chapter 1 Tests and an Open-Ended Assessment task available in the *Chapter 1 Resource Masters.*

Chapter 1 Tests			
Form	**Type**	**Level**	**Pages**
1	MC	basic	55–56
2A	MC	average	57–58
2B	MC	average	59–60
2C	FR	average	61–62
2D	FR	average	63–64
3	FR	advanced	65–66

MC = multiple-choice questions
FR = free-response questions

Open-Ended Assessment
Performance tasks for Chapter 1 can be found on p. 67 of the *Chapter 1 Resource Masters.* A sample scoring rubric for these tasks appears on p. A34.

 ExamView® Pro

Use the networkable **ExamView® Pro** to:

- Create **multiple versions** of tests.
- Create **modified** tests for *Inclusion* students.
- **Edit** existing questions and **add** your own questions.
- Use built-in **state curriculum correlations** to create tests aligned with state standards.
- Change **English** tests to **Spanish** and vice versa.

Portfolio Suggestion

Introduction Do you organize your work well enough that you can pick it up days or weeks later and understand what you were doing? Could another person pick up your work and understand what you were doing?

Ask Students Find an example of your work that you have done for Chapter 1 that is well organized, and list the qualities that make it so. Then find an example of your work that is not so well organized and list what you could have done to make it so. Place both of these in your portfolio.

Chapter 1 Standardized Test Practice

These two pages contain practice questions in the various formats that can be found on the most frequently given standardized tests.

A practice answer sheet for these two pages can be found on p. A1 of the *Chapter 1 Resource Masters*.

Standardized Test Practice
Student Recording Sheet, p. A1

Part 1 *Multiple Choice*

Select the best answer from the choices given and fill in the corresponding oval.

1. Ⓐ Ⓑ Ⓒ Ⓓ   4. Ⓐ Ⓑ Ⓒ Ⓓ   7. Ⓐ Ⓑ Ⓒ Ⓓ
2. Ⓐ Ⓑ Ⓒ Ⓓ   5. Ⓐ Ⓑ Ⓒ Ⓓ   8. Ⓐ Ⓑ Ⓒ Ⓓ
3. Ⓐ Ⓑ Ⓒ Ⓓ   6. Ⓐ Ⓑ Ⓒ Ⓓ

Part 2 *Short Response/Grid In*

Solve the problem and write your answer in the blank.

For Questions 9–11, also enter your answer by writing each number or symbol in a box. Then fill in the corresponding oval for that number or symbol.

9. _____ (grid in)
10. _____ (grid in)
11. _____ (grid in)
12. _____
13. _____
14. _____

Part 3 *Extended Response*

Record your answers for Questions 15–16 on the back of this paper.

Teaching Tip Decimal answers in grid-in questions begin with the decimal point instead of 0.

Additional Practice

See pp. 73–74 in the *Chapter 1 Resource Masters* for additional standardized test practice.

The items on the Standardized Test Practice pages were created to closely parallel those on actual state proficiency tests and college entrance exams, like PSAT, ACT and SAT.

Part 1 | Multiple Choice

Record your answers on the answer sheet provided by your teacher or on a sheet of paper.

1. The Maple Grove Warehouse measures 800 feet by 200 feet. If $\frac{3}{4}$ of the floor space is covered, how many square feet are *not* covered? (Prerequisite Skill) **B**

   Ⓐ 4000   Ⓑ 40,000
   Ⓒ 120,000   Ⓓ 160,000

2. The radius of a circular flower garden is 4 meters. How many meters of edging will be needed to surround the garden? (Prerequisite Skill) **C**

   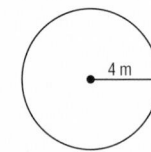
   4 m

   Ⓐ 7.14 m   Ⓑ 12.56 m
   Ⓒ 25.12 m   Ⓓ 20.24 m

3. The Johnson family spends about $80 per week on groceries. Approximately how much do they spend on groceries per year? (Prerequisite Skill) **B**

   Ⓐ $400   Ⓑ $4000
   Ⓒ $8000   Ⓓ $40,000

4. Daria is making 12 party favors for her sister's birthday party. She has 50 stickers, and she wants to use as many of them as possible. If she puts the same number of stickers in each bag, how many stickers will she have left over? (Prerequisite Skill) **A**

   Ⓐ 2   Ⓑ 4   Ⓒ 6   Ⓓ 8

Test-Taking Tip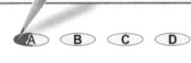

Questions 1, 3, and 8
Read each question carefully. Be sure you understand what the question asks. Look for words like *not*, *estimate*, and *approximately*.

---

5. An auto repair shop charges $36 per hour, plus the cost of replaced parts. Which of the following expressions can be used to calculate the total cost of repairing a car, where *h* represents the number of hours of work and the cost of replaced parts is $85? (Lesson 1-1) **D**

   Ⓐ $36 + h + 85$ Ⓑ $(85 \times h) + 36$
   Ⓒ $36 + 85 \times h$ Ⓓ $(36 \times h) + 85$

6. Which expression is equivalent to $3(2x + 3) + 2(x + 1)$? (Lessons 1-5 and 1-6) **D**

   Ⓐ $7x + 8$ Ⓑ $8x + 4$
   Ⓒ $8x + 9$ Ⓓ $8x + 11$

7. Find a counterexample for the following statement. (Lesson 1-7)
   If x is a positive integer, then x^2 is divisible by 2. **B**

   Ⓐ 2   Ⓑ 3   Ⓒ 4   Ⓓ 6

8. The circle graph shows the regions of birth of foreign-born persons in the United States in 2000. According to the graph, which statement is *not* true? (Lesson 1-9) **B**

   Regions of Birth

   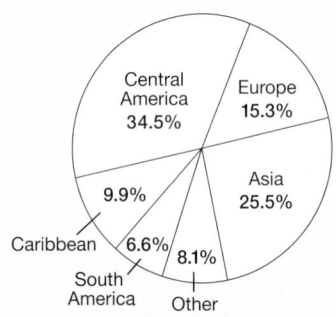

   Ⓐ More than $\frac{1}{3}$ of the foreign-born population is from Central America.

   Ⓑ More foreign-born people are from Asia than Central America.

   Ⓒ About half of the foreign-born population comes from Central America or Europe.

   Ⓓ About half of the foreign-born population comes from Central America, South America, or the Caribbean.

ExamView® Pro

Special banks of standardized test test questions similar to those on the SAT, ACT, TIMSS 8, NAEP 8, and Algebra 1 End-of-Course tests can be found on this CD-ROM.

Preparing for Standardized Tests
For test-taking strategies and more
practice, see pages 867–884.

Part 2 Short Response/Grid In

Record your answers on the answer sheet provided by your teacher or on a sheet of paper.

9. There are 32 students in the class. Five eighths of the students are girls. How many boys are in the class? (Prerequisite Skill) **12**

10. Tonya bought two paperback books. One book cost $8.99 and the other $13.99. Sales tax on her purchase was 6%. How much change should she receive if she gives the clerk $25? (Prerequisite Skill) **.64**

11. Refer to the bar graph. In which year was the difference between the number of home runs hit by the two players the least? (Prerequisite Skill) **1999**

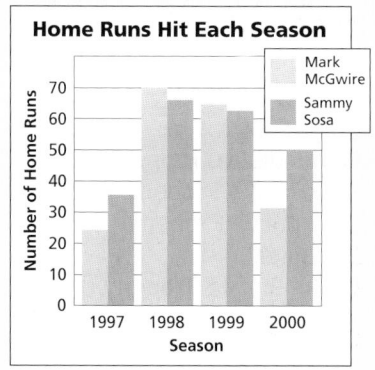

Home Runs Hit Each Season

12. Sample answer: the quotient of *x* squared and the quantity *y* plus 5

12. Write a verbal expression for $\frac{x^2}{y+5}$. (Lesson 1-1)

13. Write $7 \cdot 7 \cdot 7 \cdot a \cdot a \cdot a \cdot a \cdot a$ using exponents. (Lesson 1-1) $7^3 a^5$

14. Find the perimeter of the triangle. (Lesson 1-5) $9p - 5q + 10$

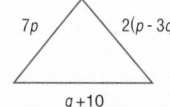

Part 3 Extended Response

Record your answers on a sheet of paper. Show your work.

15. The Lee family is going to play miniature golf. The family is composed of two adults and four children. (Lesson 1-3)

	Greens Fees	
	before 6 P.M.	after 6 P.M.
Adult (*a*)	$5.00	$6.50
Children (*c*)	$3.00	$4.50

a. Write an inequality to show the cost for the family to play miniature golf if they don't want to spend more than $30. $2a + 4c \le 30$

b. How much will it cost the family to play after 6 P.M.? **$31**

c. How much will it cost the family to play before 6 P.M.? **$22**

16. Workers are draining water from a pond. They have an old pump and a new pump. The graphs below show how each pump drains water. (Lesson 1-8) **a–c. See margin.**

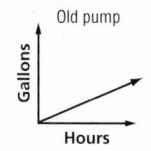 

a. Describe how the old and new pumps are different in the amount of water they pump per hour.

b. Draw a graph that shows the gallons pumped per hour by both pumps at the same time.

c. Explain what the graph below tells about how the water is pumped out.

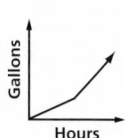

Evaluating Extended Response Questions

Extended Response questions are graded by using a multilevel rubric that guides you in assessing a student's knowledge of a particular concept.

Goal: Compare graphs of rates.

Sample Scoring Rubric: The following rubric is a sample scoring device. You may wish to add more detail to this sample to meet your individual scoring needs.

Score	Criteria
4	A correct solution that is supported by well-developed, accurate explanations
3	A generally correct solution, but may contain minor flaws in reasoning or computation
2	A partially correct interpretation and/or solution to the problem
1	A correct solution with no supporting evidence or explanation
0	An incorrect solution indicating no mathematical understanding of the concept or task, or no solution is given

Answers

16a. Sample answer: The new pump pumps many more gallons per hour than the old pump. The new pump pumps about twice as many gallons per hour as the old pump.

16b.

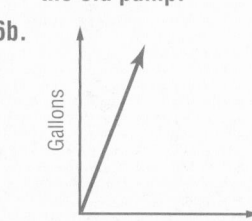

16c. This graph shows that only the old pump was pumping at first, and then after some hours the new pump started pumping also.

12. Multiplicative identity; 1

13. Multiplicative identity; 5

14. Reflexive; 5

15. Reflexive; 0.25

16. Additive identity; 0

17. Additive identity; $\frac{1}{3}$

18. Multiplicative inverse; $\frac{1}{2}$

19. Multiplicative inverse; 1

20. Substitution; 5

21. Substitution; 3

22. Multiplicative identity; 3

23. Multiplicative identity; 2

24. $\frac{3}{4}[4 \div (7 - 4)]$

$= \frac{3}{4}(4 \div 3)$ Substitution

$= \frac{3}{4} \cdot \frac{4}{3}$ Substitution

$= 1$ Multiplicative Inverse

25. $\frac{2}{3}[3 \div (2 \cdot 1)]$

$= \frac{2}{3}(3 \div 2)$ Multiplicative Identity

$= \frac{2}{3} \cdot \frac{3}{2}$ Substitution

$= 1$ Multiplicative Inverse

26. $2(3 \cdot 2 - 5) + 3 \cdot \frac{1}{3}$

$= 2(6 - 5) + 3 \cdot \frac{1}{3}$ Substitution

$= 2(1) + 3 \cdot \frac{1}{3}$ Substitution

$= 2 + 3 \cdot \frac{1}{3}$ Multiplicative Identity

$= 2 + 1$ Multiplicative Inverse

$= 3$ Substitution

27. $6 \cdot \frac{1}{6} + 5(12 \div 4 - 3)$

$= 6 \cdot \frac{1}{6} + 5(3 - 3)$ Substitution

$= 6 \cdot \frac{1}{6} + 5(0)$ Substitution

$= 6 \cdot \frac{1}{6} + 0$ Mult. Property of Zero

$= 1 + 0$ Multiplicative Inverse

$= 1$ Additive Identity

28. $3 + 5(4 - 2^2) - 1$

$= 3 + 5(4 - 4) - 1$ Substitution

$= 3 + 5(0) - 1$ Substitution

$= 3 + 0 - 1$ Mult. Property of Zero

$= 3 - 1$ Additive Identity

$= 2$ Substitution

29. $7 - 8(9 - 3^2)$

$= 7 - 8(9 - 9)$ Substitution

$= 7 - 8(0)$ Substitution

$= 7 - 0$ Mult. Property of Zero

$= 7$ Additive Identity

30. $25(5 - 3) + 80(2.5 - 1) + 40(10 - 6)$

31. $25(5 - 3) + 80(2.5 - 1) + 40(10 - 6)$

$= 25(2) + 80(2.5 - 1) + 40(10 - 6)$ Subst.

$= 25(2) + 80(1.5) + 40(10 - 6)$ Subst.

$= 25(2) + 80(1.5) + 40(4)$ Subst.

$= 50 + 120 + 160$ Subst.

$= 330$ Subst.

Page 29, Lesson 1-5

1. Sample answer: The numbers inside the parentheses are each multiplied by the number outside the parentheses then the products are added.

Page 35, Lesson 1-6

44. $2(s + t) - s$

$= 2s + 2t - s$ Distributive Property

$= 2t + 2s - s$ Commutative Property (+)

$= 2t + s(2 - 1)$ Distributive Property

$= 2t + s(1)$ Substitution

$= 2t + s$ Multiplicative Identity

$= s + 2t$ Commutative Property (+)

45. $5(xy) + 3xy$

$= 5(xy) + 3(xy)$ Associative Property ($\times$)

$= xy(5 + 3)$ Distributive Property

$= xy(8)$ Substitution

$= 8xy$ Commutative Property ($\times$)

46. $6z^2 + (7 + z^2 + 6)$

$= 6z^2 + (z^2 + 7 + 6)$ Commutative Property (+)

$= (6z^2 + z^2) + (7 + 6)$ Associative Property (+)

$= z^2(6 + 1) + (7 + 6)$ Distributive Property

$= z^2(7) + 13$ Substitution

$= 7z^2 + 13$ Commutative Property (+)

47. $6(x + y^2) - 3\left(x + \frac{1}{2}y^2\right)$

$= 6x + 6y^2 - 3x - 3\left(\frac{1}{2}y^2\right)$ Distributive Property

$= 6x - 3x + 6y^2 - \frac{3}{2}y^2$ Commutative Prop. (+)

$= x(6 - 3) + y^2\left(6 - \frac{3}{2}\right)$ Distributive Property

$= x(3) + y^2\left(4\frac{1}{2}\right)$ Substitution

$= 3x + 4\frac{1}{2}y^2$ Commutative Prop. (+)

49. You can use the Commutative and Associative Properties to rearrange and group numbers for easier calculations. Answers should include the following.

• $d = (0.4 + 1.1) + (1.5 + 1.5) + (1.9 + 1.8 + 0.8)$

Pages 46–48, Lesson 1-8

14. (0, 1), (1, 1), (2, 2), (3, 2), (4, 4), (5, 4), (6, 5), (7, 5), (8, 5), (9, 5), (10, 5), (11, 5), (12, 30), (13, 30), (14, 30), (15, 30), (16, 30), (17, 30), (18, 30), (19, 30), (20, 30), (21, 30), (22, 30), (23, 30), (24, 30), (25, 45), (26, 45), (27, 45), (28, 45), (29, 45), (30, 45), (31, 45), (32, 45), (33, 45), (34, 45), (35, 45), (36, 45)

15.

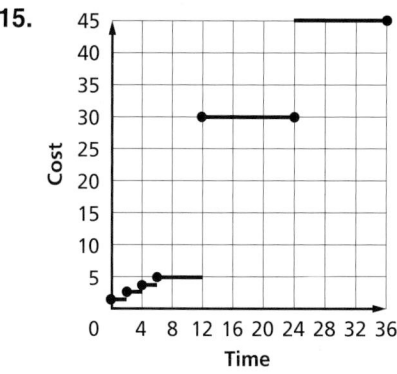

17. The independent variable is the number of sides and the dependent variable is the sum of the angle measures.

18.

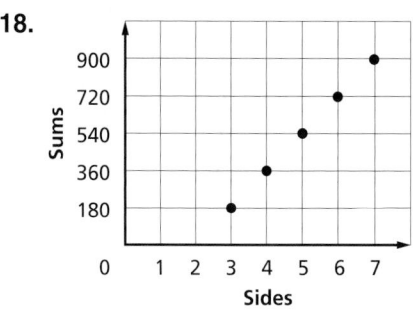

20. **21.**

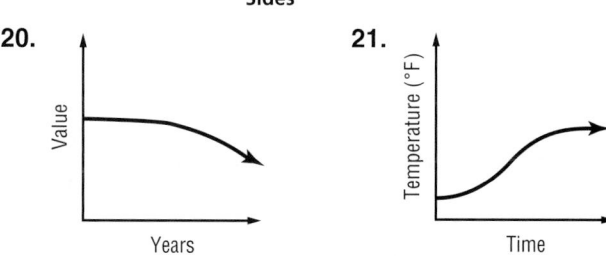

32. U.S. Commercial Radio Stations by Format, 2000

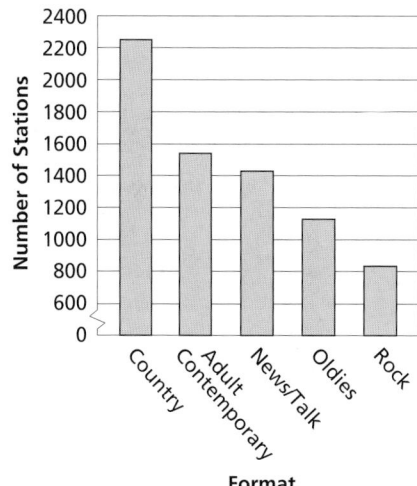

Page 49, Follow-Up of Lesson 1-8
Algebra Activity

5.

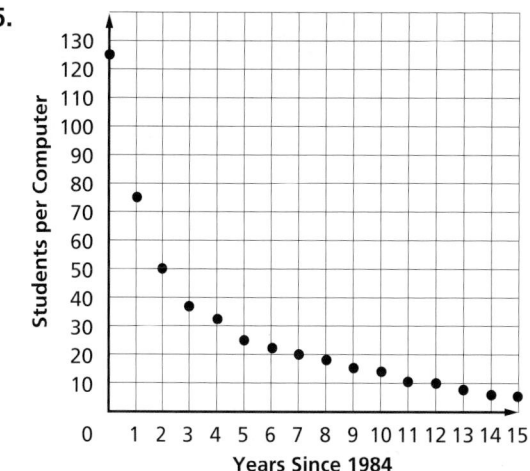

A prediction is 1 student per computer because it does not seem likely that schools would have more computers than students.

Page 56, Follow-Up of Lesson 1-9
Spreadsheet Investigation

1. Snowmobile Sales

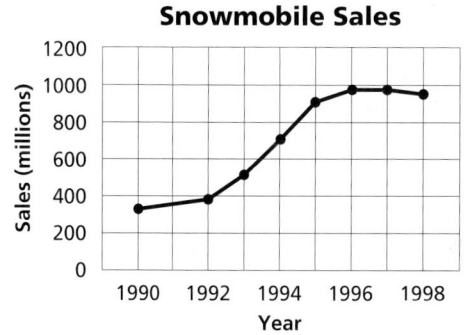

2. Snowmobile Sales

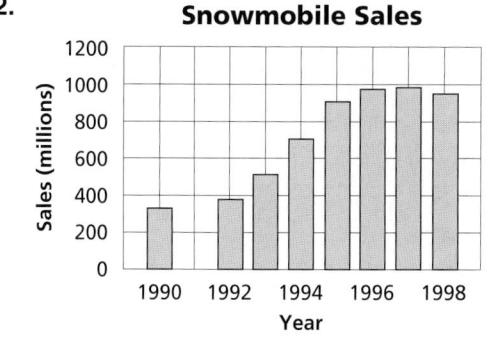

Additional Answers for Chapter 1

Year-long and two-year pacing: pages T20–T21.

LESSON OBJECTIVES

LESSON OBJECTIVES	PACING (days)			
	Regular		Block	
	Basic/ Average	Advanced	Basic/ Average	Advanced
2-1 Rational Numbers on the Number Line *(pp. 68–72)* • Graph rational numbers on a number line. • Find absolute values of rational numbers.	1	optional	0.5	optional
2-2 Adding and Subtracting Rational Numbers *(pp. 73–78)* • Add integers and rational numbers. • Subtract integers and rational numbers.	2	optional	1	optional
2-3 Multiplying Rational Numbers *(pp. 79–83)* • Multiply integers. • Multiply rational numbers.	1	optional	0.5	optional
2-4 Dividing Rational Numbers *(pp. 84–87)* • Divide integers. • Divide rational numbers.	1	optional	0.5	optional
2-5 Statistics: Displaying and Analyzing Data *(pp. 88–94)* • Interpret and create line plots and stem-and-leaf plots. • Analyze data using mean, median, and mode.	1	optional	1	optional
2-6 Probability: Simple Probability and Odds *(pp. 96–102)* • Find the probability of a simple event. • Find the odds of a simple event. *Follow-Up:* Use tables to investigate probability and Pascal's Triangle.	2 (with 2-6 Follow-Up)	optional	1 (with 2.6 Follow-Up)	optional
2-7 Square Roots and Real Numbers *(pp. 103–109)* • Find square roots. • Classify and order real numbers.	1	optional	0.5	optional
Study Guide and **Practice Test** *(pp. 110–115)* **Standardized Test Practice** *(pp. 116–117)*	1	3	0.5	1
Chapter Assessment	1	1	0.5	0
TOTAL	**11**	**4**	**6**	**1**

*An electronic version of this chapter is available on **StudentWorks**™. This backpack solution CD-ROM allows students instant access to the Student Edition, lesson worksheet pages, and web resources.*

Chapter Resource Manager

CHAPTER 2 RESOURCE MASTERS

Study Guide and Intervention	Practice (Skills and Average)	Reading to Learn Mathematics	Enrichment	Assessment	Prerequisite Skills Workbook	Applications*	Parent and Student Study Guide Workbook	5-Minute Check Transparencies	Interactive Chalkboard	AlgePASS: Tutorial Plus (lessons)	Materials
75–76	77–78	79	80		1–4, 15–16, 19–20, 45–46, 55–56, 63–66, 75–76	SM 33–36	11	2-1	2-1		
81–82	83–84	85	86	131	15–16, 19–24, 39–40, 55–60, 65–66, 75–76	GCS 26	12	2-2	2-2		
87–88	89–90	91	92		15–16, 19–20, 25–28, 39–40, 47–50, 65–66, 75–76	SC 3	13	2-3	2-3		
93–94	95–96	97	98	131, 133	15–16, 19–20, 29–32, 39–40, 47–48, 51–54, 63–66, 75–76	SC 4	14	2-4	2-4	3	
99–100	101–102	103	104		15–16, 61–62, 75–76		15	2-5	2-5		grid paper
105–106	107–108	109	110	132	17–18, 37–38, 67–70, 99–100		16	2-6	2-6		
111–112	113–114	115	116	132	75–76	GCS 25	17	2-7	2-7		grid paper
				117–130, 134–136			18				

Key to Abbreviations: GCS = Graphing Calculator and Spreadsheet Masters,
SC = School-to-Career Masters,
SM = Science and Mathematics Lab Manual

ELL Study Guide and Intervention, Skills Practice, Practice, and Parent and Student Study Guide Workbooks are also available in Spanish.

Mathematical Connections and Background

Continuity of Instruction

Prior Knowledge

In previous courses, students learned to perform the operations of adding, subtracting, multiplying, and dividing with whole numbers. They also found square roots of whole numbers. In Chapter 1, students simplified expressions using the order of operations, the Distributive, Commutative, and Associative Properties.

This Chapter

This chapter explores basic operations with rational numbers. The number line is used as a model to develop rules for addition and subtraction of real numbers. Rules for multiplying and dividing rational numbers are also explored, as well as finding square roots. Students also create and use the statistical tools of line plots and stem-and-leaf plots to solve problems involving the measures of central tendency. Probability and odds of simple events are also explored.

Future Connections

The rules for adding, subtracting, multiplying, dividing, and finding the square root of rational numbers are essential to simplifying and solving equations correctly. Creating line plots and stem-and-leaf plots will help students better understand data in the future.

2-1 Rational Numbers on the Number Line

Natural numbers, whole numbers, and integers can be shown on a number line. Rational numbers, numbers that can be expressed in the form of $\frac{a}{b}$ where b does not equal 0, can also be displayed on number lines. Positive numbers are to the right of 0, and negative numbers are to the left of 0. Number lines can help students with the concept of absolute value. When a number is graphed on a number line, students can see the distance that number is from 0. When evaluating expressions containing an absolute value, treat the absolute value bars as a grouping symbol.

2-2 Adding and Subtracting Rational Numbers

Number lines can be used to add rational numbers. Start at the first number in an expression, and then move right when adding positive numbers or left when adding negative numbers. Students soon understand that if the signs of the numbers are the same, they are to add the absolute values and the sum has the same sign as the addends. If the signs are different, subtract absolute values and the sum has the sign of the number with the greater absolute value.

The additive inverse of a rational number is its opposite. When you add a number and its additive inverse, the sum is 0. To subtract rational numbers, rewrite the expression to add the inverse of the second number. Then use a number line or the rules for addition.

2-3 Multiplying Rational Numbers

Multiplication is a representation of repeated addition of the same number. This concept can be used to arrive at the rules for multiplying rational numbers. Tables of repeated addition of the same number can be used to verify the "rules" for multiplying a positive number by either a negative or a positive number. The product of two negative numbers can be explained as the opposite of the result of a positive times a negative.

2-4 Dividing Rational Numbers

Multiplication and division are inverse operations. Therefore, they share the same rules. If the two numbers have the same sign, the quotient is positive. If the signs are different, the quotient is negative.

A fraction bar represents division. It is also considered a grouping symbol. Be sure to simplify the numerator and denominator separately before dividing the numerator by the denominator. One method for dividing is to multiply by the reciprocal of the second number.

2-5 Statistics: Displaying and Analyzing Data

Line plots are used to compare data. They resemble a number line with Xs written in columns above their corresponding numbers on the number line. The number line must contain all of the data and use a scale with equal intervals. The Xs represent the frequency of a number in a specific set of data.

Stem-and-leaf plots are another representation of frequency, but of numbers in a category, not the numbers themselves. The greatest common place value is used for the stems, and the numbers in the next greatest place value are written as the leaves.

Measures of central tendency are numbers that help analyze data. Mean, median, and mode are the most common. Carefully choose which measure of central tendency best describes a set of data. An outlier can affect the mean and not affect the median or mode. A number with a high frequency of repetition can cause the mode to be a poor representation of the data. If most numbers in a set of data are relatively close in value with a few extreme outliers, the median can be too low or too high.

2-6 Probability: Simple Probability and Odds

Probability describes the likelihood of an event happening. The list of all possible outcomes of an event is referred to as the sample space. The probability of an event is a comparison, in ratio form, of the number of favorable outcomes to the total number of possible outcomes for the event. The ratio can be expressed in fraction, decimal, or percent form. The value of the ratio is from 0 to 1. If the probability of an event is 0, then it will never occur. If the probability of an event is 1, then it will always occur.

The odds of an event is a comparison of the number of ways an event can occur to the number of ways it cannot occur.

2-7 Square Roots and Real Numbers

Finding a square root is the inverse of squaring a number. When a number is squared, it is multiplied by itself. The square root is the factor that was multiplied by itself to get the original number. All positive numbers have a positive square root and a negative square root that are additive inverses of each other. When there is no sign in front of a radical sign, find the positive or principal square root only. If a negative sign precedes the radical sign, find the negative square root. A ± sign before the radical sign indicates finding both square roots. There are no real numbers that are square roots of negative numbers.

All the numbers students have studied up to now are real numbers. All real numbers are either rational or irrational. Rational numbers can be written as a ratio and can be expressed as terminating or repeating decimals. Within the set of rational numbers are integers, whole numbers, and natural numbers. Irrational numbers cannot be expressed as terminating or repeating decimals. They go on forever with no repeating pattern. Pi is an irrational number.

Quick Review Math Handbook

Hot Words includes a glossary of terms while Hot Topics consists of explanations of key mathematical concepts with exercises to test comprehension. This valuable resource can be used as a reference in the classroom or for home study.

Lesson	Hot Topics Section	Lesson	Hot Topics Section
GS2	2.3, 2.4, 3.1, 3.4, 4.4, 6.3	2-5	2.1, 4.2, 4.3, 4.4
2-1	1.5, 2.2, 2.3, 2.5	2-6	3.4, 4.5, 4.6
2-2	1.5, 2.3, 2.4, 2.6	2-6F	4.6
2-3	1.5, 2.4, 2.6	2-7	3.2
2-4	1.5, 2.4, 2.6, 4.4		

GS = Getting Started, F = Follow-Up

 Additional mathematical information and teaching notes are available at www.algebra1.com/key_concepts.

DAILY INTERVENTION and Assessment

Key to Abbreviations:
TWE = Teacher Wraparound Edition; CRM = Chapter Resource Masters

	Type	Student Edition	Teacher Resources	Technology/Internet
INTERVENTION	Ongoing	Prerequisite Skills, pp. 67, 72, 78, 83, 87, 94, 101 Practice Quiz 1, p. 83 Practice Quiz 2, p. 101	5-Minute Check Transparencies *Prerequisite Skills Workbook,* pp. 1–4, 15–28, 31–32, 37–40, 45–54, 57–70, 75–76 Quizzes, *CRM* pp. 131–132 Mid-Chapter Test, *CRM* p. 133 Study Guide and Intervention, *CRM* pp. 75–76, 81–82, 87–88, 93–94, 99–100, 105–106, 111–112	AlgePASS: Tutorial Plus, Lesson 3 www.algebra1.com/self_check_quiz www.algebra1.com/extra_examples
	Mixed Review	pp. 72, 78, 83, 87, 94, 101, 109	Cumulative Review, *CRM* p. 134	
	Error Analysis	Find the Error, pp. 76, 98 Common Misconceptions, p. 104	Find the Error, *TWE* pp. 76, 99 Unlocking Misconceptions, *TWE* pp. 70, 91, 97	
ASSESSMENT	Standardized Test Practice	pp. 72, 78, 83, 87, 94, 101, 106, 109, 115, 116–117	*TWE* pp. 116–117 Standardized Test Practice, *CRM* pp. 135–136	Standardized Test Practice CD-ROM www.algebra1.com/standardized_test
	Open-Ended Assessment	Writing in Math, pp. 72, 78, 82, 87, 94, 100, 109 Open Ended, pp. 70, 76, 81, 86, 91, 98, 107 Standardized Test, p. 117	Modeling: *TWE* pp. 72, 109 Speaking: *TWE* pp. 78, 94 Writing: *TWE* pp. 83, 86, 101 Open-Ended Assessment, *CRM* p. 129	
	Chapter Assessment	Study Guide, pp. 110–114 Practice Test, p. 115	Multiple-Choice Tests (Forms 1, 2A, 2B), *CRM* pp. 117–122 Free-Response Tests (Forms 2C, 2D, 3), *CRM* pp. 123–128 Vocabulary Test/Review, *CRM* p. 130	ExamView® Pro (see below) MindJogger Videoquizzes www.algebra1.com/vocabulary_review www.algebra1.com/chapter_test

For more information on Yearly ProgressPro, see p. 2.

Algebra Lesson	Yearly ProgressPro Skill Lesson(s)
2-1	Rational Numbers on the Number Line Absolute Value
2-2	Adding and Subtracting Rational Numbers
2-3	Multiplying Rational Numbers Multiplying Expressions with Variables
2-4	Dividing Rational Numbers Dividing Expressions with Variables
2-5	Displaying and Analyzing Data
2-6	Simple Probability and Odds
2-7	Square Roots Compare Real Numbers

ExamView® Pro

Use the networkable **ExamView® Pro** to:
- Create **multiple versions** of tests.
- Create **modified** tests for *Inclusion* students.
- **Edit** existing questions and **add** your own questions.
- Use built-in **state curriculum correlations** to create tests aligned with state standards.
- Change **English** tests to **Spanish** and vice versa.

For more information on Intervention and Assessment, see pp. T8–T11.

Reading and Writing in Mathematics

Glencoe Algebra 1 provides numerous opportunities to incorporate reading and writing into the mathematics classroom.

Student Edition

- Foldables Study Organizer, p. 67
- Concept Check questions require students to verbalize and write about what they have learned in the lesson. (pp. 70, 76, 81, 86, 91, 98, 107)
- Reading Mathematics, p. 95
- Writing in Math questions in every lesson, pp. 68, 72, 78, 82, 87, 94, 100, 109
- Reading Study Tip, pp. 69, 96, 97, 103
- WebQuest, p. 100

Teacher Wraparound Edition

- Foldables Study Organizer, pp. 67, 110
- Study Notebook suggestions, pp. 70, 76, 81, 85, 91, 95, 99, 102, 107
- Modeling activities, pp. 72, 109
- Speaking activities, pp. 78, 94
- Writing activities, pp. 83, 86, 101
- Differentiated Instruction, (Verbal/Linguistic), p. 72
- **ELL** Resources, pp. 66, 72, 71, 77, 82, 87, 93, 95, 100, 108, 110

Additional Resources

- Vocabulary Builder worksheets require students to define and give examples for key vocabulary terms as they progress through the chapter. (*Chapter 2 Resource Masters,* pp. vii-viii)
- Reading to Learn Mathematics master for each lesson (*Chapter 2 Resource Masters*, pp. 79, 85, 91, 97, 103, 109, 115)
- *Vocabulary PuzzleMaker* software creates crossword, jumble, and word search puzzles using vocabulary lists that you can customize.
- *Teaching Mathematics with Foldables* provides suggestions for promoting cognition and language.
- *Reading and Writing in the Mathematics Classroom*
- *WebQuest and Project Resources*

For more information on Reading and Writing in Mathematics, see pp. T6–T7.

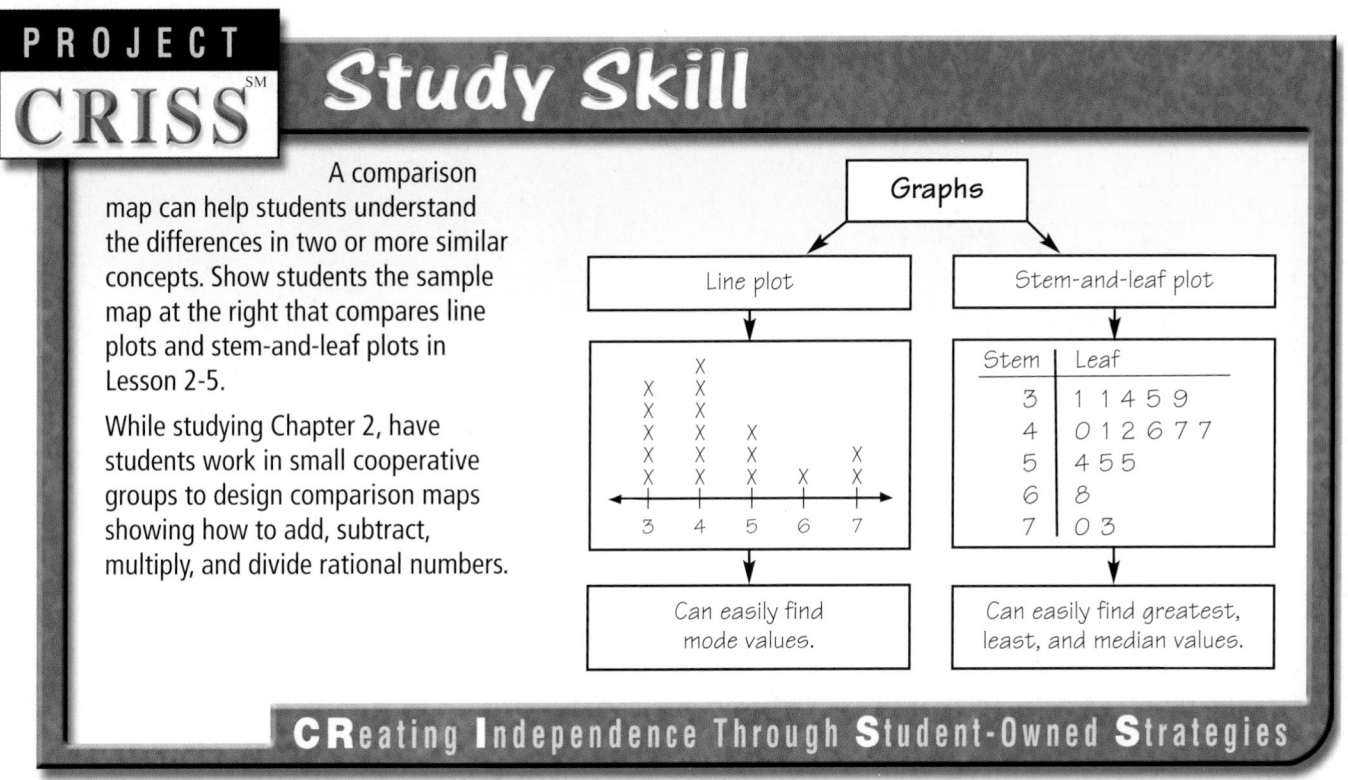

PROJECT CRISS℠ Study Skill

A comparison map can help students understand the differences in two or more similar concepts. Show students the sample map at the right that compares line plots and stem-and-leaf plots in Lesson 2-5.

While studying Chapter 2, have students work in small cooperative groups to design comparison maps showing how to add, subtract, multiply, and divide rational numbers.

CReating **I**ndependence **T**hrough **S**tudent-Owned **S**trategies

What You'll Learn

Have students read over the list of objectives and make a list of any words with which they are not familiar.

Why It's Important

Point out to students that this is only one of many reasons why each objective is important. Others are provided in the introduction to each lesson.

What You'll Learn

- **Lesson 2-1** Classify and graph rational numbers.
- **Lessons 2-2 through 2-4** Add, subtract, multiply, and divide rational numbers.
- **Lesson 2-5** Display and interpret statistical data on line graphs and stem-and-leaf plots.
- **Lesson 2-6** Determine simple probability and odds.
- **Lesson 2-7** Find square roots and compare real numbers.

Key Vocabulary

- rational number (p. 68)
- absolute value (p. 69)
- probability (p. 96)
- square root (p.103)
- real number (p. 104)

Why It's Important

The ability to work with real numbers lays the foundation for further study in mathematics and allows you to solve a variety of real-world problems. For example, temperatures in the United States vary greatly from cold arctic regions to warm tropical regions. You can use real numbers and absolute value to compare these temperature extremes. *You will use absolute value and real numbers to compare temperatures in Lessons 2-1 and 2-2.*

Lesson	NCTM Standards	Local Objectives
2-1	1, 6, 8, 9, 10	
2-2	1, 6, 8, 9, 10	
2-3	1, 6, 8, 9, 10	
2-4	1, 6, 8, 9, 10	
2-5	1, 5, 6, 8, 9, 10	
2-6	1, 5, 6, 7, 8, 9, 10	
2-6 Follow-Up	1, 5, 6, 7, 8, 9, 10	
2-7	1, 6, 8, 9, 10	

Key to NCTM Standards:

1=Number & Operations, 2=Algebra, 3=Geometry, 4=Measurement, 5=Data Analysis & Probability, 6=Problem Solving, 7=Reasoning & Proof, 8=Communication, 9=Connections, 10=Representation

Vocabulary Builder

(ELL)

The Key Vocabulary list introduces students to some of the main vocabulary terms included in this chapter. For a more thorough vocabulary list with pronunciations of new words, give students the Vocabulary Builder worksheets found on pages vii and viii of the *Chapter 2 Resource Masters*. Encourage them to complete the definition of each term as they progress through the chapter. You may suggest that they add these sheets to their study notebooks for future reference when studying for the Chapter 2 test.

Getting Started

▶ **Prerequisite Skills** To be successful in this chapter, you'll need to master these skills and be able to apply them in problem-solving situations. Review these skills before beginning Chapter 2.

For Lessons 2-1 through 2-5 Operations with Decimals and Fractions

Perform the indicated operation. *(For review, see pages 798 and 799.)*

1. $2.2 + 0.16$ **2.36** **2.** $13.4 - 4.5$ **8.9** **3.** $6.4 \cdot 8.8$ **56.32** **4.** $76.5 \div 4.25$ **18**

5. $\frac{1}{4} + \frac{2}{3}$ **$\frac{11}{12}$** **6.** $\frac{1}{2} - \frac{1}{3}$ **$\frac{1}{6}$** **7.** $\frac{5}{4} \cdot \frac{3}{10}$ **$\frac{3}{8}$** **8.** $\frac{4}{9} \div \frac{1}{3}$ **$\frac{4}{3}$ or $1\frac{1}{3}$**

For Lessons 2-1 through 2-5 Evaluate Expressions

Evaluate each expression if $a = 2$, $b = \frac{1}{4}$, $x = 7$, and $y = 0.3$. *(For review, see Lesson 1-2.)*

9. $3a - 2$ **4** **10.** $2x + 5$ **19** **11.** $8(y + 2.4)$ **21.6** **12.** $4(b + 2)$ **9**

13. $a - \frac{1}{2}$ **$1\frac{1}{2}$** **14.** $b + 3$ **$3\frac{1}{4}$** **15.** xy **2.1** **16.** $y(a \div b)$ **2.4**

For Lesson 2-5 Find Mean, Median, and Mode

Find the mean, median, and mode for each set of data. *(For review, see pages 818 and 819.)*

17. 2, 4, 7, 9, 12, 15 **$8\frac{1}{6}$; 8; none** **18.** 23, 23, 23, 12, 12, 14 **18.5** **19.** 7, 19, 2, 7, 4, 9 **8; 7; 7**

For Lesson 2-7 Square Numbers

Simplify. *(For review, see Lesson 1-1.)*

20. 11^2 **121** **21.** 0.9^2 **0.81** **22.** $\left(\frac{2}{3}\right)^2$ **$\frac{4}{9}$** **23.** $\left(\frac{4}{5}\right)^2$ **$\frac{16}{25}$**

Study Organizer

Real Numbers Make this Foldable to help you organize your notes. Begin with a sheet of grid paper.

Step 1 Fold

Fold the short sides to meet in the middle.

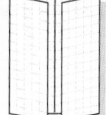

Step 2 Fold Again

Fold the top to the bottom.

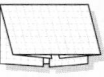

Step 3 Cut

Open. Cut along the second fold to make four tabs.

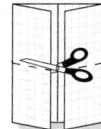

Step 4 Label

Add a number line and label the tabs as shown.

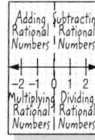

Reading and Writing As you read and study the chapter, use the number line to help you solve problems. Write examples and notes under each tab.

Chapter 2 Real Numbers 67

Getting Started

This section provides a review of the basic concepts needed before beginning Chapter 2. Page references are included for additional student help.

Additional review is provided in the *Prerequisite Skills Workbook*, pp. 1–4, 15–32, 37–40, 45–70, 75–76, 99–100.

Prerequisite Skills in the Getting Ready for the Next Lesson section at the end of each exercise set review a skill needed in the next lesson.

For Lesson	Prerequisite Skill
2-2	Adding and Subtracting Fractions, p. 72
2-3	Multiplying Fractions, p. 78
2-4	Dividing Fractions, p. 83
2-5	Mean, Median, and Mode, p. 87
2-6	Simplifying Fractions, p. 94
2-7	Evaluating Expressions, p. 101

FOLDABLES™
Study Organizer

For more information about Foldables, see *Teaching Mathematics with Foldables*.

Main Ideas and Note Taking Use this Foldable to promote student writing. Note taking is a skill that is based upon listening or reading for main ideas and then recording those ideas for future reference. Under the tabs of the Foldable, have students take notes about what they need to know to add, subtract, multiply, and divide rational numbers. Encourage students to apply these concepts by writing original addition, subtraction, multiplication, and division sentences using real numbers.

1 Focus

5-Minute Check Transparency 2-1 Use as a quiz or a review of Chapter 1.

Mathematical Background notes are available for this lesson on p. 66C.

Building on Prior Knowledge

In previous course material, students learned about fractions, decimals, and negative numbers. In this lesson, they should recognize that rational numbers are a larger set of numbers containing types of numbers that students already know.

How can you use a number line to show data?

Ask students:

- What does a positive change in river level mean? **The level of the river rose.**

- What does a negative change in river level mean? **The level of the river dropped.**

- Do you think any of these rivers are flooding? How do you know? **If any of the rivers were flooding, the river level would likely be greatly increasing.**

What You'll Learn

- Graph rational numbers on a number line.
- Find absolute values of rational numbers.

How can you use a number line to show data?

The table shows the percent of change in river depths for various rivers in Texas over a 24-hour period. You can use a number line to graph these values and compare the changes in each river.

River Report	
River	24-Hour Change (ft)
San Jacinto	+0.3
Sabine	−2.0
Neches	−0.8
Navasota	+0.1
Little	0.0
Brazos	+0.2
Colorado	−0.4
Guadalupe	−2.2

Vocabulary

- natural number
- whole number
- integers
- positive number
- negative number
- rational number
- infinity
- graph
- coordinate
- absolute value

GRAPH RATIONAL NUMBERS A number line can be used to show the sets of **natural numbers**, **whole numbers**, and **integers**. Values greater than 0, or **positive numbers**, are listed to the right of 0, and values less than 0, or **negative numbers**, are listed to the left of 0.

natural numbers:	$1, 2, 3, \ldots$
whole numbers:	$0, 1, 2, 3, \ldots$
integers:	$\ldots, -3, -2, -1, 0, 1, 2, 3, \ldots$

Another set of numbers you can display on a number line is the set of rational numbers. A **rational number** is any number that can be written in the form $\frac{a}{b}$, where a and b are integers and $b \neq 0$. Some examples of rational numbers are shown below.

$$\frac{1}{2} \qquad \frac{-2}{3} \qquad \frac{17}{5} \qquad \frac{15}{-3} \qquad \frac{-14}{-11} \qquad \frac{3}{1}$$

A rational number can also be expressed as a decimal that terminates, or as a decimal that repeats indefinitely.

$$0.5 \qquad -0.\overline{3} \qquad 3.4 \qquad 2.6767\ldots \qquad -5 \qquad 1.\overline{27} \qquad -1.23568994141\ldots$$

Concept Summary — Rational Numbers

Natural Numbers	$\{1, 2, 3, \ldots\}$
Whole Numbers	$\{0, 1, 2, 3, \ldots\}$
Integers	$\{\ldots, -2, -1, 0, 1, 2, \ldots\}$
Rational Numbers	numbers that can be expressed in the form $\frac{a}{b}$, where a and b are integers and $b \neq 0$

Rational Numbers
Integers
Whole Numbers
Natural Numbers

Later in this chapter, you will be introduced to numbers that are not rational.

Resource Manager

 **Workbook and Reproducible Masters**

Chapter 2 Resource Masters
- Study Guide and Intervention, pp. 75–76
- Skills Practice, p. 77
- Practice, p. 78
- Reading to Learn Mathematics, p. 79
- Enrichment, p. 80

Parent and Student Study Guide Workbook, p. 11
Prerequisite Skills Workbook,
pp. 1–4, 15–16, 19–20, 45–46, 55–56, 63–66, 75–76
Science and Mathematics Lab Manual,
pp. 33–36

 Transparencies

5-Minute Check Transparency 2-1
Answer Key Transparencies

 Technology

Interactive Chalkboard

To **graph** a set of numbers means to draw, or plot, the points named by those numbers on a number line. The number that corresponds to a point on a number line is called the **coordinate** of that point.

Example 1 Identify Coordinates on a Number Line

Name the coordinates of the points graphed on each number line.

a.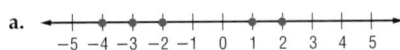
$$-5 \; -4 \; -3 \; -2 \; -1 \quad 0 \quad 1 \quad 2 \quad 3 \quad 4 \quad 5$$

The dots indicate each point on the graph.
The coordinates are $\{-4, -3, -2, 1, 2\}$.

b.
$$-1 \; -0.5 \quad 0 \quad 0.5 \quad 1 \quad 1.5 \quad 2 \quad 2.5 \quad 3$$

The bold arrow on the right means that the graph continues indefinitely in that direction. The coordinates are $\{1, 1.5, 2, 2.5, 3, …\}$.

Example 2 Graph Numbers on a Number Line

Graph each set of numbers.

a. $\{…, -4, -2, 0, 2, 4, 6\}$

$$-4 \; -3 \; -2 \; -1 \quad 0 \quad 1 \quad 2 \quad 3 \quad 4 \quad 5 \quad 6 \quad 7 \quad 8$$

b. $\left\{-\dfrac{4}{3}, -\dfrac{1}{3}, \dfrac{2}{3}, \dfrac{5}{3}\right\}$

$$-\dfrac{5}{3} \; -\dfrac{4}{3} \; -1 \; -\dfrac{2}{3} \; -\dfrac{1}{3} \quad 0 \quad \dfrac{1}{3} \quad \dfrac{2}{3} \quad 1 \quad \dfrac{4}{3} \quad \dfrac{5}{3} \quad 2 \quad \dfrac{7}{3}$$

c. {integers less than −3 or greater than or equal to 5}

$$-5 \; -4 \; -3 \; -2 \; -1 \quad 0 \quad 1 \quad 2 \quad 3 \quad 4 \quad 5 \quad 6 \quad 7$$

ABSOLUTE VALUE On a number line, 4 is four units from zero in the positive direction, and −4 is four units from zero in the negative direction. This number line illustrates the meaning of **absolute value**.

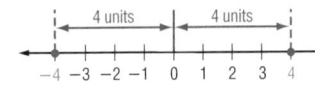
4 units   4 units
$$-4 \; -3 \; -2 \; -1 \quad 0 \quad 1 \quad 2 \quad 3 \quad 4$$

Key Concept — Absolute Value

- **Words** The absolute value of any number n is its distance from zero on a number line and is written as $|n|$.

- **Examples** $|-4| = 4$ $|4| = 4$

Since distance cannot be less than zero, absolute values are always greater than or equal to zero.

Example 3 Absolute Value of Rational Numbers

Find each absolute value.

a. $|-7|$

-7 is seven units from zero in the negative direction.

$|-7| = 7$

 www.algebra1.com/extra_examples

GRAPH RATIONAL NUMBERS

In-Class Examples PowerPoint®

Teaching Tip The real numbers also include the set of irrational numbers, which is introduced in Lesson 2-7.

1 Name the coordinates of the points graphed on each number line.

a.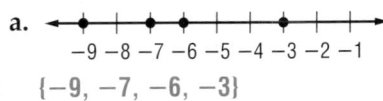
$$-9 \; -8 \; -7 \; -6 \; -5 \; -4 \; -3 \; -2 \; -1$$
$\{-9, -7, -6, -3\}$

b.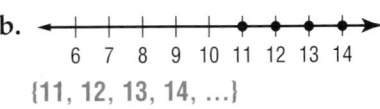
$$6 \quad 7 \quad 8 \quad 9 \quad 10 \quad 11 \quad 12 \quad 13 \quad 14$$
$\{11, 12, 13, 14, …\}$

2 Graph each set of numbers.

a. $\left\{-\dfrac{1}{2}, 0, \dfrac{1}{2}, 1\right\}$

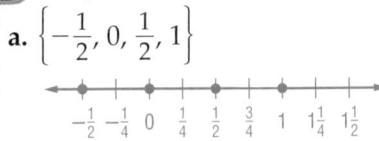
$$-\dfrac{1}{2} \; -\dfrac{1}{4} \quad 0 \quad \dfrac{1}{4} \quad \dfrac{1}{2} \quad \dfrac{3}{4} \quad 1 \quad 1\dfrac{1}{4} \quad 1\dfrac{1}{2}$$

b. $\{-1.5, 0, 1.5, …\}$

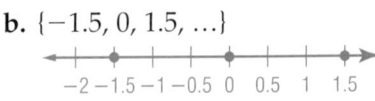
$$-2 \; -1.5 \; -1 \; -0.5 \quad 0 \quad 0.5 \quad 1 \quad 1.5$$

c. {integers less than −6, or greater than or equal to 1}

$$-7 \; -6 \; -5 \; -4 \; -3 \; -2 \; -1 \quad 0 \quad 1 \quad 2$$

ABSOLUTE VALUE

In-Class Example  PowerPoint®

3 Find each absolute value.

a. $\left|-\dfrac{5}{8}\right|$ $\dfrac{5}{8}$

b. $|0.25|$ 0.25

In-Class Example Power Point®

4 Evaluate $|y - 8| + 5$ if $y = 12$. **9**

Teaching Tip After presenting Example 4, give students the expression $|2 - x| - 7$ to evaluate for $x = 5$. **−4** Point out that while absolute values will always be positive, expressions involving absolute value may be negative.

3 Practice/Apply

Study Notebook

Have students—
• add the definitions/examples of the vocabulary terms to their Vocabulary Builder worksheets for Chapter 2.
• include the descriptions of the sets of natural numbers, whole numbers, integers, and rational numbers.
• include any other item(s) that they find helpful in mastering the skills in this lesson.

About the Exercises...

Organization by Objective
• **Graph Rational Numbers:** 18–33, 42, 58
• **Absolute Value:** 34–41, 43–57, 59

Odd/Even Assignments
Exercises 18–41 and 45–56 are structured so that students practice the same concepts whether they are assigned odd or even problems.

Assignment Guide

Basic: 19–41 odd, 42–44, 45–57 odd, 60–77

Average: 19–41 odd, 42–44, 45–57 odd, 60–77

Advanced: 18–40 even, 46–56 even, 57–69 (optional: 70–77)

---

b. $\left|\dfrac{7}{9}\right|$

$\dfrac{7}{9}$ is seven-ninths unit from zero in the positive direction.

$\left|\dfrac{7}{9}\right| = \dfrac{7}{9}$

You can also evaluate expressions involving absolute value. The absolute value bars serve as grouping symbols.

Example 4 Expressions with Absolute Value

Evaluate $15 - |x + 4|$ if $x = 8$.

$15 - |x + 4| = 15 - |8 + 4|$ Replace x with 8.

$= 15 - |12|$ $8 + 4 = 12$

$= 15 - 12$ $|12| = 12$

$= 3$ Simplify.

Check for Understanding

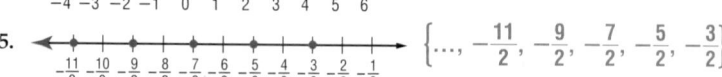

Concept Check

1–3. See pp. 117A–117B.

1. **Tell** whether the statement is *sometimes, always,* or *never* true. *An integer is a rational number.*

2. **Explain** the meaning of absolute value.

3. **OPEN ENDED** Give an example where absolute values are used in a real-life situation.

Guided Practice

GUIDED PRACTICE KEY	
Exercises	Examples
4, 5	1
6–9	2
10–13	3
14–16	4

Name the coordinates of the points graphed on each number line.

4. (number line from −4 to 6) $\{-2, 1, 2, 5\}$

5. (number line) $\left\{\dots, -\dfrac{11}{2}, -\dfrac{9}{2}, -\dfrac{7}{2}, -\dfrac{5}{2}, -\dfrac{3}{2}\right\}$

Graph each set of numbers. 6–9. See pp. 117A–117B.

6. $\{-4, -2, 1, 5, 7\}$ 7. $\{-2.8, -1.5, 0.2, 3.4\}$ 8. $\left\{-\dfrac{1}{2}, 0, \dfrac{1}{4}, \dfrac{2}{5}, \dfrac{5}{3}\right\}$

9. {integers less than or equal to -4}

Find each absolute value.

10. $|-2|$ **2**   11. $|18|$ **18**   12. $|2.5|$ **2.5**   13. $\left|-\dfrac{5}{6}\right|$ $\dfrac{5}{6}$

Evaluate each expression if $x = 18$, $y = 4$, and $z = -0.76$.

14. $57 - |x + 34|$ **5**   15. $19 + |21 - y|$ **36**   16. $|z| - 0.26$ **0.50**

Application

17. **NUMBER THEORY** Copy the Venn diagram at the right. Label the remaining sets of numbers. Then place the numbers -3, -13, 0, 53, $\dfrac{2}{3}$, $-\dfrac{1}{5}$, 0.33, 40, 2.98, -49.98, and $-\dfrac{5}{2}$ in the most specific categories. **See pp. 117A–117B.**

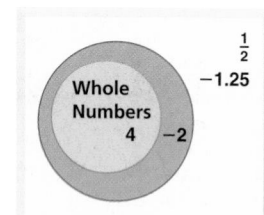

DAILY INTERVENTION **Unlocking Misconceptions**

Absolute Value Many students associate absolute value with opposites. While it is true that the absolute value of n is the opposite of n if n is negative, this definition fails if n is positive or zero. Therefore, it is important for students to think of the absolute value of a number as the distance between that number and zero on a number line.

Study Guide and Intervention, p. 75 (shown) and p. 76

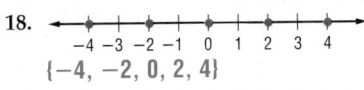

Homework Help

For Exercises	See Examples
18–23	1
24–33	2
34–41	3
42–44, 58, 59	2, 3
45–56	4

Extra Practice
See page 823.

Name the coordinates of the points graphed on each number line.

18.
$-4, -3, -2, -1, 0, 1, 2, 3, 4$
$\{-4, -2, 0, 2, 4\}$

19.
$-8, -7, -6, -5, -4, -3, -2, -1, 0$
$\{-7, -6, -5, -3, -2\}$

20.
$-2, -1, 0, 1, 2, 3, 4, 5, 6$
$\{2, 3, 4, 5, 6, \ldots\}$

21.
$0, 0.2, 0.4, 0.6, 0.8, 1.0, 1.2, 1.4, 1.6$
$\{\ldots, 0, 0.2, 0.4, 0.6, 0.8\}$

22.
$\left\{-2, -\frac{5}{3}, -1, \frac{2}{3}, 1\right\}$

23.
$\left\{\frac{1}{5}, \frac{4}{5}, \frac{7}{5}, \frac{8}{5}, 2\right\}$

Graph each set of numbers. 24–33. See pp. 117A–117B.

24. $\{-4, -2, -1, 1, 3\}$

25. $\{0, 2, 5, 6, 9\}$

26. $\{-5, -4, -3, -2, \ldots\}$

27. $\{\ldots, -2, 0, 2, 4, 6\}$

28. $\{-8.4, -7.2, -6.0, -4.8\}$

29. $\{-2.4, -1.6, -0.8, 0, \ldots\}$

30. $\left\{\ldots, -\frac{2}{3}, -\frac{1}{3}, 0, \frac{1}{3}, \frac{2}{3}, \ldots\right\}$

31. $\left\{-3\frac{2}{5}, -2\frac{1}{5}, -1\frac{4}{5}, -\frac{4}{5}, 1\right\}$

32. {integers less than -7 or greater than -1}

33. {integers greater than -5 and less than 9}

Find each absolute value.

34. $|-38|$ **38**

35. $|10|$ **10**

36. $|97|$ **97**

37. $|-61|$ **61**

38. $|3.9|$ **3.9**

39. $|-6.8|$ **6.8**

40. $\left|-\frac{23}{56}\right|$ $\frac{23}{56}$

41. $\left|\frac{35}{80}\right|$ $\frac{35}{80}$

Career Choices

Demographer

A demographer analyzes the size, nature, and movement of human populations. Many demographers specialize in one area such as health, housing, or education.

Online Research
For information about a career as a demographer, visit www.algebra1.com/careers

POPULATION For Exercises 42–44, refer to the table below. 42. See pp. 117A–117B.

Population of Various Counties, 1990–1999			
County	Percent Change	County	Percent Change
Kings, NY	−1.4	Wayne, MI	−0.2
Los Angeles, CA	5.3	Philadelphia, PA	−10.6
Cuyahoga, OH	−2.9	Suffolk, NY	4.7
Santa Clara, CA	10.0	Alameda, CA	8.5
Cook, IL	1.7	New York, NY	4.3

Source: The World Almanac

42. Use a number line to order the percents of change from least to greatest.

43. Which population had the greatest percent increase or decrease? Explain.

44. Which population had the least percent increase or decrease? Explain.

43. Philadelphia, PA; Sample answer: It had the greatest absolute value.

44. Wayne, MI; Sample answer: It had the least absolute value.

56. $\frac{15}{4}$ or $3\frac{3}{4}$

Evaluate each expression if $a = 6$, $b = \frac{2}{3}$, $c = \frac{5}{4}$, $x = 12$, $y = 3.2$, **and** $z = -5$.

45. $48 + |x - 5|$ **55**

46. $25 + |17 + x|$ **54**

47. $|17 - a| + 23$ **34**

48. $|43 - 4a| + 51$ **70**

49. $|z| + 13 - 4$ **14**

50. $28 - 13 + |z|$ **20**

51. $6.5 - |8.4 - y|$ **1.3**

52. $7.4 + |y - 2.6|$ **8**

53. $\frac{1}{6} + \left|b - \frac{7}{12}\right|$ $\frac{1}{4}$

54. $\left(b + \frac{1}{2}\right) - \left|-\frac{5}{6}\right|$ $\frac{1}{3}$

55. $|c - 1| + \frac{2}{5}$ $\frac{13}{20}$

56. $|-c| + \left(2 + \frac{1}{2}\right)$

57. **CRITICAL THINKING** Find all values for x if $|x| = -|x|$. **0**

Skills Practice, p. 77 and Practice, p. 78 (shown)

Reading to Learn Mathematics, p. 79 ELL

Enrichment, p. 80

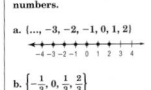
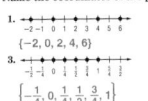
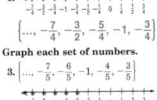

Open-Ended Assessment

Modeling Use masking tape to create a large number line on the floor in front of the classroom. Write sets of numbers on the board and have students stand on the line to "graph" the points. Also write absolute value statements on the board and have students step the "distance" equivalent to the absolute value on the number line.

Getting Ready for Lesson 2-2

PREREQUISITE SKILL Students will learn about adding and subtracting rational numbers in Lesson 2-2. They will apply the rules of adding and subtracting integers to computations with fractions. Use Exercises 70–77 to determine your students' familiarity with the addition and subtraction of fractions.

Answers

58.
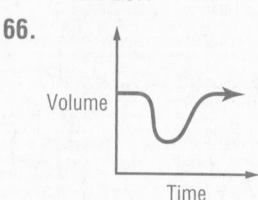
−10 0 10 20 30

59. Bismark, ND 11; Caribou, ME 5; Chicago, IL 4; Fairbanks, AK 9; International Falls, MN 13; Kansas City, MO 7; Sacramento, CA 34; Shreveport, LA 33

60. Sample answer: You can plot the data on a number line to visualize its relationship. Answers should include the following.

• Determine the least and greatest values of the data, and use those as the endpoints of the line.

• Find the absolute value of each number.

66.

Volume

Time

WEATHER For Exercises 58 and 59, use the table at the right.

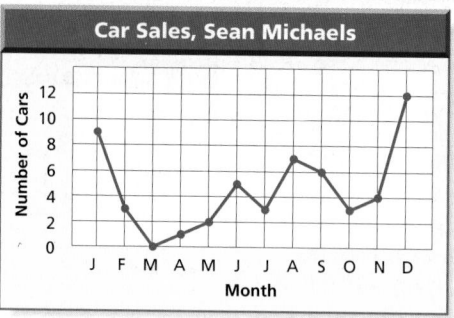

Same Day Low Temperatures for Certain U.S. Cities

City	Low Temperature (°F)
Bismarck, ND	−11
Caribou, ME	−5
Chicago, IL	−4
Fairbanks, AK	−9
International Falls, MN	−13
Kansas City, MO	7
Sacramento, CA	34
Shreveport, LA	33

Source: *The World Almanac*

58. Draw a number line and graph the set of numbers that represents the low temperatures for these cities. **58–59. See margin.**

59. Write the absolute value of the low temperature for each city.

60. **WRITING IN MATH** Answer the question that was posed at the beginning of the lesson. **See margin.**

How can you use a number line to show data?

Include the following in your answer:
• an explanation of how to choose the range for a number line, and
• an explanation of how to tell which river had the greatest increase or decrease.

Standardized Test Practice
Ⓐ Ⓑ Ⓒ Ⓓ

61. Which number is a natural number? **D**

Ⓐ −2.5   Ⓑ $5 − |5|$ Ⓒ $−|3 + 5|$ Ⓓ $|−8| − 2$

62. Which sentence is *not* true? **C**

Ⓐ All natural numbers are whole numbers.
Ⓑ Natural numbers are positive numbers.
Ⓒ Every whole number is a natural number.
Ⓓ Zero is neither positive nor negative.

Maintain Your Skills

Mixed Review **SALES** For Exercises 63–65, refer to the graph. *(Lesson 1-9)*

Car Sales, Sean Michaels

63. In which month did Mr. Michaels have the greatest sales? **December**

64. Between which two consecutive months did the greatest change in sales occur? **Nov. and Dec.**

65. In which months were sales equal? **Feb., July, Oct.**

66. **ENTERTAINMENT** Juanita has the volume on her stereo turned up. When her telephone rings, she turns the volume down. After she gets off the phone, she returns the volume to its previous level. Sketch a reasonable graph to show the volume of Juanita's stereo during this time. *(Lesson 1-8)* **See margin.**

Simplify each expression. *(Lesson 1-6)*

67. $8x + 2y + x$ **9x + 2y**

68. $7(5a + 3b) − 4a$ **31a + 21b**

69. $4[1 + 4(5x + 2y)]$ **4 + 80x + 32y**

Getting Ready for the Next Lesson
PREREQUISITE SKILL Find each sum or difference.
(To review **addition and subtraction of fractions**, see pages 798 and 799.)

70. $\frac{3}{8} + \frac{1}{8}$ $\frac{1}{2}$

71. $\frac{7}{12} − \frac{3}{12}$ $\frac{1}{3}$

72. $\frac{7}{10} + \frac{1}{5}$ $\frac{9}{10}$

73. $\frac{3}{8} + \frac{2}{3}$ $\frac{25}{24}$ or $1\frac{1}{24}$

74. $\frac{5}{6} + \frac{1}{2}$ $\frac{4}{3}$ or $1\frac{1}{3}$

75. $\frac{3}{4} − \frac{1}{3}$ $\frac{5}{12}$

76. $\frac{9}{15} − \frac{1}{2}$ $\frac{1}{10}$

77. $\frac{7}{9} − \frac{7}{18}$ $\frac{7}{18}$

DAILY
INTERVENTION   **Differentiated Instruction**   **ELL**

Verbal/Linguistic Have students look up the word *absolute* in a dictionary and find meanings that relate to the mathematical meaning. Also have them read the definitions of terms beginning with *absolute*, such as *absolute ceiling*, *absolute humidity*, or *absolute pitch*. Have students read aloud the definitions they found and invite students to define in their own words the mathematical meaning of *absolute value* based on any insights they have gained from the dictionary definitions.

Adding and Subtracting Rational Numbers

What You'll Learn

- Add integers and rational numbers.
- Subtract integers and rational numbers.

Vocabulary
- opposites
- additive inverses

How can a number line be used to show a football team's progress?

In one series of plays during Super Bowl XXXV, the New York Giants received a five-yard penalty before completing a 13-yard pass.

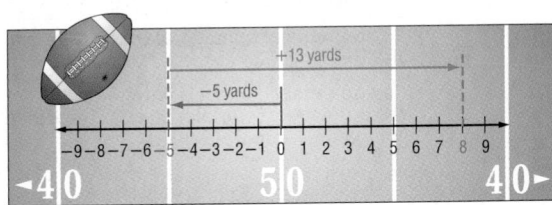

The number line shows the yards gained during this series of plays. The total yards gained was 8 yards.

ADD RATIONAL NUMBERS The number line above illustrates how to add integers on a number line. You can use a number line to add any rational numbers.

Example 1 Use a Number Line to Add Rational Numbers

Use a number line to find each sum.

a. $-3 + (-4)$

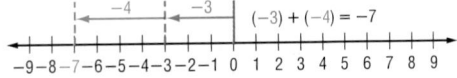

Step 1 Draw an arrow from 0 to -3.

Step 2 Then draw a second arrow 4 units to the left to represent adding -4.

Step 3 The second arrow ends at the sum -7. So, $-3 + (-4) = -7$.

b. $2.5 + (-3.5)$

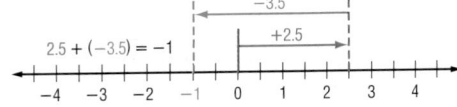

Step 1 Draw an arrow from 0 to 2.5.

Step 2 Then draw a second arrow 3.5 units to the left.

Step 3 The second arrow ends at the sum -1. So, $2.5 + (-3.5) = -1$.

---

1 Focus

 5-Minute Check Transparency 2-2 Use as a quiz or a review of Lesson 2-1.

Mathematical Background notes are available for this lesson on p. 66C.

Building on Prior Knowledge

Apply what students know already from previous courses by demonstrating adding and subtracting positive integers on a number line. In this lesson, students will extend this understanding to add and subtract all rational numbers.

How can a number line be used to show a football team's progress?

Ask students:

- How is a football field similar to a number line? Football fields have yard markers that tell the distance from the goal line, which are similar to the tic marks on a number line that tell the distance to zero.

- How are the yard markers on a football field different from the marks on a number line? The yard markers on a football field increase in number until the 50-yard line, and then they decrease until they reach the opposite goal.

Resource Manager

Workbook and Reproducible Masters

Chapter 2 Resource Masters
- Study Guide and Intervention, pp. 81–82
- Skills Practice, p. 83
- Practice, p. 84
- Reading to Learn Mathematics, p. 85
- Enrichment, p. 86
- Assessment, p. 131

Graphing Calculator and Spreadsheet Masters, p. 26
Parent and Student Study Guide Workbook, p. 12
Prerequisite Skills Workbook, pp. 15–16, 19–24, 39–40, 55–60, 65–66, 75–76

 Transparencies
5-Minute Check Transparency 2-2
Answer Key Transparencies

Technology
Interactive Chalkboard
Multimedia Applications

ADD RATIONAL NUMBERS

In-Class Examples Power Point®

Teaching Tip Tell students that when using a number line to add rational numbers, they should always start at zero. If the first number in the expression is positive, then move to the right. If it is negative, move to the left. Then, if the second number is positive, move to the right and if it is negative, move to the left. The sum is indicated by wherever they end up on the number line.

1 Use a number line to find each sum.

a. $8 + (-5)$ **3**

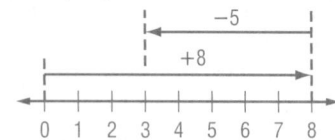

b. $-1 + (-4)$ **−5**

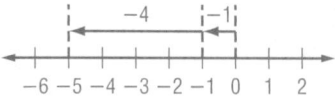

2 Find each sum.

a. $6 + (-14)$ **−8**

b. $-\frac{3}{7} + \left(-\frac{2}{7}\right)$ **$-\frac{5}{7}$**

You can use absolute value to add rational numbers.

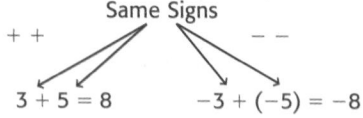 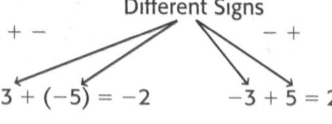

Same Signs   Different Signs
+ +   − −   + −   − +

$3 + 5 = 8$ $-3 + (-5) = -8$ $3 + (-5) = -2$ $-3 + 5 = 2$

3 and 5 are positive, so the sum is positive.

−3 and −5 are negative, so the sum is negative.

Since −5 has the greater absolute value, the sum is negative.

Since 5 has the greater absolute value, the sum is positive.

The examples above suggest the following rules for adding rational numbers.

Key Concept   Addition of Rational Numbers

- To add rational numbers with the *same sign*, add their absolute values. The sum has the same sign as the addends.
- To add rational numbers with *different signs*, subtract the lesser absolute value from the greater absolute value. The sum has the same sign as the number with the greater absolute value.

Example 2 Add Rational Numbers

Find each sum.

a. $-11 + (-7)$

$-11 + (-7) = -(|-11| + |-7|)$ Both numbers are negative, so the sum is negative.

$= -(11 + 7)$

$= -18$

b. $\frac{7}{16} + \left(-\frac{3}{8}\right)$

$\frac{7}{16} + \left(-\frac{3}{8}\right) = \frac{7}{16} + \left(-\frac{6}{16}\right)$ The LCD is 16. Replace $-\frac{3}{8}$ with $-\frac{6}{16}$.

$= +\left(\left|\frac{7}{16}\right| - \left|-\frac{6}{16}\right|\right)$ Subtract the absolute values.

$= +\left(\frac{7}{16} - \frac{6}{16}\right)$ Since the number with the greater absolute value is $\frac{7}{16}$, the sum is positive.

$= \frac{1}{16}$

SUBTRACT RATIONAL NUMBERS Every positive rational number can be paired with a negative rational number. These pairs are called **opposites**.

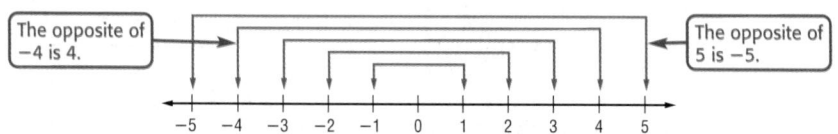

The opposite of −4 is 4.   The opposite of 5 is −5.

A number and its opposite are **additive inverses** of each other. When you add two opposites, the sum is always 0.

Study Tip

Additive Inverse
Since $0 + 0 = 0$, zero is its own additive inverse.

Key Concept — Additive Inverse Property

- **Words**   The sum of a number and its additive inverse is 0.
- **Symbols**   For every number a, $a + (-a) = 0$.
- **Examples** $2 + (-2) = 0$ $-4.25 + 4.25 = 0$ $\dfrac{1}{3} + \left(-\dfrac{1}{3}\right) = 0$

Additive inverses can be used when you subtract rational numbers.

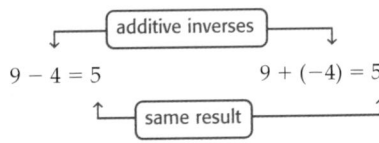

Subtraction	Addition

additive inverses

$$9 - 4 = 5 \qquad\qquad 9 + (-4) = 5$$

same result

This example suggests that subtracting a number is equivalent to adding its inverse.

Key Concept — Subtraction of Rational Numbers

- **Words**   To subtract a rational number, add its additive inverse.
- **Symbols**   For any numbers a and b, $a - b = a + (-b)$.
- **Examples** $8 - 15 = 8 + (-15)$ or -7
  $-7.6 - 12.3 = -7.6 + (-12.3)$ or -19.9

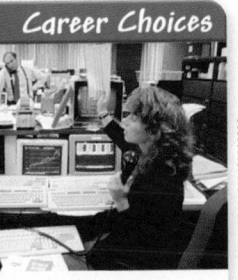

Example 3   Subtract Rational Numbers to Solve a Problem

STOCKS   During a five-day period, a telecommunications company's stock price went from $17.82 to $15.36 per share. Find the change in the price of the stock.

Explore   The stock price began at $17.82 and ended at $15.36. You need to determine the change in price for the week.

Plan   Subtract to find the change in price.

$$\underbrace{15.36}_{\text{ending price}} \;\; \underbrace{-}_{\text{minus}} \;\; \underbrace{17.82}_{\text{beginning price}}$$

Solve

$15.36 - 17.82 = 15.36 + (-17.82)$ To subtract 17.82, add its inverse.

$\qquad\qquad\qquad = -(|-17.82| - |15.36|)$ Subtract the absolute values.

$\qquad\qquad\qquad = -(17.82 - 15.36)$ The absolute value of -17.82 is greater, so the result is negative.

$\qquad\qquad\qquad = -2.46$

The price of the stock changed by $-\$2.46$.

Examine   The problem asks for the change in a stock's price from the beginning of a week to the end. Since the change was negative, the price dropped. This makes sense since the ending price is less than the beginning price.

SUBTRACT RATIONAL NUMBERS

In-Class Example   Power Point®

Teaching Tip Explain that a positive change in price indicates that the price of the stock rose. A negative change in price indicates that the price of the stock fell.

3 STOCKS In the past year, a publishing company's stock went from $52.08 per share to $70.87 per share. Find the change in the price of the stock. **The price of the stock changed by $18.79.**

Study Notebook

Have students—

- add the definitions/examples of the vocabulary terms to their Vocabulary Builder worksheets for Chapter 2.

- include worked-out examples of adding and subtracting rational numbers.

- include any other item(s) that they find helpful in mastering the skills in this lesson.

DAILY INTERVENTION **FIND THE ERROR** Remind students to review the rules for adding and subtracting rational numbers when solving this problem. Remember, when adding rational numbers with different signs, you must *subtract* the lesser absolute value from the greater absolute value. Did both Gabriella and Nick follow this rule?

About the Exercises...

Organization by Objective
- Add Rational Numbers: 17–38
- Subtract Rational Numbers: 39–56

Odd/Even Assignments
Exercises 17–56 are structured so that students practice the same concepts whether they are assigned odd or even problems.

Assignment Guide

Basic: 17–33 odd, 37–53 odd, 57–59, 63–82

Average: 17–55 odd, 57–59, 63–82

Advanced: 18–56 even, 60–76 (optional: 77–82)

Check for Understanding

Concept Check

2. Sample answer: To subtract a real number, add its opposite.

3. Gabriella; subtracting $-\frac{6}{9}$ is the same as adding $\frac{6}{9}$.

1. **OPEN ENDED** Write a subtraction expression using rational numbers that has a difference of $-\frac{2}{5}$. **Sample answer:** $\frac{1}{5} - \frac{3}{5}$

2. **Describe** how to subtract real numbers.

3. **FIND THE ERROR** Gabriella and Nick are subtracting fractions.

Gabriella

$$\left(-\frac{4}{9}\right) - \left(-\frac{2}{3}\right) = \left(-\frac{4}{9}\right) - \left(-\frac{6}{9}\right)$$
$$= \left(-\frac{4}{9}\right) + \left(\frac{6}{9}\right)$$
$$= \left(\frac{6}{9} - \frac{4}{9}\right)$$
$$= \frac{2}{9}$$

Nick

$$\left(-\frac{4}{9}\right) - \left(-\frac{2}{3}\right) = \left(-\frac{4}{9}\right) - \left(-\frac{6}{9}\right)$$
$$= \left(-\frac{4}{9}\right) + \left(-\frac{6}{9}\right)$$
$$= -\left(\frac{6}{9} + \frac{4}{9}\right)$$
$$= -\frac{10}{9}$$

Who is correct? Explain your reasoning.

Guided Practice

GUIDED PRACTICE KEY	
Exercises	Examples
4–9	1, 2
10–16	3

Find each sum.

4. $-15 + (-12)$ **−27**

5. $-24 + (-45)$ **−69**

6. $38.7 + (-52.6)$ **−13.9**

7. $-4.62 + (-12.81)$ **−17.43**

8. $\frac{4}{7} + \left(-\frac{1}{2}\right)$ $\frac{1}{14}$

9. $-\frac{5}{12} + \frac{8}{15}$ $\frac{7}{60}$

Find each difference.

10. $18 - 23$ **−5**

11. $12.7 - (-18.4)$ **31.1**

12. $(-3.86) - 1.75$ **−5.61**

13. $-32.25 - (-42.5)$ **10.25**

14. $-\frac{2}{9} - \frac{3}{10}$ $-\frac{47}{90}$

15. $\left(-\frac{7}{10}\right) - \left(-\frac{11}{12}\right)$ $\frac{13}{60}$

Application

16. **WEATHER** The highest recorded temperature in the United States was in Death Valley, California, while the lowest temperature was recorded at Prospect Creek, Alaska. What is the difference between these two temperatures? **214°**

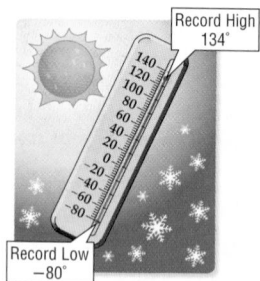

Record High 134°
Record Low −80°

★ indicates increased difficulty

Practice and Apply

Homework Help	
For Exercises	See Examples
17–38	1, 2
39–62	3

Extra Practice
See page 823.

Find each sum.

17. $-8 + 13$ **5**

18. $-11 + 19$ **8**

19. $41 + (-63)$ **−22**

20. $80 + (-102)$ **−22**

21. $-77 + (-46)$ **−123**

22. $-92 + (-64)$ **−156**

23. $-1.6 + (-3.8)$ **−5.4**

24. $-32.4 + (-4.5)$ **−36.9**

25. $-38.9 + 24.2$ **−14.7**

26. $-7.007 + 4.8$ **−2.207**

27. $43.2 + (-57.9)$ **−14.7**

28. $38.7 + (-61.1)$ **−22.4**

29. $\frac{6}{7} + \frac{2}{3}$ $\frac{32}{21}$ or $1\frac{11}{21}$

30. $\frac{3}{18} + \frac{6}{17}$ $\frac{53}{102}$

31. $-\frac{4}{11} + \frac{3}{5}$ $\frac{13}{55}$

32. $-\frac{2}{5} + \frac{17}{20}$ $\frac{9}{20}$

33. $-\frac{4}{15} + \left(-\frac{9}{16}\right)$ $-\frac{199}{240}$

34. $-\frac{16}{40} + \left(-\frac{13}{20}\right)$ $-\frac{21}{20}$ or $-1\frac{1}{20}$

★ 35. Find the sum of $4\frac{1}{8}$ and $-1\frac{1}{2}$. $2\frac{5}{8}$

★ 36. Find the sum of $1\frac{17}{50}$ and $-3\frac{17}{25}$. $-2\frac{17}{50}$

37. GAMES Sarah was playing a computer trivia game. Her scores for round one were +100, +200, +500, −300, +400, and −500. What was her total score at the end of round one? **400 points**

38. FOOTBALL The Northland Vikings' offense began a drive from their 20-yard line. They gained 6 yards on the first down, lost 8 yards on the second down, then gained 3 yards on third down. What yard line were they on at fourth down? **21-yard line**

Find each difference.

39. −19 − 8 **−27**
40. 16 − (−23) **39**
41. 9 − (−24) **33**
42. 12 − 34 **−22**
43. 22 − 41 **−19**
44. −9 − (−33) **24**
45. −58 − (−42) **−16**
46. 79.3 − (−14.1) **93.4**
47. 1.34 − (−0.458) **1.798**
48. −9.16 − 10.17 **−19.33**
49. 67.1 − (−38.2) **105.3**
50. 72.5 − (−81.3) **153.8**
51. $-\frac{1}{6} - \frac{2}{3}$ **$-\frac{5}{6}$**
52. $\frac{1}{2} - \frac{4}{5}$ **$-\frac{3}{10}$**
53. $-\frac{7}{8} - \left(-\frac{3}{16}\right)$ **$-\frac{11}{16}$**
54. $-\frac{1}{12} - \left(-\frac{3}{4}\right)$ **$\frac{2}{3}$**
★ 55. $2\frac{1}{4} - 6\frac{1}{3}$ **$-\frac{49}{12}$ or $-4\frac{1}{12}$**
★ 56. $5\frac{3}{10} - 1\frac{31}{50}$ **$\frac{92}{25}$ or $3\frac{17}{25}$**

More About. . .

Golf

In the United States, there are more than 16,000 golf courses played by 26 million people each year.
Source: Encarta Online

57. −2, −6, −4, −4
59. Under; yes, it is better than par 72.

GOLF For Exercises 57–59, use the following information.
In golf, scores are based on *par*. Par 72 means that a golfer should hit the ball 72 times to complete 18 holes of golf. A score of 67, or 5 under par, is written as −5. A score of 3 over par is written as +3. At the Masters Tournament (par 72) in April, 2001, Tiger Woods shot 70, 66, 68, and 68 during four rounds of golf.

57. Use integers to write his score for each round as over or under par.
58. Add the integers to find his overall score. **−16**
59. Was his score under or over par? Would you want to have his score? Explain.

Online Research **Data Update** Find the most recent winner of the Masters Tournament. What integer represents the winner's score for each round as over or under par? What integer represents the winner's overall score? Visit www.algebra1.com/data_update to learn more.

STOCKS For Exercises 60–62, refer to the table that shows the weekly closing values of the stock market for an eight-week period.

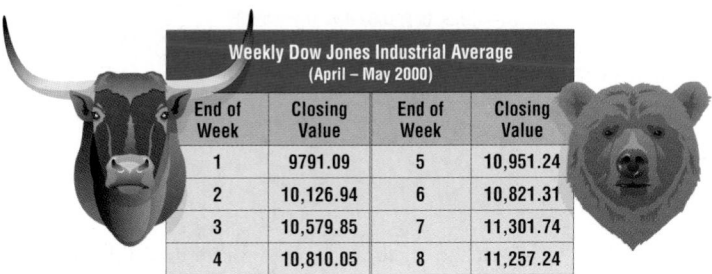

Weekly Dow Jones Industrial Average (April – May 2000)			
End of Week	Closing Value	End of Week	Closing Value
1	9791.09	5	10,951.24
2	10,126.94	6	10,821.31
3	10,579.85	7	11,301.74
4	10,810.05	8	11,257.24

Source: *The Wall Street Journal*

60. Find the change in value from week 1 to week 8. **1466.15**
61. Which week had the greatest change from the previous week? **week 7**
62. Which week had the least change from the previous week? **week 8**

63. Sometimes; the equation is false for positive values of *x*, but true for all other values of *x*.

63. **CRITICAL THINKING** Tell whether the equation $x + |x| = 0$ is *always*, *sometimes*, or *never* true. Explain.

 www.algebra1.com/self_check_quiz

Lesson 2-2 Adding and Subtracting Rational Numbers **77**

Study Guide and Intervention, p. 81 (shown) and p. 82

Add Rational Numbers

Adding Rational Numbers, Same Sign	Add the numbers. If both are positive, the sum is positive; if both are negative, the sum is negative.
Adding Rational Numbers, Different Signs	Subtract the number with the lesser absolute value from the number with the greater absolute value. The sign of the sum is the same as the sign of the number with the greater absolute value.

Example 1 Use a number line to find the sum −2 + (−3).
Step 1 Draw an arrow from 0 to −2.
Step 2 From the tip of the first arrow, draw a second arrow 3 units to the left to represent adding −3.
Step 3 The second arrow ends at the sum −5. So −2 + (−3) = −5.

Example 2 Find each sum.
a. −8 + 5
−8 + 5 = −(|−8| − |5|)
= −(8 − 5)
= −3
b. $\frac{3}{4} + \left(-\frac{1}{2}\right)$
$\frac{3}{4} + \left(-\frac{1}{2}\right) = \frac{3}{4} + \left(-\frac{2}{4}\right)$
$= +\left(\left|\frac{3}{4}\right| - \left|\frac{2}{4}\right|\right)$
$= +\left(\frac{3}{4} - \frac{2}{4}\right)$
$= \frac{1}{4}$

Exercises
Find each sum.

1. 12 + 24 **36**
2. −6 + 14 **8**
3. −12 + (−15) **−27**
4. −21.5 + 34.2 **12.7**
5. 8.2 + (−3.5) **4.7**
6. 23.5 + (−15.2) **8.3**
7. 90 + (−105) **−15**
8. 108 + (−62) **46**
9. −84 + (−90) **−174**
10. $\frac{5}{7} + \frac{1}{3}$ **$\frac{22}{21}$ or $1\frac{1}{21}$**
11. $\frac{3}{14} + \frac{6}{17}$ **$\frac{135}{238}$**
12. $-\frac{4}{9} + \frac{3}{5}$ **$\frac{7}{45}$**
13. $-\frac{2}{3} + \left(-\frac{1}{4}\right)$ **$-\frac{11}{12}$**
14. $-\frac{1}{5} + \frac{7}{11}$ **$\frac{24}{55}$**
15. $-\frac{18}{40} + \left(-\frac{10}{20}\right)$ **$-\frac{19}{20}$**
16. $-\frac{5}{5} + \left(-\frac{5}{6}\right)$ **$-\frac{43}{30}$ or $-1\frac{13}{30}$**
17. −1.6 + (−1.8) **−3.4**
18. −0.008 + (−0.25) **−0.258**

Skills Practice, p. 83 and Practice, p. 84 (shown)

Find each sum.
1. −82 + 14 **−68**
2. −33 + 47 **14**
3. −17 + (−39) **−56**
4. 8 + (−11) **−3**
5. −1.7 + 3.2 **1.5**
6. −13.3 + (−0.9) **−14.2**
7. −51.8 + 29.7 **−22.1**
8. 7.34 + (−9.06) **−1.72**
9. $\frac{5}{9} + \frac{5}{18}$ **$\frac{25}{18}$ or $1\frac{7}{18}$**
10. $\frac{3}{5} + \frac{2}{3}$ **$\frac{1}{15}$**
11. $-\frac{3}{4} + \left(-\frac{3}{5}\right)$ **$-\frac{27}{20}$ or $-1\frac{7}{20}$**
12. $\frac{3}{8} + \left(-\frac{2}{3}\right)$ **$-\frac{7}{24}$**

Find each difference.
13. 65 − 93 **−28**
14. −42 − (−17) **−25**
15. 13 − (−19) **32**
16. −8 − 43 **−51**
17. 82.8 − (−12.4) **95.2**
18. 1.27 − 2.34 **−1.07**
19. −9.26 − 12.05 **−21.31**
20. −18.1 − (−4.7) **−13.4**
21. $-\frac{1}{5} - \frac{2}{3}$ **$-\frac{13}{15}$**
22. $\frac{4}{3} - \frac{5}{6}$ **$\frac{1}{2}$**
23. $-\frac{5}{2} - \left(-\frac{3}{7}\right)$ **$-\frac{29}{14}$ or $-2\frac{1}{14}$**
24. $\frac{4}{8} - \left(-\frac{5}{6}\right)$ **$\frac{23}{24}$**

FINANCE For Exercises 25–27, use the following information.
The table shows activity in Ben's checking account. The balance before the activity was $200.00. Deposits are added to an account and checks are subtracted.

Number	Date	Transaction	Amount	Balance
	5/2	deposit	52.50	252.50
101	5/10	check to Castle Music	25.40	?
102	6/1	check to Comp U Save	235.40	?

25. What is the account balance after writing check number 101? **$227.00**
26. What is the account balance after writing check number 102? **−$8.40**
27. Realizing that he has just written a check for more than is in the account, Ben immediately deposits $425. What will this make his new account balance? **$416.60**
28. **CHEMISTRY** The melting points of krypton, radon, and sulfur in degrees Celsius are −156.6, −61.8, and 112.8, respectively. What is the difference in melting points between radon and krypton and between sulfur and krypton? **94.8°C and 269.4°C**

Reading to Learn Mathematics, p. 85 **ELL**

Pre-Activity How can a number line be used to show a football team's progress?
Read the introduction to Lesson 2-2 at the top of page 73 in your textbook.
Use *positive* or *negative* to complete the following sentences.
The five-yard penalty is shown by the **negative** number −5.
The 13-yard pass is shown by the **positive** number 13.

Reading the Lesson
1. To add two rational numbers, you can use a number line. Each number will be represented by an arrow.
   a. Where on the number line does the arrow for the first number begin? **at 0**
   b. Arrows for negative numbers will point to the **left** (left/right). Arrows for positive numbers will point to the **right** (left/right).
2. Two students added the same pair of rational numbers. Both students got the correct sum. One student used a number line. The other student used absolute value. Then they compared their work.
   a. How do the arrows show which number has the greater absolute value? **The number with the greater absolute value matches the longer arrow.**
   b. If the longer arrow points to the left, then the sum is **negative** (positive/negative). If the longer arrow points to the right, then the sum is **positive** (positive/negative).
3. If two numbers are additive inverses, what must be true about their absolute values? **The absolute values of the two numbers are equal.**
4. Write each subtraction problem as an addition problem.
   a. 12 − 4 **12 + (−4)**
   b. −15 − 7 **−15 + (−7)**
   c. 0 − 9 **0 + (−9)**
   d. −20 − 34 **−20 + (−34)**

Helping You Remember
5. Explain why knowing the rules for adding rational numbers can help you to subtract rational numbers.
Sample answer: Since subtraction is the same as adding the opposite, you can change every subtraction problem to an addition problem. Then you can use the rules for adding rational numbers to get the final answer.

Enrichment, p. 86

Rounding Fractions

Rounding fractions is more difficult than rounding whole numbers or decimals. For example, think about how you would round $\frac{4}{9}$ inches to the nearest quarter-inch. Through estimation, you might realize that $\frac{4}{9}$ is less than $\frac{1}{2}$. But, is it closer to $\frac{1}{2}$ or to $\frac{1}{4}$?

Here are two ways to round fractions. Example 1 uses only fractions; Example 2 uses decimals.

Example 1
Subtract the fraction twice. Use the two nearest quarters.
$\frac{1}{2} - \frac{4}{9} = \frac{1}{18}$ $\frac{4}{9} - \frac{1}{4} = \frac{7}{36}$
Compare the differences.
$\frac{1}{18} \quad \frac{7}{36}$

Example 2
Change the fraction and the two nearest quarters to decimals.
$\frac{4}{9} = 0.44$, $\frac{1}{2} = 0.5$, $\frac{1}{4} = 0.25$
Find the decimal halfway between the two nearest quarters.

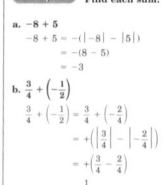

Speaking Have a student volunteer write an expression involving the addition or subtraction of rational numbers on the chalkboard or overhead projector. Have other students explain the steps involved in performing the operation. Ask the volunteer to record the steps as they are explained.

Getting Ready for Lesson 2-3

PREREQUISITE SKILL Students will learn about multiplying rational numbers in Lesson 2-3. This includes applying special rules to products involving fractions. Use Exercises 77–82 to determine your students' familiarity with the multiplication of fractions.

Assessment Options

Quiz (Lessons 2-1 and 2-2) is available on p. 131 of the *Chapter 2 Resource Masters*.

Answer

64. Sample answer: If a team gains yards, move right on the number line. If a team loses yards, move left on the number line. Answers should include the following.
 • Move right or left, depending on whether the Giants gained or lost yards on each play. Where you end will tell you how many yards the Giants lost or gained.
 • Instead of using a number line, you can use the rules for adding and subtracting rational numbers.

---

64. **WRITING IN MATH** Answer the question that was posed at the beginning of the lesson. **See margin.**

 How can a number line be used to show a football team's progress?

 Include the following in your answer:
 • an explanation of how you could use a number line to determine the yards gained or lost by the Giants on their next three plays, and
 • a description of how to determine the total yards gained or lost without using a number line.

Standardized Test Practice
Ⓐ Ⓑ Ⓒ Ⓓ

65. What is the value of n in $-57 - n = -144$? **C**
 Ⓐ -201 Ⓑ -87 Ⓒ 87 Ⓓ 201

66. Which expression is equivalent to $5 - (-8)$? **B**
 Ⓐ $(-5) + 8$ Ⓑ $8 + 5$ Ⓒ $8 - 5$ Ⓓ $5 - 8$

Maintain Your Skills

Mixed Review   Evaluate each expression if $x = 4.8$, $y = -7.4$, and $z = 10$.   *(Lesson 2-1)*
67. $12.2 + |8 - x|$ **15.4**   68. $|y| + 9.4 - 3$ **13.8**   69. $24.2 - |18.3 - z|$ **15.9**

For Exercises 70 and 71, refer to the graph.   *(Lesson 1-9)*

70. Sample answer: a category labeled "other" representing 8%

70. If you wanted to make a circle graph of the data, what additional category would you have to include so that the circle graph would not be misleading?

71. Construct a circle graph that displays the data accurately. **See pp. 117A–117B.**

Find the solution sets for each inequality if the replacement sets are $a = \{2, 3, 4, 5, 6\}$, $b = \{0.3, 0.4, 0.5, 0.6, 0.7\}$, **and** $c = \left\{\frac{1}{4}, \frac{1}{2}, \frac{3}{4}, 1, 1\frac{1}{4}\right\}$.   *(Lesson 1-3)*

72. $b + 1.3 \geq 1.8$ **{0.5, 0.6, 0.7}**

73. $3a - 5 > 7$ **{5, 6}**

74. $c + \frac{1}{2} < 2\frac{1}{4}$ $\left\{\frac{1}{4}, \frac{1}{2}, \frac{3}{4}, 1, 1\frac{1}{4}\right\}$

Write an algebraic expression for each verbal phrase.   *(Lesson 1-1)*
75. eight less than the square of q 76. 37 less than 2 times a number k
 $q^2 - 8$ $2k - 37$

USA TODAY Snapshots®

Most drink the cereal milk
What adults do with the milk in the bowl after the cereal is eaten:

Drink it
67%

Leave it
25%

Source: Gallup Organization for Wheat Foods Council

By Cindy Hall and Sam Ward, USA TODAY

Getting Ready for the Next Lesson   **PREREQUISITE SKILL   Find each product.**
*(To review **multiplication of fractions**, see pages 800 and 801.)*

77. $\frac{1}{2} \cdot \frac{2}{3}$ $\frac{1}{3}$ 78. $\frac{1}{4} \cdot \frac{2}{5}$ $\frac{1}{10}$ 79. $\frac{3}{4} \cdot \frac{5}{6}$ $\frac{5}{8}$

80. $4 \cdot \frac{3}{5}$ $2\frac{2}{5}$ 81. $8 \cdot \frac{5}{8}$ 5 82. $\frac{7}{9} \cdot 12$ $9\frac{1}{3}$

Multiplying Rational Numbers

What You'll Learn

- Multiply integers.
- Multiply rational numbers.

How do consumers use multiplication of rational numbers?

Stores often offer coupons to encourage people to shop in their stores. The receipt shows a purchase of four CDs along with four coupons for $1.00 off each CD. How could you determine the amount saved by using the coupons?

```
        CD SHOP

CD..................13.99
CD..................12.99
CD..................14.99
CD..................14.99
COUPON............−1.00
COUPON............−1.00
COUPON............−1.00
COUPON............−1.00
TAX.................0.31

TOTAL DUE..........53.27
CASH...............55.00

CHANGE.............1.73
```

MULTIPLY INTEGERS   One way to find the savings from the coupons is to use repeated addition.

$$-\$1.00 + (-\$1.00) + (-\$1.00) + (-\$1.00) = -\$4.00$$

An easier way to find the savings would be to multiply $-\$1.00$ by 4.

$$4(-\$1.00) = -\$4.00$$

Suppose the coupons were expired and had to be removed from the total. You can represent this by multiplying $-\$1.00$ by -4.

$$(-4)(-\$1.00) = \$4.00$$

In other words, $4.00 would be added back to the total.

These examples suggest the following rules for multiplying integers.

Study Tip

Multiplying Integers
When multiplying integers, if there are an even number of negative integers, the product is positive. If there are an odd number of negative integers, the product is negative.

Key Concept	Multiplication of Integers

- **Words** The product of two numbers having the *same sign* is positive.
  The product of two numbers having *different signs* is negative.

- **Examples** $(-12)(-7) = 84$ same signs → positive product
  $15(-8) = -120$ different signs → negative product

Example 1 Multiply Integers

Find each product.

a. **4(−5)**

   $4(-5) = -20$ different signs → negative product

b. **(−12)(−14)**

   $(-12)(-14) = 168$ same signs → positive product

---

1 Focus

5-Minute Check Transparency 2-3 Use as a quiz or a review of Lesson 2-2.

Mathematical Background notes are available for this lesson on p. 66C.

How do consumers use multiplication of rational numbers?

Ask students:

- What is the total value of the coupons used in this transaction? **$4**

- What are two ways that you could find the total value of the coupons? **You can add the amounts of the coupons, or since the amount is the same for all four coupons, you can multiply the amount of one coupon by 4.**

- Why might multiplying the amount of one coupon by 4 be easier than adding all the values? **Multiplying involves fewer numbers.**

Resource Manager

Workbook and Reproducible Masters

Chapter 2 Resource Masters
- Study Guide and Intervention, pp. 87–88
- Skills Practice, p. 89
- Practice, p. 90
- Reading to Learn Mathematics, p. 91
- Enrichment, p. 92

Parent and Student Study Guide Workbook, p. 13
Prerequisite Skills Workbook,
pp. 15–16, 19–20, 25–28, 39–40, 47–50, 65–66, 75–76
School-to-Career Masters, p. 3

 Transparencies
5-Minute Check Transparency 2-3
Real-World Transparency 2
Answer Key Transparencies

 Technology
Interactive Chalkboard

MULTIPLY INTEGERS

In-Class Examples Power Point®

Reading Tip Remind students to look carefully at the signs of both numbers before deciding on the sign of the product.

1 Find each product.

a. $(-8)(-6)$ **48**

b. $(10)(-11)$ **−110**

Teaching Tip The same multiplication rules apply whether or not variables are involved in the multiplication.

2 Simplify the expression $13x + (-6)(4x)$. **−11x**

MULTIPLY RATIONAL NUMBERS

In-Class Examples Power Point®

3 Find $\left(-\frac{2}{3}\right)\left(-\frac{3}{4}\right)$. $\frac{1}{2}$

4 **STOCKS** The value of a company's stock dropped by $1.25 per share. By what amount did the total value of the company's stock change if the company has issued 500,000 shares of stock? **−$625,000**

5 Evaluate $\left(-\frac{3}{7}\right)x^3$ if $x = \left(-\frac{1}{2}\right)$. $\frac{3}{56}$

You can simplify expressions by applying the rules of multiplication.

Example 2 *Simplify Expressions*

Simplify the expression $4(-3y) - 15y$.

$$4(-3y) - 15y = 4(-3)y - 15y \quad \text{Associative Property } (\times)$$
$$= -12y - 15y \quad \text{Substitution}$$
$$= (-12 - 15)y \quad \text{Distributive Property}$$
$$= -27y \quad \text{Simplify.}$$

MULTIPLY RATIONAL NUMBERS Multiplying rational numbers is similar to multiplying integers.

Example 3 *Multiply Rational Numbers*

Find $\left(-\frac{3}{4}\right)\left(\frac{3}{8}\right)$.

$$\left(-\frac{3}{4}\right)\left(\frac{3}{8}\right) = -\frac{9}{32} \quad \text{different signs} \rightarrow \text{negative product}$$

Example 4 *Multiply Rational Numbers to Solve a Problem*

BASEBALL Fenway Park, home of the Boston Red Sox, is the oldest ball park in professional baseball. It has a seating capacity of about 34,000. Determine the approximate total ticket sales for a sold-out game.

Log on for:
- Updated data
- More activities on writing equations
www.algebra1.com/usa_today

To find the approximate total ticket sales, multiply the number of tickets sold by the average price.

$$34,000 \cdot 24.05 = 817,770$$

same signs → positive product

The total ticket sales for a sold-out game are about $817,770.

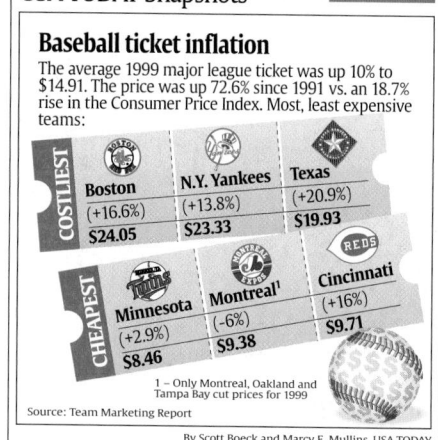

USA TODAY Snapshots®

Baseball ticket inflation
The average 1999 major league ticket was up 10% to $14.91. The price was up 72.6% since 1991 vs. an 18.7% rise in the Consumer Price Index. Most, least expensive teams:

COSTLIEST
Boston (+16.6%) $24.05
N.Y. Yankees (+13.8%) $23.33
Texas (+20.9%) $19.93

CHEAPEST
Minnesota (+2.9%) $8.46
Montreal¹ (-6%) $9.38
Cincinnati (+16%) $9.71

1 – Only Montreal, Oakland and Tampa Bay cut prices for 1999
Source: Team Marketing Report
By Scott Boeck and Marcy E. Mullins, USA TODAY

You can evaluate expressions that contain rational numbers.

Example 5 *Evaluate Expressions*

Evaluate $n^2\left(-\frac{5}{8}\right)$ if $n = -\frac{2}{5}$.

$$n^2\left(-\frac{5}{8}\right) = \left(-\frac{2}{5}\right)^2\left(-\frac{5}{8}\right) \quad \text{Substitution}$$
$$= \left(\frac{4}{25}\right)\left(-\frac{5}{8}\right) \quad \left(-\frac{2}{5}\right)^2 = \left(-\frac{2}{5}\right)\left(-\frac{2}{5}\right) \text{ or } \frac{4}{25}$$
$$= -\frac{20}{200} \text{ or } -\frac{1}{10} \quad \text{different signs} \rightarrow \text{negative product}$$

Online Lesson Plans

USA TODAY Education's Online site offers resources and interactive features connected to each day's newspaper. *Experience TODAY*, USA TODAY's daily lesson plan, is available on the site and delivered daily to subscribers. This plan provides instruction for integrating USA TODAY graphics and key editorial features into your mathematics classroom. Log on to **www.education.usatoday.com**.

In Lesson 1-4, you learned about the Multiplicative Identity Property, which states that any number multiplied by 1 is equal to the number. Another important property is the Multiplicative Property of -1.

Check for Understanding

Concept Check

1. **List** the conditions under which the product ab is negative. Give examples to support your answer. **1–3. See margin**

2. **OPEN ENDED** Describe a real-life situation in which you would multiply a positive rational number by a negative rational number. Write a corresponding multiplication expression.

3. **Explain** why the product of two negative numbers is positive.

Guided Practice **Find each product.**

GUIDED PRACTICE KEY	
Exercises	Examples
4–9	1, 3
10, 11	2
12–14	5
15	4

4. $(-6)(3)$ **-18**
5. $(5)(-8)$ **-40**
6. $(4.5)(2.3)$ **10.35**
7. $(-8.7)(-10.4)$ **90.48**
8. $\left(\frac{5}{3}\right)\left(-\frac{2}{7}\right)$ **$-\frac{10}{21}$**
9. $\left(-\frac{4}{9}\right)\left(\frac{7}{15}\right)$ **$-\frac{28}{135}$**

Simplify each expression.

10. $5s(-6t)$ **$-30st$**
11. $6x(-7y) + (-15xy)$ **$-57xy$**

Evaluate each expression if $m = -\frac{2}{3}$, $n = \frac{1}{2}$, and $p = -3\frac{3}{4}$.

12. $6m$ **-4**
13. np **$-\frac{15}{8}$ or $-1\frac{7}{8}$**
14. $n^2(m + 2)$ **$\frac{1}{3}$**

Application 15. **NATURE** The average worker honeybee makes about $\frac{1}{12}$ teaspoon of honey in its lifetime. How much honey do 675 honeybees make? **$56\frac{1}{4}$ t**

★ indicates increased difficulty

Practice and Apply

Homework Help	
For Exercises	See Examples
16–33	1, 3
34–39	2
40, 41	4
42–49	5
50–54	4

Extra Practice
See page 823.

Find each product.

16. $5(18)$ **90**
17. $8(22)$ **176**
18. $-12(15)$ **-180**
19. $-24(8)$ **-192**
20. $-47(-29)$ **1363**
21. $-81(-48)$ **3888**
22. $\left(\frac{4}{5}\right)\left(\frac{3}{8}\right)$ **$\frac{3}{10}$**
23. $\left(\frac{5}{12}\right)\left(\frac{4}{9}\right)$ **$\frac{5}{27}$**
24. $\left(-\frac{3}{5}\right)\left(\frac{5}{6}\right)$ **$-\frac{1}{2}$**
25. $\left(-\frac{2}{5}\right)\left(\frac{6}{7}\right)$ **$-\frac{12}{35}$**
26. $\left(-3\frac{1}{5}\right)\left(-7\frac{1}{2}\right)$ **24**
27. $\left(-1\frac{4}{5}\right)\left(-2\frac{1}{2}\right)$ **$4\frac{1}{2}$**
28. $7.2(0.2)$ **1.44**
29. $6.5(0.13)$ **0.845**
30. $(-5.8)(2.3)$ **-13.34**
31. $(-0.075)(6.4)$ **-0.48**
★ 32. $\frac{3}{5}(-5)(-2)$ **6**
★ 33. $\frac{2}{11}(-11)(-4)$ **8**

Simplify each expression.

34. $6(-2x) - 14x$ **$-26x$**
35. $5(-4n) - 25n$ **$-45n$**
36. $5(2x - x)$ **$5x$**
37. $-7(3d + d)$ **$-28d$**
38. $-2a(-3c) + (-6y)(6r)$ **$6ac\ -36ry$**
39. $7m(-3n) + 3s(-4t)$ **$-21mn\ -12st$**

www.algebra1.com/extra_examples

STOCK PRICES For Exercises 40 and 41, use the table that lists the closing prices of a company's stock over a one-week period.

Closing Stock Price ($)	
Day	Price
1	64.38
2	63.66
3	61.66
4	61.69
5	62.34

40. What was the change in price of 35 shares of this stock from day 2 to day 3?   **−$70**

41. If you bought 100 shares of this stock on day 1 and sold half of them on day 4, how much money did you gain or lose on those shares?   **−$134.50**

Evaluate each expression if $a = -2.7$, $b = 3.9$, $c = 4.5$, and $d = -0.2$.

42. $-5c^2$ **−101.25**
43. $-2b^2$ **−30.42**
44. $-4ab$ **42.12**
45. $-5cd$ **4.5**
46. $ad - 8$ **−7.46**
47. $ab - 3$ **−13.53**
★ 48. $d^2(b - 2a)$ **0.372**
★ 49. $b^2(d - 3c)$ **−208.377**

50. **CIVICS** In a United States flag, the length of the union is $\frac{2}{5}$ of the fly, and the width is $\frac{7}{13}$ of the hoist. If the fly is 6 feet, how long is the union? $2\frac{2}{5}$ ft

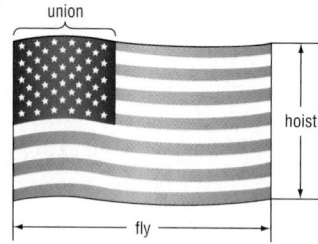
union / hoist / fly

51. **COMPUTERS** The price of a computer dropped $34.95 each month for 7 months. If the starting price was $1450, what was the price after 7 months?   **$1205.35**

52. **BALLOONING** The temperature drops about 2°F for every rise of 530 feet in altitude. Per Lindstrand achieved the altitude record of 64,997 feet in a hot-air balloon over Laredo, Texas, on June 6, 1988. About how many degrees difference was there between the ground temperature and the air temperature at that altitude?   **Source:** The Guinness Book of Records   **about −245°F**

ECOLOGY For Exercises 53 and 54, use the following information.
Americans use about 2.5 million plastic bottles every hour.
Source: www.savethewater.com

53. About how many plastic bottles are used in one day?   **60 million**
54. About how many bottles are used in one week?   **420 million**

55. **CRITICAL THINKING** An even number of negative numbers is multiplied. What is the sign of the product? Explain your reasoning.

56. **WRITING IN MATH** Answer the question that was posed at the beginning of the lesson.   **See margin.**

How do consumers use multiplication of rational numbers?

Include the following in your answer:
• an explanation of why the amount of a coupon is expressed as a negative value, and
• an explanation of how you could use multiplication to find your total discount if you bought 3 CDs for $13.99 each and there was a discount of $1.50 on each CD.

More About . . .

Civics •··········

The Marine Corps War Memorial in Washington, D.C., is dedicated to all Marines who have defended the United States since 1775. It is the most famous memorial that is centered around the flag.

Source: The United States National Park Service

55. Positive; the product of two negative numbers is positive and all even numbers can be divided into groups of two.

57. Which expression can be simplified as $-8xy$? **B**

(A) $2y - 4x$ (B) $-2x(4y)$ (C) $(-4)^2xy$ (D) $-4x(-2y)$

58. Find the value of m if $m = -2ab$, $a = -4$, and $b = 6$. **B**

(A) 8   (B) 48   (C) 12   (D) -48

Maintain Your Skills

Mixed Review   **Find each sum or difference.** *(Lesson 2-2)*

59. $-6.5 + (-5.6)$ **60.** $\frac{4}{5} + \left(-\frac{3}{4}\right)$ $\frac{1}{20}$ **61.** $42 - (-14)$ **56**   **62.** $-14.2 - 6.7$
-12.1 -20.9

Graph each set of numbers on a number line. *(Lesson 2-1)* **63–65. See margin.**

63. $\{\ldots, -3, -1, 1, 3, 5\}$ **64.** $\{-2.5, -1.5, 0.5, 4.5\}$ **65.** $\left\{-1, -\frac{1}{3}, \frac{2}{3}, 2\right\}$

66. Identify the graph below that best represents the following situation. Brandon has a deflated balloon. He slowly fills the balloon up with air. Without tying the balloon, he lets it go. *(Lesson 1-8)* **C**

a.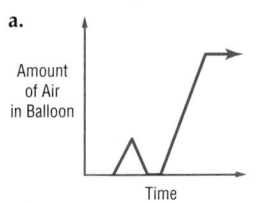

b.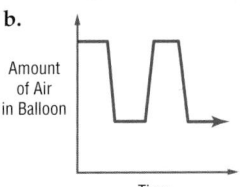

c.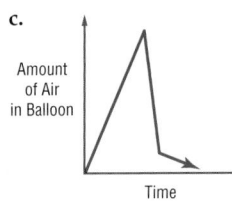

67–68. Sample answers are given.
Write a counterexample for each statement. *(Lesson 1-7)*

67. If $2x - 4 \geq 6$, then $x > 5$. $x = 5$ **68.** If $|a| > 3$, then $a > 3$. $a = -4$

Getting Ready for
the Next Lesson   **PREREQUISITE SKILL**   **Find each quotient.**
*(To review **division of fractions**, see pages 800 and 801.)*

69. $\frac{5}{8} \div 2$ $\frac{5}{16}$ **70.** $\frac{2}{3} \div 4$ $\frac{1}{6}$ **71.** $5 \div \frac{3}{4}$ $6\frac{2}{3}$ **72.** $1 \div \frac{2}{5}$ $2\frac{1}{2}$

73. $\frac{1}{2} \div \frac{3}{8}$ $1\frac{1}{3}$ **74.** $\frac{7}{9} \div \frac{5}{6}$ $\frac{14}{15}$ **75.** $\frac{4}{5} \div \frac{6}{5}$ $\frac{2}{3}$ **76.** $\frac{7}{8} \div \frac{2}{3}$ $1\frac{5}{16}$

Practice Quiz 1   Lessons 2-1 through 2-3

1. Name the set of points graphed on the number line. *(Lesson 2-1)* $\{-4, -1, 1, 6\}$

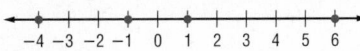

2. Evaluate $32 - |x + 8|$ if $x = 15$. *(Lesson 2-1)* **9**

Find each sum or difference. *(Lesson 2-2)*

3. $-15 + 7$ -8 **4.** $27 - (-12)$ **39**   **5.** $-6.05 + (-2.1)$ -8.15 **6.** $-\frac{3}{4} - \left(-\frac{2}{5}\right)$ $-\frac{7}{20}$

Find each product. *(Lesson 2-3)*

7. $-9(-12)$ **108**   **8.** $(3.8)(-4.1)$ -15.58

9. Simplify $(-8x)(-2y) + (-3y)(z)$. *(Lesson 2-3)* $16xy - 3yz$

10. Evaluate $mn + 5$ if $m = 2.5$ and $n = -3.2$. *(Lesson 2-3)* -3

 www.algebra1.com/self_check_quiz   **Lesson 2-3** Multiplying Rational Numbers   **83**

---

4 Assess

Open-Ended Assessment

Writing Have students write an explanation of why the product of two negative numbers is positive.

Getting Ready for Lesson 2-4

PREREQUISITE SKILL Students will learn about dividing rational numbers in Lesson 2-4. Use Exercises 69–76 to determine your students' familiarity with the division of fractions, which are part of the set of rational numbers.

Assessment Options

Practice Quiz 1 The quiz provides students with a brief review of the concepts and skills in Lessons 2-1 through 2-3. Lesson numbers are given to the right of the exercises or instruction lines so students can review concepts not yet mastered.

Answers

56. Sample answer: Multiplying lets consumers calculate quickly the total of several similar items. Answers should include the following.

- Coupons are negative values because adding a negative number is the same as subtracting a positive number.
- Multiply 13.99 and -1.50 by three, then add the products.

63.

64.

65.

2-4 Dividing Rational Numbers

1 Focus

5-Minute Check Transparency 2-4 Use as a quiz or review of Lesson 2-3.

Mathematical Background notes are available for this lesson on p. 66D.

How can you use the division of rational numbers to describe data?

Ask students:

* What is another word for mean as it is used in this problem? **average**

* How do you find the average or mean of a set of numbers? **Add the numbers and then divide the sum by the number of data items in the set.**

* If you add the numbers in the Change column in the table, will the sum be positive or negative? **negative**

What You'll Learn

* Divide integers.
* Divide rational numbers.

How can you use division of rational numbers to describe data?

TEACHING TIP

Additional practice for finding the mean is provided on pages 818 and 819.

Each year, many sea turtles are stranded on the Texas Gulf Coast. The number of sea turtles stranded from 1997 to 2000 and the changes in number from the previous years are shown in the table. The following expression can be used to find the *mean* change per year of the number of stranded turtles.

$$\text{mean} = \frac{(-127) + 54 + (-65)}{3}$$

Stranded Sea Turtles Texas Gulf Coast

Year	Number of Turtles	Change
1997	523	——
1998	396	−127
1999	450	+54
2000	385	−65

Source: www.ridleyturtles.org

DIVIDE INTEGERS Since multiplication and division are inverse operations, the rule for finding the sign of the quotient of two numbers is similar to the rule for finding the sign of a product of two numbers.

Key Concept
Division of Integers

* **Words** The quotient of two numbers having the *same sign* is positive. The quotient of two numbers having *different signs* is negative.

* **Examples** $(-60) \div (-5) = 12$ same signs → positive quotient
  $32 \div (-8) = -4$ different signs → negative quotient

Example 1 *Divide Integers*

Find each quotient.

a. $-77 \div 11$

$-77 \div 11 = -7$ negative quotient

b. $\dfrac{-51}{-3}$

$\dfrac{-51}{-3} = -51 \div (-3)$ Divide.
$= 17$ positive quotient

When simplifying fractions, recall that the fraction bar is a grouping symbol.

Example 2 *Simplify Before Dividing*

Simplify $\dfrac{-3(-12 + 8)}{7 + (-5)}$.

$\dfrac{-3(-12 + 8)}{7 + (-5)} = \dfrac{-3(-4)}{7 + (-5)}$ Simplify the numerator first.

$= \dfrac{12}{7 + (-5)}$ Multiply.

$= \dfrac{12}{2}$ or 6 same signs → positive quotient

Resource Manager

📂 Workbook and Reproducible Masters

Chapter 2 Resource Masters
* Study Guide and Intervention, pp. 93–94
* Skills Practice, p. 95
* Practice, p. 96
* Reading to Learn Mathematics, p. 97
* Enrichment, p. 98
* Assessment, pp. 131, 133

Parent and Student Study Guide Workbook, p. 14
Prerequisite Skills Workbook, pp. 15–16, 19–20, 29–32, 39–40, 47–48, 51–54, 63–66, 75–76
School-to-Career Masters, p. 4

 Transparencies

5-Minute Check Transparency 2-4
Answer Key Transparencies

 Technology

AlgePASS: Tutorial Plus, Lesson 3
Interactive Chalkboard

DIVIDE RATIONAL NUMBERS The rules for dividing positive and negative integers also apply to division with rational numbers. Remember that to divide by any nonzero number, multiply by the reciprocal of that number.

Example 3 Divide Rational Numbers

Find each quotient.

a. $245.66 \div (-14.2)$

$245.66 \div (-14.2) = -17.3$ Use a calculator.
                                different signs → negative quotient

b. $-\dfrac{2}{5} \div \dfrac{1}{4}$

$-\dfrac{2}{5} \div \dfrac{1}{4} = -\dfrac{2}{5} \cdot \dfrac{4}{1}$ Multiply by $\dfrac{4}{1}$, the reciprocal of $\dfrac{1}{4}$.

$\qquad = -\dfrac{8}{5}$ or $-1\dfrac{3}{5}$ different signs → negative quotient

Example 4 Divide Rational Numbers to Solve a Problem

ARCHITECTURE The Pentagon in Washington, D.C., has an outside perimeter of 4608 feet. Find the length of each outside wall.

To find the length of each wall, divide the perimeter by the number of sides.

$4608 \div 5 = 921.6$ same signs → positive quotient

The length of each outside wall is 921.6 feet.

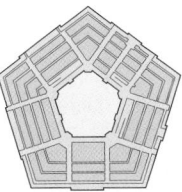
The Pentagon

You can use the Distributive Property to simplify fractional expressions.

Example 5 Simplify Algebraic Expressions

Simplify $\dfrac{24 - 6a}{3}$.

$\dfrac{24 - 6a}{3} = (24 - 6a) \div 3$ The fraction bar indicates division.

$\qquad = (24 - 6a)\left(\dfrac{1}{3}\right)$ Multiply by $\dfrac{1}{3}$, the reciprocal of 3.

$\qquad = 24\left(\dfrac{1}{3}\right) - 6a\left(\dfrac{1}{3}\right)$ Distributive Property

$\qquad = 8 - 2a$ Simplify.

Example 6 Evaluate Algebraic Expressions

Evaluate $\dfrac{ab}{c^2}$ if $a = -7.8$, $b = 5.2$, and $c = -3$. Round to the nearest hundredth.

$\dfrac{ab}{c^2} = \dfrac{(-7.8)(5.2)}{(-3)^2}$ Replace a with -7.8, b with 5.2, and c with -3.

$\qquad = \dfrac{-40.56}{9}$ Find the numerator and denominator separately.

$\qquad \approx -4.51$ Use a calculator. different signs → negative quotient

---

DIVIDE INTEGERS

In-Class Examples   Power Point®

1 Find each quotient.

a. $-60 \div (-5)$ **12**

b. $\dfrac{-108}{18}$ **−6**

2 Simplify $\dfrac{2(1 - 5)}{17 + (-13)}$. **−2**

DIVIDE RATIONAL NUMBERS

In-Class Examples   Power Point®

3 Find each quotient.

a. $-112.23 \div 8.7$ **−12.9**

b. $-\dfrac{3}{8} \div \left(-\dfrac{1}{3}\right)$ **$\dfrac{9}{8}$ or $1\dfrac{1}{8}$**

4 **BASEBALL** The perimeter of a square baseball diamond is 360 feet. Find the length of one side of the diamond. **90 ft**

Teaching Tip You may also want to show Example 5 as the difference of two fractions with the same denominator.

$\dfrac{24 - 6a}{3} = \dfrac{24}{3} - \dfrac{6a}{3} = 8 - 2a$

5 Simplify $\dfrac{-39b + 65}{13}$. **−3b + 5**

6 Evaluate $\dfrac{wx}{y^2}$ if $w = 2$, $x = -9.1$ and $y = 4$. **−1.1375**

3 Practice/Apply

Study Notebook

Have students—
• record the rules for dividing integers.
• include any other item(s) that they find helpful in mastering the skills in this lesson.

Concept Check
1. **Compare and contrast** multiplying and dividing rational numbers. **See margin.**

2. **OPEN ENDED** Find a value for x if $\frac{1}{x} > x$. **Sample answer:** $\frac{1}{2}$

3. **Explain** how to divide any rational number by another rational number.
   To divide by a rational number, multiply by its reciprocal.

Guided Practice

Find each quotient.

GUIDED PRACTICE KEY	
Exercises	Examples
4–9	1, 3
10–12	2, 5
13–15	6
16	4

4. $96 \div (-6)$ **−16**
5. $-36 \div 4$ **−9**
6. $-64 \div 5$ **−12.8**
7. $64.4 \div 2.5$ **25.76**
8. $-\frac{2}{3} \div 12$ **$-\frac{1}{18}$**
9. $-\frac{2}{3} \div \frac{4}{5}$ **$-\frac{5}{6}$**

Simplify each expression.

10. $\frac{25 + 3}{-4}$ **−7**
11. $\frac{-650a}{10}$ **−65a**
12. $\frac{6b + 18}{-2}$ **−3b − 9**

Evaluate each expression if $a = 3$, $b = -4.5$, and $c = 7.5$. Round to the nearest hundredth.

13. $\frac{2ab}{-ac}$ **1.2**
14. $\frac{cb}{4a}$ **−2.81**
15. $-\frac{a}{b} \div \frac{a}{c}$ **1.67**

Application
16. **ONLINE SHOPPING** During the 2000 holiday season, the sixth most visited online shopping site recorded 419,000 visitors. This is eight times as many visitors as in 1999. About how many visitors did the site have in 1999? **52,375**

★ indicates increased difficulty

Homework Help

For Exercises	See Examples
17–36	1, 3
37–44	5
45, 46, 55–57	4
47–54	6

Extra Practice
See page 824.

Find each quotient.

17. $-64 \div (-8)$ **8**
18. $-78 \div (-4)$ **19.5**
19. $-78 \div (-1.3)$ **60**
20. $108 \div (-0.9)$ **−120**
21. $42.3 \div (-6)$ **−7.05**
22. $68.4 \div (-12)$ **−5.7**
23. $-23.94 \div 10.5$ **−2.28**
24. $-60.97 \div 13.4$ **−4.55**
25. $-32.25 \div (-2.5)$ **12.9**
26. $-98.44 \div (-4.6)$ **21.4**
27. $-\frac{1}{3} \div 4$ **$-\frac{1}{12}$**
28. $-\frac{3}{4} \div 12$ **$-\frac{1}{16}$**
29. $-7 \div \frac{3}{5}$ **$-\frac{35}{3}$ or $-11\frac{2}{3}$**
30. $-5 \div \frac{2}{7}$ **$-\frac{35}{2}$ or $-17\frac{1}{2}$**
31. $\frac{16}{36} \div \frac{24}{60}$ **$\frac{10}{9}$ or $1\frac{1}{9}$**
32. $-\frac{24}{56} \div \frac{31}{63}$ **$-\frac{27}{31}$**
★ 33. $\frac{14}{32} \div \left(-\frac{12}{25}\right)$ **$-\frac{175}{192}$**
★ 34. $\frac{80}{25} \div \left(-\frac{2}{3}\right)$ **$-\frac{24}{5}$ or $-4\frac{4}{5}$**

35. Find the quotient of -74 and $-\frac{5}{3}$. **$\frac{222}{5}$ or $44\frac{2}{5}$**

36. Find the quotient of -156 and $-\frac{3}{8}$. **416**

Simplify each expression.

37. $\frac{81c}{9}$ **9c**
38. $\frac{105g}{5}$ **21g**
39. $\frac{8r + 24}{-8}$ **$-r - 3$**
40. $\frac{7h + 35}{-7}$ **$-h - 5$**
41. $\frac{40a - 50b}{20a - 25b}$ **2**
42. $\frac{42c - 18d}{14c - 6d}$ **3**
★ 43. $\frac{-8f + (-16g)}{-f - 2g}$ **8**
★ 44. $\frac{-5x + (-10y)}{-x - 2y}$ **5**

45. **CRAFTS** Hannah is making pillows. The pattern states that she needs $1\frac{3}{4}$ yards of fabric for each pillow. If she has $4\frac{1}{2}$ yards of fabric, how many pillows can she make? **2**

46. **BOWLING** Bowling centers in the United States made $2,800,000,000 in 1990. Their receipts in 1998 were $2,764,000,000. What was the average change in revenue for each of these 8 years? **Source:** U.S. Census Bureau **−$4,500,000**

86   Chapter 2   Real Numbers

Answer

1. Sample answer: Dividing and multiplying numbers with the same signs both result in a positive answer while dividing or multiplying numbers with different signs results in a negative answer. However, when you divide rational numbers in fractional form, you must multiply by a reciprocal.

About the Exercises...

Organization by Objective
- **Divide Integers:** 17, 18, 37–44
- **Divide Rational Numbers:** 19–36, 45–54

Odd/Even Assignments
Exercises 17–54 are structured so that students practice the same concepts whether they are assigned odd or even problems.

Assignment Guide

Basic: 17–31 odd, 35–41 odd, 45–51 odd, 55, 58–77

Average: 17–55 odd, 58–77

Advanced: 18–54 even, 56–73 (optional: 74–77)

4 Assess

Open-Ended Assessment

Writing Display an expression similar to that found in Example 6. Have one group of students evaluate the numerator while another evaluates the denominator. Have each group explain their results and then together find the quotient.

Getting Ready for Lesson 2-5

PREREQUISITE SKILL Students will learn about displaying and analyzing data in Lesson 2-5, including analyzing means, medians, and modes. Use Exercises 74–77 to determine your students' familiarity with finding mean, median, and mode.

Assessment Options

Quiz (Lessons 2-3 and 2-4) is available on p. 131 of the *Chapter 2 Resource Masters*.

Mid-Chapter Test (Lessons 2-1 through 2-4) is available on p. 133 of the *Chapter 2 Resource Masters*.

Evaluate each expression if $m = -8$, $n = 6.5$, $p = 3.2$, and $q = -5.4$.
Round to the nearest hundredth.

47. $\frac{mn}{p}$ -16.25 **48.** $\frac{np}{m}$ -2.6 **49.** $mq \div np$ 2.08   **50.** $pq \div mn$ 0.33

51. $\frac{n+p}{m}$ -1.21 **52.** $\frac{m+p}{q}$ 0.89   ★ **53.** $\frac{m-2n}{-n+q}$ 1.76   ★ **54.** $\frac{p-3q}{-q-m}$ 1.45

55. BUSINESS The president of a small business is looking at her profit/loss statement for the past year. The loss in income for the last year was $23,985. On average, what was the loss per month last year? **$1998.75**

JEWELRY For Exercises 56 and 57, use the following information.
The gold content of jewelry is given in karats. For example, 24-karat gold is pure gold, and 18-karat gold is $\frac{18}{24}$ or 0.75 gold. **56.** $\frac{5}{12}$; $\frac{7}{12}$

56. What fraction of 10-karat gold is pure gold? What fraction is not gold?

57. If a piece of jewelry is $\frac{2}{3}$ gold, how would you describe it using karats?
16-karat gold

58. CRITICAL THINKING What is the least positive integer that is divisible by all whole numbers from 1 to 9? **2520**

59. WRITING IN MATH   Answer the question that was posed at the beginning of the lesson. **See margin.**

How can you use division of rational numbers to describe data?

Include the following in your answer:
- an explanation of how you could use the mean of a set of data to describe changes in the data over time, and
- reasons why you think the change from year to year is not consistent.

Standardized Test Practice
Ⓐ Ⓑ Ⓒ Ⓓ

60. If the rod is cut as shown, how many inches long will each piece be? **D**

← 6.25 ft →

Ⓐ 0.625 in.   Ⓑ 1.875 in.
Ⓒ 5.2 in.   Ⓓ 7.5 in.

61. If $\frac{17}{3} = x$, then what is the value of $6x + 1$? **B**

Ⓐ 32   Ⓑ 33   Ⓒ 35   Ⓓ 44

Maintain Your Skills

Mixed Review   **Find each product.** *(Lesson 2-3)*

62. $-4(11)$ -44 **63.** $-2.5(-1.2)$ 3   **64.** $\frac{1}{4}(-5)$ $-1\frac{1}{4}$ **65.** $1.6(0.3)$ 0.48

Find each difference. *(Lesson 2-2)*

66. $8 - (-6)$ 14   **67.** $15 - 21$ -6 **68.** $-7.5 - 4.8$ -12.3 **69.** $-\frac{5}{8} - \left(-\frac{1}{6}\right)$ $-\frac{11}{24}$

70. Name the property illustrated by $2(1.2 + 3.8) = 2 \cdot 5$. **Subs.**

Simplify each expression. If not possible, write *simplified.* *(Lesson 1-5)*

71. $8b + 12(b + 2)$ **72.** $6(5a + 3b - 2b)$ **73.** $3(x + 2y) - 2y$
   $20b + 24$ $30a + 6b$ $3x + 4y$

Getting Ready for the Next Lesson   **PREREQUISITE SKILL** Find the mean, median, and mode for each set of data.
*(To review **mean**, **median**, and **mode**, see pages 818 and 819.)*

74. 40, 34, 40, 28, 38 **36; 38; 40**   **75.** 3, 9, 0, 2, 11, 8, 14, 3 **6.25; 5.5; 3**

76. 1.2, 1.7, 1.9, 1.8, 1.2, 1.0, 1.5   **77.** 79, 84, 81, 84, 75, 73, 80, 78
           1.5; 1.5; 1.2   **79.25; 79.5; 84**

Answer

59. Sample answer: You use division to find the mean of a set of data. Answers should include the following.
- You could track the mean number of turtles stranded each year and note if the value increases or decreases.
- Weather or pollution could affect the turtles.

Study Guide and Intervention, p. 93 (shown) and p. 94

Divide Integers The rules for finding the sign of a quotient are similar to the rules for finding the sign of a product.

Dividing Two Numbers with the Same Sign	The quotient of two numbers having the same sign is positive.
Dividing Two Numbers with Different Signs	The quotient of two numbers having different signs is negative.

Example 1 Find each quotient.
a. $-88 \div (-4)$
$-88 \div (-4) = 22$ same signs → positive quotient
b. $\frac{-64}{8}$
$\frac{-64}{8} = -8$ different signs → negative quotient

Example 2 Simplify $\frac{-4(-10+2)}{-3+(-1)}$.
$\frac{-4(-10+2)}{-3+(-1)} = \frac{-4(-8)}{-3+(-1)}$
$= \frac{32}{-3+(-1)}$
$= \frac{32}{-4}$
$= -8$

Exercises

Find each quotient.
1. $-80 \div (-10)$ 8
2. $-32 \div 16$ -2
3. $80 \div 5$ 16
4. $18 \div (-3)$ -6
5. $-12 \div (-3)$ 4
6. $8 \div (-2)$ -4
7. $-15 \div (-3)$ 5
8. $121 \div (-11)$ -11
9. $-24 \div 1.5$ -16
10. $0 \div (-8)$ 0
11. $-125 \div (-25)$ 5
12. $-104 \div 4$ -26

Simplify.
13. $\frac{-2+(-4)}{(-2)+(-1)}$ 2
14. $\frac{5(-10+(-2))}{-2+1}$ 60
15. $\frac{-6(-6+2)}{-10+(-2)}$ -2
16. $\frac{-12(2+(-3))}{-4+1}$ -4
17. $\frac{-4(-8+(-4))}{-3+(-3)}$ -8
18. $\frac{4(-12+4)}{-2(8)}$ 2

Skills Practice, p. 95 and Practice, p. 96 (shown)

Find each quotient.
1. $75 \div (-15)$ -5
2. $-323 \div (-17)$ 19
3. $-88 \div 16$ -5.5
4. $65.7 \div (-9)$ -7.3
5. $-36.08 \div 8$ -4.51
6. $-40.05 \div (-2.5)$ 16.02
7. $-9 \div \frac{3}{5}$ -15
8. $-\frac{5}{6} \div \left(-\frac{3}{8}\right)$ $\frac{20}{9}$ or $2\frac{2}{9}$
9. $\frac{14}{63} \div \left(-\frac{49}{54}\right)$ $-\frac{12}{49}$

Simplify each expression.
10. $\frac{168p}{-14}$ $-12p$
11. $\frac{25-5x}{5}$ $5-x$
12. $\frac{3t+12}{-3}$ $-t+(-4)$
13. $\frac{18x+12y}{-6}$ $-3x+(-2y)$
14. $\frac{8k-12h}{4}$ $2k-3h$
15. $\frac{-4c+(-16d)}{4}$ $-c+(-4d)$

Evaluate each expression if $p = -6$, $q = 4.5$, $r = 3.6$, and $s = -5.2$. Round to the nearest hundredth.
16. $\frac{qr}{p}$ -2.7
17. $\frac{rs}{q}$ -4.16
18. $ps \div qr$ 1.93
19. $rs \div pq$ 0.69
20. $\frac{p-q}{r}$ -2.92
21. $\frac{r+s}{q}$ -0.36

22. EXERCISE Ashley walks $2\frac{1}{2}$ miles around a lake three times a week. If Ashley walks around the lake in $\frac{3}{4}$ hour, what is her rate of speed? (*Hint:* Use the formula $r = \frac{d}{t}$, where r is rate, d is distance, and t is time.) $3\frac{1}{3}$ mi/h

23. PUBLICATION A production assistant must divide a page of text into two columns. If the page is $6\frac{3}{4}$ inches wide, how wide will each column be? $3\frac{3}{8}$ in.

ROLLER COASTERS For Exercises 24 and 25, use the following information.
The formula for acceleration is $a = \frac{f-s}{t}$, where a is acceleration, f is final speed, s is starting speed, and t is time.

24. The Hypersonic XLC roller coaster in Virginia goes from zero to 80 miles per hour in 1.8 seconds. What is its acceleration in miles per hour per second to the nearest tenth? **Source:** www.rcdb.com about 44.4 mi/h per second

25. What is the acceleration in feet per second per second? (*Hint:* Convert miles per hour and hours to seconds, then apply the formula for acceleration. 1 mile = 5280 feet) about 65.2 ft/s per second

Reading to Learn Mathematics, p. 97   ELL

Pre-Activity How can you use division of rational numbers to describe data?
Read the introduction to Lesson 2-4 at the top of page 84 in your textbook.
- What is meant by the term *mean*?
the sum of a set of data items divided by the number of data items.
- In the expression $\frac{(-127)+54+(-65)}{3}$, will the numerator be positive or negative?
negative

Reading the Lesson

1. Explain what the term *inverse operations* means to you.
Sample answer: Inverse operations are operations that undo one another.

2. Write *negative* or *positive* to describe the quotient. Explain your answer.

Expression	Negative or Positive?	Explanation
a. $\frac{36}{-7}$	negative	The signs of the two numbers are different.
b. $\frac{-78}{-13}$	positive	The signs of the two numbers are the same.
c. $\frac{(-5.6)(-2.4)}{1.92}$	positive	After multiplying, the signs of the numbers being divided are the same.

Helping You Remember

3. Explain how knowing the rules for multiplying rational numbers can help you remember the rules for dividing rational numbers.
Sample answer: Both rules state that the *answer* (product for multiplication, quotient for division) is positive if the signs are the same and negative if the signs are different.

Enrichment, p. 98

Other Kinds of Means

There are many different types of means besides the arithmetic mean. A mean for a set of numbers has these two properties.
a. It typifies or represents the set.
b. It is not less than the least number and it is not greater than the greatest number.

Here are the formulas for the arithmetic mean and three other means.

Arithmetic Mean
Add the numbers in the set. Then divide the sum by n, the number of elements in the set.
$$\frac{x_1 + x_2 + x_3 + \cdots + x_n}{n}$$

Geometric Mean
Multiply all the numbers in the set. Then find the nth root of their product.
$$\sqrt[n]{x_1 \cdot x_2 \cdot x_3 \cdot \cdots \cdot x_n}$$

Harmonic Mean
Divide the number of elements in the set by the reciprocals of...

Quadratic Mean
Add the squares of the numbers. Divide...

1 Focus

 **5-Minute Check Transparency 2-5** Use as a quiz or review of Lesson 2-4.

Mathematical Background notes are available for this lesson on p. 66D. This lesson covers *univariate data*, which means data depending on only one random variable.

Building on Prior Knowledge

In Chapter 1, students learned how graphs can be used to visualize data. In this lesson, students will learn about other types of graphs for visualizing data.

How are line plots and averages used to make decisions?

Ask students:

- What was the most popular boys' name in all five decades? How can you tell? The most popular boys' name in all five decades was Michael because it is in the first column for all five decades.

- Were any girls' names as popular as Michael? How can you tell? No, because no girl's name appears twice in any of the five columns.

What You'll Learn

- Interpret and create line plots and stem-and-leaf plots.
- Analyze data using mean, median, and mode.

How are line plots and averages used to make decisions?

How many people do you know with the same first name? Some names are more popular than others. The table below lists the top five most popular names for boys and girls born in each decade from 1950 to 1999.

Top Five First Names of America

Boys Girls						
1950-59	Michael	James	Robert	John	David
	Deborah	Mary	Linda	Patricia	Susan
1960-69	Michael	John	David	James	Robert
	Lisa	Deborah	Mary	Karen	Michelle
1970-79	Michael	Christopher	Jason	David	James
	Jennifer	Michelle	Amy	Melissa	Kimberly
1980-89	Michael	Christopher	Matthew	Joshua	David
	Jessica	Jennifer	Ashley	Sarah	Amanda
1990-99	Michael	Christopher	Matthew	Joshua	Nicholas
	Ashley	Jessica	Sarah	Brittany	Emily

Source: *The World Almanac*

To help determine which names appear most frequently, these data could be displayed graphically.

Vocabulary
- line plot
- frequency
- stem-and-leaf plot
- back-to-back stem-and-leaf plot
- measures of central tendency

CREATE LINE PLOTS AND STEM-AND-LEAF PLOTS In some cases, data can be presented using a **line plot**. Most line plots have a number line labeled with a scale to include all the data. Then an × is placed above a data point each time it occurs to represent the **frequency** of the data.

Example 1 *Create a Line Plot*

Draw a line plot for the data.

−2 4 3 2 6 10 7 4 −2 0 10 8 7 10 7 4 −1 9 −1 3

Step 1 The values of the data range from −2 to 10, so construct a number line containing those points.

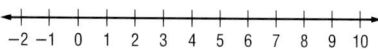

Step 2 Then place an × above a number each time it occurs.

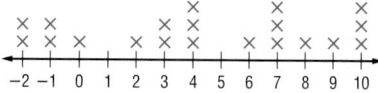

Resource Manager

Workbook and Reproducible Masters

Chapter 2 Resource Masters
- Study Guide and Intervention, pp. 99–100
- Skills Practice, p. 101
- Practice, p. 102
- Reading to Learn Mathematics, p. 103
- Enrichment, p. 104

Parent and Student Study Guide Workbook, p. 15
Prerequisite Skills Workbook, pp. 15–16, 61–62, 75–76

 Transparencies
5-Minute Check Transparency 2-5
Answer Key Transparencies

 Technology
Interactive Chalkboard

Line plots are a convenient way to organize data for comparison.

Example 2 Use a Line Plot to Solve a Problem

ANIMALS The speeds (mph) of 20 of the fastest land animals are listed below.

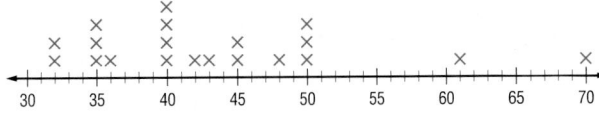

| 45 | 70 | 43 | 45 | 32 | 42 | 40 | 40 | 35 | 50 |
| 40 | 35 | 61 | 48 | 35 | 32 | 50 | 36 | 50 | 40 |

Source: *The World Almanac*

a. Make a line plot of the data.
The lowest value is 30, and the highest value is 70, so use a scale that includes those values. Place an × above each value for each occurrence.

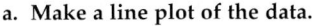

b. Which speed occurs most frequently?
Looking at the line plot, we can easily see that 40 miles per hour occurs most frequently.

Another way to organize and display data is by using a **stem-and-leaf plot**. In a stem-and-leaf plot, the greatest common place value is used for the *stems*. The numbers in the next greatest place value are used to form the *leaves*. In Example 2, the greatest place value is tens. Thus, 32 miles per hour would have a stem of 3 and a leaf of 2. A complete stem-and-leaf plot for the data in Example 2 is shown below.

Stem	Leaf
3	2 2 5 5 5 6
4	0 0 0 0 2 3 5 5 8
5	0 0 0
6	1
7	0

$3|2 = 32$
↑
key

Example 3 Create a Stem-and-Leaf Plot

Use the data below to make a stem-and-leaf plot.

| 108 | 104 | 86 | 82 | 80 | 72 | 70 | 62 | 64 | 68 | 84 | 64 | 98 | 96 | 98 |
| 103 | 87 | 65 | 83 | 79 | 97 | 96 | 112 | 62 | 80 | 62 | 83 | 76 | 66 | 97 |

The greatest common place value is tens, so the digits in the tens place are the stems.

Stem	Leaf
6	2 2 2 4 4 5 6 8
7	0 2 6 9
8	0 0 2 3 3 4 6 7
9	6 6 7 7 8 8
10	3 4 8
11	2

$10|3 = 103$

A **back-to-back stem-and-leaf plot** can be used to compare two related sets of data.

www.algebra1.com/extra_examples

Lesson 2-5 Statistics: Displaying and Analyzing Data **89**

Study Tip

Stem-and-Leaf Plots
A key is included on stem-and-leaf plots to indicate what the stems and leaves represent when read.

---

2 Teach

CREATE LINE PLOTS AND STEM-AND-LEAF PLOTS

In-Class Examples Power Point®

Reading Tip Explain that the *frequency* of the data is how many times a given number occurs. For example, in Example 1, the number 4 occurs 3 times, so its frequency is 3.

1 Draw a line plot for the data.
11 −2 10 −2 7 2 7 4 9 0
 6   9 7 2 0 4 10 7 6 9

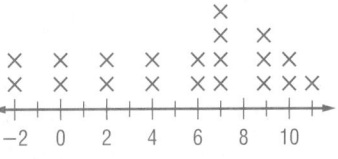

2 **TRAFFIC** The highway patrol did a radar survey of the speeds of cars along a stretch of highway for 1 minute. The speeds (in miles per hour) of the 20 cars that passed are listed below.
72 70 72 74 68 69 70
72 74 75 79 75 74 72
70 64 69 66 68 67

a. Make a line plot of the data.

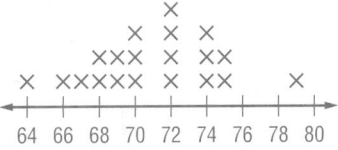

b. Which speed occurs most frequently? **72 mph**

---

3 Use the data below to make a stem-and-leaf plot.

85	115	126	92	104	107
78	131	114	92	85	116
100	121	123	131	88	97
99	116	79	90	110	129
108	93	84	75	70	132

Stem	Leaf
7	0 5 8 9
8	4 5 5 8
9	0 2 2 3 7 9
10	0 4 7 8
11	0 4 5 6 6
12	1 3 6 9
13	1 1 2 11|5 = 115

4 **WEATHER** Monique wants to compare the monthly average high temperatures of Dallas and Atlanta before she decides to which city she wants to move. The table shows the monthly average high temperatures (°F) for both cities.

Monthly Average High Temperature	
Dallas	**Atlanta**
54 59 68 77	50 55 64 72
83 91 95 95	75 85 88 87
87 78 66 57	81 72 63 54

a. Make a stem-and-leaf plot to compare the data.

Dallas	Stem	Atlanta
9 7 4	5	0 4 5
8 6	6	3 4
8 7	7	2 2 5
7 3	8	1 5 7 8
5 5 1	9	

8\|6 = 68   7\|2 = 72

b. What is the difference between the highest average temperatures in each city? **7°F**

c. Which city has higher average temperatures? **Dallas has a greater number of average high temperatures above 80°F.**

Example 4 Back-to-Back Stem-and-Leaf Plot

Mrs. Evans wants to compare recent test scores from her two algebra classes. The table shows the scores for both classes.

Algebra Test Scores

Class 1
83 79 93 79 72
98 76 86 94 68
90 85 79 89 77
82 87 68 78 89
93 86 93 74 67

Class 2
86 95 88 78 85
86 88 100 83 75
89 95 78 76 83
85 96 80 62 87
80 92 76 92 75

a. Make a stem-and-leaf plot to compare the data.
To compare the data, we can use a back-to-back stem-and-leaf plot. Since the data represent similar measurements, the plot will share a common stem.

Class 1	Stem	Class 2
8 8 7	6	2
9 9 9 8 7 6 4 2	7	5 5 6 6 8 8
9 9 7 6 6 5 3 2	8	0 0 3 3 5 5 6 6 7 8 8 9
8 4 3 3 3 0	9	2 2 5 5 6
7|6 = 67	10	0 6|2 = 62

b. What is the difference between the highest score in each class?
100 − 98 or 2 points

c. Which class scored higher overall on the test?
Looking at the scores of 80 and above, we see that class 2 has a greater number of scores at or above 80 than class 1.

ANALYZE DATA When analyzing data, it is helpful to have one number that describes the set of data. Numbers known as **measures of central tendency** are often used to describe sets of data because they represent a centralized, or middle, value. Three of the most commonly used measures of central tendency are the mean, median, and mode.

When you use a measure of central tendency to describe a set of data, it is important that the measure you use best represents all of the data.

- Extremely high or low values can affect the mean, while not affecting the median or mode.
- A value with a high frequency can cause the mode to be misleading.
- Data that is clustered with a few values separate from the cluster can cause the median to be too low or too high.

Example 5 Analyze Data

Which measure of central tendency best represents the data?
Determine the mean, median, and mode.

		Stem	Leaf
		7	7 8 9
		8	2 2 2 2 2 3 4 4 6
		9	
		10	8
		11	6 8 7|9 = 0.79

The mean is about 0.88.   Add the data and divide by 15.
The median is 0.82.   The middle value is 0.82.
The mode is 0.82.   The most frequent value is 0.82.

Either the median or the mode best represent the set of data since both measures are located in the center of the majority of the data. In this instance, the mean is too high.

Study Tip

Look Back
To review **finding mean**, **median**, and **mode**, see pages 818 and 819.

Example 6 Determine the Best Measure of Central Tendency

PRESIDENTS The numbers below show the ages of the U.S. Presidents since 1900 at the time they were inaugurated. Which measure of central tendency best represents the data?

42 51 56 55 51 54 51 60 62
43 55 56 61 52 69 64 46 54

The mean is about 54.6.   Add the data and divide by 18.

The median is 54.5.   The middle value is 54.5.

The mode is 51.   The most frequent value is 51.

The mean or the median can be used to best represent the data. The mode for the data is too low.

Check for Understanding

Concept Check

1. They describe the data as a whole.

1. **Explain** why it is useful to find the mean, median, and mode of a set of data.
2. Mitchell says that a line plot and a line graph are the same thing. Show that he is incorrect. **See pp. 117A–117B.**
3. **OPEN ENDED** Write a set of data for which the median is a better representation than the mean. **Sample answer: 13, 14, 14, 28**

Guided Practice

4. Use the data to make a line plot. **See pp. 117A–117B.**

22 19 14 15 14 21 19 16 22 19 10 15 19 14 19

GUIDED PRACTICE KEY	
Exercises	Examples
4, 5	1, 2
6, 7, 9, 10, 12, 13	5, 6
8, 11	3, 4

For Exercises 5–7, use the list that shows the number of hours students in Mr. Ricardo's class spent online last week.

7 4 7 11 3 1 5 10 10 0 9 4 0 14 13 4
11 3 1 12 0 9 13 14 7 6 10 5 12 0 6 5

5. Make a line plot of the data. **See pp. 117A–117B.**
6. Which value occurs most frequently? **0**
7. Does the mean, median, or mode best represent the data? Explain. **See pp. 117A–117B.**
8. Use the data to make a stem-and-leaf plot. **See pp. 117A–117B.**

68 66 68 88 76 71 88 93 86 64 73 80 81 72 68

For Exercises 9 and 10, use the data in the stem-and-leaf plot.

Stem	Leaf
9	3 5 5
10	2 2 5 8
11	5 8 8 9 9 9
12	0 1 7 8 9 9|3 = 9.3

9. What is the difference between the least and greatest values? **3.6**
10. Which measure of central tendency best describes the data? Explain.
Median; most of the data clusters higher, near the median.

Application

BUILDINGS For Exercises 11–13, use the data below that represents the number of stories in the 25 tallest buildings in the world.

88 88 110 88 80 69 102 78 70 54 80 85
83 100 60 90 77 55 73 55 56 61 75 64 105

13. The mode is not the best measure as it is higher than most of the values.

11. Make a stem-and-leaf plot of the data. **See pp. 117A–117B.**
12. Which value occurs most frequently? **88**
13. Does the mode best describe the set of data? Explain.

Lesson 2-5 Statistics: Displaying and Analyzing Data **91**

In-Class Examples

5 Which measure of central tendency best represents the data?

Stem	Leaf
4	1 1 2 4 4 4 5 8
5	0
6	2 5 7
7	3 9
8	1 6|2 = 6.2

The mean is about 5.5.
The median is 4.8.
The mode is 4.4.
Either the median or the mode best represent the data. The mean is too high.

6 **POLITICS** The number of electoral votes for the 12 most populous states in the 2000 Presidential election are listed below. Which measure of central tendency best represents the data?
21 22 18 23 15 25
14 32 13 33 13 54

The mean is about 23.6.
The median is 21.5.
The mode is 13.
Either the mean or median can be used to represent the data. The mode is too low.

3 Practice/Apply

Study Notebook

Have students—

- add the definitions/examples of the vocabulary terms to their Vocabulary Builder worksheets for Chapter 2.
- create examples of a line plot and a stem-and-leaf plot, along with the data used to create the plots. They can even use the same set of data to create both plots.
- include any other item(s) that they find helpful in mastering the skills in this lesson.

DAILY INTERVENTION
Unlocking Misconceptions

Mean and Median Mean and median are two mathematical terms that are often confused. Remind students that the mean is the arithmetic average of a set of data and the median is the number that is in the middle of the set of data. The mean and median can be very similar if the values in the data set are evenly spread between the lowest and highest value. But a few very high or very low values in a data set can cause the mean and median to have significantly different values.

About the Exercises...

Organization by Objective
• **Create Line Plots and Stem–and–Leaf Plots:** 14–16, 20–22, 28, 32, 35
• **Analyze Data:** 17–19, 23–25, 27, 29–31, 33–34, 36–37, 39–41

Odd/Even Assignments
Exercises 14–15 and 20–21 are structured so that students practice the same concepts whether they are assigned odd or even problems.

Alert! Exercise 25 involves research on the Internet or other reference materials.

Assignment Guide
Basic: 15–19, 21–27, 38, 42–64
Average: 15, 21, 25–34, 38–64
Advanced: 14, 20, 35–56 (optional: 57–64)

Answers

14.

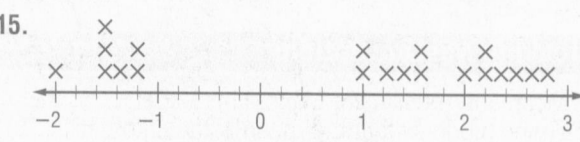

36 38 40 42 44 46 48 50 52 54

15. See below right.

16.

```
        ×
        × ×
        × ×
        × × ×
        × × ×
        × × ×
        × × × × ×
        × × × × ×
        × × × × ×                  ×
        × × × × × × ×               ×
   1    3    5    7    9
```

20.

Stem	Leaf
5	8 9
6	0 3 5 6 9
7	0 1 1 2 3

$5|8 = 5.8$

21.

Stem	Leaf
1	8 8
2	2 3 6 6 6 8 9
3	0 1 1 2 3 4
4	7

$1|8 = 18$

Practice and Apply

Homework Help

For Exercises	See Examples
14–18	1, 2
20–22, 28, 29, 32, 33, 35, 36	3, 4
19, 23–27, 30, 31, 34, 37	5, 6

Extra Practice
See page 824.

Use each set of data to make a line plot. 14–15. See margin.

14. 43 36 48 52 41 54 45 48 49 52 35 44 53 46 38 41 53

15. 1.0 −1.5 1.5 2.0 −1.5 2.1 −2.0 2.4 1.5 −1.4 2.5 1.4 −1.2 1.3 1.0 2.2 2.3 −1.2 −1.5 2.1

BASKETBALL For Exercises 16–19, use the table that shows the seeds, or rank, of the NCAA men's basketball Final Four from 1991 to 2001.

16. Make a line plot of the data. **See margin.**

17. How many of the teams in the Final Four were *not* number 1 seeds? **23**

18. How many teams were seeded higher than third? (*Hint*: Higher seeds have lesser numerical value.) **29**

19. Which measure of central tendency best describes the data? Explain. **Sample answer: Median; most of the data are near 2.**

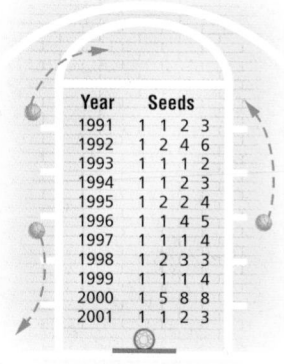

Year	Seeds
1991	1 1 2 3
1992	1 2 4 6
1993	1 1 1 2
1994	1 1 2 3
1995	1 2 2 4
1996	1 1 4 5
1997	1 1 1 4
1998	1 2 3 3
1999	1 1 1 4
2000	1 5 8 8
2001	1 1 2 3

Source: www.espn.com

Use each set of data to make a stem-and-leaf plot. 20–21. See margin.

20. 6.5 6.3 6.9 7.1 7.3 5.9 6.0 7.0 7.2 6.6 7.1 5.8

21. 31 30 28 26 22 34 26 31 47 32 18 33 26 23 18 29

WEATHER For Exercises 22–24, use the list of the highest recorded temperatures in each of the 50 states.

112	100	128	120	134	118	106	110	109	112
100	118	117	116	118	121	114	114	105	109
107	112	114	115	118	117	118	125	106	110
122	108	110	121	113	120	119	111	104	111
120	113	120	117	105	110	118	112	114	114

Source: *The World Almanac*

22. Make a stem-and-leaf plot of the data. **See pp. 117A–117B.**

23. Which temperature occurs most frequently? **118**

24. Does the mode best represent the data? Explain. **No; the mode is higher than most of the data.**

25. RESEARCH Use the Internet or another source to find the total number of each CD sold over the past six months to reach number one. Which measure of central tendency best describes the average number of top selling CDs sold? Explain. **See students' work.**

GEOLOGY For Exercises 26 and 27, refer to the stem-and-leaf plot that shows the magnitudes of earthquakes occurring in 2000 that measured at least 5.0 on the Richter scale.

26. What was the most frequent magnitude of these earthquakes? **7.5**

27. Which measure of central tendency best describes this set of data? Explain. **Mean or median; both are centrally located and the mode is too high.**

Stem	Leaf
5	1 2 2 3 4 8 8 9 9
6	1 1 2 3 4 5 6 7 7 8
7	0 1 1 2 2 3 5 5 5 6 8 8
8	0 0 2 $5|1 = 5.1$

Source: National Geophysical Data Center

15.

```
              ×
        × ×                    ×   ×   ×
  ×     × × ×                  × × × ×   × × × × ×
 -2     -1       0      1       2       3
```

OLYMPICS For Exercises 28–31, use the information in the table that shows the number of medals won by the top ten countries during the 2000 Summer Olympics in Sydney, Australia.

Sydney Olympics Total Medals by Country

Country	Gold	Silver	Bronze	Total
United States	40	24	33	97
Russia	32	28	28	88
China	28	16	15	59
Australia	16	25	17	58
Germany	13	17	26	56
France	13	14	11	38
Italy	14	8	13	35
Cuba	11	11	7	29
Britain	11	10	7	28
Korea	8	10	10	28

Source: www.espn.com

28. Make a line plot showing the number of gold medals won by the countries. **See pp. 117A–117B.**

29. How many countries won fewer than 25 gold medals? **7**

30. What was the median number of gold medals won by a country? **13.5**

31. Is the median the best measure to describe this set of data? Explain. **Sample answer: Yes; most of the data are near the median.**

CARS For Exercises 32–34, use the list of the fuel economy of various vehicles in miles per gallon.

25	28	29	30	24	28	29	31	34	30
33	47	34	43	33	36	37	29	30	30
29	26	29	22	23	19	18	20	23	21
20	20	19	16	18	21	20	19	28	20

Source: United States Environmental Protection Agency

32. Make a stem-and-leaf plot of the data. **See pp. 117A–117B.**

33. How many of the vehicles get more than 25 miles per gallon? **22**

34. Which measure of central tendency would you use to describe the fuel economy of the vehicles? Explain your reasoning. **Sample answer: Mean; the median is too high, and the modes are either too high or too low.**

EDUCATION For Exercises 35–37, use the table that shows the top ten public libraries in the United States by population served.

Top Libraries

Location	Number of Branches	Location	Number of Branches
Brooklyn, NY	59	Los Angeles County, CA	84
Broward County, FL	34	Miami, FL	30
Chicago, IL	77	New York, NY	85
Houston, TX	37	Philadelphia, PA	52
Los Angeles, CA	67	Queens Borough, NY	62

35. Make a stem-and-leaf plot to show the number of library branches. **See pp. 117A–117B.**

36. Which interval has the most values? **30–39**

37. What is the mode of the data? **no mode**

38. **CRITICAL THINKING** Construct a set of twelve numbers with a mean of 7, a median of 6, and a mode of 8. **Sample answer: 4, 4, 4, 5, 5, 5, 7, 8, 8, 8, 8, 18**

www.algebra1.com/self_check_quiz

Lesson 2-5 Statistics: Displaying and Analyzing Data 93

More About . . .

Education •

In 1848, the Boston Public Library became the first public library to allow users to borrow books and materials.
Source: The Boston Public Library

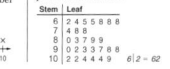
Lesson 2-5 Statistics: Displaying and Analyzing Data 93

Open-Ended Assessment

Speaking Draw several line plots and stem-and-leaf plots on the chalkboard. Make sure that some of your plots have skewed data. Ask students to comment on how they think the data in the plots will affect the measures of central tendency.

Getting Ready for Lesson 2-6

PREREQUISITE SKILL Students will learn about simple probability and odds in Lesson 2-6. Probability and odds are often expressed as fractions in simplest form. Use Exercises 57–64 to determine your students' familiarity with simplifying fractions.

Teaching Tip You may want to teach box-and-whisker plots after this lesson. These can be found in Lesson 13-5.

Answer

42. Sample answer: They can be used in marketing or sales to sell the most products to a specific group. Answers should include the following.
   - a line plot showing the number of males with the names from the beginning of the lesson
   - By finding out the most popular names you can use the popular names on more of your items.

---

39. High school: $10,123; College: $11,464; Bachelor's Degree: $18,454; Doctoral Degree: $21,608

40. Sample answer: The higher the education, the higher the income.

41. Sample answer: Because the range in salaries is often very great with extreme values on both the high end and low end.

SALARIES For Exercises 39–41, refer to the bar graph that shows the median income of males and females based on education levels.

39. What are the differences between men's and women's salaries at each level of education?

40. What do these graphs say about the difference between salaries and education levels?

41. Why do you think that salaries are usually represented by the median rather than the mean?

42.  Answer the question that was posed at the beginning of the lesson.

   How are line plots and averages used to make decisions? See margin.

   Include the following in your answer:
   - a line plot to show how many male students in your class have the most popular names for the decade in which they were born, and
   - a convincing argument that explains how you would use this information to sell personalized T-shirts.

Education
(25 or older) ☐ Male ☐ Female

High school graduate
$33,184
$23,061

Some college
$39,221
$27,757

Bachelor's degree
$60,201
$41,747

Doctoral degree
$81,687
$60,079

Source: USA TODAY

Standardized Test Practice
Ⓐ Ⓑ Ⓒ Ⓓ

For Exercises 43 and 44, refer to the line plot.

43. What is the average wingspan for these types of butterflies? **C**
   - Ⓐ 7.6 in.
   - Ⓑ 7.9 in.
   - Ⓒ 8.2 in.
   - Ⓓ 9.1 in.

44. Which sentence is *not* true? **C**
   - Ⓐ The difference between the greatest and least wingspan is 3.5 inches.
   - Ⓑ Most of the wingspans are in the 7.5 inch to 8.5 inch interval.
   - Ⓒ Most of the wingspans are greater than 8 inches.
   - Ⓓ The mode of the data is 7.5 inches.

Wingspan (in.) of Ten Largest Butterflies

```
        ×
        ×  ×
        ×  ×
     ×  ×  ×     ×              ×
  +--+--+--+--+--+--+--+--+--+
  7  7.5 8  8.5 9  9.5 10 10.5 11
```

Maintain Your Skills

Mixed Review **Find each quotient.** *(Lesson 2-4)*

45. $56 \div (-14)$ **−4**   46. $-72 \div (-12)$ **6**   47. $-40.5 \div 3$ **−13.5**   48. $102 \div 6.8$ **15**

Simplify each expression. *(Lesson 2-3)*

49. $-2(6x) - 5x$ **−17x**   50. $3x(-7y) - 4x(5y)$ **−41xy**   51. $5(3t - 2t) - 2(4t)$ **−3t**

52. Write an algebraic expression to represent the amount of money in Kara's savings account if she has d dollars and adds x dollars per week for 12 weeks. *(Lesson 1-1)* $d + 12x$

Evaluate each expression if $x = 5$, $y = 16$, and $z = 9$. *(Lesson 1-2)*

53. $y - 3x$ **1**   54. $xz \div 3$ **15**   55. $2x - x + (y \div 4)$ **9**   56. $\dfrac{x^2 - z}{2y}$ **½**

Getting Ready for the Next Lesson

PREREQUISITE SKILL Write each fraction in simplest form.
(To review simplifying fractions, see pages 798 and 799.)

57. $\dfrac{12}{18}$ **⅔**   58. $\dfrac{54}{60}$ **9/10**   59. $\dfrac{21}{30}$ **7/10**   60. $\dfrac{42}{48}$ **⅞**

61. $\dfrac{32}{64}$ **½**   62. $\dfrac{28}{52}$ **7/13**   63. $\dfrac{16}{36}$ **4/9**   64. $\dfrac{84}{90}$ **14/15**

Reading Mathematics

Interpreting Statistics

The word *statistics* is associated with the collection, analysis, interpretation, and presentation of numerical data. Sometimes, when presenting data, *notes* and *unit indicators* are included to help you interpret the data.

Headnotes give information about the table as a whole.

If the numerical data are too large, *unit indicators* are used to save space.

Public Elementary and Secondary School Enrollment, 1994–1998
[(in thousands) 44,111 represents 44,111,000.]
As of fall year, Kindergarten includes nursery schools.

Grade	1994	1995	1996	1997	1998, prel.
Pupils enrolled	**44,111**	**44,840**	**45,611**	**46,127**	**46,535**
Kindergarten and grades 1 to 8 .	31,898	32,341	32,764	33,073	33,344
Kindergarten	4047	4173	4202	4198	4171
First	3593	3671	3770	3755	3727
Second	3440	3507	3600	3689	3682
Third	3439	3445	3524	3597	3696
Fourth	3426	3431	3454	3507	3592
Fifth	3372	3438	3453	3458	3520
Sixth	3381	3395	3494	3492	3497
Seventh	3404	3422	3464	3520	3530
Eighth	3302	3356	3403	3415	3480
Unclassified[1]	494	502	401	442	460
Grades 9 to 12	12,213	12,500	12,847	13,054	13,191
Ninth	3604	3704	3801	3819	3856
Tenth	3131	3237	3323	3376	3382
Eleventh	2748	2826	2930	2972	3018
Twelfth	2488	2487	2586	2673	2724
Unclassified[1]	242	245	206	214	211

[1] Includes ungraded and special education.
Source: U.S. Census Bureau

Footnotes give information about specific items within the table.

Sources reference the origin of the data. Today, a lot of data is found on the Internet.

Suppose you need to find the number of students enrolled in the 9th grade in 1997. The following steps can be used to determine this information.

Step 1 Locate the number in the table. The number that corresponds to 1997 and 9th grade is 3819.

Step 2 Determine the unit indicator. The *unit indicator* is thousands.

Step 3 If the unit indicator is not 1 unit, multiply to find the data value. In this case, multiply 3819 by 1000.

Step 4 State the data value. The number of students enrolled in the 9th grade in 1997 was 3,819,000.

Reading to Learn

Use the information in the table to answer each question. 1–2. See margin.

1. Describe the data.
2. What information is given by the footnote?
3. How current is the data? **1999**
4. What is the unit indicator? **thousands**
5. How many acres of state parks and recreation areas does New York have? **1,016,000 acres**
6. Which of the states shown had the greatest number of visitors? How many people visited that state's parks and recreation areas in 1999?
California; 76,736,000 visitors

State Parks and Recreation Areas for Selected States, 1999

State	Acreage (1000)	Visitors (1000)[1]
United States	**12,916**	**766,842**
Alaska	3291	3855
California	1376	76,736
Florida	513	14,645
Indiana	178	18,652
New York	1016	61,960
North Carolina	158	13,269
Oregon	94	38,752
South Carolina	82	9563
Texas	628	21,446

Source: U.S. Census Bureau   [1] Includes overnight visitors.

Answers

1. Sample answer: The data show the acreage and number of visitors in thousands for selected state parks and recreation areas in 1999.

2. Sample answer: The footnote indicates that the number of visitors includes those staying overnight.

Getting Started

Ask students if they have ever used abbreviations when writing. What are some of the abbreviations that students use often? Why do they use them? How do they indicate to others what the abbreviations mean? How do they learn the meaning of abbreviations when they read them?

Teach

Reading Graphs Many people make important decisions in their lives based on how they analyze the statistics involved. In order to properly analyze statistics, you have to understand what the statistics mean. This is especially true when statistics are presented in graphical or tabular form.

Make sure students understand why unit indicators are used. As well as saving space, they also clarify a table. On the board, rewrite some of the data without the unit indicator so students can see how all the extra zeroes make the table more difficult to read.

Assess

Study Notebook

Ask students to summarize what they have learned about interpreting statistics.

ELL English Language Learners may benefit from writing key concepts from this activity in their Study Notebooks in their native language and then in English.

1 Focus

5-Minute Check Transparency 2-6 Use as a quiz or a review of Lesson 2-5.

Mathematical Background notes are available for this lesson on p. 66D.

Why is probability important in sports?

Ask students:

* Who is more likely to make a free throw, a player who makes 75% of her shots, or one who makes 50% of her shots? **the one who makes 75%**

* If you are a coach, which player would you rather have making a potentially game-tying shot? **the player with the higher free throw average**

* Why do you think probability is important in sports? **Probability can help a coach decide which player or players to use when making a shot is important.**

What You'll Learn

* Find the probability of a simple event.
* Find the odds of a simple event.

Vocabulary
* probability
* simple event
* sample space
* equally likely
* odds

Why is probability important in sports?

A basketball player is at the free throw line. Her team is down by one point. If she makes an average of 75% of her free throws, what is the probability that she will tie the game with her first shot?

PROBABILITY   One way to describe the likelihood of an event occurring is with probability. The **probability** of a **simple event**, like a coin landing heads up when it is tossed, is a ratio of the number of favorable outcomes for the event to the total number of possible outcomes of the event. The probability of an event can be expressed as a fraction, a decimal, or a percent.

Suppose you wanted to find the probability of rolling a 4 on a die. When you roll a die, there are six possible outcomes, 1, 2, 3, 4, 5, or 6. This list of all possible outcomes is called the **sample space**. Of these outcomes, only one, a 4, is favorable. So, the probability of rolling a 4 is $\frac{1}{6}$, $0.1\overline{6}$, or about 16.7%.

Study Tip

Reading Math
$P(a)$ is read *the probability of a.*

Key Concept   Probability

The probability of an event a can be expressed as

$$P(a) = \frac{\text{number of favorable outcomes}}{\text{total number of possible outcomes}}.$$

Example 1   Find Probabilities of Simple Events

a. Find the probability of rolling an even number on a die.

There are six possible outcomes. Three of the outcomes are favorable. That is, three of the six outcomes are even numbers.

Sample space: 1, 2, 3, 4, 5, 6   — 3 even numbers — $\frac{3}{6}$ — 6 total possible outcomes —

So, $P(\text{even number}) = \frac{3}{6}$ or $\frac{1}{2}$.

b. A bowl contains 5 red chips, 7 blue chips, 6 yellow chips, and 10 green chips. One chip is randomly drawn. Find $P(\text{blue})$.

There are 7 blue chips and 28 total chips.

$P(\text{blue chip}) = \dfrac{7}{28}$ ← number of favorable outcomes
                                       ← number of possible outcomes

$= \dfrac{1}{4}$ or 0.25   Simplify.

The probability of selecting a blue chip is $\frac{1}{4}$ or 25%.

Resource Manager

Workbook and Reproducible Masters

Chapter 2 Resource Masters
* Study Guide and Intervention, pp. 105–106
* Skills Practice, p. 107
* Practice, p. 108
* Reading to Learn Mathematics, p. 109
* Enrichment, p. 110
* Assessment, p. 132

Parent and Student Study Guide Workbook, p. 16
Prerequisite Skills Workbook,
   pp. 17–18, 37–38, 67–70, 99–100

Transparencies
5-Minute Check Transparency 2-6
Answer Key Transparencies

Technology
Interactive Chalkboard

c. A bowl contains 5 red chips, 7 blue chips, 6 yellow chips, and 10 green chips. One chip is randomly drawn. Find P(red or yellow).

There are 5 ways to pick a red chip and 6 ways to pick a yellow chip. So there are $5 + 6$ or 11 ways to pick a red or a yellow chip.

$$P(\text{red or yellow}) = \frac{11}{28} \quad \begin{array}{l} \leftarrow \text{number of favorable outcomes} \\ \leftarrow \text{number of possible outcomes} \end{array}$$

$$\approx 0.39 \quad \text{Divide.}$$

The probability of selecting a red chip or a yellow chip is $\frac{11}{28}$ or about 39%.

d. A bowl contains 5 red chips, 7 blue chips, 6 yellow chips, and 10 green chips. One chip is randomly drawn. Find P(not green).

There are $5 + 7 + 6$ or 18 chips that are not green.

$$P(\text{not green}) = \frac{18}{28} \quad \begin{array}{l} \leftarrow \text{number of favorable outcomes} \\ \leftarrow \text{number of possible outcomes} \end{array}$$

$$\approx 0.64 \quad \text{Divide.}$$

The probability of selecting a chip that is not green is $\frac{9}{14}$ or about 64%.

Study Tip

Reading Math
Inclusive means that the end values are included.

Notice that the probability that an event will occur is somewhere between 0 and 1 inclusive. If the probability of an event is 0, that means that it is impossible for the event to occur. A probability equal to 1 means that the event is certain to occur.

When there are n outcomes and the probability of each one is $\frac{1}{n}$, we say that the outcomes are **equally likely**. For example, when you roll a die, the 6 possible outcomes are equally likely because each outcome has a probability of $\frac{1}{6}$.

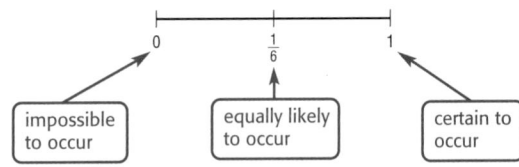

ODDS Another way to express the chance of an event occurring is with **odds**.

Key Concept   **Odds**

The odds of an event occurring is the ratio that compares the number of ways an event can occur (successes) to the number of ways it cannot occur (failures).

Study Tip

Odds
Odds are usually written in the form *number of successes : number of failures.*

Example 2   *Odds of an Event*

Find the odds of rolling a number less than 3.

There are 6 possible outcomes, 2 are successes and 4 are failures.

Sample space: 1, 2, 3, 4, 5, 6   2 numbers less than 3 → $\frac{2}{4}$ or $\frac{1}{2}$ 4 numbers not less than 3

So, the odds of rolling a number less than three are $\frac{1}{2}$ or 1:2.

www.algebra1.com/extra_examples   **Lesson 2-6** Probability: Simple Probability and Odds **97**

---

2 Teach

PROBABILITY

Tips for New Teachers

Some students confuse the numbers on a die with the probability of rolling a particular number. Once they see that the probability of rolling 6 is $\frac{1}{6}$, they are more likely to think, for example, that the probability of rolling 5 is $\frac{1}{5}$. Consider using dice with symbols on the sides rather than numbers to teach probability.

In-Class Example   Power Point®

1 **a.** Find the probability of rolling a number greater than two on a die. $\frac{4}{6}$ or $\frac{2}{3}$

  b. A class contains 6 students with black hair, 8 with brown hair, 4 with blonde hair, and 2 with red hair. Find P(black). $\frac{3}{10}$ or 0.3

  c. A class contains 6 students with black hair, 8 with brown hair, 4 with blonde hair, and 2 with red hair. Find P(red or brown). $\frac{1}{2}$ or 0.5

  d. A class contains 6 students with black hair, 8 with brown hair, 4 with blonde hair, and 2 with red hair. Find P(not blonde). $\frac{4}{5}$ or 0.8

D A I L Y

INTERVENTION   **Unlocking Misconceptions**

Odds and Probability Odds and probability are very often confused and the terms are mistakenly used interchangeably in the media. One characteristic to remember is that a probability will never be greater than one but odds can be greater than one. Remind students to read problems and label their answers very carefully when working with odds and probability.

Teaching Tip To point out the difference between probability and odds, lead students to understand why the probability of rolling a number less than three is $\frac{1}{3}$, while the odds of rolling a number less than three is $\frac{1}{2}$.

2 Find the odds of rolling a number greater than two.
$\frac{2}{1}$ or 2:1

3 A card is selected at random from a standard deck of 52 cards. What are the odds against selecting a 2 or a 3?
$\frac{11}{2}$

4 **TRAVEL** Melvin is waiting to board a flight to Washington, D.C. According to the airline, the flight he is waiting for is on time 80% of the times it flies. What are the odds that the plane will be on time? 4:1

Answer

1. Sample answers: impossible event: a number greater than 6; certain event: a number from 1 to 6; equally likely event: even number

The odds *against* an event occurring are the odds that the event will *not* occur.

Example 3 **Odds Against an Event**

A card is selected at random from a standard deck of 52 cards. What are the odds against selecting a 3?

There are four 3s in a deck of cards, and there are $52 - 4$ or 48 cards that are not a 3.

odds against a $3 = \frac{48}{4}$ ← number of ways to *not* pick a 3

The odds against selecting a 3 from a deck of cards are 12:1.

Example 4 **Probability and Odds**

WEATHER A weather forecast states that the probability of rain the next day is 40%. What are the odds that it will rain?

The probability that it will rain is 40%, so the probability that it will not rain is 60%.

odds of rain = 40:60 or 2:3

The odds that it will rain tomorrow are 2:3.

Check for Understanding

Concept Check

2. The probability is $\frac{3}{5}$, which means there are 3 favorable outcomes and $5 - 3$ or 2 unfavorable outcomes. Thus, the odds are 3:2.

1. **OPEN ENDED** Give an example of an impossible event, a certain event, and an equally likely event when a die is rolled. **See margin.**

2. **Describe** how to find the odds of an event occurring if the probability that the event will occur is $\frac{3}{5}$.

3. **FIND THE ERROR** Mark and Doug are finding the probability of picking a red card from a standard deck of cards.

Mark	Doug
$P(\text{red card}) = \frac{26}{26}$ or $\frac{1}{1}$	$P(\text{red card}) = \frac{26}{52}$ or $\frac{1}{2}$

Who is correct? Explain your reasoning. **Doug; Mark determined the odds in favor of picking a red card.**

Guided Practice

GUIDED PRACTICE KEY	
Exercises	Examples
4–7, 12, 13	1
8–11	2, 3

A card is selected at random from a standard deck of cards. Determine each probability.

4. $P(5)$ $\frac{1}{13}$

5. $P(\text{red 10})$ $\frac{1}{26}$

6. $P(\text{odd number})$ $\frac{4}{13}$

7. $P(\text{queen of hearts or jack of diamonds})$ $\frac{1}{26}$

Find the odds of each outcome if the spinner is spun once.

8. multiple of 3 **3:7**

9. even number less than 8 **3:7**

10. odd number or blue **7:3**

11. red or yellow **6:4**

Application

NUMBER THEORY One of the factors of 48 is chosen at random.

12. What is the probability that the chosen factor is not a multiple of 4? $\frac{2}{5}$

13. What is the probability that the number chosen has 4 and 6 as two of its factors? $\frac{3}{10}$

DAILY INTERVENTION **Differentiated Instruction**

Interpersonal Give groups of students marbles or colored cubes. Ask them to model probabilities and then odds. Have students take turns in the group modeling probabilities and odds until all group members understand both concepts and the difference between them.

Homework Help

For Exercises	See Examples
14–35, 51, 54, 56	1
36–47, 52, 53, 55	2, 3
48, 49	4

Extra Practice
See page 824.

One coin is randomly selected from a jar containing 70 nickels, 100 dimes, 80 quarters, and 50 1-dollar coins. Find each probability.

14. P(quarter) $\frac{4}{15} \approx 27\%$

15. P(dime) $\frac{1}{3} \approx 33\%$

16. P(nickel or dollar) $\frac{2}{5} = 40\%$

17. P(quarter or nickel) $\frac{1}{2} = 50\%$

18. P(value less than \$1.00) $\frac{5}{6} \approx 83\%$

19. P(value greater than \$0.10) $\frac{13}{30} \approx 43\%$

20. P(value at least \$0.25) $\frac{13}{30} \approx 43\%$

21. P(value at most \$1.00) $1 = 100\%$

Two dice are rolled, and their sum is recorded. Find each probability.

22. P(sum less than 7) $\frac{5}{12} \approx 42\%$

23. P(sum less than 8) $\frac{7}{12} \approx 58\%$

24. P(sum is greater than 12) $0 = 0\%$

25. P(sum is greater than 1) $1 = 100\%$

26. P(sum is between 5 and 10) $\frac{5}{9} \approx 56\%$

27. P(sum is between 2 and 9) $\frac{25}{36} \approx 69\%$

One of the polygons is chosen at random. Find each probability.

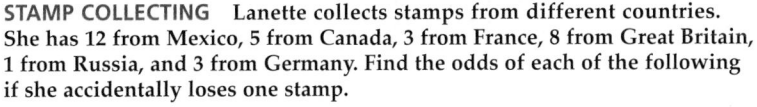

28. P(triangle) $\frac{1}{2} = 50\%$

29. P(pentagon) $\frac{1}{6} \approx 17\%$

30. P(not a triangle) $\frac{1}{2} = 50\%$

31. P(not a quadrilateral) $\frac{2}{3} \approx 67\%$

32. P(more than three sides) $\frac{1}{2} = 50\%$

33. P(more than one right angle) $\frac{1}{2} = 50\%$

34. $\frac{1}{30} \approx 3\%$

34. If a person's birthday is in April, what is the probability that it is the 29th?

35. If a person's birthday is in July, what is the probability that it is after the 16th? $\frac{15}{31} \approx 48\%$

Find the odds of each outcome if a computer randomly picks a letter in the name *The United States of America.*

36. the letter *a* 3:21 or 1:7

37. the letter *t* 4:20 or 1:5

38. a vowel 11:13

39. a consonant 13:11

40. an uppercase letter 4:20 or 1:5

41. a lowercase vowel 9:15 or 3:5

More About...

STAMP COLLECTING Lanette collects stamps from different countries. She has 12 from Mexico, 5 from Canada, 3 from France, 8 from Great Britain, 1 from Russia, and 3 from Germany. Find the odds of each of the following if she accidentally loses one stamp.

42. the stamp is from Canada 5:27

43. the stamp is from Mexico 12:20 or 3:5

44. the stamp is not from France 29:3

45. the stamp is not from a North American country 15:17

46. the stamp is from Germany or Russia 4:28 or 1:7

47. the stamp is from Canada or Great Britain 13:19

Stamp Collecting

Stamp collecting can be a very inexpensive hobby. Most stamp collectors start by saving stamps from letters, packages, and postcards.
Source: United States Postal Service

48. If the probability that an event will occur is $\frac{3}{7}$, what are the odds that it will occur? 3:4

49. If the probability that an event will occur is $\frac{2}{3}$, what are the odds against it occurring? 1:2

Teacher to Teacher

Shawntay Moore   Jupiter Community H.S., Jupiter, FL

"I have my students count the number of jelly beans in a package or cup and then find the probability and odds of choosing a specific color. I also have students collect the data and represent their findings through charts and graphs."

Study Notebook

Have students—
• add the definitions/examples of the vocabulary terms to their Vocabulary Builder worksheets for Chapter 2.
• add a description comparing and contrasting probability and odds.
• include any other item(s) that they find helpful in mastering the skills in this lesson.

DAILY INTERVENTION

FIND THE ERROR To solve this problem, students must be able to differentiate between probability and odds. Remind students that for probability to equal 1, or 100%, the event must always occur. Are all the cards in a standard deck of cards red?

About the Exercises...
Organization by Objective
• **Probability:** 14–35, 51, 54, 57
• **Odds:** 36–50, 52, 53, 55, 56, 58

Odd/Even Assignments
Exercises 14–49 are structured so that students practice the same concepts whether they are assigned odd or even problems.

Assignment Guide
Basic: 15–49 odd, 51–53, 59–82
Average: 15–49 odd, 51–56, 59–82
Advanced: 14–50 even, 54–74 (optional: 75–82)
All: Practice Quiz 2 (1–10)

Probability The **probability** of a **simple event** is a ratio that tells how likely it is that the event will take place. It is the ratio of the number of favorable outcomes of the event to the number of possible outcomes of the event. You can express the probability either as a fraction, as a decimal, or as a percent.

Probability of a Simple Event	For an event a, $P(a) = \dfrac{\text{number of favorable outcomes}}{\text{number of possible outcomes}}$

Example 1 Mr. Babcock chooses 5 out of 25 students in his algebra class at random for a special project. What is the probability of being chosen?

$P(\text{being chosen}) = \dfrac{\text{number of students chosen}}{\text{total number of students}}$

The probability of being chosen is $\dfrac{5}{25}$ or $\dfrac{1}{5}$.

Example 2 A bowl contains 3 pears, 4 bananas, and 2 apples. If you take a piece of fruit at random, what is the probability that it is *not* a banana?

There are $3 + 4 + 2$ or 9 pieces of fruit. There are $3 + 2$ or 5 pieces of fruit that are not bananas.

$P(\text{not banana}) = \dfrac{\text{number of other pieces of fruit}}{\text{total number of pieces of fruit}}$

$= \dfrac{5}{9}$

The probability of *not* choosing a banana is $\dfrac{5}{9}$.

Exercises

A card is selected at random from a standard deck of 52 cards. Determine each probability.

1. $P(10)$ $\dfrac{1}{13}$ 2. $P(\text{red 2})$ $\dfrac{1}{26}$ 3. $P(\text{king or queen})$ $\dfrac{2}{13}$

4. $P(\text{black card})$ $\dfrac{1}{2}$ 5. $P(\text{ace of spades})$ $\dfrac{1}{52}$ 6. $P(\text{spade})$ $\dfrac{1}{4}$

Two dice are rolled and their sum is recorded. Find each probability.

7. $P(\text{sum is 1})$ 0 8. $P(\text{sum is 6})$ $\dfrac{5}{36}$ 9. $P(\text{sum less than 4})$ $\dfrac{1}{12}$

10. $P(\text{sum greater than 11})$ $\dfrac{1}{36}$ 11. $P(\text{sum less than 15})$ 1 12. $P(\text{sum greater than 8})$ $\dfrac{5}{18}$

A bowl contains 4 red chips, 3 blue chips, and 8 green chips. You choose one chip at random. Find each probability.

13. $P(\text{not a red chip})$ $\dfrac{11}{15}$ 14. $P(\text{red or blue chip})$ $\dfrac{7}{15}$ 15. $P(\text{not a green chip})$ $\dfrac{7}{15}$

A number is selected at random from the list {1, 2, 3, ..., 10}. Find each probability.

16. $P(\text{even number})$ $\dfrac{1}{2}$ 17. $P(\text{multiple of 3})$ $\dfrac{3}{10}$ 18. $P(\text{less than 4})$ $\dfrac{3}{10}$

19. A computer randomly chooses a letter from the word *COMPUTER*. Find the probability that the letter is a vowel. $\dfrac{3}{8}$

Skills Practice, p. 107 and Practice, p. 108 (shown)

One chip is randomly selected from a jar containing 13 blue chips, 8 yellow chips, 15 brown chips, and 6 green chips. Find each probability.

1. $P(\text{brown})$ $\dfrac{5}{14} \approx 36\%$ 2. $P(\text{green})$ $\dfrac{1}{7} \approx 14\%$

3. $P(\text{blue or yellow})$ $\dfrac{1}{2} = 50\%$ 4. $P(\text{not yellow})$ $\dfrac{17}{21} \approx 81\%$

A card is selected at random from a standard deck of 52 cards. Find each probability.

5. $P(\text{heart})$ $\dfrac{1}{4} = 25\%$ 6. $P(\text{black card})$ $\dfrac{1}{2} = 50\%$

7. $P(\text{jack})$ $\dfrac{1}{13} \approx 8\%$ 8. $P(\text{red jack})$ $\dfrac{1}{26} \approx 4\%$

Two dice are rolled and their sum is recorded. Find each probability.

9. $P(\text{sum less than 6})$ $\dfrac{5}{18} \approx 28\%$ 10. $P(\text{sum less than 2})$ $0 = 0\%$

11. $P(\text{sum greater than 10})$ $\dfrac{1}{12} \approx 8\%$ 12. $P(\text{sum greater than 9})$ $\dfrac{1}{6} \approx 17\%$

Find the odds of each outcome if a computer randomly picks a letter in the name *The Badlands of North Dakota*.

13. the letter d 3:21 or 1:7 14. the letter a 4:20 or 1:5

15. the letter h 2:22 or 1:11 16. a consonant 16:8 or 2:1

CLASS PROJECTS For Exercises 17–20, use the following information.
Students in a biology class can choose a semester project from the following list: animal behavior (4), cellular processes (2), ecology (6), health (7), and physiology (3). Find each of the odds if a student selects a topic at random.

17. the topic is ecology 6:16 or 3:8

18. the topic is animal behavior 4:18 or 2:9

19. the topic is not cellular processes 20:2 or 10:1

20. the topic is not health 15:7

SCHOOL ISSUES For Exercises 21 and 22, use the following information.
A news team surveyed students in grades 9–12 on whether to change the time school begins. One student will be selected at random to be interviewed on the evening news. The table gives the results.

Grade	9	10	11	12
No change	6	2	5	3
Hour later	10	7	9	8

21. What is the probability the student selected will be in the 9th grade? $\dfrac{8}{25} = 32\%$

22. What are the odds the student selected wants no change? 16:34 or 8:17

Reading to Learn Mathematics, p. 109 — ELL

Pre-Activity Why is probability important in sports?

Read the introduction to Lesson 2-6 at the top of page 96 in your textbook.

Look up the definition of the word *probability* in a dictionary. Rewrite the definition in your own words.

Sample answer: the likelihood of something happening

Reading the Lesson

1. Write whether each statement is *true* or *false*. If false, replace the underlined word or number to make a true statement.

   a. Probability can be written as a fraction, a decimal, or a percent. **true**

   b. The sample space of flipping one coin is heads or tails. **true**

   c. The probability of an impossible event is 1. **false; 0**

   d. The odds against an event occurring are the odds that the event will occur. **false; will not**

2. Explain why the probability of an event cannot be greater than 1 while the odds of an event can be greater than 1.

   Sample answer: To find the probability of an event, you compare a part of the sample space to the whole sample space. When you find the odds of an event, you compare the number of favorable outcomes to the number of unfavorable outcomes. In some situations, there may be more favorable than unfavorable outcomes.

Helping You Remember

3. Probabilities are usually written as fractions, decimals, or percents. Odds are usually written with a colon (for example, 1:3). How can the spelling of the word *colon* help you remember this?

   Sample answer: The word *colon* has the letter "o" as its only vowel, and the word *odds* also has the letter "o" as its only vowel.

---

50. **CONTESTS** Every Tuesday, Mike's Submarine Shop has a business card drawing for a free lunch. Four coworkers from InvoAccounting put their business cards in the bowl for the drawing. If there are 80 cards in the bowl, what are the odds that one of the coworkers will win a free lunch? **1:19**

GAMES For Exercises 51–53, use the following information.
A game piece is randomly placed on the board shown at the right by blindfolded players.

51. What is the probability that a game piece is placed on a shaded region? $\dfrac{19}{40} = \textbf{47.5\%}$

52. What are the odds against placing a game piece on a shaded region? **21:19**

53. What are the odds that a game piece will be placed within the green rectangle? **7:13**

BASEBALL For Exercises 54–56, use the following information.
The stem-and-leaf plot shows the number of home runs hit by the top major league baseball players in the 2000 season. **Source:** www.espn.com

Stem	Leaf
3	0 0 0 0 1 1 1 1 1 1 1 2 2 2 3
	3 4 4 4 5 5 5 6 6 6 7 7 8 8 9
4	0 1 1 1 1 2 2 3 3 3 4 4 7 7 9
5	0 3|0 = 30

54. What is the probability that one of these players picked at random hit more than 35 home runs? $\dfrac{12}{23} \approx \textbf{52\%}$

55. What are the odds that a randomly selected player hit fewer than 45 home runs? **42:4 or 21:2**

56. If a player batted 439 times and hit 38 home runs, what is the probability that the next time the player bats he will hit a home run? $\dfrac{38}{439} \approx \textbf{9\%}$

CONTESTS For Exercises 57 and 58, use the following information.
A fast-food restaurant is holding a contest in which the grand prize is a new sports car. Each customer is given a game card with their order. The contest rules state that the odds of winning the grand prize are 1:1,000,000.

57. For any randomly-selected game card, what is the probability that it is the winning game card for the grand prize? $\dfrac{1}{1,000,001}$

58. Do your odds of winning the grand prize increase significantly if you have several game cards? Explain. **See margin.**

59. **CRITICAL THINKING** Three coins are tossed, and a tail appears on at least one of them. What is the probability that at least one head appears? $\dfrac{6}{7} \approx \textbf{86\%}$

60. **WRITING IN MATH** Answer the question that was posed at the beginning of the lesson. **See pp. 117A–117B.**

   Why is probability important in sports?

   Include the following in your answer:
   - examples of two sports in which probability is used and an explanation of each sport's importance, and
   - examples of methods other than probability used to show chance.

WebQuest

You can use real-world data to find the probability that a person will live to be 100. Visit www.algebra1.com/webquest to continue work on your WebQuest project.

Enrichment, p. 110

Geometric Probability

If a dart, thrown at random, hits the triangular board shown at the right, what is the probability that it will hit the shaded region? This can be determined by comparing the area of the shaded region to the area of the entire board. This ratio indicates what fraction of the tosses should hit in the shaded region.

$\dfrac{\text{area of shaded region}}{\text{area of triangular board}} = \dfrac{\frac{1}{2}(4 \times 6)}{\frac{1}{2}(8 \times 6)}$

$= \dfrac{12}{24}$ or $\dfrac{1}{2}$

In general, if S is a subregion of some region R, then the probability, $P(S)$, that a point, chosen at random, belongs to subregion S is given by the following:

$$P(S) = \dfrac{\text{area of subregion } S}{\text{area or region } R}$$

61. If the probability that an event will occur is $\frac{12}{25}$, what are the odds that the event will *not* occur? **B**

(A) 12:13   (B) 13:12   (C) 13:25   (D) 25:12

62. What is the probability that a number chosen at random from the domain $\{-6, -5, -4, -3, -2, -1, 0, 1, 2, 3, 4, 5, 6, 7, 8\}$ will satisfy the inequality $3x + 2 \le 17$? **D**

(A) 20%   (B) 27%   (C) 73%   (D) 80%

Maintain Your Skills

Mixed Review

63. WEATHER The following data represents the average daily temperature in Fahrenheit for Sacramento, California, for two weeks during the month of May. Organize the data using a stem-and-leaf plot. *(Lesson 2-5)* **See margin.**

| 58.3 | 64.3 | 66.7 | 65.1 | 68.7 | 67.0 | 69.3 |
| 70.0 | 72.8 | 77.4 | 77.4 | 73.2 | 75.8 | 65.5 |

Evaluate each expression if $a = -\frac{1}{3}$, $b = \frac{2}{5}$, and $c = \frac{1}{2}$. *(Lesson 2-4)*

64. $b \div c$ $\frac{4}{5}$ **65.** $2a \div b$ $-\frac{5}{3}$ or $-1\frac{2}{3}$ **66.** $\frac{ab}{c}$ $-\frac{4}{15}$

Find each sum. *(Lesson 2-2)*

67. $4.3 + (-8.2)$ **−3.9**   **68.** $-12.2 + 7.8$ **−4.4**   **69.** $-\frac{1}{4} + \left(-\frac{3}{8}\right)$ **−$\frac{5}{8}$**   **70.** $\frac{7}{12} + \left(-\frac{5}{6}\right)$ **−$\frac{1}{4}$**

Find each absolute value. *(Lesson 2-1)*

71. $|4.25|$ **4.25**   **72.** $|-8.4|$ **8.4**   **73.** $\left|-\frac{2}{3}\right|$ **$\frac{2}{3}$**   **74.** $\left|\frac{1}{6}\right|$ **$\frac{1}{6}$**

Getting Ready for the Next Lesson

PREREQUISITE SKILL Evaluate each expression.
(To review evaluating expressions, see Lesson 1-2.)

75. 6^2 **36**   **76.** 17^2 **289**   **77.** $(-8)^2$ **64**   **78.** $(-11.5)^2$ **132.25**

79. 1.6^2 **2.56**   **80.** $\left(\frac{5}{12}\right)^2$ **$\frac{25}{144}$**   **81.** $\left(-\frac{4}{9}\right)^2$ **$\frac{16}{81}$**   **82.** $\left(-\frac{16}{15}\right)^2$ **$\frac{256}{225}$**

Practice Quiz 2

Lessons 2-4 through 2-6

Find each quotient. *(Lesson 2-4)*

1. $-136 \div (-8)$ **17**   **2.** $15 \div \left(-\frac{3}{8}\right)$ **−40**   **3.** $(-46.8) \div 4$ **−11.7**

Simplify each expression. *(Lesson 2-4)*

4. $\frac{3a + 9}{3}$ **$a + 3$**   **5.** $\frac{4x + 32}{4}$ **$x + 8$**   **6.** $\frac{15n - 20}{-5}$ **$-3n + 4$**

7. State the scale you would use to make a line plot for the following data. Then draw the line plot. *(Lesson 2-5)* **See margin.**

| 1.9 | 1.1 | 3.2 | 5.0 | 4.3 | 2.7 | 2.5 | 1.1 | 1.4 | 1.8 | 1.8 | 1.6 |
| 4.3 | 2.9 | 1.4 | 1.7 | 3.6 | 2.9 | 1.9 | 0.4 | 1.3 | 0.9 | 0.7 | 1.9 |

Determine each probability if two dice are rolled. *(Lesson 2-6)*

8. $P(\text{sum of } 10)$ **$\frac{1}{12}$**   **9.** $P(\text{sum} \ge 6)$ **$\frac{13}{18}$**   **10.** $P(\text{sum} < 10)$ **$\frac{5}{6}$**

Open-Ended Assessment

Writing Have students write a short essay comparing and contrasting probability and odds. Have students use examples in their comparisons.

Getting Ready for Lesson 2-7

PREREQUISITE SKILL Students will learn about square roots and real numbers in Lesson 2-7. Finding square roots is the opposite of squaring a number. Use Exercises 75–82 to determine your students' familiarity with squaring rational numbers.

Assessment Options

Practice Quiz 2 The quiz provides students with a brief review of the concepts and skills in Lessons 2-4 through 2-6. Lesson numbers are given to the right of the exercises or instruction lines so students can review concepts not yet mastered.

Quiz (Lessons 2-5 and 2-6) is available on p. 132 of the *Chapter 2 Resource Masters*.

Answers

58. No; even with 100 game cards the odds of winning are only 100: 999,901. It would require several hundred thousand cards to significantly increase the odds of winning.

63.

Stem	Leaf
5	8.3
6	4.3 5.1 5.5 6.7 7.0
	8.7 9.3
7	0.0 2.8 3.2 5.8 7.4 7.4

$5|8.3 = 58.3$

Answer

7. Sample answer: scale 0–5.0

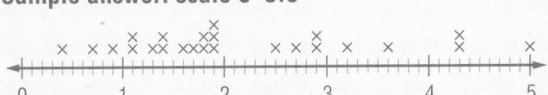

Getting Started

Objective Investigate the use of Pascal's triangle for predicting probabilities.

Teach

Explain to students that this activity is not so much about finding probability as they learned in Lesson 2-6, as it is about counting possible outcomes. To translate these outcomes into probabilities, you must read the table carefully. Each column in the table shows the total number of outcomes for the given situation. So, to find the probability that a 2-child family will have one boy and one girl, look at how many possible outcomes there are in this column: 2. There are four total possible outcomes, so the probability is $\frac{2}{4}$ or $\frac{1}{2}$.

Assess

In **Exercise 7**, students should correctly extend the pattern in Pascal's triangle. A given number in the table is the sum of the two numbers above and to the left and right. If a given number has only one number above it, the number is 1.

Study Notebook

You may wish to have students summarize this activity and what they learned from it.

Answer

6. Sample answer: Each number in each row shows the number of ways to have boys and girls for a given number of children.

Investigating Probability and Pascal's Triangle

Collect the Data

- If a family has one child, you know that the child is either a boy or a girl. You can make a simple table to show this type of family.

1 boy	1 girl
B	G

You can see that there are 2 possibilities for a one-child family.

- If a family has two children, the table below shows the possibilities for two children, including the order of birth. For example, BG means that a boy is born first and a girl second.

2 boys, 0 girls	1 boy, 1 girl	0 boys, 2 girls
BB	BG	GG
	GB	

There are 4 possibilities for the two-child family: BB, BG, GB, or GG.

Analyze the Data

1. Copy and complete the table that shows the possibilities for a three-child family.
2. Make your own table to show the possibilities for a four-child family. **See pp. 117A–117B.**
3. List the total number of possibilities for a one-child, two-child, three-child, and four-child family. How many possibilities do you think there are for a five-child family? a six-child family? Describe the pattern of the numbers you listed.

3 boys	2 boys, 1 girl	1 boy, 2 girls	3 girls
BBB	BBG	BGG	GGG
	BGB	GBG	
	GBB	GGB	

3. 2, 4, 8, 16; 32; 64; The pattern represents powers of 2.

4. Find the probability that a three-child family has 2 boys and 1 girl. $\frac{3}{8}$
5. Find the probability that a four-child family has 2 boys and 2 girls. $\frac{6}{16}$ or $\frac{3}{8}$

Make a Conjecture

6. Blaise Pascal was a French mathematician who lived in the 1600s. He is known for this triangle of numbers, called Pascal's triangle, although the pattern was known by other mathematicians before Pascal's time.

				1					Row 0
			1		1				Row 1
		1		2		1			Row 2
	1		3		3		1		Row 3
1		4		6		4		1	Row 4

Explain how Pascal's triangle relates to the possibilities for the make-up of families. (*Hint:* The first row indicates that there is 1 way to have 0 children.) **See margin.**

7. Use Pascal's triangle to find the probability that a four-child family has 1 boy. **use Row 4;** $\frac{4}{16}$ **or** $\frac{1}{4}$

Resource Manager

📁 *Teaching Algebra with Manipulatives*
- p. 49 (student recording sheet)

2-7 Square Roots and Real Numbers

What You'll Learn

- Find square roots.
- Classify and order real numbers.

Vocabulary

- square root
- perfect square
- radical sign
- principal square root
- irrational numbers
- real numbers
- rational approximations

How can using square roots determine the surface area of the human body?

In the 2000 Summer Olympics, Australian sprinter Cathy Freeman wore a special running suit that covered most of her body. The surface area of the human body may be found using the formula below, where height is measured in centimeters and weight is in kilograms.

$$\text{Surface Area} = \sqrt{\frac{\text{height} \times \text{weight}}{3600}} \text{ square meters}$$

The symbol $\sqrt{}$ designates a square root.

Study Tip

Reading Math

$\pm\sqrt{64}$ is read *plus or minus the square root of 64.*
Exponents can also be used to indicate the square root. $9^{\frac{1}{2}}$ means the same thing as $\sqrt{9}$. $9^{\frac{1}{2}}$ is read *nine to the one half power.* $9^{\frac{1}{2}} = 3.$

SQUARE ROOTS A **square root** is one of two equal factors of a number. For example, one square root of 64 is 8 since $8 \cdot 8$ or 8^2 is 64. Another square root of 64 is -8 since $(-8) \cdot (-8)$ or $(-8)^2$ is also 64. A number like 64, whose square root is a rational number is called a **perfect square**.

The symbol $\sqrt{}$, called a **radical sign**, is used to indicate a nonnegative or **principal square root** of the expression under the radical sign.

$$\sqrt{64} = 8 \quad \longleftarrow \quad \boxed{\sqrt{64} \text{ indicates the } \textit{principal} \text{ square root of 64.}}$$

$$-\sqrt{64} = -8 \quad \longleftarrow \quad \boxed{-\sqrt{64} \text{ indicates the } \textit{negative} \text{ square root of 64.}}$$

$$\pm\sqrt{64} = \pm 8 \quad \longleftarrow \quad \boxed{\pm\sqrt{64} \text{ indicates } \textit{both} \text{ square roots of 64.}}$$

Note that $-\sqrt{64}$ is not the same as $\sqrt{-64}$. The notation $-\sqrt{64}$ represents the negative square root of 64. The notation $\sqrt{-64}$ represents the square root of -64, which is not a real number since no real number multiplied by itself is negative.

Example 1 Find Square Roots

Find each square root.

a. $-\sqrt{\dfrac{49}{256}}$

$-\sqrt{\dfrac{49}{256}}$ represents the negative square root of $\dfrac{49}{256}$.

$\dfrac{49}{256} = \left(\dfrac{7}{16}\right)^2 \rightarrow -\sqrt{\dfrac{49}{256}} = -\dfrac{7}{16}$

Lesson 2-7 Square Roots and Real Numbers **103**

2-7 Lesson Notes

1 Focus

 5-Minute Check Transparency 2-7 Use as a quiz or a review of Lesson 2-6.

Mathematical Background notes are available for this lesson on p. 66D.

Building on Prior Knowledge

In Chapter 1, students reviewed squares and other powers. In this lesson, they should recognize that finding square roots is the opposite of finding squares.

How can using square roots determine the surface area of the human body?

Ask students:

- What is the opposite of addition? subtraction
- What is the opposite of multiplication? division
- How might the name of the operation "square root" help you determine its opposite operation? Sample answer: The term "square" might indicate that finding the square root is the opposite of finding the square.

Resource Manager

📁 Workbook and Reproducible Masters

Chapter 2 Resource Masters
- Study Guide and Intervention, pp. 111–112
- Skills Practice, p. 113
- Practice, p. 114
- Reading to Learn Mathematics, p. 115
- Enrichment, p. 116
- Assessment, p. 132

Graphing Calculator and Spreadsheet Masters, p. 25
Parent and Student Study Guide Workbook, p. 17
Prerequisite Skills Workbook, pp. 75–76

 Transparencies
5-Minute Check Transparency 2-7
Answer Key Transparencies

💿 Technology
Interactive Chalkboard

SQUARE ROOTS

1 Find each square root.

a. $\pm\sqrt{\dfrac{16}{9}}$ $\pm\dfrac{4}{3}$

b. $\sqrt{0.0144}$ **0.12**

CLASSIFY AND ORDER NUMBERS

2 Name the set or sets of numbers to which each real number belongs.

a. $\sqrt{17}$

Because $\sqrt{17} = 4.1231056…$, which is neither a repeating nor terminating decimal, this number is irrational.

b. $\dfrac{1}{6}$

Because 1 and 6 are integers and $1 \div 6 = 0.1666…$ is a repeating decimal, the number is a rational number.

c. $\sqrt{169}$

Because $\sqrt{169} = 13$, this number is a natural number, a whole number, an integer, and a rational number.

d. -327

This number is an integer and a rational number.

---

b. $\pm\sqrt{0.81}$

$\pm\sqrt{0.81}$ represents the positive and negative square roots of 0.81.

$0.81 = 0.9^2$ and $0.81 = (-0.9)^2$

$\pm\sqrt{0.81} = \pm 0.9$

CLASSIFY AND ORDER NUMBERS Recall that rational numbers are numbers that can be expressed as terminating or repeating decimals, or in the form $\dfrac{a}{b}$, where a and b are integers and $b \neq 0$.

As you have seen, the square roots of perfect squares are rational numbers. However, numbers such as $\sqrt{3}$ and $\sqrt{24}$ are the square roots of numbers that are not perfect squares. Numbers like these cannot be expressed as a terminating or repeating decimal.

$$\sqrt{3} = 1.73205080…$$

$$\sqrt{24} = 4.89897948…$$

Numbers that cannot be expressed as terminating or repeating decimals, or in the form $\dfrac{a}{b}$, where a and b are integers and $b \neq 0$, are called **irrational numbers**. Irrational numbers and rational numbers together form the set of **real numbers**.

Concept Summary — Real Numbers

The set of real numbers consists of the set of rational numbers and the set of irrational numbers.

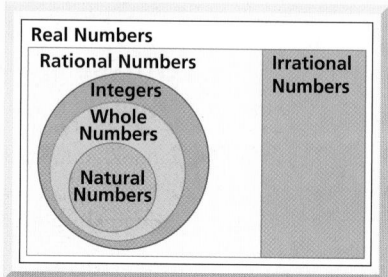

Example 2 Classify Real Numbers

Name the set or sets of numbers to which each real number belongs.

a. $\dfrac{5}{22}$

Because 5 and 22 are integers and $5 \div 22 = 0.2272727…$, which is a repeating decimal, this number is a rational number.

b. $\sqrt{121}$

Because $\sqrt{121} = 11$, this number is a natural number, a whole number, an integer, and a rational number.

c. $\sqrt{56}$

Because $\sqrt{56} = 7.48331477…$, which is not a repeating or terminating decimal, this number is irrational.

d. $-\dfrac{36}{4}$

Because $-\dfrac{36}{4} = -9$, this number is an integer and a rational number.

In Lesson 2-1 you graphed rational numbers on a number line. However, the rational numbers alone do not complete the number line. By including irrational numbers, the number line is complete. This is illustrated by the **Completeness Property** which states that each point on the number line corresponds to exactly one real number.

Recall that inequalities like $x < 7$ are open sentences. To solve the inequality, determine what replacement values for x make the sentence true. This can be shown by the solution set {all real numbers less than 7}. Not only does this set include integers like 5 and -2, but it also includes rational numbers like $\frac{3}{8}$ and $-\frac{12}{13}$ and irrational numbers like $\sqrt{40}$ and π.

Example 3 Graph Real Numbers

Graph each solution set.

a. $x > -2$

The heavy arrow indicates that all numbers to the right of -2 are included in the graph. The circle at -2 indicates -2 is *not* included in the graph.

b. $a \leq 4.5$

The heavy arrow indicates that all points to the left of 4.5 are included in the graph. The dot at 4.5 indicates that 4.5 *is* included in the graph.

To express irrational numbers as decimals, you need to use a rational approximation. A **rational approximation** of an irrational number is a rational number that is close to, but not equal to, the value of the irrational number. For example, a rational approximation of $\sqrt{2}$ is 1.41 when rounded to the nearest hundredth.

Example 4 Compare Real Numbers

Replace each ● with <, >, or = to make each sentence true.

a. $\sqrt{19}$ ● $3.\overline{8}$

Find two perfect squares closest to $\sqrt{19}$ and write an inequality.

$16 < 19 < 25$ 19 is between 16 and 25.
$\sqrt{16} < \sqrt{19} < \sqrt{25}$ Find the square root of each number.
$4 < \sqrt{19} < 5$ $\sqrt{19}$ is between 4 and 5.

Since $\sqrt{19}$ is between 4 and 5, it must be greater than $3.\overline{8}$.
So, $\sqrt{19} > 3.\overline{8}$.

b. $7.\overline{2}$ ● $\sqrt{52}$

You can use a calculator to find an approximation for $\sqrt{52}$.
$\sqrt{52} = 7.211102551\ldots$
$7.\overline{2} = 7.222\ldots$
Therefore, $7.\overline{2} > \sqrt{52}$.

www.algebra1.com/extra_examples

Lesson 2-7 Square Roots and Real Numbers **105**

Tips for New Teachers

Estimating Square Roots

You can use perfect squares to estimate square roots that are irrational. To determine where $\sqrt{27}$ lies on a number line, ask students between which two perfect squares 27 lies. Since $25 < 27 < 36$, $\sqrt{25} < \sqrt{27} < \sqrt{36}$ or $5 < \sqrt{27} < 6$. Also, since 27 is closer to 25 than 36, you know that $\sqrt{27}$ is closer to 5 than 6. In fact, $\sqrt{27}$ is about 5.2. Estimating square roots mentally can help students master problems like Example 5 more easily.

In-Class Examples

Power Point®

5 Write $\frac{12}{5}$, $\sqrt{6}$, $2.\overline{4}$, and $\frac{61}{25}$ in order from least to greatest.

$\frac{12}{5}$, $\frac{61}{25}$, $2.\overline{4}$, $\sqrt{6}$

6 For what value of x is $\sqrt{x} < 1 < \frac{1}{\sqrt{x}}$ true? **C**

A -5

B 0

C $\frac{1}{5}$

D 5

Answer

2. Rational numbers are numbers that when written as decimals terminate or repeat. Irrational numbers do not terminate nor do they repeat.

You can write a set of real numbers in order from greatest to least or from least to greatest. To do so, find a decimal approximation for each number in the set and compare.

Example 5 Order Real Numbers

Write $2.\overline{63}$, $-\sqrt{7}$, $\frac{8}{3}$, $\frac{53}{-20}$ in order from least to greatest.

Write each number as a decimal.

$2.\overline{63} = 2.6363636\ldots$ or about 2.636.

$-\sqrt{7} = -2.64575131\ldots$ or about -2.646.

$\frac{8}{3} = 2.66666666\ldots$ or about 2.667.

$\frac{53}{-20} = -2.65$

$-2.65 < -2.646 < 2.636 < 2.667$

The numbers arranged in order from least to greatest are $\frac{53}{-20}$, $-\sqrt{7}$, $2.\overline{63}$, $\frac{8}{3}$.

You can use rational approximations to test the validity of some algebraic statements involving real numbers.

Standardized Test Practice
Ⓐ Ⓑ Ⓒ Ⓓ

Example 6 Rational Approximation

Multiple-Choice Test Item

For what value of x is $\frac{1}{\sqrt{x}} > \sqrt{x} > x$ true?

Ⓐ $\frac{1}{2}$ Ⓑ 0 Ⓒ -2 Ⓓ 3

Read the Test Item

The expression $\frac{1}{\sqrt{x}} > \sqrt{x} > x$ is an open sentence, and the set of choices $\left\{\frac{1}{2}, 0, -2, 3\right\}$ is the replacement set.

Test-Taking Tip

You could stop when you find that A is a solution. But testing the other values is a good check.

Solve the Test Item

Replace x in $\frac{1}{\sqrt{x}} > \sqrt{x} > x$ with each given value.

Ⓐ $x = \frac{1}{2}$

$\frac{1}{\sqrt{\frac{1}{2}}} \overset{?}{>} \sqrt{\frac{1}{2}} \overset{?}{>} \frac{1}{2}$ Use a calculator.

$1.41 > 0.71 > 0.5$ ✓   True

Ⓑ $x = 0$

$\frac{1}{\sqrt{0}} \overset{?}{>} \sqrt{0} \overset{?}{>} 0$

False; $\frac{1}{\sqrt{0}}$ is not a real number.

Ⓒ $x = -2$

$\frac{1}{\sqrt{-2}} \overset{?}{>} \sqrt{-2} \overset{?}{>} -2$

False; $\frac{1}{\sqrt{-2}}$ and $\sqrt{-2}$ are not real numbers.

Ⓓ $x = 3$

$\frac{1}{\sqrt{3}} \overset{?}{>} \sqrt{3} \overset{?}{>} 3$ Use a calculator.

~~$0.58 > 1.73 > 3$~~   False

The inequality is true for $x = \frac{1}{2}$, so the correct answer is A.

Standardized Test Practice
Ⓐ Ⓑ Ⓒ Ⓓ

Example 6 Advise students to examine the answer choices before substituting them into the inequality. Choice B can be eliminated because $0 = \sqrt{0}$, making $\frac{1}{\sqrt{x}}$ an undefined term.

Since C is negative and the square root of a negative number is undefined for the real number set, it can be eliminated. Therefore, the only choices remaining to evaluate are A and D.

Concept Check

1. Sometimes; the square root of a number can be negative, such as $\sqrt{16} = 4$ and $-\sqrt{16} = -4$.

1. **Tell** whether the square root of any real number is *always*, *sometimes* or *never* positive. Explain your answer.

2. **OPEN ENDED** Describe the difference between rational numbers and irrational numbers. Give examples of both. **See margin.**

3. **Explain** why you cannot evaluate $\sqrt{-25}$ using real numbers. **There is no real number that can be multiplied by itself to result in a negative product.**

Guided Practice

GUIDED PRACTICE KEY	
Exercises	Examples
4–7	1
8–11	2
12, 13	3
14–16	4
17, 18	5
19	6

Find each square root. If necessary, round to the nearest hundredth.

4. $-\sqrt{25}$ -5
5. $\sqrt{1.44}$ 1.2
6. $\pm\sqrt{\dfrac{16}{49}}$ $\pm\dfrac{4}{7}$
7. $\sqrt{32}$ 5.66

Name the set or sets of numbers to which each real number belongs.

8. $-\sqrt{64}$ integers, rationals
9. $\dfrac{8}{3}$ rationals
10. $\sqrt{28}$ irrationals
11. $\dfrac{56}{7}$ naturals, wholes, integers, rationals

Graph each solution set. 12–13. See margin.

12. $x < -3.5$
13. $x \geq -7$

Replace each ⬤ with <, >, or = to make each sentence true.

14. 0.3 ⬤ $\dfrac{1}{3}$ <
15. $\dfrac{2}{9}$ ⬤ $0.\overline{2}$ =
16. $\dfrac{1}{6}$ ⬤ $\sqrt{6}$ <

Write each set of numbers in order from least to greatest.

17. $\dfrac{1}{8}, \sqrt{\dfrac{1}{8}}, 0.\overline{15}, -15$ $-15, \dfrac{1}{8}, 0.\overline{15}, \sqrt{\dfrac{1}{8}}$
18. $\sqrt{30}, 5\dfrac{4}{9}, 13, \dfrac{1}{\sqrt{30}}$ $\dfrac{1}{\sqrt{30}}, 5\dfrac{4}{9}, \sqrt{30}, 13$

Standardized Test Practice Ⓐ Ⓑ Ⓒ Ⓓ

19. For what value of a is $-\sqrt{a} < -\dfrac{1}{\sqrt{a}}$ true? **C**

Ⓐ $\dfrac{1}{3}$ Ⓑ -4 Ⓒ 2   Ⓓ 1

★ indicates increased difficulty

Practice and Apply

Homework Help	
For Exercises	See Examples
20–31, 50, 51	1
32–49	2
52–57	3
58–63	4
64–69	5

Extra Practice
See page 825.

32–49. See pp. 117A–117B.

Find each square root. If necessary, round to the nearest hundredth.

20. $\sqrt{49}$ 7
21. $\sqrt{81}$ 9
22. $\sqrt{5.29}$ 2.3
23. $\sqrt{6.25}$ 2.5
24. $-\sqrt{78}$ -8.83
25. $-\sqrt{94}$ -9.70
26. $\pm\sqrt{\dfrac{36}{81}}$ $\pm\dfrac{2}{3}$
27. $\pm\sqrt{\dfrac{100}{196}}$ $\pm\dfrac{5}{7}$
28. $\sqrt{\dfrac{9}{14}}$ 0.80
29. $\sqrt{\dfrac{25}{42}}$ 0.77
30. $\pm\sqrt{820}$ ±28.64
31. $\pm\sqrt{513}$ ±22.65

Name the set or sets of numbers to which each real number belongs.

32. $-\sqrt{22}$
33. $\dfrac{36}{6}$
34. $\dfrac{1}{3}$
35. $-\dfrac{5}{12}$
36. $\sqrt{\dfrac{82}{20}}$
37. $-\sqrt{46}$
38. $\sqrt{10.24}$
39. $\dfrac{-54}{19}$
40. $-\dfrac{3}{4}$
41. $\sqrt{20.25}$
42. $\dfrac{18}{3}$
43. $\sqrt{2.4025}$
44. $\dfrac{-68}{35}$
45. $\dfrac{6}{11}$
46. $\sqrt{5.5696}$
47. $\sqrt{\dfrac{78}{42}}$
48. $-\sqrt{9.16}$
★ 49. π

www.algebra1.com/self_check_quiz

3 Practice/Apply

Study Notebook

Have students—

- complete the definitions/examples for the remaining terms on their Vocabulary Builder worksheets for Chapter 2.
- copy the concept summary for Real Numbers, along with an explanation of how to find both square roots of a number.
- include any other item(s) that they find helpful in mastering the skills in this lesson.

About the Exercises...

Organization by Objective
- **Square Roots:** 20–31, 50
- **Classify and Order Numbers:** 32–49, 52–69

Odd/Even Assignments
Exercises 20–69 are structured so that students practice the same concepts whether they are assigned odd or even problems.

Assignment Guide

Basic: 21–47 odd, 51–55 odd, 59, 61, 65–69 odd, 73, 77–88

Average: 21–69 odd, 70–73, 77–88

Advanced: 20–68 even, 73–88

Answers

12.

13.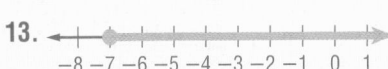

DAILY INTERVENTION

Differentiated Instruction

Intrapersonal This is the last lesson of this chapter. The chapter contains numerous concepts which may have been unfamiliar to students. Encourage each student to use their Foldables and the vocabulary list on p. 110 of the student edition to pinpoint any concepts with which students still feel unsure.

50. **PHYSICAL SCIENCE** The time it takes for a falling object to travel a certain distance d is given by the equation $t = \sqrt{\dfrac{d}{16}}$, where t is in seconds and d is in feet. If Krista dropped a ball from a window 28 feet above the ground, how long would it take for the ball to reach the ground? **1.32 s**

More About...

Tourism •
Built in 1758, the Sambro Island Lighthouse at Halifax Harbor is the oldest operational lighthouse in North America.

Source: Canadian Coast Guard

51. **LAW ENFORCEMENT** Police can use the formula $s = \sqrt{24d}$ to estimate the speed s of a car in miles per hour by measuring the distance d in feet a car skids on a dry road. On his way to work, Jerome skidded trying to stop for a red light and was involved in a minor accident. He told the police officer that he was driving within the speed limit of 35 miles per hour. The police officer measured his skid marks and found them to be $43\dfrac{3}{4}$ feet long. Should the officer give Jerome a ticket for speeding? Explain. **No; Jerome was traveling at about 32.4 mph.**

Graph each solution set. 52–57. See margin.

52. $x > −12$
53. $x \leq 8$
54. $x \geq −10.2$
55. $x < −0.25$
★ 56. $x \neq −2$
★ 57. $x \neq \pm\sqrt{36}$

Replace each ● with <, >, or = to make each sentence true.

58. $5.\overline{72}$ ● $\sqrt{5}$ >
59. $2.\overline{63}$ ● $\sqrt{8}$ <
60. $\dfrac{1}{7}$ ● $\dfrac{1}{\sqrt{7}}$ <
61. $\dfrac{2}{3}$ ● $\dfrac{2}{\sqrt{3}}$ <
★ 62. $\dfrac{1}{\sqrt{31}}$ ● $\dfrac{\sqrt{31}}{31}$ =
★ 63. $\dfrac{\sqrt{2}}{2}$ ● $\dfrac{1}{2}$ >

Write each set of numbers in order from least to greatest.

64. $\sqrt{0.42}, 0.\overline{63}, \dfrac{\sqrt{4}}{3}$ $0.\overline{63}, \sqrt{0.42}, \dfrac{\sqrt{4}}{3}$
65. $\sqrt{0.06}, 0.\overline{24}, \dfrac{\sqrt{9}}{12}$ $0.\overline{24}, \sqrt{0.06}, \dfrac{\sqrt{9}}{12}$
66. $−1.\overline{46}, −\dfrac{1}{6}, 0.2, \sqrt{2}$ $−1.\overline{46}, 0.2, \sqrt{2}, −\dfrac{1}{6}$
67. $−4.\overline{83}, −\dfrac{3}{8}, 0.4, \sqrt{8}$ $−4.\overline{83}, 0.4, \sqrt{8}, −\dfrac{3}{8}$
68. $−\sqrt{65}, −6\dfrac{2}{5}, −\sqrt{27}$ $−\sqrt{65}, −6\dfrac{2}{5}, −\sqrt{27}$
69. $\sqrt{122}, 7\dfrac{4}{9}, \sqrt{200}$ $7\dfrac{4}{9}, \sqrt{122}, \sqrt{200}$

TOURISM For Exercises 70–72, use the following information.
The formula to determine the distance d in miles that an object can be seen on a clear day on the surface of a body of water is $d = 1.4\sqrt{h}$, where h is the height in feet of the viewer's eyes above the surface of the water.

70. A charter plane is used to fly tourists on a sightseeing trip along the coast of North Carolina. If the plane flies at an altitude of 1500 feet, how far can the tourists see? **about 54.2 mi**

71. Dillan and Marissa are parasailing while on vacation. Marissa is 135 feet above the ocean while Dillan is 85 feet above the ocean. How much farther can Marissa see than Dillan? **about 3.4 mi**

72. The observation deck of a lighthouse stands 120 feet above the ocean surface. Can the lighthouse keeper see a boat that is 17 miles from the lighthouse? Explain. **No; the lighthouse keeper can only see about 15.3 mi.**

73. **CRITICAL THINKING** Determine when the following statements are all true for real numbers q and r. **They are true if q and r are positive and $q > r$.**
   a. $q^2 > r^2$
   b. $\dfrac{1}{q} < \dfrac{1}{r}$
   c. $\sqrt{q} > \sqrt{r}$
   d. $\dfrac{1}{\sqrt{q}} < \dfrac{1}{\sqrt{r}}$

66. $−1.\overline{46}, −\dfrac{1}{6}, 0.2, \sqrt{2}$

67. $−4.\overline{83}, −\dfrac{3}{8}, 0.4, \sqrt{8}$

68. $−\sqrt{65}, −6\dfrac{2}{5}, −\sqrt{27}$

69. $7\dfrac{4}{9}, \sqrt{122}, \sqrt{200}$

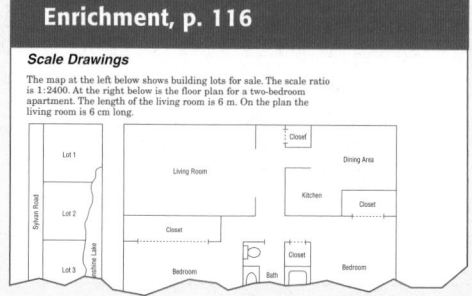

GEOMETRY For Exercises 74–76, use the table.

Squares		
Area (units²)	Side Length	Perimeter
1	1	4
4	2	8
9	3	12
16	4	16
25	5	20

74. Copy and complete the table. Determine the length of each side of each square described. Then determine the perimeter of each square.

75. The length of the side is the square root of the area.

75. Describe the relationship between the lengths of the sides and the area.

76. Write an expression you can use to find the perimeter of a square whose area is a units². **$4\sqrt{a}$**

77. WRITING IN MATH   Answer the question that was posed at the beginning of the lesson. **See margin.**

How can using square roots determine the surface area of the human body?

Include the following in your answer:
- an explanation of the order of operations that must be followed to calculate the surface area of the human body,
- a description of other situations in which you might need to calculate the surface area of the human body, and
- examples of real-world situations involving square roots.

Standardized Test Practice
(A) (B) (C) (D)

78. Which point on the number line is closest to $-\sqrt{7}$? **B**

R   ST   U
–4   –3   –2   –1   0

(A) R
(B) S
(C) T
(D) U

79. Which of the following is a true statement? **B**

(A) $-\frac{6}{3} > \frac{3}{6}$ (B) $-\frac{3}{6} > -\frac{6}{3}$ (C) $-\frac{3}{6} < -\frac{6}{3}$ (D) $\frac{6}{3} < \frac{3}{6}$

Maintain Your Skills

Mixed Review   Find the odds of each outcome if a card is randomly selected from a standard deck of cards. *(Lesson 2-6)*

80. red 4 **1:25**
81. even number **5:8**
82. against a face card **10:3**
83. against an ace **12:1**

84. **AUTO RACING**   Jeff Gordon's finishing places in the 2000 season races are listed below. Which measure of central tendency best represents the data? Explain. *(Lesson 2-5)* **Sample answer: Mean; the median and mode are too low.**

34 10 28 9 8 8 25 4 1 11 14 10 32 14 8 1 4
10 5 3 33 23 36 23 4 1 6 9 5 39 4 2 7 7

Simplify each expression. *(Lesson 2-3)* **88. $-7xy + 14xz$**

85. $4(-7) - 3(11)$ **-61**
86. $3(-4) + 2(-7)$ **-26**
87. $1.2(4x - 5y) - 0.2(-1.5x + 8y)$
$5.1x - 7.6y$
88. $-4x(y - 2z) + x(6z - 3y)$

Open-Ended Assessment
Modeling   Arrange 16 square tiles into a 4-by-4 grid and show how the side length models $\sqrt{16}$. Now give students other square numbers of tiles and have them model the square root.

Assessment Options
Quiz (Lesson 2-7) is available on p. 132 of the *Chapter 2 Resource Masters*.

Answers

52.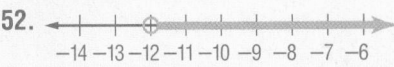
–14 –13 –12 –11 –10 –9 –8 –7 –6

53.
1 2 3 4 5 6 7 8 9

54.
–10   –9

55.
–2   –1   0

56.
–5 –4 –3 –2 –1 0 1 2 3 4

57.
–8 –6 –4 –2 0 2 4 6 8

77. Sample answer: By using the formula
$$\text{Surface Area} = \sqrt{\frac{\text{height} \times \text{weight}}{3600}},$$
you need to use square roots to calculate the quantity. Answers should include the following.

- You must multiply height by weight first. Divide that product by 3600. Then determine the square root of that result.
- Sample answers: exposure to radiation or chemicals; heat loss; scuba suits
- Sample answers: determining height, distance

Chapter 2 · Study Guide and Review

Vocabulary and Concept Check

• This alphabetical list of vocabulary terms in Chapter 2 includes a page reference where each term was introduced.

• **Assessment** A vocabulary test/review for Chapter 2 is available on p. 130 of the *Chapter 2 Resource Masters*.

Lesson-by-Lesson Review

For each lesson,

• the main ideas are summarized,

• additional examples review concepts, and

• practice exercises are provided.

Vocabulary PuzzleMaker

ELL The Vocabulary PuzzleMaker software improves students' mathematics vocabulary using four puzzle formats—crossword, scramble, word search using a word list, and word search using clues. Students can work on a computer screen or from a printed handout.

MindJogger Videoquizzes

ELL MindJogger Videoquizzes provide an alternative review of concepts presented in this chapter. Students work in teams in a game show format to gain points for correct answers. The questions are presented in three rounds.

Round 1 Concepts (5 questions)
Round 2 Skills (4 questions)
Round 3 Problem Solving (4 questions)

Vocabulary and Concept Check

absolute value (p. 69)	irrational number (p. 104)	probability (p. 96)
additive inverses (p. 74)	line plot (p. 88)	radical sign (p. 103)
back-to-back stem-and-leaf plot (p. 89)	measures of central tendency (p. 90)	rational approximation (p. 105)
Completeness Property (p. 105)	natural number (p. 68)	rational number (p. 68)
coordinate (p. 69)	negative number (p.68)	real number (p. 104)
equally likely (p. 97)	odds (p. 97)	sample space (p. 96)
frequency (p. 88)	opposites (p. 74)	simple event (p. 96)
graph (p. 69)	perfect square (p. 103)	square root (p. 103)
infinity (p. 68)	positive number (p. 68)	stem-and-leaf plot (p. 89)
integers (p. 68)	principal square root (p. 103)	whole number (p. 68)

State whether each sentence is *true* or *false*. If false, replace the underlined term or number to make a true sentence.

1. The absolute value of -26 is <u>26</u>. **true**
2. Terminating decimals are <u>rational</u> numbers. **true**
3. The principal square root of 144 is <u>12</u>. **true**
4. $-\sqrt{576}$ is an <u>irrational number</u>. **false; rational number**
5. 225 is a <u>perfect square</u>. **true**
6. <u>-3.1</u> is an integer. **false; sample answer: -3**
7. <u>0.666</u> is a repeating decimal. **false; sample answer: $0.\overline{6}$ or 0.666…**
8. The product of two numbers with different signs is <u>negative</u>. **true**

Lesson-by-Lesson Review

2-1 Rational Numbers on the Number Line

See pages 68–72.

Concept Summary

• A set of numbers can be graphed on a number line by drawing points.
• To evaluate expressions with absolute value, treat the absolute value symbols as grouping symbols.

Example Graph $\{\dots, -5, -4, -3\}$.

The bold arrow means that the graph continues indefinitely in that direction.

Exercises Graph each set of numbers. *See Example 2 on page 69.* **9–11. See margin.**

9. $\{5, 3, -1, -3\}$
10. $\left\{-1\frac{1}{2}, -\frac{1}{2}, \frac{1}{2}, 1\frac{1}{2}, \dots\right\}$
11. {integers less than -4 and greater than or equal to 2}

Evaluate each expression if $x = -4$, $y = 8$, and $z = -9$. *See Example 4 on page 70.*

12. $32 - |y - 3|$ **27**
13. $3|x| - 7$ **5**
14. $4 + |z|$ **13**
15. $46 - y|x|$ **14**

 www.algebra1.com/vocabulary_review

FOLDABLES™ Study Organizer

For more information about Foldables, see *Teaching Mathematics with Foldables.*

Have students review their Foldables to be sure they have included notes on every lesson in this chapter.

Encourage students to refer to their Foldables while completing the Study Guide and Review and to use them in preparing for the Chapter Test.

2-2 Adding and Subtracting Rational Numbers

See pages 73–78.

Concept Summary

- To add rational numbers with the *same* sign, add their absolute values. The sum has the same sign as the addends.
- To add rational numbers with *different* signs, subtract the lesser absolute value from the greater absolute value. The sum has the same sign as the number with the greater absolute value.
- To subtract a rational number, add its additive inverse.

Examples

1 Find $-4 + (-3)$.

$-4 + (-3)$
$= -(|-4| + |-3|)$ Both numbers are negative, so the sum is negative.
$= -(4 + 3)$
$= -7$

2 Find $12 - 18$.

$12 - 18$ To subtract 18, add its inverse.
$= 12 + (-18)$
$= -(|-18| - |12|)$ The absolute value of 18 is greater, so the result is negative.
$= -(18 - 12)$
$= -6$

Exercises Find each sum or difference. *See Examples 1–3 on pages 73–75.*

16. $4 + (-4)$ **0**
17. $2 + (-7)$ **−5**
18. $-0.8 + (-1.2)$ **−2**
19. $-3.9 + 2.5$ **−1.4**
20. $-\frac{1}{4} + \left(-\frac{1}{8}\right)$ **$-\frac{3}{8}$**
21. $\frac{5}{6} + \left(-\frac{1}{3}\right)$ **$\frac{1}{2}$**
22. $-2 - 10$ **−12**
23. $9 - (-7)$ **16**
24. $1.25 - 0.18$ **1.07**
25. $-7.7 - (-5.2)$ **−2.5**
26. $\frac{9}{2} - \left(-\frac{1}{2}\right)$ **5**
27. $-\frac{1}{8} - \left(-\frac{2}{3}\right)$ **$\frac{13}{24}$**

2-3 Multiplying Rational Numbers

See pages 79–83.

Concept Summary

- The product of two numbers having the same sign is positive.
- The product of two numbers having different signs is negative.

Example Multiply $\left(-2\frac{1}{7}\right)\left(3\frac{2}{3}\right)$.

$\left(-2\frac{1}{7}\right)\left(3\frac{2}{3}\right) = \frac{-15}{7} \cdot \frac{11}{3}$ Write as improper fractions.

$= \frac{-55}{7}$ or $-7\frac{6}{7}$ Simplify.

Exercises Find each product. *See Examples 1 and 3 on pages 79 and 80.*

28. $(-11)(9)$ **−99**
29. $12(-3)$ **−36**
30. $-8.2(4.5)$ **−36.9**
31. $-2.4(-3.6)$ **8.64**
32. $\frac{3}{4} \cdot \frac{7}{12}$ **$\frac{7}{16}$**
33. $\left(-\frac{1}{3}\right)\left(-\frac{9}{10}\right)$ **$\frac{3}{10}$**

Simplify each expression. *See Example 2 on page 80.*

34. $8(-3x) + 12x$ **−12x**
35. $-5(-2n) - 9n$ **n**
36. $-4(6a) - (-3)(-7a)$ **−45a**

2-4 Dividing Rational Numbers

See pages 84–87.

Concept Summary

- The quotient of two positive numbers is positive.
- The quotient of two negative numbers is positive.
- The quotient of a positive number and a negative number is negative.

Example Simplify $\dfrac{-3(4)}{-2-3}$.

$$\frac{-3(4)}{-2-3} = \frac{-12}{-2-3} \qquad \text{Simplify the numerator.}$$

$$= \frac{-12}{-5} \qquad \text{Simplify the denominator.}$$

$$= 2\frac{2}{5} \qquad \text{same signs} \rightarrow \text{positive quotient}$$

Exercises   Find each quotient.   *See Examples 1–3 on pages 84 and 85.*

37. $\dfrac{-54}{6}$ **−9**

38. $-\dfrac{74}{8}$ **−9.25**

39. $21.8 \div (-2)$ **−10.9**

40. $-7.8 \div (-6)$ **1.3**

41. $-15 \div \left(\dfrac{3}{4}\right)$ **−20**

42. $\dfrac{21}{24} \div \dfrac{1}{3}$ **$\dfrac{21}{8}$ or $2\dfrac{5}{8}$**

Simplify each expression.   *See Example 5 on page 85.*

43. $\dfrac{14 - 28x}{-7}$ **−2 + 4x**

44. $\dfrac{-5 + 25x}{5}$ **−1 + 5x**

45. $\dfrac{-4x + 24y}{4}$ **−x + 6y**

Evaluate each expression if $x = -4$, $y = 2.4$, and $z = 3$.   *See Example 6 on page 85.*

46. $xz - 2y$ **−16.8**

47. $-2\left(\dfrac{2y}{z}\right)$ **−3.2**

48. $\dfrac{2x - z}{4} + 3y$ **4.45**

2-5 Statistics: Displaying and Analyzing Data

See pages 88–94.

Concept Summary

- A set of numerical data can be displayed in a line plot or stem-and-leaf plot.
- A measure of central tendency represents a centralized value of a set of data. Examine each measure of central tendency to choose the one most representative of the data.

Examples **1** Draw a line plot for the data.

2   8   6   4   5   9   13   12   5   2   5   5   2

The value of the data ranges from 2 to 13. Construct a number line containing those points. Then place an × above a number each time it occurs.

2 **SCHOOL** Melinda's scores on the 25-point quizzes in her English class are 20, 21, 12, 21, 22, 22, 22, 21, 20, 20, and 21. Which measure of central tendency best represents her grade?

mean: 20.2   Add the data and divide by 11.

median: 21   The middle value is 21.

mode: 21   The most frequent value is 21.

The median and mode are both representative of the data. The mean is less than most of the data.

Exercises

49. Draw a line plot for the data. Then make a stem-and-leaf plot.
See Examples 1–3 on pages 88 and 89. **See margin.**

28	17	16	18	19	21	26	15
19	19	16	14	21	12	26	17
30	17	13	18	14	22	20	12
19	19	15	12	15	21	15	17

50. **BUSINESS** Of the 42 employees at Pirate Printing, four make $6.50 an hour, sixteen make $6.75 an hour, six make $6.85 an hour, thirteen make $7.25 an hour, and three make $8.85 an hour. Which measure best describes the average wage? Explain. *See Examples 5 and 6 on pages 90 and 91.* **See margin.**

51. **HOCKEY** Professional hockey uses a point system based on wins, losses and ties, to determine teams' rank. The stem-and-leaf plot shows the number of points earned by each of the 30 teams in the National Hockey League during the 2000–2001 season. Which measure of central tendency best describes the average number of points earned? Explain.
See Example 5 on page 90. **Sample answer: Median; it is closest in value to most of the data.**

Stem	Leaf
11	1 1 8
10	0 3 6 9
9	0 0 0 2 3 5 6 6 8
8	0 8 8
7	0 1 1 2 3
6	0 6 6 8
5	2 9 $11\,|\,1 = 111$

49.

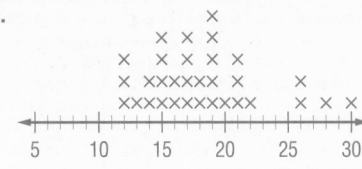

Stem	Leaf
1	2 2 2 3 4 4 5 5 5 5 6 6 7 7 7 7 8 8 9 9 9 9 9
2	0 1 1 1 2 6 6 8
3	0

$1\,|\,2 = 12$

50. Sample answer: Mean; the median and mode are too low.

2-6 Probability: Simple Probability and Odds

See pages 96–101.

Concept Summary

- The probability of an event *a* can be expressed as

$$P(a) = \frac{\text{number of favorable outcomes}}{\text{total number of possible outcomes}}.$$

- The odds of an event can be expressed as the ratio of the number of successful outcomes to the number of unsuccessful outcomes.

Examples **1** Find the probability of randomly choosing the letter *I* in the word *MISSISSIPPI*.

$$P(\text{letter I}) = \frac{4}{11} \quad \begin{array}{l} \leftarrow \text{number of favorable outcomes} \\ \leftarrow \text{number of possible outcomes} \end{array}$$

$$\approx 0.36$$

The probability of choosing an I is $\frac{4}{11}$ or about 36%.

Study Guide and Review

Chapter 2 For More ...
• Extra Practice, see pages 823–825.
• Mixed Problem Solving, see page 854.

Answers

64. rationals

65. naturals, wholes, integers, rationals

66. irrationals

Answers (p. 115)

31.

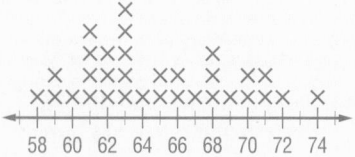

```
                    ×
              ×  ×
              ×××            ×
        ×   ×××   ××  ×  ××
        ××××××××××××××××  ×
       ├─┼─┼─┼─┼─┼─┼─┼─┼─┼─┼─┼─┤
        58  60  62  64  66  68  70  72  74
```

32. Sample answer: The median and mode can be used to best represent the data. The mean is too high.

---

2 Find the odds that you will randomly select a letter that is *not* S in the word *MISSISSIPPI.*

number of successes : number of failures = 7:4

The odds of not selecting an S are 7:4.

Exercises Find the probability of each outcome if a computer randomly chooses a letter in the word *REPRESENTING.* *See Example 1 on pages 96 and 97.*

52. $P(S)$ $\frac{1}{12}$ 53. $P(E)$ $\frac{1}{4}$ 54. $P(\text{not N})$ $\frac{5}{6}$ 55. $P(\text{R or P})$ $\frac{1}{4}$

Find the odds of each outcome if you randomly select a coin from a jar containing 90 pennies, 75 nickels, 50 dimes, and 30 quarters.
See Examples 2 and 3 on pages 97 and 98.

56. a dime 10:39   57. a penny 18:31   58. *not* a nickel   59. a nickel or a dime
                                                              34:15   25:24

2-7 Square Roots and Real Numbers

See pages 103–109.

Concept Summary

• A square root is one of two equal factors of a number.
• The symbol $\sqrt{}$ is used to indicate the nonnegative square root of a number.

Example Find $\sqrt{169}$.

$\sqrt{169}$ represents the square root of 169.

$169 = 13^2 \quad \rightarrow \quad \sqrt{169} = 13$

Exercises Find each square root. If necessary, round to the nearest hundredth.
See Example 1 on page 103.

60. $\sqrt{196}$ 14   61. $\pm\sqrt{1.21}$ ± 1.1 62. $-\sqrt{160}$ -12.65 63. $\pm\sqrt{\dfrac{4}{225}}$ $\pm\dfrac{2}{15}$

Name the set or sets of numbers to which each real number belongs.
See Example 2 on page 104. 64–66. See margin.

64. $\dfrac{16}{25}$ 65. $\dfrac{\sqrt{64}}{2}$ 66. $-\sqrt{48.5}$

Replace each ● with <, >, or = to make each sentence true. *See Example 4 on page 105.*

67. $\dfrac{1}{8}$ ● $\dfrac{1}{\sqrt{49}}$ <   68. $\sqrt{\dfrac{2}{3}}$ ● $\dfrac{4}{9}$ >   69. $\sqrt{\dfrac{3}{4}}$ ● $\sqrt{\dfrac{1}{3}}$ >

70. **WEATHER** Meteorologists can use the formula $t = \sqrt{\dfrac{d^3}{216}}$ to estimate the amount of time t in hours a storm of diameter d will last. Suppose the eye of a hurricane, which causes the greatest amount of destruction, is 9 miles in diameter. To the nearest tenth of an hour, how long will the worst part of the hurricane last?
See Example 1 on pages 103 and 104. 1.8 h

Vocabulary and Concepts

Choose the correct term to complete each sentence.

1. The (*absolute value*, square) of a number is its distance from zero on a number line.

2. A number that can be written as a fraction where the numerator and denominator are integers and the denominator does not equal zero is a (repeating, *rational*) number.

3. The list of all possible outcomes is called the (simple event, *sample space*).

Skills and Applications

Evaluate each expression.

4. $-|x| - 38$ if $x = -2$ **−40**

5. $34 - |x + 21|$ if $x = -7$ **20**

6. $-12 + |x - 8|$ if $x = 1.5$ **−5.5**

Find each sum or difference.

7. $-19 + 12$ **−7**

8. $-21 - (-34)$ **13**

9. $16.4 + (-23.7)$ **−7.3**

10. $6.32 - (-7.41)$ **13.73**

11. $-\frac{7}{16} + \frac{3}{8}$ **−$\frac{1}{16}$**

12. $-\frac{7}{12} - \left(-\frac{5}{9}\right)$ **−$\frac{1}{36}$**

Find each quotient or product.

13. $-5(19)$ **−95**

14. $-56 \div (-7)$ **8**

15. $96 \div (-0.8)$ **−120**

16. $(-7.8)(5.6)$ **−43.68**

17. $-\frac{1}{8} \div -5$ **$\frac{1}{40}$**

18. $-\frac{15}{32} \div \frac{3}{4}$ **−$\frac{5}{8}$**

Simplify each expression. **21. $28mn - 12cd$**

19. $5(-3x) - 12x$ **−27x**

20. $7(6h - h)$ **35h**

21. $-4m(-7n) + (3d)(-4c)$

22. $\frac{36k}{4}$ **9k**

23. $\frac{9a + 27}{-3}$ **−3a − 9**

24. $\frac{70x - 30y}{-5}$ **−14x + 6y**

Find each square root. If necessary, round to the nearest hundredth.

25. $-\sqrt{64}$ **−8**

26. $\sqrt{3.61}$ **1.9**

27. $\pm\sqrt{\frac{16}{81}}$ **$\pm\frac{4}{9}$**

Replace each ● with <, >, or = to make each sentence true.

28. $\frac{1}{\sqrt{3}}$ ● $\frac{1}{3}$ **>**

29. $\sqrt{\frac{1}{2}}$ ● $\frac{8}{11}$ **<**

30. $\sqrt{0.56}$ ● $\frac{\sqrt{3}}{2}$ **<**

STATISTICS For Exercises 31 and 32, use the following information. **31–32. See margin.**
The height, in inches, of the students in a health class are 65, 63, 68, 66, 72, 61, 62, 63, 59, 58, 61, 74, 65, 63, 71, 70, 60, 62, 63, 71, 70, 59, 66, 61, 62, 68, 69, 64, 63, 70, 61, 68, and 67.

31. Make a line plot of the data.

32. Which measure of central tendency best describes the data? Explain.

33. **STANDARDIZED TEST PRACTICE** During a 20-song sequence on a radio station, 8 soft-rock, 7 hard-rock, and 5 rap songs are played at random. Assume that all of the songs are the same length. What is the probability that when you turn on the radio, a hard-rock song will be playing? **B**

Ⓐ $\frac{1}{4}$
Ⓑ $\frac{7}{20}$
Ⓒ $\frac{2}{5}$
Ⓓ $\frac{13}{20}$
Ⓔ $\frac{7}{10}$

 www.algebra1.com/chapter_test

Chapter 2 Practice Test **115**

Assessment Options

Vocabulary Test A vocabulary test/review for Chapter 2 can be found on p. 130 of the *Chapter 2 Resource Masters*.

Chapter Tests There are six Chapter 2 Tests and an Open-Ended Assessment task available in the *Chapter 2 Resource Masters*.

Chapter 2 Tests			
Form	**Type**	**Level**	**Pages**
1	MC	basic	117–118
2A	MC	average	119–120
2B	MC	average	121–122
2C	FR	average	123–124
2D	FR	average	125–126
3	FR	advanced	127–128

MC = multiple-choice questions
FR = free-response questions

Open-Ended Assessment
Performance tasks for Chapter 2 can be found on p. 129 of the *Chapter 2 Resource Masters*. A sample scoring rubric for these tasks appears on p. A28.

 ExamView® Pro

Use the networkable **ExamView® Pro** to:

- Create **multiple versions** of tests.
- Create **modified** tests for *Inclusion* students.
- **Edit** existing questions and **add** your own questions.
- Use built-in **state curriculum correlations** to create tests aligned with state standards.
- Change **English** tests to **Spanish** and vice versa.

Portfolio Suggestion

Introduction Where will you use integers in the world outside your algebra classroom? Are integers common or does the outside world more often use fractions or decimals?

Ask Students Golf is an example of a game that uses integers in its scoring. Have students investigate the game of golf and how it is scored. Then have them report on how integers are used to keep score in a golf tournament. How do the integers indicate which player is the winner?

These two pages contain practice questions in the various formats that can be found on the most frequently given standardized tests.

A practice answer sheet for these two pages can be found on p. A1 of the *Chapter 2 Resource Masters*.

Standardized Test Practice
Student Recording Sheet, p. A1

Part 1 Multiple Choice

Select the best answer from the choices given and fill in the corresponding oval.

1 Ⓐ Ⓑ Ⓒ Ⓓ   4 Ⓐ Ⓑ Ⓒ Ⓓ   7 Ⓐ Ⓑ Ⓒ Ⓓ

2 Ⓐ Ⓑ Ⓒ Ⓓ   5 Ⓐ Ⓑ Ⓒ Ⓓ   8 Ⓐ Ⓑ Ⓒ Ⓓ

3 Ⓐ Ⓑ Ⓒ Ⓓ   6 Ⓐ Ⓑ Ⓒ Ⓓ   9 Ⓐ Ⓑ Ⓒ Ⓓ

Part 2 Short Response/Grid In

Solve the problem and write your answer in the blank.

For Questions 11, 12, 15, 16, and 19, also enter your answer by writing each number or symbol in a box. Then fill in the corresponding oval for that number or symbol.

10 _____
11 _____ (grid in)
12 _____ (grid in)
13 _____
14 _____
15 _____ (grid in)
16 _____ (grid in)
17 _____
18 _____ (grid in)
19 _____ (grid in)

Part 3 Extended Response

Record your answers for Questions 20–21 on the back of this paper.

Additional Practice

See pp. 135–136 in the *Chapter 2 Resource Masters* for additional standardized test practice.

Teaching Tip Exercises 10–14 are all short answer questions. However, only Exercises 11 and 12 might appear as grid-in questions.

Part 1 | Multiple Choice

Record your answers on the answer sheet provided by your teacher or on a sheet of paper.

1. Darryl works 9 days at the State Fair and earns $518.40. If he works 8 hours each day, what is his hourly pay? (Prerequisite Skill) **B**

   Ⓐ $6.48   Ⓑ $7.20

   Ⓒ $30.50   Ⓓ $57.60

2. The graph below shows how many toy trains are assembled at a factory at the end of 10-minute intervals. What is the best prediction for the number of products assembled per hour? (Prerequisite Skill) **C**

   Ⓐ 80

   Ⓑ 100

   Ⓒ 120

   Ⓓ 130

   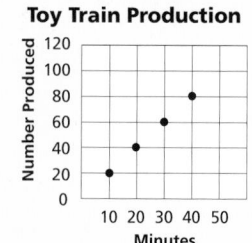
   Toy Train Production

3. Which graph shows the integers greater than −2 and less than or equal to 3? (Lesson 2-1) **C**

   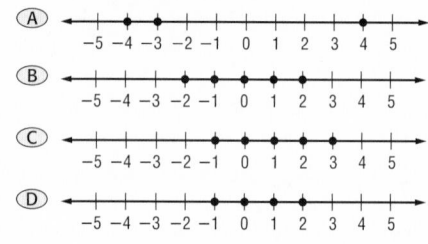

   Ⓐ
   Ⓑ
   Ⓒ
   Ⓓ

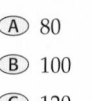

Test-Taking Tip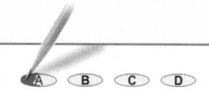
Question 1
If you don't know how to solve a problem, eliminate the answer choices you know are incorrect and then guess from the remaining choices. Even eliminating only one answer choice greatly increases your chance of guessing the correct answer.

116   Chapter 2   Real Numbers

---

4. Which number is the greatest? (Lesson 2-1) **D**

   Ⓐ $|-4|$ Ⓑ $|4|$

   Ⓒ $|7|$ Ⓓ $|-9|$

5. What is $-3.8 + 4.7$? (Lesson 2-2) **A**

   Ⓐ 0.9   Ⓑ −0.9

   Ⓒ 8.5   Ⓓ −8.5

6. Simplify $3(-2m) - 7m$. (Lesson 2-3) **D**

   Ⓐ $-12m$ Ⓑ $-m$

   Ⓒ $-2m$ Ⓓ $-13m$

7. Which statement about the stem-and-leaf plot is *not* true? (Lesson 2-5) **D**

Stem	Leaf
3	1 1 5 6 8 8
4	2 2 2 4
5	0 0
6	0 3 7 8 9 9
7	4 7|4 = 74

   Ⓐ The greatest value is 74.

   Ⓑ The mode is 42.

   Ⓒ Seven of the values are greater than 50.

   Ⓓ The least value is 38.

8. There are 4 boxes. If you choose a box at random, what are the odds that you will choose the one box with a prize? (Lesson 2-6) **A**

   Ⓐ 1:3   Ⓑ 1:4

   Ⓒ 3:1   Ⓓ 3:4

9. Which point on the number line is closest to $\sqrt{10}$? (Lesson 2-7) **B**

   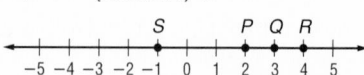

   Ⓐ point P Ⓑ point Q

   Ⓒ point R Ⓓ point S

ExamView® Pro

Special banks of standardized test questions similar to those on the SAT, ACT, TIMSS 8, NAEP 8, and Algebra 1 End-of-Course tests can be found on this CD-ROM.

Part 2 | Short Response/Grid In

Record your answers on the answer sheet provided by your teacher or on a sheet of paper.

10. Ethan needs to wrap a label around a jar of homemade jelly so that there is no overlap. Find the length of the label. (Prerequisite Skill) **25.13 cm**

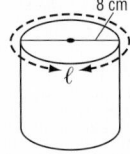

11. Evaluate $\dfrac{5-1}{4+12 \div 3 \times 2}$. (Lesson 1-2) **1/3**

12. Find the solution of $4m - 3 = 9$ if the replacement set is $\{0, 2, 3, 5\}$. (Lesson 1-3) **3**

13. Write an algebraic expression for *2p plus three times the difference of m and n*. (Lesson 1-6) **$3(m - n) + 2p$**

14. State the hypothesis in the statement *If $3x + 3 > 24$, then $x > 7$.* (Lesson 1-7) **$3x + 3 > 24$**

15. A survey of 1756 students at Prospect High School was taken, and the results are shown in the circle graph. About how many students drink water with dinner? (Lesson 1-8) **632**

What Do You Drink With Dinner?

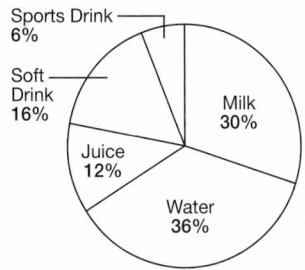

16. Augustus was the first emperor of Rome. He was born in the year 62 B.C. and died in 14 A.D. How old was Augustus when he died? (Lesson 2-2) **76**

 www.algebra1.com/standardized_test

17. The population of Ohio in 1990 was 10,847,115. It rose to 11,353,140 in 2000. What was the average change in population for each of the 10 years? (Lesson 2-4)
Source: U.S. Census Bureau **about 50,603**

18. Two dice are rolled, and their difference is recorded. Find the probability of rolling a difference of less than 2. (Lesson 2-6)
4/9 or 0.44

19. Find $\sqrt{\dfrac{25}{125}}$ to the nearest hundredth.
(Lesson 2-7) **0.45**

Part 3 | Extended Response

Record your answers on a sheet of paper. Show your work.

20. Mia has created the chart below to compare the three cellular phone plans she is considering. (Lessons 2-2 and 2-3)

Plan	Monthly Fee	Cost/Minute
A	$5.95	$0.30
B	$12.95	$0.10
C	$19.99	$0.08

a. Write an algebraic expression that Mia can use to figure the monthly cost of each plan. Use C for the total monthly cost, m for the cost per minute, x for the monthly fee, and y for the minutes used per month. **a–b. See margin.**

b. If Mia uses 150 minutes of calls each month, which plan will be least expensive? Explain.

21. The stem-and-leaf plot lists the annual profit for seven small businesses. (Lesson 2-5)
a–b. See margin.

Stem	Leaf
3	2 9
4	1 1 3 5
5	0

a. Explain how the absence of a key could lead to misinterpreting the data.

b. How do the keys below affect how the data should be interpreted?
$3 \mid 2 = 3.2$ $\quad$ $3 \mid 2 = 0.32$

Chapter 2 Standardized Test Practice **117**

Evaluating Extended Response Questions

Extended Response questions are graded by using a multilevel rubric that guides you in assessing a student's knowledge of a particular concept.

Goal: Identify what is wrong with a stem-and-leaf plot, and compare cellular phone service plans.

Sample Scoring Rubric: The following rubric is a sample scoring device. You may wish to add more detail to this sample to meet your individual scoring needs.

Score	Criteria
4	A correct solution that is supported by well-developed, accurate explanations
3	A generally correct solution, but may contain minor flaws in reasoning or computation
2	A partially correct interpretation and/or solution to the problem
1	A correct solution with no supporting evidence or explanation
0	An incorrect solution indicating no mathematical understanding of the concept or task, or no solution is given

Answers

20a. $C = x + my$

20b. Plan B is the least expensive. It costs $27.95 for 150 minutes. Plan A costs $50.95 and Plan C costs $31.99.

21a. Without a key, you cannot determine what the values are.

21b. If the key is $3 \mid 2 = 3.2$, then the data are ten times as great as they would be if the key is $3 \mid 2 = 0.32$.

Pages 70–72, Lesson 2-1

1. always

2. Sample answer: Absolute value is how far from zero a number is.

3. Sample answer: Describing directions such as north versus south, or left versus right.

6.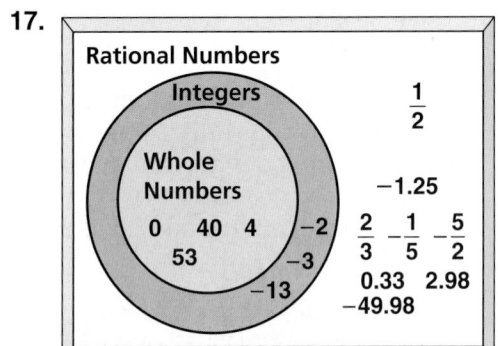
$$-5\,-4\,-3\,-2\,-1\;\;0\;\;1\;\;2\;\;3\;\;4\;\;5\;\;6\;\;7\;\;8$$

7.
$$-4\;\;-3\;\;-2\;\;-1\;\;0\;\;1\;\;2\;\;3\;\;4$$

8.
$$-1\quad -\tfrac{1}{2}\quad 0\ \tfrac{1}{4}\,\tfrac{2}{5}\quad 1\qquad \tfrac{5}{3}$$

9.
$$-9\,-8\,-7\,-6\,-5\,-4\,-3\,-2\,-1\;\;0\;\;1$$

17.

Rational Numbers

Integers

Whole Numbers

0   40   4
53

−2
−3
−13

$\dfrac{1}{2}$

−1.25

$\dfrac{2}{3}\quad -\dfrac{1}{5}\quad -\dfrac{5}{2}$

0.33   2.98
−49.98

24.
$$-5\,-4\,-3\,-2\,-1\;\;0\;\;1\;\;2\;\;3\;\;4$$

25.
$$-1\;\;0\;\;1\;\;2\;\;3\;\;4\;\;5\;\;6\;\;7\;\;8\;\;9\;\;10$$

26.
$$-7\quad -6\quad -5\quad -4\quad -3\quad -2$$

27.
$$-2\,-1\;\;0\;\;1\;\;2\;\;3\;\;4\;\;5\;\;6$$

28.
$$-9\;-8\;-7\;-6\;-5\;-4\;-3\;-2$$

29.
$$-7\;-6\;-5\;-4\;-3\;-2\;-1\;\;0$$

30.
$$-1\,-\tfrac{2}{3}\,-\tfrac{1}{3}\;\;0\;\;\tfrac{1}{3}\;\;\tfrac{2}{3}\;\;1\;\;1\tfrac{1}{3}\;\;1\tfrac{2}{3}\;\;2$$

31.
$$-4\;-3\;-2\;-1\;\;0\;\;1\;\;2\;\;3$$

32.
$$-9\,-8\,-7\,-6\,-5\,-4\,-3\,-2\,-1\;\;0\;\;1$$

33.
$$-6\;\;-4\;\;-2\;\;0\;\;2\;\;4\;\;6\;\;8\;\;10$$

42.
$$-10\,-8\,-6\,-4\,-2\;\;0\;\;2\;\;4\;\;6\;\;8\;\;10$$

Page 78, Lesson 2-2

71.

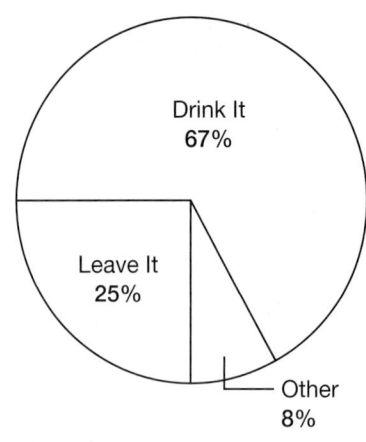

Cereal Milk

Drink It 67%

Leave It 25%

Other 8%

Pages 91–93, Lesson 2-5

2. Sample answer:

Line Plot:

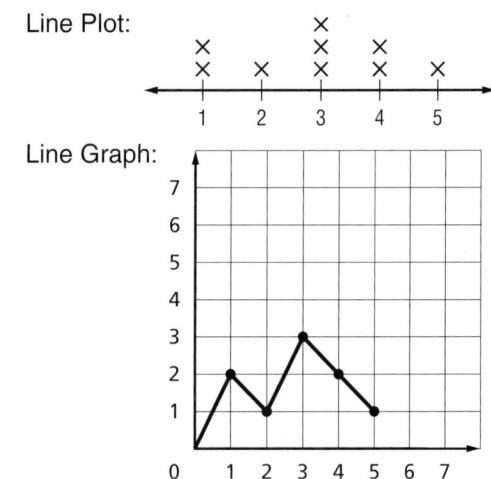

Line Graph:

4.
$$10\;\;12\;\;14\;\;16\;\;18\;\;20\;\;22\;\;24$$

5.
$$0\;\;2\;\;4\;\;6\;\;8\;\;10\;\;12\;\;14$$

7. The mean and the median both represent the data accurately as they are fairly central.

8.

Stem	Leaf
6	4 6 8 8 8
7	1 2 3 6
8	0 1 6 8 8
9	3

$6\,|\,4 = 64$

11.

Stem	Leaf
5	4 5 5 6
6	0 1 4 9
7	0 3 5 7 8
8	0 0 3 5 8 8 8
9	0
10	0 2 5
11	0

$5|4 = 54$

22.

Stem	Leaf
10	0 0 4 5 5 6 6 7 8 9 9
11	0 0 0 0 1 1 2 2 2 2 3 3 4 4 4 4 4 5
	6 7 7 7 8 8 8 8 8 8 9
12	0 0 0 0 1 1 2 5 8
13	4

$10|0 = 100$

28.

32.

Stem	Leaf
1	6 8 8 9 9 9
2	0 0 0 0 0 1 1 2 3 3 4 5 6 8 8 8 8 9 9 9 9 9
3	0 0 0 0 1 3 3 4 4 6 7
4	3 7

$1|6 = 16$

35.

Stem	Leaf
3	0 4 7
4	
5	2 9
6	2 7
7	7
8	4 5

$3|0 = 30$

Page 100–101, Lesson 2-6

60. Sample answer: Probabilities are often used for strategy like placing a certain pitcher against a batter who has a low probability of hitting a pitch from that pitcher. Answers should include the following.

- baseball: using the probability that a team can get base runners out; basketball: the probability that a player can make a basket from a certain place on the court; auto racing: the probability that a set of tires will hold out for the remainder of a race

- Odds in favor of an event and odds against an event are frequently used.

Page 102, Algebra Activity

2.

4 boys	3 boys, 1 girl	2 boys, 2 girls	1 boy, 3 girls	4 girls
BBBB	BBBG	BBGG	BGGG	GGGG
	BBGB	BGBG	GBGG	
	BGBB	BGGB	GGBG	
	GBBB	GBBG	GGGB	
		GBGB		
		GGBB		

Page 107, Lesson 2-7

32. irrationals

33. naturals, wholes, integers, rationals

34. rationals

35. rationals

36. irrationals

37. irrationals

38. rationals

39. rationals

40. rationals

41. rationals

42. naturals, wholes, integers, rationals

43. rationals

44. rationals

45. rationals

46. rationals

47. irrationals

48. irrationals

49. irrationals

Solving Linear Equations
Chapter Overview and Pacing

*An electronic version of this chapter is available on **StudentWorks**™. This backpack solution CD-ROM allows students instant access to the Student Edition, lesson worksheet pages, and web resources.*

Year-long and two-year pacing: pages T20–T21.

LESSON OBJECTIVES

		PACING (days)			
		Regular		**Block**	
		Basic/ Average	Advanced	Basic/ Average	Advanced
3-1	**Writing Equations** *(pp. 120–126)* • Translate verbal sentences into equations. • Translate equations into verbal sentences.	1	optional	0.5	optional
3-2	**Solving Equations by Using Addition and Subtraction** *(pp. 127–134)* *Preview:* Use algebra tiles to solve addition and subtraction equations. • Solve equations by using addition. • Solve equations by using subtraction.	2	optional	1	optional
3-3	**Solving Equations by Using Multiplication and Division** *(pp. 135–140)* • Solve equations by using multiplication. • Solve equations by using division.	1	optional	1 (with 3-4 Preview)	optional
3-4	**Solving Multi-Step Equations** *(pp. 141–148)* *Preview:* Use algebra tiles to solve multi-step equations. • Solve problems by working backward. • Solve equations involving more than one operation.	3 (with 3-4 Preview)	optional	0.5	optional
3-5	**Solving Equations with the Variable on Each Side** *(pp. 149–154)* • Solve equations with the variable on each side. • Solve equations involving grouping symbols.	1	optional	0.5	optional
3-6	**Ratios and Proportions** *(pp. 155–159)* • Determine whether two ratios form a proportion. • Solve proportions.	1	optional	0.5	optional
3-7	**Percent of Change** *(pp. 160–164)* • Find percents of increase and decrease. • Solve problems involving percents of change.	1	optional	0.5	optional
3-8	**Solving Equations and Formulas** *(pp. 166–170)* • Solve equations for given variables. • Use formulas to solve real-world problems.	2	optional	1	optional
3-9	**Weighted Averages** *(pp. 171–178)* • Solve mixture problems. • Solve uniform motion problems. *Follow-Up:* Use a spreadsheet to find a weighted average.	2	optional	1	optional
	Study Guide and **Practice Test** *(pp. 179–185)* **Standardized Test Practice** *(pp. 186–187)*	1	3	1 (with 3-9 Follow-Up)	1
	Chapter Assessment	1	1	0.5	0
	TOTAL	16	4	8	1

Chapter Resource Manager

| CHAPTER 3 RESOURCE MASTERS | | | | | | | | | | | |
Study Guide and Intervention	Practice (Skills and Average)	Reading to Learn Mathematics	Enrichment	Assessment	Prerequisite Skills Workbook	Applications*	Parent and Student Study Guide Workbook	5-Minute Check Transparencies	Interactive Chalkboard	AlgePASS: Tutorial Plus (lessons)	Materials
137–138	139–140	141	142				19	3-1	3-1		scissors, rectangular box
143–144	145–146	147	148		21–22, 59–60		20	3-2	3-2		(*Preview:* algebra tiles, equation mat)
149–150	151–152	153	154	205	9–12, 51–52		21	3-3	3-3		
155–156	157–158	159	160		77–78	SC 5, SM 37–40	22	3-4	3-4	4	(*Preview:* algebra tiles, equation mat)
161–162	163–164	165	166	205, 207	23–24	GCS 27	23	3-5	3-5	5	
167–168	169–170	171	172		27–28, 67–74	SC 6	24	3-6	3-6	6	
173–174	175–176	177	178	206	17–18, 41–44, 71–72, 77–78	GCS 28	25	3-7	3-7		
179–180	181–182	183	184		81–82		26	3-8	3-8	7, 8	
185–186	187–188	189	190	206			27	3-9	3-9		
				191–204, 208–210			28				

*Key to Abbreviations: GCS = Graphing Calculator and Spreadsheet Masters,
SC = School-to-Career Masters,
SM = Science and Mathematics Lab Manual

ELL Study Guide and Intervention, Skills Practice, Practice, and Parent and Student Study Guide Workbooks are also available in Spanish.

Mathematical Connections and Background

Continuity of Instruction

Prior Knowledge

In previous courses, students did work with ratios. They also found percents, and converted percents to decimals and decimals to percents. In Chapter 1, students wrote mathematical expressions for verbal expressions and vice versa. In Chapter 2, students performed mathematical operations with rational numbers.

This Chapter

Students obtain the crucial skills necessary for solving equations. Algebra tiles are used as models to develop an understanding of the Addition and Subtraction Properties of Equality. They expand this same understanding to the Multiplication and Division Properties of Equality. Students apply this knowledge to solving proportions and formulas.

Future Connections

Solving linear equations is a major mathematical concept that is used throughout all of the math courses the students will study in the future.

3-1 Writing Equations

Writing equations from verbal sentences is an essential tool for solving real-world problems. Variables are used to represent unspecified amounts. There are key words to assist in writing the mathematical equations, such as *equals, is, times, and, sum, difference, less, more,* and so on. Use the Four-Step Problem-Solving Plan to solve problems. Always examine the solution to make sure the answer is reasonable. Translating equations to verbal sentences can help give meaning to the equations.

3-2 Solving Equations by Using Addition and Subtraction

Solving an equation means finding all the values of the variable in the equation that make the statement true. To solve an equation, isolate the variable so that it has a coefficient of 1 on one side of the equation. If a number is being added to or subtracted from the variable in the original equation, use the inverse function to isolate the variable. Use the Addition or Subtraction Property of Equality to preserve equality. These properties stress the importance of performing the same operation on each side of the equation to result in an equivalent equation.

3-3 Solving Equations by Using Multiplication and Division

You also solve equations in which the variable is multiplied or divided by a rational number by using the inverse operation. The Multiplication and Division Properties of Equality state that you can multiply or divide each side of an equation by the same number and preserve equality.

3-4 Solving Multi-Step Equations

To solve some problems, the problem-solving strategy of working backward is helpful. This strategy is used to solve multi-step equations. Working backward and using inverse operations undo the order of operations. First, like terms must be combined. Then, the opposite of the order of operations is used: the Addition or Subtraction Property of Equality is performed before the Multiplication or Division Property of Equality.

3-5 Solving Equations with the Variable on Each Side

To solve any equation, no matter how complex, the variable must always be isolated. First apply the Distributive Property if necessary. Then combine like terms on each side of the equation. Move all variable terms to one side of the equation and all numeric terms to the other side using the Addition and/or Subtraction Properties of Equality. Then apply the Multiplication or Division Property of Equality.

There is no solution if the two sides of the equation cannot be equal. This occurs when all variable terms are eliminated and the two sides of the equation are not equal numbers. If both sides are identical at any point in the solution process, then the equation is an identity. In this case, all numbers are solutions.

3-6 Ratios and Proportions

A ratio is a comparison of two numbers by division. The numbers of a ratio can be written side by side with "to" or a colon between them, or they may be written to resemble a fraction. If the two numbers of a ratio represent two different measures, such as miles and hours, the ratio is called a rate. When using a rate to make a model or drawing that is larger or smaller than the original, the rate is called a scale.

A proportion is an equation stating that two ratios are equal. One way to determine if two ratios are equivalent is to use cross products. The product of the means of a proportion equals the product of its extremes. If the products are not equal, then the ratios do not form a proportion.

If a proportion contains a variable, the proportion can be solved for that variable by setting the product of the means equal to the product of the extremes. Then solve the resulting equation using the Division Property of Equality.

3-7 Percent of Change

Percent of change is the percent amount a number increases or decreases. If the new number is greater than the original number, the percent of change is called a percent of increase. If the new number is less than the original number, it is called a percent of decrease. Percent is found by dividing a part by its corresponding whole amount. Percent of change is found by solving a proportion. The ratio of the amount of change to the original number equals the ration of the percent to 100.

3-8 Solving Equations and Formulas

Some equations contain more than one variable. The process for solving one-step or multi-step equations is applied to solve these equations for one of the variables in terms of the other terms. Formulas are written as equations with multiple variables. They can be solved for one of the variables to make computation easier.

3-9 Weighted Averages

A weighted average is the sum of the product of the number of units in a set of data and the value per unit divided by the sum of the number of units. Two or more parts are combined into a whole in mixture problems. Weighted averages are used to solve mixture problems.

Uniform motion problems also use weighted averages. The distance formula is used to solve these problems. You solve the distance formula for the variable that the two movements have in common. A table is sometimes helpful when organizing these problems.

Quick Review Math Handbook

Hot Words includes a glossary of terms while Hot Topics consists of explanations of key mathematical concepts with exercises to test comprehension. This valuable resource can be used as a reference in the classroom or for home study.

Lesson	Hot Topics Section	Lesson	Hot Topics Section
GS3	2.8, 6.1, 6.3	3-5	2.1, 6.4
3-1	2.3, 2.5, 6.1	3-6	2.8, 6.5
3-2P	6.4	3-7	2.8, 6.4, 6.5
3-2	2.4, 2.6, 6.4	3-8	6.2, 6.4
3-3	1.3, 6.4	3-9	6.4, 6.5
3-4P	6.4	3-9F	6.5
3-4	6.2, 6.4		

GS = Getting Started, P = Preview, F = Follow-Up

 Additional mathematical information and teaching notes are available at www.algebra1.com/key_concepts.

DAILY
INTERVENTION and Assessment

Key to Abbreviations:
TWE = Teacher Wraparound Edition; CRM = Chapter Resource Masters

Type	Student Edition	Teacher Resources	Technology/Internet
INTERVENTION Ongoing	Prerequisite Skills, pp. 119, 126, 134, 140, 148, 154, 159, 164, 170 Practice Quiz 1, p. 140 Practice Quiz 2, p. 164	5-Minute Check Transparencies *Prerequisite Skills Workbook,* pp. 9–12, 17–18, 21–24, 27–28, 41–44, 51–52, 59–60, 67–74, 77–78, 81–82 Quizzes, *CRM* pp. 205–206 Mid-Chapter Test, *CRM* p. 207 Study Guide and Intervention, *CRM* pp. 137–138, 143–144, 149–150, 155–156, 161–162, 167–168, 173–174, 179–180, 185–186	AlgePASS: Tutorial Plus, Lessons 4, 5, 6, 7, and 8 www.algebra1.com/self_check_quiz www.algebra1.com/extra_examples
Mixed Review	pp. 126, 134, 140, 148, 154, 159, 164, 170, 177	Cumulative Review, *CRM* p. 208	
Error Analysis	Find the Error, pp. 138, 162	Find the Error, *TWE* pp. 138, 162 Unlocking Misconceptions, *TWE* p. 129 Tips for New Teachers, *TWE* pp. 136, 156	
Standardized Test Practice	pp. 126, 134, 140, 147, 151, 152, 154, 159, 164, 170, 177, 185, 186–187	*TWE* pp. 186–187 Standardized Test Practice, *CRM* pp. 209–210	Standardized Test Practice CD-ROM www.algebra1.com/standardized_test
ASSESSMENT Open-Ended Assessment	Writing in Math, pp. 126, 134, 140, 147, 154, 159, 164, 170, 177 Open Ended, pp. 123, 131, 138, 145, 152, 158, 162, 168, 174 Standardized Test, p. 187	Modeling: *TWE* pp. 140, 159 Speaking: *TWE* pp. 126, 148, 164 Writing: *TWE* pp. 134, 154, 170, 177 Open-Ended Assessment, *CRM* p. 203	
Chapter Assessment	Study Guide, pp. 179–184 Practice Test, p. 185	Multiple-Choice Tests (Forms 1, 2A, 2B), *CRM* pp. 191–196 Free-Response Tests (Forms 2C, 2D, 3), *CRM* pp. 197–202 Vocabulary Test/Review, *CRM* p. 204	ExamView® Pro (see below) MindJogger Videoquizzes www.algebra1.com/vocabulary_review www.algebra1.com/chapter_test

For more information on Yearly ProgressPro, see p. 2.

Algebra Lesson	Yearly ProgressPro Skill Lesson(s)
3-1	Writing Equations
3-2	Solving Equations by Using Addition and Subtraction
3-3	Solving Equations by Using Multiplication and Division
3-4	Solving Multi-Step Equations Consecutive Integer Problems
3-5	Solving Equations with the Variable on Each Side
3-6	Ratios and Proportions
3-7	Percent of Change
3-8	Solving Equations and Formulas
3-9	Weighted Averages

ExamView® Pro

Use the networkable **ExamView® Pro** to:
- Create **multiple versions** of tests.
- Create **modified** tests for *Inclusion* students.
- **Edit** existing questions and **add** your own questions.
- Use built-in **state curriculum correlations** to create tests aligned with state standards.
- Change **English** tests to **Spanish** and vice versa.

For more information on Intervention and Assessment, see pp. T8–T11.

Reading and Writing in Mathematics

Glencoe Algebra 1 provides numerous opportunities to incorporate reading and writing into the mathematics classroom.

Student Edition

- Foldables Study Organizer, p. 119
- Concept Check questions require students to verbalize and write about what they have learned in the lesson. (pp. 123, 131, 138, 145, 151, 158, 162, 168, 174)
- Reading Mathematics, p. 165
- Writing in Math questions in every lesson, pp. 126, 134, 140, 147, 154, 159, 164, 170, 177
- Reading Study Tip, pp. 121, 129, 155
- WebQuest, pp. 159, 177

Teacher Wraparound Edition

- Foldables Study Organizer, pp. 119, 179
- Study Notebook suggestions, pp. 123, 127, 131, 138, 141, 145, 152, 157, 162, 165, 168, 174, 178
- Modeling activities, pp. 140, 159
- Speaking activities, pp. 126, 148, 164
- Writing activities, pp. 134, 154, 170, 177
- Differentiated Instruction, (Verbal/Linguistic), p. 121
- **ELL** Resources, pp. 118, 121, 125, 133, 139, 147, 153, 156, 158, 163, 165, 169, 176, 179

Additional Resources

- Vocabulary Builder worksheets require students to define and give examples for key vocabulary terms as they progress through the chapter. (*Chapter 3 Resource Masters*, pp. vii-viii)
- Reading to Learn Mathematics master for each lesson (*Chapter 3 Resource Masters*, pp. 141, 147, 153, 159, 165, 171, 177, 183, 189)
- *Vocabulary PuzzleMaker* software creates crossword, jumble, and word search puzzles using vocabulary lists that you can customize.
- *Teaching Mathematics with Foldables* provides suggestions for promoting cognition and language.
- *Reading and Writing in the Mathematics Classroom*
- *WebQuest and Project Resources*

For more information on Reading and Writing in Mathematics, see pp. T6–T7.

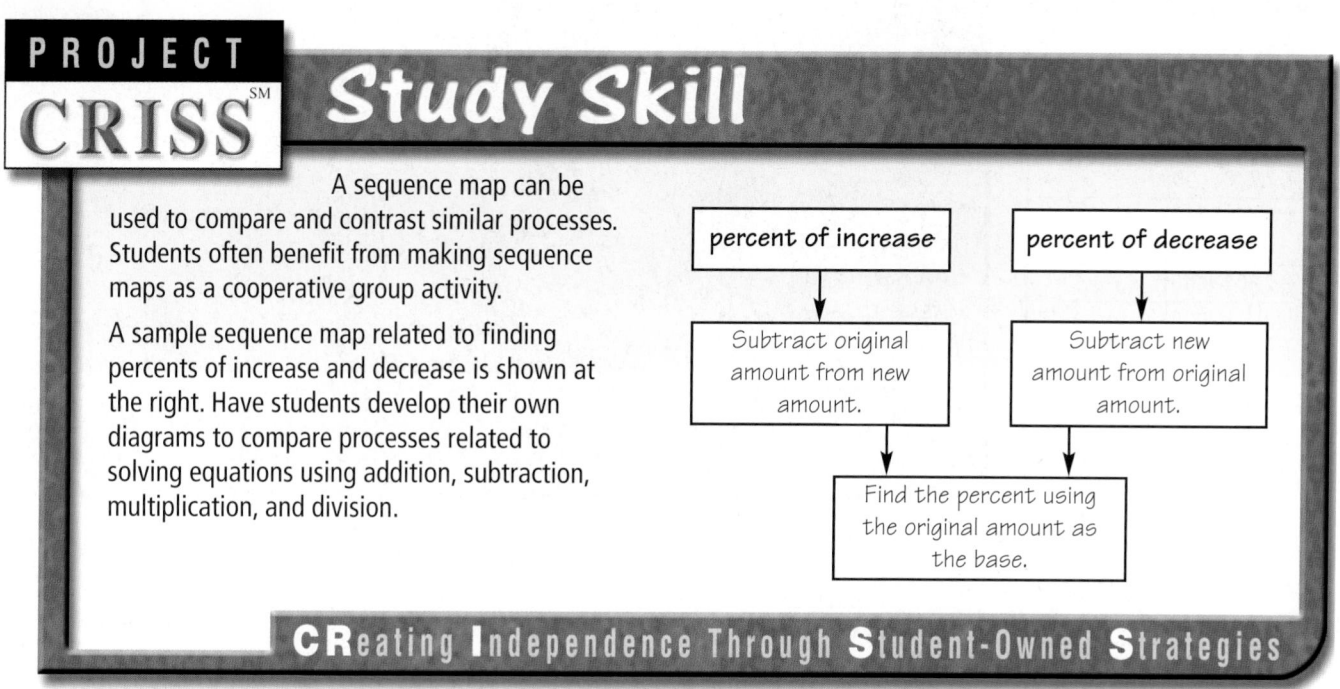

PROJECT CRISS^{SM} **Study Skill**

A sequence map can be used to compare and contrast similar processes. Students often benefit from making sequence maps as a cooperative group activity.

A sample sequence map related to finding percents of increase and decrease is shown at the right. Have students develop their own diagrams to compare processes related to solving equations using addition, subtraction, multiplication, and division.

percent of increase	percent of decrease
Subtract original amount from new amount.	Subtract new amount from original amount.

Find the percent using the original amount as the base.

CReating **I**ndependence **T**hrough **S**tudent-Owned **S**trategies

What You'll Learn

Have students read over the list of objectives and make a list of any words with which they are not familiar.

Why It's Important

Point out to students that this is only one of many reasons why each objective is important. Others are provided in the introduction to each lesson.

Lesson	NCTM Standards	Local Objectives
3-1	1, 2, 6, 8, 9, 10	
3-2 Preview	1, 2, 10	
3-2	1, 2, 6, 8, 9, 10	
3-3	1, 2, 6, 8, 9, 10	
3-4 Preview	1, 2, 10	
3-4	1, 2, 6, 8, 9, 10	
3-5	1, 2, 6, 8, 9, 10	
3-6	1, 2, 3, 6, 8, 9, 10	
3-7	1, 2, 6, 8, 9, 10	
3-8	1, 2, 6, 8, 9, 10	
3-9	1, 2, 6, 8, 9, 10	
3-9 Follow-Up	1, 2, 6, 9	

Key to NCTM Standards:

1=Number & Operations, 2=Algebra, 3=Geometry, 4=Measurement, 5=Data Analysis & Probability, 6=Problem Solving, 7=Reasoning & Proof, 8=Communication, 9=Connections, 10=Representation

Chapter 3 Solving Linear Equations

What You'll Learn

- **Lesson 3-1** Translate verbal sentences into equations and equations into verbal sentences.
- **Lessons 3-2 through 3-6** Solve equations and proportions.
- **Lesson 3-7** Find percents of change.
- **Lesson 3-8** Solve equations for given variables.
- **Lesson 3-9** Solve mixture and uniform motion problems.

Key Vocabulary

- equivalent equations (p. 129)
- identity (p. 150)
- proportion (p. 155)
- percent of change (p. 160)
- mixture problem (p. 171)

Why It's Important

Linear equations can be used to solve problems in every facet of life from planning a garden, to investigating trends in data, to making wise career choices. One of the most frequent uses of linear equations is solving problems involving mixtures or motion. For example, in the National Football League, a quarterback's passing performance is rated using an equation based on a mixture, or weighted average, of five factors, including passing attempts and completions. *You will learn how this rating system works in Lesson 3-9.*

Vocabulary Builder

ELL

The Key Vocabulary list introduces students to some of the main vocabulary terms included in this chapter. For a more thorough vocabulary list with pronunciations of new words, give students the Vocabulary Builder worksheets found on pages vii and viii of the *Chapter 3 Resource Masters*. Encourage them to complete the definition of each term as they progress through the chapter. You may suggest that they add these sheets to their study notebooks for future reference when studying for the Chapter 3 test.

Getting Started

Getting Started

▶ **Prerequisite Skills** To be successful in this chapter, you'll need to master these skills and be able to apply them in problem-solving situations. Review these skills before beginning Chapter 3.

For Lesson 3-1   **Write Mathematical Expressions**

Write an algebraic expression for each verbal expression. *(For review, see Lesson 1-1.)*

1. five greater than half of a number t $\frac{1}{2}t + 5$
2. the product of seven and s divided by the product of eight and y $7s \div 8y$
3. the sum of three times a and the square of b $3a + b^2$
4. w to the fifth power decreased by 37 $w^5 - 37$
5. nine times y subtracted from 95 $95 - 9y$
6. the quantity of r plus six divided by twelve $(r + 6) \div 12$

For Lesson 3-4   **Use the Order of Operations**

Evaluate each expression. *(For review, see Lesson 1-2.)*

7. $3 \cdot 6 - \frac{12}{4}$ **15**   8. $5(13 - 7) - 22$ **8**   9. $5(7 - 2) - 3^2$ **16**   10. $\frac{2 \cdot 6 - 4}{2}$ **4**

11. $(25 - 4) \div (2^2 - 1)$ **7**   12. $36 \div 4 - 2 + 3$ **10**   13. $\frac{19 - 5}{7} + 3$ **5**   14. $\frac{1}{4}(24) - \frac{1}{2}(12)$ **0**

For Lesson 3-7   **Find the Percent**

Find each percent. *(For review, see pages 802 and 803.)*

15. Five is what percent of 20?   **25%**   16. What percent of 300 is 21?   **7%**
17. What percent of 5 is 15?   **300%**   18. Twelve is what percent of 60?   **20%**
19. Sixteen is what percent of 10?   **160%**   20. What percent of 50 is 37.5?   **75%**

 **FOLDABLES™** **Study Organizer**

Solving Linear Equations Make this Foldable to help you organize your notes. Begin with 4 sheets of plain $8\frac{1}{2}$" by 11" paper.

Step 1   **Fold**

Fold in half along the width.

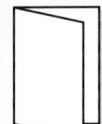

Step 2   **Open and Fold Again**

Fold the bottom to form a pocket. Glue the edges.

Step 3   **Repeat Steps 1 and 2**

Repeat three times and glue all four pieces together.

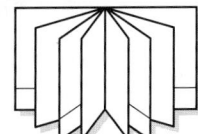

Step 4   **Label**

Label each pocket. Place an index card in each pocket.

Solving Linear Equations

Reading and Writing As you read and study the chapter, you can write notes and examples on each index card.

This section provides a review of the basic concepts needed before beginning Chapter 3. Page references are included for additional student help.

Additional review is provided in the *Prerequisite Skills Workbook*, pp. 9–12, 17–18, 21–24, 27–28, 41–44, 51–52, 59–60, 67–74, 77–78, 81–82.

Prerequisite Skills in the Getting Ready for the Next Lesson section at the end of each exercise set review a skill needed in the next lesson.

For Lesson	Prerequisite Skill
3-2 and 3-3	Operations with Fractions (pp. 126, 134)
3-4	Order of Operations (p. 140)
3-5	Simplifying Expressions (p. 148)
3-6	Simplifying Fractions (p. 154)
3-7	Finding Percents (p. 159)
3-8	Solving Equations (p. 164)
3-9	Distributive Property (p. 170)

FOLDABLES™ **Study Organizer**

For more information about Foldables, see *Teaching Mathematics with Foldables*.

Organization of Data Students will need 3 inch-by-5 inch index cards or sheets of notebook paper cut into fourths to use as study cards. In Lesson 3-1, have students write an equation on one side of each card and its verbal equivalent on the other side. Store these cards in the first pocket of the Foldable, labeled "3-1: Writing Equations." With each lesson, use the study cards to take notes, solve equations, or record and define vocabulary words and concepts. There are 8 pockets. Place Lessons 3-8 and 3-9 in the same pocket.

3-1 Writing Equations

1 Focus

5-Minute Check Transparency 3-1 Use as a quiz or review of Chapter 2.

Mathematical Background notes are available for this lesson on p. 118C.

How are equations used to describe heights?

Ask students:

• You could say that the total height of the statue, 305 feet, is equal to the sum of what two quantities? **the height of the statue and the height of the pedestal**

• Why is the height of the statue represented by a variable? **The height of the statue is not stated in the problem, so it must be represented by a variable.**

• What is another equation that could be used to represent the situation? $305 - s = 154$ or $305 - 154 = s$

3-1 Writing Equations

What You'll Learn

• Translate verbal sentences into equations.
• Translate equations into verbal sentences.

Vocabulary
• four-step problem-solving plan
• defining a variable
• formula

How are equations used to describe heights?

The Statue of Liberty sits on a pedestal that is 154 feet high. The height of the pedestal and the statue is 305 feet. If s represents the height of the statue, then the following equation represents the situation.

$$154 + s = 305$$

Source: *World Book Encyclopedia*

WRITE EQUATIONS When writing equations, use variables to represent the unspecified numbers or measures referred to in the sentence or problem. Then write the verbal expressions as algebraic expressions. Some verbal expressions that suggest the *equals sign* are listed below.

• is
• equals
• is equal to
• is the same as
• is as much as
• is identical to

Study Tip

Look Back
To review **translating verbal expressions to algebraic expressions**, see Lesson 1-1.

Example 1 Translate Sentences into Equations

Translate each sentence into an equation.

a. Five times the number a is equal to three times the sum of b and c.

Five	times	a	is equal to	three	times	the sum of b and c.
5	×	a	=	3	×	$(b + c)$

The equation is $5a = 3(b + c)$.

b. Nine times y subtracted from 95 equals 37.

Rewrite the sentence so it is easier to translate.

95	less	nine times y	equals	37.
95	−	$9y$	=	37

The equation is $95 - 9y = 37$.

Resource Manager

📁 Workbook and Reproducible Masters

Chapter 3 Resource Masters
• Study Guide and Intervention, pp. 137–138
• Skills Practice, p. 139
• Practice, p. 140
• Reading to Learn Mathematics, p. 141
• Enrichment, p. 142

Parent and Student Study Guide Workbook, p. 19
Teaching Algebra with Manipulatives Masters, p. 56

📺 Transparencies

5-Minute Check Transparency 3-1
Answer Key Transparencies

💿 Technology

Interactive Chalkboard

Using the **four-step problem-solving plan** can help you solve any word problem.

Key Concept — Four-Step Problem-Solving Plan

Step 1 Explore the problem.

Step 2 Plan the solution.

Step 3 Solve the problem.

Step 4 Examine the solution.

Each step of the plan is important.

Step 1 **Explore the Problem**
To solve a verbal problem, first read the problem carefully and explore what the problem is about.
- Identify what information is given.
- Identify what you are asked to find.

Step 2 **Plan the Solution**
One strategy you can use to solve a problem is to write an equation. Choose a variable to represent one of the unspecific numbers in the problem. This is called **defining a variable**. Then use the variable to write expressions for the other unspecified numbers in the problem. *You will learn to use other strategies throughout this book.*

Step 3 **Solve the Problem**
Use the strategy you chose in Step 2 to solve the problem.

Step 4 **Examine the Solution**
Check your answer in the context of the original problem.
- Does your answer make sense?
- Does it fit the information in the problem?

More About. . .

Ice Cream

The first ice cream plant was established in 1851 by Jacob Fussell. Today, 2,000,000 gallons of ice cream are produced in the United States each day.
Source: *World Book Encyclopedia*

Example 2 Use the Four-Step Plan

ICE CREAM Use the information at the left. In how many days can 40,000,000 gallons of ice cream be produced in the United States?

Explore You know that 2,000,000 gallons of ice cream are produced in the United States each day. You want to know how many days it will take to produce 40,000,000 gallons of ice cream.

Plan Write an equation to represent the situation. Let d represent the number of days needed to produce the ice cream.

2,000,000	times	the number of days	equals	40,000,000.
2,000,000	$\times$	d	$=$	40,000,000

Solve $2,000,000d = 40,000,000$ Find d mentally by asking, "What number times 2,000,000 equals 40,000,000?"
$d = 20$

It will take 20 days to produce 40,000,000 gallons of ice cream.

Examine If 2,000,000 gallons of ice cream are produced in one day, $2,000,000 \times 20$ or 40,000,000 gallons are produced in 20 days. The answer makes sense.

---

2 Teach

WRITE EQUATIONS

In-Class Examples Power Point®

Reading Tip Remind students that the language of math sentences is not always as obvious as in the examples.

1 Translate each sentence into an equation.

a. A number b divided by three is equal to six less than c.
$\frac{b}{3} = c - 6$

b. Fifteen more than z times 6 is y times 2 minus eleven.
$15 + 6z = 2y - 11$

2 **JELLYBEANS** A popular jellybean manufacturer produces 1,250,000 jellybeans per hour. How many hours does it take them to produce 10,000,000 jellybeans? **8 hours**

Interactive Chalkboard

PowerPoint®
Presentations

This CD-ROM is a customizable Microsoft® PowerPoint® presentation that includes:

- Step-by-step, dynamic solutions of each In-Class Example from the Teacher Wraparound Edition
- Additional, Your Turn exercises for each example
- The 5-Minute Check Transparencies
- Hot links to Glencoe Online Study Tools

DAILY INTERVENTION

Differentiated Instruction   ELL

Verbal/Linguistic Some students will likely translate sentences into equations easily. Pair those students with others who are having trouble translating sentences. Have the pairs work several example problems.

3 *Teaching Tip* Some students may have the formula for the perimeter of a rectangle memorized from previous mathematics courses. Have these students work backward from their memorized formula to confirm that it is a correct translation of the given sentence.

Translate the sentence into a formula.

The perimeter of a square equals four times the length of the side. $P = 4s$

WRITE VERBAL SENTENCES

Reading Tip Remind students that there is often more than one way to translate an equation into a verbal sentence. For example, $3m + 5 = 14$ could also be translated as, "The sum of three times *m* and 5 is 14."

4 Translate each equation into a verbal sentence.

a. $12 - 2x = -5$ Twelve minus two times *x* equals negative five.

b. $a^2 + 3b = \dfrac{c}{6}$ *a* squared plus three times *b* equals *c* divided by 6.

Answers

3. Sample answer: After sixteen people joined the drama club, there were 30 members. How many members did the club have before the new members?

10. Sample answer: The original cost of a suit is *c*. After a $25 discount, the suit costs $150. What is the original cost of the suit?

A **formula** is an equation that states a rule for the relationship between certain quantities. Sometimes you can develop a formula by making a model.

Algebra Activity

Surface Area

- Mark each side of a rectangular box as the length ℓ, the width *w*, or the height *h*.
- Use scissors to cut the box so that each surface or face of the box is a separate piece.

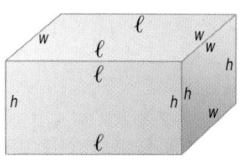

Analyze

Write an expression for the area of each side of the box.

1. front ℓh 2. back ℓh 3. left side wh

4. right side wh 5. top ℓw 6. bottom ℓw

7. The surface area of a rectangular box is the sum of all the areas of the faces of the box. If *S* represents surface area, write a formula for the surface area of a rectangular box. $S = 2\ell h + 2wh + 2\ell w$

Make a Conjecture

8. If *s* represents the length of the side of a cube, write a formula for the surface area of a cube. $S = 6s^2$

Example 3 *Write a Formula*

Translate the sentence into a formula.

The perimeter of a rectangle equals two times the length plus two times the width.

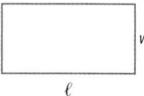

Words   Perimeter equals two times the length plus two times the width.

Variables   Let P = perimeter, ℓ = length, and *w* = width.

	Perimeter	equals	two times the length	plus	two times the width.
Formula	P	$=$	2ℓ	$+$	$2w$

The formula for the perimeter of a rectangle is $P = 2\ell + 2w$.

WRITE VERBAL SENTENCES   You can also translate equations into verbal sentences or make up your own verbal problem if you are given an equation.

Example 4 *Translate Equations into Sentences*

Translate each equation into a verbal sentence.

a. $3m + 5 = 14$

$3m$	$+$	5	$=$	14
Three times *m*	plus	five	equals	fourteen.

Algebra Activity

Materials: scissors, rectangular box

- Suggest that in addition to marking the box sides with length, width, or height, students should also label the sides as front, back, side 1, side 2, top, and bottom.
- By cutting the sides of the box into individual rectangles, students can more easily see all six components (sides) that make up the surface area of the box.

b. $w + v = y^2$

$$\underbrace{w + v}_{\text{The sum of } w \text{ and } v} \quad \underbrace{=}_{\text{equals}} \quad \underbrace{y^2}_{\text{the square of } y.}$$

Example 5 · Write a Problem

Write a problem based on the given information.

a = Rafael's age $a + 5$ = Tierra's age $a + 2(a + 5) = 46$

You know that a represents Rafael's age and $a + 5$ represents Tierra's age. The equation adds a plus twice $(a + 5)$ to get 46.

Sample problem:
Tierra is 5 years older than Rafael. The sum of Rafael's age and twice Tierra's age equals 46. How old is Rafael?

Check for Understanding

Concept Check

1. Explore the problem, plan the solution, solve the problem, and examine the solution.

2d. No; 1900 + 52(30) = 3460, which is less than 3500.

1. **List** the four steps used in solving problems.

2. **Analyze** the following problem.   **2b.** $300; $600

Misae has $1900 in the bank. She wishes to increase her account to a total of $3500 by depositing $30 per week from her paycheck. Will she reach her savings goal in one year?

   a. How much money did Misae have in her account at the beginning? **$1900**

   b. How much money will Misae add to her account in 10 weeks? in 20 weeks?

   c. Write an expression representing the amount added to the account after w weeks have passed. **30w**

   d. What is the answer to the question? Explain.

3. **OPEN ENDED** Write a problem that can be answered by solving $x + 16 = 30$.
See margin.

Guided Practice

GUIDED PRACTICE KEY	
Exercises	Examples
4, 5	1
6, 7	3
8, 9	4
10	5
11, 12	2

Translate each sentence into an equation.

4. Two times a number t decreased by eight equals seventy. **$2t - 8 = 70$**

5. Five times the sum of m and n is the same as seven times n. **$5(m + n) = 7n$**

Translate each sentence into a formula. **6.** $A = \frac{1}{2}bh$

6. The area A of a triangle equals one half times the base b times the height h.

7. The circumference C of a circle equals the product of two, pi, and the radius r.
   $C = 2\pi r$

Translate each equation into a verbal sentence.

8. $14 + d = 6d$ **14 plus d equals 6 times d.** **9.** $\frac{1}{3}b - \frac{3}{4} = 2a$ **$\frac{1}{3}$ of b minus $\frac{3}{4}$ equals 2 times a.**

10. **Write a problem** based on the given information. **See margin.**

   c = cost of a suit $c - 25 = 150$

Application

WRESTLING For Exercises 11 and 12, use the following information.
Darius is training to prepare for wrestling season. He weighs 155 pounds now. He wants to gain weight so that he starts the season weighing 160 pounds.

11. If g represents the number of pounds he wants to gain, write an equation to represent the situation. **$155 + g = 160$**

12. How many pounds does Darius need to gain to reach his goal? **5 lb**

Teaching Tip Explain to students that when they are trying to write a problem based on given information, the purpose of the problem is to solve for a variable, or unknown information. In this case, the unknown information is Rafael's age.

5 Write a problem based on the given information.
f = cost of fries
$f + 1.50$ = cost of a burger
$4(f + 1.50) - f = 8.25$
The cost of a burger is $1.50 more than the cost of fries. Four times the cost of a burger minus the cost of fries equals $8.25. How much do fries cost?

3 Practice/Apply

Study Notebook

Have students—

• add the definitions/examples of the vocabulary terms to their Vocabulary Builder worksheets for Chapter 3.

• write the steps of the four-step problem-solving plan in their study notebooks. In addition to the steps, students should include examples of what each step means.

• include any other item(s) that they find helpful in mastering the skills in this lesson.

★ indicates increased difficulty

Practice and Apply

Homework Help

For Exercises	See Examples
13–22	1
23–28	3
29–38	4
39, 40	5
41–51	2

Extra Practice
See page 825.

Translate each sentence into an equation.

13. Two hundred minus three times x is equal to nine. $200 - 3x = 9$

14. The sum of twice r and three times s is identical to thirteen. $2r + 3s = 13$

15. The sum of one-third q and 25 is as much as twice q. $\frac{1}{3}q + 25 = 2q$

16. The square of m minus the cube of n is sixteen. $m^2 - n^3 = 16$

17. Two times the sum of v and w is equal to two times z. $2(v + w) = 2z$

★ 18. Half of the sum of nine and p is the same as p minus three. $\frac{1}{2}(9 + p) = p - 3$

★ 19. The number g divided by the number h is the same as seven more than twice the sum of g and h. $g \div h = 2(g + h) + 7$

20. Five-ninths the square of the sum of a, b, and c equals the sum of the square of a and the square of c. $\frac{5}{9}(a + b + c)^2 = a^2 + c^2$

21. **GEOGRAPHY** The Pacific Ocean covers about 46% of Earth. If P represents the area of the Pacific Ocean and E represents the area of Earth, write an equation for this situation. $0.46E = P$

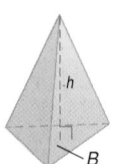
Pacific Ocean
46% of Earth's Surface

Source: *World Book Encyclopedia*

22. **GARDENING** Mrs. Patton is planning to place a fence around her vegetable garden. The fencing costs $1.75 per yard. She buys f yards of fencing and pays $3.50 in tax. If the total cost of the fencing is $73.50, write an equation to represent the situation. $1.75f + 3.50 = 73.50$

Translate each sentence into a formula.

23. The area A of a parallelogram is the base b times the height h. $A = bh$

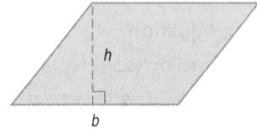

24. The volume V of a pyramid is one-third times the product of the area of the base B and its height h. $V = \frac{1}{3}Bh$

25. The perimeter P of a parallelogram is twice the sum of the lengths of the two adjacent sides, a and b. $P = 2(a + b)$

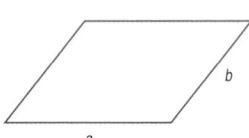

26. The volume V of a cylinder equals the product of π, the square of the radius r of the base, and the height. $V = \pi r^2 h$

27. In a right triangle, the square of the measure of the hypotenuse c is equal to the sum of the squares of the measures of the legs, a and b. $c^2 = a^2 + b^2$

28. The temperature in degrees Fahrenheit F is the same as nine-fifths of the degrees Celsius C plus thirty-two. $F = \frac{9}{5}C + 32$

29. *d* minus 14 equals 5.

30. 2 times *f* plus 6 equals 19.

31. *k* squared plus 17 equals 53 minus *j*.

32. 2 times *a* equals 7 times *a* minus *b*.

33. $\frac{3}{4}$ of *p* plus $\frac{1}{2}$ equals *p*.

34. $\frac{2}{5}$ times *w* equals $\frac{1}{2}$ times *w* plus 3.

35. 7 times the sum of *m* and *n* equals 10 times *n* plus 17.

36. 4 times the quantity *t* minus *s* equals 5 times *s* plus 12.

37. The area *A* of a trapezoid equals one-half times the product of the height *h* and the sum of the bases, *a* and *b*.

Translate each equation into a verbal sentence.

29. $d - 14 = 5$ **30.** $2f + 6 = 19$ **31.** $k^2 + 17 = 53 - j$

32. $2a = 7a - b$ **33.** $\frac{3}{4}p + \frac{1}{2} = p$ **34.** $\frac{2}{5}w = \frac{1}{2}w + 3$

35. $7(m + n) = 10n + 17$ **36.** $4(t - s) = 5s + 12$

37. GEOMETRY If *a* and *b* represent the lengths of the bases of a trapezoid and *h* represents its height, then the formula for the area *A* of the trapezoid is $A = \frac{1}{2}h(a + b)$. Write the formula in words.

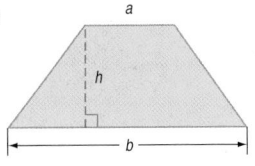

38. SCIENCE If *r* represents rate, *t* represents time, and *d* represents distance, then $rt = d$. Write the formula in words. **Rate times time equals distance.**

39–40. See margin.

WRITE A PROBLEM Write a problem based on the given information.

39. *y* = Yolanda's height in inches
y + 7 = Lindsey's height in inches
$2y + (y + 7) = 193$

40. *p* = price of a new backpack
0.055*p* = tax
$p + 0.055p = 31.65$

GEOMETRY For Exercises 41 and 42, use the following information.
The volume *V* of a cone equals one-third times the product of π, the square of the radius *r* of the base, and the height *h*.

41. Write the formula for the volume of a cone. $V = \frac{1}{3}\pi r^2 h$

42. Find the volume of a cone if *r* is 10 centimeters and *h* is 30 centimeters. **about 3142 cm³**

GEOMETRY For Exercises 43 and 44, use the following information.
The volume *V* of a sphere is four-thirds times π times the radius *r* of the sphere cubed.

43. Write a formula for the volume of a sphere. $V = \frac{4}{3}\pi r^3$

44. Find the volume of a sphere if *r* is 4 inches. **about 268 in³**

LITERATURE For Exercises 45–47, use the following information.
Edgar Rice Burroughs is the author of the *Tarzan of the Apes* stories. He published his first Tarzan story in 1912. Some years later, the town in southern California where he lived was named Tarzana. **46.** $1912 + y = 1928$

45. Let *y* represent the number of years after 1912 that the town was named Tarzana. Write an expression for the year the town was named. $1912 + y$

46. The town was named in 1928. Write an equation to represent the situation.

★ **47.** Use what you know about numbers to determine the number of years between the first Tarzan story and the naming of the town. **16 yr**

TELEVISION For Exercises 48–51, use the following information.
During a highly rated one-hour television program, the entertainment portion lasted 15 minutes longer than 4 times the advertising portion.

★ **48.** If *a* represents the time spent on advertising, write an expression for the entertainment portion. $4a + 15$

★ **49.** Write an equation to represent the situation. $a + (4a + 15) = 60$

★ **50.** Use your equation and the guess-and-check strategy to determine the number of minutes spent on advertising. Choose different values of *a* and evaluate to find the solution. **9 min**

★ **51.** Time the entertainment and advertising portions of a one-hour television program you like to watch. Describe what you found. Are the results of this problem similar to your findings? **See students' work.**

www.algebra1.com/self_check_quiz

Lesson 3-1 Writing Equations **125**

Open-Ended Assessment

Speaking Translating sentences into equations and vice versa presents an excellent opportunity for students to practice their speaking skills. Ask volunteers to translate sentences into equations and equations into sentences aloud for the entire class to hear.

Getting Ready for Lesson 3-2

PREREQUISITE SKILL In Lesson 3-2, students will learn how to solve equations using addition and subtraction. In addition to solving equations involving integers, students solve equations involving decimals and fractions. Use Exercises 69–76 to determine your students' familiarity with finding sums and differences of decimals and fractions.

Answer

53. Equations can be used to describe the relationships of the heights of various parts of a structure. Answers should include the following.

- The equation representing the Sears Tower is $1454 + a = 1707$.

---

52. **CRITICAL THINKING** The surface area of a prism is the sum of the areas of the faces of the prism. Write a formula for the surface area of the triangular prism at the right. $S = 3ah + \dfrac{a^2\sqrt{3}}{2}$

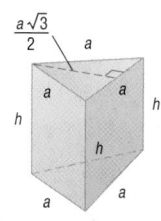

53. **WRITING IN MATH** Answer the question that was posed at the beginning of the lesson. **See margin.**

How are equations used to describe heights?

Include the following in your answer:

- an equation relating the Sears Tower, which is 1454 feet tall; the twin antenna towers on top of the building, which are a feet tall; and a total height, which is 1707 feet, and

- an equation representing the height of a building of your choice.

Standardized Test Practice

Ⓐ Ⓑ Ⓒ Ⓓ

54. Which equation represents the following sentence? **B**
One fourth of a number plus five equals the number minus seven.

Ⓐ $\frac{1}{4}n + 7 = n - 5$ Ⓑ $\frac{1}{4}n + 5 = n - 7$

Ⓒ $4n + 7 = n - 5$ Ⓓ $4n + 5 = n - 7$

55. Which sentence can be represented by $7(x + y) = 35$? **D**

Ⓐ Seven times x plus y equals 35.

Ⓑ One seventh of the sum of x and y equals 35.

Ⓒ Seven plus x and y equals 35.

Ⓓ Seven times the sum of x and y equals 35.

Maintain Your Skills

Mixed Review Find each square root. Use a calculator if necessary. Round to the nearest hundredth if the result is not a whole number or a simple fraction. *(Lesson 2-7)*

56. $\sqrt{8100}$ **90**   57. $-\sqrt{\dfrac{25}{36}}$ $-\dfrac{5}{6}$ 58. $\sqrt{90}$ **9.49**   59. $-\sqrt{55}$ **−7.42**

Find the probability of each outcome if a die is rolled. *(Lesson 2-6)*

60. a 6 $\dfrac{1}{6}$ 61. an even number $\dfrac{1}{2}$ 62. a number greater than 2 $\dfrac{2}{3}$

Simplify each expression. *(Lesson 1-5)*

63. $12d + 3 - 4d$ **$8d + 3$**   64. $7t^2 + t + 8t$ **$7t^2 + 9t$**   65. $3(a + 2b) + 5a$ **$8a + 6b$**

Evaluate each expression. *(Lesson 1-2)*

66. $5(8 - 3) + 7 \cdot 2$ **39**   67. $6(4^3 + 2^2)$ **408**   68. $7(0.2 + 0.5) - 0.6$ **4.3**

Getting Ready for the Next Lesson **PREREQUISITE SKILL** Find each sum or difference.
*(To review **operations with fractions**, see pages 798 and 799.)*

69. $5.67 + 3.7$ **9.37**   70. $0.57 + 2.8$ **3.37**   71. $5.28 - 3.4$ **1.88**   72. $9 - 7.35$ **1.65**

73. $\dfrac{2}{3} + \dfrac{1}{5}$ $\dfrac{13}{15}$ 74. $\dfrac{1}{6} + \dfrac{2}{3}$ $\dfrac{5}{6}$ 75. $\dfrac{7}{9} - \dfrac{2}{3}$ $\dfrac{1}{9}$ 76. $\dfrac{3}{4} - \dfrac{1}{6}$ $\dfrac{7}{12}$

Algebra Activity

A Preview of Lesson 3-2

Solving Addition and Subtraction Equations

You can use algebra tiles to solve equations. To solve an equation means to find the value of the variable that makes the equation true. After you model the equation, the goal is to get the x tile by itself on one side of the mat using the rules stated below.

Rules for Equation Models	
You can remove or add the same number of identical algebra tiles to each side of the mat without changing the equation.	◄ 1 1 1 1 = 1 1 1 1 ►
One positive tile and one negative tile of the same unit are a **zero pair**. Since $1 + (-1) = 0$, you can remove or add zero pairs to the equation mat without changing the equation.	◄ -1 1 1 1 = 1 1 ►

Use an equation model to solve $x - 3 = 2$.

Step 1 *Model the equation.*

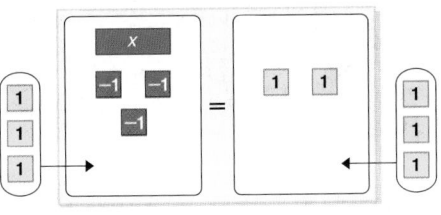

$$x - 3 = 2$$
$$x - 3 + 3 = 2 + 3$$

Place 1 x tile and 3 negative 1 tiles on one side of the mat. Place 2 positive 1 tiles on the other side of the mat. Then add 3 positive 1 tiles to each side.

Step 2 *Isolate the x term.*

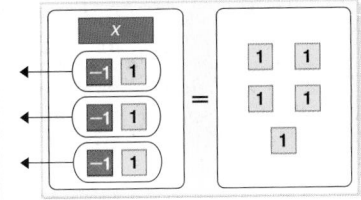

$$x = 5$$

Group the tiles to form zero pairs. Then remove all the zero pairs. The resulting equation is $x = 5$.

Model and Analyze

Use algebra tiles to solve each equation.

1. $x + 5 = 7$ **2**
2. $x + (-2) = 28$ **30**
3. $x + 4 = 27$ **23**
4. $x + (-3) = 4$ **7**
5. $x + 3 = -4$ **−7**
6. $x + 7 = 2$ **−5**

Make a Conjecture

7. If $a = b$, what can you say about $a + c$ and $b + c$? $a + c = b + c$
8. If $a = b$, what can you say about $a - c$ and $b - c$? $a - c = b - c$

Getting Started

Objective Use equation mats and algebra tiles to model solving equations.

Materials
equation mats and algebra tiles

Teach

- Remind students that when they are modeling subtraction with algebra tiles, they must add negative tiles.

- Explain to students that they can remove or add the same number of identical algebra tiles to each side of the mat or they can remove or add a zero pair to one side of the mat.

- There are not enough negative 1 tiles on the right side of the mat, so that 3 negative 1 tiles can be removed from each side as in Example 1. In this case, add 3 positive 1 tiles to both sides to create three zero-pairs on the left side.

Assess

After **Exercises 1–6**, students need to recognize that zero pairs must be formed.

Exercises 7–8 provide a symbolic representation for the activity.

Resource Manager

📁 **Teaching Algebra with Manipulatives**
- pp. 10–11 (masters for algebra tiles)
- p. 16 (master for equation mat)
- p. 59 (student recording sheet)

Glencoe Mathematics Classroom Manipulative Kit
- algebra tiles
- equation mat

Study Notebook

You may wish to have students summarize this activity and what they learned from it.

1 Focus

5-Minute Check Transparency 3-2 Use as a quiz or review of Lesson 3-1.

Mathematical Background notes are available for this lesson on p. 118C.

Building on Prior Knowledge

In the Algebra Activity on page 127, students learned that adding or subtracting the same tiles from each side of the equation mat results in an equation that is still true. In this lesson students will define these actions as the addition and subtraction properties of equality.

How can equations be used to compare data?

Ask students:

- Is the percent growth for medical assistants shown on the graph? **no**

- Why is the percent growth for medical assistants represented by a variable? **The percent growth for medical assistants is unknown, so it is represented by the variable m.**

- Is the value of m greater than or less than 66? Explain your answer. **The value of m is greater than 66 because the difference between m and 66 is a positive number, 5.**

What You'll Learn

- Solve equations by using addition.
- Solve equations by using subtraction.

Vocabulary
- equivalent equation
- solve an equation

How can equations be used to compare data?

The graph shows some of the fastest-growing occupations from 1992 to 2005.

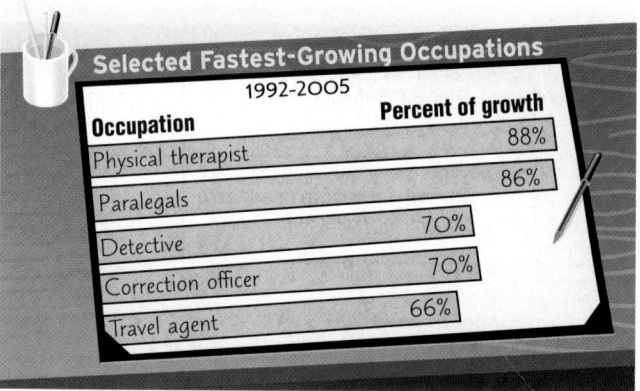

Selected Fastest-Growing Occupations
1992-2005

Occupation	Percent of growth
Physical therapist	88%
Paralegals	86%
Detective	70%
Correction officer	70%
Travel agent	66%

Source: Bureau of Labor Statistics

The difference between the percent of growth for medical assistants and the percent of growth for travel agents in these years is 5%. An equation can be used to find the percent of growth expected for medical assistants. If m is the percent of growth for medical assistants, then $m - 66 = 5$. You can use a property of equality to find the value of m.

SOLVE USING ADDITION Suppose your school's boys' soccer team has 15 members and the girls' soccer team has 15 members. If each team adds 3 new players, the number of members on the boys' and girls' teams would still be equal.

$15 = 15$	Each team has 15 members before adding the new players.
$15 + 3 = 15 + 3$	Each team adds 3 new members.
$18 = 18$	Each team has 18 members after adding the new members.

This example illustrates the **Addition Property of Equality**.

Key Concept — Addition Property of Equality

- **Words** — If an equation is true and the same number is added to each side, the resulting equation is true.

- **Symbols** — For any numbers a, b, and c, if $a = b$, then $a + c = b + c$.

- **Examples**

$$7 = 7 \qquad\qquad 14 = 14$$
$$7 + 3 = 7 + 3 \qquad 14 + (-6) = 14 + (-6)$$
$$10 = 10 \qquad\qquad 8 = 8$$

Resource Manager

 Workbook and Reproducible Masters

Chapter 3 Resource Masters
- Study Guide and Intervention, pp. 143–144
- Skills Practice, p. 145
- Practice, p. 146
- Reading to Learn Mathematics, p. 147
- Enrichment, p. 148

Parent and Student Study Guide Workbook, p. 20
Prerequisite Skills Workbook,
  pp. 21–22, 59–60

 **Transparencies**
5-Minute Check Transparency 3-2
Answer Key Transparencies

Technology
Interactive Chalkboard

If the same number is added to each side of an equation, then the result is an equivalent equation. **Equivalent equations** have the same solution.

$$t + 3 = 5 \qquad \text{The solution of this equation is 2.}$$
$$t + 3 + 2 = 5 + 2 \qquad \text{Using the Addition Property of Equality, add 2 to each side.}$$
$$t + 5 = 7 \qquad \text{The solution of this equation is also 2.}$$

To **solve an equation** means to find all values of the variable that make the equation a true statement. One way to do this is to isolate the variable having a coefficient of 1 on one side of the equation. You can sometimes do this by using the Addition Property of Equality.

Example 1 Solve by Adding a Positive Number

Solve $m - 48 = 29$. Then check your solution.

$m - 48 = 29$	Original equation
$m - 48 + 48 = 29 + 48$	Add 48 to each side.
$m = 77$	$-48 + 48 = 0$ and $29 + 48 = 77$

To check that 77 is the solution, substitute 77 for m in the original equation.

CHECK	$m - 48 = 29$	Original equation
	$77 - 48 \stackrel{?}{=} 29$	Substitute 77 for m.
	$29 = 29 \checkmark$	Subtract.

The solution is 77.

Example 2 Solve by Adding a Negative Number

Solve $21 + q = -18$. Then check your solution.

$21 + q = -18$	Original equation
$21 + q + (-21) = -18 + (-21)$	Add -21 to each side.
$q = -39$	$21 + (-21) = 0$ and $-18 + (-21) = -39$

CHECK	$21 + q = -18$	Original equation
	$21 + (-39) \stackrel{?}{=} -18$	Substitute -39 for q.
	$-18 = -18 \checkmark$	Add.

The solution is -39.

SOLVE USING SUBTRACTION Similar to the Addition Property of Equality, there is a **Subtraction Property of Equality** that may be used to solve equations.

Key Concept   **Subtraction Property of Equality**

- **Words**   If an equation is true and the same number is subtracted from each side, the resulting equation is true.
- **Symbols**   For any numbers a, b, and c, if $a = b$, then $a - c = b - c$.
- **Examples**
$17 = 17$	$3 = 3$
$17 - 9 = 17 - 9$	$3 - 8 = 3 - 8$
$8 = 8$	$-5 = -5$

 www.algebra1.com/extra_examples   **Lesson 3-2** Solving Equations by Using Addition and Subtraction   **129**

SOLVE USING SUBTRACTION

Teaching Tip Before introducing the Subtraction Property of Equality, ask students whether the Addition Property of Equality could be revised to include subtraction. Students should notice that when using the Addition Property of Equality, adding a negative number is the same as subtracting that number. So, if $a = b$, then $a + (-c) = b + (-c)$ is the same as $a - c = b - c$.

DAILY
INTERVENTION   Unlocking Misconceptions

Isolating Variables Explain to students that when isolating a variable, it does not matter whether the variable ends up on the left or right side of an equation. For example, the solution of $8 = 15 + z$ is still -7, even though the final step may be $-7 = z$.

In-Class Examples Power Point®

3 Solve $c + 102 = 36$. Then check your solution. $c = -66$

4 Solve $y + \dfrac{4}{5} = \dfrac{2}{3}$ in two ways.

$y = -\dfrac{2}{15}$

Teaching Tip Tell students that they may use whichever method is most comfortable for them when solving equations.

✓ Concept Check

Solving Equations Ask students to describe the types of equations they would solve using the Subtraction Property and what types they would solve using the Addition Property. Look for logical choices that make computation simpler.

In-Class Example Power Point®

Teaching Tip Students may try to skip a step and solve the problem without first writing an equation. Tell students that they will make fewer mistakes in solving equations if they first translate the sentence and write down the equation, before trying to solve it.

5 Write an equation for the problem. Then solve the equation and check your solution.
Fourteen more than a number is equal to twenty-seven. Find the number.
$14 + n = 27$
$n = 13$

Example 3 **Solve by Subtracting**

Solve $142 + d = 97$. Then check your solution.

$142 + d = 97$	Original equation
$142 + d - 142 = 97 - 142$	Subtract 142 from each side.
$d = -45$	$142 - 142 = 0$ and $97 - 142 = -45$

CHECK

$142 + d = 97$	Original equation
$142 + (-45) \stackrel{?}{=} 97$	Substitute −45 for d.
$97 = 97$ ✓	Add.

The solution is −45.

Remember that subtracting a number is the same as adding its inverse.

Example 4 **Solve by Adding or Subtracting**

Solve $g + \dfrac{3}{4} = -\dfrac{1}{8}$ in two ways.

Method 1 Use the Subtraction Property of Equality.

$g + \dfrac{3}{4} = -\dfrac{1}{8}$	Original equation
$g + \dfrac{3}{4} - \dfrac{3}{4} = -\dfrac{1}{8} - \dfrac{3}{4}$	Subtract $\dfrac{3}{4}$ from each side.
$g = -\dfrac{7}{8}$	$\dfrac{3}{4} - \dfrac{3}{4} = 0$ and $-\dfrac{1}{8} - \dfrac{3}{4} = -\dfrac{1}{8} - \dfrac{6}{8}$ or $-\dfrac{7}{8}$

The solution is $-\dfrac{7}{8}$.

Method 2 Use the Addition Property of Equality.

$g + \dfrac{3}{4} = -\dfrac{1}{8}$	Original equation
$g + \dfrac{3}{4} + \left(-\dfrac{3}{4}\right) = -\dfrac{1}{8} + \left(-\dfrac{3}{4}\right)$	Add $-\dfrac{3}{4}$ to each side.
$g = -\dfrac{7}{8}$	$\dfrac{3}{4} + \left(-\dfrac{3}{4}\right) = 0$ and $-\dfrac{1}{8} + \left(-\dfrac{3}{4}\right) = -\dfrac{1}{8} + \left(-\dfrac{6}{8}\right)$ or $-\dfrac{7}{8}$

The solution is $-\dfrac{7}{8}$.

Example 5 **Write and Solve an Equation**

Write an equation for the problem. Then solve the equation and check your solution.

A number increased by 5 is equal to 42. Find the number.

A number	increased by	5	is equal to	42.
n	$+$	5	$=$	42

$n + 5 = 42$	Original equation
$n + 5 - 5 = 42 - 5$	Subtract 5 from each side.
$n = 37$	$5 - 5 = 0$ and $42 - 5 = 37$

CHECK

$n + 5 = 42$	Original equation
$37 + 5 \stackrel{?}{=} 42$	Substitute 37 for n.
$42 = 42$ ✓	

The solution is 37.

Study Tip

Checking Solutions
You should always check your solution in the context of the original problem. For instance, in Example 5, is 37 increased by 5 equal to 42? The solution checks.

D A I L Y
INTERVENTION | **Differentiated Instruction**

Visual/Spatial Students will most easily grasp the concept of solving equations by addition or subtraction if they physically observe adding or removing objects from both sides of the equals sign. Use the procedures from the Algebra Activity on page 127 to solve simple equations.

Example 6 Write an Equation to Solve a Problem

HISTORY Refer to the information at the right.

In the fourteenth century, the part of the Great Wall of China that was built during Qui Shi Huangdi's time was repaired, and the wall was extended. When the wall was completed, it was 2500 miles long. How much of the wall was added during the 1300s?

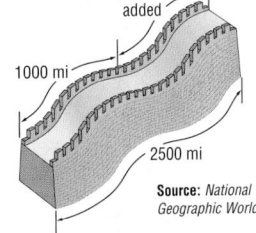

Amount added

1000 mi

2500 mi

Source: *National Geographic World*

Words   The original length plus the additional length equals 2500.

Variable   Let a = the additional length.

The original length	plus	the additional length	equals	2500.
1000	+	a	=	2500

Equation

$$1000 + a = 2500 \qquad \text{Original equation}$$
$$1000 + a - 1000 = 2500 - 1000 \qquad \text{Subtract 1000 from each side.}$$
$$a = 1500 \qquad 1000 - 1000 = 0 \text{ and } 2500 - 1000 = 1500.$$

The Great Wall of China was extended 1500 miles in the 1300s.

---

6 HISTORY The Washington Monument in Washington, D.C., was built in two phases. During the first phase, from 1848–1854, the monument was built to a height of 152 feet. From 1854 until 1878, no work was done. Then from 1878 to 1888, the additional construction resulted in its final height of 555 feet. How much of the monument was added during the second construction phase? Write an equation to solve the problem.
$152 + a = 555; a = 403$ ft

Check for Understanding

Concept Check

1. Sample answers: $n = 13$, $n + 16 = 29$, $n + 12 = 25$

1. **OPEN ENDED** Write three equations that are equivalent to $n + 14 = 27$.

2. **Compare and contrast** the Addition Property of Equality and the Subtraction Property of Equality. **See margin.**

3. **Show** two ways to solve $g + 94 = 75$.
   (1) Add −94 to each side. (2) Subtract 94 from each side.

Guided Practice

GUIDED PRACTICE KEY	
Exercises	Examples
4–9	1–4
10, 11	5
12–14	6

Solve each equation. Then check your solution.

4. $t - 4 = -7$ **−3**
5. $p + 19 = 6$ **−13**
6. $15 + r = 71$ **56**
7. $104 = y - 67$ **171**
8. $h - 0.78 = 2.65$ **3.43**
9. $\frac{2}{3} + w = 1\frac{1}{2}$ **$\frac{5}{6}$**

Write an equation for each problem. Then solve the equation and check your solution.

10. Twenty-one subtracted from a number is −8. Find the number. $n - 21 = -8$; **13**

11. A number increased by −37 is −91. Find the number. $n + (-37) = -91$; **−54**

Application

CARS For Exercises 12–14, use the following information.

The average time it takes to manufacture a car in the United States is equal to the average time it takes to manufacture a car in Japan plus 8.1 hours. The average time it takes to manufacture a car in the United States is 24.9 hours.

12. Write an addition equation to represent the situation. $\ell + 8.1 = 24.9$

13. What is the average time to manufacture a car in Japan? **16.8 h**

14. The average time it takes to manufacture a car in Europe is 35.5 hours. What is the difference between the average time it takes to manufacture a car in Europe and the average time it takes to manufacture a car in Japan? **18.7 h**

---

3 Practice/Apply

Study Notebook

Have students—
• add the definitions/examples of the vocabulary terms to their Vocabulary Builder worksheets for Chapter 3.
• include any other item(s) that they find helpful in mastering the skills in this lesson.

Answers

2. The Addition Property of Equality and the Subtraction Property of Equality can both be used to solve equations. The Addition Property of Equality says you can add the same number to each side of an equation. The Subtraction Property of Equality says you can subtract the same number from each side of an equation. Since subtracting a number is the same as adding its inverse, either property can be used to solve any addition equation or subtraction equation.

★ indicates increased difficulty

Practice and Apply

Solve each equation. Then check your solution. 29. −2.58

15. $v - 9 = 14$ **23**
16. $s - 19 = -34$ **−15**
17. $g + 5 = 33$ **28**
18. $18 + z = 44$ **26**
19. $a - 55 = -17$ **38**
20. $t - 72 = -44$ **28**
21. $-18 = -61 + d$ **43**
22. $-25 = -150 + q$ **125**
23. $r - (-19) = -77$ **−96**
24. $b - (-65) = 15$ **−50**
25. $18 - (-f) = 91$ **73**
26. $125 - (-p) = 88$ **−37**
27. $-2.56 + c = 0.89$ **3.45**
28. $k + 0.6 = -3.84$ **−4.44**
29. $-6 = m + (-3.42)$
30. $6.2 = -4.83 + y$ **11.03**
31. $t - 8.5 = 7.15$ **15.65**
32. $q - 2.78 = 4.2$ **6.98**
33. $x - \frac{3}{4} = \frac{5}{6}$ **$1\frac{7}{12}$**
34. $a - \frac{3}{5} = -\frac{7}{10}$ **$-\frac{1}{10}$**
35. $-\frac{1}{2} + p = \frac{5}{8}$ **$1\frac{1}{8}$**
36. $\frac{2}{3} + r = -\frac{4}{9}$ **$-1\frac{1}{9}$**
37. $\frac{2}{3} = v + \frac{4}{5}$ **$-\frac{2}{15}$**
38. $\frac{2}{5} = w + \frac{3}{4}$ **$-\frac{7}{20}$**

★ **39.** If $x - 7 = 14$, what is the value of $x - 2$? **19**

★ **40.** If $t + 8 = -12$, what is the value of $t + 1$? **−19**

GEOMETRY For Exercises 41 and 42, use the rectangle at the right.

41. $x + 55 = 78; 23$

41. Write an equation you could use to solve for x and then solve for x.

42. Write an equation you could use to solve for y and then solve for y. **$y - 17 = 24; 41$**

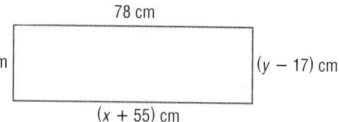

78 cm · 24 cm · $(y - 17)$ cm · $(x + 55)$ cm

Write an equation for each problem. Then solve the equation and check your solution.

43. $n - 18 = 31; 49$

43. Eighteen subtracted from a number equals 31. Find the number.

44. What number decreased by 77 equals −18? $n - 77 = -18; 59$

45. A number increased by −16 is −21. Find the number. $n + (-16) = -21; -5$

46. The sum of a number and −43 is 102. What is the number? $n + (-43) = 102; 145$

47. $n - \frac{1}{2} = -\frac{3}{4}; -\frac{1}{4}$

★ **47.** What number minus one-half is equal to negative three-fourths?

★ **48.** The sum of 19 and 42 and a number is equal to 87. What is the number? **$19 + 42 + n = 87; 26$**

49. Determine whether $x + x = x$ is *sometimes*, *always*, or *never* true. Explain. **Sometimes; if $x = 0$, $x + x = x$ is true.**

50. Determine whether $x + 0 = x$ is *sometimes*, *always*, or *never* true. Explain. **Always; any number plus 0 is always the number.**

GAS MILEAGE For Exercises 51–55, use the following information.
A midsize car with a 4-cylinder engine goes 10 miles more on a gallon of gasoline than a luxury car with an 8-cylinder engine. A midsize car consumes one gallon of gas for every 34 miles driven.

51. Write an addition equation to represent the situation. **$\ell + 10 = 34$**

52. How many miles does a luxury car travel on a gallon of gasoline? **24 mi**

53. A subcompact car with a 3-cylinder engine goes 13 miles more than a luxury car on one gallon of gas. How far does a subcompact car travel on a gallon of gasoline? **37 mi**

54. How many more miles does a subcompact travel on a gallon of gasoline than a midsize car? **3 mi**

55. Estimate how many miles a full-size car with a 6-cylinder engine goes on one gallon of gasoline. Explain your reasoning. **Sample answer: 29 mi; 29 is the average of 24 (for the 8-cylinder engine) and 34 (for the 4-cylinder engine).**

Online Lesson Plans

USA TODAY Education's Online site offers resources and interactive features connected to each day's newspaper. *Experience TODAY*, USA TODAY's daily lesson plan, is available on the site and delivered daily to subscribers. This plan provides instruction for integrating USA TODAY graphics and key editorial features into your mathematics classroom. Log on to www.education.usatoday.com.

HISTORY For Exercises 56 and 57, use the following information.
Over the years, the height of the Great Pyramid at Giza, Egypt, has decreased.

56. Write an addition equation to represent the situation. $450 + d = 481$

57. What was the decrease in the height of the pyramid? 31 ft

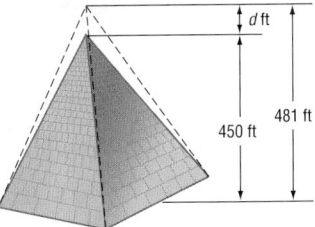

Source: World Book Encyclopedia

LIBRARIES For Exercises 58–61, use the graph at the right to write an equation for each situation. Then solve the equation.

58. $13.6 + x = 24.0$; 10.4 million volumes ★ **58.** How many more volumes does the Library of Congress have than the Harvard University Library?

59. $11.4 + x = 13.6$; 2.2 million volumes ★ **59.** How many more volumes does the Harvard University Library have than the New York Public Library?

60. $11.4 + x = 24.0$; 12.6 million volumes ★ **60.** How many more volumes does the Library of Congress have than the New York Public Library?

61. $24.0 + 13.6 + 11.4 = x$; 49.0 million volumes ★ **61.** What is the total number of volumes in the three largest U.S. libraries?

USA TODAY Snapshots®

USA's largest libraries
Among public and academic libraries in the USA, here are the largest:

Volumes (millions)

Library of Congress	24.0
Harvard University	13.6
New York Public	11.4
Yale University	9.9
Queens, N.Y., Public	9.2
University of Illinois (Urbana)	9.0

Source: American Library Association

By Anne R. Carey and Quin Tian, USA TODAY

ANIMALS For Exercises 62–64, use the information below to write an equation for each situation. Then solve the equation.
Wildlife authorities monitor the population of animals in various regions. One year's deer population in Dauphin County, Pennsylvania, is shown in the graph below.

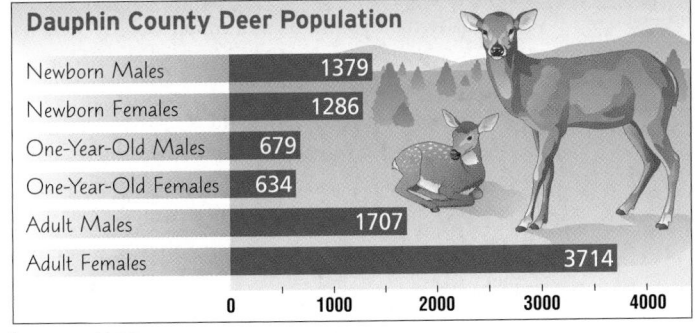

Dauphin County Deer Population

Newborn Males	1379
Newborn Females	1286
One-Year-Old Males	679
One-Year-Old Females	634
Adult Males	1707
Adult Females	3714

Source: www.visi.com

62. $679 + 634 + x = 1379 + 1286$; 1352 ★ **62.** How many more newborns are there than one-year-olds?

63. $1379 + 679 + 1707 + x = 1286 + 634 + 3714$; 1869 ★ **63.** How many more females are there than males?

★ **64.** What is the total deer population? $t = 1379 + 1286 + 679 + 634 + 1707 + 3714$; 9399

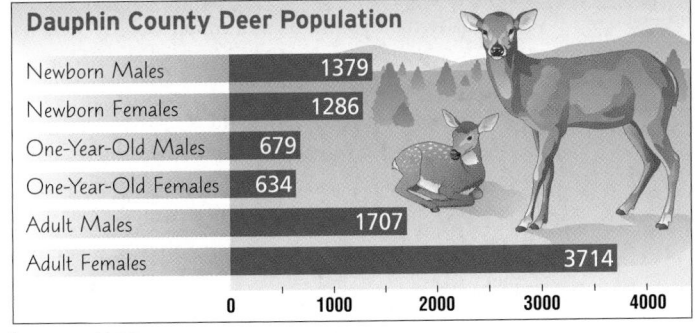www.algebra1.com/self_check_quiz

Lesson 3-2 Solving Equations by Using Addition and Subtraction **133**

Open-Ended Assessment

Writing Have students pick an example problem from the exercises of this lesson, and explain in writing how to solve the problem using addition or subtraction.

Getting Ready for Lesson 3-3

PREREQUISITE SKILL Students will learn how to solve equations using multiplication and division in Lesson 3-3. In addition to integers, they will solve equations involving decimals and fractions. Use Exercises 82–89 to determine your students' familiarity with finding products and quotients of decimals and fractions.

Answers

66. Equations can be used to describe the relationships of growth and decline in job opportunities. Answers should include the following.

   • To solve the equation, add 66 to each side. The solution is $m = 71$.

   • An example such as "The percent increase in growth for paralegals is 16 more than the percent increase in growth for detectives. If the growth rate for paralegals is 86%, what is the growth rate for detectives? $d + 16 = 86$; 70%"

78. $4(16 \div 4^2)$
   $= 4(16 \div 16)$ Subst. Property
   $= 4(1)$ Substitution Property
   $= 4$ Multiplicative Identity

79. $(2^5 - 5^2) + (4^2 - 2^4)$
   $= (32 - 25) + (16 - 16)$ Substitution Property
   $= 7 + 0$ Substitution Property
   $= 7$ Additive Identity

---

65. **CRITICAL THINKING** If $a - b = x$, what values of a, b, and x would make the equation $a + x = b + x$ true? $a = b$, $x = 0$

66. **WRITING IN MATH** Answer the question that was posed at the beginning of the lesson. **See margin.**

   How can equations be used to compare data?

   Include the following in your answer:
   • an explanation of how to solve the equation to find the growth rate for medical assistants, and
   • a sample problem and related equation using the information in the graph.

Standardized Test Practice
Ⓐ Ⓑ Ⓒ Ⓓ

67. Which equation is *not* equivalent to $b - 15 = 32$? **C**
   Ⓐ $b + 5 = 52$　　　　Ⓑ $b - 20 = 27$
   Ⓒ $b - 13 = 30$　　　　Ⓓ $b = 47$

68. What is the solution of $x - 167 = -52$? **A**
   Ⓐ 115　　　　　　　　Ⓑ -115
   Ⓒ 219　　　　　　　　Ⓓ -219

Maintain Your Skills

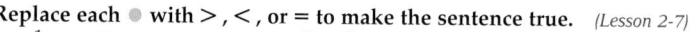

Mixed Review

GEOMETRY For Exercises 69 and 70, use the following information.
The area of a circle is the product of π times the radius r squared. *(Lesson 3-1)*

69. Write the formula for the area of the circle. $A = \pi r^2$

70. If a circle has a radius of 16 inches, find its area. **about 804 in²**

Replace each ● with $>$, $<$, or $=$ to make the sentence true. *(Lesson 2-7)*

71. $\frac{1}{2}$ ● $\sqrt{2}$ $<$　　　72. $\frac{3}{4}$ ● $\frac{2}{3}$ $>$　　　73. 0.375 ● $\frac{3}{8}$ $=$

Use each set of data to make a stem-and-leaf plot. *(Lesson 2-5)*

74. Stem	Leaf
3	1 2 4 5 6
4	0 1 2 3
5	2 4 6

$3 \mid 1 = 31$

74. 54, 52, 43, 41, 40, 36, 35, 31, 32, 34, 42, 56

75. Stem	Leaf
0	5 8
1	1 2 4 7
2	3 6 8 9
3	
4	1 5

$0 \mid 5 = 0.5$

75. 2.3, 1.4, 1.7, 1.2, 2.6, 0.8, 0.5, 2.8, 4.1, 2.9, 4.5, 1.1

Identify the hypothesis and conclusion of each statement. *(Lesson 1-7)*

76. For $y = 2$, $4y - 6 = 2$. **H: $y = 2$; C: $4y - 6 = 2$**

77. There is a science quiz every Friday.
   H: it is Friday; C: there will be a science quiz

Evaluate each expression. Name the property used in each step. *(Lesson 1-4)*

78. $4(16 \div 4^2)$ **4**　　　　79. $(2^5 - 5^2) + (4^2 - 2^4)$ **7**
78–79. See margin for properties used in each step.

Find the solution set for each inequality, given the replacement set. *(Lesson 1-3)*

80. $3x + 2 > 2$; {0, 1, 2} **{1, 2}**　　　　81. $2y^2 - 1 > 0$; {1, 3, 5} **{1, 3, 5}**

Getting Ready for the Next Lesson

PREREQUISITE SKILL Find each product or quotient.
(To review operations with fractions, see pages 800 and 801.) **83. 10.545**

82. 6.5×2.8 **18.2**　　83. 70.3×0.15　　84. $17.8 \div 2.5$ **7.12**　　85. $0.33 \div 1.5$ **0.22**

86. $\frac{2}{3} \times \frac{5}{8}$ **$\frac{5}{12}$**　　87. $\frac{5}{9} \times \frac{3}{10}$ **$\frac{1}{6}$**　　88. $\frac{1}{2} \div \frac{2}{5}$ **$1\frac{1}{4}$**　　89. $\frac{8}{9} \div \frac{4}{15}$ **$3\frac{1}{3}$**

Solving Equations by Using Multiplication and Division

What You'll Learn

- Solve equations by using multiplication.
- Solve equations by using division.

How can equations be used to find how long it takes light to reach Earth?

It may look like all seven stars in the Big Dipper are the same distance from Earth, but in fact, they are not. The diagram shows the distance between each star and Earth.

Light travels at a rate of about 5,870,000,000,000 miles per year. In general, the rate at which something travels times the time equals the distance ($rt = d$). The following equation can be used to find the time it takes light to reach Earth from the closest star in the Big Dipper.

$$rt = d$$
$$5,870,000,000,000t = 311,110,000,000,000$$

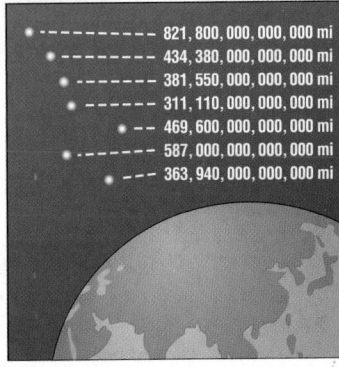

821,800,000,000,000 mi
434,380,000,000,000 mi
381,550,000,000,000 mi
311,110,000,000,000 mi
469,600,000,000,000 mi
587,000,000,000,000 mi
363,940,000,000,000 mi

Source: *National Geographic World*

SOLVE USING MULTIPLICATION

To solve equations such as the one above, you can use the **Multiplication Property of Equality**.

Key Concept — Multiplication Property of Equality

- **Words**: If an equation is true and each side is multiplied by the same number, the resulting equation is true.
- **Symbols**: For any numbers a, b, and c, if $a = b$, then $ac = bc$.
- **Examples**:

$6 = 6$	$9 = 9$	$10 = 10$
$6 \times 2 = 6 \times 2$	$9 \times (-3) = 9 \times (-3)$	$10 \times \frac{1}{2} = 10 \times \frac{1}{2}$
$12 = 12$	$-27 = -27$	$5 = 5$

Example 1 — Solve Using Multiplication by a Positive Number

Solve $\frac{t}{30} = \frac{7}{10}$. Then check your solution.

$$\frac{t}{30} = \frac{7}{10} \quad \text{Original equation}$$

$$30\left(\frac{t}{30}\right) = 30\left(\frac{7}{10}\right) \quad \text{Multiply each side by 30.}$$

$$t = 21 \quad \frac{t}{30}(30) = t \text{ and } \frac{7}{10}(30) = 21$$

(continued on the next page)

---

1 Focus

5-Minute Check Transparency 3-3 Use as a quiz or review of Lesson 3-2.

Mathematical Background notes are available for this lesson on p. 118C.

How can equations be used to find how long it takes light to reach Earth?

Ask students:

- What is the unknown quantity in the equation given in the example? **how much time it takes for light from the star to reach Earth**

- What variable represents the unknown quantity in the equation? **t**

- What do you need to accomplish to solve this equation? **isolate the variable on one side of the equation**

- **Space Flight** The manned Apollo missions to the moon traveled from Earth at a rate of about 25,000 miles per hour (219,000,000 miles per year). What equation could be used to find the time it would take a spacecraft traveling at that speed to reach the closest star in the Big Dipper? **$219,000,000t = 311,110,000,000,000$**

Resource Manager

Workbook and Reproducible Masters

Chapter 3 Resource Masters
- Study Guide and Intervention, pp. 149–150
- Skills Practice, p. 151
- Practice, p. 152
- Reading to Learn Mathematics, p. 153
- Enrichment, p. 154
- Assessment, p. 205

Parent and Student Study Guide Workbook, p. 21
Prerequisite Skills Workbook, pp. 9–12, 51–52

 Transparencies
5-Minute Check Transparency 3-3
Answer Key Transparencies

 **Technology**
Interactive Chalkboard

Building on Prior Knowledge

In Lesson 3-2, students learned that to solve an equation, the variable must be isolated on one side of the equation. Because the numbers were added to or subtracted from the variable, they added (or subtracted) the same quantity to each side of the equation to accomplish this. Ask students how the number is "connected" to the variable (multiplication). Then ask what is the opposite operation of multiplication.

SOLVE USING MULTIPLICATION

In-Class Examples
Power Point®

Teaching Tip Remind students that the goal is to multiply the coefficient of the variable by a number so that the resulting coefficient is 1.

1 Solve $\frac{s}{12} = \frac{3}{4}$. Then check your solution. **9**

Teaching Tip Remind students that the product of a fraction and its reciprocal is 1.

2 Solve $-3\frac{3}{8}k = 1\frac{4}{5}$. **$-\frac{8}{15}$**

3 Solve $-75 = -15b$. **5**

Tips for New Teachers

Intervention Students are sometimes confused about what to do with a variable in an equation like $-x = 27$. Remind students that the variable actually has a coefficient of -1 in this case. Remembering that the product of two negative numbers is positive, you can multiply each side of the equation by -1.

$$(-1)(-x) = (-1)27$$
$$x = -27$$

CHECK

$$\frac{t}{30} = \frac{7}{10} \qquad \text{Original equation}$$

$$\frac{21}{30} \stackrel{?}{=} \frac{7}{10} \qquad \text{Substitute 21 for } t.$$

$$\frac{7}{10} = \frac{7}{10} \checkmark \quad \text{The solution is 21.}$$

Example 2 Solve Using Multiplication by a Fraction

Solve $\left(2\frac{1}{4}\right)g = 1\frac{1}{2}$.

$$\left(2\frac{1}{4}\right)g = 1\frac{1}{2} \qquad \text{Original equation}$$

$$\left(\frac{9}{4}\right)g = \frac{3}{2} \qquad \text{Rewrite each mixed number as an improper fraction.}$$

$$\frac{4}{9}\left(\frac{9}{4}\right)g = \frac{4}{9}\left(\frac{3}{2}\right) \qquad \text{Multiply each side by } \frac{4}{9}, \text{ the reciprocal of } \frac{9}{4}.$$

$$g = \frac{12}{18} \text{ or } \frac{2}{3} \quad \text{Check this result.}$$

The solution is $\frac{2}{3}$.

Example 3 Solve Using Multiplication by a Negative Number

Solve $42 = -6m$.

$$42 = -6m \qquad \text{Original equation}$$

$$-\frac{1}{6}(42) = -\frac{1}{6}(-6m) \qquad \text{Multiply each side by } -\frac{1}{6}, \text{ the reciprocal of } -6.$$

$$-7 = m \qquad \text{Check this result.}$$

The solution is -7.

You can write an equation to represent a real-world problem. Then use the equation to solve the problem.

Example 4 Write and Solve an Equation Using Multiplication

SPACE TRAVEL Refer to the information about space travel at the left. The weight of anything on the moon is about one-sixth its weight on Earth. What was the weight of Neil Armstrong's suit and life-support backpacks on Earth?

Words One sixth times the weight on Earth equals the weight on the moon.

Variable Let w = the weight on Earth.

One sixth	times	the weight on Earth	equals	the weight on the moon.
$\frac{1}{6}$	·	w	=	33

Equation

$$\frac{1}{6}w = 33 \qquad \text{Original equation}$$

$$6\left(\frac{1}{6}w\right) = 6(33) \qquad \text{Multiply each side by 6.}$$

$$w = 198 \qquad \frac{1}{6}(6) = 1 \text{ and } 33(6) = 198$$

The weight of Neil Armstrong's suit and life-support backpacks on Earth was about 198 pounds.

More About. . .

Space Travel
On July 20, 1969, Neil Armstrong stepped on the surface of the moon. On the moon, his suit and life-support backpacks weighed about 33 pounds.
Source: NASA

SOLVE USING DIVISION The equation in Example 3, $42 = -6m$, was solved by multiplying each side by $-\frac{1}{6}$. The same result could have been obtained by dividing each side by -6. This method uses the **Division Property of Equality**.

In-Class Example | Power Point®

4 **SPACE TRAVEL** Using information from Example 4 in the Student Edition, what would be the weight of Neil Armstrong's suit and life-support backpack on Mars if three times the Mars weight equals the Earth weight? **66 lb**

Key Concept — Division Property of Equality

- **Words** — If an equation is true and each side is divided by the same nonzero number, the resulting equation is true.

TEACHING TIP
Ask students why $c \neq 0$.

- **Symbols** — For any numbers a, b, and c, with $c \neq 0$, if $a = b$, then $\frac{a}{c} = \frac{b}{c}$.

- **Examples**

$$15 = 15 \qquad 28 = 28$$
$$\frac{15}{3} = \frac{15}{3} \qquad \frac{28}{-7} = \frac{28}{-7}$$
$$5 = 5 \qquad -4 = -4$$

SOLVE USING DIVISION

In-Class Examples | Power Point®

Example 5 — Solve Using Division by a Positive Number

Solve $13s = 195$. Then check your solution.

$13s = 195$ Original equation

$\frac{13s}{13} = \frac{195}{13}$ Divide each side by 13.

$s = 15$ $\frac{13s}{13} = s$ and $\frac{195}{13} = 15$

CHECK $13s = 195$ Original equation

$13(15) \stackrel{?}{=} 195$ Substitute 15 for s.

$195 = 195$ ✓

The solution is 15.

5 Solve $11w = 143$. Then check your solution. **13**

6 Solve $-8x = 96$. **−12**

7 Write an equation for the problem below. Then solve the equation.
Negative fourteen times a number equals 224.
−14n = 224; −16

Study Tip

Alternative Method
You can also solve equations like those in Examples 5, 6, and 7 by using the Multiplication Property of Equality. For instance, in Example 6, you could multiply each side by $-\frac{1}{3}$.

Example 6 — Solve Using Division by a Negative Number

Solve $-3x = 12$.

$-3x = 12$ Original equation

$\frac{-3x}{-3} = \frac{12}{-3}$ Divide each side by -3.

$x = -4$ $\frac{-3x}{-3} = x$ and $\frac{12}{-3} = -4$

The solution is -4.

Example 7 — Write and Solve an Equation Using Division

Write an equation for the problem below. Then solve the equation.
Negative eighteen times a number equals -198.

Negative eighteen	times	a number	equals	-198.
-18	$\times$	n	$=$	-198

$-18n = -198$ Original equation

$\frac{-18n}{-18} = \frac{-198}{-18}$ Divide each side by -18.

$n = 11$ Check this result.

The solution is 11.

DAILY INTERVENTION

Differentiated Instruction

Auditory/Musical Have students all clap twice per second for five seconds. Write on the chalkboard: 5 seconds = 10 claps. Have students clap twice per second for 10 seconds. Write $\times 2$ under each side of the equation. Then write 10 seconds = 20 claps. Point out that each side of the equation doubled but the equation is still correct. In an equation, as long as you perform the same operation on each side, the equation remains correct.

Study Notebook

Have students—
• add the definitions/examples of the vocabulary terms to their Vocabulary Builder worksheets for Chapter 3.
• include any other item(s) that they find helpful in mastering the skills in this lesson.

DAILY
INTERVENTION **FIND THE ERROR**
Tell students to think of what operation must be performed to "undo" the operation in the equation. Then emphasize that they should always check their solution by substituting the value of the variable in the original equation.

About the Exercises...
Organization by Objective
• Solve Using Multiplication: 13–49
• Solve Using Division: 13–49

Odd/Even Assignments
Exercises 13–38 are structured so that students practice the same concepts whether they are assigned odd or even problems.

Assignment Guide
Basic: 13–29 odd, 33, 35, 39–41, 43–45, 50–70
Average: 13–37 odd, 39–41, 43–45, 50–70
Advanced: 14–38 even, 43–66 (optional: 67–70)
All: Practice Quiz 1 (1–10)

Concept Check

1. Sample answer: $4x = -12$

2. Dividing each side of an equation by a number is the same as multiplying each side of the equation by the number's reciprocal.

1. **OPEN ENDED** Write a multiplication equation that has a solution of -3.

2. **Explain** why the Multiplication Property of Equality and the Division Property of Equality can be considered the same property.

3. **FIND THE ERROR** Casey and Juanita are solving $8n = -72$.

Casey	Juanita
$8n = -72$	$8n = -72$
$8n(8) = -72(8)$	$\dfrac{8n}{8} = \dfrac{-72}{8}$
$n = -576$	$n = -9$

Who is correct? Explain your reasoning.

Juanita; to find an equivalent equation with $1n$ on one side of the equation, you must divide each side by 8 or multiply each side by $\frac{1}{8}$.

Guided Practice

GUIDED PRACTICE KEY	
Exercises	Examples
4–9	1–3, 5, 6
10, 11	7
12	4

Solve each equation. Then check your solution.

4. $-2g = -84$ **42**

5. $\dfrac{t}{7} = -5$ **−35**

6. $\dfrac{a}{36} = \dfrac{4}{9}$ **16**

7. $\dfrac{4}{5}k = \dfrac{8}{9}$ **$1\frac{1}{9}$**

8. $3.15 = 1.5y$ **2.1**

9. $\left(3\frac{1}{4}\right)p = 2\frac{1}{2}$ **$\frac{10}{13}$**

Write an equation for each problem. Then solve the equation.

10. Five times a number is 120. What is the number? $5n = 120$; **24**

11. Two fifths of a number equals -24. Find the number. $\frac{2}{5}n = -24$; **−60**

Application

12. **GEOGRAPHY** The discharge of a river is defined as the width of the river times the average depth of the river times the speed of the river. At one location in St. Louis, the Mississippi River is 533 meters wide, its speed is 0.6 meter per second, and its discharge is 3198 cubic meters per second. How deep is the Mississippi River at this location? **10 m**

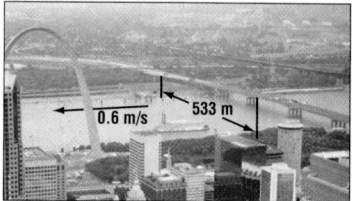

★ indicates increased difficulty

Homework Help	
For Exercises	See Examples
13–32	1–3, 5, 6
33–38	7
39–49	4

Extra Practice
See page 826.

Solve each equation. Then check your solution.

13. $-5r = 55$ **−11**

14. $8d = 48$ **6**

15. $-910 = -26a$ **35**

16. $-1634 = 86s$ **−19**

17. $\dfrac{b}{7} = -11$ **−77**

18. $-\dfrac{v}{5} = -45$ **225**

19. $\dfrac{2}{3}n = 14$ **21**

20. $\dfrac{2}{5}g = -14$ **−35**

21. $\dfrac{8}{24} = \dfrac{5}{12}$ **10**

22. $\dfrac{z}{45} = \dfrac{2}{5}$ **18**

23. $1.9f = -11.78$ **−6.2**

24. $0.49k = 6.272$ **12.8**

25. $-2.8m = 9.8$ **−3.5**

26. $-5.73q = 97.41$ **−17**

27. $\left(-2\frac{3}{5}\right)t = -22$ **$8\frac{6}{13}$**

28. $\left(3\frac{2}{3}\right)x = -5\frac{1}{2}$ **$-1\frac{1}{2}$**

29. $-5h = -3\frac{2}{3}$ **$\frac{11}{15}$**

30. $3p = 4\frac{1}{5}$ **$1\frac{2}{5}$**

★ 31. If $4m = 10$, what is the value of $12m$? **30**

★ 32. If $15b = 55$, what is the value of $3b$? **11**

Write an equation for each problem. Then solve the equation.

36. $-\frac{3}{8}n = 12;\ -32$

37. $2\frac{1}{2}n = 1\frac{1}{5};\ \frac{12}{25}$

38. $\left(1\frac{1}{3}\right)n = -4.82;$ -3.615

40. 50 people

33. Seven times a number equals -84. What is the number? $7n = -84;\ -12$

34. Negative nine times a number is -117. Find the number. $-9n = -117;\ 13$

35. One fifth of a number is 12. Find the number. $\frac{1}{5}n = 12;\ 60$

36. Negative three eighths times a number equals 12. What is the number?

★ 37. Two and one half times a number equals one and one fifth. Find the number.

★ 38. One and one third times a number is -4.82. What is the number?

GENETICS For Exercises 39–41, use the following information.
Research conducted by a daily U.S. newspaper has shown that about one seventh of people in the world are left-handed.

39. Write a multiplication equation relating the number of left-handed people ℓ and the total number of people p. $\ell = \frac{1}{7}p$

40. About how many left-handed people are there in a group of 350 people?

41. If there are 65 left-handed people in a group, about how many people are in that group? **455 people**

42. **WORLD RECORDS** In 1993, a group of people in Utica, New York, made a very large round jelly doughnut which broke the world record for doughnut size. It weighed 1.5 tons and had a circumference of 50 feet. What was the diameter of the doughnut? (*Hint: C = πd*) **about 16 ft**

BASEBALL For Exercises 43–45, use the following information.
In baseball, if all other factors are the same, the speed of a four-seam fastball is faster than a two-seam fastball. The distance from the pitcher's mound to home plate is 60.5 feet.

43. How long does it take a two-seam fastball to go from the pitcher's mound to home plate? Round to the nearest hundredth. (*Hint: rt = d*) **0.48 s**

44. How long does it take a four-seam fastball to go from the pitcher's mound to home plate? Round to the nearest hundredth. **0.46 s**

45. How much longer does it take for a two-seam fastball to reach home plate than a four-seam fastball? **about 0.02 s**

Two-Seam Fastball 126 ft/s

Four-Seam Fastball 132 ft/s

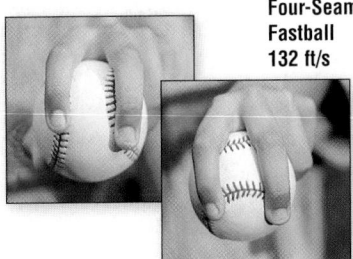

Source: *Baseball and Mathematics*

PHYSICAL SCIENCE For Exercises 46–49, use the following information.
In science lab, Devin and his classmates are asked to determine how many grams of hydrogen and how many grams of oxygen are in 477 grams of water. Devin used what he learned in class to determine that for every 8 grams of oxygen in water, there is 1 gram of hydrogen.

★ 46. If x represents the number of grams of hydrogen, write an expression to represent the number of grams of oxygen. **8x**

★ 47. Write an equation to represent the situation. **$x + 8x = 477$**

★ 48. How many grams of hydrogen are in 477 grams of water? **53 g**

★ 49. How many grams of oxygen are in 477 grams of water? **424 g**

50. **CRITICAL THINKING** If $6y - 7 = 4$, what is the value of $18y - 21$? **12**

www.algebra1.com/self_check_quiz   Lesson 3-3 Solving Equations by Using Multiplication and Division   **139**

 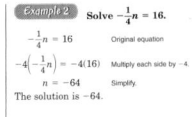

4 Assess

Open-Ended Assessment

Modeling Write an equation that involves multiplication or division on the chalkboard or overhead projector. Have students first identify the operation in the equation. Then, based on the operation they identify, have students suggest which operation might be used to solve the equation.

Assessment Options

Practice Quiz 1 The quiz provides students with a brief review of the concepts and skills in Lessons 3-1 through 3-3. Lesson numbers are given to the right of exercises or instruction lines so students can review concepts not yet mastered.

Quiz (Lessons 3-1 through 3-3) is available on p. 205 of the *Chapter 3 Resource Masters*.

Getting Ready for Lesson 3-4

PREREQUISITE SKILL Students will learn how to solve multi-step equations in Lesson 3-4. The key to solving multi-step equations is knowing the order in which to "undo" operations. This order is the opposite of the usual order of operations. Use Exercises 67–70 to determine your students' familiarity with order of operations.

Answers

51. You can use the distance formula and the speed of light to find the time it takes light from the stars to reach Earth. Answers should include the following.

- Solve the equation by dividing each side of the equation by 5,870,000,000,000. The answer is 53 years.

- The equation 5,870,000,000,000*t* = 821,800,000,000,000 describes the situation for the star in the Big Dipper farthest from Earth.

---

51. 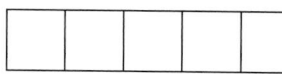 Answer the question that was posed at the beginning of the lesson. **See margin.**

How can equations be used to find how long it takes light to reach Earth?

Include the following in your answer:
- an explanation of how to find the length of time it takes light to reach Earth from the closest star in the Big Dipper, and
- an equation describing the situation for the farthest star in the Big Dipper.

Standardized Test Practice
(A) (B) (C) (D)

52. The rectangle at the right is divided into 5 identical squares. If the perimeter of the rectangle is 48 inches, what is the area of each square? **C**

(A) 4 in^2 (B) 9.8 in^2 (C) 16 in^2 (D) 23.04 in^2

53. Which equation is equivalent to $4t = 20$? **A**

(A) $-2t = -10$ (B) $t = 80$ (C) $2t = 5$ (D) $-8t = 40$

Maintain Your Skills

Mixed Review **Solve each equation. Then check your solution.** *(Lesson 3-2)*

54. $m + 14 = 81$ **67**   55. $d - 27 = -14$ **13**   56. $17 - (-w) = -55$ **−72**

57. Translate the following sentence into an equation. *(Lesson 3-1)*
Ten times a number a is equal to 5 times the sum of b and c. $10a = 5(b + c)$

Find each product. *(Lesson 2-3)*

58. $(-5)(12)$ **−60**   59. $(-2.93)(-0.003)$ **0.00879**   60. $(-4)(0)(-2)(-3)$ **0**

Graph each set of numbers on a number line. *(Lesson 2-1)* **61–64. See margin.**

61. $\{-4, -3, -1, 3\}$ 62. {integers between -6 and 10}

63. {integers less than -4}   64. {integers less than 0 and greater than -6}

Name the property illustrated by each statement. *(Lesson 1-6)*

65. $67 + 3 = 3 + 67$ **Comm. Prop. (+)**   66. $(5 \cdot m) \cdot n = 5 \cdot (m \cdot n)$ **Assoc. Prop. (×)**

Getting Ready for the Next Lesson **PREREQUISITE SKILL** Use the order of operations to find each value.
*(To review the **order of operations**, see Lesson 1-2.)*

67. $2 \times 8 + 9$ **25**   68. $24 \div 3 - 8$ **0**   69. $\frac{3}{8}(17 + 7)$ **9**   70. $\frac{15 - 9}{26 + 12}$ **$\frac{3}{19}$**

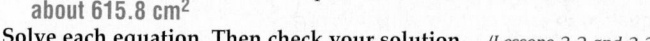

Practice Quiz 1   Lessons 3-1 through 3-3

GEOMETRY   For Exercises 1 and 2, use the following information.
The surface area S of a sphere equals four times π times the square of the radius r. *(Lesson 3-1)*

1. Write the formula for the surface area of a sphere. $S = 4\pi r^2$

2. What is the surface area of a sphere if the radius is 7 centimeters?
about 615.8 cm^2

Solve each equation. Then check your solution. *(Lessons 3-2 and 3-3)*

3. $d + 18 = -27$ **−45**   4. $m - 77 = -61$ **16**   5. $-12 + a = -36$ **−24**   6. $t - (-16) = 9$ **−7**

7. $\frac{2}{3}p = 18$ **27**   8. $-17y = 391$ **−23**   9. $5x = -45$ **−9**   10. $-\frac{2}{5}d = -10$ **25**

140   Chapter 3 Solving Linear Equations

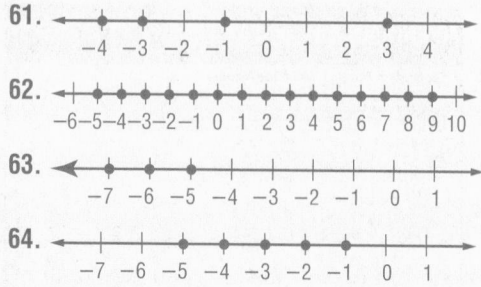

61.
62.
63.
64.

Algebra Activity

Algebra Activity

Solving Multi-Step Equations

You can use an equation model to solve multi-step equations.

Solve $3x + 5 = -7$.

Step 1 Model the equation.

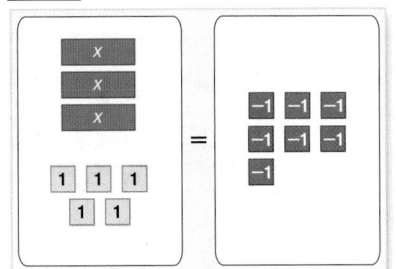

$3x + 5 = -7$

Place 3 x tiles and 5 positive 1 tiles on one side of the mat. Place 7 negative 1 tiles on the other side of the mat.

Step 2 Isolate the x term.

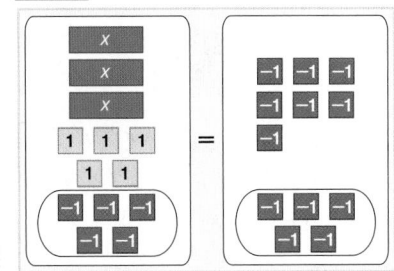

$3x + 5 - 5 = -7 - 5$

Since there are 5 positive 1 tiles with the x tiles, add 5 negative 1 tiles to each side to form zero pairs.

Step 3 Remove zero pairs.

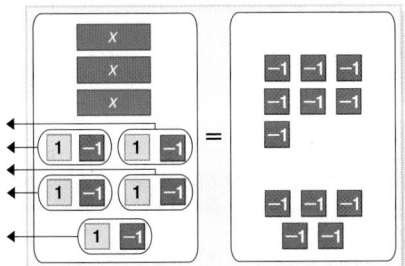

$3x = -12$

Group the tiles to form zero pairs and remove the zero pairs.

Step 4 Group the tiles.

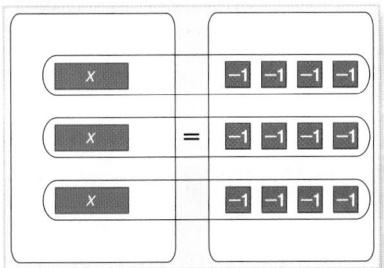

$$\frac{3x}{3} = \frac{-12}{3}$$

Separate the tiles into 3 equal groups to match the 3 x tiles. Each x tile is paired with 4 negative 1 tiles. Thus, $x = -4$.

Model Use algebra tiles to solve each equation.

1. $2x - 3 = -9$ **−3**
2. $3x + 5 = 14$ **3**
3. $3x - 2 = 10$ **4**
4. $-8 = 2x + 4$ **−6**
5. $3 + 4x = 11$ **2**
6. $2x + 7 = 1$ **−3**
7. $9 = 4x - 7$ **4**
8. $7 + 3x = -8$ **−5**

9. **MAKE A CONJECTURE** What steps would you use to solve $7x - 12 = -61$?
First add 12 to each side, and then divide each side by 7.

Algebra Activity   Solving Multi-Step Equations   **141**

Getting Started

Objective Use equation mats and algebra tiles to model solving equations with more than one operation.

Materials
equation mats
algebra tiles

Teach

- You may need to review forming zero pairs before beginning the example.
- Explain that, in Step 4, separating the x tiles and 1 tiles into 3 equivalent groups is a pictorial representation of dividing each side of the equation by 3.

Assess

In **Exercises 1–8**, students should
- discover which side of the equation directs the method of solution by locating the variable, and
- understand that addition and subtraction is done before multiplication and division when isolating the variable.

In **Exercise 9**, have students discuss how the steps in solving the equation is similar to or different from the order of operations.

Resource Manager

📁 **Teaching Algebra with Manipulatives**
- pp. 10-11 (masters for algebra tiles)
- p. 16 (master for equation mat)
- p. 68 (student recording sheet)

Glencoe Mathematics Classroom Manipulative Kit
- algebra tiles
- equation mat

Study Notebook

You may wish to have students summarize this activity and what they learned from it.

3-4 Solving Multi-Step Equations

1 Focus

How can equations be used to estimate the age of an animal?

Ask students:

- What does the number 8 represent in the expression $8 + 12a$? **eight inches, the length of an alligator hatchling**

- What does the $12a$ represent in the expression $8 + 12a$? **Twelve represents the number of inches the alligator grows per year, and *a* represents the number of years of growth.**

- What does this expression assume about the growth of an alligator over its lifetime? **An alligator continues to grow at a constant rate during its entire life.**

3-4 Solving Multi-Step Equations

What You'll Learn

- Solve problems by working backward.
- Solve equations involving more than one operation.

Vocabulary
- work backward
- multi-step equations
- consecutive integers
- number theory

How can equations be used to estimate the age of an animal?

An American alligator hatchling is about 8 inches long. These alligators grow about 12 inches per year. Therefore, the expression $8 + 12a$ represents the length in inches of an alligator that is *a* years old.

10 feet 4 inches
$8 + 12a$

Since 10 feet 4 inches equals $10(12) + 4$ or 124 inches, the equation $8 + 12a = 124$ can be used to estimate the age of the alligator in the photograph. Notice that this equation involves more than one operation.

WORK BACKWARD **Work backward** is one of many *problem-solving strategies* that you can use. Here are some other problem-solving strategies.

Problem-Solving Strategies	
draw a diagram	solve a simpler (or similar) problem
make a table or chart	eliminate the possibilities
make a model	look for a pattern
guess and check	act it out
check for hidden assumptions	list the possibilities
use a graph	identify the subgoals

Example 1 Work Backward to Solve a Problem

Solve the following problem by working backward.

After cashing her paycheck, Tara paid her father the $20 she had borrowed. She then spent half of the remaining money on a concert ticket. She bought lunch for $4.35 and had $10.55 left. What was the amount of the paycheck?

Start at the end of the problem and undo each step.

Statement	Undo the Statement
She had $10.55 left.	$10.55
She bought lunch for $4.35.	$10.55 + $4.35 = $14.90
She spent half of the money on a concert ticket.	$14.90 × 2 = $29.80
She paid her father $20.	$29.80 + $20.00 = $49.80

The paycheck was for $49.80. *Check this answer in the context of the problem.*

SOLVE MULTI-STEP EQUATIONS

To solve equations with more than one operation, often called **multi-step equations**, undo operations by working backward.

Example 2 Solve Using Addition and Division

Solve $7m - 17 = 60$. Then check your solution.

$$7m - 17 = 60 \qquad \text{Original equation}$$
$$7m - 17 + 17 = 60 + 17 \qquad \text{Add 17 to each side.}$$
$$7m = 77 \qquad \text{Simplify.}$$
$$\frac{7m}{7} = \frac{77}{7} \qquad \text{Divide each side by 7.}$$
$$m = 11 \qquad \text{Simplify.}$$

CHECK
$$7m - 17 = 60 \qquad \text{Original equation}$$
$$7(11) - 17 \stackrel{?}{=} 60 \qquad \text{Substitute 11 for } m.$$
$$77 - 17 \stackrel{?}{=} 60 \qquad \text{Multiply.}$$
$$60 = 60 \checkmark \qquad \text{The solution is 11.}$$

You have seen a multi-step equation in which the first, or *leading*, coefficient is an integer. You can use the same steps if the leading coefficient is a fraction.

Example 3 Solve Using Subtraction and Multiplication

Solve $\frac{t}{8} + 21 = 14$. Then check your solution.

$$\frac{t}{8} + 21 = 14 \qquad \text{Original equation}$$
$$\frac{t}{8} + 21 - 21 = 14 - 21 \qquad \text{Subtract 21 from each side.}$$
$$\frac{t}{8} = -7 \qquad \text{Simplify.}$$
$$8\left(\frac{t}{8}\right) = 8(-7) \qquad \text{Multiply each side by 8.}$$
$$t = -56 \qquad \text{Simplify.}$$

CHECK
$$\frac{t}{8} + 21 = 14 \qquad \text{Original equation}$$
$$\frac{-56}{8} + 21 \stackrel{?}{=} 14 \qquad \text{Substitute } -56 \text{ for } t.$$
$$-7 + 21 \stackrel{?}{=} 14 \qquad \text{Divide.}$$
$$14 = 14 \checkmark \qquad \text{The solution is } -56.$$

Example 4 Solve Using Multiplication and Addition

Solve $\frac{p - 15}{9} = -6$.

$$\frac{p - 15}{9} = -6 \qquad \text{Original equation}$$
$$9\left(\frac{p - 15}{9}\right) = 9(-6) \qquad \text{Multiply each side by 9.}$$
$$p - 15 = -54 \qquad \text{Simplify.}$$
$$p - 15 + 15 = -54 + 15 \qquad \text{Add 15 to each side.}$$
$$p = -39 \qquad \text{The solution is } -39.$$

 www.algebra1.com/extra_examples

---

2 Teach

WORK BACKWARD

In-Class Example Power Point®

1 Solve the following problem by working backward.

Danny took some rope with him on his camping trip. He used 32 feet of rope to tie his canoe to a log on the shore. He then gave $\frac{1}{3}$ of the remaining rope to some fellow campers who also needed to tie a canoe. The next night, he used half of the remaining rope to secure his tent during a thunderstorm. On the last day, he used 7 feet as a fish stringer to keep the fish that he caught. After the camping trip, he had 9 feet left. How much rope did he have at the beginning of the camping trip? **80 ft**

SOLVE MULTI-STEP EQUATIONS

In-Class Examples Power Point®

2 Solve $5q - 13 = 37$. Then check your solution. **10**

3 Solve $\frac{s}{12} - 9 = -11$. Then check your solution. **−24**

4 Solve $\frac{r + 8}{-3} = -2$. **−2**

✓ Concept Check

Multi-Step Equations Ask students: why do you multiply each side by 9 in Example 4 *before* you add 15 to each side, which is different from what you did in Examples 2 and 3?

This equation is like $\frac{a}{9} = -6$, where $a = p - 15$. To solve $\frac{a}{9} = -6$, you multiply each side by 9 first.

In-Class Examples

Power Point®

5 Write an equation for the problem below. Then solve the equation.
Eight more than five times a number is negative 62.
$5n + 8 = -62; n = -14$

Teaching Tip Ask students to explain why an equation to find consecutive odd integers looks like an equation to find consecutive even integers. Odds (or evens) are both calculated by adding 2 to the previous odd (or even).

6 **NUMBER THEORY** Write an equation for the problem below. Then solve the equation and answer the problem.
Find three consecutive odd integers whose sum is 57.
$n + (n + 2) + (n + 4) = 57$ or $3n + 6 = 57$. The consecutive integers are 17, 19, and 21.

Example 5 Write and Solve a Multi-Step Equation

Write an equation for the problem below. Then solve the equation.
Two-thirds of a number minus six is −10.

Two-thirds	of	a number	minus	six	is	−10.
$\frac{2}{3}$	$\cdot$	n	$-$	6	$=$	-10

$$\frac{2}{3}n - 6 = -10 \qquad \text{Original equation}$$

$$\frac{2}{3}n - 6 + 6 = -10 + 6 \qquad \text{Add 6 to each side.}$$

$$\frac{2}{3}n = -4 \qquad \text{Simplify.}$$

$$\frac{3}{2}\left(\frac{2}{3}n\right) = \frac{3}{2}(-4) \qquad \text{Multiply each side by } \frac{3}{2}.$$

$$n = -6 \qquad \text{Simplify.}$$

The solution is −6.

Consecutive integers are integers in counting order, such as 7, 8, and 9. Beginning with an even integer and counting by two will result in *consecutive even integers*. For example, −4, −2, 0, and 2 are consecutive even integers. Beginning with an odd integer and counting by two will result in *consecutive odd integers*. For example, −3, −1, 1, 3 and 5 are consecutive odd integers. The study of numbers and the relationships between them is called **number theory**.

Example 6 Solve a Consecutive Integer Problem

NUMBER THEORY Write an equation for the problem below. Then solve the equation and answer the problem.

Find three consecutive even integers whose sum is −42.

Let n = the least even integer.

Then $n + 2$ = the next greater even integer, and

$n + 4$ = the greatest of the three even integers.

The sum of three consecutive even integers	is	−42.
$n + (n + 2) + (n + 4)$	$=$	-42

$$n + (n + 2) + (n + 4) = -42 \qquad \text{Original equation}$$

$$3n + 6 = -42 \qquad \text{Simplify.}$$

$$3n + 6 - 6 = -42 - 6 \qquad \text{Subtract 6 from each side.}$$

$$3n = -48 \qquad \text{Simplify.}$$

$$\frac{3n}{3} = \frac{-48}{3} \qquad \text{Divide each side by 3.}$$

$$n = -16 \qquad \text{Simplify.}$$

$$n + 2 = -16 + 2 \text{ or } -14 \qquad n + 4 = -16 + 4 \text{ or } -12$$

The consecutive even integers are −16, −14, and −12.

CHECK −16, −14, and −12 are consecutive even integers.
$-16 + (-14) + (-12) = -42$ ✓

Study Tip

Representing Consecutive Integers
You can use the same expressions to represent either consecutive even integers or consecutive odd integers. It is the value of n—odd or even—that differs between the two expressions.

DAILY INTERVENTION

Differentiated Instruction

Logical Some students will identify with the orderly way in which multi-step equations are solved by undoing the steps in reverse of the order of operations. Suggest that students make a table with the steps to follow to solve multi-step equations. For example:

For $ax + b = c$, subtract b from each side, then divide each side by a.
For $ax - b = c$, add b to each side, then divide each side by a.

Concept Check

1. **OPEN ENDED** Give two examples of multi-step equations that have a solution of −2. **Sample answers: $2x + 3 = -1$, $3x - 1 = -7$**

2. **(1) Add 4 to each side. (2) Multiply each side by 5. (3) Subtract 3 from each side.**

2. **List** the steps used to solve $\dfrac{w + 3}{5} - 4 = 6$.

3. **Write** an expression for the odd integer before odd integer n. **$n - 2$**

4. **Justify** each step.

$$\frac{4 - 2d}{5} + 3 = 9$$

$\dfrac{4 - 2d}{5} + 3 - 3 = 9 - 3$	a. ?
$\dfrac{4 - 2d}{5} = 6$	b. ? Simplify.
$\dfrac{4 - 2d}{5}(5) = 6(5)$	c. ?
$4 - 2d = 30$	d. ? Simplify.
$4 - 2d - 4 = 30 - 4$	e. ?
$-2d = 26$	f. ? Simplify.
$\dfrac{-2d}{-2} = \dfrac{26}{-2}$	g. ?
$d = -13$	h. ? Simplify.

a. Subtract 3 from each side.
c. Multiply each side by 5.
e. Subtract 4 from each side.
g. Divide each side by −2.

Guided Practice

GUIDED PRACTICE KEY

Exercises	Examples
4, 7–12	2–4
5, 6	1
13–15	5, 6

Solve each problem by working backward.

5. A number is multiplied by seven, and then the product is added to 13. The result is 55. What is the number? **6**

6. **LIFE SCIENCE** A bacteria population triples in number each day. If there are 2,187,000 bacteria on the seventh day, how many bacteria were there on the first day? **3000 bacteria**

Solve each equation. Then check your solution.

7. $4g - 2 = -6$ **−1**

8. $18 = 5p + 3$ **3**

9. $\dfrac{3}{2}a - 8 = 11$ **$12\frac{2}{3}$**

10. $\dfrac{b + 4}{-2} = -17$ **30**

11. $0.2n + 3 = 8.6$ **28**

12. $3.1y - 1.5 = 5.32$ **2.2**

Write an equation and solve each problem. **13. $12 - 2n = -34$; 23**

13. Twelve decreased by twice a number equals −34. Find the number.

14. Find three consecutive integers whose sum is 42.
$n + (n + 1) + (n + 2) = 42$; 13, 14, 15

Application

15. **WORLD CULTURES** The English alphabet contains 2 more than twice as many letters as the Hawaiian alphabet. How many letters are there in the Hawaiian alphabet? **12 letters**

★ indicates increased difficulty

Solve each problem by working backward.

16. A number is divided by 4, and then the quotient is added to 17. The result is 25. Find the number. **32**

17. Nine is subtracted from a number, and then the difference is multiplied by 5. The result is 75. What is the number? **24**

 www.algebra1.com/self_check_quiz

Study Notebook

Have students—
• add the definitions/examples of the vocabulary terms to their Vocabulary Builder worksheets for Chapter 3.
• copy the Problem-Solving Strategies chart from p. 142.
• include any other item(s) that they find helpful in mastering the skills in this lesson.

About the Exercises...

Organization by Objective
Work Backward: 16–21
Solve Multi-Step Equations: 22–54

Odd/Even Assignments
Exercises 16–47 are structured so that students practice the same concepts whether they are assigned odd or even problems.

Alert! Exercises 59–64 require the use of a graphing calculator.

Assignment Guide
Basic: 17–39 odd, 43–49 odd, 51–53, 55–58, 65–89

Average: 17–49 odd, 51–53, 55–58, 65–89 (optional: 59–64)

Advanced: 16–50 even, 54–83 (optional: 84–89)

Answer

56. By using the length at birth, the amount of growth each year, and the current length, you can write and solve an equation to find the age of the animal. Answers should include the following.

- To solve the equation, subtract 8 from each side and then divide each side by 12.
- The alligator is about $9\frac{2}{3}$ or 10 years old.

Homework Help

For Exercises	See Examples
16–21	1
22–41	2–4
42–54	5, 6

Extra Practice
See page 826.

Solve each problem by working backward.

18. **GAMES** In the Trivia Bowl, each finalist must answer four questions correctly. Each question is worth twice as much as the question before it. The fourth question is worth $6000. How much is the first question worth? **$750**

19. **ICE SCULPTING** Due to melting, an ice sculpture loses one-half its weight every hour. After 8 hours, it weighs $\frac{5}{16}$ of a pound. How much did it weigh in the beginning? **80 lb**

20. **FIREFIGHTING** A firefighter spraying water on a fire stood on the middle rung of a ladder. The smoke lessened, so she moved up 3 rungs. It got too hot, so she backed down 5 rungs. Later, she went up 7 rungs and stayed until the fire was out. Then, she climbed the remaining 4 rungs and went into the building. How many rungs does the ladder have? **19 rungs**

21. **MONEY** Hugo withdrew some money from his bank account. He spent one third of the money for gasoline. Then he spent half of what was left for a haircut. He bought lunch for $6.55. When he got home, he had $13.45 left. How much did he withdraw from the bank? **$60**

Solve each equation. Then check your solution. 35. −42.72   36. 0.2

22. $5n + 6 = -4$ **−2**   23. $7 + 3c = -11$ **−6**   24. $15 = 4a - 5$ **5**

25. $-63 = 7g - 14$ **−7**   26. $\frac{c}{-3} + 5 = 7$ **−6**   27. $\frac{y}{5} + 9 = 6$ **−15**

28. $3 - \frac{a}{7} = -2$ **35**   29. $-9 - \frac{p}{4} = 5$ **−56**   30. $\frac{t}{8} - 6 = -12$ **−48**

31. $\frac{m}{-5} + 6 = 31$ **−125**   32. $\frac{17 - s}{4} = -10$ **57**   33. $\frac{-3j - (-4)}{-6} = 12$ **$25\frac{1}{3}$**

34. $-3d - 1.2 = 0.9$ **−0.7**   35. $-2.5r - 32.7 = 74.1$ 36. $-0.6 + (-4a) = -1.4$

37. $\frac{p}{-7} - 0.5 = 1.3$ **−12.6**   38. $3.5x + 5 - 1.5x = 8$ **1.5**   39. $\frac{9z + 4}{5} - 8 = 5.4$ **7**

★ 40. If $3a - 9 = 6$, what is the value of $5a + 2$? **27**

★ 41. If $2x + 1 = 5$, what is the value of $3x - 4$? **2**

Write an equation and solve each problem.

42. Six less than two thirds of a number is negative ten. Find the number.

43. Twenty-nine is thirteen added to four times a number. What is the number?

44. Find three consecutive odd integers whose sum is 51.

45. Find three consecutive even integers whose sum is −30.

46. Find four consecutive integers whose sum is 94.

47. Find four consecutive odd integers whose sum is 8.
$n + (n + 2) + (n + 4) + (n + 6) = 8; -1, 1, 3, 5$

42. $\frac{2}{3}n - 6 = -10;$ **−6**

43. $29 = 13 + 4n;$ **4**

44. $n + (n + 2) + (n + 4) = 51;$ **15, 17, 19**

45. $n + (n + 2) + (n + 4) = -30;$ **−12, −10, −8**

46. $n + (n + 1) + (n + 2) + (n + 3) = 94;$ **22, 23, 24, 25**

48. **BUSINESS** Adele Jones is on a business trip and plans to rent a subcompact car from Speedy Rent-A-Car. Her company has given her a budget of $60 per day for car rental. What is the maximum distance Ms. Jones can drive in one day and still stay within her budget? **450.5 mi**

Speedy Rent-A-Car Price List

Subcompact
$14.95 per day plus $0.10 per mile

Compact
$19.95 per day plus $0.12 per mile

Full Size
$22.95 per day plus $0.15 per mile

49. GEOMETRY The measures of the three sides of a triangle are consecutive even integers. The perimeter of the triangle is 54 centimeters. What are the lengths of the sides of the triangle? **16 cm, 18 cm, 20 cm**

50. MOUNTAIN CLIMBING A general rule for those climbing more than 7000 feet above sea level is to allow a total of $\left(\dfrac{a - 7000}{2000} + 2\right)$ weeks of camping during the ascension. In this expression, *a* represents the altitude in feet. If a group of mountain climbers have allowed for 9 weeks of camping in their schedule, how high can they climb without worrying about altitude sickness? **21,000 ft**

SHOE SIZE For Exercises 51 and 52, use the following information.
If ℓ represents the length of a person's foot in inches, the expression $2\ell - 12$ can be used to estimate his or her shoe size.

51. What is the approximate length of the foot of a person who wears size 8? **10 in.**

52. Measure your foot and use the expression to determine your shoe size. How does this number compare to the size of shoe you are wearing? **See students' work.**

53. SALES Trever Goetz is a salesperson who is paid a monthly salary of $500 plus a 2% commission on sales. How much must Mr. Goetz sell to earn $2000 this month? **$75,000**

★ **54. GEOMETRY** A rectangle is cut from the corner of a 10-inch by 10-inch of paper. The area of the remaining piece of paper is $\dfrac{4}{5}$ of the area of the original piece of paper. If the width of the rectangle removed from the paper is 4 inches, what is the length of the rectangle? **5 in.**

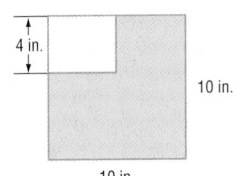

55. CRITICAL THINKING Determine whether the following statement is *sometimes, always,* or *never* true.

The sum of two consecutive even numbers equals the sum of two consecutive odd numbers. **never**

56. **WRITING IN MATH** Answer the question that was posed at the beginning of the lesson. **See margin.**

How can equations be used to estimate the age of an animal?

Include the following in your answer:
- an explanation of how to solve the equation representing the age of the alligator, and
- an estimate of the age of the alligator.

57. Which equation represents the following problem? **B**

Fifteen minus three times a number equals negative twenty-two. Find the number.

Ⓐ $3n - 15 = -22$　　　　Ⓑ $15 - 3n = -22$
Ⓒ $3(15 - n) = -22$　　　Ⓓ $3(n - 15) = -22$

58. Which equation has a solution of -5? **D**

Ⓐ $2a - 6 = 4$　　　　　Ⓑ $3a + 7 = 8$
Ⓒ $\dfrac{3a - 7}{4} = 2$　　　　Ⓓ $\dfrac{3}{5}a + 19 = 16$

Lesson 3-4 Solving Multi-Step Equations **147**

More About...

Mountain Climbing

Many mountain climbers experience altitude sickness caused by a decrease in oxygen. Climbers can acclimate themselves to these higher altitudes by camping for one or two weeks at various altitudes as they ascend the mountain.

Source: *Shape*

Lesson 3-4 Solving Multi-Step Equations **147**

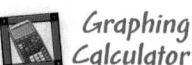

4 Assess

Open-Ended Assessment

Speaking Have one student volunteer read a word problem similar to Example 1, while another volunteer describes how to solve the problem, either by working backward or by writing and solving a two-step equation.

Getting Ready for Lesson 3-5

PREREQUISITE SKILL Students will learn how to solve equations with the variable on both sides in Lesson 3-5. This requires students to add or subtract expressions involving a variable from each side of the equation. Use Exercises 84–89 to determine your students' familiarity with simplifying expressions. Students need to know how to simplify these sums or differences readily.

Graphing Calculator

EQUATION SOLVER You can use a graphing calculator to solve equations that are rewritten as expressions that equal zero.

Step 1 Write the equation so that one side is equal to 0.

Step 2 On a TI-83 Plus, press [MATH] and choose 0, for solve.

Step 3 Enter the equation after 0=. Use [ALPHA] to enter the variables. Press [ENTER].

Step 4 Press [ALPHA] [SOLVE] to reveal the solution. Use the [▲] key to begin entering a new equation.

Use a graphing calculator to solve each equation.

59. $0 = 11y + 33$ **−3**

60. $\frac{w + 2}{5} - 4 = 0$ **18**

61. $6 = -12 + \frac{h}{-7}$ **−126**

62. $\frac{p - (-5)}{-2} = 6$ **−17**

63. $0.7 = \frac{r - 0.8}{6}$ **5**

64. $4.91 + 7.2t = 38.75$ **4.7**

Maintain Your Skills

Mixed Review

Solve each equation. Then check your solution. *(Lesson 3-3)*

65. $-7t = 91$ **−13**

66. $\frac{r}{15} = -8$ **−120**

67. $-\frac{2}{3}b = -1\frac{1}{2}$ **$2\frac{1}{4}$**

TRANSPORTATION For Exercises 68 and 69, use the following information.
In the year 2000, there were 18 more models of sport utility vehicles than there were in the year 1990. There were 47 models of sport utility vehicles in 2000. *(Lesson 3-2)*

68. Write an addition equation to represent the situation. **$m + 18 = 47$**

69. How many models of sport utility vehicles were there in 1990? **29 models**

Find the odds of each outcome if you spin the spinner at the right. *(Lesson 2-6)*

70. spinning a number divisible by 3 **1:3**

71. spinning a number equal to or greater than 5 **1:1**

72. spinning a number less than 7 **3:1**

Find each quotient. *(Lesson 2-4)* **75.** $-\frac{3}{4}a + 4$

73. $-\frac{6}{7} \div 3$ **$-\frac{2}{7}$**

74. $\frac{\frac{2}{3}}{8}$ **$\frac{1}{12}$**

75. $\frac{-3a + 16}{4}$

76. $\frac{15t - 25}{-5}$ **$5 - 3t$**

Use the Distributive Property to find each product. *(Lesson 1-5)*

77. $17 \cdot 9$ **153**

78. $13(101)$ **1313**

79. $16\left(1\frac{1}{4}\right)$ **20**

80. $18\left(2\frac{1}{9}\right)$ **38**

Write an algebraic expression for each verbal expression. *(Lesson 1-1)*

81. the product of 5 and m plus half of n **$5m + \frac{n}{2}$**

82. the quantity 3 plus b divided by y **$(3 + b) \div y$**

83. the sum of 3 times a and the square of b **$3a + b^2$**

Getting Ready for the Next Lesson

PREREQUISITE SKILL Simplify each expression.
*(To review **simplifying expressions**, see Lesson 1-5.)*

84. $5d - 2d$ **3d**

85. $11m - 5m$ **6m**

86. $8t + 6t$ **14t**

87. $7g - 15g$ **−8g**

88. $-9f + 6f$ **−3f**

89. $-3m + (-7m)$ **−10m**

Solving Equations with the Variable on Each Side

What You'll Learn

- Solve equations with the variable on each side.
- Solve equations involving grouping symbols.

Vocabulary
- identity

How can an equation be used to determine when two populations are equal?

In 1995, there were 18 million Internet users in North America. Of this total, 12 million were male, and 6 million were female. During the next five years, the number of male Internet users on average increased 7.6 million per year, and the number of female Internet users increased 8 million per year. If this trend continues, the following expressions represent the number of male and female Internet users x years after 1995.

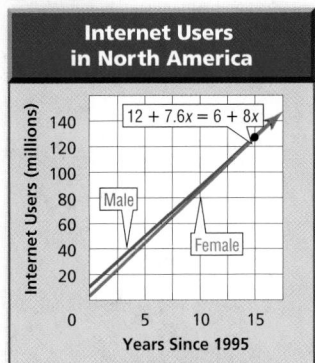

Internet Users in North America

$12 + 7.6x = 6 + 8x$

Male Internet Users: $12 + 7.6x$
Female Internet Users: $6 + 8x$

The equation $12 + 7.6x = 6 + 8x$ represents the time at which the number of male and female Internet users are equal. Notice that this equation has the variable x on each side.

VARIABLES ON EACH SIDE   Many equations contain variables on each side. To solve these types of equations, first use the Addition or Subtraction Property of Equality to write an equivalent equation that has all of the variables on one side.

Example 1 Solve an Equation with Variables on Each Side

Solve $-2 + 10p = 8p - 1$. Then check your solution.

$-2 + 10p = 8p - 1$	Original equation
$-2 + 10p - 8p = 8p - 1 - 8p$	Subtract $8p$ from each side.
$-2 + 2p = -1$	Simplify.
$-2 + 2p + 2 = -1 + 2$	Add 2 to each side.
$2p = 1$	Simplify.
$\dfrac{2p}{2} = \dfrac{1}{2}$	Divide each side by 2.
$p = \dfrac{1}{2}$ or 0.5	Simplify.

CHECK

$-2 + 10p = 8p - 1$	Original equation
$-2 + 10(0.5) \stackrel{?}{=} 8(0.5) - 1$	Substitute 0.5 for p.
$-2 + 5 \stackrel{?}{=} 4 - 1$	Multiply.
$3 = 3 \checkmark$	The solution is $\dfrac{1}{2}$ or 0.5.

1 Focus

 5-Minute Check Transparency 3-5 Use as a quiz or review of Lesson 3-4.

Mathematical Background notes are available for this lesson on p. 118D.

How can an equation be used to determine when two populations are equal?

Ask students:

- In the example, the expression $12 + 7.6x$ represents male Internet users. In this expression, what do the 12 and $7.6x$ represent? **12 represents 12 million male Internet users in 1995. 7.6x represents an addition of 7.6 million male Internet users per year for x years.**

- In the example, the expression $6 + 8x$ represents female Internet users. In this expression, what do the 6 and $8x$ represent? **6 represents the 6 million female Internet users in 1995. 8x represents an addition of 8 million female Internet users per year for x years.**

- From the graph, in how many years from 1995 will the number of female Internet users equal the number of male Internet users? **15 years**

- How many male and female Internet users will there be in 15 years? **126 million male and 126 million female**

Resource Manager

Workbook and Reproducible Masters

Chapter 3 Resource Masters
- Study Guide and Intervention, pp. 161–162
- Skills Practice, p. 163
- Practice, p. 164
- Reading to Learn Mathematics, p. 165
- Enrichment, p. 166
- Assessment, pp. 205, 207

Graphing Calculator and Spreadsheet Masters, p. 27
Parent and Student Study Guide Workbook, p. 23
Prerequisite Skills Workbook, pp. 23–24

 Transparencies
5-Minute Check Transparency 3-5
Answer Key Transparencies

Technology
AlgePASS: Tutorial Plus, Lesson 5
Interactive Chalkboard

VARIABLES ON EACH SIDE

In-Class Example Power Point®

Teaching Tip Explain to students that the side of the equation on which the variable is isolated does not matter. In Example 1, $10p$ could be subtracted from each side of the equation to end up with $-2p$ on the right side. Challenge students to solve the equation this way to see that the result is the same.

1 Solve $8 + 5s = 7s - 2$. Then check your solution. **5**

GROUPING SYMBOLS

In-Class Examples Power Point®

Teaching Tip To remind students of how they use the Distributive Property, you may want to add a step in the solution in Example 2.

$$4(2r - 8) = \frac{1}{7}(49r + 70)$$

$$4(2r) + 4(-8) = \frac{1}{7}(49r) + \frac{1}{7}(70)$$

$$8r - 32 = 7r + 10$$

2 Solve $\frac{1}{3}(18 + 12q) = 6(2q - 7)$. Then check your solution. **6**

Teaching Tip Emphasize that there are two possible outcomes when the variable can be eliminated from an equation: either the equation has no solution (false statement) or the equation is an identity (true statement).

3 Solve $8(5c - 2) = 10(32 + 4c)$. **no solution**

4 Solve $4(t + 20) = \frac{1}{5}(20t + 400)$. **all numbers**

GROUPING SYMBOLS When solving equations that contain grouping symbols, first use the Distributive Property to remove the grouping symbols.

Example 2 *Solve an Equation with Grouping Symbols*

Solve $4(2r - 8) = \frac{1}{7}(49r + 70)$. Then check your solution.

$4(2r - 8) = \frac{1}{7}(49r + 70)$	Original equation
$8r - 32 = 7r + 10$	Distributive Property
$8r - 32 - 7r = 7r + 10 - 7r$	Subtract $7r$ from each side.
$r - 32 = 10$	Simplify.
$r - 32 + 32 = 10 + 32$	Add 32 to each side.
$r = 42$	Simplify.

CHECK

$4(2r - 8) = \frac{1}{7}(49r + 70)$	Original equation
$4[2(42) - 8] \stackrel{?}{=} \frac{1}{7}[49(42) + 70]$	Substitute 42 for r.
$4(84 - 8) \stackrel{?}{=} \frac{1}{7}(2058 + 70)$	Multiply.
$4(76) \stackrel{?}{=} \frac{1}{7}(2128)$	Add and subtract.
$304 = 304 \checkmark$	

The solution is 42.

Study Tip

Look Back
To review the **Distributive Property**, see Lesson 1-5.

Some equations with the variable on each side may have no solution. That is, there is no value of the variable that will result in a true equation.

Example 3 *No Solutions*

Solve $2m + 5 = 5(m - 7) - 3m$.

$2m + 5 = 5(m - 7) - 3m$	Original equation
$2m + 5 = 5m - 35 - 3m$	Distributive Property
$2m + 5 = 2m - 35$	Simplify.
$2m + 5 - 2m = 2m - 35 - 2m$	Subtract $2m$ from each side.
$5 = -35$	This statement is false.

Since $5 = -35$ is a false statement, this equation has no solution.

An equation that is true for every value of the variable is called an **identity**.

Example 4 *An Identity*

Solve $3(r + 1) - 5 = 3r - 2$.

$3(r + 1) - 5 = 3r - 2$	Original equation
$3r + 3 - 5 = 3r - 2$	Distributive Property
$3r - 2 = 3r - 2$	Reflexive Property of Equality

Since the expressions on each side of the equation are the same, this equation is an identity. The statement $3(r + 1) - 5 = 3r - 2$ is true for all values of r.

DAILY INTERVENTION   **Differentiated Instruction**

Kinesthetic Students will benefit from manipulating or moving objects to help them solve equations with variables on both sides. Allow students to use equation mats and algebra tiles to model simple equations. Manipulating the tiles will give students a different way to learn the concepts in this lesson.

Concept Summary — Steps for Solving Equations

Step 1 Use the Distributive Property.

Step 2 Simplify the expressions on each side.

Step 3 Use the Addition and/or Subtraction Properties of Equality to get the variables on one side and the numbers without variables on the other side.

Step 4 Simplify the expressions on each side of the equals sign.

Step 5 Use the Multiplication or Division Property of Equality to solve.

In-Class Example

5 **Multiple-Choice Test Item**
Solve
$8(b + 1) + 4 = 3(2b - 8) - 16$.
D

A 13
B -13
C 26
D -26

Standardized Test Practice
Ⓐ Ⓑ Ⓒ Ⓓ

Example 5 Use Substitution to Solve an Equation

Multiple-Choice Test Item

> Solve $2(b - 3) + 5 = 3(b - 1)$.
> Ⓐ -2 Ⓑ 2 Ⓒ -3 Ⓓ 3

Read the Test Item

You are asked to solve an equation.

Solve the Test Item

You can solve the equation or substitute each value into the equation and see if it makes the equation true. We will solve by substitution.

Test-Taking Tip
If you are asked to solve a complicated equation, it sometimes takes less time to check each possible answer rather than to actually solve the equation.

A $2(b - 3) + 5 = 3(b - 1)$

$2(-2 - 3) + 5 \stackrel{?}{=} 3(-2 - 1)$

$2(-5) + 5 \stackrel{?}{=} 3(-3)$

$-10 + 5 \stackrel{?}{=} -9$

$-5 \neq -9$

B $2(b - 3) + 5 = 3(b - 1)$

$2(2 - 3) + 5 \stackrel{?}{=} 3(2 - 1)$

$2(-1) + 5 \stackrel{?}{=} 3(1)$

$-2 + 5 \stackrel{?}{=} 3$

$3 = 3 \;\checkmark$

Since the value 2 results in a true statement, you do not need to check -3 and 3. The answer is B.

Check for Understanding

Concept Check

1a. Incorrect; the 2 must be distributed over both g and 5; 6.

1. **Determine** whether each solution is correct. If the solution is not correct, find the error and give the correct solution.

a. $2(g + 5) = 22$
$2g + 5 = 22$
$2g + 5 - 5 = 22 - 5$
$2g = 17$
$\dfrac{2g}{2} = \dfrac{17}{2}$
$g = 8.5$

b. $5d = 2d - 18$
$5d - 2d = 2d - 18 - 2d$
$3d = -18$
$\dfrac{3d}{3} = \dfrac{-18}{3}$
$d = -6$
correct

c. $-6z + 13 = 7z$
$-6z + 13 - 6z = 7z - 6z$
$13 = z$
Incorrect; to eliminate $-6z$ on the left side of the equals sign, $6z$ must be added to each side of the equation; 1.

www.algebra1.com/extra_examples

Standardized Test Practice
Ⓐ Ⓑ Ⓒ Ⓓ

Example 5 Caution students to be very careful when checking possible answers on test items. It is very easy to make a substitution or arithmetic error when checking possible answers. Often, some of the incorrect possible answers are similar to the correct answers, such as -2 and 2 in Example 5. It would be easy to substitute 2 in the equation and then inadvertently choose -2 as the answer.

Study Notebook

Have students—
- add the definitions/examples of the vocabulary terms to their Vocabulary Builder worksheets for Chapter 3.
- copy the Concept Summary for Solving Equations into their study notebooks.
- include any other item(s) that they find helpful in mastering the skills in this lesson.

About the Exercises...

Organization by Objective
- **Variables on Each Side:** 14–21, 30, 31, 34–37, 40, 41, 46
- **Grouping Symbols:** 22–29, 32, 33, 38, 39, 42–45, 47, 48

Odd/Even Assignments
Exercises 14–47 are structured so that students practice the same concepts whether they are assigned odd or even problems.

Assignment Guide

Basic: 15–45 odd, 49–75

Average: 15–47 odd, 49–75

Advanced: 14–46 even, 48–67 (optional: 68–75)

---

2. If both sides of the equation are always equal, the equation is an identity.

2. **Explain** how to determine whether an equation is an identity.

3. **OPEN ENDED** Find a counterexample to the statement *all equations have a solution.* Sample answer: $2x - 5 = 2x + 5$

Guided Practice

GUIDED PRACTICE KEY	
Exercises	Examples
4–12	1–4
13	5

4. Justify each step.

$$6n + 7 = 8n - 13$$
$$6n + 7 - 6n = 8n - 13 - 6n \quad \text{a.} \quad \underline{\ ?\ }$$

a. Subtract $6n$ from each side. $\qquad 7 = 2n - 13 \quad$ **b.** $\underline{\ ?\ }$ Simplify.

c. Add 13 to each side. $\qquad 7 + 13 = 2n - 13 + 13 \quad$ **c.** $\underline{\ ?\ }$

$\qquad\qquad\qquad\qquad 20 = 2n \quad$ **d.** $\underline{\ ?\ }$ Simplify.

e. Divide each side by 2. $\qquad \dfrac{20}{2} = \dfrac{2n}{2} \quad$ **e.** $\underline{\ ?\ }$

$\qquad\qquad\qquad\qquad 10 = n \quad$ **f.** $\underline{\ ?\ }$ Simplify.

Solve each equation. Then check your solution.

5. $20c + 5 = 5c + 65$ **4**

6. $\dfrac{3}{8} - \dfrac{1}{4}t = \dfrac{1}{2}t - \dfrac{3}{4}$ $1\frac{1}{2}$

7. $3(a - 5) = -6$ **3**

8. $7 - 3r = r - 4(2 + r)$ **no solution**

9. $6 = 3 + 5(d - 2)$ **2.6**

10. $\dfrac{c+1}{8} = \dfrac{c}{4}$ **1**

11. $5h - 7 = 5(h - 2) + 3$ **all numbers**

12. $5.4w + 8.2 = 9.8w - 2.8$ **2.5**

Standardized Test Practice

13. Solve $75 - 9t = 5(-4 + 2t)$. **D**

(A) -5 (B) -4 (C) 4 (D) 5

★ indicates increased difficulty

Practice and Apply

Homework Help	
For Exercises	See Examples
14–48	1–4
51, 52	5

Extra Practice
See page 826.

14a. Multiply each side by 10.
14b. Simplify.
14c. Distrib. Prop.
14d. Add 4 to each side.
14e. Simplify.
14f. Divide each side by 6.
14g. Simplify.

Justify each step.

14. $\qquad \dfrac{3m - 2}{5} = \dfrac{7}{10}$

$\dfrac{3m-2}{5}(10) = \dfrac{7}{10}(10) \quad$ **a.** $\underline{\ ?\ }$

$(3m - 2)2 = 7 \quad$ **b.** $\underline{\ ?\ }$

$6m - 4 = 7 \quad$ **c.** $\underline{\ ?\ }$

$6m - 4 + 4 = 7 + 4 \quad$ **d.** $\underline{\ ?\ }$

$6m = 11 \quad$ **e.** $\underline{\ ?\ }$

$\dfrac{6m}{6} = \dfrac{11}{6} \quad$ **f.** $\underline{\ ?\ }$

$m = 1\dfrac{5}{6} \quad$ **g.** $\underline{\ ?\ }$

15. $v + 9 = 7v + 9$

$v + 9 - v = 7v + 9 - v \quad$ **a.** $\underline{\ ?\ }$

$9 = 6v + 9 \quad$ **b.** $\underline{\ ?\ }$

$9 - 9 = 6v + 9 - 9 \quad$ **c.** $\underline{\ ?\ }$

a. Subtract v from each side. $\quad 0 = 6v \quad$ **d.** $\underline{\ ?\ }$

b. Simplify. $\qquad \dfrac{0}{6} = \dfrac{6v}{6} \quad$ **e.** $\underline{\ ?\ }$

c. Subtract 9 from each side. $\quad 0 = v \quad$ **f.** $\underline{\ ?\ }$

d. Simplify. e. Divide each side by 6. f. Simplify.

Solve each equation. Then check your solution.

16. $3 - 4q = 10q + 10$ **−0.5**

17. $3k - 5 = 7k - 21$ **4**

18. $5t - 9 = -3t + 7$ **2**

19. $8s + 9 = 7s + 6$ **−3**

20. $\dfrac{3}{4}n + 16 = 2 - \dfrac{1}{8}n$ **−16**

21. $\dfrac{1}{4} - \dfrac{2}{3}y = \dfrac{3}{4} - \dfrac{1}{3}y$ $-1\frac{1}{2}$

22. $8 = 4(3c + 5)$ **−1**

23. $7(m - 3) = 7$ **4**

24. $6(r + 2) - 4 = -10$ **−3**

25. $5 - \dfrac{1}{2}(x - 6) = 4$ **8**

26. $4(2a - 1) = -10(a - 5)$ **3**

27. $4(f - 2) = 4f$ **no solution**

28. $3(1 + d) - 5 = 3d - 2$ **all numbers**

29. $2(w - 3) + 5 = 3(w - 1)$ **2**

30. $\frac{3}{2}y - y = 4 + \frac{1}{2}y$ **no solution**   31. $3 + \frac{2}{5}b = 11 - \frac{2}{5}b$ **10**

32. $\frac{1}{4}(7 + 3g) = -\frac{g}{8}$ **−2**   33. $\frac{1}{6}(a - 4) = \frac{1}{3}(2a + 4)$ **−4**

34. $28 - 2.2x = 11.6x + 262.6$ **−17**   35. $1.03p - 4 = -2.15p + 8.72$ **4**

36. $18 - 3.8t = 7.36 - 1.9t$ **5.6**   37. $13.7v - 6.5 = -2.3v + 8.3$ **0.925**

★ 38. $2[s + 3(s - 1)] = 18$ **3**

39. $-3(2n - 5) = 0.5(-12n + 30)$
all numbers

40. One half of a number increased by 16 is four less than two thirds of the number. Find the number. **120**

41. The sum of one half of a number and 6 equals one third of the number. What is the number? **−36**

42. **NUMBER THEORY** Twice the greater of two consecutive odd integers is 13 less than three times the lesser number. Find the integers. **17, 19**

43. **NUMBER THEORY** Three times the greatest of three consecutive even integers exceeds twice the least by 38. What are the integers? **26, 28, 30**

44. **HEALTH** When exercising, a person's pulse rate should not exceed a certain limit, which depends on his or her age. This maximum rate is represented by the expression $0.8(220 - a)$, where a is age in years. Find the age of a person whose maximum pulse is 152. **30 years**

45. **HARDWARE** Traditionally, nails are given names such as 2-penny, 3-penny, and so on. These names describe the lengths of the nails. What is the name of a nail that is $2\frac{1}{2}$ inches long? **8-penny**

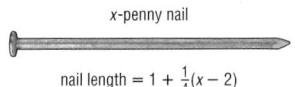
x-penny nail

nail length $= 1 + \frac{1}{4}(x - 2)$

Source: *World Book Encyclopedia*

★ 46. **TECHNOLOGY** About 4.9 million households had one brand of personal computers in 2001. The use of these computers grew at an average rate of 0.275 million households a year. In 2001, about 2.5 million households used another type of computer. The use of these computers grew at an average rate of 0.7 million households a year. How long will it take for the two types of computers to be in the same number of households? **about 5.6 yr**

★ 47. **GEOMETRY** The rectangle and square shown below have the same perimeter. Find the dimensions of each figure.

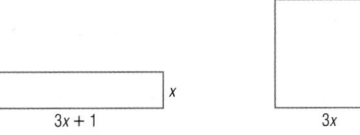

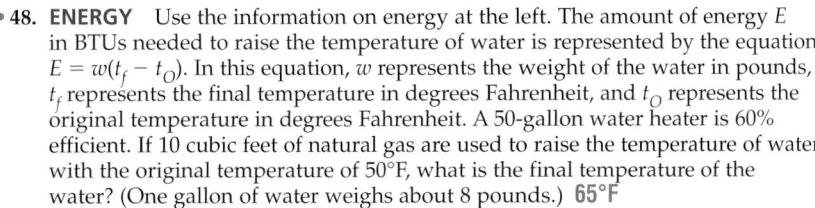

$3x + 1$ x $3x$

2.5 by 0.5 and 1.5 by 1.5

★ 48. **ENERGY** Use the information on energy at the left. The amount of energy E in BTUs needed to raise the temperature of water is represented by the equation $E = w(t_f - t_O)$. In this equation, w represents the weight of the water in pounds, t_f represents the final temperature in degrees Fahrenheit, and t_O represents the original temperature in degrees Fahrenheit. A 50-gallon water heater is 60% efficient. If 10 cubic feet of natural gas are used to raise the temperature of water with the original temperature of 50°F, what is the final temperature of the water? (One gallon of water weighs about 8 pounds.) **65°F**

49. **Sample answer:** $3(x + 1) = x - 1$

49. **CRITICAL THINKING** Write an equation that has one or more grouping symbols, the variable on each side of the equals sign, and a solution of −2.

www.algebra1.com/self_check_quiz   **Lesson 3-5** Solving Equations with the Variable on Each Side   **153**

Open-Ended Assessment

Writing Have students solve the equation $3x + 2 = 5x - 8$. Beside each step, have students write one or two sentences explaining and justifying their method.

Getting Ready for Lesson 3-6

PREREQUISITE SKILL Students will learn about ratios and proportions in Lesson 3-6. Ratios are fractions and proportions are equations involving fractions. Students should be able to simplify fractions readily before beginning Lesson 3-6. Use Exercises 68–75 to determine your students' familiarity with simplifying fractions.

Assessment Options

Quiz (Lessons 3-4 and 3-5) is available on p. 205 of the *Chapter 3 Resource Masters*.

Mid-Chapter Test (Lessons 3-1 through 3-5) is available on p. 207 of the *Chapter 3 Resource Masters*.

Answers

50. Set two expressions equal to each other and solve the equation. Answers should include the following.

- The steps used to solve the equation are (1) subtract 7.6x from each side, (2) subtract 6 from each side, and (3) divide each side by 0.4.

- The number of male and female Internet users will be the same in 2010.

- If two expressions that represent the growth in use of two items are set equal to each other, the solution to the equation can predict when the number of items in use will be equal.

---

50. [WRITING IN MATH] Answer the question that was posed at the beginning of the lesson. **See margin.**

How can an equation be used to determine when two populations are equal?

Include the following in your answer:
- a list of the steps needed to solve the equation,
- the year when the number of female Internet users will equal the number of male Internet users according to the model, and
- an explanation of why this method can be used to predict future events.

Standardized Test Practice
Ⓐ Ⓑ Ⓒ Ⓓ

51. Solve $8x - 3 = 5(2x + 1)$. **D**
   Ⓐ 4   Ⓑ 2   Ⓒ -2 Ⓓ -4

52. Solve $5n + 4 = 7(n + 1) - 2n$. **C**
   Ⓐ 0   Ⓑ -1 Ⓒ no solution   Ⓓ all numbers

Maintain Your Skills

Mixed Review

Solve each equation. Then check your solution. *(Lesson 3-4)*

53. $\frac{2}{9}v - 6 = 14$ **90**   **54.** $\frac{x - 3}{7} = -2$ **-11**   **55.** $5 - 9w = 23$ **-2**

HEALTH For Exercises 56 and 57, use the following information.
Ebony burns 4.5 Calories per minute pushing a lawn mower. *(Lesson 3-3)*

56. Write a multiplication equation representing the number of Calories C burned if Ebony pushes the lawn mower for m minutes. **$C = 4.5m$**

57. How long will it take Ebony to burn 150 Calories mowing the lawn? **$33\frac{1}{3}$ min**

Use each set of data to make a line plot. *(Lesson 2-5)* **58–59. See margin.**

58. 13, 15, 11, 15, 16, 17, 12, 12, 13, 15, 16, 15

59. 22, 25, 19, 21, 22, 24, 22, 25, 28, 21, 24, 22

Find each sum or difference. *(Lesson 2-2)*

60. $-10 + (-17)$ **-27**   **61.** $-12 - (-8)$ **-4**   **62.** $6 - 14$ **-8**

Write a counterexample for each statement. *(Lesson 1-7)*

63. Sample answer: $1 + 3 = 4$

63. If the sum of two numbers is even, then both addends are even.

64. If you are baking cookies, you will need chocolate chips. **Sample answer: You could bake sugar cookies, which do not require chocolate chips.**

Evaluate each expression when $a = 5$, $b = 8$, $c = 7$, $x = 2$, and $y = 1$. *(Lesson 1-2)*

65. $\frac{3a^2}{b + c}$ **5**   **66.** $x(a + 2b) - y$ **41**   **67.** $5(x + 2y) - 4a$ **0**

Getting Ready for the Next Lesson

PREREQUISITE SKILL Simplify each fraction.
(To review simplifying fractions, see pages 798 and 799.)

68. $\frac{12}{15}$ **$\frac{4}{5}$**   **69.** $\frac{28}{49}$ **$\frac{4}{7}$**   **70.** $\frac{36}{60}$ **$\frac{3}{5}$**   **71.** $\frac{8}{120}$ **$\frac{1}{15}$**

72. $\frac{108}{9}$ **12**   **73.** $\frac{28}{42}$ **$\frac{2}{3}$**   **74.** $\frac{16}{40}$ **$\frac{2}{5}$**   **75.** $\frac{19}{57}$ **$\frac{1}{3}$**

58.

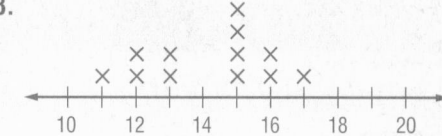

59.

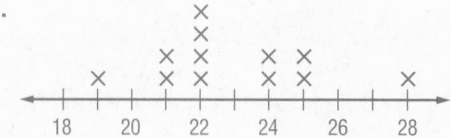

Ratios and Proportions

What You'll Learn

- Determine whether two ratios form a proportion.
- Solve proportions.

Vocabulary

- ratio
- proportion
- extremes
- means
- rate
- scale

How are ratios used in recipes?

The ingredients in the recipe will make 4 servings of honey frozen yogurt. Keri can use ratios and equations to find the amount of each ingredient needed to make enough yogurt for her club meeting.

Honey Frozen Yogurt	
2 cups 2% milk	2 eggs, beaten
$\frac{3}{4}$ cup honey	2 cups plain low-fat
1 dash salt	yogurt
	1 tablespoon vanilla

RATIOS AND PROPORTIONS

A **ratio** is a comparison of two numbers by division. The ratio of x to y can be expressed in the following ways.

$$x \text{ to } y \qquad x{:}y \qquad \frac{x}{y}$$

Ratios are often expressed in simplest form. For example, the recipe above states that for 4 servings you need 2 cups of milk. The ratio of servings to milk may be written as 4 to 2, 4:2, or $\frac{4}{2}$. Written in simplest form, the ratio of servings to milk can be written as 2 to 1, 2:1, or $\frac{2}{1}$.

Suppose you wanted to double the recipe to have 8 servings. The amount of milk required would be 4 cups. The ratio of servings to milk is $\frac{8}{4}$. When this ratio is simplified, the ratio is $\frac{2}{1}$. Notice that this ratio is equal to the original ratio.

> **Study Tip**
>
> *Reading Math*
> A ratio that is equivalent to a whole number is written with a denominator of 1.

$$\overset{\div 2}{\frac{4}{2}} = \frac{2}{1} \underset{\div 2}{} \qquad \overset{\div 4}{\frac{8}{4}} = \frac{2}{1} \underset{\div 4}{}$$

An equation stating that two ratios are equal is called a **proportion**. So, we can state that $\frac{4}{2} = \frac{8}{4}$ is a proportion.

Example 1 Determine Whether Ratios Form a Proportion

Determine whether the ratios $\frac{4}{5}$ and $\frac{24}{30}$ form a proportion.

$$\overset{\div 1}{\frac{4}{5}} = \frac{4}{5} \underset{\div 1}{} \qquad \overset{\div 6}{\frac{24}{30}} = \frac{4}{5} \underset{\div 6}{}$$

The ratios are equal. Therefore, they form a proportion.

---

1 *Focus*

5-Minute Check Transparency 3-6 Use as a quiz or review of Lesson 3-5.

Mathematical Background notes are available for this lesson on p. 118D.

How are ratios used in recipes?

Ask students:

- The recipe is for 4 servings. If you want to double the recipe to make 8 servings, what would you do to the amounts for each ingredient? **Double each amount.**

- What would you do to the amount for each ingredient if you wanted to make enough frozen yogurt for two servings? **Halve the amount of each ingredient.**

- Suppose you want to make enough frozen yogurt for six servings. How much more is six servings than four? **Six is $1\frac{1}{2}$ times as much as four.**

- By what number would you multiply the amount of each ingredient to make six servings? **You would multiply each amount by $1\frac{1}{2}$.**

Resource Manager

Workbook and Reproducible Masters

Chapter 3 Resource Masters
- Study Guide and Intervention, pp. 167–168
- Skills Practice, p. 169
- Practice, p. 170
- Reading to Learn Mathematics, p. 171
- Enrichment, p. 172

Parent and Student Study Guide Workbook, p. 24
Prerequisite Skills Workbook, pp. 27–28, 67–74
School-to-Career Masters, p. 6

 Transparencies
5-Minute Check Transparency 3-6
Answer Key Transparencies

 **Technology**
AlgePASS: Tutorial Plus, Lesson 6
Interactive Chalkboard
Multimedia Applications

RATIOS AND PROPORTIONS

In-Class Examples Power Point®

Teaching Tip Students may notice that two ratios form a proportion when the numerator and denominator of the less simplified ratio are products of the numerator and denominator of the more simplified ratio by the same factor. In Example 1, $\frac{4}{5} \times \frac{6}{6} = \frac{24}{30}$.

 Determine whether the ratios $\frac{7}{8}$ and $\frac{49}{56}$ form a proportion.

The ratios are equal when expressed in simplest form. Therefore, they form a proportion.

2 Use cross products to determine whether each pair of ratios form a proportion.

a. $\frac{0.25}{0.6}, \frac{1.25}{2}$ **not a proportion**

b. $\frac{4}{5}, \frac{16}{20}$ **a proportion**

SOLVE PROPORTIONS

In-Class Example Power Point®

3 Solve the proportion $\frac{n}{12} = \frac{3}{8}$.
4.5

Study Tip

Cross Products
When you find cross products, you are said to be *cross multiplying*.

Another way to determine whether two ratios form a proportion is to use cross products. If the cross products are equal, then the ratios form a proportion.

Example 2 **Use Cross Products**

Use cross products to determine whether each pair of ratios form a proportion.

a. $\frac{0.4}{0.8}, \frac{0.7}{1.4}$

$\frac{0.4}{0.8} \stackrel{?}{=} \frac{0.7}{1.4}$ Write the equation.

$0.4(1.4) \stackrel{?}{=} 0.8(0.7)$ Find the cross products.

$0.56 = 0.56$ Simplify.

The cross products are equal, so $\frac{0.4}{0.8} = \frac{0.7}{1.4}$. Since the ratios are equal, they form a proportion.

b. $\frac{6}{8}, \frac{24}{28}$

$\frac{6}{8} \stackrel{?}{=} \frac{24}{28}$ Write the equation.

$6(28) \stackrel{?}{=} 8(24)$ Find the cross products.

$168 \neq 192$ Simplify.

The cross products are not equal, so $\frac{6}{8} \neq \frac{24}{28}$. The ratios do not form a proportion.

In the proportion $\frac{0.4}{0.8} = \frac{0.7}{1.4}$ above, 0.4 and 1.4 are called the **extremes**, and 0.8 and 0.7 are called the **means**.

Key Concept **Means–Extremes Property of Proportion**

- **Words** In a proportion, the product of the extremes is equal to the product of the means.

- **Symbols** If $\frac{a}{b} = \frac{c}{d}$, then $ad = bc$.

- **Examples** Since $\frac{2}{4} = \frac{1}{2}$, $2(2) = 4(1)$ or $4 = 4$.

SOLVE PROPORTIONS   You can write proportions that involve a variable. To solve the proportion, use cross products and the techniques used to solve other equations.

Example 3 **Solve a Proportion**

Solve the proportion $\frac{n}{15} = \frac{24}{16}$.

$\frac{n}{15} = \frac{24}{16}$ Original equation

$16(n) = 15(24)$ Find the cross products.

$16n = 360$ Simplify.

$\frac{16n}{16} = \frac{360}{16}$ Divide each side by 16.

$n = 22.5$ Simplify.

156   **Chapter 3**   Solving Linear Equations

Tips for New Teachers

ELL Explain to students that the definitions of extremes and means are not arbitrary. In the proportion $\frac{a}{b} = \frac{c}{d}$, a and d are the extremes, and b and c are the means. Remind students that ratios can also be written in the form $x:y$. If you rewrite the proportion above in this form, you have $a:b = c:d$. Looking at this proportion, a and d are the extremes because they are on the outside, and *extreme* is a synonym for outside. Similarly, b and c are the means because they are in the middle, and *mean* is often a synonym for middle.

The ratio of two measurements having different units of measure is called a **rate**. For example, a price of $1.99 per dozen eggs, a speed of 55 miles per hour, and a salary of $30,000 per year are all rates. Proportions are often used to solve problems involving rates.

Example 4 Use Rates

BICYCLING Trent goes on a 30-mile bike ride every Saturday. He rides the distance in 4 hours. At this rate, how far can he ride in 6 hours?

Explore Let m represent the number of miles Trent can ride in 6 hours.

Plan Write a proportion for the problem.

$$\begin{array}{l} \text{miles} \rightarrow \\ \text{hours} \rightarrow \end{array} \quad \frac{30}{4} = \frac{m}{6} \quad \begin{array}{l} \leftarrow \text{miles} \\ \leftarrow \text{hours} \end{array}$$

Solve

$$\frac{30}{4} = \frac{m}{6} \qquad \text{Original proportion}$$

$$30(6) = 4(m) \qquad \text{Find the cross products.}$$

$$180 = 4m \qquad \text{Simplify.}$$

$$\frac{180}{4} = \frac{4m}{4} \qquad \text{Divide each side by 4.}$$

$$45 = m \qquad \text{Simplify.}$$

Examine If Trent rides 30 miles in 4 hours, he rides 7.5 miles in 1 hour. So, in 6 hours, Trent can ride 6×7.5 or 45 miles. The answer is correct.

Since the rates are equal, they form a proportion. So, Trent can ride 45 miles in 6 hours.

A ratio or rate called a **scale** is used when making a model or drawing of something that is too large or too small to be conveniently drawn at actual size. The scale compares the model to the actual size of the object using a proportion. Maps and blueprints are two commonly used scale drawings.

Example 5 Use a Scale Drawing

CRATER LAKE The scale of a map for Crater Lake National Park is 2 inches = 9 miles. The distance between Discovery Point and Phantom Ship Overlook on the map is about $1\frac{3}{4}$ inches. What is the distance between these two places?

Let d represent the actual distance.

$$\begin{array}{l} \text{scale} \rightarrow \\ \text{actual} \rightarrow \end{array} \quad \frac{2}{9} = \frac{1\frac{3}{4}}{d} \quad \begin{array}{l} \leftarrow \text{scale} \\ \leftarrow \text{actual} \end{array}$$

$$2(d) = 9\left(1\frac{3}{4}\right) \qquad \text{Find the cross products.}$$

$$2d = \frac{63}{4} \qquad \text{Simplify.}$$

$$2d \div 2 = \frac{63}{4} \div 2 \qquad \text{Divide each side by 2.}$$

$$d = \frac{63}{8} \text{ or } 7\frac{7}{8} \qquad \text{Simplify.}$$

The actual distance is about $7\frac{7}{8}$ miles.

More About. . .

Crater Lake

Crater Lake is a volcanic crater in Oregon that was formed by an explosion 42 times the blast of Mount St. Helens.

Source: travel.excite.com

www.algebra1.com/extra_examples

4 BICYCLING The gear on a bicycle is 8:5. This means that for every 8 turns of the pedals, the wheel turns 5 times. Suppose the bicycle wheel turns about 2435 times during a trip. How many times would you have to crank the pedals during the trip? **about 3896 times**

5 MAP In a road atlas, the scale for the map of Connecticut is 5 inches = 41 miles. The scale for the map of Texas is 5 inches = 144 miles. What are the distances in miles represented by $2\frac{1}{2}$ inches on each map? **Connecticut $20\frac{1}{2}$ mi; Texas 72 mi**

3 Practice/Apply

Study Notebook

Have students—
- add the definitions/examples of the vocabulary terms to their Vocabulary Builder worksheets for Chapter 3.
- include any other item(s) that they find helpful in mastering the skills in this lesson.

About the Exercises...

Organization by Objective
- **Ratios and Proportions:** 11–18
- **Solve Proportions:** 19–35

Odd/Even Assignments
Exercises 11–34 are structured so that students practice the same concepts whether they are assigned odd or even problems.

Assignment Guide

Basic: 11–23 odd, 31, 33, 36–58
Average: 11–35 odd, 36–58
Advanced: 12–34 even, 36–54 (optional: 55–58)

DAILY
INTERVENTION
Differentiated Instruction

Interpersonal Place students in small groups to work through the Check For Understanding problems. Have a student from each group report on that group's progress, and areas in which the group may need further assistance.

Study Guide and Intervention, p. 167 (shown) and p. 168

Ratios and Proportions A **ratio** is a comparison of two numbers by division. The ratio of x to y can be expressed as x to y, $x:y$ or $\frac{x}{y}$. Ratios are usually expressed in simplest form. An equation stating that two ratios are equal is called a **proportion**. To determine whether two ratios form a proportion, express both ratios in simplest form or check cross products.

Example 1 Determine whether the ratios $\frac{24}{36}$ and $\frac{12}{18}$ form a proportion.

$\frac{24}{36} = \frac{2}{3}$ when expressed in simplest form.

$\frac{12}{18} = \frac{2}{3}$ when expressed in simplest form.

The ratios $\frac{24}{36}$ and $\frac{12}{18}$ form a proportion because they are equal when expressed in simplest form.

Example 2 Use cross products to determine whether $\frac{10}{18}$ and $\frac{25}{45}$ form a proportion.

$\frac{10}{18} \stackrel{?}{=} \frac{25}{45}$ Write the proportion.

$10(45) \stackrel{?}{=} 18(25)$ Cross products

$450 = 450$ Simplify

The cross products are equal, so $\frac{10}{18} = \frac{25}{45}$. Since the ratios are equal, they form a proportion.

Exercises

Use cross products to determine whether each pair of ratios forms a proportion.

1. $\frac{1}{2}, \frac{16}{32}$ yes
2. $\frac{5}{8}, \frac{10}{15}$ no
3. $\frac{10}{20}, \frac{25}{49}$ no
4. $\frac{25}{36}, \frac{15}{20}$ no
5. $\frac{12}{32}, \frac{3}{16}$ no
6. $\frac{4}{9}, \frac{12}{27}$ yes
7. $\frac{0.1}{1}, \frac{5}{100}$ yes
8. $\frac{15}{20}, \frac{9}{12}$ yes
9. $\frac{14}{21}, \frac{20}{30}$ yes
10. $2:3, 20:30$ yes
11. 5 to $9, 25$ to 45 yes
12. $\frac{72}{64}, \frac{9}{8}$ yes
13. $5:5, 30:20$ no
14. 18 to $24, 50$ to 75 no
15. $100:75, 44:33$ yes
16. $\frac{0.05}{1}, \frac{1}{20}$ yes
17. $\frac{1.5}{2}, \frac{6}{8}$ yes
18. $\frac{0.1}{0.2}, \frac{0.45}{0.9}$ yes

Skills Practice, p. 169 and Practice, p. 170 (shown)

Use cross products to determine whether each pair of ratios forms a proportion. Write *yes* or *no.*

1. $\frac{7}{6}, \frac{52}{48}$ no
2. $\frac{3}{11}, \frac{15}{66}$ no
3. $\frac{18}{24}, \frac{36}{48}$ yes
4. $\frac{12}{11}, \frac{108}{99}$ yes
5. $\frac{8}{9}, \frac{72}{81}$ yes
6. $\frac{1.5}{6}, \frac{1}{4}$ yes
7. $\frac{3.4}{5.2}, \frac{7.14}{10.92}$ yes
8. $\frac{1.7}{1.2}, \frac{2.9}{2.4}$ no
9. $\frac{7.6}{1.8}, \frac{3.9}{0.9}$ no

Solve each proportion. If necessary, round to the nearest hundredth.

10. $\frac{5}{a} = \frac{30}{54}$ 9
11. $\frac{v}{46} = \frac{34}{23}$ 68
12. $\frac{40}{56} = \frac{k}{7}$ 5
13. $\frac{28}{49} = \frac{4}{w}$ 7
14. $\frac{3}{u} = \frac{27}{162}$ 18
15. $\frac{y}{3} = \frac{48}{9}$ 16
16. $\frac{2}{y} = \frac{10}{60}$ 12
17. $\frac{5}{11} = \frac{35}{x}$ 77
18. $\frac{3}{51} = \frac{z}{17}$ 1
19. $\frac{6}{61} = \frac{12}{h}$ 122
20. $\frac{g}{16} = \frac{6}{4}$ 24
21. $\frac{14}{49} = \frac{2}{y}$ 7
22. $\frac{7}{9} = \frac{8}{c}$ $10\frac{2}{7}$
23. $\frac{3}{5} = \frac{6}{b}$ $3\frac{3}{5}$
24. $\frac{m}{6} = \frac{6}{8}$ $3\frac{3}{4}$
25. $\frac{v}{0.23} = \frac{7}{1.61}$ 1
26. $\frac{3}{0.72} = \frac{12}{1.61}$ 2.88
27. $\frac{6}{8} = \frac{3}{0.51}$ 1.02
28. $\frac{7}{a-4} = \frac{14}{8}$ 7
29. $\frac{3}{12} = \frac{2}{y+6}$ 2
30. $\frac{m-1}{8} = \frac{4}{5}$ 5
31. $\frac{5}{12} = \frac{x+1}{4} \cdot \frac{2}{3}$
32. $\frac{r+2}{7} = \frac{5}{7} \cdot 3$
33. $\frac{3}{7} = \frac{x-2}{6} \cdot 4\frac{4}{7}$

34. **PAINTING** Ysidra paints a room that has 400 square feet of wall space in $2\frac{1}{2}$ hours. At this rate, how long will it take her to paint a room that has 720 square feet of wall space? $4\frac{1}{2}$ h

35. **VACATION PLANS** Walker is planning a summer vacation. He wants to visit Petrified National Forest and Meteor Crater, Arizona, the 50,000-year-old impact site of a large meteor. On a map with a scale where 2 inches equals 75 miles, the two areas are about $1\frac{1}{2}$ inches apart. What is the distance between Petrified National Forest and Meteor Crater? about 56.25 mi

Reading to Learn Mathematics, p. 171   ELL

Pre-Activity How are ratios used in recipes?

Read the introduction to Lesson 3-6 at the top of page 155 in your textbook.

• How many servings of honey frozen yogurt are made by this recipe? 4 servings

• How many recipes would be needed to make enough honey frozen yogurt for all the students in your class? See students' work.

Reading the Lesson

1. Complete the following sentence.

A ratio is a comparison of two numbers by _division_.

2. Describe two ways to decide whether the sentence $\frac{2}{5} = \frac{8}{20}$ is a proportion.

Express the ratios in simplest form to see if they are equal. Check to see whether the cross products are equal.

3. For each proportion, tell what the extremes are and what the means are.

a. $\frac{14}{35} = \frac{6}{15}$ Extremes: ___14 and 15___   Means: ___35 and 6___

b. $\frac{6}{8} = \frac{12}{16}$ Extremes: ___6 and 16___   Means: ___8 and 12___

4. A jet flying at a steady speed traveled 825 miles in 2 hours. If you solved the proportion $\frac{825}{2} = \frac{x}{1.5}$, what would the answer tell you about the jet?

how far the jet traveled in 1.5 h

Helping You Remember

5. Write how you would explain solving a proportion to a friend who missed Lesson 3-6.

Use cross products. Write an equation with the product of the extremes on the left side and the product of the means on the right side. Then solve this second equation.

Check for Understanding

Concept Check

1. See students' work.

2–3. See margin.

1. **OPEN ENDED** Find an example of ratios used in advertisements.

2. **Explain** the difference between a ratio and a proportion.

3. **Describe** how to solve a proportion if one of the ratios contains a variable.

Guided Practice

GUIDED PRACTICE KEY	
Exercises	Examples
4–6	1, 2
7–9	3
10	4, 5

Use cross products to determine whether each pair of ratios form a proportion. Write *yes* or *no.*

4. $\frac{4}{11}, \frac{12}{33}$ yes
5. $\frac{16}{17}, \frac{8}{9}$ no
6. $\frac{2.1}{3.5}, \frac{0.5}{0.7}$ no

Solve each proportion. If necessary, round to the nearest hundredth.

7. $\frac{3}{4} = \frac{6}{x}$ 8
8. $\frac{a}{45} = \frac{5}{15}$ 15
9. $\frac{0.6}{1.1} = \frac{n}{8.47}$ 4.62

Application

10. **TRAVEL** The Lehmans' minivan requires 5 gallons of gasoline to travel 120 miles. How much gasoline will they need for a 350-mile trip? about 14.6 gal

★ indicates increased difficulty

Practice and Apply

Homework Help	
For Exercises	See Examples
11–18	1, 2
19–30	3
31, 32	4
33, 34	5

Extra Practice
See page 827.

Use cross products to determine whether each pair of ratios form a proportion. Write *yes* or *no.*

11. $\frac{3}{2}, \frac{21}{14}$ yes
12. $\frac{8}{9}, \frac{12}{18}$ no
13. $\frac{2.3}{3.4}, \frac{3.0}{3.6}$ no
14. $\frac{4.2}{5.6}, \frac{1.68}{2.24}$ yes
15. $\frac{21.1}{14.4}, \frac{1.1}{1.2}$ no
16. $\frac{5}{2}, \frac{4}{1.6}$ yes

SPORTS For Exercises 17 and 18, use the graph at the right.

17. Write a ratio of the number of gold medals won to the total number of medals won for each country.

17. USA: $\frac{871}{2116}$;

USSR/Russia: $\frac{498}{1278}$;

Germany: $\frac{374}{1182}$;

GB: $\frac{180}{638}$; France: $\frac{188}{598}$;

Italy: $\frac{179}{479}$;

Sweden: $\frac{136}{469}$

18. Do any two of the ratios you wrote for Exercise 17 form a proportion? If so, explain the real-world meaning of the proportion. No; if two of these ratios formed a proportion, the two countries would have the same part of their medals as gold medals.

USA TODAY Snapshots®

USA stands atop all-time medals table

The USA, which led the 2000 Summer Olympics with 97 medals, has dominated the medal standings over the years. The all-time Summer Olympics medal standings:

	Gold	Silver	Bronze	Total
USA	**871**	**659**	**586**	**2,116**
USSR/Russia[1]	498	409	371	1,278
Germany[2]	374	392	416	1,182
Great Britain	180	233	225	638
France	188	193	217	598
Italy	179	143	157	479
Sweden	136	156	177	469

1 – Competed as the Unified Team in 1992 after the breakup of the Soviet Union
2 – Totals include medals won by both East and West Germany.
Source: The Ultimate Book of Sports Lists

By Ellen J. Horrow and Marcy E. Mullins, USA TODAY

Solve each proportion. If necessary, round to the nearest hundredth.

19. $\frac{4}{x} = \frac{2}{10}$ 20
20. $\frac{1}{y} = \frac{3}{15}$ 5
21. $\frac{6}{5} = \frac{x}{15}$ 18
22. $\frac{20}{28} = \frac{n}{21}$ 15
23. $\frac{6}{8} = \frac{7}{a}$ $9\frac{1}{3}$
24. $\frac{16}{7} = \frac{9}{b}$ $3\frac{15}{16}$
★ 25. $\frac{1}{0.19} = \frac{12}{n}$ 2.28
26. $\frac{2}{0.21} = \frac{8}{n}$ 0.84
27. $\frac{2.405}{3.67} = \frac{s}{1.88}$ 1.23
★ 28. $\frac{7}{1.066} = \frac{z}{9.65}$ 63.37
29. $\frac{6}{14} = \frac{7}{x-3}$ $19\frac{1}{3}$
30. $\frac{5}{3} = \frac{6}{x+2}$ $1\frac{3}{5}$

Enrichment, p. 172

Angles of a Triangle

In geometry, many statements about physical space are proven to be true. Such statements are called **theorems**. Here are two examples of geometric theorems.

a. The sum of the measures of the angles of a triangle is 180°.

b. If two sides of a triangle have equal measure, then the two angles opposite those sides also have equal measure.

For each of the triangles, write an equation and then solve for x. (A tick mark on two or more sides of a triangle indicates that the sides have equal measure.)

1. $x = 60°$
2. $x = 45°$
3. $x = 45°$
4. $x = 20°$

31. WORK Seth earns $152 in 4 days. At that rate, how many days will it take him to earn $532? **14 days**

32. DRIVING Lanette drove 248 miles in 4 hours. At that rate, how long will it take her to drive an additional 93 miles? $1\frac{1}{2}$ **h**

33. BLUEPRINTS A blueprint for a house states that 2.5 inches equals 10 feet. If the length of a wall is 12 feet, how long is the wall in the blueprint? **3 in.**

34. MODELS A collector's model racecar is scaled so that 1 inch on the model equals $6\frac{1}{4}$ feet on the actual car. If the model is $\frac{2}{3}$ inch high, how high is the actual car? $4\frac{1}{6}$ **ft**

★ **35. PETS** A research study shows that three out of every twenty pet owners got their pet from a breeder. Of the 122 animals cared for by a veterinarian, how many would you expect to have been bought from a breeder? **18**

36. CRITICAL THINKING Consider the proportion $a:b:c = 3:1:5$. What is the value of $\frac{2a + 3b}{4b + 3c}$? (*Hint:* Choose different values of a, b, and c for which the proportion is true and evaluate the expression.) $\frac{9}{19}$

37. WRITING IN MATH Answer the question that was posed at the beginning of the lesson. **See margin.**

How are ratios used in recipes?

Include the following in your answer:
- an explanation of how to use a proportion to determine how much honey is needed if you use 3 eggs, and
- a description of how to alter the recipe to get 5 servings.

Standardized Test Practice
Ⓐ Ⓑ Ⓒ Ⓓ

38. Which ratio is *not* equal to $\frac{9}{12}$? **D**

Ⓐ $\frac{18}{24}$ Ⓑ $\frac{3}{4}$ Ⓒ $\frac{15}{20}$ Ⓓ $\frac{18}{27}$

39. In the figure at the right, $x:y = 2:3$ and $y:z = 3:5$. If $x = 10$, find the value of z. **C**

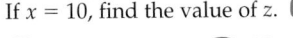

Ⓐ 15   Ⓑ 20   Ⓒ 25   Ⓓ 30

Maintain Your Skills

Mixed Review
41. no solution

Solve each equation. Then check your solution. *(Lessons 3-4 and 3-5)*

40. $8y - 10 = -3y + 2$ $1\frac{1}{11}$ **41.** $17 + 2n = 21 + 2n$ **42.** $-7(d - 3) = -4$ $3\frac{4}{7}$

43. $5 - 9w = 23$ -2 **44.** $\frac{m}{-5} + 6 = 31$ -125 **45.** $\frac{z - 7}{5} = -3$ -8

Find each product. *(Lesson 2-3)*

46. $(-7)(-6)$ **42**   **47.** $\left(-\frac{8}{9}\right)\left(\frac{9}{8}\right)$ -1 **48.** $\left(\frac{3}{7}\right)\left(\frac{3}{7}\right)$ $\frac{9}{49}$ **49.** $(-0.075)(-5.5)$ **0.4125**

Find each absolute value. *(Lesson 2-1)*

50. $|-33|$ **33**   **51.** $|77|$ **77**   **52.** $|2.5|$ **2.5**   **53.** $|-0.85|$ **0.85**

54. Sketch a reasonable graph for the temperature in the following statement. *In August, you enter a hot house and turn on the air conditioner.* *(Lesson 1-8)* **See margin.**

Getting Ready for the Next Lesson

PREREQUISITE SKILL Find each percent. *(To review percents, see pages 802 and 803.)*

55. Eighteen is what percent of 60? **30%**   **56.** What percent of 14 is 4.34? **31%**

57. Six is what percent of 15? **40%**   **58.** What percent of 2 is 8? **400%**

www.algebra1.com/self_check_quiz   **Lesson 3-6** Ratios and Proportions   **159**

Open-Ended Assessment

Modeling Give students coins, paper clips, or other manipulatives and have them model a simple proportion such as $\frac{2}{3} = \frac{6}{9}$.

Getting Ready for Lesson 3-7

PREREQUISITE SKILL Students will learn about percent of change in Lesson 3-7. Students use a proportion to find percent of change but need to understand how to find percents in order to set the proportion up correctly. Use Exercises 55–58 to determine your students' familiarity with finding percents.

Answers

2. A ratio is a comparison of two numbers and a proportion is an equation of two equal ratios.

3. Find the cross products and divide by the value with the variable.

37. Sample answer: Ratios are used to determine how much of each ingredient to use for a given number of servings. Answers should include the following.

- To determine how much honey is needed if you use 3 eggs, write and solve the proportion $2:\frac{3}{4} = 3:h$, where h is the amount of honey.

- To alter the recipe to get 5 servings, multiply each amount by $1\frac{1}{4}$.

54.

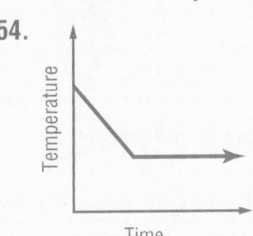

---

1 Focus

5-Minute Check Transparency 3-7 Use as a quiz or review of Lesson 3-6.

Mathematical Background notes are available for this lesson on p. 118D.

How can percents describe growth over time?

Ask students:

• What do the numbers 84, 171, and 285 represent on the graph? **The number 84 represents the number of area codes in 1947, 171 was the number of area codes in 1996, and 285 was the number of area codes in 1999.**

• Are these numbers percents? Why do you think so? **No, these numbers are not percents because they are not followed by the percent sign.**

• Do you think 171 is at least 100% more than 84? Explain your reasoning. **100% of 84 is 84. So, 84 + 84 is 168. Since 171 is greater than 168, then 171 must be at least 100% more than 84.**

What You'll Learn

• Find percents of increase and decrease.
• Solve problems involving percents of change.

Vocabulary
• percent of change
• percent of increase
• percent of decrease

How can percents describe growth over time?

Phone companies began using area codes in 1947. The graph shows the number of area codes in use in different years. The growth in the number of area codes can be described by using a percent of change.

Area codes on the rise
285
171
84
1947 1996 1999

Source: Associated Press

Study Tip

Look Back
To review the **percent proportion**, see page 802.

PERCENT OF CHANGE When an increase or decrease is expressed as a percent, the percent is called the **percent of change**. If the new number is greater than the original number, the percent of change is a **percent of increase**. If the new number is less than the original, the percent of change is a **percent of decrease**.

Example 1 Find Percent of Change

State whether each percent of change is a percent of increase or a percent of decrease. Then find each percent of change.

a. original: 25
new: 28

Find the *amount* of change. Since the new amount is greater than the original, the percent of change is a percent of increase.

$$28 - 25 = 3$$

Find the percent using the original number, 25, as the base.

$$\text{change} \rightarrow \frac{3}{25} = \frac{r}{100} \leftarrow \text{original amount}$$
$$3(100) = 25(r)$$
$$300 = 25r$$
$$\frac{300}{25} = \frac{25r}{25}$$
$$12 = r$$

The percent of increase is 12%.

b. original: 30
new: 12

The percent of change is a percent of decrease because the new amount is less than the original. Find the change.

$$30 - 12 = 18$$

Find the percent using the original number, 30, as the base.

$$\text{change} \rightarrow \frac{18}{30} = \frac{r}{100} \leftarrow \text{original amount}$$
$$18(100) = 30(r)$$
$$1800 = 30r$$
$$\frac{1800}{30} = \frac{30r}{30}$$
$$60 = r$$

The percent of decrease is 60%.

Resource Manager

 Workbook and Reproducible Masters

Chapter 3 Resource Masters
• Study Guide and Intervention, pp. 173–174
• Skills Practice, p. 175
• Practice, p. 176
• Reading to Learn Mathematics, p. 177
• Enrichment, p. 178
• Assessment, p. 206

Graphing Calculator and Spreadsheet Masters, p. 28
Parent and Student Study Guide Workbook, p. 25
Prerequisite Skills Workbook,
pp. 17–18, 41–44, 71–72, 77–78

Transparencies
5-Minute Check Transparency 3-7
Real-World Transparency 3
Answer Key Transparencies

Technology
Interactive Chalkboard

More About...

Football •.................

On November 12, 1892, the Allegheny Athletic Association paid William "Pudge" Heffelfinger $500 to play football. This game is considered the start of professional football.

Source: *World Book Encyclopedia*

Example 2 *Find the Missing Value*

• **FOOTBALL** The National Football League's (NFL) fields are 120 yards long. The Canadian Football League's (CFL) fields are 25% longer. What is the length of a CFL field?

Let ℓ = the length of a CFL field. Since 25% is a percent of increase, an NFL field is shorter than a CFL field. Therefore, $\ell - 120$ represents the amount of change.

$$\begin{array}{ll} \text{change} \rightarrow \dfrac{\ell - 120}{120} = \dfrac{25}{100} & \text{Percent proportion} \\[2mm] (\ell - 120)(100) = 120(25) & \text{Find the cross products.} \\[2mm] 100\ell - 12{,}000 = 3000 & \text{Distributive Property} \\[2mm] 100\ell - 12{,}000 + 12{,}000 = 3000 + 12{,}000 & \text{Add 12,000 to each side.} \\[2mm] 100\ell = 15{,}000 & \text{Simplify.} \\[2mm] \dfrac{100\ell}{100} = \dfrac{15{,}000}{100} & \text{Divide each side by 100.} \\[2mm] \ell = 150 & \text{Simplify.} \end{array}$$

The length of the field used by the CFL is 150 yards.

SOLVE PROBLEMS Two applications of percent of change are sales tax and discounts. Sales tax is a tax that is added to the cost of the item. It is an example of a percent of increase. Discount is the amount by which the regular price of an item is reduced. It is an example of a percent of decrease.

Example 3 *Find Amount After Sales Tax*

SALES TAX A concert ticket costs $45. If the sales tax is 6.25%, what is the total price of the ticket?

The tax is 6.25% of the price of the ticket.

6.25% of $\$45 = 0.0625 \times 45$ 6.25% = 0.0625

$\qquad\qquad\qquad = 2.8125$ Use a calculator.

Round $2.8125 to $2.81. Add this amount to the original price.

$\$45.00 + \$2.81 = \$47.81$

The total price of the ticket is $47.81.

Example 4 *Find Amount After Discount*

DISCOUNT A sweater is on sale for 35% off the original price. If the original price of the sweater is $38, what is the discounted price?

The discount is 35% of the original price.

35% of $\$38 = 0.35 \times 38$ 35% = 0.35

$\qquad\qquad\qquad = 13.30$ Use a calculator.

Subtract $13.30 from the original price.

$\$38.00 - \$13.30 = \$24.70$

The discounted price of the sweater is $24.70.

 www.algebra1.com/extra_examples

Lesson 3-7   Percent of Change   **161**

---

2 Teach

PERCENT OF CHANGE

In-Class Examples Power Point®

1 State whether each percent of change is a percent of increase or a percent of decrease. Then find each percent of change.

a. original: 32
   new: 40
   percent of increase; 25%

b. original: 20
   new: 4
   percent of decrease; 80%

2 **SALES** The price a used-book store pays to buy a book is $5. The store sells the book for 28% above the price that it pays for the book. What is the selling price of the $5 book? **$6.40**

SOLVE PROBLEMS

In-Class Examples Power Point®

3 **SALES TAX** A meal for two at a restaurant costs $32.75. If the sales tax is 5%, what is the total price of the meal? **$34.39**

4 **DISCOUNT** A dog toy is on sale for 20% off the original price. If the original price of the toy is $3.80, what is the discounted price? **$3.04**

D A I L Y
INTERVENTION   **Differentiated Instruction**

Naturalist Have students make a list of three items for which they know the exact price. The items can be gifts they want to buy for themselves or everyday household items. Then have students calculate the price of each item if each price were discounted 15%.

Study Notebook

Have students—
• add the definitions/examples of the vocabulary terms to their Vocabulary Builder worksheets for Chapter 3.
• include any other item(s) that they find helpful in mastering the skills in this lesson.

D A I L Y
INTERVENTION **FIND THE ERROR**
The only difference between Laura's and Cory's work is the number in the denominator of the first ratio in the proportion. Laura has put 20, which is the original number in the problem, and Cory has put 30, which is the new number in the problem. Suggest that students review Examples 1 and 2 to help them find the error. Then remind them that the ratio to use is the amount of change to the original amount.

About the Exercises...

Organization by Objective
Percent of Change: 14–30, 46–48
Solve Problems: 31–45

Odd/Even Assignments
Exercises 14–29 and 31–44 are structured so that students practice the same concepts whether they are assigned odd or even problems.

Alert! Exercise 48 involves the use of the Internet or other reference materials.

Assignment Guide

Basic: 15–27 odd, 31–41 odd, 49–71
Average: 15–45 odd, 46, 47, 49–71
Advanced: 14–42 even, 43–65 (optional: 66–71)
All: Practice Quiz 2 (1–10)

Check for Understanding

Concept Check

1. Percent of increase and percent of decrease are both percents of change. If the new number is greater than the original number, the percent of change is a percent of increase. If the new number is less than the original number, the percent of change is a percent of decrease.

1. **Compare and contrast** percent of increase and percent of decrease.

2. **OPEN ENDED** Give a counterexample to the statement *The percent of change must always be less than 100%*. **See margin.**

3. **FIND THE ERROR** Laura and Cory are writing proportions to find the percent of change if the original number is 20 and the new number is 30.

Laura	Cory
Amount of change: $30 - 20 = 10$	Amount of change: $30 - 20 = 10$
$\dfrac{10}{20} = \dfrac{r}{100}$	$\dfrac{10}{30} = \dfrac{r}{100}$

Who is correct? Explain your reasoning. **Laura; Cory used the new number as the base instead of the original number.**

Guided Practice

GUIDED PRACTICE KEY	
Exercises	Examples
4–7, 12, 13	1
8, 9	3
10, 11	4

State whether each percent of change is a percent of increase or a percent of decrease. Then find each percent of change. Round to the nearest whole percent.

4. original: 72
   new: 36 **decrease; 50%**

5. original: 45
   new: 50 **increase; 11%**

6. original: 14
   new: 16 **increase; 14%**

7. original: 150
   new: 120 **decrease; 20%**

Find the total price of each item.

8. software: $39.50
   sales tax: 6.5% **$42.07**

9. compact disc: $15.99
   sales tax: 5.75% **$16.91**

Find the discounted price of each item.

10. jeans: $45.00
    discount: 25% **$33.75**

11. book: $19.95
    discount: 33% **$13.37**

Application

EDUCATION For Exercises 12 and 13, use the following information.
According to the Census Bureau, the average income of a person with a bachelor's degree is $40,478. For a person with a high school diploma, it is $22,895.

12. Write an equation that could be used to find the percent of increase from the average income for a person with a high school diploma to the average income for a person with a bachelor's degree. $\dfrac{40{,}478 - 22{,}895}{22{,}895} = \dfrac{x}{100}$

13. What is the percent of increase? **about 77%**

★ indicates increased difficulty

Practice and Apply

Homework Help	
For Exercises	See Examples
14–27	1
28–30, 46, 47	2
31–36	3
37–42	4
43–45	3, 4

Extra Practice
See page 827.

State whether each percent of change is a percent of increase or a percent of decrease. Then find each percent of change. Round to the nearest whole percent.

14. original: 50
    new: 70 **inc.; 40%**

15. original: 25
    new: 18 **dec.; 28%**

16. original: 66
    new: 30 **dec.; 55%**

17. original: 58
    new: 152 **inc.; 162%**

18. original: 13.7
    new: 40.2 **inc.; 193%**

19. original: 15.6
    new: 11.4 **dec.; 27%**

20. original: 132
    new: 150 **inc.; 14%**

21. original: 85
    new: 90 **inc.; 6%**

22. original: 32.5
    new: 30 **dec.; 8%**

23. original: 9.8
    new: 12.1 **inc.; 23%**

24. original: 40
    new: 32.5 **dec.; 19%**

25. original: 25
    new: 21.5 **dec.; 14%**

Answers

2. Sample answer: If the original number is 10 and the new number is 30, the percent proportion is $\dfrac{30 - 10}{10} = \dfrac{r}{100}$ and the percent of change is 200%, which is greater than 100%.

49. $x\%$ of $y \Rightarrow \dfrac{x}{100} = \dfrac{P}{y}$ or $P = \dfrac{xy}{100}$

$y\%$ of $x \Rightarrow \dfrac{y}{100} = \dfrac{P}{x}$ or $P = \dfrac{xy}{100}$

26. **THEME PARKS** In 1990, 253 million people visited theme parks in the United States. In 2000, the number of visitors increased to 317 million people. What was the percent of increase? **about 25%**

27. **MILITARY** In 1987, the United States had 2 million active-duty military personnel. By 2000, there were only 1.4 million active-duty military personnel. What was the percent of decrease? **30%**

★ 28. The percent of increase is 16%. If the new number is 522, find the original number. **450**

★ 29. **FOOD** In order for a food to be marked "reduced fat," it must have at least 25% less fat than the same full-fat food. If one ounce of reduced fat chips has 6 grams of fat, what is the least amount of fat in one ounce of regular chips? **8 g**

★ 30. **TECHNOLOGY** From January, 1996, to January, 2001, the number of internet hosts increased by 1054%. There were 109.6 million internet hosts in January, 2001. Find the number of internet hosts in January, 1996.
about 9.5 million internet hosts

Find the total price of each item.

31. umbrella: $14.00
tax: 5.5% **$14.77**

32. backpack: $35.00
tax: 7% **$37.45**

33. candle: $7.50
tax: 5.75% **$7.93**

34. hat: $18.50
tax: 6.25% **$19.66**

35. clock radio: $39.99
tax: 6.75% **$42.69**

36. sandals: $29.99
tax: 5.75% **$31.71**

Find the discounted price of each item.

37. shirt: $45.00
discount: 40% **$27.00**

38. socks: $6.00
discount: 20% **$4.80**

39. watch: $37.55
discount: 35% **$24.41**

40. gloves: $24.25
discount: 33% **$16.25**

41. suit: $175.95
discount: 45% **$96.77**

42. coat: $79.99
discount: 30% **$55.99**

Find the final price of each item.

★ 43. lamp: $120.00
discount: 20%
tax: 6% **$101.76**

★ 44. dress: $70.00
discount: 30%
tax: 7% **$52.43**

★ 45. camera: $58.00
discount: 25%
tax: 6.5% **$46.33**

POPULATION For Exercises 46 and 47, use the following table.

Country	1997 Population (billions)	Projected Percent of Increase for 2050
China	1.24	22.6%
India	0.97	57.8%
United States	0.27	44.4%

Source: *USA TODAY*

46. What are the projected 2050 populations for each country in the table?

★ 47. Which of these three countries is projected to be the most populous in 2050? **India**

48. **RESEARCH** Use the Internet or other reference to find the tuition for the last several years at a college of your choice. Find the percent of change for the tuition during these years. Predict the tuition for the year you plan to graduate from high school. **See students' work.**

49. **CRITICAL THINKING** Are the following expressions *sometimes*, *always*, or *never* equal? Explain your reasoning. **Always; see margin for explanation.**

$$x\% \text{ of } y \qquad\qquad y\% \text{ of } x$$

Career Choices

Military •••••••••••••••

A military career can involve many different duties like working in a hospital, programming computers, or repairing helicopters. The military provides training and work in these fields and others for the Army, Navy, Marine Corps, Air Force, Coast Guard, and the Air and Army National Guard.

Online Research
For information about a career in the military, visit: www.algebra1.com/careers

46. China: about 1.52 billion people; India: about 1.53 billion people; United States: about 0.39 billion people

Speaking Give students pairs of numbers. Tell which number is the original. Have students determine whether the percent of increase or the percent of decrease is needed to find the other number.

Getting Ready for Lesson 3-8

PREREQUISITE SKILL Students will solve equations and formulas for a given variable in Lesson 3–8. This requires algebraic manipulation, which they used in solving equations in one variable. Use Exercises 66–71 to determine your students' familiarity with solving equations.

Assessment Options

Practice Quiz 2 The quiz provides students with a brief review of the concepts and skills in Lessons 3-4 through 3-7. Lesson numbers are given to the right of exercises or instruction lines so students can review concepts not yet mastered.

Quiz (Lessons 3-6 and 3-7) is available on p. 206 of the *Chapter 3 Resource Masters.*

Answer

50. Find the amount of change and express this change as a percent of the original number. Answers should include the following.
   - To find the percent of increase, first find the amount of increase. Then find what percent the amount of increase is of the original number.
   - The percent of increase from 1996 to 1999 is about 67%.
   - An increase of 100 is a very large increase if the original number is 50, but a very small increase if the original number is 100,000. The percent of change will indicate whether the change is large or small relative to the original.

---

50. **WRITING IN MATH** Answer the question that was posed at the beginning of the lesson. **See margin.**

How can percents describe growth over time?

Include the following in your answer:
- the percent of increase in the number of area codes from 1996 to 1999, and
- an explanation of why knowing a percent of change can be more informative than knowing how much the quantity changed.

Standardized Test Practice
Ⓐ Ⓑ Ⓒ Ⓓ

51. The number of students at Franklin High School increased from 840 to 910 over a 5-year period. Which proportion represents the percent of change? **B**

Ⓐ $\frac{70}{910} = \frac{r}{100}$ Ⓑ $\frac{70}{840} = \frac{r}{100}$ Ⓒ $\frac{r}{910} = \frac{70}{100}$ Ⓓ $\frac{r}{840} = \frac{70}{100}$

52. The list price of a television is $249.00. If it is on sale for 30% off the list price, what is the sale price of the television? **C**

Ⓐ $74.70 Ⓑ $149.40 Ⓒ $174.30 Ⓓ $219.00

Maintain Your Skills

Mixed Review **Solve each proportion.** *(Lesson 3-6)*

53. $\frac{a}{45} = \frac{3}{15}$ **9**
54. $\frac{2}{3} = \frac{8}{d}$ **12**
55. $\frac{5.22}{13.92} = \frac{t}{48}$ **18**

Solve each equation. Then check your solution. *(Lesson 3-5)*

56. $6n + 3 = -3$ **−1**
57. $7 + 5c = -23$ **−6**
58. $18 = 4a - 2$ **5**

Find each quotient. *(Lesson 2-4)*

59. $\frac{2}{5} \div 4$ **$\frac{1}{10}$**
60. $-\frac{4}{5} \div \frac{2}{3}$ **$-1\frac{1}{5}$**
61. $-\frac{1}{9} \div \left(-\frac{3}{4}\right)$ **$\frac{4}{27}$**

State whether each equation is *true* or *false* for the value of the variable given. *(Lesson 1-3)*

62. $a^2 + 5 = 17 - a, a = 3$ **true**
63. $2v^2 + v = 65, v = 5$ **false**
64. $8y - y^2 = y + 10, y = 4$ **false**
65. $16p - p = 15p, p = 2.5$ **true**

Getting Ready for the Next Lesson **PREREQUISITE SKILL** Solve each equation. Then check your solution.
*(To review **solving equations**, see Lesson 3-5.)*

66. $-43 - 3t = 2 - 6t$ **15**
67. $7y + 7 = 3y - 5$ **−3**
68. $7(d - 3) - 2 = 5$ **4**
69. $6(p + 3) = 4(p - 1)$ **−11**
70. $-5 = 4 - 2(a - 5)$ **9.5**
71. $8x - 4 = -10x + 50$ **3**

Practice Quiz 2 *Lessons 3-4 through 3-7*

Solve each equation. Then check your solution. *(Lessons 3-4 and 3-5)*

1. $-3x - 7 = 18$ **$-8\frac{1}{3}$**
2. $5 = \frac{m-5}{4}$ **25**
3. $4h + 5 = 11$ **1.5**
4. $5d - 6 = 3d + 9$ **7.5**
5. $7 + 2(w + 1) = 2w + 9$ **all numbers**
6. $-8(4 + 9r) = 7(-2 - 11r)$ **3.6**

Solve each proportion. *(Lesson 3-6)*

7. $\frac{2}{10} = \frac{1}{a}$ **5**
8. $\frac{3}{5} = \frac{24}{x}$ **40**
9. $\frac{y}{4} = \frac{y+5}{8}$ **5**

10. **POSTAGE** In 1975, the cost of a first-class stamp was 10¢. In 2001, the cost of a first-class stamp became 34¢. What is the percent of increase in the price of a stamp? *(Lesson 3-7)* **240%**

Teacher to Teacher

Barbara Szymczak Bayonne H.S., Bayonne, NJ

"When teaching percents, I have students cut out sales advertisements and make posters showing savings. They also cut out car ads to compute interest they would pay and compare companies for the best deals."

Reading Mathematics

Sentence Method and Proportion Method

Recall that you can solve percent problems using two different methods. With either method, it is helpful to use "clue" words such as *is* and *of*. In the sentence method, *is* means equals and *of* means multiply. With the proportion method, the "clue" words indicate where to place the numbers in the proportion.

Sentence Method

15% of 40 is what number?

$0.15 \cdot 40 = ?$

Proportion Method

15% of 40 is what number?

$$\frac{\text{(is) } P}{\text{(of) } B} = \frac{R(\text{percent})}{100} \rightarrow \frac{P}{40} = \frac{15}{100}$$

You can use the proportion method to solve percent of change problems. In this case, use the proportion $\frac{\text{difference}}{\text{original}} = \frac{\%}{100}$. When reading a percent of change problem, or any other word problem, look for the important numerical information.

Example In chemistry class, Kishi heated 20 milliliters of water. She let the water boil for 10 minutes. Afterward, only <u>17 milliliters of water remained</u>, due to evaporation. What is the <u>percent of decrease</u> in the amount of water?

$$\frac{\text{difference}}{\text{original}} = \frac{\%}{100} \rightarrow \frac{20-17}{20} = \frac{r}{100} \quad \text{Percent proportion}$$

$$\frac{3}{20} = \frac{r}{100} \qquad \text{Simplify.}$$

$$3(100) = 20(r) \qquad \text{Find the cross products.}$$

$$300 = 20r \qquad \text{Simplify.}$$

$$\frac{300}{20} = \frac{20r}{20} \qquad \text{Divide each side by 20.}$$

$$15 = r \qquad \text{Simplify.}$$

There was a 15% decrease in the amount of water.

1–3. See margin for original number, amount of change, and percent proportion.

Reading to Learn

Give the original number and the amount of change. Then write and solve a percent proportion.

1. Monsa needed to lose weight for wrestling. At the start of the season, he weighed 166 pounds. By the end of the season, he weighed 158 pounds. What is the percent of decrease in Monsa's weight? **about 5%**

2. On Carla's last Algebra test, she scored 94 points out of 100. On her first Algebra test, she scored 75 points out of 100. What is the percent of increase in her score? **about 25%**

3. In a catalog distribution center, workers processed an average of 12 orders per hour. After a reward incentive was offered, workers averaged 18 orders per hour. What is the percent of increase in production? **50%**

Answers

1. original number: 166 lb; amount of change: 166 − 158 or 8 lb; $\frac{8}{166} = \frac{r}{100}$

2. original number: 75 points; amount of change: 94 − 75 or 19 points; $\frac{19}{75} = \frac{r}{100}$

3. original number: 12 orders; amount of change: 18 − 12 or 6 orders; $\frac{6}{12} = \frac{r}{100}$

3-8 **Solving Equations and Formulas**

1 Focus

5-Minute Check Transparency 3-8 Use as a quiz or review of Lesson 3-7.

Mathematical Background notes are available for this lesson on p. 118D.

How are equations used to design roller coasters?

Ask students:

• What are the known quantities in the roller coaster equation? *g* is the acceleration due to gravity, and *v* is the velocity of the roller coaster at the top of the second hill

• What is the unknown quantity in the roller coaster equation? *h*, the height of the second hill

• Can Ron Toomer's problem about the height of the second hill be solved with the given information? Explain why or why not. Yes, the problem can be solved because the values for *g* and *v* are given.

Solving Equations and Formulas

What You'll Learn

• Solve equations for given variables.
• Use formulas to solve real-world problems.

Vocabulary
• dimensional analysis

How are equations used to design roller coasters?

Ron Toomer designed the Magnum XL-200. This roller coaster starts with a vertical drop of 195 feet and then ascends a second shorter hill.

Suppose when designing this coaster, Mr. Toomer decided he wanted to adjust the height of the second hill so that the coaster would have a speed of 49 feet per second when it reached its top.

If we ignore friction, the equation $g(195 - h) = \frac{1}{2}v^2$ can be used to find the height of the second hill. In this equation, g represents the acceleration due to gravity (32 feet per second squared), h is the height of the second hill, and v is the velocity of the coaster when it reaches the top of the second hill.

195 ft   49 ft/s   h

SOLVE FOR VARIABLES Some equations such as the one above contain more than one variable. At times, you will need to solve these equations for one of the variables.

Example 1 Solve an Equation for a Specific Variable

Solve $3x - 4y = 7$ for y.

$3x - 4y = 7$	Original equation
$3x - 4y - 3x = 7 - 3x$	Subtract $3x$ from each side.
$-4y = 7 - 3x$	Simplify.
$\dfrac{-4y}{-4} = \dfrac{7 - 3x}{-4}$	Divide each side by -4.
$y = \dfrac{7 - 3x}{-4}$ or $\dfrac{3x - 7}{4}$	Simplify.

The value of y is $\dfrac{3x - 7}{4}$.

It is sometimes helpful to use the Distributive Property to isolate the variable for which you are solving an equation or formula.

Resource Manager

 Workbook and Reproducible Masters

Chapter 3 Resource Masters
• Study Guide and Intervention, pp. 179–180
• Skills Practice, p. 181
• Practice, p. 182
• Reading to Learn Mathematics, p. 183
• Enrichment, p. 184

Parent and Student Study Guide Workbook, p. 26
Prerequisite Skills Workbook, pp. 81–82

Transparencies
5-Minute Check Transparency 3-8
Answer Key Transparencies

Technology
AlgePASS: Tutorial Plus, Lessons 7, 8
Interactive Chalkboard
Multimedia Applications

Example 2 Solve an Equation for a Specific Variable

Solve $2m - t = sm + 5$ for m.

$2m - t = sm + 5$	Original equation
$2m - t - sm = sm + 5 - sm$	Subtract sm from each side.
$2m - t - sm = 5$	Simplify.
$2m - t - sm + t = 5 + t$	Add t to each side.
$2m - sm = 5 + t$	Simplify.
$m(2 - s) = 5 + t$	Use the Distributive Property.
$\dfrac{m(2 - s)}{2 - s} = \dfrac{5 + t}{2 - s}$	Divide each side by $2 - s$.
$m = \dfrac{5 + t}{2 - s}$	Simplify.

The value of m is $\dfrac{5 + t}{2 - s}$. Since division by 0 is undefined, $2 - s \neq 0$ or $s \neq 2$.

USE FORMULAS Many real-world problems require the use of formulas. Sometimes solving a formula for a specific variable will help you solve the problem.

Example 3 Use a Formula to Solve Problems

WEATHER Use the information about the Kansas City hailstorm at the left. The formula for the circumference of a circle is $C = 2\pi r$, where C represents circumference and r represents radius.

a. Solve the formula for r.

$C = 2\pi r$	Formula for circumference
$\dfrac{C}{2\pi} = \dfrac{2\pi r}{2\pi}$	Divide each side by 2π.
$\dfrac{C}{2\pi} = r$	Simplify.

b. Find the radius of one of the largest hailstones that fell on Kansas City in 1898.

$\dfrac{C}{2\pi} = r$	Formula for radius
$\dfrac{9.5}{2\pi} = r$	$C = 9.5$
$1.5 \approx r$	The largest hailstones had a radius of about 1.5 inches.

When using formulas, you may want to use dimensional analysis. **Dimensional analysis** is the process of carrying units throughout a computation.

Example 4 Use Dimensional Analysis

PHYSICAL SCIENCE The formula $s = \frac{1}{2}at^2$ represents the distance s that a free-falling object will fall near a planet or the moon in a given time t. In the formula, a represents the acceleration due to gravity.

a. Solve the formula for a.

$s = \dfrac{1}{2}at^2$	Original formula
$\dfrac{2}{t^2}(s) = \dfrac{2}{t^2}\left(\dfrac{1}{2}at^2\right)$	Multiply each side by $\dfrac{2}{t^2}$.
$\dfrac{2s}{t^2} = a$	Simplify.

www.algebra1.com/extra_examples

More About...

---

2 Teach

SOLVE FOR VARIABLES

Teaching Tip Sometimes it is helpful for students to circle the term containing the requested variable or highlight it with color so they can remember which variable they are trying to isolate.

In-Class Examples Power Point®

1 Solve $5b + 12c = 9$ for b.
$b = \dfrac{9 - 12c}{5}$

2 Solve $7x - 2z = 4 - xy$ for x.
$x = \dfrac{4 + 2z}{7 + y}$

USE FORMULAS

In-Class Examples Power Point®

3 **FUEL ECONOMY** A car's fuel economy E (miles per gallon) is given by the formula $E = \dfrac{m}{g}$, where m is the number of miles driven and g is the number of gallons of fuel used.

a. Solve the formula for m.
$m = Eg$

b. If Claudia's car has an average fuel consumption of 30 miles per gallon and she used 9.5 gallons, how far did she drive? **285 mi**

4 **GEOMETRY** The formula for the volume of a cylinder is $V = \pi r^2 h$, were r is the radius of the cylinder and h is the height.

a. Solve the formula for h.
$h = \dfrac{V}{\pi r^2}$

b. What is the height of a cylindrical swimming pool that has a radius of 12 feet and a volume of 1810 cubic feet? **about 4 ft**

b. A free-falling object near the moon drops 20.5 meters in 5 seconds. What is the value of a for the moon?

$a = \dfrac{2s}{t^2}$ Formula for a

$a = \dfrac{2(20.5 \text{ m})}{(5 \text{ s})^2}$ $s = 20.5$ m and $t = 5$ s.

$a = \dfrac{1.64 \text{ m}}{s^2}$ or 1.64 m/s²   Use a calculator.

The acceleration due to gravity on the moon is 1.64 meters per second squared.

Check for Understanding

Concept Check

1. **List** the steps you would use to solve $ax - y = az + w$ for a. **See margin.**

2. **Describe** the possible values of t if $s = \dfrac{r}{t-2}$. *t can be any number except 2.*

3. **OPEN ENDED** Write a formula for A, the area of a geometric figure such as a triangle or rectangle. Then solve the formula for a variable other than A.
Sample answer for a triangle: $A = \frac{1}{2}bh$; $b = \dfrac{2A}{h}$

Guided Practice

Solve each equation or formula for the variable specified.

GUIDED PRACTICE KEY	
Exercises	Examples
4–9	1, 2
10–12	3, 4

4. $-3x + b = 6x$, for x $x = \dfrac{b}{9}$

5. $-5a + y = -54$, for a $a = \dfrac{54 + y}{5}$

6. $4z + b = 2z + c$, for z $z = \dfrac{c - b}{2}$

7. $\dfrac{y + a}{3} = c$, for y $y = 3c - a$

8. $p = a(b + c)$, for a $a = \dfrac{p}{b + c}$

9. $mw - t = 2w + 5$, for w $w = \dfrac{5 + t}{m - 2}$

Application

GEOMETRY For Exercises 10–12, use the formula for the area of a triangle.

10. Find the area of a triangle with a base of 18 feet and a height of 7 feet. **63 ft²**

11. Solve the formula for h. $h = \dfrac{2A}{b}$

12. What is the height of a triangle with area of 28 square feet and base of 8 feet? **7 ft**

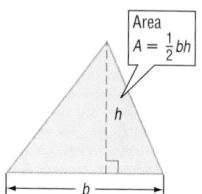

Area
$A = \frac{1}{2}bh$

★ indicates increased difficulty

Practice and Apply

Homework Help

For Exercises	See Examples
13–30	1, 2
31–41	3, 4

Extra Practice
See page 827.

Solve each equation or formula for the variable specified.

13. $5g + h = g$, for g $g = -\dfrac{h}{4}$

14. $8t - r = 12t$, for t $t = -\dfrac{r}{4}$

15. $y = mx + b$, for m $m = \dfrac{y - b}{x}$

16. $v = r + at$, for a $a = \dfrac{v - r}{t}$

17. $3y + z = am - 4y$, for y $y = \dfrac{am - z}{7}$

18. $9a - 2b = c + 4a$, for a $a = \dfrac{2b + c}{5}$

19. $km + 5x = 6y$, for m $m = \dfrac{6y - 5x}{k}$

20. $4b - 5 = -t$, for b $b = \dfrac{5 - t}{4}$

21. $\dfrac{3ax - n}{5} = -4$, for x $x = \dfrac{n - 20}{3a}$

22. $\dfrac{5x + y}{a} = 2$, for a $a = \dfrac{5x + y}{2}$

23. $\dfrac{by + 2}{3} = c$, for y $y = \dfrac{3c - 2}{b}$

24. $\dfrac{6c - t}{7} = b$, for c $c = \dfrac{7b + t}{6}$

25. $c = \dfrac{3}{4}y + b$, for y $y = \dfrac{4}{3}(c - b)$

26. $\dfrac{3}{5}m + a = b$, for m $m = \dfrac{5}{3}(b - a)$

★ 27. $S = \dfrac{n}{2}(A + t)$, for A $A = \dfrac{2S - nt}{n}$

28. $p(t + 1) = -2$, for t $t = \dfrac{-2 - p}{p}$

★ 29. $at + b = ar - c$, for a $a = \dfrac{c + b}{r - t}$

30. $2g - m = 5 - gh$, for g $g = \dfrac{5 + m}{2 + h}$

About the Exercises...

Organization by Objective
- Solve for Variables: 13–33
- Use Formulas: 34–41

Odd/Even Assignments
Exercises 13–32 are structured so that students practice the same concepts whether they are assigned odd or even problems.

Assignment Guide

Basic: 13–25 odd, 34–39, 42–66

Average: 13–29 odd, 34–39, 42–66

Advanced: 14–30 even, 31–33, 38–60 (optional: 61–66)

Answer

1. (1) Subtract az from each side. (2) Add y to each side. (3) Use the Distributive Property to write $ax - az$ as $a(x - z)$. (4) Divide each side by $x - z$.

Study Notebook

Have students—
- add the definitions/examples of the vocabulary terms to their Vocabulary Builder worksheets for Chapter 3.
- include any other item(s) that they find helpful in mastering the skills in this lesson.

DAILY
INTERVENTION

Differentiated Instruction

Intrapersonal Write *Watch Out!* at the top of the chalkboard before students begin working the Check for Understanding problems. Invite students to compile a collective list of mistakes to watch out for as they work these problems. For each mistake, have students suggest a way they could work differently to avoid the mistake.

31. $t - 5 = r + 6$;
$t = r + 11$

Write an equation and solve for the variable specified.

★ **31.** Five less than a number t equals another number r plus six. Solve for t.

★ **32.** Five minus twice a number p equals six times another number q plus one.
Solve for p. $5 - 2p = 6q + 1$; $p = 2 - 3q$

★ **33.** Five eighths of a number x is three more than one half of another number y.
Solve for y. $\frac{5}{8}x = \frac{1}{2}y + 3$; $y = \frac{5}{4}x - 6$

GEOMETRY For Exercises 34 and 35, use the
formula for the area of a trapezoid.

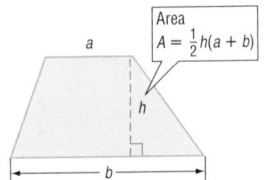
Area $A = \frac{1}{2}h(a + b)$

34. Solve the formula for h. $h = \dfrac{2A}{a + b}$

35. What is the height of a trapezoid with
an area of 60 square meters and bases
of 8 meters and 12 meters? **6 m**

WORK For Exercises 36 and 37, use the following information.

The formula $s = \dfrac{w - 10e}{m}$ is often used by placement services to find keyboarding
speeds. In the formula, s represents the speed in words per minute, w represents
the number of words typed, e represents the number of errors, and m represents the
number of minutes typed.

36. Solve the formula for e. $e = \dfrac{w - sm}{10}$

37. If Miguel typed 410 words in 5 minutes and received a keyboard speed of
76 words per minute, how many errors did he make? **3 errors**

FLOORING For Exercises 38 and 39, use the following information.

The formula $P = \dfrac{1.2W}{H^2}$ represents the amount of pressure exerted on the floor by the
heel of a shoe. In this formula, P represents the pressure in pounds per square inch,
W represents the weight of a person wearing the shoe in pounds, and H is the width
of the heel of the shoe in inches.

38. Solve the formula for W. $W = \dfrac{H^2P}{1.2}$

39. Find the weight of the person if the heel is 3 inches wide and the pressure
exerted is 30 pounds per square inch. **225 lb**

40. ROCKETRY In the book *October Sky*, high school students were experimenting
with different rocket designs. One formula they used was $R = \dfrac{S + F + P}{S + P}$, which
relates the mass ratio R of a rocket to the mass of the structure S, the mass of the
fuel F, and the mass of the payload P. The students needed to determine how
much fuel to load in the rocket. How much fuel should be loaded in a rocket
whose basic structure and payload each have a mass of 900 grams, if the mass
ratio is to be 6? **9000 g**

★ **41. PACKAGING** The Yummy Ice Cream
Company wants to package ice cream
in cylindrical containers that have a
volume of 5453 cubic centimeters. The
marketing department decides the
diameter of the base of the containers
should be 20 centimeters. How tall
should the containers be?
(*Hint*: $V = \pi r^2 h$) **about 17.4 cm**

Volume = 5453 cm³
Yummy vanilla ice cream
— 20 cm —

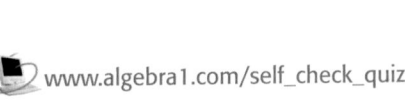
www.algebra1.com/self_check_quiz

Lesson 3-8 Solving Equations and Formulas **169**

Lesson 3-8 Solving Equations and Formulas **169**

Open-Ended Assessment

Writing Have students pick a formula that was not used in this lesson, perhaps from a science class, and explain the variables in the formula and what the formula is used to find. Then have students solve the formula for the different variables.

Getting Ready for Lesson 3-9

PREREQUISITE SKILL Students will learn about weighted averages in Lesson 3-9. Weighted average problems frequently require students to use the Distributive Property to simplify equations containing expressions in parentheses. Use Exercises 61–66 to determine your students' familiarity with the Distributive Property.

Answer

43. Equations from physics can be used to determine the height needed to produce the desired results. Answers should include the following.

- Use the following steps to solve for h. (1) Use the Distributive Property to write the equation in the form $195g - hg = \frac{1}{2}mv^2$. (2) Subtract $195g$ from each side. (3) Divide each side by $-g$.
- The second hill should be 157 ft.

---

42. CRITICAL THINKING Write a formula for the area of the arrow. $A = \frac{5}{2}s^2$

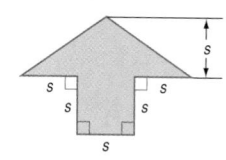

43. **WRITING IN MATH** Answer the question that was posed at the beginning of the lesson. **See margin.**

How are equations used to design roller coasters?

Include the following in your answer:
- a list of steps you could use to solve the equation for h, and
- the height of the second hill of the roller coaster.

Standardized Test Practice
(A) (B) (C) (D)

44. If $2x + y = 5$, what is the value of $4x$? **B**

  (A) $10 - y$

  (B) $10 - 2y$

  (C) $\dfrac{5 - y}{2}$

  (D) $\dfrac{10 - y}{2}$

45. What is the area of the triangle? **C**

  (A) $23\ m^2$

  (B) $28\ m^2$

  (C) $56\ m^2$

  (D) $112\ m^2$

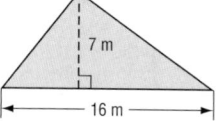

Maintain Your Skills

Mixed Review Find the discounted price of each item. *(Lesson 3-7)*

46. camera: $85.00
discount: 20% **$68.00**

47. scarf: $15.00
discount: 35% **$9.75**

48. television: $299.00
discount: 15% **$254.15**

Solve each proportion. *(Lesson 3-6)*

49. $\dfrac{2}{9} = \dfrac{5}{a}$ **22.5**

50. $\dfrac{15}{32} = \dfrac{t}{8}$ **3.75**

51. $\dfrac{x+1}{8} = \dfrac{3}{4}$ **5**

Write the numbers in each set in order from least to greatest. *(Lesson 2-7)*

52. $\dfrac{1}{4}, \sqrt{\dfrac{1}{4}}, 0.\overline{5}, 0.2$ **$0.2, \dfrac{1}{4}, \sqrt{\dfrac{1}{4}}, 0.\overline{5}$**

53. $\sqrt{5}, 3, \dfrac{2}{3}, 1.1$ **$\dfrac{2}{3}, 1.1, \sqrt{5}, 3$**

Find each sum or difference. *(Lesson 2-2)*

54. $2.18 + (-5.62)$ **-3.44**

55. $-\dfrac{1}{2} - \left(-\dfrac{3}{4}\right)$ **$\dfrac{1}{4}$**

56. $-\dfrac{2}{3} - \dfrac{2}{5}$ **$-1\dfrac{1}{15}$**

Name the property illustrated by each statement. *(Lesson 1-4)*

58. Symm. Prop. (=)

57. $mnp = 1mnp$ **Mult. Id. Prop.**

58. If $6 = 9 - 3$, then $9 - 3 = 6$.

59. $32 + 21 = 32 + 21$ **Ref. Prop.**

60. $8 + (3 + 9) = 8 + 12$ **Subst. Prop.**

Getting Ready for the Next Lesson
PREREQUISITE SKILL Use the Distributive Property to rewrite each expression without parentheses. *(To review the Distributive Property, see Lesson 1-5.)*

61. $6(2 - t)$ **$12 - 6t$**

62. $(5 + 2m)3$ **$15 + 6m$**

63. $-7(3a + b)$ **$-21a - 7b$**

64. $\dfrac{2}{3}(6h - 9)$ **$4h - 6$**

65. $-\dfrac{3}{5}(15 - 5t)$ **$-9 + 3t$**

66. $0.25(6p + 12)$ **$1.5p + 3$**

What You'll Learn

- Solve mixture problems.
- Solve uniform motion problems.

Vocabulary
- weighted average
- mixture problem
- uniform motion problem

How are scores calculated in a figure skating competition?

In individual figure skating competitions, the score for the long program is worth twice the score for the short program. Suppose Olympic gold medal winner Ilia Kulik scores 5.5 in the short program and 5.8 in the long program at a competition. His final score is determined using a weighted average.

$$\frac{5.5(1) + 5.8(2)}{1 + 2} = \frac{5.5 + 11.6}{3}$$

$$= \frac{17.1}{3} \text{ or } 5.7 \quad \text{His final score would be 5.7.}$$

MIXTURE PROBLEMS Ilia Kulik's average score is an example of a weighted average. The **weighted average** M of a set of data is the sum of the product of the number of units and the value per unit divided by the sum of the number of units.

Mixture problems are problems in which two or more parts are combined into a whole. They are solved using weighted averages.

Example 1 Solve a Mixture Problem with Prices

TRAIL MIX Assorted dried fruit sells for $5.50 per pound. How many pounds of mixed nuts selling for $4.75 per pound should be mixed with 10 pounds of dried fruit to obtain a trail mix that sells for $4.95 per pound?

Let w = the number of pounds of mixed nuts in the mixture. Make a table.

	Units (lb)	Price per Unit (lb)	Total Price
Dried Fruit	10	$5.50	5.50(10)
Mixed Nuts	w	$4.75	4.75w
Trail Mix	10 + w	$4.95	4.95(10 + w)

Price of dried fruit	plus	price of nuts	equals	price of trail mix.
5.50(10)	+	4.75w	=	4.95(10 + w)

$5.50(10) + 4.75w = 4.95(10 + w)$	Original equation
$55.00 + 4.75w = 49.50 + 4.95w$	Distributive Property
$55.00 + 4.75w - 4.75w = 49.50 + 4.95w - 4.75w$	Subtract 4.75w from each side.
$55.00 = 49.50 + 0.20w$	Simplify.
$55.00 - 49.50 = 49.50 + 0.20w - 49.50$	Subtract 49.50 from each side.
$5.50 = 0.20w$	Simplify.
$\dfrac{5.50}{0.20} = \dfrac{0.20w}{0.20}$	Divide each side by 0.20.
$27.5 = w$	Simplify.

27.5 pounds of nuts should be mixed with 10 pounds of dried fruit.

---

1 Focus

5-Minute Check Transparency 3-9 Use as a quiz or review of Lesson 3-8.

Mathematical Background notes are available for this lesson on p. 118D.

How are scores calculated in a figure skating competition?

Ask students:

- How would you find the unweighted average of the two scores? **Add the two scores and divide the sum by the number of scores, which is two.**
- What is the unweighted average of the two scores? **5.65**
- How is the weighted average similar to adding another score? **Since the score for the long program is counted twice, and the sum is divided by three, it is as if a third score has been added before the average is taken.**
- Did the weighted average help or hurt Ilia Kulik's score? Would this always be the case? **Because Ilia Kulik scored higher in the long program than in the short program, the weighted average made his average score higher. If he had scored lower in the long program, then the weighted average would have hurt his score. If he scored the same in both programs, the weighted average would have had no effect.**

Resource Manager

Workbook and Reproducible Masters

Chapter 3 Resource Masters
- Study Guide and Intervention, pp. 185–186
- Skills Practice, p. 187
- Practice, p. 188
- Reading to Learn Mathematics, p. 189
- Enrichment, p. 190
- Assessment, p. 206

Parent and Student Study Guide Workbook, p. 27

Transparencies
5-Minute Check Transparency 3-9
Answer Key Transparencies

 **Technology**
Interactive Chalkboard

MIXTURE PROBLEMS

Teaching Tip Explain to students that the object of this problem is to come up with a mixture of higher-priced dried fruit and cheaper nuts that has an average price of $4.95 per pound.

1 PETS Jeri likes to feed her cat gourmet cat food that costs $1.75 per pound. However, food at that price is too expensive so she combines it with cheaper cat food that costs $0.50 per pound. How many pounds of cheaper food should Jeri buy to go with 5 pounds of gourmet food, if she wants the average price to be $1.00 per pound? **Jeri should buy 7.5 lb of cheaper food.**

2 AUTO MAINTENANCE To provide protection against freezing, a car's radiator should contain a solution of 50% antifreeze. Darryl has 2 gallons of a 35% antifreeze solution. How many gallons of 100% antifreeze should Darryl add to his solution to produce a solution of 50% antifreeze? **Darryl should add 0.6 gal of 100% antifreeze to the solution.**

Teaching Tip Once students have learned the concept of weighted average, challenge them to describe a weighted average in terms of weights on a balance. How do the weights help to "tip" the balance?

Study Tip

Mixture Problems
When you organize the information in mixture problems, remember that the final mixture must contain the sum of the parts in the correct quantities and at the correct percents.

Sometimes mixture problems are expressed in terms of percents.

Example 2 *Solve a Mixture Problem with Percents*

SCIENCE A chemistry experiment calls for a 30% solution of copper sulfate. Kendra has 40 milliliters of 25% solution. How many milliliters of 60% solution should she add to obtain the required 30% solution?

Let x = the amount of 60% solution to be added. Make a table.

	Amount of Solution (mL)	Amount of Copper Sulfate
25% Solution	40	0.25(40)
60% Solution	x	0.60x
30% Solution	40 + x	0.30(40 + x)

Write and solve an equation using the information in the table.

Amount of copper sulfate in 25% solution	plus	amount of copper sulfate in 60% solution	equals	amount of copper sulfate in 30% solution.
0.25(40)	+	0.60x	=	0.30(40 + x)

$0.25(40) + 0.60x = 0.30(40 + x)$	Original equation
$10 + 0.60x = 12 + 0.30x$	Distributive Property
$10 + 0.60x - 0.30x = 12 + 0.30x - 0.30x$	Subtract 0.30x from each side.
$10 + 0.30x = 12$	Simplify.
$10 + 0.30x - 10 = 12 - 10$	Subtract 10 from each side.
$0.30x = 2$	Simplify.
$\dfrac{0.30x}{0.30} = \dfrac{2}{0.30}$	Divide each side by 0.30.
$x \approx 6.67$	Simplify.

Kendra should add 6.67 milliliters of the 60% solution to the 40 milliliters of the 25% solution.

UNIFORM MOTION PROBLEMS Motion problems are another application of weighted averages. **Uniform motion problems** are problems where an object moves at a certain speed, or rate. The formula $d = rt$ is used to solve these problems. In the formula, d represents distance, r represents rate, and t represents time.

Example 3 *Solve for Average Speed*

TRAVEL On Alberto's drive to his aunt's house, the traffic was light, and he drove the 45-mile trip in one hour. However, the return trip took him two hours. What was his average speed for the round trip?

To find the average speed for each leg of the trip, rewrite $d = rt$ as $r = \dfrac{d}{t}$.

Going

$r = \dfrac{d}{t}$

$= \dfrac{45 \text{ miles}}{1 \text{ hour}}$ or 45 miles per hour

Returning

$r = \dfrac{d}{t}$

$= \dfrac{45 \text{ miles}}{2 \text{ hours}}$ or 22.5 miles per hour

You may think that the average speed of the trip would be $\frac{45 + 22.5}{2}$ or 33.75 miles per hour. However, Alberto did not drive at these speeds for equal amounts of time. You must find the weighted average for the trip.

Round Trip

$M = \dfrac{45(1) + 22.5(2)}{1 + 2}$ Definition of weighted average

$= \dfrac{90}{3}$ or 30   Simplify.

Alberto's average speed was 30 miles per hour.

Sometimes a table is useful in solving uniform motion problems.

Example 4 Solve a Problem Involving Speeds of Two Vehicles

• **SAFETY** Use the information about sirens at the left. A car and an emergency vehicle are heading toward each other. The car is traveling at a speed of 30 miles per hour or about 44 feet per second. The emergency vehicle is traveling at a speed of 50 miles per hour or about 74 feet per second. If the vehicles are 1000 feet apart and the conditions are ideal, in how many seconds will the driver of the car first hear the siren?

Draw a diagram. The driver can hear the siren when the total distance traveled by the two vehicles equals $1000 - 440$ or 560 feet.

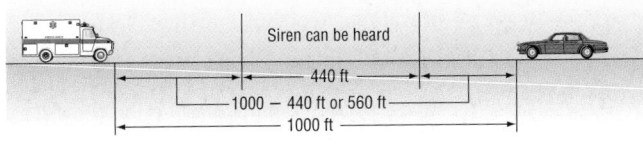

Let t = the number of seconds until the driver can hear the siren. Make a table of the information.

	r	t	$d = rt$
Car	44	t	$44t$
Emergency Squad	74	t	$74t$

Write an equation.

Distance traveled by car	plus	distance traveled by emergency vehicle	equals	560 feet.
$44t$	$+$	$74t$	$=$	560

Solve the equation.

$44t + 74t = 560$ Original equation

$118t = 560$ Simplify.

$\dfrac{118t}{118} = \dfrac{560}{118}$ Divide each side by 118.

$t \approx 4.75$ Round to the nearest hundredth.

The driver of the car will hear the siren in about 4.75 seconds.

More About. . .

Safety
Under ideal conditions, a siren can be heard from up to 440 feet. However, under normal conditions, a siren can be heard from only 125 feet.
Source: U.S. Department of Transportation

 www.algebra1.com/extra_examples

In-Class Examples   Power Point®

Teaching Tip An alternate way to solve Example 3 is to think of the total distance of the trip, 90 miles, divided by the total time spent traveling, 3 hours. The result is the average speed for the entire trip, or 30 miles per hour.

3 **AIR TRAVEL** Mirasol took a non-stop flight to visit her grandmother. The 750-mile trip took three hours and 45 minutes. Because of bad weather, the return trip took four hours and 45 minutes. What was her average speed for the round trip? **The average speed for the round trip was about 176 mi/h.**

4 **RESCUE** A railroad switching operator has discovered that two trains are heading toward each other on the same track. Currently, the trains are 53 miles apart. One train is traveling at 75 miles per hour and the other train is traveling at 40 miles per hour. The faster train will require 5 miles to stop safely, and the slower train will require 3 miles to stop safely. About how many minutes does the operator have to warn the train engineers to stop their trains? **about 23 min**

Study Notebook

Have students—
- complete the definitions/examples for the remaining terms on their Vocabulary Builder worksheets for Chapter 3.
- include any other item(s) that they find helpful in mastering the skills in this lesson.

About the Exercises...

Organization by Objective
- **Mixture Problems:** 11–18, 22–25, 27–29, 33
- **Uniform Motion Problems:** 19–21, 26, 30–32, 34

Alert! Exercise 35 includes an Internet research extension question.

Assignment Guide

Basic: 11–14, 19–21, 23–31 odd, 36–50

Average: 11–14, 19–21, 23–35 odd, 36–50

Advanced: 15–21, 22–32 even, 33–50

Check for Understanding

Concept Check

1. Sample answer: grade point average

1. **OPEN ENDED** Give a real-world example of a weighted average.

2. **Write** the formula used to solve uniform motion problems and tell what each letter represents. $d = rt$; d = distance, r = rate, t = time

3. **Make a table** that can be used to solve the following problem. *Lakeisha has $2.55 in dimes and quarters. She has 8 more dimes than quarters. How many quarters does she have?* **See margin.**

Guided Practice

GUIDED PRACTICE KEY	
Exercises	Examples
4–9	1, 2
10	3, 4

FOOD For Exercises 4–7, use the following information.
How many quarts of pure orange juice should Michael add to a 10% orange drink to create 6 quarts of a 40% orange juice mixture? Let p represent the number of quarts of pure orange juice he should add to the orange drink.

4. Copy and complete the table representing the problem.

	Quarts	Amount of Orange Juice
10% Juice	$6 - p$	$0.10(6 - p)$
100% Juice	p	$1.00p$
40% Juice	6	$0.40(6)$

5. Write an equation to represent the problem. $0.10(6 - p) + 1.00p = 0.40(6)$

6. How much pure orange juice should Michael use? **2 qt**

7. How much 10% juice should Michael use? **4 qt**

8. **BUSINESS** The Nut Shoppe sells walnuts for $4.00 a pound and cashews for $7.00 a pound. How many pounds of cashews should be mixed with 10 pounds of walnuts to obtain a mixture that sells for $5.50 a pound? **10 lb**

9. **GRADES** Many schools base a student's grade point average, or GPA, on the student's grade and the class credit rating. Brittany's grade card for this semester is shown. Find Brittany's GPA if a grade of A equals 4 and a B equals 3. **about 3.56**

Grade Card		
Class	Credit Rating	Grade
Algebra 1	1	A
Science	1	B
English	1	A
Spanish	1	B
Phys. Ed.	$\frac{1}{2}$	A

10. **CYCLING** Two cyclists begin traveling in the same direction on the same bike path. One travels at 20 miles per hour, and the other travels at 14 miles per hour. After how much time will the cyclists be 15 miles apart? **2.5 h**

★ indicates increased difficulty

Practice and Apply

Homework Help	
For Exercises	See Examples
11–18, 22–25, 27–29, 33	1, 2
19–21, 26, 30–32, 34	3, 4
Extra Practice See page 828.	

BUSINESS For Exercises 11–14, use the following information.
Cookies Inc. sells peanut butter cookies for $6.50 per dozen and chocolate chip cookies for $9.00 per dozen. Yesterday, they sold 85 dozen more peanut butter cookies than chocolate chip cookies. The total sales for both types of cookies were $4055.50. Let p represent the number of dozens of peanut butter cookies sold.

11. Copy and complete the table representing the problem.

	Number of Dozens	Price per Dozen	Total Price
Peanut Butter Cookies	p	$6.50	$6.50p$
Chocolate Chip Cookies	$p - 85$	$9.00	$9.00(p - 85)$

12. Write an equation to represent the problem. $6.50p + 9.00(p - 85) = 4055.50$

13. How many dozen peanut butter cookies were sold? **311 doz**

14. How many dozen chocolate chip cookies were sold? **226 doz**

Answer

3.

	Number of Coins	Value of Each Coin	Total Value
Dimes	d	$0.10	$0.10d$
Quarters	$d - 8$	$0.25	$0.25(d - 8)$

METALS   For Exercises 15–18, use the following information.
In 2000, the international price of gold was $270 per ounce, and the international price of silver was $5 per ounce. Suppose gold and silver were mixed to obtain 15 ounces of an alloy worth $164 per ounce. Let g represent the amount of gold used in the alloy.

15. Copy and complete the table representing the problem.

	Number of Ounces	Price per Ounce	Value
Gold	g	$270	$270g$
Silver	$15 - g$	$5	$5(15 - g)$
Alloy	15	$164	$164(15)$

16. Write an equation to represent the problem. $270g + 5(15 - g) = 164(15)$

17. How much gold was used in the alloy? **9 oz**

18. How much silver was used in the alloy? **6 oz**

TRAVEL   For Exercises 19–21, use the following information.
Two trains leave Pittsburgh at the same time, one traveling east and the other traveling west. The eastbound train travels at 40 miles per hour, and the westbound train travels at 30 miles per hour. Let t represent the amount of time since their departure.

19. Copy and complete the table representing the situation.

	r	t	$d = rt$
Eastbound Train	40	t	$40t$
Westbound Train	30	t	$30t$

20. Write an equation that could be used to determine when the trains will be 245 miles apart. $40t + 30t = 245$

21. In how many hours will the trains be 245 miles apart? $3\frac{1}{2}$ h

22. **FUND-RAISING**   The Madison High School marching band sold gift wrap. The gift wrap in solid colors sold for $4.00 per roll, and the print gift wrap sold for $6.00 per roll. The total number of rolls sold was 480, and the total amount of money collected was $2340. How many rolls of each kind of gift wrap were sold? **270 rolls of solid wrap, 210 rolls of print wrap**

23. **COFFEE**   Charley Baroni owns a specialty coffee store. He wants to create a special mix using two coffees, one priced at $6.40 per pound and the other priced at $7.28 per pound. How many pounds of the $7.28 coffee should he mix with 9 pounds of the $6.40 coffee to sell the mixture for $6.95 per pound? **15 lb**

24. **FOOD**   Refer to the graphic at the right. How much whipping cream and 2% milk should be mixed to obtain 35 gallons of milk with 4% butterfat? **10 gal of cream, 25 gal of 2% milk**

25. **METALS**   An alloy of metals is 25% copper. Another alloy is 50% copper. How much of each alloy should be used to make 1000 grams of an alloy that is 45% copper? **200 g of 25% alloy, 800 g of 50% alloy**

26. **TRAVEL**   An airplane flies 1000 miles due east in 2 hours and 1000 miles due south in 3 hours. What is the average speed of the airplane? **400 mph**

Study Guide and Intervention, p. 185 (shown) and p. 186

Mixture Problems

Weighted Average	The weighted average M of a set of data is the sum of the product of each number in the set and its weight divided by the sum of all the weights.

Mixture Problems are problems where two or more parts are combined into a whole. They involve weighted averages. In a mixture problem, the weight is usually a price or a percent of something.

Example Delectable Cookie Company sells chocolate chip cookies for $6.95 per pound and white chocolate cookies for $5.95 per pound. How many pounds of chocolate chip cookies should be mixed with 4 pounds of white chocolate cookies to obtain a mixture that sells for $6.75 per pound.

Let w = the number of pounds of chocolate chip cookies

	Number of Pounds	Price per Pound	Total Price
Chocolate Chip	w	6.95	6.95w
White Chocolate	4	5.95	4(5.95)
Mixture	w + 4	6.75	6.75(w + 4)

Equation: 6.95w + 4(5.95) = 6.75(w + 4)
Solve the equation.

6.95w + 4(5.95) = 6.75(w + 4)	Original equation
6.95w + 23.80 = 6.75w + 27	Simplify.
6.95w + 23.80 − 6.75w = 6.75w + 27 − 6.75w	Subtract 6.75w from each side.
0.2w + 23.80 = 27	Simplify.
0.2w + 23.80 − 23.80 = 27 − 23.80	Subtract 23.80 from each side.
0.2w = 3.2	Simplify.
w = 16	Simplify.

16 pounds of chocolate chip cookies should be mixed with 4 pounds of white chocolate cookies.

Exercises

1. **SOLUTIONS** How many grams of sugar must be added to 60 grams of a solution that is 32% sugar to obtain a solution that is 50% sugar? **21.6 g**

2. **NUTS** The Quik Mart has two kinds of nuts. Pecans sell for $1.55 per pound and walnuts sell for $1.95 per pound. How many pounds of walnuts must be added to 15 pounds of pecans to make a mixture that sells for $1.75 per pound? **15 lb**

3. **INVESTMENTS** Alice Gleason invested a portion of $32,000 at 9% interest and the balance at 11% interest. How much did she invest at each rate if her total income from both investments was $3,200. **$16,000 at 9% and $16,000 at 11%**

4. **MILK** Whole milk is 4% butterfat. How much skim milk with 0% butterfat should be added to 32 ounces of whole milk to obtain a mixture that is 2.5% butterfat? **19.2 oz**

Skills Practice, p. 187 and Practice, p. 188 (shown)

GRASS SEED For Exercises 1–4, use the following information.

A nursery sells Kentucky Blue Grass seed for $5.75 per pound and Tall Fescue seed for $4.50 per pound. The nursery sells a mixture of the two kinds of seed for $5.25 per pound. Let k represent the amount of Kentucky Blue Grass seed the nursery uses in 5 pounds of the mixture.

1. Complete the table representing the problem.

	Number of Pounds	Price per Pound	Cost
Kentucky Blue Grass	k	$5.75	5.75k
Tall Fescue	5 − k	$4.50	4.50(5 − k)
Mixture	5	$5.25	5.25(5)

2. Write an equation to represent the problem. **5.75k + 4.50(5 − k) = 5.25(5)**

3. How much Kentucky Blue Grass does the nursery use in 5 pounds of the mixture? **3 lb**

4. How much Tall Fescue does the nursery use in 5 pounds of the mixture? **2 lb**

TRAVEL For Exercises 5–7, use the following information.

Two commuter trains carry passengers between two cities, one traveling east, and the other west, on different tracks. Their respective stations are 150 miles apart. Both trains leave at the same time, one traveling at an average speed of 55 miles per hour and the other at an average speed of 65 miles per hour. Let t represent the time until the trains pass each other.

5. Copy and complete the table representing the problem.

	r	t	d = rt
First Train	55	t	55t
Second Train	65	t	65t

6. Write an equation using t that describes the distances traveled. **55t + 65t = 150**

7. How long after departing will the trains pass each other? **1.25 h**

8. **TRAVEL** Two trains leave Raleigh at the same time, one traveling north, and the other south. The first train travels at 50 miles per hour and the second at 60 miles per hour. In how many hours will the trains be 275 miles apart? **2.5 h**

9. **JUICE** A pineapple drink contains 15% pineapple juice. How much pure pineapple juice should be added to 8 quarts of the drink to obtain a mixture containing 50% pineapple juice? **5.6 qt**

Reading to Learn Mathematics, p. 189 **ELL**

Pre-Activity How are scores calculated in a figure skating competition?

Read the introduction to Lesson 3-9 at the top of page 171 in your textbook.

Why is the sum of Ilia Kulik's scores divided by 3?
Her first score is counted once and her second score is counted twice.

Reading the Lesson

1. Read the definition of *weighted average* on page 171 of your textbook. What is meant by the weight of a number in a set of data?
the number of times the number occurs in the set of data

2. Linda's quiz scores in science are 90, 85, 85, 75, 85, and 90. What is the weight of the score 85? **3**

3. Suppose Clint drives at 50 miles per hour for 2 hours. Then he drives at 60 miles per hour for 3 hours.

a. Write his speed for each hour of the trip.

Speed	50	50	60	60	60
Hour	1	2	3	4	5

b. What is the weight of each of the two speeds? **50 mph: 2; 60 mph: 3**

Helping You Remember

4. Making a table can be helpful in solving mixture problems. In your own words, explain how you use a table to solve mixture problems.
Complete each row to write an expression in the last column for each part of the problem and for the combination, then write an equation using those expressions from the last column.

---

27. 120 mL of 25% solution, 20 mL of 60% solution

28. 60 gal of 40% antifreeze, 40 gal of 60% antifreeze

32. No; the sprinter would catch his opponent in 40 s or after he has run 328 m.

36. Sample answer: How many grams of salt must be added to 40 grams of a 28% salt solution to obtain a 40% salt solution?

---

27. **SCIENCE** Hector is performing a chemistry experiment that requires 140 milliliters of a 30% copper sulfate solution. He has a 25% copper sulfate solution and a 60% copper sulfate solution. How many milliliters of each solution should he mix to obtain the needed solution?

28. **CAR MAINTENANCE** One type of antifreeze is 40% glycol, and another type of antifreeze is 60% glycol. How much of each kind should be used to make 100 gallons of antifreeze that is 48% glycol?

29. **GRADES** In Ms. Martinez's science class, a test is worth three times as much as a quiz. If a student has test grades of 85 and 92 and quiz grades of 82, 75, and 95, what is the student's average grade? **87**

30. **RESCUE** A fishing trawler has radioed the Coast Guard for a helicopter to pick up an injured crew member. At the time of the emergency message, the trawler is 660 kilometers from the helicopter and heading toward it. The average speed of the trawler is 30 kilometers per hour, and the average speed of the helicopter is 300 kilometers per hour. How long will it take the helicopter to reach the trawler? **2 h**

31. **ANIMALS** A cheetah is 300 feet from its prey. It starts to sprint toward its prey at 90 feet per second. At the same time, the prey starts to sprint at 70 feet per second. When will the cheetah catch its prey? **15 s**

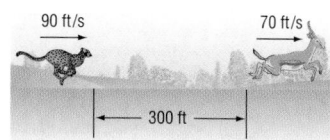

90 ft/s   70 ft/s   300 ft

32. **TRACK AND FIELD** A sprinter has a bad start, and his opponent is able to start 1 second before him. If the sprinter averages 8.2 meters per second and his opponent averages 8 meters per second, will he be able to catch his opponent before the end of the 200-meter race? Explain.

★ 33. **CAR MAINTENANCE** A car radiator has a capacity of 16 quarts and is filled with a 25% antifreeze solution. How much must be drained off and replaced with pure antifreeze to obtain a 40% antifreeze solution? **3.2 qt**

★ 34. **TRAVEL** An express train travels 80 kilometers per hour from Ironton to Wildwood. A local train, traveling at 48 kilometers per hour, takes 2 hours longer for the same trip. How far apart are Ironton and Wildwood? **240 km**

★ 35. **FOOTBALL** NFL quarterbacks are rated for their passing performance by a type of weighted average as described in the formula below.
$$R = [50 + 2000(C \div A) + 8000(T \div A) - 10{,}000(I \div A) + 100(Y \div A)] \div 24$$
In this formula,

- R represents the rating,
- C represents number of completions,
- A represents the number of passing attempts,
- T represents the number of touchdown passes,
- I represents the number of interceptions, and
- Y represents the number of yards gained by passing.

In the 2000 season, Daunte Culpepper had 297 completions, 474 passing attempts, 33 touchdown passes, 16 interceptions, and 3937 passing yards. What was his rating for that year? **about 98.0**

 Online Research **Data Update** What is the current passing rating for your favorite quarterback? Visit www.algebra1.com/data_update to get statistics on quarterbacks.

36. **CRITICAL THINKING** Write a mixture problem for the equation
$$1.00x + 0.28(40) = 0.40(x + 40).$$

Enrichment, p. 190

Diophantine Equations

The first great algebraist, Diophantus of Alexandria (about A.D. 300), devoted much of his work to the solving of indeterminate equations. An indeterminate equation has more than one variable and an unlimited number of solutions. An example is x + 2y = 4.

When the coefficients of an indeterminate equation are integers and you are asked to find solutions that must be integers, the equation is called *diophantine*. Such equations can be quite difficult to solve, often involving trial and error—and some luck!

Solve each diophantine equation by finding at least one pair of positive integers that makes the equation true. Some hints are given to help you.

1. 2x + 5y = 32

a. First solve the equation for x. $x = 16 - \dfrac{5y}{2}$

b. Why must y be an even number? If y is odd, then x won't be an integer.

37. WRITING IN MATH   Answer the question that was posed at the beginning of the lesson. **See margin.**

How are scores calculated in a figure skating competition?

Include the following in your answer:
- an explanation of how a weighted average can be used to find a skating score, and
- a demonstration of how to find the weighted average of a skater who received a 4.9 in the short program and a 5.2 in the long program.

Standardized Test Practice
Ⓐ Ⓑ Ⓒ Ⓓ

38. Eula Jones is investing $6000 in two accounts, part at 4.5% and the remainder at 6%. If d represents the number of dollars invested at 4.5%, which expression represents the amount of interest earned in one year by the account paying 6%? **D**

Ⓐ $0.06d$ Ⓑ $0.06(d - 6000)$

Ⓒ $0.06(d + 6000)$ Ⓓ $0.06(6000 - d)$

39. Todd drove from Boston to Cleveland, a distance of 616 miles. His breaks, gasoline, and food stops took 2 hours. If his trip took 16 hours altogether, what was his average speed? **C**

Ⓐ 38.5 mph   Ⓑ 40 mph   Ⓒ 44 mph   Ⓓ 47.5 mph

Maintain Your Skills

Mixed Review   **Solve each equation for the variable specified.** *(Lesson 3-8)*

40. $3t - 4 = 6t - s$, for t $t = \dfrac{s-4}{3}$ **41.** $a + 6 = \dfrac{b-1}{4}$, for b $b = 4a + 25$

State whether each percent of change is a percent of increase or a percent of decrease. Then find the percent of change. Round to the nearest whole percent. *(Lesson 3-7)*

42. original: 25   **43.** original: 35   **44.** original: 244
new: 14   new: 42   new: 300
decrease; 44%   **increase; 20%**   **increase; 23%**

45. If the probability that an event will occur is $\frac{2}{3}$, what are the odds that the event will occur? *(Lesson 2-6)* **2:1**

Simplify each expression. *(Lesson 2-3)*

46. $(2b)(-3a)$ **$-6ab$**   **47.** $3x(-3y) + (-6x)(-2y)$ **48.** $5s(-6t) + 2s(-8t)$
                                         $3xy$ **$-46st$**

Name the set of numbers graphed. *(Lesson 2-1)*

49.

−2 −1 0 1 2 3 4 5 6 7
{…, −2, −1, 0, 1, 2, 3}

50.

−1 0 1 2 3 4 5 6 7 8
{0, 2, 5, 6, 8}

 Web Quest   **Internet Project**

Can You Fit 100 Candles on a Cake?

It's time to complete your project. Use the information and data you have gathered about living to be 100 to prepare a portfolio or Web page. Be sure to include graphs and/or tables in the presentation.

www.algebra1.com/webquest

---

4 Assess

Open-Ended Assessment

Writing Ask students whether any of their teachers use weighted averages to calculate student grades. For example, a teacher might count homework assignments once, tests twice, and final exams three times. Have students describe the weighted average systems used by their teachers and whether the weighted averages help or hurt their scores.

Assessment Options

Quiz (Lessons 3-8 and 3-9) is available on p. 206 of the *Chapter 3 Resource Masters*.

Answer

37. A weighted average is used to determine a skater's average. Answers should include the following.
- The score of the short program is added to twice the score of the long program. The sum is divided by 3.
- $\dfrac{4.9(1) + 5.2(2)}{1 + 2} = 5.1$

Spreadsheet Investigation

Spreadsheet Investigation

Getting Started

Objective Find a weighted average using a computer spreadsheet.

Materials
computer
spreadsheet software

Teach

- Suggest that students work in pairs, with students taking turns reading aloud the data while the partner types in the data.

- The spreadsheet on the student page shows the formulas to calculate the income. Instead of typing the cell name, such as B4, students can click on the cell.

- In order for the spreadsheet to calculate the formulas correctly, students should type an equals sign at the beginning of any cell that contains a calculation formula.

Assess

Exercises 1–4 After students work these exercises, ask them what advantages computer spreadsheets have over pen and paper calculations.

Study Notebook

You may wish to have students summarize this activity and what they learned from it.

Finding a Weighted Average

You can use a computer spreadsheet program to calculate weighted averages. A spreadsheet allows you to make calculations and print almost anything that can be organized in a table.

The basic unit in a spreadsheet is called a **cell**. A cell may contain numbers, words, or a formula. Each cell is named by the column and row that describe its location. For example, cell B4 is in column B, row 4.

Example

Greta Norris manages the Java Roaster Coffee Shop. She has entered the price per pound and the number of pounds sold in October for each type of coffee in a spreadsheet. What was the average price per pound of coffee sold?

	October Sales			
	A	B	C	D
1	Product	Price per Pound	Pounds Sold	Income
2	Hawaiian Cafe	16.95	59	=B2*C2
3	Mocha Java	12.59	85	=B3*C3
4	House Blend	10.75	114	=B4*C4
5	Decaf Espresso	10.15	75	=B5*C5
6	Breakfast Blend	11.25	93	=B6*C6
7	Italian Roast	9.95	55	=B7*C7
8	Total		=SUM(C2:C7)	=SUM(D2:D7)
9	Weighted Average	=D8 / C8		
10				

Sheet1 / Sheet2 / Sheet3 /

The spreadsheet shows the formula that will calculate the weighted average. The formula multiplies the price of each product by its volume and calculates its sum for all the products. Then it divides that value by the sum of the volume for all products together. To the nearest cent, the weighted average of a pound of coffee is $11.75.

2. It increases by $1.00.

3. It increases by 10%.

Exercises

For Exercises 1–4, use the spreadsheet of coffee prices.

1. What is the average price of a pound of coffee for the November sales shown in the table at the right? **$11.79**

2. How does the November weighted average change if all of the coffee prices are increased by $1.00?

3. How does the November weighted average change if all of the coffee prices are increased by 10%?

4. Find the weighted average of a pound of coffee if the shop sold 50 pounds of each type of coffee. How does the weighted average compare to the average of the per-pound coffee prices? Explain. **See margin.**

November Sales	
Product	**Pounds Sold**
Hawaiian Cafe	56
Mocha Java	97
House Blend	124
Decaf Espresso	71
Breakfast Blend	69
Italian Roast	45

178 Chapter 3 Solving Linear Equations

Answer

4. The average of the prices per pound is the same as the weighted average if the same number of pounds of each type are sold. This is because each price is multiplied by the same weight, and then that weight is divided out.

Vocabulary and Concept Check

Addition Property of Equality (p. 128)
consecutive integers (p. 144)
defining a variable (p. 121)
dimensional analysis (p. 167)
Division Property of Equality (p. 137)
equivalent equation (p. 129)
extremes (p. 156)
formula (p. 122)
four-step problem-solving plan (p. 121)

identity (p. 150)
means (p. 156)
mixture problem (p. 171)
Multiplication Property of Equality (p. 135)
multi-step equations (p. 143)
number theory (p. 144)
percent of change (p. 160)
percent of decrease (p. 160)
percent of increase (p. 160)

proportion (p. 155)
rate (p. 157)
ratio (p. 155)
scale (p. 157)
solve an equation (p. 129)
Subtraction Property of Equality (p. 129)
uniform motion problem (p. 172)
weighted average (p. 171)
work backward (p. 142)

Choose the correct term to complete each sentence.

1. According to the *(Addition, Multiplication)* Property of Equality, if $a = b$, then $a + c = b + c$.

2. A *(means, ratio)* is a comparison of two numbers by division.

3. A rate is the ratio of two measurements with *(the same, different)* units of measure.

4. The first step in the four-step problem-solving plan is to *(explore, solve)* the problem.

5. $2x + 1 = 2x + 1$ is an example of a(n) *(identity, formula)*.

6. An equivalent equation for $3x + 5 = 7$ is *(3x = 2, 3x = 12)*.

7. If the original amount was 80 and the new amount is 90, then the percent of *(decrease, increase)* is 12.5%.

8. *(Defining the variable, Dimensional analysis)* is the process of carrying units throughout a computation.

9. The *(weighted average, rate)* of a set of data is the sum of the product of each number in the set and its weight divided by the sum of all the weights.

10. An example of consecutive integers is *(8 and 9, 8 and 10)*.

Lesson-by-Lesson Review

3-1 Writing Equations

See pages 120–126.

Concept Summary
- Variables are used to represent unknowns when writing equations.
- Formulas given in sentence form can be written as algebraic equations.

Example Translate the following sentence into an equation.
The sum of x and y equals 2 plus two times the product of x and y.

The sum of x and y	equals	2	plus	two times the product of x and y
$x + y$	$=$	2	$+$	$2xy$

The equation is $x + y = 2 + 2xy$.

Chapter 3

Study Guide and Review

Vocabulary and Concept Check

- This alphabetical list of vocabulary terms in Chapter 3 includes a page reference where each term was introduced.

- **Assessment** A vocabulary test/review for Chapter 3 is available on p. 204 of the *Chapter 3 Resource Masters.*

Lesson-by-Lesson Review

For each lesson,
- the main ideas are summarized,
- additional examples review concepts, and
- practice exercises are provided.

Vocabulary PuzzleMaker

ELL The Vocabulary PuzzleMaker software improves students' mathematics vocabulary using four puzzle formats—crossword, scramble, word search using a word list, and word search using clues. Students can work on a computer screen or from a printed handout.

MindJogger Videoquizzes

ELL MindJogger Videoquizzes provide an alternative review of concepts presented in this chapter. Students work in teams in a game show format to gain points for correct answers. The questions are presented in three rounds.

Round 1 Concepts (5 questions)
Round 2 Skills (4 questions)
Round 3 Problem Solving (4 questions)

Exercises   Translate each sentence into an equation.   *See Example 1 on page 120.*

11. Three times a number n decreased by 21 is 57. $3n - 21 = 57$

12. Four minus three times z is equal to z decreased by 2. $4 - 3z = z - 2$

13. The sum of the square of a and the cube of b is 16. $a^2 + b^3 = 16$

14. Translate the equation $16 - 9r = r$ into a verbal sentence.   *See Example 4 on pages 122 and 123.*   **Sixteen minus the product of 9 and a number r is equal to r.**

3-2 Solving Equations by Using Addition and Subtraction

See pages 128–134.

Concept Summary

- **Addition Property of Equality**   For any numbers a, b, and c, if $a = b$, then $a + c = b + c$.
- **Subtraction Property of Equality**   For any numbers a, b, and c, if $a = b$, then $a - c = b - c$.

Example   Solve $x - 13 = 45$. Then check your solution.

$$x - 13 = 45 \qquad \text{Original equation}$$
$$x - 13 + 13 = 45 + 13 \qquad \text{Add 13 to each side.}$$
$$x = 58 \qquad \text{Simplify.}$$

CHECK $x - 13 = 45$ Original equation

$58 - 13 \stackrel{?}{=} 45$ Substitute 58 for x.

$45 = 45$ ✓   Simplify.   The solution is 58.

Exercises   Solve each equation. Then check your solution.
See Examples 1–4 on pages 129 and 130.

15. $r - 21 = -37$ -16
16. $14 + c = -5$ -19
17. $27 = 6 + p$ 21
18. $b + (-14) = 6$ 20
19. $d - (-1.2) = -7.3$ -8.5
20. $r + \left(-\dfrac{1}{2}\right) = -\dfrac{3}{4}$ $-\dfrac{1}{4}$

3-3 Solving Equations by Using Multiplication and Division

See pages 135–140.

Concept Summary

- **Multiplication Property of Equality**   For any numbers a, b, and c, if $a = b$, then $ac = bc$.
- **Division Property of Equality**   For any numbers a, b, and c, with $c \neq 0$, if $a = b$, then $\dfrac{a}{c} = \dfrac{b}{c}$.

Example   Solve $\dfrac{4}{9}t = -72$.

$$\frac{4}{9}t = -72 \qquad \text{Original equation}$$
$$\frac{9}{4}\left(\frac{4}{9}t\right) = \frac{9}{4}(-72) \qquad \text{Multiply each side by } \frac{9}{4}.$$
$$t = -162 \qquad \text{Simplify.}$$

CHECK $\dfrac{4}{9}t = -72$ Original equation

$\dfrac{4}{9}(-162) \stackrel{?}{=} -72$ Substitute -162 for t.

$-72 = -72$ ✓   Simplify.

The solution is -162.

Exercises Solve each equation. Then check your solution.

See Examples 1–3 on pages 135 and 136.

21. $6x = -42$ **−7**

22. $-7w = -49$ **7**

23. $\frac{3}{4}n = 30$ **40**

24. $-\frac{3}{5}y = -50$ **$83\frac{1}{3}$**

25. $\frac{5}{2}a = -25$ **−10**

26. $5 = \frac{r}{2}$ **10**

3-4 Solving Multi-Step Equations

See pages 142–148.

Concept Summary

- Multi-step equations can be solved by undoing the operations in reverse of the order of operations.

Example Solve $34 = 8 - 2t$. Then check your solution.

$34 = 8 - 2t$	Original equation
$34 - 8 = 8 - 2t - 8$	Subtract 8 from each side.
$26 = -2t$	Simplify.
$\dfrac{26}{-2} = \dfrac{-2t}{-2}$	Divide each side by −2.
$-13 = t$	Simplify.

CHECK	$34 = 8 - 2t$	Original equation
	$34 \stackrel{?}{=} 8 - 2(-13)$	Substitute −13 for t.
	$34 = 34$ ✓	The solution is −13.

Exercises Solve each equation. Then check your solution.

See Examples 2–4 on page 143.

27. $4p - 7 = 5$ **3**

28. $6 = 4v + 2$ **1**

29. $\frac{y}{3} + 6 = -45$ **−153**

30. $\frac{c}{-4} - 8 = -42$ **136**

31. $\frac{4d + 5}{7} = 7$ **11**

32. $\frac{7n + (-1)}{8} = 8$ **$9\frac{2}{7}$**

3-5 Solving Equations with the Variable on Each Side

See pages 149–154.

Concept Summary

Steps for Solving Equations

Step 1 Use the Distributive Property to remove the grouping symbols.

Step 2 Simplify the expressions on each side of the equals sign.

Step 3 Use the Addition and/or Subtraction Properties of Equality to get the variables on one side of the equals sign and the numbers without variables on the other side of the equals sign.

Step 4 Simplify the expressions on each side of the equals sign.

Step 5 Use the Multiplication and/or Division Properties of Equalities to solve.

Example Solve $\frac{3}{4}q - 8 = \frac{1}{4}q + 9$.

$$\frac{3}{4}q - 8 = \frac{1}{4}q + 9 \qquad \text{Original equation}$$

$$\frac{3}{4}q - 8 - \frac{1}{4}q = \frac{1}{4}q + 9 - \frac{1}{4}q \qquad \text{Subtract } \frac{1}{4}q \text{ from each side.}$$

$$\frac{1}{2}q - 8 = 9 \qquad \text{Simplify.}$$

$$\frac{1}{2}q - 8 + 8 = 9 + 8 \qquad \text{Add 8 to each side.}$$

$$\frac{1}{2}q = 17 \qquad \text{Simplify.}$$

$$2\left(\frac{1}{2}q\right) = 2(17) \qquad \text{Multiply each side by 2.}$$

$$q = 34 \qquad \text{Simplify.}$$

The solution is 34.

Exercises Solve each equation. Then check your solution.
See Examples 1–4 on pages 149 and 150.

33. $n - 2 = 4 - 2n$ **2**   **34.** $3t - 2(t + 3) = t$ **35.** $3 - \frac{5}{6}y = 2 + \frac{1}{6}y$ **1**
                                         no solution

36. $\frac{x - 2}{6} = \frac{x}{2}$ **−1**   **37.** $2(b - 3) = 3(b - 1)$ **−3** **38.** $8.3h - 2.2 = 6.1h - 8.8$ **−3**

3-6 *Ratios and Proportions*

See pages 155–159.

Concept Summary

- A ratio is a comparison of two numbers by division.
- A proportion is an equation stating that two ratios are equal.
- A proportion can be solved by finding the cross products.

If $\frac{a}{b} = \frac{c}{d}$, then $ad = bc$.

Example Solve the proportion $\frac{8}{7} = \frac{a}{1.75}$.

$$\frac{8}{7} = \frac{a}{1.75} \qquad \text{Original equation}$$

$$8(1.75) = 7(a) \qquad \text{Find the cross products.}$$

$$14 = 7a \qquad \text{Simplify.}$$

$$\frac{14}{7} = \frac{7a}{7} \qquad \text{Divide each side by 7.}$$

$$2 = a \qquad \text{Simplify.}$$

Exercises Solve each proportion. *See Example 3 on page 156.*

39. $\frac{6}{15} = \frac{n}{45}$ **18**   **40.** $\frac{x}{11} = \frac{35}{55}$ **7**   **41.** $\frac{12}{d} = \frac{20}{15}$ **9**

42. $\frac{14}{20} = \frac{21}{m}$ **30**   **43.** $\frac{2}{3} = \frac{b + 5}{9}$ **1**   **44.** $\frac{6}{8} = \frac{9}{s - 4}$ **16**

3-7 Percent of Change

See pages
160–164.

Concept Summary

- The proportion $\dfrac{\textit{amount of change}}{\textit{original amount}} = \dfrac{r}{100}$ is used to find percents of change.

Example   Find the percent of change.   original: $120

new: $114

First, subtract to find the amount of change.

$120 − $114 = $6   Note that since the new amount is less than the original, the percent of change will be a percent of decrease.

Then find the percent using the original number, 120, as the base.

$$\begin{array}{ll} \text{change} \to \\ \text{original amount} \to \end{array} \quad \dfrac{6}{120} = \dfrac{r}{100} \quad \text{Percent proportion}$$

$$6(100) = 120(r) \quad \text{Find the cross products.}$$

$$600 = 120r \quad \text{Simplify.}$$

$$\dfrac{600}{120} = \dfrac{120r}{120} \quad \text{Divide each side by 120.}$$

$$5 = r \quad \text{Simplify.}$$

The percent of decrease is 5%.

Exercises   State whether each percent of change is a percent of increase or a percent of decrease. Then find the percent of change. Round to the nearest whole percent.   *See Example 1 on page 160.*

45. original: 40
new: 32 **dec.; 20%**

46. original: 50
new: 88 **inc.; 76%**

47. original: 35
new: 37.1 **inc.; 6%**

48. Find the total price of a book that costs $14.95 plus 6.25% sales tax.
See Example 3 on page 161. **$15.88**

49. A T-shirt priced at $12.99 is on sale for 20% off. What is the discounted price?
See Example 4 on page 161. **$10.39**

3-8 Solving Equations and Formulas

See pages
166–170.

Concept Summary

- For equations with more than one variable, you can solve for one of the variables by using the same steps as solving equations with one variable.

Example   Solve $\dfrac{x + y}{b} = c$ for x.

$$\dfrac{x + y}{b} = c \quad \text{Original equation}$$

$$b\left(\dfrac{x + y}{b}\right) = b(c) \quad \text{Multiply each side by } b.$$

$$x + y = bc \quad \text{Simplify.}$$

$$x + y - y = bc - y \quad \text{Subtract } y \text{ from each side.}$$

$$x = bc - y \quad \text{Simplify.}$$

Study Guide and Review

Chapter **3** For More …   • Extra Practice, see pages 825–828.
                              • Mixed Problem Solving, see page 855.

Exercises   Solve each equation or formula for the variable specified.
See Examples 1 and 2 on pages 166 and 167.

50. $5x = y$, for x $x = \dfrac{y}{5}$

51. $ay - b = c$, for y $y = \dfrac{b + c}{a}$

52. $yx - a = cx$, for x $x = \dfrac{a}{y - c}$

53. $\dfrac{2y - a}{3} = \dfrac{a + 3b}{4}$, for y $y = \dfrac{7a + 9b}{8}$

3-9 **Weighted Averages**

See pages 171–177.

Concept Summary

- The weighted average of a set of data is the sum of the product of each number in the set and its weight divided by the sum of all the weights.
- The formula $d = rt$ is used to solve uniform motion problems.

Example   **SCIENCE**   Mai Lin has a 35 milliliters of 30% solution of copper sulfate. How much of a 20% solution of copper sulfate should she add to obtain a 22% solution?

Let x = amount of 20% solution to be added. Make a table.

	Amount of Solution (mL)	Amount of Copper Sulfate
30% Solution	35	0.30(35)
20% Solution	x	0.20x
22% Solution	35 + x	0.22(35 + x)

$0.30(35) + 0.20x = 0.22(35 + x)$	Write and solve an equation.
$10.5 + 0.20x = 7.7 + 0.22x$	Distributive Property
$10.5 + 0.20x - 0.20x = 7.7 + 0.22x - 0.20x$	Subtract 0.20x fom each side.
$10.5 = 7.7 + 0.02x$	Simplify.
$10.5 - 7.7 = 7.7 + 0.02x - 7.7$	Subtract 7.7 from each side.
$2.8 = 0.02x$	Simplify.
$\dfrac{2.8}{0.02} = \dfrac{0.02x}{0.02}$	Divide each side by 0.02.
$140 = x$	Simplify.

Mai Lin should add 140 milliliters of the 20% solution.

Exercises

54. **COFFEE**   Ms. Anthony wants to create a special blend using two coffees, one priced at $8.40 per pound and the other at $7.28 per pound. How many pounds of the $7.28 coffee should she mix with 9 pounds of the $8.40 coffee to sell the mixture for $7.95 per pound?   *See Example 1 on page 171.*   **6 lb**

55. **TRAVEL**   Two airplanes leave Dallas at the same time and fly in opposite directions. One airplane travels 80 miles per hour faster than the other. After three hours, they are 2940 miles apart. What is the speed of each airplane?   *See Example 3 on pages 172 and 173.*   **450 mph, 530 mph**

Practice Test

Vocabulary and Concepts

Choose the correct term to complete each sentence.

1. The study of numbers and the relationships between them is called (*consecutive*, *number*) theory.

2. An equation that is true for (*every*, *only one*) value of the variable is called an identity.

3. When a new number is (*greater than*, *less than*) the original number, the percent of change is called a percent of increase.

Skills and Applications

Translate each sentence into an equation.

4. The sum of twice x and three times y is equal to thirteen. $2x + 3y = 13$

5. Two thirds of a number is negative eight fifths. $\frac{2}{3}n = -\frac{8}{5}$

Solve each equation. Then check your solution.

6. $-15 + k = 8$ **23**

7. $-1.2x = 7.2$ **−6**

8. $k - 16 = -21$ **−5**

9. $\frac{t - 7}{4} = 11$ **51**

10. $\frac{3}{4}y = -27$ **−36**

11. $-12 = 7 - \frac{y}{3}$ **57**

12. $t - (-3.4) = -5.3$ **−8.7**

13. $-3(x + 5) = 8x + 18$ **−3**

14. $5a = 125$ **25**

15. $\frac{r}{5} - 3 = \frac{2r}{5} + 16$ **−95**

16. $0.1r = 19$ **190**

17. $-\frac{2}{3}z = -\frac{4}{9}$ **$\frac{2}{3}$**

18. $-w + 11 = 4.6$ **6.4**

19. $2p + 1 = 5p - 11$ **4**

20. $25 - 7w = 46$ **−3**

Solve each proportion.

21. $\frac{36}{t} = \frac{9}{11}$ **44**

22. $\frac{n}{4} = \frac{3.25}{52}$ **0.25**

23. $\frac{5}{12} = \frac{10}{x - 1}$ **25**

State whether each percent of change is a percent of increase or a percent of decrease. Then find the percent of change. Round to the nearest whole percent.

24. original: 45
    new: 9 **decrease; 80%**

25. original: 12
    new: 20 **increase; 67%**

Solve each equation or formula for the variable specified.

26. $h = at - 0.25vt^2$, for a $a = \dfrac{h + 0.25vt^2}{t}$

27. $a(y + 1) = b$, for y $y = \dfrac{b - a}{a}$

28. **SALES** Suppose the Central Perk coffee shop sells a cup of espresso for $2.00 and a cup of cappuccino for $2.50. On Friday, Destiny sold 30 more cups of cappuccino than espresso for a total of $178.50 worth of espresso and cappuccino. How many cups of each were sold? **espresso: 23 cups, cappuccino: 53 cups**

29. **BOATING** *The Yankee Clipper* leaves the pier at 9:00 A.M. at 8 knots (nautical miles per hour). A half hour later, *The River Rover* leaves the same pier in the same direction traveling at 10 knots. At what time will *The River Rover* overtake *The Yankee Clipper*? **11:30 A.M.**

30. **STANDARDIZED TEST PRACTICE** If $\frac{4}{5}$ of $\frac{3}{4} = \frac{2}{5}$ of $\frac{x}{4}$, find the value of x. **B**

   (A) 12   (B) 6   (C) 3   (D) $\frac{3}{2}$

 www.algebra1.com/chapter_test

Assessment Options

Vocabulary Test A vocabulary test/review for Chapter 3 can be found on p. 204 of the *Chapter 3 Resource Masters*.

Chapter Tests There are six Chapter 3 Tests and an Open-Ended Assessment task available in the *Chapter 3 Resource Masters*.

Chapter 3 Tests			
Form	Type	Level	Pages
1	MC	basic	191–192
2A	MC	average	193–194
2B	MC	average	195–196
2C	FR	average	197–198
2D	FR	average	199–200
3	FR	advanced	201–202

MC = multiple-choice questions
FR = free-response questions

Open-Ended Assessment Performance tasks for Chapter 3 can be found on p. 203 of the *Chapter 3 Resource Masters*. A sample scoring rubric for these tasks appears on p. A34.

Unit 1 Test A unit test/review can be found on pp. 211–212 of the *Chapter 3 Resource Masters*.

 ExamView® Pro

Use the networkable **ExamView® Pro** to:

- Create **multiple versions** of tests.
- Create **modified** tests for *Inclusion* students.
- **Edit** existing questions and **add** your own questions.
- Use built-in **state curriculum correlations** to create tests aligned with state standards.
- Change **English** tests to **Spanish** and vice versa.

Portfolio Suggestion

Introduction Even after working through a chapter of material, you can get to the end and still feel uncertain about a problem that you still cannot solve, or that you are worried you might not be able to solve on a test.

Ask Students Write out the question that you still cannot solve and as much of the solution as you can until you get to the hard part. Then explain what it is that keeps you from solving the problem. Be clear and precise. Place this in your portfolio.

Chapter 3 Standardized Test Practice

These two pages contain practice questions in the various formats that can be found on the most frequently given standardized tests.

A practice answer sheet for these two pages can be found on p. A1 of the *Chapter 3 Resource Masters*.

Standardized Test Practice
Student Recording Sheet, p. A1

Part 1 Multiple Choice

Select the best answer from the choices given and fill in the corresponding oval.

1 Ⓐ Ⓑ Ⓒ Ⓓ   4 Ⓐ Ⓑ Ⓒ Ⓓ   7 Ⓐ Ⓑ Ⓒ Ⓓ
2 Ⓐ Ⓑ Ⓒ Ⓓ   5 Ⓐ Ⓑ Ⓒ Ⓓ   8 Ⓐ Ⓑ Ⓒ Ⓓ
3 Ⓐ Ⓑ Ⓒ Ⓓ   6 Ⓐ Ⓑ Ⓒ Ⓓ

Part 2 Short Response/Grid In

Solve the problem and write your answer in the blank.

For Questions 10, 13, 14, and 15, also enter your answer by writing each number or symbol in a box. Then fill in the corresponding oval for that number or symbol.

9 _____
10 _____ (grid in)
11 _____
12 _____
13 _____ (grid in)
14 _____ (grid in)
15 _____ (grid in)
16 _____
17 _____

Part 3 Extended Response

Record your answers for Questions 18–20 on the back of this paper.

Additional Practice

See pp. 209–210 in the *Chapter 3 Resource Masters* for additional standardized test practice.

Part 1   Multiple Choice

Record your answers on the answer sheet provided by your teacher or on a sheet of paper.

1. Bailey planted a rectangular garden that is 6 feet wide by 15 feet long. What is the perimeter of the garden?   (Prerequisite Skill) **C**

   Ⓐ 21 ft   Ⓑ 27 ft
   Ⓒ 42 ft   Ⓓ 90 ft

2. Which of the following is true about 65 percent of 20?   (Prerequisite Skill) **C**

   Ⓐ It is greater than 20.
   Ⓑ It is less than 10.
   Ⓒ It is less than 20.
   Ⓓ Can't tell from the information given

3. For a science project, Kelsey measured the height of a plant grown from seed. She made the bar graph below to show the height of the plant at the end of each week. Which is the most reasonable estimate of the plant's height at the end of the sixth week?   (Lesson 1-8) **B**

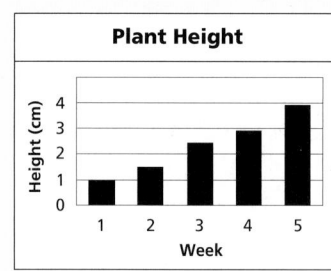

   Plant Height

   Height (cm) vs Week

   Ⓐ 2 to 3.5 cm   Ⓑ 4 to 5.5 cm
   Ⓒ 6 to 7 cm   Ⓓ 8 to 8.5 cm

4. WEAT predicted a 25% chance of snow. WFOR said the chance was 1 in 4. Myweather.com showed the chance of snow as $\frac{1}{5}$, and Allweather.com listed the chance as 0.3. Which forecast predicted the greatest chance of snow?   (Lesson 2-7) **D**

   Ⓐ WEAT   Ⓑ WFOR
   Ⓒ Myweather.com   Ⓓ Allweather.com

---

5. Amber owns a business that transfers photos to CD-ROMs. She charges her customers $24.95 for each CD-ROM. Her expenses include $575 for equipment and $0.80 for each blank CD-ROM. Which of these equations could be used to calculate her profit p for creating n CD-ROMs?   (Lesson 3-1) **A**

   Ⓐ $p = (24.95 - 0.8)n - 575$
   Ⓑ $p = (24.95 + 0.8)n + 575$
   Ⓒ $p = 24.95n - 574.2$
   Ⓓ $p = 24.95n + 575$

6. Which of the following equations has the same solution as $8(x + 2) = 12$?   (Lesson 3-4) **D**

   Ⓐ $8x + 2 = 12$
   Ⓑ $x + 2 = 4$
   Ⓒ $8x = 10$
   Ⓓ $2x + 4 = 3$

7. Eduardo is buying pizza toppings for a birthday party. His recipe uses 8 ounces of shredded cheese for 6 servings. How many ounces of cheese are needed for 27 servings?   (Lesson 3-6) **C**

   Ⓐ 27   Ⓑ 32
   Ⓒ 36   Ⓓ 162

8. The sum of x and $\frac{1}{y}$ is 0, and y does not equal 0. Which of the following is true?   (Lesson 3-8) **D**

   Ⓐ $x = -y$ Ⓑ $\frac{x}{y} = 0$
   Ⓒ $x = 1 - y$ Ⓓ $x = -\frac{1}{y}$

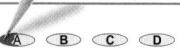

> **Test-Taking Tip**
> **Questions 2, 6 , 8**
> Always read every answer choice, particularly in questions that ask, "Which of the following is true?"

ExamView® Pro

Special banks of standardized test questions similar to those on the SAT, ACT, TIMSS 8, NAEP 8, and Algebra 1 End-of-Course tests can be found on this CD-ROM.

Part 2 | Short Response/Grid In

Record your answers on the answer sheet provided by your teacher or on a sheet of paper.

9. Let $x = 2$ and $y = -3$. Find the value of $\frac{x(xy + 5)}{4}$. (Lesson 1-2) **−0.5**

10. Use the formula $F = \frac{9}{5}C + 32$ to convert temperatures from Celsius (C) to Fahrenheit (F). If it is $-5°$ Celsius, what is the temperature in degrees Fahrenheit? (Lesson 2-3) **23**

11. The stem-and-leaf plot shows the high temperatures, in degrees Fahrenheit, during Mieko's two-week vacation. What was the median temperature during the two weeks? (Lesson 2-5) **93.5°F**

Stem	Leaf
8	8 9
9	0 0 1 1 2 5 5 5 9
10	0 1 1

$8 | 8 = 88°F$

12. Darnell keeps his cotton socks folded in pairs in his drawer. Five pairs are black, 2 pairs are navy, and 1 pair is brown. In the dark, he pulls out one pair at random. What are the odds that it is black? (Lesson 2-6) **5:3**

13. The sum of the ages of the Kruger sisters is 39. Their ages can be represented as three consecutive integers. What is the age of the middle sister? (Lesson 3-4) **13**

14. On a car trip, Tyson drove 65 miles more than half the number of miles Pete drove. Together they drove 500 miles. How many miles did Tyson drive? (Lesson 3-4) **210**

15. Solve $7(x + 2) + 4(2x - 3) = 47$ for x. (Lesson 3-5) **3**

16. A bookshop sells used hardcover books with a 45% discount. The price of a book was $22.95 when it was new. What is the discounted price for that book? (Lesson 3-7) **$12.62**

www.algebra1.com/standardized_test

17. The perimeter P of a rectangle with length ℓ and width w is $P = 2\ell + 2w$. Solve the formula for ℓ. (Lesson 3-8)

$$\ell = \frac{P - 2w}{2}$$

Part 3 | Extended Response

Record your answers on a sheet of paper.

18. Kirby's pickup truck travels at a rate of 6 miles every 10 minutes. Nola's SUV travels at a rate of 15 miles every 25 minutes. The speed limit on the street is 40 miles per hour. (Lesson 3-6)

a. Is either vehicle or are both vehicles exceeding the speed limit? Explain. **Neither; see margin for explanation.**

b. How many miles per minute would Kirby or Nola have to drive to reach a speed limit of 40 miles per hour? **about 0.7**

19. A chemist has one solution of citric acid that is 20% acid and another solution of citric acid that is 80% acid. She plans to mix these solutions together to make 200 liters of a solution that is 50% acid. (Lesson 3-9)

a. Complete the table to show the liters of 20% and 80% solutions that will be used to make the 50% solution. Use x to represent the number of liters of the 80% solution that will be used to make the 50% solution.

	Liters of Solution	Liters of Acid
20% Solution	$200 - x$	$0.20(200 - x)$
80% Solution	x	$0.80x$
50% Solution	200	$0.50(200)$

b. Write an equation that represents the number of liters of acid in the solution. **$0.20(200 - x) + 0.80x = 0.50(200)$**

c. How many liters of the 20% solution and how many of the 80% solution will the chemist need to mix together to make 200 liters of a 50% solution? **100 L of 20%, 100 L of 80%**

Chapter 3 Standardized Test Practice **187**

Evaluating Extended Response Questions

Extended Response questions are graded by using a multilevel rubric that guides you in assessing a student's knowledge of a particular concept.

Goal: Analyze rate data to determine vehicle speed and travel time.

Sample Scoring Rubric: The following rubric is a sample scoring device. You may wish to add more detail to this sample to meet your individual scoring needs.

Score	Criteria
4	A correct solution that is supported by well-developed, accurate explanations
3	A generally correct solution, but may contain minor flaws in reasoning or computation
2	A partially correct interpretation and/or solution to the problem
1	A correct solution with no supporting evidence or explanation
0	An incorrect solution indicating no mathematical understanding of the concept or task, or no solution is given

Answer

18a. When you calculate the miles per hour rate for each vehicle, both the pickup and the SUV are traveling at 36 mph. Therefore, neither is exceeding the speed limit.

Introduction

In this unit, students will explore data to determine whether a linear relationship exists. They will learn to represent a linear relationship as points on a coordinate plane, and as an equation representing a line.

Students will analyze how the equation and the graph of a line are related. They will extend their knowledge of linear graphing to inequalities and systems of linear equations.

Assessment Options

Unit 2 Test Pages 453–454 of the *Chapter 7 Resource Masters* may be used as a test or review for Unit 2. This assessment contains both multiple-choice and short answer items.

ExamView® Pro

This CD-ROM can be used to create additional unit tests and review worksheets.

An online, research-based instructional, assessment, and intervention tool that provides specific feedback on student mastery of state and national standards, instant remediation, and a data management system to track performance. For more information, contact mhdigitallearning.com.

UNIT
2

Many real-world situations such as Olympic race times can be represented using functions. In this unit, you will learn about linear functions and equations.

Linear Functions

Chapter 4
Graphing Relations and Functions

Chapter 5
Analyzing Linear Equations

Chapter 6
Solving Linear Inequalities

Chapter 7
Solving Systems of Linear Equations and Inequalities

Real-Life Math Videos

What's Math Got to Do With It? Real-Life Math Videos engage students by showing them how math is used in everyday situations. Use Video 2 with this unit.

Have students study the USA TODAY Snapshot.

- Ask them if it is possible to represent this data on a coordinate plane. If so, how would they graph the data? **not possible on a coordinate plane**

- Which sport seems to foster the most top medalists? **swimming**

- Point out to students that in their WebQuest they will be analyzing other statistics dealing with Olympic swimming.

Additional USA TODAY Snapshots appearing in Unit 2:

Chapter 4 Farmers growing bumper crop (p. 210)

Chapter 5 Dining out (p. 258)
　　　　　 Waiting on weddings (p. 284)

Chapter 6 Girls gear up for high school sports (p. 318)
　　　　　 Environment first (p. 350)

Chapter 7 India's exploding population (p. 386)

WebQuest Internet Project

The Spirit of the Games

The first Olympic Games featured only one event— a foot race. The 2004 Games will include thousands of competitors in about 300 events. In this project, you will explore how linear functions can be illustrated by the Olympics.

 Log on to www.algebra1.com/webquest. Begin your WebQuest by reading the Task.

Then continue working on your WebQuest as you study Unit 2.

Lesson	4-6	5-7	6-6	7-1
Page	230	304	357	373

USA TODAY Snapshots®

America's top medalists

Americans with most Summer Games medals:
Mark Spitz, Matt Biondi (swimming),
Carl Osburn (shooting)
11

Ray Ewry (track and field)
10

Carl Lewis, Martin Sheridan (track and field)
9

Shirley Babashoff, Charles Daniels (swimming)
8

Source: U.S. Olympic Committee

By Scott Boeck and Julie Stacey, USA TODAY

Unit 2　Linear Functions　189

WebQuest Internet Project

Problem-Based Learning A WebQuest is an online project in which students do research on the Internet, gather data, and make presentations using word processing, graphing, page-making, or presentation software. In each chapter, students advance to the next step in their WebQuest. At the end of Chapter 7, the project culminates with a presentation of their findings.

Teaching notes and sample answers are available in the *WebQuest and Project Resources.*

Graphing Relations and Functions
Chapter Overview and Pacing

Year-long and two-year pacing: pages T20–T21.

LESSON OBJECTIVES	PACING (days)			
	Regular		Block	
	Basic/ Average	Advanced	Basic/ Average	Advanced
4-1 The Coordinate Plane *(pp. 192–196)* • Locate points on the coordinate plane. • Graph points on a coordinate plane.	1	1	0.5	0.5
4-2 Transformations on the Coordinate Plane *(pp. 197–203)* • Transform figures by using reflections, translations, dilations, and rotations. • Transform figures on a coordinate plane by using reflections, translations, dilations, and rotations.	2	2	1	1
4-3 Relations *(pp. 204–211)* *Preview:* Use a graphing calculator to graph relations. • Represent relations as sets of ordered pairs, tables, mappings, and graphs. • Find the inverse of a relation.	2 (with 4-3 Preview)	2	1	1
4-4 Equations as Relations *(pp. 212–217)* • Use an equation to determine the range for a given domain. • Graph the solution set for a given domain.	1	1	0.5	0.5
4-5 Graphing Linear Equations *(pp. 218–225)* • Determine whether an equation is linear. • Graph linear equations. *Follow-Up:* Use a graphing calculator to graph linear equations.	2 (with 4-5 Follow-Up)	2	1	1
4-6 Functions *(pp. 226–231)* • Determine whether a relation is a function. • Find function values.	1	1	0.5	0.5
4-7 Arithmetic Sequences *(pp. 232–238)* *Preview:* Use a spreadsheet to generate number sequences and patterns. • Recognize arithmetic sequences. • Extend and write formulas for arithmetic sequences.	2 (with 4-7 Preview)	2	1	1
4-8 Writing Equations from Patterns *(pp. 240–245)* • Look for a pattern. • Write an equation given some of the solutions.	1	1	0.5	0.5
Study Guide and **Practice Test** *(pp. 246–251)* **Standardized Test Practice** *(pp. 252–253)*	1	1	0.5	0.5
Chapter Assessment	1	1	0.5	0.5
TOTAL	14	14	7	7

*An electronic version of this chapter is available on **StudentWorks**™. This backpack solution CD-ROM allows students instant access to the Student Edition, lesson worksheet pages, and web resources.*

Chapter Resource Manager

Timesaving Tools

TeacherWorks™

All-In-One Planner and Resource Center

See pages T5 and T21.

CHAPTER 4 RESOURCE MASTERS

Study Guide and Intervention	Practice (Skills and Average)	Reading to Learn Mathematics	Enrichment	Assessment	Prerequisite Skills Workbook	Applications*	Parent and Student Study Guide Workbook	5-Minute Check Transparencies	Interactive Chalkboard	AlgePASS: Tutorial Plus (lessons)	Materials
213–214	215–216	217	218				29	4-1	4-1		
219–220	221–222	223	224	275		GCS 29	30	4-2	4-2		
225–226	227–228	229	230			SC 7, SM 45–50	31	4-3	4-3		colored pencils, grid paper, graphing calculator
231–232	233–234	235	236	275, 277			32	4-4	4-4		
237–238	239–240	241	242			GCS 30	33	4-5	4-5	9	(*Follow-Up:* graphing calculator
243–244	245–246	247	248	276		SC 8, SM 139–144	34	4-6	4-6	10	
249–250	251–252	253	254		5–8		35	4-7	4-7		
255–256	257–258	259	260	276			36	4-8	4-8		scissors, string
				261–274, 278–280			37				

Key to Abbreviations: GCS = Graphing Calculator and Spreadsheet Masters,
SC = School-to-Career Masters,
SM = Science and Mathematics Lab Manual

ELL Study Guide and Intervention, Skills Practice, Practice, and Parent and Student Study Guide Workbooks are also available in Spanish.

Mathematical Connections and Background

Continuity of Instruction

Prior Knowledge

Students located and identified points on the coordinate plane in previous courses. In Chapter 1, students interpreted and drew graphs of functions from tables. They solved equations and formulas for given variables in Chapter 3.

This Chapter

This chapter connects algebraic equations to their geometric models. Students identify coordinates, locate points, and perform transformations of figures on a coordinate plane. They also identify relations, functions, the domain, the range, and the inverse of a relation. Students explore graphing linear relations using intercepts and tables. They learn to recognize, extend, and write arithmetic sequences, and then write equations from patterns.

Future Connections

The concept of functions is used throughout all mathematics, from algebra to beyond calculus. Functions are used to model many real-world situations that relate two variables. Looking for patterns helps find a trend in data. Many analysts use this concept to determine trends in various fields, such as finance, business, and sociology.

4-1 The Coordinate Plane

A coordinate plane contains two perpendicular number lines that intersect at their zero points, called the origin. These number lines, called axes, separate the plane into four quadrants, numbered I, II, III, and IV. Quadrant I is the top, right-hand quadrant, and the rest follow in a counterclockwise direction.

The location of points on a plane is described using the numbers on the axes that are vertically and horizontally aligned with the point. The numbers make an ordered pair written as (x, y). An ordered pair is named such because the order in which the coordinates are written is important. The corresponding number from the horizontal axis, the x-coordinate, is written first, followed by the y-coordinate. When graphing an ordered pair, start at $(0, 0)$, the origin. The x-coordinate indicates how many units to move right (positive) or left (negative). The y-coordinate indicates the number of units to move up (positive) or down (negative).

4-2 Transformations on the Coordinate Plane

Transformations of figures include reflections, translations, dilations, and rotations. The preimage is the original figure and the image is the transformed figure. A reflection is a flip over a line. A translation is the sliding of a figure in any direction. In a dilation, a figure is enlarged or reduced. When a figure is turned about a point, it is a called a rotation.

There are rules to help find the coordinates of an image when you know the coordinates of the preimage. To find the coordinates of a reflection, either the x- or y-coordinate is multiplied by -1. To translate a figure, add the amount of a translation to the coordinates to find the image. Each coordinate is multiplied by a scale factor in a dilation. In rotations, you sometimes switch the coordinates and multiply one or both of them by -1.

4-3 Relations

Students have learned in the past that a relation is a set of ordered pairs. Relations can also be presented as a table, a graph, or a mapping. Mappings demonstrate how each element of the domain is paired with elements of the range using arrows. The inverse of a relation is found by switching the coordinates in each ordered pair. In other words, the domain becomes the range and the range becomes the domain.

4-4 Equations as Relations

An equation written in two variables is a relation. Ordered pairs that make a statement true when substituted into the equation are solutions of the equation. The independent variables are the x-values of each ordered pair in the solution set. They represent the domain. The dependent variables are the y-values of each ordered pair in the solution set. They represent the range.

When equations are not written so that a variable is isolated on one side of the equal sign, solve for one variable. This variable is the dependent variable. Its value depends on the value of the independent variable substituted into the equation.

4-5 Graphing Linear Equations

The standard form of a linear equation is $Ax + By = C$. If the Properties of Equality can be applied to an equation to rewrite it in standard form, then the equation is linear. To graph a linear equation, first find coordinate pairs that make the statement true. Then plot the points and draw a line through the points. Another graphing method is to find the x- and y-intercepts by alternately replacing x and y with 0. Graph these points, then draw the line that contains these two points. All of the ordered pairs that lie on the line are solutions of the equation.

4-6 Functions

A function is a relation in which each element of the range is paired with exactly one element of the domain. This means that an x-coordinate cannot be repeated. To check if a graph is a function, make sure the graph does not touch any vertical line more than once. This is called the vertical line test.

Equations can be written using function notation. Solve the equation for the dependent variable, then replace that variable with f(independent variable), such as $f(x)$. The form $\ll$independent variable$\gg$, is used on some standardized tests.

4-7 Arithmetic Sequences

A sequence is a set of numbers in a specific order. If the terms of a sequence increase or decrease at a constant rate, it is called it is called an arithmetic sequence. The constant rate or value is called the common difference. The formula for finding a specific term in an arithmetic sequence is $a_n = a_1 + (n - 1)d$. This means to find a specific term, find the sum of the first term and the product of the common difference times one less than the number of the specific term.

4-8 Writing Equations from Patterns

Inductive reasoning is used when the problem-solving strategy of looking for a pattern is applied. There can be patterns in sequences of figures or of numbers. To write an equation for a list of data with two variables, use a ratio to compare the common difference of the range variables to the common difference of the domain variables. Next, write the equation as:

dependent variable
 = constant ratio(independent variable)

Quick Review Math Handbook

Hot Words includes a glossary of terms while Hot Topics consists of explanations of key mathematical concepts with exercises to test comprehension. This valuable resource can be used as a reference in the classroom or for home study.

Lesson	Hot Topics Section	Lesson	Hot Topics Section
GS4	6.2, 6.3, 6.4, 6.6	4-5	6.2, 6.7
4-1	6.2, 6.7	4-5F	6.7
4-2	6.7, 7.3	4-6	1.5, 2.3, 6.7
4-3P	6.7	4-7P	9.4
4-3	6.7	4-7	6.7
4-4	6.4, 6.7	4-8	6.1

GS = Getting Started, P = Preview, F = Follow-Up

 Additional mathematical information and teaching notes are available at www.algebra1.com/key_concepts.

Chapter 4

DAILY INTERVENTION and Assessment

Key to Abbreviations:
TWE = Teacher Wraparound Edition; CRM = Chapter Resource Masters

	Type	Student Edition	Teacher Resources	Technology/Internet
INTERVENTION	Ongoing	Prerequisite Skills, pp. 191, 196, 203, 211, 217, 223, 231, 238 Practice Quiz 1, p. 211 Practice Quiz 2, p. 231	5-Minute Check Transparencies *Prerequisite Skills Workbook*, pp. 5–8 Quizzes, *CRM* pp. 275–276 Mid-Chapter Test, *CRM* p. 277 Study Guide and Intervention, *CRM* pp. 213–214, 219–220, 225–226, 231–232, 237–238, 243–244, 249–250, 255–256	AlgePASS: Tutorial Plus, Lessons 9 and 10 www.algebra1.com/self_check_quiz www.algebra1.com/extra_examples
	Mixed Review	pp. 196, 203, 211, 217, 223, 231, 238, 245	Cumulative Review, *CRM* p. 278	
	Error Analysis	Find the Error, pp. 214, 236	Find the Error, *TWE* pp. 215, 236 Tips for New Teachers, *TWE* p. 220	
ASSESSMENT	Standardized Test Practice	pp. 196, 203, 210, 216, 223, 227, 228, 231, 238, 245, 251, 252–253	*TWE* pp. 252–253 Standardized Test Practice, *CRM* pp. 279–280	Standardized Test Practice CD-ROM www.algebra1.com/ standardized_test
	Open-Ended Assessment	Writing in Math, pp. 196, 203, 210, 216, 222, 231, 238, 245 Open Ended, pp. 194, 200, 208, 214, 221, 228, 236, 243 Standardized Test, p. 253	Modeling: *TWE* pp. 196, 203, 238, 245 Speaking: *TWE* pp. 217, 231 Writing: *TWE* pp. 211, 223 Open-Ended Assessment, *CRM* p. 273	
	Chapter Assessment	Study Guide, pp. 246–250 Practice Test, p. 251	Multiple-Choice Tests (Forms 1, 2A, 2B), *CRM* pp. 261–266 Free-Response Tests (Forms 2C, 2D, 3), *CRM* pp. 267–272 Vocabulary Test/Review, *CRM* p. 274	ExamView® Pro (see below) MindJogger Videoquizzes www.algebra1.com/ vocabulary_review www.algebra1.com/chapter_test

For more information on Yearly ProgressPro, see p. 188.

Algebra Lesson	Yearly ProgressPro Skill Lesson
4-1	The Coordinate Plane
4-2	Transformations on the Coordinate Plane
4-3	Relations
4-4	Equations as Relations
4-5	Graphing Linear Equations
4-6	Functions
4-7	Arithmetic Sequences
4-8	Writing Equations from Patterns

ExamView® Pro

Use the networkable **ExamView® Pro** to:
- Create **multiple versions** of tests.
- Create **modified** tests for *Inclusion* students.
- **Edit** existing questions and **add** your own questions.
- Use built-in **state curriculum correlations** to create tests aligned with state standards.
- Change **English** tests to **Spanish** and vice versa.

For more information on Intervention and Assessment, see pp. T8–T11.

Reading and Writing in Mathematics

Glencoe Algebra 1 provides numerous opportunities to incorporate reading and writing into the mathematics classroom.

Student Edition

- Foldables Study Organizer, p. 191
- Concept Check questions require students to verbalize and write about what they have learned in the lesson. (pp. 194, 200, 208, 214, 221, 228, 236, 243)
- Reading Mathematics, p. 239
- Writing in Math questions in every lesson, pp. 196, 203, 210, 216, 222, 231, 238, 245
- Reading Study Tip, pp. 198, 199, 227, 230, 233, 234
- WebQuest, p. 230

Teacher Wraparound Edition

- Foldables Study Organizer, pp. 191, 246
- Study Notebook suggestions, pp. 194, 200, 208, 215, 221, 229, 232, 236, 239, 243
- Modeling activities, pp. 196, 203, 238, 245
- Speaking activities, pp. 217, 231
- Writing activities, pp. 211, 223
- Differentiated Instruction, (Verbal/Linguistic), pp. 196, 213
- **ELL** Resources, pp. 190, 195, 196, 201, 209, 213, 216, 222, 230, 237, 239, 244, 246

Additional Resources

- Vocabulary Builder worksheets require students to define and give examples for key vocabulary terms as they progress through the chapter. (*Chapter 4 Resource Masters,* pp. vii-viii)
- Reading to Learn Mathematics master for each lesson (*Chapter 4 Resource Masters,* pp. 217, 223, 229, 235, 241, 247, 253, 259)
- *Vocabulary PuzzleMaker* software creates crossword, jumble, and word search puzzles using vocabulary lists that you can customize.
- *Teaching Mathematics with Foldables* provides suggestions for promoting cognition and language.
- *Reading and Writing in the Mathematics Classroom*
- *WebQuest and Project Resources*

For more information on Reading and Writing in Mathematics, see pp. T6–T7.

ENGLISH LANGUAGE LEARNERS

Lesson 4-2
Language Experience Approach to Illustrations

Have groups create, compare, and contrast graphic organizers of the four transformations in the lesson on a sheet of paper. Students should make the organizer with four columns showing how they are alike, how they are different, an example of each transformation, similarities and differences among the four, and a conclusion.

Lesson 4-6
Higher-Level Thinking

Give students in groups several index cards with relations in different forms. Have them find the domain and range of each relation. Then have them determine whether each relation represents a function and explain their reasoning.

Lesson 4-8
Peer Tutoring

Have students work in pairs to translate sequences into equations. If possible, pair English-Language Learners with a bilingual student. Help students to see the connection between the domain and range, and the linear relationship. Have the students write the difference between x and y values on the table or graph.

What You'll Learn

Have students read over the list of objectives and make a list of any words with which they are not familiar.

Why It's Important

Point out to students that this is only one of many reasons why each objective is important. Others are provided in the introduction to each lesson.

What You'll Learn

- **Lessons 4-1, 4-4, and 4-5** Graph ordered pairs, relations, and equations.
- **Lesson 4-2** Transform figures on a coordinate plane.
- **Lesson 4-3** Find the inverse of a relation.
- **Lesson 4-6** Determine whether a relation is a function.
- **Lessons 4-7 and 4-8** Look for patterns and write formulas for sequences.

Key Vocabulary

- coordinate plane (p. 192)
- transformation (p. 197)
- inverse (p. 206)
- function (p. 226)
- arithmetic sequence (p. 233)

Why It's Important

The concept of a function is used throughout higher mathematics, from algebra to calculus. A function is a rule or a formula. You can use a function to describe real-world situations like converting between currencies. For example, if you are in Mexico, you can calculate that an item that costs 100 pesos is equivalent to about 11 U.S. dollars. *You will learn how to convert different currencies in Lesson 4-4.*

190 Chapter 4 Graphing Relations and Functions

Lesson	NCTM Standards	Local Objectives
4-1	2, 3, 6, 8, 9, 10	
4-2	2, 3, 6, 8, 9, 10	
4-3 Preview	3, 8	
4-3	2, 3, 6, 8, 9, 10	
4-4	2, 3, 6, 8, 9, 10	
4-5	2, 3, 6, 8, 9, 10	
4-5 Follow-Up	2, 3, 10	
4-6	2, 3, 6, 8, 9, 10	
4-7 Preview	1, 2, 6	
4-7	1, 2, 6, 8, 9, 10	
4-8	1, 2, 3, 6, 8, 9, 10	

Key to NCTM Standards:

1=Number & Operations, 2=Algebra,
3=Geometry, 4=Measurement,
5=Data Analysis & Probability, 6=Problem Solving, 7=Reasoning & Proof,
8=Communication, 9=Connections,
10=Representation

Vocabulary Builder

The Key Vocabulary list introduces students to some of the main vocabulary terms included in this chapter. For a more thorough vocabulary list with pronunciations of new words, give students the Vocabulary Builder worksheets found on pages vii and viii of the *Chapter 4 Resource Masters*. Encourage them to complete the definition of each term as they progress through the chapter. You may suggest that they add these sheets to their study notebooks for future reference when studying for the Chapter 4 test.

▶ **Prerequisite Skills** To be successful in this chapter, you'll need to master these skills and be able to apply them in problem-solving situations. Review these skills before beginning Chapter 4.

For Lesson 4-1   Graph Real Numbers

Graph each set of numbers. *(For review, see Lesson 2-1.)* **1–4. See margin.**

1. $\{1, 3, 5, 7\}$ **2.** $\{-3, 0, 1, 4\}$ **3.** $\{-8, -5, -2, 1\}$ **4.** $\left\{\frac{1}{2}, 1, 1\frac{1}{2}, 2\right\}$

For Lesson 4-2   Distributive Property

Rewrite each expression using the Distributive Property. *(For review, see Lesson 1-5.)*

5. $3(7 - t)$ $21 - 3t$ **6.** $-4(w + 2)$ **7.** $-5(3b - 2)$ **8.** $\frac{1}{2}(2z + 4)$ $z + 2$
                       $-4w - 8$ $-15b + 10$

For Lessons 4-4 and 4-5   Solve Equations for a Specific Variable

Solve each equation for y. *(For review, see Lesson 3-8.)*

9. $2x + y = 1$ $y = 1 - 2x$ **10.** $x = 8 - y$ $y = 8 - x$ **11.** $6x - 3y = 12$ $y = 2x - 4$

12. $2x + 3y = 9$ **13.** $9 - \frac{1}{2}y = 4x$ **14.** $\frac{y + 5}{3} = x + 2$
     $y = -\frac{2}{3}x + 3$ $y = 18 - 8x$ $y = 3x + 1$

For Lesson 4-6   Evaluate Expressions

Evaluate each expression if $a = -1$, $b = 4$, and $c = -3$. *(For review, see Lesson 2-3.)*

15. $a + b - c$ **6**   **16.** $2c - b$ -10 **17.** $c - 3a$ **0**

18. $3a - 6b - 2c$ -21 **19.** $8a + \frac{1}{2}b - 3c$ **3**   **20.** $6a + 8b + \frac{2}{3}c$ **24**

FOLDABLES™ Study Organizer

Graphing Relations and Functions Make this Foldable to help you organize your notes. Begin with four sheets of grid paper.

Step 1 Fold

Fold each sheet of grid paper in half from top to bottom.

Step 2 Cut and Staple

Cut along each fold. Staple the eight half-sheets together to form a booklet.

Step 3 Cut Tabs into Margin

The top tab is 4 lines wide, the next tab is 8 lines wide, and so on.

Step 4 Label

Label each of the tabs with a lesson number.

Reading and Writing As you read and study the chapter, use each page to write notes and to graph examples.

This section provides a review of the basic concepts needed before beginning Chapter 4. Page references are included for additional student help.

Additional review is provided in the *Prerequisite Skills Workbook*, pp. 5–8.

Prerequisite Skills in the Getting Ready for the Next Lesson section at the end of each exercise set review a skill needed in the next lesson.

For Lesson	Prerequisite Skill
4-2	Using the Distributive Property (p. 196)
4-3	Writing Ordered Pairs (p. 203)
4-4	Finding Solution Sets (p. 211)
4-5	Solving Equations (p. 217)
4-6	Evaluating Expressions (p. 223)
4-7	Subtracting Integers (p. 231)
4-8	Writing Ordered Pairs (p. 238)

Answers

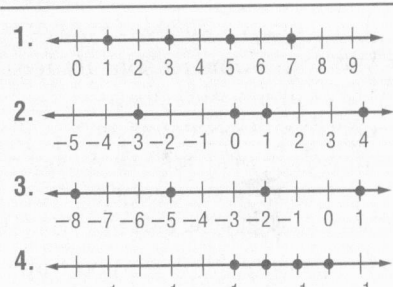

1.

2.

3.

4.

FOLDABLES™ Study Organizer

For more information about Foldables, see *Teaching Mathematics with Foldables*.

Summarizing Use this Foldable for student writing about graphing relations and functions. After students make their Foldable, have them label a tab for each lesson in this chapter. Students use their Foldable to take notes, record concepts, and define terms. At the end of each lesson, ask students to write a summary of the lesson in their own words. Summaries are useful for condensing data. Ask students what summaries and algebraic equations have in common.

4-1

The Coordinate Plane

1 Focus

Mathematical Background notes are available for this lesson on p. 190C.

Building on Prior Knowledge

In Chapter 2, students learned to graph on a number line. In this lesson, they should recognize that graphing on a coordinate plane is comparable to graphing on two perpendicular number lines.

How do archaeologists use coordinate systems?

Ask students:

- When archaeologists use a grid system to excavate an archaeological site, what does the grid simulate? **a map of the site**

- What are some reasons underwater archaeologists use a coordinate system at an archaeological site? **as a point of reference and to record the location of objects they find**

- **Geography** How do you think the grid on a map is similar to the grid system that archaeologists use? **The grid on a map is used to locate places on the map, just as the archaeologists' grid system is used to locate where objects were found.**

What You'll Learn

- Locate points on the coordinate plane.
- Graph points on a coordinate plane.

Vocabulary

- coordinate plane
- quadrant
- graph

How do archaeologists use coordinate systems?

Underwater archaeologists use a grid system to map excavation sites of sunken ships. The grid is used as a point of reference on the ocean floor.

The coordinate system is also used to record the location of objects they find. Knowing the position of each object helps archaeologists reconstruct how the ship sank and where to find other artifacts.

IDENTIFY POINTS In mathematics, points are located in reference to the *x*-axis and *y*-axis on a coordinate system or **coordinate plane**.

Example 1 Name an Ordered Pair

Write the ordered pair for each point.

a. point *G*

- Begin at point *G*.

- Follow along a vertical line through the point to find the *x*-coordinate on the *x*-axis. The *x*-coordinate is -4.

- Follow along a horizontal line through the point to find the *y*-coordinate on the *y*-axis. The *y*-coordinate is 3.

- So, the ordered pair for point *G* is $(-4, 3)$. This can also be written as $G(-4, 3)$.

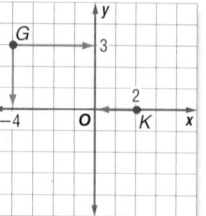

Unless marked otherwise, you can assume that each division on the axes represents 1 unit.

b. point *K*

- Begin at point *K*.

- *K* is on the *x*-axis 2 units from the origin. The *x*-coordinate is 2.

- The *y*-coordinate is 0 because point *K* is on the *x*-axis.

- Thus, the ordered pair for *K* is $(2, 0)$ or $K(2, 0)$.

Resource Manager

📁 Workbook and Reproducible Masters

Chapter 4 Resource Masters
- Study Guide and Intervention, pp. 213–214
- Skills Practice, p. 215
- Practice, p. 216
- Reading to Learn Mathematics, p. 217
- Enrichment, p. 218

Parent and Student Study Guide Workbook, p. 29

Transparencies

5-Minute Check Transparency 4-1
Answer Key Transparencies

Technology

Interactive Chalkboard

The x-axis and y-axis separate the coordinate plane into four regions, called **quadrants**. Notice which quadrants contain positive and negative x-coordinates and which quadrants contain positive and negative y-coordinates. The axes are not located in any of the quadrants.

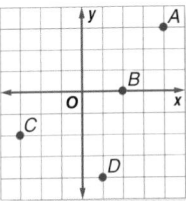

Example 2 Identify Quadrants

Write ordered pairs for points A, B, C, and D. Name the quadrant in which each point is located.

Use a table to help find the coordinates of each point.

Point	x-Coordinate	y-Coordinate	Ordered Pair	Quadrant
A	4	3	(4, 3)	I
B	2	0	(2, 0)	none
C	−3	−2	(−3, −2)	III
D	1	−4	(1, −4)	IV

GRAPH POINTS To **graph** an ordered pair means to draw a dot at the point on the coordinate plane that corresponds to the ordered pair. This is sometimes called *plotting a point*. When graphing an ordered pair, start at the origin. The x-coordinate indicates how many units to move right (positive) or left (negative). The y-coordinate indicates how many units to move up (positive) or down (negative).

Example 3 Graph Points

Plot each point on a coordinate plane.

a. $R(-4, 1)$
  - Start at the origin.
  - Move left 4 units since the x-coordinate is −4.
  - Move up 1 unit since the y-coordinate is 1.
  - Draw a dot and label it R.

b. $S(0, -5)$
  - Start at the origin.
  - Since the x-coordinate is 0, the point will be located on the y-axis.
  - Move down 5 units.
  - Draw a dot and label it S.

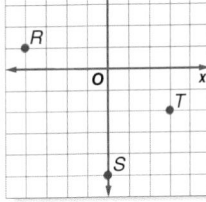

c. $T(3, -2)$
  - Start at the origin.
  - Move right 3 units and down 2 units.
  - Draw a dot and label it T.

www.algebra1.com/extra_examples

2 Teach

IDENTIFY POINTS

In-Class Examples

Power Point®

1 Write the ordered pair for each point.
  a. point A (3, −2)
  b. point B (0, −2)

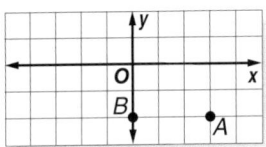

2 Write ordered pairs for points A, B, C, and D. Name the quadrant in which each point is located.

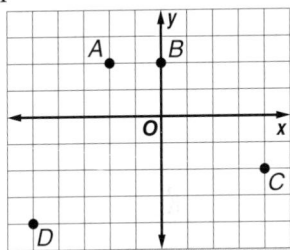

Point	Ordered Pair	Quadrant
A	(−2, 2)	II
B	(0, 2)	none
C	(4, −2)	IV
D	(−5, −4)	III

GRAPH POINTS

In-Class Example

Power Point®

3 Plot each point on a coordinate plane.
  a. $A(3, 1)$
  b. $B(-2, 0)$
  c. $C(2, -5)$

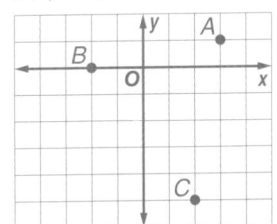

Teacher to Teacher

Larry Romary Heritage H.S., Monroeville, IN

"I have students trace a picture of an animal from a coloring book (as it will be well outlined) onto a piece of graph paper. Students select about 40–50 points on the figure that would define the outline of the animal. They write the ordered pairs so that when graphed and connected the animal's picture would result. I give their ordered pairs to my other classes to plot and discover what the animal is."

In-Class Example

Power Point®

4 **GEOGRAPHY** Use the map in Example 4 to answer the following questions.

a. Name the city at about (33°, 80°). **Charleston**

b. Estimate the latitude and longitude of Las Vegas. (37°, 115°)

---

3 Practice/Apply

Study Notebook

Have students—

• add the definitions/examples of the vocabulary terms to their Vocabulary Builder worksheets for Chapter 4.

• draw a coordinate plane labeling the parts with the vocabulary terms from this lesson.

• include any other item(s) that they find helpful in mastering the skills in this lesson.

About the Exercises...

Organization by Objective
• **Identify Points:** 13–24, 37–43
• **Graph Points:** 25–30

Odd/Even Assignments
Exercises 13–36 are structured so that students practice the same concepts whether they are assigned odd or even problems.

Assignment Guide

Basic: 13–21 odd, 25–43 odd, 44–47, 51–71

Average: 13–43 odd, 44–47, 51–71 (optional: 48–50)

Advanced: 14–42 even, 44–65 (optional: 66–71)

Example 4 Use a Coordinate System

GEOGRAPHY Latitude and longitude lines form a system of coordinates to designate locations on Earth. Latitude lines run east and west and are the first coordinate of the ordered pairs. Longitude lines run north and south and are the second coordinate of the ordered pairs.

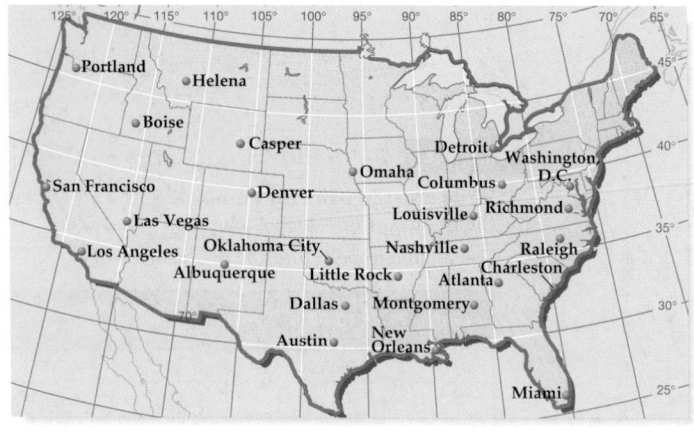

a. Name the city at (40°, 105°).
Locate the latitude line at 40°. Follow the line until it intersects with the longitude line at 105°. The city is Denver.

b. Estimate the latitude and longitude of Washington, D.C.
Locate Washington, D.C., on the map. It is close to 40° latitude and 75° longitude. There are 5° between each line, so a good estimate is 39° for the latitude and 77° for the longitude.

TEACHING TIP
Point out to students that on maps, the vertical measurement is named first, followed by the horizontal measurement. In the traditional x, y coordinate plane, the horizontal distance will always be named first.

Check for Understanding

Concept Check

1. See margin.

1. **Draw** a coordinate plane. Label the origin, x-axis, y-axis, and the quadrants.

2. **Explain** why (−1, 4) does not name the same point as (4, −1). **See margin.**

3. **OPEN ENDED** Give the coordinates of a point for each quadrant in the coordinate plane. **Sample answer: I(3, 3), II(−3, 3), III(−3, −3), IV(3, −3).**

Guided Practice

Write the ordered pair for each point shown at the right. Name the quadrant in which the point is located.

GUIDED PRACTICE KEY

Exercises	Examples
4–7	1, 2
8–11	3
12	4

4. E (−2, −5); III
5. F (−1, 1); II
6. G (4, 4); I
7. H (−4, −2); III

Plot each point on a coordinate plane. **8–11. See right.**

8. J(2, 5)
9. K(−1, 4)
10. L(0, −3)
11. M(−2, −2)

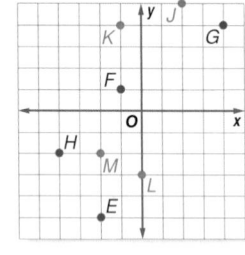

Application

12. **ARCHITECTURE** Chun Wei has sketched the southern view of a building. If A is located on a coordinate system at (−40, 10), locate the coordinates of the other vertices.
B(0, 10), C(0, 20), D(−20, 20), E(−40, 40)

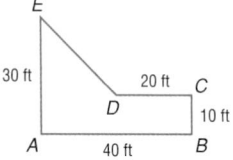

Answers

1.
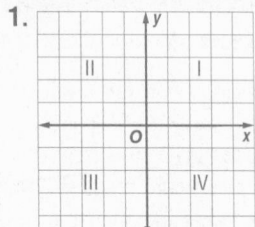

2. To graph (−1, 4) move 1 unit left from the origin and 4 units up. This point is in quadrant II. To graph (4, −1) move 4 units right from the origin and 1 unit down. This point is in quadrant IV.

★ indicates increased difficulty

Practice and Apply

Homework Help

For Exercises	See Examples
13–24, 39	1, 2
25–36	3
37, 38, 40–43	4

Extra Practice
See page 828.

Write the ordered pair for each point shown at the right. Name the quadrant in which the point is located.

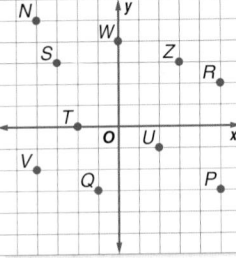

13. N (−4, 5); II
14. P (5, −3); IV
15. Q (−1, −3); III
16. R (5, 2); I
17. S (−3, 3); II
18. T (−2, 0); none
19. U (2, −1); IV
20. V (−4, −2); III
21. W (0, 4); none
22. Z (3, 3); I

★ 23. Write the ordered pair that describes a point 12 units down from and 7 units to the right of the origin. **(7, −12)**

★ 24. Write the ordered pair for a point that is 9 units to the left of the origin and lies on the x-axis. **(−9, 0)**

Plot each point on a coordinate plane. 25–36. **See margin.**

25. $A(3, 5)$
26. $B(−2, 2)$
27. $C(4, −2)$
28. $D(0, −1)$
29. $E(−2, 5)$
30. $F(−3, −4)$
31. $G(4, 4)$
32. $H(−4, 4)$
33. $I(3, 1)$
34. $J(−1, −3)$
35. $K(−4, 0)$
36. $L(2, −4)$

GEOGRAPHY For Exercises 37 and 38, use the map on page 194.

37. Name two cities that have approximately the same latitude.

38. Name two cities that have approximately the same longitude.
Sample answer: Austin and Oklahoma City

37. Sample answer: Louisville and Richmond

39. **ARCHAEOLOGY** The diagram at the right shows the positions of artifacts found on the ocean floor. Write the coordinates of the location for each object: coins, plate, goblet, and vase. **coins, (3, 5); plate, (7, 2); goblet, (8, 4); vase, (5, 9)**

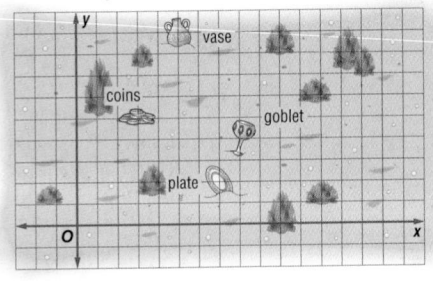

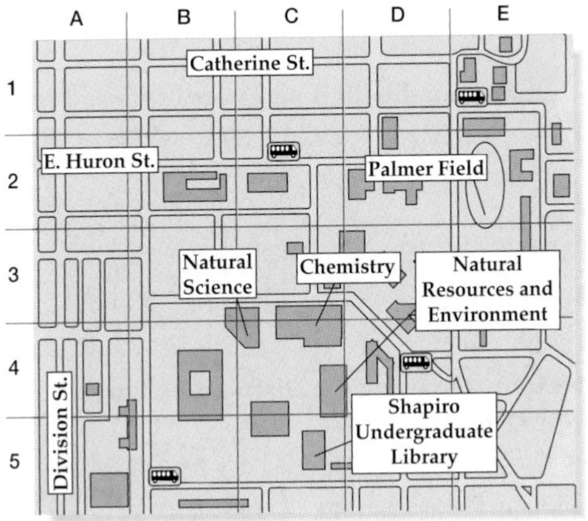

MAPS For Exercises 40–43, use the map of the University of Michigan at the left.
On many maps, letters and numbers are used to define a region or sector. For example, Palmer Field is located in sector E2. **41. C4**

40. In what sector is the Undergraduate Library? **C5**

41. In what sector are most of the science buildings?

42. Which street goes from sector (A, 2) to (D, 2)?

43. Name the sectors that have bus stops.
42. E. Huron St.   43. B5, C2, D4, E1

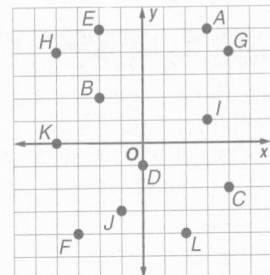

44. **CRITICAL THINKING** Describe the possible locations, in terms of quadrants or axes, for the graph of (x, y) given each condition.
a. $xy > 0$ **I, III**   b. $xy < 0$ **II, IV**   c. $xy = 0$
c. x-axis, y-axis, origin

25–36.

Enrichment, p. 218

Study Guide and Intervention, p. 213 (shown) and p. 214
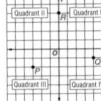

Identify Points In the diagram at the right, points are located in reference to two perpendicular number lines called **axes**. The horizontal number line is the **x-axis**, and the vertical number line is the **y-axis**. The plane containing the x- and y-axes is called the **coordinate plane**. Points in the coordinate plane are named by ordered pairs of the form (x, y). The first number, or **x-coordinate** corresponds to a number on the x-axis. The second number, or **y-coordinate**, corresponds to a number on the y-axis.

The axes divide the coordinate plane into Quadrants I, II, III, and IV, as shown. The point where the axes intersect is called the **origin**. The origin has coordinates (0, 0).

Example 1 Write an ordered pair for point R above.
The x-coordinate is 0 and the y-coordinate is 4. Thus the ordered pair for R is (0, 4).

Example 2 Write ordered pairs for points P and Q above. Then name the quadrant in which each point is located.
The x-coordinate of P is −3 and the y-coordinate is −2. Thus the ordered pair for P is (−3, −2). P is in Quadrant III.

The x-coordinate of Q is 4 and the y-coordinate is −1. Thus the ordered pair for Q is (4, −1). Q is in Quadrant IV.

Exercises

Write the ordered pair for each point shown at the right. Name the quadrant in which the point is located.

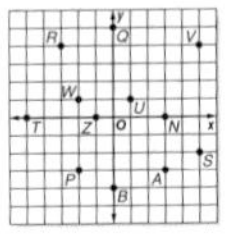

1. N (3, 0), none
2. P (−2, 3), III
3. Q (0, 5), none
4. R (−3, 4), II
5. S (5, −2), IV
6. T (−5, 0), none
7. U (1, 1), I
8. V (5, 4), I
9. W (−2, 1), II
10. Z (−1, 0), none
11. A (3, −3), IV
12. B (0, −4), none

13. Write the ordered pair that describes a point 4 units down from and 3 units to the right of the origin. (3, −4)

14. Write the ordered pair that is 8 units to the left of the origin and lies on the x-axis. (−8, 0)

Skills Practice, p. 215 and Practice, p. 216 (shown)

Write the ordered pair for each point shown at the right. Name the quadrant in which the point is located.

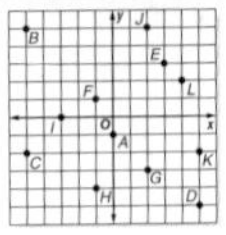

1. A (0, −1); none
2. B (−5, 5); II
3. C (−5, −2); III
4. D (5, −5); IV
5. E (3, 3); I
6. F (−1, 1); II
7. G (2, −3); IV
8. H (−1, −4); III
9. I (−3, 0); none
10. J (2, 5); I
11. K (5, −2); IV
12. L (4, 2); I

Plot each point on the coordinate plane at the right. 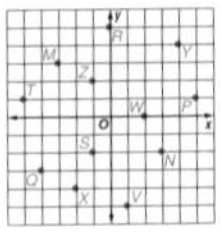
13. M(−3, 3)
14. N(3, −2)
15. P(5, 1)
16. Q(−4, −3)
17. R(0, 5)
18. S(−1, −2)
19. T(−5, 1)
20. V(1, −5)
21. W(2, 0)
22. X(−2, −4)
23. Y(4, 4)
24. Z(−1, 2)

25. **CHESS** Letters and numbers are used to show the positions of chess pieces and to describe their moves. For example, in the diagram at the right, a white pawn is located at f5. Name the positions of each of the remaining chess pieces.
white pawns: a7, c6; black pawns: b4, d7; white king: g3; black king: e8
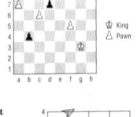

ARCHAEOLOGY For Exercises 26 and 27, use the grid at the right that shows the location of arrowheads excavated at a **midden**—a place where people in the past dumped trash, food remains, and other discarded items.
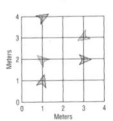
26. Write the coordinates of each arrowhead. (1, 1), (3, 2), (1, 4)
27. Suppose an archaeologist discovers two other arrowheads located at (1, 2) and (3, 3). Draw an arrowhead at each of these locations on the grid.

Reading to Learn Mathematics, p. 217   **ELL**
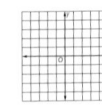

Pre-Activity How do archaeologists use coordinate systems?
Read the introduction to Lesson 4-1 at the top of page 192 in your textbook.
What do the terms *grid system*, *grid*, and *coordinate system* mean to you? See students' work.

Reading the Lesson
1. Use the coordinate plane shown at the right.
a. Label the origin O.
b. Label the y-axis y.
c. Label the x-axis x.

2. Explain why the coordinates of the origin are (0, 0).
Sample answer: The origin is the intersection of two number lines at their common zero point.

3. Use the ordered pair (−2, 3).
a. Explain how to identify the x- and y-coordinates. The x-coordinate is the first number, the y-coordinate is the second number.
b. Name the x- and y-coordinates. The x-coordinate is −2, the y-coordinate is 3.
c. Describe the steps you would use to locate the point (−2, 3) on the coordinate plane. Start at the origin. Move left 2 units. Then move up 3 units.

4. What does the term *quadrant* mean? Sample answer: one of the four regions in the coordinate plane

Helping You Remember
5. Explain how the way the axes are labeled on the coordinate plane can help you remember how to plot the point for an ordered pair. Sample answer: The right side of the horizontal axis is labeled with the letter x. This is the side of the horizontal number line where you find positive numbers. The top end of the vertical number line is labeled with the letter y. This is the part of the vertical number line where you find positive numbers.

Midpoint
The *midpoint* of a line segment is the point that lies exactly halfway between the two endpoints of the segment. The coordinates of the midpoint of a line segment whose endpoints are (x_1, y_1) and (x_2, y_2) are given by $\left(\dfrac{x_1 + x_2}{2}, \dfrac{y_1 + y_2}{2}\right)$.

Find the midpoint of each line segment with the given endpoints.
1. (7, 1) and (−3, 1)
(2, 1)
2. (5, −2) and (9, −8)
(7, −5)
3. (−4, 4) and (4, −4)
(0, 0)
4. (−3, −6) and (−10, −15)
(−6.5, −10.5)

Open-Ended Assessment

Modeling Have students draw a map of their dream bedroom on a coordinate plane. The map should include some of the objects and furnishings in the room, but the objects should not be labeled. Students should identify the objects on the map with the ordered pair that makes up the coordinates of each object.

Getting Ready for Lesson 4-2

PREREQUISITE SKILL Students will learn about transformations on the coordinate plane in Lesson 4-2. Dilations are one type of transformation. In dilations, the scale factor is distributed by multiplication over each coordinate in an ordered pair. Use Exercises 66–71 to determine your students' familiarity with the Distributive Property.

Answer

45. Archaeologists used coordinate systems as a mapping guide and as a system to record locations of artifacts. Answers should include the following.

- The grid gives archaeologists a point of reference so they can identify and explain to others the location of artifacts in a site they are excavating. You can divide the space so more people can work at the same time in different areas.

- Knowing the exact location of artifacts helps archaeologists reconstruct historical events.

---

45. **WRITING IN MATH** Answer the question that was posed at the beginning of the lesson. **See margin.**

How do archaeologists use coordinate systems?

Include the following in your answer:

- an explanation of how dividing an excavation site into sectors can be helpful in excavating a site, and
- a reason why recording the exact location of an artifact is important.

Standardized Test Practice
Ⓐ Ⓑ Ⓒ Ⓓ

For Exercises 46 and 47, refer to the figure at the right.

46. $ABCD$ is a rectangle with its center at the origin. If the coordinates of vertex B are $(3, 2)$, what are the coordinates of vertex A? **C**

    Ⓐ $(-3, -2)$ Ⓑ $(3, -2)$

    Ⓒ $(-3, 2)$ Ⓓ $(3, 2)$

47. What is the length of $\overline{AD}$? **B**

    Ⓐ 6 units   Ⓑ 4 units

    Ⓒ 5 units   Ⓓ 3 units

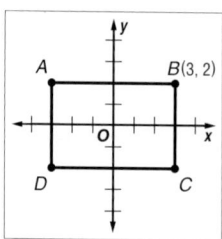

Extending the Lesson

The **midpoint** of a line segment is the point that lies exactly halfway between the two endpoints. The midpoint of a line segment whose endpoints are at (a, b) and (c, d) is at $\left(\dfrac{a+c}{2}, \dfrac{b+d}{2}\right)$. **Find the midpoint of each line segment whose endpoints are given.**

48. $(7, 1)$ and $(-3, 1)$ 49. $(5, -2)$ and $(9, -8)$ 50. $(-4, 4)$ and $(4, -4)$
     (2, 1)   **(7, -5)**   **(0, 0)**

Maintain Your Skills

Mixed Review

51. **AIRPLANES** At 1:30 P.M., an airplane leaves Tucson for Baltimore, a distance of 2240 miles. The plane flies at 280 miles per hour. A second airplane leaves Tucson at 2:15 P.M. and is scheduled to land in Baltimore 15 minutes before the first airplane. At what rate must the second airplane travel to arrive on schedule? *(Lesson 3-9)* **320 mph**

Solve each equation or formula for the variable specified. *(Lesson 3-8)*

52. $3x + b = 2x + 5$ for x $x = 5 - b$ 53. $10c = 2(2d + 3c)$ for d $d = c$

54. $6w - 3h = b$ for h $h = \dfrac{6w - b}{3}$ 55. $\dfrac{3(a - t)}{4} = 2t$ for t $t = \dfrac{3a}{11}$

Find each square root. Round to the nearest hundredth if necessary. *(Lesson 2-7)*

56. $-\sqrt{81}$ **−9**   57. $\sqrt{63}$ **7.94**   58. $\sqrt{180}$ **13.42**   59. $-\sqrt{256}$ **−16**

Evaluate each expression. *(Lesson 2-1)*

60. $52 + |18 - 7|$ **63**   61. $|81 - 47| + 17$ **51**   62. $42 - |60 - 74|$ **28**

63. $36 - |15 - 21|$ **30**   64. $|10 - 16 + 27|$ **21**   65. $|38 - 65 - 21|$ **48**

Getting Ready for the Next Lesson

PREREQUISITE SKILL Rewrite each expression using the Distributive Property. Then simplify. *(To review the **Distributive Property**, see Lesson 1-5.)*

66. $4(x + y)$ $4x + 4y$ 67. $-1(x + 3)$ $-x - 3$ 68. $3(1 - 6y)$ $3 - 18y$

69. $-3(2x - 5)$ $-6x + 15$ 70. $\frac{1}{3}(2x + 6y)$ $\frac{2}{3}x + 2y$ 71. $\frac{1}{4}(5x - 2y)$ $\frac{5}{4}x - \frac{1}{2}y$

196 **Chapter 4** Graphing Relations and Functions

Transformations on the Coordinate Plane

What You'll Learn

- Transform figures by using reflections, translations, dilations, and rotations.
- Transform figures on a coordinate plane by using reflections, translations, dilations, and rotations.

Vocabulary
- transformation
- preimage
- image
- reflection
- translation
- dilation
- rotation

How are transformations used in computer graphics?

Computer programs can create movements that mimic real-life situations. A new CD-ROM-based flight simulator replicates an actual flight experience so closely that the U.S. Navy is using it for all of their student aviators. The movements of the on-screen graphics are accomplished by using mathematical transformations.

TRANSFORM FIGURES **Transformations** are movements of geometric figures. The **preimage** is the position of the figure before the transformation, and the **image** is the position of the figure after the transformation.

reflection
a figure is flipped over a line

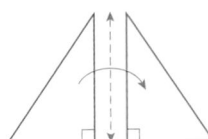

translation
a figure is slid in any direction

dilation
a figure is enlarged or reduced

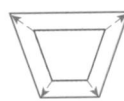

rotation
a figure is turned around a point

Example 1 Identify Transformations

Identify each transformation as a *reflection, translation, dilation,* or *rotation.*

a.    b. 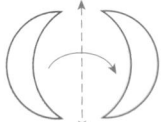   c. 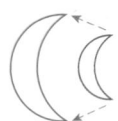   d.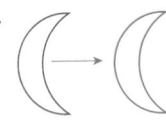

a. The figure has been turned around a point. This is a rotation.
b. The figure has been flipped over a line. This is a reflection.
c. The figure has been increased in size. This is a dilation.
d. The figure has been shifted horizontally to the right. This is a translation.

---

1 Focus

5-Minute Check Transparency 4-2 Use as a quiz or review of Lesson 4-1.

Mathematical Background notes are available for this lesson on p. 190C.

Building on Prior Knowledge

Students may have experienced these geometric transformations under the names *flip, slide, turn,* and *enlarge* or *shrink.* Check students' familiarity with these terms before presenting the more formal terminology.

How are transformations used in computer graphics?

Ask students:

- How can actual movement, such as airplane flight, be simulated on a computer screen? **Sample answer: Objects on the screen can be made to move to simulate the way objects on the ground appear to move as the plane flies by.**

- **Aviation** Why might computer flight simulators be a good way to train beginning student pilots? **Sample answer: Student pilots can use the simulator to become familiar with the operation and controls of an airplane without actually flying one.**

Resource Manager

Workbook and Reproducible Masters

Chapter 4 Resource Masters
- Study Guide and Intervention, pp. 219–220
- Skills Practice, p. 221
- Practice, p. 222
- Reading to Learn Mathematics, p. 223
- Enrichment, p. 224
- Assessment, p. 275

Graphing Calculator and Spreadsheet Masters, p. 29
Parent and Student Study Guide Workbook, p. 30

Transparencies
5-Minute Check Transparency 4-2
Answer Key Transparencies

Technology
Interactive Chalkboard

TRANSFORM FIGURES

1 Identify each transformation as a *reflection, translation, dilation,* or *rotation.*

a. 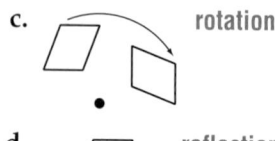 dilation

b. translation

c. rotation

d. reflection

TRANSFORM FIGURES ON THE COORDINATE PLANE

2 A trapezoid has vertices $W(-1, 4)$, $X(4, 4)$, $Y(4, 1)$, and $Z(-3, 1)$.

a. Trapezoid $WXYZ$ is reflected over the y-axis. Find the coordinates of the vertices of the image. $W'(1, 4)$, $X'(-4, 4)$, $Y'(-4, 1)$, $Z'(3, 1)$

b. Graph trapezoid $WXYZ$ and its image $W'X'Y'Z'$.

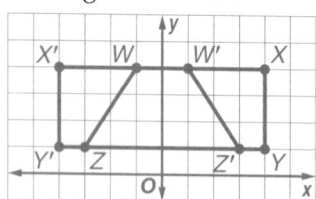

TRANSFORM FIGURES ON THE COORDINATE PLANE You can perform transformations on a coordinate plane by changing the coordinates of the points on a figure. The points on the translated figure are indicated by the prime symbol ′ to distinguish them from the original points.

Key Concept — Transformations on the Coordinate Plane

Name	Words	Symbols	Model
Reflection	To reflect a point over the *x*-axis, multiply the *y*-coordinate by −1.	reflection over *x*-axis: $(x, y) \rightarrow (x, -y)$	
	To reflect a point over the *y*-axis, multiply the *x*-coordinate by −1.	reflection over *y*-axis: $(x, y) \rightarrow (-x, y)$	
Translation	To translate a point by an ordered pair (a, b), add a to the *x*-coordinate and b to the *y*-coordinate.	$(x, y) \rightarrow (x + a, y + b)$	
Dilation	To dilate a figure by a scale factor k, multiply both coordinates by k. If $k > 1$, the figure is enlarged. If $0 < k < 1$, the figure is reduced.	$(x, y) \rightarrow (kx, ky)$	
Rotation	To rotate a figure 90° *counterclockwise* about the origin, switch the coordinates of each point and then multiply the new first coordinate by −1.	90° rotation: $(x, y) \rightarrow (-y, x)$	
	To rotate a figure 180° about the origin, multiply both coordinates of each point by −1.	180° rotation: $(x, y) \rightarrow (-x, -y)$	

Study Tip

Reading Math
The *vertices* of a polygon are the endpoints of the angles.

Example 2 *Reflection*

A parallelogram has vertices $A(-4, 3)$, $B(1, 3)$, $C(0, 1)$, and $D(-5, 1)$.

a. Parallelogram *ABCD* is reflected over the *x*-axis. Find the coordinates of the vertices of the image.

To reflect the figure over the *x*-axis, multiply each *y*-coordinate by −1.

$(x, y) \rightarrow (x, -y)$ $(x, y) \rightarrow (x, -y)$
$A(-4, 3) \rightarrow A'(-4, -3)$ $C(0, 1) \rightarrow C'(0, -1)$
$B(1, 3) \rightarrow B'(1, -3)$ $D(-5, 1) \rightarrow D'(-5, -1)$

The coordinates of the vertices of the image are $A'(-4, -3)$, $B'(1, -3)$, $C'(0, -1)$, and $D'(-5, -1)$.

DAILY INTERVENTION — Unlocking Misconceptions

Rotations Rotations are traditionally expressed in a *counterclockwise* direction. This may give students the false impression that figures can only be rotated counterclockwise. To rotate figures 90° *clockwise* about the origin, switch the two coordinates of each point, and then multiply the new *second* coordinate by −1. The direction of a 180° rotation about the origin does not matter because whether the figure is rotated clockwise or counterclockwise, the final figure will be in the same position.

Reading Math
Parallelogram *ABCD* and its image *A'B'C'D'* are said to be **symmetric** about the *x*-axis. The *x*-axis is called the **line of symmetry**.

b. **Graph parallelogram** *ABCD* **and its image** *A'B'C'D'*.

Graph each vertex of the parallelogram *ABCD*. Connect the points.

Graph each vertex of the reflected image *A'B'C'D'*. Connect the points.

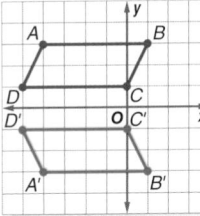

Example 3 Translation

Triangle *ABC* **has vertices** *A*(−2, 3), *B*(4, 0), **and** *C*(2, −5).

a. **Find the coordinates of the vertices of the image if it is translated 3 units to the left and 2 units down.**

To translate the triangle 3 units to the left, add −3 to the *x*-coordinate of each vertex. To translate the triangle 2 units down, add −2 to the *y*-coordinate of each vertex.

$$(x, y) \to (x - 3, y - 2)$$
$$A(-2, 3) \to A'(-2 - 3, 3 - 2) \to A'(-5, 1)$$
$$B(4, 0) \to B'(4 - 3, 0 - 2) \to B'(1, -2)$$
$$C(2, -5) \to C'(2 - 3, -5 - 2) \to C'(-1, -7)$$

The coordinates of the vertices of the image are *A'*(−5, 1), *B'*(1, −2), and *C'*(−1, −7).

b. **Graph triangle** *ABC* **and its image.**

The preimage is △*ABC*.
The translated image is △*A'B'C'*.

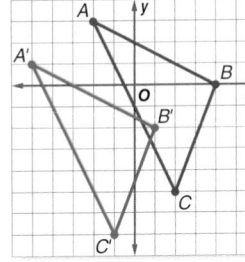

Example 4 Dilation

A trapezoid has vertices *L*(−4, 1), *M*(1, 4), *N*(7, 0), **and** *P*(−3, −6).

a. **Find the coordinates of the dilated trapezoid** *L'M'N'P'* **if the scale factor is** $\frac{3}{4}$.

To dilate the figure multiply the coordinates of each vertex by $\frac{3}{4}$.

$$(x, y) \to \left(\frac{3}{4}x, \frac{3}{4}y\right)$$
$$L(-4, 1) \to L'\left(\frac{3}{4} \cdot (-4), \frac{3}{4} \cdot 1\right) \to L'\left(-3, \frac{3}{4}\right)$$
$$M(1, 4) \to M'\left(\frac{3}{4} \cdot 1, \frac{3}{4} \cdot 4\right) \to M'\left(\frac{3}{4}, 3\right)$$
$$N(7, 0) \to N'\left(\frac{3}{4} \cdot 7, \frac{3}{4} \cdot 0\right) \to N'\left(5\frac{1}{4}, 0\right)$$
$$P(-3, -6) \to P'\left(\frac{3}{4} \cdot (-3), \frac{3}{4} \cdot (-6)\right) \to P'\left(-2\frac{1}{4}, -4\frac{1}{2}\right)$$

The coordinates of the vertices of the image are $L'\left(-3, \frac{3}{4}\right)$, $M'\left(\frac{3}{4}, 3\right)$, $N'\left(5\frac{1}{4}, 0\right)$, and $P'\left(-2\frac{1}{4}, -4\frac{1}{2}\right)$.

(continued on the next page)

www.algebra1.com/extra_examples

DAILY
INTERVENTION

Differentiated Instruction

Visual/Spatial Some students need to manipulate figures physically to perceive the concepts in this lesson. Have students model each transformation on a large grid with cutouts of the figure. Have them color one side blue and one side red so they can flip, slide, and rotate figures about the plane.

3 Triangle *ABC* has vertices *A*(−2, 1), *B*(2, 4), and *C*(1, 1).

a. Find the coordinates of the vertices of the image if it is translated 3 units to the right and 5 units down. *A'*(1, −4), *B'*(5, −1), *C'*(4, −4)

b. Graph triangle *ABC* and its image.

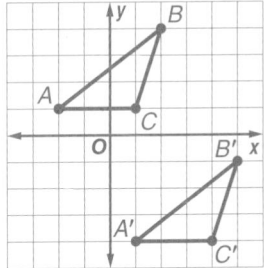

4 A trapezoid has vertices *E*(−1, 2), *F*(2, 1), *G*(2, −1), and *H*(−1, −2).

a. Find the coordinates of the dilated trapezoid *E'F'G'H'* if the scale factor is 2. *E'*(−2, 4), *F'*(4, 2), *G'*(4, −2), *H'*(−2, −4)

b. Graph the preimage and its image.

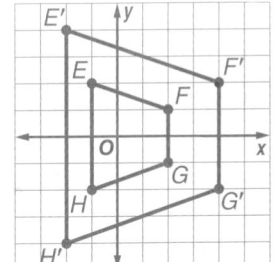

Interactive Chalkboard
PowerPoint® Presentations

This CD-ROM is a customizable Microsoft® PowerPoint® presentation that includes:

- Step-by-step, dynamic solutions of each In-Class Example from the Teacher Wraparound Edition
- Additional, Your Turn exercises for each example
- The 5-Minute Check Transparencies
- Hot links to Glencoe Online Study Tools

Teaching Tip In this age of digital timepieces, some students may not be familiar with *clockwise* and *counterclockwise*. Have them use their fingers to draw an imaginary circle in a counterclockwise direction.

5 Triangle *ABC* has vertices *A*(1, −3), *B*(3, 1), and *C*(5, −2).

a. Find the coordinates of the image of △*ABC* after it is rotated 180° about the origin. *A'*(−1, 3), *B'*(−3, −1), *C'*(−5, 2)

b. Graph the preimage and its image.

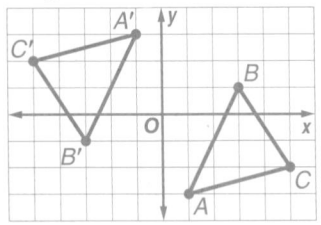

---

b. Graph the preimage and its image.

The preimage is trapezoid *LMNP*.

The image is trapezoid *L'M'N'P'*.

Notice that the image has sides that are three-fourths the length of the sides of the original figure.

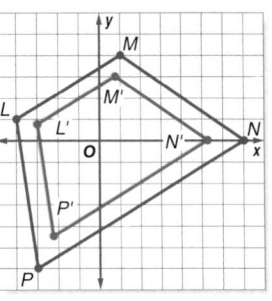

Example 5 Rotation

Triangle *XYZ* has vertices *X*(1, 5), *Y*(5, 2), and *Z*(−1, 2).

a. Find the coordinates of the image of △*XYZ* after it is rotated 90° counterclockwise about the origin.

To find the coordinates of the vertices after a 90° rotation, switch the coordinates of each point and then multiply the new first coordinate by −1.

$(x, y) \rightarrow (-y, x)$

$X(1, 5) \rightarrow X'(-5, 1)$

$Y(5, 2) \rightarrow Y'(-2, 5)$

$Z(-1, 2) \rightarrow Z'(-2, -1)$

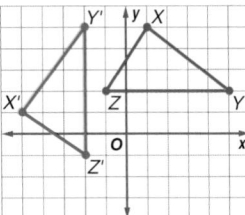

b. Graph the preimage and its image.

The image is △*XYZ*.

The rotated image is △*X'Y'Z'*.

---

3 Practice/Apply

Study Notebook

Have students—
- add the definitions/examples of the vocabulary terms to their Vocabulary Builder worksheets for Chapter 4.
- make drawings to illustrate each transformation.
- include any other item(s) that they find helpful in mastering the skills in this lesson.

Check for Understanding

Concept Check
1. **Compare and contrast** the size, shape, and orientation of a preimage and an image for each type of transformation. **See margin.**

2. **OPEN ENDED** Draw a figure on the coordinate plane. Then show a dilation of the object that is an enlargement and a dilation of the object that is a reduction. **See margin.**

Guided Practice **Identify each transformation as a *reflection, translation, dilation,* or *rotation*.**

GUIDED PRACTICE KEY	
Exercises	Examples
3, 4	1
5–10	2–5

3. 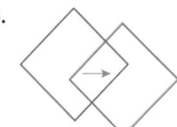 translation

4.  rotation

Find the coordinates of the vertices of each figure after the given transformation is performed. Then graph the preimage and its image.

5–8. See pp.253A–253H for graphs.

5. *P'*(1, −2), *Q'*(4, −4), *R'*(2, 3)

5. triangle *PQR* with *P*(1, 2), *Q*(4, 4), and *R*(2, −3) reflected over the *x*-axis

6. quadrilateral *ABCD* with *A*(4, 2), *B*(4, −2), *C*(−1, −3), and *D*(−3, 2) translated 3 units up *A'*(4, 5), *B'*(4, 1), *C'*(−1, 0), *D'*(−3, 5)

7. parallelogram *EFGH* with *E*(−1, 4), *F*(5, −1), *G*(2, −4), and *H*(−4, 1) dilated by a scale factor of 2 *E'*(−2, 8), *F'*(10, −2), *G'*(4, −8), *H'*(−8, 2)

8. triangle *JKL* with *J*(0, 0), *K*(−2, −5), and *L*(−4, 5) rotated 90° counterclockwise about the origin *J'*(0, 0), *K'*(5, −2), *L'*(−5, −4)

Answers

1.

Transformation	Size	Shape	Orientation
Reflection	same	same	changes
Rotation	same	same	changes
Translation	same	same	same
Dilation	changes	same	same

2. Sample answer:

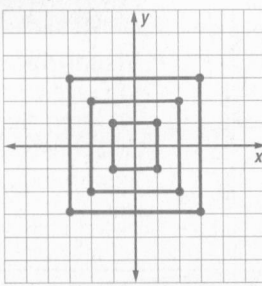

Application **NAVIGATION** **For Exercises 9 and 10, use the following information.**
A ship was heading on a chartered route when it was blown off course by a storm.
The ship is now ten miles west and seven miles south of its original destination.

9. Using a coordinate grid, make a drawing to show the original destination *A* and
   the current position *B* of the ship. **See margin.**

10. Using coordinates (*x, y*) to represent the original destination of the ship, write an
    ordered pair to show its current location. (*x* − 10, *y* − 7)

★ indicates increased difficulty

Practice and Apply

Homework Help

For Exercises	See Examples
11–16, 37, 38	1
17–36	2–5

Extra Practice
See page 828.

Identify each transformation as a *reflection, translation, dilation,* or *rotation*.

11.  translation

12.  rotation

13. 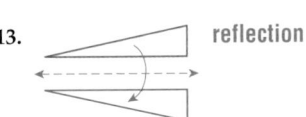 reflection

14.  dilation

15. 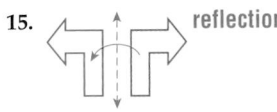 reflection

16. 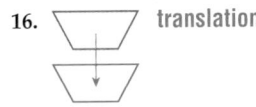 translation

For Exercises 17–26, complete parts a and b. 17–26. See pp. 253A–253H for graphs.

a. **Find the coordinates of the vertices of each figure after the given
   transformation is performed.**

b. **Graph the preimage and its image.**

17. *R*′(−2, 0), *S*′(2, −3), *T*′(2, 3)
    17. triangle *RST* with *R*(2, 0), *S*(−2, −3), and *T*(−2, 3) reflected over the *y*-axis

18. trapezoid *ABCD* with *A*(2, 3), *B*(5, 3), *C*(6, 1), and *D*(−2, 1) reflected over the
    x-axis *A*′(2, −3), *B*′(5, −3), *C*′(6, −1), *D*′(−2, −1)

19. quadrilateral *RSTU* with *R*(−6, 3), *S*(−4, 2), *T*(−1, 5), and *U*(−3, 7) translated
    8 units right *R*′(2, 3), *S*′(4, 2), *T*′(7, 5), *U*′(5, 7)

20. parallelogram *MNOP* with *M*(−6, 0), *N*(−4, 3), *O*(−1, 3), and *P*(−3, 0) translated
    3 units right and 2 units down *M*′(−3, −2), *N*′(−1, 1), *O*′(2, 1), *P*′(0, −2)

21. trapezoid *JKLM* with *J*(−4, 2), *K*(−2, 4), *L*(4, 4), and *M*(−4, −4) dilated by a scale
    factor of $\frac{1}{2}$ *J*′(−2, 1), *K*′(−1, 2), *L*′(2, 2), *M*′(−2, −2)

22. square *ABCD* with *A*(−2, 1), *B*(2, 2), *C*(3, −2), and *D*(−1, −3) dilated by a scale
    factor of 3 *A*′(−6, 3), *B*′(6, 6), *C*′(9, −6), *D*′(−3, −9)

23. *F*′(3, −2), *G*′(−2, −5), *H*′(−6, −3)
    23. triangle *FGH* with *F*(−3, 2), *G*(2, 5), and *H*(6, 3) rotated 180° about the origin

24. quadrilateral *TUVW* with *T*(−4, 2), *U*(−2, 4), *V*(0, 2), and *W*(−2, −4) rotated 90°
    25. *W*′(−1, −2), *X*′(3, −2), *Y*′(0, 4), *Z*′(−4, 4)
    counterclockwise about the origin *T*′(−2, −4), *U*′(−4, −2), *V*′(−2, 0), *W*′(4, −2)

★ 25. parallelogram *WXYZ* with *W*(−1, 2), *X*(3, 2), *Y*(0, −4), and *Z*(−4, −4) reflected
    over the *y*-axis, then rotated 180° about the origin

26. *P*′(−2, −4), *Q*′(1, −3), *R*′(0, 0), *S*′(−4, 0), *T*′(−5, −3)
    ★ 26. pentagon *PQRST* with *P*(0, 5), *Q*(3, 4), *R*(2, 1), *S*(−2, 1), and *T*(−3, 4) reflected
    over the *x*-axis, then translated 2 units left and 1 unit up

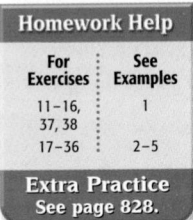Lesson 4-2 Transformations on the Coordinate Plane **201**

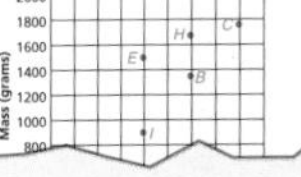

9.

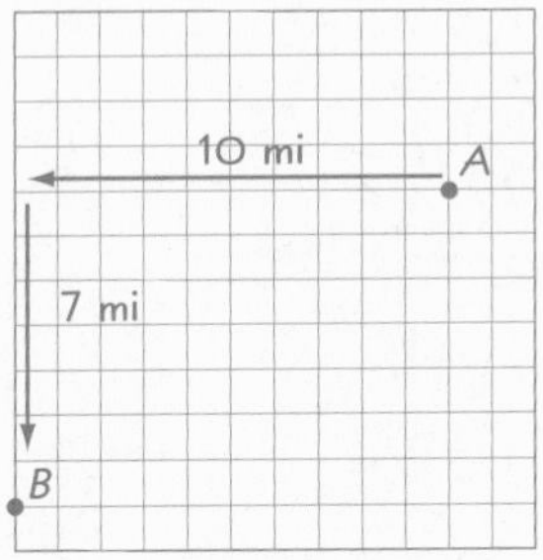

Study Guide and Intervention,
p. 219 (shown) and p. 220

Transform Figures Transformations are movements of geometric figures. The
preimage is the position of the figure before the transformation, and the **image** is the
position of the figure after the transformation.

Reflection	A figure is flipped over a line.
Translation	A figure is slid horizontally, vertically, or both.
Dilation	A figure is enlarged or reduced.
Rotation	A figure is turned around a point.

Example Determine whether each transformation is a *reflection, translation,
dilation,* or *rotation.*

a. The figure has been flipped over a line, so this is a reflection.

b.  The figure has been turned around a point, so this is a rotation.

c. The figure has been reduced in size, so this is a dilation.

d.  The figure has been shifted horizontally to the right, so this is a
translation.

Exercises

Determine whether each transformation is a *reflection, translation, dilation,* or
rotation.

1. 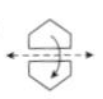 reflection
2. dilation
3.  rotation
4. translation
5. 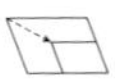 dilation
6.  rotation

**Skills Practice, p. 221 and
Practice, p. 222 (shown)**

Identify each transformation as a *reflection, translation, dilation,* or *rotation.*

1. 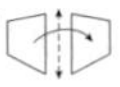  reflection 2.  translation 3.  rotation

For Exercises 4–6, complete parts a and b.
a. Find the coordinates of the vertices of each figure after the given
transformation is performed.
b. Graph the preimage and its image.

4. triangle *DEF* with *D*(2, 3), *E*(4, 1), and *F*(1, −1) translated 4 units left and 1 unit down *D*′(−2, 0), *E*′(0, −2), *F*′(−3, −4) 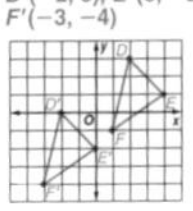
5. trapezoid *EFGH* with *E*(3, 2), *F*(3, −3), *G*(1, −2), and *H*(1, 1) reflected over the *y*-axis *E*′(−3, 2), *F*′(−3, −3), *G*′(−1, −2), *H*′(−1, 1) 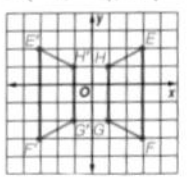
6. triangle *XYZ* with *X*(3, 1), *Y*(4, −2), and *Z*(1, −3) rotated 90° counterclockwise about the origin *X*′(−1, 3), *Y*′(2, 4), *Z*′(3, 1)

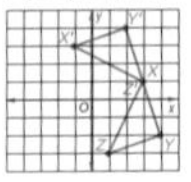

GRAPHICS For Exercises 7–9, use the diagram at the right
and the following information.
A designer wants to dilate the rocket by a scale factor of $\frac{1}{2}$, and
then translate it $5\frac{1}{2}$ units up. 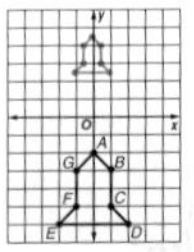
7. Write the coordinates for the vertices of the rocket.
A(0, −2), *B*(1, −3), *C*(1, −5), *D*(2, −6), *E*(−2, −6),
F(−1, −5), *G*(−1, −3)
8. Find the coordinates of the final position of the rocket.
A′(0, 4½), *B*′(½, 4), *C*′(½, 3), *D*′(1, 2½), *E*′(−1, 2½), *F*′(−½, 3), *G*′(−½, 4)
9. Graph the image on the coordinate plane.
10. **DESIGN** Ramona transformed figure *ABCDEF* to design a
pattern for a quilt. Name two different sets of transformations
she could have used to design the pattern. Sample answer:
reflection over the *x*-axis, 90° counterclockwise
rotation, and then reflection over the *y*-axis; three 90°
counterclockwise rotations

**Reading to Learn
Mathematics, p. 223**   ELL

Pre-Activity How are transformations used in computer graphics?

Read the introduction to Lesson 4-2 at the top of page 197 in your textbook.

In the sentence, "Computer graphic designers can create movement that
mimics real-life situations," what phrase indicates the use of
transformations? create movement

Reading the Lesson

1. Suppose you look at a diagram that shows two figures *ABCDE* and *A′B′C′D′E′*. If one
figure was obtained from the other by using a transformation, how do you tell which is
the original figure? The letters that have no prime symbols are used for
vertices of the original figure.

2. Write the letter of the term and the Roman numeral of the figure that best matches each
statement.
a. A figure is flipped over a line. __C, I__   A. dilation   I. 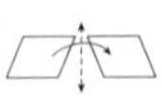
b. A figure is turned around a point. __D, III__   B. translation   II.
c. A figure is enlarged or reduced. __A, II__   C. reflection   III.
d. A figure is slid horizontally, vertically, or both. __B, IV__   D. rotation   IV.

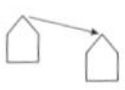

Helping You Remember

3. Give examples of things in everyday life that can help you remember what reflections,
dilations, and rotations are. Sample answer: For a reflection, think of looking
at yourself in a mirror. For a dilation, think of how your hand looks if you
hold it far from your face and then move it straight in, very close to your
face. For a rotation, think of twisting the top of a jar to open the jar.

Enrichment, p. 224

The Legendary City of Ur

The city of Ur was founded more than five thousand years ago in
Mesopotamia (modern-day Iraq). It was one of the world's first cities.
Between 1922 and 1934, archeologists discovered many treasures from
this ancient city. A large cemetery from the 26th century B.C. was
found to contain large quantities of gold, silver, bronze, and jewels. The
many cultural artifacts that were found, such as musical instruments,
weapons, mosaics, and statues, have provided historians with valuable
clues about the civilization that existed in early Mesopotamia.

1. Suppose that the ordered pairs below represent the
volume (cm³) and mass (grams) of ten artifacts from
the city of Ur. Plot each point on the graph.
A(10, 150)
B(150, 1350)
C(200, 1760)
D(50, 525)
E(100, 1500)

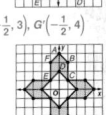

Answer

37.

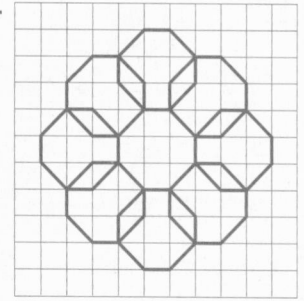

27. $A(-5, -1)$, $B(-3, -3)$, $C(-5, -5)$, $D(-5, -4)$, $E(-8, -4)$, $F(-8, -2)$, $G(-5, -2)$

28. $A'(-3, 1)$, $B'(-1, 3)$, $C'(-3, 5)$, $D'(-3, 4)$, $E'(-6, 4)$, $F'(-6, 2)$, $G'(-3, 2)$

ANIMATION For Exercises 27–29, use the diagram at the right.
An animator places an arrow representing an airplane on a coordinate grid. She wants to move the arrow 2 units right and then reflect it across the x-axis.

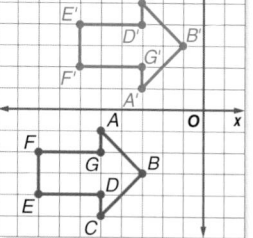

27. Write the coordinates for the vertices of the arrow.

28. Find the coordinates of the final position of the arrow.

29. Graph the image. **See right.**

30. Trapezoid $JKLM$ with $J(-6, 0)$, $K(-1, 5)$, $L(-1, 1)$, and $M(-3, -1)$ is translated to $J'K'L'M'$ with $J'(-3, -2)$, $K'(2, 3)$, $L'(2, -1)$, $M'(0, -3)$. Describe this translation. **3 units right, 2 units down**

31. Triangle QRS with vertices $Q(-2, 6)$, $R(8, 0)$, and $S(6, 4)$ is dilated. If the image $Q'R'S'$ has vertices $Q'(-1, 3)$, $R'(4, 0)$, and $S'(3, 2)$, what is the scale factor? $\frac{1}{2}$

★ 32. Describe the transformation of parallelogram $WXYZ$ with $W(-5, 3)$, $X(-2, 5)$, $Y(0, 3)$, and $Z(-3, 1)$ if the coordinates of its image are $W'(5, 3)$, $X'(2, 5)$, $Y'(0, 3)$, and $Z'(3, 1)$. **reflection over the y-axis**

★ 33. Describe the transformation of triangle XYZ with $X(2, -1)$, $Y(-5, 3)$, and $Z(4, 0)$ if the coordinates of its image are $X'(1, 2)$, $Y'(-3, -5)$, and $Z'(0, 4)$. **90° counterclockwise rotation**

DIGITAL PHOTOGRAPHY For Exercises 34–36, use the following information.
Soto wants to enlarge a digital photograph that is 1800 pixels wide and 1600 pixels high (1800 × 1600) by a scale factor of $2\frac{1}{2}$.

34. What will be the dimensions of the new digital photograph? **4500 × 4000**

35. Use a coordinate grid to draw a picture representing the 1800 × 1600 digital photograph. Place one corner of the photograph at the origin and write the coordinates of the other three vertices. **See pp. 253A–253H.**

36. Draw the enlarged photograph and write its coordinates. **See pp. 253A–253H.**

ART For Exercises 37 and 38, use the following information.
On grid paper, draw an octagon like the one shown.

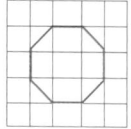

★ 37. Reflect the octagon over each of its sides. Describe the pattern that results.

38. Could this same pattern be drawn using any of the other transformations? If so, which kind? **yes; translation**

39. **CRITICAL THINKING** Make a conjecture about the coordinates of a point (x, y) that has been rotated 90° *clockwise* about the origin. $(y, -x)$

40. **CRITICAL THINKING** Determine whether the following statement is *sometimes*, *always*, or *never* true.

A reflection over the x-axis followed by a reflection over the y-axis gives the same result as a rotation of 180°. **always**

41. WRITING IN MATH   Answer the question that was posed at the beginning of the lesson. **See margin.**

How are transformations used in computer graphics?

Include the following in your answer:
- examples of movements that could be simulated by transformations, and
- types of other industries that might use transformations in computer graphics to simulate movement.

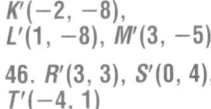

Standardized Test Practice
Ⓐ Ⓑ Ⓒ Ⓓ

42. The coordinates of the vertices of quadrilateral $QRST$ are $Q(-2, 4)$, $R(3, 7)$, $S(4, -2)$, and $T(-5, -3)$. If the quadrilateral is moved up 3 units and right 1 unit, which point below has the correct coordinates? **C**

Ⓐ $Q'(1, 5)$ Ⓑ $R'(4, 4)$ Ⓒ $S'(5, 1)$ Ⓓ $T'(-6, 0)$

43. x is $\frac{2}{3}$ of y and y is $\frac{1}{4}$ of z. If $x = 14$, then $z = $ **C**

Ⓐ 48.   Ⓑ 72.   Ⓒ 84.   Ⓓ 96.

Extending the Lesson

44. $A'(3, 4)$, $B'(2, 2)$, $C'(3, -2)$, $D'(4, 0)$

45. $J'(-3, -5)$, $K'(-2, -8)$, $L'(1, -8)$, $M'(3, -5)$

46. $R'(3, 3)$, $S'(0, 4)$, $T'(-4, 1)$

Graph the image of each figure after a reflection over the graph of the given equation. Find the coordinates of the vertices.

44. $x = 0$

45. $y = -3$

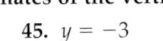

46. $y = x$

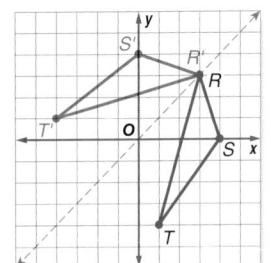

Maintain Your Skills

Mixed Review

Plot each point on a coordinate plane. *(Lesson 4-1)* **47–52. See margin.**

47. $A(2, -1)$ **48.** $B(-4, 0)$ **49.** $C(1, 5)$
50. $D(-1, -1)$ **51.** $E(-2, 3)$ **52.** $F(4, -3)$

53. CHEMISTRY   Jamaal needs a 25% solution of nitric acid. He has 20 milliliters of a 30% solution. How many milliliters of a 15% solution should he add to obtain the required 25% solution? *(Lesson 3-9)* **10 mL**

58. {(1, 9.95), (2, 11.45), (3, 12.95), (4, 14.45), (5, 15.95), (6, 17.45)}

Two dice are rolled and their sum is recorded. Find each probability. *(Lesson 2-6)*

54. $P(\text{sum is less than 9})$ $\frac{13}{18} \approx 72\%$ **55.** $P(\text{sum is greater than 10})$ $\frac{1}{12} \approx 8\%$
56. $P(\text{sum is less than 7})$ $\frac{5}{12} \approx 42\%$ **57.** $P(\text{sum is greater than 4})$ $\frac{5}{6} \approx 83\%$

Getting Ready for the Next Lesson

PREREQUISITE SKILL   Write a set of ordered pairs that represents the data in the table. *(To review ordered pairs, see Lesson 1-8.)*

58.

Number of toppings	1	2	3	4	5	6
Cost of large pizza ($)	9.95	11.45	12.95	14.45	15.95	17.45

59. {(0, 100), (5, 90), (10, 81), (15, 73), (20, 66), (25, 60), (30, 55)}

59.

Time (minutes)	0	5	10	15	20	25	30
Temperature of boiled water as it cools (°C)	100	90	81	73	66	60	55

Open-Ended Assessment

Modeling Draw a coordinate plane on the chalkboard or overhead projector. Give a student volunteer a cardboard cutout figure to place on the coordinate plane. Once the student volunteer has placed the figure on the coordinate plane, ask the student to model one of the transformations described in this lesson.

Getting Ready for Lesson 4-3

PREREQUISITE SKILL Students will learn about relations in Lesson 4-3. Students will learn that a relation is a set of ordered pairs. Use Exercises 58–59 to determine your students' familiarity with writing ordered pairs.

Assessment Options

Quiz (Lessons 4-1 and 4-2) is available on p. 275 of the *Chapter 4 Resource Masters.*

Answers

41. Artists use computer graphics to simulate movement, change the size of objects, and create designs. Answers should include the following.

- Objects can appear to move by using a series of translations. Moving forward can be simulated by enlarging objects using dilations so they appear to be getting closer.
- Computer graphics are used in special effects in movies, animated cartoons, and web design.

47–52.

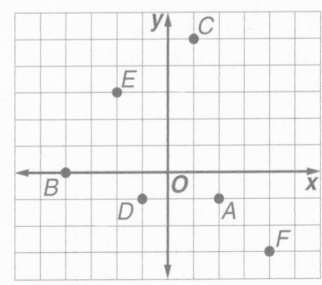

Graphs of Relations

You can represent a relation as a graph using a TI-83 Plus graphing calculator.

Graph the relation {(3, 7), (−8, 12), (−5, 7), (11, −1)}.

Step 1 *Enter the data.*

- Enter the *x*-coordinates in L1 and the *y*-coordinates in L2.

  KEYSTROKES: [STAT] [ENTER] 3 [ENTER] −8 [ENTER] −5 [ENTER] 11 [ENTER] ▶ 7 [ENTER] 12 [ENTER] 7 [ENTER] −1 [ENTER]

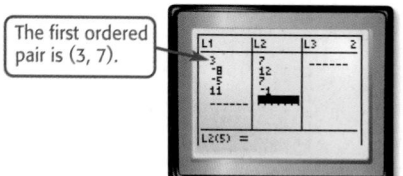

> The first ordered pair is (3, 7).

Step 2 *Format the graph.*

- Turn on the statistical plot.

  KEYSTROKES: [2nd] [STAT PLOT] [ENTER] [ENTER]

- Select the scatter plot, L1 as the Xlist and L2 as the Ylist.

  KEYSTROKES: ▼ [ENTER] ▼ [2nd] [L1] [ENTER] [2nd] [L2] [ENTER]

Step 3 *Choose the viewing window.*

- Be sure you can see all of the points. [−10, 15] scl: 1 by [−5, 15] scl: 1

  KEYSTROKES: [WINDOW] −10 [ENTER] 15 [ENTER] 1 [ENTER] −5 [ENTER] 15 [ENTER] 1

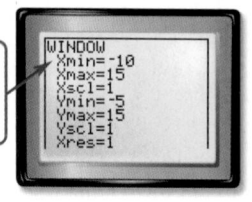

> The *x*-axis will go from −10 to 15 with a tick mark at every unit.

Step 4 *Graph the relation.*

- Display the graph.

  KEYSTROKES: [GRAPH]

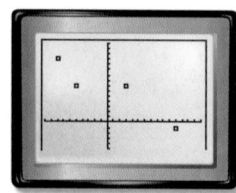

[−10, 15] scl: 1 by [−5, 15] scl: 1

Exercises

Graph each relation. Sketch the result. 1–4. See pp. 253A-253H.

1. {(10, 10), (0, −6), (4, 7), (5, −2)}

2. {(−4, 1), (3, −5), (4, 5), (−5, 1)}

3. {(12, 15), (10, −16), (11, 7), (−14, −19)}

4. {(45, 10), (23, 18), (22, 26), (35, 26)}

5. MAKE A CONJECTURE How are the values of the domain and range used to determine the scale of the viewing window? **See margin.**

 www.algebra1.com/other_calculator_keystrokes

Answer

5. The scale of the *x*-axis should include the least and greatest values in the domain and the scale of the *y*-axis should include the least and greatest values in the range.

Getting Started

Clear Lists In order for the investigation directions to work properly, all previous data lists must be cleared from memory using the following keystrokes: [2nd] [MEM] 4 [ENTER]. In the display, you should see:

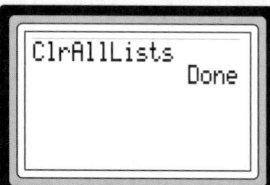

> ClrAllLists
> Done

Teach

- **Step 1** In Edit mode, students can navigate between lists by using the arrow keys. Make sure students enter negative numbers with the [(−)] key, and not the [−] key.

- **Step 2** Students should compare their screens to the screen in their textbooks. Most likely, their screens will match those shown.

- **Steps 3 and 4** Students must set Xmin, Xmax, Ymin, and Ymax as shown or their graphs will not look like the one shown in Step 4.

Assess

Have students look at the *x* and *y* values for Exercises 3 and 4. Explain what they will have to do to be able to view properly the graphs of these relations. **Change the viewing window.**

4-3 Relations

What You'll Learn

- Represent relations as sets of ordered pairs, tables, mappings, and graphs.
- Find the inverse of a relation.

Vocabulary
- mapping
- inverse

How can relations be used to represent baseball statistics?

Ken Griffey, Jr.'s, batting statistics for home runs and strikeouts can be represented as a set of ordered pairs. The number of home runs are the first coordinates, and the number of strikeouts are the second coordinates.

You can plot the ordered pairs on a graph to look for patterns.

Ken Griffey, Jr.		
Year	Home Runs	Strikeouts
1994	40	73
1995	17	53
1996	49	104
1997	56	121
1998	56	121
1999	48	108
2000	40	117
2001	22	72

Study Tip

Look Back
To review **relations**, see Lesson 1-8.

REPRESENT RELATIONS Recall that a *relation* is a set of ordered pairs. A relation can be represented by a set of ordered pairs, a table, a graph, or a **mapping**. A mapping illustrates how each element of the domain is paired with an element in the range. Study the different representations of the same relation below.

Ordered Pairs
(1, 2)
(−2, 4)
(0, −3)

Table

x	y
1	2
−2	4
0	−3

Graph

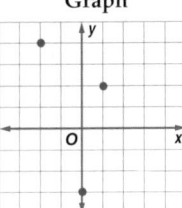

Mapping

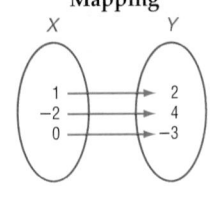

Example 1 Represent a Relation

a. Express the relation {(3, 2), (−1, 4), (0, −3), (−3, 4), (−2, −2)} as a table, a graph, and a mapping.

Table

List the set of *x*-coordinates in the first column and the corresponding *y*-coordinates in the second column.

x	y
3	2
−1	4
0	−3
−3	4
−2	−2

Graph

Graph each ordered pair on a coordinate plane.

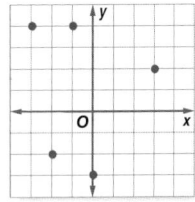

(continued on the next page)

---

1 Focus

5-Minute Check Transparency 4-3 Use as a quiz or review of Lesson 4-2.

Mathematical Background notes are available for this lesson on p. 190C.

How can relations be used to represent baseball statistics?

Ask students:

- Give an example of an ordered pair from the data table shown. **Sample answer: (56, 121), assuming the *x* value is home runs and the *y* value is strikeouts.**

- Why might plotting the data on a graph help a person analyze this data? **Sample answer: Looking at the data graphically might reveal patterns that are not easy to detect when simply looking at the numbers.**

Resource Manager

Workbook and Reproducible Masters

Chapter 4 Resource Masters
- Study Guide and Intervention, pp. 225–226
- Skills Practice, p. 227
- Practice, p. 228
- Reading to Learn Mathematics, p. 229
- Enrichment, p. 230

Parent and Student Study Guide Workbook, p. 31
School-to-Career Masters, p. 7
Science and Mathematics Lab Manual, pp. 45–50
Teaching Algebra with Manipulatives Masters, pp. 1, 86

 Transparencies
5-Minute Check Transparency 4-3
Answer Key Transparencies

 Technology
Interactive Chalkboard

REPRESENT RELATIONS

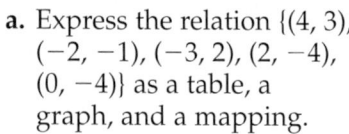

Teaching Tip Point out to students that the letters D and R are often used to name the sets of numbers representing the domain and range.

1 **a.** Express the relation {(4, 3), (−2, −1), (−3, 2), (2, −4), (0, −4)} as a table, a graph, and a mapping.

x	y
4	3
−2	−1
−3	2
2	−4
0	−4

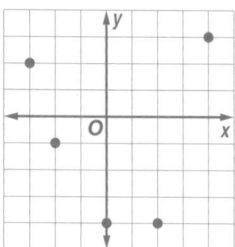

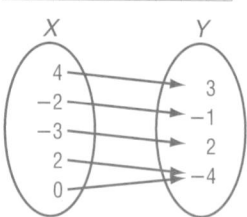

b. Determine the domain and range.
D = {−3, −2, 0, 2, 4};
R = {−4, −1, 2, 3}

Study Tip

Domain and Range
When writing the elements of the domain and range, if a value is repeated, you need to list it only once.

More About. . .

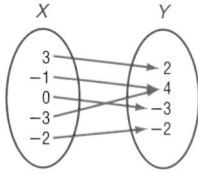

Bald Eagles
The bald eagle is not really bald. Its name comes from the Old English meaning of bald, "having white feathers on the head."

Source: *Webster's Dictionary*

Mapping

List the *x* values in set *X* and the *y* values in set *Y*. Draw an arrow from each *x* value in *X* to the corresponding *y* value in *Y*.

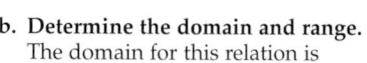

b. Determine the domain and range.
The domain for this relation is {−3, −2, −1, 0, 3}.
The range is {−3, −2, 2, 4}.

When graphing relations that represent real-life situations, you may need to select values for the *x*- or *y*-axis that do not begin with 0 and do not have units of 1.

Example 2 Use a Relation

BALD EAGLES In 1990, New York purchased 12,000 acres for the protection of bald eagles. The table shows the number of eagles observed in New York during the annual mid-winter bald eagle survey from 1993 to 2000.

Bald Eagle Survey								
Year	1993	1994	1995	1996	1997	1998	1999	2000
Number of Eagles	102	116	144	174	175	177	244	350

Source: New York Department of Environmental Conservation

a. Determine the domain and range of the relation.
The domain is {1993, 1994, 1995, 1996, 1997, 1998, 1999, 2000}.
The range is {102, 116, 144, 174, 175, 177, 244, 350}.

b. Graph the data.
- The values of the *x*-axis need to go from 1993 to 2000. It is not practical to begin the scale at 0. Begin at 1992 and extend to 2001 to include all of the data. The units can be 1 unit per grid square.
- The values on the *y*-axis need to go from 102 to 350. In this case, it is possible to begin the scale at 0. Begin at 0 and extend to 400. You can use units of 50.

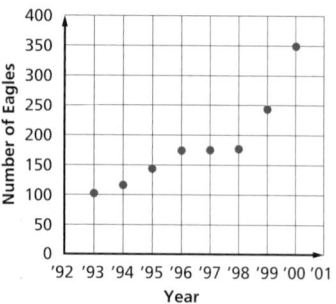

c. What conclusions might you make from the graph of the data?
The number of eagles has increased each year. This may be due to the efforts of those who are protecting the eagles in New York.

INVERSE RELATIONS The **inverse** of any relation is obtained by switching the coordinates in each ordered pair.

Key Concept   Inverse of a Relation

Relation *Q* is the inverse of relation *S* if and only if for every ordered pair (*a*, *b*) in *S*, there is an ordered pair (*b*, *a*) in *Q*.

DAILY INTERVENTION

Differentiated Instruction

Auditory/Musical If students have difficulty with the concept of a mapping, have those who are familiar with music make a mapping of the relation between different notes and the number of beats the notes contain. For example, a whole note has 4 beats, and a half note has 2 beats. In this case, the notes would be the domain and the number of beats would be the range.

Relation	Inverse
(2, 5)	(5, 2)
(−3, 2)	(2, −3)
(6, 7)	(7, 6)
(5, −1)	(−1, 5)

Notice that the domain of a relation becomes the range of the inverse and the range of a relation becomes the domain of the inverse.

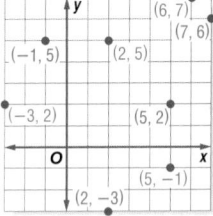

Example 3 Inverse Relation

Express the relation shown in the mapping as a set of ordered pairs. Then write the inverse of the relation.

Relation Notice that both 2 and 3 in the domain are paired with −4 in the range.
{(2, −4), (3, −4), (5, −7), (6, −8)}

Inverse Exchange x and y in each ordered pair to write the inverse relation.
{(−4, 2), (−4, 3), (−7, 5), (−8, 6)}

The mapping of the inverse is shown at the right. Compare this to the mapping of the relation.

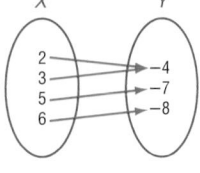

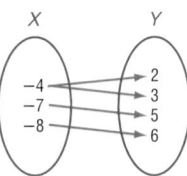

Algebra Activity

Relations and Inverses

- Graph the relation {(3, 4), (−2, 5), (−4, −3), (5, −6), (−1, 0), (0, 2)} on grid paper using a colored pencil. Connect the points in order using the same colored pencil.
- Use a different colored pencil to graph the inverse of the relation, connecting the points in order.
- Fold the grid paper through the origin so that the positive y-axis lies on top of the positive x-axis. Hold the paper up to a light so that you can see all of the points you graphed.

Analyze

1. What do you notice about the location of the points you graphed when you looked at the folded paper? The inverse of each point matches the point.
2. Unfold the paper. Describe the transformation of each point and its inverse. reflection across fold
3. What do you think are the ordered pairs that represent the points on the fold line? Describe these in terms of x and y.
   Sample ordered pairs: (−1, −1), (0, 0), (2, 2); for each (x, y), $x = y$

Make a Conjecture

4. How could you graph the inverse of a function without writing ordered pairs first? Reflect the points across the line in which the x-coordinate equals the y-coordinate.

---

2 **OPINION POLLS** The table shows the percent of people satisfied with the way things were going in the U.S. at the time of the survey.

Year	1992	1995	1998	2001
Percent Satisfied	21	32	60	51

a. Determine the domain and range of the relation.
   D = {1992, 1995, 1998, 2001};
   R = {21, 32, 51, 60}

b. Graph the data.

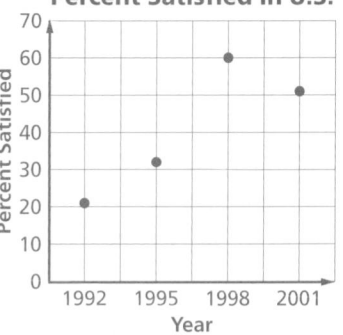

c. What conclusions might you make from the graph of the data? Americans became more satisfied with the country from 1992–1998, but the percentage dropped from 1998–2001.

INVERSE RELATIONS

In-Class Example Power Point®

3 Express the relation shown in the mapping as a set of ordered pairs. Then write the inverse of the relation.

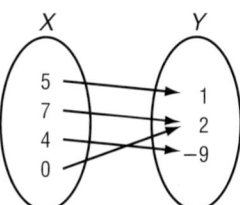

Relation:
{(5, 1), (7, 2), (4, −9), (0, 2)}
Inverse:
{(1, 5), (2, 7), (−9, 4), (2, 0)}

Algebra Activity

Materials: grid paper, colored pencils

- It might be easier for students to connect the points in order as they graph them. For example, after students graph (3, 4) and (−2, 5), draw a line between them. Then, after they graph (−4, −3), draw a line between (−2, 5) and (−4, −3).
- Explain that the fold is along a line through the center of quadrant I, the origin, and quadrant III.

Teaching Tip Make sure students do not confuse inverse with negative when finding inverse relations.

3 Practice/Apply

Study Notebook

Have students—
- add the definitions/examples of the vocabulary terms to their Vocabulary Builder worksheets for Chapter 4.
- include any other item(s) that they find helpful in mastering the skills in this lesson.

Answers

2. Sample answer: {(1, 2), (3, 4), (5, 6), (7, 8), (9, 8)}

3. The domain of a relation is the range of the inverse, and the range of a relation is the domain of the inverse.

12. {(−1, 2), (2, 4), (3, −3), (4, −1)}; {(2, −1), (4, 2), (−3, 3), (−1, 4)}

13. {(−4, −4), (−3, 0), (0, −3), (2, 1), (2, −1)}; {(−4, −4), (0, −3), (−3, 0), (1, 2), (−1, 2)}

36. {(−3, 3), (−2, 2), (−1, 1), (1, −1), (2, −2), (3, −3)}; {(3, −3), (2, −2), (1, −1), (−1, 1), (−2, 2), (−3, 3)}

37. {(−3, −1), (−3, −3), (−3, −5), (0, 3), (2, 3), (4, 3)}; {(−1, −3), (−3, −3), (−5, −3), (3, 0), (3, 2), (3, 4)}

Check for Understanding

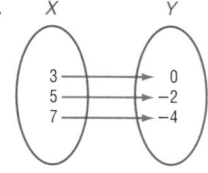

Concept Check

1. A relation can be represented as a set of ordered pairs, a table, a graph, or a mapping.

1. **Describe** the different ways a relation can be represented.

2. **OPEN ENDED** Give an example of a set of ordered pairs that has five elements in its domain and four elements in its range. **See margin.**

3. **State** the relationship between the domain and range of a relation and the domain and range of its inverse. **See margin.**

Guided Practice

GUIDED PRACTICE KEY	
Exercises	Examples
4–7	1
8–13	2
14–17	3

Express each relation as a table, a graph, and a mapping. Then determine the domain and range. 4–7. See pp. 253A-253H.

4. {(5, −2), (8, 3), (−7, 1)}
5. {(6, 4), (3, −3), (−1, 9), (5, −3)}
6. {(7, 1), (3, 0), (−2, 5)}
7. {(−4, 8), (−1, 9), (−4, 7), (6, 9)}

Express the relation shown in each table, mapping, or graph as a set of ordered pairs. Then write the inverse of the relation.

8. {(3, −2), (−6, 7), (4, 3), (−6, 5)}; {(−2, 3), (7, −6), (3, 4), (5, −6)}

9. {(−4, 9), (2, 5), (−2, −2), (11, 12)}; {(9, −4), (5, 2), (−2, −2), (12, 11)}

10. {(3, 0), (5, −2), (7, −4)}; {(0, 3), (−2, 5), (−4, 7)}

12–13. See margin.

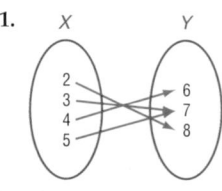

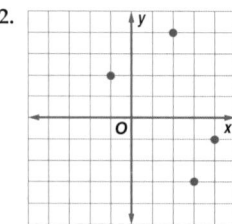

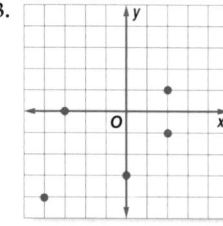

11.

{(2, 8), (3, 7), (4, 6), (5, 7)}; {(8, 2), (7, 3), (6, 4), (7, 5)}

12–13.

Application

14. Sample answer: (1989, 25), (1991, 20), (1996, 10)

15. {1989, 1990, 1991, 1992, 1993, 1994, 1995, 1996, 1997, 1998, 1999}

17. There are fewer students per computer in more recent years. So the number of computers in schools has increased.

TECHNOLOGY For Exercises 14–17, use the graph of the average number of students per computer in U.S. public schools.

14. Name three ordered pairs from the graph.

15. Determine the domain of the relation.

16. What are the least value and the greatest value in the range? **5.7; 25**

17. What conclusions can you make from the graph of the data?

Online Research **Data Update** What is the average number of students per computer in your state? Visit www.algebra1.com/data_update to learn more.

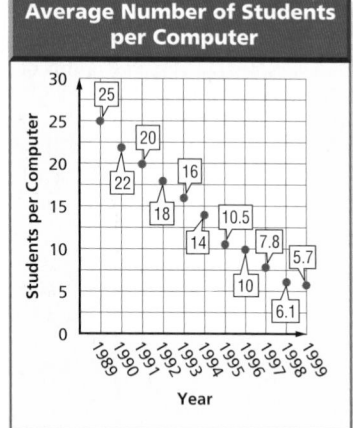

Source: Quality Education Data

Practice and Apply

Homework Help

For Exercises	See Examples
18–25	1
26–37	3
38–48	2

Extra Practice
See page 829.

Express each relation as a table, a graph, and a mapping. Then determine the domain and range. 18–25. See pp. 253A–253H.

18. {(4, 3), (1, −7), (1, 3), (2, 9)}

19. {(5, 2), (−5, 0), (6, 4), (2, 7)}

20. {(0, 0), (6, −1), (5, 6), (4, 2)}

21. {(3, 8), (3, 7), (2, −9), (1, −9)}

22. {(4, −2), (3, 4), (1, −2), (6, 4)}

23. {(0, 2), (−5, 1), (0, 6), (−1, 9)}

24. {(3, 4), (4, 3), (2, 2), (5, −4), (−4, 5)}

25. {(7, 6), (3, 4), (4, 5), (−2, 6), (−3, 2)}

Express the relation shown in each table, mapping, or graph as a set of ordered pairs. Then write the inverse of the relation.

28. {(6, −2), (4, 5), (3, −3), (1, 7)}; {(−2, 6), (5, 4), (−3, 3), (7, 1)}

30. {(−4, −2), (−2, −1), (2, 4), (2, −3)}; {(−2, −4), (−1, −2), (4, 2), (−3, 2)}

31. {(−3, 3), (1, 3), (4, 2), (−1, −5)}; {(3, −3), (3, 1), (2, 4), (−5, −1)}

33. {(1, 16.50), (1.75, 28.30), (2.5, 49.10), (3.25, 87.60), (4, 103.40)}; {(16.50, 1), (28.30, 1.75), (49.10, 2.5), (87.60, 3.25), (103.40, 4)}

34. {(−3, 2), (−3, −8), (6, 5), (7, 4), (11, 4)}; {(2, −3), (−8, −3), (5, 6), (4, 7), (4, 11)}

35. {(2, 0), (2, 4), (3, 7), (5, 0), (5, 8), (−7, 7)}; {(0, 2), (4, 2), (7, 3), (0, 5), (8, 5), (7, −7)}

36–37. See margin.

26.
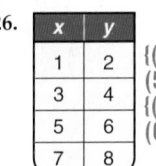

x	y
1	2
3	4
5	6
7	8

{(1, 2), (3, 4), (5, 6), (7, 8)}; {(2, 1), (4, 3), (6, 5), (8, 7)}

27.
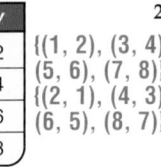

x	y
0	3
−5	2
4	7
−3	2

{(0, 3), (−5, 2), (4, 7), (−3, 2)}; {(3, 0), (2, −5), (7, 4), (2, −3)}

28.
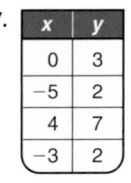

{(0, 3), (−5, 2), (4, 7), (−3, 2)}; {(3, 0), (2, −5), (7, 4), (2, −3)}

29.
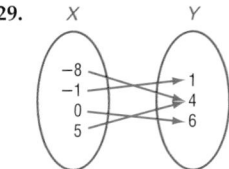

{(−8, 4), (−1, 1), (0, 6), (5, 4)}; {(4, −8), (1, −1), (6, 0), (4, 5)}

30.
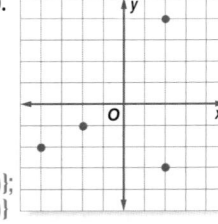

31.
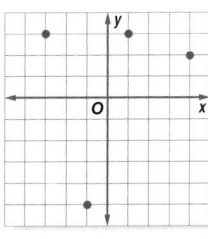

32.
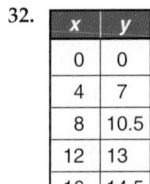

x	y
0	0
4	7
8	10.5
12	13
16	14.5

{(0, 0), (4, 7), (8, 10.5), (12, 13), (16, 14.5)}; {(0, 0), (7, 4), (10.5, 8), (13, 12), (14.5, 16)}

33.
x	y
1	16.50
1.75	28.30
2.5	49.10
3.25	87.60
4	103.40

34.
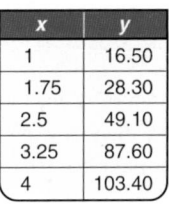

35.
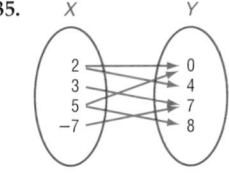

36.
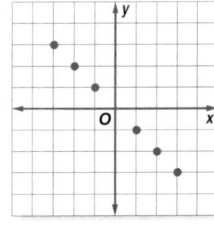

37.
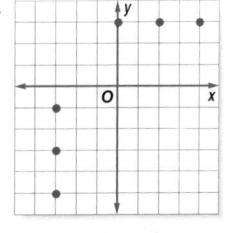

COOKING For Exercises 38–40, use the table that shows the boiling point of water at various altitudes. Many recipes have different cooking times for high altitudes. This is due to the fact that water boils at a lower temperature in higher altitudes.

38. Graph the relation. 38–40. See pp. 253A–253H.

39. Write the inverse as a set of ordered pairs.

40. How could you estimate your altitude by finding the boiling point of water at your location?

Altitude (feet)	Boiling Point of Water (°F)
0	212.0
1000	210.2
2000	208.4
3000	206.5
5000	201.9
10,000	193.7

Source: Stevens Institute of Technology

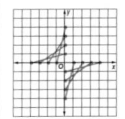 www.algebra1.com/self_check_quiz

Lesson 4-3 Relations 209

Study Guide and Intervention, p. 225 (shown) and p. 226

Represent Relations A relation is a set of ordered pairs. A relation can be represented by a set of ordered pairs, a table, a graph, or a mapping. A mapping illustrates how each element of the domain is paired with an element in the range.

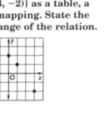

Example 1 Express the relation {(1, 1), (0, 2), (3, −2)} as a table, a graph, and a mapping. Then determine the domain and range of the relation.

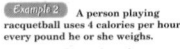 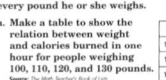

Example 2 A person playing racquetball uses 4 calories per hour for every pound he or she weighs.

a. Make a table to show the relation between weight and calories burned in one hour for people weighing 100, 110, 120, and 130 pounds.

x	y
100	400
110	440
120	480
130	520

b. Give the domain and range.
domain: {100, 110, 120, 130}
range: {400, 440, 480, 520}

c. Graph the relation.

The domain for this relation is {0, 1, 3}.
The range for this relation is {−2, 1, 2}.

Exercises

1. Express the relation {(−2, −1), (3, 3), (4, 3)} as a table, a graph, and a mapping. Then determine the domain and range.
domain: {−2, 3, 4}; range: {−1, 3}

2. The temperature in a house drops 2° for every hour the air conditioner is on between the hours of 6 A.M. and 11 A.M. Make a table to show the relationship between time and temperature if the temperature at 6 A.M. was 82°F.

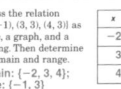 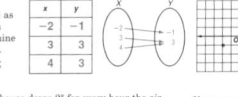

Skills Practice, p. 227 and Practice, p. 228 (shown)

Express each relation as a table, a graph, and a mapping. Then determine the domain and range.

1. {(4, 3), (−1, 4), (3, −2), (2, 3), (−2, 1)}

x	y
4	3
−1	4
3	−2
−2	1

D = {−2, −1, 3, 4}; R = {−2, 1, 3, 4}

Express the relation shown in each table, mapping, or graph as a set of ordered pairs. Then write the inverse of the relation.

2.
x	y
−8	3
2	−6
1	4

{(0, 9), (−8, 3), (2, −6), (1, 4)}; {(9, 0), (3, −8), (−6, 2), (4, 1)}

3.
{(9, 5), (9, 3), (−6, −5), (4, 3), (8, −5), (8, 7)}; {(5, 9), (3, 9), (−5, −6), (3, 4), (−5, 8), (7, 8)}

4.
{(−3, −1), (−2, −2), (−1, −3), (1, 1), (2, 1), (3, 1)}; {(−1, −3), (−2, −2), (−3, −1), (1, 1), (1, 2), (1, 3)}

BASEBALL For Exercises 5 and 6, use the graph that shows the batting average for Barry Bonds of the San Francisco Giants. Source: www.sfgiants.com

5. Find the domain and estimate the range.
D = {1996, 1997, 1998, 1999, 2000, 2001};
R = {.262, .291, .303, .306, .308, .328}

6. Which seasons did Bonds have the lowest and highest batting averages? lowest: 1999, highest: 2001

METEORS For Exercises 7 and 8, use the table that shows the number of meteors Ann observed each hour during a meteor shower.

Time (A.M.)	Number of Meteors
12	15
1	26
2	28
3	28
4	15

7. What are the domain and range?
D = {12, 1, 2, 3, 4}; R = {15, 26, 28}

8. Graph the relation.

Reading to Learn Mathematics, p. 229 ELL

Pre-Activity How can relations be used to represent baseball statistics?

Read the introduction to Lesson 4-3 at the top of page 205 in your textbook.
In 1997, Ken Griffey, Jr. had __56__ home runs and __121__ strikeouts.
This can be represented with the ordered pair (__56__, __121__).

Reading the Lesson

1. Look at page 205 in your textbook. There you see the same relation represented by a set of ordered pairs, a table, a graph, and a mapping.

a. In the list of ordered pairs, where do you see the numbers for the domain? the numbers for the range? before the commas; after the commas

b. What parts of the table show the domain and the range? The column of numbers under the letter x shows the domain, and the column of numbers under the letter y shows the range.

c. How do the table, the graph, and the mapping show that there are three ordered pairs in the relation? The table has three rows of numbers, the graph shows three points marked with dots, and the mapping uses three arrows.

2. Which tells you more about a relation, a list of the ordered pairs in the relation or the domain and range of the relation? Explain. Sample answer: A list of the ordered pairs tells you more. You can use it to find the domain and the range, and you know exactly how the numbers are paired. If you only know the domain and the range, you cannot be sure how the numbers are paired.

3. Describe how you would find the inverse of the relation {(1, 2), (2, 4), (3, 6), (4, 8)}. Switch the coordinates in each ordered pair to get {(2, 1), (4, 2), (6, 3), (8, 4)}.

Helping You Remember

4. The first letters in two words and their order in the alphabet can sometimes help you remember their mathematical meaning. Two key terms in this lesson are *domain* and *range*. Describe how the alphabet method could help you remember their meaning. Sample answer: d comes first for the first coordinate, r comes second for the second coordinate.

Enrichment, p. 230

Inverse Relations

On each grid below, plot the points in Sets A and B. Then connect the points in Set A with the corresponding points in Set B. Then find the inverses of Set A and Set B, plot the two sets, and connect those points.

Set A	Set B
(−4, 0)	(0, 1)
(−3, 0)	(0, 2)
(−2, 0)	(0, 3)
(−1, 0)	(0, 4)

Inverse
Set A	Set B
1. (0, −4)	(1, 0)
2. (0, −3)	(2, 0)
3. (0, −2)	(3, 0)
4. (0, −1)	(4, 0)

Answers

41. D = {1991, 1992, 1993, 1994, 1995, 1996, 1997, 1998, 1999, 2000}; R = {6.3, 7.5, 9.2, 9.5, 9.8, 10, 10.4}

43. The production seems to go up and down every other year; however, from 1995 through 1998, farmers have produced more corn each year.

50. Expressing real-world data as relations shows how the members of a domain relate to the members of the range. For example, a table helps to organize the data or a graph may show a pattern in the data. Answers should include the following.

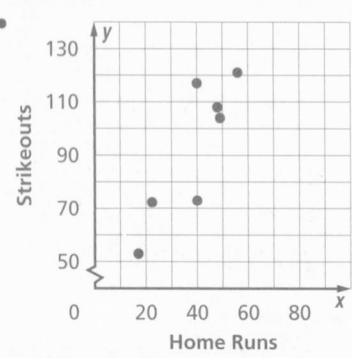

- There seems to be a positive

42. 1993; 2000

45. D = {100, 105, 110, 115, 120, 125, 130}; R = {40, 42, 44, 46, 48, 50, 52}

47. D = {40, 42, 44, 46, 48, 50, 52}; R = {100, 105, 110, 115, 120, 125, 130}

49. Sample answer: F = {(−1, 1), (−2, 2), (−3, 3)}, G = {(1, −2), (2, −3), (3, −1)}; The elements in the domain and range of F should be paired differently in G.

Standardized Test Practice
Ⓐ Ⓑ Ⓒ Ⓓ

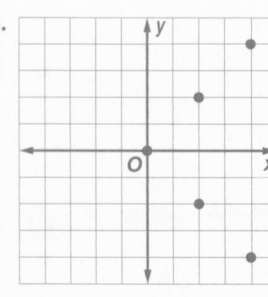

Graphing Calculator

FOOD For Exercises 41–43, use the graph that shows the annual production of corn from 1991–2000.

41. Estimate the domain and range of the relation. **See margin.**

42. Which year had the lowest production? the highest?

43. Describe any pattern you see. **See margin.**

HEALTH For Exercises 44–48, use the following information.
A person's muscle weight is about 2 pounds of muscle for each 5 pounds of body weight.

44. Make a table to show the relation between body and muscle weight for people weighing 100, 105, 110, 115, 120, 125, and 130 pounds. **See pp. 253A–253H.**

45. What are the domain and range?

46. Graph the relation. **See pp. 253A–253H.**

47. What are the domain and range of the inverse?

48. Graph the inverse relation. **See pp. 253A–253H.**

49. **CRITICAL THINKING** Find a counterexample to disprove the following.
The domain of relation F contains the same elements as the range of relation G. The range of relation F contains the same elements as the domain of relation G. Therefore, relation G must be the inverse of relation F.

50. **WRITING IN MATH** Answer the question that was posed at the beginning of the lesson. **See margin.**

How can relations be used to represent baseball statistics?

Include the following in your answer:
- a graph of the relation of the number of Ken Griffey, Jr.'s, home runs and his strikeouts, and
- an explanation of any relationship between the number of home runs hit and the number of strikeouts.

For Exercises 51 and 52, use the graph at the right.
51. State the domain and range of the relation. **B**
  Ⓐ D = {0, 2, 4}; R = {−4, −2, 0, 2, 4}
  Ⓑ D = {−4, −2, 0, 2, 4}; R = {0, 2, 4}
  Ⓒ D = {0, 2, 4}; R = {−4, −2, 0}
  Ⓓ D = {−4, −2, 0, 2, 4}; R = {−4, −2, 0, 2, 4}

52. **SHORT RESPONSE** Graph the inverse of the relation. **See margin.**

For Exercises 53–56, use a graphing calculator. **53–56. See pp. 253A–253H.**
a. Graph each relation.
b. State the WINDOW settings that you used.
c. Write the coordinates of the inverse. Then graph the inverse.
d. Name the quadrant in which each point of the relation and its inverse lies.

53. {(0, 10), (2, −8), (6, 6), (9, −4)}
54. {(−1, 18), (−2, 23), (−3, 28), (−4, 33)}
55. {(35, 12), (48, 25), (60, 52)}
56. {(−92, −77), (−93, 200), (19, −50)}

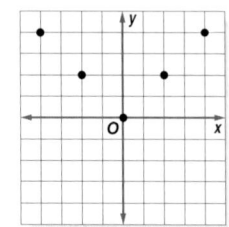

relationship between the number of home runs and strikeouts. In years where Griffey hit more home runs, he also struck out more.

52.

Mixed Review   Identify each transformation as a *reflection, translation, dilation,* or *rotation.*
(Lesson 4-2)

57.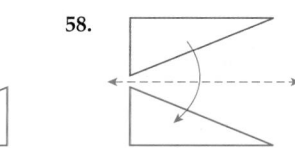
58.
59.

rotation   reflection   translation

Write the ordered pair for each point shown at
the right. Name the quadrant in which the point
is located.   *(Lesson 4-1)*

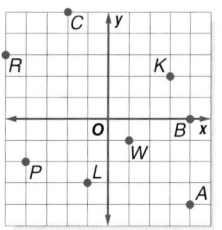

60. *A* (4, −4); IV
61. *K* (3, 2); I
62. *L* (−1, −3); III
63. *W* (1, −1); IV
64. *B* (4, 0); none
65. *P* (−4, −2); III
66. *R* (−5, 3); II
67. *C* (−2, 5); II

68. **HOURLY PAY**   Dominique earns $9.75 per hour. Her employer is increasing
her hourly rate to $10.15 per hour. What is the percent of increase in her salary?
(Lesson 3-7)   about 4.1%

Simplify each expression.   *(Lesson 2-4)*

69. $72 \div 9$ 8
70. $105 \div 15$ 7
71. $3 \div \frac{1}{3}$ 9
72. $16 \div \frac{1}{4}$ 64
73. $\frac{54n + 78}{6}$ $9n + 13$
74. $\frac{98x - 35y}{7}$ $14x - 5y$

Getting Ready for
the Next Lesson   **PREREQUISITE SKILL**   Find the solution set for each equation if the replacement
set is {3, 4, 5, 6, 7, 8}.   *(To review **solution sets**, see Lesson 1-3.)*

75. $a + 15 = 20$ {5}
76. $r - 6 = 2$ {8}
77. $9 = 5n - 6$ {3}
78. $3 + 8w = 35$ {4}
79. $\frac{g}{3} + 15 = 17$ {6}
80. $\frac{m}{5} + \frac{3}{5} = 2$ {7}

Practice Quiz 1   *Lessons 4-1 through 4-3*

Plot each point on a coordinate plane.   *(Lesson 4-1)*   **1–4. See margin.**

1. $Q(2, 3)$
2. $R(-4, -4)$
3. $S(5, -1)$
4. $T(-1, 3)$

**Find the coordinates of the vertices of each figure after the given transformation
is performed. Then graph the preimage and its image.**   *(Lesson 4-2)* **5–6. See pp. 253A–253H for graphs.**

5. triangle *ABC* with *A*(4, 8), *B*(7, 5), and *C*(2, −1) reflected over the *x*-axis *A*′(4, −8), *B*′(7, −5), *C*′(2, 1)
6. quadrilateral *WXYZ* with *W*(1, 0), *X*(2, 3), *Y*(4, 1), and *Z*(3, −3) translated 5 units
to the left and 4 units down *W*′(−4, −4), *X*′(−3, −1), *Y*′(−1, −3), *Z*′(−2, −7)

State the domain, range, and inverse of each relation.   *(Lesson 4-3)* **7–10. See margin.**

7. {(1, 3), (4, 6), (2, 3), (1, 5)}
8. {(−2, 6), (0, 3), (4, 2), (8, −5)}
9. {(11, 5), (15, 3), (−8, 22), (11, 31)}
10. {(−5, 8), (−1, 0), (−1, 4), (2, 7), (6, 3)}

   **Online Lesson Plans**

USA TODAY Education's Online site offers resources and
interactive features connected to each day's newspaper.
Experience TODAY, USA TODAY's daily lesson plan, is
available on the site and delivered daily to subscribers.
This plan provides instruction for integrating USA TODAY
graphics and key editorial features into your mathematics
classroom. Log on to www.education.usatoday.com.

Open-Ended Assessment

Writing Have students write a
paragraph describing how
inverse relations can be found
using reflections rather than
writing the ordered pairs, based
on the concept they learned in
the Algebra Activity in this lesson.

Getting Ready for
Lesson 4-4

PREREQUISITE SKILL Students will
learn about equations as relations
in Lesson 4-4. They will find a
range value for each given domain
value by substituting domain
values (the replacement set) into
the equation. Use Exercises 75–80
to determine students' familiarity
with finding solution sets from
replacement sets.

Assessment Options

Practice Quiz 1 The quiz provides
students with a brief review of the
concepts and skills in Lessons 4-1
through 4-3. Lesson numbers are
given to the right of exercises or
instruction lines so students can
review concepts not yet mastered.

Answers

1–4.

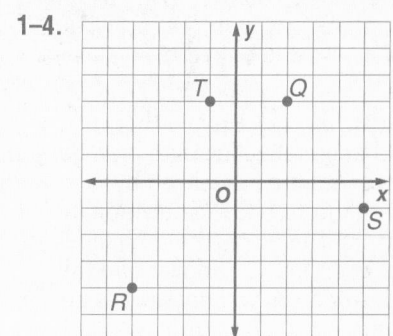

7. D = {1, 2, 4}; R = {3, 5, 6};
   I = {(3, 1), (6, 4), (3, 2), (5, 1)}
8. D = {−2, 0, 4, 8}; R = {−5, 2, 3, 6};
   I = {(6, −2), (3, 0), (2, 4), (−5, 8)}
9. D = {−8, 11, 15};
   R = {3, 5, 22, 31}; I = {(5, 11),
   (3, 15), (22, −8), (31, 11)}
10. D = {−5, −1, 2, 6};
   R = {0, 3, 4, 7, 8}; I = {(8, −5),
   (0, −1), (4, −1), (7, 2), (3, 6)}

1 Focus

5-Minute Check Transparency 4-4 Use as a quiz or review of Lesson 4-3.

Mathematical Background notes are available for this lesson on p. 190D.

Why are equations of relations important in traveling?

Ask students:

- According to the exchange rate listed, is one dollar worth more or less than one pound? **One dollar is worth less than one pound.**

- How many pounds equal one dollar? **0.69 pound = 1 dollar**

- How many dollars equal one pound? **about $1.45 = 1 pound**

- **Travel** Suppose Eric arrives at the airport in England and goes to a currency exchange booth to exchange $100. Should he expect more or less than 100 pounds? Explain. **He should expect less than 100 pounds because 1 dollar = 0.69 pound. In fact, he would receive 69 pounds.**

Teaching Tip Explain that currency exchange rates fluctuate on a daily basis and are influenced by numerous worldwide economic factors. Therefore, the exchange rate between the U. S. dollar and the British pound will not always be 1 dollar = 0.69 pound.

What You'll Learn

- Use an equation to determine the range for a given domain.
- Graph the solution set for a given domain.

Vocabulary
- equation in two variables
- solution

Why are equations of relations important in traveling?

During the summer, Eric will be taking a trip to England. He has saved $500 for his trip, and he wants to find how much that will be worth in British pounds sterling. The exchange rate today is 1 dollar = 0.69 pound. Eric can use the equation $p = 0.69d$ to convert dollars d to pounds p.

SOLVE EQUATIONS The equation $p = 0.69d$ is an example of an **equation in two variables**. A **solution** of an equation in two variables is an ordered pair that results in a true statement when substituted into the equation.

Example 1 Solve Using a Replacement Set

Find the solution set for $y = 2x + 3$, given the replacement set $\{(-2, -1), (-1, 3), (0, 4), (3, 9)\}$.

Make a table. Substitute each ordered pair into the equation.

The ordered pairs $(-2, -1)$ and $(3, 9)$ result in true statements. The solution set is $\{(-2, -1), (3, 9)\}$.

x	y	$y = 2x + 3$	True or False?
-2	-1	$-1 = 2(-2) + 3$ $-1 = -1$	true ✓
-1	3	$3 = 2(-1) + 3$ $3 = 1$	false
0	4	$4 = 2(0) + 3$ $4 = 3$	false
3	9	$9 = 2(3) + 3$ $9 = 9$	true ✓

Since the solutions of an equation in two variables are ordered pairs, the equation describes a relation. So, in an equation involving x and y, the set of x values is the domain, and the corresponding set of y values is the range.

Study Tip

Variables
Unless the variables are chosen to represent real quantities, when variables other than x and y are used in an equation, assume that the letter that comes first in the alphabet is the domain.

Example 2 Solve Using a Given Domain

Solve $b = a + 5$ if the domain is $\{-3, -1, 0, 2, 4\}$.

Make a table. The values of a come from the domain. Substitute each value of a into the equation to determine the values of b in the range.

The solution set is $\{(-3, 2), (-1, 4), (0, 5), (2, 7), (4, 9)\}$.

a	$a + 5$	b	(a, b)
-3	$-3 + 5$	2	$(-3, 2)$
-1	$-1 + 5$	4	$(-1, 4)$
0	$0 + 5$	5	$(0, 5)$
2	$2 + 5$	7	$(2, 7)$
4	$4 + 5$	9	$(4, 9)$

Resource Manager

📁 Workbook and Reproducible Masters

Chapter 4 Resource Masters
- Study Guide and Intervention, pp. 231–232
- Skills Practice, p. 233
- Practice, p. 234
- Reading to Learn Mathematics, p. 235
- Enrichment, p. 236
- Assessment, pp. 275, 277

Parent and Student Study Guide Workbook, p. 32

Transparencies
5-Minute Check Transparency 4-4
Answer Key Transparencies

💿 Technology
Interactive Chalkboard

GRAPH SOLUTION SETS You can graph the ordered pairs in the solution set for an equation in two variables. The domain contains values represented by the *independent variable*. The range contains the corresponding value represented by the *dependent variable*.

Study Tip

Look Back
To review **independent and dependent variables**, see Lesson 1-8.

Example 3 Solve and Graph the Solution Set

Solve $4x + 2y = 10$ if the domain is $\{-1, 0, 2, 4\}$. Graph the solution set.

First solve the equation for y in terms of x. This makes creating a table of values easier.

$4x + 2y = 10$	Original equation
$4x + 2y - 4x = 10 - 4x$	Subtract $4x$ from each side.
$2y = 10 - 4x$	Simplify.
$\dfrac{2y}{2} = \dfrac{10 - 4x}{2}$	Divide each side by 2.
$y = 5 - 2x$	Simplify.

Substitute each value of x from the domain to determine the corresponding values of y in the range.

x	$5 - 2x$	y	(x, y)
-1	$5 - 2(-1)$	7	$(-1, 7)$
0	$5 - 2(0)$	5	$(0, 5)$
2	$5 - 2(2)$	1	$(2, 1)$
4	$5 - 2(4)$	-3	$(4, -3)$

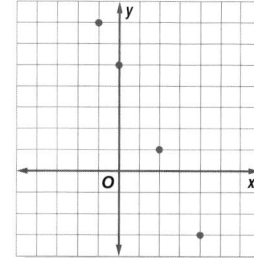

Graph the solution set $\{(-1, 7), (0, 5), (2, 1), (4, -3)\}$.

When you solve an equation for a given variable, that variable becomes the dependent variable. That is, its value depends upon the domain values chosen for the other variable.

Example 4 Solve for a Dependent Variable

Refer to the application at the beginning of the lesson. Eric has made a list of the expenses he plans to incur while in England. Use the conversion rate to find the equivalent U.S. dollars for these amounts given in pounds (£) and graph the ordered pairs.

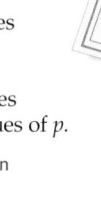

Daily Expenses
Hotel   £40
Meals   £30
Transportation £15
Entertainment £6

Explore In the equation $p = 0.69d$, d represents U.S. dollars and p represents British pounds. However, we are given values in pounds and want to find values in dollars. Solve the equation for d since the values of d depend on the given values of p.

$p = 0.69d$	Original equation
$\dfrac{p}{0.69} = \dfrac{0.69d}{0.69}$	Divide each side by 0.69.
$1.45p = d$	Simplify and round to the nearest hundredth.

(continued on the next page)

---

2 Teach

Building on Prior Knowledge

Students learned how to solve multi-step equations in Lesson 3-4. Although equations in that lesson had only one variable, the principle of solving equations in two variables is the same. You work in the reverse of the order of operations to isolate one of the variables.

SOLVE EQUATIONS

In-Class Examples Power Point®

1 Find the solution set for $y = 7 + 3x$, given the replacement set $\{(-5, 0), (-3, -2), (2, 13), (4, 19)\}$. $\{(-3, -2), (2, 13), (4, 19)\}$

2 Solve $d = 8 - c$ if the domain is $\{-2, 0, 3, 5, 8\}$. **The solution set is $\{(-2, 10), (0, 8), (3, 5), (5, 3), (8, 0)\}$.**

Teaching Tip Explain that since the domain is given, it is easier to find the solution set by solving the equation for y. If the range was given, it would be easier to find the solution set by solving the equation for x.

GRAPH SOLUTION SETS

In-Class Examples Power Point®

3 Solve $9x + 3y = 15$ if the domain is $\{0, 1, 2, 3\}$. Graph the solution set. $\{(0, 5), (1, 2), (2, -1), (3, -4)\}$

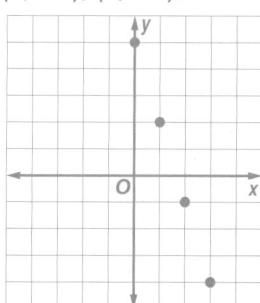

4 continued on next page

4 **TRAVEL** In 2002, 12 countries in Europe made the switch to a single currency, the euro. Suppose the exchange rate between U.S. dollars and euros is one dollar = 1.11 euros. The equation $E = 1.11D$ can be used to convert U.S. dollars to euros. If a traveler is going to spend the following amounts per day while in Europe, find the equivalent U.S. dollars for the amounts given in euros (EUR). Graph the ordered pairs.

Hotel	90 EUR	$81
Food	50 EUR	$45
Transportation	30 EUR	$27
Gifts	20 EUR	$18

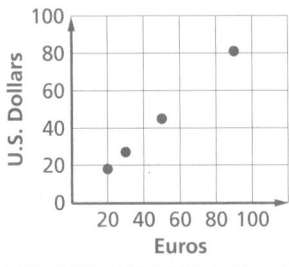

Answers

6. {(−3, −7), (−1, −3), (0, −1), (2, 3)}

7. {(−3, 7), (−1, 5), (0, 4), (2, 2)}

8. {(−3, 9), (−1, 7), (0, 6), (2, 4)}

9. {(−3, 11), (−1, 8), (0, 6.5), (2, 3.5)}

10. {(−3, −9), (−2, −6), (−1, −3), (0, 0), (1, 3), (2, 6), (3, 9)}

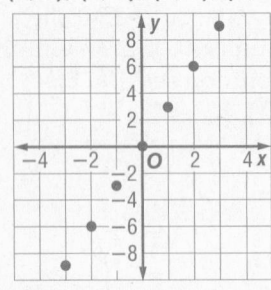

Plan   The values of p, {40, 30, 15, 6}, are the domain. Use the equation $d = 1.45p$ to find the values for the range.

Solve   Make a table of values. Substitute each value of p from the domain to determine the corresponding values of d. Round to the nearest dollar.

p	1.45p	d	(p, d)
40	1.45(40)	58.00	(40, 58)
30	1.45(30)	43.50	(30, 44)
15	1.45(15)	21.75	(15, 22)
6	1.45(6)	8.70	(6, 9)

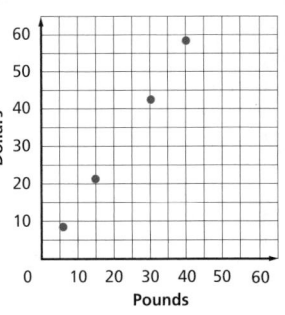

Graph the ordered pairs. Notice that the values for the independent variable p are graphed along the horizontal axis, and the values for dependent variable d are graphed along the vertical axis.

Examine   Look at the values in the range. The cost in dollars is higher than the cost in pounds. Do the results make sense?

Expense	Pounds	Dollars
Hotel	40	58
Meals	30	43
Entertainment	15	22
Transportation	6	9

Check for Understanding

Concept Check

1. Substitute the values for *y* and solve for *x*.

3. Bryan; *x* represents the domain and *y* represents the range. So, replace *x* with 5 and *y* with 1.

1. **Describe** how to find the domain of an equation if you are given the range.

2. **OPEN ENDED** Give an example of an equation in two variables and state two solutions for your equation. **Sample answer: $y = x − 5$; (9, 4), (10, 5)**

3. **FIND THE ERROR** Malena says that (5, 1) is a solution of $y = 2x + 3$. Bryan says it is not a solution.

Malena
$y = 2x + 3$
$5 = 2(1) + 3$
$5 = 5$

Bryan
$y = 2x + 3$
$1 = 2(5) + 3$
$1 \neq 13$

Who is correct? Explain your reasoning.

Guided Practice

GUIDED PRACTICE KEY	
Exercises	Examples
4, 5	1
6–9	2
10, 11	3
12, 13	4

Find the solution set for each equation, given the replacement set.

4. $y = 3x + 4$; {(−1, 1), (2, 10), (3, 12), (7, 1)} **{(−1, 1), (2, 10)}**

5. $2x − 5y = 1$; {(−7, −3), (7, 3), (2, 1), (−2, −1)} **{(−7, −3), (−2, −1)}**

Solve each equation if the domain is {−3, −1, 0, 2}. 6–9. See margin.

6. $y = 2x − 1$ 7. $y = 4 − x$

8. $2y + 2x = 12$ 9. $3x + 2y = 13$

10–11. See margin.

Solve each equation for the given domain. Graph the solution set.

10. $y = 3x$ for $x = \{−3, −2, −1, 0, 1, 2, 3\}$

11. $2y = x + 2$ for $x = \{−4, −2, 0, 2, 4\}$

11. {(−4, −1), (−2, 0), (0, 1), (2, 2), (4, 3)}

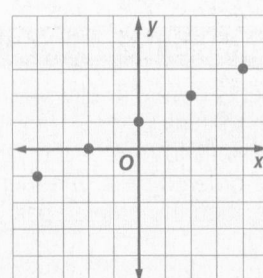

JEWELRY For Exercises 12 and 13, use the following information.
Since pure gold is very soft, other metals are often added to it to make an alloy that is stronger and more durable. The relative amount of gold in a piece of jewelry is measured in karats. The formula for the relationship is $g = \frac{25k}{6}$, where k is the number of karats and g is the percent of gold in the jewelry.

12. Find the percent of gold if the domain is {10, 14, 18, 24}. Make a table of values and graph the function. **See pp. 253A–253H.**

13. How many karats are in a ring that is 50% gold? **12 karats**

Practice and Apply

Homework Help

For Exercises	See Examples
14–19	1
20–31	2
32–39	3
40–45	4

Extra Practice
See page 829.

21. {(−2, −1), (−1, 1), (1, 5), (3, 9), (4, 11)}

22. {(−2, −6), (−1, −5), (1, −3), (3, −1), (4, 0)}

23. {(−2, 9), (−1, 8), (1, 6), (3, 4), (4, 3)}

24. {(−2, −10), (−1, −8), (1, −4), (3, 0), (4, 2)}

25. {(−2, −9), (−1, −3), (1, 9), (3, 21), (4, 27)}

26. {(−2, 7), (−1, 5), (1, 1), (3, −3), (4, −5)}

27. {(−2, −2), (−1, −1), (1, 1), (3, 3), (4, 4)}

28. {(−2, −3), (−1, −2.5), (1, −1.5), (3, −0.5), (4, 0)}

29. {(−2, 10), (−1, 8.5), (1, 5.5), (3, 2.5), (4, 1)}

30. {(−2, 20), (−1, 18), (1, 14), (3, 10), (4, 8)}

31. {(−2, −24), (−1, −18), (1, −6), (3, 6), (4, 12)}

Find the solution set for each equation, given the replacement set.

14. $y = 4x + 1$; {(2, −1), (1, 5), (9, 2), (0, 1)} **{(1, 5), (0, 1)}**

15. $y = 8 − 3x$; {(4, −4), (8, 0), (2, 2), (3, 3)} **{(4, −4), (2, 2)}**

16. $x − 3y = −7$; {(−1, 2), (2, −1), (2, 4), (2, 3)} **{(−1, 2), (2, 3)}**

17. $2x + 2y = 6$; {(3, 0), (2, 1), (−2, −1), (4, −1)} **{(3, 0), (2, 1), (4, −1)}**

18. $3x − 8y = −4$; {(0, 0.5), (4, 1), (2, 0.75), (2, 4)} **{(0, 0.5)}**

19. $2y + 4x = 8$; {(0, 2), (−3, 0.5), (0.25, 3.5), (1, 2)} **{(0.25, 3.5), (1, 2)}**

20. {(−2, 14), (−1, 9), (1, −1), (3, −11), (4, −16)}
Solve each equation if the domain is {−2, −1, 1, 3, 4}.

20. $y = 4 − 5x$

21. $y = 2x + 3$

22. $x = y + 4$

23. $x = 7 − y$

24. $6x − 3y = 18$

25. $6x − y = −3$

26. $8x + 4y = 12$

27. $2x − 2y = 0$

28. $5x − 10y = 20$

29. $3x + 2y = 14$

30. $x + \frac{1}{2}y = 8$

31. $2x − \frac{1}{3}y = 4$

32–37. See pp. 253A–253H.
Solve each equation for the given domain. Graph the solution set.

32. $y = 2x + 3$ for $x = \{−3, −2, −1, 1, 2, 3\}$

33. $y = 3x − 1$ for $x = \{−5, −2, 1, 3, 4\}$

34. $3x − 2y = 5$ for $x = \{−3, −1, 2, 4, 5\}$

35. $5x + 4y = 8$ for $x = \{−4, −1, 0, 2, 4, 6\}$

36. $\frac{1}{2}x + y = 2$ for $x = \{−4, −1, 1, 4, 7, 8\}$

37. $y = \frac{1}{4}x − 3$ for $x = \{−4, −2, 0, 2, 4, 6\}$

38. The domain for $3x + y = 8$ is {−1, 2, 5, 8}. Find the range. **{−16, −7, 2, 11}**

39. The range for $2y − x = 6$ is {−4, −3, 1, 6, 7}. Find the domain.
{−14, −12, −4, 6, 8}

TRAVEL For Exercises 40 and 41, use the following information.
Heinrich and his brother live in Germany. They are taking a trip to the United States. They are unfamiliar with the Fahrenheit scale, so they would like to convert U.S. temperatures to Celsius. The equation $F = 1.8C + 32$ relates the temperature in degrees Celsius C to degrees Fahrenheit F.

City	Temperature (°F)
New York	34
Chicago	23
San Francisco	55
Miami	72
Washington, D.C.	40

40. Solve the equation for C. $C = \frac{F − 32}{1.8}$

41. Find the temperatures in degrees Celsius for each city. **See margin.**

Answer
41. New York: 1.1°C, Chicago: −5°C, San Francisco: 12.8°C, Miami: 22.2°C, Washington, D.C.: 4.4°C

Study Notebook
Have students—
• add the definitions/examples of the vocabulary terms to their Vocabulary Builder worksheets for Chapter 4.
• include any other item(s) that they find helpful in mastering the skills in this lesson.

DAILY
INTERVENTION   **FIND THE ERROR**
Remind students that it is important to make sure they substitute the correct values for x and y when finding solutions.

About the Exercises...
Organization by Objective
• **Solve Equations:** 14–37, 40, 42, 44
• **Graph Solution Sets:** 32–37, 45

Odd/Even Assignments
Exercises 14–37 are structured so that students practice the same concepts whether they are assigned odd or even problems.

Alert! Exercise 46 requires the Internet or other research materials. Exercises 52–55 require a graphing calculator.

Assignment Guide
Basic: 15–39 odd, 40–44, 47–51, 56–76

Average: 15–39 odd, 40–45, 47–51, 56–76 (optional: 52–55)

Advanced: 14–38 even, 42–44, 46–70 (optional: 71–76)

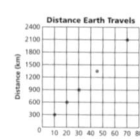
GEOMETRY For Exercises 42–44, use the following information.
The equation for the perimeter of a rectangle is $P = 2\ell + 2w$. Suppose the perimeter of rectangle $ABCD$ is 24 centimeters.

42. Solve the equation for ℓ. $\ell = 12 - w$
43. State the independent and dependent variables. w is independent; ℓ is dependent.
44. Choose five values for w and find the corresponding values of ℓ.
Sample answer: $\{(1, 11), (2, 10), (3, 9), (4, 8), (5, 7)\}$

45. **ANTHROPOLOGY** When the remains of ancient people are discovered, usually only a few bones are found. Anthropologists can determine a person's height by using a formula that relates the length of the tibia T (shin bone) to the person's height H, both measured in centimeters. The formula for males is $H = 81.7 + 2.4T$ and for females is $H = 72.6 + 2.5T$. Copy and complete the tables below. Then graph each set of ordered pairs. **See margin for graph.**

Male			Female		
Length of Tibia (cm)	Height (cm)	(T, H)	Length of Tibia (cm)	Height (cm)	(T, H)
30.5	154.9	$(30.5, 154.9)$	30.5	148.9	$(30.5, 148.9)$
34.8	165.2	$(34.8, 165.2)$	34.8	159.6	$(34.8, 159.6)$
36.3	168.8	$(36.3, 168.8)$	36.3	163.4	$(36.3, 163.4)$
37.9	172.7	$(37.9, 172.7)$	37.9	167.4	$(37.9, 167.4)$

46. **RESEARCH** Choose a country that you would like to visit. Use the Internet or other reference to find the cost of various services such as hotels, meals, and transportation. Use the currency exchange rate to determine how much money in U.S. dollars you will need on your trip. **See students' work.**

47. **CRITICAL THINKING** Find the domain values of each relation if the range is $\{0, 16, 36\}$.
   a. $y = x^2$ $\{-6, -4, 0, 4, 6\}$ b. $y = |4x| - 16$ $\{-13, -8, -4, 4, 8, 13\}$ c. $y = |4x - 16|$ $\{-5, 0, 4, 8, 13\}$

48. **CRITICAL THINKING** Select five values for the domain and find the range of $y = x + 4$. Then look at the range and domain of the inverse relation. Make a conjecture about the equation that represents the inverse relation. $y = x - 4$

49. **WRITING IN MATH** Answer the question that was posed at the beginning of the lesson. **See margin.**

Why are equations of relations important in traveling?

Include the following in your answer:
• an example of how you would keep track of how much you were spending in pounds and the equivalent amount in dollars, and
• an explanation of your spending power if the currency exchange rate is 0.90 pound compared to one U.S. dollar or 1.04 pounds compared to one dollar.

Standardized Test Practice

50. If $3x - y = 18$ and $y = 3$, then $x =$ **D**
   Ⓐ 4. Ⓑ 5. Ⓒ 6. Ⓓ 7.

51. If the perimeter of a rectangle is 14 units and the area is 12 square units, what are the dimensions of the rectangle? **C**
   Ⓐ 2×6 Ⓑ 3×3
   Ⓒ 3×4 Ⓓ 1×12

Answer

45.
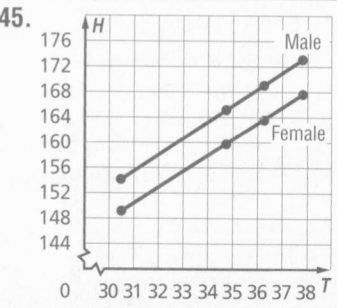

 **Graphing Calculator**

TABLE FEATURE You can enter selected x values in the TABLE feature of a graphing calculator, and it will calculate the corresponding y values for a given equation. To do this, enter an equation into the Y= list. Go to TBLSET and highlight **Ask** under the Independent variable. Now you can use the TABLE function to enter any domain value and the corresponding range value will appear in the second column.

Use a graphing calculator to find the solution set for the given equation and domain.

53. {(−8, 94), (−5, 74.5), (0, 42), (3, 22.5), (7, −3.5), (12, −36)}

52. $y = 3x − 4$; $x = \{−11, 15, 23, 44\}$ {(−11, −37), (15, 41), (23, 65), (44, 128)}

53. $y = −6.5x + 42$; $x = \{−8, −5, 0, 3, 7, 12\}$

54. $y = 3x + 12$ for $x = \{0.4, 0.6, 1.8, 2.2, 3.1\}$

54. {(0.4, 13.2), (0.6, 13.8), (1.8, 17.4), (2.2, 18.6), (3.1, 21.3)}

55. $y = 1.4x − 0.76$ for $x = \{−2.5, −1.75, 0, 1.25, 3.33\}$
{(−2.5, −4.26), (−1.75, −3.21), (0, −0.76), (1.25, 0.99), (3.33, 3.90)}

Maintain Your Skills

Mixed Review

Express the relation shown in each table, mapping, or graph as a set of ordered pairs. Then write the inverse of the relation. *(Lesson 4-3)*

58. {(−3, −2), (−2, 3), (3, −3), (4, 2)}; {(−2, −3), (3, −2), (−3, 3), (2, 4)}

56.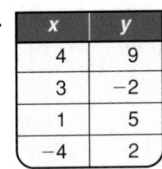

x	y
4	9
3	−2
1	5
−4	2

{(4, 9), (3, −2), (1, 5), (−4, 2)}; {(9, 4), (−2, 3), (5, 1), (2, −4)}

57.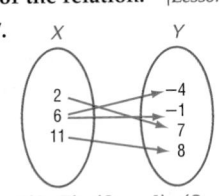

{(2, 7), (6, −4), (6, −1), (11, 8)}; {(7, 2), (−4, 6), (−1, 6), (8, 11)}

58.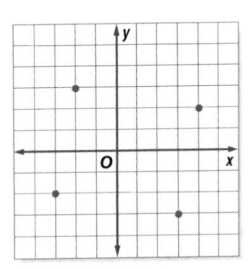

59–60. See margin for graphs.

59. $X'(6, 4)$, $Y'(5, 0)$, $Z'(−3, 3)$

Find the coordinates of the vertices of each figure after the given transformation is performed. Then graph the preimage and its image. *(Lesson 4-2)*

59. triangle XYZ with $X(−6, 4)$, $Y(−5, 0)$, and $Z(3, 3)$ reflected over the y-axis

60. quadrilateral $QRST$ with $Q(2, 2)$, $R(3, −3)$, $S(−1, −4)$ and $T(−4, −3)$ rotated 90° counterclockwise about the origin $Q'(−2, 2)$, $R'(3, 3)$, $S'(4, −1)$, $T'(3, −4)$

Use cross products to determine whether each pair of ratios forms a proportion. Write yes or no. *(Lesson 3-6)*

61. $\dfrac{6}{15}$, $\dfrac{18}{45}$ yes

62. $\dfrac{11}{12}$, $\dfrac{33}{34}$ no

63. $\dfrac{8}{22}$, $\dfrac{20}{55}$ yes

64. $\dfrac{6}{8}$, $\dfrac{3}{4}$ yes

65. $\dfrac{3}{5}$, $\dfrac{9}{25}$ no

66. $\dfrac{26}{35}$, $\dfrac{12}{15}$ no

Identify the hypothesis and conclusion of each statement. *(Lesson 1-7)*

67. If it is hot, then we will go swimming. H: it is hot; C: we will go swimming

68. H: you do your chores; C: you get an allowance

68. If you do your chores, then you get an allowance.

69. If $3n − 7 = 17$, then $n = 8$. H: $3n − 7 = 17$; C: $n = 8$

70. If $a > b$ and $b > c$, then $a > c$. H: $a > b$ and $b > c$; C: $a > c$

Getting Ready for the Next Lesson

PREREQUISITE SKILL Solve each equation. *(To review solving equations, see Lesson 3-4.)*

71. $a + 15 = 20$ 5

72. $r − 9 = 12$ 21

73. $−4 = 5n + 6$ −2

74. $3 − 8w = 35$ −4

75. $\dfrac{g}{4} + 2 = 5$ 12

76. $\dfrac{m}{5} + \dfrac{3}{5} = 2$ 7

59.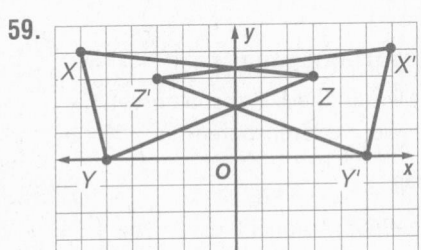

60.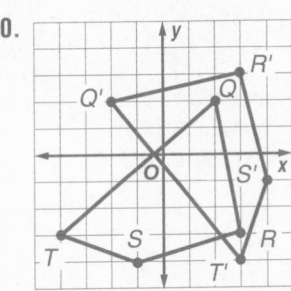

Open-Ended Assessment

Speaking Have students explain how to tell if an ordered pair is a solution of an equation with two variables.

Getting Ready for Lesson 4-5

PREREQUISITE SKILL Students will learn about graphing linear equations in Lesson 4-5. It is often easier to find ordered pairs for the solution set if the equation has been solved for the domain variable. Use Exercises 71–76 to determine your students' familiarity with solving equations.

Assessment Options

Quiz (Lessons 4-3 and 4-4) is available on p. 275 of the *Chapter 4 Resource Masters*.

Mid-Chapter Test (Lessons 4-1 through 4-4) is available on p. 277 of the *Chapter 4 Resource Masters*.

Answers

49. When traveling to other countries, currency and measurement systems are often different. You need to convert these systems to the system with which you are familiar. Answers should include the following.

- At the current exchange rate, 15 pounds is roughly 10 dollars and 10 pounds is roughly 7 dollars. Keeping track of every 15 pounds you spend would be relatively easy.

- If the exchange rate is 0.90 compared to the dollar, then items will cost less in dollars. For example, an item that is 10 in local currency is equivalent to $9.00. If the exchange rate is 1.04, then items will cost more in dollars. For example, an item that costs 10 in local currency is equivalent to $10.40.

1 Focus

5-Minute Check Transparency 4-5 Use as a quiz or review of Lesson 4-4.

Mathematical Background notes are available for this lesson on p. 190D.

How can linear equations be used in nutrition?

Ask students:

- If a person consumes an average of 2000 Calories per day, how many grams of fat should the person consume? **66 g**

- How did you find that amount? **Substitute 2000 for *C* and solve for *f*.**

- How could you use the graph to answer the first question above? **Find 2000 on the *C*-axis and then look up to where it meets the line. Then move horizontally to the *f*-axis to read the value.**

Teaching Tip You may want to show how $0.3\left(\dfrac{C}{9}\right)$ and $\dfrac{C}{30}$ are equivalent expressions.

What You'll Learn

- Determine whether an equation is linear.
- Graph linear equations.

Vocabulary

- linear equation
- standard form
- *x*-intercept
- *y*-intercept

How can linear equations be used in nutrition?

Nutritionists recommend that no more than 30% of a person's daily caloric intake come from fat. Each gram of fat contains nine Calories. To determine the most grams of fat *f* you should have, find the total number of Calories *C* you consume each day and use the equation $f = 0.3\left(\dfrac{C}{9}\right)$ or $f = \left(\dfrac{C}{30}\right)$. The graph of this equation shows the maximum number of grams of fat you can consume based on the total number of Calories consumed.

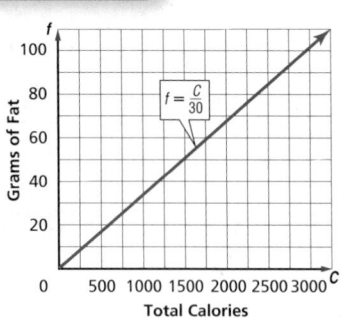

IDENTIFY LINEAR EQUATIONS   A **linear equation** is the equation of a line. Linear equations can often be written in the form $Ax + By = C$. This is called the **standard form** of a linear equation.

> **Key Concept** | *Standard Form of a Linear Equation*
>
> The standard form of a linear equation is
>
> $$Ax + By = C,$$
>
> where $A \geq 0$, *A* and *B* are not both zero, and *A*, *B*, and *C* are integers whose greatest common factor is 1.

Example 1 *Identify Linear Equations*

Determine whether each equation is a linear equation. If so, write the equation in standard form.

a. $y = 5 - 2x$

   First rewrite the equation so that both variables are on the same side of the equation.

   $$y = 5 - 2x \qquad \text{Original equation}$$
   $$y + 2x = 5 - 2x + 2x \qquad \text{Add 2x to each side.}$$
   $$2x + y = 5 \qquad \text{Simplify.}$$

   The equation is now in standard form where $A = 2$, $B = 1$, and $C = 5$. This is a linear equation.

b. $2xy - 5y = 6$

   Since the term $2xy$ has two variables, the equation cannot be written in the form $Ax + By = C$. Therefore, this is not a linear equation.

Resource Manager

 Workbook and Reproducible Masters

Chapter 4 Resource Masters
- Study Guide and Intervention, pp. 237–238
- Skills Practice, p. 239
- Practice, p. 240
- Reading to Learn Mathematics, p. 241
- Enrichment, p. 242

Graphing Calculator and Spreadsheet Masters, p. 30
Parent and Student Study Guide Workbook, p. 33

 Transparencies

5-Minute Check Transparency 4-5
Answer Key Transparencies

Technology

AlgePASS: Tutorial Plus, Lesson 9
Interactive Chalkboard

c. $3x + 9y = 15$

Since the GCF of 3, 9, and 15 is not 1, the equation is not written in standard form. Divide each side by the GCF.

$3x + 9y = 15$ Original equation

$3(x + 3y) = 15$ Factor the GCF.

$\dfrac{3(x + 3y)}{3} = \dfrac{15}{3}$ Divide each side by 3.

$x + 3y = 5$ Simplify.

The equation is now in standard form where $A = 1$, $B = 3$, and $C = 5$.

d. $\dfrac{1}{3}y = -1$

To write the equation with integer coefficients, multiply each term by 3.

$\dfrac{1}{3}y = -1$ Original equation

$3\left(\dfrac{1}{3}\right)y = 3(-1)$ Multiply each side of the equation by 3.

$y = -3$ Simplify.

The equation $y = -3$ can be written as $0x + y = -3$. Therefore, it is a linear equation in standard form where $A = 0$, $B = 1$, and $C = -3$.

GRAPH LINEAR EQUATIONS The graph of a linear equation is a continuous line. It extends beyond the endpoints in each direction and represents all the solutions of the linear equation. Also, every ordered pair on this line satisfies the equation.

Example 2 *Graph by Making a Table*

Graph $x + 2y = 6$.

In order to find values for y more easily, solve the equation for y.

$x + 2y = 6$ Original equation

$x + 2y - x = 6 - x$ Subtract x from each side.

$2y = 6 - x$ Simplify.

$\dfrac{2y}{2} = \dfrac{6 - x}{2}$ Divide each side by 2.

$y = 3 - \dfrac{1}{2}x$ Simplify.

Select five values for the domain and make a table. Then graph the ordered pairs.

x	$3 - \dfrac{1}{2}x$	y	(x, y)
-2	$3 - \dfrac{1}{2}(-2)$	4	$(-2, 4)$
0	$3 - \dfrac{1}{2}(0)$	3	$(0, 3)$
2	$3 - \dfrac{1}{2}(2)$	2	$(2, 2)$
4	$3 - \dfrac{1}{2}(4)$	1	$(4, 1)$
6	$3 - \dfrac{1}{2}(6)$	0	$(6, 0)$

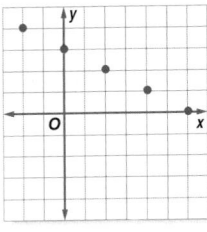

(continued on the next page)

Unlocking Misconceptions

Graphs of Linear Equations When students graph linear equations by making a table and plotting points, make sure that the line they draw extends beyond the end points, with an arrow at each end. Explain that the arrows on the end of the line signify that the line continues on infinitely in each direction. This is because no matter how far you go along the line in either direction, the points on the line will still be solutions of the equation.

---

2 Teach

IDENTIFY LINEAR EQUATIONS

In-Class Example

Teaching Tip Point out to students that there are no restrictions on the value of B. This means that B could be negative. So, an equation like $3x - 4y = 7$ is a linear equation.

1 Determine whether each equation is a linear equation. If so, write the equation in standard form.

a. $5x + 3y = z + 2$
not a linear equation

b. $\dfrac{3}{4}x = y + 8$

linear equation; $3x - 4y = 32$

c. $3x - 6y = 27$
linear equation; $x - 2y = 9$

d. $\dfrac{1}{4}x = -7$

linear equation; $x = -28$

GRAPH LINEAR EQUATIONS

In-Class Example

2 Graph $\dfrac{1}{2}y - x = 1$.

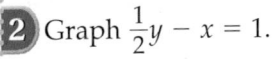

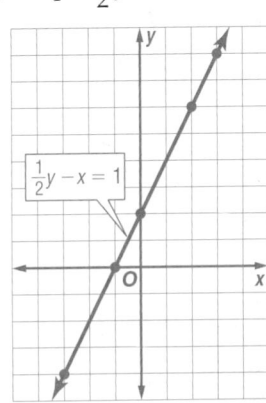

Teaching Tip Explain that the graph for Example 3 does not extend below the origin because negative values would not make sense in this problem. Carlos could not swim for a negative amount of time, nor could he burn a negative number of Calories.

3 Shiangtai walks his dog 2.5 miles around the lake every day.

a. Graph $m = 2.5d$, where m represents the number of miles walked and d represents the number of days of walking.

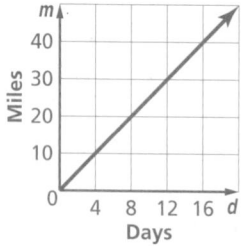

b. Suppose Shiangtai wanted to walk 50 miles, how many days would it take him? **20 days**

4 Determine the x-intercept and y-intercept of $4x - y = 4$. Then graph the equation. **The x-intercept is 1 and the y-intercept is −4.**

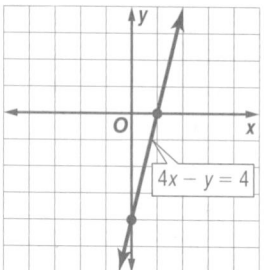

Intervention If students find that one of the intercepts of the graph is not a whole number, they might find it easier to graph the line if they find another point on the line that is a solution of the equation in which both coordinates are whole numbers.

Study Tip

Graphing Equations
When you graph an equation, use arrows at both ends to show that the graph continues. You should also label the graph with the equation.

More About . . .

Physical Fitness
In a triathlon competition, athletes swim 1.5 kilometers, bicycle 40 kilometers, and run 10 kilometers.
Source: www.usatriathlon.org

When you graph the ordered pairs, a pattern begins to form. The domain of $y = 3 - \frac{1}{2}x$ is the set of all real numbers, so there are an infinite number of solutions of the equation. Draw a line through the points. This line represents all of the solutions of $y = 3 - \frac{1}{2}x$.

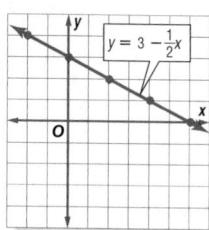

Example 3 *Use the Graph of a Linear Equation*

PHYSICAL FITNESS Carlos swims every day. He burns approximately 10.6 Calories per minute when swimming laps.

a. Graph the equation $C = 10.6t$, where C represents the number of Calories burned and t represents the time in minutes spent swimming.

Select five values for t and make a table. Graph the ordered pairs and connect them to draw a line.

t	$10.6t$	C	(t, C)
10	10.6(10)	106	(10, 106)
15	10.6(15)	159	(15, 159)
20	10.6(20)	212	(20, 212)
30	10.6(30)	318	(30, 318)

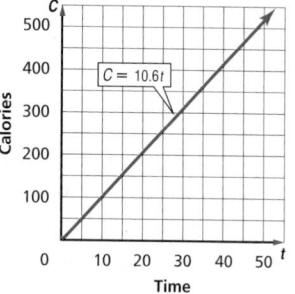

b. Suppose Carlos wanted to burn 350 Calories. Approximately how long should he swim?

Since any point on the line is a solution of the equation, use the graph to estimate the value of the x-coordinate in the ordered pair that contains 350 as the y-coordinate. The ordered pair (33, 350) appears to be on the line so Carlos should swim for 33 minutes to burn 350 Calories. *Check this solution algebraically by substituting (33, 350) into the original equation.*

Since two points determine a line, a simple method of graphing a linear equation is to find the points where the graph crosses the x-axis and the y-axis. The x-coordinate of the point at which it crosses the x-axis is the **x-intercept**, and the y-coordinate of the point at which the graph crosses the y-axis is called the **y-intercept**.

Example 4 *Graph Using Intercepts*

Determine the x-intercept and y-intercept of $3x + 2y = 9$. Then graph the equation.

To find the x-intercept, let $y = 0$.

$3x + 2y = 9$ Original equation
$3x + 2(0) = 9$ Replace y with 0.
$3x = 9$ Divide each side by 3.
$x = 3$

To find the y-intercept, let $x = 0$.

$3x + 2y = 9$ Original equation
$3(0) + 2y = 9$ Replace x with 0.
$2y = 9$ Divide each side by 2.
$y = 4.5$

DAILY INTERVENTION

Differentiated Instruction

Kinesthetic If students have difficulty graphing equations using intercepts, consider having them work in small groups to work on problems like Example 4. Make a large coordinate grid on a tiled floor. Assign one or two group members to find the intercepts. Then have students stand on the intercepts and hold string between them to model the line.

The x-intercept is 3, so the graph intersects the x-axis at (3, 0). The y-intercept is 4.5, so the graph intersects the y-axis at (0, 4.5). Plot these points. Then draw a line that connects them.

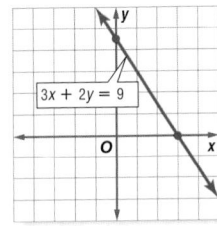

Study Notebook

Have students—
• add the definitions/examples of the vocabulary terms to their Vocabulary Builder worksheets for Chapter 4.
• include any other item(s) that they find helpful in mastering the skills in this lesson.

Check for Understanding

Concept Check

1. The former will be a graph of four points and the latter will be a graph of a line.

1. **Explain** how the graph of $y = 2x + 1$ for the domain {1, 2, 3, 4} differs from the graph of $y = 2x + 1$ for the domain of all real numbers.

2. **OPEN ENDED** Give an example of a linear equation in the form $Ax + By = C$ for each of the following conditions. **a–c. Sample answers given.**

   a. $A = 0$ $y = 8$ **b.** $B = 0$ $x = 5$ **c.** $C = 0$ $x - y = 0$

3. **Explain** how to graph an equation using the x- and y-intercepts. **See margin.**

Guided Practice

GUIDED PRACTICE KEY	
Exercises	Examples
4–7	1
8–13	2, 4
14, 15	3

Determine whether each equation is a linear equation. If so, write the equation in standard form.

4. $x + y^2 = 25$ **no**

5. $3y + 2 = 0$ **yes; $3y = -2$**

6. $\frac{3}{5}x - \frac{2}{5}y = 5$ **yes; $3x - 2y = 25$**

7. $x + \frac{1}{y} = 7$ **no**

Graph each equation. **8–13. See pp. 253A–253H.**

8. $x = 3$

9. $x - y = 0$

10. $y = 2x + 8$

11. $y = -3 - x$

12. $x + 4y = 10$

13. $4x + 3y = 12$

Application

TAXI FARE For Exercises 14 and 15, use the following information.
A taxi company charges a fare of $2.25 plus $0.75 per mile traveled. The cost of the fare c can be described by the equation $c = 0.75m + 2.25$, where m is the number of miles traveled.

14. Graph the equation. **See margin.**

15. If you need to travel 18 miles, how much will the taxi fare cost? **$15.75**

★ indicates increased difficulty

Practice and Apply

Homework Help	
For Exercises	See Examples
16–25	1
26–45	2, 4
46–56	3

Extra Practice
See page 829.

Determine whether each equation is a linear equation. If so, write the equation in standard form.

16. $3x = 5y$ **yes; $3x - 5y = 0$**

17. $6 - y = 2x$ **yes; $2x + y = 6$**

18. $6xy + 3x = 4$ **no**

19. $y + 5 = 0$ **yes; $y = -5$**

20. $7y = 2x + 5x$ **yes; $x - y = 0$**

21. $y = 4x^2 - 1$ **no**

22. $\frac{3}{x} + \frac{4}{y} = 2$ **no**

23. $\frac{x}{2} = 10 + \frac{2y}{3}$ **yes; $3x - 4y = 60$**

24. $7n - 8m = 4 - 2m$ **yes; $6m - 7n = -4$**

25. $3a + b - 2 = b$ **yes; $3a = 2$**

Graph each equation. **26–37. See pp. 253A–253H.**

26. $y = -1$

27. $y = 2x$

28. $y = 5 - x$

29. $y = 2x - 8$

30. $y = 4 - 3x$

31. $y = x - 6$

32. $x = 3y$

33. $x = 4y - 6$

34. $x - y = -3$

35. $x + 3y = 9$

36. $4x + 6y = 8$

37. $3x - 2y = 15$

www.algebra1.com/self_check_quiz

About the Exercises...

Organization by Objective
• Identify Linear Equations: 16–25
• Graph Linear Equations: 26–43, 48, 50

Odd/Even Assignments
Exercises 16–43 are structured so that students practice the same concepts whether they are assigned odd or even problems.

Assignment Guide

Basic: 17–41 odd, 45–51, 57–84

Average: 17–45 odd, 49–53, 57–84

Advanced: 16–44 even, 52–78 (optional: 79–84)

Answers

3. Determine the point at which the graph intersects the x-axis by letting $y = 0$ and solving for x. Likewise, determine the point at which the graph intersects the y-axis by letting $x = 0$ and solving for y. Draw a line through the two points.

14.

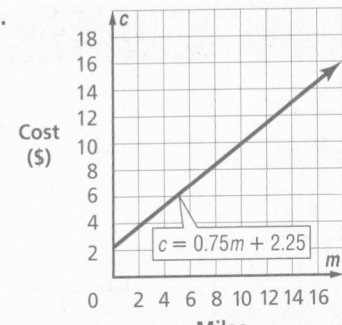

Identify Linear Equations A **linear equation** is an equation that can be written in the form $Ax + By = C$. This is called the **standard form** of a linear equation.

Standard Form of a Linear Equation	$Ax + By = C$, where $A \geq 0$, A and B are not both zero, and A, B, and C are integers whose GCF is 1.

Example 1 Determine whether $y = 6 - 3x$ is a linear equation. If so, write the equation in standard form.

First rewrite the equation so both variables are on the same side of the equation.
$y = 6 - 3x$ Original equation
$y + 3x = 6 - 3x + 3x$ Add $3x$ to each side.
$3x + y = 6$ Simplify.
The equation is now in standard form, with $A = 3$, $B = 1$ and $C = 6$. This is a linear equation.

Example 2 Determine whether $3xy + y = 4 + 2x$ is a linear equation. If so, write the equation in standard form.

Since the term $3xy$ has two variables, the equation cannot be written in the form $Ax + By = C$. Therefore, this is not a linear equation.

Exercises

Determine whether each equation is a linear equation. If so, write the equation in standard form.

1. $2x = 4y$ yes; $2x - 4y = 0$
2. $6 + y = 8$ yes; $y = 2$
3. $4x - 2y = -1$ yes; $4x - 2y = -1$
4. $3xy + 8 = 4y$ no
5. $3x - 4 = 12$ yes; $3x = 16$
6. $y = x^2 + 7$ no
7. $y - 4x = 9$ yes; $4x - y = -9$
8. $x + 8 = 0$ yes; $x = -8$
9. $-2x + 3 = 4y$ yes; $2x + 4y = 3$
10. $2 + \frac{1}{2}x = y$ yes; $x - 2y = -4$
11. $\frac{1}{2}y = 12 - 4x$ yes; $16x + y = 48$
12. $3xy - y = 8$ no
13. $6x + 4y - 3 = 0$ yes; $6x + 4y = 3$
14. $yx - 2 = 8$ no
15. $6a - 2b = 8 + b$ yes; $6a - 3b = 8$
16. $\frac{1}{4}x - 12y = 1$ yes; $x - 48y = 4$
17. $3 + x + x^2 = 0$ no
18. $x^2 = 2xy$ no

Determine whether each equation is a linear equation. If so, write the equation in standard form.

1. $4xy + 2y = 9$ no
2. $8x - 3y = 6 - 4x$ yes; $4x - y = 2$
3. $7x + y + 3 = y$ yes; $7x = -3$
4. $5 - 2y = 3x$ yes; $3x + 2y = 5$
5. $4y + x = 9x$ yes; $8x - 4y = 0$
6. $a + \frac{1}{5}b = 2$ yes; $5a + b = 10$
7. $6x = 2y$ yes; $6x - 2y = 0$
8. $\frac{x}{4} - \frac{y}{3} = 1$ yes; $3x - 4y = 12$
9. $\frac{5}{x} - \frac{2}{y} = 7$ no

Graph each equation.

10. $\frac{1}{3}x - y = 2$
11. $5x - 2y = 7$
12. $1.5x + 3y = 9$

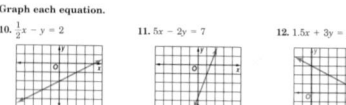

COMMUNICATIONS For Exercises 13–15, use the following information.
A telephone company charges $4.95 per month for long distance calls plus $0.05 per minute. The monthly cost c of long distance calls can be described by the equation $c = 0.05m + 4.95$, where m is the number of minutes.

13. Find the y-intercept of the graph of the equation. $(0, 4.95)$
14. Graph the equation.
15. If you talk 140 minutes, what is the monthly cost for long distance? $11.95

MARINE BIOLOGY For Exercises 16 and 17, use the following information.
Killer whales usually swim at a rate of 3.2–9.7 kilometers per hour, though they can travel up to 48.4 kilometers per hour. Suppose a migrating killer whale is swimming at an average rate of 4.5 kilometers per hour. The distance d the whale has traveled in t hours can be predicted by the equation $d = 4.5t$.

16. Graph the equation.
17. Use the graph to predict the time it takes the killer whale to travel 30 kilometers. between 6 h and 7 h

Pre-Activity How can linear equations be used in nutrition?
Read the introduction to Lesson 4-5 at the top of page 218 in your textbook.
In the equation $f = 0.3\left(\frac{C}{9}\right)$, what are the independent and dependent variables? C is independent, f is dependent.

Reading the Lesson
1. Describe the graph of a linear equation. The graph is a straight line.

2. Determine whether each equation is a linear equation. Explain.

	Equation	Linear or non-linear?	Explanation
a.	$2x = 3y + 1$	linear	The equation can be written as $2x - 3y = 1$.
b.	$4xy + 2y = 7$	non-linear	$4xy$ has two variables.
c.	$2x^2 = 4y - 3$	non-linear	The variable x has an exponent of 2.
d.	$\frac{x}{5} = \frac{4y}{3} = 2$	linear	The equation can be written as $3x - 20y = 30$.

3. What do the terms x-intercept and y-intercept mean? The x-intercept is the x-coordinate of the point where the graph of an equation crosses the x-axis, and the y-intercept is the y-coordinate of the point where the graph crosses the y-axis.

Helping You Remember
4. Describe the method you would use to graph $4x + 2y = 8$. Sample answer: Find the x- and y-intercepts, which are 2 and 4. Plot the points for the ordered pairs $(2, 0)$ and $(0, 4)$, and draw a line that connects them.

Graph each equation. 38–43. See pp. 253A–253H.

38. $1.5x + y = 4$
39. $2.5x + 5y = 75$
40. $\frac{1}{2}x + y = 4$
41. $x - \frac{2}{3}y = 1$
★ 42. $\frac{4x}{3} = \frac{3y}{4} + 1$
★ 43. $y + \frac{1}{3} = \frac{1}{4}x - 3$

44. Find the x- and y-intercept of the graph of $4x - 7y = 14$. $\frac{7}{2}, -2$

45. Write an equation in standard form of the line with an x-intercept of 3 and a y-intercept of 5. $5x + 3y = 15$

GEOMETRY For Exercises 46–48, refer to the figure.
The perimeter P of a rectangle is given by $2\ell + 2w = P$, where ℓ is the length of the rectangle and w is the width.

46. If the perimeter of the rectangle is 30 inches, write an equation for the perimeter in standard form. $2x + y = 15$

47. What are the x- and y-intercepts of the graph of the equation? 7.5, 15

48. Graph the equation. See margin.

METEOROLOGY For Exercises 49–51, use the following information.
As a thunderstorm approaches, you see lightning as it occurs, but you hear the accompanying sound of thunder a short time afterward. The distance d in miles that sound travels in t seconds is given by the equation $d = 0.21t$.

49. Make a table of values. See margin.
50. Graph the equation. See margin.
51. Estimate how long it will take to hear the thunder from a storm 3 miles away. about 14 s

BIOLOGY For Exercises 52 and 53, use the following information.
The amount of blood in the body can be predicted by the equation $y = 0.07w$, where y is the number of pints of blood and w is the weight of a person in pounds.

52. Graph the equation. See pp. 253A–253H.
53. Predict the weight of a person whose body holds 12 pints of blood. about 171 lb

• **OCEANOGRAPHY** For Exercises 54–56, use the information at left and below.
Under water, pressure increases 4.3 pounds per square inch (psi) for every 10 feet you descend. This can be expressed by the equation $p = 0.43d + 14.7$, where p is the pressure in pounds per square inch and d is the depth in feet.

54. Graph the equation. See pp. 253A–253H.
55. Divers cannot work at depths below about 400 feet. What is the pressure at this depth? 186.7 psi
★ 56. How many times as great is the pressure at 400 feet as the pressure at sea level? 12.7 times
57. **CRITICAL THINKING** Explain how you can determine whether a point at (x, y) is *above*, *below*, or *on* the line given by $2x - y = 8$ without graphing it. Give an example of each. See margin.

58. **WRITING IN MATH** Answer the question that was posed at the beginning of the lesson. See margin.

How can linear equations be used in nutrition?

Include the following in your answer:
- an explanation of how you could use the Nutrition Information labels on packages to limit your fat intake, and
- an equation you could use to find how many grams of protein you should have each day if you wanted 10% of your diet to consist of protein. (*Hint:* Protein contains 4 Calories per gram.)

More About . . .

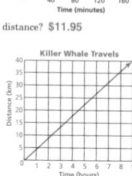

Oceanography •
How heavy is air? The atmospheric pressure is a measure of the weight of air. At sea level, air pressure is 14.7 pounds per square inch.
Source: www.brittanica.com

Taxicab Graphs

You have used a rectangular coordinate system to graph equations such as $y = x - 1$ on a coordinate plane. In a coordinate plane, the numbers in an ordered pair (x, y) can be any two real numbers.

A **taxicab plane** is different from the usual coordinate plane. The only points allowed are those that exist along the horizontal and vertical grid lines. You may think of the points as taxicabs that must stay on the streets.

The taxicab graph shows the equations $y = -2$ and $y = x - 1$. Notice that one of the graphs is no longer a straight line. It is now a collection of separate points.

Graph these equations on the taxicab plane at the right.
1. $y = x + 1$
2. $y = -2x + 3$
3. $y = 2.5$
4. $x = -4$

48.

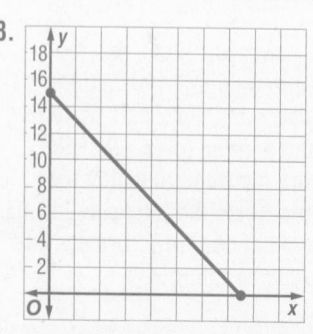

Standardized Test Practice
Ⓐ Ⓑ Ⓒ Ⓓ

59. Which point lies on the line given by $y = 3x - 5$? **A**
   - Ⓐ $(1, -2)$
   - Ⓑ $(0, 5)$
   - Ⓒ $(1, 2)$
   - Ⓓ $(4, 3)$

60. In the graph at the right, $(0, 1)$ and $(4, 3)$ lie on the line. Which ordered pair also lies on the line? **B**
   - Ⓐ $(1, 1)$
   - Ⓑ $(2, 2)$
   - Ⓒ $(3, 3)$
   - Ⓓ $(4, 4)$

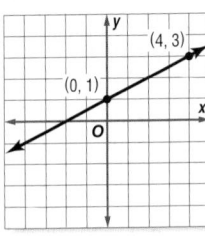

Maintain Your Skills

Mixed Review

61. $\{(-3, -8), (-1, -6), (2, -3), (5, 0), (8, 3)\}$

62. $\{(-3, -5), (-1, -1), (2, 5), (5, 11), (8, 17)\}$

63. $\{(-3, 21), (-1, 15), (2, 6), (5, -3), (8, -12)\}$

64. $\{(-3, -3), (-1, 1), (2, 7), (5, 13), (8, 19)\}$

65. $\{(-3, -30), (-1, -18), (2, 0), (5, 18), (8, 36)\}$

66. $\{(-3, -6), (-1, 6), (2, 24), (5, 42), (8, 60)\}$

Solve each equation if the domain is $\{-3, -1, 2, 5, 8\}$. *(Lesson 4-4)*

61. $y = x - 5$
62. $y = 2x + 1$
63. $3x + y = 12$
64. $2x - y = -3$
65. $3x - \frac{1}{2}y = 6$
66. $-2x + \frac{1}{3}y = 4$

Express each relation as a table, a graph, and a mapping. Then determine the domain and range. *(Lesson 4-3)* **67–70. See pp. 253A–253H.**

67. $\{(3, 5), (-4, -1), (-3, 2), (3, 1)\}$
68. $\{(4, 0), (2, -3), (-1, -3), (4, 4)\}$
69. $\{(1, 4), (3, 0), (-1, -1), (3, 5)\}$
70. $\{(4, 5), (2, 5), (4, -1), (3, 2)\}$

Solve each equation. Then check your solution. *(Lesson 3-5)*

71. $2(x - 2) = 3x - (4x - 5)$ **3**
72. $3a + 8 = 2a - 4$ **−12**
73. $3n - 12 = 5n - 20$ **4**
74. $6(x + 3) = 3x$ **−6**

ANIMALS For Exercises 75–78, use the table below that shows the average life spans of 20 different animals. *(Lesson 2-5)*

Animal	Life Span (years)	Animal	Life Span (years)	Animal	Life Span (years)
Baboon	20	Lion	15	Squirrel	10
Camel	12	Monkey	15	Tiger	16
Cow	15	Mouse	3	Wolf	5
Elephant	40	Opossum	1	Zebra	15
Fox	7	Pig	10		
Gorilla	20	Rabbit	5		
Hippopotamus	25	Sea Lion	12		
Kangaroo	7	Sheep	12		

75. See pp. 253A–253H.

75. Make a line plot of the average life spans of the animals in the table.
76. How many animals live between 7 and 16 years? **12 animals**
77. Which number occurred most frequently? **15 yr**
78. How many animals live at least 20 years? **4 animals**

Getting Ready for the Next Lesson

PREREQUISITE SKILL Evaluate each expression.
(To review evaluating expressions, see Lesson 1-2.)

79. $19 + 5 \cdot 4$ **39**
80. $(25 - 4) \div (2^2 - 1^3)$ **7**
81. $12 \div 4 + 15 \cdot 3$ **48**
82. $12(19 - 15) - 3 \cdot 8$ **24**
83. $6(4^3 + 2^2)$ **408**
84. $7[4^3 - 2(4 + 3)] \div 7 + 2$ **52**

Lesson 4-5 Graphing Linear Equations **223**

Open-Ended Assessment

Writing Have students give an example of a situation in which an ordered pair is a solution for a linear equation, but not a solution for the problem that is modeled by the situation. If students have difficulty thinking of such a situation, have them review Example 3.

Getting Ready for Lesson 4-6

PREREQUISITE SKILL Students will learn about functions in Lesson 4-6. To evaluate functions for a given value, students must be able to simplify expressions. Use Exercises 79–84 to determine your students' familiarity with evaluating expressions.

Answers

57. Substitute the values for x and y into the equation $2x - y = 8$. If the value of $2x - y$ is less than 8, then the point lies *above* the line. If the value of $2x - y$ is greater than 8, then the point lies *below* the line. If the value of $2x - y$ equals 8, then the point lies *on* the line. Sample answers: $(1, 5)$ lies above the line, $(5, 1)$ lies below the line, $(6, 4)$ lies on the line.

58. You can graph an equation that represents how many Calories and nutrients your diet should contain. Since your diet is different every day, it is easier to use the graph to determine your goal instead of making calculations every day. Answers should include the following.
   - Nutrition information labels provide facts about how many grams of fat are in each serving and/or how many Calories are from fat.
   - The number of grams of protein would equal 10% of the total number of Calories divided by 4 Calories per gram or $p = 0.025C$.

49.

t	d	t	d
0	0	10	2.1
2	0.42	12	2.52
4	0.84	14	2.94
6	1.26	16	3.36
8	1.68		

50.

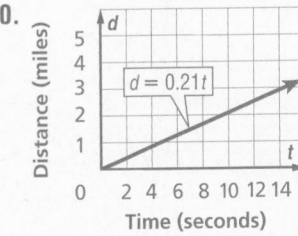

$d = 0.21t$

Distance (miles) vs Time (seconds)

Graphing Calculator Investigation

A Follow-Up of Lesson 4-5

Getting Started

Know Your Calculator The graphing calculator has the ability to make the graphs appear differently on the screen. The symbol before each Y= entry shows how the line will appear. Highlight the symbol and press ENTER repeatedly until the line type you want appears.

Standard Viewing Window The standard viewing is selected by pressing ZOOM 6. This is a [−10, 10] by [−10, 10] screen with Xscl and Yscl of 1.

Suppressing Graphs You can keep an equation in the Y= list and have it not appear on the graphing screen by highlighting the = sign and pressing ENTER.

Answers

1.
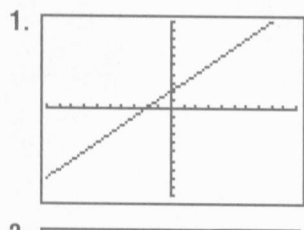

2.
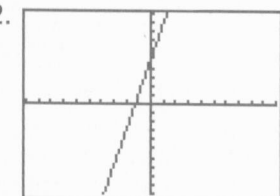

3.
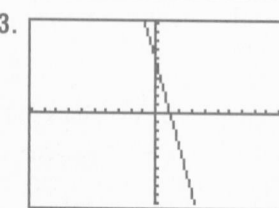

4.
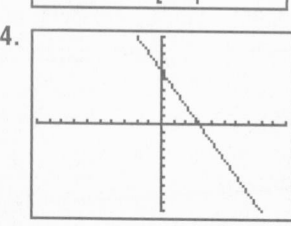

Graphing Linear Equations

The power of a graphing calculator is the ability to graph different types of equations accurately and quickly. Often linear equations are graphed in the standard viewing window. The **standard viewing window** is [−10, 10] by [−10, 10] with a scale of 1 on both axes. To quickly choose the standard viewing window on a TI-83 Plus, press ZOOM 6.

Example 1

Graph $2x − y = 3$ on a TI-83 Plus graphing calculator.

Step 1 *Enter the equation in the Y= list.*

- The Y= list shows the equation or equations that you will graph.
- Equations must be entered with the y isolated on one side of the equation. Solve the equation for y, then enter it into the calculator.

$2x − y = 3$	Original equation
$2x − y − 2x = 3 − 2x$	Subtract 2x from each side.
$−y = −2x + 3$	Simplify.
$y = 2x − 3$	Multiply each side by −1.

KEYSTROKES: Y= 2 X,T,θ,n − 3

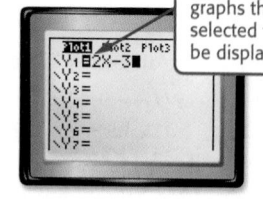

The equals sign appears shaded for graphs that are selected to be displayed.

Step 2 *Graph the equation in the standard viewing window.*

Graph the selected equations.

KEYSTROKES: ZOOM 6

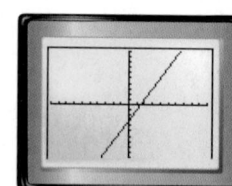

[−10, 10] scl: 1 by [−10, 10] scl: 1

Notice that the graph of $2x − y = 3$ above is a complete graph because all of these points are visible.

Sometimes a complete graph is not displayed using the standard viewing window. A **complete graph** includes all of the important characteristics of the graph on the screen. These include the origin, and the x- and y-intercepts.

When a complete graph is not displayed using the standard viewing window, you will need to change the viewing window to accommodate these important features. You can use what you have learned about intercepts to help you choose an appropriate viewing window.

224 Chapter 4 Graphing Relations and Functions

5.
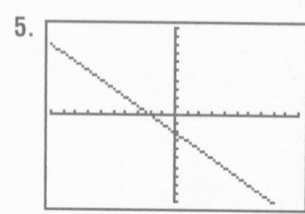

6.
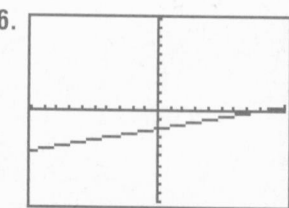

Investigation

Example 2

Graph $y = 3x - 15$ on a graphing calculator.

Step 1 *Enter the equation in the Y= list and graph in the standard viewing window.*

Clear the previous equation from the Y= list. Then enter the new equation and graph.

KEYSTROKES: [Y=] [CLEAR] 3 [X,T,θ,*n*] [−] 15 [ZOOM] 6

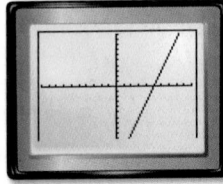

[−10, 10] scl: 1 by [−10, 10] scl: 1

Step 2 *Modify the viewing window and graph again.*

The origin and the *x*-intercept are displayed in the standard viewing window. But notice that the *y*-intercept is outside of the viewing window. Find the *y*-intercept.

$y = 3x - 15$ Original equation

$y = 3(0) - 15$ Replace *x* with 0.

$y = -15$ Simplify.

Since the *y*-intercept is −15, choose a viewing window that includes a number less than −15. The window [−10, 10] by [−20, 5] with a scale of 1 on each axis is a good choice.

KEYSTROKES: [WINDOW] −10 [ENTER] 10 [ENTER] 1 [ENTER]
−20 [ENTER] 5 [ENTER] 1 [GRAPH]

This window allows the complete graph, including the *y*-intercept, to be displayed.

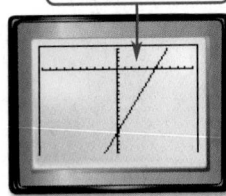

[−10, 10] scl: 1 by [−20, 5] scl: 1

Exercises

Use a graphing calculator to graph each equation in the standard viewing window. Sketch the result. **1–6. See margin.**

1. $y = x + 2$
2. $y = 4x + 5$
3. $y = 6 - 5x$

4. $2x + y = 6$
5. $x + y = -2$
6. $x - 4y = 8$

Graph each linear equation in the standard viewing window. Determine whether the graph is complete. If the graph is not complete, choose a viewing window that will show a complete graph and graph the equation again. **7–12. See pp. 253A–253H.**

7. $y = 5x + 9$
8. $y = 10x - 6$
9. $y = 3x - 18$

10. $3x - y = 12$
11. $4x + 2y = 21$
12. $3x + 5y = -45$

For Exercises 13–15, consider the linear equation $y = 2x + b$.

13. Choose several different positive and negative values for *b*. Graph each equation in the standard viewing window. **See students' work.**

14. For which values of *b* is the complete graph in the standard viewing window? **−10 < b < 10**

15. How is the value of *b* related to the *y*-intercept of the graph of $y = 2x + b$? **b is the y-intercept of the graph.**

 www.algebra1.com/other_calculator_keystrokes

Graphing Calculator Investigation **225**

Teach

- If students see any existing equations when they press the [Y=] key, they must first clear these equations before they enter the equations in Steps 1 and 2.
- Remind students that the *y*-intercept, where the line intersects the *y*-axis, occurs when *x* = 0.
- Suggest that students keep the scale on the axes the same so that the appearance of the graph is not distorted.

Assess

In **Exercises 1–6**, students should first isolate *y* in each equation.

In **Exercises 7–12**, students show how to change the viewing window.

In **Exercise 15**, students should realize that *b* in the equation represents the *y*-intercept.

1 Focus

5-Minute Check Transparency 4-6 Use as a quiz or review of Lesson 4-5.

Mathematical Background notes are available for this lesson on p. 190D.

How are functions used in meteorology?

Ask students:

- If you look at the data in this table as a set of ordered pairs, could the ordered pairs be represented by a linear equation? Explain why or why not. **No, because when the ordered pairs are graphed, they do not form a straight line.**

- If you represented the ordered pairs in this table as a mapping with temperature being the domain and pressure being the range, what would the mapping reveal? **There are fewer range values than domain values because there are two different temperatures associated with the pressure values of 995 and 1006 millibars.**

What You'll Learn

- Determine whether a relation is a function.
- Find function values.

Vocabulary
- function
- vertical line test
- function notation

How are functions used in meteorology?

The table shows barometric pressures and temperatures recorded by the National Climatic Data Center over a three-day period.

Pressure (millibars)	1013	1006	997	995	995	1000	1006	1011	1016	1019
Temperature (°C)	3	4	10	13	8	4	1	−2	−6	−9

Notice that when the pressure is 995 and 1006 millibars, there is more than one value for the temperature.

IDENTIFY FUNCTIONS Recall that relations in which each element of the domain is paired with exactly one element of the range are called **functions**.

Study Tip

Functions
In a function, knowing the value of x tells you the value of y.

Key Concept — Function

A function is a relation in which each element of the domain is paired with *exactly* one element of the range.

Example 1 Identify Functions

Determine whether each relation is a function. Explain.

a.

X → Y
−4, −1, 1, 3 → 9, −6, 11

This mapping represents a function since, for each element of the domain, there is only one corresponding element in the range. It does not matter if two elements of the domain are paired with the same element in the range.

b.

x	y
−3	6
2	5
3	1
2	4

This table represents a relation that is not a function. The element 2 in the domain is paired with both 5 and 4 in the range. If you are given that x is 2, you cannot determine the value of y.

c. {(−2, 4), (1, 5), (3, 6), (5, 8), (7, 10)}

Since each element of the domain is paired with exactly one element of the range, this relation is a function. If you are given that x is −3, you can determine that the value of y is 6 since 6 is the only value of y that is paired with $x = 3$.

Resource Manager

📁 Workbook and Reproducible Masters

Chapter 4 Resource Masters
- Study Guide and Intervention, pp. 243–244
- Skills Practice, p. 245
- Practice, p. 246
- Reading to Learn Mathematics, p. 247
- Enrichment, p. 248
- Assessment, p. 276

Parent and Student Study Guide Workbook, p. 34
School-to-Career Masters, p. 8
Science and Mathematics Lab Manual, pp. 139–144

Transparencies
5-Minute Check Transparency 4-6
Real-World Transparency 4
Answer Key Transparencies

Technology
AlgePASS: Tutorial Plus, Lesson 10
Interactive Chalkboard

You can use the **vertical line test** to see if a graph represents a function. If no vertical line can be drawn so that it intersects the graph more than once, then the graph is a function. If a vertical line can be drawn so that it intersects the graph at two or more points, the relation is not a function.

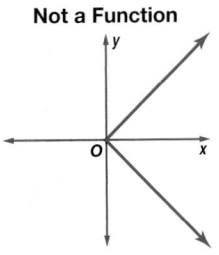

Function

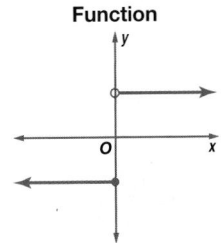

Not a Function

Function

One way to perform the vertical line test is to use a pencil.

Example 2 *Equations as Functions*

Determine whether $2x - y = 6$ is a function.

Graph the equation using the x- and y-intercepts.

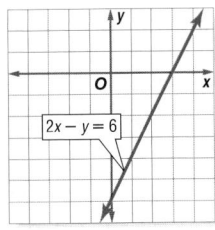

Since the equation is in the form $Ax + By = C$, the graph of the equation will be a line. Place your pencil at the left of the graph to represent a vertical line. Slowly move the pencil to the right across the graph.

For each value of x, this vertical line passes through no more than one point on the graph. Thus, the line represents a function.

FUNCTION VALUES Equations that are functions can be written in a form called **function notation**. For example, consider $y = 3x - 8$.

equation	function notation
$y = 3x - 8$	$f(x) = 3x - 8$

Study Tip

Reading Math
The symbol $f(x)$ is read f of x.

In a function, x represents the elements of the domain, and $f(x)$ represents the elements of the range. Suppose you want to find the value in the range that corresponds to the element 5 in the domain. This is written $f(5)$ and is read "f of 5." The value $f(5)$ is found by substituting 5 for x in the equation.

Example 3 *Function Values*

If $f(x) = 2x + 5$, find each value.

a. $f(-2)$

$f(-2) = 2(-2) + 5$ Replace x with -2.

      $= -4 + 5$ Multiply.

      $= 1$ Add.

b. $f(1) + 4$

$f(1) + 4 = [2(1) + 5] + 4$ Replace x with 1.

      $= 7 + 4$ Simplify.

      $= 11$ Add.

 www.algebra1.com/extra_examples

DAILY
INTERVENTION

Differentiated Instruction

Interpersonal Have pairs of students write a relation that is a function and a relation that is not a function. Students can write each relation as a table, a set of ordered pairs, or an equation.

---

2 *Teach*

IDENTIFY FUNCTIONS

In-Class Examples Power Point®

1 Determine whether each relation is a function. Explain.

a.

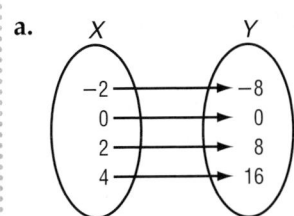

This is a function because the mapping shows each element of the domain paired with exactly one member of the range.

b.

x	y
-7	-12
-4	-9
2	-3
5	0

This table represents a function because the table shows each element of the domain paired with exactly one member of the range.

c. $\{(-5, 2), (-2, 5), (0, 7), (0, 9)\}$
This relation is not a function because the element 0 in the domain is paired with both 7 and 9 in the range.

2 Determine whether $x = -2$ is a function.

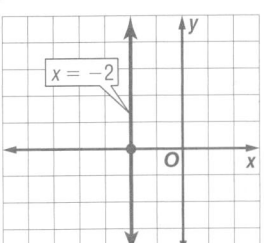

This graph does not pass the vertical line test, so the equation is not a function.

3 See p. 228.

FUNCTION VALUES

Teaching Tip Function notation is sometimes difficult for students to comprehend. Stress that $f(x)$ does not mean the product of f and x.

3 If $f(x) = 3x - 4$, find each value.

a. $f(4)$ 8

b. $f(-5)$ -19

c. $f(2 - x)$ $2 - 3x$

4 If $k(m) = m^2 - 4m + 5$, find each value.

a. $k(-3)$ 26

b. $k(6z)$ $36z^2 - 24z + 5$

c. $-4[k(y)]$ $-4y^2 + 16y - 20$

Teaching Tip Explain to students that various symbols can be used for nonstandard function notation.

5 If $\ll x \gg = 3x^2 + x - 1$, then $\ll -5 \gg =$ **A**

A 69.   **B** 70.

C 79.   **D** 81.

Answer

1. y is not a function of x since 3 in the domain is paired with 2 and -3 in the range. x is not a function of y since -3 in the domain of the inverse is paired with 4 and 3 in the range.

---

c. $f(x + 3)$

$$f(x + 3) = 2(x + 3) + 5 \quad \text{Replace } x \text{ with } x + 3.$$
$$= 2x + 6 + 5 \quad \text{Distributive Property}$$
$$= 2x + 11 \quad \text{Simplify.}$$

The functions we have studied thus far have been linear functions. However, many functions are not linear. You can find the value of these functions in the same way.

Example 4 Nonlinear Function Values

Study Tip

Reading Math
Other letters such as g and h can be used to represent functions, for example, $g(x)$ or $h(z)$.

If $h(z) = z^2 + 3z - 4$, find each value.

a. $h(-4)$

$$h(-4) = (-4)^2 + 3(-4) - 4 \quad \text{Replace } z \text{ with } -4.$$
$$= 16 - 12 - 4 \quad \text{Multiply.}$$
$$= 0 \quad \text{Simplify.}$$

b. $h(5a)$

$$h(5a) = (5a)^2 + 3(5a) - 4 \quad \text{Replace } z \text{ with } 5a.$$
$$= 25a^2 + 15a - 4 \quad \text{Simplify.}$$

c. $2[h(g)]$

$$2[h(g)] = 2[(g)^2 + 3(g) - 4] \quad \text{Evaluate } h(g) \text{ by replacing } z \text{ with } g.$$
$$= 2(g^2 + 3g - 4) \quad \text{Multiply the value of } h(g) \text{ by 2.}$$
$$= 2g^2 + 6g - 8 \quad \text{Simplify.}$$

On some standardized tests, an arbitrary symbol may be used to represent a function.

Standardized Test Practice
Ⓐ Ⓑ Ⓒ Ⓓ

Example 5 Nonstandard Function Notation

Multiple-Choice Test Item

If $\ll x \gg = x^2 - 4x + 2$, then $\ll 3 \gg =$

Ⓐ -2.   Ⓑ -1.   Ⓒ 1.   Ⓓ 2.

Read the Test Item

The symbol $\ll x \gg$ is just a different notation for $f(x)$.

Solve the Test Item

Replace x with 3.

$$\ll x \gg = x^2 - 4x + 2 \quad \text{Think: } \ll x \gg = f(x)$$
$$\ll 3 \gg = (3)^2 - 4(3) + 2 \quad \text{Replace } x \text{ with 3.}$$
$$= 9 - 12 + 2 \text{ or } -1 \quad \text{The answer is B.}$$

Check for Understanding

Concept Check

2. Sample answer: $\# x \# = x + 1$

1. **Study** the following set of ordered pairs that describe a relation between x and y: $\{(1, -1), (-1, 2), (4, -3), (3, 2), (-2, 4), (3, -3)\}$. Is y a function of x? Is x a function of y? Explain your answer. **See margin.**

2. **OPEN ENDED** Define a function using nonstandard function notation.

3. **Find a counterexample** to disprove the following statement. *All linear equations are functions.* $x = c$, where c is any constant

---

Standardized Test Practice
Ⓐ Ⓑ Ⓒ Ⓓ

Example 5 When taking standardized tests, students may be used to substituting answer choices for the variable(s) in equations to find the correct solution. However, this method will not work for function problems like the one in Example 5. Closer inspection reveals that this particular problem asks students to solve the function for 3. Tell students to look over the problem carefully before substituting values from the answer choices.

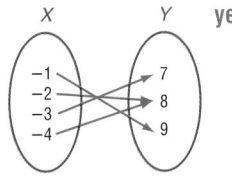
Guided Practice

Determine whether each relation is a function.

GUIDED PRACTICE KEY	
Exercises	Examples
4–9	1, 2
10–15	3, 4
16	5

4. 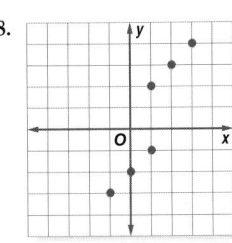 **yes**

5. **no**

x	y
−3	0
2	1
2	4
6	5

6. {(24, 1), (21, 4), (3, 22), (24, 5)} **no**

7. $y = x + 3$ **yes**

8. 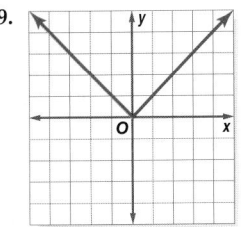 **no**

9. **yes**

If $f(x) = 4x − 5$ and $g(x) = x^2 + 1$, find each value.

10. $f(2)$ **3**

11. $g(−1)$ **2**

12. $f(c)$ **$4c − 5$**

13. $g(t) − 4$ **$t^2 − 3$**

14. $f(3a^2)$ **$12a^2 − 5$**

15. $f(x + 5)$ **$4x + 15$**

Standardized Test Practice
Ⓐ Ⓑ Ⓒ Ⓓ

16. If $x^{**} = 2x − 1$, then $5^{**} − 2^{**} =$ **D**

Ⓐ 3.　　　Ⓑ 4.　　　Ⓒ 5.　　　Ⓓ 6.

★ **indicates increased difficulty**

Practice and Apply

Homework Help	
For Exercises	**See Examples**
17–31, 44	1, 2
32–43, 45–51	3–5

Extra Practice
See page 830.

Determine whether each relation is a function.

17. X　Y **no**　**18.** X　Y **yes**　**19.** **yes**

x	y
2	7
4	9
5	5
8	−1

20. **no**

x	y
−9	−5
−4	0
3	6
7	1
6	−5
3	2

21. 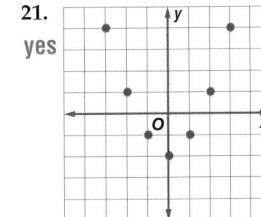 **yes**

22. 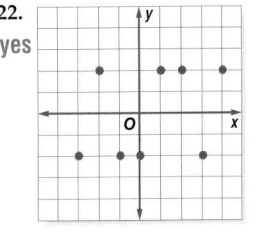 **yes**

23. {(5, −7), (6, −7), (−8, −1), (0, −1)} **yes**　**24.** {(4, 5), (3, −2), (−2, 5), (4, 7)} **no**

25. $y = −8$ **yes**

26. $x = 15$ **no**

27. $y = 3x − 2$ **yes**

28. $y = 3x + 2y$ **yes**

www.algebra1.com/self_check_quiz

Study Guide and Intervention, p. 243 (shown) and p. 244

Identify Functions Relations in which each element of the domain is paired with exactly one element of the range are called **functions**.

Example 1 Determine whether the relation {(6, −3), (4, 1), (7, −2), (−3, 1)} is a function. Explain.

Since each element of the domain is paired with exactly one element of the range, this relation is a function.

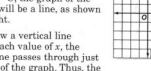

Example 2 Determine whether $3x - y = 6$ is a function.

Since the equation is in the form $Ax + By = C$, the graph of the equation will be a line, as shown at the right.

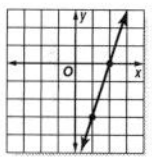

If you draw a vertical line through each value of x, the vertical line passes through just one point of the graph. Thus, the line represents a function.

Exercises

Determine whether each relation is a function.

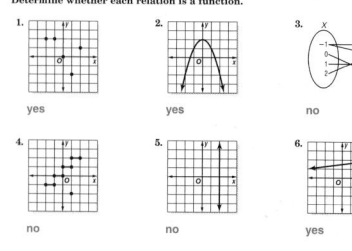

1. yes 2. yes 3. 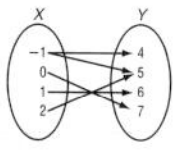 no

4. no 5. no 6. yes

7. {(4, 2), (2, 3), (6, 1)} yes
8. {(−3, −3), (−3, 4), (−2, 4)} no
9. {(−1, 0), (1, 0)} yes

10. $-2x + 4y = 0$ yes
11. $x^2 + y^2 = 8$ no
12. $x = -4$ no

Skills Practice, p. 245 and Practice, p. 246 (shown)

Determine whether each relation is a function.

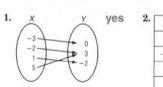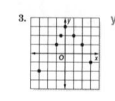

1. yes 2. no 3. yes

4. {(1, 4), (2, −2), (3, −6), (−6, 3), (−3, 6)} yes
5. {(6, −4), (2, −4), (−4, 2), (4, 6), (2, 6)} no
6. $x = -2$ no
7. $y = 2$ yes

If $f(x) = 2x - 6$ and $g(x) = x - 2x^2$, find each value.

8. $f(2)$ −2
9. $f\left(-\frac{1}{2}\right)$ −7
10. $g(-1)$ −3
11. $g\left(-\frac{1}{3}\right)$ −$\frac{5}{9}$
12. $f(7) - 9$ −1
13. $g(-3) + 13$ −8
14. $f(h + 9)$ $2h + 12$
15. $g(3y)$ $3y - 18y^2$
16. $2[g(b) + 1]$ $2b - 4b^2 + 2$

WAGES For Exercises 17 and 18, use the following information.
Martin earns $7.50 per hour proofreading ads at a local newspaper. His weekly wage w can be described by the equation $w = 7.5h$, where h is the number of hours worked.

17. Write the equation in functional notation. $f(h) = 7.5h$

18. Find $f(15)$, $f(20)$, and $f(25)$. 112.50, 150, 187.50

ELECTRICITY For Exercises 19–21, use the following information.
The table shows the relationship between resistance R and current I in a circuit.

Resistance (ohms)	120	80	48	6	4
Current (amperes)	0.1	0.15	0.25	2	3

19. Is the relationship a function? Explain. Yes; for each value in the domain, there is only one value in the range.

20. If the relation can be represented by the equation $IR = 12$, rewrite the equation in functional notation so that the resistance R is a function of the current I. $f(I) = \frac{12}{I}$

21. What is the resistance in a circuit when the current is 0.5 ampere? 24 ohms

Reading to Learn Mathematics, p. 247   ELL

Pre-Activity How are functions used in meteorology?
Read the introduction to Lesson 4-6 at the top of page 226 in your textbook.

If pressure is the independent variable and temperature is the dependent variable, what are the ordered pairs for this set of data? {(1013, 3), (1006, 4), (997, 10), (995, 13), (995, 8), (1000, 4), (1006, 1), (1011, −2), (1016, −6), (1019, −9)}

Reading the Lesson

1. The statement, "Relations in which each element of the _range_ is paired with exactly one element of the _domain_ are called functions," is false. How can you change the underlined words to make the statement true? Change _range_ to _domain_ and _domain_ to _range_.

2. Describe how each method shows that the relation represented is a function.

a. mapping
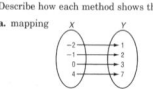
The elements of the domain are paired with corresponding elements in the range. Each element of the domain has only one arrow going from it.

b. vertical line test 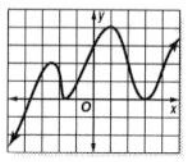
No vertical line passes through more than one point of the graph.

Helping You Remember

3. A student who was trying to help a friend remember how functions are different from relations that are not functions gave the following advice: _Just remember that functions are very strict and never give you a choice._ Explain how this might help you remember what a function is. Sample answer: A function always pairs each element in the domain with exactly one element in the range. If two people start with the same element of the domain, they are forced to pair it with the same element in the range. The second person cannot pick a different number from the first person.

Determine whether each relation is a function.

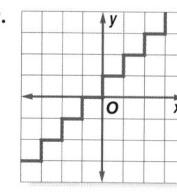 29. 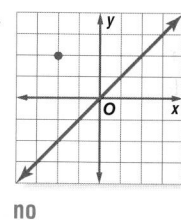 30. 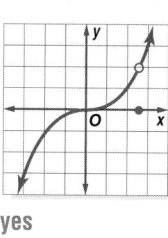 31.

no   no   yes

If $f(x) = 3x + 7$ and $g(x) = x^2 - 2x$, find each value.

32. $f(3)$ **16**
33. $f(-2)$ **1**
34. $g(5)$ **15**
35. $g(0)$ **0**
36. $g(-3) + 1$ **16**
37. $f(8) - 5$ **26**
38. $g(2c)$ **$4c^2 - 4c$**
39. $f(a^2)$ **$3a^2 + 7$**
40. $f(k + 2)$ **$3k + 13$**
41. $f(2m - 5)$ **$6m - 8$**
★ 42. $3[g(x) + 4]$ **$3x^2 - 6x + 12$**
★ 43. $2[f(x^2) - 5]$ **$6x^2 + 4$**

★ 44. **PARKING** The rates for a parking garage are $2.00 for the first hour, $2.75 for the second hour, $3.50 for the third hour, $4.25 for the fourth hour, and $5.00 for any time over four hours. Choose the graph that best represents the information and determine whether the graph represents a function. Explain.

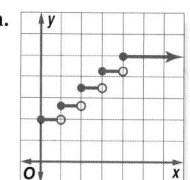 a. 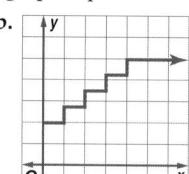 b. 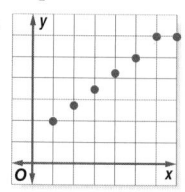 c.

a; See margin for explanation.

CLIMATE For Exercises 45–48, use the following information.
The temperature of the atmosphere decreases about 5°F for every 1000 feet increase in altitude. Thus, if the temperature at ground level is 77°F, the temperature at a given altitude is found by using the equation $t = 77 - 0.005h$, where h is the height in feet.

45. Write the equation in function notation. **$f(h) = 77 - 0.005h$**

46. Find $f(100)$, $f(200)$, and $f(1000)$. **76.5, 76, 72**

47. Graph the equation. **See margin.**

48. Use the graph of the function to determine the temperature at 4000 feet. **57°**

EDUCATION For Exercises 49–51, use the following information.
The National Assessment of Educational Progress tests 4th, 8th, and 12th graders in the United States. The average math test scores for 17-year-olds can be represented as a function of the science scores by $f(s) = 0.8s + 72$, where $f(s)$ is the math score and s is the science score.

49. Graph this function. **See margin.**

50. What is the science score that corresponds to a math score of 308? **295**

★ 51. Krista scored 260 in science and 320 in math. How does her math score compare to the average score of other students who scored 260 in science? Explain your answer.

52. **CRITICAL THINKING** State whether the following is _sometimes_, _always_, or _never_ true.
   The inverse of a function is also a function. **sometimes**

Study Tip

Reading Math
The graph shown in Part a of Exercise 44 is also called a _step function_.

WebQuest

A graph of the winning Olympic swimming times will help you determine whether the winning time is a function of the year. Visit www.algebra1.com/webquest to continue work on your WebQuest project.

51. Krista's math score is above the average because the point at (260, 320) lies above the graph of the line for $f(s)$.

Enrichment, p. 248

Composite Functions
Three things are needed to have a function—a set called the domain, a set called the range, and a rule that matches each element in the domain with only one element in the range. Here is an example.

Rule: $f(x) = 2x + 1$

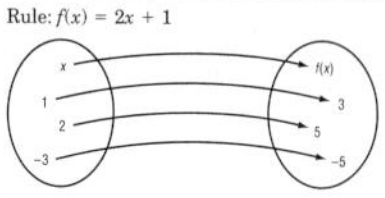

$f(x) = 2x + 1$
$f(1) = 2(1) + 1 = 2 + 1 = 3$
$f(2) = 2(2) + 1 = 4 + 1 = 5$
$f(23) = 2(-3) + 1 = -6 + 1 = -5$

Suppose we have three sets A, B, and C and two functions described as shown below.

Rule: $f(x) = 2x + 1$ Rule: $g(y) = 3y - 4$

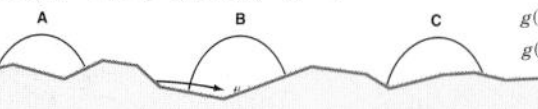

$g(y) = 3y - 4$
$g(3) = 3(3) - 4 = 5$

Answer

44. The cost is the same for 0–1 hour, excluding 0. Then it jumps after 1 hour and remains the same up to 2 hours. So the line is constant for x values between 0 and 1, then it jumps at 1. This trend continues at each hourly interval until 5 hours; then the cost is constant.

53. WRITING IN MATH Answer the question that was posed at the beginning of the lesson. **See margin.**

How are functions used in meteorology?

Include the following in your answer:
- a description of the relationship between pressure and temperature, and
- an explanation of whether the relation is a function.

Standardized Test Practice
Ⓐ Ⓑ Ⓒ Ⓓ

54. If $f(x) = 20 - 2x$, find $f(7)$. **A**

  Ⓐ 6   Ⓑ 7   Ⓒ 13   Ⓓ 14

55. If $f(x) = 2x$, which of the following statements must be true? **A**

  I. $f(3x) = 3[f(x)]$

  II. $f(x + 3) = f(x) + 3$

  III. $f(x^2) = [f(x)]^2$

  Ⓐ I only   Ⓑ II only   Ⓒ I and II only   Ⓓ I, II, and III

Maintain Your Skills

Mixed Review Graph each equation. *(Lesson 4-5)* **56–58. See pp. 253A–253H.**

56. $y = x + 3$ **57.** $y = 2x - 4$ **58.** $2x + 5y = 10$

Find the solution set for each equation, given the replacement set. *(Lesson 4-4)*

59. $y = 5x - 3$; $\{(3, 12), (1, -2), (-2, -7), (-1, -8)\}$ $\{(3, 12), (-1, -8)\}$

60. $y = 2x + 6$; $\{(3, 0), (-1, 4), (6, 0), (5, -1)\}$ $\{(-1, 4)\}$

61. RUNNING Adam is training for an upcoming 26-mile marathon. He can run a 10K race (about 6.2 miles) in 45 minutes. If he runs the marathon at the same pace, how long will it take him to finish? *(Lesson 3-6)* **approximately 3 h 9 min**

Name the property used in each equation. Then find the value of n.
(Lesson 1-4)

62. $16 = n + 16$ **63.** $3.5 + 6 = n + 6$ **64.** $\frac{3}{5}n = \frac{3}{5}$ **Mult. Identity; 1**
  Additive Identity; 0   **Reflexive; 3.5**

Getting Ready for the Next Lesson PREREQUISITE SKILL Find each difference.
*(To review **subtracting integers**, see Lesson 2-2.)*

65. $12 - 16$ **−4**   **66.** $-5 - (-8)$ **3**   **67.** $16 - (-4)$ **20**

68. $-9 - 6$ **−15**   **69.** $\frac{3}{4} - \frac{1}{8}$ **$\frac{5}{8}$**   **70.** $3\frac{1}{2} - \left(-1\frac{2}{3}\right)$ **$5\frac{1}{6}$**

Practice Quiz 2   *Lessons 4-4 through 4-6*

Solve each equation if the domain is $\{-3, -1, 0, 2, 4\}$. *(Lesson 4-4)* **1–3. See pp. 253A–253H.**

1. $y = x + 5$ **2.** $y = 3x + 4$ **3.** $x + 2y = 8$

Graph each equation. *(Lesson 4-5)* **4–5. See pp. 253A–253H.**

4. $y = x - 2$ **5.** $3x + 2y = 6$

Determine whether each relation is a function. *(Lesson 4-6)*

6. $\{(3, 4), (5, 3), (-1, 4), (6, 2)\}$ **yes**   **7.** $\{(-1, 4), (-2, 5), (7, 2), (3, 9), (-2, 1)\}$ **no**

If $f(x) = 3x + 5$, find each value. *(Lesson 4-6)*

8. $f(-4)$ **−7**   **9.** $f(2a)$ **$6a + 5$**   **10.** $f(x + 2)$ **$3x + 11$**

47.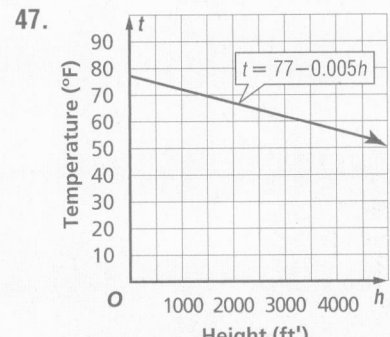

49.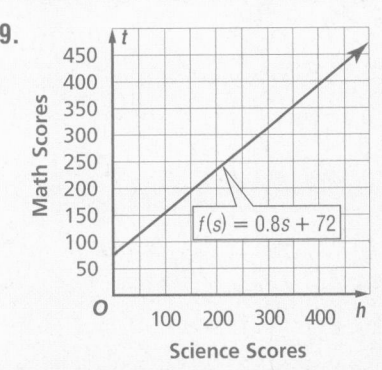

Open-Ended Assessment

Speaking Ask students to describe the various methods used to check whether relations or equations are functions. Which methods do students find easiest to use, and why?

Getting Ready for Lesson 4-7

PREREQUISITE SKILL Students will learn about arithmetic sequences in Lesson 4-7. To determine if a sequence is arithmetic, students must find the difference between consecutive terms in the sequence. Use Exercises 65–70 to determine your students' familiarity with finding differences.

Assessment Options

Practice Quiz 2 The quiz provides students with a brief review of the concepts and skills in Lessons 4-4 through 4-6. Lesson numbers are given to the right of exercises or instruction lines so students can review concepts not yet mastered.

Quiz (Lessons 4-5 and 4-6) is available on p. 276 of the *Chapter 4 Resource Masters*.

Answers

53. Functions can be used in meteorology to determine if there is a relationship between certain weather conditions. This can help to predict future weather patterns. Answers should include the following.
- As barometric pressure decreases, temperature increases. As barometric pressure increases, temperature decreases.
- The relation is not a function since there is more than one temperature for a given barometric pressure. However, there is still a pattern in the data and the two variables are related.

Getting Started

Menu Commands Note that the menu command described in the text is only for Microsoft Excel® spreadsheets. Students using other spreadsheets may need to explore the menu choice for a comparable procedure.

Teach

- Make sure students understand that "step" refers to the fixed interval between values.

- Another way to "teach" the spreadsheet sequence desired is to enter the values for 2 or 3 successive cells. Then highlight the cells and drag them downward. The software can analyze the pattern and extend it to fill the cells you dragged across.

- Make sure students understand that the subscripts are just an alternative way of labeling the variables. Students should not confuse subscripts with exponents.

Assess

Have students work in small groups for **Exercises 3-5**. Observe to determine if they are able to translate the sequence into the algebraic formula.

Study Notebook

You may wish to have students summarize this activity and what they learned from it.

Number Sequences

You can use a spreadsheet to generate number sequences and patterns. The simplest type of sequence is one in which the difference between successive terms is constant. This type of sequence is called an **arithmetic sequence**.

Example

Use a spreadsheet to generate a sequence of numbers from an initial value of 10 to 90 with a fixed interval of 8.

Step 1   Enter the initial value 10 in cell A1.

Step 2   Highlight the cells in column A. Under the Edit menu, choose the Fill option and then Series.

Step 3   A command box will appear on the screen asking for the Step value and the Stop value. The Step value is the fixed interval between each number, which in this case is 8. The Stop value is the last number in your sequence, 90. Enter these numbers and click OK. The column is filled with the numbers in the sequence from 10 to 90 at intervals of 8.

	A	B
1	10	
2	18	
3	26	
4	34	
5	42	
6	50	
7	58	
8	66	
9	74	
10	82	
11	90	
12		
13		
14		

Exercises

For Exercises 1–5, use a sequence of numbers from 7 to 63 with a fixed interval of 4.   1. 7, 11, 15, 19, 23, 27, 31, 35, 39, 43, 47, 51, 55, 59, 63

1. Use a spreadsheet to generate the sequence. Write the numbers in the sequence.

2. How many numbers are in the sequence?   **15**

MAKE A CONJECTURE   Let a_n represent each number in a sequence if n is the position of the number in the sequence. For example, a_1 = the first number in the sequence, a_2 = the second number, a_3 = the third number, and so on.

3. Write a formula for a_2 in terms of a_1. Write similar formulas for a_3 and a_4 in terms of a_1. $a_2 = a_1 + 4$; $a_3 = a_1 + 4 + 4$; $a_4 = a_1 + 4 + 4 + 4$

4. Look for a pattern. Write an equation that can be used to find the nth term of a sequence. $a_n = a_1 + (n - 1)4$

5. Use the equation from Exercise 4 to find the 21st term in the sequence.   **87**

What You'll Learn

- Recognize arithmetic sequences.
- Extend and write formulas for arithmetic sequences.

How are arithmetic sequences used to solve problems in science?

A probe to measure air quality is attached to a hot-air balloon. The probe has an altitude of 6.3 feet after the first second, 14.5 feet after the next second, 22.7 feet after the third second, and so on. You can make a table and look for a pattern in the data.

Time (s)	1	2	3	4	5	6	7	8
Altitude (ft)	6.3	14.5	22.7	30.9	39.1	47.3	55.5	63.7

+ 8.2   + 8.2   + 8.2   + 8.2   + 8.2   + 8.2   + 8.2

Vocabulary

- sequence
- terms
- arithmetic sequence
- common difference

RECOGNIZE ARITHMETIC SEQUENCES A **sequence** is a set of numbers in a specific order. The numbers in the sequence are called **terms**. If the difference between successive terms is constant, then it is called an **arithmetic sequence**. The difference between the terms is called the **common difference**.

terms

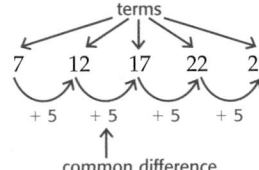

7   12   17   22   27

+ 5   + 5   + 5   + 5

↑

common difference

Key Concept   Arithmetic Sequence

An arithmetic sequence is a numerical pattern that increases or decreases at a constant rate or value called the common difference.

Example 1 *Identify Arithmetic Sequences*

Determine whether each sequence is arithmetic. Justify your answer.

a. 1, 2, 4, 8, ...

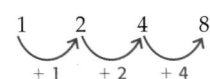

1   2   4   8

+ 1   + 2   + 4

This is not an arithmetic sequence because the difference between terms is not constant.

b. $\frac{1}{2}, \frac{1}{4}, 0, -\frac{1}{4}, ...$

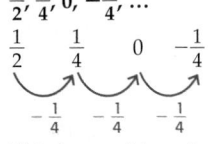

$\frac{1}{2}$ $\frac{1}{4}$ 0 $-\frac{1}{4}$

$-\frac{1}{4}$ $-\frac{1}{4}$ $-\frac{1}{4}$

This is an arithmetic sequence because the difference between terms is constant.

Study Tip

Reading Math
The three dots after the last number in a sequence are called an *ellipsis*. The ellipsis indicates that there are more terms in the sequence that are not listed.

---

1 *Focus*

5-Minute Check Transparency 4-7 Use as a quiz or review of Lesson 4-6.

Mathematical Background notes are available for this lesson on p. 190D.

How are arithmetic sequences used to solve problems in science?

Ask students:

- What pattern do you see in the data table? **After the first second, the balloon rises 8.2 feet every second.**

- Why might the balloon not have risen 8.2 feet in the first second? **Sample answer: Perhaps overcoming the force of gravity initially caused it not to rise as far in the first second.**

- What will the altitude of the balloon be after 9 seconds? **71.9 feet**

- How can you find the altitude of the balloon after 12 seconds? **Sample answer: 63.7 + 4(8.2)**

Resource Manager

📁 Workbook and Reproducible Masters

Chapter 4 Resource Masters
- Study Guide and Intervention, pp. 249–250
- Skills Practice, p. 251
- Practice, p. 252
- Reading to Learn Mathematics, p. 253
- Enrichment, p. 254

Parent and Student Study Guide Workbook, p. 35
Prerequisite Skills Workbook, pp. 5–8

 Transparencies
5-Minute Check Transparency 4-7
Answer Key Transparencies

💿 Technology
Interactive Chalkboard

RECOGNIZE ARITHMETIC SEQUENCES

Building on Prior Knowledge

Ask a student volunteer to count from zero by twos. Ask another volunteer to count from zero by threes. Finally, ask a third volunteer to count from zero by fives. Explain to students that when they count by a certain number, whether 1, 2, 3, or 5, they are using an arithmetic sequence because there is a common difference.

In-Class Example | Power Point®

1 Determine whether each sequence is arithmetic. Justify your answer.

a. $-15, -13, -11, -9, \ldots$
This is an arithmetic sequence because the difference between terms is constant.

b. $\dfrac{7}{8}, \dfrac{5}{8}, \dfrac{1}{8}, -\dfrac{5}{8}, \ldots$
This is not an arithmetic sequence because the difference between terms is not constant.

WRITE ARITHMETIC SEQUENCES

In-Class Example | Power Point®

2 Find the next three terms of the arithmetic sequence $-8, -11, -14, -17, \ldots.$
$-20, -23, -26$

WRITE ARITHMETIC SEQUENCES You can use the common difference of an arithmetic sequence to find the next term in the sequence.

Key Concept | Writing Arithmetic Sequences

- **Words**   Each term of an arithmetic sequence after the first term can be found by adding the common difference to the preceding term.
- **Symbols**   An arithmetic sequence can be found as follows
$$a_1, a_1 + d, a_2 + d, a_3 + d, \ldots,$$
where d is the common difference, a_1 is the first term, a_2 is the second term, and so on.

Example 2 | **Extend a Sequence**

Find the next three terms of the arithmetic sequence 74, 67, 60, 53, ...

Find the common difference by subtracting successive terms.

74   67   60   53   ?   ?   ?
$-7 \quad -7 \quad -7 \quad -7 \quad -7 \quad -7$

The common difference is -7.

Add -7 to the last term of the sequence to get the next term in the sequence. Continue adding -7 until the next three terms are found.

53   46   39   32
$-7 \quad -7 \quad -7$

The next three terms are 46, 39, 32.

Each term in an arithmetic sequence can be expressed in terms of the first term a_1 and the common difference d.

Term	Symbol	In Terms of a_1 and d	Numbers
first term	a_1	a_1	8
second term	a_2	$a_1 + d$	$8 + 1(3) = 11$
third term	a_3	$a_1 + 2d$	$8 + 2(3) = 14$
fourth term	a_4	$a_1 + 3d$	$8 + 3(3) = 17$
⋮	⋮	⋮	⋮
nth term	a_n	$a_1 + (n - 1)d$	$8 + (n - 1)(3)$

Study Tip

Reading Math
The formula for the nth term of an arithmetic sequence is called a *recursive formula*. This means that each succeeding term is formulated from one or more of the previous terms.

The following formula generalizes this pattern and can be used to find any term in an arithmetic sequence.

Key Concept | nth Term of an Arithmetic Sequence

The nth term a_n of an arithmetic sequence with first term a_1 and common difference d is given by
$$a_n = a_1 + (n - 1)d,$$
where n is a positive integer.

 **Example 3** Find a Specific Term

Find the 14th term in the arithmetic sequence 9, 17, 25, 33, …

In this sequence, the first term, a_1, is 9. You want to find the 14th term, so $n = 14$. Find the common difference.

9   17   25   33

+ 8   + 8   + 8   The common difference is 8.

Use the formula for the nth term of an arithmetic sequence.

$a_n = a_1 + (n - 1)d$ Formula for the nth term
$a_{14} = 9 + (14 - 1)8$ $a_1 = 9, n = 14, d = 8$
$a_{14} = 9 + 104$ Simplify.
$a_{14} = 113$ The 14th term in the sequence is 113.

Example 4 Write an Equation for a Sequence

Consider the arithmetic sequence 12, 23, 34, 45, …

a. Write an equation for the nth term of the sequence.

In this sequence, the first term, a_1, is 12. Find the common difference.

12   23   34   45

+ 11   + 11   + 11   The common difference is 11.

Use the formula for the nth term to write an equation.

$a_n = a_1 + (n - 1)d$ Formula for nth term
$a_n = 12 + (n - 1)11$ $a_1 = 12, d = 11$
$a_n = 12 + 11n - 11$ Distributive Property
$a_n = 11n + 1$ Simplify.

CHECK   For $n = 1$, $11(1) + 1 = 12$.
         For $n = 2$, $11(2) + 1 = 23$.
         For $n = 3$, $11(3) + 1 = 34$, and so on.

b. Find the 10th term in the sequence.

Replace n with 10 in the equation written in part **a**.

$a_n = 11n + 1$ Equation for the nth term
$a_{10} = 11(10) + 1$ Replace n with 10.
$a_{10} = 111$ Simplify.

c. Graph the first five terms of the sequence.

n	$11n + 1$	a_n	(n, a_n)
1	$11(1) + 1$	12	(1, 12)
2	$11(2) + 1$	23	(2, 23)
3	$11(3) + 1$	34	(3, 34)
4	$11(4) + 1$	45	(4, 45)
5	$11(5) + 1$	56	(5, 56)

Notice that the points fall on a line. The graph of an arithmetic sequence is linear.

Teaching Tip Make sure students carefully keep track of the variables in the equation $a_n = a_1 + (n - 1)d$ as it is easy to mistakenly substitute the wrong variable when using this equation.

3 Find the 9th term in the arithmetic sequence 7, 11, 15, 19, … **The 9th term in the sequence is 39.**

4 Consider the arithmetic sequence $-8, 1, 10, 19, …$

a. Write an equation for the nth term of the sequence. $a_n = 9n - 17$

b. Find the 12th term in the sequence. $a_{12} = 91$

c. Graph the first five terms of the sequence.

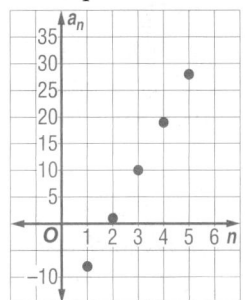

DAILY
INTERVENTION

Differentiated Instruction

Naturalist Sequences are often visible in nature. Have students research different sequences in nature, and determine whether the sequence is arithmetic. One particular sequence, called the Fibonacci series, appears in reproduction rates, the arrangement of seeds in a sunflower head, the arrangements of leaves, and many other natural phenomena. Students can use an Internet search engine and the words "Fibonacci series nature" to find numerous references.

Study Notebook

Have students—

- add the definitions/examples of the vocabulary terms to their Vocabulary Builder worksheets for Chapter 4.
- write the formula for the nth term of an arithmetic sequence and identify each component of the formula.
- include any other item(s) that they find helpful in mastering the skills in this lesson.

DAILY
INTERVENTION **FIND THE ERROR**
The common difference is found by subtracting the first term in the sequence from the second term. Ask students to check the arithmetic to make sure Marisela and Richard correctly subtracted the negative amount.

About the Exercises...

Organization by Objective
- **Recognize Arithmetic Sequences:** 15–20
- **Write Arithmetic Sequences:** 21–44

Odd/Even Assignments
Exercises 15–44 are structured so that students practice the same concepts whether they are assigned odd or even problems.

Assignment Guide

Basic: 15–35 odd, 39, 41, 45–49, 56–80

Average: 15–43 odd, 45–49, 56–80

Advanced: 16–44 even, 50–74 (optional: 75–80)

Check for Understanding

Concept Check

1. **OPEN ENDED** Write an arithmetic sequence whose common difference is −10. **Sample answer: 2, −8, −18, −28, …**

2. **Find** the common difference and the first term in the sequence defined by $a_n = 5n + 2$. **5, 7**

3. **FIND THE ERROR** Marisela and Richard are finding the common difference for the arithmetic sequence −44, −32, −20, −8.

Marisela	Richard
−32 − (−44) = 12	−44 − (−32) = −12
−20 − (−32) = 12	−32 − (−20) = −12
−8 − (−20) = 12	−20 − (−8) = −12

Who is correct? Explain your reasoning. **Marisela; to find the common difference, subtract the first term from the second term.**

Guided Practice

Determine whether each sequence is an arithmetic sequence. If it is, state the common difference.

GUIDED PRACTICE KEY

Exercises	Examples
4, 5	1
6, 7	2
8–11, 14	3
12, 13	4

4. 24, 16, 8, 0, … **yes; −8**
5. 3, 6, 12, 24, … **no**

Find the next three terms of each arithmetic sequence.

6. 7, 14, 21, 28, … **35, 42, 49**
7. 34, 29, 24, 19, … **14, 9, 4**

Find the nth term of each arithmetic sequence described.

8. $a_1 = 3, d = 4, n = 8$ **31**
9. $a_1 = 10, d = -5, n = 21$ **−90**
10. 23, 25, 27, 29, … for $n = 12$ **45**
11. −27, −19, −11, −3, … for $n = 17$ **101**

Write an equation for the nth term of each arithmetic sequence. Then graph the first five terms of the sequence. **12–13. See margin for graphs.**

12. 6, 12, 18, 24, … $a_n = 6n$
13. 12, 17, 22, 27, … $a_n = 5n + 7$

Application

14. **FITNESS** Latisha is beginning an exercise program that calls for 20 minutes of walking each day for the first week. Each week thereafter, she has to increase her walking by 7 minutes a day. Which week of her exercise program will be the first one in which she will walk over an hour a day? **the seventh week**

★ indicates increased difficulty

Practice and Apply

Determine whether each sequence is an arithmetic sequence. If it is, state the common difference.

Homework Help

For Exercises	See Examples
15–20, 43, 44	1
21–26	2
27–38, 45–49, 54, 55	3
39–42, 50–53	4

Extra Practice
See page 830.

15. 7, 6, 5, 4, … **yes; −1**
16. 10, 12, 15, 18, … **no**
17. 9, 5, −1, −5, … **no**
18. −15, −11, −7, −3, … **yes; 4**
19. −0.3, 0.2, 0.7, 1.2, … **yes; 0.5**
20. 2.1, 4.2, 8.4, 17.6, … **no**

Find the next three terms of each arithmetic sequence. **23. −82, −86, −90**

21. 4, 7, 10, 13, … **16, 19, 22**
22. 18, 24, 30, 36, … **42, 48, 54**
23. −66, −70, −74, −78, …
24. −31, −22, −13, −4, … **5, 14, 23**
25. $2\frac{1}{3}, 2\frac{2}{3}, 3, 3\frac{1}{3}, …$ **$3\frac{2}{3}, 4, 4\frac{1}{3}$**
★ 26. $\frac{7}{12}, 1\frac{1}{3}, 2\frac{1}{12}, 2\frac{5}{6}, …$ **See margin.**

236 **Chapter 4** Graphing Relations and Functions

Answers

12.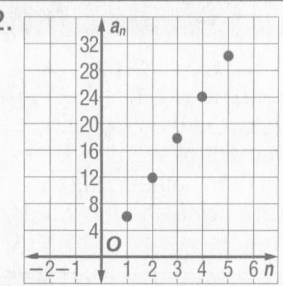

13.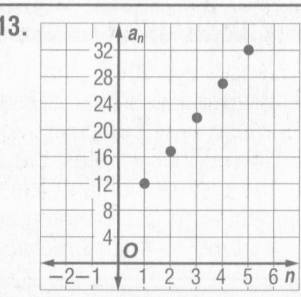

26. $3\frac{7}{12}, 4\frac{1}{3}, 5\frac{1}{12}$

Find the nth term of each arithmetic sequence described.

27. $a_1 = 5, d = 5, n = 25$ **125**   28. $a_1 = 8, d = 3, n = 16$ **53**

29. $a_1 = 52, d = 12, n = 102$ **1264**   30. $a_1 = 34, d = 15, n = 200$ **3019**

31. $a_1 = \frac{5}{8}, d = \frac{1}{8}, n = 22$ $3\frac{1}{4}$ 32. $a_1 = 1\frac{1}{2}, d = 2\frac{1}{4}, n = 39$ **87**

33. $-9, -7, -5, -3, \dots$ for $n = 18$ **25**   34. $-7, -3, 1, 5, \dots$ for $n = 35$ **129**

35. $0.5, 1, 1.5, 2, \dots$ for $n = 50$ **25**   36. $5.3, 5.9, 6.5, 7.1, \dots$ for $n = 12$ **11.9**

★ 37. 200 is the ___?___ th term of 24, 35, 46, 57, … **17**

★ 38. -34 is the ___?___ th term of 30, 22, 14, 6, … **9**

Write an equation for the nth term of each arithmetic sequence. Then graph the first five terms in the sequence. 39–42. See pp. 253A–253H for graphs.

39. $-3, -6, -9, -12, \dots$ $a_n = -3n$ 40. $8, 9, 10, 11, \dots$ $a_n = n + 7$

41. $2, 8, 14, 20, \dots$ $a_n = 6n - 4$ 42. $-18, -16, -14, -12, \dots$
$a_n = 2n - 20$

★ 43. Find the value of y that makes $y + 4, 6, y, \dots$ an arithmetic sequence. **4**

★ 44. Find the value of y that makes $y + 8, 4y + 6, 3y, \dots$ an arithmetic sequence. **−1**

GEOMETRY For Exercises 45 and 46, use the diagram below that shows the perimeter of the pattern consisting of trapezoids.

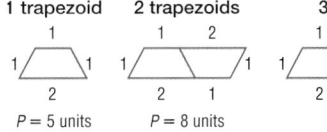

1 trapezoid	2 trapezoids	3 trapezoids	4 trapezoids
$P = 5$ units	$P = 8$ units	$P = 11$ units	$P = 14$ units

45. Write a formula that can be used to find the perimeter of a pattern containing n trapezoids. $P(n) = 3n + 2$

46. What is the perimeter of the pattern containing 12 trapezoids? **38**

THEATER For Exercises 47–49, use the following information.
The Coral Gables Actors' Playhouse has 76 seats in the last row of the orchestra section of the theater, 68 seats in the next row, 60 seats in the next row, and so on. There are 7 rows of seats in the section. On opening night, 368 tickets were sold for the orchestra section.

47. Write a formula to find the number of seats in any given row of the orchestra section of the theater. $a_n = 8n + 20$

48. How many seats are in the first row? **28**

49. Was this section oversold? **Yes, the section was oversold by 4 seats.**

PHYSICAL SCIENCE For Exercises 50–53, use the following information.
Taylor and Brooklyn are recording how far a ball rolls down a ramp during each second. The table below shows the data they have collected.

Time (s)	1	2	3	4	5	6
Distance traveled (cm)	9	13	17	21	25	29

50. Do the distances traveled by the ball form an arithmetic sequence? Justify your answer. **Yes, the constant difference between terms is 4.**

51. Write an equation for the sequence. $a_n = 4n + 5$

52. How far will the ball travel during the 35th second? **145 cm**

53. Graph the sequence. **See pp. 253A-253H.**

www.algebra1.com/self_check_quiz

Lesson 4-7 Arithmetic Sequences **237**

More About...

Theater

The open-air theaters of ancient Greece held about 20,000 people. They became the models for amphitheaters, Roman coliseums, and modern sports arenas.

Source: www.encarta.msn.com

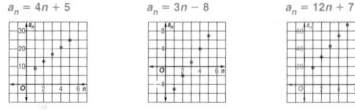
Lesson 4-7 Arithmetic Sequences **237**

Open-Ended Assessment

Modeling Ask student volunteers to demonstrate arithmetic sequences with algebra tiles. Have them identify the common differences and the next three terms without using tiles.

Getting Ready for Lesson 4-8

PREREQUISITE SKILL Students will learn to write equations from patterns in Lesson 4-8. One of the patterns involves analyzing differences in coordinates of ordered pairs. Use Exercises 75–80 to determine your students' familiarity with writing ordered pairs.

Answer

58. By finding a pattern in a sequence of numbers, scientists can predict results of large numbers that they are not able to observe. Answers should include the following.
- The formula $a_t = 8.2t - 1.9$ represents the altitude a_t of the probe after t seconds.
- Replace t with 15 in the equation for a_t to find that the altitude of the probe after 15 seconds is 121.1 feet.

Answers (page 239)

1. Sample answer: Inductive reasoning uses examples or past experience to make conclusions; deductive reasoning uses rules to make conclusions. Looking at a pattern of numbers to decide the next number is an example of inductive reasoning. Using the formula $A = \ell w$ and the length and width of a rectangle to find the area of a rectangle is an example of deductive reasoning.

2. Deductive reasoning; he is applying a general rule about men's heights to a specific case.

GAMES For Exercises 54 and 55, use the following information.
Contestants on a game show win money by answering 10 questions. The value of each question increases by $1500.

54. If the first question is worth $2500, find the value of the 10th question. **$16,000**

55. If the contestant answers all ten questions correctly, how much money will he or she win? **$92,500**

56. **CRITICAL THINKING** Is $2x + 5, 4x + 5, 6x + 5, 8x + 5 \ldots$ an arithmetic sequence? Explain your answer.

56. Yes; $4x + 5 - (2x + 5) = 2x$, $6x + 5 - (4x + 5) = 2x$, $8x + 5 - (6x + 5) = 2x$. The common difference is $2x$.

57. **CRITICAL THINKING** Use an arithmetic sequence to find how many multiples of 7 are between 29 and 344. **45**

58.  **WRITING IN MATH** Answer the question that was posed at the beginning of the lesson. **See margin.**

How are arithmetic sequences used to solve problems in science?

Include the following in your answer:
- a formula for the arithmetic sequence that represents the altitude of the probe after each second, and
- an explanation of how you could use this information to predict the altitude of the probe after 15 seconds.

Standardized Test Practice
Ⓐ Ⓑ Ⓒ Ⓓ

59. Luis puts $25 a week into a savings account from his part-time job. If he has $350 in savings now, how much will he have 12 weeks from now? **C**
- Ⓐ $600
- Ⓑ $625
- Ⓒ $650
- Ⓓ $675

60. In an arithmetic sequence a_n, if $a_1 = 2$ and $a_4 = 11$, find a_{20}. **B**
- Ⓐ 40
- Ⓑ 59
- Ⓒ 78
- Ⓓ 97

Maintain Your Skills

Mixed Review If $f(x) = 3x - 2$ and $g(x) = x^2 - 5$, find each value. *(Lesson 4-6)*

61. $f(4)$ **10**　　62. $g(-3)$ **4**　　63. $2[f(6)]$ **32**

Determine whether each equation is a linear equation. If so, write the equation in standard form. *(Lesson 4-5)* 65. yes; $x + y = 18$　66. yes; $2x - y = 3$

64. $x^2 + 3x - y = 8$ **no**　　65. $y - 8 = 10 - x$　　66. $2y = y + 2x - 3$

Translate each sentence into an algebraic equation. *(Lesson 3-1)*

67. Two hundred minus three times x is equal to nine. **$200 - 3x = 9$**

68. The sum of twice r and three times s is identical to thirteen. **$2r + 3s = 13$**

Find each product. *(Lesson 2-3)*

69. $7(-3)$ **-21**　　70. $-11 \cdot 15$ **-165**　　71. $-8(-1.5)$ **12**

72. $6\left(\frac{2}{3}\right)$ **4**　　73. $\left(-\frac{5}{8}\right)\left(\frac{4}{7}\right)$ **$-\frac{5}{14}$**　　74. $5 \cdot 3\frac{1}{2}$ **$17\frac{1}{2}$**

Getting Ready for the Next Lesson **PREREQUISITE SKILL** Write the ordered pair for each point shown at the right.
*(To review **graphing points**, see Lesson 4-1.)*

75. H **$(-2, 2)$**　　76. J **$(3, 0)$**

77. K **$(-4, -2)$**　　78. L **$(-3, -4)$**

79. M **$(3, 5)$**　　80. N **$(5, -1)$**

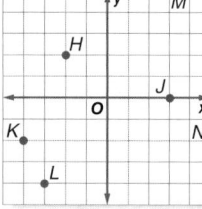

---

3. Inductive reasoning; you are observing specific pairs of terms and discovering a common difference, and you conclude that the common difference applies to the sequence in general.

4. Deductive reasoning; you are using the general formula for the nth term and applying it to a particular term of a particular series.

5b. 3, 9, 7, 1, 3, 9, 7, 1, 3, …

5c. 1; 100 is divisible by 4. According to the pattern, all powers with exponents divisible by 4 have 1 in the ones place. Inductive reasoning.

6. Deductive reasoning; the conclusion was based on a given rule.

Reading Mathematics

Reading Mathematics

Reasoning Skills

Throughout your life, you have used reasoning skills, possibly without even knowing it. As a child, you used inductive reasoning to conclude that your hand would hurt if you touched the stove while it was hot. Now, you use inductive reasoning when you decide, after many trials, that one of the worst ways to prepare for an exam is by studying only an hour before you take it. **Inductive reasoning** is used to derive a general rule after observing many individual events.

Inductive reasoning involves . . .
- observing many examples
- looking for a pattern
- making a conjecture
- checking the conjecture
- discovering a likely conclusion

With **deductive reasoning**, you use a general rule to help you decide about a specific event. You come to a conclusion by accepting facts. There is no conjecturing involved. Read the two statements below.

1) If a person wants to play varsity sports, he or she must have a C average in academic classes.

2) Jolene is playing on the varsity tennis team.

If these two statements are accepted as facts, then the obvious conclusion is that Jolene has at least a C average in her academic classes. This is an example of deductive reasoning.

Reading to Learn 1–6. See margin.

1. Explain the difference between *inductive* and *deductive* reasoning. Then give an example of each.

2. When Sherlock Holmes reaches a conclusion about a murderer's height because he knows the relationship between a man's height and the distance between his footprints, what kind of reasoning is he using? Explain.

3. When you examine a sequence of numbers and decide that it is an arithmetic sequence, what kind of reasoning are you using? Explain.

4. Once you have found the common difference for an arithmetic sequence, what kind of reasoning do you use to find the 100th term in the sequence?

5. **a.** Copy and complete the following table.

3^1	3^2	3^3	3^4	3^5	3^6	3^7	3^8	3^9
3	9	27	81	243	729	2187	6561	19,683

   b. Write the sequence of numbers representing the numbers in the ones place.

   c. Find the number in the ones place for the value of 3^{100}. Explain your reasoning. State the type of reasoning that you used.

6. A sequence contains all numbers less than 50 that are divisible by 5. You conclude that 35 is in the sequence. Is this an example of inductive or deductive reasoning? Explain.

Reading Mathematics Reasoning Skills **239**

Getting Started

Ask students to explain the types of thoughts they have when they solve a problem. If students have trouble coming up with ideas, give them a situation. Ask them how they would solve the problem of opening a locked door if they had a key ring with 100 keys on it.

Teach

Induce Explain to students that the root of inductive is *induce*. Induce is a verb that means to call forth or bring about by influence, or to cause the formation of. After students read the description of inductive reasoning, have them relate the principle of inductive reasoning to the definition of the word induce.

Deduce The root of deductive is *deduce*. Deduce is a verb that means to infer from a general principle. Ask students to relate the principle of deductive reasoning to the definition of the word deduce.

Assess

Reading to Learn Ask students whether predicting the next term in a sequence of numbers is done by trial and error, or by interpreting given information with a set of rules.

Study Notebook

Ask students to summarize what they have learned about inductive and deductive reasoning.

4-8 Writing Equations from Patterns

Vocabulary

- look for a pattern
- inductive reasoning

Study Tip

Look Back
To review **deductive reasoning**, see Lesson 1-7.

What You'll Learn

- Look for a pattern.
- Write an equation given some of the solutions.

Why is writing equations from patterns important in science?

Water is one of the few substances that expands when it freezes. The table shows different volumes of water and the corresponding volumes of ice.

Volume of Water (ft³)	11	22	33	44	55
Volume of Ice (ft³)	12	24	36	48	60

The relation in the table can be represented by a graph. Let w represent the volume of water, and let c represent the volume of ice. When the ordered pairs are graphed, they form a linear pattern. This pattern can be described by an equation.

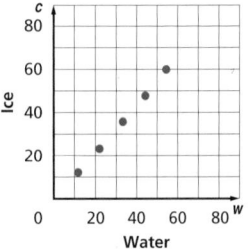

LOOK FOR PATTERNS A very useful problem-solving strategy is **look for a pattern**. When you make a conclusion based on a pattern of examples, you are using **inductive reasoning**. Recall that *deductive reasoning* uses facts, rules, or definitions to reach a conclusion.

Example 1 *Extend a Pattern*

Study the pattern below.

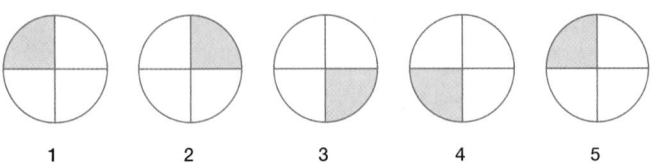

a. **Draw the next three figures in the pattern.**

The pattern consists of circles with one-fourth shaded. The section that is shaded is rotated in a clockwise direction. The next three figures are shown.

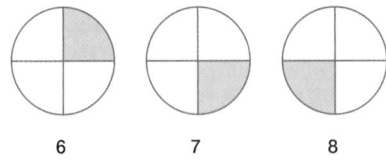

b. Draw the 27th circle in the pattern.

The pattern repeats every fourth design. Therefore designs 4, 8, 12, 16, and so on, will all be the same. Since 24 is the greatest number less than 27 that is a multiple of 4, the 25th circle in the pattern will be the same as the first circle.

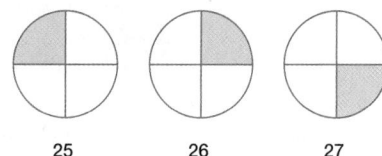

Other sequences besides arithmetic sequences can follow a pattern.

Example 2 *Patterns in a Sequence*

Find the next three terms in the sequence 3, 6, 12, 24, … .

Study the pattern in the sequence.

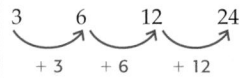

You can use inductive reasoning to find the next term in a sequence. Notice the pattern 3, 6, 12, … The difference between each term doubles in each successive term. To find the next three terms in the sequence, continue doubling each successive difference. Add 24, 48, and 96.

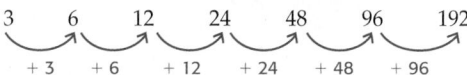

The next three terms are 48, 96, and 192.

Algebra Activity

Looking for Patterns

- You will need several pieces of string.
- Loop a piece of string around one of the cutting edges of the scissors and cut. How many pieces of string do you have as a result of this cut? Discard those pieces. **3**
- Use another piece of string to make 2 loops around the scissors and cut. How many pieces of string result? **4**
- Continue making loops and cutting until you see a pattern.

Analyze

1. Describe the pattern and write a sequence that describes the number of loops and the number of pieces of string.
2. Write an expression that you could use to find the number of pieces of string you would have if you made *n* loops. $n + 2$
3. How many pieces of string would you have if you made 20 loops? **22**

1. The number of pieces is 2 more than the number of loops; 3, 4, 5, 6, 7, … .

WRITE EQUATIONS Sometimes a pattern can lead to a general rule. If the relationship between the domain and range of a relation is linear, the relationship can be described by a linear equation.

 www.algebra1.com/extra_examples

Lesson 4-8 Writing Equations from Patterns **241**

Algebra Activity

Materials: scissors, string

- Draw students' attention to the art. Point out that with one loop around the scissor blade, the scissors are about to close on two pieces of string.
- Students should hold the string while they are cutting, so that the lengths do not fall during the cutting.

Lesson 4-8 Writing Equations from Patterns **241**

---

2 Teach

LOOK FOR PATTERNS

In-Class Examples 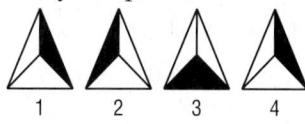 Power Point®

1 Study the pattern below.

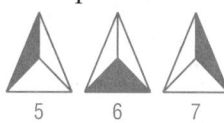

a. Draw the next three figures in the pattern.

b. Draw the 17th triangle in the pattern.

2 Find the next three terms in the sequence −3, −1, 3, 9, … .
17, 27, 39

3 **ENERGY** The table shows the number of miles driven for each hour of driving.

Hours	1	2	3	4
Miles	50	100	150	200

a. Graph the data. What conclusion can you make about the relationship between the number of hours of driving, h, and the number of miles driven, m?

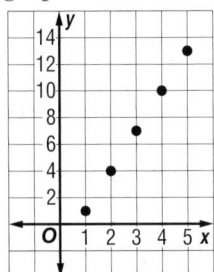

The graph shows a linear relationship between the number of hours of driving and the number of miles driven.

b. Write an equation to describe this relationship. $f(h) = 50h$, where $f(h)$ represents the number of miles driven.

4 Write an equation in function notation for the relation graphed below.

First make a table of ordered pairs, find the domain and range differences, and finally write an equation in function notation.

x	1	2	3	4	5
y	1	4	7	10	13

The pattern suggests that y is always 2 less than 3 times x. So, the equation is $f(x) = 3x - 2$.

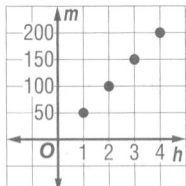

More About. . .

Fuel Economy

Not all cars use gasoline. Many alternative fuels are being used today in place of fossil fuels like oil.

Source: U.S. Department of Energy

Example 3 *Write an Equation from Data*

FUEL ECONOMY The table below shows the average amount of gas Rogelio's car uses depending on how many miles he drives.

Gallons of gasoline	1	2	3	4	5
Miles driven	28	56	84	112	140

a. Graph the data. What conclusion can you make about the relationship between the number of gallons used and the number of miles driven?

The graph shows a linear relationship between the number of gallons used g and the number of miles driven m.

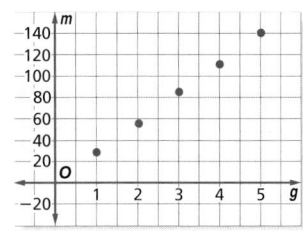

b. Write an equation to describe this relationship.

Look at the relationship between the domain and range to find a pattern that can be described by an equation.

$$+1 \quad +1 \quad +1 \quad +1$$

Gallons of gasoline	1	2	3	4	5
Miles driven	28	56	84	112	140

$$+28 \quad +28 \quad +28 \quad +28$$

The difference of the values for g is 1, and the difference of the values for m is 28. This suggests that $m = 28g$. Check to see if this equation is correct by substituting values of g into the equation.

CHECK If $g = 1$, then $m = 28(1)$ or 28. ✓
If $g = 2$, then $m = 28(2)$ or 56. ✓
If $g = 3$, then $m = 28(3)$ or 84. ✓

The equation checks. Since this relation is also a function, we can write the equation as $f(g) = 28g$, where $f(g)$ represents the number of miles driven.

Example 4 *Write an Equation with a Constant*

Write an equation in function notation for the relation graphed at the right.

Make a table of ordered pairs for several points on the graph.

$$+1 +1 +1 +1$$

x	1	2	3	4	5
y	5	7	9	11	13

$$+2 +2 +2 +2$$

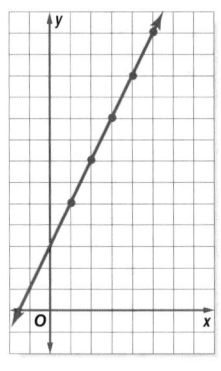

The difference of the x values is 1, and the difference of the y values is 2. The difference in y values is twice the difference of x values. This suggests that $y = 2x$. Check this equation.

DAILY
INTERVENTION   **Differentiated Instruction**

Intrapersonal Some students may be aware that they are having trouble with a difficult concept, but they may not be willing to voice their concern unless they are prompted to do so. Make sure you make yourself available to answer questions that students might have. Seek out the quiet students who seem to be showing signs of trouble and let them privately share their concerns.

CHECK If $x = 1$, then $y = 2(1)$ or 2. But the y value for $x = 1$ is 5. This is a difference of 3. Try some other values in the domain to see if the same difference occurs.

x	1	2	3	4	5
2x	2	4	6	8	10
y	5	7	9	11	13

y is always 3 more than $2x$.

This pattern suggests that 3 should be added to one side of the equation in order to correctly describe the relation. Check $y = 2x + 3$.

If $x = 2$, then $y = 2(2) + 3$ or 7.
If $x = 3$, then $y = 2(3) + 3$, or 9.

Thus, $y = 2x + 3$ correctly describes this relation. Since this relation is also a function, we can write the equation in function notation as $f(x) = 2x + 3$.

Check for Understanding

Concept Check

1. Once you recognize a pattern, you can find a general rule that can be written as an algebraic expression.

1. Explain how you can use inductive reasoning to write an equation from a pattern.

2. OPEN ENDED Write a sequence for which the first term is 4 and the second term is 8. Explain the pattern that you used. **See margin.**

3. Explain how you can determine whether an equation correctly represents a relation given in a table. **See margin.**

Guided Practice

GUIDED PRACTICE KEY

Exercises	Examples
4	1
5, 6	2
7, 8	3
9–11	4

4. Find the next two items for the pattern. Then find the 16th figure in the pattern.

  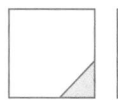 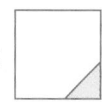 ;

Find the next three terms in each sequence.

5. 1, 2, 4, 7, 11, ... **16, 22, 29**

6. 5, 9, 6, 10, 7, 11, ... **8, 12, 9**

Write an equation in function notation for each relation.

7. 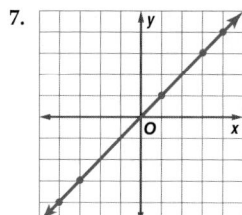 $f(x) = x$

8. 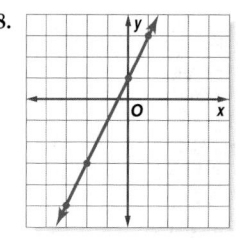 $f(x) = 2x + 1$

Application **GEOLOGY** For Exercises 9–11, use the table below that shows the underground temperature of rocks at various depths below Earth's surface.

Depth (km)	1	2	3	4	5	6
Temperature (°C)	55	90	125	160	195	230

9. Graph the data. **See margin.**

10. Write an equation in function notation for the relation. $f(x) = 35x + 20$

11. Find the temperature of a rock that is 10 kilometers below the surface. **370°C**

Lesson 4-8 Writing Equations from Patterns **243**

3 Practice/Apply

Study Notebook

Have students—
• complete the definitions/examples for the remaining terms on their Vocabulary Builder worksheets for Chapter 4.
• include any other item(s) that they find helpful in mastering the skills in this lesson.

About the Exercises...

Organization by Objective
• **Look for Patterns:** 12–19, 26–28
• **Write Equations:** 20–25, 29, 32

Odd/Even Assignments
Exercises 12–25 are structured so that students practice the same concepts whether they are assigned odd or even problems.

Assignment Guide
Basic: 13–23 odd, 27–28, 31–42
Average: 13–25 odd, 27–28, 31–42
Advanced: 12–26 even, 27–42

Answers

2. Sample answer: 4, 8, 16, 32, 64, ...; each successive term doubles.

3. Test the values of the domain in the equation. If the resulting values match the range, the equation is correct.

9.

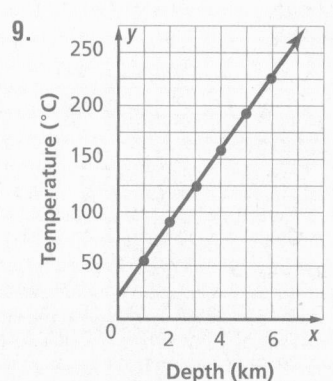

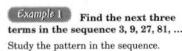
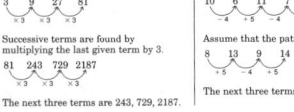
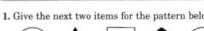

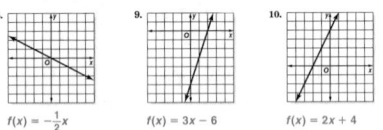
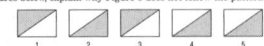
★ indicates increased difficulty

Practice and Apply

Find the next two items for each pattern. Then find the 21st figure in the pattern.

12.
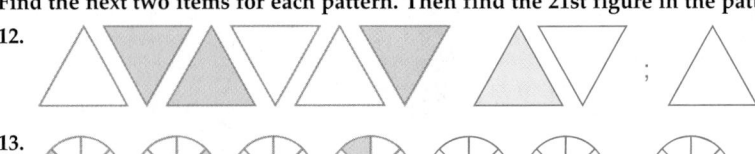

13.
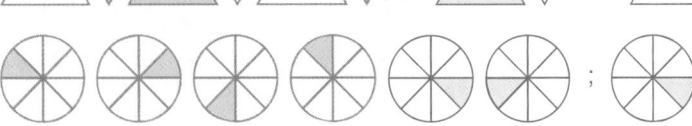

Find the next three terms in each sequence.

14. 0, 2, 6, 12, 20, ... **30, 42, 56**
15. 9, 7, 10, 8, 11, 9, 12, ... **10, 13, 11**
16. 1, 4, 9, 16, ... **25, 36, 49**
17. 0, 2, 5, 9, 14, 20, ... **27, 35, 44**
18. $a + 1, a + 2, a + 3, ...$
    $a + 4, a + 5, a + 6$
19. $x + 1, 2x + 1, 3x + 1, ...$
    $4x + 1, 5x + 1, 6x + 1$

Write an equation in function notation for each relation.

20. $f(x) = −2x$
21. $f(x) = \frac{1}{2}x$
22. $f(x) = x + 2$

20.
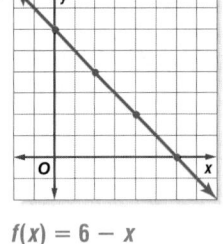

21.
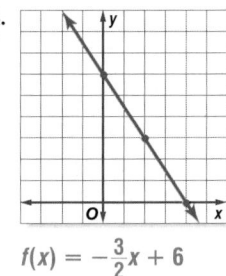

22.
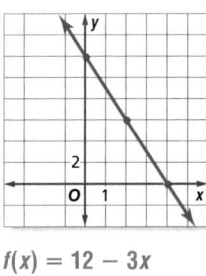

23.
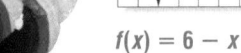

24. ★

25. ★

$f(x) = 6 − x$ $f(x) = −\frac{3}{2}x + 6$ $f(x) = 12 − 3x$

26. **TRAVEL** On an island cruise in Hawaii, each passenger is given a flower chain. A crew member hands out 3 red, 3 blue, and 3 green chains in that order. If this pattern is repeated, what color chain will the 50th person receive? **blue**

NUMBER THEORY For Exercises 27 and 28, use the following information.
In 1201, Leonardo Fibonacci introduced his now famous pattern of numbers called the Fibonacci sequence.

$$1, 1, 2, 3, 5, 8, 13, ...$$

Notice the pattern in this sequence. After the second number, each number in the sequence is the sum of the two numbers that precede it. That is $2 = 1 + 1, 3 = 2 + 1, 5 = 3 + 2$, and so on. 27. **1, 1, 2, 3, 5, 8, 13, 21, 34, 55, 89, 144**

27. Write the first 12 terms of the Fibonacci sequence.

28. Notice that every third term is divisible by 2. What do you notice about every fourth term? every fifth term? **See margin.**

244   **Chapter 4**   Graphing Relations and Functions

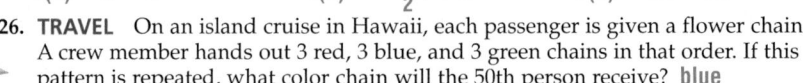
Answer

28. Every fourth term is divisible by 3; every fifth term is divisible by 5.

FITNESS For Exercises 29 and 30, use the table below that shows the maximum heart rate to maintain, for different ages, during aerobic activities such as running, biking, or swimming.

Age (yr)	20	30	40	50	60	70
Pulse rate (beats/min)	175	166	157	148	139	130

Source: Ontario Association of Sport and Exercise Sciences

★ 29. Write an equation in function notation for the relation. $f(a) = -0.9a + 193$

★ 30. What would be the maximum heart rate to maintain in aerobic training for a 10-year old? an 80-year old? **184 beats/min; 121 beats/min**

CRITICAL THINKING For Exercises 31–33, use the following information.
Suppose you arrange a number of regular pentagons so that only one side of each pentagon touches. Each side of each pentagon is 1 centimeter.

  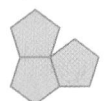 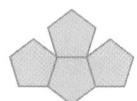

| 1 pentagon | 2 pentagons | 3 pentagons | 4 pentagons |

31. For each arrangement of pentagons, compute the perimeter. **5, 8, 11, 14 cm**

32. Write an equation in function form to represent the perimeter $f(n)$ of n pentagons.

33. What is the perimeter if 24 pentagons are used? **74 cm** $f(n) = 3n + 2$

34. **WRITING IN MATH** Answer the question that was posed at the beginning of the lesson. **See margin.**

Why is writing equations from patterns important in science?

Include the following in your answer:
- an explanation of the relationship between the volume of water and the volume of ice, and
- a reasonable estimate of the size of a container that had 99 cubic feet of water, if it was going to be frozen.

Standardized Test Practice
Ⓐ Ⓑ Ⓒ Ⓓ

35. Find the next two terms in the sequence 3, 4, 6, 9, … . **B**
- Ⓐ 12, 15
- Ⓑ 13, 18
- Ⓒ 14, 19
- Ⓓ 15, 21

36. After P pieces of candy are divided equally among 5 children, 4 pieces remain. How many would remain if $P + 4$ pieces of candy were divided equally among the 5 children? **D**
- Ⓐ 0
- Ⓑ 1
- Ⓒ 2
- Ⓓ 3

Maintain Your Skills

Mixed Review Find the next three terms of each arithmetic sequence. *(Lesson 4-7)*

37. 1, 4, 7, 10, … **13, 16, 19**
38. 9, 5, 1, −3, … **−7, −11, −15**
39. −25, −19, −13, −7, … **−1, 5, 11**
40. 22, 34, 46, 58, … **70, 82, 94**

41. Determine whether the relation graphed at the right is a function. *(Lesson 4-6)* **no**

42. **GEOGRAPHY** The world's tallest waterfall is Angel Falls in Venezuela at 3212 feet. It is 102 feet higher than Tulega Falls in South Africa. How high is Tulega Falls?
(Lesson 3-2) **3110 ft**

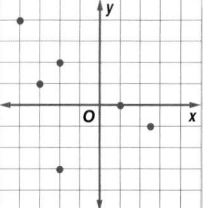

---

4 Assess

Open-Ended Assessment
Modeling Have students describe a geometric pattern like those in Example 1 and have other students illustrate the pattern with pictures, blocks, or other manipulatives.

Assessment Options
Quiz (Lessons 4-7 and 4-8) is available on p. 276 of the *Chapter 4 Resource Masters*.

Answer

34. In scientific experiments you try to find a relationship or develop a formula from observing the results of your experiment. Answers should include the following.
- For every 11 cubic feet the volume of water increases, the volume of ice increases 12 cubic feet.
- The container should have a volume of at least 108 cubic feet.

Chapter 4 — Study Guide and Review

Vocabulary and Concept Check

Vocabulary and Concept Check

arithmetic sequence (p. 233)   graph (p. 193)   preimage (p. 197)   terms (p. 233)
common difference (p. 233)   image (p. 197)   quadrant (p. 193)   transformation (p. 197)
coordinate plane (p. 192)   inductive reasoning (p. 240)   reflection (p. 197)   translation (p. 197)
dilation (p. 197)   inverse (p. 206)   rotation (p. 197)   vertical line test (p. 227)
equation in two variables (p. 212)   linear equation (p. 218)   sequence (p. 233) x-intercept (p. 220)
function (p. 226)   look for a pattern (p. 240)   solution (p. 212) y-intercept (p. 220)
function notation (p. 227)   mapping (p. 205)   standard form (p. 218)

Choose the letter of the term that best matches each statement or phrase.

1. In the coordinate plane, the axes intersect at the __?__ . **e**
2. A(n) __?__ is a set of ordered pairs. **g**
3. A(n) __?__ flips a figure over a line. **d**
4. In a coordinate system, the __?__ is a horizontal number line. **h**
5. In the ordered pair, $A(2, 7)$, 7 is the __?__ . **k**
6. The coordinate axes separate a plane into four __?__ . **f**
7. A(n) __?__ has a graph that is a nonvertical straight line. **c**
8. In the relation $\{(4, -2), (0, 5), (6, 2), (-1, 8)\}$, the __?__ is $\{-1, 0, 4, 6\}$. **a**
9. A(n) __?__ enlarges or reduces a figure. **b**
10. In a coordinate system, the __?__ is a vertical number line. **i**

a. domain
b. dilation
c. linear function
d. reflection
e. origin
f. quadrants
g. relation
h. x-axis
i. y-axis
j. x-coordinate
k. y-coordinate

Lesson-by-Lesson Review

4-1 **The Coordinate Plane**

See pages 192–196.

Concept Summary

- The first number, or x-coordinate, of an ordered pair corresponds to the numbers on the x-axis.
- The second number, or y-coordinate, corresponds to the numbers on the y-axis.

Example   Plot $T(3, -2)$ on a coordinate plane. Name the quadrant in which the point is located.

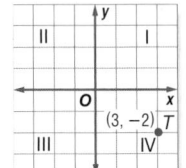

$T(3, -2)$ is located in Quadrant IV.

11–16. See margin.

Exercises   Plot each point on a coordinate plane. *See Example 3 on page 193.*

11. $A(4, 2)$ 12. $B(-1, 3)$ 13. $C(0, -5)$
14. $D(-3, -2)$ 15. $E(-4, 0)$ 16. $F(2, -1)$

 www.algebra1.com/vocabulary_revie

Sidebar (left column)

Vocabulary and Concept Check

- This alphabetical list of vocabulary terms in Chapter 4 includes a page reference where each term was introduced.
- **Assessment** A vocabulary test/review for Chapter 4 is available on p. 274 of the *Chapter 4 Resource Masters*.

Lesson-by-Lesson Review

For each lesson,

- the main ideas are summarized,
- additional examples review concepts, and
- practice exercises are provided.

Vocabulary PuzzleMaker

ELL The Vocabulary PuzzleMaker software improves students' mathematics vocabulary using four puzzle formats—crossword, scramble, word search using a word list, and word search using clues. Students can work on a computer screen or from a printed handout.

MindJogger Videoquizzes

ELL MindJogger Videoquizzes provide an alternative review of concepts presented in this chapter. Students work in teams in a game show format to gain points for correct answers. The questions are presented in three rounds.

Round 1 Concepts (5 questions)
Round 2 Skills (4 questions)
Round 3 Problem Solving (4 questions)

FOLDABLES Study Organizer

For more information about Foldables, see *Teaching Mathematics with Foldables.*

Have students review the examples and drawings they made on their Foldables. Encourage students to refer to their Foldables while completing the Study Guide and Review and to use them in preparing for the Chapter Test.

4-2 Transformations on the Coordinate Plane

See pages 197–203.

Concept Summary

- A reflection is a flip.
- A translation is a slide.
- A dilation is a reduction or enlargement.
- A rotation is a turn.

Example A quadrilateral with vertices $W(1, 2)$, $X(2, 3)$, $Y(5, 2)$, and $Z(2, 1)$ is reflected over the y-axis. Find the coordinates of the vertices of the image. Then graph quadrilateral $WXYZ$ and its image $W'X'Y'Z'$.

Multiply each x-coordinate by -1.

$W(1, 2) \rightarrow W'(-1, 2)$ $Y(5, 2) \rightarrow Y'(-5, 2)$

$X(2, 3) \rightarrow X'(-2, 3)$ $Z(2, 1) \rightarrow Z'(-2, 1)$

The coordinates of the image are $W'(-1, 2)$, $X'(-2, 3)$, $Y'(-5, 2)$, and $Z'(-2, 1)$.

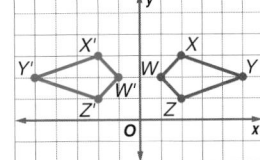

Exercises Find the coordinates of the vertices of each figure after the given transformation is performed. Then graph the preimage and its image.
See Examples 2–5 on pages 198–200. **17–20. See margin.**

17. triangle ABC with $A(3, 3)$, $B(5, 4)$, and $C(4, -3)$ reflected over the x-axis

18. quadrilateral $PQRS$ with $P(-2, 4)$, $Q(0, 6)$, $R(3, 3)$, and $S(-1, -4)$ translated 3 units down

19. parallelogram $GHIJ$ with $G(2, 2)$, $H(6, 0)$, $I(6, 2)$, and $J(2, 4)$ dilated by a scale factor of $\frac{1}{2}$

20. trapezoid $MNOP$ with $M(2, 0)$, $N(4, 3)$, $O(6, 3)$, and $P(8, 0)$ rotated 90° counterclockwise about the origin

4-3 Relations

See pages 205–211.

Concept Summary

- A relation can be expressed as a set of ordered pairs, a table, a graph, or a mapping.

Example Express the relation {(3, 2), (5, 3), (4, 3), (5, 2)} as a table, a graph, and a mapping.

Table	Graph	Mapping
List the set of x-coordinates and corresponding y-coordinates.	Graph each ordered pair on a coordinate plane.	List the x and y values. Draw arrows to show the relation.

x	y
3	2
5	3
4	3
5	2

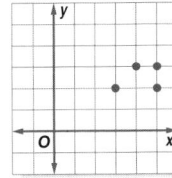

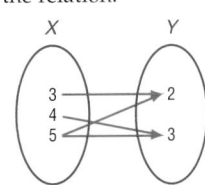

Answers

11–16.

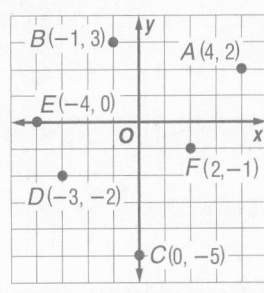

17. $A'(3, -3)$, $B'(5, -4)$, $C'(4, 3)$

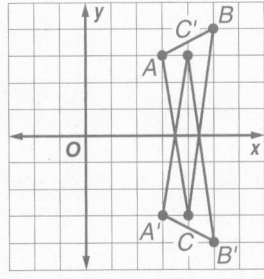

18. $P'(-2, 1)$, $Q'(0, 3)$, $R'(3, 0)$, $S'(-1, -7)$

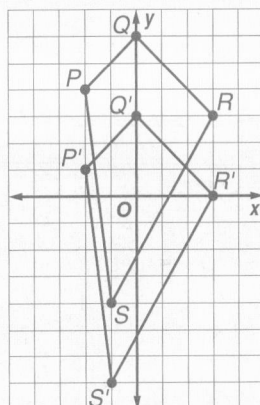

19. $G'(1, 1)$, $H'(3, 0)$, $I'(3, 1)$, $J'(1, 2)$

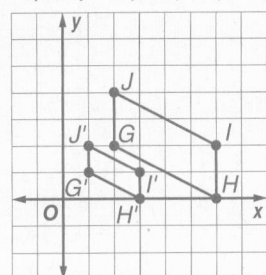

20. $M'(0, 2)$, $N'(-3, 4)$, $O'(-3, 6)$, $P'(0, 8)$

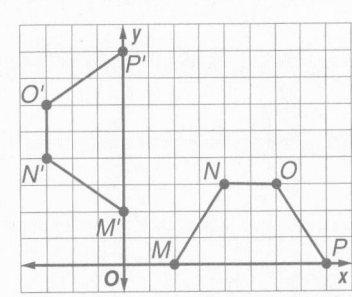

Answers

21. $D = \{-2, 3, 4\}$, $R = \{-2, 0, 6\}$

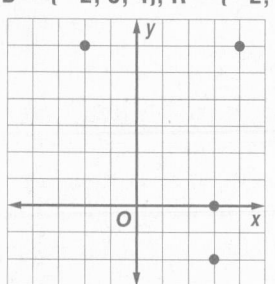

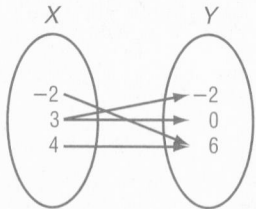

22. $D = \{-1, 3, 6\}$, $R = \{0, 2\}$

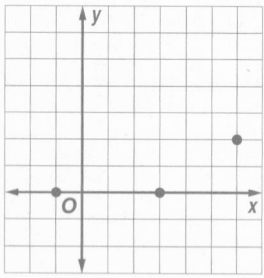

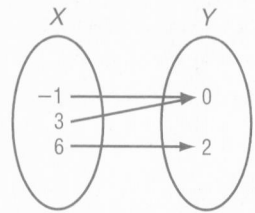

23. $D = \{-3, 3, 5, 9\}$, $R = \{3, 8\}$

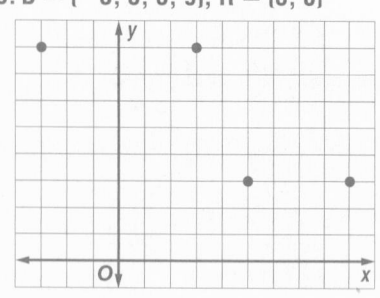

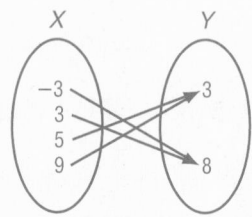

24. $D = \{-3, 2, 4\}$, $R = \{-2, 1, 3, 5\}$

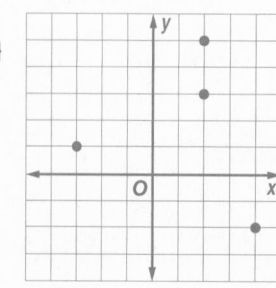

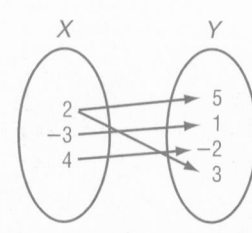

21–24. See margin.

Exercises Express each relation as a table, a graph, and a mapping. Then determine the domain and range.   *See Example 1 on page 205.*

21. $\{(-2, 6), (3, -2), (3, 0), (4, 6)\}$ **22.** $\{(-1, 0), (3, 0), (6, 2)\}$

23. $\{(3, 8), (9, 3), (-3, 8), (5, 3)\}$ **24.** $\{(2, 5), (-3, 1), (4, -2), (2, 3)\}$

4-4 Equations as Relations

See pages 212–217.

Concept Summary

- In an equation involving x and y, the set of x values is the domain, and the corresponding set of y values is the range.

Example Solve $2x + y = 8$ if the domain is $\{3, 2, 1\}$. Graph the solution set.

First solve the equation for y in terms of x.

$$2x + y = 8 \qquad \text{Original equation}$$

$$y = 8 - 2x \quad \text{Subtract } 2x \text{ from each side.}$$

Substitute each value of x from the domain to determine the corresponding values of y in the range. Then graph the solution set $\{(3, 2), (2, 4), (1, 6)\}$.

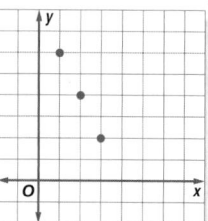

x	$8 - 2x$	y	(x, y)
3	$8 - 2(3)$	2	$(3, 2)$
2	$8 - 2(2)$	4	$(2, 4)$
1	$8 - 2(1)$	6	$(1, 6)$

Exercises Solve each equation if the domain is $\{-4, -2, 0, 2, 4\}$. Graph the solution set.   *See Example 3 on page 213.* **25–30. See margin.**

25. $y = x - 9$ **26.** $y = 4 - 2x$ **27.** $4x - y = -5$

28. $2x + y = 8$ **29.** $3x + 2y = 9$ **30.** $4x - 3y = 0$

4-5 Graphing Linear Equations

See pages 218–223.

Concept Summary

- Standard form: $Ax + By = C$, where $A \geq 0$ and A and B are not both zero, and A, B, and C are integers whose greatest common factor is 1.
- To find the x-intercept, let $y = 0$. To find the y-intercept, let $x = 0$.

Example Determine the x- and y-intercepts of $3x - y = 4$. Then graph the equation.

To find the x-intercept, let $y = 0$.

$$3x - y = 4 \quad \text{Original equation}$$

$$3x - 0 = 4 \quad \text{Replace } y \text{ with 0.}$$

$$3x = 4 \quad \text{Simplify.}$$

$$x = \frac{4}{3} \quad \text{Divide each side by 3.}$$

To find the y-intercept, let $x = 0$.

$$3x - y = 4 \quad \text{Original equation}$$

$$3(0) - y = 4 \quad \text{Replace } x \text{ with 0.}$$

$$-y = 4 \quad \text{Simplify.}$$

$$y = -4 \quad \text{Divide each side by } -1.$$

The x-intercept is $\frac{4}{3}$, so the graph intersects the x-axis at $\left(\frac{4}{3}, 0\right)$.

The y-intercept is -4, so the graph intersects the y-axis at $(0, -4)$.

Plot these points, then draw a line that connects them.

31–36. See pp. 253A–253H.

Exercises Graph each equation. *See Examples 2 and 4 on pages 219 and 220.*

31. $y = -x + 2$
32. $x + 5y = 4$
33. $2x - 3y = 6$

34. $5x + 2y = 10$
35. $\frac{1}{2}x + \frac{1}{3}y = 3$
36. $y - \frac{1}{3} = \frac{1}{3}x + \frac{2}{3}$

4-6 Functions

See pages 226–231.

Concept Summary

- A relation is a function if each element of the domain is paired with exactly one element of the range.
- Substitute values for x to determine $f(x)$ for a specific value.

Examples

1 Determine whether the relation $\{(0, -4), (1, -1), (2, 2), (6, 3)\}$ is a function.

Since each element of the domain is paired with exactly one element of the range, the relation is a function.

2 If $g(x) = 2x - 1$, find $g(-6)$.

$g(-6) = 2(-6) - 1$ Replace x with -6.
$\quad\quad = -12 - 1$ Multiply.
$\quad\quad = -13$ Subtract.

Exercises Determine whether each relation is a function. *See Example 1 on page 226.*

37. 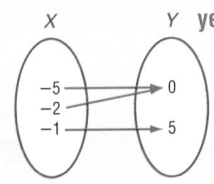 **yes**

38. **no**

x	y
5	3
1	4
-6	5
1	6
-2	7

39. $\{(2, 3), (-3, -4), (-1, 3)\}$ **yes**

If $g(x) = x^2 - x + 1$, find each value. *See Examples 3 and 4 on pages 227 and 228.*

40. $g(2)$ **3**
41. $g(-1)$ **3**
42. $g\left(\frac{1}{2}\right)$ $\frac{3}{4}$

43. $g(5) - 3$ **18**
44. $g(a)$ $a^2 - a + 1$
45. $g(-2a)$ $4a^2 + 2a + 1$

4-7 Arithmetic Sequences

See pages 233–238.

Concept Summary

- An arithmetic sequence is a numerical pattern that increases or decreases at a constant rate or value called the common difference.
- To find the next term in an arithmetic sequence, add the common difference to the last term.

27. $\{(-4, -11), (-2, -3), (0, 5), (2, 13), (4, 21)\}$

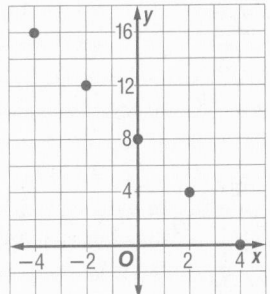

28. $\{(-4, 16), (-2, 12), (0, 8), (2, 4), (4, 0)\}$

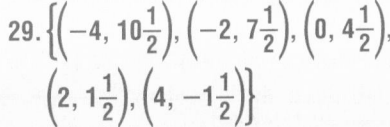

29. $\left\{\left(-4, 10\frac{1}{2}\right), \left(-2, 7\frac{1}{2}\right), \left(0, 4\frac{1}{2}\right), \left(2, 1\frac{1}{2}\right), \left(4, -1\frac{1}{2}\right)\right\}$

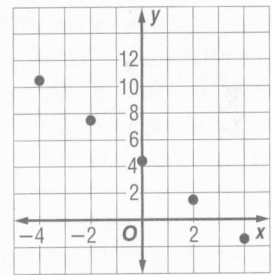

30. $\left\{\left(-4, -5\frac{1}{3}\right), \left(-2, -2\frac{2}{3}\right), (0, 0), \left(2, 2\frac{2}{3}\right), \left(4, 5\frac{1}{3}\right)\right\}$

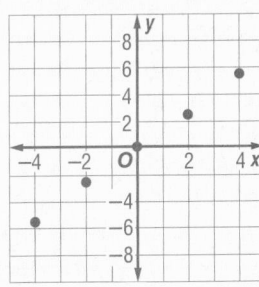

25. $\{(-4, -13), (-2, -11), (0, -9), (2, -7), (4, -5)\}$

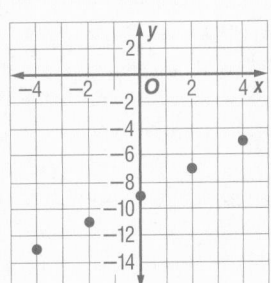

26. $\{(-4, 12), (-2, 8), (0, 4), (2, 0), (4, -4)\}$

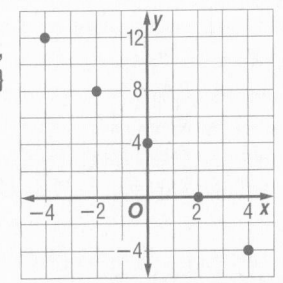

Study Guide and Review

Chapter 4   For More ...
• Extra Practice, see pages 828–830.
• Mixed Problem Solving, see page 856.

Answers (page 251)

4.

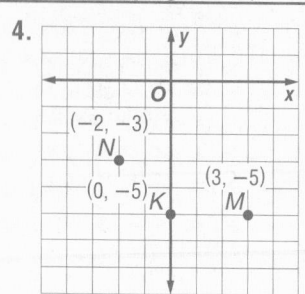

6.

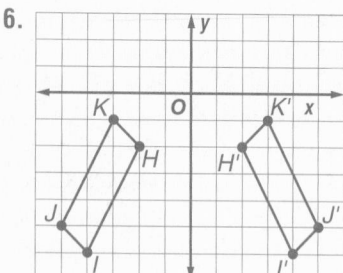

7.

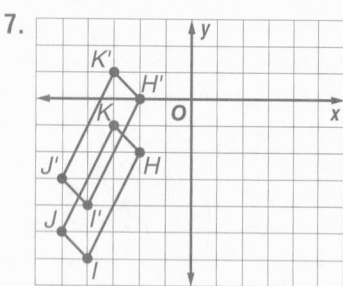

8. {(0, −1), (2, 4), (4, 5), (6, 10)};
I = {(−1, 0), (4, 2), (5, 4), (10, 6)}

9. {(−1, 2), (−2, −2), (−3, 2)};
I = {(2, −1), (−2, −2), (2, −3)}

10. {(−1, −1), (0, −3), (1, 0), (4, 2)};
I = {(−1, −1), (−3, 0), (0, 1), (2, 4)}

14.

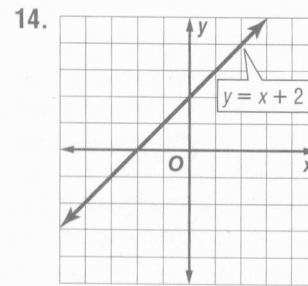

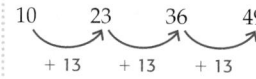 **Example**   Find the next three terms of the arithmetic sequence 10, 23, 36, 49, … .

Find the common difference.

10   23   36   49
+ 13 + 13 + 13

So, $d = 13$.

Add 13 to the last term of the sequence to get the next term. Continue adding 13 until the next three terms are found.

49   62   75   88
+ 13 + 13 + 13

The next three terms are 62, 75, and 88.

Exercises   Find the next three terms of each arithmetic sequence.
See Example 2 on page 234.   **46.** 45, 54, 63   **47.** 26, 31, 36   **48.** 54, 65, 76

46. 9, 18, 27, 36, …   **47.** 6, 11, 16, 21, …   **48.** 10, 21, 32, 43, …

49. 14, 12, 10, 8, …   **50.** −3, −11, −19, −27, …   **51.** −35, −29, −23, −17, …
6, 4, 2   −35, −43, −51   −11, −5, 1

4-8 Writing Equations from Patterns

See pages 240–245.

Concept Summary

• Look for a pattern in data. If the relationship between the domain and range is linear, the relationship can be described by an equation.

Example   Write an equation in function notation for the relation graphed at the right.

Make a table of ordered pairs for several points on the graph.

x	1	2	3	4	5
y	3	5	7	9	11

The difference in y values is twice the difference of x values. This suggests that $y = 2x$. However, $3 \neq 2(1)$. Compare the values of y to the values of $2x$.

The difference between y and $2x$ is always 1. So the equation is $y = 2x + 1$. Since this relation is also a function, it can be written as $f(x) = 2x + 1$.

x	1	2	3	4	5
2x	2	4	6	8	10
y	3	5	7	9	11

y is always 3 more than $2x$.

Exercises   Write an equation in function notation for each relation.
See Example 4 on pages 242 and 243.

52. 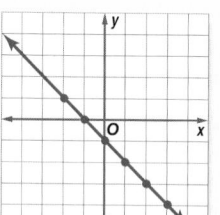 $f(x) = 3x$ **53.** $f(x) = -x - 1$

15.

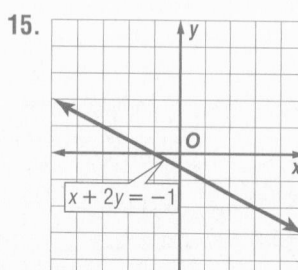

16.

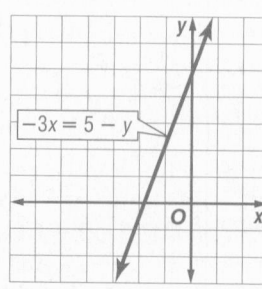

29. $C = K − 273$; independent is K, dependent is C; see students' work.

Vocabulary and Concepts

Choose the letter that best matches each description.

1. a figure turned around a point **b**
2. a figure slid horizontally, vertically, or both **c**
3. a figure flipped over a line **a**

a. reflection
b. rotation
c. translation

Skills and Applications

4. Graph $K(0, -5)$, $M(3, -5)$, and $N(-2, -3)$. **See margin.**
5. Name the quadrant in which $P(25, 1)$ is located. **I**

For Exercises 6 and 7, use the following information.
A parallelogram has vertices $H(-2, -2)$, $I(-4, -6)$, $J(-5, -5)$, and $K(-3, -1)$. **6–7. See margin.**

6. Reflect parallelogram $HIJK$ over the y-axis and graph its image.
7. Translate parallelogram $HIJK$ up 2 units and graph its image.

Express the relation shown in each table, mapping, or graph as a set of ordered pairs. Then write the inverse of the relation. 8–10. See margin.

8.

x	f(x)
0	−1
2	4
4	5
6	10

9.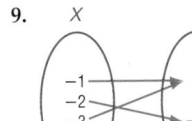

10.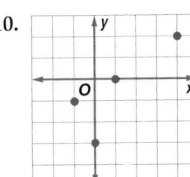

11. $\{(-2, 18), (-1, 14), (0, 10), (2, 2), (4, -6)\}$ 12. $\{(-2, -16), (-1, -13), (0, -10), (2, -4), (4, 2)\}$

Solve each equation if the domain is $\{-2, -1, 0, 2, 4\}$. Graph the solution set. 11–13. See pp. 253A–253H for graphs.

11. $y = -4x + 10$

12. $3x - y = 10$

13. $\frac{1}{2}x - y = 5$

Graph each equation. 14–16. See margin.

13. $\left\{(-2, -6), \left(-1, -5\frac{1}{2}\right), (0, -5), (2, -4), (4, -3)\right\}$

14. $y = x + 2$

15. $x + 2y = -1$

16. $-3x = 5 - y$

Determine whether each relation is a function.

17. $\{(2, 4), (3, 2), (4, 6), (5, 4)\}$ **yes** 18. $\{(3, 1), (2, 5), (4, 0), (3, -2)\}$ **no** 19. $8y = 7 + 3x$ **yes**

If $f(x) = -2x + 5$ and $g(x) = x^2 - 4x + 1$, find each value. 22. $9a^2 - 12a + 2$

20. $g(-2)$ **13**

21. $f\left(\frac{1}{2}\right)$ **4**

22. $g(3a) + 1$

23. $f(x + 2)$ **$-2x + 1$**

Determine whether each sequence is an arithmetic sequence. If it is, state the common difference.

24. 16, 24, 32, 40, … **yes; 8**

25. 99, 87, 76, 65, … **no**

26. 5, 17, 29, 41, … **yes; 12**

Find the next three terms in each sequence.

27. 5, −10, 15, −20, 25, … **−30, 35, −40**

28. 5, 5, 6, 8, 11, 15, … **20, 26, 33**

29. **TEMPERATURE** The equation to convert Celsius temperature to Kelvin temperature is $K = C + 273$. Solve the equation for C. State the independent and dependent variables. Choose five values for K and their corresponding values for C. **See margin.**

30. **STANDARDIZED TEST PRACTICE** If $f(x) = 3x - 2$, find $f(8) - f(-5)$. **D**
   (A) 7
   (B) 9
   (C) 37
   (D) 39

 www.algebra1.com/chapter_test

Assessment Options

Vocabulary Test A vocabulary test/review for Chapter 4 can be found on p. 274 of the *Chapter 4 Resource Masters*.

Chapter Tests There are six Chapter 4 Tests and an Open-Ended Assessment task available in the *Chapter 4 Resource Masters*.

Chapter 4 Tests			
Form	Type	Level	Pages
1	MC	basic	261–262
2A	MC	average	263–264
2B	MC	average	265–266
2C	FR	average	267–268
2D	FR	average	269–270
3	FR	advanced	271–272

MC = multiple-choice questions
FR = free-response questions

Open-Ended Assessment
Performance tasks for Chapter 4 can be found on p. 273 of the *Chapter 4 Resource Masters*. A sample scoring rubric for these tasks appears on p. A31.

 ExamView® Pro

Use the networkable **ExamView® Pro** to:

- Create **multiple versions** of tests.
- Create **modified** tests for *Inclusion* students.
- **Edit** existing questions and **add** your own questions.
- Use built-in **state curriculum correlations** to create tests aligned with state standards.
- Change **English** tests to **Spanish** and vice versa.

Portfolio Suggestion

Introduction Suppose you have been asked to show another student how to graph an equation, but you must do so only in writing.

Ask Students Select one of the graphing assignments from this chapter and list the steps involved in graphing the equation. Give this description to another student who will follow the written steps. Collect his or her graph and check for accuracy. Place both of these in your portfolio.

These two pages contain practice questions in the various formats that can be found on the most frequently given standardized tests.

A practice answer sheet for these two pages can be found on p. A1 of the *Chapter 4 Resource Masters*.

Standardized Test Practice Student Recording Sheet, p. A1

Part 1 *Multiple Choice*

Select the best answer from the choices given and fill in the corresponding oval.

1 Ⓐ Ⓑ Ⓒ Ⓓ	4 Ⓐ Ⓑ Ⓒ Ⓓ	7 Ⓐ Ⓑ Ⓒ Ⓓ
2 Ⓐ Ⓑ Ⓒ Ⓓ	5 Ⓐ Ⓑ Ⓒ Ⓓ	8 Ⓐ Ⓑ Ⓒ Ⓓ
3 Ⓐ Ⓑ Ⓒ Ⓓ	6 Ⓐ Ⓑ Ⓒ Ⓓ	9 Ⓐ Ⓑ Ⓒ Ⓓ

Part 2 *Short Response/Grid In*

Solve the problem and write your answer in the blank.

For Questions 10, 13, 14, 15, and 19, also enter your answer by writing each number or symbol in a box. Then fill in the corresponding oval for that number or symbol.

10 _____ (grid in)	10 ... 13 ... 14 ...
11 _____	
12 _____	
13 _____ (grid in)	
14 _____ (grid in)	
15 _____ (grid in)	15 ... 19 ...
16 _____	
17 _____	
18 _____	
19 _____ (grid in)	

Part 3 *Extended Response*

Record your answers for Questions 20–21 on the back of this paper.

Additional Practice

See pp. 279–280 in the *Chapter 4 Resource Masters* for additional standardized test practice.

Part 1 | **Multiple Choice**

Record your answers on the answer sheet provided by your teacher or on a sheet of paper.

1. The number of students in Highview School is currently 315. The school population is predicted to increase by 2% next year. According to the prediction, how many students will attend next year?
(Prerequisite Skill) **B**

   Ⓐ 317   Ⓑ 321

   Ⓒ 378   Ⓓ 630

2. In 2001, two women skied 1675 miles in 89 days across the land mass of Antarctica. They still had to ski 508 miles across the Ross Ice Shelf to reach McMurdo Station. About what percent of their total distance remained?
(Prerequisite Skill) **C**

   Ⓐ 2%   Ⓑ 17%

   Ⓒ 23%   Ⓓ 30%

3. Only 2 out of 5 students surveyed said they eat five servings of fruits or vegetables daily. If there are 470 students in a school, how many would you predict eat five servings of fruits or vegetables daily? (Lesson 2-6) **B**

   Ⓐ 94   Ⓑ 188

   Ⓒ 235   Ⓓ 282

4. Solve $13x = 2(5x + 3)$ for x. (Lesson 3-4) **B**

   Ⓐ 0   Ⓑ 2   Ⓒ 3   Ⓓ 4

Test-Taking Tip Ⓐ Ⓑ Ⓒ Ⓓ

Questions 4 and 14
Some multiple-choice questions ask you to solve an equation or inequality. You can check your solution by replacing the variable in the equation or inequality with your answer. The answer choice that results in a true statement is the correct answer.

5. The circle shown below passes through points at $(1, 4)$, $(-2, 1)$, $(-5, 4)$, and $(-2, 7)$. Which point represents the center of the circle?
(Lesson 4-1) **B**

   Ⓐ $(-2, -4)$

   Ⓑ $(-2, 4)$

   Ⓒ $(-4, 2)$

   Ⓓ $(4, -2)$

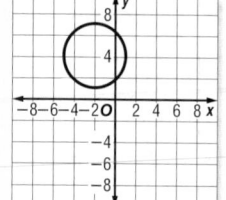

6. Which value of x would cause the relation $\{(2, 5), (x, 8), (7, 10)\}$ *not* to be a function?
(Lesson 4-4) **B**

   Ⓐ 1   Ⓑ 2   Ⓒ 5   Ⓓ 8

7. Which ordered pair (x, y) is a solution of $3x + 4y = 12$? (Lesson 4-4) **D**

   Ⓐ $(-2, 4)$ Ⓑ $(0, -3)$

   Ⓒ $(1, 2)$ Ⓓ $(4, 0)$

8. Which missing value for y would make this relation a linear relation? (Lesson 4-7) **C**

   Ⓐ -2

   Ⓑ 0

   Ⓒ 1

   Ⓓ 2

x	y
1	−3
2	−1
3	?
4	3

9. Which equation describes the data in the table? (Lesson 4-8) **C**

   Ⓐ $y = -2x + 1$

   Ⓑ $y = x + 1$

   Ⓒ $y = -x + 3$

   Ⓓ $y = x - 5$

x	y
−2	5
1	2
4	−1
6	−3

ExamView® Pro

Special banks of standardized test questions similar to those on the SAT, ACT, TIMSS 8, NAEP 8, and Algebra 1 End-of-Course tests can be found on this CD-ROM.

Preparing for Standardized Tests
For test-taking strategies and more
practice, see pages 867–884.

Part 2 Short Response/Grid In

Record your answers on the answer sheet provided by your teacher or on a sheet of paper.

10. The lengths of the corresponding sides of these two rectangles are proportional. What is the width w? (Lesson 2-6) $8/5 = 1.6$

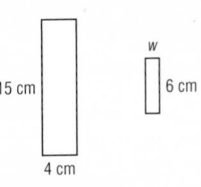

15 cm 4 cm w 6 cm

11. The PTA at Fletcher's school sold raffle tickets for a television set. Two thousand raffle tickets were sold. Fletcher's family bought 25 raffle tickets. What is the probability that his family will win the television? Express the answer as a percent. (Lesson 2-7) 1.25%

12. The sum of three integers is 52. The second integer is 3 more than the first. The third integer is 1 more than twice the first. What are the integers? (Lessons 3-1 and 3-4) $12, 15, 25$

13. Solve $5(x - 2) - 3(x + 4) = 10$ for x. (Lesson 3-4) 16

14. A CD player originally cost $160. It is now on sale for $120. What is the percent of decrease in its price? (Lesson 3-5) 25

15. A swimming pool holds 1800 cubic feet of water. It is 6 feet deep and 20 feet long. How many feet wide is the pool? ($V = \ell wh$) (Lesson 3-8) 15

16. Write the ordered pair that describes a point 7 units up from and 3 units to the left of the origin. (Lesson 4-1) $(-3, 7)$

17. A triangle that has vertices $D(1, 3)$, $E(7, 2)$, and $F(-3, 4)$ is reflected over the x-axis. Find the coordinates of the vertices of the image. (Lesson 4-2) $D'(1, -3)$, $E'(7, -2)$, $F'(-3, -4)$

www.algebra1.com/standardized_test

18. The range for $2x + y = -5$ is $\{1, -13, -5, -7\}$. Find the domain. (Lesson 4-4) $\{-3, 4, 0, 1\}$

19. Garth used toothpicks to form a pattern of triangles as shown below. If he continues this pattern, what is the total number of toothpicks that he will use to form a pattern of 7 triangles? (Lessons 4-7 and 4-8) 15

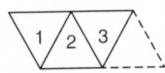

1 2 3

Part 3 Extended Response

Record your answers on a sheet of paper. Show your work.

20. A car company lists the stopping distances of a car at different speeds. Does the table of values represent a function? Explain. (Lesson 4-6) **Yes, because each element of the domain is paired with exactly one element of the range.**

Speed (ft/s)	Minimum Stopping Distance (ft)
10	2
20	8
40	31
60	70
100	194

21. Latoya bought 48 one-foot-long sections of fencing. She plans to use the fencing to enclose a rectangular area for a garden. (Lesson 3-8)

  a. Using ℓ for the length and w for the width of the garden, write an equation for its perimeter. $2\ell + 2w = 48$

  b. If the length ℓ in feet and width w in feet are positive integers, what is the greatest possible area of this garden? 144 ft^2

  c. If the length and width in feet are positive integers what is the least possible area of the garden? 23 ft^2

  d. How do the shapes of the gardens with the greatest and least areas compare?

21d. **The garden with the greatest area is square. The garden with the least area is long and narrow.**

Chapter 4 Standardized Test Practice 253

Evaluating Extended Response Questions

Extended Response questions are graded by using a multilevel rubric that guides you in assessing a student's knowledge of a particular concept.

Goal: Determine the dimensions of a rectangular garden for a given perimeter.

Sample Scoring Rubric: The following rubric is a sample scoring device. You may wish to add more detail to this sample to meet your individual scoring needs.

Score	Criteria
4	A correct solution that is supported by well-developed, accurate explanations
3	A generally correct solution, but may contain minor flaws in reasoning or computation
2	A partially correct interpretation and/or solution to the problem
1	A correct solution with no supporting evidence or explanation
0	An incorrect solution indicating no mathematical understanding of the concept or task, or no solution is given

Pages 200–203, Lesson 4-2

5.

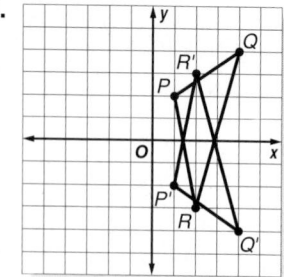

6.

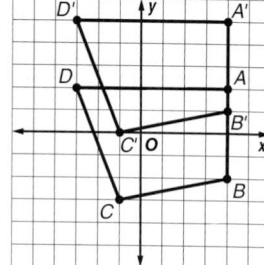

7.

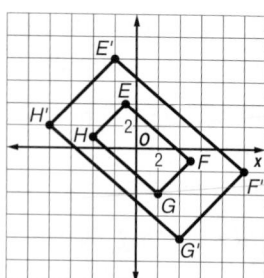

8.

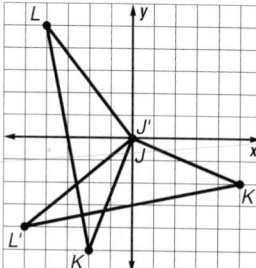

17.

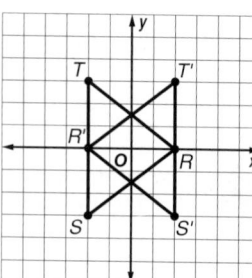

18.

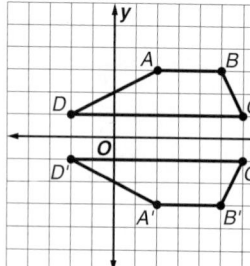

19.

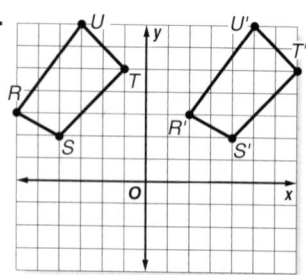

20.

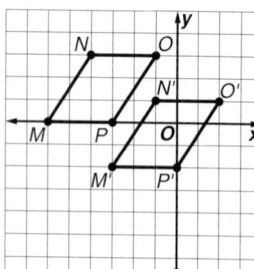

21.

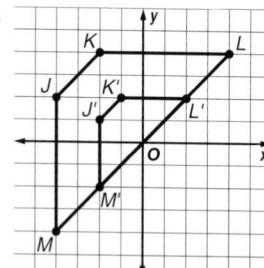

22.

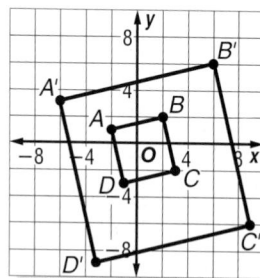

23.

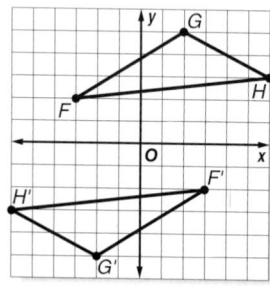

24.

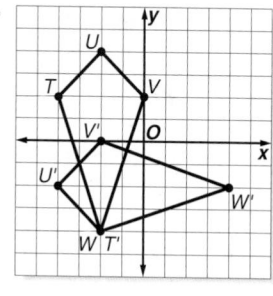

25.

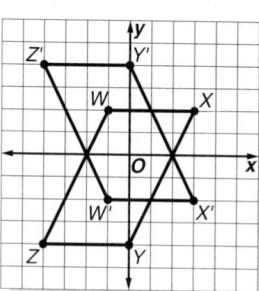

26.

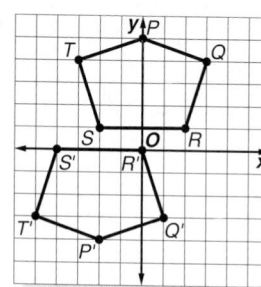

35–36.

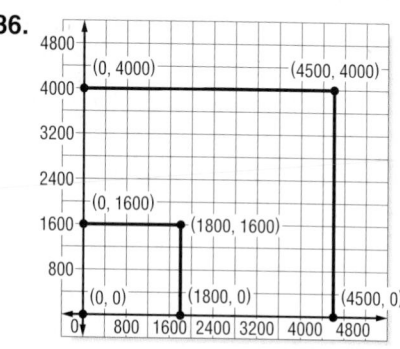

Page 204, Preview of Lesson 4-3
Graphing Calculator Investigation

1.

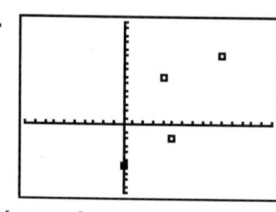

[−10, 15] scl: 1 by [−10, 15] scl: 1

2.

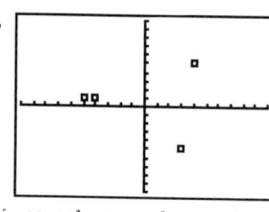

[−10, 10] scl: 1 by [−10, 10] scl: 1

3.

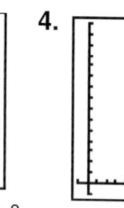

[−15, 15] scl: 2 by [−20, 20] scl: 2

4.

[−2, 50] scl: 2 by [−2, 30] scl: 2

Pages 208–211, Lesson 4-3

4. D = {−7, 5, 8}; R = {−2, 1, 3}

x	y
5	−2
8	3
−7	1

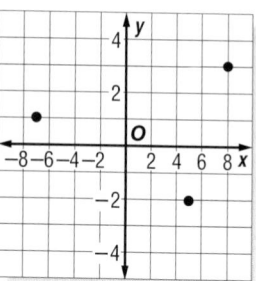

5. D = {−1, 3, 5, 6}; R = {−3, 4, 9}

x	y
6	4
3	−3
−1	9
5	−3

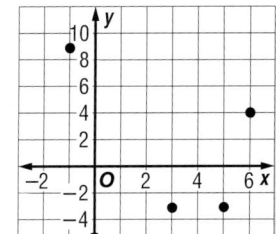

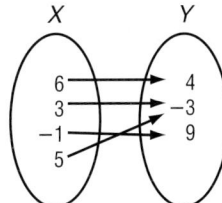

6. D = {−2, 3, 7}; R = {0, 1, 5}

x	y
7	1
3	0
−2	5

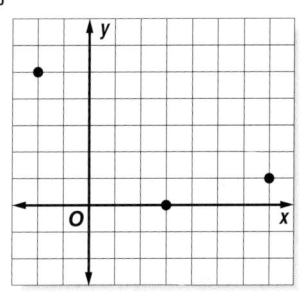

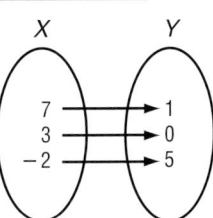

7. D = {−4, −1, 6}; R = {7, 8, 9}

x	y
−4	8
−1	9
−4	7
6	9

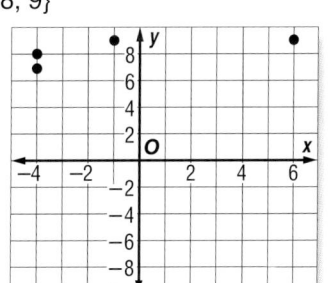

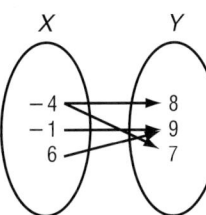

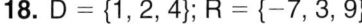

18. D = {1, 2, 4}; R = {−7, 3, 9}

x	y
4	3
1	−7
1	3
2	9

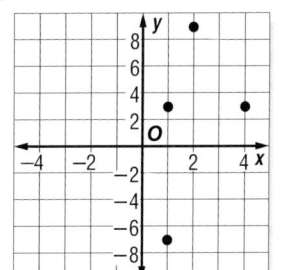

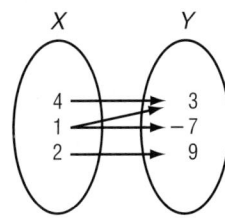

19. D = {−5, 2, 5, 6}; R = {0, 2, 4, 7}

x	y
5	2
−5	0
6	4
2	7

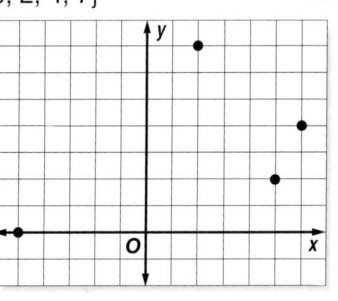

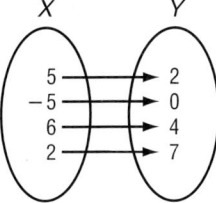

20. D = {0, 4, 5, 6}; R = {−1, 0, 2, 6}

x	y
0	0
6	−1
5	6
4	2

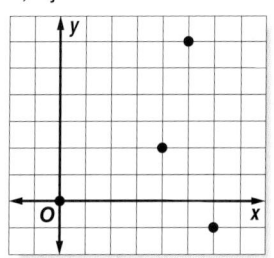

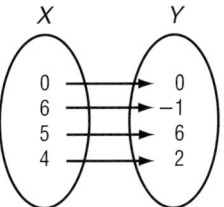

21. D = {1, 2, 3}; R = {−9, 7, 8}

x	y
3	8
3	7
2	−9
1	−9

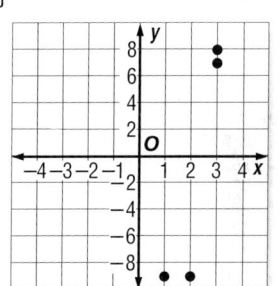

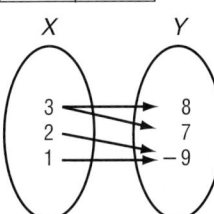

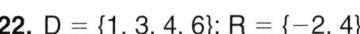

22. D = {1, 3, 4, 6}; R = {−2, 4}

x	y
4	−2
3	4
1	−2
6	4

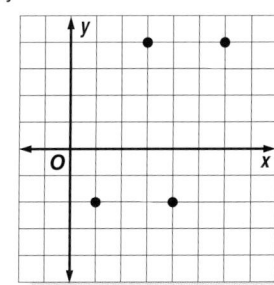

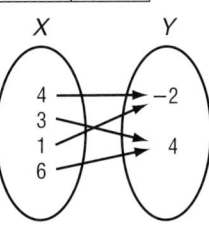

23. D = {−5, −1, 0}; R = {1, 2, 6, 9}

x	y
0	2
−5	1
0	6
−1	9

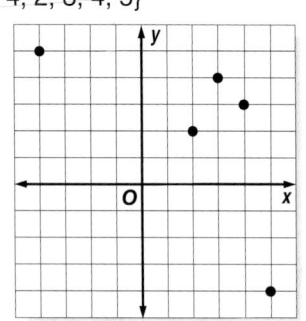

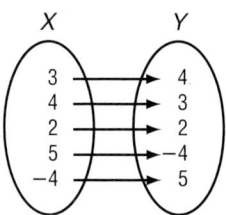

24. D = {−4, 2, 3, 4, 5}; R = {−4, 2, 3, 4, 5}

x	y
3	4
4	3
2	2
5	−4
−4	5

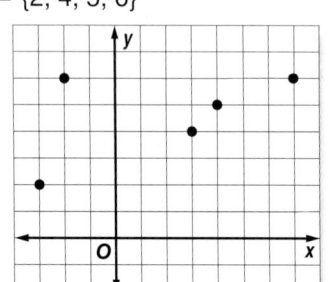

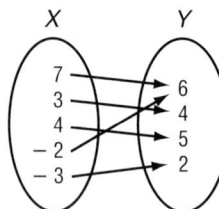

25. D = {−3, −2, 3, 4, 7}; R = {2, 4, 5, 6}

x	y
7	6
3	4
4	5
−2	6
−3	2

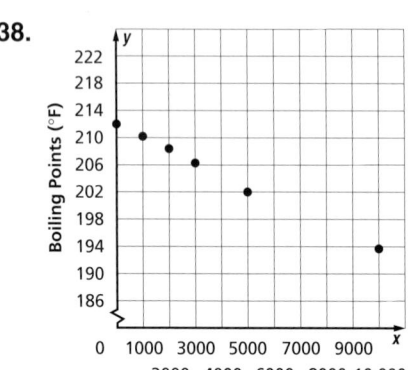

38.

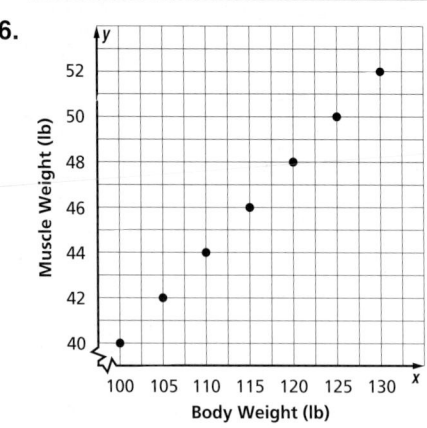

39. {(212.0, 0), (210.2, 1000), (208.4, 2000), (206.5, 3000), (201.9, 5000), (193.7, 10,000)}

40. Use the inverse relation to find the corresponding altitude for a given boiling point.

44.

Body Weight (lb)	100	105	110	115	120	125	130
Muscle Weight (lb)	40	42	44	46	48	50	52

46.

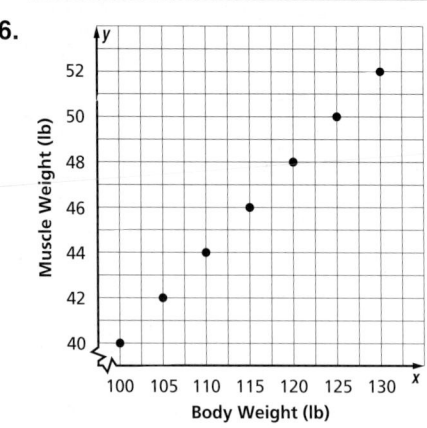

48.

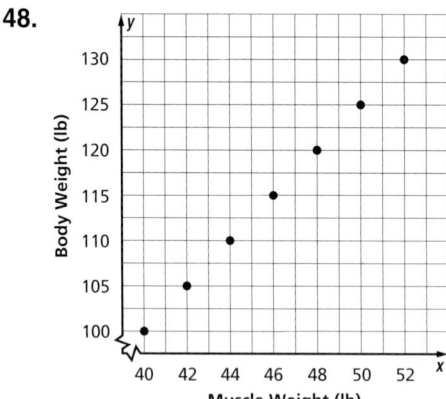

53a.

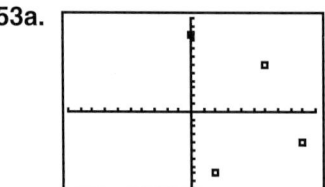

53b. [−10, 10] scl: 1 by [−10, 12] scl: 1

53c. {(10, 0), (−8, 2), (6, 6), (−4, 9)}

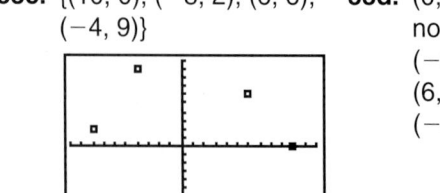

53d. (0, 10), none; (10, 0), none; (2, −8), IV; (−8, 2), II; (6, 6), I; (6, 6), I; (9, −4), IV; (−4, 9), II

54a.

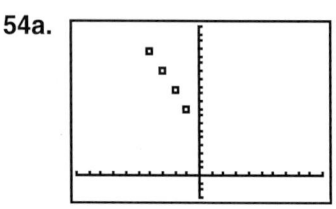

54b. [−10, 10] scl: 1 by [−6, 40] scl: 2

54c. {(18, −1), (23, −2), (28, −3), (33, −4)}

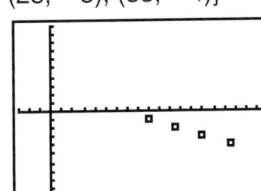

54d. (−1, 18), (−2, 23), (−3, 28), and (−4, 33) are all in II. (18, −1), (23, −2), (28, −3), and (33, −4) are all in IV.

55a.

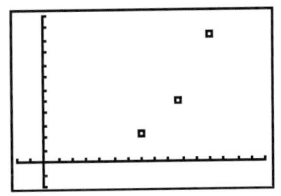

55b. [−10, 80] scl: 5 by [−10, 60] scl: 5

55c. {(12, 35), (25, 48), (52, 60)}

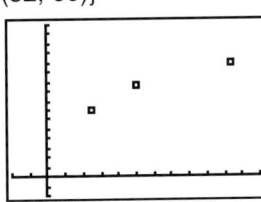

55d. (35, 12), (48, 25), and (60, 52) are all in I. (12, 35), (25, 48), and (52, 60) are all in I.

56a.

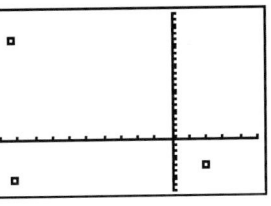

56b. [−100, 50] scl: 10; [−100, 250] scl: 10

56c. {(−77, −92), (200, −93) (−50, 19)}

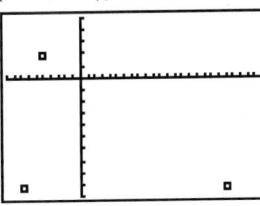

56d. (−92, −77), III; (−77, −92), III; (−93, 200), II; (200, −93), IV; (19, −50), IV; (−50, 19), II

Page 211, Practice Quiz 1

5. A′(4, −8), B′(7, −5), C′(2, 1)

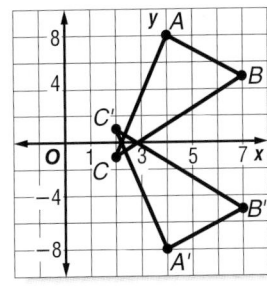

6. W′(−4, −4), X′(−3, −1), Y′(−1, −3), Z′(−2, −7)

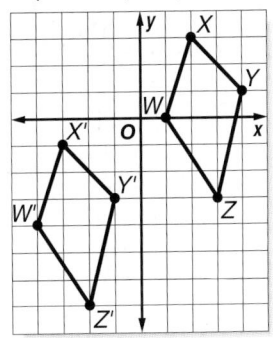

Pages 214–217, Lesson 4-4

12.

k	g
10	41.67
14	58.33
18	75
24	100

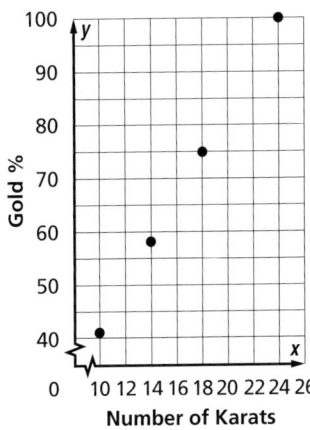

32. {(−3, −3), (−2, −1), (−1, 1), (1, 5), (2, 7), (3, 9)}

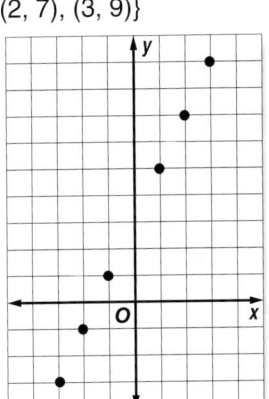

33. {(−5, −16), (−2, −7), (1, 2), (3, 8), (4, 11)}

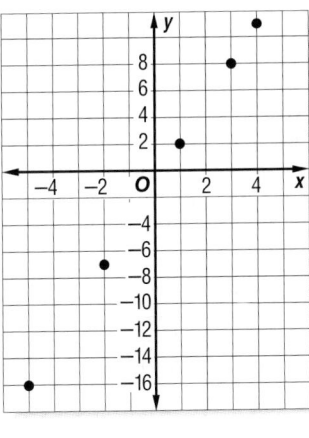

34. {(−3, −7), (−1, −4), (2, 0.5), (4, 3.5), (5, 5)}

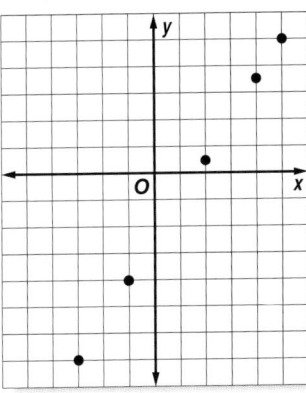

35. {(−4, 7), (−1, 3.25), (0, 2), (2, −0.5), (4, −3), (6, −5.5)}

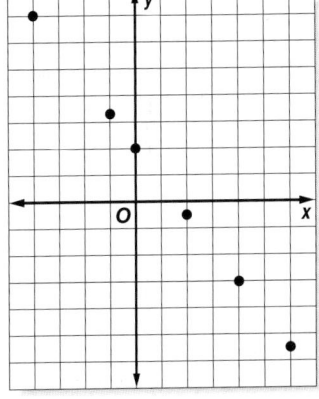

36. {(−4, 4), (−1, 2.5), (1, 1.5), (4, 0), (7, −1.5), (8, −2)}

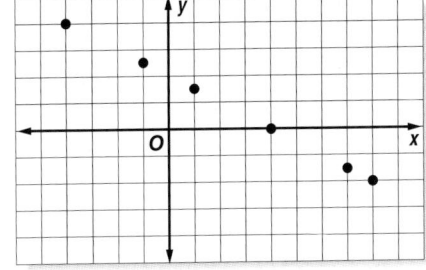

37. $\{(-4, -4), (-2, -3.5),$
$(0, -3), (2, -2.5),$
$(4, -2), (6, -1.5)\}$

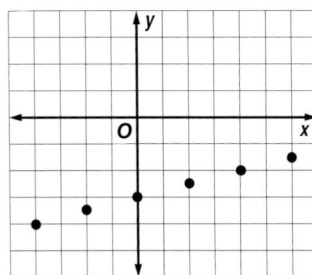

Pages 221–223, Lesson 4-5

8.
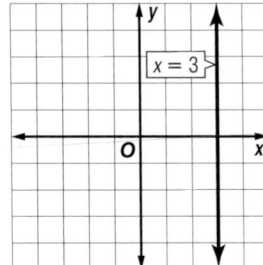

9.
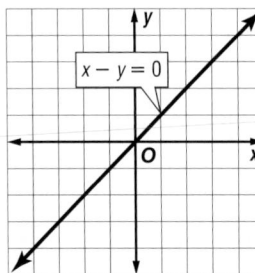

10.
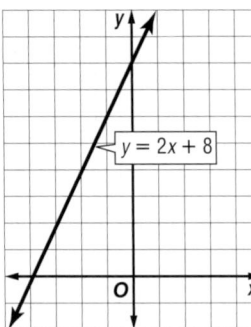

11.
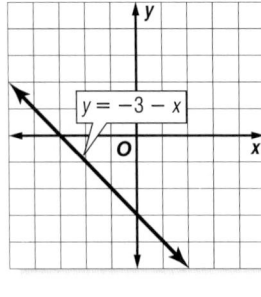

12.
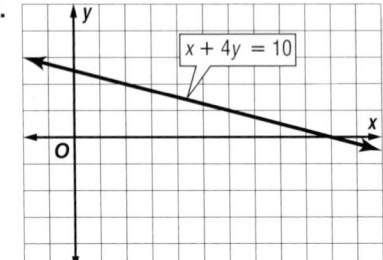

13.
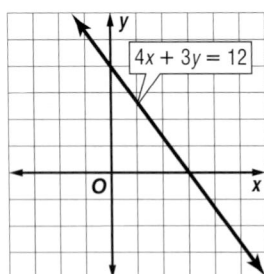

26.
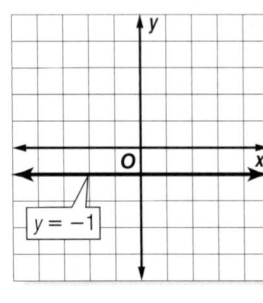

27.
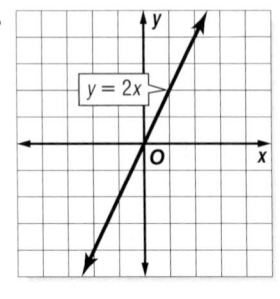

28.
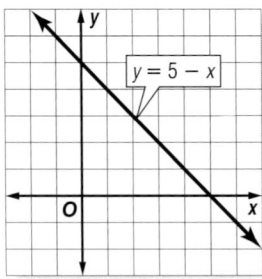

29.
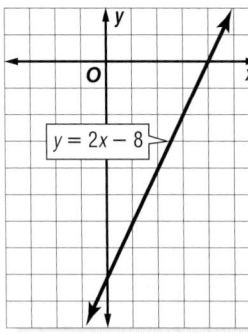

30.
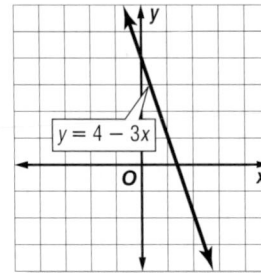

31.
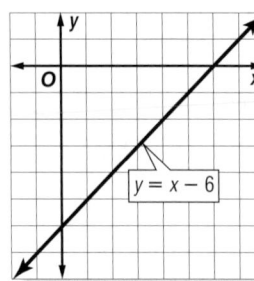

32.
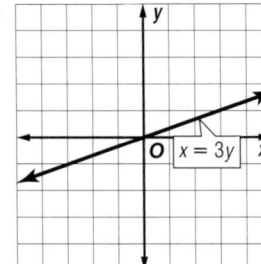

33.
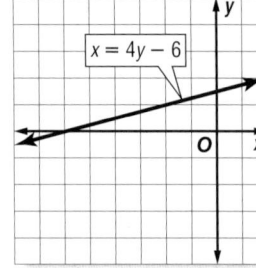

34.
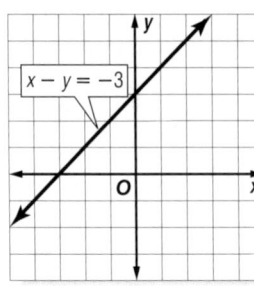

35.
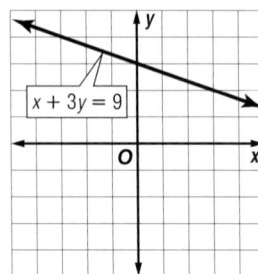

36.
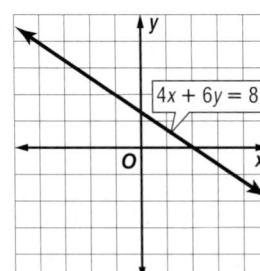

37.
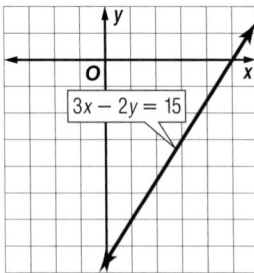

38.
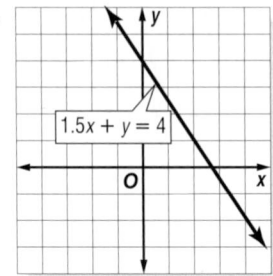

39.
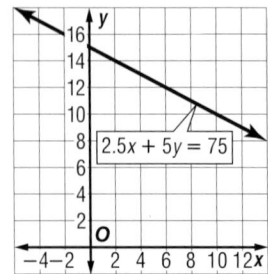

40.

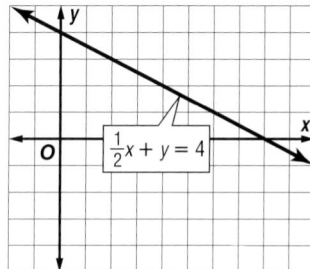

$\frac{1}{2}x + y = 4$

41.

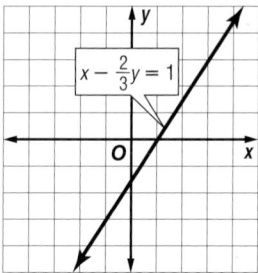

$x - \frac{2}{3}y = 1$

42.

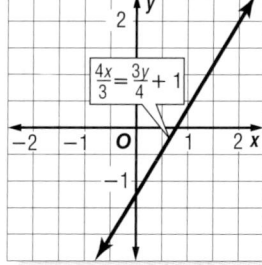

$\frac{4x}{3} = \frac{3y}{4} + 1$

43.

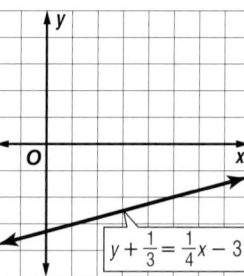

$y + \frac{1}{3} = \frac{1}{4}x - 3$

52.

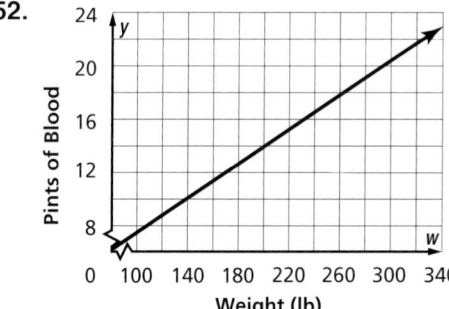

54.

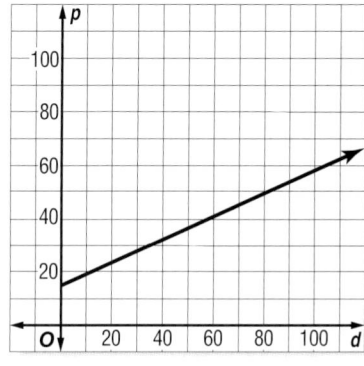

67. D = {−4, −3, 3}; R = {−1, 1, 2, 5}

x	y
3	5
−4	−1
−3	2
3	1

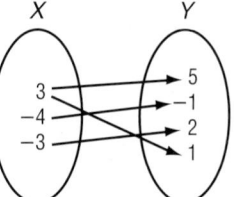

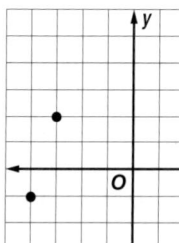

68. D = {−1, 2, 4}; R = {−3, 0, 4}

x	y
4	0
2	−3
−1	−3
4	4

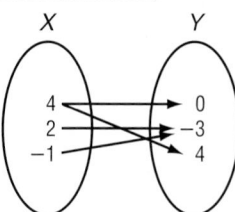

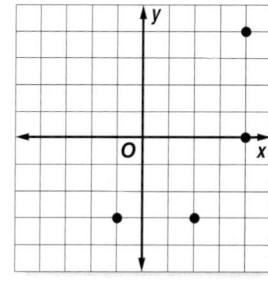

69. D = {−1, 1, 3}; R = {−1, 0, 4, 5}

x	y
1	4
3	0
−1	−1
3	5

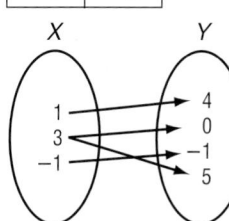

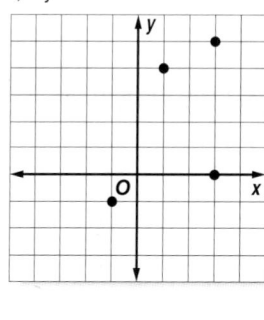

70. D = {2, 3, 4}; R = {−1, 2, 5}

x	y
4	5
2	5
4	−1
3	2

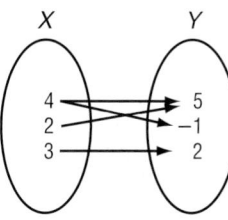

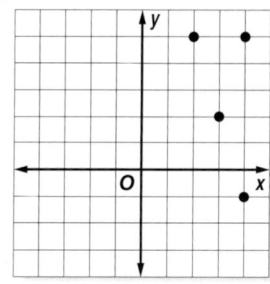

75.

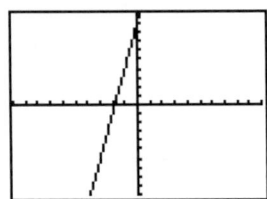

(number line dot plot, marks at values 0 through 40)

Pages 224–225, Follow-Up of Lesson 4-5
Graphing Calculator Investigation

7. Sample answer:

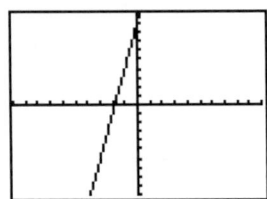

8. Sample answer:

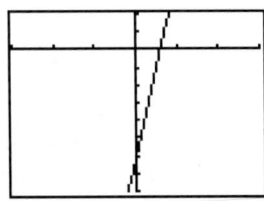

9. Sample answer:

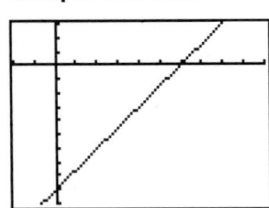

10. Sample answer:

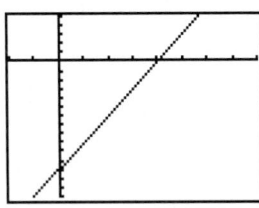

11. Sample answer:

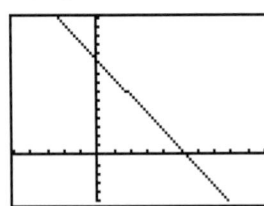

12. Sample answer:

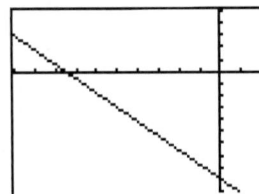

Pages 228–231, Lesson 4-6

56.

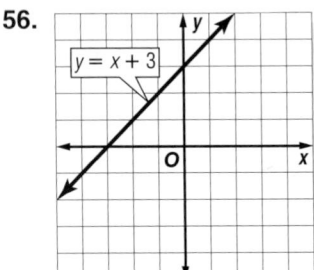

$y = x + 3$

57.

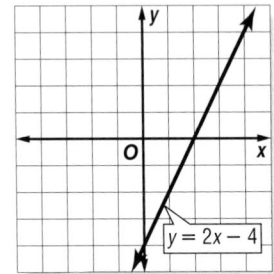

$y = 2x - 4$

58.

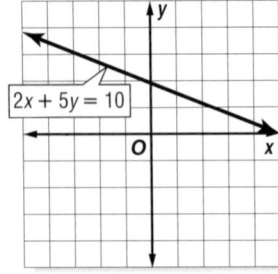

$2x + 5y = 10$

Page 231, Practice Quiz 2

1. {(−3, 2), (−1, 4), (0, 5), (2,7), (4, 9)}

2. {(−3, −5), (−1, 1), (0, 4), (2, 10), (4, 16)}

3. {(−3, 5.5), (−1, 4.5), (0, 4), (2, 3), (4, 2)}

4.

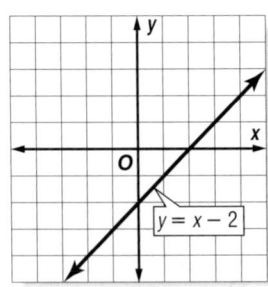

$y = x - 2$

5.

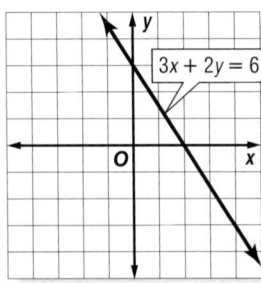

$3x + 2y = 6$

Pages 236–238, Lesson 4-7

39.

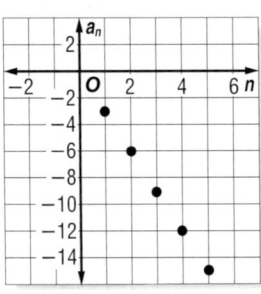

40.

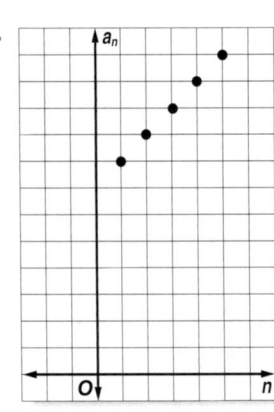

41.

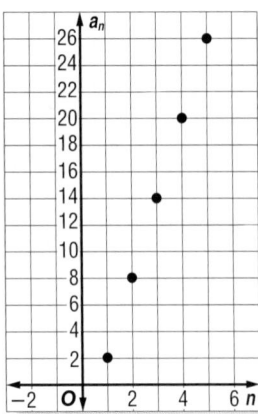

42.

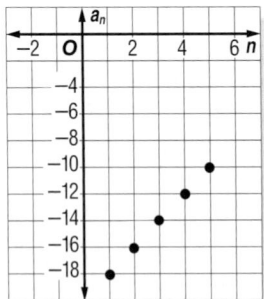

53.

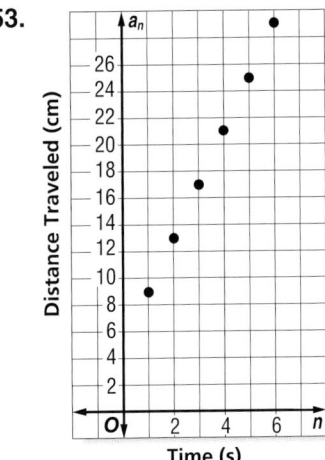

Page 249, Study Guide and Review

31.

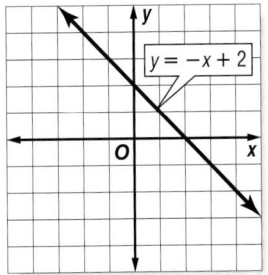

32.

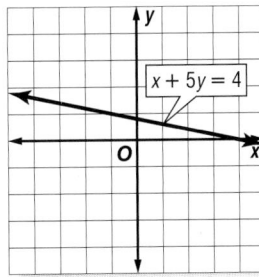

33.

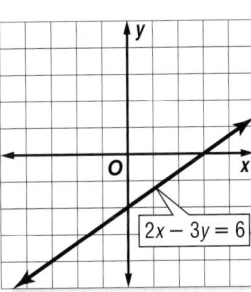

34.

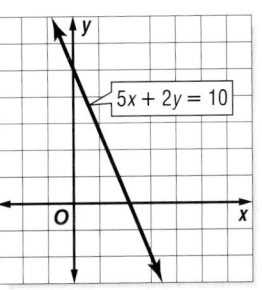

35.

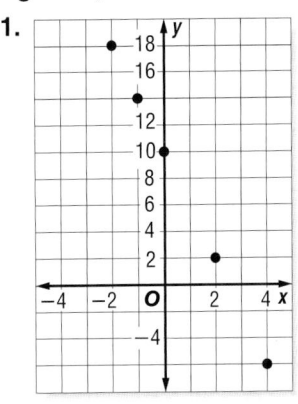

36.

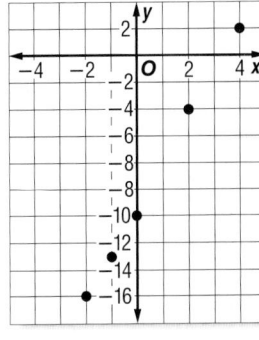

Page 251, Practice Test

11.

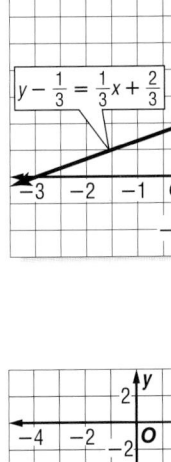

12.

13.

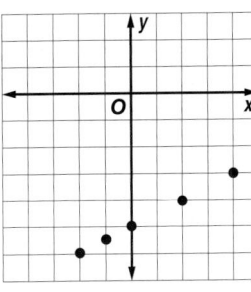

Analyzing Linear Equations
Chapter Overview and Pacing

Year-long and two-year pacing: pages T20–T21.

LESSON OBJECTIVES	PACING (days)			
	Regular		**Block**	
	Basic/ Average	Advanced	Basic/ Average	Advanced
5-1 Slope (pp. 256–262) • Find the slope of a line. • Use rate of change to solve problems.	1	1	0.5	0.5
5-2 Slope and Direct Variation (pp. 264–270) • Write and graph direct variation equations. • Solve problems involving direct variation.	1	1	0.5	0.5
5-3 Slope-Intercept Form (pp. 271–279) *Preview:* Use manipulatives to investigate slope-intercept form. • Write and graph linear equations in slope-intercept form. • Model real-world data with an equation in slope-intercept form. *Follow-Up:* Use a graphing calculator to identify families of linear graphs.	2 (with 5-3 Preview)	2 (with 5-3 Follow-Up)	1	1 (with 5-3 Follow-Up)
5-4 Writing Equations in Slope-Intercept Form (pp. 280–285) • Write an equation of a line given the slope and one point on a line. • Write an equation of a line given two points on the line.	2	2	1	1
5-5 Writing Equations in Point-Slope Form (pp. 286–291) • Write the equation of a line in point-slope form. • Write linear equations in different forms.	1	2	0.5	1 (with 5-4 Follow-Up)
5-6 Geometry: Parallel and Perpendicular Lines (pp. 292–297) • Write an equation of the line that passes through a given point, parallel to a given line. • Write an equation of the line that passes through a given point, perpendicular to a given line.	2	1	1	0.5
5-7 Statistics: Scatter Plots and Lines of Fit (pp. 298–307) • Interpret points on a scatter plot. • Write equations for lines of fit. *Follow-Up:* Use a graphing calculator to find a median-fit line.	3 (with 5-7 Follow-Up)	2 (with 5-7 Follow-Up)	1	1
Study Guide and **Practice Test** (pp. 308–313) **Standardized Test Practice** (pp. 314–315)	1	1	1 (with 5-7 Follow-Up)	1 (with 5-7 Follow-Up)
Chapter Assessment	1	1	0.5	0.5
TOTAL	14	13	7	7

An electronic version of this chapter is available on **StudentWorks**™. *This backpack solution CD-ROM allows students instant access to the Student Edition, lesson worksheet pages, and web resources.*

Chapter Resource Manager

CHAPTER 5 RESOURCE MASTERS

Study Guide and Intervention	Practice (Skills and Average)	Reading to Learn Mathematics	Enrichment	Assessment	Prerequisite Skills Workbook	Applications*	Parent and Student Study Guide Workbook	5-Minute Check Transparencies	Interactive Chalkboard	AlgePASS: Tutorial Plus (lessons)	Materials
281–282	283–284	285	286		39–40, 63–64	38	5-1	5-1			uncooked spaghetti, transparency showing coordinate plane
287–288	289–290	291	292	337	29–30	SM 41–44	39	5-2	5-2		graphing calculator
293–294	295–296	297	298			SC 9	40	5-3	5-3		(*Preview:* scissors, plastic sandwich bags, long rubber bands, tape, centimeter ruler, metal washers) (*Follow-Up:* graphing calculator)
299–300	301–302	303	304	337, 339		SC 10	41	5-4	5-4	11	
305–306	307–308	309	310			GCS 31	42	5-5	5-5	12	
311–312	313–314	315	316	338			43	5-6	5-6	13	grid paper, scissors, graphing calculator
317–318	319–320	321	322	338		GCS 32, SM 51–56	44	5-7	5-7		
				323–336, 340–342			45				

Key to Abbreviations: GCS = Graphing Calculator and Spreadsheet Masters,
SC = School-to-Career Masters,
SM = Science and Mathematics Lab Manual

ELL Study Guide and Intervention, Skills Practice, Practice, and Parent and Student Study Guide Workbooks are also available in Spanish.

Mathematical Connections and Background

Continuity of Instruction

Prior Knowledge

In Chapter 3, students learned to solve equations for a given variable (algebraic manipulation). In Chapter 4, students graphed and analyzed points that composed a relation or function. They learned that two points determine a specific line. They also plotted points that represent real-world data.

This Chapter

Students closely examine the equations that represent the linear functions they graphed in Chapter 4. They learn to graph equations without finding two specific points. They use their skills in algebraic manipulation to rewrite linear equations in various forms. Students use their equation-writing skills to describe relationships in real-world data they have graphed.

Future Connections

Slope is a key concept that spans mathematics through calculus and beyond. By knowing the characteristics of linear equations, students can determine what type(s) of solutions a system of equations might have. The concept of a best-fit line (or curve) is used again in Algebra 2 and Statistics courses.

5-1 Slope

The slope of a straight line is one of the most important characteristics of the line. The slope, a ratio of the vertical change in the line to the horizontal change, can be expressed in many ways. One common definition is $\frac{\text{rise}}{\text{run}}$, which can frequently be observed from graphed lines. On lines in which two points have been identified, you can also use the algebraic definition, $\frac{y_2 - y_1}{x_2 - x_1}$, for which (x_1, y_1) and (x_2, y_2) represent the coordinates of points on that line.

Rate of change describes how rapidly a line rises or falls. It also is used in the real-world context to express the relationship between two quantities, for example number of words typed in each minute.

5-2 Slope and Direct Variation

The concept of direct variation grows from the meaning of ratio (Lesson 3-6). If the ratio of two variables is a constant, then direct variation is the way of expressing the relationship between the two variables. That is, $\frac{y}{x} = k$, where y and x are variables and k is a constant (number). If you multiply each side of the equation by x, you get $y = kx$. This represents an equation of a line and the k is the same value as the slope of the line. So when you graph a direct variation, you are graphing lines with slope k. All of these lines pass through the origin. In real-world applications, most direct variation graphs only occupy the first quadrant.

5-3 Slope-Intercept Form

Slope-intercept form is $y = mx + b$, where m is the slope and b is the y-value where the line crosses the y-axis. The slope-intercept form offers two ways to graph a line. One can select two values for x and very easily calculate the corresponding values of y to create two ordered pairs that can be used to graph points on the line. Then the line is drawn that contains those two points. One can also use the slope and intercept to graph the line directly. The intercept gives a starting point on the y-axis. Use the slope to determine the distance and direction you go up/down and right/left to find another point on the line. Then draw the line.

5-4 Writing Equations in Slope-Intercept Form

It is important to understand what an equation represents and how to use it as a tool. The general expression for slope-intercept form is $y = mx + b$. This is the starting point for creating an equation from different types of information given. The goal is to use the given information to find values for m and b, so that you can rewrite the general form with x and y being the only unknowns.

5-5 Writing Equations in Point-Slope Form

Point-slope form is derived from the definition of slope using the coordinates of two points on a line. Suppose one point is given as (x_1, y_1) and another point is unknown (x, y). Using the definition of slope, you get $m = \frac{y - y_1}{x - x_1}$. Multiply each side by $(x - x_1)$ and use the symmetric property of equality. You get $y - y_1 = m(x - x_1)$, which is the point-slope form of a linear equation.

You can also manipulate equations in point-slope form and slope-intercept form to express them in standard form, $Ax + By = C$.

5-6 Geometry: Parallel and Perpendicular Lines

This is a part of mathematics often called *coordinate geometry* or *analytic geometry*. In coordinate geometry, you use graphing and properties of graphs to prove geometric concepts. What properties, besides not intersecting, do parallel lines have? They lie in the same plane and have the same slope. Now consider perpendicular lines. We know they intersect, so they cannot have the same slope. Actually, they slope in opposite directions. That is, if one is vertical, the other is horizontal; if one slopes upward, the other slopes downward. A comparison of slopes of the two lines will lead you to discover that they are negative reciprocals of each other.

To write the equation of a line that is parallel to or perpendicular to a given line, you must realize that you are still using the equation-writing skills presented in the previous lessons. You still need the slope and the coordinates of one of the points on the line to write the equation. Using the properties of parallel and perpendicular lines helps you to determine what slope you are using and the point is usually given to you.

5-7 Statistics: Scatter Plots and Lines of Fit

A scatter plot includes graphs of ordered pairs that belong to a set in which the first coordinate represents one real-world measurement and the second coordinate represents another. Scatter plots can be used to visually identify trends, if they exist, and determine how strong that trend is.

At this point in their studies, students do not have the mathematical background to attempt to write the equation of a best-fit line by using statistical formulas. So, they draw a line that seems characteristic of the data, select two points on that line, and then use those points to write an equation. Using this method, there are many correct best-fit lines that can be drawn. This should be understood so that students realize that predictions are totally dependent on the line drawn and have no factual rule for determining them.

Quick Review Math Handbook

Hot Words includes a glossary of terms while Hot Topics consists of explanations of key mathematical concepts with exercises to test comprehension. This valuable resource can be used as a reference in the classroom or for home study.

Lesson	Hot Topics Section	Lesson	Hot Topics Section
GS5	2.1, 6.3, 6.7	5-4	1.5, 6.8
5-1	2.4, 6.8	5-5	6.8
5-2	6.4, 6.8	5-6	6.8
5-3P	6.8	5-7	4.3
5-3	6.7, 6.8	5-7F	4.3
5-3F	6.7, 6.8		

GS = Getting Started, P = Preview, F = Follow-Up

 Additional mathematical information and teaching notes are available at www.algebra1.com/key_concepts.

DAILY INTERVENTION and Assessment

Key to Abbreviations:
TWE = Teacher Wraparound Edition; CRM = Chapter Resource Masters

	Type	Student Edition	Teacher Resources	Technology/Internet
INTERVENTION	Ongoing	Prerequisite Skills, pp. 255, 262, 270, 277, 285, 291, 297 Practice Quiz 1, p. 270 Practice Quiz 2, p. 297	5-Minute Check Transparencies *Prerequisite Skills Workbook*, pp. 29–30, 39–40, 63–64 Quizzes, *CRM* pp. 337–338 Mid-Chapter Test, *CRM* p. 339 Study Guide and Intervention, *CRM* pp. 281–282, 287–288, 293–294, 299–300, 305–306, 311–312, 317–318	AlgePASS: Tutorial Plus, Lessons 11, 12, and 13 www.algebra1.com/self_check_quiz www.algebra1.com/extra_examples
	Mixed Review	pp. 262, 270, 277, 285, 291, 297, 305	Cumulative Review, *CRM* p. 340	
	Error Analysis	Find the Error, pp. 259, 289 Common Misconceptions, p. 257	Find the Error, *TWE* pp. 259, 289 Unlocking Misconceptions, *TWE* p. 257 Tips for New Teachers, *TWE* pp. 262, 287	
ASSESSMENT	Standardized Test Practice	pp. 262, 269, 277, 281, 283, 285, 291, 297, 304, 313, 314–315	*TWE* pp. 314–315 Standardized Test Practice, *CRM* pp. 341–342	Standardized Test Practice CD-ROM www.algebra1.com/standardized_test
	Open-Ended Assessment	Writing in Math, pp. 262, 269, 277, 285, 291, 297, 304 Open Ended, pp. 259, 267, 275, 283, 289, 291, 295, 301 Standardized Test, p. 315	Modeling: *TWE* pp. 262, 297 Speaking: *TWE* pp. 277, 285 Writing: *TWE* pp. 270, 291, 305 Open-Ended Assessment, *CRM* p. 335	
	Chapter Assessment	Study Guide, pp. 308–312 Practice Test, p. 313	Multiple-Choice Tests (Forms 1, 2A, 2B), *CRM* pp. 323–328 Free-Response Tests (Forms 2C, 2D, 3), *CRM* pp. 329–334 Vocabulary Test/Review, *CRM* p. 336	ExamView® Pro (see below) MindJogger Videoquizzes www.algebra1.com/vocabulary_review www.algebra1.com/chapter_test

For more information on Yearly ProgressPro, see p. 188.

Algebra Lesson	Yearly ProgressPro Skill Lesson
5-1	Slope
5-2	Slope and Direct Variation
5-3	Slope-Intercept Form
5-4	Writing Equations in Slope-Intercept Form
5-5	Writing Equations in Point-Slope Form
5-6	Geometry: Parallel and Perpendicular Lines
5-7	Scatter Plots and Lines of Fit

ExamView® Pro

Use the networkable **ExamView® Pro** to:
- Create **multiple versions** of tests.
- Create **modified** tests for *Inclusion* students.
- **Edit** existing questions and **add** your own questions.
- Use built-in **state curriculum correlations** to create tests aligned with state standards.
- Change **English** tests to **Spanish** and vice versa.

For more information on Intervention and Assessment, see pp. T8–T11.

Reading and Writing in Mathematics

Glencoe Algebra 1 provides numerous opportunities to incorporate reading and writing into the mathematics classroom.

Student Edition

- Foldables Study Organizer, p. 255
- Concept Check questions require students to verbalize and write about what they have learned in the lesson. (pp. 259, 267, 275, 283, 289, 291, 295, 301)
- Reading Mathematics, p. 263
- Writing in Math questions in every lesson, pp. 262, 269, 277, 285, 291, 297, 304
- Reading Study Tip, p. 256
- WebQuest, p. 304

Teacher Wraparound Edition

- Foldables Study Organizer, pp. 255, 308
- Study Notebook suggestions, pp. 259, 263, 267, 271, 275, 283, 289, 295, 301
- Modeling activities, pp. 262, 297
- Speaking activities, pp. 277, 285
- Writing activities, pp. 270, 291, 305
- Differentiated Instruction, (Verbal/Linguistic), p. 288
- **ELL** Resources, pp. 254, 261, 263, 268, 274, 276, 284, 288, 290, 296, 303, 308

For more information on Reading and Writing in Mathematics, see pp. T6–T7.

Additional Resources

- Vocabulary Builder worksheets require students to define and give examples for key vocabulary terms as they progress through the chapter. (*Chapter 5 Resource Masters,* pp. vii-viii)
- Reading to Learn Mathematics master for each lesson (*Chapter 5 Resource Masters,* pp. 285, 291, 297, 303, 309, 315, 321)
- *Vocabulary PuzzleMaker* software creates crossword, jumble, and word search puzzles using vocabulary lists that you can customize.
- *Teaching Mathematics with Foldables* provides suggestions for promoting cognition and language.
- *Reading and Writing in the Mathematics Classroom*
- *WebQuest and Project Resources*

ELL ENGLISH LANGUAGE LEARNERS

Lesson 5-2
Using Multisensory Activities

Have pairs of students use graphing calculators. Demonstrate processes step-by-step for those that don't have experience in using graphing calculators. Show students how to input ordered pairs using the list function of the calculator. Once the calculator has graphed the data, you may wish to refer students to the menu on the calculator that will give them a linear regression equation for the data. Ask the students to write the linear equation and identify the slope and y-intercept of the equation.

Lesson 5-5
Peer Tutoring

If possible, pair each English-Language Learner with a bilingual student. Give pairs of students several equations. Have them express the equations in slope-intercept form, point-slope form, and standard form. Then, have them graph each line on graph paper.

Lesson 5-7
Using Manipulatives

Demonstrate on an overhead transparency how to determine a line of best fit using a piece of dry spaghetti. Have students graph a set of data and use the spaghetti to model the line of best fit. Using the spaghetti helps students determine a positive or negative relationship for the given values. Once they have agreed on a best line for a set of data, they can find the slope and y-intercept for the line.

What You'll Learn

Have students read over the list of objectives and make a list of any words with which they are not familiar.

Why It's Important

Point out to students that this is only one of many reasons why each objective is important. Others are provided in the introduction to each lesson.

What You'll Learn

- **Lesson 5-1** Find the slope of a line.
- **Lesson 5-2** Write direct variation equations.
- **Lessons 5-3 through 5-5** Write linear equations in slope-intercept and point-slope forms.
- **Lesson 5-6** Write equations for parallel and perpendicular lines.
- **Lesson 5-7** Draw a scatter plot and write the equations of a line of fit.

Key Vocabulary

- slope (p. 256)
- rate of change (p. 258)
- direct variation (p. 264)
- slope-intercept form (p. 272)
- point-slope form (p. 286)

Why It's Important

Linear equations are used to model a variety of real-world situations. The concept of slope allows you to analyze how a quantity changes over time.

You can use a linear equation to model the cost of the space program. The United States began its exploration of space in January, 1958, when it launched its first satellite into orbit. In the 1970s, NASA developed the space shuttle to reduce costs by inventing the first reusable spacecraft.

You will use a linear equation to model the cost of the space program in Lesson 5-7.

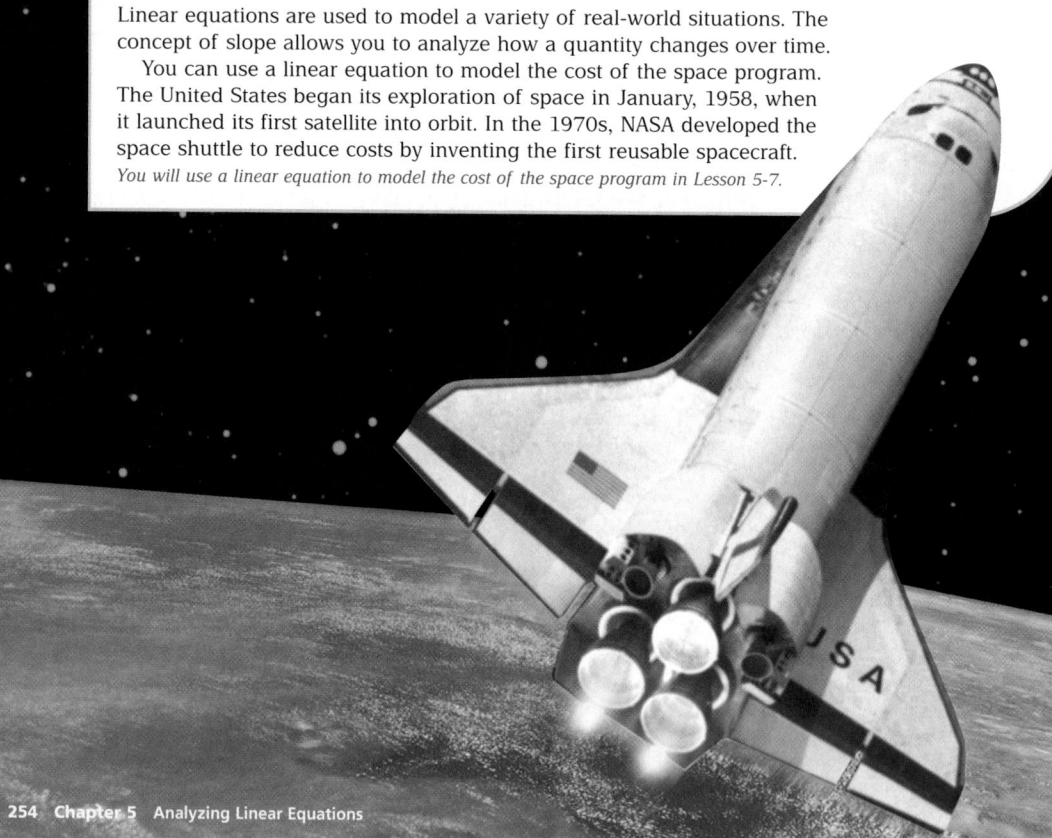

254 Chapter 5 Analyzing Linear Equations

Lesson	NCTM Standards	Local Objectives
5-1	2, 3, 4, 6, 7, 8, 9, 10	
5-2	2, 4, 8, 9, 10	
5-3 Preview	2, 3, 4, 8, 9, 10	
5-3	2, 3, 4, 6, 8, 9, 10	
5-3 Follow-Up	2, 6, 7, 8, 10	
5-4	2, 6, 8, 9, 10	
5-5	2, 6, 8, 9, 10	
5-6	2, 3, 6, 7, 8, 9, 10	
5-7	2, 5, 6, 7, 8, 9, 10	
5-7 Follow-Up	2, 5, 7, 8, 9, 10	

Key to NCTM Standards:

1=Number & Operations, 2=Algebra, 3=Geometry, 4=Measurement, 5=Data Analysis & Probability, 6=Problem Solving, 7=Reasoning & Proof, 8=Communication, 9=Connections, 10=Representation

Vocabulary Builder   ELL

The Key Vocabulary list introduces students to some of the main vocabulary terms included in this chapter. For a more thorough vocabulary list with pronunciations of new words, give students the Vocabulary Builder worksheets found on pages vii and viii of the *Chapter 5 Resource Masters*. Encourage them to complete the definition of each term as they progress through the chapter. You may suggest that they add these sheets to their study notebooks for future reference when studying for the Chapter 5 test.

▶ **Prerequisite Skills** To be successful in this chapter, you'll need to master these skills and be able to apply them in problem-solving situations. Review these skills before beginning Chapter 5.

For Lesson 5-1   Simplify Fractions

Simplify. *(For review, see pages 798 and 799.)*

1. $\frac{2}{10}$ $\frac{1}{5}$
2. $\frac{8}{12}$ $\frac{2}{3}$
3. $\frac{2}{-8}$ $-\frac{1}{4}$
4. $\frac{-4}{8}$ $-\frac{1}{2}$
5. $\frac{-5}{-15}$ $\frac{1}{3}$
6. $\frac{-7}{-28}$ $\frac{1}{4}$
7. $\frac{9}{3}$ 3
8. $\frac{18}{12}$ $1\frac{1}{2}$

For Lesson 5-2   Evaluate Expressions

Evaluate $\frac{a-b}{c-d}$ for each set of values. *(For review, see Lesson 1-2.)*

9. $a = 6, b = 5, c = 8, d = 4$ $\frac{1}{4}$
10. $a = 5, b = -1, c = 2, d = -1$ 2
11. $a = -2, b = 1, c = 4, d = 0$ $-\frac{3}{4}$
12. $a = 8, b = -2, c = -1, d = 1$ −5
13. $a = -3, b = -3, c = 4, d = 7$ 0
14. $a = \frac{1}{2}, b = \frac{3}{2}, c = 7, d = 9$ $\frac{1}{2}$

For Lessons 5-3 through 5-7   Identify Points on a Coordinate Plane

Write the ordered pair for each point.
(For review, see Lesson 4-1.)

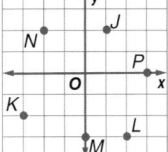

15. J (1, 2)
16. K (−3, −2)
17. L (2, −3)
18. M (0, −3)
19. N (−2, 2)
20. P (3, 0)

FOLDABLES™
Study Organizer

Writing Linear Equations Make this Foldable to help you organize your notes. Begin with four sheets of grid paper.

Step 1 Fold and Cut

Fold each sheet of grid paper in half along the width. Then cut along the crease.

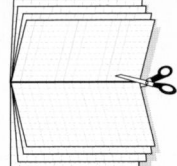

Step 2 Staple

Staple the eight half-sheets together to form a booklet.

Step 3 Cut Tabs

Cut seven lines from the bottom of the top sheet, six lines from the second sheet, and so on.

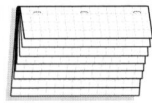

Step 4 Label

Label each of the tabs with a lesson number. The last tab is for the vocabulary.

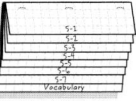

Reading and Writing As you read and study the chapter, use each page to write notes and to graph examples for each lesson.

Chapter 5 Analyzing Linear Equations 255

Getting Started

This section provides a review of the basic concepts needed before beginning Chapter 5. Page references are included for additional student help.

Additional review is provided in the *Prerequisite Skills Workbook*, pp. 29–30, 39–40, 63–64.

Prerequisite Skills in the Getting Ready for the Next Lesson section at the end of each exercise set review a skill needed in the next lesson.

For Lesson	Prerequisite Skill
5-2	Dividing Fractions (p. 262)
5-3	Rewriting Equations (p. 270)
5-4	Finding Slope (p. 277)
5-5	Subtracting Integers (p. 285)
5-6	Writing Multiplicative Inverses (p. 291)
5-7	Slope-Intercept Form (p. 297)

FOLDABLES™
Study Organizer

For more information about Foldables, see *Teaching Mathematics with Foldables.*

Descriptive Writing and Organizing Data After students make their Foldable, have them label a tab for each lesson in this chapter. At the end of each lesson, ask students to write a descriptive paragraph about their experiences with the concepts, computational skills, and the graphs presented. For example, students might write about how they felt when they were first asked to find the slope of a line or how the lesson appeared to them visually before they understood the concepts presented and how it appeared after mastery.

1 Focus

5-Minute Check Transparency 5-1 Use as a quiz or review of Chapter 4.

Mathematical Background notes are available for this lesson on p. 254C.

Building on Prior Knowledge

In Chapter 4, students learned that points on a line have coordinates that satisfy a given equation. In this lesson, they should recognize that there is another relationship that exists between any two points on a line.

Why is slope important in architecture?

Ask students:

- What is the slope of the roof if the rise is 10 and the run is 6? $\frac{5}{3}$

- Which has a steeper slope, a roof whose rise is greater than the run or one whose run is greater than the rise? **rise > run**

- **Geography** The steepness of roofs on buildings is often associated with certain climates. Very steep roofs are used in rainy or snowy climates, while flatter roofs are often found in arid regions. What type of roof would be most common in our community? **Answers may vary.**

5-1 # Slope

What You'll Learn

- Find the slope of a line.
- Use rate of change to solve problems.

Vocabulary

- slope
- rate of change

Why is slope important in architecture?

The slope of a roof describes how steep it is. It is the number of units the roof rises for each unit of run. In the photo, the roof rises 8 feet for each 12 feet of run.

$$\text{slope} = \frac{\text{rise}}{\text{run}}$$

$$= \frac{8}{12} \text{ or } \frac{2}{3}$$

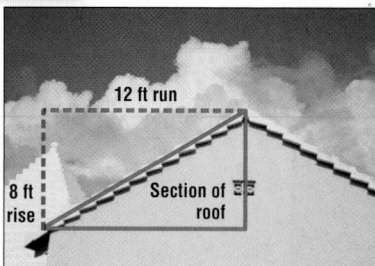

12 ft run

8 ft rise

Section of roof

FIND SLOPE The **slope** of a line is a number determined by any two points on the line. This number describes how steep the line is. The greater the absolute value of the slope, the steeper the line. Slope is the ratio of the change in the *y*-coordinates (rise) to the change in the *x*-coordinates (run) as you move from one point to the other.

The graph shows a line that passes through (1, 3) and (4, 5).

$$\text{slope} = \frac{\text{rise}}{\text{run}}$$

$$= \frac{\text{change in } y\text{-coordinates}}{\text{change in } x\text{-coordinates}}$$

$$= \frac{5 - 3}{4 - 1} \text{ or } \frac{2}{3}$$

So, the slope of the line is $\frac{2}{3}$.

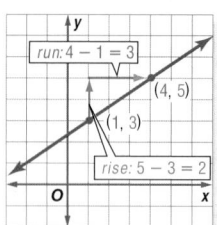

run: 4 − 1 = 3

(4, 5)

(1, 3)

rise: 5 − 3 = 2

Study Tip

Reading Math
In x_1, the 1 is called a *subscript*. It is read *x sub 1*.

Key Concept — Slope of a Line

- **Words** The slope of a line is the ratio of the rise to the run.

- **Symbols** The slope *m* of a nonvertical line through any two points, (x_1, y_1) and (x_2, y_2), can be found as follows.

  $m = \dfrac{y_2 - y_1}{x_2 - x_1}$ ← change in *y*

  ← change in *x*

- **Model**

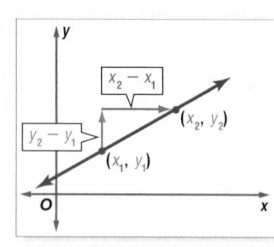

$x_2 - x_1$

(x_2, y_2)

$y_2 - y_1$

(x_1, y_1)

Resource Manager

📁 Workbook and Reproducible Masters

Chapter 5 Resource Masters
- Study Guide and Intervention, pp. 281–282
- Skills Practice, p. 283
- Practice, p. 284
- Reading to Learn Mathematics, p. 285
- Enrichment, p. 286

Parent and Student Study Guide Workbook, p. 38
Prerequisite Skills Workbook, pp. 39–40, 63–64

📀 Transparencies

5-Minute Check Transparency 5-1
Answer Key Transparencies

💿 Technology

Interactive Chalkboard

Example 1 *Positive Slope*

Find the slope of the line that passes through $(-1, 2)$ and $(3, 4)$.

Let $(-1, 2) = (x_1, y_1)$ and $(3, 4) = (x_2, y_2)$.

$$m = \frac{y_2 - y_1}{x_2 - x_1} \qquad \frac{\text{rise}}{\text{run}}$$

$$= \frac{4 - 2}{3 - (-1)} \qquad \text{Substitute.}$$

$$= \frac{2}{4} \text{ or } \frac{1}{2} \qquad \text{Simplify.}$$

The slope is $\frac{1}{2}$.

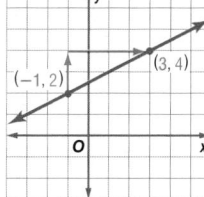

Example 2 *Negative Slope*

Find the slope of the line that passes through $(-1, -2)$ and $(-4, 1)$.

Let $(-1, -2) = (x_1, y_1)$ and $(-4, 1) = (x_2, y_2)$.

$$m = \frac{y_2 - y_1}{x_2 - x_1} \qquad \frac{\text{rise}}{\text{run}}$$

$$= \frac{1 - (-2)}{-4 - (-1)} \qquad \text{Substitute.}$$

$$= \frac{3}{-3} \text{ or } -1 \qquad \text{Simplify.}$$

The slope is -1.

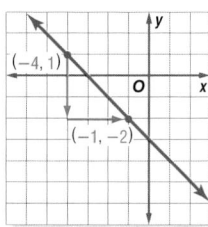

Example 3 *Zero Slope*

Find the slope of the line that passes through $(1, 2)$ and $(-1, 2)$.

Let $(1, 2) = (x_1, y_1)$ and $(-1, 2) = (x_2, y_2)$.

$$m = \frac{y_2 - y_1}{x_2 - x_1} \qquad \frac{\text{rise}}{\text{run}}$$

$$= \frac{2 - 2}{-1 - 1} \qquad \text{Substitute.}$$

$$= \frac{0}{-2} \text{ or } 0 \qquad \text{Simplify.}$$

The slope is zero.

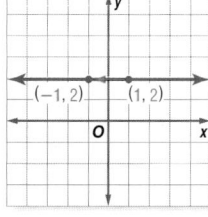

Example 4 *Undefined Slope*

Find the slope of the line that passes through $(1, -2)$ and $(1, 3)$.

Let $(1, -2) = (x_1, y_1)$ and $(1, 3) = (x_2, y_2)$.

$$m = \frac{y_2 - y_1}{x_2 - x_1} \qquad \frac{\text{rise}}{\text{run}}$$

$$= \frac{3 - (-2)}{1 - 1} \text{ or } \cancel{\frac{5}{0}}$$

Since division by zero is undefined, the slope is undefined.

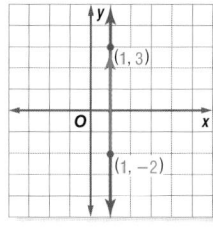

---

2 Teach

FIND SLOPE

In-Class Examples Power Point®

1 Find the slope of the line that passes through $(-3, 2)$ and $(5, 5)$. $\frac{3}{8}$

2 Find the slope of the line that passes through $(-3, -4)$ and $(-2, -8)$. -4

3 Find the slope of the line that passes through $(-3, 4)$ and $(4, 4)$. 0

Teaching Tip Ask students how they would determine if two points lie on a horizontal line without graphing the points.

4 Find the slope of the line that passes through $(-2, -4)$ and $(-2, 3)$.   undefined

✓ Concept Check

Slope Ask students to give the slope of a very steep line and then the slope of one that is almost horizontal. Make sure students acknowledge that negative slopes are acceptable to meet these criteria.

Sample answers: $6, -\frac{2}{5}; -5, -\frac{2}{15}$

Interactive Chalkboard
PowerPoint® Presentations

This CD-ROM is a customizable Microsoft® PowerPoint® presentation that includes:

• Step-by-step, dynamic solutions of each In-Class Example from the Teacher Wraparound Edition

• Additional, Your Turn exercises for each example

• The 5-Minute Check Transparencies

• Hot links to Glencoe Online Study Tools

In-Class Example

Teaching Tip Watch for students who try to find the cross product mentally and forget to multiply both 10 and $-r$ by -3.

5 Find the value of r so that the line through $(6, 3)$ and $(r, 2)$ has a slope of $\frac{1}{2}$. **4**

RATE OF CHANGE

In-Class Example

6 **TRAVEL** The graph below shows the number of U.S. passports issued in 1991, 1995, and 1999.

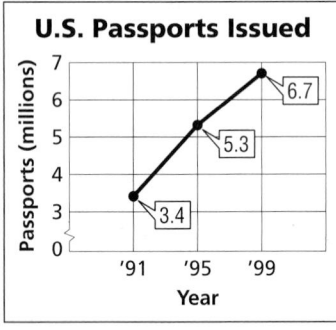

U.S. Passports Issued

Source: U.S. State Department

a. Find the rates of change for 1991–1995 and 1995–1999. **475,000/yr; 350,000/yr**

b. Explain the meaning of the slope in each case. **'91–'95: The number of U.S. passports issued increased about 475,000 each year. '95–'99: The number of U.S. passports issued increased about 350,000 each year.**

c. How are the different rates of change shown on the graph? **There is a greater rate of change from '91–'95 than from '95–'99. So the '91–'95 segment has the steeper slope.**

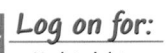
Concept Summary — Classifying Lines

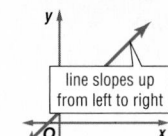 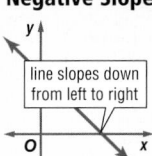 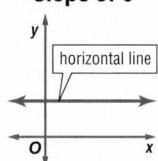 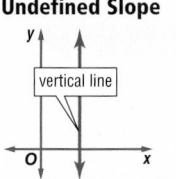

Positive Slope	Negative Slope	Slope of 0	Undefined Slope
line slopes up from left to right	line slopes down from left to right	horizontal line	vertical line

If you know the slope of a line and the coordinates of one of the points on a line, you can find the coordinates of other points on the line.

Example 5 Find Coordinates Given Slope

Find the value of r so that the line through $(r, 6)$ and $(10, -3)$ has a slope of $-\frac{3}{2}$.

Let $(r, 6) = (x_1, y_1)$ and $(10, -3) = (x_2, y_2)$.

$$m = \frac{y_2 - y_1}{x_2 - x_1} \qquad \text{Slope formula}$$

$$-\frac{3}{2} = \frac{-3 - 6}{10 - r} \qquad \text{Substitute.}$$

$$-\frac{3}{2} = \frac{-9}{10 - r} \qquad \text{Subtract.}$$

$$-3(10 - r) = 2(-9) \qquad \text{Find the cross products.}$$

$$-30 + 3r = -18 \qquad \text{Simplify.}$$

$$-30 + 3r + 30 = -18 + 30 \qquad \text{Add 30 to each side.}$$

$$3r = 12 \qquad \text{Simplify.}$$

$$\frac{3r}{3} = \frac{12}{3} \qquad \text{Divide each side by 3.}$$

$$r = 4 \qquad \text{Simplify.}$$

RATE OF CHANGE Slope can be used to describe a rate of change. The **rate of change** tells, on average, how a quantity is changing over time.

Example 6 Find a Rate of Change

DINING OUT The graph shows the amount spent on food and drink at U.S. restaurants in recent years.

a. Find the rates of change for 1980–1990 and 1990–2000.

Use the formula for slope.

$$\frac{\text{rise}}{\text{run}} = \frac{\text{change in quantity}}{\text{change in time}} \quad \begin{array}{l} \leftarrow \text{billion \$} \\ \leftarrow \text{years} \end{array}$$

USA TODAY Snapshots®

Dining out
Food and drink sales at U.S. restaurants by year (in billions):

1980: $120
1990: $239
2000: $376

Source: National Restaurant Association
By Hilary Wasson and Alejandro Gonzalez, USA TODAY

1980–1990: $\dfrac{\text{change in quantity}}{\text{change in time}} = \dfrac{239 - 120}{1990 - 1980}$ Substitute.

$ = \dfrac{119}{10}$ or 11.9 Simplify.

Spending on food and drink increased by \$119 billion in a 10-year period for a rate of change of \$11.9 billion per year.

1990–2000: $\dfrac{\text{change in quantity}}{\text{change in time}} = \dfrac{376 - 239}{2000 - 1990}$ Substitute.

$ = \dfrac{137}{10}$ or 13.7 Simplify.

Over this 10-year period, spending increased by \$137 billion, for a rate of change of \$13.7 billion per year.

b. Explain the meaning of the slope in each case.

For 1980–1990, on average, \$11.9 billion more was spent each year than the last. For 1990–2000, on average, \$13.7 billion more was spent each year than the last.

c. How are the different rates of change shown on the graph?

There is a greater vertical change for 1990–2000 than for 1980–1990. Therefore, the section of the graph for 1990–2000 has a steeper slope.

Check for Understanding

Concept Check

1. Sample answer: Use $(-1, -3)$ as (x_1, y_1) and $(3, -5)$ as (x_2, y_2) in the slope formula.

3. The difference in the x values is always 0, and division by 0 is undefined.

4. Carlos; Allison switched the order of the x-coordinates, resulting in an incorrect sign.

1. Explain how you would find the slope of the line at the right.

2. OPEN ENDED Draw the graph of a line having each slope. **See students' work.**
   a. positive slope   b. negative slope
   c. slope of 0   d. undefined slope

3. Explain why the formula for determining slope using the coordinates of two points does not apply to vertical lines.

4. FIND THE ERROR Carlos and Allison are finding the slope of the line that passes through $(2, 6)$ and $(5, 3)$.

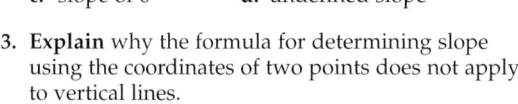

Carlos

$\dfrac{3 - 6}{5 - 2} = \dfrac{-3}{3}$ or -1

Allison

$\dfrac{6 - 3}{5 - 2} = \dfrac{3}{3}$ or 1

Who is correct? Explain your reasoning.

Guided Practice

GUIDED PRACTICE KEY	
Exercises	Examples
5–10	1–4
11, 12	5
13, 14	6

Find the slope of the line that passes through each pair of points.

5. $(1, 1), (3, 4)$ $\dfrac{3}{2}$

6. $(0, 0), (5, 4)$ $\dfrac{4}{5}$

7. $(-2, 2), (-1, -2)$ -4

8. $(7, -4), (9, -1)$ $\dfrac{3}{2}$

9. $(3, 5), (-2, 5)$ 0

10. $(-1, 3), (-1, 0)$ undefined

Find the value of r so the line that passes through each pair of points has the given slope.

11. $(6, -2), (r, -6), m = 4$ 5

12. $(9, r), (6, 3), m = -\dfrac{1}{3}$ 2

Lesson 5-1 Slope 259

3 Practice/Apply

Study Notebook

Have students—

• add the definitions/examples of the vocabulary terms to their Vocabulary Builder worksheets for Chapter 5.

• copy their drawings for Exercise 2 and write notes about each type of graph.

• include any other item(s) that they find helpful in mastering the skills in this lesson.

DAILY

INTERVENTION **FIND THE ERROR**
   If students are having difficulty with writing the coordinates in the correct order, have them complete the slope formula by filling in each ordered pair, instead of each pair of y or x values. Fill in the first ordered pair, $\dfrac{y}{x} \rightarrow \dfrac{6 -}{2 -}$. Then fill in the second ordered pair, $\dfrac{6 - 3}{2 - 5}$.

Teacher to Teacher

Ruth Casey   Anderson County H.S., Lawrenceburg, KY

"I like to introduce the Greek letter Δ (delta) to represent 'change in' with my students when studying slope. The definition of slope becomes $m = \dfrac{\Delta y}{\Delta x}$, the change in the y-coordinate over the change in the x-coordinate."

Answer

50.

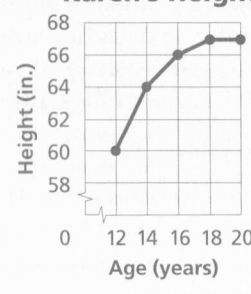

Karen's Height

Application   **CABLE TV**   For Exercises 13 and 14, use the graph at the right.

13. 1.5 million subscribers per year

13. Find the rate of change for 1990–1992.

14. Without calculating, find a 2-year period that had a greater rate of change than 1990–1992. Explain your reasoning.
Sample answer: '92–'94; steeper segment means greater rate of change.

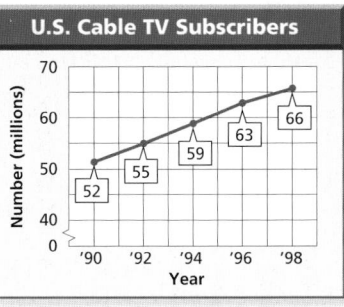

U.S. Cable TV Subscribers

★ indicates increased difficulty

Practice and Apply

Find the slope of the line that passes through each pair of points.

15. 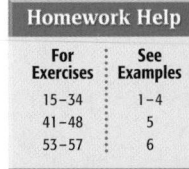 $\frac{3}{4}$

16. 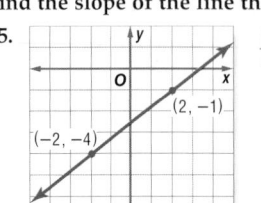 $-\frac{1}{3}$

17. $(-4, -1), (-3, -3)$ **−2**

18. $(-3, 3), (1, 3)$ **0**

19. $(-2, 1), (-2, 3)$ **undefined**

20. $(2, 3), (9, 7)$ $\frac{4}{7}$

21. $(5, 7), (-2, -3)$ $\frac{10}{7}$

22. $(-3, 6), (2, 4)$ $-\frac{2}{5}$

23. $(-3, -4), (5, -1)$ $\frac{3}{8}$

24. $(2, -1), (5, -3)$ $-\frac{2}{3}$

25. $(-5, 4), (-5, -1)$ **undefined**

26. $(2, 6), (-1, 3)$ **1**

27. $(-2, 3), (8, 3)$ **0**

28. $(-3, 9), (-7, 6)$ $\frac{3}{4}$

29. $(-8, 3), (-6, 2)$ $-\frac{1}{2}$

30. $(-2, 0), (1, -1)$ $-\frac{1}{3}$

★ 31. $(4.5, -1), (5.3, 2)$ $\frac{15}{4}$

★ 32. $(0.75, 1), (0.75, -1)$ **undefined**

★ 33. $\left(2\frac{1}{2}, -1\frac{1}{2}\right), \left(-\frac{1}{2}, \frac{1}{2}\right)$ $-\frac{2}{3}$

★ 34. $\left(\frac{3}{4}, 1\frac{1}{4}\right), \left(-\frac{1}{2}, -1\right)$ $\frac{9}{5}$

ARCHITECTURE   Use a ruler to estimate the slope of each roof.

35. Sample answer: $\frac{8}{11}$

36. Sample answer: $\frac{1}{3}$

35.

36.

37. Find the slope of the line that passes through the origin and (r, s). $\frac{s}{r}$, if $r \neq 0$

38. What is the slope of the line that passes through (a, b) and $(a, -b)$? **undefined**

39. **PAINTING**   A ladder reaches a height of 16 feet on a wall. If the bottom of the ladder is placed 4 feet away from the wall, what is the slope of the ladder as a positive number? **4**

40. PART-TIME JOBS In 1991, the federal minimum wage rate was $4.25 per hour. In 1997, it was increased to $5.15. Find the annual rate of change in the federal minimum wage rate from 1991 to 1997. **$0.15 per year**

Find the value of r so the line that passes through each pair of points has the given slope.

41. $(6, 2)$, $(9, r)$, $m = -1$ **−1**

42. $(4, -5)$, $(3, r)$, $m = 8$ **−13**

43. $(5, r)$, $(2, -3)$, $m = \frac{4}{3}$ **1**

44. $(-2, 7)$, $(r, 3)$, $m = \frac{4}{3}$ **−5**

★ 45. $\left(\frac{1}{2}, -\frac{1}{4}\right)$, $\left(r, -\frac{5}{4}\right)$, $m = 4$ **$\frac{1}{4}$**

★ 46. $\left(\frac{2}{3}, r\right)$, $\left(1, \frac{1}{2}\right)$, $m = \frac{1}{2}$ **$\frac{1}{3}$**

★ 47. $(4, r)$, $(r, 2)$, $m = -\frac{5}{3}$ **7**

★ 48. $(r, 5)$, $(-2, r)$, $m = -\frac{2}{9}$ **7**

49. $(-4, -5)$ is in Quadrant III and $(4, 5)$ is in Quadrant I. The segment connecting them goes from lower left to upper right, which is a positive slope.

★ **49. CRITICAL THINKING** Explain how you know that the slope of the line through $(-4, -5)$ and $(4, 5)$ is positive without calculating.

HEALTH For Exercises 50–52, use the table that shows Karen's height from age 12 to age 20.

Age (years)	12	14	16	18	20
Height (inches)	60	64	66	67	67

50. Make a broken-line graph of the data. **See margin.**

51. Use the graph to determine the two-year period when Karen grew the fastest. Explain your reasoning. **12–14; steepest part of the graph**

52. Explain the meaning of the horizontal section of the graph. **There was no change in height.**

SCHOOL For Exercises 53–55, use the graph that shows public school enrollment.

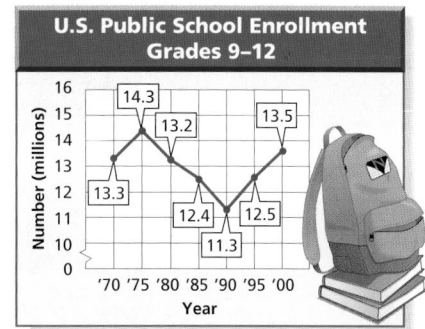
U.S. Public School Enrollment Grades 9–12

53. For which 5-year period was the rate of change the greatest? When was the rate of change the least? **'90–'95; '80–'85**

54. Find the rate of change from 1985 to 1990. **−0.22**

55. Explain the meaning of the part of the graph with a negative slope. **a decline in enrollment**

56. RESEARCH Use the Internet or other reference to find the population of your city or town in 1930, 1940, . . . , 2000. For which decade was the rate of change the greatest? **See students' work.**

57. CONSTRUCTION The slope of a stairway determines how easy it is to climb the stairs. Suppose the vertical distance between two floors is 8 feet 9 inches. Find the total run of the ideal stairway in feet and inches. **13 ft 9 in.**

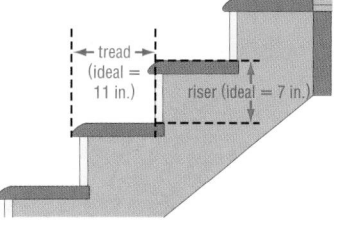

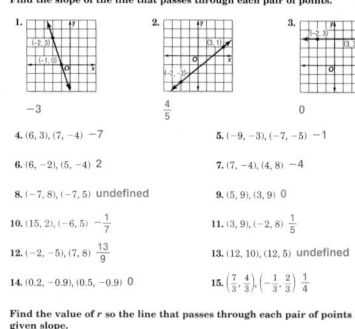
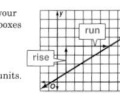

Open-Ended Assessment

Modeling Use a transparency of a coordinate plane and a piece of thin spaghetti to create a "line" on the overhead projector. Ask students to determine whether the slope of that line is positive, negative, zero, or undefined and then calculate the actual slope. Repeat until all types of slope have been addressed.

Tips for New Teachers

Intervention If there is any doubt whether your students thoroughly understand slope, consider spending an extra day on this lesson. Use the Extra Practice on p. 831, the Study Guide and Intervention masters, or the Practice masters in the *Chapter 5 Resource Masters* to reinforce this concept.

Getting Ready for Lesson 5-2

PREREQUISITE SKILL Lesson 5-2 presents direct variation in which students must find quotients of numbers to determine the constant of variation. Exercises 77–85 should be used to determine your students' familiarity with finding quotients involving fractions.

Answers

58. Sample answer: Analysis of the slope of a roof might help to determine the materials of which it should be made and its functionality. Answers should include the following.
   • To find the slope of the roof, find a vertical line that passes through the peak of the roof and a horizontal line that passes through the eave. Find the distances from the intersection of those two lines to the peak and to the eave. Use those measures as the rise and run to calculate the slope.

---

58. **WRITING IN MATH** Answer the question that was posed at the beginning of the lesson.

    Why is slope important in architecture?
    Include the following in your answer: **See margin.**
    • an explanation of how to find the slope of a roof, and
    • a comparison of the appearance of roofs with different slopes.

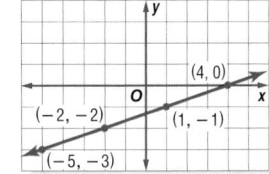

Standardized Test Practice

59. The slope of the line passing through (5, −4) and (5, −10) is **D**
    Ⓐ positive.　　Ⓑ negative.　　Ⓒ zero.　　Ⓓ undefined.

60. The slope of the line passing through (a, b) and (c, d) is **B**
    Ⓐ $\frac{d-c}{b-a}$.　　Ⓑ $\frac{b-d}{a-c}$.　　Ⓒ $\frac{d-b}{a-c}$.　　Ⓓ $\frac{a-c}{b-d}$.

Extending the Lesson

61. Choose four different pairs of points from those labeled on the graph. Find the slope of the line using the coordinates of each pair of points. Describe your findings.
    $\frac{1}{3}$; The slope is the same regardless of points chosen.

62. **MAKE A CONJECTURE** Determine whether Q(2, 3), R(−1, −1), and S(−4, −2) lie on the same line. Explain your reasoning. **See margin.**

Maintain Your Skills

Mixed Review

Write an equation for each function. *(Lesson 4-8)*

63.

x	1	2	3	4	5
f(x)	5	10	15	20	25

$f(x) = 5x$

64.

x	−2	−1	1	2	4
f(x)	13	12	10	9	7

$f(x) = 11 - x$

Determine whether each relation is a function. *(Lesson 4-6)*

65. $y = -15$　yes
66. $x = 5$　no
67. {(1, 0), (1, 4), (−1, 1)}　no
68. {(6, 3), (5, −2), (2, 3)}　yes

69. Graph $x - y = 0$. *(Lesson 4-4)* **See margin.**

70. What number is 40% of 37.5? *(Prerequisite Skill)* **15**

Find each product. *(Lesson 2-4)*

71. 7(−3) **−21**
72. (−4)(−2) **8**
73. (9)(−4) **−36**
74. (−8)(3.7) **−29.6**
75. $\left(-\frac{7}{8}\right)\left(\frac{1}{3}\right)$ **$-\frac{7}{24}$**
76. $\left(\frac{1}{4}\right)\left(\frac{1}{2}\right)(-14)$ **$-1\frac{3}{4}$**

Getting Ready for the Next Lesson

PREREQUISITE SKILL Find each quotient.
*(To review **dividing fractions**, see pages 800 and 801.)*

77. $6 \div \frac{2}{3}$ **9**
78. $12 \div \frac{1}{4}$ **48**
79. $10 \div \frac{3}{8}$ **$26\frac{2}{3}$**
80. $\frac{1}{2} \div \frac{1}{3}$ **$1\frac{1}{2}$**
81. $\frac{3}{4} \div \frac{1}{6}$ **$4\frac{1}{2}$**
82. $\frac{3}{4} \div 6$ **$\frac{1}{8}$**
83. $18 \div \frac{7}{8}$ **$20\frac{4}{7}$**
84. $\frac{3}{8} \div \frac{2}{5}$ **$\frac{15}{16}$**
85. $2\frac{2}{3} \div \frac{1}{4}$ **$10\frac{2}{3}$**

• A roof that is steeper than one with a rise of 6 and a run of 12 would be one with a rise greater than 6 and the same run. A roof with a steeper slope appears taller than one with a less steep slope.

62. No, they do not. Slope of $\overline{QR}$ is $\frac{4}{3}$ and slope of $\overline{RS}$ is $\frac{1}{3}$. If they lie on the same line, the slopes should be the same.

69.

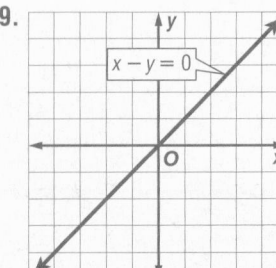

Reading Mathematics

Mathematical Words and Everyday Words

You may have noticed that many words used in mathematics are also used in everyday language. You can use the everyday meaning of these words to better understand their mathematical meaning. The table shows two mathematical words along with their everyday and mathematical meanings.

Word	Everyday Meaning	Mathematical Meaning
expression	1. something that expresses or communicates in words, art, music, or movement 2. the manner in which one expresses oneself, especially in speaking, depicting, or performing	one or more numbers or variables along with one or more arithmetic operations
function	1. the action for which one is particularly fitted or employed 2. an official ceremony or a formal social occasion 3. something closely related to another thing and dependent on it for its existence, value, or significance	a relationship in which the output depends upon the input

Source: *The American Heritage Dictionary of the English Language*

Notice that the mathematical meaning is more specific, but related to the everyday meaning. For example, the mathematical meaning of *expression* is closely related to the first everyday definition. In mathematics, an expression communicates using symbols.

Reading to Learn

1. How does the mathematical meaning of *function* compare to the everyday meaning?

2. **RESEARCH** Use the Internet or other reference to find the everyday meaning of each word below. How might these words apply to mathematics? Make a table like the one above and note the mathematical meanings that you learn as you study Chapter 5. **a–c. See pp. 315A–315B for sample answers.**

   a. slope

   b. intercept

   c. parallel

1. Sample answer: The mathematical meaning of function is most closely related to the third definition in the everyday meanings.

Getting Started

Before using this page, ask students if there are any words they know that have more than one meaning, depending on how they are used. Some examples might be:

bolt: a fastener; a roll of cloth measured to a specified length

bow: a decorative knot formed by a ribbon or piece of cloth; a weapon made of curved material and a cord

row: a line of seats or objects; using a paddle to move a boat through water

Teach

Word Association Explain to students that if they can relate a word they are trying to learn to something with which they are already familiar, it makes it easier to remember what that word means. This is a technique taught to business people to improve their recollection of names and business contacts. By relating mathematical terms to everyday things, they can recall their meanings more readily.

Assess

Study Notebook

Ask students to summarize what they have learned about mathematical words and everyday words.

ELL English Language Learners may benefit from writing key concepts from this activity in their Study Notebooks in their native language and then in English.

5-2 Slope and Direct Variation

Vocabulary

- direct variation
- constant of variation
- family of graphs
- parent graph

What You'll Learn

- Write and graph direct variation equations.
- Solve problems involving direct variation.

How is slope related to your shower?

A standard showerhead uses about 6 gallons of water per minute. If you graph the ordered pairs from the table, the slope of the line is 6.

x (minutes)	y (gallons)
0	0
1	6
2	12
3	18
4	24

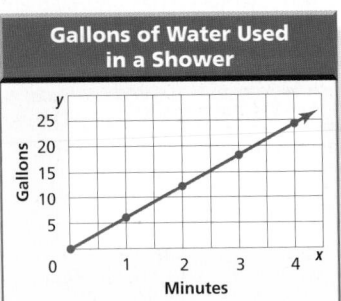

Gallons of Water Used in a Shower

The equation is $y = 6x$. The number of gallons of water y depends *directly* on the amount of time in the shower x.

DIRECT VARIATION A **direct variation** is described by an equation of the form $y = kx$, where $k \neq 0$. We say that *y varies directly with x* or *y varies directly as x*. In the equation $y = kx$, k is the **constant of variation**.

Example 1 Slope and Constant of Variation

Name the constant of variation for each equation. Then find the slope of the line that passes through each pair of points.

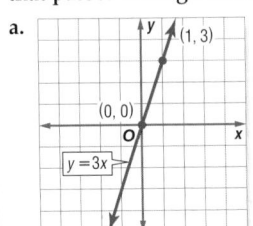

a. (1, 3), (0, 0), $y = 3x$

The constant of variation is 3.

$m = \dfrac{y_2 - y_1}{x_2 - x_1}$ Slope formula

$m = \dfrac{3 - 0}{1 - 0}$ $(x_1, y_1) = (0, 0)$
$(x_2, y_2) = (1, 3)$

$m = 3$ The slope is 3.

b. $y = -2x$, (0, 0), (1, -2)

The constant of variation is -2.

$m = \dfrac{y_2 - y_1}{x_2 - x_1}$ Slope formula

$m = \dfrac{-2 - 0}{1 - 0}$ $(x_1, y_1) = (0, 0)$
$(x_2, y_2) = (1, -2)$

$m = -2$ The slope is -2.

Compare the constant of variation with the slope of the graph for each example. Notice that the slope of the graph of $y = kx$ is k.

The ordered pair (0, 0) is a solution of $y = kx$. Therefore, the graph of $y = kx$ passes through the origin. You can use this information to graph direct variation equations.

Example 2 Direct Variation with $k > 0$

Graph $y = 4x$.

Step 1 Write the slope as a ratio.

$$4 = \frac{4}{1} \quad \frac{\text{rise}}{\text{run}}$$

Step 2 Graph (0, 0).

Step 3 From the point (0, 0), move up 4 units and right 1 unit. Draw a dot.

Step 4 Draw a line containing the points.

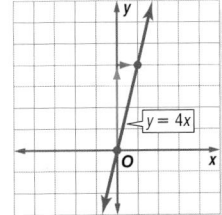

Example 3 Direct Variation with $k < 0$

Graph $y = -\frac{1}{3}x$.

Step 1 Write the slope as a ratio.

$$-\frac{1}{3} = \frac{-1}{3} \quad \frac{\text{rise}}{\text{run}}$$

Step 2 Graph (0, 0).

Step 3 From the point (0, 0), move down 1 unit and right 3 units. Draw a dot.

Step 4 Draw a line containing the points.

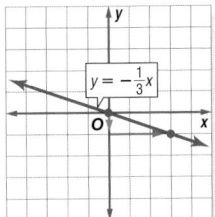

A **family of graphs** includes graphs and equations of graphs that have at least one characteristic in common. The **parent graph** is the simplest graph in a family.

Graphing Calculator Investigation

Family of Graphs

The calculator screen shows the graphs of $y = x$, $y = 2x$, and $y = 4x$.

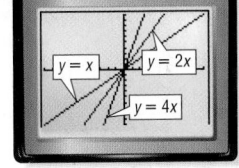

[−10, 10] scl: 1 by [−10, 10] scl: 1

Think and Discuss

1. Describe any similarities among the graphs.

2. Describe any differences among the graphs.

3. Write an equation whose graph has a steeper slope than $y = 4x$. Check your answer by graphing $y = 4x$ and your equation.

4. Write an equation whose graph lies between the graphs of $y = x$ and $y = 2x$. Check your answer by graphing the equations.

5. Write a description of this family of graphs. What characteristics do the graphs have in common? How are they different?

6. The equations whose graphs are in this family are all of the form $y = mx$. How does the graph change as the absolute value of m increases?
   As |m| increases, the graph becomes more steep.

 www.algebra1.com/extra_examples

Lesson 5-2 Slope and Direct Variation **265**

Graphing Calculator Investigation

Family of Graphs Graphing calculators are ideal for studying families of graphs. The **Y=** screen allows students to enter many functions so they can experiment while investigating Questions 3 and 4.

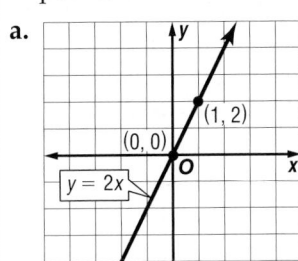
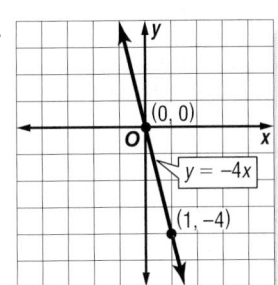

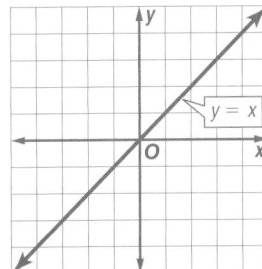
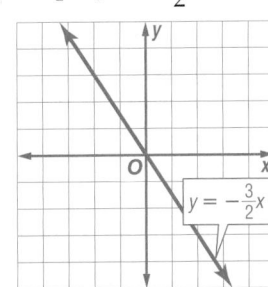

Teaching Tip Be sure students do not interchange the values of *x* and *y* when substituting values into an equation.

4 Suppose *y* varies directly as *x*, and *y* = 9 when *x* = −3.

a. Write a direct variation equation that relates *x* and *y*.
$y = -3x$

b. Use the direct variation equation to find *x* when *y* = 15. **−5**

SOLVE PROBLEMS

In-Class Example   Power Point®

5 **TRAVEL** The Ramirez family is driving cross-country on vacation. They drive 330 miles in 5.5 hours.

a. Write a direct variation equation to find the distance driven for any number of hours. $d = 60t$

b. Graph the equation.

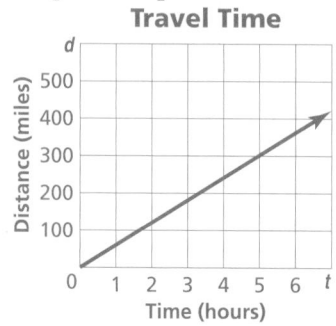

Travel Time

c. Estimate how many hours it would take to drive 600 miles.
10 h

- Direct variation equations are of the form $y = kx$, where $k \neq 0$.
- The graph of $y = kx$ always passes through the origin.

• The slope can be positive. $k > 0$	• The slope can be negative. $k < 0$
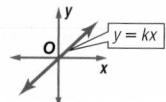	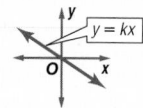

If you know that *y* varies directly as *x*, you can write a direct variation equation that relates the two quantities.

Example 4 *Write and Solve a Direct Variation Equation*

Suppose *y* varies directly as *x*, and *y* = 28 when *x* = 7.

a. Write a direct variation equation that relates *x* and *y*.

Find the value of *k*.

$y = kx$ Direct variation formula

$28 = k(7)$ Replace *y* with 28 and *x* with 7.

$\dfrac{28}{7} = \dfrac{k(7)}{7}$ Divide each side by 7.

$4 = k$ Simplify.

Therefore, $y = 4x$.

b. Use the direct variation equation to find *x* when *y* = 52.

$y = 4x$ Direct variation equation

$52 = 4x$ Replace *y* with 52.

$\dfrac{52}{4} = \dfrac{4x}{4}$ Divide each side by 4.

$13 = x$ Simplify.

Therefore, $x = 13$ when $y = 52$.

SOLVE PROBLEMS One of the most common uses of direct variation is the formula for distance, $d = rt$. In the formula, distance *d* varies directly as time *t*, and the rate *r* is the constant of variation.

Example 5 *Direct Variation Equation*

BIOLOGY A flock of snow geese migrated 375 miles in 7.5 hours.

a. Write a direct variation equation for the distance flown in any time.

Words   The distance traveled is 375 miles, and the time is 7.5 hours.

Variables   Let *r* = rate.

	Distance	equals	rate	times	time.
Equation	375 mi	=	*r*	×	7.5 h

Solve for the rate.

$375 = r(7.5)$ Original equation

$\dfrac{375}{7.5} = \dfrac{r(7.5)}{7.5}$ Divide each side by 7.5.

$50 = r$ Simplify.

Therefore, the direct variation equation is $d = 50t$.

More About. . .

Biology •

Snow geese migrate more than 3000 miles from their winter home in the southwest United States to their summer home in the Canadian arctic.

Source: Audubon Society

DAILY
INTERVENTION   **Differentiated Instruction**

Interpersonal Have small groups of students use a triple-beam balance and 4 stacks of identical washers. Each stack should contain a different number of washers tied together so students cannot weigh just one washer. Record the number of washers *n* in each stack. Have students weigh one stack and then predict the weights *W* of the other stacks. How do they think this relates to the equation $W = kn$? **See students' work.** What does *k* represent? **the weight of each washer**

b. Graph the equation.

The graph of $d = 50t$ passes through the origin with slope 50.

$$m = \frac{50}{1} \quad \frac{rise}{run}$$

c. Estimate how many hours of flying time it would take the geese to migrate 3000 miles.

$d = 50t$	Original equation
$3000 = 50t$	Replace d with 3000.
$\dfrac{3000}{50} = \dfrac{50t}{50}$	Divide each side by 50.
$t = 60$	Simplify.

At this rate, it will take 60 hours of flying time to migrate 3000 miles.

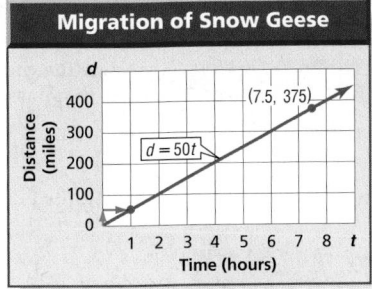

Migration of Snow Geese

(7.5, 375)

$d = 50t$

Distance (miles)

Time (hours)

Check for Understanding

Concept Check

2. b, constant of variation = 4;
c, constant of variation = $\frac{1}{3}$

1. **OPEN ENDED** Write a general equation for y varies directly as x. $y = kx$

2. **Choose** the equations that represent direct variations. Then find the constant of variation for each direct variation.

   a. $15 = rs$ **b.** $4a = b$ **c.** $z = \frac{1}{3}x$ **d.** $s = \frac{9}{t}$

3. **Explain** how the constant of variation and the slope are related in a direct variation equation. **They are equal.**

Guided Practice

Name the constant of variation for each equation. Then determine the slope of the line that passes through each pair of points.

GUIDED PRACTICE KEY	
Exercises	Examples
4–8	1–3
9–11	4
12–14	5

4.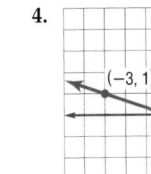
(−3, 1)
(0, 0)
$y = -\frac{1}{3}x$
 $-\frac{1}{3}, -\frac{1}{3}$

5.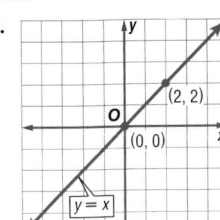
(2, 2)
(0, 0)
$y = x$
 1; 1

Graph each equation. **6–8. See margin.**

6. $y = 2x$ 7. $y = -3x$ 8. $y = \frac{1}{2}x$

Write a direct variation equation that relates x and y. Assume that y varies directly as x. Then solve.

9. If $y = 27$ when $x = 6$, find x when $y = 45$. $y = \frac{9}{2}x$; 10

10. $y = \frac{10}{9}x$; 8.1

10. If $y = 10$ when $x = 9$, find x when $y = 9$.

11. If $y = -7$ when $x = -14$, find y when $x = 20$. $y = \frac{1}{2}x$; 10

Application

JOBS For Exercises 12–14, use the following information.
Suppose you work at a job where your pay varies directly as the number of hours you work. Your pay for 7.5 hours is $45.

12. Write a direct variation equation relating your pay to the hours worked. $y = 6x$

13. Graph the equation. **See margin.**

14. Find your pay if you work 30 hours. **$180**

Lesson 5-2 Slope and Direct Variation **267**

6.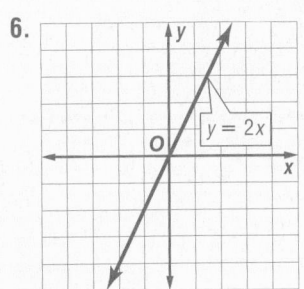
$y = 2x$

7.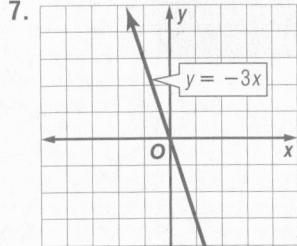
$y = -3x$

8.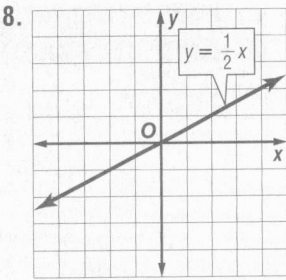
$y = \frac{1}{2}x$

13.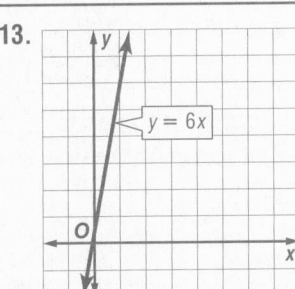
$y = 6x$

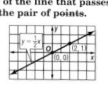 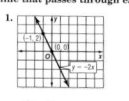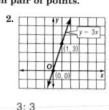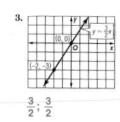
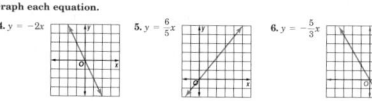
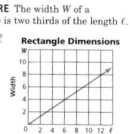
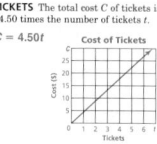
Practice and Apply

Name the constant of variation for each equation. Then determine the slope of the line that passes through each pair of points.

15. 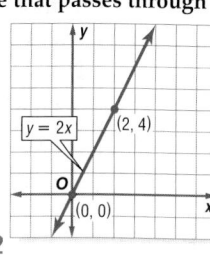   16. 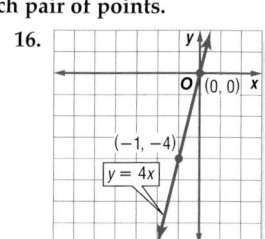   17.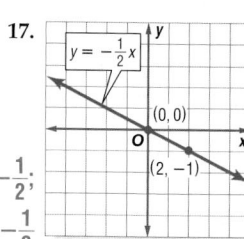

2; 2   4; 4 $-\frac{1}{2}; -\frac{1}{2}$

18. 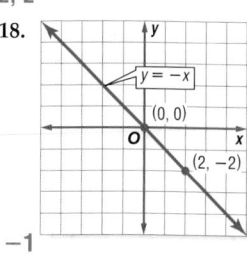   19. 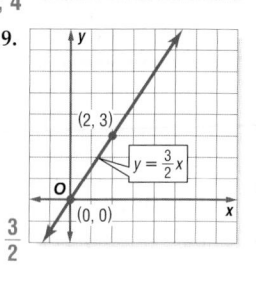   20.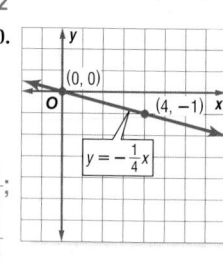

$-1; -1$ $\frac{3}{2}; \frac{3}{2}$ $-\frac{1}{4}; -\frac{1}{4}$

Graph each equation. 21–32. See pp. 315A–315B.

21. $y = x$ 22. $y = 3x$ 23. $y = -x$ 24. $y = -4x$

25. $y = \frac{1}{4}x$ 26. $y = \frac{3}{5}x$ 27. $y = \frac{5}{2}x$ 28. $y = \frac{7}{5}x$

29. $y = \frac{1}{5}x$ 30. $y = -\frac{2}{3}x$ 31. $y = -\frac{4}{3}x$ 32. $y = -\frac{9}{2}x$

Write a direct variation equation that relates x and y. Assume that y varies directly as x. Then solve.

33. If $y = 8$ when $x = 4$, find y when $x = 5$. $y = 2x; 10$

34. If $y = 36$ when $x = 6$, find x when $y = 42$. $y = 6x; 7$

35. If $y = -16$ when $x = 4$, find x when $y = 20$. $y = -4x; -5$

36. If $y = -18$ when $x = 6$, find x when $y = 6$. $y = -3x; -2$

37. If $y = 4$ when $x = 12$, find y when $x = -24$. $y = \frac{1}{3}x; -8$

38. If $y = 12$ when $x = 15$, find x when $y = 21$. $y = \frac{4}{5}x; 26.25$

39. If $y = 2.5$ when $x = 0.5$, find y when $x = 20$. $y = 5x; 100$

40. If $y = -6.6$ when $x = 9.9$, find y when $x = 6.6$. $y = -\frac{2}{3}x; -4.4$

41. If $y = 2\frac{2}{3}$ when $x = \frac{1}{4}$, find x when $y = 1\frac{1}{8}$. $y = \frac{32}{3}x; 12$

42. If $y = 6$ when $x = \frac{2}{3}$, find x when $y = 12$. $y = 9x; \frac{4}{3}$

Write a direct variation equation that relates the variables. Then graph the equation.

43–46. See margin for graphs.

43. $C = 3.14d$

45. $C = 0.99n$

46. $C = 14.49p$

43. **GEOMETRY** The circumference C of a circle is about 3.14 times the diameter d.

44. **GEOMETRY** The perimeter P of a square is 4 times the length of a side s. $P = 4s$

45. **SEWING** The total cost is C for n yards of ribbon priced at $0.99 per yard.

46. **RETAIL** Kona coffee beans are $14.49 per pound. The total cost of p pounds is C.

47. It also doubles. If $\frac{y}{x} = k$, and x is multiplied by 2, y must also be multiplied by 2 to maintain the value of k.

47. CRITICAL THINKING Suppose y varies directly as x. If the value of x is doubled, what happens to the value of y? Explain.

BIOLOGY Which line in the graph represents the sprinting speeds of each animal?

48. elephant, 25 mph **4**

49. reindeer, 32 mph **2**

50. lion, 50 mph **1**

51. grizzly bear, 30 mph **3**

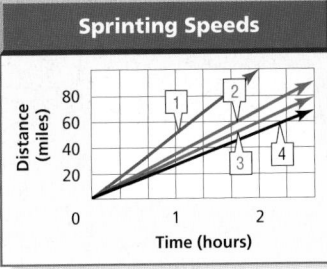
Sprinting Speeds

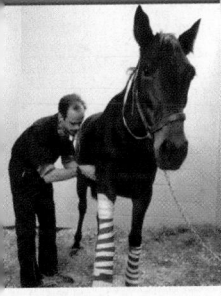

SPACE For Exercises 52 and 53, use the following information.
The weight of an object on the moon varies directly with its weight on Earth. With all of his equipment, astronaut Neil Armstrong weighed 360 pounds on Earth, but weighed only 60 pounds on the moon. **52.** $m = \frac{1}{6}e$

52. Write an equation that relates weight on the moon m with weight on Earth e.

53. Suppose you weigh 138 pounds on Earth. What would you weigh on the moon? **23 lb**

ANIMALS For Exercises 54 and 55, use the following information.
Most animals age more rapidly than humans do. The chart shows equivalent ages for horses and humans.

Horse age (x)	0	1	2	3	4	5
Human age (y)	0	3	6	9	12	15

54. Write an equation that relates human age to horse age. $y = 3x$

55. Find the equivalent horse age for a human who is 16 years old. **5 yr 4 mo**

56. WRITING IN MATH   Answer the question that was posed at the beginning of the lesson. **See margin.**

How is slope related to your shower?

Include the following in your answer:
• an equation that relates the number of gallons y to the time spent in the shower x for a low-flow showerhead that uses only 2.5 gallons of water per minute, and
• a comparison of the steepness of the graph of this equation to the graph at the top of page 264.

60. They all pass through (0, 0), but these have negative slopes.

57. Which equation best describes the graph at the right? **D**
Ⓐ $y = 2x$
Ⓑ $y = -2x$
Ⓒ $y = \frac{1}{2}x$
Ⓓ $y = -\frac{1}{2}x$

58. Which equation does *not* model a direct variation? **C**
Ⓐ $y = 4x$
Ⓑ $y = 22x$
Ⓒ $y = 3x + 1$
Ⓓ $y = \frac{1}{2}x$

FAMILIES OF GRAPHS For Exercises 59–62, use the graphs of $y = -1x$, $y = -2x$, and $y = -4x$, which form a family of graphs.

59. Graph $y = -1x$, $y = -2x$, and $y = -4x$ on the same screen. **See margin.**

60. How are these graphs similar to the graphs in the Graphing Calculator Investigation on page 265? How are they different?

Answers

43.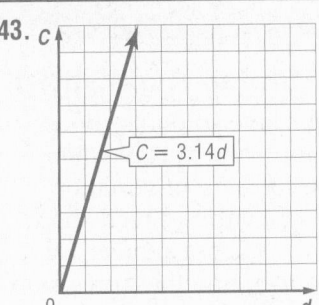
$C = 3.14d$

44.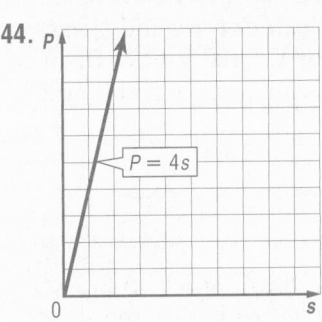
$P = 4s$

45.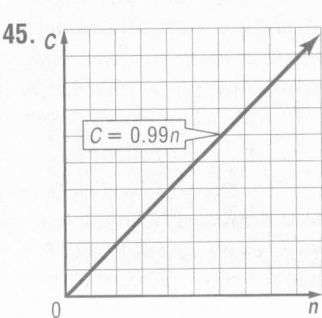
$C = 0.99n$

46.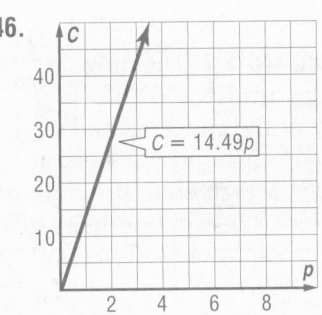
$C = 14.49p$

56. The slope of the equation that relates time and water use is the number of gallons used per minute in the shower. Answers should include the following.
• $y = 2.5x$
• Less steep; the slope is less than the slope of the graph on page 268.

59.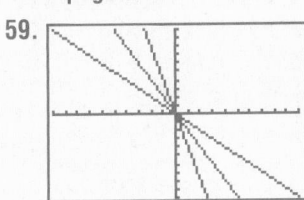

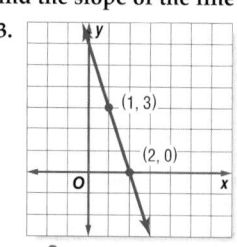

4 Assess

Open-Ended Assessment

Writing Have students choose values for y and x. Have them find the constant of variation, assuming y varies directly as x. Have them choose another value of x and then find the corresponding value of y. Next, have students choose values for y and k, and solve for x. Finally, have them choose values for x and k, and solve for y.

Getting Ready for Lesson 5-3

PREREQUISITE SKILL In Lesson 5-3, students identify the slope and y-intercept from an equation written in the form $y = mx + b$. To rewrite some equations in this form, students must be able to solve a linear equation for y. Exercises 73–78 can be used to determine if students need additional review in solving equations for a given variable.

Assessment Options

Practice Quiz 1 The quiz provides students with a brief review of the concepts and skills in Lessons 5-1 and 5-2. Lesson numbers are given to the right of exercises or instruction lines so students can review concepts not yet mastered.

Quiz (Lessons 5-1 and 5-2) is available on p. 337 of the *Chapter 5 Resource Masters*.

Answers

62. Sample answer: Find the absolute value of k in each equation. The one with the greatest value of $|k|$ has the steeper slope.

---

61. Sample answer: $y = -5x$

61. Write an equation whose graph has a steeper slope than $y = -4x$.

62. MAKE A CONJECTURE Explain how you can tell without graphing which of two direct variation equations has the graph with a steeper slope. **See margin.**

Maintain Your Skills

Mixed Review Find the slope of the line that passes through each pair of points. *(Lesson 5-1)*

63.
-3

64.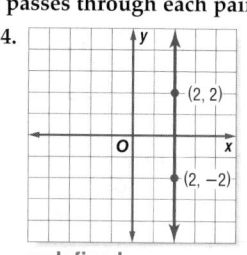
undefined

65.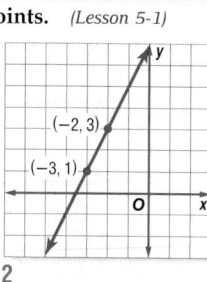
2

66. Find the value of r so that the line that passes through $(1, 7)$ and $(r, 3)$ has a slope of 2. *(Lesson 5-1)* -1

Each table below represents points on a linear graph. Copy and complete each table. *(Lesson 4-8)*

67.

x	0	1	2	3	4	5
y	1	5	9	13	17	21

68.

x	2	4	6	8	10	12
y	8	6	4	2	0	-2

Add or subtract. *(Lesson 2-2)*

69. $15 + (-12)$ **3**   **70.** $8 - (-5)$ **13**   **71.** $-9 - 6$ **-15**   **72.** $-18 - 12$ **-30**

Getting Ready for the Next Lesson

PREREQUISITE SKILL Solve each equation for y.
*(To review **rewriting equations**, see Lesson 3-8.)* **73.** $y = 3x + 8$ **74.** $y = -2x + 7$

73. $-3x + y = 8$ **74.** $2x + y = 7$ **75.** $4x = y + 3$ $y = 4x - 3$

76. $2y = 4x + 10$ **77.** $9x + 3y = 12$ **78.** $x - 2y = 5$ $y = \dfrac{x - 5}{2}$
$y = 2x + 5$ $y = -3x + 4$

Practice Quiz 1   Lessons 5-1 and 5-2

Find the slope of the line that passes through each pair of points. *(Lesson 5-1)*

1. $(-4, -6), (-3, -8)$ **-2** **2.** $(8, 3), (-11, 3)$ **0** **3.** $(-4, 8), (5, 9)$ $\dfrac{1}{9}$ **4.** $(0, 1), (7, 11)$ $\dfrac{10}{7}$

Find the value of r so the line that passes through each pair of points has the given slope. *(Lesson 5-1)*

5. $(5, -3), (r, -5), m = 2$ **4**   **6.** $(6, r), (-4, 9), m = \dfrac{3}{2}$ **24**

Graph each equation. *(Lesson 5-2)* **7–8. See margin.**

7. $y = -7x$ **8.** $y = \dfrac{3}{4}x$

Write a direct variation equation that relates x and y. Assume that y varies directly as x. Then solve. *(Lesson 5-2)* **9.** $y = 3x; -9$ **10.** $y = -\dfrac{2}{3}x; 9$

9. If $y = 24$ when $x = 8$, find y when $x = -3$.   **10.** If $y = -10$ when $x = 15$, find x when $y = -6$.

7.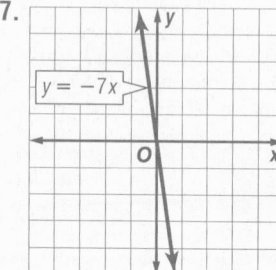

8.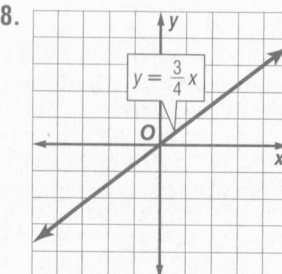

Algebra Activity
A Preview of Lesson 5-3

Investigating Slope-Intercept Form

Collect the Data
- Cut a small hole in a top corner of a plastic sandwich bag. Loop a long rubber band through the hole.
- Tape the free end of the rubber band to the desktop.
- Use a centimeter ruler to measure the distance from the desktop to the end of the bag. Record this distance for 0 washers in the bag using a table like the one below.

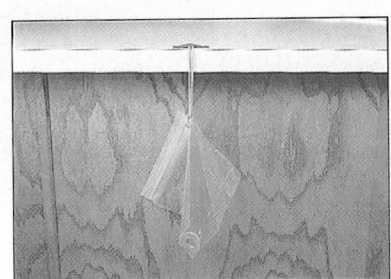

Number of Washers x	Distance y
0	
1	

- Place one washer in the plastic bag. Then measure and record the new distance from the desktop to the end of the bag.
- Repeat the experiment, adding different numbers of washers to the bag. Each time, record the number of washers and the distance from the desktop to the end of the bag.

Analyze the Data
1. The domain contains values represented by the independent variable, washers. The range contains values represented by the dependent variable, distance. On grid paper, graph the ordered pairs (washers, distance). **See students' work.**

2. Write a sentence that describes the points on the graph. **Sample answer: It is a linear pattern.**

3. Describe the point that represents the trial with no washers in the bag. **It is the y-intercept.**

4. The rate of change can be found by using the formula for slope.

$$\frac{rise}{run} = \frac{change\ in\ distance}{change\ in\ number\ of\ washers}$$

Find the rate of change in the distance from the desktop to the end of the bag as more washers are added. **See students' work. Sample answer: 1.5**

5. Explain how the rate of change is shown on the graph.
The slope represents the rate of change.

Make a Conjecture 6–8. See pp. 315A–315B.

The graph shows sample data from a rubber band experiment. Draw a graph for each situation.

6. A bag that hangs 10.5 centimeters from the desktop when empty and lengthens at the rate of the sample.

7. A bag that has the same length when empty as the sample and lengthens at a faster rate.

8. A bag that has the same length when empty as the sample and lengthens at a slower rate.

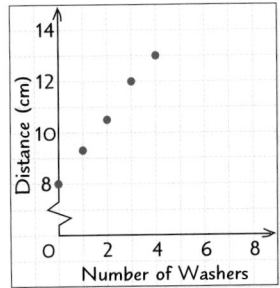

Distance (cm) vs Number of Washers

Algebra Activity Investigating Slope-Intercept Form **271**

A Preview of Lesson 5-3

Getting Started

Objective To discover the linear relationship between the length of a rubber band and the number of washers hanging from the rubber band.

Materials
plastic sandwich bag
long rubber band   scissors
tape   grid paper
centimeter ruler   washers

Teach

- You may want to show students how to measure carefully and accurately with the centimeter ruler.
- Urge students to work logically, recording their data carefully. One careless recording will prevent students from seeing a pattern.
- Ask students to find a rule that gives "directions" for how to get from one point to the next on the graph (i.e., up how many units, right how many units).

Assess

In **Exercises 1–5**, students should
- discover that the graphed points form a linear pattern
- find the rate of change
- understand that the rate of change is the slope of the line connecting the points.

Resource Manager

📁 **Teaching Algebra with Manipulatives**
- p. 1 (master for grid paper)
- p. 98 (student recording sheet)

Glencoe Mathematics Classroom Manipulative Kit
- rulers
- tape measures

Study Notebook
You may wish to have students summarize this activity and what they learned from it.

5-3 Lesson Notes

1 Focus

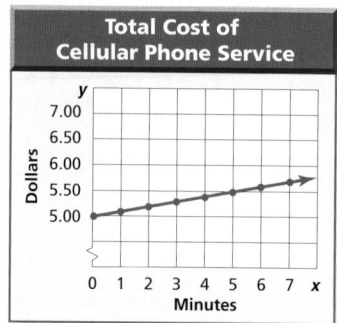

5-Minute Check Transparency 5-3 Use as a quiz or review of Lesson 5-2.

Mathematical Background notes are available for this lesson on p. 254C.

How is a *y*-intercept related to a flat fee?

Ask students:

- Does this line have a positive slope or a negative slope? **positive**

- What do *x* and *y* represent in the equation $y = 0.1x + 5$? **x is the number of minutes, and y is the total amount spent for cellular service.**

- **Banking** One of the checking plans offered by a local bank includes a $10 monthly service fee and $0.20 per check or withdrawal for accounts with an average daily balance of less than $2000. What equation describes this plan? **Sample answer:** $P = 0.20c + 10$

5-3 Slope-Intercept Form

What You'll Learn

- Write and graph linear equations in slope-intercept form.
- Model real-world data with an equation in slope-intercept form.

Vocabulary
- slope-intercept form

How is a *y*-intercept related to a flat fee?

A cellular phone service provider charges $0.10 per minute plus a flat fee of $5.00 each month.

x (minutes)	y (dollars)
0	5.00
1	5.10
2	5.20
3	5.30
4	5.40
5	5.50
6	5.60
7	5.70

Total Cost of Cellular Phone Service

The slope of the line is 0.1. It crosses the *y*-axis at (0, 5). The equation of the line is $y = 0.1x + 5$.

charge per minute, $0.10 ⌐   ⌐ flat fee, $5.00

TEACHING TIP
Point out that the *y*-intercept is the value on the *y*-axis where the line crosses that axis.

Study Tip

Look Back
To review **intercepts**, see Lesson 4-5.

SLOPE-INTERCEPT FORM An equation of the form $y = mx + b$ is in **slope-intercept form**. When an equation is written in this form, you can identify the slope and *y*-intercept of its graph.

Key Concept   Slope-Intercept Form

- **Words** The linear equation $y = mx + b$ is written in slope-intercept form, where *m* is the slope and *b* is the *y*-intercept.

- **Model**

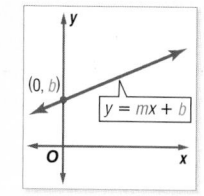

- **Symbols** $y = mx + b$
  slope ⌐   ⌐ y-intercept

Example 1 Write an Equation Given Slope and y-Intercept

Write an equation of the line whose slope is 3 and whose *y*-intercept is 5.

$y = mx + b$ Slope-intercept form

$y = 3x + 5$ Replace *m* with 3 and *b* with 5.

Resource Manager

📁 Workbook and Reproducible Masters

Chapter 5 Resource Masters
- Study Guide and Intervention, pp. 293–294
- Skills Practice, p. 295
- Practice, p. 296
- Reading to Learn Mathematics, p. 297
- Enrichment, p. 298

Parent and Student Study Guide Workbook, p. 40
School-to-Career Masters, p. 9

🖥 Transparencies

5-Minute Check Transparency 5-3
Real-World Transparency 5
Answer Key Transparencies

💿 Technology

Interactive Chalkboard
Multimedia Applications

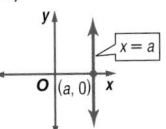
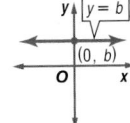
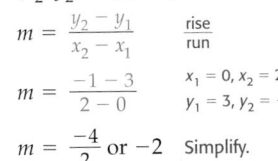

Example 2 Write an Equation Given Two Points

Write an equation of the line shown in the graph.

Step 1 You know the coordinates of two points on the line. Find the slope. Let $(x_1, y_1) = (0, 3)$ and $(x_2, y_2) = (2, -1)$.

$$m = \frac{y_2 - y_1}{x_2 - x_1} \qquad \frac{\text{rise}}{\text{run}}$$

$$m = \frac{-1 - 3}{2 - 0} \qquad \begin{array}{l} x_1 = 0, x_2 = 2 \\ y_1 = 3, y_2 = -1 \end{array}$$

$$m = \frac{-4}{2} \text{ or } -2 \quad \text{Simplify.}$$

The slope is -2.

Step 2 The line crosses the *y*-axis at $(0, 3)$. So, the *y*-intercept is 3.

Step 3 Finally, write the equation.

$$y = mx + b \qquad \text{Slope-intercept form}$$

$$y = -2x + 3 \qquad \text{Replace } m \text{ with } -2 \text{ and } b \text{ with 3.}$$

The equation of the line is $y = -2x + 3$.

One advantage of the slope-intercept form is that it allows you to graph an equation quickly.

Example 3 Graph an Equation in Slope-Intercept Form

Graph $y = -\frac{2}{3}x + 1$.

Step 1 The *y*-intercept is 1. So, graph $(0, 1)$.

Step 2 The slope is $-\frac{2}{3}$ or $\frac{-2}{3}$. $\frac{\text{rise}}{\text{run}}$

From $(0, 1)$, move down 2 units and right 3 units. Draw a dot.

Step 3 Draw a line connecting the points.

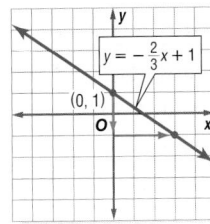

Example 4 Graph an Equation in Standard Form

Graph $5x - 3y = 6$.

Step 1 Solve for *y* to find the slope-intercept form.

$$5x - 3y = 6 \qquad \text{Original equation}$$

$$5x - 3y - 5x = 6 - 5x \qquad \text{Subtract } 5x \text{ from each side.}$$

$$-3y = 6 - 5x \qquad \text{Simplify.}$$

$$-3y = -5x + 6 \qquad 6 - 5x = 6 + (-5x) \text{ or } -5x + 6$$

$$\frac{-3y}{-3} = \frac{-5x + 6}{-3} \qquad \text{Divide each side by } -3.$$

$$\frac{-3y}{-3} = \frac{-5x}{-3} + \frac{6}{-3} \qquad \text{Divide each term in the numerator by } -3.$$

$$y = \frac{5}{3}x - 2 \qquad \text{Simplify.}$$

(continued on the next page)

www.algebra1.com/extra_examples

Lesson 5-3 Slope-Intercept Form 273

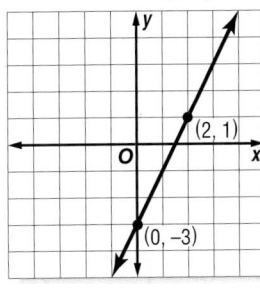
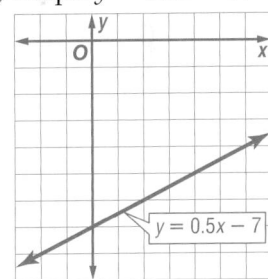
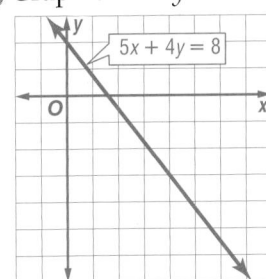

MODEL
REAL-WORLD DATA

In-Class Example Power Point®

5 **HEALTH** The ideal maximum heart rate for a 25-year-old who is exercising to burn fat is 117 beats per minute. For every 5 years older than 25, that ideal rate drops 3 beats per minute.

a. Write a linear equation to find the ideal maximum heart rate for anyone over 25 who is exercising to burn fat.

$R = -\frac{3}{5}a + 117$, where R is the ideal heart rate and a is the number of years older than 25

b. Graph the equation.

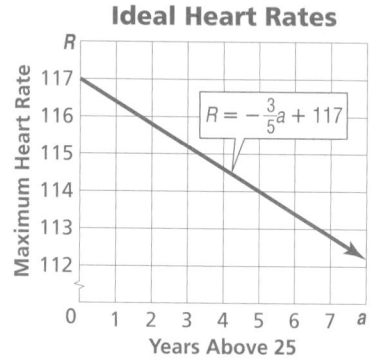

Ideal Heart Rates

$R = -\frac{3}{5}a + 117$

(y-axis: Maximum Heart Rate, 112–117; x-axis: Years Above 25, 0–7, labeled a)

c. Find the ideal maximum heart rate for a person exercising to burn fat who is 55 years old.

99 beats per minute

Step 2 The y-intercept of $y = \frac{5}{3}x - 2$ is -2. So, graph $(0, -2)$.

Step 3 The slope is $\frac{5}{3}$. From $(0, -2)$, move up 5 units and right 3 units. Draw a dot.

Step 4 Draw a line containing the points.

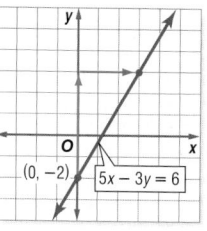

$(0, -2)$ $5x - 3y = 6$

MODEL REAL-WORLD DATA If a quantity changes at a constant rate over time, it can be modeled by a linear equation. The y-intercept represents a starting point, and the slope represents the rate of change.

Example 5 *Write an Equation in Slope-Intercept Form*

AGRICULTURE The natural sweeteners used in foods include sugar, corn sweeteners, syrup, and honey. Use the information at the left about natural sweeteners.

a. The amount of natural sweeteners consumed has increased by an average of 2.6 pounds per year. Write a linear equation to find the average consumption of natural sweeteners in any year after 1989.

Words The consumption increased 2.6 pounds per year, so the rate of change is 2.6 pounds per year. In the first year, the average consumption was 133 pounds.

Variables Let C = average consumption.
Let n = number of years after 1989.

Equation

Average consumption	equals	rate of change	times	number of years after 1989	plus	amount at start.
C	$=$	2.6	$\cdot$	n	$+$	133

b. Graph the equation.

The graph passes through $(0, 133)$ with slope 2.6.

c. Find the number of pounds of natural sweeteners consumed by each person in 1999.

The year 1999 is 10 years after 1989. So, $n = 10$.

$C = 2.6n + 133$ Consumption equation
$C = 2.6(10) + 133$ Replace n with 10.
$C = 159$ Simplify.

So, the average person consumed 159 pounds of natural sweeteners in 1999.

CHECK Notice that $(10, 159)$ lies on the graph.

Consumption of Natural Sweeteners

(y-axis: Pounds, 130–160; x-axis: Years Since 1989, 0–10, labeled n)
$(10, 159)$
$C = 2.6n + 133$

More About . . .

Agriculture •

In 1989, each person in the United States consumed an average of 133 pounds of natural sweeteners.
Source: USDA *Agricultural Outlook*

DAILY
INTERVENTION   **Differentiated Instruction**   **ELL**

Visual/Spatial Word problems may be difficult for visual learners because they cannot picture what the problem is trying to communicate. Sometimes it is easier for a visual learner to graph or draw a picture of the given information before they can write the equation. In In-Class Example 5, you may wish to do part **b** first by using the starting point and the rate of change to determine other points on the graph. Then write the equation that describes the line formed.

Concept Check

1. Sample answer:
   $y = 7x + 2$

1. **OPEN ENDED** Write an equation for a line with a slope of 7.

2. **Explain** why equations of vertical lines cannot be written in slope-intercept form, but equations of horizontal lines can.

3. **Tell** which part of the slope-intercept form represents the rate of change. **slope**

2. Vertical lines have undefined slope. Horizontal lines have a slope of 0.

Guided Practice

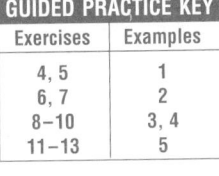

GUIDED PRACTICE KEY	
Exercises	Examples
4, 5	1
6, 7	2
8–10	3, 4
11–13	5

Write an equation of the line with the given slope and y-intercept.

4. slope: -3, y-intercept: 1 $y = -3x + 1$ 5. slope: 4, y-intercept: -2 $y = 4x - 2$

Write an equation of the line shown in each graph.

6.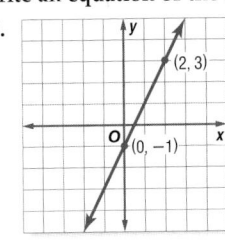

$y = 2x - 1$

7.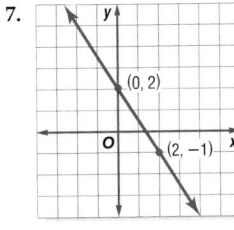

$y = -\frac{3}{2}x + 2$

Graph each equation. 8–10. See margin.

8. $y = 2x - 3$ 9. $y = -3x + 1$ 10. $2x + y = 5$

Application

MONEY For Exercises 11–13, use the following information.
Suppose you have already saved $50 toward the cost of a new television set. You plan to save $5 more each week for the next several weeks. 11. $T = 50 + 5w$

11. Write an equation for the total amount T you will have w weeks from now.

12. Graph the equation. **See margin.**

13. Find the total amount saved after 7 weeks. **$85**

Practice and Apply

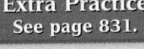

Homework Help	
For Exercises	See Examples
14–19	1
20–27	2
28–39	3, 4
40–43	5

Extra Practice
See page 831.

20. $y = 3x + 1$

21. $y = \frac{3}{2}x - 4$

22. $y = -4x + 2$

Write an equation of the line with the given slope and y-intercept.

14. slope: 2, y-intercept: -6 $y = 2x - 6$ 15. slope: 3, y-intercept: -5 $y = 3x - 5$

16. slope: $\frac{1}{2}$, y-intercept: 3 $y = \frac{1}{2}x + 3$ 17. slope: $-\frac{3}{5}$, y-intercept: 0 $y = -\frac{3}{5}x$

18. slope: -1, y-intercept: 10
    $y = -x + 10$

19. slope: 0.5; y-intercept: 7.5
    $y = 0.5x + 7.5$

Write an equation of the line shown in each graph.

20.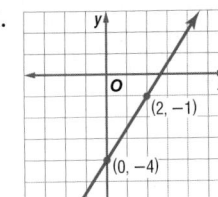

21.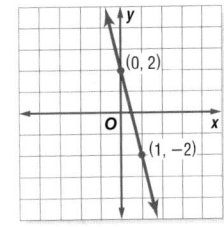

22.

www.algebra1.com/self_check_quiz

Study Notebook

Have students—
• add the definitions/examples of the vocabulary terms to their Vocabulary Builder worksheets for Chapter 5.
• include any other item(s) that they find helpful in mastering the skills in this lesson.

About the Exercises...

Organization by Objective
• Slope-Intercept Form: 14–39
• Model Real-World Data: 40–43, 45–49

Odd/Even Assignments
Exercises 14–39 are structured so that students practice the same concepts whether they are assigned odd or even problems.

Assignment Guide
Basic: 15–43 odd, 44–46, 50–52, 56–67

Average: 15–43 odd, 44–46, 50–52, 56–67 (optional: 53–55)

Advanced: 14–42 even, 44–64 (optional: 65–67)

Answer

12.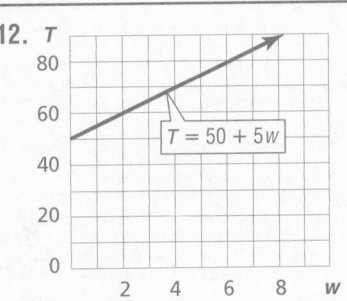

8.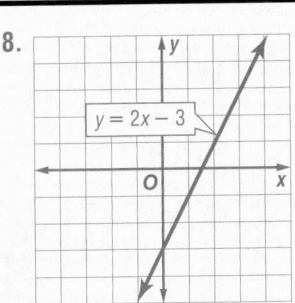

9.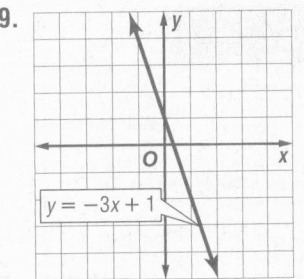

10.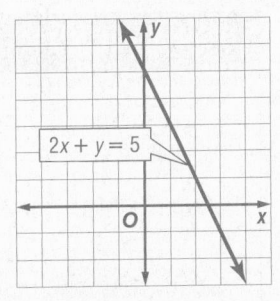

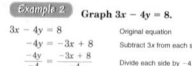

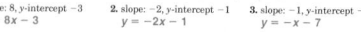
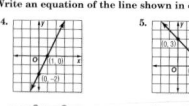 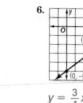

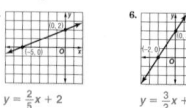 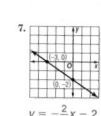
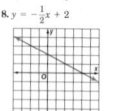 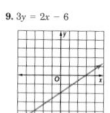 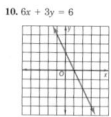
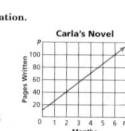
Write an equation of the line shown in each graph.

23.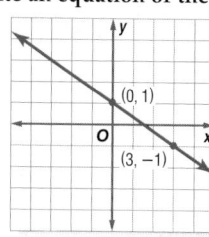
(0, 1)
(3, −1)
$y = -\frac{2}{3}x + 1$

24.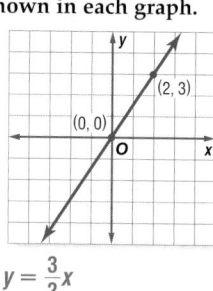
(2, 3)
(0, 0)
$y = \frac{3}{2}x$

25.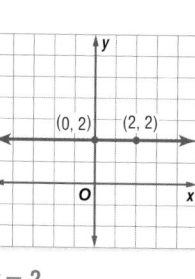
(0, 2)   (2, 2)
$y = 2$

26. Write an equation of a horizontal line that crosses the y-axis at $(0, -5)$. $y = -5$

27. Write an equation of a line that passes through the origin with slope 3. $y = 3x$

Graph each equation. 28–39. See pp. 315A–315B.

28. $y = 3x + 1$ 29. $y = x - 2$ 30. $y = -4x + 1$
31. $y = -x + 2$ 32. $y = \frac{1}{2}x + 4$ 33. $y = -\frac{1}{3}x - 3$
34. $3x + y = -2$ 35. $2x - y = -3$ 36. $3y = 2x + 3$
37. $-2y = 6x - 4$ 38. $2x + 3y = 6$ 39. $4x - 3y = 3$

Write a linear equation in slope-intercept form to model each situation.

40. You rent a bicycle for $20 plus $2 per hour. $C = 20 + 2t$

41. An auto repair shop charges $50 plus $25 per hour. $C = 50 + 25h$

42. A candle is 6 inches tall and burns at a rate of $\frac{1}{2}$ inch per hour. $H = 6 - \frac{1}{2}t$

43. The temperature is 15° and is expected to fall 2° each hour during the night. $T = 15 - 2h$

44. **CRITICAL THINKING** The equations $y = 2x + 3$, $y = 4x + 3$, $y = -x + 3$, and $y = -10x + 3$ form a family of graphs. What characteristic do their graphs have in common? **They all have a y-intercept of 3.**

SALES For Exercises 45 and 46, use the following information and the graph at the right.
In 1991, book sales in the United States totaled $16 billion. Sales increased by about $1 billion each year until 1999.

45. Write an equation to find the total sales S for any number of years t since 1991. $S = 16 + t$

46. If the trend continues, what will sales be in 2005? **$30 billion**

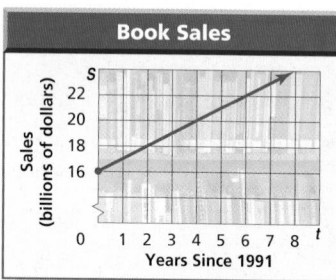

Book Sales

Source: Association of American Publishers

TRAFFIC For Exercises 47–49, use the following information.
In 1966, the traffic fatality rate in the United States was 5.5 fatalities per 100 million vehicle miles traveled. Between 1966 and 1999, the rate decreased by about 0.12 each year.

47. Write an equation to find the fatality rate R for any number of years t since 1966. $R = 5.5 - 0.12t$

48. Graph the equation. **See margin.**

49. Find the fatality rate in 1999. **1.54**

Answer

48. R

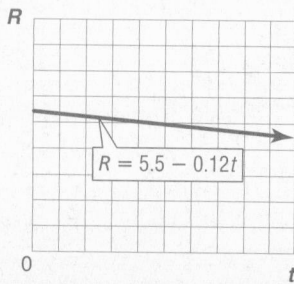

$R = 5.5 - 0.12t$

50. WRITING IN MATH   Answer the question that was posed at the beginning of the lesson. **See margin.**

How is a *y*-intercept related to a flat fee?

Include the following in your answer:
- the point at which the graph would cross the *y*-axis if your cellular phone service provider charges a rate of $0.07 per minute plus a flat fee of $5.99,
- and a description of a situation in which the *y*-intercept of its graph is $25.

Standardized Test Practice

51. Which equation does *not* have a *y*-intercept of 5? **D**

   Ⓐ $2x = y - 5$ Ⓑ $3x + y = 5$

   Ⓒ $y = x + 5$ Ⓓ $2x - y = 5$

52. Which situation below is modeled by the graph? **B**

   Ⓐ You have $100 and plan to spend $5 each week.

   Ⓑ You have $100 and plan to save $5 each week.

   Ⓒ You need $100 for a new CD player and plan to save $5 each week.

   Ⓓ You need $100 for a new CD player and plan to spend $5 each week.

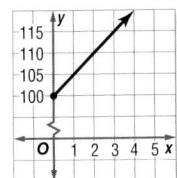

Extending the Lesson

53. The standard form of a linear equation is $Ax + By = C$, where *A*, *B*, and *C* are integers, $A \geq 0$, and *A* and *B* are not both zero. Solve $Ax + By = C$ for *y*. Your answer is written in slope-intercept form.

53. $y = -\dfrac{A}{B}x + \dfrac{C}{B}$, where $B \neq 0$

54. Use the slope-intercept equation in Exercise 53 to write expressions for the slope and *y*-intercept in terms of *A*, *B*, and *C*.

54. $m = -\dfrac{A}{B}$, $b = \dfrac{C}{B}$, where $B \neq 0$

55. Use the expressions in Exercise 54 to find the slope and *y*-intercept of each equation.

   a. $2x + y = -4$ **b.** $3x + 4y = 12$ **c.** $2x - 3y = 9$

     $m = -2, b = -4$ $m = -\dfrac{3}{4}, b = 3$ $m = \dfrac{2}{3}, b = -3$

Maintain Your Skills

Mixed Review   Write a direct variation equation that relates *x* and *y*. Assume that *y* varies directly as *x*. Then solve.   *(Lesson 5-2)*

56. If $y = 45$ when $x = 60$, find *x* when $y = 8$. $y = \dfrac{3}{4}x$, $10\dfrac{2}{3}$

57. If $y = 15$ when $x = 4$, find *y* when $x = 10$. $y = \dfrac{15}{4}x$, $37\dfrac{1}{2}$

Find the slope of the line that passes through each pair of points.   *(Lesson 5-1)*

58. $(-3, 0), (-4, 6)$ **−6**   **59.** $(3, -1), (3, -4)$ **undefined**   **60.** $(5, -5), (9, 2)$ $\dfrac{7}{4}$

61. $-0.5, \dfrac{3}{4}, \dfrac{7}{8}, 2.5$

61. Write the numbers $2.5, \dfrac{3}{4}, -0.5, \dfrac{7}{8}$ in order from least to greatest.   *(Lesson 2-7)*

Solve each equation.   *(Lesson 1-3)*

62. $x = \dfrac{15 - 9}{2}$ **3**   **63.** $3(7) + 2 = b$ **23**   **64.** $q = 6^2 - 2^2$ **32**

Getting Ready for the Next Lesson   PREREQUISITE SKILL   Find the slope of the line that passes through each pair of points.   *(To review slope, see Lesson 5-1.)*

65. $(-1, 2), (1, -2)$ **−2**   **66.** $(5, 8), (-2, 8)$ **0**   **67.** $(1, -1), (10, -13)$ $-\dfrac{4}{3}$

Lesson 5-3 Slope-Intercept Form   **277**

---

4 Assess

Open-Ended Assessment

Speaking Have students summarize how they can draw the graph of an equation without finding points that satisfy the equation.

Getting Ready for Lesson 5-4

PREREQUISITE SKILL In Lesson 5-1, students found the slope of a line using two points on that line. This same skill is vital in Lesson 5-4, in which students use points on the line to determine the information necessary to write an equation in slope-intercept form. Exercises 65–67 should be used to determine your students' familiarity with finding the slope of a line from two points on that line.

Answer

50. The *y*-intercept is the flat fee in an equation that represents a price. Answers should include the following.
- The graph crosses the *y*-axis at 5.99.
- Sample answer: A mechanic charges $25 plus $40 per hour to work on your car.

Getting Started

Know Your Calculator The graphing calculator has the ability to make the graphs appear differently on the screen. The symbol before each Y= entry shows how the line will appear. Highlight the symbol and press ENTER repeatedly until the line type you want appears.

Standard Viewing Window The standard viewing is selected by pressing ZOOM 6. This is a $[-10, 10]$ by $[-10, 10]$ screen with Xscl and Yscl of 1.

Suppressing Graphs You can keep an equation in the Y= list and have it not appear on the graphing screen by highlighting the = sign and pressing ENTER.

Teach

- Make sure students have cleared or suppressed any equations in the Y= list other than those they wish to graph.

Families of Linear Graphs

A family of people is a group of people related by birth, marriage, or adoption. Recall that a *family of graphs* includes graphs and equations of graphs that have at least one characteristic in common.

Families of linear graphs fall into two categories—those with the same slope and those with the same *y*-intercept. A graphing calculator is a useful tool for studying a group of graphs to determine whether they form a family.

Example 1

Graph $y = x$, $y = x + 4$, and $y = x - 2$ in the standard viewing window. Describe any similarities and differences among the graphs. Write a description of the family.

Enter the equations in the Y= list as Y1, Y2, and Y3. Then graph the equations.

  KEYSTROKES: *Review graphing on pages 224 and 225.*

- The graph of $y = x$ has a slope of 1 and a *y*-intercept of 0.
- The graph of $y = x + 4$ has a slope of 1 and a *y*-intercept of 4.
- The graph of $y = x - 2$ has a slope of 1 and a *y*-intercept of -2.

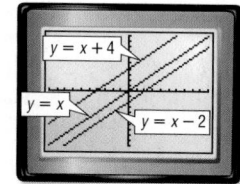

$[-10, 10]$ scl: 1 by $[-10, 10]$ scl: 1

Notice that the graph of $y = x + 4$ is the same as the graph of $y = x$, moved 4 units up. Also, the graph of $y = x - 2$ is the same as the graph of $y = x$, moved 2 units down. All graphs have the same slope and different intercepts.

Because they all have the same slope, this family of graphs can be described as linear graphs with a slope of 1.

Example 2

Graph $y = x + 1$, $y = 2x + 1$, and $y = -\frac{1}{3}x + 1$ in the standard viewing window. Describe any similarities and differences among the graphs. Write a description of the family.

Enter the equations in the Y= list and graph.

- The graph of $y = x + 1$ has a slope of 1 and a *y*-intercept of 1.
- The graph of $y = 2x + 1$ has a slope of 2 and a *y*-intercept of 1.
- The graph of $y = -\frac{1}{3}x + 1$ has a slope of $-\frac{1}{3}$ and a *y*-intercept of 1.

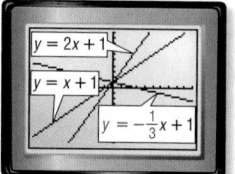

$[-10, 10]$ scl: 1 by $[-10, 10]$ scl: 1

These graphs have the same intercept and different slopes. This family of graphs can be described as linear graphs with a *y*-intercept of 1.

Investigation

Nonlinear functions can also be defined in terms of a family of graphs. Consider the **absolute value function** $y = |x|$, where $y \geq 0$ for all values of x.

Example 3

Graph $y = |x|$, $y = |x| + 2$, and $y = |x + 3|$ in the standard viewing window. Describe any similarities or differences among the graphs.

Enter the equations in the Y= list and graph.

KEYSTROKES: Y= MATH ▶ 1 X,T,θ,n ENTER
MATH ▶ 1 X,T,θ,n)) + 2 ENTER
MATH ▶ 1 X,T,θ,n + 3) ZOOM 6

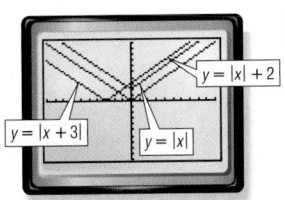

$y = |x| + 2$
$y = |x + 3|$
$y = |x|$

[−10, 10] scl: 1 by [−10, 10] scl: 1

- The graph of $y = |x|$ is v-shaped with its vertex at the origin.
- The graph of $y = |x| + 2$ is v-shaped with its vertex at $(0, 2)$.
- The graph of $y = |x + 3|$ is v-shaped with its vertex at $(-3, 0)$.

These graphs have the same shape, but they are positioned in different places on the coordinate plane.

Exercises

Graph each set of equations on the same screen. Describe any similarities or differences among the graphs. If the graphs are part of the same family, describe the family. 1–6. See pp. 315A–315B. 7–9. See margin.

1. $y = -4$
$y = 0$
$y = 7$

2. $y = -x + 1$
$y = 2x + 1$
$y = \frac{1}{4}x + 1$

3. $y = x + 4$
$y = 2x + 4$
$y = 2x - 4$

4. $y = \frac{1}{2}x + 2$
$y = \frac{1}{3}x + 3$
$y = \frac{1}{4}x + 4$

5. $y = -2x - 2$
$y = 2x - 2$
$y = \frac{1}{2}x - 2$

6. $y = 3x$
$y = 3x + 6$
$y = 3x - 7$

7. $y = |x|$
$y = -3|x|$
$y = |-3x|$

8. $y = |x|$
$y = |x| + 3$
$y = |x| - 2$

9. $y = |x|$
$y = |2x| + 4$
$y = 3|x| - 5$

10. MAKE A CONJECTURE Write a paragraph explaining how the values of m and b in the slope-intercept form affect the graph of a linear equation. **See margin.**

11. Families of graphs are also called **classes of functions**. Describe the similarities and differences in the class of functions $f(x) = x + c$, where c is any real number.

12. Describe the similarities and differences in the classes of functions $f(x) = |x| + c$ and $f(x) = |x + c|$, where c is any real number. **See margin.**

www.algebra1.com/other_calculator_keystrokes

Graphing Calculator Investigation 279

11. This class of functions has graphs that are lines with slope 1. Their y-intercepts are all different.

Answers

10. Sample answer: The value of m determines the steepness and direction of the graph. If the graph has a positive slope, it slants upward from left to right. A graph with a negative slope slants downward from left to right. The greater the absolute value of the slope, the steeper the line. Lines with the same slope are parallel. The value of b determines where the line crosses the y-axis. Lines with the same value of b form a family of lines that intersect at that intercept. The values of b in a family of parallel lines determine how far the lines are apart on the y-axis.

12. The graph of $y = |x| + c$ is the same as the graph of $y = |x|$, translated vertically c units. If c is positive, the translation is up; if c is negative, the translation is down. The graph of $y = |x + c|$ is the same as the graph of $y = |x|$, translated horizontally c units. If c is positive, the translation is to the left; if c is negative, the translation is to the right.

7.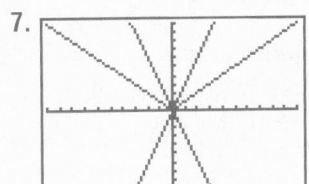

8.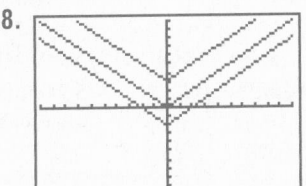

9.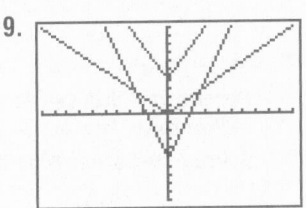

1 *Focus*

5-Minute Check Transparency 5-4 Use as a quiz or review of Lesson 5-3.

Mathematical Background notes are available for this lesson on p. 254D.

How can slope-intercept form be used to make predictions?

Ask students:

• How do you know that the slope is 2000? **The *y* values increase 2000 for each unit on the *x*-axis.**

• What would be the *y* value for *x* = 1997? **179,000**

• **Biology** Suppose a population of bacteria has an average growth of 200 bacteria per hour. Describe the graph that demonstrates the growth pattern of the bacteria. **The line would have a slope of 200 and begin at (0, *p*) where *p* is the initial population.**

5-4 Writing Equations in Slope-Intercept Form

What You'll Learn

• Write an equation of a line given the slope and one point on a line.

• Write an equation of a line given two points on the line.

Vocabulary
• linear extrapolation

How can slope-intercept form be used to make predictions?

In 1995, the population of Orlando, Florida, was about 175,000. At that time, the population was growing at a rate of about 2000 per year.

x (year)	y (population)
⋮	⋮
1994	173,000
1995	175,000
1996	177,000
⋮	⋮

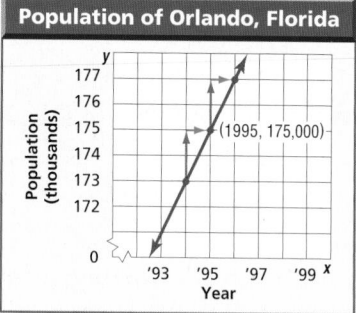

Population of Orlando, Florida

If you could write an equation based on the slope, 2000, and the point (1995, 175,000), you could predict the population for another year.

WRITE AN EQUATION GIVEN THE SLOPE AND ONE POINT You have learned how to write an equation of a line when you know the slope and a specific point, the *y*-intercept. The following example shows how to write an equation when you know the slope and any point on the line.

Example 1 *Write an Equation Given Slope and One Point*

Write an equation of a line that passes through (1, 5) with slope 2.

Step 1 The line has slope 2. To find the *y*-intercept, replace *m* with 2 and (*x, y*) with (1, 5) in the slope-intercept form. Then, solve for *b*.

$$y = mx + b \qquad \text{Slope-intercept form}$$
$$5 = 2(1) + b \qquad \text{Replace } m \text{ with 2, } y \text{ with 5, and } x \text{ with 1.}$$
$$5 = 2 + b \qquad \text{Multiply.}$$
$$5 - 2 = 2 + b - 2 \qquad \text{Subtract 2 from each side.}$$
$$3 = b \qquad \text{Simplify.}$$

Step 2 Write the slope-intercept form using *m* = 2 and *b* = 3.

$$y = mx + b \qquad \text{Slope-intercept form}$$
$$y = 2x + 3 \qquad \text{Replace } m \text{ with 2 and } b \text{ with 3.}$$

Therefore, the equation is $y = 2x + 3$.

Resource Manager

 Workbook and Reproducible Masters

Chapter 5 Resource Masters
• Study Guide and Intervention, pp. 299–300
• Skills Practice, p. 301
• Practice, p. 302
• Reading to Learn Mathematics, p. 303
• Enrichment, p. 304
• Assessment, pp. 337, 339

Parent and Student Study Guide Workbook, p. 41
School-to-Career Masters, p. 10

Transparencies
5-Minute Check Transparency 5-4
Answer Key Transparencies

 Technology
AlgePASS: Tutorial Plus, Lesson 11
Interactive Chalkboard

CHECK You can check your result by graphing $y = 2x + 3$ on a graphing calculator. Use the **CALC** menu to verify that it passes through $(1, 5)$.

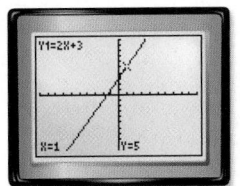

[−10, 10] scl: 1 by [−10, 10] scl: 1

WRITE AN EQUATION GIVEN TWO POINTS Sometimes you do not know the slope of a line, but you know two points on the line. In this case, find the slope of the line. Then follow the steps in Example 1.

Standardized Test Practice
ⒶⒷⒸⒹ

Example 2 Write an Equation Given Two Points

Multiple-Choice Test Item

The table of ordered pairs shows the coordinates of the two points on the graph of a function. Which equation describes the function?

x	y
−3	−1
6	−4

Ⓐ $y = -\frac{1}{3}x - 2$ Ⓑ $y = 3x - 2$

Ⓒ $y = -\frac{1}{3}x + 2$ Ⓓ $y = \frac{1}{3}x - 2$

Read the Test Item

The table represents the ordered pairs $(-3, -1)$ and $(6, -4)$.

Solve the Test Item

Step 1 Find the slope of the line containing the points. Let $(x_1, y_1) = (-3, -1)$ and $(x_2, y_2) = (6, -4)$.

$m = \dfrac{y_2 - y_1}{x_2 - x_1}$ Slope formula

$m = \dfrac{-4 - (-1)}{6 - (-3)}$ $x_1 = -3, x_2 = 6, y_1 = -1, y_2 = -4$

$m = \dfrac{-3}{9}$ or $-\dfrac{1}{3}$ Simplify.

Step 2 You know the slope and two points. Choose one point and find the y-intercept. In this case, we chose $(6, -4)$.

$y = mx + b$ Slope-intercept form

$-4 = -\dfrac{1}{3}(6) + b$ Replace m with $-\frac{1}{3}$, x with 6, and y with -4.

$-4 = -2 + b$ Multiply.

$-4 + 2 = -2 + b + 2$ Add 2 to each side.

$-2 = b$ Simplify.

Step 3 Write the slope-intercept form using $m = -\dfrac{1}{3}$ and $b = -2$.

$y = mx + b$ Slope-intercept form

$y = -\dfrac{1}{3}x - 2$ Replace m with $-\frac{1}{3}$ and b with -2.

Therefore, the equation is $y = -\dfrac{1}{3}x - 2$. The answer is A.

Test-Taking Tip
You can check your result by graphing. The line should pass through $(-3, -1)$ and $(6, -4)$.

www.algebra1.com/extra_examples

---

2 Teach

WRITE AN EQUATION GIVEN THE SLOPE AND ONE POINT

In-Class Example Power Point®

Teaching Tip Remind students that the x and y in an equation represent any pairs of x and y values that satisfy the equation. The coordinates of the given point are one pair of these values.

❶ Write an equation of a line that passes through $(2, -3)$ with slope $\frac{1}{2}$. $y = \frac{1}{2}x - 4$

WRITE AN EQUATION GIVEN TWO POINTS

In-Class Example Power Point®

Teaching Tip Point out that students can check their solution by substituting the given coordinates into their equation.

❷ The table of ordered pairs shows the coordinates of two points on the graph of a function. Which equation describes the function? **D**

x	y
−3	−4
−2	−8

A $5y = 12x - 16$
B $y = 4x - 16$
C $y = -4x + 16$
D $y = -4x - 16$

Standardized Test Practice
ⒶⒷⒸⒹ

Example 2 Point out to students that there are several ways to approach this question. While the example shows how to find the actual equation, students can save time by examining the choices once they have found the slope, $-\frac{1}{3}$. Only choices A and C have equations with the correct slope.

Teaching Tip Make sure students understand that while two points can be used to write an equation, real-life prediction equations involve many more data points.

3 ECONOMY In 2000, the cost of many items increased because of the increase in the cost of petroleum. In Chicago, a gallon of self-serve regular gasoline cost $1.76 in May and $2.13 in June. Write a linear equation to predict the cost of gasoline in any month in 2000, using 1 to represent January. **$y = 0.37x - 0.09$**

4 ECONOMY The Yellow Cab Company budgeted $7000 for the July gasoline supply. On average, they use 3000 gallons of gasoline per month. Use the prediction equation in In-Class Example 3 to determine if they will have to add to their budget. Explain. **If gas increases at the same rate, a gallon will cost $2.50 in July. 3000 gallons at this price is $7500, so they will have to add $500 to their budget.**

More About . . .

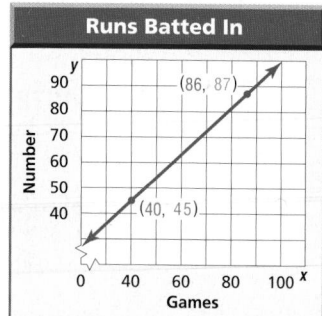

Baseball ·········
Mark McGwire is best known for breaking Roger Maris' single-season home run record of 61. In the 1998 season, McGwire hit 70 home runs.
Source: *USA TODAY*

TEACHING TIP
Ask students what extracurricular activities are. Establish that these are activities *outside* the normal school day. Associate this with *extrapolation* by saying that they are predicting values *outside* the given range of data.

Example 3 *Write an Equation to Solve a Problem*

BASEBALL In the middle of the 1998 baseball season, Mark McGwire seemed to be on track to break the record for most runs batted in. After 40 games, McGwire had 45 runs batted in. After 86 games, he had 87 runs batted in. Write a linear equation to estimate the number of runs batted in for any number of games that season.

Explore You know the number of runs batted in after 40 and 86 games.

Plan Let x represent the number of games. Let y represent the number of runs batted in. Write an equation of the line that passes through (40, 45) and (86, 87).

Runs Batted In

[graph: y-axis labeled "Number" from 40 to 90; x-axis labeled "Games" from 0 to 100; line through points (40, 45) and (86, 87)]

Solve Find the slope.

$m = \dfrac{y_2 - y_1}{x_2 - x_1}$ Slope formula

$m = \dfrac{87 - 45}{86 - 40}$ Let $(x_1, y_1) = (40, 45)$ and $(x_2, y_2) = (86, 87)$.

$m = \dfrac{42}{46}$ or about 0.91 Simplify.

Choose (40, 45) and find the y-intercept of the line.

$y = mx + b$ Slope-intercept form

$45 = 0.91(40) + b$ Replace m with 0.91, x with 40, and y with 45.

$45 = 36.4 + b$ Multiply.

$45 - 36.4 = 36.4 + b - 36.4$ Subtract 36.4 from each side.

$8.6 = b$ Simplify.

Write the slope-intercept form using $m = 0.91$, and $b = 8.6$.

$y = mx + b$ Slope-intercept form

$y = 0.91x + 8.6$ Replace m with 0.91 and b with 8.6.

Therefore, the equation is $y = 0.91x + 8.6$.

Examine Check your result by substituting the coordinates of the point not chosen, (86, 87), into the equation.

$y = 0.91x + 8.6$ Original equation

$87 \stackrel{?}{=} 0.91(86) + 8.6$ Replace y with 87 and x with 86.

$87 \stackrel{?}{=} 78.26 + 8.6$ Multiply.

$87 \approx 86.86$ ✓ The slope was rounded, so the answers vary slightly.

282 Chapter 5 Analyzing Linear Equations

DAILY
INTERVENTION   **Differentiated Instruction**

Logical The reality of learning many different formulas for one aspect of algebra may seem threatening and confusing to some students. The logical learner is capable of relating new concepts in terms of what they have already learned. Have students use the definition of slope to develop the slope-intercept form of an equation. Revisit this approach in Lesson 5-5 for the point-slope form of an equation.

<table>
<tr><td colspan="2">Concept Summary</td><td>Writing Equations</td></tr>
</table>

Concept Summary — Writing Equations

Given the Slope and One Point

Step 1 Substitute the values of m, x, and y into the slope-intercept form and solve for b.

Step 2 Write the slope-intercept form using the values of m and b.

Given Two Points

Step 1 Find the slope.

Step 2 Choose one of the two points to use.

Step 3 Then, follow the steps for writing an equation given the slope and one point.

When you use a linear equation to predict values that are beyond the range of the data, you are using **linear extrapolation**.

Example 4 — Linear Extrapolation

SPORTS The record for most runs batted in during a single season is 190. Use the equation in Example 3 to decide whether a baseball fan following the 1998 season would have expected McGwire to break the record in the 162 games played that year.

$y = 0.91x + 8.6$ Original equation

$y = 0.91(162) + 8.6$ Replace x with 162.

$y \approx 156$ Simplify.

Since the record is 190 runs batted in, a fan would have predicted that Mark McGwire would not break the record.

Be cautious when making a prediction using just two given points. The model may be *approximately* correct, but still give inaccurate predictions. For example, in 1998, Mark McGwire had 147 runs batted in, which was nine less than the prediction.

Check for Understanding

Concept Check

1, 3. See margin.

1. **Compare and contrast** the process used to write an equation given the slope and one point with the process used for two points.

2. **OPEN ENDED** Write an equation in slope-intercept form of a line that has a y-intercept of 3. **Sample answer:** $y = 2x + 3$

3. **Tell** whether the statement is *sometimes, always,* or *never* true. Explain.
You can write the equation of a line given its x- and y-intercepts.

Guided Practice

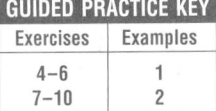

GUIDED PRACTICE KEY

Exercises	Examples
4–6	1
7–10	2

Write an equation of the line that passes through each point with the given slope.

4. $(4, -2)$, $m = 2$
$y = 2x - 10$

5. $(3, 7)$, $m = -3$
$y = -3x + 16$

6. $(-3, 5)$, $m = -1$
$y = -x + 2$

Write an equation of the line that passes through each pair of points.

7. $(5, 1)$, $(8, -2)$
$y = -x + 6$

8. $(6, 0)$, $(0, 4)$
$y = -\frac{2}{3}x + 4$

9. $(5, 2)$, $(-7, -4)$
$y = \frac{1}{2}x - \frac{1}{2}$

Standardized Test Practice

10. The table of ordered pairs shows the coordinates of the two points on the graph of a line. Which equation describes the line? **A**

x	y
−5	2
0	7

   (A) $y = x + 7$ (B) $y = x - 7$

   (C) $y = -5x + 2$ (D) $y = 5x + 2$

---

3 Practice/Apply

Study Notebook

Have students—

• add the definitions/examples of the vocabulary terms to their Vocabulary Builder worksheets for Chapter 5.

• include the answer to Exercise 1 as a summary of the concepts in this lesson.

• include any other item(s) that they find helpful in mastering the skills in this lesson.

About the Exercises...

Organization by Objective

• Write an Equation Given the Slope and One Point: 11–18

• Write an Equation Given Two Points: 19–34, 36, 38, 41

Odd/Even Assignments

Exercises 11–33 are structured so that students practice the same concepts whether they are assigned odd or even problems.

Assignment Guide

Basic: 11–27 odd, 38, 39, 44–62

Average: 11–33 odd, 34–39, 44–62

Advanced: 12–32 even, 38–56 (optional: 57–62)

Answers

1. When you have the slope and one point, you can substitute these values in for x, y, and m to find b. When you are given two points, you must first find the slope and then use the first procedure.

3. Sometimes; if the x- and y-intercepts are both zero, you cannot write the equation of the graph.

Study Guide and Intervention, p. 299 (shown) and p. 300

Write an Equation Given the Slope and One Point

Example 1 Write an equation of a line that passes through (−4, 2) with slope 3.

The line has slope 3. To find the y-intercept, replace m with 3 and (x, y) with (−4, 2) in the slope-intercept form. Then solve for b.

$y = mx + b$ Slope-intercept form
$2 = 3(−4) + b$ $m = 3, y = 2,$ and $x = −4$
$2 = −12 + b$ Multiply.
$14 = b$ Add 12 to each side.

Therefore, the equation is $y = 3x + 14$.

Example 2 Write an equation of the line that passes through (−2, −1) with slope $\frac{1}{4}$.

The line has slope $\frac{1}{4}$. Replace m with $\frac{1}{4}$ and (x, y) with (−2, −1) in the slope-intercept form.

$y = mx + b$ Slope-intercept form
$−1 = \frac{1}{4}(−2) + b$ $m = \frac{1}{4}, y = −1,$ and $x = −2$
$−1 = −\frac{1}{2} + b$ Multiply.
$−\frac{1}{2} = b$ Add $\frac{1}{2}$ to each side.

Therefore, the equation is $y = \frac{1}{4}x − \frac{1}{2}$.

Exercises

Write an equation of the line that passes through each point with the given slope.

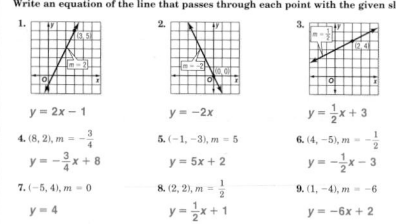

1. $y = 2x − 1$
2. $y = −2x$
3. $y = \frac{1}{2}x + 3$

4. (8, 2), $m = −\frac{3}{4}$ $y = −\frac{3}{4}x + 8$
5. (−1, −3), $m = 5$ $y = 5x + 2$
6. (4, −5), $m = −\frac{1}{2}$ $y = −\frac{1}{2}x − 3$

7. (−5, 4), $m = 0$ $y = 4$
8. (2, 2), $m = \frac{1}{2}$ $y = \frac{1}{2}x + 1$
9. (1, −4), $m = −6$ $y = −6x + 2$

10. Write an equation of a line that passes through the y-intercept −3 with slope 2.
$y = 2x − 3$

11. Write an equation of a line that passes through the x-intercept 4 with slope −3.
$y = −3x + 12$

12. Write an equation of a line that passes through the point (0, 350) with slope $\frac{1}{5}$.
$y = \frac{1}{5}x + 350$

Skills Practice, p. 301 and Practice, p. 302 (shown)

Write an equation of the line that passes through each point with the given slope.

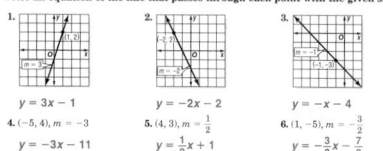

1. $y = 3x − 1$
2. $y = −2x − 2$
3. $y = −x − 4$

4. (−5, 4), $m = −3$ $y = −3x − 11$
5. (4, 3), $m = \frac{1}{2}$ $y = \frac{1}{2}x + 1$
6. (1, −5), $m = −\frac{3}{2}$ $y = −\frac{3}{2}x − \frac{7}{2}$

Write an equation of the line that passes through each pair of points.

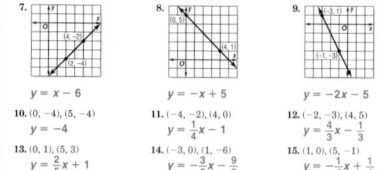

7. $y = x − 6$
8. $y = −x + 5$
9. $y = −2x − 5$

10. (0, −4), (5, −4) $y = −4$
11. (−4, −2), (4, 0) $y = \frac{1}{4}x − 1$
12. (−2, −3), (4, 5) $y = \frac{4}{3}x − \frac{1}{3}$

13. (0, 1), (5, 3) $y = \frac{2}{5}x + 1$
14. (−3, 0), (1, −6) $y = −\frac{3}{2}x − \frac{9}{2}$
15. (1, 0), (5, −1) $y = −\frac{1}{4}x + \frac{1}{4}$

Write an equation of the line that has each pair of intercepts.

16. x-intercept: 2, y-intercept: −5 $y = \frac{5}{2}x − 5$
17. x-intercept: 2, y-intercept: 10 $y = −5x + 10$
18. x-intercept: −2, y-intercept: 1 $y = \frac{1}{2}x + 1$
19. x-intercept: −4, y-intercept: −3 $y = −\frac{3}{4}x − 3$

20. **DANCE LESSONS** The cost for 7 dance lessons is $82. The cost for 11 lessons is $122. Write a linear equation to find the total cost C for ℓ lessons. Then use the equation to find the cost of 4 lessons. $C = 10ℓ + 12; \$52$

21. **WEATHER** It is 76°F at the 6000-foot level of a mountain, and 49°F at the 12,000-foot level of the mountain. Write a linear equation to find the temperature T at an elevation e on the mountain, where e is in thousands of feet. $T = −4.5e + 103$

Reading to Learn Mathematics, p. 303   ELL

Pre-Activity How can slope-intercept form be used to make predictions?

Read the introduction to Lesson 5-4 at the top of page 284 in your textbook.

• What is the rate of change per year? **about 2000 per year**

• Study the pattern on the graph. How would you find the population in 1997? **Add 2000 to the 1996 population, which gives 179,000.**

Reading the Lesson

1. Suppose you are given that a line goes through (2, 5) and has a slope of −2. Use this information to complete the following equation.

$y = mx + b$
$5 = −2 \cdot 2 + b$

2. What must you first do if you are not given the slope in the problem?
Use the information given (two points) to find the slope.

3. What is the first step in answering any standardized test practice question?
Read the problem.

4. What are four steps you can use in solving a word problem?
Explore, Plan, Solve, Examine

5. Define the term linear extrapolation.
Linear extrapolation means using a linear equation to predict values that are outside the two given data points.

Helping You Remember

6. In your own words, explain how you would answer a question that asks you to write the slope-intercept form of an equation. Sample answer: Determine what information you are given. If you have a point and the slope, you can substitute the x- and y-values and the slope into $y = mx + b$ to find the value of b. Then use the values of m and b to write the equation. If you have two points, use them to find the slope, and then use the method for a point and the slope.

Practice and Apply

Write an equation of the line that passes through each point with the given slope.

11. 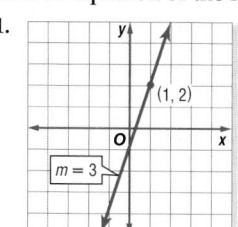 $y = 3x − 1$
12. 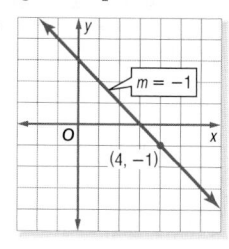 $y = −x + 3$

13. $y = 3x − 17$
14. $y = −5x + 29$
15. $y = −2x + 6$
16. $y = \frac{1}{2}x + \frac{1}{2}$
17. $y = −\frac{2}{3}x − 3$
18. $y = −\frac{5}{3}x − 10$

13. (5, −2), $m = 3$
14. (5, 4), $m = −5$
15. (3, 0), $m = −2$
16. (5, 3), $m = \frac{1}{2}$
17. (−3, −1), $m = −\frac{2}{3}$
18. (−3, −5), $m = −\frac{5}{3}$

Write an equation of the line that passes through each pair of points.

19. 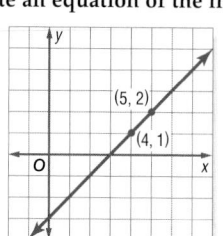 $y = x − 3$
20. 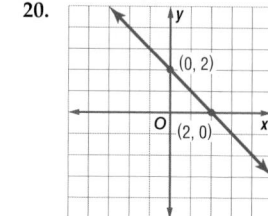 $y = −x + 2$

21. $y = x − 2$
22. $y = 2x − 8$
23. $y = −2x + 1$
24. $y = 4x − 10$
25. $y = −2$
26. $y = 5$

21. (4, 2), (−2, −4)
22. (3, −2), (6, 4)
23. (−1, 3), (2, −3)
24. (2, −2), (3, 2)
25. (7, −2), (−4, −2)
26. (0, 5), (−3, 5)
27. (1, 1), (7, 4) $y = \frac{1}{2}x + \frac{1}{2}$
28. (5, 7), (0, 6) $y = \frac{1}{5}x + 6$
★ 29. $\left(−\frac{5}{4}, 1\right), \left(−\frac{1}{4}, \frac{3}{4}\right)$ $y = −\frac{1}{4}x + \frac{11}{16}$

30. $y = \frac{5}{3}x + 5$
31. $y = −\frac{4}{3}x + 4$
32. $y = −\frac{1}{2}x + 3$
33. $y = x − 2$

Write an equation of the line that has each pair of intercepts.

★ 30. x-intercept: −3, y-intercept: 5
★ 31. x-intercept: 3, y-intercept: 4
★ 32. x-intercept: 6, y-intercept: 3
★ 33. x-intercept: 2, y-intercept: −2

MARRIAGE AGE For Exercises 34–37, use the information in the graphic.

34. $M = \frac{1}{8}t − 223.05$

34. Write a linear equation to predict the median age that men marry M for any year t.

35. about 27.6 yr

35. Use the equation to predict the median age of men who marry for the first time in 2005.

36. about $W = \frac{3}{20}t − 274.7$

36. Write a linear equation to predict the median age that women marry W for any year t.

37. Use the equation to predict the median age of women who marry for the first time in 2005.
about 26.05 yr

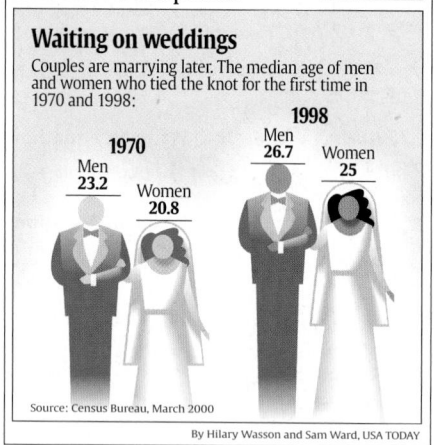

USA TODAY Snapshots®

Waiting on weddings

Couples are marrying later. The median age of men and women who tied the knot for the first time in 1970 and 1998:

1970: Men 23.2, Women 20.8
1998: Men 26.7, Women 25

Source: Census Bureau, March 2000

By Hilary Wasson and Sam Ward, USA TODAY

Enrichment, p. 304

Celsius and Kelvin Temperatures

If you blow up a balloon and put it in the refrigerator, the balloon will shrink as the temperature of the air in the balloon decreases.

The volume of a certain gas is measured at 30° Celsius. The temperature is decreased and the volume is measured again.

Temperature (t)	Volume (V)
30°C	202 mL
21°C	196 mL
0°C	182 mL
212°C	174 mL
227°C	164 mL

1. Graph this table on the coordinate plane provided below.

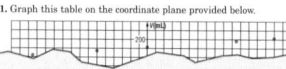

Answer

45. Answers should include the following.

• Linear extrapolation is when you use a linear equation to predict values that are outside of the given points on the graph.

• You can use the slope-intercept form of the equation to find the y-value for any requested x-value.

POPULATION For Exercises 38 and 39, use the data at the top of page 280.

38. $y = 2000x - 3,815,000$

38. Write a linear equation to find Orlando's population for any year.

39. Predict what Orlando's population will be in 2010. **205,000**

40. CANOE RENTAL If you rent a canoe for 3 hours, you will pay $45. Write a linear equation to find the total cost C of renting the canoe for h hours. $C = 10h + 15$

CANOE RENTALS
DAILY RATE PLUS
$10 PER
HOUR

For Exercises 41–43, consider line ℓ that passes through (14, 2) and (28, 6).

41. Write an equation for line ℓ. $y = \frac{2}{7}x - 2$

42. What is the slope of line ℓ? $\frac{2}{7}$

43. Where does line ℓ intersect the x-axis? the y-axis? **(7, 0), (0, −2)**

44. CRITICAL THINKING The x-intercept of a line is p, and the y-intercept is q. Write an equation of the line. $y = -\frac{q}{p}x + q$, where $p \neq 0$

45. [WRITING IN MATH] Answer the question that was posed at the beginning of the lesson. **See margin.**

How can slope-intercept form be used to make predictions?

Include the following in your answer:
- a definition of linear extrapolation, and
- an explanation of how slope-intercept form is used in linear extrapolation.

Standardized Test Practice
Ⓐ Ⓑ Ⓒ Ⓓ

46. Which is an equation for the line with slope $\frac{1}{3}$ through $(-2, 1)$? **B**

Ⓐ $y = \frac{1}{3}x + 1$　Ⓑ $y = \frac{1}{3}x + \frac{5}{3}$　Ⓒ $y = \frac{1}{3}x - \frac{5}{3}$　Ⓓ $y = \frac{1}{3}x + \frac{1}{3}$

47. About 20,000 fewer babies were born in California in 1996 than in 1995. In 1995, about 560,000 babies were born. Which equation can be used to predict the number of babies y (in thousands), born x years after 1995? **B**

Ⓐ $y = 20x + 560$　　　Ⓑ $y = -20x + 560$
Ⓒ $y = -20x - 560$　　　Ⓓ $y = 20x - 560$

Maintain Your Skills

Mixed Review **Graph each equation.** *(Lesson 5-3)* **48–50. See margin.**

48. $y = 3x - 2$　　**49.** $x + y = 6$　　**50.** $x + 2y = 8$

51. HEALTH Each time your heart beats, it pumps 2.5 ounces of blood through your heart. Write a direct variation equation that relates the total volume of blood V with the number of times your heart beats b. *(Lesson 5-2)* $V = 2.5b$

State the domain of each relation. *(Lesson 4-3)*

52. $\{(0, 8), (9, -2), (4, 2)\}$ **{0, 4, 9}**　　**53.** $\{(-2, 1), (5, 1), (-2, 7), (0, -3)\}$ **{−2, 0, 5}**

Replace each ● with $<$, $>$, or $=$ to make a true sentence. *(Lesson 2-7)*

54. $-3 ● -5$ **>**　　**55.** $4 ● \frac{16}{3}$ **<**　　**56.** $\frac{3}{4} ● \frac{2}{3}$ **>**

Getting Ready for the Next Lesson **PREREQUISITE SKILL Find each difference.**
(To review subtracting integers, see Lesson 2-2.)

57. $4 - 7$ **−3**　　**58.** $5 - 12$ **−7**　　**59.** $2 - (-3)$ **5**

60. $-1 - 4$ **−5**　　**61.** $-7 - 8$ **−15**　　**62.** $-5 - (-2)$ **−3**

Online Lesson Plans

USA TODAY Education's Online site offers resources and interactive features connected to each day's newspaper. *Experience TODAY*, USA TODAY's daily lesson plan, is available on the site and delivered daily to subscribers. This plan provides instruction for integrating USA TODAY graphics and key editorial features into your mathematics classroom. Log on to **www.education.usatoday.com**.

 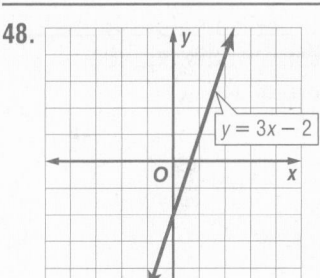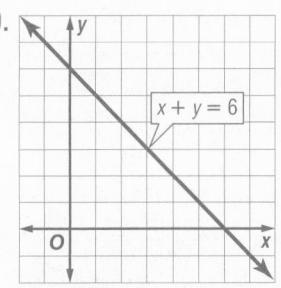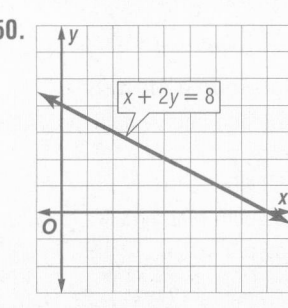

1 Focus

5-Minute Check Transparency 5-5 Use as a quiz or review of Lesson 5-4.

Mathematical Background notes are available for this lesson on p. 254D.

How can you use the slope formula to write an equation of a line?

Ask students:

- How does the final form of the equation relate to the given slope and point? **Sample answer: Each coordinate and the slope appear as numbers in the equation.**

- How would the equation change if the given point were (4, 6)? $y - 6 = 2(x - 4)$

- What equation do you get if you substitute x_1, y_1, and m for the numerical values in the final form of the equation? $y - y_1 = m(x - x_1)$

What You'll Learn

- Write the equation of a line in point-slope form.
- Write linear equations in different forms.

Vocabulary

- point-slope form

How can you use the slope formula to write an equation of a line?

The graph shows a line with slope 2 that passes through (3, 4). Another point on the line is (x, y).

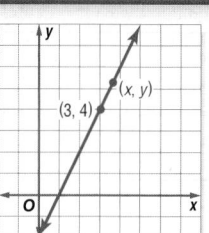

$$m = \frac{y_2 - y_1}{x_2 - x_1} \quad \text{Slope formula}$$

$$2 = \frac{y - 4}{x - 3} \quad \begin{array}{l}(x_2, y_2) = (x, y) \\ (x_1, y_1) = (3, 4)\end{array}$$

$$2(x - 3) = \frac{y - 4}{x - 3}(x - 3) \quad \text{Multiply each side by } (x - 3).$$

$$2(x - 3) = y - 4 \quad \text{Simplify.}$$

$$y - 4 = 2(x - 3) \quad \text{Symmetric Property of Equality}$$

↑ slope ↑ x-coordinate
y-coordinate

POINT-SLOPE FORM The equation above was generated using the coordinates of a known point and the slope of the line. It is written in **point-slope form**.

Key Concept — Point-Slope Form

- **Words** The linear equation $y - y_1 = m(x - x_1)$ is written in point-slope form, where (x_1, y_1) is a given point on a nonvertical line and m is the slope of the line.

- **Model**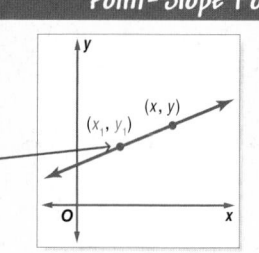

- **Symbols** $y - y_1 = m(x - x_1)$ given point

Study Tip

Point-Slope Form
Remember, (x_1, y_1) represents the *given* point, and (x, y) represents *any other* point on the line.

Example 1 Write an Equation Given Slope and a Point

Write the point-slope form of an equation for a line that passes through (−1, 5) with slope −3.

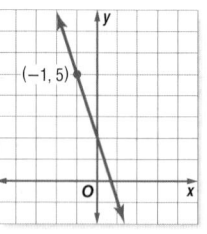

$$y - y_1 = m(x - x_1) \quad \text{Point-slope form}$$

$$y - 5 = -3[x - (-1)] \quad (x_1, y_1) = (-1, 5)$$

$$y - 5 = -3(x + 1) \quad \text{Simplify.}$$

Therefore, the equation is $y - 5 = -3(x + 1)$.

Resource Manager

📁 Workbook and Reproducible Masters

Chapter 5 Resource Masters
- Study Guide and Intervention, pp. 305–306
- Skills Practice, p. 307
- Practice, p. 308
- Reading to Learn Mathematics, p. 309
- Enrichment, p. 310

Graphing Calculator and Spreadsheet Masters, p. 31
Parent and Student Study Guide Workbook, p. 42

🖥 Transparencies

5-Minute Check Transparency 5-5
Answer Key Transparencies

💿 Technology

AlgePASS: Tutorial Plus, Lesson 12
Interactive Chalkboard

Vertical lines cannot be written in point-slope form because the slope is undefined. However, since the slope of a horizontal line is 0, horizontal lines can be written in point-slope form.

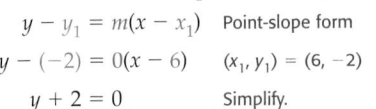 **Write an Equation of a Horizontal Line**

Write the point-slope form of an equation for a horizontal line that passes through (6, −2).

$$y - y_1 = m(x - x_1) \quad \text{Point-slope form}$$
$$y - (-2) = 0(x - 6) \quad (x_1, y_1) = (6, -2)$$
$$y + 2 = 0 \quad \text{Simplify.}$$

Therefore, the equation is $y + 2 = 0$.

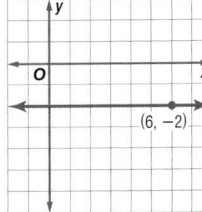

FORMS OF LINEAR EQUATIONS You have learned about three of the most common forms of linear equations.

Concept Summary		Forms of Linear Equations
Form	**Equation**	**Description**
Slope-Intercept	$y = mx + b$	m is the slope, and b is the y-intercept.
Point-Slope	$y - y_1 = m(x - x_1)$	m is the slope and (x_1, y_1) is a given point.
Standard	$Ax + By = C$	A and B are not both zero. Usually A is nonnegative and A, B, and C are integers whose greatest common factor is 1.

Study Tip

Look Back
To review **standard form**, see Lesson 4-5.

Linear equations in point-slope form can be written in slope-intercept or standard form.

Example 3 **Write an Equation in Standard Form**

Write $y + 5 = -\frac{5}{4}(x - 2)$ in standard form.

In standard form, the variables are on the left side of the equation. A, B, and C are all integers.

$$y + 5 = -\frac{5}{4}(x - 2) \quad \text{Original equation}$$
$$4(y + 5) = 4\left(-\frac{5}{4}\right)(x - 2) \quad \text{Multiply each side by 4 to eliminate the fraction.}$$
$$4y + 20 = -5(x - 2) \quad \text{Distributive Property}$$
$$4y + 20 = -5x + 10 \quad \text{Distributive Property}$$
$$4y + 20 - 20 = -5x + 10 - 20 \quad \text{Subtract 20 from each side.}$$
$$4y = -5x - 10 \quad \text{Simplify.}$$
$$4y + 5x = -5x - 10 + 5x \quad \text{Add 5x to each side.}$$
$$5x + 4y = -10 \quad \text{Simplify.}$$

The standard form of the equation is $5x + 4y = -10$.

 www.algebra1.com/extra_examples

---

2 Teach

POINT-SLOPE FORM

In-Class Examples Power Point®

1 Write the point-slope form of an equation for a line that passes through $(-2, 0)$ with slope $-\frac{3}{2}$. $y = -\frac{3}{2}(x + 2)$

Teaching Tip Students may look at the graph and the point given and say the equation is $y = -2$. Remind them that while this is an equation of the line, it is *not* an equation in point-slope form.

2 Write the point-slope form of an equation for a horizontal line that passes through $(0, 5)$. $y - 5 = 0$

FORMS OF LINEAR EQUATIONS

In-Class Example Power Point®

Teaching Tip Emphasize that in standard form, A, B, and C are all integers. This example is an exercise in algebraic manipulation.

3 Write $y = \frac{3}{4}x - 5$ in standard form. $3x - 4y = 20$

 **Classroom Management** If *point-slope form* is not required by your district or state guidelines, this lesson may be considered optional. Students have already learned to write an equation given the slope and a point. However, the point-slope form is good experience for writing equations in a form that will be used in later chapters to describe transformations on the coordinate plane.

Teaching Tip Another way for students to write this equation in slope-intercept form is to identify the slope m and a point on the line from the equation. Use that information to find b in the slope-intercept form.

4 Write $y - 5 = \frac{4}{3}(x - 3)$ in slope-intercept form.
$y = \frac{4}{3}x + 1$

5 **GEOMETRY** The figure shows trapezoid $ABCD$, with bases $\overline{AB}$ and $\overline{CD}$.

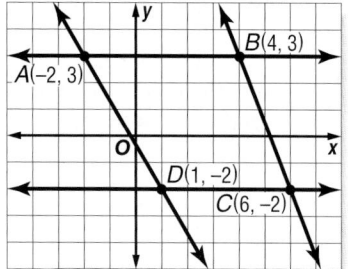

a. Write the point-slope form of the lines containing the bases of the trapezoid.
$\overline{AB}: y - 3 = 0$, $\overline{CD}: y + 2 = 0$

b. Write each equation in standard form. $y = 3$, $y = -2$

Write $y - 2 = \frac{1}{2}(x + 5)$ in slope-intercept form.

In slope-intercept form, y is on the left side of the equation. The constant and x are on the right side.

$y - 2 = \frac{1}{2}(x + 5)$	Original equation
$y - 2 = \frac{1}{2}x + \frac{5}{2}$	Distributive Property
$y - 2 + 2 = \frac{1}{2}x + \frac{5}{2} + 2$	Add 2 to each side.
$y = \frac{1}{2}x + \frac{9}{2}$	$2 = \frac{4}{2}$ and $\frac{4}{2} + \frac{5}{2} = \frac{9}{2}$

The slope-intercept form of the equation is $y = \frac{1}{2}x + \frac{9}{2}$.

You can draw geometric figures on a coordinate plane and use the point-slope form to write equations of the lines.

Example 5 *Write an Equation in Point-Slope Form*

GEOMETRY The figure shows right triangle ABC.

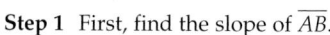

a. Write the point-slope form of the line containing the hypotenuse $\overline{AB}$.

Step 1 First, find the slope of $\overline{AB}$.

$m = \frac{y_2 - y_1}{x_2 - x_1}$ Slope formula

$= \frac{4 - 1}{6 - 2}$ or $\frac{3}{4}$ $(x_1, y_1) = (2, 1), (x_2, y_2) = (6, 4)$

Step 2 You can use either point for (x_1, y_1) in the point-slope form.

Method 1 Use (6, 4).	**Method 2** Use (2, 1).
$y - y_1 = m(x - x_1)$	$y - y_1 = m(x - x_1)$
$y - 4 = \frac{3}{4}(x - 6)$	$y - 1 = \frac{3}{4}(x - 2)$

b. Write each equation in standard form.

$y - 4 = \frac{3}{4}(x - 6)$	Original equation	$y - 1 = \frac{3}{4}(x - 2)$
$4(y - 4) = 4\left(\frac{3}{4}\right)(x - 6)$	Multiply each side by 4.	$4(y - 1) = 4\left(\frac{3}{4}\right)(x - 2)$
$4y - 16 = 3(x - 6)$	Multiply.	$4y - 4 = 3(x - 2)$
$4y - 16 = 3x - 18$	Distributive Property	$4y - 4 = 3x - 6$
$4y = 3x - 2$	Add to each side.	$4y = 3x - 2$
$-3x + 4y = -2$	Subtract 3x from each side.	$-3x + 4y = -2$
$3x - 4y = 2$	Multiply each side by -1.	$3x - 4y = 2$

Regardless of which point was used to find the point-slope form, the standard form results in the same equation.

288 Chapter 5 Analyzing Linear Equations

DAILY INTERVENTION   **Differentiated Instruction**   **ELL**

Verbal/Linguistic Give students several exercises that ask them to write a particular type of equation. Have them describe or write how they would solve each type of problem. Then have them summarize the technique they think works best for each given situation (point and slope, two points, rewriting equations in various forms).

Check for Understanding

Concept Check

1. They are the coordinates of any point on the graph of the equation.

2. Akira; $(-2, -6)$ and $(1, 6)$ are both on the line, so either could be substituted into point-slope form to find a correct equation.

1. **Explain** what x_1 and y_1 in the point-slope form of an equation represent.

2. **FIND THE ERROR** Tanya and Akira wrote the point-slope form of an equation for a line that passes through $(-2, -6)$ and $(1, 6)$. Tanya says that Akira's equation is wrong. Akira says they are both correct. Who is correct? Explain.

Tanya	Akira
$y + 6 = 4(x + 2)$	$y - 6 = 4(x - 1)$

3. **OPEN ENDED** Write an equation in point-slope form. Then write an equation for the same line in slope-intercept form. **Sample answer:** $y - 2 = 4(x + 1)$; $y = 4x + 6$

Guided Practice

Write the point-slope form of an equation for a line that passes through each point with the given slope.

GUIDED PRACTICE KEY	
Exercises	Examples
4–6	1
7–9	2
10–12	3
13, 14	4

4.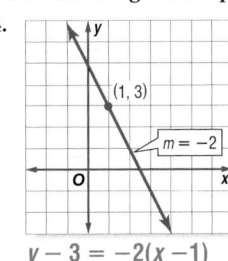
$y - 3 = -2(x - 1)$

5.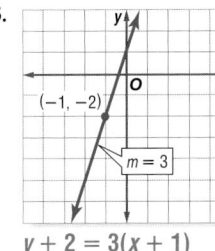
$y + 2 = 3(x + 1)$

6.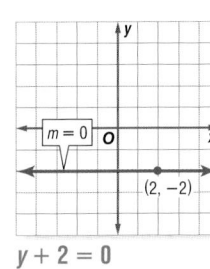
$y + 2 = 0$

Write each equation in standard form.

7. $y - 5 = 4(x + 2)$
$4x - y = -13$

8. $y + 3 = -\frac{3}{4}(x - 1)$
$3x + 4y = -9$

9. $y - 3 = 2.5(x + 1)$
$5x - 2y = -11$

Write each equation in slope-intercept form.

10. $y + 6 = 2(x - 2)$
$y = 2x - 10$

11. $y + 3 = -\frac{2}{3}(x - 6)$
$y = -\frac{2}{3}x + 1$

12. $y - \frac{7}{2} = \frac{1}{2}(x - 4)$
$y = \frac{1}{2}x + \frac{3}{2}$

Application

13. $y - 3 = 2(x + 1)$ or $y + 1 = 2(x + 3)$

GEOMETRY For Exercises 13 and 14, use parallelogram $ABCD$.
A parallelogram has opposite sides parallel.

13. Write the point-slope form of the line containing $\overline{AD}$.

14. Write the standard form of the line containing $\overline{AD}$. $2x - y = -5$

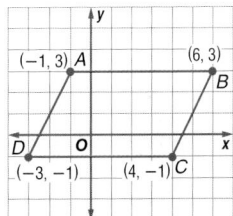

Practice and Apply

Homework Help	
For Exercises	See Examples
15–26	1
27–28	2
29–40	3
41–52	4

Extra Practice
See page 832.

Write the point-slope form of an equation for a line that passes through each point with the given slope. 15–26. See margin.

15. $(3, 8)$, $m = 2$

16. $(-4, -3)$, $m = 1$

17. $(-2, 4)$, $m = -3$

18. $(-6, 1)$, $m = -4$

19. $(-3, 6)$, $m = 0$

20. $(9, 1)$, $m = \frac{2}{3}$

21. $(8, -3)$, $m = \frac{3}{4}$

22. $(-6, 3)$, $m = -\frac{2}{3}$

23. $(1, -3)$, $m = -\frac{5}{8}$

24. $(9, -5)$, $m = 0$

25. $(-4, 8)$, $m = \frac{7}{2}$

26. $(1, -4)$, $m = -\frac{8}{3}$

Study Notebook

Have students—
• add the definitions/examples of the vocabulary terms to their Vocabulary Builder worksheets for Chapter 5.
• include any other item(s) that they find helpful in mastering the skills in this lesson.

DAILY INTERVENTION **FIND THE ERROR**
Students may assume that one of the two examples has to be incorrect. This is not necessarily the case, as in Exercise 2.

About the Exercises...

Organization by Objective
• Point-Slope Form: 15–28
• Forms of Linear Equations: 29–54

Odd/Even Assignments
Exercises 15–54 are structured so that students practice the same concepts whether they are assigned odd or even problems.

Assignment Guide
Basic: 15–53 odd, 55–57, 61–67, 72–87
Average: 15–53 odd, 58–67, 72–87 (optional: 68–71)
Advanced: 16–54 even, 58–79 (optional: 80–87)

Answers

15. $y - 8 = 2(x - 3)$

16. $y + 3 = x + 4$

17. $y - 4 = -3(x + 2)$

18. $y - 1 = -4(x + 6)$

19. $y - 6 = 0$

20. $y - 1 = \frac{2}{3}(x - 9)$

21. $y + 3 = \frac{3}{4}(x - 8)$

22. $y - 3 = -\frac{2}{3}(x + 6)$

23. $y + 3 = -\frac{5}{8}(x - 1)$

24. $y + 5 = 0$

25. $y - 8 = \frac{7}{2}(x + 4)$

26. $y + 4 = -\frac{8}{3}(x - 1)$

Point-Slope Form

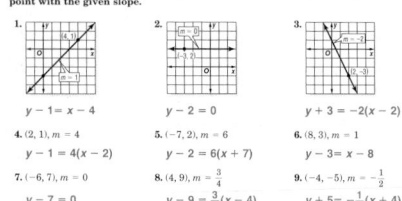

| Point-Slope Form | $y - y_1 = m(x - x_1)$, where (x_1, y_1) is a given point on a nonvertical line and m is the slope of the line |

Example 1 Write the point-slope form of an equation for a line that passes through $(6, 1)$ and has a slope of $-\frac{5}{2}$.

$y - y_1 = m(x - x_1)$ Point-slope form
$y - 1 = -\frac{5}{2}(x - 6)$ $m = -\frac{5}{2}; (x_1, y_1) = (6, 1)$

Therefore, the equation is $y - 1 = -\frac{5}{2}(x - 6)$.

Example 2 Write the point-slope form of an equation for a horizontal line that passes through $(4, -1)$.

$y - y_1 = m(x - x_1)$ Point-slope form
$y - (-1) = 0(x - 4)$ $m = 0; (x_1, y_1) = (4, -1)$
$y + 1 = 0$ Simplify

Therefore, the equation is $y + 1 = 0$.

Exercises

Write the point-slope form of an equation for a line that passes through each point with the given slope.

1. $y - 1 = x - 4$ 2. $y - 2 = 0$ 3. $y + 3 = -2(x - 2)$

4. $(2, 1), m = 4$ 5. $(-7, 2), m = 6$ 6. $(8, 3), m = 1$
$y - 1 = 4(x - 2)$ $y - 2 = 6(x + 7)$ $y - 3 = x - 8$

7. $(-6, 7), m = 0$ 8. $(4, 9), m = \frac{3}{4}$ 9. $(-4, -5), m = -\frac{1}{2}$
$y - 7 = 0$ $y - 9 = \frac{3}{4}(x - 4)$ $y + 5 = -\frac{1}{2}(x + 4)$

10. Write the point-slope form of an equation for the horizontal line that passes through $(4, -2)$. $y + 2 = 0$

11. Write the point-slope form of an equation for the horizontal line that passes through $(-5, 6)$. $y - 6 = 0$

12. Write the point-slope form of an equation for the horizontal line that passes through $(5, 0)$. $y = 0$

Write the point-slope form of an equation for a line that passes through each point with the given slope.

1. $(2, 2), m = -3$ 2. $(1, -6), m = -1$ 3. $(-3, -4), m = 0$
$y - 2 = -3(x - 2)$ $y + 6 = -(x - 1)$ $y + 4 = 0$

4. $(1, 3), m = -\frac{3}{4}$ 5. $(-8, 5), m = -\frac{2}{5}$ 6. $(3, -3), m = \frac{1}{3}$
$y - 3 = -\frac{3}{4}(x - 1)$ $y - 5 = -\frac{2}{5}(x + 8)$ $y + 3 = \frac{1}{3}(x - 3)$

Write each equation in standard form.

7. $y - 11 = 3(x - 2)$ 8. $y - 10 = -(x - 2)$ 9. $y + 7 = 2(x + 5)$
$3x - y = -5$ $x + y = 12$ $2x - y = -3$

10. $y - 5 = \frac{3}{2}(x + 4)$ 11. $y + 2 = -\frac{3}{4}(x + 1)$ 12. $y - 6 = \frac{4}{3}(x - 3)$
$3x - 2y = -22$ $3x + 4y = -11$ $4x - 3y = -6$

13. $y + 4 = 1.5(x + 2)$ 14. $y - 3 = -2.4(x - 5)$ 15. $y - 3 = 2.5(x + 3)$
$3x - 2y = 2$ $12x + 5y = 75$ $5x - 2y = -23$

Write each equation in slope-intercept form.

16. $y + 2 = 4(x + 2)$ 17. $y + 1 = -7(x + 1)$ 18. $y - 3 = -5(x + 12)$
$y = 4x + 6$ $y = -7x - 8$ $y = -5x - 57$

19. $y - 5 = \frac{3}{2}(x + 4)$ 20. $y - \frac{1}{4} = -3(x + \frac{1}{4})$ 21. $y - \frac{2}{3} = -2(x - \frac{1}{4})$
$y = \frac{3}{2}x + 11$ $y = -3x - \frac{1}{2}$ $y = -2x + \frac{7}{6}$

CONSTRUCTION For Exercises 22-24, use the following information.
A construction company charges $15 per hour for debris removal, plus a one-time fee for the use of a trash dumpster. The total fee for 9 hours of service is $195.

22. Write the point-slope form of an equation to find the total fee y for any number of hours x.
$y - 195 = 15(x - 9)$

23. Write the equation in slope-intercept form. $y = 15x + 60$

24. What is the fee for the use of a trash dumpster? $60

MOVING For Exercises 25-27, use the following information.
There is a set daily fee for renting a moving truck, plus a charge of $0.50 per mile driven. It costs $64 to rent the truck on a day when it is driven 48 miles.

25. Write the point-slope form of an equation to find the total charge y for any number of miles x for a one-day rental. $y - 64 = 0.5(x - 48)$

26. Write the equation in slope-intercept form. $y = 0.5x + 40$

27. What is the daily fee? $40

Pre-Activity How can you use the slope formula to write an equation of a line?

Read the introduction to Lesson 5-5 at the top of page 290 in your textbook.

Note that in the final equation there is a value subtracted from x and from y. What are these values?
The value subtracted from x is the x-coordinate of the given point. The value subtracted from y is the y-coordinate of the given point.

Reading the Lesson

1. In the formula $y - y_1 = m(x - x_1)$, what do x_1 and y_1 represent?
x_1 and y_1 represent the coordinates of any given point on the graph of the line.

2. Complete the chart below by listing three forms of equations. Then write the formula for each form. Finally, write three examples of equations in those forms. Sample examples are given.

Form of Equation	Formula	Example
slope-intercept	$y = mx + b$	$y = 3x + 2$
point-slope	$y - y_1 = m(x - x_1)$	$y - 2 = 4(x + 3)$
standard	$Ax + By = C$	$3x - 5y = 15$

3. Refer to Example 5 on page 292 of your textbook. What do you think the *hypotenuse* of a right triangle is? Sample answers: The hypotenuse is the longest side of the right triangle. The hypotenuse is the side opposite the right angle in a right triangle.

Helping You Remember

4. Suppose you could not remember all three formulas listed in the table above. Which of the forms would you concentrate on for writing linear equations? Explain why you chose that form. Sample answer: Point-slope form; the slope-intercept form can be written from the point-slope form. This is so because the y-intercept lets you write the coordinates of the point where the line crosses the y-axis. You can use that point as the given point in the point-slope formula.

---

27. Write the point-slope form of an equation for a horizontal line that passes through $(5, -9)$. $y + 9 = 0$

28. A horizontal line passes through $(0, 7)$. Write the point-slope form of its equation. $y - 7 = 0$

Write each equation in standard form.

29. $y - 13 = 4(x - 2)$ 30. $y + 3 = 3(x + 5)$ 31. $y - 5 = -2(x + 6)$

32. $y + 3 = -5(x + 1)$ 33. $y + 7 = \frac{1}{2}(x + 2)$ 34. $y - 1 = \frac{5}{6}(x - 4)$

35. $y - 2 = -\frac{2}{5}(x - 8)$ 36. $y + 4 = -\frac{1}{3}(x - 12)$ 37. $y + 2 = \frac{5}{3}(x + 6)$

38. $y + 6 = \frac{3}{2}(x - 4)$ 39. $y - 6 = 1.3(x + 7)$ 40. $y - 2 = -2.5(x - 1)$
$3x - 2y = 24$ $13x - 10y = -151$ $5x + 2y = 9$

Write each equation in slope-intercept form.

41. $y - 2 = 3(x - 1)$ 42. $y - 5 = 6(x + 1)$ 43. $y + 2 = -2(x - 5)$

44. $y - 1 = -7(x - 3)$ 45. $y + 3 = \frac{1}{2}(x + 4)$ 46. $y - 1 = \frac{2}{3}(x + 9)$

47. $y + 3 = -\frac{1}{4}(x + 2)$ 48. $y - 5 = -\frac{2}{5}(x + 15)$ 49. $y + \frac{1}{2} = x - \frac{1}{2}$

50. $y - \frac{1}{3} = -2(x + \frac{1}{3})$ 51. $y + \frac{1}{4} = -3(x + \frac{1}{2})$ 52. $y + \frac{3}{5} = -4(x - \frac{1}{2})$
$y = -2x - \frac{1}{3}$ $y = -3x - \frac{7}{4}$ $y = -4x + \frac{7}{5}$

53. Write the point-slope form, slope-intercept form, and standard form of an equation for a line that passes through $(5, -3)$ with slope 10. **See margin.**

54. Line ℓ passes through $(1, -6)$ with slope $\frac{3}{2}$. Write the point-slope form, slope-intercept form, and standard form of an equation for line ℓ. **See margin.**

BUSINESS For Exercises 55-57, use the following information.
A home security company provides security systems for $5 per week, plus an installation fee. The total fee for 12 weeks of service is $210.

55. Write the point-slope form of an equation to find the total fee y for any number of weeks x. $y - 210 = 5(x - 12)$

56. Write the equation in slope-intercept form. $y = 5x + 150$

57. What is the flat fee for installation? $150

MOVIES For Exercises 58-60, use the following information.
Between 1990 and 1999, the number of movie screens in the United States increased by about 1500 each year. In 1996, there were 29,690 movie screens.

58. Write the point-slope form of an equation to find the total number of screens y for any year x. **58-60. See margin.**

59. Write the equation in slope-intercept form.

60. Predict the number of movie screens in the United States in 2005.

 Online Research Data Update What has happened to the number of movie screens since 1999? Visit www.algebra1.com/data_update to learn more.

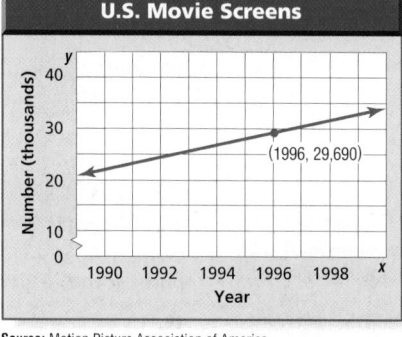

U.S. Movie Screens

Number (thousands) vs. Year, showing point $(1996, 29,690)$.

Source: Motion Picture Association of America

More About. . .

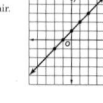

Movies

In 1907, movie theaters were called nickelodeons. There were about 5000 movie screens, and the average movie ticket cost 5 cents.

Source: National Association of Theatre Owners

---

29. $4x - y = -5$
30. $3x - y = -12$
31. $2x + y = -7$
32. $5x + y = -8$
33. $x - 2y = 12$
34. $5x - 6y = 14$
35. $2x + 5y = 26$
36. $x + 3y = 0$
37. $5x - 3y = -24$
41. $y = 3x - 1$
42. $y = 6x + 11$
43. $y = -2x + 8$
44. $y = -7x + 22$
45. $y = \frac{1}{2}x - 1$
46. $y = \frac{2}{3}x + 7$
47. $y = -\frac{1}{4}x - \frac{7}{2}$
48. $y = -\frac{2}{5}x - 1$
49. $y = x - 1$

Collinearity

You have learned how to find the slope between two points on a line. Does it matter which two points you use? How does your choice of points affect the slope-intercept form of the equation of the line?

1. Choose three different pairs of points from the graph at the right. Write the slope-intercept form of the line using each pair.
$y = 1x + 1$

2. How are the equations related?
They are the same.

GEOMETRY For Exercises 61–63, use square *PQRS*.

61–64. See pp. 315A–315B.

61. Write a point-slope equation of the line containing each side.

62. Write the slope-intercept form of each equation.

63. Write the standard form of each equation.

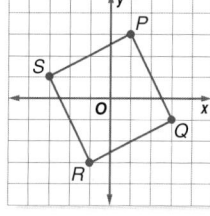

64. CRITICAL THINKING A line contains the points (9, 1) and (5, 5). Write a convincing argument that the same line intersects the *x*-axis at (10, 0).

65. WRITING IN MATH   Answer the question that was posed at the beginning of the lesson. **See margin.**

How can you use the slope formula to write an equation of a line?

Include the following in your answer:

• an explanation of how you can use the slope formula to write the point-slope form.

Standardized Test Practice
Ⓐ Ⓑ Ⓒ Ⓓ

66. Which equation represents a line that *neither* passes through (0, 1) *nor* has a slope of 3? **D**

Ⓐ $-2x + y = 1$

Ⓑ $y + 1 = 3(x + 6)$

Ⓒ $y - 3 = 3(x - 6)$

Ⓓ $x - 3y = -15$

67. SHORT RESPONSE Write the slope-intercept form of an equation of a line that passes through (2, −5). $y = mx - 2m - 5$

Extending the Lesson   For Exercises 68–71, use the graph at the right.

68–71. See margin.

68. Choose three different pairs of points from the graph. Write the slope-intercept form of the line using each pair.

69. Describe how the equations are related.

70. Choose a different pair of points from the graph and predict the equation of the line determined by these points. Check your conjecture by finding the equation.

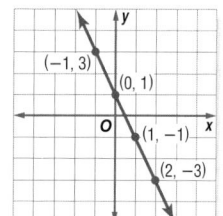

71. MAKE A CONJECTURE What conclusion can you draw from this activity?

Maintain Your Skills

Mixed Review

Write the slope-intercept form of an equation of the line that satisfies each condition.   *(Lessons 5-3 and 5-4)*

72. $y = -2x - 5$
73. $y = 3x + 10$

72. slope −2 and *y*-intercept –5

73. passes through (−2, 4) with slope 3

74. passes through (2, −4) and (0, 6) $y = -5x + 6$

75. a horizontal line through (1, −1) $y = -1$

Solve each equation.   *(Lesson 3-4)*

76. $4a - 5 = 15$ **5**

77. $7 + 3c = -11$ **−6**

78. $\frac{2}{9}v - 6 = 14$ **90**

79. Evaluate $(25 - 4) \div (2^2 - 1^3)$.   *(Lesson 1-3)*   **7**

Getting Ready for the Next Lesson

PREREQUISITE SKILL Write the multiplicative inverse of each number.
(For review of multiplicative inverses, see pages 800 and 801.)

80. $2\frac{1}{2}$

81. $10\frac{1}{10}$

82. 1 **1**

83. -1 **−1**

84. $\frac{2}{3}$ $\frac{3}{2}$

85. $-\frac{1}{9}$ **−9**

86. $\frac{5}{2}$ $\frac{2}{5}$

87. $-\frac{2}{3}$ $-\frac{3}{2}$

Open-Ended Assessment

Writing Prepare two paper bags containing pieces of paper: one with a value for the slope on each piece, one with an ordered pair. Each student can select either a slope and an ordered pair, or two ordered pairs. Have them write the three forms of linear equations discussed in this lesson.

Getting Ready for Lesson 5-6

PREREQUISITE SKILL Lesson 5-6 explores the equations of parallel and perpendicular lines. To find the slopes of perpendicular lines, you must be familiar with the negative reciprocal of a number. Exercises 80-87 should be used to determine your students' familiarity with finding multiplicative inverses, also known as reciprocals.

Answers

65. Answers should include the following.

• Write the definition of the slope using (*x, y*) as one point and (x_1, y_1) as the other. Then solve the equation so that the *y*s are on one side and the slope and *x*s are on the other.

68. (−1, 3) and (0, 1) → $y = -2x + 1$; (0, 1) and (1, −1) → $y = -2x + 1$; (1, −1) and (2, −3) → $y = -2x + 1$

69. All of the equations are the same.

70. The equation will be $y = -2x + 1$; see students' work.

71. Regardless of which two points on a line you select, the slope-intercept form of the equation will always be the same.

Answers

53. $y + 3 = 10(x - 5)$; $y = 10x - 53$; $10x - y = 53$

54. $y + 6 = \frac{3}{2}(x - 1)$; $y = \frac{3}{2}x - \frac{15}{2}$; $3x - 2y = 15$

58. $y - 29{,}690 = 1500(x - 1996)$

59. $y = 1500x - 2{,}964{,}310$

60. 43,190

5-6 Geometry: Parallel and Perpendicular Lines

1 Focus

5-Minute Check Transparency 5-6 Use as a quiz or review of Lesson 5-5.

Mathematical Background notes are available for this lesson on p. 254D.

Building on Prior Knowledge

Students may already be familiar with the terms *parallel* and *perpendicular*. Before covering the examples, you may want students to use rulers or a corner of their books to draw parallel and perpendicular lines on graph paper.

How can you determine whether two lines are parallel?

Ask students:

- How would the graph of $y = x + 5$ relate to the graphs shown? **It would be parallel to them.**

- How would the appearance of the lines change if the slopes were 2? **The lines would be steeper, but they would still be parallel.**

- **Geometry** Describe the slopes of the sides of a rectangle whose vertices are $A(0, 0)$, $B(2, 0)$, $C(2, 6)$, and $D(0, 6)$. $\overline{AB}$ and $\overline{CD}$ **have slope 0 and are parallel.** $\overline{AD}$ **and** $\overline{BC}$ **are vertical, so their slope is undefined. They are also parallel.**

Geometry: Parallel and Perpendicular Lines

What You'll Learn

- Write an equation of the line that passes through a given point, parallel to a given line.
- Write an equation of the line that passes through a given point, perpendicular to a given line.

Vocabulary
- parallel lines
- perpendicular lines

How can you determine whether two lines are parallel?

The graphing calculator screen shows a family of linear graphs whose slope is 1. Notice that the lines do not appear to intersect.

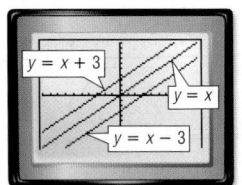

PARALLEL LINES   Lines in the same plane that do not intersect are called **parallel lines**. Parallel lines have the same slope.

Key Concept — Parallel Lines in a Coordinate Plane

- **Words**   Two nonvertical lines are parallel if they have the same slope. All vertical lines are parallel.

- **Model**

You can write the equation of a line parallel to a given line if you know a point on the line and an equation of the given line.

Example 1   Parallel Line Through a Given Point

Write the slope-intercept form of an equation for the line that passes through $(-1, -2)$ and is parallel to the graph of $y = -3x - 2$.

The line parallel to $y = -3x - 2$ has the same slope, -3. Replace m with -3, and (x_1, y_1) with $(-1, -2)$ in the point-slope form.

$$y - y_1 = m(x - x_1) \quad \text{Point-slope form}$$
$$y - (-2) = -3[x - (-1)] \quad \text{Replace } m \text{ with } -3, y \text{ with } -2, \text{ and } x \text{ with } -1.$$
$$y + 2 = -3(x + 1) \quad \text{Simplify.}$$
$$y + 2 = -3x - 3 \quad \text{Distributive Property}$$
$$y + 2 - 2 = -3x - 3 - 2 \quad \text{Subtract 2 from each side.}$$
$$y = -3x - 5 \quad \text{Write the equation in slope-intercept form.}$$

Therefore, the equation is $y = -3x - 5$.

Resource Manager

📂 Workbook and Reproducible Masters

Chapter 5 Resource Masters
- Study Guide and Intervention, pp. 311–312
- Skills Practice, p. 313
- Practice, p. 314
- Reading to Learn Mathematics, p. 315
- Enrichment, p. 316
- Assessment, p. 338

Parent and Student Study Guide Workbook, p. 43
Teaching Algebra With Manipulatives Masters, pp. 1, 104

Transparencies
5-Minute Check Transparency 5-6
Answer Key Transparencies

💿 Technology
AlgePASS: Tutorial Plus, Lesson 13
Interactive Chalkboard

CHECK You can check your result by graphing both equations. The lines appear to be parallel. The graph of $y = -3x - 5$ passes through $(-1, -2)$.

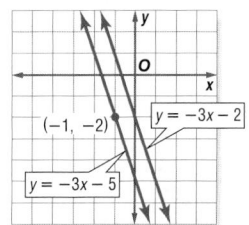

PERPENDICULAR LINES Lines that intersect at right angles are called **perpendicular lines**. There is a relationship between the slopes of perpendicular lines.

Algebra Activity

Perpendicular Lines

Model

- A scalene triangle is one in which no two sides are equal. Cut out a scalene right triangle *ABC* so that $\angle C$ is a right angle. Label the vertices and the sides as shown.
- Draw a coordinate plane on grid paper. Place $\triangle ABC$ on the coordinate plane so that *A* is at the origin and side *b* lies along the positive *x*-axis.

Analyze 1–4. Sample answers are given.

1. Name the coordinates of *B*. (3, 6)
2. What is the slope of side *c*? 2
3. Rotate the triangle 90° counterclockwise so that *A* is still at the origin and side *b* is along the positive *y*-axis. Name the coordinates of *B*. (-6, 3)
4. What is the slope of side *c*? $-\dfrac{1}{2}$
5. Repeat the activity for two other different scalene triangles.
6. For each triangle and its rotation, what is the relationship between the first position of side *c* and the second? They are perpendicular.
7. For each triangle and its rotation, describe the relationship between the coordinates of *B* in the first and second positions.
8. Describe the relationship between the slopes of *c* in each position.

Make a Conjecture

9. Describe the relationship between the slopes of any two perpendicular lines.

5. See students' work.

7. The *x*- and *y*-coordinates are reversed and the *x*-coordinate is multiplied by -1.

8. They are opposite reciprocals.

9. Their product is -1.

Key Concept

Perpendicular Lines in a Coordinate Plane

- **Words** Two nonvertical lines are perpendicular if the product of their slopes is -1. That is, the slopes are *opposite reciprocals* of each other. Vertical lines and horizontal lines are also perpendicular.
- **Model**

Lesson 5-6 Geometry: Parallel and Perpendicular Lines 293

---

2 Teach

PARALLEL LINES

In-Class Example Power Point®

Teaching Tip Students can also use their graphing calculators to check their equations.

1 Write the slope-intercept form of an equation for the line that passes through $(4, -2)$ and is parallel to the graph of $y = \dfrac{1}{2}x - 7$. $y = \dfrac{1}{2}x - 4$

Algebra Activity

Materials: grid paper, scissors

- To save time, you may want to have students work in groups and provide them with scalene triangles precut from lightweight cardboard.
- The term "negative reciprocal" may not be familiar to your students. Make sure your students know that the multiplicative inverse is another name for reciprocal.

Lesson 5-6 Geometry: Parallel and Perpendicular Lines 293

PERPENDICULAR LINES

2 GEOMETRY The height of a trapezoid is measured on a segment that is perpendicular to a base. In trapezoid $ARTP$, $\overline{RT}$ and $\overline{AP}$ are bases. Can $\overline{EZ}$ be used to measure the height of the trapezoid? Explain.

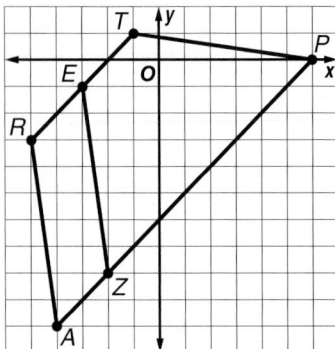

No, the slope of $\overline{RT}$ is 1 and the slope of $\overline{EZ}$ is -7. $1 \cdot -7 \neq -1$. $\overline{EZ}$ is not perpendicular to $\overline{RT}$ so it cannot be used to measure height.

Teaching Tip Encourage students to understand the process used, instead of the mechanics. For example, what do they know from the given information? What do they know about perpendicular lines? What do they need to know to write a new equation?

3 Write the slope-intercept form for an equation of a line that passes through $(4, -1)$ and is perpendicular to the graph of $7x - 2y = 3$. $y = -\frac{2}{7}x + \frac{1}{7}$

4 Write the slope-intercept form for an equation of a line perpendicular to the graph of $2y + 5x = 2$ that passes through $(0, 6)$. $y = \frac{2}{5}x + 6$

More About . . .

Kites •
In India, kite festivals mark *Makar Sankranti*, when the Sun moves into the northern hemisphere.
Source: www.cam-india.com

Study Tip

Graphing Calculator
The lines will not appear to be perpendicular on a graphing calculator if the scales on the axes are not set correctly. After graphing, press
[ZOOM] 5 to set the axes for a correct representation.

Example 2 Determine Whether Lines are Perpendicular

KITES The outline of a kite is shown on a coordinate plane. Determine whether $\overline{AC}$ is perpendicular to $\overline{BD}$.

A (5, 5) *B (8, 4)* *D (0, 0)* *C (7, 1)*

Find the slope of each segment.

Slope of $\overline{AC}$: $m = \dfrac{5-1}{5-7}$ or -2

Slope of $\overline{BD}$: $m = \dfrac{4-0}{8-0}$ or $\dfrac{1}{2}$

The line segments are perpendicular because $\dfrac{1}{2}(-2) = -1$.

You can write the equation of a line perpendicular to a given line if you know a point on the line and the equation of the given line.

Example 3 Perpendicular Line Through a Given Point

Write the slope-intercept form for an equation of the line that passes through $(-3, -2)$ and is perpendicular to the graph of $x + 4y = 12$.

Step 1 Find the slope of the given line.

$x + 4y = 12$	Original equation
$x + 4y - x = 12 - x$	Subtract 1x from each side.
$4y = -1x + 12$	Simplify.
$\dfrac{4y}{4} = \dfrac{-1x + 12}{4}$	Divide each side by 4.
$y = -\dfrac{1}{4}x + 3$	Simplify.

Step 2 The slope of the given line is $-\dfrac{1}{4}$. So, the slope of the line perpendicular to this line is the opposite reciprocal of $-\dfrac{1}{4}$, or 4.

Step 3 Use the point-slope form to find the equation.

$y - y_1 = m(x - x_1)$	Point-slope form
$y - (-2) = 4[x - (-3)]$	$(x_1, y_1) = (-3, -2)$ and $m = 4$
$y + 2 = 4(x + 3)$	Simplify.
$y + 2 = 4x + 12$	Distributive Property
$y + 2 - 2 = 4x + 12 - 2$	Subtract 2 from each side.
$y = 4x + 10$	Simplify.

Therefore, the equation of the line is $y = 4x + 10$.

CHECK Graph both equations on a graphing calculator. Use the **CALC** menu to verify that $y = 4x + 10$ passes through $(-3, -2)$.

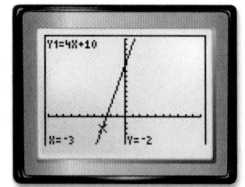

$[-15.16..., 15.16...]$ scl: 1 by $[-10, 10]$ scl: 1

DAILY
INTERVENTION   **Differentiated Instruction**

Naturalist Have students collect items in nature or pictures of those items that display parallel and perpendicular segments. Ask them to sketch or trace the item on grid paper. Then have students calculate the slopes of the segments to determine if they are truly parallel or truly perpendicular.

Example 4 *Perpendicular Line Through a Given Point*

Write the slope-intercept form for an equation of a line perpendicular to the graph of $y = -\frac{1}{3}x + 2$ and passes through the x-intercept of that line.

Step 1 Find the slope of the perpendicular line. The slope of the given line is $-\frac{1}{3}$, therefore a perpendicular line has slope 3 because $-\frac{1}{3} \cdot 3 = -1$.

Step 2 Find the x-intercept of the given line.

$y = -\frac{1}{3}x + 2$ Original equation

$0 = -\frac{1}{3}x + 2$ Replace y with 0.

$-2 = -\frac{1}{3}x$ Subtract 2 from each side.

$6 = x$ Multiply each side by -3.

The x-intercept is at (6, 0).

Step 3 Substitute the slope and the given point into the point-slope form of a linear equation. Then write the equation in slope-intercept form.

$y - y_1 = m(x - x_1)$ Point-slope form

$y - 0 = 3(x - 6)$ Replace x with 6, y with 0, and m with 3.

$y = 3x - 18$ Distributive Property

Check for Understanding

Concept Check

1, 3. See margin.

2. Sample answer: 2, $-\frac{1}{2}$

1. **Explain** how to find the slope of a line that is perpendicular to the line shown in the graph.

2. **OPEN ENDED** Give an example of two numbers that are negative reciprocals.

3. **Define** *parallel lines* and *perpendicular lines*.

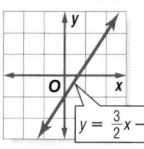
$y = \frac{3}{2}x - 1$

Guided Practice

GUIDED PRACTICE KEY	
Exercises	Examples
4–7	1
8	2
9–11	3
12	4

Write the slope-intercept form of an equation of the line that passes through the given point and is parallel to the graph of each equation.

4. 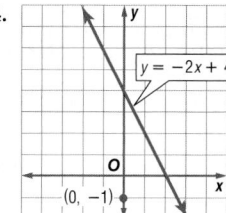 $y = -2x - 1$
$y = -2x + 4$
$(0, -1)$

5. 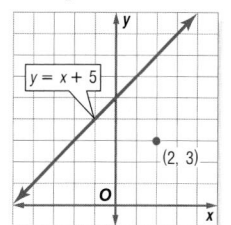 $y = x + 1$
$y = x + 5$
$(2, 3)$

6. $(1, -3)$, $y = 2x - 1$ $y = 2x - 5$

7. $(-2, 2)$, $-3x + y = 4$ $y = 3x + 8$

8. **GEOMETRY** Quadrilateral $ABCD$ has vertices $A(-2, 1)$, $B(3, 3)$, $C(5, 7)$, and $D(0, 5)$. Determine whether $\overline{AC}$ is perpendicular to $\overline{BD}$. **See margin.**

9. $y = -3x - 8$

10. $y = -\frac{5}{3}x + 8$

11. $y = \frac{1}{2}x - 3$

Write the slope-intercept form of an equation that passes through the given point and is perpendicular to the graph of each equation.

9. $(-3, 1)$, $y = \frac{1}{3}x + 2$ 10. $(6, -2)$, $y = \frac{3}{5}x - 4$ 11. $(2, -2)$, $2x + y = 5$

Lesson 5-6 Geometry: Parallel and Perpendicular Lines   295

Study Notebook

Have students—
• add the definitions/examples of the vocabulary terms to their Vocabulary Builder worksheets for Chapter 5.
• include any other item(s) that they find helpful in mastering the skills in this lesson.

About the Exercises...
Organization by Objective
• **Parallel Lines:** 13–27
• **Perpendicular Lines:** 28–41

Odd/Even Assignments
Exercises 13–24 and 28–39 are structured so that students practice the same concepts whether they are assigned odd or even problems.

Assignment Guide
Basic: 13–37 odd, 41, 46–60
Average: 13–45 odd, 46–60
Advanced: 14–44 even, 46–54 (optional: 55–60)
All: Practice Quiz 2 (1–5)

Answers

1. The slope is $\frac{3}{2}$, so the slope of a line perpendicular to the given line is $-\frac{2}{3}$.

3. Parallel lines lie in the same plane and never intersect. Perpendicular lines intersect at right angles.

8. Slope of $\overline{AC} = \frac{1 - 7}{-2 - 5}$ or $\frac{6}{7}$; slope of $\overline{BD} = \frac{3 - 5}{3 - 0}$ or $-\frac{2}{3}$; they are not perpendicular.

Study Guide and Intervention, p. 311 (shown) and p. 312

Parallel Lines Two nonvertical lines are **parallel** if they have the same slope. All vertical lines are parallel.

Example **Write the slope-intercept form for an equation of the line that passes through (−1, 6) and is parallel to the graph of $y = 2x + 12$.**

A line parallel to $y = 2x + 12$ has the same slope, 2. Replace m with 2 and (x_1, y_1) with (−1, 6) in the point-slope form.

$y - y_1 = m(x - x_1)$	Point-slope form
$y - 6 = 2(x - (-1))$	$m = 2$; $(x_1, y_1) = (-1, 6)$
$y - 6 = 2(x + 1)$	Simplify.
$y - 6 = 2x + 2$	Distributive Property
$y = 2x + 8$	Slope-intercept form

Therefore, the equation is $y = 2x + 8$.

Exercises

Write the slope-intercept form for an equation of the line that passes through the given point and is parallel to the graph of each equation.

1.

$y = x - 4$

2.

$y = -\frac{1}{2}x + 3$

3.

$y = \frac{4}{3}x + 7$

4. (−2, 2), $y = 4x - 2$ — $y = 4x + 10$
5. (6, 4), $y = \frac{1}{3}x + 1$ — $y = \frac{1}{3}x + 2$
6. (4, −2), $y = -2x + 3$ — $y = -2x + 6$
7. (−2, 4), $y = -3x + 10$ — $y = -3x - 2$
8. (−1, 6), $3x + y = 12$ — $y = -3x + 3$
9. (4, −6), $x + 2y = 5$ — $y = -\frac{1}{2}x - 4$
10. Find an equation of the line that has a y-intercept of 2 that is parallel to the graph of the line $4x + 2y = 8$. $y = -2x + 2$
11. Find an equation of the line that has a y-intercept of −1 that is parallel to the graph of the line $x - 3y = 6$. $y = \frac{1}{3}x - 1$
12. Find an equation of the line that has a y-intercept of −4 that is parallel to the graph of the line $y = 6$. $y = -4$

Skills Practice, p. 313 and Practice, p. 314 (shown)

Write the slope-intercept form of an equation of the line that passes through the given point and is parallel to the graph of each equation.

1. (3, 2), $y = x + 5$ — $y = x - 1$
2. (−2, 5), $y = -4x + 2$ — $y = -4x - 3$
3. (4, −6), $y = -\frac{3}{4}x + 1$ — $y = -\frac{3}{4}x - 3$
4. (5, 4), $y = \frac{2}{5}x - 2$ — $y = \frac{2}{5}x + 2$
5. (12, 3), $y = \frac{4}{3}x + 5$ — $y = \frac{4}{3}x - 13$
6. (3, 1), $2x + y = 5$ — $y = -2x + 7$
7. (−3, 4), $3y = 2x - 3$ — $y = \frac{2}{3}x + 6$
8. (−1, −2), $3x - y = 5$ — $y = 3x + 1$
9. (−8, 2), $5x - 4y = 1$ — $y = \frac{5}{4}x + 12$
10. (−1, −4), $9x + 3y = 8$ — $y = -3x - 7$
11. (−5, 6), $4x + 3y = 1$ — $y = -\frac{4}{3}x - \frac{2}{3}$
12. (3, 1), $2x + 5y = 7$ — $y = -\frac{2}{5}x + \frac{11}{5}$

Write the slope-intercept form of an equation of the line that passes through the given point and is perpendicular to the graph of each equation.

13. (−2, −2), $y = -\frac{1}{3}x + 9$ — $y = 3x + 4$
14. (−6, 5), $x - y = 5$ — $y = -x - 1$
15. (−4, −3), $4x + y = 7$ — $y = \frac{1}{4}x - 2$
16. (0, 1), $x + 5y = 15$ — $y = 5x + 1$
17. (2, 4), $x - 6y = 2$ — $y = -6x + 16$
18. (−1, −7), $3x + 12y = -6$ — $y = 4x - 3$
19. (−4, 1), $4x + 7y = 6$ — $y = \frac{7}{4}x + 8$
20. (10, 5), $5x + 4y = 8$ — $y = \frac{4}{5}x - 3$
21. (4, −5), $2x - 5y = -10$ — $y = -\frac{5}{2}x + 5$
22. (1, 1), $3x + 2y = -7$ — $y = \frac{2}{3}x + \frac{1}{3}$
23. (−6, −5), $4x + 3y = -6$ — $y = \frac{3}{4}x - \frac{1}{2}$
24. (−3, 5), $5x - 6y = 9$ — $y = -\frac{6}{5}x + \frac{7}{5}$
25. **GEOMETRY** Quadrilateral $ABCD$ has diagonals $\overline{AC}$ and $\overline{BD}$. Determine whether $\overline{AC}$ is perpendicular to $\overline{BD}$. Explain.
Yes; they are perpendicular because their slopes are 7 and $-\frac{1}{7}$, which are negative reciprocals.

26. **GEOMETRY** Triangle ABC has vertices $A(0, 4)$, $B(1, 2)$, and $C(4, 6)$. Determine whether triangle ABC is a right triangle. Explain.
Yes; sides $\overline{AB}$ and $\overline{AC}$ are perpendicular because their slopes are −2 and $\frac{1}{2}$, which are negative reciprocals.

Reading to Learn Mathematics, p. 315 ELL

Pre-Activity **How can you determine whether two lines are parallel?**

Read the introduction to Lesson 5-6 at the top of page 296 in your textbook.

- What is a family of graphs? A group of graphs that have at least one characteristic in common, such as slope or y-intercept.
- Do you think lines that do not appear to intersect are parallel or perpendicular? parallel

Reading the Lesson

1. Refer to the Key Concept box on page 296. Why does the definition use the term *nonvertical* when talking about lines with the same slope? Vertical lines have slopes that are undefined so we cannot say they have the same slope.
2. What is a right angle? Sample answers: A right angle is one that measures 90°. It is an angle formed by perpendicular lines.
3. Refer to the Key Concept box on page 297. Describe how you find the opposite reciprocal of a number. Sample answer: The reciprocal of a given number is the number formed when you switch the numerator and denominator. Then you give it the opposite sign of the original number.
4. Write the opposite reciprocal of each number.
   a. 2 $-\frac{1}{2}$ b. −3 $\frac{1}{3}$ c. $\frac{12}{13}$ $-\frac{13}{12}$ d. $-\frac{1}{5}$ 5

Helping You Remember

5. One way to remember how slopes of parallel lines are related is to say "same direction, same slope." Try to think of a phrase to help you remember that perpendicular lines have slopes that are opposite reciprocals.
Sample answer: Nicely right angles formed, use opposite reciprocals.

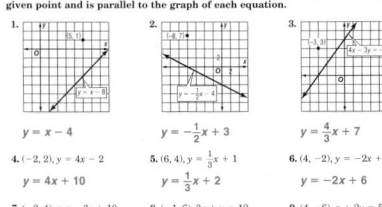

Application

12. **GEOMETRY** The line with equation $y = 3x - 4$ contains side $\overline{AC}$ of right triangle ABC. If the vertex of the right angle C is at (3, 5), what is an equation of the line that contains side $\overline{BC}$?
$y = -\frac{1}{3}x + 6$

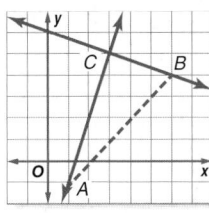

★ indicates increased difficulty

Practice and Apply

Homework Help	
For Exercises	See Examples
13–24	1
26	2
28–39	3, 4

Extra Practice
See page 832.

Write the slope-intercept form of an equation of the line that passes through the given point and is parallel to the graph of each equation.

13. (2, −7), $y = x - 2$
14. (2, −1), $y = 2x + 2$
15. (−3, 2), $y = x - 6$
16. (4, −1), $y = 2x + 1$
17. (−5, −4), $y = \frac{1}{2}x + 1$
18. (3, 3), $y = \frac{2}{3}x - 1$
19. (−4, −3), $y = -\frac{1}{3}x + 3$
20. (−1, 2), $y = -\frac{1}{2}x - 4$
21. (−3, 0), $2y = x - 1$
22. (2, 2), $3y = -2x + 6$
23. (−2, 3), $6x + y = 4$
24. (2, 2), $3x - 4y = -4$

13. $y = x - 9$
14. $y = 2x - 5$
15. $y = x + 5$
16. $y = 2x - 9$
17. $y = \frac{1}{2}x - \frac{3}{2}$
18. $y = \frac{2}{3}x + 1$
19. $y = -\frac{1}{3}x - \frac{13}{3}$
20. $y = -\frac{1}{2}x + \frac{3}{2}$
21. $y = \frac{1}{2}x + \frac{3}{2}$
22. $y = -\frac{2}{3}x + \frac{10}{3}$
23. $y = -6x - 9$
24. $y = \frac{3}{4}x + \frac{1}{2}$

25. **GEOMETRY** A *parallelogram* is a quadrilateral in which opposite sides are parallel. Is $ABCD$ a parallelogram? Explain. See margin.

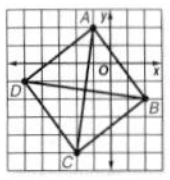

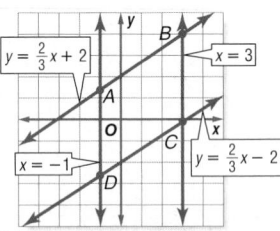

26. Write an equation of the line parallel to the graph of $y = 5x - 3$ and through the origin. $y = 5x$
27. Write an equation of the line with y-intercept −6 that is parallel to the graph of $x - 3y = 8$. $y = \frac{1}{3}x - 6$

Write the slope-intercept form of an equation that passes through the given point and is perpendicular to the graph of each equation. 28–39. See margin.

28. (−2, 0), $y = x - 6$
29. (1, 1), $y = 4x + 6$
30. (−3, 1), $y = -3x + 7$
31. (0, 5), $y = -8x + 4$
32. (1, −3), $y = \frac{1}{2}x + 4$
33. (4, 7), $y = \frac{2}{3}x - 1$
34. (0, 4), $3x + 8y = 4$
35. (−2, 7), $2x - 5y = 3$
36. (6, −1), $3y + x = 3$
37. (0, −1), $5x - y = 3$
38. (8, −2), $5x - 7 = 3y$
★ 39. (3, −3), $3x + 7 = 2x$

40. Find an equation of the line that has a y-intercept of −2 and is perpendicular to the graph of $3x + 6y = 2$. $y = 2x - 2$
41. Write an equation of the line that is perpendicular to the line through (9, 10) and (3, −2) and passes through the x-intercept of that line. $y = -\frac{1}{2}x + 2$

Determine whether the graphs of each pair of equations are *parallel*, *perpendicular*, or *neither*.

★ 42. $y = -2x + 11$
$y + 2x = 23$ parallel
★ 43. $3y = 2x + 14$
$2x - 3y = 2$ parallel
★ 44. $y = -5x$
$y = 5x - 18$ neither

45. They are ⊥, because the slopes are 3 and $-\frac{1}{3}$.

★ 45. **GEOMETRY** The diagonals of a square are segments that connect the opposite vertices. Determine the relationship between the diagonals $\overline{AC}$ and $\overline{BD}$ of square $ABCD$.

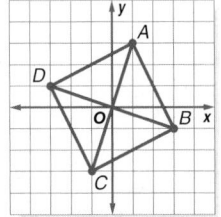

46. **CRITICAL THINKING** What is a if the lines with equations $y = ax + 5$ and $2y = (a + 4)x - 1$ are parallel? 4

Enrichment, p. 316

Pencils of Lines

All of the lines that pass through a single point in the same plane are called a **pencil of lines**.

All lines with the same slope, but different intercepts, are also called a "pencil," a **pencil of parallel lines**.

Graph some of the lines in each pencil.

1. A pencil of lines through the point (1, 3)

2. A pencil of lines described by $y - 4 = m(x - 2)$, where m is any real number

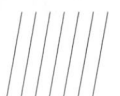

Answer

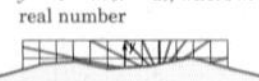

25. The lines for $x = 3$ and $x = -1$ are parallel because all vertical lines are parallel. The lines for $y = \frac{2}{3}x + 2$ and $y = \frac{2}{3}x - 3$ are parallel because they have the same slope. Thus, both pairs of opposite sides are parallel and the figure is a parallelogram.

296 Chapter 5 Analyzing Linear Equations

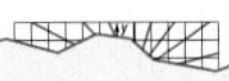

47. WRITING IN MATH Answer the question that was posed at the beginning of the lesson. **See margin.**

How can you determine whether two lines are parallel?

Include the following in your answer:
- an equation whose graph is parallel to the graph of $y = -5x$, with an explanation of your reasoning, and
- an equation whose graph is perpendicular to the graph of $y = -5x$, with an explanation of your reasoning.

48. What is the slope of a line perpendicular to the graph of $3x + 4y = 24$? **D**

 Ⓐ $-\dfrac{4}{3}$ Ⓑ $-\dfrac{3}{4}$ Ⓒ $\dfrac{3}{4}$ Ⓓ $\dfrac{4}{3}$

49. How can the graph of $y = 3x + 4$ be used to graph $y = 3x + 2$? **C**

 Ⓐ Move the graph of the line right 2 units.
 Ⓑ Change the slope of the graph from 4 to 2.
 Ⓒ Change the y-intercept from 4 to 2.
 Ⓓ Move the graph of the line left 2 units.

Maintain Your Skills

Mixed Review   Write the point-slope form of an equation for a line that passes through each point with the given slope. *(Lesson 5-5)*

50. $(3, 5)$, $m = -2$ **51.** $(-4, 7)$, $m = 5$ **52.** $(-1, -3)$, $m = -\dfrac{1}{2}$
$y - 5 = -2(x - 3)$ $y - 7 = 5(x + 4)$ $y + 3 = -\dfrac{1}{2}(x + 1)$

TELEPHONE For Exercises 53 and 54, use the following information.
An international calling plan charges a rate per minute plus a flat fee. A 10-minute call to the Czech Republic costs \$3.19. A 15-minute call costs \$4.29. *(Lesson 5-4)*

53. Write a linear equation in slope-intercept form to find the total cost C of an m-minute call. $C = 0.22m + 0.99$

54. Find the cost of a 12-minute call. **\$3.63**

55. $y = -\dfrac{1}{2}x + \dfrac{3}{2}$ **56.** $y = -\dfrac{1}{4}x + 2$ **57.** $y = -5x + 11$

Getting Ready for the Next Lesson   **PREREQUISITE SKILL** Write the slope-intercept form of an equation of the line that passes through each pair of points. *(To review slope-intercept form, see Lesson 5-4.)*

55. $(5, -1)$, $(-3, 3)$ **56.** $(0, 2)$, $(8, 0)$ **57.** $(2, 1)$, $(3, -4)$

58. $(5, 5)$, $(8, -1)$ **59.** $(6, 9)$, $(4, 9)$ **60.** $(-6, 4)$, $(2, -2)$
$y = -2x + 15$ $y = 9$ $y = -\dfrac{3}{4}x - \dfrac{1}{2}$

Practice Quiz 2   Lessons 5-3 through 5-6

Write the slope-intercept form for an equation of the line that satisfies each condition.

1. slope 4 and y-intercept -3 *(Lesson 5-3)* $y = 4x - 3$
2. passes through $(1, -3)$ with slope 2 *(Lesson 5-4)* $y = 2x - 5$
3. passes through $(-1, -2)$ and $(1, 3)$ *(Lesson 5-4)* $y = \dfrac{5}{2}x + \dfrac{1}{2}$
4. parallel to the graph of $y = 2x - 2$ and passes through $(-2, 3)$ *(Lesson 5-6)* $y = 2x + 7$
            5. $x - 2y = -11$, $y = \dfrac{1}{2}x + \dfrac{11}{2}$
5. Write $y - 4 = \dfrac{1}{2}(x + 3)$ in standard form and in slope-intercept form. *(Lesson 5-5)*

www.algebra1.com/self_check_quiz   Lesson 5-6   Geometry: Parallel and Perpendicular Lines   **297**

---

28. $y = -x - 2$ **32.** $y = -2x - 1$ **36.** $y = 3x - 19$

29. $y = -\dfrac{1}{4}x + \dfrac{5}{4}$ **33.** $y = -\dfrac{3}{2}x + 13$ **37.** $y = -\dfrac{1}{5}x - 1$

30. $y = \dfrac{1}{3}x + 2$ **34.** $y = \dfrac{8}{3}x + 4$ **38.** $y = -\dfrac{3}{5}x + \dfrac{14}{5}$

31. $y = \dfrac{1}{8}x + 5$ **35.** $y = -\dfrac{5}{2}x + 2$ **39.** $y = -3$

5-7 Statistics: Scatter Plots and Lines of Fit

1 Focus

5-Minute Check Transparency 5-7 Use as a quiz or review of Lesson 5-6.

Mathematical Background notes are available for this lesson on p. 254D.

Building on Prior Knowledge

In Lesson 5-1, students learned that the direction of the line corresponded to a positive or negative slope. That same logic applies to determining a positive correlation or a negative correlation in data.

How do scatter plots help identify trends in data?

Ask students:

• What type of slope does the line have? **positive**

• What would you do to find the equation of that line? **Use two points on the line to write the equation.**

• **Travel** What type of graph would show that the longer you drive the less gas is left in your gas tank? **a line with negative slope**

What You'll Learn

• Interpret points on a scatter plot.

• Write equations for lines of fit.

Vocabulary

• scatter plot
• positive correlation
• negative correlation
• line of fit
• best-fit line
• linear interpolation

How do scatter plots help identify trends in data?

The points of a set of real-world data do not always lie on one line. But, you may be able to draw a line that seems to be close to all the points.

The line in the graph shows a linear relationship between the year x and the number of bushels of apples y. As the years increase, the number of bushels of apples also increases.

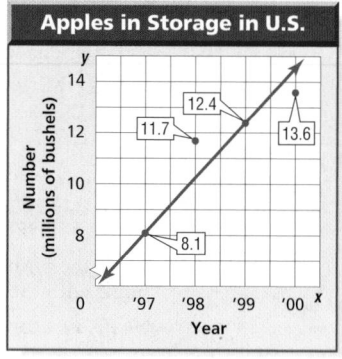

Apples in Storage in U.S.

Source: U.S. Apple Association

INTERPRET POINTS ON A SCATTER PLOT A **scatter plot** is a graph in which two sets of data are plotted as ordered pairs in a coordinate plane. Scatter plots are used to investigate a relationship between two quantities.

• In the first graph below, there is a **positive correlation** between x and y. That is, as x increases, y increases.

• In the second graph below, there is a **negative correlation** between x and y. That is, as x increases, y decreases.

• In the third graph below, there is *no correlation* between x and y. That is, x and y are not related.

If the pattern in a scatter plot is linear, you can draw a line to summarize the data. This can help identify trends in the data.

Key Concept — **Scatter Plots**

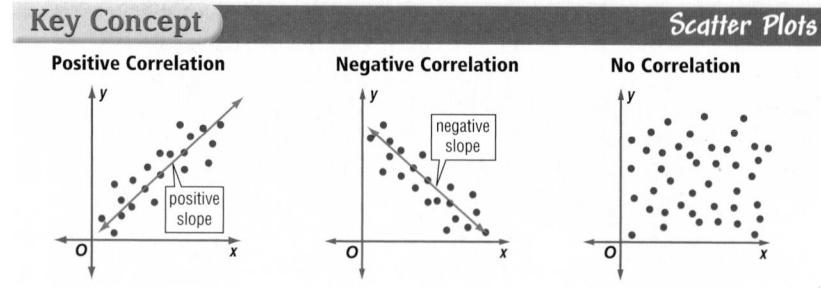

Positive Correlation   Negative Correlation   No Correlation

Resource Manager

 Workbook and Reproducible Masters

Chapter 5 Resource Masters
• Study Guide and Intervention, pp. 317–318
• Skills Practice, p. 319
• Practice, p. 320
• Reading to Learn Mathematics, p. 321
• Enrichment, p. 322
• Assessment, p. 338

Graphing Calculator and Spreadsheet Masters, p. 32
Parent and Student Study Guide Workbook, p. 44
Science and Mathematics Lab Manual, pp. 51–56
Teaching Algebra With Manipulatives Masters, pp. 1, 24, 105

 Transparencies

5-Minute Check Transparency 5-7
Answer Key Transparencies

Technology

Interactive Chalkboard

Example 1 **Analyze Scatter Plots**

Determine whether each graph shows a *positive correlation*, **a** *negative correlation*, **or** *no correlation*. **If there is a positive or negative correlation, describe its meaning in the situation.**

a. **NUTRITION** The graph shows fat grams and Calories for selected choices at a fast-food restaurant.

The graph shows a positive correlation. As the number of fat grams increases, the number of Calories increases.

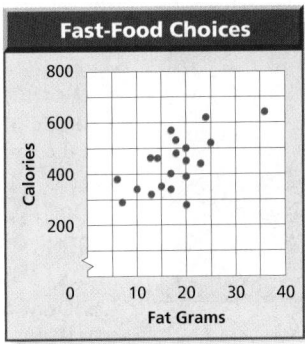

Fast-Food Choices

Source: Olen Publishing Co.

b. **CARS** The graph shows the weight and the highway gas mileage of selected cars.

The graph shows a negative correlation. As the weight of the automobile increases, the gas mileage decreases.

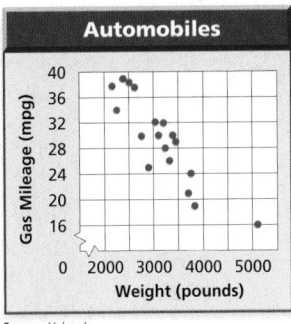

Automobiles

Source: Yahoo!

TEACHING TIP

Make sure that students understand that you can have a negative correlation without having negative numbers in your data.

Is there a relationship between the length of a person's foot and his or her height? Make a scatter plot and then look for a pattern.

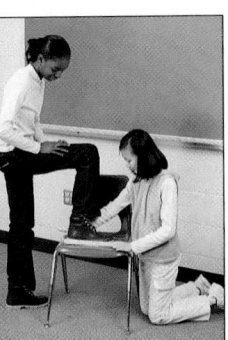

Algebra Activity
Making Predictions

Collect the Data
- Measure your partner's foot and height in centimeters. Then trade places.
- Add the points (foot length, height) to a class scatter plot.

Analyze the Data 1–3. See students' work.
1. Is there a correlation between foot length and height for the members of your class? If so, describe it.
2. Draw a line that summarizes the data and shows how the height changes as the foot length changes.

Make a Conjecture
3. Use the line to predict the height of a person whose foot length is 25 centimeters. Explain your method.

 www.algebra1.com/extra_examples

Lesson 5-7 Statistics: Scatter Plots and Lines of Fit **299**

INTERPRET POINTS ON A SCATTER PLOT

In-Class Example Power Point®

1. Determine whether each graph shows a *positive correlation*, a *negative correlation*, or *no correlation*. If there is a positive or negative correlation, describe it.

a. The graph shows average personal income for U.S. citizens.

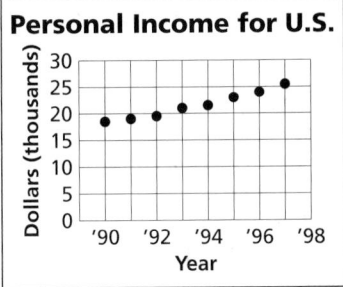

Personal Income for U.S.

Source: U.S. Department of Commerce

Positive correlation; with each year, the average personal income rose.

b. The graph shows the average students per computer in U.S. public schools.

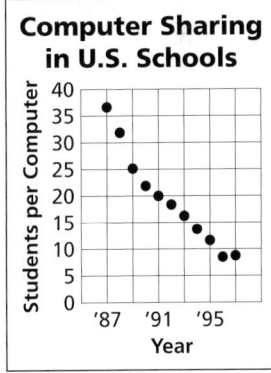

Computer Sharing in U.S. Schools

Source: QED National Education Database

Negative correlation; with each year, more computers are in the schools, making the students per computer rate smaller.

Algebra Activity

Materials: centimeter ruler or meterstick, grid paper
- You could also give pairs of students identical grids on transparencies to plot their two data points. Lay all the grids together on the overhead projector to get a quick compilation of the data points.
- Allow students to skip this activity if they are uncomfortable having their feet measured.

Lesson 5-7 Statistics: Scatter Plots and Lines of Fit **299**

LINES OF FIT

2 The table shows the world population growing at a rapid rate.

Year	Population (millions)
1650	500
1850	1000
1930	2000
1975	4000
1998	5900

Source: *The World Almanac*

a. Draw a scatter plot and determine what relationship exists, if any, in the data.
There is a positive correlation between years and population.

b. Draw a line of fit for the scatter plot.

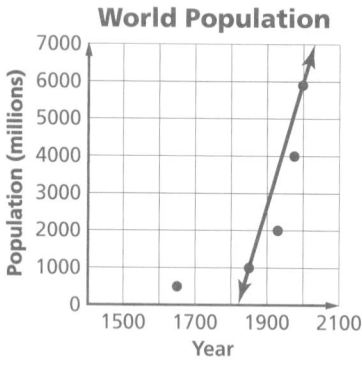

World Population

c. Write the slope-intercept form of an equation for the line of fit. **Using (1850, 1000) and (1998, 5900), $y \approx 33.1x - 60,235$.**

More About . . .

Birds · · · · · · · · · · ·

The bald eagle was listed as an endangered species in 1963, when the number of breeding pairs had dropped below 500.
Source: U.S. Fish and Wildlife Service

Study Tip

Lines of Fit
When you use the graphical method, the line of fit is an approximation. So, you may draw another line of fit using other points that is equally valid. Some valid lines of fit may not contain any of the data points.

LINES OF FIT   If the data points do not all lie on a line, but are close to a line, you can draw a **line of fit**. This line describes the trend of the data. Once you have a line of fit, you can find an equation of the line.

In this lesson, you will use a graphical method to find a line of fit. In the follow-up to Lesson 5-7, you will use a graphing calculator to find a line of fit. The calculator uses a statistical method to find the line that most closely approximates the data. This line is called the **best-fit line**.

Example 2 *Find a Line of Fit*

BIRDS   The table shows an estimate for the number of bald eagle pairs in the United States for certain years since 1985.

Years since 1985	3	5	7	9	11	14
Bald Eagle Pairs	2500	3000	3700	4500	5000	5800

Source: U.S. Fish and Wildlife Service

a. Draw a scatter plot and determine what relationship exists, if any, in the data.

Let the independent variable x be the number of years since 1985, and let the dependent variable y be the number of bald eagle pairs.

As the number of years increases, the number of bald eagle pairs increases. There is a positive correlation between the two variables.

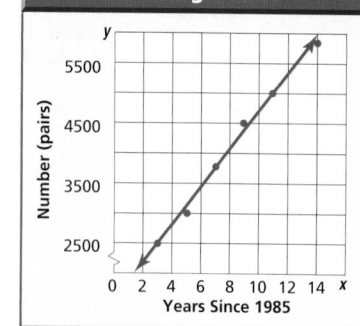

b. Draw a line of fit for the scatter plot.

No one line will pass through all of the data points. Draw a line that passes close to the points. A line of fit is shown in the scatter plot at the right.

c. Write the slope-intercept form of an equation for the line of fit.

The line of fit shown above passes through the data points (3, 2500) and (11, 5000).

Step 1 Find the slope.

$$m = \frac{y_2 - y_1}{x_2 - x_1} \qquad \text{Slope formula}$$

$$m = \frac{5000 - 2500}{11 - 3} \qquad \text{Let } (x_1, y_1) = (3, 2500) \text{ and } (x_2, y_2) = (11, 5000).$$

$$m = \frac{2500}{8} \text{ or } 312.5 \qquad \text{Simplify.}$$

Step 2 Use $m = 312.5$ and either the point-slope form or the slope-intercept form to write the equation. You can use either data point. We chose (3, 2500).

Point-slope form	**Slope-intercept form**
$y - y_1 = m(x - x_1)$	$y = mx + b$
$y - 2500 = 312.5(x - 5)$	$2500 = 312.5(3) + b$
$y - 2500 = 312.5x - 937.5$	$2500 = 937.5 + b$
$y = 312.5x + 1562.5$	$1562.5 = b$
	$y = 312.5x + 1562.5$

Using either method, $y = 312.5x + 1562.5$.

CHECK Check your result by substituting (11, 5000) into $y = 312.5x + 1562.5$.

$$y = 312.5x + 1562.5 \quad \text{Line of fit equation}$$
$$5000 \stackrel{?}{=} 312.5(11) + 1562.5 \quad \text{Replace } x \text{ with 11 and } y \text{ with 5000.}$$
$$5000 \stackrel{?}{=} 3437.5 + 1562.5 \quad \text{Multiply.}$$
$$5000 = 5000 \checkmark \quad \text{Add.}$$

The solution checks.

In Lesson 5-4, you learned about linear extrapolation, which is predicting values that are *outside* the range of the data. You can also use a linear equation to predict values that are *inside* the range of the data. This is called **linear interpolation**.

Example 3 *Linear Interpolation*

BIRDS Use the equation for the line of fit in Example 2 to estimate the number of bald eagle pairs in 1998.

Use the equation $y = 312.5x + 1562.5$, where x is the number of years since 1985 and y is the number of bald eagle pairs.

$$y = 312.5x + 1562.5 \quad \text{Original equation}$$
$$y = 312.5(13) + 1562.5 \quad \text{Replace } x \text{ with 1998 − 1985 or 13.}$$
$$y = 5625 \quad \text{Simplify.}$$

There were about 5625 bald eagle pairs in 1998.

Check for Understanding

Concept Check
1. **Explain** how to determine whether a scatter plot has a positive or negative correlation. **1–3. See margin.**

2. **OPEN ENDED** Sketch scatter plots that have each type of correlation.
   a. positive
   b. negative
   c. no correlation

3. **Compare and contrast** linear interpolation and linear extrapolation.

Guided Practice Determine whether each graph shows a *positive correlation*, a *negative correlation*, or *no correlation*. If there is a positive or negative correlation, describe its meaning in the situation.

GUIDED PRACTICE KEY	
Exercises	Examples
4, 5	1
6–8	2
9	3

4. Positive; the longer you study, the better your test score.

5. Negative; the more TV you watch, the less you exercise.

4.
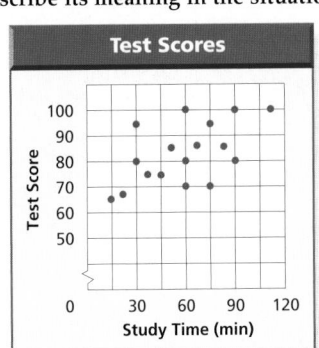

5.
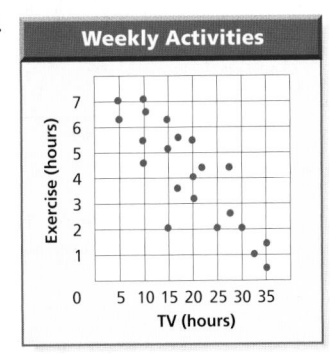

Answers

1. If the data points form a linear pattern such that *y* increases as *x* increases, there is a positive correlation. If the linear pattern shows that *y* decreases as *x* increases, there is a negative correlation.

2a.
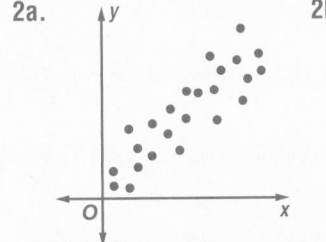

2b.
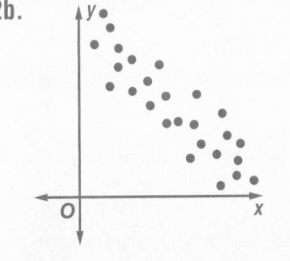

3. Linear extrapolation predicts values outside the range of the data set. Linear interpolation predicts values inside the range of the data.

Teaching Tip Remind students that any prediction is only as valid as the equation used to find it. Therefore, there are as many predictions as there are equations that can be written from pairs of points.

3 Use the prediction equation in In-Class Example 2 to predict the world population in 2010. **6281 million**

3 Practice/Apply

Study Notebook

Have students—
* complete the definitions/examples for the remaining terms on their Vocabulary Builder worksheets for Chapter 5.
* include their sketches from Exercise 2.
* include any other item(s) that they find helpful in mastering the skills in this lesson.

Answers

2c.

Answers

6–7. positive correlation

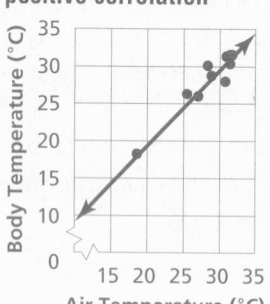

18–19.

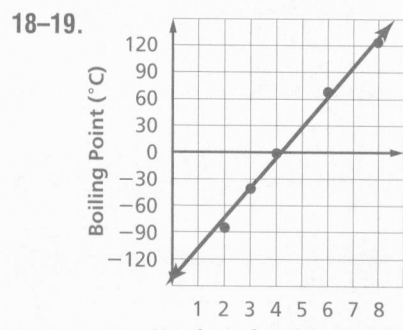

24–25.

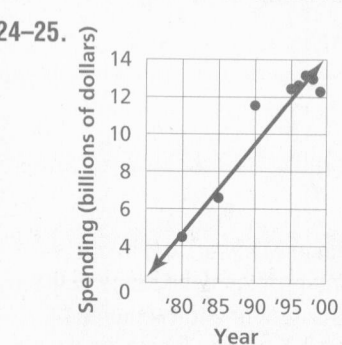

Application   **BIOLOGY**   For Exercises 6–9, use the table that shows the average body temperature in degrees Celsius of 9 insects at a given air temperature.

Temperature (°C)								
Air	25.7	30.4	28.7	31.2	31.5	26.2	30.1	31.5	18.2
Body	27.0	31.5	28.9	31.0	31.5	25.6	28.4	31.7	18.7

6. Draw a scatter plot and determine what relationship exists, if any, in the data. **See margin.**

7. Draw a line of fit for the scatter plot. **See margin.**

8. using (26.2, 25.6) and (31.2, 31.0) and rounding, $y = x - 3$

8. Write the slope-intercept form of an equation for the line of fit.

9. Predict the body temperature of an insect if the air temperature is 40.2°C. **40.1°C**

Practice and Apply

10. Negative; as time goes by, fewer people return their census forms.

11. no correlation

12. Positive; as time goes on, more people use electronic tax returns.

13. Positive; the higher the sugar content, the more Calories.

Determine whether each graph shows a *positive correlation*, a *negative correlation*, or *no correlation*. If there is a positive or negative correlation, describe its meaning in the situation.

10.

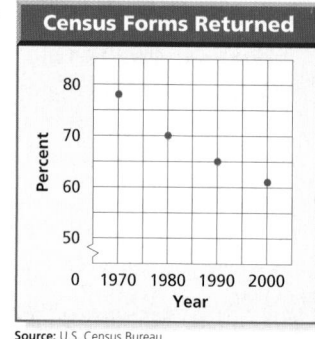

Source: U.S. Census Bureau

11.

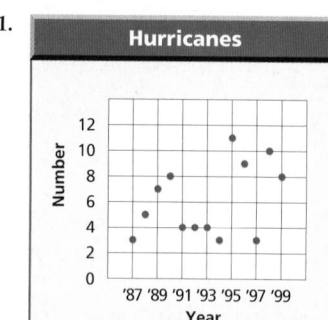

Source: *USA TODAY*

12.

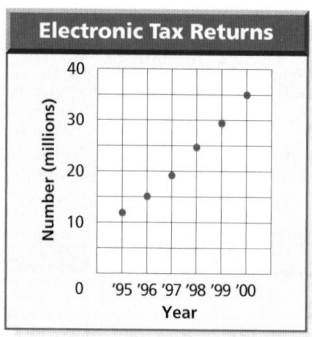

Source: IRS

13.

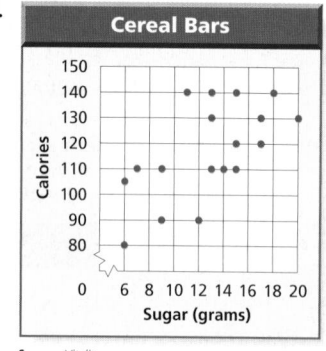

Source: *Vitality*

FARMING   For Exercises 14 and 15, refer to the graph at the top of page 298 about apple storage.

14. Use the points (1997, 8.1) and (1999, 12.4) to write the slope-intercept form of an equation for the line of fit. **$y = 2.15x - 4285.45$**

15. Predict the number of bushels of apples in storage in 2002. **18.85 million**

USED CARS For Exercises 16 and 17, use the scatter plot that shows the ages and prices of used cars from classified ads.

16. Use the points (2, 9600) and (5, 6000) to write the slope-intercept form of an equation for the line of fit shown in the scatter plot.

17. Predict the price of a car that is 7 years old. **$3600**

16. $y = -1200x + 12{,}000$

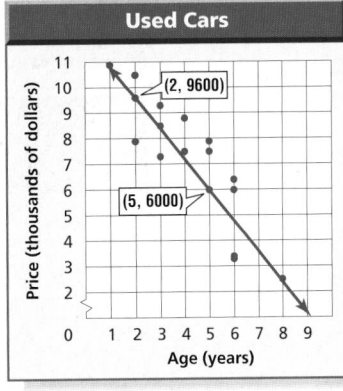

Used Cars

(2, 9600)

(5, 6000)

Price (thousands of dollars) / Age (years)

Source: *Columbus Dispatch*

PHYSICAL SCIENCE For Exercises 18–23, use the following information. Hydrocarbons are composed of only carbon and hydrogen atoms. The table gives the number of carbon atoms and the boiling points for several hydrocarbons.

18. Draw a scatter plot comparing the numbers of carbon atoms to the boiling points. **See margin.**

19. Draw a line of fit for the data. **See margin.** **20–23. Sample answers given.**

20. Write the slope-intercept form of an equation for the line of fit. $y = 37x - 153$

21. Predict the boiling point for methane (CH_4), which has 1 carbon atom. **−116°C**

22. Predict the boiling point for pentane (C_5H_{12}), which has 5 carbon atoms. **32°C**

23. The boiling point of heptane is 98.4°C. Use the equation of the line of fit to predict the number of carbon atoms in heptane. **7**

	Hydrocarbons		
Name	**Formula**	**Number of Carbon Atoms**	**Boiling Point (°C)**
Ethane	C_2H_6	2	−89
Propane	C_3H_8	3	−42
Butane	C_4H_{10}	4	−1
Hexane	C_6H_{12}	6	69
Octane	C_8H_{18}	8	126

SPACE For Exercises 24–28, use the table that shows the amount the United States government has spent on space and other technologies in selected years.

Federal Spending on Space and Other Technologies								
Year	1980	1985	1990	1995	1996	1997	1998	1999
Spending (billions of dollars)	4.5	6.6	11.6	12.6	12.7	13.1	12.9	12.4

Source: U.S. Office of Management and Budget

24. Draw a scatter plot and determine what relationship, if any, exists in the data. **See margin.**

25. Draw a line of fit for the scatter plot. **See margin.**

26. Let x represent the number of years since 1980. Let y represent the spending in billions of dollars. Write the slope-intercept form of the equation for the line of fit. **Sample answer: using (0, 4.5) and (16, 12.7), $y = 0.5125x + 4.5$**

27. **Sample answer: about $17.3 billion**

27. Predict the amount that will be spent on space and other technologies in 2005.

28. **Sample answer: less**

28. The government projects spending of $14.3 billion in space and other technologies in 2005. How does this compare to your prediction?

www.algebra1.com/self_check_quiz

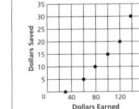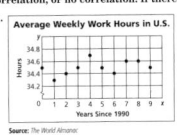
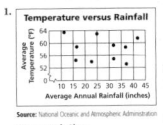

Answers

29–30.

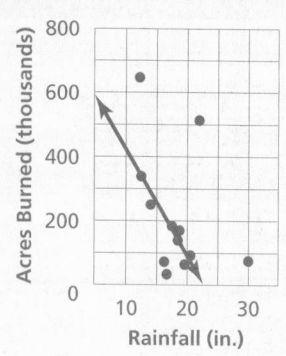

34.

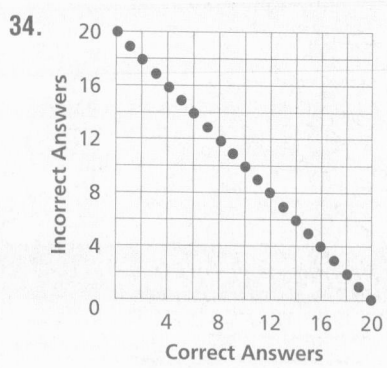

37. You can visualize a line to determine whether the data has a positive or negative correlation. Answers should include the following.

• Write a linear equation for the line of fit. Then substitute the person's height and solve for the corresponding age.

---

31. using (12.7, 340) and (17.5, 194) and rounding,
$y = -30.4x + 726.3$

WebQuest

You can use a line of fit to describe the trend in winning Olympic times. Visit www.algebra1.com/webquest to continue work on your WebQuest project.

33. The data point lies beyond the main grouping of data points. It can be ignored as an extreme value.

Standardized Test Practice
Ⓐ Ⓑ Ⓒ Ⓓ

FORESTRY For Exercises 29–33, use the table that shows the number of acres burned by wildfires in Florida each year and the corresponding number of inches of spring rainfall.

Florida's Burned Acreage and Spring Rainfall

Year	Rainfall (inches)	Acres (thousands)	Year	Rainfall (inches)	Acres (thousands)
1988	17.5	194	1994	18.1	180
1989	12.0	645	1995	16.3	46
1990	14.0	250	1996	20.4	94
1991	30.1	87	1997	18.5	146
1992	16.0	83	1998	22.2	507
1993	19.6	80	1999	12.7	340

Source: Florida Division of Forestry

29–30. See margin.

29. Draw a scatter plot with rainfall on the *x*-axis and acres on the *y*-axis.

30. Draw a line of fit for the data.

31. Write the slope-intercept form of an equation for the line of fit.

32. In 2000, there was only 8.25 inches of spring rainfall. Estimate the number of acres burned by wildfires in 2000. **about 476 thousand acres**

33. In 1998, there was 22.2 inches of rainfall, yet 507,000 acres were burned. Where was this data graphed in the scatter plot? How did this affect the line of fit?

Online Research **Data Update** What has happened to the number of acres burned by wildfires in Florida since 1999? Visit www.algebra1.com/data_update to learn more.

34. CRITICAL THINKING A test contains 20 true-false questions. Draw a scatter plot that shows the relationship between the number of correct answers *x* and the number of incorrect answers *y*. **See margin.**

RESEARCH For Exercises 35 and 36, choose a topic to research that you believe may be correlated, such as arm span and height. Find existing data or collect your own.

35. Draw a line of fit for the data. **35–36. See students' work.**

36. Use the line to make a prediction about the data.

37. **WRITING IN MATH** Answer the question that was posed at the beginning of the lesson. **See margin.**

How do scatter plots help identify trends in data?

Include the following in your answer:

• a scatter plot that shows a person's height and his or her age, with a description of any trends, and

• an explanation of how you could use the scatter plot to predict a person's age given his or her height.

38. Which graph is the best example of data that show a negative linear relationship between the variables *x* and *y*? **D**

Ⓐ 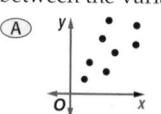 Ⓑ 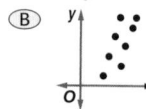 Ⓒ 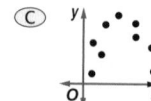 Ⓓ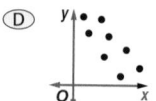

Differentiated Instruction

Intrapersonal Have students make a list of concepts from this chapter that they feel they know well and some they may need to review. Have students review their lists after they complete the Study Guide and reevaluate what topics they need to study more before the chapter test.

39. Choose the equation for the line that best fits the data in the table at the right. **B**

    Ⓐ $y = x + 4$

    Ⓑ $y = 2x + 3$

    Ⓒ $y = 7$

    Ⓓ $y = 4x - 5$

x	y
1	5
2	7
3	7
4	11

Extending the Lesson

GEOGRAPHY For Exercises 40–44, use the following information.
The *latitude* of a place on Earth is the measure of its distance from the equator.

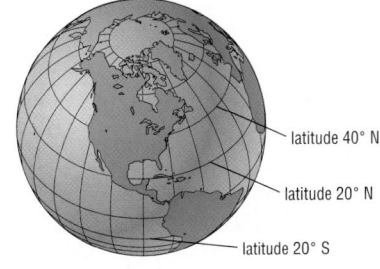

latitude 40° N

latitude 20° N

latitude 20° S

40. Sample answer: Cities with greater north latitudes have lower January temperatures.

41–44. See students' work.

40. MAKE A CONJECTURE What do you think is the relationship between a city's latitude and its January temperature?

41. RESEARCH Use the Internet or other reference to find the latitude of 15 cities in the northern hemisphere and the corresponding January mean temperatures.

42. Make a scatter plot and draw a line of fit for the data.

43. Write an equation for the line of fit.

44. MAKE A CONJECTURE Find the latitude of your city and use the equation to predict its mean January temperature. Check your prediction by using another source such as the newspaper.

Maintain Your Skills

Mixed Review

Write the slope-intercept form of an equation for the line that satisfies each condition. *(Lesson 5-6)*

45. $y = -4x - 3$

46. $y = -\frac{1}{2}x$

45. parallel to the graph of $y = -4x + 5$ and passes through $(-2, 5)$

46. perpendicular to the graph of $y = 2x + 3$ and passes through $(0, 0)$

Write the point-slope form of an equation for a line that passes through each point with the given slope. *(Lesson 5-5)*

47. $y - 3 = -2(x + 2)$

48. $y + 2 = 3(x - 1)$

49. $y + 3 = x + 3$

47.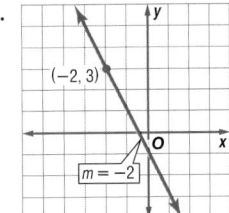

48.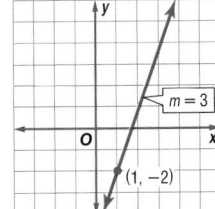

49.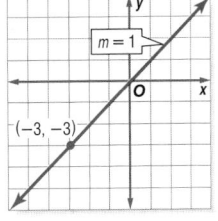

Find the *x*- and *y*-intercepts of the graph of each equation. *(Lesson 4-5)*

50. $3x + 4y = 12$ **4, 3**   **51.** $2x - 5y = 8$ **4, −1.6**   **52.** $y = 3x + 6$ **−2, 6**

Solve each equation. Then check your solution. *(Lesson 3-4)*

53. $\frac{r + 7}{-4} = \frac{r + 2}{6}$ **−5**   **54.** $\frac{n - (-4)}{-3} = 7$ **−25**   **55.** $\frac{2x - 1}{5} = \frac{4x - 5}{7}$ **3**

4 Assess

Open-Ended Assessment

Writing Have students describe a situation in which a scatter plot would be a better representation of the data than a broken line graph.

Assessment Options

Quiz (Lesson 5-7) is available on p. 338 of the *Chapter 5 Resource Masters*.

Graphing Calculator
A Follow-Up of Lesson 5-7

Know Your Calculator The graphing calculator has two models to compute the equation of a best-fit line —

LinReg (ax+b) linear regression
Med-Med   median-fit line

The linear regression method uses a least-squares fit method to determine the values for a and b. This utilizes calculus involving the distance each point is from the best-fit line.

The median-fit method calculates the medians of the coordinates of the data points.

Correlation Coefficient The calculator also displays values for r^2 and r. The closer $|r|$ is to 1, the better the equation fits the data.

• Make sure students have cleared the L1 and L2 lists before entering new data.

• Have students complete Exercises 1–5.

Regression and Median-Fit Lines

One type of equation of best-fit you can find is a linear **regression equation**. Linear regression is sometimes called the *method of least squares*.

EARNINGS The table shows the average hourly earnings of U.S. production workers for selected years.

Year	1960	1965	1970	1975	1980	1985	1990	1995	1999
Earnings	$2.09	2.46	3.23	4.53	6.66	8.57	10.01	11.43	13.24

Source: Bureau of Labor Statistics

Find and graph a linear regression equation. Then predict the average hourly earnings in 2010.

Step 1 *Find a regression equation.*

• Enter the years in L1 and the earnings in L2.
  KEYSTROKES: *Review entering a list on page 204.*

• Find the regression equation by selecting LinReg(ax+b) on the STAT CALC menu.
  KEYSTROKES: $\boxed{\text{STAT}}$ 4 $\boxed{\text{ENTER}}$

The equation is in the form $y = ax + b$.

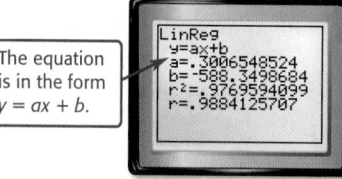

The equation is about $y = 0.30x - 588.35$.

r is the **linear correlation coefficient**. The closer the absolute value of r is to 1, the better the equation models the data. Because the r value is close to 1, the model fits the data well.

Step 2 *Graph the regression equation.*

• Use STAT PLOT to graph the scatter plot.
  KEYSTROKES: *Review statistical plots on page 204.*

• Copy the equation to the Y= list and graph.
  KEYSTROKES: $\boxed{\text{Y=}}$ $\boxed{\text{VARS}}$ 5   1 $\boxed{\text{GRAPH}}$

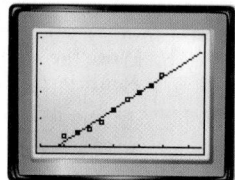

[1950, 2020] scl: 10 by [0, 20] scl: 5

The *residual* is the difference between actual and predicted data. The predicted earnings in 1970 using this model were $3.94. (To calculate, press $\boxed{\text{2nd}}$ [CALC] 1 1970 $\boxed{\text{ENTER}}$.) So the residual for 1970 was $3.94 – $3.23 or $0.71.

Step 3 *Predict using the regression equation.*

• Find y when $x = 2010$ using **value** on the CALC menu.
  KEYSTROKES: $\boxed{\text{2nd}}$ [CALC] 1 2010 $\boxed{\text{ENTER}}$

According to the regression equation, the average hourly earnings in 2010 will be about $15.97.

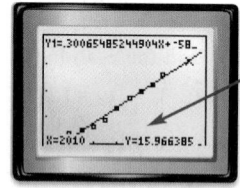

The graph and the coordinates of the point are shown.

Investigation

A second type of best-fit line that can be found using a graphing calculator is a **median-fit line**. The equation of a median-fit line is calculated using the medians of the coordinates of the data points.

Find and graph a median-fit equation for the data on hourly earnings. Then predict the average hourly earnings in 2010. Compare this prediction to the one made using the regression equation.

Step 1 *Find a median-fit equation.*

- The data are already in Lists 1 and 2. Find the median-fit equation by using **Med-Med** on the **STAT CALC** menu.

  KEYSTROKES: STAT ▶ 3 ENTER

The median-fit equation is $y = 0.299x - 585.17$.

Step 2 *Graph the median-fit equation.*

- Copy the equation to the Y= list and graph.

  KEYSTROKES: Y= CLEAR VARS 5 ▶ ▶ 1
  GRAPH

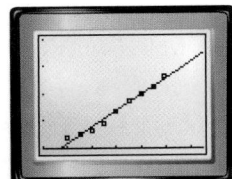

[1950, 2010] scl: 10 by [0, 20] scl: 5

Step 3 *Predict using the median-fit equation.*

  KEYSTROKES: 2nd [CALC] 1 2010 ENTER

According to the median-fit equation, the average hourly earnings in 2010 will be about $15.82. This is slightly less than the predicted value found using the regression equation.

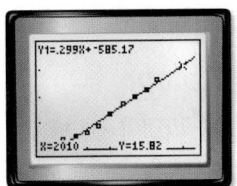

Exercises

Exercises

Refer to the data on bald eagles in Example 2 on pages 300 and 301.

1. Find regression and median-fit equations for the data. 1–5. See margin.

2. What is the correlation coefficient of the regression equation? What does it tell you about the data?

3. Use the regression and median-fit equations to predict the number of bald eagle pairs in 1998. Compare these to the number found in Example 3 on page 301.

For Exercises 4 and 5, use the table that shows the number of votes cast for the Democratic presidential candidate in selected North Carolina counties in the 1996 and 2000 elections.

4. Find regression and median-fit equations for the data.

5. In 1996, New Hanover County had 22,839 votes for the Democratic candidate. Use the regression and median-fit equations to estimate the number of votes for the Democratic candidate in that county in 2000. How do the predictions compare to the actual number of 29,292?

1996	2000
14,447	16,284
19,458	19,281
28,674	30,921
31,658	38,545
32,739	38,626
46,543	52,457
49,186	53,907
69,208	80,787
103,429	126,911
103,574	123,466

Source: NC State Board of Elections

www.algebra1.com/other_calculator_keystrokes

Graphing Calculator Investigation 307

Chapter 5 Study Guide and Review

Vocabulary and Concept Check

Vocabulary and Concept Check

- This alphabetical list of vocabulary terms in Chapter 5 includes a page reference where each term was introduced.

- **Assessment** A vocabulary test/review for Chapter 5 is available on p. 336 of the *Chapter 5 Resource Masters*.

Lesson-by-Lesson Review

For each lesson,
- the main ideas are summarized,
- additional examples review concepts, and
- practice exercises are provided.

Vocabulary PuzzleMaker

ELL The Vocabulary PuzzleMaker software improves students' mathematics vocabulary using four puzzle formats—crossword, scramble, word search using a word list, and word search using clues. Students can work on a computer screen or from a printed handout.

MindJogger Videoquizzes

ELL MindJogger Videoquizzes provide an alternative review of concepts presented in this chapter. Students work in teams in a game show format to gain points for correct answers. The questions are presented in three rounds.

Round 1 Concepts (5 questions)
Round 2 Skills (4 questions)
Round 3 Problem Solving (4 questions)

Vocabulary and Concept Check

best-fit line (p. 300)	line of fit (p. 300)	positive correlation (p. 298)
constant of variation (p. 264)	negative correlation (p. 298)	rate of change (p. 258)
direct variation (p. 264)	parallel lines (p. 292)	scatter plot (p. 298)
family of graphs (p. 265)	parent graph (p. 265)	slope (p. 256)
linear extrapolation (p. 283)	perpendicular lines (p. 293)	slope-intercept form (p. 272)
linear interpolation (p. 301)	point-slope form (p. 286)	

Exercises Choose the correct term to complete each sentence.

1. An equation of the form $y = kx$, where $k \neq 0$, describes a (*direct variation*, *linear extrapolation*).

2. The ratio of (*rise*, *run*), or vertical change, to the (*rise*, *run*), or horizontal change, as you move from one point on a line to another, is the slope of a nonvertical line.

3. The lines with equations $y = -2x + 7$ and $y = -2x - 6$ are (*parallel*, *perpendicular*).

4. The equation $y - 2 = -3(x - 1)$ is written in (*point-slope*, *slope-intercept*) form.

5. The equation $y = -\frac{1}{3}x + 6$ is written in (*slope-intercept*, *standard*) form.

6. The (*x-intercept*, *y-intercept*) of the equation $-x - 4y = 2$ is $-\frac{1}{2}$.

Lesson-by-Lesson Review

5-1 *Slope*

See pages 256–262.

Concept Summary

- The slope of a nonvertical line is the ratio of the rise to the run.
- $m = \dfrac{y_2 - y_1}{x_2 - x_1}$

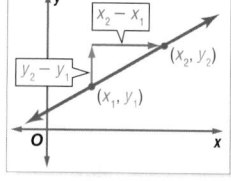

Example Determine the slope of the line that passes through $(0, -4)$ and $(3, 2)$.

Let $(0, -4) = (x_1, y_1)$ and $(3, 2) = (x_2, y_2)$.

$m = \dfrac{y_2 - y_1}{x_2 - x_1}$ Slope formula

$m = \dfrac{2 - (-4)}{3 - 0}$ $x_1 = 0, x_2 = 3, y_1 = -4, y_2 = 2$

$m = \dfrac{6}{3}$ or 2   Simplify.

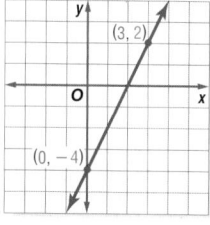

Exercises Find the slope of the line that passes through each pair of points.
See Examples 1–4 on page 257.

7. $(1, 3), (-2, -6)$ **3**
8. $(0, 5), (6, 2)$ $-\dfrac{1}{2}$
9. $(-6, 4), (-6, -2)$ **undefined**
10. $(8, -3), (-2, -3)$ **0**
11. $(2.9, 4.7), (0.5, 1.1)$ **1.5**
12. $\left(\dfrac{1}{2}, 1\right), \left(-1, \dfrac{2}{3}\right)$ $\dfrac{2}{9}$

 www.algebra1.com/vocabulary_review

FOLDABLES™

Study Organizer

For more information about Foldables, see *Teaching Mathematics with Foldables.*

Have students look through the chapter to make sure they have included examples in their Foldables for each lesson of the chapter.

Encourage students to refer to their Foldables while completing the Study Guide and Review and to use them in preparing for the Chapter Test.

5-2 Slope and Direct Variation

See pages 264–270.

Concept Summary

- A direct variation is described by an equation of the form $y = kx$, where $k \neq 0$.
- In $y = kx$, k is the constant of variation. It is also the slope of the related graph.

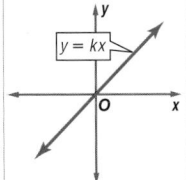

Example Suppose y varies directly as x, and $y = -24$ when $x = 8$. Write a direct variation equation that relates x and y.

$y = kx$ Direct variation equation

$-24 = k(8)$ Replace y with -24 and x with 8.

$\dfrac{-24}{8} = \dfrac{k(8)}{8}$ Divide each side by 8.

$-3 = k$ Simplify.

Therefore, $y = -3x$.

Exercises Graph each equation. *See Examples 2 and 3 on page 265.* **13–18. See margin.**

13. $y = 2x$ 14. $y = -4x$ 15. $y = \dfrac{1}{3}x$

16. $y = -\dfrac{1}{4}x$ 17. $y = \dfrac{3}{2}x$ 18. $y = -\dfrac{4}{3}x$

Suppose y varies directly as x. Write a direct variation equation that relates x and y. *See Example 4 on page 266.*

19. $y = -6$ when $x = 9$ 20. $y = 15$ when $x = 2$ 21. $y = 4$ when $x = -4$

22. $y = -6$ when $x = -18$ 23. $y = -10$ when $x = 5$ 24. $y = 7$ when $x = -14$

19. $y = -\dfrac{2}{3}x$

20. $y = \dfrac{15}{2}x$

21. $y = -x$

22. $y = \dfrac{1}{3}x$

23. $y = -2x$

24. $y = -\dfrac{1}{2}x$

5-3 Slope-Intercept Form

See pages 272–277.

Concept Summary

- The linear equation $y = mx + b$ is written in slope-intercept form, where m is the slope, and b is the y-intercept.
- Slope-intercept form allows you to graph an equation quickly.

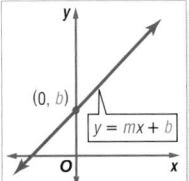

Example Graph $-3x + y = -1$.

$-3x + y = -1$ Original equation

$-3x + y + 3x = -1 + 3x$ Add $3x$ to each side.

$y = 3x - 1$ Simplify.

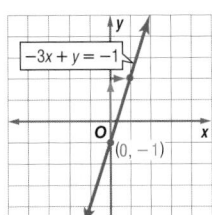

Step 1 The y-intercept is -1. So, graph $(0, -1)$.

Step 2 The slope is 3 or $\dfrac{3}{1}$. From $(0, -1)$, move up 3 units and right 1 unit. Then draw a line.

Answers

13.

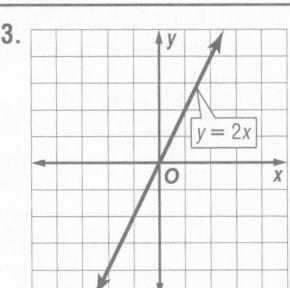

14.

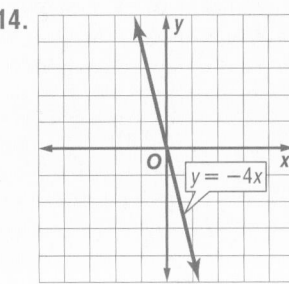

15.

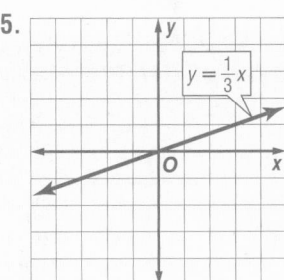

16.

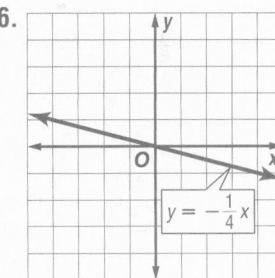

17.

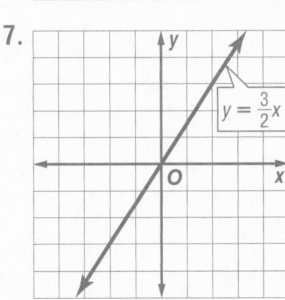

18.

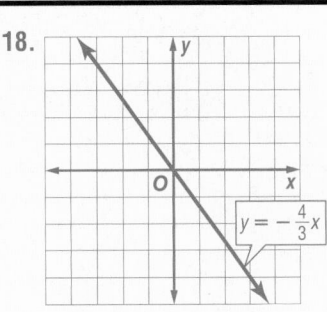

Answers

31.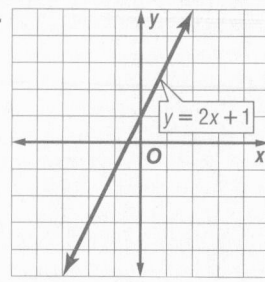

32.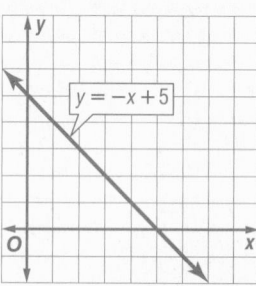

33.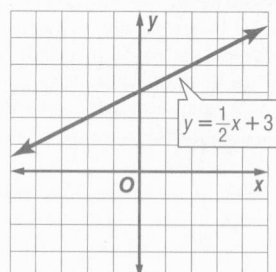

34.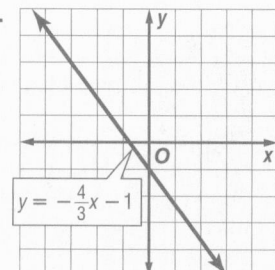

35.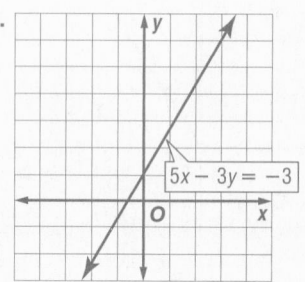

Exercises   Write an equation of the line with the given slope and *y*-intercept.
See Examples 1 and 2 on pages 272 and 273.

25. slope: 3, *y*-intercept: 2 $y = 3x + 2$ **26.** slope: 1, *y*-intercept: −3 $y = x - 3$

27. slope: 0, *y*-intercept: 4 $y = 4$ **28.** slope: $\frac{1}{3}$, *y*-intercept: 2 $y = \frac{1}{3}x + 2$

29. slope: 0.5, *y*-intercept: −0.3
$y = 0.5x - 0.3$

30. slope: −1.3, *y*-intercept: 0.4
$y = -1.3x + 0.4$

Graph each equation.   *See Examples 3 and 4 on pages 273 and 274.* **31–36. See margin.**

31. $y = 2x + 1$ **32.** $y = -x + 5$ **33.** $y = \frac{1}{2}x + 3$

34. $y = -\frac{4}{3}x - 1$ **35.** $5x - 3y = -3$ **36.** $6x + 2y = 9$

5-4   Writing Equations in Slope-Intercept Form

See pages 280–285.

Concept Summary

- To write an equation given the slope and one point, substitute the values of *m*, *x*, and *y* into the slope-intercept form and solve for *b*. Then, write the slope-intercept form using the values of *m* and *b*.
- To write an equation given two points, find the slope. Then follow the steps above.

Example   Write an equation of a line that passes through (−2, −3) with slope $\frac{1}{2}$.

$y = mx + b$ Slope-intercept form

$-3 = \frac{1}{2}(-2) + b$ Replace *m* with $\frac{1}{2}$, *y* with −3, and *x* with −2.

$-3 = -1 + b$ Multiply.

$-3 + 1 = -1 + b + 1$ Add 1 to each side.

$-2 = b$ Simplify.

Therefore, the equation is $y = \frac{1}{2}x - 2$.

Exercises   Write an equation of the line that satisfies each condition.
See Examples 1 and 2 on pages 280 and 281.

37. passes through (−3, 3)
with slope 1 $y = x + 6$

38. passes through (0, 6)
with slope −2 $y = -2x + 6$

39. passes through (1, 6)
with slope $\frac{1}{2}$ $y = \frac{1}{2}x + \frac{11}{2}$

40. passes through (4, −3)
with slope $-\frac{3}{5}$ $y = -\frac{3}{5}x - \frac{3}{5}$

41. passes through (−4, 2)
and (1, 12) $y = 2x + 10$

42. passes through (5, 0)
and (4, 5) $y = -5x + 25$

43. passes through (8, −1)
with slope 0 $y = -1$

44. passes through (4, 6)
and has slope 0 $y = 6$

36.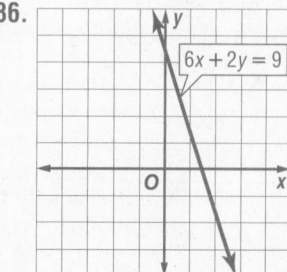

5-5 Writing Equations in Point-Slope Form

See pages
286–291.

Concept Summary

- The linear equation $y - y_1 = m(x - x_1)$ is written in point-slope form, where (x_1, y_1) is a given point on a nonvertical line and m is the slope.

Example Write the point-slope form of an equation for a line that passes through $(-2, 5)$ with slope 3.

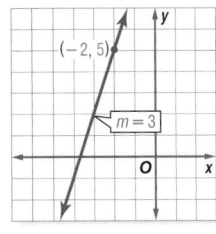

$y - y_1 = m(x - x_1)$ Use the point-slope form.

$y - 5 = 3[x - (-2)]$ $(x_1, y_1) = (-2, 5)$

$y - 5 = 3(x + 2)$ Subtract.

45. $y - 6 = 5(x - 4)$ **46.** $y - 4 = -2(x + 1)$

47. $y + 3 = \dfrac{1}{2}(x - 5)$ **48.** $y + 4 = -\dfrac{5}{2}(x - 1)$

Exercises Write the point-slope form of an equation for a line that passes through each point with the given slope. *See Example 2 on page 287.*

49. $y + 2 = 3\left(x - \dfrac{1}{4}\right)$

45. $(4, 6)$, $m = 5$	**46.** $(-1, 4)$, $m = -2$ **47.** $(5, -3)$, $m = \dfrac{1}{2}$
48. $(1, -4)$, $m = -\dfrac{5}{2}$	**49.** $\left(\dfrac{1}{4}, -2\right)$, $m = 3$ **50.** $(4, -2)$, $m = 0$

$y + 2 = 0$

Write each equation in standard form. *See Example 3 on page 287.*

51. $y - 1 = 2(x + 1)$ **52.** $y + 6 = \dfrac{1}{3}(x - 9)$ **53.** $y + 4 = 1.5(x - 4)$

$2x - y = -3$ $x - 3y = 27$ $3x - 2y = 20$

5-6 Geometry: Parallel and Perpendicular Lines

See pages
292–297.

Concept Summary

- Two nonvertical lines are parallel if they have the same slope.
- Two nonvertical lines are perpendicular if the product of their slopes is -1.

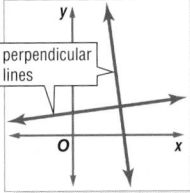

Example Write the slope-intercept form for an equation of the line that passes through $(5, -2)$ and is parallel to $y = 2x + 7$.

The line parallel to $y = 2x + 7$ has the same slope, 2.

$y - y_1 = m(x - x_1)$ Point-slope form

$y - (-2) = 2(x - 5)$ Replace m with 2, y with -2, and x with 5.

$y + 2 = 2x - 10$ Simplify.

$y = 2x - 12$ Subtract 2 from each side.

Chapter 5 Study Guide and Review **311**

Study Guide and Review

Chapter
5 For More ...
• Extra Practice, see pages 831–833.
• Mixed Problem Solving, see page 857.

Answer

66–67.

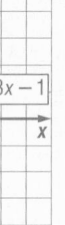

Graph: Weight (long tons) on y-axis (0–60), Length (ft) on x-axis (35–60), with scatter points and line of fit.

Answers (page 313)

2.

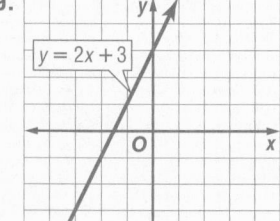

8.

$y = 3x - 1$

9.

$y = 2x + 3$

10.

$2x + 3y = 9$

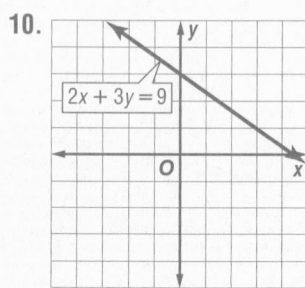

21–22.

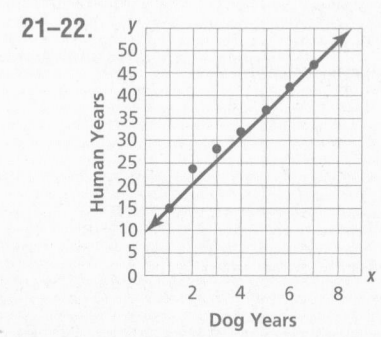

Graph: Human Years (y-axis 0–50) vs Dog Years (x-axis 2–8).

Exercises Write the slope-intercept form for an equation of the line parallel to the graph of the given equation and passing through the given point.
See Example 1 on page 292. 54. $y = 3x - 6$ 55. $y = -2x + 6$ 56. $y = -6x + 8$

54. $y = 3x - 2, (4, 6)$ 55. $y = -2x + 4, (6, -6)$ 56. $y = -6x - 1, (1, 2)$

57. $y = \frac{5}{12}x + 2, (0, 4)$ 58. $4x - y = 7, (2, -1)$ 59. $3x + 9y = 1, (3, 0)$
$\quad\; y = \frac{5}{12}x + 4$ $\quad\; y = 4x - 9$ $\quad\; y = -\frac{1}{3}x + 1$

Write the slope-intercept form for an equation of the line perpendicular to the graph of the given equation and passing through the given point.   *See Example 3 on page 294.*

60. $y = 4x + 2, (1, 3)$ 61. $y = -2x - 7, (0, -3)$ 62. $y = 0.4x + 1, (2, -5)$
63. $2x - 7y = 1, (-4, 0)$ 64. $8x - 3y = 7, (4, 5)$ 65. $5y = -x + 1, (2, -5)$

60. $y = -\frac{1}{4}x + \frac{13}{4}$ 61. $y = \frac{1}{2}x - 3$ 62. $y = -2.5x$ 63. $y = -\frac{7}{2}x - 14$

64. $y = -\frac{3}{8}x + \frac{13}{2}$
65. $y = 5x - 15$

5-7 Statistics: Scatter Plots and Lines of Fit

See pages 298–305.

Concept Summary

• If y increases as x increases, then there is a positive correlation between x and y.

• If y decreases as x increases, then there is a negative correlation between x and y.

• If there is no relationship between x and y, then there is no correlation between x and y.

• A line of fit describes the trend of the data.

• You can use the equation of a line of fit to make predictions about the data.

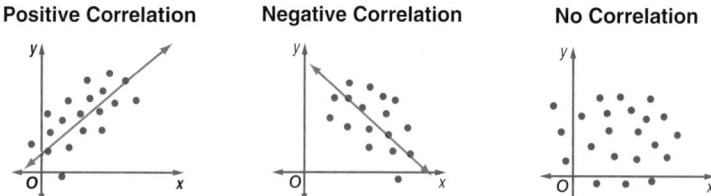

Positive Correlation   **Negative Correlation**   **No Correlation**

Exercises For Exercises 66–70, use the table that shows the length and weight of several humpback whales.   *See Examples 2 and 3 on pages 300 and 301.* 66–67. **See margin.**

Length (ft)	40	42	45	46	50	52	55
Weight (long tons)	25	29	34	35	43	45	51

66. Draw a scatter plot with length on the x-axis and weight on the y-axis.

67. Draw a line of fit for the data.   **Sample answer:**

68. Write the slope-intercept form of an equation for the line of fit. $W = \frac{5}{3}\ell - \frac{125}{3}$

69. Predict the weight of a 48-foot humpback whale. $38\frac{1}{3}$ long tons

70. Most newborn humpback whales are about 12 feet in length. Use the equation of the line of fit to predict the weight of a newborn humpback whale. Do you think your prediction is accurate? Explain. $-21\frac{2}{3}$ long tons; No, a negative weight is not reasonable.

Vocabulary and Concepts

1. **Explain** why the equation of a vertical line cannot be in slope-intercept form. **Vertical lines have no slope.**
2. **Draw** a scatter plot that shows a positive correlation. **See margin.**
3. **Name** the part of the slope-intercept form that represents the rate of change. **slope**

Skills and Applications

Find the slope of the line that passes through each pair of points.

4. $(5, 8), (-3, 7)$ $\dfrac{1}{8}$

5. $(5, -2), (3, -2)$ **0**

6. $(6, -3), (6, 4)$ **undefined**

7. **BUSINESS** A web design company advertises that it will design and maintain a website for your business for $9.95 per month. Write a direct variation equation to find the total cost C for any number of months m. $C = 9.95m$

Graph each equation. **8–10. See margin.**

8. $y = 3x - 1$

9. $y = 2x + 3$

10. $2x + 3y = 9$

11. **WEATHER** The temperature is 16°F at midnight and is expected to fall 2° each hour during the night. Write the slope-intercept form of an equation to find the temperature T for any hour h after midnight. $T = -2h + 16$

Suppose y varies directly as x. Write a direct variation equation that relates x and y.

12. $y = 6$ when $x = 9$ $y = \dfrac{2}{3}x$

13. $y = -12$ when $x = 4$ $y = -3x$

14. $y = -8$ when $x = 8$ $y = -x$

Write the slope-intercept form of an equation of the line that satisfies each condition.

15. has slope -4 and y-intercept 3 $y = -4x + 3$

16. passes through $(-2, -5)$ and $(8, -3)$ $y = \dfrac{1}{5}x - 4\dfrac{3}{5}$

17. parallel to $3x + 7y = 4$ and passes through $(5, -2)$ $y = -\dfrac{3}{7}x + \dfrac{1}{7}$

18. a horizontal line passing through $(5, -8)$ $y = -8$

19. perpendicular to the graph of $5x - 3y = 9$ and passes through the origin $y = -\dfrac{3}{5}x$

20. Write the point-slope form of an equation for a line that passes through $(-4, 3)$ with slope -2. $y - 3 = -2(x + 4)$

ANIMALS For Exercises 21–24, use the table that shows the relationship between dog years and human years.

Dog Years	1	2	3	4	5	6	7
Human Years	15	24	28	32	37	42	47

21. Draw a scatter plot and determine what relationship, if any, exists in the data. **21–22. See margin.**
22. Draw a line of fit for the scatter plot.
23. Write the slope-intercept form of an equation for the line of fit. **using $(1, 15)$ and $(7, 47)$, $y = \dfrac{16}{3}x + \dfrac{29}{3}$**
24. Determine how many human years are comparable to 13 dog years. **79**

25. **STANDARDIZED TEST PRACTICE** A line passes through $(0, 4)$ and $(3, 0)$. Which equation does *not* represent the equation of this line? **B**

   Ⓐ $y - 4 = -\dfrac{4}{3}(x - 0)$

   Ⓑ $y = -\dfrac{4}{3}x + 3$

   Ⓒ $\dfrac{x}{3} + \dfrac{y}{4} = 1$

   Ⓓ $y - 0 = -\dfrac{4}{3}(x - 3)$

   Ⓔ $4x + 3y = 12$

 www.algebra1.com/chapter_test

---

Assessment Options

Vocabulary Test A vocabulary test/review for Chapter 5 can be found on p. 336 of the *Chapter 5 Resource Masters*.

Chapter Tests There are six Chapter 5 Tests and an Open-Ended Assessment task available in the *Chapter 5 Resource Masters*.

Chapter 5 Tests			
Form	Type	Level	Pages
1	MC	basic	323–324
2A	MC	average	325–326
2B	MC	average	327–328
2C	FR	average	329–330
2D	FR	average	331–332
3	FR	advanced	333–334

MC = multiple-choice questions
FR = free-response questions

Open-Ended Assessment
Performance tasks for Chapter 5 can be found on p. 335 of the *Chapter 5 Resource Masters*. A sample scoring rubric for these tasks appears on p. A28.

 ExamView® Pro

Use the networkable **ExamView® Pro** to:

- Create **multiple versions** of tests.
- Create **modified** tests for *Inclusion* students.
- **Edit** existing questions and **add** your own questions.
- Use built-in **state curriculum correlations** to create tests aligned with state standards.
- Change **English** tests to **Spanish** and vice versa.

Portfolio Suggestion

Introduction There is often more than one way to graph a line. Sometimes you use two points, sometimes you use a point and a slope, and sometimes you use the *x*- and *y*-intercepts.

Ask Students Find an equation from your work in this chapter and describe at least three ways in which to graph it. Place your descriptions in your portfolio.

These two pages contain practice questions in the various formats that can be found on the most frequently given standardized tests.

A practice answer sheet for these two pages can be found on p. A1 of the *Chapter 5 Resource Masters*.

Standardized Test Practice
Student Recording Sheet, p. A1

Part 1 *Multiple Choice*

Select the best answer from the choices given and fill in the corresponding oval.

1 Ⓐ Ⓑ Ⓒ Ⓓ   4 Ⓐ Ⓑ Ⓒ Ⓓ   7 Ⓐ Ⓑ Ⓒ Ⓓ
2 Ⓐ Ⓑ Ⓒ Ⓓ   5 Ⓐ Ⓑ Ⓒ Ⓓ   8 Ⓐ Ⓑ Ⓒ Ⓓ
3 Ⓐ Ⓑ Ⓒ Ⓓ   6 Ⓐ Ⓑ Ⓒ Ⓓ   9 Ⓐ Ⓑ Ⓒ Ⓓ

Part 2 *Short Response/Grid In*

Solve the problem and write your answer in the blank.

For Questions 10, 12, and 14, also enter your answer by writing each number or symbol in a box. Then fill in the corresponding oval for that number or symbol.

10 _____ (grid in)
11 _____
12 _____ (grid in)
13 _____
14 _____ (grid in)
15 _____
16 _____
17 _____

Part 3 *Extended Response*

Record your answers for Questions 18–19 on the back of this paper.

Additional Practice

See pp. 341–342 in the *Chapter 5 Resource Masters* for additional standardized test practice.

Part 1 Multiple Choice

Record your answers on the answer sheet provided by your teacher or on a sheet of paper.

1. If a person's weekly salary is x and she saves y, what fraction of her weekly salary does she spend? (Lesson 1-1) **B**

Ⓐ $\frac{x}{y}$ Ⓑ $\frac{x-y}{x}$

Ⓒ $\frac{x-y}{y}$ Ⓓ $\frac{y-x}{x}$

2. Evaluate $-2x + 7y$ if $x = -5$ and $y = 4$. (Lesson 2-6) **A**

Ⓐ 38   Ⓑ 43
Ⓒ 227   Ⓓ 243

3. Find x, if $5x + 6 = 10$. (Lesson 3-3) **D**

Ⓐ $-\frac{5}{4}$ Ⓑ $\frac{1}{10}$

Ⓒ $\frac{5}{16}$ Ⓓ $\frac{4}{5}$

4. According to the data in the table, which of the following statements is true? (Lesson 3-7) **C**

Age	Frequency
8	1
10	3
14	2
16	1
17	2

Ⓐ mean age = median age
Ⓑ mean age > median age
Ⓒ mean age < median age
Ⓓ median age < mode age

314 **Chapter 5** Analyzing Linear Equations

---

5. What relationship exists between the x- and y-coordinates of each of the data points shown in the table? (Lesson 4-8) **D**

x	y
−3	4
−2	3
0	1
1	0
3	−2
5	−4

Ⓐ x and y are opposites.

Ⓑ The sum of x and y is 2.

Ⓒ The y-coordinate is 1 more than the square of the x-coordinate.

Ⓓ The y-coordinate is 1 more than the opposite of the x-coordinate.

6. What is the y-intercept of the line with equation $\frac{x}{3} - \frac{y}{2} = 1$? (Lesson 4-5) **B**

Ⓐ -3 Ⓑ -2

Ⓒ $\frac{2}{3}$ Ⓓ $\frac{3}{2}$

7. Find the slope of a line that passes through $(2, 4)$ and $(-4, 7)$. (Lesson 5-1) **A**

Ⓐ $-\frac{1}{2}$ Ⓑ $\frac{1}{2}$

Ⓒ -2 Ⓓ 2

8. Which equation represents the line that passes through $(3, 7)$ and $(10, 21)$? (Lesson 5-4) **C**

Ⓐ $x + y = 10$ Ⓑ $y = \frac{1}{2}x + \frac{11}{2}$

Ⓒ $y = 2x + 1$ Ⓓ $y = 3x - 2$

9. Choose the equation of a line parallel to the graph of $y = 3x + 4$. (Lesson 5-6) **D**

Ⓐ $y = -\frac{1}{3}x + 4$ Ⓑ $y = -3x + 4$

Ⓒ $y = -x + 1$ Ⓓ $y = 3x + 5$

 ExamView® Pro

Special banks of standardized test questions similar to those on the SAT, ACT, TIMSS 8, NAEP 8, and Algebra 1 End-of-Course tests can be found on this CD-ROM.

Part 2 Short Response/Grid In

Record your answers on the answer sheet provided by your teacher or on a sheet of paper.

10. While playing a game with her friends, Ellen scored 12 points less than twice the lowest score. She scored 98. What was the lowest score in the game? (Lesson 3-4) **55**

11. Find the x- and y-intercepts of $3x - 2y = 12$. (Lesson 4-5) **4, −6**

12. Find the slope of a line that passes through $(5, 2)$ and $(-7, -3)$. (Lesson 5-1) **5/12**

13. Suppose y varies directly as x, and $y = -9$ when $x = 3$. Find x when $y = 18$. (Lesson 5-2) **−6**

14. The graph of $3x + 2y = 3$ is shown at the right. What is the y-intercept? (Lesson 5-3) **1.5**

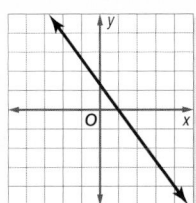

15. The table of ordered pairs shows the coordinates of some of the points on the graph of a function.

What is the y-coordinate of a point $(5, y)$ that lies on the graph of the function? (Lesson 5-4) **−6**

x	y
−1	6
0	4
1	2
2	0
3	−2

16. The equation $y - 3 = -2(x + 5)$ is written in point-slope form. What is the slope of the line? (Lesson 5-5) **−2**

17. Find the slope-intercept form of an equation that passes through $(5, -8)$ and is perpendicular to the graph of $-5x + 2y = 14$. (Lesson 5-6) $y = -\dfrac{2}{5}x - 6$

 www.algebra1.com/standardized_test

Part 3 Extended Response

Record your answers on a sheet of paper. Show your work.

18. A friend wants to enroll for cellular phone service. Three different plans are available. (Lesson 5-3)

Plan 1 charges $0.59 per minute.

Plan 2 charges a monthly fee of $10, plus $0.39 per minute.

Plan 3 charges a monthly fee of $59.95.

a. For each plan, write an equation that represents the monthly cost C for m number of minutes per month. **See pp. 315A–315B.**

b. Graph each of the three equations. **See pp. 315A–315B.**

c. Your friend expects to use 100 minutes per month. In which plan do you think that your friend should enroll? Explain. **Plan 2; when $m = 100$, the cost is least for Plan 2.**

19. A record company is designing a new CD case in the shape of a parallelogram. (Lesson 5-5)

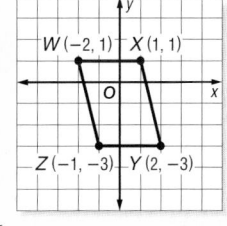

a. Find the point-slope form of the equation of the line containing side $\overline{WZ}$.
$y - 1 = -4(x + 2)$ or $y + 3 = -4(x + 1)$

b. Find the standard form of the equation of the line containing side $\overline{WZ}$.
$4x + y = -7$

Test-Taking Tip Ⓐ Ⓑ Ⓒ Ⓓ

Questions 9 and 17
Recall that graphs of linear equations that are parallel have the same slope. Graphs of linear equations that are perpendicular have slopes that are opposite reciprocals of each other.

Evaluating Extended Response Questions

Extended Response questions are graded by using a multilevel rubric that guides you in assessing a student's knowledge of a particular concept.

Goal: Analyze the given data to determine the best cellular phone service plan.

Sample Scoring Rubric: The following rubric is a sample scoring device. You may wish to add more detail to this sample to meet your individual scoring needs.

Score	Criteria
4	A correct solution that is supported by well-developed, accurate explanations
3	A generally correct solution, but may contain minor flaws in reasoning or computation
2	A partially correct interpretation and/or solution to the problem
1	A correct solution with no supporting evidence or explanation
0	An incorrect solution indicating no mathematical understanding of the concept or task, or no solution is given

Page 263, Reading Mathematics

	Term	Everyday Meaning	Mathematical Meaning
2a.	slope	1. to diverge from the vertical or horizontal; incline 2. to move on a slant; ascend or descend	the ratio of the rise to the run
2b.	intercept	to stop, deflect, or interrupt the progress or intended course of	the coordinate at which a graph intersects an axis
2c.	parallel	of, relating to, or carrying out the simultaneous performance of separate tasks	lines that never intersect; nonvertical lines that have the same slope

Pages 267–270, Lesson 5-2

21.

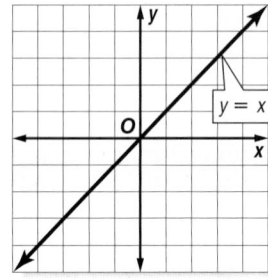

22.

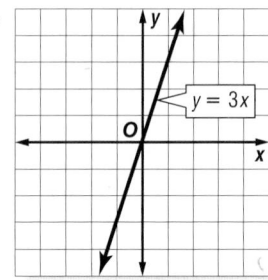

23.

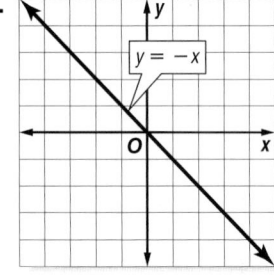

24.

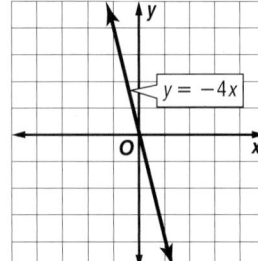

25.

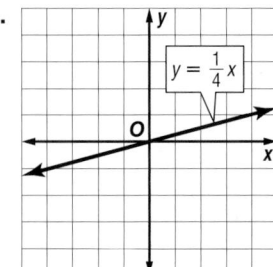

26.

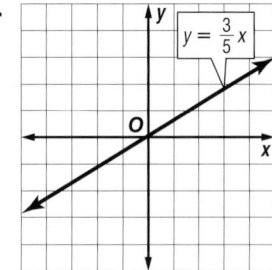

27.

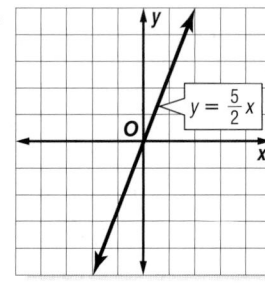

28.

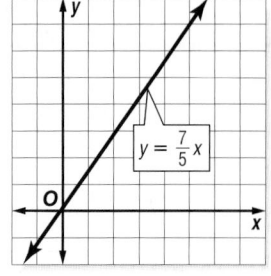

29.

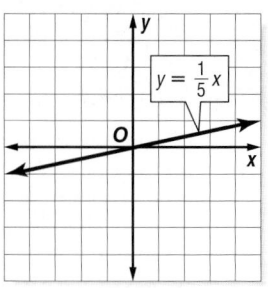

30.

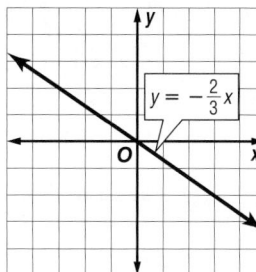

31.

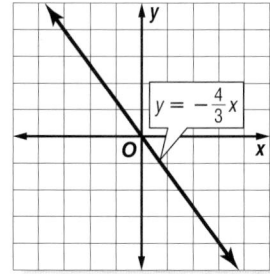

32.

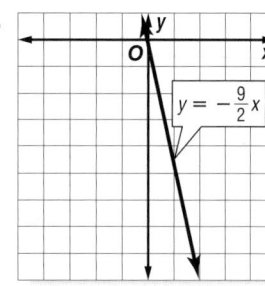

Page 271, Preview of Lesson 5-3

6.

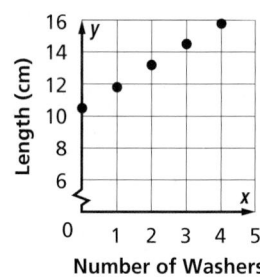

7.

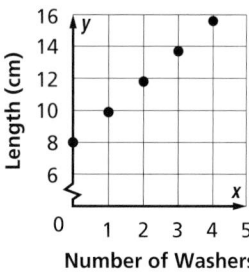

8.

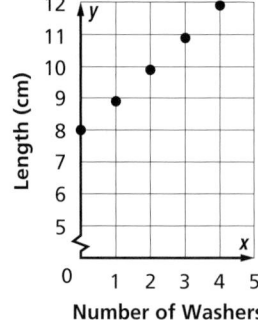

Pages 275–277, Lesson 5-3

28.

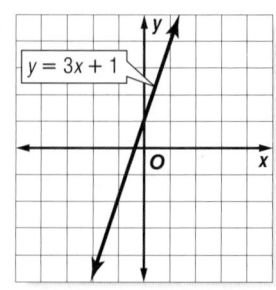

29.

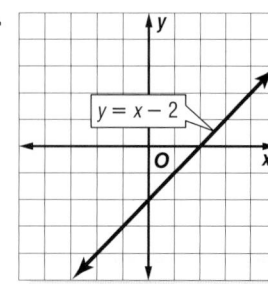

30.

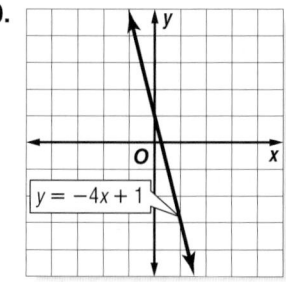

31.

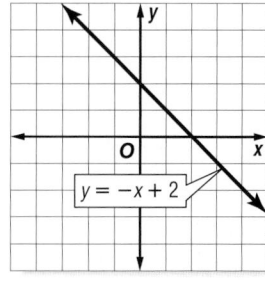

32.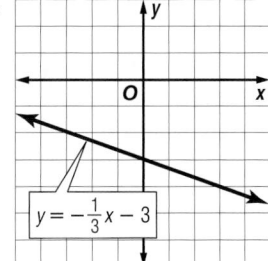
$y = \frac{1}{2}x + 4$

33.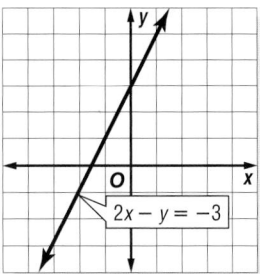
$y = -\frac{1}{3}x - 3$

34.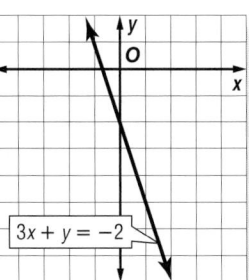
$3x + y = -2$

35.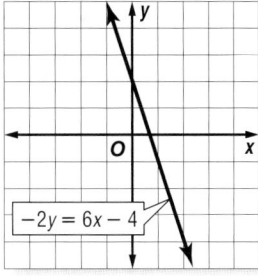
$2x - y = -3$

36.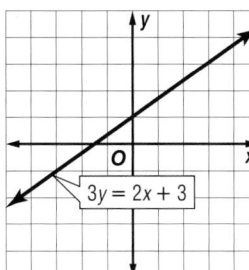
$3y = 2x + 3$

37.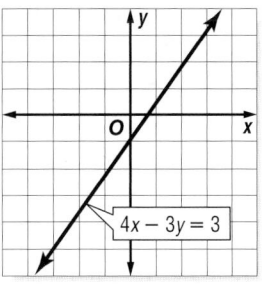
$-2y = 6x - 4$

38.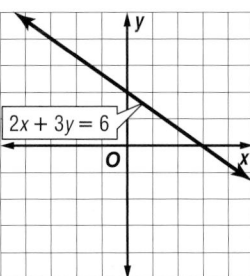
$2x + 3y = 6$

39.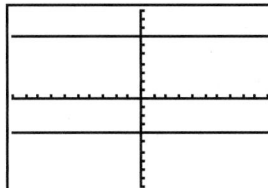
$4x - 3y = 3$

Page 279, Follow-Up of Lesson 5-3
Graphing Calculator Investigation

1. All same slope of 0, different intercepts; the family is linear equations with slope of 0.

2. All same y-intercept of 1, different slopes; the family is linear equations with y-intercept of 1.

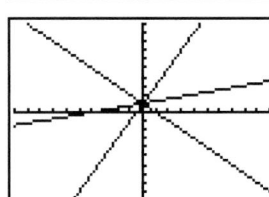

3. All positive slopes, different intercepts; the equations are not in the same family.

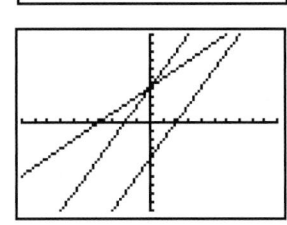

4. All positive slopes, different intercepts; the equations are not in the same family.

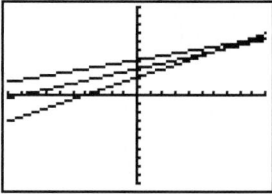

5. All same y-intercept of -2, different slopes; the family is linear equations with y-intercept of -2.

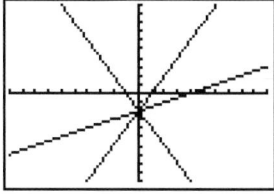

6. All same slope of 3, different intercepts; the family is linear equations with slope of 3.

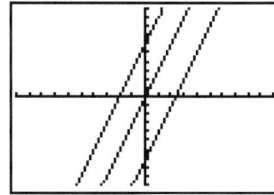

Pages 289–291, Lesson 5-5

61. $\overline{RQ}$: $y + 3 = \frac{1}{2}(x + 1)$ or $y + 1 = \frac{1}{2}(x - 3)$;

$\overline{QP}$: $y + 1 = -2(x - 3)$ or $y - 3 = -2(x - 1)$;

$\overline{PS}$: $y - 3 = \frac{1}{2}(x - 1)$ or $y - 1 = \frac{1}{2}(x + 3)$;

$\overline{RS}$: $y + 3 = -2(x + 1)$ or $y - 1 = -2(x + 3)$

62. $\overline{RQ}$: $y = \frac{1}{2}x - \frac{5}{2}$; $\overline{QP}$: $y = -2x + 5$; $\overline{PS}$: $y = \frac{1}{2}x + \frac{5}{2}$;

$\overline{RS}$: $y = -2x - 5$

63. $\overline{RQ}$: $x - 2y = 5$; $\overline{QP}$: $2x + y = 5$; $\overline{PS}$: $x - 2y = -5$;
$\overline{RS}$: $2x + y = -5$

64. Sample answer: The point-slope form of the equation is $y - 1 = -(x - 9)$. Let $x = 10$ and $y = 0$. The equation becomes $0 - 1 = -(10 - 9)$ or $-1 = -1$. Since the equation holds true, $(10, 0)$ is a point on the line passing through $(9, 1)$ and $(5, 5)$.

Pages 314–315,
Standardized Test Practice

18a. Plan 1: $C = 0.59m$; Plan 2: $C = 0.39m + 10$; Plan 3: $C = 59.95$

18b.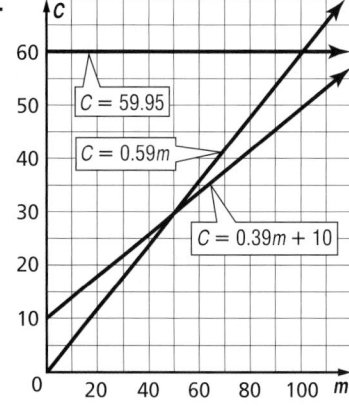

Solving Linear Inequalities
Chapter Overview and Pacing

Year-long and two-year pacing: pages T20–T21.

LESSON OBJECTIVES	PACING (days)			
	Regular		**Block**	
	Basic/ Average	Advanced	Basic/ Average	Advanced
6-1 Solving Inequalities by Addition and Subtraction *(pp. 318–323)* • Solve linear inequalities by using addition. • Solve linear inequalities by using subtraction.	1	1	0.5	0.5
6-2 Solving Inequalities by Multiplication and Division *(pp. 324–331)* *Preview:* Use algebra tiles to solve inequalities. • Solve linear inequalities by using multiplication. • Solve linear inequalities by using division.	2 (with 6-2 Preview)	1	1 (with 6-2 Preview)	0.5
6-3 Solving Multi-Step Inequalities *(pp. 332–337)* • Solve linear inequalities involving more that one operation. • Solve linear inequalities involving the Distributive Property.	1	1	1	0.5
6-4 Solving Compound Inequalities *(pp. 339–344)* • Solve compound inequalities containing the word *and* and graph their solution sets. • Solve compound inequalities containing the word *or* and graph their solution sets.	2	2	1	1
6-5 Solving Open Sentences Involving Absolute Value *(pp. 345–351)* • Solve absolute value equations. • Solve absolute value inequalities.	2	2	1	1
6-6 Graphing Inequalities in Two Variables *(pp. 352–358)* • Graph inequalities on the coordinate plane. • Solve real-world problems involving linear inequalities. *Follow-Up:* Use a graphing calculator to investigate graphs of inequalities.	2	2 (with 6-6 Follow-Up)	1	1.5 (with 6-6 Follow-Up)
Study Guide and **Practice Test** *(pp. 359–363)* **Standardized Test Practice** *(pp. 364–365)*	1	1	1 (with 6-6 Follow-Up)	0.5
Chapter Assessment	1	1	0.5	0.5
TOTAL	12	11	7	6

*An electronic version of this chapter is available on **StudentWorks**™. This backpack solution CD-ROM allows students instant access to the Student Edition, lesson worksheet pages, and web resources.*

Chapter Resource Manager

| CHAPTER 6 RESOURCE MASTERS | | | | | | | Applications* | | | | | Materials |
Study Guide and Intervention	Practice (Skills and Average)	Reading to Learn Mathematics	Enrichment	Assessment	Prerequisite Skills Workbook		Parent and Student Study Guide Workbook	5-Minute Check Transparencies	Interactive Chalkboard	AlgePASS: Tutorial Plus (lessons)		
343–344	345–346	347	348			SC 11	46	6-1	6-1			
349–350	351–352	353	354	393		SC 12	47	6-2	6-2			(*Preview:* algebra tiles, equation mat, self-adhesive notes)
355–356	357–358	359	360	393, 395			48	6-3	6-3	14		graphing calculator
361–362	363–364	365	366				49	6-4	6-4	15		
367–368	369–370	371	372	394	79–80, 83–84	GCS 33	50	6-5	6-5			stopwatch
373–374	375–376	377	378	394		GCS 34	51	6-6	6-6			(*Follow-Up:* graphing calculator)
				379–392, 396–398			52					

Key to Abbreviations: GCS = Graphing Calculator and Spreadsheet Masters,
SC = School-to-Career Masters,
SM = Science and Mathematics Lab Manual

 Study Guide and Intervention, Skills Practice, Practice, and Parent and Student Study Guide Workbooks are also available in Spanish.

Chapter 6
Mathematical Connections and Background

Continuity of Instruction

Prior Knowledge

Students solved open sentence inequalities in Chapter 1. Chapter 2 had them graphing rational numbers and exploring absolute value. Solving single-step and multi-step equations was developed in Chapter 3. Students learned to graph linear equations in Chapter 4.

This Chapter

Students develop the properties for solving inequalities. They apply the Addition and Subtraction Properties of Inequalities to solve inequalities. They also use the Multiplication and Division Properties of Inequalities, where the sign is sometimes reversed, to solve inequalities. They solve single-step and multi-step inequalities. Students solve compound inequalities, as well as equations and inequalities that contain absolute values. The chapter ends with graphing inequalities in two variables.

Future Connections

In future math studies, students solve and graph inequalities of other types of functions, such as quadratics. They also apply solving and graphing inequalities in Algebra 2 to linear programming where the maximum profit for a situation is determined. Inequalities are used in many biological areas, such as determining appropriate parameters for populations of species in various regions.

6-1 Solving Inequalities by Addition and Subtraction

To solve an equation, isolate the variable so that it has a coefficient of 1 on one side of the equal sign. An inequality is solved the same way. The Addition Property of Inequality is used in the same way as the Addition Property of Equality. It states that any number can be added to each side of an inequality and the result is a true inequality. The same is true for the Subtraction Property of Inequality: a number can be subtracted from each side of an inequality and the result is a true inequality.

There are infinitely many solutions to an inequality. The solutions to inequalities can be written in set builder notation, for example $\{x|x > 3\}$. This is read as *the set of all numbers x such that x is greater than 3*.

The number found when solving an inequality is a boundary that is sometimes included in the solution and sometimes not. It is included in the solution if the inequality sign is $\leq$ or $\geq$, but it is not included if the symbol is $<$ or $>$. If the boundary number is included, a solid dot is placed at that point on the number line. If the number is not included, use an open circle. Then draw an arrow to the right if the rest of the solution set is greater than the boundary, or to the left if the rest of the solution set is less than the boundary.

6-2 Solving Inequalities by Multiplication and Division

Inequalities that include multiplication or division of the variable can also be solved. The same principles as found in the Multiplication and Division Properties of Equality are used, with one main difference. If an inequality is multiplied or divided by the same negative number on each side, the inequality symbol is reversed. The symbol must be reversed to result in a true inequality. The inequality sign is not reversed if each side is multiplied or divided by the same positive number. You multiply or divide by a negative number only if the coefficient of the variable is negative.

6-3 Solving Multi-Step Inequalities

Solve multi-step inequalities using the same process as for solving multi-step equations. Work backward using inverse operations to undo the operations. After each side is simplified using the Distributive Property and/or combining like terms, work in the opposite order of the order of operations. The Addition and Subtraction Properties of Inequality are applied first, followed by the Multiplication and Division Properties of Inequalities.

If the solution is an untrue statement, such as $4 > 8$, there is no solution. If the solution results in a statement that is always true, such as $5 > 3$, then the solution is the set of all real numbers. A solution can always be checked by substituting it back into the inequality.

 6-4 Solving Compound Inequalities

In a compound inequality, one variable is related to two different amounts with two inequality signs. The signs may be the same or they may be different. If *and* is written between the inequalities, or the variable expression is between the two inequality signs, the graph is the intersection of the two inequalities. This is because the solution must be true for both inequalities. If *or* is written between the two inequalities, the graph is the union of the two inequalities. This is because the solution can be true for either inequality.

 6-5 Solving Open Sentences Involving Absolute Value

An absolute value open sentence can be an equation or an inequality. The value inside the absolute value symbols could be positive or negative. The absolute value represents the distance a number is from zero on a number line. Absolute value equations can be solved by graphing them or by writing them as a compound sentence and solving algebraically. To solve algebraically, write the expression inside the symbol as equal to the given value and then equal to the opposite of the given value. Solve each equation. Write both solutions inside one set of brackets.

An absolute value inequality is written as a compound inequality. If the absolute value is on the left and the inequality symbol is $<$ or $\leq$, the compound sentence is written with *and*. If the absolute value is on the left and the inequality symbol is $>$ or $\geq$, the compound sentence is written with *or*.

To solve the first case, write the expression from inside the absolute value symbol, the $<$ or $\leq$, and the value to the right of the sign. Then write the expression, the opposite inequality sign, and the opposite value. Solve both inequalities and write the solution set as an intersection. To solve the second case you follow the same process, only write the solution set as a union using *or* before solving both inequalities.

 6-6 Graphing Inequalities in Two Variables

The solution set of an inequality, like that of an equation, is all ordered pairs that make the statement true. Similar to the solution set of an equation in two variables, the solution set of an inequality in two variables is graphed on a coordinate plane. However, the solution set of an inequality is not linear. It does have a linear boundary, but it covers a region called a half-plane.

First graph the inequality as if it contained an equal sign like an equation. This is the boundary line. If the inequality is $<$ or $>$, then the line is dashed. A solid line is graphed for $\leq$ and $\geq$. These relate to the circle and dot on a number line. Select a point in either half-plane and test it in the inequality. $(0, 0)$ is a good point to use if it is not on the boundary line. If the resulting statement is true, shade the half-plane that contains the point. If the statement is false, shade the other half plane.

Quick Review Math Handbook *hot* **words** *hot* **topics**

Hot Words includes a glossary of terms while Hot Topics consists of explanations of key mathematical concepts with exercises to test comprehension. This valuable resource can be used as a reference in the classroom or for home study.

Lesson	Hot Topics Section	Lesson	Hot Topics Section
GS6	6.4, 6.8	6-3	6.6
6-1	6.4, 6.6	6-4	6.6
6-2P	6.6	6-5	6.4
6-2	6.4, 6.6		

GS = Getting Started, P = Preview

 Additional mathematical information and teaching notes are available at www.algebra1.com/key_concepts.

DAILY INTERVENTION and Assessment

Key to Abbreviations:
TWE = Teacher Wraparound Edition; CRM = Chapter Resource Masters

	Type	Student Edition	Teacher Resources	Technology/Internet
INTERVENTION	Ongoing	Prerequisite Skills, pp. 317, 323, 331, 337, 344, 351 Practice Quiz 1, p. 331 Practice Quiz 2, p. 344	5-Minute Check Transparencies *Prerequisite Skills Workbook*, pp. 79–80, 83–84 Quizzes, *CRM* pp. 393–394 Mid-Chapter Test, *CRM* p. 395 Study Guide and Intervention, *CRM* pp. 343–344, 349–350, 355–356, 361–362, 367–368, 373–374	AlgePASS: Tutorial Plus, Lessons 14 and 15 www.algebra1.com/self_check_quiz www.algebra1.com/extra_examples
	Mixed Review	pp. 323, 331, 337, 344, 351, 357	Cumulative Review, *CRM* p. 396	
	Error Analysis	Find the Error, pp. 329, 348 Common Misconceptions, p. 326	Find the Error, *TWE* pp. 329, 348 Unlocking Misconceptions, *TWE* pp. 321, 334 Tips for New Teachers, *TWE* pp. 323, 334	
ASSESSMENT	Standardized Test Practice	pp. 323, 328, 329, 331, 337, 343, 351, 357, 363, 364–365	*TWE* pp. 364–365 Standardized Test Practice, *CRM* pp. 397–398	Standardized Test Practice CD-ROM www.algebra1.com/standardized_test
	Open-Ended Assessment	Writing in Math, pp. 323, 331, 337, 343, 351, 357 Open Ended, pp. 321, 328, 334, 341, 348, 355 Standardized Test, p. 365	Modeling: *TWE* pp. 323, 351 Speaking: *TWE* pp. 337, 357 Writing: *TWE* pp. 331, 344 Open-Ended Assessment, *CRM* p. 391	
	Chapter Assessment	Study Guide, pp. 359–362 Practice Test, p. 363	Multiple-Choice Tests (Forms 1, 2A, 2B), *CRM* pp. 379–384 Free-Response Tests (Forms 2C, 2D, 3), *CRM* pp. 385–390 Vocabulary Test/Review, *CRM* p. 392	ExamView® Pro (see below) MindJogger Videoquizzes www.algebra1.com/vocabulary_review www.algebra1.com/chapter_test

For more information on Yearly ProgressPro, see p. 188.

Algebra Lesson	Yearly ProgressPro Skill Lesson(s)
6-1	Solving Inequalities by Addition and Subtraction Graphing Inequalities
6-2	Solving Inequalities by Multiplication and Division
6-3	Solving Multi-Step Inequalities
6-4	Solving Compound Inequalities Graphing Compound Inequalities
6-5	Solving Open Sentences Involving Absolute Value
6-6	Graphing Inequalities in Two Variables

ExamView® Pro

Use the networkable **ExamView® Pro** to:
- Create **multiple versions** of tests.
- Create **modified** tests for *Inclusion* students.
- **Edit** existing questions and **add** your own questions.
- Use built-in **state curriculum correlations** to create tests aligned with state standards.
- Change **English** tests to **Spanish** and vice versa.

For more information on Intervention and Assessment, see pp. T8–T11.

Reading and Writing in Mathematics

Glencoe Algebra 1 provides numerous opportunities to incorporate reading and writing into the mathematics classroom.

Student Edition

- Foldables Study Organizer, p. 317
- Concept Check questions require students to verbalize and write about what they have learned in the lesson. (pp. 321, 328, 334, 341, 348, 355)
- Reading Mathematics, p. 338
- Writing in Math questions in every lesson, pp. 323, 331, 337, 343, 351, 357
- Reading Study Tip, pp. 319, 339, 340
- WebQuest, p. 357

Teacher Wraparound Edition

- Foldables Study Organizer, pp. 317, 359
- Study Notebook suggestions, pp. 321, 324, 328, 334, 338, 341, 348, 355
- Modeling activities, pp. 323, 351
- Speaking activities, pp. 337, 357
- Writing activities, pp. 331, 344
- Differentiated Instruction, (Verbal/Linguistic), p. 320
- **ELL** Resources, pp. 316, 320, 322, 330, 336, 338, 343, 350, 356, 359

For more information on Reading and Writing in Mathematics, see pp. T6–T7.

Additional Resources

- Vocabulary Builder worksheets require students to define and give examples for key vocabulary terms as they progress through the chapter. (*Chapter 6 Resource Masters,* pp. vii-viii)
- Reading to Learn Mathematics master for each lesson (*Chapter 6 Resource Masters,* pp. 347, 353, 359, 365, 371, 377)
- *Vocabulary PuzzleMaker* software creates crossword, jumble, and word search puzzles using vocabulary lists that you can customize.
- *Teaching Mathematics with Foldables* provides suggestions for promoting cognition and language.
- *Reading and Writing in the Mathematics Classroom*
- *WebQuest and Project Resources*

PROJECT CRISS℠ Study Skill

Taking good notes will help students become actively involved in the learning process. For each lesson, have students read and then write notes about the topic.

You may wish to show them the sample notes for Lesson 6-5 at the right to use as a guide. Afterward, allow class time for students to discuss their notes. Encourage students to talk about the procedures used in the lesson for solving the problems and how they addressed those procedures in their notes.

> **Lesson 6-5**
>
> Set up an absolute value inequality.
>
> Example: $|x + 8| < 10$
>
> **Case 1:** The value inside the absolute value symbols is less than 10.
> $x + 8 < 10$
>
> **Case 2:** The value inside the absolute value symbols is greater than −10.
> $x - 8 > -10$

CReating **I**ndependence **T**hrough **S**tudent-**O**wned **S**trategies

Chapter

6 Solving Linear Inequalities

What You'll Learn

Have students read over the list of objectives and make a list of any words with which they are not familiar.

Why It's Important

Point out to students that this is only one of many reasons why each objective is important. Others are provided in the introduction to each lesson.

What You'll Learn

- **Lessons 6-1 through 6-3** Solve linear inequalities.
- **Lesson 6-4** Solve compound inequalities and graph their solution sets.
- **Lesson 6-5** Solve absolute value equations and inequalities.
- **Lesson 6-6** Graph inequalities in the coordinate plane.

Key Vocabulary

- set-builder notation (p. 319)
- compound inequality (p. 339)
- intersection (p. 339)
- union (p. 340)
- half-plane (p. 353)

Why It's Important

Inequalities are used to represent various real-world situations in which a quantity must fall within a range of possible values. For example, figure skaters and gymnasts frequently want to know what they need to score to win a competition. That score can be represented by an inequality. *You will learn how a competitor can determine what score is needed to win in Lesson 6-1.*

Lesson	NCTM Standards	Local Objectives
6-1	2, 6, 8, 9, 10	
6-2 Preview	2, 6, 8, 9, 10	
6-2	2, 6, 8, 9, 10	
6-3	2, 6, 8, 9, 10	
6-4	2, 4, 6, 8, 9, 10	
6-5	2, 4, 6, 8, 9, 10	
6-6	2, 6, 8, 9, 10	
6-6 Follow-Up	2, 6, 8, 9, 10	

Key to NCTM Standards:

1=Number & Operations, 2=Algebra, 3=Geometry, 4=Measurement, 5=Data Analysis & Probability, 6=Problem Solving, 7=Reasoning & Proof, 8=Communication, 9=Connections, 10=Representation

Vocabulary Builder

ELL

The Key Vocabulary list introduces students to some of the main vocabulary terms included in this chapter. For a more thorough vocabulary list with pronunciations of new words, give students the Vocabulary Builder worksheets found on pages vii and viii of the *Chapter 6 Resource Masters*. Encourage them to complete the definition of each term as they progress through the chapter. You may suggest that they add these sheets to their study notebooks for future reference when studying for the Chapter 6 test.

Prerequisite Skills To be successful in this chapter, you'll need to master these skills and be able to apply them in problem-solving situations. Review these skills before beginning Chapter 6.

For Lessons 6-1 and 6-3 — Solve Equations

Solve each equation. *(For review, see Lessons 3-2, 3-4, and 3-5.)* **6. −19**

1. $t + 31 = 84$ **53** **2.** $b - 17 = 23$ **40** **3.** $18 = 27 + f$ **−9** **4.** $d - \frac{2}{3} = \frac{1}{2}$ $1\frac{1}{6}$

5. $3r - 45 = 4r$ **−45** **6.** $5m + 7 = 4m - 12$ **7.** $3y + 4 = 16$ **4** **8.** $2a + 5 - 3a = 4$ **1**

9. $\frac{1}{2}k - 4 = 7$ **22** **10.** $4.3b + 1.8 = 8.25$ **1.5** **11.** $6s - 12 = 2(s + 2)$ **4** **12.** $n - 3 = \frac{n+1}{2}$ **7**

For Lesson 6-5 — Evaluate Absolute Values

Find each value. *(For review, see Lesson 2-1.)*

13. $|-8|$ **8** **14.** $|20|$ **20** **15.** $|-30|$ **30** **16.** $|-1.5|$ **1.5**

17. $|14 - 7|$ **7** **18.** $|1 - 16|$ **15** **19.** $|2 - 3|$ **1** **20.** $|7 - 10|$ **3**

For Lesson 6-6 — Graph Equations with Two Variables

Graph each equation. *(For review, see Lesson 4-5.)* **21–28. See pp. 365A–365D.**

21. $2x + 2y = 6$ **22.** $x - 3y = -3$ **23.** $y = 2x - 3$ **24.** $y = -4$

25. $x = -\frac{1}{2}y$ **26.** $3x - 6 = 2y$ **27.** $15 = 3(x + y)$ **28.** $2 - x = 2y$

Study Organizer

Solving Linear Inequalities Make this Foldable to help you organize your notes. Begin with two sheets of notebook paper.

Step 1 Fold and Cut

Fold one sheet in half along the width. Cut along the fold from each edge to the margin.

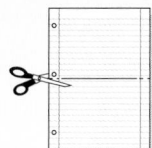

Step 2 Fold a New Paper and Cut

Fold in half along the width. Cut along the fold between the margins.

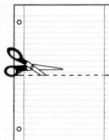

Step 3 Fold

Insert the first sheet through the second sheet and align the folds.

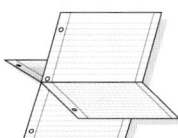

Step 4 Label

Label each page with a lesson number and title.

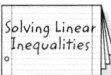

Reading and Writing As you read and study the chapter, fill the journal with notes, diagrams, and examples of linear inequalities.

This section provides a review of the basic concepts needed before beginning Chapter 6. Page references are included for additional student help.

Additional review is provided in the *Prerequisite Skills Workbook*, pp. 79–80 and 83–84.

Prerequisite Skills in the Getting Ready for the Next Lesson section at the end of each exercise set review a skill needed in the next lesson.

For Lesson	Prerequisite Skill
6-2	Multiplication and division equations (p. 323)
6-3	Multi-step equations (p. 331)
6-4	Graphing integers on a number line (p. 337)
6-5	Absolute values (p. 344)
6-6	Graphing linear equations (p. 351)

Study Organizer

For more information about Foldables, see *Teaching Mathematics with Foldables.*

Organization of Data and Journal Writing After students make their Foldable journals, have them label each page to correspond to a lesson in the chapter. Students can use their Foldables to take notes, record concepts, and define terms. They can also use them to record the direction and progress of learning, to describe positive and negative experiences during learning, to write about personal associations and experiences, and to list examples of ways in which new knowledge has or will be used in their daily life.

1 Focus

5-Minute Check Transparency 6-1 Use as a quiz or a review of Chapter 5.

Mathematical Background notes are available for this lesson on p. 316C.

Building on Prior Knowledge

In Chapter 3, students learned to solve equations using addition and subtraction. In this lesson, they should recognize that solving inequalities by addition and subtraction is a very similar process.

How are inequalities used to describe school sports?

Ask students:

• Is the number of schools that offer volleyball greater than or less than the number of schools that offer track and field? **less than**

• Suppose 1200 schools added track and field, and 1200 added volleyball. Would there be more schools offering track and field, or volleyball? **track and field**

• **Sports** The kinds of sports offered in schools often reflects the sports that are popular in the region. Which sports are offered at your school? Which have the most participants?

What You'll Learn

• Solve linear inequalities by using addition.
• Solve linear inequalities by using subtraction.

Vocabulary
• set-builder notation

How are inequalities used to describe school sports?

In the 1999–2000 school year, more high schools offered girls' track and field than girls' volleyball.

$$14{,}587 > 13{,}426$$

If 20 schools added girls' track and field and 20 schools added girls' volleyball the next school year, there would still be more schools offering girls' track and field than schools offering girls' volleyball.

$$14{,}587 + 20 \quad \underline{?} \quad 13{,}426 + 20$$

$$14{,}607 > 13{,}446$$

USA TODAY Snapshots®

Girls gear up for high school sports

High school girls are playing sports in record numbers, almost 2.7 million in the 1999-2000 school year. Most popular girls sports by number of schools offering each program:

16,526 Basketball
14,587 Track and field
13,426 Volleyball
13,009 Softball
11,277 Cross country

Source: National Federation of State High School Associations

By Ellen J. Horrow and Alejandro Gonzalez, USA TODAY

Study Tip
Look Back
To review **inequalities**, see Lesson 1-3.

SOLVE INEQUALITIES BY ADDITION The sports application illustrates the **Addition Property of Inequalities**.

Key Concept — Addition Property of Inequalities

• **Words** If any number is added to each side of a true inequality, the resulting inequality is also true.

• **Symbols** For all numbers a, b, and c, the following are true.
   1. If $a > b$, then $a + c > b + c$.
   2. If $a < b$, then $a + c < b + c$.

• **Example** $2 < 7$
   $2 + 6 < 7 + 6$
   $8 < 13$

This property is also true when $>$ and $<$ are replaced with $\geq$ and $\leq$.

Example 1 Solve by Adding

Solve $t - 45 \leq 13$. **Then check your solution.**

$$t - 45 \leq 13 \qquad \text{Original inequality}$$
$$t - 45 + 45 \leq 13 + 45 \qquad \text{Add 45 to each side.}$$
$$t \leq 58 \qquad \text{This means all numbers less than or equal to 58.}$$

CHECK Substitute 58, a number less than 58, and a number greater than 58.

Let $t = 58$.
$$58 - 45 \overset{?}{\leq} 13$$
$$13 \leq 13 \checkmark$$

Let $t = 50$.
$$50 - 45 \overset{?}{\leq} 13$$
$$5 \leq 13 \checkmark$$

Let $t = 60$.
$$60 - 45 \overset{?}{\leq} 13$$
$$15 \nleq 13$$

The solution is the set {all numbers less than or equal to 58}.

Resource Manager

Workbook and Reproducible Masters

Chapter 6 Resource Masters
• Study Guide and Intervention, pp. 343–344
• Skills Practice, p. 345
• Practice, p. 346
• Reading to Learn Mathematics, p. 347
• Enrichment, p. 348

Parent and Student Study Guide
Workbook, p. 46
School-to-Career Masters, p. 11

Transparencies

5-Minute Check Transparency 6-1
Answer Key Transparencies

Technology

Interactive Chalkboard

The solution of the inequality in Example 1 was expressed as a set. A more concise way of writing a solution set is to use **set-builder notation**. The solution in set-builder notation is $\{t \mid t \le 58\}$.

The solution to Example 1 can also be represented on a number line.

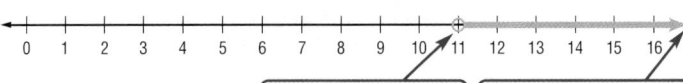

The heavy arrow pointing to the left shows that the inequality includes all numbers less than 58.

The dot at 58 shows that 58 is included in the inequality.

Example 2 *Graph the Solution*

Solve $7 < x - 4$. Then graph it on a number line.

$7 < x - 4$ Original inequality
$7 + 4 < x - 4 + 4$ Add 4 to each side.
$11 < x$ Simplify.

Since $11 < x$ is the same as $x > 11$, the solution set is $\{x \mid x > 11\}$.

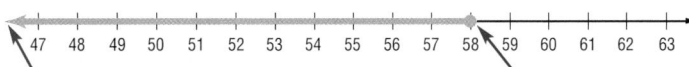

The circle at 11 shows that 11 is *not* included in the inequality.

The heavy arrow pointing to the right shows that the inequality includes all numbers greater than 11.

SOLVE INEQUALITIES BY SUBTRACTION   Subtraction can also be used to solve inequalities.

Key Concept   *Subtraction Property of Inequalities*

- **Words**   If any number is subtracted from each side of a true inequality, the resulting inequality is also true.

- **Symbols**   For all numbers a, b, and c, the following are true.
  1. If $a > b$, then $a - c > b - c$.
  2. If $a < b$, then $a - c < b - c$.

- **Example** $17 > 8$
  $17 - 5 > 8 - 5$
  $12 > 3$

This property is also true when $>$ and $<$ are replaced with $\ge$ and $\le$.

Example 3 *Solve by Subtracting*

Solve $19 + r \ge 16$. Then graph the solution.

$19 + r \ge 16$ Original inequality
$19 + r - 19 \ge 16 - 19$ Subtract 19 from each side.
$r \ge -3$ Simplify.

The solution set is $\{r \mid r \ge -3\}$.

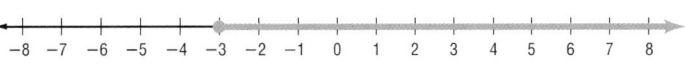

 www.algebra1.com/extra_examples   **Lesson 6-1** Solving Inequalities by Addition and Subtraction   **319**

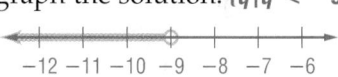

Online Lesson Plans

USA TODAY Education's Online site offers resources and interactive features connected to each day's newspaper. *Experience TODAY*, USA TODAY's daily lesson plan, is available on the site and delivered daily to subscribers. This plan provides instruction for integrating USA TODAY graphics and key editorial features into your mathematics classroom. Log on to **www.education.usatoday.com**.

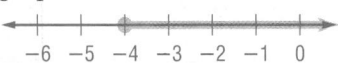
4 Solve $12n - 4 \le 13n$. Then graph the solution. $\{n \mid n \ge -4\}$

$-6 \quad -5 \quad -4 \quad -3 \quad -2 \quad -1 \quad 0$

Teaching Tip When students solve inequalities with variables on both sides, suggest that they subtract the term with the lesser coefficient from each side so the remaining coefficient of the variable will be positive.

5 Write an inequality for the sentence below. Then solve the inequality.

Seven times a number is greater than six times that number minus two.

$7a > 6a - 2$; $\{a \mid a > -2\}$

6 ENTERTAINMENT Alicia wants to buy season passes to two theme parks. If one season pass costs $54.99, and Alicia has $100 to spend on passes, the second season pass must cost no more than what amount? **The second season pass must cost no more than $45.01.**

☑ Concept Check

Solving Inequalities Ask students what the one phrase is that they will never see in a verbal inequality problem.
Sample answer: equal, or is equal to

---

320 Chapter 6 Solving Linear Inequalities

Terms with variables can also be subtracted from each side to solve inequalities.

Example 4 *Variables on Both Sides*

Solve $5p + 7 > 6p$. Then graph the solution.

$5p + 7 > 6p$	Original inequality
$5p + 7 - 5p > 6p - 5p$	Subtract $5p$ from each side.
$7 > p$	Simplify.

Since $7 > p$ is the same as $p < 7$, the solution set is $\{p \mid p < 7\}$.

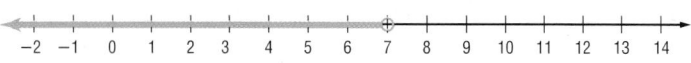
$-2 \quad -1 \quad 0 \quad 1 \quad 2 \quad 3 \quad 4 \quad 5 \quad 6 \quad 7 \quad 8 \quad 9 \quad 10 \quad 11 \quad 12 \quad 13 \quad 14$

Verbal problems containing phrases like *greater than* or *less than* can often be solved by using inequalities. The following chart shows some other phrases that indicate inequalities.

Inequalities			
<	>	≤	≥
• less than	• greater than	• at most	• at least
• fewer than	• more than	• no more than	• no less than
		• less than or equal to	• greater than or equal to

Example 5 *Write and Solve an Inequality*

Write an inequality for the sentence below. Then solve the inequality.

Four times a number is no more than three times that number plus eight.

Four times a number	is no more than	three times that number	plus	eight.
$4n$	$\le$	$3n$	$+$	8

$4n \le 3n + 8$	Original inequality
$4n - 3n \le 3n + 8 - 3n$	Subtract $3n$ from each side.
$n \le 8$	Simplify.

The solution set is $\{n \mid n \le 8\}$.

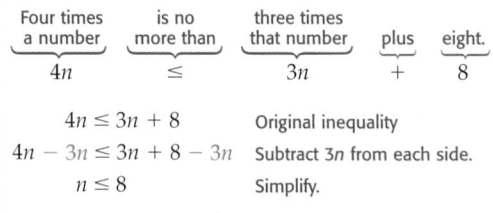

More About...

Olympics •
Yulia Barsukova of the Russian Federation won the gold medal in rhythmic gymnastics at the 2000 Summer Olympics in Sydney, and Yulia Raskina of Belarus won the silver medal.
Source: www.olympic.org

Example 6 *Write an Inequality to Solve a Problem*

OLYMPICS Yulia Raskina scored a total of 39.548 points in the four events of rhythmic gymnastics. Yulia Barsukova scored 9.883 in the rope competition, 9.900 in the hoop competition, and 9.916 in the ball competition. How many points did Barsukova need to score in the ribbon competition to surpass Raskina and win the gold medal?

Words   Barsukova's total must be greater than Raskina's total.

Variable   Let r = Barsukova's score in the ribbon competition.

Barsukova's total	is greater than	Raskina's total.
Inequality $9.883 + 9.900 + 9.916 + r$	$>$	39.548

Solve the inequality.

$$9.883 + 9.900 + 9.916 + r > 39.548 \qquad \text{Original inequality}$$
$$29.699 + r > 39.548 \qquad \text{Simplify.}$$
$$29.699 + r - 29.699 > 39.548 - 29.699 \qquad \text{Subtract 29.699 from each side.}$$
$$r > 9.849 \qquad \text{Simplify.}$$

Barsukova needed to score more than 9.849 points to win the gold medal.

Check for Understanding

Concept Check

1. Sample answers: $y + 1 < -2$, $y - 1 < -4$, $y + 3 < 0$

1. **OPEN ENDED** List three inequalities that are equivalent to $y < -3$.

2. **Compare and contrast** the graphs of $a < 4$ and $a \le 4$. **See margin.**

3. **Explain** what $\{b \,|\, b \ge -5\}$ means. **The set of all numbers b such that b is greater than or equal to -5.**

Guided Practice

4. Which graph represents the solution of $m + 3 > 7$? **a**

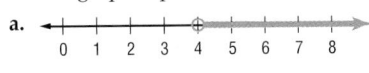

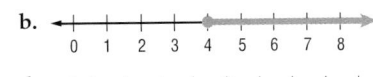

GUIDED PRACTICE KEY	
Exercises	Examples
4–10	1–4
11, 12	5
13	6

5–10. See pp. 365A–365D.

Solve each inequality. Then check your solution, and graph it on a number line.

5. $a + 4 < 2$ $\{a \,|\, a < -2\}$
6. $9 \le b + 4$ $\{b \,|\, b \ge 5\}$
7. $t - 7 \ge 5$ $\{t \,|\, t \ge 12\}$
8. $y - 2.5 > 3.1$ $\{y \,|\, y > 5.6\}$
9. $5.2r + 6.7 \ge 6.2r$ $\{r \,|\, r \le 6.7\}$
10. $7p \le 6p - 2$ $\{p \,|\, p \le -2\}$

Define a variable, write an inequality, and solve each problem. Then check your solution. 11–12. Sample answer: Let n = the number.

11. A number decreased by 8 is at most 14. $n - 8 \le 14$; $\{n \,|\, n \le 22\}$

12. A number plus 7 is greater than 2. $n + 7 > 2$; $\{n \,|\, n > -5\}$

Application

13. **HEALTH** Chapa's doctor recommended that she limit her fat intake to no more than 60 grams per day. This morning, she ate two breakfast bars with 3 grams of fat each. For lunch she ate pizza with 21 grams of fat. If she follows her doctor's advice, how many grams of fat can she have during the rest of the day? **no more than 33 g**

★ indicates increased difficulty

Practice and Apply

Homework Help	
For Exercises	See Examples
14–39	1–4
40–45	5
46–55	6

Extra Practice
See page 833.

Match each inequality with its corresponding graph.

14. $x - 3 \ge -2$ **d**
15. $x + 7 \le 6$ **f**
16. $4x > 3x - 1$ **a**
17. $8 + x < 9$ **c**
18. $5 \le x + 6$ **e**
19. $x - 1 > 0$ **b**

a. [number line −4 to 4, open circle at −1, shaded right]
b. [number line −4 to 4, open circle at 1, shaded right]
c. [number line −4 to 4, open circle at 1, shaded left]
d. [number line −4 to 4, closed dot at 1, shaded right]
e. [number line −4 to 4, closed dot at −1, shaded right]
f. [number line −4 to 4, closed dot at −1, shaded left]

www.algebra1.com/self_check_quiz

Lesson 6-1 Solving Inequalities by Addition and Subtraction **321**

Study Notebook

Have students—
- add the definitions/examples of the vocabulary terms to their Vocabulary Builder worksheets for Chapter 6.
- write a solution set in set-builder notation with an explanation of how to read it.
- include an explanation of the difference between an inequality graph with a dot and one with a circle.
- include any other item(s) that they find helpful in mastering the skills in this lesson.

About the Exercises...

Organization by Objective
- Solve Inequalities by Addition: 14–51
- Solve Inequalities by Subtraction: 14–51

Odd/Even Assignments
Exercises 14–51 are structured so that students practice the same concepts whether they are assigned odd or even problems.

Assignment Guide

Basic: 15–31 odd, 41–53 odd, 56–76

Average: 15–53 odd, 56–76

Advanced: 14–52 even, 53–68 (optional: 69–76)

Answer

2. In both graphs, the line is darkened to the left. In the graph of $a < 4$, there is a circle at 4 to indicate that 4 is not included in the graph. In the graph of $a \le 4$, there is a dot at 4 to indicate that 4 is included in the graph.

DAILY INTERVENTION
Unlocking Misconceptions

Rewriting Inequalities An equation such as $x = 5$ can be rewritten as $5 = x$ because of the Symmetric Property of Equality. Because of this property, students may incorrectly assume that they can rewrite an inequality such as $3 > y$ as $y > 3$. Remind students that the inequality sign always points to the smaller value. In $3 > y$, it points to y, so to write the expression with y on the left, use $y < 3$.

20–37. See pp. 365A–365D.

28. $\{y \mid y > -8\}$
31. $\{w \mid w \geq 1\}$
32. $\{v \mid v > -1\}$
33. $\{a \mid a \leq -5\}$
34. $\{h \mid h > -0.36\}$
35. $\{x \mid x \geq 0.6\}$
36. $\left\{a \mid a > -\frac{1}{8}\right\}$
37. $\left\{p \mid p \leq 1\frac{1}{9}\right\}$

42. $30 \leq n + (-8)$; $\{n \mid n \geq 38\}$
43. $2n > n + 14$; $\{n \mid n > 14\}$
44. $n + (-7) \leq 18$; $\{n \mid n \leq 25\}$

Solve each inequality. Then check your solution, and graph it on a number line.

20. $t + 14 \geq 18$ $\{t \mid t \geq 4\}$ 21. $d + 5 \leq 7$ $\{d \mid d \leq 2\}$ 22. $n - 7 < -3$ $\{n \mid n < 4\}$

23. $s - 5 > -1$ $\{s \mid s > 4\}$ 24. $5 < 3 + g$ $\{g \mid g > 2\}$ 25. $4 > 8 + r$ $\{r \mid r < -4\}$

26. $-3 \geq q - 7$ $\{q \mid q \leq 4\}$ 27. $2 \leq m - 1$ $\{m \mid m \geq 3\}$ 28. $2y > -8 + y$

29. $3f < -3 + 2f$ $\{f \mid f < -3\}$ 30. $3b \leq 2b - 5$ $\{b \mid b \leq -5\}$ 31. $4w \geq 3w + 1$

★ 32. $v - (-4) > 3$ ★ 33. $a - (-2) \leq -3$ ★ 34. $-0.23 < h - (-0.13)$

★ 35. $x + 1.7 \geq 2.3$ ★ 36. $a + \frac{1}{4} > \frac{1}{8}$ ★ 37. $p - \frac{2}{3} \leq \frac{4}{9}$

★ 38. If $d + 5 \geq 17$, then complete each inequality.

   a. $d \geq$?   12   b. $d +$? ≥ 20 8   c. $d - 5 \geq$?   7

★ 39. If $z - 2 \leq 10$, then complete each inequality.

   a. $z \leq$?   12   b. $z -$? ≤ 5 7   c. $z + 4 \leq$?   16

Define a variable, write an inequality, and solve each problem. Then check your solution. 40–45. Sample answer: Let $n =$ the number.

40. The sum of a number and 13 is at least 27. $n + 13 \geq 27$; $\{n \mid n \geq 14\}$

41. A number decreased by 5 is less than 33. $n - 5 < 33$; $\{n \mid n < 38\}$

42. Thirty is no greater than the sum of a number and -8.

43. Twice a number is more than the sum of that number and 14.

44. The sum of two numbers is at most 18, and one of the numbers is -7.

45. Four times a number is less than or equal to the sum of three times the number and -2. $4n \leq 3n + (-2)$; $\{n \mid n \leq -2\}$

46. **BIOLOGY** Adult Nile crocodiles weigh up to 2200 pounds. If a young Nile crocodile weighs 157 pounds, how many pounds might it be expected to gain in its lifetime? no more than 2043 lb

47. **ASTRONOMY** There are at least 200 billion stars in the Milky Way. If 1100 of these stars can be seen in a rural area without the aid of a telescope, how many stars in the galaxy cannot be seen in this way? at least 199,999,998,900 stars

48. **BIOLOGY** There are 3500 species of bees and more than 600,000 species of insects. How many species of insects are not bees? more than 596,500 species

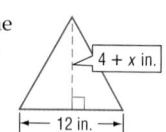

More About. . .

Biology •
One common species of bees is the honeybee. A honeybee colony may have 60,000 to 80,000 bees.

Source: Penn State, Cooperative Extension Service

49. **BANKING** City Bank requires a minimum balance of $1500 to maintain free checking services. If Mr. Hayashi knows he must write checks for $1300 and $947, how much money should he have in his account before writing the checks? at least $3747

50. **GEOMETRY** The length of the base of the triangle at the right is less than the height of the triangle. What are the possible values of x? more than 8 in.

4 + x in.
12 in.

51. **SHOPPING** Terrell has $65 to spend at the mall. He bought a T-shirt for $18 and a belt for $14. If Terrell still wants to buy a pair of jeans, how much can he spend on the jeans? no more than $33

★ 52. **SOCCER** The Centerville High School soccer team plays 18 games in the season. The team has a goal of winning at least 60% of its games. After the first three weeks of the season, the team has won 4 games. How many more games must the team win to meet their goal? at least 7 more games

322   Chapter 6   Solving Linear Inequalities

53. CRITICAL THINKING Determine whether each statement is *always*, *sometimes*, or *never* true.

    a. If $a < b$ and $c < d$, then $a + c < b + d$. **always**

    b. If $a < b$ and $c < d$, then $a + c \geq b + d$. **never**

    c. If $a < b$ and $c < d$, then $a - c = b - d$. **sometimes**

HEALTH **For Exercises 54 and 55, use the following information.**
Hector's doctor told him that his cholesterol level should be below 200. Hector's cholesterol is 225.

54. Let p represent the number of points Hector should lower his cholesterol. Write an inequality with $225 - p$ on one side. $225 - p < 200$

★ **55.** Solve the inequality. $\{p \mid p > 25\}$

56. WRITING IN MATH Answer the question that was posed at the beginning of the lesson. **See pp. 365A–365D.**

    How are inequalities used to describe school sports?

    Include the following in your answer:

    • an inequality describing the number of schools needed to add girls' track and field so that the number is greater than the number of schools currently participating in girls' basketball.

Standardized Test Practice
Ⓐ Ⓑ Ⓒ Ⓓ

57. Which inequality is *not* equivalent to $x \leq 12$? **C**

    Ⓐ $x - 7 \leq 5$ Ⓑ $x + 4 \leq 16$ Ⓒ $x - 1 \leq 13$ Ⓓ $12 \geq x$

58. Which statement is modeled by $n + 6 \geq 5$? **A**

    Ⓐ The sum of a number and six is at least five.

    Ⓑ The sum of a number and six is at most five.

    Ⓒ The sum of a number and six is greater than five.

    Ⓓ The sum of a number and six is no greater than five.

Maintain Your Skills

Mixed Review **59.** Would a scatter plot for the relationship of a person's height to the person's grade on the last math test show a *positive*, *negative*, or *no correlation*? *(Lesson 5-7)* **no**

Write an equation in slope-intercept form of the line that passes through the given point and is parallel to the graph of each equation. *(Lesson 5-6)*

60. $(1, -3)$; $y = 3x - 2$ **61.** $(0, 4)$; $x + y = -3$ **62.** $(-1, 2)$; $2x - y = 1$
     $y = 3x - 6$ $y = -x + 4$ $y = 2x + 4$

66. $\{(-1, 2), (3, -6),$ **Find the next two terms in each sequence.** *(Lesson 4-8)*
(5, -10)\}

67. $\{(-1, 8), (3, 4),$ **63.** 7, 13, 19, 25, …   **64.** 243, 81, 27, 9, …   **65.** 3, 6, 12, 24, …
(5, 2)\}   **31, 37**   **3, 1**   **48, 96**

68. $\{(-1, -8), (3, 0),$ **Solve each equation if the domain is $\{-1, 3, 5\}$.** *(Lesson 4-4)*
(5, 4)\}

     66. $y = -2x$ **67.** $y = 7 - x$ **68.** $2x - y = 6$

Getting Ready for the Next Lesson **PREREQUISITE SKILL** Solve each equation.
*(For review of **multiplication and division equations**, see Lesson 3-3.)*

69. $6g = 42$ **7**   **70.** $\dfrac{t}{9} = 14$ **126**   **71.** $\dfrac{2}{3}y = 14$ **21**   **72.** $3m = 435$ **145**

73. $\dfrac{4}{7}x = 28$ **49**   **74.** $5.3g = 11.13$ **2.1**   **75.** $\dfrac{a}{3.5} = 7$ **24.5**   **76.** $8p = 35$ **4.375**

Lesson 6-1 Solving Inequalities by Addition and Subtraction **323**

4 Assess

Open-Ended Assessment

Modeling Draw a large number line on an overhead transparency. Using a washer or a coin, and a ribbon or a strip of paper, graph several different inequalities on the overhead. Use the coin to indicate a dot on the number line and the washer to indicate a circle. The ribbon is the ray representing points greater or less than the starting value. Have students identify the inequalities you graph, identifying the significance of the circle or dot.

Tips for New Teachers

Intervention Students should always check their solutions, but they often hurry to finish their assignments and omit this step. Remind students that checking solutions is especially important with inequalities because the direction of the inequality sign often gets changed when writing solutions in set-builder notation.

Getting Ready for Lesson 6-2

PREREQUISITE SKILL In Lesson 6-2, students learn how to solve inequalities using multiplication and division. The process is almost identical to the process for solving *equations* using multiplication and division. Use Exercises 69–76 to determine your students' familiarity with solving these types of equations.

Algebra Activity

A Preview of Lesson 6-2

Objective Use algebra tiles to solve inequalities.

Materials
algebra tiles
equation mat
self-adhesive notes

Teach

- You may wish to do the example as a demonstration.
- Make sure the inequality sign on the self-adhesive note is pointed in the correct direction to match the inequality.
- Once they have isolated the x tiles, remind students to separate the 1 tiles into equal groups to correspond to the number of x tiles.
- If the x tiles end up on the right side of the inequality, students may rotate the mat 180 degrees to read the inequality with the variable on the left side.

Assess

Have students work in small groups for **Exercises 1–7**. Observe to determine if they are able to verbalize the activities in **Exercises 1–4**. Students should conclude after **Exercises 6–7** that when they multiply or divide both sides of an inequality by a negative number, the direction of the inequality sign changes.

Study Notebook

You may wish to have students summarize this activity and what they learned from it.

Solving Inequalities

You can use algebra tiles to solve inequalities.

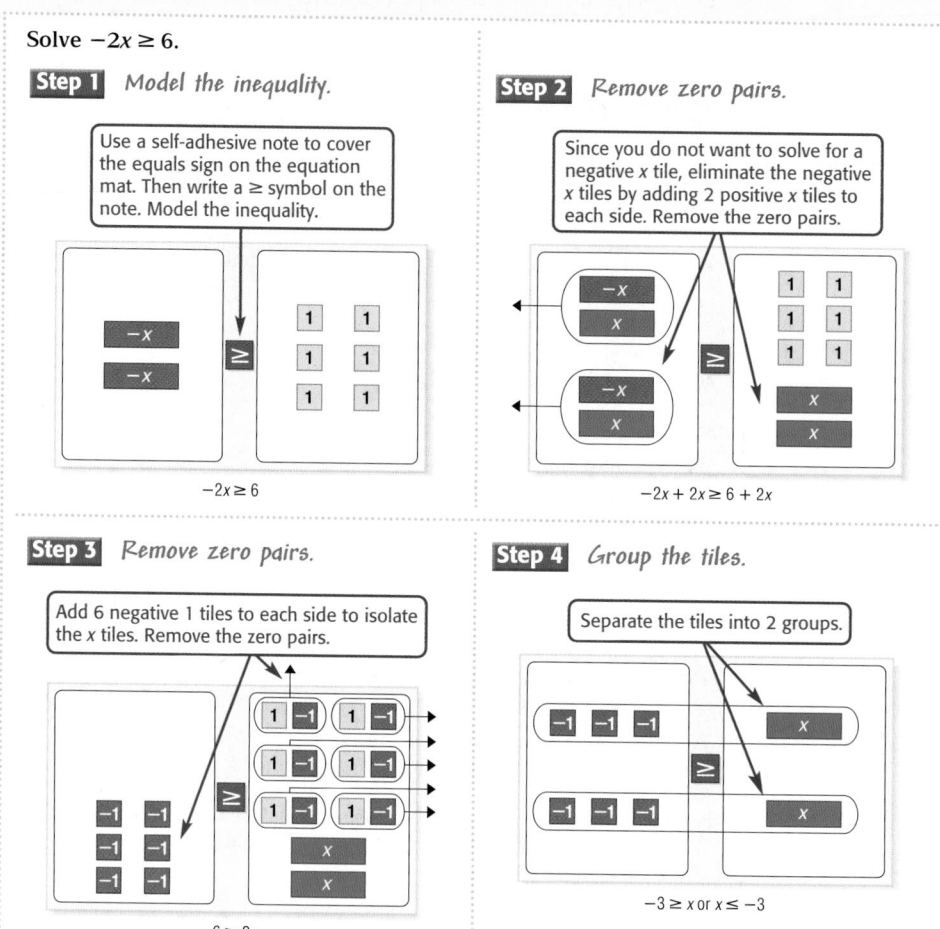

Solve $-2x \geq 6$.

Step 1 Model the inequality.

Use a self-adhesive note to cover the equals sign on the equation mat. Then write a $\geq$ symbol on the note. Model the inequality.

$-2x \geq 6$

Step 2 Remove zero pairs.

Since you do not want to solve for a negative x tile, eliminate the negative x tiles by adding 2 positive x tiles to each side. Remove the zero pairs.

$-2x + 2x \geq 6 + 2x$

Step 3 Remove zero pairs.

Add 6 negative 1 tiles to each side to isolate the x tiles. Remove the zero pairs.

$-6 \geq 2x$

Step 4 Group the tiles.

Separate the tiles into 2 groups.

$-3 \geq x$ or $x \leq -3$

Model and Analyze

Use algebra tiles to solve each inequality.

1. $-4x < 12$ $\{x \mid x > -3\}$ 2. $-2x > 8$ $\{x \mid x < -4\}$ 3. $-3x \geq -6$ $\{x \mid x \leq 2\}$ 4. $-5x \leq -5$ $\{x \mid x \geq 1\}$

5. In Exercises 1–4, is the coefficient of x in each inequality positive or negative? **negative**

6. Compare the inequality symbols and locations of the variable in Exercises 1–4 with those in their solutions. What do you find? **6–7. See pp. 365A–365D.**

7. Model the solution for $2x \geq 6$. What do you find? How is this different from solving $-2x \geq 6$?

324 Chapter 6 Solving Linear Inequalities

Resource Manager

📁 **Teaching Algebra with Manipulatives**

- pp. 10–11 (master for algebra tiles)
- p. 16 (master for equation mat)
- p. 115 (student recording sheet)

Glencoe Mathematics Classroom Manipulative Kit

- algebra tiles
- equation mat

Solving Inequalities by Multiplication and Division

What You'll Learn

- Solve linear inequalities by using multiplication.
- Solve linear inequalities by using division.

Why are inequalities important in landscaping?

Isabel Franco is a landscape architect. To beautify a garden, she plans to build a decorative wall of either bricks or blocks. Each brick is 3 inches high, and each block is 12 inches high. Notice that $3 < 12$.

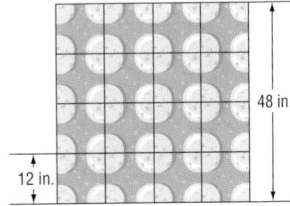

3 in. — | 12 in.

12 in. | 48 in.

A wall 4 bricks high would be lower than a wall 4 blocks high.

$$3 \times 4 \underline{} 12 \times 4$$
$$12 < 48$$

SOLVE INEQUALITIES BY MULTIPLICATION

If each side of an inequality is multiplied by a positive number, the inequality remains true.

$8 > 5$	$5 < 9$
$8(2) \underline{} 5(2)$ Multiply each side by 2.	$5(4) \underline{} 9(4)$ Multiply each side by 4.
$16 > 10$	$20 < 36$

This is *not* true when multiplying by negative numbers.

$5 > 3$	$-6 < 8$
$5(-2) \underline{} 3(-2)$ Multiply each side by -2.	$-6(-5) \underline{} 8(-5)$ Multiply each side by -5.
$-10 < -6$	$30 > -40$

If each side of an inequality is multiplied by a negative number, the direction of the inequality symbol changes. These examples illustrate the **Multiplication Property of Inequalities**.

Key Concept — Multiplying by a Positive Number

- **Words** If each side of a true inequality is multiplied by the same positive number, the resulting inequality is also true.

- **Symbols** If a and b are any numbers and c is a positive number, the following are true.
  If $a > b$, then $ac > bc$, and if $a < b$, then $ac < bc$.

Lesson 6-2 Solving Inequalities by Multiplication and Division **325**

---

1 Focus

 **5-Minute Check Transparency 6-2** Use as a quiz or a review of Lesson 6-1.

Mathematical Background notes are available for this lesson on p. 316C.

Building on Prior Knowledge

The process of solving inequalities is identical to the process of solving equations *except* when multiplying or dividing by a negative value. Students should understand that they do not have to learn a whole new process, but just a special rule when using negatives.

Why are inequalities important in landscaping?

Ask students:

- What is similar about the two walls? What is different? **Both walls are 4 rows high. Each row of bricks is 3 inches high and each row of blocks is 12 inches high.**

- By what number are both sides of the inequality $3 < 12$ multiplied to yield $12 < 48$? **4**

- After you multiply both sides of the inequality $3 < 12$ by the same number to yield $12 < 48$, is the inequality still true? Explain. **Yes; 12 is less than 48.**

Resource Manager

Workbook and Reproducible Masters

Chapter 6 Resource Masters
- Study Guide and Intervention, pp. 349–350
- Skills Practice, p. 351
- Practice, p. 352
- Reading to Learn Mathematics, p. 353
- Enrichment, p. 354
- Assessment, p. 393

Parent and Student Study Guide Workbook, p. 47
School-to-Career Masters, p. 12

 Transparencies
5-Minute Check Transparency 6-2
Answer Key Transparencies

 **Technology**
Interactive Chalkboard

SOLVE INEQUALITIES BY MULTIPLICATION

In-Class Examples Power Point®

Teaching Tip Remind students that $\frac{b}{7}$ is the same as $\frac{1}{7}b$. To isolate b, multiply by the reciprocal of $\frac{1}{7}$, which is 7.

1 Solve $\frac{g}{3} < 12$. Then check your solution. $\{g \mid g < 36\}$

2 Solve $-\frac{3}{4}d \geq 6$. $\{d \mid d \leq -8\}$

3 Write an inequality for the sentence below. Then solve the inequality. *Four-fifths of a number is at most twenty.*
$\frac{4}{5}r \leq 20$; $\{r \mid r \leq 25\}$

Key Concept — Multiplying by a Negative Number

- **Words** If each side of a true inequality is multiplied by the same negative number, the direction of the inequality symbol must be *reversed* so that the resulting inequality is also true.

- **Symbols** If a and b are any numbers and c is a negative number, the following are true.
  If $a > b$, then $ac < bc$, and if $a < b$, then $ac > bc$.

This property also holds for inequalities involving $\geq$ and $\leq$.

You can use this property to solve inequalities.

Example 1 Multiply by a Positive Number

Solve $\frac{b}{7} \geq 25$. Then check your solution.

$\frac{b}{7} \geq 25$ Original inequality

$(7)\frac{b}{7} \geq (7)25$ Multiply each side by 7. Since we multiplied by a positive number, the inequality symbol stays the same.

$b \geq 175$

CHECK To check this solution, substitute 175, a number less than 175, and a number greater than 175 into the inequality.

Let $b = 175$.	Let $b = 140$.	Let $b = 210$.
$\frac{175}{7} \overset{?}{\geq} 25$	$\frac{140}{7} \overset{?}{\geq} 25$	$\frac{210}{7} \overset{?}{\geq} 25$
$25 \geq 25$ ✓	$20 \ngeq 25$	$30 \geq 25$ ✓

The solution set is $\{b \mid b \geq 175\}$.

Example 2 Multiply by a Negative Number

Solve $-\frac{2}{5}p < -14$.

$-\frac{2}{5}p < -14$ Original inequality

$\left(-\frac{5}{2}\right)\left(-\frac{2}{5}p\right) > \left(-\frac{5}{2}\right)(-14)$ Multiply each side by $-\frac{5}{2}$ and change $<$ to $>$.

$p > 35$ The solution set is $\{p \mid p > 35\}$.

Example 3 Write and Solve an Inequality

Write an inequality for the sentence below. Then solve the inequality.

One fourth of a number is less than −7.

One fourth,	of	a number,	is less than,	−7.
$\frac{1}{4}$	$\times$	n	$<$	-7

$\frac{1}{4}n < -7$ Original inequality

$(4)\frac{1}{4}n < (4)(-7)$ Multiply each side by 4 and do not change the inequality's direction.

$n < -28$ The solution set is $\{n \mid n < -28\}$.

SOLVE INEQUALITIES BY DIVISION Dividing each side of an inequality by the same number is similar to multiplying each side of an equality by the same number. Consider the inequality $6 < 15$.

Divide each side by 3.

$$6 < 15$$
$$6 \div 3 \ \underline{\ ?\ } \ 15 \div 3$$
$$2 < 5$$

Since each side is divided by a positive number, the direction of the inequality symbol remains the same.

Divide each side by -3.

$$6 < 15$$
$$6 \div (-3) \ \underline{\ ?\ } \ 15 \div (-3)$$
$$-2 > -5$$

Since each side is divided by a negative number, the direction of the inequality symbol is reversed.

These examples illustrate the **Division Property of Inequalities**.

> ### Key Concept   Dividing by a Positive Number
>
> - **Words**   If each side of a true inequality is divided by the same positive number, the resulting inequality is also true.
>
> - **Symbols**   If a and b are any numbers and c is a positive number, the following are true.
>   If $a > b$, then $\frac{a}{c} > \frac{b}{c}$, and if $a < b$, then $\frac{a}{c} < \frac{b}{c}$.
>
> ### Dividing by a Negative Number
>
> - **Words**   If each side of a true inequality is divided by the same negative number, the direction of the inequality symbol must be *reversed* so that the resulting inequality is also true.
>
> - **Symbols**   If a and b are any numbers and c is a negative number, the following are true.
>   If $a > b$, then $\frac{a}{c} < \frac{b}{c}$, and if $a < b$, then $\frac{a}{c} > \frac{b}{c}$.

This property also holds for inequalities involving $\geq$ and $\leq$.

Example 4 *Divide by a Positive Number*

Solve $14h > 91$.

$14h > 91$	Original inequality
$\dfrac{14h}{14} > \dfrac{91}{14}$	Divide each side by 14 and do not change the direction of the inequality sign.
$h > 6.5$	

CHECK   Let $h = 6.5$.   Let $h = 7$.   Let $h = 6$.

$$14h > 91 \qquad\qquad 14h > 91 \qquad\qquad 14h > 91$$
$$14(6.5) \overset{?}{>} 91 \qquad 14(7) \overset{?}{>} 91 \qquad 14(6) \overset{?}{>} 91$$
$$91 \not> 91 \qquad\qquad 98 > 91 \ \checkmark \qquad\quad 84 \not> 91$$

The solution set is $\{h \,|\, h > 6.5\}$.

Since dividing is the same as multiplying by the reciprocal, there are two methods to solve an inequality that involve multiplication.

SOLVE INEQUALITIES BY DIVISION

Assessment
Challenge students to explain how they might already know how to solve inequalities by division. Students should suggest that since they know how to solve inequalities by multiplication, and since division is the same as multiplying by a reciprocal, then they already know how to solve inequalities by division.

In-Class Example   Power Point®

Teaching Tip Point out to students that the rules for the Division Property of Inequalities state that each side of an inequality can be divided by a positive or negative number. In neither case is zero included because division by zero is an undefined operation.

4 Solve $12s \geq 60$. $\{s \,|\, s \geq 5\}$

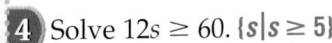

DAILY INTERVENTION

Differentiated Instruction

Kinesthetic Have students write an inequality involving a negative coefficient of the variable on their paper, using a self-adhesive note for the inequality symbol, such as $-12x > 24$. Tell them that they are going to change all the signs in the inequality, so everything is its opposite. The expression becomes $+12x < -24$. Students now can divide without having to worry about the inequality sign.

Teaching Tip Point out to students that it may be easier to solve an inequality using division when the inequality involves whole numbers, and easier to solve using multiplication by reciprocals when the inequality involves fractions.

5 Solve $-8q < 136$ using two methods. $\{q \mid q > -17\}$

Teaching Tip Another way to check the solution is to rework the problem using a different method.

6 Which inequality does *not* have the solution $\{x \mid x > 6\}$? **B**

A $-2x < -12$

B $-6x > -72$

C $\frac{5}{6}x > 5$

D $-\frac{1}{8}x < -\frac{3}{4}$

3 Practice/Apply

Study Notebook

Have students—

• add the definitions/examples of the vocabulary terms to their Vocabulary Builder worksheets for Chapter 6.

• copy the rules for the Multiplication Property of Inequalities and Division Property of Inequalities.

• include any other item(s) that they find helpful in mastering the skills in this lesson.

Answer

1. You could solve the inequality by multiplying each side by $-\frac{1}{7}$ or by dividing each side by -7. In either case, you must reverse the direction of the inequality symbol.

Example 5 Divide by a Negative Number

Solve $-5t \geq 275$ using two methods.

Method 1 Divide.

$-5t \geq 275$ Original inequality

$\dfrac{-5t}{-5} \leq \dfrac{275}{-5}$ Divide each side by -5 and change $\geq$ to $\leq$.

$t \leq -55$ Simplify.

Method 2 Multiply by the multiplicative inverse.

$-5t \geq 275$ Original inequality

$\left(-\dfrac{1}{5}\right)(-5t) \leq \left(-\dfrac{1}{5}\right)275$ Multiply each side by $-\dfrac{1}{5}$ and change $\geq$ to $\leq$.

$t \leq -55$ Simplify.

The solution set is $\{t \mid t \leq -55\}$.

You can use the Multiplication Property and the Division Property for Inequalities to solve standardized test questions.

Standardized Test Practice
Ⓐ Ⓑ Ⓒ Ⓓ

Example 6 The Word "not"

Multiple-Choice Test Item

> Which inequality does *not* have the solution $\{y \mid y \leq -5\}$?
>
> Ⓐ $-7y \geq 35$ Ⓑ $2y \leq -10$ Ⓒ $\dfrac{7}{5}y \geq -7$ Ⓓ $-\dfrac{y}{4} \geq \dfrac{5}{4}$

Read the Test Item

You want to find the inequality that does *not* have the solution set $\{y \mid y \leq -5\}$.

Solve the Test Item

Consider each possible choice.

Ⓐ $-7y \geq 35$

$\dfrac{-7y}{-7} \leq \dfrac{35}{-7}$

$y \leq -5$ ✓

Ⓑ $2y \leq -10$

$\dfrac{2y}{2} \leq \dfrac{-10}{2}$

$y \leq -5$ ✓

Ⓒ $\dfrac{7}{5}y \geq -7$

$\left(\dfrac{5}{7}\right)\dfrac{7}{5}y \geq \left(\dfrac{5}{7}\right)(-7)$

$y \geq -5$

Ⓓ $-\dfrac{y}{4} \geq \dfrac{5}{4}$

$(-4)\left(-\dfrac{y}{4}\right) \leq (-4)\dfrac{5}{4}$

$y \leq -5$ ✓

The answer is C.

Test-Taking Tip

Always look for the word *not* in the questions. This indicates that you are looking for the one incorrect answer, rather than looking for the one correct answer. The word *not* is usually in italics or uppercase letters to draw your attention to it.

Check for Understanding

Concept Check

1. **Explain** why you can use either the Multiplication Property of Inequalities or the Division Property of Inequalities to solve $-7r \leq 28$. **See margin.**

2. Sample answer: Three fourths of a number is greater than 9.

2. **OPEN ENDED** Write a problem that can be represented by the inequality $\frac{3}{4}c > 9$.

 *Standardized Test Practice*
Ⓐ Ⓑ Ⓒ Ⓓ

Example 6 Some questions can be answered without solving each equation or inequality given. Have students examine each inequality in Example 6 to determine what inequality sign should be included in the solution set without working it out. For A and D, the sign becomes $\leq$. For B, it stays $\leq$. C is the remaining choice.

3. Ilonia; when you divide each side of an inequality by a negative number, you must reverse the direction of the inequality symbol.

3. FIND THE ERROR Ilonia and Zachary are solving $-9b \leq 18$.

Ilonia	Zachary
$-9b \leq 18$	$-9b \leq 18$
$\dfrac{-9b}{-9} \geq \dfrac{18}{-9}$	$\dfrac{-9b}{-9} \leq \dfrac{18}{-9}$
$b \geq -2$	$b \leq -2$

Who is correct? Explain your reasoning.

Guided Practice

GUIDED PRACTICE KEY

Exercises	Examples
4, 5, 10, 11	3
6–9	1, 2, 4, 5
12	6

4. Which statement is represented by $7n \geq 14$? **a**

  a. Seven times a number is at least 14.

  b. Seven times a number is greater than 14.

  c. Seven times a number is at most 14.

  d. Seven times a number is less than 14.

5. Which inequality represents *five times a number is less than 25*? **c**

  a. $5n > 25$ **b.** $5n \geq 25$ **c.** $5n < 25$ **d.** $5n \leq 25$

Solve each inequality. Then check your solution.

  6. $-15g > 75$ **7.** $\dfrac{t}{9} < -12$ **8.** $-\dfrac{2}{3}b \leq -9$ **9.** $25f \geq 9$

  $\{g \mid g < -5\}$ $\{t \mid t < -108\}$ $\{b \mid b \geq 13.5\}$ $\{f \mid f \geq 0.36\}$

Define a variable, write an inequality, and solve each problem. Then check your solution. 10–11. Sample answer: Let n = the number.

  10. The opposite of four times a number is more than 12. $-4n > 12$; $\{n \mid n < -3\}$

  11. Half of a number is at least 26. $\dfrac{1}{2}n \geq 26$; $\{n \mid n \geq 52\}$

Standardized Test Practice
Ⓐ Ⓑ Ⓒ Ⓓ

12. Which inequality does *not* have the solution set $\{x \mid x > 4\}$? **B**

  Ⓐ $-5x < -20$ Ⓑ $6x < 24$ Ⓒ $\dfrac{1}{5}x > \dfrac{4}{5}$ Ⓓ $-\dfrac{3}{4}x < -3$

★ indicates increased difficulty

Practice and Apply

Homework Help

For Exercises	See Examples
13–18, 39–44	3
19–38	1, 2, 4, 5
45–51	6

Extra Practice
See page 833.

Match each inequality with its corresponding statement.

  13. $\dfrac{1}{5}n > 10$ **d**   **a.** Five times a number is less than or equal to ten.

  14. $5n \leq 10$ **a**   **b.** One fifth of a number is no less than ten.

  15. $5n > 10$ **e**   **c.** Five times a number is less than ten.

  16. $-5n < 10$ **f**   **d.** One fifth of a number is greater than ten.

  17. $\dfrac{1}{5}n \geq 10$ **b**   **e.** Five times a number is greater than ten.

  18. $5n < 10$ **c**   **f.** Negative five times a number is less than ten.

Solve each inequality. Then check your solution. 19–34. See margin.

  19. $6g \leq 144$ **20.** $7t > 84$ **21.** $-14d \geq 84$ **22.** $-16z \leq -64$

  23. $\dfrac{m}{5} \geq 7$ **24.** $\dfrac{b}{10} \leq 5$ **25.** $-\dfrac{r}{7} < -7$ **26.** $-\dfrac{a}{11} > 9$

  27. $\dfrac{5}{8}y \geq -15$ **28.** $\dfrac{2}{3}v < 6$ **29.** $-\dfrac{3}{4}q \leq -33$ **30.** $-\dfrac{2}{5}p > 10$

  ★ **31.** $-2.5w < 6.8$ ★ **32.** $-0.8s > 6.4$ ★ **33.** $\dfrac{15c}{-7} > \dfrac{3}{14}$ ★ **34.** $\dfrac{4m}{5} < \dfrac{-3}{15}$

Answers

  19. $\{g \mid g \leq 24\}$

  20. $\{t \mid t > 12\}$

  21. $\{d \mid d \leq -6\}$

  22. $\{z \mid z \geq 4\}$

  23. $\{m \mid m \geq 35\}$

  24. $\{b \mid b \leq 50\}$

  25. $\{r \mid r > 49\}$

  26. $\{a \mid a < -99\}$

  27. $\{y \mid y \geq -24\}$

  28. $\{v \mid v < 9\}$

  29. $\{q \mid q \geq 44\}$

  30. $\{p \mid p < -25\}$

  31. $\{w \mid w > -2.72\}$

  32. $\{s \mid s < -8\}$

  33. $\left\{c \mid c < -\dfrac{1}{10}\right\}$

  34. $\left\{m \mid m < -\dfrac{1}{4}\right\}$

DAILY
INTERVENTION **FIND THE ERROR**
Tell students to look first at the solutions from Ilonia and Zachary. The only difference is the inequality symbol. Since the solution involves division by a negative number, the inequality symbol of the solution must be reversed from the original inequality.

About the Exercises...
Organization by Objective
• Solve Inequalities by Multiplication: 13–50
• Solve Inequalities by Division: 13–50

Odd/Even Assignments
Exercises 13–50 are structured so that students practice the same concepts whether they are assigned odd or even problems.

Assignment Guide
Basic: 13–29 odd, 35, 39, 41, 45, 47, 49, 52, 55–78
Average: 13–51 odd, 52, 53, 55–78
Advanced: 14–54 even, 55–72 (optional: 73–78)
All: Practice Quiz 1 (1–10)

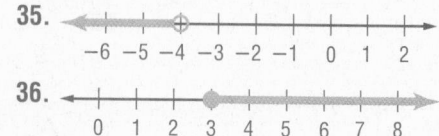

35. Solve $-\frac{y}{8} > \frac{1}{2}$. Then graph the solution. $\{y \mid y < -4\}$; See margin for graph.

36. Solve $-\frac{m}{9} \leq -\frac{1}{3}$. Then graph the solution. $\{m \mid m \geq 3\}$; See margin for graph.

★ 37. If $2a \geq 7$, then complete each inequality.

a. $a \geq$ ___?___ 3.5   b. $-4a \leq$ ___?___ -14 c. ___?___ $a \leq -21$ -6

★ 38. If $4t < -2$, then complete each inequality.

a. $t <$ ___?___ -0.5 b. $-8t >$ ___?___ 4   c. ___?___ $t > 14$ -28

Define a variable, write an inequality, and solve each problem. Then check your solution. 39–44. Sample answer: Let $n =$ the number.

39. Seven times a number is greater than 28. $7n > 28$; $\{n \mid n > 4\}$

40. Negative seven times a number is at least 14. $-7n \geq 14$; $\{n \mid n \leq -2\}$

41. Twenty-four is at most a third of a number. $24 \leq \frac{1}{3}n$; $\{n \mid n \geq 72\}$

42. Two thirds of a number is less than -15. $\frac{2}{3}n < -15$; $\{n \mid n < -22.5\}$

43. $0.25n \geq 90$; $\{n \mid n \geq 360\}$

★ 43. Twenty-five percent of a number is greater than or equal to 90.

★ 44. Forty percent of a number is less than or equal to 45. $0.40n \leq 45$; $\{n \mid n \leq 112.5\}$

45. **GEOMETRY** The area of a rectangle is less than 85 square feet. The length of the rectangle is 20 feet. What is the width of the rectangle? less than $4\frac{1}{4}$ ft

46. **FUND-RAISING** The Middletown Marching Mustangs want to make at least $2000 on their annual mulch sale. The band makes $2.50 on each bag of mulch that is sold. How many bags of mulch should the band sell? at least 800 bags

47. **LONG-DISTANCE COSTS** Juan's long-distance phone company charges him 9¢ for each minute or any part of a minute. He wants to call his friend, but he does not want to spend more than $2.50 on the call. How long can he talk to his friend? no more than 27 min

48. **EVENT PLANNING** The Country Corner Reception Hall does not charge a rental fee as long as at least $4000 is spent on food. Shaniqua is planning a class reunion. If she has chosen a buffet that costs $28.95 per person, how many people must attend the reunion to avoid a rental fee for the hall? at least 139 people

49. **LANDSCAPING** Matthew is planning a circular flower garden with a low fence around the border. If he can use up to 38 feet of fence, what radius can he use for the garden? (*Hint:* $C = 2\pi r$) up to about 6 ft

50. **DRIVING** Average speed is calculated by dividing distance by time. If the speed limit on the interstate is 65 miles per hour, how far can a person travel legally in $1\frac{1}{2}$ hours? no more than $97\frac{1}{2}$ mi

★ 51. **ZOOS** The yearly membership to the San Diego Zoo for a family with 2 adults and 2 children is $144. The regular admission to the zoo is $18 for each adult and $8 for each child. How many times should such a family plan to visit the zoo in a year to make a membership less expensive than paying regular admission? at least 3 times

52a. Sample answer: $2 > -3$, but $4 < 9$.

52b. Sample answer: $-1 < 2$ and $-3 < -2$, but $3 > -4$.

52. **CRITICAL THINKING** Give a counterexample to show that each statement is not always true.

a. If $a > b$, then $a^2 > b^2$.   b. If $a < b$ and $c < d$, then $ac < bd$.

★ 53. **CITY PLANNING** The city of Santa Clarita requires that a parking lot can have no more than 20% of the parking spaces limited to compact cars. If a certain parking lot has 35 spaces for compact cars, how many spaces must the lot have to conform to the code? at least 175 spaces

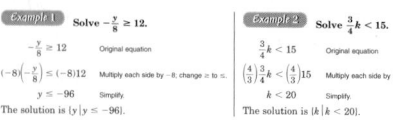

More About. . .

Zoos

Dr. Harry Wegeforth founded the San Diego Zoo in 1916 with just 50 animals. Today, the zoo has over 3800 animals.

Source: www.sandiegozoo.org

Answers

35.

-6 -5 -4 -3 -2 -1 0 1 2

36.

0 1 2 3 4 5 6 7 8

★ 54. **CIVICS** For a candidate to run for a county office, he or she must submit a petition with at least 6000 signatures of registered voters. Usually only 85% of the signatures are valid. How many signatures should a candidate seek on a petition? **at least 7059 signatures**

55. **WRITING IN MATH** Answer the question that was posed at the beginning of the lesson. **See margin.**

Why are inequalities important in landscaping?

Include the following in your answer:
- an inequality representing a brick wall that can be no higher than 4 feet, and
- an explanation of how to solve the inequality.

Standardized Test Practice
Ⓐ Ⓑ Ⓒ Ⓓ

56. The solution set for which inequality is *not* represented by the following graph?

-9-8-7-6-5-4-3-2-1 0 1 2 3 4 5 6 7 8 9   **B**

Ⓐ $-\dfrac{x}{5} \le 1$ Ⓑ $\dfrac{x}{5} \le -1$ Ⓒ $-9x \le 45$ Ⓓ $2.5x \ge -12.5$

57. Solve $-\dfrac{7}{8}t < \dfrac{14}{15}$. **C**

Ⓐ $\left\{t \middle| t > \dfrac{16}{15}\right\}$ Ⓑ $\left\{t \middle| t < \dfrac{16}{15}\right\}$ Ⓒ $\left\{t \middle| t > -\dfrac{16}{15}\right\}$ Ⓓ $\left\{t \middle| t < -\dfrac{16}{15}\right\}$

Maintain Your Skills

Mixed Review **Solve each inequality. Then check your solution, and graph it on a number line.** *(Lesson 6-1)* **58–60. See margin for graphs.**

58. $s - 7 < 12$ $\{s | s < 19\}$ 59. $g + 3 \le -4$ $\{g | g \le -7\}$ 60. $7 > n + 2$ $\{n | n < 5\}$

61. Draw a scatter plot that shows a positive correlation. *(Lesson 5-7)* See pp. 365A–365D.

Write an equation of the line that passes through each pair of points. *(Lesson 5-4)*

62. $(-1, 3), (2, 4)$ $y = \dfrac{1}{3}x + \dfrac{10}{3}$ 63. $(5, -2), (-1, -2)$ $y = -2$ 64. $(3, 3), (-1, 2)$ $y = \dfrac{1}{4}x + \dfrac{9}{4}$

If $h(x) = 3x + 2$, find each value. *(Lesson 4-6)*

65. $h(-4)$ **−10** 66. $h(2)$ **8** 67. $h(w)$ **3w + 2** 68. $h(r - 6)$ **3r − 16**

Solve each proportion. *(Lesson 3-6)*

69. $\dfrac{3}{4} = \dfrac{x}{8}$ **6** 70. $\dfrac{t}{1.5} = \dfrac{2.4}{1.6}$ **2.25** 71. $\dfrac{w + 2}{5} = \dfrac{7}{5}$ **5** 72. $\dfrac{x}{3} = \dfrac{x + 5}{15}$ **$1\dfrac{1}{4}$**

Getting Ready for the Next Lesson **PREREQUISITE SKILL Solve each equation.**
*(To review **multi-step equations**, see Lessons 3-4 and 3-5.)*

73. $5x - 3 = 32$ **7** 74. $4t + 9 = 14$ **1.25** 75. $6y - 1 = 4y + 23$ **12**

76. $\dfrac{14g + 5}{6} = 9$ **3.5** 77. $5a + 6 = 9a - (7a + 18)$ **−8** 78. $2(p - 4) = 7(p + 3)$ **−5.8**

Practice Quiz 1 *Lessons 6-1 and 6-2*

1–5. See pp. 365A–365D for graphs.
Solve each inequality. Then check your solution, and graph it on a number line. *(Lesson 6-1)*

1. $h - 16 > -13$ $\{h | h > 3\}$
2. $r + 3 \le -1$ $\{r | r \le -4\}$
3. $4 \ge p + 9$ $\{p | p \le -5\}$
4. $-3 < a - 5$ $\{a | a > 2\}$
5. $7g \le 6g - 1$ $\{g | g \le -1\}$

Solve each inequality. Then check your solution. *(Lesson 6-2)* **6–10. See pp. 365A–365D.**

6. $15z \ge 105$ 7. $\dfrac{v}{5} < 7$ 8. $-\dfrac{3}{7}q > 15$ 9. $-156 < 12r$ 10. $-\dfrac{2}{5}w \le -\dfrac{1}{2}$

Open-Ended Assessment

Writing Have students write a one-paragraph summary of what they think is the most important thing to remember about solving inequalities by multiplication or division. Students will likely suggest that the most important thing to remember is to change the direction of the inequality symbol when multiplying or dividing by negative numbers. Ask student volunteers to read their paragraphs to the class.

Getting Ready for Lesson 6-3

PREREQUISITE SKILL Lesson 6-3 presents multi-step inequalities, which builds on what students have learned about solving multi-step equations. Use Exercises 73–78 to determine your students' familiarity with solving multi-step equations.

Assessment Options

Practice Quiz 1 The quiz provides students with a brief review of the concepts and skills in Lessons 6-1 and 6-2. Lesson numbers are given to the right of the exercises or instruction lines so students can review concepts not yet mastered.

Quiz (Lessons 6-1 and 6-2) is available on p. 393 of the *Chapter 6 Resource Masters*.

Answers

55. Inequalities can be used to compare the heights of walls. Answers should include the following.
- If *x* represents the number of bricks and the wall must be no higher than 4 ft or 48 in., then $3x \le 48$.
- To solve this inequality, divide each side by 3 and do not change the direction of the inequality. The wall must be 16 bricks high or fewer.

58.
15 16 17 18 19 20 21 22 23

59.
−8 −7 −6 −5 −4 −3 −2 −1 0

60.
0 1 2 3 4 5 6 7 8

6-3 Solving Multi-Step Inequalities

1 Focus

5-Minute Check Transparency 6-3 Use as a quiz or a review of Lesson 6-2.

Mathematical Background notes are available for this lesson on p. 316C.

Building on Prior Knowledge

Solving multi-step inequalities is no different from solving multi-step equations *except* when multiplying or dividing by a negative value. Students should understand that they don't have to learn a whole new process, but just a special rule when using negatives.

How are linear inequalities used in science?

Ask students:

• What would the inequality $F < -31$ represent? **The temperatures at which chlorine is not a gas.**

• What expression was substituted for F to represent the temperature of the boiling point of chlorine in degrees Celsius? $\frac{9}{5}C + 32$

What You'll Learn

• Solve linear inequalities involving more than one operation.
• Solve linear inequalities involving the Distributive Property.

How are linear inequalities used in science?

The boiling point of a substance is the temperature at which the element changes from a liquid to a gas. The boiling point of chlorine is $-31°F$. That means chlorine will be a gas for all temperatures greater than $-31°F$. If F represents temperature in degrees Fahrenheit, the inequality $F > -31$ represents the temperatures for which chlorine is a gas.

If C represents degrees Celsius, then $F = \frac{9}{5}C + 32$. You can solve $\frac{9}{5}C + 32 > -31$ to find the temperatures in degrees Celsius for which chlorine is a gas.

Boiling Points

argon	$-303°F$
chlorine	$-31°F$
bromine	$138°F$
water	$212°F$
iodine	$363°F$

Source: *World Book Encyclopedia*

SOLVE MULTI-STEP INEQUALITIES The inequality $\frac{9}{5}C + 32 > -31$ involves more than one operation. It can be solved by undoing the operations in the same way you would solve an equation with more than one operation.

Example 1 *Solve a Real-World Problem*

SCIENCE Find the temperatures in degrees Celsius for which chlorine is a gas.

$\frac{9}{5}C + 32 > -31$	Original inequality
$\frac{9}{5}C + 32 - 32 > -31 - 32$	Subtract 32 from each side.
$\frac{9}{5}C > -63$	Simplify.
$\left(\frac{5}{9}\right)\frac{9}{5}C > \left(\frac{5}{9}\right)(-63)$	Multiply each side by $\frac{5}{9}$.
$C > -35$	Simplify.

Chlorine will be a gas for all temperatures greater than $-35°C$.

When working with inequalities, do not forget to reverse the inequality sign whenever you multiply or divide each side by a negative number.

Example 2 *Inequality Involving a Negative Coefficient*

Solve $-7b + 19 < -16$. Then check your solution.

$-7b + 19 < -16$	Original inequality
$-7b + 19 - 19 < -16 - 19$	Subtract 19 from each side.
$-7b < -35$	Simplify.
$\frac{-7b}{-7} > \frac{-35}{-7}$	Divide each side by -7 and change $<$ to $>$.
$b > 5$	Simplify.

Resource Manager

Workbook and Reproducible Masters

Chapter 6 Resource Masters
• Study Guide and Intervention, pp. 355–356
• Skills Practice, p. 357
• Practice, p. 358
• Reading to Learn Mathematics, p. 359
• Enrichment, p. 360
• Assessment, pp. 393, 395

Parent and Student Study Guide Workbook, p. 48

Transparencies
5-Minute Check Transparency 6-3
Answer Key Transparencies

Technology

AlgePASS: Tutorial Plus, Lesson 14
Interactive Chalkboard
Multimedia Applications

CHECK To check this solution, substitute 5, a number less than 5, and a number greater than 5.

Let $b = 5$.

$-7b + 19 < -16$
$-7(5) + 19 \overset{?}{<} -16$
$-35 + 19 \overset{?}{<} -16$
$-16 \not< -16$

Let $b = 4$.

$-7b + 19 < -16$
$-7(4) + 19 \overset{?}{<} -16$
$-28 + 19 \overset{?}{<} -16$
$-9 \not< -16$

Let $b = 6$.

$-7b + 19 < -16$
$-7(6) + 19 \overset{?}{<} -16$
$-42 + 19 \overset{?}{<} -16$
$-23 < -16$ ✓

The solution set is $\{b \mid b > 5\}$.

Example 3 Write and Solve an Inequality

Write an inequality for the sentence below. Then solve the inequality.
Three times a number minus eighteen is at least five times the number plus twenty-one.

Three times a number	minus	eighteen	is at least	five times the number	plus	twenty one.
$3n$	$-$	18	$\geq$	$5n$	$+$	21

$3n - 18 \geq 5n + 21$ Original inequality

$3n - 18 - 5n \geq 5n + 21 - 5n$ Subtract $5n$ from each side.

$-2n - 18 \geq 21$ Simplify.

$-2n - 18 + 18 \geq 21 + 18$ Add 18 to each side.

$-2n \geq 39$ Simplify.

$\dfrac{-2n}{-2} \leq \dfrac{39}{-2}$ Divide each side by -2 and change $\geq$ to $\leq$.

$n \leq -19.5$ Simplify.

The solution set is $\{n \mid n \leq -19.5\}$.

A graphing calculator can be used to solve inequalities.

Graphing Calculator Investigation

Solving Inequalities

You can find the solution of an inequality in one variable by using a graphing calculator. On a TI-83 Plus, clear the Y= list. Enter $6x + 9 < -4x + 29$ as Y1. (The symbol $<$ is item 5 on the TEST menu.)
Press GRAPH .

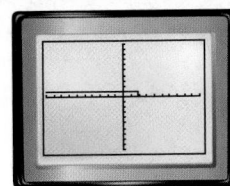

[10, 10] scl: 1 by [10, 10] scl: 1

Think and Discuss

1. Describe what is shown on the screen. **part of the graph of $y = 1$**
2. Use the TRACE function to scan the values along the graph. What do you notice about the values of y on the graph? **$y = 1$ if $x < 2$; otherwise, $y = 0$**
3. Solve the inequality algebraically. How does your solution compare to the pattern you noticed in Exercise 2?

3. $x < 2$; $y = 1$ for those values of x for which the inequality is true; $y = 0$ for those values of x for which the inequality is not true.

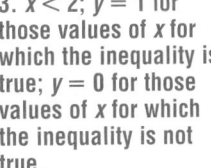

www.algebra1.com/extra_examples

Lesson 6-3 Solving Multi-Step Inequalities **333**

SOLVE MULTI-STEP INEQUALITIES

In-Class Examples Power Point®

1 **SCIENCE** The inequality $F > 212$ represents the temperatures in degrees Fahrenheit for which water is a gas (steam). Similarly, the inequality $\frac{9}{5}C + 32 > 212$ represents the temperatures in degrees Celsius for which water is a gas. Find the temperatures in degrees Celsius for which water is a gas. **Water will be a gas for all temperatures greater than 100°C.**

2 Solve $13 - 11d \geq 79$. Then check your solution. $\{d \mid d \leq -6\}$

Teaching Tip Examples 1 and 2 were solved in two steps. Example 3 requires three steps. Other problems will require even more steps. Remind students that when they solve multi-step inequalities, they should always undo operations in the reverse of the order of operations. This means undoing addition or subtraction first to isolate the variable, then multiplying or dividing to make the coefficient 1.

3 Write an inequality for the sentence below. Then solve the inequality. *Four times a number plus twelve is less than a number minus 3.* $4n + 12 < n - 3$; $\{n \mid n < -5\}$

Graphing Calculator Investigation

Solving Inequalities Graphed on a number line, $6x + 9 < -4x + 29$ would have a circle at 2, and $6x + 9 \leq -4x + 29$ would have a dot at 2. Since the calculator does not make this distinction on the graph, have students use the **TABLE** feature. For an x-value of 2, the table shows that the corresponding y-value is 0, meaning the graph does not include 2 (which is the same as having a circle at 2).

Tips for New Teachers

Intervention Before you introduce solving inequalities involving the Distributive Property, review the Distributive Property with students. Have volunteers explain the Distributive Property in their own words, and give examples on the chalkboard or overhead projector.

SOLVE INEQUALITIES INVOLVING THE DISTRIBUTIVE PROPERTY

In-Class Examples

 Power Point®

④ Solve $8 - (c + 3) \leq 6c + 3(2 - c)$. $\left\{c \mid c \geq -\frac{1}{4}\right\}$

⑤ Solve $-7(s + 4) + 11s \geq 8s - 2(2s + 1)$. $\varnothing$

✓ Concept Check

Distributive Property Ask students to identify the first step they must do when solving inequalities that have grouping symbols. **Use the Distributive Property to remove the grouping symbols.**

3 Practice/Apply

Study Notebook

Have students—
• copy Example 4 or a similar problem to show how to solve inequalities using the Distributive Property.
• include any other item(s) that they find helpful in mastering the skills in this lesson.

SOLVE INEQUALITIES INVOLVING THE DISTRIBUTIVE PROPERTY

When solving equations that contain grouping symbols, first use the Distributive Property to remove the grouping symbols.

Example 4 Distributive Property

Solve $3d - 2(8d - 9) > 3 - (2d + 7)$.

$3d - 2(8d - 9) > 3 - (2d + 7)$	Original inequality
$3d - 16d + 18 > 3 - 2d - 7$	Distributive Property
$-13d + 18 > -2d - 4$	Combine like terms.
$-13d + 18 + 13d > -2d - 4 + 13d$	Add 13d to each side.
$18 > 11d - 4$	Simplify.
$18 + 4 > 11d - 4 + 4$	Add 4 to each side.
$22 > 11d$	Simplify.
$\dfrac{22}{11} > \dfrac{11d}{11}$	Divide each side by 11.
$2 > d$	Simplify.

Since $2 > d$ is the same as $d < 2$, the solution set is $\{d \mid d < 2\}$.

If solving an inequality results in a statement that is always true, the solution is all real numbers. If solving an inequality results in a statement that is never true, the solution is the empty set $\varnothing$. The empty set has no members.

Example 5 Empty Set

Solve $8(t + 2) - 3(t - 4) < 5(t - 7) + 8$.

$8(t + 2) - 3(t - 4) < 5(t - 7) + 8$	Original inequality
$8t + 16 - 3t + 12 < 5t - 35 + 8$	Distributive Property
$5t + 28 < 5t - 27$	Combine like terms.
$5t + 28 - 5t < 5t - 27 - 5t$	Subtract 5t from each side.
$28 < -27$	This statement is false.

Since the inequality results in a false statement, the solution set is the empty set $\varnothing$.

Check for Understanding

Concept Check
1. **Compare and contrast** the method used to solve $-5h + 6 = -7$ and the method used to solve $-5h + 6 \leq -7$. **See margin.**

2. **OPEN ENDED** Write a multi-step inequality with the solution graphed below.

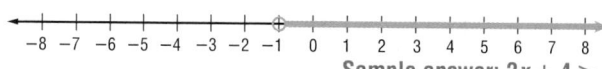

Sample answer: $2x + 4 > 2$

Guided Practice
3. Justify each indicated step.

$3(a - 7) + 9 \leq 21$
$3a - 21 + 9 \leq 21$ a. __?__ **Distributive Property**
$3a - 12 \leq 21$
$3a - 12 + 12 \leq 21 + 12$ b. __?__ **Add 12 to each side.**
$3a \leq 33$
$\dfrac{3a}{3} \leq \dfrac{33}{3}$ c. __?__ **Divide each side by 3.**
$a \leq 11$

GUIDED PRACTICE KEY

Exercises	Examples
3	1–5
4–8	2, 4, 5
9	3
10	1

DAILY INTERVENTION

Unlocking Misconceptions

Students may incorrectly assume that the solution of all inequalities in which the variable has been eliminated is the empty set $\varnothing$. Remind students that they must simplify the inequality to see whether it is a true statement. If the inequality is true, the solution set is all real numbers. Only when the inequality is untrue is the solution set the empty set.

Solve each inequality. Then check your solution.

4. $\{y \mid y > -10.5\}$
5. $\{r \mid r \geq -18\}$
6. $\{b \mid b < 12\}$

4. $-4y - 23 < 19$ 5. $\frac{2}{3}r + 9 \geq -3$ 6. $7b + 11 > 9b - 13$

7. $-5(g + 4) > 3(g - 4)$ $\{g \mid g < -1\}$ 8. $3 + 5t \leq 3(t + 1) - 4(2 - t)$ $\{t \mid t \geq 4\}$

9. Define a variable, write an inequality, and solve the problem below. Then check your solution.
Seven minus two times a number is less than three times the number plus thirty-two.
Sample answer: Let n = the number; $7 - 2n < 3n + 32$; $\{n \mid n > -5\}$.

Application

10. **SALES** A salesperson is paid \$22,000 a year plus 5% of the amount of sales made. What is the amount of sales needed to have an annual income greater than \$35,000? **more than \$260,000**

★ indicates increased difficulty

Practice and Apply

Homework Help

For Exercises	See Examples
11–14	1–5
15–34	2, 4, 5
35–38	3
39–52	1.

Extra Practice
See page 834.

Justify each indicated step.

11. $\frac{2}{5}w + 7 \leq -9$

$\frac{2}{5}w + 7 - 7 \leq -9 - 7$ a. ___?___

$\frac{2}{5}w \leq -16$

$\left(\frac{5}{2}\right)\frac{2}{5}w \leq \left(\frac{5}{2}\right)(-16)$ b. ___?___

$w \leq -40$

11a. Subtract 7 from each side.
11b. Multiply each side by $\frac{5}{2}$.

12. $m > \frac{15 - 2m}{-3}$ **See margin.**

$(-3)m < (-3)\frac{15 - 2m}{-3}$ a. ___?___

$-3m < 15 - 2m$

$-3m + 2m < 15 - 2m + 2m$ b. ___?___

$-m < 15$

$(-1)(-m) > (-1)15$ c. ___?___

$m > -15$

13. Solve $4(t - 7) \leq 2(t + 9)$. Show each step and justify your work. $\{t \mid t \leq 23\}$

14. Solve $-5(k + 4) > 3(k - 4)$. Show each step and justify your work. $\{k \mid k < -1\}$
13–14. See margin and pp. 365A–365D for steps and justifications.

Solve each inequality. Then check your solution.

16. $\{f \mid f < -8\}$
17. $\{d \mid d > -125\}$
18. $\{w \mid w > 56\}$
19. $\left\{q \mid q \leq 3\frac{1}{3}\right\}$
20. $\{a \mid a \geq -9\}$
21. $\{r \mid r \geq -9\}$
22. $\{k \mid k > 8\}$
27. $\{t \mid t \geq -1\}$
28. $\{h \mid h < -79\}$
30. $\{b \mid b$ is a real number.$\}$

15. $-3t + 6 \leq -3$ $\{t \mid t \geq 3\}$ 16. $-5 - 8f > 59$ 17. $-2 - \frac{d}{5} < 23$

18. $\frac{w}{8} - 13 > -6$ 19. $7q - 1 + 2q \leq 29$ 20. $8a + 2 - 10a \leq 20$

21. $9r + 15 \leq 24 + 10r$ 22. $13k - 11 > 7k + 37$ 23. $\frac{2v - 3}{5} \geq 7$ $\{v \mid v \geq 19\}$

24. $\frac{3a + 8}{2} < 10$ $\{a \mid a < 4\}$ 25. $\frac{3w + 5}{4} \geq 2w$ $\{w \mid w \leq 1\}$ 26. $\frac{5b + 8}{3} < 3b$ $\{b \mid b > 2\}$

★27. $7 + 3t \leq 2(t + 3) - 2(-1 - t)$ 28. $5(2h - 6) - 7(h + 7) > 4h$

★29. $3y + 4 > 2(y + 3) + y$ $\varnothing$ 30. $3 - 3(b - 2) < 13 - 3(b - 6)$

★31. $3.1v - 1.4 \geq 1.3v + 6.7$ $\{v \mid v \geq 4.5\}$ 32. $0.3(d - 2) - 0.8d > 4.4$ $\{d \mid d < -10\}$

★33. Solve $4(y + 1) - 3(y - 5) \geq 3(y - 1)$. Then graph the solution. $\{y \mid y \leq 11\}$

★34. Solve $5(x + 4) - 2(x + 6) \geq 5(x + 1) - 1$. Then graph the solution. $\{x \mid x \leq 2\}$
33–34. See pp. 365A–365D for graphs.

Define a variable, write an inequality, and solve each problem. Then check your solution. **35–38. Sample answer: Let n = the number.**

35. $\frac{1}{8}n - 5 \geq 30$; $\{n \mid n \geq 280\}$
36. $\frac{2}{3}n + 8 > 12$; $\{n \mid n > 6\}$

35. One eighth of a number decreased by five is at least thirty.

36. Two thirds of a number plus eight is greater than twelve.

37. Negative four times a number plus nine is no more than the number minus twenty-one. $-4n + 9 \leq n - 21$; $\{n \mid n \geq 6\}$

38. Three times the sum of a number and seven is greater than five times the number less thirteen. $3(n + 7) > 5n - 13$; $\{n \mid n < 17\}$

www.algebra1.com/self_check_quiz

DAILY INTERVENTION

Differentiated Instruction

Interpersonal Some students benefit from working with a partner so that they can talk through the process being used. Group students in pairs to solve inequalities. Once both students agree on the solution, have them test several values to help verify that their solution is correct.

About the Exercises...

Organization by Objective

- **Solve Multi-Step Inequalities:** 11, 12, 15–26, 31, 35–37, 39–42, 45, 48–52
- **Solve Inequalities Involving the Distributive Property:** 13, 14, 27–30, 32–34, 38, 43, 44, 47

Odd/Even Assignments

Exercises 11–38 are structured so that students practice the same concepts whether they are assigned odd or even problems.

Alert! Exercises 56–58 require a graphing calculator.

Assignment Guide

Basic: 11–25 odd, 35, 37, 39–42, 46, 53–82

Average: 11–37 odd, 43–46, 53–82

Advanced: 12–38 even, 46–73 (optional: 74–82)

Answers

1. To solve both the equation and the inequality, you first subtract 6 from each side and then divide each side by -5. In the equation, the equal sign does not change. In the inequality, the inequality symbol is reversed because you divided by a negative number.

12a. Multiply each side by -3 and change $>$ to $<$.

12b. Add $2m$ to each side.

12c. Multiply each side by -1 and change $<$ to $>$.

13. $4(t - 7) \leq 2(t + 9)$ *Original inequality*
$4t - 28 \leq 2t + 18$ *Distributive Property*
$4t - 28 - 2t \leq 2t + 18 - 2t$ *Subtract 2t from each side.*
$2t - 28 \leq 18$ *Simplify.*
$2t - 28 + 28 \leq 18 + 28$ *Add 28 to each side.*
$2t \leq 46$ *Simplify.*
$\frac{2t}{2} \leq \frac{46}{2}$ *Divide each side by 2.*
$t \leq 23$ *Simplify.*
$\{t \mid t \leq 23\}$

Solve Multi-Step Inequalities To solve linear inequalities involving more than one operation, undo the operations in reverse of the order of operations, just as you would solve an equation with more than one operation.

Example 1 Solve $6x - 4 \leq 2x + 12$.

$$6x - 4 \leq 2x + 12 \quad \text{Original inequality}$$
$$6x - 4 - 2x \leq 2x + 12 - 2x \quad \text{Subtract } 2x \text{ from each side.}$$
$$4x - 4 \leq 12 \quad \text{Simplify.}$$
$$4x - 4 + 4 \leq 12 + 4 \quad \text{Add 4 to each side.}$$
$$4x \leq 16 \quad \text{Simplify.}$$
$$\frac{4x}{4} \leq \frac{16}{4} \quad \text{Divide each side by 4.}$$
$$x \leq 4 \quad \text{Simplify.}$$
The solution is $\{x \mid x \leq 4\}$.

Example 2 Solve $3a - 15 > 4 + 5a$.

$$3a - 15 > 4 + 5a \quad \text{Original inequality}$$
$$3a - 15 - 5a > 4 + 5a - 5a \quad \text{Subtract } 5a \text{ from each side.}$$
$$-2a - 15 > 4 \quad \text{Simplify.}$$
$$-2a - 15 + 15 > 4 + 15 \quad \text{Add 15 to each side.}$$
$$-2a > 19 \quad \text{Simplify.}$$
$$\frac{-2a}{-2} < \frac{19}{-2} \quad \text{Divide each side by } -2 \text{ and change } > \text{ to } <.$$
$$a < -9\frac{1}{2} \quad \text{Simplify.}$$
The solution is $\left\{a \mid a < -9\frac{1}{2}\right\}$.

Exercises

Solve each inequality. Then check your solution.

1. $11y + 13 \geq -1$
$\left\{y \mid y \geq -1\frac{3}{11}\right\}$

2. $8n - 10 < 6 - 2n$
$\left\{n \mid n < 1\frac{3}{5}\right\}$

3. $\frac{q}{7} + 1 > -5$
$\{q \mid q > -42\}$

4. $6n + 12 < 8 + 8n$
$\{n \mid n > 2\}$

5. $-12 - d > -12 + 4d$
$\{d \mid d < 0\}$

6. $5r - 6 > 8r - 18$
$\{r \mid r < 4\}$

7. $\frac{-3x + 6}{2} \leq 12$
$\{x \mid x \geq -6\}$

8. $7.3y - 14.4 > 4.9y$
$\{y \mid y > 6\}$

9. $-8m - 3 < 18 - m$
$\{m \mid m > -3\}$

10. $-4y - 10 > 19 - 2y$
$\left\{y \mid y < -14\frac{1}{2}\right\}$

11. $9n - 24n + 45 > 0$
$\{n \mid n < 3\}$

12. $\frac{4x - 2}{5} \geq -4$
$\left\{x \mid x \geq -4\frac{1}{2}\right\}$

Define a variable, write an inequality, and solve each problem. Then check your solution. 13–15. Sample answer: Let n = the number.

13. Negative three times a number plus four is no more than the number minus eight.
$-3n + 4 \leq n - 8$; $\{n \mid n \geq 6\}$

14. One fourth of a number decreased by three is at least two. $\frac{1}{4}n - 3 \geq 2$; $\{n \mid n \geq 20\}$

15. The sum of twelve and a number is no greater than the sum of twice the number and −8.
$12 + n \leq 2n + (-8)$; $\{n \mid n \geq 20\}$

Justify each indicated step.

1. $x > \frac{5x - 12}{8}$

$8x > (8)\frac{5x - 12}{8}$ a. _?_
$8x > 5x - 12$
$8x - 5x > 5x - 12 - 5x$ b. _?_
$3x > -12$
$\frac{3x}{3} > \frac{-12}{3}$ c. _?_
$x > -4$

a. Multiply each side by 8.
b. Subtract 5x from each side.
c. Divide each side by 3.

2. $2(2h + 2) < 2(3h + 5) - 12$
$4h + 4 < 6h + 10 - 12$ a. _?_
$4h + 4 < 6h - 2$
$4h + 4 - 6h < 6h - 2 - 6h$ b. _?_
$-2h + 4 < -2$
$-2h + 4 - 4 < -2 - 4$ c. _?_
$-2h < -6$
$\frac{-2h}{-2} > \frac{-6}{-2}$ d. _?_
$h > 3$

a. Distributive Property
b. Subtract 6h from each side.
c. Subtract 4 from each side.
d. Divide each side by −2 and change < to >.

Solve each inequality. Then check your solution.

3. $-5 - \frac{t}{6} \geq -9$
$\{t \mid t \leq 24\}$

4. $4u - 6 \geq 6u - 20$
$\{u \mid u \leq 7\}$

5. $13 > \frac{2}{3}a - 1$
$\{a \mid a < 21\}$

6. $\frac{w + 3}{2} < -8$
$\{w \mid w < -19\}$

7. $\frac{3f - 10}{5} > 7$
$\{f \mid f > 15\}$

8. $h \leq \frac{6h + 3}{5}$
$\{h \mid h \geq -3\}$

9. $3(z + 1) + 11 < -2(z + 13)$
$\{z \mid z < -8\}$

10. $3e + 2(4e + 2) \leq 2(6e + 1)$
$\{e \mid e \geq 2\}$

11. $5n - 3(n - 6) \geq 0$
$\{n \mid n \geq -9\}$

Define a variable, write an inequality, and solve each problem. Then check your solution. 12–13. Sample answer: Let n = the number.

12. A number is less than one fourth the sum of three times the number and four.
$n < \frac{3n + 4}{4}$; $\{n \mid n < 4\}$

13. Two times the sum of a number and four is no more than three times the sum of the number and seven decreased by four. $2(n + 4) \leq 3(n + 7) - 4$; $\{n \mid n \geq -9\}$

14. **GEOMETRY** The area of a triangular garden can be no more than 120 square feet. The base of the triangle is 16 feet. What is the height of the triangle? no more than 15 ft

15. **MUSIC PRACTICE** Nabuko practices the violin at least 12 hours per week. She practices for three fourths of an hour each session. If Nabuko has already practiced 3 hours in one week, how many sessions remain to meet or exceed her weekly practice goal? at least 12 sessions

Pre-Activity How are linear inequalities used in science?

Read the introduction to Lesson 6-3 at the top of page 332 in your textbook.
Then write an inequality that could be used to find the temperatures in degrees Celsius for which each substance is a gas.

Argon: $\frac{9}{5}C + 32 > -303$ Bromine: $\frac{9}{5}C + 32 > 138$

Reading the Lesson

1. What does the phrase "undoing the operations in reverse of the order of operations" mean?
Sample answer: First add or subtract to undo subtraction or addition, then multiply or divide to undo division or multiplication.

2. Describe how checking the solution of an inequality is different from checking the solution of an equation.
Sample answer: Instead of substituting one value for the variable, there are infinitely many values that can be used to check. It is a good idea to use a value that is less than, the value equal to, and a value greater than the number in the solution to check an inequality.

3. Describe how the Distributive Property can be used to remove the grouping symbols in the inequality $4x - 7(2x + 8) \leq 3x - 5$.
Multiply −7 by both 2x and 8.

4. Is it possible to have no solution when you solve an inequality? Explain your answer and give an example.
Sample answer: Yes; if solving results in an inequality that is never true (and the signs have been reversed if necessary), then there is no solution. Example: $3(t - 4) - 8 > 3(t + 4) - 8$

Helping You Remember

5. Make a checklist of steps you can use when solving inequalities.
(1) Use the Distributive Property to remove any grouping symbols.
(2) Combine any like terms.
(3) Add or subtract the same variable terms or constants on both sides.
(4) Multiply or divide to undo operations.
(5) Reverse the direction of the inequality symbol if both sides were multiplied or divided by a negative number.
(6) Be sure the variable is by itself on one side of the final inequality.

GEOMETRY For Exercises 39 and 40, use the following information.
By definition, the measure of any acute angle is less than 90 degrees. Suppose the measure of an acute angle is $3a - 15$.

39. Write an inequality to represent the situation. $3a - 15 < 90$

40. Solve the inequality. $\{a \mid a < 35\}$

SCHOOL For Exercises 41 and 42, use the following information.
Carmen's scores on three math tests were 91, 95, and 88. The fourth and final test of the grading period is tomorrow. She needs an average (mean) of at least 92 to receive an A for the grading period.   41. $\frac{91 + 95 + 88 + s}{4} \geq 92$

41. If s is her score on the fourth test, write an inequality to represent the situation.

42. If Carmen wants an A in math, what must she score on the test? at least 94

PHYSICAL SCIENCE For Exercises 43 and 44, use the information at the left and the information below.
The melting point for an element is the temperature where the element changes from a solid to a liquid. If C represents degrees Celsius and F represents degrees Fahrenheit, then $C = \frac{5(F - 32)}{9}$.   43. $\frac{5(F - 32)}{9} < -38$

43. Write an inequality that can be used to find the temperatures in degrees Fahrenheit for which mercury is a solid.

44. For what temperatures will mercury be a solid? temperatures less than −36.4°F

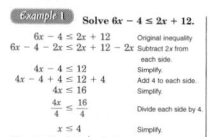

More About . . .

Physical Science

Mercury is a metal that is a liquid at room temperature. In fact, its melting point is −38°C. Mercury is used in thermometers because it expands evenly as it is heated.

Source: World Book Encyclopedia

45. **HEALTH** Keith weighs 200 pounds. He wants to weigh less than 175 pounds. If he can lose an average of 2 pounds per week on a certain diet, how long should he stay on his diet to reach his goal weight? more than $12\frac{1}{2}$ weeks

46. **CRITICAL THINKING** Write a multi-step inequality that has no solution and one that has infinitely many solutions.
Sample answers: $2x + 5 < 2x + 3$; $2x + 5 > 2x + 3$

★ 47. **PERSONAL FINANCES** Nicholas wants to order a pizza. He has a total of $13.00 to pay the delivery person. The pizza costs $7.50 plus $1.25 per topping. If he plans to tip 15% of the total cost of the pizza, how many toppings can he order? 3 or fewer toppings

LABOR For Exercises 48–50, use the following information.
A union worker made $500 per week. His union sought a one-year contract and went on strike. Once the new contract was approved, it provided for a 4% raise.

★ 48. Assume that the worker was not paid during the strike. Given his raise in salary, how many weeks could he strike and still make at least as much for the next 52 weeks as he would have made without a strike? no more than 2 weeks

★ 49. How would your answer to Exercise 48 change if the worker had been making $600 per week? no change

★ 50. How would your answer to Exercise 48 change if the worker's union provided him with $150 per week during the strike? up to 2.8 weeks

★ 51. **NUMBER THEORY** Find all sets of two consecutive positive odd integers whose sum is no greater than 18. 7, 9; 5, 7; 3, 5; 1, 3

★ 52. **NUMBER THEORY** Find all sets of three consecutive positive even integers whose sum is less than 40. 10, 12, 14; 8, 10, 12; 6, 8, 10; 4, 6, 8; 2, 4, 6

Carlos Montezuma

During his lifetime, Carlos Montezuma (1865?–1923) was one of the most influential Native Americans in the United States. He was recognized as a prominent physician and was also a passionate advocate of the rights of Native American peoples. The exercises that follow will help you learn some interesting facts about Dr. Montezuma's life.

Solve each inequality. The word or phrase next to the equivalent inequality will complete the statement correctly.

1. $-2k > 10$
Montezuma was born in the state of _?_.
a. $k < -5$ Arizona
b. $k > -5$ Montana
c. $k > 12$ Utah

2. $5 \geq r - 9$
He was a Native American of the Yavapais, who are a _?_ people.
a. $r \leq -4$ Navajo
b. $r \geq -4$ Mohawk
c. $r \leq 14$ Mohave-Apache

53. WRITING IN MATH Answer the question that was posed at the beginning of the lesson. **See margin.**

How are linear inequalities used in science?

Include the following in your answer:
- an inequality for the temperatures in degrees Celsius for which bromine is a gas, and
- a description of a situation in which a scientist might use an inequality.

 Standardized Test Practice

54. What is the first step in solving $\frac{y-5}{9} \geq 13$? **D**

Ⓐ Add 5 to each side.　　　Ⓑ Subtract 5 from each side.
Ⓒ Divide each side by 9.　　Ⓓ Multiply each side by 9.

55. Solve $4t + 2 < 8t - (6t - 10)$. **C**

Ⓐ $\{t \mid t < -6\}$　　Ⓑ $\{t \mid t > -6\}$　　Ⓒ $\{t \mid t < 4\}$　　Ⓓ $\{t \mid t > 4\}$

 Graphing Calculator   Use a graphing calculator to solve each inequality.

56. $3x + 7 > 4x + 9$　　　**57.** $13x - 11 \leq 7x + 37$　　　**58.** $2(x - 3) < 3(2x + 2)$
$\{x \mid x < -2\}$　　　　　　$\{x \mid x \leq 8\}$　　　　　　　　$\{x \mid x > -3\}$

Maintain Your Skills

Mixed Review

59. BUSINESS   The charge per mile for a compact rental car at Great Deal Rentals is $0.12. Mrs. Ludlow must rent a car for a business trip. She has a budget of $50 for mileage charges. How many miles can she travel without going over her budget? *(Lesson 6-2)* **up to 416 mi**

Solve each inequality. Then check your solution, and graph it on a number line. *(Lesson 6-1)* **60–62. See margin for graphs.**

60. $d + 13 \geq 22$ $\{d \mid d \geq 9\}$　**61.** $t - 5 < 3$ $\{t \mid t < 8\}$　**62.** $4 > y + 7$ $\{y \mid y < -3\}$

Write the point-slope form of an equation for a line that passes through each point with the given slope. *(Lesson 5-5)*

63. $(1, -3), m = 2$　　**64.** $(-2, -1), m = -\frac{2}{3}$　**65.** $(3, 6), m = 0$ $y - 6 = 0$
$y + 3 = 2(x - 1)$　　　$y + 1 = -\frac{2}{3}(x + 2)$

Determine the slope of the line that passes through each pair of points. *(Lesson 5-1)*

66. $(3, -1), (4, -6)$ **−5**　**67.** $(-2, -4), (1, 3)$ $\frac{7}{3}$　**68.** $(0, 3), (-2, -5)$ **4**

Determine whether each equation is a linear equation. If an equation is linear, rewrite it in the form $Ax + By = C$. *(Lesson 4-5)*

69. $4x = 7 + 2y$　　**70.** $2x^2 - y = 7$ **no**　　**71.** $x = 12$ **yes;** $x + 0y = 12$
yes; $4x - 2y = 7$

Solve each equation. Then check your solution. *(Lesson 3-5)*

72. $2(x - 2) = 3x - (4x - 5)$ **3**　　**73.** $5t - 7 = t + 3$ **2.5**

Getting Ready for the Next Lesson

PREREQUISITE SKILL   Graph each set of numbers on a number line.
*(To review **graphing integers on a number line**, see Lesson 2-1.)* **74–82. See pp. 365A–365D.**

74. $\{-2, 3, 5\}$　　　　**75.** $\{-1, 0, 3, 4\}$　　　　**76.** $\{-5, -4, -1, 1\}$
77. {integers less than 5}　　　**78.** {integers greater than −2}
79. {integers between 1 and 6}　　**80.** {integers between −4 and 2}
81. {integers greater than or equal to −4}
82. {integers less than 6 but greater than −1}

Lesson 6-3 Solving Multi-Step Inequalities   337

---

4 Assess

Open-Ended Assessment

Speaking Have students explain to the class the different methods they now know for solving inequalities, including those learned in previous lessons. Ask them to start with the simplest methods and progress to the more complex. Record student responses on the chalkboard or overhead projector. As each student describes a method, call on another student to give an example of how to use the method. Record this example along with the corresponding method.

Getting Ready for Lesson 6-4

PREREQUISITE SKILL Students will learn how to solve compound inequalities and graph them in Lesson 6-4. Use Exercises 74–82 to determine your students' familiarity with graphing sets of integers on a number line.

Assessment Options

Quiz (Lesson 6-3) is available on p. 393 of the *Chapter 6 Resource Masters*.

Mid-Chapter Test (Lessons 6-1 through 6-3) is available on p. 395 of the *Chapter 6 Resource Masters*.

Answers

53. Inequalities can be used to describe the temperatures for which an element is a gas or a solid. Answers should include the following.
- The inequality for temperatures in degrees Celsius for which bromine is a gas is $\frac{9}{5}C + 32 > 138$.

- Sample answer: Scientists may use inequalities to describe the temperatures for which an element is a solid.

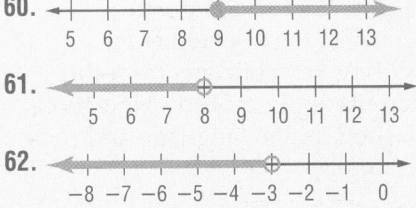

60.
61.
62.

Getting Started

Discuss the meaning of the adjective *compound*. Ask students the meaning of the word and to give an example of something that is compound.

Review the polygons listed on this page. In order to determine whether compound statements are true, students must be familiar with the number of sides each polygon has.

Teach

Sentence Structure Ask students to recall the definition of a compound sentence from their language arts studies. Students should recall that a compound sentence has two independent clauses that are joined by a coordinating conjunction, punctuation, or both.

Explain that the compound statements in this activity are compound sentences in which the two independent clauses are joined by the coordinating conjunctions *and* or *or*.

Assess

Study Notebook

Ask students to summarize what they have learned about compound statements.

ELL English Language Learners may benefit from writing key concepts from this activity in their Study Notebooks in their native language and then in English.

Compound Statements

Two simple statements connected by the words *and* or *or* form a compound statement. Before you can determine whether a compound statement is true or false, you must understand what the words *and* and *or* mean. Consider the statement below.

A triangle has three sides, *and* a hexagon has five sides.
For a compound statement connected by the word *and* to be true, both simple statements must be true. In this case, it is true that a triangle has three sides. However, it is false that a hexagon has five sides; it has six. Thus, the compound statement is false.

A compound statement connected by the word *or* may be *exclusive* or *inclusive*. For example, the statement "With your dinner, you may have soup *or* salad," is exclusive. In everyday language, *or* means one or the other, but not both. However, in mathematics, *or* is inclusive. It means one or the other or both. Consider the statement below.

A triangle has three sides, *or* a hexagon has five sides.
For a compound statement connected by the word *or* to be true, at least one of the simple statements must be true. Since it is true that a triangle has three sides, the compound statement is true.

Triangle

Square

Pentagon

Hexagon

Octagon

Reading to Learn

Determine whether each compound statement is *true* or *false*. Explain your answer. 1–12. See margin for explanations.

1. A hexagon has six sides, *or* an octagon has seven sides. **true**

2. An octagon has eight sides, *and* a pentagon has six sides. **false**

3. A pentagon has five sides, *and* a hexagon has six sides. **true**

4. A triangle has four sides, *or* an octagon does *not* have seven sides. **true**

5. A pentagon has three sides, *or* an octagon has ten sides. **false**

6. A square has four sides, *or* a hexagon has six sides. **true**

7. $5 < 4$ or $8 < 6$ **false**

8. $-1 > 0$ and $1 < 5$ **false**

9. $4 > 0$ and $-4 < 0$ **true**

10. $0 = 0$ or $-2 > -3$ **true**

11. $5 \neq 5$ or $-1 > -4$ **true**

12. $0 > 3$ and $2 > -2$ **false**

338 Chapter 6 Solving Linear Inequalities

Answers

1. true <u>or</u> false	5. false <u>or</u> false	9. true <u>and</u> true
2. true <u>and</u> false	6. true <u>or</u> true	10. true <u>or</u> true
3. true <u>and</u> true	7. false <u>or</u> false	11. false <u>or</u> true
4. false <u>or</u> true	8. false <u>and</u> true	12. false <u>and</u> true

Solving Compound Inequalities

What You'll Learn

- Solve compound inequalities containing the word *and* and graph their solution sets.
- Solve compound inequalities containing the word *or* and graph their solution sets.

Vocabulary
- compound inequality
- intersection
- union

How are compound inequalities used in tax tables?

Richard Kelley is completing his income tax return. He uses the table to determine the amount he owes in federal income tax.

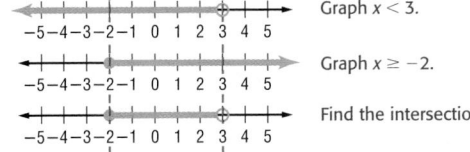

2002 Tax Tables

If taxable income is—		Single	Married filing jointly	Married filing separately	Head of a household
At least	Less than				
41,000	41,050	7423	5554	7975	6083
41,050	41,100	7436	5561	7988	6096
41,100	41,150	7450	5569	8002	6110
41,150	41,200	7463	5576	8015	6123
41,200	41,250	7477	5584	8029	6137
41,250	41,300	7490	5591	8042	6150
41,300	41,350	7504	5599	8056	6164
41,350	41,400	7517	5606	8069	6177
41,400	41,450	7531	5614	8083	6191
41,450	41,500	7544	5621	8096	6204
41,500	41,550	7558	5629	8110	6218
41,550	41,600	7571	5636	8123	6231

Source: IRS

Let c represent the amount of Mr. Kelley's income. His income is at least $41,350 and it is less than $41,400. This can be written as $c \geq 41,350$ and $c < 41,400$. When considered together, these two inequalities form a **compound inequality**. This compound inequality can be written without using *and* in two ways.

$$41,350 \leq c < 41,400 \text{ or } 41,400 > c \geq 41,350$$

Study Tip

Reading Math
The statement
$41,350 \leq c < 41,400$ can be read *41,350 is less than or equal to c, which is less than 41,400.*

INEQUALITIES CONTAINING *AND* A compound inequality containing *and* is true only if both inequalities are true. Thus, the graph of a compound inequality containing *and* is the **intersection** of the graphs of the two inequalities. In other words, the solution must be a solution of *both* inequalities.

The intersection can be found by graphing each inequality and then determining where the graphs overlap.

Example 1 Graph an Intersection

Graph the solution set of $x < 3$ and $x \geq -2$.

Graph $x < 3$.

Graph $x \geq -2$.

Find the intersection.

The solution set is $\{x \mid -2 \leq x < 3\}$. Note that the graph of $x \geq -2$ includes the point -2. The graph of $x < 3$ does *not* include 3.

---

1 Focus

 5-Minute Check Transparency 6-4 Use as a quiz or a review of Lesson 6-3.

Mathematical Background notes are available for this lesson on p. 316D.

Building on Prior Knowledge

In Lesson 6-1, students learned to graph inequalities on a number line. Those same skills will be used in this lesson to graph two inequalities and determine which part(s) of their graphs satisfy the given compound inequality.

How are compound inequalities used in tax tables?

Ask students:

- What inequality symbol represents the term *at least*, when we say that Mr. Kelley's income is *at least* $41,350? **greater than or equal to (≥)**
- What is the least amount his income could be? **$41,350**
- What is the greatest amount his income could be? **$41,399.99**

Resource Manager

📂 Workbook and Reproducible Masters

Chapter 6 Resource Masters
- Study Guide and Intervention, pp. 361–362
- Skills Practice, p. 363
- Practice, p. 364
- Reading to Learn Mathematics, p. 365
- Enrichment, p. 366

Parent and Student Study Guide Workbook, p. 49

Transparencies
5-Minute Check Transparency 6-4
Real-World Transparency 6
Answer Key Transparencies

Technology
AlgePASS: Tutorial Plus, Lesson 15
Interactive Chalkboard

2 Teach

INEQUALITIES CONTAINING *AND*

Teaching Tip The symbol for intersection is ∩. The solution set in Example 1 could be written as $\{x|x < 3\} \cap \{x|x \geq -2\}$.

1 Graph the solution set of $y \geq 5$ and $y < 12$. The solution set is $\{y|5 \leq y < 12\}$

4 5 6 7 8 9 10 11 12 13 14

Teaching Tip Students may benefit from rewriting the compound inequality as two separate inequalities before they attempt to solve it.

2 Solve $7 < z + 2 \leq 11$. Then graph the solution set. $\{z|5 < z \leq 9\}$

4 5 6 7 8 9 10 11 12 13 14

INEQUALITIES CONTAINING *OR*

3 **TRAVEL** A ski resort has several types of hotel rooms and several types of cabins. The hotel rooms cost at most $89 per night, and the cabins cost at least $109 per night. Write and graph a compound inequality that describes the amount a guest would pay per night at the resort. $\{n|n \leq 89$ or $n \geq 109\}$, where n is the amount a guest pays per night

84 90 96 102 108 114

Career Choices

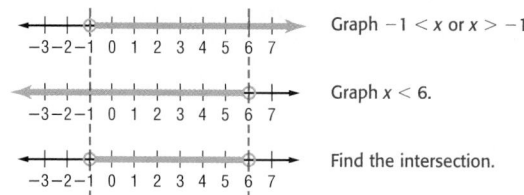

Pilot

Pilots check aviation weather forecasts to choose a route and altitude that will provide the smoothest flight.

Online Research
For information about a career as a pilot, visit:
www.algebra1.com/careers

Example 2 *Solve and Graph an Intersection*

Solve $-5 < x - 4 < 2$. Then graph the solution set.

First express $-5 < x - 4 < 2$ using *and*. Then solve each inequality.

$$-5 < x - 4 \qquad \text{and} \qquad x - 4 < 2$$
$$-5 + 4 < x - 4 + 4 \qquad \qquad x - 4 + 4 < 2 + 4$$
$$-1 < x \qquad\qquad\qquad x < 6$$

The solution set is the intersection of the two graphs.

Graph $-1 < x$ or $x > -1$.

Graph $x < 6$.

Find the intersection.

The solution set is $\{x \,|\, -1 < x < 6\}$.

INEQUALITIES CONTAINING *OR* Another type of compound inequality contains the word *or*. A compound inequality containing *or* is true if one or more of the inequalities is true. The graph of a compound inequality containing *or* is the **union** of the graphs of the two inequalities. In other words, the solution of the compound inequality is a solution of *either* inequality, not necessarily both.

The union can be found by graphing each inequality.

Example 3 *Write and Graph a Compound Inequality*

AVIATION An airplane is experiencing heavy turbulence while flying at 30,000 feet. The control tower tells the pilot that he should increase his altitude to at least 33,000 feet or decrease his altitude to no more than 26,000 feet to avoid the turbulence. Write and graph a compound inequality that describes the altitude at which the airplane should fly.

Words   The pilot has been told to fly at an altitude of at least 33,000 feet or no more than 26,000 feet.

Variables   Let *a* be the plane's altitude.

The plane's altitude	is at least	33,000 feet	or	the altitude	is no more than	26,000 feet.
Inequality a	$\geq$	33,000	or	a	$\leq$	26,000

Now, graph the solution set.

Graph $a \geq 33,000$.

Graph $a \leq 26,000$.

Find the union.

$a \geq 33,000$ or $a \leq 26,000$

340   Chapter 6   Solving Linear Inequalities

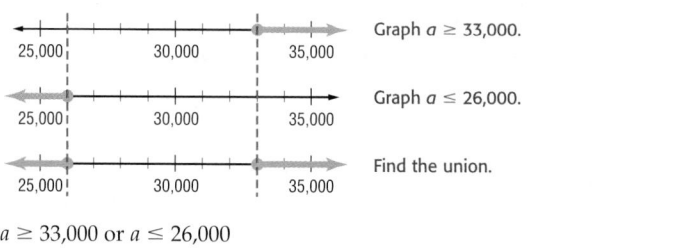

Example **4** Solve and Graph a Union

Solve $-3h + 4 < 19$ or $7h - 3 > 18$. Then graph the solution set.

$$-3h + 4 < 19 \qquad \text{or} \qquad 7h - 3 > 18$$
$$-3h + 4 - 4 < 19 - 4 \qquad 7h - 3 + 3 > 18 + 3$$
$$-3h < 15 \qquad\qquad 7h > 21$$
$$\frac{-3h}{-3} > \frac{15}{-3} \qquad\qquad \frac{7h}{7} > \frac{21}{7}$$
$$h > -5 \qquad\qquad h > 3$$

The solution set is the union of the two graphs.

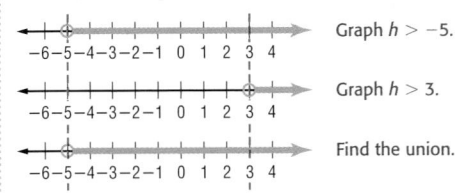

Graph $h > -5$.

Graph $h > 3$.

Find the union.

Notice that the graph of $h > -5$ contains every point in the graph of $h > 3$. So, the union is the graph of $h > -5$. The solution set is $\{h \mid h > -5\}$.

In-Class Example

Teaching Tip The symbol for union is $\cup$. The solution set in Example 4 could be written as $\{h \mid h > -5\} \cup \{h \mid h > 3\}$.

4 Solve $4k - 7 \le 25$ or $12 - 9k \ge 30$. Then graph the solution set. $\{k \mid k \le 8\}$

3 Practice/Apply

Study Notebook

Have students—
• add the definitions/examples of the vocabulary terms to their Vocabulary Builder worksheets for Chapter 6.
• include an example of an inequality containing "and," and the graph of the inequality.
• include an example of an inequality containing "or," and the graph of the inequality.
• include any other item(s) that they find helpful in mastering the skills in this lesson.

Check for Understanding

Concept Check
1. **Describe** the difference between a compound inequality containing *and* and a compound inequality containing *or*. **See margin.**

2. **Write** 7 *is less than t, which is less than* 12 as a compound inequality. $7 < t < 12$

3. **OPEN ENDED** Give an example of a compound inequality containing *and* that has no solution. **Sample answer:** $x < -2$ **and** $x > 3$

Guided Practice

GUIDED PRACTICE KEY	
Exercises	Examples
4–7	1
8–12	2, 4
13	3

8–11. See margin for graphs.
8. $\{w \mid 3 < w < 8\}$
9. $\{n \mid n \le 2 \text{ or } n \ge 8\}$

Graph the solution set of each compound inequality. 4–5. See margin.

4. $a \le 6$ and $a \ge -2$

5. $y > 12$ or $y < 9$

Write a compound inequality for each graph.

6.
$-3 < x \le 1$

7.
$x \le -1$ or $x \ge 5$

Solve each compound inequality. Then graph the solution set.

8. $6 < w + 3$ and $w + 3 < 11$

9. $n - 7 \le -5$ or $n - 7 \ge 1$

10. $3z + 1 < 13$ or $z \le 1$ $\{z \mid z < 4\}$

11. $-8 < x - 4 \le -3$ $\{x \mid -4 < x \le 1\}$

12. Define a variable, write a compound inequality, and solve the following problem.
Three times a number minus 7 is less than 17 and greater than 5.
Sample answer: Let n **= the number;** $5 < 3n - 7 < 17$; $\{n \mid 4 < n < 8\}$.

Application
13. **PHYSICAL SCIENCE** According to Hooke's Law, the force F in pounds required to stretch a certain spring x inches beyond its natural length is given by $F = 4.5x$. If forces between 20 and 30 pounds, inclusive, are applied to the spring, what will be the range of the increased lengths of the stretched spring? **about** $4.44 \le x \le 6.67$

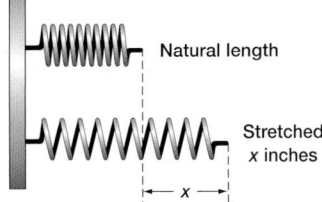

Natural length

Stretched x inches

x

 www.algebra1.com/extra_examples

Answers

1. A compound inequality containing *and* is true if and only if both inequalities are true. A compound inequality containing *or* is true if and only if at least one of the inequalities is true.

4.

5.

8.

9.

10.

11.

Practice and Apply

About the Exercises...

Organization by Objective
- **Inequalities Containing and:** 14, 15, 18–21, 26, 28, 29, 32–35, 38, 39, 42, 43, 46–48
- **Inequalities Containing or:** 16, 17, 22–25, 27, 30, 31, 36, 37, 40, 41, 44, 45

Odd/Even Assignments
Exercises 14–47 are structured so that students practice the same concepts whether they are assigned odd or even problems.

Alert! Exercise 53 involves research on the Internet or other reference materials. Exercise 57 requires a graphing calculator.

Assignment Guide

Basic: 15–23 odd, 27–37 odd, 43–49 odd, 53–80
Average: 15–49 odd, 53–80
Advanced: 14–48 even, 49–72 (optional: 73–80)
All: Practice Quiz 2 (1–10)

Answers

14.
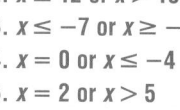

15.

16.

17.

18.

19.

Homework Help

For Exercises	See Examples
14–27	1
28–45	2, 4
46–48	3

Extra Practice
See page 834.

21. $-7 < x < -3$
22. $x \le 12$ or $x > 15$
23. $x \le -7$ or $x \ge -6$
24. $x = 0$ or $x \le -4$
25. $x = 2$ or $x > 5$

28–41. See pp. 365A–365D for graphs.
28. $\{k \mid 10 < k \le 16\}$
29. $\{f \mid -13 \le f \le -5\}$
30. $\{d \mid d \le 5$ or $d > 7\}$
31. $\{h \mid h < -1\}$
35. $\{q \mid -1 < q < 6\}$
36. $\{x \mid x$ is a real number$\}$
38. $\{p \mid 3 \le p \le 5\}$
42. $5 \le n - 8 \le 14$; $\{n \mid 13 \le n \le 22\}$
43. $-8 < 3n + 4 < 10$; $\{n \mid -4 < n < 2\}$
44. $-5n > 35$ or $-5n < 10$; $\{n \mid n < -7$ or $n > -2\}$
45. $0 < \frac{1}{2}n \le 1$; $\{n \mid 0 < n \le 2\}$

Graph the solution set of each compound inequality. 14–19. See margin.

14. $x > 5$ and $x \le 9$
15. $s < -7$ and $s \le 0$
16. $r < 6$ or $r > 6$
17. $m \ge -4$ or $m > 6$
18. $7 < d < 11$
19. $-1 \le g < 3$

Write a compound inequality for each graph.

20.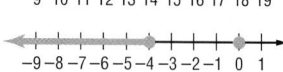
21.
22.
23.
★ 24.
★ 25.

26. **WEATHER** The Fujita Scale (F-scale) is the official classification system for tornado damage. One factor used to classify a tornado is wind speed. Use the information in the table to write an inequality for the range of wind speeds of an F3 tornado. **$158 \le w \le 206$**

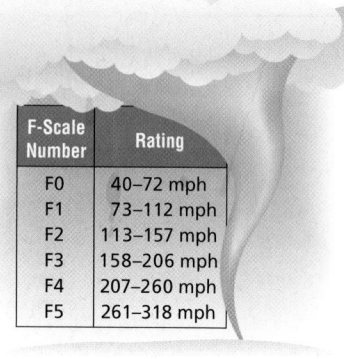

F-Scale Number	Rating
F0	40–72 mph
F1	73–112 mph
F2	113–157 mph
F3	158–206 mph
F4	207–260 mph
F5	261–318 mph

27. **BIOLOGY** Each type of fish thrives in a specific range of temperatures. The optimum temperatures for sharks range from 18°C to 22°C, inclusive. Write an inequality to represent temperatures where sharks will *not* thrive. **$t \le 18$ or $t \ge 22$**

Solve each compound inequality. Then graph the solution set.

28. $k + 2 > 12$ and $k + 2 \le 18$
29. $f + 8 \le 3$ and $f + 9 \ge -4$
30. $d - 4 > 3$ or $d - 4 \le 1$
31. $h - 10 < -21$ or $h + 3 < 2$
32. $3 < 2x - 3 < 15$ $\{x \mid 3 < x < 9\}$
33. $4 < 2y - 2 < 10$ $\{y \mid 3 < y < 6\}$
34. $3t - 7 \ge 5$ and $2t + 6 \le 12$ ∅
35. $8 > 5 - 3q$ and $5 - 3q > -13$
36. $-1 + x \le 3$ or $-x \le -4$
37. $3n + 11 \le 13$ or $-3n \ge -12$ $\{n \mid n \le 4\}$
★ 38. $2p - 2 \le 4p - 8 \le 3p - 3$
39. $3g + 12 \le 6 + g \le 3g - 18$ ∅
★ 40. $4c < 2c - 10$ or $-3c < -12$ $\{c \mid c < -5$ or $c > 4\}$
41. $0.5b > -6$ or $3b + 16 < -8 + b$ $\{b \mid b < -12$ or $b > -12\}$

Define a variable, write an inequality, and solve each problem. 42–45. Sample answer: Let n = the number.

42. Eight less than a number is no more than 14 and no less than 5.
43. The sum of 3 times a number and 4 is between -8 and 10.
44. The product of -5 and a number is greater than 35 or less than 10.
45. One half a number is greater than 0 and less than or equal to 1.

46. **HEALTH** About 20% of the time you sleep is spent in rapid eye movement (REM) sleep, which is associated with dreaming. If an adult sleeps 7 to 8 hours, how much time is spent in REM sleep? **between 1.4 and 1.6 hours inclusive**

47. **SHOPPING** A store is offering a $30 mail-in rebate on all color printers. Luisana is looking at different color printers that range in price from $175 to $260. How much can she expect to spend after the mail-in rebate? **between $145 and $230 inclusive**

48. FUND-RAISING Rashid is selling chocolates for his school's fund-raiser. He can earn prizes depending on how much he sells. So far, he has sold $70 worth of chocolates. How much more does he need to sell to earn a prize in category D? **between $51 and $110 inclusive**

Sales ($)	Prize
0–25	A
26–60	B
61–120	C
121–180	D
180+	E

49. CRITICAL THINKING Write a compound inequality that represents the values of x which make the following expressions *false*.

  a. $x < 5$ or $x > 8$ $x \geq 5$ and $x \leq 8$ **b.** $x \leq 6$ and $x \geq 1$ $x > 6$ or $x < 1$

HEARING For Exercises 50–52, use the following information.
Humans hear sounds with sound waves within the 20 to 20,000 hertz range. Dogs hear sounds in the 15 to 50,000 hertz range.

50. Write a compound inequality for the hearing range of humans and one for the hearing range of dogs. $20 \leq h \leq 20{,}000$; $15 \leq d \leq 50{,}000$

51. $\{h \mid 15 \leq h \leq 50{,}000\}$; **51.** What is the union of the two solution sets? the intersection?
$\{h \mid 20 \leq h \leq 20{,}000\}$; ★ **52.** Write an inequality or inequalities for the range of sounds that dogs can hear, but humans cannot. $15 \leq h < 20$ or $20{,}000 < h \leq 50{,}000$

53. RESEARCH Use the Internet or other resource to find the altitudes in miles of the layers of Earth's atmosphere, troposphere, stratosphere, mesosphere, thermosphere, and exosphere. Write inequalities for the range of altitudes for each layer. **Sample answer: troposphere: $a \leq 10$, stratosphere: $10 < a \leq 30$, mesosphere: $30 < a \leq 50$, thermosphere: $50 < a \leq 400$, exosphere: $a > 400$**

54. WRITING IN MATH Answer the question that was posed at the beginning of the lesson. **See pp. 365A–365D.**

How are compound inequalities used in tax tables?

Include the following in your answer:
- a description of the intervals used in the tax table shown at the beginning of the lesson, and
- a compound inequality describing the income of a head of a household paying $7024 in taxes.

Standardized Test Practice
(A) (B) (C) (D)

55. Ten pounds of fresh tomatoes make between 10 and 15 cups of cooked tomatoes. How many cups does one pound of tomatoes make? **A**
  (A) between 1 and $1\frac{1}{2}$ cups   (B) between 1 and 5 cups
  (C) between 2 and 3 cups   (D) between 2 and 4 cups

56. Solve $-7 < x + 2 < 4$. **B**
  (A) $-5 < x < 6$ (B) $-9 < x < 2$
  (C) $-5 < x < 2$ (D) $-9 < x < 6$

Graphing Calculator

57. SOLVE COMPOUND INEQUALITIES In Lesson 6-3, you learned how to use a graphing calculator to find the values of x that make a given inequality true. You can also use this method to test compound inequalities. The words *and* and *or* can be found in the **LOGIC** submenu of the **TEST** menu of a TI-83 Plus. Use this method to solve each of the following compound inequalities using your graphing calculator. **a. $\{x \mid x < -6$ or $x > -1\}$ b. $\{x \mid -2 \leq x \leq 8\}$**
  a. $x + 4 < -2$ or $x + 4 > 3$ **b.** $x - 3 \leq 5$ and $x + 6 \geq 4$

www.algebra1.com/self_check_quiz

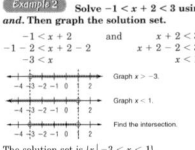

Open-Ended Assessment

Writing Have students write a paragraph comparing and contrasting compound inequalities containing *and* with inequalities containing *or*. The paragraph should contain examples of the different types of inequalities and their graphs.

Getting Ready for Lesson 6-5

PREREQUISITE SKILL Students will learn how to solve open sentences involving absolute value in Lesson 6-5. A good grasp of what absolute value means will help them understand how this concept applies to expressions in open sentences. Use Exercises 73–80 to determine your students' familiarity with finding absolute values.

Assessment Options

Practice Quiz 2 The quiz provides students with a brief review of the concepts and skills in Lessons 6-3 and 6-4. Lesson numbers are given to the right of the exercises or instruction lines so students can review concepts not yet mastered.

Answers

7.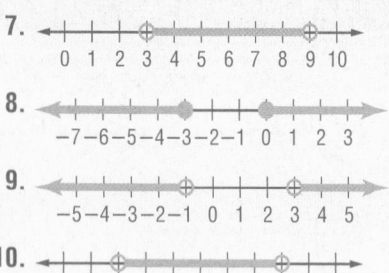

8.

9.

10.

Mixed Review

58. FUND-RAISING A university is running a drive to raise money. A corporation has promised to match 40% of whatever the university can raise from other sources. How much must the school raise from other sources to have a total of at least $800,000 after the corporation's donation? *(Lesson 6-3)* **at least $571,428.57**

Solve each inequality. Then check your solution. *(Lesson 6-2)*

59. $18d \geq 90$ **60.** $-7v < 91$ **61.** $\frac{t}{13} < 13$ **62.** $-\frac{3}{8}b > 9$

$\{d \mid d \geq 5\}$ $\{v \mid v > -13\}$ $\{t \mid t < 169\}$ $\{b \mid b < -24\}$

Solve. Assume that *y* varies directly as *x*. *(Lesson 5-2)*

63. If $y = -8$ when $x = -3$, find x when $y = 6$. **2.25**

64. If $y = 2.5$ when $x = 0.5$, find y when $x = 20$. **100**

Express the relation shown in each mapping as a set of ordered pairs. Then state the domain, range, and inverse. *(Lesson 4-3)*

65. $\{(6, 0), (-3, 5),$
$(2, -2), (-3, 3)\};$
$\{-3, 2, 6\}; \{-2, 0, 3, 5\};$
$\{(0, 6), (5, -3),$
$(-2, 2), (3, -3)\}$

66. $\{(5, 2), (-3, 1),$
$(2, 2), (1, 7)\};$
$\{-3, 1, 2, 5\}; \{1, 2, 7\};$
$\{(2, 5), (1, -3),$
$(2, 2), (7, 1)\}$

67. $\{(3, 4), (3, 2),$
$(2, 9), (5, 4) (5, 8),$
$(-7, 2)\}; \{-7, 2, 3, 5\};$
$\{2, 4, 8, 9\}; \{(4, 3),$
$(2, 3), (9, 2), (4, 5),$
$(8, 5), (2, -7)\}$

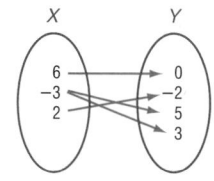

Find the odds of each outcome if a die is rolled. *(Lesson 2-6)*

68. a number greater than 2 **2:1**   **69.** not a 3 **5:1**

Find each product. *(Lesson 2-3)*

70. $-\frac{5}{6}\left(-\frac{2}{5}\right) \frac{1}{3}$ **71.** $-100(4.7)$ **−470**   **72.** $-\frac{7}{12}\left(\frac{6}{7}\right)\left(-\frac{3}{4}\right) \frac{3}{8}$

Getting Ready for the Next Lesson

PREREQUISITE SKILL Find each value. *(To review **absolute value**, see Lesson 2-1.)*

73. $|-7|$ **7**   **74.** $|10|$ **10**   **75.** $|-1|$ **1**   **76.** $|-3.5|$ **3.5**

77. $|12 - 6|$ **6**   **78.** $|5 - 9|$ **4**   **79.** $|20 - 21|$ **1**   **80.** $|3 - 18|$ **15**

Practice Quiz 2   *Lessons 6-3 and 6-4*

Solve each inequality. Then check your solution. *(Lesson 6-3)*

1. $5 - 4b > -23$ $\{b \mid b < 7\}$ **2.** $\frac{1}{2}n + 3 \geq -5$ $\{n \mid n \geq -16\}$

3. $3(t + 6) < 9$ $\{t \mid t < -3\}$ **4.** $9x + 2 > 20$ $\{x \mid x > 2\}$

5. $2m + 5 \leq 4m - 1$ $\{m \mid m \geq 3\}$ **6.** $a < \frac{2a - 15}{3}$ $\{a \mid a < -15\}$

Solve each compound inequality. Then graph the solution set. *(Lesson 6-4)* **7–10. See margin for graphs.**

7. $x - 2 < 7$ and $x + 2 > 5$ $\{x \mid 3 < x < 9\}$ **8.** $2b + 5 \leq -1$ or $b - 4 \geq -4$ $\{b \mid b \leq -3$ or $b \geq 0\}$

9. $4m - 5 > 7$ or $4m - 5 < -9$
$\{m \mid m > 3$ or $m < -1\}$ **10.** $a - 4 < 1$ and $a + 2 > 1$ $\{a \mid -1 < a < 5\}$

Solving Open Sentences Involving Absolute Value

What You'll Learn

- Solve absolute value equations.
- Solve absolute value inequalities.

How is absolute value used in election polls?

Voters in Hamilton will vote on a new tax levy in the next election. A poll conducted before the election found that 47% of the voters surveyed were for the tax levy, 45% were against the tax levy, and 8% were undecided. The poll has a 3-point margin of error.

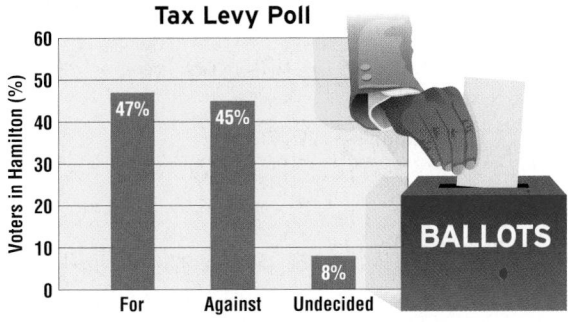

Tax Levy Poll

The margin of error means that the result may be 3 percentage points higher or lower. So, the number of people in favor of the tax levy may be as high as 50% or as low as 44%. This can be written as an inequality using absolute value.

$|x - 47| \leq 3$ The difference between the actual number and 47 is within 3 points.

Study Tip

Look Back
To review **absolute value**, see Lesson 2-1.

ABSOLUTE VALUE EQUATIONS   There are three types of open sentences that can involve absolute value.

$$|x| = n \qquad |x| < n \qquad |x| > n$$

Consider the case of $|x| = n$. $|x| = 5$ means the distance between 0 and x is 5 units.

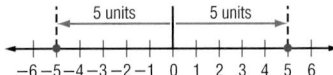

If $|x| = 5$, then $x = -5$ or $x = 5$. The solution set is $\{-5, 5\}$.

When solving equations that involve absolute value, there are two cases to consider.

Case 1   The value inside the absolute value symbols is positive.

Case 2   The value inside the absolute value symbols is negative.

Equations involving absolute value can be solved by graphing them on a number line or by writing them as a compound sentence and solving it.

---

1 Focus

5-Minute Check Transparency 6-5 Use as a quiz or a review of Lesson 6-4.

Mathematical Background notes are available for this lesson on p. 316D.

How is absolute value used in election polls?

Ask students:

- With a 3-point margin of error, the percent of people who are against the tax levy could be how high and how low? **48% and 42%**

- How would you represent the percent of people, x, who are against the tax levy, with an absolute value inequality? $|x - 45| \leq 3$

- Why is it necessary to represent the percent of people who may be for the tax levy with the inequality $|x - 47| \leq 3$? **The percent of people who are for the tax levy could be *less than* 47. Assume that 46% actually vote for the levy. Substituting 46 for *x* in the inequality would yield $46 - 47 \leq 3$. While this inequality is true, because $-1 \leq 3$, the margin of error cannot be negative. So adding the absolute value symbols makes the margin of error positive.**

Resource Manager

Workbook and Reproducible Masters

Chapter 6 Resource Masters
- Study Guide and Intervention, pp. 367–368
- Skills Practice, p. 369
- Practice, p. 370
- Reading to Learn Mathematics, p. 371
- Enrichment, p. 372
- Assessment, p. 394

Graphing Calculator and Spreadsheet Masters, p. 33
Parent and Student Study Guide Workbook, p. 50
Prerequisite Skills Workbook, pp. 79–80, 83–84

Transparencies
5-Minute Check Transparency 6-5
Answer Key Transparencies

Technology
Interactive Chalkboard

2 Teach

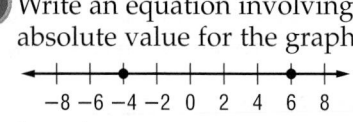

In-Class Examples Power Point®

1 Solve $|b + 6| = 5$.
$\{-1, -11\}$

2 Write an equation involving absolute value for the graph.

-8 -6 -4 -2 0 2 4 6 8

$|y - 1| = 5$

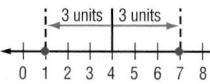

Example 1 Solve an Absolute Value Equation

Solve $|a - 4| = 3$.

Method 1 Graphing

$|a - 4| = 3$ means that the distance between a and 4 is 3 units. To find a on the number line, start at 4 and move 3 units in either direction.

3 units | 3 units
0 1 2 3 4 5 6 7 8

The distance from 4 to 1 is 3 units.
The distance from 4 to 7 is 3 units.

The solution set is {1, 7}.

Method 2 Compound Sentence

Write $|a - 4| = 3$ as $a - 4 = 3$ or $a - 4 = -3$.

Case 1

$a - 4 = 3$
$a - 4 + 4 = 3 + 4$ Add 4 to each side.
$a = 7$ Simplify.

Case 2

$a - 4 = -3$
$a - 4 + 4 = -3 + 4$ Add 4 to each side.
$a = 1$ Simplify.

The solution set is {1, 7}.

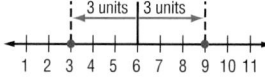

Example 2 Write an Absolute Value Equation

Write an equation involving absolute value for the graph.

1 2 3 4 5 6 7 8 9 10 11

Find the point that is the same distance from 3 as the distance from 9. The midpoint between 3 and 9 is 6.

3 units | 3 units
1 2 3 4 5 6 7 8 9 10 11

The distance from 6 to 3 is 3 units.
The distance from 6 to 9 is 3 units.

So, an equation is $|x - 6| = 3$.

CHECK Substitute 3 and 9 into $|x - 6| = 3$.

$|x - 6| = 3$ $|x - 6| = 3$
$|3 - 6| \stackrel{?}{=} 3$ $|9 - 6| \stackrel{?}{=} 3$
$|-3| \stackrel{?}{=} 3$ $|3| \stackrel{?}{=} 3$
$3 = 3$ ✓ $3 = 3$ ✓

ABSOLUTE VALUE INEQUALITIES Consider the inequality $|x| < n$. $|x| < 5$ means that the distance from 0 to x is less than 5 units.

5 units   5 units
-6 -5 -4 -3 -2 -1 0 1 2 3 4 5 6

Therefore, $x > -5$ and $x < 5$. The solution set is $\{x | -5 < x < 5\}$.

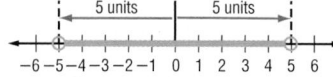

DAILY INTERVENTION Differentiated Instruction

Logical Some students may respond better to rewriting absolute value equations by applying the two situations (positive and negative) to the expression within the absolute value symbols. For example, $|x| = 4$ can be written as $x = 4$ or $-x = 4$, which yields $x = -4$. Example 1 can be written as $a - 4 = 3$ or $-(a - 4) = 3$. Then students can solve each equation.

The Algebra Activity explores an inequality of the form $|x| < n$.

Algebra Activity
Absolute Value

Collect the Data
- Work in pairs. One person is the timekeeper.
- Start timing. The other person tells the timekeeper to stop timing after he or she thinks that one minute has elapsed.
- Write down the time in seconds.
- Switch places. Make a table that includes the results of the entire class.

Analyze the Data 1. See students' work.
1. Determine the error by subtracting 60 seconds from each student's time.
2. What does a negative error represent? a positive error?
3. The *absolute error* is the absolute value of the error. Since absolute value cannot be negative, the absolute error is positive. If the absolute error is 6 seconds, write two possibilities for a student's estimated time of one minute. **54 s or 66 s**
4. What estimates would have an absolute error less than 6 seconds?
5. Graph the responses and highlight all values such that $|60 - x| < 6$. How many guesses were within 6 seconds? **See students' work.**

2. A negative error indicates that the time guessed was less than 1 min. A positive error indicates that the time guessed was more than 1 min.

4. estimate greater than 54 s and less than 66 s

When solving inequalities of the form $|x| < n$, find the intersection of these two cases.

Case 1 The value inside the absolute value symbols is less than the positive value of n.

Case 2 The value inside the absolute value symbols is greater than the negative value of n.

Example 3 Solve an Absolute Value Inequality ($<$)

Solve $|t + 5| < 9$. Then graph the solution set.

Write $|t + 5| < 9$ as $t + 5 < 9$ and $t + 5 > -9$.

Case 1
$$t + 5 < 9$$
$$t + 5 - 5 < 9 - 5 \qquad \text{Subtract 5 from each side.}$$
$$t < 4 \qquad \text{Simplify.}$$

Case 2
$$t + 5 > -9$$
$$t + 5 - 5 > -9 - 5 \qquad \text{Subtract 5 from each side.}$$
$$t > -14 \qquad \text{Simplify.}$$

The solution set is $\{t \mid -14 < t < 4\}$.

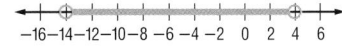

Consider the inequality $|x| > n$. $|x| > 5$ means that the distance from 0 to x is greater than 5 units.

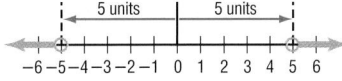

Therefore, $x < -5$ or $x > 5$. The solution set is $\{x \mid x < -5 \text{ or } x > 5\}$.

 www.algebra1.com/extra_examples

Lesson 6-5 Solving Open Sentences Involving Absolute Value **347**

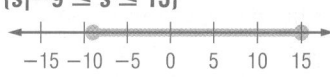

Algebra Activity

Materials: clock or watch that displays seconds
- Explain to students that the purpose of this activity is not to see which student can guess closest to the length of a minute, but to collect data for the rest of the activity.
- If students do not understand why the error cannot be negative, refer them to the example involving election poll results at the beginning of the lesson.

Lesson 6-5 Solving Open Sentences Involving Absolute Value **347**

In-Class Example

Teaching Tip Point out to students that when they graph absolute value inequalities, the circles that indicate the points on the graph will either be both open or both closed.

4 Solve $|3y - 3| > 9$. Then graph the solution set. $\{y \mid y < -2 \text{ or } y > 4\}$

-3 -2 -1 0 1 2 3 4 5

✓ **Concept Check**

Absolute Value Ask students what the values inside the absolute value symbols are compared to in absolute value inequalities. **The values inside the inequalities are compared to n and $-n$.**

3 Practice/Apply

Study Notebook

Have students—

• record the three rules to remember when solving equations and inequalities involving absolute values.

• include any other item(s) that they find helpful in mastering the skills in this lesson.

DAILY

INTERVENTION **FIND THE ERROR** Suggest that students determine whether Leslie and Holly are considering the correct two cases for each absolute value. Students should notice that Holly's second case, $x + 3 = 2$ is incorrect. It should also be noted that if Holly's second case equation was $-x - 3 = 2$, she would come up with the correct solution.

When solving inequalities of the form $|x| > n$, find the union of these two cases.

Case 1 The value inside the absolute value symbols is greater than the positive value of n.

Case 2 The value inside the absolute value symbols is less than the negative value of n.

Study Tip

Greater Than
When the absolute value is on the left and the inequality symbol is $>$ or $\geq$, the compound sentence uses *or*.

Example 4 *Solve an Absolute Value Inequality (>)*

Solve $|2x + 8| \geq 6$. Then graph the solution set.

Write $|2x + 8| \geq 6$ as $2x + 8 \geq 6$ or $2x + 8 \leq -6$.

Case 1

$$2x + 8 \geq 6$$
$$2x + 8 - 8 \geq 6 - 8 \qquad \text{Subtract 8 from each side.}$$
$$2x \geq -2 \qquad \text{Simplify.}$$
$$\frac{2x}{2} \geq \frac{-2}{2} \qquad \text{Divide each side by 2.}$$
$$x \geq -1 \qquad \text{Simplify.}$$

Case 2

$$2x + 8 \leq -6$$
$$2x + 8 - 8 \leq -6 - 8 \qquad \text{Subtract 8 from each side.}$$
$$2x \leq -14 \qquad \text{Simplify.}$$
$$\frac{2x}{2} \leq \frac{-14}{2} \qquad \text{Divide each side by 2.}$$
$$x \leq -7 \qquad \text{Simplify.}$$

The solution set is $\{x \mid x \leq -7 \text{ or } x \geq -1\}$.

-9 -8 -7 -6 -5 -4 -3 -2 -1 0 1

In general, there are three rules to remember when solving equations and inequalities involving absolute value.

Concept Summary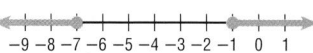

If $|x| = n$, then $x = -n$ or $x = n$.

If $|x| < n$, then $x < n$ and $x > -n$.

If $|x| > n$, then $x > n$ or $x < -n$.

These properties are also true when $>$ or $<$ is replaced with $\geq$ or $\leq$.

Check for Understanding

Concept Check **1.** **Compare and contrast** the solution of $|x - 2| > 6$ and the solution of $|x - 2| < 6$. **1–2. See margin.**

2. **OPEN ENDED** Write an absolute value inequality and graph its solution set.

3. **FIND THE ERROR** Leslie and Holly are solving $|x + 3| = 2$.

Leslie	Holly
$x + 3 = 2$ or $x + 3 = -2$	$x + 3 = 2$ or $x - 3 = 2$
$x + 3 - 3 = 2 - 3 \qquad x + 3 - 3 = -2 - 3$	$x + 3 - 3 = 2 - 3 \qquad x - 3 + 3 = 2 + 3$
$x = -1 \qquad x = -5$	$x = -1 \qquad x = 5$

Who is correct? Explain your reasoning. **Leslie; see margin for explanation.**

348 Chapter 6 Solving Linear Inequalities

Answers

1. The solution of $|x - 2| > 6$ includes all values that are less than -4 or greater than 8. The solution of $|x - 2| < 6$ includes all values that are greater than -4 and less than 8.

2. Sample answer: $|x| > 2$

   -5 -4 -3 -2 -1 0 1 2 3 4 5

3. You need to consider the case when the value inside the absolute value symbols is positive and the case when the value inside the absolute value symbols is negative. So $x + 3 = 2$ or $x + 3 = -2$.

GUIDED PRACTICE KEY

Exercises	Examples
4, 6, 13	3
5	4
7–10	1, 3, 4
11, 12	2

4. Which graph represents the solution of $|k| \leq 3$? **a**

a. ![number line from -5 to 5]
-5 -4 -3 -2 -1 0 1 2 3 4 5

b. ![number line from -5 to 5]
-5 -4 -3 -2 -1 0 1 2 3 4 5

c. ![number line from -5 to 5]
-5 -4 -3 -2 -1 0 1 2 3 4 5

d. ![number line from -5 to 5]
-5 -4 -3 -2 -1 0 1 2 3 4 5

5. Which graph represents the solution of $|x - 4| > 2$? **c**

a. ![number line from -3 to 7]
-3 -2 -1 0 1 2 3 4 5 6 7

b. ![number line from -3 to 7]
-3 -2 -1 0 1 2 3 4 5 6 7

c. ![number line from -3 to 7]
-3 -2 -1 0 1 2 3 4 5 6 7

d. ![number line from -3 to 7]
-3 -2 -1 0 1 2 3 4 5 6 7

6. Express the statement in terms of an inequality involving absolute value. Do not solve. $|g - 832| \leq 46$
A jar contains 832 gumballs. Amanda's guess was within 46 pieces.

Solve each open sentence. Then graph the solution set.

7–10. See margin for graphs.

7. $|r + 3| = 10$ {−13, 7}

8. $|c - 2| < 6$ {$c | -4 < c < 8$}

9. $|10 - w| > 15$ {$w | w < -5$ or $w > 25$}

10. $|2g + 5| \geq 7$ {$g | g \leq -6$ or $g \geq 1$}

For each graph, write an open sentence involving absolute value.

11. $|x - 1| = 3$

12. $|x - 8| > 4$

11. ![number line from -4 to 6]
-4 -3 -2 -1 0 1 2 3 4 5 6

12. ![number line from 3 to 13]
3 4 5 6 7 8 9 10 11 12 13

Application

13. {$d | 1.499 \leq d \leq 1.501$}

13. MANUFACTURING A manufacturer produces bolts which must have a diameter within 0.001 centimeter of 1.5 centimeters. What are the acceptable measurements for the diameter of the bolts?

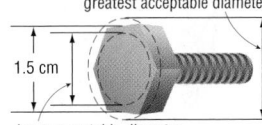
greatest acceptable diameter
1.5 cm
least acceptable diameter

★ indicates increased difficulty

Practice and Apply

Homework Help

For Exercises	See Examples
14–19, 24–39, 46–51	1, 3, 4
20–23	3
40–45	2

Extra Practice
See page 834.

Match each open sentence with the graph of its solution set.

14. $|x + 5| \leq 3$ **c**

15. $|x - 4| > 4$ **f**

16. $|2x - 8| = 6$ **a**

17. $|x + 3| \geq -1$ **b**

18. $|x| < 2$ **e**

19. $|8 - x| = 2$ **d**

a. ![number line from -1 to 9]
-1 0 1 2 3 4 5 6 7 8 9

b. ![number line from -5 to 5]
-5 -4 -3 -2 -1 0 1 2 3 4 5

c. ![number line from -9 to 1]
-9 -8 -7 -6 -5 -4 -3 -2 -1 0 1

d. ![number line from 2 to 12]
2 3 4 5 6 7 8 9 10 11 12

e. ![number line from -5 to 5]
-5 -4 -3 -2 -1 0 1 2 3 4 5

f. ![number line from -1 to 9]
-1 0 1 2 3 4 5 6 7 8 9

Express each statement using an inequality involving absolute value. Do *not* solve.

20. $|p - 7.3| \leq 0.002$
20. The pH of a buffered eye solution must be within 0.002 of a pH of 7.3.

21. $|t - 38| \leq 1.5$
21. The temperature inside a refrigerator should be within 1.5 degrees of 38°F.

22. $|s - 98| \leq 6$
22. Ramona's bowling score was within 6 points of her average score of 98.

23. The cruise control of a car set at 55 miles per hour should keep the speed within 3 miles per hour of 55. $|s - 55| \leq 3$

www.algebra1.com/self_check_quiz

Answers

7. ![number line answer]
-14 -12 -10 -8 -6 -4 -2 0 2 4 6 8

8. ![number line answer]
-10 -8 -6 -4 -2 0 2 4 6 8 10

9. ![number line answer]
-15 -10 -5 0 5 10 15 20 25 30 35

10. ![number line answer]
-8 -7 -6 -5 -4 -3 -2 -1 0 1 2

Teacher to Teacher

Laurie Newton   Crossler M.S., Salem, OR

"To help students understand what their solution set to an absolute inequality represents, I have students check their work by testing numbers in all of the regions of the number line prescribed by the inequality. In Example 3, I have them test a number less than −2, −2 itself, a number greater than −2 and less than 7, 7 itself, and a number greater than 7."

24–39. See margin for graphs.

40. $|x| = 5$
41. $|x - 3| = 5$
42. $|x| \leq 3$
43. $|x + 3| < 4$
44. $|x - 1| > 2$
45. $|x + 10| \geq 2$

50. 49–55%
51. $\{p \mid 28 \leq p \leq 32\}$

Solve each open sentence. Then graph the solution set. 36. $\left\{d \mid -1 \leq d \leq 8\frac{1}{3}\right\}$

24. $|x - 5| = 8$ $\{-3, 13\}$
25. $|b + 9| = 2$ $\{-11, -7\}$
26. $|2p - 3| = 17$ $\{-7, 10\}$
27. $|5c - 8| = 12$ $\{-0.8, 4\}$
28. $|z - 2| \leq 5$ $\{z \mid -3 \leq z \leq 7\}$
29. $|t + 8| < 2$ $\{t \mid -10 < t < -6\}$
30. $|v + 3| > 1$ $\{v \mid v < -4 \text{ or } v > -2\}$
31. $|w - 6| \geq 3$ $\{w \mid w \leq 3 \text{ or } w \geq 9\}$
32. $|3s + 2| > -7$ $\{s \mid s \text{ is a real number.}\}$
33. $|3k + 4| \geq 8$ $\left\{k \mid k \leq -4 \text{ or } k \geq 1\frac{1}{3}\right\}$
34. $|2n + 1| < 9$ $\{n \mid -5 < n < 4\}$
35. $|6r + 8| < -4$ $\varnothing$
★ 36. $|6 - (3d - 5)| \leq 14$
37. $|8 - (w - 1)| \leq 9$ $\{w \mid 0 \leq w \leq 18\}$
★ 38. $\left|\frac{5h + 2}{6}\right| = 7$ $\left\{-8\frac{4}{5}, 8\right\}$
39. $\left|\frac{2 - 3x}{5}\right| \geq 2$ $\left\{x \mid x \leq -2\frac{2}{3} \text{ or } x \geq 4\right\}$

For each graph, write an open sentence involving absolute value.

40.
41.
42.
43.
44.
45.

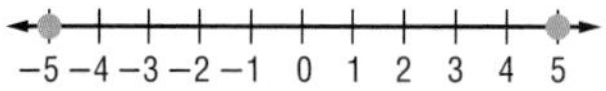

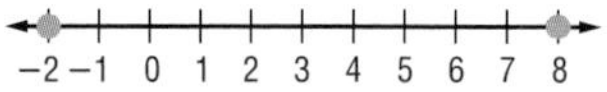

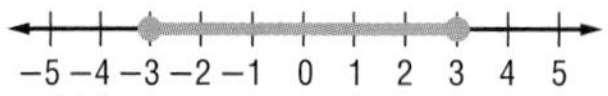

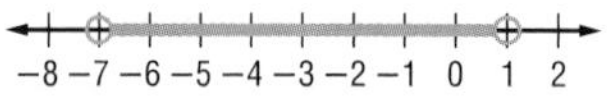

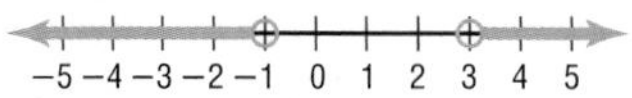

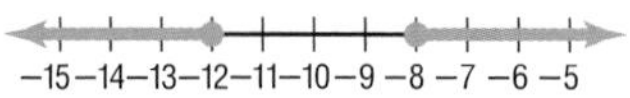

HEALTH For Exercises 46 and 47, use the following information.
The *average* length of a human pregnancy is 280 days. However, a healthy, full-term pregnancy can be 14 days longer or shorter. 46. $|d - 280| \leq 14$

46. Write an absolute value inequality for the length of a full-term pregnancy.

47. Solve the inequality for the length of a full-term pregnancy. $\{d \mid 266 \leq d \leq 294\}$

48. **FIRE SAFETY** The pressure of a typical fire extinguisher should be within 25 pounds per square inch (psi) of 195 psi. Write the range of pressures for safe fire extinguishers. $\{p \mid 170 < p < 220\}$

49. **HEATING** A thermostat with a 2-degree differential will keep the temperature within 2 degrees Fahrenheit of the temperature set point. Suppose your home has a thermostat with a 3-degree differential. If you set the thermostat at $68°F$, what is the range of temperatures in the house? $\{t \mid 65 \leq t \leq 71\}$

50. **ENERGY** Use the margin of error indicated in the graph at the right to find the range of the percent of people who say protection of the environment should have priority over developing energy supplies.

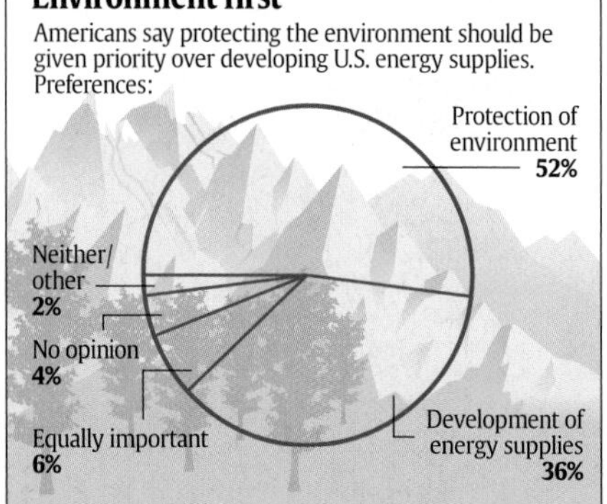

51. **TIRE PRESSURE** Tire pressure is measured in pounds per square inch (psi). Tires should be kept within 2 psi of the manufacturer's recommended tire pressure. If the recommended inflation pressure for a tire is 30 psi, what is the range of acceptable pressures?

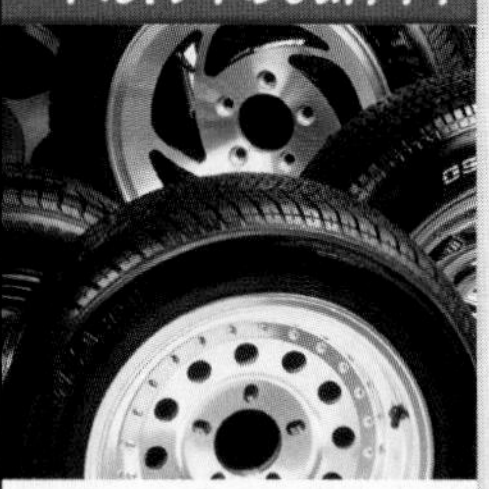

52. **CRITICAL THINKING** State whether each open sentence is *always*, *sometimes*, or *never* true.

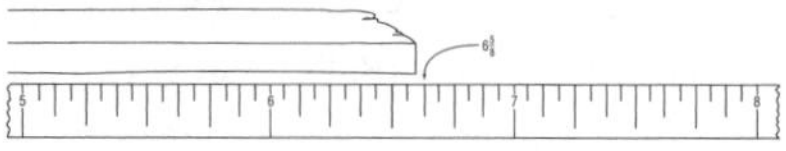

a. $|x + 3| < -5$ never
b. $|x - 6| > -1$ always
c. $|x + 2| = 0$ sometimes

53. $\{a \mid 2.5 \le a \le 3.5\}$

53. PHYSICAL SCIENCE Li-Cheng must add 3.0 milliliters of sodium chloride to a solution. The sodium chloride must be within 0.5 milliliter of the required amount. How much sodium chloride can she add and obtain the correct results?

★ **54. ENTERTAINMENT** Luis Gomez is a contestant on a television game show. He must guess within $1500 of the actual price of a car without going over to win the car. The actual price of the car is $18,000. What is the range of guesses in which Luis can win the vehicle? $\{p \mid 16{,}500 \le p \le 18{,}000\}$

55. CRITICAL THINKING The symbol $\pm$ means *plus* or *minus*.

  a. If $x = 3 \pm 1.2$, what are the values of x? **1.8, 4.2**

  b. Write $x = 3 \pm 1.2$ as an expression involving absolute value. $|x - 3| = 1.2$

56. **WRITING IN MATH** Answer the question that was posed at the beginning of the lesson. **See margin.**

  How is absolute value used in election polls?

  Include the following in your answer:

  • an explanation of how to solve the inequality describing the percent of people who are against the tax levy, and

  • a prediction of whether you think the tax levy will pass and why.

57. Choose the replacement set that makes $|x + 5| = 2$ true. **B**

  Ⓐ $\{-3, 3\}$ Ⓑ $\{-3, -7\}$ Ⓒ $\{2, -2\}$ Ⓓ $\{3, -7\}$

58. What can you conclude about x if $-6 < |x| < 6$? **C**

  Ⓐ $-x \ge 0$ Ⓑ $x \le 0$ Ⓒ $-x < 6$ Ⓓ $-x > 6$

Maintain Your Skills

Mixed Review

59. FITNESS To achieve the maximum benefits from aerobic activity, your heart rate should be in your target zone. Your target zone is the range between 60% and 80% of your maximum heart rate. If Rafael's maximum heart rate is 190 beats per minute, what is his target zone? *(Lesson 6-4)*
between 114 and 152 beats per min

Solve each inequality. Then check your solution. *(Lesson 6-3)*

61. $\left\{x \mid x \le -1\frac{1}{3}\right\}$

60. $2m + 7 > 17$ **61.** $-2 - 3x \ge 2$ **62.** $\frac{2}{3}w - 3 \le 7$ $\{w \mid w \le 15\}$
$\{m \mid m > 5\}$

Find the slope and y-intercept of each equation. *(Lesson 5-4)*

63. $2x + y = 4$ **-2; 4**   **64.** $2y - 3x = 4$ **$\frac{3}{2}$; 2**   **65.** $\frac{1}{2}x + \frac{3}{4}y = 0$ **$-\frac{2}{3}$; 0**

Solve each equation or formula for the variable specified. *(Lesson 3-8)*

67. $x = \dfrac{3z + 2y}{e}$

66. $I = prt$, for r $r = \dfrac{I}{pt}$ **67.** $ex - 2y = 3z$, for x **68.** $\dfrac{a + 5}{3} = 7x$, for x $x = \dfrac{a + 5}{21}$

Find each sum or difference. *(Lesson 2-2)*

69. $-13 + 8$ **-5**   **70.** $-13.2 - 6.1$ **-19.3**   **71.** $-4.7 - (-8.9)$ **4.2**

Name the property illustrated by each statement. *(Lesson 1-6)*

72. $10x + 10y = 10(x + y)$ **73.** $(2 + 3)a + 7 = 5a + 7$
  Distributive Property   **Substitution Property**

Getting Ready for the Next Lesson

PREREQUISITE SKILL Graph each equation.

*(To review **graphing linear equations**, see Lesson 4-5.)* **74–79. See pp. 365A–365D.**

74. $y = 3x + 4$ **75.** $y = -2$ **76.** $x + y = 3$

77. $y - 2x = -1$ **78.** $2y - x = -6$ **79.** $2(x + y) = 10$

---

1 Focus

5-Minute Check Transparency 6-6 Use as a quiz or a review of Lesson 6-5.

Mathematical Background notes are available for this lesson on p. 316D.

Building on Prior Knowledge

In Chapter 4, students learned how to graph equations on the coordinate plane. In this lesson, they will graph a line and then decide which side of the line represents an inequality.

How are inequalities used in budgets?

Ask students:

- What does the 3 in the quantity $3x$ represent? **her average cost of a cafeteria lunch, which is $3**

- What does the 4 in the quantity $4y$ represent? **her average cost of restaurant lunches, which is $4**

- Why can't this problem be represented with an inequality containing only one variable? **Because the amount Hannah spends on cafeteria lunches and the amount she spends on restaurant lunches are not the same.**

What You'll Learn

- Graph inequalities on the coordinate plane.
- Solve real-world problems involving linear inequalities.

Vocabulary
- half-plane
- boundary

How are inequalities used in budgets?

Hannah budgets $30 a month for lunch. On most days, she brings her lunch. She can also buy lunch at the cafeteria or at a fast-food restaurant. She spends an average of $3 for lunch at the cafeteria and an average of $4 for lunch at a restaurant. How many times a month can Hannah buy her lunch and remain within her budget?

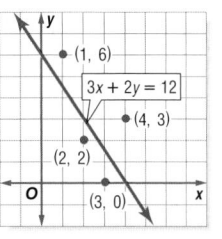

	My Monthly Budget	
○	Lunch (school days)	$30
	Entertainment	$55
	Clothes	$50
○	Fuel	$60

Let x represent the number of days she buys lunch at the cafeteria, and let y represent the number of days she buys lunch at a restaurant. Then the following inequality can be used to represent the situation.

The cost of eating in the cafeteria	plus	the cost of eating in a restaurant	is less than or equal to	$30.
$3x$	$+$	$4y$	$\leq$	30

There are many solutions of this inequality.

GRAPH LINEAR INEQUALITIES The solution set of an inequality in two variables is the set of all ordered pairs that satisfy the inequality. Like a linear equation in two variables, the solution set is graphed on a coordinate plane.

Example 1 Ordered Pairs that Satisfy an Inequality

From the set $\{(1, 6), (3, 0), (2, 2), (4, 3)\}$, which ordered pairs are part of the solution set for $3x + 2y < 12$?

Use a table to substitute the x and y values of each ordered pair into the inequality.

x	y	$3x + 2y < 12$	True or False
1	6	$3(1) + 2(6) < 12$ $15 < 12$	false
3	0	$3(3) + 2(0) < 12$ $9 < 12$	true
2	2	$3(2) + 2(2) < 12$ $10 < 12$	true
4	3	$3(4) + 2(3) < 12$ $18 < 12$	false

The ordered pairs $\{(3, 0), (2, 2)\}$ are part of the solution set of $3x + 2y < 12$. In the graph, notice the location of the two ordered pairs that are solutions for $3x + 2y < 12$ in relation to the line.

Resource Manager

Workbook and Reproducible Masters

Chapter 6 Resource Masters
- Study Guide and Intervention, pp. 373–374
- Skills Practice, p. 375
- Practice, p. 376
- Reading to Learn Mathematics, p. 377
- Enrichment, p. 378
- Assessment, p. 394

Graphing Calculator and Spreadsheet Masters, p. 34
Parent and Student Study Guide Workbook, p. 51

Transparencies
5-Minute Check Transparency 6-6
Answer Key Transparencies

Technology
Interactive Chalkboard

The solution set for an inequality in two variables contains many ordered pairs when the domain and range are the set of real numbers. The graphs of all of these ordered pairs fill a region on the coordinate plane called a **half-plane**. An equation defines the **boundary** or edge for each half-plane.

Key Concept — Half-Planes and Boundaries

- **Words** Any line in the plane divides the plane into two regions called half-planes. The line is called the boundary of each of the two half-planes.

- **Model**

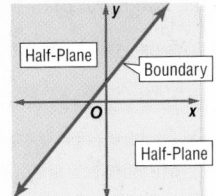

GRAPH LINEAR INEQUALITIES

In-Class Examples Power Point®

1 From the set {(3, 3), (0, 2), (2, 4), (1, 0)}, which ordered pairs are part of the solution set for $4x + 2y > 8$?
{(3, 3), (2, 4)}

Teaching Tip Students may need a quick refresher on slope-intercept form before they graph inequalities. Remind students that slope-intercept form is $y = mx + b$.

2 Graph $2y - 4x > 6$.

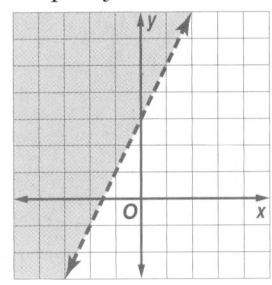

Consider the graph of $y > 4$. First determine the boundary by graphing $y = 4$, the equation you obtain by replacing the inequality sign with an equals sign. Since the inequality involves y-values greater than 4, but not equal to 4, the line should be dashed. The boundary divides the coordinate plane into two half-planes.

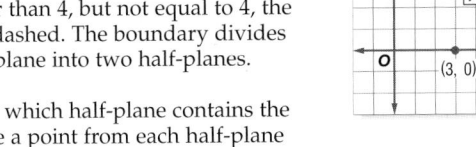

To determine which half-plane contains the solution, choose a point from each half-plane and test it in the inequality.

Try (3, 0).

$y > 4$ $y = 0$

$0 > 4$ false

Try (5, 6).

$y > 4$ $y = 6$

$6 > 4$ true

The half-plane that contains (5, 6) contains the solution. Shade that half-plane.

Example 2 Graph an Inequality

Graph $y - 2x \le -4$.

Step 1 Solve for y in terms of x.

$$y - 2x \le -4 \qquad \text{Original inequality}$$

$$y - 2x + 2x \le -4 + 2x \qquad \text{Add 2x to each side.}$$

$$y \le 2x - 4 \qquad \text{Simplify.}$$

Step 2 Graph $y = 2x - 4$. Since $y \le 2x - 4$ means $y < 2x - 4$ or $y = 2x - 4$, the boundary is included in the solution set. The boundary should be drawn as a solid line.

(continued on the next page)

 www.algebra1.com/extra_examples

Lesson 6-6 Graphing Inequalities in Two Variables **353**

DAILY INTERVENTION

Differentiated Instruction

Intrapersonal Before students work Example 3, suggest that they first explore the problem and try to write a mathematically correct answer. Students will likely write an inequality in one variable or they may create a table of possible answers. Then work through Example 3 as a class, so students can appreciate how the solution is described by the inequality graph. Afterward, give students time to compare their original reasoning to the method shown in Example 3.

In-Class Example

Power Point®

3 Journalism Lee Cooper writes and edits short articles for a local newspaper. It generally takes her an hour to write an article and about a half-hour to edit an article. If Lee works up to 8 hours a day, how many articles can she write and edit in one day?

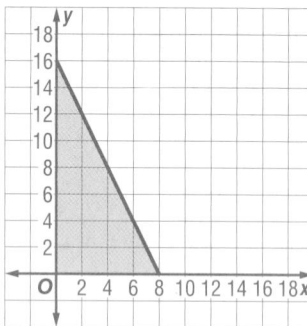

One solution is (2, 3), meaning she could write two articles and edit three articles.

Answers (p. 355)

1. The graph of $y = x + 2$ is a line. The graph of $y < x + 2$ does not include the boundary $y = x + 2$, and it includes all ordered pairs in the half-plane that contains the origin.

2. Sample answer: $x > y$

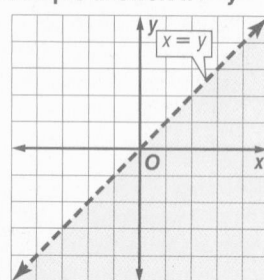

3. If the test point results in a true statement, shade the half-plane that contains the point. If the test point results in a false statement, shade the other half-plane.

Study Tip

Origin as the Test Point
Use the origin as a standard test point because the values are easy to substitute into the inequality.

More About. . .

Advertising

A typical one-hour program on television contains 40 minutes of the program and 20 minutes of commercials. During peak periods, a 30-second commercial can cost an average of $2.3 million.

Source: www.superbowl-ads.com

Step 3 Select a point in one of the half-planes and test it. Let's use (0, 0).

$$y - 2x \le -4 \qquad \text{Original inequality}$$
$$0 \le 2(0) - 4 \quad x = 0, y = 0$$
$$0 \le -4 \qquad \text{false}$$

Since the statement is false, the half-plane containing the origin is not part of the solution. Shade the other half-plane.

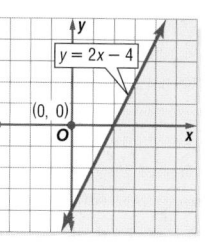

CHECK Test a point in the other half plane, for example, (3, −3).

$$y - 2x \le -4 \qquad \text{Original inequality}$$
$$-3 \le 2(3) - 4 \quad x = 3, y = -3$$
$$-3 \le 2 \quad \checkmark$$

Since the statement is true, the half-plane containing (3, −3) should be shaded. The graph of the solution is correct.

SOLVE REAL-WORLD PROBLEMS When solving real-world inequalities, the domain and range of the inequality are often restricted to nonnegative numbers or whole numbers.

Example 3 Write and Solve an Inequality

ADVERTISING Rosa Padilla sells radio advertising in 30-second and 60-second time slots. During every hour, there are up to 15 minutes available for commercials. How many commercial slots can she sell for one hour of broadcasting?

Step 1 Let x equal the number of 30-second commercials. Let y equal the number of 60-second or 1-minute commercials. Write an open sentence representing this situation.

$\frac{1}{2}$ min	times	the number of 30-s commercials	plus	the number of 1-min commercials	is up to	15 min.
$\frac{1}{2}$	$\cdot$	x	$+$	y	$\le$	15

Step 2 Solve for y in terms of x.

$$\frac{1}{2}x + y \le 15 \qquad \text{Original inequality}$$
$$\frac{1}{2}x + y - \frac{1}{2}x \le 15 - \frac{1}{2}x \quad \text{Subtract } \frac{1}{2}x \text{ from each side.}$$
$$y \le 15 - \frac{1}{2}x \quad \text{Simplify.}$$

Step 3 Since the open sentence includes the equation, graph $y = 15 - \frac{1}{2}x$ as a solid line. Test a point in one of the half-planes, for example (0, 0). Shade the half-plane containing (0, 0) since $0 \le 15 - \frac{1}{2}(0)$ is true.

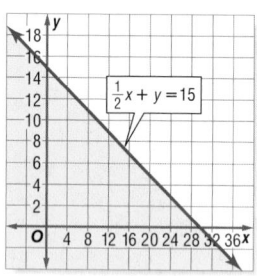

7.
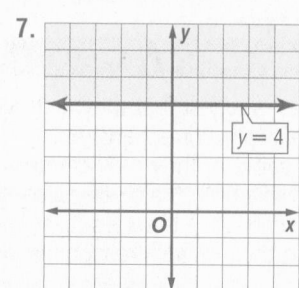

8.
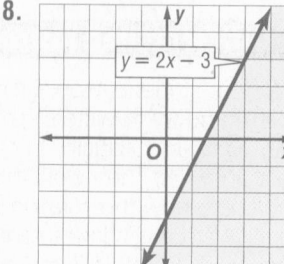

9.
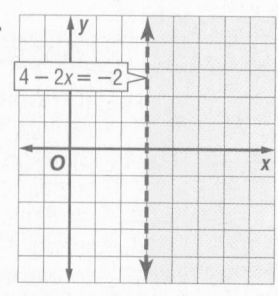

Step 4 Examine the solution.

- Rosa cannot sell a negative number of commercials. Therefore, the domain and range contain only nonnegative numbers.
- She also cannot sell half of a commercial. Thus, only points in the shaded half-plane whose x- and y-coordinates are whole numbers are possible solutions.

One solution is (12, 8). This represents twelve 30-second commercials and eight 60-second commercials in a one hour period.

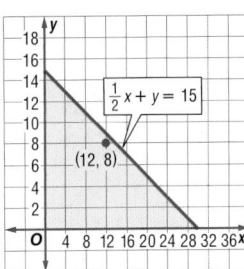

$$\tfrac{1}{2}x + y = 15$$

(12, 8)

Check for Understanding

Concept Check

1–3. See margin.

1. **Compare and contrast** the graph of $y = x + 2$ and the graph of $y < x + 2$.

2. **OPEN ENDED** Write an inequality in two variables and graph it.

3. **Explain** why it is usually only necessary to test one point when graphing an inequality.

Guided Practice

GUIDED PRACTICE KEY	
Exercises	**Examples**
4, 5	1
6–10	2
11	3

Determine which ordered pairs are part of the solution set for each inequality.

4. $y \leq x + 1$, {(−1, 0), (3, 2), (2, 5), (−2, 1)} **{(−1, 0), (3, 2)}**

5. $y > 2x$, {(2, 6), (0, −1), (3, 5), (−1, −2)} **{(2, 6)}**

6. Which graph represents $y - 2x \geq 2$? **b**

a. 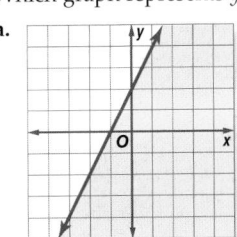   b. 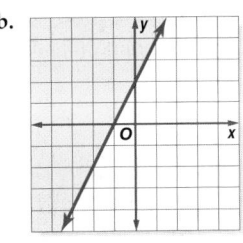   c.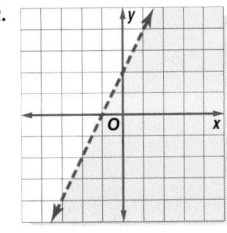

Graph each inequality. **7–10. See margin.**

7. $y \geq 4$

8. $y \leq 2x - 3$

9. $4 - 2x < -2$

10. $1 - y > x$

Application

11. **ENTERTAINMENT** Coach Riley wants to take her softball team out for pizza and soft drinks after the last game of the season. She doesn't want to spend more than $60. Write an inequality that represents this situation and graph the solution set.
$12x + 3y \leq 60$; See margin for graph.

Welcome to
Angelo's Pizza!

Large Pizza $12

Pitcher of
soft drink $3

Study Notebook

Have students—

- *complete the definitions/examples for the remaining terms on their Vocabulary Builder worksheets for Chapter 6.*
- *include any other item(s) that they find helpful in mastering the skills in this lesson.*

About the Exercises...

Organization by Objective
- **Graph Linear Inequalities:** 12–37
- **Solve Real-World Problems:** 38–44

Odd/Even Assignments
Exercises 12–37 are structured so that students practice the same concepts whether they are assigned odd or even problems.

Assignment Guide
Basic: 13–17 odd, 21–35 odd, 38–39, 45–63
Average: 13–37 odd, 38–41, 45–63
Advanced: 12–36 even, 40–63

10.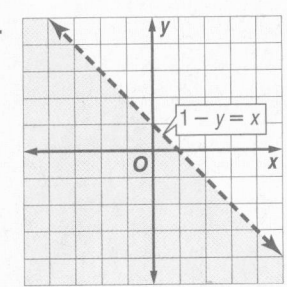

$1 - y = x$

11.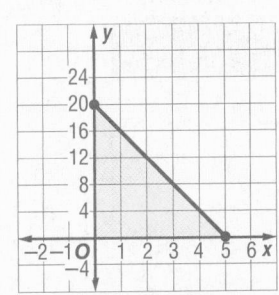

Study Guide and Intervention, p. 373 (shown) and p. 374

Graph Linear Inequalities The solution set of an inequality that involves two variables is graphed by graphing a related linear equation that forms a boundary of a **half-plane**. The graph of the ordered pairs that make up the solution set of the inequality fill a region of the coordinate plane on one side of the half-plane.

Example Graph $y \le -3x - 2$.

Graph $y = -3x - 2$.
Since $y \le -3x - 2$ is the same as $y < -3x - 2$ and $y = -3x - 2$, the boundary is included in the solution set and the graph should be drawn as a solid line.
Select a point in each half plane and test it. Choose $(0, 0)$ and $(-2, -2)$.

$y \le -3x - 2$	$y \le -3x - 2$
$0 \le -3(0) - 2$	$-2 \le -3(-2) - 2$
$0 \le -2$ is false.	$-2 \le 6 - 2$
	$-2 \le 4$ is true.

The half-plane that contains $(-2, -2)$ contains the solution. Shade that half-plane.

Exercises

Graph each inequality.

1. $y < 4$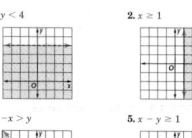

2. $x \ge 1$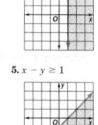

3. $3x \le y$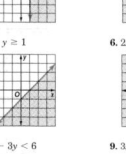

4. $-x > y$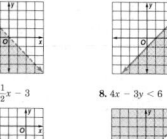

5. $x - y \ge 1$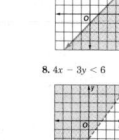

6. $2x - 3y \le 6$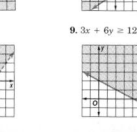

7. $y < -\frac{1}{2}x - 3$

8. $4x - 3y < 6$

9. $3x + 6y \ge 12$

Skills Practice, p. 375 and Practice, p. 376 (shown)

Determine which ordered pairs are part of the solution set for each inequality.

1. $3x + y \ge 6$, $\{(4, 3), (-2, 4), (-5, -3), (3, -3)\}$ $\{(4, 3), (3, -3)\}$

2. $y \ge x + 3$, $\{(6, 3), (-3, 2), (3, -2), (4, 3)\}$ $\{(-3, 2)\}$

3. $3x - 2y < 5$, $\{(4, -4), (3, 5), (5, 2), (-3, 4)\}$ $\{(3, 5), (-3, 4)\}$

Match each inequality with its graph.

4. $5y - 2x \le 10$ **d**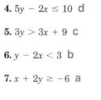

5. $3y > 3x + 9$ **c**

6. $y - 2x < 3$ **b**

7. $x + 2y \ge -6$ **a**

Graph each inequality.

8. $2y - x < -4$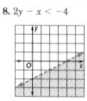

9. $2x - 2y \ge 8$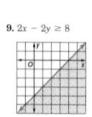

10. $3y > 2x - 3$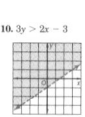

11. MOVING A moving van has an interior height of 7 feet (84 inches). You have boxes in 12 inch and 15 inch heights, and want to stack them as high as possible to fit. Write an inequality that represents this situation. $12x + 15y \le 84$

BUDGETING For Exercises 12 and 13, use the following information.
Satchi found a used bookstore that sells pre-owned videos and CDs. Videos cost $9 each, and CDs cost $7 each. Satchi can spend no more than $35.

12. Write an inequality that represents this situation. $9x + 7y \le 35$

13. Does Satchi have enough money to buy 2 videos and 3 CDs?
No, the purchases will be $39, which is greater than $35.

Reading to Learn Mathematics, p. 377 ELL

Pre-Activity How are inequalities used in budgets?
Read the introduction to Lesson 6-6 at the top of page 352 in your textbook.
What do 3 and 4 represent in the terms $3x$ and $4y$?
the average amount spent on a cafeteria lunch and a fast-food lunch

Reading the Lesson

1. Complete the chart to show which type of line is needed for each symbol.

Symbol	Type of Line	Boundary Part of Solution?
$<$	dashed	no
$>$	dashed	no
$\le$	solid	yes
$\ge$	solid	yes

2. If a test point results in a false statement, what do you know about the graph?
The half-plane containing the test point is not part of the solution and is not shaded.

3. If a test point results in a true statement, what do you know about the graph?
The half-plane containing the test point is part of the solution and is shaded.

4. When can the origin *not* be used as a test point?
The origin cannot be used as a test point when it is on the boundary.

Helping You Remember

5. The two-variable inequalities in this lesson can be solved for y in terms of x to get a sentence in slope-intercept form. It looks much like a slope-intercept equation, but it has an inequality symbol instead of an equals sign. For example, $4x + 2y \le 5$ can be written as $y \le -2x + \frac{5}{2}$. Explain how to graph an inequality once it is written in slope-intercept form. Use the idea that *greater* can mean *above* and *less* can mean *below*.
Draw the boundary line. If the inequality symbol is $>$ or $<$, make the boundary dashed. If the symbol is $\ge$ or $\le$, make the boundary line solid. If the symbol in the slope-intercept inequality is $<$ or $\le$, shade below the boundary to indicate smaller values of y. If the symbol is $>$ or $\ge$, shade above the boundary to indicate greater values of y.

Practice and Apply

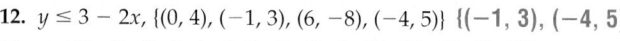

Homework Help

For Exercises	See Examples
12–19	1
20–37	2
38–44	3

Extra Practice
See page 835.

Determine which ordered pairs are part of the solution set for each inequality.

12. $y \le 3 - 2x$, $\{(0, 4), (-1, 3), (6, -8), (-4, 5)\}$ $\{(-1, 3), (-4, 5)\}$

13. $y < 3x$, $\{(-3, 1), (-3, 2), (1, 1), (1, 2)\}$ $\{(1, 1), (1, 2)\}$

14. $x + y < 11$, $\{(5, 7), (-13, 10), (4, 4), (-6, -2)\}$ $\{(-13, 10), (4, 4), (-6, -2)\}$

15. $2x - 3y > 6$, $\{(3, 2), (-2, -4), (6, 2), (5, 1)\}$ $\{(-2, -4), (5, 1)\}$

16. $4y - 8 \ge 0$, $\{(5, -1), (0, 2), (2, 5), (-2, 0)\}$ $\{(0, 2), (2, 5)\}$

17. $3x + 4y < 7$, $\{(1, 1), (2, -1), (-1, 1), (-2, 4)\}$ $\{(2, -1), (-1, 1)\}$

★ **18.** $|x - 3| \ge y$, $\{(6, 4), (-1, 8), (-3, 2), (5, 7)\}$ $\{(-3, 2)\}$

★ **19.** $|y + 2| < x$, $\{(2, -4), (-1, -5), (6, -7), (0, 0)\}$ $\{(6, -7)\}$

Match each inequality with its graph.

20. $2y + x \le 6$ **c**

21. $\frac{1}{2}x - y > 4$ **a**

22. $y > 3 + \frac{1}{2}x$ **d**

23. $4y + 2x \ge 16$ **b**

a.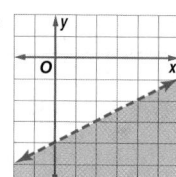

b.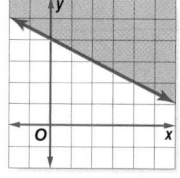

c.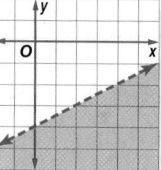

d.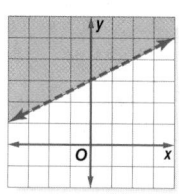

24. Is the point $A(2, 3)$ on, above, or below the graph of $-2x + 3y = 5$? **on**

25. Is the point $B(0, 1)$ on, above, or below the graph of $4x - 3y = 4$? **above**

Graph each inequality. 26–37. See pp. 365A–365D.

26. $y < -3$

27. $x \ge 2$

28. $5x + 10y > 0$

29. $y < x$

30. $2y - x \le 6$

31. $6x + 3y > 9$

32. $3y - 4x \ge 12$

33. $y \le -2x - 4$

34. $8x - 6y < 10$

35. $3x - 1 \ge y$

★ **36.** $3(x + 2y) > -18$

37. $\frac{1}{2}(2x + y) < 2$

POSTAGE For Exercises 38 and 39, use the following information.
The U.S. Postal Service limits the size of packages to those in which the length of the longest side plus the distance around the thickest part is less than or equal to 108 inches.

38. Write an inequality that represents this situation. $\ell + d \le 108$

39. Are there any restrictions on the domain or range?
The solution set is limited to pairs of positive numbers.

Online Research **Data Update** What are the current postage rates and regulations? Visit www.algebra1.com/data_update to learn more.

SHIPPING For Exercises 40 and 41, use the following information.
A delivery truck is transporting televisions and microwaves to an appliance store. The weight limit for the truck is 4000 pounds. The televisions weigh 77 pounds, and the microwaves weigh 55 pounds.

40. Write an inequality for this situation. $77t + 55m \le 4000$

41. Will the truck be able to deliver 35 televisions and 25 microwaves at once?
No, the weight will be greater than 4000 pounds.

Enrichment, p. 378

Using Equations: Ideal Weight

You can find your ideal weight as follows.

A woman should weigh 100 pounds for the first 5 feet of height and 5 additional pounds for each inch over 5 feet (5 feet = 60 inches).
A man should weigh 106 pounds for the first 5 feet of height and 6 additional pounds for each inch over 5 feet. These formulas apply to people with normal bone structures.

To determine your bone structure, wrap your thumb and index finger around the wrist of your other hand. If the thumb and finger just touch, you have normal bone structure. If they overlap, you are small-boned. If they don't overlap, you are large-boned. Small-boned people should decrease their calculated ideal weight by 10%. Large-boned people should increase the value by 10%.

Calculate the ideal weights of these people.

1. woman, 5 ft 4 in., normal-boned
120 lb

2. man, 5 ft 11 in., large-boned
189.2 lb

FALL DANCE For Exercises 42–44, use the following information.

Tickets for the fall dance are $5 per person or $8 for couples. In order to cover expenses, at least $1200 worth of tickets must be sold.

42. Write an inequality that represents this situation. $5s + 8c \geq 1200$

43. Graph the inequality. **See margin.**

44. If 100 single tickets and 125 couple tickets are sold, will the committee cover its expenses? **yes**

A linear inequality can be used to represent trends in Olympic times. Visit www.algebra1.com/webquest to continue work on your WebQuest project.

45. **CRITICAL THINKING** Graph the intersection of the graphs of $y \leq x - 1$ and $y \geq -x$. **See margin.**

46. WRITING IN MATH Answer the question that was posed at the beginning of the lesson. **See margin.**

How are inequalities used in budgets?

Include the following in your answer:
- an explanation of the restrictions placed on the domain and range of the inequality used to describe the number of times Hannah can buy her lunch, and
- three possible solutions of the inequality.

Standardized Test Practice

47. Which ordered pair is *not* a solution of $y - 2x < -5$? **D**
    (A) $(2, -2)$ (B) $(-1, -8)$ (C) $(4, 1)$ (D) $(5, 6)$

48. Which inequality is represented by the graph at the right? **B**
    (A) $2x + y < 1$ (B) $2x + y > 1$
    (C) $2x + y \leq 1$ (D) $2x + y \geq 1$

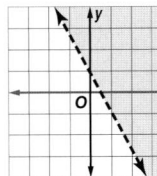

Maintain Your Skills

Mixed Review

49–53. See margin for graphs.

Solve each open sentence. Then graph the solution set. *(Lesson 6-5)*

49. $|3 + 2t| = 11$ $\{-7, 4\}$
50. $|x + 8| < 6$ $\{x \mid -14 < x < -2\}$
51. $|2y + 5| \geq 3$ $\{y \mid y \leq -4 \text{ or } y \geq -1\}$

Solve each compound inequality. Then graph the solution. *(Lesson 6-4)*

52. $y + 6 > -1$ and $y - 2 < 4$ $\{y \mid -7 < y < 6\}$
53. $m + 4 < 2$ or $m - 2 > 1$ $\{m \mid m < -2 \text{ or } m > 3\}$

State whether each percent of change is a percent of *increase* or *decrease*. Then find the percent of change. Round to the nearest whole percent. *(Lesson 3-7)*

54. original: 200   new: 172 **decrease; 14%**
55. original: 100   new: 142 **increase; 42%**
56. original: 53   new: 75 **increase; 42%**

Solve each equation. *(Lesson 3-4)*

57. $\frac{d-2}{3} = 7$ **23**
58. $3n + 6 = -15$ **−7**
59. $35 + 20h = 100$ **3.25**

Simplify. *(Lesson 2-4)*

60. $\frac{-64}{4}$ **−16**
61. $\frac{27c}{-9}$ **−3c**
62. $\frac{12a - 14b}{-2}$ **−6a + 7b**
63. $\frac{18y - 9}{3}$ **6y − 3**

Lesson 6-6 Graphing Inequalities in Two Variables **357**

43.
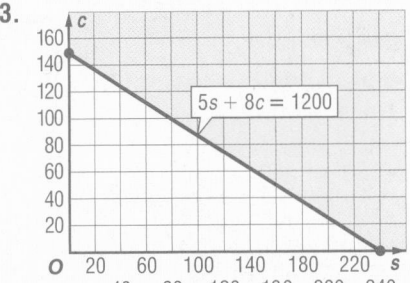

45.
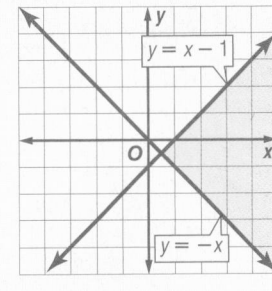

Open-Ended Assessment

Speaking Have students explain why, when they use linear inequalities to solve real-world problems, the solution is often not the entire half-plane. The explanations should include an example.

Assessment Options

Quiz (Lesson 6-6) is available on p. 394 of the *Chapter 6 Resource Masters*.

Answers

46. The amount of money spent in each category must be less than or equal to the budgeted amount. How much you spend on individual items can vary. Answers should include the following.

- The domain and range must be positive integers.
- Sample answers: Hannah could buy 5 cafeteria lunches and 3 restaurant lunches, 2 cafeteria lunches and 5 restaurant lunches, or 8 cafeteria lunches and 1 restaurant lunch.

49.

50.

51.

52.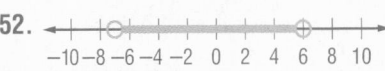

53.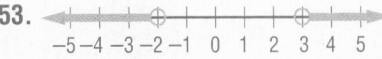

A Follow-Up of Lesson 6-6

Getting Started

Reset the Calculator Have students enter 2nd DRAW 1 ENTER to clear any stored drawings. You may also need students to reset the viewing windows. Have them enter ZOOM 6 to the graph in the standard viewing window.

Teach

- Tell students that when using the **DRAW** function, the first boundary they enter is always the lower boundary. The comma separates the lower and upper boundaries.
- An alternative method to graphing inequalities is to enter the function in the Y= table at Y₁=. Then highlight the symbol in front of the Y= entry and press ENTER until either shading above or below appears.

Assess

Make sure students understand that the solutions for the inequalities can be anywhere in the shaded area of the graph, including the lines themselves.

Answers

1. $y \leq 3x + 1$ is shaded below the line $y = 3x + 1$. $y \geq 3x + 1$ is shaded above the line $y = 3x + 1$.

3c.

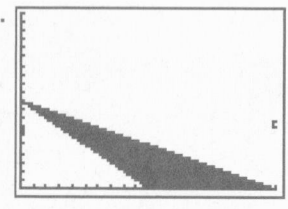

Graphing Inequalities

You can use a TI-83 Plus graphing calculator to investigate the graphs of inequalities. Since graphing calculators only shade between two functions, enter a lower boundary as well as an upper boundary for each inequality.

Graph two different inequalities on your graphing calculator.

Step 1 Graph $y \leq 3x + 1$.

- Clear all functions from the Y= list.

  KEYSTROKES: Y= CLEAR

- Graph $y \leq 3x + 1$ in the standard window.

  KEYSTROKES: 2nd [DRAW] 7 (−) 10 , 3 X,T,θ,n + 1) ENTER

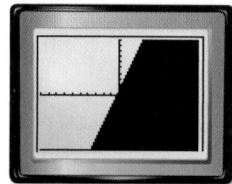

The lower boundary is Ymin or −10. The upper boundary is $y = 3x + 1$. All ordered pairs for which y is *less than or equal to* $3x + 1$ lie *below or on* the line and are solutions.

Step 2 Graph $y - 3x \geq 1$.

- Clear the drawing that is currently displayed.

  KEYSTROKES: 2nd [DRAW] 1

- Rewrite $y - 3x \geq 1$ as $y \geq 3x + 1$ and graph it.

  KEYSTROKES: 2nd [DRAW] 7 3 X,T,θ,n + 1 , 10) ENTER

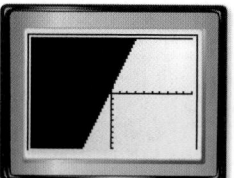

This time, the lower boundary is $y = 3x + 1$. The upper boundary is Ymax or 10. All ordered pairs for which y is *greater than or equal to* $3x + 1$ lie *above or on* the line and are solutions.

Exercises 2b. Sample answer: {(0, 4), (−1, 7), (2, 6), (4.2, −1.5)}

1. Compare and contrast the two graphs shown above. **See margin.**

2. Graph the inequality $y \geq -2x + 4$ in the standard viewing window.
   a. What functions do you enter as the lower and upper boundaries? $y = -2x + 4$; Ymax or 10
   b. Using your graph, name four solutions of the inequality.

3. Suppose student movie tickets cost $4 and adult movie tickets cost $8. You would like to buy at least 10 tickets, but spend no more than $80.
   a. Let x = number of student tickets and y = number of adult tickets. Write two inequalities, one representing the total number of tickets and the other representing the total cost of the tickets. $x + y \geq 10$; $4x + 8y \leq 80$
   b. Which inequalities would you use as the lower and upper boundaries? $y \geq -x + 10$; $y \leq -0.5x + 10$
   c. Graph the inequalities. Use the viewing window [0, 20] scl: 1 by [0, 20] scl: 1. **See margin.**
   d. Name four possible combinations of student and adult tickets. Sample answer: {(8, 5), (10, 4), (14, 2), (20, 0)}

www.algebra1.com/other_calculator_keystrokes

Vocabulary and Concept Check

Addition Property of Inequalities (p. 318)
boundary (p. 353)
compound inequality (p. 339)
Division Property of Inequalities (p. 327)

half-plane (p. 353)
intersection (p. 339)
Multiplication Property of Inequalities (p. 325)

set-builder notation (p. 319)
Subtraction Property of Inequalities (p. 319)
union (p. 340)

Choose the letter of the term that best matches each statement, algebraic expression, or algebraic sentence.

1. $\{w \mid w \geq -14\}$ **f**
2. If $x \leq y$, then $-5x \geq -5y$. **e**
3. $p > -5$ and $p \leq 0$ **d**
4. If $a < b$, then $a + 2 < b + 2$. **a**
5. the graph on one side of a boundary **c**
6. If $s \geq t$, then $s - 7 \geq t - 7$. **g**
7. $g \geq 7$ or $g < 2$ **h**
8. If $m > n$, then $\frac{m}{7} > \frac{n}{7}$. **b**

a. Addition Property of Inequalities
b. Division Property of Inequalities
c. half-plane
d. intersection
e. Multiplication Property of Inequalities
f. set-builder notation
g. Subtraction Property of Inequalities
h. union

Lesson-by-Lesson Review

6-1 Solving Inequalities by Addition and Subtraction

See pages 318–323.

Concept Summary

• If any number is added to each side of a true inequality, the resulting inequality is also true.
• If any number is subtracted from each side of a true inequality, the resulting inequality is also true.

Examples Solve each inequality.

1. $f + 9 \leq -23$

$f + 9 \leq -23$ Original inequality
$f + 9 - 9 \leq -23 - 9$ Subtract.
$f \leq -32$ Simplify.
The solution set is $\{f \mid f \leq -32\}$.

2. $v - 19 > -16$

$v - 19 > -16$ Original inequality
$v - 19 + 19 > -16 + 19$ Add.
$v > 3$ Simplify.
The solution set is $\{v \mid v > 3\}$.

Exercises Solve each inequality. Then check your solution, and graph it on a number line. *See Examples 1–5 on pages 318–320.* **9–16. See pp. 365A–365D.**

9. $c + 51 > 32$
10. $r + 7 > -5$
11. $w - 14 \leq 23$
12. $a - 6 > -10$
13. $-0.11 \geq n - (-0.04)$
14. $2.3 < g - (-2.1)$
15. $7h \leq 6h - 1$
16. $5b > 4b + 5$

17. Define a variable, write an inequality, and solve the problem. Then check your solution. *Twenty-one is no less than the sum of a number and negative two.*

Sample answer: Let n = the number; $21 \geq n + (-2)$; $\{n \mid n \leq 23\}$.

www.algebra1.com/vocabulary_review   Chapter 6 Study Guide and Review **359**

Chapter 6

Study Guide and Review

Vocabulary and Concept Check

• This alphabetical list of vocabulary terms in Chapter 6 includes a page reference where each term was introduced.

• **Assessment** A vocabulary test/review for Chapter 6 is available on p. 392 of the *Chapter 6 Resource Masters*.

Lesson-by-Lesson Review

For each lesson,

• the main ideas are summarized,
• additional examples review concepts, and
• practice exercises are provided.

Vocabulary PuzzleMaker

ELL The Vocabulary PuzzleMaker software improves students' mathematics vocabulary using four puzzle formats—crossword, scramble, word search using a word list, and word search using clues. Students can work on a computer screen or from a printed handout.

MindJogger Videoquizzes

ELL MindJogger Videoquizzes provide an alternative review of concepts presented in this chapter. Students work in teams in a game show format to gain points for correct answers. The questions are presented in three rounds.

Round 1 Concepts (5 questions)
Round 2 Skills (4 questions)
Round 3 Problem Solving (4 questions)

FOLDABLES™
Study Organizer

For more information about Foldables, see *Teaching Mathematics with Foldables.*

Have students look through the chapter to make sure they have included examples in their Foldable journal for each type of inequality they learned to solve.

Encourage students to refer to their Foldable journal while completing the Study Guide and Review and to use them in preparing for the Chapter Test.

6-2 Solving Inequalities by Multiplication and Division

See pages 325–331.

Concept Summary

- If each side of a true inequality is multiplied or divided by the same positive number, the resulting inequality is also true.
- If each side of a true inequality is multiplied or divided by the same negative number, the direction of the inequality must be *reversed*.

Examples   Solve each inequality.

1 $-14g \geq 126$

$-14g \geq 126$ Original inequality

$\dfrac{-14g}{-14} \leq \dfrac{126}{-14}$ Divide and change $\geq$ to $\leq$.

$g \leq -9$ Simplify.

The solution set is $\{g \,|\, g \leq -9\}$.

2 $\dfrac{3}{4}d < 15$

$\dfrac{3}{4}d < 15$ Original inequality

$\left(\dfrac{4}{3}\right)\dfrac{3}{4}d < \left(\dfrac{4}{3}\right)15$ Multiply each side by $\dfrac{4}{3}$.

$d < 20$ Simplify.

The solution set is $\{d \,|\, d < 20\}$.

Exercises   Solve each inequality. Then check your solution.
See Examples 1–5 on pages 326–328.

18. $15v > 60$ **19.** $12r \leq 72$ **20.** $-15z \geq -75$ **21.** $-9m < 99$

22. $\dfrac{b}{-12} \leq 3$ **23.** $\dfrac{d}{-13} > -5$ **24.** $\dfrac{2}{3}w > -22$ **25.** $\dfrac{3}{5}p \leq -15$

26. Define a variable, write an inequality, and solve the problem. Then check your solution. *Eighty percent of a number is greater than or equal to 24.* **Sample answer:** Let $n =$ the number; $0.80n \geq 24$; $\{n \,|\, n \geq 30\}$.

18. $\{v \,|\, v > 4\}$
19. $\{r \,|\, r \leq 6\}$
20. $\{z \,|\, z \leq 5\}$
21. $\{m \,|\, m > -11\}$
22. $\{b \,|\, b \geq -36\}$
23. $\{d \,|\, d < 65\}$
24. $\{w \,|\, w > -33\}$
25. $\{p \,|\, p \leq -25\}$

6-3 Solving Multi-Step Inequalities

See pages 332–337.

Concept Summary

- Multi-step inequalities can be solved by undoing the operations.
- Remember to reverse the inequality sign when multiplying or dividing each side by a negative number.
- When solving equations that contain grouping symbols, first use the Distributive Property to remove the grouping symbols.

Example   Solve $4(n - 1) < 7n + 8$.

$4(n - 1) < 7n + 8$ Original inequality

$4n - 4 < 7n + 8$ Distributive Property

$4n - 4 - 7n < 7n + 8 - 7n$ Subtract $7n$ from each side.

$-3n - 4 < 8$ Simplify.

$-3n - 4 + 4 < 8 + 4$ Add 4 to each side.

$-3n < 12$ Simplify.

$\dfrac{-3n}{-3} > \dfrac{12}{-3}$ Divide each side by -3 and change $<$ to $>$.

$n > -4$ Simplify.

The solution set is $\{n \,|\, n > -4\}$.

Exercises Solve each inequality. Then check your solution.

See Examples 1–5 on pages 332–334.

27. $-4h + 7 > 15$ **28.** $5 - 6n > -19$ **29.** $-5x + 3 < 3x + 19$

30. $15b - 12 > 7b + 60$ **31.** $-5(q + 12) < 3q - 4$ **32.** $7(g + 8) < 3(g + 2) + 4g$ $\varnothing$

33. $\dfrac{2(x + 2)}{3} \geq 4$ $\{x \mid x \geq 4\}$ **34.** $\dfrac{1 - 7n}{5} > 10$ $\{n \mid n < -7\}$

35. Define a variable, write an inequality, and solve the problem. Then check your solution. *Two thirds of a number decreased by 27 is at least 9.* **Sample answer:**
Let $n =$ the number; $\frac{2}{3}n - 27 \geq 9$; $\{n \mid n \geq 54\}$.

27. $\{h \mid h < -2\}$ **28.** $\{n \mid n < 4\}$ **29.** $\{x \mid x > -2\}$ **30.** $\{b \mid b > 9\}$ **31.** $\{q \mid q > -7\}$

6-4 Solving Compound Inequalities

See pages 339–344.

Concept Summary

- The solution of a compound inequality containing *and* is the intersection of the graphs of the two inequalities.
- The solution of a compound inequality containing *or* is the union of the graphs of the two inequalities.

Examples Graph the solution set of each compound inequality.

1 $x \geq -1$ and $x > 3$

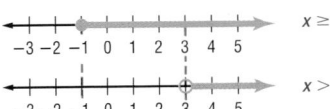

Find the intersection.

The solution set is $\{x \mid x > 3\}$.

2 $x \leq 8$ or $x < 2$

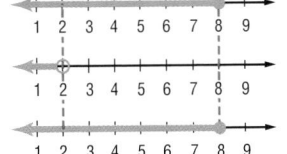

Find the union.

The solution set is $\{x \mid x \leq 8\}$.

Exercises Solve each compound inequality. Then graph the solution set.

See Examples 1–4 on pages 339–341. **36–41. See margin for graphs.**

36. $-1 < p + 3 < 5$
$\{p \mid -4 < p < 2\}$

37. $-3 < 2k - 1 < 5$
$\{k \mid -1 < k < 3\}$

38. $3w + 8 < 2$ or $w + 12 > 2 - w$ $\{w \mid w$ is a real number.$\}$

39. $a - 3 \leq 8$ or $a + 5 \geq 21$
$\{a \mid a \leq 11$ or $a \geq 16\}$

40. $m + 8 < 4$ and $3 - m < 5$ $\varnothing$

41. $10 - 2y > 12$ and $7y < 4y + 9$
$\{y \mid y < -1\}$

6-5 Solving Open Sentences Involving Absolute Value

See pages 345–351.

Concept Summary

- If $|x| = n$, then $x = -n$ or $x = n$.

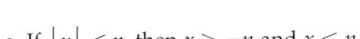

- If $|x| < n$, then $x > -n$ and $x < n$.

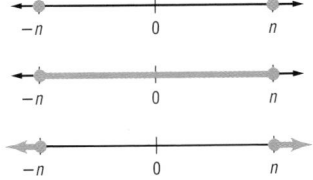

- If $|x| > n$, then $x < -n$ or $x > n$.

Answers

36.

-5 -4 -3 -2 -1 0 1 2 3 4 5

37.

-5 -4 -3 -2 -1 0 1 2 3 4 5

38.

-5 -4 -3 -2 -1 0 1 2 3 4 5

39.

9 10 11 12 13 14 15 16 17 18 19

40.

-5 -4 -3 -2 -1 0 1 2 3 4 5

41.

-5 -4 -3 -2 -1 0 1 2 3 4 5

Study Guide and Review

Chapter **6** For More ...
• Extra Practice, see pages 833–835.
• Mixed Problem Solving, see page 858.

Answers

42.

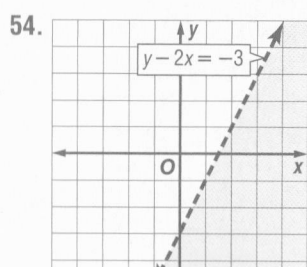

−12 −8 −4 0 4 8 12 16 20 24 28

43.

−9 −8 −7 −6 −5 −4 −3 −2 −1 0 1

44.

−16 −14 −12 −10 −8 −6 −4 −2 0 2 4

45.

−10 −9 −8 −7 −6 −5 −4 −3 −2 −1 0

46.

−15 −14 −13 −12 −11 −10 −9 −8 −7 −6 −5

47.

−9 −8 −7 −6 −5 −4 −3 −2 −1 0 1

48.

−8 −7 −6 −5 −4 −3 −2 −1 0 1 2

49.

−6 −5 −4 −3 −2 −1 0 1 2 3 4

54.

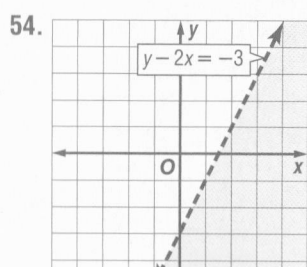

$y − 2x = −3$

55.

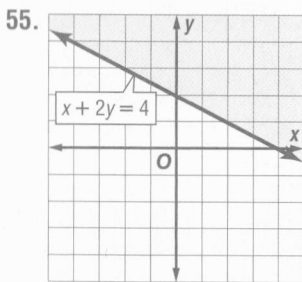

$x + 2y = 4$

56.

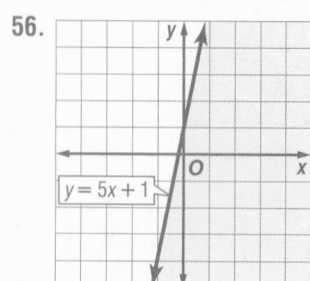

$y = 5x + 1$

---

42. $\{−4, 20\}$
43. $\{−7, −3\}$
44. $\{h \mid h < −12$ or $h > 2\}$
45. $\{w \mid w \le −9$ or $w \ge −7\}$

Example

Solve $|x + 6| = 15$.

$$|x + 6| = 15$$

$$x + 6 = 15 \quad \text{or} \quad x + 6 = −15$$
$$x + 6 − 6 = 15 − 6 \qquad x + 6 − 6 = −15 − 6$$
$$x = 9 \qquad\qquad x = −21$$

The solution set is $\{−21, 9\}$.

Exercises Solve each open sentence. Then graph the solution set.
See Examples 1, 3, and 4 on pages 346–348. **42–49. See margin for graphs.**

42. $|w − 8| = 12$ **43.** $|q + 5| = 2$ **44.** $|h + 5| > 7$ **45.** $|w + 8| \ge 1$

46. $|r + 10| < 3$ **47.** $|t + 4| \le 3$ **48.** $|2x + 5| < 4$ **49.** $|3d + 4| < 8$

$\{r \mid −13 < r < −7\}$ $\{t \mid −7 \le t \le −1\}$ $\left\{x \mid −4\frac{1}{2} < x < −\frac{1}{2}\right\}$ $\left\{d \mid −4 < d < 1\frac{1}{3}\right\}$

6-6 ## Graphing Inequalities in Two Variables

See pages 352–357.

Concept Summary

• To graph an inequality in two variables:

  Step 1 Determine the boundary and draw a dashed or solid line.

  Step 2 Select a test point. Test that point.

  Step 3 Shade the half-plane that contains the solution.

Example

Graph $y \ge x − 2$.

Since the boundary is included in the solution, draw a solid line.

Test the point $(0, 0)$.

$y \ge x − 2$ Original inequality

$0 \ge 0 − 2$ $x = 0, y = 0$

$0 \ge −2$ true

The half plane that contains $(0, 0)$ should be shaded.

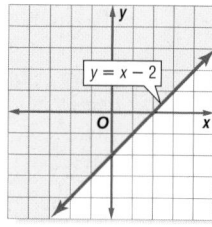

$y = x − 2$

Exercises Determine which ordered pairs are part of the solution set for each inequality. *See Example 1 on page 352.*

50. $3x + 2y < 9$, $\{(1, 3), (3, 2), (−2, 7), (−4, 11)\}$ $\{(−2, 7)\}$

51. $5 − y \ge 4x$, $\left\{(2, −5), \left(\frac{1}{2}, 7\right), (−1, 6), (−3, 20)\right\}$ $\{(2, −5), (−1, 6)\}$

52. $\frac{1}{2}y \le 6 − x$, $\{(−4, 15), (5, 1), (3, 8), (−2, 25)\}$ $\{(−4, 15), (5, 1)\}$

53. $−2x < 8 − y$, $\{(5, 10), (3, 6), (−4, 0), (−3, 6)\}$ $\{(5, 10), (3, 6)\}$

Graph each inequality. *See Example 2 on pages 353 and 354.* **54–57. See margin.**

54. $y − 2x < −3$ **55.** $x + 2y \ge 4$ **56.** $y \le 5x + 1$ **57.** $2x − 3y > 6$

362 Chapter 6 Solving Linear Inequalities

57.

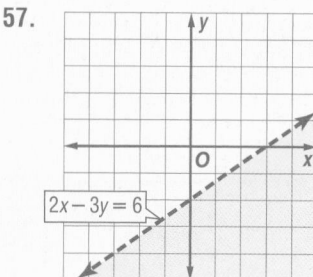

$2x − 3y = 6$

Vocabulary and Concepts

1. **Write** *the set of all numbers t such that t is greater than or equal to 17* in set-builder notation. $\{t \mid t \geq 17\}$

2. **Show** how to solve $6(a + 5) < 2a + 8$. Justify your work. **See pp. 365A–365D.**

3. **OPEN ENDED** Give an example of a compound inequality that is an **Sample answers:** intersection and an example of a compound inequality that is a union. $2 < x < 8; x < 2$ or $x > 8$

4. **Compare and contrast** the graphs of $|x| \leq 3$ and $|x| \geq 3$. **Both graphs have dots at 3 and −3. The graph of $|x| \leq 3$ is darkened between the two dots. The graph of $|x| \geq 3$ is darkened to the right of the dot at 3 and to the left of the dot at −3.**

Skills and Applications

Solve each inequality. Then check your solution.

5. $-23 \geq g - 6$ $\{g \mid g \leq -17\}$

6. $9p < 8p - 18$ $\{p \mid p < -18\}$

7. $d - 5 < 2d - 14$ $\{d \mid d > 9\}$

8. $\frac{7}{8}w \geq -21$ $\{w \mid w \geq -24\}$

9. $-22b \leq 99$ $\{b \mid b \geq -4.5\}$

10. $4m - 11 \geq 8m + 7$ $\{m \mid m \leq -4.5\}$

11. $-3(k - 2) > 12$ $\{k \mid k < -2\}$

12. $\frac{f-5}{3} > -3$ $\{f \mid f > -4\}$

13. $0.3(y - 4) \leq 0.8(0.2y + 2)$ $\{y \mid y \leq 20\}$

14. **REAL ESTATE** A homeowner is selling her house. She must pay 7% of the selling price to her real estate agent after the house is sold. To the nearest dollar, what must be the selling price of her house to have at least $110,000 after the agent is paid? **at least $118,280**

15. Solve $6 + |r| = 3$. $\varnothing$

16. Solve $|d| > -2$. $\{d \mid d$ is a real number.$\}$

Solve each compound inequality. Then graph the solution set. 17–22. See pp. 365A–365D for graphs.

17. $r + 3 > 2$ and $4r < 12$ $\{r \mid -1 < r < 3\}$

18. $3n + 2 \geq 17$ or $3n + 2 \leq -1$ $\{n \mid n \leq -1$ or $n \geq 5\}$

19. $9 + 2p > 3$ and $-13 > 8p + 3$ $\{p \mid -3 < p < -2\}$

20. $|2a - 5| < 7$ $\{a \mid -1 < a < 6\}$

21. $|7 - 3s| \geq 2$ $\left\{s \mid s \leq 1\frac{2}{3} \text{ or } s \geq 3\right\}$

22. $|7 - 5z| > 3$ $\{z \mid z < 0.8$ or $z > 2\}$

Define a variable, write an inequality, and solve each problem. Then check your solution. 23–25. Sample answer: Let n = the number.

23. One fourth of a number is no less than −3. $\frac{1}{4}n \geq -3; \{n \mid n \geq -12\}$

24. Three times a number subtracted from 14 is less than two. $14 - 3n < 2; \{n \mid n > 4\}$

25. Five less than twice a number is between 13 and 21. $13 < 2n - 5 < 21; \{n \mid 9 < n < 13\}$

26. **TRAVEL** Megan's car gets between 18 and 21 miles per gallon of gasoline. If her car's tank holds 15 gallons, what is the range of distance that Megan can drive her car on one tank of gasoline? **between 270 and 315 mi**

Graph each inequality. 27–29. See pp. 365A–365D.

27. $y \geq 3x - 2$

28. $2x + 3y < 6$

29. $x - 2y > 4$

30. **STANDARDIZED TEST PRACTICE** Which inequality is represented by the graph? **B**

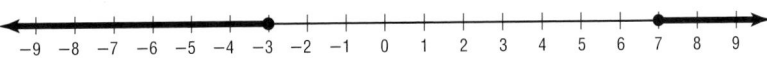

(A) $|x - 2| \leq 5$ (B) $|x - 2| \geq 5$ (C) $|x + 2| \leq 5$ (D) $|x + 2| \geq 5$

 www.algebra1.com/chapter_test

Portfolio Suggestion

Introduction In mathematics, there is often more than one way to solve a problem. In order to solve an inequality, for example, you can write a solution set or graph the inequality.

Ask Students Find an inequality from your work in this chapter and show two different ways to solve it. Place your work in your portfolio.

Assessment Options

Vocabulary Test A vocabulary test/review for Chapter 6 can be found on p. 392 of the *Chapter 6 Resource Masters*.

Chapter Tests There are six Chapter 6 Tests and an Open-Ended Assessment task available in the *Chapter 6 Resource Masters*.

Chapter 6 Tests			
Form	**Type**	**Level**	**Pages**
1	MC	basic	379–380
2A	MC	average	381–382
2B	MC	average	383–384
2C	FR	average	385–386
2D	FR	average	387–388
3	FR	advanced	389–390

MC = multiple-choice questions
FR = free-response questions

Open-Ended Assessment Performance tasks for Chapter 6 can be found on p. 391 of the *Chapter 6 Resource Masters*. A sample scoring rubric for these tasks appears on p. A25.

First Semester Test A test for Chapters 1–6 can be found on pp. 399–402 of the *Chapter 6 Resource Masters*.

 ExamView® Pro

Use the networkable **ExamView® Pro** to:

- Create **multiple versions** of tests.
- Create **modified** tests for *Inclusion* students.
- **Edit** existing questions and **add** your own questions.
- Use built-in **state curriculum correlations** to create tests aligned with state standards.
- Change **English** tests to **Spanish** and vice versa.

These two pages contain practice questions in the various formats that can be found on the most frequently given standardized tests.

A practice answer sheet for these two pages can be found on p. A1 of the *Chapter 6 Resource Masters*.

Standardized Test Practice
Student Recording Sheet, p. A1

Part 1 *Multiple Choice*

Select the best answer from the choices given and fill in the corresponding oval.

1 Ⓐ Ⓑ Ⓒ Ⓓ   4 Ⓐ Ⓑ Ⓒ Ⓓ   7 Ⓐ Ⓑ Ⓒ Ⓓ
2 Ⓐ Ⓑ Ⓒ Ⓓ   5 Ⓐ Ⓑ Ⓒ Ⓓ   8 Ⓐ Ⓑ Ⓒ Ⓓ
3 Ⓐ Ⓑ Ⓒ Ⓓ   6 Ⓐ Ⓑ Ⓒ Ⓓ   9 Ⓐ Ⓑ Ⓒ Ⓓ

Part 2 *Short Response/Grid In*

Solve the problem and write your answer in the blank.

For Questions 11 and 15, also enter your answer by writing each number or symbol in a box. Then fill in the corresponding oval for that number or symbol.

10 _____
11 _____ (grid in)
12 _____
13 _____
14 _____
15 _____ (grid in)
16 _____
17 _____
18 _____

Part 3 *Extended Response*

Record your answers for Questions 19–21 on the back of this paper.

Additional Practice

See pp. 397–398 in the *Chapter 6 Resource Masters* for additional standardized test practice.

Part 1 Multiple Choice

Record your answers on the answer sheet provided by your teacher or on a sheet of paper.

1. Which of the following is a correct statement? (Lesson 2-4) **B**

   Ⓐ $-\frac{9}{3} > \frac{3}{9}$ Ⓑ $-\frac{3}{9} > -\frac{9}{3}$

   Ⓒ $-\frac{3}{9} < -\frac{9}{3}$ Ⓓ $\frac{9}{3} < \frac{3}{9}$

2. $(-6)(-7) =$ (Lesson 2-3) **D**

   Ⓐ -42 Ⓑ -13

   Ⓒ 13 Ⓓ 42

3. A cylindrical can has a volume of 5625π cubic centimeters. Its height is 25 centimeters. What is the radius of the can? Use the formula $V = \pi r^2 h$. (Lessons 2-8 and 3-8) **C**

   Ⓐ 4.8 cm   Ⓑ 7.5 cm

   Ⓒ 15 cm   Ⓓ 47.1 cm

4. A furnace repair service charged a customer $80 for parts and $65 per hour worked. The bill totaled $177.50. About how long did the repair technician work on the furnace? (Lessons 3-1 and 3-4) **B**

   Ⓐ 0.5 hour   Ⓑ 1.5 hours

   Ⓒ 2 hours   Ⓓ 4 hours

5. The formula $P = \frac{4(220 - A)}{5}$ determines the recommended maximum pulse rate P during exercise for a person who is A years old. Cameron is 15 years old. What is his recommended maximum pulse rate during exercise? (Lesson 3-8) **B**

   Ⓐ 162   Ⓑ 164

   Ⓒ 173   Ⓓ 263

6. The graph of the function $y = 2x - 1$ is shown. If the graph is translated 3 units up, which equation will best represent the new line? (Lesson 4-2) **A**

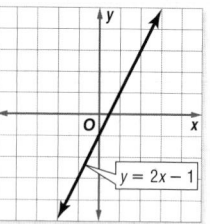

   Ⓐ $y = 2x + 2$ Ⓑ $y = 2x - 3$

   Ⓒ $y = 2x + 3$ Ⓓ $y = 2x - 4$

7. The table shows a set of values for x and y. Which equation best represents this set of data? (Lesson 4-8) **D**

x	−4	−1	2	5	8
y	−16	−4	8	20	32

   Ⓐ $y = 3x - 4$ Ⓑ $y = 3x + 2$

   Ⓒ $y = 2x - 10$ Ⓓ $y = 4x$

8. Ali's grade depends on 4 test scores. On the first 3 tests, she earned scores of 78, 82, and 75. She wants to average at least 80. Which inequality can she use to find the score x that she needs on the fourth test in order to earn a final grade of at least 80? (Lesson 6-3) **B**

   Ⓐ $\frac{78 + 82 + 75 + x}{3} \geq 80$

   Ⓑ $\frac{78 + 82 + 75 + x}{4} \geq 80$

   Ⓒ $\frac{78 + 82 + 75 - x}{4} \geq 80$

   Ⓓ $\frac{78 + 82 + 75 + x}{4} \leq 80$

9. Which inequality is represented by the graph? (Lesson 6-4) **C**

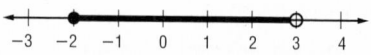

   Ⓐ $-2 < x < 3$ Ⓑ $-2 < x \leq 3$

   Ⓒ $-2 \leq x < 3$ Ⓓ $-2 \leq x \leq 3$

 ExamView® Pro

Special banks of standardized test questions similar to those on the SAT, ACT, TIMSS 8, NAEP 8, and Algebra 1 End-of-Course tests can be found on this CD-ROM.

Preparing for Standardized Tests
For test-taking strategies and more
practice, see pages 867–884.

Part 2 | Short Response/Grid In

Record your answers on the answer sheet provided by your teacher or on a sheet of paper.

10. A die is rolled. What are the odds of rolling a number less than 5? (Lesson 2-6)
4:2 or 2:1

11. A car is traveling at an average speed of 54 miles per hour. How many minutes will it take the car to travel 117 miles? (Lesson 3-6)
130

12. The price of a tape player was cut from $48 to $36. What was the percent of decrease? (Lesson 3-7)
25%

13. Quadrilateral $MNOP$ has vertices $M(0, -4)$, $N(-2, 8)$, $O(5, 3)$, and $P(2, -9)$. Find the coordinates of the vertices of the image if it is reflected over the y-axis. (Lesson 4-2)
$M'(0, -4)$, $N'(2, 8)$, $O'(-5, 3)$, $P'(-2, -9)$

14. Write an equation in slope-intercept form that describes the graph. (Lesson 5-4)
$y = -x + 3$

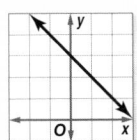

15. A line is parallel to the graph of the equation $\frac{1}{3}y = \frac{2}{3}x - 1$. What is the slope of the parallel line? (Lessons 5-4 and 5-6) **2**

16. Solve $\frac{1}{2}(10x - 8) - 3(x - 1) \geq 15$ for x.
(Lesson 6-3) **$x \geq 8$**

21d. The solution set is limited to nonnegative numbers because the vendor cannot sell less than zero product.

www.algebra1.com/standardized_test

17. Find all values of x that make the inequality $|x - 3| > 5$ true. (Lesson 6-5)
$\{x \mid x < -2$ or $x > 8\}$

18. Graph the equation $y = -2x + 4$ and indicate which region represents $y < -2x + 4$. (Lesson 6-6)
See margin.

Part 3 | Extended Response

Record your answers on a sheet of paper. Show your work.

19. The Carlson family is building a house on a lot that is 91 feet long and 158 feet wide.
(Lessons 6-1, 6-2, and 6-4)

   a. Town law states that the sides of a house cannot be closer than 10 feet to the edges of a lot. Write an inequality for the possible lengths of the Carlson family's house, and solve the inequality.
   $\ell \leq 91 - 20$; $\ell \leq 71$

   b. The Carlson family wants their house to be at least 2800 square feet and no more than 3200 square feet. They also want their house to have the maximum possible length. Write an inequality for the possible widths of their house, and solve the inequality. Round your answer to the nearest whole number of feet.
   $2800 \leq 71w \leq 3200$; $39 \leq w \leq 45$

20. For the graph below, write an open sentence involving absolute value. (Lesson 6-5)
Sample answer: $|x + 2| \leq 3$

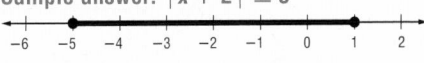

21. A street vendor sells hot dogs for $3 each and bratwurst for $5 each. In order to cover his daily expenses, he must sell at least $400 worth of food. (Lesson 6-6)

   a. Write an inequality that represents this situation. **$3h + 5b \geq 400$**

   b. If 68 hot dogs and 38 bratwursts are sold, will the street vendor cover his costs?
   no

   c. Find a number of hotdogs and bratwursts that could be sold and cover the daily costs. **Sample answer: 100 hot dogs and 21 bratwursts**

   d. Are there any restrictions on the domain and range? Explain. **See margin.**

Evaluating Extended Response Questions

Extended Response questions are graded by using a multilevel rubric that guides you in assessing a student's knowledge of a particular concept.

Goal: Write inequalities to describe the possible dimensions of a house.

Sample Scoring Rubric: The following rubric is a sample scoring device. You may wish to add more detail to this sample to meet your individual scoring needs.

Score	Criteria
4	A correct solution that is supported by well-developed, accurate explanations
3	A generally correct solution, but may contain minor flaws in reasoning or computation
2	A partially correct interpretation and/or solution to the problem
1	A correct solution with no supporting evidence or explanation
0	An incorrect solution indicating no mathematical understanding of the concept or task, or no solution is given

Answer

18.

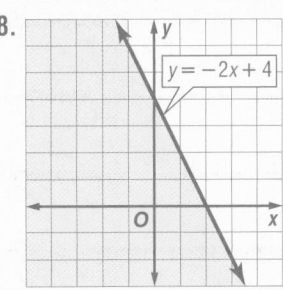

21d. The solution set is limited to nonnegative numbers because the vendor cannot sell less than zero products.

Page 317, Chapter 6 Getting Started

21.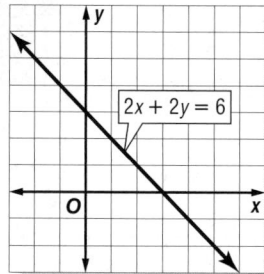

22.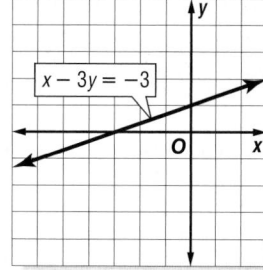

23.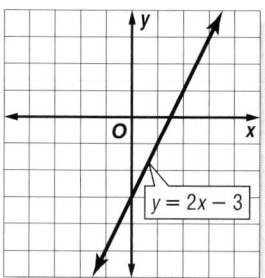

24.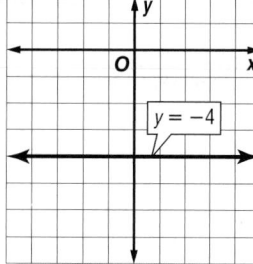

25.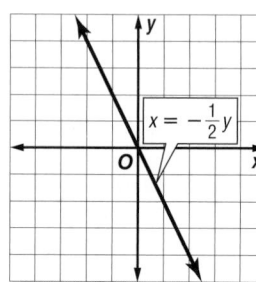

26.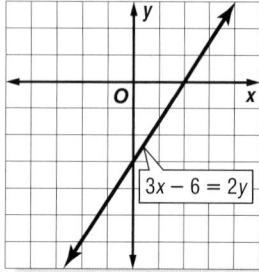

27.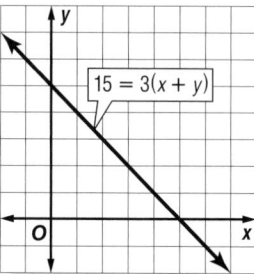

28.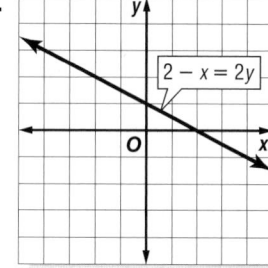

Pages 321–323, Lesson 6-1

5.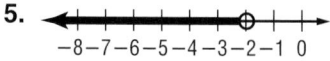
$-8\,-7\,-6\,-5\,-4\,-3\,-2\,-1\ \ 0$

6.
$0\ \ 1\ \ 2\ \ 3\ \ 4\ \ 5\ \ 6\ \ 7\ \ 8$

7.
$0\ \ 2\ \ 4\ \ 6\ \ 8\ \ 10\ \ 12\ \ 14\ \ 16$

8.
$0\ \ 1\ \ 2\ \ 3\ \ 4\ \ 5\ \ 6\ \ 7\ \ 8$

9.
$0\ \ 1\ \ 2\ \ 3\ \ 4\ \ 5\ \ 6\ \ 7\ \ 8$

10.
$-4\,-3\,-2\,-1\ \ 0\ \ 1\ \ 2\ \ 3\ \ 4$

20.
$0\ \ 1\ \ 2\ \ 3\ \ 4\ \ 5\ \ 6\ \ 7\ \ 8$

21.
$0\ \ 1\ \ 2\ \ 3\ \ 4\ \ 5\ \ 6\ \ 7\ \ 8$

22.
$0\ \ 1\ \ 2\ \ 3\ \ 4\ \ 5\ \ 6\ \ 7\ \ 8$

23.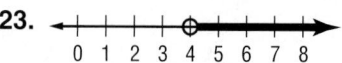
$0\ \ 1\ \ 2\ \ 3\ \ 4\ \ 5\ \ 6\ \ 7\ \ 8$

24.
$0\ \ 1\ \ 2\ \ 3\ \ 4\ \ 5\ \ 6\ \ 7\ \ 8$

25.
$-8\,-7\,-6\,-5\,-4\,-3\,-2\,-1\ \ 0$

26.
$0\ \ 1\ \ 2\ \ 3\ \ 4\ \ 5\ \ 6\ \ 7\ \ 8$

27.
$0\ \ 1\ \ 2\ \ 3\ \ 4\ \ 5\ \ 6\ \ 7\ \ 8$

28.
$-8\,-7\,-6\,-5\,-4\,-3\,-2\,-1\ \ 0$

29.
$-8\,-7\,-6\,-5\,-4\,-3\,-2\,-1\ \ 0$

30.
$-8\,-7\,-6\,-5\,-4\,-3\,-2\,-1\ \ 0$

31.
$-4\,-3\,-2\,-1\ \ 0\ \ 1\ \ 2\ \ 3\ \ 4$

32.
$-4\,-3\,-2\,-1\ \ 0\ \ 1\ \ 2\ \ 3\ \ 4$

33.
$-8\,-7\,-6\,-5\,-4\,-3\,-2\,-1\ \ 0$

34.
$-4\,-3\,-2\,-1\ \ 0\ \ 1\ \ 2\ \ 3\ \ 4$

35.
$-4\,-3\,-2\,-1\ \ 0\ \ 1\ \ 2\ \ 3\ \ 4$

36.
$-4\,-3\,-2\,-1\ \ 0\ \ 1\ \ 2\ \ 3\ \ 4$

37.
$-4\,-3\,-2\,-1\ \ 0\ \ 1\ \ 2\ \ 3\ \ 4$

56. Inequalities can be used to compare the number of schools participating in certain sports, to compare the number of participating schools if sports are added or discontinued in a certain number of schools, and to determine how many schools need to add a certain sport to surpass the number participating in another sport. Answers should include the following.

   - To find how many schools must add girls track and field to surpass the current number of schools participating in girls basketball, solve $16{,}526 < 14{,}587 + x$. More than 1939 schools must add girls track and field.

Page 324, Lesson 6-2A
Algebra Activity

6. The symbols in the solutions point in the opposite direction with relationship to the variable than the symbols in the original problem.

7.

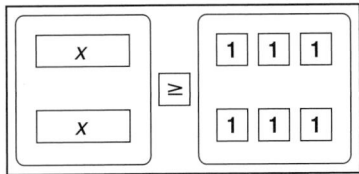

$2x \geq 6$

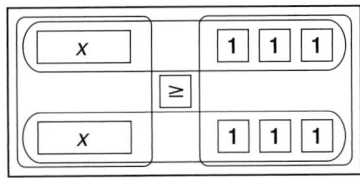

$x \geq 3$

There are no negative x-tiles, so the variable remains on the left and the symbol remains $\geq$.

Page 331, Lesson 6-2

61. Sample answer:

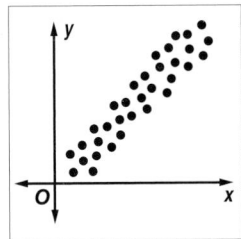

Page 331, Practice Quiz 1

1.
0 1 2 3 4 5 6 7 8

2.
−8 −7 −6 −5 −4 −3 −2 −1 0

3.
−8 −7 −6 −5 −4 −3 −2 −1 0

4.
0 1 2 3 4 5 6 7 8

5.
−4 −3 −2 −1 0 1 2 3 4

6. $\{z|z \geq 7\}$

7. $\{v|v < 35\}$

8. $\{q|q < -35\}$

9. $\{r|r > -13\}$

10. $\left\{w|w \geq \dfrac{5}{4}\right\}$

Pages 335–337, Lesson 6-3

14.

$-5(k + 4) > 3(k - 4)$	Original inequality
$-5k - 20 > 3k - 12$	Distributive Property
$-5k - 20 + 5k > 3k - 12 + 5k$	Add 5k to each side.
$-20 > 8k - 12$	Simplify.
$-20 + 12 > 8k - 12 + 12$	Add 12 to each side.
$-8 > 8k$	Simplify.
$\dfrac{-8}{8} > \dfrac{8k}{8}$	Divide each side by 8.
$-1 > k$	Simplify.

$\{k|k < -1\}$

33.
5 6 7 8 9 10 11 12 13

34.
−4 −3 −2 −1 0 1 2 3 4

74.
−3 −2 −1 0 1 2 3 4 5

75.
−3 −2 −1 0 1 2 3 4 5

76.
−6 −5 −4 −3 −2 −1 0 1 2

77.
−3 −2 −1 0 1 2 3 4 5

78.
−4 −3 −2 −1 0 1 2 3 4

79.
0 1 2 3 4 5 6 7 8

80.
−5 −4 −3 −2 −1 0 1 2 3

81.
−5 −4 −3 −2 −1 0 1 2 3

82.
−2 −1 0 1 2 3 4 5 6

Pages 342–343, Lesson 6-4

28.
8 9 10 11 12 13 14 15 16 17 18

29.
−14 −13 −12 −11 −10 −9 −8 −7 −6 −5 −4

30.
0 1 2 3 4 5 6 7 8 9 10

31.
−5 −4 −3 −2 −1 0 1 2 3 4 5

32.
0 1 2 3 4 5 6 7 8 9 10

33.
0 1 2 3 4 5 6 7 8 9 10

34.
−5 −4 −3 −2 −1 0 1 2 3 4 5

35.
−3 −2 −1 0 1 2 3 4 5 6 7

36.

![number line from -5 to 5, shaded entire line]

37.

![number line from 0 to 10, shaded from left to 4 closed]

38.

![number line from 0 to 10, shaded from 3 to 5 closed dots]

39.

![number line from -5 to 5, no shading shown]

40.

![number line from -5 to 5, open circles at -4 and 4, shaded outside]

41.

![number line from -18 to 2, open circle at -11, shaded entire]

54. The tax table gives intervals of income and how much a taxpayer with taxable income in each interval must pay in taxes. These intervals can be expressed as compound inequalities. Answers should include the following.

- The incomes are in $50 intervals.
- $41,100 \le x < 41,150$ represents the possible incomes of a head of a household paying $7024 in taxes.

Pages 350–351, Lesson 6-5

24.

![number line from -6 to 14, closed dots at -4 and 12]

25.

![number line from -13 to -3, closed dots at -11 and -7]

26.

![number line from -5 to 5, shaded entire line]

27.

![number line from -5 to 5, closed dots at -2 and 3]

28.

![number line from -3 to 7, closed dots at -3 and 6]

29.

![number line from -10 to 0, open circles at -9 and -7]

30.

![number line from -8 to 2, open circles at -3 and -2, shaded outside]

31.

![number line from 0 to 10, closed dots at 2 and 8]

32.

![number line from -5 to 5, shaded entire line]

33.

![number line from -5 to 5, closed dots at -4 and 2]

34.

![number line from -5 to 5, open circles at -4 and 4]

35.

![number line from -5 to 5, no shading shown]

36.

![number line from -1 to 9, closed dots at 0 and 7]

37.

![number line from 0 to 20, closed dots at 2 and 16]

38.

![number line from -10 to 10, closed dots at -10 and 6]

39.

![number line from -5 to 5, closed dots at -3 and 3]

74.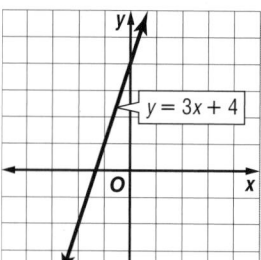

$y = 3x + 4$

75.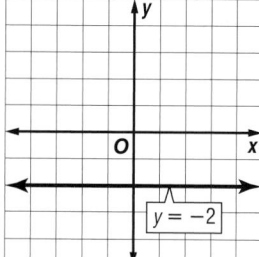

$y = -2$

76.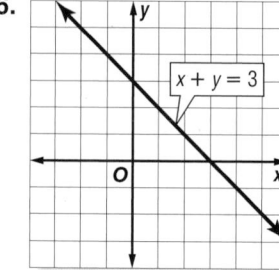

$x + y = 3$

77.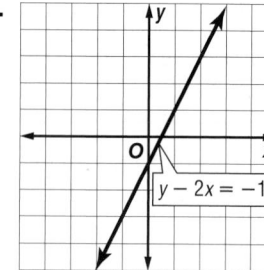

$y - 2x = -1$

78.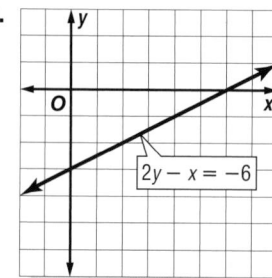

$2y - x = -6$

79.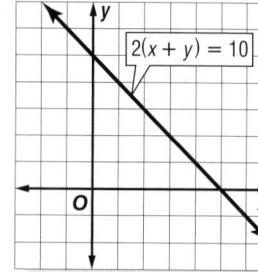

$2(x + y) = 10$

Page 356, Lesson 6-6

26.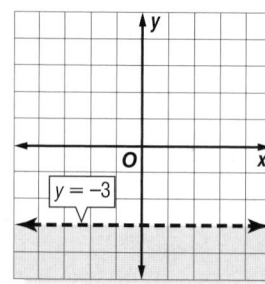

$y = -3$

27.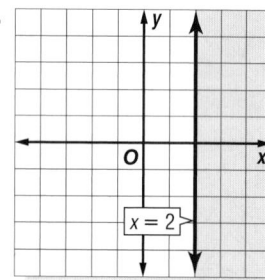

$x = 2$

28.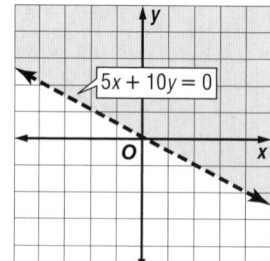

$5x + 10y = 0$

29.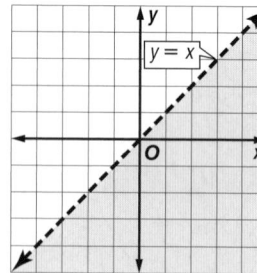

$y = x$

30.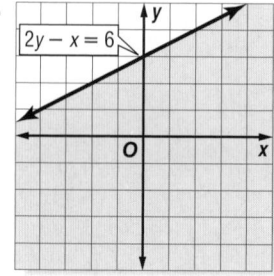

$2y - x = 6$

31.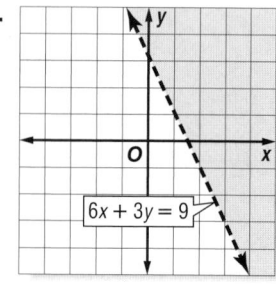

$6x + 3y = 9$

32.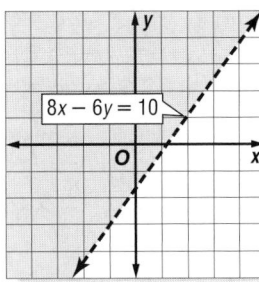

33.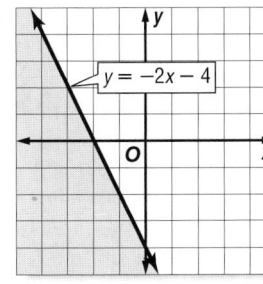

34.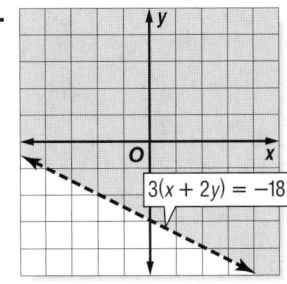

35.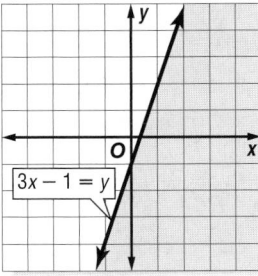

36.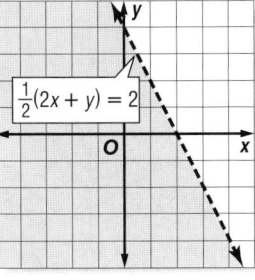

37.

2.

$6(a + 5) < 2a + 8$	*Original equation*
$6a + 30 < 2a + 8$	*Distributive Property*
$6a + 30 - 2a < 2a + 8 - 2a$	*Subtract 2a from each side.*
$4a + 30 < 8$	*Simplify.*
$4a + 30 - 30 < 8 - 30$	*Subtract 30 from each side.*
$4a < -22$	*Simplify.*
$\dfrac{4a}{4} < \dfrac{-22}{4}$	*Divide each side by 4.*
$a < -5.5$	*Simplify.*

$\{a \mid a < -5.5\}$

17.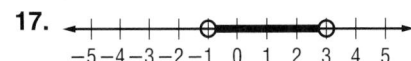

18.

19.

20.

21.

22.

Page 359, Chapter 6 Study Guide and Review

9. $\{c \mid c > -19\}$

10. $\{r \mid r > -12\}$

11. $\{w \mid w \le 37\}$

12. $\{a \mid a > -4\}$

13. $\{n \mid n \le -0.15\}$

14. $\{g \mid g > 0.2\}$

15. $\{h \mid h \le -1\}$

16. $\{b \mid b > 5\}$

27.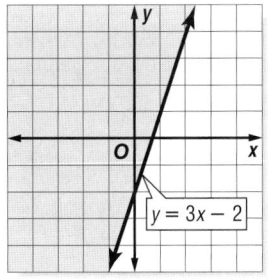

28.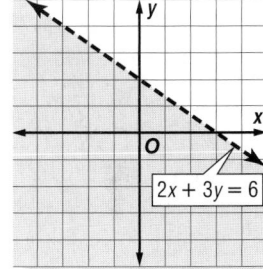

29.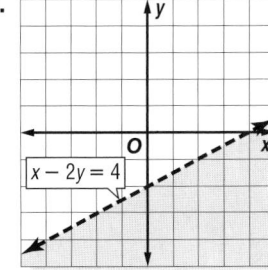

Solving Systems of Linear Equations and Inequalities
Chapter Overview and Pacing

Year-long and two-year pacing: pages T20–T21.

LESSON OBJECTIVES

	PACING (days)			
	Regular		**Block**	
	Basic/ Average	Advanced	Basic/ Average	Advanced
7-1 Graphing Systems of Equations (pp. 368–375) *Preview:* Use a spreadsheet to investigate when two quantities will be equal. • Determine whether a system of linear equations has 0, 1, or infinitely many solutions. • Solve systems of equations by graphing. *Follow-Up:* Use a graphing calculator to solve a system of equations.	2 (with 7-1 Follow-Up)	2 (with 7-1 Preview and Follow-Up)	1.5 (with 7-1 Preview and Follow-Up)	1.5 (with 7-1 Preview and Follow-Up)
7-2 Substitution (pp. 376–381) • Solve systems of equations by using substitution. • Solve real-world problems involving systems of equations.	2	2	1	1
7-3 Elimination Using Addition and Subtraction (pp. 382–386) • Solve systems of equations by using elimination with addition. • Solve systems of equations by using elimination with subtraction.	2	2	1	1
7-4 Elimination Using Multiplication (pp. 387–392) • Solve systems of equations by using elimination with multiplication. • Determine the best method for solving systems of equations.	2	2	1	1
7-5 Graphing Systems of Inequalities (pp. 394–398) • Solve systems of inequalities by graphing. • Solve real-world problems involving systems of inequalities.	1	1	0.5	0.5
Study Guide and **Practice Test** (pp. 399–403) **Standardized Test Practice** (pp. 404–405)	1	1	0.5	0.5
Chapter Assessment	1	1	0.5	0.5
TOTAL	11	11	6	6

*An electronic version of this chapter is available on **StudentWorks™**. This backpack solution CD-ROM allows students instant access to the Student Edition, lesson worksheet pages, and web resources.*

Chapter Resource Manager

Study Guide and Intervention	Practice (Skills and Average)	Reading to Learn Mathematics	Enrichment	Assessment	Prerequisite Skills Workbook	Applications*	Parent and Student Study Guide Workbook	5-Minute Check Transparencies	Interactive Chalkboard	AlgePASS: Tutorial Plus (lessons)	Materials
403–404	405–406	407	408			SC 13	53	7-1	7-1		(*Follow-Up:* graphing calculator)
409–410	411–412	413	414	447	27–28	SM 63–66	54	7-2	7-2	16	algebra tiles, equation mat
415–416	417–418	419	420	447, 449		GCS 36	55	7-3	7-3		
421–422	423–424	425	426	448		SC 14	56	7-4	7-4		
427–428	429–430	431	432	448		GCS 35	57	7-5	7-5	17	graphing calculator
				433–446, 450–452			58				

Key to Abbreviations: GCS = Graphing Calculator and Spreadsheet Masters,
SC = School-to-Career Masters,
SM = Science and Mathematics Lab Manual

ELL Study Guide and Intervention, Skills Practice, Practice, and Parent and Student Study Guide Workbooks are also available in Spanish.

Mathematical Connections and Background

Continuity of Instruction

Prior Knowledge

In Chapter 2, students learned that when you add additive inverses, the sum is always 0. They used the Addition, Subtraction, Multiplication, and Division Properties of Equality to solve equations throughout Chapter 3. Students graph linear equations in Chapter 5 and graph linear inequalities in Chapter 6.

This Chapter

Chapter 7 introduces students to systems of linear equations. They first solve the systems by graphing and then classify the systems as consistent or inconsistent, and as independent or dependent. Students also learn to apply the algebraic methods to solving the systems. These methods include substitution, elimination using addition or subtraction, and elimination using multiplication first. Students must determine which method is best for different systems. The chapter ends with students solving systems of inequalities by graphing.

Future Connections

Business analysts use systems of linear equations to determine where break-even points are and to analyze trends for predicting future events. There are not only systems of linear equations and inequalities, but also systems of all types of functions including quadratic, absolute value, and sine. These systems can mix any types of functions. The solutions of these systems are not only used in business, but also in science and other fields.

7-1 Graphing Systems of Equations

A solution of a system of equations is the set of points that satisfy each equation in the system. Carefully graph each equation on the same coordinate plane. There is only one solution if the graphs of the lines intersect, since the intersection is at only one point. There is no solution if the lines are parallel. The lines never intersect, so no one point is common to both graphs. If the graphs are the same line, the system has an infinite number of solutions.

If there is one solution or infinitely many solutions, the system of equations is described as consistent. Systems with one solution are said to be independent, while those with infinitely many solutions are said to be dependent. If there is no solution, the system is described as inconsistent.

7-2 Substitution

It is sometimes difficult to determine the exact solution of a system of equations from a graph. Therefore, an algebraic method may be used to find the exact solution. Substitution is an algebraic method. First solve one equation for one variable in terms of the other. Substitute the expression into the other equation so that one variable is eliminated. Solve for the remaining variable. Substitute this value into either equation and solve for the other variable. The two values make up the solution of the system. They are written in the form (x, y) to represent the point where the two lines intersect if graphed.

If a solution results in an identity, for example $2 = 2$, the system has an infinite number of solutions. If the result is a false statement, such as $5 = 3$, there is no solution. If you incur either of these situations during any part of the solution process, you may stop solving and write either infinitely many solutions or no solution.

7-3 Elimination Using Addition and Subtraction

Elimination is another algebraic method used to solve systems of equations. The objective is to combine the two equations to eliminate one of the variables. If the coefficients of one variable are additive inverses of each other, use addition. If the coefficients of one variable are the same, use subtraction. Because the Addition and Subtraction Properties of Equality state that equal amounts can be added to or subtracted from each side of an equation, you can add or subtract one equation with the other. This step eliminates one variable. Then solve for the other variable. Substitute this value into either original equation to find the value of the variable that was eliminated. The two values are the solution of the system.

7-4 Elimination Using Multiplication

If the coefficients of one variable are neither additive inverses nor equal, one or both equations must be changed so that the elimination method can be applied to solve the system of equations. Change either one, or both, of the equations by applying the Multiplication Property of Equality. Every term of the equation is multiplied by the same number, or both equations are multiplied by different numbers, in order to make one pair of coefficients of a variable either additive inverses or the same. Then follow the steps for solving the system using the elimination method.

Five methods for solving systems of equations have been seen in this chapter. They are graphing, substitution, elimination using addition, elimination using subtraction, and elimination using multiplication. Graphing is used only if an estimation is needed, since it is difficult to get an exact solution. Use substitution if one of the variables has a coefficient of 1 or -1. Elimination using addition is used when one of the variables has coefficients that are additive inverses of each other, and elimination using subtraction is best used when one of the variables has the same coefficient. Apply elimination using multiplication if none of the above situations occur.

7-5 Graphing Systems of Inequalities

A solution of a system of inequalities is all the points that satisfy both inequalities. Use the methods learned in Lesson 6-6 to graph each inequality. The points that are solutions of both inequalities lie in the region where the graphs overlap, or intersect. A system of inequalities has no solution if the boundary lines are parallel and the shaded regions do not overlap. Otherwise, there are infinitely many solutions since the overlapping shaded region extends on indefinitely.

Quick Review Math Handbook

Hot Words includes a glossary of terms while Hot Topics consists of explanations of key mathematical concepts with exercises to test comprehension. This valuable resource can be used as a reference in the classroom or for home study.

Lesson	Hot Topics Section	Lesson	Hot Topics Section
GS7	6.2, 6.3, 6.7, 6.8	7-2	6.2
7-1P	9.4	7-3	6.2
7-1	6.4	7-4	6.6

GS = Getting Started, P = Preview

 Additional mathematical information and teaching notes are available at www.algebra1.com/key_concepts.

DAILY INTERVENTION and Assessment

Key to Abbreviations:
TWE = Teacher Wraparound Edition; CRM = Chapter Resource Masters

Type	Student Edition	Teacher Resources	Technology/Internet
INTERVENTION Ongoing	Prerequisite Skills, pp. 367, 374, 381, 386, 392 Practice Quiz 1, p. 381 Practice Quiz 2, p. 392	5-Minute Check Transparencies *Prerequisite Skills Workbook,* pp. 27–28 Quizzes, *CRM* pp. 447–448 Mid-Chapter Test, *CRM* p. 449 Study Guide and Intervention, *CRM* pp. 403–404, 409–410, 415–416, 421–422, 427–428	AlgePASS: Tutorial Plus, Lessons 16 and 17 www.algebra1.com/self_check_quiz www.algebra1.com/extra_examples
Mixed Review	pp. 374, 381, 386, 392, 398	Cumulative Review, *CRM* p. 450	
Error Analysis	Find the Error, pp. 384, 396	Find the Error, *TWE* pp. 384, 396 Unlocking Misconceptions, *TWE* p. 372 Tips for New Teachers, *TWE* pp. 367, 384	
Standardized Test Practice	pp. 374, 381, 384, 385, 386, 392, 398, 403, 404–405	*TWE* pp. 404–405 Standardized Test Practice, *CRM* pp. 451–452	Standardized Test Practice CD-ROM www.algebra1.com/ standardized_test
ASSESSMENT Open-Ended Assessment	Writing in Math, pp. 374, 381, 386, 392, 398 Open Ended, pp. 371, 379, 384, 390, 396 Standardized Test, p. 405	Modeling: *TWE* pp. 374 Speaking: *TWE* pp. 381, 392 Writing: *TWE* pp. 386, 398 Open-Ended Assessment, *CRM* p. 445	
Chapter Assessment	Study Guide, pp. 399–402 Practice Test, p. 403	Multiple-Choice Tests (Forms 1, 2A, 2B), *CRM* pp. 433–438 Free-Response Tests (Forms 2C, 2D, 3), *CRM* pp. 439–444 Vocabulary Test/Review, *CRM* p. 446	ExamView® Pro (see below) MindJogger Videoquizzes www.algebra1.com/ vocabulary_review www.algebra1.com/chapter_test

Yearly ProgressPro

For more information on Yearly ProgressPro, see p. 188.

Algebra Lesson	Yearly ProgressPro Skill Lesson(s)
7-1	Graphing Systems of Equations
7-2	Substitution Solving a System of Equations
7-3	Elimination Solving a System of Equations
7-4	Elimination Solving a System of Equations
7-5	Graphing Systems of Inequalities

ExamView® Pro

Use the networkable **ExamView® Pro** to:
- Create **multiple versions** of tests.
- Create **modified** tests for *Inclusion* students.
- **Edit** existing questions and **add** your own questions.
- Use built-in **state curriculum correlations** to create tests aligned with state standards.
- Change **English** tests to **Spanish** and vice versa.

For more information on Intervention and Assessment, see pp. T8–T11.

Reading and Writing in Mathematics

Glencoe Algebra 1 provides numerous opportunities to incorporate reading and writing into the mathematics classroom.

Student Edition

- Foldables Study Organizer, p. 367
- Concept Check questions require students to verbalize and write about what they have learned in the lesson. (pp. 371, 379, 384, 390, 396)
- Reading Mathematics, p. 393
- Writing in Math questions in every lesson, pp. 374, 381, 386, 392, 398
- WebQuest, pp. 373, 398

Teacher Wraparound Edition

- Foldables Study Organizer, pp. 367, 399
- Study Notebook suggestions, pp. 372, 379, 384, 390, 393, 396
- Modeling activities, p. 374
- Speaking activities, pp. 381, 392
- Writing activities, pp. 386, 398
- Differentiated Instruction, (Verbal/Linguistic), p. 389
- **ELL** Resources, pp. 366, 373, 380, 385, 389, 391, 393, 397, 399

Additional Resources

- Vocabulary Builder worksheets require students to define and give examples for key vocabulary terms as they progress through the chapter. (*Chapter 7 Resource Masters*, pp. vii-viii)
- Reading to Learn Mathematics master for each lesson (*Chapter 7 Resource Masters*, pp. 407, 413, 419, 425, 431)
- *Vocabulary PuzzleMaker* software creates crossword, jumble, and word search puzzles using vocabulary lists that you can customize.
- *Teaching Mathematics with Foldables* provides suggestions for promoting cognition and language.
- *Reading and Writing in the Mathematics Classroom*
- *WebQuest and Project Resources*

For more information on Reading and Writing in Mathematics, see pp. T6–T7.

 **ENGLISH LANGUAGE LEARNERS**

Lesson 7-1
Higher-Level Thinking

Show students examples of systems of equations with 0, 1, and infinitely many solutions and their corresponding graphs. After showing students several examples, ask them to write a conjecture on the number of solutions possible for each type of graph. Lead a discussion on the similarities and differences of each type of system.

Lesson 7-4
Using Authentic Assessment

Make a poster to display the three ways (graphing, substitution, and elimination) to solve a system of linear equations. Ask students to study the three methods and examples of each and ask a series of questions: What are the similarities among the three methods? What do they have in common? Which method do you think is easiest? Which method would you use to solve $x - 2y = 0$ and $2x + 10y = 27$? Explain.

Lesson 7-5
Building on Prior Knowledge

Using information learned from Lessons 6-6 and 7-1, ask students how they would solve a system of equations. Then relate this method to how they would solve a system of inequalities. Ask them how they would represent their answers. Show examples of how solutions to systems of inequalities would have to be shown on a graph. Ask students what the intersection of the two graphs represents. Depending on the inequality, the intersection of the two lines may or may not be part of the solution.

Solving Systems of Linear Equations and Inequalities

Have students read over the list of objectives and make a list of any words with which they are not familiar.

Point out to students that this is only one of many reasons why each objective is important. Others are provided in the introduction to each lesson.

What You'll Learn

- **Lesson 7-1**   Solve systems of linear equations by graphing.
- **Lessons 7-2 through 7-4**   Solve systems of linear equations algebraically.
- **Lesson 7-5**   Solve systems of linear inequalities by graphing.

Key Vocabulary
- system of equations (p. 369)
- substitution (p. 376)
- elimination (p. 382)
- system of inequalities (p. 394)

Why It's Important

Business decision makers often use systems of linear equations to model a real-world situation in order to predict future events. Being able to make an accurate prediction helps them plan and manage their businesses.

Trends in the travel industry change with time. For example, in recent years, the number of tourists traveling to South America, the Caribbean, and the Middle East is on the rise. *You will use a system of linear equations to model the trends in tourism in Lesson 7-2.*

Lesson	NCTM Standards	Local Objectives
7-1 Preview	1, 2, 6, 9, 10	
7-1	2, 6, 8, 9, 10	
7-1 Follow-Up	2, 6	
7-2	2, 6, 8, 9, 10	
7-3	2, 6, 8, 9, 10	
7-4	2, 6, 8, 9, 10	
7-5	2, 6, 8, 9, 10	

Key to NCTM Standards:

1=Number & Operations, 2=Algebra, 3=Geometry, 4=Measurement, 5=Data Analysis & Probability, 6=Problem Solving, 7=Reasoning & Proof, 8=Communication, 9=Connections, 10=Representation

Vocabulary Builder   **ELL**

The Key Vocabulary list introduces students to some of the main vocabulary terms included in this chapter. For a more thorough vocabulary list with pronunciations of new words, give students the Vocabulary Builder worksheets found on pages vii and viii of the *Chapter 7 Resource Masters*. Encourage them to complete the definition of each term as they progress through the chapter. You may suggest that they add these sheets to their study notebooks for future reference when studying for the Chapter 7 test.

Getting Started

Getting Started

▶ **Prerequisite Skills** To be successful in this chapter, you'll need to master these skills and be able to apply them in problem-solving situations. Review these skills before beginning Chapter 7.

For Lesson 7-1   Graph Linear Equations

Graph each equation. *(For review, see Lesson 4-5.)* **1–6. See pp. 405A–405D.**

1. $y = 1$
2. $y = -2x$
3. $y = 4 - x$
4. $y = 2x + 3$
5. $y = 5 - 2x$
6. $y = \frac{1}{2}x + 2$

For Lesson 7-2   Solve for a Given Variable

Solve each equation or formula for the variable specified. *(For review, see Lesson 3-8.)*

7. $4x + a = 6x$, for x $x = \dfrac{a}{2}$
8. $8a + y = 16$, for a $a = \dfrac{16 - y}{8}$
9. $\dfrac{7bc - d}{10} = 12$, for b $b = \dfrac{120 + d}{7c}$
10. $\dfrac{7m + n}{q} = 2m$, for q $q = \dfrac{7m + n}{2m}$

For Lessons 7-3 and 7-4   Simplify Expressions

Simplify each expression. If not possible, write *simplified*. *(For review, see Lesson 1-5.)*

11. $(3x + y) - (2x + y)$ **x**
12. $(7x - 2y) - (7x + 4y)$ **$-6y$**
13. $(16x - 3y) + (11x + 3y)$ **$27x$**
14. $(8x - 4y) + (-8x + 5y)$ **y**
15. $4(2x + 3y) - (8x - y)$ **$13y$**
16. $3(x - 4y) + (x + 12y)$ **$4x$**
17. $2(x - 2y) + (3x + 4y)$ **$5x$**
18. $5(2x - y) - 2(5x + 3y)$ **$-11y$**
19. $3(x + 4y) + 2(2x - 6y)$ **$7x$**

FOLDABLES™
Study Organizer

Solving Systems of Equations and Inequalities Make this Foldable to help you organize your notes. Begin with five sheets of grid paper.

Step 1 **Fold**

Fold each sheet in half along the width.

Step 2 **Cut**

Unfold and cut four rows from the left side of each sheet, from the top to the crease.

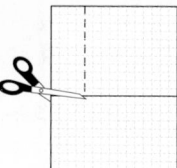

Step 3 **Stack and Staple**

Stack the sheets and staple to form a booklet.

Step 4 **Label**

Label each page with a lesson number and title.

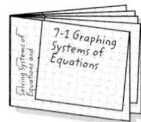

Reading and Writing As you read and study the chapter, unfold each page and fill the journal with notes, graphs, and examples for systems of equations and inequalities.

Getting Started

This section provides a review of the basic concepts needed before beginning Chapter 7. Page references are included for additional student help.

Additional review is provided in the *Prerequisite Skills Workbook*, pp. 27–28.

Prerequisite Skills in the Getting Ready for the Next Lesson section at the end of each exercise set review a skill needed in the next lesson.

For Lesson	Prerequisite Skill
7-2	Solving Equations for a Specified Value, p. 374
7-3	Simplifying Expressions, p. 381
7-4	Distributive Property, p. 386
7-5	Graphing Inequalities, p. 392

Tips for New Teachers In addition to reviewing graphing as in Exercises 1–6, you may want to review slope-intercept form. These are two skills essential for students' success in this chapter.

FOLDABLES™
Study Organizer

For more information about Foldables, see *Teaching Mathematics with Foldables.*

Organization of Data: Visualization Journal After students make their visualization journal, have them label the top of each front page with a lesson number. Under the tabs of their Foldable, students take notes and define terms presented in each lesson. At the end of each lesson, ask students to design a visual (graph, diagram, picture, chart) that presents the lesson information in a concise, easy-to-study format. Encourage students to clearly label their visuals.

Spreadsheet Investigation

A Preview of Lesson 7-1

Getting Started

Copying Formulas Once the spreadsheet formulas are entered for one sales amount, those formulas can be dragged to copy for all the other sales amounts. Students must take their time creating the first formulas as any errors will be duplicated to all the other cells.

Teach

- In Excel, you create a graph by using the Chart Wizard button on the standard toolbar. If using another spreadsheet software program, consult the Help feature for instructions on creating graphs (charts).

- Remind students that spreadsheet software cannot interpret an expression such as $0.1x$. Students must type the multiplication sign implied.

- Urge students not to assume that the software will apply the order of operations. Students should use parentheses to insure that operations are performed in the correct order.

- You may wish to extend the activity by discussing the pros and cons of different sales commissions. Students who can imagine themselves as salespeople can relate personally to the amounts calculated and to the process of using equations to explore pay rates.

Assess

Exercises 1–2 Students should write the correct expressions to translate the real-world scenario into an algebraic representation.

Exercise 4 Students should be able to translate between the mathematical solution and its real-world meaning.

Systems of Equations

You can use a spreadsheet to investigate when two quantities will be equal. Enter each formula into the spreadsheet and look for the row in which both formulas have the same result.

Example

Bill Winters is considering two job offers in telemarketing departments. The salary at the first job is $400 per week plus 10% commission on Mr. Winters' sales. At the second job, the salary is $375 per week plus 15% commission. For what amount of sales would the weekly salary be the same at either job?

Enter different amounts for Mr. Winters' weekly sales in column A. Then enter the formula for the salary at the first job in each cell in column B. In each cell of column C, enter the formula for the salary at the second job.

	Job Salaries		
	A	**B**	**C**
1	Sales	Salary 1	Salary 2
2	0	400	375
3	100	410	390
4	200	420	405
5	300	430	420
6	400	440	435
7	500	450	450
8	600	460	465
9	700	470	480
10	800	480	495
11	900	490	510
12	1000	500	525
13			

Sheet1

The spreadsheet shows that for sales of $500 the total weekly salary for each job is $450.

4. (500, 450); If Mr. Winters makes $500 in sales, he will make $450 for either job.
5. Sample answer: Write and graph two linear equations. Find the point where the graphs intersect.

Exercises

For Exercises 1–4, use the spreadsheet of weekly salaries above.

1. If x is the amount of Mr. Winters' weekly sales and y is his total weekly salary, write a linear equation for the salary at the first job. $y = 400 + 0.1x$

2. Write a linear equation for the salary at the second job. $y = 375 + 0.15x$

3. Which ordered pair is a solution for both of the equations you wrote for Exercises 1 and 2? **c**
   a. (100, 410)　　　b. (300, 420)　　　c. (500, 450)　　　d. (900, 510)

4. Use the graphing capability of the spreadsheet program to graph the salary data using a line graph. At what point do the two lines intersect? What is the significance of that point in the real-world situation?

5. How could you find the sales for which Mr. Winters' salary will be equal without using a spreadsheet?

368　Chapter 7 Solving Systems of Linear Equations and Inequalities

What You'll Learn

- Determine whether a system of linear equations has 0, 1, or infinitely many solutions.
- Solve systems of equations by graphing.

Vocabulary

- system of equations
- consistent
- inconsistent
- independent
- dependent

How can you use graphs to compare the sales of two products?

During the 1990s, sales of cassette singles decreased, and sales of CD singles increased. Assume that the sales of these singles were linear functions. If x represents the years since 1991 and y represents the sales in millions of dollars, the following equations represent the sales of these singles.

Cassette singles: $y = 69 - 6.9x$
CD singles: $y = 5.7 + 6.3x$

These equations are graphed at the right.

The point at which the two graphs intersect represents the time when the sales of cassette singles equaled the sales of CD singles. The ordered pair of this point is a solution of both equations.

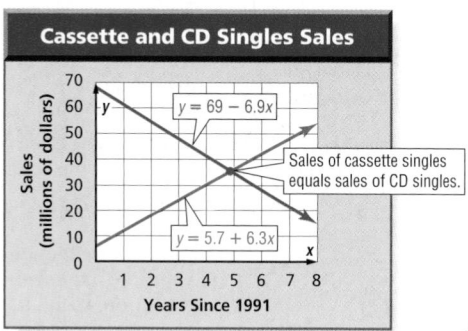

Cassette and CD Singles Sales

$y = 69 - 6.9x$

Sales of cassette singles equals sales of CD singles.

$y = 5.7 + 6.3x$

Sales (millions of dollars)

Years Since 1991

NUMBER OF SOLUTIONS Two equations, such as $y = 69 - 6.9x$ and $y = 5.7 + 6.3x$, together are called a **system of equations**. A solution of a system of equations is an ordered pair of numbers that satisfies both equations. A system of two linear equations can have 0, 1, or an infinite number of solutions.

- If the graphs intersect or coincide, the system of equations is said to be **consistent**. That is, it has at least one ordered pair that satisfies both equations.
- If the graphs are parallel, the system of equations is said to be **inconsistent**. There are *no* ordered pairs that satisfy both equations.
- Consistent equations can be **independent** or **dependent**. If a system has exactly one solution, it is independent. If the system has an infinite number of solutions, it is dependent.

Concept Summary — Systems of Equations

	Intersecting Lines	Same Line	Parallel Lines
Graph of a System			
Number of Solutions	exactly one solution	infinitely many	no solutions
Terminology	consistent and independent	consistent and dependent	inconsistent

1 Focus

5-Minute Check Transparency 7-1 Use as a quiz or review of Chapter 6.

Mathematical Background notes are available for this lesson on p. 366C.

How can you use graphs to compare the sales of two products?

Ask students:

- The graph that is sloping downward represents sales of which product? **cassette singles**
- The graph that is sloping upward represents sales of which product? **CD singles**
- In what year were the sales of cassette and CD singles equal? **1996; Note: The *x*-value of 0 represents the year 1991.**
- You are told to assume that the sales are linear functions. What does this mean? **It means that sales either increase or decrease by the same amount every year. Also, the graphs of linear functions are straight lines.**

Resource Manager

Workbook and Reproducible Masters

Chapter 7 Resource Masters
- Study Guide and Intervention, pp. 403–404
- Skills Practice, p. 405
- Practice, p. 406
- Reading to Learn Mathematics, p. 407
- Enrichment, p. 408

Parent and Student Study Guide Workbook, p. 53
School-to-Career Masters, p. 13

 Transparencies
5-Minute Check Transparency 7-1
Real-World Transparency 7
Answer Key Transparencies

 **Technology**
Interactive Chalkboard

Building on Prior Knowledge

In Chapter 4, students learned to graph linear equations. In this lesson, they should recognize that graphing systems of equations simply involves graphing more than one linear equation on the same coordinate grid.

NUMBER OF SOLUTIONS

In-Class Example   **Power Point®**

Reading Tip Tell students to pay close attention to the labels on the graph. If any lines are labeled with more than one equation, then the two equations will have infinitely many solutions.

 Use the graph to determine whether each system has *no* solution, *one* solution, or *infinitely many* solutions.

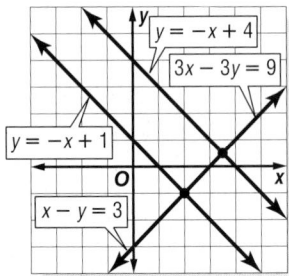

a. $y = -x + 1$
$y = -x + 4$

The graphs are parallel, so there are no solutions.

b. $3x - 3y = 9$
$y = -x + 1$

The graphs are intersecting lines, so there is one solution.

c. $x - y = 3$
$3x - 3y = 9$

The graphs coincide, so there are infinitely many solutions.

Example 1 *Number of Solutions*

Use the graph at the right to determine whether each system has *no* solution, *one* solution, or *infinitely many* solutions.

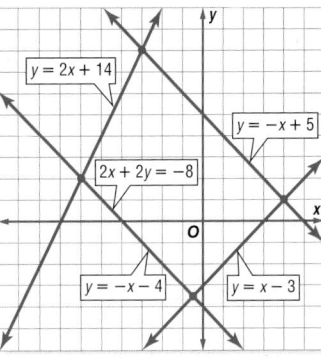

a. $y = -x + 5$
$y = x - 3$

Since the graphs of $y = -x + 5$ and $y = x - 3$ are intersecting lines, there is one solution.

b. $y = -x + 5$
$2x + 2y = -8$

Since the graphs of $y = -x + 5$ and $2x + 2y = -8$ are parallel, there are no solutions.

c. $2x + 2y = -8$
$y = -x - 4$

Since the graphs of $2x + 2y = -8$ and $y = -x - 4$ coincide, there are infinitely many solutions.

SOLVE BY GRAPHING One method of solving systems of equations is to carefully graph the equations on the same coordinate plane.

Example 2 *Solve a System of Equations*

Graph each system of equations. Then determine whether the system has *no* solution, *one* solution, or *infinitely many* solutions. If the system has one solution, name it.

a. $y = -x + 8$
$y = 4x - 7$

The graphs appear to intersect at the point with coordinates $(3, 5)$. Check this estimate by replacing x with 3 and y with 5 in each equation.

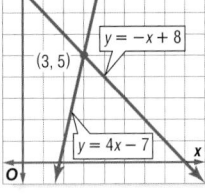

CHECK

$y = -x + 8$	$y = 4x - 7$
$5 \stackrel{?}{=} -3 + 8$	$5 \stackrel{?}{=} 4(3) - 7$
$5 = 5$ ✓	$5 \stackrel{?}{=} 12 - 7$
	$5 = 5$ ✓

The solution is $(3, 5)$.

b. $x + 2y = 5$
$2x + 4y = 2$

The graphs of the equations are parallel lines. Since they do not intersect, there are no solutions to this system of equations. Notice that the lines have the same slope but different y-intercepts. *Recall that a system of equations that has no solution is said to be inconsistent.*

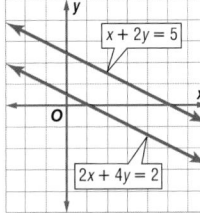

Study Tip

Look Back
To review **graphing linear equations**, see Lesson 4-5.

DAILY INTERVENTION   **Differentiated Instruction**

Logical Before students graph a system of equations, have them write the two equations in slope-intercept form and compare slopes and intercepts. Different slopes mean the lines intersect and there is one solution. Same slope, same intercept means they are the same line and there are infinite solutions. Same slope, different intercepts indicates parallel lines and no solution.

Example 3 Write and Solve a System of Equations

WORLD RECORDS Use the information on Guy Delage's swim at the left. If Guy can swim 3 miles per hour for an extended period and the raft drifts about 1 mile per hour, how many hours did he spend swimming each day?

Words You have information about the amount of time spent swimming and floating. You also know the rates and the total distance traveled.

Variables Let s = the number of hours Guy swam, and let f = the number of hours he floated each day. Write a system of equations to represent the situation.

Equations

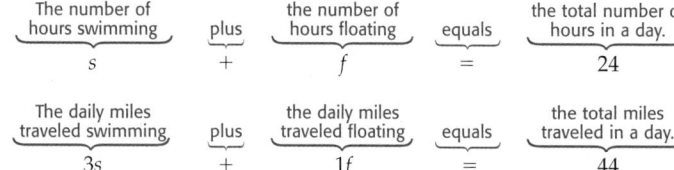

The number of hours swimming	plus	the number of hours floating	equals	the total number of hours in a day.
s	$+$	f	$=$	24

The daily miles traveled swimming	plus	the daily miles traveled floating	equals	the total miles traveled in a day.
$3s$	$+$	$1f$	$=$	44

Graph the equations $s + f = 24$ and $3s + f = 44$. The graphs appear to intersect at the point with coordinates $(10, 14)$. Check this estimate by replacing s with 10 and f with 14 in each equation.

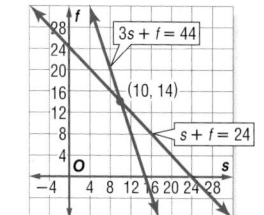

CHECK

$$s + f = 24 \qquad\qquad 3s + f = 44$$
$$10 + 14 \overset{?}{=} 24 \qquad 3(10) + 14 \overset{?}{=} 44$$
$$24 = 24 \ \checkmark \qquad\quad 30 + 14 \overset{?}{=} 44$$
$$44 = 44 \ \checkmark$$

Guy Delage spent about 10 hours swimming each day.

Check for Understanding

Concept Check

1–3. See pp. 405A–405D.

1. **OPEN ENDED** Draw the graph of a system of equations that has one solution at $(-2, 3)$.

2. **Determine** whether a system of equations with $(0, 0)$ and $(2, 2)$ as solutions *sometimes*, *always*, or *never* has other solutions. Explain.

3. **Find a counterexample** for the following statement.
   If the graphs of two linear equations have the same slope, then the system of equations has no solution.

Guided Practice

GUIDED PRACTICE KEY

Exercises	Examples
4–7	1
8–13	2
14	3

Use the graph at the right to determine whether each system has *no solution*, *one solution*, or *infinitely many* solutions.

4. $y = x - 4$
   $y = \frac{1}{3}x - 2$ **one**

5. $y = \frac{1}{3}x + 2$ **no solution**
   $y = \frac{1}{3}x - 2$

6. $x - y = 4$
   $y = x - 4$ **infinitely many**

7. $x - y = 4$
   $y = -\frac{1}{3}x + 4$ **one**

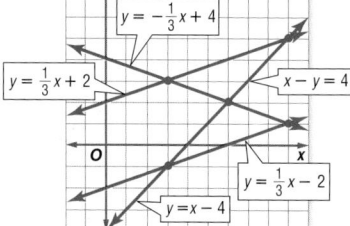

www.algebra1.com/extra_examples

Lesson 7-1 Graphing Systems of Equations 371

SOLVE BY GRAPHING

In-Class Examples

2 Graph each system of equations. Then determine whether the system has *no* solution, *one* solution, or *infinitely many* solutions. If the system has one solution, name it.

a. $2x - y = -3$ **infinitely many**
   $8x - 4y = -12$ **solutions**

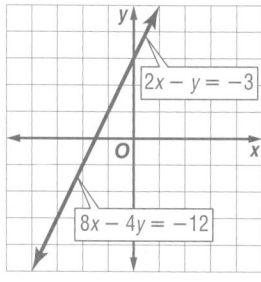

b. $x - 2y = 4$
   $x - 2y = -2$ **no solution**

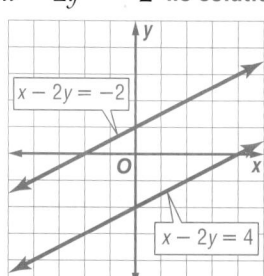

3 **BICYCLING** Tyler and Pearl went on a 20-kilometer bike ride that lasted 3 hours. Because there were many steep hills on the bike ride, they had to walk for most of the trip. Their walking speed was 4 kilometers per hour. Their riding speed was 12 kilometers per hour. How much time did they spend walking?

Let r = the number of hours they rode and w = the number of hours they walked.

$r + w = 3$
$12r + 4w = 20$

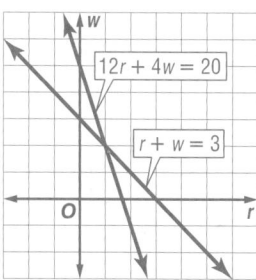

They walked for 2 hours.

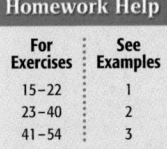
Graph each system of equations. Then determine whether the system has *no* solution, *one* solution, or *infinitely many* solutions. If the system has one solution, name it.   8–13. See pp. 405A–405D for graphs.

8. $y = -x$
   $y = 2x$ **one; (0, 0)**

9. $x + y = 8$
   $x - y = 2$ **one; (5, 3)**

10. $2x + 4y = 2$ **infinitely**
    $3x + 6y = 3$ **many**

11. $x + y = 4$
    $x + y = 1$ **no solution**

12. $x - y = 2$
    $3y + 2x = 9$ **one; (3, 1)**

13. $x + y = 2$
    $y = 4x + 7$ **one; (−1, 3)**

Application

14. **RESTAURANTS** A restaurant charges one price for adults and another price for children. The Rodriguez family has two adults and three children, and their bill was $40.50. The Wong family has three adults and one child. Their bill was $38. Determine the price of the buffet for an adult and the price for a child.
$10.50; $6.50

★ indicates increased difficulty

Practice and Apply

Homework Help

For Exercises	See Examples
15–22	1
23–40	2
41–54	3

Extra Practice
See page 835.

Use the graph at the right to determine whether each system has *no* solution, *one* solution, or *infinitely many* solutions.

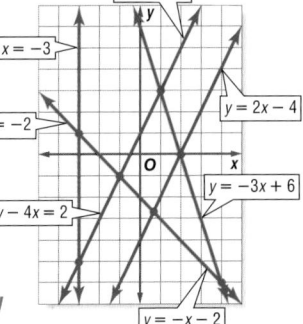

15. $x = -3$
    $y = 2x + 1$ **one**

16. $y = -x - 2$
    $y = 2x - 4$ **one**

17. $y + x = -2$ **inf.**
    $y = -x - 2$ **many**

18. $y = 2x + 1$
    $y = 2x - 4$ **no solution**

19. $y = -3x + 6$
    $y = 2x - 4$ **one**

20. $2y - 4x = 2$
    $y = 2x - 4$ **no solution**

21. $2y - 4x = 2$
    $y = -3x + 6$ **one**

22. $2y - 4x = 2$
    $y = 2x + 1$ **infinitely many**

Graph each system of equations. Then determine whether the system has *no* solution, *one* solution, or *infinitely many* solutions. If the system has one solution, name it.   23–40. See pp. 405A–405D for graphs.

23. $y = -6$
    $4x + y = 2$ **one; (2, −6)**

24. $x = 2$
    $3x - y = 8$ **one; (2, −2)**

25. $y = \frac{1}{2}x$
    $2x + y = 10$ **one; (4, 2)**

26. $y = -x$
    $y = 2x - 6$ **one; (2, −2)**

27. $y = 3x - 4$
    $y = -3x - 4$ **one; (0, −4)**

28. $y = 2x + 6$
    $y = -x - 3$ **one; (−3, 0)**

29. $x - 2y = 2$
    $3x + y = 6$ **one; (2, 0)**

30. $x + y = 2$
    $2y - x = 10$ **one; (−2, 4)**

31. $3x + 2y = 12$
    $3x + 2y = 6$ **no solution**

32. $2x + 3y = 4$ **infinitely**
    $-4x - 6y = -8$ **many**

33. $2x + y = -4$
    $5x + 3y = -6$ **one; (−6, 8)**

34. $4x + 3y = 24$ **one; (3, 4)**
    $5x - 8y = -17$

35. $3x + y = 3$ **infinitely**
    $2y = -6x + 6$ **many**

36. $y = x + 3$
    $3y + x = 5$ **one; (−1, 2)**

37. $2x + 3y = -17$
    $y = x - 4$ **one; (−1, −5)**

★ 38. $y = \frac{2}{3}x - 5$
    $3y = 2x$ **no solution**

39. $6 - \frac{3}{8}y = x$ **infinitely**
    $\frac{2}{3}x + \frac{1}{4}y = 4$ **many**

40. $\frac{1}{2}x + \frac{1}{3}y = 6$
    $y = \frac{1}{2}x + 2$ **one; (8, 6)**

41. **GEOMETRY** The length of the rectangle at the right is 1 meter less than twice its width. What are the dimensions of the rectangle?
13 m by 7 m

ℓ

Perimeter = 40 m w

About the Exercises...

Organization by Objective
- **Number of Solutions:** 15–22
- **Solve by Graphing:** 23–54

Odd/Even Assignments
Exercises 15–40 are structured so that students practice the same concepts whether they are assigned odd or even problems.

Assignment Guide

Basic: 15–41 odd, 42–47, 55–68

Average: 15–41 odd, 42–47, 55–68

Advanced: 16–40 even, 48–64 (optional: 65–68)

Study Notebook

Have students—
- add the definitions/examples of the vocabulary terms to their Vocabulary Builder worksheets for Chapter 7.
- include examples of graphs that have exactly one solution, infinitely many solutions, and no solution.
- include any other item(s) that they find helpful in mastering the skills in this lesson.

DAILY INTERVENTION

Unlocking Misconceptions

Infinitely Many Solutions Though two equations may look different because variables are on different sides of the equals sign, or because all terms are multiplied by a common factor, any two equations that have the same graph are equivalent. The easiest way to tell whether two equations have the same graph, and thus infinitely many solutions, is to rewrite both equations in slope-intercept form.

GEOMETRY For Exercises 42 and 43, use the graphs of $y = 2x + 6$, $3x + 2y = 19$, and $y = 2$, which contain the sides of a triangle.

42. Find the coordinates of the vertices of the triangle. $(-2, 2), (5, 2), (1, 8)$

43. Find the area of the triangle. **21 units²**

WebQuest

You can graph a system of equations to predict when men's and women's Olympic times will be the same. Visit www.algebra1.com/ webquest to continue work on your WebQuest project.

BALLOONING For Exercises 44 and 45, use the information in the graphic at the right.

44. In how many minutes will the balloons be at the same height? **4 min**

45. How high will the balloons be at that time? **70 m**

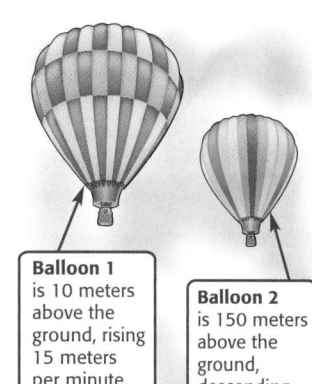

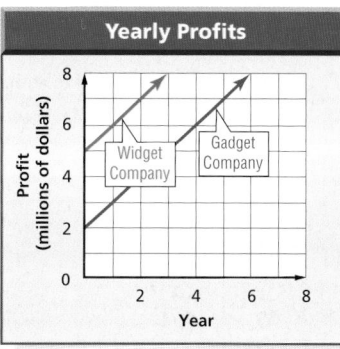

Balloon 1 is 10 meters above the ground, rising 15 meters per minute.

Balloon 2 is 150 meters above the ground, descending 20 meters per minute.

SAVINGS For Exercises 46 and 47, use the following information.
Monica and Michael Gordon both want to buy a scooter. Monica has already saved $25 and plans to save $5 per week until she can buy the scooter. Michael has $16 and plans to save $8 per week.

46. In how many weeks will Monica and Michael have saved the same amount of money? **3 weeks**

47. How much will each person have saved at that time? **$40**

BUSINESS For Exercises 48–50, use the graph at the right.

48. Which company had the greater profit during the ten years? **Widget Company**

49. Which company had a greater rate of growth? **neither**

50. If the profit patterns continue, will the profits of the two companies ever be equal? Explain. **No; the graphs are parallel so the lines will never meet and there is no year when the profits will be equal.**

Yearly Profits

Profit (millions of dollars) vs *Year*

Widget Company, Gadget Company

POPULATION For Exercises 51–54, use the following information.
The U.S. Census Bureau divides the country into four sections. They are the Northeast, the Midwest, the South, and the West.

51. $p = 60 + 0.4t$

★ **51.** In 1990, the population of the Midwest was about 60 million. During the 1990s, the population of this area increased an average of about 0.4 million per year. Write an equation to represent the population of the Midwest for the years since 1990.

52. $p = 53 + 1t$ or $p = 53 + t$

★ **52.** The population of the West was about 53 million in 1990. The population of this area increased an average of about 1 million per year during the 1990s. Write an equation to represent the population of the West for the years since 1990.

★ **53.** Graph the population equations. **See pp. 405A–405D.**

★ **54.** Assume that the rate of growth of each of these areas remains the same. Estimate when the population of the West would be equal to the population of the Midwest. **in about 11.7 years or sometime in 2001**

55. CRITICAL THINKING The solution of the system of equations $Ax + y = 5$ and $Ax + By = 20$ is $(2, -3)$. What are the values of A and B? $A = 4, B = -4$

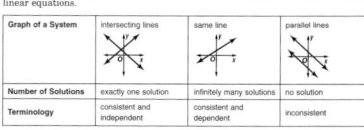
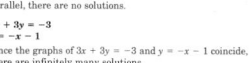

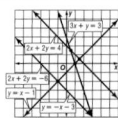
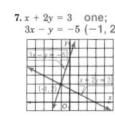

Open-Ended Assessment

Modeling Model a line on a coordinate plane with string, spaghetti, or a similar item. Then ask volunteers to come up and model another line that would represent a system of equations with one solution. Do the same for systems of equations with no solutions and with infinitely many solutions.

Getting Ready for Lesson 7-2

PREREQUISITE SKILL Students will learn to solve systems of equations by substitution in Lesson 7-2. The process of substitution involves solving equations for a specific variable. Use Exercises 65–68 to determine your students' familiarity with solving equations for a specific variable.

Answer

56. Graphs can show when the sales of one item is greater than the sales of the other item and when the sales of the items are equal. Answers should include the following.
 • The sales of cassette singles equaled the sales of CD singles in about 5 years or by the end of 1995.
 • The graph of each equation contains all of the points whose coordinates satisfy the equation. If a point is contained in both lines, then its coordinates satisfy both equations.

---

56. **WRITING IN MATH** Answer the question that was posed at the beginning of the lesson. **See margin.**

 How can you use graphs to compare the sales of two products?

 Include the following in your answer:
 • an estimate of the year in which the sales of cassette singles equaled the sales of CD singles, and
 • an explanation of why graphing works.

Standardized Test Practice
Ⓐ Ⓑ Ⓒ Ⓓ

57. Which graph represents a system of equations with no solution? **B**

Ⓐ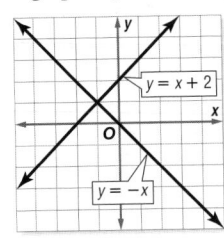

Ⓑ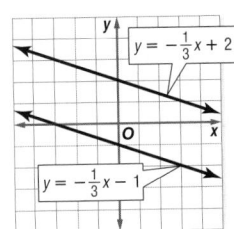

Ⓒ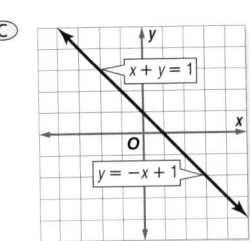

Ⓓ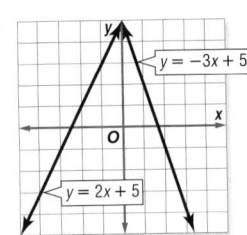

58. How many solutions exist for the system of equations below? **B**

$$4x + y = 7$$
$$3x - y = 0$$

 Ⓐ no solution   Ⓑ one solution
 Ⓒ infinitely many solutions   Ⓓ cannot be determined

Maintain Your Skills

Mixed Review Determine which ordered pairs are part of the solution set for each inequality. *(Lesson 6-6)*

59. $y \le 2x$, {(1, 4), (−1, 5), (5, −6), (−7, 0)} {(5, −6)}

60. $y < 8 − 3x$, {(−4, 2), (−3, 0), (1, 4), (1, 8)} {(−4, 2), (−3, 0), (1, 4)}

61. **MANUFACTURING** The inspector at a perfume manufacturer accepts a bottle if it is less than 0.05 ounce above or below 2 ounces. What are the acceptable numbers of ounces for a perfume bottle? *(Lesson 6-5)* {$n \mid 1.95 < n < 2.05$}

Write each equation in standard form. *(Lesson 5-5)*

62. $y − 1 = 4(x − 5)$
  $4x − y = 19$

63. $y + 2 = \frac{1}{3}(x + 3)$
  $x − 3y = 3$

64. $y − 4 = −6(x + 2)$
  $6x + y = −8$

Getting Ready for the Next Lesson **PREREQUISITE SKILL** Solve each equation for the variable specified. *(To review solving equations for a specified variable, see Lesson 3-8.)*

65. $12x − y = 10x$, for y $y = 2x$

66. $6a + b = 2a$, for a $a = -\frac{1}{4}b$

67. $\frac{7m − n}{q} = 10$, for q $q = \frac{7m − n}{10}$

68. $\frac{5tz − s}{2} = 6$, for z $z = \frac{12 + s}{5t}$

Graphing Calculator Investigation

A Follow-Up of Lesson 7-1

Systems of Equations

You can use a TI-83 Plus graphing calculator to solve a system of equations.

Example

Solve the system of equations. State the decimal solution to the nearest hundredth.

$2.93x + y = 6.08$
$8.32x - y = 4.11$

Step 1 Solve each equation for y to enter them into the calculator.

$2.93x + y = 6.08$	First equation
$2.93x + y - 2.93x = 6.08 - 2.93x$	Subtract 2.93x from each side.
$y = 6.08 - 2.93x$	Simplify.

$8.32x - y = 4.11$	Second equation
$8.32x - y - 8.32x = 4.11 - 8.32x$	Subtract 8.32x from each side.
$-y = 4.11 - 8.32x$	Simplify.
$(-1)(-y) = (-1)(4.11 - 8.32x)$	Multiply each side by −1.
$y = -4.11 + 8.32x$	Simplify.

Step 2 Enter these equations in the **Y=** list and graph.

KEYSTROKES: *Review on pages 224–225.*

Step 3 Use the **CALC** menu to find the point of intersection.

KEYSTROKES: [2nd] [CALC] 5 [ENTER] [ENTER] [ENTER]

The solution is approximately (0.91, 3.43).

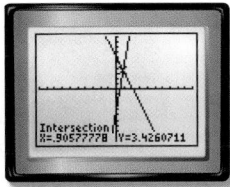

[10, 10] scl: 1 by [−10, 10] scl: 1

Exercises

Use a graphing calculator to solve each system of equations. Write decimal solutions to the nearest hundredth.

1. $y = 3x - 4$
$y = -0.5x + 6$ **(2.86, 4.57)**

2. $y = 2x + 5$
$y = -0.2x - 4$ **(−4.09, −3.18)**

3. $x + y = 5.35$
$3x - y = 3.75$ **(2.28, 3.08)**

4. $0.35x - y = 1.12$
$2.25x + y = -4.05$ **(−1.13, −1.51)**

5. $1.5x + y = 6.7$
$5.2x - y = 4.1$ **(1.61, 4.28)**

6. $5.4x - y = 1.8$
$6.2x + y = -3.8$ **(−0.17, −2.73)**

7. $5x - 4y = 26$
$4x + 2y = 53.3$ **(10.2, 6.25)**

8. $2x + 3y = 11$
$4x + y = -6$ **(−2.9, 5.6)**

9. $0.22x + 0.15y = 0.30$
$-0.33x + y = 6.22$ **(−2.35, 5.44)**

10. $125x - 200y = 800$
$65x - 20y = 140$ **(1.14, −3.29)**

www.algebra1.com/other_calculator_keystrokes

Graphing Calculator Investigation 375

Getting Started

Entering Equations The equations must be solved for y before they are entered in the calculator.

Teach

- **Step 2** Remind students to clear all previous equations from the **Y=** list first.

  Have students graph each system using the standard viewing window. If the intersection is not visible, have students adjust the window to an area suggested by the directions of the lines.

- **Step 3** The **GUESS** feature that appears after the second [ENTER] gives students an opportunity to use the arrow keys to estimate the solution and then check their estimate by pressing [ENTER] the third time.

Assess

Ask students how they can verify that their solution is correct. They should respond that substitution of values into the original equations will confirm solutions.

1 Focus

5-Minute Check Transparency 7-2 Use as a quiz or review of Lesson 7-1.

Mathematical Background notes are available for this lesson on p. 366C.

How can a system of equations be used to predict media use?

Ask students:

- Which is changing at a greater rate: the number of newspaper readers, or the number of people online? **the number of people online**

- According to the graph, in about what year will the number of hours online per person equal time spent reading newspapers? **in about 2003**

- If the two equations weren't labeled, how would you know which was which? **The one with negative slope represents newspaper readers because the time spent reading newspapers is declining.**

4. On an equation mat, use algebra tiles to model $4x + 3y = 10$ using 1 positive x tile and 1 positive 1 tile to represent each y. Use what you know about equation mats to solve for x. Use the value of x and $y = x + 1$ to solve for y. The solution is $(1, 2)$.

7-2 Substitution

How

- Solve systems of equations by using substitution.
- Solve real-world problems involving systems of equations.

Vocabulary
- substitution

How can a system of equations be used to predict media use?

Americans spend more time online than they spend reading daily newspapers. If x represents the number of years since 1993 and y represents the average number of hours per person per year, the following system represents the situation.

reading daily newspapers: $\quad y = -2.8x + 170$
online: $\qquad\qquad\qquad\quad y = 14.4x + 2$

The solution of the system represents the year that the number of hours spent on each activity will be the same. To solve this system, you could graph the equations and find the point of intersection. However, the exact coordinates of the point would be very difficult to determine from the graph. You could find a more accurate solution by using algebraic methods.

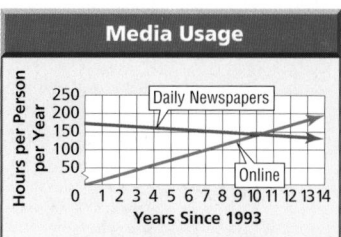

SUBSTITUTION The exact solution of a system of equations can be found by using algebraic methods. One such method is called **substitution**.

Algebra Activity

Using Substitution

Use algebra tiles and an equation mat to solve the system of equations.
$3x + y = 8$ and $y = x - 4$

Model and Analyze

Since $y = x - 4$, use 1 positive x tile and 4 negative 1 tiles to represent y. Use algebra tiles to represent $3x + y = 8$.

1. Use what you know about equation mats to solve for x. What is the value of x? **3**
2. Use $y = x - 4$ to solve for y. **−1**
3. What is the solution of the system of equations? $(3, -1)$

Make a Conjecture

4. Explain how to solve the following system of equations using algebra tiles.
   $4x + 3y = 10$ and $y = x + 1$ **You substitute a representation of y for y.**
5. Why do you think this method is called substitution?

Resource Manager

📁 Workbook and Reproducible Masters

Chapter 7 Resource Masters
- Study Guide and Intervention, pp. 409–410
- Skills Practice, p. 411
- Practice, p. 412
- Reading to Learn Mathematics, p. 413
- Enrichment, p. 414
- Assessment, p. 447

Parent and Student Study Guide Workbook, p. 54
Prerequisite Skills Workbook, pp. 27–28
Science and Mathematics Lab Manual, pp. 63–66
Teaching Algebra With Manipulatives Masters, pp. 10–11, 16, 125

📇 Transparencies
5-Minute Check Transparency 7-2
Answer Key Transparencies

💿 Technology
AlgePASS: Tutorial Plus, Lesson 16
Interactive Chalkboard

Example 1 Solve Using Substitution

Use substitution to solve the system of equations.

$y = 3x$
$x + 2y = -21$

Since $y = 3x$, substitute $3x$ for y in the second equation.

$x + 2y = -21$	Second equation
$x + 2(3x) = -21$	$y = 3x$
$x + 6x = -21$	Simplify.
$7x = -21$	Combine like terms.
$\dfrac{7x}{7} = \dfrac{-21}{7}$	Divide each side by 7.
$x = -3$	Simplify.

Use $y = 3x$ to find the value of y.

$y = 3x$	First equation
$y = 3(-3)$	$x = -3$
$y = -9$	The solution is $(-3, -9)$.

Study Tip

Look Back
To review **solving linear equations**, see Lesson 3-5.

Example 2 Solve for One Variable, Then Substitute

Use substitution to solve the system of equations.

$x + 5y = -3$
$3x - 2y = 8$

Solve the first equation for x since the coefficient of x is 1.

$x + 5y = -3$	First equation
$x + 5y - 5y = -3 - 5y$	Subtract 5y from each side.
$x = -3 - 5y$	Simplify.

Find the value of y by substituting $-3 - 5y$ for x in the second equation.

$3x - 2y = 8$	Second equation
$3(-3 - 5y) - 2y = 8$	$x = -3 - 5y$
$-9 - 15y - 2y = 8$	Distributive Property
$-9 - 17y = 8$	Combine like terms.
$-9 - 17y + 9 = 8 + 9$	Add 9 to each side.
$-17y = 17$	Simplify.
$\dfrac{-17y}{-17} = \dfrac{17}{-17}$	Divide each side by -17.
$y = -1$	Simplify.

Substitute -1 for y in either equation to find the value of x.
Choose the equation that is easier to solve.

$x + 5y = -3$	First equation
$x + 5(-1) = -3$	$y = -1$
$x - 5 = -3$	Simplify.
$x = 2$	Add 5 to each side.

The solution is $(2, -1)$. The graph verifies the solution.

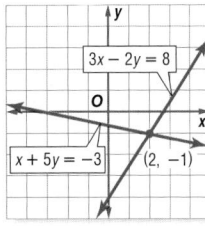

SUBSTITUTION

In-Class Examples   Power Point®

Teaching Tip Explain that the purpose of the substitution method is that once you find one of the values (either x or y), you can then substitute it into either of the original equations to find the other value. In Example 1, the value of y is given in terms of x because $y = 3x$. So, substitute $3x$ for y in the second equation and solve.

1 Use substitution to solve the system of equations.
$x = 4y$
$4x - y = 75$ **(20, 5)**

Teaching Tip You must solve for one variable first because neither equation gives one variable in terms of the other as in Example 1. The easiest choice in Example 2 is to solve the first equation for x by subtracting $5y$ from both sides.

2 Use substitution to solve the system of equations.
$4x + y = 12$
$-2x - 3y = 14$ **(5, -8)**

www.algebra1.com/extra_examples

Algebra Activity

Materials: algebra tiles, equation mat

- Remind students that anything they add to one side of the equation mat must also be added to the other side of the mat.
- Remind students that the purpose is to eliminate zero pairs.
- Once a value is found for x, have students use that value to find y.

In-Class Example

Teaching Tip If there are infinitely many solutions, then the two equations represent the same line. If you solve both equations for y, then you will see this is true. If there are no solutions, then the equations represent two parallel lines. If you solve both equations for y, the equations will have the same slope but a different y-intercept.

3 Use substitution to solve the system of equations.

$2x + 2y = 8$
$x + y = -2$

no solution

REAL-WORLD PROBLEMS

In-Class Example

4 **GOLD** Gold is alloyed with different metals to make it hard enough to be used in jewelry. The amount of gold present in a gold alloy is measured in 24ths called karats. 24-karat gold is $\frac{24}{24}$ or 100% gold. Similarly, 18-karat gold is $\frac{18}{24}$ or 75% gold. How many ounces of 18-karat gold should be added to an amount of 12-karat gold to make 4 ounces of 14-karat gold?

$1\frac{1}{3}$ ounces of 18-karat gold and

$2\frac{2}{3}$ ounces of 12-karat gold

378 Chapter 7 Solving Systems of Linear Equations and Inequalities

---

Study Tip

Alternative Method
Using a system of equations is an alternative method for solving the weighted average problems that you studied in Lesson 3-9.

Example 3 *Dependent System*

Use substitution to solve the system of equations.

$6x - 2y = -4$
$y = 3x + 2$

Since $y = 3x + 2$, substitute $3x + 2$ for y in the first equation.

$\quad 6x - 2y = -4$ First equation

$6x - 2(3x + 2) = -4$ $y = 3x + 2$

$\quad 6x - 6x - 4 = -4$ Distributive Property

$\quad\quad\quad\quad -4 = -4$ Simplify.

The statement $-4 = -4$ is true. This means that there are infinitely many solutions of the system of equations. This is true because the slope-intercept form of both equations is $y = 3x + 2$. That is, the equations are equivalent, and they have the same graph.

In general, if you solve a system of linear equations and the result is a true statement (an identity such as $-4 = -4$), the system has an infinite number of solutions. However, if the result is a false statement (for example, $-4 = 5$), the system has no solution.

REAL-WORLD PROBLEMS   Sometimes it is helpful to organize data before solving a problem. Some ways to organize data are to use tables, charts, different types of graphs, or diagrams.

Example 4 *Write and Solve a System of Equations*

METAL ALLOYS A metal alloy is 25% copper. Another metal alloy is 50% copper. How much of each alloy should be used to make 1000 grams of a metal alloy that is 45% copper?

Let a = the number of grams of the 25% copper alloy and b = the number of grams of the 50% copper alloy. Use a table to organize the information.

	25% Copper	50% Copper	45% Copper
Total Grams	a	b	1000
Grams of Copper	$0.25a$	$0.50b$	$0.45(1000)$

The system of equations is $a + b = 1000$ and $0.25a + 0.50b = 0.45(1000)$. Use substitution to solve this system.

$\quad a + b = 1000$ First equation

$a + b - b = 1000 - b$ Subtract b from each side.

$\quad\quad a = 1000 - b$ Simplify.

$\quad\quad 0.25a + 0.50b = 0.45(1000)$ Second equation

$0.25(1000 - b) + 0.50b = 0.45(1000)$ $a = 1000 - b$

$\quad 250 - 0.25b + 0.50b = 450$ Distributive Property

$\quad\quad\quad 250 + 0.25b = 450$ Combine like terms.

$\quad 250 + 0.25b - 250 = 450 - 250$ Subtract 250 from each side.

$\quad\quad\quad\quad 0.25b = 200$ Simplify.

$\quad\quad\quad\quad \dfrac{0.25b}{0.25} = \dfrac{200}{0.25}$ Divide each side by 0.25.

$\quad\quad\quad\quad\quad b = 800$ Simplify.

DAILY
INTERVENTION

Differentiated Instruction

Intrapersonal If students have difficulty solving systems of equations by using substitution, ask them to indicate where they get confused in the process before doing another example. Encourage students to think through each step.

$$a + b = 1000 \qquad \text{First equation}$$
$$a + 800 = 1000 \qquad b = 800$$
$$a + 800 - 800 = 1000 - 800 \qquad \text{Subtract 800 from each side.}$$
$$a = 200 \qquad \text{Simplify.}$$

200 grams of the 25% alloy and 800 grams of the 50% alloy should be used.

3 **Practice/Apply**

Check for Understanding

Concept Check

1. **Explain** why you might choose to use substitution rather than graphing to solve a system of equations. **Substitution may result in a more accurate solution.**

2. **Describe** the graphs of two equations if solving the system of equations yields the equation $4 = 2$. **They are parallel lines.**

3. **OPEN-ENDED** Write a system of equations that has infinitely many solutions. **Sample answer:** $y = x + 3, 2y = 2x + 6$

Guided Practice

Use substitution to solve each system of equations. If the system does *not* have exactly one solution, state whether it has *no* solution or *infinitely many* solutions.

GUIDED PRACTICE KEY	
Exercises	Examples
4–9	1–3
10	4

4. $x = 2y$
   $4x + 2y = 15$ **(3, 1.5)**

5. $y = 3x - 8$
   $y = 4 - x$ **(3, 1)**

6. $2x + 7y = 3$
   $x = 1 - 4y$ **(5, −1)**

7. $6x - 2y = -4$
   $y = 3x + 2$ **infinitely many**

8. $x + 3y = 12$
   $x - y = 8$ **(9, 1)**

9. $y = \frac{3}{5}x$ **no solution**
   $3x - 5y = 15$

Application

10. **TRANSPORTATION** The Thrust SSC is the world's fastest land vehicle. Suppose the driver of a car whose top speed is 200 miles per hour requests a race against the SSC. The car gets a head start of one-half hour. If there is unlimited space to race, at what distance will the SSC pass the car? **about 135.5 mi**

Thrust SSC top speed is 763 mph.

★ indicates increased difficulty

Practice and Apply

Homework Help	
For Exercises	See Examples
11–28	1–3
29–37	4

Extra Practice
See page 835.

Use substitution to solve each system of equations. If the system does *not* have exactly one solution, state whether it has *no* solution or *infinitely many* solutions.

11. $y = 5x$
    $2x + 3y = 34$ **(2, 10)**

12. $x = 4y$
    $2x + 3y = 44$ **(16, 4)**

13. $x = 4y + 5$
    $x = 3y - 2$ **(−23, −7)**

14. $y = 2x + 3$
    $y = 4x - 1$ **(2, 7)**

15. $4c = 3d + 3$
    $c = d - 1$ **(6, 7)**

16. $4x + 5y = 11$
    $y = 3x - 13$ **(4, −1)**

17. $8x + 2y = 13$
    $4x + y = 11$ **no solution**

18. $2x - y = -4$
    $-3x + y = -9$ **(13, 30)**

19. $3x - 5y = 11$
    $x - 3y = 1$ **(7, 2)**

20. $2x + 3y = 1$
    $-3x + y = 15$ **(−4, 3)**

21. $c - 5d = 2$
    $2c + d = 4$ **(2, 0)**

22. $5r - s = 5$
    $-4r + 5s = 17$ **(2, 5)**

23. $3x - 2y = 12$
    $x + 2y = 6$ $\left(4\frac{1}{2}, \frac{3}{4}\right)$

24. $x - 3y = 0$
    $3x + y = 7$ $\left(2\frac{1}{10}, \frac{7}{10}\right)$

25. $-0.3x + y = 0.5$
    $0.5x - 0.3y = 1.9$ **(5, 2)**

26. $0.5x - 2y = 17$
    $2x + y = 104$ **(50, 4)**

27. $y = \frac{1}{2}x + 3$
    $y = 2x - 1$ $\left(2\frac{2}{3}, 4\frac{1}{3}\right)$

28. $x = \frac{1}{2}y + 3$
    $2x - y = 6$ **infinitely many**

www.algebra1.com/self_check_quiz

Study Notebook

Have students—
- add the definitions/examples of the vocabulary terms to their Vocabulary Builder worksheets for Chapter 7.
- include examples of how to solve a system of equations by using substitution.
- include any other item(s) that they find helpful in mastering the skills in this lesson.

About the Exercises...

Organization by Objective
- **Substitution:** 11–28
- **Real–World Problems:** 29–37

Odd/Even Assignments

Exercises 11–32 are structured so that students practice the same concepts whether they are assigned odd or even problems.

Alert! Exercise 38 requires the Internet or other research materials.

Assignment Guide

Basic: 11–33 odd, 34, 35, 39–53

Average: 11–33 odd, 34, 35, 37, 39–53

Advanced: 12–32 even, 36–49 (optional: 50–53)

All: Practice Quiz 1 (1–5)

29. **GEOMETRY** The base of the triangle is 4 inches longer than the length of one of the other sides. Use a system of equations to find the length of each side of the triangle. **14 in., 14 in., 18 in.**

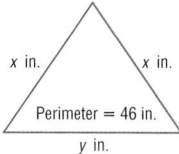

x in. x in.
Perimeter = 46 in.
y in.

30. **FUND-RAISING** The Future Teachers of America Club at Paint Branch High School is making a healthy trail mix to sell to students during lunch. The mix will have three times the number of pounds of raisins as sunflower seeds. Sunflower seeds cost $4.00 per pound, and raisins cost $1.50 per pound. If the group has $34.00 to spend on the raisins and sunflower seeds, how many pounds of each should they buy? **4 lb of sunflower seeds, 12 lb of raisins**

31. **CHEMISTRY** MX Labs needs to make 500 gallons of a 34% acid solution. The only solutions available are a 25% acid solution and a 50% acid solution. How many gallons of each solution should be mixed to make the 34% solution? **320 gal of 25% acid, 180 gal of 50% acid**

32. **GEOMETRY** Supplementary angles are two angles whose measures have the sum of 180 degrees. Angles X and Y are supplementary, and the measure of angle X is 24 degrees greater than the measure of angle Y. Find the measures of angles X and Y. **$m\angle X = 102$, $m\angle Y = 78$**

33. **SPORTS** At the end of the 2000 baseball season, the New York Yankees and the Cincinnati Reds had won a total of 31 World Series. The Yankees had won 5.2 times as many World Series as the Reds. How many World Series did each team win? **Yankees: 26, Reds: 5**

JOBS For Exercises 34 and 35, use the following information.
Shantel Jones has two job offers as a car salesperson. At one dealership, she will receive $600 per month plus a commission of 2% of the total price of the automobiles she sells. At the other dealership, she will receive $1000 per month plus a commission of 1.5% of her total sales.

34. What is the total price of the automobiles that Ms. Jones must sell each month to make the same income from either dealership? **$80,000**

35. Explain which job offer is better. **The second offer is better if she sells less than $80,000. The first offer is better if she sells more than $80,000.**

★ 36. **LANDSCAPING** A blue spruce grows an average of 6 inches per year. A hemlock grows an average of 4 inches per year. If a blue spruce is 4 feet tall and a hemlock is 6 feet tall, when would you expect the trees to be the same height? **in 12 years**

★ 37. **TOURISM** In 2000, approximately 40.3 million tourists visited South America and the Caribbean. The number of tourists to that area had been increasing at an average rate of 0.8 million tourists per year. In the same year, 17.0 million tourists visited the Middle East. The number of tourists to the Middle East had been increasing at an average rate of 1.8 million tourists per year. If the trend continues, when would you expect the number of tourists to South America and the Caribbean to equal the number of tourists to the Middle East? **during the year 2023**

38. **RESEARCH** Use the Internet or other resources to find the pricing plans for various cell phones. Determine the number of minutes you would need to use the phone for two plans to cost the same amount of money. Support your answer with a table, a graph, and/or an equation. **See students' work.**

More About . . .

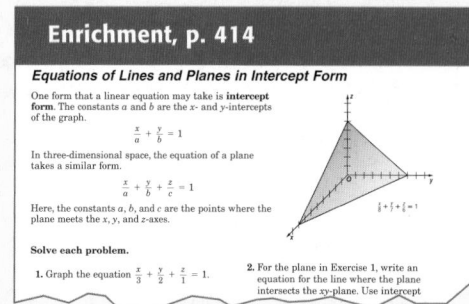

Tourism
Every year, multitudes of visitors make their way to South America to stand in awe of Machu Picchu, the spectacular ruins of the Lost City of the Incas.
Source: www.about.com

39. CRITICAL THINKING Solve the system of equations. Write the solution as an ordered triple of the form (x, y, z).

$$2x + 3y - z = 17$$
$$y = -3z - 7$$
$$2x = z + 2 \quad (-1, 5, -4)$$

40. WRITING IN MATH Answer the question that was posed at the beginning of the lesson. **See margin.**

How can a system of equations be used to predict media use?

Include the following in your answer:

- an explanation of solving a system of equations by using substitution, and
- the year when the number of hours spent reading daily newspapers is the same as the hours spent online.

Standardized Test Practice
Ⓐ Ⓑ Ⓒ Ⓓ

41. When solving the following system, which expression could be substituted for x?

$$x + 4y = 1$$
$$2x - 3y = -9 \quad \text{B}$$

    Ⓐ $4y - 1$ Ⓑ $1 - 4y$ Ⓒ $3y - 9$ Ⓓ $-9 - 3y$

42. If $x - 3y = -9$ and $5x - 2y = 7$, what is the value of x? **C**

    Ⓐ 1   Ⓑ 2   Ⓒ 3   Ⓓ 4

Maintain Your Skills

Mixed Review Graph each system of equations. Then determine whether the system has *no* solution, *one* solution, or *infinitely many* solutions. If the system has one solution, name it. *(Lesson 7-1)* **43–45. See pp. 405A–405D for graphs.**

43. $x + y = 3$
$x + y = 4$ **no solution**

44. $x + 2y = 1$
$2x + y = 5$ **one; (3, −1)**

45. $2x + y = 3$ **infinitely**
$4x + 2y = 6$ **many**

Graph each inequality. *(Lesson 6-6)* **46–48. See pp. 405A–405D.**

46. $y < -5$

47. $x \geq 4$

48. $2x + y > 6$

49. RECYCLING When a pair of blue jeans is made, the leftover denim scraps can be recycled. One pound of denim is left after making every five pair of jeans. How many pounds of denim would be left from 250 pairs of jeans? *(Lesson 3-6)* **50 lb**

Getting Ready for the Next Lesson **PREREQUISITE SKILL** Simplify each expression.
*(To review **simplifying expressions**, see Lesson 1-5.)*

50. $6a - 9a$ **$-3a$**   **51.** $8t + 4t$ **12t**   **52.** $-7g - 8g$ **$-15g$**   **53.** $7d - (2d + b)$ **$5d - b$**

Practice Quiz 1   Lessons 7-1 and 7-2

1–2. See margin for graphs.
Graph each system of equations. Then determine whether the system has *no* solution, *one* solution, or *infinitely many* solutions. If the system has one solution, name it. *(Lesson 7-1)*

1. $x + y = 3$
$x - y = 1$ **one; (2, 1)**

2. $3x - 2y = -6$
$3x - 2y = 6$ **no solution**

Use substitution to solve each system of equations. If the system does *not* have exactly one solution, state whether it has *no* solution or *infinitely many* solutions. *(Lesson 7-2)*

3. $x + y = 0$
$3x + y = -8$ **(−4, 4)**

4. $x - 2y = 5$
$3x - 5y = 8$ **(−9, −7)**

5. $x + y = 2$
$y = 2 - x$ **infinitely many**

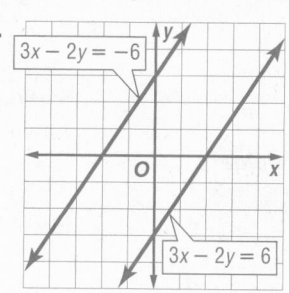

1.
$x + y = 3$
$x - y = 1$
$(2, 1)$

2.
$3x - 2y = -6$
$3x - 2y = 6$

Open-Ended Assessment

Speaking Write a system of equations on the chalkboard. Have students explain how they would check this system of equations to find out whether it has no solution, one solution, or infinitely many solutions. Then use student suggestions to solve the system.

Getting Ready for Lesson 7-3

PREREQUISITE SKILL Students will learn to solve systems of equations by elimination using addition and subtraction in Lesson 7-3. This method includes simplifying expressions. Use Exercises 50–53 to determine your students' familiarity with simplifying expressions.

Assessment Options

Practice Quiz 1 The quiz provides students with a brief review of the concepts and skills in Lessons 7-1 and 7-2. Lesson numbers are given to the right of exercises or instruction lines so students can review concepts not yet mastered.

Quiz (Lessons 7-1 and 7-2) is available on p. 447 of the *Chapter 7 Resource Masters*.

Answer

40. When problems about technology involve a system of equations, the problem can be solved by substitution. Answers should include the following.

- To solve a system of equations using substitution, solve one equation for one unknown. Substitute this value for the unknown in the other equation and solve the equation. Use this number to find the other unknown.

- The number of hours will be the same about 9.8 years after 1993. That represents the year 2002.

Elimination Using Addition and Subtraction

What You'll Learn

- Solve systems of equations by using elimination with addition.
- Solve systems of equations by using elimination with subtraction.

Vocabulary
- elimination

How can you use a system of equations to solve problems about weather?

On the winter solstice, there are fewer hours of daylight in the Northern Hemisphere than on any other day. On that day in Seward, Alaska, the difference between the number of hours of darkness n and the number of hours of daylight d is 12. The following system of equations represents the situation.

$$n + d = 24$$
$$n - d = 12$$

Notice that if you add these equations, the variable d is eliminated.

$$\begin{array}{r} n + d = 24 \\ (+)\,n - d = 12 \\ \hline 2n \quad\;\; = 36 \end{array}$$

ELIMINATION USING ADDITION Sometimes adding two equations together will eliminate one variable. Using this step to solve a system of equations is called **elimination**.

Example 1 *Elimination Using Addition*

Use elimination to solve each system of equations.

$3x - 5y = -16$
$2x + 5y = 31$

Since the coefficients of the y terms, -5 and 5, are additive inverses, you can eliminate the y terms by adding the equations.

$$\begin{array}{rl} 3x - 5y = -16 & \text{Write the equations in column form and add.} \\ (+)\,2x + 5y = 31 \\ \hline 5x = 15 & \text{Notice that the } y \text{ variable is eliminated.} \\ \dfrac{5x}{5} = \dfrac{15}{5} & \text{Divide each side by 5.} \\ x = 3 & \text{Simplify.} \end{array}$$

Now substitute 3 for x in either equation to find the value of y.

$$\begin{array}{rl} 3x - 5y = -16 & \text{First equation} \\ 3(3) - 5y = -16 & \text{Replace } x \text{ with 3.} \\ 9 - 5y = -16 & \text{Simplify.} \\ 9 - 5y - 9 = -16 - 9 & \text{Subtract 9 from each side.} \\ -5y = -25 & \text{Simplify.} \\ \dfrac{-5y}{-5} = \dfrac{-25}{-5} & \text{Divide each side by } -5. \\ y = 5 & \text{Simplify.} \end{array}$$

The solution is $(3, 5)$.

Example 2 Write and Solve a System of Equations

Twice one number added to another number is 18. Four times the first number minus the other number is 12. Find the numbers.

Let x represent the first number and y represent the second number.

Twice one number	added to	another number	is	18.
$2x$	$+$	y	$=$	18

Four times the first number	minus	the other number	is	12.
$4x$	$-$	y	$=$	12

Use elimination to solve the system.

$$
\begin{array}{rl}
2x + y = 18 \\
(+)\ 4x - y = 12 \\
\hline
6x\ \ \ \ \ = 30
\end{array}
$$
Write the equations in column form and add.

Notice that the variable y is eliminated.

$\dfrac{6x}{6} = \dfrac{30}{6}$ Divide each side by 6.

$x = 5$ Simplify.

Now substitute 5 for x in either equation to find the value of y.

$4x - y = 12$	Second equation
$4(5) - y = 12$	Replace x with 5.
$20 - y = 12$	Simplify.
$20 - y - 20 = 12 - 20$	Subtract 20 from each side.
$-y = -8$	Simplify.
$\dfrac{-y}{-1} = \dfrac{-8}{-1}$	Divide each side by -1.
$y = 8$	The numbers are 5 and 8.

ELIMINATION USING SUBTRACTION
Sometimes subtracting one equation from another will eliminate one variable.

Example 3 Elimination Using Subtraction

Use elimination to solve the system of equations.

$5s + 2t = 6$
$9s + 2t = 22$

Since the coefficients of the t terms, 2 and 2, are the same, you can eliminate the t terms by subtracting the equations.

$$
\begin{array}{rl}
5s + 2t = \ \ \ 6 \\
(-)\ 9s + 2t = \ \ 22 \\
\hline
-4s\ \ \ \ \ = -16
\end{array}
$$
Write the equations in column form and subtract.

Notice that the variable t is eliminated.

$\dfrac{-4s}{-4} = \dfrac{-16}{-4}$ Divide each side by -4.

$s = 4$ Simplify.

Now substitute 4 for s in either equation to find the value of t.

$5s + 2t = 6$	First equation
$5(4) + 2t = 6$	$s = 4$
$20 + 2t = 6$	Simplify.
$20 + 2t - 20 = 6 - 20$	Subtract 20 from each side.
$2t = -14$	Simplify.
$\dfrac{2t}{2} = \dfrac{-14}{2}$	Divide each side by 2.
$t = -7$	The solution is $(4, -7)$.

2 Teach

Building on Prior Knowledge

In Lesson 7-2 students learned to solve a system of equations by using substitution. Even though they are learning different methods for solving systems of equations in this lesson, they still must use substitution as part of those methods.

ELIMINATION USING ADDITION

In-Class Examples Power Point®

Teaching Tip Explain that, when using the elimination method, either the x or y coefficients must be the same.

1 Use elimination to solve the system of equations.
$-3x + 4y = 12$
$3x - 6y = 18$ **(−24, −15)**

2 Four times one number minus three times another number is 12. Two times the first number added to three times the second number is 6. Find the numbers. **The numbers are 3 and 0.**

✓ Concept Check

Ask students to explain why the system, $2x + y = 7$ and $7x + y = 32$, cannot be solved with elimination using addition. **Adding these two equations will not eliminate a variable.**

ELIMINATION USING SUBTRACTION

In-Class Example Power Point®

3 Use elimination to solve the system of equations.
$4x + 2y = 28$
$4x - 3y = 18$ **(6, 2)**

Intervention
Since subtraction is the same as adding the inverse, you might suggest that students change the signs of the terms and then add to eliminate the variable.

Power Point®

4 MULTIPLE CHOICE TEST ITEM If $8x + y = 16$ and $-6x + y = -26$, what is the value of y? **C**

A $(3, -8)$ **B** 3
C -8 **D** $(-8, 3)$

3 Practice/Apply

Study Notebook

Have students—
• add the definitions/examples of the vocabulary terms to their Vocabulary Builder worksheets for Chapter 7.
• include examples of how to solve a system of equations by using elimination with addition or subtraction.
• include any other item(s) that they find helpful in mastering the skills in this lesson.

DAILY
INTERVENTION **FIND THE ERROR**
Tell students to look at the original system of equations before they evaluate the students' work. Do they need to use addition or subtraction to eliminate s?

Standardized Test Practice
Ⓐ Ⓑ Ⓒ Ⓓ

Example 4 **Elimination Using Subtraction**

Multiple-Choice Test Item

If $x - 3y = 7$ and $x + 2y = 2$, what is the value of x?
Ⓐ 4 Ⓑ -1 Ⓒ $(-1, 4)$ Ⓓ $(4, -1)$

Test-Taking Tip
Always read the question carefully. Ask yourself, "What does the question ask?" Then answer that question.

Read the Test Item
You are given a system of equations, and you are asked to find the value of x.

Solve the Test Item
You can eliminate the x terms by subtracting one equation from the other.

$$\begin{array}{ll} x - 3y = 7 & \text{Write the equations in column form and subtract.} \\ (-)\ x + 2y = 2 & \\ \hline -5y = 5 & \text{Notice the } x \text{ variable is eliminated.} \end{array}$$

$$\dfrac{-5y}{-5} = \dfrac{5}{-5} \qquad \text{Divide each side by } -5.$$

$$y = -1 \qquad \text{Simplify.}$$

Now substitute -1 for y in either equation to find the value of x.

$$\begin{array}{ll} x + 2y = 2 & \text{Second equation} \\ x + 2(-1) = 2 & y = -1 \\ x - 2 = 2 & \text{Simplify.} \\ x - 2 + 2 = 2 + 2 & \text{Add 2 to each side.} \\ x = 4 & \text{Simplify.} \end{array}$$

Notice that B is the value of y and D is the solution of the system of equations. However, the question asks for the value of x. The answer is A.

Check for Understanding

Concept Check
2. a system in which one variable has the same coefficient

3. Michael; in order to eliminate the s-terms, you must add the two equations.

1. **OPEN ENDED** Write a system of equations that can be solved by using addition to eliminate one variable. **Sample answer:** $2a + b = 5$; $a - b = 4$

2. **Describe** a system of equations that can be solved by using subtraction to eliminate one variable.

3. **FIND THE ERROR** Michael and Yoomee are solving a system of equations.

Michael	Yoomee
$2r + s = 5$	$2r + s = 5$
$(+)\ r - s = 1$	$(-)r - s =$
$3r \quad = 6$	$r \quad = 4$
$r = 2$	
	$r - s = 1$
$2r + s = 5$	$4 - s = 1$
$2(2) + s = 5$	$-s = -3$
$4 + s = 5$	$s = 3$
$s = 1$	
The solution is $(2, 1)$.	The solution is $(4, 3)$.

Who is correct? Explain your reasoning.

Standardized Test Practice
Ⓐ Ⓑ Ⓒ Ⓓ

Example 4 is an example of a test item in which too much information is given in some of the answer choices. Always carefully compare the answer choices with the question before marking your final answer. By doing so, you can eliminate choices C and D because the question asks for the value of x, and choices C and D are solution sets.

Guided Practice

GUIDED PRACTICE KEY	
Exercises	Examples
4–9	1, 3
10	2
11	4

Use elimination to solve each system of equations. 9. $\left(-2\frac{1}{2}, -2\right)$

4. $x - y = 14$
   $x + y = 20$ **(17, 3)**

5. $2a - 3b = -11$
   $a + 3b = 8$ **(−1, 3)**

6. $4x + y = -9$ **(−2, −1)**
   $4x + 2y = -10$

7. $6x + 2y = -10$
   $2x + 2y = -10$ **(0, −5)**

8. $2a + 4b = 30$ **(6.5, 4.25)**
   $-2a - 2b = -21.5$

9. $-4m + 2n = 6$
   $-4m + n = 8$

10. The sum of two numbers is 24. Five times the first number minus the second number is 12. What are the two numbers? **6, 18**

Standardized Test Practice

11. If $2x + 7y = 17$ and $2x + 5y = 11$, what is the value of $2y$? **D**

   (A) −4   (B) −2   (C) 3   (D) 6

★ indicates increased difficulty

Practice and Apply

Homework Help

For Exercises	See Examples
12–29	1, 3
30–39	2
42, 43	4

Extra Practice
See page 836.

Use elimination to solve each system of equations. 26. **(1.75, 2.5)** 27. **(15.8, 3.4)**

12. $x + y = -3$
    $x - y = 1$ **(−1, −2)**

13. $s - t = 4$
    $s + t = 2$ **(3, −1)**

14. $3m - 2n = 13$
    $m + 2n = 7$ **(5, 1)**

15. $-4x + 2y = 8$
    $4x - 3y = -10$ **(−1, 2)**

16. $3a + b = 5$
    $2a + b = 10$ **(−5, 20)**

17. $2m - 5n = -6$
    $2m - 7n = -14$ **(7, 4)**

18. $3r - 5s = -35$
    $2r - 5s = -30$ **(−5, 4)**

19. $13a + 5b = -11$
    $13a + 11b = 7$ **(−2, 3)**

20. $3x - 5y = 16$
    $-3x + 2y = -10$ **(2, −2)**

21. $6s + 5t = 1$
    $6s - 5t = 11$ **(1, −1)**

22. $4x - 3y = 12$
    $4x + 3y = 24$ $\left(4\frac{1}{2}, 2\right)$

23. $a - 2b = 5$
    $3a - 2b = 9$ $\left(2, -1\frac{1}{2}\right)$

★ 24. $4x + 5y = 7$
    $8x + 5y = 9$ $\left(\frac{1}{2}, 1\right)$

25. $8a + b = 1$
    $8a - 3b = 3$ $\left(\frac{3}{16}, -\frac{1}{2}\right)$

26. $1.44x - 3.24y = -5.58$
    $1.08x + 3.24y = 9.99$

★ 27. $7.2m + 4.5n = 129.06$
    $7.2m + 6.7n = 136.54$

28. $\frac{3}{5}c - \frac{1}{5}d = 9$
    $\frac{7}{5}c + \frac{1}{5}d = 11$ **(10, −15)**

29. $\frac{2}{3}x - \frac{1}{2}y = 14$
    $\frac{5}{6}x - \frac{1}{2}y = 18$ **(24, 4)**

30. The sum of two numbers is 48, and their difference is 24. What are the numbers? **36, 12**

31. Find the two numbers whose sum is 51 and whose difference is 13. **32, 19**

32. Three times one number added to another number is 18. Twice the first number minus the other number is 12. Find the numbers. **6, 0**

33. One number added to twice another number is 23. Four times the first number added to twice the other number is 38. What are the numbers? **5, 9**

34. **BUSINESS** In 1999, the United States produced about 2 million more motor vehicles than Japan. Together, the two countries produced about 22 million motor vehicles. How many vehicles were produced in each country? **U.S.: about 12 million vehicles, Japan: about 10 million vehicles**

35. **PARKS** A youth group and their leaders visited Mammoth Cave. Two adults and 5 students in one van paid $77 for the Grand Avenue Tour of the cave. Two adults and 7 students in a second van paid $95 for the same tour. Find the adult price and the student price of the tour. **adult: $16, student: $9**

36. **FOOTBALL** During the National Football League's 1999 season, Troy Aikman, the quarterback for the Dallas Cowboys, earned $0.467 million more than Deion Sanders, the Cowboys cornerback. Together they cost the Cowboys $12.867 million. How much did each player make? **Aikman: $6.667 million, Sanders: $6.200 million**

★ 37. Let x represent the number of years since 2000 and y represent population in billions. Write an equation to represent the population of China. **$y = 0.0048x + 1.28$**

38. $y = 0.0104x + 1.01$

★ 38. Write an equation to represent the population of India.

★ 39. Use elimination to find the year when the populations of China and India are predicted to be the same. What is the predicted population at that time? **2048; 1.51 billion**

40. **CRITICAL THINKING**   The graphs of $Ax + By = 15$ and $Ax - By = 9$ intersect at $(2, 1)$. Find A and B. **$A = 6$, $B = 3$**

41. **WRITING IN MATH**   Answer the question that was posed at the beginning of the lesson. **See pp. 405A–405D.**

How can you use a system of equations to solve problems about weather?

Include the following in your answer:
- an explanation of how to use elimination to solve a system of equations, and
- a step-by-step solution of the Seward daylight problem.

Standardized Test Practice
Ⓐ Ⓑ Ⓒ Ⓓ

42. If $2x - 3y = -9$ and $3x - 3y = -12$, what is the value of y? **B**
   Ⓐ -3 Ⓑ 1 Ⓒ $(-3, 1)$ Ⓓ $(1, -3)$

43. What is the solution of $4x + 2y = 8$ and $2x + 2y = 2$? **C**
   Ⓐ $(-2, 3)$ Ⓑ $(3, 2)$ Ⓒ $(3, -2)$ Ⓓ $(12, -3)$

Maintain Your Skills

Mixed Review   Use substitution to solve each system of equations. If the system does *not* have exactly one solution, state whether it has *no* solution or *infinitely many* solutions.   *(Lesson 7-2)*

44. $y = 5x$
    $x + 2y = 22$ **(2, 10)**

45. $x = 2y + 3$
    $3x + 4y = -1$ **(1, -1)**

46. $2y - x = -5$
    $4y - 3x = -1$ **(-9, -7)**

Graph each system of equations. Then determine whether the system has *no* solution, *one* solution, or *infinitely many* solutions. If the system has one solution, name it.   *(Lesson 7-1)*   47–49. See pp. 405A–405D for graphs.   49. infinitely many

47. $x - y = 3$
    $3x + y = 1$ **one; (1, -2)**

48. $2x - 3y = 7$
    $3y = 7 + 2x$ **no solution**

49. $4x + y = 12$
    $x = 3 - \frac{1}{4}y$

50. Write an equation of a line that is parallel to the graph of $y = \frac{5}{4}x - 3$ and passes through the origin.   *(Lesson 5-6)* $y = \frac{5}{4}x$

Getting Ready for the Next Lesson   **PREREQUISITE SKILL**   Use the Distributive Property to rewrite each expression without parentheses.   *(To review the Distributive Property, see Lesson 1-5.)*

51. $2(3x + 4y)$
    $6x + 8y$

52. $6(2a - 5b)$
    $12a - 30b$

53. $-3(-2m + 3n)$
    $6m - 9n$

54. $-5(4t - 2s)$
    $-20t + 10s$

About the Exercises...
Organization by Objective
- **Elimination Using Addition:** 12–15, 20–22, 26, 28, 30–32, 34, 36
- **Elimination Using Subtraction:** 16–19, 23–25, 27, 29, 33, 35

Odd/Even Assignments
Exercises 12–35 are structured so that students practice the same concepts whether they are assigned odd or even problems.

Assignment Guide
Basic: 13–25 odd, 29–35 odd, 40–54

Average: 13–35 odd, 40–54

Advanced: 12–36 even, 37–50 (optional: 51–54)

---

4 Assess

Open-Ended Assessment
Writing Have students write a real-world problem that can be solved with elimination using addition and subtraction.

Getting Ready for Lesson 7-4
PREREQUISITE SKILL Students will learn to solve systems of equations by elimination using multiplication in Lesson 7-4. This method will include multiplying whole equations and simplifying them using the Distributive Property. Use Exercises 51–54 to determine your students' familiarity with rewriting expressions using the Distributive Property.

Assessment Options
Quiz (Lesson 7-3) is available on p. 447 of the *Chapter 7 Resource Masters.*

Mid-Chapter Test (Lessons 7-1 through 7-3) is available on p. 449 of the *Chapter 7 Resource Masters.*

Teacher to Teacher

Lou Jane Tynan   Sacred Heart Model School, Louisville, KY

"Many students will forget to distribute the negative sign over the entire equation being subtracted in Example 3. I require my students to change the signs of the equation being subtracted and then add the two equations."

$$5s + 2t = 6$$
$$(-) \; 9s + 2t = 22$$
$$\Rightarrow$$
$$5s + 2t = 6$$
$$(+) \; -9s - 2t = -22$$

Elimination Using Multiplication

What You'll Learn

- Solve systems of equations by using elimination with multiplication.
- Determine the best method for solving systems of equations.

How can a manager use a system of equations to plan employee time?

The Finneytown Bakery is making peanut butter cookies and loaves of quick bread. The preparation and baking times for each are given in the table below.

For these two items, the management has allotted 800 minutes of employee time and 900 minutes of oven time. If c represents the number of batches of cookies and b represents the number of loaves of bread, the following system of equations can be used to determine how many of each to bake.

$$20c + 10b = 800$$
$$10c + 30b = 900$$

	Cookies (per batch)	Bread (per loaf)
Preparation	20 min	10 min
Baking	10 min	30 min

ELIMINATION USING MULTIPLICATION   Neither variable in the system above can be eliminated by simply adding or subtracting the equations. However, you can use the Multiplication Property of Equality so that adding or subtracting eliminates one of the variables.

Example 1 Multiply One Equation to Eliminate

Use elimination to solve the system of equations.

$$3x + 4y = 6$$
$$5x + 2y = -4$$

Multiply the second equation by -2 so the coefficients of the y terms are additive inverses. Then add the equations.

$$3x + 4y = 6$$
$$5x + 2y = -4 \quad \text{Multiply by } -2.$$

$$
\begin{array}{rcl}
3x + 4y &=& 6 \\
(+) \; -10x - 4y &=& 8 \\
\hline
-7x &=& 14 \quad \text{Add the equations.}
\end{array}
$$

$$\frac{-7x}{-7} = \frac{14}{-7} \quad \text{Divide each side by } -7.$$

$$x = -2 \quad \text{Simplify.}$$

Now substitute -2 for x in either equation to find the value of y.

$$3x + 4y = 6 \quad \text{First equation}$$
$$3(-2) + 4y = 6 \quad x = -2$$
$$-6 + 4y = 6 \quad \text{Simplify.}$$
$$-6 + 4y + 6 = 6 + 6 \quad \text{Add 6 to each side.}$$
$$4y = 12 \quad \text{Simplify.}$$
$$\frac{4y}{4} = \frac{12}{4} \quad \text{Divide each side by 4.}$$
$$y = 3 \quad \text{The solution is } (-2, 3).$$

1 Focus

 5-Minute Check Transparency 7-4 Use as a quiz or review of Lesson 7-3.

Mathematical Background notes are available for this lesson on p. 366D.

How can a manager use a system of equations to plan employee time?

Ask students:

- Explain what the first equation in the system of equations represents. **The first equation represents preparation time because the cookies take 20 minutes to prepare, the bread takes 10 minutes to prepare, and the bakery has allotted 800 minutes of employee time for preparation.**

- Explain what the second equation in the system of equations represents. **The second equation represents baking time because the cookies take 10 minutes to bake, the bread takes 30 minutes to bake, and the bakery has allotted 900 minutes of oven time for preparation.**

Resource Manager

Workbook and Reproducible Masters

Chapter 7 Resource Masters
- Study Guide and Intervention, pp. 421–422
- Skills Practice, p. 423
- Practice, p. 424
- Reading to Learn Mathematics, p. 425
- Enrichment, p. 426
- Assessment, p. 448

Parent and Student Study Guide Workbook, p. 56
School-to-Career Masters, p. 14

 **Transparencies**
5-Minute Check Transparency 7-4
Answer Key Transparencies

Technology
Interactive Chalkboard

1 Use elimination to solve the system of equations.
$2x + y = 23$
$3x + 2y = 37$ **(9, 5)**

2 Use elimination to solve the system of equations.
$4x + 3y = 8$
$3x - 5y = -23$ **(−1, 4)**

For some systems of equations, it is necessary to multiply each equation by a different number in order to solve the system by elimination. You can choose to eliminate either variable.

Example 2 Multiply Both Equations to Eliminate

Use elimination to solve the system of equations.
$3x + 4y = -25$
$2x - 3y = 6$

Method 1   Eliminate x.

$3x + 4y = -25$ Multiply by 2.
$2x - 3y = 6$ Multiply by −3.

$\quad\quad 6x + 8y = -50$
$(+)\ -6x + 9y = -18$
$\quad\quad\quad\quad 17y = -68$ Add the equations.
$\quad\quad\quad\quad \dfrac{17y}{17} = \dfrac{-68}{17}$ Divide each side by 17.
$\quad\quad\quad\quad y = -4$ Simplify.

Now substitute −4 for y in either equation to find the value of x.

$2x - 3y = 6$ Second equation
$2x - 3(-4) = 6$ $y = -4$
$2x + 12 = 6$ Simplify.
$2x + 12 - 12 = 6 - 12$ Subtract 12 from each side.
$2x = -6$ Simplify.
$\dfrac{2x}{2} = \dfrac{-6}{2}$ Divide each side by 2.
$x = -3$ Simplify.

The solution is $(-3, -4)$.

Method 2   Eliminate y.

$3x + 4y = -25$ Multiply by 3.
$2x - 3y = 6$ Multiply by 4.

$\quad\quad 9x + 12y = -75$
$(+)\ 8x - 12y = \quad 24$
$\quad\quad 17x \quad\quad\quad = -51$ Add the equations.
$\quad\quad \dfrac{17x}{17} = \dfrac{-51}{17}$ Divide each side by 17.
$\quad\quad x = -3$ Simplify.

Now substitute −3 for x in either equation to find the value of y.

$2x - 3y = 6$ Second equation
$2(-3) - 3y = 6$ $x = -3$
$-6 - 3y = 6$ Simplify.
$-6 - 3y + 6 = 6 + 6$ Add 6 to each side.
$-3y = 12$ Simplify.
$\dfrac{-3y}{-3} = \dfrac{12}{-3}$ Divide each side by −3.
$y = -4$ Simplify.

The solution is $(-3, -4)$, which matches the result obtained with Method 1.

Study Tip

Using Multiplication
There are many other combinations of multipliers that could be used to solve the system in Example 2. For instance, the first equation could be multiplied by −2 and the second by 3.

DETERMINE THE BEST METHOD You have learned five methods for solving systems of linear equations.

Concept Summary	Solving Systems of Equations
Method	**The Best Time to Use**
Graphing	to estimate the solution, since graphing usually does not give an exact solution
Substitution	if one of the variables in either equation has a coefficient of 1 or −1
Elimination Using Addition	if one of the variables has opposite coefficients in the two equations
Elimination Using Subtraction	if one of the variables has the same coefficient in the two equations
Elimination Using Multiplication	if none of the coefficients are 1 or −1 and neither of the variables can be eliminated by simply adding or subtracting the equations

Example 3 Determine the Best Method

Determine the best method to solve the system of equations. Then solve the system.

$4x − 3y = 12$
$x + 2y = 14$

- For an exact solution, an algebraic method is best.
- Since neither the coefficients of x nor the coefficients of y are the same or additive inverses, you cannot use elimination using addition or subtraction.
- Since the coefficient of x in the second equation is 1, you can use the substitution method. You could also use elimination using multiplication.

The following solution uses substitution.   *Which method would you prefer?*

$$x + 2y = 14 \qquad \text{Second equation}$$
$$x + 2y − 2y = 14 − 2y \qquad \text{Subtract } 2y \text{ from each side.}$$
$$x = 14 − 2y \qquad \text{Simplify.}$$

$$4x − 3y = 12 \qquad \text{First equation}$$
$$4(14 − 2y) − 3y = 12 \qquad x = 14 − 2y$$
$$56 − 8y − 3y = 12 \qquad \text{Distributive Property}$$
$$56 − 11y = 12 \qquad \text{Combine like terms.}$$
$$56 − 11y − 56 = 12 − 56 \qquad \text{Subtract 56 from each side.}$$
$$−11y = −44 \qquad \text{Simplify.}$$
$$\frac{−11y}{−11} = \frac{−44}{−11} \qquad \text{Divide each side by } −11.$$
$$y = 4 \qquad \text{Simplify.}$$

$$x + 2y = 14 \qquad \text{Second equation}$$
$$x + 2(4) = 14 \qquad y = 4$$
$$x + 8 = 14 \qquad \text{Simplify.}$$
$$x + 8 − 8 = 14 − 8 \qquad \text{Subtract 8 from each side.}$$
$$x = 6 \qquad \text{Simplify.}$$

The solution is (6, 4).

Study Tip

Alternative Method
This system could also be solved easily by multiplying the second equation by 4 and then subtracting the equations.

DETERMINE THE BEST METHOD

In-Class Example Power Point®

3 Determine the best method to solve the system of equations. Then solve the system.

$x + 5y = 4$
$3x − 7y = −10$

The best method to use is substitution because the coefficient of x in the first equation is 1. (−1, 1)

DAILY INTERVENTION

Differentiated Instruction   ELL

Verbal/Linguistic Place students in pairs or small groups and assign systems of equations for them to solve. Tell students to use the Concept Summary on p. 389 to discuss which method is the best to use to solve the system of equations they have been assigned. Make sure all group members participate in the discussion.

4 **TRANSPORTATION** A fishing boat travels 10 miles downstream in 30 minutes. The return trip takes the boat 40 minutes. Find the rate of the boat in still water. **17.5 mi/h**

3 Practice/Apply

Study Notebook

Have students—
• add the definitions/examples of the vocabulary terms to their Vocabulary Builder worksheets for Chapter 7.
• include examples of how to solve a system of equations by using elimination with multiplication.
• include any other item(s) that they find helpful in mastering the skills in this lesson.

About the Exercises...

Organization by Objective
• Elimination Using Multiplication: 13–26
• Determine the Best Method: 27–43

Odd/Even Assignments
Exercises 13–38 are structured so that students practice the same concepts whether they are assigned odd or even problems.

Assignment Guide

Basic: 13–39 odd, 40, 44–57

Average: 13–39 odd, 40, 41, 43–57

Advanced: 14–42 even, 43–53 (optional: 54–57)

All: Practice Quiz 2 (1–5)

More About. . .

Transportation •
About 203 million tons of freight are transported on the Ohio River each year making it the second most used commercial river in the United States.
Source: *World Book Encyclopedia*

Example 4 **Write and Solve a System of Equations**

TRANSPORTATION A coal barge on the Ohio River travels 24 miles upstream in 3 hours. The return trip takes the barge only 2 hours. Find the rate of the barge in still water.

Let b = the rate of the barge in still water and c = the rate of the current. Use the formula rate × time = distance, or $rt = d$.

	r	t	d	$rt = d$
Downstream	$b + c$	2	24	$2b + 2c = 24$
Upstream	$b - c$	3	24	$3b - 3c = 24$

This system cannot easily be solved using substitution. It cannot be solved by just adding or subtracting the equations.

The best way to solve this system is to use elimination using multiplication. Since the problem asks for b, eliminate c.

$2b + 2c = 24$ Multiply by 3. $6b + 6c = 72$
$3b - 3c = 24$ Multiply by 2. $(+)\ 6b - 6c = 48$

$$12b = 120 \quad \text{Add the equations.}$$
$$\frac{12b}{12} = \frac{120}{12} \quad \text{Divide each side by 12.}$$
$$b = 10 \quad \text{Simplify.}$$

The rate of the barge in still water is 10 miles per hour.

Check for Understanding

Concept Check
1. **Explain** why multiplication is sometimes needed to solve a system of equations by elimination. **See margin.**

2. **OPEN ENDED** Write a system of equations that could be solved by multiplying one equation by 5 and then adding the two equations together to eliminate one variable. **Sample answer: $3x + 2y = 5$, $4x - 10y = -6$**

3. **Describe** two methods that could be used to solve the following system of equations. Which method do you prefer? Explain. **See pp. 405A–405D.**
$$a - b = 5$$
$$2a + 3b = 15$$

Guided Practice

GUIDED PRACTICE KEY	
Exercises	Examples
4–7	1–2
8–11	3
12	4

Use elimination to solve each system of equations.

4. $2x - y = 6$
   $3x + 4y = -2$ **(2, −2)**

5. $x + 5y = 4$
   $3x - 7y = -10$ **(−1, 1)**

6. $4x + 7y = 6$
   $6x + 5y = 20$ **(5, −2)**

7. $4x + 2y = 10.5$
   $2x + 3y = 10.75$ **(1.25, 2.75)**

Determine the best method to solve each system of equations. Then solve the system.

8. $4x + 3y = 19$
   $3x - 4y = 8$ **elimination (×); (4, 1)**

9. $3x - 7y = 6$
   $2x + 7y = 4$ **elimination (+); (2, 0)**

10. $y = 4x + 11$
    $3x - 2y = -7$ **substitution; (−3, −1)**

11. $5x - 2y = 12$ **elimination (−);**
    $3x - 2y = -2$ **(7, 11.5)**

Answer

1. If one of the variables cannot be eliminated by adding or subtracting the equations, you must multiply one or both of the equations by numbers so that a variable will be eliminated when the equations are added or subtracted.

Application 12. **BUSINESS** The owners of the River View Restaurant have hired enough servers to handle 17 tables of customers, and the fire marshal has approved the restaurant for a limit of 56 customers. How many two-seat tables and how many four-seat tables should the owners purchase? **6 two-seat tables, 11 four-seat tables**

★ indicates increased difficulty

Practice and Apply

Homework Help

For Exercises	See Examples
13–26	1, 2
27–38	3
39–43	4

Extra Practice
See page 836.

Use elimination to solve each system of equations.

13. $-5x + 3y = 6$
    $x - y = 4$ $(-9, -13)$

14. $x + y = 3$
    $2x - 3y = 16$ $(5, -2)$

15. $2x + y = 5$
    $3x - 2y = 4$ $(2, 1)$

16. $4x - 3y = 12$
    $x + 2y = 14$ $(6, 4)$

17. $5x - 2y = -15$
    $3x + 8y = 37$ $(-1, 5)$

18. $8x - 3y = -11$
    $2x - 5y = 27$ $(-4, -7)$

19. $4x - 7y = 10$
    $3x + 2y = -7$ $(-1, -2)$

20. $2x - 3y = 2$
    $5x + 4y = 28$ $(4, 2)$

21. $1.8x - 0.3y = 14.4$
    $x - 0.6y = 2.8$ $(10, 12)$

22. $0.4x + 0.5y = 2.5$
    $1.2x - 3.5y = 2.5$ $(5, 1)$

23. $3x - \frac{1}{2}y = 10$
    $5x + \frac{1}{4}y = 8$ $(2, -8)$

24. $2x + \frac{2}{3}y = 4$
    $x - \frac{1}{2}y = 7$ $(4, -6)$

25. Seven times a number plus three times another number equals negative one. The sum of the two numbers is negative three. What are the numbers? **2, −5**

26. Five times a number minus twice another number equals twenty-two. The sum of the numbers is three. Find the numbers. **4, −1**

Determine the best method to solve each system of equations. Then solve the system. **27. elimination (×); (−2, 1) 28. elimination (+); (2, −3)**

29. substitution; (2, 6)

30. substitution; no solution

31. elimination (+); $\left(8, \frac{4}{3}\right)$

33. elimination (×) or substitution; (3, 1)

34. substitution; infinitely many solutions

35. elimination (−); no solution

27. $3x - 4y = -10$
    $5x + 8y = -2$

28. $9x - 8y = 42$
    $4x + 8y = -16$

29. $y = 3x$
    $3x + 4y = 30$

30. $x = 4y + 8$
    $2x - 8y = -3$

31. $2x - 3y = 12$
    $x + 3y = 12$

32. $4x - 2y = 14$
    $y = x$ substitution; (7, 7)

33. $x - y = 2$
    $5x + 3y = 18$

34. $y = 2x + 9$
    $2x - y = -9$

35. $6x - y = 9$
    $6x - y = 11$

36. $x = 8y$ subst.; (16, 2)
    $2x + 3y = 38$

37. $\frac{2}{3}x - \frac{1}{2}y = 14$
    $\frac{5}{6}x - \frac{1}{2}y = 18$
    elimin. (−); (24, 4)

38. $\frac{1}{2}x - \frac{2}{3}y = \frac{7}{3}$
    $\frac{3}{2}x + 2y = -25$
    elimin. (×); (−6, −8)

39. **BASKETBALL** In basketball, a free throw is 1 point and a field goal is either 2 points or 3 points. Suppose a professional basketball player scored a total of 1938 points in one season. The total number of 2-point field goals and 3-point field goals was 701, and he made 475 of the 557 free throws that he attempted. Find the number of 2-point field goals and 3-point field goals the player made that season. **640 2-point field goals, 61 3-point field goals**

 Online Research Data Update What are the current statistics for your favorite basketball player? Visit www.algebra1.com/data_update to learn more.

40. **CRITICAL THINKING** The solution of the system $4x + 5y = 2$ and $6x - 2y = b$ is $(3, a)$. Find the values of a and b. **$a = -2$, $b = 22$**

★ 41. **CAREERS** Mrs. Henderson discovered that she had accidentally reversed the digits of a test and shorted a student 36 points. Mrs. Henderson told the student that the sum of the digits was 14 and agreed to give the student his correct score plus extra credit if he could determine his actual score without looking at his test. What was his actual score on the test? **95**

 www.algebra1.com/self_check_quiz

Lesson 7-4 Elimination Using Multiplication **391**

Open-Ended Assessment

Speaking Using the Concept Summary from p. 389, write on the board a list of the different methods for solving systems of equations. For each method, have a volunteer explain in his or her own words when it is appropriate to use the method.

Getting Ready for Lesson 7-5

PREREQUISITE SKILL Students will learn to graph systems of inequalities in Lesson 7-5. Students must be comfortable graphing inequalities before beginning this lesson because otherwise they will find it very confusing to have different shaded regions. Use Exercises 54–57 to determine your students' familiarity with graphing inequalities.

Assessment Options

Practice Quiz 2 The quiz provides students with a brief review of the concepts and skills in Lessons 7-3 and 7-4. Lesson numbers are given to the right of exercises or instruction lines so students can review concepts not yet mastered.

Quiz (Lesson 7-4) is available on p. 448 of the *Chapter 7 Resource Masters.*

Answers

54.

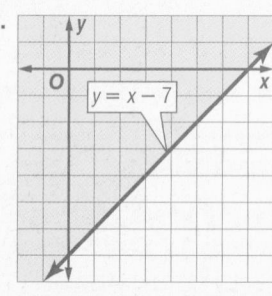

★ 42. **NUMBER THEORY** The sum of the digits of a two-digit number is 14. If the digits are reversed, the new number is 18 less than the original number. Find the original number. **86**

★ 43. **TRANSPORTATION** Traveling against the wind, a plane flies 2100 miles from Chicago to San Diego in 4 hours and 40 minutes. The return trip, traveling with a wind that is twice as fast, takes 4 hours. Find the rate of the plane in still air. **475 mph**

44. WRITING IN MATH Answer the question that was posed at the beginning of the lesson. **See pp. 405A–405D.**

How can a manager use a system of equations to plan employee time?

Include the following in your answer:
- a demonstration of how to solve the system of equations concerning the cookies and bread, and
- an explanation of how a restaurant manager would schedule oven and employee time.

Standardized Test Practice

Ⓐ Ⓑ Ⓒ Ⓓ

45. If $5x + 3y = 12$ and $4x - 5y = 17$, what is the value of y? **A**

Ⓐ -1 Ⓑ 3 Ⓒ $(-1, 3)$ Ⓓ $(3, -1)$

46. Determine the number of solutions of the system $x + 2y = -1$ and $2x + 4y = -2$. **D**

Ⓐ 0 Ⓑ 1 Ⓒ 2 Ⓓ infinitely many

Maintain Your Skills

Mixed Review Use elimination to solve each system of equations. *(Lesson 7-3)*

47. $x + y = 8$
$x - y = 4$ **(6, 2)**

48. $2r + s = 5$
$r - s = 1$ **(2, 1)**

49. $x + y = 18$
$x + 2y = 25$ **(11, 7)**

Use substitution to solve each system of equations. If the system does *not* have exactly one solution, state whether it has *no* solution or *infinitely many* solutions. *(Lesson 7-2)*

50. $2x + 3y = 3$
$x = -3y$ **(3, −1)**

51. $x + y = 0$
$3x + y = -8$ **(−4, 4)**

52. $x - 2y = 7$
$-3x + 6y = -21$
infinitely many

53. **CAREERS** A store manager is paid $32,000 a year plus 4% of the revenue the store makes above quota. What is the amount of revenue above quota needed for the manager to have an annual income greater than $45,000? *(Lesson 6-3)*
more than $325,000

Getting Ready for the Next Lesson **PREREQUISITE SKILL** Graph each inequality.
*(To review **graphing inequalities**, see Lesson 6-6.)* **54–57. See margin.**

54. $y \geq x - 7$ 55. $x + 3y \geq 9$ 56. $-y \leq x$ 57. $-3x + y \geq -1$

Practice Quiz 2   Lessons 7-3 and 7-4

Use elimination to solve each system of equations. *(Lessons 7-3 and 7-4)*

1. $5x + 4y = 2$
$3x - 4y = 14$
(2, −2)

2. $2x - 3y = 13$
$2x + 2y = -2$
(2, −3)

3. $6x - 2y = 24$
$3x + 4y = 27$
(5, 3)

4. $5x + 2y = 4$
$10x + 4y = 9$
no solution

5. The price of a cellular telephone plan is based on peak and nonpeak service. Kelsey used 45 peak minutes and 50 nonpeak minutes and was charged $27.75. That same month, Mitch used 70 peak minutes and 30 nonpeak minutes for a total charge of $36. What are the rates per minute for peak and nonpeak time? *(Lesson 7-4)* **$0.45; $0.15**

392 Chapter 7 Solving Systems of Linear Equations and Inequalities

55.

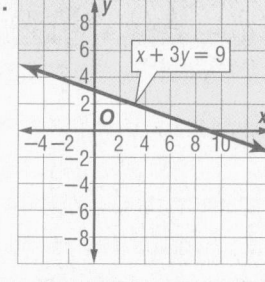

56.

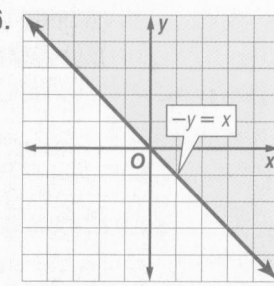

57.

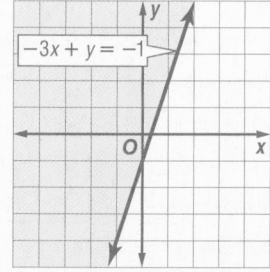

Reading Mathematics

Making Concept Maps

After completing a chapter, it is wise to review each lesson's main topics and vocabulary. In Lesson 7-1, the new vocabulary words were *system of equations*, *consistent*, *inconsistent*, *independent*, and *dependent*. They are all related in that they explain how many and what kind of solutions a system of equations has.

A graphic organizer called a *concept map* is a convenient way to show these relationships. A concept map is shown below for the vocabulary words for Lesson 7-1. The main ideas are placed in boxes. Any information that describes how to move from one box to the next is placed along the arrows.

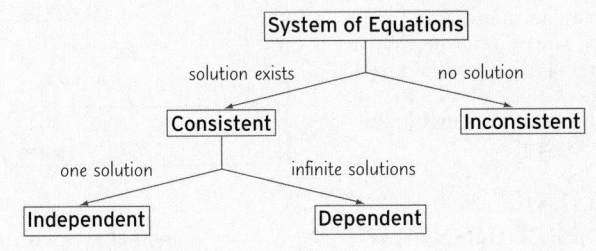

Concept maps are used to organize information. They clearly show how ideas are related to one another. They also show the flow of mental processes needed to solve problems.

Reading to Learn

Review Lessons 7-2, 7-3, and 7-4. 1–4. See margin.

1. Write a couple of sentences describing the information in the concept map above.
2. How do you decide whether to use substitution or elimination? Give an example of a system that you would solve using each method.
3. How do you decide whether to multiply an equation by a factor?
4. How do you decide whether to add or subtract two equations?
5. Copy and complete the concept map below for solving systems of equations by using either substitution or elimination.

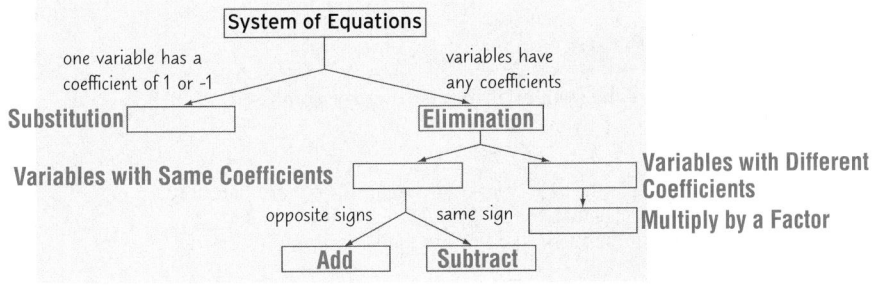

Ask students how they organize information such as vocabulary words when they study for tests. Write down several examples. Then ask students to comment on whether visual arrangements of information (as opposed to lists or paragraphs) helps them remember the information better.

Teach

Creating Concept Maps After students examine the sample concept map shown, have them create their own concept map. Have them create the map over an unrelated task such as the school lunch menu or beginning of class procedures. Ask students to share their maps when they are complete.

Assess

Study Notebook

Ask students to summarize what they have learned about concept maps.

ELL English Language Learners may benefit from writing key concepts from this activity in their Study Notebooks in their native language and then in English.

Answers

1. There are two types of systems of equations, consistent and inconsistent. Consistent systems have one or more solutions and inconsistent systems have no solutions. If consistent systems have one solution, they are called independent. If consistent systems have infinite solutions, they are called dependent.

2. Use substitution if an expression for one variable is given or if the coefficient of a variable is ± 1. Otherwise, use elimination.

   Sample answers:

   system to solve using substitution
   $$y = 3x + 3$$
   $$5x + 2y = 6$$

   system to solve using elimination
   $$4x + 3y = 9$$
   $$6x - y = 10$$

3. Multiply by a factor if neither variable has the same or opposite coefficients in the two equations.

4. Add if one of the variables has opposite coefficients in the two equations. Subtract if one of the variables has the same coefficient in the two equations.

1 Focus

5-Minute Check Transparency 7-5 Use as a quiz or review of Lesson 7-4.

Mathematical Background notes are available for this lesson on p. 366D.

Building on Prior Knowledge

In Chapter 6, students learned to graph linear inequalities. In this lesson, they should recognize that graphing systems of inequalities simply involves graphing more than one inequality on the same coordinate grid and then shading the regions that overlap.

How can you use a system of inequalities to plan a sensible diet?

Ask students:

- Does Joshua need to eat the exact same amount of Calories and fat each day? Explain. **No, but his Calorie and fat intake should be within the green area of the graph.**

- Suppose Joshua eats 2600 Calories one day, but only 55 grams of fat. Is this an appropriate intake of Calories and fat? How do you know? **It is not appropriate because it does not fall within the green section of the graph.**

Resource Manager

Workbook and Reproducible Masters

Chapter 7 Resource Masters
- Study Guide and Intervention, pp. 427–428
- Skills Practice, p. 429
- Practice, p. 430
- Reading to Learn Mathematics, p. 431
- Enrichment, p. 432
- Assessment, pp. 448, 453–454

Graphing Calculator and Spreadsheet Masters, p. 35
Parent and Student Study Guide Workbook, p. 57

Transparencies
5-Minute Check Transparency 7-5
Answer Key Transparencies

Technology
AlgePASS: Tutorial Plus, Lesson 17
Interactive Chalkboard
Multimedia Applications

7-5 Graphing Systems of Inequalities

What You'll Learn

- Solve systems of inequalities by graphing.
- Solve real-world problems involving systems of inequalities.

Vocabulary
- system of inequalities

How can you use a system of inequalities to plan a sensible diet?

Joshua watches what he eats. His doctor told him to eat between 2000 and 2400 Calories per day. The doctor also wants him to keep his daily fat intake between 60 and 75 grams. The graph indicates the appropriate amounts of Calories and fat for Joshua. The graph is of a system of inequalities. He should try to keep his Calorie and fat intake to amounts represented in the green section.

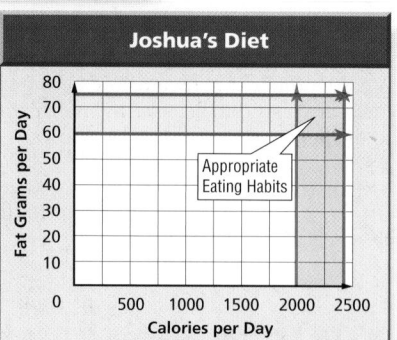

Joshua's Diet

SYSTEMS OF INEQUALITIES To solve a **system of inequalities**, you need to find the ordered pairs that satisfy all the inequalities involved. One way to do this is to graph the inequalities on the same coordinate plane. The solution set is represented by the intersection, or overlap, of the graphs.

Example 1 Solve by Graphing

Solve the system of inequalities by graphing.

$y < -x + 1$
$y \leq 2x + 3$

The solution includes the ordered pairs in the intersection of the graphs of $y < -x + 1$ and $y \leq 2x + 3$. This region is shaded in green at the right. The graphs of $y = -x + 1$ and $y = 2x + 3$ are boundaries of this region. The graph of $y = -x + 1$ is dashed and is *not* included in the graph of $y < -x + 1$. The graph of $y = 2x + 3$ is included in the graph of $y \leq 2x + 3$.

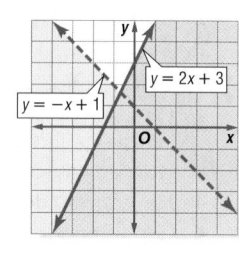

Example 2 No Solution

Solve the system of inequalities by graphing.

$x - y < -1$
$x - y > 3$

The graphs of $x - y = -1$ and $x - y = 3$ are parallel lines. Because the two regions have no points in common, the system of inequalities has no solution.

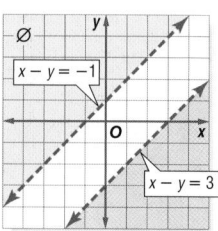

You can use a TI-83 Plus to solve systems of inequalities.

Graphing Calculator Investigation
Graphing Systems of Inequalities

To graph the system $y \geq 4x - 3$ and $y \leq -2x + 9$ on a TI-83 Plus, select the SHADE feature in the DRAW menu. Enter the function that is the lower boundary of the region to be shaded, followed by the upper boundary. (Note that inequalities that have $>$ or $\geq$ are lower boundaries and inequalities that have $<$ or $\leq$ are upper boundaries.)

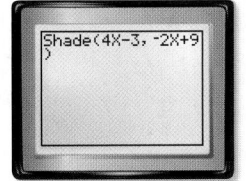

Think and Discuss 2, 4. See pp. 405A–405D.

1. To graph the system $y \leq 3x + 1$ and $y \geq -2x - 5$ on a graphing calculator, which function should you enter first? $y \geq -2x - 5$

2. Use a graphing calculator to graph the system $y \leq 3x + 1$ and $y \geq -2x - 5$.

3. Explain how you could use a graphing calculator to graph the system $2x + y \geq 7$ and $x - 2y \geq 5$.

4. Use a graphing calculator to graph the system $2x + y \geq 7$ and $x - 2y \geq 5$.

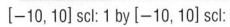
[−10, 10] scl: 1 by [−10, 10] scl: 1

3. Solve each inequality for y. Then enter the function that is the lower boundary ($y \geq 7 - 2x$), a comma, and the function that is the upper boundary ($y \leq 0.5x - 2.5$).

REAL-WORLD PROBLEMS In real-life problems involving systems of inequalities, sometimes only whole-number solutions make sense.

Example 3 Use a System of Inequalities to Solve a Problem

COLLEGE The middle 50% of first-year students attending Florida State University score between 520 and 620, inclusive, on the verbal portion of the SAT and between 530 and 630, inclusive, on the math portion. Graph the scores that a student would need to be in the middle 50% of FSU freshmen.

Words The verbal score is between 520 and 620, inclusive. The math score is between 530 and 630, inclusive.

Variables If v = the verbal score and m = the math score, the following inequalities represent the middle 50% of Florida State University freshmen.

Inequalities
The verbal score is between 520 and 620, inclusive.
$$520 \leq v \leq 620$$

The math score is between 530 and 630, inclusive.
$$530 \leq m \leq 630$$

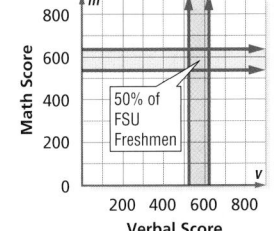

The solution is the set of all ordered pairs whose graphs are in the intersection of the graphs of these inequalities. However, since SAT scores are whole numbers, only whole-number solutions make sense in this problem.

 www.algebra1.com/extra_examples

Lesson 7-5 Graphing Systems of Inequalities 395

Graphing Calculator Investigation

Graphing Systems of Inequalities Extra applications can be downloaded from the Internet for the TI-83 Plus calculator, including an inequality application that automates and simplifies inequality graphing.

---

2 Teach

SYSTEMS OF INEQUALITIES

In-Class Examples   Power Point®

1 Solve the system of inequalities by graphing.
$y < 2x + 2$
$y \geq -x - 3$

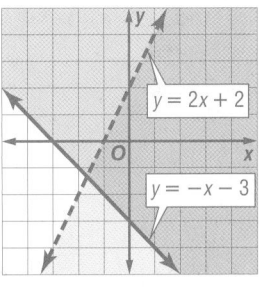

2 Solve the system of inequalities by graphing.
$y \geq -3x + 1$
$y \leq -3x - 2$ ∅

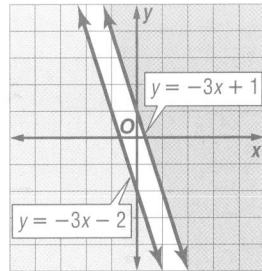

REAL-WORLD PROBLEMS

In-Class Example   Power Point®

3 SERVICE A college service organization requires that its members maintain at least a 3.0 grade point average, and volunteer at least 10 hours a week. Graph these requirements.

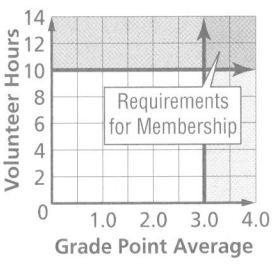

---

4 EMPLOYMENT Jamail mows grass after school but his job pays only $3 per hour. He has been offered another job as a library assistant for $6 per hour. Because of school, his parents allow him to work at most 15 hours per week. How many hours can Jamail mow grass and work in the library and still make at least $60 per week?

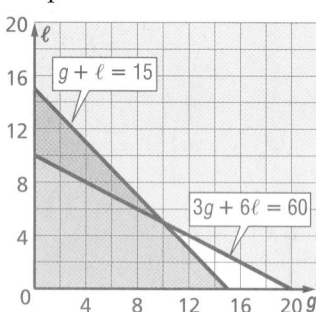

Jamail can work any combination of hours in the darker shaded area of the graph.

3 Practice/Apply

Study Notebook

Have students—
• complete the definitions/examples for the remaining terms on their Vocabulary Builder worksheets for Chapter 7.
• include any other item(s) that they find helpful in mastering the skills in this lesson.

Example 4 Use a System of Inequalities

AGRICULTURE To ensure a growing season of sufficient length, Mr. Hobson has at most 16 days left to plant his corn and soybean crops. He can plant corn at a rate of 250 acres per day and soybeans at a rate of 200 acres per day. If he has at most 3500 acres available, how many acres of each type of crop can he plant?

Let c = the number of days that corn will be planted and s = the number of days that soybeans will be planted. Since both c and s represent a number of days, neither can be a negative number. The following system of inequalities can be used to represent the conditions of this problem.

$c \geq 0$

$s \geq 0$

$c + s \leq 16$

$250c + 200s \leq 3500$

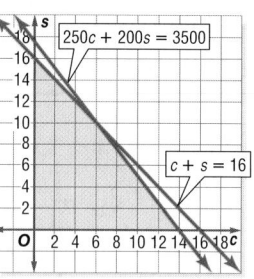

The solution is the set of all ordered pairs whose graphs are in the intersection of the graphs of these inequalities. This region is shown in green at the right. Only the portion of the region in the first quadrant is used since $c \geq 0$ and $s \geq 0$.

Any point in this region is a possible solution. For example, since (7, 8) is a point in the region, Mr. Hobson could plant corn for 7 days and soybeans for 8 days. In this case, he would use 15 days to plant 250(7) or 1750 acres of corn and 200(8) or 1600 acres of soybeans.

Check for Understanding

Concept Check

1. See margin for sample answer.

3. Kayla; the graph of $x + 2y \geq -2$ is the region representing $x + 2y = -2$ and the half-plane above it.

1. **OPEN ENDED** Draw the graph of a system of inequalities that has no solution.

2. **Determine** which of the following ordered pairs represent a solution of the system of inequalities graphed at the right.

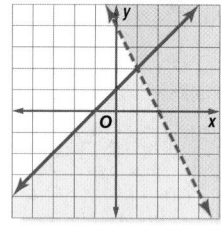

   a. (3, 1) **yes**   b. (−1, −3) **no**

   c. (2, 3) **yes**   d. (4, −2) **yes**

   e. (3, −2) **no**   f. (1, 4) **no**

3. **FIND THE ERROR** Kayla and Sonia are solving the system of inequalities $x + 2y \geq -2$ and $x - y > 1$.

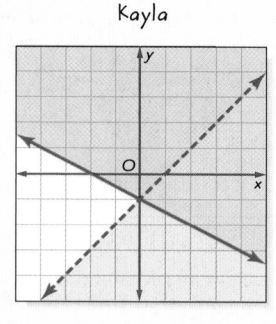
Kayla

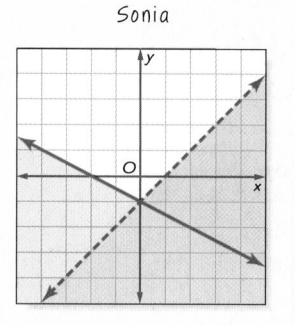
Sonia

Who is correct? Explain your reasoning.

Guided Practice

Solve each system of inequalities by graphing. 4–9. See pp. 405A–405D.

GUIDED PRACTICE KEY	
Exercises	Examples
4–9	1, 2
10, 11	3, 4

4. $x > 5$
$y \leq 4$

5. $y > 3$
$y > -x + 4$

6. $y \leq -x + 3$
$y \leq x + 3$

7. $2x + y \geq 4$
$y \leq -2x - 1$

8. $2y + x < 6$
$3x - y > 4$

9. $x - 2y \leq 2$
$3x + 4y \leq 12$
$x \geq 0$

Application

HEALTH For Exercises 10 and 11, use the following information.
Natasha walks and jogs at least 3 miles every day. Natasha walks 4 miles per hour and jogs 8 miles per hour. She only has a half-hour to exercise. **10. See pp. 405A–405D.**

10. Draw a graph of the possible amounts of time she can spend walking and jogging.

11. List three possible solutions. **Sample answers: walk: 15 min, jog: 15 min; walk: 10 min, jog: 20 min; walk: 5 min, jog: 25 min**

★ indicates increased difficulty

Practice and Apply

Solve each system of inequalities by graphing. 12–26. See pp. 405A–405D.

Homework Help	
For Exercises	See Examples
12–28	1–2
29–31, 33–35	3–4

Extra Practice
See page 836.

12. $y < 0$
$x \geq 0$

13. $x > -4$
$y \leq -1$

14. $y \geq -2$
$y - x < 1$

15. $x \geq 2$
$y + x \leq 5$

16. $x \leq 3$
$x + y > 2$

17. $y \geq 2x + 1$
$y \leq -x + 1$

18. $y < 2x + 1$
$y \geq -x + 3$

19. $y - x < 1$
$y - x > 3$

20. $y - x < 3$
$y - x \geq 2$

21. $2x + y \leq 4$
$3x - y \geq 6$

22. $3x - 4y < 1$
$x + 2y \leq 7$

23. $x + y > 4$
$-2x + 3y < -12$

24. $2x + y \geq -4$
$-5x + 2y < 1$

★ **25.** $y \leq x + 3$
$2x - 7y \leq 4$
$3x + 2y \leq 6$

★ **26.** $x < 2$
$4y > x$
$2x - y > -9$
$x + 3y < 9$

Write a system of inequalities for each graph.

★ **27.** 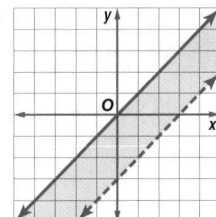 $y \leq x,$
$y > x - 3$

28. 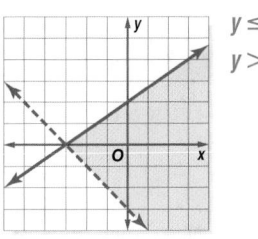 $y \leq \frac{2}{3}x + 2,$
$y > -x - 3$

29. See pp. 405A–405D.

ART For Exercises 29 and 30, use the following information.
A painter has exactly 32 units of yellow dye and 54 units of blue dye. She plans to mix the dyes to make two shades of green. Each gallon of the lighter shade of green requires 4 units of yellow dye and 1 unit of blue dye. Each gallon of the darker shade of green requires 1 unit of yellow dye and 6 units of blue dye.

29. Make a graph showing the numbers of gallons of the two greens she can make.

30. List three possible solutions. **Sample answers: 2 light, 8 dark; 6 light, 8 dark; 7 light, 4 dark**

31. HEALTH The LDL or "bad" cholesterol of a teenager should be less than 110. The HDL or "good" cholesterol of a teenager should be between 35 and 59. Make a graph showing appropriate levels of cholesterol for a teenager. **See pp. 405A–405D.**

32. CRITICAL THINKING Write a system of inequalities equivalent to $|x| \leq 4$.
$x \geq -4$ and $x \leq 4$

www.algebra1.com/self_check_quiz

Lesson 7-5 Graphing Systems of Inequalities **397**

Career Choices

Visual Artist
Visual artists create art to communicate ideas. The work of fine artists is made for display. Illustrators and graphic designers produce art for clients.

Online Research
For information about a career as a visual artist, visit: www.algebra1.com/careers

 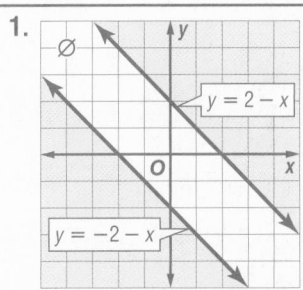
Study Guide and Intervention, p. 427 (shown) and p. 428

Systems of Inequalities The solution of a **system of inequalities** is the set of all ordered pairs that satisfy both inequalities. If you graph the inequalities in the same coordinate plane, the solution is the region where the graphs overlap.

Example 1 Solve the system of inequalities by graphing.
$y > x + 2$
$y \leq -2x - 1$

The solution includes the ordered pairs in the intersection of the graphs. This region is shaded at the right. The graphs of $y = x + 2$ and $y = -2x - 1$ are boundaries of this region. The graph of $y = x + 2$ is dashed and is not included in the graph of $y > x + 2$.

Example 2 Solve the system of inequalities by graphing.
$x + y > 4$
$x + y < -1$

The graphs of $x + y = 4$ and $x + y = -1$ are parallel. Because the two regions have no points in common, the system of inequalities has no solution.

Exercises

Solve each system of inequalities by graphing.

1. $y > -1$
$x < 0$

2. $y > -2x + 2$
$y \leq x + 1$

3. $y < x + 1$
$3x + 4y \geq 12$

4. $2x + y \geq 1$
$x - y \geq -2$

5. $y \leq 2x + 3$
$y \geq -1 + 2x$

6. $5x - 2y < 6$
$y > -x + 1$

Skills Practice, p. 429 and Practice, p. 430 (shown)

Solve each system of inequalities by graphing.

1. $y > x - 2$
$y \leq x$

2. $y \geq x + 2$
$y > 2x + 3$

3. $x + y \geq 1$
$x + 2y > 1$

4. $y < 2x - 1$
$y > 2 - x$

5. $y > x - 4$
$2x + y \leq 2$

6. $2x - y \geq 2$
$x - 2y \geq 2$

FITNESS For Exercises 7 and 8, use the following information.
Diego started an exercise program in which each week he works out at the gym between 4.5 and 6 hours and walks between 9 and 12 miles.

7. Make a graph to show the number of hours Diego works out at the gym and the number of miles he walks per week.

8. List three possible combinations of working out and walking that meet Diego's goals. **Sample answers: gym 5 h, walk 9 mi; gym 6 h, walk 10 mi; gym 5.5 h, walk 11 mi**

SOUVENIRS For Exercises 9 and 10, use the following information.
Emily wants to buy turquoise stones on her trip to New Mexico to give to at least 4 of her friends. The gift shop sells stones for either $4 or $6 per stone. Emily has no more than $30 to spend.

9. Make a graph showing the numbers of each price of stone Emily can purchase.

10. List three possible solutions. **Sample answer: one $4 stone and four $6 stones; three $4 stones and three $6 stones; five $4 stones and one $6 stone**

Reading to Learn Mathematics, p. 431   **ELL**

Pre-Activity How can you use a system of inequalities to plan a sensible diet?
Read the introduction to Lesson 7-5 at the top of page 394 in your textbook.
The green section on the graph represents a range of 2000 to 2400 Calories a day and 60 to 75 grams of fat per day.

Reading the Lesson

Write the inequality symbols that you need to get a system whose graph looks like the one shown. Use <, ≤, >, or ≥.

1.
$y \geq x + 2$
$y \geq -2x - 1$

2.
$y \leq x + 2$
$y \leq -2x - 1$

3.
$y \geq x + 2$
$y \leq -2x - 1$

4.
$y \leq x + 2$
$y \geq -2x - 1$

Helping You Remember

5. Describe how you would explain the process of using a graph to solve a system of inequalities to a friend who missed Lesson 7-5. Graph each inequality on the same coordinate plane. The solutions are the ordered pairs for the points in both graphs.

Enrichment, p. 432

Describing Regions

The shaded region inside the triangle can be described with a system of three inequalities.

$y < 2x + 1$
$y > \frac{1}{3}x - 3$
$y > 29x - 31$

Write systems of inequalities to describe each region. You may first need to divide a region into triangles or quadrilaterals.

About the Exercises...

Organization by Objective
- **Systems of Inequalities:** 12–28
- **Real-World Problems:** 29–31, 33–35

Odd/Even Assignments
Exercises 12–28 are structured so that students practice the same concepts whether they are assigned odd or even problems.

Alert! Exercises 36–38 require a graphing calculator.

Assignment Guide

Basic: 13–23 odd, 29–32, 35, 39–49

Average: 13–27 odd, 29–32, 35, 39–49 (optional: 36–38)

Advanced: 12–28 even, 32–49

4 Assess

Open-Ended Assessment

Writing Have students describe in words the method for determining whether to shade above or below a line when graphing an inequality, and how to determine the common solutions when graphing a system of inequalities.

Assessment Options

Quiz (Lesson 7-5) is available on p. 448 of the *Chapter 7 Resource Masters*.

Answers

33. Furniture Manufacturing

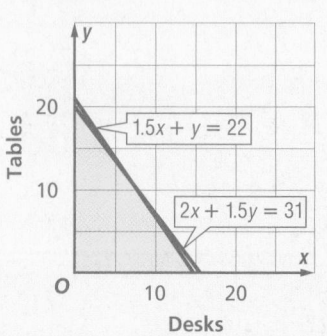

MANUFACTURING For Exercises 33 and 34, use the following information.
The Natural Wood Company has machines that sand and varnish desks and tables. The table gives the time requirements of the machines.

Machine	Hours per Desk	Hours per Table	Total Hours Available Each Week
Sanding	2	1.5	31
Varnishing	1.5	1	22

33. Make a graph showing the number of desks and the number of tables that can be made in a week. **See margin.**

34. List three possible solutions. **Sample answers: 8 desks, 10 tables; 6 desks, 12 tables; 4 desks, 14 tables**

35.  **WRITING IN MATH** Answer the question that was posed at the beginning of the lesson. **See pp. 405A–405D.**

How can you use a system of inequalities to plan a sensible diet?

Include the following in your answer:
- two appropriate Calorie and fat intakes for a day, and
- the system of inequalities that is represented by the graph.

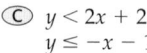 *Graphing Calculator*

GRAPHING SYSTEMS OF INEQUALITIES Use a graphing calculator to solve each system of inequalities. Sketch the results. **36–38. See margin.**

36. $y \le x + 9$
$y \ge -x - 4$

37. $y \le 2x + 10$
$y \ge 7x + 15$

38. $3x - y \le 6$
$x - y \ge -1$

Standardized Test Practice
Ⓐ Ⓑ Ⓒ Ⓓ

39. Which ordered pair does *not* satisfy the system $x + 2y > 5$ and $3x - y < -2$? **D**
Ⓐ $(-3, 7)$ Ⓑ $(0, 5)$ Ⓒ $(-1, 4)$ Ⓓ $(0, 2.5)$

40. Which system of inequalities is represented by the graph? **A**
Ⓐ $y \le 2x + 2$
$y > -x - 1$

Ⓑ $y \ge 2x + 2$
$y < -x - 1$

Ⓒ $y < 2x + 2$
$y \le -x - 1$

Ⓓ $y > 2x + 2$
$y \le -x - 1$

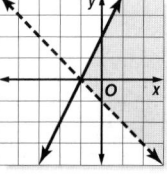

Maintain Your Skills

Mixed Review

Use elimination to solve each system of equations. *(Lessons 7-3 and 7-4)*

41. $2x + 3y = 1$
$4x - 5y = 13$ **$(2, -1)$**

42. $5x - 2y = -3$
$3x + 6y = -9$ **$(-1, -1)$**

43. $-3x + 2y = 12$
$2x - 3y = -13$ **$(-2, 3)$**

44. $6x - 2y = 4$
$5x - 3y = -2$ **$(2, 4)$**

45. $2x + 5y = 13$
$3x - 5y = -18$ **$(-1, 3)$**

46. $3x - y = 6$
$3x + 2y = 15$ **$(3, 3)$**

Write an equation of the line that passes through each point with the given slope. *(Lesson 5-4)* **47.** $y = 2x - 9$ **48.** $y = -6x + 6$ **49.** $y = \frac{1}{3}x - \frac{11}{3}$

47. $(4, -1)$, $m = 2$ **48.** $(1, 0)$, $m = -6$ **49.** $(5, -2)$, $m = \frac{1}{3}$

 WebQuest **Internet Project**

The Spirit of the Games

It's time to complete your project. Use the information and data you have gathered about the Olympics to prepare a portfolio or Web page. Be sure to include graphs and/or tables in your project.

www.algebra1.com/webquest

36.

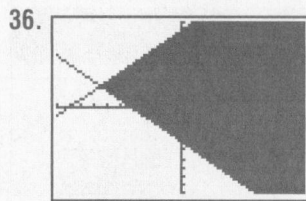

$[-10, 10]$ scl: 1 by
$[-10, 10]$ scl: 1

37.

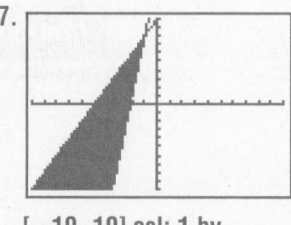

$[-10, 10]$ scl: 1 by
$[-10, 10]$ scl: 1

38.

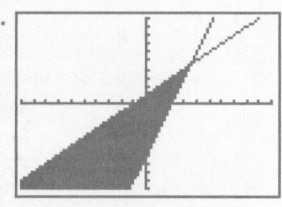

$[-10, 10]$ scl: 1 by
$[-10, 10]$ scl: 1

Study Guide and Review

Vocabulary and Concept Check

consistent (p. 369)	elimination (p. 382)	independent (p. 369)	system of equations (p. 369)
dependent (p. 369)	inconsistent (p. 369)	substitution (p. 376)	system of inequalities (p. 394)

Choose the correct term to complete each statement.

1. If a system of equations has exactly one solution, it is (*dependent*, <u>*independent*</u>).

2. If the graph of a system of equations is parallel lines, the system is (*consistent*, <u>*inconsistent*</u>).

3. A system of equations that has infinitely many solutions is (<u>*dependent*</u>, *independent*).

4. If the graphs of the equations in a system have the same slope and different *y*-intercepts, the graph of the system is a pair of (*intersecting lines*, <u>*parallel lines*</u>).

5. If the graphs of the equations in a system have the same slope and *y*-intercept(s), the system has (*exactly one*, <u>*infinitely many*</u>) solution(s).

6. The solution of a system of equations is $(3, -5)$. The system is (<u>*consistent*</u>, *inconsistent*).

Lesson-by-Lesson Review

7-1 Graphing Systems of Inequalities

See pages 369–374.

Concept Summary

	Intersecting Lines	Same Line	Parallel Lines
Graph of a System			
Number of Solutions	exactly one solution	infinitely many	no solutions
Terminology	consistent and independent	consistent and dependent	inconsistent

Example **Graph the system of equations. Then determine whether the system has *no* solution, *one* solution, or *infinitely many* solutions. If the system has one solution, name it.**

$3x + y = -4$
$6x + 2y = -8$

When the lines are graphed, they coincide. There are infinitely many solutions.

Exercises **Graph each system of equations. Then determine whether the system of equations has *one* solution, *no* solution, or *infinitely many* solutions. If the system has one solution, name it.** *See Example 2 on page 370.* **7–10. See margin for graphs.**

7. $x - y = 9$
   $x + y = 11$
   one; (10, 1)

8. $9x + 2 = 3y$
   $y - 3x = 8$
   no solution

9. $2x - 3y = 4$
   $6y = 4x - 8$
   infinitely many

10. $3x - y = 8$
    $3x = 4 - y$
    one; (2, −2)

Chapter 7 Study Guide and Review

Vocabulary and Concept Check

- This alphabetical list of vocabulary terms in Chapter 7 includes a page reference where each term was introduced.

- **Assessment** A vocabulary test/review for Chapter 7 is available on p. 446 of the *Chapter 7 Resource Masters*.

Lesson-by-Lesson Review

For each lesson,

- the main ideas are summarized,
- additional examples review concepts, and
- practice exercises are provided.

Vocabulary PuzzleMaker

ELL The Vocabulary PuzzleMaker software improves students' mathematics vocabulary using four puzzle formats—crossword, scramble, word search using a word list, and word search using clues. Students can work on a computer screen or from a printed handout.

MindJogger Videoquizzes

ELL MindJogger Videoquizzes provide an alternative review of concepts presented in this chapter. Students work in teams in a game show format to gain points for correct answers. The questions are presented in three rounds.

Round 1 Concepts (5 questions)
Round 2 Skills (4 questions)
Round 3 Problem Solving (4 questions)

See p. 400 for the graphs for Exercises 7–10.

FOLDABLES ™
Study Organizer

For more information about Foldables, see *Teaching Mathematics with Foldables*.

Have students look through the chapter to make sure they have included examples in their Foldables for each method of solving systems of equations they learned.

Encourage students to refer to their Foldables while completing the Study Guide and Review and to use them in preparing for the Chapter Test.

Answers

7.

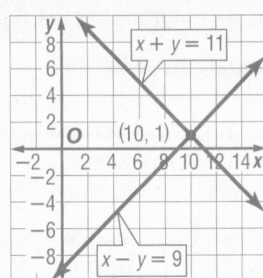

8.

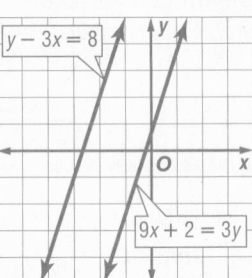

9.

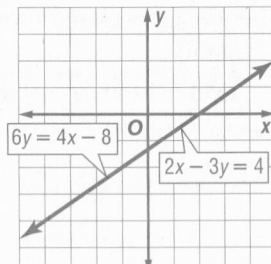

10.

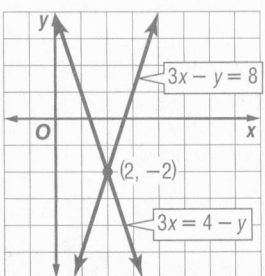

7-2 Substitution

See pages 376–381.

Concept Summary

- In a system of equations, solve one equation for a variable, and then substitute that expression into the second equation to solve.

Example   Use substitution to solve the system of equations.

$y = x - 1$
$4x - y = 19$

Since $y = x - 1$, substitute $x - 1$ for y in the second equation.

$4x - y = 19$	Second equation
$4x - (x - 1) = 19$	$y = x - 1$
$4x - x + 1 = 19$	Distributive Property
$3x + 1 = 19$	Combine like terms.
$3x = 18$	Subtract 1 from each side.
$x = 6$	Divide each side by 3.

Use $y = x - 1$ to find the value of y.

$y = x - 1$	First equation
$y = 6 - 1$	$x = 6$
$y = 5$	The solution is (6, 5).

Exercises   Use substitution to solve each system of equations. If the system does *not* have exactly one solution, state whether it has *no* solutions or *infinitely many* solutions.   *See Examples 1–3 on pages 377 and 378.*

11. $2m + n = 1$
$m - n = 8$
(3, −5)

12. $x = 3 - 2y$
$2x + 4y = 6$
infinitely many solutions

13. $3x - y = 1$
$2x + 4y = 3$
$\left(\dfrac{1}{2}, \dfrac{1}{2}\right)$

14. $0.6m - 0.2n = 0.9$
$n = 4.5 - 3m$
(1.5, 0)

7-3 Elimination Using Addition and Subtraction

See pages 382–386.

Concept Summary

- Sometimes adding or subtracting two equations will eliminate one variable.

Example   Use elimination to solve the system of equations.

$2m - n = 4$
$m + n = 2$

You can eliminate the n terms by adding the equations.

$2m - n = 4$	Write the equations in column form and add.
$(+)\ m + n = 2$	
$3m\ = 6$	Notice the variable n is eliminated.
$m = 2$	Divide each side by 3.

Now substitute 2 for m in either equation to find n.

$m + n = 2$	Second equation
$2 + n = 2$	$m = 2$
$2 + n - 2 = 2 - 2$	Subtract 2 from each side.
$n = 0$	Simplify.

The solution is $(2, 0)$.

Exercises   Use elimination to solve each system of equations.
See Examples 1–3 on pages 382 and 383.

15. $x + 2y = 6$
$x - 3y = -4$
$(2, 2)$

16. $2m - n = 5$
$2m + n = 3$
$(2, -1)$

17. $3x - y = 11$
$x + y = 5$
$(4, 1)$

18. $3x + 1 = -7y$
$6x + 7y = 0$
$\left(\dfrac{1}{3}, -\dfrac{2}{7}\right)$

7-4 *Elimination Using Multiplication*

See pages
387–392.

Concept Summary

- Multiplying one equation by a number or multiplying each equation by a different number is a strategy that can be used to solve a system of equations by elimination.

- There are five methods for solving systems of equations.

Method	The Best Time to Use
Graphing	to estimate the solution, since graphing usually does not give an exact solution
Substitution	if one of the variables in either equation has a coefficient of 1 or −1
Elimination Using Addition	if one of the variables has opposite coefficients in the two equations
Elimination Using Subtraction	if one of the variables has the same coefficient in the two equations
Elimination Using Multiplication	if none of the coefficients are 1 or −1 and neither of the variables can be eliminated by simply adding or subtracting the equations

Example   Use elimination to solve the system of equations.

$x + 2y = 8$
$3x + y = 1.5$

Multiply the second equation by -2 so the coefficients of the y terms are additive inverses. Then add the equations.

$x + 2y = 8$
$3x + y = 1.5$ Multiply by −2.

$$\begin{array}{rl} x + 2y = & 8 \\ (+) -6x - 2y = & -3 \\ \hline -5x \quad\quad = & 5 \end{array}$$ Add the equations.

$\dfrac{-5x}{-5} = \dfrac{5}{-5}$ Divide each side by −5.

$x = -1$ Simplify.

(continued on the next page)

Chapter 7 Study Guide and Review **401**

Study Guide and Review

Chapter 7 **For More …**
• Extra Practice, see pages 835–836.
• Mixed Problem Solving, see page 859.

Answers

27.

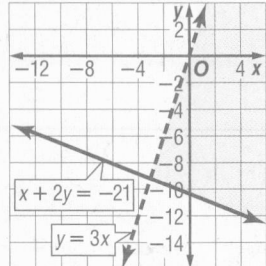

28.

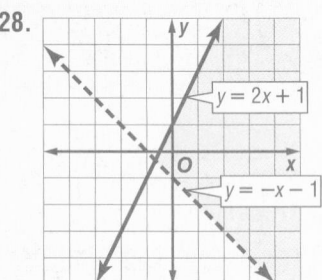

29.

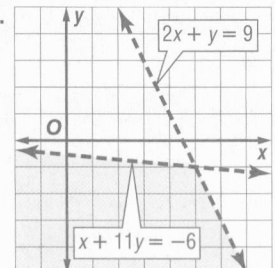

30.

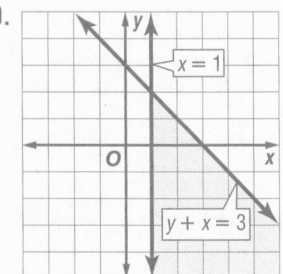

Answers (page 403)

4.

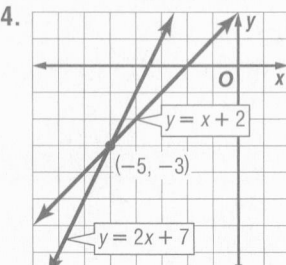

$x + 2y = 8$ First equation

$-1 + 2y = 8$ $x = -1$

$-1 + 2y + 1 = 8 + 1$ Add 1 to each side.

$2y = 9$ Simplify.

$\dfrac{2y}{2} = \dfrac{9}{2}$ Divide each side by 2.

$y = 4.5$ Simplify.

The solution is $(-1, 4.5)$.

Exercises   Use elimination to solve each system of equations.
See Examples 1 and 2 on pages 387 and 388.

19. $x - 5y = 0$
$2x - 3y = 7$ **(5, 1)**

20. $x - 2y = 5$
$3x - 5y = 8$ **(−9, −7)**

21. $2x + 3y = 8$
$x - y = 2$ $\left(2\dfrac{4}{5}, \dfrac{4}{5}\right)$

22. $-5x + 8y = 21$
$10x + 3y = 15$ $\left(\dfrac{3}{5}, 3\right)$

Determine the best method to solve each system of equations. Then solve the system.   *See Example 3 on page 389.*

23. $y = 2x$
$x + 2y = 8$ **substitution;** $\left(1\dfrac{3}{5}, 3\dfrac{1}{5}\right)$

24. $9x + 8y = 7$
$18x - 15y = 14$ **elimination (×);** $\left(\dfrac{7}{9}, 0\right)$

25. $3x + 5y = 2x$
$x + 3y = y$ **substitution; (0, 0)**

26. $2x + y = 3x - 15$
$x + 5 = 4y + 2x$ **substitution; (13, −2)**

7-5 Graphing Systems of Inequalities

See pages 394–398.

Concept Summary

• Graph each inequality on a coordinate plane to determine the intersection of the graphs.

Example   Solve the system of inequalities.

$x \geq -3$
$y \leq x + 2$

The solution includes the ordered pairs in the intersection of the graphs $x \geq -3$ and $y \leq x + 2$. This region is shaded in green. The graphs of $x \geq -3$ and $y \leq x + 2$ are boundaries of this region.

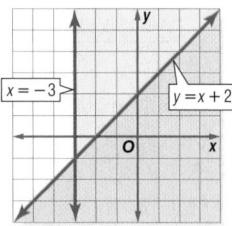

Exercises   Solve each system of inequalities by graphing.
See Examples 1 and 2 on page 394. **27–30. See margin.**

27. $y < 3x$
$x + 2y \geq -21$

28. $y > -x - 1$
$y \leq 2x + 1$

29. $2x + y < 9$
$x + 11y < -6$

30. $x \geq 1$
$y + x \leq 3$

5.

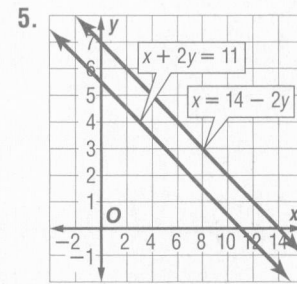

6.

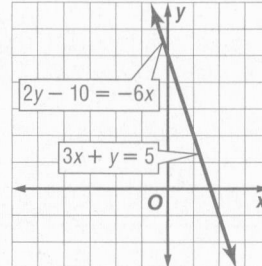

Vocabulary and Concepts

Choose the letter that best matches each description.

1. a system of equations with two parallel lines **c**
2. a system of equations with at least one ordered pair that satisfies both equations **a**
3. a system of equations may be solved using this method **b**

> a. consistent
> b. elimination
> c. inconsistent

Skills and Applications

Graph each system of equations. Then determine whether the system has *no* solution, *one* solution, or *infinitely many* solutions. If the system has one solution, name it. **4–6. See margin for graphs.**

4. $y = x + 2$
   $y = 2x + 7$ **one; (−5, −3)**

5. $x + 2y = 11$
   $x = 14 − 2y$ **no solution**

6. $3x + y = 5$
   $2y − 10 = −6x$ **infinitely many**

Use substitution or elimination to solve each system of equations.

7. $2x + 5y = 16$
   $5x − 2y = 11$ **(3, 2)**

8. $y + 2x = −1$
   $y − 4 = −2x$ **no solution**

9. $2x + y = −4$
   $5x + 3y = −6$ **(−6, 8)**

10. $y = 7 − x$
    $x − y = −3$ **(2, 5)**

11. $x = 2y − 7$
    $y − 3x = −9$ **(5, 6)**

12. $x + y = 10$
    $x − y = 2$ **(6, 4)**

13. $3x − y = 11$
    $x + 2y = −36$ **(−2, −17)**

14. $3x + y = 10$
    $3x − 2y = 16$ **(4, −2)**

15. $5x − 3y = 12$
    $−2x + 3y = −3$ **(3, 1)**

16. $2x + 5y = 12$
    $x − 6y = −11$ **(1, 2)**

17. $x + y = 6$
    $3x − 3y = 13$ $\left(5\frac{1}{6}, \frac{5}{6}\right)$

18. $3x + \frac{1}{3}y = 10$
    $2x − \frac{5}{3}y = 35$ **(5, −15)**

19. **NUMBER THEORY** The units digit of a two-digit number exceeds twice the tens digit by 1. Find the number if the sum of its digits is 10. **37**

20. **GEOMETRY** The difference between the length and width of a rectangle is 7 centimeters. Find the dimensions of the rectangle if its perimeter is 50 centimeters. **16 cm by 9 cm**

Solve each system of inequalities by graphing. **21–23. See pp. 405A–405D.**

21. $y > −4$
    $y < −1$

22. $y \le 3$
    $y > −x + 2$

23. $x \le 2y$
    $2x + 3y \le 7$

24. **FINANCE** Last year, Jodi invested \$10,000, part at 6% annual interest and the rest at 8% annual interest. If she received \$760 in interest at the end of the year, how much did she invest at each rate? **\$2000 at 6%, \$8000 at 8%**

25. **STANDARDIZED TEST PRACTICE** Which graph represents the system of inequalities $y > 2x + 1$ and $y < −x − 2$? **D**

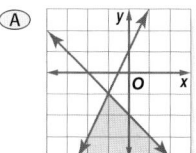 (A)

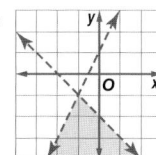 (B)
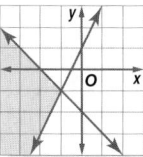 (C)
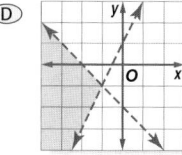 (D)

www.algebra1.com/chapter_test

Chapter 7 · Practice Test

Assessment Options

Vocabulary Test A vocabulary test/review for Chapter 7 can be found on p. 446 of the *Chapter 7 Resource Masters*.

Chapter Tests There are six Chapter 7 Tests and an Open-Ended Assessment task available in the *Chapter 7 Resource Masters*.

Chapter 7 Tests			
Form	Type	Level	Pages
1	MC	basic	433–434
2A	MC	average	435–436
2B	MC	average	437–438
2C	FR	average	439–440
2D	FR	average	441–442
3	FR	advanced	443–444

MC = multiple-choice questions
FR = free-response questions

Open-Ended Assessment
Performance tasks for Chapter 7 can be found on p. 445 of the *Chapter 7 Resource Masters*. A sample scoring rubric for these tasks appears on p. A22.

Unit 2 Test A unit test/review can be found on pp. 453–454 of the *Chapter 7 Resource Masters*.

 ExamView® Pro

Use the networkable **ExamView® Pro** to:

• Create **multiple versions** of tests.
• Create **modified** tests for *Inclusion* students.
• **Edit** existing questions and **add** your own questions.
• Use built-in **state curriculum correlations** to create tests aligned with state standards.
• Change **English** tests to **Spanish** and vice versa.

Portfolio Suggestion

Introduction Have you ever found that your preference for completing a task may be different from those of others?

Ask Students Select one of the systems of equations from this chapter that could be solved by various methods. Demonstrate how to solve it using some of the methods you learned in this chapter. Write some pros and cons for using each method. Which method do you prefer, and why?

These two pages contain practice questions in the various formats that can be found on the most frequently given standardized tests.

A practice answer sheet for these two pages can be found on p. A1 of the *Chapter 7 Resource Masters*.

Standardized Test Practice
Student Recording Sheet, p. A1

Part 1 Multiple Choice

Select the best answer from the choices given and fill in the corresponding oval.

1 Ⓐ Ⓑ Ⓒ Ⓓ   4 Ⓐ Ⓑ Ⓒ Ⓓ   7 Ⓐ Ⓑ Ⓒ Ⓓ   9 Ⓐ Ⓑ Ⓒ Ⓓ
2 Ⓐ Ⓑ Ⓒ Ⓓ   5 Ⓐ Ⓑ Ⓒ Ⓓ   8 Ⓐ Ⓑ Ⓒ Ⓓ   10 Ⓐ Ⓑ Ⓒ Ⓓ
3 Ⓐ Ⓑ Ⓒ Ⓓ   6 Ⓐ Ⓑ Ⓒ Ⓓ

Part 2 Short Response/Grid In

Solve the problem and write your answer in the blank.

For Questions 11–13, also enter your answer by writing each number or symbol in a box. Then fill in the corresponding oval for that number or symbol.

11 _____ (grid in)
12 _____ (grid in)
13 _____ (grid in)
14 _____
15 _____
16 _____
17 _____

Part 3 Extended Response

Record your answers for Questions 18–19 on the back of this paper.

Additional Practice

See pp. 451–452 in the *Chapter 7 Resource Masters* for additional standardized test practice.

Part 1 Multiple Choice

Record your answers on the answer sheet provided by your teacher or on a sheet of paper.

1. What is the solution of $4x - 2(x - 2) - 8 = 0$? (Lesson 3-4) **B**

   Ⓐ -2 Ⓑ 2

   Ⓒ 5 Ⓓ 6

2. Noah paid $17.11 for a CD, including tax. If the tax rate is 7%, then what was the price of the CD before tax? (Lesson 3-5) **C**

   Ⓐ $10.06   Ⓑ $11.98

   Ⓒ $15.99   Ⓓ $17.04

3. What is the range of $f(x) = 2x - 3$ when the domain is {3, 4, 5}? (Lesson 4-3) **B**

   Ⓐ {0, 1, 2}   Ⓑ {3, 5, 7}

   Ⓒ {6, 8, 10}   Ⓓ {9, 11, 13}

4. Jolene kept a log of the numbers of birds that visited a birdfeeder over periods of several hours. In the table below, she recorded the number of hours she watched and the cumulative number of birds that she saw each session. Which equation best represents the data set shown in the table? (Lesson 4-8) **D**

Number of hours, x	1	3	4	6
Number of birds, y	6	14	18	26

   Ⓐ $y = x + 5$ Ⓑ $y = 3x + 3$

   Ⓒ $y = 3x + 5$ Ⓓ $y = 4x + 2$

5. Which equation describes the graph? (Lesson 5-3) **C**

   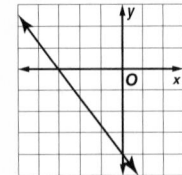

   Ⓐ $3y - 4x = -12$

   Ⓑ $4y + 3x = -16$

   Ⓒ $3y + 4x = -12$

   Ⓓ $3y + 4x = -9$

6. Which equation represents a line parallel to the line given by $y - 3x = 6$? (Lesson 5-6) **B**

   Ⓐ $y = -3x + 4$ Ⓑ $y = 3x - 2$

   Ⓒ $y = \frac{1}{3}x + 6$ Ⓓ $y = -\frac{1}{3}x + 4$

7. Tamika has $185 in her bank account. She needs to deposit enough money so that she can withdraw $230 for her car payment and still have at least $200 left in the account. Which inequality describes d, the amount she needs to deposit? (Lesson 6-1) **D**

   Ⓐ $d(185 - 230) \geq 200$

   Ⓑ $185 - 230d \geq 200$

   Ⓒ $185 + 230 + d \geq 200$

   Ⓓ $185 + d - 230 \geq 200$

8. The perimeter of a rectangular garden is 68 feet. The length of the garden is 4 more than twice the width. Which system of equations will determine the length ℓ and the width w of the garden? (Lesson 7-2) **B**

   Ⓐ $2\ell + 2w = 68$ Ⓑ $2\ell + 2w = 68$
      $\ell = 4 - 2w$ $\ell = 2w + 4$

   Ⓒ $2 + 2w = 68$ Ⓓ $2\ell + 2w = 68$
      $2\ell - w = 4$ $w = 2\ell + 4$

9. Ernesto spent a total of $64 for a pair of jeans and a shirt. The jeans cost $6 more than the shirt. What was the cost of the jeans? (Lesson 7-2) **C**

   Ⓐ $26   Ⓑ $29

   Ⓒ $35   Ⓓ $58

10. What is the value of y in the following system of equations? (Lesson 7-3) **C**

    $3x + 4y = 8$
    $3x + 2y = -2$

    Ⓐ -2 Ⓑ 4

    Ⓒ 5 Ⓓ 6

ExamView® Pro

Special banks of standardized test questions similar to those on the SAT, ACT, TIMSS 8, NAEP 8, and Algebra 1 End-of-Course tests can be found on this CD-ROM.

Preparing for Standardized Tests
For test-taking strategies and more
practice, see pages 867–884.

Part 2 | Short Response/Grid In

Record your answers on the answer sheet
provided by your teacher or on a sheet of
paper.

11. The diagram shows the dimensions of the
cargo area of a delivery truck.

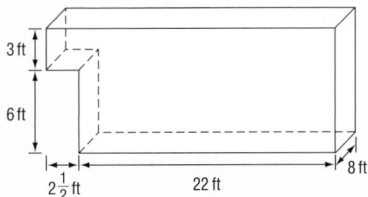

What is the maximum volume of cargo,
in cubic feet, that can fit in the truck?
(Prerequisite Skill) **1644**

12. The perimeter of the square below is 204 feet.
What is the value of x? (Lesson 3-4) **9**

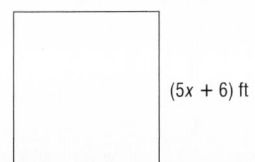

$(5x + 6)$ ft

13. What is the x-intercept of the graph of
$4x + 3y = 12$? (Lesson 4-5) **3**

14. What are the slope and the y-intercept of
the graph of the equation $4x - 2y = 5$?
(Lesson 5-4) $m = 2, b = -\dfrac{5}{2}$

15. Solve the following system of equations.
(Lesson 7-2) $(3, 5)$

$$5x - y = 10$$
$$7x - 2y = 11$$

> **Test-Taking Tip** Ⓐ Ⓑ Ⓒ Ⓓ
>
> **Questions 11 and 12**
> To prepare for a standardized test, make flash cards of
> key mathematical terms, such as "perimeter" and
> "volume." Use the glossary of your textbook to determine
> the important terms and their correct definitions.

www.algebra1.com/standardized_test

16. Two times one number minus three times
another number is -11. The sum of the first
number and three times the second number
is 8. What are the two numbers? (Lesson 7-4)
$-1, 3$

17. Write a system of inequalities for the graph.
(Lesson 7-5)

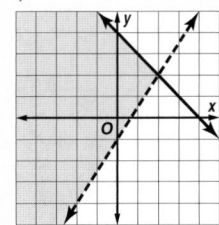

$y > \dfrac{3}{2}x - 1, y \le -x + 4$

Part 3 | Extended Response

Record your answers on a sheet of paper.
Show your work.

18. During a work-out session, Mark either ran
at a speed of 7 miles per hour or walked at
a speed of 3 miles per hour. He completed
20 miles in 3 hours. (Lesson 7-1)

a. Let r represent the number of miles Mark
ran and w represent the number of miles
Mark walked. Write a system of
equations that represents the situation.
$r + w = 3, 7r + 3w = 20$

b. Solve the system of equations to find
how much time Mark spent running.
2.75 h or 2 h 45 min

19. The manager of a movie theater found that
Saturday's sales were \$3675. He knew
that a total of 650 tickets were sold Saturday.
Adult tickets cost \$7.50, and children's tickets
cost \$4.50. (Lesson 7-2) **a–b. See margin.**

a. Write equations to represent the number
of tickets sold and the amount of money
collected.

b. How many of each kind of ticket were
sold? Show your work. Include all steps.

Chapter 7 Standardized Test Practice **405**

Evaluating Extended Response Questions

Extended Response questions
are graded by using a multilevel
rubric that guides you in
assessing a student's knowledge
of a particular concept.

Goal: Use a system of equations
to find ticket sales and money
earned from sales.

Sample Scoring Rubric: The following rubric is a sample scoring
device. You may wish to add
more detail to this sample to meet
your individual scoring needs.

Score	Criteria
4	A correct solution that is supported by well-developed, accurate explanations
3	A generally correct solution, but may contain minor flaws in reasoning or computation
2	A partially correct interpretation and/or solution to the problem
1	A correct solution with no supporting evidence or explanation
0	An incorrect solution indicating no mathematical understanding of the concept or task, or no solution is given

Answers

19a. $A + C = 650,$
$7.5A + 4.5C = 3675$

19b.
$$A + C = 650$$
$$A + C - C = 650 - C$$
$$A = 650 - C$$
$$7.5A + 4.5C = 3675$$
$$7.5(650 - C) + 4.5C = 3675$$
$$4875 - 7.5C + 4.5C = 3675$$
$$4875 - 3C = 3675$$
$$4875 - 3C - 4875 = 3675 - 4875$$
$$-3C = -1200$$
$$\frac{-3C}{-3} = \frac{-1200}{-3}$$
$$C = 400$$

$A = 650 - C$
$A = 650 - 400$ or $A = 250$

250 adult tickets and 400 child tickets

Page 367, Chapter 7 Getting Started

1.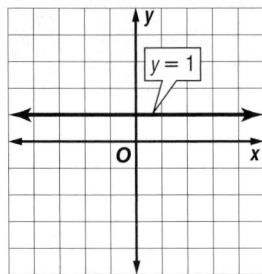

2.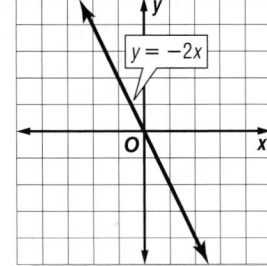

3.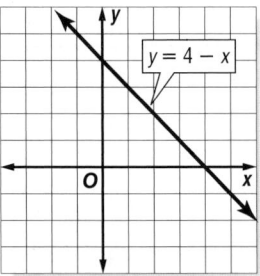

4.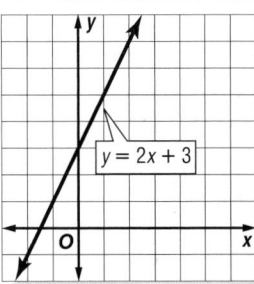

5.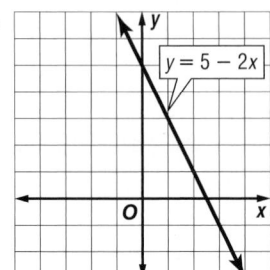

6.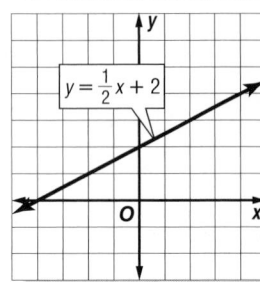

Page 371–374, Lesson 7-1

1. Sample answer:

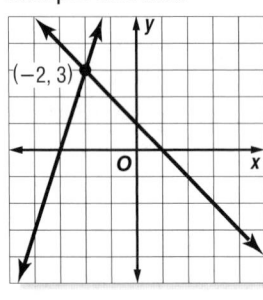

2. Always; if the system of linear equations has 2 solutions, their graphs are the same line and there are infinitely many solutions.

3. Sample answer: The graphs of the equations $x + y = 3$ and $2x + 2y = 6$ have a slope of -1. Since the graphs of the equations coincide, there are infinitely many solutions.

8.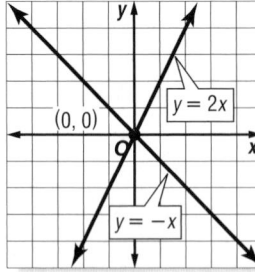

9.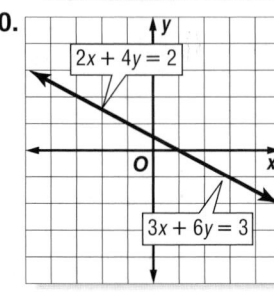

10.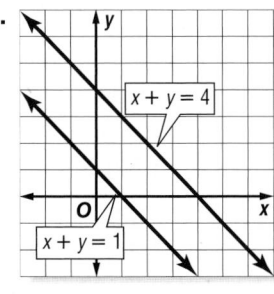

11.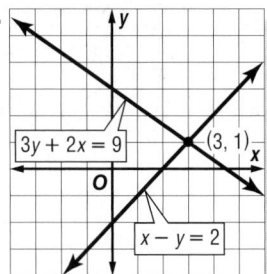

12.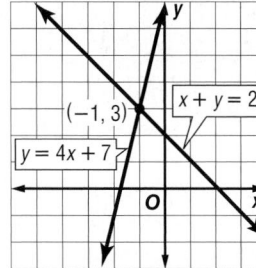

13.

23.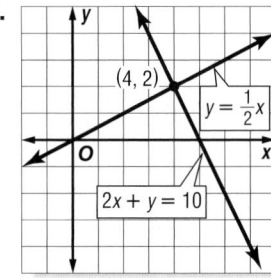

24.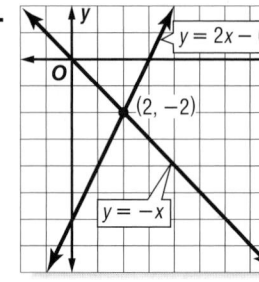

25.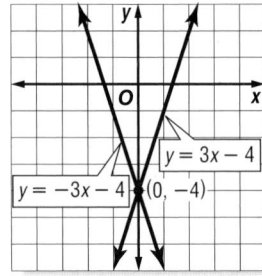

26.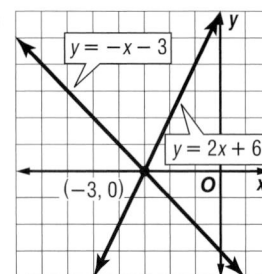

27.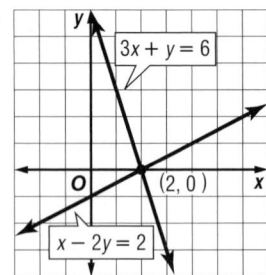

28.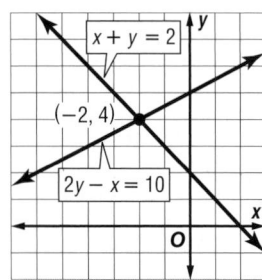

29.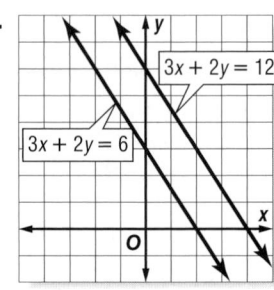

30.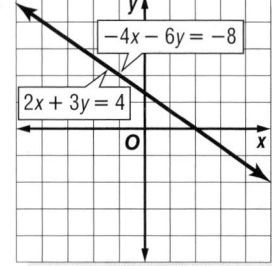

31.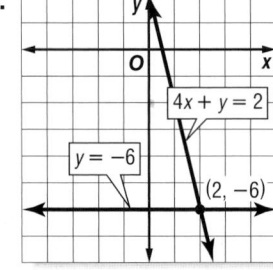

32.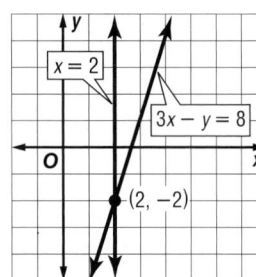

33.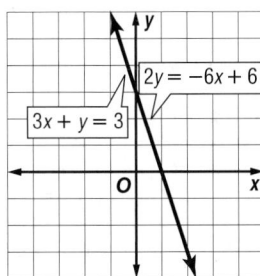

34.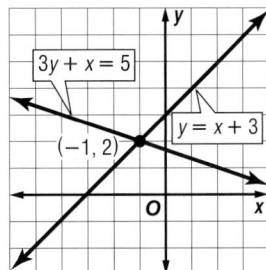

35.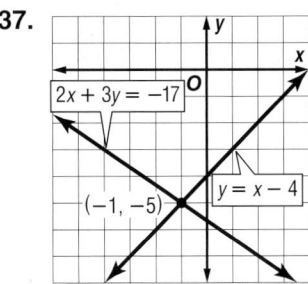

36.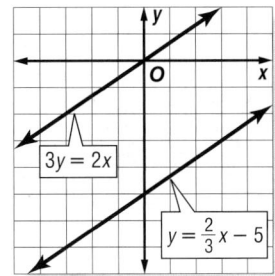

37.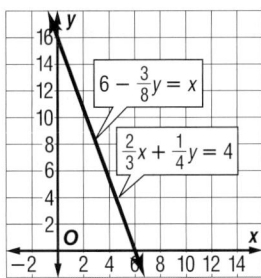

38.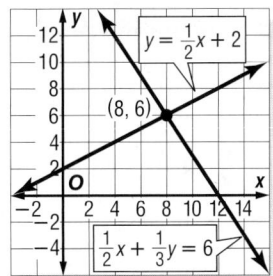

39.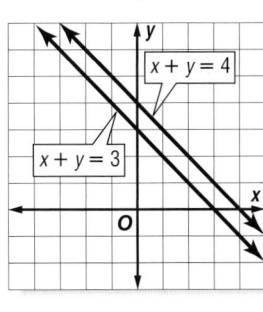

40.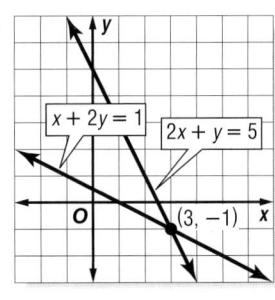

53.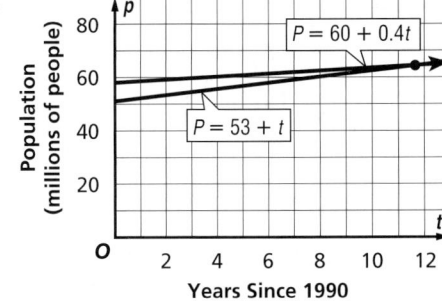

Pages 379–381, Lesson 7-2

43.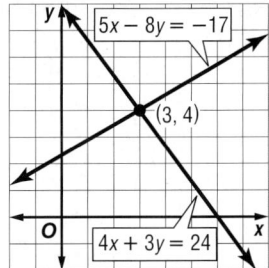

44.

45.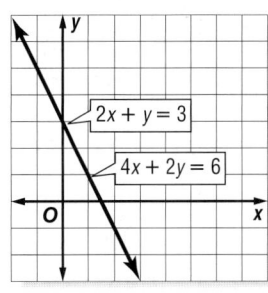

46.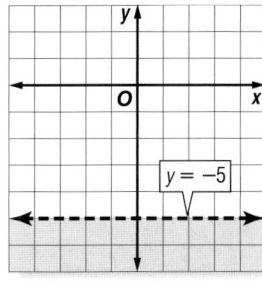

47.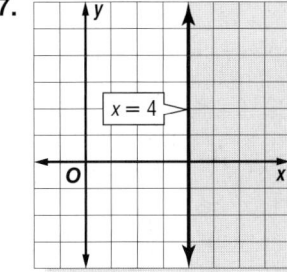

48.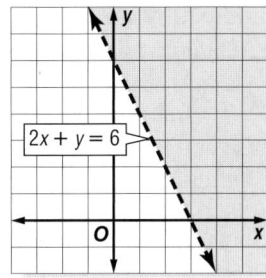

Pages 384–386, Lesson 7-3

41. Elimination can be used to solve problems about meteorology if the coefficients of one variable are the same or are additive inverses. Answers should include the following.

- The two equations in the system of equations are added or subtracted so that one of the variables is eliminated. You then solve for the remaining variable. This number is substituted into one of the original equations, and that equation is solved for the other variable.

-

$$\begin{aligned} n + d &= 24 \\ (+) \; n - d &= 12 \\ \hline 2n &= 36 \end{aligned}$$ Write the equations in column form and add. Notice the d variable is eliminated.

$$\frac{2n}{2} = \frac{36}{2}$$ Divide each side by 2.

$n = 18$ Simplify.

$n + d = 24$ First equation

$18 + d = 24$ $n = 18$

$18 + d - 18 = 24 - 18$ Subtract 18 from each side.

$d = 6$ Simplify.

On the winter solstice, Seward, Alaska, has 18 hours of nighttime and 6 hours of daylight.

47.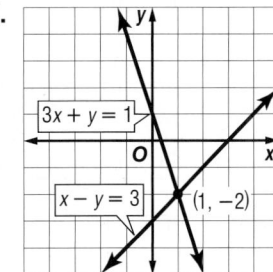

48.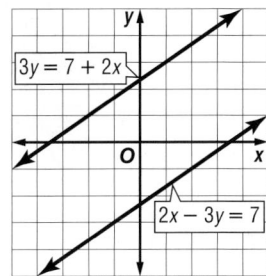

49.

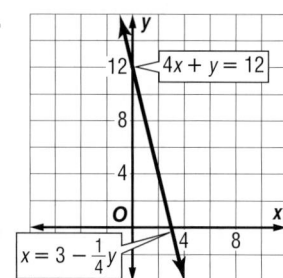

Pages 390–392, Lesson 7-4

3. Sample answer: (1) You could solve the first equation for a and substitute the resulting expression for a in the second equation. Then find the value of b. Use this value for b and one of the original equations to find the value of a. (2) You could multiply the first equation by 3 and add this new equation to the second equation. This will eliminate the b term. Find the value of a. Use this value for a and one of the original equations to find the value of b. See student's work for their preference and explanation.

44. By having two equations that represent the time restraints, a manager can determine the best use of employee time. Answers should include the following.

- $20c + 10b = 800 \rightarrow \quad 20c + 10b = \quad 800$
  $10c + 30b = 900 \rightarrow \underline{-20c - 60b = -1800}$
  $$-50b = -1000$$
  $$\frac{-50b}{-50} = \frac{-1000}{-50}$$
  $$b = 20$$

  $$20c + 10b = 800$$
  $$20c + 10(20) = 800$$
  $$20c + 200 = 800$$
  $$20c + 200 - 200 = 800 - 200$$
  $$20c = 600$$
  $$\frac{20c}{20} = \frac{600}{20}$$
  $$c = 30$$

- In order to make the most of the employee and oven time, the manager should make assignments to bake 30 batches of cookies and 20 loaves of bread.

Page 395, Graphing Calculator Investigation

2.

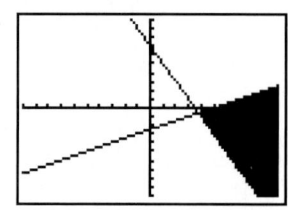

[−10, 10] scl: 1 by
[−10, 10] scl: 1

4.

[−10, 10] scl: 1 by
[−10, 10] scl: 1

Pages 396–398, Lesson 7-5

4.

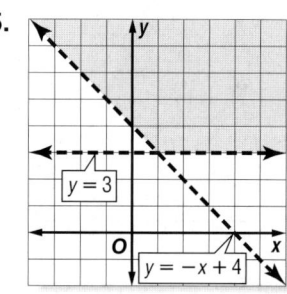

5.

6.

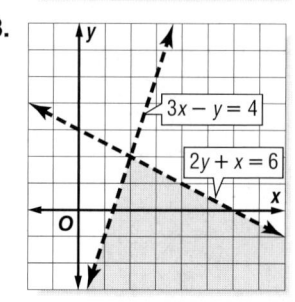

7.

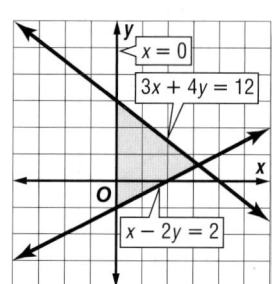

8.

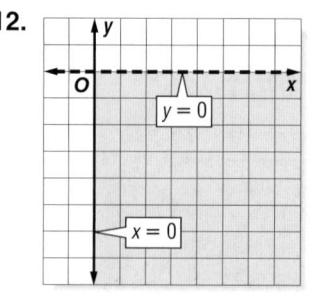

9.

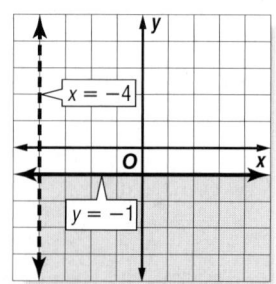

10. **Natasha's Daily Exercise**

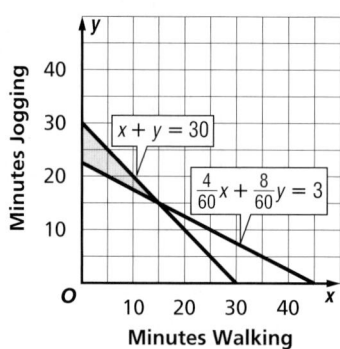

12.

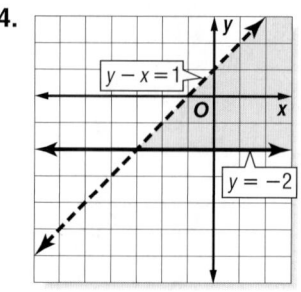

13.

14.

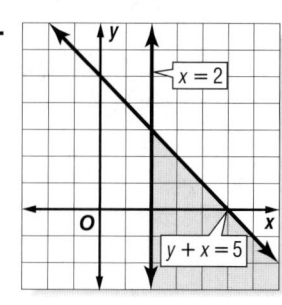

15.

16.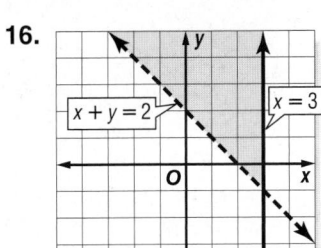

17.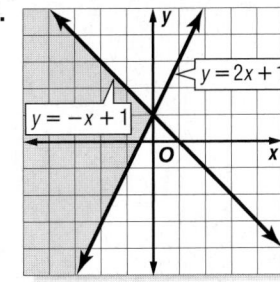

18.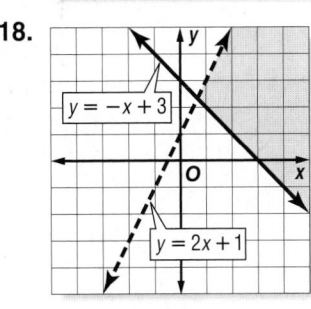

19.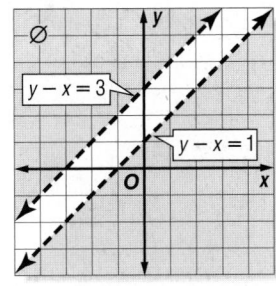

20.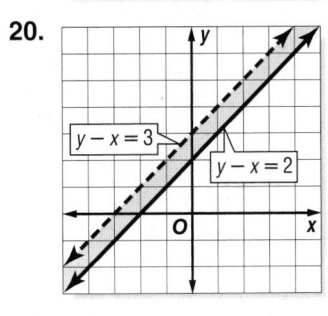

21.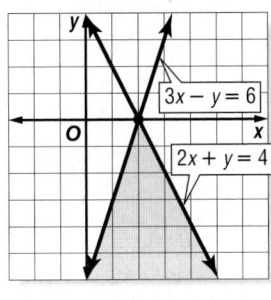

22.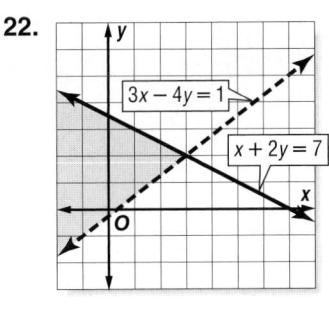

23.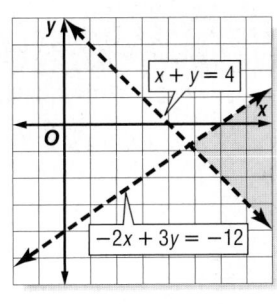

24.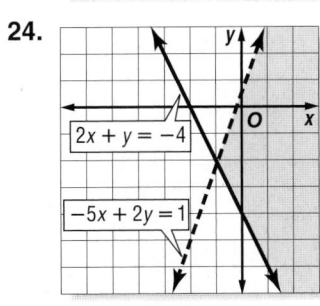

25.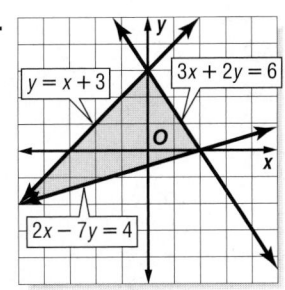

26.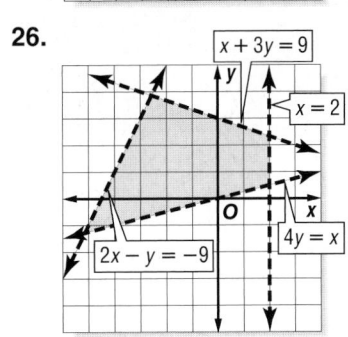

29. Green Paint

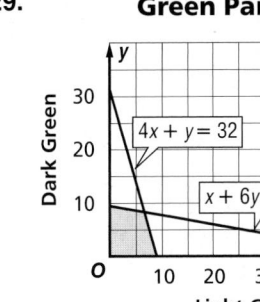

31. Appropriate Cholesterol Levels

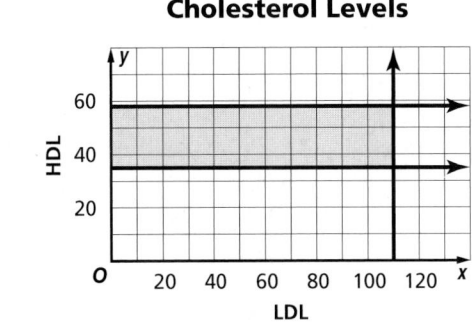

35. By graphing a system of equations, you can see the appropriate range of Calories and fat intake. Answers should include the following.

- Two sample appropriate Calorie and fat intakes are 2200 Calories and 60 g of fat and 2300 Calories and 65 g of fat.

- The graph represents $2000 \le c \le 2400$ and $60 \le f \le 75$.

Page 403, Practice Test

21.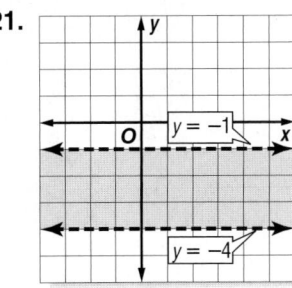

22.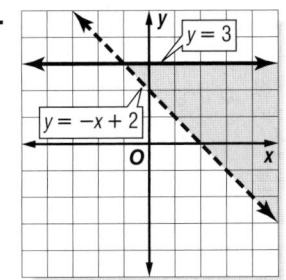

23.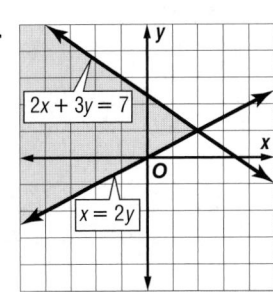

Introduction

In this unit, students will be introduced to nonlinear functions. Students will first learn about polynomials and operations involving monomials and polynomials. Students then learn various methods of factoring, and are finally introduced to quadratic and exponential functions.

Assessment Options

Unit 3 Test Pages 641–642 of the *Chapter 10 Resource Masters* may be used as a test or review for Unit 3. This assessment contains both multiple-choice and short answer items.

ExamView® Pro

This CD-ROM can be used to create additional unit tests and review worksheets.

Yearly Progress Pro

An online, research-based, instructional, assessment, and intervention tool that provides specific feedback on student mastery of state and national standards, instant remediation, and a data management system to track performance. For more information, contact mhdigitallearning.com.

UNIT 3

Not all real-world situations can be modeled using a linear function. In this unit, you will learn about polynomials and nonlinear functions.

Polynomials and Nonlinear Functions

Chapter 8
Polynomials

Chapter 9
Factoring

Chapter 10
Quadratic and Exponential Functions

Real-Life Math Videos

What's Math Got to Do With It? Real-Life Math Videos engage students by showing them how math is used in everyday situations. Use Video 3 with this unit.

Teaching Suggestions

Have students study the USA TODAY Snapshot.

- Ask students what fraction of people believe that evidence will be discovered that life exists in this or other galaxies. $\frac{2}{3}$

- Take an informal poll in the class and compare the results to the USA TODAY results.

- Point out to students that in their WebQuest they will be designing a display about the planets in the solar system.

Additional USA TODAY Snapshots appearing in Unit 3:

Chapter 8   A sweet holiday season (p. 427)

Chapter 9   Number of domain registrations climbs (p. 494)

Chapter 10   Spending more on eating out (p. 561)

           Making gains (p. 563)

           Grand Canyon Visitors (p. 564)

WebQuest   Internet Project

Pluto Is Falling From Status as Distant Planet

Source: *USA TODAY,* March 28, 2001

"Like any former third-grader, Catherine Beyhl knows that the solar system has nine planets, and she knows a phrase to help remember their order: 'My Very Educated Mother Just Served Us Nine Pizzas.' But she recently visited the American Museum of Natural History's glittering new astronomy hall at the Hayden Planetarium and found only eight scale models of the planets. No Pizza—no Pluto." In this project, you will examine how scientific notation, factors, and graphs are useful in presenting information about the planets.

Log on to www.algebra1.com/webquest. Begin your WebQuest by reading the Task.

Then continue working on your WebQuest as you study Unit 3.

Lesson	8-3	9-1	10-2
Page	429	479	537

USA TODAY Snapshots®

Are we alone in the universe?

Adults who believe that during the next century evidence will be discovered that shows:

- Life exists only on Earth — 28%
- Other life in this or other galaxies — 66%
- Don't know — 6%

Source: The Gallup Organization for the John Templeton Foundation

By Cindy Hall and Sam Ward, USA TODAY

WebQuest   Internet Project

Problem-Based Learning   A WebQuest is an online project in which students do research on the Internet, gather data, and make presentations using word processing, graphing, page-making, or presentation software. In each chapter, students advance to the next step in their WebQuest. At the end of Chapter 10, the project culminates with a presentation of their findings.

Teaching notes and sample answers are available in the *WebQuest and Project Resources.*

Polynomials
Chapter Overview and Pacing

Year-long and two-year pacing: pages T20–T21.

LESSON OBJECTIVES	PACING (days)			
	Regular		**Block**	
	Basic/ Average	Advanced	Basic/ Average	Advanced
8-1 Multiplying Monomials (pp. 410–416) • Multiply monomials. • Simplify expressions involving powers of monomials. *Follow-Up:* Use paper prisms to investigate surface area and volume.	2 (with 8-1 Follow-Up)	2 (with 8-1 Follow-Up)	0.5	0.5
8-2 Dividing Monomials (pp. 417–423) • Simplify expressions involving the quotient of monomials. • Simplify expressions containing negative exponents.	2	2	1.5 (with 8-1 Follow-Up)	1.5 (with 8-1 Follow-Up)
8-3 Scientific Notation (pp. 425–430) • Express numbers in scientific notation and standard notation. • Find products and quotients of numbers expressed in scientific notation.	1	1	0.5	0.5
8-4 Polynomials (pp. 431–436) *Preview:* Use algebra tiles to model polynomials. • Find the degree of a polynomial. • Arrange the terms of a polynomial in ascending or descending order.	2 (with 8-4 Preview)	1	1 (with 8-4 Preview)	0.5
8-5 Adding and Subtracting Polynomials (pp. 437–443) *Preview:* Use algebra tiles to add and subtract polynomials. • Add polynomials. • Subtract polynomials.	2	2	1	1
8-6 Multiplying a Polynomial by a Monomial (pp. 444–449) • Find the product of a monomial and a polynomial. • Solve equations involving polynomials.	2	1	1	0.5
8-7 Multiplying Polynomials (pp. 450–457) *Preview:* Use algebra tiles to find the product of two binomials. • Multiply two binomials by using the FOIL method. • Multiply two polynomials by using the Distributive Property.	2 (with 8-7 Preview)	2	1 (with 8-7 Preview)	1
8-8 Special Products (pp. 458–463) • Find squares of sums and differences. • Find the product of a sum and a difference.	1	1	0.5	0.5
Study Guide and **Practice Test** (pp. 464–469) **Standardized Test Practice** (pp. 470–471)	1	1	0.5	0.5
Chapter Assessment	1	1	0.5	0.5
TOTAL	16	14	8	7

*An electronic version of this chapter is available on **StudentWorks**™. This backpack solution CD-ROM allows students instant access to the Student Edition, lesson worksheet pages, and web resources.*

Chapter Resource Manager

CHAPTER 8 RESOURCE MASTERS

Study Guide and Intervention	Practice (Skills and Average)	Reading to Learn Mathematics	Enrichment	Assessment	Prerequisite Skills Workbook	Applications*	Parent and Student Study Guide Workbook	5-Minute Check Transparencies	Interactive Chalkboard	AlgePASS: Tutorial Plus (lessons)	Materials
455–456	457–458	459	460				59	8-1	8-1	18	(*Follow-Up:* centimeter grid paper)
461–462	463–464	465	466	517			60	8-2	8-2	19	graphing calculator
467–468	469–470	471	472		33–36	SC 15, SM 67–70	61	8-3	8-3	20	graphing calculator
473–474	475–476	477	478	517, 519		GCS 37	62	8-4	8-4		(*Preview:* algebra tiles)
479–480	481–482	483	484				63	8-5	8-5		(*Preview:* algebra tiles)
485–486	487–488	489	490	518		SC 16	64	8-6	8-6	21	
491–492	493–494	495	496			GCS 38	65	8-7	8-7	22	(*Preview:* algebra tiles, product mat)
497–498	499–500	501	502	518			66	8-8	8-8	23	
				503–516, 520–522			67				

Key to Abbreviations: GCS = Graphing Calculator and Spreadsheet Masters,
SC = School-to-Career Masters,
SM = Science and Mathematics Lab Manual

ELL Study Guide and Intervention, Skills Practice, Practice, and Parent and Student Study Guide Workbooks are also available in Spanish.

Mathematical Connections and Background

Continuity of Instruction

Prior Knowledge

In Chapter 1, students apply the order of operations, and the Distributive, Commutative, and Associative Properties to simplify expressions. Students perform operations with real numbers in Chapter 2.

This Chapter

This chapter helps students master operations with monomials and polynomials. It begins with connecting the multiplication and division of monomials with variables and exponents to multiplying and dividing real numbers. Students convert numbers from standard notation to scientific notation, and vice versa, then multiply and divide numbers written in scientific notation. Polynomials are defined, and students learn to perform operations with them. Finally, students learn patterns for finding products of some special polynomials.

Future Connections

Students will apply their knowledge of multiplying and dividing monomials and polynomials to factoring polynomials in Chapter 9. The concepts are essential to simplifying and solving many problems involving upper level mathematics and science.

8-1 Multiplying Monomials

A monomial is a number, variable, or a product of a number and one or more variables. Monomials do not involve the addition, subtraction, or division of variables. Monomials that only involve real numbers are called constants. This is because their value does not change.

When multiplying monomials, use the Commutative and Associative Properties to group constants together and group powers with the same base together. To multiply powers with the same base, add the exponents. Multiply the exponents to find a power of a power. When finding the power of a product, find the power of each factor. A monomial expression is simplified when each base appears exactly once, there are no powers of powers, and all fractions are in simplest form.

8-2 Dividing Monomials

Exponents are subtracted when dividing two powers that have the same base. To find the power of a quotient, find the power of both the numerator and the denominator. If the numerator and denominator of a fraction are the same, the value of the fraction is 1. Therefore, if both the numerator and denominator have the same base raised to the same exponent, the value of the fraction is 1. Using the Quotient of Powers Property, the exponents of the original fraction are subtracted and the fraction simplifies to the base raised to the zero power. So it follows that any base raised to the zero power equals one.

A positive number raised to a negative power represents the reciprocal of the number with the opposite or positive exponent. Likewise, if a negative exponent appears in the denominator of a fraction, this power is equivalent to a fraction with this same base raised to the opposite power in its numerator.

8-3 Scientific Notation

When a number is written in scientific notation, the power of 10 is the number of places the decimal moves. To convert a number that is in scientific notation to one in standard form, move the decimal the number of places indicated by the exponent. A positive exponent is used to represent a number that is greater than or equal to 10 in standard form. A negative exponent represents a number that is less than 1 in standard form. To translate a number in standard form to scientific notation, first move the decimal to the right of the first non-zero digit. Then write the appropriate power of 10 to the right of the number. Keep in mind what the sign of the power indicates.

Numbers in scientific notation can be multiplied or divided. First multiply or divide the decimals. Then apply

either the Product of Powers or the Quotient of Powers Property to simplify the powers of 10. Next, rewrite the decimal in scientific notation and simplify the powers of 10. The result is in scientific notation, but it can also be presented in standard form if preferred.

8-4 Polynomials

A polynomial is a monomial, or a sum of monomials. Remember that subtraction can be rewritten as addition. A monomial has only one term and is considered a type of polynomial. Some polynomials that contain more than one monomial, or term, have special names. A binomial has two terms and a trinomial has three terms. All others are just referred to as polynomials. The degree of a monomial is the sum of the exponents of all its variables. The term with the greatest degree determines the degree of a polynomial. Usually the terms of a polynomial are arranged so that the powers of one variable are in ascending (increasing) or descending (decreasing) order. This aids in reading and understanding the polynomial.

8-5 Adding and Subtracting Polynomials

To add polynomials, combine like terms. Like terms have the same variable bases with the same exponents. The coefficients of like terms are added using the rules for adding real numbers. The bases and exponents of these terms, however, remain the same. The rule for subtracting polynomials is the same as the rule for subtracting integers. First replace each term of the second polynomial with its additive inverse or opposite. Then combine like terms using the rules for adding real numbers.

8-6 Multiplying a Polynomial by a Monomial

To multiply a polynomial by a monomial, apply the Distributive Property by multiplying each term in the polynomial by the monomial. Use the rules for multiplying monomials. If the monomial is negative, don't forget to apply the rules for multiplying real numbers. Be sure to simplify by combining any like terms.

Equations may contain polynomials. To solve these equations, first simplify each side using the order of operations by multiplying, adding, and subtracting as indicated. Then apply the rules for solving multi-step equations and equations with variables on both sides.

8-7 Multiplying Polynomials

The Distributive Property is applied twice when multiplying two binomials. Multiply the first term of the first binomial by each term of the second binomial. Do the same with the second term of the first binomial. Then combine like terms. This results in a multiplying pattern called the FOIL method. You multiply the First terms, Outer terms, Inside terms, and Last terms of the binomials. The Distributive Property is used to multiply any two polynomials. The product is not in simplest terms until all like terms have been combined.

8-8 Special Products

The Distributive Property and FOIL method can always be used to multiply polynomials. However, some binomial products have patterns that make their multiplication simpler. One product involves the multiplying of two identical binomials, called the square of a sum. The pattern is $(a + b)(a + b) = a^2 + 2ab + b^2$. There is also a pattern for the square of a difference: $(a - b)(a - b) = a^2 - 2ab + b^2$. Note that the only difference in the two patterns is the sign before the middle term. A third pattern exists for the product of a sum and a difference: $(a + b)(a - b) = a^2 - b^2$. The products of the Outer terms and the Inner terms add to zero. While it is not essential to learn these patterns, identifying when to use them can make simplifying these products quicker and less laborious.

Quick Review Math Handbook

Hot Words includes a glossary of terms while Hot Topics consists of explanations of key mathematical concepts with exercises to test comprehension. This valuable resource can be used as a reference in the classroom or for home study.

Lesson	Hot Topics Section	Lesson	Hot Topics Section
GS8	3.1, 3.4, 7.5, 7.7, 7.8	8-4	6.2
8-1	2.1	8-5	6.2
8-2	3.4	8-6	6.2
8-3	3.3, 6.3	8-7	3.2, 3.4

GS = Getting Started

 Additional mathematical information and teaching notes are available at www.algebra1.com/key_concepts.

DAILY
INTERVENTION and Assessment

Key to Abbreviations:
TWE = Teacher Wraparound Edition; CRM = Chapter Resource Masters

	Type	Student Edition	Teacher Resources	Technology/Internet
INTERVENTION	Ongoing	Prerequisite Skills, pp. 409, 415, 423, 430, 436, 443, 449, 457 Practice Quiz 1, p. 430 Practice Quiz 2, p. 449	5-Minute Check Transparencies *Prerequisite Skills Workbook*, pp. 33–36 Quizzes, *CRM* pp. 517–518 Mid-Chapter Test, *CRM* p. 519 Study Guide and Intervention, *CRM* pp. 455–456, 461–462, 467–468, 473–474, 479–480, 485–486, 491–492, 497–498	AlgePASS: Tutorial Plus, Lessons 18, 19, 20, 21, 22, and 23 www.algebra1.com/self_check_quiz www.algebra1.com/extra_examples
	Mixed Review	pp. 415, 423, 430, 436, 443, 449, 457, 463	Cumulative Review, *CRM* p. 520	
	Error Analysis	Find the Error, pp. 413, 421, 441 Common Misconceptions, pp. 420, 432, 454	Find the Error, *TWE* pp. 413, 421 Unlocking Misconceptions, *TWE* pp. 421, 433 Tips for New Teachers, *TWE* pp. 426, 459	
	Standardized Test Practice	pp. 415, 420, 421, 423, 430, 436, 443, 448, 457, 463, 469, 470–471	*TWE* pp. 470–471 Standardized Test Practice, *CRM* pp. 521–522	Standardized Test Practice CD-ROM www.algebra1.com/standardized_test
ASSESSMENT	Open-Ended Assessment	Writing in Math, pp. 415, 423, 430, 436, 443, 448, 457, 463 Open Ended, pp. 413, 421, 428, 434, 441, 446, 455, 461 Standardized Test, p. 471	Modeling: *TWE* pp. 415, 436, 449 Speaking: *TWE* pp. 423, 457 Writing: *TWE* pp. 430, 443, 463 Open-Ended Assessment, *CRM* p. 515	
	Chapter Assessment	Study Guide, pp. 464–468 Practice Test, p. 469	Multiple-Choice Tests (Forms 1, 2A, 2B), *CRM* pp. 503–508 Free-Response Tests (Forms 2C, 2D, 3), *CRM* pp. 509–514 Vocabulary Test/Review, *CRM* p. 516	ExamView® Pro (see below) MindJogger Videoquizzes www.algebra1.com/vocabulary_review www.algebra1.com/chapter_test

For more information on Yearly ProgressPro, see p. 406.

Algebra Lesson	Yearly ProgressPro Skill Lesson(s)
8-1	Multiplying Monomials
8-2	Dividing Monomials Dividing Monomials with Zero and Negative Exponents
8-3	Scientific Notation
8-4	Polynomials
8-5	Adding and Subtracting Polynomials
8-6	Multiplying a Polynomial by a Monomial Solving Equations with Monomials and Polynomials
8-7	Multiplying Polynomials
8-8	Special Products

ExamView® Pro

Use the networkable **ExamView® Pro** to:
- Create **multiple versions** of tests.
- Create **modified** tests for *Inclusion* students.
- **Edit** existing questions and **add** your own questions.
- Use built-in **state curriculum correlations** to create tests aligned with state standards.
- Change **English** tests to **Spanish** and vice versa.

For more information on Intervention and Assessment, see pp. T8–T11.

Reading and Writing in Mathematics

Glencoe Algebra 1 provides numerous opportunities to incorporate reading and writing into the mathematics classroom.

Student Edition

- Foldables Study Organizer, p. 409
- Concept Check questions require students to verbalize and write about what they have learned in the lesson. (pp. 413, 421, 428, 434, 441, 446, 455, 461)
- Reading Mathematics, p. 424
- Writing in Math questions in every lesson, pp. 415, 423, 430, 436, 443, 448, 457, 463
- Reading Study Tip, pp. 410, 425
- WebQuest, p. 429

Teacher Wraparound Edition

- Foldables Study Organizer, pp. 409, 464
- Study Notebook suggestions, pp. 413, 416, 421, 424, 428, 431, 434, 438, 446, 451, 455, 461
- Modeling activities, pp. 415, 436, 449
- Speaking activities, pp. 423, 457
- Writing activities, pp. 430, 443, 463
- Differentiated Instruction, (Verbal/Linguistic), p. 460
- **ELL** Resources, pp. 408, 414, 422, 424, 429, 435, 442, 448, 456, 460, 462, 464

Additional Resources

- Vocabulary Builder worksheets require students to define and give examples for key vocabulary terms as they progress through the chapter. (*Chapter 8 Resource Masters*, pp. vii-viii)
- Reading to Learn Mathematics master for each lesson (*Chapter 8 Resource Masters*, pp. 459, 465, 471, 477, 483, 489, 495, 501)
- *Vocabulary PuzzleMaker* software creates crossword, jumble, and word search puzzles using vocabulary lists that you can customize.
- *Teaching Mathematics with Foldables* provides suggestions for promoting cognition and language.
- *Reading and Writing in the Mathematics Classroom*
- *WebQuest and Project Resources*

For more information on Reading and Writing in Mathematics, see pp. T6–T7.

PROJECT CRISS^SM Study Skill

Writing out the steps in a mathematical process using a point-by-point format with an example can help students better understand that process. In order to explain a process, they must not only understand how to perform each step, but they must also understand the reasoning behind each step. Provide students with the description below as an example of using a point-by-point format to explain how to multiply a polynomial by a monomial. After reading Lessons 8-7 and 8-8, have students write a description of how to multiply two binomials using the FOIL method.

Main Idea	Point-by-Point Steps	Example: $7x(x^2 - 5x^3 + 3x - 7)$
Multiplying a Polynomial by a Monomial	1. Use the Distributive Property to multiply the monomial by each term of the polynomial. 2. Multiply the coefficients of each term. 3. Use the Product of Powers to simplify the variables. 4. Add like terms. 5. Write the terms of the resulting polynomial in ascending order of the powers of one variable.	1. $7x(x^2) - 7x(5x^3) + 7x(3x) - 7x(7)$ 2. $7x(x^2) - 35x(x^3) + 21x(x) - 49x$ 3. $7x^3 - 35x^4 + 21x^2 - 49x$ 4. $7x^3 - 35x^4 + 21x^2 - 49x$ 5. $-35x^4 + 7x^3 + 21x^2 - 49x$

CReating **I**ndependence **T**hrough **S**tudent-**O**wned **S**trategies

Have students read over the list of objectives and make a list of any words with which they are not familiar.

Why It's Important

Point out to students that this is only one of many reasons why each objective is important. Others are provided in the introduction to each lesson.

Lesson	NCTM Standards	Local Objectives
8-1	2, 6, 8, 9, 10	
8-1 Follow-Up	2, 3, 6, 7	
8-2	2, 6, 8, 9, 10	
8-3	1, 6, 8, 9, 10	
8-4 Preview	2, 10	
8-4	2, 6, 8, 9, 10	
8-5 Preview	2, 10	
8-5	2, 6, 8, 9, 10	
8-6	2, 6, 8, 9, 10	
8-7 Preview	2, 10	
8-7	2, 6, 8, 9, 10	
8-8	2, 6, 8, 9, 10	

Key to NCTM Standards:

1=Number & Operations, 2=Algebra,
3=Geometry, 4=Measurement,
5=Data Analysis & Probability, 6=Problem Solving, 7=Reasoning & Proof,
8=Communication, 9=Connections,
10=Representation

Chapter 8 Polynomials

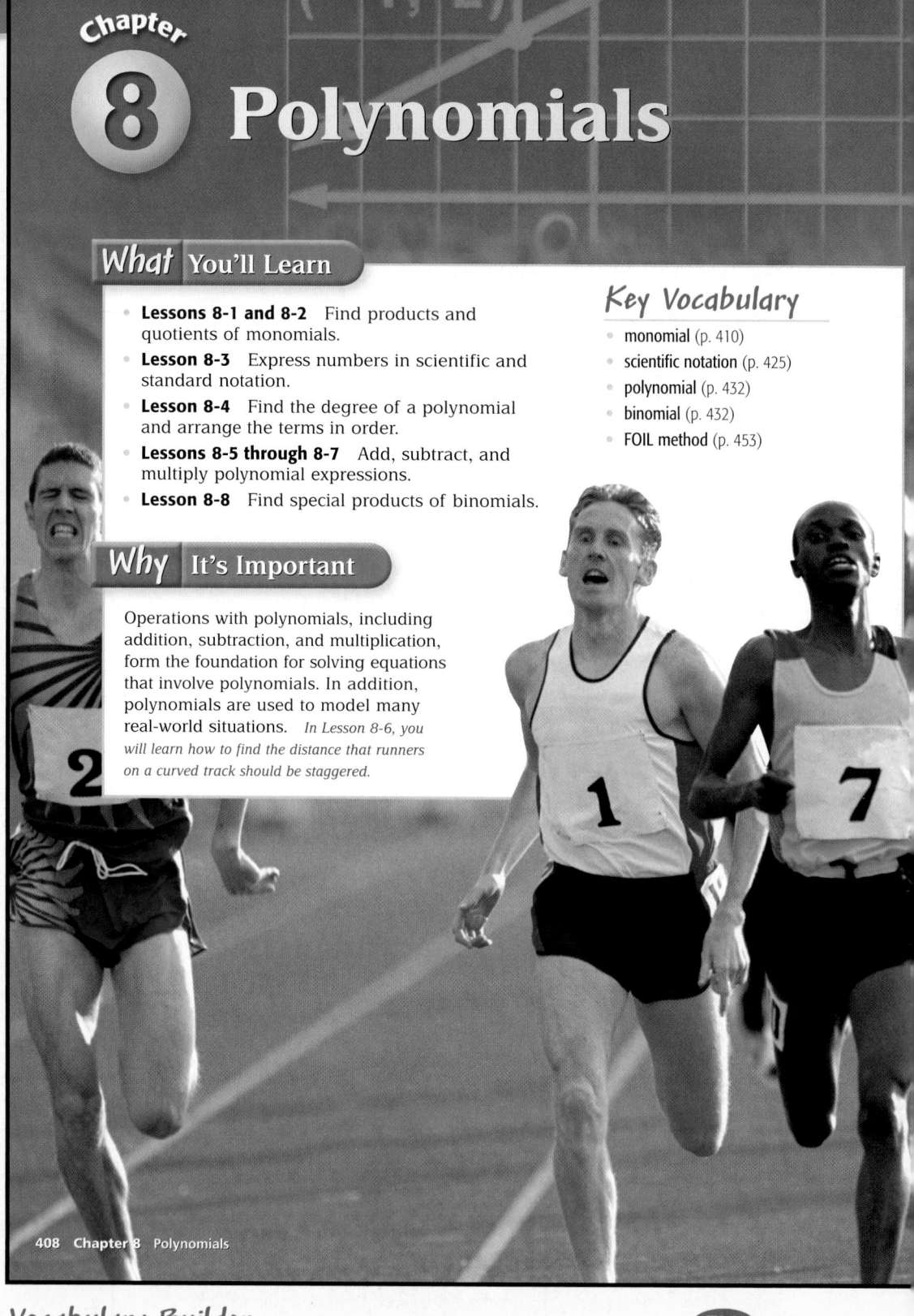

What You'll Learn

- **Lessons 8-1 and 8-2** Find products and quotients of monomials.
- **Lesson 8-3** Express numbers in scientific and standard notation.
- **Lesson 8-4** Find the degree of a polynomial and arrange the terms in order.
- **Lessons 8-5 through 8-7** Add, subtract, and multiply polynomial expressions.
- **Lesson 8-8** Find special products of binomials.

Key Vocabulary

- monomial (p. 410)
- scientific notation (p. 425)
- polynomial (p. 432)
- binomial (p. 432)
- FOIL method (p. 453)

Why It's Important

Operations with polynomials, including addition, subtraction, and multiplication, form the foundation for solving equations that involve polynomials. In addition, polynomials are used to model many real-world situations. *In Lesson 8-6, you will learn how to find the distance that runners on a curved track should be staggered.*

Vocabulary Builder   ELL

The Key Vocabulary list introduces students to some of the main vocabulary terms included in this chapter. For a more thorough vocabulary list with pronunciations of new words, give students the Vocabulary Builder worksheets found on pages vii and viii of the *Chapter 8 Resource Masters*. Encourage them to complete the definition of each term as they progress through the chapter. You may suggest that they add these sheets to their study notebooks for future reference when studying for the Chapter 8 test.

Prerequisite Skills To be successful in this chapter, you'll need to master these skills and be able to apply them in problem-solving situations. Review these skills before beginning Chapter 8.

For Lessons 8-1 and 8-2 Exponential Notation

Write each expression using exponents. *(For review, see Lesson 1-1.)*

1. $2 \cdot 2 \cdot 2 \cdot 2 \cdot 2$ 2^5 2. $3 \cdot 3 \cdot 3 \cdot 3$ 3^4 3. $5 \cdot 5$ 5^2 4. $x \cdot x \cdot x$ x^3

5. $a \cdot a \cdot a \cdot a \cdot a \cdot a$ a^6 6. $x \cdot x \cdot y \cdot y \cdot y$ $x^2 y^3$ 7. $\frac{1}{2} \cdot \frac{1}{2} \cdot \frac{1}{2} \cdot \frac{1}{2} \cdot \frac{1}{2}$ $\left(\frac{1}{2}\right)^5$ 8. $\frac{a}{b} \cdot \frac{a}{b} \cdot \frac{c}{d} \cdot \frac{c}{d} \cdot \frac{c}{d}$

$\left(\frac{a}{b}\right)^2 \left(\frac{c}{d}\right)^3$

For Lessons 8-1 and 8-2 Evaluating Powers

Evaluate each expression. *(For review, see Lesson 1-1.)*

9. 3^2 9 10. 4^3 64 11. 5^2 25 12. 10^4 10,000

13. $(-6)^2$ 36 14. $(-3)^3$ -27 15. $\left(\frac{2}{3}\right)^4$ $\frac{16}{81}$ 16. $\left(-\frac{7}{8}\right)^2$ $\frac{49}{64}$

For Lessons 8-1, 8-2, and 8-5 through 8-8 Area and Volume

Find the area or volume of each figure shown below. *(For review, see pages 813–817.)*

17. 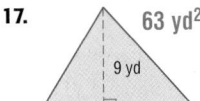 63 yd²

9 yd, 14 yd

18. 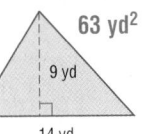 6m 36π m² or about 113.04 m²

19. 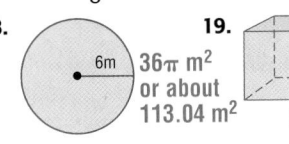 4 ft, 7 ft, 3 ft

20. 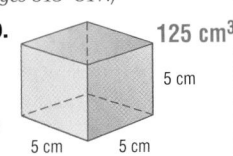 125 cm³, 5 cm, 5 cm, 5 cm, 84 ft³

FOLDABLES™ Study Organizer

Polynomials Make this Foldable to help you organize your notes. Begin with a sheet of 11" by 17" paper.

Step 1 Fold
Fold in thirds lengthwise.

Step 2 Open and Fold
Fold a 2" tab along the width. Then fold the rest in fourths.

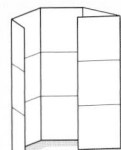

Step 3 Label
Draw lines along the folds and label as shown.

+ | − | × | ÷
Mon.
Poly.

Reading and Writing As you read and study the chapter, write examples and notes for each operation.

This section provides a review of the basic concepts needed before beginning Chapter 8. Page references are included for additional student help.

Additional review is provided in the *Prerequisite Skills Workbook*, pp. 33–36.

Prerequisite Skills in the Getting Ready for the Next Lesson section at the end of each exercise set review a skill needed in the next lesson.

For Lesson	Prerequisite Skill
8-2	Simplifying Fractions (p. 415)
8-3	Products of Powers (p. 423)
8-4	Evaluating Expressions (p. 430)
8-5	Simplifying Expressions (p. 436)
8-6	Distributive Property (p. 443)
8-7	Products of Powers (p. 449)
8-8	Power of a Power, Power of a Product (p. 457)

FOLDABLES™ Study Organizer

For more information about Foldables, see *Teaching Mathematics with Foldables.*

Organization of Data using a Table to Make Comparisons
After students make their Foldable tables, have them label the columns and rows as illustrated. Students use their Foldables to take notes and write examples for each operation. Have students compare different functions. For example, compare adding monomials and adding polynomials. Remind students that comparing involves determining a trait to be compared and then finding the similarities and differences in that trait.

1 Focus

5-Minute Check Transparency 8-1 Use as a quiz or review of Chapter 7.

Mathematical Background notes are available for this lesson on p. 408C.

Why does doubling speed quadruple braking distance?

Ask students:

- What does the term quadrupled mean? **increased by 4 times, or multiplied by 4**

- Why isn't the braking distance 4 times the speed? **The expression for finding the braking distance, where *s* is speed in mph, is $\frac{1}{20}s^2$, not 4*s*.**

- Based on the chart, what would be the braking distance for a car traveling 80 mph? **320 ft** 120 mph? **720 ft**

- **Drag Racing** Suppose a sports car on a drag strip can reach 100 miles per hour in a quarter of a mile. Using the braking distance graph, calculate how far the car would travel on the drag strip, from start to stop, if the driver started braking when the car reached 100 miles per hour. A mile is 5280 feet. **1820 ft**

8-1 Multiplying Monomials

What You'll Learn

- Multiply monomials.
- Simplify expressions involving powers of monomials.

Vocabulary
- monomial
- constant

Why does doubling speed quadruple braking distance?

The table shows the braking distance for a vehicle at certain speeds. If *s* represents the speed in miles per hour, then the approximate number of feet that the driver must apply the brakes is $\frac{1}{20}s^2$. Notice that when speed is doubled, the braking distance is quadrupled.

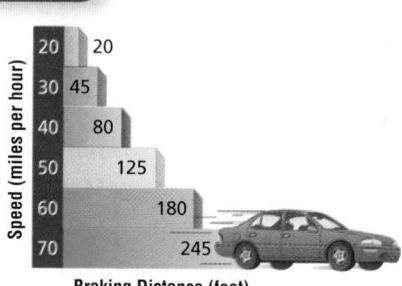

Speed (miles per hour)	Braking Distance (feet)
20	20
30	45
40	80
50	125
60	180
70	245

Source: *British Highway Code*

MULTIPLY MONOMIALS An expression like $\frac{1}{20}s^2$ is called a monomial. A **monomial** is a number, a variable, or a product of a number and one or more variables. An expression involving the division of variables is not a monomial. Monomials that are real numbers are called **constants**.

Example 1 Identify Monomials

Determine whether each expression is a monomial. Explain your reasoning.

	Expression	Monomial?	Reason
a.	-5	yes	-5 is a real number and an example of a constant.
b.	$p + q$	no	The expression involves the addition, not the product, of two variables.
c.	x	yes	Single variables are monomials.
d.	$\frac{c}{d}$	no	The expression is the quotient, not the product, of two variables.
e.	$\frac{abc^8}{5}$	yes	$\frac{abc^8}{5} = \frac{1}{5}abc^8$. The expression is the product of a number, $\frac{1}{5}$, and three variables.

Recall that an expression of the form x^n is called a *power* and represents the product you obtain when x is used as a factor n times. The number x is the *base*, and the number n is the *exponent*.

Study Tip

Reading Math
The expression x^n is read x to the nth power.

$$\text{exponent} \longrightarrow \overbrace{2^5 = 2 \cdot 2 \cdot 2 \cdot 2 \cdot 2}^{5 \text{ factors}} \text{ or } 32$$
$$\text{base} \longrightarrow$$

In the following examples, the definition of a power is used to find the products of powers. Look for a pattern in the exponents.

Resource Manager

Workbook and Reproducible Masters

Chapter 8 Resource Masters
- Study Guide and Intervention, pp. 455–456
- Skills Practice, p. 457
- Practice, p. 458
- Reading to Learn Mathematics, p. 459
- Enrichment, p. 460

Parent and Student Study Guide Workbook, p. 59

 Transparencies
5-Minute Check Transparency 8-1
Answer Key Transparencies

 Technology
AlgePASS: Tutorial Plus, Lesson 18
Interactive Chalkboard

$$2^3 \cdot 2^5 = \overbrace{2 \cdot 2 \cdot 2}^{3 \text{ factors}} \cdot \overbrace{2 \cdot 2 \cdot 2 \cdot 2 \cdot 2}^{5 \text{ factors}} \text{ or } 2^8 \qquad 3^2 \cdot 3^4 = \overbrace{3 \cdot 3}^{2 \text{ factors}} \cdot \overbrace{3 \cdot 3 \cdot 3 \cdot 3}^{4 \text{ factors}} \text{ or } 3^6$$

$$\underbrace{}_{3 + 5 \text{ or } 8 \text{ factors}} \qquad \underbrace{}_{2 + 4 \text{ or } 6 \text{ factors}}$$

These and other similar examples suggest the property for multiplying powers.

Key Concept — Product of Powers

- **Words** To multiply two powers that have the same base, add the exponents.
- **Symbols** For any number a and all integers m and n, $a^m \cdot a^n = a^{m+n}$.
- **Example** $a^4 \cdot a^{12} = a^{4+12}$ or a^{16}

Example 2 Product of Powers

Simplify each expression.

a. $(5x^7)(x^6)$

$$
\begin{aligned}
(5x^7)(x^6) &= (5)(1)(x^7 \cdot x^6) && \text{Commutative and Associative Properties} \\
&= (5 \cdot 1)(x^{7+6}) && \text{Product of Powers} \\
&= 5x^{13} && \text{Simplify.}
\end{aligned}
$$

Study Tip

Power of 1
Recall that a variable with no exponent indicated can be written as a power of 1. For example, $x = x^1$ and $ab = a^1b^1$.

b. $(4ab^6)(-7a^2b^3)$

$$
\begin{aligned}
(4ab^6)(-7a^2b^3) &= (4)(-7)(a \cdot a^2)(b^6 \cdot b^3) && \text{Commutative and Associative Properties} \\
&= -28(a^{1+2})(b^{6+3}) && \text{Product of Powers} \\
&= -28a^3b^9 && \text{Simplify.}
\end{aligned}
$$

POWERS OF MONOMIALS You can also look for a pattern to discover the property for finding the power of a power.

$$
\begin{aligned}
(4^2)^5 &= \overbrace{(4^2)(4^2)(4^2)(4^2)(4^2)}^{5 \text{ factors}} & (z^8)^3 &= \overbrace{(z^8)(z^8)(z^8)}^{3 \text{ factors}} \\
&= 4^{2+2+2+2+2} & &= z^{8+8+8} \\
&= 4^{10} & &= z^{24}
\end{aligned}
$$

$\longleftarrow$ Apply rule for Product of Powers. $\longrightarrow$

Therefore, $(4^2)^5 = 4^{10}$ and $(z^8)^3 = z^{24}$. These and other similar examples suggest the property for finding the power of a power.

Key Concept — Power of a Power

- **Words** To find the power of a power, multiply the exponents.
- **Symbols** For any number a and all integers m and n, $(a^m)^n = a^{m \cdot n}$.
- **Example** $(k^5)^9 = k^{5 \cdot 9}$ or k^{45}

Study Tip

Look Back
To review **using a calculator to find a power of a number**, see Lesson 1-1.

Example 3 Power of a Power

Simplify $[(3^2)^3]^2$.

$$
\begin{aligned}
[(3^2)^3]^2 &= (3^{2 \cdot 3})^2 && \text{Power of a Power} \\
&= (3^6)^2 && \text{Simplify.} \\
&= 3^{6 \cdot 2} && \text{Power of a Power} \\
&= 3^{12} \text{ or } 531,441 && \text{Simplify.}
\end{aligned}
$$

 www.algebra1.com/extra_examples

---

2 Teach

Building on Prior Knowledge

In Chapter 1, students learned that an algebraic expression is an expression consisting of one or more numbers and variables along with one or more arithmetic operations. All monomials are expressions, but not all expressions are monomials.

MULTIPLY MONOMIALS

In-Class Examples Power Point®

1 Determine whether each expression is a monomial. Explain your reasoning.

a. $17 - s$
This is not a monomial because it involves subtraction, not multiplication.

b. $8f^2g$
This is a monomial because it is the product of a number and two variables.

c. $\dfrac{3}{4}$
This is a monomial because it is a real number.

d. xy
This is a monomial because it is the product of two variables.

Teaching Tip Make sure students read the Study Tip in the margin next to Example 2. In order for students to find the products of powers correctly, they must remember that the expression x is understood to mean x^1. Suggest that students rewrite variables without exponents with an exponent of 1.

2 Simplify each expression.
a. $(r^4)(-12r^7)$ $-12r^{11}$
b. $(6cd^5)(5c^5d^2)$ $30c^6d^7$

Teacher to Teacher

Patricia Lund   Divide County H.S., Crosby, ND

"The paragraph at the top of page 410 interests students because many of them are preparing to drive. I like to graph this data on a coordinate plane so we review ordered pairs and graphing points. We analyze the graph to determine whether or not it is linear and if it is a function. We also review function notation to name the graph suggested by these points."

POWERS OF MONOMIALS

3 Simplify $[(2^3)^3]^2$.
2^{18} or 262,144

4 **GEOMETRY** Find the volume of a cube with a side length $s = 5xyz$. $(5xyz)^3 = 125x^3y^3z^3$

Teaching Tip Remind students that when multiple sets of grouping symbols are used in an expression, the outermost set is usually a pair of brackets [ ]. The expression $[(xy)^2]^4$ is the same as $((xy)^2)^4$.

5 Simplify $[(8g^3h^4)^2](2gh^5)^4$.
$65,536g^{16}h^{36}$

✓ Concept Check

Simplifying Expressions Janice simplified $\frac{4}{6}(x^2y^5)^3[2(xy)^7]$ into $\frac{8}{6}x^{13}y^{22}$. Explain whether her simplification is complete.
The simplification is not complete because the fraction is not in simplest form.

Answers

2a. $(5m)^2 = 25m^2$

2b. The power of a product is the product of the powers.

2c. $(-3a)^2 = 9a^2$

2d. $2(c^7)^3 = 2c^{21}$

3. When finding the product of powers with the same base, keep the same base and add the exponents. Do not multiply the bases.

4. $5 - 7d$ shows subtraction as well as multiplication.

5. $\frac{4a}{3b}$ shows division as well as multiplication.

6. A single variable is a monomial.

Study Tip

Powers of Monomials
Sometimes the rules for the Power of a Power and the Power of a Product are combined into one rule.
$(a^m b^n)^p = a^{mp} b^{np}$

Look for a pattern in the examples below.

$$(xy)^4 = (xy)(xy)(xy)(xy)$$
$$= (x \cdot x \cdot x \cdot x)(y \cdot y \cdot y \cdot y)$$
$$= x^4 y^4$$

$$(6ab)^3 = (6ab)(6ab)(6ab)$$
$$= (6 \cdot 6 \cdot 6)(a \cdot a \cdot a)(b \cdot b \cdot b)$$
$$= 6^3 a^3 b^3 \text{ or } 216a^3 b^3$$

These and other similar examples suggest the following property for finding the power of a product.

Key Concept — Power of a Product

- **Words** To find the power of a product, find the power of each factor and multiply.

- **Symbols** For all numbers a and b and any integer m, $(ab)^m = a^m b^m$.

- **Example** $(-2xy)^3 = (-2)^3 x^3 y^3$ or $-8x^3 y^3$

Example 4 — Power of a Product

GEOMETRY Express the area of the square as a monomial.

$$\text{Area} = s^2 \qquad \text{Formula for the area of a square}$$
$$= (4ab)^2 \qquad s = 4ab$$
$$= 4^2 a^2 b^2 \qquad \text{Power of a Product}$$
$$= 16a^2 b^2 \qquad \text{Simplify.}$$

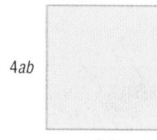

4ab

4ab

The area of the square is $16a^2 b^2$ square units.

The properties can be used in combination to simplify more complex expressions involving exponents.

Concept Summary — Simplifying Monomial Expressions

To *simplify* an expression involving monomials, write an equivalent expression in which:

- each base appears exactly once,
- there are no powers of powers, and
- all fractions are in simplest form.

Example 5 — Simplify Expressions

Simplify $\left(\frac{1}{3}xy^4\right)^2[(-6y)^2]^3$.

$$\left(\frac{1}{3}xy^4\right)^2[(-6y)^2]^3 = \left(\frac{1}{3}xy^4\right)^2(-6y)^6 \qquad \text{Power of a Power}$$

$$= \left(\frac{1}{3}\right)^2 x^2 (y^4)^2 (-6)^6 y^6 \qquad \text{Power of a Product}$$

$$= \frac{1}{9}x^2 y^8 (46,656)y^6 \qquad \text{Power of a Power}$$

$$= \frac{1}{9}(46,656)x^2 \cdot y^8 \cdot y^6 \qquad \text{Commutative Property}$$

$$= 5184x^2 y^{14} \qquad \text{Product of Powers}$$

DAILY
INTERVENTION

Differentiated Instruction

Logical Give students a term such as $144a^{10}b^8$ and challenge them to write 20 unique combinations of monomials that would produce this product if multiplied.

Concept Check

1a–c. Sample answers are given.

1a. $n^2(n^5) = n^7$

1b. $(n^2)^5 = n^{10}$

1c. $(nm^2)^5 = n^5n^{10}$

2a–d. See margin for explanations.

1. **OPEN ENDED** Give an example of an expression that can be simplified using each property. Then simplify each expression.

   a. Product of Powers   **b.** Power of a Power   **c.** Power of a Product

2. **Determine** whether each pair of monomials is equivalent. Explain.

   a. $5m^2$ and $(5m)^2$ **no**   **b.** $(yz)^4$ and y^4z^4 **yes**

   c. $-3a^2$ and $(-3a)^2$ **no**   **d.** $2(c^7)^3$ and $8c^{21}$ **no**

3. **FIND THE ERROR** Nathan and Poloma are simplifying $(5^2)(5^9)$.

Nathan	Poloma
$(5^2)(5^9) = (5 \cdot 5)^{2+9}$	$(5^2)(5^9) = 5^{2+9}$
$= 25^{11}$	$= 5^{11}$

   Who is correct? Explain your reasoning. **Poloma; see margin for explanation.**

Guided Practice

Determine whether each expression is a monomial. Write *yes* or *no*. Explain.

4. $5 - 7d$ **no**   5. $\frac{4a}{3b}$ **no**   6. n **yes**

4–6. See margin for explanations.

Simplify.

7. $x(x^4)(x^6)$ x^{11} 8. $(4a^4b)(9a^2b^3)$ $36a^6b^4$ 9. $[(2^3)^2]^3$ 2^{18} or 262,144

10. $(3y^5z)^2$ $9y^{10}z^2$ 11. $(-4mn^2)(12m^2n)$ $-48m^3n^3$ 12. $(-2v^3w^4)^3(-3vw^3)^2$ $-72v^{11}w^{18}$

Application

GEOMETRY Express the area of each triangle as a monomial.

13. $5n^5$

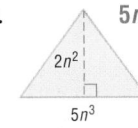

$2n^2$

$5n^3$

14. $6a^5b^6$

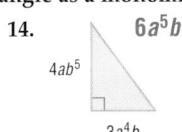

$4ab^5$

$3a^4b$

★ indicates increased difficulty

Practice and Apply

Determine whether each expression is a monomial. Write *yes* or *no*. Explain.

15. 12 **yes**   16. $4x^3$ **yes**   17. $a - 2b$ **no**

18. $4n + 5m$ **no**   19. $\frac{x}{y^2}$ **no**   20. $\frac{1}{5}abc^{14}$ **yes**

15–20. See margin for explanations.

Simplify.

21. $(ab^4)(ab^2)$ a^2b^6 22. $(p^5q^4)(p^2q)$ p^7q^5

23. $(-7c^3d^4)(4cd^3)$ $-28c^4d^7$ 24. $(-3j^7k^5)(-8jk^8)$ $24j^8k^{13}$

25. $(5a^2b^3c^4)(6a^3b^4c^2)$ $30a^5b^7c^6$ 26. $(10xy^5z^3)(3x^4y^6z^3)$ $30x^5y^{11}z^6$

27. $(9pq^7)^2$ $81p^2q^{14}$ 28. $(7b^3c^6)^3$ $343b^9c^{18}$

29. $[(3^2)^4]^2$ 3^{16} or 43,046,721   30. $[(4^2)^3]^2$ 4^{12} or 16,777,216

31. $(0.5x^3)^2$ $0.25x^6$ 32. $(0.4h^5)^3$ $0.064h^{15}$

33. $\left(-\frac{3}{4}c\right)^3$ $-\frac{27}{64}c^3$ 34. $\left(\frac{4}{5}a^2\right)^2$ $\frac{16}{25}a^4$

35. $(4cd)^2(-3d^2)^3$ $-432c^2d^8$ 36. $(-2x^5)^3(-5xy^6)^2$ $-200x^{17}y^{12}$

37. $(2ag^2)^4(3a^2g^3)^2$ $144a^8g^{14}$ 38. $(2m^2n^3)^3(3m^3n)^4$ $648m^{18}n^{13}$

★ 39. $(8y^3)(-3x^2y^2)\left(\frac{3}{8}xy^4\right)$ $-9x^3y^9$ ★ 40. $\left(\frac{4}{7}m\right)^2(49m)(17p)\left(\frac{1}{34}p^5\right)$ $8m^3p^6$

Study Notebook

Have students—
- add the definitions/examples of the vocabulary terms to their Vocabulary Builder worksheets for Chapter 8.
- include any other item(s) that they find helpful in mastering the skills in this lesson.

DAILY
INTERVENTION **FIND THE ERROR**
Both Nathan and Poloma added the exponents 2 and 9, which is the correct procedure when finding a product of powers. However, tell students to notice how Nathan and Poloma handled the bases. Suggest that students substitute a variable for 5 and then examine which method is correct.

About the Exercises...

Organization by Objective
- **Multiply Monomials:** 15–26
- **Powers of Monomials:** 27–54

Odd/Even Assignments
Exercises 15–42 are structured so that students practice the same concepts whether they are assigned odd or even problems.

Assignment Guide

Basic: 15–37 odd, 43–47 odd, 49–52, 55–82

Average: 15–47 odd, 51–82

Advanced: 16–50 even, 53–74 (optional: 75–82)

Answers

15. 12 is a real number and therefore a monomial.

16. $4x^3$ is the product of a number and three variables.

17. $a - 2b$ shows subtraction, not multiplication of variables.

18. $4n + 5m$ shows addition, not multiplication of variables.

19. $\frac{x}{y^2}$ shows division, not multiplication of variables.

20. $\frac{1}{5}abc^{14}$ is the product of a number, $\frac{1}{5}$, and several variables.

★ 41. Simplify the expression $(-2b^3)^4 - 3(-2b^4)^3$. $40b^{12}$

★ 42. Simplify the expression $2(-5y^3)^2 + (-3y^3)^3$. $50y^6 - 27y^9$

GEOMETRY   **Express the area of each figure as a monomial.**

43. $15f^5g^5$ 44. a^4b^2 45. $(49x^8)\pi$

$3fg^2$ $5f^4g^3$ a^2b a^2b $7x^4$

GEOMETRY   **Express the volume of each solid as a monomial.**

46. $64k^9$ 47. x^3y^5 48. $16\pi n^5$

$4k^3$ $4k^3$ $4k^3$ x^2y y xy^3 $2n$ $4n^3$

TELEPHONES   **For Exercises 49 and 50, use the following information.**
The first transatlantic telephone cable has 51 amplifiers along its length. Each amplifier strengthens the signal on the cable 10^6 times.

49. After it passes through the second amplifier, the signal has been boosted $10^6 \cdot 10^6$ times. Simplify this expression. 10^{12} or 1 trillion

50. Represent the number of times the signal has been boosted after it has passed through the first four amplifiers as a power of 10^6. Then simplify the expression. $(10^6)^4$ or 10^{24}

DEMOLITION DERBY   **For Exercises 51 and 52, use the following information.**
When a car hits an object, the damage is measured by the collision impact. For a certain car, the collision impact I is given by $I = 2s^2$, where s represents the speed in kilometers per minute.

51. What is the collision impact if the speed of the car is 1 kilometer per minute? 2 kilometers per minute? 4 kilometers per minute?   2; 8; 32

52. As the speed doubles, explain what happens to the collision impact.
The collision impact quadruples, since $2(2s)^2$ is $4(2s^2)$.

TEST TAKING   **For Exercises 53 and 54, use the following information.**
A history test covers two chapters. There are 2^{12} ways to answer the 12 true-false questions on the first chapter and 2^{10} ways to answer the 10 true-false questions on the second chapter.

53. How many ways are there to answer all 22 questions on the test?
(*Hint:* Find the product of 2^{12} and 2^{10}.) 2^{22} or 4,194,304 ways

54. If a student guesses on each question, what is the probability of answering all questions correctly? $\frac{1}{4,194,304}$

CRITICAL THINKING   **Determine whether each statement is *true* or *false*. If true, explain your reasoning. If false, give a counterexample.**

55. For any real number a, $(-a)^2 = -a^2$.   false

56. For all real numbers a and b, and all integers m, n, and p, $(a^m b^n)^p = a^{mp} b^{np}$.   true

57. For all real numbers a, b, and all integers n, $(a + b)^n = a^n + b^n$.   false

55–57. See margin for explanations or counterexamples.

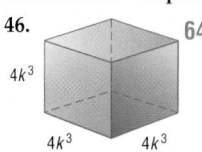

More About. . .

Demolition Derby

In a demolition derby, the winner is not the car that finishes first but the last car still moving under its own power.

Source: *Smithsonian Magazine*

58.  Answer the question that was posed at the beginning of the lesson. **See margin.**

Why does doubling speed quadruple braking distance?

Include the following in your answer:
- the ratio of the braking distance required for a speed of 40 miles per hour and the braking distance required for a speed of 80 miles per hour, and
- a comparison of the expressions $\frac{1}{20}s^2$ and $\frac{1}{20}(2s)^2$.

Standardized Test Practice
Ⓐ Ⓑ Ⓒ Ⓓ

59. $4^2 \cdot 4^5 = ?$ **D**

   Ⓐ 16^7 Ⓑ 8^7 Ⓒ 4^{10} Ⓓ 4^7

60. Which of the following expressions represents the volume of the cube? **D**

   Ⓐ $15x^3$ Ⓑ $25x^2$

   Ⓒ $25x^3$ Ⓓ $125x^3$

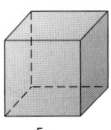
$5x$

Maintain Your Skills

Mixed Review   Solve each system of inequalities by graphing. *(Lesson 7-5)*

61–63. See pp. 471A–471B.

61. $y \le 2x + 2$
$y \ge -x - 1$

62. $y \ge x - 2$
$y < 2x - 1$

63. $x > -2$
$y < x + 3$

Use elimination to solve each system of equations. *(Lesson 7-4)*

64. $-4x + 5y = 2$
$x + 2y = 6$ **(2, 2)**

65. $3x + 4y = -25$
$2x - 3y = 6$ **(−3, −4)**

66. $x + y = 20$ **(4, 16)**
$0.4x + 0.15y = 4$

Solve each compound inequality. Then graph the solution set. *(Lesson 6-4)*

67–70. See margin for graphs.

67. $4 + h \le -3$ or $4 + h \ge 5$ $\{h | h \le -7$ or $h \ge 1\}$

68. $4 < 4a + 12 < 24$ $\{a | -2 < a < 3\}$

69. $14 < 3h + 2 < 2$ $\varnothing$

70. $2m - 3 > 7$ or $2m + 7 > 9$ $\{m | m > 1\}$

Determine whether each transformation is a *reflection, translation, dilation,* or *rotation.* *(Lesson 4-2)*

71.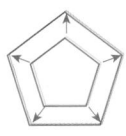

72.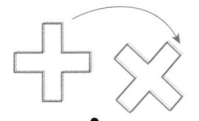

73. 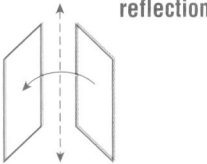 reflection

    dilation   rotation

74. TRANSPORTATION Two trains leave York at the same time, one traveling north, the other south. The northbound train travels at 40 miles per hour and the southbound at 30 miles per hour. In how many hours will the trains be 245 miles apart? *(Lesson 3-7)* $3\frac{1}{2}$ h

Getting Ready for the Next Lesson   **PREREQUISITE SKILL**   **Simplify.** *(To review **simplifying fractions**, see pages 798 and 799.)*

75. $\frac{2}{6}$ $\frac{1}{3}$ **76.** $\frac{3}{15}$ $\frac{1}{5}$ **77.** $\frac{10}{5}$ 2   **78.** $\frac{27}{9}$ 3

79. $\frac{14}{36}$ $\frac{7}{18}$ **80.** $\frac{9}{48}$ $\frac{3}{16}$ **81.** $\frac{44}{32}$ $\frac{11}{8}$ **82.** $\frac{45}{18}$ $\frac{5}{2}$

Answers

55. If $a = 4$, then $(-4)^2 = 16$ and $-4^2 = -16$.

56. $(a^m b^n)^p = (a^m)^p (b^n)^p$ Power of a Product
     $= a^{mp} b^{np}$ Power of a Power

57. Let $a = 3$, $b = 4$, and $n = 2$. Then $(a + b)^n = (3 + 4)^2$ or 49 and $a^n + b^n = 3^2 + 4^2$ or 25.

---

4 Assess

Open-Ended Assessment

Modeling Write an expression such as $(2x^3y)^3(3x^2y^4)^2$ on the chalkboard, but write the exponents on self-adhesive notes. Ask student volunteers to simplify the expression, using more self-adhesive notes to show the multiplication and addition of exponents in each step of the simplification process.

Getting Ready for Lesson 8-2

PREREQUISITE SKILL Students will learn about dividing monomials in Lesson 8-2. Part of dividing monomials involves simplifying fractions formed by dividing coefficients. Use Exercises 75–82 to determine your students' familiarity with simplifying fractions.

Answers

58. Answers should include the following.
- the ratio $\frac{80 \text{ feet}}{320 \text{ feet}}$, which simplifies to a ratio of 1 to 4
- If s is replaced by $2s$ in the formula for the breaking distance required for a car traveling s miles per hour the result is $\frac{1}{20}(2s)^2$. Using the Power of a Product and Power of a Power Properties, this simplifies to $4 \cdot \left(\frac{1}{20}s^2\right)$. This means that doubling the speed of a car multiplies the breaking distance by 4.

67.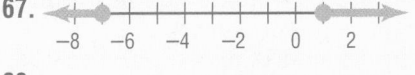

68.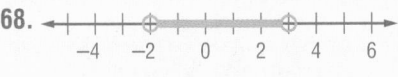

69.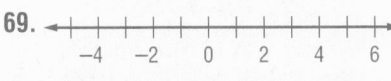

70.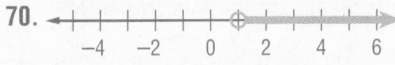

Getting Started

Objective Determine surface area ratio and volume ratio of rectangular prisms when dimensions are multiplied by *a*.

Materials
centimeter grid paper
scissors
tape

Teach

- Any size grid paper will work for this activity because the units are not important.

- Before students begin this activity, direct their attention to the data table. Ask students to make a conjecture about the surface area and volume of the prism when each dimension is multiplied by two, and by three. Write student predictions on the chalkboard to use in a discussion after the activity has been completed.

- Have students verify the formula for the surface area of a prism by counting the squares on the surface of their prism.

Assess

Students should determine that if the length, width, and height of a rectangular prism are each multiplied by *a*, the resulting surface area will be a^2 times the original surface area, and the resulting volume will be a^3 times the original volume.

Study Notebook

You may wish to have students summarize this activity and what they learned from it.

Investigating Surface Area and Volume

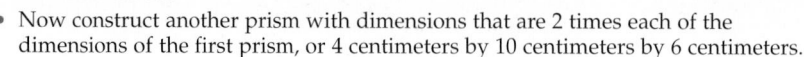

Collect the Data

- Cut out the pattern shown from a sheet of centimeter grid paper. Fold along the dashed lines and tape the edges together to form a rectangular prism with dimensions 2 centimeters by 5 centimeters by 3 centimeters.

- Find the surface area *SA* of the prism by counting the squares on all the faces of the prism or by using the formula $SA = 2w\ell + 2wh + 2\ell h$, where *w* is the width, ℓ is the length, and *h* is the height of the prism. **62 cm²**

- Find the volume *V* of the prism by using the formula $V = \ell wh$. **30 cm³**

- Now construct another prism with dimensions that are 2 times each of the dimensions of the first prism, or 4 centimeters by 10 centimeters by 6 centimeters.

- Finally, construct a third prism with dimensions that are 3 times each of the dimensions of the first prism, or 6 centimeters by 15 centimeters by 9 centimeters.

Analyze the Data

1. Copy and complete the table using the prisms you made.

Prism	Dimensions	Surface Area (cm²)	Volume (cm³)	Surface Area Ratio ($\frac{SA \text{ of New}}{SA \text{ of Original}}$)	Volume Ratio ($\frac{V \text{ of New}}{V \text{ of Original}}$)
Original	2 by 5 by 3	62	30	——	——
A	4 by 10 by 6	248	240	$\frac{248}{62} = 4$	$\frac{240}{30} = 8$
B	6 by 15 by 9	558	810	$\frac{558}{62} = 9$	$\frac{810}{30} = 27$

2. Make a prism with different dimensions from any in this activity. Repeat the steps in **Collect the Data**, and make a table similar to the one in Exercise 1. **See pp. 471A–471B.**

Make a Conjecture

3. Suppose you multiply each dimension of a prism by 2. What is the ratio of the surface area of the new prism to the surface area of the original prism? What is the ratio of the volumes? **4; 8**

4. If you multiply each dimension of a prism by 3, what is the ratio of the surface area of the new prism to the surface area of the original? What is the ratio of the volumes? **9; 27**

5. Suppose you multiply each dimension of a prism by *a*. Make a conjecture about the ratios of surface areas and volumes. a^2; a^3

Extend the Activity

6. Repeat the steps in **Collect the Data** and **Analyze the Data** using cylinders. To start, make a cylinder with radius 4 centimeters and height 5 centimeters. To compute surface area *SA* and volume *V*, use the formulas $SA = 2\pi r^2 + 2\pi rh$ and $V = \pi r^2 h$, where *r* is the radius and *h* is the height of the cylinder. Do the conjectures you made in Exercise 5 hold true for cylinders? Explain. **See pp. 471A–471B.**

416 Chapter 8 Polynomials

Resource Manager

Teaching Algebra with Manipulatives
- p. 2 (master for centimeter grid paper)
- p. 135 (student recording sheet)

Glencoe Mathematics Classroom Manipulative Kit
- scissors

What You'll Learn

- Simplify expressions involving the quotient of monomials.
- Simplify expressions containing negative exponents.

Vocabulary
- zero exponent
- negative exponent

How can you compare pH levels?

To test whether a solution is a *base* or an *acid*, chemists use a pH test. This test measures the concentration c of hydrogen ions (in moles per liter) in the solution.

$$c = \left(\frac{1}{10}\right)^{pH}$$

The table gives examples of solutions with various pH levels. You can find the quotient of powers and use negative exponents to compare measures on the pH scale.

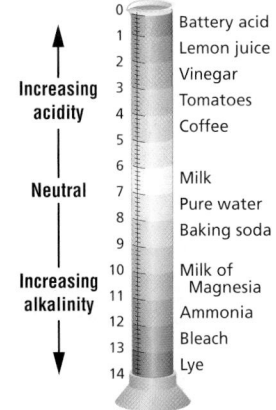

0	Battery acid
1	Lemon juice
2	Vinegar
3	Tomatoes
4	Coffee
5	
6	Milk
7	Pure water
8	Baking soda
9	
10	Milk of Magnesia
11	Ammonia
12	Bleach
13	Lye
14	

Increasing acidity / Neutral / Increasing alkalinity

Source: U.S. Geological Survey

QUOTIENTS OF MONOMIALS

In the following examples, the definition of a power is used to find quotients of powers. Look for a pattern in the exponents.

5 factors

$$\frac{4^5}{4^3} = \frac{\overset{1}{\cancel{4}} \cdot \overset{1}{\cancel{4}} \cdot \overset{1}{\cancel{4}} \cdot 4 \cdot 4}{\underset{1}{\cancel{4}} \cdot \underset{1}{\cancel{4}} \cdot \underset{1}{\cancel{4}}} = 4 \cdot 4 \text{ or } 4^2$$

3 factors   5 − 3 or 2 factors

6 factors

$$\frac{3^6}{3^2} = \frac{\overset{1}{\cancel{3}} \cdot \overset{1}{\cancel{3}} \cdot 3 \cdot 3 \cdot 3 \cdot 3}{\underset{1}{\cancel{3}} \cdot \underset{1}{\cancel{3}}} = 3 \cdot 3 \cdot 3 \cdot 3 \text{ or } 3^4$$

2 factors   6 − 2 or 4 factors

These and other similar examples suggest the following property for dividing powers.

Key Concept — Quotient of Powers

- **Words** — To divide two powers that have the same base, subtract the exponents.
- **Symbols** — For all integers m and n and any nonzero number a, $\dfrac{a^m}{a^n} = a^{m-n}$.
- **Example** — $\dfrac{b^{15}}{b^7} = b^{15-7}$ or b^8

TEACHING TIP
Ask students why a and b cannot be 0.

Example 1 — Quotient of Powers

Simplify $\dfrac{a^5 b^8}{ab^3}$. Assume that a and b are not equal to zero.

$$\frac{a^5 b^8}{ab^3} = \left(\frac{a^5}{a}\right)\left(\frac{b^8}{b^3}\right) \qquad \text{Group powers that have the same base.}$$

$$= (a^{5-1})(b^{8-3}) \qquad \text{Quotient of Powers}$$

$$= a^4 b^5 \qquad \text{Simplify.}$$

---

1 Focus

 5-Minute Check Transparency 8-2 Use as a quiz or review of Lesson 8-1.

Mathematical Background notes are available for this lesson on p. 408C.

How can you compare pH levels?

Ask students:

- Using the formula $c = \left(\dfrac{1}{10}\right)^{pH}$, what is the concentration of hydrogen ions in a solution with pH 1? **0.1 moles/liter**

- Using the same formula, what is the concentration of hydrogen ions in a solution with pH 2? **0.01 moles/liter**

- As the pH increases by 1, what happens to the hydrogen ion concentration? **It gets 10 times as small.**

- According to the scale, ammonia has a pH of 12. Would this indicate that ammonia has a very large or very small concentration of hydrogen ions? **a very small concentration**

Resource Manager

Workbook and Reproducible Masters

Chapter 8 Resource Masters
- Study Guide and Intervention, pp. 461–462
- Skills Practice, p. 463
- Practice, p. 464
- Reading to Learn Mathematics, p. 465
- Enrichment, p. 466
- Assessment, p. 517

Parent and Student Study Guide Workbook, p. 60

 Transparencies
5-Minute Check Transparency 8-2
Answer Key Transparencies

Technology
AlgePASS: Tutorial Plus, Lesson 19
Interactive Chalkboard

Remind students that multiplying and dividing are inverse or opposite operations. With that in mind, ask students to make a conjecture about dividing monomials based on what they know about multiplying monomials.

QUOTIENTS OF MONOMIALS

In-Class Examples Power Point®

1 Simplify $\dfrac{x^7y^{12}}{x^6y^3}$. Assume that x and y are not equal to zero. xy^9

Teaching Tip Remind students not to forget to find the powers of the constant terms of the monomials.

2 Simplify $\left(\dfrac{4c^3d^2}{5e^4f^7}\right)^3$. Assume that e and f are not equal to zero.

$\dfrac{64c^9d^6}{125e^{12}f^{21}}$

Study Tip

Graphing Calculator
To express a value as a fraction, press
[MATH] [ENTER]
[ENTER].

In the following example, the definition of a power is used to compute the power of a quotient. Look for a pattern in the exponents.

$$\left(\frac{2}{5}\right)^3 = \underbrace{\left(\frac{2}{5}\right)\left(\frac{2}{5}\right)\left(\frac{2}{5}\right)}_{\text{3 factors}} = \frac{\overbrace{2 \cdot 2 \cdot 2}^{\text{3 factors}}}{\underbrace{5 \cdot 5 \cdot 5}_{\text{3 factors}}} \text{ or } \frac{2^3}{5^3}$$

This and other similar examples suggest the following property.

Key Concept — **Power of a Quotient**

- **Words** To find the power of a quotient, find the power of the numerator and the power of the denominator.
- **Symbols** For any integer m and any real numbers a and b, $b \neq 0$, $\left(\dfrac{a}{b}\right)^m = \dfrac{a^m}{b^m}$.
- **Example** $\left(\dfrac{c}{d}\right)^5 = \dfrac{c^5}{d^5}$

Example 2 *Power of a Quotient*

Simplify $\left(\dfrac{2p^2}{3}\right)^4$.

$\left(\dfrac{2p^2}{3}\right)^4 = \dfrac{(2p^2)^4}{3^4}$ Power of a Quotient

$= \dfrac{2^4(p^2)^4}{3^4}$ Power of a Product

$= \dfrac{16p^8}{81}$ Power of a Power

NEGATIVE EXPONENTS A graphing calculator can be used to investigate expressions with 0 as an exponent as well as expressions with negative exponents.

Graphing Calculator Investigation

Zero Exponent and Negative Exponents

Use the △ key on a TI-83 Plus to evaluate expressions with exponents.

Think and Discuss 2a–d. They are reciprocals. 3. $\dfrac{1}{5}$

1. Copy and complete the table below.

Power	2^4	2^3	2^2	2^1	2^0	2^{-1}	2^{-2}	2^{-3}	2^{-4}
Value	16	8	4	2	1	$\dfrac{1}{2}$	$\dfrac{1}{4}$	$\dfrac{1}{8}$	$\dfrac{1}{16}$

2. Describe the relationship between each pair of values.
  a. 2^4 and 2^{-4} **b.** 2^3 and 2^{-3} **c.** 2^2 and 2^{-2} **d.** 2^1 and 2^{-1}

3. Make a Conjecture as to the fractional value of 5^{-1}. Verify your conjecture using a calculator.

4. What is the value of 5^0? 1

5. What happens when you evaluate 0^0? An error message appears.

Graphing Calculator Investigation

Zero and Negative Exponents Make sure students understand that 2^4 and 2^{-4} are reciprocals of each other.

After answering Exercise 5, ask students to write an expression involving division that is equivalent to 0^0. A sample answer is $\dfrac{0^6}{0^6}$. Show students that $\dfrac{0^6}{0^6} = \dfrac{0}{0}$ and remind them that division by zero is undefined.

To understand why a calculator gives a value of 1 for 2^0, study the two methods used to simplify $\frac{2^4}{2^4}$.

Method 1	**Method 2**
$\frac{2^4}{2^4} = 2^{4-4}$ Quotient of Powers	$\frac{2^4}{2^4} = \frac{\overset{1}{2} \cdot \overset{1}{2} \cdot \overset{1}{2} \cdot \overset{1}{2}}{\underset{1}{2} \cdot \underset{1}{2} \cdot \underset{1}{2} \cdot \underset{1}{2}}$ Definition of powers
$= 2^0$ Subtract.	$= 1$ Simplify.

Since $\frac{2^4}{2^4}$ cannot have two different values, we can conclude that $2^0 = 1$.

Key Concept   *Zero Exponent*

- **Words**   Any nonzero number raised to the zero power is 1.
- **Symbols**   For any nonzero number a, $a^0 = 1$.
- **Example** $(-0.25)^0 = 1$

Example 3   *Zero Exponent*

Simplify each expression. Assume that x and y are not equal to zero.

a. $\left(-\frac{3x^5y}{8xy^7}\right)^0$

   $\left(-\frac{3x^5y}{8xy^7}\right)^0 = 1$ $a^0 = 1$

b. $\frac{t^3s^0}{t}$

   $\frac{t^3s^0}{t} = \frac{t^3(1)}{t}$ $a^0 = 1$

       $= \frac{t^3}{t}$ Simplify.

       $= t^2$ Quotient of Powers

To investigate the meaning of a negative exponent, we can simplify expressions like $\frac{8^2}{8^5}$ in two ways.

Method 1	**Method 2**
$\frac{8^2}{8^5} = 8^{2-5}$ Quotient of Powers	$\frac{8^2}{8^5} = \frac{\overset{1}{8} \cdot \overset{1}{8}}{8 \cdot 8 \cdot \underset{1}{8} \cdot \underset{1}{8} \cdot 8}$ Definition of powers
$= 8^{-3}$ Subtract.	$= \frac{1}{8^3}$ Simplify.

Since $\frac{8^2}{8^5}$ cannot have two different values, we can conclude that $8^{-3} = \frac{1}{8^3}$.

Key Concept   *Negative Exponent*

- **Words**   For any nonzero number a and any integer n, a^{-n} is the reciprocal of a^n. In addition, the reciprocal of a^{-n} is a^n.
- **Symbols**   For any nonzero number a and any integer n, $a^{-n} = \frac{1}{a^n}$ and $\frac{1}{a^{-n}} = a^n$.
- **Examples** $5^{-2} = \frac{1}{5^2}$ or $\frac{1}{25}$ $\frac{1}{m^{-3}} = m^3$

NEGATIVE EXPONENTS

Teaching Tip Ask students why the negative sign does not affect the outcome. Students should explain that any nonzero number raised to the zero power is 1, and a negative number is a nonzero number.

3 Simplify each expression. Assume that m and n are not equal to zero.

a. $\left(\frac{12m^8n^7}{8m^5n^{10}}\right)^0$ 1

b. $\frac{m^0n^3}{n^2}$ n

Differentiated Instruction

Naturalist When one-celled organisms reproduce, the population increases by a factor of 2. Population can be counted by multiplying by powers of 2. Use this pattern to show values of negative powers of 2.

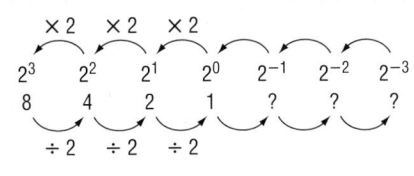

Teaching Tip Point out to students that rewriting a polynomial as a product of fractions makes applying the Negative Exponent Property easier. Fractions that have negative exponents can be rewritten as their reciprocals.

4 Simplify each expression. Assume that no denominator is equal to zero.

a. $\dfrac{x^{-6}}{y^{-4}z^9} \quad \dfrac{y^4}{x^6z^9}$

b. $\dfrac{75p^3q^{-5}}{15p^5q^{-4}r^{-8}} \quad \dfrac{5r^8}{p^2q}$

Teaching Tip Make sure students realize that the diameter of the circle is the same measure as the length of a side of the square. It is very important that students recognize that the area of the square is $(2r)^2$ and not $2r^2$.

5 **TEST ITEM** Refer to the figure in Example 5 of the Student Edition. Write the ratio of the circumference of the circle to the area of the square in simplest form. **C**

A $\dfrac{2r}{\pi}$ **B** $\dfrac{2\pi}{r}$

C $\dfrac{\pi}{2r}$ **D** $\dfrac{2\pi r}{1}$

Answer

3. A factor is moved from the numerator of a fraction to the denominator or vice versa only if the *exponent* of the factor is negative; $-4 \neq \dfrac{1}{4}$.

An expression involving exponents is not considered simplified if the expression contains negative exponents.

Example 4 **Negative Exponents**

Simplify each expression. Assume that no denominator is equal to zero.

a. $\dfrac{b^{-3}c^2}{d^{-5}}$

$\dfrac{b^{-3}c^2}{d^{-5}} = \left(\dfrac{b^{-3}}{1}\right)\left(\dfrac{c^2}{1}\right)\left(\dfrac{1}{d^{-5}}\right)$ Write as a product of fractions.

$= \left(\dfrac{1}{b^3}\right)\left(\dfrac{c^2}{1}\right)\left(\dfrac{d^5}{1}\right)$ $a^{-n} = \dfrac{1}{a^n}$

$= \dfrac{c^2d^5}{b^3}$ Multiply fractions.

b. $\dfrac{-3a^{-4}b^7}{21a^2b^7c^{-5}}$

$\dfrac{-3a^{-4}b^7}{21a^2b^7c^{-5}} = \left(\dfrac{-3}{21}\right)\left(\dfrac{a^{-4}}{a^2}\right)\left(\dfrac{b^7}{b^7}\right)\left(\dfrac{1}{c^{-5}}\right)$ Group powers with the same base.

$= \dfrac{-1}{7}(a^{-4-2})(b^{7-7})(c^5)$ Quotient of Powers and Negative Exponent Properties

$= \dfrac{-1}{7}a^{-6}b^0c^5$ Simplify.

$= \dfrac{-1}{7}\left(\dfrac{1}{a^6}\right)(1)c^5$ Negative Exponent and Zero Exponent Properties

$= -\dfrac{c^5}{7a^6}$ Multiply fractions.

Example 5 **Apply Properties of Exponents**

Multiple-Choice Test Item

Write the ratio of the area of the circle to the area of the square in simplest form.

Ⓐ $\dfrac{\pi}{2}$ Ⓑ $\dfrac{\pi}{4}$ Ⓒ $\dfrac{2\pi}{1}$ Ⓓ $\dfrac{\pi}{3}$

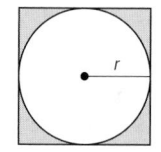

Read the Test Item

A ratio is a comparison of two quantities. It can be written in fraction form.

Test-Taking Tip
Some problems can be solved using estimation. The area of the circle is less than the area of the square. Therefore, the ratio of the two areas must be less than 1. Use 3 as an approximate value for π to determine which of the choices is less than 1.

Solve the Test Item

- area of circle = πr^2
  length of square = diameter of circle or $2r$
  area of square = $(2r)^2$

- $\dfrac{\text{area of circle}}{\text{area of square}} = \dfrac{\pi r^2}{(2r)^2}$ Substitute.

  $= \dfrac{\pi}{4}r^{2-2}$ Quotient of Powers

  $= \dfrac{\pi}{4}r^0 \text{ or } \dfrac{\pi}{4}$ $r^0 = 1$

The answer is B.

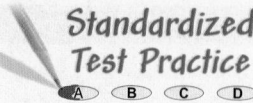
Standardized Test Practice
Ⓐ Ⓑ Ⓒ Ⓓ

Example 5 Remind students that most of the answer choices in multiple-choice test items are answers that result from an arithmetic or other mistake when solving the problem. For example, answer choice A in Example 5 is $\dfrac{\pi}{2}$, which is the answer you get if you use $2r^2$ as the area of the square.

Check for Understanding

Concept Check

1. Sample answer:
$9xy$ and $6xy^2$

2. $\dfrac{a^3b^5}{ab^2} = a^3a^{-1}b^5b^{-2}$
$= a^{3-1}b^{5-2}$
$= a^2b^3$

1. OPEN ENDED Name two monomials whose product is $54x^2y^3$.

2. Show a method of simplifying $\dfrac{a^3b^5}{ab^2}$ using negative exponents instead of the Quotient of Powers Property.

3. FIND THE ERROR Jamal and Emily are simplifying $\dfrac{-4x^3}{x^5}$.

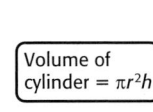

Jamal

$\dfrac{-4x^3}{x^5} = -4x^{3-5}$

$= -4x^{-2}$

$= \dfrac{-4}{x^2}$

Emily

$\dfrac{-4x^3}{x^5} = \dfrac{x^{3-5}}{4}$

$= \dfrac{x^{-2}}{4}$

$= \dfrac{1}{4x^2}$

Who is correct? Explain your reasoning. **Jamal; see margin for explanation.**

Guided Practice

GUIDED PRACTICE KEY

Exercises	Examples
4–12	1–4
13	5

Simplify. Assume that no denominator is equal to zero.

4. $\dfrac{7^8}{7^2}$ 7^6 or $117{,}649$

5. $\dfrac{x^8y^{12}}{x^2y^7}$ x^6y^5

6. $\left(\dfrac{2c^3d}{7z^2}\right)^3$ $\dfrac{8c^9d^3}{343z^6}$

7. $y^0(y^5)(y^{-9})$ $\dfrac{1}{y^4}$

8. 13^{-2} $\dfrac{1}{169}$

9. $\dfrac{c^{-5}}{d^3g^{-8}}$ $\dfrac{g^8}{d^3c^5}$

10. $\dfrac{-5pq^7}{10p^6q^3}$ $-\dfrac{q^4}{2p^5}$

11. $\dfrac{(cd^{-2})^3}{(c^4d^9)^{-2}}$ $c^{11}d^{12}$

12. $\dfrac{(4m^{-3}n^5)^0}{mn}$ $\dfrac{1}{mn}$

Standardized Test Practice
Ⓐ Ⓑ Ⓒ Ⓓ

13. Find the ratio of the volume of the cylinder to the volume of the sphere. **C**

Ⓐ $\dfrac{1}{2}$

Ⓑ 1

Ⓒ $\dfrac{3}{2}$

Ⓓ $\dfrac{3\pi}{2}$

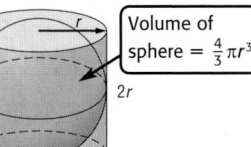

Volume of sphere = $\dfrac{4}{3}\pi r^3$

Volume of cylinder = $\pi r^2 h$

★ indicates increased difficulty

Practice and Apply

Homework Help

For Exercises	See Examples
14–21	1, 2
22–37	1–4

Extra Practice
See page 837.

Simplify. Assume that no denominator is equal to zero.

14. $\dfrac{4^{12}}{4^2}$ 4^{10} or $1{,}048{,}576$

15. $\dfrac{3^{13}}{3^7}$ 3^6 or 729

16. $\dfrac{p^7n^3}{p^4n^2}$ p^3n

17. $\dfrac{y^3z^9}{yz}$ y^2z^7

18. $\left(\dfrac{5b^4n}{2a^6}\right)^2$ $\dfrac{25b^8n^2}{4a^{12}}$

19. $\left(\dfrac{3m^7}{4x^5y^3}\right)^4$ $\dfrac{81m^{28}}{256x^{20}y^{12}}$

20. $\dfrac{-2a^3}{10a^8}$ $-\dfrac{1}{5a^5}$

21. $\dfrac{15b}{45b^5}$ $\dfrac{1}{3b^4}$

22. $x^3y^0x^{-7}$ $\dfrac{1}{x^4}$

23. $n^2(p^{-4})(n^{-5})$ $\dfrac{1}{n^3p^4}$

24. 6^{-2} $\dfrac{1}{36}$

25. 5^{-3} $\dfrac{1}{125}$

26. $\left(\dfrac{4}{5}\right)^{-2}$ $\dfrac{25}{16}$

27. $\left(\dfrac{3}{2}\right)^{-3}$ $\dfrac{8}{27}$

28. $\dfrac{28a^7c^{-4}}{7a^3b^0c^{-8}}$ $4a^4c^4$

29. $\dfrac{30h^{-2}k^{14}}{5hk^{-3}}$ $\dfrac{6k^{17}}{h^3}$

30. $\dfrac{18x^3y^4z^7}{-2x^2yz}$ $-9xy^3z^6$

31. $\dfrac{-19y^0z^4}{-3z^{16}}$ $\dfrac{19}{3z^{12}}$

32. $\dfrac{(5r^{-2})^{-2}}{(2r^3)^2}$ $\dfrac{1}{100r^2}$

33. $\dfrac{p^{-4}q^{-3}}{(p^5q^2)^{-1}}$ $\dfrac{p}{q}$

34. $\left(\dfrac{r^{-2}t^5}{t^{-1}}\right)^0$ 1

35. $\left(\dfrac{4c^{-2}d}{b^{-2}c^3d^{-1}}\right)^0$ 1

★ 36. $\left(\dfrac{5b^{-2}n^4}{n^2z^{-3}}\right)^{-1}$ $\dfrac{b^2}{5n^2z^3}$

★ 37. $\left(\dfrac{2a^{-2}bc^{-1}}{3ab^{-2}}\right)^{-3}$ $\dfrac{27a^9c^3}{8b^9}$

www.algebra1.com/self_check_quiz

Lesson 8-2 Dividing Monomials **421**

Study Notebook

Study Notebook

Have students—
• add the definitions/examples of the vocabulary terms to their Vocabulary Builder worksheets for Chapter 8.
• include any other item(s) that they find helpful in mastering the skills in this lesson.

DAILY INTERVENTION FIND THE ERROR
It appears that Emily was so busy thinking about what to do with negative exponents that she accidentally rewrote -4 as $\dfrac{1}{4}$. Remind students that a negative number is different from a number raised to a negative exponent.

About the Exercises…
Organization by Objective
• **Quotients of Monomials:** 14–21, 38–39
• **Negative Exponents:** 22–37, 40–45

Odd/Even Assignments
Exercises 14–39 are structured so that students practice the same concepts whether they are assigned odd or even problems.

Alert! You may wish to have students use calculators to aid them in computation of numerical powers.

Assignment Guide
Basic: 15–35 odd, 39–42, 47–77
Average: 15–39 odd, 40–44, 47–77
Advanced: 14–38 even, 43–71 (optional : 72–77)

DAILY INTERVENTION Unlocking Misconceptions

• **Powers of Negative Numbers** Students may assume that the expression -6^3 means $(-6)(-6)(-6)$. Explain that -6^3 means $-(6^3)$. To express -6 to the third power, they must use parentheses, $(-6)^3$.

• **Zero Exponents** The Zero Exponent property states that any nonzero number raised to the zero power is equal to 1. So, $(-6)^0 = 1$. However, $-(6^0) = -1$. The expression $-(6^0)$ means the opposite of 6 raised to the zero power. So, the opposite of 1 is -1.

Lesson 8-2 Dividing Monomials **421**

Study Guide and Intervention, p. 461 (shown) and p. 462

Quotients of Monomials To divide two powers with the same base, subtract the exponents.

Quotient of Powers	For all integers m and n and any nonzero number a, $\frac{a^m}{a^n} = a^{m-n}$.
Power of a Quotient	For any integer m and any real numbers a and b, $b \ne 0$, $\left(\frac{a}{b}\right)^m = \frac{a^m}{b^m}$.

Example 1 Simplify $\frac{a^4 b^7}{ab^2}$. Assume neither a nor b is equal to zero.

$\frac{a^4 b^7}{ab^2} = \left(\frac{a^4}{a}\right)\left(\frac{b^7}{b^2}\right)$ Group powers with the same base.
$= (a^{4-1})(b^{7-2})$ Quotient of Powers
$= a^3 b^5$ Simplify.

The quotient is $a^3 b^5$.

Example 2 Simplify $\left(\frac{2a^3 b^5}{3b^2}\right)^3$. Assume that b is not equal to zero.

$\left(\frac{2a^3 b^5}{3b^2}\right)^3 = \frac{(2a^3 b^5)^3}{(3b^2)^3}$ Power of a Quotient
$= \frac{2^3 a^9 (b^5)^3}{(3)^3 (b^2)^3}$ Power of a Product
$= \frac{8a^9 b^{15}}{27 b^6}$ Power of a Power
$= \frac{8a^9 b^9}{27}$ Quotient of Powers

The quotient is $\frac{8a^9 b^9}{27}$.

Exercises

Simplify. Assume that no denominator is equal to zero.

1. $\frac{5^5}{5^2}$ 5^3 or 125
2. $\frac{m^6}{m^4}$ m^2
3. $\frac{p^5 n^4}{p^2 n}$ $p^3 n^3$
4. $\frac{a^2}{a}$ a
5. $\frac{x^5 y^3}{x^4 y^2}$ y
6. $\frac{-2y^7}{14y^5}$ $-\frac{1}{7}y^2$
7. $\frac{xy^6}{y^4 x}$ y^2
8. $\left(\frac{2a^3 b}{a}\right)^3$ $8a^6 b^3$
9. $\left(\frac{4p^4 q^4}{3p^2 q^2}\right)^3$ $\frac{64}{27}p^6 q^6$
10. $\left(\frac{2v^5 w^3}{v^4 w^3}\right)^4$ $16v^4$
11. $\left(\frac{3r^6 s^3}{2r^5 s}\right)^4$ $\frac{81}{16}r^4 s^8$
12. $\frac{r^7 u^7 t^2}{s^3 r^3 t^2}$ $r^4 s^4$

Skills Practice, p. 463 and Practice, p. 464 (shown)

Simplify. Assume that no denominator is equal to zero.

1. $\frac{8^8}{8^4}$ 8^4 or 4096
2. $\frac{a^4 b^4}{ab^3}$ $a^3 b^3$
3. $\frac{xy^3}{xy}$ y
4. $\frac{m^5 np}{m^4 p}$ mn
5. $\frac{5c^4 d^3}{-4c^2 d}$ $-\frac{5d^2}{4}$
6. $\frac{8y^7 z^6}{4y^5 z^5}$ $2yz$
7. $\left(\frac{4j^5 k}{3h^6}\right)^3$ $\frac{64j^9 g^3}{27h^{18}}$
8. $\left(\frac{6u^5}{7p^5 s^3}\right)^2$ $\frac{36u^{10}}{49p^{12} s^8}$
9. $\frac{-4c^2}{24c^5}$ $-\frac{1}{6c^3}$
10. $x^3(y^{-5})(x^{-8})$ $\frac{1}{x^5 y^5}$
11. $p(q^{-2})(r^{-3})$ $\frac{p}{q^2 r^3}$
12. 12^{-2} $\frac{1}{144}$
13. $\left(\frac{3}{7}\right)^{-2}$ $\frac{49}{9}$
14. $\left(\frac{4}{3}\right)^{-4}$ $\frac{81}{256}$
15. $\frac{22r^3 s^2}{11r^2 s^{-3}}$ $2rs^5$
16. $\frac{-15u^9 u^{-1}}{5u^3}$ $-\frac{3}{u^4}$
17. $\frac{8c^3 d^7 f^4}{4c^{-1} d^2 f^{-3}}$ $2c^4 f^7$
18. $\left(\frac{x^{-5} y^3}{4^{-3}}\right)^0$ 1
19. $\frac{6f^{-2} g^3 h^5}{54f^{-3} g^{-5} h^3}$ $\frac{g^8 h^2}{9}$
20. $\frac{-12t^{-1} u^5 v^{-4}}{2t^{-3} u^5}$ $-\frac{6t^2 u^4}{v^9}$
21. $\frac{r^4}{(3r^3)^{-1}}$ $\frac{r}{27}$
22. $\frac{m^{-2} n^{-5}}{(m^4 n^5)^{-1}}$ $\frac{m^2}{n^2}$
23. $\frac{(j^{-1} k^2)^{-4}}{j^3 k^5}$ $\frac{j}{k^{15}}$
24. $\frac{(2a^{-2} b)^{-3}}{5a^3 b^4}$ $\frac{a^4}{40b^7}$
25. $\frac{(q^{-1} r^3)^{-5}}{qr^{-2}}$ $\frac{q^{10}}{r^{25}}$
26. $\frac{7c^{-3} d^4}{c^5 d e^{-4}}$ $\frac{c^8}{7d^2 e^4}$
27. $\frac{2x^5 y^2 z}{3x^4 y z^{-3}}$ $\frac{9x^2}{4y^2 z^6}$

28. **BIOLOGY** A lab technician draws a sample of blood. A cubic millimeter of the blood contains 22^3 white blood cells and 22^5 red blood cells. What is the ratio of white blood cells to red blood cells? $\frac{1}{484}$

29. **COUNTING** The number of three-letter "words" that can be formed with the English alphabet is 26^3. The number of five-letter "words" that can be formed is 26^5. How many times more five-letter "words" can be formed than three-letter "words"? 676

Reading to Learn Mathematics, p. 465 **ELL**

Pre-Activity How can you compare pH levels?

Read the introduction to Lesson 8-2 at the top of page 417 in your textbook.
- In the formula $c = \left(\frac{1}{10}\right)^{\text{pH}}$, identify the base and the exponent.
  base $= \frac{1}{10}$, exponent = pH
- How do you think c will change as the exponent increases?
  c will decrease.

Reading the Lesson

1. Explain what the statement $\frac{a^m}{a^n} = a^{m-n}$ means.
   To divide two powers that have the same base, subtract the exponents.

2. To find c in the formula $c = \left(\frac{1}{10}\right)^{\text{pH}}$, you can find the power of the numerator, the power of the denominator, and divide. This is an example of what property?
   Power of a Quotient Property

3. Use the Quotient of Powers Property to explain why $3^0 = 1$. Sample answer: $\frac{3^4}{3^4} = 1$. The Quotient of Powers Property says that when you divide two powers that have the same base, you subtract the exponents. So $\frac{3^4}{3^4} = 3^0$.

4. Consider the expression 4^{-3}.
   a. Explain why the expression 4^{-3} is not simplified. An expression involving exponents is not considered simplified if the expression contains negative exponents.
   b. Define the term reciprocal. The reciprocal of a number is 1 divided by the number.
   c. 4^{-3} is the reciprocal of what power of 4? 4^3
   d. What is the simplified form of 4^{-3}? $\frac{1}{4^3}$ or $\frac{1}{64}$

Helping You Remember

5. Describe how you would help a friend who needs to simplify the expression $\frac{4x^2}{2x^5}$.
   Divide the constants and group powers with the same base to get $\left(\frac{4}{2}\right)\left(\frac{x^2}{x^5}\right)$. Use the Quotient of Powers Property to get $(2)(x^{2-5})$ or $(2)(x^{-3})$. To simplify $(2)(x^{-3})$, use the Negative Exponent Property to get $(2)\left(\frac{1}{x^3}\right)$, or $\frac{2}{x^3}$.

---

38. The area of the rectangle is $24x^5 y^3$ square units. Find the length of the rectangle. **$3x^2 y$ units**

$8x^3 y^2$

39. The area of the triangle is $100a^3 b$ square units. Find the height of the triangle. **$10ab$ units**

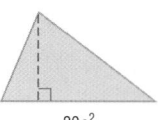

$20a^2$

•• SOUND For Exercises 40–42, use the following information.
The intensity of sound can be measured in watts per square meter. The table gives the watts per square meter for some common sounds.

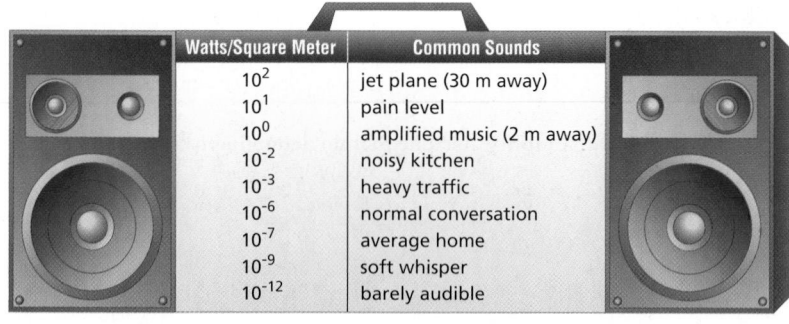

Watts/Square Meter	Common Sounds
10^2	jet plane (30 m away)
10^1	pain level
10^0	amplified music (2 m away)
10^{-2}	noisy kitchen
10^{-3}	heavy traffic
10^{-6}	normal conversation
10^{-7}	average home
10^{-9}	soft whisper
10^{-12}	barely audible

40. How many times more intense is the sound from heavy traffic than the sound from normal conversation? **10^3 or 1000**

41. What sound is 10,000 times as loud as a noisy kitchen? **jet plane**

42. How does the intensity of a whisper compare to that of normal conversation? **$\frac{1}{1000}$**

PROBABILITY For Exercises 43 and 44, use the following information.
If you toss a coin, the probability of getting heads is $\frac{1}{2}$. If you toss a coin 2 times, the probability of getting heads each time is $\frac{1}{2} \cdot \frac{1}{2}$ or $\left(\frac{1}{2}\right)^2$.

43. Write an expression to represent the probability of tossing a coin n times and getting n heads.

44. Express your answer to Exercise 43 as a power of 2. **2^{-n}**

LIGHT For Exercises 45 and 46, use the table below.

45. Express the range of the wavelengths of visible light using positive exponents. Then evaluate each expression.

46. Express the range of the wavelengths of X-rays using positive exponents. Then evaluate each expression.

Spectrum of Electromagnetic Radiation	
Region	**Wavelength (cm)**
Radio	greater than 10
Microwave	10^1 to 10^{-2}
Infrared	10^{-2} to 10^{-5}
Visible	10^{-5} to 10^{-4}
Ultraviolet	10^{-4} to 10^{-7}
X-rays	10^{-7} to 10^{-9}
Gamma Rays	less than 10^{-9}

More About. . .

Sound •·········

Timbre is the quality of the sound produced by a musical instrument. Sound quality is what distinguishes the sound of a note played on a flute from the sound of the same note played on a trumpet with the same frequency and intensity.

Source: www.school.discovery.com

43. $\left(\frac{1}{2}\right)^n$

45. $\frac{1}{10^5}$ to $\frac{1}{10^4}$ cm;

$\frac{1}{100,000}$ to $\frac{1}{10,000}$ cm

46. $\frac{1}{10^7}$ to $\frac{1}{10^9}$ cm;

$\frac{1}{10,000,000}$ to $\frac{1}{1,000,000,000}$ cm

Enrichment, p. 466

Patterns with Powers

Use your calculator, if necessary, to complete each pattern.

a.
$2^{10} = $ 1024
$2^9 = $ 512
$2^8 = $ 256
$2^7 = $ 128
$2^6 = $ 64
$2^5 = $ 32
$2^4 = $ 16
$2^3 = $ 8
$2^2 = $ 4
$2^1 = $ 2

b.
$5^{10} = $ 9,765,625
$5^9 = $ 1,953,125
$5^8 = $ 390,625
$5^7 = $ 78,125
$5^6 = $ 15,625
$5^5 = $ 3125
$5^4 = $ 625
$5^3 = $ 125
$5^2 = $ 25
$5^1 = $ 5

c.
$4^{10} = $ 1,048,576
$4^9 = $ 262,144
$4^8 = $ 65,536
$4^7 = $ 16,384
$4^6 = $ 4096
$4^5 = $ 1024
$4^4 = $ 256
$4^3 = $ 64
$4^2 = $ 16
$4^1 = $ 4

CRITICAL THINKING Simplify. Assume that no denominator is equal to zero.

47. $a^n(a^3)$ a^{n+3}

48. $(5^{4x-3})(5^{2x+1})$ 5^{6x-2}

49. $\dfrac{c^{x+7}}{c^{x-4}}$ c^{11}

50. $\dfrac{3b^{2n-9}}{b^{3(n-3)}}$ $\dfrac{3}{b^n}$

51. **WRITING IN MATH** Answer the question that was posed at the beginning of the lesson. **See pp. 471A–471B.**

   How can you compare pH levels?

   Include the following in your answer:
   - an example comparing two pH levels using the properties of exponents.

52. What is the value of $\dfrac{2^2 \cdot 2^3}{2^{-2} \cdot 2^{-3}}$? **A**

   Ⓐ 2^{10} Ⓑ 2^{12} Ⓒ -1 Ⓓ $\dfrac{1}{2}$

53. **EXTENDED RESPONSE** Write a convincing argument to show why $3^0 = 1$ using the following pattern.
   $3^5 = 243, 3^4 = 81, 3^3 = 27, 3^2 = 9, \ldots$ **Since each number is obtained by dividing the previous number by 3, $3^1 = 3$ and $3^0 = 1$.**

Maintain Your Skills

Mixed Review Simplify. *(Lesson 8-1)*

54. $(m^3n)(mn^2)$ m^4n^3

55. $(3x^4y^3)(4x^4y)$ $12x^8y^4$

56. $(a^3x^2)^4$ $a^{12}x^8$

57. $(3cd^5)^2$ $9c^2d^{10}$

58. $[(2^3)^2]^2$ 2^{12} or 4096

59. $(-3ab)^3(2b^3)^2$ $-108a^3b^9$

NUTRITION For Exercises 60 and 61, use the following information.
Between the ages of 11 and 18, you should get at least 1200 milligrams of calcium each day. One ounce of mozzarella cheese has 147 milligrams of calcium, and one ounce of Swiss cheese has 219 milligrams. Suppose you wanted to eat no more than 8 ounces of cheese. *(Lesson 7-5)*

60. Draw a graph showing the possible amounts of each type of cheese you can eat and still get your daily requirement of calcium. Let x be the amount of mozzarella cheese and y be the amount of Swiss cheese. **See margin.**

61. List three possible solutions. **Sample answers: 3 oz of mozzarella, 4 oz of Swiss; 4 oz of mozzarella, 3 oz of Swiss; 5 oz of mozzarella, 3 oz of Swiss**

Write an equation of the line with the given slope and y-intercept. *(Lesson 5-3)*

63. $y = -2x + 3$

62. slope: 1, y-intercept: -4 $y = x - 4$

63. slope: -2, y-intercept: 3

64. $y = -\dfrac{1}{3}x - 1$

64. slope: $-\dfrac{1}{3}$, y-intercept: -1

65. slope: $\dfrac{3}{2}$, y-intercept: 2

65. $y = \dfrac{3}{2}x + 2$

Graph each equation by finding the x- and y-intercepts. *(Lesson 4-5)*

66. $2y = x + 10$ 67. $4x - y = 12$ 68. $2x = 7 - 3y$
66–68. See margin.

Find each square root. If necessary, round to the nearest hundredth. *(Lesson 2-7)*

69. $\pm\sqrt{121}$ ± 11

70. $\sqrt{3.24}$ 1.8

71. $-\sqrt{52}$ -7.21

Getting Ready for the Next Lesson **PREREQUISITE SKILL** Write each product in the form 10^n.
*(To review **Products of Powers**, see Lesson 8-1.)*

72. $10^2 \times 10^3$ 10^5

73. $10^{-8} \times 10^{-5}$ 10^{-13}

74. $10^{-6} \times 10^9$ 10^3

75. $10^8 \times 10^{-1}$ 10^7

76. $10^4 \times 10^{-4}$ 10^0 or 1

77. $10^{-12} \times 10$ 10^{-11}

Open-Ended Assessment

Speaking Write an expression from one of the Practice and Apply problems on the chalkboard or overhead projector. Have two students come up to the front of the classroom to simplify the expression. One of the students will actually do the simplification and the other one will explain what the partner is doing for each step of the simplification.

Getting Ready for Lesson 8-3

PREREQUISITE SKILL Students will learn about scientific notation in Lesson 8-3. Calculations with scientific notation involve products of powers of 10. Use Exercises 72–77 to determine your students' familiarity with products of powers of 10.

Assessment Options

Quiz (Lessons 8-1 and 8-2) is available on p. 517 of the *Chapter 8 Resource Masters*.

Answers

60.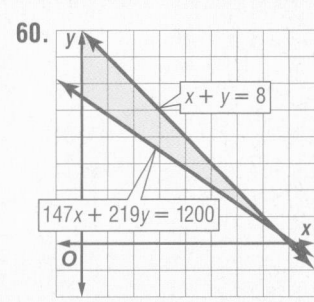

66.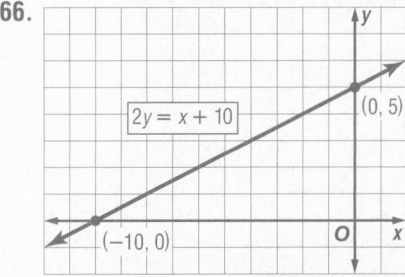

67.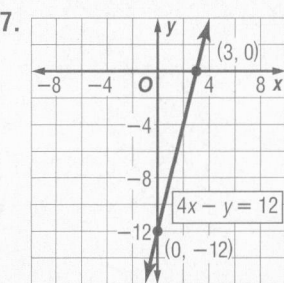

68.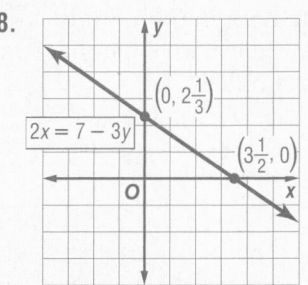

Reading Mathematics

Getting Started

Before using this page, ask students the difference between a bicycle and a tricycle. As students answer, write references to two and three on the chalkboard or overhead projector along with the words bicycle and tricycle.

Teach

Prefixes Discuss with students the meaning of each prefix. Then divide the class into three or four groups and challenge each group to brainstorm as many words as they can that begin with mono-, bi-, tri-, and poly-. Give each group five minutes and then have groups compare answers.

Students can use dictionaries to find more words with these prefixes. Encourage students to record the spellings and definitions of new words they learn from the dictionary.

Assess

Study Notebook

Ask students to summarize what they have learned about prefixes.

ELL English Language Learners may benefit from writing key concepts from this activity in their Study Notebooks in their native language and then in English.

Mathematical Prefixes and Everyday Prefixes

You may have noticed that many prefixes used in mathematics are also used in everyday language. You can use the everyday meaning of these prefixes to better understand their mathematical meaning. The table shows four mathematical prefixes along with their meaning and an example of an everyday word using that prefix.

Prefix	Everyday Meaning	Example
mono-	1. one; single; alone	**monologue** A continuous series of jokes or comic stories delivered by one comedian.
bi-	1. two 2. both 3. both sides, parts, or directions	**bicycle** A vehicle consisting of a light frame mounted on two wire-spoked wheels one behind the other and having a seat, handlebars for steering, brakes, and two pedals or a small motor by which it is driven.
tri-	1. three 2. occurring at intervals of three 3. occurring three times during	**trilogy** A group of three dramatic or literary works related in subject or theme.
poly-	1. more than one; many; much	**polygon** A closed plane figure bounded by three or more line segments.

Source: *The American Heritage Dictionary of the English Language*

You can use your everyday understanding of prefixes to help you understand mathematical terms that use those prefixes.

Reading to Learn

1. Give an example of a geometry term that uses one of these prefixes. Then define that term. **Sample answer: triangle; a three-sided polygon**

2. **MAKE A CONJECTURE** Given your knowledge of the meaning of the word monomial, make a conjecture as to the meaning of each of the following mathematical terms. **See students' work.**
   a. binomial   **b.** trinomial   **c.** polynomial

3. Research the following prefixes and their meanings.
   a. semi- half   **b.** hexa- six   **c.** octa- eight

What You'll Learn

- Express numbers in scientific notation and standard notation.
- Find products and quotients of numbers expressed in scientific notation.

Vocabulary

- scientific notation

Why is scientific notation important in astronomy?

Astronomers often work with very large numbers, such as the masses of planets. The mass of each planet in our solar system is given in the table. Notice that each value is written as the product of a number and a power of 10. These values are written in scientific notation.

Planet	Mass (kilograms)
Mercury	3.30×10^{23}
Venus	4.87×10^{24}
Earth	5.97×10^{24}
Mars	6.42×10^{23}
Jupiter	1.90×10^{27}
Saturn	5.69×10^{26}
Uranus	8.68×10^{25}
Neptune	1.02×10^{26}
Pluto	1.27×10^{22}

Source: NASA

SCIENTIFIC NOTATION When dealing with very large or very small numbers, keeping track of place value can be difficult. For this reason, numbers such as these are often expressed in **scientific notation**.

Key Concept — Scientific Notation

- **Words** A number is expressed in scientific notation when it is written as a product of a factor and a power of 10. The factor must be greater than or equal to 1 and less than 10.

- **Symbols** A number in scientific notation is written as $a \times 10^n$, where $1 \le a < 10$ and n is an integer.

Study Tip

Reading Math
Standard notation is the way in which you are used to seeing a number written, where the decimal point determines the place value for each digit of the number.

The following examples show one way of expressing a number that is written in scientific notation in its decimal or standard notation. Look for a relationship between the power of 10 and the position of the decimal point in the standard notation of the number.

$$6.59 \times 10^4 = 6.59 \times 10,000$$

$$4.81 \times 10^{-6} = 4.81 \times \frac{1}{10^6}$$
$$= 4.81 \times 0.000001$$

$$= 65,900$$

$$= 0.00000481$$

The decimal point moved 4 places to the right.

The decimal point moved 6 places to the left.

These examples suggest the following rule for expressing a number written in scientific notation in standard notation.

SCIENTIFIC NOTATION

Teaching Tip You may want to review how to enter or find numbers in scientific notation on a calculator. For example, on a graphing calculator, you can set it for scientific mode, enter a number in standard notation, press ENTER and it will display the decimal with what exponent of 10 is used. Likewise, in normal mode, they can use the 10^x function to change a number in scientific notation to standard notation.

In-Class Examples

Teaching Tip Caution students to count decimal place moves carefully because it is very easy to add or drop a zero when converting numbers from scientific notation to standard notation.

1 Express each number in standard notation.

a. 7.48×10^{-3} **0.00748**

b. 2.19×10^5 **219,000**

2 Express each number in scientific notation.

a. 0.000000672 **6.72×10^{-7}**

b. 3,022,000,000,000 **3.022×10^{12}**

Tips for New Teachers

Intervention Students may have previously encountered scientific notation in a science class. Often in science, numbers are rounded to two decimal places when they are converted from standard to scientific notation. For example, 0.0002569 would be rounded to 2.57×10^{-4} when it is converted to scientific notation. Make sure students do not automatically round numbers to two decimal places when they convert to scientific notation in this lesson.

Concept Summary | Scientific to Standard Notation

Use these steps to express a number of the form $a \times 10^n$ in standard notation.

1. Determine whether $n > 0$ or $n < 0$.
2. If $n > 0$, move the decimal point in a to the right n places.
   If $n < 0$, move the decimal point in a to the left n places.
3. Add zeros, decimal point, and/or commas as needed to indicate place value.

Example 1 Scientific to Standard Notation

Express each number in standard notation.

a. 2.45×10^8

$2.45 \times 10^8 = 245,000,000$ $n = 8$; move decimal point 8 places to the right.

b. 3×10^{-5}

$3 \times 10^{-5} = 0.00003$ $n = -5$; move decimal point 5 places to the left.

To express a number in scientific notation, reverse the process used above.

Concept Summary | Standard to Scientific Notation

Use these steps to express a number in scientific notation.

1. Move the decimal point so that it is to the right of the first nonzero digit. The result is a decimal number a.
2. Observe the number of places n and the direction in which you moved the decimal point.
3. If the decimal point moved to the left, write as $a \times 10^n$.
   If the decimal point moved to the right, write as $a \times 10^{-n}$.

Example 2 Standard to Scientific Notation

Express each number in scientific notation.

a. 30,500,000

$30,500,000 \rightarrow 3.0500000 \times 10^n$ Move decimal point 7 places to the left.

$30,500,000 = 3.05 \times 10^7$ $a = 3.05$ and $n = 7$

b. 0.000781

$0.000781 \rightarrow 00007.81 \times 10^n$ Move decimal point 4 places to the right.

$0.000781 = 7.81 \times 10^{-4}$ $a = 7.81$ and $n = -4$

Study Tip

Scientific Notation Notice that when a number is in scientific notation, no more than one digit is to the left of the decimal point.

You will often see large numbers in the media written using a combination of a number and a word, such as 3.2 million. To write this number in standard notation, rewrite the word *million* as 10^6. The exponent 6 indicates that the decimal point should be moved 6 places to the right.

$$3.2 \text{ million} = 3,200,000$$

DAILY INTERVENTION | Differentiated Instruction

Kinesthetic Have students write each digit of the number they are trying to convert on a note card. Also have them make several zero cards to use as placeholders. Using a penny as the decimal point, students can physically move the decimal point and count the number of places it moved.

Example 3 Use Scientific Notation

The graph shows chocolate and candy sales during a recent holiday season.

a. **Express the sales of candy canes, chocolates, and all candy in standard notation.**

Candy canes:
$120 million = $120,000,000

Chocolates:
$300 million = $300,000,000

All candy:
$1.45 billion = $1,450,000,000

b. **Write each of these sales figures in scientific notation.**

Candy canes:
$120,000,000 = 1.2×10^8

Chocolates:
$300,000,000 = 3.0×10^8

All candy: $1,450,000,000 = 1.45×10^9

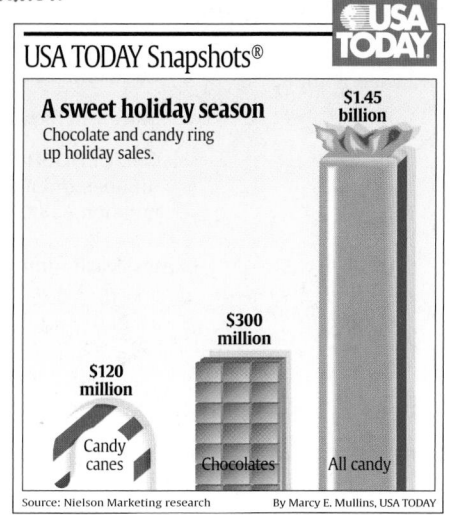

USA TODAY Snapshots®

A sweet holiday season
Chocolate and candy ring up holiday sales.

$120 million — Candy canes
$300 million — Chocolates
$1.45 billion — All candy

Source: Nielson Marketing research   By Marcy E. Mullins, USA TODAY

Log on for:
• Updated data
• More activities on scientific notation
www.algebra1.com/usa_today

TEACHING TIP
A billion in the U.S. and France means 10^9. A billion in Great Britain and Germany means 10^{12}.

PRODUCTS AND QUOTIENTS WITH SCIENTIFIC NOTATION

You can use scientific notation to simplify computation with very large and/or very small numbers.

Example 4 Multiplication with Scientific Notation

Evaluate $(5 \times 10^{-8})(2.9 \times 10^2)$. Express the result in scientific and standard notation.

$(5 \times 10^{-8})(2.9 \times 10^2)$

$= (5 \times 2.9)(10^{-8} \times 10^2)$ Commutative and Associative Properties

$= 14.5 \times 10^{-6}$ Product of Powers

$= (1.45 \times 10^1) \times 10^{-6}$ $14.5 = 1.45 \times 10^1$

$= 1.45 \times (10^1 \times 10^{-6})$ Associative Property

$= 1.45 \times 10^{-5}$ or 0.0000145   Product of Powers

Example 5 Division with Scientific Notation

Evaluate $\frac{1.2789 \times 10^9}{5.22 \times 10^5}$. Express the result in scientific and standard notation.

$\frac{1.2789 \times 10^9}{5.22 \times 10^5} = \left(\frac{1.2789}{5.22}\right)\left(\frac{10^9}{10^5}\right)$ Associative Property

$= 0.245 \times 10^4$ Quotient of Powers

$= (2.45 \times 10^{-1}) \times 10^4$ $0.245 = 2.45 \times 10^{-1}$

$= 2.45 \times (10^{-1} \times 10^4)$ Associative Property

$= 2.45 \times 10^3$ or 2450   Product of Powers

 www.algebra1.com/extra_examples

 ### Online Lesson Plans

USA TODAY Education's Online site offers resources and interactive features connected to each day's newspaper. *Experience TODAY*, USA TODAY's daily lesson plan, is available on the site and delivered daily to subscribers. This plan provides instruction for integrating USA TODAY graphics and key editorial features into your mathematics classroom. Log on to **www.education.usatoday.com**.

Study Notebook

Have students—
- add the definitions/examples of the vocabulary terms to their Vocabulary Builder worksheets for Chapter 8.
- include examples that show how to move the decimal point when writing numbers in scientific notation and vice versa.
- include any other item(s) that they find helpful in mastering the skills in this lesson.

About the Exercises...

Organization by Objective
- Scientific Notation: 18–43
- Products and Quotients with Scientific Notation: 44–59

Odd/Even Assignments
Exercises 18–59 are structured so that students practice the same concepts whether they are assigned odd or even problems.

Alert! Exercises 64–67 require a graphing calculator.

Assignment Guide

Basic: 19–23 odd, 27–39 odd, 43–57 odd, 60–63, 68–82

Average: 19–59 odd, 60–63, 68–82 (optional: 64–67)

Advanced: 18–58 even, 60–76 (optional: 77–82)

All: Practice Quiz 1 (1–10)

Check for Understanding

Concept Check
1–2. See margin.

1. **Explain** how you know to use a positive or a negative exponent when writing a number in scientific notation.

2. **State** whether 65.2×10^3 is in scientific notation. Explain your reasoning.

3. **OPEN ENDED** Give an example of a large number written using a decimal number and a word. Write this number in standard and then in scientific notation. **Sample answer: 6.5 million; 6,500,000; 6.5×10^6**

Guided Practice

GUIDED PRACTICE KEY	
Exercises	Examples
4–7	1
8–11	2
12–15	3, 4
16, 17	5

Express each number in standard notation.

4. 2×10^{-8} **0.00000002**
5. 4.59×10^3 **4590**
6. 7.183×10^{14} **718,300,000,000,000**
7. 3.6×10^{-5} **0.000036**

Express each number in scientific notation.

8. 56,700,000 **5.67×10^7**
9. 0.00567 **5.67×10^{-3}**
10. 0.00000000004 **4×10^{-11}**
11. 3,002,000,000,000,000 **3.002×10^{15}**

Evaluate. Express each result in scientific and standard notation.

12–15. See margin.

12. $(5.3 \times 10^2)(4.1 \times 10^5)$
13. $(2 \times 10^{-5})(9.4 \times 10^{-3})$
14. $\dfrac{1.5 \times 10^2}{2.5 \times 10^{12}}$
15. $\dfrac{1.25 \times 10^4}{2.5 \times 10^{-6}}$

Application

16. 1,650,000,000; 1.65×10^9; 1,540,000,000,000; 1.54×10^{12}

CREDIT CARDS For Exercises 16 and 17, use the following information. During the year 2000, 1.65 billion credit cards were in use in the United States. During that same year, $1.54 trillion was charged to these cards. (*Hint:* 1 trillion = 1×10^{12}) **Source:** U.S. Department of Commerce

16. Express each of these values in standard and then in scientific notation.

17. Find the average amount charged per credit card. **$933.33**

★ indicates increased difficulty

Practice and Apply

Homework Help	
For Exercises	See Examples
18–29	1
30–43	2
44–55	3, 4
56–59	5

Extra Practice
See page 837.

27. 238,900
28. 0.00000000000000000000000000167265
30. 5.04×10^{10}
31. 3.4402×10^7
33. 9.0465×10^{-4}

Express each number in standard notation.

18. 5×10^{-6} **0.000005**
19. 6.1×10^{-9} **0.0000000061**
20. 7.9×10^4 **79,000**
21. 8×10^7 **80,000,000**
22. 1.243×10^{-7} **0.0000001243**
23. 2.99×10^{-1} **0.299**
24. 4.782×10^{13} **47,820,000,000,000**
★ 25. 6.89×10^0 **6.89**

PHYSICS Express the number in each statement in standard notation.

26. There are 2×10^{11} stars in the Andromeda Galaxy. **200,000,000,000**

27. The center of the moon is 2.389×10^5 miles away from the center of Earth.

28. The mass of a proton is 1.67265×10^{-27} kilograms.

29. The mass of an electron is 9.1095×10^{-31} kilograms. **0.00000000000000000000000000000091095**

Express each number in scientific notation.

30. 50,400,000,000
31. 34,402,000
32. 0.000002 **2×10^{-6}**
33. 0.00090465
34. 25.8 **2.58×10**
35. 380.7 **3.807×10^2**
36. 622×10^6 **6.22×10^8**
37. 87.3×10^{11} **8.73×10^{12}**
38. 0.5×10^{-4} **5×10^{-5}**
39. 0.0081×10^{-3} **8.1×10^{-6}**
★ 40. 94×10^{-7} **9.4×10^{-6}**
★ 41. 0.001×10^{12} **1×10^9**

Answers

1. When numbers between 0 and 1 are written in scientific notation, the exponent is negative. If the number is not between 0 and 1, use a positive exponent.

2. 65.2×10^3 is not written in scientific notation. The number 65.2 is greater than 10.

12. 2.173×10^8; 217,300,000
13. 1.88×10^{-7}; 0.000000188
14. 6×10^{-11}; 0.00000000006
15. 5×10^9; 5,000,000,000

50. 1.5×10^5; 150,000
51. 4×10^{-4} 0.0004
52. 6.2×10^{-7} 0.00000062
53. 2.3×10^{-6}; 0.0000023
54. 6.5×10^{-5}; 0.000065
55. 9.3×10^{-7}; 0.00000093

The distances of the planets from the Sun can be written in scientific notation. Visit www.algebra1.com/webquest to continue work on your WebQuest project.

44. 3.56×10^8; 356,000,000

45. 1.71×10^9; 1,710,000,000

46. 4.3×10^{-4}; 0.00043

47. 1.44×10^{-8}; 0.0000000144

48. 2.135×10^0; 2.135

49. 2.548×10^5; 254,800

Baseball

The contract Alex Rodriguez signed with the Texas Rangers on December 11, 2000, guarantees him $25.2 million a year for 10 seasons.

Source: Associated Press

42. STARS In the 1930s, the Indian physicist Subrahmanyan Chandrasekhar and others predicted the existence of neutron stars. These stars can have a density of 10 billion tons per teaspoonful. Express this density in scientific notation. 1×10^{10} tons

43. PHYSICAL SCIENCE The unit of measure for counting molecules is a *mole*. One mole of a substance is the amount that contains about 602,214,299,000,000,000,000,000 molecules. Write this number in scientific notation. $6.02214299 \times 10^{23}$

Evaluate. Express each result in scientific and standard notation.

44. $(8.9 \times 10^4)(4 \times 10^3)$

45. $(3 \times 10^6)(5.7 \times 10^2)$

46. $(5 \times 10^{-2})(8.6 \times 10^{-3})$

47. $(1.2 \times 10^{-5})(1.2 \times 10^{-3})$

48. $(3.5 \times 10^7)(6.1 \times 10^{-8})$

49. $(2.8 \times 10^{-2})(9.1 \times 10^6)$

50. $\dfrac{7.2 \times 10^9}{4.8 \times 10^4}$

51. $\dfrac{7.2 \times 10^3}{1.8 \times 10^7}$

52. $\dfrac{3.162 \times 10^{-4}}{5.1 \times 10^2}$

53. $\dfrac{1.035 \times 10^{-2}}{4.5 \times 10^3}$

54. $\dfrac{2.795 \times 10^{-8}}{4.3 \times 10^{-4}}$

55. $\dfrac{4.65 \times 10^{-1}}{5 \times 10^5}$

50–55. See margin.

56. HAIR GROWTH The usual growth rate of human hair is 3.3×10^{-4} meter per day. If an individual hair grew for 10 years, how long would it be in meters? (Assume 365 days in a year.) **about 1.2 m**

57. NATIONAL DEBT In April 2001, the national debt was about $5.745 trillion, and the estimated U.S. population was 283.9 million. About how much was each U.S. citizen's share of the national debt at that time? **about $20,236**

 Online Research Data Update What is the current U.S. population and amount of national debt? Visit www.algebra1.com/data_update to learn more.

58. BASEBALL The table below lists the greatest yearly salary for a major league baseball player for selected years.

Baseball Salary Milestones

Year	Player	Yearly Salary
1979	Nolan Ryan	$1 million
1982	George Foster	$2.04 million
1990	Jose Canseco	$4.7 million
1992	Ryne Sandberg	$7.1 million
1996	Ken Griffey, Jr.	$8.5 million
1997	Pedro Martinez	$12.5 million
2000	Alex Rodriguez	$25.2 million

Source: USA TODAY

About how many times as great was the yearly salary of Alex Rodriguez in 2000 as that of George Foster in 1982? **about 12 times**

★ 59. ASTRONOMY The Sun burns about 4.4×10^6 tons of hydrogen per second. How much hydrogen does the Sun burn in one year? (*Hint*: First, find the number of seconds in a year and write this number in scientific notation.) **about 1.4×10^{14} or 140 trillion tons**

60. CRITICAL THINKING Determine whether each statement is *sometimes*, *always*, or *never* true. Explain your reasoning. **a–b. See pp. 471A–471B.**

  a. If $1 \le a < 10$ and n and p are integers, then $(a \times 10^n)^p = a^p \times 10^{np}$.

  b. The expression $a^p \times 10^{np}$ in part **a** is in scientific notation.

Open-Ended Assessment

Writing Have students look through their science book and find numbers expressed in scientific notation. Ask students to write a sentence explaining what each number represents in science.

Getting Ready for Lesson 8-4

PREREQUISITE SKILL Students will learn about polynomials in Lesson 8-4. They will identify, write, and simplify polynomials and must know how to evaluate expressions. Use Exercises 77–82 to determine your students' familiarity with evaluating expressions.

Assessment Options

Practice Quiz 1 The quiz provides students with a brief review of the concepts and skills in Lesson 8-1 through 8-3. Lesson numbers are given to the right of the exercises or instruction lines so students can review concepts not yet mastered.

Answers

74.

$-18 \quad -16 \quad -14 \quad -12 \quad -10$

75.
$12 \quad 14 \quad 18 \quad 20 \quad 22$

76.
$-38 \quad -36 \quad -34 \quad -32 \quad -30$

---

61. **WRITING IN MATH** Answer the question that was posed at the beginning of the lesson. **See pp. 471A–471B.**

Why is scientific notation important in astronomy?

Include the following in your answer:
- the mass of each of the planets in standard notation, and
- an explanation of how scientific notation makes presenting and computing with large numbers easier.

Standardized Test Practice

62. Which of the following is equivalent to 360×10^{-4}? **C**

   (A) 3.6×10^3 (B) 3.6×10^2 (C) 3.6×10^{-2} (D) 3.6×10^{-3}

63. **SHORT RESPONSE** There are an average of 25 billion red blood cells in the human body and about 270 million hemoglobin molecules in each red blood cell. Find the average number of hemoglobin molecules in the human body. **6.75×10^{18}**

Graphing Calculator

SCIENTIFIC NOTATION You can use a graphing calculator to solve problems involving scientific notation. First, put your calculator in scientific mode. To enter 4.5×10^9, enter 4.5 $\boxed{\times}$ 10 $\boxed{\wedge}$ 9.

64. $(4.5 \times 10^9)(1.74 \times 10^{-2})$ **7.83×10^7**   65. $(7.1 \times 10^{-11})(1.2 \times 10^5)$ **8.52×10^{-6}**

66. $(4.095 \times 10^5) \div (3.15 \times 10^8)$ **1.3×10^{-3}**   67. $(6 \times 10^{-4}) \div (5.5 \times 10^{-7})$ **1.09×10^3**

Maintain Your Skills

Mixed Review

Simplify. Assume no denominator is equal to zero. *(Lesson 8-2)*

68. $\dfrac{49a^4b^7c^2}{7ab^4c^3}$ **$\dfrac{7a^3b^3}{c}$**   69. $\dfrac{-4n^3p^{-5}}{n^{-2}}$ **$-\dfrac{4n^5}{p^5}$**   70. $\dfrac{(8n^7)^2}{(3n^2)^{-3}}$ **$1728n^{20}$**

Determine whether each expression is a monomial. Write *yes* or *no*. *(Lesson 8-1)*

71. $3a + 4b$ **no**   72. $\dfrac{6}{n}$ **no**   73. $\dfrac{v^2}{3}$ **yes**

Solve each inequality. Then check your solution and graph it on a number line. *(Lesson 6-1)* **74–76. See margin for graphs.**

74. $m - 3 < -17$ $\{m \mid m < -14\}$ 75. $-9 + d > 9$ $\{d \mid d > 18\}$ 76. $-x - 11 \geq 23$ $\{x \mid x \leq -34\}$

Getting Ready for the Next Lesson

PREREQUISITE SKILL Evaluate each expression when $a = 5$, $b = -2$, and $c = 3$.
*(To review **evaluating expressions**, see Lesson 1-2.)*

77. $5b^2$ **20**   78. $c^2 - 9$ **0**   79. $b^3 + 3ac$ **37**

80. $a^2 + 2a - 1$ **34**   81. $-2b^4 - 5b^3 - b$ **10**   82. $3.2c^3 + 0.5c^2 - 5.2c$ **75.3**

Practice Quiz 1   Lessons 8-1 through 8-3

Simplify. *(Lesson 8-1)*

1. $n^3(n^4)(n)$ **n^8**   2. $4ad(3a^3d)$ **$12a^4d^2$**   3. $(-2w^3z^4)^3(-4wz^3)^2$ **$-128w^{11}z^{18}$**

Simplify. Assume that no denominator is equal to zero. *(Lesson 8-2)*

4. $\dfrac{25p^{10}}{15p^3}$ **$\dfrac{5p^7}{3}$**   5. $\left(\dfrac{6k^3}{7np^4}\right)^2$ **$\dfrac{36k^6}{49n^2p^8}$**   6. $\dfrac{4x^0y^2}{(3y^{-3}z^5)^{-2}}$ **$\dfrac{36z^{10}}{y^4}$**

Evaluate. Express each result in scientific and standard notation. *(Lesson 8-3)* **7–10. See margin.**

7. $(6.4 \times 10^3)(7 \times 10^2)$ 8. $(4 \times 10^2)(15 \times 10^{-6})$ 9. $\dfrac{9.2 \times 10^3}{2.3 \times 10^5}$ 10. $\dfrac{3.6 \times 10^7}{1.2 \times 10^{-2}}$

Answers

7. 4.48×10^6; 4,480,000

8. 6×10^{-3}; 0.006

9. 4×10^{-2}; 0.04

10. 3×10^9; 3,000,000,000

Polynomials

Algebra tiles can be used to model polynomials. A polynomial is a monomial or the sum of monomials. The diagram at the right shows the models.

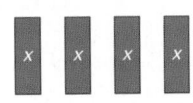

Polynomial Models	
Polynomials are modeled using three types of tiles.	1 x x^2
Each tile has an opposite.	-1 $-x$ $-x^2$

Use algebra tiles to model each polynomial.

- **4x**
  To model this polynomial, you will need 4 green x tiles.

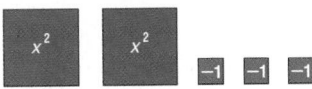

- **2x^2 − 3**
  To model this polynomial, you will need 2 blue x^2 tiles and 3 red −1 tiles.

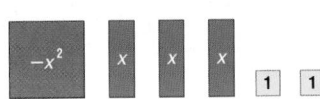

- **−x^2 + 3x + 2**
  To model this polynomial, you will need 1 red −x^2 tile, 3 green x tiles, and 2 yellow 1 tiles.

Model and Analyze

Use algebra tiles to model each polynomial. Then draw a diagram of your model. 1–4. See pp. 471A–471B.

1. $-2x^2$ **2.** $5x - 4$ **3.** $3x^2 - x$ **4.** $x^2 + 4x + 3$

Write an algebraic expression for each model.

5.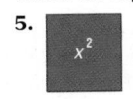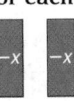

$3x^2 - 2x$

6.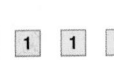

$-x^2 + x + 4$

7.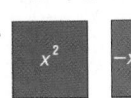

$-2x^2 + 3x - 1$

8.

$x^2 - 2x + 3$

9. MAKE A CONJECTURE Write a sentence or two explaining why algebra tiles are sometimes called *area tiles*. x^2, x, and 1 represent the areas of the tiles.

A Preview of Lesson 8-4

Getting Started

Objective Use algebra tiles to model polynomials.

Materials
algebra tiles

Teach

- Prior to the activity, make sure students easily recognize each type of algebra tile. Remind them that constants are represented by the 1 and −1 tiles, variables without exponents are represented by the x tiles, and x^2 tiles represent variables with an exponent of 2.

- Make sure students understand that the number of x and x^2 tiles represent the coefficients of x and x^2, respectively. The number of 1 tiles represents the constant in the expression.

- Tell students to be careful to use the tiles with the correct sign. It is easy to accidentally substitute an x tile when you should use a −x tile.

Assess

Speak a polynomial and have students model the polynomial.

Study Notebook

You may wish to have students summarize this activity and what they learned from it.

Resource Manager

📁 **Teaching Algebra with Manipulatives**
- pp. 10–11 (master for algebra tiles)
- p. 136 (student recording sheet)

Glencoe Mathematics Classroom Manipulative Kit
- algebra tiles

8-4 **Polynomials**

1 Focus

5-Minute Check Transparency 8-4 Use as a quiz or review of Lesson 8-3.

Mathematical Background notes are available for this lesson on p. 408D.

How **are polynomials useful in modeling data?**

Ask students:

- What is the value of t for the year 1994? **2** What would be the value of t for the year 1997? **5**

- Using the equation, find the value of H for the year 1997. **34**

- Why does the value of H for the year 1997 differ from the value in the table? **The polynomial model approximates but does not necessarily match the real values exactly.**

Vocabulary

- polynomial
- binomial
- trinomial
- degree of a monomial
- degree of a polynomial

Study Tip

Common Misconception
Before deciding if an expression is a polynomial, write each term of the expression so that there are no variables in the denominator. Then look for negative exponents. Recall that the exponents of a monomial must be nonnegative integers.

TEACHING TIP

Remind students to combine any like terms before deciding if a polynomial is a monomial, binomial, or trinomial.

What **You'll Learn**

- Find the degree of a polynomial.
- Arrange the terms of a polynomial in ascending or descending order.

How **are polynomials useful in modeling data?**

The number of hours H spent per person per year playing video games from 1992 through 1997 is shown in the table. These data can be modeled by the equation

$$H = \frac{1}{4}(t^4 - 9t^3 + 26t^2 - 18t + 76),$$

where t is the number of years since 1992. The expression $t^4 - 9t^3 + 26t^2 - 18t + 76$ is an example of a polynomial.

Video Game Usage

Year	Hours spent per person
1992	19
1993	19
1994	22
1995	24
1996	26
1997	36

Source: U.S. Census Bureau

DEGREE OF A POLYNOMIAL A **polynomial** is a monomial or a sum of monomials. Some polynomials have special names. A **binomial** is the sum of *two* monomials, and a **trinomial** is the sum of *three* monomials. Polynomials with more than three terms have no special names.

Monomial	Binomial	Trinomial
7	$3 + 4y$	$x + y + z$
$13n$	$2a + 3c$	$p^2 + 5p + 4$
$-5z^3$	$6x^2 + 3xy$	$a^2 - 2ab - b^2$
$4ab^3c^2$	$7pqr + pq^2$	$3v^2 - 2w + ab^3$

Example 1 **Identify Polynomials**

State whether each expression is a polynomial. If it is a polynomial, identify it as a *monomial, binomial,* or *trinomial.*

	Expression	Polynomial?	Monomial, Binomial, or Trinomial?
a.	$2x - 3yz$	Yes, $2x - 3yz = 2x + (-3yz)$. The expression is the sum of two monomials.	binomial
b.	$8n^3 + 5n^{-2}$	No. $5n^{-2} = \frac{5}{n^2}$, which is not a monomial.	none of these
c.	-8	Yes. -8 is a real number.	monomial
d.	$4a^2 + 5a + a + 9$	Yes. The expression simplifies to $4a^2 + 6a + 9$, so it is the sum of three monomials.	trinomial

---

Resource Manager

 Workbook and Reproducible Masters

Chapter 8 Resource Masters
- Study Guide and Intervention, pp. 473–474
- Skills Practice, p. 475
- Practice, p. 476
- Reading to Learn Mathematics, p. 477
- Enrichment, p. 478
- Assessment, pp. 517, 519

Graphing Calculator and Spreadsheet Masters, p. 37
Parent and Student Study Guide Workbook, p. 62

 Transparencies

5-Minute Check Transparency 8-4
Answer Key Transparencies

Technology

Interactive Chalkboard

Polynomials can be used to express geometric relationships.

GEOMETRY Write a polynomial to represent the area of the shaded region.

Words	The area of the shaded region is the area of the rectangle minus the area of the circle.

Variables	area of shaded region = A
	width of rectangle = $2r$
	rectangle area = $b(2r)$
	circle area = πr^2

Equation	area of shaded region = rectangle area − circle area
	$A = b(2r) - \pi r^2$
	$A = 2br - \pi r^2$

The polynomial representing the area of the shaded region is $2br - \pi r^2$.

TEACHING TIP
The number 0 has no degree.

The **degree of a monomial** is the sum of the exponents of all its variables.

The **degree of a polynomial** is the greatest degree of any term in the polynomial. To find the degree of a polynomial, you must find the degree of each term.

Monomial	Degree
$8y^4$	4
$3a$	1
$-2xy^2z^3$	$1 + 2 + 3$ or 6
7	0

 **Degree of a Polynomial**

Find the degree of each polynomial.

	Polynomial	Terms	Degree of Each Term	Degree of Polynomial
a.	$5mn^2$	$5mn^2$	3	3
b.	$-4x^2y^2 + 3x^2 + 5$	$-4x^2y^2, 3x^2, 5$	4, 2, 0	4
c.	$3a + 7ab - 2a^2b + 16$	$3a, 7ab, 2a^2b, 16$	1, 2, 3, 0	3

Study Tip

Degrees of 1 and 0
- Since $a = a^1$, the monomial $3a$ can be rewritten as $3a^1$. Thus $3a$ has degree 1.
- Since $x^0 = 1$, the monomial 7 can be rewritten as $7x^0$. Thus 7 has degree 0.

WRITE POLYNOMIALS IN ORDER The terms of a polynomial are usually arranged so that the powers of one variable are in *ascending* (increasing) order or *descending* (decreasing) order.

 Arrange Polynomials in Ascending Order

Arrange the terms of each polynomial so that the powers of x are in ascending order.

a. $7x^2 + 2x^4 - 11$

$7x^2 + 2x^4 - 11 = 7x^2 + 2x^4 - 11x^0$ $x^0 = 1$

$= -11 + 7x^2 + 2x^4$ Compare powers of x: $0 < 2 < 4$.

b. $2xy^3 + y^2 + 5x^3 - 3x^2y$

$2xy^3 + y^2 + 5x^3 - 3x^2y$

$= 2x^1y^3 + y^2 + 5x^3 - 3x^2y^1$ $x = x^1$

$= y^2 + 2xy^3 - 3x^2y + 5x^3$ Compare powers of x: $0 < 1 < 2 < 3$.

DAILY
INTERVENTION   **Unlocking Misconceptions**

Degree of Polynomials Make sure students do not confuse the degree of a polynomial with the number of terms. For example, $x^3 + 1$ is a binomial, but the degree is *three*, not two, because the greatest degree of any of the terms is three.

---

2 Teach

DEGREE OF A POLYNOMIAL

In-Class Examples   Power Point®

Teaching Tip Since students must recall the definition of a monomial in order to define a polynomial, review the definition of a polynomial from Lesson 8-1. Remind students that monomials are the *product* of a number and one or more variables, so expressions such as $\frac{1}{b^2}$ are not monomials.

1 State whether each expression is a polynomial. If it is a polynomial, identify it as a *monomial*, *binomial*, or *trinomial*.

a. $6 - 4$ **yes, binomial**

b. $x^2 + 2xy - 7$ **yes, trinomial**

c. $\frac{14d + 19e^2}{5d^4}$ **no**

d. $26b^5$ **yes, monomial**

2 **GEOMETRY** Write a polynomial to represent the area of the shaded region.

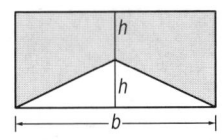 $2bh - \frac{1}{2}bh$

3 Find the degree of each polynomial.

a. $12 + 5b + 6bc + 8bc^2$ **3**

b. $9x^2 - 2x - 4$ **2**

c. $14g^2h^5i$ **8**

WRITE POLYNOMIALS IN ORDER

In-Class Example   Power Point®

4 Arrange the terms of each polynomial so that the powers of x are in ascending order.

a. $16 + 14x^3 + 2x - x^2$
$16 + 2x - x^2 + 14x^3$

b. $7y^2 + 4x^3 + 2xy^3 - x^2y^2$
$7y^2 + 2xy^3 - x^2y^2 + 4x^3$

In-Class Example Power Point®

5 Arrange the terms of each polynomial so that the powers of x are in descending order.

a. $8 + 7x^2 - 12xy^3 - 4x^3y$
$-4x^3y + 7x^2 - 12xy^3 + 8$

b. $a^4 + ax^2 - 2a^3xy^3 - 9x^4y$
$-9x^4y + ax^2 - 2a^3xy^3 + a^4$

3 Practice/Apply

Study Notebook

Have students—
• add the definitions/examples of the vocabulary terms to their Vocabulary Builder worksheets for Chapter 8.
• include any other item(s) that they find helpful in mastering the skills in this lesson.

Answer

2. A variable with a negative power would indicate the quotient of a number, 1, and a variable. Monomials can only be a number, variable, or the product of a number and one or more variables. If one of the terms of an expression is not a monomial, then the expression is not a polynomial.

Example 5 *Arrange Polynomials in Descending Order*

Arrange the terms of each polynomial so that the powers of x are in descending order.

a. $6x^2 + 5 - 8x - 2x^3$

$6x^2 + 5 - 8x - 2x^3 = 6x^2 + 5x^0 - 8x^1 - 2x^3$ $x^0 = 1$ and $x = x^1$

$\qquad = -2x^3 + 6x^2 - 8x + 5$ $3 > 2 > 1 > 0$

b. $3a^3x^2 - a^4 + 4ax^5 + 9a^2x$

$3a^3x^2 - a^4 + 4ax^5 + 9a^2x = 3a^3x^2 - a^4x^0 + 4a^1x^5 + 9a^2x^1$ $a = a^1, x^0 = 1$, and $x = x^1$

$\qquad = 4ax^5 + 3a^3x^2 + 9a^2x - a^4$ $5 > 2 > 1 > 0$

Check for Understanding

Concept Check

1. **OPEN ENDED**   Give an example of a monomial of degree zero.   Sample answer: -8

2. See margin.

2. **Explain** why a polynomial cannot contain a variable raised to a negative power.

3. **Determine** whether each statement is *true* or *false*. If false, give a counterexample.
   a. All binomials are polynomials. **true**
   b. All polynomials are monomials. **false; $3x + 5$**
   c. All monomials are polynomials. **true**

Guided Practice

State whether each expression is a polynomial. If the expression is a polynomial, identify it as a *monomial*, a *binomial*, or a *trinomial*.

GUIDED PRACTICE KEY	
Exercises	Examples
4–6	1
7–9	3
10, 11	4
12, 13	5
14	2

4. $5x - 3xy + 2x$
   yes; binomial

5. $\frac{2z}{5}$ **yes; monomial**

6. $9a^2 + 7a - 5$
   yes; trinomial

Find the degree of each polynomial.

7. 1 **0**

8. $3x + 2$ **1**

9. $2x^2y^3 + 6x^4$ **5**

Arrange the terms of each polynomial so that the powers of x are in ascending order.

10. $6x^3 - 12 + 5x$ **$-12 + 5x + 6x^3$**

11. $-7a^2x^3 + 4x^2 - 2ax^5 + 2a$
    $2a + 4x^2 - 7a^2x^3 - 2ax^5$

Arrange the terms of each polynomial so that the powers of x are in descending order.

12. $2c^5 + 9cx^2 + 3x$ **$9cx^2 + 3x + 2c^5$**

13. $y^3 + x^3 + 3x^2y + 3xy^2$
    $x^3 + 3x^2y + 3xy^2 + y^3$

Application

14. **GEOMETRY**   Write a polynomial to represent the area of the shaded region. **$2cd - \pi d^2$**

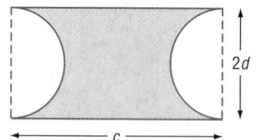

★ indicates increased difficulty

Practice and Apply

State whether each expression is a polynomial. If the expression is a polynomial, identify it as a *monomial*, a *binomial*, or a *trinomial*.

15. 14 **yes; monomial**

16. $\frac{6m^2}{p} + p^3$ **no**

17. $7b - 3.2c + 8b$ **yes; binomial**

18. $\frac{1}{3}x^2 + x - 2$ **yes; trinomial**

19. $6gh^2 - 4g^2h + g$ **yes; trinomial**

20. $-4 + 2a + \frac{5}{a^2}$ **no**

DAILY
INTERVENTION   **Differentiated Instruction**

Auditory/Musical Have students work in pairs. Give them a polynomial and a rhythm instrument (or have them tap on their desks). For each monomial have them tap out each exponent as a beat. Have the partner record the total number of beats for each monomial. Then decide the degree of the polynomial based on the monomial with the greatest number of beats.

GEOMETRY Write a polynomial to represent the area of each shaded region.

21. 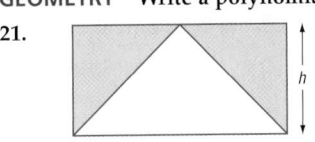 $0.5bh$

22. 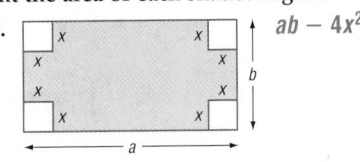 $ab - 4x^2$

23. 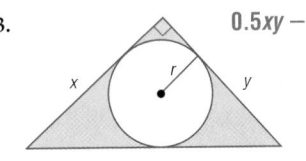 $0.5xy - \pi r^2$

★ 24. 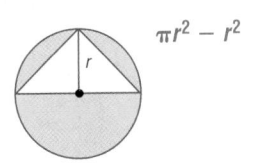 $\pi r^2 - r^2$

Find the degree of each polynomial.

25. $5x^3$ **3**
26. $9y$ **1**
27. $4ab$ **2**
28. -13 **0**
29. $c^4 + 7c^2$ **4**
30. $6n^3 - n^2p^2$ **4**
31. $15 - 8ag$ **2**
32. $3a^2b^3c^4 - 18a^5c$ **9**
33. $2x^3 - 4y + 7xy$ **3**
34. $3z^5 - 2x^2y^3z - 4x^2z$ **6**
35. $7 + d^5 - b^2c^2d^3 + b^6$ **7**
36. $11r^2t^4 - 2s^4t^5 + 24$ **9**

Arrange the terms of each polynomial so that the powers of x are in ascending order. 41. $4 - 5a^7 + 2ax^2 + 3ax^5$

37. $2x + 3x^2 - 1$ $-1 + 2x + 3x^2$
38. $9x^3 + 7 - 3x^5$ $7 + 9x^3 - 3x^5$
39. $c^2x^3 - c^3x^2 + 8c$ $8c - c^3x^2 + c^2x^3$
40. $x^3 + 4a + 5a^2x^6$ $4a + x^3 + 5a^2x^6$
41. $4 + 3ax^5 + 2ax^2 - 5a^7$
42. $10x^3y^2 - 3x^9y + 5y^4 + 2x^2$
43. $3xy^2 - 4x^3 + x^2y + 6y$ $6y + 3xy^2 + x^2y - 4x^3$
44. $-8a^5x + 2ax^4 - 5 - a^2x^2$ $-5 - 8a^5x - a^2x^2 + 2ax^4$

Arrange the terms of each polynomial so that the powers of x are in descending order.

45. $5 + x^5 + 3x^3$ $x^5 + 3x^3 + 5$
46. $2x - 1 + 6x^2$ $6x^2 + 2x - 1$
47. $4a^3x^2 - 5a + 2a^2x^3$ $2a^2x^3 + 4a^3x^2 - 5a$
48. $b^2 + x^2 - 2xb$ $x^2 - 2xb + b^2$
49. $c^2 + cx^3 - 5c^3x^2 + 11x$
50. $9x^2 + 3 + 4ax^3 - 2a^2x$
51. $8x - 9x^2y + 7y^2 - 2x^4$ $-2x^4 - 9x^2y + 8x + 7y^2$
52. $4x^3y + 3xy^4 - x^2y^3 + y^4$ $4x^3y - x^2y^3 + 3xy^4 + y^4$

53. **MONEY** Write a polynomial to represent the value of q quarters, d dimes, and n nickels. $0.25q + 0.10d + 0.05n$

• 54. **MULTIPLE BIRTHS** The number of quadruplet births Q in the United States from 1989 to 1998 can be modeled by $Q = -0.5t^3 + 11.7t^2 - 21.5t + 218.6$, where t represents the number of years since 1989. For what values of t does this model no longer give realistic data? Explain your reasoning. $t > 23$; For $t > 23$, the model predicts a negative number of quadruplet births.

PACKAGING For Exercises 55 and 56, use the following information.
A convenience store sells milkshakes in cups with semispherical lids. The volume of a cylinder is the product of π, the square of the radius r, and the height h. The volume of a sphere is the product of $\frac{4}{3}$, π, and the cube of the radius. 55. $\pi r^2 h + \frac{2}{3}\pi r^3$

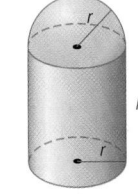

★ 55. Write a polynomial that represents the volume of the container.

★ 56. If the height of the container is 6 inches and the radius is 2 inches, find the volume of the container. **about 92.15 in³**

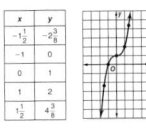

Organization by Objective
- **Degree of a Polynomial:** 15–36, 53–56
- **Writing Polynomials in Order:** 37–52

Odd/Even Assignments
Exercises 15–52 are structured so that students practice the same concepts whether they are assigned odd or even problems.

Assignment Guide
Basic: 15–53 odd, 57–76
Average: 15–53 odd, 55–76
Advanced: 16–54 even, 55–71 (optional: 72–76)

4 Assess

Open-Ended Assessment
Modeling Write several monomials of different degrees on large pieces of paper. Ask student volunteers to stand in front of the class holding the monomials for the class to see. Have the class arrange the volunteers in ascending and then descending order, according to the degree of the monomial that they are holding.

Getting Ready for Lesson 8-5

PREREQUISITE SKILL Students will learn how to add and subtract polynomials in Lesson 8-5. This will include simplifying expressions and combining like terms. Use Exercises 72–76 to determine your students' familiarity with simplifying expressions.

Assessment Options

Quiz (Lessons 8-3 and 8-4) is available on p. 517 of the *Chapter 8 Resource Masters*.

Mid-Chapter Test (Lessons 8-1 through 8-4) is available on p. 519 of the *Chapter 8 Resource Masters*.

---

57. **CRITICAL THINKING** Tell whether the following statement is *true* or *false*. Explain your reasoning. **True; see margin for explanation.**
The degree of a binomial can never be zero.

58. **WRITING IN MATH** Answer the question that was posed at the beginning of the lesson. **See pp. 471A–471B.**

   How are polynomials useful in modeling data?

   Include the following in your answer:
   - a discussion of the accuracy of the equation by evaluating the polynomial for $t = \{0, 1, 2, 3, 4, 5\}$, and
   - an example of how and why someone might use this equation.

Standardized Test Practice

59. If $x = -1$, then $3x^3 + 2x^2 + x + 1 = $ **B**
   - Ⓐ -5.
   - Ⓑ -1.
   - Ⓒ 1.
   - Ⓓ 2.

60. Which polynomial has a degree of 6? **C**
   - Ⓐ $5x^2y + 8xy^4 - y^2 + 6xy - x^3$
   - Ⓑ $6xy + y^2 + y^5 - 5x - 4x^3y + 2xy^3$
   - Ⓒ $2x^2y^4 - 3xy^2 + 4y + 7x - 6$
   - Ⓓ $6x$

Maintain Your Skills

Mixed Review

Express each number in scientific notation. *(Lesson 8-3)*
61. 12,300,000 1.23×10^7
62. 0.00345 3.45×10^{-3}
63. 12×10^6 1.2×10^7
64. 0.77×10^{-10} 7.7×10^{-11}

Simplify. Assume that no variable is equal to zero. *(Lesson 8-2)*
65. $a^0b^{-2}c^{-1}$ $\dfrac{1}{b^2c}$
66. $\dfrac{-5n^5}{n^8}$ $\dfrac{-5}{n^3}$
67. $\left(\dfrac{4x^3y^2}{3z}\right)^2$ $\dfrac{16x^6y^4}{9z^2}$
68. $\dfrac{(-y)^5m^8}{y^3m^{-7}}$ $-y^2m^{15}$

Determine whether each relation is a function. *(Lesson 4-6)*

69. 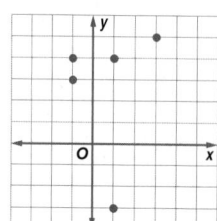 **no**

70. **yes**

x	y
-2	-2
0	1
3	4
5	-2

71. **PROBABILITY** A card is selected at random from a standard deck of 52 cards. What is the probability of selecting a black card? *(Lesson 2-6)* $\dfrac{1}{2}$

Getting Ready for the Next Lesson

PREREQUISITE SKILL Simplify each expression. If not possible, write *simplified*.
(To review simplifying expressions, see Lesson 1-5.)
74. **simplified**

72. $3n + 5n$ **8n**
73. $9a^2 + 3a - 2a^2$ $7a^2 + 3a$
74. $12x^2 + 8x - 6$
75. $-3a + 5b + 4a - 7b$ $a - 2b$
76. $4x + 3y - 6 + 7x + 8 - 10y$ $11x - 7y + 2$

Answer

57. For the degree of a binomial to be zero, the highest degree of both terms would need to be zero. Then the terms would be like terms. With these like terms combined, the expression is not a binomial, but a monomial. Therefore, the degree of a binomial can never be zero. Only a monomial can have a degree of zero.

Adding and Subtracting Polynomials

Monomials such as $5x$ and $-3x$ are called *like terms* because they have the same variable to the same power. When you use algebra tiles, you can recognize like terms because the individual tiles have the same size and shape.

Polynomial Models	
Like terms are represented by tiles that have the same shape and size.	$\boxed{x}$ $\boxed{x}$ $\boxed{-x}$ like terms
A *zero pair* may be formed by pairing one tile with its opposite. You can remove or add zero pairs without changing the polynomial.	$\boxed{x}$ $\boxed{-x}$ → 0

Getting Started

Objective Use algebra tiles to add and subtract polynomials.

Materials
algebra tiles

Teach

- Stress the concept of a *zero pair*. Have students form zero pairs using 1 tiles, x tiles, and x^2 tiles. The concept of a zero pair is essential in future modeling activities.

- **Activity 1** Tell students that it is easier to use the tiles to model the polynomials if they arrange the tiles in the same order that the monomials are arranged within each polynomial. In this case, the monomials are arranged in descending order. Therefore, arrange the tiles in descending order from left to right on the mat. The x^2 tiles go on the left, the x tiles go in the middle, and the 1 tiles go on the right.

- Show students how the result of the model can show a way to add the polynomials.

$$\begin{array}{r} 3x^2 - 2x + 1 \\ (+)\ 1x^2 + 4x - 3 \\ \hline 4x^2 + 2x - 2 \end{array}$$

Activity 1 Use algebra tiles to find $(3x^2 - 2x + 1) + (x^2 + 4x - 3)$.

Step 1 Model each polynomial.

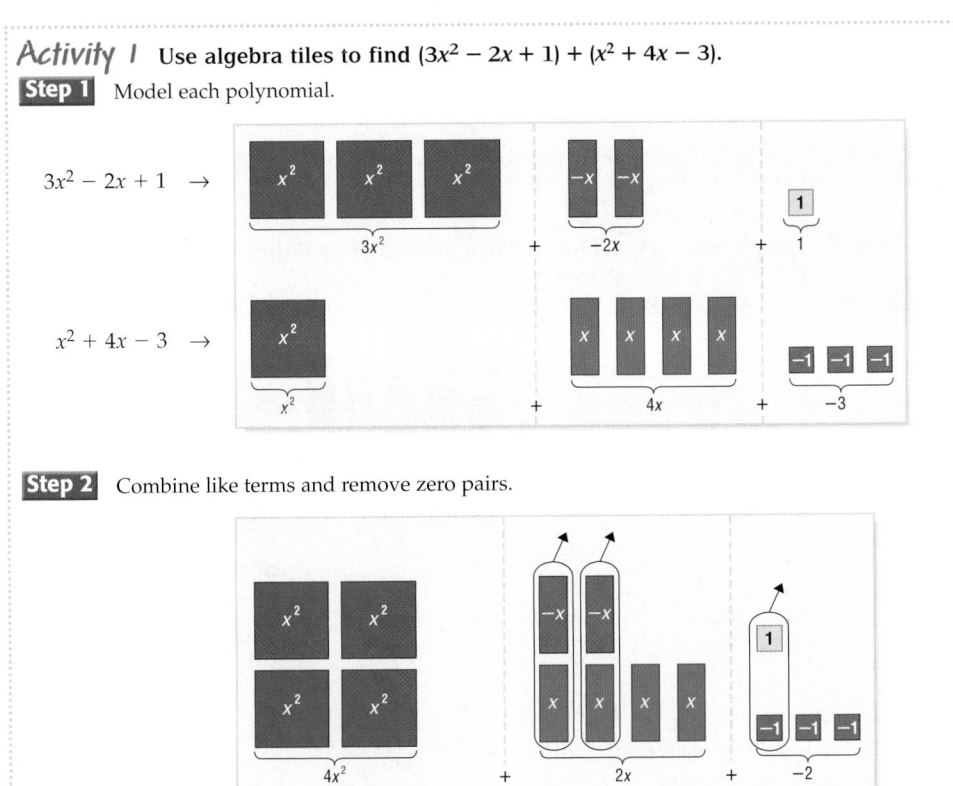

Step 2 Combine like terms and remove zero pairs.

Step 3 Write the polynomial for the tiles that remain.
$(3x^2 - 2x + 1) + (x^2 + 4x - 3) = 4x^2 + 2x - 2$

Algebra Activity Adding and Subtracting Polynomials **437**

Resource Manager

📁 **Teaching Algebra with Manipulatives**
- pp. 10–11 (master for algebra tiles)
- p. 137 (student recording sheet)

Glencoe Mathematics Classroom Manipulative Kit
- algebra tiles

- **Activity 2** Explain that adding a zero pair to the polynomial does not change its value because the zero pairs are equal to zero. After adding the two zero pairs, there are enough red x tiles to remove to satisfy the operation. The seven remaining green x tiles represent $7x$.

- Write the difference vertically so students can see that each pair of like terms is subtracted.

$$\begin{array}{r} 5x + 4 \\ (-)\ -2x + 3 \\ \hline 7x + 1 \end{array}$$

$$5 - (-2) \quad 4 - 3$$

- **Activity 3** Students may find that it is easier to add the additive inverse when using algebra tiles. By doing so, they can avoid having to add zero pairs as they had to do in Activity 2.

- Have students rework Example 3 using the subtraction method in Example 2 to confirm the result. Then rework Example 2 using the additive inverse method.

Assess

Ask students to discuss which method seems easier for subtracting polynomials. Give students an exercise to find the sum or difference without using models. Have students who answer incorrectly use models to determine where they erred.

Activity 2 Use algebra tiles to find $(5x + 4) - (-2x + 3)$.

Step 1 Model the polynomial $5x + 4$.

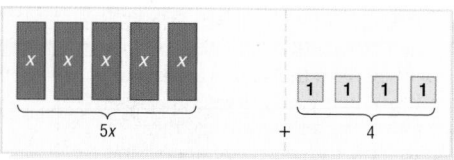

Step 2 To subtract $-2x + 3$, you must remove 2 red $-x$ tiles and 3 yellow 1 tiles. You can remove the yellow 1 tiles, but there are no red $-x$ tiles. Add 2 zero pairs of x tiles. Then remove the 2 red $-x$ tiles.

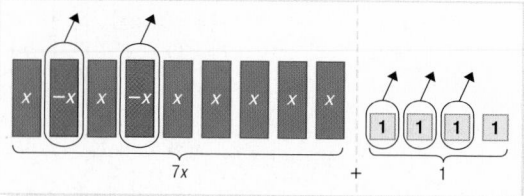

Step 3 Write the polynomial for the tiles that remain.
$(5x + 4) - (-2x + 3) = 7x + 1$

Recall that you can subtract a number by adding its additive inverse or opposite. Similarly, you can subtract a polynomial by adding its opposite.

Activity 3 Use algebra tiles and the additive inverse, or opposite, to find $(5x + 4) - (-2x + 3)$.

Step 1 To find the difference of $5x + 4$ and $-2x + 3$, add $5x + 4$ and the opposite of $-2x + 3$.

$5x + 4 \rightarrow$

The opposite of $\rightarrow$
$-2x + 3$ is $2x - 3$.

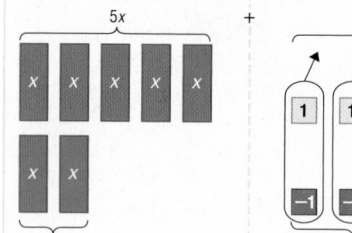

Step 2 Write the polynomial for the tiles that remain.
$(5x + 4) - (-2x + 3) = 7x + 1$ Notice that this is the same answer as in Activity 2.

Model and Analyze

Use algebra tiles to find each sum or difference. 1–6. See margin.

1. $(5x^2 + 3x - 4) + (2x^2 - 4x + 1)$
2. $(2x^2 + 5) + (3x^2 - 2x + 6)$
3. $(-4x^2 + x) + (5x - 2)$
4. $(3x^2 + 4x + 2) - (x^2 - 5x - 5)$
5. $(-x^2 + 7x) - (2x^2 + 3x)$
6. $(8x + 4) - (6x^2 + x - 3)$

7. Find $(2x^2 - 3x + 1) - (2x + 3)$ using each method from Activity 2 and Activity 3. Illustrate with drawings and explain in writing how zero pairs are used in each case. **See pp. 471A–471B.**

438 Chapter 8 Polynomials

Study Notebook

You may wish to have students summarize this activity and what they learned from it.

Answers

1. $7x^2 - x - 3$

2. $5x^2 - 2x + 11$

3. $-4x^2 + 6x - 2$

4. $2x^2 + 9x + 7$

5. $-3x^2 + 4x$

6. $-6x^2 + 7x + 7$

Adding and Subtracting Polynomials

What You'll Learn

- Add polynomials.
- Subtract polynomials.

How can adding polynomials help you model sales?

From 1996 to 1999, the amount of sales (in billions of dollars) of video games V and traditional toys R in the United States can be modeled by the following equations, where t is the number of years since 1996.

Source: *Toy Industry Fact Book*

$$V = -0.05t^3 + 0.05t^2 + 1.4t + 3.6$$
$$R = 0.5t^3 - 1.9t^2 + 3t + 19$$

The total toy sales T is the sum of the video game sales V and traditional toy sales R.

ADD POLYNOMIALS   To add polynomials, you can group like terms horizontally or write them in column form, aligning like terms.

Example 1 Add Polynomials

Find $(3x^2 - 4x + 8) + (2x - 7x^2 - 5)$.

Method 1   Horizontal
Group like terms together.

$(3x^2 - 4x + 8) + (2x - 7x^2 - 5)$

$= [3x^2 + (-7x^2)] + (-4x + 2x) + [8 + (-5)]$ Associative and Commutative Properties

$= -4x^2 - 2x + 3$ Add like terms.

Method 2   Vertical
Align the like terms in columns and add.

$$
\begin{array}{r}
3x^2 - 4x + 8 \\
(+)\ -7x^2 + 2x - 5 \\
\hline
-4x^2 - 2x + 3
\end{array}
$$

Notice that terms are in descending order with like terms aligned.

SUBTRACT POLYNOMIALS   Recall that you can subtract a rational number by adding its opposite or additive inverse. Similarly, you can subtract a polynomial by adding its additive inverse.

To find the additive inverse of a polynomial, replace each term with its additive inverse or opposite.

Polynomial	Additive Inverse
$-5m + 3n$	$5m - 3n$
$2y^2 - 6y + 11$	$-2y^2 + 6y - 11$
$7a + 9b - 4$	$-7a - 9b + 4$

 www.algebra1.com/extra_examples

---

2 Teach

ADD POLYNOMIALS

1 Find $(7y^2 + 2y - 3) + (2 - 4y + 5y^2)$. $12y^2 - 2y - 1$

Teaching Tip Some students may benefit by marking through like terms as they mentally combine them. This saves time spent rewriting terms so like terms are grouped.

SUBTRACT POLYNOMIALS

Teaching Tip Explain to students that in order to combine like terms when subtracting polynomials, you *must* add the additive inverse.

2 Find $(6y^2 + 8y^4 - 5y) - (9y^4 - 7y + 2y^2)$. $-y^4 + 4y^2 + 2y$

3 **GEOMETRY** The measure of the perimeter of the triangle shown is $37s + 42$.

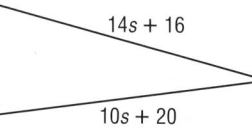

14s + 16

10s + 20

a. Find the polynomial that represents the third side of the triangle. $13s + 6$

b. Find the length of the third side of the triangle if $s = 3$ meters. 45 m

Answers

1. The powers of x and y are not the same.
12. $4n^2 + 5$
13. $13z - 10z^2$
14. $2a^2 - 6a + 8$
15. $-2n^2 + 7n + 5$
16. $5x + 2y + 3$
17. $5b^3 - 8b^2 - 4b$
18. $10d^2 + 8$

19. $2g^3 - 9g$
20. $-8y^3 - 3y^2 - y + 17$
21. $-2x - 3xy$
22. $-2x^2 + 8x + 8$
23. $3ab^2 + 11ab - 4$
24. $x^3 + 2x^2 + 2x - 6$
25. $3x^2 - 12x + 5ax + 3a^2$

Study Tip

Inverse of a Polynomial
When finding the additive inverse of a polynomial, remember to find the additive inverse of *every* term.

Career Choices

Teacher · · · · · · · ·

The educational requirements for a teaching license vary by state. In 2001, the average public K–12 teacher salary was $44,400.

Online Research
For information about a career as a teacher, visit:
www.algebra1.com/careers

Example 2 Subtract Polynomials

Find $(3n^2 + 13n^3 + 5n) - (7n + 4n^3)$.

Method 1 Horizontal
Subtract $7n + 4n^3$ by adding its additive inverse.

$(3n^2 + 13n^3 + 5n) - (7n + 4n^3)$

$= (3n^2 + 13n^3 + 5n) + (-7n - 4n^3)$ The additive inverse of $7n + 4n^3$ is $-7n - 4n^3$.

$= 3n^2 + [13n^3 + (-4n^3)] + [5n + (-7n)]$ Group like terms.

$= 3n^2 + 9n^3 - 2n$ Add like terms.

Method 2 Vertical
Align like terms in columns and subtract by adding the additive inverse.

$$3n^2 + 13n^3 + 5n$$
$$(-) \qquad\quad 4n^3 + 7n$$

Add the opposite.

$$3n^2 + 13n^3 + 5n$$
$$(+) \qquad\quad -4n^3 - 7n$$
$$\overline{3n^2 + \;\;9n^3 - 2n}$$

Thus, $(3n^2 + 13n^3 + 5n) - (7n + 4n^3) = 3n^2 + 9n^3 - 2n$ or, arranged in descending order, $9n^3 + 3n^2 - 2n$.

When polynomials are used to model real-world data, their sums and differences can have real-world meaning too.

Example 3 Subtract Polynomials

EDUCATION The total number of public school teachers T consists of two groups, elementary E and secondary S. From 1985 through 1998, the number (in thousands) of secondary teachers and total teachers could be modeled by the following equations, where n is the number of years since 1985.

$$S = 11n + 942$$
$$T = 44n + 2216$$

a. Find an equation that models the number of elementary teachers E for this time period.

Subtract the polynomial for S from the polynomial for T.

Total	$44n + 2216$
$-$ Secondary	$(-)\; 11n + \;\;942$
Elementary	

Add the opposite.

$$44n + 2216$$
$$(+)\; -11n - \;\;942$$
$$\overline{33n + 1274}$$

An equation is $E = 33n + 1274$.

b. Use the equation to predict the number of elementary teachers in the year 2010.

The year 2010 is $2010 - 1985$ or 25 years after the year 1985.

If this trend continues, the number of elementary teachers in 2010 would be $33(25) + 1274$ thousand or about 2,099,000.

Concept Check

1. **Explain** why $5xy^2$ and $3x^2y$ are *not* like terms. **See margin.**

2. Sample answer: $6x^2 + 4x + 7$ and $4x^2 + 3x + 4$

2. **OPEN ENDED** Write two polynomials whose difference is $2x^2 + x + 3$.

3. Kendra; Esteban added the additive inverses of both polynomials when he should have added the opposite of the polynomial being subtracted.

3. **FIND THE ERROR** Esteban and Kendra are finding $(5a - 6b) - (2a + 5b)$.

Esteban	Kendra
$(5a - 6b) - (2a + 5b)$	$(5a - 6b) - (2a + 5b)$
$= (-5a + 6b) + (-2a - 5b)$	$= (5a - 6b) + (-2a - 5b)$
$= -7a + b$	$= 3a - 11b$

Who is correct? Explain your reasoning.

Guided Practice

5. $9y^2 - 3y - 1$
6. $10cd - 3d + 4c - 6$
7. $11a^2 + 6a + 1$

Find each sum or difference.

4. $(4p^2 + 5p) + (-2p^2 + p)$ $2p^2 + 6p$

5. $(5y^2 - 3y + 8) + (4y^2 - 9)$

6. $(8cd - 3d + 4c) + (-6 + 2cd)$

7. $(6a^2 + 7a - 9) - (-5a^2 + a - 10)$

8. $(g^3 - 2g^2 + 5g + 6) - (g^2 + 2g)$
   $g^3 - 3g^2 + 3g + 6$

9. $(3ax^2 - 5x - 3a) - (6a - 8a^2x + 4x)$
   $3ax^2 - 9x - 9a + 8a^2x$

Application

POPULATION For Exercises 10 and 11, use the following information.
From 1990 through 1999, the female population F and the male population M of the United States (in thousands) are modeled by the following equations, where n is the number of years since 1990. **Source:** U.S. Census Bureau

GUIDED PRACTICE KEY	
Exercises	Examples
4–9	1, 2
10, 11	3

$$F = 1247n + 126{,}971 \qquad M = 1252n + 120{,}741$$

10. Find an equation that models the total population T in thousands of the United States for this time period. $T = 2499n + 247{,}712$

11. If this trend continues, what will the population of the United States be in 2010?
    about 297,692,000

★ indicates increased difficulty

Practice and Apply

Homework Help	
For Exercises	See Examples
12–31	1, 2
32, 33	3

Extra Practice
See page 838.

Find each sum or difference. 12–25. See margin.

12. $(6n^2 - 4) + (-2n^2 + 9)$

13. $(9z - 3z^2) + (4z - 7z^2)$

14. $(3 + a^2 + 2a) + (a^2 - 8a + 5)$

15. $(-3n^2 - 8 + 2n) + (5n + 13 + n^2)$

16. $(x + 5) + (2y + 4x - 2)$

17. $(2b^3 - 4b + b^2) + (-9b^2 + 3b^3)$

18. $(11 + 4d^2) - (3 - 6d^2)$

19. $(4g^3 - 5g) - (2g^3 + 4g)$

20. $(-4y^3 - y + 10) - (4y^3 + 3y^2 - 7)$

21. $(4x + 5xy + 3y) - (3y + 6x + 8xy)$

22. $(3x^2 + 8x + 4) - (5x^2 - 4)$

23. $(5ab^2 + 3ab) - (2ab^2 + 4 - 8ab)$

24. $(x^3 - 7x + 4x^2 - 2) - (2x^2 - 9x + 4)$

25. $(5x^2 + 3a^2 - 5x) - (2x^2 - 5ax + 7x)$

26. $(3a + 2b - 7c) + (6b - 4a + 9c) + (-7c - 3a - 2b)$ $-4a + 6b - 5c$

27. $(5x^2 - 3) + (x^2 - x + 11) + (2x^2 - 5x + 7)$ $8x^2 - 6x + 15$

★ 28. $(3y^2 - 8) + (5y + 9) - (y^2 + 6y - 4)$ $2y^2 - y + 5$

★ 29. $(9x^3 + 3x - 13) - (6x^2 - 5x) + (2x^3 - x^2 - 8x + 4)$ $11x^3 - 7x^2 - 9$

GEOMETRY The measures of two sides of a triangle are given. If P is the perimeter, find the measure of the third side.

★ 30. $P = 7x + 3y$ $4x + 2y$
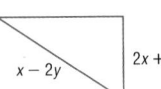
$x - 2y$ $2x + 3y$

★ 31. $P = 10x^2 - 5x + 16$ $6x^2 - 15x + 12$
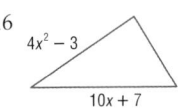
$4x^2 - 3$ $10x + 7$

Study Notebook

Have students—
- select an exercise and show two methods for finding the sum or difference.
- include any other item(s) that they find helpful in mastering the skills in this lesson.

DAILY
INTERVENTION   **FIND THE ERROR**
Have students check each step of Esteban and Kendra's work. Remind students that since this is a subtraction problem, Esteban and Kendra need to add the additive inverse.

About the Exercises...

Organization by Objective
- **Add Polynomials:** 12–17, 26, 27, 34–40
- **Subtract Polynomials:** 18–25, 28–33

Odd/Even Assignments
Exercises 12–31 are structured so that students practice the same concepts whether they are assigned odd or even problems.

Assignment Guide

Basic: 13–27 odd, 32, 33, 41, 44–68

Average: 13–31 odd, 34–38, 41–68

Advanced: 12–30 even, 36–62 (optional: 63–68)

Teaching Tip You may want students to make the box described in Exercises 36–40.

DAILY
INTERVENTION   **Differentiated Instruction**

Interpersonal To reinforce the concepts of the lesson, place students in pairs and have the students take turns completing the Check for Understanding Exercises. As one student works the problem, have the other student offer guidance and suggestions. Make sure students offer constructive reinforcement to each other and that each student completes at least one exercise.

Movies •·············

In 1998, attendance at movie theaters was at its highest point in 40 years with 1.48 billion tickets sold for a record $6.95 billion in gross income.

Source: The National Association of Theatre Owners

MOVIES   For Exercises 32 and 33, use the following information.

From 1990 to 1999, the number of indoor movie screens I and total movie screens T in the U.S. could be modeled by the following equations, where n is the number of years since 1990.

$$I = 161.6n^2 - 20n + 23{,}326 \qquad T = 160.3n^2 - 26n + 24{,}226$$

32. Find an equation that models the number of outdoor movie screens D in the U.S. for this time period. $D = -1.3n^2 - 6n + 900$

33. If this trend continues, how many outdoor movie screens will there be in the year 2010? **260 outdoor screens**

NUMBER TRICK   For Exercises 34 and 35, use the following information.

Think of a two-digit number whose ones digit is greater than its tens digit. Multiply the difference of the two digits by 9 and add the result to your original number. Repeat this process for several other such numbers. **34–35. See margin.**

34. What observation can you make about your results?

35. Justify that your observation holds for all such two-digit numbers by letting x equal the tens digit and y equal the ones digit of the original number. (*Hint:* The original number is then represented by $10x + y$.)

POSTAL SERVICE   For Exercises 36–40, use the information below and in the figure at the right.

The U.S. Postal Service restricts the sizes of boxes shipped by parcel post. The sum of the length and the girth of the box must not exceed 108 inches.

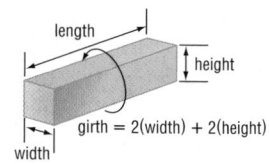

girth = 2(width) + 2(height)

Suppose you want to make an open box using a 60-by-40 inch piece of cardboard by cutting squares out of each corner and folding up the flaps. The lid will be made from another piece of cardboard. You do not know how big the squares should be, so for now call the length of the side of each square x.

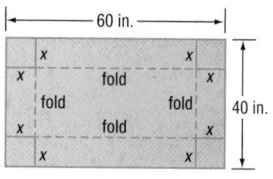
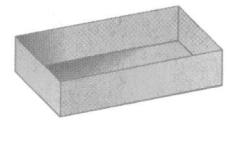

36. Write a polynomial to represent the length of the box formed. $60 - 2x$

37. Write a polynomial to represent the width of the box formed. $40 - 2x$

38. Write a polynomial to represent the girth of the box formed. $80 - 2x$

★ 39. Write and solve an inequality to find the least possible value of x you could use in designing this box so it meets postal regulations. $140 - 4x \le 108$; 8 in.

★ 40. What is the greatest integral value of x you could use to design this box if it does not have to meet regulations? **19 in.**

CRITICAL THINKING   For Exercises 41–43, suppose x is an integer.

41. Write an expression for the next integer greater than x. $x + 1$

★ 42. Show that the sum of two consecutive integers, x and the next integer after x, is always odd. (*Hint:* A number is considered even if it is divisible by 2.) **See margin.**

★ 43. What is the least number of consecutive integers that must be added together to always arrive at an even integer? **4**

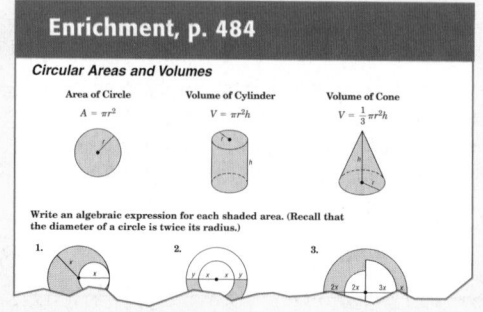

44. **WRITING IN MATH** 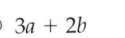 Answer the question that was posed at the beginning of the lesson. **See margin.**

How can adding polynomials help you model sales?

Include the following in your answer:
- an equation that models total toy sales, and
- an example of how and why someone might use this equation.

Standardized
Test Practice
Ⓐ Ⓑ Ⓒ Ⓓ

45. The perimeter of the rectangle shown at the right is $16a + 2b$. Which of the following expressions represents the length of the rectangle? **A**

$5a - b$

  Ⓐ $3a + 2b$ Ⓑ $10a + 2b$
  Ⓒ $2a - 3b$ Ⓓ $6a + 4b$

46. If $a^2 - 2ab + b^2 = 36$ and $a^2 - 3ab + b^2 = 22$, find ab. **D**

  Ⓐ 6   Ⓑ 8   Ⓒ 12   Ⓓ 14

Maintain Your Skills

Mixed Review   **Find the degree of each polynomial.** *(Lesson 8-4)*

47. $15t^3y^2$ **5**   **48.** 24 **0**   **49.** $m^2 + n^3$ **3**   **50.** $4x^2y^3z - 5x^3z$ **6**

Express each number in standard notation. *(Lesson 8-3)*

51. 8×10^6 **52.** 2.9×10^5 **53.** 5×10^{-4} **54.** 4.8×10^{-7}
   8,000,000   **290,000**   **0.0005**   **0.00000048**

KEYBOARDING For Exercises 55–59, use the table below that shows the keyboarding speeds and experience of 12 students. *(Lesson 5-2)*

Experience (weeks)	4	7	8	1	6	3	5	2	9	6	7	10
Keyboarding Speed (wpm)	33	45	46	20	40	30	38	22	52	44	42	55

55–56. See margin.
55. Make a scatter plot of these data.

56. Draw a best-fit line for the data.

57. Find the equation of the line. **Sample answer:** $y = 4x + 17$

58. Use the equation to predict the keyboarding speed of a student after a 12-week course. **about 65 wpm**

59. Can this equation be used to predict the speed for any number of weeks of experience? Explain. **No; there's a limit as to how fast one can keyboard.**

State the domain and range of each relation. *(Lesson 4-3)*

60. $\{(-2, 5), (0, -2), (-6, 3)\}$
    $D = \{-2, 0, -6\}; R = \{5, -2, 3\}$

61. $\{(-4, 2), (-1, -3), (5, 0), (-4, 1)\}$
    $D = \{-4, -1, 5\}; R = \{2, -3, 0, 1\}$

62. MODEL TRAINS One of the most popular sizes of model trains is called the HO. Every dimension of the HO model measures $\frac{1}{87}$ times that of a real engine. The HO model of a modern diesel locomotive is about 8 inches long. About how many feet long is the real locomotive? *(Lesson 3-6)* **58**

Getting Ready for   **PREREQUISITE SKILL**   **Simplify.** *(To review the **Distributive Property**, see Lesson 1-7.)*
the Next Lesson
65. $35p - 28q$ **63.** $6(3x - 8)$ **18x − 48**   **64.** $-2(b + 9)$ **−2b − 18**   **65.** $-7(-5p + 4q)$

66. $9(3a + 5b - c)$ **67.** $8(x^2 + 3x - 4)$ **68.** $-3(2a^2 - 5a + 7)$
    27a + 45b − 9c   **8x² + 24x − 32**   **−6a² + 15a − 21**

Lesson 8-5 Adding and Subtracting Polynomials   **443**

Answers

34. The result is always the original number with its digits swapped.

35. Original number = $10x + y$; show that the new number will always be represented by $10y + x$.

    new number = $9(y - x) + (10x + y)$
               $= 9y - 9x + 10x + y$
               $= 10y + x$

---

4 Assess

Open-Ended Assessment

Writing Have students write a short essay describing how to subtract monomials using the additive inverse. Make sure students include an example with their descriptions.

Getting Ready for Lesson 8-6

PREREQUISITE SKILL Students will learn how to multiply a polynomial by a monomial in Lesson 8-6. This process is an application of the Distributive Property. Use Exercises 63–68 to determine your students' familiarity with the Distributive Property.

Answers

42. $\dfrac{x + (x + 1)}{2} = \dfrac{2x + 1}{2}$

             $= \dfrac{2x}{2} + \dfrac{1}{2}$ or $x + \dfrac{1}{2}$

    $x + (x + 1)$ when divided by 2 has a remainder of $\dfrac{1}{2}$, therefore the sum of two consecutive integers is odd.

44. In order to find the sum of the video games sales and the traditional toy sales, you must add the two polynomial models V and R, which represent each of these sales from 1996 to 1999.

- $T = 0.45t^3 - 1.85t^2 + 4.4t + 22.6$

- If a person was looking to invest in a toy company, they might want to look at the trend in toy sales over the last several years and try to predict toy sales for the future.

55–56.

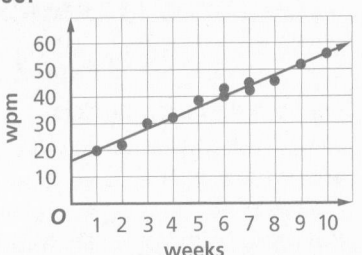

8-6 Lesson Notes

8-6 Multiplying a Polynomial by a Monomial

1 Focus

5-Minute Check Transparency 8-6 Use as a quiz or review of Lesson 8-5.

Mathematical Background notes are available for this lesson on p. 408D.

How is finding the product of a monomial and a polynomial related to finding the area of a rectangle?

Ask students:

- What is the formula for finding the area of a rectangle? **The area of a rectangle is $A = \ell \times w$, where ℓ is the length and w is the width.**

- What are ℓ and w for the rectangle shown? **ℓ is $x + 3$ and w is $2x$.**

- What is the area of the rectangle? **$2x^2 + 6x$**

- Substitute the given values for A, ℓ, and w to write an equation for the area of this rectangle. **$2x^2 + 6x = (x + 3)(2x)$**

What You'll Learn

- Find the product of a monomial and a polynomial.
- Solve equations involving polynomials.

How is finding the product of a monomial and a polynomial related to finding the area of a rectangle?

The algebra tiles shown are grouped together to form a rectangle with a width of $2x$ and a length of $x + 3$. Notice that the rectangle consists of 2 blue x^2 tiles and 6 green x tiles. The area of the rectangle is the sum of these algebra tiles or $2x^2 + 6x$.

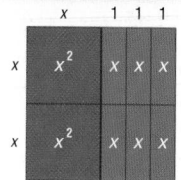

PRODUCT OF MONOMIAL AND POLYNOMIAL The Distributive Property can be used to multiply a polynomial by a monomial.

Study Tip

Look Back
To review the **Distributive Property**, see Lesson 1-5.

Example 1 Multiply a Polynomial by a Monomial

Find $-2x^2(3x^2 - 7x + 10)$.

Method 1 Horizontal

$-2x^2(3x^2 - 7x + 10)$

$= -2x^2(3x^2) - (-2x^2)(7x) + (-2x^2)(10)$ Distributive Property

$= -6x^4 - (-14x^3) + (-20x^2)$ Multiply.

$= -6x^4 + 14x^3 - 20x^2$ Simplify.

Method 2 Vertical

$3x^2 - 7x + 10$

$(\times) \qquad\qquad -2x^2$ Distributive Property

$-6x^4 + 14x^3 - 20x^2$ Multiply.

When expressions contain like terms, simplify by combining the like terms.

Example 2 Simplify Expressions

Simplify $4(3d^2 + 5d) - d(d^2 - 7d + 12)$.

$4(3d^2 + 5d) - d(d^2 - 7d + 12)$

$= 4(3d^2) + 4(5d) + (-d)(d^2) - (-d)(7d) + (-d)(12)$ Distributive Property

$= 12d^2 + 20d + (-d^3) - (-7d^2) + (-12d)$ Product of Powers

$= 12d^2 + 20d - d^3 + 7d^2 - 12d$ Simplify.

$= -d^3 + (12d^2 + 7d^2) + (20d - 12d)$ Commutative and Associative Properties

$= -d^3 + 19d^2 + 8d$ Combine like terms.

444 Chapter 8 Polynomials

Resource Manager

📁 Workbook and Reproducible Masters

Chapter 8 Resource Masters
- Study Guide and Intervention, pp. 485–486
- Skills Practice, p. 487
- Practice, p. 488
- Reading to Learn Mathematics, p. 489
- Enrichment, p. 490
- Assessment, p. 518

Parent and Student Study Guide Workbook, p. 64
School-to-Career Masters, p. 16

🖥 Transparencies

5-Minute Check Transparency 8-6
Answer Key Transparencies

💿 Technology

AlgePASS: Tutorial Plus, Lesson 21
Interactive Chalkboard

Example 3 *Use Polynomial Models*

PHONE SERVICE Greg pays a fee of $20 a month for local calls. Long-distance rates are 6¢ per minute for in-state calls and 5¢ per minute for out-of-state calls. Suppose Greg makes 300 minutes of long-distance phone calls in January and m of those minutes are for in-state calls.

a. **Find an expression for Greg's phone bill for January.**

Words The bill is the sum of the monthly fee, in-state charges, and the out-of-state charges.

Variables If m = number of minutes of in-state calls, then $300 - m$ = number of minutes of out-of-state calls. Let B = phone bill for the month of January.

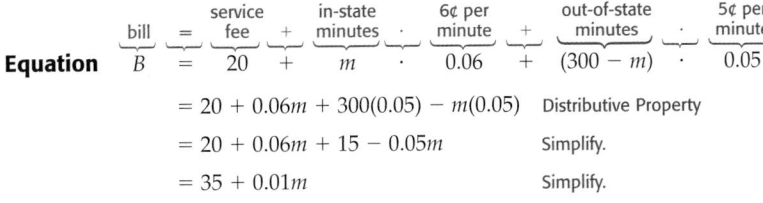

| bill | = | service fee | + | in-state minutes | · | 6¢ per minute | + | out-of-state minutes | · | 5¢ per minute |

Equation
$$B = 20 + m \cdot 0.06 + (300 - m) \cdot 0.05$$
$$= 20 + 0.06m + 300(0.05) - m(0.05) \quad \text{Distributive Property}$$
$$= 20 + 0.06m + 15 - 0.05m \quad \text{Simplify.}$$
$$= 35 + 0.01m \quad \text{Simplify.}$$

An expression for Greg's phone bill for January is $35 + 0.01m$, where m is the number of minutes of in-state calls.

b. **Evaluate the expression to find the cost if Greg had 37 minutes of in-state calls in January.**

$$35 + 0.01m = 35 + 0.01(37) \quad m = 37$$
$$= 35 + 0.37 \quad \text{Multiply.}$$
$$= \$35.37 \quad \text{Add.}$$

Greg's bill was $35.37.

SOLVE EQUATIONS WITH POLYNOMIAL EXPRESSIONS
Many equations contain polynomials that must be added, subtracted, or multiplied before the equation can be solved.

Example 4 *Polynomials on Both Sides*

Solve $y(y - 12) + y(y + 2) + 25 = 2y(y + 5) - 15.$

$$y(y - 12) + y(y + 2) + 25 = 2y(y + 5) - 15 \quad \text{Original equation}$$
$$y^2 - 12y + y^2 + 2y + 25 = 2y^2 + 10y - 15 \quad \text{Distributive Property}$$
$$2y^2 - 10y + 25 = 2y^2 + 10y - 15 \quad \text{Combine like terms.}$$
$$-10y + 25 = 10y - 15 \quad \text{Subtract } 2y^2 \text{ from each side.}$$
$$-20y + 25 = -15 \quad \text{Subtract } 10y \text{ from each side.}$$
$$-20y = -40 \quad \text{Subtract 25 from each side.}$$
$$y = 2 \quad \text{Divide each side by } -20.$$

The solution is 2.

CHECK $\quad y(y - 12) + y(y + 2) + 25 = 2y(y + 5) - 15 \quad$ Original equation
$$2(2 - 12) + 2(2 + 2) + 25 \stackrel{?}{=} 2(2)(2 + 5) - 15 \quad y = 2$$
$$2(-10) + 2(4) + 25 \stackrel{?}{=} 4(7) - 15 \quad \text{Simplify.}$$
$$-20 + 8 + 25 \stackrel{?}{=} 28 - 15 \quad \text{Multiply.}$$
$$13 = 13 \checkmark \quad \text{Add and subtract.}$$

DAILY INTERVENTION

Differentiated Instruction

Visual/Spatial Have students analyze the rectangle shown.

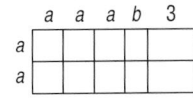

$$a \quad a \quad a \quad b \quad 3$$

Ask: What is the width and length? Write the area as a product. Label each part of the figure by its area. Compare these areas with the product.

---

2 Teach

PRODUCT OF MONOMIAL AND POLYNOMIAL

In-Class Examples Power Point®

Teaching Tip Explain to students that the two methods shown are actually two forms of the same method.

Teaching Tip If students are having difficulty multiplying by a negative monomial in Example 1, you may want to have students apply the negative first (by multiplying all terms by -1) and then multiply by $2x^2$.

1 Find $6y(4y^2 - 9y - 7)$.
$24y^3 - 54y^2 - 42y$

Teaching Tip Remind students that they must follow the order of operations when simplifying expressions. In Example 2, you must multiply before you can add.

2 Simplify $3(2t^2 - 4t - 15) + 6t(5t + 2)$. $36t^2 - 45$

3 **ENTERTAINMENT** Admission to the Super Fun Amusement Park is $10. Once in the park, super rides are an additional $3 each and regular rides are an additional $2. Sarita goes to the park and rides 15 rides, of which s of those 15 are super rides.

a. Find an expression for how much money Sarita spent at the park. $40 + s$

b. Evaluate the expression to find the cost if Sarita rode 9 super rides. $49

SOLVE EQUATIONS WITH POLYNOMIAL EXPRESSIONS

In-Class Example  Power Point®

4 Solve $b(12 + b) - 7 = 2b + b(-4 + b)$ $\frac{1}{2}$

Study Notebook

Have students—
- list skills from other lessons that they use in solving polynomial equations.
- include any other item(s) that they find helpful in mastering the skills in this lesson.

Answers

2. The three monomials that make up the trinomial are similar to the three digits that make up the 3-digit number. The single monomial is similar to a 1-digit number. With each procedure you perform 3 multiplications. The difference is that polynomial multiplication involves variables and the resulting product is often the sum of two or more monomials while numerical multiplication results in a single number.

15. $5r^2 + r^3$

16. $2w^4 - 9w^3$

17. $-32x - 12x^2$

18. $-10y^3 - 35y^2$

19. $7ag^4 + 14a^2g^2$

20. $-3n^3p + 6np^2$

21. $-6b^4 + 8b^3 - 18b^2$

22. $30x^3 + 18x^4 - 66x^5$

23. $40x^3y + 16x^2y^3 - 24x^2y$

24. $-3cd^3 - 2c^3d^3 + 4c^2d^2$

25. $-15hk^4 - \dfrac{15}{4}h^2k^2 + 6hk^2$

26. $4a^5b - \dfrac{8}{3}a^3b^2 + 6a^2b^3$

27. $-10a^3b^2 - 25a^4b^2 + 5a^3b^3 - 5a^6b$

28. $8p^4q^2 - 4p^2q^4 + 36p^5q^2 + 12p^2q^3$

Check for Understanding

Concept Check

1. **State** the property used in each step to multiply $2x(4x^2 + 3x - 5)$.

$2x(4x^2 + 3x - 5) = 2x(4x^2) + 2x(3x) - 2x(5)$ ___?___   Distributive Property

$= 8x^{1+2} + 6x^{1+1} - 10x$ ___?___   Product of Powers Property

$= 8x^3 + 6x^2 - 10x$ Simplify.

2. **Compare and contrast** the procedure used to multiply a trinomial by a monomial using the vertical method with the procedure used to multiply a three-digit number by a two-digit number. **See margin.**

3. **OPEN ENDED** Write a monomial and a trinomial involving a single variable. Then find their product. **Sample answer: $4x$ and $x^2 + 2x + 3$; $4x^3 + 8x^2 + 12x$**

Guided Practice

GUIDED PRACTICE KEY	
Exercises	Examples
4–7	1
8, 9	2
10, 11	4
12–14	3

Find each product. 5. $18b^5 - 27b^4 + 9b^3 - 72b^2$

4. $-3y(5y + 2)$ $-15y^2 - 6y$

5. $9b^2(2b^3 - 3b^2 + b - 8)$

6. $2x(4a^4 - 3ax + 6x^2)$
   $8a^4x - 6ax^2 + 12x^3$

7. $-4xy(5x^2 - 12xy + 7y^2)$
   $-20x^3y + 48x^2y^2 - 28xy^3$

Simplify.

8. $t(5t - 9) - 2t$ $5t^2 - 11t$

9. $5n(4n^3 + 6n^2 - 2n + 3) - 4(n^2 + 7n)$
   $20n^4 + 30n^3 - 14n^2 - 13n$

Solve each equation.

10. $-2(w + 1) + w = 7 - 4w$ 3

11. $x(x + 2) - 3x = x(x - 4) + 5$ $\dfrac{5}{3}$

Application

SAVINGS For Exercises 12–14, use the following information.

Kenzie's grandmother left her $10,000 for college. Kenzie puts some of the money into a savings account earning 4% per year, and with the rest, she buys a certificate of deposit (CD) earning 7% per year.

12. If Kenzie puts x dollars into the savings account, write an expression to represent the amount of the CD. **$10,000 - x$**

13. Write an equation for the total amount of money T Kenzie will have saved for college after one year. **$T = 10,700 - 0.03x$**

14. If Kenzie puts $3000 in savings, how much money will she have after one year?
    $10,610

★ indicates increased difficulty

Practice and Apply

Homework Help	
For Exercises	See Examples
15–28	1
29–38	2
39–48	4
49–54, 58–62	3

Extra Practice
See page 838.

Find each product. 15–28. See margin.

15. $r(5r + r^2)$

16. $w(2w^3 - 9w^2)$

17. $-4x(8 + 3x)$

18. $5y(-2y^2 - 7y)$

19. $7ag(g^3 + 2ag)$

20. $-3np(n^2 - 2p)$

21. $-2b^2(3b^2 - 4b + 9)$

22. $6x^3(5 + 3x - 11x^2)$

23. $8x^2y(5x + 2y^2 - 3)$

24. $-cd^2(3d + 2c^2d - 4c)$

25. $-\dfrac{3}{4}hk^2(20k^2 + 5h - 8)$

26. $\dfrac{2}{3}a^2b(6a^3 - 4ab + 9b^2)$

27. $-5a^3b(2b + 5ab - b^2 + a^3)$

★ 28. $4p^2q^2(2p^2 - q^2 + 9p^3 + 3q)$

Simplify. 31. $20w^2 - 18w + 10$ 32. $10n^4 + 5n^3 - n^2 + 44n$

29. $d(-2d + 4) + 15d$ $-2d^2 + 19d$

30. $-x(4x^2 - 2x) - 5x^3$ $-9x^3 + 2x^2$

31. $3w(6w - 4) + 2(w^2 - 3w + 5)$

32. $5n(2n^3 + n^2 + 8) + n(4 - n)$

33. $10(4m^3 - 3m + 2) - 2m(-3m^2 - 7m + 1)$ $46m^3 + 14m^2 - 32m + 20$

34. $4y(y^2 - 8y + 6) - 3(2y^3 - 5y^2 + 2)$ $-2y^3 - 17y^2 + 24y - 6$

35. $-3c^2(2c + 7) + 4c(3c^2 - c + 5) + 2(c^2 - 4)$ $6c^3 - 23c^2 + 20c - 8$

36. $4x^2(x + 2) + 3x(5x^2 + 2x - 6) - 5(3x^2 - 4x)$ $19x^3 - x^2 + 2x$

446 Chapter 8 Polynomials

GEOMETRY Find the area of each shaded region in simplest form.

★ 37.

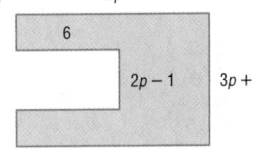

$6x^2 + 8x$

★ 38.

$15p^2 + 8p + 6$

Solve each equation.

39. $2(4x - 7) = 5(-2x - 9) - 5$ **-2**

40. $2(5a - 12) = -6(2a - 3) + 2$ **2**

41. $4(3p + 9) - 5 = -3(12p - 5)$ **$-\frac{1}{3}$**

42. $7(8w - 3) + 13 = 2(6w + 7)$ **$\frac{1}{2}$**

43. $d(d - 1) + 4d = d(d - 8)$ **0**

44. $c(c + 3) - c(c - 4) = 9c - 16$ **8**

45. $y(y + 12) - 8y = 14 + y(y - 4)$ **$\frac{7}{4}$**

46. $k(k - 7) + 10 = 2k + k(k + 6)$ **$\frac{2}{3}$**

★ **47.** $2n(n + 4) + 18 = n(n + 5) + n(n - 2) - 7$ **-5**

★ **48.** $3g(g - 4) - 2g(g - 7) = g(g + 6) - 28$ **7**

SAVINGS For Exercises 49 and 50, use the following information.
Marta has $6000 to invest. She puts x dollars of this money into a savings account that earns 3% per year, and with the rest, she buys a certificate of deposit that earns 6% per year.

49. Write an equation for the total amount of money T Marta will have after one year. $T = -0.03x + 6360$

50. Suppose at the end of one year, Marta has a total of $6315. How much money did Marta invest in each account?
savings account: $1500; certificate of deposit: $4500

51. GARDENING A gardener plants corn in a garden with a length-to-width ratio of 5:4. Next year, he plans to increase the garden's area by increasing its length by 12 feet. Write an expression for this new area.
$20x^2 + 48x$

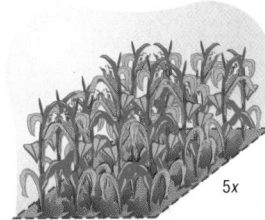

52. CLASS TRIP Mr. Smith's American History class will take taxis from their hotel in Washington, D.C., to the Lincoln Memorial. The fare is $2.75 for the first mile and $1.25 for each additional mile. If the distance is m miles and t taxis are needed, write an expression for the cost to transport the group. $1.50t + 1.25mt$

NUMBER THEORY For Exercises 53 and 54, let x be an odd integer.

53. Write an expression for the next odd integer. $x + 2$

54. Find the product of x and the next odd integer. $x^2 + 2x$

CRITICAL THINKING For Exercises 55–57, use the following information.
An even number can be represented by $2x$, where x is any integer.

55. Show that the product of two even integers is always even. See margin.

56. Write a representation for an odd integer. $2x + 1$ or $2x - 1$

57. Show that the product of an even and an odd integer is always even. See margin.

More About . . .

Class Trip

Inside the Lincoln Memorial is a 19-foot marble statue of the United States' 16th president. The statue is flanked on either side by the inscriptions of Lincoln's Second Inaugural Address and Gettysburg Address.

Source: www.washington.org

About the Exercises...
Organization by Objective
• **Product of Monomial and Polynomial:** 15–38, 51–54, 58–61
• **Solve Equations with Polynomial Expressions:** 39–50, 62

Odd/Even Assignments
Exercises 15–48 are structured so that students practice the same concepts whether they are assigned odd or even problems.

Assignment Guide
Basic: 15–35 odd, 39–45 odd, 49–51, 55–57, 63–87
Average: 15–47 odd, 51, 53, 55–57, 63–87
Advanced: 16–48 even, 55–81 (optional: 82–87)
All: Practice Quiz 2 (1–10)

55. Let x and y be integers. Then $2x$ and $2y$ are even numbers, and $(2x)(2y) = 4xy$. $4xy$ is divisible by 2 since one of its factors, 4, is divisible by 2. Therefore $4xy$ is an even number.

57. Let x and y be integers. Then $2x$ is an even number and $2y + 1$ is an odd number. Their product, $2x(2y + 1)$, is always even since one of its factors is 2.

Study Guide and Intervention, p. 485 (shown) and p. 486

Product of Monomial and Polynomial The Distributive Property can be used to multiply a polynomial by a monomial. You can multiply horizontally or vertically. Sometimes multiplying results in like terms. The products can be simplified by combining like terms.

Example 1 Find $-3x^2(4x^2 + 6x - 8)$.

Horizontal Method
$-3x^2(4x^2 + 6x - 8)$
$= -3x^2(4x^2) + (-3x^2)(6x) - (-3x^2)(8)$
$= -12x^4 + (-18x^3) - (-24x^2)$
$= -12x^4 - 18x^3 + 24x^2$

Vertical Method
$\quad 4x^2 + 6x - 8$
$(\times)\qquad\quad -3x^2$
$\overline{-12x^4 - 18x^3 + 24x^2}$
The product is $-12x^4 - 18x^3 + 24x^2$.

Example 2 Simplify $-2(4x^2 + 5x) - x(x^2 + 6x)$.

$-2(4x^2 + 5x) - x(x^2 + 6x)$
$= -2(4x^2) + (-2)(5x) + (-x)(x^2) + (-x)(6x)$
$= -8x^2 + (-10x) + (-x^3) + (-6x^2)$
$= (-x^3) + [-8x^2 + (-6x^2)] + (-10x)$
$= -x^3 - 14x^2 - 10x$

Exercises

Find each product.

1. $x(5x + x^2)$
$5x^2 + x^3$

2. $x(4x^2 + 3x + 2)$
$4x^3 + 3x^2 + 2x$

3. $-2xy(2y + 4x^2)$
$-4xy^2 - 8x^3y$

4. $-2g(g^2 - 2g + 2)$
$-2g^3 + 4g^2 - 4g$

5. $3x(x^4 + x^3 + x^2)$
$3x^5 + 3x^4 + 3x^3$

6. $-4x(2x^3 - 2x + 3)$
$-8x^4 + 8x^2 - 12x$

7. $-4cx(10 + 3x)$
$-40cx - 12cx^2$

8. $3y(-4x - 6x^3 - 2y)$
$-12xy - 18x^3y - 6y^2$

9. $2x^2y^2(3xy + 2y + 5x)$
$6x^3y^3 + 4x^2y^3 + 10x^3y^2$

Simplify.

10. $x(3x - 4) - 5x$
$3x^2 - 9x$

11. $-x(2x^2 - 4x) - 6x^2$
$-2x^3 - 2x^2$

12. $6a(2a - b) + 2a(-4a + 5b)$
$4a^2 + 4ab$

13. $4r(2r^2 - 3r + 5) + 6r(4r^2 + 2r + 8)$
$32r^3 + 68r$

14. $4n(3n^2 + n - 4) - n(3 - n)$
$12n^3 + 5n^2 - 19n$

15. $2b(b^2 + 4b + 8) - 3b(3b^2 + 9b - 18)$
$-7b^3 - 19b^2 + 70b$

16. $-2z(4z^2 - 3z + 1) - z(3z^2 + 2z - 1)$
$-11z^3 + 4z^2 - z$

17. $2(4x^2 - 2x) - 3(-6x^2 + 4) + 2x(x - 1)$
$28x^2 - 6x - 12$

Skills Practice, p. 487 and Practice, p. 488 (shown)

Find each product.

1. $2h(-7h^2 - 4h)$
$-14h^3 - 8h^2$

2. $6pq(3p^2 + 4q)$
$18p^3q + 24pq^2$

3. $-2u^2n(4u - 2n)$
$-8u^3n + 4u^2n^2$

4. $5jk(3jk + 2k)$
$15j^2k^2 + 10jk^2$

5. $-3ra(-2s^2 + 3r)$
$6rs^3 - 9r^2s$

6. $4mg^2(2mg + 4g)$
$8m^2g^3 + 16mg^3$

7. $-\frac{1}{4}m(8m^2 + m - 7)$
$-2m^3 - \frac{1}{4}m^2 + \frac{7}{4}m$

8. $-\frac{2}{3}n^3(-9n^2 + 3n + 6)$
$6n^4 - 2n^3 - 4n^2$

Simplify.

9. $-2\ell(3\ell - 4) + 7\ell$
$-6\ell^2 + 15\ell$

10. $5w(-7w + 3) + 2w(-2w^2 + 19w + 2)$
$-4w^3 + 3w^2 + 19w$

11. $6t(2t - 3) - 5(2t^2 + 9t - 3)$
$2t^2 - 63t + 15$

12. $-2(3m^3 + 5m + 6) + 3m(2m^2 + 3m + 1)$
$9m^2 - 7m - 12$

13. $-3g(7g - 2) + 3(g^2 + 2g + 1) - 3g(-5g + 3)$
$-3g^2 + 3g + 3$

14. $3z^3(z - 7) - 5z(z^2 - 2z - 2) + 3z(4z - 2)$
$-z^3 - 6z^2 + 4z$

Solve each equation.

15. $5(2s - 1) + 3 = 3(3s + 2)$ 8

16. $3(3u + 2) + 5 = 2(2u - 2) - 3$

17. $4(8n + 3) - 5 = 2(6n + 8) + 1$ $\frac{1}{2}$

18. $8(3h + 1) = 4(b + 3) - 9 - \frac{1}{4}$

19. $h(h - 3) - 2h = h(h - 2) - 12$ 4

20. $w(w + 6) + 4w = -7 + w(w + 9) -7$

21. $t(t + 4) - 1 = t(t + 2) + 2$ $\frac{3}{2}$

22. $u(u - 5) + 8u = u(u + 2) - 4$ -4

23. **NUMBER THEORY** Let x be an integer. What is the product of twice the integer added to three times the next consecutive integer? $5x + 3$

INVESTMENTS For Exercises 24–26, use the following information.
Kent invested $5,000 in a retirement plan. He allocated x dollars of the money to a bond account that earns 4% interest per year and the rest to a traditional account that earns 5% interest per year.

24. Write an expression that represents the amount of money invested in the traditional account. $5,000 - x$

25. Write a polynomial model in simplest form for the total amount of money T Kent has invested after one year. (Hint: Each account has $A + IA$ dollars, where A is the original amount in the account and I is its interest rate.) $T = 5,250 - 0.01x$

26. If Kent put $500 in the bond account, how much money does he have in his retirement plan after one year? $5,245

Reading to Learn Mathematics, p. 489   ELL

Pre-Activity How is finding the product of a monomial and a polynomial related to finding the area of a rectangle?

Read the introduction to Lesson 8-6 at the top of page 444 in your textbook.

You may recall that the formula for the area of a rectangle is $A = \ell w$. In this rectangle, $\ell = \underline{\quad x + 3 \quad}$ and $w = \underline{\quad 2x \quad}$. How would you substitute these values in the area formula?

$A = (x + 3)(2x)$

Reading the Lesson

1. Refer to Lesson 8-6.
   a. How is the Distributive Property used to multiply a polynomial by a monomial?
      The monomial is multiplied by each term in the polynomial.
   b. Use the Distributive Property to complete the following.

   $2y^3(3y^2 + 2y - 7) = 2y^3(\underline{3y^2}) + 2y^3(\underline{2y}) - 2y^3(\underline{7})$
   $\qquad = \underline{6y^4} + \underline{4y^3} - \underline{14y^2}$

   $-3x^3(x^3 - 2x^2 + 3) = \underline{-3x^3(x^3)} - \underline{(-3x^3)(2x^2)} + \underline{(-3x^3)(3)}$
   $\qquad = \underline{-3x^6} + \underline{6x^5} - \underline{9x^3}$

2. What is the difference between simplifying an expression and solving an equation?
   Simplifying an expression is combining like terms. Solving an equation is finding the value of the variable that makes the equation true.

Helping You Remember

3. Use the equation $2x(x - 5) + 3x(x + 3) = 5x(x + 7) - 9$ to show how you would explain the process of solving equations with polynomial expressions to another algebra student.
   Use the Distributive Property. $\quad 2x^2 - 10x + 3x^2 + 9x = 5x^2 + 35x - 9$
   Combine like terms. $\qquad\qquad\qquad 5x^2 - x = 5x^2 + 35x - 9$
   Subtract $5x^2$ from both sides. $\qquad\quad -x = 35x - 9$
   Subtract $35x$ from both sides. $\qquad\quad -36x = -9$
   Divide each side by -36. $\qquad\qquad\quad x = 0.25$

• **VOLUNTEERING** For Exercises 58 and 59, use the following information.
Laura is making baskets of apples and oranges for homeless shelters. She wants to place a total of 10 pieces of fruit in each basket. Apples cost 25¢ each, and oranges cost 20¢ each.

58. If a represents the number of apples Laura uses, write a polynomial model in simplest form for the total amount of money T Laura will spend on the fruit for each basket. $T = 2 + 0.05a$

59. If Laura uses 4 apples in each basket, find the total cost for fruit. $2.20

SALES For Exercises 60 and 61, use the following information.
A store advertises that all sports equipment is 30% off the retail price. In addition, the store asks customers to select and pop a balloon to receive a coupon for an additional n percent off the already marked down price of one of their purchases.

60. Write an expression for the cost of a pair of inline skates with retail price p after receiving both discounts. $0.7p - 0.007np$

61. Use this expression to calculate the cost, not including sales tax, of a $200 pair of inline skates for an additional 10 percent off. $126

★ 62. **SPORTS** You may have noticed that when runners race around a curved track, their starting points are staggered. This is so each contestant runs the same distance to the finish line.

If the radius of the inside lane is x and each lane is 2.5 feet wide, how far apart should the officials start the runners in the two inside lanes? (*Hint*: Circumference of a circle: $C = 2\pi r$, where r is the radius of the circle)
2.5π or about 7.9 ft

63. **WRITING IN MATH**   Answer the question that was posed at the beginning of the lesson. See pp. 471A–471B.

How is finding the product of a monomial and a polynomial related to finding the area of a rectangle?

Include the following in your answer:
- the product of $2x$ and $x + 3$ derived algebraically, and
- a representation of another product of a monomial and a polynomial using algebra tiles and multiplication.

64. Simplify $[(3x^2 - 2x + 4) - (x^2 + 5x - 2)](x + 2)$. **B**
   (A) $2x^3 + 7x^2 + 8x + 4$
   (B) $2x^3 - 3x^2 - 8x + 12$
   (C) $4x^3 + 11x^2 + 8x + 4$
   (D) $-4x^3 - 11x^2 - 8x - 4$

65. A plumber charges $70 for the first thirty minutes of each house call plus $4 for each additional minute that she works. The plumber charges Ke-Min $122 for her time. What amount of time, in minutes, did the plumber work? **A**
   (A) 43
   (B) 48
   (C) 58
   (D) 64

Standardized Test Practice
(A) (B) (C) (D)

Enrichment, p. 490

Figurate Numbers

Pentagonal Numbers

The numbers below are called **pentagonal numbers**. They are the numbers of dots or disks that can be arranged as pentagons.

1   5   12   22

1. Find the product $\frac{1}{2}n(3n - 1)$. $\frac{3n^2}{2} - \frac{n}{2}$

2. Evaluate the product in Exercise 1 for values of n from 1 through 4. 1, 5, 12, 22

3. What do you notice? They are the first four pentagonal numbers.

Mixed Review **Find each sum or difference.** *(Lesson 8-5)* 67. $-4y^2 + 5y + 3$

66. $(4x^2 + 5x) + (-7x^2 + x)$ $-3x^2 + 6x$ 67. $(3y^2 + 5y - 6) - (7y^2 - 9)$

68. $(5b - 7ab + 8a) - (5ab - 4a)$ 69. $(6p^3 + 3p^2 - 7) + (p^3 - 6p^2 - 2p)$
$5b - 12ab + 12a$ $7p^3 - 3p^2 - 2p - 7$

State whether each expression is a polynomial. If the expression is a polynomial, identify it as a *monomial*, a *binomial*, or a *trinomial*. *(Lesson 8-4)*

70. $4x^2 - 10ab + 6$ 71. $4c + ab - c$ 72. $\dfrac{7}{y} + y^2$ **no**   73. $\dfrac{n^2}{3}$
yes; trinomial   **yes; binomial**   **yes; monomial**

Define a variable, write an inequality, and solve each problem. Then check your solution. *(Lesson 6-3)* 74. $6 + 10n < 9n$; $\{n \mid n < -6\}$

74. Six increased by ten times a number is less than nine times the number.

75. Nine times a number increased by four is no less than seven decreased by thirteen times the number. $9n + 4 \geq 7 - 13n$; $\left\{n \mid n \geq \dfrac{3}{22}\right\}$

Write an equation of the line that passes through each pair of points. *(Lesson 5-4)*

78. $y = -\dfrac{1}{2}x + \dfrac{1}{2}$ 76. $(-3, -8)$, $(1, 4)$ 77. $(-4, 5)$, $(2, -7)$ 78. $(3, -1)$, $(-3, 2)$
$y = 3x + 1$ $y = -2x - 3$

79. **EXPENSES** Kristen spent one fifth of her money on gasoline to fill up her car. Then she spent half of what was left for a haircut. She bought lunch for $7. When she got home, she had $13 left. How much money did Kristen have originally? *(Lesson 3-4)* **$50**

For Exercises 80 and 81, use each set of data to make a stem-and-leaf plot.
(Lesson 2-5)

80. 49 51 55 62 47 32 56 57 48 47 33 68 53 45 30

81. 21 18 34 30 20 15 14 10 22 21 18 43 44 20 18
80–81. See margin.

Getting Ready for the Next Lesson **PREREQUISITE SKILL** **Simplify.** *(To review products of powers, see Lesson 8-1.)*

82. $(a)(a)$ a^2 83. $2x(3x^2)$ $6x^3$

84. $-3y^2(8y^2)$ $-24y^4$ 85. $4y(3y) - 4y(6)$ $12y^2 - 24y$

86. $-5n(2n^2) - (-5n)(8n) + (-5n)(4)$ 87. $3p^2(6p^2) - 3p^2(8p) + 3p^2(12)$
$-10n^3 + 40n^2 - 20n$ $18p^4 - 24p^3 + 36p^2$

Practice Quiz 2   **Lessons 8-4 through 8-6**

Find the degree of each polynomial. *(Lesson 8-4)*

1. $5x^4$ **4**   2. $-9n^3p^4$ **7**   3. $7a^2 - 2ab^2$ **3**   4. $-6 - 8x^2y^2 + 5y^3$ **4**

Arrange the terms of each polynomial so that the powers of x are in ascending order. *(Lesson 8-4)*

5. $4x^2 + 9x - 12 + 5x^3$ 6. $2xy^4 + x^3y^5 + 5x^5y - 13x^2$
$-12 + 9x + 4x^2 + 5x^3$ $2xy^4 - 13x^2 + x^3y^5 + 5x^5y$

Find each sum or difference. *(Lesson 8-5)*

7. $(7n^2 - 4n + 10) + (3n^2 - 8)$ 8. $(3g^3 - 5g) - (2g^3 + 5g^2 - 3g + 1)$
$10n^2 - 4n + 2$ $g^3 - 5g^2 - 2g - 1$

Find each product. *(Lesson 8-6)*

9. $5a^2(3a^3b - 2a^2b^2 + 6ab^3)$ 10. $7x^2y(5x^2 - 3xy + y)$ $35x^4y - 21x^3y^2 + 7x^2y^2$

$15a^5b - 10a^4b^2 + 30a^3b^3$

Lesson 8-6 Multiplying a Polynomial by a Monomial **449**

Getting Started

Objective Use algebra tiles to multiply polynomials.

Materials
algebra tiles
product mat

Teach

- Some students may benefit from laying tiles along the top and side of the product mat to model each expression. Then have them remove the two factors before determining their final product.

- **Activity 1** Make sure students mark the dimensions properly on the product mat. Since x tiles are rectangular, remind students that the long side is the correct side to use to mark a value of x on the mat.

- When students are filling in the mats with the tiles, remind them to look carefully at both the horizontal and vertical dimensions of each tile on the product mat. If both dimensions have a value of x, then use an x^2 tile. If one dimension is x and the other is 1, then use an x tile. If both dimensions are 1, then use a 1 tile.

Multiplying Polynomials

You can use algebra tiles to find the product of two binomials.

Activity 1 Use algebra tiles to find $(x + 2)(x + 5)$.

The rectangle will have a width of $x + 2$ and a length of $x + 5$. Use algebra tiles to mark off the dimensions on a product mat. Then complete the rectangle with algebra tiles.

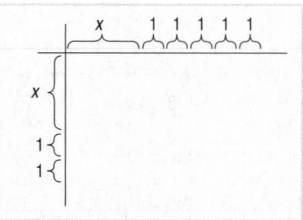  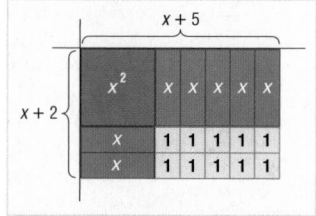

The rectangle consists of 1 blue x^2 tile, 7 green x tiles, and 10 yellow 1 tiles. The area of the rectangle is $x^2 + 7x + 10$. Therefore, $(x + 2)(x + 5) = x^2 + 7x + 10$.

Activity 2 Use algebra tiles to find $(x - 1)(x - 4)$.

Step 1 The rectangle will have a width of $x - 1$ and a length of $x - 4$. Use algebra tiles to mark off the dimensions on a product mat. Then begin to make the rectangle with algebra tiles.

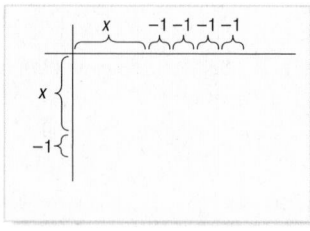  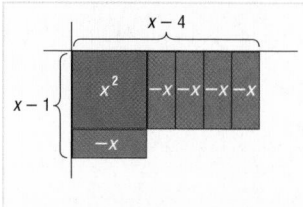

Step 2 Determine whether to use 4 yellow 1 tiles or 4 red -1 tiles to complete the rectangle. Remember that the numbers at the top and side give the dimensions of the tile needed. The area of each tile is the product of -1 and -1 or 1. This is represented by a yellow 1 tile. Fill in the space with 4 yellow 1 tiles to complete the rectangle.

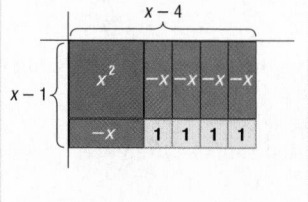

The rectangle consists of 1 blue x^2 tile, 5 red $-x$ tiles, and 4 yellow 1 tiles. The area of the rectangle is $x^2 - 5x + 4$. Therefore, $(x - 1)(x - 4) = x^2 - 5x + 4$.

450 Chapter 8 Polynomials

Resource Manager

📁 **Teaching Algebra with Manipulatives**

- pp. 10–11 (master for algebra tiles)
- p. 16 (master for equation mat)
- p. 144 (student recording sheet)

Glencoe Mathematics Classroom Manipulative Kit

- algebra tiles
- equation mat

Activity 3 Use algebra tiles to find $(x - 3)(2x + 1)$.

Step 1 The rectangle will have a width of $x - 3$ and a length of $2x + 1$. Mark off the dimensions on a product mat. Then begin to make the rectangle with algebra tiles.

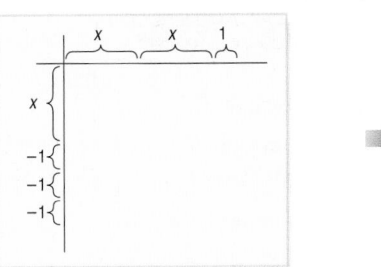 →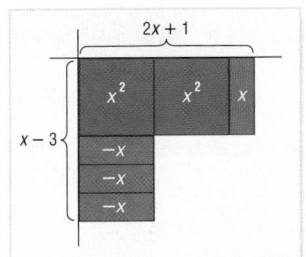

Step 2 Determine what color x tiles and what color 1 tiles to use to complete the rectangle. The area of each x tile is the product of x and -1. This is represented by a red $-x$ tile. The area of the 1 tile is represented by the product of 1 and -1 or -1. This is represented by a red -1 tile. Complete the rectangle with 3 red $-x$ tiles and 3 red -1 tiles.

Step 3 Rearrange the tiles to simplify the polynomial you have formed. Notice that a zero pair is formed by one positive and one negative x tile.

There are 2 blue x^2 tiles, 5 red $-x$ tiles, and 3 red -1 tiles left. In simplest form, $(x - 3)(2x + 1) = 2x^2 - 5x - 3$.

Model and Analyze

Use algebra tiles to find each product. 1. $x^2 + 5x + 6$ 2. $x^2 - 4x + 3$

1. $(x + 2)(x + 3)$
2. $(x - 1)(x - 3)$
3. $(x + 1)(x - 2)$ $x^2 - x - 2$
4. $(x + 1)(2x + 1)$ $2x^2 + 3x + 1$
5. $(x - 2)(2x - 3)$ $2x^2 - 7x + 6$
6. $(x + 3)(2x - 4)$ $2x^2 + 2x - 12$

7. You can also use the Distributive Property to find the product of two binomials. The figure at the right shows the model for $(x + 3)(x + 4)$ separated into four parts. Write a sentence or two explaining how this model shows the use of the Distributive Property. **See margin.**

- **Activity 2** Remind students to pay close attention to whether the dimensions for each tile are positive or negative, as this affects which tile to use. Determining whether to use a positive or negative tile is just like determining whether a product is positive or negative. If both dimensions are positive, then the tile is positive. If one is positive and the other is negative, then the tile is negative. If both are negative then the tile is positive.

- **Activity 3** As an alternative to removing zero pairs, have students write the expression based on the tiles without removing zero pairs. They can then simplify the expression by combining like terms.

Assess

For **Exercise 7**, help students to see that when using the Distributive Property to multiply polynomials, each term from the first polynomial is multiplied by each term from the second polynomial.

Study Notebook

You may wish to have students summarize this activity and what they learned from it.

Answer

7. By the Distributive Property, $(x + 3)(x + 4) = x(x + 4) + 3(x + 4)$. The top row represents $x(x + 4)$ or $x^2 + 4x$. The bottom row represents $3(x + 4)$ or $3x + 12$.

1 Focus

5-Minute Check Transparency 8-7 Use as a quiz or review of Lesson 8-6.

Mathematical Background notes are available for this lesson on p. 408D.

Building on Prior Knowledge

Students have learned how to use the Distributive Property to multiply a polynomial by a monomial. Make sure students realize that they are applying the same process in multiplying polynomials.

How is multiplying binomials similar to multiplying two-digit numbers?

Ask students:

- Explain how the Distributive Property was used in the first step of this problem. **The number 6 in 36 was multiplied by 20 and 4.**

- Explain how the Distributive Property was used in the second step of this problem. **The number 30 in 36 was multiplied by 20 and 4.**

- How is the third step in this multiplication process similar to combining like terms when working with polynomials? **The digits in each place value are combined: first the ones, then the tens, and finally the hundreds.**

What You'll Learn

- Multiply two binomials by using the FOIL method.
- Multiply two polynomials by using the Distributive Property.

Vocabulary
- FOIL method

How is multiplying binomials similar to multiplying two-digit numbers?

To compute 24×36, we multiply each digit in 24 by each digit in 36, paying close attention to the place value of each digit.

Step 1 Multiply by the ones.	**Step 2** Multiply by the tens.	**Step 3** Add like place values.
$\begin{array}{r} 24 \\ \times\, 36 \\ \hline 144 \end{array}$	$\begin{array}{r} 24 \\ \times\, 36 \\ \hline 144 \\ 720 \end{array}$	$\begin{array}{r} 24 \\ \times\, 36 \\ \hline 144 \\ +\,720 \\ \hline 864 \end{array}$
$6 \times 24 = 6(20 + 4)$ $= 120 + 24 \text{ or } 144$	$30 \times 24 = 30(20 + 4)$ $= 600 + 120 \text{ or } 720$	

You can multiply two binomials in a similar way.

MULTIPLY BINOMIALS   To multiply two binomials, apply the Distributive Property twice as you do when multiplying two-digit numbers.

> **Study Tip**
>
> **Look Back**
> To review the **Distributive Property**, see Lesson 1-7.

Example 1   The Distributive Property

Find $(x + 3)(x + 2)$.

Method 1   Vertical

Multiply by 2.	Multiply by x.	Add like terms.
$\begin{array}{r} x + 3 \\ (\times)\, x + 2 \\ \hline 2x + 6 \end{array}$	$\begin{array}{r} x + 3 \\ (\times)\, x + 2 \\ \hline 2x + 6 \\ x^2 + 3x \end{array}$	$\begin{array}{r} x + 3 \\ (\times)\, x + 2 \\ \hline 2x + 6 \\ x^2 + 3x \\ \hline x^2 + 5x + 6 \end{array}$
$2(x + 3) = 2x + 6$	$x(x + 3) = x^2 + 3x$	

Method 2   Horizontal

$$
\begin{aligned}
(x + 3)(x + 2) &= x(x + 2) + 3(x + 2) && \text{Distributive Property} \\
&= x(x) + x(2) + 3(x) + 3(2) && \text{Distributive Property} \\
&= x^2 + 2x + 3x + 6 && \text{Multiply.} \\
&= x^2 + 5x + 6 && \text{Combine like terms.}
\end{aligned}
$$

An alternative method for finding the product of two binomials can be shown using algebra tiles.

Resource Manager

📁 Workbook and Reproducible Masters

Chapter 8 Resource Masters
- Study Guide and Intervention, pp. 491–492
- Skills Practice, p. 493
- Practice, p. 494
- Reading to Learn Mathematics, p. 495
- Enrichment, p. 496

Graphing Calculator and Spreadsheet Masters, p. 38
Parent and Student Study Guide Workbook, p. 65

 Transparencies

5-Minute Check Transparency 8-7
Answer Key Transparencies

 Technology

AlgePASS: Tutorial Plus, Lesson 22
Interactive Chalkboard
Multimedia Applications

Consider the product of $x + 3$ and $x - 2$. The rectangle shown below has a length of $x + 3$ and a width of $x - 2$. Notice that this rectangle can be broken up into four smaller rectangles.

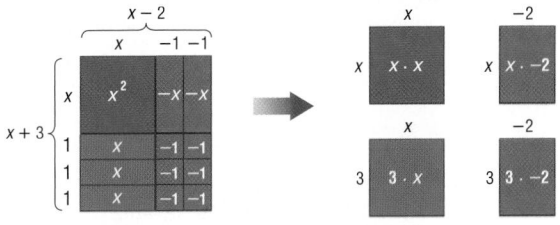

The product of $(x - 2)$ and $(x + 3)$ is the sum of these four areas.

$$(x + 3)(x - 2) = (x \cdot x) + (x \cdot -2) + (3 \cdot x) + (3 \cdot -2) \quad \text{Sum of the four areas}$$
$$= x^2 + (-2x) + 3x + (-6) \quad \text{Multiply.}$$
$$= x^2 + x - 6 \quad \text{Combine like terms.}$$

This example illustrates a shortcut of the Distributive Property called the **FOIL method**. You can use the FOIL method to multiply two binomials.

> **Key Concept**   *FOIL Method for Multiplying Binomials*
>
> - **Words**   To multiply two binomials, find the sum of the products of
>
>   F   the *First* terms,
>
>   O   the *Outer* terms,
>
>   I   the *Inner* terms, and
>
>   L   the *Last* terms.
>
> - **Example**
>
>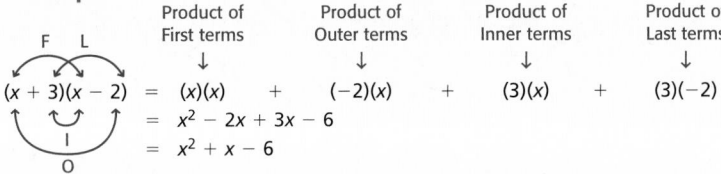
>
> | | Product of First terms | | Product of Outer terms | | Product of Inner terms | | Product of Last terms |
> |---|---|---|---|---|---|---|---|
> | | ↓ | | ↓ | | ↓ | | ↓ |
> | $(x + 3)(x - 2)$ = | $(x)(x)$ | + | $(-2)(x)$ | + | $(3)(x)$ | + | $(3)(-2)$ |
>
> $$= x^2 - 2x + 3x - 6$$
> $$= x^2 + x - 6$$

Example 2   FOIL Method

Find each product.

a. $(x - 5)(x + 7)$

$$(x - 5)(x + 7) = (x)(x) + (x)(7) + (-5)(x) + (-5)(7) \quad \text{FOIL method}$$
$$= x^2 + 7x - 5x - 35 \quad \text{Multiply.}$$
$$= x^2 + 2x - 35 \quad \text{Combine like terms.}$$

b. $(2y + 3)(6y - 7)$

$$(2y + 3)(6y - 7)$$
$$= (2y)(6y) + (2y)(-7) + (3)(6y) + (3)(-7) \quad \text{FOIL method}$$
$$= 12y^2 - 14y + 18y - 21 \quad \text{Multiply.}$$
$$= 12y^2 + 4y - 21 \quad \text{Combine like terms.}$$

www.algebra1.com/extra_examples

Lesson 8-7 Multiplying Polynomials   **453**

Study Tip

Checking Your Work
You can check your products in Examples 2a and 2b by reworking each problem using the Distributive Property.

---

2 Teach

MULTIPLY BINOMIALS

In-Class Examples   Power Point®

Teaching Tip Students who are less familiar with the Distributive Property may wish to use the vertical method for multiplying binomials because it is similar to multiplying two-digit numbers. Suggest that students use the method with which they are most comfortable.

1 Find $(y + 8)(y - 4)$.
$y^2 + 4y - 32$

2 Find each product.

a. $(z - 6)(z - 12)$ $z^2 - 18z + 72$

b. $(5x - 4)(2x + 8)$
$10x^2 + 32x - 32$

Teaching Tip Remind students that the FOIL method only works for multiplying two binomials. To multiply any other polynomials, you must use the Distributive Property directly, rather than taking a shortcut.

DAILY INTERVENTION

Differentiated Instruction

Auditory/Musical Music can be a powerful memory tool. Suggest that groups of students make up a song or rap to explain how to use the FOIL method to multiply binomials. Have the groups perform their songs in front of the class when they are finished.

In-Class Example Power Point®

Teaching Tip Tell students that they must find the sum of the bases first before they can multiply by one-half the height. This is why $b_1 + b_2$ is written within parentheses when the problem is translated from the words into an equation.

③ GEOMETRY The area A of a triangle is one-half the height h times the base. Write an expression for the area of the triangle. $3x^2 - 19x - 14$ units²

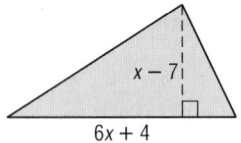

MULTIPLY POLYNOMIALS

In-Class Example Power Point®

④ Find each product.

a. $(3a + 4)(a^2 - 12a + 1)$
$3a^3 - 32a^2 - 45a + 4$

b. $(2b^2 + 7b + 9)(b^2 + 3b - 1)$
$2b^4 + 13b^3 + 28b^2 + 20b - 9$

Answer

1.

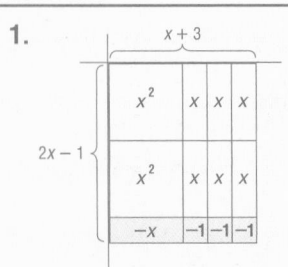

2a. $(3x + 4)(2x - 5)$
$= 3x(2x - 5) + 4(2x - 5)$
$= 6x^2 - 15x + 8x - 20$
$= 6x^2 - 7x - 20$

2b. $(3x + 4)(2x - 5)$
$= 3x(2x) + 3x(-5) + 4(2x) + 4(-5)$
$= 6x^2 - 15x + 8x - 20$
$= 6x^2 - 7x - 20$

2c.
$$\begin{array}{r} 3x + 4 \\ (\times)\, 2x - 5 \\ \hline -15x - 20 \\ 6x^2 + 8x \\ \hline 6x^2 - 7x - 20 \end{array}$$

2d.

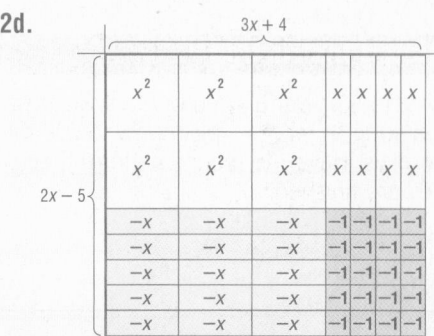

Example 3 *FOIL Method*

GEOMETRY The area A of a trapezoid is one-half the height h times the sum of the bases, b_1 and b_2. Write an expression for the area of the trapezoid.

Identify the height and bases.

$h = x + 2$

$b_1 = 3x - 7$

$b_2 = 2x + 1$

Now write and apply the formula.

Area	equals	one-half	height	times	sum of bases,
A	$=$	$\frac{1}{2}$	$\cdot$ h	$\cdot$	$(b_1 + b_2)$

$A = \frac{1}{2}h(b_1 + b_2)$ Original formula

$\quad = \frac{1}{2}(x + 2)[(3x - 7) + (2x + 1)]$ Substitution

$\quad = \frac{1}{2}(x + 2)(5x - 6)$ Add polynomials in the brackets.

$\quad = \frac{1}{2}[x(5x) + x(-6) + 2(5x) + 2(-6)]$ FOIL method

$\quad = \frac{1}{2}(5x^2 - 6x + 10x - 12)$ Multiply.

$\quad = \frac{1}{2}(5x^2 + 4x - 12)$ Combine like terms.

$\quad = \frac{5}{2}x^2 + 2x - 6$ Distributive Property

The area of the trapezoid is $\frac{5}{2}x^2 + 2x - 6$ square units.

Study Tip

Common Misconception
A common mistake when multiplying polynomials horizontally is to combine terms that are not alike. For this reason, you may prefer to multiply polynomials in column form, aligning like terms.

MULTIPLY POLYNOMIALS The Distributive Property can be used to multiply any two polynomials.

Example 4 *The Distributive Property*

Find each product.

a. $(4x + 9)(2x^2 - 5x + 3)$

$(4x + 9)(2x^2 - 5x + 3)$

$\quad = 4x(2x^2 - 5x + 3) + 9(2x^2 - 5x + 3)$ Distributive Property

$\quad = 8x^3 - 20x^2 + 12x + 18x^2 - 45x + 27$ Distributive Property

$\quad = 8x^3 - 2x^2 - 33x + 27$ Combine like terms.

b. $(y^2 - 2y + 5)(6y^2 - 3y + 1)$

$(y^2 - 2y + 5)(6y^2 - 3y + 1)$

$\quad = y^2(6y^2 - 3y + 1) - 2y(6y^2 - 3y + 1) + 5(6y^2 - 3y + 1)$ Distributive Property

$\quad = 6y^4 - 3y^3 + y^2 - 12y^3 + 6y^2 - 2y + 30y^2 - 15y + 5$ Distributive Property

$\quad = 6y^4 - 15y^3 + 37y^2 - 17y + 5$ Combine like terms.

Concept Check

1. **Draw a diagram** to show how you would use algebra tiles to find the product of $2x - 1$ and $x + 3$. **See margin.**

2. **Show** how to find $(3x + 4)(2x - 5)$ using each method. **2a–d. See margin.**

   a. Distributive Property   b. FOIL method

   c. vertical or column method   d. algebra tiles

3. **OPEN ENDED** State which method of multiplying binomials you prefer and why. **See students' work.**

Guided Practice

Find each product. **4–11. See margin.**

GUIDED PRACTICE KEY	
Exercises	Examples
4–11	1, 2, 4
12	3

4. $(y + 4)(y + 3)$ 5. $(x - 2)(x + 6)$ 6. $(a - 8)(a + 5)$

7. $(4h + 5)(h + 7)$ 8. $(9p - 1)(3p - 2)$ 9. $(2g + 7)(5g - 8)$

10. $(3b - 2c)(6b + 5c)$

11. $(3k - 5)(2k^2 + 4k - 3)$

Application

12. **GEOMETRY** The area A of a triangle is half the product of the base b times the height h. Write a polynomial expression that represents the area of the triangle at the right.

$\dfrac{6x^2 + 7x - 3}{2}$ or $3x^2 + \dfrac{7}{2}x - \dfrac{3}{2}$

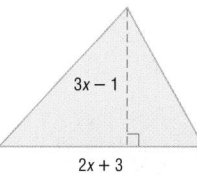

$3x - 1$

$2x + 3$

★ indicates increased difficulty

Homework Help

For Exercises	See Examples
13–38	1, 2, 4
39–42	3

Extra Practice
See page 839.

Find each product. **31–38. See margin.**

13. $(b + 8)(b + 2)$ 14. $(n + 6)(n + 7)$ 15. $(x - 4)(x - 9)$

16. $(a - 3)(a - 5)$ 17. $(y + 4)(y - 8)$ 18. $(p + 2)(p - 10)$

19. $(2w - 5)(w + 7)$ 20. $(k + 12)(3k - 2)$ 21. $(8d + 3)(5d + 2)$

22. $(4g + 3)(9g + 6)$ 23. $(7x - 4)(5x - 1)$ 24. $(6a - 5)(3a - 8)$

25. $(2n + 3)(2n + 3)$ 26. $(5m - 6)(5m - 6)$ 27. $(10r - 4)(10r + 4)$

28. $(7t + 5)(7t - 5)$ 29. $(8x + 2y)(5x - 4y)$ 30. $(11a - 6b)(2a + 3b)$

31. $(p + 4)(p^2 + 2p - 7)$ 32. $(a - 3)(a^2 - 8a + 5)$

33. $(2x - 5)(3x^2 - 4x + 1)$ 34. $(3k + 4)(7k^2 + 2k - 9)$

35. $(n^2 - 3n + 2)(n^2 + 5n - 4)$ 36. $(y^2 + 7y - 1)(y^2 - 6y + 5)$

37. $(4a^2 + 3a - 7)(2a^2 - a + 8)$ 38. $(6x^2 - 5x + 2)(3x^2 + 2x + 4)$

GEOMETRY Write an expression to represent the area of each figure.

39.

$2x^2 + 3x - 20$ units^2

40.

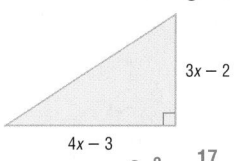

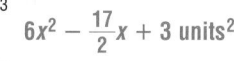

$6x^2 - \dfrac{17}{2}x + 3$ units^2

41.

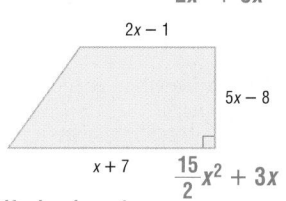

$\dfrac{15}{2}x^2 + 3x - 24$ units^2

★ 42.

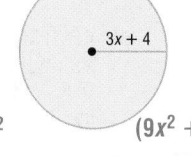

$3x + 4$

$(9x^2 + 24x + 16)\pi$ units^2

www.algebra1.com/self_check_quiz

Lesson 8-7 Multiplying Polynomials **455**

Answers

13. $b^2 + 10b + 16$

14. $n^2 + 13n + 42$

15. $x^2 - 13x + 36$

16. $a^2 - 8a + 15$

17. $y^2 - 4y - 32$

18. $p^2 - 8p - 20$

19. $2w^2 + 9w - 35$

20. $3k^2 + 34k - 24$

21. $40d^2 + 31d + 6$

22. $36g^2 + 51g + 18$

23. $35x^2 - 27x + 4$

24. $18a^2 - 63a + 40$

25. $4n^2 + 12n + 9$

26. $25m^2 - 60m + 36$

27. $100r^2 - 16$

28. $49t^2 - 25$

29. $40x^2 - 22xy - 8y^2$

30. $22a^2 + 21ab - 18b^2$

Answers

4. $y^2 + 7y + 12$ 8. $27p^2 - 21p + 2$

5. $x^2 + 4x - 12$ 9. $10g^2 + 19g - 56$

6. $a^2 - 3a - 40$ 10. $18b^2 + 3bc - 10c^2$

7. $4h^2 + 33h + 35$ 11. $6k^3 + 2k^2 - 29k + 15$

Answers

31. $p^3 + 6p^2 + p - 28$

32. $a^3 - 11a^2 + 29a - 15$

33. $6x^3 - 23x^2 + 22x - 5$

34. $21k^3 + 34k^2 - 19k - 36$

35. $n^4 + 2n^3 - 17n^2 + 22n - 8$

36. $y^4 + y^3 - 38y^2 + 41y - 5$

37. $8a^4 + 2a^3 + 15a^2 + 31a - 56$

38. $18x^4 - 3x^3 + 20x^2 - 16x + 8$

Study Guide and Intervention, p. 491 (shown) and p. 492

Multiply Binomials To multiply two binomials, you can apply the Distributive Property twice. A useful way to keep track of terms in the product is to use the FOIL method as illustrated in Example 2.

Example 1 Find $(x + 3)(x - 4)$.

Horizontal Method
$(x + 3)(x - 4)$
$= x(x - 4) + 3(x - 4)$
$= (x)(x) + x(-4) + 3(x) + 3(-4)$
$= x^2 - 4x + 3x - 12$
$= x^2 - x - 12$

Vertical Method
$x + 3$
$(\times) \quad x - 4$
$\underline{-4x - 12}$
$\underline{x^2 + 3x}$
$x^2 - x - 12$

The product is $x^2 - x - 12$.

Example 2 Find $(x - 2)(x + 5)$ using the FOIL method.

$(x - 2)(x + 5)$
    First   Outer   Inner   Last
$= (x)(x) + (x)(5) + (-2)(x) + (-2)(5)$
$= x^2 + 5x + (-2x) - 10$
$= x^2 + 3x - 10$

The product is $x^2 + 3x - 10$.

Exercises

Find each product.

1. $(x + 2)(x + 3)$
$x^2 + 5x + 6$

2. $(x - 4)(x + 1)$
$x^2 - 3x - 4$

3. $(x - 6)(x - 2)$
$x^2 - 8x + 12$

4. $(p - 4)(p + 2)$
$p^2 - 2p - 8$

5. $(y + 5)(y + 2)$
$y^2 + 7y + 10$

6. $(2x - 1)(x + 5)$
$2x^2 + 9x - 5$

7. $(3n - 4)(3n - 4)$
$9n^2 - 24n + 16$

8. $(8m - 2)(8m + 2)$
$64m^2 - 4$

9. $(k + 4)(5k - 1)$
$5k^2 + 19k - 4$

10. $(3x + 1)(4x + 3)$
$12x^2 + 13x + 3$

11. $(x - 8)(-3x + 1)$
$-3x^2 + 25x - 8$

12. $(5t + 4)(2t - 6)$
$10t^2 - 22t - 24$

13. $(5m - 3n)(4m - 2n)$
$20m^2 - 22mn + 6n^2$

14. $(a - 3b)(2a - 5b)$
$2a^2 - 11ab + 15b^2$

15. $(8x - 5)(8x + 5)$
$64x^2 - 25$

16. $(2n - 4)(2n + 5)$
$4n^2 + 2n - 20$

17. $(4m - 3)(5m - 5)$
$20m^2 - 35m + 15$

18. $(7g - 4)(7g + 4)$
$49g^2 - 16$

Skills Practice, p. 493 and Practice, p. 494 (shown)

Find each product.

1. $(q + 6)(q + 5)$
$q^2 + 11q + 30$

2. $(x + 7)(x + 4)$
$x^2 + 11x + 28$

3. $(s + 5)(s - 6)$
$s^2 - s - 30$

4. $(n - 4)(n - 6)$
$n^2 - 10n + 24$

5. $(a - 5)(a - 8)$
$a^2 - 13a + 40$

6. $(w - 6)(w - 9)$
$w^2 - 15w + 54$

7. $(4c + 6)(c - 4)$
$4c^2 - 10c - 24$

8. $(2x - 9)(2x + 4)$
$4x^2 - 10x - 36$

9. $(4d - 5)(2d - 3)$
$8d^2 - 22d + 15$

10. $(4b + 3)(3b - 4)$
$12b^2 - 7b - 12$

11. $(4m + 2)(4m - 3)$
$16m^2 - 4m - 6$

12. $(5c - 9)(7c + 9)$
$35c^2 + 10c - 45$

13. $(6a - 3)(7a - 4)$
$42a^2 - 45a + 12$

14. $(6h - 3)(4h - 2)$
$24h^2 - 24h + 6$

15. $(2x - 2)(5x - 4)$
$10x^2 - 18x + 8$

16. $(3a - b)(2a - b)$
$6a^2 - 5ab + b^2$

17. $(4g + 3h)(2g + 3h)$
$8g^2 + 18gh + 9h^2$

18. $(4x + y)(4x + y)$
$16x^2 + 8xy + y^2$

19. $(m + 5)(m^2 + 4m - 8)$
$m^3 + 9m^2 + 12m - 40$

20. $(t + 3)(t^2 + 4t + 7)$
$t^3 + 7t^2 + 19t + 21$

21. $(2h + 3)(2h^2 + 3h + 4)$
$4h^3 + 12h^2 + 17h + 12$

22. $(3d + 3)(2d^2 + 5d - 2)$
$6d^3 + 21d^2 + 9d - 6$

23. $(3g + 2)(9g^2 - 12g + 4)$
$27g^3 - 18g^2 - 12g + 8$

24. $(3r + 2)(9r^2 + 6r + 4)$
$27r^3 + 36r^2 + 24r + 8$

25. $(3c^2 + 2c - 1)(2c^2 + c + 9)$
$6c^4 + 7c^3 + 27c^2 + 17c - 9$

26. $(2\ell + \ell + 4)(4\ell^2 + 2\ell - 2)$
$8\ell^4 + 8\ell^3 + 10\ell^2 + 4\ell - 6$

27. $(2x^2 - 2x - 3)(2x^2 - 4x + 3)$
$4x^4 - 12x^3 + 8x^2 + 6x - 9$

28. $(3y^2 + 2y + 2)(3y^2 - 4y - 5)$
$9y^4 - 6y^3 - 17y^2 - 18y - 10$

GEOMETRY Write an expression to represent the area of each figure.

29. 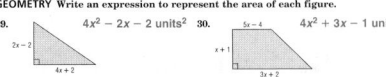 $4x^2 - 2x - 2$ units^2

30. $4x^2 + 3x - 1$ units^2

31. **NUMBER THEORY** Let x be an even integer. What is the product of the next two consecutive even integers? $x^2 + 6x + 8$

32. **GEOMETRY** The volume of a rectangular pyramid is one third the product of the area of its base and its height. Find an expression for the volume of a rectangular pyramid whose base has an area of $3x^2 + 12x + 9$ square feet and whose height is $x + 3$ feet.
$x^3 + 7x^2 + 15x + 9$ feet^3

Reading to Learn Mathematics, p. 495   **ELL**

Pre-Activity How is multiplying binomials similar to multiplying two-digit numbers?

Read the introduction to Lesson 8-7 at the top of page 452 in your textbook.

In your own words, explain how the distributive property is used twice to multiply two-digit numbers.
The ones of the first factor are multiplied by the tens and the ones of the other factor. Then the tens of the first factor are multiplied by the tens and ones of the other factor.

Reading the Lesson

1. How is multiplying binomials similar to multiplying two-digit numbers?
Binomials have two terms and each term of one binomial is multiplied by each term of the other binomial.

2. Complete the table using the FOIL method.

	Product of First Terms	+	Product of Outer Terms	+	Product of Inner Terms	+	Product of Last Terms
$(x + 5)(x - 3)$	$(x)(x)$	+	$(x)(-3)$	+	$(5)(x)$	+	$(5)(-3)$
=	x^2	+	$-3x$	+	$5x$	+	-15
=	x^2	+	$2x$	−	15		
$(3y + 6)(y - 2)$	$(3y)(y)$	+	$(3y)(-2)$	+	$(6)(y)$	+	$(6)(-2)$
=	$3y^2$	+	$-6y$	+	$6y$	+	-12
=	$3y^2$	−	12				

Helping You Remember

3. Think of a method for remembering all the product combinations used in the FOIL method of multiplying two binomials. Describe your method using words or a diagram.
Sample answer: Imagine that the two binomials are written on the floor. For FOIL, think of all the possible ways you could have your left foot on a term of the first binomial and your right foot on a term of the second binomial. Your feet could be on the first terms, the outer terms, the inner terms, or the last terms.

GEOMETRY The volume V of a prism equals the area of the base B times the height h. Write an expression to represent the volume of each prism.

★ 43.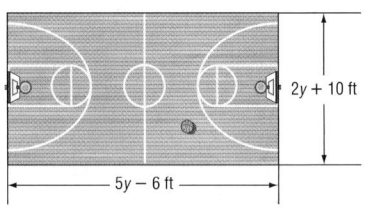
$2a^3 + 10a^2 - 2a - 10$ units^3

★ 44.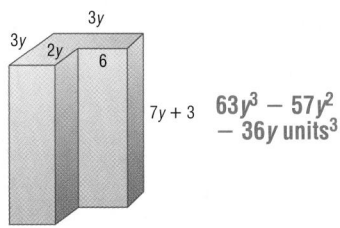
$63y^3 - 57y^2 - 36y$ units^3

NUMBER THEORY For Exercises 45–47, consider three consecutive integers. Let the least of these integers be a. **45.** $a^3 + 3a^2 + 2a$

45. Write a polynomial representing the product of these three integers.

46. Choose an integer for a. Find their product. **Sample answer: $a = 1$; $1(2)(3) = 6$**

47. Evaluate the polynomial in Exercise 45 for the value of a you chose in Exercise 46. Describe the result.
Sample answer: 6; The result is the same as the product in Exercise 46.

48. **BASKETBALL** The dimensions of a professional basketball court are represented by a width of $2y + 10$ feet and a length of $5y - 6$ feet. Find an expression for the area of the court. $10y^2 + 38y - 60$ ft^2

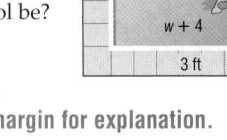

2y + 10 ft

5y − 6 ft

OFFICE SPACE For Exercises 49–51, use the following information.
Latanya's modular office is square. Her office in the company's new building will be 2 feet shorter in one direction and 4 feet longer in the other.

49. Write expressions for the dimensions of Latanya's new office. $x - 2$, $x + 4$

50. Write a polynomial expression for the area of her new office. $x^2 + 2x - 8$

51. Suppose her office is presently 9 feet by 9 feet. Will her new office be bigger or smaller than her old office and by how much? **bigger; 10 ft^2**

★ 52. **MENTAL MATH** One way to mentally multiply 25 and 18 is to find $(20 + 5)(20 - 2)$. Show how the FOIL method can be used to find each product.

  a. $35(19)$ **b.** $67(102)$ **c.** $8\frac{1}{2} \cdot 6\frac{3}{4}$ **d.** $12\frac{3}{5} \cdot 10\frac{2}{3}$
a–d. See margin.

★ 53. **POOL CONSTRUCTION** A homeowner is installing a swimming pool in his backyard. He wants its length to be 4 feet longer than its width. Then he wants to surround it with a concrete walkway 3 feet wide. If he can only afford 300 square feet of concrete for the walkway, what should the dimensions of the pool be? **20 ft by 24 ft**

54. **CRITICAL THINKING** Determine whether the following statement is *sometimes*, *always*, or *never* true. Explain your reasoning. **Sometimes; see margin for explanation.**

The product of a binomial and a trinomial is a polynomial with four terms.

More About. . .

Basketball •

More than 200 million people a year pay to see basketball games. That is more admissions than for any other American sport.

Source: *Compton's Encyclopedia*

Enrichment, p. 496

Pascal's Triangle

This arrangement of numbers is called Pascal's Triangle. It was first published in 1665, but was known hundreds of years earlier.

```
        1
      1   1
    1   2   1
  1   3   3   1
1   4   6   4   1
```

1. Each number in the triangle is found by adding two numbers. What two numbers were added to get the 6 in the 5th row?
3 and 3

2. Describe how to create the 6th row of Pascal's Triangle.
The first and last numbers are 1. Evaluate $1 + 4$, $4 + 6$, $6 + 4$, and $4 + 1$ to find the other numbers.

3. Write the numbers for rows 6 through 10 of the triangle.
Row 6:   1   5   10   10   5   1
Row 7:   1   6   15   20   15   6   1
       21   35

55.  **WRITING IN MATH** Answer the question that was posed at the beginning of the lesson. **See margin.**

How is multiplying binomials similar to multiplying two-digit numbers?

Include the following in your answer:
- a demonstration of a horizontal method for multiplying 24×36, and
- an explanation of the meaning of "like terms" in the context of vertical two-digit multiplication.

Standardized Test Practice
A B C D

56. $(x + 2)(x - 4) - (x + 4)(x - 2) =$ **C**

    (A) 0   (B) $2x^2 + 4x - 16$ (C) $-4x$ (D) $4x$

57. The expression $(x - y)(x^2 + xy + y^2)$ is equivalent to which of the following? **B**

    (A) $x^2 - y^2$ (B) $x^3 - y^3$ (C) $x^3 - xy^2$ (D) $x^3 - x^2y + y^2$

Maintain Your Skills

Mixed Review   **Find each product.** *(Lesson 8-6)*

58. $3d(4d^2 - 8d - 15)$ **59.** $-4y(7y^2 - 4y + 3)$ **60.** $2m^2(5m^2 - 7m + 8)$
     $12d^3 - 24d^2 - 45d$ $-28y^3 + 16y^2 - 12y$ $10m^4 - 14m^3 + 16m^2$

Simplify. *(Lesson 8-6)*

61. $3x(2x - 4) + 6(5x^2 + 2x - 7)$ **62.** $4a(5a^2 + 2a - 7) - 3(2a^2 - 6a - 9)$
     $36x^2 - 42$ $20a^3 + 2a^2 - 10a + 27$

GEOMETRY   **For Exercises 63 and 64, use the following information.**
The sum of the degree measures of the angles of a triangle is 180. *(Lesson 8-5)*

63. Write an expression to represent the measure of the third angle of the triangle. $(181 - 7x)°$

64. If $x = 15$, find the measures of the three angles of the triangle. $31°, 73°, 76°$

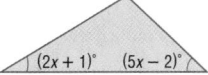
$(2x + 1)°$ $(5x - 2)°$

65. Use the graph at the right to determine whether the system below has *no* solution, *one* solution, or *infinitely many* solutions. If the system has one solution, name it. *(Lesson 7-1)*

$x + 2y = 0$
$y + 3 = -x$ one; $(-6, 3)$

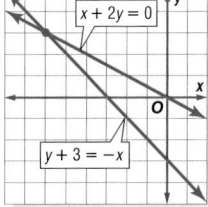
$x + 2y = 0$
$y + 3 = -x$

If $f(x) = 2x - 5$ and $g(x) = x^2 + 3x$, find each value. *(Lesson 4-6)*

66. $f(-4)$ -13 **67.** $g(-2) + 7$ 5 **68.** $f(a + 3)$ $2a + 1$

Solve each equation or formula for the variable specified. *(Lesson 3-8)*

69. $a = \dfrac{v}{t}$ for t $t = \dfrac{v}{a}$ **70.** $ax - by = 2cz$ for y **71.** $4x + 3y = 7$ for y
                              $y = \dfrac{ax - 2cz}{b}$ $y = -\dfrac{4}{3}x + \dfrac{7}{3}$

Getting Ready for the Next Lesson   **PREREQUISITE SKILL   Simplify.**
*(To review **Power of a Power** and **Power of a Product** Properties, see Lesson 8-1.)*

72. $(6a)^2$ $36a^2$ **73.** $(7x)^2$ $49x^2$ **74.** $(9b)^2$ $81b^2$

75. $(4y^2)^2$ $16y^4$ **76.** $(2v^3)^2$ $4v^6$ **77.** $(3g^4)^2$ $9g^8$

Lesson 8-7 Multiplying Polynomials **457**

---

4 Assess

Open-Ended Assessment
Speaking Have student volunteers explain orally how the FOIL method for multiplying binomials works, and use it to solve a problem.

Getting Ready for Lesson 8-8

PREREQUISITE SKILL Students will learn squares and products of sums and differences in Lesson 8-8. They need to be able to find squares of monomials mentally to efficiently compute these special products. Use Exercises 72–77 to determine your students' familiarity with powers of powers and powers of products.

Answers

54. The product of $x + 1$ and $x^2 + 2x + 3$ is $x^3 + 3x^2 + 5x + 3$, which has 4 terms; the product of $y + 1$ and $x^3 + 2x^2 + 3x$ is $x^3y + 2x^2y + 3xy + x^3 + 2x^2 + 3x$, which has 6 terms.

55. Multiplying binomials and two-digit numbers each involve the use of the Distributive Property twice. Each procedure involves four multiplications and the addition of like terms. Answers should include the following.

- 24×36
  $= (4 + 20)(6 + 30)$
  $= (4 + 20)6 + (4 + 20)30$
  $= (24 + 120) + (120 + 600)$
  $= 144 + 720$
  $= 864$

- The like terms in vertical two-digit multiplication are digits with the same place value.

52a. Sample answer:
$(30 + 5)(10 + 9) = (30)(10) + 30(9) + 5(10) + 5(9)$
$\qquad\qquad = 300 + 270 + 50 + 45 = 665$

52b. Sample answer:
$(60 + 7)(100 + 2) = 60(100) + 60(2) + 7(100) + 7(2)$
$\qquad\qquad = 6000 + 120 + 700 + 14 = 6834$

52c. Sample answer:
$\left(8 + \dfrac{1}{2}\right)\left(6 + \dfrac{3}{4}\right) = 8(6) + 8\left(\dfrac{3}{4}\right) + \dfrac{1}{2}(6) + \dfrac{1}{2}\left(\dfrac{3}{4}\right)$
$\qquad\qquad = 48 + 6 + 3 + \dfrac{3}{8} = 57\dfrac{3}{8}$

52d. Sample answer:
$\left(12 + \dfrac{3}{5}\right)\left(10 + \dfrac{2}{3}\right) = 12(10) + 12\left(\dfrac{2}{3}\right) + \dfrac{3}{5}(10) + \dfrac{3}{5}\left(\dfrac{2}{3}\right)$
$\qquad\qquad = 120 + 8 + 6 + \dfrac{2}{5} = 134\dfrac{2}{5}$

1 Focus

5-Minute Check Transparency 8-8 Use as a quiz or review of Lesson 8-7.

Mathematical Background notes are available for this lesson on p. 408D.

When is the product of two binomials also a binomial?

Ask students:

• Looking at the second example, what sometimes happens when using the FOIL method to multiply binomials that produces a binomial product? **The like *x* terms combine to produce a zero pair, which causes the term to drop out of the product.**

What You'll Learn

• Find squares of sums and differences.
• Find the product of a sum and a difference.

Vocabulary
• difference of squares

When is the product of two binomials also a binomial?

In the previous lesson, you learned how to multiply two binomials using the FOIL method. You may have noticed that the *Outer* and *Inner* terms often combine to produce a trinomial product.

$$\begin{array}{cccc} & \text{F} & \text{O} & \text{I} & \text{L} \end{array}$$
$$(x + 5)(x - 3) = x^2 - 3x + 5x - 15$$
$$= x^2 + 2x - 15 \qquad \text{Combine like terms.}$$

This is not always the case, however. Examine the product below.

$$\begin{array}{cccc} & \text{F} & \text{O} & \text{I} & \text{L} \end{array}$$
$$(x + 3)(x - 3) = x^2 - 3x + 3x - 9$$
$$= x^2 + 0x - 9 \qquad \text{Combine like terms.}$$
$$= x^2 - 9 \qquad \text{Simplify.}$$

Notice that the product of $x + 3$ and $x - 3$ is a binomial.

SQUARES OF SUMS AND DIFFERENCES While you can always use the FOIL method to find the product of two binomials, some pairs of binomials have products that follow a specific pattern. One such pattern is the *square of a sum*, $(a + b)^2$ or $(a + b)(a + b)$. You can use the diagram below to derive the pattern for this special product.

$$(a + b)^2 \quad = \quad a^2 \quad + \quad ab \quad + \quad ab \quad + \quad b^2$$
$$= a^2 + 2ab + b^2$$

Key Concept   *Square of a Sum*

• **Words**   The square of $a + b$ is the square of a plus twice the product of a and b plus the square of b.

• **Symbols** $(a + b)^2 = (a + b)(a + b)$
$$= a^2 + 2ab + b^2$$

• **Example** $(x + 7)^2 = x^2 + 2(x)(7) + 7^2$
$$= x^2 + 14x + 49$$

Resource Manager

📁 Workbook and Reproducible Masters

Chapter 8 Resource Masters
• Study Guide and Intervention, pp. 497–498
• Skills Practice, p. 499
• Practice, p. 500
• Reading to Learn Mathematics, p. 501
• Enrichment, p. 502
• Assessment, p. 518

Parent and Student Study Guide
  Workbook, p. 66

📽 Transparencies

5-Minute Check Transparency 8-8
Answer Key Transparencies

💿 Technology

AlgePASS: Tutorial Plus, Lesson 23
Interactive Chalkboard

Example 1 Square of a Sum

Find each product.

a. $(4y + 5)^2$

$$(a + b)^2 = a^2 + 2ab + b^2 \qquad \text{Square of a Sum}$$
$$(4y + 5)^2 = (4y)^2 + 2(4y)(5) + 5^2 \qquad a = 4y \text{ and } b = 5$$
$$= 16y^2 + 40y + 25 \qquad \text{Simplify.}$$

CHECK Check your work by using the FOIL method.

$$(4y + 5)^2 = (4y + 5)(4y + 5)$$

$$ \quad \overset{F}{} \quad \overset{O}{} \quad \overset{I}{} \quad \overset{L}{}$$
$$= (4y)(4y) + (4y)(5) + 5(4y) + 5(5)$$
$$= 16y^2 + 20y + 20y + 25$$
$$= 16y^2 + 40y + 25 \checkmark$$

b. $(8c + 3d)^2$

$$(a + b)^2 = a^2 + 2ab + b^2 \qquad \text{Square of a Sum}$$
$$(8c + 3d)^2 = (8c)^2 + 2(8c)(3d) + (3d)^2 \qquad a = 8c \text{ and } b = 3d$$
$$= 64c^2 + 48cd + 9d^2 \qquad \text{Simplify.}$$

To find the pattern for the *square of a difference*, $(a - b)^2$, write $a - b$ as $a + (-b)$ and square it using the square of a sum pattern.

$$(a - b)^2 = [a + (-b)]^2$$
$$= a^2 + 2(a)(-b) + (-b)^2 \qquad \text{Square of a Sum}$$
$$= a^2 - 2ab + b^2 \qquad \text{Simplify. Note that } (-b)^2 = (-b)(-b) \text{ or } b^2.$$

The square of a difference can be found by using the following pattern.

Key Concept — Square of a Difference

- **Words** The square of $a - b$ is the square of a minus twice the product of a and b plus the square of b.

- **Symbols** $(a - b)^2 = (a - b)(a - b)$
  $$= a^2 - 2ab + b^2$$

- **Example** $(x - 4)^2 = x^2 - 2(x)(4) + 4^2$
  $$= x^2 - 8x + 16$$

Example 2 Square of a Difference

Find each product.

a. $(6p - 1)^2$

$$(a - b)^2 = a^2 - 2ab + b^2 \qquad \text{Square of a Difference}$$
$$(6p - 1)^2 = (6p)^2 - 2(6p)(1) + 1^2 \qquad a = 6p \text{ and } b = 1$$
$$= 36p^2 - 12p + 1 \qquad \text{Simplify.}$$

b. $(5m^3 - 2n)^2$

$$(a - b)^2 = a^2 - 2ab + b^2 \qquad \text{Square of a Difference}$$
$$(5m^3 - 2n)^2 = (5m^3)^2 - 2(5m^3)(2n) + (2n)^2 \qquad a = 5m^3 \text{ and } b = 2n$$
$$= 25m^6 - 20m^3n + 4n^2 \qquad \text{Simplify.}$$

 www.algebra1.com/extra_examples

SQUARES OF SUMS AND DIFFERENCES

In-Class Examples · Power Point®

Teaching Tip Remind students that when a or b are expressions with numbers and variables, they must square both the constant and variable parts of the term.

1 Find each product.

a. $(7z + 2)^2$ $49z^2 + 28z + 4$

b. $(5q + 9r)^2$ $25q^2 + 90qr + 81r^2$

2 Find each product.

a. $(3c - 4)^2$ $9c^2 - 24c + 16$

b. $(6e - 6f)^2$ $36e^2 - 72ef + 36f^2$

Tips for New Teachers

Intervention Since the square of a sum and a square of the difference are the same except for the sign of the middle term, the risk of making a careless mistake when finding the sum of a square or difference is high. Tell students that they must pay close attention to the signs when finding squares of sums or differences.

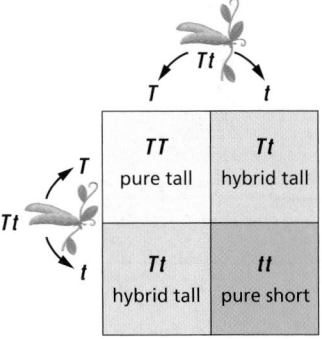

Career Choices

Geneticist

Laboratory geneticists work in medicine to find cures for disease, in agriculture to breed new crops and livestock, and in police work to identify criminals.

Online Research
For information about a career as a geneticist, visit: www.algebra1.com/careers

Example 3 Apply the Sum of a Square

GENETICS The Punnett square shows the possible gene combinations of a cross between two pea plants. Each plant passes along one *dominant* gene T for tallness and one *recessive* gene t for shortness.

Show how combinations can be modeled by the square of a binomial. Then determine what percent of the offspring will be pure tall, hybrid tall, and pure short.

Each parent has half the genes necessary for tallness and half the genes necessary for shortness. The makeup of each parent can be modeled by $0.5T + 0.5t$. Their offspring can be modeled by the product of $0.5T + 0.5t$ and $0.5T + 0.5t$ or $(0.5T + 0.5t)^2$.

If we expand this product, we can determine the possible heights of the offspring.

$(a + b)^2 = a^2 + 2ab + b^2$	Square of a Sum
$(0.5T + 0.5t)^2 = (0.5T)^2 + 2(0.5T)(0.5t) + (0.5t)^2$	$a = 0.5T$ and $b = 0.5t$
$= 0.25T^2 + 0.5Tt + 0.25t^2$	Simplify.
$= 0.25TT + 0.5Tt + 0.25tt$	$T^2 = TT$ and $t^2 = tt$

Thus, 25% of the offspring are TT or pure tall, 50% are Tt or hybrid tall, and 25% are tt or pure short.

PRODUCT OF A SUM AND A DIFFERENCE You can use the diagram below to find the pattern for the product of a sum and a difference of the *same two terms*, $(a + b)(a - b)$. Recall that $a - b$ can be rewritten as $a + (-b)$.

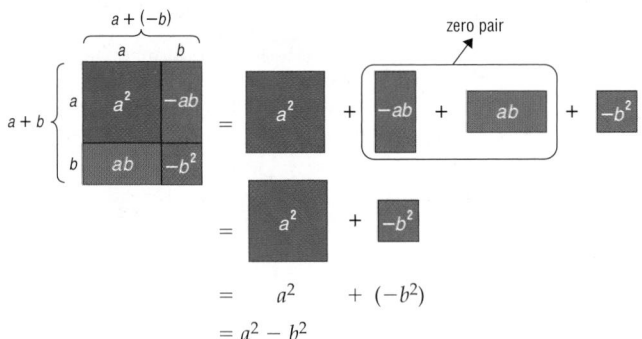

$$= a^2 + (-b^2)$$
$$= a^2 - b^2$$

The resulting product, $a^2 - b^2$, has a special name. It is called a **difference of squares**. Notice that this product has no middle term.

Key Concept   Product of a Sum and a Difference

- **Words** The product of $a + b$ and $a - b$ is the square of a minus the square of b.
- **Symbols** $(a + b)(a - b) = (a - b)(a + b)$
  $$= a^2 - b^2$$
- **Example** $(x + 9)(x - 9) = x^2 - 9^2$
  $$= x^2 - 81$$

460 Chapter 8 Polynomials

Example 4 *Product of a Sum and a Difference*

Find each product.

a. $(3n + 2)(3n - 2)$

$(a + b)(a - b) = a^2 - b^2$ Product of a Sum and a Difference

$(3n + 2)(3n - 2) = (3n)^2 - 2^2$ $a = 3n$ and $b = 2$

$= 9n^2 - 4$ Simplify.

b. $(11v - 8w^2)(11v + 8w^2)$

$(a - b)(a + b) = a^2 - b^2$ Product of a Sum and a Difference

$(11v - 8w^2)(11v + 8w^2) = (11v)^2 - (8w^2)^2$ $a = 11v$ and $b = 8w^2$

$= 121v^2 - 64w^4$ Simplify.

The following list summarizes the special products you have studied.

Key Concept   **Special Products**

- **Square of a Sum** $(a + b)^2 = a^2 + 2ab + b^2$
- **Square of a Difference** $(a - b)^2 = a^2 - 2ab + b^2$
- **Product of a Sum and a Difference** $(a - b)(a + b) = a^2 - b^2$

Check for Understanding

Concept Check
1–3. See margin.

1. **Compare and contrast** the pattern for the square of a sum with the pattern for the square of a difference.

2. **Explain** how the square of a difference and the difference of squares differ.

3. **Draw a diagram** to show how you would use algebra tiles to model the product of $x - 3$ and $x - 3$, or $(x - 3)^2$.

4. **OPEN ENDED** Write two binomials whose product is a difference of squares.
Sample answer: $x - 1$ and $x + 1$

Guided Practice

GUIDED PRACTICE KEY	
Exercises	Examples
5–10	1, 2, 4
11, 12	3

Find each product.

5. $(a + 6)^2$ $a^2 + 12a + 36$

6. $(4n - 3)(4n - 3)$ $16n^2 - 24n + 9$

7. $(8x - 5)(8x + 5)$ $64x^2 - 25$

8. $(3a + 7b)(3a - 7b)$ $9a^2 - 49b^2$

9. $(x^2 - 6y)^2$ $x^4 - 12x^2y + 36y^2$

10. $(9 - p)^2$ $81 - 18p + p^2$

Application

GENETICS For Exercises 11 and 12, use the following information.
In hamsters, golden coloring G is dominant over cinnamon coloring g. Suppose a purebred cinnamon male is mated with a purebred golden female.

Golden

Cinnamon

11. Write an expression for the genetic makeup of the hamster pups. **1.0Gg**

12. What is the probability that the pups will have cinnamon coloring? Explain your reasoning.
0%; All pups will be golden since only Gg combinations are possible.

Lesson 8-8   Special Products   **461**

Study Notebook

Have students—
- complete the definitions/examples for the remaining terms on their Vocabulary Builder worksheets for Chapter 8.
- include any other item(s) that they find helpful in mastering the skills in this lesson.

About the Exercises...
Organization by Objective
- **Squares of Sums and Differences:** 13–16, 19–22, 25–28, 31–32, 35–36, 39–46
- **Product of a Sum and a Difference:** 17–18, 23–24, 29–30, 33–34, 37–38, 47

Odd/Even Assignments
Exercises 13–38 are structured so that students practice the same concepts whether they are assigned odd or even problems.

Assignment Guide
Basic: 13–35 odd, 39–44, 48–50, 52–70
Average: 13–37 odd, 39–44, 47–50, 52–70 (optional: 51)
Advanced: 14–38 even, 45–70

Answers

1. The patterns are the same except for their middle terms. The middle terms have different signs.

2. The square of a difference is $(a - b)^2$, which equals $a^2 - 2ab + b^2$. The difference of squares is the product of $a - b$ and $a + b$ or $a^2 - b^2$.

3.

	$x - 3$			
x^2	$-x$	$-x$	$-x$
$-x$	1	1	1
$-x$	1	1	1
$-x$	1	1	1

★ indicates increased difficulty

Practice and Apply

14. $k^2 + 16k + 64$
15. $a^2 - 10a + 25$
16. $n^2 - 24n + 144$
19. $4g^2 + 20g + 25$
20. $81x^2 + 54x + 9$
21. $49 - 56y + 16y^2$
22. $16 - 48h + 36h^2$
23. $121r^2 - 64$
24. $144p^2 - 9$

Find each product. 25–38. See margin.

13. $(y + 4)^2$ $y^2 + 8y + 16$
14. $(k + 8)(k + 8)$
15. $(a - 5)(a - 5)$
16. $(n - 12)^2$
17. $(b + 7)(b - 7)$ $b^2 - 49$
18. $(c - 2)(c + 2)$ $c^2 - 4$
19. $(2g + 5)^2$
20. $(9x + 3)^2$
21. $(7 - 4y)^2$
22. $(4 - 6h)^2$
23. $(11r + 8)(11r - 8)$
24. $(12p - 3)(12p + 3)$
25. $(a + 5b)^2$
26. $(m + 7n)^2$
27. $(2x - 9y)^2$
28. $(3n - 10p)^2$
29. $(5w + 14)(5w - 14)$
30. $(4d - 13)(4d + 13)$
31. $(x^3 + 4y)^2$
32. $(3a^2 - b^2)^2$
33. $(8a^2 - 9b^3)(8a^2 + 9b^3)$
34. $(5x^4 - y)(5x^4 + y)$
35. $\left(\frac{2}{3}x - 6\right)^2$
36. $\left(\frac{4}{5}x + 10\right)^2$
★ 37. $(2n + 1)(2n - 1)(n + 5)$
★ 38. $(p + 3)(p - 4)(p - 3)(p + 4)$

GENETICS For Exercises 39 and 40, use the following information.
Pam has brown eyes and Bob has blue eyes. Brown genes B are dominant over blue genes b. A person with genes BB or Bb has brown eyes. Someone with genes bb has blue eyes. Suppose Pam's genes for eye color are Bb.   **39. $0.5Bb + 0.5bb$**

39. Write an expression for the possible eye coloring of Pam and Bob's children.

40. What is the probability that a child of Pam and Bob would have blue eyes? $\frac{1}{2}$

MAGIC TRICK For Exercises 41–44, use the following information.
Julie says that she can perform a magic trick with numbers. She asks you to pick a whole number, any whole number. Square that number. Then, add twice your original number. Next add 1. Take the square root of the result. Finally, subtract your original number. Then Julie exclaims with authority, "Your answer is 1!"

41. Sample answer: 2; yes

43. $(a + 1)^2$

41. Pick a whole number and follow Julie's directions. Is your result 1?

42. Let a represent the whole number you chose. Then, find a polynomial representation for the first three steps of Julie's directions. $a^2 + 2a + 1$

43. The polynomial you wrote in Exercise 42 is the square of what binomial sum?

44. Take the square root of the perfect square you wrote in Exercise 43, then subtract a, your original number. What is the result? **1**

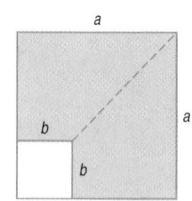
••**ARCHITECTURE** For Exercises 45 and 46, use the following information.
A diagram of a portion of the Gwennap Pit is shown at the right. Suppose the radius of the stage is s meters. **45. $s + 2, s + 3$**

★ 45. Use the information at the left to find binomial representations for the radii of the second and third seating levels.

★ 46. Find the area of the shaded region representing the third seating level. **about $(6.3s + 15.7)$ m²**

★ 47. **GEOMETRY** The area of the shaded region models the difference of two squares, $a^2 - b^2$. Show that the area of the shaded region is also equal to $(a - b)(a + b)$. (*Hint*: Divide the shaded region into two trapezoids as shown.) **See pp. 471A–471B.**

48. WRITING IN MATH Answer the question that was posed at the beginning of the lesson. **See margin.**

When is the product of two binomials also a binomial?

Include the following in your answer:
- an example of two binomials whose product is a binomial, and
- an example of two binomials whose product is not a binomial.

Standardized Test Practice
Ⓐ Ⓑ Ⓒ Ⓓ

49. If $a^2 + b^2 = 40$ and $ab = 12$, find the value of $(a - b)^2$. **C**
　Ⓐ 1　　　　Ⓑ 121　　　　Ⓒ 16　　　　Ⓓ 28

50. If $x - y = 10$ and $x + y = 20$, find the value of $x^2 - y^2$. **B**
　Ⓐ 400　　　Ⓑ 200　　　Ⓒ 100　　　Ⓓ 30

Extending the Lesson
51. Does a pattern exist for the cube of a sum, $(a + b)^3$? **a.** $a^3 + 3a^2b + 3ab^2 + b^3$
　a. Investigate this question by finding the product of $(a + b)(a + b)(a + b)$.
　b. Use the pattern you discovered in part **a** to find $(x + 2)^3$. $x^3 + 6x^2 + 12x + 8$
　c. Draw a diagram of a geometric model for the cube of a sum. **See margin.**

Maintain Your Skills

Mixed Review **Find each product.** *(Lesson 8-7)*

52. $x^2 + 9x + 14$
53. $c^2 - 6c - 27$
54. $20y^2 - 29y + 6$

52. $(x + 2)(x + 7)$　　　**53.** $(c - 9)(c + 3)$　　　**54.** $(4y - 1)(5y - 6)$

55. $(3n - 5)(8n + 5)$　　**56.** $(x - 2)(3x^2 - 5x + 4)$　　**57.** $(2k + 5)(2k^2 - 8k + 7)$
$24n^2 - 25n - 25$　　　　$3x^3 - 11x^2 + 14x - 8$　　$4k^3 - 6k^2 - 26k + 35$

Solve. *(Lesson 8-6)*

58. $6(x + 2) + 4 = 5(3x - 4)$ **4**　　　　**59.** $-3(3a - 8) + 2a = 4(2a + 1)$ $\frac{4}{3}$
60. $p(p + 2) + 3p = p(p - 3)$ **0**　　　　**61.** $y(y - 4) + 2y = y(y + 12) - 7$ $\frac{1}{2}$

Use elimination to solve each system of equations. *(Lessons 7-3 and 7-4)*

62. $\frac{3}{4}x + \frac{1}{5}y = 5$ **(0, 25)**　　**63.** $2x - y = 10$ **(3, −4)**　　**64.** $2x = 4 - 3y$ **(5, −2)**
　　$\frac{3}{4}x - \frac{1}{5}y = -5$　　　　　　$5x + 3y = 3$　　　　　　　$3y - x = -11$

Write the slope-intercept form of an equation that passes through the given point and is perpendicular to the graph of each equation. *(Lesson 5-6)*

65. $5x + 5y = 35, (-3, 2)$　　**66.** $2x - 5y = 3, (-2, 7)$　　**67.** $5x + y = 2, (0, 6)$
　$y = x + 5$　　　　　　　　$y = -2.5x + 2$　　　　　　　　$y = \frac{1}{5}x + 6$

Find the nth term of each arithmetic sequence described. *(Lesson 4-7)*

68. $a_1 = 3, d = 4, n = 18$ **71**　　　　**69.** $-5, 1, 7, 13, \ldots$ for $n = 12$ **61**

70. PHYSICAL FITNESS Mitchell likes to exercise regularly. He likes to warm up by walking two miles. Then he runs five miles. Finally, he cools down by walking for another mile. Identify the graph that best represents Mitchell's heart rate as a function of time. *(Lesson 1-8)* **b**

a. 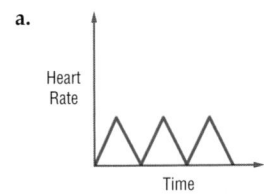　　**b.** 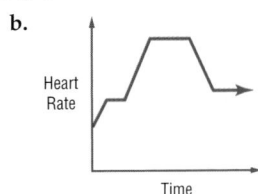　　**c.**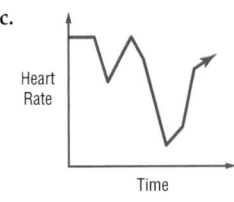

Open-Ended Assessment

Writing Have students write a short explanation of why knowing the special products that they learned in this lesson could be important.

Assessment Options

Quiz (Lessons 8-7 and 8-8) is available on p. 518 of the *Chapter 8 Resource Masters*.

Answers

25. $a^2 + 10ab + 25b^2$

26. $m^2 + 14mn + 49n^2$

27. $4x^2 - 36xy + 81y^2$

28. $9n^2 - 60np + 100p^2$

29. $25w^2 - 196$

30. $16d^2 - 169$

31. $x^6 + 8x^3y + 16y^2$

32. $9a^4 - 6a^2b^2 + b^4$

33. $64a^4 - 81b^6$

34. $25x^8 - y^2$

35. $\frac{4}{9}x^2 - 8x + 36$

36. $\frac{16}{25}x^2 + 16x + 100$

37. $4n^3 + 20n^2 - n - 5$

38. $p^4 - 25p^2 + 144$

48. The product of two binomials is also a binomial when the two binomials are the sum and the difference of the same two terms. Answers should include the following.
- Sample answer: $(2x - 13)(2x + 13)$
- Sample answer: $(10x + 11)(10x + 11)$

51c. $(a + b)^3$

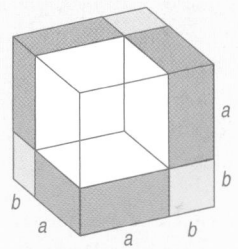

Vocabulary and Concept Check

binomial (p. 432)	monomial (p. 410)	Product of Powers (p. 411)
constant (p. 410)	negative exponent (p. 419)	Quotient of Powers (p. 417)
degree of a monomial (p. 433)	polynomial (p. 432)	scientific notation (p. 425)
degree of a polynomial (p. 433)	Power of a Power (p. 411)	trinomial (p. 432)
difference of squares (p. 460)	Power of a Product (p. 412)	zero exponent (p. 419)
FOIL method (p. 453)	Power of a Quotient (p. 418)	

Choose a term from the vocabulary list that best matches each example.

1. $4^{-3} = \frac{1}{4^3}$ **negative exponent**

2. $(n^3)^5 = n^{15}$ **Power of a Power**

3. $\frac{4x^2y}{8xy^3} = \frac{x}{2y^2}$ **Quotient of Powers**

4. $4x^2$ **monomial**

5. $x^2 - 3x + 1$ **trinomial**

6. $2^0 = 1$ **zero exponent**

7. $x^4 - 3x^3 + 2x^2 - 1$ **polynomial**

8. $(x + 3)(x - 4) = x^2 - 4x + 3x - 12$ **FOIL method**

9. $x^2 + 2$ **binomial**

10. $(a^3b)(2ab^2) = 2a^4b^3$ **Product of Powers**

Lesson-by-Lesson Review

8-1 Multiplying Monomials

See pages 410–415.

Concept Summary

- A monomial is a number, a variable, or a product of a number and one or more variables.
- To multiply two powers that have the same base, add exponents.
- To find the power of a power, multiply exponents.
- The power of a product is the product of the powers.

Examples

$6x^2$, -5, $\frac{2c}{3}$

$a^2 \cdot a^3 = a^5$

$(a^2)^3 = a^6$

$(ab^2)^3 = a^3b^6$

Examples 1 Simplify $(2ab^2)(3a^2b^3)$.

$(2ab^2)(3a^2b^3) = (2 \cdot 3)(a \cdot a^2)(b^2 \cdot b^3)$ Commutative Property

$= 6a^3b^5$ Product of Powers

2 Simplify $(2x^2y^3)^3$.

$(2x^2y^3)^3 = 2^3(x^2)^3(y^3)^3$ Power of a Product

$= 8x^6y^9$ Power of a Power

Exercises **Simplify.** *See Examples 2, 3, and 5 on pages 411 and 412.*

11. $y^3 \cdot y^3 \cdot y$ y^7 12. $(3ab)(-4a^2b^3)$ $-12a^3b^4$ 13. $(-4a^2x)(-5a^3x^4)$ $20a^5x^5$

14. $(4a^2b)^3$ $64a^6b^3$ 15. $(-3xy)^2(4x)^3$ $576x^5y^2$ 16. $(-2c^2d)^4(-3c^2)^3$ $-432c^{14}d^4$

17. $-\frac{1}{2}(m^2n^4)^2$ $-\frac{1}{2}m^4n^8$ 18. $(5a^2)^3 + 7(a^6)$ $132a^6$ 19. $[(3^2)^2]^3$ $531,441$

 www.algebra1.com/vocabulary_review

---

Vocabulary and Concept Check

- This alphabetical list of vocabulary terms in Chapter 8 includes a page reference where each term was introduced.
- **Assessment** A vocabulary test/review for Chapter 8 is available on p. 516 of the *Chapter 8 Resource Masters*.

Lesson-by-Lesson Review

For each lesson,
- the main ideas are summarized,
- additional examples review concepts, and
- practice exercises are provided.

Vocabulary PuzzleMaker

ELL The Vocabulary PuzzleMaker software improves students' mathematics vocabulary using four puzzle formats— crossword, scramble, word search using a word list, and word search using clues. Students can work on a computer screen or from a printed handout.

MindJogger Videoquizzes

ELL MindJogger Videoquizzes provide an alternative review of concepts presented in this chapter. Students work in teams in a game show format to gain points for correct answers. The questions are presented in three rounds.

Round 1 Concepts (5 questions)
Round 2 Skills (4 questions)
Round 3 Problem Solving (4 questions)

Study Organizer

For more information about Foldables, see *Teaching Mathematics with Foldables*.

Have students look through the chapter to make sure they have included examples in their Foldables for each type of polynomial and monomial operation they learned.

Encourage students to refer to their Foldables while completing the Study Guide and Review and to use them in preparing for the Chapter Test.

8-2 Dividing Monomials

See pages 417–423.

Concept Summary

- To divide two powers that have the same base, subtract the exponents.
- To find the power of a quotient, find the power of the numerator and the power of the denominator.
- Any nonzero number raised to the zero power is 1.
- For any nonzero number a and any integer n,
$$a^{-n} = \frac{1}{a^n} \text{ and } \frac{1}{a^{-n}} = a^n.$$

Examples

$\frac{a^5}{a^3} = a^2$

$\left(\frac{a}{b}\right)^2 = \frac{a^2}{b^2}$

$(3a^3b^2)^0 = 1$

$a^{-3} = \frac{1}{a^3}$

Example Simplify $\frac{2x^6y}{8x^2y^2}$. **Assume that x and y are not equal to zero.**

$\frac{2x^6y}{8x^2y^2} = \left(\frac{2}{8}\right)\left(\frac{x^6}{x^2}\right)\left(\frac{y}{y^2}\right)$ Group the powers with the same base.

$= \left(\frac{1}{4}\right)(x^{6-2})(y^{1-2})$ Quotient of Powers

$= \frac{x^4}{4y}$ Simplify.

Exercises Simplify. **Assume that no denominator is equal to zero.**
See Examples 1–4 on pages 417–420.

20. $\frac{(3y)^0}{6a}$ $\frac{1}{6a}$

21. $\left(\frac{3bc^2}{4d}\right)^3$ $\frac{27b^3c^6}{64d^3}$

22. $x^{-2}y^0z^3 \cdot \frac{z^3}{x^2}$

23. $\frac{27b^{-2}}{14b^{-3}}$ $\frac{27b}{14}$

24. $\frac{(3a^3bc^2)^2}{18a^2b^3c^4}$ $\frac{a^4}{2b}$

25. $\frac{-16a^3b^2x^4y}{-48a^4bxy^3}$ $\frac{bx^3}{3ay^2}$

26. $\frac{(-a)^5b^8}{a^5b^2}$ $-b^6$

27. $\frac{(4a^{-1})^{-2}}{(2a^4)^2}$ $\frac{1}{64a^6}$

28. $\left(\frac{5xy^{-2}}{35x^{-2}y^{-6}}\right)^0$ 1

8-3 Scientific Notation

See pages 425–430.

Concept Summary

- A number is expressed in scientific notation when it is written as a product of a factor and a power of 10. The factor must be greater than or equal to 1 and less than 10.

$$a \times 10^n, \text{ where } 1 \le a < 10 \text{ and } n \text{ is an integer.}$$

Examples   **1**   **Express 5.2×10^7 in standard notation.**

$5.2 \times 10^7 = 52,000,000$ $n = 7$; move decimal point 7 places to the right.

2   **Express 0.0021 in scientific notation.**

$0.0021 \rightarrow 0002.1 \times 10^n$ Move decimal point 3 places to the right.

$0.0021 = 2.1 \times 10^{-3}$ $a = 2.1$ and $n = -3$

3 Evaluate $(2 \times 10^2)(5.2 \times 10^6)$. Express the result in scientific and standard notation.

$$
\begin{aligned}
(2 \times 10^2)(5.2 \times 10^6) &= (2 \times 5.2)(10^2 \times 10^6) && \text{Associative Property} \\
&= 10.4 \times 10^8 && \text{Product of Powers} \\
&= (1.04 \times 10^1) \times 10^8 && 10.4 = 1.04 \times 10^1 \\
&= 1.04 \times (10^1 \times 10^8) && \text{Associative Property} \\
&= 1.04 \times 10^9 \text{ or } 1{,}040{,}000{,}000 && \text{Product of Powers}
\end{aligned}
$$

Exercises Express each number in standard notation. *See Example 1 on page 426.*

29. 2.4×10^5 **240,000**   **30.** 3.14×10^{-4} **0.000314**   **31.** 4.88×10^9 **4,880,000,000**

Express each number in scientific notation. *See Example 2 on page 426.*

32. 0.00000187
1.87×10^{-6}

33. 796×10^3
7.96×10^5

34. 0.0343×10^{-2}
3.43×10^{-4}

Evaluate. Express each result in scientific and standard notation.
See Examples 3 and 4 on page 427.

35. $(2 \times 10^5)(3 \times 10^6)$
6×10^{11};
600,000,000,000

36. $\dfrac{8.4 \times 10^{-6}}{1.4 \times 10^{-9}}$
6×10^3; 6000

37. $(3 \times 10^2)(5.6 \times 10^{-8})$
1.68×10^{-5};
0.0000168

8-4 Polynomials

See pages
432–436.

Concept Summary

- A polynomial is a monomial or a sum of monomials.
- A binomial is the sum of *two* monomials, and a trinomial is the sum of *three* monomials.
- The degree of a monomial is the sum of the exponents of all its variables.
- The degree of the polynomial is the greatest degree of any term. To find the degree of a polynomial, you must find the degree of each term.

Examples

1 Find the degree of $2xy^3 + x^2y$.

Polynomial	Terms	Degree of Each Term	Degree of Polynomial
$2xy^3 + x^2y$	$2xy^3, x^2y$	4, 3	4

2 Arrange the terms of $4x^2 + 9x^3 - 2 - x$ so that the powers of x are in descending order.

$$
\begin{aligned}
4x^2 + 9x^3 - 2 - x &= 4x^2 + 9x^3 - 2x^0 - x^1 && x^0 = 1 \text{ and } x = x^1 \\
&= 9x^3 + 4x^2 - x - 2 && 3 > 2 > 1 > 0
\end{aligned}
$$

Exercises Find the degree of each polynomial. *See Example 3 on page 433.*

38. $n - 2p^2$ **2**   **39.** $29n^2 + 17n^2t^2$ **4**   **40.** $4xy + 9x^3z^2 + 17rs^3$ **5**

41. $-6x^5y - 2y^4 + 4 - 8y^2$ **6**   **42.** $3ab^3 - 5a^2b^2 + 4ab$ **4**   **43.** $19m^3n^4 + 21m^5n$ **7**

Arrange the terms of each polynomial so that the powers of x are in descending order. *See Example 5 on page 433.*

45. $-4x^4 + 5x^3y^2 - 2x^2y^3 + xy - 27$

44. $3x^4 - x + x^2 - 5$ $3x^4 + x^2 - x - 5$ **45.** $-2x^2y^3 - 27 - 4x^4 + xy + 5x^3y^2$

8-5 Adding and Subtracting Polynomials

See pages 439–443.

Concept Summary

- To add polynomials, group like terms horizontally or write them in column form, aligning like terms vertically.
- Subtract a polynomial by adding its additive inverse. To find the additive inverse of a polynomial, replace each term with its additive inverse.

Example   Find $(7r^2 + 9r) - (12r^2 - 4)$.

$$\begin{aligned}
(7r^2 + 9r) - (12r^2 - 4) &= 7r^2 + 9r + (-12r^2 + 4) && \text{The additive inverse of } 12r^2 - 4 \text{ is } -12r^2 + 4.\\
&= (7r^2 - 12r^2) + 9r + 4 && \text{Group like terms.}\\
&= -5r^2 + 9r + 4 && \text{Add like terms.}
\end{aligned}$$

Exercises   Find each sum or difference.   *See Examples 1 and 2 on pages 439 and 440.*

46. $(2x^2 - 5x + 7) - (3x^3 + x^2 + 2)$ 47. $(x^2 - 6xy + 7y^2) + (3x^2 + xy - y^2)$

48. $(7z^2 + 4) - (3z^2 + 2z - 6)$ 49. $(13m^4 - 7m - 10) + (8m^4 - 3m + 9)$

50. $(11m^2n^2 + 4mn - 6) + (5m^2n^2 + 6mn + 17)$ **$16m^2n^2 + 10mn + 11$**

51. $(-5p^2 + 3p + 49) - (2p^2 + 5p + 24)$ **$-7p^2 - 2p + 25$**

46. $-3x^3 + x^2 - 5x + 5$ 47. $4x^2 - 5xy + 6y^2$ 48. $4z^2 - 2z + 10$ 49. $21m^4 - 10m - 1$

8-6 Multiplying a Polynomial by a Monomial

See pages 444–449.

Concept Summary

- The Distributive Property can be used to multiply a polynomial by a monomial.

Examples   **1   Simplify $x^2(x + 2) + 3(x^3 + 4x^2)$.**

$$\begin{aligned}
x^2(x + 2) + 3(x^3 + 4x^2) &= x^2(x) + x^2(2) + 3(x^3) + 3(4x^2) && \text{Distributive Property}\\
&= x^3 + 2x^2 + 3x^3 + 12x^2 && \text{Multiply.}\\
&= 4x^3 + 14x^2 && \text{Combine like terms.}
\end{aligned}$$

2   Solve $x(x - 10) + x(x + 2) + 3 = 2x(x + 1) - 7$.

$$\begin{aligned}
x(x - 10) + x(x + 2) + 3 &= 2x(x + 1) - 7 && \text{Original equation}\\
x^2 - 10x + x^2 + 2x + 3 &= 2x^2 + 2x - 7 && \text{Distributive Property}\\
2x^2 - 8x + 3 &= 2x^2 + 2x - 7 && \text{Combine like terms.}\\
-8x + 3 &= 2x - 7 && \text{Subtract } 2x^2 \text{ from each side.}\\
-10x + 3 &= -7 && \text{Subtract } 2x \text{ from each side.}\\
-10x &= -10 && \text{Subtract 3 from each side.}\\
x &= 1 && \text{Divide each side by } -10.
\end{aligned}$$

Exercises   Simplify.   *See Example 2 on page 444.* 53. **$10x^2 - 19x + 63$**

52. $b(4b - 1) + 10b$ **$4b^2 + 9b$**   53. $x(3x - 5) + 7(x^2 - 2x + 9)$

54. $8y(11y^2 - 2y + 13) - 9(3y^3 - 7y + 2)$ 55. $2x(x - y^2 + 5) - 5y^2(3x - 2)$

  $61y^3 - 16y^2 + 167y - 18$ **$2x^2 - 17xy^2 + 10x + 10y^2$**

Solve each equation.   *See Example 4 on page 445.*

56. $m(2m - 5) + m = 2m(m - 6) + 16$ **2** 57. $2(3w + w^2) - 6 = 2w(w - 4) + 10$ **$1\frac{1}{7}$**

Study Guide and Review

Chapter 8 | **For More ...**

• Extra Practice, see pages 837–839.
• Mixed Problem Solving, see page 860.

8-7 Multiplying Polynomials

See pages 452–457.

Concept Summary

• The FOIL method is the sum of the products of the first terms F, the outer terms O, the inner terms I, and the last terms L.
• The Distributive Property can be used to multiply any two polynomials.

Examples

1 Find $(3x + 2)(x - 2)$.

$$(3x + 2)(x - 2) = (3x)(x) + (3x)(-2) + (2)(x) + (2)(-2)$$ FOIL Method
$$= 3x^2 - 6x + 2x - 4$$ Multiply.
$$= 3x^2 - 4x - 4$$ Combine like terms.

2 Find $(2y - 5)(4y^2 + 3y - 7)$.

$(2y - 5)(4y^2 + 3y - 7)$
$= 2y(4y^2 + 3y - 7) - 5(4y^2 + 3y - 7)$ Distributive Property
$= 8y^3 + 6y^2 - 14y - 20y^2 - 15y + 35$ Distributive Property
$= 8y^3 - 14y^2 - 29y + 35$ Combine like terms.

58. $r^2 + 4r - 21$ 59. $4a^2 + 13a - 12$ 60. $18x^2 - 0.125$

Exercises Find each product.   *See Examples 1, 2, and 4 on pages 452–454.*

58. $(r - 3)(r + 7)$ 59. $(4a - 3)(a + 4)$ 60. $(3x + 0.25)(6x - 0.5)$
61. $(5r - 7s)(4r + 3s)$ 62. $(2k + 1)(k^2 + 7k - 9)$ 63. $(4p - 3)(3p^2 - p + 2)$

$20r^2 - 13rs - 21s^2$ $2k^3 + 15k^2 - 11k - 9$ $12p^3 - 13p^2 + 11p - 6$

8-8 Special Products

See pages 458–463.

Concept Summary

• Square of a Sum: $(a + b)^2 = a^2 + 2ab + b^2$
• Square of a Difference: $(a - b)^2 = a^2 - 2ab + b^2$
• Product of a Sum and a Difference: $(a + b)(a - b) = (a - b)(a + b) = a^2 - b^2$

Examples

1 Find $(r - 5)^2$.

$(a - b)^2 = a^2 - 2ab + b^2$ Square of a Difference
$(r - 5)^2 = r^2 - 2(r)(5) + 5^2$ $a = r$ and $b = 5$
$= r^2 - 10r + 25$ Simplify.

2 Find $(2c + 9)(2c - 9)$.

$(a + b)(a - b) = a^2 - b^2$ Product of a Sum and a Difference
$(2c + 9)(2c - 9) = (2c)^2 - 9^2$ $a = 2c$ and $b = 9$
$= 4c^2 - 81$ Simplify.

65. $16x^2 + 56x + 49$ 66. $64x^2 - 80x + 25$

Exercises Find each product.   *See Examples 1, 2, and 4 on pages 459 and 461.*

64. $(x - 6)(x + 6)$ $x^2 - 36$ 65. $(4x + 7)^2$ 66. $(8x - 5)^2$
67. $(5x - 3y)(5x + 3y)$ 68. $(6a - 5b)^2$ 69. $(3m + 4n)^2$

$25x^2 - 9y^2$ $36a^2 - 60ab + 25b^2$ $9m^2 + 24mn + 16n^2$

Vocabulary and Concepts

1. **Explain** why $(4^2)(4^3) \neq 16^5$. $(4^2)(4^3) = (4 \cdot 4)(4 \cdot 4 \cdot 4) = 4 \cdot 4 \cdot 4 \cdot 4 \cdot 4$ or 4^5 and $16^5 \neq 4^5$.
2. **Write** $\frac{1}{5}$ using a negative exponent. 5^{-1}
3. **Define and give an example** of a monomial. **Sample answer: A monomial is a number, variable, or product of numbers and variables; $6x^2$.**

Skills and Applications

Simplify. Assume that no denominator is equal to zero. 5. $-48a^3b^5c$

4. $(a^2b^4)(a^3b^5)$ a^5b^9
5. $(-12abc)(4a^2b^4)$
6. $\left(\frac{3}{5}m\right)^2$ $\frac{9}{25}m^2$
7. $(-3a)^4(a^5b)^2$ $81a^{14}b^2$

8. $(-5a^2)(-6b^3)^2$ $-180a^2b^6$
9. $\frac{mn^4}{m^3n^2}$ $\frac{n^2}{m^2}$
10. $\frac{9a^2bc^2}{63a^4bc}$ $\frac{c}{7a^2}$
11. $\frac{48a^2bc^5}{(3ab^3c^2)^2}$ $\frac{16c}{3b^5}$

Express each number in scientific notation.

12. 46,300 4.63×10^4
13. 0.003892 3.892×10^{-3}
14. 284×10^3 2.84×10^5
15. 52.8×10^{-9} 5.28×10^{-8}

Evaluate. Express each result in scientific notation and standard notation.

16. $(3 \times 10^3)(2 \times 10^4)$ 6×10^7; 60,000,000
17. $\frac{14.72 \times 10^{-4}}{3.2 \times 10^{-3}}$ 4.6×10^{-1}; 0.46
18. $(15 \times 10^{-7})(3.1 \times 10^4)$ 4.65×10^{-2}; 0.0465

19. **SPACE EXPLORATION** A space probe that is 2.85×10^9 miles away from Earth sends radio signals to NASA. If the radio signals travel at the speed of light (1.86×10^5 miles per second), how long will it take the signals to reach NASA? **about 1.53×10^4 s or 4.25 h**

Find the degree of each polynomial. Then arrange the terms so that the powers of y are in descending order.

20. $2y^2 + 8y^4 + 9y$ $4; 8y^4 + 2y^2 + 9y$
21. $5xy - 7 + 2y^4 - x^2y^3$ $5; 2y^4 - x^2y^3 + 5xy - 7$

Find each sum or difference.

22. $(5a + 3a^2 - 7a^3) + (2a - 8a^2 + 4)$ $7a - 5a^2 - 7a^3 + 4$
23. $(x^3 - 3x^2y + 4xy^2 + y^3) - (7x^3 + x^2y - 9xy^2 + y^3)$ $-6x^3 - 4x^2y + 13xy^2$

24. **GEOMETRY** The measures of two sides of a triangle are given. If the perimeter is represented by $11x^2 - 29x + 10$, find the measure of the third side. $5x^2 - 23x - 23$

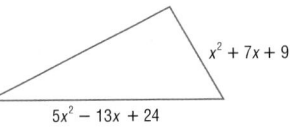

$x^2 + 7x + 9$

$5x^2 - 13x + 24$

Simplify.

25. $(h - 5)^2$ $h^2 - 10h + 25$
26. $(4x - y)(4x + y)$ $16x^2 - y^2$
27. $3x^2y^3(2x - xy^2)$ $6x^3y^3 - 3x^3y^5$
28. $(2a^2b + b^2)^2$ $4a^4b^2 + 4a^2b^3 + b^4$
29. $(4m + 3n)(2m - 5n)$ $8m^2 - 14mn - 15n^2$
30. $(2c + 5)(3c^2 - 4c + 2)$ $6c^3 + 7c^2 - 16c + 10$

Solve each equation.

31. $2x(x - 3) = 2(x^2 - 7) + 2$ 2
32. $3a(a^2 + 5) - 11 = a(3a^2 + 4)$ 1

33. **STANDARDIZED TEST PRACTICE** If $x^2 + 2xy + y^2 = 8$, find $3(x + y)^2$. **C**

   Ⓐ 2   Ⓑ 4
   Ⓒ 24   Ⓓ cannot be determined

 www.algebra1.com/chapter_test

Chapter 8 Practice Test **469**

Assessment Options

Vocabulary Test A vocabulary test/review for Chapter 8 can be found on p. 516 of the *Chapter 8 Resource Masters*.

Chapter Tests There are six Chapter 8 Tests and an Open-Ended Assessment task available in the *Chapter 8 Resource Masters*.

Chapter 8 Tests			
Form	Type	Level	Pages
1	MC	basic	503–504
2A	MC	average	505–506
2B	MC	average	507–508
2C	FR	average	509–510
2D	FR	average	511–512
3	FR	advanced	513–514

MC = multiple-choice questions
FR = free-response questions

Open-Ended Assessment Performance tasks for Chapter 8 can be found on p. 515 of the *Chapter 8 Resource Masters*. A sample scoring rubric for these tasks appears on p. A31.

 ExamView® Pro

Use the networkable **ExamView® Pro** to:

- Create **multiple versions** of tests.
- Create **modified** tests for *Inclusion* students.
- **Edit** existing questions and **add** your own questions.
- Use built-in **state curriculum correlations** to create tests aligned with state standards.
- Change **English** tests to **Spanish** and vice versa.

Portfolio Suggestion

Introduction Error analysis shows common mistakes that happen when performing an operation. An example of a error when multiplying like bases is $4^3 \cdot 4^4 = 16^7$. Actually, $4^3 \cdot 4^4 = 4^7$. The error occurred by multiplying the bases while adding the exponents. The base should stay the same while adding the exponents.

Ask Students From the material in this chapter, find a problem that occurs often and write an error analysis for it. Describe the situation, give the correct method for that example, and write a paragraph about it. Place this in your portfolio.

These two pages contain practice questions in the various formats that can be found on the most frequently given standardized tests.

A practice answer sheet for these two pages can be found on p. A1 of the *Chapter 8 Resource Masters*.

Standardized Test Practice
Student Recording Sheet, p. A1

Part 1 *Multiple Choice*

Select the best answer from the choices given and fill in the corresponding oval.

1 Ⓐ Ⓑ Ⓒ Ⓓ   4 Ⓐ Ⓑ Ⓒ Ⓓ   7 Ⓐ Ⓑ Ⓒ Ⓓ   9 Ⓐ Ⓑ Ⓒ Ⓓ
2 Ⓐ Ⓑ Ⓒ Ⓓ   5 Ⓐ Ⓑ Ⓒ Ⓓ   8 Ⓐ Ⓑ Ⓒ Ⓓ   10 Ⓐ Ⓑ Ⓒ Ⓓ
3 Ⓐ Ⓑ Ⓒ Ⓓ   6 Ⓐ Ⓑ Ⓒ Ⓓ

Part 2 *Short Response/Grid In*

Solve the problem and write your answer in the blank.
For Questions 11 and 13, also enter your answer by writing each number or symbol in a box. Then fill in the corresponding oval for that number or symbol.

11 _____ (grid in)   11   13
12 _____
13 _____ (grid in)
14 _____
15 _____
16 _____
17 _____
18 _____
19 _____
20 _____

Part 3 *Extended Response*

Record your answers for Questions 21–23 on the back of this paper.

Additional Practice

See pp. 521–522 in the *Chapter 8 Resource Masters* for additional standardized test practice.

Teaching Tip Urge students to check their answer to Question 7 by substituting it back into the original question.

Part 1 | Multiple Choice

Record your answers on the answer sheet provided by your teacher or on a sheet of paper.

1. A basketball team scored the following points during the first five games of the season: 70, 65, 75, 70, 80. During the sixth game, they scored only 30 points. Which of these measures changed the most as a result of the sixth game? (Lessons 2-2 and 2-5) **A**

   Ⓐ mean

   Ⓑ median

   Ⓒ mode

   Ⓓ They all changed the same amount.

2. A machine produces metal bottle caps. The number of caps it produces is proportional to the number of minutes the machine operates. The machine produces 2100 caps in 60 minutes. How many minutes would it take the machine to produce 5600 caps? (Lesson 2-6) **D**

   Ⓐ 35   Ⓑ 58.3   Ⓒ 93.3   Ⓓ 160

3. The odometer on Juliana's car read 20,542 miles when she started a trip. After 4 hours of driving, the odometer read 20,750 miles. Which equation can be used to find r, her average rate of speed for the 4 hours? (Lesson 3-1) **D**

   Ⓐ $r = 20{,}750 - 20{,}542$

   Ⓑ $r = 4(20{,}750 - 20{,}542)$

   Ⓒ $r = \dfrac{20{,}750}{4}$

   Ⓓ $r = \dfrac{20{,}750 - 20{,}542}{4}$

4. Which equation best describes the graph? (Lesson 5-4) **A**

   Ⓐ $y = -\dfrac{1}{5}x + 1$

   Ⓑ $y = -5x + 1$

   Ⓒ $y = \dfrac{1}{5}x + 5$

   Ⓓ $y = -5x - 5$

470 **Chapter 8** Polynomials

5. Which equation represents the line that passes through the point at $(-1, 4)$ and has a slope of -2? (Lesson 5-5) **B**

   Ⓐ $y = -2x - 2$ Ⓑ $y = -2x + 2$
   Ⓒ $y = -2x + 6$ Ⓓ $y = -2x + 7$

6. Mr. Puram is planning an addition to the school library. The budget is $7500. Each bookcase costs $125, and each set of table and chairs costs $550. If he buys 4 sets of tables and chairs, which inequality shows the number of bookcases b he can buy? (Lesson 6-6) **A**

   Ⓐ $4(550) + 125b \leq 7500$

   Ⓑ $125b \leq 7500$

   Ⓒ $4(550 + 125)b \leq 7500$

   Ⓓ $4(125) + 550b \leq 7500$

7. Sophia and Allie went shopping and spent $122 altogether. Sophia spent $25 less than twice as much as Allie. How much did Allie spend? (Lesson 7-2) **B**

   Ⓐ $39   Ⓑ $49   Ⓒ $53   Ⓓ $73

8. The product of $2x^3$ and $4x^4$ is (Lesson 8-1) **D**

   Ⓐ $8x^{12}$.   Ⓑ $6x^{12}$.   Ⓒ $6x^7$.   Ⓓ $8x^7$.

9. If 0.00037 is expressed as 3.7×10^n, what is the value of n? (Lesson 8-3) **B**

   Ⓐ -5 Ⓑ -4 Ⓒ 4   Ⓓ 5

10. When $x^2 - 2x + 1$ is subtracted from $3x^2 - 4x + 5$, the result will be (Lesson 8-5) **A**

    Ⓐ $2x^2 - 2x + 4$.   Ⓑ $2x^2 - 6x + 4$.
    Ⓒ $3x^2 - 6x + 6$.   Ⓓ $4x^2 - 6x + 6$.

Test-Taking Tip   Ⓐ Ⓑ Ⓒ Ⓓ

Question 5
When you write an equation, check that the given values make a true statement. For example, in Question 5, substitute the values of the coordinates $(-1, 4)$ into your equation to check.

 ExamView® Pro

Special banks of standardized test questions similar to those on the SAT, ACT, TIMSS 8, NAEP 8, and Algebra 1 End-of-Course tests can be found on this CD-ROM.

Preparing for Standardized Tests
For test-taking strategies and more
practice, see pages 867–884.

Part 2 | Short Response/Grid In

Record your answers on the answer sheet
provided by your teacher or on a sheet of
paper.

11. Find the 15th term in the arithmetic sequence
$-20, -11, -2, 7, \ldots$. (Lesson 4-7) **106**

12. Write a function that includes all of the
ordered pairs in the table. (Lesson 4-8)

x	−3	−1	1	3	4
y	12	4	−4	−12	−16

$y = -4x$ or $f(x) = -4x$

13. Find the y-intercept of the line represented
by $3x - 2y + 8 = 0$. (Lesson 5-4) **4**

14. Graph the solution of the linear inequality
$3x - y \le 2$. (Lesson 6-6) **See margin.**

15. Write the area of the triangle as a monomial.
(Lesson 8-1) **$15x^4y^5$**

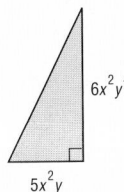

$6x^2y^4$

$5x^2y$

16. Simplify $\dfrac{r^5s^2t^{-3}}{r^{-4}s^5t^{-1}}$. (Lesson 8-2) $\dfrac{r^9}{s^3t^2}$

17. Evaluate $(9.4 \times 10^{12})(7.5 \times 10^{-5})$. Express
your result in scientific and standard
notation. (Lesson 8-3) **7.05×10^8,
705,000,000**

18. Let $P = 3x^2 - 2x - 1$ and $Q = -x^2 + 2x - 2$.
Find $P + Q$. (Lesson 8-5) **$2x^2 - 3$**

19. Find $(x^2 + 1)(x - 3)$. (Lesson 8-7)
$x^3 - 3x^2 + x - 3$

20. To find the amount of force being applied
on an object, multiply the mass of the
object times its acceleration when the force
is applied. Suppose a couch that weighs
$(x + 9)$ kilograms is being accelerated at a
rate of $(x - 4)$ meters per second squared.
Find the amount of force being applied to
the couch. (Lesson 8-8) **$x^2 + 5x - 36$**

 www.algebra1.com/standardized_test

Part 3 | Extended Response

Record your answers on a sheet of paper.
Show your work.

21. The length of a spring varies directly with
the amount of weight attached to it. When a
weight of 8 grams is attached, the spring
stretches to 20 centimeters. (Lesson 5-2)

  a. Write an equation that relates the
weight x and the length y of the spring.
$y = 2.5x$

  b. Find the number of grams of a weight
that stretches a spring 35 centimeters.
14 g

22. Use the rectangular prism below to solve
the following problems. (Lessons 8-1 and 8-7)

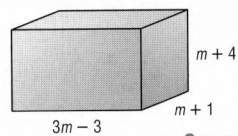

$m + 4$

$m + 1$

$3m - 3$

c. See margin.

  a. Write a polynomial expression that
represents the surface area of the top of
the prism. **$3m^2 - 3$**

  b. Write a polynomial expression that
represents the surface area of the front of
the prism. **$3m^2 + 9m - 12$**

  c. Write a polynomial expression that
represents the volume of the prism.

  d. If $m = 2$ centimeters, then what is the
volume of the prism? **54 cm³**

23. Two cars leave at the same time and both
drive to Nashville. The cars' distance from
Knoxville, in miles, can be represented by
the two equations below, where t represents
time in hours. (Lesson 8-5)

Car A: $A = 65t + 10$ Car B: $B = 55t + 20$

  a. Which car is faster? Explain.
**Car A is faster because it has a greater speed
(slope).**

  b. How far did Car B travel after 2 hours?
130 mi

  c. Find an expression that models the
distance between the two cars. **$10t - 10$**

  d. How far apart are the cars after $3\frac{1}{2}$ hours?
25 mi

Evaluating Extended Response Questions

Extended Response questions are
graded by using a multilevel
rubric that guides you in
assessing a student's knowledge
of a particular concept.

Goal: Write polynomial expressions to describe surface area and
volume of a prism.

Sample Scoring Rubric: The following rubric is a sample scoring
device. You may wish to add more
detail to this sample to meet your
individual scoring needs.

Score	Criteria
4	A correct solution that is supported by well-developed, accurate explanations
3	A generally correct solution, but may contain minor flaws in reasoning or computation
2	A partially correct interpretation and/or solution to the problem
1	A correct solution with no supporting evidence or explanation
0	An incorrect solution indicating no mathematical understanding of the concept or task, or no solution is given

Answers

14.

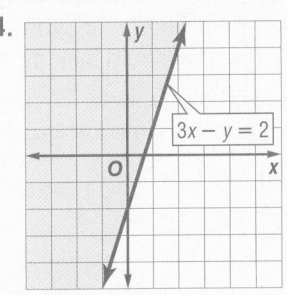

$3x - y = 2$

22c. $3m^3 + 12m^2 - 3m - 12$

Pages 413–415, Lesson 8-1

61.

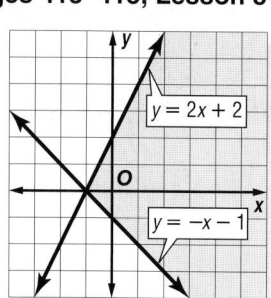

$y = 2x + 2$
$y = -x - 1$

62.

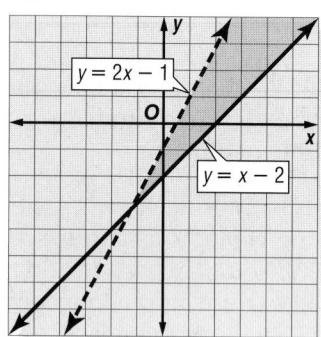

$y = 2x - 1$
$y = x - 2$

63.

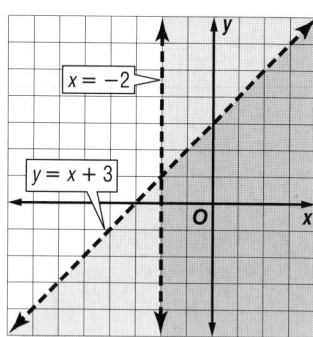

$x = -2$
$y = x + 3$

Page 416, Follow-Up of Lesson 8-1

2. Sample answer:

Prism	Dimensions	S.A.	Vol.	S.A. Ratio	Vol. Ratio
Original	4 by 6 by 9	228	216	—	—
A	8 by 12 by 18	912	1728	$\frac{912}{228} = 4$	$\frac{1728}{216} = 8$
B	12 by 18 by 27	2052	5832	$\frac{2052}{228} = 9$	$\frac{5832}{216} = 27$

6. Yes, the conjectures hold. If the ratio of the dimensions of two cylinders is a, then the ratio of the surface areas is a^2 and the ratio of the volumes is a^3.

Pages 421–423, Lesson 8-2

51. You can compare pH levels by finding the ratio of one pH level to another written in terms of the concentration c of hydrogen ions, $c = \left(\frac{1}{10}\right)^{pH}$. Answers should include the following.

- Sample answer: To compare a pH of 8 with a pH of 9 requires simplifying the quotient of powers,

$$\frac{\left(\frac{1}{10}\right)^8}{\left(\frac{1}{10}\right)^9} \cdot \frac{\left(\frac{1}{10}\right)^8}{\left(\frac{1}{10}\right)^9} = \left(\frac{1}{10}\right)^{8-9}$$

$$= \left(\frac{1}{10}\right)^{-1}$$

$$= \frac{1}{\left(\frac{1}{10}\right)^1} \quad \text{Negative Exponent Property}$$

$$= 10$$

Thus, a pH of 8 is ten times more acidic than a pH of 9.

Pages 428–430, Lesson 8-3

60a. always

$$(a \times 10^p) = a^p \times (10^n)^p \quad \text{Product of Powers}$$
$$= a^p \times 10^{np} \quad \text{Power of a Product}$$

60b. Sometimes; $a^p \times 10^{np}$ is only in scientific notation if $1 \le a^p < 10$. Counterexample: $(5 \times 10^3)^2 = 5^2 \times 10^6$ or 25×10^6, but 25×10^6 is not in scientific notation since 25 is greater than 10.

61. Astronomers work with very large numbers such as the masses of planets. Scientific notation allows them to more easily perform calculations with these numbers. Answers should include the following.

-

Planet	Mass (kg)
Mercury	330,000,000,000,000,000,000,000
Venus	4,870,000,000,000,000,000,000,000
Earth	5,970,000,000,000,000,000,000,000
Mars	642,000,000,000,000,000,000,000
Jupiter	1,900,000,000,000,000,000,000,000,000
Saturn	569,000,000,000,000,000,000,000,000
Uranus	86,800,000,000,000,000,000,000,000
Neptune	102,000,000,000,000,000,000,000,000
Pluto	12,700,000,000,000,000,000,000

- Scientific notation allows you to fit numbers such as these into a smaller table. It allows you to compare large values quickly by comparing the powers of 10 instead of counting zeros to find place value. For computation, scientific notation allows you work with fewer place values and to express your answers in a compact form.

Page 431, Preview of Lesson 8-4

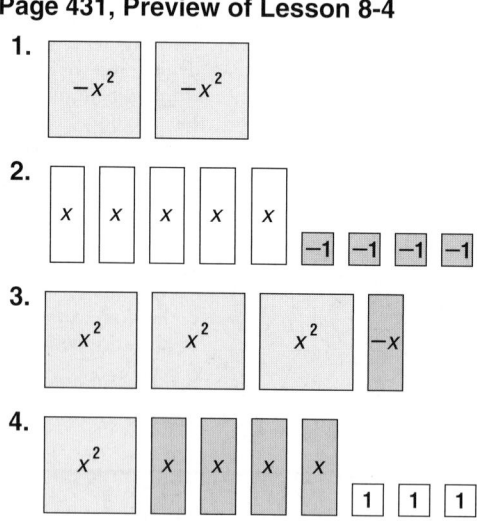

1.

$-x^2$ $-x^2$

2.

x x x x x
-1 -1 -1 -1

3.

x^2 x^2 x^2 $-x$

4.

x^2 x x x x
1 1 1

Pages 434–436, Lesson 8-4

58. A polynomial model of a set of data can be used to predict future trends in data. Answers should include the following.

t	H	Actual Data Values
0	19	19
1	19	19
2	22	22
3	23.5	24
4	25	26
5	34	36

The polynomial function models the data exactly for the first 3 values of t, and then closely for the next 3 values.

- Someone might point to this model as evidence that the time people spend playing video games is on the rise. This model may assist video game manufacturers in predicting production needs.

Page 438, Preview of Lesson 8-5

7. Method from Activity 2:

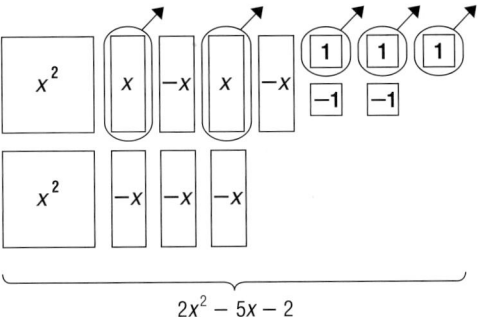

$$2x^2 - 5x - 2$$

You need to add zero pairs so that you can remove 2 green x tiles and 3 yellow 1 tiles.

Method from Activity 3:

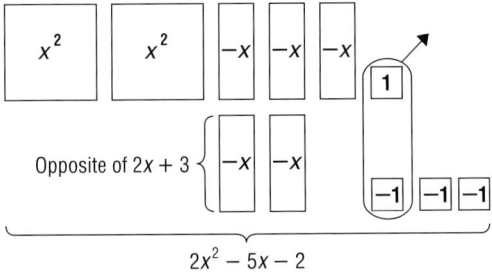

$$2x^2 - 5x - 2$$

You remove all zero pairs to find the difference in simplest form.

Page 446–449, Lesson 8-6

63. Answers should include the following.
- The product of a monomial and a polynomial can be modeled using an area model. The area of the figure shown at the beginning of the lesson is the product of its length $2x$ and width $(x + 3)$. This product is $2x(x + 3)$, which when the Distributive Property is applied becomes $2x(x) + 2x(3)$ or $2x^2 + 6x$. This is the same result obtained when the areas of the algebra tiles are added together.

- Sample answer: $(3x)(2x + 1)$
$$(3x)(2x + 1) = (3x)(2x) + (3x)(1)$$
$$= 6x^2 + 3x$$

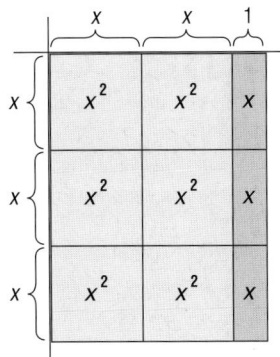

Pages 461–463, Lesson 8-8

47.

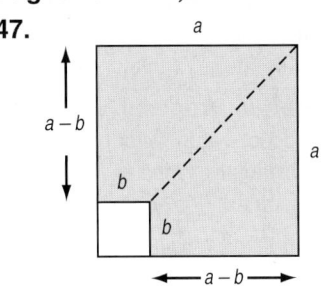

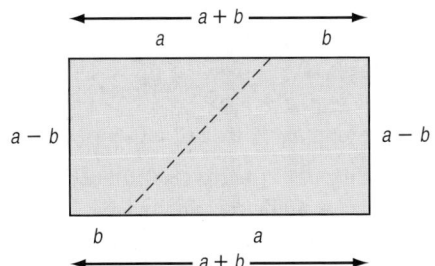

Area of rectangle $= (a - b)(a + b)$

or

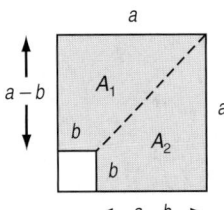

Area of a trapezoid $= \frac{1}{2}(\text{height})(\text{base 1} + \text{base 2})$

$$A_1 = \frac{1}{2}(a - b)(a + b)$$

$$A_2 = \frac{1}{2}(a - b)(a + b)$$

Total area of shaded region
$$= \left[\frac{1}{2}(a - b)(a + b)\right] + \left[\frac{1}{2}(a - b)(a + b)\right]$$
$$= (a - b)(a + b)$$

Factoring
Chapter Overview and Pacing

Year-long and two-year pacing: pages T20–T21.

LESSON OBJECTIVES

	PACING (days)			
	Regular		Block	
LESSON OBJECTIVES	Basic/Average	Advanced	Basic/Average	Advanced
9-1 Factors and Greatest Common Factors *(pp. 474–479)* • Find prime factorizations of integers and monomials. • Find the greatest common factors of integers and monomials.	1	1	0.5	0.5
9-2 Factoring Using the Distributive Property *(pp. 480–486)* *Preview:* Use algebra tiles and a product mat to factor binomials. • Factor polynomials by using the Distributive Property. • Solve quadratic equations of the form $ax^2 + bx = 0$.	2 (with 9-2 Preview)	1	1	0.5
9-3 Factoring Trinomials: $x^2 + bx + c$ *(pp. 487–494)* *Preview:* Use algebra tiles to factor trinomials. • Factor trinomials of the form $x^2 + bx + c$. • Solve equations of the form $x^2 + bx + c = 0$.	3 (with 9-3 Preview)	2	2 (with 9-3 Preview)	1
9-4 Factoring Trinomials: $ax^2 + bx + c$ *(pp. 495–500)* • Factor trinomials of the form $ax^2 + bx + c$. • Solve equations of the form $ax^2 + bx + c = 0$.	2	2	1	1
9-5 Factoring Differences of Squares *(pp. 501–506)* • Factor binomials that are the differences of squares. • Solve equations involving the differences of squares.	2	2	1	1
9-6 Perfect Squares and Factoring *(pp. 508–514)* • Factor perfect square trinomials. • Solve equations involving perfect squares.	2	2	1	1
Study Guide and **Practice Test** *(pp. 515–519)* **Standardized Test Practice** *(pp. 520–521)*	1	1	1	0.5
Chapter Assessment	1	1	0.5	0.5
TOTAL	14	12	8	6

*An electronic version of this chapter is available on **StudentWorks™**. This backpack solution CD-ROM allows students instant access to the Student Edition, lesson worksheet pages, and web resources.*

Chapter Resource Manager

CHAPTER 9 RESOURCE MASTERS

Study Guide and Intervention	Practice (Skills and Average)	Reading to Learn Mathematics	Enrichment	Assessment	Prerequisite Skills Workbook	Applications *	Parent and Student Study Guide Workbook	5-Minute Check Transparencies	Interactive Chalkboard	AlgePASS: Tutorial Plus (lessons)	Materials
523–524	525–526	527	528		13–14		68	9-1	9-1		
529–530	531–532	533	534	573	13–14	SC 17	69	9-2	9-2		(*Preview:* algebra tiles, product mat)
535–536	537–538	539	540	573, 575			70	9-3	9-3	24, 25	(*Preview:* algebra tiles, product mat), graphing calculator
541–542	543–544	545	546		13–14	GCS 39	71	9-4	9-4	26	
547–548	549–550	551	552	574	13–14	GCS 40, SC 18, SM 71–76	72	9-5	9-5		straightedge, scissors, graph paper
553–554	555–556	557	558	574			73	9-6	9-6	27	
				559–572, 576–578			74				

Key to Abbreviations: GCS = Graphing Calculator and Spreadsheet Masters,
SC = School-to-Career Masters,
SM = Science and Mathematics Lab Manual

ELL Study Guide and Intervention, Skills Practice, Practice, and Parent and Student Study Guide Workbooks are also available in Spanish.

Mathematical Connections and Background

Continuity of Instruction

Prior Knowledge

Students studied prime numbers and greatest common factors in previous courses. They also found the prime factorization of numbers. In Chapter 8, students learned the rules for dividing monomials.

This Chapter

This chapter covers the factoring of integers, monomials and polynomials. Students learn to find the greatest common factor of the monomials in a polynomial. They use the GCF and the Distributive Property to factor polynomials. Students also apply the Zero Product Property to solve quadratic equations.

Future Connections

Factoring polynomials is used to solve many real-world problems. It is basic to studying more about polynomial equations and functions.

9-1 Factors and Greatest Common Factors

The factors of a given number are all the numbers that divide the number evenly. This includes the number itself and 1. The factors of a number can be found by determining all the pairs of numbers whose product is that number. Natural numbers greater than 1 are classified as either prime or composite. Prime numbers have exactly two factors while composite numbers have more than two factors. The number 1 is neither prime nor composite. A prime factorization is the expression of a number as the product of factors that are all prime numbers. The prime factorization of a negative integer is expressed as the product -1 and prime numbers. Monomials can be written in factored form. A monomial in factored form is the product of prime numbers and variables. Variables, however, cannot have an exponent greater than 1. So x^3 must be written as $x \cdot x \cdot x$ in factored form.

Prime factorizations are used to determine the greatest common factor (GCF) of two or more integers or monomials. The GCF is the product of all the common prime factors of the two integers or monomials. If 1 is the only common factor, then they are relatively prime.

9-2 Factoring Using the Distributive Property

Many polynomials also have factors. Some polynomials are the product of a polynomial and a monomial. Reverse the process of multiplying a polynomial by a monomial to factor using the Distributive Property. First find the greatest common factor of the terms of the polynomial. If the GCF is not 1, then rewrite each term as the product of the GCF and its remaining factors. Then use the Distributive Property to factor out the GCF.

If a polynomial has four or more terms you can factor by grouping. Group terms in pairs that have common factors. Use the Distributive Property to factor the GCF from each pair of terms. The binomials in each pair of factored terms should be identical. Use the Distributive Property to factor out the common binomial factor. The remaining factors are grouped to form a second binomial. It may appear that the factored pairs do not have identical binomials, but one may be the additive inverse of the other. Write one as the product of -1 and its additive inverse. Then multiply the GCF of that pair by -1.

If the product of two factors is 0, then at least one of them is 0 according to the Zero Product Property. If an equation has the form $ab = 0$ or can be written in this form by factoring, then the Zero Product Property can be applied to solve the equation. Set each factor equal to 0 and solve each resulting equation.

9-3 Factoring Trinomials: $x^2 + bx + c$

The FOIL method was used to multiply two binomials. Reverse the FOIL method to factor a quadratic polynomial of the form $x^2 + bx + c$ into two binomials. Find two numbers m and n whose product is c and whose sum is b. The two numbers are the last terms of the two binomials $(x + m)$ and $(x + n)$.

If b is negative and c is positive then m and n must both be negative. If c is negative, then m and n must have different signs. This is because the product of two numbers with different signs is negative.

The Zero Product Property can be used to solve some quadratic equations written in the form $x^2 + bx + c = 0$. Factor the trinomial, and then set each factor equal to 0. Solve each equation to find the solution of the quadratic equation. Be sure to check the solutions in the original equation.

9-4 Factoring Trinomials: $ax^2 + bx + c$

To factor a trinomial in which the coefficient of x^2 is not 1, first check to see if the terms of the polynomial have a GCF. If so, factor it out. If the coefficient of x^2 is still not 1, or there is no GCF, factor $ax^2 + bx + c$ by making an organized list of the factors of the product of a and c. For example, to factor $8x^2 - 5x - 3$, make an organized list of the factors of $8 \cdot (-3)$, or -24. Look for a pair of factors, m and n, whose sum is equal to b in the trinomial. Then rewrite the trinomial, replacing bx with $mx + nx$. The new polynomial has four terms. Use the factoring by grouping technique shown in Lesson 9-2 to factor this polynomial into two binomial factors. A polynomial that cannot be factored is a prime polynomial. Use the above method and the Zero Product Property to solve equations in the form $ax^2 + bx + c = 0$.

9-5 Factoring Differences of Squares

Lesson 8-8 discussed the pattern for the product of a sum and a difference: $(a + b)(a - b) = a^2 - b^2$. The binomial $a^2 - b^2$ is called the difference of two squares and can be factored as the product of a sum and a difference: $a^2 - b^2 = (a - b)(a + b)$. To do this, identify a and b, the square roots of the first and last terms, respectively. Then apply the pattern.

Other aspects of factoring to watch for are factoring out a common factor, applying a technique more than once, and applying several techniques. Use any of the appropriate techniques and the Zero Product Property to solve many polynomial equations.

9-6 Perfect Squares and Factoring

Some trinomials have patterns that make their factoring easier. In Lesson 8-8, students learned about patterns for the square of a sum, $(a + b)^2 = a^2 + 2ab + b^2$, and the square of a difference, $(a - b)^2 = a^2 - 2ab + b^2$. These products, $a^2 + 2ab + b^2$ and $a^2 + 2ab + b^2$, are called perfect square trinomials, because they are the result of squaring a binomial. To recognize a perfect square trinomial, first determine if the first and last terms are perfect squares. Then find the square roots of the first and last terms, checking to see if twice the product of these square roots is equal to the middle term of the trinomial. If the trinomial is a perfect square, and the middle term is positive use the pattern $a^2 + 2ab + b^2 = (a + b)^2$ to factor it. If the middle term is negative, use the pattern $a^2 - 2ab + b^2 = (a - b)^2$. It is important to note that the last term of a perfect square trinomial cannot be negative.

If one side of an equation is a perfect square or can be written as a perfect square, then the Square Root Property can be applied to solve the equation. The Square Root Property allows you to take the square root of each side of an equation, so long as both the positive and negative square roots of a number are taken into account. So, for any number n that is greater than 0, if $x^2 = n$, then $x = \pm\sqrt{n}$. Two solutions result from such equations, one using the positive square root and one using the negative square root.

Quick Review Math Handbook

Hot Words includes a glossary of terms while Hot Topics consists of explanations of key mathematical concepts with exercises to test comprehension. This valuable resource can be used as a reference in the classroom or for home study.

Lesson	Hot Topics Section	Lesson	Hot Topics Section
GS9	6.2	9-2P	1.2
9-1	6.2	9-4	3.2

GS = Getting Started, P = Preview

 Additional mathematical information and teaching notes are available at www.algebra1.com/key_concepts.

DAILY
INTERVENTION and Assessment

Key to Abbreviations:
TWE = Teacher Wraparound Edition; CRM = Chapter Resource Masters

	Type	Student Edition	Teacher Resources	Technology/Internet
INTERVENTION	Ongoing	Prerequisite Skills, pp. 473, 479, 486, 494, 500, 506 Practice Quiz 1, p. 486 Practice Quiz 2, p. 500	5-Minute Check Transparencies *Prerequisite Skills Workbook*, pp. 13–14 Quizzes, *CRM* pp. 573–574 Mid-Chapter Test, *CRM* p. 575 Study Guide and Intervention, *CRM* pp. 523–524, 529–530, 535–536, 541–542, 547–548, 553–554	AlgePASS: Tutorial Plus, Lessons 24, 25, 26, and 27 www.algebra1.com/self_check_quiz www.algebra1.com/extra_examples
	Mixed Review	pp. 479, 486, 494, 500, 506, 514	Cumulative Review, *CRM* p. 576	
	Error Analysis	Find the Error, pp. 492, 498, 504 Common Misconceptions, pp. 483, 502	Find the Error, *TWE* pp. 492, 498, 504 Unlocking Misconceptions, *TWE* p. 497 Tips for New Teachers, *TWE* pp. 490, 509	
ASSESSMENT	Standardized Test Practice	pp. 479, 486, 494, 500, 503, 505, 514, 519, 520–521	*TWE* pp. 520–521 Standardized Test Practice, *CRM* pp. 577–578	Standardized Test Practice CD-ROM www.algebra1.com/standardized_test
	Open-Ended Assessment	Writing in Math, pp. 479, 485, 494, 500, 506, 514 Open Ended, pp. 477, 484, 492, 498, 504, 512 Standardized Test, p. 521	Modeling: *TWE* pp. 479, 506 Speaking: *TWE* pp. 486, 494 Writing: *TWE* pp. 500, 514 Open-Ended Assessment, *CRM* p. 571	
	Chapter Assessment	Study Guide, pp. 515–518 Practice Test, p. 519	Multiple-Choice Tests (Forms 1, 2A, 2B), *CRM* pp. 559–564 Free-Response Tests (Forms 2C, 2D, 3), *CRM* pp. 565–570 Vocabulary Test/Review, *CRM* p. 572	ExamView® Pro (see below) MindJogger Videoquizzes www.algebra1.com/vocabulary_review www.algebra1.com/chapter_test

For more information on Yearly ProgressPro, see p. 406.

Algebra Lesson	Yearly ProgressPro Skill Lesson
9-1	Factors and Greatest Common Factors
9-2	Factoring Using the Distributive Property
9-3	Factoring Trinomials $x^2 + bx + c$
9-4	Factoring Trinomials $ax^2 + bx + c$
9-5	Factoring Differences of Squares
9-6	Perfect Squares and Factoring

ExamView® Pro

Use the networkable **ExamView® Pro** to:
- Create **multiple versions** of tests.
- Create **modified** tests for *Inclusion* students.
- **Edit** existing questions and **add** your own questions.
- Use built-in **state curriculum correlations** to create tests aligned with state standards.
- Change **English** tests to **Spanish** and vice versa.

For more information on Intervention and Assessment, see pp. T8–T11.

Reading and Writing in Mathematics

Glencoe Algebra 1 provides numerous opportunities to incorporate reading and writing into the mathematics classroom.

Student Edition

- Foldables Study Organizer, p. 473
- Concept Check questions require students to verbalize and write about what they have learned in the lesson. (pp. 477, 484, 492, 498, 504, 512)
- Reading Mathematics, p. 507
- Writing in Math questions in every lesson, pp. 479, 485, 494, 500, 506, 514
- Reading Study Tip, pp. 489, 511
- WebQuest, p. 479

Teacher Wraparound Edition

- Foldables Study Organizer, pp. 473, 515
- Study Notebook suggestions, pp. 477, 480, 484, 488, 492, 498, 504, 507, 512
- Modeling activities, pp. 479, 506
- Speaking activities, pp. 486, 494
- Writing activities, pp. 500, 514
- Differentiated Instruction, (Verbal/Linguistic), p. 475
- **ELL** Resources, pp. 472, 475, 478, 485, 493, 499, 505, 507, 513, 515

Additional Resources

- Vocabulary Builder worksheets require students to define and give examples for key vocabulary terms as they progress through the chapter. (*Chapter 9 Resource Masters*, pp. vii-viii)
- Reading to Learn Mathematics master for each lesson (*Chapter 9 Resource Masters*, pp. 527, 533, 539, 545, 551, 559)
- *Vocabulary PuzzleMaker* software creates crossword, jumble, and word search puzzles using vocabulary lists that you can customize.
- *Teaching Mathematics with Foldables* provides suggestions for promoting cognition and language.
- *Reading and Writing in the Mathematics Classroom*
- *WebQuest and Project Resources*

For more information on Reading and Writing in Mathematics, see pp. T6–T7.

 **ENGLISH LANGUAGE LEARNERS**

Lesson 9-1
Building on Prior Knowledge

Have groups of students find the greatest common factor (GCF) of two numbers. For example, find the GCF of 54 and 72.
$$54 = ②·③·③· 3$$
$$72 = ②· 2· 2 ·③·③$$
Circle common prime factors.
So, $2 · 3 · 3 = 18$.
Then, show students how to find the GCF of a set of monomials. Have students note similarities in the procedures.

Lesson 9-3
Flexible Groups

Give groups of four students a set of four cards with one trinomial on each card. Each group should receive a trinomial where b and c are positive, b is positive and c is negative, b is negative and c is positive, and b and c are negative. Have groups develop rules of how to find the factors of b and c and how to ultimately find the factors of the trinomial. Allow groups to share their findings with other groups.

Lesson 9-6
Peer Tutoring

Give students a set of trinomials. You can use Exercises 17–22 on page 512 or make up your own. Have students work with a partner to analyze each problem and state whether it is a perfect square trinomial. Students can then factor each trinomial and find a solution set.

What You'll Learn

Have students read over the list of objectives and make a list of any words with which they are not familiar.

Why It's Important

Point out to students that this is only one of many reasons why each objective is important. Others are provided in the introduction to each lesson.

What You'll Learn

- **Lesson 9-1** Find the prime factorizations of integers and monomials.
- **Lesson 9-1** Find the greatest common factors (GCF) for sets of integers and monomials.
- **Lessons 9-2 through 9-6** Factor polynomials.
- **Lessons 9-2 through 9-6** Use the Zero Product Property to solve equations.

Key Vocabulary

- factored form (p. 475)
- factoring by grouping (p. 482)
- prime polynomial (p. 497)
- difference of squares (p. 501)
- perfect square trinomials (p. 508)

Why It's Important

The factoring of polynomials can be used to solve a variety of real-world problems and lays the foundation for the further study of polynomial equations. Factoring is used to solve problems involving vertical motion. For example, the height h in feet of a dolphin that jumps out of the water traveling at 20 feet per second is modeled by a polynomial equation. Factoring can be used to determine how long the dolphin is in the air. *You will learn how to solve polynomial equations in Lesson 9-2.*

472 Chapter 9 Factoring

Lesson	NCTM Standards	Local Objectives
9-1	1, 2, 6, 8, 9, 10	
9-2 Preview	2, 6, 8, 10	
9-2	2, 6, 8, 9, 10	
9-3 Preview	2, 6, 8, 10	
9-3	2, 6, 8, 9, 10	
9-4	2, 6, 8, 9, 10	
9-5	2, 3, 6, 8, 9, 10	
9-6	2, 6, 8, 9, 10	

Key to NCTM Standards:

1=Number & Operations, 2=Algebra, 3=Geometry, 4=Measurement, 5=Data Analysis & Probability, 6=Problem Solving, 7=Reasoning & Proof, 8=Communication, 9=Connections, 10=Representation

Vocabulary Builder   ELL

The Key Vocabulary list introduces students to some of the main vocabulary terms included in this chapter. For a more thorough vocabulary list with pronunciations of new words, give students the Vocabulary Builder worksheets found on pages vii and viii of the *Chapter 9 Resource Masters.* Encourage them to complete the definition of each term as they progress through the chapter. You may suggest that they add these sheets to their study notebooks for future reference when studying for the Chapter 9 test.

Getting Started

▶ **Prerequisite Skills** To be successful in this chapter, you'll need to master these skills and be able to apply them in problem-solving situations. Review these skills before beginning Chapter 9.

For Lessons 9-2 through 9-6   **Distributive Property**

Rewrite each expression using the Distributive Property. Then simplify.
(For review, see Lesson 1-5.)

1. $3(4 - x)$ $12 - 3x$ **2.** $a(a + 5)$ $a^2 + 5a$ **3.** $-7(n^2 - 3n + 1)$ **4.** $6y(-3y - 5y^2 + y^3)$

$-7n^2 + 21n - 7$ $-18y^2 - 30y^3 + 6y^4$

For Lessons 9-3 and 9-4   **Multiplying Binomials**

Find each product.   *(For review, see Lesson 8-7.)*

5. $(x + 4)(x + 7)$ **6.** $(3n - 4)(n + 5)$ **7.** $(6a - 2b)(9a + b)$ **8.** $(-x - 8y)(2x - 12y)$

$x^2 + 11x + 28$ $3n^2 + 11n - 20$ $54a^2 - 12ab - 2b^2$ $-2x^2 - 4xy + 96y^2$

For Lessons 9-5 and 9-6   **Special Products**

Find each product.   *(For review, see Lesson 8-8.)*

9. $(y + 9)^2$ **10.** $(3a - 2)^2$ **11.** $(n - 5)(n + 5)$ **12.** $(6p + 7q)(6p - 7q)$

$y^2 + 18y + 81$ $9a^2 - 12a + 4$ $n^2 - 25$ $36p^2 - 49q^2$

For Lesson 9-6   **Square Roots**

Find each square root.   *(For review, see Lesson 2-7.)*

13. $\sqrt{121}$ **11**   **14.** $\sqrt{0.0064}$ **0.08**   **15.** $\sqrt{\dfrac{25}{36}}$ $\dfrac{5}{6}$ **16.** $\sqrt{\dfrac{8}{98}}$ $\dfrac{2}{7}$

Factoring Make this Foldable to help you organize your notes. Begin with a sheet of plain $8\frac{1}{2}"$ by 11" paper.

Step 1   **Fold in Sixths**

Fold in thirds and then in half along the width.

Step 2   **Fold Again**

Open. Fold lengthwise, leaving a $\frac{1}{2}"$ tab on the right.

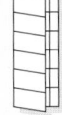

Step 3   **Cut**

Open. Cut the short side along the folds to make tabs.

Step 4   **Label**

Label each tab as shown.

Reading and Writing As you read and study the chapter, write notes and examples for each lesson under its tab.

This section provides a review of the basic concepts needed before beginning Chapter 9. Page references are included for additional student help.

Additional review is provided in the *Prerequisite Skills Workbook*, pp. 13–14.

Prerequisite Skills in the Getting Ready for the Next Lesson section at the end of each exercise set review a skill needed in the next lesson.

For Lesson	Prerequisite Skill
9-2	Distributive Property, p. 479
9-3	Multiplying Polynomials, p. 486
9-4	Factoring by Grouping, p. 494
9-5	Square Roots, p. 500
9-6	Special Products, p. 506

Organization of Data and Questioning Before beginning each lesson, ask students to think of one question that comes to mind as they skim through the lesson. Write the question on the front of the corresponding lesson tab. As students read and work through the lesson, ask them to record the answer to their question under the tab. Students can also use their Foldables to take notes, record concepts, define terms, and record other questions that arise about factoring.

For more information about Foldables, see *Teaching Mathematics with Foldables*.

9-1 Factors and Greatest Common Factors

1 Focus

Mathematical Background notes are available for this lesson on p. 472C.

How are prime numbers related to the search for extraterrestrial life?

Ask students:

- What is a prime number?
  A prime number is any whole number, greater than one, whose only factors are one and itself.

- Why might a radio signal from space composed of prime numbers be significant?
  Sample answer: A signal composed of only prime numbers would seem to signify that it was sent by intelligent beings.

What You'll Learn

- Find prime factorizations of integers and monomials.
- Find the greatest common factors of integers and monomials.

Vocabulary
- prime number
- composite number
- prime factorization
- factored form
- greatest common factor (GCF)

How are prime numbers related to the search for extraterrestrial life?

In the search for extraterrestrial life, scientists listen to radio signals coming from faraway galaxies. How can they be sure that a particular radio signal was deliberately sent by intelligent beings instead of coming from some natural phenomenon? What if that signal began with a series of beeps in a pattern comprised of the first 30 prime numbers ("beep-beep," "beep-beep-beep," and so on)?

PRIME FACTORIZATION Recall that when two or more numbers are multiplied, each number is a *factor* of the product. Some numbers, like 18, can be expressed as the product of different pairs of whole numbers. This can be shown geometrically. Consider all of the possible rectangles with whole number dimensions that have areas of 18 square units.

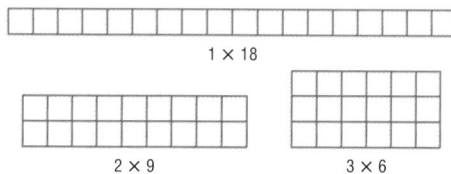

1 × 18

2 × 9   3 × 6

The number 18 has 6 factors, 1, 2, 3, 6, 9, and 18. Whole numbers greater than 1 can be classified by their number of factors.

TEACHING TIP
An alternative definition is that a prime number is a positive integer with exactly two different factors. You may want to point out that 2 is the only even prime number.

Key Concept — Prime and Composite Numbers

Words	Examples
A whole number, greater than 1, whose only factors are 1 and itself, is called a **prime number**.	2, 3, 5, 7, 11, 13, 17, 19
A whole number, greater than 1, that has more than two factors is called a **composite number**.	4, 6, 8, 9, 10, 12, 14, 15, 16, 18

0 and 1 are neither prime nor composite.

Study Tip

Listing Factors
Notice that in Example 1, 6 is listed as a factor of 36 only once.

Example 1 Classify Numbers as Prime or Composite

Factor each number. Then classify each number as *prime* or *composite*.

a. 36

To find the factors of 36, list all pairs of whole numbers whose product is 36.

1×36 2×18 3×12 4×9 6×6

Therefore, the factors of 36, in increasing order, are 1, 2, 3, 4, 6, 9, 12, 18, and 36. Since 36 has more than two factors, it is a composite number.

Resource Manager

📁 Workbook and Reproducible Masters

Chapter 9 Resource Masters
- Study Guide and Intervention, pp. 523–524
- Skills Practice, p. 525
- Practice, p. 526
- Reading to Learn Mathematics, p. 527
- Enrichment, p. 528

Parent and Student Study Guide Workbook, p. 68
Prerequisite Skills Workbook, pp. 13–14

📺 Transparencies

5-Minute Check Transparency 9-1
Answer Key Transparencies

💿 Technology

Interactive Chalkboard

b. 23

The only whole numbers that can be multiplied together to get 23 are 1 and 23. Therefore, the factors of 23 are 1 and 23. Since the only factors of 23 are 1 and itself, 23 is a prime number.

When a whole number is expressed as the product of factors that are all prime numbers, the expression is called the **prime factorization** of the number.

Example 2 *Prime Factorization of a Positive Integer*

Find the prime factorization of 90.

Method 1

$90 = 2 \cdot 45$ The least prime factor of 90 is 2.

$ = 2 \cdot 3 \cdot 15$ The least prime factor of 45 is 3.

$ = 2 \cdot 3 \cdot 3 \cdot 5$ The least prime factor of 15 is 3.

All of the factors in the last row are prime. Thus, the prime factorization of 90 is $2 \cdot 3 \cdot 3 \cdot 5$.

Method 2

Use a factor tree.

```
      90
     /  \
 ▶ 9  ·  10      90 = 9 · 10
  /\    /\
 3·3·2·5        9 = 3 · 3 and 10 = 2 · 5
```

All of the factors in the last branch of the factor tree are prime. Thus, the prime factorization of 90 is $2 \cdot 3 \cdot 3 \cdot 5$ or $2 \cdot 3^2 \cdot 5$.

Usually the factors are ordered from the least prime factor to the greatest.

A negative integer is factored completely when it is expressed as the product of -1 and prime numbers.

Example 3 *Prime Factorization of a Negative Integer*

Find the prime factorization of -140.

$-140 = -1 \cdot 140$ Express -140 as -1 times 140.

$ = -1 \cdot 2 \cdot 70$ $140 = 2 \cdot 70$

$ = -1 \cdot 2 \cdot 7 \cdot 10$ $70 = 7 \cdot 10$

$ = -1 \cdot 2 \cdot 7 \cdot 2 \cdot 5$ $10 = 2 \cdot 5$

Thus, the prime factorization of -140 is $-1 \cdot 2 \cdot 2 \cdot 5 \cdot 7$ or $-1 \cdot 2^2 \cdot 5 \cdot 7$.

A monomial is in **factored form** when it is expressed as the product of prime numbers and variables and no variable has an exponent greater than 1.

 www.algebra1.com/extra_examples

Lesson 9-1 Factors and Greatest Common Factors **475**

---

2 Teach

PRIME FACTORIZATION

In-Class Examples Power Point®

1 Factor each number. Then classify each number as *prime* or *composite*.

a. 22   The factors are 1, 2, 11, and 22, so the number is composite.

b. 31   The factors are 1 and 31, so the number is prime.

Teaching Tip Explain that the prime factorization for each number is unique, so as long as you divide by prime numbers, you will get the same prime factorization. For example:

$90 = 3 \cdot 30$

$ = 3 \cdot 3 \cdot 10$

$ = 3 \cdot 3 \cdot 2 \cdot 5,$

which is the same as $2 \cdot 3 \cdot 3 \cdot 5$ that was found in Example 2.

2 Find the prime factorization of 84. $2 \cdot 2 \cdot 3 \cdot 7$ or $2^2 \cdot 3 \cdot 7$

3 Find the prime factorization of -132. $-1 \cdot 2^2 \cdot 3 \cdot 11$

✓ Concept Check

Prime Factorization José and Latecia both found the prime factorization of 60. José got $2^2 \cdot 3 \cdot 5$, and Latecia got $3 \cdot 2^2 \cdot 5$. Explain which is correct. **Both are correct. Each number has a unique prime factorization.**

In-Class Example

Power Point®

4 Factor each monomial completely.

a. $18x^3y^3$

$2 \cdot 3^2 \cdot x \cdot x \cdot x \cdot y \cdot y \cdot y$

b. $-26rst^2$ $-1 \cdot 2 \cdot 13 \cdot r \cdot s \cdot t \cdot t$

Teaching Tip Remind students that prime factorization of a constant can have exponents greater than 1, but prime factorization of variable values cannot.

GREATEST COMMON FACTOR

In-Class Examples

Power Point®

5 Find the GCF of each set of monomials.

a. 12 and 18 **The GCF is 6**

b. $27a^2b$ and $15ab^2c$ **The GCF is** $3ab$

6 **CRAFTS** Rene has crocheted 32 squares for an afghan. Each square is 1 foot square. She is not sure how she will arrange the squares but does know it will be rectangular and have a ribbon trim. What is the maximum amount of ribbon she might need to finish the afghan? **66 ft**

Interactive Chalkboard

PowerPoint® **Presentations**

This CD-ROM is a customizable Microsoft® PowerPoint® presentation that includes:

- Step-by-step, dynamic solutions of each In-Class Example from the Teacher Wraparound Edition
- Additional, Your Turn exercises for each example
- The 5-Minute Check Transparencies
- Hot links to Glencoe Online Study Tools

Example 4 Prime Factorization of a Monomial

Factor each monomial completely.

a. $12a^2b^3$

$12a^2b^3 = 2 \cdot 6 \cdot a \cdot a \cdot b \cdot b \cdot b$ $12 = 2 \cdot 6, a^2 = a \cdot a,$ and $b^3 = b \cdot b \cdot b$

$= 2 \cdot 2 \cdot 3 \cdot a \cdot a \cdot b \cdot b \cdot b$ $6 = 2 \cdot 3$

Thus, $12a^2b^3$ in factored form is $2 \cdot 2 \cdot 3 \cdot a \cdot a \cdot b \cdot b \cdot b$.

b. $-66pq^2$

$-66pq^2 = -1 \cdot 66 \cdot p \cdot q \cdot q$ Express -66 as -1 times 66.

$= -1 \cdot 2 \cdot 33 \cdot p \cdot q \cdot q$ $66 = 2 \cdot 33$

$= -1 \cdot 2 \cdot 3 \cdot 11 \cdot p \cdot q \cdot q$ $33 = 3 \cdot 11$

Thus, $-66pq^2$ in factored form is $-1 \cdot 2 \cdot 3 \cdot 11 \cdot p \cdot q \cdot q$.

GREATEST COMMON FACTOR Two or more numbers may have some common prime factors. Consider the prime factorization of 48 and 60.

$$48 = ②·②· 2 · 2 ·③$$ Factor each number.

$$60 = ②·②·③· 5$$ Circle the common prime factors.

The integers 48 and 60 have two 2s and one 3 as common prime factors. The product of these common prime factors, $2 \cdot 2 \cdot 3$ or 12, is called the **greatest common factor (GCF)** of 48 and 60. The GCF is the greatest number that is a factor of both original numbers.

Key Concept   Greatest Common Factor (GCF)

- The GCF of two or more integers is the product of the prime factors common to the integers.
- The GCF of two or more monomials is the product of their common factors when each monomial is in factored form.
- If two or more integers or monomials have a GCF of 1, then the integers or monomials are said to be *relatively prime*.

Study Tip

Alternative Method

You can also find the greatest common factor by listing the factors of each number and finding which of the common factors is the greatest. Consider Example 5a.

15: ①, 3, 5, 15
16: ①, 2, 4, 8, 16

The only common factor, and therefore, the greatest common factor, is 1.

Example 5 GCF of a Set of Monomials

Find the GCF of each set of monomials.

a. 15 and 16

$15 = 3 \cdot 5$ Factor each number.

$16 = 2 \cdot 2 \cdot 2 \cdot 2$ Circle the common prime factors, if any.

There are no common prime factors, so the GCF of 15 and 16 is 1. This means that 15 and 16 are relatively prime.

b. $36x^2y$ and $54xy^2z$

$36x^2y = ②· 2 ·③·③·ⓧ· x ·ⓨ$ Factor each number.

$54xy^2z = ②·③·③· 3 ·ⓧ·ⓨ· y · z$ Circle the common prime factors.

The GCF of $36x^2y$ and $54xy^2z$ is $2 \cdot 3 \cdot 3 \cdot x \cdot y$ or $18xy$.

Teacher to Teacher

Lisa Cook   Kaysville Jr. H.S., Kaysville, UT

"To help in identifying prime factors, I like to have my students explore the Sieve of Eratosthenes. Use a 10-by-10 grid with the numbers 1-100 on it. Cross out 1 since prime numbers are greater than 1. Circle 2 and cross out all multiples of 2. Circle 3 and cross out multiples of 3. Continue with the next odd number until all multiples have been eliminated. The circled numbers are the prime numbers less than 100."

Example 6 Use Factors

GEOMETRY The area of a rectangle is 28 square inches. If the length and width are both whole numbers, what is the maximum perimeter of the rectangle?

Find the factors of 28, and draw rectangles with each length and width. Then find each perimeter.

The factors of 28 are 1, 2, 4, 7, 14, and 28.

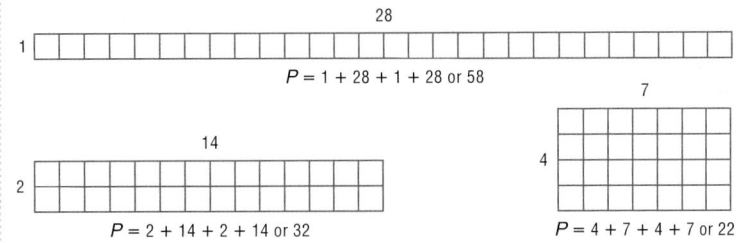

$P = 1 + 28 + 1 + 28$ or 58

$P = 2 + 14 + 2 + 14$ or 32

$P = 4 + 7 + 4 + 7$ or 22

The greatest perimeter is 58 inches. The rectangle with this perimeter has a length of 28 inches and a width of 1 inch.

Check for Understanding

Concept Check

1. **Determine** whether the following statement is *true* or *false*. If false, provide a counterexample.
   All prime numbers are odd. **false; 2**

2. **Explain** what it means for two numbers to be relatively prime. **Their GCF is 1.**

3. **OPEN ENDED** Name two monomials whose GCF is $5x^2$.
   Sample answer: $5x^2$ and $10x^3$

Guided Practice

GUIDED PRACTICE KEY	
Exercises	Examples
4–6	1
7–9	2, 3
10–12	4
13–18	5
19	6

Find the factors of each number. Then classify each number as *prime* or *composite*.

4. 8 **1, 2, 4, 8; composite**   5. 17 **1, 17; prime**   6. 112 **1, 2, 4, 7, 8, 14, 16, 28, 56, 112; composite**

Find the prime factorization of each integer.

7. 45 $3^2 \cdot 5$ 8. -32 $-1 \cdot 2^5$ 9. -150 $-1 \cdot 2 \cdot 3 \cdot 5^2$

Factor each monomial completely.

10. $4p^2$ $2 \cdot 2 \cdot p \cdot p$ 11. $39b^3c^2$ $3 \cdot 13 \cdot b \cdot b \cdot b \cdot c \cdot c$ 12. $-100x^3yz^2$

12. $-1 \cdot 2 \cdot 2 \cdot 5 \cdot 5 \cdot x \cdot x \cdot x \cdot y \cdot z \cdot z$

Find the GCF of each set of monomials.

13. 10, 15 **5**   14. $18xy, 36y^2$ **$18y$**   15. 54, 63, 180 **9**

16. $25n, 21m$ **1 (relatively prime)**   17. $12a^2b, 90a^2b^2c$ **$6a^2b$**   18. $15r^2, 35s^2, 70rs$ **5**

Application

19. **GARDENING** Ashley is planting 120 tomato plants in her garden. In what ways can she arrange them so that she has the same number of plants in each row, at least 5 rows of plants, and at least 5 plants in each row?

19. 5 rows of 24 plants, 6 rows of 20 plants, 8 rows of 15 plants, 10 rows of 12 plants, 12 rows of 10 plants, 15 rows of 8 plants, 20 rows of 6 plants or 24 rows of 5 plants   ★ indicates increased difficulty

Practice and Apply

Find the factors of each number. Then classify each number as *prime* or *composite*.

20–27. See margin.

20. 19	**21.** 25	**22.** 80	**23.** 61
24. 91	**25.** 119	**26.** 126	**27.** 304

Answers

20. 1, 19; prime

21. 1, 5, 25; composite

22. 1, 2, 4, 5, 8, 10, 16, 20, 40, 80; composite

23. 1, 61; prime

24. 1, 7, 13, 91; composite

25. 1, 7, 17, 119; composite

26. 1, 2, 3, 6, 7, 9, 14, 18, 21, 42, 63, 126; composite

27. 1, 2, 4, 8, 16, 19, 38, 76, 152, 304; composite

Study Notebook

Have students—
- add the definitions/examples of the vocabulary terms to their Vocabulary Builder worksheets for Chapter 9.
- include explanations on how to factor numbers, find prime factorizations, and find the greatest common factor.
- include any other item(s) that they find helpful in mastering the skills in this lesson.

About the Exercises...

Organization by Objective
- **Prime Factorization:** 20–27, 32–39
- **Greatest Common Factor:** 48–61

Odd/Even Assignments
Exercises 20–29 and 32–61 are structured so that students practice the same concepts whether they are assigned odd or even problems.

Assignment Guide

Basic: 21–29 odd, 30, 31, 33–61 odd, 68–86

Average: 21–29 odd, 33–61 odd, 63–66, 68–86

Advanced: 20–28 even, 32–62 even, 63–80 (optional: 81–86)

Prime Factorization When two or more numbers are multiplied, each number is called a **factor** of the product.

	Definition	Example
Prime Number	A prime number is a whole number, greater than 1, whose only factors are 1 and itself.	5
Composite Number	A composite number is a whole number, greater than 1, that has more than two factors.	10
Prime Factorization	Prime factorization occurs when a whole number is expressed as a product of factors that are all prime numbers.	$45 = 3^2 \cdot 5$

Example 1 Factor each number. Then classify each number as *prime* or *composite*.

a. 28
To find the factors of 28, list all pairs of whole numbers whose product is 28.
$1 \times 28 \quad 2 \times 14 \quad 4 \times 7$
Therefore, the factors of 28 are 1, 2, 4, 7, 14, and 28. Since 28 has more than 2 factors, it is a composite number.

b. 31
To find the factors of 31, list all pairs of whole numbers whose product is 31.
1×31
Therefore, the factors of 31 are 1 and 31. Since the only factors of 31 are itself and 1, it is a prime number.

Example 2 Find the prime factorization of 200.

Method 1
$200 = 2 \cdot 100$
$= 2 \cdot 2 \cdot 50$
$= 2 \cdot 2 \cdot 2 \cdot 25$
$= 2 \cdot 2 \cdot 2 \cdot 5 \cdot 5$
All the factors in the last row are prime, so the prime factorization of 200 is $2^3 \cdot 5^2$.

Method 2
Use a factor tree.
All of the factors in each last branch of the factor tree are prime, so the prime factorization of 200 is $2^3 \cdot 5^2$.

Exercises

Find the factors of each number. Then classify the number as *prime* or *composite*.

1. 41 1, 41; prime
2. 121 1, 11, 121; composite
3. 90 1, 2, 3, 5, 6, 9, 10, 15, 18, 30, 45, 90; composite
4. 2865 1, 3, 5, 15, 191, 573, 955, 2865; composite

Find the prime factorization of each integer.

5. 600 $2^3 \cdot 3 \cdot 5^2$
6. 175 $5^2 \cdot 7$
7. −150 $−1 \cdot 2 \cdot 3 \cdot 5^2$

Factor each monomial completely.

8. $32x^2$ $2 \cdot 2 \cdot 2 \cdot 2 \cdot 2 \cdot x \cdot x$
9. $18m^2n$ $2 \cdot 3 \cdot 3 \cdot m \cdot m \cdot n$
10. $49a^3b^2$ $7 \cdot 7 \cdot a \cdot a \cdot a \cdot b \cdot b$

Find the factors of each number. Then classify the number as *prime* or *composite*.

1. 18 1, 2, 3, 6, 9, 18; composite
2. 37 1, 37; prime
3. 48 1, 2, 3, 4, 6, 8, 12, 16, 24, 48; composite
4. 116 1, 2, 4, 29, 58, 116; composite
5. 138 1, 2, 3, 6, 23, 46, 69, 138; composite
6. 211 1, 211; prime

Find the prime factorization of each integer.

7. 52 $2^2 \cdot 13$
8. −96 $−1 \cdot 2^5 \cdot 3$
9. 108 $2^2 \cdot 3^3$
10. 225 $3^2 \cdot 5^2$
11. 286 $2 \cdot 11 \cdot 13$
12. −384 $−1 \cdot 2^7 \cdot 3$

Factor each monomial completely.

13. $30d^6$ $2 \cdot 3 \cdot 5 \cdot d \cdot d \cdot d \cdot d \cdot d \cdot d$
14. $−72mn$ $−1 \cdot 2 \cdot 2 \cdot 2 \cdot 3 \cdot 3 \cdot m \cdot n$
15. $81b^2c^3$ $3 \cdot 3 \cdot 3 \cdot b \cdot c \cdot c \cdot c$
16. $145abc^3$ $5 \cdot 29 \cdot a \cdot b \cdot c \cdot c \cdot c$
17. $168pq^2r$ $2 \cdot 2 \cdot 2 \cdot 3 \cdot 7 \cdot p \cdot q \cdot q \cdot r$
18. $−121x^2yz^2$ $−1 \cdot 11 \cdot 11 \cdot x \cdot x \cdot y \cdot z \cdot z$

Find the GCF of each set of monomials.

19. 18, 49 1
20. 18, 45, 63 9
21. 16, 24, 48 8
22. 12, 30, 114 6
23. 9, 27, 77 1
24. 24, 72, 108 12
25. $24fg^5, 56f^3g$ $8fg$
26. $72x^2z^2, 36rs^3$ $36rs^2$
27. $15a^2b, 35ab^2$ $5ab$
28. $28m^3n^2, 45pq^2$ 1
29. $40xy^2, 56x^3y^2, 124x^2y^3$ $4xy^2$
30. $88a^3d, 40c^3d^2, 32c^2d$ $8c^2d$

GEOMETRY For Exercises 31 and 32, use the following information.
The area of a rectangle is 84 square inches. Its length and width are both whole numbers.

31. What is the minimum perimeter of the rectangle? 38 in.

32. What is the maximum perimeter of the rectangle? 170 in.

RENOVATION For Exercises 33 and 34, use the following information.
Ms. Baxter wants to tile a wall to serve as a splashguard above a basin in the basement. She plans to use equal-sized tiles to cover an area that measures 48 inches by 36 inches.

33. What is the maximum-size square tile Ms. Baxter can use and not have to cut any of the tiles? 12-in. square

34. How many tiles of this size will she need? 12

Pre-Activity How are prime numbers related to the search for extraterrestrial life?

Read the introduction to Lesson 9-1 at the top of page 474 in your textbook.
If each "beep" counts as one, what are the first two prime numbers?
2 and 3

Reading the Lesson

1. Every whole number greater than 1 is either composite or ___prime___.

2. Complete each statement.
   a. In the prime factorization of a whole number, each factor is a ___prime___ number.
   b. In the prime factorization of a negative integer, all the factors are prime except the factor ___−1___.

3. Explain why the monomial $5x^2y$ is *not* in factored form.
   The variable x has an exponent that is greater than 1.

4. Explain the steps used below to find the greatest common factor (GCF) of 84 and 120.
   $84 = 2 \cdot 2 \cdot 3 \cdot 7$ Write the prime factorization of 84.
   $120 = 2 \cdot 2 \cdot 2 \cdot 3 \cdot 5$ Write the prime factorization of 120.
   Common prime factors: 2, 2, 3 Identify common prime factors of 84 and 120.
   $2 \cdot 2 \cdot 3 = 12$ Multiply the common factors to find the GCF of 84 and 120.

Helping You Remember

5. How can the two words that make up the term *prime factorization* help you remember what the term means?
   Sample answer: The word *factorization* reminds you that the number must be expressed as a product of factors. The word *prime* reminds you that with the possible exception of −1, all of the factors used must be prime numbers.

For Exercises	See Examples
20–27, 62, 65, 66	1
32–39	2, 3
40–47	4
48–61, 63, 64	5
28–31, 67	6

Extra Practice
See page 839.

GEOMETRY For Exercises 28 and 29, consider a rectangle whose area is 96 square millimeters and whose length and width are both whole numbers.

28. What is the minimum perimeter of the rectangle? Explain your reasoning. 40 mm

29. What is the maximum perimeter of the rectangle? Explain your reasoning. 194 mm   28–29. See margin for explanations.

COOKIES For Exercises 30 and 31, use the following information.
A bakery packages cookies in two sizes of boxes, one with 18 cookies and the other with 24 cookies. A small number of cookies are to be wrapped in cellophane before they are placed in a box. To save money, the bakery will use the same size cellophane packages for each box.

30. How many cookies should the bakery place in each cellophane package to maximize the number of cookies in each package? 6 cookies

31. How many cellophane packages will go in each size box?
    3 packages in the box of 18 cookies and 4 packages in the box of 24 cookies.

Find the prime factorization of each integer.

32. 39 $3 \cdot 13$
33. −98 $−1 \cdot 2 \cdot 7^2$
34. 117 $3^2 \cdot 13$
35. 102 $2 \cdot 3 \cdot 17$
36. −115 $−1 \cdot 5 \cdot 23$
37. 180 $2^2 \cdot 3^2 \cdot 5$
38. 360 $2^3 \cdot 3^2 \cdot 5$
39. −462 $−1 \cdot 2 \cdot 3 \cdot 7 \cdot 11$

Factor each monomial completely. 40–47. See margin.

40. $66d^4$
41. $85x^2y^2$
42. $49a^3b^2$
43. $50gh$
44. $128pq^2$
45. $243n^3m$
46. $−183xyz^3$
47. $−169a^2bc^2$

Find the GCF of each set of monomials.

48. 27, 72 9
49. 18, 35 1
50. 32, 48 16
51. 84, 70 14
52. 16, 20, 64 4
53. 42, 63, 105 21
54. $15a, 28b^2$ 1
55. $24d^2, 30c^2d$ $6d$
56. $20gh, 36g^2h^2$ $4gh$
57. $21p^2q, 32r^2t$ 1
58. $18x, 30xy, 54y$ 6
59. $28a^2, 63a^3b^2, 91b^3$ 7
60. $14m^2n^2, 18mn, 2m^2n^3$ $2mn$
61. $80a^2b, 96a^2b^3, 128a^2b^2$ $16a^2b$

62. **NUMBER THEORY** *Twin primes* are two consecutive odd numbers that are prime. The first pair of twin primes is 3 and 5. List the next five pairs of twin primes. 5, 7; 11, 13; 17, 19; 29, 31; 41, 43

MARCHING BANDS For Exercises 63 and 64, use the following information.
Central High's marching band has 75 members, and the band from Northeast High has 90 members. During the halftime show, the bands plan to march into the stadium from opposite ends using formations with the same number of rows.

63. If the bands want to match up in the center of the field, what is the maximum number of rows? 15

64. How many band members will be in each row after the bands are combined? 11

NUMBER THEORY For Exercises 65 and 66, use the following information.
One way of generating prime numbers is to use the formula $2^p - 1$, where p is a prime number. Primes found using this method are called *Mersenne primes*. For example, when $p = 2$, $2^2 - 1 = 3$. The first Mersenne prime is 3.

65. Find the next two Mersenne primes. 7, 31

★ 66. Will this formula generate all possible prime numbers? Explain your reasoning.
    No, it does not generate the first prime number, 2.

Online Research Data Update What is the greatest known prime number? Visit www.algebra1.com/data_update to learn more.

More About. . .

Marching Bands

Drum Corps International (DCI) is a nonprofit youth organization serving junior drum and bugle corps around the world. Members of these marching bands range from 14 to 21 years of age.
Source: www.dci.org

Finding the GCF by Euclid's Algorithm

Finding the greatest common factor of two large numbers can take a long time using prime factorizations. This method can be avoided by using Euclid's Algorithm as shown in the following example.

Example Find the GCF of 209 and 532.

Divide the greater number, 532, by the lesser, 209.

Divide the remainder into the divisor above.
Repeat this process until the remainder is zero. The last nonzero remainder is the GCF.

Answers

28. The factors of 96 whose sum when doubled is the least are 12 and 18.

29. The factors of 96 whose sum when doubled is the greatest are 1 and 96.

★ **67. GEOMETRY** The area of a triangle is 20 square centimeters. What are possible whole-number dimensions for the base and height of the triangle? **See margin.**

68. CRITICAL THINKING Suppose 6 is a factor of ab, where a and b are natural numbers. Make a valid argument to explain why each assertion is true or provide a counterexample to show that an assertion is false.

  a. 6 must be a factor of a or of b.

  b. 3 must be a factor of a or of b. **True; see margin for explanation.**

  c. 3 must be a factor of a and of b. **false; counterexample: $a = 3$, $b = 1082$**

68a. false;
counterexample:
$a = 3$, $b = 4$

69. WRITING IN MATH Answer the question that was posed at the beginning of the lesson. **See p. 521A.**

  How are prime numbers related to the search for extraterrestrial life?

  Include the following in your answer:
  • a list of the first 30 prime numbers and an explanation of how you found them, and
  • an explanation of why a signal of this kind might indicate that an extraterrestrial message is to follow.

Standardized Test Practice
Ⓐ Ⓑ Ⓒ Ⓓ

70. Miko claims that there are at least four ways to design a 120-square-foot rectangular space that can be tiled with 1-foot by 1-foot tiles. Which statement best describes this claim? **D**

  Ⓐ Her claim is false because 120 is a prime number.

  Ⓑ Her claim is false because 120 is not a perfect square.

  Ⓒ Her claim is true because 240 is a multiple of 120.

  Ⓓ Her claim is true because 120 has at least eight factors.

71. Suppose Ψ_x is defined as the largest prime factor of x. For which of the following values of x would Ψ_x have the greatest value? **A**

  Ⓐ 53   Ⓑ 74   Ⓒ 99   Ⓓ 117

Maintain Your Skills

Mixed Review **Find each product.** *(Lessons 8-7 and 8-8)* **73. $9a^2 - 25$ 74. $49p^4 + 56p^2 + 16$**

  72. $(2x - 1)^2$ $4x^2 - 4x + 1$ **73.** $(3a + 5)(3a - 5)$ **74.** $(7p^2 + 4)(7p^2 + 4)$

  75. $(6r + 7)(2r - 5)$ **76.** $(10h + k)(2h + 5k)$ **77.** $(b + 4)(b^2 + 3b - 18)$
  $12r^2 - 16r - 35$ $20h^2 + 52hk + 5k^2$ $b^3 + 7b^2 - 6b - 72$

Find the value of r so that the line that passes through the given points has the given slope. *(Lesson 5-1)*

  78. $(1, 2), (-2, r), m = 3$ -7 **79.** $(-5, 9), (r, 6), m = -\frac{3}{5}$ 0

80. RETAIL SALES A department store buys clothing at wholesale prices and then marks the clothing up 25% to sell at retail price to customers. If the retail price of a jacket is $79, what was the wholesale price? *(Lesson 3-7)* **$63.20**

Getting Ready for the Next Lesson **PREREQUISITE SKILL** Use the Distributive Property to rewrite each expression. *(To review the Distributive Property, see Lesson 1-5.)*

  81. $5(2x + 8)$ $10x + 40$ **82.** $a(3a + 1)$ $3a^2 + a$ **83.** $2g(3g - 4)$ $6g^2 - 8g$

84. $-12y^2 + 24y$ **84.** $-4y(3y - 6)$ **85.** $7b + 7c$ $7(b + c)$ **86.** $2x + 3x$ $(2 + 3)x$

Open-Ended Assessment

Modeling Write a number and each step of its prime factorization (using the factor tree method) on note cards. Each factor, including the intermediate factors, should be on separate note cards. Then draw some arrows on other note cards. Tape the cards at random on the chalkboard. Have student volunteers come up and arrange the factors to find the prime factorization of the number.

Getting Ready for Lesson 9-2

PREREQUISITE SKILL Students will learn to factor polynomials using the Distributive Property in Lesson 9-2. Students should know how to rewrite expressions using the Distributive Property so they can factor polynomials. Use Exercises 81–86 to determine your students' familiarity with the Distributive Property.

Answers

40. $2 \cdot 3 \cdot 11 \cdot d \cdot d \cdot d \cdot d$

41. $5 \cdot 17 \cdot x \cdot x \cdot y \cdot y$

42. $7 \cdot 7 \cdot a \cdot a \cdot a \cdot b \cdot b$

43. $2 \cdot 5 \cdot 5 \cdot g \cdot h$

44. $2 \cdot 2 \cdot 2 \cdot 2 \cdot 2 \cdot 2 \cdot 2 \cdot p \cdot q \cdot q$

45. $3 \cdot 3 \cdot 3 \cdot 3 \cdot 3 \cdot n \cdot n \cdot n \cdot m$

46. $-1 \cdot 3 \cdot 61 \cdot x \cdot y \cdot z \cdot z \cdot z$

47. $-1 \cdot 13 \cdot 13 \cdot a \cdot a \cdot b \cdot c \cdot c$

67. base 1 cm, height 40 cm; base 2 cm, height 20 cm; base 4 cm, height 10 cm; base 5 cm, height 8 cm; base 8 cm, height 5 cm; base 10 cm, height 4 cm; base 20 cm, height 2 cm; base 40 cm, height 1 cm

68b. If 6 is a factor of ab, then the prime factorization of ab must contain $2 \cdot 3$ So, 3 must be a factor of either a or b.

Algebra Activity

A Preview of Lesson 9-2

Getting Started

Objective Factor polynomials with algebra tiles.

Materials
algebra tiles
product mat

Teach

- Remind students that they used rectangles at the beginning of Lesson 9-1 to find factors of whole numbers. The procedure for finding the factors of polynomials with algebra tiles is very similar. The length and width of a modeled polynomial represent the factors of the polynomial.

Assess

- In **Exercises 1–4**, students need to recognize that they must arrange the tiles into a rectangle with a width greater than one in order to find the factors.

- In **Exercises 5–9**, students should recognize that the binomials that cannot be factored can only be modeled in a rectangle with a width of one.

Study Notebook

You may wish to have students summarize this activity and what they learned from it.

Factoring Using the Distributive Property

Sometimes you know the product of binomials and are asked to find the factors. This is called factoring. You can use algebra tiles and a product mat to factor binomials.

Activity 1 Use algebra tiles to factor $3x + 6$.

Step 1 Model the polynomial $3x + 6$.

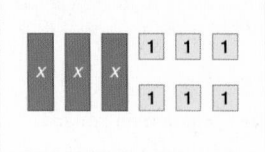

Step 2 Arrange the tiles into a rectangle. The total area of the rectangle represents the product, and its length and width represent the factors.

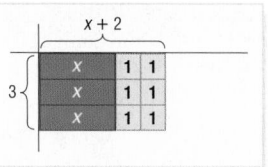

The rectangle has a width of 3 and a length of $x + 2$. So, $3x + 6 = 3(x + 2)$.

Activity 2 Use algebra tiles to factor $x^2 - 4x$.

Step 1 Model the polynomial $x^2 - 4x$.

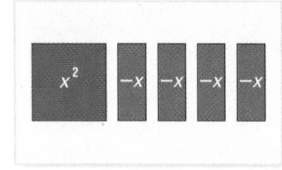

Step 2 Arrange the tiles into a rectangle.

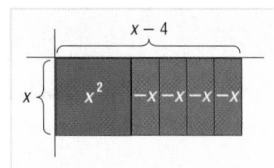

The rectangle has a width of x and a length of $x - 4$. So, $x^2 - 4x = x(x - 4)$.

Model and Analyze

9. Binomials can be factored if they can be represented by a rectangle. Examples: $2x + 2$ can be factored and $2x + 1$ cannot be factored.

Use algebra tiles to factor each binomial.

1. $2x + 10$ $2(x + 5)$ 2. $6x - 8$ $2(3x - 4)$ 3. $5x^2 + 2x$ $x(5x + 2)$ 4. $9 - 3x$ $3(3 - x)$

Tell whether each binomial can be factored. Justify your answer with a drawing.

5. $4x - 10$ **yes**   6. $3x - 7$ **no**   7. $x^2 + 2x$ **yes**   8. $2x^2 + 3$ **no**
5–8. See pp. 521A–521B for drawings.

9. **MAKE A CONJECTURE** Write a paragraph that explains how you can use algebra tiles to determine whether a binomial can be factored. Include an example of one binomial that can be factored and one that cannot.

Resource Manager

📁 **Teaching Algebra with Manipulatives**
- pp. 10–11 (master for algebra tiles)
- p. 17 (master for product mat)
- p. 156 (student recording sheet)

Glencoe Mathematics Classroom Manipulative Kit
- algebra tiles
- product mat

Factoring Using the Distributive Property

What You'll Learn

- Factor polynomials by using the Distributive Property.
- Solve quadratic equations of the form $ax^2 + bx = 0$.

Vocabulary
- factoring
- factoring by grouping

How can you determine how long a baseball will remain in the air?

Nolan Ryan, the greatest strike-out pitcher in the history of baseball, had a fastball clocked at 98 miles per hour or about 151 feet per second. If he threw a ball directly upward with the same velocity, the height h of the ball in feet above the point at which he released it could be modeled by the formula $h = 151t - 16t^2$, where t is the time in seconds. You can use factoring and the Zero Product Property to determine how long the ball would remain in the air before returning to his glove.

Study Tip

Look Back
To review the **Distributive Property**, see Lesson 1-5.

FACTOR BY USING THE DISTRIBUTIVE PROPERTY
In Chapter 8, you used the Distributive Property to multiply a polynomial by a monomial.

$$2a(6a + 8) = 2a(6a) + 2a(8)$$
$$= 12a^2 + 16a$$

You can reverse this process to express a polynomial as the product of a monomial factor and a polynomial factor.

$$12a^2 + 16a = 2a(6a) + 2a(8)$$
$$= 2a(6a + 8)$$

Thus, a *factored form* of $12a^2 + 16a$ is $2a(6a + 8)$.

Factoring a polynomial means to find its *completely* factored form. The expression $2a(6a + 8)$ is not completely factored since $6a + 8$ can be factored as $2(3a + 4)$.

Example 1 Use the Distributive Property

Use the Distributive Property to factor each polynomial.

a. $12a^2 + 16a$

First, find the GCF of $12a^2$ and $16a$.

$12a^2 = $ ②·②· 3 ·ⓐ· a Factor each number.
$16a = $ ②·②· 2 · 2 ·ⓐ   Circle the common prime factors.
GCF: $2 \cdot 2 \cdot a$ or $4a$

Write each term as the product of the GCF and its remaining factors. Then use the Distributive Property to factor out the GCF.

$12a^2 + 16a = 4a(3 \cdot a) + 4a(2 \cdot 2)$ Rewrite each term using the GCF.
$= 4a(3a) + 4a(4)$ Simplify remaining factors.
$= 4a(3a + 4)$ Distributive Property

Thus, the completely factored form of $12a^2 + 16a$ is $4a(3a + 4)$.

1 Focus

5-Minute Check Transparency 9-2 Use as a quiz or review of Lesson 9-1.

Mathematical Background notes are available for this lesson on p. 472C.

Building on Prior Knowledge

In Chapter 1, students were introduced to the Distributive Property and learned how to use it to simplify expressions. In Chapter 8, students learned to multiply a polynomial by a monomial using the Distributive Property. In this lesson, students will reverse that process to factor polynomials.

How can you determine how long a baseball will remain in the air?

Ask students:

- What is the greatest common factor (GCF) of two numbers? **The GCF is the greatest number that is a factor of both original numbers.**

- What is the GCF of $151t$ and $16t^2$? **t**

- What is the height of the ball when $t = 0$? **0 ft**

- What is the height of the ball when $t = 1$? **135 ft**

Resource Manager

Workbook and Reproducible Masters

Chapter 9 Resource Masters
- Study Guide and Intervention, pp. 529–530
- Skills Practice, p. 531
- Practice, p. 532
- Reading to Learn Mathematics, p. 533
- Enrichment, p. 534
- Assessment, p. 573

Parent and Student Study Guide Workbook, p. 69
Prerequisite Skills Workbook, pp. 13–14
School-to-Career Masters, p. 17

Transparencies
5-Minute Check Transparency 9-2
Answer Key Transparencies

Technology
Interactive Chalkboard

FACTOR BY USING THE DISTRIBUTIVE PROPERTY

In-Class Examples Power Point®

Teaching Tip Tell students that one way to find the remaining factors is to divide each term by the GCF.

1 Use the Distributive Property to factor each polynomial.

a. $15x + 25x^2$ $5x(3 + 5x)$

b. $12xy + 24xy^2 - 30x^2y^4$ $6xy(2 + 4y - 5xy^3)$

Teaching Tip Remind students that when using the FOIL method, they multiply the First terms, Outer terms, Inner terms, and Last terms.

2 Factor $2xy + 7x - 2y - 7$. $(x - 1)(2y + 7)$

3 Factor $15a - 3ab + 4b - 20$. $(-3a + 4)(b - 5)$

✔ Concept Check

Factoring Using the Distributive Property Malcolm and Fatima each factored the polynomial $2ax + 6cx + ab + 3bc$. Malcolm's answer was $(2x + b)(a + 3c)$ and Fatima's was $(a + 3c)(2x + b)$. Which is correct? Explain your answer.
Both are correct. The order in which factors are multiplied does not affect the product.

---

b. $18cd^2 + 12c^2d + 9cd$

$18cd^2 = 2 \cdot ③ \cdot 3 \cdot ⓒ \cdot ⓓ \cdot d$ Factor each number.
$12c^2d = 2 \cdot 2 \cdot ③ \cdot ⓒ \cdot c \cdot ⓓ$ Circle the common prime factors.
$9cd = ③ \cdot 3 \cdot ⓒ \cdot ⓓ$

GCF: $3 \cdot c \cdot d$ or $3cd$

$18cd^2 + 12c^2d + 9cd = 3cd(6d) + 3cd(4c) + 3cd(3)$ Rewrite each term using the GCF.
$= 3cd(6d + 4c + 3)$ Distributive Property

The Distributive Property can also be used to factor some polynomials having four or more terms. This method is called **factoring by grouping** because pairs of terms are grouped together and factored. The Distributive Property is then applied a second time to factor a common binomial factor.

Example 2 Use Grouping

Factor $4ab + 8b + 3a + 6$.

$4ab + 8b + 3a + 6$
$= (4ab + 8b) + (3a + 6)$ Group terms with common factors.
$= 4b(a + 2) + 3(a + 2)$ Factor the GCF from each grouping.
$= (a + 2)(4b + 3)$ Distributive Property

CHECK Use the FOIL method.

$$
\begin{array}{cccc}
& F & O & I & L \\
(a + 2)(4b + 3) = (a)(4b) & + & (a)(3) & + & (2)(4b) & + & (2)(3) \\
= 4ab & + & 3a & + & 8b & + & 6 \checkmark
\end{array}
$$

Recognizing binomials that are additive inverses is often helpful when factoring by grouping. For example, $7 - y$ and $y - 7$ are additive inverses. By rewriting $7 - y$ as $-1(y - 7)$, factoring by grouping is possible in the following example.

Example 3 Use the Additive Inverse Property

Factor $35x - 5xy + 3y - 21$.

$35x - 5xy + 3y - 21 = (35x - 5xy) + (3y - 21)$ Group terms with common factors.
$= 5x(7 - y) + 3(y - 7)$ Factor the GCF from each grouping.
$= 5x(-1)(y - 7) + 3(y - 7)$ $7 - y = -1(y - 7)$
$= -5x(y - 7) + 3(y - 7)$ $5x(-1) = -5x$
$= (y - 7)(-5x + 3)$ Distributive Property

Concept Summary   Factoring by Grouping

- **Words**   A polynomial can be factored by grouping if all of the following situations exist.
  - There are four or more terms.
  - Terms with common factors can be grouped together.
  - The two common factors are identical or are additive inverses of each other.

- **Symbols** $ax + bx + ay + by = x(a + b) + y(a + b)$
  $= (a + b)(x + y)$

SOLVE EQUATIONS BY FACTORING Some equations can be solved by factoring. Consider the following products.

$$6(0) = 0 \qquad 0(-3) = 0 \qquad (5 - 5)(0) = 0 \qquad -2(-3 + 3) = 0$$

Notice that in each case, *at least one* of the factors is zero. These examples illustrate the **Zero Product Property**.

Key Concept — Zero Product Property

- **Words**   If the product of two factors is 0, then at least one of the factors must be 0.

- **Symbols**   For any real numbers a and b, if $ab = 0$, then either $a = 0$, $b = 0$, or both a and b equal zero.

Example 4 *Solve an Equation in Factored Form*

Solve $(d - 5)(3d + 4) = 0$. Then check the solutions.

If $(d - 5)(3d + 4) = 0$, then according to the Zero Product Property either $d - 5 = 0$ or $3d + 4 = 0$.

$(d - 5)(3d + 4) = 0$	Original equation
$d - 5 = 0 \quad$ or $\quad 3d + 4 = 0$	Set each factor equal to zero.
$d = 5 \qquad\qquad 3d = -4$	Solve each equation.
$d = -\dfrac{4}{3}$	

The solution set is $\left\{5, -\dfrac{4}{3}\right\}$.

CHECK   Substitute 5 and $-\dfrac{4}{3}$ for d in the original equation.

$$(d - 5)(3d + 4) = 0 \qquad\qquad (d - 5)(3d + 4) = 0$$

$$(5 - 5)[3(5) + 4] \stackrel{?}{=} 0 \qquad\qquad \left(-\tfrac{4}{3} - 5\right)\left[3\left(-\tfrac{4}{3}\right) + 4\right] \stackrel{?}{=} 0$$

$$(0)(19) \stackrel{?}{=} 0 \qquad\qquad\qquad \left(-\tfrac{19}{3}\right)(0) \stackrel{?}{=} 0$$

$$0 = 0 \ \checkmark \qquad\qquad\qquad\qquad 0 = 0 \ \checkmark$$

If an equation can be written in the form $ab = 0$, then the Zero Product Property can be applied to solve that equation.

Study Tip

Common Misconception
You may be tempted to try to solve the equation in Example 5 by dividing each side of the equation by x. Remember, however, that x is an *unknown* quantity. If you divide by x, you may actually be dividing by zero, which is undefined.

Example 5 *Solve an Equation by Factoring*

Solve $x^2 = 7x$. Then check the solutions.

Write the equation so that it is of the form $ab = 0$.

$x^2 = 7x$	Original equation
$x^2 - 7x = 0$	Subtract $7x$ from each side.
$x(x - 7) = 0$	Factor the GCF of x^2 and $-7x$, which is x.
$x = 0 \quad$ or $\quad x - 7 = 0$	Zero Product Property
$x = 7$	Solve each equation.

The solution set is $\{0, 7\}$. Check by substituting 0 and 7 for x in the original equation.

 www.algebra1.com/extra_examples

SOLVE EQUATIONS BY FACTORING

In-Class Examples   Power Point®

Teaching Tip If students think using the Zero Product Property to set factors equal to zero is somewhat arbitrary, have them multiply the two factors to obtain a polynomial, and set the polynomial equal to zero. Then have students substitute the two solutions into the polynomial to see that they produce a true sentence.

4 Solve $(x - 2)(4x - 1) = 0$. Then check the solutions. $\left\{2, \dfrac{1}{4}\right\}$

Teaching Tip Remind students that for the Zero Product Property to work, one of two factors is equal to zero. Therefore, students must factor $x^2 - 7x$ before they can assume that one term is equal to zero.

5 Solve $4y = 12y^2$. Then check the solutions. $\left\{0, \dfrac{1}{3}\right\}$

DAILY INTERVENTION

Differentiated Instruction

Visual/Spatial When students solve factored equations, have them write each factor on a separate sheet of scrap paper, followed by "= 0" on a third sheet of scrap paper. Then, have students remove one of the factors and solve the remaining equation. Once the first solution is found, have students place the other factor equal to zero and solve for the second solution.

Study Notebook

Have students—

• add the definitions/examples of the vocabulary terms to their Vocabulary Builder worksheets for Chapter 9.

• include explanations on how to factor polynomials using the distributive property, and how to solve equations using factoring.

• include any other item(s) that they find helpful in mastering the skills in this lesson.

About the Exercises...

Organization by Objective
• Factor by Using the Distributive Property: 16–39
• Solve Equations by Factoring: 48–59

Odd/Even Assignments
Exercises 16–39 and 44–59 are structured so that students practice the same concepts whether they are assigned odd or even problems.

Assignment Guide

Basic: 17–39 odd, 40–43, 47–59 odd, 62–81

Average: 17–39 odd, 42, 43, 45, 47–61 odd, 62–81

Advanced: 16–38 even, 44, 45, 46–60 even, 62–75 (optional: 76–81)

All: Practice Quiz 1 (1–10)

Check for Understanding

Concept Check

1. **Write** $4x^2 + 12x$ as a product of factors in three different ways. Then decide which of the three is the completely factored form. Explain your reasoning. **See margin.**

2. **OPEN ENDED** Give an example of the type of equation that can be solved by using the Zero Product Property.

3. **Explain** why $(x - 2)(x + 4) = 0$ cannot be solved by dividing each side by $x - 2$. **The division would eliminate 2 as a solution.**

2. an equation that can be written as a product of factors that equal 0

Guided Practice

Factor each polynomial. 7. $2ab(a^2b + 4 + 8ab^2)$

GUIDED PRACTICE KEY	
Exercises	Examples
4–9	1–3
10–15	4, 5

4. $9x^2 + 36x$ $9x(x + 4)$

5. $16xz - 40xz^2$ $8xz(2 - 5z)$

6. $24m^2np^2 + 36m^2n^2p$ $12m^2np(2p + 3n)$

7. $2a^3b^2 + 8ab + 16a^2b^3$

8. $5y^2 - 15y + 4y - 12$ $(5y + 4)(y - 3)$

9. $5c - 10c^2 + 2d - 4cd$
$(5c + 2d)(1 - 2c)$

Solve each equation. Check your solutions.

10. $h(h + 5) = 0$ $\{0, -5\}$

11. $(n - 4)(n + 2) = 0$
$\{-2, 4\}$

12. $5m = 3m^2$ $\left\{0, \frac{5}{3}\right\}$

Application

PHYSICAL SCIENCE For Exercises 13–15, use the information below and in the graphic.

A flare is launched from a life raft. The height h of the flare in feet above the sea is modeled by the formula $h = 100t - 16t^2$, where t is the time in seconds after the flare is launched.

13. At what height is the flare when it returns to the sea? **0 ft**

14. Let $h = 0$ in the equation $h = 100t - 16t^2$ and solve for t. **0, 6.25**

15. How many seconds will it take for the flare to return to the sea? Explain your reasoning. **6.25 s; The answer 0 is not reasonable since it represents the time at which the flare is launched.**

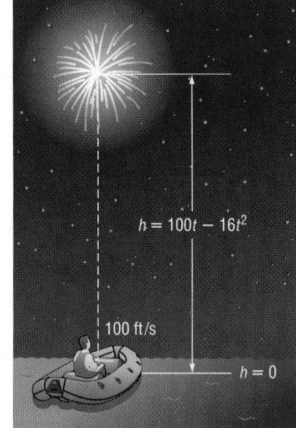

$h = 100t - 16t^2$

100 ft/s

$h = 0$

★ indicates increased difficulty

Practice and Apply

Homework Help	
For Exercises	See Examples
16–29, 40–47	1
30–39	2, 3
48–61	4, 5

Extra Practice
See page 840.

Factor each polynomial. 16–39. See p. 521A.

16. $5x + 30y$

17. $16a + 4b$

18. $a^5b - a$

19. $x^3y^2 + x$

20. $21cd - 3d$

21. $14gh - 18h$

22. $15a^2y - 30ay$

23. $8bc^2 + 24bc$

24. $12x^2y^2z + 40xy^3z^2$

25. $18a^2bc^2 - 48abc^3$

26. $a + a^2b^2 + a^3b^3$

27. $15x^2y^2 + 25xy + x$

28. $12ax^3 + 20bx^2 + 32cx$

29. $3p^3q - 9pq^2 + 36pq$

30. $x^2 + 2x + 3x + 6$

31. $x^2 + 5x + 7x + 35$

32. $4x^2 + 14x + 6x + 21$

33. $12y^2 + 9y + 8y + 6$

34. $6a^2 - 15a - 8a + 20$

35. $18x^2 - 30x - 3x + 5$

36. $4ax + 3ay + 4bx + 3by$

37. $2my + 7x + 7m + 2xy$

38. $8ax - 6x - 12a + 9$

39. $10x^2 - 14xy - 15x + 21y$

GEOMETRY For Exercises 40 and 41, use the following information.
A quadrilateral has 4 sides and 2 diagonals. A pentagon has 5 sides and 5 diagonals. You can use $\frac{1}{2}n^2 - \frac{3}{2}n$ to find the number of diagonals in a polygon with n sides.

40. Write this expression in factored form. $\frac{1}{2}n(n - 3)$

41. Find the number of diagonals in a decagon (10-sided polygon). **35**

484 Chapter 9 Factoring

Answers

1. Sample answers: $4(x^2 + 3x)$, $x(4x + 12)$, or $4x(x + 3)$; $4x(x + 3)$; $4x$ is the GCF of $4x^2$ and $12x$.

63. Answers should include the following.

• Let $h = 0$ in the equation $h = 151t - 16t^2$. To solve $0 = 151t - 16t^2$, factor the right-hand side as $t(151 - 16t)$. Then, since $t(151 - 16t) = 0$, either $t = 0$ or $151 - 16t = 0$. Solving each equation for t, we find that $t = 0$ or $t \approx 9.44$.

• The solution $t = 0$ represents the point at which the ball was initially thrown into the air. The solution $t \approx 9.44$ represents how long it took after the ball was thrown for it to return to the same height at which it was thrown.

SOFTBALL For Exercises 42 and 43, use the following information.

Albertina is scheduling the games for a softball league. To find the number of games she needs to schedule, she uses the equation $g = \frac{1}{2}n^2 - \frac{1}{2}n$, where g represents the number of games needed for each team to play each other team exactly once and n represents the number of teams.

42. Write this equation in factored form. $g = \frac{1}{2}n(n - 1)$

43. How many games are needed for 7 teams to play each other exactly 3 times?
63 games

GEOMETRY Write an expression in factored form for the area of each shaded region.

44.

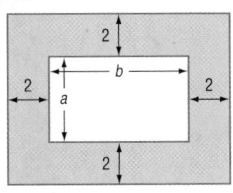

$4(a + b + 4)$

★ 45.

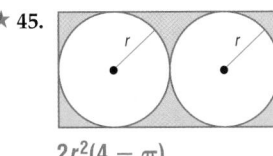

$2r^2(4 - \pi)$

GEOMETRY Find an expression for the area of a square with the given perimeter.

46. $P = 12x + 20y$ in.
$9x^2 + 30xy + 25y^2$ in^2

47. $P = 36a - 16b$ cm
$81a^2 - 72ab + 16b^2$ cm^2

Solve each equation. Check your solutions.

48. $x(x - 24) = 0$ $\{0, 24\}$

49. $a(a + 16) = 0$ $\{-16, 0\}$

50. $(q + 4)(3q - 15) = 0$ $\{-4, 5\}$

51. $(3y + 9)(y - 7) = 0$ $\{-3, 7\}$

52. $(2b - 3)(3b - 8) = 0$ $\left\{\frac{3}{2}, \frac{8}{3}\right\}$

53. $(4n + 5)(3n - 7) = 0$ $\left\{-\frac{5}{4}, \frac{7}{3}\right\}$

54. $3z^2 + 12z = 0$ $\{-4, 0\}$

55. $7d^2 - 35d = 0$ $\{0, 5\}$

56. $2x^2 = 5x$ $\left\{0, \frac{5}{2}\right\}$

57. $7x^2 = 6x$ $\left\{0, \frac{6}{7}\right\}$

58. $6x^2 = -4x$ $\left\{-\frac{2}{3}, 0\right\}$

59. $20x^2 = -15x$ $\left\{-\frac{3}{4}, 0\right\}$

Career Choices

Marine Biologist

Marine biologists study factors that affect organisms living in and near the ocean.

📖 **Online Research**
For information about a career as a marine biologist, visit:
www.algebra1.com/careers

Source: National Sea Grant Library

60. **MARINE BIOLOGY** In a pool at a water park, a dolphin jumps out of the water traveling at 20 feet per second. Its height h, in feet, above the water after t seconds is given by the formula $h = 20t - 16t^2$. How long is the dolphin in the air before returning to the water? **1.25 s**

61. **BASEBALL** Malik popped a ball straight up with an initial upward velocity of 45 feet per second. The height h, in feet, of the ball above the ground is modeled by the equation $h = 2 + 45t - 16t^2$. How long was the ball in the air if the catcher catches the ball when it is 2 feet above the ground? **about 2.8 s**

62. **CRITICAL THINKING** Factor $a^{x + y} + a^x b^y - a^y b^x - b^{x + y}$. $(a^x - b^x)(a^y + b^y)$

63. **WRITING IN MATH** Answer the question that was posed at the beginning of the lesson. **See margin.**

How can you determine how long a baseball will remain in the air?

Include the following in your answer:
- an explanation of how to use factoring and the Zero Product Property to find how long the ball would be in the air, and
- an interpretation of each solution in the context of the problem.

www.algebra1.com/self_check_quiz

Open-Ended Assessment

Speaking Ask a volunteer to describe the similarities and differences between factoring using grouping, and factoring using the additive inverse property. Encourage other students to ask questions.

Getting Ready for Lesson 9-3

PREREQUISITE SKILL Students will learn to factor trinomials in Lesson 9-3. It is important that students recall how to multiply polynomials to check that they correctly factored trinomials. Use Exercises 76–81 to determine your students' familiarity with multiplying polynomials.

Assessment Options

Practice Quiz 1 The quiz provides students with a brief review of the concepts and skills in Lessons 9-1 and 9-2. Lesson numbers are given to the right of the exercises or instruction lines so students can review concepts not yet mastered.

Quiz (Lessons 9-1 and 9-2) is available on p. 573 of the *Chapter 9 Resource Masters*.

Answer

1. 1, 3, 5, 9, 15, 25, 45, 75, 225; composite

Standardized Test Practice
ⒶⒷⒸⒹ

64. The total number of feet in x yards, y feet, and z inches is **A**

Ⓐ $3x + y + \dfrac{z}{12}$.

Ⓑ $12(x + y + z)$.

Ⓒ $x = 3y + 36z$.

Ⓓ $\dfrac{x}{36} + \dfrac{y}{12} + z$.

65. Lola is batting for her school's softball team. She hit the ball straight up with an initial upward velocity of 47 feet per second. The height h of the softball in feet above ground after t seconds can be modeled by the equation $h = -16t^2 + 47t + 3$. How long was the softball in the air before it hit the ground? **C**

Ⓐ 0.06 s

Ⓑ 2.5 s

Ⓒ 3 s

Ⓓ 3.15 s

Maintain Your Skills

Mixed Review

66. 1, 3, 41, 123; composite
67. 1, 2, 3, 4, 5, 6, 10, 12, 15, 20, 25, 30, 50, 60, 75, 100, 150, 300; composite
71. $9k^2 + 48k + 64$

Find the factors of each number. Then classify each number as *prime* or *composite*. *(Lesson 9-1)*

66. 123

67. 300

68. 67 **1, 67; prime**

Find each product. *(Lesson 8-8)* **69.** $16s^6 + 24s^3 + 9$ **70.** $4p^2 - 25q^2$

69. $(4s^3 + 3)^2$

70. $(2p + 5q)(2p - 5q)$

71. $(3k + 8)(3k + 8)$

Simplify. Assume that no denominator is equal to zero. *(Lesson 8-2)*

72. $\dfrac{s^4}{s^{-7}}$ $\;s^{11}$

73. $\dfrac{18x^3y^{-1}}{12x^2y^4}$ $\;\dfrac{3x}{2y^5}$

74. $\dfrac{34p^7q^2r^{-5}}{17(p^3qr^{-1})^2}$ $\;\dfrac{2p}{r^3}$

75. FINANCE Michael uses at most 60% of his annual FlynnCo stock dividend to purchase more shares of FlynnCo stock. If his dividend last year was $885 and FlynnCo stock is selling for $14 per share, what is the greatest number of shares that he can purchase? *(Lesson 6-2)* **37 shares**

Getting Ready for the Next Lesson

76. $n^2 + 11n + 24$
77. $x^2 - 9x + 20$
78. $b^2 - 3b - 70$

PREREQUISITE SKILL **Find each product.**
*(To review **multiplying polynomials**, see Lesson 8-7.)*

76. $(n + 8)(n + 3)$

77. $(x - 4)(x - 5)$

78. $(b - 10)(b + 7)$

79. $(3a + 1)(6a - 4)$
$\qquad 18a^2 - 6a - 4$

80. $(5p - 2)(9p - 3)$
$\qquad 45p^2 - 33p + 6$

81. $(2y - 5)(4y + 3)$
$\qquad 8y^2 - 14y - 15$

Practice Quiz 1 — Lessons 9-1 and 9-2

1. Find the factors of 225. Then classify the number as *prime* or *composite*. *(Lesson 9-1)* **See margin.**

2. Find the prime factorization of -320. *(Lesson 9-1)* $-1 \cdot 2^6 \cdot 5$

3. Factor $78a^2bc^3$ completely. *(Lesson 9-1)* $2 \cdot 3 \cdot 13 \cdot a \cdot a \cdot b \cdot c \cdot c \cdot c$

4. Find the GCF of $54x^3$, $42x^2y$, and $30xy^2$. *(Lesson 9-1)* $6x$

Factor each polynomial. *(Lesson 9-2)*

5. $4xy^2 - xy$ $\;xy(4y - 1)$

6. $32a^2b + 40b^3 - 8a^2b^2$
$\quad 8b(4a^2 + 5b^2 - a^2b)$

7. $6py + 16p - 15y - 40$
$\quad (2p - 5)(3y + 8)$

Solve each equation. Check your solutions. *(Lesson 9-2)*

8. $(8n + 5)(n - 4) = 0$ $\left\{-\dfrac{5}{8}, 4\right\}$

9. $9x^2 - 27x = 0$ $\{0, 3\}$

10. $10x^2 = -3x$ $\left\{-\dfrac{3}{10}, 0\right\}$

Factoring Trinomials

You can use algebra tiles to factor trinomials. If a polynomial represents the area of a rectangle formed by algebra tiles, then the rectangle's length and width are *factors* of the area.

Activity 1 Use algebra tiles to factor $x^2 + 6x + 5$.

Step 1 Model the polynomial $x^2 + 6x + 5$.

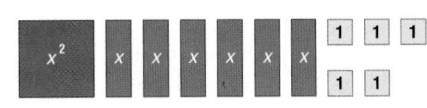

Step 2 Place the x^2 tile at the corner of the product mat. Arrange the 1 tiles into a rectangular array. Because 5 is prime, the 5 tiles can be arranged in a rectangle in one way, a 1-by-5 rectangle.

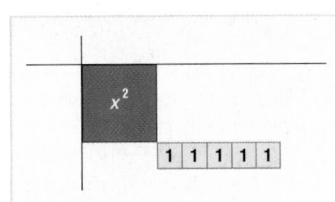

Step 3 Complete the rectangle with the x tiles.

The rectangle has a width of $x + 1$ and a length of $x + 5$. Therefore, $x^2 + 6x + 5 = (x + 1)(x + 5)$.

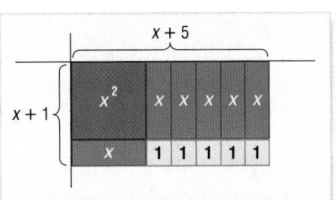

Activity 2 Use algebra tiles to factor $x^2 + 7x + 6$.

Step 1 Model the polynomial $x^2 + 7x + 6$.

Step 2 Place the x^2 tile at the corner of the product mat. Arrange the 1 tiles into a rectangular array. Since $6 = 2 \times 3$, try a 2-by-3 rectangle. Try to complete the rectangle. Notice that there are two extra x tiles.

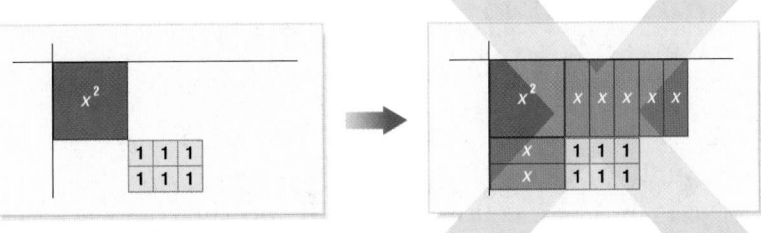

(continued on the next page)

Algebra Activity Factoring Trinomials **487**

Resource Manager

📂 *Teaching Algebra with Manipulatives*

• pp. 10–11 (master for algebra tiles)
• p. 17 (master for product mat)
• p. 159 (student recording sheet)

Glencoe Mathematics Classroom Manipulative Kit

• algebra tiles
• product mat

Algebra Activity

A Preview of Lesson 9-3

Getting Started

Objective Factor trinomials with algebra tiles.

Materials
algebra tiles
product mat

Teach

• Remind students that they used algebra tiles in an activity prior to Lesson 9-2 to factor polynomials. Ask students to tell you what they must be able to form with the tiles in order to factor a polynomial. **a rectangle**

• **Activity 1** Remind students to read the width of the tiles along the edge of the rectangle. The x^2 tile has a width of x and the x tiles have a width of one.

• **Activity 2** Encourage students to try several different arrangements until they can form a rectangle. While the x^2 tile should be in the corner, there is more than one correct way to arrange the tiles into a rectangle.

- **Activity 3** Remind students to pay close attention to the sign of the tiles. It would be very easy to mistake the factors as $(x + 3)(x + 3)$ if they do not pay attention to the signs.
- Students may need to be reminded that adding a zero pair is similar to adding the same number to both sides of an equation. Be sure that students are careful to add one x tile and one $-x$ tile when they add a zero pair.

Assess

- After students complete **Exercises 1–8**, ask them whether they notice a correlation between the need to use zero pairs to factor the trinomial, and the appearance of the resulting factors. **Sample answer: When zero pairs are used, the signs of the factors are opposite. When zero pairs are not used, the signs of the factors are the same.**

Study Notebook

You may wish to have students summarize this activity and what they learned from it.

Step 3 Arrange the 1 tiles into a 1-by-6 rectangular array. This time you can complete the rectangle with the x tiles.

The rectangle has a width of $x + 1$ and a length of $x + 6$. Therefore, $x^2 + 7x + 6 = (x + 1)(x + 6)$.

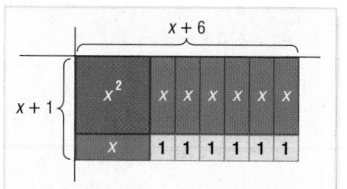

Activity 3 Use algebra tiles to factor $x^2 - 2x - 3$.

Step 1 Model the polynomial $x^2 - 2x - 3$.

Step 2 Place the x^2 tile at the corner of the product mat. Arrange the 1 tiles into a 1-by-3 rectangular array as shown.

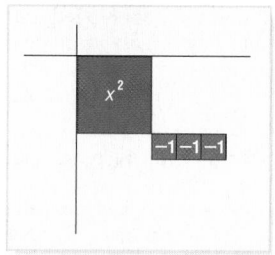

Step 3 Place the x tile as shown. Recall that you can add zero-pairs without changing the value of the polynomial. In this case, add a zero pair of x tiles.

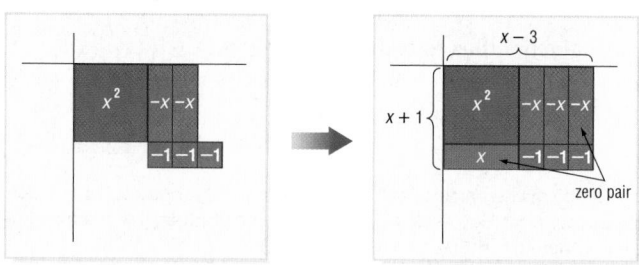

The rectangle has a width of $x + 1$ and a length of $x - 3$. Therefore, $x^2 - 2x - 3 = (x + 1)(x - 3)$.

Model 1. $(x + 3)(x + 1)$ 2. $(x + 4)(x + 1)$ 3. $(x - 3)(x + 2)$ 4. $(x - 2)(x - 1)$

Use algebra tiles to factor each trinomial.

1. $x^2 + 4x + 3$ 2. $x^2 + 5x + 4$ 3. $x^2 - x - 6$ 4. $x^2 - 3x + 2$

5. $x^2 + 7x + 12$ 6. $x^2 - 4x + 4$ 7. $x^2 - x - 2$ 8. $x^2 - 6x + 8$
   $(x + 4)(x + 3)$ $(x - 2)(x - 2)$ $(x + 1)(x - 2)$ $(x - 4)(x - 2)$

What You'll Learn

- Factor trinomials of the form $x^2 + bx + c$.
- Solve equations of the form $x^2 + bx + c = 0$.

How can factoring be used to find the dimensions of a garden?

Tamika has enough bricks to make a 30-foot border around the rectangular vegetable garden she is planting. The booklet she got from the nursery says that the plants will need a space of 54 square feet to grow. What should the dimensions of her garden be? To solve this problem, you need to find two numbers whose product is 54 and whose sum is 15, half the perimeter of the garden.

$A = 54 \text{ ft}^2$

$P = 30 \text{ ft}$

FACTOR $x^2 + bx + c$ In Lesson 9-1, you learned that when two numbers are multiplied, each number is a factor of the product. Similarly, when two binomials are multiplied, each binomial is a factor of the product.

To factor some trinomials, you will use the pattern for multiplying two binomials. Study the following example.

$$
\begin{array}{llll}
& \text{F} \quad \text{O} \quad \text{I} \quad \text{L} & \\
(x + 2)(x + 3) = (x \cdot x) + (x \cdot 3) + (x \cdot 2) + (2 \cdot 3) & \text{Use the FOIL method.} \\
= x^2 + 3x + 2x + 6 & \text{Simplify.} \\
= x^2 + (3 + 2)x + 6 & \text{Distributive Property} \\
= x^2 + 5x + 6 & \text{Simplify.}
\end{array}
$$

Observe the following pattern in this multiplication.

$$
\begin{array}{ll}
(x + 2)(x + 3) = x^2 + (3 + 2)x + (2 \cdot 3) \\
(x + m)(x + n) = x^2 + (n + m)x + mn \\
\qquad\qquad = x^2 + \underline{(m + n)}x + \underline{mn} \\
\qquad x^2 + \quad bx \quad + \quad c & b = m + n \text{ and } c = mn
\end{array}
$$

Notice that the coefficient of the middle term is the sum of m and n and the last term is the product of m and n. This pattern can be used to factor quadratic trinomials of the form $x^2 + bx + c$.

Study Tip

Reading Math
A *quadratic trinomial* is a trinomial of degree 2. This means that the greatest exponent of the variable is 2.

Key Concept — Factoring $x^2 + bx + c$

- **Words**   To factor quadratic trinomials of the form $x^2 + bx + c$, find two integers, m and n, whose sum is equal to b and whose product is equal to c. Then write $x^2 + bx + c$ using the pattern $(x + m)(x + n)$.

- **Symbols** $x^2 + bx + c = (x + m)(x + n)$ when $m + n = b$ and $mn = c$.

- **Example** $x^2 + 5x + 6 = (x + 2)(x + 3)$, since $2 + 3 = 5$ and $2 \cdot 3 = 6$.

---

1 Focus

5-Minute Check Transparency 9-3 Use as a quiz or review of Lesson 9-2.

Mathematical Background notes are available for this lesson on p. 472D.

How can factoring be used to find the dimensions of a garden?

Ask students:

- Why do you need to find two numbers whose product is 54 to find the dimensions of the garden? **The garden is a rectangle with an area of 54 ft². The area of a rectangle is equal to the length times the width. Since the area is 54 ft², the length and the width must be two numbers whose product is 54.**

- What two integers have a product of 54? **1 and 54, 2 and 27, 3 and 18, 6 and 9**

- Which pair has a sum of 15? **6 and 9**

- What are the dimensions of the vegetable garden? **The garden is 6 ft by 9 ft.**

Resource Manager

Workbook and Reproducible Masters

Chapter 9 Resource Masters
- Study Guide and Intervention, pp. 535–536
- Skills Practice, p. 537
- Practice, p. 538
- Reading to Learn Mathematics, p. 539
- Enrichment, p. 540
- Assessment, pp. 573, 575

Parent and Student Study Guide Workbook, p. 70

 Transparencies

5-Minute Check Transparency 9-3
Answer Key Transparencies

 Technology

AlgePASS: Tutorial Plus, Lessons 24, 25
Interactive Chalkboard

FACTOR $x^2 + bx + c$

The concept of factoring trinomials as introduced in this lesson may seem somewhat abstract to some students. Whenever you introduce abstract concepts, it is good to reinforce them with a concrete example. After introducing factoring trinomials, refer students back to the lesson opener problem. Ask students to describe any similarities they notice between finding the dimensions of the garden and factoring a trinomial.

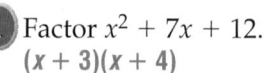
In-Class Examples   Power Point®

Teaching Tip Tell students that the order in which they record the factors does not matter. So, $(x + 4)(x + 2)$ is also correct.

1 Factor $x^2 + 7x + 12$.
$(x + 3)(x + 4)$

Teaching Tip If students use the graphing calculator to check their factoring, make sure they clear all other functions from the Y= list, and clear all other drawings from the draw menu.

2 Factor $x^2 - 12x + 27$.
$(x - 3)(x - 9)$

To determine m and n, find the factors of c and use a guess-and-check strategy to find which pair of factors has a sum of b.

Example 1 b and c Are Positive

Factor $x^2 + 6x + 8$.

In this trinomial, $b = 6$ and $c = 8$. You need to find two numbers whose sum is 6 and whose product is 8. Make an organized list of the factors of 8, and look for the pair of factors whose sum is 6.

Factors of 8	Sum of Factors
1, 8	9
2, 4	6

The correct factors are 2 and 4.

$$x^2 + 6x + 8 = (x + m)(x + n) \quad \text{Write the pattern.}$$
$$= (x + 2)(x + 4) \quad m = 2 \text{ and } n = 4$$

CHECK You can check this result by multiplying the two factors.

$$\overset{\text{F} \quad \text{O} \quad \text{I} \quad \text{L}}{(x + 2)(x + 4)} = x^2 + 4x + 2x + 8 \quad \text{FOIL method}$$
$$= x^2 + 6x + 8 \checkmark \quad \text{Simplify.}$$

When factoring a trinomial where b is negative and c is positive, you can use what you know about the product of binomials to help narrow the list of possible factors.

Example 2 b Is Negative and c Is Positive

Factor $x^2 - 10x + 16$.

In this trinomial, $b = -10$ and $c = 16$. This means that $m + n$ is negative and mn is positive. So m and n must both be negative. Therefore, make a list of the negative factors of 16, and look for the pair of factors whose sum is -10.

Factors of 16	Sum of Factors
$-1, -16$	-17
$-2, -8$	-10
$-4, -4$	-8

The correct factors are -2 and -8.

$$x^2 - 10x + 16 = (x + m)(x + n) \quad \text{Write the pattern.}$$
$$= (x - 2)(x - 8) \quad m = -2 \text{ and } n = -8$$

CHECK You can check this result by using a graphing calculator. Graph $y = x^2 - 10x + 16$ and $y = (x - 2)(x - 8)$ on the same screen. Since only one graph appears, the two graphs must coincide. Therefore, the trinomial has been factored correctly. ✓

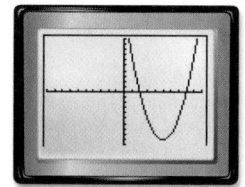

$[-10, 10]$ scl: 1 by $[-10, 10]$ scl: 1

You will find that keeping an organized list of the factors you have tested is particularly important when factoring a trinomial like $x^2 + x - 12$, where the value of c is negative.

Differentiated Instruction

Kinesthetic As students are learning the rules for factoring trinomials, encourage them to use algebra tiles to confirm their results. Students should soon realize that the greater the values of b and c in the trinomials, the more cumbersome algebra tiles become, which should reinforce the importance of learning to factor using the method in the text.

Example 3 | b Is Positive and c Is Negative

Factor $x^2 + x - 12$.

In this trinomial, $b = 1$ and $c = -12$. This means that $m + n$ is positive and mn is negative. So either m or n is negative, but not both. Therefore, make a list of the factors of -12, where one factor of each pair is negative. Look for the pair of factors whose sum is 1.

Factors of -12	Sum of Factors
1, -12	-11
-1, 12	11
2, -6	-4
-2, 6	4
3, -4	-1
-3, 4	1

The correct factors are -3 and 4.

$$x^2 + x - 12 = (x + m)(x + n) \quad \text{Write the pattern.}$$
$$= (x - 3)(x + 4) \quad m = -3 \text{ and } n = 4$$

Example 4 | b Is Negative and c Is Negative

Factor $x^2 - 7x - 18$.

Since $b = -7$ and $c = -18$, $m + n$ is negative and mn is negative. So either m or n is negative, but not both.

Factors of -18	Sum of Factors
1, -18	-17
-1, 18	17
2, -9	-7

The correct factors are 2 and -9.

$$x^2 - 7x - 18 = (x + m)(x + n) \quad \text{Write the pattern.}$$
$$= (x + 2)(x - 9) \quad m = 2 \text{ and } n = -9$$

SOLVE EQUATIONS BY FACTORING Some equations of the form $x^2 + bx + c = 0$ can be solved by factoring and then using the Zero Product Property.

Example 5 | Solve an Equation by Factoring

Solve $x^2 + 5x = 6$. Check your solutions.

$x^2 + 5x = 6$	Original equation
$x^2 + 5x - 6 = 0$	Rewrite the equation so that one side equals 0.
$(x - 1)(x + 6) = 0$	Factor.
$x - 1 = 0$ or $x + 6 = 0$	Zero Product Property
$x = 1 \qquad x = -6$	Solve each equation.

The solution set is $\{1, -6\}$.

CHECK Substitute 1 and -6 for x in the original equation.

$$x^2 + 5x = 6 \qquad\qquad x^2 + 5x = 6$$
$$(1)^2 + 5(1) \stackrel{?}{=} 6 \qquad (-6)^2 + 5(-6) \stackrel{?}{=} 6$$
$$6 = 6 \; \checkmark \qquad\qquad 6 = 6 \; \checkmark$$

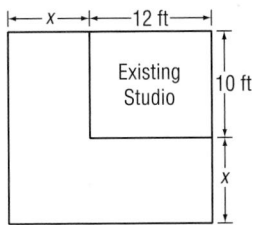

Study Notebook

Have students—
• include explanations on how to factor trinomials.
• include any other item(s) that they find helpful in mastering the skills in this lesson.

DAILY INTERVENTION **FIND THE ERROR**
Ask students to recall how many answers they usually get when solving a trinomial equation.

About the Exercises...

Organization by Objective
• Factor $x^2 + bx + c$: 17–34
• Solve Equations by Factoring: 37–53

Odd/Even Assignments
Exercises 17–53 are structured so that students practice the same concepts whether they are assigned odd or even problems.

Alert! Exercises 66–69 require a graphing calculator.

Assignment Guide

Basic: 17–33 odd, 37–51 odd, 55, 57–60, 63–65, 70–83

Average: 17–55 odd, 57–60, 63–65, 70–83 (optional: 66–69)

Advanced: 18–56 even, 57–77 (optional: 78–83)

Answers

1. In this trinomial, $b = 6$ and $c = 9$. This means that $m + n$ is positive and mn is positive. Only two positive numbers have both a positive sum and product. Therefore, negative factors of 9 need not be considered.

Example 6 *Solve a Real-World Problem by Factoring*

YEARBOOK DESIGN A sponsor for the school yearbook has asked that the length and width of a photo in their ad be increased by the same amount in order to double the area of the photo. If the photo was originally 12 centimeters wide by 8 centimeters long, what should the new dimensions of the enlarged photo be?

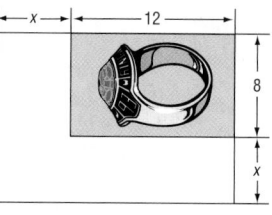

Explore Begin by making a diagram like the one shown above, labeling the appropriate dimensions.

Plan Let $x =$ the amount added to each dimension of the photo.

The new length,	times	the new width,	equals	the new area,
$x + 12$	$\cdot$	$x + 8$	$=$	$2(8)(12)$
				old area

Solve
$(x + 12)(x + 8) = 2(8)(12)$ Write the equation.
$x^2 + 20x + 96 = 192$ Multiply.
$x^2 + 20x - 96 = 0$ Subtract 192 from each side.
$(x + 24)(x - 4) = 0$ Factor.

$x + 24 = 0$ or $x - 4 = 0$ Zero Product Property
$x = -24$ $x = 4$ Solve each equation.

Examine The solution set is $\{-24, 4\}$. Only 4 is a valid solution, since dimensions cannot be negative. Thus, the new length of the photo should be $4 + 12$ or 16 centimeters, and the new width should be $4 + 8$ or 12 centimeters.

Check for Understanding

Concept Check
1. **Explain** why, when factoring $x^2 + 6x + 9$, it is not necessary to check the sum of the factor pairs -1 and -9 or -3 and -3. **See margin.**

2. Sample answer: $x^2 - 14x + 40 = 0$; $\{4, 10\}$

2. **OPEN ENDED** Give an example of an equation that can be solved using the factoring techniques presented in this lesson. Then, solve your equation.

3. **FIND THE ERROR** Peter and Aleta are solving $x^2 + 2x = 15$.

Peter
$x^2 + 2x = 15$
$x(x + 2) = 15$
$x = 15$ or $x + 2 = 15$
$x = 13$

Aleta
$x^2 + 2x = 15$
$x^2 + 2x - 15 = 0$
$(x - 3)(x + 5) = 0$
$x - 3 = 0$ or $x + 5 = 0$
$x = 3$ $x = -5$

Who is correct? Explain your reasoning. **Aleta; to use the Zero Product Property, one side of the equation must equal zero.**

GUIDED PRACTICE KEY	
Exercises	Examples
4–9	1–4
10–15	5
16	6

Guided Practice
Factor each trinomial.   4. $(x + 3)(x + 8)$ 5. $(c - 1)(c - 2)$ 6. $(n - 3)(n + 16)$
4. $x^2 + 11x + 24$ 5. $c^2 - 3c + 2$ 6. $n^2 + 13n - 48$
7. $p^2 - 2p - 35$ 8. $72 + 27a + a^2$ 9. $x^2 - 4xy + 3y^2$
    $(p + 5)(p - 7)$ $(a + 3)(a + 24)$ $(x - 3y)(x - y)$

---

10. $\{-1, -6\}$

11. $\{-9, 4\}$

12. $\{-2, 21\}$

13. $\{-9, -1\}$

14. $\{-11, 2\}$

15. $\{-7, 10\}$

17. $(a + 3)(a + 5)$

18. $(x + 3)(x + 9)$

19. $(c + 5)(c + 7)$

20. $(y + 10)(y + 3)$

21. $(m - 1)(m - 21)$

22. $(d - 5)(d - 2)$

23. $(p - 8)(p - 9)$

24. $(g - 4)(g - 15)$

25. $(x - 1)(x + 7)$

26. $(b - 4)(b + 5)$

27. $(h - 5)(h + 8)$

28. $(n - 6)(n + 9)$

29. $(y - 7)(y + 6)$

30. $(z + 2)(z - 20)$

31. $(w + 12)(w - 6)$

32. $(x - 2)(x + 15)$

33. $(a + b)(a + 4b)$

34. $(x - 4y)(x - 9y)$

Solve each equation. Check your solutions. **10–15. See margin.**

10. $n^2 + 7n + 6 = 0$ **11.** $a^2 + 5a - 36 = 0$ **12.** $p^2 - 19p - 42 = 0$

13. $y^2 + 9 = -10y$ **14.** $9x + x^2 = 22$ **15.** $d^2 - 3d = 70$

Application   **16. NUMBER THEORY**   Find two consecutive integers whose product is 156.
12 and 13 or −13 and −12

★ indicates increased difficulty

Practice and Apply

Factor each trinomial. **17–34. See margin.**

17. $a^2 + 8a + 15$ **18.** $x^2 + 12x + 27$ **19.** $c^2 + 12c + 35$

20. $y^2 + 13y + 30$ **21.** $m^2 - 22m + 21$ **22.** $d^2 - 7d + 10$

23. $p^2 - 17p + 72$ **24.** $g^2 - 19g + 60$ **25.** $x^2 + 6x - 7$

26. $b^2 + b - 20$ **27.** $h^2 + 3h - 40$ **28.** $n^2 + 3n - 54$

29. $y^2 - y - 42$ **30.** $z^2 - 18z - 40$ **31.** $-72 + 6w + w^2$

32. $-30 + 13x + x^2$ **33.** $a^2 + 5ab + 4b^2$ **34.** $x^2 - 13xy + 36y^2$

Homework Help

For Exercises	See Examples
17–36	1–4
37–53	5
54–56, 61, 62	6

Extra Practice
See page 840.

GEOMETRY   Find an expression for the perimeter of a rectangle with the given area.

★ **35.** area $= x^2 + 24x - 81$ **4x + 48**   ★ **36.** area $= x^2 + 13x - 90$ **4x + 26**

Solve each equation. Check your solutions.

37. $x^2 + 16x + 28 = 0$ **38.** $b^2 + 20b + 36 = 0$ **39.** $y^2 + 4y - 12 = 0$ **{−6, 2}**

40. $d^2 + 2d - 8 = 0$ **{−4, 2}**   **41.** $a^2 - 3a - 28 = 0$ **{−4, 7}**   **42.** $g^2 - 4g - 45 = 0$ **{−5, 9}**

43. $m^2 - 19m + 48 = 0$ **44.** $n^2 - 22n + 72 = 0$ **45.** $z^2 = 18 - 7z$ **{2, −9}**

46. $h^2 + 15 = -16h$ **47.** $24 + k^2 = 10k$ **{4, 6}**   **48.** $x^2 - 20 = x$ **{−4, 5}**

49. $c^2 - 50 = -23c$ **{−25, 2}**   **50.** $y^2 - 29y = -54$ **{2, 27}**   **51.** $14p + p^2 = 51$ **{−17, 3}**

★ **52.** $x^2 - 2x - 6 = 74$ **{−8, 10}**   ★ **53.** $x^2 - x + 56 = 17x$ **{4, 14}**

37. {−14, −2}
38. {−18, −2}
43. {3, 16}
44. {4, 18}
46. {−15, −1}

54. SUPREME COURT   When the Justices of the Supreme Court assemble to go on the Bench each day, each Justice shakes hands with each of the other Justices for a total of 36 handshakes. The total number of handshakes h possible for n people is given by $h = \dfrac{n^2 - n}{2}$. Write and solve an equation to determine the number of Justices on the Supreme Court. $36 = \dfrac{n^2 - n}{2}$; **9**

55. NUMBER THEORY   Find two consecutive even integers whose product is 168.
−14 and −12 or 12 and 14

56. GEOMETRY   The triangle has an area of 40 square centimeters. Find the height h of the triangle. **5 cm**

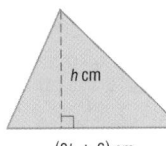

h cm

$(2h + 6)$ cm

More About. . .

Supreme Court

The "Conference handshake" has been a tradition since the late 19th century.

Source: www.supremecourtus.gov

CRITICAL THINKING   Find all values of k so that each trinomial can be factored using integers.

57. $x^2 + kx - 19$ **−18, 18**   **58.** $x^2 + kx + 14$ **−15, −9, 9, 15**

59. $x^2 - 8x + k$, $k > 0$ **7, 12, 15, 16**   **60.** $x^2 - 5x + k$, $k > 0$ **4, 6**

RUGBY   For Exercises 61 and 62, use the following information.
The length of a Rugby League field is 52 meters longer than its width w.

61. Write an expression for the area of the rectangular field. **[w(w + 52)] m²**

62. The area of a Rugby League field is 8160 square meters. Find the dimensions of the field. **120 m by 68 m**

www.algebra1.com/self_check_quiz

Lesson 9-3   Factoring Trinomials: $x^2 + bx + c$ **493**

Open-Ended Assessment

Speaking Ask volunteers to brainstorm a mnemonic device that will help them remember how to factor trinomials with different positive and negative values of b and c. Then write example trinomials on the chalkboard and have students factor them using the mnemonic devices as a guide.

Getting Ready for Lesson 9-4

PREREQUISITE SKILL Students will learn to factor additional types of trinomials in Lesson 9-4 using factoring by grouping. Use Exercises 78–83 to determine your students' familiarity with factoring by grouping.

Assessment Options

Quiz (Lesson 9-3) is available on p. 573 of the *Chapter 9 Resource Masters*.

Mid-Chapter Test (Lessons 9-1 through 9-3) is available on p. 575 of the *Chapter 9 Resource Masters*.

Answer

63. Answers should include the following.
   • You would use a guess-and-check process, listing the factors of 54, checking to see which pairs added to 15.
   • To factor a trinomial of the form $x^2 + ax + c$, you also use a guess-and-check process, list the factors of c, and check to see which ones add to a.

---

63.  **WRITING IN MATH** Answer the question that was posed at the beginning of the lesson. **See margin.**

How can factoring be used to find the dimensions of a garden?

Include the following in your answer:
   • a description of how you would find the dimensions of the garden, and
   • an explanation of how the process you used is related to the process used to factor trinomials of the form $x^2 + bx + c$.

 *Standardized Test Practice*
Ⓐ Ⓑ Ⓒ Ⓓ

64. Which is the factored form of $x^2 - 17x + 42$? **C**
   Ⓐ $(x - 1)(y - 42)$ Ⓑ $(x - 2)(x - 21)$
   Ⓒ $(x - 3)(x - 14)$ Ⓓ $(x - 6)(x - 7)$

65. **GRID IN** What is the positive solution of $p^2 - 13p - 30 = 0$? **15**

Graphing Calculator Use a graphing calculator to determine whether each factorization is correct. Write *yes* or *no*. If no, state the correct factorization.

66. $x^2 - 14x + 48 = (x + 6)(x + 8)$ 67. $x^2 - 16x - 105 = (x + 5)(x - 21)$ **yes**
68. $x^2 + 25x + 66 = (x + 33)(x + 2)$ 69. $x^2 + 11x - 210 = (x + 10)(x - 21)$
66. no; $(x - 6)(x - 8)$ 68. no; $(x + 22)(x + 3)$ 69. no; $(x - 10)(x + 21)$

Maintain Your Skills

Mixed Review

70. $\left\{-3, \dfrac{5}{2}\right\}$

Solve each equation. Check your solutions. *(Lesson 9-2)*

70. $(x + 3)(2x - 5) = 0$ 71. $b(7b - 4) = 0$ $\left\{0, \dfrac{4}{7}\right\}$ 72. $5y^2 = -9y$ $\left\{-\dfrac{9}{5}, 0\right\}$

Find the GCF of each set of monomials. *(Lesson 9-1)*

73. $24, 36, 72$ **12**   74. $9p^2q^5, 21p^3q^3$ **$3p^2q^3$**   75. $30x^4y^5, 20x^2y^7, 75x^3y^4$
$5x^2y^4$

INTERNET For Exercises 76 and 77, use the graph at the right. *(Lessons 3-7 and 8-3)*

76. Find the percent increase in the number of domain registrations from 1997 to 2000. **1731%**

77. Use your answer from Exercise 76 to verify the claim that registrations grew more than 18-fold from 1997 to 2000 is correct. $1(1.54) + 17.31(1.54) = (1 + 17.31)(1.54)$ or $18.31(1.54)$

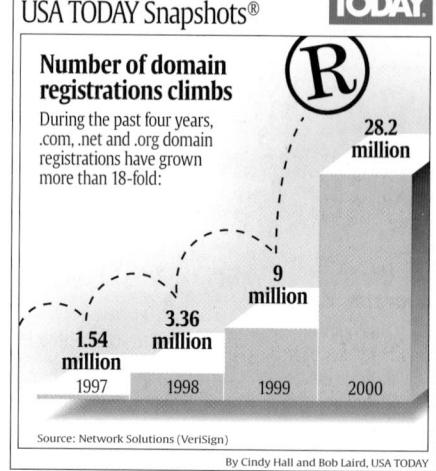

USA TODAY Snapshots®

Number of domain registrations climbs

During the past four years, .com, .net and .org domain registrations have grown more than 18-fold:

28.2 million
9 million
3.36 million
1.54 million

1997   1998   1999   2000

Source: Network Solutions (VeriSign)

By Cindy Hall and Bob Laird, USA TODAY

78. $(y + 3)(3y + 2)$
79. $(a + 4)(3a + 2)$
80. $(x + 2)(4x + 3)$

Getting Ready for the Next Lesson

PREREQUISITE SKILL Factor each polynomial.
(To review factoring by grouping, see Lesson 9-2.)

78. $3y^2 + 2y + 9y + 6$ 79. $3a^2 + 2a + 12a + 8$ 80. $4x^2 + 3x + 8x + 6$
81. $2p^2 - 6p + 7p - 21$ 82. $3b^2 + 7b - 12b - 28$ 83. $4g^2 - 2g - 6g + 3$
$(2p + 7)(p - 3)$ $(b - 4)(3b + 7)$ $(2g - 3)(2g - 1)$

 **Online Lesson Plans**

USA TODAY Education's Online site offers resources and interactive features connected to each day's newspaper. *Experience TODAY*, USA TODAY's daily lesson plan, is available on the site and delivered daily to subscribers. This plan provides instruction for integrating USA TODAY graphics and key editorial features into your mathematics classroom. Log on to **www.education.usatoday.com**.

Factoring Trinomials: $ax^2 + bx + c$

What You'll Learn

- Factor trinomials of the form $ax^2 + bx + c$.
- Solve equations of the form $ax^2 + bx + c = 0$.

Vocabulary
- prime polynomial

How can algebra tiles be used to factor $2x^2 + 7x + 6$?

The factors of $2x^2 + 7x + 6$ are the dimensions of the rectangle formed by the algebra tiles shown below.

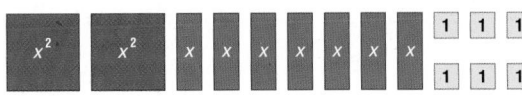

The process you use to form the rectangle is the same mental process you can use to factor this trinomial algebraically.

FACTOR $ax^2 + bx + c$ For trinomials of the form $x^2 + bx + c$, the coefficient of x^2 is 1. To factor trinomials of this form, you find the factors of c whose sum is b. We can modify this approach to factor trinomials whose leading coefficient is not 1.

Study Tip

Look Back
To review **factoring by grouping**, see Lesson 9-2.

$$(2x + 5)(3x + 1) = 6x^2 + 2x + 15x + 5 \quad \text{Use the FOIL method.}$$

F O I L

$2 \cdot 15 = 30$

$6 \cdot 5 = 30$

Observe the following pattern in this product.

$6x^2 + 2x + 15x + 5 \qquad\qquad ax^2 + mx + nx + c$
$6x^2 + 17x + 5 \qquad\qquad\quad ax^2 + bx + c$

$2 + 15 = 17$ and $2 \cdot 15 = 6 \cdot 5$ $\qquad m + n = b$ and $mn = ac$

You can use this pattern and the method of factoring by grouping to factor $6x^2 + 17x + 5$. Find two numbers, m and n, whose product is $6 \cdot 5$ or 30 and whose sum is 17.

Factors of 30	Sum of Factors
1, 30	31
2, 15	17

The correct factors are 2 and 15.

$6x^2 + 17x + 5 = 6x^2 + mx + nx + 5$ Write the pattern.
$\qquad\qquad\quad = 6x^2 + 2x + 15x + 5$ $m = 2$ and $n = 15$
$\qquad\qquad\quad = (6x^2 + 2x) + (15x + 5)$ Group terms with common factors.
$\qquad\qquad\quad = 2x(3x + 1) + 5(3x + 1)$ Factor the GCF from each grouping.
$\qquad\qquad\quad = (3x + 1)(2x + 5)$ $3x + 1$ is the common factor.

Therefore, $6x^2 + 17x + 5 = (3x + 1)(2x + 5)$.

---

1 Focus

 5-Minute Check Transparency 9-4 Use as a quiz or review of Lesson 9-3.

Mathematical Background notes are available for this lesson on p. 472D.

How can algebra tiles be used to factor $2x^2 + 7x + 6$?

Ask students:

- When you form a rectangle with algebra tiles to model a trinomial such as the one given, how do you know the factors? **The length of the rectangle is one factor, and the height is the other factor.**

- How is the trinomial $2x^2 + 7x + 6$ different from those that you learned how to factor in Lesson 9-3? **The x^2 term is multiplied by a constant (2).**

- What would the rectangle formed by the given algebra tiles look like? What are the factors of the trinomial?

x^2	x^2	x	x	x
x	x	1	1	1
x	x	1	1	1

$(2x + 3)(x + 2)$

Resource Manager

Workbook and Reproducible Masters

Chapter 9 Resource Masters
- Study Guide and Intervention, pp. 541–542
- Skills Practice, p. 543
- Practice, p. 544
- Reading to Learn Mathematics, p. 545
- Enrichment, p. 546

Graphing Calculator and Spreadsheet Masters, p. 39
Parent and Student Study Guide Workbook, p. 71
Prerequisite Skills Workbook, pp. 13–14

Transparencies
5-Minute Check Transparency 9-4
Answer Key Transparencies

Technology
AlgePASS: Tutorial Plus, Lesson 26
Interactive Chalkboard

FACTOR $ax^2 + bx + c$

In-Class Examples

Power Point®

Teaching Tip In Example 1b of the Student Edition, mn is a large number, which has quite a few factors. Have students start listing the factors that can easily be determined by mental math. More than likely, the factors that equal $m + n$ can be found this way, without too much calculation.

a. Factor $5x^2 + 27x + 10$.
$(5x + 2)(x + 5)$

b. Factor $24x^2 - 22x + 3$.
$(4x - 3)(6x - 1)$

Teaching Tip Remind students not to forget to record the common factor that they factored out of the trinomial when they record the other two factors.

2 Factor $4x^2 + 24x + 32$.
$4(x + 2)(x + 4)$

Study Tip

Finding Factors
Factor pairs in an organized list so you do not miss any possible pairs of factors.

Example 1 Factor $ax^2 + bx + c$

a. **Factor $7x^2 + 22x + 3$.**

In this trinomial, $a = 7$, $b = 22$ and $c = 3$. You need to find two numbers whose sum is 22 and whose product is $7 \cdot 3$ or 21. Make an organized list of the factors of 21 and look for the pair of factors whose sum is 22.

Factors of 21	Sum of Factors
1, 21	22

The correct factors are 1 and 21.

$$
\begin{aligned}
7x^2 + 22x + 3 &= 7x^2 + mx + nx + 3 && \text{Write the pattern.} \\
&= 7x^2 + 1x + 21x + 3 && m = 1 \text{ and } n = 21 \\
&= (7x^2 + 1x) + (21x + 3) && \text{Group terms with common factors.} \\
&= x(7x + 1) + 3(7x + 1) && \text{Factor the GCF from each grouping.} \\
&= (7x + 1)(x + 3) && \text{Distributive Property}
\end{aligned}
$$

CHECK You can check this result by multiplying the two factors.

$$
\begin{aligned}
& \quad\quad\quad\;\; \text{F} \quad\; \text{O} \quad\; \text{I} \quad \text{L} \\
(7x + 1)(x + 3) &= 7x^2 + 21x + x + 3 && \text{FOIL method} \\
&= 7x^2 + 22x + 3 \;\checkmark && \text{Simplify.}
\end{aligned}
$$

b. **Factor $10x^2 - 43x + 28$.**

In this trinomial, $a = 10$, $b = -43$ and $c = 28$. Since b is negative, $m + n$ is negative. Since c is positive, mn is positive. So m and n must both be negative. Therefore, make a list of the negative factors of $10 \cdot 28$ or 280, and look for the pair of factors whose sum is -43.

Factors of 280	Sum of Factors
$-1, -280$	-281
$-2, -140$	-142
$-4, -70$	-74
$-5, -56$	-61
$-7, -40$	-47
$-8, -35$	-43

The correct factors are -8 and -35.

$$
\begin{aligned}
10x^2 - 43x + 28 & \\
&= 10x^2 + mx + nx + 28 && \text{Write the pattern.} \\
&= 10x^2 + (-8)x + (-35)x + 28 && m = -8 \text{ and } n = -35 \\
&= (10x^2 - 8x) + (-35x + 28) && \text{Group terms with common factors.} \\
&= 2x(5x - 4) + 7(-5x + 4) && \text{Factor the GCF from each grouping.} \\
&= 2x(5x - 4) + 7(-1)(5x - 4) && -5x + 4 = (-1)(5x - 4) \\
&= 2x(5x - 4) + (-7)(5x - 4) && 7(-1) = -7 \\
&= (5x - 4)(2x - 7) && \text{Distributive Property}
\end{aligned}
$$

Sometimes the terms of a trinomial will contain a common factor. In these cases, first use the Distributive Property to factor out the common factor. Then factor the trinomial.

Example 2 Factor When a, b, and c Have a Common Factor

Factor $3x^2 + 24x + 45$.

Notice that the GCF of the terms $3x^2$, $24x$, and 45 is 3. When the GCF of the terms of a trinomial is an integer other than 1, you should first factor out this GCF.

$$3x^2 + 24x + 45 = 3(x^2 + 8x + 15) \quad \text{Distributive Property}$$

DAILY

INTERVENTION

Differentiated Instruction

Interpersonal Place students in groups to factor polynomials such as those in Examples 1 and 2. Have each group member find one or two factors for mn, depending on the number of factors and number of students in the group. By dividing the labor, students should be able to quickly find the factors for mn that sum to $m + n$. Once they find the factors, have students complete the factoring as a group.

Now factor $x^2 + 8x + 15$. Since the lead coefficient is 1, find two factors of 15 whose sum is 8.

Factors of 15	Sum of Factors	
1, 15	16	
3, 5	8	The correct factors are 3 and 5.

So, $x^2 + 8x + 15 = (x + 3)(x + 5)$. Thus, the complete factorization of $3x^2 + 24x + 45$ is $3(x + 3)(x + 5)$.

Study Tip

Factoring Completely
Always check for a GCF first before trying to factor a trinomial.

A polynomial that cannot be written as a product of two polynomials with integral coefficients is called a **prime polynomial**.

Example 3 *Determine Whether a Polynomial Is Prime*

Factor $2x^2 + 5x - 2$.

In this trinomial, $a = 2$, $b = 5$ and $c = -2$. Since b is positive, $m + n$ is positive. Since c is negative, mn is negative. So either m or n is negative, but not both. Therefore, make a list of the factors of $2 \cdot -2$ or -4, where one factor in each pair is negative. Look for a pair of factors whose sum is 5.

Factors of -4	Sum of Factors
1, -4	-3
-1, 4	3
-2, 2	0

There are no factors whose sum is 5. Therefore, $2x^2 + 5x - 2$ cannot be factored using integers. Thus, $2x^2 + 5x - 2$ is a prime polynomial.

SOLVE EQUATIONS BY FACTORING Some equations of the form $ax^2 + bx + c = 0$ can be solved by factoring and then using the Zero Product Property.

Example 4 *Solve Equations by Factoring*

Solve $8a^2 - 9a - 5 = 4 - 3a$. Check your solutions.

$8a^2 - 9a - 5 = 4 - 3a$	Original equation
$8a^2 - 6a - 9 = 0$	Rewrite so that one side equals 0.
$(4a + 3)(2a - 3) = 0$	Factor the left side.

$4a + 3 = 0 \quad$ or $\quad 2a - 3 = 0 \quad$ Zero Product Property
$4a = -3 \qquad\qquad 2a = 3 \qquad$ Solve each equation.
$a = -\dfrac{3}{4} \qquad\qquad a = \dfrac{3}{2}$

The solution set is $\left\{ -\dfrac{3}{4}, \dfrac{3}{2} \right\}$.

CHECK Check each solution in the original equation.

$8a^2 - 9a - 5 = 4 - 3a$

$8\left(-\dfrac{3}{4}\right)^2 - 9\left(-\dfrac{3}{4}\right) - 5 \stackrel{?}{=} 4 - 3\left(-\dfrac{3}{4}\right)$

$\dfrac{9}{2} + \dfrac{27}{4} - 5 \stackrel{?}{=} 4 + \dfrac{9}{4}$

$\dfrac{25}{4} = \dfrac{25}{4} \checkmark$

$8a^2 - 9a - 5 = 4 - 3a$

$8\left(\dfrac{3}{2}\right)^2 - 9\left(\dfrac{3}{2}\right) - 5 \stackrel{?}{=} 4 - 3\left(\dfrac{3}{2}\right)$

$18 - \dfrac{27}{2} - 5 \stackrel{?}{=} 4 - \dfrac{9}{2}$

$-\dfrac{1}{2} = -\dfrac{1}{2} \checkmark$

In-Class Example Power Point®

Teaching Tip Make sure students list all possible factors of mn, including both positive and negative factors, before they decide the polynomial is prime.

3 Factor $3x^2 + 7x - 5$. **prime**

SOLVE EQUATIONS BY FACTORING

In-Class Examples Power Point®

Teaching Tip Remind students that when a polynomial has two factors, there are two solutions. Check each solution by substituting it into the original equation.

4 Solve $18b^2 - 19b - 8 = 3b^2 - 5b$. $\left\{ -\dfrac{2}{5}, \dfrac{4}{3} \right\}$

5 MODEL ROCKETS Ms. Nguyen's science class built an air-launched model rocket for a competition. When they test-launched their rocket outside the classroom, the rocket landed in a nearby tree. If the launch pad was 2 feet above the ground, the initial velocity of the rocket was 64 feet per second, and the rocket landed 30 feet above the ground, how long was the rocket in flight? Use the equation $h = -16t^2 + vt + s$. **3.5 seconds**

D A I L Y
INTERVENTION **Unlocking Misconceptions**

Dividing Students may assume that because they cannot divide each side of $x(x + 2) = 0$ by x, they may never divide both sides of an equation set equal to zero by anything. Make sure they realize that they can divide each side by a known number, as in Example 5, but they cannot divide each side by a variable that may equal zero.

Study Notebook

Have students—

- add the definitions/examples of the vocabulary terms to their Vocabulary Builder worksheets for Chapter 9.
- include explanations on how to factor trinomials of the form $ax^2 + bx + c$.
- include any other item(s) that they find helpful in mastering the skills in this lesson.

DAILY INTERVENTION FIND THE ERROR

Students should first look at the numbers for which Dasan and Craig are finding factors. This clue should immediately tell them which student is correct. Then, challenge students to find another error in Dasan's work. Students should notice that he factored a 2 out of $2x^2 + 11x + 18$, which is not possible.

About the Exercises...

Organization by Objective
- Factor $ax^2 + bx + c$: 14–34
- Solve Equations by Factoring: 35–48

Odd/Even Assignments
Exercises 14–48 are structured so that students practice the same concepts whether they are assigned odd or even problems.

Assignment Guide

Basic: 15–29 odd, 33–43 odd, 49, 50, 53–70

Average: 15–47 odd, 49–51, 53–70

Advanced: 14–48 even, 52–62 (optional: 63–70)

All: Practice Quiz 2 (1–10)

A *model for the vertical motion of a projected object* is given by the equation $h = -16t^2 + vt + s$, where h is the height in feet, t is the time in seconds, v is the initial upward velocity in feet per second, and s is the starting height of the object in feet.

Example 5 *Solve Real-World Problems by Factoring*

PEP RALLY At a pep rally, small foam footballs are launched by cheerleaders using a sling-shot. How long is a football in the air if a student in the stands catches it on its way down 26 feet above the gym floor?

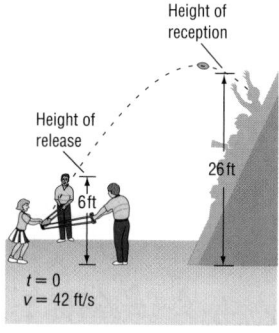

Use the model for vertical motion.

$h = -16t^2 + vt + s$	Vertical motion model
$26 = -16t^2 + 42t + 6$	$h = 26, v = 42, s = 6$
$0 = -16t^2 + 42t - 20$	Subtract 26 from each side.
$0 = -2(8t^2 - 21t + 10)$	Factor out -2.
$0 = 8t^2 - 21t + 10$	Divide each side by -2.
$0 = (8t - 5)(t - 2)$	Factor $8t^2 - 21t + 10$.
$8t - 5 = 0$ or $t - 2 = 0$	Zero Product Property
$8t = 5$ $t = 2$	Solve each equation.
$t = \dfrac{5}{8}$	

The solutions are $\dfrac{5}{8}$ second and 2 seconds. The first time represents how long it takes the football to reach a height of 26 feet on its way up. The later time represents how long it takes the ball to reach a height of 26 feet again on its way down. Thus, the football will be in the air for 2 seconds before the student catches it.

Study Tip

Factoring When a Is Negative
When factoring a trinomial of the form $ax^2 + bx + c$, where a is negative, it is helpful to factor out a negative monomial.

Check for Understanding

Concept Check

1. **Explain** how to determine which values should be chosen for m and n when factoring a polynomial of the form $ax^2 + bx + c$.

2. **OPEN ENDED** Write a trinomial that can be factored using a pair of numbers whose sum is 9 and whose product is 14. **Sample answer:** $2x^2 + 9x + 7$

3. **FIND THE ERROR** Dasan and Craig are factoring $2x^2 + 11x + 18$.

1. m and n are the factors of ac that add to b.

Dasan

Factors of 18	Sum
1, 18	19
3, 6	9
9, 2	11

$2x^2 + 11x + 18$
$= 2(x^2 + 11x + 18)$
$= 2(x + 9)(x + 2)$

Craig

Factors of 36	Sum
1, 36	37
2, 18	20
3, 12	15
4, 9	13
6, 6	12

$2x^2 + 11x + 18$ is prime.

GUIDED PRACTICE KEY

Exercises	Examples
4–9	1–3
10–12	4
13	5

Who is correct? Explain your reasoning. **Craig; see margin for explanation.**

Guided Practice Factor each trinomial, if possible. If the trinomial cannot be factored using integers, write *prime*. **4.** $(3a + 2)(a + 2)$ **6.** $2(p + 3)(p + 4)$

4. $3a^2 + 8a + 4$ **5.** $2a^2 - 11a + 7$ **prime**   **6.** $2p^2 + 14p + 24$

7. $2x^2 + 13x + 20$ **8.** $6x^2 + 15x - 9$ **9.** $4n^2 - 4n - 35$
$(x + 4)(2x + 5)$ $3(2x - 1)(x + 3)$ $(2n + 5)(2n - 7)$

Answers

3. When factoring a trinomial of the form $ax^2 + bx + c$, where $a \neq 1$, you must find the factors of ac, not of c.

14. $(2x + 5)(x + 1)$

15. $(3x + 2)(x + 1)$

16. $(2p + 3)(3p - 2)$

17. $(5d - 4)(d + 2)$

18. prime

19. $(3g - 2)(3g - 2)$

20. $(2a + 3)(a - 6)$

21. $(x - 4)(2x + 5)$

22. $(5c - 7)(c - 2)$

23. prime

24. $(2y - 3)(4y + 3)$

25. $(5n + 2)(2n - 3)$

26. $(5z + 9)(3z - 2)$

27. $(2x + 3)(7x - 4)$

28. $2(3r + 2)(r - 3)$

29. $5(3x + 2)(2x - 3)$

30. $(3x + 5y)(3x + 5y)$

31. $(12a - 5b)(3a + 2b)$

10. $\left\{-3, -\dfrac{2}{3}\right\}$

Solve each equation. Check your solutions.

10. $3x^2 + 11x + 6 = 0$ 11. $10p^2 - 19p + 7 = 0$ 12. $6n^2 + 7n = 20$ $\left\{-\dfrac{5}{2}, \dfrac{4}{3}\right\}$
$\left\{\dfrac{1}{2}, \dfrac{7}{5}\right\}$

Application 13. **GYMNASTICS** When a gymnast making a vault leaves the horse, her feet are 8 feet above the ground traveling with an initial upward velocity of 8 feet per second. Use the model for vertical motion to find the time t in seconds it takes for the gymnast's feet to reach the mat. (*Hint*: Let $h = 0$, the height of the mat.) **1 s**

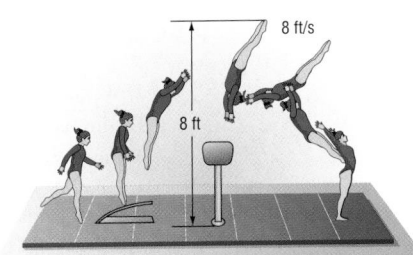

8 ft/s

8 ft

★ indicates increased difficulty

Practice and Apply

Homework Help

For Exercises	See Examples
14–31	1–3
35–48	4
49–52	5

Extra Practice
See page 840.

Factor each trinomial, if possible. If the trinomial cannot be factored using integers, write *prime*. 14–31. See margin.

14. $2x^2 + 7x + 5$
15. $3x^2 + 5x + 2$
16. $6p^2 + 5p - 6$
17. $5d^2 + 6d - 8$
18. $8k^2 - 19k + 9$
19. $9g^2 - 12g + 4$
20. $2a^2 - 9a - 18$
21. $2x^2 - 3x - 20$
22. $5c^2 - 17c + 14$
23. $3p^2 - 25p + 16$
24. $8y^2 - 6y - 9$
25. $10n^2 - 11n - 6$
26. $15z^2 + 17z - 18$
27. $14x^2 + 13x - 12$
28. $6r^2 - 14r - 12$
29. $30x^2 - 25x - 30$
★ 30. $9x^2 + 30xy + 25y^2$
★ 31. $36a^2 + 9ab - 10b^2$

CRITICAL THINKING Find all values of k so that each trinomial can be factored as two binomials using integers.

32. $2x^2 + kx + 12$
$\pm 25, \pm 14, \pm 11, \pm 10$
33. $2x^2 + kx + 15$
$\pm 31, \pm 17, \pm 13, \pm 11$
34. $2x^2 + 12x + k, k > 0$
$10, 16, 18$

Solve each equation. Check your solutions. 35–48. See p. 521A.

35. $5x^2 + 27x + 10 = 0$
36. $3x^2 - 5x - 12 = 0$
37. $24x^2 - 11x - 3 = 3x$
38. $17x^2 - 11x + 2 = 2x^2$
39. $14n^2 = 25n + 25$
40. $12a^2 - 13a = 35$
41. $6x^2 - 14x = 12$
42. $21x^2 - 6 = 15x$
43. $24x^2 - 30x + 8 = -2x$
44. $24x^2 - 46x = 18$
★ 45. $\dfrac{x^2}{12} - \dfrac{2x}{3} - 4 = 0$
★ 46. $t^2 - \dfrac{t}{6} = \dfrac{35}{6}$
★ 47. $(3y + 2)(y + 3) = y + 14$
★ 48. $(4a - 1)(a - 2) = 7a - 5$

GEOMETRY For Exercises 49 and 50, use the following information.
A rectangle with an area of 35 square inches is formed by cutting off strips of equal width from a rectangular piece of paper.

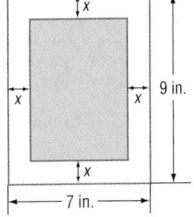

x x x 9 in. x 7 in.

49. Find the width of each strip. **1 in.**
50. Find the dimensions of the new rectangle. **5 in. by 7 in.**

51. **CLIFF DIVING** Suppose a diver leaps from the edge of a cliff 80 feet above the ocean with an initial upward velocity of 8 feet per second. How long will it take the diver to enter the water below? **2.5 s**

Lesson 9-4   Factoring Trinomials: $ax^2 + bx + c$ **499**

Lesson 9-4   Factoring Trinomials: $ax^2 + bx + c$ **499**

Open-Ended Assessment
Writing Place students in pairs. Have each student pick a problem that involves solving an equation by factoring and intentionally make a mistake while solving the problem. Then have students exchange problems. Students should write a description of what is incorrect, and how to solve the problem correctly. Have students share their explanations and correct solutions with the class.

Getting Ready for Lesson 9-5

PREREQUISITE SKILL Students will learn to factor binomials that are differences of squares in Lesson 9-5. Factoring differences of squares requires students to be able to quickly find the principal square roots of perfect squares. Use Exercises 63–70 to determine your students' familiarity with finding square roots.

Assessment Options

Practice Quiz 2 The quiz provides students with a brief review of the concepts and skills in Lessons 9-3 and 9-4. Lesson numbers are given to the right of the exercises or instruction lines so students can review concepts not yet mastered.

Answer

53. You can use algebra tiles to factor $2x^2 + 7x + 6$ by finding the dimensions of the rectangle that is formed by the tiles for $2x^2 + 7x + 6$. Answers should include the following.
- $2x + 3$ by $x + 2$
- With algebra tiles, you can try various ways to make a rectangle with the necessary tiles. Once you make the rectangle, however, the dimensions of the rectangle are the factors of the polynomial. In a way, you have to go through the guess-and-check process whether you are factoring algebraically or geometrically (using algebra tiles.)

---

52. **CLIMBING** Damaris launches a grappling hook from a height of 6 feet with an initial upward velocity of 56 feet per second. The hook just misses the stone ledge of a building she wants to scale. As it falls, the hook anchors on the ledge, which is 30 feet above the ground. How long was the hook in the air? **3 s**

53. **WRITING IN MATH** Answer the question that was posed at the beginning of the lesson. **See margin.**

How can algebra tiles be used to factor $2x^2 + 7x + 6$?

Include the following in your answer:
- the dimensions of the rectangle formed, and
- an explanation, using words and drawings, of how this geometric guess-and-check process of factoring is similar to the algebraic process described on page 495.

Standardized Test Practice

54. What are the solutions of $2p^2 - p - 3 = 0$? **D**
   Ⓐ $-\frac{2}{3}$ and 1   Ⓑ $\frac{2}{3}$ and -1 Ⓒ $-\frac{3}{2}$ and 1   Ⓓ $\frac{3}{2}$ and -1

55. Suppose a person standing atop a building 398 feet tall throws a ball upward. If the person releases the ball 4 feet above the top of the building, the ball's height h, in feet, after t seconds is given by the equation $h = -16t^2 + 48t + 402$. After how many seconds will the ball be 338 feet from the ground? **B**
   Ⓐ 3.5   Ⓑ 4   Ⓒ 4.5   Ⓓ 5

Maintain Your Skills

Mixed Review **Factor each trinomial, if possible. If the trinomial cannot be factored using integers, write** *prime*. *(Lesson 9-3)*

56. $a^2 - 4a - 21$ 57. $t^2 + 2t + 2$ 58. $d^2 + 15d + 44$
   $(a + 3)(a - 7)$ prime $(d + 4)(d + 11)$

Solve each equation. Check your solutions. *(Lesson 9-2)*

59. $\left\{-\frac{7}{5}, 4\right\}$

60. $\left\{-\frac{9}{2}, -\frac{2}{3}\right\}$

59. $(y - 4)(5y + 7) = 0$ 60. $(2k + 9)(3k + 2) = 0$ 61. $12u = u^2$ **{0, 12}**

62. **BUSINESS** Jake's Garage charges $83 for a two-hour repair job and $185 for a five-hour repair job. Write a linear equation that Jake can use to bill customers for repair jobs of any length of time. *(Lesson 5-3)* $y = 34x + 15$

Getting Ready for the Next Lesson **PREREQUISITE SKILL** **Find the principal square root of each number.**
(To review **square roots***, see Lesson 2-7.)*

63. 16 **4**   64. 49 **7**   65. 36 **6**   66. 25 **5**
67. 100 **10**   68. 121 **11**   69. 169 **13**   70. 225 **15**

Practice Quiz 2 — Lessons 9-3 and 9-4

Factor each trinomial, if possible. If the trinomial cannot be factored using integers, write *prime*. *(Lessons 9-3 and 9-4)*

1. $x^2 - 14x - 72$ $(x + 4)(x - 18)$ 2. $8p^2 - 6p - 35$ $(2p - 5)(4p + 7)$ 3. $16a^2 - 24a + 5$ $(4a - 1)(4a - 5)$
4. $n^2 - 17n + 52$ $(n - 13)(n - 4)$ 5. $24c^2 + 62c + 18$ 6. $3y^2 + 33y + 54$ $3(y + 2)(y + 9)$
                                          $2(3c + 1)(4c + 9)$

Solve each equation. Check your solutions. *(Lessons 9-3 and 9-4)*

7. $b^2 + 14b - 32 = 0$ {−16, 2}   8. $x^2 + 45 = 18x$ {3, 15}
9. $12y^2 - 7y - 12 = 0$ $\left\{-\frac{3}{4}, \frac{4}{3}\right\}$ 10. $6a^2 = 25a - 14$ $\left\{\frac{2}{3}, \frac{7}{2}\right\}$

Guess $(2x + 1)(x + 3)$ incorrect because 8 x tiles are needed to complete the rectangle

x^2	x	x	x
x^2	x	x	x
x	1	1	1
	1	1	1

x^2	x	x
x^2	x	x
x	1	1
x	1	1
x	1	1

Factoring Differences of Squares

What You'll Learn

- Factor binomials that are the differences of squares.
- Solve equations involving the differences of squares.

How can you determine a basketball player's hang time?

A basketball player's *hang time* is the length of time he is in the air after jumping. Given the maximum height h a player can jump, you can determine his hang time t in seconds by solving $4t^2 - h = 0$. If h is a perfect square, this equation can be solved by factoring using the pattern for the difference of squares.

FACTOR $a^2 - b^2$ A geometric model can be used to factor the difference of squares.

Algebra Activity

Difference of Squares

Step 1 Use a straightedge to draw two squares similar to those shown below. Choose any measures for a and b.

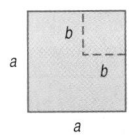

Notice that the area of the large square is a^2, and the area of the small square is b^2.

Step 2 Cut the small square from the large square.

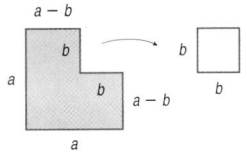

The area of the remaining irregular region is $a^2 - b^2$.

Step 3 Cut the irregular region into two congruent pieces as shown below.

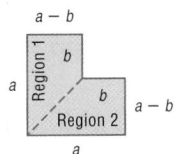

Step 4 Rearrange the two congruent regions to form a rectangle with length $a + b$ and width $a - b$.

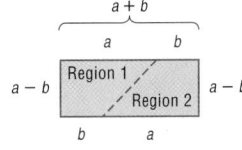

Make a Conjecture

1. Write an expression representing the area of the rectangle. $(a + b)(a - b)$
2. Explain why $a^2 - b^2 = (a + b)(a - b)$. Since $a^2 - b^2$ and $(a + b)(a - b)$ describe the same area, $a^2 - b^2 = (a + b)(a - b)$.

Study Tip

Look Back
To review the **product of a sum and a difference**, see Lesson 8-8.

---

1 *Focus*

 5-Minute Check Transparency 9-5 Use as a quiz or review of Lesson 9-4.

Mathematical Background notes are available for this lesson on p. 472D.

Building on Prior Knowledge

In Chapter 8, students learned about a special binomial product called a difference of squares. Specifically, a difference of squares is the product of two binomials of the form $(a + b)(a - b)$, and the product is of the form $a^2 - b^2$. In this lesson, students will learn to factor differences of squares, and use the factoring of differences of squares to solve equations.

How can you determine a basketball player's hang time?

Ask students:

- What is a perfect square? **A perfect square is a rational number whose square root is a rational number.**
- Is $4t^2$ a perfect square? If so, what is its principal square root? **Yes, the principal square root is $2t$.**
- If a basketball player can jump 4 feet, what would be her hang time? **1 second**

Resource Manager

Workbook and Reproducible Masters

Chapter 9 Resource Masters
- Study Guide and Intervention, pp. 547–548
- Skills Practice, p. 549
- Practice, p. 550
- Reading to Learn Mathematics, p. 551
- Enrichment, p. 552
- Assessment, p. 574

Prerequisite Skills Workbook, pp. 13–14

Graphing Calculator and Spreadsheet Masters, p. 40
Parent and Student Study Guide Workbook, p. 72
School-to-Career Masters, p. 18
Science and Mathematics Lab Manual, pp. 71–76
Teaching Algebra With Manipulatives Masters, pp. 24, 167

 Transparencies
5-Minute Check Transparency 9-5
Answer Key Transparencies

 Technology
Interactive Chalkboard

FACTOR $a^2 - b^2$

 Power Point®

Teaching Tip Students may check their factoring by multiplying the factors using the FOIL method. The first-degree term will always drop out when the product is a difference of squares.

1 Factor each binomial.

a. $m^2 - 64$ $(m + 8)(m - 8)$

b. $16y^2 - 81z^2$ $(4y + 9z)(4y - 9z)$

2 Factor $3b^3 - 27b$.
$3b(b + 3)(b - 3)$

Teaching Tip Students should notice that when the difference of squares factoring technique has been applied once, one of the factors should be prime.

3 Factor $4y^4 - 2500$.
$4(y^2 + 25)(y + 5)(y - 5)$

4 Factor $6x^3 + 30x^2 - 24x - 120$.
$6(x + 2)(x - 2)(x + 5)$

Study Tip

Common Misconception
Remember that the sum of two squares, like $x^2 + 9$, is not factorable using the difference of squares pattern. $x^2 + 9$ is a prime polynomial.

Key Concept	Difference of Squares

- **Symbols** $a^2 - b^2 = (a + b)(a - b)$ or $(a - b)(a + b)$
- **Example** $x^2 - 9 = (x + 3)(x - 3)$ or $(x - 3)(x + 3)$

We can use this pattern to factor binomials that can be written in the form $a^2 - b^2$.

Example 1 Factor the Difference of Squares

Factor each binomial.

a. $n^2 - 25$

$n^2 - 25 = n^2 - 5^2$ Write in the form $a^2 - b^2$.

$= (n + 5)(n - 5)$ Factor the difference of squares.

b. $36x^2 - 49y^2$

$36x^2 - 49y^2 = (6x)^2 - (7y)^2$ $36x^2 = 6x \cdot 6x$ and $49y^2 = 7y \cdot 7y$

$= (6x + 7y)(6x - 7y)$ Factor the difference of squares.

If the terms of a binomial have a common factor, the GCF should be factored out first before trying to apply any other factoring technique.

Example 2 Factor Out a Common Factor

Factor $48a^3 - 12a$.

$48a^3 - 12a = 12a(4a^2 - 1)$ The GCF of $48a^3$ and $-12a$ is $12a$.

$= 12a[(2a)^2 - 1^2]$ $4a^2 = 2a \cdot 2a$ and $1 = 1 \cdot 1$

$= 12a(2a + 1)(2a - 1)$ Factor the difference of squares.

Occasionally, the difference of squares pattern needs to be applied more than once to factor a polynomial completely.

Example 3 Apply a Factoring Technique More Than Once

Factor $2x^4 - 162$.

$2x^4 - 162 = 2(x^4 - 81)$ The GCF of $2x^4$ and -162 is 2.

$= 2[(x^2)^2 - 9^2]$ $x^4 = x^2 \cdot x^2$ and $81 = 9 \cdot 9$

$= 2(x^2 + 9)(x^2 - 9)$ Factor the difference of squares.

$= 2(x^2 + 9)(x^2 - 3^2)$ $x^2 = x \cdot x$ and $9 = 3 \cdot 3$

$= 2(x^2 + 9)(x + 3)(x - 3)$ Factor the difference of squares.

Example 4 Apply Several Different Factoring Techniques

Factor $5x^3 + 15x^2 - 5x - 15$.

$5x^3 + 15x^2 - 5x - 15$ Original polynomial

$= 5(x^3 + 3x^2 - x - 3)$ Factor out the GCF.

$= 5[(x^3 - x) + (3x^2 - 3)]$ Group terms with common factors.

$= 5[x(x^2 - 1) + 3(x^2 - 1)]$ Factor each grouping.

$= 5(x^2 - 1)(x + 3)$ $x^2 - 1$ is the common factor.

$= 5(x + 1)(x - 1)(x + 3)$ Factor the difference of squares, $x^2 - 1$, into $(x + 1)(x - 1)$.

Algebra Activity

Materials: straightedge, scissors

- Using graph paper, students are more likely to draw straight squares, which will make the final product appear more like a rectangle.
- Make sure students label their figures as shown. Explain that the sides of the original square have length of a, and when the b square is cut out, the remaining sides have lengths of $a - b$.

SOLVE EQUATIONS BY FACTORING You can apply the Zero Product Property to an equation that is written as the product of any number of factors set equal to 0.

Example 5 Solve Equations by Factoring

Solve each equation by factoring. Check your solutions.

a. $p^2 - \dfrac{9}{16} = 0$

$$p^2 - \dfrac{9}{16} = 0 \qquad \text{Original equation}$$

$$p^2 - \left(\dfrac{3}{4}\right)^2 = 0 \qquad p^2 = p \cdot p \text{ and } \dfrac{9}{16} = \dfrac{3}{4} \cdot \dfrac{3}{4}$$

$$\left(p + \dfrac{3}{4}\right)\left(p - \dfrac{3}{4}\right) = 0 \qquad \text{Factor the difference of squares.}$$

$$p + \dfrac{3}{4} = 0 \quad \text{or} \quad p - \dfrac{3}{4} = 0 \quad \text{Zero Product Property}$$

$$p = -\dfrac{3}{4} \qquad\qquad p = \dfrac{3}{4} \quad \text{Solve each equation.}$$

The solution set is $\left\{-\dfrac{3}{4}, \dfrac{3}{4}\right\}$. Check each solution in the original equation.

b. $18x^3 = 50x$

$$18x^3 = 50x \qquad \text{Original equation}$$

$$18x^3 - 50x = 0 \qquad \text{Subtract } 50x \text{ from each side.}$$

$$2x(9x^2 - 25) = 0 \qquad \text{The GCF of } 18x^3 \text{ and } -50x \text{ is } 2x.$$

$$2x(3x + 5)(3x - 5) = 0 \qquad 9x^2 = 3x \cdot 3x \text{ and } 25 = 5 \cdot 5$$

Applying the Zero Product Property, set each factor equal to 0 and solve the resulting three equations.

$$2x = 0 \quad \text{or} \quad 3x + 5 = 0 \quad \text{or} \quad 3x - 5 = 0$$

$$x = 0 \qquad\qquad 3x = -5 \qquad\qquad 3x = 5$$

$$x = -\dfrac{5}{3} \qquad\qquad x = \dfrac{5}{3}$$

The solution set is $\left\{-\dfrac{5}{3}, 0, \dfrac{5}{3}\right\}$. Check each solution in the original equation.

Standardized Test Practice
Ⓐ Ⓑ Ⓒ Ⓓ

Example 6 Use Differences of Two Squares

Extended-Response Test Item

A corner is cut off a 2-inch by 2-inch square piece of paper. The cut is x inches from a corner as shown.

a. Write an equation in terms of x that represents the area A of the paper after the corner is removed.

b. What value of x will result in an area that is $\dfrac{7}{9}$ the area of the original square piece of paper? Show how you arrived at your answer.

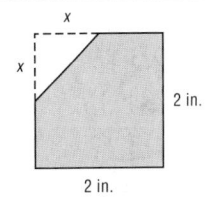

Read the Test Item

A is the area of the square minus the area of the triangular corner to be removed.

(continued on the next page)

> **Study Tip**
>
> **Alternative Method**
> The fraction could also be cleared from the equation in Example 5a by multiplying each side of the equation by 16.
>
> $$p^2 - \dfrac{9}{16} = 0$$
> $$16p^2 - 9 = 0$$
> $$(4p + 3)(4p - 3) = 0$$
> $$4p + 3 = 0 \text{ or } 4p - 3 = 0$$
> $$p = -\dfrac{3}{4} \qquad p = \dfrac{3}{4}$$

> **Test-Taking Tip**
>
> Look to see if the area of an oddly-shaped figure can be found by subtracting the areas of more familiar shapes, such as triangles, rectangles, or circles.

Teaching Tip Students may not be used to thinking of fractions as perfect squares. Remind them that if both the numerator and denominator are perfect squares, then the fraction itself is a perfect square. Also, if students are uncomfortable finding square roots of fractions, point out the Study Tip in the text.

5 Solve each equation by factoring. Check your solutions.

a. $q^2 - \dfrac{4}{25} = 0 \quad \left\{\dfrac{2}{5}, -\dfrac{2}{5}\right\}$

b. $48y^3 = 3y \quad \left\{-\dfrac{1}{4}, 0, \dfrac{1}{4}\right\}$

6 **EXTENDED RESPONSE** A square with side length x is cut from the right triangle shown below.

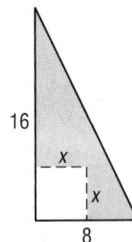

a. Write an equation in terms of x that represents the area A of the figure after the corner is removed. $A = 64 - x^2$

b. What value of x will result in a figure that is $\dfrac{3}{4}$ of the area of the original triangle? Show how you arrived at your answer. 4; solve $48 = 64 - x^2$.

Standardized Test Practice
Ⓐ Ⓑ Ⓒ Ⓓ

Example 6 Explain to students that when they complete extended response test items, it is very important to show all the steps in working out the problem, rather than just writing the answer. Often, full credit is not given for an extended response item unless all of the steps are shown. Conversely, students may receive partial credit for an incorrect answer, if their work shows only an arithmetic error, but the problem was solved using the correct method.

Study Notebook

Have students—

- add the definitions/examples of the vocabulary terms to their Vocabulary Builder worksheets for Chapter 9.
- include explanations on how to factor differences of squares.
- include any other item(s) that they find helpful in mastering the skills in this lesson.

DAILY
INTERVENTION **FIND THE ERROR**
Make sure students can explain what Jessica did wrong. Stress that Jessica's error is a common one. Ask students what they can do to avoid making the same mistake themselves.

About the Exercises...

Organization by Objective
- Factor $a^2 - b^2$: 16–33
- Solve Equations by Factoring: 34–45

Odd/Even Assignments
Exercises 16–45 are structured so that students practice the same concepts whether they are assigned odd or even problems.

Assignment Guide

Basic: 17–31 odd, 35–43 odd, 46, 47, 49, 51–70

Average: 17–43 odd, 46, 47, 49, 51–70

Advanced: 16–50 even, 51–64 (optional: 65–70)

Solve the Test Item

a. The area of the square is $2 \cdot 2$ or 4 square inches, and the area of the triangle is $\frac{1}{2} \cdot x \cdot x$ or $\frac{1}{2}x^2$ square inches. Thus, $A = 4 - \frac{1}{2}x^2$.

b. Find x so that A is $\frac{7}{9}$ the area of the original square piece of paper, A_o.

$$A = \frac{7}{9}A_o \qquad \text{Translate the verbal statement.}$$

$$4 - \frac{1}{2}x^2 = \frac{7}{9}(4) \qquad A = 4 - \frac{1}{2}x^2 \text{ and } A_o \text{ is 4.}$$

$$4 - \frac{1}{2}x^2 = \frac{28}{9} \qquad \text{Simplify.}$$

$$4 - \frac{1}{2}x^2 - \frac{28}{9} = 0 \qquad \text{Subtract } \frac{28}{9} \text{ from each side.}$$

$$\frac{8}{9} - \frac{1}{2}x^2 = 0 \qquad \text{Simplify.}$$

$$16 - 9x^2 = 0 \qquad \text{Multiply each side by 18 to remove fractions.}$$

$$(4 + 3x)(4 - 3x) = 0 \qquad \text{Factor the difference of squares.}$$

$$4 + 3x = 0 \quad \text{or} \quad 4 - 3x = 0 \qquad \text{Zero Product Property}$$

$$x = -\frac{4}{3} \qquad\qquad x = \frac{4}{3} \qquad \text{Solve each equation.}$$

Since length cannot be negative, the only reasonable solution is $\frac{4}{3}$.

Check for Understanding

Concept Check

1. The binomial is the difference of two terms, each of which is a perfect square.

3. Yes; $3n^2 - 48 = 3(n^2 - 16) = 3(n + 4)(n - 4)$.

1. **Describe** a binomial that is the difference of two squares.

2. **OPEN ENDED** Write a binomial that is the difference of two squares. Then factor your binomial. **Sample answer:** $x^2 - 25 = (x + 5)(x - 5)$

3. **Determine** whether the difference of squares pattern can be used to factor $3n^2 - 48$. Explain your reasoning.

4. **FIND THE ERROR** Manuel and Jessica are factoring $64x^2 + 16y^2$.

Manuel	Jessica
$64x^2 + 16y^2$	$64x^2 + 16y^2$
$= 16(4x^2 + y^2)$	$= 16(4x^2 + y^2)$
	$= 16(2x + y)(2x - y)$

Who is correct? Explain your reasoning. **Manuel;** $4x^2 + y^2$ is not the *difference* of squares.

Guided Practice

Factor each polynomial, if possible. If the polynomial cannot be factored, write *prime*. 8. $2(4x^2 + y^2)(2x + y)(2x - y)$

GUIDED PRACTICE KEY	
Exercises	Examples
5–10	1–4
11–14	5
15	6

5. $n^2 - 81$ $(n + 9)(n - 9)$

6. $4 - 9a^2$ $(2 + 3a)(2 - 3a)$

7. $2x^5 - 98x^3$ $2x^3(x + 7)(x - 7)$

8. $32x^4 - 2y^4$

9. $4t^2 - 27$ prime

10. $x^3 - 3x^2 - 9x + 27$ $(x + 3)(x - 3)(x - 3)$

Solve each equation by factoring. Check your solutions.

11. $4y^2 = 25$ $\left\{-\frac{5}{2}, \frac{5}{2}\right\}$

12. $17 - 68k^2 = 0$ $\left\{-\frac{1}{2}, \frac{1}{2}\right\}$

13. $x^2 - \frac{1}{36} = 0$ $\left\{-\frac{1}{6}, \frac{1}{6}\right\}$

14. $121a = 49a^3$ $\left\{-\frac{11}{7}, 0, \frac{11}{7}\right\}$

DAILY
INTERVENTION **Differentiated Instruction**

Intrapersonal Consider having students complete the Check for Understanding problems on one day, and then check their own work on the next day, examining their work and answers. Letting their own work sit for a day often allows students to see mistakes or problems in their work that they otherwise might not have noticed. It may also give students more of a chance to ask for help on difficult problems.

15. OPEN ENDED The area of the shaded part of the square at the right is 72 square inches. Find the dimensions of the square. **12 in. by 12 in.**

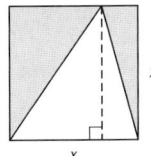

★ indicates increased difficulty

Practice and Apply

Homework Help

For Exercises	See Examples
16–33	1–4
34–45	5
47–50	6

Extra Practice
See page 841.

Factor each polynomial, if possible. If the polynomial cannot be factored, write prime. 19. $(5 + 2p)(5 - 2p)$ 20. $(7h + 4)(7h - 4)$

16. $x^2 - 49$ $(x + 7)(x - 7)$ **17.** $n^2 - 36$ $(n + 6)(n - 6)$ **18.** $81 + 16k^2$ **prime**

19. $25 - 4p^2$

20. $-16 + 49h^2$

21. $-9r^2 + 121$

22. $100c^2 - d^2$

23. $9x^2 - 10y^2$ **prime**

24. $144a^2 - 49b^2$

25. $169y^2 - 36z^2$

26. $8d^2 - 18$

27. $3x^2 - 75$

28. $8z^2 - 64$ $8(z^2 - 8)$

29. $4g^2 - 50$

30. $18a^4 - 72a^2$

31. $20x^3 - 45xy^2$
$5x(2x - 3y)(2x + 3y)$

★ **32.** $n^3 + 5n^2 - 4n - 20$
$(n + 2)(n - 2)(n + 5)$

★ **33.** $(a + b)^2 - c^2$
$(a + b + c)(a + b - c)$

21. $(11 + 3r)(11 - 3r)$
22. $(10c + d)$
$(10c - d)$
24. $(12a + 7b)$
$(12a - 7b)$
25. $(13y + 6z)$
$(13y - 6z)$
26. $2(2d + 3)(2d - 3)$
27. $3(x - 5)(x + 5)$
29. $2(2g^2 - 25)$
30. $18a^2(a + 2)$
$(a - 2)$

Solve each equation by factoring. Check your solutions.

34. $25x^2 = 36$ $\left\{\pm\frac{6}{5}\right\}$

35. $9y^2 = 64$ $\left\{\pm\frac{8}{3}\right\}$

36. $12 - 27n^2 = 0$ $\left\{\pm\frac{2}{3}\right\}$

37. $50 - 8a^2 = 0$ $\left\{\pm\frac{5}{2}\right\}$

38. $w^2 - \frac{4}{49} = 0$ $\left\{\pm\frac{2}{7}\right\}$

39. $\frac{81}{100} - p^2 = 0$ $\left\{\pm\frac{9}{10}\right\}$

40. $36 - \frac{1}{9}r^2 = 0$ $\{\pm18\}$

41. $\frac{1}{4}x^2 - 25 = 0$ $\{\pm10\}$

42. $12d^3 - 147d = 0$ $\left\{-\frac{7}{2}, 0, \frac{7}{2}\right\}$

43. $18n^3 - 50n = 0$ $\left\{-\frac{5}{3}, 0, \frac{5}{3}\right\}$

★ **44.** $x^3 - 4x = 12 - 3x^2$
$\{-3, -2, 2\}$

★ **45.** $36x - 16x^3 = 9x^2 - 4x^4$ $\left\{-\frac{3}{2}, 0, \frac{3}{2}, 4\right\}$

46. CRITICAL THINKING Show that $a^2 - b^2 = (a + b)(a - b)$ algebraically. (Hint: Rewrite $a^2 - b^2$ as $a^2 - ab + ab - b^2$.) **See margin.**

47. BOATING The United States Coast Guard's License Exam includes questions dealing with the breaking strength of a line. The basic breaking strength b in pounds for a natural fiber line is determined by the formula $900c^2 = b$, where c is the circumference of the line in inches. What circumference of natural line would have 3600 pounds of breaking strength? **2 in.**

48. AERODYNAMICS The formula for the pressure difference P above and below a wing is described by the formula $P = \frac{1}{2}dv_1^2 - \frac{1}{2}dv_2^2$, where d is the density of the air, v_1 is the velocity of the air passing above, and v_2 is the velocity of the air passing below. Write this formula in factored form. $P = \frac{1}{2}d(v_1 + v_2)(v_1 - v_2)$

49. LAW ENFORCEMENT If a car skids on dry concrete, police can use the formula $\frac{1}{24}s^2 = d$ to approximate the speed s of a vehicle in miles per hour given the length d of the skid marks in feet. If the length of skid marks on dry concrete are 54 feet long, how fast was the car traveling when the brakes were applied? **36 mph**

★ **50. PACKAGING** The width of a box is 9 inches more than its length. The height of the box is 1 inch less than its length. If the box has a volume of 72 cubic inches, what are the dimensions of the box? **3 in. by 12 in. by 2 in.**

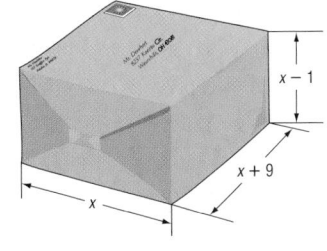

More About. . .

Aerodynamics •••••••

Lift works on the principle that as the speed of a gas increases, the pressure decreases. As the velocity of the air passing over a curved wing increases, the pressure above the wing decreases, lift is created, and the wing rises.
Source: www.gleim.com

Lesson 9-5 Factoring Differences of Squares **505**

Answer

46. Use factoring by grouping.
$$a^2 - b^2 = a^2 - ab + ab - b^2$$
$$= (a^2 - ab) + (ab - b^2)$$
$$= a(a - b) + b(a - b)$$
$$= (a - b)(a + b)$$

Study Guide and Intervention,
p. 547 (shown) and p. 548

Factor $a^2 - b^2$ The binomial expression $a^2 - b^2$ is called the **difference of two squares**. The following pattern shows how to factor the difference of squares.

Difference of Squares	$a^2 - b^2 = (a - b)(a + b) = (a + b)(a - b)$

Example 1 Factor each binomial.

a. $n^2 - 64$
$n^2 - 64$
$= n^2 - 8^2$ Write in the form $a^2 - b^2$.
$= (n + 8)(n - 8)$ Factor.

b. $4m^2 - 81n^2$
$4m^2 - 81n^2$
$= (2m)^2 - (9n)^2$ Write in the form $a^2 - b^2$.
$= (2m - 9n)(2m + 9n)$ Factor.

Example 2 Factor each polynomial.

a. $50a^2 - 72$
$50a^2 - 72$
$= 2(25a^2 - 36)$ Find the GCF.
$= 2[(5a)^2 - 6^2]$ $25a^2 = 5a \cdot 5a$ and $36 = 6 \cdot 6$
$= 2(5a + 6)(5a - 6)$ Factor the difference of squares.

b. $4x^4 + 8x^3 - 4x^2 - 8x$
$4x^4 + 8x^3 - 4x^2 - 8x$ Original polynomial
$= 4x(x^3 + 2x^2 - x - 2)$ Find the GCF
$= 4x[(x^3 + 2x^2) - (x + 2)]$ Group terms
$= 4x[x^2(x + 2) - 1(x + 2)]$ Find the GCF
$= 4x[(x^2 - 1)(x + 2)]$ Factor by grouping.
$= 4x[(x - 1)(x + 1)(x + 2)]$ Factor the difference of squares.

Exercises

Factor each polynomial if possible. If the polynomial cannot be factored, write *prime*.

1. $x^2 - 81$
$(x + 9)(x - 9)$
2. $m^2 - 100$
$(m + 10)(m - 10)$
3. $16n^2 - 25$
$(4n - 5)(4n + 5)$
4. $36z^2 - 100c^2$
$(6z + 10c)(6z - 10c)$
5. $49x^2 - 32$
prime
6. $16a^2 - 9b^2$
$(4a - 3b)(4a + 3b)$
7. $225c^2 - a^2$
$(15c - a)(15c + a)$
8. $72p^2 - 50$
$2(6p + 5)(6p - 5)$
9. $-2 + 2x^2$
$2(x - 1)(x + 1)$
10. $-81 + a^4$
$(a - 3)(a + 3)(a^2 + 9)$
11. $6 - 54z^2$
$6(1 + 3a)(1 - 3a)$
12. $8y^2 - 200$
$8(y + 5)(y - 5)$
13. $4x^3 - 100x$
$4x(x + 5)(x - 5)$
14. $2y^4 - 32y^3$
$2y^3(y + 4)(y - 4)$
15. $8m^3 - 128m$
$8m(m + 4)(m - 4)$
16. $6x^2 - 25$
prime
17. $2a^3 - 98ab^2$
$2a(a - 7b)(a + 7b)$
18. $18y^3 - 72y^4$
$18y^3(1 - 2y)(1 + 2y)$
19. $169x^3 - x$
$x(13x + 1)(13x - 1)$
20. $3x^4 - 3x^2$
$3x^2(a + 1)(a - 1)$
21. $3x^4 + 6x^3 - 3x^2 - 6x$
$3x(x - 1)(x + 1)(x + 2)$

Skills Practice, p. 549 and Practice, p. 550 (shown)

Factor each polynomial, if possible. If the polynomial cannot be factored, write *prime*.

1. $k^2 - 100$
$(k + 10)(k - 10)$
2. $81 - r^2$
$(9 + r)(9 - r)$
3. $16p^2 - 36$
$(4p + 6)(4p - 6)$
4. $4x^2 + 25$
prime
5. $144 - 9f^2$
$(12 + 3f)(12 - 3f)$
6. $36g^2 - 49h^2$
$(6g + 7h)(6g - 7h)$
7. $121m^2 - 144n^2$
$(11m - 12n)(11m + 12n)$
8. $32 - 8y^2$
$8(2 - y)(2 + y)$
9. $24a^2 - 54b^2$
$6(2a - 3b)(2a + 3b)$
10. $32s^2 - 18u^2$
$2(4s - 3u)(4s + 3u)$
11. $9jf^2 - 32$
prime
12. $36z^3 - 9z$
$9z(2z + 1)(2z - 1)$
13. $45g^3 - 20g$
$5g(3g + 2)(3g - 2)$
14. $100b^3 - 36b$
$4b(5b + 3)(5b - 3)$
15. $3t^4 - 48t^2$
$3t^2(t + 4)(t - 4)$

Solve each equation by factoring. Check your solutions.

16. $4y^2 = 81$
$\left\{\pm\frac{9}{2}\right\}$
17. $64p^2 = 9$
$\left\{\pm\frac{3}{8}\right\}$
18. $98b^2 - 50 = 0$
$\left\{\pm\frac{5}{7}\right\}$
19. $32 - 162k^2 = 0$
$\left\{\pm\frac{4}{9}\right\}$
20. $x^2 - \frac{64}{121} = 0$
$\left\{\pm\frac{8}{11}\right\}$
21. $\frac{16}{49} - v^2 = 0$
$\left\{\pm\frac{4}{7}\right\}$
22. $\frac{1}{36}x^2 - 25 = 0$
$\{\pm30\}$
23. $27h^3 = 48h$
$\left\{\pm\frac{4}{3}, 0\right\}$
24. $75g^3 = 147g$
$\left\{\pm\frac{7}{5}, 0\right\}$

25. EROSION A rock breaks loose from a cliff and plunges toward the ground 400 feet below. The distance d that the rock falls in t seconds is given by the equation $d = 16t^2$. How long does it take the rock to hit the ground? **5 s**

26. FORENSICS Mr. Cooper contested a speeding ticket given to him after he applied his brakes and skidded to a halt to avoid hitting another car. In traffic court, he argued that the length of the skid marks on the pavement, 150 feet, proved that he was driving under the posted speed limit of 65 miles per hour. The ticket cited his speed at 70 miles per hour. Use the formula $\frac{1}{24}s^2 = d$, where s is the speed of the car and d is the length of the skid marks, to determine Mr. Cooper's speed when he applied the brakes. Was Mr. Cooper correct in claiming that he was not speeding when he applied the brakes? **60 mi/h; yes**

Reading to Learn Mathematics, p. 551   **ELL**

Pre-Activity **How can you determine a basketball player's hang time?**

Read the introduction to Lesson 9-5 at the top of page 501 in your textbook.

Suppose a player can jump 2 feet. Can you use the pattern for the difference of squares to solve the equation $4t^2 - 2 = 0$? Explain.

No; 2 is not a perfect square.

Reading the Lesson

1. Explain why each binomial is a difference of squares.
   a. $4x^2 - 25$
   $4x^2$ is the square of $2x$, 25 is the square of 5, and the operation sign is a minus sign.
   b. $49a^2 - 64b^2$
   $49a^2$ is the square of $7a$, $64b^2$ is the square of $8b$, and the operation sign is a minus sign.

2. Sometimes it is necessary to apply more than one technique when factoring, or to apply the same technique more than once.
   a. What should you look for first when you are factoring a binomial?
   Look for a factor or factors common to the terms of the binomial.
   b. Explain what is done in each step to factor $4x^4 - 64$.
   $4x^4 - 64$
   $= 4(x^4 - 16)$ Factor out the GCF.
   $= 4[(x^2)^2 - 4^2]$ Write $x^4 - 16$ in difference of squares form.
   $= 4(x^2 + 4)(x^2 - 4)$ Factor the difference of squares.
   $= 4(x^2 + 4)(x^2 - 2^2)$ Write $x^2 - 4$ in difference of squares form.
   $= 4(x^2 + 4)(x + 2)(x - 2)$ Factor the difference of squares.

3. Suppose you are solving the equation $16x^2 - 9 = 0$ and rewrite it as $(4x + 3)(4x - 3) = 0$. What would be your next steps in solving the equation?
   Set each factor equal to zero, then solve the resulting equations.

Helping You Remember

4. How can you remember whether a binomial can be factored as a difference of squares?
   The operation sign must be a minus sign, and the expressions before and after the minus sign must be perfect squares.

Enrichment, p. 552

Factoring Trinomials of Fourth Degree

Some trinomials of the form $a^4 + a^2b^2 + b^4$ can be written as the difference of two squares and then factored.

Example Factor $4x^4 - 37x^2y^2 + 9y^4$.

Step 1 Find the square roots of the first and last terms.
$\sqrt{4x^4} = 2x^2$ $\sqrt{9y^4} = 3y^2$

Step 2 Find twice the product of the square roots.
$2(2x^2)(3y^2) = 12x^2y^2$

Step 3 Separate the middle term into two parts. One part is either your answer to Step 2 or its opposite. The other part should be the opposite of a perfect square.
$-37x^2y^2 = -12x^2y^2 - 25x^2y^2$

Step 4 Rewrite the trinomial as the difference of two squares and then factor.
$4x^4 + 9y^4 = (...$

Lesson 9-5 Factoring Differences of Squares **505**

Open-Ended Assessment

Modeling Have students complete an area problem similar to Example 6 using grid paper. Have them demonstrate using the grid that the area and lengths they come up with using factoring a difference of squares is correct.

Getting Ready for Lesson 9-6

PREREQUISITE SKILL Students will learn to factor perfect square trinomials in Lesson 9-6. When they learn how to factor perfect square trinomials, students will have to know how to square binomials. Use Exercises 65–70 to determine your students' familiarity with finding special products, such as the square of a binomial.

Assessment Options

Quiz (Lessons 9-4 and 9-5) is available on p. 574 of the *Chapter 9 Resource Masters*.

Answers

52. Answers should include the following.

- 1 foot
- To find the hang time of a student athlete who attains a maximum height of 1 foot, solve the equation $4t^2 - 1 = 0$. You can factor the left side using the difference of squares pattern since $4t^2$ is the square of $2t$ and 1 is the square of 1. Thus the equation becomes $(2t + 1)(2t - 1) = 0$. Using the Zero Product Property, each factor can be set equal to zero, resulting in two solutions, $t = -\frac{1}{2}$ and $t = \frac{1}{2}$. Since time cannot be negative, the hang time is $\frac{1}{2}$ second.

---

51. The flaw is in line 5. Since $a = b$, $a - b = 0$. Therefore dividing by $a - b$ is dividing by zero, which is undefined.

51. CRITICAL THINKING The following statements appear to prove that 2 is equal to 1. Find the flaw in this "proof."

Suppose a and b are real numbers such that $a = b$, $a \neq 0$, $b \neq 0$.

(1)	$a = b$	Given.
(2)	$a^2 = ab$	Multiply each side by a.
(3)	$a^2 - b^2 = ab - b^2$	Subtract b^2 from each side.
(4)	$(a - b)(a + b) = b(a - b)$	Factor.
(5)	$a + b = b$	Divide each side by $a - b$.
(6)	$a + a = a$	Substitution Property; $a = b$
(7)	$2a = a$	Combine like terms.
(8)	$2 = 1$	Divide each side by a.

52.  Answer the question that was posed at the beginning of the lesson. **See margin.**

How can you determine a basketball player's hang time?

Include the following in your answer:

- a maximum height that is a perfect square and that would be considered a reasonable distance for a student athlete to jump, and
- a description of how to find the hang time for this maximum height.

Standardized Test Practice
Ⓐ Ⓑ Ⓒ Ⓓ

53. What is the factored form of $25b^2 - 1$? **A**

Ⓐ $(5b - 1)(5b + 1)$ Ⓑ $(5b + 1)(5b + 1)$
Ⓒ $(5b - 1)(5b - 1)$ Ⓓ $(25b + 1)(b - 1)$

54. **GRID IN** In the figure, the area between the two squares is 17 square inches. The sum of the perimeters of the two squares is 68 inches. How many inches long is a side of the larger square? **9 in.**

Maintain Your Skills

Mixed Review **Factor each trinomial, if possible. If the trinomial cannot be factored using integers, write prime.** *(Lesson 9-4)*

55. $2n^2 + 5n + 7$ **56.** $6x^2 - 11x + 4$ **57.** $21p^2 + 29p - 10$
prime $(2x - 1)(3x - 4)$ $(3p + 5)(7p - 2)$

Solve each equation. Check your solutions. *(Lesson 9-3)*

58. $y^2 + 18y + 32 = 0$ **59.** $k^2 - 8k = -15$ {3, 5}   **60.** $b^2 - 8 = 2b$ {−2, 4}
{−16, −2}

61. STATISTICS Amy's scores on the first three of four 100-point biology tests were 88, 90, and 91. To get a B+ in the class, her average must be between 88 and 92, inclusive, on all tests. What score must she receive on the fourth test to get a B+ in biology? *(Lesson 6-4)* **between 83 and 99, inclusive**

Solve each inequality, check your solution, and graph it on a number line.
(Lesson 6-1) 62–64. See margin for graphs.

62. $6 \leq 3d - 12$ $d \geq 6$ **63.** $-5 + 10r > 2$ $r > \dfrac{7}{10}$ **64.** $13x - 3 < 23$ $x < 2$

65. $x^2 + 2x + 1$
66. $x^2 - 12x + 36$
67. $x^2 + 16x + 64$

Getting Ready for the Next Lesson **PREREQUISITE SKILL** **Find each product.** *(To review special products, see Lesson 8-8.)*

65. $(x + 1)(x + 1)$ **66.** $(x - 6)(x - 6)$ **67.** $(x + 8)^2$
68. $(3x - 4)(3x - 4)$ **69.** $(5x - 2)^2$ **70.** $(7x + 3)^2$
     $9x^2 - 24x + 16$ $25x^2 - 20x + 4$ $49x^2 + 42x + 9$

62.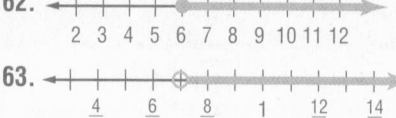

63.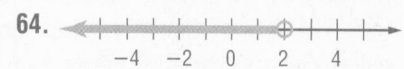

64.

Reading Mathematics

The Language of Mathematics

Mathematics is a language all its own. As with any language you learn, you must read slowly and carefully, translating small portions of it at a time. Then you must reread the entire passage to make complete sense of what you read.

In mathematics, concepts are often written in a compact form by using symbols. Break down the symbols and try to translate each piece before putting them back together. Read the following sentence.

$$a^2 + 2ab + b^2 = (a + b)^2$$

The trinomial a squared plus twice the product of a and b plus b squared equals the square of the binomial a plus b.

Below is a list of the concepts involved in that single sentence.

- The letters a and b are variables and can be replaced by monomials like 2 or $3x$ or by polynomials like $x + 3$.

- The square of the binomial $a + b$ means $(a + b)(a + b)$. So, $a^2 + 2ab + b^2$ can be written as the product of two identical factors, $a + b$ and $a + b$.

Now put these concepts together. The algebraic statement $a^2 + 2ab + b^2 = (a + b)^2$ means that any trinomial that can be written in the form $a^2 + 2ab + b^2$ can be factored as the square of a binomial using the pattern $(a + b)^2$.

When reading a lesson in your book, use these steps.

- Read the "What You'll Learn" statements to understand what concepts are being presented.

- Skim to get a general idea of the content.

- Take note of any new terms in the lesson by looking for highlighted words.

- Go back and reread in order to understand all of the ideas presented.

- Study all of the examples.

- Pay special attention to the explanations for each step in each example.

- Read any study tips presented in the margins of the lesson.

Reading to Learn 2. GCF, perfect square trinomial; $x^2 + bx + c$, $ax^2 + bx + c$

Turn to page 508 and skim Lesson 9-6.

1. List three main ideas from Lesson 9-6. Use phrases instead of whole sentences. **See margin.**

2. What factoring techniques should be tried when factoring a trinomial?

3. What should you always check for first when trying to factor any polynomial? **a greatest common factor**

4. Translate the symbolic representation of the Square Root Property presented on page 511 and explain why it can be applied to problems like $(a + 4)^2 = 49$ in Example 4a. **See margin.**

Reading Mathematics The Language of Mathematics **507**

1 Focus

Mathematical Background notes are available for this lesson on p. 472D.

How can factoring be used to design a pavilion?

Ask students:

• What does the expression $8 + 2x$ represent? **The expression represents the side length of the entire square pavilion.**

• What does 144 represent? **144 is the area of the entire square pavilion.**

• How do you know the area of the pavilion is 144 square feet? **The square mascot area has an area of 8^2, or 64 ft^2 because its side length is 8 ft. The problem states that the bricks will cover 80 ft^2, so the area of the entire structure is 64 + 80, or 144 ft^2.**

• What feature of the pavilion tells you that 144 must be a perfect square? **The building is square, so the area must be the square of the side length. Since the area is 144, $8 + 2x = 12$, and $x = 2$.**

Vocabulary
• perfect square trinomials

What You'll Learn

• Factor perfect square trinomials.
• Solve equations involving perfect squares.

How can factoring be used to design a pavilion?

The senior class has decided to build an outdoor pavilion. It will have an 8-foot by 8-foot portrayal of the school's mascot in the center. The class is selling bricks with students' names on them to finance the project. If they sell enough bricks to cover 80 square feet and want to arrange the bricks around the art, how wide should the border of bricks be? To solve this problem, you would need to solve the equation $(8 + 2x)^2 = 144$.

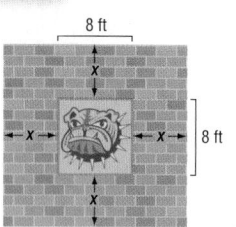

FACTOR PERFECT SQUARE TRINOMIALS Numbers like 144, 16, and 49 are perfect squares, since each can be expressed as the square of an integer.

$$144 = 12 \cdot 12 \text{ or } 12^2 \qquad 16 = 4 \cdot 4 \text{ or } 4^2 \qquad 49 = 7 \cdot 7 \text{ or } 7^2$$

Products of the form $(a + b)^2$ and $(a - b)^2$, such as $(8 + 2x)^2$, are also perfect squares. Recall that these are special products that follow specific patterns.

$$(a + b)^2 = (a + b)(a + b) \qquad\qquad (a - b)^2 = (a - b)(a - b)$$
$$= a^2 + ab + ab + b^2 \qquad\qquad = a^2 - ab - ab + b^2$$
$$= a^2 + 2ab + b^2 \qquad\qquad = a^2 - 2ab + b^2$$

These patterns can help you factor **perfect square trinomials**, trinomials that are the square of a binomial.

Squaring a Binomial	Factoring a Perfect Square
$(x + 7)^2 = x^2 + 2(x)(7) + 7^2$ $= x^2 + 14x + 49$	$x^2 + 14x + 49 = x^2 + 2(x)(7) + 7^2$ $= (x + 7)^2$
$(3x - 4)^2 = (3x)^2 - 2(3x)(4) + 4^2$ $= 9x^2 - 24x + 16$	$9x^2 - 24x + 16 = (3x)^2 - 2(3x)(4) + 4^2$ $= (3x - 4)^2$

For a trinomial to be factorable as a perfect square, three conditions must be satisfied as illustrated in the example below.

$$4x^2 + 20x + 25$$

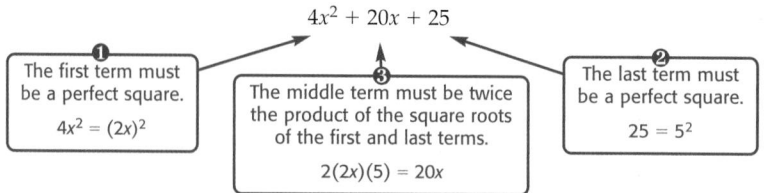

❶ The first term must be a perfect square.
$4x^2 = (2x)^2$

❸ The middle term must be twice the product of the square roots of the first and last terms.
$2(2x)(5) = 20x$

❷ The last term must be a perfect square.
$25 = 5^2$

Resource Manager

📁 Workbook and Reproducible Masters

Chapter 9 Resource Masters
• Study Guide and Intervention, pp. 553–554
• Skills Practice, p. 555
• Practice, p. 556
• Reading to Learn Mathematics, p. 557
• Enrichment, p. 558
• Assessment, p. 574

Parent and Student Study Guide Workbook, p. 73

🖥 Transparencies
5-Minute Check Transparency 9-6
Real-World Transparency 9
Answer Key Transparencies

💿 Technology
AlgePASS: Tutorial Plus, Lesson 27
Interactive Chalkboard
Multimedia Applications

Key Concept — Factoring Perfect Square Trinomials

- **Words**   If a trinomial can be written in the form $a^2 + 2ab + b^2$ or $a^2 - 2ab + b^2$, then it can be factored as $(a + b)^2$ or as $(a - b)^2$, respectively.

- **Symbols** $a^2 + 2ab + b^2 = (a + b)^2$ and $a^2 - 2ab + b^2 = (a - b)^2$

- **Example** $4x^2 - 20x + 25 = (2x)^2 - 2(2x)(5) + (5)^2$ or $(2x - 5)^2$

Example 1   Factor Perfect Square Trinomials

Determine whether each trinomial is a perfect square trinomial. If so, factor it.

a. $16x^2 + 32x + 64$

   ❶ Is the first term a perfect square?   Yes, $16x^2 = (4x)^2$.
   ❷ Is the last term a perfect square?   Yes, $64 = 8^2$.
   ❸ Is the middle term equal to $2(4x)(8)$?   No, $32x \neq 2(4x)(8)$.

$16x^2 + 32x + 64$ is not a perfect square trinomial.

b. $9y^2 - 12y + 4$

   ❶ Is the first term a perfect square?   Yes, $9y^2 = (3y)^2$.
   ❷ Is the last term a perfect square?   Yes, $4 = 2^2$.
   ❸ Is the middle term equal to $2(3y)(2)$?   Yes, $12y = 2(3y)(2)$.

$9y^2 - 12y + 4$ is a perfect square trinomial.

$9y^2 - 12y + 4 = (3y)^2 - 2(3y)(2) + 2^2$ Write as $a^2 - 2ab + b^2$.
$ = (3y - 2)^2$ Factor using the pattern.

In this chapter, you have learned to factor different types of polynomials. The Concept Summary lists these methods and can help you decide when to use a specific method.

Concept Summary — Factoring Polynomials

Number of Terms	Factoring Technique		Example
2 or more	greatest common factor		$3x^3 + 6x^2 - 15x = 3x(x^2 + 2x - 5)$
2	difference of squares	$a^2 - b^2 = (a + b)(a - b)$	$4x^2 - 25 = (2x + 5)(2x - 5)$
3	perfect square trinomial	$a^2 + 2ab + b^2 = (a + b)^2$ $a^2 - 2ab + b^2 = (a - b)^2$	$x^2 + 6x + 9 = (x + 3)^2$ $4x^2 - 4x + 1 = (2x - 1)^2$
3	$x^2 + bx + c$	$x^2 + bx + c = (x + m)(x + n)$, when $m + n = b$ and $mn = c$.	$x^2 - 9x + 20 = (x - 5)(x - 4)$
3	$ax^2 + bx + c$	$ax^2 + bx + c = ax^2 + mx + nx + c$, when $m + n = b$ and $mn = ac$. Then use factoring by grouping.	$6x^2 - x - 2 = 6x^2 + 3x - 4x - 2$ $= 3x(2x + 1) - 2(2x + 1)$ $= (2x + 1)(3x - 2)$
4 or more	factoring by grouping	$ax + bx + ay + by$ $= x(a + b) + y(a + b)$ $= (a + b)(x + y)$	$3xy - 6y + 5x - 10$ $= (3xy - 6y) + (5x - 10)$ $= 3y(x - 2) + 5(x - 2)$ $= (x - 2)(3y + 5)$

---

2 Teach

Building on Prior Knowledge

In Chapter 8, students learned how to square a binomial such as $(a + b)^2$ or $(a - b)^2$. In this lesson, students will learn how to undo this process to factor perfect square trinomials.

FACTOR PERFECT SQUARE TRINOMIALS

In-Class Example

Teaching Tip Remind students to look closely at the operation sign in front of the second term of the trinomial. This sign signifies whether the factors are in the form $(a + b)^2$ or $(a - b)^2$.

❶ Determine whether each trinomial is a perfect square trinomial. If so, factor it.

a. $25x^2 - 30x + 9$ yes; $(5x - 3)^2$

b. $49y^2 + 42y + 36$ not a perfect square trinomial

Assessment During the last lesson of a chapter, it is often good to review some of the major concepts of the chapter to assess whether students have mastered the concepts. The concept summary table on Factoring Polynomials provides a perfect opportunity for review. Briefly review each factoring technique with students. After your review, you might consider giving students a quiz on the different techniques to assess student mastery.

SOLVE EQUATIONS WITH PERFECT SQUARES

When there is a GCF other than 1, it is usually easier to factor it out first. Then, check the appropriate factoring methods in the order shown in the table. Continue factoring until you have written the polynomial as the product of a monomial and/or prime polynomial factors.

Example 2 *Factor Completely*

Factor each polynomial.

a. $4x^2 - 36$

First check for a GCF. Then, since the polynomial has two terms, check for the difference of squares.

$$
\begin{aligned}
4x^2 - 36 &= 4(x^2 - 9) && \text{4 is the GCF.}\\
&= 4(x^2 - 3^2) && x^2 = x \cdot x \text{ and } 9 = 3 \cdot 3\\
&= 4(x + 3)(x - 3) && \text{Factor the difference of squares.}
\end{aligned}
$$

b. $25x^2 + 5x - 6$

This polynomial has three terms that have a GCF of 1. While the first term is a perfect square, $25x^2 = (5x)^2$, the last term is not. Therefore, this is not a perfect square trinomial.

This trinomial is of the form $ax^2 + bx + c$. Are there two numbers m and n whose product is $25 \cdot -6$ or -150 and whose sum is 5? Yes, the product of 15 and -10 is -150 and their sum is 5.

$$
\begin{aligned}
&25x^2 + 5x - 6\\
&= 25x^2 + mx + nx - 6 && \text{Write the pattern.}\\
&= 25x^2 + 15x - 10x - 6 && m = 15 \text{ and } n = -10\\
&= (25x^2 + 15x) + (-10x - 6) && \text{Group terms with common factors.}\\
&= 5x(5x + 3) - 2(5x + 3) && \text{Factor out the GCF from each grouping.}\\
&= (5x + 3)(5x - 2) && 5x + 3 \text{ is the common factor.}
\end{aligned}
$$

SOLVE EQUATIONS WITH PERFECT SQUARES   When solving equations involving repeated factors, it is only necessary to set one of the repeated factors equal to zero.

Example 3 *Solve Equations with Repeated Factors*

Solve $x^2 - x + \dfrac{1}{4} = 0$.

$$
\begin{aligned}
x^2 - x + \tfrac{1}{4} &= 0 && \text{Original equation}\\
x^2 - 2(x)\left(\tfrac{1}{2}\right) + \left(\tfrac{1}{2}\right)^2 &= 0 && \text{Recognize } x^2 - x + \tfrac{1}{4} \text{ as a perfect square trinomial.}\\
\left(x - \tfrac{1}{2}\right)^2 &= 0 && \text{Factor the perfect square trinomial.}\\
x - \tfrac{1}{2} &= 0 && \text{Set repeated factor equal to zero.}\\
x &= \tfrac{1}{2} && \text{Solve for } x.
\end{aligned}
$$

Thus, the solution set is $\left\{\dfrac{1}{2}\right\}$. Check this solution in the original equation.

DAILY

INTERVENTION

Differentiated Instruction

Logical If students do not understand how a second-degree equation can have only one solution, suggest that they graph a perfect square trinomial on a graphing calculator. The graph will immediately reveal how this is possible. The vertex of the graph of a perfect square trinomial equation lies on the *x*-axis, hence only one solution.

You have solved equations like $x^2 - 36 = 0$ by using factoring. You can also use the definition of square root to solve this equation.

$$x^2 - 36 = 0 \qquad \text{Original equation}$$
$$x^2 = 36 \qquad \text{Add 36 to each side.}$$
$$x = \pm\sqrt{36} \qquad \text{Take the square root of each side.}$$

Remember that there are two square roots of 36, namely 6 and -6. Therefore, the solution set is $\{-6, 6\}$. This is sometimes expressed more compactly as $\{\pm 6\}$. This and other examples suggest the following property.

> **Key Concept**   **Square Root Property**
> - **Symbols** For any number $n > 0$, if $x^2 = n$, then $x = \pm\sqrt{n}$.
> - **Example** $x^2 = 9$
> $$x = \pm\sqrt{9} \text{ or } \pm 3$$

Example 4 Use the Square Root Property to Solve Equations

Solve each equation. Check your solutions.

a. $(a + 4)^2 = 49$

$$
\begin{array}{ll}
(a + 4)^2 = 49 & \text{Original equation} \\
a + 4 = \pm\sqrt{49} & \text{Square Root Property} \\
a + 4 = \pm 7 & 49 = 7 \cdot 7 \\
a = -4 \pm 7 & \text{Subtract 4 from each side.}
\end{array}
$$

$$
\begin{array}{lll}
a = -4 + 7 & \text{or} \quad a = -4 - 7 & \text{Separate into two equations.} \\
\;\;\;\;= 3 & \qquad\quad\;\; = -11 & \text{Simplify.}
\end{array}
$$

The solution set is $\{-11, 3\}$. Check each solution in the original equation.

b. $y^2 - 4y + 4 = 25$

$$
\begin{array}{ll}
y^2 - 4y + 4 = 25 & \text{Original equation} \\
(y)^2 - 2(y)(2) + 2^2 = 25 & \text{Recognize perfect square trinomial.} \\
(y - 2)^2 = 25 & \text{Factor perfect square trinomial.} \\
y - 2 = \pm\sqrt{25} & \text{Square Root Property} \\
y - 2 = \pm 5 & 25 = 5 \cdot 5 \\
y = 2 \pm 5 & \text{Add 2 to each side.}
\end{array}
$$

$$
\begin{array}{lll}
y = 2 + 5 & \text{or} \quad y = 2 - 5 & \text{Separate into two equations.} \\
\;\;\;\;= 7 & \qquad\quad\;\; = -3 & \text{Simplify.}
\end{array}
$$

The solution set is $\{-3, 7\}$. Check each solution in the original equation.

c. $(x - 3)^2 = 5$

$$
\begin{array}{ll}
(x - 3)^2 = 5 & \text{Original equation} \\
x - 3 = \pm\sqrt{5} & \text{Square Root Property} \\
x = 3 \pm \sqrt{5} & \text{Add 3 to each side.}
\end{array}
$$

Since 5 is not a perfect square, the solution set is $\{3 \pm \sqrt{5}\}$. Using a calculator, the approximate solutions are $3 + \sqrt{5}$ or about 5.24 and $3 - \sqrt{5}$ or about 0.76.

Lesson 9-6 Perfect Squares and Factoring **511**

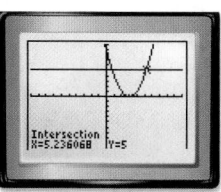

3 Practice/Apply

Study Notebook

Have students—
• complete the definitions/examples for the remaining terms on their Vocabulary Builder worksheets for Chapter 9.
• include explanations on how to factor perfect square trinomials.
• include any other item(s) that they find helpful in mastering the skills in this lesson.

About the Exercises...

Organization by Objective
• Factor Perfect Square Trinomials: 17–22
• Solve Equations With Perfect Squares: 43–48

Odd/Even Assignments
Exercises 17–53 are structured so that students practice the same concepts whether they are assigned odd or even problems.

Assignment Guide

Basic: 17–21 odd, 25–39 odd, 43–53 odd, 55–56, 60–80

Average: 17–53 odd, 55–59, 60–80

Advanced: 18–54 even, 57, 58, 60–80

Teaching Tip Remind students that any of the factoring methods they have studied thus far can be used in the exercises.

CHECK You can check your answer using a graphing calculator. Graph $y = (x - 3)^2$ and $y = 5$. Using the **INTERSECT** feature of your graphing calculator, find where $(x - 3)^2 = 5$. The check of 5.24 as one of the approximate solutions is shown at the right.

[−10, 10] scl: 1 by [−10, 10] scl: 1

Check for Understanding

Concept Check
1. See margin.

1. **Explain** how to determine whether a trinomial is a perfect square trinomial.
2. **Determine** whether the following statement is *sometimes*, *always*, or *never* true. Explain your reasoning. **never;** $(a - b)^2 = a^2 - 2ab + b^2$
   $a^2 - 2ab - b^2 = (a - b)^2, b \neq 0$
3. **OPEN ENDED** Write a polynomial that requires at least two different factoring techniques to factor it completely. **Sample answer:** $x^3 + 5x^2 - 4x - 20$

Guided Practice

GUIDED PRACTICE KEY	
Exercises	Examples
4, 5	1
6–11	2
12–16	3, 4

Determine whether each trinomial is a perfect square trinomial. If so, factor it.
4. $y^2 + 8y + 16$ **yes;** $(y + 4)^2$
5. $9x^2 - 30x + 10$ **no**

Factor each polynomial, if possible. If the polynomial cannot be factored, write *prime*.
6. $2x^2 + 18$ $2(x^2 + 9)$
7. $c^2 - 5c + 6$ $(c - 3)(c - 2)$
8. $5a^3 - 80a$ $5a(a + 4)(a - 4)$
9. $8x^2 - 18x - 35$ $(2x - 7)(4x + 5)$
10. $9g^2 + 12g - 4$ **prime**
11. $3m^3 + 2m^2n - 12m - 8n$ $(m - 2)(m + 2)(3m + 2n)$

Solve each equation. Check your solutions.
12. $4y^2 + 24y + 36 = 0$ $\{-3\}$
13. $3n^2 = 48$ $\{\pm 4\}$
14. $a^2 - 6a + 9 = 16$ $\{-1, 7\}$
15. $(m - 5)^2 = 13$ $\{5 \pm \sqrt{13}\}$

Application
16. **HISTORY** Galileo demonstrated that objects of different weights fall at the same velocity by dropping two objects of different weights from the top of the Leaning Tower of Pisa. A model for the height h in feet of an object dropped from an initial height h_o in feet is $h = -16t^2 + h_o$, where t is the time in seconds after the object is dropped. Use this model to determine approximately how long it took for the objects to hit the ground if Galileo dropped them from a height of 180 feet. **about 3.35 s**

★ indicates increased difficulty

Practice and Apply

Homework Help	
For Exercises	See Examples
17–24	1
25–42	2
43–59	3, 4

Extra Practice
See page 841.

Determine whether each trinomial is a perfect square trinomial. If so, factor it.
17. $x^2 + 9x + 81$
18. $a^2 - 24a + 144$
19. $4y^2 - 44y + 121$
20. $2c^2 + 10c + 25$
21. $9n^2 + 49 + 42n$
22. $25a^2 - 120ab + 144b^2$

17–22. See margin.

★ 23. **GEOMETRY** The area of a circle is $(16x^2 + 80x + 100)\pi$ square inches. What is the diameter of the circle? $8x + 20$

★ 24. **GEOMETRY** The area of a square is $81 - 90x + 25x^2$ square meters. If x is a positive integer, what is the least possible perimeter measure for the square? **16 m**

Answers

1. Determine if the first term is a perfect square. Then determine if the last term is a perfect square. Finally, check to see if the middle term is equal to twice the product of the square roots of the first and last terms.

17. no
18. yes; $(a - 12)^2$
19. yes; $(2y - 11)^2$
20. no
21. yes; $(3n + 7)^2$
22. yes; $(5a - 12b)^2$

Factor each polynomial, if possible. If the polynomial cannot be factored, write *prime*.

25. $4k^2 - 100$ $4(k + 5)(k - 5)$

26. $9x^2 - 3x - 20$ $(3x + 4)(3x - 5)$

27. $x^2 + 6x - 9$ prime

28. $50g^2 + 40g + 8$ $2(5g + 2)^2$

29. $9t^3 + 66t^2 - 48t$ $3t(3t - 2)(t + 8)$

30. $4a^2 - 36b^2$ $4(a - 3b)(a + 3b)$

31. $20n^2 + 34n + 6$ $2(5n + 1)(2n + 3)$

32. $5y^2 - 90$ $5(y^2 - 18)$

33. $24x^3 - 78x^2 + 45x$ $3x(4x - 3)(2x - 5)$

34. $18y^2 - 48y + 32$ $2(3y - 4)^2$

35. $90g - 27g^2 - 75$ $-3(3g - 5)^2$

36. $45c^2 - 32cd$ $c(45c - 32d)$

37. $(a^2 + 2)(4a + 3b^2)$

37. $4a^3 + 3a^2b^2 + 8a + 6b^2$

38. $5a^2 + 7a + 6b^2 - 4b$ prime

39. $x^2y^2 - y^2 - z^2 + x^2z^2$
$(y^2 + z^2)(x + 1)(x - 1)$

40. $4m^4n + 6m^3n - 16m^2n^2 - 24mn^2$
$2mn(m^2 - 4n)(2m + 3)$

★ **41. GEOMETRY** The volume of a rectangular prism is $x^3y - 63y^2 + 7x^2 - 9xy^3$ cubic meters. Find the dimensions of the prism if they can be represented by binomials with integral coefficients. $x - 3y$ m, $x + 3y$ m, $xy + 7$ m

42. $8x^2 - 22x + 14$ in^2 if $x > \frac{7}{4}$, $8x^2 - 34x + 35$ in^2 if $x < \frac{7}{4}$

★ **42. GEOMETRY** If the area of the square shown below is $16x^2 - 56x + 49$ square inches, what is the area of the rectangle in terms of x?

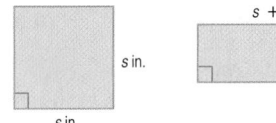

s in.

s in.

$s + 3$ in.

$\frac{1}{2}s$ in.

Solve each equation. Check your solutions.

43. $3x^2 + 24x + 48 = 0$ $\{-4\}$

44. $7r^2 = 70r - 175$ $\{5\}$

45. $49a^2 + 16 = 56a$ $\left\{\frac{4}{7}\right\}$

46. $18y^2 + 24y + 8 = 0$ $\left\{-\frac{2}{3}\right\}$

47. $y^2 - \frac{2}{3}y + \frac{1}{9} = 0$

48. $a^2 + \frac{4}{5}a + \frac{4}{25} = 0$

47. $\left\{\frac{1}{3}\right\}$ **48.** $\left\{-\frac{2}{5}\right\}$

49. $z^2 + 2z + 1 = 16$ $\{-5, 3\}$

50. $x^2 + 10x + 25 = 81$ $\{-14, 4\}$

51. $(y - 8)^2 = 7$ $\{8 \pm \sqrt{7}\}$

52. $(w + 3)^2 = 2$ $\{-3 \pm \sqrt{2}\}$

53. $p^2 + 2p + 1 = 6$ $\{-1 \pm \sqrt{6}\}$

54. $x^2 - 12x + 36 = 11$ $\{6 \pm \sqrt{11}\}$

FORESTRY For Exercises 55 and 56, use the following information.
Lumber companies need to be able to estimate the number of board feet that a given log will yield. One of the most commonly used formulas for estimating board feet is the *Doyle Log Rule*, $B = \frac{L}{16}(D^2 - 8D + 16)$, where B is the number of board feet, D is the diameter in inches, and L is the length of the log in feet.

55. Write this formula in factored form. $B = \frac{L}{16}(D - 4)^2$

56. For logs that are 16 feet long, what diameter will yield approximately 256 board feet? **20 in.**

FREE-FALL RIDE For Exercises 57 and 58, use the following information.
The height h in feet of a car above the exit ramp of an amusement park's free-fall ride can be modeled by $h = -16t^2 + s$, where t is the time in seconds after the car drops and s is the starting height of the car in feet.

57. How high above the car's exit ramp should the ride's designer start the drop in order for riders to experience free fall for at least 3 seconds? **144 ft**

58. Approximately how long will riders be in free fall if their starting height is 160 feet above the exit ramp? **3.16 s**

www.algebra1.com/self_check_quiz

Lesson 9-6 Perfect Squares and Factoring **513**

Lesson 9-6 Perfect Squares and Factoring 513

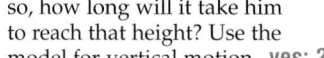

4 Assess

Open-Ended Assessment

Writing Ask students to look at the concept summary table on page 509, and decide which factoring technique they like best. Then have students write a description of how to use their favorite technique, and why they think it is a better method as compared to one or two of the other methods.

Assessment Options

Quiz (Lesson 9-6) is available on p. 574 of the *Chapter 9 Resource Masters*.

---

59. HUMAN CANNONBALL A circus acrobat is shot out of a cannon with an initial upward velocity of 64 feet per second. If the acrobat leaves the cannon 6 feet above the ground, will he reach a height of 70 feet? If so, how long will it take him to reach that height? Use the model for vertical motion. **yes; 2 s**

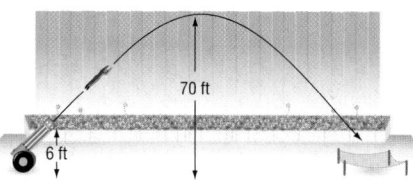

CRITICAL THINKING Determine all values of k that make each of the following a perfect square trinomial. **62. 70, −70**

60. $x^2 + kx + 64$ **16, −16**   **61.** $4x^2 + kx + 1$ **4, −4**   **62.** $25x^2 + kx + 49$

63. $x^2 + 8x + k$ **16**   **64.** $x^2 - 18x + k$ **81**   **65.** $x^2 + 20x + k$ **100**

66. ▢ **WRITING IN MATH**   Answer the question that was posed at the beginning of the lesson. **See margin.**

How can factoring be used to design a pavilion?

Include the following in your answer:

- an explanation of how the equation $(8 + 2x)^2 = 144$ models the given situation, and
- an explanation of how to solve this equation, listing any properties used, and an interpretation of its solutions.

67. During an experiment, a ball is dropped off a bridge from a height of 205 feet. The formula $205 = 16t^2$ can be used to approximate the amount of time, in seconds, it takes for the ball to reach the surface of the water of the river below the bridge. Find the time it takes the ball to reach the water to the nearest tenth of a second. **C**

(A) 2.3 s   (B) 3.4 s   (C) 3.6 s   (D) 12.8 s

68. If $\sqrt{a^2 - 2ab + b^2} = a - b$, then which of the following statements best describes the relationship between a and b? **D**

(A) $a < b$ (B) $a \leq b$ (C) $a > b$ (D) $a \geq b$

Maintain Your Skills

Mixed Review   Solve each equation. Check your solutions.   *(Lessons 9-4 and 9-5)*

69. $s^2 = 25$ **±5**   **70.** $9x^2 - 16 = 0$ $\pm\frac{4}{3}$ **71.** $49m^2 = 81$ $\pm\frac{9}{7}$

72. $8k^2 + 22k - 6 = 0$ $-3, \frac{1}{4}$ **73.** $12w^2 + 23w = -5$ $-\frac{5}{3}, -\frac{1}{4}$ **74.** $6z^2 + 7 = 17z$ $\frac{1}{2}, \frac{7}{3}$

Write the slope-intercept form of an equation that passes through the given point and is perpendicular to the graph of each equation.   *(Lesson 5-6)*

75. $(1, 4), y = 2x - 1$ $y = -\frac{1}{2}x + \frac{9}{2}$ **76.** $(-4, 7), y = -\frac{2}{3}x + 7$ $y = \frac{3}{2}x + 13$

77. NATIONAL LANDMARKS At the Royal Gorge in Colorado, an inclined railway takes visitors down to the Arkansas River. Suppose the slope is 50% or $\frac{1}{2}$ and the vertical drop is 1015 feet. What is the horizontal change of the railway? *(Lesson 5-1)* **2030 ft**

Find the next three terms of each arithmetic sequence.   *(Lesson 4-7)*

78. 17, 13, 9, 5, ...   **1, −3, −7**   **79.** −5, −4.5, −4, −3.5, ...   **−3, −2.5, −2**   **80.** 45, 54, 63, 72, ...   **81, 90, 99**

Answer

66. Answers should include the following.

- The length of each side of the pavilion is $8 + x + x$ or $8 + 2x$ feet. Thus, the area of the pavilion is $(8 + 2x)^2$ square feet. This area includes the 80 square feet of bricks and the 8^2 or 64-square foot piece of art, for a total area of 144 square feet. These two representations of the area of the pavilion must be equal, so we can write the equation $(8 + 2x)^2 = 144$.

- $(8 + 2x)^2 = 144$ Original equation
  $8 + 2x = \pm 12$ Square Root Property
  $8 + 2x = 12$ or $8 + 2x = -12$ Separate into two equations.
  $2x = 4$ $2x = -20$ Solve each equation.
  $x = 2$ $x = -10$

  Since length cannot be negative, the border should be 2 feet wide.

Study Guide and Review

Vocabulary and Concept Check

composite number (p. 474)	greatest common factor (GCF) (p. 476)	prime polynomial (p. 497)
factored form (p. 475)	perfect square trinomials (p. 508)	Square Root Property (p. 511)
factoring (p. 481)	prime factorization (p. 475)	Zero Product Property (p. 483)
factoring by grouping (p. 482)	prime number (p. 474)	

State whether each sentence is *true* or *false*. If false, replace the underlined word or number to make a true sentence.

1. The number 27 is an example of a <u>prime</u> number. **false, composite**
2. <u>$2x$</u> is the greatest common factor (GCF) of $12x^2$ and $14xy$. **true**
3. <u>66</u> is an example of a perfect square. **false, sample answer: 64**
4. 61 is a <u>factor</u> of 183. **true**
5. The prime factorization for 48 is <u>$3 \cdot 4^2$</u>. **false, $2^4 \cdot 3$**
6. $x^2 - 25$ is an example of a <u>perfect square trinomial</u>. **false, difference of squares**
7. The number 35 is an example of a <u>composite</u> number. **true**
8. <u>$x^2 - 3x - 70$</u> is an example of a prime polynomial. **false, sample answer: $x^2 + 2x + 2$**
9. Expressions with four or more unlike terms can sometimes be <u>factored by grouping</u>. **true**
10. <u>$(b - 7)(b + 7)$</u> is the factorization of a difference of squares. **true**

Lesson-by-Lesson Review

9-1 Factors and Greatest Common Factors

See pages 474–479.

Concept Summary
- The greatest common factor (GCF) of two or more monomials is the product of their common prime factors.

Example Find the GCF of $15x^2y$ and $45xy^2$.

$15x^2y = ③ ⑤ ⓧ x ⓨ$ Factor each number.
$45xy^2 = ③ 3 ⑤ ⓧ ⓨ y$ Circle the common prime factors.

The GCF is $3 \cdot 5 \cdot x \cdot y$ or $15xy$.

Exercises Find the prime factorization of each integer.
See Examples 2 and 3 on page 475.

11. 28 $2^2 \cdot 7$ 12. 33 $3 \cdot 11$ 13. 150 $2 \cdot 3 \cdot 5^2$
14. 301 $7 \cdot 43$ 15. -83 $-1 \cdot 83$ 16. -378 $-1 \cdot 2 \cdot 3^3 \cdot 7$

Find the GCF of each set of monomials. *See Example 5 on page 476.*

17. 35, 30 **5**   18. 12, 18, 40 **2**   19. $12ab, 4a^2b^2$ **$4ab$**
20. $16mrt, 30m^2r$ **$2mr$**   21. $20n^2, 25np^5$ **$5n$**   22. $60x^2y^2, 35xz^3$ **$5x$**

www.algebra1.com/vocabulary_review   **Chapter 9** Study Guide and Review **515**

Vocabulary and Concept Check

- This alphabetical list of vocabulary terms in Chapter 9 includes a page reference where each term was introduced.
- **Assessment** A vocabulary test/review for Chapter 9 is available on p. 572 of the *Chapter 9 Resource Masters*.

Lesson-by-Lesson Review

For each lesson,
- the main ideas are summarized,
- additional examples review concepts, and
- practice exercises are provided.

Vocabulary PuzzleMaker

ELL The Vocabulary PuzzleMaker software improves students' mathematics vocabulary using four puzzle formats— crossword, scramble, word search using a word list, and word search using clues. Students can work on a computer screen or from a printed handout.

MindJogger Videoquizzes

ELL MindJogger Videoquizzes provide an alternative review of concepts presented in this chapter. Students work in teams in a game show format to gain points for correct answers. The questions are presented in three rounds.

Round 1 Concepts (5 questions)
Round 2 Skills (4 questions)
Round 3 Problem Solving (4 questions)

FOLDABLES™
Study Organizer

For more information about Foldables, see *Teaching Mathematics with Foldables.*

Have students look through the chapter to make sure they have included questions and notes in their Foldables for each lesson of Chapter 9.

Encourage students to refer to their Foldables while completing the Study Guide and Review and to use them in preparing for the Chapter Test.

9-2 Factoring Using the Distributive Property

See pages 481–486.

Concept Summary

- Find the greatest common factor and then use the Distributive Property.
- With four or more terms, try factoring by grouping.
  Factoring by Grouping: $ax + bx + ay + by = x(a + b) + y(a + b) = (a + b)(x + y)$
- Factoring can be used to solve some equations.
  Zero Product Property: For any real numbers a and b, if $ab = 0$, then
  either $a = 0$, $b = 0$, or both a and b equal zero.

Example Factor $2x^2 - 3xz - 2xy + 3yz$.

$2x^2 - 3xz - 2xy + 3yz = (2x^2 - 3xz) + (-2xy + 3yz)$ Group terms with common factors.

$\hspace{4.5cm} = x(2x - 3z) - y(2x - 3z)$ Factor out the GCF from each grouping.

$\hspace{4.5cm} = (x - y)(2x - 3z)$ Factor out the common factor $2x - 3z$.

25. $2a(13b + 9c + 16a)$

Exercises Factor each polynomial. *See Examples 1 and 2 on pages 481 and 482.*

23. $13x + 26y$ $13(x + 2y)$

24. $24a^2b^2 - 18ab$ $6ab(4ab - 3)$

25. $26ab + 18ac + 32a^2$

26. $a^2 - 4ac + ab - 4bc$ $(a - 4c)(a + b)$

27. $4rs + 12ps + 2mr + 6mp$
$2(r + 3p)(2s + m)$

28. $24am - 9an + 40bm - 15bn$
$(8m - 3n)(3a + 5b)$

Solve each equation. Check your solutions. *See Examples 2 and 5 on pages 482 and 483.*

29. $x(2x - 5) = 0$ $\left\{0, \dfrac{5}{2}\right\}$

30. $(3n + 8)(2n - 6) = 0$ $\left\{-\dfrac{8}{3}, 3\right\}$

31. $4x^2 = -7x$ $\left\{0, -\dfrac{7}{4}\right\}$

9-3 Factoring Trinomials: $x^2 + bx + c$

See pages 489–494.

Concept Summary

- Factoring $x^2 + bx + c$: Find m and n whose sum is b and whose product is c.
  Then write $x^2 + bx + c$ as $(x + m)(x + n)$.

Example Solve $a^2 - 3a - 4 = 0$. Then check the solutions.

$a^2 - 3a - 4 = 0$ Original equation

$(a + 1)(a - 4) = 0$ Factor.

$a + 1 = 0$ or $a - 4 = 0$ Zero Product Property

$\hspace{0.8cm} a = -1 \hspace{1.3cm} a = 4$ Solve each equation.

The solution set is $\{-1, 4\}$.

32. $(y + 3)(y + 4)$ 33. $(x - 12)(x + 3)$

Exercises Factor each trinomial. *See Examples 1–4 on pages 490 and 491.*

32. $y^2 + 7y + 12$

33. $x^2 - 9x - 36$

34. $b^2 + 5b - 6$ $(b + 6)(b - 1)$

35. $18 - 9r + r^2$
$(r - 3)(r - 6)$

36. $a^2 + 6ax - 40x^2$
$(a + 10x)(a - 4x)$

37. $m^2 - 4mn - 32n^2$
$(m + 4n)(m - 8n)$

Solve each equation. Check your solutions. *See Example 5 on page 491.*

38. $y^2 + 13y + 40 = 0$
$\{-5, -8\}$

39. $x^2 - 5x - 66 = 0$
$\{-6, 11\}$

40. $m^2 - m - 12 = 0$ $\{-3, 4\}$

9-4 Factoring Trinomials: $ax^2 + bx + c$

See pages 495–500.

Concept Summary

- Factoring $ax^2 + bx + c$: Find m and n whose product is ac and whose sum is b. Then, write as $ax^2 + mx + nx + c$ and use factoring by grouping.

Example **Factor $12x^2 + 22x - 14$.**

First, factor out the GCF, 2: $12x^2 + 22x - 14 = 2(6x^2 + 11x - 7)$. In the new trinomial, $a = 6$, $b = 11$ and $c = -7$. Since b is positive, $m + n$ is positive. Since c is negative, mn is negative. So either m or n is negative, but not both. Therefore, make a list of the factors of $6(-7)$ or -42, where one factor in each pair is negative. Look for a pair of factors whose sum is 11.

Factors of -42	Sum of Factors
$-1,\ \ 42$	41
$1, -42$	-41
$-2,\ \ 21$	19
$2, -21$	-19
$-3,\ \ 14$	11

The correct factors are -3 and 14.

$$6x^2 + 11x - 7 = 6x^2 + mx + nx - 7 \qquad \text{Write the pattern.}$$
$$= 6x^2 - 3x + 14x - 7 \qquad m = -3 \text{ and } n = 14$$
$$= (6x^2 - 3x) + (14x - 7) \qquad \text{Group terms with common factors.}$$
$$= 3x(2x - 1) + 7(2x - 1) \qquad \text{Factor the GCF from each grouping.}$$
$$= (2x - 1)(3x + 7) \qquad 2x - 1 \text{ is the common factor.}$$

Thus, the complete factorization of $12x^2 + 22x - 14$ is $2(2x - 1)(3x + 7)$.

42. $(2m - 3)(m + 8)$ 43. $(5r + 2)(5r + 2)$

Exercises Factor each trinomial, if possible. If the trinomial cannot be factored using integers, write *prime*.   *See Examples 1–3 on pages 496 and 497.*

41. $2a^2 - 9a + 3$ **prime**   42. $2m^2 + 13m - 24$ 43. $25r^2 + 20r + 4$

44. $6z^2 + 7z + 3$ **prime**   45. $12b^2 + 17b + 6$ 46. $3n^2 - 6n - 45$
$\qquad\qquad\qquad\qquad\qquad\qquad (4b + 3)(3b + 2) \qquad 3(n - 5)(n + 3)$

Solve each equation. Check your solutions.   *See Example 4 on page 497.*

47. $2r^2 - 3r - 20 = 0$ 48. $3a^2 - 13a + 14 = 0$ 49. $40x^2 + 2x = 24$ $\left\{\dfrac{3}{4}, -\dfrac{4}{5}\right\}$
$\left\{4, -\dfrac{5}{2}\right\} \qquad\qquad\qquad \left\{2, \dfrac{7}{3}\right\}$

9-5 Factoring Differences of Squares

See pages 501–506.

Concept Summary

- Difference of Squares: $a^2 - b^2 = (a + b)(a - b)$ or $(a - b)(a + b)$
- Sometimes it may be necessary to use more than one factoring technique or to apply a factoring technique more than once.

Example **Factor $3x^3 - 75x$.**

$$3x^3 - 75x = 3x(x^2 - 25) \qquad \text{The GCF of } 3x^3 \text{ and } 75x \text{ is } 3x.$$
$$= 3x(x + 5)(x - 5) \qquad \text{Factor the difference of squares.}$$

Study Guide and Review

Chapter 9 For More ...
• Extra Practice, see pages 839–841.
• Mixed Problem Solving, see page 861.

Answers (p. 519)

22. $(a + 2)(a - 2)$
23. $(y - 5)(4m + 3p)$
24. $5a(3ab + a - 2)$
25. $(2y - 3)(3y + 2)$
26. $4(s - 5t)(s + 5t)$
27. $(x - 4)(x - 3)(x + 3)$

Exercises Factor each polynomial, if possible. If the polynomial cannot be factored, write *prime*. *See Examples 1–4 on page 502.*

50. $2y^3 - 128y$ $\quad$ 51. $9b^2 - 20$ **prime** $\quad$ 52. $\frac{1}{4}n^2 - \frac{9}{16}r^2$
$\qquad 2y(y - 8)(y + 8)$

Solve each equation by factoring. Check your solutions. *See Example 5 on page 503.*

53. $b^2 - 16 = 0$ $\{-4, 4\}$ $\quad$ 54. $25 - 9y^2 = 0$ $\left\{-\frac{5}{3}, \frac{5}{3}\right\}$ $\quad$ 55. $16a^2 - 81 = 0$ $\left\{-\frac{9}{4}, \frac{9}{4}\right\}$

52. $\left(\frac{1}{2}n - \frac{3}{4}r\right)\left(\frac{1}{2}n + \frac{3}{4}r\right)$

9-6 Perfect Squares and Factoring

See pages 508–514.

Concept Summary

• If a trinomial can be written in the form $a^2 + 2ab + b^2$ or $a^2 - 2ab + b^2$, then it can be factored as $(a + b)^2$ or as $(a - b)^2$, respectively.
• For a trinomial to be factorable as a perfect square, the first term must be a perfect square, the middle term must be twice the product of the square roots of the first and last terms, and the last term must be a perfect square.
• Square Root Property: For any number $n > 0$, if $x^2 = n$, then $x = \pm\sqrt{n}$.

Examples

1 **Determine whether $9x^2 + 24xy + 16y^2$ is a perfect square trinomial. If so, factor it.**

❶ Is the first term a perfect square? $\qquad$ Yes, $9x^2 = (3x)^2$.
❷ Is the last term a perfect square? $\qquad$ Yes, $16y^2 = (4y)^2$.
❸ Is the middle term equal to $2(3x)(4y)$? Yes, $24xy = 2(3x)(4y)$.

$9x^2 + 24xy + 16y^2 = (3x)^2 + 2(3x)(4y) + (4y)^2$ $\quad$ Write as $a^2 + 2ab + b^2$.
$\qquad\qquad\qquad\qquad\quad = (3x + 4y)^2$ $\qquad\qquad$ Factor using the pattern.

2 **Solve $(x - 4)^2 = 121$.**

$(x - 4)^2 = 121$ $\qquad\qquad$ Original equation
$x - 4 = \pm\sqrt{121}$ $\qquad$ Square Root Property
$x - 4 = \pm 11$ $\qquad\quad$ $121 = 11 \cdot 11$
$x = 4 \pm 11$ $\qquad\quad$ Add 4 to each side.
$x = 4 + 11 \quad$ or $\quad x = 4 - 11$ $\quad$ Separate into two equations.
$= 15 \qquad\qquad\quad = -7$ $\qquad$ The solution set is $\{-7, 15\}$.

Exercises Factor each polynomial, if possible. If the polynomial cannot be factored, write *prime*. *See Example 2 on page 510.*

56. $a^2 + 18a + 81$ $(a + 9)^2$ $\qquad$ 57. $9k^2 - 12k + 4$ $(3k - 2)^2$
58. $4 - 28r + 49r^2$ $(2 - 7r)^2$ $\qquad$ 59. $32n^2 - 80n + 50$ $2(4n - 5)^2$

Solve each equation. Check your solutions. *See Examples 3 and 4 on pages 510 and 511.*

60. $6b^3 - 24b^2 + 24b = 0$ $\{0, 2\}$ $\qquad$ 61. $49m^2 - 126m + 81 = 0$ $\left\{\frac{9}{7}\right\}$
62. $(c - 9)^2 = 144$ $\{-3, 21\}$ $\qquad\qquad$ 63. $144b^2 = 36$ $\left\{\pm\frac{1}{2}\right\}$

Vocabulary and Concepts

1. **Give an example** of a prime number and explain why it is prime. **Sample answer: 7; Its only factors are 1 and itself.**
2. **Write** a polynomial that is the difference of two squares. Then factor your polynomial. **Sample answer:** $n^2 - 100$; $(n + 10)(n - 10)$
3. **Describe** the first step in factoring any polynomial. **Check for a GCF other than 1 and factor it out.**

Skills and Applications

Find the prime factorization of each integer.

4. 63 $3^2 \cdot 7$
5. 81 3^4
6. -210 $-1 \cdot 2 \cdot 3 \cdot 5 \cdot 7$

Find the GCF of the given monomials.

7. 48, 64 **16**
8. 28, 75 **1, relatively prime**
9. $18a^2b^2$, $28a^3b^2$ $2a^2b^2$

Factor each polynomial, if possible. If the polynomial cannot be factored using integers, write *prime*. 14. $(a - 2b)(a - 9b)$ 17. $3x(x + 3)(2x - 1)$

10. $25y^2 - 49w^2$ $(5y - 7w)(5y + 7w)$
11. $t^2 - 16t + 64$ $(t - 8)^2$
12. $x^2 + 14x + 24$ $(x + 12)(x + 2)$
13. $28m^2 + 18m$ $2m(14m + 9)$
14. $a^2 - 11ab + 18b^2$
15. $12x^2 + 23x - 24$ $(3x + 8)(4x - 3)$
16. $2h^2 - 3h - 18$ **prime**
17. $6x^3 + 15x^2 - 9x$
18. $64p^2 - 63p + 16$ **prime**
19. $2d^2 + d - 1$ $(2d - 1)(d + 1)$
20. $36a^2b^3 - 45ab^4$ $9ab^3(4a - 5b)$
21. $36m^2 + 60mn + 25n^2$ $(6m + 5n)^2$
22. $a^2 - 4$ **22–27. See margin.**
23. $4my - 20m + 3py - 15p$
24. $15a^2b + 5a^2 - 10a$
25. $6y^2 - 5y - 6$
26. $4s^2 - 100t^2$
27. $x^3 - 4x^2 - 9x + 36$

Write an expression in factored form for the area of each shaded region.

28. 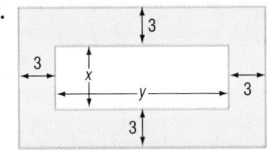 $6(x + y + 6)$
29. 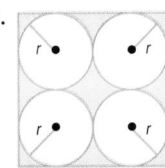 $4r^2(4 - \pi)$

Solve each equation. Check your solutions.

30. $(4x - 3)(3x + 2) = 0$ $\left\{ \frac{3}{4}, -\frac{2}{3} \right\}$
31. $18s^2 + 72s = 0$ $\{0, -4\}$
32. $4x^2 = 36$ $\{-3, 3\}$
33. $t^2 + 25 = 10t$ $\{5\}$
34. $a^2 - 9a - 52 = 0$ $\{-4, 13\}$
35. $x^3 - 5x^2 - 66x = 0$ $\{-6, 0, 11\}$
36. $2x^2 = 9x + 5$ $\left\{ -\frac{1}{2}, 5 \right\}$
37. $3b^2 + 6 = 11b$ $\left\{ \frac{2}{3}, 3 \right\}$

38. **GEOMETRY** A rectangle is 4 inches wide by 7 inches long. When the length and width are increased by the same amount, the area is increased by 26 square inches. What are the dimensions of the new rectangle? **6 in. by 9 in.**

39. **CONSTRUCTION** A rectangular lawn is 24 feet wide by 32 feet long. A sidewalk will be built along the inside edges of all four sides. The remaining lawn will have an area of 425 square feet. How wide will the walk be? **3.5 ft**

40. **STANDARDIZED TEST PRACTICE** The area of the shaded part of the square shown at the right is 98 square meters. Find the dimensions of the square. **14 m by 14 m**

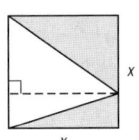

 www.algebra1.com/chapter_test

Portfolio Suggestion

Introduction Have you ever noticed that when you are learning the concepts in a chapter, such as how to factor polynomials in this chapter, that there is often more than one way to solve a problem?

Ask Students Pick a trinomial that can be factored by more than one method that you learned in this chapter, and explain how to factor it using these methods. Make sure you include a worked-out example with your descriptions in your portfolio.

Assessment Options

Vocabulary Test A vocabulary test/review for Chapter 9 can be found on p. 572 of the *Chapter 9 Resource Masters*.

Chapter Tests There are six Chapter 9 Tests and an Open-Ended Assessment task available in the *Chapter 9 Resource Masters*.

Chapter 9 Tests			
Form	Type	Level	Pages
1	MC	basic	559–560
2A	MC	average	561–562
2B	MC	average	563–564
2C	FR	average	565–566
2D	FR	average	567–568
3	FR	advanced	569–570

MC = multiple-choice questions
FR = free-response questions

Open-Ended Assessment
Performance tasks for Chapter 9 can be found on p. 571 of the *Chapter 9 Resource Masters*. A sample scoring rubric for these tasks appears on p. A25.

 ExamView® Pro

Use the networkable **ExamView® Pro** to:

- Create **multiple versions** of tests.
- Create **modified** tests for *Inclusion* students.
- **Edit** existing questions and **add** your own questions.
- Use built-in **state curriculum correlations** to create tests aligned with state standards.
- Change **English** tests to **Spanish** and vice versa.

These two pages contain practice questions in the various formats that can be found on the most frequently given standardized tests.

A practice answer sheet for these two pages can be found on p. A1 of the *Chapter 9 Resource Masters*.

Standardized Test Practice
Student Recording Sheet, p. A1

Part 1 Multiple Choice

Select the best answer from the choices given and fill in the corresponding oval.

1 Ⓐ Ⓑ Ⓒ Ⓓ   4 Ⓐ Ⓑ Ⓒ Ⓓ   7 Ⓐ Ⓑ Ⓒ Ⓓ

2 Ⓐ Ⓑ Ⓒ Ⓓ   5 Ⓐ Ⓑ Ⓒ Ⓓ   8 Ⓐ Ⓑ Ⓒ Ⓓ

3 Ⓐ Ⓑ Ⓒ Ⓓ   6 Ⓐ Ⓑ Ⓒ Ⓓ   9 Ⓐ Ⓑ Ⓒ Ⓓ

Part 2 Short Response/Grid In

Solve the problem and write your answer in the blank.

For Questions 13 and 16, also enter your answer by writing each number or symbol in a box. Then fill in the corresponding oval for that number or symbol.

10 _____   13   16
11 _____
12 _____
13 _____ (grid in)
14 _____
15 _____
16 _____ (grid in)
17 _____
18 _____
19 _____
20 _____

Part 3 Extended Response

Record your answers for Questions 21–23 on the back of this paper.

Additional Practice

See pp. 577–578 in the *Chapter 9 Resource Masters* for additional standardized test practice.

Record your answers on the answer sheet provided by your teacher or on a sheet of paper.

1. Which equation best describes the function graphed below? (Lesson 5-3) **A**

   Ⓐ $y = -\frac{3}{5}x - 3$

   Ⓑ $y = \frac{3}{5}x - 3$

   Ⓒ $y = -\frac{5}{3}x - 3$

   Ⓓ $y = \frac{5}{3}x - 3$

   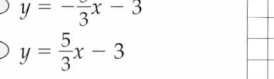

2. The school band sold tickets to their spring concert every day at lunch for one week. Before they sold any tickets, they had $80 in their account. At the end of each day, they recorded the total number of tickets sold and the total amount of money in the band's account.

Day	Total Number of Tickets Sold *t*	Total Amount in Account *a*
Monday	12	$176
Tuesday	18	$224
Wednesday	24	$272
Thursday	30	$320
Friday	36	$368

   Which equation describes the relationship between the total number of tickets sold *t* and the amount of money in the band's account *a*? (Lesson 5-4) **D**

   Ⓐ $a = \frac{1}{8}t + 80$ Ⓑ $a = \frac{t + 80}{6}$

   Ⓒ $a = 6t + 8$ Ⓓ $a = 8t + 80$

3. Which inequality represents the shaded portion of the graph? (Lesson 6-6) **A**

   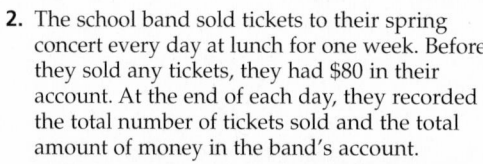

   Ⓐ $y \geq \frac{1}{3}x - 1$

   Ⓑ $y \leq \frac{1}{3}x - 1$

   Ⓒ $y \leq 3x + 1$

   Ⓓ $y \geq 3x - 1$

4. Today, the refreshment stand at the high school football game sold twice as many bags of popcorn as were sold last Friday. The total sold both days was 258 bags. Which system of equations will determine the number of bags sold today *n* and the number of bags sold last Friday *f*? (Lesson 7-2) **D**

   Ⓐ $n = f - 258$
      $f = 2n$

   Ⓑ $n = f - 258$
      $n = 2f$

   Ⓒ $n + f = 258$
      $f = 2n$

   Ⓓ $n + f = 258$
      $n = 2f$

5. Express 5.387×10^{-3} in standard notation. (Lesson 8-3) **B**

   Ⓐ 0.0005387   Ⓑ 0.005387

   Ⓒ 538.7   Ⓓ 5387

6. The quotient $\frac{16x^8}{8x^4}$, $x \neq 0$, is (Lesson 9-1) **C**

   Ⓐ $2x^2$.   Ⓑ $8x^2$.   Ⓒ $2x^4$.   Ⓓ $8x^4$.

7. What are the solutions of the equation $3x^2 - 48 = 0$? (Lesson 9-1) **A**

   Ⓐ $4, -4$ Ⓑ $4, \frac{1}{3}$

   Ⓒ $16, -16$ Ⓓ $16, \frac{1}{3}$

8. What are the solutions of the equation $x^2 - 3x + 8 = 6x - 6$? (Lesson 9-4) **D**

   Ⓐ $2, -7$ Ⓑ $-2, -4$

   Ⓒ $2, 4$ Ⓓ $2, 7$

9. The area of a rectangle is $12x^2 - 21x - 6$. The width is $3x - 6$. What is the length? (Lesson 9-5) **B**

   Ⓐ $4x - 1$ Ⓑ $4x + 1$

   Ⓒ $9x + 1$ Ⓓ $12x - 18$

Test-Taking Tip

Questions 7 and 9
When answering a multiple-choice question, first find an answer on your own. Then, compare your answer to the answer choices given in the item. If your answer does not match any of the answer choices, check your calculations.

 ExamView® Pro

Special banks of standardized test questions similar to those on the SAT, ACT, TIMSS 8, NAEP 8, and Algebra 1 End-of-Course tests can be found on this CD-ROM.

Preparing for Standardized Tests
For test-taking strategies and more
practice, see pages 867–884.

Part 2 | Short Response/Grid In

Record your answers on the answer sheet
provided by your teacher or on a sheet of
paper.

10. Write an equation of a line that has a
y-intercept of -1 and is perpendicular to
the graph of $2 - 2y = -5x$. (Lesson 5-6)
$$y = -\frac{2}{5}x - 1$$

11. Find all values of x that make the equation
$6|x - 2| = 18$ true. (Lesson 6-5) **5 and -1**

12. Graph the inequality $x + y \leq 3$. (Lesson 6-6)
See margin.

13. A movie theater charges $7.50 for each adult
ticket and $4 for each child ticket. If the
theater sold a total of 145 tickets for a total
of $790, how many adult tickets were sold?
(Lesson 7-2) **60**

14. Solve the following system of equations.
$3x + y = 8$
$4x - 2y = 14$ (Lesson 7-3) **{3, -1}**

15. Write an expression
to represent the
volume of the
rectangular prism.
(Lesson 8-7)
$8x^3 + 4x^2 - 60x$

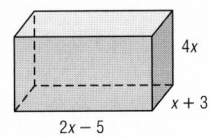

16. Jon is cutting a 64-inch-long board and a
48-inch-long board to make shelves. He
wants the shelves to be the same length
without wasting any wood. What is the
longest possible length of the shelves?
(Lesson 9-1) **16 in.**

17. Write $(x + t)x + (x + t)y$ as the product of
two factors. (Lesson 9-3) $(x + t)(x + y)$

18. The product of two consecutive odd integers
is 195. Find the integers. (Lesson 9-4)
13 and 15 or -13 and -15

19. Solve $2x^2 + 5x - 12 = 0$ by factoring.
(Lesson 9-5) $\frac{3}{2}$ or -4

20. Factor $2x^2 + 7x + 3$. (Lesson 9-5)
$(2x + 1)(x + 3)$

 www.algebra1.com/standardized_test

Part 3 | Extended Response

Record your answers on a sheet of paper.
Show your work.

21. The length and width of an advertisement
in the local newspaper had to be increased
by the same amount in order to double its
area. The original advertisement had a
length of 6 centimeters and a width of
4 centimeters. (Lesson 9-3)
a. Find an equation that represents the area
of the enlarged advertisement.
$$(x + 6)(x + 4) = 2(6)(4)$$
b. What are the new dimensions of the
advertisement? Round to the nearest
tenth. **length = 8 cm, width = 6 cm**

c. What is the new area of the
advertisement? **48 cm^2**

d. If the entire page has 200 square
centimeters of space, about what fraction
does the advertisement take up? $\frac{6}{25}$

22. Suppose the area of a rectangular plot of
land is $(6c^2 + 7c - 3)$ square miles.
(Lesson 9-4)
a. Find algebraic expressions for the length
and the width. **length = $(3c - 1)$ mi,
width = $(2c + 3)$ mi**
b. If the area is 21 square miles, find the
value of c. **1.5**

c. What are the length and the width?
3.5 mi, 6 mi

23. Madison is building a fenced, rectangular
dog pen. The width of the pen will be
3 yards less than the length. The total area
enclosed is 28 square yards. (Lesson 9-4)
a. Using L to represent the length of the
pen, write an equation showing the area
of the pen in terms of its length.

b. What is the length of the pen?

c. How many yards of fencing will
Madison need to enclose the pen
completely? **a–c. See margin.**

Evaluating Extended Response Questions

Extended Response questions are
graded by using a multilevel
rubric that guides you in
assessing a student's knowledge
of a particular concept.

Goal: Write a polynomial and
use it to find the dimensions of a
dog pen.

Sample Scoring Rubric: The following rubric is a sample scoring
device. You may wish to add
more detail to this sample to meet
your individual scoring needs.

Score	Criteria
4	A correct solution that is supported by well-developed, accurate explanations
3	A generally correct solution, but may contain minor flaws in reasoning or computation
2	A partially correct interpretation and/or solution to the problem
1	A correct solution with no supporting evidence or explanation
0	An incorrect solution indicating no mathematical understanding of the concept or task, or no solution is given

Answers

12.

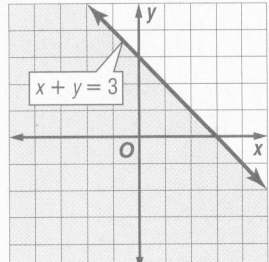

23a. a polynomial equation
equivalent to $28 = L(L - 3)$

23b. The length is 7 yards.
$$28 = L^2 - 3L$$
$$L^2 - 3L - 28 = 0$$
$$(L - 7)(L + 4) = 0$$
$$L = 7$$

23c. 22 yd

Calculate W. Calculate the
perimeter.

$W = L - 3$
$W = 7 - 3$ or 4
$P = 2L + 2W$
$P = 2(7) + 2(4)$
$P = 14 + 8$ or 22

Pages 477–479, Lesson 9-1

69. Scientists listening to radio signals would suspect that a modulated signal beginning with prime numbers would indicate a message from an extraterrestrial.

Answers should include the following.

- 2, 3, 5, 7, 11, 13, 17, 19, 23, 29, 31, 37, 41, 43, 47, 53, 59, 61, 67, 71, 79, 83, 89, 97, 101, 103, 107, 109, 113; See student's explanation.

- Sample answer: It is unlikely that any natural phenomenon would produce such an artificial and specifically mathematical pattern.

Page 480, Preview of Lesson 9-2

5.

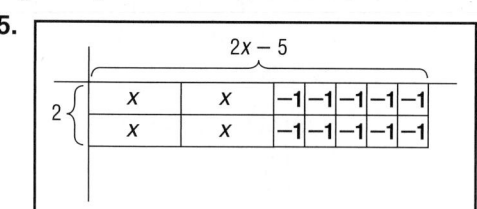

6.

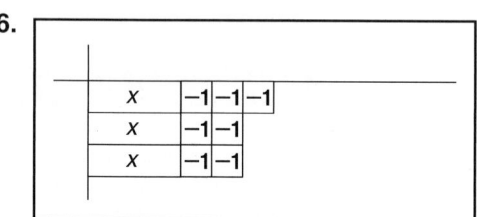

7.

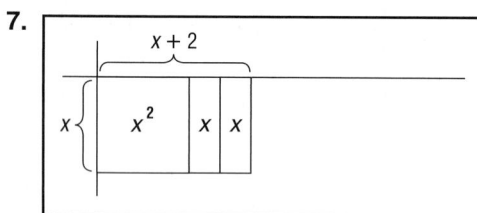

8.

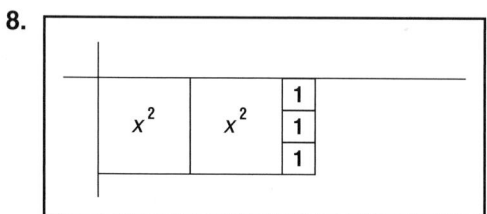

Pages 484–486, Lesson 9-2

16. $5(x + 6y)$ **17.** $4(4a + b)$

18. $a(a^4b - 1)$ **19.** $x(x^2y^2 + 1)$

20. $3d(7c - 1)$ **21.** $2h(7g - 9)$

22. $15ay(a - 2)$ **23.** $8bc(c + 3)$

24. $4xy^2z(3x + 10yz)$ **25.** $6abc^2(3a - 8c)$

26. $a(1 + ab^2 + a^2b^3)$ **27.** $x(15xy^2 + 25y + 1)$

28. $4x(3ax^2 + 5bx + 8c)$ **29.** $3pq(p^2 - 3q + 12)$

30. $(x + 3)(x + 2)$ **31.** $(x + 7)(x + 5)$

32. $(2x + 3)(2x + 7)$ **33.** $(3y + 2)(4y + 3)$

34. $(3a - 4)(2a - 5)$ **35.** $(6x - 1)(3x - 5)$

36. $(a + b)(4x + 3y)$ **37.** $(m + x)(2y + 7)$

38. $(2x - 3)(4a - 3)$ **39.** $(2x - 3)(5x - 7y)$

Pages 498–500, Lesson 9-4

35. $\left\{-5, -\dfrac{2}{5}\right\}$ **36.** $\left\{-\dfrac{4}{3}, 3\right\}$

37. $\left\{-\dfrac{1}{6}, \dfrac{3}{4}\right\}$ **38.** $\left\{\dfrac{1}{3}, \dfrac{2}{5}\right\}$

39. $\left\{-\dfrac{5}{7}, \dfrac{5}{2}\right\}$ **40.** $\left\{-\dfrac{5}{4}, \dfrac{7}{3}\right\}$

41. $\left\{-\dfrac{2}{3}, 3\right\}$ **42.** $\left\{-\dfrac{2}{7}, 1\right\}$

43. $\left\{\dfrac{1}{2}, \dfrac{2}{3}\right\}$ **44.** $\left\{-\dfrac{1}{3}, \dfrac{9}{4}\right\}$

45. $\{-4, 12\}$ **46.** $\left\{-\dfrac{7}{3}, \dfrac{5}{2}\right\}$

47. $\left\{-4, \dfrac{2}{3}\right\}$ **48.** $\left\{\dfrac{1}{2}, \dfrac{7}{2}\right\}$

Notes

Quadratic and Exponential Functions
Chapter Overview and Pacing

Year-long and two-year pacing: pages T20–T21.

LESSON OBJECTIVES	PACING (days)			
	Regular		**Block**	
	Basic/ Average	Advanced	Basic/ Average	Advanced
10-1 Graphing Quadratic Functions *(pp. 524–532)* • Graph quadratic functions. • Find the equation of the axis of symmetry and the coordinates of the vertex of a parabola. ***Follow-Up:*** Use a graphing calculator to explore families of quadratic graphs.	2	2 (with 10-1 Follow-Up)	1.5 (with 10-1 Follow-Up)	1.5 (with 10-1 Follow-Up)
10-2 Solving Quadratic Equations by Graphing *(pp. 533–538)* • Solve quadratic equations by graphing. • Estimate solutions of quadratic equations by graphing.	2	2	1	0.5
10-3 Solving Quadratic Equations by Completing the Square *(pp. 539-545)* • Solve quadratic equations by finding the square root. • Solve quadratic equations by completing the square. ***Follow-Up:*** Use a graphing calculator to graph quadratic functions in vertex form.	2	2 (with 10-3 Follow-Up)	1	1 (with 10-3 Follow-Up)
10-4 Solving Quadratic Equations by Using the Quadratic Formula *(pp. 546–553)* • Solve quadratic equations by using the Quadratic Formula. • Use the discriminant to determine the number of solutions for a quadratic equation. ***Follow-Up:*** Use a graphing calculator to solve quadratic-linear systems.	2	2 (with 10-4 Follow-Up)	1.5 (with 10-4 Follow-Up)	1 (with 10-4 Follow-Up)
10-5 Exponential Functions *(pp. 554–560)* • Graph exponential functions. • Identify data that displays exponential behavior.	2	2	1	1
10-6 Growth and Decay *(pp. 561–565)* • Solve problems involving exponential growth. • Solve problems involving exponential decay.	2	2	1	1
10-7 Geometric Sequences *(pp. 567–573)* • Recognize and extend geometric sequences. • Find geometric means. ***Follow-Up:*** Use a table to investigate rates of change.	2	2 (with 10-7 Follow-Up)	1	1 (with 10-7 Follow-Up)
Study Guide and **Practice Test** *(pp. 574–579)* **Standardized Test Practice** *(pp. 580–581)*	1	1	0.5	0.5
Chapter Assessment	1	1	0.5	0.5
TOTAL	16	16	9	8

*An electronic version of this chapter is available on **StudentWorks™**. This backpack solution CD-ROM allows students instant access to the Student Edition, lesson worksheet pages, and web resources.*

Chapter Resource Manager

CHAPTER 10 RESOURCE MASTERS

Study Guide and Intervention	Practice (Skills and Average)	Reading to Learn Mathematics	Enrichment	Assessment	Prerequisite Skills Workbook	Applications*	Parent and Student Study Guide Workbook	5-Minute Check Transparencies	Interactive Chalkboard	AlgePASS: Tutorial Plus (lessons)	Materials
579–580	581–582	583	584				75	10-1	10-1	28	grid paper, graphing calculator (*Follow-Up:* graphing calculator)
585–586	587–588	589	590	635		SC 19	76	10-2	10-2		graphing calculator
591–592	593–594	595	596				77	10-3	10-3	29	(*Follow-Up:* graphing calculator)
597–598	599–600	601	602	635, 637		SC 20	78	10-4	10-4	30, 31	graphing calculator (*Follow-Up:* graphing calculator)
603–604	605–606	607	608			GCS 42	79	10-5	10-5		grid paper, piece of string, graphing calculator
609–610	611–612	613	614	636		SM 77–80	80	10-6	10-6		
615–616	617–618	619	620	636	9–12, 47–48	GCS 41	81	10-7	10-7		(*Follow-Up:* grid paper)
				621–634, 638–640			82				

Key to Abbreviations: GCS = Graphing Calculator and Spreadsheet Masters,
SC = School-to-Career Masters,
SM = Science and Mathematics Lab Manual

ELL Study Guide and Intervention, Skills Practice, Practice, and Parent and Student Study Guide Workbooks are also available in Spanish.

Mathematical Connections and Background

Continuity of Instruction

Prior Knowledge

In Chapter 4, students graphed ordered pairs on a coordinate plane. They also analyzed arithmetic sequences. Students factored perfect square trinomials in Chapter 9.

This Chapter

This chapter introduces students to quadratic functions by having them graph the functions and determine the axis of symmetry and vertex. Students solve quadratic equations by graphing, completing the square, and using the Quadratic Formula. They use the determinant to determine the number of real roots of quadratic equations. Students graph and translate exponential functions and then relate them to growth and decay problems. Finally, students analyze geometric sequences.

Future Connections

The Quadratic Formula can be used to solve any second-degree polynomial equation in future studies of math. Exponential functions, such as growth and decay, are applied in many fields, including science and finance.

10-1 Graphing Quadratic Functions

The standard form of a quadratic function is $y = ax^2 + bx + c$, where $a \neq 0$. If $a = 0$, there would be no x^2 term, and therefore the equation would be linear. The graph of a quadratic function is a symmetrical curve called a parabola. If a is positive, the graph opens upward and the vertex is the minimum of the function. If a is negative, the graph opens downward and the vertex is the maximum of the function.

When a graph of a parabola is folded so that the two sides exactly match, the fold line is called the axis of symmetry. The vertex is the only point of a parabola that lies on its axis of symmetry. The equation for the axis of symmetry is $x = -\dfrac{b}{2a}$. The value $-\dfrac{b}{2a}$ is also the x-coordinate of the vertex. Substitute this value into the equation to find the y-coordinate of the vertex.

10-2 Solving Quadratic Equations by Graphing

Graphing can be used to find the solutions of a quadratic equation. The solutions of a quadratic equation are also called the roots of the equation. They are the x-intercepts of the graph of the related function.

Quadratic equations can have two real roots, a double real root, or no real roots. There are two real roots when the vertex is on one side of the x-axis and the curve extends to the other side. There is a double real root when the vertex is on the x-axis. There are no real roots when the entire parabola is on one side of the x-axis. Sometimes the roots are not integers and must be estimated from the graph.

10-3 Solving Quadratic Equations by Completing the Square

One way to solve some equations is to take the square root of each side. To do this, the quadratic expression on one side of the equation must be a perfect square. There are very few quadratic equations that fit this description.

For many quadratic equations, a process called completing the square is used while solving the equation. To complete the square of a quadratic expression $x^2 + bx$, find half of b and square it. Add this amount to the original expression. When solving an equation using this process, first add the square of half of b to each side of the equation. Solve by factoring and taking the square root of each side. If the coefficient of x^2 is not 1, first divide each term by this coefficient before completing the square.

10-4 Solving Quadratic Equations by Using the Quadratic Formula

Completing the square is the basis for the Quadratic Formula. Any quadratic equation can be solved using the Quadratic Formula. The coefficients a and b, and the constant c (from the standard form $ax^2 + bx + c = 0$), are substituted into the formula $x = \dfrac{-b \pm \sqrt{b^2 - 4ac}}{2a}$. Then the expression is simplified to determine the solutions.

The discriminant is the value $b^2 - 4ac$ that is inside the radical in the Quadratic Formula. This value can be used to determine the number of roots, or solutions, a quadratic equation has. A positive discriminant indicates two real roots, while a negative discriminant indicates that there are no real roots. If the discriminant is 0, there is one real root.

10-5 Exponential Functions

An exponential function has a variable as an exponent. The base of the exponent must be greater than 0, but not equal to 1. The base cannot equal 1 since 1 to any power equals 1. One way to graph an exponential function is to use ordered pairs. If the base is greater than 1, the graph rises faster and faster as the x values increase. If the base is less than 1, the graph falls more slowly as the x values increase.

The graphs of exponential functions can be translated by numbers other than the base and exponent. The y-intercept is changed if a constant is multiplied by the original expression. Adding a constant to the original expression translates the graph up or down depending on whether the constant is positive or negative.

Two ways to identify exponential functions are to look at the graph and to look for a pattern in the data. In the data, domain values at regular intervals have corresponding range values that have a common factor, not a common difference.

10-6 Growth and Decay

The general formula for exponential growth is $y = C(1 + r)^t$. The original amount C increases by the same percent r over a given period of time t. Compound interest is one application of exponential growth. Exponential decay is a variation of exponential growth. Instead of the original amount increasing by the same percent over a given period of time, it decreases. Depreciation is an application of exponential decay.

10-7 Geometric Sequences

Recall that in an arithmetic sequence, the terms increase or decrease by a constant value called the common difference. In a geometric sequence, each term is found by multiplying the previous term by the same number, called the common ratio. The common ratio is found by dividing a term by the previous term. If all the terms have the same sign, the common ratio is positive. If the terms alternate signs, the common ratio is negative.

Once you determine the common ratio, you can use the formula $a_n = a_1 \cdot r^{n-1}$ to find the nth term. In this equation, a_1 is the first term and r is the common ratio. In other words, to find a specific term, multiply the first term of the sequence by the common ratio raised to a power one less than the number of the specific term.

A term or terms between two other terms in a geometric sequence are called geometric means. Use the geometric sequence formula to find the geometric means. Solve for r. Once the common ratio is known, multiply the previous term by r to find the missing geometric mean or means.

Quick Review Math Handbook

Hot Words includes a glossary of terms while Hot Topics consists of explanations of key mathematical concepts with exercises to test comprehension. This valuable resource can be used as a reference in the classroom or for home study.

Lesson	Hot Topics Section	Lesson	Hot Topics Section
GS10	6.7, 6.8	10-4	6.3
10-1	6.8	10-5	6.3
10-3	6.3		

GS = Getting Started

 Additional mathematical information and teaching notes are available at www.algebra1.com/key_concepts.

DAILY
INTERVENTION and Assessment

Key to Abbreviations:
TWE = Teacher Wraparound Edition; CRM = Chapter Resource Masters

	Type	Student Edition	Teacher Resources	Technology/Internet
INTERVENTION	Ongoing	Prerequisite Skills, pp. 523, 530, 538, 544, 552, 560, 565 Practice Quiz 1, p. 544 Practice Quiz 2, p. 560	5-Minute Check Transparencies *Prerequisite Skills Workbook,* pp. 9–12, 47–48 Quizzes, *CRM* pp. 635–636 Mid-Chapter Test, *CRM* p. 637 Study Guide and Intervention, *CRM* pp. 579–580, 585–586, 591–592, 597–598, 603–604, 609–610, 615–616	AlgePASS: Tutorial Plus, Lessons 28, 29, 30, and 31 www.algebra1.com/self_check_quiz www.algebra1.com/extra_examples
	Mixed Review	pp. 530, 538, 544, 552, 560, 565, 572	Cumulative Review, *CRM* p. 638	
	Error Analysis	Find the Error, pp. 550, 558 Common Misconceptions, p. 534	Find the Error, *TWE* pp. 550, 558 Unlocking Misconceptions, *TWE* pp. 534, 540 Tips for New Teachers, *TWE* pp. 547, 548	
ASSESSMENT	Standardized Test Practice	pp. 527, 528, 530, 538, 543, 552, 560, 565, 572, 579, 580–581	*TWE* pp. 580–581 Standardized Test Practice, *CRM* pp. 639–640	Standardized Test Practice CD-ROM www.algebra1.com/standardized_test
	Open-Ended Assessment	Writing in Math, pp. 530, 537, 543, 552, 560, 565, 572 Open Ended, pp. 528, 536, 542, 550, 557, 563, 570 Standardized Test, p. 581	Modeling: *TWE* pp. 530, 544, 560, 572 Speaking: *TWE* p. 538 Writing: *TWE* pp. 552, 565 Open-Ended Assessment, *CRM* p. 633	
	Chapter Assessment	Study Guide, pp. 574–578 Practice Test, p. 579	Multiple-Choice Tests (Forms 1, 2A, 2B), *CRM* pp. 621–626 Free-Response Tests (Forms 2C, 2D, 3), *CRM* pp. 627–632 Vocabulary Test/Review, *CRM* p. 634	ExamView® Pro (see below) MindJogger Videoquizzes www.algebra1.com/vocabulary_review www.algebra1.com/chapter_test

For more information on *Yearly ProgressPro*, see p. 406.

Algebra Lesson	Yearly ProgressPro Skill Lesson
10-1	Graphing Quadratic Functions
10-2	Solving Quadratic Equations by Graphing
10-3	Solving Quadratic Equations by Completing the Square
10-4	Solving Quadratic Equations by Using the Quadratic Formula
10-5	Exponential Functions
10-6	Growth and Decay
10-7	Geometric Sequences

ExamView® Pro

Use the networkable **ExamView® Pro** to:
- Create **multiple versions** of tests.
- Create **modified** tests for *Inclusion* students.
- **Edit** existing questions and **add** your own questions.
- Use built-in **state curriculum correlations** to create tests aligned with state standards.
- Change **English** tests to **Spanish** and vice versa.

For more information on Intervention and Assessment, see pp. T8–T11.

Reading and Writing in Mathematics

Glencoe Algebra 1 provides numerous opportunities to incorporate reading and writing into the mathematics classroom.

Student Edition

- Foldables Study Organizer, p. 523
- Concept Check questions require students to verbalize and write about what they have learned in the lesson. (pp. 528, 535, 542, 550, 557, 563, 570)
- Reading Mathematics, p. 566
- Writing in Math questions in every lesson, pp. 530, 537, 543, 552, 560, 565, 572
- Reading Study Tip, p. 525
- WebQuest, pp. 537, 572

Teacher Wraparound Edition

- Foldables Study Organizer, pp. 523, 574
- Study Notebook suggestions, pp. 528, 536, 542, 550, 558, 563, 566, 570, 573
- Modeling activities, pp. 530, 544, 560, 572
- Speaking activities, p. 538
- Writing activities, pp. 552, 565
- Differentiated Instruction, (Verbal/Linguistic), p. 547
- **ELL** Resources, pp. 522, 529, 537, 543, 547, 551, 559, 564, 566, 571, 574

Additional Resources

- Vocabulary Builder worksheets require students to define and give examples for key vocabulary terms as they progress through the chapter. (*Chapter 10 Resource Masters*, pp. vii-viii)
- Reading to Learn Mathematics master for each lesson (*Chapter 10 Resource Masters*, pp. 583, 589, 595, 601, 607, 613, 619)
- *Vocabulary PuzzleMaker* software creates crossword, jumble, and word search puzzles using vocabulary lists that you can customize.
- *Teaching Mathematics with Foldables* provides suggestions for promoting cognition and language.
- *Reading and Writing in the Mathematics Classroom*
- *WebQuest and Project Resources*

For more information on Reading and Writing in Mathematics, see pp. T6–T7.

PROJECT CRISS℠ Study Skill

Power notes help students outline a lesson or chapter. Students often benefit from making power notes as a cooperative activity. In the outline at the right, Power 1 is the main idea, Power 2 provides details about the main idea, Power 3 provides details about Power 2 and so on. More than one detail can be placed under each power. You may have students copy the power notes at the right and complete them using the information in Chapter 10. You may also wish to have students develop another set of power notes outlining how to graph quadratic and exponential functions.

1. Solving Quadratic Equations
2. Graph the Equation
    3. zero roots; if it doesn't intersect the x-axis
    3. one root; if it touches the x-axis at one point
    3. two roots; if it intersects the x-axis at two points
2. Complete the Square
    3. Find $\frac{1}{2}$ of the coefficient of x.
    3. Square the result from above.
    3. Add the new result to each side of the original equation.
    3. Solve.
2. Use the Quadratic Formula
    3. Rewrite the equation in standard form.
    3. Substitute values into the formula.
    3. Simplify.

CReating **I**ndependence **T**hrough **S**tudent-Owned **S**trategies

Quadratic and Exponential Functions

What You'll Learn

Have students read over the list of objectives and make a list of any words with which they are not familiar.

Why It's Important

Point out to students that this is only one of many reasons why each objective is important. Others are provided in the introduction to each lesson.

What You'll Learn

- **Lesson 10-1** Graph quadratic functions.
- **Lessons 10-2 through 10-4** Solve quadratic equations.
- **Lesson 10-5** Graph exponential functions.
- **Lesson 10-6** Solve problems involving exponential growth and exponential decay.
- **Lesson 10-7** Recognize and extend geometric sequences.

Why It's Important

Quadratic functions and equations are used to solve problems about fireworks, to simulate the flight of golf balls in computer games, to describe arches, to determine hang time in football, and to help with water management. Exponential functions are used to describe changes in population, to solve compound interest problems, and to determine concentration of chemicals in a body of water after a spill. Exponential decay is one type of exponential function. Carbon dating uses exponential decay to determine the age of fossils and dinosaurs. *You will learn about carbon dating in Lesson 10-6.*

Key Vocabulary

- parabola (p. 524)
- completing the square (p. 539)
- Quadratic Formula (p. 546)
- exponential function (p. 554)
- geometric sequence (p. 567)

Lesson	NCTM Standards	Local Objectives
10-1	2, 6, 8, 9, 10	
10-1 Follow-Up	2, 6, 7, 8	
10-2	2, 6, 8, 9, 10	
10-3	2, 6, 8, 9, 10	
10-3 Follow-Up	2, 6, 7, 8	
10-4	2, 6, 8, 9, 10	
10-4 Follow-Up	2, 6	
10-5	2, 6, 8, 9, 10	
10-6	2, 6, 8, 9, 10	
10-7	1, 2, 3, 6, 8, 9, 10	
10-7 Follow-Up	1, 2, 6, 8, 9, 10	

Key to NCTM Standards:

1=Number & Operations, 2=Algebra, 3=Geometry, 4=Measurement, 5=Data Analysis & Probability, 6=Problem Solving, 7=Reasoning & Proof, 8=Communication, 9=Connections, 10=Representation

Vocabulary Builder

The Key Vocabulary list introduces students to some of the main vocabulary terms included in this chapter. For a more thorough vocabulary list with pronunciations of new words, give students the Vocabulary Builder worksheets found on pages vii and viii of the *Chapter 10 Resource Masters*. Encourage them to complete the definition of each term as they progress through the chapter. You may suggest that they add these sheets to their study notebooks for future reference when studying for the Chapter 10 test.

Getting Started

> **Prerequisite Skills** To be successful in this chapter, you'll need to master these skills and be able to apply them in problem-solving situations. Review these skills before beginning Chapter 10.

For Lesson 10-1   Graph Functions

Use a table of values to graph each equation. *(For review, see Lesson 5-3.)*   **1–8. See pp. 581A–581H.**

1. $y = x + 5$ **2.** $y = 2x - 3$ **3.** $y = 0.5x + 1$ **4.** $y = -3x - 2$

5. $2x - 3y = 12$ **6.** $5y = 10 + 2x$ **7.** $x + 2y = -6$ **8.** $3x = -2y + 9$

For Lesson 10-3   Perfect Square Trinomials

Determine whether each trinomial is a perfect square trinomial. If so, factor it.
(For review, see Lesson 9-6.) **9. yes; $(t + 6)^2$ 10. yes; $(a - 7)^2$**

9. $t^2 + 12t + 36$ **10.** $a^2 - 14a + 49$ **11.** $m^2 + 18m - 81$ **no** **12.** $y^2 + 8y + 12$ **no**

13. $9b^2 - 6b + 1$ **14.** $6x^2 + 4x + 1$ **no** **15.** $4p^2 + 12p + 9$ **16.** $16s^2 - 24s + 9$

13. yes; $(3b - 1)^2$ **15. yes; $(2p + 3)^2$**   **16. yes; $(4s - 3)^2$**

For Lesson 10-7   Arithmetic Sequences

Find the next three terms of each arithmetic sequence.   *(For review, see Lesson 4-7.)*

17. $5, 9, 13, 17, \ldots$ **21, 25, 29**   **18.** $12, 5, -2, -9, \ldots$ **−16, −23, −30**

19. $-4, -1, 2, 5, \ldots$ **8, 11, 14**   **20.** $24, 32, 40, 48, \ldots$ **56, 64, 72**

21. $-1, -6, -11, -16, \ldots$ **−21, −26, −31** **22.** $-27, -20, -13, -6, \ldots$ **1, 8, 15**

23. $5.3, 6.0, 6.7, 7.4, \ldots$ **8.1, 8.8, 9.5** **24.** $9.1, 8.8, 8.5, 8.2, \ldots$ **7.9, 7.6, 7.3**

 **Study Organizer**

Quadratic and Exponential Functions Make this Foldable to help you organize your notes. Begin with four sheets of grid paper.

Step 1   Fold in Half

Fold each sheet in half along the width.

Step 2   Tape

Unfold each sheet and tape to form one long piece.

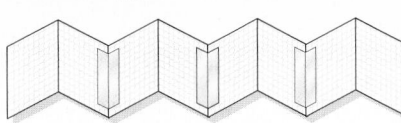

Step 3   Label

Label each page with the lesson number as shown. Refold to form a booklet.

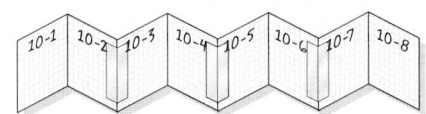

10-1 10-2 10-3 10-4 10-5 10-6 10-7 10-8

Reading and Writing As you read and study the chapter, write notes and examples for each lesson on each page of the journal.

Chapter 10 Quadratic and Exponential Functions **523**

Getting Started

This section provides a review of the basic concepts needed before beginning Chapter 10. Page references are included for additional student help.

Additional review is provided in the *Prerequisite Skills Workbook*, pp. 9–12 and 47–48.

Prerequisite Skills in the Getting Ready for the Next Lesson section at the end of each exercise set review a skill needed in the next lesson.

For Lesson	Prerequisite Skill
10-2	Finding *x*-Intercepts (p. 530)
10-3	Factoring Perfect Square Trinomials (p. 538)
10-4	Finding Square Roots (p. 544)
10-5	Evaluating Expressions with Exponents (p. 552)
10-6	Evaluating Expressions with Exponents (p. 560)
10-7	Finding Terms in Arithmetic Sequences (p. 565)

FOLDABLES™ **Study Organizer**

For more information about Foldables, see *Teaching Mathematics with Foldables.*

Organization of Data: Sequencing Information Students use their Foldable to take notes, define terms, record concepts, and write examples. Ask students to note the order in which the concepts are presented in this chapter. Ask them to write about why the concepts and computations were presented in that sequence. If students have difficulty seeing the logic in this sequence, have them outline the key concepts in their own order, and justify their reasoning in writing.

10-1 Graphing Quadratic Functions

1 Focus

5-Minute Check Transparency 10-1 Use as a quiz or review of Chapter 9.

Mathematical Background notes are available for this lesson on p. 522C.

Building on Prior Knowledge

Students were first introduced to nonlinear functions in Chapter 8. In this lesson, students will learn about one kind of nonlinear function, a quadratic function. Students will learn how to graph quadratic functions.

How can you coordinate a fireworks display with recorded music?

Ask students:

• Which is more important to the music planners, the height of the firework when it explodes, or the time at which it explodes? Explain. **The time is more important if the planners want to coordinate the explosions with music.**

• Why must the planners still know the height? **The firework explodes at approximately its highest point. When the highest point is found, the value of *t* at this point is the time at which the firework will explode.**

What You'll Learn

• Graph quadratic functions.
• Find the equation of the axis of symmetry and the coordinates of the vertex of a parabola.

Vocabulary
• quadratic function
• parabola
• minimum
• maximum
• vertex
• symmetry
• axis of symmetry

How can you coordinate a fireworks display with recorded music?

The Sky Concert in Peoria, Illinois, is a 4th of July fireworks display set to music. If a rocket (firework) is launched with an initial velocity of 39.2 meters per second at a height of 1.6 meters above the ground, the equation $h = -4.9t^2 + 39.2t + 1.6$ represents the rocket's height h in meters after t seconds. The rocket will explode at approximately the highest point.

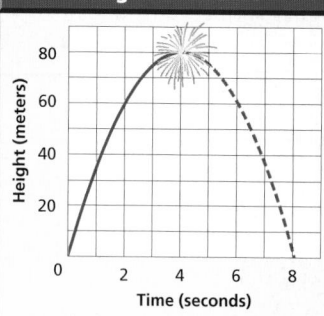

Height of Rocket

GRAPH QUADRATIC FUNCTIONS
The function describing the height of the rocket is an example of a quadratic function. A **quadratic function** can be written in the form $y = ax^2 + bx + c$, where $a \neq 0$. This form of the quadratic function is called the *standard form*. Notice that this polynomial has degree 2 and the exponents are positive. The graph of a quadratic function is called a **parabola**.

Key Concept — Quadratic Function

• **Words** A quadratic function can be described by an equation of the form $y = ax^2 + bx + c$, where $a \neq 0$.

• **Models**

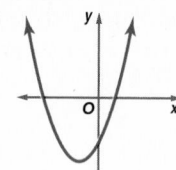 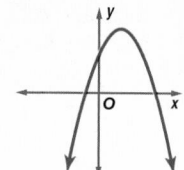

Example 1 — Graph Opens Upward

Use a table of values to graph $y = 2x^2 - 4x - 5$.

Graph these ordered pairs and connect them with a smooth curve.

x	y
-2	11
-1	1
0	-5
1	-7
2	-5
3	1
4	11

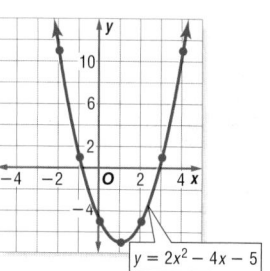

$y = 2x^2 - 4x - 5$

Resource Manager

Workbook and Reproducible Masters

Chapter 10 Resource Masters
• Study Guide and Intervention, pp. 579–580
• Skills Practice, p. 581
• Practice, p. 582
• Reading to Learn Mathematics, p. 583
• Enrichment, p. 584

Parent and Student Study Guide
Workbook, p. 75
Teaching Algebra With Manipulatives
Masters, pp. 1, 176

Transparencies

5-Minute Check Transparency 10-1
Answer Key Transparencies

Technology

AlgePASS: Tutorial Plus, Lesson 28
Interactive Chalkboard

Consider the standard form $y = ax^2 + bx + c$. Notice that the value of a in Example 1 is positive and the curve opens upward. The lowest point, or **minimum**, of the graph is located at $(1, -7)$.

Example 2 *Graph Opens Downward*

Use a table of values to graph $y = -x^2 + 4x - 1$.

Graph these ordered pairs and connect them with a smooth curve.

x	y
−1	−6
0	−1
1	2
2	3
3	2
4	−1
5	−6

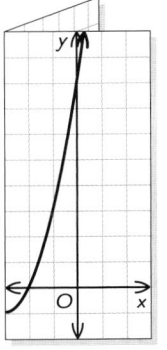

Notice that the value of a in Example 2 is negative and the curve opens downward. The highest point, or **maximum**, of the graph is located at $(2, 3)$. The maximum or minimum point of a parabola is called the **vertex**.

SYMMETRY AND VERTICES Parabolas possess a geometric property called **symmetry**. Symmetrical figures are those in which the figure can be folded in half so that each half matches the other exactly.

Algebra Activity

Symmetry of Parabolas

Model
- Graph $y = x^2 + 6x + 8$ on grid paper.
- Hold your paper up to the light and fold the parabola in half so that the two sides match exactly.
- Unfold the paper.

Make a Conjecture
1. What is the vertex of the parabola? $(-3, -1)$
2. Write an equation of the fold line. $x = -3$
3. Which point on the parabola lies on the fold line? $(-3, -1)$
4. Write a few sentences to describe the symmetry of a parabola based on your findings in this activity.

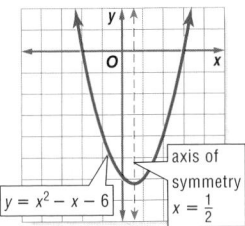

The fold line in the activity above is called the **axis of symmetry** for the parabola. Each point on the parabola that is on one side of the axis of symmetry has a corresponding point on the parabola on the other side of the axis. The vertex is the only point on the parabola that is on the axis of symmetry.

In the graph of $y = x^2 - x - 6$, the axis of symmetry is $x = \frac{1}{2}$. The vertex is $\left(\frac{1}{2}, -6\frac{1}{4}\right)$.

Notice the relationship between the values a and b and the equation of the axis of symmetry.

$y = x^2 - x - 6$

axis of symmetry $x = \frac{1}{2}$

Algebra Activity

Materials grid paper
- Tell students to make sure the sides of the parabola match before they crease the paper.
- Make sure students understand the connection between the fold line (axis of symmetry) and the vertex. The vertex of a parabola always lies on the axis of symmetry.

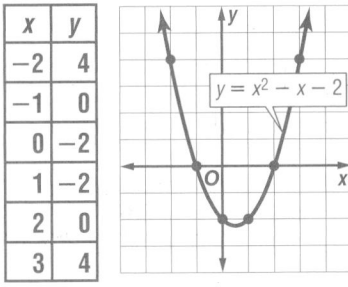
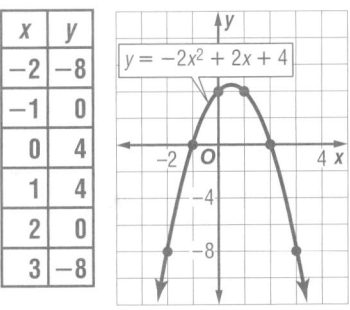

In-Class Example

Power Point®

Teaching Tip When students use symmetry to graph parabolas, they need only find a few points, and then reflect those points across the line of symmetry. You may want to suggest that students occasionally check their reflected points by substituting them into the original equation.

3 Consider the graph of $y = -2x^2 - 8x - 2$.

a. Write the equation of the axis of symmetry. $x = -2$

b. Find the coordinates of the vertex. **The coordinates of the vertex are $(-2, 6)$.**

c. Identify the vertex as a maximum or minimum. **Since the coefficient of the x^2 term is negative, the parabola opens downward and the vertex is a maximum point.**

d. Graph the function.

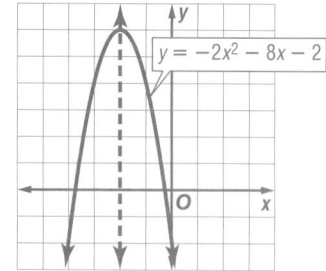

$y = -2x^2 - 8x - 2$

TEACHING TIP
The equation for the axis of symmetry can be derived by completing the square. This skill is taught in Lesson 10-3.

Key Concept *Equation of the Axis of Symmetry of a Parabola*

- **Words** The equation of the axis of symmetry for the graph of $y = ax^2 + bx + c$, where $a \neq 0$, is $x = -\dfrac{b}{2a}$.

- **Model**

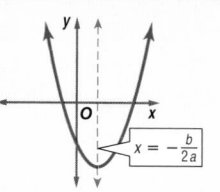

$x = -\dfrac{b}{2a}$

You can determine information about a parabola from its equation.

Example 3 Vertex and Axis of Symmetry

Consider the graph of $y = -3x^2 - 6x + 4$.

a. Write the equation of the axis of symmetry.

In $y = -3x^2 - 6x + 4$, $a = -3$ and $b = -6$.

$x = -\dfrac{b}{2a}$ Equation for the axis of symmetry of a parabola

$x = -\dfrac{-6}{2(-3)}$ or -1 $a = -3$ and $b = -6$

The equation of the axis of symmetry is $x = -1$.

Study Tip

Coordinates of Vertex
Notice that you can find the *x*-coordinate by knowing the axis of symmetry. However, to find the *y*-coordinate, you must substitute the value of *x* into the quadratic equation.

b. Find the coordinates of the vertex.

Since the equation of the axis of symmetry is $x = -1$ and the vertex lies on the axis, the *x*-coordinate for the vertex is -1.

$y = -3x^2 - 6x + 4$ Original equation

$y = -3(-1)^2 - 6(-1) + 4$ $x = -1$

$y = -3 + 6 + 4$ Simplify.

$y = 7$ Add.

The vertex is at $(-1, 7)$.

c. Identify the vertex as a maximum or minimum.

Since the coefficient of the x^2 term is negative, the parabola opens downward and the vertex is a maximum point.

d. Graph the function.

You can use the symmetry of the parabola to help you draw its graph. On a coordinate plane, graph the vertex and the axis of symmetry. Choose a value for *x* other than -1. For example, choose 1 and find the *y*-coordinate that satisfies the equation.

$y = -3x^2 - 6x + 4$ Original equation

$y = -3(1)^2 - 6(1) + 4$ Let $x = 1$.

$y = -5$ Simplify.

Graph $(1, -5)$. Since the graph is symmetrical about its axis of symmetry $x = -1$, you can find another point on the other side of the axis of symmetry. The point at $(1, -5)$ is 2 units to the right of the axis. Go 2 units to the left of the axis and plot the point $(-3, -5)$. Repeat this for several other points. Then sketch the parabola.

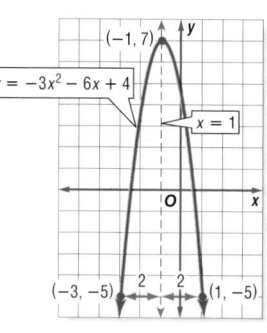

$(-1, 7)$

$y = -3x^2 - 6x + 4$

$x = 1$

$(-3, -5)$ 2   2 $(1, -5)$

DAILY INTERVENTION

Differentiated Instruction

Interpersonal Place students in small groups. Since there are several tasks involved in graphing quadratic functions, have the group members decide which of the tasks they should complete in order to graph a given function. For example, one member can be responsible for finding the equation for the axis of symmetry, another can substitute values in order to determine points on the graph, and a third member can graph the points and draw the curve of the parabola.

CHECK Does $(-3, -5)$ satisfy the equation?

$$y = -3x^2 - 6x + 4 \qquad \text{Original equation}$$
$$-5 \stackrel{?}{=} -3(-3)^2 - 6(-3) + 4 \qquad y = -5 \text{ and } x = -3$$
$$-5 = -5 \checkmark \qquad \text{Simplify.}$$

The ordered pair $(-3, -5)$ satisfies $y = -3x^2 - 6x + 4$, and the point is on the graph.

Teaching Tip Point out to students that although this equation does not look exactly like the other quadratic equations that they have graphed so far in this lesson, the equation still has a degree of 2 so it is quadratic. Furthermore, when they multiply $x + 1$ by itself, the equation takes on the more traditional form.

4 Using the item choices from Example 4 in the Student Edition, which graph corresponds to the graph of $y = -x^2 - 2x - 2$? **D**

Standardized Test Practice
Ⓐ Ⓑ Ⓒ Ⓓ

Example 4 Match Equations and Graphs

Multiple-Choice Test Item

Which is the graph of $y + 1 = (x + 1)^2$?

Ⓐ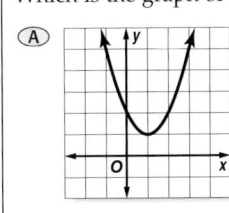

Ⓑ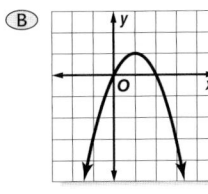

Ⓒ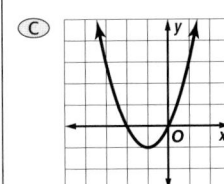

Ⓓ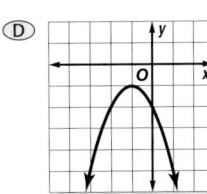

Read the Test Item

You are given a quadratic function, and you are asked to choose the graph that corresponds to it.

Solve the Test Item

First write the equation in standard form.

$$y + 1 = (x + 1)^2 \qquad \text{Original equation}$$
$$y + 1 = x^2 + 2x + 1 \qquad (x + 1)^2 = x^2 + 2x + 1$$
$$y + 1 - 1 = x^2 + 2x + 1 - 1 \qquad \text{Subtract 1 from each side.}$$
$$y = x^2 + 2x \qquad \text{Simplify.}$$

Then find the axis of symmetry of the graph of $y = x^2 + 2x$.

$$x = -\frac{b}{2a} \qquad \text{Equation for the axis of symmetry}$$
$$x = -\frac{2}{2(1)} \text{ or } -1 \qquad a = 1 \text{ and } b = 2$$

> **Test-Taking Tip**
> Sometimes you can answer a question by eliminating the incorrect choices. For example, in this test question, choices A and B are eliminated because their axes of symmetry are *not* $x = -1$.

The axis of symmetry is $x = -1$. Look at the graphs. Since only choices C and D have this as their axis of symmetry, you can eliminate choices A and B. Since the coefficient of the x^2 term is positive, the graph opens upward. Eliminate choice D. The answer is C.

Standardized Test Practice
Ⓐ Ⓑ Ⓒ Ⓓ

Example 4 When the answer choices for a test question are graphs, look for obvious clues that would make a graph incorrect. The text mentioned eliminating two of the graphs that had the incorrect axis of symmetry. You can also eliminate two of the parabolas that open in the wrong direction. Since the coefficient of the x^2 term is positive, you know that the parabola opens upward and B and D are incorrect.

About the Exercises ...

Organization by Objective
- Graph Quadratic Functions: 10–15
- Symmetry and Vertices: 16–51

Odd/Even Assignments
Exercises 10–37 are structured so that students practice the same concepts whether they are assigned odd or even problems.

Alert! Exercises 49, 54–59 require a graphing calculator.

Assignment Guide

Basic: 11–29 odd, 37–40, 50–53, 60–80

Average: 11–37 odd, 39–43, 50–53, 60–80 (optional: 54–59)

Advanced: 10–38 even, 44–74 (optional: 75–80)

Answers

1. Both types of parabolas are U shaped. A parabola with a maximum opens downward, and its corresponding equation has a negative coefficient for the x^2 term. A parabola with a minimum opens upward, and its corresponding equation has a positive coefficient for the x^2 term.

Check for Understanding

Concept Check
1–3. See margin.

1. **Compare and contrast** a parabola with a maximum and a parabola with a minimum.

2. **OPEN ENDED** Draw two different parabolas with a vertex of $(2, -1)$.

3. **Explain** how the axis of symmetry can help you graph a quadratic function.

Guided Practice

GUIDED PRACTICE KEY	
Exercises	Examples
4, 5	1, 2
6–8	3
9	4

Use a table of values to graph each function. 4–5. See pp. 581A–581H.

4. $y = x^2 - 5$

5. $y = -x^2 + 4x + 5$

Write the equation of the axis of symmetry, and find the coordinates of the vertex of the graph of each function. Identify the vertex as a maximum or minimum. Then graph the function. 6–8. See pp. 581A–581H for graphs.

6. $y = x^2 + 4x - 9$
$x = -2; (-2, -13); min$

7. $y = -x^2 + 5x + 6$
$x = 2.5; (2.5, 12.25); max$

8. $y = -(x - 2)^2 + 1$
$x = 2; (2, 1); max$

Standardized Test Practice
Ⓐ Ⓑ Ⓒ Ⓓ

9. Which is the graph of $y = -\frac{1}{2}x^2 + 1$? **B**

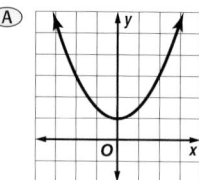
Ⓐ

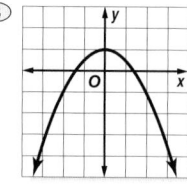
Ⓑ

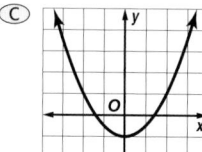
Ⓒ

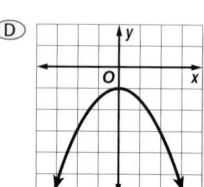
Ⓓ

18. $x = 0; (0, 0); min$
19. $x = 0; (0, 0); max$
20. $x = 0; (0, 2); min$
21. $x = 0; (0, 5); max$
22. $x = 1; (1, 4); max$

★ indicates increased difficulty

Practice and Apply

Homework Help	
For Exercises	See Examples
10–15	1, 2
16–49	3
52, 53	4

Extra Practice
See page 841.

23. $x = -3; (-3, 24); max$
24. $x = 7; (7, -36); min$
25. $x = -1; (-1, 17); min$
26. $x = -3; (-3, -29); min$
27. $x = 1; (1, 1); min$

Use a table of values to graph each function. 10–15. See pp. 581A–581H.

10. $y = x^2 - 3$
11. $y = -x^2 + 7$
12. $y = x^2 - 2x - 8$
13. $y = x^2 - 4x + 3$
14. $y = -3x^2 - 6x + 4$
15. $y = -3x^2 + 6x + 1$

16. What is the equation of the axis of symmetry of the graph of $y = -3x^2 + 2x - 5$? $x = \frac{1}{3}$

17. Find the equation of the axis of symmetry of the graph of $y = 4x^2 - 5x + 16$. $x = \frac{5}{8}$

Write the equation of the axis of symmetry, and find the coordinates of the vertex of the graph of each function. Identify the vertex as a maximum or minimum. Then graph the function. 18–35. See pp. 581A–581H for graphs.

18. $y = 4x^2$
19. $y = -2x^2$
20. $y = x^2 + 2$
21. $y = -x^2 + 5$
22. $y = -x^2 + 2x + 3$
23. $y = -x^2 - 6x + 15$
24. $y = x^2 - 14x + 13$
25. $y = x^2 + 2x + 18$
26. $y = 2x^2 + 12x - 11$
27. $y = 3x^2 - 6x + 4$
28. $y = 5 + 16x - 2x^2$
$x = 4; (4, 37); max$
29. $y = 9 - 8x + 2x^2$
$x = 2; (2, 1); min$

2. Sample answer:

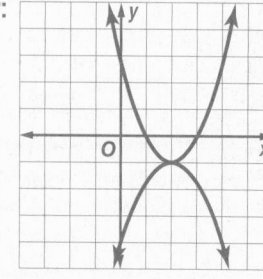

3. If you locate several points of the graph on one side of the axis of symmetry, you can locate corresponding points on the other side of the axis of symmetry to help graph the equation.

30. $x = -1$; $(-1, -20)$; min

31. $x = 4$; $(4, -3)$; max

32. $x = 5$; $(5, -2)$; min

★ **30.** $y = 3(x + 1)^2 - 20$ ★ **31.** $y = -2(x - 4)^2 - 3$ ★ **32.** $y + 2 = x^2 - 10x + 25$

★ **33.** $y + 1 = 3x^2 + 12x + 12$ ★ **34.** $y - 5 = \frac{1}{3}(x + 2)^2$ ★ **35.** $y + 1 = \frac{2}{3}(x + 1)^2$
   $x = -2$; $(-2, -1)$; min $x = -2$; $(-2, 5)$; min $x = -1$; $(-1, -1)$; min

36. The vertex of a parabola is at $(-4, -3)$. If one x-intercept is -11, what is the other x-intercept? **3**

37. What is the equation of the axis of symmetry of a parabola if its x-intercepts are -6 and 4? $x = -1$

38. SPORTS A diver follows a path that is in the shape of a parabola. Suppose the diver's foot reaches 1 meter above the height of the diving board at the maximum height of the dive. At that time, the diver's foot is also 1 meter horizontally from the edge of the diving board. What is the distance of the diver's foot from the diving board as the diver descends past the diving board? Explain.
2 m; parabolas are symmetric.

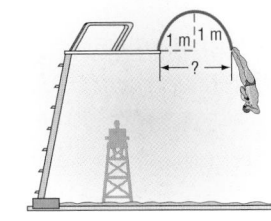

ENTERTAINMENT For Exercises 39 and 40, use the following information.
A carnival game involves striking a lever that forces a weight up a tube. If the weight reaches 20 feet to ring the bell, the contestant wins a prize. The equation $h = -16t^2 + 32t + 3$ gives the height of the weight if the initial velocity is 32 feet per second.

39. Find the maximum height of the weight. **19 ft**

40. Will a prize be won? **no**

PETS For Exercises 41–43, use the following information.
Miriam has 40 meters of fencing to build a pen for her dog. **41.** $A = x(20 - x)$ or $A = -x^2 + 20x$

41. Use the diagram at the right to write an equation for the area A of the pen.

42. What value of x will result in the greatest area? **10 m**

43. What is the greatest possible area of the pen? **100 m²**

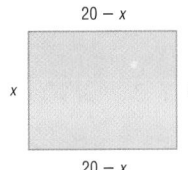
20 − x

x   x

20 − x

• ARCHITECTURE For Exercises 44–46, use the following information.
The shape of the Gateway Arch in St. Louis, Missouri, is a *catenary* curve. It resembles a parabola with the equation $h = -0.00635x^2 + 4.0005x - 0.07875$, where h is the height in feet and x is the distance from one base in feet.

★ **44.** What is the equation of the axis of symmetry? $x = 315$

★ **45.** What is the distance from one end of the arch to the other? **630 ft**

★ **46.** What is the maximum height of the arch? **630 ft**

BRIDES For Exercises 47–49, use the following information.
The equation $a = 0.003x^2 - 0.115x + 21.3$ models the average ages of women when they first married since the year 1940. In this equation, a represents the average age and x represents the years since 1940.

★ **47.** Use what you know about parabolas and their minimum values to estimate the year in which the average age of brides was the youngest. **1959**

★ **48.** Estimate the average age of the brides during that year. **about 20 years old**

★ **49.** Use a graphing calculator to check your estimates. **See margin.**

Lesson 10-1 Graphing Quadratic Functions   **529**

More About. . .

Architecture •••••••••••
The Gateway Arch is part of a tribute to Thomas Jefferson, the Louisiana Purchase, and the pioneers who settled the West. Each year about 2.5 million people visit the arch.
Source: *World Book Encyclopedia*

Answer

49.
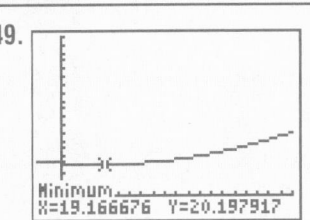
Minimum
X=19.166676   Y=20.197917

Lesson 10-1 Graphing Quadratic Functions   **529**

Modeling Model parabolas with string using a coordinate grid on an overhead projector, making sure that some graphs are not symmetric. For example, move a point one unit up, down, to the left, or right, so that the parabola looks pretty close, but is not symmetric. See if students can use what they know about the symmetry of parabolas to spot your mistakes. Have volunteers correct the parabolas.

Getting Ready for Lesson 10-2

PREREQUISITE SKILL Students will learn how to solve quadratic equations by graphing in Lesson 10-2. In order to solve quadratic equations by graphing, students will need to be able to identify the x-intercepts of the graphs. Use Exercises 75–80 to determine your students' familiarity with identifying the x-intercepts of linear graphs.

Answer

51. In order to coordinate a firework with recorded music, you must know when and how high it will explode. Answers should include the following.

- The rocket will explode when the rocket reaches the vertex or when $t = -\frac{39.2}{2(-4.9)}$ which is 4 seconds.

- The height of the rocket when it explodes is the height when $t = 4$. Therefore, $h = -4.9(4^2) + 39.2(4) + 1.6$ or 80 meters.

---

50. **CRITICAL THINKING** Write a quadratic equation that represents a graph with an axis of symmetry with equation $x = -\frac{3}{8}$. **Sample answer:** $y = 4x^2 + 3x + 5$

51.  Answer the question that was posed at the beginning of the lesson. **See margin.**

How can you coordinate a fireworks display with recorded music?

Include the following in your answer:
- an explanation of how to determine when the rocket will explode, and
- an explanation of how to determine the height of the rocket when it explodes.

Standardized Test Practice
Ⓐ Ⓑ Ⓒ Ⓓ

52. Which equation corresponds to the graph at the right? **A**

Ⓐ $y = x^2 - 4x + 5$
Ⓑ $y = -x^2 + 4x + 5$
Ⓒ $y = x^2 - 4x - 5$
Ⓓ $y = -x^2 + 4x - 5$

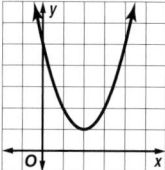

53. Which equation does *not* represent a quadratic function? **D**

Ⓐ $y = (x + 3)^2$ Ⓑ $y = 3x^2$ Ⓒ $y = 6x^2 - 1$ Ⓓ $y = x + 5$

54–59. See pp. 581A–581H for graphs.

Graphing Calculator

MAXIMUM OR MINIMUM Graph each function. Determine whether the vertex is a maximum or a minimum and give the ordered pair for the vertex.

54. minimum; (5, 0)
55. maximum; (2, 7)
56. maximum; (−2, 7)

54. $y = x^2 - 10x + 25$
55. $y = -x^2 + 4x + 3$
56. $y = -2x^2 - 8x - 1$
57. $y = 2x^2 - 40x + 214$ minimum; (10, 14)
58. $y = 0.25x^2 - 4x - 2$ minimum; (8, −18)
59. $y = -0.5x^2 - 2x + 3$ maximum; (−2, 5)

Maintain Your Skills

Mixed Review

Factor each polynomial, if possible. If the polynomial cannot be factored, write *prime*. *(Lessons 9-5 and 9-6)* 61. $(a + 11)^2$

60. $x^2 + 6x - 9$ **prime**
61. $a^2 + 22a + 121$
62. $4m^2 - 4m + 1 (2m - 1)^2$
63. $4q^2 - 9$ $(2q - 3)(2q + 3)$
64. $2a^2 - 25$ **prime**
65. $1 - 16g^2$ $(1 - 4g)(1 + 4g)$

Find each sum or difference. *(Lesson 8-5)*

66. $(13x + 9y) + 11y$ $13x + 20y$
67. $(7p^2 - p - 7) - (p^2 + 11)$ $6p^2 - p - 18$

68. **RECREATION** At a recreation and sports facility, 3 members and 3 nonmembers pay a total of $180 to take an aerobics class. A group of 5 members and 3 nonmembers pay $210 to take the same class. How much does it cost members and nonmembers to take an aerobics class? *(Lesson 7-3)* **$15 for members, $45 for nonmembers**

Solve each inequality. Then check your solution. *(Lesson 6-2)*

69. $12b > -144$ $\{b \mid b > -12\}$
70. $-5w > -125$ $\{w \mid w < 25\}$
71. $\frac{3r}{4} \le \frac{2}{3}$ $\left\{ r \mid r \le \frac{8}{9} \right\}$

Write an equation of the line that passes through each point with the given slope. *(Lesson 5-4)* 74. $y = \frac{3}{2}x + 12$

72. $(2, 13)$, $m = 4$ $y = 4x + 5$
73. $(-2, -7)$, $m = 0$ $y = -7$
74. $(-4, 6)$, $m = \frac{3}{2}$

Getting Ready for the Next Lesson

PREREQUISITE SKILL Find the x-intercept of the graph of each equation. *(To review finding x-intercepts, see Lesson 4-5.)*

75. $3x + 4y = 24$ **8**
76. $2x - 5y = 14$ **7**
77. $-2x - 4y = 7$ **−3.5**
78. $7y + 6x = 42$ **7**
79. $2y - 4x = 10$ **−2.5**
80. $3x - 7y + 9 = 0$ **−3**

Graphing Calculator Investigation

A Follow-Up of Lesson 10-1

Families of Quadratic Graphs

Recall that a *family of graphs* is a group of graphs that have at least one characteristic in common. On page 278, families of linear graphs were introduced. Families of quadratic graphs often fall into two categories—those that have the same vertex and those that have the same shape.

In each of the following families, the parent function is $y = x^2$. Graphing calculators make it easy to study the characteristics of these families of parabolas. You can enter equations for several parabolas and graph them on the same screen to compare and contrast the graphs.

Graph each group of equations on the same screen. Use the standard viewing window. Compare and contrast the graphs.

KEYSTROKES: *Review graphing equations on pages 224 and 225.*

a. $y = x^2$, $y = 2x^2$, $y = 4x^2$

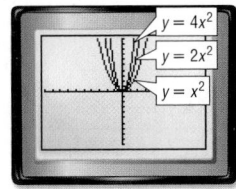

Each graph opens upward and has its vertex at the origin. The graphs of $y = 2x^2$ and $y = 4x^2$ are narrower than the graph of $y = x^2$.

b. $y = x^2$, $y = 0.5x^2$, $y = 0.2x^2$

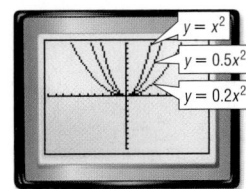

Each graph opens upward and has its vertex at the origin. The graphs of $y = 0.5x^2$ and $y = 0.2x^2$ are wider than the graph of $y = x^2$.

How does the value of a in $y = ax^2$ affect the shape of the graph?

c. $y = x^2$, $y = x^2 + 3$, $y = x^2 - 2$, $y = x^2 - 4$

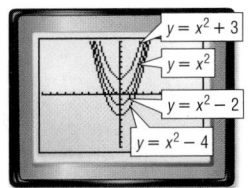

Each graph opens upward and has the same shape as $y = x^2$. However, each parabola has a different vertex, located along the y-axis. *How does the value of the constant affect the position of the graph?*

d. $y = x^2$, $y = (x - 3)^2$, $y = (x + 2)^2$, $y = (x + 4)^2$

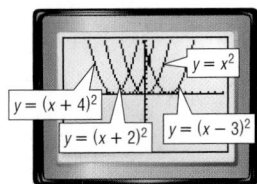

Each graph opens upward and has the same shape as $y = x^2$. However, each parabola has a different vertex located along the x-axis. *How is the location of the vertex related to the equation of the graph?*

Graphing Calculator Investigation

A Follow-Up of Lesson 10-1

Getting Started

Know Your Calculator Remind students that the $\boxed{x^2}$ key squares the quantity but does not enter x^2 into the equation. To enter $3x^2$, press 3 $\boxed{\text{X,T,}\theta\text{,}n}$ $\boxed{x^2}$.

Teach

- Remind students that to set the calculator to the standard viewing window, press $\boxed{\text{ZOOM}}$ 6.

- To help students remember how the value of a in $y = ax^2$ affects the shape of the graph, suggest that students sketch some of the parabolas from these examples, along with the equations, in their study notebooks.

- Students can use the $\boxed{\text{TRACE}}$ feature on their calculator to help them identify the different parabolas on the screen. After pressing $\boxed{\text{TRACE}}$, students can use the arrow keys to move the cursor around on the graphs. The up and down arrows switch the cursor between graphs. The left and right arrows move the cursor along the individual graphs. The graph on which the cursor lies is identified in the top left-hand corner of the screen.

Assess

- To change the scale of the viewing window, remind students to press WINDOW and change the appropriate settings, but not the **Xres** setting.

- Have students use the **TRACE** function to see that even though the parabolas look different, the graph still has the same vertex and x-intercepts.

Ask students to summarize how changes in the appearance and location of the graph are reflected in the equation. **In the equation $y = ax^2 + bx + c$, changes in the value of a affect the width of the graph. Changes in c affect the vertical position of the graph. In the equation $y = (x + c)^2$, changes in c affect the horizontal position of the graph.**

Answers

1.

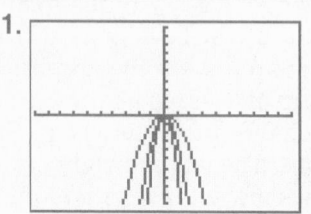

All of the graphs open downward from the origin. $y = -3x^2$ is narrower than $y = -x^2$, and $y = -6x^2$ is the narrowest.

2.

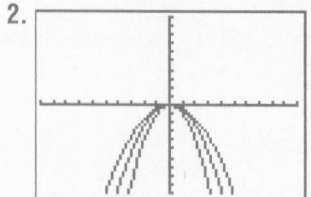

All of the graphs open downward from the origin. $y = -0.6x^2$ is wider than $y = -x^2$, and $y = -0.4x^2$ is the widest.

When analyzing or comparing the shapes of various graphs on different screens, it is important to compare the graphs using the same window with the same scale factors. Suppose you graph the same equation using a different window for each. How will the appearance of the graph change?

Graph $y = x^2 - 7$ in each viewing window. What conclusions can you draw about the appearance of a graph in the window used?

a. standard viewing window

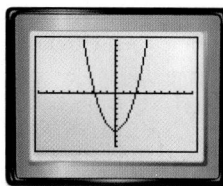

b. $[-10, 10]$ scl: 1 by $[-200, 200]$ scl: 50

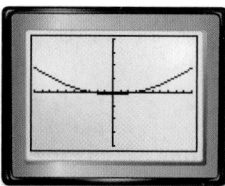

c. $[-50, 50]$ scl: 5 by $[-10, 10]$ scl: 1

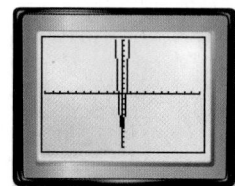

d. $[-0.5, 0.5]$ scl: 0.1 by $[-10, 10]$ scl: 1

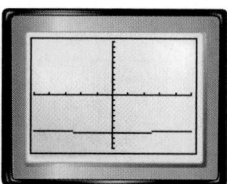

The window greatly affects the appearance of the parabola. Without knowing the window, graph **b** might be of the family $y = ax^2$, where $0 < a < 1$. Graph **c** looks like a member of $y = ax^2 - 7$, where $a > 1$. Graph **d** looks more like a line. However, all are graphs of the same equation.

Exercises

Graph each family of equations on the same screen. Compare and contrast the graphs. 1–4. See margin.

1. $y = -x^2$
$y = -3x^2$
$y = -6x^2$

2. $y = -x^2$
$y = -0.6x^2$
$y = -0.4x^2$

3. $y = -x^2$
$y = -(x + 5)^2$
$y = -(x - 4)^2$

4. $y = -x^2$
$y = -x^2 + 7$
$y = -x^2 - 5$

Use the families of graphs on page 531 and Exercises 1–4 above to predict the appearance of the graph of each equation. Then draw the graph. 5–8. See pp. 581A–581H.

5. $y = -0.1x^2$ **6.** $y = (x + 1)^2$ **7.** $y = 4x^2$ **8.** $y = x^2 - 6$

Describe how each change in $y = x^2$ would affect the graph of $y = x^2$. Be sure to consider all values of a, h, and k. 9–12. See pp. 581A–581H.

9. $y = ax^2$ **10.** $y = (x + h)^2$ **11.** $y = x^2 + k$ **12.** $y = (x + h)^2 + k$

532 Chapter 10 Quadratic and Exponential Functions

 www.algebra1.com/other_calculator_keystrokes

3.

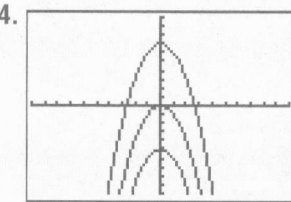

All of the graphs open downward, have the same shape, and have vertices along the x-axis. However, each vertex is different.

4.

All of the graphs open downward, have the same shape, and have vertices along the y-axis. However, each vertex is different.

Solving Quadratic Equations by Graphing

What You'll Learn

- Solve quadratic equations by graphing.
- Estimate solutions of quadratic equations by graphing.

Vocabulary
- quadratic equation
- roots
- zeros

How can quadratic equations be used in computer simulations?

A golf ball follows a path much like a parabola. Because of this property, quadratic functions can be used to simulate parts of a computer golf game. One of the x-intercepts of the quadratic function represents the location where the ball will hit the ground.

SOLVE BY GRAPHING

Recall that a quadratic function has standard form $f(x) = ax^2 + bx + c$. In a **quadratic equation**, the value of the related quadratic function is 0. So for the quadratic equation $0 = x^2 - 2x - 3$, the related quadratic function is $f(x) = x^2 - 2x - 3$. You have used factoring to solve equations like $x^2 - 2x - 3 = 0$. You can also use graphing to determine the solutions of equations like this.

The solutions of a quadratic equation are called the **roots** of the equation. The roots of a quadratic equation can be found by finding the x-intercepts or **zeros** of the related quadratic function.

Example 1 Two Roots

Solve $x^2 + 6x - 7 = 0$ by graphing.

Graph the related function $f(x) = x^2 + 6x - 7$. The equation of the axis of symmetry is $x = -\dfrac{6}{2(1)}$ or $x = -3$. When x equals -3, $f(x)$ equals $(-3)^2 + 6(-3) - 7$ or -16. So, the coordinates of the vertex are $(-3, -16)$. Make a table of values to find other points to sketch the graph.

x	f(x)
−8	9
−6	−7
−4	−15
−3	−16
−2	−15
0	−7
2	9

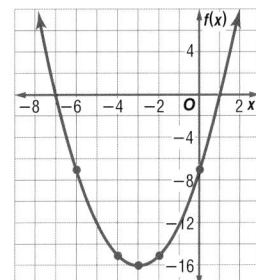

To solve $x^2 + 6x - 7 = 0$, you need to know where the value of $f(x)$ is 0. This occurs at the x-intercepts. The x-intercepts of the parabola appear to be -7 and 1.

(continued on the next page)

Lesson 10-2 Solving Quadratic Equations by Graphing **533**

1 Focus

5-Minute Check Transparency 10-2 Use as a quiz or review of Lesson 10-1.

Mathematical Background notes are available for this lesson on p. 522C.

Building on Prior Knowledge

In Chapter 9, students learned how to solve quadratic trinomial equations using factoring. In this lesson, students will apply what they already know about solving quadratic equations to check the solutions they found by graphing.

How can quadratic equations be used in computer simulations?

Ask students:

- If one of the x-intercepts represents where the ball hits the ground, what represents the ground? **the x-axis**

- Suppose the green is uphill from the tee. How would this affect the value of the y-coordinate of the location where the ball lands? How would a downhill shot affect the ball's y-coordinate? **Assuming that the ground at the tee is represented by the x-axis, the y-coordinate of the landing spot would be positive if the shot was uphill, and negative if the shot was downhill.**

Study Notebook

Have students—

• add the definitions/examples of the vocabulary terms to their Vocabulary Builder worksheets for Chapter 10.

• include examples of how to solve quadratic equations by graphing.

• include any other item(s) that they find helpful in mastering the skills in this lesson.

About the Exercises ...

Organization by Objective
• Solve by Graphing: 11–20, 35–40
• Estimate Solutions: 21–34, 41–46

Odd/Even Assignments
Exercises 11–34 are structured so that students practice the same concepts whether they are assigned odd or even problems.

Alert! Exercises 51–52 require a graphing calculator.

Assignment Guide

Basic: 11–33 odd, 35–37, 39, 47–50, 53–68

Average: 11–33 odd, 35–39, 41, 42, 47–50, 53–68 (optional: 51, 52)

Advanced: 12–34 even, 35, 36, 38, 40–62 (optional: 63–68)

Answer

3. Sample answer:

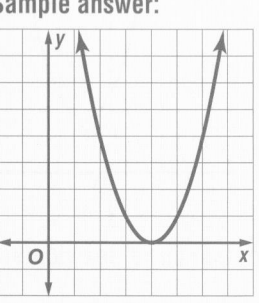

---

3. **OPEN ENDED** Draw a graph to show a counterexample to the following statement.
   All quadratic equations have two different solutions. **See margin.**

Guided Practice

Solve each equation by graphing. 4–9. See pp. 581A–581H for graphs.

4. $x^2 - 7x + 6 = 0$ **1, 6**   5. $a^2 - 10a + 25 = 0$ **5**   6. $c^2 + 3 = 0$ **∅**

GUIDED PRACTICE KEY	
Exercises	Examples
4–6	1–3
7–9	4
10	5

Solve each equation by graphing. If integral roots cannot be found, estimate the roots by stating the consecutive integers between which the roots lie.

7. $t^2 + 9t + 5 = 0$
$-9 < t < -8, -1 < t < 0$

8. $x^2 - 16 = 0$ **−4, 4**

9. $w^2 - 3w = 5$
$-2 < w < -1, 4 < w < 5$

Application

10. **NUMBER THEORY** Two numbers have a sum of 4 and a product of −12. Use a quadratic equation to determine the two numbers. **−2, 6**

★ indicates increased difficulty

Practice and Apply

Homework Help

For Exercises	See Examples
11–20	1–3
21–34	4
35–46	5

Extra Practice
See page 842.

Solve each equation by graphing. 11–16. See pp. 581A–581H for graphs.

11. $c^2 - 5c - 24 = 0$ **−3, 8** 12. $5n^2 + 2n + 6 = 0$ **∅** 13. $x^2 + 6x + 9 = 0$ **−3**

14. $b^2 - 12b + 36 = 0$ **6** 15. $x^2 + 2x + 5 = 0$ **∅** 16. $r^2 + 4r - 12 = 0$ **−6, 2**

17. The roots of a quadratic equation are −2 and −6. The minimum point of the graph of its related function is at (−4, −2). Sketch the graph of the function. **See pp. 581A**

18. The roots of a quadratic equation are −6 and 0. The maximum point of the graph of its related function is at (−3, 4). Sketch the graph of the function. **See pp. 581A**

19. **NUMBER THEORY** The sum of two numbers is 9, and their product is 20. Use a quadratic equation to determine the two numbers. **4, 5**

20. **NUMBER THEORY** Use a quadratic equation to find two numbers whose sum is 5 and whose product is −24. **−3, 8**

Solve each equation by graphing. If integral roots cannot be found, estimate the roots by stating the consecutive integers between which the roots lie.

21. $a^2 - 12 = 0$ 22. $n^2 - 7 = 0$ 23. $2c^2 + 20c + 32 = 0$

24. $3s^2 + 9s - 12 = 0$ 25. $x^2 + 6x + 6 = 0$ 26. $y^2 - 4y + 1 = 0$

27. $a^2 - 8a = 4$ 28. $x^2 + 6x = -7$ 29. $m^2 - 10m = -21$

30. $p^2 + 16 = 8p$ 31. $12n^2 - 26n = 30$ 32. $4x^2 - 35 = -4x$

21–32. See pp. 581A–581H.

33. One root of a quadratic equation is between −4 and −3, and the other root is between 1 and 2. The maximum point of the graph of the related function is at (−1, 6). Sketch the graph of the function. See pp. 581A–581H.

34. One root of a quadratic equation is between −1 and 0, and the other root is between 6 and 7. The minimum point of the graph of the related function is at (3, −5). Sketch the graph of the function. See pp. 581A–581H.

DESIGN For Exercises 35–39, use the following information.
An art gallery has walls that are sculptured with arches that can be represented by the quadratic function $f(x) = -x^2 - 4x + 12$, where x is in feet. The wall space under each arch is to be painted a different color from the arch itself.

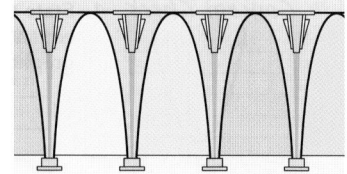

35. See pp. 581A–581H for graph; −6, 2.

35. Graph the quadratic function and determine its x-intercepts.

36. What is the length of the segment along the floor of each arch? **8 ft**

---

48. Since quadratic functions can be used to model a golf ball after it is hit, solving the related quadratic equation will determine where the ball hits the ground. Answers should include the following.

• In the golf problem, one intercept represents the ball's original location and the other intercept represents where the ball hits the ground.

• Using the quadratic function $y = -0.0015x^2 + 0.3x$, the ball will hit the ground 200 yd from the starting point.

37. What is the height of the arch? **16 ft**

38. The formula $A = \frac{2}{3}bh$ can be used to estimate the area under a parabola. In this formula, A represents area, b represents the length of the base, and h represents the height. Calculate the area that needs to be painted. **about $85\frac{1}{3}$ ft²**

39. How much would the paint for the walls under 12 arches cost if the paint is $27 per gallon, the painter applies 2 coats, and the manufacturer states that each gallon will cover 200 square feet? (*Hint*: Remember that you cannot buy part of a gallon.) **$297**

40. **COMPUTER GAMES** Suppose the function $-0.005d^2 + 0.22d = h$ is used to simulate the path of a football at the kickoff of a computer football game. In this equation, h is the height of the ball and d is the horizontal distance in yards. What is the horizontal distance the ball will travel before it hits the ground? **44 yd**

HIKING For Exercises 41 and 42, use the following information.
Monya and Kishi are hiking in the mountains and stop for lunch on a ledge 1000 feet above the valley below. Kishi decides to climb to another ledge 20 feet above Monya. Monya throws an apple up to Kishi, but Kishi misses it. The equation $h = -16t^2 + 30t + 1000$ represents the height in feet of the apple t seconds after it was thrown.

★ 41. How long did it take for the apple to reach the ground? **about 9 s**

★ 42. If it takes 3 seconds to react, will the girls have time to call down and warn any hikers below? Assume that sound travels about 1000 feet per second. Explain. **Yes; there are $9 - 3 - 1$ or 5 s to warn them.**

WORK For Exercises 43–46, use the following information.
Kirk and Montega have accepted a job mowing the soccer playing fields. They must mow an area 500 feet long and 400 feet wide. They agree that each will mow half the area. They decide that Kirk will mow around the edge in a path of equal width until half the area is left.

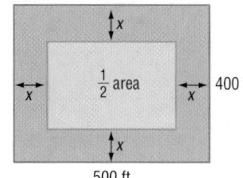

43. What is the area each person will mow? **100,000 ft²**

★ 44. Write a quadratic equation that could be used to find the width x that Kirk should mow. **$(500 - 2x)(400 - 2x) = 100,000$ or $4x^2 - 1800x + 100,000 = 0$**

★ 45. What width should Kirk mow? **about 65 ft**

★ 46. The mower can mow a path 5 feet wide. To the nearest whole number, how many times should Kirk go around the field? **13 times**

47. **CRITICAL THINKING** Where does the graph of $f(x) = \frac{x^3 + 2x^2 - 3x}{x + 5}$ intersect the x-axis? **$-3, 0, 1$**

48. **WRITING IN MATH** Answer the question that was posed at the beginning of the lesson. **See margin.**

How can quadratic equations be used in computer simulations?

Include the following in your answer:
- the meaning of the two roots of a simulation equation for a computer golf game, and
- the approximate location at which the ball will hit the ground if the equation of the path of the ball is $y = -0.0015x^2 + 0.3x$, where y and x are in yards.

www.algebra1.com/self_check_quiz

Lesson 10-2 Solving Quadratic Equations by Graphing **537**

Study Guide and Intervention, p. 585 (shown) and p. 586

Solve by Graphing

| Quadratic Equation | an equation of the form $ax^2 + bx + c = 0$, where $a \neq 0$ |

The solutions of a quadratic equation are called the **roots** of the equation. The roots of a quadratic equation can be found by graphing the related quadratic function $f(x) = ax^2 + bx + c$ and finding the x-intercepts or **zeros** of the function.

Example 1 Solve $x^2 + 4x + 3 = 0$ by graphing.
Graph the related function $f(x) = x^2 + 4x + 3$. The equation of the axis of symmetry is $x = -\frac{4}{2(1)}$ or -2. The vertex is at $(-2, -1)$. Graph the vertex and several other points on either side of the axis of symmetry.

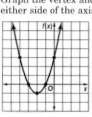

To solve $x^2 + 4x + 3 = 0$, you need to know where the value of $f(x) = 0$. This occurs at the x-intercepts, -3 and -1. The solutions are -3 and -1.

Example 2 Solve $x^2 - 6x + 9 = 0$ by graphing.
Graph the related function $f(x) = x^2 - 6x + 9$. The equation of the axis of symmetry is $x = \frac{6}{2(1)}$ or 3. The vertex is at $(3, 0)$. Graph the vertex and several other points on either side of the axis of symmetry.

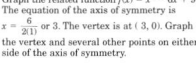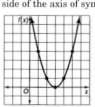

To solve $x^2 - 6x + 9 = 0$, you need to know where the value of $f(x) = 0$. The vertex of the parabola is the x-intercept. Thus, the only solution is 3.

Exercises

Solve each equation by graphing.

1. $x^2 + 7x + 12 = 0$ 2. $x^2 - x - 12 = 0$ 3. $x^2 - 4x + 5 = 0$

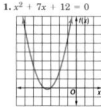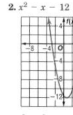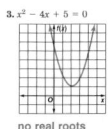

$-3; -4$ **$4, -3$**   **no real roots**

Skills Practice, p. 587 and Practice, p. 588 (shown)

Solve each equation by graphing.

1. $x^2 - 5x + 6 = 0$ **2, 3**   2. $w^2 + 6w + 9 = 0$ **-3**   3. $b^2 - 4b + 5 = 0$ **∅**

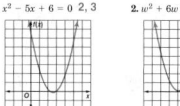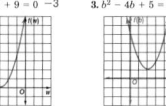

Solve each equation by graphing. If integral roots cannot be found, estimate the roots by stating the consecutive integers between which the roots lie.

4. $p^2 + 4p = 3$ 5. $2m^2 + 5 = 10m$ 6. $2v^2 + 8v = -7$

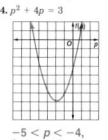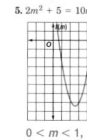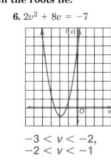

$-5 < p < -4$, $0 < p < 1$ **$0 < m < 1$, $4 < m < 5$**   **$-3 < v < -2$, $-2 < v < -1$**

NUMBER THEORY For Exercises 7 and 8, use the following information.
Two numbers have a sum of 2 and a product of -8. The quadratic equation $-n^2 + 2n + 8 = 0$ can be used to determine the two numbers.

7. Graph the related function $f(n) = -n^2 + 2n + 8$ and determine its x-intercepts. **$-2, 4$**

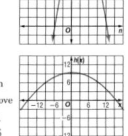

8. What are the two numbers? **-2 and 4**

DESIGN For Exercises 9 and 10, use the following information.
A footbridge is suspended from a parabolic support. The function $h(x) = -\frac{1}{25}x^2 + 9$ represents the height in feet of the support above the walkway, where $x = 0$ represents the midpoint of the bridge.

9. Graph the function and determine its x-intercepts. **$-15, 15$**

10. What is the length of the walkway between the two supports? **30 ft**

Reading to Learn Mathematics, p. 589   **ELL**

Pre-Activity How can quadratic equations be used in computer simulations?

Read the introduction to Lesson 10-2 at the top of page 533 in your textbook.

If one of the x-intercepts represents the location where the ball will hit the ground, what does the other x-intercept represent? **The location where the ball is hit.**

Reading the Lesson

1. The x-intercepts of the graph of a quadratic function are the x-coordinates of the points where the graph of the function intersects the x-axis. At those points, the y-coordinates are equal to **0**. This explains why the x-intercepts are called **zeros** of the quadratic function.

2. The graphs of three functions are shown below. Use the graphs to provide the requested information about the related quadratic equations.

A. $f(x) = x^2 - 6x + 9$ B. $f(x) = x^2 + 2x + 3$ C. $f(x) = x^2 + x - 2$

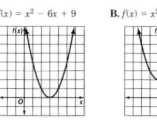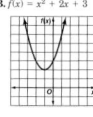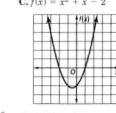

a. For Graph A, the related quadratic equation is **$x^2 - 6x + 9 = 0$**
   How many solutions are there? **one**
   Name any solutions. **3**

b. For Graph B, the related quadratic equation is **$x^2 + 2x + 3 = 0$**
   How many solutions are there? **none**
   Name any solutions. **none**

c. For Graph C, the related quadratic equation is **$x^2 + x - 2 = 0$**
   How many solutions are there? **two**
   Name any solutions. **-2 and 1**

Helping You Remember

3. Describe how you can remember that the word *zero* is used when you are talking about functions, but the word *root* is used when you are talking about equations. **Sample answer: Some functions can have a value of zero. Equations can be true or false, but they do not have a number value.**

Enrichment, p. 590

Odd Numbers and Parabolas
The solid parabola and the dashed stair-step graph are related. The parabola intersects the stair steps at their inside corners.

Use the figure for Exercises 1–3.

1. What is the equation of the parabola?
   $y = x^2$

2. Describe the horizontal sections of the stair-step graph.
   Each is 1 unit wide.

3. Describe the vertical sections of the stair-step graph.
   They form the sequence 1, 3, 5, 7.

Lesson 10-2 Solving Quadratic Equations by Graphing **537**

Open-Ended Assessment

Speaking Have students describe how to solve a quadratic equation by graphing, as if they were teaching the procedure. Make sure students include any tips or hints that they use when they solve by graphing.

Getting Ready for Lesson 10-3

PREREQUISITE SKILL Students will learn how to solve quadratic equations by completing the square in Lesson 10-3. Using this method requires that students know how to transform quadratic expressions into perfect squares. Use Exercises 63–68 to determine your students' familiarity with identifying and factoring perfect square trinomials.

Assessment Options

Quiz (Lessons 10-1 and 10-2) is available on p. 635 of the *Chapter 10 Resource Masters*.

Answers

53.

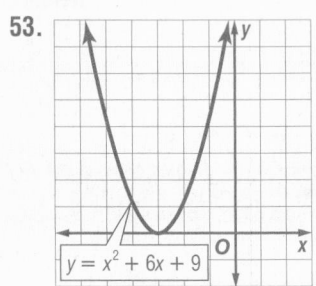

$y = x^2 + 6x + 9$

54.

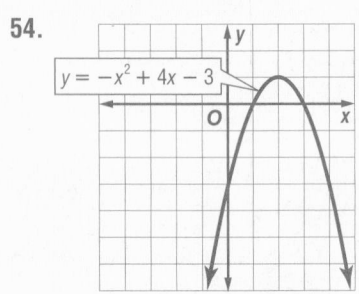

$y = -x^2 + 4x - 3$

---

49. Which graph represents a function whose corresponding quadratic equation has no solutions? **C**

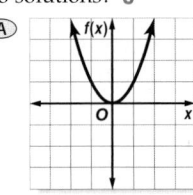
(A)

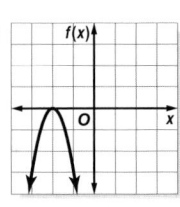
(B)

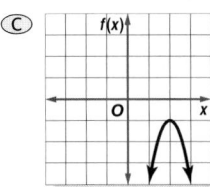
(C)

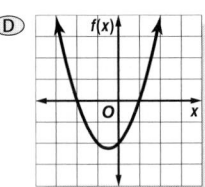
(D)

50. What are the root(s) of the quadratic equation whose related function is graphed at the right? **A**

(A) $-2, 2$ (B) 0

(C) 4 (D) $0, 4$

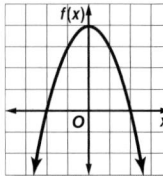

Graphing Calculator

CUBIC EQUATIONS An equation of the form $ax^3 + bx^2 + cx + d = 0$ is called a **cubic equation**. You can use a graphing calculator to graph and solve cubic equations.

Use the graph of the related function of each cubic equation to estimate the roots of the equation.

51. $x^3 - x^2 - 4x + 4 = 0$ **−2, 1, 2**   **52.** $2x^3 - 11x^2 + 13x - 4 = 0$ $\frac{1}{2}$, **1, 4**

Maintain Your Skills

Mixed Review

53. $x = -3$; $(-3, 0)$; minimum

54. $x = 2$; $(2, 1)$; maximum

55. $x = 6$; $(6, -13)$; minimum

Write the equation of the axis of symmetry, and find the coordinates of the vertex of the graph of each function. Identify the vertex as a maximum or minimum. Then graph the function. *(Lesson 10-1)* **53–55. See margin for graphs.**

53. $y = x^2 + 6x + 9$ **54.** $y = -x^2 + 4x - 3$ **55.** $y = 0.5x^2 - 6x + 5$

Solve each equation. Check your solutions. *(Lesson 9-6)*

56. $m^2 - 24m = -144$ {12}   **57.** $7r^2 = 70r - 175$ {5}   **58.** $4d^2 + 9 = -12d$ {−1.5}

Simplify. Assume that no denominator is equal to zero. *(Lesson 8-2)*

59. $\frac{10m^4}{30m} \cdot \frac{m^3}{3}$ **60.** $\frac{22a^2b^5c^7}{-11abc^2}$ $-2ab^4c^5$ **61.** $\frac{-9m^3n^5}{27m^{-2}n^5y^{-4}}$ $-\frac{m^5y^4}{3}$

62. SHIPPING An empty book crate weighs 30 pounds. The weight of a book is 1.5 pounds. For shipping, the crate must weigh at least 55 pounds and no more than 60 pounds. What is the acceptable number of books that can be packed in the crate? *(Lesson 6-4)* **17 to 20 books**

63. $(a + 7)^2$

64. $(m - 5)^2$

Getting Ready for the Next Lesson

66. $(2y + 3)^2$

68. $(5x - 1)^2$

PREREQUISITE SKILL Determine whether each trinomial is a perfect square trinomial. If so, factor it. *(To review perfect square trinomials, see Lesson 9-6.)*

63. $a^2 + 14a + 49$ **yes**   **64.** $m^2 - 10m + 25$ **yes**   **65.** $t^2 + 16t - 64$ **no**

66. $4y^2 + 12y + 9$ **yes**   **67.** $9d^2 - 12d - 4$ **no**   **68.** $25x^2 - 10x + 1$ **yes**

538 **Chapter 10** Quadratic and Exponential Functions

55.

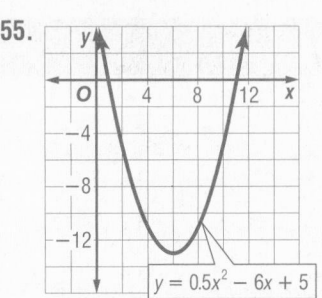

$y = 0.5x^2 - 6x + 5$

Solving Quadratic Equations by Completing the Square

What You'll Learn

• Solve quadratic equations by finding the square root.

• Solve quadratic equations by completing the square.

Vocabulary

• completing the square

How did ancient mathematicians use squares to solve algebraic equations?

Al-Khwarizmi, born in Baghdad in 780, is considered to be one of the foremost mathematicians of all time. He wrote some of the oldest works on arithmetic and algebra. He wrote algebra in sentences instead of using equations, and he explained the work with geometric sketches. Al-Khwarizmi would have described $x^2 + 8x = 35$ as "A square and 8 roots are equal to 35 units." He would solve the problem using the following sketch.

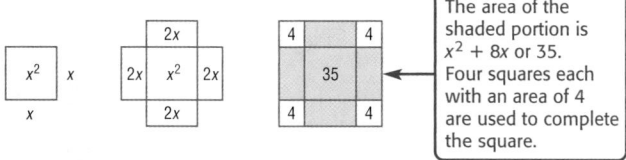

The area of the shaded portion is $x^2 + 8x$ or 35. Four squares each with an area of 4 are used to complete the square.

To solve problems this way today, you might use algebra tiles or a method called completing the square.

FIND THE SQUARE ROOT Some equations can be solved by taking the square root of each side.

Example 1 Irrational Roots

Solve $x^2 - 10x + 25 = 7$ by taking the square root of each side. Round to the nearest tenth if necessary.

$x^2 - 10x + 25 = 7$ Original equation

$(x - 5)^2 = 7$ $x^2 - 10x + 25$ is a perfect square trinomial.

$\sqrt{(x - 5)^2} = \sqrt{7}$ Take the square root of each side.

$|x - 5| = \sqrt{7}$ Simplify.

$x - 5 = \pm\sqrt{7}$ Definition of absolute value

$x - 5 + 5 = \pm\sqrt{7} + 5$ Add 5 to each side.

$x = 5 \pm \sqrt{7}$ Simplify.

Use a calculator to evaluate each value of x.

$x = 5 + \sqrt{7}$ or $x = 5 - \sqrt{7}$

≈ 7.6 ≈ 2.4

The solution set is {2.4, 7.6}.

COMPLETE THE SQUARE To use the method shown in Example 1, the quadratic expression on one side of the equation must be a perfect square. However, few quadratic expressions are perfect squares. To make any quadratic expression a perfect square, a method called **completing the square** may be used.

---

1 Focus

 5-Minute Check Transparency 10-3 Use as a quiz or review of Lesson 10-2.

Mathematical Background notes are available for this lesson on p. 522C.

Building on Prior Knowledge

In Chapter 9, students learned how to factor trinomials, including perfect square trinomials. In this lesson, students will build upon that knowledge and learn how to complete the square to solve quadratic equations.

How did ancient mathematicians use squares to solve algebraic equations?

Ask students:

• Look at the completed square. What is the side length of the square? Remember, each of the smaller squares are made up of 4 unit squares. **side length = $x + 4$**

• Given the side length you just found, what is the area of the square? **$(x + 4)^2$ or $x^2 + 8x + 16$**

• Graphically, 16 unit squares were added to the original figure to complete the square. How would you change the original equation to represent this addition? **$x^2 + 8x + 16 = 35 + 16$**

Resource Manager

Workbook and Reproducible Masters

Chapter 10 Resource Masters
• Study Guide and Intervention, pp. 591–592
• Skills Practice, p. 593
• Practice, p. 594
• Reading to Learn Mathematics, p. 595
• Enrichment, p. 596

Parent and Student Study Guide Workbook, p. 77

 Transparencies
5-Minute Check Transparency 10-3
Answer Key Transparencies

Technology
AlgePASS: Tutorial Plus, Lesson 29
Interactive Chalkboard

FIND THE SQUARE ROOT

In-Class Example Power Point®

Teaching Tip Remind students that when taking the square root of a number, there are two square roots, one positive and one negative. That's why the plus or minus sign is placed in front of the square root of 7 when the absolute value signs are removed. Also, quadratic equations often have two solutions. Without the plus or minus sign, there would be only one solution.

1 Solve $x^2 + 6x + 9 = 5$ by taking the square root of each side. Round to the nearest tenth if necessary. {$-5.2, -0.8$}

COMPLETE THE SQUARE

In-Class Examples Power Point®

2 Find the value of c that makes $x^2 - 12x + c$ a perfect square. *c* must be 36 for the expression to be a perfect square.

Teaching Tip Remind students that any amount that they add to the left side of the equation to complete the square must also be added to the right side of the equation.

3 Solve $x^2 - 18x + 5 = -12$ by completing the square. {1, 17}

Study Tip

Look Back
To review **perfect square trinomials**, see Lesson 9-6.

TEACHING TIP
Encourage students to find the length of each side to verify that the figure at the right is a square.

Consider the pattern for squaring a binomial such as $x + 6$.

$$(x + 6)^2 = x^2 + 2(6)(x) + 6^2$$
$$= x^2 + 12x + 36$$
$$\left(\frac{12}{2}\right)^2 \rightarrow 6^2 \quad \text{Notice that one half of 12 is 6 and } 6^2 \text{ is 36.}$$

Key Concept Completing the Square

To complete the square for a quadratic expression of the form $x^2 + bx$, you can follow the steps below.

Step 1 Find $\frac{1}{2}$ of b, the coefficient of x.

Step 2 Square the result of Step 1.

Step 3 Add the result of Step 2 to $x^2 + bx$, the original expression.

Example 2 Complete the Square

Find the value of c that makes $x^2 + 6x + c$ a perfect square.

Method 1 Use algebra tiles.

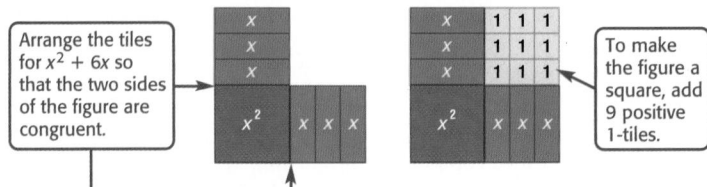

$x^2 + 6x + 9$ is a perfect square.

Method 2 Complete the square.

Step 1 Find $\frac{1}{2}$ of 6. $\frac{6}{2} = 3$

Step 2 Square the result of Step 1. $3^2 = 9$

Step 3 Add the result of Step 2 to $x^2 + 6x$. $x^2 + 6x + 9$

Thus, $c = 9$. Notice that $x^2 + 6x + 9 = (x + 3)^2$.

Example 3 Solve an Equation by Completing the Square

Solve $a^2 - 14a + 3 = -10$ by completing the square.

Step 1 Isolate the a^2 and a terms.

$$a^2 - 14a + 3 = -10 \quad \text{Original equation}$$
$$a^2 - 14a + 3 - 3 = -10 - 3 \quad \text{Subtract 3 from each side.}$$
$$a^2 - 14a = -13 \quad \text{Simplify.}$$

Step 2 Complete the square and solve.

$$a^2 - 14a + 49 = -13 + 49 \quad \text{Since } \left(\frac{-14}{2}\right)^2 = 49, \text{ add 49 to each side.}$$
$$(a - 7)^2 = 36 \quad \text{Factor } a^2 - 14a + 49.$$
$$a - 7 = \pm 6 \quad \text{Take the square root of each side.}$$
$$a - 7 + 7 = \pm 6 + 7 \quad \text{Add 7 to each side.}$$
$$a = 7 \pm 6 \quad \text{Simplify.}$$

540 **Chapter 10** Quadratic and Exponential Functions

DAILY
INTERVENTION   **Unlocking Misconceptions**

Point out to students that completing the square to solve a quadratic equation does not necessarily mean that the solutions will be integers. If the equation already has a constant term, it is very likely that after completing the square, the constant will not be a perfect square, and the solutions will be irrational.

$$a = 7 + 6 \quad \text{or} \quad a = 7 - 6$$
$$= 13 \qquad\qquad = 1$$

CHECK Substitute each value for a in the original equation.

$$a^2 - 14a + 3 = -10 \qquad\qquad a^2 - 14a + 3 = -10$$
$$1^2 - 14(1) + 3 \stackrel{?}{=} -10 \qquad 13^2 - 14(13) + 3 \stackrel{?}{=} -10$$
$$1 - 14 + 3 \stackrel{?}{=} -10 \qquad\quad 169 - 182 + 3 \stackrel{?}{=} -10$$
$$-10 = -10 \ \checkmark \qquad\qquad\quad -10 = -10 \ \checkmark$$

The solution set is {1, 13}.

This method of completing the square cannot be used unless the coefficient of the first term is 1. To solve a quadratic equation in which the leading coefficient is not 1, first divide each term by the coefficient. Then follow the steps for completing the square.

Example 4 · Solve a Quadratic Equation in Which a ≠ 1

ENTERTAINMENT The path of debris from a firework display on a windy evening can be modeled by a quadratic function. A function for the path of the fireworks when the wind is about 15 miles per hour is $h = -0.04x^2 + 2x + 8$, where h is the height and x is the horizontal distance in feet. How far away from the launch site will the debris land?

Explore You know the function that relates the horizontal and vertical distances. You want to know how far away from the launch site the debris will land.

Plan The debris will hit the ground when $h = 0$. Use completing the square to solve $-0.04x^2 + 2x + 8 = 0$.

Solve

$-0.04x^2 + 2x + 8 = 0$	Equation for where debris will land
$\dfrac{-0.04x^2 + 2x + 8}{-0.04} = \dfrac{0}{-0.04}$	Divide each side by -0.04.
$x^2 - 50x - 200 = 0$	Simplify.
$x^2 - 50x - 200 + 200 = 0 + 200$	Add 200 to each side.
$x^2 - 50x = 200$	Simplify.
$x^2 - 50x + 625 = 200 + 625$	Since $\left(\dfrac{50}{2}\right)^2 = 625$, add 625 to each side.
$x^2 - 50x + 625 = 825$	Simplify.
$(x - 25)^2 = 825$	Factor $x^2 - 50x + 625$.
$x - 25 = \pm\sqrt{825}$	Take the square root of each side.
$x - 25 + 25 = \pm\sqrt{825} + 25$	Add 25 to each side.
$x = 25 \pm \sqrt{825}$	Simplify.

Use a calculator to evaluate each value of x.

$$x = 25 + \sqrt{825} \quad \text{or} \quad x = 25 - \sqrt{825}$$
$$\approx 53.7 \qquad\qquad\qquad \approx -3.7$$

Examine Since you are looking for a distance, ignore the negative number. The debris will land about 53.7 feet from the launch site.

www.algebra1.com/extra_examples

Lesson 10-3 Solving Quadratic Equations by Completing the Square **541**

More About. . .

Entertainment
One of the exploded fireworks for the Lake Toya Festival in Japan on July 15, 1988, broke a world record. The diameter of the burst was 3937 feet.
Source: *The Guinness Book of Records*

Teaching Tip Tell students not to automatically throw out negative solutions to real-world problems. They must first examine the problem to see if the solution fits the situation. In Example 4, a negative distance does not make sense but in other situations, a negative solution may be appropriate.

4 BOATING Suppose the rate of flow of an 80-foot-wide river is given by the equation $r = -0.01x^2 + 0.8x$, where r is the rate in miles per hour, and x is the distance from the shore in feet. Joacquim does not want to paddle his canoe against a current faster than 5 miles per hour. At what distance from the river bank must he paddle in order to avoid a current of 5 miles per hour? He must stay within about 7 ft of either bank. Note: The solutions to the equation are about 7 ft and about 73 ft. The solutions are distances from the one shore. Since the river is 80 ft wide, $80 - 73 = 7$.

DAILY INTERVENTION

Differentiated Instruction

Visual/Spatial Have students graph the equation in Example 4 and discuss how it corresponds to the application. Make sure they understand that this is the picture of height in relation to time and *does not* model the actual path of the fireworks.

Lesson 10-3 Solving Quadratic Equations by Completing the Square **541**

Study Notebook

Have students—

- add the definitions/examples of the vocabulary terms to their Vocabulary Builder worksheets for Chapter 10.
- include examples of how to solve quadratic equations by completing the square.
- include any other item(s) that they find helpful in mastering the skills in this lesson.

About the Exercises ...

Organization by Objective
- **Find the Square Root:** 15–20
- **Complete the Square:** 21–52

Odd/Even Assignments

Exercises 15–50 are structured so that students practice the same concepts whether they are assigned odd or even problems.

Assignment Guide

Basic: 15–25 odd, 29–45 odd, 49, 51, 53–75

Average: 15–51 odd, 53–75

Advanced: 16–48 even, 50–71 (optional: 72–75)

All: Practice Quiz 1 (1–10)

Answer

1. Sample answer:

x	1	1
x	1	1
x^2	x	x

$x^2 + 4x + 4$

Check for Understanding

Concept Check

1. **OPEN ENDED** Make a square using one or more of each of the following types of tiles.
   - x^2 tile
   - x tile
   - 1 tile

   Write an expression for the area of your square. **See margin.**

2. Graphing $f(x) = x^2 - 5x - 7$ would not result in an exact answer and $x^2 - 5x - 7$ cannot be factored.

2. **Explain** why completing the square to solve $x^2 - 5x - 7 = 0$ is a better strategy than graphing the related function or factoring.

3. **Describe** the first step needed to solve $5x^2 + 12x = 15$ by completing the square. **Divide each side by 5.**

Guided Practice

GUIDED PRACTICE KEY	
Exercises	Examples
4, 5	1
6, 7	2
8–14	3, 4

Solve each equation by taking the square root of each side. Round to the nearest tenth if necessary.

4. $b^2 - 6b + 9 = 25$ **−2, 8**   5. $m^2 + 14m + 49 = 20$ **−11.5, −2.5**

Find the value of c that makes each trinomial a perfect square.

6. $a^2 - 12a + c$ **36**   7. $t^2 + 5t + c$ **$\frac{25}{4}$**

Solve each equation by completing the square. Round to the nearest tenth if necessary.

8. $c^2 - 6c = 7$ **−1, 7**   9. $x^2 + 7x = -12$ **−4, −3**   10. $v^2 + 14v - 9 = 6$ **−15, 1**
11. $r^2 - 4r = 2$ **−0.4, 4.4**   12. $a^2 - 24a + 9 = 0$ **0.4, 23.6**   13. $2p^2 - 5p + 8 = 7$ **0.2, 2.3**

Application 14. **GEOMETRY** The area of a square can be doubled by increasing the length by 6 inches and the width by 4 inches. What is the length of the side of the square? **12 in.**

★ indicates increased difficulty

Practice and Apply

Homework Help	
For Exercises	See Examples
15–20	1
21–28	2
29–52	3, 4

Extra Practice
See page 842.

Solve each equation by taking the square root of each side. Round to the nearest tenth if necessary. **17. 2.6, 5.4**

15. $b^2 - 4b + 4 = 16$ **−2, 6** 16. $t^2 + 2t + 1 = 25$ **−6, 4** 17. $g^2 - 8g + 16 = 2$
18. $y^2 - 12y + 36 = 5$ **3.8, 8.2**   19. $w^2 + 16w + 64 = 18$ **−12.2, −3.8**   20. $a^2 + 18a + 81 = 90$ **−18.5, 0.5**

Find the value of c that makes each trinomial a perfect square.

21. $s^2 - 16s + c$ **64**   22. $y^2 - 10y + c$ **25**   23. $w^2 + 22w + c$ **121**
24. $a^2 + 34a + c$ **289**   25. $p^2 - 7p + c$ **$\frac{49}{4}$**   26. $k^2 + 11k + c$ **$\frac{121}{4}$**

★ 27. Find all values of c that make $x^2 + cx + 81$ a perfect square. **−18, 18**

★ 28. Find all values of c that make $x^2 + cx + 144$ a perfect square. **−24, 24**

Solve each equation by completing the square. Round to the nearest tenth if necessary. **31. −3, 22   32. −27, 7   43. −2.5, 0.5**

29. $s^2 - 4s - 12 = 0$ **−2, 6** 30. $d^2 + 3d - 10 = 0$ **−5, 2** 31. $y^2 - 19y + 4 = 70$
32. $d^2 + 20d + 11 = 200$ 33. $a^2 - 5a = -4$ **1, 4**   34. $p^2 - 4p = 21$ **−3, 7**
35. $x^2 + 4x + 3 = 0$ **−3, −1** 36. $d^2 - 8d + 7 = 0$ **1, 7**   37. $s^2 - 10s = 23$ **−1.9, 11.9**
38. $m^2 - 8m = 4$ **−0.5, 8.5** 39. $9r^2 + 49 = 42r$ **$2\frac{1}{3}$**   40. $4h^2 + 25 = 20h$ **$2\frac{1}{2}$**
41. $0.3t^2 + 0.1t = 0.2$ **−1, $\frac{2}{3}$** 42. $0.4v^2 + 2.5 = 2v$ **$2\frac{1}{2}$**   43. $5x^2 + 10x - 7 = 0$
44. $9w^2 - 12w - 1 = 0$ **−0.1, 1.4**   45. $\frac{1}{2}d^2 - \frac{5}{4}d - 3 = 0$ **$-1\frac{1}{2}$, 4**   46. $\frac{1}{3}f^2 - \frac{7}{6}f + \frac{1}{2} = 0$ **$\frac{1}{2}$, 3**

Solve each equation for x by completing the square.

★ 47. $x^2 + 4x + c = 0$ $\quad -2 \pm \sqrt{4 - c}$ ★ 48. $x^2 - 6x + c = 0$ $\quad 3 \pm \sqrt{9 - c}$

49. **PARK PLANNING** A plan for a park has a rectangular plot of wild flowers that is 9 meters long by 6 meters wide. A pathway of constant width goes around the plot of wild flowers. If the area of the path is equal to the area of the plot of wild flowers, what is the width of the path? **1.5 m**

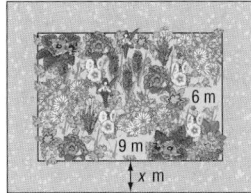
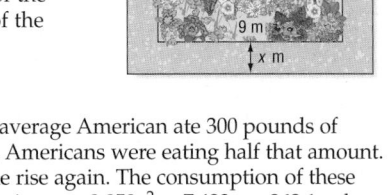

6 m

9 m

x m

50. **EATING HABITS** In the early 1900s, the average American ate 300 pounds of bread and cereal every year. By the 1960s, Americans were eating half that amount. However, eating cereal and bread is on the rise again. The consumption of these types of foods can be modeled by the function $y = 0.059x^2 - 7.423x + 362.1$, where y represents the bread and cereal consumption in pounds and x represents the number of years since 1900. If this trend continues, in what future year will the average American consume 300 pounds of bread and cereal? **about 2017**

Online Research **Data Update** What are the eating habits of Americans? Visit www.algebra1.com/data_update to learn more.

51. **CRITICAL THINKING** Describe the solution of $x^2 + 4x + 12 = 0$. Explain your reasoning. **There are no real solutions since completing the square results in $(x + 2)^2 = -8$ and the square of a number cannot be negative.**

52. **PHOTOGRAPHY** Emilio is placing a photograph behind a 12-inch-by-12-inch piece of matting. The photograph is to be positioned so that the matting is twice as wide at the top and bottom as it is at the sides. If the area of the photograph is to be 54 square inches, what are the dimensions? **9 in. by 6 in.**

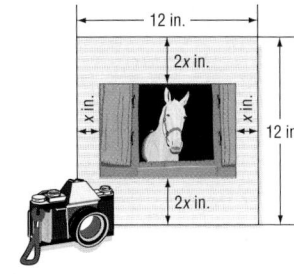

12 in.

2x in.

x in. x in.

12 in.

2x in.

53. **WRITING IN MATH** Answer the question that was posed at the beginning of the lesson. **See pp. 581A–581H.**

How did ancient mathematicians use squares to solve algebraic equations?

Include the following in your answer:
- an explanation of Al-Khwarizmi's drawings for $x^2 + 8x = 35$, and
- a step-by-step algebraic solution with justification for each step of the equation.

Standardized Test Practice
Ⓐ Ⓑ Ⓒ Ⓓ

54. Determine which trinomial is *not* a perfect square trinomial. **C**

Ⓐ $a^2 - 26a + 169$ Ⓑ $a^2 + 32a + 256$
Ⓒ $a^2 + 30a - 225$ Ⓓ $a^2 - 44a + 484$

55. Which equation is equivalent to $x^2 + 5x = 14$? **A**

Ⓐ $\left(x + \dfrac{5}{2}\right)^2 = \dfrac{81}{4}$ Ⓑ $\left(x - \dfrac{5}{2}\right)^2 = \dfrac{45}{4}$

Ⓒ $\left(x + \dfrac{5}{2}\right)^2 = -\dfrac{5}{4}$ Ⓓ $\left(x - \dfrac{5}{2}\right)^2 = -\dfrac{5}{4}$

www.algebra1.com/self_check_quiz

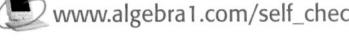

Study Guide and Intervention, p. 591 (shown) and p. 592

Find the Square Root An equation such as $x^2 - 4x + 4 = 5$ can be solved by taking the square root of each side.

Example 1 Solve $x^2 - 2x + 1 = 9$. Round to the nearest tenth if necessary.
$x^2 - 2x + 1 = 9$
$(x - 1)^2 = 9$
$\sqrt{(x - 1)^2} = \sqrt{9}$
$|x - 1| = \sqrt{9}$
$x - 1 = \pm 3$
$x - 1 + 1 = \pm 3 + 1$
$x = 1 \pm 3$
$x = 1 + 3$ or $x = 1 - 3$
$= 4$ $\qquad = -2$
The solution set is $\{-2, 4\}$.

Example 2 Solve $x^2 - 4x + 4 = 5$. Round to the nearest tenth if necessary.
$x^2 - 4x + 4 = 5$
$(x - 2)^2 = 5$
$\sqrt{(x - 2)^2} = \sqrt{5}$
$|x - 2| = \sqrt{5}$
$x - 2 = \pm\sqrt{5}$
$x - 2 + 2 = \pm\sqrt{5} + 2$
$x = 2 \pm \sqrt{5}$
Use a calculator to evaluate each value of x.
$x = 2 + \sqrt{5}$ or $x = 2 - \sqrt{5}$
≈ 4.2 $\qquad \approx -0.2$
The solution set is $\{-0.2, 4.2\}$.

Exercises
Solve each equation by taking the square root of each side. Round to the nearest tenth if necessary.

1. $x^2 + 4x + 4 = 9$ −5, 1
2. $m^2 + 12m + 36 = 1$ −7, −5
3. $r^2 - 6r + 9 = 16$ −1, 7
4. $x^2 - 2x + 1 = 25$ −4, 6
5. $x^2 - 8x + 16 = 5$ 1.8, 6.2
6. $x^2 - 10x + 25 = 8$ 2.2, 7.8
7. $c^2 - 4c + 4 = 7$ −0.6, 4.6
8. $p^2 + 16p + 64 = 3$ −9.7, −6.3
9. $x^2 + 8x + 16 = 9$ −7, −1
10. $x^2 + 6x + 9 = 4$ −5, −1
11. $a^2 + 8a + 16 = 10$ −7.2, −0.8
12. $y^2 - 12y + 36 = 5$ 3.8, 8.2
13. $x^2 + 10x + 25 = 1$ −6, −4
14. $y^2 + 14y + 49 = 6$ −9.4, −4.6
15. $m^2 - 8m + 16 = 2$ 2.6, 5.4
16. $x^2 + 12x + 36 = 10$ −9.2, −2.8
17. $a^2 - 14a + 49 = 3$ 5.3, 8.7
18. $y^2 + 8y + 16 = 7$ −6.6, −1.4

Skills Practice, p. 593 and Practice, p. 594 (shown)

Solve each equation by taking the square root of each side. Round to the nearest tenth if necessary.

1. $b^2 - 14b + 49 = 64$ −1, 15
2. $s^2 + 16s + 64 = 100$ −18, 2
3. $h^2 - 8h + 16 = 15$ 0.1, 7.9
4. $a^2 + 6a + 9 = 27$ −8.2, 2.2
5. $p^2 - 20p + 100 = 28$ 4.7, 15.3
6. $u^2 + 10u + 25 = 90$ −14.5, 4.5

Find the value of c that makes each trinomial a perfect square.

7. $t^2 - 24t + c$ 144
8. $b^2 + 28b + c$ 196
9. $y^2 + 40y + c$ 400
10. $m^2 + 3m + c$ $\dfrac{9}{4}$
11. $g^2 - 9g + c$ $\dfrac{81}{4}$
12. $v^2 - v + c$ $\dfrac{1}{4}$

Solve each equation by completing the square. Round to the nearest tenth if necessary.

13. $w^2 - 14w + 24 = 0$ 2, 12
14. $p^2 + 12p = 13$ −13, 1
15. $s^2 - 30s + 56 = -25$ 3, 27
16. $v^2 + 8v + 9 = 0$ −6.6, −1.4
17. $t^2 - 10t + 6 = -7$ 1.5, 8.5
18. $n^2 + 18n + 50 = 9$ −15.3, −2.7
19. $3u^2 + 15u - 3 = 0$ −5.2, 0.2
20. $4c^2 - 72 = 24c$ −2.2, 8.2
21. $0.9a^2 + 5.4a - 4 = 0$ $-6\frac{2}{3}, \frac{2}{3}$
22. $0.4h^2 + 0.8h = 0.2$ −2.2, 0.2
23. $\frac{1}{2}x^2 - \frac{1}{2}x - 10 = 0$ −4, 5
24. $\frac{1}{4}x^2 + \frac{3}{4}x - 2 = 0$ −7.1, 1.1

BUSINESS For Exercises 25 and 26, use the following information.
Jaime owns a business making decorative boxes to store jewelry, mementos, and other valuables. The function $y = x^2 + 50x + 1800$ models the profit y that Jaime has made in month x for the first two years of his business.

25. Write an equation representing the month in which Jaime's profit is $2400. $x^2 + 50x + 1800 = 2400$
26. Use completing the square to find out in which month Jaime's profit is $2400.   the tenth month

27. **PHYSICS** From a height of 256 feet above a lake on a cliff, Mikaela throws a rock over the lake. The height H of the rock t seconds after Mikaela throws it is represented by the equation $H = -16t^2 + 32t + 256$. To the nearest tenth of a second, how long will it take the rock to reach the lake below? (*Hint*: Replace H with 0.)   5.1 s

Reading to Learn Mathematics, p. 595   **ELL**

Pre-Activity How did ancient mathematicians use squares to solve algebraic equations?

Read the introduction to Lesson 10-3 at the top of page 539 in your textbook.

To solve the problem, how many "units" would Al-Khwarizmi have added to each side of the equation? **16**

Reading the Lesson

1. Draw a line under each quadratic equation that you could solve by taking the square root of each side.

$\underline{x^2 + 6x + 9 = 100}$ $x^2 - 14x + 40 = 25$ $\underline{x^2 - 16x + 64 = 26}$
$x^2 - 20x + 80 = 16$ $x^2 + 10x + 36 = 49$ $\underline{x^2 - 12x + 36 = 6}$

2. How can you tell whether it is possible to solve a quadratic equation by taking the square root of each side?
Sample answer: Check to be sure that all terms that contain the variable are on the same side of the equation. Next, check whether the quadratic expression is a perfect square. Finally, check that the number on the side that contains no variables is greater than or equal to 0.

3. Explain how to find what number is needed for the ■ in order to make $x^2 - 20x + ■$ a perfect square.
Find one half of −20, which is −10, and square it. The result, which is 100, is the required number.

4. To solve $3x^2 - 6x = 54$ by completing the square, why does it help first to divide both sides by 3?
Sample answer: If you divide both sides by 3, the coefficient of x^2 will be 1. It is then easy to use the coefficient of x to decide what number you need to add to both sides to make the left side a perfect square trinomial.

Helping You Remember

5. The method of completing the square might be easier to remember if you can connect it to what you know about perfect square trinomials. How is completing the square related to the method you use to determine whether a trinomial is a perfect square trinomial?
Sample answer: If the first and last terms of a trinomial are perfect squares, you *multiply* the product of their *square roots* by 2 to get the middle term. In completing the square, you check that the coefficient of x^2 is 1. Then you divide the coefficient of the x term by 2 and square the result to get the third term.

Enrichment, p. 596

Parabolas Through Three Given Points

If you know two points on a straight line, you can find the equation of the line. To find the equation of a parabola, you need three points on the curve.

Here is how to approximate an equation of the parabola through the points $(0, -2)$, $(3, 0)$, and $(5, 2)$.

Use the general equation $y = ax^2 + bx + c$. By substituting the given values for x and y, you get three equations.

$(0, -2)$: $-2 = c$
$(3, 0)$: $0 = 9a + 3b + c$
$(5, 2)$: $2 = 25a + 5b + c$

First, substitute -2 for c in the second and third equations. Then solve those two equations as you would any system of two equations. Multiply the second equation by 5 and the third equation by -3.

$0 = 9a + 3b - 2$ Multiply by 5. $0 = 45a + 15b - 10$
$0 = 25a + 5b - 2$ Multiply by -3. $-6 = -75a - 15b + 6$

Open-Ended Assessment

Modeling Have students use algebra tiles to model how completing the square makes it possible to solve a quadratic equation.

Getting Ready for Lesson 10-4

PREREQUISITE SKILL Students will learn how to solve quadratic equations using the quadratic formula in Lesson 10-4. Using this method requires that students know how to find square roots of polynomials. Use Exercises 72–75 to determine your students' familiarity with finding square roots of polynomials.

Assessment Options

Practice Quiz 1 The quiz provides students with a brief review of the concepts and skills in Lessons 10-1 through 10-3. Lesson numbers are given to the right of exercises or instruction lines so students can review concepts not yet mastered.

Answers

56.

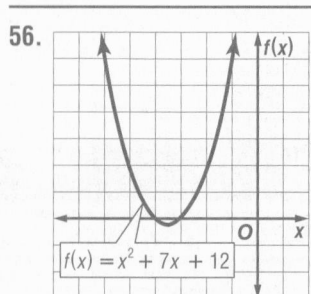

57.

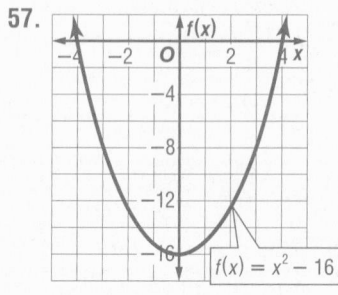

Maintain Your Skills

Mixed Review

Solve each equation by graphing. *(Lesson 10-2)* **56–58. See margin for graphs.**

56. $x^2 + 7x + 12 = 0$ **−4, −3** 57. $x^2 − 16 = 0$ **−4, 4** 58. $x^2 − 2x + 6 = 0$ ∅

Use a table of values to graph each equation. *(Lesson 10-1)* **59–61. See pp. 581A–58**

59. $y = 4x^2 + 16$ 60. $y = x^2 − 3x − 10$ 61. $y = −x^2 + 3x − 4$

Find each GCF of the given monomials. *(Lesson 9-1)*

62. $14a^2b^3, 20a^3b^2c, 35ab^3c^2$ **ab^2** 63. $32m^2n^3, 8m^2n, 56m^3n^2$ **$8m^2n$**

Use substitution to solve each system of equations. If the system does not have exactly one solution, state whether it has no solution or infinitely many solutions. *(Lesson 7-2)*

64. $y = 2x$ 65. $x = y + 3$ 66. $x − 2y = 3$
    $x + y = 9$ **(3, 6)** $2x − 3y = 5$ **(4, 1)** $3x + y = 23$ **(7, 2)**

Write a compound inequality for each graph. *(Lesson 6-4)*

67.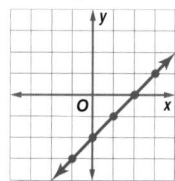
    $−3 < x < 1$

68.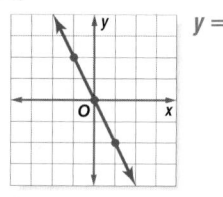
    $x ≤ −2$ or $x > 1$

69. Write the slope-intercept form of an equation that passes through $(8, −2)$ and is perpendicular to the graph of $5x − 3y = 7$. *(Lesson 5-6)* $y = −\frac{3}{5}x + \frac{14}{5}$

Write an equation for each relation. *(Lesson 4-8)*

70.
$y = x − 2$

71.
$y = −2x$

Getting Ready for the Next Lesson

PREREQUISITE SKILL Evaluate $\sqrt{b^2 − 4ac}$ for each set of values. Round to the nearest tenth if necessary. *(To review finding square roots, see Lesson 2-7.)*

72. $a = 1, b = −2, c = −15$ **8** 73. $a = 2, b = 7, c = 3$ **5**

74. $a = 1, b = 5, c = −2$ **5.7** 75. $a = −2, b = 7, c = 5$ **9.4**

Practice Quiz 1
Lessons 10-1 through 10-3

Write the equation of the axis of symmetry and find the coordinates of the vertex of the graph of each function. Identify the vertex as a maximum or minimum. Then graph the function. *(Lesson 10-1)* **1–6. See pp. 581A–581H for graphs.**

1. $y = x^2 − x − 6$
   $x = 0.5$; $(0.5, −6.25)$; minimum

2. $y = 2x^2 + 3$
   $x = 0$; $(0, 3)$; minimum

3. $y = −3x^2 − 6x + 5$
   $x = −1$; $(−1, 8)$; maximum

Solve each equation by graphing. If integral roots cannot be found, estimate the roots by stating the consecutive integers between which the roots lie. *(Lesson 10-2)*

4. $x^2 + 6x + 10 = 0$ ∅

5. $x^2 − 2x − 1 = 0$
   $−1 < x < 0, 2 < x < 3$

6. $x^2 − 5x − 6 = 0$ **−1, 6**

Solve each equation by completing the square. Round to the nearest tenth if necessary. *(Lesson 10-3)*

7. $s^2 + 8s = −15$ **−5, −3**
8. $a^2 − 10a = −24$ **4, 6**
9. $y^2 − 14y + 49 = 5$ **4.8, 9.2**
10. $2b^2 − b − 7 = 14$ **−3, 3.5**

544 Chapter 10 Quadratic and Exponential Functions

58.

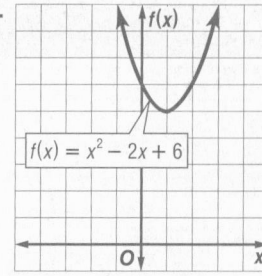

Graphing Calculator Investigation

A Follow-Up of Lesson 10-3

Graphing Quadratic Functions in Vertex Form

Quadratic functions written in the form $y = a(x - h)^2 + k$ are said to be in **vertex form**.

Graph each group of equations on the same screen. Use the standard viewing window. Compare and contrast the graphs.

a. $y = x^2$
$y = (x - 3)^2 + 5$
$y = (x + 2)^2 + 6$
$y = (x - 5)^2 - 4$

b. $y = -2x^2$
$y = -2(x - 1)^2 + 3$
$y = -2(x + 3)^2 + 1$
$y = -2(x - 5)^2 - 2$

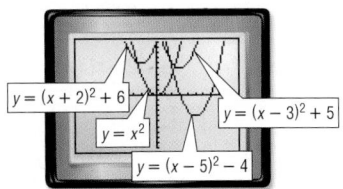

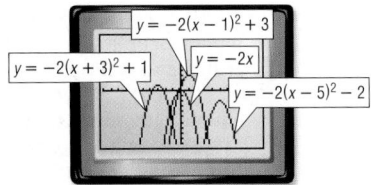

Each graph opens upward and has the same shape. However, the vertices are different.

Equation	Vertex
$y = x^2$	$(0, 0)$
$y = (x - 3)^2 + 5$	$(3, 5)$
$y = (x + 2)^2 + 6$	$(-2, 6)$
$y = (x - 5)^2 - 4$	$(5, -4)$

Each graph opens downward and has the same shape. However, the vertices are different.

Equation	Vertex
$y = -2x^2$	$(0, 0)$
$y = -2(x - 1)^2 + 3$	$(1, 3)$
$y = -2(x + 3)^2 + 1$	$(-3, 1)$
$y = -2(x - 5)^2 - 2$	$(5, -2)$

Exercises

1. Study the relationship between the equations in vertex form and their vertices. What is the vertex of the graph of $y = a(x - h)^2 + k$? **(h, k)**

2. Completing the square can be used to change a quadratic equation to vertex form. Copy and complete the steps needed to rewrite $y = x^2 - 2x - 3$ in vertex form.
$y = x^2 - 2x - 3$
$y = (x^2 - 2x + \underline{\ ?\ }) - 3 - \underline{\ ?\ }$ **1, 1**
$y = (x - \underline{\ ?\ })^2 - \underline{\ ?\ }$ **1, 4**

3–5. See margin for graphs.

Complete the square to rewrite each quadratic equation in vertex form. Then determine the vertex of the graph of the equation and sketch the graph.

3. $y = x^2 + 2x - 7$
$y = (x + 1)^2 - 8;\ (-1, -8)$

4. $y = x^2 - 4x + 8$
$y = (x - 2)^2 + 4;\ (2, 4)$

5. $y = x^2 + 6x - 1$
$y = (x + 3)^2 - 10;\ (-3, -10)$

www.algebra1.com/other_calculator_keystrokes

Graphing Calculator Investigation **545**

Getting Started

Know Your Calculator Remind students to clear all previously entered functions before entering functions for this activity. To use the standard viewing window, press ZOOM 6.

Teach

- In part **a**, students can use the calculator to find the minimum of each function, which will reveal the location of the vertex. Select minimum in the **CALC** menu. Then use the up and down arrow keys to jump between the different graphs. Use the left and right arrow keys to set the left and right bounds for the minimum calculation for each graph.

- In part **b**, students use the same procedures as above except with the maximum function to find the vertex of each graph.

Assess

Have students explain what they know about the vertex of a graph of a function in the form $y = a(x - h)^2 + k$. **The vertex is (h, k).**

3.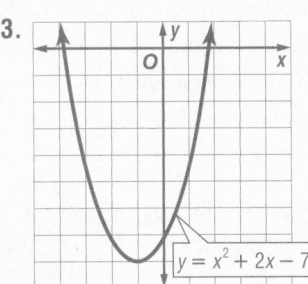

4.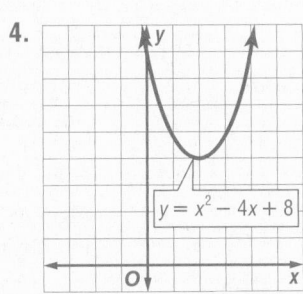

5.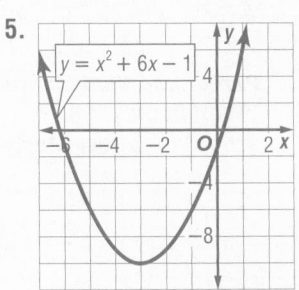

Solving Quadratic Equations by Using the Quadratic Formula

10-4

1 Focus

5-Minute Check Transparency 10-4 Use as a quiz or review of Lesson 10-3.

Mathematical Background notes are available for this lesson on p. 522D.

How can the Quadratic Formula be used to solve problems involving population trends?

Ask students:

• Since this population trend is represented by a quadratic equation, what does it assume about the percent of people who were born in other countries in the past? **The percent must have been higher in the past, then bottomed out a few decades ago, and has now been rising ever since.**

• Why would the equation be difficult to solve using factoring or completing the square? **The fractional values of the coefficients will make using the methods very difficult if not impossible.**

What You'll Learn

• Solve quadratic equations by using the Quadratic Formula.
• Use the discriminant to determine the number of solutions for a quadratic equation.

Vocabulary
• Quadratic Formula
• discriminant

How can the Quadratic Formula be used to solve problems involving population trends?

In the past few decades, there has been a dramatic increase in the percent of people living in the United States who were born in other countries. This trend can be modeled by the quadratic function $P = 0.006t^2 - 0.080t + 5.281$, where P is the percent born outside the United States and t is the number of years since 1960.

To predict when 15% of the population will be people who were born outside of the U.S., you can solve the equation $15 = 0.006t^2 - 0.080t + 5.281$. This equation would be impossible or difficult to solve using factoring, graphing, or completing the square.

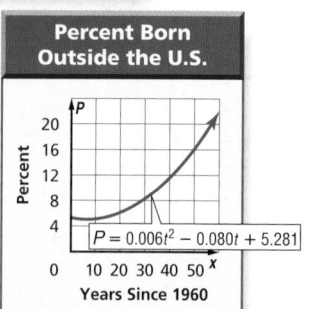

Percent Born Outside the U.S.

$P = 0.006t^2 - 0.080t + 5.281$

Years Since 1960

QUADRATIC FORMULA You can solve the standard form of the quadratic equation $ax^2 + bx + c = 0$ for x. The result is called the **Quadratic Formula**.

TEACHING TIP
The Quadratic Formula will be derived in Lesson 11-1.

Key Concept *The Quadratic Formula*

The solutions of a quadratic equation in the form $ax^2 + bx + c = 0$, where $a \neq 0$, are given by the Quadratic Formula.

$$x = \frac{-b \pm \sqrt{b^2 - 4ac}}{2a}$$

You can solve quadratic equations by factoring, graphing, completing the square, or using the Quadratic Formula.

Study Tip

Look Back
To review **solving equations by factoring,** see Chapter 9.

Example 1 Integral Roots

Use two methods to solve $x^2 - 2x - 24 = 0$.

Method 1 Factoring

$x^2 - 2x - 24 = 0$ Original equation

$(x + 4)(x - 6) = 0$ Factor $x^2 - 2x - 24$.

$x + 4 = 0$ or $x - 6 = 0$ Zero Product Property

$x = -4$ $x = 6$ Solve for x.

Resource Manager

📁 Workbook and Reproducible Masters

Chapter 10 Resource Masters
• Study Guide and Intervention, pp. 597–598
• Skills Practice, p. 599
• Practice, p. 600
• Reading to Learn Mathematics, p. 601
• Enrichment, p. 602
• Assessment, pp. 635, 637

Parent and Student Study Guide Workbook, p. 78
School-to-Career Masters, p. 20

🖥 Transparencies

5-Minute Check Transparency 10-4
Answer Key Transparencies

💿 Technology

AlgePASS: Tutorial Plus, Lessons 30, 31
Interactive Chalkboard

Method 2 Quadratic Formula

For this equation, $a = 1$, $b = -2$, and $c = -24$.

$$x = \frac{-b \pm \sqrt{b^2 - 4ac}}{2a} \qquad \text{Quadratic Formula}$$

$$= \frac{-(-2) \pm \sqrt{(-2)^2 - 4(1)(-24)}}{2(1)} \qquad a = 1, b = -2, \text{ and } c = -24$$

$$= \frac{2 \pm \sqrt{4 + 96}}{2} \qquad \text{Multiply.}$$

$$= \frac{2 \pm \sqrt{100}}{2} \qquad \text{Add.}$$

$$= \frac{2 \pm 10}{2} \qquad \text{Simplify.}$$

$$x = \frac{2 - 10}{2} \quad \text{or} \quad x = \frac{2 + 10}{2}$$

$$= -4 \qquad\qquad = 6$$

The solution set is $\{-4, 6\}$.

Example 2 *Irrational Roots*

Solve $24x^2 - 14x = 6$ by using the Quadratic Formula. Round to the nearest tenth if necessary.

Step 1 Rewrite the equation in standard form.

$$24x^2 - 14x = 6 \qquad \text{Original equation}$$
$$24x^2 - 14x - 6 = 6 - 6 \qquad \text{Subtract 6 from each side.}$$
$$24x^2 - 14x - 6 = 0 \qquad \text{Simplify.}$$

Step 2 Apply the Quadratic Formula.

$$x = \frac{-b \pm \sqrt{b^2 - 4ac}}{2a} \qquad \text{Quadratic Formula}$$

$$= \frac{-(-14) \pm \sqrt{(-14)^2 - 4(24)(-6)}}{2(24)} \qquad a = 24, b = -14, \text{ and } c = -6$$

$$= \frac{14 \pm \sqrt{196 + 576}}{48} \qquad \text{Multiply.}$$

$$= \frac{14 \pm \sqrt{772}}{48} \qquad \text{Add.}$$

$$x = \frac{14 - \sqrt{772}}{48} \quad \text{or} \quad x = \frac{14 + \sqrt{772}}{48}$$

$$\approx -0.3 \qquad\qquad\qquad \approx 0.9$$

Check the solutions by using the **CALC** menu on a graphing calculator to determine the zeros of the related quadratic function.

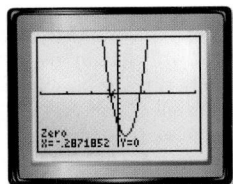 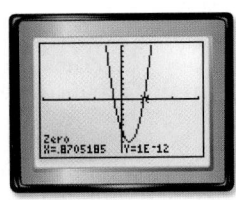

[−3, 3] scl: 1 by [−10. 10] scl: 1   [−3, 3] scl: 1 by [−10. 10] scl: 1

The approximate solution set is $\{-0.3, 0.9\}$.

Lesson 10-4 Solving Quadratic Equations by Using the Quadratic Formula   **547**

---

2 Teach

QUADRATIC FORMULA

Tips for New Teachers

Students may be curious about how the Quadratic Formula is derived. The text explains that it is simply a standard quadratic equation solved for x, but the solution goes beyond the scope of this lesson. When students want to know more about a concept that exceeds the scope of a given lesson, challenge them to research the concept using the library or Internet. When students find the answer, ask them to share it with the class. Students are much more likely to retain a concept that they had to research and explain, than if you simply explain it for them.

In-Class Examples

 Power Point®

Teaching Tip Some students may notice that the trinomial $x^2 - 2x - 24$ can be factored. Explain that for this example, an equation that could be factored was specifically used to demonstrate that the Quadratic Formula produces the correct solutions. Tell students that if they see an easier way (such as factoring) to solve a quadratic equation, then they should use the easier method.

1 Use two methods to solve $x^2 - 2x - 35 = 0$. $\{-5, 7\}$

2 Solve $15x^2 - 8x = 4$ by using the Quadratic Formula. Round to the nearest tenth if necessary. $\{-0.3, 0.8\}$

DAILY INTERVENTION

Differentiated Instruction — ELL

Verbal/Linguistic Have students come up with a riddle, poem, rap, or some other mnemonic device to help them remember how to use the Quadratic Formula, and how to interpret the discriminant. Ask students to share their mnemonic devices with the class.

While the chart on this page offers suggestions for when to use each quadratic method, do not hold students firm to using all methods. Some students do not yet have the mathematical maturity to analyze each equation and the best method to use to save time.

Teaching Tip Tell students that it is best to simplify the Quadratic Formula one step at a time, after the values from the problem have been substituted. For example, it is probably best to simplify under the radical sign first, then find the square root, then simplify the numerator, denominator, and finally perform the division. Trying to skip steps is likely to introduce errors.

3 **SPACE TRAVEL** Two possible future destinations of astronauts are the planet Mars and a moon of the planet Jupiter, Europa. The gravitational acceleration on Mars is about 3.7 meters per second squared and on Europa, it is only 1.3 meters per second squared. Using the information and equation from Example 3 in the text, find how much longer baseballs thrown on Mars and on Europa will stay above the ground than a similarly thrown baseball on Earth. **The ball thrown on Mars will stay aloft about 3.4 seconds longer than the ball thrown on Earth. The ball thrown on Europa will stay aloft 13.4 seconds longer than the ball thrown on Earth.**

You have studied four methods for solving quadratic equations. The table summarizes these methods.

Concept Summary — **Solving Quadratic Equations**

Method	Can Be Used	Comments
graphing	always	Not always exact; use only when an approximate solution is sufficient.
factoring	sometimes	Use if constant term is 0 or factors are easily determined.
completing the square	always	Useful for equations of the form $x^2 + bx + c = 0$, where b is an even number.
Quadratic Formula	always	Other methods may be easier to use in some cases, but this method always gives accurate solutions.

Example 3 **Use the Quadratic Formula to Solve a Problem**

SPACE TRAVEL The height H of an object t seconds after it is propelled upward with an initial velocity v is represented by $H = -\frac{1}{2}gt^2 + vt + h$, where g is the gravitational pull and h is the initial height. Suppose an astronaut on the Moon throws a baseball upward with an initial velocity of 10 meters per second, letting go of the ball 2 meters above the ground. Use the information at the left to find how much longer the ball will stay in the air than a similarly-thrown baseball on Earth.

In order to find when the ball hits the ground, you must find when $H = 0$. Write two equations to represent the situation on the Moon and on Earth.

Baseball Thrown on the Moon

$H = -\frac{1}{2}gt^2 + vt + h$

$0 = -\frac{1}{2}(1.6)t^2 + 10t + 2$

$0 = -0.8t^2 + 10t + 2$

Baseball Thrown on Earth

$H = -\frac{1}{2}gt^2 + vt + h$

$0 = -\frac{1}{2}(9.8)t^2 + 10t + 2$

$0 = -4.9t^2 + 10t + 2$

These equations cannot be factored, and completing the square would involve a lot of computation. To find accurate solutions, use the Quadratic Formula.

$t = \dfrac{-b \pm \sqrt{b^2 - 4ac}}{2a}$

$= \dfrac{-10 \pm \sqrt{10^2 - 4(-0.8)(2)}}{2(-0.8)}$

$= \dfrac{-10 \pm \sqrt{106.4}}{-1.6}$

$t \approx 12.7$ or $t \approx -0.2$

$t = \dfrac{-b \pm \sqrt{b^2 - 4ac}}{2a}$

$= \dfrac{-10 \pm \sqrt{10^2 - 4(-4.9)(2)}}{2(-4.9)}$

$= \dfrac{-10 \pm \sqrt{139.2}}{-9.8}$

$t \approx 2.2$ or $t \approx -0.2$

Since a negative number of seconds is not reasonable, use the positive solutions. Therefore, the baseball will stay in the air about 12.7 seconds on the Moon and about 2.2 seconds on Earth. The baseball will stay in the air about $12.7 - 2.2$ or 10.5 seconds longer on the Moon.

THE DISCRIMINANT In the Quadratic Formula, the expression under the radical sign, $b^2 - 4ac$, is called the **discriminant**. The value of the discriminant can be used to determine the number of real roots for a quadratic equation.

More About . . .

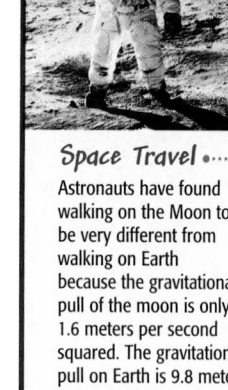

Space Travel

Astronauts have found walking on the Moon to be very different from walking on Earth because the gravitational pull of the moon is only 1.6 meters per second squared. The gravitational pull on Earth is 9.8 meters per second squared.
Source: *World Book Encyclopedia*

Teacher to Teacher

Linda Hayek   Ralston Public Schools, Omaha, NE

"I like for my students to discuss all the different ways that a quadratic equation can be solved before presenting the Concept Summary on page 548. We conduct a class discussion, listing the possibilities and when each type might be used. Then we write our summary in our Foldables."

Discriminant	negative	zero	positive
Example	$2x^2 + x + 3 = 0$ $x = \dfrac{-1 \pm \sqrt{1^2 - 4(2)(3)}}{2(2)}$ $= \dfrac{-1 \pm \sqrt{-23}}{4}$ There are no real roots since no real number can be the square root of a negative number.	$x^2 + 6x + 9 = 0$ $x = \dfrac{-6 \pm \sqrt{6^2 - 4(1)(9)}}{2(1)}$ $= \dfrac{-6 \pm \sqrt{0}}{2}$ $= \dfrac{-6}{2}$ or -3 There is a double root, -3.	$x^2 - 5x + 2 = 0$ $x = \dfrac{-(-5) \pm \sqrt{(-5)^2 - 4(1)(2)}}{2(1)}$ $= \dfrac{5 \pm \sqrt{17}}{2}$ There are two roots, $\dfrac{5 + \sqrt{17}}{2}$ and $\dfrac{5 - \sqrt{17}}{2}$.
Graph of Related Function	$f(x) = 2x^2 + x + 3$ The graph does not cross the x-axis.	$f(x) = x^2 + 6x + 9$ The graph touches the x-axis in one place.	$f(x) = x^2 - 5x + 2$ The graph crosses the x-axis twice.
Number of Real Roots	0	1	2

Example 4   **Use the Discriminant**

State the value of the discriminant for each equation. Then determine the number of real roots of the equation.

a. $2x^2 + 10x + 11 = 0$

$b^2 - 4ac = 10^2 - 4(2)(11)$ $a = 2, b = 10,$ and $c = 11$

         $= 12$ Simplify.

Since the discriminant is positive, the equation has two real roots.

b. $4t^2 - 20t + 25 = 0$

$b^2 - 4ac = (-20)^2 - 4(4)(25)$ $a = 4, b = -20,$ and $c = 25$

         $= 0$ Simplify.

Since the discriminant is 0, the equation has one real root.

c. $3m^2 + 4m = -2$

Step 1   Rewrite the equation in standard form.

           $3m^2 + 4m = -2$ Original equation

     $3m^2 + 4m + 2 = -2 + 2$ Add 2 to each side.

       $3m^2 + 4m + 2 = 0$ Simplify.

Step 2   Find the discriminant.

     $b^2 - 4ac = 4^2 - 4(3)(2)$ $a = 3, b = 4,$ and $c = 2$

            $= -8$ Simplify.

Since the discriminant is negative, the equation has no real roots.

THE DISCRIMINANT

In-Class Example   Power Point®

Teaching Tip Remind students to be careful to include any negative signs when finding the discriminant. One missed negative sign can turn the discriminant from positive to negative, yielding an incorrect result.

4 State the value of the discriminant for each equation. Then determine the number of real roots of the equation.

a. $4x^2 - 2x + 14 = 0$
The discriminant is -220 so the equation has no real roots.

b. $x^2 + 24x = -144$
The discriminant is 0 so the equation has one real root.

c. $3x^2 + 10x = 12$
The discriminant is 244 so the equation has two real roots.

Check for Understanding

Concept Check

2. Sample answer: $x^2 - x + 5 = 0$

3. Juanita; you must first write the equation in the form $ax^2 + bx + c = 0$ to determine the values of a, b, and c. Therefore, the value of c is -2, not 2.

1. **Describe** three different ways to solve $x^2 - 2x - 15 = 0$. Which method do you prefer and why? **See margin.**

2. **OPEN ENDED** Write a quadratic equation with no real solutions.

3. **FIND THE ERROR** Lakeisha and Juanita are determining the number of solutions of $5y^2 - 3y = 2$.

Lakeisha
$5y^2 - 3y = 2$
$b^2 - 4ac = (-3)^2 - 4(5)(2)$
$= -31$
Since the discriminant is negative, there are no real solutions.

Juanita
$5y^2 - 3y = 2$
$5y^2 - 3y - 2 = 0$
$b^2 - 4ac = (-3)^2 - 4(5)(-2)$
$= 49$
Since the discriminant is positive, there are two real roots.

Who is correct? Explain your reasoning.

Guided Practice

GUIDED PRACTICE KEY

Exercises	Examples
4–9	1, 2
10–12	4
13	3

Solve each equation by using the Quadratic Formula. Round to the nearest tenth if necessary. **6. −8.6, −1.4**

4. $x^2 + 7x + 6 = 0$ **−6, −1** 5. $t^2 + 11t = 12$ **−12, 1** 6. $r^2 + 10r + 12 = 0$

7. $3v^2 + 5v + 11 = 0$ **∅** 8. $4x^2 + 2x = 17$ **−2.3, 1.8** 9. $w^2 + \frac{2}{25} = \frac{3}{5}w$ **$\frac{1}{5}, \frac{2}{5}$**

State the value of the discriminant for each equation. Then determine the number of real roots of the equation.

10. $m^2 + 5m - 6 = 0$ **49; 2 real roots** 11. $s^2 + 8s + 16 = 0$ **0; 1 real root** 12. $2z^2 + z = -50$ **−399; no real roots**

Application 13. **MANUFACTURING** A pan is to be formed by cutting 2-centimeter-by-2-centimeter squares from each corner of a square piece of sheet metal and then folding the sides. If the volume of the pan is to be 441 cubic centimeters, what should the dimensions of the original piece of sheet metal be? **about 18.8 cm by 18.8 cm**

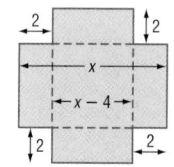

★ indicates increased difficulty

Practice and Apply

Homework Help

For Exercises	See Examples
14–37	1, 2
38–45	4
46–53	3

Extra Practice
See page 842.

26. $-3, -\frac{1}{2}$

27. $-\frac{3}{4}, \frac{5}{6}$

Solve each equation by using the Quadratic Formula. Round to the nearest tenth if necessary. **15. −10, −2** **16. $-1\frac{2}{3}$, 4** **22. −2.9, 2.4** **23. −0.4, 3.9**

14. $x^2 + 3x - 18 = 0$ **−6, 3** 15. $v^2 + 12v + 20 = 0$ 16. $3t^2 - 7t - 20 = 0$

17. $5y^2 - y - 4 = 0$ **$-\frac{4}{5}$, 1** 18. $x^2 - 25 = 0$ **−5, 5** 19. $r^2 + 25 = 0$ **∅**

20. $2x^2 + 98 = 28x$ **7** 21. $4s^2 + 100 = 40s$ **5** 22. $2r^2 + r - 14 = 0$

23. $2n^2 - 7n - 3 = 0$ 24. $5v^2 - 7v = 1$ **−0.1, 1.5** 25. $11z^2 - z = 3$ **−0.5, 0.6**

26. $2w^2 = -(7w + 3)$ 27. $2(12g^2 - g) = 15$ 28. $1.34d^2 - 1.1d = -1.02$ **∅**

29. $-2x^2 + 0.7x = -0.3$ **−0.3, 0.6** 30. $2y^2 - \frac{5}{4}y = \frac{1}{2}$ **−0.3, 0.9** 31. $\frac{1}{2}v^2 - v = \frac{3}{4}$ **−0.6, 2.6**

32. **GEOMETRY** The perimeter of a rectangle is 60 inches. Find the dimensions of the rectangle if its area is 221 square inches. **13 in. by 17 in.**

Answer

1. Sample answer: (1) Factor $x^2 - 2x - 15$ as $(x + 3)(x - 5)$. Then according to the Zero Product Property, either $x + 3 = 0$ or $x - 5 = 0$. Solving these equations, $x = -3$ or $x = 5$. (2) Rewrite the equation as $x^2 - 2x = 15$. Then add 1 to each side of the equation to complete the square on the left side. Then $(x - 1)^2 = 16$. Taking the square root of each side, $x - 1 = \pm 4$. Therefore, $x = 1 \pm 4$ and $x = -3$ or $x = 5$. (3) Use the Quadratic Formula.

Therefore, $x = \dfrac{2 \pm \sqrt{2^2 - 4(1)(-15)}}{2(1)}$ or $x = \dfrac{2 \pm \sqrt{64}}{2}$.

Simplifying the expression, $x = -3$ or $x = 5$. See students' preferences.

33. GEOMETRY Rectangle $ABCD$ has a perimeter of 42 centimeters. What are the dimensions of the rectangle if its area is 80 square centimeters? **5 cm by 16 cm**

34. NUMBER THEORY Find two consecutive odd integers whose product is 255. **−17 and −15 or 15 and 17**

35. NUMBER THEORY The sum of the squares of two consecutive odd numbers is 130. What are the numbers? **−9 and −7 or 7 and 9**

36. Without graphing, determine the x-intercepts of the graph of $f(x) = 4x^2 - 9x + 4$. **about 0.6 and 1.6**

37. Without graphing, determine the x-intercepts of the graph of $f(x) = 13x^2 - 16x - 4$. **about −0.2 and 1.4**

State the value of the discriminant for each equation. Then determine the number of real roots of the equation.

38. $x^2 + 3x - 4 = 0$ **25; 2 real roots**

39. $y^2 + 3y + 1 = 0$

40. $4p^2 + 10p = -6.25$

41. $1.5m^2 + m = -3.5$ **−20; no real roots**

42. $2r^2 = \frac{1}{2}r - \frac{2}{3}$

43. $\frac{4}{3}n^2 + 4n = -3$ **0; 1 real root**

44. Without graphing, determine the number of x-intercepts of the graph of $f(x) = 7x^2 - 3x - 1$. **2**

45. Without graphing, determine the number of x-intercepts of the graph of $f(x) = x^2 + 4x + 7$. **0**

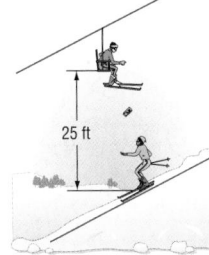

RECREATION For Exercises 46 and 47, use the following information.
As Darius is skiing down a ski slope, Jorge is on the chair lift on the same slope. The chair lift has stopped. Darius stops directly below Jorge and attempts to toss a disposable camera up to him. If the camera is thrown with an initial velocity of 35 feet per second, the equation for the height of the camera is $h = -16t^2 + 35t + 5$, where h represents the height in feet and t represents the time in seconds.

25 ft

46. If the chair lift is 25 feet above the ground, will Jorge have 0, 1, or 2 chances to catch the camera? **0**

47. If Jorge is unable to catch the camera, when will it hit the ground? **about 2.3 s**

48. PHYSICAL SCIENCE A projectile is shot vertically up in the air from ground level. Its distance s, in feet, after t seconds is given by $s = 96t - 16t^2$. Find the values of t when s is 96 feet. **about 1.3 s and 4.7 s**

49. WATER MANAGEMENT Cox's formula for measuring velocity of water draining from a reservoir through a horizontal pipe is $4v^2 + 5v - 2 = \frac{1200HD}{L}$, where v represents the velocity of the water in feet per second, H represents the height of the reservoir in feet, D represents the diameter of the pipe in inches, and L represents the length of the pipe in feet. How fast is water flowing through a pipe 20 feet long with a diameter of 6 inches that is draining a swimming pool with a depth of 10 feet? **about 29.4 ft/s**

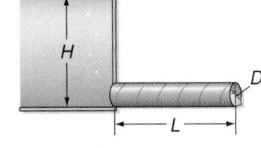

50. CRITICAL THINKING If the graph of $f(x) = ax^2 + 10x + 3$ intersects the x-axis in two places, what must be true about the value of a? $a < 8\frac{1}{3}$

39. 5; 2 real roots
40. 0; 1 real root
42. $-\frac{61}{12}$, no real roots

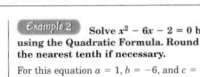

Open-Ended Assessment

Writing Make three large columns on the chalkboard. At the top of the columns, write "Two Real Roots," "One Real Root," and "No Real Roots." Challenge students to come up and write a quadratic equation that fits in the column of your choosing. After each student writes his or her equation, have the class use the discriminant to check whether the student was correct, then use the Quadratic Formula to find the roots (for equations that have real roots).

Getting Ready for Lesson 10-5

PREREQUISITE SKILL Students will learn how to graph exponential functions and identify exponential behavior in Lesson 10-5. In order to graph exponential functions, students must be able to evaluate expressions with exponents. Use Exercises 72–74 to determine your students' familiarity with evaluating expressions with exponents.

Assessment Options

Quiz (Lessons 10-3 and 10-4) is available on p. 635 of the *Chapter 10 Resource Masters*.

Mid-Chapter Test (Lessons 10-1 through 10-4) is available on p. 637 of the *Chapter 10 Resource Masters*.

Answers

60.

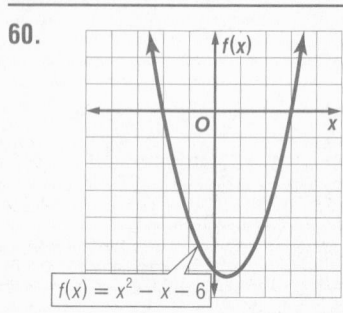

CANCER STATISTICS For Exercises 51–53, use the following information.
A decrease in smoking in the United States has resulted in lower death rates caused by cancer. In 1965, 42% of adults smoked, compared with less than 25% in 1995. The number of deaths per 100,000 people y can be approximated by $y = -0.048x^2 + 1.87x + 154$, where x represents the number of years after 1970.

★ 51. Use the Quadratic Formula to solve for x when $y = 150$. **about 41 yr**

★ 52. In what year would you expect the death rate from cancer to be 150 per 100,000? **2011**

53. 2049; Sample answer: No; the death rate from cancer will never be 0 unless a cure is found. If and when a cure will be found cannot be predicted.

★ 53. According to the quadratic function, when will the death rate from cancer be 0 per 100,000? Do you think that the prediction is valid? Why or why not?

54.  Answer the question that was posed at the beginning of the lesson. **See pp. 581A–581H.**

How can the Quadratic Formula be used to solve problems involving population trends?

Include the following in your answer:
- a step-by-step solution of $15 = 0.0055t^2 - 0.0796t + 5.2810$ with justification of each step, and
- an explanation for why the Quadratic Formula is the best way to solve this equation.

Standardized Test Practice
Ⓐ Ⓑ Ⓒ Ⓓ

55. Determine the number of solutions of $x^2 - 5x + 8 = 0$. **A**
- Ⓐ 0
- Ⓑ 1
- Ⓒ 2
- Ⓓ infinitely many

56. Which expression represents the solutions of $2x^2 + 5x + 1 = 0$? **C**
- Ⓐ $\dfrac{5 \pm \sqrt{17}}{4}$
- Ⓑ $\dfrac{5 \pm \sqrt{33}}{4}$
- Ⓒ $\dfrac{-5 \pm \sqrt{17}}{4}$
- Ⓓ $\dfrac{-5 \pm \sqrt{33}}{4}$

Maintain Your Skills

Mixed Review

Solve each equation by completing the square. Round to the nearest tenth if necessary. *(Lesson 10-3)*

57. $x^2 - 8x = -7$ **1, 7**
58. $a^2 + 2a + 5 = 20$ **−5, 3**
59. $n^2 - 12n = 5$ **−0.4, 12.4**

60–62. See margin for graphs.

Solve each equation by graphing. If integral roots cannot be found, estimate the roots by stating the consecutive integers between which the roots lie. *(Lesson 10-2)*

60. $x^2 - x = 6$ **−2, 3**
61. $2x^2 + x = 2$ **$-2 < x < -1, 0 < x < 1$**
62. $-x^2 + 3x + 6 = 0$ **$-2 < x < -1, 4 < x < 5$**

Factor each polynomial. *(Lesson 9-2)*

63. $15xy^3 + y^4$ **$y^3(15x + y)$**
64. $2ax + 6xc + ba + 3bc$ **$(2x + b)(a + 3c)$**

65. **SCIENCE** The mass of a proton is 0.00000000000000000000001672 milligram. Write this number in scientific notation. *(Lesson 8-3)* **1.672×10^{-21}**

Graph each system of inequalities. *(Lesson 7-5)* **66–68. See pp. 581A–581H.**

66. $x \le 2$
$y + 4 \ge 5$

67. $x + y > 2$
$x - y \le 2$

68. $y > x$
$y \le x + 4$

70. $\left\{x \mid x \le -1\tfrac{1}{3}\right\}$

Solve each inequality. Then check your solution. *(Lesson 6-3)*

69. $2m + 7 > 17$
$\{m \mid m > 5\}$
70. $-2 - 3x \ge 2$
71. $-20 \ge 8 + 7k$
$\{k \mid k \le -4\}$

Getting Ready for the Next Lesson

PREREQUISITE SKILL Evaluate $c(a^x)$ for each of the given values.
(To review evaluating expressions with exponents, see Lesson 1-1.)

72. $a = 2, c = 1, x = 4$ **16**
73. $a = 7, c = 3, x = 2$ **147**
74. $a = 5, c = 2, x = 3$ **250**

61.

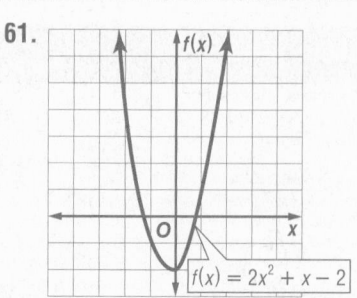

62.

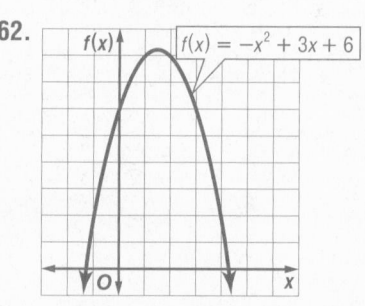

Graphing Calculator Investigation

A Follow-Up of Lesson 10-4

Solving Quadratic-Linear Systems

Since you can graph multiple functions on a graphing calculator, it is a useful tool when finding the intersection points or solutions of a system of equations in which one equation is quadratic and one is linear.

Solve the following quadratic-linear system of equations.
$$y + 1 = x$$
$$y = -x^2 + 2x + 5$$

Step 1 *Solve each equation for y.*
- $y + 1 = x$
  $$y = x - 1$$
- $y = -x^2 + 2x + 5$

Step 2 *Graph the equations on the same screen.*
- Enter $y = x - 1$ as Y₁.
- Enter $y = -x^2 + 2x + 5$ as Y₂.
- Graph both in the standard viewing window.

Step 3 *Approximate the intersection point.*
- Use the intersect option on the **CALC** menu to approximate the first intersection point.

  KEYSTROKES: [2nd] [CALC] 5 [ENTER] [ENTER] [ENTER]

Step 4 *Approximate the other intersection point.*
- Use the **TRACE** feature with the right and left arrow keys to move the cursor near the other intersection point.
- Use the **intersect** option on the **CALC** menu to approximate the other intersection point.

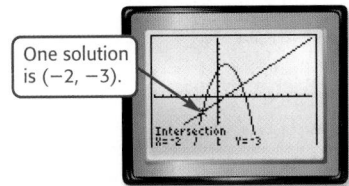

One solution is (−2, −3).

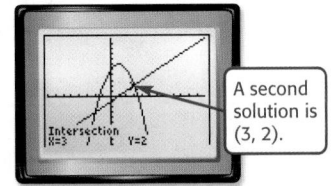

A second solution is (3, 2).

Thus, the solutions of the quadratic-linear system are (−2, −3) and (3, 2).

Exercises

Use the intersect feature to solve each quadratic-linear system of equations. State any decimal solutions to the nearest tenth.

1. $y = -2(2x + 3)$
   $y = x^2 + 2x + 3$ **(−3, 6)**

2. $y - 5 = 0$
   $y = -x^2$ **no solution**

3. $1.8x + y = 3.6$
   $y = x^2 - 3x - 1$ **(−1.6, 6.5), (2.8, −1.5)**

4. $y = -1.4x - 2.88$
   $y = x^2 + 0.4x - 3.14$ **(−1.9, −0.2), (0.1, −3.1)**

5. $y = x^2 - 3.5x + 2.2$
   $y = 2x - 5.3625$ **(2.8, 0.1)**

6. $y = 0.35x - 1.648$
   $y = -0.2x^2 + 0.28x + 1.01$
   (−3.8, −3.0), (3.5, −0.4)

 www.algebra1.com/other_calculator_keystrokes

Graphing Calculator Investigation 553

Getting Started

Know Your Calculator It is important for students to differentiate between the ⊟ and ⊟ keys when entering equations. To enter the expression $x - 1$, press [X,T,θ,n] ⊟ 1. However, to enter $-x^2$, press ⊟ [X,T,θ,n] [x²].

Teach

- Tell students to select the intersection that they want the calculator to estimate by moving the cursor after pressing [2nd] [CALC] 5. Then press [ENTER] [ENTER] [ENTER].

Assess

Have students explain what must occur for there to be no solutions to a quadratic-linear system of equations. **The graph of the linear equation must be either above the vertex of the quadratic graph if the parabola opens downward, or below the vertex if the parabola opens upward.**

10-5 Exponential Functions

1 Focus

5-Minute Check Transparency 10-5 Use as a quiz or review of Lesson 10-4.

Mathematical Background notes are available for this lesson on p. 522D.

How can exponential functions be used in art?

Ask students:

• What happens to the number of pliers in each level? **It doubles.**

• How many pliers would there be in a ninth level? In a tenth level? **There would be 512 pliers in a ninth level and 1024 in a tenth level.**

• Suppose Mr. Warther carved pliers for powers of 3. By how much would the number of pliers increase at each level? **The number of pliers would increase by three times in each level.**

• How many pliers would be on the eighth level if each level is a power of three? **6561 pliers**

10-5 Exponential Functions

What You'll Learn

• Graph exponential functions.
• Identify data that displays exponential behavior.

Vocabulary

• exponential function

How can exponential functions be used in art?

Earnest "Mooney" Warther was a whittler and a carver. For one of his most unusual carvings, Mooney carved a large pair of pliers in a tree.

From this original carving, he carved another pair of pliers in each handle of the original. Then he carved another pair of pliers in each of those handles. He continued this pattern to create the original pliers and 8 more layers of pliers. Even more amazing is the fact that all of the pliers work.

The number of pliers on each level is given in the table below.

Level	Number of Pliers	Power of 2
Original	1	2^0
First	$1(2) = 2$	2^1
Second	$2(2) = 4$	2^2
Third	$2(2)(2) = 8$	2^3
Fourth	$2(2)(2)(2) = 16$	2^4
Fifth	$2(2)(2)(2)(2) = 32$	2^5
Sixth	$2(2)(2)(2)(2)(2) = 64$	2^6
Seventh	$2(2)(2)(2)(2)(2)(2) = 128$	2^7
Eighth	$2(2)(2)(2)(2)(2)(2)(2) = 256$	2^8

GRAPH EXPONENTIAL FUNCTIONS Study the Power of 2 column. Notice that the exponent number matches the level. So we can write an equation to describe y, the number of pliers for any given level x as $y = 2^x$. This type of function, in which the variable is the exponent, is called an **exponential function**.

Key Concept	Exponential Function

An exponential function is a function that can be described by an equation of the form $y = a^x$, where $a > 0$ and $a \neq 1$.

As with other functions, you can use ordered pairs to graph an exponential function.

Resource Manager

 **Workbook and Reproducible Masters**

Chapter 10 Resource Masters
• Study Guide and Intervention, pp. 603–604
• Skills Practice, p. 605
• Practice, p. 606
• Reading to Learn Mathematics, p. 607
• Enrichment, p. 608

Graphing Calculator and Spreadsheet Masters, p. 42
Parent and Student Study Guide Workbook, p. 79

 Transparencies

5-Minute Check Transparency 10-5
Answer Key Transparencies

 Technology

Interactive Chalkboard

Example 1 *Graph an Exponential Function with a > 1*

a. Graph $y = 4^x$. State the y-intercept.

x	4^x	y
−2	4^{-2}	$\frac{1}{16}$
−1	4^{-1}	$\frac{1}{4}$
0	4^0	1
1	4^1	4
2	4^2	16
3	4^3	64

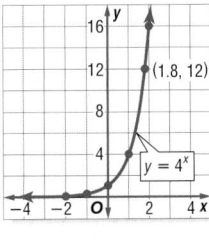

Graph the ordered pairs and connect the points with a smooth curve. The y-intercept is 1. *Notice that the y values change little for small values of x, but they increase quickly as the values of x become greater.*

b. Use the graph to determine the approximate value of $4^{1.8}$.

The graph represents all real values of x and their corresponding values of y for $y = 4^x$. So, the value of y is about 12 when $x = 1.8$. Use a calculator to confirm this value.

$$4^{1.8} \approx 12.12573252$$

The graphs of functions of the form $y = a^x$, where $a > 1$, all have the same shape as the graph in Example 1, rising faster and faster as you move from left to right.

Example 2 *Graph Exponential Functions with 0 < a < 1*

a. Graph $y = \left(\frac{1}{2}\right)^x$. State the y-intercept.

x	$\left(\frac{1}{2}\right)^x$	y
−3	$\left(\frac{1}{2}\right)^{-3}$	8
−2	$\left(\frac{1}{2}\right)^{-2}$	4
−1	$\left(\frac{1}{2}\right)^{-1}$	2
0	$\left(\frac{1}{2}\right)^0$	1
1	$\left(\frac{1}{2}\right)^1$	$\frac{1}{2}$
2	$\left(\frac{1}{2}\right)^2$	$\frac{1}{4}$

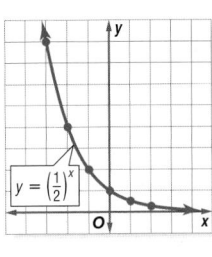

Graph the ordered pairs and connect the points with a smooth curve. The y-intercept is 1. *Notice that the y values decrease less rapidly as x increases.*

b. Use the graph to determine the approximate value of $\left(\frac{1}{2}\right)^{-2.5}$.

The value of y is about $5\frac{1}{2}$ when $x = -2.5$. Use a calculator to confirm this value.

$$\left(\frac{1}{2}\right)^{-2.5} \approx 5.656854249$$

 www.algebra1.com/extra_examples

GRAPH EXPONENTIAL FUNCTIONS

In-Class Examples Power Point®

Teaching Tip Make sure students understand that the graph of this exponential function never actually touches the x-axis. It is acceptable for hand-drawn graphs to show the graph just above and about parallel to the x-axis as long as students understand that it gets infinitely closer to the axis without touching it.

1

a. Graph $y = 3^x$. State the y-intercept. 1

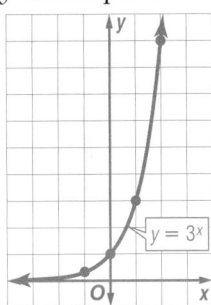

b. Use the graph to determine the approximate value of $3^{1.5}$. about 5

2

a. Graph $y = \left(\frac{1}{4}\right)^x$. State the y-intercept. 1

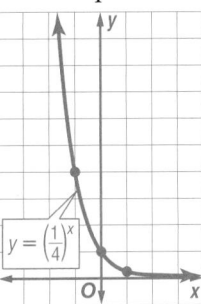

b. Use the graph to determine the approximate value of $\left(\frac{1}{4}\right)^{-1.5}$. 8

3 DEPRECIATION People joke that the value of a new car decreases as soon as it is driven off the dealer's lot. The function $V = 25{,}000 \cdot 0.82^t$ models the depreciation of the value of a new car that originally cost \$25,000. V represents the value of the car and t represents the time in years from the time the car was purchased.

a. Graph the function. What values of V and t are meaningful in the function?

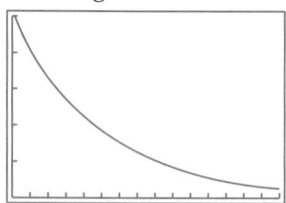

[0,15] scl: 1 by [0,25000] scl: 5000

Only values of $V \leq 25{,}000$ and $t \geq 0$ are meaningful in the problem.

b. What is the value of the car after one year? **After one year the car's value is about \$20,500.**

c. What is the value of the car after five years? **After five years the car's value is about \$9,270.**

Graphing Calculator Investigation

Transformations of Exponential Functions

You can use a graphing calculator to study families of graphs of exponential functions. For example, the graph at the right shows the graphs of $y = 2^x$, $y = 3 \cdot 2^x$, and $y = 0.5 \cdot 2^x$. Notice that the y-intercept of $y = 2^x$ is 1, the y-intercept of $y = 3 \cdot 2^x$ is 3, and the y-intercept of $y = 0.5 \cdot 2^x$ is 0.5. The graph of $y = 3 \cdot 2^x$ is steeper than the graph of $y = 2^x$. The graph of $y = 0.5 \cdot 2^x$ is not as steep as the graph of $y = 2^x$.

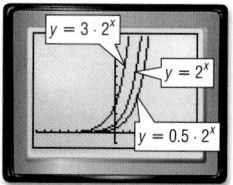

[−10, 10] scl: 1 by [−1, 10] scl: 1

Think and Discuss

Graph each family of equations on the same screen. Compare and contrast the graphs. 1–4. See pp. 581A–581H.

1. $y = 2^x$
$y = 2^x + 3$
$y = 2^x - 4$

2. $y = 2^x$
$y = 2^{x+5}$
$y = 2^{x-4}$

3. $y = 2^x$
$y = 3^x$
$y = 5^x$

4. $y = 3 \cdot 2^x$
$y = 3(2^x - 1)$
$y = 3(2^x + 1)$

Example 3 *Use Exponential Functions to Solve Problems*

MOTION PICTURES Movies tend to have their best ticket sales the first weekend after their release. The sales then follow a decreasing exponential function each successive weekend after the opening. The function $E = 49.9 \cdot 0.692^w$ models the earnings of a popular movie. In this equation, E represents earnings in millions of dollars and w represents the weekend number.

a. Graph the function. What values of E and w are meaningful in the context of the problem?

Use a graphing calculator to graph the function. Only values where $E \leq 49.9$ and $w > 0$ are meaningful in the context of the problem.

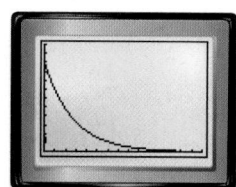

[0, 15] scl: 1 by [0, 60] scl: 5

b. How much did the movie make on the first weekend?

$E = 49.9 \cdot 0.692^w$ Original equation

$E = 49.9 \cdot 0.692^1$ $w = 1$

$E = 34.5308$ Use a calculator.

On the first weekend, the movie grossed about \$34.53 million.

c. How much did it make on the fifth weekend?

$E = 49.9 \cdot 0.692^w$ Original equation

$E = 49.9 \cdot 0.692^5$ $w = 5$

$E \approx 7.918282973$ Use a calculator.

On the fifth weekend, the movie grossed about \$7.92 million.

More About. . .

Motion Pictures

The first successful photographs of motion were made in 1877. Today, the motion picture industry is big business, with the highest-grossing movie making \$600,800,000.

Source: *World Book Encyclopedia*

Graphing Calculator Investigation

Transformations of Exponential Functions Most of the graphs in this investigation will be visible in the standard viewing window, which is set by pressing ZOOM 6.

Suggest that students record their findings in their Study Notebooks, to help them remember how manipulating the exponential function affects the exponential graphs.

IDENTIFY EXPONENTIAL BEHAVIOR How do you know if a set of data is exponential? One method is to observe the shape of the graph. But the graph of an exponential function may resemble part of the graph of a quadratic function. Another way is to use the problem-solving strategy *look for a pattern* with the data.

Example 4 Identify Exponential Behavior

Determine whether each set of data displays exponential behavior.

a.

x	0	10	20	30	40	50
y	80	40	20	10	5	2.5

Method 1 Look for a Pattern

The domain values are at regular intervals of 10. Let's see if there is a common factor among the range values.

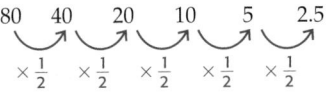

Since the domain values are at regular intervals and the range values have a common factor, the data are probably exponential. The equation for the data may involve $\left(\frac{1}{2}\right)^x$.

Method 2 Graph the Data

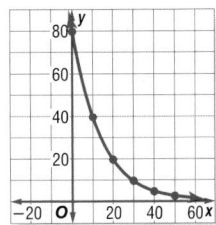

The graph shows a rapidly decreasing value of y as x increases. This is a characteristic of exponential behavior.

b.

x	0	10	20	30	40	50
y	15	21	27	33	39	45

Method 1 Look for a Pattern

The domain values are at regular intervals of 10. The range values have a common difference 6.

The data do not display exponential behavior, but rather linear behavior.

Method 2 Graph the Data

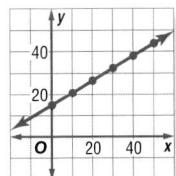

This is a graph of a line, not an exponential function.

Check for Understanding

Concept Check **1. Determine** whether the graph of $y = a^x$, where $a > 0$ and $a \neq 1$, *sometimes*, *always*, or *never* has an x-intercept. **never**

2. OPEN ENDED Write an exponential function and graph the function. Describe the graph. **See margin.**

Lesson 10-5 Exponential Functions **557**

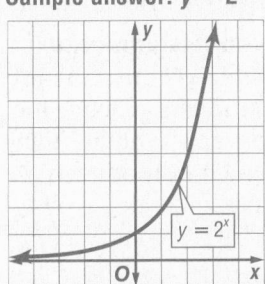

DAILY
INTERVENTION **FIND THE ERROR**
If students have trouble with this problem, suggest that they multiply $\frac{1}{3} \times \frac{1}{3}$ and then $\frac{1}{3} \times \frac{1}{3} \times \frac{1}{3}$. Does the product get larger or smaller as the exponent increases?

About the Exercises …
Organization by Objective
• **Graph Exponential Functions:** 13–26, 34
• **Identify Exponential Behavior:** 27–32

Odd/Even Assignments
Exercises 13–32 are structured so that students practice the same concepts whether they are assigned odd or even problems.

Assignment Guide
Basic: 13–21 odd, 25–31 odd, 33–35, 42–64

Average: 13–31 odd, 37–39, 42–64

Advanced: 14–32 even, 36–60 (optional: 61–64)

All: Practice Quiz 2 (1–5)

---

3. Kiski; the graph of $y = \left(\frac{1}{3}\right)^x$ decreases as x increases.

3. **FIND THE ERROR** Amalia and Kiski are graphing $y = \left(\frac{1}{3}\right)^x$.

Amalia 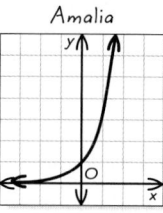   Kiski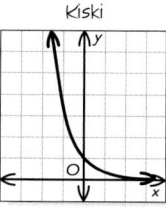

Who is correct? Explain your reasoning.

Guided Practice

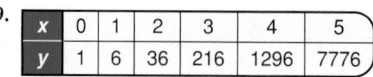

GUIDED PRACTICE KEY

Exercises	Examples
4–8	1, 2
9, 10	4
11, 12	3

4–8. See pp. 581A–581H for graphs.

Graph each function. State the y-intercept. Then use the graph to determine the approximate value of the given expression. Use a calculator to confirm the value.

4. $y = 3^x$; $3^{1.2}$ **1; 3.7**   5. $y = \left(\frac{1}{4}\right)^x$; $\left(\frac{1}{4}\right)^{1.7}$ **1; 0.1**   6. $y = 9^x$; $9^{0.8}$ **1; 5.8**

Graph each function. State the y-intercept.

7. $y = 2 \cdot 3^x$ **2**   8. $y = 4(5^x - 10)$ **−36**

Determine whether the data in each table display exponential behavior. Explain why or why not.

9.

x	0	1	2	3	4	5
y	1	6	36	216	1296	7776

Yes; the domain values are at regular intervals and the range values have a common factor 6.

10.

x	4	6	8	10	12	14
y	5	9	13	17	21	25

No; the domain values are at regular intervals and the range values have a common difference 4.

Application

FOLKLORE For Exercises 11 and 12, use the following information.
A wise man asked his ruler to provide rice for feeding his people. Rather than receiving a constant daily supply of rice, the wise man asked the ruler to give him 2 grains of rice for the first square on a chessboard, 4 grains for the second, 8 grains for the third, 16 for the fourth, and so on doubling the amount of rice with each square of the board.

11. How many grains of rice will the wise man receive for the last (64th) square on the chessboard? **about 1.84×10^{19} grains**

12. If one pound of rice has approximately 24,000 grains, how many tons of rice will the wise man receive on the last day? (*Hint:* one ton = 2000 pounds) **about 3.84×10^{11} tons**

★ indicates increased difficulty

Practice and Apply

Homework Help

For Exercises	See Examples
13–26	1, 2
27–32	4
33–41	3

Extra Practice
See page 843.

Graph each function. State the y-intercept. Then use the graph to determine the approximate value of the given expression. Use a calculator to confirm the value.

13. $y = 5^x$; $5^{1.1}$ **1; 5.9**   14. $y = 10^x$; $10^{0.3}$ **1; 2.0**   15. $y = \left(\frac{1}{10}\right)^x$; $\left(\frac{1}{10}\right)^{-1.3}$ **1; 20.0**

16. $y = \left(\frac{1}{5}\right)^x$; $\left(\frac{1}{5}\right)^{0.5}$ **1; 0.4**   17. $y = 6^x$; $6^{0.3}$ **1; 1.7**   18. $y = 8^x$; $8^{0.8}$ **1; 5.3**

13–18. See pp. 581A–581H for graphs.

Graph each function. State the y-intercept. 19–26. See pp. 581A–581H for graphs.

19. $y = 5(2^x)$ **5**   20. $y = 3(5^x)$ **3**   21. $y = 3^x - 7$ **−6**   22. $y = 2^x + 4$ **5**

★ 23. $y = 2(3^x) - 1$ **1**   24. $y = 5(2^x) + 4$ **9**   25. $y = 2(3^x + 1)$ **4**   26. $y = 3(2^x - 5)$ **−12**

558 **Chapter 10** Quadratic and Exponential Functions

Answers

34.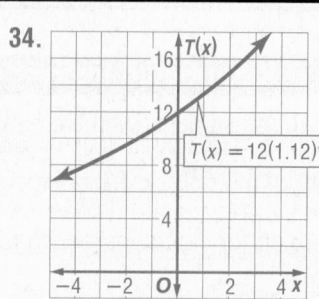

$T(x) = 12(1.12)^x$

42. a reflection over the y-axis

43. a translation 2 units up

44. a translation 4 units down

27. No; the domain values are at regular intervals and the range values have a common difference 3.

28. Yes; the domain values are at regular intervals and the range values have a common factor 0.5.

29. Yes; the domain values are at regular intervals and the range values have a common factor 0.75.

30. No; the domain values are at regular intervals, but the range values do not have a positive common factor.

31. No; the domain values are at regular intervals, but the range values do not change.

More About...

Training •••••
The first Boston Marathon was held in 1896. The distance of this race was based on the Greek legend that Pheidippides ran 24.8 miles from Marathon to Athens to bring the news of victory over the Persian army.

Source: www.bostonmarathon.org

32. Yes; the domain values are at regular intervals and the range values have a common ratio 0.5.

33. about $37.27 million; about $41.74 million; about $46.75 million

---

Determine whether the data in each table display exponential behavior. Explain why or why not.

27.

x	−2	−1	0	1
y	−5	−2	1	4

28.

x	0	1	2	3
y	1	0.5	0.25	0.125

29.

x	10	20	30	40
y	16	12	9	6.75

30.

x	−1	0	1	2
y	−0.5	1.0	−2.0	4.0

31.

x	3	6	9	12
y	5	5	5	5

32.

x	5	3	1	−1
y	32	16	8	4

BUSINESS For Exercises 33–35, use the following information.
The amount of money spent at West Outlet Mall in Midtown continues to increase. The total $T(x)$ in millions of dollars can be estimated by the function $T(x) = 12(1.12)^x$, where x is the number of years after it opened in 1995.

33. According to the function, find the amount of sales for the mall in the years 2005, 2006, and 2007.

34. Graph the function and name the y-intercept. **See margin for graph; 12.**

35. What does the y-intercept represent in this problem? **$12 million sales in 1995**

36. BIOLOGY Mitosis is a process of cell reproduction in which one cell divides into two identical cells. *E. coli* is a fast-growing bacterium that is often responsible for food poisoning in uncooked meat. It can reproduce itself in 15 minutes. If you begin with 100 *E. coli* bacteria, how many will there be in one hour? **1600 bacteria**

TOURNAMENTS For Exercises 37–39, use the following information.
In a regional quiz bowl competition, three schools compete and the winner advances to the next round. Therefore, after each round, only $\frac{1}{3}$ of the schools remain in the competition for the next round. Suppose 729 schools start the competition.

37. Write an exponential function to describe the number of schools remaining after x rounds. $y = 729\left(\frac{1}{3}\right)^x$

38. How many schools are left after 3 rounds? **27 schools**

★ **39.** How many rounds will it take to declare a champion? **6 rounds**

••• **TRAINING** For Exercises 40 and 41, use the following information.
A runner is training for a marathon, running a total of 20 miles per week on a regular basis. She plans to increase the distance $D(x)$ in miles according to the function $D(x) = 20(1.1)^x$, where x represents the number of weeks of training.

40. Copy and complete the table showing the number of miles she plans to run.

★ **41.** The runner's goal is to work up to 50 miles per week. What is the first week that the total will be 50 miles or more? **10th week**

Week	Distance (miles)
1	22
2	24.2
3	26.62
4	29.282

CRITICAL THINKING Describe the graph of each equation as a transformation of the graph of $y = 5^x$. **42–44. See margin.**

42. $y = \left(\frac{1}{5}\right)^x$

43. $y = 5^x + 2$

44. $y = 5^x - 4$

www.algebra1.com/self_check_quiz

Lesson 10-5 Exponential Functions **559**

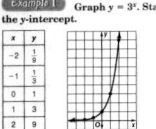
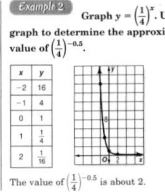
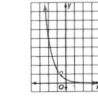
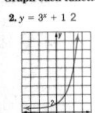  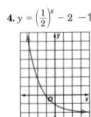
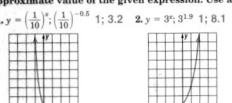 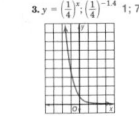
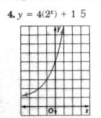 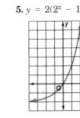 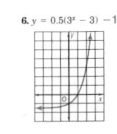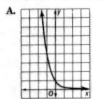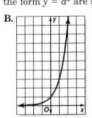

Lesson 10-5 Exponential Functions **559**

Open-Ended Assessment

Modeling Using a piece of string and a coordinate grid, model different exponential functions on an overhead projector. Have students identify the y-intercept and try to identify the actual functions that you have graphed.

Getting Ready for Lesson 10-6

PREREQUISITE SKILL Students will learn about growth and decay in Lesson 10-6. Growth and decay problems involve exponential functions. Use Exercises 61–64 to determine your students' familiarity with evaluating expressions with exponents.

Assessment Options

Practice Quiz 2 The quiz provides students with a brief review of the concepts and skills in Lessons 10-4 and 10-5. Lesson numbers are given to the right of exercises or instruction lines so students can review concepts not yet mastered.

Answers

45. If the number of items on each level of a piece of art is a given number times the number of items on the previous level, an exponential function can be used to describe the situation. Answers should include the following.
   - For the carving of the pliers, $y = 2^x$.
   - For this situation, x is an integer between 0 and 8 inclusive. The values of y are 1, 2, 4, 8, 16, 32, 64, 128, and 256.
   -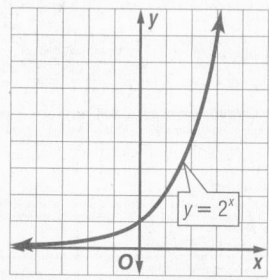

---

45. **WRITING IN MATH** Answer the question that was posed at the beginning of the lesson. **See margin.**

   How can exponential functions be used in art?

   Include the following in your answer:
   - the exponential function representing the pliers,
   - an explanation of which x and y values are meaningful, and
   - the graph of this function.

Standardized Test Practice Ⓐ Ⓑ Ⓒ Ⓓ

46. Which function is an exponential function? **B**
   - Ⓐ $f(x) = x^2$
   - Ⓒ $f(x) = x^5$
   - Ⓑ $f(x) = 6^x$
   - Ⓓ $f(x) = x^3 + 2x^2 - x + 5$

47. Compare the graphs of $y = 2^x$ and $y = 6^x$. **A**
   - Ⓐ The graph of $y = 6^x$ steeper than the graph of $y = 2^x$.
   - Ⓑ The graph of $y = 2^x$ steeper than the graph of $y = 6^x$.
   - Ⓒ The graph of $y = 6^x$ is the graph of $y = 2^x$ translated 4 units up.
   - Ⓓ The graph of $y = 6^x$ is the graph of $y = 2^x$ translated 3 units up.

Maintain Your Skills

Mixed Review Solve each equation by using the Quadratic Formula. Round to the nearest tenth if necessary. *(Lesson 10-4)* **48. −3, 12   49. −1.8, 0.3**

48. $x^2 - 9x - 36 = 0$ 49. $2t^2 + 3t - 1 = 0$ 50. $5y^2 + 3 = y$ **∅**

Solve each equation by completing the square. Round to the nearest tenth if necessary. *(Lesson 10-3)* **52. −0.2, 12.2   53. −5.4, −0.6**

51. $x^2 - 7x = -10$ **2, 5**   52. $a^2 - 12a = 3$ 53. $t^2 + 6t + 3 = 0$

Factor each trinomial, if possible. If the trinomial cannot be factored using integers, write *prime*. *(Lesson 9-3)* **54. $(m - 4)(m - 10)$ 56. $(z - 8)(z + 3)$**

54. $m^2 - 14m + 40$ 55. $t^2 - 2t + 35$ **prime**   56. $z^2 - 5z - 24$

57. Three times one number equals twice a second number. Twice the first number is 3 more than the second number. Find the numbers. *(Lesson 7-4)* **6, 9**

Solve each inequality. *(Lesson 6-1)*

58. $x + 7 > 2$ $\{x \mid x > -5\}$ 59. $10 \geq x + 8$ $\{x \mid x \leq 2\}$ 60. $y - 7 < -12$ $\{y \mid y < -5\}$

Getting Ready for the Next Lesson **PREREQUISITE SKILL** Evaluate $p(1 + r)^t$ for each of the given values.
*(To review **evaluating expressions with exponents**, see Lesson 1-1.)*

61. $p = 5, r = \frac{1}{2}, t = 2$ **11.25**   62. $p = 300, r = \frac{1}{4}, t = 3$ **585.9375**

63. $p = 100, r = 0.2, t = 2$ **144**   64. $p = 6, r = 0.5, t = 3$ **20.25**

Practice Quiz 2 | Lessons 10-4 and 10-5

Solve each equation by using the Quadratic Formula. Round to the nearest tenth if necessary. *(Lesson 10-4)*

1. $x^2 + 2x = 35$ **−7, 5**   2. $2n^2 - 3n + 5 = 0$ **∅**   3. $2v^2 - 4v = 1$ **−0.2, 2.2**

Graph each function. State the y-intercept. *(Lesson 10-5)* **4–5. See margin for graphs.**

4. $y = 0.5(4^x)$ **0.5**   5. $y = 5^x - 4$ **−3**

Answers, Practice Quiz 2

4.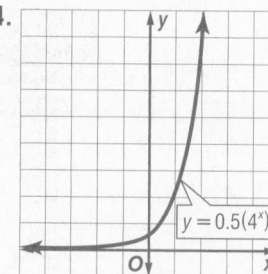

5.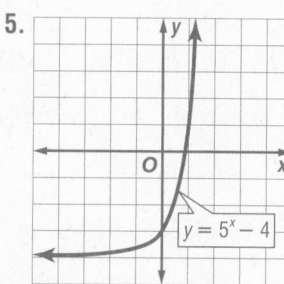

What You'll Learn

- Solve problems involving exponential growth.
- Solve problems involving exponential decay.

Vocabulary
- exponential growth
- compound interest
- exponential decay

How can exponential growth be used to predict future sales?

The graph shows that the average household in the United States has increased its spending for restaurant meals. In fact, the amount grew at an annual rate of about 4.6% between 1994 and 1998. Let y represent the average amount spent on restaurant meals, and let t represent the number of years since 1994. Then the average amount spent on restaurant meals can be modeled by $y = 1698(1 + 0.046)^t$ or $y = 1698(1.046)^t$.

USA TODAY Snapshots®

Spending more on eating out
Annual spending on eating out, by year, for an average household of 2.5 people:

$1,698 $1,702 $1,823 $1,921 $2,030

1994 1995 1996 1997 1998

Source: Bureau of Labor Statistics consumer expenditure surveys

By Mark Pearson and Sam Ward, USA TODAY

EXPONENTIAL GROWTH The equation for the average amount spent on restaurant meals is in the form $y = C(1 + r)^t$. This is the general equation for **exponential growth** in which the initial amount C increases by the same percent over a given period of time.

Key Concept   General Equation for Exponential Growth

The general equation for exponential growth is $y = C(1 + r)^t$ where y represents the final amount, C represents the initial amount, r represents the rate of change expressed as a decimal, and t represents time.

Example 1 Exponential Growth

SPORTS In 1971, there were 294,105 females participating in high school sports. Since then, that number has increased an average of 8.5% per year.

a. **Write an equation to represent the number of females participating in high school sports since 1971.**

$y = C(1 + r)^t$ General equation for exponential growth

$y = 294{,}105(1 + 0.085)^t$ $C = 294{,}105$ and $r = 8.5\%$ or 0.085

$y = 294{,}105(1.085)^t$ Simplify.

An equation to represent the number of females participating in high school sports is $y = 294{,}105(1.085)^t$, where y represents the number of female athletes and t represents the number of years since 1971.

(continued on the next page)

 www.algebra1.com/extra_examples   **Lesson 10-6** Growth and Decay   **561**

Workbook and Reproducible Masters

Chapter 10 Resource Masters
- Study Guide and Intervention, pp. 609–610
- Skills Practice, p. 611
- Practice, p. 612
- Reading to Learn Mathematics, p. 613
- Enrichment, p. 614
- Assessment, p. 636

Parent and Student Study Guide Workbook, p. 80
Science and Mathematics Lab Manual, p. 77–80

1 Focus

5-Minute Check Transparency 10-6 Use as a quiz or review of Lesson 10-5.

Mathematical Background notes are available for this lesson on p. 522D.

How can exponential growth be used to predict future sales?

Ask students:

- Looking at the graph, the function looks very linear. How do you know it is not linear? **The y value increases by the factor 1.046 each year. Since the values increase by a common factor, the function is exponential.**

- Explain why the function looks so linear on the graph, even though it is an exponential function. **The function looks linear because the common factor is so close to one, and the range of x values is small.**

Resource Manager

 Transparencies
5-Minute Check Transparency 10-6
Real-World Transparency 10
Answer Key Transparencies

Technology
Interactive Chalkboard

EXPONENTIAL GROWTH

In-Class Examples Power Point®

1 POPULATION In 2000, the United States had a population of about 280 million, and a growth rate of about 0.85% per year.

a. Write an equation to represent the population of the United States since the year 2000.
$y = 280,000,000(1.0085)^t$

b. According to the equation, what will be the population of the United States in the year 2010? **about 304,731,295**

2 COMPOUND INTEREST When Jing May was born, her grandparents invested $1000 in a fixed rate savings account at a rate of 7% compounded annually. The money will go to Jing May when she turns 18 to help with her college expenses. What amount of money will Jing May receive from the investment? **She will receive about $3380.**

EXPONENTIAL DECAY

In-Class Example Power Point®

3 CHARITY During an economic recession, a charitable organization found that its donations dropped by 1.1% per year. Before the recession, its donations were $390,000.

a. Write an equation to represent the charity's donations since the beginning of the recession.
$A = 390,000(0.989)^t$

b. Estimate the amount of the donations 5 years after the start of the recession. **about $369,017**

---

b. According to the equation, how many females participated in high school sports in the year 2001?

$y = 294,105(1.085)^t$ Equation for females participating in sports

$y = 294,105(1.085)^{30}$ $t = 2001 - 1971$ or 30

$y \approx 3,399,340$ In 2001, about 3,399,340 females participated.

One special application of exponential growth is **compound interest**. The equation for compound interest is $A = P\left(1 + \dfrac{r}{n}\right)^{nt}$, where A represents the amount of the investment, P is the principal (initial amount of the investment), r represents the annual rate of interest expressed as a decimal, n represents the number of times that the interest is compounded each year, and t represents the number of years that the money is invested.

Example 2 Compound Interest

HISTORY Use the information at the left. If the money the Native Americans received for Manhattan had been invested at 6% per year compounded semiannually, how much money would there be in the year 2026?

$A = P\left(1 + \dfrac{r}{n}\right)^{nt}$ Compound interest equation

$A = 24\left(1 + \dfrac{0.06}{2}\right)^{2(400)}$ $P = 24, r = 6\%$ or 0.06, $n = 2$, and $t = 400$

$A = 24(1.03)^{800}$ Simplify.

$A \approx 4.47 \times 10^{11}$ There would be about $447,000,000,000.

EXPONENTIAL DECAY A variation of the growth equation can be used as the general equation for **exponential decay**. In exponential decay, the original amount decreases by the same percent over a period of time.

Key Concept   *General Equation for Exponential Decay*

The general equation for exponential decay is $y = C(1 - r)^t$ where y represents the final amount, C represents the initial amount, r represents the rate of decay expressed as a decimal, and t represents time.

Example 3 Exponential Decay

ENERGY In 1950, the use of coal by residential and commercial users was 114.6 million tons. Many businesses now use cleaner sources of energy. As a result, the use of coal has decreased by 6.6% per year.

a. Write an equation to represent the use of coal since 1950.

$y = C(1 - r)^t$ General equation for exponential decay

$y = 114.6(1 - 0.066)^t$ $C = 114.6$ and $r = 6.6\%$ or 0.066

$y = 114.6(0.934)^t$ Simplify.

An equation to represent the use of coal is $y = 114.6(0.934)^t$, where y represents tons of coal used annually and t represents the number of years since 1950.

b. Estimate the estimated amount of coal that will be used in 2015.

$y = 114.6(0.934)^t$ Equation for coal use

$y = 114.6(0.934)^{65}$ $t = 2015 - 1950$ or 65

$y \approx 1.35$ The amount of coal should be about 1.35 million tons.

More About. . .

History •

In 1626, Peter Minuit, governor of the colony of New Netherland, bought the island of Manhattan from the Native Americans for beads, cloth, and trinkets worth 60 Dutch guilders ($24).

Source: *World Book Encyclopedia*

D A I L Y

INTERVENTION   **Differentiated Instruction**

Kinesthetic Have students make graphs for the functions in the Example problems. Since none of these examples have graphs, the process of making the graphs may help students develop a better understanding of the concepts of exponential growth and decay.

Sometimes items decrease in value or *depreciate*. For example, most cars and office equipment depreciate as they get older. You can use the exponential decay formula to determine the value of an item at a given time.

Example 4 **Depreciation**

FARMING A farmer buys a tractor for $50,000. If the tractor depreciates 10% per year, find the value of the tractor in 7 years.

$y = C(1 - r)^t$ General equation for exponential decay

$y = 50{,}000(1 - 0.10)^7$ $C = 50{,}000, r = 10\%$ or 0.10, and $t = 7$

$y = 50{,}000(0.90)^7$ Simplify.

$y \approx 23{,}914.85$ Use a calculator.

The tractor will be worth about $23,914.85 or less than half its original value.

Check for Understanding

Concept Check

1–3. See margin.

1. **Explain** the difference between *exponential growth* and *exponential decay*.

2. **OPEN ENDED** Write a compound interest problem that could be solved by the equation $A = 500\left(1 + \dfrac{0.07}{4}\right)^{4(6)}$.

3. **Draw** a graph representing exponential decay.

Guided Practice

GUIDED PRACTICE KEY

Exercises	Examples
4, 5	1
6	2
7	3
8	4

INCOME For Exercises 4 and 5, use the graph at the right and the following information.
The median household income in the United States increased an average of 0.5% each year between 1979 and 1999. Assume this pattern continues. **4.** $I = 37{,}060(1.005)^t$

4. Write an equation for the median household income for t years after 1979.

5. Predict the median household income in 2009. **about $43,041**

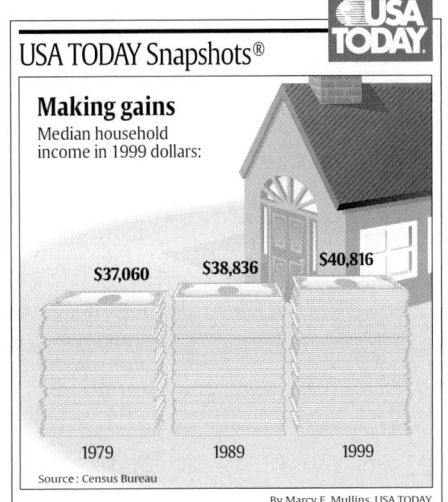

USA TODAY Snapshots®

Making gains
Median household income in 1999 dollars:

$37,060 $38,836 $40,816

1979   1989   1999

Source: Census Bureau

By Marcy E. Mullins, USA TODAY

Applications

6. **INVESTMENTS** Determine the amount of an investment if $400 is invested at an interest rate of 7.25% compounded quarterly for 7 years. **about $661.44**

7. about 1,767,128 people

7. **POPULATION** In 1995, the population of West Virginia reached 1,821,000, its highest in the 20th century. For the next 5 years, its population decreased 0.2% each year. If this trend continues, predict the population of West Virginia in 2010.

8. **TRANSPORTATION** A car sells for $16,000. If the rate of depreciation is 18%, find the value of the car after 8 years. **about $3270.63**

★ indicates increased difficulty

Practice and Apply

TECHNOLOGY For Exercises 9 and 10, use the following information.
Computer use around the world has risen 19% annually since 1980.

9. If 18.9 million computers were in use in 1980, write an equation for the number of computers in use for t years after 1980. **$C = 18.9(1.19)^t$**

10. Predict the number of computers in 2015. **about 8329.24 million computers**

www.algebra1.com/self_check_quiz

Answers

1. Exponential growth is an increase by the same percent over a period of time, while exponential decay is a decrease by the same percent over a period of time.

2. Determine the amount of the investment if $500 is invested at an interest rate of 7% compounded quarterly for 6 years.

3.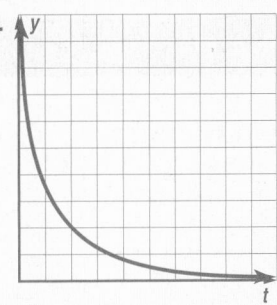

In-Class Example   Power Point®

Teaching Tip Remind students that the amount inside the parentheses will be greater than one for growth, and less than one for decay.

4 **DEPRECIATION** Jackson and Elizabeth bought a house when they first married ten years ago. Since that time the value of the real estate in their neighborhood has declined 3% per year. If they initially paid $179,000 for their house, what is its value today? **about $131,999**

3 Practice/Apply

Study Notebook

Have students—
• add the definitions/examples of the vocabulary terms to their Vocabulary Builder worksheets for Chapter 10.
• include examples of exponential growth and decay functions.
• include any other item(s) that they find helpful in mastering the skills in this lesson.

About the Exercises ...

Organization by Objective
• **Exponential Growth:** 9–15, 18, 21, 22
• **Exponential Decay:** 16, 17, 19, 20, 25–28

Odd/Even Assignments
Exercises 13–20 are structured so that students practice the same concepts whether they are assigned odd or even problems.

Assignment Guide
Basic: 9–12, 13–19 odd, 23–24, 29–48
Average: 9–12, 13–19 odd, 23–24, 29–48
Advanced: 11–12, 14–20 even, 21–45 (optional: 46–48)

Lesson 10-6 Growth and Decay **563**

Study Guide and Intervention, p. 609 (shown) and p. 610

Exponential Growth Population increases and growth of monetary investments are examples of **exponential growth**. This means that an initial amount increases at a steady rate over time.

| Exponential Growth | The general equation for exponential growth is $y = C(1 + r)^t$.
• y represents the final amount.
• C represents the initial amount.
• r represents the rate of change expressed as a decimal.
• t represents time. |

Example 1 **POPULATION** The population of Johnson City in 1995 was 25,000. Since then, the population has grown at an average rate of 3.2% each year.

a. Write an equation to represent the population of Johnson City since 1995.

The rate 3.2% can be written as 0.032.
$y = C(1 + r)^t$
$y = 25,000(1 + 0.032)^t$
$y = 25,000(1.032)^t$

b. According to the equation, what will the population of Johnson City be in the year 2005?

In 2005, t will equal $2005 - 1995$ or 10. Substitute 10 for t in the equation from part a.
$y = 25,000(1.032)^{10}$ $t = 10$
$\approx 34,256$
In 2005, the population of Johnson City will be about 34,256.

Example 2 **INVESTMENT** The Garcias have $12,000 in a savings account. The bank pays 3.5% interest on savings accounts, compounded monthly. Find the balance in 3 years.

The rate 3.5% can be written as 0.035.

The special equation for compound interest is $A = P\left(1 + \frac{r}{n}\right)^{nt}$, where A represents the balance, P is the initial amount, r represents the annual rate expressed as a decimal, n represents the number of times the interest is compounded each year, and t represents the number of years the money is invested.

$A = P\left(1 + \frac{r}{n}\right)^{nt}$
$A = 12,000\left(1 + \frac{0.035}{12}\right)^{36}$
$A = 12,000(1.00292)^{36}$
$A \approx 13,328.09$

In three years, the balance of the account will be $13,328.09.

Exercises

1. **POPULATION** The population of the United States has been increasing at an average annual rate of 0.91%. If the population of the United States was about 284,905,400 in the year 2001, predict the U.S. population in the year 2005. *Source: U.S. Census Bureau* **about 295,418,375**

2. **INVESTMENT** Determine the amount of an investment of $2500 if it is invested at in interest rate of 5.25% compounded monthly for 4 years. **$3082.78**

3. **POPULATION** It is estimated that the population of the world is increasing at an average annual rate of 1.3%. If the population of the world was about 6,167,007,000 in the year 2001, predict the world population in the year 2010. *Source: U.S. Census Bureau* **about 6,927,227,483**

4. **INVESTMENT** Determine the amount of an investment of $100,000 if it is invested at an interest rate of 5.2% compounded quarterly for 12 years. **$185,888.87**

Skills Practice, p. 611 and Practice, p. 612 (shown)

COMMUNICATIONS For Exercises 1 and 2, use the following information.
Commercial non-music radio stations increased at an average annual rate of 3.1% from 1996 to 2000. Commercial radio stations in this format numbered 1262 in 1996. *Source: M Street Corporation, Nashville, TN*

1. Write an equation for the number of radio stations for t years after 1996.
$R = 1262(1.031)^t$

2. If the trend continues, predict the number of radio stations in this format for the year 2006. **about 1713 stations**

3. **INVESTMENTS** Determine the amount of an investment if $500 is invested at an interest rate of 4.25% compounded quarterly for 12 years. **$830.41**

4. **INVESTMENTS** Determine the amount of an investment if $300 is invested at an interest rate of 6.75% compounded semiannually for 20 years. **$1131.73**

5. **HOUSING** The Greens bought a condominium for $110,000 in 2000. If its value appreciates at an average rate of 6% per year, what will the value be in 2005? **about $147,205**

DEFORESTATION For Exercises 6 and 7, use the following information.
During the 1990s, the forested area of Guatemala decreased at an average rate of 1.7%. *Source: www.worldbank.org*

6. If the forested area in Guatemala in 1990 was about 34,400 square kilometers, write an equation for the forested area for t years after 1990. $C = 34,400(0.983)^t$

7. If this trend continues, predict the forested area in 2015. **about 22,400 km²**

8. **BUSINESS** A piece of machinery valued at $25,000 depreciates at a steady rate of 10% yearly. What will the value of the piece of machinery be after 7 years? **about $11,957**

9. **TRANSPORTATION** A new car costs $18,000. It is expected to depreciate at an average rate of 12% per year. Find the value of the car in 8 years. **about $6473**

10. **POPULATION** The population of Osaka, Japan declined at an average annual rate of 0.05% for the five years between 1995 and 2000. If the population of Osaka was 11,013,000 in 2000 and it continues to decline at the same rate, predict the population in 2050. **about 10,741,000**

Reading to Learn Mathematics, p. 613   ELL

Pre-Activity **How can exponential growth be used to predict future sales?**
Read the introduction to Lesson 10-6 at the top of page 561 in your textbook.

Suppose you want to predict the amount of money an average household will spend on restaurant meals in the year 2005. What number should be substituted for t? **11**

Reading the Lesson

Match an equation to each situation, and then indicate whether the situation is an example of exponential growth or decay.

1. A coin had a value of $1.17 in 1995. Its value has been increasing at a rate of 9% per year. **A; growth**
   A. $y = 1.17(1.09)^t$ **B.** $y = 1.17(0.91)^t$

2. A business owner has just paid $6000 for a computer. It depreciates at a rate of 22% per year. How much will it be worth in 5 years? **B; decay**
   A. $A = 6000(1.22)^5$ **B.** $A = 6000(0.78)^5$

3. A city had a population of 14,358 residents in 1999. Since then, its population has been decreasing at a rate of about 5.5% per year. **B; decay**
   A. $A = 14,358(1.055)^t$ **B.** $A = 14,358(0.945)^t$

4. Gina deposited $1500 in an account that pays 4% interest compounded quarterly. What will be the worth of the account in 2 years if she makes no deposits and no withdrawals? **B; growth**
   A. $A = 1500(1.02)^2$ **B.** $A = 1500(1.02)^8$

Helping You Remember

5. How can you use what you know about raising a number to the 0 power to help you remember what C represents in the exponential growth equation $A = C(1 + r)^t$ and the exponential decay equation $A = C(1 - r)^t$?
Sample answer: The initial amount is the amount before any time has passed, that is, when $t = 0$. When $t = 0$, $C(1 + r)^t = C(1 + r)^0 = C(1) = C$ and $C(1 - r)^t = C(1 - r)^0 = C(1) = C$. So C represents the initial amount.

WEIGHT TRAINING For Exercises 11 and 12, use the following information.
In 1997, there were 43.2 million people who used free weights.

11. Assuming the use of free weights increases 6% annually, write an equation for the number of people using free weights t years from 1997. $W = 43.2(1.06)^t$

12. Predict the number of people using free weights in 2007. **12. about 77.36 million people**

13. **POPULATION** The population of Mexico has been increasing at an annual rate of 1.7%. If the population of Mexico was 100,350,000 in the year 2000, predict its population in 2012. **about 122,848,204 people**

14. **INVESTMENTS** Determine the amount of an investment if $500 is invested at an interest rate of 5.75% compounded monthly for 25 years. **about $2097.86**

15. **INVESTMENTS** Determine the amount of an investment if $250 is invested at an interest rate of 10.3% compounded quarterly for 40 years. **about $14,607.78**

16. **POPULATION** The country of Latvia has been experiencing a 1.1% annual decrease in population. In 2000, its population was 2,405,000. If the trend continues, predict Latvia's population in 2015. **about 2,037,321 people**

17. **MUSIC** In 1994, the sales of music cassettes reached its peak at $2,976,400,000. Since then, cassette sales have been declining. If the annual percent of decrease in sales is 18.6%, predict the sales of cassettes in the year 2009. **17. about $135,849,289**

18. **GRAND CANYON** The increase in the number of visitors to the Grand Canyon National Park is similar to an exponential function. If the average visitation has increased 5.63% annually since 1920, use the graph to predict the number of visitors to the park in 2020. **18. about 17,125,650 visitors**

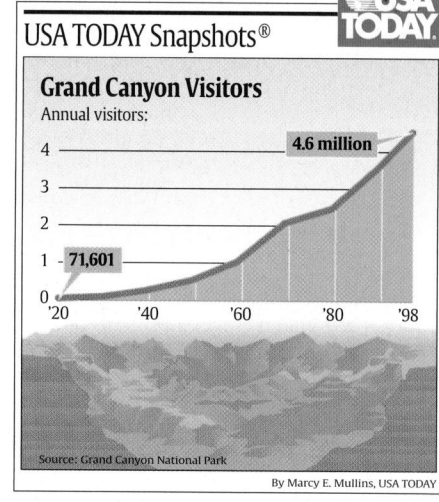

USA TODAY Snapshots®

Grand Canyon Visitors
Annual visitors:

4.6 million

71,601

'20   '40   '60   '80   '98

Source: Grand Canyon National Park

By Marcy E. Mullins, USA TODAY

19. **BUSINESS** A piece of office equipment valued at $25,000 depreciates at a steady rate of 10% per year. What is the value of the equipment in 8 years? **19. about $10,761.68**

20. **TRANSPORTATION** A new car costs $23,000. It is expected to depreciate 12% each year. Find the value of the car in 5 years. **20. about $12,137.83**

POPULATION For Exercises 21 and 22, use the following information.
The percent of the population that is 65 years old or older continues to rise. The percent of the U.S. population P that is at least 65 years old can be approximated by $P = 3.86(1.013)^t$, where t represents the number of years since 1900.

21. What percent of the population will be 65 years of age or older in the year 2010? **21. about 15.98%**

★ 22. Predict the year in which people ages 65 or older will represent 20% of the population if this trend continues. (*Hint:* Make a table.) **about 2028**

CRITICAL THINKING Each equation represents an exponential rate of change if t is time in years. Determine whether each equation represents growth or decay. Give the annual rate of change as a percent.

23. $y = 500(1.026^t)$ **growth; 2.6% increase**   24. $y = 500(0.761^t)$ **decay; 23.9% decrease**

Homework Help

For Exercises	See Examples
9–13, 18 21, 22	1
14, 15	2
16, 17, 25–28	3
19, 20	4

Extra Practice See page 843.

564   Chapter 10   Quadratic and Exponential Functions

Enrichment, p. 614

Curious Circles

Two circles can be arranged in four ways: one circle can be inside the other, they can be separate, they can overlap, or they can coincide.

In how many ways can a given number of circles be either separate or inside each other? (The situations in which the circles overlap or coincide are not counted here.)

For 3 circles, there are 4 different possibilities.

Solve each problem. Make drawings to show your answers.

1. Show the different ways in which 2 circles can be separate or inside each other. How many ways are there? **two ways**

ARCHAEOLOGY For Exercises 25–28, use the following information.
The *half-life* of a radioactive element is the time that it takes for one-half a quantity of the element to decay. Carbon-14 is found in all living organisms and has a half-life of 5730 years. Archaeologists use this fact to estimate the age of fossils. Consider an organism with an original Carbon-14 content of 256 grams. The number of grams remaining in the organism's fossil after t years is $256(0.5)^{\frac{t}{5730}}$.

25. 128 g

26. about 226.83 g

27. about 76.36 g

25. If the organism died 5730 years ago, what is the amount of Carbon-14 today?

★ **26.** If the organism died 1000 years ago, what is the amount of Carbon-14 today?

★ **27.** If the organism died 10,000 years ago, what is the amount of Carbon-14 today?

★ **28.** If the fossil has 32 grams of Carbon-14 remaining, how long ago did it live? (*Hint*: Make a table.) **17,190 years ago**

29. RESEARCH Find the enrollment of your school district each year for the last decade. Find the rate of change from one year to the next. Then, determine the average annual rate of change for those years. Use this information to estimate the enrollment for your school district in ten years. **See students' work.**

30.  **WRITING IN MATH** Answer the question that was posed at the beginning of the lesson. **See margin.**

How can exponential growth be used to predict future sales?

Include the following in your answer:
- an explanation of the equation $y = 1698(1 + 0.046)^t$, and
- an estimate of the average family's spending for restaurant meals in 2010.

Standardized Test Practice
Ⓐ Ⓑ Ⓒ Ⓓ

31. Which equation represents exponential growth? **C**
- Ⓐ $y = 50x^3$
- Ⓑ $y = 30x^2 + 10$
- Ⓒ $y = 35(1.05^x)$
- Ⓓ $y = 80(0.92^x)$

32. Lorena is investing a $5000 inheritance from her aunt in a certificate of deposit that matures in 4 years. The interest rate is 8.25% compounded quarterly. What is the balance of the account after 4 years? **D**
- Ⓐ $5412.50
- Ⓑ $6865.65
- Ⓒ $6908.92
- Ⓓ $6931.53

Maintain Your Skills

Mixed Review
33–35. See margin for graphs.

Graph each function. State the y-intercept. *(Lesson 10-5)*

33. $y = \left(\frac{1}{8}\right)^x$ **1**   **34.** $y = 2^x - 5$ **−4**   **35.** $y = 4(3^x - 6)$ **−20**

Solve each equation by using the Quadratic Formula. Round to the nearest tenth if necessary. *(Lesson 10-4)* **36. −1, 10**

36. $m^2 - 9m - 10 = 0$ **37.** $2t^2 - 4t = 3$ **−0.6, 2.6** **38.** $7x^2 + 3x + 1 = 0$ **∅**

Simplify. *(Lesson 8-1)*

39. $m^7(m^3b^2)$ $m^{10}b^2$ **40.** $-3(ax^3y)^2$ $-3a^2x^6y^2$ **41.** $(0.3x^3y^2)^2$ $0.09x^6y^4$

Solve each open sentence. *(Lesson 6-5)* **44.** $\{t \mid t \le -7 \text{ or } t \ge -1\}$

42. $|7x + 2| = -2$ ∅   **43.** $|3 - 3x| = 0$ {1}   **44.** $|t + 4| \ge 3$

45. SKIING A course for cross-country skiing is regulated so that the slope of any hill cannot be greater than 0.33. A hill rises 60 meters over a horizontal distance of 250 meters. Does the hill meet the requirements? *(Lesson 5-1)* **yes**

Getting Ready for the Next Lesson

PREREQUISITE SKILL Find the next three terms in each arithmetic sequence.
*(To review **arithmetic sequences**, see Lesson 4-7.)*

46. 8, 11, 14, 17, ...   **47.** 7, 4, 1, −2, ...   **48.** 1.5, 2.6, 3.7, 4.8, ...
   20, 23, 27   **−5, −8, −11**   **5.9, 7.0, 8.1**

Answer

30. If the sales are growing by the same percent each year, an exponential equation can be used to model sales and predict future sales. Answers should include the following.
- The equation states that the new value equals the amount in the year 1994 or $1698 times the sum of 1 plus 4.6% raised to the power that is equal to the number of years since 1994.
- According to the equation, the average family will spend about $3486.94 for restaurant meals in 2010.

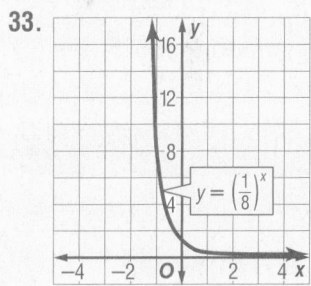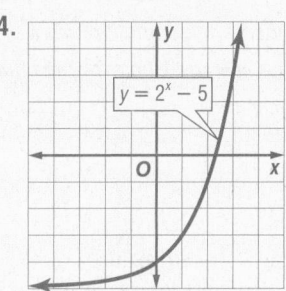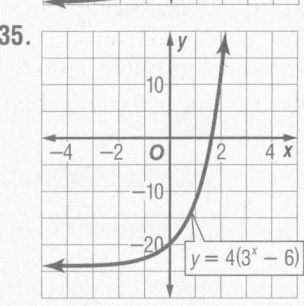

Growth and Decay Formulas

Growth and decay problems may be confusing, unless you read them in a simplified, generalized form. The growth and decay formulas that you used in Lesson 10-6 are based on the idea that an initial amount is multiplied by a rate raised to a power of time, which is equivalent to a final amount. If you remember the following formula, all other formulas will be easier to remember.

$$final\ amount = initial\ amount \cdot rate^{time}$$

Below, we will review the general equation for exponential growth to see how it is related to the generalized formula above.

The final amount	equals	an initial amount	times	the quantity one plus a rate raised to the power of time.
y	$=$	C	$\cdot$	$(1 + r)^t$

The only difference from the generalized formula is that rate equals $1 + r$. *Why?*

One represents 100%. If you multiply C by 100%, the final amount is the same as the initial amount. We *add* 1 to the rate r so that the final amount is the initial amount plus the increase.

You can break each growth and decay formula into the following pieces:

- final amount,
- initial amount,
- rate, and
- time.

Reading to Learn 1–2. See pp. 581A–581H.

1. Write the general equation for exponential decay. Discuss how it is related to the generalized formula. Why is the rate equal to $1 - r$?

2. Write the formula for compound interest. How is it related to the generalized formula? Why does the rate equal $\left(1 + \frac{r}{n}\right)$? Why does the time equal nt?

3. Suppose that $\underline{\$2500}$ is invested at an $\underline{annual\ rate\ of\ 6\%}$. If the interest is $\underline{compounded\ quarterly}$, find the value of the account $\underline{after\ 5\ years}$.
   a. Copy the problem and underline all important numerical data.
   b. Choose the appropriate formula and solve the problem. **See margin.**

4. Angela bought a car for $\underline{\$18,500}$. If the $\underline{rate\ of\ depreciation\ is\ 11\%}$, find the value of the car $\underline{in\ 4\ years}$.
   a. Copy the problem and underline all important numerical data.
   b. Choose the appropriate formula and solve the problem. **See margin.**

5. The population of Centerville is increasing at an average $\underline{annual\ rate\ of\ 3.5\%}$. If its current population is $\underline{12,500}$, predict its population in $\underline{5\ years}$.
   a. Copy the problem and underline all important numerical data.
   b. Choose the appropriate formula and solve the problem. **See margin.**

566 Chapter 10 Quadratic and Exponential Functions

Answers

3b. $A = P\left(1 + \frac{r}{n}\right)^{nt}$; $A = 2500\left(1 + \frac{0.06}{4}\right)^{4(5)}$ or about $3367.14

4b. $y = C(1 - r)^t$; $18{,}500(1 - 0.11)^4$ or about $11,607.31

5b. $y = C(1 + r)^t$; $y = 12{,}500(1 + 0.035)^5$ or about 14,846 people

10-7 Geometric Sequences

What You'll Learn

- Recognize and extend geometric sequences.
- Find geometric means.

Vocabulary

- geometric sequence
- common ratio
- geometric means

How can a geometric sequence be used to describe a bungee jump?

A thrill ride is set up with a bungee rope that will stretch when a person jumps from the platform. The ride continues as the person bounces back and forth closer to the stopping place of the rope. Each bounce is only $\frac{3}{4}$ as far from the stopping length as the preceding bounce. If the initial drop is 80 feet past the stopping length of the rope, the following table gives the distance of the first four bounces.

Bounce	Distance (ft)
1	80
2	$\frac{3}{4} \cdot 80$ or 60
3	$\frac{3}{4} \cdot 60$ or 45
4	$\frac{3}{4} \cdot 45$ or $33\frac{3}{4}$

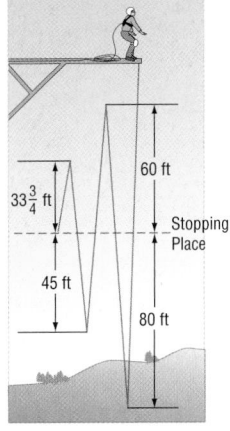

60 ft
$33\frac{3}{4}$ ft
Stopping Place
45 ft
80 ft

GEOMETRIC SEQUENCES

The distance of each bounce is found by multiplying the previous term by $\frac{3}{4}$. The successive distances of the bounces is an example of a **geometric sequence**. The number by which each term is multiplied is called the **common ratio**.

Key Concept — Geometric Sequence

- **Words**   A geometric sequence is a sequence in which each term after the nonzero first term is found by multiplying the previous term by a constant called the common ratio r, where $r \neq 0, 1$.

- **Symbols** a, ar, $(ar)r$ or ar^2, $(ar^2)r$ or ar^3, ...   ($a \neq 0$; $r \neq 0, 1$)

- **Examples**   1, 3, 9, 27, 81, ...

Example 1   Recognize Geometric Sequences

Determine whether each sequence is geometric.

a. 0, 5, 10, 15, 20, ...

Determine the pattern.

0   5   10   15   20
   +5   +5   +5   +5

In this sequence, each term is found by adding 5 to the previous term. This sequence is arithmetic, *not* geometric.

Study Tip

Look Back
To review **arithmetic sequences**, see Lesson 4-7.

10-7 Lesson Notes

1 Focus

5-Minute Check Transparency 10-7   Use as a quiz or review of Lesson 10-6.

Mathematical Background notes are available for this lesson on p. 522D.

Building on Prior Knowledge

In Lesson 4-7, students learned to recognize arithmetic sequences, as well as how to extend arithmetic sequences and how to write formulas for arithmetic sequences. In this lesson, students will learn similar concepts about geometric sequences, beginning with differentiating between arithmetic and geometric sequences.

How can a geometric sequence be used to describe a bungee jump?

Ask students:

- If you used the bounce numbers as x-coordinates, and the height of the bounce as y-coordinates and graphed the function, what would the graph resemble? **The graph would resemble an exponential function.**

- What about the values of the heights of the bounces tells you that this is indeed an exponential function? **The values are decreased by a common factor each bounce.**

Resource Manager

Workbook and Reproducible Masters

Chapter 10 Resource Masters
- Study Guide and Intervention, pp. 615–616
- Skills Practice, p. 617
- Practice, p. 618
- Reading to Learn Mathematics, p. 619
- Enrichment, p. 620
- Assessment, p. 636

Graphing Calculator and Spreadsheet Masters, p. 41
Parent and Student Study Guide Workbook, p. 81
Prerequisite Skills Workbook, pp. 9–12, 47–48
Teaching Algebra With Manipulatives Masters, p. 181

Transparencies
5-Minute Check Transparency 10-7
Answer Key Transparencies

Technology
Interactive Chalkboard

GEOMETRIC SEQUENCES

In-Class Examples · · · · [Power Point®]

Teaching Tip Students should immediately recognize that the first series is not geometric because the first term is zero.

1 Determine whether each sequence is geometric.

a. 1, 4, 16, 64, 256, … **yes**

b. 1, 3, 5, 7, 9, 11, …
no; arithmetic

2 Find the next three terms in each geometric sequence.

a. 20, −28, 39.2, …
−54.88, 76.832, −107.5648

b. 64, 48, 36, …
27, 20.25, 15.1875

3 **GEOGRAPHY** The population of the African country of Liberia was about 2,900,000 in 1999. If the population grows at a rate of about 5% per year, what will the population be in the years 2003, 2004, and 2005? **The population of Liberia in the years 2003, 2004, 2005 will be about 3,524,968, 3,701,217, and 3,886,277, respectively.**

---

b. 1, 5, 25, 125, 625

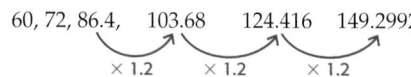

In this sequence, each term is found by multiplying the previous term times 5. This sequence is geometric.

The common ratio of a geometric sequence can be found by dividing any term by the preceding term.

Example 2 *Continue Geometric Sequences*

Find the next three terms in each geometric sequence.

a. 4, −8, 16, …

$\dfrac{-8}{4} = -2$ Divide the second term by the first.

The common factor is −2. Use this information to find the next three terms.

4, −8, 16,   −32   64   −128
× (−2)   × (−2)   × (−2)

The next three terms are −32, 64, and −128.

b. 60, 72, 86.4, …

$\dfrac{72}{60} = 1.2$ Divide the second term by the first.

The common factor is 1.2. Use this information to find the next three terms.

60, 72, 86.4,   103.68   124.416   149.2992
× 1.2   × 1.2   × 1.2

The next three terms are 103.68, 124.416, and 149.2992.

Example 3 *Use Geometric Sequences to Solve a Problem*

GEOGRAPHY Madagascar's population has been increasing at an average annual rate of 3%. Use the information at the left to determine the population of Madagascar in 2001, 2002, and 2003.

The population is a geometric sequence in which the first term is 15,500,000 and the common ratio is 1.03.

Year	Population
2000	15,500,000
2001	15,500,000(1.03) or 15,965,000
2002	15,965,000(1.03) or 16,443,950
2003	16,443,950(1.03) or about 16,937,269

The population of Madagascar in the years 2001, 2002, and 2003 will be 15,965,000, 16,443,950, and about 16,937,269, respectively.

As with arithmetic sequences, you can name the terms of a geometric sequence using $a_1, a_2, a_3,$ and so on. Then the nth term is represented as a_n. Each term of a geometric sequence can also be represented using r and its previous term. A third way to represent each term is by using r and the first term a_1.

568   Chapter 10   Quadratic and Exponential Functions

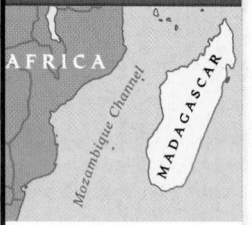

More About. . .

AFRICA

Mozambique Channel

MADAGASCAR

Geography •··········

Madagascar is a country just east of mainland Africa. It consists of the third largest island in the world and many tiny islands. In 2000, the population of Madagascar was about 15,500,000.

Source: *World Book Encyclopedia*

D A I L Y

INTERVENTION   **Differentiated Instruction**

Logical Challenge students to use the general equation for exponential growth to find the answer to Example 3. Have students explain how the equation is related to a geometric sequence.

Sequence	number	2	6	18	54	...	
	symbols	a_1	a_2	a_3	a_4	...	a_n
Expressed in Terms of r and Previous Term	number	2	2(3)	6(3)	18(3)	...	
	symbols	a_1	$a_1 \cdot r$	$a_2 \cdot r$	$a_3 \cdot r$	...	$a_{n-1} \cdot r$
Expressed in Terms of r and First Term	number	2 or $2(3^0)$	2(3) or $2(3^1)$	2(9) or $2(3^2)$	2(27) or $2(3^3)$	...	
	symbols	$a_1 \cdot r^0$	$a_1 \cdot r^1$	$a_1 \cdot r^2$	$a_1 \cdot r^3$	...	$a_1 \cdot r^{n-1}$

The three values in the last column of the table all describe the nth term of a geometric sequence.

In-Class Example Power Point®

Teaching Tip Make sure students raise r to the power $n - 1$ instead of n.

4 Find the eighth term of a geometric sequence in which $a_1 = 7$ and $r = 3$. **15,309**

Study Tip

Recursive Formulas
When the nth term of a sequence is expressed in terms of the previous term, as in $a_n = a_{n-1} \cdot r$, the formula is called a *recursive formula*.

Key Concept — Formula for the nth Term of a Geometric Sequence

The nth term a_n of a geometric sequence with the first term a_1 and common ratio r is given by $a_n = a_1 \cdot r^{n-1}$.

Example 4 — nth Term of a Geometric Sequence

Find the sixth term of a geometric sequence in which $a_1 = 3$ and $r = -5$.

$a_n = a_1 \cdot r^{n-1}$ Formula for the nth term of a geometric sequence

$a_6 = 3 \cdot (-5)^{6-1}$ $n = 6$, $a_1 = 3$, and $r = -5$

$a_6 = 3 \cdot (-5)^5$ $6 - 1 = 5$

$a_6 = 3 \cdot (-3125)$ $(-5)^5 = -3125$

$a_6 = -9375$ $3 \cdot (-3125) = -9375$

The sixth term of the geometric sequence is -9375.

Geometric sequences are related to exponential functions.

Algebra Activity

Graphs of Geometric Sequences

You can graph a geometric sequence by graphing the coordinates (n, a_n). For example, consider the sequence 2, 6, 18, 54, ... To graph this sequence, graph the points at (1, 2), (2, 6), (3, 18), and (4, 54).

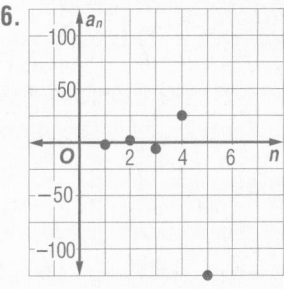

Model 1–6. See margin for graphs.

Graph each geometric sequence. Name each common ratio.

1. 1, 2, 4, 8, 16, ...   **2**   **2.** 1, −2, 4, −8, 16, ...   **−2**

3. 81, 27, 9, 3, 1, ... $\frac{1}{3}$ **4.** −81, 27, −9, 3, −1, ... $-\frac{1}{3}$

5. 0.2, 1, 5, 25, 125, ...   **5**   **6.** −0.2, 1, −5, 25, −125, ...   **−5**

Analyze

7. Which graphs appear to be similar to an exponential function?   **1, 3, 5**

8. Compare and contrast the graphs of geometric sequences with $r > 0$ and $r < 0$.

9. Compare the formula for an exponential function $y = c(a^x)$ to the value of the nth term of a geometric sequence.

8. Both types of graphs show rapid change. If $r > 0$, the graph of the geometric sequence is similar to an exponential function. If $r < 0$, the graph of the geometric sequence has points above and below the n-axis and is not similar to an exponential function.

9. The two values $c(a^x)$ and $a_1 r^{n-1}$ are very similar. Both have a number multiplied by another number that is raised to a power.

Answers

1.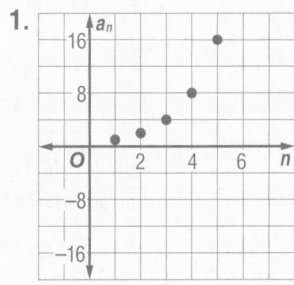

2.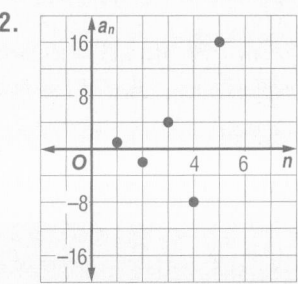

3.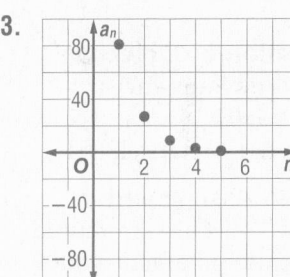

4.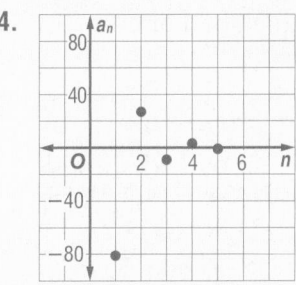

5.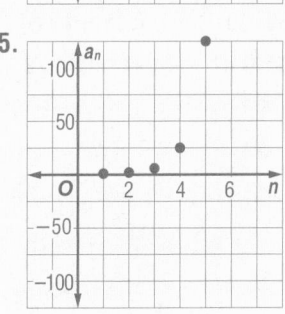

6.

Algebra Activity

Since the value of a_n can increase greatly in the graph of a geometric sequence, make sure students allow for large numbers on the vertical axis of their graphs, both in the positive and negative directions.

GEOMETRIC MEANS

5 Find the geometric mean in the sequence 7, ____, 112. **±28**

3 Practice/Apply

Study Notebook

Have students—

- complete the definitions/examples for the remaining terms on their Vocabulary Builder worksheets for Chapter 10.
- include examples of geometric sequences.
- include any other item(s) that they find helpful in mastering the skills in this lesson.

About the Exercises ...

Organization by Objective
- **Geometric Sequences:** 17–42, 55–63
- **Geometric Means:** 43–54

Odd/Even Assignments
Exercises 17–54 are structured so that students practice the same concepts whether they are assigned odd or even problems.

Assignment Guide

Basic: 17–21 odd, 25–29 odd, 33–39 odd, 43–51 odd, 53, 55, 61–65, 69–74

Average: 17–55 odd, 56, 57, 61–65, 69–74 (optional: 66–68)

Advanced: 18–54 even, 56–74

GEOMETRIC MEANS Missing term(s) between two nonconsecutive terms in a geometric sequence are called **geometric means**. In the sequence 100, 20, 4, …, the geometric mean between 100 and 4 is 20. You can use the formula for the nth term of a geometric sequence to find a geometric mean.

Example 5 Find Geometric Means

Find the geometric mean in the sequence 2, ____, 18.

In the sequence, $a_1 = 2$ and $a_3 = 18$. To find a_2, you must first find r.

$$a_n = a_1 \cdot r^{n-1} \qquad \text{Formula for the } n\text{th term of a geometric sequence}$$
$$a_3 = a_1 \cdot r^{3-1} \qquad n = 3$$
$$18 = 2 \cdot r^2 \qquad a_3 = 18 \text{ and } a_1 = 2$$
$$\frac{18}{2} = \frac{2r^2}{2} \qquad \text{Divide each side by 2.}$$
$$9 = r^2 \qquad \text{Simplify.}$$
$$\pm 3 = r \qquad \text{Take the square root of each side.}$$

If $r = 3$, the geometric mean is $2(3)$ or 6. If $r = -3$, the geometric mean is $2(-3)$ or -6. Therefore, the geometric mean is 6 or -6.

Check for Understanding

Concept Check
1–2. See margin.

1. **Compare and contrast** an arithmetic sequence and a geometric sequence.

2. **Explain** why the definition of a geometric sequence restricts the values of the common ratio to numbers other than 0 and 1.

3. **OPEN ENDED** Give an example of a sequence that is neither arithmetic nor geometric. **Sample answer: 1, 4, 9, 16, 25, 36, …**

Guided Practice

GUIDED PRACTICE KEY	
Exercises	Examples
4–6	1
7–9	2
10–12	4
13–15	5
16	3

Determine whether each sequence is geometric.

4. 5, 15, 45, 135, … **yes**
5. 56, −28, 14, −7, … **yes**
6. 25, 20, 15, 10, … **no**

Find the next three terms in each geometric sequence.

7. 5, 20, 80, 320, … **1280, 5120, 20,480**
8. 176, −88, 44, −22, … **11, −5.5, 2.75**
9. −8, 12, −18, 27, … **−40.5, 60.75, −91.125**

Find the nth term of each geometric sequence.

10. $a_1 = 3, n = 5, r = 4$ **768**
11. $a_1 = -1, n = 6, r = 2$ **−32**
12. $a_1 = 4, n = 7, r = -3$ **2916**

Find the geometric means in each sequence.

13. 7, ____, 28 **±14**
14. 48, ____, 3 **±12**
15. −4, ____, −100 **±20**

Application

16. **GEOMETRY** Consider the inscribed equilateral triangles at the right. The perimeter of each triangle is one-half of the perimeter of the next larger triangle. What is the perimeter of the smallest triangle? **7.5 cm**

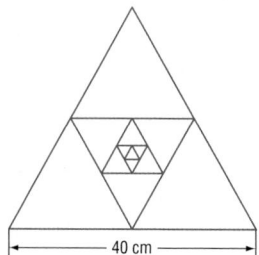

40 cm

Answers

1. Both arithmetic sequences and geometric sequences are lists of related numbers. In an arithmetic sequence, each term is found by adding the previous term to a constant called the common difference. In a geometric sequence, each term is found by multiplying the previous term by a constant called the common ratio.

2. If a common ratio equals 0, all of the terms except the first term will equal 0, since any number times 0 equals 0. If a common ratio equals 1, all of the terms will equal the first term, since 1 is the multiplicative identity.

Practice and Apply

Homework Help

For Exercises	See Examples
17–24	1
25–34	2
35–42	4
43–54	5
55–62	3

Extra Practice
See page 843.

Determine whether each sequence is geometric. **19. no** **22. yes**

17. 2, 6, 18, 54, ... **yes**   **18.** 7, 17, 27, 37, ... **no**   **19.** $-19, -16, -13, -10, ...$

20. 640, 160, 40, 10, ... **yes**   **21.** 36, 25, 16, 9, ... **no**   **22.** $-567, -189, -63, -21, ...$

★ **23.** 20, -90, 405, -1822.5, ... **yes**   **24.** -50, 110, -242, 532.4, ... **yes**

Find the next three terms in each geometric sequence. **25. 256, -1024, 4096**

25. 1, -4, 16, -64, ...   **26.** $-1, -6, -36, -216, ...$ **27.** 1024, 512, 256, 128, ...

28. 224, 112, 56, 28, ...   **29.** -80, 20, -5, 1.25, ...   **30.** 10,000, -200, 4, -0.08, ...

★ **31.** $\frac{1}{2}, \frac{1}{3}, \frac{2}{9}, \frac{4}{27}, ... \quad \frac{8}{81}, \frac{16}{243}, \frac{32}{729}$ **32.** $\frac{3}{4}, \frac{1}{2}, \frac{1}{3}, \frac{2}{9}, ... \quad \frac{4}{27}, \frac{8}{81}, \frac{16}{243}$

26. $-1296, -7776, -46,656$

27. 64, 32, 16

28. 14, 7, 3.5

29. -0.3125, 0.078125, -0.01953125

30. 0.0016, -0.000032, 0.00000064

40. -1280

58. 848, 636, 477, 357.75, 268.3125, 201.234375, 150.92578125

33. **GEOMETRY** A rectangle is 6 inches by 8 inches. The rectangle is cut in half, and one half is discarded. The remaining rectangle is cut in half, and one half is discarded. This is repeated twice. List the areas of the five rectangles formed. **48 in², 24 in², 12 in², 6 in², 3 in²**

34. **GEOMETRY** To bisect an angle means to cut it into two angles with the same measure. Suppose a 160° angle is bisected. Then one of the new angles is bisected. This is repeated twice. List the measures of the four sizes of angles. **160°, 80°, 40°, 20°**

Find the nth term of each geometric sequence. **37. 250** **38. -3072** **39. -288**

35. $a_1 = 5, n = 7, r = 2$ **320**   **36.** $a_1 = 4, n = 5, r = 3$ **324**   **37.** $a_1 = -2, n = 4, r = -5$

38. $a_1 = 3, n = 6, r = -4$ **39.** $a_1 = -8, n = 3, r = 6$ **40.** $a_1 = -10, n = 8, r = 2$

★ **41.** $a_1 = 300, n = 10, r = 0.5$ **0.5859375**   **42.** $a_1 = 14, n = 6, r = 1.5$ **106.3125**

Find the geometric means in each sequence.

43. 5, ___, 20 **±10**   **44.** 6, ___, 54 **±18**   **45.** -9, ___, -225 **±45**

46. -5, ___, -80 **±20**   **47.** 128, ___, 8 **±32**   **48.** 180, ___, 5 **±30**

49. -2, ___, -98 **±14**   **50.** -6, ___, -384 **±48**   **51.** 7, ___, 1.75 **±3.5**

★ **52.** 3, ___, 0.75 **±1.5**   **53.** $\frac{3}{5}$, ___, $\frac{3}{20}$ **±$\frac{3}{10}$**   **54.** $\frac{2}{5}$, ___, $\frac{2}{45}$ **±$\frac{2}{15}$**

55. A ball is thrown vertically. It is allowed to return to the ground and rebound without interference. If each rebound is 60% of the previous height, give the heights of the three rebounds after the initial rebound of 10 meters. **6 m, 3.6 m, 2.16 m**

QUIZ GAMES For Exercises 56 and 57, use the following information.
Radio station WXYZ has a special game for its listeners. A trivia question is asked, and the player scores 10 points for the first correct answer. Every correct answer after that doubles the player's score.

56. List the scores after each of the first 6 correct answers. **10, 20, 40, 80, 160, 320**

★ **57.** Suppose the player needs to answer the question worth more than a million points to win the grand prize of a car. How many questions must be answered correctly in order to earn the car? **18 questions**

POLLUTION For Exercise 58–60, use the following information.
A lake was closed because of an accidental pesticide spill. The concentration of the pesticide after the spill was 848 parts per million. Each day the water is tested, and the amount of pesticide is found to be about 75% of what was there the day before.

58. List the level of pesticides in the water during the first week.

★ **59.** If a safe level of pesticides is considered to be 12 parts per million or less, when will the lake be considered safe? **in 16 days**

★ **60.** Do you think the lake will ever be completely free of the pesticide? Explain.

More About. . .

Pollution •·············
On March 23, 1989, 250,000 barrels of oil were spilled affecting 1300 miles of Alaskan coastline. This was the largest oil spill in the United States.
Source: www.oilspill.state.ak.us

60. Sample answer: Although the amount of pesticide will become very small, 75% of something will always be something. Therefore, there will always be pesticides according to this model.

www.algebra1.com/self_check_quiz

Modeling Drop a tennis ball at the front of the classroom and ask students to describe how the bouncing of the ball can be modeled by a geometric sequence. Have students give an example of a sequence that might model the bouncing ball.

Assessment Options

Quiz (Lesson 10-7) is available on p. 636 of the *Chapter 10 Resource Masters*.

Answer

63. Since the distance of each bounce is $\frac{3}{4}$ times the distance of the last bounce, the list of the distances from the stopping place is a geometric sequence. Answers should include the following.
- To find the 10th term, multiply the first term 80 by $\frac{3}{4}$ to the 9th power.
- The 17th bounce will be the first bounce less than 1 ft from the resting place.

CRITICAL THINKING   For Exercises 61 and 62, suppose a sequence is geometric.

61. If each term of the sequence is multiplied by the same nonzero real number, is the new sequence *always*, *sometimes*, or *never* a geometric sequence? **always**

62. If the same nonzero number is added to each term of the sequence, is the new sequence *always*, *sometimes*, or *never* a geometric sequence? **never**

63.    Answer the question that was posed at the beginning of the lesson. **See margin.**

How can a geometric sequence be used to describe a bungee jump?

Include the following in your answer:
- an explanation of how to determine the tenth term in the sequence, and
- the number of rebounds the first time the distance from the stopping place is less than one foot, which would trigger the end of the ride.

Standardized Test Practice

64. Which number is next in the geometric sequence 40, 100, 250, 625, ... ? **C**
   (A) 900   (B) 1250   (C) 1562.5   (D) 1875

65. **GRID IN**   Find the next term in the following geometric sequence. 343, 49, 7, 1, ... **1/7**

Extending the Lesson

For Exercises 66–68, consider the *n*th term of the sequence $2, 1, \frac{1}{2}, \frac{1}{4}, \frac{1}{8}, \frac{1}{16}, \frac{1}{32}, \frac{1}{64}, \dots$

66. As *n* approaches infinity, what value will the *n*th term approach? **0**

67. In mathematics, a **limit** is a number that something approaches, but never reaches. What would you consider the limit of the values of the sequence? **0**

68. If *n* approaches infinity, how is the *n*th term of a geometric sequence where $0 < r < 1$ different than the *n*th term of a geometric sequence where $r > 1$?

68. If $0 < r < 1$, the *n*th term will approach 0. If $r > 1$, the *n*th term will approach infinity.

Maintain Your Skills

Mixed Review

69. **INVESTMENTS**   Determine the value of an investment if $1500 is invested at an interest rate of 6.5% compounded monthly for 3 years.   *(Lesson 10-6)* **about $1822.01**

Determine whether the data in each table display exponential behavior. Explain why or why not.   *(Lesson 10-5)*

70. No; the domain values are at regular intervals and the range values have a common difference 2.

71. Yes; the domain values are at regular intervals and the range values have a common factor 3.

70.

x	3	5	7	9
y	10	12	14	16

71.

x	2	5	8	11
y	0.5	1.5	4.5	13.5

Factor each trinomial, if possible. If the trinomial cannot be factored using integers, write *prime*.   *(Lesson 9-4)*

72. $7a^2 + 22a + 3$
   $(7a + 1)(a + 3)$

73. $2x^2 - 5x - 12$
   $(2x + 3)(x - 4)$

74. $3c^2 - 3c - 5$ **prime**

WebQuest   Internet Project

Pluto Is Falling from Status as a Distant Planet

It is time to complete your project. Use the information and data you have gathered about the solar system to prepare a brochure, poster, or Web page. Be sure to include the three graphs, tables, diagrams, or calculations in the presentation.

www.algebra1.com/webquest

Algebra Activity

A Follow-Up of Lesson 10-7

Investigating Rates of Change

Getting Started

Objective Analyze the Richter scale for rates of change.

Materials
grid paper

Collect the Data

- The Richter scale is used to measure the force of an earthquake. The table below shows the increase in magnitude for the values on the Richter scale.

Richter Number (x)	Increase in Magnitude (y)	Rate of Change (slope)
1	1	—
2	10	9
3	100	90
4	1000	900
5	10,000	9000
6	100,000	90,000
7	1,000,000	900,000

Source: *The New York Public Library Science Desk Reference*

- On grid paper, plot the ordered pairs (Richter number, increase in magnitude).
- Copy the table for the Richter scale and fill in the rate of change from one value to the next. For example, the rate of change for (1, 1) and (2, 10) is $\frac{10 - 1}{2 - 1}$ or 9.

Analyze the Data

1. The graph begins by increasing slowly and then increases rapidly for the last few values.

1. Describe the graph you made of the Richter scale data.
2. Is the rate of change between any two points the same? no
3. No; the rate of change between any two points is always a different value.

Make a Conjecture

3. Can the data be represented by a linear equation? Why or why not?
4. Describe the pattern shown in the rates of change in Column 3.
   To move from one rate of change to the next, you multiply by 10.

Extend the Investigation 5. $y = 0.1(10^x)$

5. Use a graphing calculator or graphing software to find a regression equation for the Richter scale data. (*Hint:* If you are using the TI-83 Plus, use **ExpReg**.)

6. Graph the following set of data that shows the amount of energy released for each Richter scale value. Describe the graph. Fill in the third column and describe the rates of change. Find a regression equation for this set of data. See pp. 581A–581H.

Richter Number (x)	Energy Released (y)	Rate of Change (slope)
1	0.00017 metric ton	
2	0.006 metric ton	0.00583
3	0.179 metric ton	0.173
4	5 metric tons	4.821
5	179 metric tons	174
6	5643 metric tons	5464
7	179,100 metric tons	173,457

Source: *The New York Public Library Science Desk Reference*

Teach

- Point out to students that they are going to have to make a very large scale on the y-axis of their graphs in order to plot the points.

Assess

Before students answer Exercise 3, have them plot only the first three points on a coordinate plane with a y-axis from 0 to 100. Then ask them to look at this partial graph and describe whether the graph is linear. **Sample answer: The graph is not linear because the slope between the first and second points is very different from the slope between the second and third points.**

Study Notebook

You may wish to have students summarize this activity and what they learned from it.

Resource Manager

📁 Teaching Algebra with Manipulatives
- p. 1 (master for grid paper)
- p. 182 (student recording sheet)

Glencoe Mathematics Classroom Manipulative Kit
- coordinate grid stamp

Vocabulary and Concept Check

- This alphabetical list of vocabulary terms in Chapter 10 includes a page reference where each term was introduced.
- **Assessment** A vocabulary test/review for Chapter 10 is available on p. 634 of the *Chapter 10 Resource Masters*.

Lesson-by-Lesson Review

For each lesson,
- the main ideas are summarized,
- additional examples review concepts, and
- practice exercises are provided.

Vocabulary PuzzleMaker

ELL The Vocabulary PuzzleMaker software improves students' mathematics vocabulary using four puzzle formats—crossword, scramble, word search using a word list, and word search using clues. Students can work on a computer screen or from a printed handout.

MindJogger Videoquizzes

ELL MindJogger Videoquizzes provide an alternative review of concepts presented in this chapter. Students work in teams in a game show format to gain points for correct answers. The questions are presented in three rounds.

Round 1 Concepts (5 questions)
Round 2 Skills (4 questions)
Round 3 Problem Solving (4 questions)

Vocabulary and Concept Check

axis of symmetry (p. 525)	exponential growth (p. 561)	Quadratic Formula (p. 546)
common ratio (p. 567)	geometric means (p. 570)	quadratic function (p. 524)
completing the square (p. 539)	geometric sequence (p. 567)	roots (p. 533)
compound interest (p. 562)	maximum (p. 525)	symmetry (p. 525)
discriminant (p. 548)	minimum (p. 525)	vertex (p. 525)
exponential decay (p. 562)	parabola (p. 524)	zeros (p. 533)
exponential function (p. 554)	quadratic equation (p. 533)	

Choose the letter of the term that best matches each equation or phrase.

1. $y = C(1 + r)^t$ **d**
2. $f(x) = ax^2 + bx + c$ **g**
3. a geometric property of parabolas **i**
4. $x = -\frac{b}{2a}$ **a**
5. $y = a^x$ **c**
6. maximum or minimum point of a parabola **j**
7. $y = C(1 - r)^t$ **b**
8. solutions of a quadratic equation **h**
9. $x = \frac{-b \pm \sqrt{b^2 - 4ac}}{2a}$ **f**
10. the graph of a quadratic function **e**

a. equation of axis of symmetry
b. exponential decay equation
c. exponential function
d. exponential growth equation
e. parabola
f. Quadratic Formula
g. quadratic function
h. roots
i. symmetry
j. vertex

Lesson-by-Lesson Review

10-1 Graphing Quadratic Functions

See pages 524–530.

Concept Summary
- The standard form of a quadratic function is $y = ax^2 + bx + c$.
- Complete a table of values to graph a quadratic function.
- The equation of the axis of symmetry for the graph of $y = ax^2 + bx + c$, where $a \neq 0$, is $x = -\frac{b}{2a}$.
- The vertex of a parabola is on the axis of symmetry.

Example Consider the graph of $y = x^2 - 8x + 12$.

a. **Write the equation of the axis of symmetry.**

In the equation $y = x^2 - 8x + 12$, $a = 1$ and $b = -8$. Substitute these values into the equation of the axis of symmetry.

$x = -\frac{b}{2a}$ Equation of the axis of symmetry

$= -\frac{-8}{2(1)}$ or 4 $a = 1$ and $b = -8$

The equation of the axis of symmetry is $x = 4$.

 www.algebra1.com/vocabulary_revie

FOLDABLES™

Study Organizer

For more information about Foldables, see *Teaching Mathematics with Foldables.*

Have students review their Foldables to make sure that they have included information for every lesson page in the Foldable. Now is a good time to ask if students have any questions about the concepts that they recorded.

Encourage students to refer to their Foldables while completing the Study Guide and Review and to use them in preparing for the Chapter Test.

b. Find the coordinates of the vertex of the graph.

The x-coordinate of the vertex is 4.

$y = x^2 - 8x + 12$ Original equation

$y = (4)^2 - 8(4) + 12$ $x = 4$

$y = 16 - 32 + 12$ Simplify.

$y = -4$ The coordinates of the vertex are $(4, -4)$.

11–16. See margin.
Exercises   Write the equation of the axis of symmetry, and find the coordinates of the vertex of the graph of each function. Identify the vertex as a maximum or minimum. Then graph the function.   *See Example 3 on pages 526 and 527.*

11. $y = x^2 + 2x$ **12.** $y = -3x^2 + 4$ **13.** $y = x^2 - 3x - 4$
14. $y = 3x^2 + 6x - 17$ **15.** $y = -2x^2 + 1$ **16.** $y = -x^2 - 3x$

10-2 Solving Quadratic Equations by Graphing

See pages 533–538.

Concept Summary

• The roots of a quadratic equation are the x-intercepts of the related quadratic function.

Example   Solve $x^2 - 3x - 4 = 0$ by graphing.

Graph the related function
$f(x) = x^2 - 3x - 4$.

The x-intercepts are -1 and 4. Therefore, the solutions are -1, and 4.

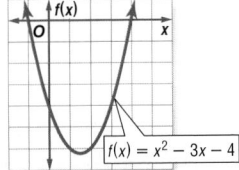

17–22. See margin for graphs.
Exercises   Solve each equation by graphing. If integral roots cannot be found, estimate the roots by stating the consecutive integers between which the roots lie.
See Examples 1–4 on pages 533–535. **19.** $-5 < x < -4, 0 < x < 1$

17. $x^2 - x - 12 = 0$ $-3, 4$ **18.** $x^2 + 6x + 9 = 0$ -3 **19.** $x^2 + 4x - 3 = 0$
20. $2x^2 - 5x + 4 = 0$ $\varnothing$ **21.** $x^2 - 10x = -21$ $3, 7$ **22.** $6x^2 - 13x = 15$
$-1 < x < 0, 3$

10-3 Solving Quadratic Equations by Completing the Square

See pages 539–544.

Concept Summary

• Complete the square to make a quadratic expression a perfect square.
• Use the following steps to complete the square of $x^2 + bx$.

Step 1   Find $\frac{1}{2}$ of b, the coefficient of x.

Step 2   Square the result of Step 1.

Step 3   Add the result of Step 2 to $x^2 + bx$, the original expression.

11. $x = -1$; $(-1, -1)$; minimum   **12.** $x = 0$; $(0, 4)$; maximum

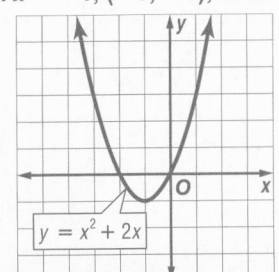

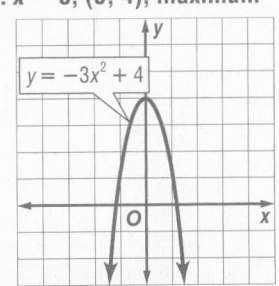

Answers

13. $x = 1\frac{1}{2}$; $\left(1\frac{1}{2}, -6\frac{1}{4}\right)$; minimum

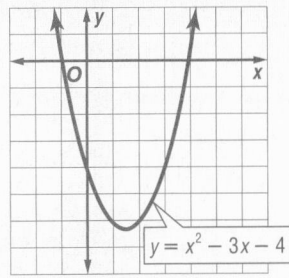

14. $x = -1$; $(-1, -20)$; minimum

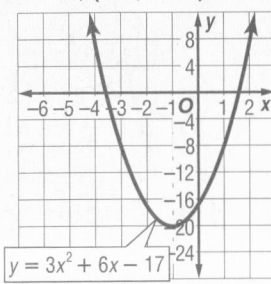

15. $x = 0$; $(0, 1)$; maximum

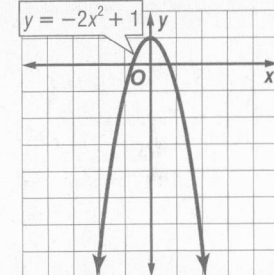

16. $x = -1\frac{1}{2}$; $\left(-1\frac{1}{2}, 2\frac{1}{4}\right)$; maximum

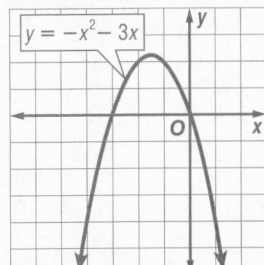

17.

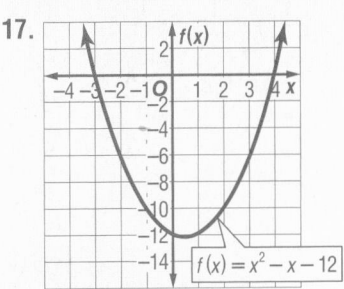

(continued on next page)

Answers

(continued from p. 575)

18.

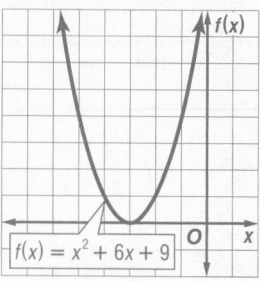

$f(x) = x^2 + 6x + 9$

19.

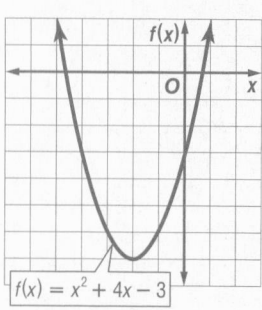

$f(x) = x^2 + 4x - 3$

20.

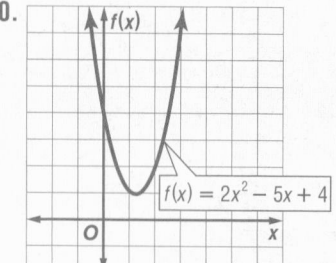

$f(x) = 2x^2 - 5x + 4$

21.

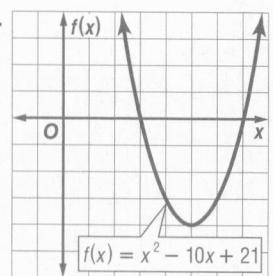

$f(x) = x^2 - 10x + 21$

22.

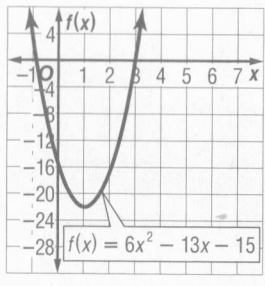

$f(x) = 6x^2 - 13x - 15$

Example   Solve $y^2 + 6y + 2 = 0$ by completing the square. Round to the nearest tenth if necessary.

$y^2 + 6y + 2 = 0$ Original equation

$y^2 + 6y + 2 - 2 = 0 - 2$ Subtract 2 from each side.

$y^2 + 6y = -2$ Simplify.

$y^2 + 6y + 9 = -2 + 9$ Since $\left(\frac{6}{2}\right)^2 = 9$, add 9 to each side.

$(y + 3)^2 = 7$ Factor $y^2 + 6y + 9$.

$y + 3 = \pm\sqrt{7}$ Take the square root of each side.

$y + 3 - 3 = \pm\sqrt{7} - 3$ Subtract 3 from each side.

$y = -3 \pm \sqrt{7}$ Simplify.

Use a calculator to evaluate each value of y.

$y = -3 + \sqrt{7}$ or $y = -3 - \sqrt{7}$

$y \approx -0.4$ $y \approx -5.6$

The solution set is $\{-5.6, -0.4\}$.

Exercises   Solve each equation by completing the square. Round to the nearest tenth if necessary.   *See Example 3 on pages 540 and 541.*   **24. 2.3, 13.7**

23. $-3x^2 + 4 = 0$ **−1.2, 1.2**   **24.** $x^2 - 16x + 32 = 0$ **25.** $m^2 - 7m = 5$ **−0.7, 7.7**

26. $4a^2 + 16a + 15 = 0$ **27.** $\frac{1}{2}y^2 + 2y - 1 = 0$ **28.** $n^2 - 3n + \frac{5}{4} = 0$

    −2.5, −1.5   **−4.4, 0.4**   **0.5, 2.5**

10-4   **Solving Quadratic Equations by Using the Quadratic Formula**

See pages 546–552.

Concept Summary

- The solutions of a quadratic equation in the form $ax^2 + bx + c = 0$, where $a \neq 0$, are given by the Quadratic Formula, $x = \dfrac{-b \pm \sqrt{b^2 - 4ac}}{2a}$.

Example   Solve $2x^2 + 7x - 15 = 0$ by using the Quadratic Formula.

For this equation, $a = 2$, $b = 7$, and $c = -15$.

$x = \dfrac{-b \pm \sqrt{b^2 - 4ac}}{2a}$ Quadratic Formula

$x = \dfrac{-7 \pm \sqrt{7^2 - 4(2)(-15)}}{2(2)}$ $a = 2$, $b = 7$, and $c = -15$

$x = \dfrac{-7 \pm \sqrt{169}}{4}$ Simplify.

$x = \dfrac{-7 + 13}{4}$ or $x = \dfrac{-7 - 13}{4}$

$x = 1\frac{1}{2}$ $x = -5$ The solution set is $\left\{-5, 1\frac{1}{2}\right\}$.

Exercises Solve each equation by using the Quadratic Formula. Round to the nearest tenth if necessary. *See Examples 1 and 2 on pages 546 and 547.* **30. −9, −1**

29. $x^2 - 8x = 20$ **−2, 10**   **30.** $r^2 + 10r + 9 = 0$ **31.** $4p^2 + 4p = 15$ **−2.5, 1.5**

32. $2y^2 + 3 = -8y$ **33.** $2d^2 + 8d + 3 = 3$ **34.** $21a^2 + 5a - 7 = 0$

−3.6, −0.4   **−4, 0**   **−0.7, 0.5**

10-5 Exponential Functions

See pages 554–560.

Concept Summary

- An exponential function is a function that can be described by the equation of the form $y = a^x$, where $a > 0$ and $a \neq 1$.

Example   Graph $y = 2^x - 3$. State the y-intercept.

x	y
−3	−2.875
−2	−2.75
−1	−2.5
0	−2
1	−1
2	1
3	5

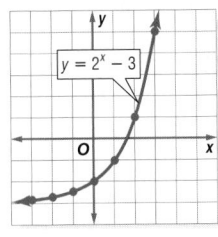

Graph the ordered pairs and connect the points with a smooth curve. The y-intercept is −2.

Exercises Graph each function. State the y-intercept. *See Examples 1 and 2 on page 555.* **35–37. See margin for graphs.**

35. $y = 3^x + 6$ **7**   **36.** $y = 3^{x+2}$ **9**   **37.** $y = 2\left(\frac{1}{2}\right)^x$ **2**

35.
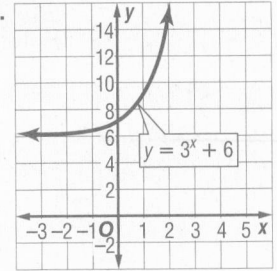

36.
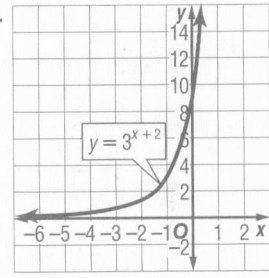

37.
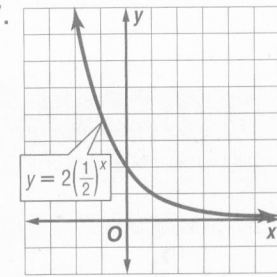

10-6 Growth and Decay

See pages 561–565.

Concept Summary

- Exponential Growth: $y = C(1 + r)^t$, where y represents the final amount, C represents the initial amount, r represents the rate of change expressed as a decimal, and t represents time.

- Compound Interest: $A = P\left(1 + \frac{r}{n}\right)^{nt}$, where A represents the amount of the investment, P represents the principal, r represents the annual rate of interest expressed as a decimal, n represents the number of times that the interest is compounded each year, and t represents the number of years that the money is invested.

- Exponential Decay: $y = C(1 - r)^t$, where y represents the final amount, C represents the initial amount, r represents the rate of decay expressed as a decimal, and t represents time.

Study Guide and Review

Chapter **10** For More ...
- Extra Practice, see pages 841–843.
- Mixed Problem Solving, see page 862.

Answers (p. 579)

4.
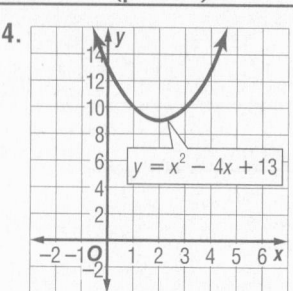
$y = x^2 - 4x + 13$

5.
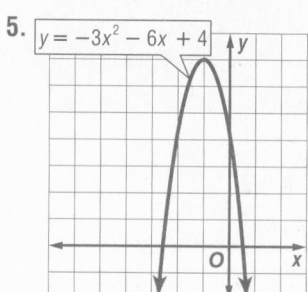
$y = -3x^2 - 6x + 4$

6.
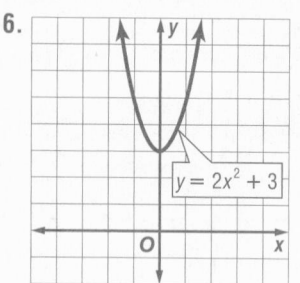
$y = 2x^2 + 3$

7.
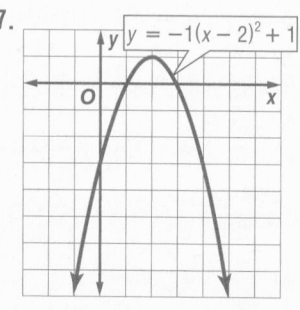
$y = -1(x - 2)^2 + 1$

8.
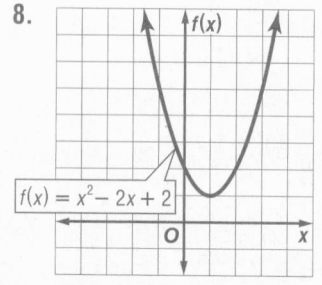
$f(x) = x^2 - 2x + 2$

Example Find the final amount of an investment if \$1500 is invested at an interest rate of 7.5% compounded quarterly for 10 years.

$A = P\left(1 + \dfrac{r}{n}\right)^{nt}$ Compound interest equation

$A = 1500\left(1 + \dfrac{0.075}{4}\right)^{4 \cdot 10}$ $P = 1500, r = 7.5\%$ or $0.075, n = 4$, and $t = 10$

$A \approx 3153.52$ Simplify.

The final amount in the account is about \$3153.52.

Exercises Determine the final amount for each investment.
See Example 2 on page 562.

	Principal	Annual Interest Rate	Time	Type of Compounding	
38.	\$2000	8%	8 years	quarterly	\$3769.08
39.	\$5500	5.25%	15 years	monthly	\$12,067.68
40.	\$15,000	7.5%	25 years	monthly	\$97,243.21
41.	\$500	9.75%	40 years	daily	\$24,688.36

10-7 Geometric Sequences

See pages 567–572.

Concept Summary

- A geometric sequence is a sequence in which each term after the nonzero first term is found by multiplying the previous term by a constant called the common ratio r, where $r \neq 0$ or 1.
- The nth term a_n of a geometric sequence with the first term a_1, and a common ratio r is given by $a_n = a_1 \cdot r^{n-1}$.

Example Find the next three terms in the geometric sequence 7.5, 15, 30, ...

$\dfrac{15}{7.5} = 2$ Divide the second term by the first.

The common ratio is 2. Find the next three terms.

7.5, 15, 30, 60, 120, 240
        ×2   ×2   ×2

The next three terms are 60, 120, and 240.

Exercises Find the nth term of each geometric sequence.
See Example 4 on page 569.

42. $a_1 = 2, n = 5, r = 2$ **32** **43.** $a_1 = 7, n = 4, r = \dfrac{2}{3}$ **$\dfrac{56}{27}$** **44.** $a_1 = 243, n = 5, r = -\dfrac{1}{3}$ **3**

Find the geometric means in each sequence.   *See Example 5 on page 570.*

45. 5, ___, 20 **±10**   **46.** −12, ___, −48 **±24**   **47.** 1, ___, $\dfrac{1}{4}$ **±$\dfrac{1}{2}$**

578   **Chapter 10**   Quadratic and Exponential Functions

9.
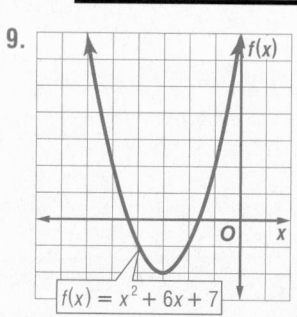
$f(x) = x^2 + 6x + 7$

10.
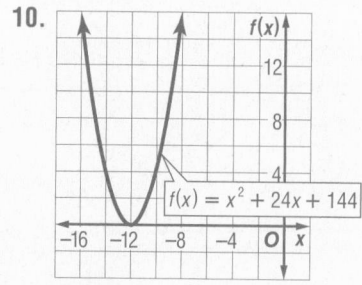
$f(x) = x^2 + 24x + 144$

11.
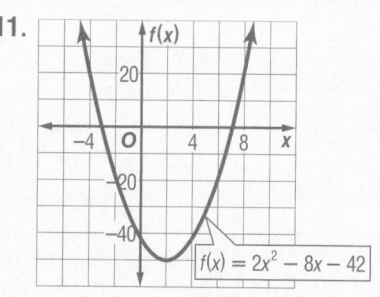
$f(x) = 2x^2 - 8x - 42$

Vocabulary and Concepts

Choose the letter of the term that matches each formula.

1. $x = \dfrac{-b \pm \sqrt{b^2 - 4ac}}{2a}$ **c**

2. $y = C(1 + r)^t$ **b**

3. $y = C(1 - r)^t$ **a**

> a. exponential decay equation
> b. exponential growth equation
> c. Quadratic Formula

Skills and Applications

Write the equation of the axis of symmetry, and find the coordinates of the vertex of the graph of each function. Identify the vertex as a maximum or minimum. Then graph the function. 4–7. See margin for graphs.

4. $y = x^2 - 4x + 13$ $x = 2$; (2, 9); min

5. $y = -3x^2 - 6x + 4$ $x = -1$; (−1, 7); max

6. $y = 2x^2 + 3$ $x = 0$; (0, 3); min

7. $y = -1(x - 2)^2 + 1$ $x = 2$; (2, 1); max

Solve each equation by graphing. If integral roots cannot be found, estimate the roots by stating the consecutive integers between which the roots lie. 8–11. See margin for graphs.

8. $x^2 - 2x + 2 = 0$ $\varnothing$

9. $x^2 + 6x = -7$ $-5 < x < -4$; $-2 < x < -1$

10. $x^2 + 24x + 144 = 0$ **−12**

11. $2x^2 - 8x = 42$ **−3, 7**

Solve each equation. Round to the nearest tenth if necessary.

12. $x^2 + 7x + 6 = 0$ **−6, −1**

13. $2x^2 - 5x - 12 = 0$ $-1\frac{1}{2}$, 4

14. $6n^2 + 7n = 20$ $-2\frac{1}{2}$, $1\frac{1}{3}$

15. $3k^2 + 2k = 5$ $-1\frac{2}{3}$, 1

16. $y^2 - \frac{3}{5}y + \frac{2}{25} = 0$ $\frac{1}{5}$, $\frac{2}{5}$

17. $-3x^2 + 5 = 14x$ -5, $\frac{1}{3}$

18. $z^2 - 13z = 32$ **−2.1, 15.1**

19. $3x^2 + 4x = 8$ **−2.4, 1.1**

20. $7m^2 = m + 5$ **−0.8, 0.9**

Graph each function. State the y-intercept. 21–23. See pp. 581A–581H for graphs.

21. $y = \left(\dfrac{1}{2}\right)^x$ **1**

22. $y = 4 \cdot 2^x$ **4**

23. $y = \left(\dfrac{1}{3}\right)^x - 3$ **−2**

Find the nth term of each geometric sequence.

24. $a_1 = 12, n = 6, r = 2$ **384**

25. $a_1 = 20, n = 4, r = 3$ **540**

Find the geometric means in each sequence.

26. 7, ____, 63 **±21**

27. $-\dfrac{1}{3}$, ____, −12 **±2**

28. **CARS** Ley needs to replace her car. If she leases a car, she will pay $410 a month for 2 years and then has the option to buy the car for $14,458. The current price of the car is $17,369. If the car depreciates at 16% per year, how will the depreciated price compare with the buyout price of the lease? **$2202 less than the buyout price**

29. **FINANCE** Find the total amount after $1500 is invested for 10 years at a rate of 6%, compounded quarterly. **about $2721.03**

30. **STANDARDIZED TEST PRACTICE** Which value is the next value in the pattern −4, 12, −36, 108, … ? **A**

(A) −324   (B) 324   (C) −432   (D) 432

 www.algebra1.com/chapter_test

Assessment Options

Vocabulary Test A vocabulary test/review for Chapter 10 can be found on p. 634 of the *Chapter 10 Resource Masters*.

Chapter Tests There are six Chapter 10 Tests and an Open-Ended Assessment task available in the *Chapter 10 Resource Masters*.

Chapter 10 Tests			
Form	Type	Level	Pages
1	MC	basic	621–622
2A	MC	average	623–624
2B	MC	average	625–626
2C	FR	average	627–628
2D	FR	average	629–630
3	FR	advanced	631–632

MC = multiple-choice questions
FR = free-response questions

Open-Ended Assessment
Performance tasks for Chapter 10 can be found on p. 633 of the *Chapter 10 Resource Masters*. A sample scoring rubric for these tasks appears on p. A28.

Unit 3 Test A unit test/review can be found on pp. 641–642 of the *Chapter 10 Resource Masters*.

 ExamView® Pro

Use the networkable **ExamView® Pro** to:

- Create **multiple versions** of tests.
- Create **modified** tests for *Inclusion* students.
- **Edit** existing questions and **add** your own questions.
- Use built-in **state curriculum correlations** to create tests aligned with state standards.
- Change **English** tests to **Spanish** and vice versa.

Portfolio Suggestion

Introduction If you had to solve a quadratic function in the future, which method would you use? Do you have a favorite method?

Ask Students How do the different methods work? At which times are the two methods most useful? Explain which one is your favorite, giving reasons why you like it. Pick two methods of solving a quadratic function, one being your favorite method, and compare and contrast the methods.

These two pages contain practice questions in the various formats that can be found on the most frequently given standardized tests.

A practice answer sheet for these two pages can be found on p. A1 of the *Chapter 10 Resource Masters*.

Standardized Test Practice
Student Recording Sheet, p. A1

Part 1 Multiple Choice

Select the best answer from the choices given and fill in the corresponding oval.

1 Ⓐ Ⓑ Ⓒ Ⓓ	4 Ⓐ Ⓑ Ⓒ Ⓓ	7 Ⓐ Ⓑ Ⓒ Ⓓ
2 Ⓐ Ⓑ Ⓒ Ⓓ	5 Ⓐ Ⓑ Ⓒ Ⓓ	8 Ⓐ Ⓑ Ⓒ Ⓓ
3 Ⓐ Ⓑ Ⓒ Ⓓ	6 Ⓐ Ⓑ Ⓒ Ⓓ	9 Ⓐ Ⓑ Ⓒ Ⓓ

Part 2 Short Response/Grid In

Solve the problem and write your answer in the blank.

For Questions 16, 17, 18, and 20, also enter your answer by writing each number or symbol in a box. Then fill in the corresponding oval for that number or symbol.

10 _____
11 _____
12 _____
13 _____
14 _____
15 _____
16 _____ (grid in)
17 _____ (grid in)
18 _____ (grid in)
19 _____
20 _____ (grid in)

Part 3 Extended Response

Record your answers for Questions 21–22 on the back of this paper.

Additional Practice

See pp. 639–640 in the *Chapter 10 Resource Masters* for additional standardized test practice.

Part 1 Multiple Choice

Record your answers on the answer sheet provided by your teacher or on a sheet of paper.

1. The graph of $y = 3x$ is shown. If the line is translated 2 units down, which equation will describe the new line? (Lesson 4-2) **B**

Ⓐ $y = -6x$
Ⓑ $y = 3x - 2$
Ⓒ $y = 3x + 2$
Ⓓ $y = 3(x - 2)$

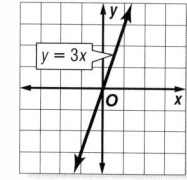

2. Suppose a varies directly as b, and $a = 21$ when $b = 6$. Find a when $b = 28$. (Lesson 5-2) **C**

Ⓐ 4.5
Ⓑ 8
Ⓒ 98
Ⓓ 126

3. Which equation is represented by the graph? (Lesson 5-5) **A**

Ⓐ $y = -2x - 10$
Ⓑ $y = -2x - 5$
Ⓒ $y = 2x + 10$
Ⓓ $y = 2x - 5$

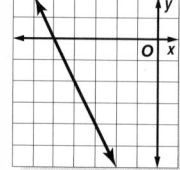

4. At a farm market, apples cost 20¢ each and grapefruit cost 25¢ each. A shopper bought twice as many apples as grapefruit and spent a total of $1.95. How many apples did he buy? (Lesson 7-2) **D**

Ⓐ 3   Ⓑ 4   Ⓒ 5   Ⓓ 6

5. A rectangle has a length of $2x + 3$ and a width of $2x - 6$. Which expression describes the area of the rectangle? (Lesson 8-7) **C**

Ⓐ $4x - 3$
Ⓑ $4x^2 - 18$
Ⓒ $4x^2 - 6x - 18$
Ⓓ $4x^2 + 18x - 18$

---

6. The solution set for the equation $x^2 + x - 12 = 0$ is (Lesson 9-3) **B**

Ⓐ $\{-4, -3\}$.
Ⓑ $\{-4, 3\}$.
Ⓒ $\{4, -3\}$.
Ⓓ $\{4, 3\}$.

7. Which equation best represents the data in the table? (Lesson 10-1) **B**

x	y
-3	0
-1	8
0	9
2	5
3	0
4	-7

Ⓐ $y = -x^2 + 3$
Ⓑ $y = -x^2 + 9$
Ⓒ $y = x^2 - 3$
Ⓓ $y = x^2 + 9$

8. Which equation best represents the parabola graphed below? (Lesson 10-1) **B**

Ⓐ $y = x^2 - 2x - 4$
Ⓑ $y = x^2 - 2x - 3$
Ⓒ $y = x^2 + 2x - 3$
Ⓓ $y = x^2 + 2x + 3$

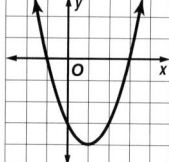

9. At which points does the graph of $f(x) = 2x^2 + 8x + 6$ intersect the x-axis? (Lesson 10-2) **B**

Ⓐ $(-3, 0)$ and $(-2, 0)$
Ⓑ $(-3, 0)$ and $(-1, 0)$
Ⓒ $(1, 0)$ and $(3, 0)$
Ⓓ $(2, 0)$ and $(3, 0)$

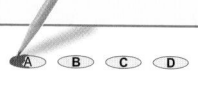

Test-Taking Tip   Ⓐ Ⓑ Ⓒ Ⓓ

Questions 1 and 7
Sketching the graph of a function or a transformation may help you see which answer choice is correct.

ExamView® Pro

Special banks of standardized test questions similar to those on the SAT, ACT, TIMSS 8, NAEP 8, and Algebra 1 End-of-Course tests can be found on this CD-ROM.

Part 2 Short Response/Grid In

Record your answers on the answer sheet provided by your teacher or on a sheet of paper. **11.** $y = -\frac{1}{2}x + 4$

10. Monica earned $18.50, $23.00, and $15.00 mowing lawns for 3 consecutive weeks. She wanted to earn an average of at least $18 per week. What is the minimum she should earn during the 4th week to meet her goal? (Lesson 3-4) **$15.50**

11. Write an equation in slope-intercept form of the line that is perpendicular to the line represented by $8x - 4y + 9 = 0$ and passes through the point at $(2, 3)$. (Lesson 5-6)

12. Name an inequality that matches the graph. (Lesson 6-6)
$y \leq -2$

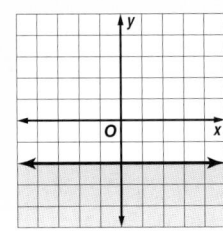

13. If $5a + 4b = 25$ and $3a - 8b = 41$, solve for a and b. (Lesson 7-4) $a = 7, b = -2\frac{1}{2}$

14. Simplify $\left(\dfrac{4d^3}{3a^7}\right)^{-3}$. (Lesson 8-2) $\dfrac{27a^{21}}{64d^9}$

15. Complete the square of $x^2 + 4x - 5$ by finding numbers h and k such that $x^2 + 4x - 5 = (x + h)^2 + k$. (Lesson 10-2)
$h = 2, k = -9$

16. At how many points does the graph of $y = 6x^2 + 11x + 4$ intersect the x-axis?
(Lesson 10-3) **2**

17. The length and width of a rectangle that measures 8 inches by 6 inches are both increased by the same amount. The area of the larger rectangle is twice the area of the original rectangle. How much was added to each dimension of the original rectangle? Round to the nearest hundredth of an inch.
(Lesson 10-4) **2.85**

 www.algebra1.com/standardized_test

18. What is the y-intercept of the graph of $y = 5(6 - 9^x)$? (Lesson 10-5) **25**

19. Mr. Ramirez bought a car for $27,000. If the car depreciates 13% per year, what is the value of the car after 8 years? (Lesson 10-5)
$8861.72

20. Find the geometric mean in the sequence 3, _____, 48. (Lesson 10-7) **12**

Part 3 Extended Response

Record your answers on a sheet of paper. Show your work.

21. Analyze the graph of $y = -4x^2 + 8x - \frac{15}{4}$.
(Lessons 10-1, 10-3)

  a. Show that the equation $-4x^2 + 8x - \frac{15}{4} = -4(x - 1)^2 + \frac{1}{4}$ is always true by expanding the right side. **See margin.**

  b. Find the equation of the axis of symmetry of the graph of
  $y = -4x^2 + 8x - \frac{15}{4}$. $x = 1$

  c. Does the parabola open upward or downward? Explain how you determined this. **See margin.**

  d. Find the values of x, if any, where the graph crosses the x-axis. Write as rational numbers. $\frac{3}{4}, 1\frac{1}{4}$

  e. Find the coordinates of the maximum or minimum point on this parabola. $\left(1, \frac{1}{4}\right)$

  f. Sketch the graph of the equation. Label the maximum or minimum point and the roots. **See margin.**

22. Annika Sorenstam hit a golf ball and its path through the air is modeled by the equation $h = -16t^2 + 80t + 1$, where h is the height in feet of the golf ball and t is the time in seconds. (Lesson 10-2)

  a. Approximately how long was the ball in the air? **5.01 s**

  b. How high was the ball at its highest point? **101.0 ft**

Evaluating Extended Response Questions

Extended Response questions are graded by using a multilevel rubric that guides you in assessing a student's knowledge of a particular concept.

Goal: Analyze features of a parabola using the concepts learned in this chapter.

Sample Scoring Rubric: The following rubric is a sample scoring device. You may wish to add more detail to this sample to meet your individual scoring needs.

Score	Criteria
4	A correct solution that is supported by well-developed, accurate explanations
3	A generally correct solution, but may contain minor flaws in reasoning or computation
2	A partially correct interpretation and/or solution to the problem
1	A correct solution with no supporting evidence or explanation
0	An incorrect solution indicating no mathematical understanding of the concept or task, or no solution is given

---

Answers

21a. $-4x^2 + 8x - \frac{15}{4} \overset{?}{=} -4(x - 1)^2 + \frac{1}{4}$

$-4x^2 + 8x - \frac{15}{4} \overset{?}{=} -4(x^2 - 2x + 1) + \frac{1}{4}$

$-4x^2 + 8x - \frac{15}{4} \overset{?}{=} -4x^2 + 8x - 4 + \frac{1}{4}$

$-4x^2 + 8x - \frac{15}{4} = -4x^2 + 8x - \frac{15}{4}$

21c. Since the coefficient of the x^2 term is negative, the parabola opens downward.

21f.

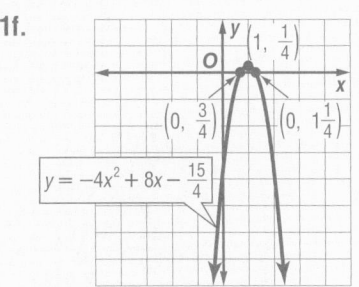

Page 523, Chapter 10 Getting Started

1. Sample answer:

x	y
−6	−1
−4	1
−2	3
0	5
2	7

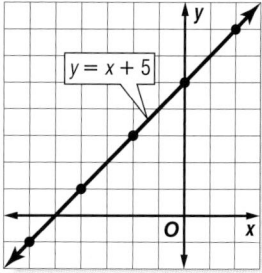

2. Sample answer:

x	y
0	−3
1	−1
2	1
3	3

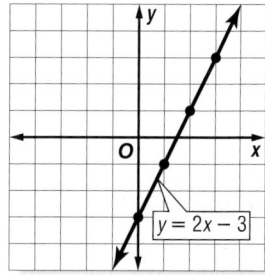

3. Sample answer:

x	y
−4	−1
−2	0
0	1
2	2
4	3

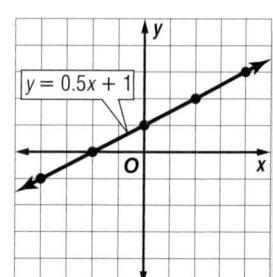

4. Sample answer:

x	y
−2	4
−1	1
0	−2

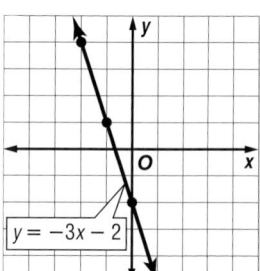

5. Sample answer:

x	y
0	−4
3	−2
6	0

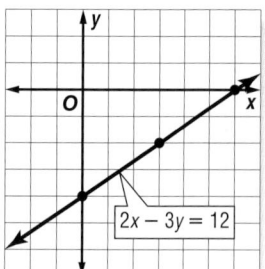

6. Sample answer:

x	y
−5	0
0	2

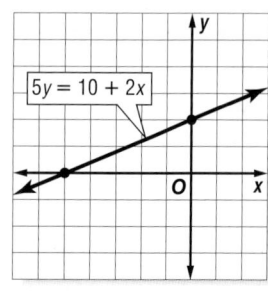

7. Sample answer:

x	y
−6	0
−4	−1
−2	−2
0	−3
2	−4

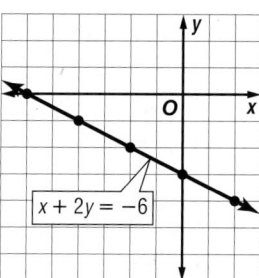

8. Sample answer:

x	y
−1	6
1	3
3	0

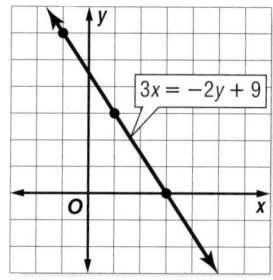

Pages 528–530 Lesson 10-1

4.

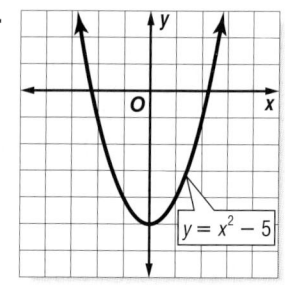

5.

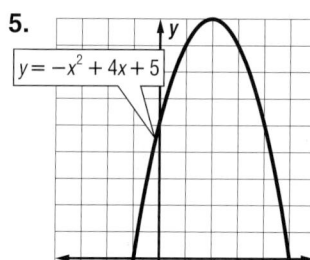

6.

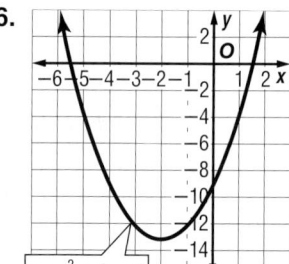

7.

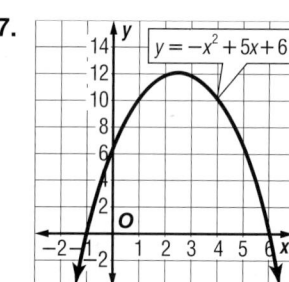

8.

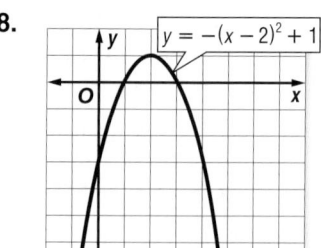

10.

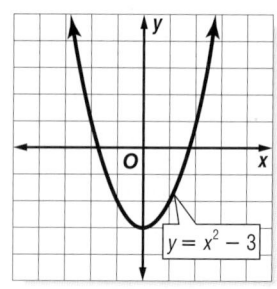

11.

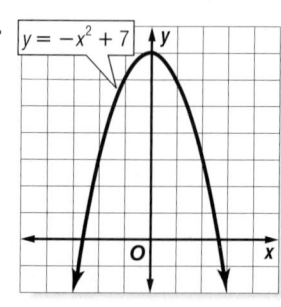

12.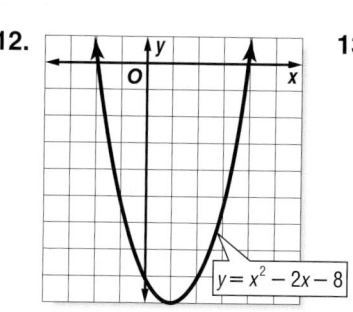
$y = x^2 - 2x - 8$

13.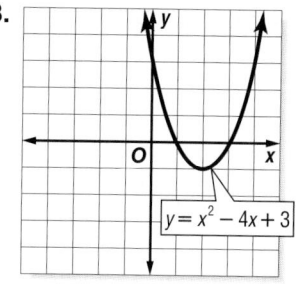
$y = x^2 - 4x + 3$

14.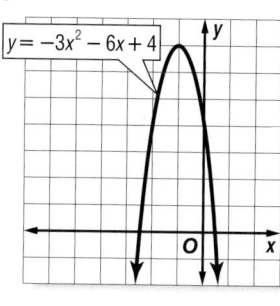
$y = -3x^2 - 6x + 4$

15.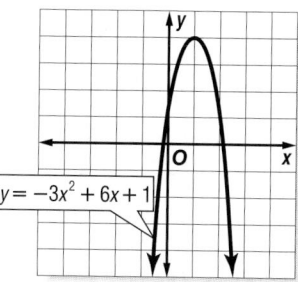
$y = -3x^2 + 6x + 1$

18.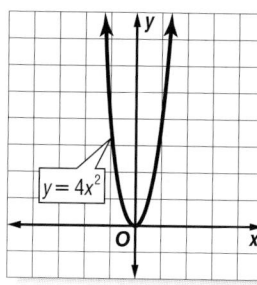
$y = 4x^2$

19.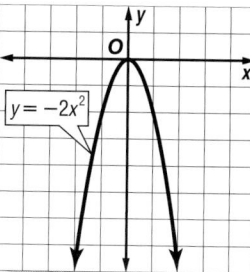
$y = -2x^2$

20.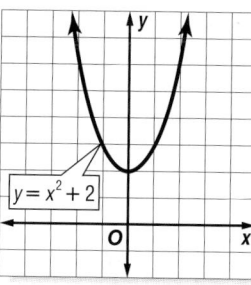
$y = x^2 + 2$

21.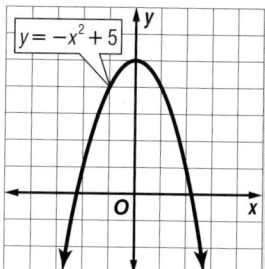
$y = -x^2 + 5$

22.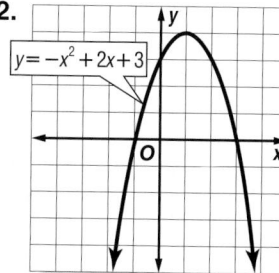
$y = -x^2 + 2x + 3$

23.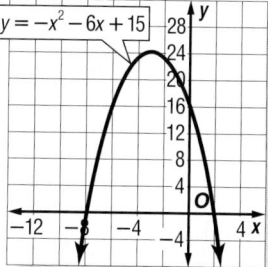
$y = -x^2 - 6x + 15$

24.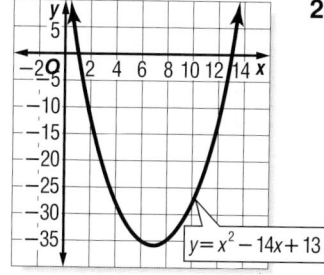
$y = x^2 - 14x + 13$

25.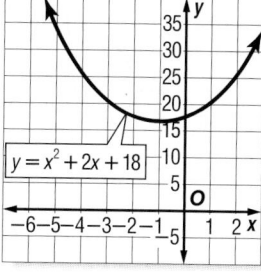
$y = x^2 + 2x + 18$

26.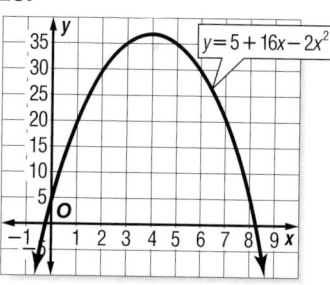
$y = 2x^2 + 12x - 11$

27.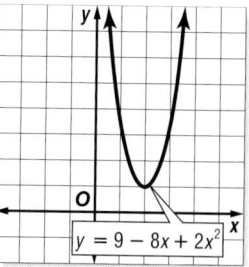
$y = 3x^2 - 6x + 4$

28.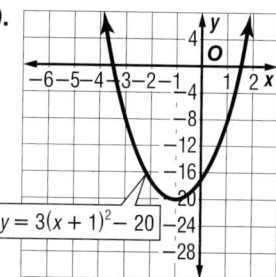
$y = 5 + 16x - 2x^2$

29.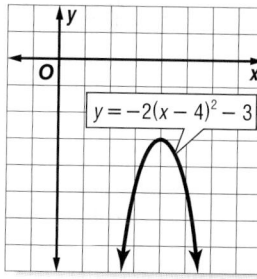
$y = 9 - 8x + 2x^2$

30.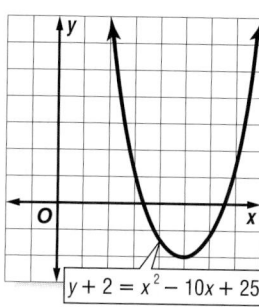
$y = 3(x + 1)^2 - 20$

31.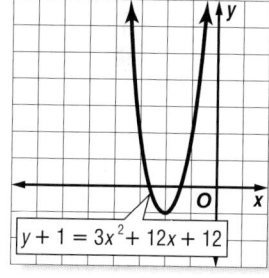
$y = -2(x - 4)^2 - 3$

32.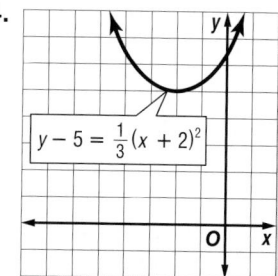
$y + 2 = x^2 - 10x + 25$

33.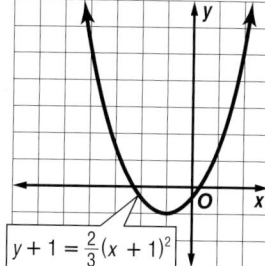
$y + 1 = 3x^2 + 12x + 12$

34.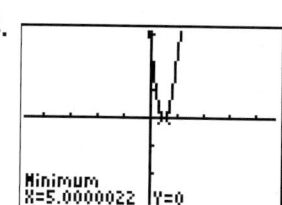
$y - 5 = \frac{1}{3}(x + 2)^2$

35.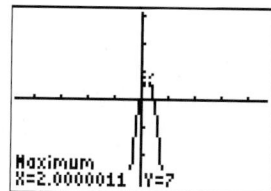
$y + 1 = \frac{2}{3}(x + 1)^2$

54.
Minimum
X=5.0000022 Y=0

55.
Maximum
X=2.0000011 Y=7

56.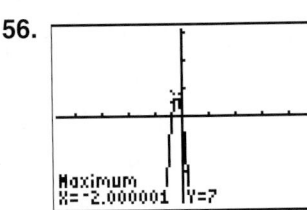
Maximum
X=-2.000001 Y=7

57. Minimum
X=10.000001 Y=14

58.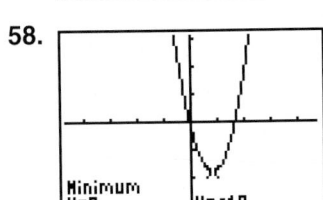
Minimum
X=8 Y=-18

59. Maximum
X=-2.000002 Y=5

Page 532, Follow-Up of Lesson 10-1
Graphing Calculator Investigation

5. The graph will have a vertex at the origin, open downward, and be wider than $y = -x^2$.

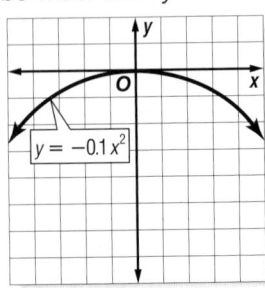
$y = -0.1x^2$

6. The graph will open upward and have the same shape as $y = x^2$, but the vertex will be at $(-1, 0)$.

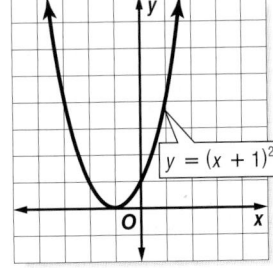
$y = (x + 1)^2$

7. The graph will open upward, have a vertex at the origin, and be narrower than $y = x^2$.

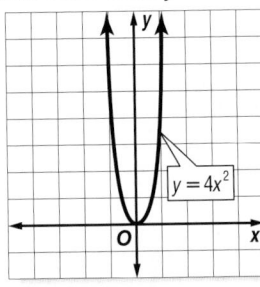
$y = 4x^2$

8. The graph will open upward and have the same shape as $y = x^2$, but its vertex will be at $(0, -6)$.

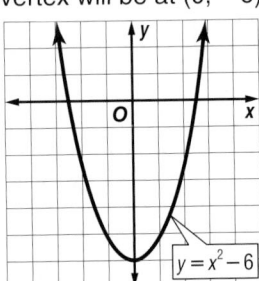
$y = x^2 - 6$

9. If $|a| > 1$, the graph is narrower than the graph of $y = x^2$. If $0 < |a| < 1$, the graph is wider than the graph of $y = x^2$. If $a < 0$, it opens downward. If $a > 0$, it opens upward.

10. The graph has the same shape as $y = x^2$, but is shifted h units (left if $h > 0$, right if $h < 0$).

11. The graph has the same shape as $y = x^2$, but is shifted k units (up if $k > 0$, down if $k < 0$).

12. The graph has the same shape as $y = x^2$, but is shifted h units left or right and k units up or down as prescribed in Exercises 10 and 11.

Pages 535–538 Lesson 10-2

4.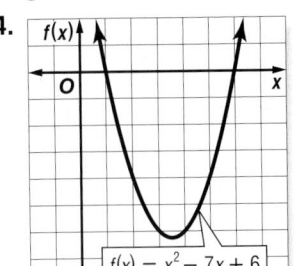
$f(x) = x^2 - 7x + 6$

5.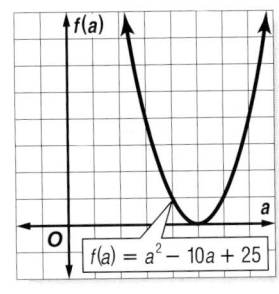
$f(a) = a^2 - 10a + 25$

6.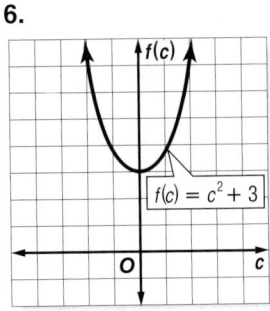
$f(c) = c^2 + 3$

7.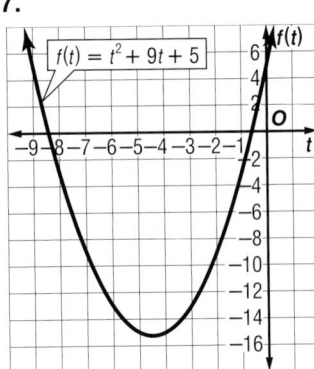
$f(t) = t^2 + 9t + 5$

8.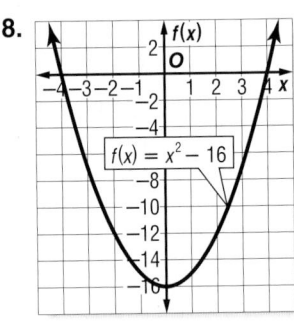
$f(x) = x^2 - 16$

9.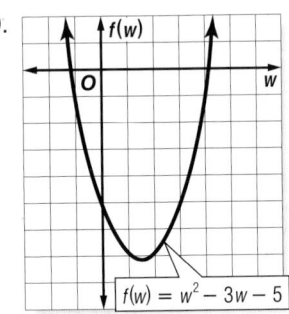
$f(w) = w^2 - 3w - 5$

11.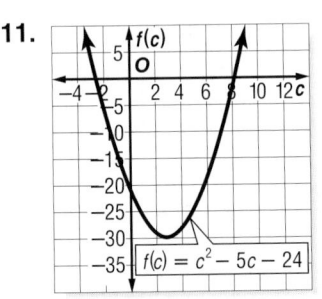
$f(c) = c^2 - 5c - 24$

12.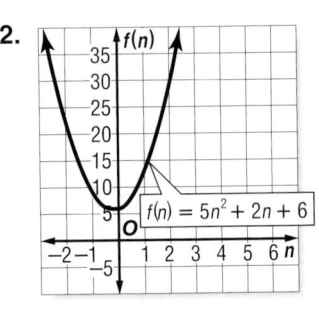
$f(n) = 5n^2 + 2n + 6$

13.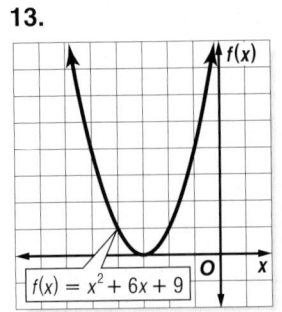
$f(x) = x^2 + 6x + 9$

14.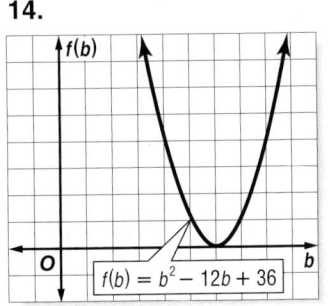
$f(b) = b^2 - 12b + 36$

15.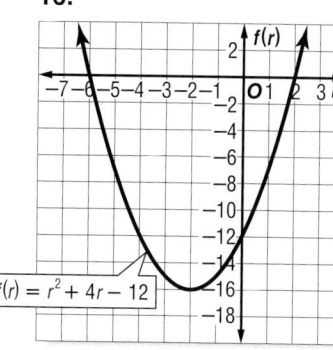

$f(x) = x^2 + 2x + 5$

16.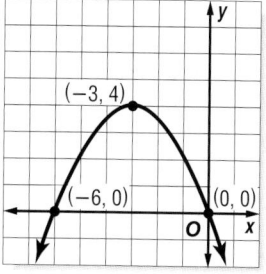

$f(r) = r^2 + 4r - 12$

17.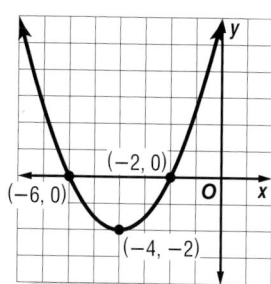

$(-2, 0)$
$(-6, 0)$
$(-4, -2)$

18.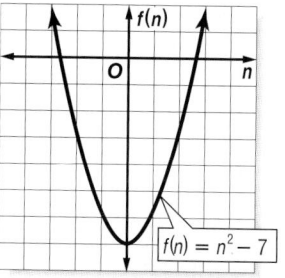

$(-3, 4)$
$(-6, 0)$
$(0, 0)$

21.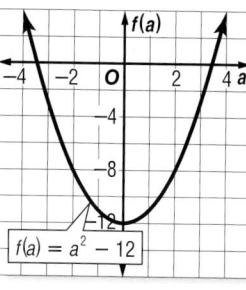

$f(a) = a^2 - 12$

$-4 < a < -3, 3 < a < 4$

22.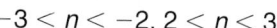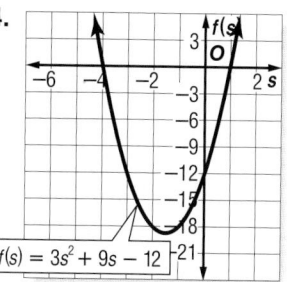

$f(n) = n^2 - 7$

$-3 < n < -2, 2 < n < 3$

23.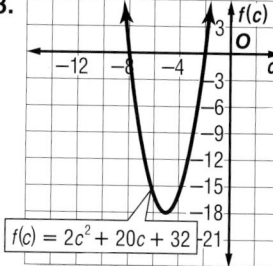

$f(c) = 2c^2 + 20c + 32$

$-8, -2$

24.

$f(s) = 3s^2 + 9s - 12$

$-4, 1$

25.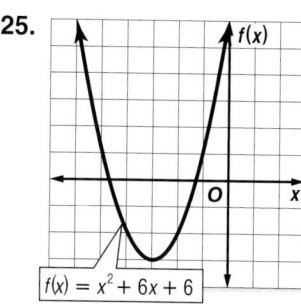

$f(x) = x^2 + 6x + 6$

$-5 < x < -4, -2 < x < -1$

26.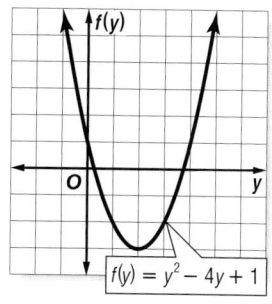

$f(y) = y^2 - 4y + 1$

$0 < y < 1, 3 < y < 4$

27.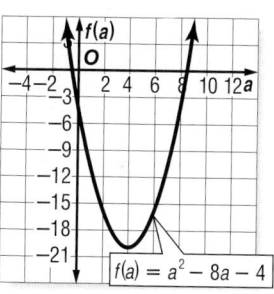

$f(a) = a^2 - 8a - 4$

$-1 < a < 0, 8 < a < 9$

28.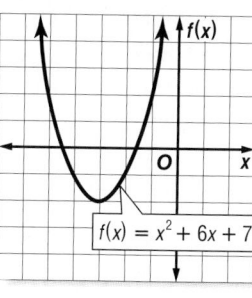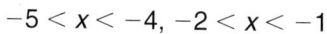

$f(x) = x^2 + 6x + 7$

$-5 < x < -4, -2 < x < -1$

29.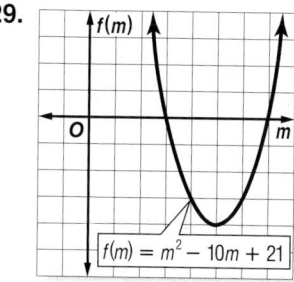

$f(m) = m^2 - 10m + 21$

$3, 7$

30.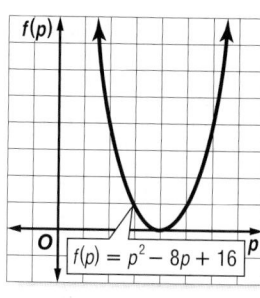

$f(p) = p^2 - 8p + 16$

4

31.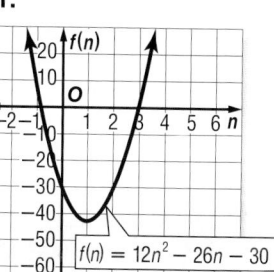

$f(n) = 12n^2 - 26n - 30$

$-1 < n < 0, 3$

32.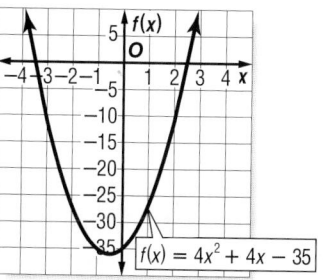

$f(x) = 4x^2 + 4x - 35$

$-4 < x < -3, 2 < x < 3$

33. Sample answer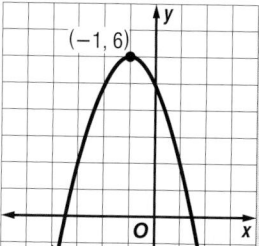

$(-1, 6)$

34. Sample answer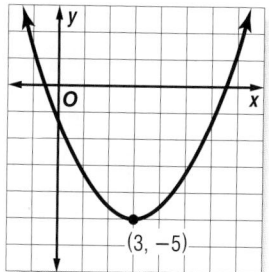

$(3, -5)$

35.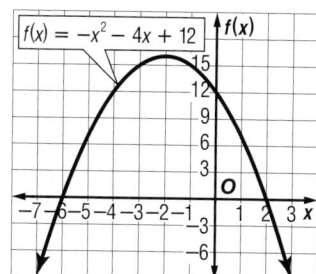

$f(x) = -x^2 - 4x + 12$

53. Al-Khwarizmi used squares to geometrically represent quadratic equations. Answers should include the following.

- Al-Khwarizmi represented x^2 by a square whose sides were each x units long. To this square, he added 4 rectangles with length x units long and width $\frac{8}{4}$ or 2 units long. This area represents 35. To make this a square, four 4×4 squares must by added.

- To solve $x^2 + 8x = 35$ by completing the square, use the following steps.

$x^2 + 8x = 35$	Original equation
$x^2 + 8x + 16 = 35 + 16$	Since $\left(\frac{8}{2}\right)^2 = 16$, add 16 to each side.
$(x + 4)^2 = 51$	Factor $x^2 + 8x + 16$.
$x + 4 = \pm\sqrt{51}$	Take the square root of each side.
$x + 4 - 4 = \pm\sqrt{51} - 4$	Subtract 4 from each side.
$x = -4 \pm \sqrt{51}$	Simplify.

$x = -4 - \sqrt{51}$ or $x = -4 + \sqrt{51}$
$x \approx -11.14$ $x \approx 3.14$

The solution set is $\{-11.14, 3.14\}$.

59.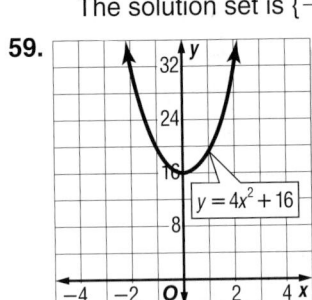

60.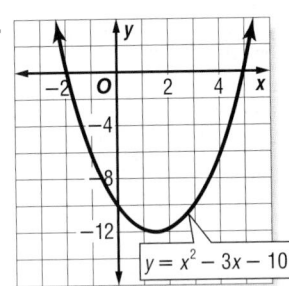

61.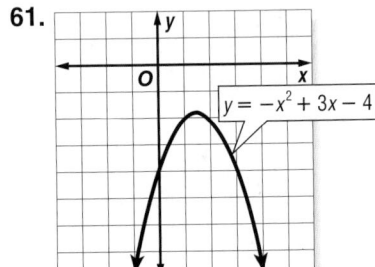

Page 544, Practice Quiz 1

1.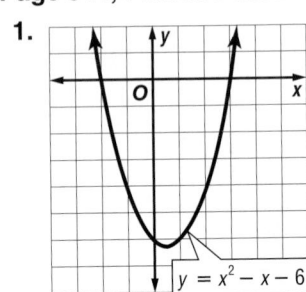

2.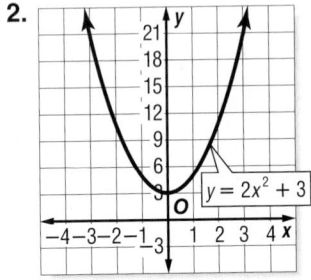

3.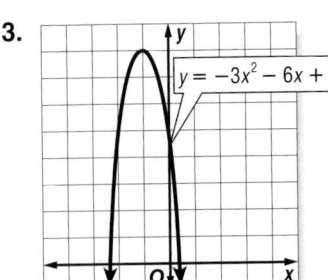

4.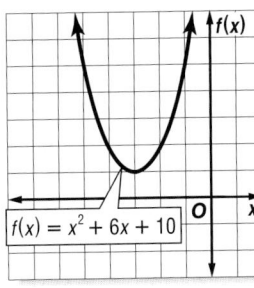

5.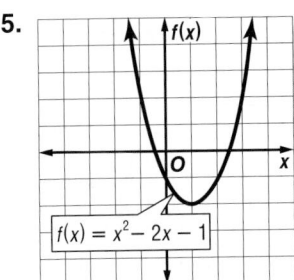

6.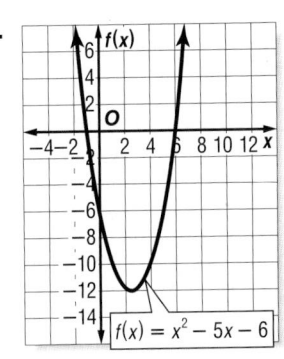

54. If a population trend can be modeled by a quadratic function, the Quadratic Formula can be used to solve when the function equals a particular value. Answers should include the following.

- $15 = 0.0055t^2 - 0.0796t + 5.2810$ Original equation

$15 - 15 = 0.0055t^2 - 0.0796t + 5.2810 - 15$
       Subtract 15 from each side.

$0 = 0.0055t^2 - 0.0796t - 9.7190$ Simplify.

$t = \dfrac{-b \pm \sqrt{b^2 - 4ac}}{2a}$ Quadratic Formula

$t = \dfrac{-(-0.0796) \pm \sqrt{(-0.0796)^2 - 4(0.0055)(-9.7190)}}{2(0.0055)}$

     $a = 0.0055$, $b = -0.0796$, and $c = -9.7190$

$t = \dfrac{0.0796 \pm \sqrt{0.22015416}}{0.011}$ Simplify.

$t = \dfrac{0.0796 - \sqrt{0.22015416}}{0.011}$ or $t = \dfrac{0.0796 + \sqrt{0.22015416}}{0.011}$

$t \approx -35.42$ $t \approx 49.89$

- Graphing the related function would not give precise solutions. The quadratic equation cannot be factored and completing the square would involve difficult computations.

66.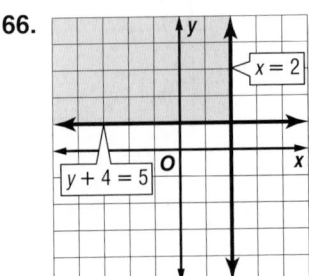

67.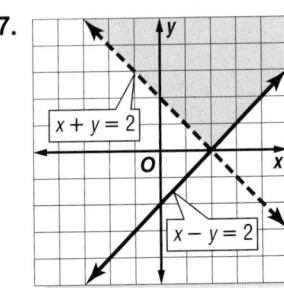

68.

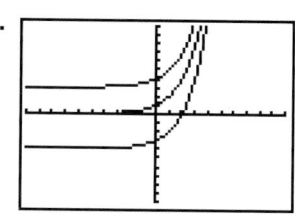

Page 556, Lesson 10-5
Graphing Calculator Investigation

1.

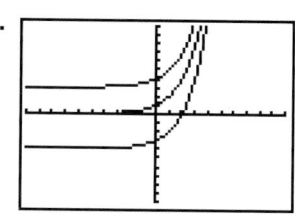

$[-10, 10]$ scl: 1
by $[-10, 10]$ scl: 1

The graphs are the same shape. The graph of $y = 2^x + 3$ is the graph of $y = 2^x$ translated 3 units up. The graph of $y = 2^x - 4$ is the graph of $y = 2^x$ translated 4 units down.

2.

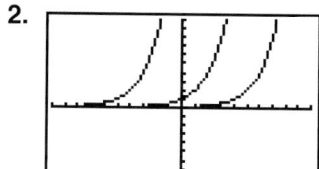

$[-10, 10]$ scl: 1
by $[-10, 10]$ scl: 1

The graphs are the same shape. The graph of $y = 2^{x+5}$ is the graph of $y = 2^x$ translated 5 units to the left. The graph of $y = 2^{x-4}$ is the graph of $y = 2^x$ translated 4 units to the right.

3.

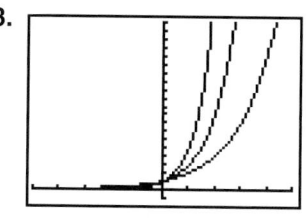

$[-5, 5]$ scl: 1
by $[-1, 20]$ scl: 1

All of the graphs cross the y-axis at 1. The graph of $y = 3^x$ is steeper than the graph of $y = 2^x$, and the graph of $y = 5^x$ is steeper yet.

4.

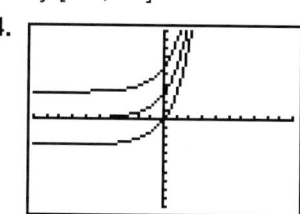

$[-10, 10]$ scl: 1
by $[-10, 10]$ scl: 1

The graphs are the same shape. The graph of $y = 3(2^x - 1)$ is the graph of $y = 3(2^x)$ translated 3 units down. The graph of $y = 3(2^x + 1)$ is the graph of $y = 3(2^x)$ translated 3 units up.

Pages 557–560, Lesson 10-5

4.

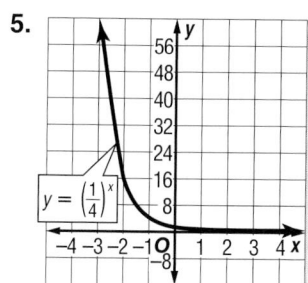

6.

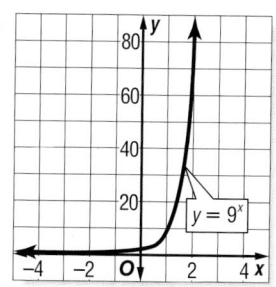

7.

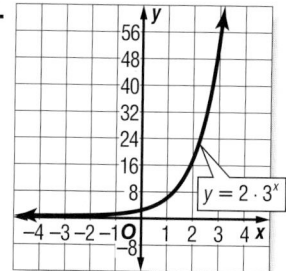

8.

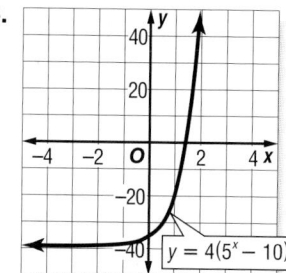

13.

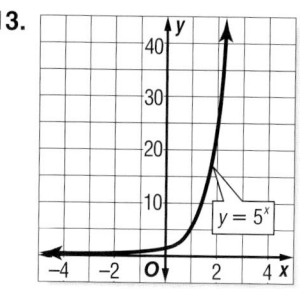

14.

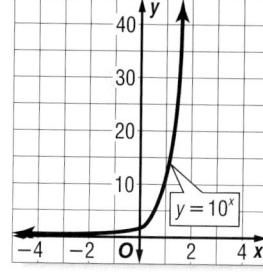

15.

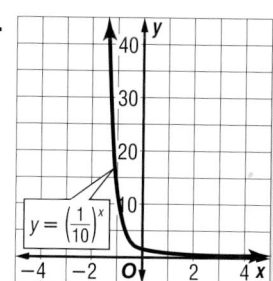

16.

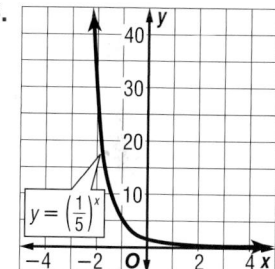

17.

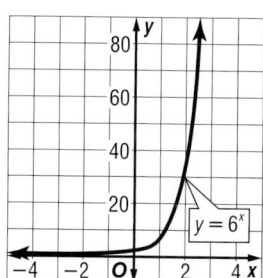

18.

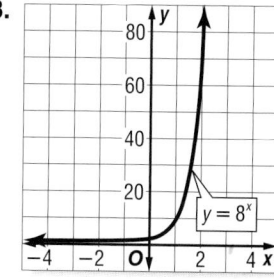

19.

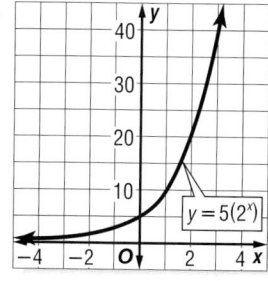

20.

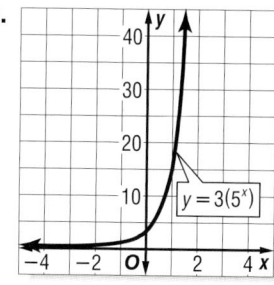

21.

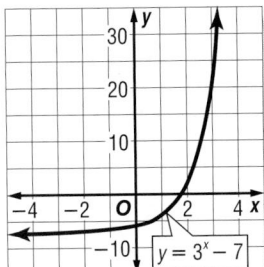

$y = 3^x - 7$

22.

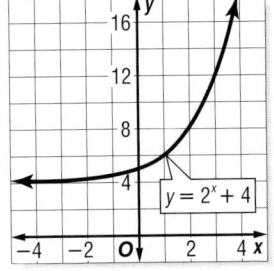

$y = 2^x + 4$

23.

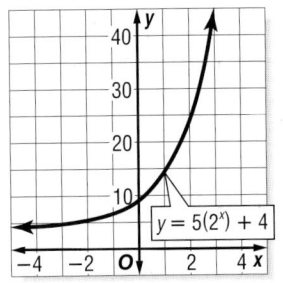

$y = 2(3^x) - 1$

24.

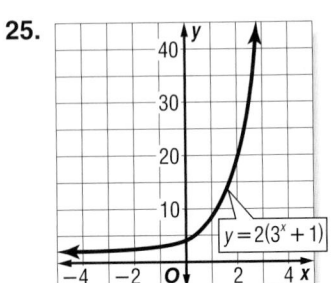

$y = 5(2^x) + 4$

25.

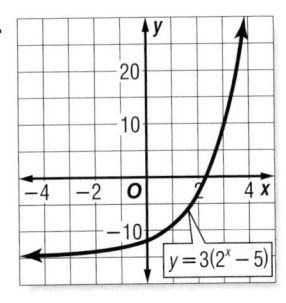

$y = 2(3^x + 1)$

26.

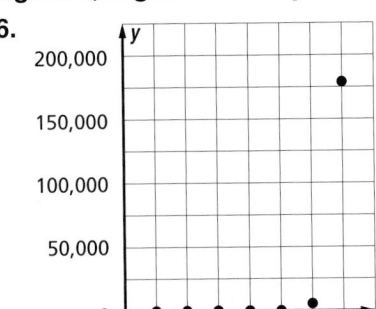

$y = 3(2^x - 5)$

Page 566, Chapter 10 Reading Mathematics

1. $y = C(1 - r)^t$; Since the final amount is less than the initial amount, the initial amount is multiplied by a number less than 1. If an amount is decreased by r percent, then $1 - r$ percent will remain.

2. $A = P\left(1 + \dfrac{r}{n}\right)^{nt}$; since the final amount is greater than the initial amount, P is multiplied by a number greater than 1. Also, the annual rate is divided by the number of times it is compounded per year. Time is equal to nt because this is the total number of times that the interest is compounded over the course of t years.

Page 573, Algebra Activity

6.

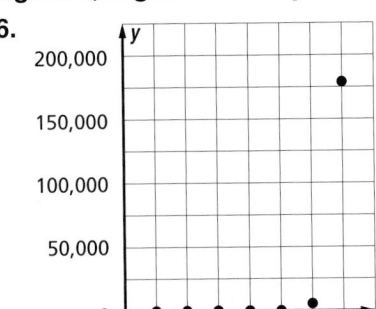

The graph begins increasing slowly and then increases rapidly for the last few values. The values in the Rate of Change column are 0.00583, 0.173, 4.821, 174, 5464, and 173,457. There is no constant value that can be multiplied by each rate of change to obtain the next value. A regression equation that approximates the data is $y = 0.0000055(31.7^x)$.

Page 579, Chapter 10 Practice Test

21.

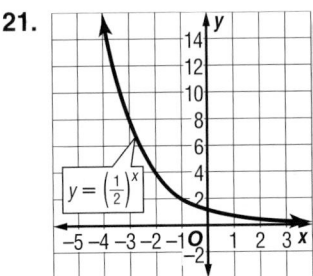

$y = \left(\dfrac{1}{2}\right)^x$

22.

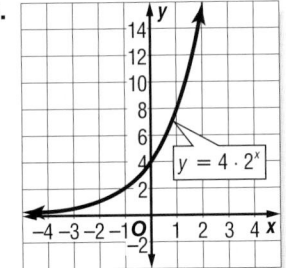

$y = 4 \cdot 2^x$

23.

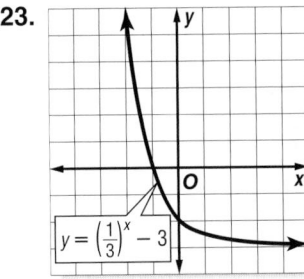

$y = \left(\dfrac{1}{3}\right)^x - 3$

Notes

Introduction

In this unit, students will be introduced to additional nonlinear functions such as radical and rational equations. Students learn how to simplify radical and rational expressions, and how to solve equations involving these expressions.

Students also explore triangles through the Pythagorean Theorem and trigonometric ratios.

Assessment Options

 Unit 4 Test Pages 779–780 of the *Chapter 12 Resource Masters* may be used as a test or review for Unit 4. This assessment contains both multiple-choice and short answer items.

ExamView® Pro
This CD-ROM can be used to create additional unit tests and review worksheets.

An online, research-based, instructional, assessment, and intervention tool that provides specific feedback on student mastery of state and national standards, instant remediation, and a data management system to track performance. For more information, contact

mhdigitallearning.com.

UNIT
4

Radical and Rational Functions

Nonlinear functions such as radical and rational functions can be used to model real-world situations such as the speed of a roller coaster. In this unit, you will learn about radical and rational functions.

Chapter 11
Radical Expressions and Triangles

Chapter 12
Rational Expressions and Equations

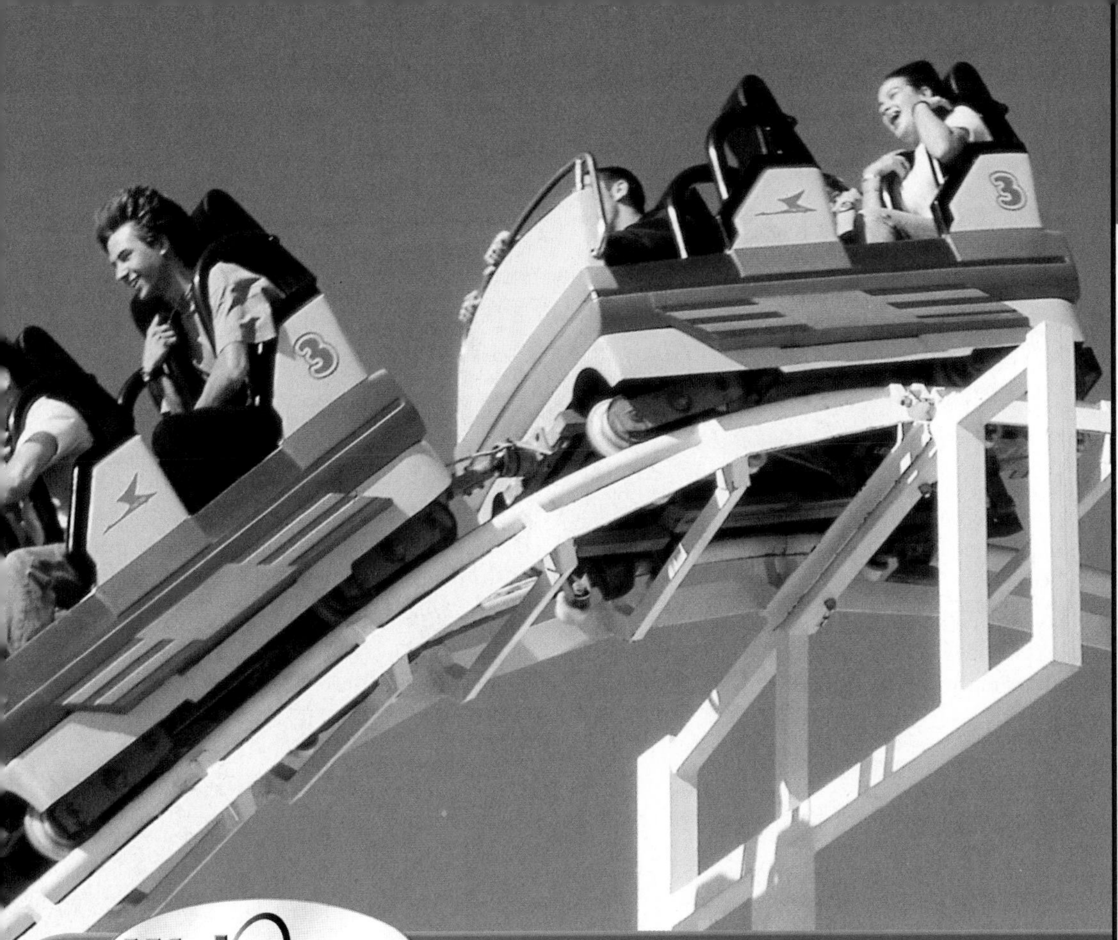

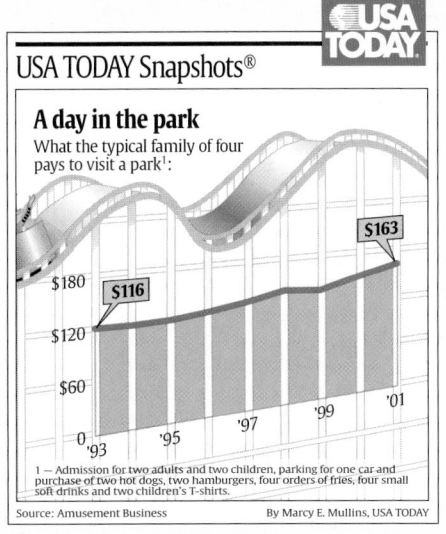

WebQuest Internet Project

Building the Best Roller Coaster

Each year, amusement park owners compete to earn part of the billions of dollars Americans spend at amusement parks. Often the parks draw customers with new taller and faster roller coasters. In this project, you will explore how radical and rational functions are related to buying and building a new roller coaster.

Log on to www.algebra1.com/webquest. Begin your WebQuest by reading the Task.

Then continue working on your WebQuest as you study Unit 4.

Lesson	11-1	12-2
Page	590	652

USA TODAY
USA TODAY Snapshots®
A day in the park
What the typical family of four pays to visit a park[1]:
$163
$180
$116
$120
$60
0
'93
'95
'97
'99
'01
1 — Admission for two adults and two children, parking for one car and purchase of two hot dogs, two hamburgers, four orders of fries, four small soft drinks and two children's T-shirts.
Source: Amusement Business
By Marcy E. Mullins, USA TODAY

Teaching Suggestions

Have students study the USA TODAY Snapshot.

- Ask students how the data in the graph differs from that of a linear function. **The data in the graph does not follow a straight line, therefore it is not linear.**
- Why might math be important to a roller coaster designer? **Sample answer: A roller coaster designer might use math to calculate the speed of a roller coaster before it is built to make sure it is safe.**

Additional USA TODAY Snapshots appearing in Unit 4:

Chapter 11 Global spending on construction (p. 615)

Chapter 12 Most Americans have one or two credit cards (p. 672)

Cost of parenthood rising (p. 689)

WebQuest Internet Project

Problem-Based Learning A WebQuest is an online project in which students do research on the Internet, gather data, and make presentations using word processing, graphing, page-making, or presentation software. In each chapter, students advance to the next step in their WebQuest. At the end of Chapter 12, the project culminates with a presentation of their findings.

Teaching notes and sample answers are available in the *WebQuest and Project Resources.*

Chapter 11 Radical Expressions and Triangles
Chapter Overview and Pacing

Year-long and two-year pacing: pages T20–T21.

LESSON OBJECTIVES

LESSON OBJECTIVES	Regular Basic/Average	Regular Advanced	Block Basic/Average	Block Advanced
11-1 Simplifying Radical Expressions (pp. 586–592) • Simplify radical expressions using the Product Property of Square Roots. • Simplify radical expressions using the Quotient Property of Square Roots.	2	2	1.5	1.5
11-2 Operations with Radical Expressions (pp. 593–597) • Add and subtract radical expressions. • Multiply radical expressions.	2	2	1	1
11-3 Radical Equations (pp. 598–604) • Solve radical equations. • Solve radical equations with extraneous solutions. *Follow-Up:* Use a graphing calculator to graph radical equations.	2	3 (with 11-3 Follow-Up)	1	2
11-4 The Pythagorean Theorem (pp. 605–610) • Solve problems by using the Pythagorean Theorem. • Determine whether a triangle is a right triangle.	1	1	0.5	0.5
11-5 The Distance Formula (pp. 611–615) • Find the distance between two points on the coordinate plane. • Find a point that is a given distance from a second point in a plane.	1	1	0.5	0.5
11-6 Similar Triangles (pp. 616–621) • Determine whether two triangles are similar. • Find the unknown measures of sides of two similar triangles.	1	1	0.5	0.5
11-7 Trigonometric Ratios (pp. 622–630) *Preview:* Use paper triangles to investigate trigonometric ratios. • Define the sine, cosine, and tangent ratios. • Use trigonometric ratios to solve right triangles.	2	2	1	1
Study Guide and **Practice Test** (pp. 632–637) **Standardized Test Practice** (pp. 638–639)	1	1	0.5	0.5
Chapter Assessment	1	1	0.5	0.5
TOTAL	13	14	7	8

*An electronic version of this chapter is available on **StudentWorks™**. This backpack solution CD-ROM allows students instant access to the Student Edition, lesson worksheet pages, and web resources.*

584A Chapter 11 Radical Expressions and Triangles

Chapter Resource Manager

CHAPTER 11 RESOURCE MASTERS

Study Guide and Intervention	Practice (Skills and Average)	Reading to Learn Mathematics	Enrichment	Assessment	Prerequisite Skills Workbook	Applications*	Parent and Student Study Guide Workbook	5-Minute Check Transparencies	Interactive Chalkboard	AlgePASS: Tutorial Plus (lessons)	Materials
643–644	645–646	647	648			SC 21	83	11-1	11-1		graphing calculator
649–650	651–652	653	654	699	37–38		84	11-2	11-2		
655–656	657–658	659	660			GCS 43	85	11-3	11-3		graphing calculator (*Follow-Up:* graphing calculator)
661–662	663–664	665	666	699, 701		GCS 44, SC 22	86	11-4	11-4	32	
667–668	669–670	671	672			SM 85–90	87	11-5	11-5		
673–674	675–676	677	678	700	61–62		88	11-6	11-6		
679–680	681–682	683	684	700			89	11-7	11-7		(*Follow-Up:* ruler, grid paper, protractor), string, drinking straw, paper clip, protractor, tape, meter sticks or tape measure
				685–698, 702–704			90				

Key to Abbreviations: GCS = Graphing Calculator and Spreadsheet Masters,
SC = School-to-Career Masters,
SM = Science and Mathematics Lab Manual

ELL Study Guide and Intervention, Skills Practice, Practice, and Parent and Student Study Guide Workbooks are also available in Spanish.

Chapter 11 — Mathematical Connections and Background

Continuity of Instruction

Prior Knowledge

In Chapter 2, students learned to find principal square roots. They solved proportions in Chapter 3. Students found the factors of the difference of squares in Chapter 8.

This Chapter

In this chapter, students simplify and perform operations with radical expressions. They apply these skills to solving radical equations. The Pythagorean Theorem is used to solve problems involving right triangles. The Distance Formula is introduced as an application of the Pythagorean Theorem. Similar triangles and trigonometric ratios are used to find missing measures in triangles.

Future Connections

The basics of trigonometry and the study of triangles are explored in this chapter. These basics will be applied to deeper studies of triangles in later mathematics courses. Many of these concepts are used in construction and engineering.

11-1 Simplifying Radical Expressions

A radical expression contains a square root. The expression is in simplest form if the expression inside the radical sign, or radicand, has only 1 as a perfect square factor. The Product Property of Square Roots states that the square root of a product equals the product of each square root. Prime factorizations combined with the Product Property of Square Roots can be used to simplify radical expressions. Principal square roots are never negative, so absolute value symbols must be used to signify that some results are not negative. The Quotient Property of Square Roots states that the square root of a quotient equals the quotient of each square root. The Quotient Property of Square Roots can be used to derive the Quadratic Formula.

A fraction does not have a radical in its denominator if it is in simplest form. Since squaring and taking a square root are inverse functions, you multiply the numerator and the denominator by the same number so that the denominator contains a perfect square. Remember that the numerator must be multiplied by the same amount so that the whole fraction is being multiplied by a value of 1. This process is called *rationalizing the denominator*. After rationalizing the denominator, check for coefficients of the radical in the numerator that will simplify with the denominator. If the denominator is an expression containing a radical, multiply by the conjugate. For example, if the denominator is $a + \sqrt{b}$, multiply by $a - \sqrt{b}$.

11-2 Operations with Radical Expressions

Use the process of combining like terms to simplify expressions in which radicals are added or subtracted. For terms to be combined, their radicands must be the same. As in combining monomials with variables, only the coefficients of the radicals are combined. Be sure to simplify all radicals first. When multiplying radical expressions, first multiply the coefficients, and then use the Product Property of Square Roots to multiply the radicals. Simplify each term and then combine like terms as necessary.

11-3 Radical Equations

Equations that contain variables in the radicand are called radical equations. To solve radical equations, the radical must first be isolated on one side. Then square each side. This will eliminate the radical. This process sometimes produces results that are not solutions of the original equation. These are called *extraneous solutions*. All solutions must be substituted back into the original equation to check their validity.

11-4 The Pythagorean Theorem

The two sides of a right triangle that form the right angle are the legs of the triangle. The third, and longest, side is the hypotenuse. The hypotenuse is the longest side because it is always across from the angle with the greatest measure. The Pythagorean Theorem states that the sum of the squares of the legs equals the square of the hypotenuse. The formula is $c^2 = a^2 + b^2$, where a and b are the measures of the legs and c is the measure of the hypotenuse. This formula can be used to find the length of any missing side of a right triangle if the lengths of the other two sides are known. Any three whole numbers that satisfy this equation are known as a Pythagorean Triple. These triples represent side lengths that always form right triangles. It follows that if three numbers do not satisfy the Pythagorean Theorem, then sides of their length will not form a right triangle.

11-5 The Distance Formula

If the Pythagorean Theorem is solved for c, the result is the Distance Formula. The variable a is expressed as the difference of the x-coordinates of the endpoints of the hypotenuse and b is expressed as the difference of the y-coordinates. This formula is used to find the distance between any two points. You can also find one missing coordinate of an endpoint if you know the other coordinate, the coordinates of the other endpoint, and the distance between the two points.

11-6 Similar Triangles

Similar triangles have the same shape, but are not necessarily the same size. All of the corresponding angles will have equal measures, and the corresponding sides will all be proportional. If the sides have a 1 to 1 ratio of proportionality, then the similar triangles are the same size. When determining whether triangles are similar, all you need to check is if the corresponding angles have the same measure. If all the angle measures cannot be determined, then check the corresponding sides to see if they are proportional.

Proportions can be used to find the lengths of missing sides of similar triangles. You must know the lengths of at least one pair of corresponding sides and the length of the side that corresponds to the missing side's length. Set up the proportion, and then cross multiply. Solve the resulting equation.

11-7 Trigonometric Ratios

Trigonometry is the mathematical study of angles and triangles. Ratios comparing the measures of two sides of a right triangle are called trigonometric ratios. The three most common trigonometric ratios are sine, cosine, and tangent. These ratios can be used to find the measures of missing sides or the measures of the acute angles. The relationship of the two sides necessary for the problem to a specific acute angle determines which ratio is used. If the measures of just two sides of a triangle or the measures of one side and one acute angle are known, then the measures of all of the rest of the sides and angles can be found. This is called *solving the triangle*. Trigonometric ratios are used to find distances in problems involving angles of elevation and angles of depression.

Quick Review Math Handbook

Hot Words includes a glossary of terms while Hot Topics consists of explanations of key mathematical concepts with exercises to test comprehension. This valuable resource can be used as a reference in the classroom or for home study.

Lesson	Hot Topics Section	Lesson	Hot Topics Section
11-1	3.2	11-6	8.6
11-2	3.2	11-7P	7.10
11-4	7.9	11-7	7.10

P = Preview

 Additional mathematical information and teaching notes are available at www.algebra1.com/key_concepts.

Key to Abbreviations:
TWE = Teacher Wraparound Edition; CRM = Chapter Resource Masters

	Type	Student Edition	Teacher Resources	Technology/Internet
INTERVENTION	Ongoing	Prerequisite Skills, pp. 585, 592, 597, 603, 610, 615, 621 Practice Quiz 1, p. 603 Practice Quiz 2, p. 621	5-Minute Check Transparencies *Prerequisite Skills Workbook*, pp. 37–38, 61–62 Quizzes, *CRM* pp. 699–700 Mid-Chapter Test, *CRM* p. 701 Study Guide and Intervention, *CRM* pp. 643–644, 649–650, 655–656, 661–662, 667–668, 673–674, 679–680	AlgePASS: Tutorial Plus, Lesson 32 www.algebra1.com/self_check_quiz www.algebra1.com/extra_examples
	Mixed Review	pp. 592, 597, 603, 610, 615, 621, 630	Cumulative Review, *CRM* p. 702	
	Error Analysis	Find the Error, pp. 600, 618	Find the Error, *TWE* pp. 600, 618 Unlocking Misconceptions, *TWE* p. 612 Tips for New Teachers, *TWE* pp. 587, 624	
	Standardized Test Practice	pp. 591, 597, 602, 606, 608, 610, 615, 620, 630, 637, 638–639	*TWE* pp. 638–639 Standardized Test Practice, *CRM* pp. 703–704	Standardized Test Practice CD-ROM www.algebra1.com/standardized_test
ASSESSMENT	Open-Ended Assessment	Writing in Math, pp. 591, 597, 602, 610, 614, 620, 630 Open Ended, pp. 589, 595, 600, 607, 612, 618, 627 Standardized Test, p. 639	Modeling: *TWE* pp. 603, 610, 621 Speaking: *TWE* pp. 597, 615 Writing: *TWE* pp. 592, 630 Open-Ended Assessment, *CRM* p. 697	
	Chapter Assessment	Study Guide, pp. 632–636 Practice Test, p. 637	Multiple-Choice Tests (Forms 1, 2A, 2B), *CRM* pp. 685–690 Free-Response Tests (Forms 2C, 2D, 3), *CRM* pp. 691–696 Vocabulary Test/Review, *CRM* p. 698	ExamView® Pro (see below) MindJogger Videoquizzes www.algebra1.com/vocabulary_review www.algebra1.com/chapter_test

For more information on Yearly ProgressPro, see p. 582.

Algebra Lesson	Yearly ProgressPro Skill Lesson(s)
11-1	Simplifying Radical Expressions Simplifying Rational Expressions with Radicals in the Denominator
11-2	Operations with Radical Expressions
11-3	Radical Equations
11-4	The Pythagorean Theorem
11-5	The Distance Formula
11-6	Similar Triangles
11-7	Trigonometric Ratios Applying Trigonometric Ratios

ExamView® Pro

Use the networkable **ExamView® Pro** to:
- Create **multiple versions** of tests.
- Create **modified** tests for *Inclusion* students.
- **Edit** existing questions and **add** your own questions.
- Use built-in **state curriculum correlations** to create tests aligned with state standards.
- Change **English** tests to **Spanish** and vice versa.

For more information on Intervention and Assessment, see pp. T8–T11.

Reading and Writing in Mathematics

Glencoe Algebra 1 provides numerous opportunities to incorporate reading and writing into the mathematics classroom.

Student Edition

- Foldables Study Organizer, p. 585
- Concept Check questions require students to verbalize and write about what they have learned in the lesson. (pp. 589, 595, 600, 607, 612, 618, 627)
- Reading Mathematics, p. 631
- Writing in Math questions in every lesson, pp. 591, 597, 602, 610, 614, 620, 630
- Reading Study Tip, pp. 586, 611, 623
- WebQuest, p. 590

Teacher Wraparound Edition

- Foldables Study Organizer, pp. 585, 632
- Study Notebook suggestions, pp. 589, 595, 600, 608, 613, 618, 627, 631
- Modeling activities, pp. 603, 610, 621
- Speaking activities, pp. 597, 615
- Writing activities, pp. 592, 630
- Differentiated Instruction, (Verbal/Linguistic), p. 599
- **ELL** Resources, pp. 584, 591, 596, 599, 602, 609, 614, 620, 629, 631, 632

Additional Resources

- Vocabulary Builder worksheets require students to define and give examples for key vocabulary terms as they progress through the chapter. (*Chapter 11 Resource Masters*, pp. vii-viii)
- Reading to Learn Mathematics master for each lesson (*Chapter 11 Resource Masters*, pp. 647, 653, 659, 665, 671, 677, 683)
- *Vocabulary PuzzleMaker* software creates crossword, jumble, and word search puzzles using vocabulary lists that you can customize.
- *Teaching Mathematics with Foldables* provides suggestions for promoting cognition and language.
- *Reading and Writing in the Mathematics Classroom*
- *WebQuest and Project Resources*
- *Hot Words/Hot Topics* Sections 3.2, 7.9, 7.10, 8.6

For more information on Reading and Writing in Mathematics, see pp. T6–T7.

PROJECT CRISS℠   Study Skill

Encourage students to create frames to organize their notes. The math frame below describes the Distance Formula, which students study in Lesson 11-5. Creating frames helps students understand topics by explaining them in their own words. Frames also allow students to quickly review information in the chapter.

Term/Concept	Definition (in your own words)	Formula	Original Question with Answer
The Distance Formula	A formula to find the distance between any two points on a coordinate plane.	The distance between two points with coordinates (x_1, y_1) and (x_2, y_2) is $d = \sqrt{(x_2 - x_1)^2 + (y_2 - y_1)^2}$.	Find the distance between $(-7, 7)$ and $(2, -5)$. $d = \sqrt{[2 - (-7)]^2 + (-5 - 7)^2}$ $= \sqrt{81 + 144}$ $= 15$

CReating **I**ndependence **T**hrough **S**tudent-Owned **S**trategies

Radical Expressions and Triangles

What You'll Learn

Have students read over the list of objectives and make a list of any words with which they are not familiar.

Why It's Important

Point out to students that this is only one of many reasons why each objective is important. Others are provided in the introduction to each lesson.

What You'll Learn

- **Lessons 11-1 and 11-2** Simplify and perform operations with radical expressions.
- **Lesson 11-3** Solve radical equations.
- **Lessons 11-4 and 11-5** Use the Pythagorean Theorem and Distance Formula.
- **Lessons 11-6 and 11-7** Use similar triangles and trigonometric ratios.

Key Vocabulary

- radical expression (p. 586)
- radical equation (p. 598)
- Pythagorean Theorem (p. 605)
- Distance Formula (p. 611)
- trigonometric ratios (p. 623)

Why It's Important

Physics problems are among the many applications of radical equations. Formulas that contain the value for the acceleration due to gravity, such as free-fall times, escape velocities, and the speeds of roller coasters, can all be written as radical equations. *You will learn how to calculate the time it takes for a skydiver to fall a given distance in Lesson 11-3.*

584 Chapter 11 Radical Expressions and Triangles

Lesson	NCTM Standards	Local Objectives
11-1	1, 2, 6, 8, 9, 10	
11-2	1, 6, 8, 9, 10	
11-3	2, 6, 8, 9, 10	
11-3 Follow-Up	2, 6, 8	
11-4	1, 2, 3, 6, 8, 9, 10	
11-5	1, 2, 3, 6, 8, 9, 10	
11-6	1, 2, 3, 6, 8, 9, 10	
11-7 Preview	1, 3, 7	
11-7	3, 6, 8, 9, 10	

Key to NCTM Standards:

1=Number & Operations, 2=Algebra, 3=Geometry, 4=Measurement, 5=Data Analysis & Probability, 6=Problem Solving, 7=Reasoning & Proof, 8=Communication, 9=Connections, 10=Representation

Vocabulary Builder ⓔⓛⓛ

The Key Vocabulary list introduces students to some of the main vocabulary terms included in this chapter. For a more thorough vocabulary list with pronunciations of new words, give students the Vocabulary Builder worksheets found on pages vii and viii of the *Chapter 11 Resource Masters*. Encourage them to complete the definition of each term as they progress through the chapter. You may suggest that they add these sheets to their study notebooks for future reference when studying for the Chapter 11 test.

Getting Started

Prerequisite Skills

To be successful in this chapter, you'll need to master these skills and be able to apply them in problem-solving situations. Review these skills before beginning Chapter 11.

For Lessons 11-1 and 11-4   Find Square Roots

Find each square root. If necessary, round to the nearest hundredth.
(For review, see Lesson 2-7.)

1. $\sqrt{25}$ **5**   **2.** $\sqrt{80}$ **8.94**   **3.** $\sqrt{56}$ **7.48**   **4.** $\sqrt{324}$ **18**

For Lesson 11-2   Combine Like Terms

Simplify each expression.   *(For review, see Lesson 1-6.)*

5. $3a + 7b - 2a$ $\boldsymbol{a + 7b}$ **6.** $14x - 6y + 2y$ $\boldsymbol{14x - 4y}$

7. $(10c - 5d) + (6c + 5d)$ $\boldsymbol{16c}$ **8.** $(21m + 15n) - (9n - 4m)$ $\boldsymbol{25m + 6n}$

For Lesson 11-3   Solve Quadratic Equations

Solve each equation.   *(For review, see Lesson 9-3.)*

9. $x(x - 5) = 0$ $\{0, 5\}$ **10.** $x^2 + 10x + 24 = 0$ $\{-6, -4\}$

11. $x^2 - 6x - 27 = 0$ $\{-3, 9\}$ **12.** $2x^2 + x + 1 = 2$ $\left\{\frac{1}{2}, -1\right\}$

For Lesson 11-6   Proportions

Use cross products to determine whether each pair of ratios forms a proportion. Write *yes* or *no*.   *(For review, see Lesson 3-6.)*

13. $\frac{2}{3}, \frac{8}{12}$ **yes**   **14.** $\frac{4}{5}, \frac{16}{25}$ **no**   **15.** $\frac{8}{10}, \frac{12}{16}$ **no**   **16.** $\frac{6}{30}, \frac{3}{15}$ **yes**

FOLDABLES™ Study Organizer

Radical Expressions and Equations Make this Foldable to help you organize your notes. Begin with a sheet of plain $8\frac{1}{2}''$ by 11" paper.

Step 1   Fold in Half

Fold in half lengthwise.

Step 2   Fold Again

Fold the top to the bottom.

Step 3   Cut

Open. Cut along the second fold to the center to make two tabs.

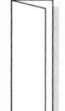

Step 4   Label

Label each tab as shown.

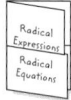

Radical Expressions
Radical Equations

Reading and Writing As you read and study the chapter, write notes and examples for each lesson under each tab.

Getting Started

This section provides a review of the basic concepts needed before beginning Chapter 11. Page references are included for additional student help.

Additional review is provided in the *Prerequisite Skills Workbook,* pp. 37–38 and 61–62.

Prerequisite Skills in the Getting Ready for the Next Lesson section at the end of each exercise set review a skill needed in the next lesson.

For Lesson	Prerequisite Skill
11-2	Multiplying Binomials (p. 592)
11-3	Finding Special Products (p. 597)
11-4	Evaluating Radical Expressions (p. 603)
11-5	Simplifying Radical Expressions (p. 610)
11-6	Solving Proportions (p. 615)
11-7	Evaluating Expressions (p. 621)

FOLDABLES™ Study Organizer

For more information about Foldables, see *Teaching Mathematics with Foldables.*

Organization of Data: Annotating As students read and work through the chapter, have them make annotations under the tabs of their Foldable. Explain to them that annotations are usually notes taken in the margins of books we own to organize the text for review or studying. Annotations often include questions that arise as we read the chapter, reader comments and reactions, sentence length summaries, steps or data numbered by the reader, and key points highlighted or underlined.

11-1 Lesson Notes

1 Focus

 5-Minute Check Transparency 11-1 Use as a quiz or review of Chapter 10.

Mathematical Background notes are available for this lesson on p. 584C.

Building on Prior Knowledge

Students were introduced to the Quadratic Formula in Lesson 10-4 and they learned how to use it to solve quadratic equations. In this lesson, students learn how to derive the Quadratic Formula from the standard form of a quadratic equation using the Quotient Property of Square Roots.

How are radical expressions used in space exploration?

Ask students:

- In the formula for escape velocity, what does the radical sign mean? **The radical sign means that you must find the square root of the value under the radical sign.**

- Based on what you know about the order of operations, how do you think you should simplify the radical expression in the escape velocity formula? **You should simplify the expression under the radical sign before finding the square root.**

11-1 Simplifying Radical Expressions

What You'll Learn

- Simplify radical expressions using the Product Property of Square Roots.
- Simplify radical expressions using the Quotient Property of Square Roots.

Vocabulary
- radical expression
- radicand
- rationalizing the denominator
- conjugate

How are radical expressions used in space exploration?

A spacecraft leaving Earth must have a velocity of at least 11.2 kilometers per second (25,000 miles per hour) to enter into orbit. This velocity is called the *escape velocity*. The escape velocity of an object is given by the radical expression

$\sqrt{\dfrac{2GM}{R}}$, where G is the gravitational constant, M is the mass of the planet or star, and R is the radius of the planet or star. Once values are substituted for the variables, the formula can be simplified.

PRODUCT PROPERTY OF SQUARE ROOTS A **radical expression** is an expression that contains a square root. A **radicand**, the expression under the radical sign, is in simplest form if it contains no perfect square factors other than 1. The following property can be used to simplify square roots.

> **Key Concept** *Product Property of Square Roots*
>
> - **Words** For any numbers a and b, where $a \geq 0$ and $b \geq 0$, the square root of the product ab is equal to the product of each square root.
>
> - **Symbols** $\sqrt{ab} = \sqrt{a} \cdot \sqrt{b}$ • **Example** $\sqrt{4 \cdot 25} = \sqrt{4} \cdot \sqrt{25}$

The Product Property of Square Roots and prime factorization can be used to simplify radical expressions in which the radicand is not a perfect square.

> **Example 1** *Simplify Square Roots*
>
> **Simplify.**
>
> a. $\sqrt{12}$
>
> $\sqrt{12} = \sqrt{2 \cdot 2 \cdot 3}$ Prime factorization of 12
>
> $= \sqrt{2^2} \cdot \sqrt{3}$ Product Property of Square Roots
>
> $= 2\sqrt{3}$ Simplify.
>
> b. $\sqrt{90}$
>
> $\sqrt{90} = \sqrt{2 \cdot 3 \cdot 3 \cdot 5}$ Prime factorization of 90
>
> $= \sqrt{3^2} \cdot \sqrt{2 \cdot 5}$ Product Property of Square Roots
>
> $= 3\sqrt{10}$ Simplify.

Study Tip

Reading Math
$2\sqrt{3}$ is read *two times the square root of 3* or *two radical three.*

Resource Manager

Workbook and Reproducible Masters

Chapter 11 Resource Masters
- Study Guide and Intervention, pp. 643–644
- Skills Practice, p. 645
- Practice, p. 646
- Reading to Learn Mathematics, p. 647
- Enrichment, p. 648

Parent and Student Study Guide Workbook, p. 83
School-to-Career Masters, p. 21

Transparencies
5-Minute Check Transparency 11-1
Answer Key Transparencies

Technology
Interactive Chalkboard

The Product Property can also be used to multiply square roots.

Example 2 *Multiply Square Roots*

Find $\sqrt{3} \cdot \sqrt{15}$.

$\sqrt{3} \cdot \sqrt{15} = \sqrt{3} \cdot \sqrt{3} \cdot \sqrt{5}$ Product Property of Square Roots

$= \sqrt{3^2} \cdot \sqrt{5}$ Product Property

$= 3\sqrt{5}$ Simplify.

When finding the principal square root of an expression containing variables, be sure that the result is not negative. Consider the expression $\sqrt{x^2}$. It may seem that $\sqrt{x^2} = x$. Let's look at $x = -2$.

$$\sqrt{x^2} \stackrel{?}{=} x$$
$$\sqrt{(-2)^2} \stackrel{?}{=} -2 \quad \text{Replace } x \text{ with } -2.$$
$$\sqrt{4} \stackrel{?}{=} -2 \quad (-2)^2 = 4$$
$$2 \neq -2 \quad \sqrt{4} = 2$$

For radical expressions where the exponent of the variable inside the radical is *even* and the resulting simplified exponent is odd, you must use absolute value to ensure nonnegative results.

$$\sqrt{x^2} = |x| \qquad \sqrt{x^3} = x\sqrt{x} \qquad \sqrt{x^4} = x^2 \qquad \sqrt{x^5} = x^2\sqrt{x} \qquad \sqrt{x^6} = |x^3|$$

Example 3 *Simplify a Square Root with Variables*

Simplify $\sqrt{40x^4y^5z^3}$.

$\sqrt{40x^4y^5z^3} = \sqrt{2^3 \cdot 5 \cdot x^4 \cdot y^5 \cdot z^3}$ Prime factorization

$= \sqrt{2^2} \cdot \sqrt{2} \cdot \sqrt{5} \cdot \sqrt{x^4} \cdot \sqrt{y^4} \cdot \sqrt{y} \cdot \sqrt{z^2} \cdot \sqrt{z}$ Product Property

$= 2 \cdot \sqrt{2} \cdot \sqrt{5} \cdot x^2 \cdot y^2 \cdot \sqrt{y} \cdot |z| \cdot \sqrt{z}$ Simplify.

$= 2x^2y^2|z|\sqrt{10yz}$ The absolute value of z ensures a nonnegative result.

QUOTIENT PROPERTY OF SQUARE ROOTS You can divide square roots and simplify radical expressions that involve division by using the Quotient Property of Square Roots.

Key Concept   *Quotient Property of Square Roots*

- **Words**   For any numbers a and b, where $a \geq 0$ and $b > 0$, the square root of the quotient $\frac{a}{b}$ is equal to the quotient of each square root.

- **Symbols** $\sqrt{\dfrac{a}{b}} = \dfrac{\sqrt{a}}{\sqrt{b}}$ • **Example** $\sqrt{\dfrac{49}{4}} = \dfrac{\sqrt{49}}{\sqrt{4}}$

You can use the Quotient Property of Square Roots to derive the Quadratic Formula by solving the quadratic equation $ax^2 + bx + c = 0$.

$$ax^2 + bx + c = 0 \quad \text{Original equation}$$
$$x^2 + \frac{b}{a}x + \frac{c}{a} = 0 \quad \text{Divide each side by } a, a \neq 0.$$

(continued on the next page)

 www.algebra1.com/extra_examples

Lesson 11-1 Simplifying Radical Expressions   **587**

4 Simplify.

a. $\dfrac{\sqrt{12}}{\sqrt{5}}$ $\dfrac{2\sqrt{15}}{5}$

b. $\dfrac{\sqrt{11y}}{\sqrt{27}}$ $\dfrac{\sqrt{33y}}{9}$

c. $\dfrac{\sqrt{3}}{\sqrt{8}}$ $\dfrac{\sqrt{6}}{4}$

$$x^2 + \frac{b}{a}x = -\frac{c}{a}$$ Subtract $\frac{c}{a}$ from each side.

$$x^2 + \frac{b}{a}x + \frac{b^2}{4a^2} = -\frac{c}{a} + \frac{b^2}{4a^2}$$ Complete the square; $\left(\frac{b}{2a}\right)^2 = \frac{b^2}{4a^2}$.

$$\left(x + \frac{b}{2a}\right)^2 = \frac{-4ac + b^2}{4a^2}$$ Factor $x^2 + \frac{b}{a}x + \frac{b^2}{4a^2}$.

$$\left|x + \frac{b}{2a}\right| = \sqrt{\frac{b^2 - 4ac}{4a^2}}$$ Take the square root of each side.

$$x + \frac{b}{2a} = \pm\sqrt{\frac{b^2 - 4ac}{4a^2}}$$ Remove the absolute value symbols and insert $\pm$.

$$x + \frac{b}{2a} = \pm\frac{\sqrt{b^2 - 4ac}}{\sqrt{4a^2}}$$ Quotient Property of Square Roots

$$x + \frac{b}{2a} = \pm\frac{\sqrt{b^2 - 4ac}}{2a}$$ $\sqrt{4a^2} = 2a$

$$x = \frac{-b \pm \sqrt{b^2 - 4ac}}{2a}$$ Subtract $\frac{b}{2a}$ from each side.

Thus, we have derived the Quadratic Formula.

> **Study Tip**
>
> **Plus or Minus Symbol**
> The $\pm$ symbol is used with the radical expression since both square roots lead to solutions.

A fraction containing radicals is in simplest form if no prime factors appear under the radical sign with an exponent greater than 1 and if no radicals are left in the denominator. **Rationalizing the denominator** of a radical expression is a method used to eliminate radicals from the denominator of a fraction.

Example 4 *Rationalizing the Denominator*

Simplify.

a. $\dfrac{\sqrt{10}}{\sqrt{3}}$

b. $\dfrac{\sqrt{7x}}{\sqrt{8}}$

$\dfrac{\sqrt{10}}{\sqrt{3}} = \dfrac{\sqrt{10}}{\sqrt{3}} \cdot \dfrac{\sqrt{3}}{\sqrt{3}}$ Multiply by $\frac{\sqrt{3}}{\sqrt{3}}$.

$\dfrac{\sqrt{7x}}{\sqrt{8}} = \dfrac{\sqrt{7x}}{\sqrt{2 \cdot 2 \cdot 2}}$ Prime factorization

$= \dfrac{\sqrt{30}}{3}$ Product Property of Square Roots

$= \dfrac{\sqrt{7x}}{2\sqrt{2}} \cdot \dfrac{\sqrt{2}}{\sqrt{2}}$ Multiply by $\frac{\sqrt{2}}{\sqrt{2}}$.

$= \dfrac{\sqrt{14x}}{4}$ Product Property of Square Roots

c. $\dfrac{\sqrt{2}}{\sqrt{6}}$

$\dfrac{\sqrt{2}}{\sqrt{6}} = \dfrac{\sqrt{2}}{\sqrt{6}} \cdot \dfrac{\sqrt{6}}{\sqrt{6}}$ Multiply by $\frac{\sqrt{6}}{\sqrt{6}}$.

$= \dfrac{\sqrt{12}}{6}$ Product Property of Square Roots

$= \dfrac{\sqrt{2 \cdot 2 \cdot 3}}{6}$ Prime factorization

$= \dfrac{2\sqrt{3}}{6}$ $\sqrt{2^2} = 2$

$= \dfrac{\sqrt{3}}{3}$ Divide the numerator and denominator by 2.

DAILY INTERVENTION

Differentiated Instruction

Logical Have students use the same method that is shown for the derivation of the Quadratic Formula to solve actual quadratic equations. Have students turn back to Lesson 10-4 and solve an example problem using this method.

Binomials of the form $p\sqrt{q} + r\sqrt{s}$ and $p\sqrt{q} - r\sqrt{s}$ are called **conjugates**. For example, $3 + \sqrt{2}$ and $3 - \sqrt{2}$ are conjugates. Conjugates are useful when simplifying radical expressions because if p, q, r, and s are rational numbers, their product is always a rational number with no radicals. Use the pattern $(a - b)(a + b) = a^2 - b^2$ to find their product.

$$(3 + \sqrt{2})(3 - \sqrt{2}) = 3^2 - (\sqrt{2})^2 \quad a = 3, b = \sqrt{2}$$
$$= 9 - 2 \text{ or } 7 \quad (\sqrt{2})^2 = \sqrt{2} \cdot \sqrt{2} \text{ or } 2$$

Example 5 Use Conjugates to Rationalize a Denominator

Simplify $\dfrac{2}{6 - \sqrt{3}}$.

$$\frac{2}{6 - \sqrt{3}} = \frac{2}{6 - \sqrt{3}} \cdot \frac{6 + \sqrt{3}}{6 + \sqrt{3}} \qquad \frac{6 + \sqrt{3}}{6 + \sqrt{3}} = 1$$

$$= \frac{2(6 + \sqrt{3})}{6^2 - (\sqrt{3})^2} \qquad (a - b)(a + b) = a^2 - b^2$$

$$= \frac{12 + 2\sqrt{3}}{36 - 3} \qquad (\sqrt{3})^2 = 3$$

$$= \frac{12 + 2\sqrt{3}}{33} \qquad \text{Simplify.}$$

When simplifying radical expressions, check the following conditions to determine if the expression is in simplest form.

Concept Summary   Simplest Radical Form

A radical expression is in simplest form when the following three conditions have been met.

1. No radicands have perfect square factors other than 1.

2. No radicands contain fractions.

3. No radicals appear in the denominator of a fraction.

Check for Understanding

Concept Check

1. **Explain** why absolute value is not necessary for $\sqrt{x^4} = x^2$. See margin.

2. **Show** that $\dfrac{1}{\sqrt{a}} = \dfrac{\sqrt{a}}{a}$ for $a > 0$. $\dfrac{1}{\sqrt{a}} \cdot \dfrac{\sqrt{a}}{\sqrt{a}} = \dfrac{\sqrt{a}}{a}$

3. **OPEN ENDED** Give an example of a binomial in the form $a\sqrt{b} + c\sqrt{d}$ and its conjugate. Then find their product. **Sample answer:** $2\sqrt{2} + 3\sqrt{3}$ and $2\sqrt{2} - 3\sqrt{3}$; -19

Guided Practice

Simplify. 8. $2x^2|y^3|\sqrt{15x}$

GUIDED PRACTICE KEY	
Exercises	Examples
4	1
5, 6, 13	2
7, 8	3
9, 10, 14	4
11, 12	5

4. $\sqrt{20}$ $2\sqrt{5}$

5. $\sqrt{2} \cdot \sqrt{8}$ 4

6. $3\sqrt{10} \cdot 4\sqrt{10}$ 120

7. $\sqrt{54a^2b^2}$ $3|ab|\sqrt{6}$

8. $\sqrt{60x^5y^6}$

9. $\dfrac{4}{\sqrt{6}}$ $\dfrac{2\sqrt{6}}{3}$

10. $\sqrt{\dfrac{3}{10}}$ $\dfrac{\sqrt{30}}{10}$

11. $\dfrac{8}{3 - \sqrt{2}}$ $\dfrac{8(3 + \sqrt{2})}{7}$

12. $\dfrac{2\sqrt{5}}{-4 + \sqrt{8}}$ $\dfrac{-2\sqrt{5} - \sqrt{10}}{2}$

In-Class Example

 Power Point®

5 Simplify $\dfrac{3}{5 - \sqrt{2}}$. $\dfrac{15 + 3\sqrt{2}}{23}$

3 Practice/Apply

Study Notebook

Have students—

• add the definitions/examples of the vocabulary terms to their Vocabulary Builder worksheets for Chapter 11.

• include examples of how to use the Product and Quotient Properties of Square Roots to simplify radical expressions.

• include examples of how to rationalize denominators, with and without conjugates.

• include any other item(s) that they find helpful in mastering the skills in this lesson.

Answer

1. Both x^4 and x^2 are positive even if x is a negative number.

Answer

51. A lot of formulas and calculations that are used in space exploration contain radical expressions. Answers should include the following.

- To determine the escape velocity of a planet, you would need to know its mass and the radius. It would be very important to know the escape velocity of a planet before you landed on it so you would know if you had enough fuel and velocity to launch from it to get back into space.

- The astronomical body with the smaller radius would have a greater escape velocity. As the radius decreases, the escape velocity increases.

Applications

13. **GEOMETRY** A square has sides each measuring $2\sqrt{7}$ feet. Determine the area of the square. **28 ft²**

14. **PHYSICS** The period of a pendulum is the time required for it to make one complete swing back and forth. The formula of the period P of a pendulum is $P = 2\pi\sqrt{\dfrac{\ell}{32}}$, where ℓ is the length of the pendulum in feet. If a pendulum in a clock tower is 8 feet long, find the period. Use 3.14 for π. **3.14 s**

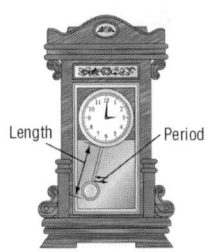

Length   Period

★ indicates increased difficulty

Practice and Apply

Homework Help

For Exercises	See Examples
15–18, 41, 44–46	1
19–22, 39, 40, 48, 49	2
23–26	3
27–32, 42, 43, 47	4
33–38	5

Extra Practice
See page 844.

Simplify. 25. $7|x^3y^3|\sqrt{3}$ 26. $6|x|y^2z^2\sqrt{2xz}$

15. $\sqrt{18}$ $3\sqrt{2}$

16. $\sqrt{24}$ $2\sqrt{6}$

17. $\sqrt{80}$ $4\sqrt{5}$

18. $\sqrt{75}$ $5\sqrt{3}$

19. $\sqrt{5}\cdot\sqrt{6}$ $\sqrt{30}$

20. $\sqrt{3}\cdot\sqrt{8}$ $2\sqrt{6}$

21. $7\sqrt{30}\cdot 2\sqrt{6}$ $84\sqrt{5}$

22. $2\sqrt{3}\cdot 5\sqrt{27}$ 90

23. $\sqrt{40a^4}$ $2a^2\sqrt{10}$

24. $\sqrt{50m^3n^5}$ $5|m|n^2\sqrt{2mn}$

25. $\sqrt{147x^6y^7}$

26. $\sqrt{72x^3y^4z^5}$

27. $\sqrt{\dfrac{2}{7}}\cdot\sqrt{\dfrac{7}{3}}$ $\dfrac{\sqrt{6}}{3}$

28. $\sqrt{\dfrac{3}{5}}\cdot\sqrt{\dfrac{6}{4}}$ $\dfrac{3\sqrt{10}}{10}$

29. $\sqrt{\dfrac{t}{8}}$ $\dfrac{\sqrt{2t}}{4}$

30. $\sqrt{\dfrac{27}{p^2}}$ $\dfrac{3\sqrt{3}}{|p|}$

31. $\sqrt{\dfrac{5c^5}{4d^5}}$ $\dfrac{c^2\sqrt{5cd}}{2|d^3|}$

32. $\dfrac{\sqrt{9x^5y}}{\sqrt{12x^2y^6}}$

32. $\dfrac{|x|\sqrt{3xy}}{2|y^3|}$

34. $\dfrac{-2\sqrt{5}-\sqrt{10}}{2}$

35. $2\sqrt{7}-2\sqrt{2}$

36. $\dfrac{2\sqrt{6}-2\sqrt{3}}{3}$

33. $\dfrac{18}{6-\sqrt{2}}$ $\dfrac{54+9\sqrt{2}}{17}$

34. $\dfrac{2\sqrt{5}}{-4+\sqrt{8}}$

35. $\dfrac{10}{\sqrt{7}+\sqrt{2}}$

36. $\dfrac{2}{\sqrt{3}+\sqrt{6}}$

37. $\dfrac{4}{4-3\sqrt{3}}$

★38. $\dfrac{3\sqrt{7}}{5\sqrt{3}+3\sqrt{5}}$

37. $\dfrac{-16-12\sqrt{3}}{11}$

38. $\dfrac{5\sqrt{21}-3\sqrt{35}}{10}$

39. **GEOMETRY** A rectangle has width $3\sqrt{5}$ centimeters and length $4\sqrt{10}$ centimeters. Find the area of the rectangle. **$60\sqrt{2}$ or about 84.9 cm²**

40. **GEOMETRY** A rectangle has length $\sqrt{\dfrac{a}{8}}$ meters and width $\sqrt{\dfrac{a}{2}}$ meters. What is the area of the rectangle? **$\dfrac{a}{4}$ m²**

41. **GEOMETRY** The formula for the area A of a square with side length s is $A = s^2$. Solve this equation for s, and find the side length of a square having an area of 72 square inches. **$s = \sqrt{A}$; $6\sqrt{2}$ in.**

PHYSICS For Exercises 42 and 43, use the following information.
The formula for the kinetic energy of a moving object is $E = \frac{1}{2}mv^2$, where E is the kinetic energy in joules, m is the mass in kilograms, and v is the velocity in meters per second.

42. Solve the equation for v. **$v = \sqrt{\dfrac{2E}{m}}$**

43. Find the velocity of an object whose mass is 0.6 kilogram and whose kinetic energy is 54 joules. **$6\sqrt{5}$ or about 13.4 m/s**

44. **SPACE EXPLORATION** Refer to the application at the beginning of the lesson. Find the escape velocity for the Moon in kilometers per second if $G = \dfrac{6.7\times 10^{-20}\text{ km}}{s^2\text{ kg}}$, $M = 7.4\times 10^{22}$ kg, and $R = 1.7\times 10^3$ km. How does this compare to the escape velocity for Earth? **2.4 km/s; The Moon has a much lower escape velocity than Earth.**

Teacher to Teacher

Judy Buchholtz   Dublin Scioto H.S., Dublin, OH

"To make algebra more meaningful to my students, I bring in the school police officer to discuss the formula used in Exercises 45–47."

INVESTIGATION For Exercises 45–47, use the following information.

Police officers can use the formula $s = \sqrt{30fd}$ to determine the speed s that a car was traveling in miles per hour by measuring the distance d in feet of its skid marks. In this formula, f is the coefficient of friction for the type and condition of the road.

45. Write a simplified expression for the speed if $f = 0.6$ for a wet asphalt road. $3\sqrt{2d}$

46. What is a simplified expression for the speed if $f = 0.8$ for a dry asphalt road?

47. An officer measures skid marks that are 110 feet long. Determine the speed of the car for both wet road conditions and for dry road conditions. **about 44.5 mph, about 51.4 mph**

46. $2\sqrt{6d}$

GEOMETRY For Exercises 48 and 49, use the following information.

Hero's Formula can be used to calculate the area A of a triangle given the three side lengths a, b, and c.

$$A = \sqrt{s(s-a)(s-b)(s-c)}, \text{ where } s = \frac{1}{2}(a+b+c)$$

48. Find the value of s if the side lengths of a triangle are 13, 10, and 7 feet. **15**

49. Determine the area of the triangle. $20\sqrt{3}$ or about 34.6 ft²

50. **CRITICAL THINKING** Simplify $\dfrac{1}{a-1+\sqrt{a}} \cdot \dfrac{a-1-\sqrt{a}}{a^2-3a+1}$.

51. **WRITING IN MATH** Answer the question that was posed at the beginning of the lesson. **See margin.**

How are radical expressions used in space exploration?

Include the following in your answer:

• an explanation of how you could determine the escape velocity for a planet and why you would need this information before you landed on the planet, and

• a comparison of the escape velocity for two astronomical bodies with the same mass, but different radii.

Standardized
Test Practice

52. If the cube has a surface area of $96a^2$, what is its volume? **C**

   Ⓐ $32a^3$ Ⓑ $48a^3$

   Ⓒ $64a^3$ Ⓓ $96a^3$

53. If $x = 81b^2$ and $b > 0$, then $\sqrt{x} = $ **B**

   Ⓐ $-9b$.   Ⓑ $9b$.

   Ⓒ $3b\sqrt{27}$.   Ⓓ $27b\sqrt{3}$.

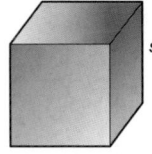
Surface area
of a cube = $6s^2$

Graphing
Calculator

WEATHER For Exercises 54 and 55, use the following information.

The formula $y = 91.4 - (91.4 - t)\left[0.478 + 0.301\left(\sqrt{x} - 0.02\right)\right]$ can be used to find the windchill factor. In this formula, y represents the windchill factor, t represents the air temperature in degrees Fahrenheit, and x represents the wind speed in miles per hour. Suppose the air temperature is 12°.

54. Use a graphing calculator to find the wind speed to the nearest mile per hour if it feels like $-9°$ with the windchill factor. **7 mph**

55. What does it feel like to the nearest degree if the wind speed is 4 miles per hour? **6°F**

Open-Ended Assessment

Writing Have students copy the Concept Summary on p. 589 into their Study Notebooks. For each of the three conditions listed, have students provide an example of an expression that does not satisfy the condition and then show how they simplified the expression to satisfy the condition.

Getting Ready for Lesson 11-2

PREREQUISITE SKILL Students will learn how to perform operations with radical expressions in Lesson 11-2. In order to perform operations with radical expressions, students must be able to use the Distributive Property to multiply binomials. Use Exercises 84–89 to determine your students' familiarity with multiplying binomials.

Extending the Lesson Radical expressions can be represented with fractional exponents. For example, $x^{\frac{1}{2}} = \sqrt{x}$. Using the properties of exponents, simplify each expression.

56. $x^{\frac{1}{2}} \cdot x^{\frac{1}{2}}$ **x**

57. $\left(x^{\frac{1}{2}}\right)^4$ **x^2**

58. $\dfrac{x^{\frac{5}{2}}}{x}$ **$x^{\frac{3}{2}}$ or $x\sqrt{x}$**

★ 59. Simplify the expression $\dfrac{\sqrt{a}}{a\sqrt[3]{a}}$. **$a^{-\frac{5}{6}}$ or $\dfrac{\sqrt[6]{a}}{a}$**

★ 60. Solve the equation $|y^3| = \dfrac{1}{3\sqrt{3}}$ for y. **$\pm\dfrac{\sqrt{3}}{3}$**

★ 61. Write $\left(s^2 t^{\frac{1}{2}}\right)^8 \sqrt{s^5 t^4}$ in simplest form. **$s^{18} t^6 \sqrt{s}$**

Maintain Your Skills

Mixed Review **Find the next three terms in each geometric sequence.** *(Lesson 10-7)*

62. 2, 6, 18, 54 **162, 486, 1458**

63. 1, −2, 4, −8 **16, −32, 64**

64. 384, 192, 96, 48 **24, 12, 6**

65. $\frac{1}{9}, \frac{2}{3}, 4, 24$ **144, 864, 5184**

66. $3, \frac{3}{4}, \frac{3}{16}, \frac{3}{64}$ **$\frac{3}{256}, \frac{3}{1024}, \frac{3}{4096}$**

67. 50, 10, 2, 0.4 **0.08, 0.016, 0.0032**

68. **BIOLOGY**   A certain type of bacteria, if left alone, doubles its number every 2 hours. If there are 1000 bacteria at a certain point in time, how many bacteria will there be 24 hours later? *(Lesson 10-6)* **4,096,000**

69. **PHYSICS**   According to Newton's Law of Cooling, the difference between the temperature of an object and its surroundings decreases in time exponentially. Suppose a cup of coffee is 95°C and it is in a room that is 20°C. The cooling of the coffee can be modeled by the equation $y = 75(0.875)^t$, where y is the temperature difference and t is the time in minutes. Find the temperature of the coffee after 15 minutes. *(Lesson 10-6)* **84.9°C**

Factor each trinomial, if possible. If the trinomial cannot be factored using integers, write *prime*. *(Lesson 9-4)*

70. $6x^2 + 7x - 5$ **$(3x + 5)(2x - 1)$**

71. $35x^2 - 43x + 12$ **$(5x - 4)(7x - 3)$**

72. $5x^2 + 3x + 31$ **prime**

73. $3x^2 - 6x - 105$ **$3(x - 7)(x + 5)$**

74. $4x^2 - 12x + 15$ **prime**

75. $8x^2 - 10x + 3$ **$(4x - 3)(2x - 1)$**

Find the solution set for each equation, given the replacement set. *(Lesson 4-4)*

76. $y = 3x + 2$; {(1, 5), (2, 6), (−2, 2), (−4, −10)} **{(1, 5), (−4, −10)}**

77. $5x + 2y = 10$; {(3, 5), (2, 0), (4, 2), (1, 2.5)} **{(2, 0), (1, 2.5)}**

78. $3a + 2b = 11$; {(−3, 10), (4, 1), (2, 2.5), (3, −2)} **{(−3, 10), (2, 2.5)}**

79. $5 - \frac{3}{2}x = 2y$; $\left\{(0, 1), (8, 2), \left(4, -\frac{1}{2}\right), (2, 1)\right\}$ **$\left\{\left(4, -\frac{1}{2}\right), (2, 1)\right\}$**

Solve each equation. Then check your solution. *(Lesson 3-3)*

80. $40 = -5d$ **−8**

81. $20.4 = 3.4y$ **6**

82. $\dfrac{h}{-11} = -25$ **275**

83. $-65 = \dfrac{r}{29}$ **−1885**

Getting Ready for the Next Lesson **PREREQUISITE SKILL   Find each product.**
*(To review **multiplying binomials**, see Lesson 8-7.)*

84. $(x - 3)(x + 2)$ **$x^2 - x - 6$**

85. $(a + 2)(a + 5)$ **$a^2 + 7a + 10$**

86. $(2t + 1)(t - 6)$ **$2t^2 - 11t - 6$**

87. $(4x - 3)(x + 1)$ **$4x^2 + x - 3$**

88. $(5x + 3y)(3x - y)$ **$15x^2 + 4xy - 3y^2$**

89. $(3a - 2b)(4a + 7b)$ **$12a^2 + 13ab - 14b^2$**

Operations with Radical Expressions

What You'll Learn

- Add and subtract radical expressions.
- Multiply radical expressions.

How can you use radical expressions to determine how far a person can see?

The formula $d = \sqrt{\dfrac{3h}{2}}$ represents the distance d in miles that a person h feet high can see. To determine how much farther a person can see from atop the Sears Tower than from atop the Empire State Building, we can substitute the heights of both buildings into the equation.

World's Tall Structures

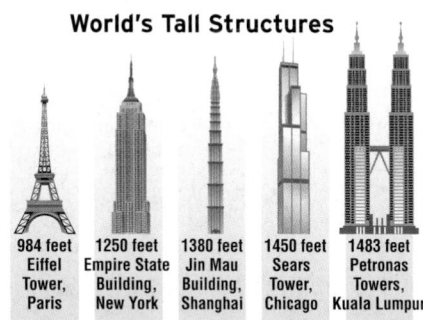

| 984 feet | 1250 feet | 1380 feet | 1450 feet | 1483 feet |
| Eiffel Tower, Paris | Empire State Building, New York | Jin Mau Building, Shanghai | Sears Tower, Chicago | Petronas Towers, Kuala Lumpur |

ADD AND SUBTRACT RADICAL EXPRESSIONS Radical expressions in which the radicands are alike can be added or subtracted in the same way that monomials are added or subtracted.

Monomials	Radical Expressions
$2x + 7x = (2 + 7)x$	$2\sqrt{11} + 7\sqrt{11} = (2 + 7)\sqrt{11}$
$= 9x$	$= 9\sqrt{11}$
$15y - 3y = (15 - 3)y$	$15\sqrt{2} - 3\sqrt{2} = (15 - 3)\sqrt{2}$
$= 12y$	$= 12\sqrt{2}$

Notice that the Distributive Property was used to simplify each radical expression.

Example 1 Expressions with Like Radicands

Simplify each expression.

a. $4\sqrt{3} + 6\sqrt{3} - 5\sqrt{3}$

$4\sqrt{3} + 6\sqrt{3} - 5\sqrt{3} = (4 + 6 - 5)\sqrt{3}$ Distributive Property

$= 5\sqrt{3}$ Simplify.

b. $12\sqrt{5} + 3\sqrt{7} + 6\sqrt{7} - 8\sqrt{5}$

$12\sqrt{5} + 3\sqrt{7} + 6\sqrt{7} - 8\sqrt{5} = 12\sqrt{5} - 8\sqrt{5} + 3\sqrt{7} + 6\sqrt{7}$ Commutative Property

$= (12 - 8)\sqrt{5} + (3 + 6)\sqrt{7}$ Distributive Property

$= 4\sqrt{5} + 9\sqrt{7}$ Simplify.

In Example 1b, $4\sqrt{5} + 9\sqrt{7}$ cannot be simplified further because the radicands are different. There are no common factors, and each radicand is in simplest form. If the radicals in a radical expression are not in simplest form, simplify them first.

1 Focus

5-Minute Check Transparency 11-2 Use as a quiz or review of Lesson 11-1.

Mathematical Background notes are available for this lesson on p. 584C.

How can you use radical expressions to determine how far a person can see?

Ask students:

- What is an assumption that the formula makes? **Sample answer: That there are no obstructions that would block a person from seeing the entire distance.**

- Assuming that nothing blocks the view, how much farther can a person atop the Sears Tower see than a person atop the Empire State Building? **about 3.3 miles farther**

- **Mountain Climbing** Mount Everest, the tallest mountain in the world, is about 12,000 feet above the plateau out of which it rises. How far would a climber be able to see from the peak of Mount Everest? **about 134 miles**

Resource Manager

Workbook and Reproducible Masters

Chapter 11 Resource Masters
- Study Guide and Intervention, pp. 649–650
- Skills Practice, p. 651
- Practice, p. 652
- Reading to Learn Mathematics, p. 653
- Enrichment, p. 654
- Assessment, p. 699

Parent and Student Study Guide Workbook, p. 84
Prerequisite Skills Workbook, pp. 37–38

Transparencies

5-Minute Check Transparency 11-2
Answer Key Transparencies

Technology

Interactive Chalkboard

ADD AND SUBTRACT RADICAL EXPRESSIONS

In-Class Examples

1 Simplify each expression.
   a. $6\sqrt{5} + 2\sqrt{5} - 5\sqrt{5}$ $3\sqrt{5}$
   b. $7\sqrt{2} + 8\sqrt{11} - 4\sqrt{11} - 6\sqrt{2}$
      $\sqrt{2} + 4\sqrt{11}$

2 $6\sqrt{27} + 8\sqrt{12} + 2\sqrt{75}$
   $44\sqrt{3}$

MULTIPLY RADICAL EXPRESSIONS

In-Class Example

3 Find the area of a rectangle with a width of $4\sqrt{6} - 2\sqrt{10}$ and a length of $5\sqrt{3} + 7\sqrt{5}$.
   $18\sqrt{30} - 10\sqrt{2}$

Example 2 *Expressions with Unlike Radicands*

Simplify $2\sqrt{20} + 3\sqrt{45} + \sqrt{180}$.

$$2\sqrt{20} + 3\sqrt{45} + \sqrt{180} = 2\sqrt{2^2 \cdot 5} + 3\sqrt{3^2 \cdot 5} + \sqrt{6^2 \cdot 5}$$
$$= 2(\sqrt{2^2} \cdot \sqrt{5}) + 3(\sqrt{3^2} \cdot \sqrt{5}) + \sqrt{6^2} \cdot \sqrt{5}$$
$$= 2(2\sqrt{5}) + 3(3\sqrt{5}) + 6\sqrt{5}$$
$$= 4\sqrt{5} + 9\sqrt{5} + 6\sqrt{5}$$
$$= 19\sqrt{5}$$

The simplified form is $19\sqrt{5}$.

You can use a calculator to verify that a simplified radical expression is equivalent to the original expression. Consider Example 2. First, find a decimal approximation for the original expression.

KEYSTROKES: 2 [2nd] [√] 20 [ )] [+] 3 [2nd] [√] 45 [ )] [+] [2nd] [√]
180 [ )] [ENTER]   42.48529157

Next, find a decimal approximation for the simplified expression.

KEYSTROKES: 19 [2nd] [√] 5 [ENTER]   42.48529157

Since the approximations are equal, the expressions are equivalent.

MULTIPLY RADICAL EXPRESSIONS   Multiplying two radical expressions with different radicands is similar to multiplying binomials.

Example 3 *Multiply Radical Expressions*

Find the area of the rectangle in simplest form.

To find the area of the rectangle multiply the measures of the length and width.

$$(4\sqrt{5} - 2\sqrt{3})(3\sqrt{6} - \sqrt{10})$$

| First terms | Outer terms | Inner terms | Last terms |

$$= (4\sqrt{5})(3\sqrt{6}) + (4\sqrt{5})(-\sqrt{10}) + (-2\sqrt{3})(3\sqrt{6}) + (-2\sqrt{3})(-\sqrt{10})$$
$$= 12\sqrt{30} - 4\sqrt{50} - 6\sqrt{18} + 2\sqrt{30} \qquad \text{Multiply.}$$
$$= 12\sqrt{30} - 4\sqrt{5^2 \cdot 2} - 6\sqrt{3^2 \cdot 2} + 2\sqrt{30} \qquad \text{Prime factorization}$$
$$= 12\sqrt{30} - 20\sqrt{2} - 18\sqrt{2} + 2\sqrt{30} \qquad \text{Simplify.}$$
$$= 14\sqrt{30} - 38\sqrt{2} \qquad \text{Combine like terms.}$$

The area of the rectangle is $14\sqrt{30} - 38\sqrt{2}$ square units.

Study Tip

Look Back
To review the **FOIL method**, see Lesson 8-7.

$4\sqrt{5} - 2\sqrt{3}$

$3\sqrt{6} - \sqrt{10}$

DAILY INTERVENTION

Differentiated Instruction

Visual/Spatial Have students write all the perfect squares from 1 to 100 on an index card using a colored pen or pencil. Then have them rework Example 3. After they multiply the binomials, have students use their colored pen or pencil to circle the terms inside radicals that have perfect square factors. Using the same color, have students write the factorization in the line below each radical expression that can be factored.

Concept Check

1. **Explain** why you should simplify each radical in a radical expression before adding or subtracting. **to determine if there are any like radicands**

2. **Explain** how you use the Distributive Property to simplify like radicands that are added or subtracted. **See margin.**

3. **OPEN ENDED** Choose values for x and y. Then find $(\sqrt{x} + \sqrt{y})^2$.
Sample answer: $(\sqrt{2} + \sqrt{3})^2 = 2 + 2\sqrt{6} + 3$ or $5 + 2\sqrt{6}$

Guided Practice

Simplify each expression.

GUIDED PRACTICE KEY	
Exercises	Examples
4, 5	1
6–9	2
10–13	3

4. $4\sqrt{3} + 7\sqrt{3}$ $11\sqrt{3}$

5. $2\sqrt{6} - 7\sqrt{6}$ $-5\sqrt{6}$

6. $5\sqrt{5} - 3\sqrt{20}$ $-\sqrt{5}$

7. $2\sqrt{3} + \sqrt{12}$ $4\sqrt{3}$

8. $3\sqrt{5} + 5\sqrt{6} + 3\sqrt{20}$ $9\sqrt{5} + 5\sqrt{6}$

9. $8\sqrt{3} + \sqrt{3} + \sqrt{9}$ $9\sqrt{3} + 3$

Find each product.

10. $\sqrt{2}(\sqrt{8} + 4\sqrt{3})$ $4 + 4\sqrt{6}$

11. $(4 + \sqrt{5})(3 + \sqrt{5})$ $17 + 7\sqrt{5}$

Applications

12. **GEOMETRY** Find the perimeter and the area of a square whose sides measure $4 + 3\sqrt{6}$ feet. $P = 16 + 12\sqrt{6}$ ft; $A = 70 + 24\sqrt{6}$ ft^2

13. **ELECTRICITY** The voltage V required for a circuit is given by $V = \sqrt{PR}$, where P is the power in watts and R is the resistance in ohms. How many more volts are needed to light a 100-watt bulb than a 75-watt bulb if the resistance for both is 110 ohms? $10\sqrt{110} - 5\sqrt{330} \approx 14.05$ volts

★ indicates increased difficulty

Practice and Apply

Homework Help	
For Exercises	See Examples
14–21	1
22–29	2
30–48	3

Extra Practice
See page 844.

20. $13\sqrt{3} + \sqrt{2}$

21. $4\sqrt{6} - 6\sqrt{2} + 5\sqrt{17}$

34. $10\sqrt{3} + 16$

Simplify each expression.

14. $8\sqrt{5} + 3\sqrt{5}$ $11\sqrt{5}$

15. $3\sqrt{6} + 10\sqrt{6}$ $13\sqrt{6}$

16. $2\sqrt{15} - 6\sqrt{15} - 3\sqrt{15}$ $-7\sqrt{15}$

17. $5\sqrt{19} + 6\sqrt{19} - 11\sqrt{19}$ 0

18. $16\sqrt{x} + 2\sqrt{x}$ $18\sqrt{x}$

19. $3\sqrt{5b} - 4\sqrt{5b} + 11\sqrt{5b}$ $10\sqrt{5b}$

20. $8\sqrt{3} - 2\sqrt{2} + 3\sqrt{2} + 5\sqrt{3}$

21. $4\sqrt{6} + \sqrt{17} - 6\sqrt{2} + 4\sqrt{17}$

22. $\sqrt{18} + \sqrt{12} + \sqrt{8}$ $5\sqrt{2} + 2\sqrt{3}$

23. $\sqrt{6} + 2\sqrt{3} + \sqrt{12}$ $\sqrt{6} + 4\sqrt{3}$

24. $3\sqrt{7} - 2\sqrt{28}$ $-\sqrt{7}$

25. $2\sqrt{50} - 3\sqrt{32}$ $-2\sqrt{2}$

★ 26. $\sqrt{2} + \sqrt{\frac{1}{2}}$ $\frac{3\sqrt{2}}{2}$

★ 27. $\sqrt{10} - \sqrt{\frac{2}{5}}$ $\frac{4\sqrt{10}}{5}$

★ 28. $3\sqrt{3} - \sqrt{45} + 3\sqrt{\frac{1}{3}}$ $4\sqrt{3} - 3\sqrt{5}$

★ 29. $6\sqrt{\frac{7}{4}} + 3\sqrt{28} - 10\sqrt{\frac{1}{7}}$ $\frac{53\sqrt{7}}{7}$

Find each product.

30. $\sqrt{6}(\sqrt{3} + 5\sqrt{2})$ $3\sqrt{2} + 10\sqrt{3}$

31. $\sqrt{5}(2\sqrt{10} + 3\sqrt{2})$ $10\sqrt{2} + 3\sqrt{10}$

32. $(3 + \sqrt{5})(3 - \sqrt{5})$ 4

33. $(7 - \sqrt{10})^2$ $59 - 14\sqrt{10}$

★ 34. $(\sqrt{6} + \sqrt{8})(\sqrt{24} + \sqrt{2})$

★ 35. $(\sqrt{5} - \sqrt{2})(\sqrt{14} + \sqrt{35})$ $3\sqrt{7}$

★ 36. $(2\sqrt{10} + 3\sqrt{15})(3\sqrt{3} - 2\sqrt{2})$ $19\sqrt{5}$

★ 37. $(5\sqrt{2} + 3\sqrt{5})(2\sqrt{10} - 3)$ $15\sqrt{2} + 11\sqrt{5}$

38. **GEOMETRY** Find the perimeter of a rectangle whose length is $8\sqrt{7} + 4\sqrt{5}$ inches and whose width is $5\sqrt{7} - 3\sqrt{5}$ inches. $26\sqrt{7} + 2\sqrt{5}$ in.

 www.algebra1.com/extra_examples

Lesson 11-2 Operations with Radical Expressions **595**

3 Practice/Apply

Study Notebook

Have students—
• include examples of how to add, subtract, and multiply radical expressions.
• include any other item(s) that they find helpful in mastering the skills in this lesson.

About the Exercises ...

Organization by Objective
• Add and Subtract Radical Expressions: 14–29
• Multiply Radical Expressions: 30–37

Odd/Even Assignments
Exercises 14–39 are structured so that students practice the same concepts whether they are assigned odd or even problems.

Alert! Exercise 42 requires the use of the Internet or other research materials.

Assignment Guide

Basic: 15–25 odd, 31, 33, 39, 41, 42, 49–76

Average: 15–39 odd, 41–44, 49–76

Advanced: 14–40 even, 45–70 (optional: 71–76)

Answer

2. The Distributive Property allows you to add like terms. Radicals with like radicands can be added or subtracted.

Add and Subtract Radical Expressions When adding or subtracting radical expressions, use the Associative and Distributive Properties to simplify the expressions. If radical expressions are not in simplest form, simplify them.

Example 1 Simplify $10\sqrt{6} - 5\sqrt{3} + 6\sqrt{3} - 4\sqrt{6}$.

$10\sqrt{6} - 5\sqrt{3} + 6\sqrt{3} - 4\sqrt{6} = (10 - 4)\sqrt{6} + (-5 + 6)\sqrt{3}$ Associative and Distributive Properties
$= 6\sqrt{6} + \sqrt{3}$ Simplify.

Example 2 Simplify $3\sqrt{12} + 5\sqrt{75}$.

$3\sqrt{12} + 5\sqrt{75} = 3\sqrt{2^2 \cdot 3} + 5\sqrt{5^2 \cdot 3}$ Simplify.
$= 3 \cdot 2\sqrt{3} + 5 \cdot 5\sqrt{3}$ Simplify.
$= 6\sqrt{3} + 25\sqrt{3}$ Simplify.
$= 31\sqrt{3}$ Distributive Property

Exercises

Simplify each expression.

1. $2\sqrt{5} + 4\sqrt{5}$ $6\sqrt{5}$
2. $\sqrt{6} - 4\sqrt{6}$ $-3\sqrt{6}$
3. $\sqrt{8} - \sqrt{2}$ $\sqrt{2}$
4. $3\sqrt{75} + 2\sqrt{5}$ $15\sqrt{3} + 2\sqrt{5}$
5. $\sqrt{20} + 2\sqrt{5} - 3\sqrt{5}$ $\sqrt{5}$
6. $2\sqrt{3} + \sqrt{6} - 5\sqrt{3}$ $-3\sqrt{3} + \sqrt{6}$
7. $\sqrt{12} + 2\sqrt{3} - 5\sqrt{3}$ $-\sqrt{3}$
8. $3\sqrt{6} + 3\sqrt{2} - \sqrt{50} + \sqrt{24}$ $5\sqrt{6} - 2\sqrt{2}$
9. $\sqrt{8a} - \sqrt{2a} + 5\sqrt{2a}$ $6\sqrt{2a}$
10. $\sqrt{54} + \sqrt{24}$ $5\sqrt{6}$
11. $\sqrt{3} + \sqrt{\frac{1}{3}}$ $\frac{4\sqrt{3}}{3}$
12. $\sqrt{12} + \sqrt{\frac{1}{3}}$ $\frac{7\sqrt{3}}{3}$
13. $\sqrt{54} - \sqrt{\frac{1}{6}}$ $\frac{17\sqrt{6}}{6}$
14. $\sqrt{80} - \sqrt{20} + \sqrt{180}$ $8\sqrt{5}$
15. $\sqrt{50} + \sqrt{18} - \sqrt{75} + \sqrt{27}$ $8\sqrt{2} - 2\sqrt{3}$
16. $2\sqrt{3} - 4\sqrt{45} + 2\sqrt{\frac{1}{3}}$ $\frac{8\sqrt{3}}{3} - 12\sqrt{5}$
17. $\sqrt{125} - 2\sqrt{\frac{1}{5}} + \sqrt{\frac{1}{3}}$ $\frac{23\sqrt{5}}{5} + \frac{\sqrt{3}}{3}$
18. $\sqrt{\frac{2}{3}} + 3\sqrt{3} - 4\sqrt{\frac{1}{12}}$ $\frac{\sqrt{6}}{3} + \frac{28\sqrt{3}}{12}$

Simplify each expression.

1. $8\sqrt{30} - 4\sqrt{30}$ $4\sqrt{30}$
2. $2\sqrt{5} + 7\sqrt{5} - 5\sqrt{5}$ $4\sqrt{5}$
3. $7\sqrt{13x} - 14\sqrt{13x} + 2\sqrt{13x}$ $-5\sqrt{13x}$
4. $2\sqrt{45} + 4\sqrt{20}$ $14\sqrt{5}$
5. $\sqrt{40} - \sqrt{10} + \sqrt{90}$ $4\sqrt{10}$
6. $2\sqrt{32} + 3\sqrt{50} - 3\sqrt{18}$ $14\sqrt{2}$
7. $\sqrt{27} + \sqrt{18} + \sqrt{300}$ $3\sqrt{2} + 13\sqrt{3}$
8. $5\sqrt{8} + 3\sqrt{20} - \sqrt{32}$ $6\sqrt{2} + 6\sqrt{5}$
9. $\sqrt{14} - \sqrt{\frac{6}{7}}$ $\frac{6\sqrt{14}}{7}$
10. $\sqrt{50} + \sqrt{32} - \sqrt{\frac{1}{2}}$ $\frac{17\sqrt{2}}{2}$
11. $5\sqrt{19} + 4\sqrt{28} - 8\sqrt{19} + \sqrt{63}$
   $-3\sqrt{19} + 11\sqrt{7}$
12. $3\sqrt{10} + \sqrt{75} - 2\sqrt{40} - 4\sqrt{12}$
   $-\sqrt{10} - 3\sqrt{3}$

Find each product.

13. $\sqrt{6}(\sqrt{10} + \sqrt{15})$ $2\sqrt{15} + 3\sqrt{10}$
14. $\sqrt{5}(\sqrt{2} - 4\sqrt{8})$ $-3\sqrt{10}$
15. $2\sqrt{7}(3\sqrt{12} + 5\sqrt{8})$ $12\sqrt{21} + 20\sqrt{14}$
16. $(5 - \sqrt{15})^2$ $40 - 10\sqrt{15}$
17. $(\sqrt{10} + \sqrt{6})(\sqrt{30} - \sqrt{18})$ $4\sqrt{3}$
18. $(\sqrt{8} + \sqrt{12})(\sqrt{48} + \sqrt{18})$ $36 + 14\sqrt{6}$
19. $(\sqrt{2} + 2\sqrt{8})(3\sqrt{6} - \sqrt{5})$
   $30\sqrt{3} - 5\sqrt{10}$
20. $(4\sqrt{3} - 2\sqrt{5})(3\sqrt{10} + 5\sqrt{6})$
   $2\sqrt{30} + 30\sqrt{2}$

SOUND For Exercises 21 and 22, use the following information.
The speed of sound V in meters per second near Earth's surface is given by $V = 20\sqrt{t + 273}$, where t is the surface temperature in degrees Celsius.

21. What is the speed of sound near Earth's surface at 15°C and at 2°C in simplest form?
   $240\sqrt{2}$ m/s, $100\sqrt{11}$ m/s

22. How much faster is the speed of sound at 15°C than at 2°C?
   $240\sqrt{2} - 100\sqrt{11} \approx 7.75$ m/s

GEOMETRY For Exercises 23 and 24, use the following information.
A rectangle is $5\sqrt{7} + 2\sqrt{3}$ centimeters long and $6\sqrt{7} - 3\sqrt{3}$ centimeters wide.

23. Find the perimeter of the rectangle in simplest form. $22\sqrt{7} - 2\sqrt{3}$ cm

24. Find the area of the rectangle in simplest form. $192 - 3\sqrt{21}$ cm²

Pre-Activity How can you use radical expressions to determine how far a person can see?

Read the introduction to Lesson 11-2 at the top of page 593 in your textbook.

Suppose you substitute the heights of the Sears Tower and the Empire State Building into the formula to find how far you can see from atop each building. What operation should you then use to determine how much farther you can see from the Sears Tower than from the Empire State Building?
subtraction

Reading the Lesson

1. Indicate whether the following expressions are in simplest form. Explain your answer.
   a. $6\sqrt{3} - \sqrt{12}$
   No; 12 can be simplified to $\sqrt{2^2} \cdot \sqrt{3}$ or $2\sqrt{3}$.

   b. $12\sqrt{6} + 7\sqrt{10}$
   Yes; both the addends are radical expressions in simplest form, the radicands are different, and there are no common factors.

2. Below the words First terms, Outer terms, Inner terms, and Last terms, write the products you would use to simplify the expression $(2\sqrt{15} + 3\sqrt{5})(6\sqrt{3} - 5\sqrt{2})$.

First terms	Outer terms	Inner terms	Last terms
$(2\sqrt{15})(6\sqrt{3})$	$(2\sqrt{15})(-5\sqrt{2})$	$(3\sqrt{5})(6\sqrt{3})$	$(3\sqrt{5})(-5\sqrt{2})$

Helping You Remember

3. How can you use what you know about adding and subtracting monomials to help you remember how to add and subtract radical expressions?
   Sample answer: Check that the addends have been simplified. Next, group addends that involve like radicals. Then use the Distributive Property to combine the addends that involve like radicals.

---

39. **GEOMETRY** The perimeter of a rectangle is $2\sqrt{3} + 4\sqrt{11} + 6$ centimeters, and its length is $2\sqrt{11} + 1$ centimeters. Find the width. $\sqrt{3} + 2$ cm

40. **GEOMETRY** A formula for the area A of a rhombus can be found using the formula $A = \frac{1}{2}d_1d_2$, where d_1 and d_2 are the lengths of the diagonals of the rhombus. What is the area of the rhombus at the right? $15\sqrt{6}$ cm²

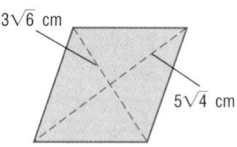

$3\sqrt{6}$ cm
$5\sqrt{4}$ cm

DISTANCE For Exercises 41 and 42, refer to the application at the beginning of the lesson.

41. How much farther can a person see from atop the Sears Tower than from atop the Empire State Building? $5\sqrt{87} - 25\sqrt{3} \approx 3.34$ mi

42. A person atop the Empire State Building can see approximately 4.57 miles farther than a person atop the Texas Commerce Tower in Houston. Find the height of the Texas Commerce Tower. Explain how you found the answer.   **See margin.**

 Online Research **Data Update** What are the tallest buildings and towers in the world today? Visit www.algebra1.com/data_update to learn more.

ENGINEERING For Exercises 43 and 44, use the following information.
The equation $r = \sqrt{\frac{F}{5\pi}}$ relates the radius r of a drainpipe in inches to the flow rate F of water passing through it in gallons per minute.

43. Find the radius of a pipe that can carry 500 gallons of water per minute. Round to the nearest whole number.   **6 in.**

44. An engineer determines that a drainpipe must be able to carry 1000 gallons of water per minute and instructs the builder to use an 8-inch radius pipe. Can the builder use two 4-inch radius pipes instead? Justify your answer.
   No, each pipe would need to carry 500 gallons per minute, so the pipes would need a radius greater than 5.6 in.

MOTION For Exercises 45–47, use the following information.
The velocity of an object dropped from a certain height can be found using the formula $v = \sqrt{2gd}$, where v is the velocity in feet per second, g is the acceleration due to gravity, and d is the distance in feet the object drops.

45. Find the speed of an object that has fallen 25 feet and the speed of an object that has fallen 100 feet. Use 32 feet per second squared for g.   **40 ft/s; 80 ft/s**

46. When you increased the distance by 4 times, what happened to the velocity?
   The velocity doubled.

47. **MAKE A CONJECTURE** Estimate the velocity of an object that has fallen 225 feet. Then use the formula to verify your answer. **The velocity should be $\sqrt{9}$ or 3 times the velocity of an object falling 25 feet; $3 \cdot 40 = 120$ ft/s, $\sqrt{2(32)(225)} = 120$ ft/s.**

48. **WATER SUPPLY** The relationship between a city's size and its capacity to supply water to its citizens can be described by the expression $1020\sqrt{P}(1 - 0.01\sqrt{P})$, where P is the population in thousands and the result is the number of gallons per minute required. If a city has a population of 55,000 people, how many gallons per minute must the city's pumping station be able to supply?
   about 7003.5 gal/min

The Wheel of Theodorus

The Greek mathematicians were intrigued by problems of representing different numbers and expressions using geometric constructions.

Theodorus, a Greek philosopher who lived about 425 B.C., is said to have discovered a way to construct the sequence $\sqrt{1}, \sqrt{2}, \sqrt{3}, \sqrt{4}, \ldots$.

The beginning of his construction is shown. You start with an isosceles right triangle with sides 1 unit long.

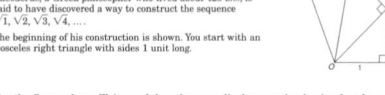

Use the figure above. Write each length as a radical expression in simplest form.

1. line segment AO $\sqrt{1}$
2. line segment BO $\sqrt{2}$
3. line segment CO $\sqrt{3}$
4. line segment DO $\sqrt{4}$

Answer

42. Approximately 1000 feet; solve

$$\sqrt{\frac{3(1250)}{2}} - \sqrt{\frac{3h}{2}} = 4.57;$$

may use guess and test, graphical, or analytical methods.

More About . . .

Distance

The Sears Tower was the tallest building in the world from 1974 to 1996. You can see four states from its roof: Michigan, Indiana, Illinois, and Wisconsin.

Source: www.the-skydeck.com

49. CRITICAL THINKING Find a counterexample to disprove the following statement. **Sample answer:** $a = 4$, $b = 9$: $\sqrt{4 + 9} \neq \sqrt{4} + \sqrt{9}$
For any numbers a and b, where a > 0 and b > 0, $\sqrt{a + b} = \sqrt{a} + \sqrt{b}$.

50. CRITICAL THINKING Under what conditions is $(\sqrt{a + b})^2 = (\sqrt{a})^2 + (\sqrt{b})^2$ true? $a = 0$ or $b = 0$ or both

51. WRITING IN MATH   Answer the question that was posed at the beginning of the lesson. **See margin.**

How can you use radical expressions to determine how far a person can see?

Include the following in your answer:
- an explanation of how this information could help determine how far apart lifeguard towers should be on a beach, and
- an example of a real-life situation where a lookout position is placed at a high point above the ground.

Standardized Test Practice
Ⓐ Ⓑ Ⓒ Ⓓ

52. Find the difference of $9\sqrt{7}$ and $2\sqrt{28}$. **C**
- Ⓐ $\sqrt{7}$
- Ⓑ $4\sqrt{7}$
- Ⓒ $5\sqrt{7}$
- Ⓓ $7\sqrt{7}$

53. Simplify $\sqrt{3}(4 + \sqrt{12})^2$. **D**
- Ⓐ $4\sqrt{3} + 6$
- Ⓑ $28\sqrt{3}$
- Ⓒ $28 + 16\sqrt{3}$
- Ⓓ $48 + 28\sqrt{3}$

Maintain Your Skills

Mixed Review
56. $-14|x|y\sqrt{y}$

Simplify. *(Lesson 11-1)*

54. $\sqrt{40}$ $2\sqrt{10}$

55. $\sqrt{128}$ $8\sqrt{2}$

56. $-\sqrt{196x^2y^3}$

57. $\dfrac{\sqrt{50}}{\sqrt{8}}$ $\dfrac{5}{2}$

58. $\sqrt{\dfrac{225c^4d}{18c^2}}$ $\dfrac{5|c|\sqrt{2d}}{2}$

59. $\sqrt{\dfrac{63a}{128a^3b^2}}$ $\dfrac{3\sqrt{14}}{16|ab|}$

Find the *n*th term of each geometric sequence. *(Lesson 10-7)*

60. $a_1 = 4$, $n = 6$, $r = 4$
4096

61. $a_1 = -7$, $n = 4$, $r = 9$
−5103

62. $a_1 = 2$, $n = 8$, $r = -0.8$
−0.4194304

Solve each equation by factoring. Check your solutions. *(Lesson 9-5)*

63. $81 = 49y^2$ $\left\{\pm\dfrac{9}{7}\right\}$

64. $q^2 - \dfrac{36}{121} = 0$ $\left\{\pm\dfrac{6}{11}\right\}$

65. $48n^3 - 75n = 0$ $\left\{-\dfrac{5}{4}, 0, \dfrac{5}{4}\right\}$

66. $5x^3 - 80x = 240 - 15x^2$ $\{-4, -3, 4\}$

Solve each inequality. Then check your solution. *(Lesson 6-2)*

67. $8n \geq 5$ $n \geq \dfrac{5}{8}$

68. $\dfrac{w}{9} < 14$ $w < 126$

69. $\dfrac{7k}{2} > \dfrac{21}{10}$ $k > \dfrac{3}{5}$

70. PROBABILITY A student rolls a die three times. What is the probability that each roll is a 1? *(Lesson 2-6)* $\dfrac{1}{216}$

Getting Ready for the Next Lesson
PREREQUISITE SKILL Find each product. *(To review special products, see Lesson 8-8.)*

71. $(x - 2)^2$ $x^2 - 4x + 4$

72. $(x + 5)^2$ $x^2 + 10x + 25$

73. $(x + 6)^2$ $x^2 + 12x + 36$

74. $(3x - 1)^2$ $9x^2 - 6x + 1$

75. $(2x - 3)^2$ $4x^2 - 12x + 9$

76. $(4x + 7)^2$ $16x^2 + 56x + 49$

Lesson 11-2 Operations with Radical Expressions **597**

---

4 *Assess*

Open-Ended Assessment

Speaking Ask students to compare and contrast adding, subtracting, and multiplying radical expressions and variable expressions. What are the similarities? What are the differences? Allow students to give examples on the chalkboard if they wish.

Getting Ready for Lesson 11-3

PREREQUISITE SKILL Students will learn how to solve radical equations in Lesson 11-3. In order to solve radical equations, students will need to be able to recognize and find special products. Use Exercises 71–76 to determine your students' familiarity with finding special products.

Assessment Options

Quiz (Lessons 11-1 and 11-2) is available on p. 699 of the *Chapter 11 Resource Masters*.

Answer

51. The distance a person can see is related to the height of the person using $d = \sqrt{\dfrac{3h}{2}}$. Answers should include the following.

- You can find how far each lifeguard can see from the height of the lifeguard tower. Each tower should have some overlap to cover the entire beach area.

- On early ships, a lookout position (Crow's nest) was situated high on the foremast. Sailors could see farther from this position than from the ship's deck.

11-3 Radical Equations

1 Focus

5-Minute Check Transparency 11-3 Use as a quiz or review of Lesson 11-2.

Mathematical Background notes are available for this lesson on p. 584D.

How are radical equations used to find free-fall times?

Ask students:

• Is $\dfrac{\sqrt{h}}{4}$ in simplest form?
  Explain. **Yes, since there is no radical in the denominator, the expression is in simplest form.**

• How would you solve $t = \dfrac{x}{4}$ for x? **Multiply each side by 4.**

• What do you think might be a way to remove the radical sign from $4t = \sqrt{h}$? **Square each side of the equation.**

What You'll Learn

• Solve radical equations.
• Solve radical equations with extraneous solutions.

Vocabulary
• radical equation
• extraneous solution

How are radical equations used to find free-fall times?

Skydivers fall 1050 to 1480 feet every 5 seconds, reaching speeds of 120 to 150 miles per hour at *terminal velocity*. It is the highest speed they can reach and occurs when the air resistance equals the force of gravity. With no air resistance, the time t in seconds that it takes an object to fall h feet can be determined by the equation $t = \dfrac{\sqrt{h}}{4}$. How would you find the value of h if you are given the value of t?

RADICAL EQUATIONS Equations like $t = \dfrac{\sqrt{h}}{4}$ that contain radicals with variables in the radicand are called **radical equations**. To solve these equations, first isolate the radical on one side of the equation. Then square each side of the equation to eliminate the radical.

Example 1 *Radical Equation with a Variable*

FREE-FALL HEIGHT Two objects are dropped simultaneously. The first object reaches the ground in 2.5 seconds, and the second object reaches the ground 1.5 seconds later. From what heights were the two objects dropped?

Find the height of the first object. Replace t with 2.5 seconds.

$$t = \frac{\sqrt{h}}{4} \qquad \text{Original equation}$$

$$2.5 = \frac{\sqrt{h}}{4} \qquad \text{Replace } t \text{ with 2.5.}$$

$$10 = \sqrt{h} \qquad \text{Multiply each side by 4.}$$

$$10^2 = (\sqrt{h})^2 \qquad \text{Square each side.}$$

$$100 = h \qquad \text{Simplify.}$$

CHECK $t = \dfrac{\sqrt{h}}{4} \qquad \text{Original equation}$

$t \overset{?}{=} \dfrac{\sqrt{100}}{4} \qquad h = 100$

$t \overset{?}{=} \dfrac{10}{4} \qquad \sqrt{100} = 10$

$t = 2.5 \qquad \text{Simplify.}$

The first object was dropped from 100 feet.

Resource Manager

📁 **Workbook and Reproducible Masters**

Chapter 11 Resource Masters
• Study Guide and Intervention, pp. 655–656
• Skills Practice, p. 657
• Practice, p. 658
• Reading to Learn Mathematics, p. 659
• Enrichment, p. 660

Graphing Calculator and Spreadsheet Masters, p. 43
Parent and Student Study Guide Workbook, p. 85

📀 **Transparencies**
5-Minute Check Transparency 11-3
Answer Key Transparencies

💿 **Technology**
Interactive Chalkboard
Multimedia Applications

The time it took the second object to fall was 2.5 + 1.5 seconds or 4 seconds.

$$t = \frac{\sqrt{h}}{4}$$ Original equation

$$4 = \frac{\sqrt{h}}{4}$$ Replace t with 4.

$$16 = \sqrt{h}$$ Multiply each side by 4.

$$16^2 = (\sqrt{h})^2$$ Square each side.

$$256 = h$$ Simplify.

The second object was dropped from 256 feet. *Check this solution.*

Example 2 *Radical Equation with an Expression*

Solve $\sqrt{x + 1} + 7 = 10$.

$$\sqrt{x + 1} + 7 = 10$$ Original equation

$$\sqrt{x + 1} = 3$$ Subtract 7 from each side.

$$(\sqrt{x + 1})^2 = 3^2$$ Square each side.

$$x + 1 = 9 \quad (\sqrt{x + 1})^2 = x + 1$$

$$x = 8$$ Subtract 1 from each side.

The solution is 8. *Check this result.*

EXTRANEOUS SOLUTIONS   Squaring each side of an equation sometimes produces extraneous solutions. An **extraneous solution** is a solution derived from an equation that is not a solution of the original equation. Therefore, you must check all solutions in the original equation when you solve radical equations.

Example 3 *Variable on Each Side*

Solve $\sqrt{x + 2} = x - 4$.

$$\sqrt{x + 2} = x - 4$$ Original equation

$$(\sqrt{x + 2})^2 = (x - 4)^2$$ Square each side.

$$x + 2 = x^2 - 8x + 16$$ Simplify.

$$0 = x^2 - 9x + 14$$ Subtract x and 2 from each side.

$$0 = (x - 7)(x - 2)$$ Factor.

$$x - 7 = 0 \quad \text{or} \quad x - 2 = 0$$ Zero Product Property

$$x = 7 \qquad\qquad x = 2$$ Solve.

CHECK

$$\sqrt{x + 2} = x - 4 \qquad\qquad \sqrt{x + 2} = x - 4$$

$$\sqrt{7 + 2} \stackrel{?}{=} 7 - 4 \quad x = 7 \qquad \sqrt{2 + 2} \stackrel{?}{=} 2 - 4 \quad x = 2$$

$$\sqrt{9} \stackrel{?}{=} 3 \qquad\qquad\qquad \sqrt{4} \stackrel{?}{=} -2$$

$$3 = 3 \;\checkmark \qquad\qquad\qquad 2 \neq -2 \;\times$$

Since 2 does not satisfy the original equation, 7 is the only solution.

Study Tip

Look Back
To review **Zero Product Property**, see Lesson 9-2.

---

2 Teach

RADICAL EQUATIONS

In-Class Examples   Power Point®

1 **FREE-FALL HEIGHT** An object is dropped from an unknown height and reaches the ground in 5 seconds. From what height is it dropped? **The object is dropped from 400 ft.**

Teaching Tip Remind students that they must isolate the radical part of the expression before squaring each side.

2 Solve $\sqrt{x - 3} + 8 = 15$. **52**

EXTRANEOUS SOLUTIONS

Building on Prior Knowledge

In Chapter 10, students learned that there are two solutions to most quadratic equations. In this lesson, students will learn that when solving radical equations, it is possible to introduce a second solution when squaring both sides of an equation. However, since the original equation was not quadratic, one of the solutions will be extraneous.

In-Class Example   Power Point®

3 Solve $\sqrt{2 - y} = y$. **1**

DAILY INTERVENTION

Differentiated Instruction   ELL

Verbal/Linguistic Have students write a short paragraph in their own words explaining why checking solutions is important when solving radical equations. Students should include an example of a radical equation that has an extraneous solution.

Study Notebook

Have students—
• include examples of how to solve radical equations.
• include any other item(s) that they find helpful in mastering the skills in this lesson.

DAILY
INTERVENTION **FIND THE ERROR**
This problem may require close inspection for students to find the error. Tell students to focus on checking the given solutions. One solution produces an impossible radicand. Also point out that Alex and Victor could have begun by multiplying each side by -1 to eliminate the negative signs.

Answer

1.
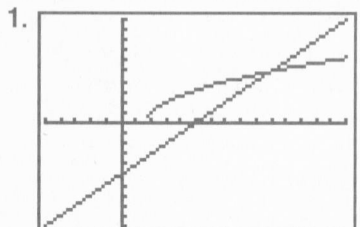

---

2. (10, 5)
3. $x = 10$; the solution is the same as the solution from the graph. However, when solving algebraically, you have to check that $x = 3$ is an extraneous solution.

Graphing Calculator Investigation
Solving Radical Equations

You can use a TI-83 Plus graphing calculator to solve radical equations such as $\sqrt{3x - 5} = x - 5$. Clear the Y= list. Enter the left side of the equation as $Y1 = \sqrt{3x - 5}$. Enter the right side of the equation as $Y2 = x - 5$. Press GRAPH.

Think and Discuss
1. Sketch what is shown on the screen. See margin.
2. Use the intersect feature on the CALC menu, to find the point of intersection.
3. Solve the radical equation algebraically. How does your solution compare to the solution from the graph?

Check for Understanding

Concept Check

1. Isolate the radical on one side of the equation. Square each side of the equation and simplify. Then check for extraneous solutions.

4. Alex; the square of $-\sqrt{x-5}$ is $x - 5$.

1. **Describe** the steps needed to solve a radical equation.

2. **Explain** why it is necessary to check for extraneous solutions in radical equations. The solution may not satisfy the original equation.

3. **OPEN ENDED** Give an example of a radical equation. Then solve the equation for the variable. Sample answer: $\sqrt{x + 1} = 8$; 63

4. **FIND THE ERROR** Alex and Victor are solving $-\sqrt{x - 5} = -2$.

Alex	Victor
$-\sqrt{x - 5} = -2$	$-\sqrt{x - 5} = -2$
$(-\sqrt{x - 5})^2 = (-2)^2$	$(-\sqrt{x - 5})^2 = (-2)^2$
$x - 5 = 4$	$-(x - 5) = 4$
$x = 9$	$-x + 5 = 4$
	$x = 1$

Who is correct? Explain your reasoning.

Guided Practice

Solve each equation. Check your solution.

5. $\sqrt{x} = 5$ 25
6. $\sqrt{2b} = -8$ no solution
7. $\sqrt{7x} = 7$ 7
8. $\sqrt{-3a} = 6$ −12
9. $\sqrt{8s + 1} = 5$ 2
10. $\sqrt{7x + 18} = 9$ 9
11. $\sqrt{5x + 1} + 2 = 6$ 3
12. $\sqrt{6x - 8} = x - 4$ 6
13. $4 + \sqrt{x - 2} = x$ 6

Application

GUIDED PRACTICE KEY	
Exercises	Examples
5–8, 14–16	1
9–11	2
12, 13	3

OCEANS For Exercises 14–16, use the following information.
Tsunamis, or large tidal waves, are generated by undersea earthquakes in the Pacific Ocean. The speed of the tsunami in meters per second is $s = 3.1\sqrt{d}$, where d is the depth of the ocean in meters. **15. about 5994 m**

14. Find the speed of the tsunami if the depth of the water is 10 meters. about 9.8 m/s

15. Find the depth of the water if a tsunami's speed is 240 meters per second.

16. A tsunami may begin as a 2-foot high wave traveling 450–500 miles per hour. It can approach a coastline as a 50-foot wave. How much speed does the wave lose if it travels from a depth of 10,000 meters to a depth of 20 meters?
approximately 296 m/s

Graphing Calculator Investigation

Solving Radical Equations An alternative to graphing each side of the equation separately is to graph the single equation as it is. Move the $x - 5$ to the left side of the equation and then enter the equation as $Y1 = \sqrt{3x - 5} - x + 5$. Then press 2nd [CALC] 2 to calculate the zero point of the graph. The zero point is the solution, which for this equation is 10.

Practice and Apply

Homework Help

For Exercises	See Examples
17–34	1, 2
35–47	3
48–59	1–3

Extra Practice
See page 844.

Solve each equation. Check your solution.

17. $\sqrt{a} = 10$ **100**

18. $\sqrt{-k} = 4$ **−16**

19. $5\sqrt{2} = \sqrt{x}$ **50**

20. $3\sqrt{7} = \sqrt{-y}$ **−63**

21. $3\sqrt{4a} - 2 = 10$ **4**

22. $3 + 5\sqrt{n} = 18$ **9**

23. $\sqrt{x + 3} = -5$ **no solution**

24. $\sqrt{x - 5} = 2\sqrt{6}$ **29**

25. $\sqrt{3x + 12} = 3\sqrt{3}$ **5**

26. $\sqrt{2c - 4} = 8$ **34**

27. $\sqrt{4b + 1} - 3 = 0$ **2**

28. $\sqrt{3r - 5} + 7 = 3$ **no solution**

29. $\sqrt{\dfrac{4x}{5}} - 9 = 3$ **180**

30. $5\sqrt{\dfrac{4t}{3}} - 2 = 0$ $\dfrac{3}{25}$

31. $\sqrt{x^2 + 9x + 14} = x + 4$ **2**

32. $y + 2 = \sqrt{y^2 + 5y + 4}$ **0**

33. The square root of the sum of a number and 7 is 8. Find the number. **57**

34. The square root of the quotient of a number and 6 is 9. Find the number. **486**

Solve each equation. Check your solution.

35. $x = \sqrt{6 - x}$ **2**

36. $x = \sqrt{x + 20}$ **5**

37. $\sqrt{5x - 6} = x$ **2, 3**

38. $\sqrt{28 - 3x} = x$ **4**

39. $\sqrt{x + 1} = x - 1$ **3**

40. $\sqrt{1 - 2b} = 1 + b$ **0**

41. $4 + \sqrt{m - 2} = m$ **6**

42. $\sqrt{3d - 8} = d - 2$ **3, 4**

43. $x + \sqrt{6 - x} = 4$ **2**

44. $\sqrt{6 - 3x} = x + 16$ **−10**

45. $\sqrt{2r^2 - 121} = r$ **11**

46. $\sqrt{5p^2 - 7} = 2p$ $\sqrt{7}$

47. State whether the following equation is *sometimes*, *always*, or *never* true.

$\sqrt{(x - 5)^2} = x - 5$ **sometimes**

Aviation

Piloted by A. Scott Crossfield on November 20, 1953, the Douglas D-558-2 Skyrocket became the first aircraft to fly faster than Mach 2, twice the speed of sound.

Source: National Air and Space Museum

AVIATION For Exercises 48 and 49, use the following information.
The formula $L = \sqrt{kP}$ represents the relationship between a plane's length L in feet and the pounds P its wings can lift, where k is a constant of proportionality calculated for a plane.

48. The length of the Douglas D-558-II, called the Skyrocket, was approximately 42 feet, and its constant of proportionality was $k = 0.1669$. Calculate the maximum takeoff weight of the Skyrocket. **10,569 lb**

49. A Boeing 747 is 232 feet long and has a takeoff weight of 870,000 pounds. Determine the value of k for this plane. **about 0.0619**

GEOMETRY For Exercises 50–53, use the figure below. The area A of a circle is equal to πr^2 where r is the radius of the circle.

50. Write an equation for r in terms of A. $r = \sqrt{\dfrac{A}{\pi}}$

51. The area of the larger circle is 96π square meters. Find the radius. $4\sqrt{6}$ or about 9.8 m

52. The area of the smaller circle is 48π square meters. Find the radius. $4\sqrt{3}$ or about 6.9 m

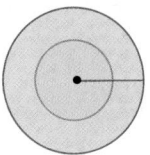

★ **53.** If the area of a circle is doubled, what is the change in the radius? **It increases by a factor of $\sqrt{2}$.**

About the Exercises …

Organization by Objective
• Radical Equations: 17–34
• Extraneous Solutions: 35–47

Odd/Even Assignments
Exercises 17–46 are structured so that students practice the same concepts whether they are assigned odd or even problems.

Assignment Guide
Basic: 17–47 odd, 48, 49, 60–63, 70–89

Average: 17–47 odd, 48–53, 60–63, 70–89 (optional: 64–69)

Advanced: 18–46 even, 50–85 (optional: 86–89)

All: Practice Quiz 1 (1–10)

PHYSICAL SCIENCE For Exercises 54–56, use the following information.

The formula $P = 2\pi\sqrt{\dfrac{\ell}{32}}$ gives the period of a pendulum of length ℓ feet. The period P is the number of seconds it takes for the pendulum to swing back and forth once.

54. Suppose we want a pendulum to complete three periods in 2 seconds. How long should the pendulum be? **about 0.36 ft**

55. Two clocks have pendulums of different lengths. The first clock requires 1 second for its pendulum to complete one period. The second clock requires 2 seconds for its pendulum to complete one period. How much longer is one pendulum than the other? **about 2.43 ft**

★ 56. Repeat Exercise 55 if the pendulum periods are t and $2t$ seconds. **$\dfrac{24t^2}{\pi^2}$**

SOUND For Exercises 57–59, use the following information.
The speed of sound V near Earth's surface can be found using the equation $V = 20\sqrt{t + 273}$, where t is the surface temperature in degrees Celsius.

57. Find the temperature if the speed of sound V is 356 meters per second. **43.84°C**

58. The speed of sound at Earth's surface is often given at 340 meters per second, but that is only accurate at a certain temperature. On what temperature is this figure based? **16°C**

★ 59. What is the speed of sound when the surface temperature is below 0°C? **$V < 330.45$ m/s**

60. **CRITICAL THINKING** Solve $\sqrt{h + 9} - \sqrt{h} = \sqrt{3}$. **3**

61.  Answer the question that was posed at the beginning of the lesson. **See margin.**

   How are radical equations used to find free-fall times?

   Include the following in your answer:
   - the time it would take a skydiver to fall 10,000 feet if he falls 1200 feet every 5 seconds and the time using the equation $t = \dfrac{\sqrt{h}}{4}$, with an explanation of why the two methods find different times, and
   - ways that a skydiver can increase or decrease his speed.

62. Solve the equation $8 + \sqrt{x + 1} = 2$. **A**

   Ⓐ no solution   Ⓑ −35

   Ⓒ −6   Ⓓ 6

   Ⓔ 35

63. The surface area S of a cone can be found by using $S = \pi r\sqrt{r^2 + h^2}$, where r is the radius of the base and h is the height of the cone. Find the height of the cone at the right. **C**

   Ⓐ 2.70 in.   Ⓑ 11.03 in.

   Ⓒ 12.84 in.   Ⓓ 13.30 in.

   Ⓔ 53.65 in.

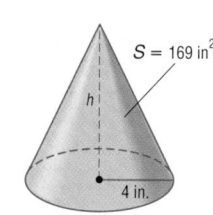

$S = 169$ in^2

4 in.

Standardized Test Practice
Ⓐ Ⓑ Ⓒ Ⓓ

More About. . .

Physical Science ••••

The Foucault pendulum appears to change its path during the day, but it moves in a straight line. The path under the pendulum changes because Earth is rotating beneath it.

Source: California Academy of Sciences

 **Graphing Calculator** RADICAL EQUATIONS   Use a graphing calculator to solve each radical equation. Round to the nearest hundredth.

64. $3 + \sqrt{2x} = 7$ **8**

65. $\sqrt{3x - 8} = 5$ **11**

66. $\sqrt{x + 6} - 4 = x$ **−2**

67. $\sqrt{4x + 5} = x - 7$ **15.08**

68. $x + \sqrt{7 - x} = 4$ **1.70**

69. $\sqrt{3x - 9} = 2x + 6$ **no solution**

Maintain Your Skills

Mixed Review   Simplify each expression.   *(Lesson 11-2)*

70. $5\sqrt{6} + 12\sqrt{6}$ **17√6**

71. $\sqrt{12} + 6\sqrt{27}$ **20√3**

72. $\sqrt{18} + 5\sqrt{2} - 3\sqrt{32}$ **−4√2**

Simplify.   *(Lesson 11-1)*

73. $\sqrt{192}$ **8√3**

74. $\sqrt{6} \cdot \sqrt{10}$ **2√15**

75. $\dfrac{21}{\sqrt{10} + \sqrt{3}}$ **3(√10 − √3)**

Determine whether each trinomial is a perfect square trinomial. If so, factor it.
(Lesson 9-6)

76. $d^2 + 50d + 225$ **no**

77. $4n^2 - 28n + 49$ **yes; $(2n - 7)^2$**

78. $16b^2 - 56bc + 49c^2$ **yes; $(4b - 7c)^2$**

Find each product.   *(Lesson 8-7)*

79. $(r + 3)(r - 4)$ **$r^2 - r - 12$**

80. $(3z + 7)(2z + 10)$ **$6z^2 + 44z + 70$**

81. $(2p + 5)(3p^2 - 4p + 9)$ **$6p^3 + 7p^2 - 2p + 45$**

82. PHYSICAL SCIENCE   A European-made hot tub is advertised to have a temperature of 35°C to 40°C, inclusive. What is the temperature range for the hot tub in degrees Fahrenheit? Use $F = \frac{9}{5}C + 32$.   *(Lesson 6-4)*   **$95° \le F \le 104°$**

Write each equation in standard form.   *(Lesson 5-5)*

83. $y = 2x + \frac{3}{7}$ **$14x - 7y = -3$**

84. $y - 3 = -2(x - 6)$ **$2x + y = 15$**

85. $y + 2 = 7.5(x - 3)$ **$15x - 2y = 49$**

Getting Ready for the Next Lesson   PREREQUISITE SKILL   Evaluate $\sqrt{a^2 + b^2}$ for each value of a and b.
(To review evaluating expressions, see Lesson 1-2.)

86. $a = 3, b = 4$ **5**

87. $a = 24, b = 7$ **25**

88. $a = 1, b = 1$ **√2**

89. $a = 8, b = 12$ **4√13**

Practice Quiz 1

Lessons 11-1 through 11-3

Simplify.   *(Lesson 11-1)*

1. $\sqrt{48}$ **4√3**

2. $\sqrt{3} \cdot \sqrt{6}$ **3√2**

3. $\dfrac{3}{2 + \sqrt{10}}$ **$\dfrac{-2 + \sqrt{10}}{2}$**

Simplify.   *(Lesson 11-2)*

4. $6\sqrt{5} + 3\sqrt{11} + 5\sqrt{5}$ **$11\sqrt{5} + 3\sqrt{11}$**

5. $2\sqrt{3} + 9\sqrt{12}$ **20√3**

6. $(3 - \sqrt{6})^2$ **$15 - 6\sqrt{6}$**

7. GEOMETRY   Find the area of a square whose side measure is $2 + \sqrt{7}$ centimeters.   *(Lesson 11-2)*   **$11 + 4\sqrt{7}$ or 21.6 cm²**

Solve each equation. Check your solution.   *(Lesson 11-3)*

8. $\sqrt{15 - x} = 4$ **−1**

9. $\sqrt{3x^2 - 32} = x$ **4**

10. $\sqrt{2x - 1} = 2x - 7$ **5**

 www.algebra1.com/self_check_quiz

Lesson 11-3   Radical Equations   **603**

---

4 Assess

Open-Ended Assessment

Modeling   Write radical equations on the overhead projector, using a cut-out overlay for the radical. Have students explain what must be done to the equation in order to "remove" the radical. When students explain the correct procedure, remove the overlay and solve the equation.

Getting Ready for Lesson 11-4

PREREQUISITE SKILL   Students will learn about the Pythagorean Theorem in Lesson 11-4. In order to use the Pythagorean Theorem, students must be able to evaluate radical expressions for given values. Use Exercises 86–89 to determine your students' familiarity with evaluating radical expressions.

Assessment Options

Practice Quiz 1   The quiz provides students with a brief review of the concepts and skills in Lessons 11-1 through 11-3. Lesson numbers are given to the right of exercises or instruction lines so students can review concepts not yet mastered.

Answer

61. You can determine the time it takes an object to fall from a given height using a radical equation. Answers should include the following.

- It would take a skydiver approximately 42 seconds to fall 10,000 feet. Using the equation, it would take 25 seconds. The time is different in the two calculations because air resistance slows the skydiver.

- A skydiver can increase the speed of his fall by lowering air resistance. This can be done by pulling his arms and legs close to his body. A skydiver can decrease his speed by holding his arms and legs out, which increases the air resistance.

Lesson 11-3   Radical Equations   **603**

Graphing
Calculator
Investigation

Graphing Calculator
Investigation
A Follow-Up of Lesson 11-3

A Follow-Up of Lesson 11-3

Getting Started

Know Your Calculator The ZoomFit option in the ZOOM menu will let the calculator automatically zoom the viewing window to fit the graph. Suggest that students use this option with the examples in this investigation to get a better view of the shape of the graph of a radical equation.

Teach

- Have students use the CALC Value function to find the value of the function at different *x*-values. Press 2nd [CALC] 1 and then enter an *x* value. Students should quickly see that as the cursor moves along the curve, the value of the function is the square root of the radicand of the function.

Assess

Ask: The graph of $y = \sqrt{x}$ looks somewhat flat, as though it is approaching a specific *y* value. Does it? Explain why or why not. **No; as the value of *x* increases, the value of *y*, which is the square root of *x*, should continue to increase as well. There is no horizontal asymptote.**

Graphs of Radical Equations

In order for a square root to be a real number, the radicand cannot be negative. When graphing a radical equation, determine when the radicand would be negative and exclude those values from the domain.

Example 1

Graph $y = \sqrt{x}$. State the domain of the graph.

Enter the equation in the Y= list.

KEYSTROKES: Y= 2nd [√] X,T,θ,*n*) GRAPH

From the graph, you can see that the domain of *x* is $\{x \mid x \geq 0\}$.

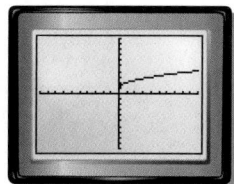

[−10, 10] scl: 1 by [−10, 10] scl: 1

Example 2

Graph $y = \sqrt{x + 4}$. State the domain of the graph.

Enter the equation in the Y= list.

KEYSTROKES: Y= 2nd [√] X,T,θ,*n* + 4) GRAPH

The value of the radicand will be positive when $x + 4 \geq 0$, or when $x \geq -4$. So the domain of *x* is $\{x \mid x \geq -4\}$.

This graph looks like the graph of $y = \sqrt{x}$ shifted left 4 units.

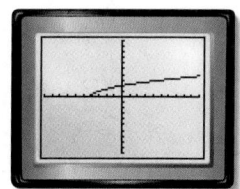

[−10, 10] scl: 1 by [−10, 10] scl: 1

Exercises 1–9. See pp. 639A–639B.

Graph each equation and sketch the graph on your paper. State the domain of the graph. Then describe how the graph differs from the parent function $y = \sqrt{x}$.

1. $y = \sqrt{x} + 1$ **2.** $y = \sqrt{x} - 3$ **3.** $y = \sqrt{x + 2}$

4. $y = \sqrt{x - 5}$ **5.** $y = \sqrt{-x}$ **6.** $y = \sqrt{3x}$

7. $y = -\sqrt{x}$ **8.** $y = \sqrt{1 - x} + 6$ **9.** $y = \sqrt{2x + 5} - 4$

10. Is the graph of $x = y^2$ a function? Explain your reasoning. **10–11. See margin.**

11. Does the equation $x^2 + y^2 = 1$ determine *y* as a function of *x*? Explain.

12. Graph $y = |x| \pm \sqrt{1 - x^2}$ in the window defined by [−2, 2] scl: 1 by [−2, 2] scl: 1. Describe the graph. **heart**

 www.algebra1.com/other_calculator_keystrokes

Answers

10. No; you must consider the graph of $y = \sqrt{x}$ and the graph of $y = -\sqrt{x}$. This graph fails the vertical line test. For every value of $x > 0$, there are two values for *y*.

11. No; the equation $y = \pm\sqrt{1 - x^2}$ is not a function since there are both positive and negative values for *y* for each value of *x*.

The Pythagorean Theorem

What You'll Learn

- Solve problems by using the Pythagorean Theorem.
- Determine whether a triangle is a right triangle.

Vocabulary
- hypotenuse
- legs
- Pythagorean triple
- corollary

How is the Pythagorean Theorem used in roller coaster design?

The roller coaster *Superman: Ride of Steel* in Agawam, Massachusetts, is one of the world's tallest roller coasters at 208 feet. It also boasts one of the world's steepest drops, measured at 78 degrees, and it reaches a maximum speed of 77 miles per hour. You can use the Pythagorean Theorem to estimate the length of the first hill.

THE PYTHAGOREAN THEOREM

In a right triangle, the side opposite the right angle is called the **hypotenuse**. This side is always the longest side of a right triangle. The other two sides are called the **legs** of the triangle.

To find the length of any side of a right triangle when the lengths of the other two are known, you can use a formula developed by the Greek mathematician Pythagoras.

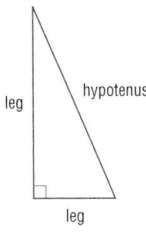

Study Tip

Triangles
Sides of a triangle are represented by lowercase letters a, b, and c.

Key Concept   The Pythagorean Theorem

- **Words**   If a and b are the lengths of the legs of a right triangle and c is the length of the hypotenuse, then the square of the length of the hypotenuse is equal to the sum of the squares of the lengths of the legs.

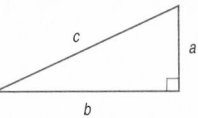

- **Symbols** $c^2 = a^2 + b^2$

Example 1   Find the Length of the Hypotenuse

Find the length of the hypotenuse of a right triangle if $a = 8$ and $b = 15$.

$c^2 = a^2 + b^2$ Pythagorean Theorem

$c^2 = 8^2 + 15^2$ $a = 8$ and $b = 15$

$c^2 = 289$ Simplify.

$c = \pm\sqrt{289}$ Take the square root of each side.

$c = \pm 17$ Disregard -17. Why?

The length of the hypotenuse is 17 units.

---

1 Focus

 5-Minute Check Transparency 11-4 Use as a quiz or review of Lesson 11-3.

Mathematical Background notes are available for this lesson on p. 584D.

How is the Pythagorean Theorem used in roller coaster design?

Ask students:

- What shape is being used to estimate the length of the first hill? **a right triangle**
- What information in the problem is most likely useful in finding the length of the hill? What information is extraneous? **The height of the hill and the angle of the drop are probably useful, and the maximum speed is probably not useful.**

Resource Manager

📁 Workbook and Reproducible Masters

Chapter 11 Resource Masters
- Study Guide and Intervention, pp. 661–662
- Skills Practice, p. 663
- Practice, p. 664
- Reading to Learn Mathematics, p. 665
- Enrichment, p. 666
- Assessment, pp. 699, 701

Graphing Calculator and Spreadsheet Masters, p. 44
Parent and Student Study Guide Workbook, p. 86
School-to-Career Masters, p. 22

Transparencies

5-Minute Check Transparency 11-4
Real-World Transparency 11
Answer Key Transparencies

🔘 Technology

AlgePASS: Tutorial Plus, Lesson 32
Interactive Chalkboard

THE PYTHAGOREAN THEOREM

In-Class Examples Power Point®

1 Find the length of the hypotenuse of a right triangle if $a = 18$ and $b = 24$. **The length of the hypotenuse is 30 units.**

2 Find the length of the missing side.

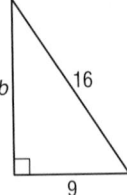

The length of the leg is approximately 13.23 units.

3 What is the area of triangle XYZ? **C**

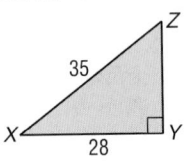

A 94 units²
B 128 units²
C 294 units²
D 588 units²

✓ Concept Check

Pythagorean Theorem Ask students to rewrite the formula for the Pythagorean Theorem in terms of c. $c = \sqrt{a^2 + b^2}$

Example 2 *Find the Length of a Side*

Find the length of the missing side.

In the triangle, $c = 25$ and $b = 10$ units.

$$c^2 = a^2 + b^2 \quad \text{Pythagorean Theorem}$$
$$25^2 = a^2 + 10^2 \quad b = 10 \text{ and } c = 25$$
$$625 = a^2 + 100 \quad \text{Evaluate squares.}$$
$$525 = a^2 \quad \text{Subtract 100 from each side.}$$
$$\pm\sqrt{525} = a \quad \text{Use a calculator to evaluate } \sqrt{525}.$$
$$22.91 \approx a \quad \text{Use the positive value.}$$

To the nearest hundredth, the length of the leg is 22.91 units.

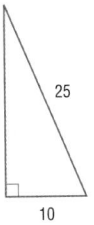

Whole numbers that satisfy the Pythagorean Theorem are called **Pythagorean triples**. Multiples of Pythagorean triples also satisfy the Pythagorean Theorem. Some common triples are (3, 4, 5), (5, 12, 13), (8, 15, 17), and (7, 24, 25).

Standardized Test Practice Ⓐ Ⓑ Ⓒ Ⓓ

Example 3 *Pythagorean Triples*

Multiple-Choice Test Item

What is the area of triangle *ABC*?

Ⓐ 96 units² Ⓑ 120 units²
Ⓒ 160 units² Ⓓ 196 units²

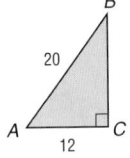

Read the Test Item

The area of a triangle is $A = \frac{1}{2}bh$. In a right triangle, the legs form the base and height of the triangle. Use the measures of the hypotenuse and the base to find the height of the triangle.

Solve the Test Item

Step 1 Check to see if the measurements of this triangle are a multiple of a common Pythagorean triple. The hypotenuse is $4 \cdot 5$ units, and the leg is $4 \cdot 3$ units. This triangle is a multiple of a (3, 4, 5) triangle.

$$4 \cdot 3 = 12$$
$$4 \cdot 4 = 16$$
$$4 \cdot 5 = 20$$

The height of the triangle is 16 units.

Step 2 Find the area of the triangle.

$$A = \frac{1}{2}bh \quad \text{Area of a triangle}$$
$$A = \frac{1}{2} \cdot 12 \cdot 16 \quad b = 12 \text{ and } h = 16$$
$$A = 96 \quad \text{Simplify.}$$

The area of the triangle is 96 square units. Choice A is correct.

Test-Taking Tip
Memorize the common Pythagorean triples and check for multiples such as (6, 8, 10). This will save you time when evaluating square roots.

Standardized Test Practice Ⓐ Ⓑ Ⓒ Ⓓ

Example 3 Caution students that this is a two-step problem. First they must find the missing side length, then they must calculate the area of the triangle. Also stress to students that it is important to read each answer choice carefully before selecting the correct answer. In Example 3, choices B and C look very similar, and one could mistakenly choose D, 196, when the correct answer is A, 96.

RIGHT TRIANGLES A statement that can be easily proved using a theorem is often called a **corollary**. The following corollary, based on the Pythagorean Theorem, can be used to determine whether a triangle is a right triangle.

Key Concept — **Corollary to the Pythagorean Theorem**

If a and b are measures of the shorter sides of a triangle, c is the measure of the longest side, and $c^2 = a^2 + b^2$, then the triangle is a right triangle.

If $c^2 \neq a^2 + b^2$, then the triangle is not a right triangle.

Example 4 Check for Right Triangles

Determine whether the following side measures form right triangles.

a. 20, 21, 29

Since the measure of the longest side is 29, let $c = 29$, $a = 20$, and $b = 21$. Then determine whether $c^2 = a^2 + b^2$.

$c^2 = a^2 + b^2$ Pythagorean Theorem

$29^2 \stackrel{?}{=} 20^2 + 21^2$ $a = 20$, $b = 21$, and $c = 29$

$841 \stackrel{?}{=} 400 + 441$ Multiply.

$841 = 841$ Add.

Since $c^2 = a^2 + b^2$, the triangle is a right triangle.

b. 8, 10, 12

Since the measure of the longest side is 12, let $c = 12$, $a = 8$, and $b = 10$. Then determine whether $c^2 = a^2 + b^2$.

$c^2 = a^2 + b^2$ Pythagorean Theorem

$12^2 \stackrel{?}{=} 8^2 + 10^2$ $a = 8$, $b = 10$, and $c = 12$

$144 \stackrel{?}{=} 64 + 100$ Multiply.

$144 \neq 164$ Add.

Since $c^2 \neq a^2 + b^2$, the triangle is not a right triangle.

Check for Understanding

Concept Check

1. **OPEN ENDED** Draw a right triangle and label each side and angle. Be sure to indicate the right angle. **See margin.**

2. **Explain** how you can determine which angle is the right angle of a right triangle if you are given the lengths of the three sides. **See margin.**

GUIDED PRACTICE KEY	
Exercises	Examples
4–9	1, 2
10, 11	4
12	3

3. **Write** an equation you could use to find the length of the diagonal d of a square with side length s. $d = \sqrt{2s^2}$ or $d = s\sqrt{2}$

Guided Practice   **Find the length of each missing side. If necessary, round to the nearest hundredth.**

4. 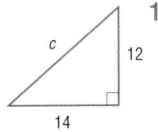   18.44   (c, 12, 14)

5. 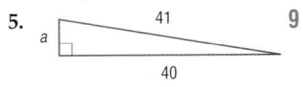   (a, 41, 40, 9)

 www.algebra1.com/extra_examples

---

In-Class Example Power Point®

Teaching Tip Point out to students that with Pythagorean triples, the greatest value is always the measure of the hypotenuse, and the two lesser values are the measures of the two legs.

4 Determine whether the following side measures form right triangles.

a. 7, 12, 15   not a right triangle

b. 27, 36, 45   right triangle

Answers

1.
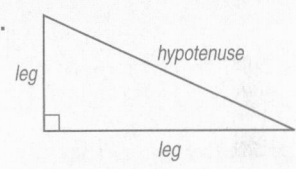

2. Compare the lengths of the sides. The hypotenuse is the longest side, which is always the side opposite the right angle.

DAILY
INTERVENTION   **Differentiated Instruction**

Kinesthetic Give students blocks, algebra tiles, or some other square or cube-shaped manipulatives. Have them use the manipulatives and what they know about the Pythagorean Theorem and Pythagorean triples to construct a right triangle, placing the manipulatives along the outside of the triangle. Have students construct the triangle on a piece of paper, then trace inside the blocks to transfer the triangle to the paper. Then ask them to use a protractor to confirm that the right angle is 90°.

3 Practice/Apply

About the Exercises ...

Organization by Objective
• **The Pythagorean Theorem:** 13–30, 37–40
• **Right Triangles:** 31–36

Odd/Even Assignments
Exercises 13–36 are structured so that students practice the same concepts whether they are assigned odd or even problems.

Alert! Exercise 44 requires the use of the Internet or another reference source.

Assignment Guide

Basic: 13–37 odd, 41–43, 49–68

Average: 13–39 odd, 41–43, 45, 48–68

Advanced: 14–40 even, 44, 46–62 (optional: 63–68)

If c is the measure of the hypotenuse of a right triangle, find each missing measure. If necessary, round to the nearest hundredth.

6. $a = 10, b = 24, c = ?$ **26**

7. $a = 11, c = 61, b = ?$ **60**

8. $b = 13, c = \sqrt{233}, a = ?$ **8**

9. $a = 7, b = 4, c = ?$ $\sqrt{65} \approx 8.06$

Determine whether the following side measures form right triangles. Justify your answer.

10. 4, 6, 9 No; $4^2 + 6^2 \neq 9^2$.

11. 16, 30, 34 Yes; $16^2 + 30^2 = 34^2$.

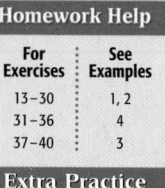
Standardized Test Practice
Ⓐ Ⓑ Ⓒ Ⓓ

12. In right triangle XYZ, the length of $\overline{YZ}$ is 6, and the length of the hypotenuse is 8. Find the area of the triangle. **A**

Ⓐ $6\sqrt{7}$ units²   Ⓑ 30 units²   Ⓒ 40 units²   Ⓓ 48 units²

★ indicates increased difficulty

Practice and Apply

Find the length of each missing side. If necessary, round to the nearest hundredth.

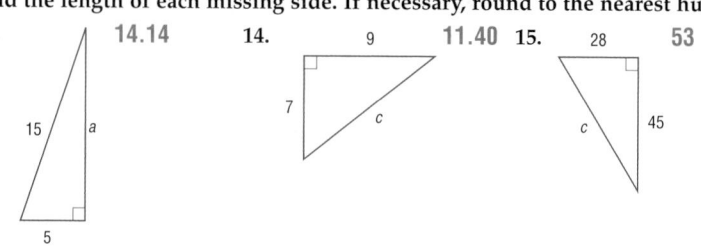

13. 14.14   **14.** 11.40   **15.** 53

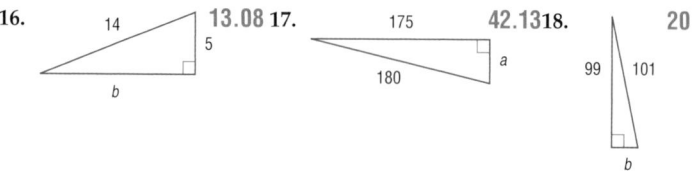

16. 13.08   **17.** 42.13   **18.** 20

If c is the measure of the hypotenuse of a right triangle, find each missing measure. If necessary, round to the nearest hundredth.

19. $a = 16, b = 63, c = ?$ **65**

20. $a = 16, c = 34, b = ?$ **30**

21. $b = 3, a = \sqrt{112}, c = ?$ **11**

22. $a = \sqrt{15}, b = \sqrt{10}, c = ?$ **5**

23. $c = 14, a = 9, b = ?$ $\sqrt{115} \approx 10.72$

24. $a = 6, b = 3, c = ?$ $\sqrt{45} \approx 6.71$

25. $b = \sqrt{77}, c = 12, a = ?$ $\sqrt{67} \approx 8.19$

26. $a = 4, b = \sqrt{11}, c = ?$ $\sqrt{27} \approx 5.20$

27. $\sqrt{253} \approx 15.91$

28. $\sqrt{124} \approx 11.14$

27. $a = \sqrt{225}, b = \sqrt{28}, c = ?$

28. $a = \sqrt{31}, c = \sqrt{155}, b = ?$

29. $a = 8x, b = 15x, c = ?$ **17x**

30. $b = 3x, c = 7x, a = ?$ $\sqrt{40}x \approx 6.32x$

Determine whether the following side measures form right triangles. Justify your answer.

31. 30, 40, 50 Yes; $30^2 + 40^2 = 50^2$.

32. 6, 12, 18 No; $6^2 + 12^2 \neq 18^2$.

33. 24, 30, 36 No; $24^2 + 30^2 \neq 36^2$.

34. 45, 60, 75 Yes; $45^2 + 60^2 = 75^2$.

35. 15, $\sqrt{31}$, 16 Yes; $15^2 + \left(\sqrt{31}\right)^2 = 16^2$.

36. 4, 7, $\sqrt{65}$ Yes; $4^2 + 7^2 = \left(\sqrt{65}\right)^2$.

Use an equation to solve each problem. If necessary, round to the nearest hundredth.

37. Find the length of a diagonal of a square if its area is 162 square feet. **18 ft**

Answer

48. The area of the largest semicircle is $\dfrac{\pi c^2}{4} = \dfrac{\pi}{4}c^2$.

The sum of the other two areas is $\dfrac{\pi}{4}(a^2 + b^2)$. Using the Pythagorean Theorem, $c^2 = a^2 + b^2$, we can show that the sum of the two small areas is equal to the area of the largest semicircle.

★ 38. A right triangle has one leg that is 5 centimeters longer than the other leg. The hypotenuse is 25 centimeters long. Find the length of each leg of the triangle. **15 cm, 20 cm**

★ 39. Find the length of the diagonal of the cube if each side of the cube is 4 inches long. **$4\sqrt{3}$ in. or about 6.93 in.**

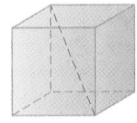

★ 40. The ratio of the length of the hypotenuse to the length of the *shorter* leg in a right triangle is 8:5. The hypotenuse measures 144 meters. Find the length of the *longer* leg. **about 112.41 m**

ROLLER COASTERS For Exercises 41–43, use the following information and the figure.
Suppose a roller coaster climbs 208 feet higher than its starting point making a horizontal advance of 360 feet. When it comes down, it makes a horizontal advance of 44 feet.

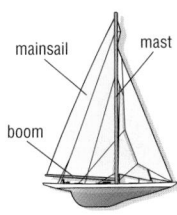

41. How far will it travel to get to the top of the ride? **about 415.8 ft**

42. How far will it travel on the downhill track? **about 212.6 ft**

43. Compare the total horizontal advance, vertical height, and total track length. **The roller coaster makes a total horizontal advance of 404 feet, reaches a vertical height of 208 feet, and travels a total track length of about 628.4 feet.**

44. **RESEARCH** Use the Internet or other reference to find the measurements of your favorite roller coaster or a roller coaster that is at an amusement park close to you. Draw a model of the first drop. Include the height of the hill, length of the vertical drop, and steepness of the hill. **See students' work.**

45. **SAILING** A sailboat's mast and boom form a right angle. The sail itself, called a *mainsail*, is in the shape of a right triangle. If the edge of the mainsail that is attached to the mast is 100 feet long and the edge of the mainsail that is attached to the boom is 60 feet long, what is the length of the longest edge of the mainsail? **about 116.6 ft**

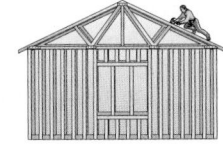
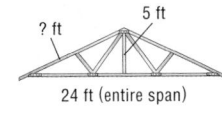

ROOFING For Exercises 46 and 47, refer to the figures below.

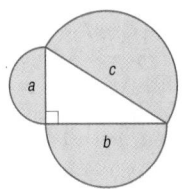

46. Determine the missing length shown in the rafter. **13 ft**

47. If the roof is 30 feet long and it hangs an additional 2 feet over the garage walls, how many square feet of shingles are needed for the entire garage roof? **900 ft²**

★ 48. **CRITICAL THINKING** Compare the area of the largest semicircle to the areas of the two smaller semicircles. Justify your reasoning. **See margin.**

 www.algebra1.com/self_check_quiz

Lesson 11-4 The Pythagorean Theorem **609**

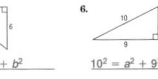

Open-Ended Assessment
Modeling Have students use pencils, uncooked spaghetti, or twigs to model right triangles. Ask students to explain the Pythagorean Theorem and relate it to their triangle.

Getting Ready for Lesson 11-5
PREREQUISITE SKILL Students will learn about the Distance Formula in Lesson 11-5. In order to use the Distance Formula, students must be able to simplify radical expressions. Use Exercises 63–68 to determine your students' familiarity with simplifying radical expressions.

Assessment Options
Quiz (Lessons 11-3 and 11-4) is available on p. 699 of the *Chapter 11 Resource Masters.*

Mid-Chapter Test (Lessons 11-1 through 11-4) is available on p. 701 of the *Chapter 11 Resource Masters.*

Answer

50. Engineers can use the Pythagorean Theorem to find the total length of the track, which determines how much material and land area they need to build the attraction. Answers should include the following.

- A tall hill requires more track length both going uphill and downhill, which will add to the total length of the tracks. Tall, steep hills will increase the speed of the roller coaster. So a coaster with a tall, steep first hill will have more speed and a longer track length.

- The steepness of the hill and speed are limited for safety and to keep the cars on the track.

49. **CRITICAL THINKING** A model of a part of a roller coaster is shown. Determine the total distance traveled from start to finish and the maximum height reached by the roller coaster. **1081.7 ft, 324.5 ft**

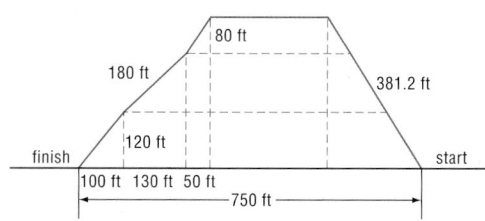

50. **WRITING IN MATH** Answer the question that was posed at the beginning of the lesson. **See margin.**

How is the Pythagorean Theorem used in roller coaster design?

Include the following in your answer:

- an explanation of how the height, speed, and steepness of a roller coaster are related, and
- a description of any limitations you can think of in the design of a new roller coaster.

Standardized Test Practice

51. Find the area of $\triangle XYZ$. **C**

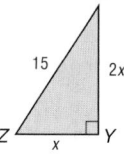

   Ⓐ $6\sqrt{5}$ units²   Ⓑ $18\sqrt{5}$ units²

   Ⓒ 45 units²   Ⓓ 90 units²

52. Find the perimeter of a square whose diagonal measures 10 centimeters. **B**

   Ⓐ $10\sqrt{2}$ cm   Ⓑ $20\sqrt{2}$ cm

   Ⓒ $25\sqrt{2}$ cm   Ⓓ 80 cm

Maintain Your Skills

Mixed Review

Solve each equation. Check your solution. *(Lesson 11-3)*

53. $\sqrt{y} = 12$ **144**   54. $3\sqrt{s} = 126$ **1764**   55. $4\sqrt{2v+1} - 3 = 17$ **12**

Simplify each expression. *(Lesson 11-2)*

56. $\sqrt{72}$ **$6\sqrt{2}$**   57. $7\sqrt{z} - 10\sqrt{z}$ **$-3\sqrt{z}$**   58. $\sqrt{\frac{3}{7}} + \sqrt{21}$ **$\frac{8\sqrt{21}}{7}$**

Simplify. Assume that no denominator is equal to zero. *(Lesson 8-2)*

59. $\frac{5^8}{5^3}$ **5^5 or 3125**   60. d^{-7} **$\frac{1}{d^7}$**   61. $\frac{-26a^4b^7c^{-5}}{-13a^2b^4c^3}$ **$\frac{2a^2b^3}{c^8}$**

62. **AVIATION** Flying with the wind, a plane travels 300 miles in 40 minutes. Flying against the wind, it travels 300 miles in 45 minutes. Find the air speed of the plane. *(Lesson 7-4)* **425 mph**

Getting Ready for the Next Lesson

PREREQUISITE SKILL **Simplify each expression.**
*(To review **simplifying radical expressions**, see Lesson 11-1.)*

63. $\sqrt{(6-3)^2 + (8-4)^2}$ **5**   64. $\sqrt{(10-4)^2 + (13-5)^2}$ **10**

65. $\sqrt{(5-3)^2 + (2-9)^2}$ **$\sqrt{53}$**   66. $\sqrt{(-9-5)^2 + (7-3)^2}$ **$2\sqrt{53}$**

67. $\sqrt{(-4-5)^2 + (-4-3)^2}$ **$\sqrt{130}$**   68. $\sqrt{(20-5)^2 + (-2-6)^2}$ **17**

What You'll Learn

- Find the distance between two points on the coordinate plane.
- Find a point that is a given distance from a second point in a plane.

How can the distance between two points be determined?

Consider two points A and B in the coordinate plane. Notice that a right triangle can be formed by drawing lines parallel to the axes through the points at A and B. These lines intersect at C forming a right angle. The hypotenuse of this triangle is the distance between A and B. You can determine the length of the legs of this triangle and use the Pythagorean Theorem to find the distance between the two points. Notice that AC is the difference of the y-coordinates, and BC is the difference of the x-coordinates.

So, $(AB)^2 = (AC)^2 + (BC)^2$, and $AB = \sqrt{(AC)^2 + (BC)^2}$.

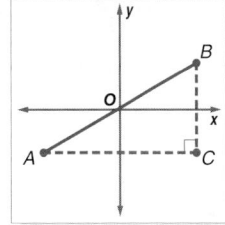

Study Tip

Reading Math
AC is the measure of $\overline{AC}$ and BC is the measure of $\overline{BC}$.

THE DISTANCE FORMULA You can find the distance between any two points in the coordinate plane using a similar process. The result is called the **Distance Formula**.

Key Concept — The Distance Formula

- **Words** The distance d between any two points with coordinates (x_1, y_1) and (x_2, y_2) is given by $d = \sqrt{(x_2 - x_1)^2 + (y_2 - y_1)^2}$.

- **Model**

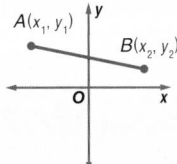

Example 1 Distance Between Two Points

Find the distance between the points at $(2, 3)$ and $(-4, 6)$.

$d = \sqrt{(x_2 - x_1)^2 + (y_2 - y_1)^2}$ Distance Formula

$\quad = \sqrt{(-4 - 2)^2 + (6 - 3)^2}$ $(x_1, y_1) = (2, 3)$ and $(x_2, y_2) = (-4, 6)$

$\quad = \sqrt{(-6)^2 + 3^2}$ Simplify.

$\quad = \sqrt{45}$ Evaluate squares and simplify.

$\quad = 3\sqrt{5}$ or about 6.71 units

1 Focus

 5-Minute Check Transparency 11-5 Use as a quiz or review of Lesson 11-4.

Mathematical Background notes are available for this lesson on p. 584D.

How can the distance between two points be determined?

Ask students:

- What must you know in order to use the Pythagorean Theorem to determine the distance between the two points? **You must know the lengths of the two legs in order to find the distance between the two points, which is the hypotenuse.**

- How do you find the length of the vertical leg? **Find the difference in the y-coordinates of A and B.**

- How do you find the length of the horizontal leg? **Find the difference in the x-coordinates of A and B.**

Resource Manager

Workbook and Reproducible Masters

Chapter 11 Resource Masters
- Study Guide and Intervention, pp. 667–668
- Skills Practice, p. 669
- Practice, p. 670
- Reading to Learn Mathematics, p. 671
- Enrichment, p. 672

Parent and Student Study Guide Workbook, p. 87
Science and Mathematics Lab Manual, pp. 85–90

 Transparencies
5-Minute Check Transparency 11-5
Answer Key Transparencies

 Technology
Interactive Chalkboard

THE DISTANCE FORMULA

Teaching Tip Point out to students that it does not matter which of the two points are designated (x_1, y_1) or (x_2, y_2).

1 Find the distance between the points at $(1, 2)$ and $(-3, 0)$. **The distance is $2\sqrt{5}$, or about 4.47 units.**

2 BIATHLON Julianne is sighting in her rifle for an upcoming biathlon competition. Her first shot is 2 inches to the right and 7 inches below the bull's-eye. What is the distance between the bull's-eye and where her first shot hit the target? **The distance is $\sqrt{53}$ or about 7.28 inches.**

FIND COORDINATES

3 Find the value of a if the distance between the points at $(2, -1)$ and $(a, -4)$ is 5 units. **−2 or 6**

Answers

1. The values that are subtracted are squared before being added and the square of a negative number is always positive. The sum of two positive numbers is positive, so the distance will never be negative.

2. See students' graph; the distance from A to B equals the distance from B to A. Using the Distance Formula, the solution is the same no matter which ordered pair is used first.

3. See students' diagrams; there are exactly two points that lie on the line $y = -3$ that are 10 units from the point $(7, 5)$.

More About. . .

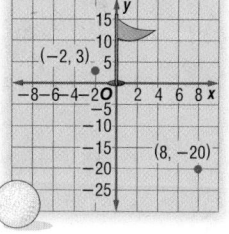

Golf ·············

There are four major tournaments that make up the "grand slam" of golf: Masters, U.S. Open, British Open, and PGA Championship. In 2000, Tiger Woods became the youngest player to win the four major events (called a career grand slam) at age 24.
Source: PGA

Example 2 *Use the Distance Formula*

• GOLF Tracy hits a golf ball that lands 20 feet short and 8 feet to the right of the cup. On her first putt, the ball lands 2 feet to the left and 3 feet beyond the cup. Assuming that the ball traveled in a straight line, how far did the ball travel on her first putt?

Draw a model of the situation on a coordinate grid. If the cup is at $(0, 0)$, then the location of the ball after the first hit is $(8, -20)$. The location of the ball after the first putt is $(-2, 3)$. Use the Distance Formula.

$$d = \sqrt{(x_2 - x_1)^2 + (y_2 - y_1)^2} \quad \text{Distance Formula}$$

$$= \sqrt{(-2 - 8)^2 + [3 - (-20)]^2} \quad \begin{array}{l}(x_1, y_1) = (8, -20), \\ (x_2, y_2) = (-2, 3)\end{array}$$

$$= \sqrt{(-10)^2 + 23^2} \quad \text{Simplify.}$$

$$= \sqrt{629} \text{ or about 25 feet}$$

FIND COORDINATES Suppose you know the coordinates of a point, one coordinate of another point, and the distance between the two points. You can use the Distance Formula to find the missing coordinate.

Example 3 *Find a Missing Coordinate*

Find the value of a if the distance between the points at $(7, 5)$ and $(a, -3)$ is 10 units.

$$d = \sqrt{(x_2 - x_1)^2 + (y_2 - y_1)^2} \quad \text{Distance Formula}$$

$$10 = \sqrt{(a - 7)^2 + (-3 - 5)^2} \quad \begin{array}{l}\text{Let } x_2 = a, x_1 = 7, y_2 = -3, y_1 = 5, \end{array}$$

$$10 = \sqrt{(a - 7)^2 + (-8)^2} \quad \text{and } d = 10.$$

$$10 = \sqrt{a^2 - 14a + 49 + 64} \quad \text{Evaluate squares.}$$

$$10 = \sqrt{a^2 - 14a + 113} \quad \text{Simplify.}$$

$$10^2 = \left(\sqrt{a^2 - 14a + 113}\right)^2 \quad \text{Square each side.}$$

$$100 = a^2 - 14a + 113 \quad \text{Simplify.}$$

$$0 = a^2 - 14a + 13 \quad \text{Subtract 100 from each side.}$$

$$0 = (a - 1)(a - 13) \quad \text{Factor.}$$

$$a - 1 = 0 \quad \text{or} \quad a - 13 = 0 \quad \text{Zero Product Property}$$

$$a = 1 \qquad\qquad a = 13 \quad \text{The value of } a \text{ is 1 or 13.}$$

Check for Understanding

Concept Check

1–3. See margin.

1. **Explain** why the value calculated under the radical sign in the Distance Formula will never be negative.

2. **OPEN ENDED** Plot two ordered pairs and find the distance between their graphs. Does it matter which ordered pair is first when using the Distance Formula? Explain.

3. **Explain** why there are two values for a in Example 3. Draw a diagram to support your answer.

612 Chapter 11 Radical Expressions and Triangles

DAILY INTERVENTION

Unlocking Misconceptions

Not only does it not matter which point is designated (x_1, y_1) and (x_2, y_2) when using the Distance Formula, it also does not matter in which order the x- and y-coordinates are subtracted. For example,

$\sqrt{(x_2 - x_1)^2 + (y_2 - y_1)^2}$ will produce the same results as

$\sqrt{(x_1 - x_2)^2 + (y_1 - y_2)^2}$ or $\sqrt{(x_1 - x_2)^2 + (y_2 - y_1)^2}$. Have students test each method with two points.

Guided Practice

Find the distance between each pair of points whose coordinates are given. Express in simplest radical form and as decimal approximations rounded to the nearest hundredth if necessary.

4. $(5, -1), (11, 7)$ **10**

5. $(3, 7), (-2, -5)$ **13**

6. $(2, 2), (5, -1)$ $3\sqrt{2} \approx 4.24$

7. $(-3, -5), (-6, -4)$ $\sqrt{10} \approx 3.16$

Find the possible values of a if the points with the given coordinates are the indicated distance apart.

8. $(3, -1), (a, 7); d = 10$ **9 or -3**

9. $(10, a), (1, -6); d = \sqrt{145}$ **2 or -14**

Applications

10. GEOMETRY An isosceles triangle has two sides of equal length. Determine whether triangle ABC with vertices $A(-3, 4)$, $B(5, 2)$, and $C(-1, -5)$ is an isosceles triangle. **yes; $AB = \sqrt{68}$, $BC = \sqrt{85}$, $AC = \sqrt{85}$**

FOOTBALL For Exercises 11 and 12, use the information at the right.

11. 25.5 yd, 25 yd

11. A quarterback can throw the football to one of the two receivers. Find the distance from the quarterback to each receiver.

12. What is the distance between the two receivers? **about 20.6 yd**

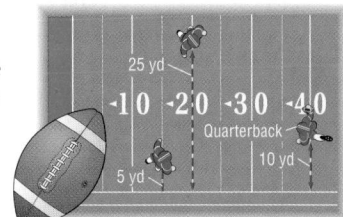

★ indicates increased difficulty

Practice and Apply

Find the distance between each pair of points whose coordinates are given. Express in simplest radical form and as decimal approximations rounded to the nearest hundredth if necessary.

13. $(12, 3), (-8, 3)$ **20**

14. $(0, 0), (5, 12)$ **13**

15. $(6, 8), (3, 4)$ **5**

16. $(-4, 2), (4, 17)$ **17**

17. $(-3, 8), (5, 4)$ $4\sqrt{5} \approx 8.94$

18. $(9, -2), (3, -6)$ $2\sqrt{13} \approx 7.21$

19. $(-8, -4), (-3, -8)$ $\sqrt{41} \approx 6.40$

20. $(2, 7), (10, -4)$ $\sqrt{185} \approx 13.60$

21. $(4, 2), \left(6, -\frac{2}{3}\right)$ $\frac{10}{3} \approx 3.33$

22. $\left(5, \frac{1}{4}\right), (3, 4)$ $\frac{17}{4}$ or 4.25

23. $\left(\frac{4}{5}, -1\right), \left(2, -\frac{1}{2}\right)$ $\frac{13}{10}$ or 1.30

24. $\left(3, \frac{3}{7}\right), \left(4, -\frac{2}{7}\right)$ $\frac{\sqrt{74}}{7} \approx 1.23$

25. $\left(4\sqrt{5}, 7\right), \left(6\sqrt{5}, 1\right)$ $2\sqrt{14} \approx 7.48$

26. $\left(5\sqrt{2}, 8\right), \left(7\sqrt{2}, 10\right)$ $2\sqrt{3} \approx 3.46$

Find the possible values of a if the points with the given coordinates are the indicated distance apart.

27. $(4, 7), (a, 3); d = 5$ **1 or 7**

28. $(-4, a), (4, 2); d = 17$ **17 or -13**

29. $(5, a), (6, 1); d = \sqrt{10}$ **-2 or 4**

30. $(a, 5), (-7, 3); d = \sqrt{29}$ **-2 or -12**

31. $(6, -3), (-3, a); d = \sqrt{130}$ **-10 or 4**

32. $(20, 5), (a, 9); d = \sqrt{340}$ **2 or 38**

★ **33.** Triangle ABC has vertices at $A(7, -4)$, $B(-1, 2)$, and $C(5, -6)$. Determine whether the triangle has three, two, or no sides that are equal in length. **two; $AB = BC = 10$**

34. $\sqrt{157} \neq \sqrt{101}$; The trapezoid is not isosceles.

★ **34.** If the diagonals of a trapezoid have the same length, then the trapezoid is isosceles. Find the lengths of the diagonals of trapezoid $ABCD$ with vertices $A(-2, 2)$, $B(10, 6)$, $C(9, 8)$, and $D(0, 5)$ to determine if it is isosceles.

 www.algebra1.com/extra_examples

Lesson 11-5 The Distance Formula **613**

The Distance Formula The Pythagorean Theorem can be used to derive the **Distance Formula** shown below. The Distance Formula can then be used to find the distance between any two points in the coordinate plane.

Distance Formula	The distance between any two points with coordinates (x_1, y_1) and (x_2, y_2) is given by $d = \sqrt{(x_2 - x_1)^2 + (y_2 - y_1)^2}$.

Example 1 Find the distance between the points at $(-5, 2)$ and $(4, 5)$.

$d = \sqrt{(x_2 - x_1)^2 + (y_2 - y_1)^2}$ Distance Formula
$= \sqrt{(4 - (-5))^2 + (5 - 2)^2}$ $(x_1, y_1) = (-5, 2), (x_2, y_2) = (4, 5)$
$= \sqrt{9^2 + 3^2}$ Simplify.
$= \sqrt{81 + 9}$ Evaluate squares and simplify.
$= \sqrt{90}$
The distance is $\sqrt{90}$, or about 9.49 units.

Example 2 Jill draws a line segment from point $(1, 4)$ on her computer screen to point $(98, 49)$. How long is the segment?

$d = \sqrt{(x_2 - x_1)^2 + (y_2 - y_1)^2}$
$= \sqrt{(98 - 1)^2 + (49 - 4)^2}$
$= \sqrt{97^2 + 45^2}$
$= \sqrt{9409 + 2025}$
$= \sqrt{11,434}$
The segment is about 106.93 units long.

Exercises

Find the distance between each pair of points whose coordinates are given. Express answers in simplest radical form and as decimal approximations rounded to the nearest hundredth if necessary.

1. $(1, 5), (3, 1)$
   $2\sqrt{5}$; 4.47
2. $(0, 0), (6, 8)$
   10
3. $(-2, -8), (7, -3)$
   $\sqrt{106}$; 10.30

4. $(6, -7), (-2, 8)$
   17
5. $(1, 5), (-8, 4)$
   $\sqrt{82}$; 9.06
6. $(3, -4), (-4, -4)$
   7

7. $(-1, 4), (3, 2)$
   $2\sqrt{5}$; 4.47
8. $(0, 0), (-3, 5)$
   $\sqrt{34}$; 5.83
9. $(2, -6), (-7, 1)$
   $\sqrt{130}$; 11.40

10. $(-2, -5), (0, 8)$
    $\sqrt{173}$; 13.15
11. $(3, 4), (0, 0)$
    5
12. $(3, -4), (-4, -16)$
    $\sqrt{193}$; 13.89

13. $(1, -1), (3, -2)$
    $\sqrt{5}$; 2.24
14. $(-2, 0), (-3, -9)$
    $\sqrt{82}$; 9.06
15. $(-9, 0), (-2, 5)$
    $\sqrt{74}$; 8.60

16. $(2, -7), (-2, -2)$
    $\sqrt{41}$; 6.40
17. $(1, -3), (-8, 21)$
    $\sqrt{657}$; 25.63
18. $(-3, -5), (1, -8)$
    5

Find the distance between each pair of points whose coordinates are given. Express answers in simplest radical form and as decimal approximations rounded to the nearest hundredth if necessary.

1. $(4, 7), (1, 3)$ 5
2. $(0, 9), (-7, -2)$ $\sqrt{170} \approx 13.04$
3. $(4, -6), (3, -9)$ $\sqrt{10} \approx 3.16$
4. $(-3, -8), (-7, 2)$ $2\sqrt{29} \approx 10.77$
5. $(0, -4), (3, 2)$ $3\sqrt{5} \approx 6.71$
6. $(-13, -9), (-1, -5)$ $4\sqrt{10} \approx 12.65$
7. $(6, 2), \left(4, \frac{1}{2}\right)$ $\frac{5}{2}$ or 2.50
8. $(-1, 7), \left(\frac{1}{3}, 6\right)$ $\frac{5}{3} \approx 1.67$
9. $\left(2, -\frac{1}{3}\right), \left(1, \frac{1}{3}\right)$ $\sqrt{2} \approx 1.41$
10. $\left(\frac{2}{3}, -1\right), \left(2, \frac{1}{3}\right)$ $\frac{4\sqrt{2}}{3} \approx 1.89$
11. $(\sqrt{3}, 3), (2\sqrt{3}, 5)$ $\sqrt{7} \approx 2.65$
12. $(2\sqrt{2}, -1), (3\sqrt{2}, 2)$ $3\sqrt{2} \approx 4.24$

Find the possible values of a if the points with the given coordinates are the indicated distance apart.

13. $(4, -1), (a, 5); d = 10$ $a = -4$ or 12
14. $(2, -5), (a, 7); d = 15$ $a = -7$ or 11
15. $(6, -7), (a, -4); d = \sqrt{18}$ $a = 3$ or 9
16. $(-4, 1), (a, 8); d = \sqrt{50}$ $a = -5$ or -3
17. $(8, -5), (a, 4); d = \sqrt{85}$ $a = 6$ or 10
18. $(-9, 7), (a, 5); d = \sqrt{29}$ $a = -14$ or -4

BASEBALL For Exercises 19–21, use the following information.
Three players are warming up for a baseball game. Player B stands 9 feet to the right and 18 feet in front of Player A. Player C stands 8 feet to the left and 13 feet in front of Player A.

19. Draw a model of the situation on the coordinate grid. Assume that Player A is located at $(0, 0)$.

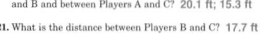

20. To the nearest tenth, what is the distance between Players A and B and between Players A and C? 20.1 ft; 15.3 ft

21. What is the distance between Players B and C? 17.7 ft

22. **MAPS** Maria and Jackson live in adjacent neighborhoods. If they superimpose a coordinate grid on the map of their neighborhoods, Maria lives at $(-9, 1)$ and Jackson lives at $(5, -4)$. If each unit on the grid is equal to approximately 0.132 mile, how far apart do Maria and Jackson live? about 1.96 mi

Pre-Activity How can the distance between two points be determined?
Read the introduction to Lesson 11-5 at the top of page 611 in your textbook.
What are the coordinates of points A, B, and C?
$A = (4, 3), B = (-3, -2),$ and $C = (4, -2)$

Reading the Lesson

1. Suppose you want to use the Distance Formula to find the distance between $(6, 4)$ and $(2, 1)$. Use $(x_1, y_1) = (6, 4)$ and $(x_2, y_2) = (2, 1)$. Complete the equations by writing the correct numbers in the blanks.

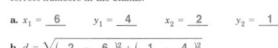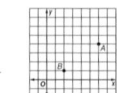

a. $x_1 = \underline{6}$ $y_1 = \underline{4}$ $x_2 = \underline{2}$ $y_2 = \underline{1}$
b. $d = \sqrt{(\underline{2} - \underline{6})^2 + (\underline{1} - \underline{4})^2}$

2. Suppose you want to use the Distance Formula to find the distance between $(3, 7)$ and $(9, -2)$. Use $(x_1, y_1) = (3, 7)$ and $(x_2, y_2) = (9, -2)$. Complete the equations by writing the correct numbers in the blanks.

a. $x_1 = \underline{3}$ $y_1 = \underline{7}$ $x_2 = \underline{9}$ $y_2 = \underline{-2}$
b. $d = \sqrt{(\underline{9} - \underline{3})^2 + (\underline{-2} - \underline{7})^2}$

3. A classmate is using the Distance Formula to find the distance between two points. She has done everything correctly so far, and her equation is $d = \sqrt{(-2 - 5)^2 + (7 - 11)^2}$. This equation will give her the distance between what two points?
$(5, 11)$ and $(-2, 7)$

Helping You Remember

4. Sometimes it is easier to remember a formula if you can state it in words. How can you state the Distance Formula in easy-to-remember words?
Sample answer: Square the difference between the x-coordinates, then add that to the square of the difference between the y-coordinates. Take the square root of the sum to find the distance between the two points.

★ 35. Triangle LMN has vertices at $L(-4, -3)$, $M(2, 5)$, and $N(-13, 10)$. If the distance from point $P(x, -2)$ to L equals the distance from P to M, what is the value of x? 3

★ 36. Plot the points $Q(1, 7)$, $R(3, 1)$, $S(9, 3)$, and $T(7, d)$. Find the value of d that makes each side of $QRST$ have the same length. 9

37. **FREQUENT FLYERS** To determine the mileage between cities for their frequent flyer programs, some airlines superimpose a coordinate grid over the United States. An ordered pair on the grid represents the location of each airport. The units of this grid are approximately equal to 0.316 mile. So, a distance of 3 units on the grid equals an actual distance of 3(0.316) or 0.948 mile. Suppose the locations of two airports are at $(132, 428)$ and $(254, 105)$. Find the actual distance between these airports to the nearest mile. 109 mi

COLLEGE For Exercises 38 and 39, use the map of a college campus.

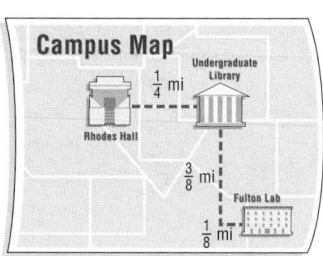

38. Kelly has her first class in Rhodes Hall and her second class in Fulton Lab. How far does she have to walk between her first and second class? about 0.53 mi

39. She has 12 minutes between the end of her first class and the start of her second class. If she walks an average of 3 miles per hour, will she make it to her second class on time? Yes; it will take her about 10.6 minutes to walk between the two buildings.

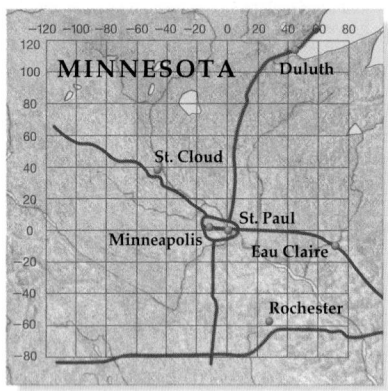

GEOGRAPHY For Exercises 40–42, use the map at the left that shows part of Minnesota and Wisconsin.
A coordinate grid has been superimposed on the map with the origin at St. Paul. The grid lines are 20 miles apart. Minneapolis is at $(-7, 3)$.

40. Estimate the coordinates for Duluth, St. Cloud, Eau Claire, and Rochester. Duluth, (44, 116); St. Cloud, (−46, 39); Eau Claire, (71, −8); Rochester, (27, −58)

41. Find the distance between the following pairs of cities: Minneapolis and St. Cloud, St. Paul and Rochester, Minneapolis and Eau Claire, and Duluth and St. Cloud.

42. A radio station in St. Paul has a broadcast range of 75 miles. Which cities shown on the map can receive the broadcast? all cities except Duluth

41. Minneapolis-St. Cloud, 53 mi; St. Paul-Rochester, 64 mi; Minneapolis-Eau Claire, 79 mi; Duluth-St. Cloud, 118 mi

43. **CRITICAL THINKING** Plot $A(-4, 4)$, $B(-7, -3)$, and $C(4, 0)$, and connect them to form triangle ABC. Demonstrate two different ways to show whether ABC is a right triangle. See margin.

44. **WRITING IN MATH** Answer the question that was posed at the beginning of the lesson. See margin.
How can the distance between two points be determined?
Include the following in your answer:
- an explanation how the Distance Formula is derived from the Pythagorean Theorem, and
- an explanation why the Distance Formula is not needed to find the distance between points $P(-24, 18)$ and $Q(-24, 10)$.

614   Chapter 11   Radical Expressions and Triangles

A Space-Saving Method

Two arrangements for cookies on a 32 cm by 40 cm cookie sheet are shown at the right. The cookies have 8-cm diameters after they are baked. The centers of the cookies are on the vertices of squares in the top arrangement. In the other, the centers are on the vertices of equilateral triangles. Which arrangement is more economical? The triangle arrangement is more economical, because it contains one more cookie.

In the square arrangement, rows are placed every 8 cm. At what intervals are rows placed in the triangle arrangement?

Look at the right triangle labeled a, b, and c. A leg of the triangle is the radius of a cookie, or 4 cm. The hypotenuse c is the sum of two radii, or 8 cm. Use the Pythagorean theorem to find b, the interval of the rows.

$c^2 = a^2 + b^2$
$8^2 = 4^2 + b^2$

45. Find the distance between points at (6, 11) and (−2, −4). **B**
  Ⓐ 16 units
  Ⓑ 17 units
  Ⓒ 18 units
  Ⓓ 19 units

46. Find the perimeter of a square $ABCD$ if two of the vertices are $A(3, 7)$ and $B(−3, 4)$. **B**
  Ⓐ 12 units
  Ⓑ $12\sqrt{5}$ units
  Ⓒ $9\sqrt{5}$ units
  Ⓓ 45 units

Maintain Your Skills

Mixed Review

If c is the measure of the hypotenuse of a right triangle, find each missing measure. If necessary, round to the nearest hundredth. *(Lesson 11-4)*

47. $a = 7, b = 24, c = ?$ **25**
48. $b = 30, c = 34, a = ?$ **16**
49. $a = \sqrt{7}, c = \sqrt{16}, b = ?$ **3**
50. $a = \sqrt{13}, b = \sqrt{50}, c = ?$
  $3\sqrt{7} \approx 7.94$

Solve each equation. Check your solution. *(Lesson 11-3)*

51. $\sqrt{p-2} + 8 = p$ **11**
52. $\sqrt{r+5} = r - 1$ **4**
53. $\sqrt{5t^2 + 29} = 2t + 3$
  {2, 10}

COST OF DEVELOPMENT For Exercises 54–56, use the graph that shows the amount of money being spent on worldwide construction.
(Lesson 8-3)

54. Write the value shown for each continent or region listed in standard notation.

55. Write the value shown for each continent or region in scientific notation.

56. How much more money is being spent in Asia than in Latin America? **$8.72 × 10^{11}$ or $872 billion**

USA TODAY Snapshots®

Global spending on construction
The worldwide construction industry, valued at $3.41 trillion in 2000, grew 5.8% since 1998. Breakdown by region:

$1.113 trillion — Asia
$1.016 trillion — Europe
$884 billion — U.S./Canada
$241 billion — Latin America
$101.2 billion — Middle East
$56.1 billion — Africa

Source: Engineering News Record
By Shannon Reilly and Frank Pompa, USA TODAY

54. Asia, 1,113,000,000,000; Europe, 1,016,000,000,000; U.S./Canada, 884,000,000,000; Latin America, 241,000,000,000; Middle East, 101,200,000,000; Africa, 56,100,000,000.

55. Asia, $1.113 × 10^{12}$; Europe, $1.016 × 10^{12}$; U.S./Canada, $8.84 × 10^{11}$; Latin America, $2.41 × 10^{11}$; Middle East, $1.012 × 10^{11}$; Africa, $5.61 × 10^{10}$.

Solve each inequality. Then check your solution and graph it on a number line. *(Lesson 6-1)* **57–62. See pp. 639A–639B for graphs.**

57. $8 \le m - 1$ $\{m \mid m \ge 9\}$
58. $3 > 10 + k$ $\{k \mid k < -7\}$
59. $3x \le 2x - 3$ $\{x \mid x \le -3\}$
60. $v - (-4) > 6$ $\{v \mid v > 2\}$
61. $r - 5.2 \ge 3.9$ $\{r \mid r \ge 9.1\}$
62. $s + \frac{1}{6} \le \frac{2}{3}$ $\{s \mid s \le \frac{1}{2}\}$

Getting Ready for the Next Lesson

PREREQUISITE SKILL Solve each proportion. *(To review **proportions**, see Lesson 3-6.)*

63. $\frac{x}{4} = \frac{3}{2}$ **6**
64. $\frac{20}{x} = \frac{-5}{2}$ **−8**
65. $\frac{6}{9} = \frac{8}{x}$ **12**
66. $\frac{10}{12} = \frac{x}{18}$ **15**
67. $\frac{x+2}{7} = \frac{3}{7}$ **1**
68. $\frac{2}{3} = \frac{6}{x+4}$ **5**

---

4 Assess

Open-Ended Assessment

Speaking Have students describe a real-world situation in which the Distance Formula could be used to find the distance between two points. If students have trouble thinking of situations, suggest that they think of anything that involves measurement such as construction, art, sports, and so on. Have them explain how the Distance Formula is used in the situation.

Getting Ready for Lesson 11-6

PREREQUISITE SKILL Students will learn about similar triangles in Lesson 11-6. In order to determine whether triangles are similar, they must be able to solve proportions. Use Exercises 63–68 to determine your students' familiarity with solving proportions.

Answer

43. Compare the slopes of the two potential legs to determine whether the slopes are negative reciprocals of each other. You can also compute the lengths of the three sides and determine whether the square of the longest side length is equal to the sum of the squares of the other two side lengths. Neither test holds true in this case because the triangle is not a right triangle.

11-6 Similar Triangles

1 Focus

5-Minute Check Transparency 11-6 Use as a quiz or review of Lesson 11-5.

Mathematical Background notes are available for this lesson on p. 584D.

Building on Prior Knowledge

In Lesson 3-6, students learned how to solve proportions. In this lesson, students will use their knowledge of proportions to determine whether two triangles are similar.

How are similar triangles related to photography?

Ask students:

• If you photograph two people from the same distance, one of whom is twice the height of the other, what are the heights of their images in the photograph? **One image will be twice the height of the other.**

• How would you describe this relationship using ratios? **The ratio of the heights of the people is the same as the ratio of the heights of the images.**

• What do you call an equation that states two ratios are equal? **a proportion**

Vocabulary
• similar triangles

What You'll Learn

• Determine whether two triangles are similar.

• Find the unknown measures of sides of two similar triangles.

How are similar triangles related to photography?

When you take a picture, the image of the object being photographed is projected by the camera lens onto the film. The height of the image on the film can be related to the height of the object using similar triangles.

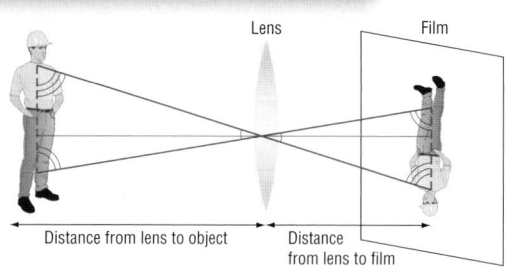

SIMILAR TRIANGLES **Similar triangles** have the same shape, but not necessarily the same size. There are two main tests for similarity.

• If the angles of one triangle and the corresponding angles of a second triangle have equal measures, then the triangles are similar.

• If the measures of the sides of two triangles form equal ratios, or are *proportional*, then the triangles are similar.

The triangles below are similar. This is written as $\triangle ABC \sim \triangle DEF$. The vertices of similar triangles are written in order to show the corresponding parts.

Study Tip

Reading Math
The symbol $\sim$ is read *is similar to.*

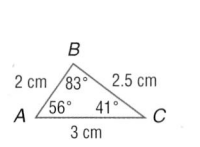
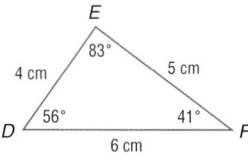

corresponding angles	corresponding sides
$\angle A$ and $\angle D$	$\overline{AB}$ and $\overline{DE} \rightarrow \dfrac{AB}{DE} = \dfrac{2}{4} = \dfrac{1}{2}$
$\angle B$ and $\angle E$	$\overline{BC}$ and $\overline{EF} \rightarrow \dfrac{BC}{EF} = \dfrac{2.5}{5} = \dfrac{1}{2}$
$\angle C$ and $\angle F$	$\overline{AC}$ and $\overline{DF} \rightarrow \dfrac{AC}{DF} = \dfrac{3}{6} = \dfrac{1}{2}$

TEACHING TIP

Arcs are used to show angles that have equal measures.

Key Concept · Similar Triangles

• **Words** If two triangles are similar, then the measures of their corresponding sides are proportional, and the measures of their corresponding angles are equal.

• **Symbols** If $\triangle ABC \sim \triangle DEF$, then $\dfrac{AB}{DE} = \dfrac{BC}{EF} = \dfrac{AC}{DF}$.

• **Model**

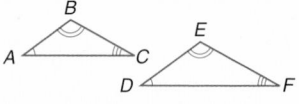

Resource Manager

Workbook and Reproducible Masters

Chapter 11 Resource Masters
• Study Guide and Intervention, pp. 673–674
• Skills Practice, p. 675
• Practice, p. 676
• Reading to Learn Mathematics, p. 677
• Enrichment, p. 678
• Assessment, p. 700

Parent and Student Study Guide Workbook, p. 88
Prerequisite Skills Workbook, pp. 61–62

Transparencies
5-Minute Check Transparency 11-6
Answer Key Transparencies

Technology
Interactive Chalkboard

Example 1 Determine Whether Two Triangles Are Similar

Determine whether the pair of triangles is similar. Justify your answer.

Remember that the sum of the measures of the angles in a triangle is 180°.

The measure of $\angle P$ is $180° - (51° + 51°)$ or 78°.

In $\triangle MNO$, $\angle N$ and $\angle O$ have the same measure.

Let x = the measure of $\angle N$ and $\angle O$.

$x + x + 78° = 180°$

$2x = 102°$

$x = 51°$

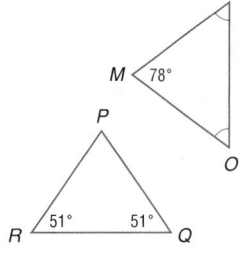

So $\angle N = 51°$ and $\angle O = 51°$. Since the corresponding angles have equal measures, $\triangle MNO \sim \triangle PQR$.

FIND UNKNOWN MEASURES Proportions can be used to find the measures of the sides of similar triangles when some of the measurements are known.

Example 2 Find Missing Measures

Find the missing measures if each pair of triangles below is similar.

a. Since the corresponding angles have equal measures, $\triangle TUV \sim \triangle WXY$. The lengths of the corresponding sides are proportional.

$\dfrac{WX}{TU} = \dfrac{XY}{UV}$ Corresponding sides of similar triangles are proportional.

$\dfrac{a}{3} = \dfrac{16}{4}$ $WX = a$, $XY = 16$, $TU = 3$, $UV = 4$

$4a = 48$ Find the cross products.

$a = 12$ Divide each side by 4.

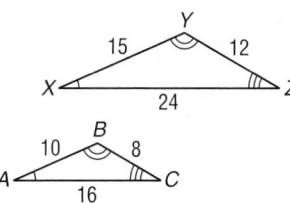

$\dfrac{WY}{TV} = \dfrac{XY}{UV}$ Corresponding sides of similar triangles are proportional.

$\dfrac{b}{6} = \dfrac{16}{4}$ $WY = b$, $XY = 16$, $TV = 6$, $UV = 4$

$4b = 96$ Find the cross products.

$b = 24$ Divide each side by 4.

The missing measures are 12 and 24.

b. $\triangle ABE \sim \triangle ACD$

$\dfrac{BE}{CD} = \dfrac{AE}{AD}$ Corresponding sides of similar triangles are proportional.

$\dfrac{10}{x} = \dfrac{6}{9}$ $BE = 10$, $CD = x$, $AE = 6$, $AD = 9$

$90 = 6x$ Find the cross products.

$15 = x$ Divide each side by 6.

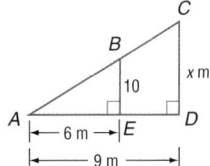

The missing measure is 15.

Lesson 11-6 Similar Triangles **617**

Study Tip

Corresponding Vertices
Always use the corresponding order of the vertices to write proportions for similar triangles.

Teaching Tip Tell students to look closely at all the angles and sides of the two triangles for clues about whether the triangles are similar. In Example 1, the same angles are not marked on both triangles, but there is sufficient information to determine that the angles are congruent.

1 Determine whether the pair of triangles is similar. Justify your answer.

The corresponding sides of the triangles are proportional, so the triangles are similar.

FIND UNKNOWN MEASURES

In-Class Example Power Point®

2 Find the missing measures if each pair of triangles below is similar.

a.

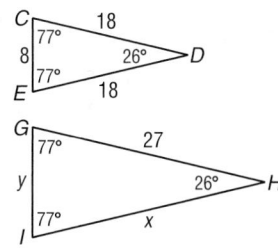

The missing measures are 27 and 12.

b.

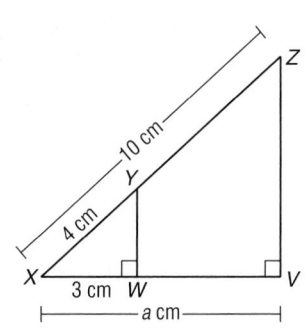

The missing measure is 7.5.

Lesson 11-6 Similar Triangles **617**

In-Class Example
Power Point®

3 SHADOWS Richard is standing next to the General Sherman Giant Sequoia tree in Sequoia National Park. The shadow of the tree is 22.5 meters, and Richard's shadow is 53.6 centimeters. If Richard's height is 2 meters, how tall is the tree?
The tree is about 84 m tall.

3 Practice/Apply

Study Notebook

Have students—
• add the definitions/examples of the vocabulary terms to their Vocabulary Builder worksheets for Chapter 11.
• include examples of how to determine whether two triangles are similar, and how to find unknown measures using triangles.
• include any other item(s) that they find helpful in mastering the skills in this lesson.

DAILY
INTERVENTION **FIND THE ERROR**
Remind students to pay close attention to the arcs that denote which angles are congruent.

Answers

3. Consuela; the arcs indicate which angles correspond. The vertices of the triangles are written in order to show the corresponding parts.

More About . . .

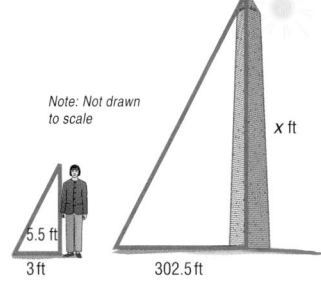

Washington Monument

The monument has a shape of an Egyptian *obelisk*. A pyramid made of solid aluminum caps the top of the monument.

Example 3 Use Similar Triangles to Solve a Problem

SHADOWS Jenelle is standing near the Washington Monument in Washington, D.C. The shadow of the monument is 302.5 feet, and Jenelle's shadow is 3 feet. If Jenelle is 5.5 feet tall, how tall is the monument?

The shadows form similar triangles. Write a proportion that compares the heights of the objects and the lengths of their shadows.

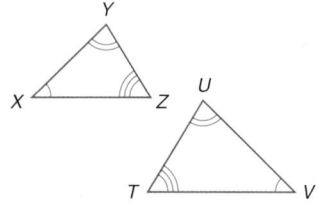

Note: Not drawn to scale

Let x = the height of the monument.

$$\begin{array}{ll} \text{Jenelle's shadow} \rightarrow & \dfrac{3}{302.5} = \dfrac{5.5}{x} \leftarrow \text{Jenelle's height} \\ \text{monument's shadow} \rightarrow & \qquad\qquad\quad \leftarrow \text{monument's height} \end{array}$$

$$3x = 1663.75 \qquad \text{Cross products}$$
$$x \approx 554.6 \text{ feet} \qquad \text{Divide each side by 3.}$$

The height of the monument is about 554.6 feet.

Check for Understanding

Concept Check

1. If the measures of the angles of one triangle equal the measures of the corresponding angles of another triangle, and the lengths of the sides are proportional, then the two triangles are similar.

1. **Explain** how to determine whether two triangles are similar.

2. **OPEN ENDED** Draw a pair of similar triangles. List the corresponding angles and the corresponding sides. **See pp. 639A–639B.**

3. **FIND THE ERROR** Russell and Consuela are comparing the similar triangles below to determine their corresponding parts. **See margin.**

Russell
$m\angle X = m\angle T$
$m\angle Y = m\angle U$
$m\angle Z = m\angle V$
$\triangle XYZ, \triangle TUV$

Consuela
$m\angle X = m\angle V$
$m\angle Y = m\angle U$
$m\angle Z = m\angle T$
$\triangle XYZ, \triangle VUT$

Who is correct? Explain your reasoning.

Guided Practice

GUIDED PRACTICE KEY	
Exercises	Examples
4, 5	1
6–9	2
10	3

Determine whether each pair of triangles is similar. Justify your answer.

4. [triangle with 84°, 46°, 46°] No; the angle measures are not equal.

5. [triangles with 55°, 35°] Yes; the angle measures are equal.

For each set of measures given, find the measures of the missing sides if $\triangle ABC \sim \triangle DEF$.

6. $c = 15, d = 7, e = 9, f = 5$ $\quad a = 21, b = 27$
7. $a = 18, c = 9, e = 10, f = 6$ $\quad b = 15, d = 12$
8. $a = 5, d = 7, f = 6, e = 5$ $\quad b = \dfrac{25}{7}, c = \dfrac{30}{7}$
9. $a = 17, b = 15, c = 10, f = 6$ $\quad d = 10.2, e = 9$

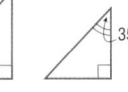

DAILY
INTERVENTION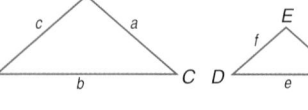

Differentiated Instruction

Naturalist Have students use the method in Example 3 to find the heights of trees that are native to your area. Make sure students record the location and type of tree along with the height. Students will need tape measures and will need to take measurements on a sunny day.

Application **10. SHADOWS** If a 25-foot flagpole casts a shadow that is 10 feet long and the nearby school building casts a shadow that is 26 feet long, how high is the building? **65 ft**

★ indicates increased difficulty

Practice and Apply

Homework Help

For Exercises	See Examples
11–16	1
17–24	2
25–32	3

Extra Practice
See page 845.

Determine whether each pair of triangles is similar. Justify your answer.

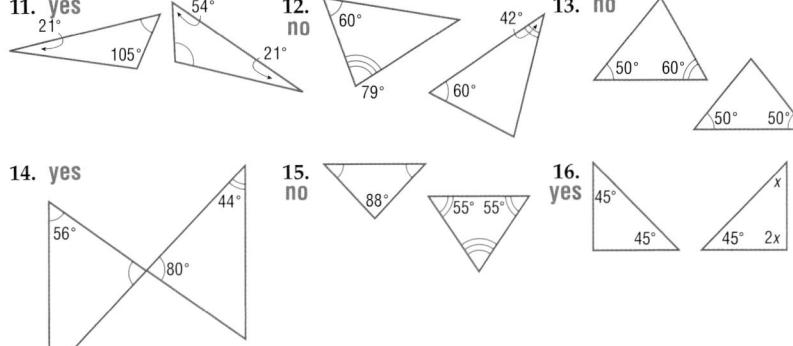

11. yes

12. no

13. no

14. yes

15. no

16. yes

11–16. See margin for justifications.

For each set of measures given, find the measures of the missing sides if $\triangle KLM \sim \triangle NOP$.

17. $k = 9, n = 6, o = 8, p = 4$ $\ell = 12, m = 6$
18. $k = 24, \ell = 30, m = 15, n = 16$ $o = 20, p = 10$
19. $m = 11, p = 6, n = 5, o = 4$ $k = \dfrac{55}{6}, \ell = \dfrac{22}{3}$
20. $k = 16, \ell = 13, m = 12, o = 7$ $n = \dfrac{112}{13}, p = \dfrac{84}{13}$
21. $n = 6, p = 2.5, \ell = 4, m = 1.25$ $k = 3, o = 8$
22. $p = 5, k = 10.5, \ell = 15, m = 7.5$ $n = 7, o = 10$
23. $n = 2.1, \ell = 4.4, p = 2.7, o = 3.3$ $k = 2.8, m = 3.6$
24. $m = 5, k = 12.6, o = 8.1, p = 2.5$ $\ell = 16.2, n = 6.3$

25. Determine whether the following statement is *sometimes, always,* or *never* true. *If the measures of the sides of a triangle are multiplied by 3, then the measures of the angles of the enlarged triangle will have the same measures as the angles of the original triangle.* **always**

26. **PHOTOGRAPHY** Refer to the diagram of a camera at the beginning of the lesson. Suppose the image of a man who is 2 meters tall is 1.5 centimeters tall on film. If the film is 3 centimeters from the lens of the camera, how far is the man from the camera? **4 m**

27. $3\dfrac{1}{3}$ in.

27. **BRIDGES** Truss bridges use triangles in their support beams. Mark plans to make a model of a truss bridge in the scale 1 inch = 12 feet. If the height of the triangles on the actual bridge is 40 feet, what will the height be on the model?

28. **BILLIARDS** Lenno is playing billiards on a table like the one shown at the right. He wants to strike the cue ball at *D*, bank it at *C*, and hit another ball at the mouth of pocket *A*. Use similar triangles to find where Lenno's cue ball should strike the rail. **24 in. from pocket *B***

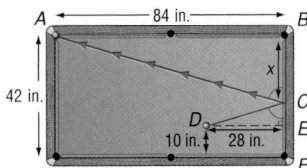

About the Exercises ...

Organization by Objective
• **Similar Triangles:** 11–16
• **Find Unknown Measures:** 17–32

Odd/Even Assignments
Exercises 11–24 are structured so that students practice the same concepts whether they are assigned odd or even problems.

Assignment Guide

Basic: 11–27 odd, 33–61

Average: 11–27 odd, 29, 30, 33–61

Advanced: 12–28 even, 29–55 (optional: 56–61)

All: Practice Quiz 2 (1–10)

Answers

11. The angle measures are equal.

12. The angle measures are not equal.

13. The angle measures are not equal.

14. The angle measures are equal.

15. The angle measures are not equal.

16. The angle measures are equal.

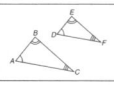
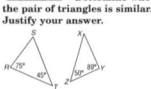
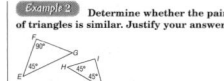 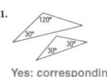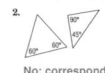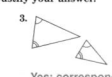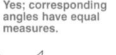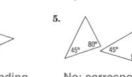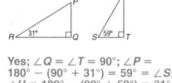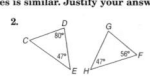
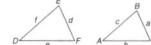 
CRAFTS For Exercises 29 and 30, use the following information.
Melinda is working on a quilt pattern containing isosceles right triangles whose sides measure 2 inches, 2 inches, and about 2.8 inches.

★ 29. She has several square pieces of material that measure 4 inches on each side. From each square piece, how many triangles with the required dimensions can she cut? **8**

★ 30. She wants to enlarge the pattern to make similar triangles for the center of the quilt. What is the largest similar triangle she can cut from the square material? **4 by 4 by about 5.6 in.**

MIRRORS For Exercises 31 and 32, use the diagram and the following information.
Viho wanted to measure the height of a nearby building. He placed a mirror on the pavement at point P, 80 feet from the base of the building. He then backed away until he saw an image of the top of the building in the mirror.

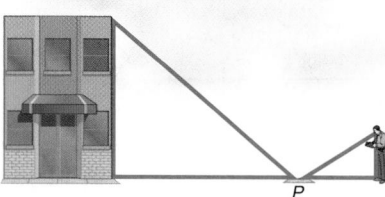

★ 31. If Viho is 6 feet tall and he is standing 9 feet from the mirror, how tall is the building? **about 53 ft**

★ 32. What assumptions did you make in solving the problem?

CRITICAL THINKING For Exercises 33–35, use the following information.
The radius of one circle is twice the radius of another. **34–35. See margin.**

33. Are the circles similar? Explain your reasoning.

34. What is the ratio of their circumferences? Explain your reasoning.

35. What is the ratio of their areas? Explain your reasoning.

36. **WRITING IN MATH** Answer the question that was posed at the beginning of the lesson. **See margin.**

How are similar triangles related to photography?

Include the following in your answer:
- an explanation of the effect of moving a camera with a zoom lens closer to the object being photographed, and
- a description of what you could do to fit the entire image of a large object on the picture.

Standardized Test Practice

For Exercises 37 and 38, use the figure at the right.

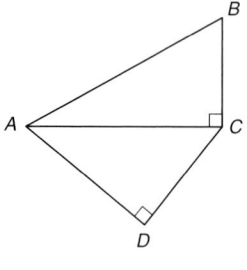

37. Which statement must be true? **D**
Ⓐ △ABC ∼ △ADC
Ⓑ △ABC ∼ △ACD
Ⓒ △ABC ∼ △CAD
Ⓓ none of the above

38. Which statement is always true? **A**
Ⓐ AB > DC
Ⓑ CB > AD
Ⓒ AC > BC
Ⓓ AC = AB

620   Chapter 11   Radical Expressions and Triangles

32. Viho's eyes are 6 feet off the ground, Viho and the building each create right angles with the ground, and the two angles with the ground at P have equal measure.

33. Yes; all circles are similar because they have the same shape.

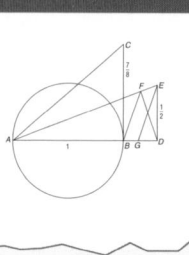

Mixed Review   Find the distance between each pair of points whose coordinates are given. Express answers in simplest radical form and as decimal approximations rounded to the nearest hundredth if necessary.   *(Lesson 11-5)*

39. $(1, 8), (-2, 4)$ **5**

40. $(6, -3), (12, 5)$ **10**

41. $(4, 7), (3, 12)$ $\sqrt{26} \approx 5.1$

42. $(1, 5\sqrt{6}), (6, 7\sqrt{6})$ **7**

Determine whether the following side measures form right triangles. Justify your answer.   *(Lesson 11-4)*

43. $25, 60, 65$ Yes; $25^2 + 60^2 = 65^2$.

44. $20, 25, 35$ No; $20^2 + 25^2 \neq 35^2$.

45. $49, 168, 175$ Yes; $49^2 + 168^2 = 175^2$.

46. $7, 9, 12$ No; $7^2 + 9^2 \neq 12^2$.

Arrange the terms of each polynomial so that the powers of the variable are in descending order.   *(Lesson 8-4)* **48.** $5x^3 - 2x^2 - 4x + 7$

47. $1 + 3x^2 - 7x$ $3x^2 - 7x + 1$

48. $7 - 4x - 2x^2 + 5x^3$

49. $6x + 3 - 3x^2$ $-3x^2 + 6x + 3$

50. $abx^2 - bcx + 34 - x^7$
$-x^7 + abx^2 - bcx + 34$

Use elimination to solve each system of equations.   *(Lesson 7-3)*

51. $2x + y = 4$ $(3, -2)$
   $x - y = 5$

52. $3x - 2y = -13$ $(-5, -1)$
   $2x - 5y = -5$

53. $0.6m - 0.2n = 0.9$ $(1.5, 0)$
   $0.3m = 0.45 - 0.1n$

54. $\frac{1}{3}x + \frac{1}{2}y = 8$ $(6, 12)$
   $\frac{1}{2}x - \frac{1}{4}y = 0$

55. AVIATION   An airplane passing over Sacramento at an elevation of 37,000 feet begins its descent to land at Reno, 140 miles away. If the elevation of Reno is 4500 feet, what should be the approximate slope of descent? (*Hint*: 1 mi = 5280 ft)   *(Lesson 5-1)* about -0.044

Getting Ready for the Next Lesson   **PREREQUISITE SKILL**   Evaluate if $a = 6$, $b = -5$, and $c = -1.5$. (*To review* **evaluating expressions**, *see Lesson 1-2*.)

56. $\frac{a}{c}$ -4

57. $\frac{b}{a}$ $-\frac{5}{6}$ or $-0.8\overline{3}$

58. $\frac{a+b}{c}$ $-\frac{2}{3}$ or $-0.\overline{6}$

59. $\frac{ac}{b}$ $\frac{9}{5}$ or 1.8

60. $\frac{b}{a+c}$ $-\frac{10}{9}$ or $-1.\overline{1}$

61. $\frac{c}{a+c}$ $-\frac{1}{3}$ or $-0.\overline{3}$

Practice Quiz 2   **Lessons 11-4 through 11-6**

If c is the measure of the hypotenuse of a right triangle, find each missing measure. If necessary, round to the nearest hundredth.   *(Lesson 11-4)*

1. $a = 14, b = 48, c = ?$ **50**

2. $a = 40, c = 41, b = ?$ **9**

3. $b = 8, c = \sqrt{84}, a = ?$ $2\sqrt{5} \approx 4.47$

4. $a = \sqrt{5}, b = \sqrt{8}, c = ?$ $\sqrt{13} \approx 3.61$

Find the distance between each pair of points whose coordinates are given.   *(Lesson 11-5)*

5. $(6, -12), (-3, 3)$ $\sqrt{306} \approx 17.49$

6. $(1, 3), (-5, 11)$ **10**

7. $(2, 5), (4, 7)$ $2\sqrt{2} \approx 2.83$

8. $(-2, -9), (-5, 4)$ $\sqrt{178} \approx 13.34$

Find the measures of the missing sides if $\triangle BCA \sim \triangle EFD$.   *(Lesson 11-6)*

9. $b = 10, d = 2, e = 1, f = 1.5$ $a = 20, c = 15$

10. $a = 12, c = 9, d = 8, e = 12$ $b = 18, f = 6$

 www.algebra1.com/self_check_quiz

4 Assess

Open-Ended Assessment

Modeling Construct a triangle using unsharpened pencils, uncooked spaghetti or other items that have a uniform length. Have students construct a triangle similar to yours and explain how they would show that the two triangles are similar.

Getting Ready for Lesson 11-7

PREREQUISITE SKILL Students will learn about trigonometric ratios in Lesson 11-7. In order to compute trigonometric ratios, students must be able to divide rational numbers. Use Exercises 56–61 to determine your students' familiarity with dividing rational numbers.

Assessment Options

Practice Quiz 2 The quiz provides students with a brief review of the concepts and skills in Lessons 11-4 through 11-6. Lesson numbers are given to the right of exercises or instruction lines so students can review concepts not yet mastered.

Quiz (Lessons 11-5 and 11-6) is available on p. 700 of the *Chapter 11 Resource Masters*.

Answers

34. 2:1; Let the first circle have radius r and the larger have radius $2r$. The circumference of the first is $2\pi r$ and the other has circumference $2\pi(2r) = 4\pi r$.

35. 4:1; The area of the first is πr^2 and the area of the other is $\pi(2r)^2 = 4\pi r^2$.

36. The size of an object on the film of a camera can be related to its actual size using similar triangles. Answers should include the following.
- Moving the lens closer to the object (and farther from the film) makes the object appear larger.
- Taking a picture of a building; you would need to be a great distance away to fit the entire building in the picture.

Algebra Activity

Getting Started

Objective Construct right triangles with legs whose lengths are equal to a specific ratio, in order to investigate the relationship between the sides and the angles as a preview of trigonometric ratios.

Materials
ruler
grid paper
protractor

Teach

- Remind students that the triangles they are drawing are similar because the ratio of the corresponding sides is the same for each triangle.

- Point out to students that because they drew the triangles by hand, the measures of the angles may not be exact, according to the protractor. However, the measures should be close to 35°, 55°, and 90°.

Assess

Ask students to conjecture why knowing the relationship between the ratios of the sides of a triangle to each other and the angles might be useful. **Sample answer: Knowing these relationships might allow you to calculate a missing side length or angle measure.**

Investigating Trigonometric Ratios

You can use paper triangles to investigate trigonometric ratios.

Collect the Data

Step 1 Use a ruler and grid paper to draw several right triangles whose legs are in a 7:10 ratio. Include a right triangle with legs 3.5 units and 5 units, a right triangle with legs 7 units and 10 units, another with legs 14 units and 20 units, and several more right triangles similar to these three. Label the vertices of each triangle as *A*, *B*, and *C*, where *C* is at the right angle, *B* is opposite the longest leg, and *A* is opposite the shortest leg.

Step 2 Copy the table below. Complete the first three columns by measuring the hypotenuse (side *AB*) in each right triangle you created and recording its length.

Step 3 Calculate and record the ratios in the middle two columns. Round to the nearest tenth, if necessary.

Step 4 Use a protractor to carefully measure angles *A* and *B* in each right triangle. Record the angle measures in the table.

Side Lengths			Ratios		Angle Measures		
side *BC*	side *AC*	side *AB*	*BC:AC*	*BC:AB*	angle *A*	angle *B*	angle *C*
3.5	5	6.1	0.7	0.574	35°	55°	90°
7	10	12.2	0.7	0.574	35°	55°	90°
14	20	24.4	0.7	0.574	35°	55°	90°
28	40	48.8	0.7	0.574	35°	55°	90°
35	50	61	0.7	0.574	35°	55°	90°
42	60	73.2	0.7	0.574	35°	55°	90°

Sample answers are given in table.

Analyze the Data

1. Examine the measures and ratios in the table. What do you notice? Write a sentence or two to describe any patterns you see.
   All ratios and angle measures are the same for any 7:10 right triangle.

Make a Conjecture

2. For any right triangle similar to the ones you have drawn here, what will be the value of the ratio of the length of the shortest leg to the length of the longest leg? **7:10**

3. If you draw a right triangle and calculate the ratio of the length of the shortest leg to the length of the hypotenuse to be approximately 0.574, what will be the measure of the larger acute angle in the right triangle? **55°**

622 Chapter 11 Radical Expressions and Triangles

Resource Manager

📁 *Teaching Algebra with Manipulatives*

- p. 1 (master for grid paper)
- p. 23 (master for protractors)
- p. 24 (master for rulers)
- p. 191 (student recording sheet)

Glencoe Mathematics Classroom Manipulative Kit

- coordinate grid stamp
- protractors
- rulers

11-7 Trigonometric Ratios

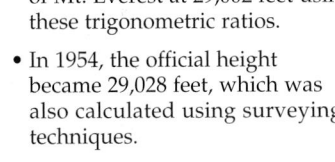

What You'll Learn

- Define the sine, cosine, and tangent ratios.
- Use trigonometric ratios to solve right triangles.

How are trigonometric ratios used in surveying?

Surveyors use triangle ratios called trigonometric ratios to determine distances that cannot be measured directly.

- In 1852, British surveyors measured the altitude of the peak of Mt. Everest at 29,002 feet using these trigonometric ratios.

- In 1954, the official height became 29,028 feet, which was also calculated using surveying techniques.

- On November 11, 1999, a team using advanced technology and the Global Positioning System (GPS) satellite measured the mountain at 29,035 feet.

Vocabulary
- trigonometric ratios
- sine
- cosine
- tangent
- solve a triangle
- angle of elevation
- angle of depression

TRIGONOMETRIC RATIOS *Trigonometry* is an area of mathematics that involves angles and triangles. If enough information is known about a right triangle, certain ratios can be used to find the measures of the remaining parts of the triangle. **Trigonometric ratios** are ratios of the measures of two sides of a right triangle. Three common trigonometric ratios are called **sine**, **cosine**, and **tangent**.

> **Study Tip**
>
> *Reading Math*
> Notice that sine, cosine, and tangent are abbreviated sin, cos, and tan respectively.

Key Concept — Trigonometric Ratios

- **Words**

  $$\text{sine of } \angle A = \frac{\text{measure of leg opposite } \angle A}{\text{measure of hypotenuse}}$$

  $$\text{cosine of } \angle A = \frac{\text{measure of leg adjacent to } \angle A}{\text{measure of hypotenuse}}$$

  $$\text{tangent of } \angle A = \frac{\text{measure of leg opposite } \angle A}{\text{measure of leg adjacent to } \angle A}$$

- **Symbols** $\sin A = \dfrac{BC}{AB}$

  $\cos A = \dfrac{AC}{AB}$

  $\tan A = \dfrac{BC}{AC}$

- **Model**

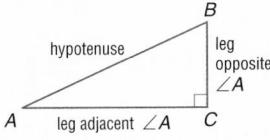

Lesson 11-7 Trigonometric Ratios **623**

---

1 Focus

5-Minute Check Transparency 11-7 Use as a quiz or review of Lesson 11-6.

Mathematical Background notes are available for this lesson on p. 584D.

How are trigonometric ratios used in surveying?

Ask students:

- In the previous lesson, you calculated the height of the Washington Monument using ratios. What is required in order to make this calculation? **Two similar triangles formed by the shadow of the monument and the shadow of a person standing next to it. You know the length of both shadows and the height of the person. You can use ratios to calculate the height of the monument.**

- Based on the Algebra Activity on the previous page, how do you suppose a surveyor could calculate the height of a mountain? **Sample answer: A surveyor could use the angle between him or herself and the top of the mountain, and the distance to the mountain to construct a similar right triangle. Then based on the side measures of that similar triangle, the height of the mountain could be calculated using ratios.**

Resource Manager

Workbook and Reproducible Masters

Chapter 11 Resource Masters
- Study Guide and Intervention, pp. 679–680
- Skills Practice, p. 681
- Practice, p. 682
- Reading to Learn Mathematics, p. 683
- Enrichment, p. 684
- Assessment, p. 700

Parent and Student Study Guide Workbook, p. 89
Teaching Algebra With Manipulatives Masters, pp. 23, 24, 192

 Transparencies
5-Minute Check Transparency 11-7
Answer Key Transparencies

Technology
Interactive Chalkboard

TRIGONOMETRIC RATIOS

Tips for New Teachers

The trigonometric ratios are a concept that students will use in other classes such as Geometry, Algebra II, and Trigonometry. Any time students are introduced to such important concepts, have them record the concepts in their Study Notebooks for future reference. Additionally, the act of recording the concepts will help the students remember them.

In-Class Example Power Point®

Teaching Tip While it is true that a fraction with radicals in the denominator is not in simplest form, it is not necessary to rationalize the denominator if students are going to use a calculator to simplify the expression. Suggest that students use a calculator to find $\frac{\sqrt{10}}{\sqrt{3}}$ and $\frac{\sqrt{30}}{3}$. Both produce the same result, and rationalization was not necessary.

1 Find the sine, cosine, and tangent of each acute angle of $\triangle DEF$. Round to the nearest ten-thousandth.

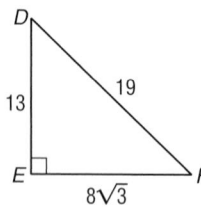

$\sin D = 0.7293$; $\cos D = 0.6842$;
$\tan D = 1.0659$; $\sin F = 0.6842$;
$\cos F = 0.7293$; $\tan F = 0.9382$

Example 1 *Sine, Cosine, and Tangent*

Find the sine, cosine, and tangent of each acute angle of $\triangle RST$. Round to the nearest ten thousandth.

Write each ratio and substitute the measures. Use a calculator to find each value.

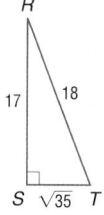

$\sin R = \dfrac{\text{opposite leg}}{\text{hypotenuse}}$

$= \dfrac{\sqrt{35}}{18}$ or 0.3287

$\cos R = \dfrac{\text{adjacent leg}}{\text{hypotenuse}}$

$= \dfrac{17}{18}$ or 0.9444

$\tan R = \dfrac{\text{opposite leg}}{\text{adjacent leg}}$

$= \dfrac{\sqrt{35}}{17}$ or 0.3480

$\sin T = \dfrac{\text{opposite leg}}{\text{hypotenuse}}$

$= \dfrac{17}{18}$ or 0.9444

$\cos T = \dfrac{\text{adjacent leg}}{\text{hypotenuse}}$

$= \dfrac{\sqrt{35}}{18}$ or 0.3287

$\tan T = \dfrac{\text{opposite leg}}{\text{adjacent leg}}$

$= \dfrac{17}{\sqrt{35}}$ or 2.8735

You can use a calculator to find the values of trigonometric functions or to find the measure of an angle. On a graphing calculator, press the trigometric function key, and then enter the value. On a nongraphing scientific calculator, enter the value, and then press the function key. In either case, be sure your calculator is in degree mode. Consider cos 50°.

Graphing Calculator	Nongraphing Scientific Calculator
KEYSTROKES: COS 50 ENTER .6427876097	**KEYSTROKES:** 50 COS .642787609

Example 2 *Find the Sine of an Angle*

Find sin 35° to the nearest ten thousandth.

KEYSTROKES: SIN 35 ENTER .5735764364

Rounded to the nearest ten thousandth, sin 35° ≈ 0.5736.

Example 3 *Find the Measure of an Angle*

Find the measure of $\angle J$ to the nearest degree.

Since the lengths of the opposite and adjacent sides are known, use the tangent ratio.

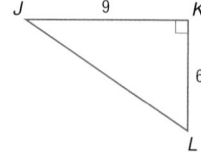

$\tan J = \dfrac{\text{opposite leg}}{\text{adjacent leg}}$ Definition of tangent

$= \dfrac{6}{9}$ $KL = 6$ and $JK = 9$

Now use the [TAN⁻¹] on a calculator to find the measure of the angle whose tangent ratio is $\frac{6}{9}$.

KEYSTROKES: 2nd [TAN⁻¹] 6 ÷ 9 ENTER 33.69006753

To the nearest degree, the measure of $\angle J$ is 34°.

624 Chapter 11 Radical Expressions and Triangles

DAILY INTERVENTION

Differentiated Instruction

Auditory/Musical Divide the class into small groups. Challenge each group to devise a rap verse, limerick, poem, or a song that they can use to remember the trigonometric ratios.

SOLVE TRIANGLES You can find the missing measures of a right triangle if you know the measure of two sides of a triangle or the measure of one side and one acute angle. Finding all of the measures of the sides and the angles in a right triangle is called **solving the triangle**.

Example 4 Solve a Triangle

Find all of the missing measures in △ABC.

You need to find the measures of $\angle B$, $\overline{AC}$, and $\overline{BC}$.

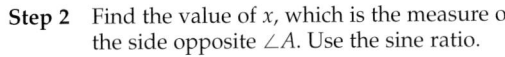

Step 1 Find the measure of $\angle B$. The sum of the measures of the angles in a triangle is 180.

$$180° - 90° - 38° = 52°$$

The measure of $\angle B$ is 52°.

Step 2 Find the value of x, which is the measure of the side opposite $\angle A$. Use the sine ratio.

$\sin 38° = \dfrac{x}{12}$ Definition of sine

$0.6157 \approx \dfrac{x}{12}$ Evaluate sin 38°.

$7.4 \approx x$ Multiply by 12.

$\overline{BC}$ is about 7.4 inches long.

Step 3 Find the value of y, which is the measure of the side adjacent to $\angle A$. Use the cosine ratio.

$\cos 38° = \dfrac{y}{12}$ Definition of cosine

$0.7880 \approx \dfrac{y}{12}$ Evaluate cos 38°.

$9.5 \approx y$ Multiply by 12.

$\overline{AC}$ is about 9.5 inches long.

So, the missing measures are 52°, 7.4 in., and 9.5 in.

Study Tip

Verifying Right Triangles
You can use the Pythagorean Theorem to verify that the sides are sides of a right triangle.

Trigonometric ratios are often used to find distances or lengths that cannot be measured directly. In these situations, you will sometimes use an angle of elevation or an angle of depression. An **angle of elevation** is formed by a horizontal line of sight and a line of sight above it. An **angle of depression** is formed by a horizontal line of sight and a line of sight below it.

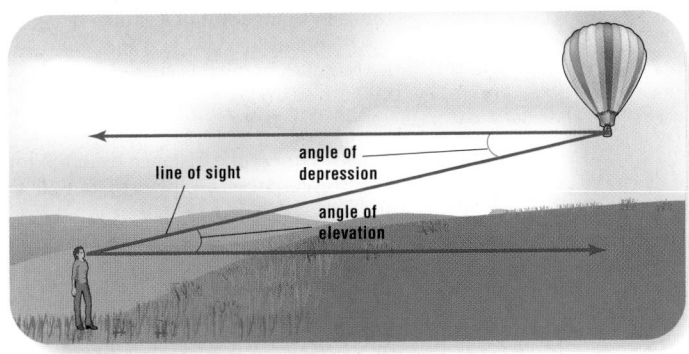

www.algebra1.com/extra_examples

Teaching Tip To make sure that their calculators are in degree mode, tell students to press MODE and then look at the third row to see whether Radian or Degree is highlighted. If Radian is highlighted, students should use the cursor to select Degree, then press ENTER.

2 Find cos 65° to the nearest ten thousandth. **0.4226**

Teaching Tip If students have trouble understanding the concept of the inverse of a trigonometric function, write $4J = \dfrac{6}{9}$ on the chalkboard. Ask students to explain how you would solve this problem. They will say to divide both sides by 4. Point out that dividing by 4 is the inverse operation of multiplying J by 4. Therefore, to solve for J in the equation $\tan J = \dfrac{6}{9}$, you perform the inverse of the tangent operation on both sides of the equation.

3 Find the measure of $\angle B$ to the nearest degree.

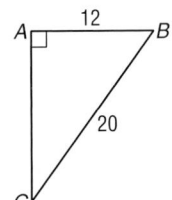

To the nearest degree, the measure of $\angle B$ is 53°.

SOLVE TRIANGLES

In-Class Example Power Point®

4 Find all of the missing measures in △DEF.

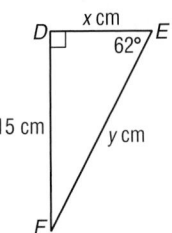

The missing measures are $m\angle F = 28°$, $x \approx 8$ cm, and $y \approx 17$ cm.

Teaching Tip Problems involving angles of depression are solved in the same manner as problems with angles of elevation. It is just a different orientation of the angle.

5 **INDIRECT MEASUREMENT**
In the diagram, Barone is flying his model airplane 400 feet above him. An angle of depression is formed by a horizontal line of sight and a line of sight below it. Find the angles of depression at points A and B to the nearest degree.

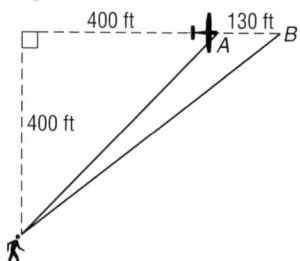

The angle of depression at point A is 45° and the angle of depression at point B is 37°.

Algebra Activity

Make a Hypsometer

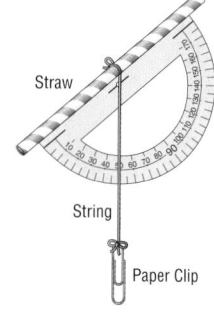

- Tie one end of a piece of string to the middle of a straw. Tie the other end of string to a paper clip.
- Tape a protractor to the side of the straw. Make sure that the string hangs freely to create a vertical or plumb line.
- Find an object outside that is too tall to measure directly, such as a basketball hoop, a flagpole, or the school building.
- Look through the straw to the top of the object you are measuring. Find the angle measure where the string and protractor intersect. Determine the angle of elevation by subtracting this measurement from 90°.
- Measure the distance from your eye level to the ground and from your foot to the base of the object you are measuring.

Analyze 1. See students' work.

1. Make a sketch of your measurements. Use the equation
   $$\tan (\text{angle of elevation}) = \frac{\text{height of object} - x}{\text{distance of object}},$$ where x represents distance from the ground to your eye level, to find the height of the object.

2. Why do you have to subtract the angle measurement on the hypsometer from 90° to find the angle of elevation?

3. Compare your answer with someone who measured the same object. Did your heights agree? Why or why not? **See students' work.**

2. The angle measured by the hypsometer is not the angle of elevation. It is the other acute angle formed in the triangle. So, to find the measure of the angle of elevation, subtract the reading on the hypsometer from 90 since the sum of the measures of the two acute angles in a right triangle is 90°.

Example 5 *Angle of Elevation*

INDIRECT MEASUREMENT At point A, Umeko measured the angle of elevation to point P to be 27 degrees. At another point B, which was 600 meters closer to the cliff, Umeko measured the angle of elevation to point P to be 31.5 degrees. Determine the height of the cliff.

Explore Draw a diagram to model the situation. Two right triangles, $\triangle BPC$ and $\triangle APC$, are formed. You know the angle of elevation for each triangle. To determine the height of the cliff, find the length of $\overline{PC}$, which is shared by both triangles.

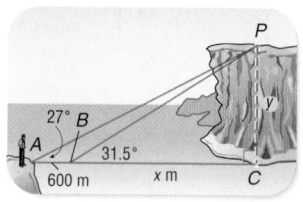

Plan Let y represent the distance from the top of the cliff P to its base C. Let x represent BC in the first triangle and let $x + 600$ represent AC.

Solve Write two equations involving the tangent ratio.

$$\tan 31.5° = \frac{y}{x} \quad \text{and} \quad \tan 27° = \frac{y}{600 + x}$$
$$x \tan 31.5° = y \qquad\qquad (600 + x)\tan 27° = y$$

Algebra Activity

Materials string, drinking straw, paper clip, protractor, tape, meter sticks or tape measure

Remind students that the angle of elevation is being measured from their eye level, not the ground. They must account for this distance when calculating the height of the object that they are measuring with their hypsometer.

Since both expressions are equal to y, use substitution to solve for x.

$$x \tan 31.5° = (600 + x) \tan 27°$$ Substitute.

$$x \tan 31.5° = 600 \tan 27° + x \tan 27°$$ Distributive Property

$$x \tan 31.5° - x \tan 27° = 600 \tan 27°$$ Subtract.

$$x(\tan 31.5° - \tan 27°) = 600 \tan 27°$$ Isolate x.

$$x = \frac{600 \tan 27°}{\tan 31.5° - \tan 27°}$$ Divide.

$$x \approx 2960 \text{ feet}$$ Use a calculator.

Use this value for x and the equation $x \tan 31.5° = y$ to solve for y.

$$x \tan 31.5° = y$$ Original equation

$$2960 \tan 31.5° \approx y$$ Replace x with 2960.

$$1814 \approx y$$ Use a calculator.

The height of the cliff is about 1814 feet.

Examine Examine the solution by finding the angles of elevation.

$$\tan B = \frac{y}{x} \qquad\qquad \tan A = \frac{y}{600 + x}$$

$$\tan B \stackrel{?}{=} \frac{1814}{2960} \qquad\qquad \tan A \stackrel{?}{=} \frac{1814}{600 + 2960}$$

$$B \approx 31.5° \qquad\qquad A \approx 27°$$

The solution checks.

Check for Understanding

Concept Check
1. **Explain** how to determine which trigonometric ratio to use when solving for an unknown measure of a right triangle. **See margin.**

2. **See margin.**
2. **OPEN ENDED** Draw a right triangle and label the measure of the hypotenuse and the measure of one acute angle. Then solve for the remaining measures.

3. **Compare** the measure of the angle of elevation and the measure of the angle of depression for two objects. What is the relationship between their measures? **They are equal.**

Guided Practice For each triangle, find sin Y, cos Y, and tan Y to the nearest ten thousandth.

GUIDED PRACTICE KEY	
Exercises	Examples
4, 5	1
6–8	2
9–14	3
15–17	4
18	5

4. 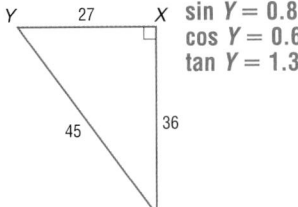 sin Y = 0.8, cos Y = 0.6, tan Y = 1.3333

5. 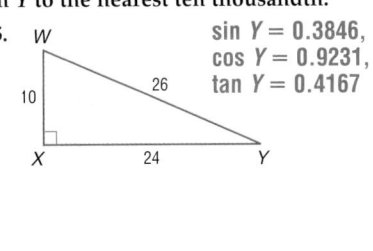 sin Y = 0.3846, cos Y = 0.9231, tan Y = 0.4167

Use a calculator to find the value of each trigonometric ratio to the nearest ten thousandth.

6. sin 60° **0.8660**   7. cos 75° **0.2588**   8. tan 10° **0.1763**

Use a calculator to find the measure of each angle to the nearest degree.

9. sin W = 0.9848 **80°**   10. cos X = 0.6157 **52°**   11. tan C = 0.3249 **18°**

Lesson 11-7 Trigonometric Ratios **627**

3 Practice/Apply

Study Notebook

Have students—
• complete the definitions/examples for the remaining terms on their Vocabulary Builder worksheets for Chapter 11.
• include examples of how to derive the trigonometric ratios from a right triangle, and how to use the ratios to solve triangles.
• include any other item(s) that they find helpful in mastering the skills in this lesson.

Answers

1. If you know the measure of the hypotenuse, use sine or cosine, depending on whether you know the measure of the adjacent side or the opposite side. If you know the measures of the two legs, use tangent.

2. Sample answer:
$A = 180° - (90° + 50°)$ or 40°

$$\sin 50° = \frac{AC}{10} \qquad \cos 50° = \frac{BC}{10}$$

$$AC = 7.66 \qquad BC = 6.43$$

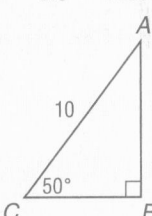

12. 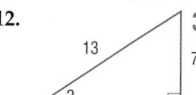 33°, 13, 7, ?

13. 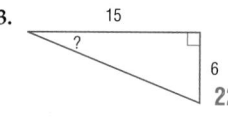 15, ?, 6, 22°

14. 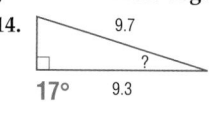 9.7, ?, 17°, 9.3

Solve each right triangle. State the side lengths to the nearest tenth and the angle measures to the nearest degree.

15.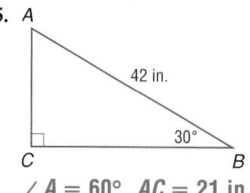
A, 42 in., 30°, C, B
∠A = 60°, AC = 21 in.,
BC ≈ 36.4 in.

16.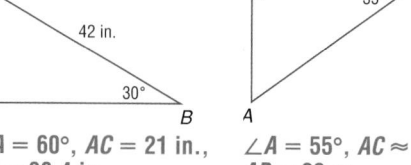
C, 18 m, B, 35°, A
∠A = 55°, AC ≈ 12.6 m,
AB ≈ 22 m

17.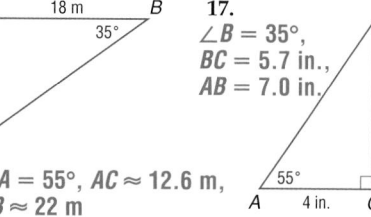
∠B = 35°,
BC = 5.7 in.,
AB = 7.0 in.
B, 55°, A, 4 in., C

Application **18. DRIVING** The percent grade of a road is the ratio of how much the road rises or falls in a given horizontal distance. If a road has a vertical rise of 40 feet for every 1000 feet horizontal distance, calculate the percent grade of the road and the angle of elevation the road makes with the horizontal. **4% grade, about 2.3°**

Trucks check brakes 6% grade

★ indicates increased difficulty

Practice and Apply

Homework Help

For Exercises	See Examples
19–24	1
25–33	2
34–51	3
52–60	4
61–65	5

Extra Practice
See page 846.

19–24. See margin.
For each triangle, find sin R, cos R, and tan R to the nearest ten thousandth.

19.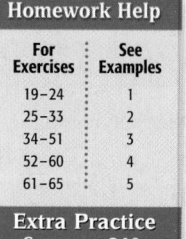
T, 10, 6, R, 8, S

20. R, 35, F, 37, 12, G

21.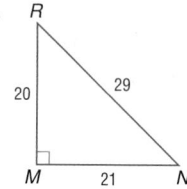
R, 20, 29, M, 21, N

22.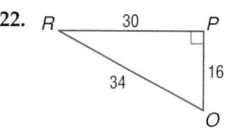
R, 30, P, 34, 16, O

23.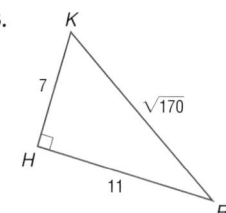
K, 7, √170, H, 11, R

24.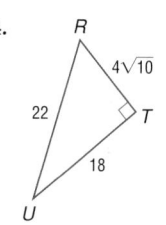
R, 4√10, 22, T, 18, U

Use a calculator to find the value of each trigonometric ratio to the nearest ten thousandth.

25. sin 30° **0.5**

26. sin 80° **0.9848**

27. cos 45° **0.7071**

28. cos 48° **0.6691**

29. tan 32° **0.6249**

30. tan 15° **0.2679**

31. tan 67° **2.3559**

32. sin 53° **0.7986**

33. cos 12° **0.9781**

Use a calculator to find the measure of each angle to the nearest degree.

34. cos V = 0.5000 **60°**

35. cos Q = 0.7658 **40°**

36. sin K = 0.9781 **78°**

37. sin A = 0.8827 **62°**

38. tan S = 1.2401 **51°**

39. tan H = 0.6473 **33°**

40. sin V = 0.3832 **23°**

41. cos M = 0.9793 **12°**

42. tan L = 3.6541 **75°**

About the Exercises ...

Organization by Objective
• **Trigonometric Ratios:** 19–51
• **Solve Triangles:** 52–65

Odd/Even Assignments
Exercises 19–60 are structured so that students practice the same concepts whether they are assigned odd or even problems.

Assignment Guide

Basic: 19–49 odd, 53–59 odd, 61, 62, 66–79

Average: 19–59 odd, 61–64, 66–79

Advanced: 20–60 even, 63–79

Answers

19. sin R = 0.6, cos R = 0.8, tan R = 0.75

20. sin R = 0.3243, cos R = 0.9459, tan R = 0.3429

21. sin R = 0.7241, cos R = 0.6897, tan R = 1.05

22. sin R = 0.4706, cos R = 0.8824, tan R = 0.5333

23. sin R = 0.5369, cos R = 0.8437, tan R = 0.6364

24. sin R = 0.8182, cos R = 0.5750, tan R = 1.4230

For each triangle, find the measure of the indicated angle to the nearest degree.

43.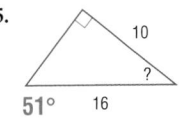

44.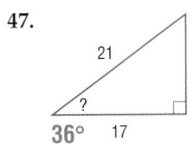

45.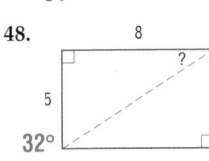

46.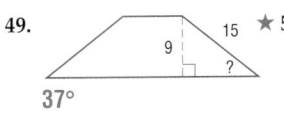

47.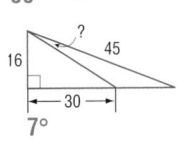

48.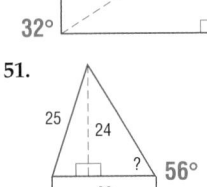

49.

★ 50.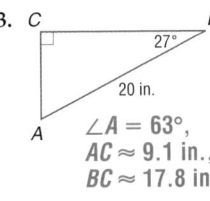

★ 51.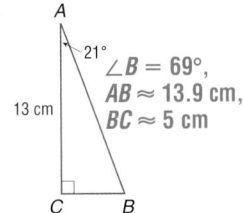

Solve each right triangle. State the side lengths to the nearest tenth and the angle measures to the nearest degree.

52.
$\angle A = 45°$,
$AB \approx 11.3$ ft,
$AC = 8$ ft

53.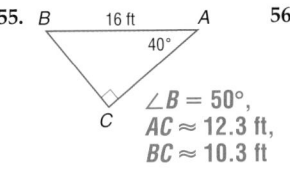
$\angle A = 63°$,
$AC \approx 9.1$ in.,
$BC \approx 17.8$ in.

54.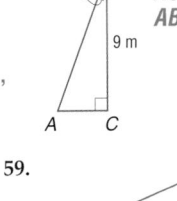
$\angle B = 69°$,
$AB \approx 13.9$ cm,
$BC \approx 5$ cm

55.
$\angle B = 50°$,
$AC \approx 12.3$ ft,
$BC \approx 10.3$ ft

56.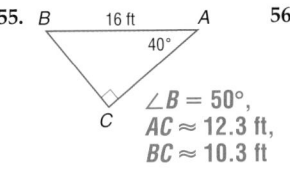
$\angle A = 70°$,
$AC \approx 3.3$ m,
$AB \approx 9.6$ m

57.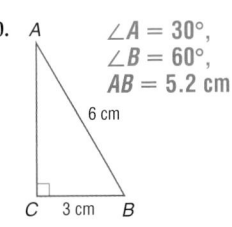
$\angle B = 52°$,
$AC \approx 30.7$ in.,
$AB \approx 39$ in.

58. $\angle A \approx 53°$,
$\angle B \approx 37°$,
$AB = 10$ ft

59.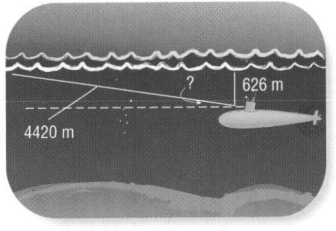
$\angle A \approx 23°$,
$\angle B \approx 67°$,
$AB = 13$ ft

60. $\angle A = 30°$,
$\angle B = 60°$,
$AB = 5.2$ cm

SUBMARINES For Exercises 61 and 62, use the following information.
A submarine is traveling parallel to the surface of the water 626 meters below the surface. The sub begins a constant ascent to the surface so that it will emerge on the surface after traveling 4420 meters from the point of its initial ascent.

61. What angle of ascent did the submarine make? **about 8.1°**

62. What horizontal distance did the submarine travel during its ascent? **4375 m**

www.algebra1.com/self_check_quiz

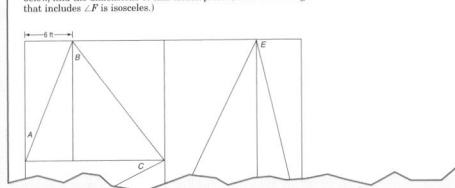
 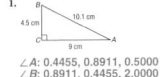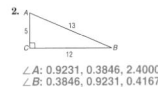
 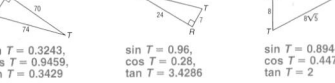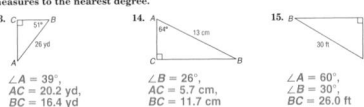

Open-Ended Assessment

Writing Ask students to sketch a right triangle, label the sides and angles with their measures, and find the trigonometric ratios for the two acute angles.

Assessment Options

Quiz (Lesson 11-7) is available on p. 700 of the *Chapter 11 Resource Masters*.

Answers

66. Let $\sin A = \dfrac{a}{c}$ and let $\cos A = \dfrac{b}{c}$, where a and b are legs of a right triangle and c is the hypotenuse. Then $\sin^2 A + \cos^2 A = \dfrac{a^2}{c^2} + \dfrac{b^2}{c^2} = \dfrac{a^2 + b^2}{c^2}$. Since the Pythagorean Theorem states that $a^2 + b^2 = c^2$, the expression becomes $\dfrac{c^2}{c^2}$ or 1. Thus $\sin^2 A + \cos^2 A = 1$.

67. If you know the distance between two points and the angles from these two points to a third point, you can determine the distance to the third point by forming a triangle and using trigonometric ratios. Answers should include the following.

- If you measure your distance from the mountain and the angle of elevation to the peak of the mountain from two different points, you can write an equation using trigonometric ratios to determine its height, similar to Example 5.

- You need to know the altitude of the two points you are measuring.

AVIATION For Exercises 63 and 64, use the following information.
Germaine pilots a small plane on weekends. During a recent flight, he determined that he was flying at an altitude of 3000 feet parallel to the ground and that the ground distance to the start of the landing strip was 8000 feet.

63. What is Germaine's angle of depression to the start of the landing strip? **about 20.6°**

64. What is the distance between the plane in the air and the landing strip on the ground? **about 8544 ft**

★ 65. **FARMING** Leonard and Alecia are building a new feed storage system on their farm. The feed conveyor must be able to reach a range of heights. It has a length of 8 meters, and its angle of elevation can be adjusted from 20° to 5°. Under these conditions, what range of heights is possible for an opening in the building through which feed can pass? **about 2.74 m to 0.7 m**

66. See margin.

66. **CRITICAL THINKING** An important trigonometric identity is $\sin^2 A + \cos^2 A = 1$. Use the sine and cosine ratios and the Pythagorean Theorem to prove this identity.

67.  Answer the question that was posed at the beginning of the lesson. **See margin.**

How are trigonometric ratios used in surveying?

Include the following in your answer:
- an explanation of how trigonometric ratios are used to measure the height of a mountain, and
- any additional information you need to know about the point from which you are measuring in order to find the altitude of a mountain.

Standardized Test Practice
Ⓐ Ⓑ Ⓒ Ⓓ

For Exercises 68 and 69, use the figure at the right.

68. *RT* is equal to *TS*. What is *RS*? **A**

Ⓐ $2\sqrt{6}$ Ⓑ $2\sqrt{3}$ Ⓒ $4\sqrt{3}$ Ⓓ $2\sqrt{2}$

69. What is the measure of $\angle Q$? **D**

Ⓐ 25°   Ⓑ 30°   Ⓒ 45°   Ⓓ 60°

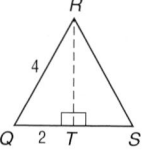

Maintain Your Skills

Mixed Review For each set of measures given, find the measures of the missing sides if $\triangle KLM \sim \triangle NOP$. *(Lesson 11-6)*

70. $k = 5,\ \ell = 3,\ m = 6,\ n = 10$ $o = 6,\ p = 12$

71. $\ell = 9,\ m = 3,\ n = 12,\ p = 4.5$
    $k = 8,\ o = 13.5$

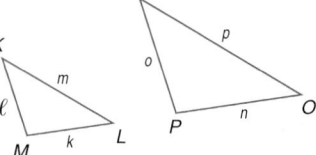

Find the possible values of a if the points with the given coordinates are the indicated distance apart. *(Lesson 11-5)*

72. $(9, 28), (a, -8); d = 39$ **−6 or 24**

73. $(3, a), (10, -1); d = \sqrt{65}$ **−5 or 3**

Find each product. *(Lesson 8-6)*

74. $c^2(c^2 + 3c)$ $c^4 + 3c^3$

75. $s(4s^2 - 9s + 12)$
    $4s^3 - 9s^2 + 12s$

76. $xy^2(2x^2 + 5xy - 7y^2)$
    $2x^3y^2 + 5x^2y^3 - 7xy^4$

Use substitution to solve each system of equations. *(Lesson 7-2)*

77. $a = 3b + 2$ **(11, 3)**
    $4a - 7b = 23$

78. $p + q = 10$ **(3, 7)**
    $3p - 2q = -5$

79. $3r + 6s = 0$ **(−2, 1)**
    $-4r - 10s = -2$

Reading Mathematics

The Language of Mathematics

The language of mathematics is a specific one, but it borrows from everyday language, scientific language, and world languages. To find a word's correct meaning, you will need to be aware of some confusing aspects of language.

Confusing Aspect	Words
Some words are used in English and in mathematics, but have distinct meanings.	factor, **leg**, prime, power, **rationalize**
Some words are used in English and in mathematics, but the mathematical meaning is more precise.	difference, even, **similar**, slope
Some words are used in science and in mathematics, but the meanings are different.	divide, **radical**, solution, variable
Some words are only used in mathematics.	decimal, **hypotenuse**, integer, quotient
Some words have more than one mathematical meaning.	base, **degree**, range, round, square
Sometimes several words come from the same root word.	polygon and polynomial, **radical** and **radicand**
Some mathematical words sound like English words.	**cosine** and cosign, **sine** and sign, **sum** and some
Some words are often abbreviated, but you must use the whole word when you read them.	**cos** for cosine, **sin** for sine, **tan** for tangent

Words in boldface are in this chapter.

Reading to Learn 1–3. See pp. 639A–639B.

1. How do the mathematical meanings of the following words compare to the everyday meanings?

    a. factor   **b.** leg   **c.** rationalize

2. State two mathematical definitions for each word. Give an example for each definition.

    a. degree   **b.** range   **c.** round

3. Each word below is shown with its root word and the root word's meaning. Find three additional words that come from the same root.

    a. domain, from the root word *domus*, which means house

    b. radical, from the root word *radix*, which means root

    c. similar, from the root word *similis*, which means like

Getting Started

Have students think of words that have more than one meaning. As students respond, make a list of the words on the chalkboard along with their multiple definitions.

Teach

- Place students in small groups. Assign each group several of the words listed in this activity to define. Have students use their textbooks, dictionaries, or the Internet to find the definitions. Then, as you discuss each group of words, ask the groups to give the definitions.

Assess

Study Notebook

Ask students to summarize what they have learned about the language of mathematics.

ELL English Language Learners may benefit from writing key concepts from this activity in their Study Notebooks in their native language and then in English.

Vocabulary and Concept Check

- This alphabetical list of vocabulary terms in Chapter 11 includes a page reference where each term was introduced.

- **Assessment** A vocabulary test/review for Chapter 11 is available on p. 698 of the *Chapter 11 Resource Masters*.

Lesson-by-Lesson Review

For each lesson,

- the main ideas are summarized,

- additional examples review concepts, and

- practice exercises are provided.

Vocabulary PuzzleMaker

ELL The Vocabulary PuzzleMaker software improves students' mathematics vocabulary using four puzzle formats—crossword, scramble, word search using a word list, and word search using clues. Students can work on a computer screen or from a printed handout.

MindJogger Videoquizzes

ELL MindJogger Videoquizzes provide an alternative review of concepts presented in this chapter. Students work in teams in a game show format to gain points for correct answers. The questions are presented in three rounds.

Round 1 Concepts (5 questions)
Round 2 Skills (4 questions)
Round 3 Problem Solving (4 questions)

Vocabulary and Concept Check

angle of depression (p. 625)	hypotenuse (p. 605)	rationalizing the denominator (p. 588)
angle of elevation (p. 625)	leg (p. 605)	similar triangles (p. 616)
conjugate (p. 589)	Pythagorean triple (p. 606)	sine (p. 623)
cosine (p. 623)	radical equation (p. 598)	solve a triangle (p. 625)
Distance Formula (p. 611)	radical expression (p. 586)	tangent (p. 623)
extraneous solution (p. 599)	radicand (p. 586)	trigonometric ratios (p. 623)

State whether each sentence is *true* or *false*. If false, replace the underlined word, number, expression, or equation to make a true sentence.

1. The binomials $-3 + \sqrt{7}$ and $\underline{3 - \sqrt{7}}$ are conjugates. **false, $-3 - \sqrt{7}$**

2. In the expression $-4\sqrt{5}$, the radicand is $\underline{5}$. **true**

3. The sine of an acute angle of a right triangle is the measure of the opposite leg divided by the measure of the $\underline{\text{hypotenuse}}$. **true**

4. The $\underline{\text{longest}}$ side of a right triangle is the hypotenuse. **true**

5. After the first step in solving $\sqrt{3x + 19} = x + 3$, you would have $\underline{3x + 19 = x^2 + 9}$. **false, $3x + 19 = x^2 + 6x + 9$**

6. The two sides that form the right angle in a right triangle are called the $\underline{\text{legs}}$ of the triangle. **true**

7. The expression $\dfrac{2x\sqrt{3x}}{\sqrt{6y}}$ is in simplest radical form. **false, $\dfrac{x\sqrt{2xy}}{y}$**

8. A triangle with sides having measures of $\underline{25, 20, \text{ and } 15}$ is a right triangle. **true**

Lesson-by-Lesson Review

11-1 Simplifying Radical Expressions

See pages 586–592.

Concept Summary

- A radical expression is in simplest form when no radicands have perfect square factors other than 1, no radicands contain fractions, and no radicals appear in the denominator of a fraction.

Example Simplify $\dfrac{3}{5 - \sqrt{2}}$.

$$\frac{3}{5 - \sqrt{2}} = \frac{3}{5 - \sqrt{2}} \cdot \frac{5 + \sqrt{2}}{5 + \sqrt{2}} \quad \text{Multiply by } \frac{5 + \sqrt{2}}{5 + \sqrt{2}} \text{ to rationalize the denominator.}$$

$$= \frac{3(5) + 3\sqrt{2}}{5^2 - (\sqrt{2})^2} \quad (a - b)(a + b) = a^2 - b^2$$

$$= \frac{15 + 3\sqrt{2}}{25 - 2} \quad (\sqrt{2})^2 = 2$$

$$= \frac{15 + 3\sqrt{2}}{23} \quad \text{Simplify.}$$

 www.algebra1.com/vocabulary_revie

FOLDABLES™ Study Organizer

Have students flip back through their Foldables to make sure they have included information for every lesson.

Encourage students to refer to their Foldables while completing the Study Guide and Review and use them in preparing for the Chapter Test.

For more information about Foldables, see *Teaching Mathematics with Foldables.*

Exercises Simplify. *See Examples 1–5 on pages 586–589.*

9. $\sqrt{\dfrac{60}{y^2}}$ $\dfrac{2\sqrt{15}}{|y|}$ 10. $\sqrt{44a^2b^5}$ $2|a|b^2\sqrt{11b}$ 11. $(3-2\sqrt{12})^2$ $57-24\sqrt{3}$

12. $\dfrac{9}{3+\sqrt{2}}$ $\dfrac{27-9\sqrt{2}}{7}$ 13. $\dfrac{2\sqrt{7}}{3\sqrt{5}+5\sqrt{3}}$ 14. $\dfrac{\sqrt{3a^3b^4}}{\sqrt{8ab^{10}}}$ $\dfrac{|a|\sqrt{6}}{4|b^3|}$

$\dfrac{5\sqrt{21}-3\sqrt{35}}{15}$

11-2 Operations with Radical Expressions

See pages 593–597.

Concept Summary

- Radical expressions with like radicands can be added or subtracted.
- Use the FOIL Method to multiply radical expressions.

Examples 1 Simplify $\sqrt{6}-\sqrt{54}+3\sqrt{12}+5\sqrt{3}$.

$\sqrt{6}-\sqrt{54}+3\sqrt{12}+5\sqrt{3}$

$=\sqrt{6}-\sqrt{3^2\cdot 6}+3\sqrt{2^2\cdot 3}+5\sqrt{3}$ Simplify radicands.

$=\sqrt{6}-(\sqrt{3^2}\cdot\sqrt{6})+3(\sqrt{2^2}\cdot\sqrt{3})+5\sqrt{3}$ Product Property of Square Roots

$=\sqrt{6}-3\sqrt{6}+3(2\sqrt{3})+5\sqrt{3}$ Evaluate square roots.

$=\sqrt{6}-3\sqrt{6}+6\sqrt{3}+5\sqrt{3}$ Simplify.

$=-2\sqrt{6}+11\sqrt{3}$ Add like radicands.

2 Find $(2\sqrt{3}-\sqrt{5})(\sqrt{10}+4\sqrt{6})$.

$(2\sqrt{3}-\sqrt{5})(\sqrt{10}+4\sqrt{6})$

     First terms   **Outer terms**   **Inner terms**   **Last terms**

$=(2\sqrt{3})(\sqrt{10})+(2\sqrt{3})(4\sqrt{6})+(-\sqrt{5})(\sqrt{10})+(-\sqrt{5})(4\sqrt{6})$

$=2\sqrt{30}+8\sqrt{18}-\sqrt{50}-4\sqrt{30}$ Multiply.

$=2\sqrt{30}+8\sqrt{3^2\cdot 2}-\sqrt{5^2\cdot 2}-4\sqrt{30}$ Prime factorization

$=2\sqrt{30}+24\sqrt{2}-5\sqrt{2}-4\sqrt{30}$ Simplify.

$=-2\sqrt{30}+19\sqrt{2}$ Combine like terms.

Exercises Simplify each expression. *See Examples 1 and 2 on pages 593 and 594.*

15. $2\sqrt{3}+8\sqrt{5}-3\sqrt{5}+3\sqrt{3}$ 16. $2\sqrt{6}-\sqrt{48}$ $2\sqrt{6}-4\sqrt{3}$

17. $4\sqrt{27}+6\sqrt{48}$ $36\sqrt{3}$ 18. $4\sqrt{7k}-7\sqrt{7k}+2\sqrt{7k}$ $-\sqrt{7k}$

19. $5\sqrt{18}-3\sqrt{112}-3\sqrt{98}$ 20. $\sqrt{8}+\sqrt{\dfrac{1}{8}}$ $\dfrac{9\sqrt{2}}{4}$

15. $5\sqrt{3}+5\sqrt{5}$ 19. $-6\sqrt{2}-12\sqrt{7}$

Find each product. *See Example 3 on page 594.* 24. $18\sqrt{10}+30+6\sqrt{2}+2\sqrt{5}$

21. $\sqrt{2}(3+3\sqrt{3})$ $3\sqrt{2}+3\sqrt{6}$ 22. $\sqrt{5}(2\sqrt{5}-\sqrt{7})$ $10-\sqrt{35}$

23. $(\sqrt{3}-\sqrt{2})(2\sqrt{2}+\sqrt{3})$ $\sqrt{6}-1$ 24. $(6\sqrt{5}+2)(3\sqrt{2}+\sqrt{5})$

Answers

31. 34

32. $2\sqrt{34} \approx 11.66$

33. $\sqrt{115} \approx 10.72$

34. $4\sqrt{195} \approx 55.86$

35. 24

36. 2

11-3 Radical Equations

See pages 598–603.

Concept Summary

- Solve radical equations by isolating the radical on one side of the equation. Square each side of the equation to eliminate the radical.

Example   Solve $\sqrt{5 - 4x} - 6 = 7$.

$$\sqrt{5 - 4x} - 6 = 7 \qquad \text{Original equation}$$

$$\sqrt{5 - 4x} = 13 \qquad \text{Add 6 to each side.}$$

$$5 - 4x = 169 \qquad \text{Square each side.}$$

$$-4x = 164 \qquad \text{Subtract 5 from each side.}$$

$$x = -41 \qquad \text{Divide each side by } -4.$$

Exercises   Solve each equation. Check your solution.   *See Examples 2 and 3 on page 599.*

25. $10 + 2\sqrt{b} = 0$ **no solution**   **26.** $\sqrt{a + 4} = 6$ **32**   **27.** $\sqrt{7x - 1} = 5$ $\dfrac{26}{7}$

28. $\sqrt{\dfrac{4a}{3}} - 2 = 0$ **3**   **29.** $\sqrt{x + 4} = x - 8$ **12**   **30.** $\sqrt{3x - 14} + x = 6$ **5**

11-4 The Pythagorean Theorem

See pages 605–610.

Concept Summary

- If a and b are the measures of the legs of a right triangle and c is the measure of the hypotenuse, then $c^2 = a^2 + b^2$.

- If a and b are measures of the shorter sides of a triangle, c is the measure of the longest side, and $c^2 = a^2 + b^2$, then the triangle is a right triangle.

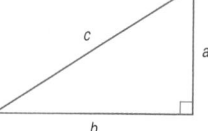

Example   Find the length of the missing side.

$$c^2 = a^2 + b^2 \qquad \text{Pythagorean Theorem}$$

$$25^2 = 15^2 + b^2 \qquad c = 25 \text{ and } a = 15$$

$$625 = 225 + b^2 \qquad \text{Evaluate squares.}$$

$$400 = b^2 \qquad \text{Subtract 225 from each side.}$$

$$20 = b \qquad \text{Take the square root of each side.}$$

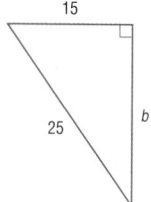

Exercises   If c is the measure of the hypotenuse of a right triangle, find each missing measure. If necessary, round answers to the nearest hundredth.
See Example 2 on page 606.   **31–36. See margin.**

31. $a = 30, b = 16, c = ?$ **32.** $a = 6, b = 10, c = ?$ **33.** $a = 10, c = 15, b = ?$

34. $b = 4, c = 56, a = ?$ **35.** $a = 18, c = 30, b = ?$ **36.** $a = 1.2, b = 1.6, c = ?$

Determine whether the following side measures form right triangles.
See Example 4 on page 607.

37. 9, 16, 20   **no**   **38.** 20, 21, 29   **yes**   **39.** 9, 40, 41   **yes**   **40.** 18, $\sqrt{24}$, 30   **no**

11-5 The Distance Formula

See pages 611–615.

Concept Summary

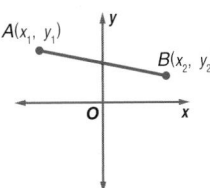

- The distance d between any two points with coordinates (x_1, y_1) and (x_2, y_2) is given by $d = \sqrt{(x_2 - x_1)^2 + (y_2 - y_1)^2}$.

Example Find the distance between the points with coordinates $(-5, 1)$ and $(1, 5)$.

$$d = \sqrt{(x_2 - x_1)^2 + (y_2 - y_1)^2} \quad \text{Distance Formula}$$
$$= \sqrt{(1 - (-5))^2 + (5 - 1)^2} \quad (x_1, y_1) = (-5, 1) \text{ and } (x_2, y_2) = (1, 5)$$
$$= \sqrt{6^2 + 4^2} \quad \text{Simplify.}$$
$$= \sqrt{36 + 16} \quad \text{Evaluate squares.}$$
$$= \sqrt{52} \text{ or about 7.21 units} \quad \text{Simplify.}$$

42. $\sqrt{58} \approx 7.62$ 43. $\sqrt{205} \approx 14.32$

Exercises Find the distance between each pair of points whose coordinates are given. Express in simplest radical form and as decimal approximations rounded to the nearest hundredth if necessary.   *See Example 1 on page 611.*

41. $(9, -2), (1, 13)$ **17**
42. $(4, 2), (7, 9)$
43. $(4, -6), (-2, 7)$
44. $(2\sqrt{5}, 9), (4\sqrt{5}, 3)$
    $2\sqrt{14} \approx 7.48$
45. $(4, 8), (-7, 12)$
    $\sqrt{137} \approx 11.70$
46. $(-2, 6), (5, 11)$
    $\sqrt{74} \approx 8.60$

Find the value of a if the points with the given coordinates are the indicated distance apart.   *See Example 3 on page 612.*

47. $(-3, 2), (1, a); d = 5$ **5 or −1**
48. $(1, 1), (4, a); d = 5$ **5 or −3**
49. $(6, -2), (5, a); d = \sqrt{145}$ **10 or −14**
50. $(5, -2), (a, -3); d = \sqrt{170}$ **18 or −8**

11-6 Similar Triangles

See pages 616–621.

Concept Summary

- Similar triangles have congruent corresponding angles and proportional corresponding sides.
- If $\triangle ABC \sim \triangle DEF$, then $\dfrac{AB}{DE} = \dfrac{BC}{EF} = \dfrac{AC}{DF}$.

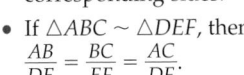

Example Find the measure of side a if the two triangles are similar.

$$\frac{10}{5} = \frac{6}{a} \quad \text{Corresponding sides of similar triangles are proportional.}$$
$$10a = 30 \quad \text{Find the cross products.}$$
$$a = 3 \quad \text{Divide each side by 10.}$$

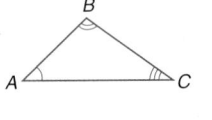

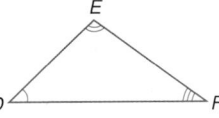

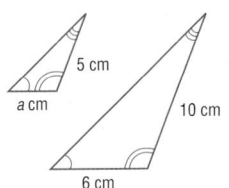

Study Guide and Review

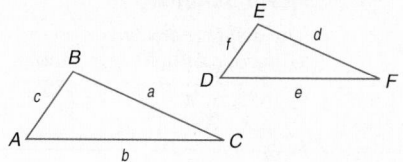

For More ...
- Extra Practice, see pages 844–846.
- Mixed Problem Solving, see page 863.

Answers

51. $d = \frac{45}{8}$, $e = \frac{27}{4}$

52. $d = 9.6$, $e = 7.2$

53. $b = \frac{44}{3}$, $d = 6$

54. $a = 17.5$, $e = 8$

Exercises For each set of measures given, find the measures of the remaining sides if $\triangle ABC \sim \triangle DEF$. *See Example 2 on page 617.* **51–54. See margin.**

51. $c = 16$, $b = 12$, $a = 10$, $f = 9$

52. $a = 8$, $c = 10$, $b = 6$, $f = 12$

53. $c = 12$, $f = 9$, $a = 8$, $e = 11$

54. $b = 20$, $d = 7$, $f = 6$, $c = 15$

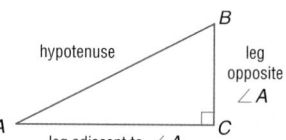

11-7 Trigonometric Ratios

See pages 623–630.

Concept Summary

Three common trigonometric ratios are sine, cosine, and tangent.

- $\sin A = \dfrac{BC}{AB}$
- $\cos A = \dfrac{AC}{AB}$
- $\tan A = \dfrac{BC}{AC}$

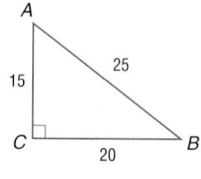

Example Find the sine, cosine, and tangent of $\angle A$. Round to the nearest ten thousandth.

$$\sin A = \frac{\text{opposite leg}}{\text{hypotenuse}}$$
$$= \frac{20}{25} \text{ or } 0.8000$$

$$\cos A = \frac{\text{adjacent leg}}{\text{hypotenuse}}$$
$$= \frac{15}{25} \text{ or } 0.6000$$

$$\tan A = \frac{\text{opposite leg}}{\text{adjacent leg}}$$
$$= \frac{20}{15} \text{ or } 1.3333$$

Exercises For $\triangle ABC$, find each value of each trigonometric ratio to the nearest ten thousandth. *See Example 1 on page 624.*

55. $\cos B$ **0.5283**

56. $\tan A$ **0.6222**

57. $\sin B$ **0.8491**

58. $\cos A$ **0.8491**

59. $\tan B$ **1.6071**

60. $\sin A$ **0.5283**

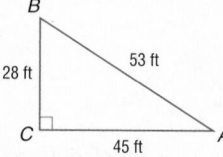

Use a calculator to find the measure of each angle to the nearest degree.
See Example 3 on page 624.

61. $\tan M = 0.8043$ **39°**   **62.** $\sin T = 0.1212$ **7°**   **63.** $\cos B = 0.9781$ **12°**

64. $\cos F = 0.7443$ **42°**   **65.** $\sin A = 0.4540$ **27°**   **66.** $\tan Q = 5.9080$ **80°**

Vocabulary and Concepts

Match each term and its definition.

1. measure of the opposite leg divided by the measure of the hypotenuse **b**
2. measure of the adjacent leg divided by the measure of the hypotenuse **a**
3. measure of the opposite leg divided by the measure of the adjacent leg **c**

a. cosine
b. sine
c. tangent

Skills and Applications

Simplify.

4. $2\sqrt{27} + \sqrt{63} - 4\sqrt{3}$ **$2\sqrt{3} + 3\sqrt{7}$**

5. $\sqrt{6} + \sqrt{\dfrac{2}{3}}$ **$\dfrac{4\sqrt{6}}{3}$**

6. $\sqrt{112x^4y^6}$ **$4x^2|y^3|\sqrt{7}$**

7. $\sqrt{\dfrac{10}{3}} \cdot \sqrt{\dfrac{4}{30}}$ **$\dfrac{2}{3}$**

8. $\sqrt{6}(4 + \sqrt{12})$ **$4\sqrt{6} + 6\sqrt{2}$**

9. $(1 - \sqrt{3})(3 + \sqrt{2})$ **$3 + \sqrt{2} - 3\sqrt{3} - \sqrt{6}$**

Solve each equation. Check your solution.

10. $\sqrt{10x} = 20$ **40**
11. $\sqrt{4s + 1} = 11$ **25**
12. $\sqrt{4x + 1} = 5$ **6**
13. $x = \sqrt{-6x - 8}$ **no solution**
14. $x = \sqrt{5x + 14}$ **7**
15. $\sqrt{4x - 3} = 6 - x$ **3**

If c is the measure of the hypotenuse of a right triangle, find each missing measure. If necessary, round to the nearest hundredth.

16. $a = 8, b = 10, c = ?$ **16. $\sqrt{164} \approx 12.81$**
17. $a = 6\sqrt{2}, c = 12, b = ?$ **17. $\sqrt{72} \approx 8.49$**
18. $b = 13, c = 17, a = ?$ **18. $\sqrt{120} \approx 10.95$**

Find the distance between each pair of points whose coordinates are given. Express in simplest radical form and as decimal approximations rounded to the nearest hundredth if necessary.

19. $(4, 7), (4, -2)$ **9**
20. $(-1, 1), (1, -5)$ **$2\sqrt{10} \approx 6.32$**
21. $(-9, 2), (21, 7)$ **$5\sqrt{37} \approx 30.41$**

For each set of measures given, find the measures of the missing sides if $\triangle ABC \sim \triangle JKH$.

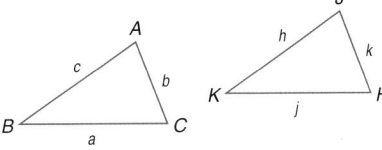

22. $c = 20, h = 15, k = 16, j = 12$ **$a = 16, b = \dfrac{64}{3}$**
23. $c = 12, b = 13, a = 6, h = 10$ **$j = 5, k = \dfrac{65}{6}$**
24. $k = 5, c = 6.5, b = 7.5, a = 4.5$ **$h = 4.\overline{3}, j = 3$**
25. $h = 1\dfrac{1}{2}, c = 4\dfrac{1}{2}, k = 2\dfrac{1}{4}, a = 3$ **$b = 6\dfrac{3}{4}, j = 1$**

Solve each right triangle. State the side lengths to the nearest tenth and the angle measures to the nearest degree.

26. 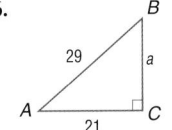 $m\angle A \approx 44°$ $m\angle B \approx 46°$ $a = 20$

27. 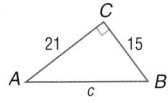 $m\angle A \approx 36°$ $m\angle B \approx 54°$ $c \approx 25.8$

28. 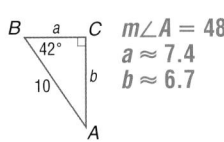 $m\angle A = 48°$ $a \approx 7.4$ $b \approx 6.7$

29. **SPORTS** A hiker leaves her camp in the morning. How far is she from camp after walking 9 miles due west and then 12 miles due north? **15 mi**

30. **STANDARDIZED TEST PRACTICE** Find the area of the rectangle. **B**

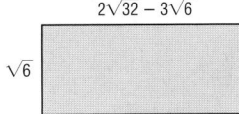

Ⓐ $16\sqrt{2} - 4\sqrt{6}$ units^2
Ⓑ $16\sqrt{3} - 18$ units^2
Ⓒ $32\sqrt{3} - 18$ units^2
Ⓓ $2\sqrt{32} - 18$ units^2

Assessment Options

Vocabulary Test A vocabulary test/review for Chapter 11 can be found on p. 698 of the *Chapter 11 Resource Masters*.

Chapter Tests There are six Chapter 11 Tests and an Open-Ended Assessment task available in the *Chapter 11 Resource Masters*.

Chapter 11 Tests			
Form	Type	Level	Pages
1	MC	basic	685–686
2A	MC	average	687–688
2B	MC	average	689–690
2C	FR	average	691–692
2D	FR	average	693–694
3	FR	advanced	695–696

MC = multiple-choice questions
FR = free-response questions

Open-Ended Assessment
Performance tasks for Chapter 11 can be found on p. 697 of the *Chapter 11 Resource Masters*. A sample scoring rubric for these tasks appears on p. A27.

ExamView® Pro
Use the networkable **ExamView® Pro** to:

- Create **multiple versions** of tests.
- Create **modified** tests for *Inclusion* students.
- **Edit** existing questions and **add** your own questions.
- Use built-in **state curriculum correlations** to create tests aligned with state standards.
- Change **English** tests to **Spanish** and vice versa.

Portfolio Suggestion

Introduction In this chapter, students are introduced to ways in which professionals such as architects and surveyors can use math to solve problems.

Ask Students Pick a profession such as architecture, surveying, or engineering and research to find out how triangles, ratios, or trigonometric ratios are used in the field. Write a short report in which you explain how these concepts are used, along with examples.

These two pages contain practice questions in the various formats that can be found on the most frequently given standardized tests.

A practice answer sheet for these two pages can be found on p. A1 of the *Chapter 11 Resource Masters*.

Standardized Test Practice
Student Recording Sheet, p. A1

Part 1 Multiple Choice

Select the best answer from the choices given and fill in the corresponding oval.

1 Ⓐ Ⓑ Ⓒ Ⓓ   4 Ⓐ Ⓑ Ⓒ Ⓓ   7 Ⓐ Ⓑ Ⓒ Ⓓ
2 Ⓐ Ⓑ Ⓒ Ⓓ   5 Ⓐ Ⓑ Ⓒ Ⓓ   8 Ⓐ Ⓑ Ⓒ Ⓓ
3 Ⓐ Ⓑ Ⓒ Ⓓ   6 Ⓐ Ⓑ Ⓒ Ⓓ   9 Ⓐ Ⓑ Ⓒ Ⓓ

Part 2 Short Response/Grid In

Solve the problem and write your answer in the blank.
For Questions 13 and 15, also enter your answer by writing each number or symbol in a box. Then fill in the corresponding oval for that number or symbol.

10 _____   13   15
11 _____
12 _____
13 _____ (grid in)
14 _____
15 _____ (grid in)
16 _____
17 _____

Part 3 Extended Response

Record your answers for Questions 18–21 on the back of this paper.

Additional Practice

See pp. 703–704 in the *Chapter 11 Resource Masters* for additional standardized test practice.

Part 1 Multiple Choice

Record your answers on the answer sheet provided by your teacher or on a sheet of paper.

1. Which equation describes the data in the table? (Lesson 4-8) **D**

x	−5	−2	1	4
y	11	5	−1	−7

Ⓐ $y = x - 6$ Ⓑ $y = 2x - 1$
Ⓒ $y = 2x + 1$ Ⓓ $y = -2x + 1$

2. The length of a rectangle is 6 feet more than the width. The perimeter is 92 feet. Which system of equations will determine the length in feet ℓ and the width in feet w of the rectangle? (Lesson 7-2) **C**

Ⓐ $w = \ell + 6$
  $2\ell + 2w = 92$

Ⓑ $\ell + w = 6$
  $\ell w = 92$

Ⓒ $\ell = w + 6$
  $2\ell + 2w = 92$

Ⓓ $\ell - w = 6$
  $\ell + w = 92$

3. A highway resurfacing project and a bridge repair project will cost $2,500,000 altogether. The bridge repair project will cost $200,000 less than twice the cost of the highway resurfacing. How much will the highway resurfacing project cost? (Lesson 7-2) **C**

Ⓐ $450,000   Ⓑ $734,000
Ⓒ $900,000   Ⓓ $1,600,000

4. If 32,800,000 is expressed in the form 3.28×10^n, what is the value of n? (Lesson 8-3) **C**

Ⓐ 5   Ⓑ 6
Ⓒ 7   Ⓓ 8

5. What are the solutions of the equation $x^2 + 7x - 18 = 0$? (Lesson 9-4) **A**

Ⓐ 2 or −9   Ⓑ −2 or 9
Ⓒ −2 or −9   Ⓓ 2 or 9

6. The function $g = t^2 - t$ represents the total number of games played by t teams in a sports league in which each team plays each of the other teams twice. The Metro League plays a total of 132 games. How many teams are in the league? (Lesson 9-4) **B**

Ⓐ 11   Ⓑ 12
Ⓒ 22   Ⓓ 33

7. One leg of a right triangle is 4 inches longer than the other leg. The hypotenuse is 20 inches long. What is the length of the shorter leg? (Lesson 11-4) **B**

Ⓐ 10 in.   Ⓑ 12 in.
Ⓒ 16 in.   Ⓓ 18 in.

8. What is the distance from one corner of the garden to the opposite corner? (Lesson 11-4) **A**

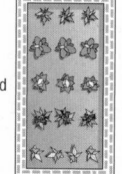

Ⓐ 13 yards
Ⓑ 14 yards
Ⓒ 15 yards
Ⓓ 17 yards

9. How many points in the coordinate plane are equidistant from both the x- and y-axes and are 5 units from the origin? (Lesson 11-5) **D**

Ⓐ 0   Ⓑ 1
Ⓒ 2   Ⓓ 4

Test-Taking Tip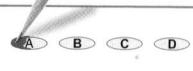

Questions 7, 21 and 22
Be sure that you know and understand the Pythagorean Theorem. References to right angles, the diagonal of a rectangle, or the hypotenuse of a triangle indicate that you may need to use the Pythagorean Theorem to find the answer to an item.

ExamView® Pro

Special banks of standardized test questions similar to those on the SAT, ACT, TIMSS 8, NAEP 8, and Algebra 1 End-of-Course tests can be found on this CD-ROM.

Preparing for Standardized Tests
For test-taking strategies and more
practice, see pages 867–884.

Part 2 Short Response/Grid In

Record your answers on the answer sheet
provided by your teacher or on a sheet of
paper.

10. A line is parallel to the line represented by
the equation $\frac{1}{2}y + \frac{3}{2}x + 4 = 0$. What is the
slope of the parallel line? (Lesson 5-6) **−3**

11. Graph the solution of the system of linear
inequalities $2x - y > 2$ and $3x + 2y < -4$.
(Lesson 6-6) **See margin.**

12. The sum of two integers is 66. The second
integer is 18 more than half of the first. What
are the integers? (Lesson 7-2) **32 and 34**

13. The function $h(t) = -16t^2 + v_0 t + h_0$
describes the height in feet above the
ground $h(t)$ of an object thrown vertically
from a height of h_0 feet, with an initial
velocity of v_0 feet per second, if there is no
air friction and t is the time in seconds since
the object was thrown. A ball is thrown
upward from a 100-foot tower at a velocity
of 60 feet per second. How many seconds
will it take for the ball to reach the ground?
(Lesson 9-5) **5**

14. Find all values of x that satisfy the equation
$x^2 - 8x + 6 = 0$. Approximate irrational
numbers to the nearest hundredth.
(Lesson 10-4) **7.16 and 0.84**

15. Simplify the expression $\sqrt[3]{3\sqrt{81}}$.
(Lesson 11-1) **3**

16. Simplify the expression $\left(x^{\frac{3}{2}}\right)^{\frac{4}{3}}\left(\frac{\sqrt{x}}{x}\right)$.
(Lesson 11-1) $x^{\frac{3}{2}}$ **or** $x\sqrt{x}$

17. The area of a rectangle is 64. The length is
$\frac{x^3}{x+1}$, and the width is $\frac{x+1}{x}$. What is x?
(Lesson 11-3) **8 or −8**

www.algebra1.com/standardized_test

Part 3 Extended Response

Record your answers on a sheet of paper.
Show your work.

18. A rectangle is $5\sqrt{7} + \sqrt{3}$ centimeters
long and $7\sqrt{7} - 2\sqrt{3}$ centimeters wide.
(Lesson 11-2)

　a. Find the perimeter of the rectangle in
　　simplest form. $24\sqrt{17} - 2\sqrt{3}$ **cm**

　b. Find the area of the rectangle in simplest
　　form. $239 - 3\sqrt{21}$ **cm²**

19. Haley hikes 3 miles north, 7 miles east, and
then 6 miles north again. (Lesson 11-4)

　a. Draw a diagram showing the direction
　　and distance of each segment of Haley's
　　hike. Label Haley's starting point, her
　　ending point, and the distance, in miles,
　　of each segment of her hike. **See margin.**

　b. To the nearest tenth of a mile, how far (in
　　a straight line) is Haley from her starting
　　point? **11.4 mi**
　　　　　　　　　　　c. See margin

　c. How did your diagram help you to find
　　Haley's distance from her starting point?

　d. Describe the direction and distance of
　　Haley's return trip back to her starting
　　position if she used the same trail. **Haley
　　would hike 6 miles south, 7 miles west, and 3 miles south.**

20. Suppose a coordinate grid is superimposed
on a city. Ben lives at $(-5, -8)$, and Sophie
lives at $(9, 1)$. Each grid unit is equal to
0.13 mile. (Lessons 11-4 and 11-5)

　a. Describe in grid units one way to travel
　　from Sophie's to Ben's.

　b. Find the distance between their two
　　houses. **about 2.16 mi**

　c. Whose house is closer to a bakery located
　　at $(-1, 5)$? **Sophie's**

21. Janelle is swimming in the ocean and sees
a cliff diver who is about to dive into the
water. The diver is 70 feet above the water,
and the angle of elevation from Janelle to
the diver is 22°. (Lesson 11-7)

　a. How far is Janelle from the diver
　　standing on top of the cliff? Round to
　　the nearest tenth. **186.9 ft**

　b. How far is Janelle from the diver when
　　he enters the water? Round to the nearest
　　tenth. **173.3 ft**

Chapter 11 Standardized Test Practice **639**

Evaluating Extended Response Questions

Extended Response questions
are graded by using a multilevel
rubric that guides you in
assessing a student's knowledge
of a particular concept.

Goal: Students use right
triangles to find a distance.

Sample Scoring Rubric: The following rubric is a sample scoring
device. You may wish to add
more detail to this sample to meet
your individual scoring needs.

Score	Criteria
4	A correct solution that is supported by well-developed, accurate explanations
3	A generally correct solution, but may contain minor flaws in reasoning or computation
2	A partially correct interpretation and/or solution to the problem
1	A correct solution with no supporting evidence or explanation
0	An incorrect solution indicating no mathematical understanding of the concept or task, or no solution is given

---

Answers

11.
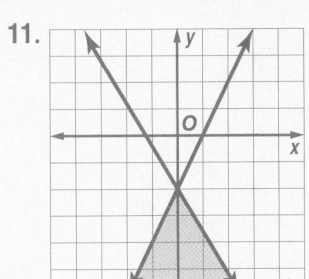

19a.
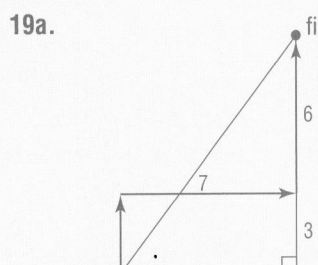

13. (20a.) Sample answer: Walk 9 blocks
south. Turn right. Walk 14 blocks west.

19c. The sketch shows that the
distance she is from her
starting point is the length of
the hypotenuse of a right
triangle with legs 7 mi and
9 mi long.

**Page 604, Follow-Up to Lesson 11-3
Graphing Calculator Investigation**

1. $\{x|x \geq 0\}$; shifted up 1

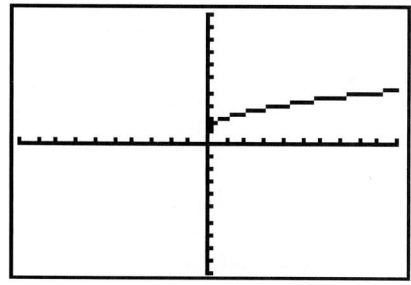

$[-10, 10]$ scl: 1 by $[-10, 10]$ scl: 1

2. $\{x|x \geq 0\}$; shifted down 3

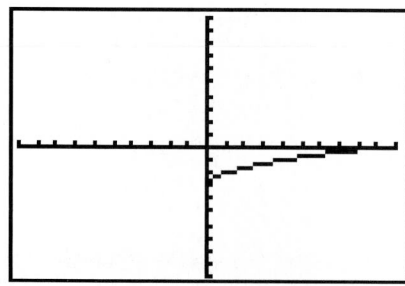

$[-10, 10]$ scl: 1 by $[-10, 10]$ scl: 1

3. $\{x|x \geq -2\}$; shifted left 2

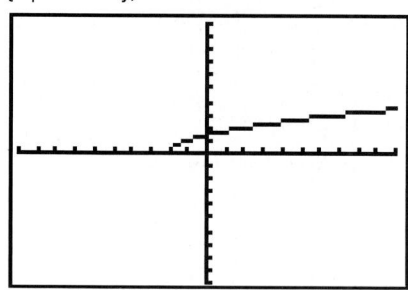

$[-10, 10]$ scl: 1 by $[-10, 10]$ scl: 1

4. $\{x|x \geq 5\}$; shifted right 5

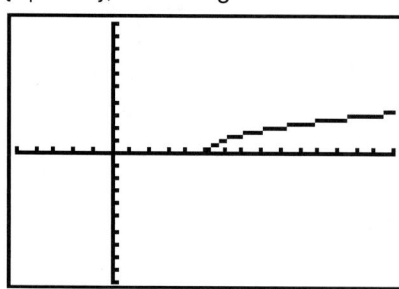

$[-5, 15]$ scl: 1 by $[-10, 10]$ scl: 1

5. $\{x|x \leq 0\}$; reflected across y-axis

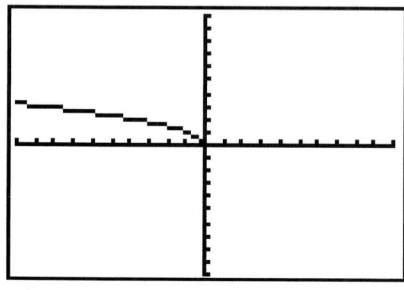

$[-10, 10]$ scl: 1 by $[-10, 10]$ scl: 1

6. $\{x|x \geq 0\}$; expanded

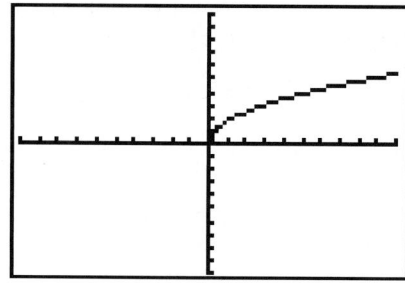

$[-10, 10]$ scl: 1 by $[-10, 10]$ scl: 1

7. $\{x|x \geq 0\}$; reflected across x-axis

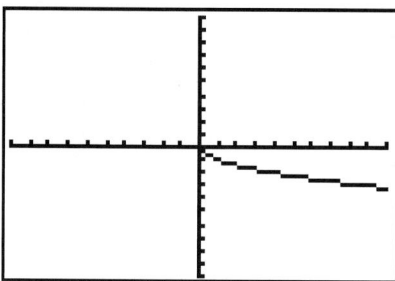

$[-10, 10]$ scl: 1 by $[-10, 10]$ scl: 1

8. $\{x|x \leq 1\}$; reflected across y-axis, shifted right 1, up 6

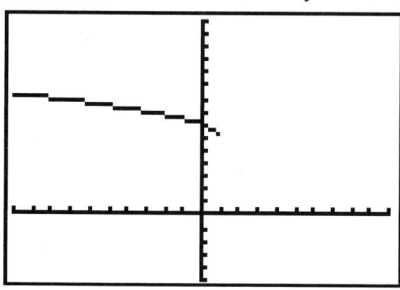

$[-10, 10]$ scl: 1 by $[-5, 15]$ scl: 1

9. $\{x|x \geq -2.5\}$; shifted left 2.5, down 4

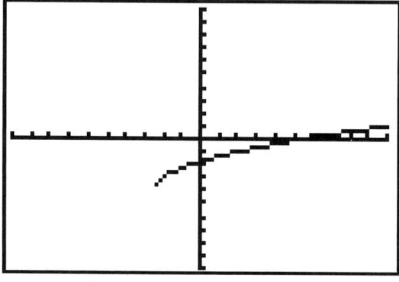

$[-10, 10]$ scl: 1 by $[-10, 10]$ scl: 1

Pages 612–615, Lesson 11-5

44. You can determine the distance between two points by forming a right triangle. Drawing a line through each point parallel to the axes forms the legs of the triangle. The hypotenuse of this triangle is the distance between the two points. You can find the lengths of each leg by subtracting the corresponding *x*- and *y*-coordinates, then use the Pythagorean Theorem. Answers should include the following.

- You can draw lines parallel to the axes through the two points that will intersect at another point forming a right triangle. The length of a leg of a triangle is the difference in the *x*- or *y*-coordinates. The length of the hypotenuse is the distance between the points. Using the Pythagorean Theorem to solve for the hypotenuse, you have the Distance Formula.

- The points are on a vertical line so you can calculate distance by determining the absolute difference between the *y*-coordinates.

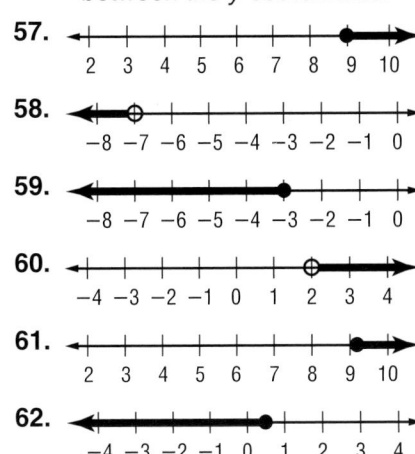

Pages 618–621, Lesson 11-6

2. Sample answer: $\triangle ABC \sim \triangle DEF$

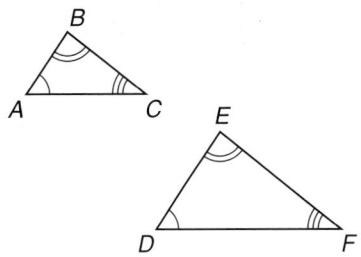

corresponding angles	corresponding sides
$\angle A$ and $\angle D$	$\overline{AB}$ and $\overline{DE}$
$\angle B$ and $\angle E$	$\overline{BC}$ and $\overline{EF}$
$\angle C$ and $\angle F$	$\overline{AC}$ and $\overline{DF}$

Page 631, Reading Mathematics

1a. Sample answer: A circumstance that brings about a result; any of two or more quantities that form a product when multiplied together; the quantities bring about a result, a product.

1b. Sample answer: The legs of an animal support the animal; one of the two shorter sides of a right triangle; the legs of a triangle support the hypotenuse.

1c. Sample answer: To devise rational explanations for one's acts without being aware that these are not the real motives; to remove the radical signs from an expression without changing its value; to justify an action without changing its intent.

2a. Sample answer: Rank as determined by the sum of a term's exponents; the degree of x^2y^2 is 4. $\frac{1}{360}$ of a circle; a semicircle measures 180°.

2b. Sample answer: The difference between the greatest and least values in a set of data; the range of 2, 3, 6 is $6 - 2$ or 4. The set of all *y*-values in a function; the range of {(2, 6), (1, 3)} is {6, 3}.

2c. Sample answer: Circular or spherical; circles are round. To abbreviate a number by replacing its ending digits with zeros; 235,611 rounded to the nearest hundred is 235,600.

3a. Sample answer: dome, domestic, domicile

3b. Sample answer: eradicate, radicand, radius

3c. Sample answer: simile, similarity, similitude

Rational Expressions and Equations

Chapter Overview and Pacing

Year-long and two-year pacing: pages T20–T21.

LESSON OBJECTIVES	PACING (days)			
	Regular		Block	
	Basic/Average	Advanced	Basic/Average	Advanced
12-1 Inverse Variation (pp. 642–647) • Graph inverse variations. • Solve problems involving inverse variation.	1	1	0.5	0.5
12-2 Rational Expressions (pp. 648–654) • Identify values excluded from the domain of a rational expression. • Simplify rational expressions. *Follow-Up:* Use a graphing calculator to check simplified rational expressions.	1	2 (with 11-2 Follow-Up)	0.5	1.5
12-3 Multiplying Rational Expressions (pp. 655–659) • Multiply rational expressions. • Use dimensional analysis with multiplication.	1	1	0.5	0.5
12-4 Dividing Rational Expressions (pp. 660–664) • Divide rational expressions. • Use dimensional analysis with division.	1	2	0.5	1
12-5 Dividing Polynomials (pp. 666–671) • Divide a polynomial by a monomial. • Divide a polynomial by a binomial.	1	2	0.5	1
12-6 Rational Expressions with Like Denominators (pp. 672–677) • Add rational expressions with like denominators. • Subtract rational expressions with like denominators.	1	1	0.5	0.5
12-7 Rational Expressions with Unlike Denominators (pp. 678–683) • Add rational expressions with unlike denominators. • Subtract rational expressions with unlike denominators.	2	2	1	1
12-8 Mixed Expressions and Complex Fractions (pp. 684–689) • Simplify mixed expressions. • Simplify complex fractions.	2	2	1	1
12-9 Solving Rational Equations (pp. 690–695) • Solve rational equations. • Eliminate extraneous solutions.	2	2	1	1
Study Guide and **Practice Test** (pp. 696–701) **Standardized Test Practice** (pp. 702–703)	1	1	0.5	0.5
Chapter Assessment	1	1	0.5	0.5
TOTAL	14	17	7	9

*An electronic version of this chapter is available on **StudentWorks**™. This backpack solution CD-ROM allows students instant access to the Student Edition, lesson worksheet pages, and web resources.*

Chapter Resource Manager

Timesaving Tools
TeacherWorks™
All-In-One Planner and Resource Center
See pages T5 and T21.

Chapter 12 Resource Masters

Study Guide and Intervention	Practice (Skills and Average)	Reading to Learn Mathematics	Enrichment	Assessment	Prerequisite Skills Workbook	Applications*	Parent and Student Study Guide Workbook	5-Minute Check Transparencies	Interactive Chalkboard	AlgePASS: Tutorial Plus (lessons)	Materials
705–706	707–708	709	710				91	12-1	12-1		
711–712	713–714	715	716			SM 81–84	92	12-2	12-2	33	(*Follow-Up:* graphing calculator)
717–718	719–720	721	722	773			93	12-3	12-3		
723–724	725–726	727	728			GCS 46	94	12-4	12-4		
729–730	731–732	733	734	773, 775			95	12-5	12-5		algebra tiles, product mat
735–736	737–738	739	740				96	12-6	12-6		
741–742	743–744	745	746	774	17–18	SC 23	97	12-7	12-7		
747–748	749–750	751	752			SC 24	98	12-8	12-8		
753–754	755–756	757	758	774		GCS 45	99	12-9	12-9		
				759–772, 776–778			100				

Key to Abbreviations: GCS = Graphing Calculator and Spreadsheet Masters,
SC = School-to-Career Masters,
SM = Science and Mathematics Lab Manual

ELL Study Guide and Intervention, Skills Practice, Practice, and Parent and Student Study Guide Workbooks are also available in Spanish.

Chapter 12 Mathematical Connections and Background

Continuity of Instruction

Prior Knowledge

In Chapter 5, students solved problems involving direct variation. In previous courses, they have simplified, added, subtracted, and multiplied fractions and mixed numbers. Students performed operations with monomials and polynomials in Chapter 8.

This Chapter

Students are introduced to inverse variation problems and compare these to direct variation problems. Through inverse variation problems, students are introduced to rational expressions. After being introduced to rational expressions, students learn to add, subtract, multiply, and divide rational expressions. Students go on to learn how to divide polynomials and simplify mixed expressions and complex fractions. The chapter ends with a lesson on how to solve rational equations.

Future Connections

Students will need to be able to solve rational equations in many real-world problem situations. Therefore, understanding all of the intricacies of rational expressions is necessary before delving into solving rational equations. Specifically, in Chapter 14, students will use rational expressions and equations when finding permutations and combinations.

12-1 Inverse Variation

Previously, students have learned that situations in which y increases as x increases are known as direct variations. However, there are also situations where y decreases as x increases, or vice versa. These are inverse variations, which can be represented by equations of the form $xy = k$, where $k \neq 0$. To graph an inverse variation, find k and make a table of values for x and y.

The product rule for inverse variations states that if (x_1, y_1) and (x_2, y_2) are solutions of an inverse variation, then $x_1y_1 = x_2y_2$ because both x_1y_1 and x_2y_2 equal k. You can use the equation $x_1y_1 = x_2y_2$ to solve for missing values of x and y.

12-2 Rational Expressions

Rational expressions are simply fractions that have polynomials for numerators and denominators. All properties that apply to rational numbers also apply to rational expressions, including the fact that the denominator cannot equal zero. Because certain values of variables in the denominator may produce a value of zero for the denominator, these values are excluded from the domain of the expression. To find theses excluded values, apply the Zero Product Property to the factors of the denominator.

Simplifying rational expressions is just like simplifying rational numbers. To simplify rational expressions in which both the numerator and denominator are monomials, divide each by the GCF. To simplify rational expressions in which both the numerator and denominator are polynomials, first factor each polynomial, and then eliminate any common factors.

12-3 Multiplying Rational Expressions

The process of multiplying rational expressions is just like that of multiplying rational numbers. Simply multiply the numerators, and multiply the denominators. If rational expressions can be factored, do so before multiplying so that simplifying will be easier. Multiplying rational expressions with unit measures to convert between units is a process known as *dimensional analysis*.

12-4 Dividing Rational Expressions

Recall that division is the inverse function of multiplication. To divide rational expressions, multiply by the reciprocal of the divisor, just like dividing rational numbers. Follow all the rules learned for multiplying and simplifying rational expressions. Dimensional analysis can also be accomplished by dividing rational expressions involving units.

12-5 Dividing Polynomials

In the process of simplifying rational expressions or solving rational equations, it may be necessary to divide polynomials. To divide a polynomial by a monomial, simply divide each term of the polynomial by the monomial. To divide a polynomial by a binomial, first try to factor the polynomial to see if there is perhaps a common binomial factor. If factoring is not possible, perform the division by long division. The procedure is similar to long division of integers. If a power is skipped in the polynomial, write the power with a coefficient of 0 to hold its place.

12-6 Rational Expressions with Like Denominators

When rational expressions have like denominators, add them by adding the numerators and writing the sum over the common denominator. If the denominators are polynomials, they must be exactly alike in all ways. Some denominators are alike, but do not appear to be. They may be inverse denominators, such as $x - 3$ and $3 - x$. Rewrite the second denominator as $-(x - 3)$, and move the negative sign to the numerator or change the operation from addition to subtraction.

Subtract rational expressions with like denominators by subtracting the numerators, then write the difference over the common denominator. Be sure to subtract each term, not just the first one. When subtracting expressions, it is often easier to think of the subtraction in terms of adding the additive inverse of the expression.

12-7 Rational Expressions with Unlike Denominators

As students learned in Lesson 12-6, rational expressions that have like denominators can be easily added or subtracted. When rational expressions have unlike denominators, a common denominator must be found before they can be added or subtracted. The least common denominator (LCD) is usually the easiest to find. The LCD is the least common multiple of the two denominators. To find the LCD, find the prime factorization of both denominators, and then use each factor the greatest number of times it appears in either of the factorizations. Once the LCD is found, change each rational expression into an equivalent expression with the LCD as the denominator. Then add or subtract. Be sure to simplify whenever possible.

12-8 Mixed Expressions and Complex Fractions

A mixed expression contains the sum of a monomial and a rational expression. To simplify mixed expressions, change them into a single rational expression by rewriting the monomial as a rational expression with the same denominator as the given rational expression.

A complex fraction is a fraction with a fraction in the numerator, denominator, or both. You can rewrite complex fractions as division sentences. Divide the numerator of the fraction by the denominator, and then write the quotient as a simple fraction.

12-9 Solving Rational Equations

All that students have learned about rational expressions can be applied to solving rational equations. Rational equations are equations that contain rational expressions. If both sides of a rational equation are single fractions, then cross products may be used to solve the equation. Or, one can multiply each side of the equation by the LCD of the fractions to eliminate the fractions, and then solve the resulting equation.

When solving rational equations, there may be two solutions. Sometimes, both solutions are correct. Other times, an incorrect one may be introduced when multiplying both sides of the equation by the LCD. Always check all solutions in the original equation to make sure they work. If a particular solution does not work, then it is an *extraneous solution*.

Quick Review Math Handbook

Hot Words includes a glossary of terms while Hot Topics consists of explanations of key mathematical concepts with exercises to test comprehension. This valuable resource can be used as a reference in the classroom or for home study.

Lesson	Hot Topics Section	Lesson	Hot Topics Section
GS12	1.4, 6.4, 6.5	12-6	1.4
12-1	1.4	12-8	6.4
12-2	8.2		

GS = Getting Started

 Additional mathematical information and teaching notes are available at www.algebra1.com/key_concepts.

D A I L Y
INTERVENTION and Assessment

Key to Abbreviations:
TWE = Teacher Wraparound Edition; CRM = Chapter Resource Masters

	Type	Student Edition	Teacher Resources	Technology/Internet
INTERVENTION	Ongoing	Prerequisite Skills, pp. 641, 647, 659, 664, 671, 683, 689 Practice Quiz 1, p. 659 Practice Quiz 2, p. 677	5-Minute Check Transparencies *Prerequisite Skills Workbook*, pp. 17–18 Quizzes, *CRM* pp. 773–774 Mid-Chapter Test, *CRM* p. 775 Study Guide and Intervention, *CRM* pp. 705–706, 711–712, 717–718, 723–724, 729–730, 735–736, 741–742, 747–748, 753–754	AlgePASS: Tutorial Plus, Lesson 33 www.algebra1.com/self_check_quiz www.algebra1.com/extra_examples
	Mixed Review	pp. 647, 653, 659, 664, 671, 677, 683, 689, 695	Cumulative Review, *CRM* p. 776	
	Error Analysis	Find the Error, pp. 657, 674, 686 Common Misconceptions, p. 673	Find the Error, *TWE* pp. 657, 674, 686 Unlocking Misconceptions, *TWE* pp. 649, 693	
ASSESSMENT	Standardized Test Practice	pp. 646, 647, 653, 659, 664, 671, 676, 680, 681, 683, 688, 695, 701, 702–703	*TWE* pp. 702–703 Standardized Test Practice, *CRM* pp. 777–778	Standardized Test Practice CD-ROM www.algebra1.com/standardized_test
	Open-Ended Assessment	Writing in Math, pp. 646, 653, 658, 664, 671, 676, 683, 688, 695 Open Ended, pp. 645, 651, 657, 662, 669, 674, 681, 686, 694 Standardized Test, p. 703	Modeling: *TWE* pp. 659, 677, 689 Speaking: *TWE* pp. 647, 671, 683 Writing: *TWE* pp. 653, 664, 695 Open-Ended Assessment, *CRM* p. 771	
	Chapter Assessment	Study Guide, pp. 696–700 Practice Test, p. 701	Multiple-Choice Tests (Forms 1, 2A, 2B), *CRM* pp. 759–764 Free-Response Tests (Forms 2C, 2D, 3), *CRM* pp. 765–770 Vocabulary Test/Review, *CRM* p. 772	ExamView® Pro (see below) MindJogger Videoquizzes www.algebra1.com/vocabulary_review www.algebra1.com/chapter_test

For more information on Yearly ProgressPro, see p. 582.

Algebra Lesson	Yearly ProgressPro Skill Lesson
12-1	Inverse Variation
12-2	Rational Expressions
12-3	Multiplying Rational Expressions
12-4	Dividing Rational Expressions
12-5	Dividing Polynomials
12-6	Rational Expressions with Like Denominators
12-7	Rational Expressions with Unlike Denominators
12-8	Mixed Expressions and Complex Fractions
12-9	Solving Rational Equations

ExamView® Pro

Use the networkable **ExamView® Pro** to:
- Create **multiple versions** of tests.
- Create **modified** tests for *Inclusion* students.
- **Edit** existing questions and **add** your own questions.
- Use built-in **state curriculum correlations** to create tests aligned with state standards.
- Change **English** tests to **Spanish** and vice versa.

For more information on Intervention and Assessment, see pp. T8–T11.

Reading and Writing in Mathematics

Glencoe Algebra 1 provides numerous opportunities to incorporate reading and writing into the mathematics classroom.

Student Edition

- Foldables Study Organizer, p. 641
- Concept Check questions require students to verbalize and write about what they have learned in the lesson. (pp. 645, 651, 657, 662, 669, 674, 681, 686, 694)
- Reading Mathematics, p. 665
- Writing in Math questions in every lesson, pp. 646, 653, 658, 664, 671, 676, 683, 688, 695
- WebQuest, pp. 652, 695

Teacher Wraparound Edition

- Foldables Study Organizer, pp. 641, 696
- Study Notebook suggestions, pp. 645, 651, 657, 662, 665, 669, 681, 686, 693
- Modeling activities, pp. 659, 677, 689
- Speaking activities, pp. 647, 671, 683
- Writing activities, pp. 653, 664, 695
- Differentiated Instruction, (Verbal/Linguistic), p. 674
- **ELL** Resources, pp. 640, 646, 652, 658, 663, 665, 670, 674, 676, 682, 688, 694, 696

For more information on Reading and Writing in Mathematics, see pp. T6–T7.

Additional Resources

- Vocabulary Builder worksheets require students to define and give examples for key vocabulary terms as they progress through the chapter. (*Chapter 12 Resource Masters*, pp. vii-viii)
- Reading to Learn Mathematics master for each lesson (*Chapter 12 Resource Masters*, pp. 709, 715, 721, 727, 733, 739, 745, 751, 757)
- *Vocabulary PuzzleMaker* software creates crossword, jumble, and word search puzzles using vocabulary lists that you can customize.
- *Teaching Mathematics with Foldables* provides suggestions for promoting cognition and language.
- *Reading and Writing in the Mathematics Classroom*
- *WebQuest and Project Resources*
- *Hot Words/Hot Topics* Sections 1.4, 6.4, 6.5, 8.2

ENGLISH LANGUAGE LEARNERS

Lesson 12-2
Language Experience Approach to Illustrations

Show students several examples of the domain of a rational expression. Have them come up with their own definition for excluded values. Once they have a definition, ask them to find the excluded values of several rational expressions, explaining how they found those values.

Lesson 12-7
Reading and Writing

After completing the lesson, have students write in their own words a process for finding the sum and difference of rational expressions with unlike denominators. Then have them share and compare their processes with a partner.

Lesson 12-8
Building on Prior Knowledge

Students who know how to simplify numerical complex fractions often have trouble simplifying algebraic complex fractions because of the variables with exponents. In order to help with this transition, have students simplify a numerical complex fraction, then an algebraic complex fraction with no exponents, and then incorporate the variables with exponents.

What You'll Learn

Have students read over the list of objectives and make a list of any words with which they are not familiar.

Why It's Important

Point out to students that this is only one of many reasons why each objective is important. Others are provided in the introduction to each lesson.

Lesson	NCTM Standards	Local Objectives
12-1	1, 2, 6, 8, 9, 10	
12-2	1, 2, 6, 8, 9, 10	
12-2 Follow-Up	2, 8	
12-3	1, 2, 6, 8, 9, 10	
12-4	1, 2, 6, 8, 9, 10	
12-5	1, 2, 6, 8, 9, 10	
12-6	1, 2, 6, 8, 9, 10	
12-7	1, 2, 6, 8, 9, 10	
12-8	1, 2, 6, 8, 9, 10	
12-9	1, 2, 6, 8, 9, 10	

Key to NCTM Standards:

1=Number & Operations, 2=Algebra,
3=Geometry, 4=Measurement,
5=Data Analysis & Probability, 6=Problem Solving, 7=Reasoning & Proof,
8=Communication, 9=Connections,
10=Representation

640   Chapter 12   Rational Expressions and Equations

Chapter **12** Rational Expressions and Equations

What You'll Learn

- **Lesson 12-1**   Solve problems involving inverse variation.
- **Lessons 12-2, 12-3, 12-4, 12-6, and 12-7** Simplify, add, subtract, multiply, and divide rational expressions.
- **Lesson 12-5**   Divide polynomials.
- **Lesson 12-8**   Simplify mixed expressions and complex fractions.
- **Lesson 12-9**   Solve rational equations.

Key Vocabulary

- inverse variation (p. 642)
- rational expression (p. 648)
- excluded values (p. 648)
- complex fraction (p. 684)
- extraneous solutions (p. 693)

Why It's Important

Performing operations on rational expressions is an important part of working with equations. For example, knowing how to divide rational expressions and polynomials can help you simplify complex expressions. You can use this process to determine the number of flags that a marching band can make from a given amount of material.   *You will divide rational expressions and polynomials in Lessons 12-4 and 12-5.*

640   Chapter 12   Rational Expressions and Equations

Vocabulary Builder   ELL

The Key Vocabulary list introduces students to some of the main vocabulary terms included in this chapter. For a more thorough vocabulary list with pronunciations of new words, give students the Vocabulary Builder worksheets found on pages vii and viii of the *Chapter 12 Resource Masters*. Encourage them to complete the definition of each term as they progress through the chapter. You may suggest that they add these sheets to their study notebooks for future reference when studying for the Chapter 12 test.

Getting Started

Getting Started

Prerequisite Skills To be successful in this chapter, you'll need to master these skills and be able to apply them in problem-solving situations. Review these skills before beginning Chapter 12.

For Lesson 12-1 **Solve Proportions**

Solve each proportion. *(For review, see Lesson 3-6.)*

1. $\frac{y}{9} = \frac{-7}{16}$ $-\frac{63}{16}$
2. $\frac{4}{x} = \frac{2}{10}$ 20
3. $\frac{3}{15} = \frac{1}{n}$ 5
4. $\frac{x}{8} = \frac{0.21}{2}$ 0.84
5. $\frac{1.1}{0.6} = \frac{8.47}{n}$ 4.62
6. $\frac{9}{8} = \frac{y}{6}$ 6.75
7. $\frac{2.7}{3.6} = \frac{8.1}{a}$ 10.8
8. $\frac{0.19}{2} = \frac{x}{24}$ 2.28

For Lesson 12-2 **Greatest Common Factor**

Find the greatest common factor for each pair of monomials. *(For review, see Lesson 9-1.)*

9. 30, 42 6
10. $60r^2, 45r^3$ $15r^2$
11. $32m^2n^3, 12m^2n$ $4m^2n$
12. $14a^2b^2, 18a^3b$ $2a^2b$

For Lessons 12-3 through 12-8 **Factor Polynomials**

Factor each polynomial. *(For review, see Lessons 9-2 and 9-3.)*

13. $3c^2d - 6c^2d^2$ $3c^2d(1 - 2d)$
14. $6mn + 15m^2$ $3m(2n + 5m)$
15. $x^2 + 11x + 24$ $(x + 3)(x + 8)$
16. $x^2 + 4x - 45$ $(x - 5)(x + 9)$
17. $2x^2 + x - 21$ $(2x + 7)(x - 3)$
18. $3x^2 - 12x + 9$ $3(x - 3)(x - 1)$

For Lesson 12-9 **Solve Equations**

Solve each equation. *(For review, see Lessons 3-4, 3-5, and 9-3.)*

19. $3x - 2 = -5$ -1
20. $5x - 8 - 3x = (2x - 3)$ no solution
21. $\frac{m + 9}{5} = \frac{m - 10}{11}$ $-\frac{149}{6}$
22. $\frac{5 + x}{x - 3} = \frac{14}{10}$ 23
23. $\frac{7n - 1}{6} = 5$ $\frac{31}{7}$
24. $\frac{4t - 5}{-9} = 7$ -14.5
25. $x^2 - x - 56 = 0$ $8, -7$
26. $x^2 + 2x = 8$ $-4, 2$

Rational Expressions and Equations Make this Foldable to help you organize your notes. Begin with a sheet of plain $8\frac{1}{2}"$ by 11" paper.

Step 1 **Fold in Half**

Fold in half lengthwise.

Step 2 **Fold Again**

Fold the top to the bottom.

Step 3 **Cut**

Open. Cut along the second fold to the center to make two tabs.

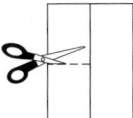

Step 4 **Label**

Label each tab as shown.

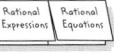

Reading and Writing As you read and study the chapter, write notes and examples under each tab. Use this Foldable to apply what you learn about simplifying rational expressions and solving rational equations.

Getting Started

This section provides a review of the basic concepts needed before beginning Chapter 12. Page references are included for additional student help.

Additional review is provided in the *Prerequisite Skills Workbook*, pp. 17–18.

Prerequisite Skills in the Getting Ready for the Next Lesson section at the end of each exercise set review a skill needed in the next lesson.

For Lesson	Prerequisite Skill
12-2	Finding Greatest Common Factors p. 647
12-3	Using Conversion Factors, p. 653
12-4	Factoring Polynomials, p. 659
12-5	Dividing Monomials, p. 664
12-6	Adding Polynomials, p. 671
12-7	Finding Least Common Multiples, p. 677
12-8	Dividing Rational Expressions, p. 683
12-9	Solving Equations, p. 689

FOLDABLES™
Study Organizer

For more information about Foldables, see *Teaching Mathematics with Foldables.*

Organization of Data and Expository Writing Ask students to use their notes to write expositions (explanations) for operations with rational expressions and solving rational equations. They should present the information in such a manner that someone who did not know about or understand rational expressions and equations would understand them after reading what the students have written. Explain that textbooks are examples of expository writing.

12-1 Inverse Variation

1 Focus

5-Minute Check Transparency 12-1 Use as a quiz or review of Chapter 11.

Mathematical Background notes are available for this lesson on p. 640C.

Building on Prior Knowledge

In Lesson 5-2 students learned how slope can be used to write and graph direct variation equations. In this lesson, students will differentiate between direct and inverse variation, and learn how to graph and solve inverse variation equations.

How is inverse variation related to the gears on a bicycle?

Ask students:

• Which gear ratio would you want to use for pedaling on a level surface? Explain. **You would want to use the 117.8 gear ratio because it requires the slowest pedaling rate. In other words, you have to pedal less to maintain your speed.**

• Which gear ratio would you want to use for pedaling up a steep hill? Explain. **You would want to use the 40.5 ratio because this requires a much faster pedaling rate to maintain your speed.**

What You'll Learn

• Graph inverse variations.
• Solve problems involving inverse variation.

Vocabulary
• inverse variation
• product rule

How is inverse variation related to the gears on a bicycle?

The number of revolutions of the pedals made when riding a bicycle at a constant speed varies inversely as the gear ratio of the bicycle. In other words, as the gear ratio *decreases*, the revolutions per minute (rpm) *increase*. This is why when pedaling up a hill, shifting to a lower gear allows you to pedal with less difficulty.

Pedaling Rates to Maintain Speed of 10 mph

Gear Ratio	Rate
117.8	89.6
108.0	97.8
92.6	114.0
76.2	138.6
61.7	171.2
49.8	212.0
40.5	260.7

Study Tip

Look Back
To review **direct variation**, see Lesson 5-2.

GRAPH INVERSE VARIATION Recall that some situations in which *y* increases as *x* increases are *direct variations*. If *y* varies directly as *x*, we can represent this relationship with an equation of the form $y = kx$, where $k \neq 0$. However, in the application above, as one value increases the other value decreases. When the product of two values remains constant, the relationship forms an **inverse variation**. We say *y varies inversely as x* or *y is inversely proportional to x*.

Key Concept — Inverse Variation

y varies inversely as *x* if there is some nonzero constant *k* such that $xy = k$.

Example 1 *Graph an Inverse Variation*

DRIVING The time *t* it takes to travel a certain distance varies inversely as the rate *r* at which you travel. The equation $rt = 250$ can be used to represent a person driving 250 miles. Complete the table and draw a graph of the relation.

r (mph)	5	10	15	20	25	30	35	40	45	50
t (hours)										

Solve for *t* when *r* = 5.

$rt = 250$ Original equation
$5t = 250$ Replace *r* with 5.
$t = \dfrac{250}{5}$ Divide each side by 5.
$t = 50$ Simplify.

Solve the equation for the other values of *r*.

r (mph)	5	10	15	20	25	30	35	40	45	50
t (hours)	50	25	16.67	12.5	10	8.33	7.14	6.25	5.56	5

Resource Manager

 Workbook and Reproducible Masters

Chapter 12 Resource Masters
• Study Guide and Intervention, pp. 705–706
• Skills Practice, p. 707
• Practice, p. 708
• Reading to Learn Mathematics, p. 709
• Enrichment, p. 710

Parent and Student Study Guide Workbook, p. 91

 Transparencies

5-Minute Check Transparency 12-1
Answer Key Transparencies

Technology

Interactive Chalkboard

Next, graph the ordered pairs: (5, 50), (10, 25), (15, 16.67), (20, 12.5), (25, 10), (30, 8.33), (35, 7.14), (40, 6.25), (45, 5.56), and (50, 5).

The graph of an inverse variation is not a straight line like the graph of a direct variation. As the rate r increases, the time t that it takes to travel the same distance decreases.

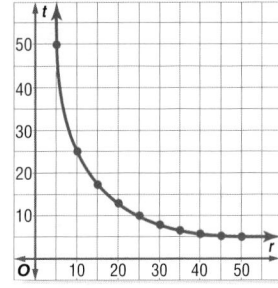

Graphs of inverse variations can also be drawn using negative values of x.

Example 2 Graph an Inverse Variation

Graph an inverse variation in which y varies inversely as x and $y = 15$ when $x = 6$.

Solve for k.

$xy = k$ Inverse variation equation

$(6)(15) = k$ $x = 6$, $y = 15$

$90 = k$ The constant of variation is 90.

Choose values for x and y whose product is 90.

x	y
−9	−10
−6	−15
−3	−30
−2	−45
0	undefined
2	45
3	30
6	15
9	10

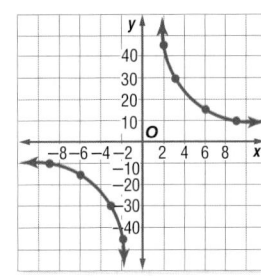

USE INVERSE VARIATION   If (x_1, y_1) and (x_2, y_2) are solutions of an inverse variation, then $x_1y_1 = k$ and $x_2y_2 = k$.

$x_1y_1 = k$ and $x_2y_2 = k$

$x_1y_1 = x_2y_2$ Substitute x_2y_2 for k.

The equation $x_1y_1 = x_2y_2$ is called the **product rule** for inverse variations. You can use this equation to form a proportion.

$x_1y_1 = x_2y_2$ Product rule for inverse variations

$\dfrac{x_1y_1}{x_2y_1} = \dfrac{x_2y_2}{x_2y_1}$ Divide each side by x_2y_1.

$\dfrac{x_1}{x_2} = \dfrac{y_2}{y_1}$ Simplify.

You can use the product rule or a proportion to solve inverse variation problems.

www.algebra1.com/extra_examples

Lesson 12-1 Inverse Variation **643**

Study Tip

Proportions
Notice that the proportion for inverse variations is different from the proportion for direct variation, $\dfrac{x_1}{x_2} = \dfrac{y_1}{y_2}$.

---

2 Teach

GRAPH INVERSE VARIATION

In-Class Examples

1 MANUFACTURING The owner of Superfast Computer Company has calculated that the time t in hours that it takes to build a particular model of computer varies inversely with the number of people p working on the computer. The equation $pt = 12$ can be used to represent the people building a computer. Complete a table and draw a graph of the relation.

p	2	4	6	8	10	12
t	6	3	2	1.5	1.2	1

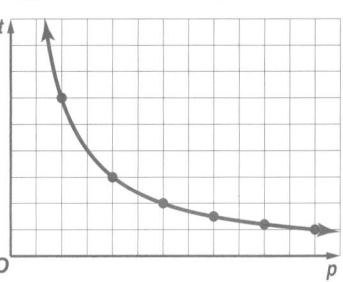

Teaching Tip Ask students why negative values are included for the inverse variation in Example 2 but not for Example 1. Negative rate and time values are not realistic in Example 1.

2 Graph an inverse variation in which y varies inversely as x, and $y = 1$ when $x = 4$.

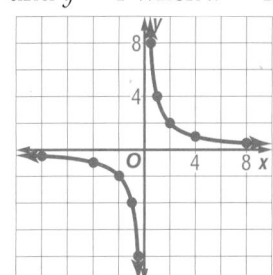

Power Point®

3 If y varies inversely as x and $y = 5$ when $x = 12$, find x when $y = 15$. **4**

4 If y varies inversely as x and $y = 8$ when $x = 6$, find y when $x = 4$. **12**

5 **PHYSICAL SCIENCE** Using the same lever and fulcrum problem from Example 5 in the Student Edition, how far should a 2-kilogram weight be from the fulcrum if a 6 kilogram weight is 3.2 meters from the fulcrum? **9.6 m**

Answers (p. 645)

2. Sample answer: Direct variation equations are in the form $y = kx$ and inverse variation equations are in the form $xy = k$. The graph of a direct variation is linear while the graph of an inverse variation is nonlinear.

4.
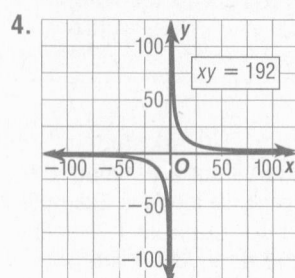

5.
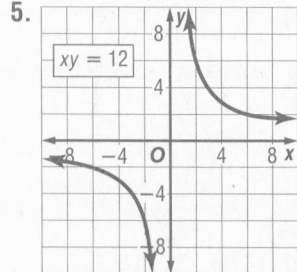

11.
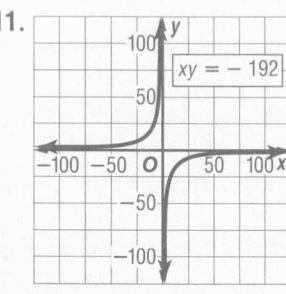

Example 3 *Solve for x*

If y varies inversely as x and $y = 4$ when $x = 7$, find x when $y = 14$.

Let $x_1 = 7$, $y_1 = 4$, and $y_2 = 14$. Solve for x_2.

Method 1 Use the product rule.

$$x_1 y_1 = x_2 y_2 \quad \text{Product rule for inverse variations}$$
$$7 \cdot 4 = x_2 \cdot 14 \quad x_1 = 7, y_1 = 4, \text{ and } y_2 = 14$$
$$\frac{28}{14} = x_2 \quad \text{Divide each side by 14.}$$
$$2 = x_2 \quad \text{Simplify.}$$

Method 2 Use a proportion.

$$\frac{x_1}{x_2} = \frac{y_2}{y_1} \quad \text{Proportion for inverse variations}$$
$$\frac{7}{x_2} = \frac{14}{4} \quad x_1 = 7, y_1 = 4, \text{ and } y_2 = 14$$
$$28 = 14x_2 \quad \text{Cross multiply.}$$
$$2 = x_2 \quad \text{Divide each side by 14.}$$

Both methods show that $x = 2$ when $y = 14$.

Example 4 *Solve for y*

If y varies inversely as x and $y = -6$ when $x = 9$, find y when $x = 6$.

Use the product rule.

$$x_1 y_1 = x_2 y_2 \quad \text{Product rule for inverse variations}$$
$$9 \cdot (-6) = 6y_2 \quad x_1 = 9, y_1 = -6, \text{ and } x_2 = 6$$
$$\frac{-54}{6} = y_2 \quad \text{Divide each side by 6.}$$
$$-9 = y_2 \quad \text{Simplify.}$$

Thus, $y = -9$ when $x = 6$.

Inverse variation is often used in real-world situations.

Example 5 *Use Inverse Variation to Solve a Problem*

PHYSICAL SCIENCE When two objects are balanced on a lever, their distances from the fulcrum are inversely proportional to their weights. In other words, the greater the weight, the less distance it should be from the fulcrum in order to maintain balance. If an 8-kilogram weight is placed 1.8 meters from the fulcrum, how far should a 12-kilogram weight be placed from the fulcrum in order to balance the lever?

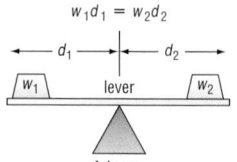

Let $w_1 = 8$, $d_1 = 1.8$, and $w_2 = 12$. Solve for d_2.

$$w_1 d_1 = w_2 d_2 \quad \text{Original equation}$$
$$8 \cdot 1.8 = 12d_2 \quad w_1 = 8, d_1 = 1.8, \text{ and } w_2 = 12$$
$$\frac{14.4}{12} = d_2 \quad \text{Divide each side by 12.}$$
$$1.2 = d_2 \quad \text{Simplify.}$$

The 12-kilogram weight should be placed 1.2 meters from the fulcrum.

644 **Chapter 12** Rational Expressions and Equations

D A I L Y
INTERVENTION **Differentiated Instruction**

Kinesthetic Borrow a fulcrum, lever, and weights from a science teacher to recreate the experiment in Example 5. After some experimentation, challenge students to calculate where to place the weights for the lever to balance.

Check for Understanding

Concept Check

3. b; Sample answer: As the price increases, the number purchased decreases.

1. **OPEN ENDED** Write an equation showing an inverse variation with a constant of 8. **Sample answer:** $xy = 8$

2. **Compare and contrast** direct variation and indirect variation equations and graphs. **See margin.**

3. **Determine** which situation is an example of inverse variation. Explain.
   a. Emily spends $2 each day for snacks on her way home from school. The total amount she spends each week depends on the number of days school was in session.
   b. A business donates $200 to buy prizes for a school event. The number of prizes that can be purchased depends upon the price of each prize.

Guided Practice

Graph each variation if y varies inversely as x. **4–5. See margin.**

GUIDED PRACTICE KEY	
Exercises	Examples
4, 5	1, 2
6–9	3, 4
10	5

4. $y = 24$ when $x = 8$

5. $y = -6$ when $x = -2$

Write an inverse variation equation that relates x and y. Assume that y varies inversely as x. Then solve.

6. If $y = 12$ when $x = 6$, find y when $x = 8$. $xy = 72; 9$

7. If $y = -8$ when $x = -3$, find y when $x = 6$. $xy = 24; 4$

8. If $y = 2.7$ when $x = 8.1$, find x when $y = 5.4$. $xy = 21.87; 4.05$

9. If $x = \frac{1}{2}$ when $y = 16$, find x when $y = 32$. $xy = 8; \frac{1}{4}$

Application

10. **MUSIC** The length of a violin string varies inversely as the frequency of its vibrations. A violin string 10 inches long vibrates at a frequency of 512 cycles per second. Find the frequency of an 8-inch string. **640 cycles per second**

★ indicates increased difficulty

Practice and Apply

Homework Help	
For Exercises	See Examples
11–16	1, 2
17–28	3, 4
29–37	5

Extra Practice
See page 846.

Graph each variation if y varies inversely as x. **11–16. See margin.**

11. $y = 24$ when $x = -8$

12. $y = 3$ when $x = 4$

13. $y = 5$ when $x = 15$

14. $y = -4$ when $x = -12$

15. $y = 9$ when $x = 8$

16. $y = 2.4$ when $x = 8.1$

Write an inverse variation equation that relates x and y. Assume that y varies inversely as x. Then solve.

17. If $y = 12$ when $x = 5$, find y when $x = 3$. $xy = 60; 20$

18. If $y = 7$ when $x = -2$, find y when $x = 7$. $xy = -14; -2$

19. If $y = 8.5$ when $x = -1$, find x when $y = -1$. $xy = -8.5; 8.5$

20. If $y = 8$ when $x = 1.55$, find x when $y = -0.62$. $xy = 12.4; -20$

21. If $y = 6.4$ when $x = 4.4$, find x when $y = 3.2$. $xy = 28.16; 8.8$

22. If $y = 1.6$ when $x = 0.5$, find x when $y = 3.2$. $xy = 0.8; 0.25$

23. If $y = 4$ when $x = 4$, find y when $x = 7$. $xy = 16; \frac{16}{7}$

24. If $y = -6$ when $x = -2$, find y when $x = 5$. $xy = 12; \frac{12}{5}$

★ 25. Find the value of y when $x = 7$ if $y = 7$ when $x = \frac{2}{3}$. $xy = \frac{14}{3}; \frac{2}{3}$

★ 26. Find the value of y when $x = 32$ if $y = 16$ when $x = \frac{1}{2}$. $xy = 8; \frac{1}{4}$

★ 27. If $x = 6.1$ when $y = 4.4$, find x when $y = 3.2$. $xy = 26.84; 8.3875$

★ 28. If $x = 0.5$ when $y = 2.5$, find x when $y = 20$. $xy = 1.25; 0.0625$

Study Notebook

Have students—
• add the definitions/examples of the vocabulary terms to their Vocabulary Builder worksheets for Chapter 12.
• include any other item(s) that they find helpful in mastering the skills in this lesson.

About the Exercises …

Organization by Objective
• **Graph Inverse Variation:** 11–16
• **Use Inverse Variation:** 17–37

Odd/Even Assignments
Exercises 11–28 are structured so that students practice the same concepts whether they are assigned odd or even problems.

Assignment Guide

Basic: 11–23 odd, 31–33, 38–60
Average: 11–31 odd, 34–60
Advanced: 12–30 even, 34–54 (optional: 55–60)

15.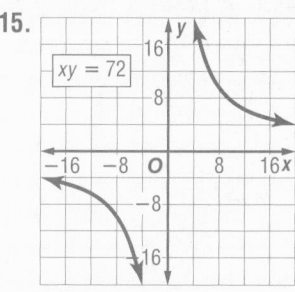

12.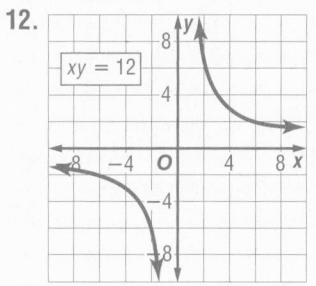

13.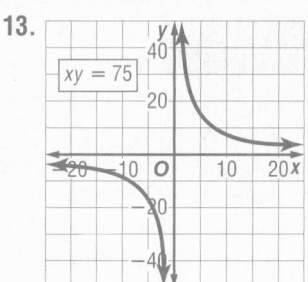

14.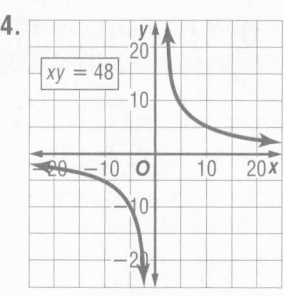

16.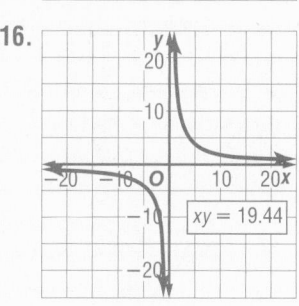

Graph Inverse Variation Situations in which the values of y decrease as the values of x increase are examples of **inverse variation**. We say that y varies inversely as x, or y is inversely proportional to x.

Inverse Variation Equation	an equation of the form $xy = k$, where $k \neq 0$

Example 1 Suppose you drive 200 miles without stopping. The time it takes to travel a distance varies inversely as the rate at which you travel. Let $x =$ speed in miles per hour and $y =$ time in hours. Graph the variation.
The equation $xy = 200$ can be used to represent the situation. Use various speeds to make a table.

x	y
10	20
20	10
30	6.7
40	5
50	4
60	3.3

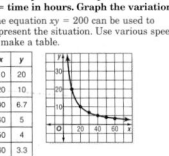

Example 2 Graph an inverse variation in which y varies inversely as x and $y = 3$ when $x = 12$.
Solve for k.
$xy = k$ Inverse variation equation
$12(3) = k$ $x = 12$ and $y = 3$
$36 = k$ Simplify
Choose values for x and y whose product is 36.

x	y
−6	−6
−3	−12
−2	−18
2	18
3	12
6	6

Exercises

Graph each variation if y varies inversely as x.

1. $y = 9$ when $x = -3$
2. $y = 12$ when $x = 4$
3. $y = -25$ when $x = 5$
4. $y = 4$ when $x = 5$
5. $y = -18$ when $x = -9$
6. $y = 4.8$ when $x = 5.4$

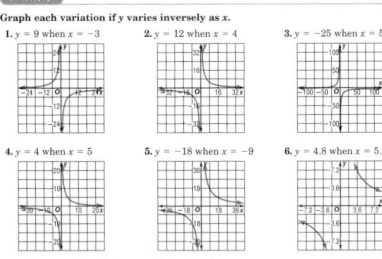

Graph each variation if y varies inversely as x.

1. $y = -2$ when $x = -12$
2. $y = -6$ when $x = -5$
3. $y = 2.5$ when $x = 2$

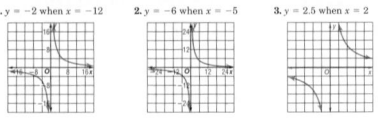

Write an inverse variation equation that relates x and y. Assume that y varies inversely as x. Then solve.

4. If $y = 124$ when $x = 12$, find y when $x = -24$. $xy = 1488; -62$
5. If $y = -8.5$ when $x = 6$, find y when $x = -2.5$. $xy = -51; 20.4$
6. If $y = 3.2$ when $x = -5.5$, find y when $x = 6.4$. $xy = -17.6; -2.75$
7. If $y = 0.6$ when $x = 7.5$, find y when $x = -1.25$. $xy = 4.5; -3.6$
8. If $y = 6$ when $x = \frac{1}{2}$, find x when $y = 4$. $xy = 3; \frac{3}{4}$
9. If $y = 8$ when $x = \frac{1}{4}$, find x when $y = -12$. $xy = 2; -\frac{1}{6}$
10. If $y = 4$ when $x = -2$, find x when $y = -10$. $xy = -8; \frac{4}{5}$
11. If $y = -7$ when $x = 4$, find x when $y = -6$. $xy = -28; \frac{14}{3}$

EMPLOYMENT For Exercises 12 and 13, use the following information.
The manager of a lumber store schedules 6 employees to take inventory in an 8-hour work period. The manager assumes all employees work at the same rate.

12. Suppose 2 employees call in sick. How many hours will 4 employees need to take inventory? **12 h**

13. If the district supervisor calls in and says she needs the inventory finished in 6 hours, how many employees should the manager assign to take inventory? **8**

14. **TRAVEL** Jesse and Joaquin can drive to their grandparents' home in 3 hours if they average 50 miles per hour. Since the road between the homes is winding and mountainous, their parents prefer they average between 40 and 45 miles per hour. How long will it take to drive to the grandparents' home at the reduced speed? **between 3 h 20 min and 3 h 45 min**

Pre-Activity How is inverse variation related to the gears on a bicycle?
Read the introduction to Lesson 12-1 at the top of page 642 in your textbook.
Given the data in the table, a bicyclist will pedal
___faster___ (faster/slower) when shifting to a lower gear and
___slower___ (faster/slower) when shifting to a higher gear.

Reading the Lesson

1. Write *direct variation*, *inverse variation*, or *neither* to describe the relationship between x and y described by each equation.

   a. $y = 3x$ **direct variation**
   b. $xy = 5$ **inverse variation**
   c. $y = -8x$ **direct variation**
   d. $y = \frac{2}{x}$ **inverse variation**
   e. $x = \frac{10}{y}$ **inverse variation**
   f. $y = 7x - 1$ **neither**

2. Why does the equation $xy = 0$ *not* describe an inverse variation? **The product of x and y must be a nonzero constant.**

3. Suppose you want to graph an inverse variation in which $y = 12$ when $x = 9$. What two things should you do before you sketch the graph? **First, find the value of k. To do this, you can multiply 9 and 12 to get 108. Second, make a table of values in which the product of x and y values is 108.**

4. For each problem, assume that y varies inversely as x. Use the Product Rule to write an equation you could use to solve the problem. Then write a proportion you could use to solve the problem.

	Problem	Product Rule	Proportion
a.	If $y = 8$ when $x = 12$, find y when $x = 4$.	$8 \cdot 12 = 4y$	$\frac{12}{4} = \frac{y}{8}$
b.	If $x = 50$ when $y = 6$, find x when $y = 30$.	$50 \cdot 6 = x \cdot 30$	$\frac{50}{x} = \frac{30}{6}$

Helping You Remember

5. To remember how to set up a proportion to solve a problem involving inverse variation, write a sentence describing the form the proportion should have. **Sample answer: The first x value divided by the second x value equals the second y value divided by the first y value.**

---

29. **GEOMETRY** A rectangle is 36 inches wide and 20 inches long. How wide is a rectangle of equal area if its length is 90 inches? **8 in.**

30. **MUSIC** The pitch of a musical note varies inversely as its wavelength. If the tone has a pitch of 440 vibrations per second and a wavelength of 2.4 feet, find the pitch of a tone that has a wavelength of 1.6 feet. **660 vibrations per second**

31. **COMMUNITY SERVICE** Students at Roosevelt High School are collecting canned goods for a local food pantry. They plan to distribute flyers to homes in the community asking for donations. Last year, 12 students were able to distribute 1000 flyers in nine hours. How long would it take if 15 students hand out the same number of flyers this year? **7.2 h**

TRAVEL For Exercises 32 and 33, use the following information.
The Zalinski family can drive the 220 miles to their cabin in 4 hours at 55 miles per hour. Son Jeff claims that they could save half an hour if they drove 65 miles per hour, the speed limit.

32. How long will it take the family if they drive 65 miles per hour? **about 3 h 23 min**

33. How much time would be saved driving at 65 miles per hour? **about 37 min**

CHEMISTRY For Exercises 34–36, use the following information.
Boyle's Law states that the volume of a gas V varies inversely with applied pressure P.

34. Write an equation to show this relationship. **$PV = k$ or $P_1 V_1 = P_2 V_2$**

35. Pressure on 60 cubic meters of a gas is raised from 1 atmosphere to 3 atmospheres. What new volume does the gas occupy? **20 m³**

36. A helium-filled balloon has a volume of 22 cubic meters at sea level where the air pressure is 1 atmosphere. The balloon is released and rises to a point where the air pressure is 0.8 atmosphere. What is the volume of the balloon at this height? **27.5 m³**

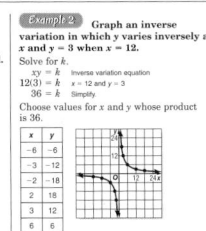

More About...

Art •

American sculptor Alexander Calder was the first artist to use mobiles as an art form.
Source: www.infoplease.com

37. **ART** Anna is designing a mobile to suspend from a gallery ceiling. A chain is attached eight inches from the end of a bar that is 20 inches long. On the shorter end of the bar is a sculpture weighing 36 kilograms. She plans to place another piece of artwork on the other end of the bar. How much should the second piece of art weigh if she wants the bar to be balanced? **24 kg**

CRITICAL THINKING For Exercises 38 and 39, assume that y varies inversely as x.

38. If the value of x is doubled, what happens to the value of y? **It is half of what it was.**

39. If the value of y is tripled, what happens to the value of x? **It is one third of what it was.**

40. **WRITING IN MATH** Answer the question that was posed at the beginning of the lesson. **See margin.**

   How is inverse variation related to the gears on a bicycle?

   Include the following in your answer:
   • an explanation of how shifting to a lower gear ratio affects speed and the pedaling rate on a certain bicycle if a rider is pedaling 73.4 revolutions per minute while traveling at 15 miles per hour, and
   • an explanation why the gear ratio affects the pedaling speed of the rider.

Standardized Test Practice
Ⓐ Ⓑ Ⓒ Ⓓ

41. Determine the constant of variation if y varies inversely as x and $y = 4.25$ when $x = -1.3$. **B**

   Ⓐ -3.269 Ⓑ -5.525 Ⓒ -0.306 Ⓓ -2.950

Direct or Indirect Variation

Fill in each table below. Then write *inversely*, or *directly* to complete each conclusion.

1.
i	2	4	8	16	32
w	4	4	4	4	4
A	8	16	32	64	128

For a set of rectangles with a width of 4, the area varies ___directly___ as the length.

2.
Hours	2	4	5	6
Speed	55	55	55	55
Distance	165	220	275	330

For a car traveling at 55 mi/h, the distance covered varies ___directly___ as the hours driven.

3.
Oat Bran	$\frac{1}{3}$ cup	$\frac{2}{3}$ cup	1 cup
Water	1 cup	2 cups	3 cups
Servings	1	2	3

4.
Hours of Work	128	128	128
People Working	2	4	8
Hours per Person	64	32	16

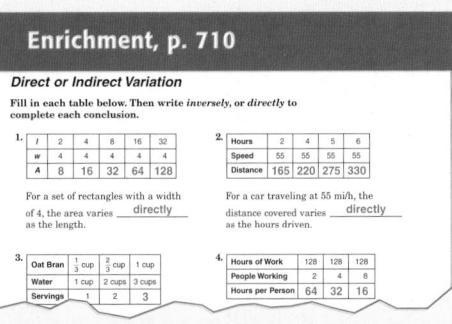

42. Identify the graph of $xy = k$ if $x = -2$ when $y = -4$. **A**

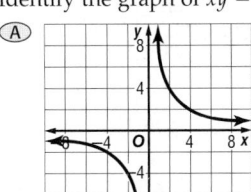 (A)

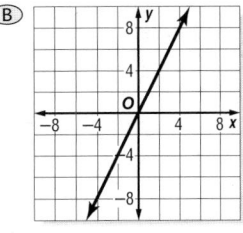 (B)

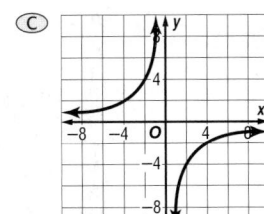 (C)

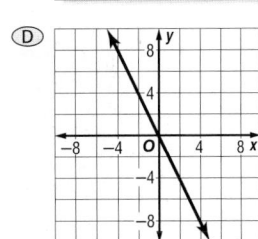 (D)

Maintain Your Skills

Mixed Review For each triangle, find the measure of the indicated angle to the nearest degree. *(Lesson 11-7)*

43. 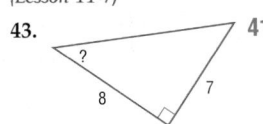 $41°$

44. 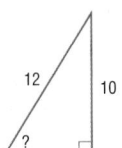 $56°$

45. 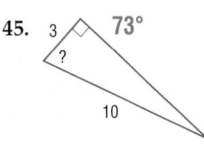 $73°$

For each set of measures given, find the measures of the missing sides if $\triangle ABC \sim \triangle DEF$. *(Lesson 11-6)*

46. $a = 3, b = 10, c = 9, d = 12$
$e = 40, f = 36$

47. $b = 8, c = 4, d = 21, e = 28$
$a = 6, f = 14$

48. MUSIC Two musical notes played at the same time produce harmony. The closest harmony is produced by frequencies with the greatest GCF. A, C, and C sharp have frequencies of 220, 264, and 275, respectively. Which pair of these notes produce the closest harmony? *(Lesson 9-1)* **A and C sharp**

Solve each equation. *(Lesson 8-6)*

49. $7(2y - 7) = 5(4y + 1)$ **−9**

50. $w(w + 2) = 2w(w - 3) + 16$ **4**

Solve each system of inequalities by graphing. *(Lesson 7-5)* **51–54. See margin.**

51. $y \leq 3x - 5$
$y > -x + 1$

52. $y \geq 2x + 3$
$2y \geq -5x - 14$

53. $x + y \leq 1$
$x - y \leq -3$
$y \geq 0$

54. $3x - 2y \geq -16$
$x + 4y < 4$
$5x - 8y < -8$

Getting Ready for the Next Lesson

PREREQUISITE SKILL Find the greatest common factor for each set of monomials.
(To review greatest common factors, see Lesson 9-1.)

55. 36, 15, 45 **3**

56. 48, 60, 84 **12**

57. 210, 330, 150 **30**

58. $17a, 34a^2$ **17a**

59. $12xy^2, 18x^2y^3$ **6xy²**

60. $12pr^2, 40p^4$ **4p**

4 Assess

Open-Ended Assessment

Speaking Ask students for an example of inverse variation. Ask students to suggest values that would be likely to occur.

Getting Ready for Lesson 12-2

PREREQUISITE SKILL Students will learn how to simplify rational expressions in Lesson 12-2. In order to simplify rational expressions, students must be able to find greatest common factors. Use Exercises 55–60 to determine your students' familiarity with finding greatest common factors.

Answers

51.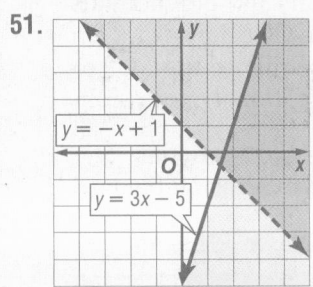

52.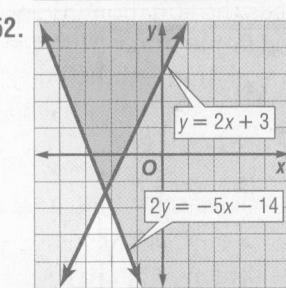

53.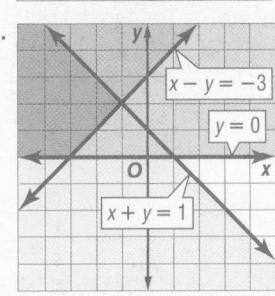

54.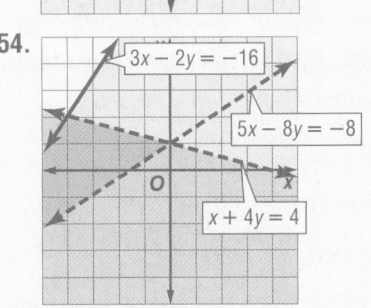

Answer

40. Sample answer: When the gear ratio is lower, the pedaling revolutions increase to keep a constant speed. Answers should include the following.

- Shifting gears will require that the rider increase pedaling revolutions.
- Lower gears at a constant rate will cause a decrease in speed, while higher gears at a constant rate will cause an increase in speed.

1 Focus

5-Minute Check Transparency 12-2 Use as a quiz or review of Lesson 12-1.

Mathematical Background notes are available for this lesson on p. 640C.

Building on Prior Knowledge

In Chapter 9, students learned how to find the greatest common factor (GCF) and how to factor monomials and polynomials using the GCF. In this lesson, students will use the GCF to simplify rational expressions.

How can a rational expression be used in a movie theater?

Ask students:

- How does the equation given in this example differ from the inverse variations studied in Lesson 12-1? **There is a squared term and the variables are on different sides of the equation instead of on the same side.**

- As the projector is moved away from the screen, what happens to the image? **The image will become larger but also dimmer.**

12-2 # Rational Expressions

What You'll Learn

- Identify values excluded from the domain of a rational expression.
- Simplify rational expressions.

Vocabulary

- rational expression
- excluded values

How can a rational expression be used in a movie theater?

The intensity I of an image on a movie screen is inversely proportional to the square of the distance d between the projector and the screen. Recall from Lesson 12-1 that this can be represented by the equation $I = \frac{k}{d^2}$, where k is a constant.

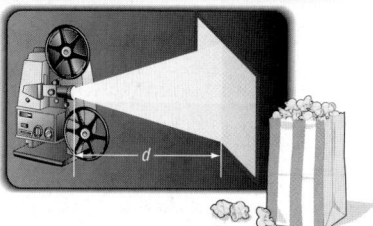

EXCLUDED VALUES OF RATIONAL EXPRESSIONS The expression $\frac{k}{d^2}$ is an example of a rational expression. A **rational expression** is an algebraic fraction whose numerator and denominator are polynomials.

Because a rational expression involves division, the denominator may not have a value of zero. Any values of a variable that result in a denominator of zero must be excluded from the domain of that variable. These are called **excluded values** of the rational expression.

Example 1 *One Excluded Value*

State the excluded value of $\frac{5m + 3}{m - 6}$.

Exclude the values for which $m - 6 = 0$.

$m - 6 = 0$ The denominator cannot equal 0.

$m = 6$ Add 6 to each side.

Therefore, m cannot equal 6.

To determine the excluded values of a rational expression, you may be able to factor the denominator first.

Example 2 *Multiple Excluded Values*

State the excluded values of $\frac{x^2 - 5}{x^2 - 5x + 6}$.

Exclude the values for which $x^2 - 5x + 6 = 0$.

$x^2 - 5x + 6 = 0$ The denominator cannot equal zero.

$(x - 2)(x - 3) = 0$ Factor.

Use the Zero Product Property to solve for x.

$x - 2 = 0$ or $x - 3 = 0$

$x = 2$ $x = 3$

Therefore, x cannot equal 2 or 3.

Resource Manager

📁 Workbook and Reproducible Masters

Chapter 12 Resource Masters
- Study Guide and Intervention, pp. 711–712
- Skills Practice, p. 713
- Practice, p. 714
- Reading to Learn Mathematics, p. 715
- Enrichment, p. 716

Parent and Student Study Guide Workbook, p. 92
Science and Mathematics Lab Manual, pp. 81–84

Ⓛ Transparencies

5-Minute Check Transparency 12-2
Real-World Transparency 12
Answer Key Transparencies

⊙ Technology

AlgePASS: Tutorial Plus, Lesson 33
Interactive Chalkboard

You can use rational expressions to solve real-world problems.

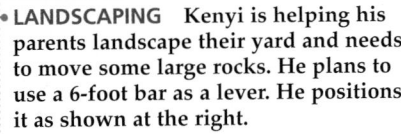

Example 3 *Use Rational Expressions*

LANDSCAPING Kenyi is helping his parents landscape their yard and needs to move some large rocks. He plans to use a 6-foot bar as a lever. He positions it as shown at the right.

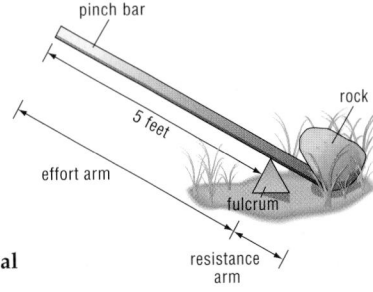

a. The mechanical advantage of a lever is $\frac{L_E}{L_R}$, where L_E is the length of the effort arm and L_R is the length of the resistance arm. Calculate the mechanical advantage of the lever Kenyi is using.

Let b represent the length of the bar and e represent the length of the effort arm. Then $b - e$ represents the length of the resistance arm.

Use the expression for mechanical advantage to write an expression for the mechanical advantage in this situation.

$$\frac{L_E}{L_R} = \frac{e}{b - e} \qquad L_E = e, L_R = b - e$$
$$= \frac{5}{6 - 5} \qquad e = 5, b = 6$$
$$= 5 \qquad \text{Simplify.}$$

The mechanical advantage is 5.

b. The force placed on the rock is the product of the mechanical advantage and the force applied to the end of the lever. If Kenyi can apply a force of 180 pounds, what is the greatest weight he can lift with the lever?

Since the mechanical advantage is 5, Kenyi can lift $5 \cdot 180$ or 900 pounds with this lever.

SIMPLIFY RATIONAL EXPRESSIONS Simplifying rational expressions is similar to simplifying fractions with numbers. To simplify a rational expression, you must eliminate any common factors of the numerator and denominator. To do this, use their greatest common factor (GCF). Remember that $\frac{ab}{ac} = \frac{a}{a} \cdot \frac{b}{c}$ and $\frac{a}{a} = 1$. So, $\frac{ab}{ac} = 1 \cdot \frac{b}{c}$ or $\frac{b}{c}$.

Example 4 *Expression Involving Monomials*

Simplify $\frac{-7a^2b^3}{21a^5b}$.

$$\frac{-7a^2b^3}{21a^5b} = \frac{(7a^2b)(-b^2)}{(7a^2b)(3a^3)} \qquad \text{The GCF of the numerator and denominator is } 7a^2b.$$

$$= \frac{\overset{1}{\cancel{(7a^2b)}}(-b^2)}{\underset{1}{\cancel{(7a^2b)}}(3a^3)} \qquad \text{Divide the numerator and denominator by } 7a^2b.$$

$$= \frac{-b^2}{3a^3} \qquad \text{Simplify.}$$

 www.algebra1.com/extra_examples

Lesson 12-2 Rational Expressions **649**

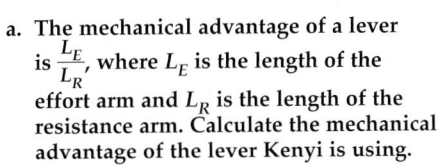
EXCLUDED VALUES OF RATIONAL EXPRESSIONS

In-Class Examples Power Point®

1 State the excluded value of $\frac{3b - 2}{b + 7}$. *b cannot equal −7.*

2 State the excluded values of $\frac{5a^2 + 2}{a^2 - a - 12}$. *a cannot equal −3 or 4.*

3 **LANDSCAPING** Refer to Example 3 in the Student Edition. Suppose Kenyi finds a rock that he cannot move with a 6 foot bar, so he gets an 8 foot bar. But this time, he places the fulcrum so that the effort arm is 6 feet long, and the resistance arm is 2 feet long.

a. Explain whether he has more or less mechanical advantage with his new setup. *Even though the bar is longer, because he moved the fulcrum he has a mechanical advantage of 3, so his mechanical advantage is less than before.*

b. If Kenyi can apply a force of 180 pounds, what is the greatest weight he can lift with the longer bar? *540 lb*

SIMPLIFY RATIONAL EXPRESSIONS

In-Class Example Power Point®

4 Simplify $\frac{32x^5y^2}{4xy^7} \cdot \frac{8x^4}{y^5}$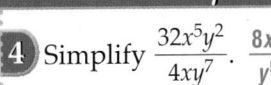

DAILY INTERVENTION

Unlocking Misconceptions

Students may assume that excluded values are determined from the simplified expression. This may or may not be true. Stress that excluded values must always be determined from the original denominator.

Teaching Tip Refer students to Chapter 9 if they need to review how to factor polynomials.

5 Simplify $\dfrac{x^2 - 9x + 14}{x^2 - 2x - 35} \cdot \dfrac{x - 2}{x + 5}$.

6 Simplify $\dfrac{4x + 16}{x^2 - 5x - 36}$. State the excluded values of x.
$\dfrac{4}{x - 9}$; The excluded values are -4 and 9.

✓ Concept Check

Simplify $\dfrac{2x + 4}{x^2 - 2x + 2}$. State the excluded values of x. The expression is in simplest form, and there are no excluded values for x.

Answers

3. Sample answer: You need to determine excluded values before simplifying. One or more factors may have been canceled in the denominator.

24. $\dfrac{5z}{2y}$; 0, 0

25. $\dfrac{a^2}{3b}$; 0, 0

26. $\dfrac{4r}{q}$; 0, 0, 0

27. $\dfrac{3x}{8z}$; 0, 0, 0

28. $\dfrac{a^2 b}{3a + 7b^2}$; $a \neq -\dfrac{7}{3}b^2$, 0, 0

29. $\dfrac{mn}{12n - 4m}$; $m \neq 3n$, 0, 0

30. $x - 4$; -5

31. $z + 8$; -2

32. $\dfrac{4}{x + 4}$; $-4, -2$

33. $\dfrac{2}{y + 5}$; $-5, 2$

34. $\dfrac{m + 6}{m + 1}$; $-1, 6$

35. $\dfrac{a + 3}{a + 9}$; $-9, 3$

You can use the same procedure to simplify a rational expression in which the numerator and denominator are polynomials.

Simplest Form
When a rational expression is in simplest form, the numerator and denominator have no common factors other than 1 or -1.

Example 5 Expressions Involving Polynomials

Simplify $\dfrac{x^2 - 2x - 15}{x^2 - x - 12}$.

$$\dfrac{x^2 - 2x - 15}{x^2 - x - 12} = \dfrac{(x + 3)(x - 5)}{(x + 3)(x - 4)} \quad \text{Factor.}$$

$$= \dfrac{\cancel{(x + 3)}(x - 5)}{\cancel{(x + 3)}(x - 4)} \quad \text{Divide the numerator and denominator by the GCF, } x + 3.$$

$$= \dfrac{x - 5}{x - 4} \quad \text{Simplify.}$$

It is important to determine the excluded values of a rational expression using the original expression rather than the simplified expression.

Example 6 Excluded Values

Simplify $\dfrac{3x - 15}{x^2 - 7x + 10}$. State the excluded values of x.

$$\dfrac{3x - 15}{x^2 - 7x + 10} = \dfrac{3(x - 5)}{(x - 2)(x - 5)} \quad \text{Factor.}$$

$$= \dfrac{3\cancel{(x - 5)}}{(x - 2)\cancel{(x - 5)}} \quad \text{Divide the numerator and denominator by the GCF, } x - 5.$$

$$= \dfrac{3}{x - 2} \quad \text{Simplify.}$$

Exclude the values for which $x^2 - 7x + 10$ equals 0.

$x^2 - 7x + 10 = 0$ The denominator cannot equal zero.

$(x - 5)(x - 2) = 0$ Factor.

$x = 5$ or $x = 2$ Zero Product Property

CHECK Verify the excluded values by substituting them into the original expression.

$$\dfrac{3x - 15}{x^2 - 7x + 10} = \dfrac{3(5) - 15}{5^2 - 7(5) + 10} \quad x = 5$$

$$= \dfrac{15 - 15}{25 - 35 + 10} \quad \text{Evaluate.}$$

$$= \dfrac{0}{0} \quad \text{Simplify.}$$

$$\dfrac{3x - 15}{x^2 - 7x + 10} = \dfrac{3(2) - 15}{2^2 - 7(2) + 10} \quad x = 2$$

$$= \dfrac{6 - 15}{4 - 14 + 10} \quad \text{Evaluate.}$$

$$= \dfrac{-9}{0} \quad \text{Simplify.}$$

The expression is undefined when $x = 5$ and $x = 2$. Therefore, $x \neq 5$ and $x \neq 2$.

D A I L Y
INTERVENTION

Differentiated Instruction

Interpersonal Place students in pairs to work through Examples 5 and 6. Have one student factor the numerator and the other student factor the denominator. Then, ask them to compare their factors to identify the GCF in order to simplify the expression.

Check for Understanding

Concept Check

1. Sample answer: Factor the denominator, set each factor equal to 0, and solve for *x*.

1. **Describe** how you would determine the values to be excluded from the expression $\frac{x + 3}{x^2 + 5x + 6}$.

2. **OPEN ENDED** Write a rational expression involving one variable for which the excluded values are −4 and −7. **Sample answer:** $\frac{1}{(x + 4)(x + 7)}$

3. **Explain** why −2 may not be the only excluded value of a rational expression that simplifies to $\frac{x - 3}{x + 2}$. **See margin.**

Guided Practice

State the excluded values for each rational expression.

GUIDED PRACTICE KEY	
Exercises	Examples
4–6	1, 2
7, 8	4, 6
9–13	5, 6
14, 15	3

4. $\frac{4a}{3 + a}$ −3

5. $\frac{x^2 - 9}{2x + 6}$ −3

6. $\frac{n + 5}{n^2 + n - 20}$ −5, 4

Simplify each expression. State the excluded values of the variables.

7. $\frac{56x^2y}{70x^3y^2}$ $\frac{4}{5xy}$; 0, 0

8. $\frac{x^2 - 49}{x + 7}$ $x - 7$; −7

9. $\frac{x + 4}{x^2 + 8x + 16}$ $\frac{1}{x + 4}$; −4

10. $\frac{x^2 - 2x - 3}{x^2 - 7x + 12}$ $\frac{x + 1}{x - 4}$; 3, 4

11. $\frac{a^2 + 4a - 12}{a^2 + 2a - 8}$ $\frac{a + 6}{a + 4}$; −4, 2

12. $\frac{2x^2 - x - 21}{2x^2 - 15x + 28}$ $\frac{x + 3}{x - 4}$; $\frac{7}{2}$, 4

13. Simplify $\frac{b^2 - 3b - 4}{b^2 - 13b + 36}$. State the excluded values of *b*. $\frac{b + 1}{b - 9}$; 4, 9

Application

AQUARIUMS For Exercises 14 and 15, use the following information.
Jenna has guppies in her aquarium. One week later, she adds four neon fish.

14. Write an expression that represents the fraction of neon fish in the aquarium. $\frac{4}{4 + g}$

15. Suppose that two months later the guppy population doubles, she still has four neons, and she buys 5 different tropical fish. Write an expression that shows the fraction of neons in the aquarium after the other fish have been added. $\frac{4}{9 + 2g}$

★ indicates increased difficulty

Practice and Apply

Homework Help	
For Exercises	See Examples
16–23	1, 2
24–27	4, 6
28–41	5, 6
42–54	3

Extra Practice
See page 846.

24–41. See margin.

State the excluded values for each rational expression.

16. $\frac{m + 3}{m - 2}$ 2

17. $\frac{3b}{b + 5}$ −5

18. $\frac{3n + 18}{n^2 - 36}$ −6, 6

19. $\frac{2x - 10}{x^2 - 25}$ −5, 5

20. $\frac{a^2 - 2a + 1}{a^2 + 2a - 3}$ −3, 1

21. $\frac{x^2 - 6x + 9}{x^2 + 2x - 15}$ −5, 3

22. $\frac{n^2 - 36}{n^2 + n - 30}$ −6, 5

23. $\frac{25 - x^2}{x^2 + 12x + 35}$ −7, −5

Simplify each expression. State the excluded values of the variables.

24. $\frac{35yz^2}{14y^2z}$

25. $\frac{14a^3b^2}{42ab^3}$

26. $\frac{64qr^2s}{16q^2rs}$

27. $\frac{9x^2yz}{24xyz^2}$

28. $\frac{7a^3b^2}{21a^2b + 49ab^3}$

29. $\frac{3m^2n^3}{36mn^3 - 12m^2n^2}$

30. $\frac{x^2 + x - 20}{x + 5}$

31. $\frac{z^2 + 10z + 16}{z + 2}$

32. $\frac{4x + 8}{x^2 + 6x + 8}$

33. $\frac{2y - 4}{y^2 + 3y - 10}$

34. $\frac{m^2 - 36}{m^2 - 5m - 6}$

35. $\frac{a^2 - 9}{a^2 + 6a - 27}$

36. $\frac{x^2 + x - 2}{x^2 - 3x + 2}$

37. $\frac{b^2 + 2b - 8}{b^2 - 20b + 64}$

38. $\frac{x^2 - x - 20}{x^3 + 10x^2 + 24x}$

39. $\frac{n^2 - 8n + 12}{n^3 - 12n^2 + 36n}$

40. $\frac{4x^2 - 6x - 4}{2x^2 - 8x + 8}$

41. $\frac{3m^2 + 9m + 6}{4m^2 + 12m + 8}$

www.algebra1.com/self_check_quiz

Answers

36. $\frac{x + 2}{x - 2}$; 1, 2

37. $\frac{(b + 4)(b - 2)}{(b - 4)(b - 16)}$; 4, 16

38. $\frac{x - 5}{x(x + 6)}$; −6, −4, 0

39. $\frac{n - 2}{n(n - 6)}$; 0, 6

40. $\frac{2x + 1}{x - 2}$; 2

41. $\frac{3}{4}$; −2, −1

Study Notebook

Have students—
• add the definitions/examples of the vocabulary terms to their Vocabulary Builder worksheets for Chapter 12.
• include examples of how to factor rational expressions, and how to identify excluded values.
• include any other item(s) that they find helpful in mastering the skills in this lesson.

About the Exercises …

Organization by Objective
• **Excluded Values of Rational Expressions:** 16–23
• **Simplify Rational Expressions:** 24–41

Odd/Even Assignments
Exercises 16–41 are structured so that students practice the same concepts whether they are assigned odd or even problems.

Assignment Guide
Basic: 17–41 odd, 42–48, 55–80
Average: 17–41 odd, 46–52, 55–80
Advanced: 16–40 even, 49–74 (optional: 75–80)

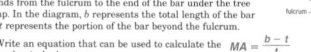
COOKING For Exercises 42–45, use the following information.
The formula $t = \frac{40(25 + 1.85a)}{50 - 1.85a}$ relates the time t in minutes that it takes to cook an average-size potato in an oven that is at an altitude of a thousands of feet.

42. What is the value of a for an altitude of 4500 feet? **4.5**

43. Calculate the time it takes to cook a potato at an altitude of 3500 feet.

44. About how long will it take to cook a potato at an altitude of 7000 feet?

45. The altitude in Exercise 44 is twice that of Exercise 43. How do your cooking times compare for those two altitudes? **The times are not doubled; the difference is 12 minutes.**

PHYSICAL SCIENCE For Exercises 46–48, use the following information.
To pry the lid off a paint can, a screwdriver that is 17.5 centimeters long is used as a lever. It is placed so that 0.4 centimeter of its length extends inward from the rim of the can.

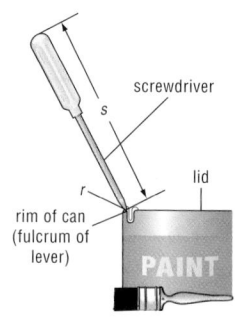

screwdriver

lid

rim of can (fulcrum of lever)

PAINT

46. Write an equation that can be used to calculate the mechanical advantage. $MA = \frac{s-r}{r}$

47. What is the mechanical advantage? **42.75**

48. If a force of 6 pounds is applied to the end of the screwdriver, what is the force placed on the lid? **256.5 lb**

FIELD TRIPS For Exercises 49–52, use the following information.
Mrs. Hoffman's art class is taking a trip to the museum. A bus that can seat up to 56 people costs $450 for the day, and group rate tickets at the museum cost $4 each.

49. If there are no more than 56 students going on the field trip, write an expression for the total cost for n students to go to the museum. **$450 + 4n$**

50. Write a rational expression that could be used to calculate the cost of the trip per student. $\frac{450 + 4n}{n}$

51. How many students must attend in order to keep the cost under $15 per student? **41**

52. How would you change the expression for cost per student if the school were to cover the cost of two adult chaperones? $\frac{450 + 4(n + 2)}{n}$

FARMING For Exercises 53 and 54, use the following information.
Some farmers use an irrigation system that waters a circular region in a field. Suppose a square field with sides of length $2x$ is irrigated from the center of the square. The irrigation system can reach a radius of x.

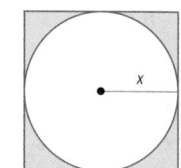

x

★ 53. Write an expression that represents the fraction of the field that is irrigated. $\frac{\pi x^2}{4x^2}$ or $\frac{\pi}{4}$

★ 54. Calculate the percent of the field that is irrigated to the nearest whole percent. **79%**

55. **CRITICAL THINKING** Two students graphed the following equations on their calculators. **See margin.**

$$y = \frac{x^2 - 16}{x - 4} \qquad\qquad y = x + 4$$

They were surprised to see that the graphs appeared to be identical.

a. Explain why the graphs appear to be the same.

b. Explain how and why the graphs are different.

652 Chapter 12 Rational Expressions and Equations

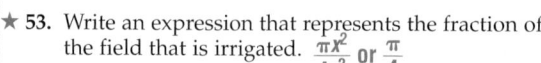

More About...

Farming

Although the amount of farmland in the United States is declining, crop production has increased steadily due in part to better irrigation practices.

Source: U.S. Department of Agriculture

56. **WRITING IN MATH** Answer the question that was posed at the beginning of the lesson. **See margin.**

How can a rational expression be used in a movie theater?

Include the following in your answer:
- a description of how you determine the excluded values of a rational expression, and
- an example of another real-world situation that could be described using a rational expression.

Standardized Test Practice
Ⓐ Ⓑ Ⓒ Ⓓ

57. Which expression is written in simplest form? **C**

Ⓐ $\dfrac{x^2 + 3x + 2}{x^2 + x - 2}$ 　　　Ⓑ $\dfrac{3x - 3}{2x^2 - 2}$

Ⓒ $\dfrac{x^2 + 7x}{x^2 + 3x - 4}$ 　　　Ⓓ $\dfrac{2x^2 - 5x - 3}{x^2 + x - 12}$

58. In which expression are 1 and 5 excluded values? **B**

Ⓐ $\dfrac{x^2 + 6x + 5}{x^2 - 3x + 2}$ 　　　Ⓑ $\dfrac{x^2 - 3x + 2}{x^2 - 6x + 5}$

Ⓒ $\dfrac{x^2 - 6x + 5}{x^2 - 3x + 2}$ 　　　Ⓓ $\dfrac{x^2 - 3x + 2}{x^2 + 6x + 5}$

Maintain Your Skills

Mixed Review Write an inverse variation equation that relates x and y. Assume that y varies inversely as x. Then solve. *(Lesson 12-1)*

59. If $y = 6$ when $x = 10$, find y when $x = -12$. $xy = 60$; -5

60. If $y = 16$ when $x = \frac{1}{2}$, find x when $y = 32$. $xy = 8$; $\frac{1}{4}$

61. If $y = -2.5$ when $x = 3$, find y when $x = -8$. $xy = -7.5$; 0.9375

Use a calculator to find the measure of each angle to the nearest degree. *(Lesson 11-7)*

62. $\sin N = 0.2347$ **14°** 　　　**63.** $\cos B = 0.3218$ **71°**

64. $\tan V = 0.0765$ **4°** 　　　**65.** $\sin A = 0.7011$ **45°**

Solve each equation. Check your solution. *(Lesson 11-3)*

66. $\sqrt{a + 3} = 2$ **1** 　　　**67.** $\sqrt{2z + 2} = z - 3$ **7**

68. $\sqrt{13 - 4p} - p = 8$ **−3** 　　　**69.** $\sqrt{3r^2 + 61} = 2r + 1$ **6**

Find the next three terms in each geometric sequence. *(Lesson 10-7)*

70. $1, 3, 9, 27, \ldots$ **81, 243, 729**

71. $6, 24, 96, 384, \ldots$ **1536, 6144, 24,576**

72. $\frac{1}{4}, -\frac{1}{2}, 1, -2, \ldots$ **4, −8, 16**

73. $4, 3, \frac{9}{4}, \frac{27}{16}, \ldots$ **$\frac{81}{64}, \frac{243}{256}, \frac{729}{1024}$**

74. **GEOMETRY** Find the area of a rectangle if the length is $2x + y$ units and the width is $x + y$ units. *(Lesson 8-7)* $2x^2 + 3xy + y^2$ **units²**

Getting Ready for the Next Lesson **BASIC SKILL** Complete.

75. 84 in. = _____ ft **7** 　　　**76.** 4.5 m = _____ cm **450**

77. 4 h 15 min = _____ s **15,300** 　　　**78.** 18 mi = _____ ft **95,040**

79. 3 days = _____ h **72** 　　　**80.** 220 mL = _____ L **0.22**

Open-Ended Assessment

Writing Have students write a paragraph explaining how to identify excluded values and give an example.

Getting Ready for Lesson 12-3

BASIC SKILL Students will learn dimensional analysis in Lesson 12-3. In order to solve dimensional analysis problems, students need a basic understanding of conversion factors between different units of measure. Use Exercises 75–80 to determine your students' familiarity with completing open sentences by using conversion factors.

Answers

55a. Sample answer: The graph appear to be identical because the second equation is the simplified form of the first equation.

55b. Sample answer: The first graph has a hole at $x = 4$ because it is an excluded value of the equation.

56. Sample answer: Use the rational expression for light intensity to help determine the brightness of the picture on the screen for the distance between the projector and the screen. Answers should include the following.
- Find the solutions for the expression in the denominator.
- Use the light intensity expression to determine the brightness of a search light.

Getting Started

Know Your Calculator When students enter two functions that should produce identical graphs, it is impossible to tell from the screen whether there are actually two graphs or one. To make sure there are two graphs, and that they overlap, have students press TRACE. Then have them use the up and down arrow keys to switch between the two graphs. Each time they press the keys, the equation in the upper left-hand corner of the screen should change.

Teach

- Make sure students enter the equations exactly as shown in the keystrokes. If students fail to put the numerator and denominator in parentheses, the resulting graph may be incorrect.

Assess

Ask students when they would use a graphing calculator to confirm the simplification of a rational expression. **Sample answer: when the simplification is very complicated**

Rational Expressions

When simplifying rational expressions, you can use a TI-83 Plus graphing calculator to support your answer. If the graphs of the original expression and the simplified expression coincide, they are equivalent. You can also use the graphs to see excluded values.

Simplify $\dfrac{x^2 - 25}{x^2 + 10x + 25}$.

Step 1 *Factor the numerator and denominator.*

- $\dfrac{x^2 - 25}{x^2 + 10x + 25} = \dfrac{(x - 5)(x + 5)}{(x + 5)(x + 5)}$

  $= \dfrac{(x - 5)}{(x + 5)}$ When $x = -5$, $x + 5 = 0$. Therefore, x cannot equal -5 because you cannot divide by zero.

Step 2 *Graph the original expression.*

- Set the calculator to **Dot** mode.
- Enter $\dfrac{x^2 - 25}{x^2 + 10x + 25}$ as Y1 and graph.

  KEYSTROKES: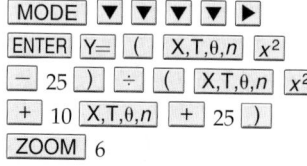

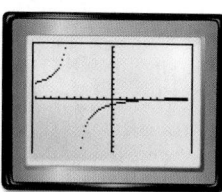

[−10, 10] scl: 1 by [−10, 10] scl: 1

Step 3 *Graph the simplified expression.*

- Enter $\dfrac{(x - 5)}{(x + 5)}$ as Y2 and graph.

  KEYSTROKES: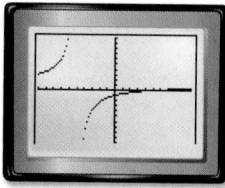

[−10, 10] scl: 1 by [−10, 10] scl: 1

Since the graphs overlap, the two expressions are equivalent.

Exercises 4a. Sample answer: Examine the values and verify that they are identical.

Simplify each expression. Then verify your answer graphically. Name the excluded values. 1–3. See margin for graphs.

1. $\dfrac{3x + 6}{x^2 + 7x + 10}$ $\dfrac{3}{x + 5}$; -5, -2

2. $\dfrac{x^2 - 9x + 8}{x^2 - 16x + 64}$ $\dfrac{x - 1}{x - 8}$; 8

3. $\dfrac{5x^2 + 10x + 5}{3x^2 + 6x + 3}$ $\dfrac{5}{3}$; -1

4. Simplify the rational expression $\dfrac{2x - 9}{4x^2 - 18x}$ and answer the following questions using the TABLE menu on your calculator.

   a. How can you use the TABLE function to verify that the original expression and the simplified expression are equivalent?

   b. How does the TABLE function show you that an x value is an excluded value?   It displays ERROR.

 www.algebra1.com/other_calculator_keystrokes

Answers

1.

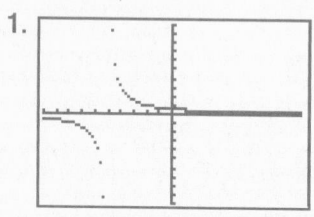

[−10, 10] scl: 1 by [−10, 10] scl: 1

2.

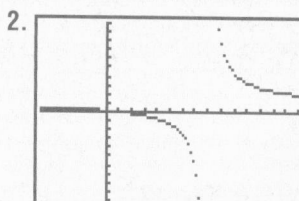

[−5, 15] scl: 1 by [−10, 10] scl: 1

3.

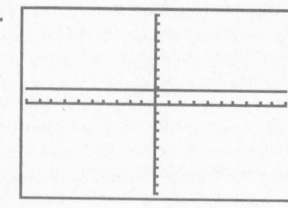

[−10, 10] scl: 1 by [−10, 10] scl:

What You'll Learn

- Multiply rational expressions.
- Use dimensional analysis with multiplication.

How can you multiply rational expressions to determine the cost of electricity?

There are 25 lights around a patio. Each light is 40 watts, and the cost of electricity is 15 cents per kilowatt-hour. You can use the expression below to calculate the cost of using the lights for *h* hours.

$$25 \text{ lights} \cdot h \text{ hours} \cdot \frac{40 \text{ watts}}{\text{light}} \cdot \frac{1 \text{ kilowatt}}{1000 \text{ watts}} \cdot \frac{15 \text{ cents}}{1 \text{ kilowatt} \cdot \text{hour}} \cdot \frac{1 \text{ dollar}}{100 \text{ cents}}$$

From this point on, you may assume that no denominator of a rational expression has a value of zero.

MULTIPLY RATIONAL EXPRESSIONS The multiplication expression above is similar to the multiplication of rational expressions. Recall that to multiply rational numbers expressed as fractions, you multiply numerators and multiply denominators. You can use this same method to multiply rational expressions.

Example 1 Expressions Involving Monomials

a. Find $\dfrac{5ab^3}{8c^2} \cdot \dfrac{16c^3}{15a^2b}$.

Method 1 Divide by the greatest common factor after multiplying.

$$\frac{5ab^3}{8c^2} \cdot \frac{16c^3}{15a^2b} = \frac{80ab^3c^3}{120a^2bc^2} \qquad \begin{array}{l} \leftarrow \text{Multiply the numerators.} \\ \leftarrow \text{Multiply the denominators.} \end{array}$$

$$= \frac{\overset{1}{40abc^2}(2b^2c)}{\underset{1}{40abc^2}(3a)} \qquad \text{The GCF is } 40abc^2.$$

$$= \frac{2b^2c}{3a} \qquad \text{Simplify.}$$

Method 2 Divide by the common factors before multiplying.

$$\frac{5ab^3}{8c^2} \cdot \frac{16c^3}{15a^2b} = \frac{\overset{1}{\cancel{5}}a\overset{b^2}{\cancel{b^3}}}{\underset{1}{\cancel{8}}\overset{}{c^2}} \cdot \frac{\overset{2}{\cancel{16}}\overset{c}{\cancel{c^3}}}{\underset{3\,a\,1}{\cancel{15}a^2\cancel{b}}} \qquad \text{Divide by common factors 5, 8, } a, b, \text{ and } c^2.$$

$$= \frac{2b^2c}{3a} \qquad \text{Multiply.}$$

b. Find $\dfrac{12xy^2}{45mp^2} \cdot \dfrac{27m^3p}{40x^3y}$.

$$\frac{12xy^2}{45mp^2} \cdot \frac{27m^3p}{40x^3y} = \frac{\overset{3}{\cancel{12}}\overset{1}{\cancel{x}}\overset{y}{\cancel{y^2}}}{\underset{5\,1\,p}{\cancel{45}\cancel{m}\cancel{p^2}}} \cdot \frac{\overset{3}{\cancel{27}}\overset{m^2}{\cancel{m^3}}\overset{1}{\cancel{p}}}{\underset{10\,x^2\,1}{\cancel{40}\cancel{x^3}\cancel{y}}} \qquad \text{Divide by common factors 4, 9, } x, y, m, \text{ and } p.$$

$$= \frac{9m^2y}{50x^2p} \qquad \text{Multiply.}$$

 www.algebra1.com/extra_examples

---

1 Focus

5-Minute Check Transparency 12-3 Use as a quiz or review of Lesson 12-2.

Mathematical Background notes are available for this lesson on p. 640C.

Building on Prior Knowledge

Students were briefly introduced to dimensional analysis in Chapter 3. In this lesson, students will learn that dimensional analysis is a process to convert between different units of measure through multiplying by rational expressions.

How can you multiply rational expressions to determine the cost of electricity?

Ask students:

- What is the simplification of the expression shown? **0.15*h* dollar**

- In what way are the units in these expressions similar to variables? **The common units in the numerator and denominator can be factored out.**

- How do you know that you ended up with the correct units at the end of the simplification? **The problem states that you want to know the cost of the electricity. The final unit left is dollars, which is the correct unit for cost.**

MULTIPLY RATIONAL EXPRESSIONS

In-Class Examples

Power Point®

Teaching Tip The text states that from this point forward, students can assume that no denominator of a rational expression has a value of zero. Ask students to discuss why this is an important assumption.

1 a. Find $\dfrac{7x^2y}{12z^3} \cdot \dfrac{14z}{49xy^4} \cdot \dfrac{x}{6y^3z^2}$

b. Find $\dfrac{5c^2d^4}{18q^3r} \cdot \dfrac{6q^5r^4}{60c^2d^2} \cdot \dfrac{d^2q^2r^3}{36}$

2 a. Find $\dfrac{x}{x+4} \cdot \dfrac{x^2-4x-32}{x^3}$.

$\dfrac{x-8}{x^2}$

b. Find $\dfrac{b+3}{4b-12} \cdot$

$\dfrac{b^2-4b+3}{b^2-7b-30} \cdot \dfrac{b-1}{4b-40}$

DIMENSIONAL ANALYSIS

In-Class Example

Power Point®

3 SPACE The velocity that a spacecraft must have in order to escape Earth's gravitational pull is called the escape velocity. The escape velocity for a spacecraft leaving Earth is about 40,320 kilometers per hour. What is this speed in meters per second? **11,200 m/s**

Study Tip

Look Back
To review **dimensional analysis**, see Lesson 3-8.

More About...

Olympics •

American sprinter Thomas Burke won the 100-meter dash at the first modern Olympics in Athens, Greece, in 1896 in 12.0 seconds.
Source: www.olympics.org

Sometimes you must factor a quadratic expression before you can simplify a product of rational expressions.

Example 2 Expressions Involving Polynomials

a. Find $\dfrac{x-5}{x} \cdot \dfrac{x^2}{x^2-2x-15}$.

$$\dfrac{x-5}{x} \cdot \dfrac{x^2}{x^2-2x-15} = \dfrac{x-5}{x} \cdot \dfrac{x^2}{(x-5)(x+3)} \quad \text{Factor the denominator.}$$

$$= \dfrac{\overset{x}{\cancel{x^2}}(\cancel{x-5})}{x(\cancel{x-5})(x+3)} \quad \text{The GCF is } x(x-5).$$

$$= \dfrac{x}{x+3} \quad \text{Simplify.}$$

b. Find $\dfrac{a^2+7a+10}{a+1} \cdot \dfrac{3a+3}{a+2}$.

$$\dfrac{a^2+7a+10}{a+1} \cdot \dfrac{3a+3}{a+2} = \dfrac{(a+5)(a+2)}{a+1} \cdot \dfrac{3(a+1)}{a+2} \quad \text{Factor the numerators.}$$

$$= \dfrac{3(a+5)(\cancel{a+2})(\cancel{a+1})}{(\cancel{a+1})(\cancel{a+2})} \quad \text{The GCF is } (a+1)(a+2).$$

$$= \dfrac{3(a+5)}{1} \quad \text{Multiply.}$$

$$= 3a+15 \quad \text{Simplify.}$$

DIMENSIONAL ANALYSIS When you multiply fractions that involve units of measure, you can divide by the units in the same way that you divide by variables. Recall that this process is called dimensional analysis.

Example 3 Dimensional Analysis

OLYMPICS In the 2000 Summer Olympics in Sydney, Australia, Maurice Green of the United States won the gold medal for the 100-meter sprint. His winning time was 9.87 seconds. What was his speed in kilometers per hour? Round to the nearest hundredth.

$$\dfrac{100 \text{ meters}}{9.87 \text{ seconds}} \cdot \dfrac{1 \text{ kilometer}}{1000 \text{ meters}} \cdot \dfrac{60 \text{ seconds}}{1 \text{ minute}} \cdot \dfrac{60 \text{ minutes}}{1 \text{ hour}}$$

$$= \dfrac{100 \text{ \cancel{meters}}}{9.87 \text{ \cancel{seconds}}} \cdot \dfrac{1 \text{ kilometer}}{1000 \text{ \cancel{meters}}} \cdot \dfrac{60 \text{ \cancel{seconds}}}{1 \text{ \cancel{minute}}} \cdot \dfrac{60 \text{ \cancel{minutes}}}{1 \text{ hour}}$$

$$= \dfrac{\overset{1}{\cancel{100}} \cdot 1 \cdot 60 \cdot 60 \text{ kilometers}}{9.87 \cdot \underset{10}{\cancel{1000}} \cdot 1 \cdot 1 \text{ hours}}$$

$$= \dfrac{60 \cdot 60 \text{ kilometers}}{9.87 \cdot 10 \text{ hours}} \quad \text{Simplify.}$$

$$= \dfrac{3600 \text{ kilometers}}{98.7 \text{ hours}} \quad \text{Multiply.}$$

$$= \dfrac{36.47 \text{ kilometers}}{1 \text{ hour}} \quad \text{Divide numerator and denominator by 98.7.}$$

His speed was 36.47 kilometers per hour.

D A I L Y

INTERVENTION | **Differentiated Instruction**

Logical Challenge students to write at least one rational expression consisting of two quadratic expressions, one divided by the other. The expression should simplify to $\dfrac{x-1}{x+2}$.

Concept Check

1. Sample answer:
$$\frac{2}{1}, \frac{1}{x}$$

2. Sample answer:
When the negative sign in front of the first expression is distributed, the numerator is $-x - 6$.

3. Amiri; sample answer: Amiri correctly divided by the GCF.

1. **OPEN ENDED** Write two rational expressions whose product is $\frac{2}{x}$.

2. **Explain** why $-\frac{x+6}{x-5}$ is not equivalent to $\frac{-x+6}{x-5}$.

3. **FIND THE ERROR** Amiri and Hoshi multiplied $\frac{x-3}{x+3}$ and $\frac{4x}{x^2-4x+3}$.

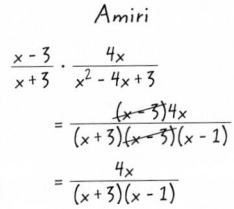

Amiri

$$\frac{x-3}{x+3} \cdot \frac{4x}{x^2-4x+3}$$
$$= \frac{(x-3)4x}{(x+3)(x-3)(x-1)}$$
$$= \frac{4x}{(x+3)(x-1)}$$

Hoshi

$$\frac{x-3}{x+3} \cdot \frac{4x}{x^2-4x+3}$$
$$= \frac{x-3}{x+3} \cdot \frac{4x}{x^2-4x+3}$$
$$= \frac{1}{x^2+3}$$

Who is correct? Explain your reasoning.

Guided Practice

GUIDED PRACTICE KEY	
Exercises	Examples
4–9	1–2
10, 11	3

Find each product.

4. $\dfrac{64y^2}{5y} \cdot \dfrac{5y}{8y}$ **8y**

5. $\dfrac{15s^2t^3}{12st} \cdot \dfrac{16st^2}{10s^3t^3}$ $\dfrac{2t}{s}$

6. $\dfrac{m+4}{3m} \cdot \dfrac{4m^2}{(m+4)(m+5)}$ $\dfrac{4m}{3(m+5)}$

7. $\dfrac{x^2-4}{2} \cdot \dfrac{4}{x-2}$ **2(x + 2)**

8. $\dfrac{n^2-16}{n+4} \cdot \dfrac{n+2}{n^2-8n+16}$ $\dfrac{n+2}{n-4}$

9. $\dfrac{x-5}{x^2-7x+10} \cdot \dfrac{x^2+x-6}{5}$ $\dfrac{x+3}{5}$

10. Find $\dfrac{24 \text{ feet}}{1 \text{ second}} \cdot \dfrac{60 \text{ seconds}}{1 \text{ minute}} \cdot \dfrac{60 \text{ minutes}}{1 \text{ hour}} \cdot \dfrac{1 \text{ mile}}{5280 \text{ feet}}$ **about 16.36 mph**

Application

11. **SPACE** The moon is about 240,000 miles from Earth. How many days would it take a spacecraft to reach the moon if it travels at an average of 100 miles per minute? $1\frac{2}{3}$ **days**

Practice and Apply

Homework Help	
For Exercises	See Examples
12–15	1
16–27	2
28–37	3

Extra Practice
See page 847.

17. $\dfrac{n-4}{n+4}$

18. $\dfrac{(z+6)(z-5)}{(z-6)(z+3)}$

19. $\dfrac{(x-1)(x+7)}{(x-7)(x+1)}$

26. $\dfrac{b+1}{(b+3)(b-3)}$

www.algebra1.com/self_check_quiz

Find each product.

12. $\dfrac{8}{x^2} \cdot \dfrac{x^4}{4x}$ **2x**

13. $\dfrac{10r^3}{6n^3} \cdot \dfrac{42n^2}{35r^3}$ $\dfrac{2}{n}$

14. $\dfrac{10y^3z^2}{6wx^3} \cdot \dfrac{12w^2x^2}{25y^2z^4}$ $\dfrac{4yw}{5xz^2}$

15. $\dfrac{3a^2b}{2gh} \cdot \dfrac{24g^2h}{15ab^2}$ $\dfrac{12ag}{5b}$

16. $\dfrac{(x-8)}{(x+8)(x-3)} \cdot \dfrac{(x+4)(x-3)}{(x-8)}$ $\dfrac{x+4}{x+8}$

17. $\dfrac{(n-1)(n+1)}{(n+1)} \cdot \dfrac{(n-4)}{(n-1)(n+4)}$

18. $\dfrac{(z+4)(z+6)}{(z-6)(z+1)} \cdot \dfrac{(z+1)(z-5)}{(z+3)(z+4)}$

19. $\dfrac{(x-1)(x+7)}{(x-7)(x-4)} \cdot \dfrac{(x-4)(x+10)}{(x+1)(x+10)}$

20. $\dfrac{x^2-25}{9} \cdot \dfrac{x+5}{x-5}$ $\dfrac{(x+5)^2}{9}$

21. $\dfrac{y^2-4}{y^2-1} \cdot \dfrac{y+1}{y+2}$ $\dfrac{y-2}{y-1}$

22. $\dfrac{1}{x^2+x-12} \cdot \dfrac{x-3}{x+5}$ $\dfrac{1}{(x+4)(x+5)}$

23. $\dfrac{x-6}{x^2+4x-32} \cdot \dfrac{x-4}{x+2}$ $\dfrac{x-6}{(x+8)(x+2)}$

24. $\dfrac{x+3}{x+4} \cdot \dfrac{x}{x^2+7x+12}$ $\dfrac{x}{(x+4)^2}$

25. $\dfrac{n}{n^2+8n+15} \cdot \dfrac{2n+10}{n^2}$ $\dfrac{2}{n(n+3)}$

26. $\dfrac{b^2+12b+11}{b^2-9} \cdot \dfrac{b+9}{b^2+20b+99}$

27. $\dfrac{a^2-a-6}{a^2-16} \cdot \dfrac{a^2+7a+12}{a^2+4a+4}$ $\dfrac{(a-3)(a+3)}{(a-4)(a+2)}$

Study Notebook

Have students—
• include examples of how to multiply rational expressions, and how to use dimensional analysis.
• include any other item(s) that they find helpful in mastering the skills in this lesson.

DAILY INTERVENTION **FIND THE ERROR** Remind students that only common factors can be eliminated from the numerator and denominator.

About the Exercises ...

Organization by Objective
• **Multiply Rational Expressions:** 12–27
• **Dimensional Analysis:** 28–31

Odd/Even Assignments
Exercises 12–31 are structured so that students practice the same concepts whether they are assigned odd or even problems.

Alert! Exercise 33 requires the Internet or other research materials.

Assignment Guide

Basic: 13–31 odd, 35–61
Average: 13–33 odd, 35–61
Advanced: 12–32 even, 34–55 (optional: 56–61)
All: Practice Quiz 1 (1–10)

Teacher to Teacher

Diane Stilwell South M.S., Morgantown, WV

"I remind my students that only common factors, not common terms, can be cancelled when simplifying rational expressions. I use Exercise 3 to determine whether my students understand the difference between the factors and the terms of a polynomial."

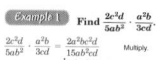

Study Guide and Intervention, p. 717 (shown) and p. 718

Multiply Rational Expressions To multiply rational expressions, you multiply the numerators and multiply the denominators. Then simplify.

Example 1 Find $\dfrac{2c^2d}{5ab^2} \cdot \dfrac{a^2b}{3cd}$.

$\dfrac{2c^2d}{5ab^2} \cdot \dfrac{a^2b}{3cd} = \dfrac{2a^2bc^2d}{15ab^2cd}$ Multiply.

$= \dfrac{(abcd)(2ac)}{(abcd)(15b)}$ Simplify.

$= \dfrac{2ac}{15b}$ Simplify.

Example 2 Find $\dfrac{x^2-16}{2x+8} \cdot \dfrac{x+4}{x^2+8x+16}$.

$\dfrac{x^2-16}{2x+8} \cdot \dfrac{x+4}{x^2+8x+16} = \dfrac{(x-4)(x+4)}{2(x+4)} \cdot \dfrac{x+4}{(x+4)(x+4)}$ Factor.

$= \dfrac{(x-4)(x+4)}{2(x+4)} \cdot \dfrac{x+4}{(x+4)(x+4)}$ Simplify.

$= \dfrac{x-4}{2x+8}$ Multiply.

Exercises

Find each product.

1. $\dfrac{6ab}{a^2b^2} \cdot \dfrac{a^2}{b^2} \quad \dfrac{6a}{b^3}$

2. $\dfrac{mn^2}{3} \cdot \dfrac{4}{mn} \quad \dfrac{4n}{3}$

3. $\dfrac{x+2}{x-4} \cdot \dfrac{x-4}{x-1} \quad \dfrac{x+2}{x-1}$

4. $\dfrac{m-5}{8} \cdot \dfrac{16}{m-5} \quad 2$

5. $\dfrac{2n-8}{n+2} \cdot \dfrac{2n+4}{n-4} \quad 4$

6. $\dfrac{x^2-16}{2x+8} \cdot \dfrac{x+4}{x^2+8x+16} \quad \dfrac{x-4}{2x+8}$

7. $\dfrac{8x+8}{x^2-2x+1} \cdot \dfrac{x-1}{2x+2} \quad \dfrac{4}{x-1}$

8. $\dfrac{a^2-25}{a+2} \cdot \dfrac{a^2-4}{a-5} \quad (a+5)(a-2)$

9. $\dfrac{x^2+6x+8}{2x^2+9x+4} \cdot \dfrac{2x^2-x-1}{x^2-3x+2} \quad \dfrac{x+2}{x-2}$

10. $\dfrac{m^2-1}{2m^2-m-1} \cdot \dfrac{2m+1}{m^2-2m+1} \quad \dfrac{m+1}{(m-1)^2}$

11. $\dfrac{n^2-1}{n^2-7n+10} \cdot \dfrac{n^2-25}{n^2+6n+5} \quad \dfrac{n-1}{n-2}$

12. $\dfrac{3p-3q}{10pq} \cdot \dfrac{20p^2q^3}{p^2-q^2} \quad \dfrac{6pq}{p+q}$

13. $\dfrac{a^2+7a+12}{a^2+3a-8} \cdot \dfrac{a^2+3a-10}{a^2+2a-8} \quad \dfrac{(a+3)(a+5)}{(a-2)(a+4)}$

14. $\dfrac{v^2-4v-21}{3v^2+6v} \cdot \dfrac{v^2+8v}{v^2+11v+24} \quad \dfrac{v-7}{3v+6}$

Skills Practice, p. 719 and Practice, p. 720 (shown)

Find each product.

1. $\dfrac{18x^2}{10y^3} \cdot \dfrac{15y^3}{24x} \quad \dfrac{9xy}{8}$

2. $\dfrac{24t^2}{8s^4t^3} \cdot \dfrac{12s^2t^2}{36s^3t} \quad \dfrac{1}{s^2}$

3. $\dfrac{14xy^2}{27m^2n} \cdot \dfrac{36m^4n^2}{7x^2y} \quad \dfrac{8m^2ny}{3x}$

4. $\dfrac{12n^2b}{4} \cdot \dfrac{4(a+2b)}{20n^2b^3} \quad \dfrac{3(a+2b)}{5b^2}$

5. $\dfrac{(x+2)(x+2)}{8} \cdot \dfrac{72}{(x+2)(x-2)} \quad \dfrac{9(x+2)}{x-2}$

6. $\dfrac{m+7}{m-6xm+2} \cdot \dfrac{(m-6xm+4)}{(m+7)} \quad \dfrac{m+4}{m+2}$

7. $\dfrac{c^2-1}{2c-6} \cdot \dfrac{c^2-9}{3c-3} \quad \dfrac{(c+1)(c+3)}{6}$

8. $\dfrac{x^2-16}{x^2-4} \cdot \dfrac{x+2}{x-4} \quad \dfrac{x+4}{x-2}$

9. $\dfrac{a-4}{a^2-a-12} \cdot \dfrac{a+3}{a-6} \quad \dfrac{1}{a-6}$

10. $\dfrac{4x+8}{x^2} \cdot \dfrac{x}{x^2-5x-14} \cdot \dfrac{4}{x(x-7)}$

11. $\dfrac{n^2+10n+16}{5n-10} \cdot \dfrac{n-2}{n^2+9n+8} \quad \dfrac{n+2}{5(n+1)}$

12. $\dfrac{3y-9}{y^2-9y+20} \cdot \dfrac{y^2-8y+16}{y-3} \quad \dfrac{3(y-4)}{y-5}$

13. $\dfrac{b^2+5b+4}{b^2-36} \cdot \dfrac{b^2+5b-6}{b^2+2b-8} \quad \dfrac{(b+1)(b-1)}{(b-6)(b-2)}$

14. $\dfrac{t^2+6t+9}{t^2-10t+25} \cdot \dfrac{t^2-t-20}{t^2+7t+12} \quad \dfrac{t+3}{t-5}$

Find each product.

15. $\dfrac{450 \text{ gallons}}{1 \text{ hour}} \cdot \dfrac{128 \text{ ounces}}{1 \text{ gallon}} \cdot \dfrac{1 \text{ hour}}{60 \text{ minutes}} \cdot \dfrac{1 \text{ minute}}{60 \text{ seconds}} \quad 16 \text{ oz/s}$

16. $\dfrac{81 \text{ kilometers}}{1 \text{ day}} \cdot \dfrac{1000 \text{ meters}}{1 \text{ kilometer}} \cdot \dfrac{1 \text{ day}}{24 \text{ hours}} \cdot \dfrac{1 \text{ hour}}{60 \text{ minutes}} \quad 56.25 \text{ m/min}$

17. **ANIMAL SPEEDS** The maximum speed of a coyote is 43 miles per hour over a distance of approximately a quarter mile. What is a coyote's maximum speed in feet per second? Round to the nearest tenth. 63.1 ft/s

18. **BIOLOGY** The heart of an average person pumps about 9000 liters of blood per day. How many quarts of blood does the heart pump per hour? (*Hint:* One quart is equal to 0.946 liter.) Round to the nearest whole number. 396 qt/h

Reading to Learn Mathematics, p. 721 — ELL

Pre-Activity How can you multiply rational expressions to determine the cost of electricity?

Read the introduction to Lesson 12-3 at the top of page 655 in your textbook.

• Why are units of measure crossed out in the expression?
to eliminate common units in the numerator and the denominator

• What is the expression after you multiply the numerators and multiply the denominators?
$\dfrac{15,000h}{100,000}$ or 0.15h dollars

Reading the Lesson

1. Complete the sentence. The product of two rational expressions can always be found by multiplying the numerators and multiplying the **denominators**.

2. When you multiply rational expressions, why do you eliminate common factors from the expression(s) above and below the fraction bar(s)?
so that the final answer will be in simplest form

3. Complete the sentence. If the numerators or denominators of two rational expressions involve quadratic expressions with two or three terms, try to **factor** these expressions before you multiply the rational expressions.

4. A student thinks that Example 2b on page 656 shows that you can multiply two rational expressions and get an answer that is not a rational expression. Do you agree? Explain.
Sample answer: No; $3a + 15$ is not in fraction form, but it is a rational expression, because it can be written as the fraction $\dfrac{3a+15}{1}$.

Helping You Remember

5. Suppose that a friend was absent when the class worked on this lesson. Tell how you can explain to your friend the procedure for multiplying rational expressions.
Sample answer: Factor the numerators and denominators of the rational expressions. Without using the Distributive Property, write a single fraction showing the product of the numerators divided by the product of the denominators. Divide numerator and denominator by the GCF. Then simplify.

Find each product.

28. $\dfrac{2.54 \text{ centimeters}}{1 \text{ inch}} \cdot \dfrac{12 \text{ inches}}{1 \text{ foot}} \cdot \dfrac{3 \text{ feet}}{1 \text{ yard}}$ **91.44 cm/yd**

29. $\dfrac{60 \text{ kilometers}}{1 \text{ hour}} \cdot \dfrac{1000 \text{ meters}}{1 \text{ kilometer}} \cdot \dfrac{1 \text{ hour}}{60 \text{ minutes}} \cdot \dfrac{1 \text{ minutes}}{60 \text{ seconds}}$ **about 16.67 m/s**

30. $\dfrac{32 \text{ feet}}{1 \text{ second}} \cdot \dfrac{60 \text{ seconds}}{1 \text{ minute}} \cdot \dfrac{60 \text{ minutes}}{1 \text{ hour}} \cdot \dfrac{1 \text{ mile}}{5280 \text{ feet}}$ **about 21.8 mi/h**

31. $10 \text{ feet} \cdot 18 \text{ feet} \cdot 3 \text{ feet} \cdot \dfrac{1 \text{ yard}^3}{27 \text{ feet}^3}$ **20 yd³**

32. **DECORATING** Alani's bedroom is 12 feet wide and 14 feet long. What will it cost to carpet her room if the carpet costs $18 per square yard? **$336**

33. **EXCHANGE RATES** While traveling in Canada, Johanna bought some gifts to bring home. She bought 2 T-shirts that cost $21.95 (Canadian). If the exchange rate at the time was 1 U.S. dollar for 1.37 Canadian dollars, how much did Johanna spend in U.S. dollars? **about $16.02**

Online Research **Data Update** Visit www.algebra1.com/data_update to find the most recent exchange rate between the United States and Canadian currency. How much does a $21.95 (Canadian) purchase cost in U.S. dollars?

34. **CITY MAINTENANCE** Street sweepers can clean 3 miles of streets per hour. A city owns 2 street sweepers, and each sweeper can be used for three hours before it comes in for an hour to refuel. How many miles of streets can be cleaned in 18 hours on the road? **108 mi**

TRAFFIC For Exercises 35–37, use the following information.
During rush hour one evening, traffic was backed up for 13 miles along a particular stretch of freeway. Assume that each vehicle occupied an average of 30 feet of space in a lane and that the freeway has three lanes.

35. Write an expression that could be used to determine the number of vehicles involved in the backup. $3 \text{ lanes} \cdot \dfrac{13 \text{ miles}}{1 \text{ lane}} \cdot \dfrac{5280 \text{ feet}}{1 \text{ mile}} \cdot \dfrac{1 \text{ vehicle}}{30 \text{ feet}}$

36. How many vehicles are involved in the backup? **6864**

37. Suppose that there are 8 exits along this stretch of freeway, and it takes each vehicle an average of 24 seconds to exit the freeway. Approximately how many hours will it take for all the vehicles in the backup to exit? **5.72 h**

38. **CRITICAL THINKING** Identify the expressions that are equivalent to $\dfrac{x}{y}$. Explain why the expressions are equivalent.

   a. $\dfrac{x+3}{y+3}$ b. $\dfrac{3-x}{3-y}$ c. $\dfrac{3x}{3y}$ d. $\dfrac{x^3}{y^3}$ e. $\dfrac{n^3x}{n^3y}$

39. **WRITING IN MATH** Answer the question that was posed at the beginning of the lesson. **See margin.**

   How can you multiply rational expressions to determine the cost of electricity?

   Include the following in your answer:
   • an expression that you could use to determine the cost of using 60-watt light bulbs instead of 40-watt bulbs, and
   • an example of a real-world situation in which you must multiply rational expressions.

658 Chapter 12 Rational Expressions and Equations

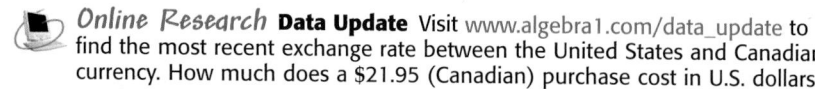

More About. . .

Exchange Rates ••••

A system of floating exchange rates among international currencies was established in 1976. It was needed because the old system of basing a currency's value on gold had become obsolete.

Source: www.infoplease.com

38. c and e;
Sample answer:
The expressions each have a GCF that can be used to simplify the expressions.

Enrichment, p. 722

Continued Fractions

The following is an example of a continued fraction. By starting at the bottom you can simplify the expression to a rational number.

$3 + \dfrac{4}{1+\dfrac{6}{7}} = 3 + \dfrac{4}{\dfrac{13}{7}}$

$= 3 + \dfrac{28}{13}$ or $\dfrac{67}{13}$

Example Express $\dfrac{48}{19}$ as a continued fraction.

$\dfrac{48}{19} = 2 + \dfrac{10}{19}$ Notice that the numerator of the last fraction must be equal to 1 before the process stops.

$= 2 + \dfrac{1}{\dfrac{19}{10}}$

Standardized Test Practice
Ⓐ Ⓑ Ⓒ Ⓓ

40. Which expression is the product of $\dfrac{13xyz}{4x^2y}$ and $\dfrac{8x^2z^2}{2y^3}$? **D**

Ⓐ $\dfrac{13xy^3}{z^3}$ Ⓑ $\dfrac{13xz^2}{y^3}$ Ⓒ $\dfrac{13xyz}{z^3}$ Ⓓ $\dfrac{13xz^3}{y^3}$

41. Identify the product of $\dfrac{4a+4}{a^2+a}$ and $\dfrac{a^2}{3a-3}$. **A**

Ⓐ $\dfrac{4a}{3(a-1)}$ Ⓑ $\dfrac{4a}{3}$ Ⓒ $\dfrac{4a}{3(a+1)}$ Ⓓ $\dfrac{4a^2}{3(a-1)}$

Maintain Your Skills

Mixed Review

State the excluded values for each rational expression. *(Lesson 12-2)*

42. $\dfrac{s+6}{s^2-36}$ **−6, 6**   43. $\dfrac{a^2-25}{a^2+3a-10}$ **−5, 2**   44. $\dfrac{x+3}{x^2+6x+9}$ **−3**

Write an inverse variation equation that relates x and y. Assume that y varies inversely as x. Then solve. *(Lesson 12-1)*

45. If $y = 9$ when $x = 8$, find x when $y = 6$. **$xy = 72$; 12**
46. If $y = 2.4$ when $x = 8.1$, find y when $x = 3.6$. **$xy = 19.44$; 5.4**
47. If $y = 24$ when $x = -8$, find y when $x = 4$. **$xy = -192$; −48**
48. If $y = 6.4$ when $x = 4.4$, find x when $y = 3.2$. **$xy = 28.16$; 8.8**

Simplify. Assume that no denominator is equal to zero. *(Lesson 8-2)*

49. $\dfrac{-7^{12}}{7^9}$ **-7^3 or −343**   50. $\dfrac{20p^6}{8p^8} \cdot \dfrac{5}{2p^2}$ 51. $\dfrac{24a^3b^4c^7}{6a^6c^2} \cdot \dfrac{4b^4c^5}{a^3}$

Solve each inequality. Then check your solution. *(Lesson 6-2)*

52. $\dfrac{g}{8} < \dfrac{7}{2}$ **$\{g \mid g < 28\}$**   53. $3.5r \geq 7.35$ **$\{r \mid r \geq 2.1\}$**   54. $\dfrac{9k}{4} > \dfrac{3}{5}$ **$\{k \mid k > \dfrac{4}{15}\}$**

55. **FINANCE** The total amount of money Antonio earns mowing lawns and doing yard work varies directly with the number of days he works. At one point, he earned $340 in 4 days. At this rate, how long will it take him to earn $935? *(Lesson 5-2)* **11 days**

Getting Ready for the Next Lesson
56. $(x + 5)(x - 8)$
57. $(n + 8)(n - 8)$

PREREQUISITE SKILL Factor each polynomial.
*(To review **factoring polynomials**, see Lessons 9-3 through 9-6.)*

56. $x^2 - 3x - 40$ 57. $n^2 - 64$ 58. $x^2 - 12x + 36$
59. $a^2 + 2a - 35$ 60. $2x^2 - 5x - 3$ 61. $3x^3 - 24x^2 + 36x$

58. $(x - 6)^2$ 59. $(a + 7)(a - 5)$ 60. $(2x + 1)(x - 3)$ 61. $3x(x - 2)(x - 6)$

Practice Quiz 1
Lessons 12-1 through 12-3

Graph each variation if y varies inversely as x. *(Lesson 12-1)* **1–2. See margin.**

1. $y = 28$ when $x = 7$ 2. $y = -6$ when $x = 9$

Simplify each expression. *(Lesson 12-2)*

3. $\dfrac{28a^2}{49ab}$ **$\dfrac{4a}{7b}$**   4. $\dfrac{y + 3y^2}{3y + 1}$ **y**   5. $\dfrac{b^2 - 3b - 4}{b^2 - 13b + 36}$ **$\dfrac{b + 1}{b - 9}$**   6. $\dfrac{3n^2 + 5n - 2}{3n^2 - 13n + 4}$ **$\dfrac{n + 2}{n - 4}$**

Find each product. *(Lesson 12-3)*   8. $\dfrac{2x}{a + 9}$ 9. $\dfrac{4}{5(n + 5)}$ 10. $\dfrac{x + 4}{x + 2}$

7. $\dfrac{3m^2}{2m} \cdot \dfrac{18m^2}{9m}$ **$3m^2$**   8. $\dfrac{5a + 10}{10x^2} \cdot \dfrac{4x^3}{a^2 + 11a + 18}$ 9. $\dfrac{4n + 8}{n^2 - 25} \cdot \dfrac{n - 5}{5n + 10}$ 10. $\dfrac{x^2 - x - 6}{x^2 - 9} \cdot \dfrac{x^2 + 7x + 12}{x^2 + 4x + 4}$

Open-Ended Assessment

Modeling Use note cards or scrap pieces of paper to write a multiplication problem involving rational expressions. Tape the pieces of paper on the board so that each numerator and denominator is on a separate piece of paper. Ask volunteers to come up and find common factors. For each common factor found, have students rewrite the expression on a piece of paper and tape it over the existing expression, until the product is found.

Getting Ready for Lesson 12-4

PREREQUISITE SKILL Students will learn to divide rational expressions in Lesson 12-4, which involves factoring polynomials. Use Exercises 56–61 to determine your students' familiarity with factoring polynomials.

Assessment Options

Practice Quiz 1 The quiz provides students with a brief review of the concepts and skills in Lessons 12-1 through 12-3. Lesson numbers are given to the right of exercises or instruction lines so students can review concepts not yet mastered.

Quiz (Lessons 12-1 through 12-3) is available on p. 773 of the *Chapter 12 Resource Masters*.

Answers

39. Sample answer: Multiply rational expressions to perform dimensional analysis. Answers should include the following.

- 25 lights · h hours · $\dfrac{60 \text{ watts}}{\text{light}}$ · $\dfrac{1 \text{ kilowatt}}{1000 \text{ watts}}$ · $\dfrac{15 \text{ cents}}{1 \text{ kilowatt} \cdot \text{hour}}$ · $\dfrac{1 \text{ dollar}}{100 \text{ cents}}$

- Sample answer: converting units of measure

1.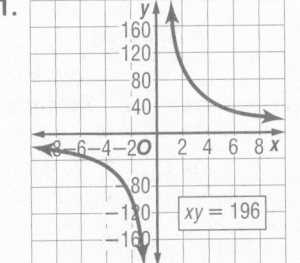

2.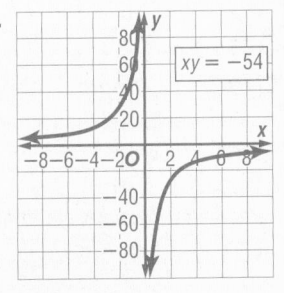

1 Focus

5-Minute Check Transparency 12-4 Use as a quiz or review of Lesson 12-3.

Mathematical Background notes are available for this lesson on p. 640C.

Building on Prior Knowledge

In Lesson 2-4, students learned that to divide rational numbers, you multiply by the reciprocal. In this lesson, students will learn that the same procedure is used for dividing rational expressions involving monomials, binomials, and polynomials.

How can you determine the number of aluminum soft drink cans made each year?

Ask students:

- Use the information in the paragraph to write an equation that represents c, the number of aluminum soft drink cans produced each year.
  $\frac{5}{8}c = 63.9$ billion

- How do you solve the equation that you just wrote for c? **Multiply both sides of the equation by the reciprocal of $\frac{5}{8}$, which is $\frac{8}{5}$.**

- About how many aluminum soft drink cans are produced each year? **102.24 billion**

Resource Manager

📁 Workbook and Reproducible Masters

Chapter 12 Resource Masters
- Study Guide and Intervention, pp. 723–724
- Skills Practice, p. 725
- Practice, p. 726
- Reading to Learn Mathematics, p. 727
- Enrichment, p. 728

Graphing Calculator and Spreadsheet Masters, p. 46
Parent and Student Study Guide Workbook, p. 94

🔲 Transparencies
5-Minute Check Transparency 12-4
Answer Key Transparencies

💿 Technology
Interactive Chalkboard

What You'll Learn

- Divide rational expressions.
- Use dimensional analysis with division.

How can you determine the number of aluminum soft drink cans made each year?

Most soft drinks come in aluminum cans. Although more cans are used today than in the 1970s, the demand for new aluminum has declined. This is due in large part to the great number of cans that are recycled. In recent years, approximately 63.9 billion cans were recycled annually. This represents $\frac{5}{8}$ of all cans produced.

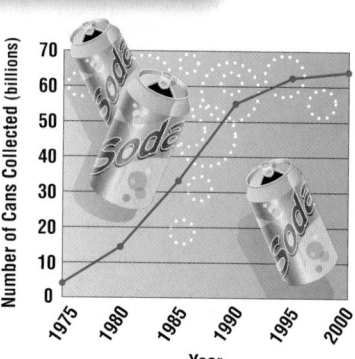

Number of Cans Collected (billions) vs. Year

DIVIDE RATIONAL EXPRESSIONS Recall that to divide rational numbers expressed as fractions you multiply by the reciprocal of the divisor. You can use this same method to divide rational expressions.

Example 1 *Expression Involving Monomials*

Find $\frac{5x^2}{7} \div \frac{10x^3}{21}$.

$\frac{5x^2}{7} \div \frac{10x^3}{21} = \frac{5x^2}{7} \cdot \frac{21}{10x^3}$ Multiply by $\frac{21}{10x^3}$, the reciprocal of $\frac{10x^3}{21}$.

$= \frac{\overset{1}{5x^2}}{\underset{1}{7}} \cdot \frac{\overset{3}{21}}{\underset{2x}{10x^3}}$ Divide by common factors 5, 7, and x^2.

$= \frac{3}{2x}$ Simplify.

Example 2 *Expression Involving Binomials*

Find $\frac{n+1}{n+3} \div \frac{2n+2}{n+4}$.

$\frac{n+1}{n+3} \div \frac{2n+2}{n+4} = \frac{n+1}{n+3} \cdot \frac{n+4}{2n+2}$ Multiply by $\frac{n+4}{2n+2}$, the reciprocal of $\frac{2n+2}{n+4}$.

$= \frac{n+1}{n+3} \cdot \frac{n+4}{2(n+1)}$ Factor $2n+2$.

$= \frac{\overset{1}{n+1}}{n+3} \cdot \frac{n+4}{2(\underset{1}{n+1})}$ The GCF is $n+1$.

$= \frac{n+4}{2(n+3)}$ or $\frac{n+4}{2n+6}$ Simplify.

Often the quotient of rational expressions involves a divisor that is a binomial.

Example 3 *Divide by a Binomial*

Find $\frac{5a + 10}{a + 5} \div (a + 2)$.

$$\frac{5a + 10}{a + 5} \div (a + 2) = \frac{5a + 10}{a + 5} \cdot \frac{1}{(a + 2)} \quad \text{Multiply by } \frac{1}{(a + 2)}, \text{ the reciprocal of } (a + 2).$$

$$= \frac{5(a + 2)}{a + 5} \cdot \frac{1}{(a + 2)} \quad \text{Factor } 5a + 10.$$

$$= \frac{5(\overset{1}{\cancel{a + 2}})}{a + 5} \cdot \frac{1}{(\underset{1}{\cancel{a + 2}})} \quad \text{The GCF is } a + 2.$$

$$= \frac{5}{a + 5} \quad \text{Simplify.}$$

Sometimes you must factor a quadratic expression before you can simplify the quotient of rational expressions.

Example 4 *Expression Involving Polynomials*

Find $\frac{m^2 + 3m + 2}{4} \div \frac{m + 2}{m + 1}$.

$$\frac{m^2 + 3m + 2}{4} \div \frac{m + 2}{m + 1} = \frac{m^2 + 3m + 2}{4} \cdot \frac{m + 1}{m + 2} \quad \text{Multiply by the reciprocal, } \frac{m + 1}{m + 2}.$$

$$= \frac{(m + 1)(m + 2)}{4} \cdot \frac{m + 1}{m + 2} \quad \text{Factor } m^2 + 3m + 2.$$

$$= \frac{(m + 1)(\overset{1}{\cancel{m + 2}})}{4} \cdot \frac{m + 1}{\underset{1}{\cancel{m + 2}}} \quad \text{The GCF is } m + 2.$$

$$= \frac{(m + 1)^2}{4} \quad \text{Simplify.}$$

DIMENSIONAL ANALYSIS You can divide rational expressions that involve units of measure by using dimensional analysis.

Example 5 *Dimensional Analysis*

SPACE In November, 1996, NASA launched the Mars Global Surveyor. It took 309 days for the orbiter to travel 466,000,000 miles from Earth to Mars. What was the speed of the spacecraft in miles per hour? Round to the nearest hundredth.

Use the formula for rate, time, and distance.

$rt = d$	rate · time = distance
$r \cdot 309 \text{ days} = 466{,}000{,}000 \text{ mi}$	$t = 309 \text{ days}, d = 466{,}000{,}000$
$r = \dfrac{466{,}000{,}000 \text{ mi}}{309 \text{ days}}$	Divide each side by 309 days.
$\quad = \dfrac{466{,}000{,}000 \text{ miles}}{309 \text{ days}} \cdot \dfrac{1 \text{ day}}{24 \text{ hours}}$	Convert days to hours.
$\quad = \dfrac{466{,}000{,}000 \text{ miles}}{7416 \text{ hours}} \text{ or about } \dfrac{62{,}837.11 \text{ miles}}{1 \text{ hour}}$	

Thus, the spacecraft traveled at a rate of about 62,837.11 miles per hour.

www.algebra1.com/extra_examples

Lesson 12-4 Dividing Rational Expressions **661**

Study Notebook

Have students—
- include examples of how to divide rational expressions
- include any other item(s) that they find helpful in mastering the skills in this lesson.

About the Exercises ...

Organization by Objective
- **Divide Rational Expressions:** 13–24, 29, 30, 31–34
- **Dimensional Analysis:** 25–28

Odd/Even Assignments
Exercises 13–36 are structured so that students practice the same concepts whether they are assigned odd or even problems.

Assignment Guide

Basic: 13–37 odd, 38, 39, 42, 45–75

Average: 13–37 odd, 40–42, 45–75

Advanced: 14–36 even, 42, 45–69 (optional: 70–75)

Check for Understanding

Concept Check

1. **OPEN ENDED** Write two rational expressions whose quotient is $\frac{5z}{xy}$.

1. Sample answer: $\frac{15z}{4y^2} \div \frac{3x}{4y}$

2. **Tell** whether the following statement is *always*, *sometimes*, or *never* true. Explain your reasoning. **Sometimes; sample answer: 0 has no reciprocal.** *Every real number has a reciprocal.*

3. **Explain** how to calculate the mass in kilograms of one cubic meter of a substance whose density is 2.16 grams per cubic centimeter. **Sample answer: Divide the density by the given volume, then perform dimensional analysis.**

Guided Practice

Find each quotient.

GUIDED PRACTICE KEY	
Exercises	Examples
4–6	1, 2
7	3
8, 9	4
10–12	5

9. $\frac{2(x-2)(x+3)}{(x+1)(x+9)}$

4. $\frac{10n^3}{7} \div \frac{5n^2}{21}$ **6n**

5. $\frac{2a}{a+3} \div \frac{a+7}{a+3}$ **$\frac{2a}{a+7}$**

6. $\frac{3m-15}{m+4} \div \frac{m-5}{6m+24}$ **18**

7. $\frac{2x+6}{x+5} \div (x+3)$ **$\frac{2}{x+5}$**

8. $\frac{k+3}{k^2+4k+4} \div \frac{2k+6}{k+2}$ **$\frac{1}{2(k+2)}$**

9. $\frac{2x-4}{x^2+11x+18} \div \frac{x+1}{x^2+5x+6}$

10. Express 85 kilometers per hour in meters per second. **about 23.61 m/s**

11. Express 32 pounds per square foot as pounds per square inch. **$\frac{2}{9}$ lb/in^2**

Application

12. **COOKING** Latisha was making candy using a two-quart pan. As she stirred the mixture, she noticed that the pan was about $\frac{2}{3}$ full. If each piece of candy has a volume of about $\frac{3}{4}$ ounce, approximately how many pieces of candy will Latisha make? **about 57 pieces**

Practice and Apply

Homework Help	
For Exercises	See Examples
13–18	1
19–22	3
23, 24	2
29–36	4
25–28, 37–41	5

Extra Practice
See page 847.

Find each quotient.

13. $\frac{a^2}{b^2} \div \frac{a}{b^3}$ **ab**

14. $\frac{n^4}{p^2} \div \frac{n^2}{p^3}$ **n^2p**

15. $\frac{4x^3}{y^4} \div \frac{8x^2}{y^2}$ **$\frac{x}{2y^2}$**

16. $\frac{10m^2}{7n^2} \div \frac{25m^4}{14n^3}$ **$\frac{4n}{5m^2}$**

17. $\frac{x^2y^3z}{s^2t^2} \div \frac{x^2yz^3}{s^3t^2}$ **$\frac{sy^2}{z^2}$**

18. $\frac{a^4bc^3}{g^2h^3} \div \frac{ab^2c^2}{g^3h^3}$ **$\frac{a^3cg}{b}$**

19. $\frac{b^2-9}{4b} \div (b-3)$ **$\frac{b+3}{4b}$**

20. $\frac{m^2-16}{5m} \div (m+4)$ **$\frac{m-4}{5m}$**

21. $\frac{3k}{k+1} \div (k-2)$ **$\frac{3k}{(k+1)(k-2)}$**

22. $\frac{5d}{d-3} \div (d+1)$ **$\frac{5d}{(d-3)(d+1)}$**

23. $\frac{3x+12}{4x-18} \div \frac{2x+8}{x+4}$ **$\frac{3(x+4)}{4(2x-9)}$**

24. $\frac{4a-8}{2a-6} \div \frac{2a-4}{a-4}$ **$\frac{a-4}{a-3}$**

Complete.

25. $24 \text{ yd}^3 =$ _____ ft^3 **648**

26. $0.35 \text{ m}^3 =$ _____ cm^3 **350,000**

27. $330 \text{ ft/s} =$ _____ mi/h **225**

28. $1730 \text{ plants/km}^2 =$ _____ plants/m^2 **0.00173**

29. What is the quotient when $\frac{2x+6}{x+5}$ is divided by $\frac{2}{x+5}$? **$x+3$**

30. Find the quotient when $\frac{m-8}{m+7}$ is divided by $m^2 - 7m - 8$. **$\frac{1}{(m+7)(m+1)}$**

Find each quotient.

31. $\dfrac{x^2 + 2x + 1}{2} \div \dfrac{x + 1}{x - 1}$ $\quad \dfrac{(x + 1)(x - 1)}{2}$

32. $\dfrac{n^2 + 3n + 2}{4} \div \dfrac{n + 1}{n + 2}$ $\quad \dfrac{(n + 2)^2}{4}$

33. $\dfrac{a^2 + 8a + 16}{a^2 - 6a + 9} \div \dfrac{2a + 8}{3a - 9}$ $\quad \dfrac{3(a + 4)}{2(a - 3)}$

34. $\dfrac{b + 2}{b^2 + 4b + 4} \div \dfrac{2b + 4}{b + 4}$ $\quad \dfrac{b + 4}{2(b + 2)^2}$

35. $\dfrac{x^2 + x - 2}{x^2 + 5x + 6} \div \dfrac{x^2 + 2x - 3}{x^2 + 7x + 12}$ $\quad \dfrac{x + 4}{x + 3}$

36. $\dfrac{x^2 + 2x - 15}{x^2 - x - 30} \div \dfrac{x^2 - 3x - 18}{x^2 - 2x - 24}$

36. $\dfrac{(x - 3)(x + 4)}{(x - 6)(x + 3)}$

37. TRIATHLONS Irena is training for an upcoming triathlon and plans to run 12 miles today. Jorge offered to ride his bicycle to help her maintain her pace. If Irena wants to keep a steady pace of 6.5 minutes per mile, how fast should Jorge ride in miles per hour? **about 9.2 mph**

39. $n = 20{,}000 \text{ yd}^3 \div$
$\left[\dfrac{5 \text{ ft}(18 \text{ ft} + 15 \text{ ft})}{2} \cdot 9 \text{ ft} \cdot \right.$
$\left. \dfrac{1 \text{ yd}^3}{27 \text{ ft}^3} \right]; 727.\overline{27}$

CONSTRUCTION For Exercises 38 and 39, use the following information.
A construction supervisor needs to determine how many truckloads of earth must be removed from a site before a foundation can be poured. The bed of the truck has the shape shown at the right.

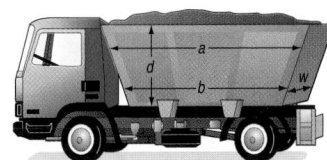

38. Use the formula $V = \dfrac{d(a + b)}{2} \cdot w$ to write an equation involving units that represents the volume of the truck bed in cubic yards if $a = 18$ feet, $b = 15$ feet, $w = 9$ feet, and $d = 5$ feet. $\quad V = \dfrac{5 \text{ ft}(18 \text{ ft} + 15 \text{ ft})}{2} \cdot 9 \text{ ft} \cdot \dfrac{1 \text{ yd}^3}{27 \text{ ft}^3}$

39. There are 20,000 cubic yards of earth that must be removed from the excavation site. Write an equation involving units that represents the number of truckloads that will be required to remove all of the earth. Then solve the equation.

TRUCKS For Exercises 40 and 41, use the following information.
The speedometer of John's truck uses the revolutions of his tires to calculate the speed of the truck.

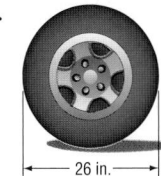
← 26 in. →

40. How many revolutions per minute do the tires make when the truck is traveling at 55 miles per hour? **about 711 rpm**

41. Suppose John buys tires with a diameter of 30 inches. When the speedometer reads 55 miles per hour, the tires would still revolve at the same rate as before. However, with the new tires, the truck travels a different distance in each revolution. Calculate the actual speed when the speedometer reads 55 miles per hour. **63.5 mph**

42. d; Sample answer:
$\dfrac{1}{x} - \dfrac{1}{2y} = \dfrac{2y - x}{2xy}$,
which is not equivalent to $\dfrac{x + 2y}{x^2 - 4y^2}$

42. CRITICAL THINKING Which expression is *not* equivalent to the reciprocal of $\dfrac{x^2 - 4y^2}{x + 2y}$? Justify your answer.

a. $\dfrac{1}{\dfrac{x^2 - 4y^2}{x + 2y}}$

b. $\dfrac{-1}{2y - x}$

c. $\dfrac{1}{x - 2y}$

d. $\dfrac{1}{x} - \dfrac{1}{2y}$

43. $\left(x - \dfrac{1}{2}\right)\left(x - \dfrac{3}{4}\right)(x)$

44. $(10 \cdot 85 \text{ pounds}) \div$
$\dfrac{\left(x - \dfrac{1}{2}\right)\left(x - \dfrac{3}{4}\right)(x)}{x^3}$

SCULPTURE For Exercises 43 and 44, use the following information.
A sculptor had a block of marble in the shape of a cube with sides x feet long. A piece that was $\dfrac{1}{2}$ foot thick was chiseled from the bottom of the block. Later, the sculptor removed a piece $\dfrac{3}{4}$ foot wide from the side of the marble block.

43. Write a rational expression that represents the volume of the block of marble that remained.

44. If the remaining marble was cut into ten pieces weighing 85 pounds each, write an expression that represents the weight of the original block of marble.

www.algebra1.com/self_check_quiz

Lesson 12-4 Dividing Rational Expressions **663**

Study Guide and Intervention, p. 723 (shown) and p. 724

Divide Rational Expressions To divide rational expressions, multiply by the reciprocal of the divisor. Then simplify.

Example 1 Find $\dfrac{12c^2d}{5a^2b^2} \div \dfrac{c^3d^2}{10ab}$.

Example 2 Find $\dfrac{x^2 + 6x - 27}{x^2 + 11x + 18} \div \dfrac{x - 3}{x^2 + x - 2}$.

Exercises

Find each quotient.

1. $\dfrac{12ab}{a^2b^2} \div \dfrac{b}{a} \cdot \dfrac{12}{b^2}$

2. $\dfrac{n}{4} \div \dfrac{n}{m} \cdot \dfrac{m}{4}$

3. $\dfrac{3xy^2}{8} \div 6xy \cdot \dfrac{y}{16}$

4. $\dfrac{m - 5}{2} \div \dfrac{m - 5}{16} \cdot 2$

5. $\dfrac{2n - 4}{2n} \div \dfrac{n^2 - 4}{n} \cdot \dfrac{1}{n + 2}$

6. $\dfrac{y^2 - 36}{y^2 - 49} \div \dfrac{y + 6}{y + 7} \cdot \dfrac{y - 6}{y - 7}$

7. $\dfrac{x^2 - 5x + 6}{5} \div \dfrac{x - 3}{15} \cdot 3(x - 2)$

8. $\dfrac{a^2b^2c}{3s^2t} \div \dfrac{6a^2bc}{8s^2tu} \cdot \dfrac{4b^2tu}{9s}$

9. $\dfrac{x^2 + 6x + 8}{x^2 + 4x + 4} \div \dfrac{x + 4}{x + 2} \cdot 1$

10. $\dfrac{m^2 - 49}{m} \div \dfrac{m^2 - 13m + 42}{3m^2} \cdot \dfrac{3m(m + 7)}{m - 6}$

11. $\dfrac{n^2 - 5n + 6}{n^2 + 3n} \div \dfrac{3 - n}{4n + 12} \cdot \dfrac{-4(n - 2)}{n}$

12. $\dfrac{p^2 - 2pq + q^2}{p + q} \div \dfrac{p^2 - q^2}{p + q} \cdot \dfrac{p - q}{p + q}$

13. $\dfrac{a^3 + 7a + 12}{a^2 + 3a - 10} \div \dfrac{a^2 - 9}{a^2 - 25} \cdot \dfrac{(a + 4)(a - 5)}{(a - 2)(a - 3)}$

14. $\dfrac{a^2 - 9}{2a^2 + 13a - 7} \div \dfrac{a + 3}{4a^2 - 1} \cdot \dfrac{(a - 3)(2a + 1)}{a + 7}$

Skills Practice, p. 725 and Practice, p. 726 (shown)

Find each quotient.

1. $\dfrac{28a^2}{7b^2} \div \dfrac{21a^3}{35b} \cdot \dfrac{20}{3ab}$

2. $\dfrac{mn^2p^3}{x^4y^2} \div \dfrac{mnp^2}{x^3y} \cdot \dfrac{np}{xy}$

3. $\dfrac{2a}{a - 1} \div (a + 1) \cdot \dfrac{2a}{(a + 1)(a - 1)}$

4. $\dfrac{z^2 - 16}{3z} \div (z - 4) \cdot \dfrac{z + 4}{3z}$

5. $\dfrac{4y + 12}{y - 3} \div \dfrac{y + 5}{2y - 6} \cdot \dfrac{8}{y + 5}$

6. $\dfrac{4x + 12}{6x - 24} \div \dfrac{x - 3}{x + 3} \cdot \dfrac{x + 3}{3(x - 4)}$

Complete.

7. $1.75 \text{ m}^2 = \_\_ \text{ cm}^2 \cdot 17{,}500$

8. $0.54 \text{ tons/yd}^3 = \_\_ \text{ lb/ft}^3 \cdot 40$

Find each quotient.

9. $\dfrac{s^2 - 8s - 20}{7} \div \dfrac{s + 2}{s - 2} \cdot \dfrac{(s - 2)(s - 10)}{7}$

10. $\dfrac{n^2 - 9n + 8}{9n - 9} \div \dfrac{n + 8}{27} \cdot \dfrac{3(n - 8)}{n + 8}$

11. $\dfrac{y^2 - 3y - 10}{y^2 - 9y + 8} \div \dfrac{2y + 4}{y - 1} \cdot \dfrac{y - 5}{2(y - 8)}$

12. $\dfrac{n - 1}{2n^2 + 2n - 15} \div \dfrac{n^2 - 6n + 5}{4n - 12} \cdot \dfrac{4}{(n + 5)(n - 5)}$

13. $\dfrac{b^2 + 2b - 8}{b^2 - 11b + 18} \div \dfrac{2b - 8}{2b - 18} \cdot \dfrac{b + 4}{b - 4}$

14. $\dfrac{3x - 3}{x^3 - 6x + 9} \div \dfrac{6x - 6}{x^2 - 3x + 6} \cdot \dfrac{x - 2}{2(x - 3)}$

15. $\dfrac{a^2 + 8a + 12}{a^2 - 7a + 10} \div \dfrac{a^2 - 4a - 12}{a^2 + 3a - 10} \cdot \dfrac{(a + 6)(a + 5)}{(a - 6)(a - 5)}$

16. $\dfrac{y^2 + 6y - 7}{y^2 + 8y - 9} \div \dfrac{y^2 + 9y + 14}{y^2 + 7y - 18} \cdot \dfrac{y - 2}{y + 2}$

TRAFFIC For Exercises 17 and 18, use the following information.
On Saturday, it took Ms. Torres 24 minutes to drive 20 miles from her home to her office. During Friday's rush hour, it took 75 minutes to drive the same distance.

17. What was Ms. Torres's speed in miles per hour on Saturday? **50 mi/h**

18. What was her speed in miles per hour on Friday? **16 mi/h**

SHOPPING For Exercises 19 and 20, use the following information.
Ashley wants to buy some treats for her dog Foo. She can purchase a $1\frac{1}{4}$-pound box of treats for $2.99. She can purchase the same treats in a 2-pound package on sale for $4.19.

19. What is the cost of each in cents per ounce? Round to the nearest tenth.
$1\frac{1}{4}$ lb: 15.0 cents/oz, 2 lb: 13.1 cents/oz

20. If a box of treats costs $3.49 at a rate of 14.5 cents per ounce, how much does the box weigh in ounces and in pounds?
about 24.1 oz, or just over $1\frac{1}{2}$ lb

Reading to Learn Mathematics, p. 727 **ELL**

Pre-Activity **How can you determine the number of aluminum soft drink cans made each year?**

Read the introduction to Lesson 12-4 at the top of page 660 in your textbook.

Write an equation that you could use to determine the number of aluminum cans, in billions, produced each year.

Sample answer: $\dfrac{5}{8}x = 63.9$

Reading the Lesson

1. Why is it important to know the reciprocal of the divisor when you divide two rational expressions?

Sample answer: To divide two rational expressions, you multiply by the reciprocal of the divisor.

2. State the reciprocal of the divisor in each of the following.

a. $\dfrac{3b + 15}{b + 1} \div (b - 2) \cdot \dfrac{1}{b - 2}$

b. $\dfrac{2c^2}{d} \div \dfrac{c}{3d} \cdot \dfrac{3d}{c}$

3. Supply the reason for each step below.

$\dfrac{y + 1}{y^2 + 5y + 6} \div \dfrac{1}{y + 3}$	Original expression
$= \dfrac{y + 1}{y^2 + 5y + 6} \cdot \dfrac{y + 3}{1}$	Multiply by the reciprocal of the divisor.
$= \dfrac{y + 1}{(y + 2)(y + 3)} \cdot \dfrac{y + 3}{1}$	Factor $y^2 + 5y + 6$.
$= \dfrac{y + 1}{(y + 2)} \cdot \dfrac{1}{1}$	Divide by the GCF.
$= \dfrac{y + 1}{y + 2}$	Multiply the fractions.

Helping You Remember

4. One way to remember something is to see how it is similar to something you already know. How is dividing rational expressions similar to dividing rational numbers that are in fraction form?

Sample answer: When you divide fractions for rational numbers, you invert and multiply. This is the same method as multiplying by the reciprocal when you divide rational expressions.

Enrichment, p. 728

Division by Zero?

You may remember being told, "division by zero is not possible" or "division by zero is undefined" or "we never divide by zero." Have you wondered why this is so? Consider the two equations below.

$$\dfrac{5}{0} = n \qquad \dfrac{0}{0} = m$$

Because multiplication is the inverse of division, these equations lead to the following.

$$0 \cdot n = 5 \qquad 0 \cdot m = 0$$

There is no number that will make the first equation true. Any number at all will satisfy the second equation.

For each expression, give the values that must be excluded from the replacement set in order to prevent division by zero.

1. $\dfrac{x + 1}{x - 1}$ $x = 1$

2. $\dfrac{2(x + 1)}{2x - 1}$ $x = \dfrac{1}{2}$

3. $\dfrac{(x + 1)(x - 1)}{(x + 2)(x - 2)}$ $x = -2$ or $x = 2$

Lesson 12-4 Dividing Rational Expressions **663**

Open-Ended Assessment

Writing Have students write a short paragraph explaining why dividing rational expressions is the same as multiplying by the reciprocal.

Getting Ready for Lesson 12-5

PREREQUISITE SKILL Students will learn to divide polynomials in Lesson 12-5. In order to divide polynomials, students must recall how to divide monomials. Use Exercises 70–75 to determine your students' familiarity with dividing monomials.

Answer

45. Sample answer: Divide the number of cans recycled by $\frac{5}{8}$ to find the total number of cans produced. Answers should include the following.

- $x = 63,900,000$ cans $\div \frac{5}{8} \cdot$ $\frac{1 \text{ pound}}{33 \text{ cans}}$

---

45. **WRITING IN MATH** Answer the question that was posed at the beginning of the lesson. **See margin.**

How can you determine the number of aluminum soft drink cans made each year?

Include the following in your answer:
- a rational expression that will give the amount of new aluminum needed to produce x aluminum cans today when $\frac{5}{8}$ of the cans are recycled and 33 cans are produced from a pound of aluminum.

Standardized Test Practice
Ⓐ Ⓑ Ⓒ Ⓓ

46. Which expression is the quotient of $\frac{3b}{5c}$ and $\frac{18b}{15c}$? **B**

Ⓐ $\frac{18b^2}{15c^2}$　　Ⓑ $\frac{1}{2}$　　Ⓒ $\frac{18b}{15c}$　　Ⓓ 2

47. Which expression could be used for the width of the rectangle? **C**

Ⓐ $x - 2$　　Ⓑ $(x + 2)(x - 2)^2$
Ⓒ $x + 2$　　Ⓓ $(x + 2)(x - 2)$

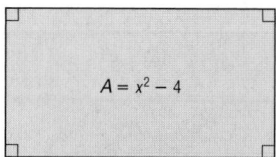

$A = x^2 - 4$

$\frac{x^2 - x - 2}{x + 1}$

Maintain Your Skills

Mixed Review **Find each product.** *(Lesson 12-3)*

48. $\frac{x - 5}{x^2 - 7x + 10} \cdot \frac{x - 2}{1}$ **1**

49. $\frac{x^2 + 3x - 10}{x^2 + 8x + 15} \cdot \frac{x^2 + 5x + 6}{x^2 + 4x + 4}$ **$\frac{x - 2}{x + 2}$**

51. $\frac{7(x + 2y)(x + 5)}{x + y}$

50. $\frac{x + 4}{4y} \cdot \frac{16y}{x^2 + 7x + 12}$ **$\frac{4}{x + 3}$**

51. $\frac{x^2 + 8x + 15}{x + y} \cdot \frac{7x + 14y}{x + 3}$

Simplify each expression. *(Lesson 12-2)*

52. $\frac{c - 6}{c^2 - 12c + 36}$ **$\frac{1}{c - 6}$**

53. $\frac{25 - x^2}{x^2 + x - 30}$ **$-\frac{x + 5}{x + 6}$**

54. $\frac{a + 3}{a^2 + 4a + 3}$ **$\frac{1}{a + 1}$**

55. $\frac{n^2 - 16}{n^2 - 8n + 16}$ **$\frac{n + 4}{n - 4}$**

Solve each equation. Check your solutions. *(Lesson 9-6)*

56. $3y^2 = 147$ **{±7}**

57. $9x^2 - 24x = -16$ **$\left\{\frac{4}{3}\right\}$**

58. $a^2 + 225 = 30a$ **{15}**

59. $(n + 6)^2 = 14$ **$\left\{-6 \pm \sqrt{14}\right\}$**

Find the degree of each polynomial. *(Lesson 8-4)*

60. $13 + \frac{1}{8}$ **0**

61. $z^3 - 2z^2 + 3z - 4$ **3**

62. $a^5b^2c^3 + 6a^3b^3c^2$ **10**

Solve each inequality. Then check your solution. *(Lesson 6-2)*

65. $\{x \mid x \geq -0.7\}$

63. $6 \leq 0.8g$ **$\{g \mid g \geq 7.5\}$**

64. $-15b < -28$ **$\left\{b \mid b > \frac{28}{15}\right\}$**

65. $-0.049 \leq 0.07x$

66. $\frac{3}{7}h < \frac{3}{49}$ **$\left\{h \mid h < \frac{1}{7}\right\}$**

67. $\frac{12r}{-4} > \frac{3}{20}$ **$\left\{r \mid r < -\frac{1}{20}\right\}$**

68. $\frac{y}{6} \geq \frac{1}{2}$ **$\{y \mid y \geq 3\}$**

69. **MANUFACTURING** Tanisha's Sporting Equipment manufactures tennis racket covers at the rate of 3250 each month. How many tennis racket covers will the company manufacture in one year? *(Lesson 5-3)* **39,000 covers**

Getting Ready for the Next Lesson　**PREREQUISITE SKILL** **Simplify.** *(To review **dividing monomials**, see Lesson 8-2.)*

70. $\frac{6x^2}{x^4}$ **$\frac{6}{x^2}$**

71. $\frac{5m^4}{25m}$ **$\frac{m^3}{5}$**

72. $\frac{18a^3}{45a^5}$ **$\frac{2}{5a^2}$**

73. $\frac{b^6c^3}{b^3c^6}$ **$\frac{b^3}{c^3}$**

74. $\frac{12x^3y^2}{28x^4y}$ **$\frac{3y}{7x}$**

75. $\frac{7x^4z^2}{z^3}$ **$\frac{7x^4}{z}$**

Rational Expressions

Several concepts need to be applied when reading rational expressions.

- A fraction bar acts as a grouping symbol, where the entire numerator is divided by the entire denominator.

Example 1 $\dfrac{6x + 4}{10}$

It is <u>correct</u> to read the expression as *the quantity six x plus four divided by ten.*

It is <u>incorrect</u> to read the expression as *six x divided by ten plus four,* or *six x plus four divided by ten.*

- If a fraction consists of two or more terms divided by a one-term denominator, the denominator divides each term.

Example 2 $\dfrac{6x + 4}{10}$

It is <u>correct</u> to write $\dfrac{6x + 4}{10} = \dfrac{6x}{10} + \dfrac{4}{10}.$

$$= \dfrac{3x}{5} + \dfrac{2}{5} \quad \text{or} \quad \dfrac{3x + 2}{5}$$

It is also <u>correct</u> to write $\dfrac{6x + 4}{10} = \dfrac{2(3x + 2)}{2 \cdot 5}.$

$$= \dfrac{\cancel{2}(3x + 2)}{\cancel{2} \cdot 5} \quad \text{or} \quad \dfrac{3x + 2}{5}$$

It is <u>incorrect</u> to write $\dfrac{6x + 4}{10} = \dfrac{6\cancel{x} + 4}{\cancel{10}} = \dfrac{3x + 4}{5}.$

Reading to Learn

Write the verbal translation of each rational expression. 1–6. See margin.

1. $\dfrac{m + 2}{4}$

2. $\dfrac{3x}{x - 1}$

3. $\dfrac{a + 2}{a^2 + 8}$

4. $\dfrac{x^2 - 25}{x + 5}$

5. $\dfrac{x^2 - 3x + 18}{x - 2}$

6. $\dfrac{x^2 + 2x - 35}{x^2 - x - 20}$

Simplify each expression.

7. $\dfrac{3x + 6}{9} \cdot \dfrac{x + 2}{3}$

8. $\dfrac{4n - 12}{8} \cdot \dfrac{n - 3}{4}$

9. $\dfrac{5x^2 - 25x}{10x} \cdot \dfrac{x - 5}{2}$

10. $\dfrac{x + 3}{x^2 + 7x + 12} \cdot \dfrac{1}{x + 4}$

11. $\dfrac{x + y}{x^2 + 2xy + y^2} \cdot \dfrac{1}{x + y}$

12. $\dfrac{x^2 - 16}{x^2 - 8x + 16} \cdot \dfrac{x + 4}{x - 4}$

Reading Mathematics Rational Expressions **665**

Answers

1. Sample answer: the quantity *m* plus two, divided by 4

2. Sample answer: three *x* divided by the quantity *x* minus 1

3. Sample answer: the quantity *a* plus 2 divided by the quantity *a* squared plus 8

4. Sample answer: the quantity *x* squared minus 25 divided by the quantity *x* plus 5

5. Sample answer: the quantity *x* squared minus 3*x* plus 18 divided by the quantity *x* minus 2

6. Sample answer: the quantity *x* squared plus 2*x* minus 35 divided by the quantity *x* squared minus *x* minus 20

12-5 Dividing Polynomials

1 Focus

5-Minute Check Transparency 12-5 Use as a quiz or review of Lesson 12-4.

Mathematical Background notes are available for this lesson on p. 640D.

Building on Prior Knowledge

In Lesson 8-2, students learned to divide by monomials. In this lesson, students will first learn how to divide binomials and polynomials by monomials, then they will learn how to divide polynomials by binomials.

How is division used in sewing?

Ask students:

• Think back to the Reading Mathematics activity on the previous page. How might you read the expression given in this example? **The quantity 36 yards minus seven and one-half yards, divided by one and one-half yards.**

• How can the fraction be written so that the denominator divides each term?

$$\frac{36 \text{ yards}}{1\frac{1}{2} \text{ yards}} - \frac{7\frac{1}{2} \text{ yards}}{1\frac{1}{2} \text{ yards}}$$

• Use a calculator to find the number of flags that can be made using the roll of fabric. **19 flags**

📂 **Workbook and Reproducible Masters**

Chapter 12 Resource Masters
• Study Guide and Intervention, pp. 729–730
• Skills Practice, p. 731
• Practice, p. 732
• Reading to Learn Mathematics, p. 733
• Enrichment, p. 734
• Assessment, pp. 773, 775

Parent and Student Study Guide Workbook, p. 95
Teaching Algebra With Manipulatives Masters, pp. 10, 11, 17, 197

🖥 **Transparencies**

5-Minute Check Transparency 12-5
Answer Key Transparencies

💿 **Technology**

Interactive Chalkboard

12-5 Dividing Polynomials

What You'll Learn

• Divide a polynomial by a monomial.
• Divide a polynomial by a binomial.

How is division used in sewing?

Marching bands often use intricate marching routines and colorful flags to add interest to their shows. Suppose a partial roll of fabric is used to make flags. The original roll was 36 yards long, and $7\frac{1}{2}$ yards of the fabric were used to make a banner for the band. Each flag requires $1\frac{1}{2}$ yards of fabric. The expression

$$\frac{36 \text{ yards} - 7\frac{1}{2} \text{ yards}}{1\frac{1}{2} \text{ yards}}$$

can be used to represent the number of flags that can be made using the roll of fabric.

DIVIDE POLYNOMIALS BY MONOMIALS

To divide a polynomial by a monomial, divide each term of the polynomial by the monomial.

Example 1 Divide a Binomial by a Monomial

Find $(3r^2 - 15r) \div 3r$.

$$(3r^2 - 15r) \div 3r = \frac{3r^2 - 15r}{3r} \quad \text{Write as a rational expression.}$$

$$= \frac{3r^2}{3r} - \frac{15r}{3r} \quad \text{Divide each term by } 3r.$$

$$= \frac{3r^2}{3r}^{r} - \frac{15r}{3r}^{5} \quad \text{Simplify each term.}$$

$$= r - 5 \quad \text{Simplify.}$$

Example 2 Divide a Polynomial by a Monomial

Find $(n^2 + 10n + 12) \div 5n$.

$$(n^2 + 10n + 12) \div 5n = \frac{n^2 + 10n + 12}{5n} \quad \text{Write as a rational expression.}$$

$$= \frac{n^2}{5n} + \frac{10n}{5n} + \frac{12}{5n} \quad \text{Divide each term by } 5n.$$

$$= \frac{n^2}{5n}^{n} + \frac{10n}{5n}^{2} + \frac{12}{5n} \quad \text{Simplify each term.}$$

$$= \frac{n}{5} + 2 + \frac{12}{5n} \quad \text{Simplify.}$$

DIVIDE POLYNOMIALS BY BINOMIALS You can use algebra tiles to model some quotients of polynomials.

Algebra Activity

Dividing Polynomials

Use algebra tiles to find $(x^2 + 3x + 2) \div (x + 1)$.

Step 1 Model the polynomial $x^2 + 3x + 2$.

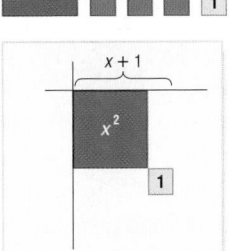

Step 2 Place the x^2 tile at the corner of the product mat. Place one of the 1 tiles as shown to make a length of $x + 1$.

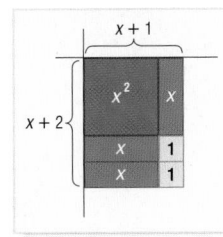

Step 3 Use the remaining tiles to make a rectangular array.

The width of the array, $x + 2$, is the quotient.

Model and Analyze

Use algebra tiles to find each quotient.

1. $(x^2 + 3x - 4) \div (x - 1)$ $(x + 4)$ **2.** $(x^2 - 5x + 6) \div (x - 2)$ $(x - 3)$

3. $(x^2 - 16) \div (x + 4)$ $(x - 4)$ **4.** $(2x^2 - 4x - 6) \div (x - 3)$ $(2x + 2)$

5. Describe what happens when you try to model $(3x^2 - 4x + 3) \div (x + 2)$. What do you think the result means? **You cannot do it. There is a remainder.**

Recall from Lesson 12-4 that when you factor, some divisions can be performed easily.

Example 3 *Divide a Polynomial by a Binomial*

Find $(s^2 + 6s - 7) \div (s + 7)$.

$$(s^2 + 6s - 7) \div (s + 7) = \frac{s^2 + 6s - 7}{(s + 7)} \quad \text{Write as a rational expression.}$$

$$= \frac{(s + 7)(s - 1)}{(s + 7)} \quad \text{Factor the numerator.}$$

$$= \frac{\overset{1}{(s + 7)}(s - 1)}{\underset{1}{(s + 7)}} \quad \text{Divide by the GCF.}$$

$$= s - 1 \quad \text{Simplify.}$$

 www.algebra1.com/extra_examples

Lesson 12-5 Dividing Polynomials **667**

2 Teach

DIVIDE POLYNOMIALS BY MONOMIALS

In-Class Examples Power Point®

Teaching Tip As an alternative to dividing each term of the polynomial by the monomial, students can factor and then eliminate the GCF.

1 Find $(4x^2 - 18x) \div 2x$.
$2x - 9$

2 Find $(2y^2 - 3y - 9) \div 3y$.
$\frac{2y}{3} - 1 - \frac{3}{y}$

DIVIDE POLYNOMIALS BY BINOMIALS

In-Class Example Power Point®

3 Find $(2r^2 + 5r - 3) \div (r + 3)$.
$2r - 1$

Algebra Activity

Materials algebra tiles and product mat

Point out to students that the divisor in this example is found along the horizontal axis, and the quotient is found along the vertical axis. Suggest that students arrange their problems in this way as they use algebra tiles in this activity.

Teaching Tip Remind students to pay close attention to the signs of the binomials as they perform the long division. Since each binomial is being subtracted, the sign of the second term in the binomial changes.

4 Find $(x^2 + 7x - 15) \div (x - 2)$. The quotient is $x + 9$ with a remainder of 3.

Teaching Tip Ask students to explain why a term with a zero coefficient is added to the polynomial. A term with a zero coefficient has a value of zero, so it does not affect the quotient. It is simply a placeholder.

5 Find $(x^3 - 34x + 45) \div (x - 5)$. The quotient is $x^2 + 5x - 9$.

✓ Concept Check

Explain which method you would use to find the quotient in the following problems.

a. $(x^2 + 9x - 2) \div (x + 1)$
Since the dividend cannot be factored, this quotient must be found through long division.

b. $(2x^2 - 13x + 15) \div (2x - 3)$
Since the dividend can be factored and one of its factors is $2x - 3$, divide by the GCF.

Answers

2. Sample answer: A remainder of zero means that the divisor is a factor of the dividend.

11. $\dfrac{x}{3} + 3 - \dfrac{7}{3x}$

12. $\dfrac{a}{7} + 1 - \dfrac{4}{a}$

In Example 3 the division could be performed easily by dividing by common factors. However, when you cannot factor, you can use a long division process similar to the one you use in arithmetic.

Example 4 Long Division

Find $(x^2 + 3x - 24) \div (x - 4)$.

The expression $x^2 + 3x - 24$ cannot be factored, so use long division.

Step 1 Divide the first term of the dividend, x^2, by the first term of the divisor, x.

$$
\begin{array}{r}
x \\
x - 4 \overline{)x^2 + 3x - 24} \\
\underline{(-)\ x^2 - 4x} \\
7x
\end{array}
$$

$x^2 \div x = x$
Multiply x and $x - 4$.
Subtract.

Step 2 Divide the first term of the partial dividend, $7x - 24$, by the first term of the divisor, x.

$$
\begin{array}{r}
x + 7 \\
x - 4 \overline{)x^2 + 3x - 24} \\
\underline{(-)\ x^2 - 4x} \\
7x - 24 \\
\underline{(-)\ 7x - 28} \\
4
\end{array}
$$

$7x \div x = 7$
Subtract and bring down the 24.
Multiply 7 and $x - 4$.
Subtract.

The quotient of $(x^2 + 3x - 24) \div (x - 4)$ is $x + 7$ with a remainder of 4, which can be written as $x + 7 + \dfrac{4}{x - 4}$. Since there is a nonzero remainder, $x - 4$ is not a factor of $x^2 + 3x - 24$.

When the dividend is an expression like $a^3 + 8a - 21$, there is no a^2 term. In such situations, you must rename the dividend using 0 as the coefficient of the missing terms.

Example 5 Polynomial with Missing Terms

Find $(a^3 + 8a - 24) \div (a - 2)$.

Rename the a^2 term using a coefficient of 0.

$(a^3 + 8a - 24) \div (a - 2) = (a^3 + 0a^2 + 8a - 24) \div (a - 2)$

$$
\begin{array}{r}
a^2 + 2a + 12 \\
a - 2 \overline{)a^3 + 0a^2 + 8a - 24} \\
\underline{(-)\ a^3 - 2a^2} \\
2a^2 + 8a \\
\underline{(-)\ 2a^2 - 4a} \\
12a - 24 \\
\underline{(-)\ 12a - 24} \\
0
\end{array}
$$

Multiply a^2 and $a - 2$.
Subtract and bring down $8a$.
Multiply $2a$ and $a - 2$.
Subtract and bring down 24.
Multiply 12 and $a - 2$.
Subtract.

Therefore, $(a^3 + 8a - 24) \div (a - 2) = a^2 + 2a + 12$.

Study Tip

Factors
When the remainder in a division problem is 0, the divisor is a factor of the dividend.

668 Chapter 12 Rational Expressions and Equations

DAILY
INTERVENTION

Differentiated Instruction

Intrapersonal Ask students to write a journal entry about what they learned in this lesson. Tell them to include the aspects of the lesson that they liked, and that they did not like. They should also explain which concepts they feel like they mastered, and which ones they are still not comfortable with. Have students share their journal entries with you privately.

Concept Check

GUIDED PRACTICE KEY

Exercises	Examples
4, 5	1, 2
6, 7	3
9, 10	4
8	5

1. **Choose** the divisors of $2x^2 - 9x + 9$ that result in a remainder of 0. **b and c**
   a. $x + 3$ b. $x - 3$ c. $2x - 3$ d. $2x + 3$

2. **Explain** the meaning of a remainder of zero in a long division of a polynomial by a binomial. **See margin.**

3. **OPEN ENDED** Write a third-degree polynomial that includes a zero term. Rewrite the polynomial so that it can be divided by $x + 5$ using long division.
   Sample answer: $x^3 + 2x^2 + 8$; $x^3 + 2x^2 + 0x + 8$

Guided Practice **Find each quotient.**

4. $(4x^3 + 2x^2 - 5) \div 2x$ $2x^2 + x - \dfrac{5}{2x}$

5. $\dfrac{14a^2b^2 + 35ab^2 + 2a^2}{7a^2b^2}$ $2 + \dfrac{5}{a} + \dfrac{2}{7b^2}$

6. $(n^2 + 7n + 12) \div (n + 3)$ $n + 4$

7. $(r^2 + 12r + 36) \div (r + 9)$ $r + 3 + \dfrac{9}{r + 9}$

8. $\dfrac{4m^3 + 5m - 21}{2m - 3}$ $2m^2 + 3m + 7$

9. $(2b^2 + 3b - 5) \div (2b - 1)$ $b + 2 - \dfrac{3}{2b - 1}$

Application

10. **ENVIRONMENT** The equation $C = \dfrac{120{,}000p}{1 - p}$ models the cost C in dollars for a manufacturer to reduce the pollutants by a given percent, written as p in decimal form. How much will the company have to pay to remove 75% of the pollutants it emits? **$360,000**

★ indicates increased difficulty

Practice and Apply

Homework Help

For Exercises	See Examples
11–14	1, 2
15–18, 23, 24	3
19–22, 25, 26	4
27–30	5

Extra Practice
See page 847.

Find each quotient. 11–22. See margin.

11. $(x^2 + 9x - 7) \div 3x$

12. $(a^2 + 7a - 28) \div 7a$

13. $\dfrac{9s^3t^2 - 15s^2t + 24t^3}{3s^2t^2}$

14. $\dfrac{12a^3b + 16ab^3 - 8ab}{4ab}$

15. $(x^2 + 9x + 20) \div (x + 5)$

16. $(x^2 + 6x - 16) \div (x - 2)$

17. $(n^2 - 2n - 35) \div (n + 5)$

18. $(s^2 + 11s + 18) \div (s + 9)$

19. $(z^2 - 2z - 30) \div (z + 7)$

20. $(a^2 + 4a - 22) \div (a - 3)$

21. $(2r^2 - 3r - 35) \div (r - 5)$

22. $(3p^2 + 20p + 11) \div (p + 6)$

23. $\dfrac{3t^2 + 14t - 24}{3t - 4}$ $t + 6$

24. $\dfrac{12n^2 + 36n + 15}{2n + 5}$ $6n + 3$

25. $\dfrac{3x^3 + 8x^2 + x - 7}{x + 2}$

26. $\dfrac{20b^3 - 27b^2 + 13b - 3}{4b - 3}$

27. $\dfrac{6x^3 - 9x^2 + 6}{2x - 3}$ $3x^2 + \dfrac{6}{2x - 3}$

28. $\dfrac{9g^3 + 5g - 8}{3g - 2}$ $3g^2 + 2g + 3 - \dfrac{2}{3g - 2}$

29. Determine the quotient when $6n^3 + 5n^2 + 12$ is divided by $2n + 3$.

30. What is the quotient when $4t^3 + 17t^2 - 1$ is divided by $4t + 1$? $t^2 + 4t - 1$

Answers (margin, left):

25. $3x^2 + 2x - 3 - \dfrac{1}{x + 2}$

26. $5b^2 - 3b + 1$

29. $3n^2 - 2n + 3 + \dfrac{3}{2n + 3}$

LANDSCAPING For Exercises 31 and 32, use the following information.
A heavy object can be lifted more easily using a lever and fulcrum. The amount that can be lifted depends upon the length of the lever, the placement of the fulcrum, and the force applied. The expression $\dfrac{W(L - x)}{x}$ represents the weight of an object that can be lifted if W pounds of force are applied to a lever L inches long with the fulcrum placed x inches from the object.

31. Suppose Leyati, who weighs 150 pounds, uses all of his weight to lift a rock using a 60-inch lever. Write an expression that could be used to determine the heaviest rock he could lift if the fulcrum is x inches from the rock. $\dfrac{150(60 - x)}{x}$

32. Use the expression to find the weight of a rock that could be lifted by a 210-pound man using a six-foot lever placed 20 inches from the rock.   **546 lb**

 www.algebra1.com/self_check_quiz

Study Notebook

Have students—
• include examples of how to divide polynomials.
• include any other item(s) that they find helpful in mastering the skills in this lesson.

About the Exercises ...

Organization by Objective
• Divide Polynomials by Monomials: 11–14
• Divide Polynomials by Binomials: 15–28, 29, 30

Odd/Even Assignments
Exercises 11–30 are structured so that students practice the same concepts whether they are assigned odd or even problems.

Assignment Guide

Basic: 11–29 odd, 31–33, 40–60

Average: 11–29 odd, 33–35, 39–60

Advanced: 12–30 even, 36–56 (optional: 57–60)

Answers

13. $3s - \dfrac{5}{t} + \dfrac{8t}{s^2}$

14. $3a^2 + 4b^2 - 2$

15. $x + 4$

16. $x + 8$

17. $n - 7$

18. $s + 2$

19. $z - 9 + \dfrac{33}{z + 7}$

20. $a + 7 - \dfrac{1}{a - 3}$

21. $2r + 7$

22. $3p + 2 - \dfrac{1}{p + 6}$

670 Chapter 12 Rational Expressions and Equations

Study Guide and Intervention, p. 729 (shown) and p. 730

Divide Polynomials by Monomials To divide a polynomial by a monomial, divide each term of the polynomial by the monomial.

Example 1 Find $(4r^2 - 12r) \div 2r$.

$(4r^2 - 12r) \div 2r = \dfrac{4r^2 - 12r}{2r}$

$= \dfrac{4r^2}{2r} - \dfrac{12r}{2r}$ Divide each term.

$= 2r - 6$ Simplify.

Example 2 Find $(3x^2 - 8x + 4) \div 4x$.

$(3x^2 - 8x + 4) \div 4x = \dfrac{3x^2 - 8x + 4}{4x}$

$= \dfrac{3x^2}{4x} - \dfrac{8x}{4x} + \dfrac{4}{4x}$

$= \dfrac{3x}{4} - 2 + \dfrac{1}{x}$

Exercises

Find each quotient.

1. $(x^3 + 2x^2 - x) \div x$ $x^2 + 2x - 1$
2. $(2x^3 + 12x^2 - 8x) \div 2x$ $x^2 + 6x - 4$
3. $(x^2 + 3x - 4) \div x$ $x + 3 - \frac{4}{x}$
4. $(4m^2 + 6m - 8) \div 2m^2$ $2 + \frac{3}{m} - \frac{4}{m^2}$
5. $(3x^3 + 15x^2 - 21x) \div 3x$ $x^2 + 5x - 7$
6. $(8m^2n^2 + 4mn - 8n) \div n$ $8m^2n + 4m - 8$
7. $(8y^4 + 16y^2 - 4) \div 4y^2$ $2y^2 + 4 - \frac{1}{y^2}$
8. $(16x^4y^3 + 24xy + 5) \div xy$ $16x^3y^2 + 24 + \frac{5}{xy}$
9. $\frac{15x^2 - 25x + 30}{5}$ $3x^2 - 5x + 6$
10. $\frac{10a^2b + 12ab - 8b}{2a}$ $5ab + 6b - \frac{4b}{a}$
11. $\frac{6x^3 + 9x^2 + 9}{3x}$ $2x^2 + 3x + \frac{3}{x}$
12. $\frac{m^2 - 12m + 42}{3m^2}$ $\frac{1}{3} - \frac{4}{m} + \frac{14}{m^2}$
13. $\frac{m^2n^2 - 5mn + 6}{m^2n^2}$ $1 - \frac{5}{mn} + \frac{6}{m^2n^2}$
14. $\frac{p^2 - 4pq + 6q^2}{pq}$ $\frac{p}{q} - 4 + \frac{6q}{p}$
15. $\frac{6a^2b^2 - 8ab + 12}{2a^2}$ $3b^2 - \frac{4b}{a} + \frac{6}{a^2}$
16. $\frac{2x^2y^3 - 4x^3y^2 - 8xy}{2xy}$ $xy^2 - 2xy - 4$
17. $\frac{9x^2y^2z - 2xyz + 12x}{xy}$ $9xyz - 2z + \frac{12}{y}$
18. $\frac{2a^3b^3 + 8a^2b^2 - 10ab + 12}{2a^2b^2}$ $ab + 4 - \frac{5}{ab} + \frac{6}{a^2b^2}$

Skills Practice, p. 731 and Practice, p. 732 (shown)

Find each quotient.

1. $(6q^2 - 18q - 9) \div 9q$ $\frac{2q}{3} - 2 - \frac{1}{q}$
2. $(y^2 + 6y + 2) \div 3y$ $\frac{y}{3} + 2 + \frac{2}{3y}$
3. $\frac{12a^3b - 3ab^2 + 42ab}{6a^2b}$ $2 - \frac{b}{2a} + \frac{7}{a}$
4. $\frac{2m^2n + 56mn - 4m^2n^3}{8m^2n}$ $\frac{n}{4} + \frac{7}{m} - \frac{n^2}{2m}$
5. $(x^2 - 3x - 40) \div (x + 5)$ $x - 8$
6. $(3m^2 - 20m + 12) \div (m - 6)$ $3m - 2$
7. $(a^2 + 5a + 20) \div (a - 3)$ $a + 8 + \frac{44}{a - 3}$
8. $(x^2 - 3x - 2) \div (x + 7)$ $x - 10 + \frac{68}{x + 7}$
9. $(t^2 + 9t + 28) \div (t + 3)$ $t + 6 + \frac{10}{t + 3}$
10. $(s^2 - 9s + 25) \div (s - 4)$ $s - 5 + \frac{5}{s - 4}$
11. $\frac{6x^2 - 5x - 56}{3r + 8}$ $2r - 7$
12. $\frac{20u^2 + 39w + 18}{5w + 6}$ $4w + 3$
13. $(x^3 + 2x^2 - 16) \div (x - 2)$ $x^2 + 4x + 8$
14. $(s^3 - 11s - 6) \div (s + 3)$ $s^2 - 3s - 2$
15. $\frac{x^3 + 6x^2 + 3x + 1}{x - 2}$ $x^2 + 8x + 19 + \frac{39}{x - 2}$
16. $\frac{6d^3 + d^2 - 2d + 17}{2d + 3}$ $3d^2 - 4d + 5 + \frac{2}{2d + 3}$
17. $\frac{2k^3 + 7k^2 - 7}{2k + 3}$ $k^2 + 2k - 3 + \frac{2}{2k + 3}$
18. $\frac{9y^3 - y - 1}{3y + 2}$ $3y^2 - 2y + 1 - \frac{3}{3y + 2}$

LANDSCAPING For Exercises 19 and 20, use the following information.
Jocelyn is designing a bed for cactus specimens at a botanical garden. The total area can be modeled by the expression $2x^2 + 7x + 3$, where x is in feet.

19. Suppose in one design the length of the cactus bed is $4x$, and in another, the length is $2x + 1$. What are the widths of the two designs? $\frac{x}{2} + \frac{7}{4} + \frac{3}{4x}$; $x + 3$

20. If $x = 3$ feet, what will be the dimensions of the cactus bed in each of the designs?   12 ft by 3.5 ft; 7 ft by 6 ft

21. **FURNITURE** Teri is upholstering the seats of four chairs and a bench. She needs $\frac{1}{4}$ square yard of fabric for each chair, and $\frac{1}{2}$ square yard for the bench. If the fabric at the store is 45 inches wide, how many yards of fabric will Teri need to cover the chairs and the bench if there is no waste? $1\frac{1}{5}$ yd

Reading to Learn Mathematics, p. 733   **ELL**

Pre-Activity How is division used in sewing?
Read the introduction to Lesson 12-5 at the top of page 666 in your textbook.

- One way to find the number of flags is to _subtract_ the terms in the numerator, and then divide by the _denominator_.
- Another way to find the number of flags is to _divide_ each term of the numerator by the _denominator_ and then _subtract_.

Reading the Lesson

Complete each sentence.

1. To divide a polynomial by a monomial, you can divide each _term_ of the polynomial by the monomial.

2. You can use factoring to divide a polynomial by a binomial if a _factor_ of the polynomial is equal to the binomial divisor.

3. If you cannot see a way to factor a polynomial, then you can divide it by a binomial by using _long division_.

4. In Example 4, the polynomial that is being divided cannot be factored. In such cases, the quotient can be written as the sum of a polynomial and a fraction whose numerator is a number and whose denominator is equal to the _binomial divisor_.

5. Tell whether the following statement is true or false. If you say that it is false, give an example that supports your answer.
To divide a polynomial by a binomial of the form $x - a$, the polynomial must have at least two terms.
False; sample answer: The monomial x^5 can be divided by $x - 3$.

6. If you are dividing a polynomial by a binomial, what number should you use to represent a missing term of the polynomial?   0

Helping You Remember

7. If you want to remember one method that you can always use to divide a polynomial by a binomial, which method should you select?   long division

---

33. **DECORATING** Anoki wants to put a decorative border 3 feet above the floor around his bedroom walls. If the border comes in 5-yard rolls, how many rolls of border should Anoki buy?   **3 rolls**

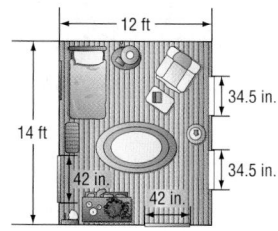

PIZZA For Exercises 34 and 35, use the following information.
The expression $\dfrac{\pi d^2}{64}$ can be used to determine the number of slices of a round pizza with diameter d.

34. Write a formula to calculate the cost per slice s of a pizza that costs C dollars.

$$34.\ s = \frac{64C}{\pi d^2}$$

35. Copy and complete the table below. Which size pizza offers the best price per slice?   **18-inch**

Size	10-inch	14-inch	18-inch
Price	$4.99	$8.99	$12.99
Number of slices	5	10	16
Cost per slice	$1.02	$0.93	$0.82

SCIENCE For Exercises 36–38, use the following information.
The *density* of a material is its mass per unit volume. **36–37. See margin.**

★ 36. Determine the densities for the materials listed in the table. Round to the nearest hundredth.

★ 37. Make a graph of the densities computed in Exercise 36.

★ 38. Interpret the line plot made in Exercise 37.
The densities are clustered around 9.

Material	Mass (g)	Volume (cm³)
aluminum	4.15	1.54
gold	2.32	0.12
silver	6.30	0.60
steel	7.80	1.00
iron	15.20	1.95
copper	2.48	0.28
blood	4.35	4.10
lead	11.30	1.00
brass	17.90	2.08
concrete	40.00	20.00

39. **GEOMETRY** The volume of a prism with a triangular base is $10w^3 + 23w^2 + 5w - 2$. The height of the prism is $2w + 1$, and the height of the triangle is $5w - 1$. What is the measure of the base of the triangle? $\left(\textit{Hint: } V = Bh\right)$ $2w + 4$

CRITICAL THINKING Find the value of k in each situation.

40. k is an integer and there is no remainder when $x^2 + 7x + 12$ is divided by $x + k$.   **3, 4**

41. When $x^2 + 7x + k$ is divided by $x + 2$, there is a remainder of 2.   **12**

42. $x + 7$ is a factor of $x^2 - 2x - k$.   **63**

More About. . .

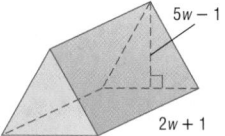

Science •··············
When air is heated it is less dense than the air surrounding it, and the heated air rises. This is why a hot air balloon is able to fly.

Source: www.howstuffworks.com

Enrichment, p. 734

Synthetic Division

You can divide a polynomial such as $3x^3 - 4x^2 - 3x - 2$ by a binomial such as $x - 3$ by a process called **synthetic division**. Compare the process with long division in the following explanation.

Example Divide $(3x^3 - 4x^2 - 3x - 2)$ by $(x - 3)$ using synthetic division.

1. Show the coefficients of the terms in descending order.
2. The divisor is $x - 3$. Since 3 is to be subtracted, write 3 in the corner.
3. Bring down the first coefficient, 3.
4. Multiply. $3 \cdot 3 = 9$
5. Add. $-4 + 9 = 5$
6. Multiply. $3 \cdot 5 = 15$
7. Add. $-3 + 15 = 12$
8. Multiply. $3 \cdot 12 = 36$
9. Add. $-2 + 36 = 34$

$3x^2 + 5x + 12$, remainder 34

Answer

36. aluminum: 2.69 g/cm³, gold: 19.33 g/cm³, silver: 10.5 g/cm³, steel: 7.8 g/cm³, iron: 7.79 g/cm³, copper: 8.86 g/cm³, blood: 1.06 g/cm³, lead: 11.3 g/cm³, brass: 8.61 g/cm³, concrete: 2 g/cm³

43. WRITING IN MATH Answer the question that was posed at the beginning of the lesson. **See margin.**

How is division used in sewing?

Include the following in your answer:

- a description showing that $\dfrac{36\text{ yards} - 7\frac{1}{2}\text{ yards}}{1\frac{1}{2}\text{ yards}}$ and $\dfrac{36\text{ yards}}{1\frac{1}{2}\text{ yards}} - \dfrac{7\frac{1}{2}\text{ yards}}{1\frac{1}{2}\text{ yards}}$

  result in the same answer, and
- a convincing explanation to show that $\dfrac{a-b}{c} = \dfrac{a}{c} - \dfrac{b}{c}$.

Standardized Test Practice
Ⓐ Ⓑ Ⓒ Ⓓ

44. Which expression represents the length of the rectangle? **D**

Ⓐ $m + 7$ Ⓑ $m - 8$

Ⓒ $m - 7$ Ⓓ $m + 8$

$A = m^2 + 4m - 32$ $m - 4$

45. What is the quotient of $x^3 + 5x - 20$ divided by $x - 3$? **B**

Ⓐ $x^2 - 3x + 14 + \dfrac{22}{x-3}$ Ⓑ $x^2 + 3x + 14 + \dfrac{22}{x-3}$

Ⓒ $x^2 + 8x + \dfrac{4}{x-3}$ Ⓓ $x^2 + 3x - 14 + \dfrac{22}{x-3}$

Maintain Your Skills

Mixed Review

Find each quotient. *(Lesson 12-4)*

46. $\dfrac{x^2 + 5x + 6}{x^2 - x - 12} \div \dfrac{x + 2}{x^2 + x - 20}$ $x + 5$ **47.** $\dfrac{m^2 + m - 6}{m^2 + 8m + 15} \div \dfrac{m^2 - m - 2}{m^2 + 9m + 20}$ $\dfrac{m+4}{m+1}$

Find each product. *(Lesson 12-3)*

48. $\dfrac{b^2 + 19b + 84}{b - 3} \cdot \dfrac{b^2 - 9}{b^2 + 15b + 36}$ $b + 7$ **49.** $\dfrac{z^2 + 16z + 39}{z^2 + 9z + 18} \cdot \dfrac{z + 5}{z^2 + 18z + 65}$ $\dfrac{1}{z+6}$

Simplify. Then use a calculator to verify your answer. *(Lesson 11-2)*

50. $3\sqrt{7} - \sqrt{7}$ **51.** $\sqrt{72} + \sqrt{32}$ **52.** $\sqrt{12} - \sqrt{18} + \sqrt{48}$
    $2\sqrt{7}$ $10\sqrt{2}$ $6\sqrt{3} - 3\sqrt{2}$

Factor each polynomial, if possible. If the polynomial cannot be factored, write *prime*. *(Lesson 9-6)*

53. $d^2 - 3d - 40$ **54.** $x^2 + 8x + 16$ **55.** $t^2 + t + 1$
    $(d + 5)(d - 8)$ $(x + 4)^2$ prime

56. BUSINESS Jorge Martinez has budgeted $150 to have business cards printed. A card printer charges $11 to set up each job and an additional $6 per box of 100 cards printed. What is the greatest number of cards Mr. Martinez can have printed? *(Lesson 6-3)* **2300 cards**

Getting Ready for the Next Lesson

PREREQUISITE SKILL Find each sum. **57.** $4m^3 + 6n^2 - n$ **58.** $4x^2 + 13xy + 2y^2$
*(To review **addition of polynomials**, see Lesson 8-5.)*

57. $(6n^2 - 6n + 10m^3) + (5n - 6m^3)$ **58.** $(3x^2 + 4xy - 2y^2) + (x^2 + 9xy + 4y^2)$
59. $(a^3 - b^3) + (-3a^3 - 2a^2b + b^2 - 2b^3)$ **60.** $(2g^3 + 6h) + (-4g^2 - 8h)$
    $-2a^3 - 2a^2b + b^2 - 3b^3$ $2g^3 - 4g^2 - 2h$

Lesson 12-5 Dividing Polynomials **671**

43. Sample answer: Division can be used to find the number of pieces of fabric available when you divide a large piece of fabric into smaller pieces. Answers should include the following.

- The two expressions are equivalent. If you use the Distributive Property, you can separate the numerator into two expressions with the same denominator.
- When you simplify the right side of the equation, the numerator is $a - b$ and the denominator is c. This is the same as the expression on the left.

4 Assess

Open-Ended Assessment

Speaking Have students work in pairs. Assign each student two polynomial division problems. Tell the students to study their problems for a few minutes to decide how the quotients should be found. Then ask the students to explain their decisions to each other, and discuss whether the methods chosen are correct.

Getting Ready for Lesson 12-6

PREREQUISITE SKILL Students will learn to add and subtract rational expressions with like denominators in Lesson 12-6. To prepare students for these concepts, make sure they understand how to add polynomials. Use Exercises 57–60 to determine your students' familiarity with adding polynomials.

Assessment Options

Quiz (Lessons 12-4 and 12-5) is available on p. 773 of the *Chapter 12 Resource Masters*.

Mid-Chapter Test (Lessons 12-1 through 12-5) is available on p. 775 of the *Chapter 12 Resource Masters*.

Answers

37.

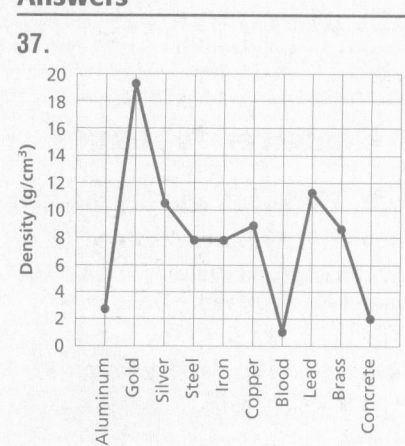

Lesson 12-5 Dividing Polynomials **671**

1 Focus

5-Minute Check Transparency 12-6 Use as a quiz or review of Lesson 12-5.

Mathematical Background notes are available for this lesson on p. 640D.

Building on Prior Knowledge

In Lesson 2-2, students first learned to add and subtract rational numbers. In this lesson, students will learn how to add and subtract rational expressions with binomials in the denominator

How can you use rational expressions to interpret graphics?

Ask students:

- What conditions must be met to add fractions? **They must have like denominators.**

- Do you really need to change percents into fractions before adding them? Explain. **No. Percents are understood to be fractions of 100, so they can be added without first converting them to fraction form.**

What You'll Learn

- Add rational expressions with like denominators.

- Subtract rational expressions with like denominators.

How can you use rational expressions to interpret graphics?

The graphic at the right shows the number of credit cards Americans have. To determine what fraction of those surveyed have no more than two credit cards, you can use addition. Remember that percents can be written as fractions with denominators of 100.

USA TODAY Snapshots®

Most Americans have one or two credit cards

One in five Americans say they have no credit cards. The number of cards among those who have them:

- One or two 33%
- Three or four 23%
- None 22%
- Five or six 11%
- Seven or more 9%

Source: Gallup Poll of 1,025 adults April 6-8.
Margin of error: ±3 percentage points.

By Marcy E. Mullins, USA TODAY

No credit cards	plus	one or two credit cards	equals	no more than two credit cards.
$\frac{22}{100}$	$+$	$\frac{33}{100}$	$=$	$\frac{55}{100}$

Thus, $\frac{55}{100}$ or 55% of those surveyed have no more than two credit cards.

ADD RATIONAL EXPRESSIONS Recall that to add fractions with like denominators you add the numerators and then write the sum over the common denominator. You can add rational expressions with like denominators in the same way.

Example 1 *Numbers in Denominator*

Find $\frac{3n}{12} + \frac{7n}{12}$.

$\frac{3n}{12} + \frac{7n}{12} = \frac{3n + 7n}{12}$ The common denominator is 12.

$= \frac{10n}{12}$ Add the numerators.

$= \frac{\overset{5}{10n}}{\underset{6}{12}}$ Divide by the common factor, 2.

$= \frac{5n}{6}$ Simplify.

Sometimes the denominators of rational expressions are binomials. As long as each rational expression has exactly the same binomial as its denominator, the process of adding is the same.

Resource Manager

 Workbook and Reproducible Masters

Chapter 12 Resource Masters
- Study Guide and Intervention, pp. 735–736
- Skills Practice, p. 737
- Practice, p. 738
- Reading to Learn Mathematics, p. 739
- Enrichment, p. 740

Parent and Student Study Guide Workbook, p. 96

Transparencies
5-Minute Check Transparency 12-6
Answer Key Transparencies

 Technology
Interactive Chalkboard

Example 2 *Binomials in Denominator*

Example 2 *Binomials in Denominator*

Find $\dfrac{2x}{x+1} + \dfrac{2}{x+1}$.

$\dfrac{2x}{x+1} + \dfrac{2}{x+1} = \dfrac{2x+2}{x+1}$ The common denominator is $x+1$.

$= \dfrac{2(x+1)}{x+1}$ Factor the numerator.

$= \dfrac{2(\cancel{x+1})}{\cancel{x+1}}$ Divide by the common factor, $x+1$.

$= \dfrac{2}{1}$ or 2 Simplify.

Example 3 *Find a Perimeter*

GEOMETRY Find an expression for the perimeter of rectangle *PQRS*.

$P = 2\ell + 2w$ Perimeter formula

$= 2\left(\dfrac{4a+5b}{3a+7b}\right) + 2\left(\dfrac{2a+3b}{3a+7b}\right)$ $\ell = \dfrac{4a+5b}{3a+7b}$, $w = \dfrac{2a+3b}{3a+7b}$

$= \dfrac{2(4a+5b) + 2(2a+3b)}{3a+7b}$ The common denominator is $3a+7b$.

$= \dfrac{8a+10b+4a+6b}{3a+7b}$ Distributive Property

$= \dfrac{12a+16b}{3a+7b}$ Combine like terms.

$= \dfrac{4(3a+4b)}{3a+7b}$ Factor.

The perimeter can be represented by the expression $\dfrac{4(3a+4b)}{3a+7b}$.

SUBTRACT RATIONAL EXPRESSIONS To subtract rational expressions with like denominators, subtract the numerators and write the difference over the common denominator. Recall that to subtract an expression, you add its additive inverse.

Example 4 *Subtract Rational Expressions*

Find $\dfrac{3x+4}{x-2} - \dfrac{x-1}{x-2}$.

$\dfrac{3x+4}{x-2} - \dfrac{x-1}{x-2} = \dfrac{(3x+4)-(x-1)}{x-2}$ The common denominator is $x-2$.

$= \dfrac{(3x+4)+[-(x-1)]}{x-2}$ The additive inverse of $(x-1)$ is $-(x-1)$.

$= \dfrac{3x+4-x+1}{x-2}$ Distributive Property

$= \dfrac{2x+5}{x-2}$ Simplify.

www.algebra1.com/extra_examples   **Lesson 12-6** Rational Expressions with Like Denominators **673**

2 Teach

ADD RATIONAL EXPRESSIONS

In-Class Examples Power Point®

Teaching Tip Remind students to avoid the temptation to simplify $\dfrac{3n}{12}$ before adding. The denominators must be the same in order to add, and simplifying the fraction will change the denominator.

1 Find $\dfrac{4b}{15} + \dfrac{16b}{15}$. $\dfrac{4b}{3}$

2 Find $\dfrac{6c}{c+2} + \dfrac{12}{c+2}$. **6**

3 **GEOMETRY** Find an expression for the perimeter of rectangle *WXYZ*.

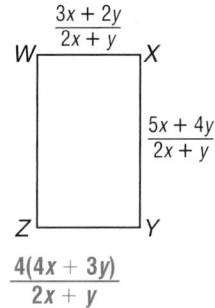

$\dfrac{4(4x+3y)}{2x+y}$

SUBTRACT RATIONAL EXPRESSIONS

In-Class Example Power Point®

4 Find $\dfrac{7x+9}{x-3} - \dfrac{x-5}{x-3}$.

$\dfrac{2(3x+7)}{x-3}$

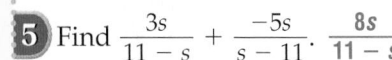

3 Practice/Apply

Sometimes you must express a denominator as its additive inverse to have like denominators.

Example 5 Inverse Denominators

Find $\dfrac{2m}{m - 9} + \dfrac{4m}{9 - m}$.

The denominator $9 - m$ is the same as $-(-9 + m)$ or $-(m - 9)$. Rewrite the second expression so that it has the same denominator as the first.

$$\dfrac{2m}{m - 9} + \dfrac{4m}{9 - m} = \dfrac{2m}{m - 9} + \dfrac{4m}{-(m - 9)} \qquad 9 - m = -(m - 9)$$

$$= \dfrac{2m}{m - 9} - \dfrac{4m}{m - 9} \qquad \text{Rewrite using like denominators.}$$

$$= \dfrac{2m - 4m}{m - 9} \qquad \text{The common denominator is } m - 9.$$

$$= \dfrac{-2m}{m - 9} \qquad \text{Subtract.}$$

Check for Understanding

Concept Check

1. **OPEN ENDED** Write two rational expressions with a denominator of $x + 2$ that have a sum of 1.

2. **Describe** how adding rational expressions with like denominators is similar to adding fractions with like denominators. **See margin.**

3. **Compare and contrast** two rational expressions whose sum is 0 with two rational expressions whose difference is 0.

4. **FIND THE ERROR** Russell and Ginger are finding the difference of $\dfrac{7x + 2}{4x - 3}$ and $\dfrac{x - 8}{3 - 4x}$.

Russell

$$\dfrac{7x + 2}{4x - 3} - \dfrac{x - 8}{3 - 4x} = \dfrac{7x + 2}{4x - 3} + \dfrac{x - 8}{4x - 3}$$

$$= \dfrac{7x + x + 2 - 8}{4x - 3}$$

$$= \dfrac{8x - 6}{4x - 3}$$

$$= \dfrac{2(4x - 3)}{4x - 3}$$

$$= 2$$

Ginger

$$\dfrac{7x + 2}{4x - 3} - \dfrac{x - 8}{3 - 4x} = \dfrac{-2 - 7x}{3 - 4x} - \dfrac{x - 8}{3 - 4x}$$

$$= \dfrac{-2 + 8 - 7x - x}{3 - 4x}$$

$$= \dfrac{-6 - 8x}{3 - 4x}$$

$$= \dfrac{-2(3 - 4x)}{3 - 4x}$$

$$= -2$$

Who is correct? Explain your reasoning.

Guided Practice Find each sum.

GUIDED PRACTICE KEY	
Exercises	Examples
5–8	1–3
9, 10, 12, 13	4
11	5

5. $\dfrac{a + 2}{4} + \dfrac{a - 2}{4}$ $\dfrac{a}{2}$

6. $\dfrac{3x}{x + 1} + \dfrac{3}{x + 1}$ 3

7. $\dfrac{2 - n}{n - 1} + \dfrac{1}{n - 1}$ $\dfrac{3 - n}{n - 1}$

8. $\dfrac{4t - 1}{1 - 4t} + \dfrac{2t + 3}{1 - 4t}$ $\dfrac{6t + 2}{1 - 4t}$

Find each difference.

9. $\dfrac{5a}{12} - \dfrac{7a}{12}$ $-\dfrac{a}{6}$

10. $\dfrac{7}{n - 3} - \dfrac{4}{n - 3}$ $\dfrac{3}{n - 3}$

11. $\dfrac{3m}{m - 2} - \dfrac{6}{2 - m}$ $\dfrac{3m + 6}{m - 2}$

12. $\dfrac{x^2}{x - y} - \dfrac{y^2}{x - y}$ $x + y$

Application **13. SCHOOL** Most schools create daily attendance reports to keep track of their students. Suppose that one day, out of 960 students, 45 were absent due to illness, 29 were participating in a wrestling tournament, 10 were excused to go to their doctors, and 12 were at a music competition. What fraction of the students were absent from school on this day? $\dfrac{1}{10}$

Practice and Apply

Find each sum.

14. $\dfrac{m}{3} + \dfrac{2m}{3}$ m

15. $\dfrac{12z}{7} + \dfrac{-5z}{7}$ z

16. $\dfrac{x+3}{5} + \dfrac{x+2}{5}$ $\dfrac{2x+5}{5}$

17. $\dfrac{n-7}{2} + \dfrac{n+5}{2}$ $n-1$

18. $\dfrac{2y}{y+3} + \dfrac{6}{y+3}$ 2

19. $\dfrac{3r}{r+5} + \dfrac{15}{r+5}$ 3

20. $\dfrac{k-5}{k-1} + \dfrac{4}{k-1}$ 1

21. $\dfrac{n-2}{n+3} + \dfrac{-1}{n+3}$ $\dfrac{n-3}{n+3}$

22. $\dfrac{4x-5}{x-2} + \dfrac{x+3}{x-2}$ $\dfrac{5x-2}{x-2}$

23. $\dfrac{2a+3}{a-4} + \dfrac{a-2}{a-4}$ $\dfrac{3a+1}{a-4}$

24. $\dfrac{5s+1}{2s+1} + \dfrac{3s-2}{2s+1}$ $\dfrac{8s-1}{2s+1}$

25. $\dfrac{9b+3}{2b+6} + \dfrac{5b+4}{2b+6}$ $\dfrac{14b+7}{2b+6}$

26. What is the sum of $\dfrac{12x-7}{3x-2}$ and $\dfrac{9x-5}{2-3x}$? 1

27. Find the sum of $\dfrac{11x-5}{2x+5}$ and $\dfrac{11x+12}{2x+5}$. $\dfrac{22x+7}{2x+5}$

Find each difference.

28. $\dfrac{5x}{7} - \dfrac{3x}{7}$ $\dfrac{2x}{7}$

29. $\dfrac{4n}{3} - \dfrac{2n}{3}$ $\dfrac{2n}{3}$

30. $\dfrac{x+4}{5} - \dfrac{x+2}{5}$ $\dfrac{2}{5}$

31. $\dfrac{a+5}{6} - \dfrac{a+3}{6}$ $\dfrac{1}{3}$

32. $\dfrac{2}{x+7} - \dfrac{-5}{x+7}$ $\dfrac{7}{x+7}$

33. $\dfrac{4}{z-2} - \dfrac{-6}{z-2}$ $\dfrac{10}{z-2}$

34. $\dfrac{5}{3x-5} - \dfrac{3x}{3x-5}$ -1

35. $\dfrac{4}{7m-2} - \dfrac{7m}{7m-2}$

36. $\dfrac{2x}{x-2} - \dfrac{2x}{2-x}$ $\dfrac{4x}{x-2}$

35. $\dfrac{4-7m}{7m-2}$

37. $\dfrac{5y}{y-3} - \dfrac{5y}{3-y}$ $\dfrac{10y}{y-3}$

38. $\dfrac{8}{3t-4} - \dfrac{6t}{3t-4}$ -2

39. $\dfrac{15x}{5x+1} - \dfrac{-3}{5x+1}$ 3

40. Find the difference of $\dfrac{10a-12}{2a-6}$ and $\dfrac{6a}{6-2a}$. $\dfrac{8a-6}{a-3}$

41. What is the difference of $\dfrac{b-15}{2b+12}$ and $\dfrac{-3b+8}{2b+12}$? $\dfrac{4b-23}{2b+12}$

42. POPULATION The United States population in 1998 is described in the table. Use this information to write the fraction of the population that is 80 years or older.

$\dfrac{8695}{269,817}$

Age	Number of People
0–19	77,525,000
20–39	79,112,000
40–59	68,699,000
60–79	35,786,000
80–99	8,634,000
100+	61,000

Source: *Statistical Abstract of the United States*

43. CONSERVATION The freshman class chose to plant spruce and pine trees at a wildlife sanctuary for a service project. Some students can plant 140 trees on Saturday, and others can plant 20 trees after school on Monday and again on Tuesday. Write an expression for the fraction of the trees that could be planted on these days if n represents the number of spruce trees and there are twice as many pine trees. $\dfrac{60}{n}$

Add Rational Expressions To add rational expressions with like denominators, add the numerators and then write the sum over the common denominator. If possible, simplify the resulting rational expression.

Example 1 Find $\frac{5n}{15} + \frac{7n}{15}$.

$\frac{5n}{15} + \frac{7n}{15} = \frac{5n + 7n}{15}$ Add the numerators.

$= \frac{12n}{15}$ Simplify.

$= \frac{12n^{4n}}{15_5}$ Divide by 3.

$= \frac{4n}{5}$ Simplify.

Example 2 Find $\frac{3x}{x+2} + \frac{6}{x+2}$.

$\frac{3x}{x+2} + \frac{6}{x+2} = \frac{3x+6}{x+2}$

$= \frac{3(x+2)}{x+2}$

$= \frac{3(x+2)^1}{x+2_1}$

$= \frac{3}{1}$ or 3

Exercises

Find each sum.

1. $\frac{3}{a} + \frac{4}{a}$ $\frac{7}{a}$

2. $\frac{x^2}{8} + \frac{x}{8}$ $\frac{x^2+x}{8}$

3. $\frac{x+3}{6} + \frac{x-2}{6}$ $\frac{2x+1}{6}$

4. $\frac{m}{2} + \frac{m+4}{2}$ $m-2$

5. $\frac{2x}{x+5} + \frac{3x}{x+5}$ $\frac{5x}{x+5}$

6. $\frac{m+4}{m-1} + \frac{m+4}{m-1}$ $\frac{2m+8}{m-1}$

7. $\frac{y+5}{y+6} + \frac{1}{y+6}$ 1

8. $\frac{3x+5}{5} + \frac{2x+10}{5}$ $x+3$

9. $\frac{2a-4}{a-4} + \frac{-a}{a-4}$ 1

10. $\frac{m+1}{2m-1} + \frac{3m-3}{2m-1}$ 2

11. $\frac{x+1}{x-2} + \frac{x-5}{x-2}$ 2

12. $\frac{5a}{3b^2} + \frac{10a}{3b^2}$ $\frac{5a}{b^2}$

13. $\frac{3x+2}{x+2} + \frac{x+6}{x+2}$ 4

14. $\frac{a-4}{a+1} + \frac{a+6}{a+1}$ 2

15. $\frac{2x+3}{x+3} + \frac{x+6}{x+3}$ 3

16. $\frac{3a^2+4a}{a} + \frac{6a^2}{a}$ $9a+4$

17. $\frac{-8x}{x-4} + \frac{4x+x^2}{x-4}$ x

18. $\frac{9a-14}{2a+1} + \frac{8a+16}{2a+1}$ $\frac{17a+2}{2a+1}$

Find each sum.

1. $\frac{n}{8} + \frac{3n}{8}$ $\frac{n}{2}$

2. $\frac{7u}{16} + \frac{5u}{16}$ $\frac{3u}{4}$

3. $\frac{w+9}{9} + \frac{w+4}{9}$ $\frac{2w+13}{9}$

4. $\frac{s-8}{4} + \frac{s-4}{4}$ $\frac{s-6}{2}$

5. $\frac{4c}{c+1} + \frac{4}{c+1}$ 4

6. $\frac{n+6}{n-2} + \frac{-8}{n-2}$ 1

7. $\frac{x-5}{x+2} + \frac{-2}{x+2}$ $\frac{x-7}{x+2}$

8. $\frac{r+5}{r-5} + \frac{2r-1}{r-5}$ $\frac{3r+4}{r-5}$

9. $\frac{4p+14}{p+4} + \frac{2p+10}{p+4}$ 6

10. $\frac{2y+1}{3y-2} + \frac{4y-5}{3y-2}$ 2

11. $\frac{5a+2}{2a-2} + \frac{2a-4}{2a-2}$ $\frac{7a-2}{2a-2}$

12. $\frac{6t-5}{3t+1} + \frac{4t+3}{3t+1}$ $\frac{10t-2}{3t+1}$

Find each difference.

13. $\frac{3y}{8} - \frac{y}{8}$ $\frac{y}{4}$

14. $\frac{9n}{5} - \frac{4n}{5}$ n

15. $\frac{r+2}{3} - \frac{r+5}{3}$ -1

16. $\frac{x-6}{2} - \frac{x-7}{2}$ $\frac{1}{2}$

17. $\frac{s+14}{5} - \frac{s-14}{5}$ $\frac{28}{5}$

18. $\frac{6}{c-1} - \frac{-2}{c-1}$ $\frac{8}{c-1}$

19. $\frac{7}{d+6} - \frac{6}{d+6}$ $\frac{1}{d+6}$

20. $\frac{2y}{2y-3} - \frac{3}{3-2y}$ 1

21. $\frac{4p}{p-5} - \frac{4p}{5-p}$ $\frac{8p}{p-5}$

22. $\frac{2y}{y-2} - \frac{7y}{2-y}$ $\frac{9y}{y-2}$

23. $\frac{6a-4}{2a+2} - \frac{4a-6}{2a+2}$ 1

24. $\frac{30t}{6t-1} - \frac{5}{1-6t}$ $\frac{30t+5}{6t-1}$

25. **GEOMETRY** Find an expression for the perimeter of rectangle $ABCD$. Use the formula $P = 2\ell + 2w$. $\frac{4(4a+3b)}{2a+b}$

26. **MUSIC** Kerrie is burning an 80-minute CD-R containing her favorite dance songs. Suppose she has burned 41 minutes of songs and has five more songs in the queue that total x minutes. When she is done, write an expression for the fraction of the CD that has been filled with music. $\frac{41+x}{80}$

Pre-Activity How can you use rational expressions to interpret graphics?

Read the introduction to Lesson 12-6 at the top of page 672 in your textbook.

Write a subtraction expression that you can evaluate to find what percent of the people surveyed have three or more credit cards.

Sample answer: $\frac{100}{100} - \frac{55}{100}$

Reading the Lesson

1. To add or subtract rational expressions with like denominators, add or subtract the __numerators__ and then write the sum or difference over the __common denominator__.

2. For each addition or subtraction problem, write the needed expression in each box on the right side of the equation.

a. $\frac{5n}{7} + 8 = \frac{5n + \boxed{8}}{7}$

b. $\frac{7x}{x-1} + \frac{x+3}{x-1} = \frac{\boxed{7x} + (x+3)}{x-1}$

c. $\frac{3}{2m+5} - \frac{6m+1}{2m+5} = \frac{3 - (\boxed{6m+1})}{2m+5}$

d. $\frac{d-c}{c+2d} - \frac{c-d}{c+2d} = \frac{\boxed{d-c} - (c-d)}{c+2d}$

e. $\frac{7}{3x-4} - \frac{5}{3-3x} = \frac{7 + \boxed{5}}{3x-4}$

f. $\frac{8}{6x-1} + \frac{9}{1-6x} = \frac{8 + \boxed{(-9)}}{6x-1}$

Helping You Remember

3. How can you use what you know about addition and subtraction of rational numbers that have like denominators to remember how to add and subtract rational expressions that have like denominators?

To add or subtract rational numbers that have like denominators, you add or subtract their numerators and keep the same denominator. You do the same to add or subtract rational expressions that have like denominators.

---

44. **GEOMETRIC DESIGN** A student center is a square room that is 25 feet wide and 25 feet long. The walls are 10 feet high and each wall is painted white with a red diagonal stripe as shown. What fraction of the walls are painted red? $\frac{1}{5}$

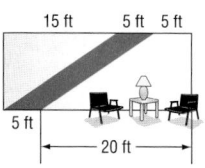

HIKING For Exercises 45 and 46, use the following information.
A tour guide recommends that hikers carry a gallon of water on hikes to the bottom of the Grand Canyon. Water weighs 62.4 pounds per cubic foot, and one cubic foot of water contains 7.48 gallons.

45. Tanika plans to carry two 1-quart bottles and four 1-pint bottles for her hike. Write a rational expression for this amount of water written as a fraction of a cubic foot. $\frac{1}{7.48}$ ft³

46. How much does this amount of water weigh?   **about 8.3 lb**

GEOMETRY For Exercises 47 and 48, use the following information.
Each figure has a perimeter of x units.

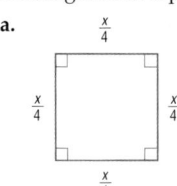 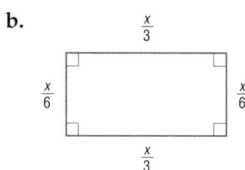 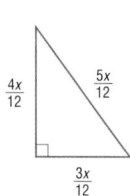

a.   b.   c.

47. Find the ratio of the area of each figure to its perimeter. $\frac{x}{16}$, $\frac{x}{18}$, $\frac{x}{24}$

48. Which figure has the greatest ratio?   **a**

49. **CRITICAL THINKING** Which of the following rational numbers is not equivalent to the others?   **c**

a. $\frac{3}{2-x}$

b. $\frac{-3}{x-2}$

c. $-\frac{3}{2-x}$

d. $-\frac{3}{x-2}$

50. **WRITING IN MATH** Answer the question that was posed at the beginning of the lesson.   **See margin.**

How can you use rational expressions to interpret graphics?

Include the following in your answer:
- an explanation of how the numbers in the graphic relate to rational expressions, and
- a description of how to add two rational expressions whose denominators are $3x - 4y$ and $4y - 3x$.

Standardized Test Practice
Ⓐ Ⓑ Ⓒ Ⓓ

51. Find $\frac{k+2}{k-7} + \frac{-3}{k-7}$.   **A**

(A) $\frac{k-1}{k-7}$

(B) $\frac{k-5}{k-7}$

(C) $\frac{k+1}{k-7}$

(D) $\frac{k+5}{k-7}$

52. Which is an expression for the perimeter of rectangle $ABCD$?   **B**

(A) $\frac{14r}{2r+6s}$

(B) $\frac{14r}{r+3s}$

(C) $\frac{14r}{r+6s}$

(D) $\frac{28r}{r+3s}$

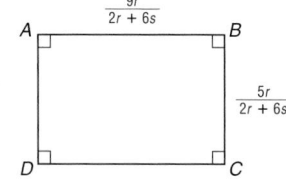

Sum and Difference of Any Two Like Powers

The sum of any two like powers can be written $a^n + b^n$, where n is a positive integer. The difference of like powers is $a^n - b^n$. Under what conditions are these expressions exactly divisible by $(a + b)$ or $(a - b)$? The answer depends on whether n is an odd or even number.

Use long division to find the following quotients. (*Hint:* Write $a^3 + b^3$ as $a^3 + 0a^2 + 0a + b^3$.) Is the numerator exactly divisible by the denominator? Write *yes* or *no*.

1. $\frac{a^3+b^3}{a+b}$ yes

2. $\frac{a^3+b^3}{a-b}$ no

3. $\frac{a^3-b^3}{a+b}$ no

4. $\frac{a^3-b^3}{a-b}$ yes

5. $\frac{a^4+b^4}{a+b}$ no

6. $\frac{a^4+b^4}{a-b}$ no

7. $\frac{a^4-b^4}{a+b}$ yes

8. $\frac{a^4-b^4}{a-b}$ yes

Hiking

Due to its popularity, the Grand Canyon is one of the most threatened natural areas in the United States.

Source: The Wildlife Foundation

Mixed Review **Find each quotient.** *(Lessons 12-4 and 12-5)*

53. $\dfrac{x^3 - 7x + 6}{x - 2}$ $x^2 + 2x - 3$

54. $\dfrac{56x^3 + 32x^2 - 63x - 36}{7x + 4}$ $8x^2 - 9$

55. $\dfrac{b^2 - 9}{4b} \div (b - 3)$ $\dfrac{b + 3}{4b}$

56. $\dfrac{x}{x + 2} \div \dfrac{x^2}{x^2 + 5x + 6}$ $\dfrac{x + 3}{x}$

Factor each trinomial. *(Lesson 9-3)*

57. $a^2 + 9a + 14$
   $(a + 7)(a + 2)$

58. $p^2 + p - 30$
   $(p + 6)(p - 5)$

59. $y^2 - 11yz + 28z^2$
   $(y - 4z)(y - 7z)$

Find each sum or difference. *(Lesson 8-5)*

60. $(3x^2 - 4x) - (7 - 9x)$
   $3x^2 + 5x - 7$

61. $(5x^2 - 6x + 14) + (2x^2 + 3x + 8)$
   $7x^2 - 3x + 22$

62. **CARPENTRY** When building a stairway, a carpenter considers the ratio of riser to tread. If each stair being built is to have a width of 1 foot and a height of 8 inches, what will be the slope of the stairway? $\dfrac{2}{3}$

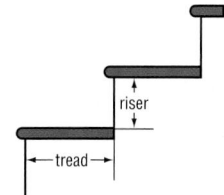
riser
tread

Getting Ready for the Next Lesson **BASIC SKILL** Find the least common multiple for each set of numbers.

63. 4, 9, 12 **36**

64. 7, 21, 5 **105**

65. 6, 12, 24 **24**

66. 45, 10, 6 **90**

67. 5, 6, 15 **30**

68. 8, 9, 12 **72**

69. 16, 20, 25 **400**

70. 36, 48, 60 **720**

71. 9, 16, 24 **144**

Practice Quiz 2 *Lessons 12-4 through 12-6*

Find each quotient. *(Lessons 12-4 and 12-5)*

1. $\dfrac{a}{a + 3} \div \dfrac{a + 11}{a + 3}$ $\dfrac{a}{a + 11}$

2. $\dfrac{4z + 8}{z + 3} \div (z + 2)$ $\dfrac{4}{z + 3}$

3. $\dfrac{x - 1}{x + 5}$

4. $3y - 5 + \dfrac{1}{xy}$

5. $x - 5 - \dfrac{1}{2x + 3}$

3. $\dfrac{(2x - 1)(x - 2)}{(x - 2)(x - 3)} \div \dfrac{(2x - 1)(x + 5)}{(x - 3)(x - 1)}$

4. $(9xy^2 - 15xy + 3) \div 3xy$

5. $(2x^2 - 7x - 16) \div (2x + 3)$

6. $\dfrac{y^2 - 19y + 9}{y - 4}$ $y - 15 - \dfrac{51}{y - 4}$

Find each sum or difference. *(Lesson 12-6)*

7. $\dfrac{2}{x + 7} + \dfrac{5}{x + 7}$ $\dfrac{7}{x + 7}$

8. $\dfrac{2m}{m + 3} - \dfrac{-6}{m + 3}$ **2**

9. $\dfrac{5x - 1}{3x + 2} - \dfrac{2x - 1}{3x + 2}$ $\dfrac{3x}{3x + 2}$

10. **MUSIC** Suppose the record shown played for 16.5 minutes on one side and the average of the radii of the grooves on the record was $3\frac{3}{4}$ inches. Write an expression involving units that represents how many inches the needle passed through the grooves while the record was being played. Then evaluate the expression.
$2\pi\left(3\frac{3}{4}\text{in.}\right) \cdot \dfrac{33\frac{1}{3} \text{ revolutions}}{1 \text{ minute}} \cdot \dfrac{16.5 \text{ minutes}}{1}$; 4125π or about 12,959 in.

$33\frac{1}{3}$ revolutions per minute

Answer

50. Sample answer: Since any rational number can be expressed as a fraction, values on graphs can be written as rational expressions for clarification. Answers should include the following.

   • The numbers in the graphic are percents that can be written as rational expressions with a denominator of 100.

   • To add the rational expressions, factor -1 out of either denominator so that it is like the other.

Open-Ended Assessment

Modeling Have students use construction paper, scrap paper, etc. to create models of rational expressions. The models need to be keyed so that they fit together like pieces of a puzzle if they have like denominators, and do not fit together if the denominators are not alike. Display students' models on a bulletin board to remind them of the properties that rational expressions must have in order to be added or subtracted.

Getting Ready for Lesson 12-7

BASIC SKILL Students will learn to add and subtract rational expressions with unlike denominators in Lesson 12-7. In order to add and subtract rational expressions with unlike denominators, students must find the least common denominator. Use Exercises 63–71 to determine your students' familiarity with finding least common multiples.

Assessment Options

Practice Quiz 2 The quiz provides students with a brief review of the concepts and skills in Lessons 12-4 through 12-6. Lesson numbers are given to the right of exercises or instruction lines so students can review concepts not yet mastered.

5-Minute Check Transparency 12-7 Use as a quiz or review of Lesson 12-6.

Mathematical Background notes are available for this lesson on p. 640D.

How can rational expressions be used to describe elections?

Ask students:

• In what year will the senator face his or her first reelection? The second reelection? **The senator will face reelection in 2010, and 2016.**

• When will the next three presidential elections take place? **2008, 2012, 2016**

• Based on this information, when will the senator's reelection fall in the same year as a presidential election? **2016**

12-7 Rational Expressions with Unlike Denominators

What You'll Learn

• Add rational expressions with unlike denominators.

• Subtract rational expressions with unlike denominators.

Vocabulary
• least common multiple (LCM)
• least common denominator (LCD)

How can rational expressions be used to describe elections?

The President of the United States is elected every four years, and senators are elected every six years. A certain senator is elected in 2004, the same year as a presidential election, and is reelected in subsequent elections. In what year is the senator's reelection the same year as a presidential election?

ADD RATIONAL EXPRESSIONS The number of years in which a specific senator's election coincides with a presidential election is related to the common multiples of 4 and 6. The least number of years that will pass until the next election for both a specific senator and the President is the least common multiple of these numbers. The **least common multiple (LCM)** is the least number that is a common multiple of two or more numbers.

Example 1 LCM of Monomials

Find the LCM of $15m^2b^3$ and $18mb^2$.

Find the prime factors of each coefficient and variable expression.

$15m^2b^3 = 3 \cdot 5 \cdot m \cdot m \cdot b \cdot b \cdot b$

$18mb^2 = 2 \cdot 3 \cdot 3 \cdot m \cdot b \cdot b$

Use each prime factor the greatest number of times it appears in any of the factorizations.

$15m^2b^3 = 3 \cdot 5 \cdot m \cdot m \cdot b \cdot b \cdot b$

$18mb^2 = 2 \cdot 3 \cdot 3 \cdot m \cdot b \cdot b$

LCM $= 2 \cdot 3 \cdot 3 \cdot 5 \cdot m \cdot m \cdot b \cdot b \cdot b$ or $90m^2b^3$

Example 2 LCM of Polynomials

Find the LCM of $x^2 + 8x + 15$ and $x^2 + x - 6$.

Express each polynomial in factored form.

$x^2 + 8x + 15 = (x + 3)(x + 5)$

$x^2 + x - 6 = (x - 2)(x + 3)$

Use each factor the greatest number of times it appears.

LCM $= (x - 2)(x + 3)(x + 5)$

Resource Manager

Workbook and Reproducible Masters

Chapter 12 Resource Masters
• Study Guide and Intervention, pp. 741–742
• Skills Practice, p. 743
• Practice, p. 744
• Reading to Learn Mathematics, p. 745
• Enrichment, p. 746
• Assessment, p. 774

Parent and Student Study Guide Workbook, p. 97
Prerequisite Skills Workbook, pp. 17–18
School-to-Career Masters, p. 23

Transparencies
5-Minute Check Transparency 12-7
Answer Key Transparencies

Technology
Interactive Chalkboard

Recall that to add fractions with unlike denominators, you need to rename the fractions using the least common multiple (LCM) of the denominators, known as the **least common denominator (LCD)**.

Key Concept — Add Rational Expressions

Use the following steps to add rational expressions with unlike denominators.

Step 1 Find the LCD.

Step 2 Change each rational expression into an equivalent expression with the LCD as the denominator.

Step 3 Add just as with rational expressions with like denominators.

Step 4 Simplify if necessary.

Example 3 Monomial Denominators

Find $\dfrac{a+1}{a} + \dfrac{a-3}{3a}$.

Factor each denominator and find the LCD.

$a = a$

$3a = 3 \cdot a$

$\text{LCD} = 3a$

Since the denominator of $\dfrac{a-3}{3a}$ is already $3a$, only $\dfrac{a+1}{a}$ needs to be renamed.

$$\dfrac{a+1}{a} + \dfrac{a-3}{3a} = \dfrac{3(a+1)}{3(a)} + \dfrac{a-3}{3a} \qquad \text{Multiply } \dfrac{a+1}{a} \text{ by } \dfrac{3}{3}.$$

$$= \dfrac{3a+3}{3a} + \dfrac{a-3}{3a} \qquad \text{Distributive Property}$$

$$= \dfrac{3a+3+a-3}{3a} \qquad \text{Add the numerators.}$$

$$= \dfrac{\overset{1}{4a}}{\underset{1}{3\cancel{a}}} \qquad \text{Divide out the common factor } a.$$

$$= \dfrac{4}{3} \qquad \text{Simplify.}$$

Example 4 Polynomial Denominators

Find $\dfrac{y-2}{y^2+4y+4} + \dfrac{y-2}{y+2}$.

$$\dfrac{y-2}{y^2+4y+4} + \dfrac{y-2}{y+2} = \dfrac{y-2}{(y+2)^2} + \dfrac{y-2}{y+2} \qquad \text{Factor the denominators.}$$

$$= \dfrac{y-2}{(y+2)^2} + \dfrac{y-2}{y+2} \cdot \dfrac{y+2}{y+2} \qquad \text{The LCD is } (y+2)^2.$$

$$= \dfrac{y-2}{(y+2)^2} + \dfrac{y^2-4}{(y+2)^2} \qquad (y-2)(y+2) = y^2 - 4$$

$$= \dfrac{y-2+y^2-4}{(y+2)^2} \qquad \text{Add the numerators.}$$

$$= \dfrac{y^2+y-6}{(y+2)^2} \text{ or } \dfrac{(y-2)(y+3)}{(y+2)^2} \qquad \text{Simplify.}$$

 www.algebra1.com/extra_examples **Lesson 12-7** Rational Expressions with Unlike Denominators **679**

---

2 Teach

ADD RATIONAL EXPRESSIONS

Building on Prior Knowledge

Students first learned to find the prime factorization of monomials in Lesson 9-1. Without this knowledge, students would not be able to find the LCM of monomials and polynomials. If students need a refresher on finding prime factorizations, refer them to Lesson 9-1.

In-Class Examples Power Point®

Teaching Tip Point out to students that it is possible for two monomials to have no common multiple other than their product and multiples of their product.

1 Find the LCM of $12b^4c^5$ and $32bc^2$. **$96\,b^4c^5$**

2 Find the LCM of $x^2 - 3x - 28$ and $x^2 - 8x + 7$. **$(x+4)(x-7)(x-1)$**

3 Find $\dfrac{z+2}{5z} + \dfrac{z-6}{z}$.

$\dfrac{2(3z-14)}{5z}$

4 Find $\dfrac{x+7}{x^2-6x+9} + \dfrac{x+3}{x-3}$.

$\dfrac{(x+2)(x-1)}{(x-3)^2}$

Teaching Tip Remind students that whatever they multiply the denominator by to produce the LCD must also be used to multiply by the numerator.

5 Find $\dfrac{c}{20 + 4c} + \dfrac{6}{5 - c}$.

$$\dfrac{-c^2 + 29c + 120}{4(5 + c)(5 - c)}$$

Teaching Tip Tell students that with a test item of this complexity, they need to work out the difference without looking at the item choices, then compare their difference with the item choices.

6 Find $\dfrac{x - 4}{(2 - x)^2} - \dfrac{x - 5}{x^2 + x - 6}$. **C**

A $\dfrac{6x + 22}{(x - 2)^2(x + 3)}$

B $\dfrac{6x - 22}{(x - 2)^2(x + 3)^2}$

C $\dfrac{6x - 22}{(x - 2)^2(x + 3)}$

D $\dfrac{6x + 22}{(x - 2)(x + 3)}$

SUBTRACT RATIONAL EXPRESSIONS As with addition, to subtract rational expressions with unlike denominators, you must first rename the expressions using a common denominator.

Example 5 Binomials in Denominators

Find $\dfrac{4}{3a - 6} - \dfrac{a}{a + 2}$.

$\dfrac{4}{3a - 6} - \dfrac{a}{a + 2} = \dfrac{4}{3(a - 2)} - \dfrac{a}{a + 2}$ Factor.

$= \dfrac{4(a + 2)}{3(a - 2)(a + 2)} - \dfrac{3a(a - 2)}{3(a + 2)(a - 2)}$ The LCD is $3(a + 2)(a - 2)$.

$= \dfrac{4(a + 2) - 3a(a - 2)}{3(a - 2)(a + 2)}$ Subtract the numerators.

$= \dfrac{4a + 8 - 3a^2 + 6a}{3(a - 2)(a + 2)}$ Multiply.

$= \dfrac{-3a^2 + 10a + 8}{3(a - 2)(a + 2)}$ or $-\dfrac{3a^2 - 10a - 8}{3(a - 2)(a + 2)}$ Simplify.

Standardized Test Practice
Ⓐ Ⓑ Ⓒ Ⓓ

Example 6 Polynomials in Denominators

Multiple-Choice Test Item

Find $\dfrac{h - 2}{h^2 + 4h + 4} - \dfrac{h - 4}{h^2 - 4}$.

Ⓐ $\dfrac{2h - 12}{(h - 2)(h + 2)^2}$

Ⓑ $\dfrac{-2h + 12}{(h - 2)(h + 2)^2}$

Ⓒ $\dfrac{2h - 12}{(h - 2)^2(h + 2)}$

Ⓓ $\dfrac{-2h + 12}{(h - 2)(h + 2)}$

Read the Test Item

The expression $\dfrac{h - 2}{h^2 + 4h + 4} - \dfrac{h - 4}{h^2 - 4}$ represents the difference of two rational expressions with unlike denominators.

Test-Taking Tip

Examine all of the answer choices carefully. Look for differences in operations, positive and negative signs, and exponents.

Solve the Test Item

Step 1 Factor each denominator and find the LCD.

$h^2 + 4h + 4 = (h + 2)^2$
$h^2 - 4 = (h + 2)(h - 2)$ The LCD is $(h - 2)(h + 2)^2$.

Step 2 Change each rational expression into an equivalent expression with the LCD. Then subtract.

$\dfrac{h - 2}{(h + 2)^2} - \dfrac{h - 4}{(h + 2)(h - 2)} = \dfrac{(h - 2)}{(h + 2)^2} \cdot \dfrac{(h - 2)}{(h - 2)} - \dfrac{(h - 4)}{(h + 2)(h - 2)} \cdot \dfrac{(h + 2)}{(h + 2)}$

$= \dfrac{(h - 2)(h - 2)}{(h + 2)^2(h - 2)} - \dfrac{(h - 4)(h + 2)}{(h + 2)^2(h - 2)}$

$= \dfrac{h^2 - 4h + 4}{(h + 2)^2(h - 2)} - \dfrac{h^2 - 2h - 8}{(h + 2)^2(h - 2)}$

$= \dfrac{(h^2 - 4h + 4) - (h^2 - 2h - 8)}{(h + 2)^2(h - 2)}$

$= \dfrac{h^2 - h^2 - 4h + 2h + 4 + 8}{(h + 2)^2(h - 2)}$

$= \dfrac{-2h + 12}{(h - 2)(h + 2)^2}$ The correct answer is B.

Standardized Test Practice
Ⓐ Ⓑ Ⓒ Ⓓ

Example 6 If students are working on a standardized test they are allowed to write on, suggest that they highlight any subtle differences that they see in the answer choices. With the differences highlighted, it may be easier for students to spot and eliminate the incorrect choices.

Concept Check

1–2. See margin.

3. Sample answer:
$\dfrac{x}{2x+6}, \dfrac{5}{x+3}$

1. **Describe** how to find the LCD of two rational expressions with unlike denominators.

2. **Explain** how to rename rational expressions using their LCD.

3. **OPEN ENDED** Give an example of two rational expressions in which the LCD is equal to twice the denominator of one of the expressions.

Guided Practice

Find the LCM for each pair of expressions.

GUIDED PRACTICE KEY	
Exercises	Examples
4	1
5, 6	2
7	3
8–10	4
11–14	5
15	6

4. $5a^2, 7a$ $35a^2$

5. $2x - 4, 3x - 6$ $6(x-2)$

6. $n^2 + 3n - 4, (n-1)^2$ $(n+4)(n-1)^2$

Find each sum.

7. $\dfrac{6}{5x} + \dfrac{7}{10x^2}$ $\dfrac{12x+7}{10x^2}$

8. $\dfrac{a}{a-4} + \dfrac{4}{a+4}$ $\dfrac{a^2+8a-16}{(a-4)(a+4)}$

9. $\dfrac{2y}{y^2-25} + \dfrac{y+5}{y-5}$ $\dfrac{y^2+12y+25}{(y-5)(y+5)}$

10. $\dfrac{a+2}{a^2+4a+3} + \dfrac{6}{a+3}$ $\dfrac{7a+8}{(a+3)(a+1)}$

Find each difference.

11. $\dfrac{3z}{6w^2} - \dfrac{z}{4w}$ $\dfrac{2z-wz}{4w^2}$

12. $\dfrac{4a}{2a+6} - \dfrac{3}{a+3}$ $\dfrac{2a-3}{a+3}$

13. $\dfrac{b+8}{b^2-16} - \dfrac{1}{b-4}$ $\dfrac{4}{(b-4)(b+4)}$

14. $\dfrac{x}{x-2} - \dfrac{3}{x^2+3x-10}$ $\dfrac{x^2+5x-3}{(x-2)(x+5)}$

Standardized Test Practice
Ⓐ Ⓑ Ⓒ Ⓓ

15. Find $\dfrac{2y}{y^2+7y+12} + \dfrac{y+2}{y+4}$. **C**

Ⓐ $\dfrac{y^2+5y+6}{(y+4)(y+3)}$

Ⓑ $\dfrac{y^2+2y+6}{(y+4)(y+3)}$

Ⓒ $\dfrac{y^2+7y+6}{(y+4)(y+3)}$

Ⓓ $\dfrac{y^2-5y+6}{(y+4)(y+3)}$

Practice and Apply

Homework Help	
For Exercises	See Examples
16, 17, 54–57	1
18–21	2
22–25	3
26–37	4
38–49	5
50–53	6

Extra Practice
See page 848.

Find the LCM for each pair of expressions. **18.** $(x-4)(x+2)$

16. a^2b, ab^3 a^2b^3

17. $7xy, 21x^2y$ $21x^2y$

18. $x-4, x+2$

19. $2n - 5, n + 2$ $(2n-5)(n+2)$

20. $x^2 + 5x - 14, (x-2)^2$ $(x+7)(x-2)^2$

21. $p^2 - 5p - 6, p + 1$ $(p+1)(p-6)$

Find each sum.

22. $\dfrac{3}{x^2} + \dfrac{5}{x}$ $\dfrac{3+5x}{x^2}$

23. $\dfrac{2}{a^3} + \dfrac{7}{a^2}$ $\dfrac{2+7a}{a^3}$

24. $\dfrac{7}{6a^2} + \dfrac{5}{3a}$ $\dfrac{7+10a}{6a^2}$

25. $\dfrac{3}{7m} + \dfrac{4}{5m^2}$ $\dfrac{15m+28}{35m^2}$

26. $\dfrac{3}{x+5} + \dfrac{4}{x-4}$ $\dfrac{7x+8}{(x+5)(x-4)}$

27. $\dfrac{n}{n+4} + \dfrac{3}{n-3}$ $\dfrac{n^2+12}{(n+4)(n-3)}$

28. $\dfrac{7a}{a+5} + \dfrac{a}{a-2}$ $\dfrac{8a^2-9a}{(a+5)(a-2)}$

29. $\dfrac{6x}{x-3} + \dfrac{x}{x+1}$ $\dfrac{7x^2+3x}{(x-3)(x+1)}$

30. $\dfrac{5}{3x-9} + \dfrac{3}{x-3}$ $\dfrac{14}{3(x-3)}$

31. $\dfrac{m}{3m+2} + \dfrac{2}{9m+6}$ $\dfrac{1}{3}$

32. $\dfrac{-3}{5-a} + \dfrac{5}{a^2-25}$ $\dfrac{3a+20}{(a-5)(a+5)}$

33. $\dfrac{18}{y^2-9} + \dfrac{-7}{3-y}$ $\dfrac{7y+39}{(y+3)(y-3)}$

34. $\dfrac{x}{x^2+2x+1} + \dfrac{1}{x+1}$ $\dfrac{2x+1}{(x+1)^2}$

35. $\dfrac{2x+1}{(x-1)^2} + \dfrac{x-2}{x^2+3x-4}$ $\dfrac{3x^2+6x+6}{(x+4)(x-1)^2}$

36. $\dfrac{x^2}{4x^2-9} + \dfrac{x}{(2x+3)^2}$ $\dfrac{2x^3+5x^2-3x}{(2x-3)(2x+3)^2}$

37. $\dfrac{a^2}{a^2-b^2} + \dfrac{a}{(a-b)^2}$ $\dfrac{a^3-a^2b+a^2+ab}{(a+b)(a-b)^2}$

Practice/Apply

Study Notebook

Have students—
- add the definitions/examples of the vocabulary terms to their Vocabulary Builder worksheets for Chapter 12.
- include examples of how to add and subtract rational expressions with unlike denominators.
- include any other item(s) that they find helpful in mastering the skills in this lesson.

About the Exercises …

Organization by Objective
- **Add Rational Expressions:** 22–37
- **Subtract Rational Expressions:** 38–53

Odd/Even Assignments
Exercises 16–53 are structured so that students practice the same concepts whether they are assigned odd or even problems.

Assignment Guide

Basic: 17–57 odd, 58–77

Average: 17–57 odd, 58–77

Advanced: 16–56 even, 58–71 (optional: 72–77)

Answers

1. Sample answer: To find the LCD, determine the least common multiple of all of the factors of the denominators.

2. Sample answer: Multiply both the numerator and denominator by factors necessary to form the LCD.

DAILY
INTERVENTION

Differentiated Instruction

Visual/Spatial Have students work Example 5 by writing each fraction with a different color. Once the two fractions have the same denominator, then switch to a third color and combine the numerators. Using different colors may help students visualize how each fraction is changed while helping students differentiate one fraction from another.

Add Rational Expressions Adding rational expressions with unlike denominators is similar to adding fractions with unlike denominators.

Adding Rational Expressions	Step 1 Find the LCD of the expressions.
	Step 2 Change each expression into an equivalent expression with the LCD as the denominator.
	Step 3 Add just as with expressions with like denominators.
	Step 4 Simplify if necessary.

Example 1 Find $\dfrac{n+3}{n} + \dfrac{8n-4}{4n}$.

Factor each denominator.

$n = n$

$4n = 4 \cdot n$

LCD = $4n$

Since the denominator of $\dfrac{8n-4}{4n}$ is already $4n$, only $\dfrac{n+3}{n}$ needs to be renamed.

$\dfrac{n+3}{n} + \dfrac{8n-4}{4n} = \dfrac{4(n+3)}{4n} + \dfrac{8n-4}{4n}$

$= \dfrac{4n+12}{4n} + \dfrac{8n-4}{4n}$

$= \dfrac{12n+8}{4n}$

$= \dfrac{3n+2}{n}$

Example 2 Find $\dfrac{1}{2x^2+6x} + \dfrac{3}{x^2}$.

$\dfrac{1}{2x^2+6x} + \dfrac{3}{x^2} = \dfrac{1}{2x(x+3)} + \dfrac{3}{x^2}$

$= \dfrac{1}{2x(x+3)} \cdot \dfrac{x}{x} + \dfrac{3}{x^2} \cdot \dfrac{2(x+3)}{2(x+3)}$

$= \dfrac{x}{2x^2(x+3)} + \dfrac{6(x+3)}{2x^2(x+3)}$

$= \dfrac{x+6x+18}{2x^2(x+3)}$

$= \dfrac{7x+18}{2x^2(x+3)}$

Exercises

Find each sum.

1. $\dfrac{1}{a} + \dfrac{7}{3a}$ $\dfrac{10}{3a}$

2. $\dfrac{1}{6x} + \dfrac{3}{8}$ $\dfrac{4+9x}{24x}$

3. $\dfrac{4}{9x} + \dfrac{5}{x^2}$ $\dfrac{4x+45}{9x^2}$

4. $\dfrac{2}{x} + \dfrac{3}{x^3}$ $\dfrac{2x+3}{x^3}$

5. $\dfrac{8}{4a^2} + \dfrac{6}{a}$ $\dfrac{2+2a}{a^2}$

6. $\dfrac{4}{h+1} + \dfrac{2}{h+2}$ $\dfrac{6h+10}{(h+1)(h+2)}$

7. $\dfrac{4}{y+6} + \dfrac{1}{y+2}$ $\dfrac{5y+14}{(y+6)(y+2)}$

8. $\dfrac{y}{y^2+4y+4} + \dfrac{2}{y+2}$ $\dfrac{3y+4}{(y+2)^2}$

9. $\dfrac{a}{a+4} + \dfrac{4}{a-4}$ $\dfrac{a^2+16}{(a+4)(a-4)}$

10. $\dfrac{6}{3(m+1)} + \dfrac{2}{3(m-1)}$ $\dfrac{8m-4}{3(m+1)(m-1)}$

11. $\dfrac{4x}{6x-2y} + \dfrac{3y}{9x-3y}$ $\dfrac{2x+y}{3x-y}$

12. $\dfrac{a-2}{a^2-4} + \dfrac{a-2}{a+2}$ $\dfrac{a-1}{a+2}$

13. $\dfrac{y+2}{y^2+5y+6} + \dfrac{2-y}{y^2+y-6}$ 0

14. $\dfrac{-q}{q^2-16} + \dfrac{q+1}{q^2+5q+4}$ $\dfrac{2q-4}{(q-4)(q+4)}$

Skills Practice, p. 743 and Practice, p. 744 (shown)

Find the LCM for each pair of expressions.

1. $3a^3b^2, 18ab^5$ $18a^3b^5$

2. $w-4, w+2$ $(w-4)(w+2)$

3. $5d-20, d-4$ $5(d-4)$

4. $6p+1, p-1$ $(6p+1)(p-1)$

5. $x^2+5x+4, (x+1)^2$ $(x+4)(x+1)^2$

6. $s^2+3s-10, s^2-4$ $(s+5)(s-2)(s+2)$

Find each sum.

7. $\dfrac{7}{6x^2y} + \dfrac{10}{3xy^2}$ $\dfrac{7y+20x}{6x^2y^2}$

8. $\dfrac{b+5}{4b} + \dfrac{b-2}{b}$ $\dfrac{5b-3}{4b}$

9. $\dfrac{n}{n+2} + \dfrac{7}{n-6}$ $\dfrac{n^2+n+14}{(n-6)(n+2)}$

10. $\dfrac{8}{n^2-9} + \dfrac{2}{2n+6}$ $\dfrac{n+5}{(n+3)(n-3)}$

11. $\dfrac{y+3}{y^2-16} + \dfrac{3y-2}{y^2+8y+16}$ $\dfrac{4y^2-7y+20}{(y+4)^2(y-4)}$

12. $\dfrac{p+1}{p^2+3p-4} + \dfrac{p}{p+4}$ $\dfrac{p^2+1}{(p+4)(p-1)}$

13. $\dfrac{2a+6}{a-5} + \dfrac{6a+24}{a^2-10a+25}$ $\dfrac{2a^2+2a-6}{(a-5)^2}$

14. $\dfrac{h-3}{h^2+6h+9} + \dfrac{h-2}{h+3}$ $\dfrac{h^2+2h-9}{(h+3)^2}$

Find each difference.

15. $\dfrac{6p}{5x^2} - \dfrac{2p}{3x}$ $\dfrac{18p-10xp}{15x^2}$

16. $\dfrac{m+4}{m-3} - \dfrac{2}{m-6}$ $\dfrac{m^2-4m-18}{(m-3)(m-6)}$

17. $\dfrac{s+1}{s^2-9} - \dfrac{2s+3}{4s+12}$ $\dfrac{-2s^2+7s+13}{4(s-3)(s+3)}$

18. $\dfrac{b-3}{b^2+6b+9} - \dfrac{-3}{b-3}$ $\dfrac{4b^2+12b+36}{(b-3)(b+3)^2}$

19. $\dfrac{t+3}{t^2-3t-10} - \dfrac{4t-8}{t^2-10t+25}$ $\dfrac{-3t^2-2t+1}{(t+2)(t-5)^2}$

20. $\dfrac{4y}{y^3-y-6} - \dfrac{3y+3}{y^2-4}$ $\dfrac{y^2-2y+9}{(y-3)(y+2)(y-2)}$

21. SERVICE Members of the ninth grade class at Pine Ridge High School are organizing into service groups. What is the minimum number of students who must participate for all students to be divided into groups of 4, 6, or 9 students with no one left out? **36**

22. SAFETY When the Cooper family goes on vacation, they set the house lights on timers from 5 P.M. until 11 P.M. The lights come on at different times in each of three rooms: every 40 minutes, every 50 minutes, and every 100 minutes, respectively. The timer turns each of them off after 30 minutes. After 5 P.M., how many times do all the lights come on at the same time in one evening? at what time(s)? **once; 8:20 P.M.**

Reading to Learn Mathematics, p. 745 **ELL**

Pre-Activity How can rational expressions be used to describe elections?

Read the introduction to Lesson 12-7 at the top of page 678 in your textbook.

- How can you find the years after 2004 when an election for senator will occur? **Sample answer: Add multiples of 6 to 2004.**
- How can you find the years after 2004 when an election for President of the United States will occur? **Sample answer: Add multiples of 4 to 2004.**

Reading the Lesson

1. Answer each question about the monomials $49k^2n^3$ and $21kn^5$.

   a. What prime numbers are factors of these monomials? **3 and 7**

   b. How many times are these prime factors used in each monomial? In $49k^2n^3$, 3 is not used, but 7 is used twice. In $21kn^5$, 3 is used once and 7 is used once.

   c. How many times should you use 3 as a factor in the LCM of the two monomials? How many times should you use 7 as a factor in the LCM? **one time; two times**

   d. How many times should you use k as a factor in the LCM? How many times should you use n as a factor in the LCM? **two times; five times**

2. How is the LCD for two rational expressions related to the LCM of the denominators? **They are equal.**

3. How does the LCD of two rational expressions help you add or subtract the expressions? **It helps you rename the expressions as rational expressions with like denominators.**

Helping You Remember

4. Making a short list of the steps in a procedure can help you remember the procedure. Make a short list of the main steps you can use to add or subtract rational expressions with unlike denominators. **Sample answer: 1. Write the prime factorization of the denominator of each expression. 2. Use the prime factorizations to write the LCM of the denominators. 3. Using the LCM as the LCD of the expressions, write each of the rational expressions to have the LCD as its denominator. 4. Add or subtract the numerators and keep the same denominator. 5. Simplify if possible.**

Find each difference.

38. $\dfrac{7}{3x} - \dfrac{3}{6x^2}$ $\dfrac{14x-3}{6x^2}$

39. $\dfrac{4}{15x^2} - \dfrac{5}{3x}$ $\dfrac{4-25x}{15x^2}$

40. $\dfrac{11x}{3y^2} - \dfrac{7x}{6y}$ $\dfrac{22x-7xy}{6y^2}$

41. $\dfrac{5a}{7x} - \dfrac{3a}{21x^2}$ $\dfrac{5ax-a}{7x^2}$

42. $\dfrac{x^2-1}{x+1} - \dfrac{x^2+1}{x-1}$ $\dfrac{-2x}{x-1}$

43. $\dfrac{k}{k+5} - \dfrac{3}{k-3}$ $\dfrac{k^2-6k-15}{(k+5)(k-3)}$

44. $\dfrac{k}{2k+1} - \dfrac{2}{k+2}$ $\dfrac{k^2-2k-2}{(2k+1)(k+2)}$

45. $\dfrac{m-1}{m+1} - \dfrac{4}{2m+5}$ $\dfrac{2m^2-m-9}{(m+1)(2m+5)}$

46. $\dfrac{2x}{x^2-5x} - \dfrac{-3x}{x-5}$ $\dfrac{2+3x}{(x-5)}$

47. $\dfrac{-3}{a-6} - \dfrac{-6}{a^2-6a}$ $\dfrac{-3a+6}{a(a-6)}$

48. $\dfrac{n}{5-n} - \dfrac{3}{n^2-25}$ $\dfrac{-n^2-5n-3}{(n-5)(n+5)}$

49. $\dfrac{3a+2}{6-3a} - \dfrac{a+2}{a^2-4}$ $\dfrac{3a+5}{-3(a-2)}$

50. $\dfrac{9x+6}{(x+1)(x+2)^2}$

50. $\dfrac{3x}{x^2+3x+2} - \dfrac{3x-6}{x^2+4x+4}$

51. $\dfrac{4a^2+2a+4}{(a+4)(a+1)(a-1)}$

51. $\dfrac{5a}{a^2+3a-4} - \dfrac{a-1}{a^2-1}$

52. $\dfrac{x^2+4x-5}{x^2-2x-3} - \dfrac{2}{x+1}$ $\dfrac{x+1}{x-3}$

53. $\dfrac{-m^3-11m^2-56m-48}{(m-4)(m+4)^2}$

53. $\dfrac{m-4}{m^2+8m+16} - \dfrac{m+4}{m-4}$

More About. . .

Pet Care

Kell, an English Mastiff owned by Tom Scott of the United Kingdom, is the heaviest dog in the world. Weighing in at 286 pounds, Kell eats a high protein diet of eggs, goat's milk, and beef.

Source: *The Guinness Book of Records*

54. MUSIC A music director wants to form a group of students to sing and dance at community events. The music they will sing is 2-part, 3-part, or 4-part harmony. The director would like to have the same number of voices on each part. What is the least number of students that would allow for an even distribution on all these parts? **12**

55. CHARITY Maya, Makalla, and Monya can walk one mile in 12, 15, and 20 minutes respectively. They plan to participate in a walk-a-thon to raise money for a local charity. Sponsors have agreed to pay $2.50 for each mile that is walked. What is the total number of miles the girls would walk in one hour and how much money would they raise? **12 mi; $30**

56. PET CARE Kendra takes care of pets while their owners are out of town. One week she has three dogs that all eat the same kind of dog food. The first dog eats a bag of food every 12 days, the second dog eats a bag every 15 days, and the third dog eats a bag every 16 days. How many bags of food should Kendra buy for one week? **2 bags**

57. AUTOMOBILES Car owners need to follow a regular maintenance schedule to keep their cars running safely and efficiently. The table shows several items that should be performed on a regular basis. If all of these items are performed when a car's odometer reads 36,000 miles, what would be the car's mileage reading the next time all of the items should be performed? **66,000 mi**

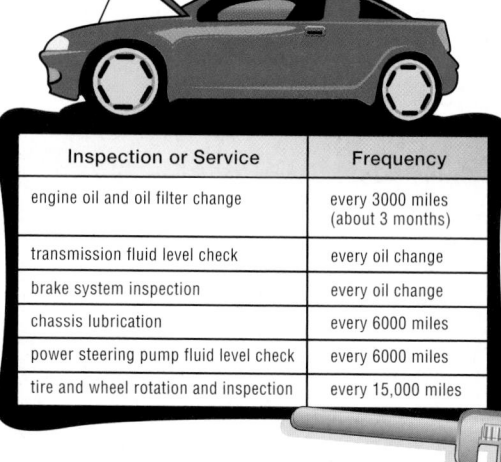

Inspection or Service	Frequency
engine oil and oil filter change	every 3000 miles (about 3 months)
transmission fluid level check	every oil change
brake system inspection	every oil change
chassis lubrication	every 6000 miles
power steering pump fluid level check	every 6000 miles
tire and wheel rotation and inspection	every 15,000 miles

Enrichment, p. 746

Graphing Circles by Completing Squares

One use for completing the square is to graph circles. The general equation for a circle with center at the origin and radius r is $x^2 + y^2 = r^2$. An equation represents a circle if it can be transformed into the sum of two squares.

$x^2 - 6x + y^2 + 4y - 3 = 0$

$(x^2 - 6x + \blacksquare) + (y^2 + 4y + \blacksquare) = 3$ $\left[\frac{1}{2}(-6)\right]^2$ and $\left[\frac{1}{2}(4)\right]^2$

$(x^2 - 6x + 9) + (y^2 + 4y + 4) = 3 + 9 + 4$ Add to both sides.

$(x-3)^2 + (y+2)^2 = 4^2$ Factor trinomials.

Notice that the center of the circle is at the point $(3, -2)$.

Transform each equation into the sum of two squares. Then graph the circle represented by the equation. Use the coordinate plane provided at the bottom of the page.

1. $x^2 - 14x + y^2 + 6y + 49 = 0$

2. $x^2 + y^2 - 8y - 9 = 0$

58. **CRITICAL THINKING** Janelle says that a shortcut for adding fractions with unlike denominators is to add the cross products for the numerator and write the denominator as the product of the denominators. She gives the following example.

$$\frac{2}{7} + \frac{5}{8} = \frac{2 \cdot 8 + 5 \cdot 7}{7 \cdot 8} = \frac{51}{56}$$

Explain why Janelle's method will always work or provide a counterexample to show that it does not always work. **See margin.**

59. **WRITING IN MATH** Answer the question that was posed at the beginning of the lesson. **See margin.**

How can rational expressions be used to describe elections?

Include the following in your answer:

- an explanation of how to determine the least common multiple of two or more rational expressions, and
- if a certain senator is elected in 2006, when is the next election in which the senator and a President will be elected?

Standardized Test Practice

60. What is the least common denominator of $\frac{6}{a^2 - 2ab + b^2}$ and $\frac{6}{a^2 - b^2}$? **D**

Ⓐ $(a - b)^2$ Ⓑ $(a - b)(a + b)$

Ⓒ $(a + b)^2$ Ⓓ $(a - b)^2(a + b)$

61. Find $\frac{x - 4}{(2 - x)^2} - \frac{x - 5}{x^2 + x - 6}$. **C**

Ⓐ $\frac{8x - 22}{(x + 3)(x - 2)^2}$ Ⓑ $\frac{x^2 - 2x - 17}{(x - 2)(x + 3)}$

Ⓒ $\frac{6x - 22}{(x + 3)(x - 2)^2}$ Ⓓ $\frac{22 - 6x}{(x + 3)(x - 2)}$

Maintain Your Skills

Mixed Review

62. $\frac{3m + 3}{2m + 1}$

63. $\frac{4x + 5}{2x + 3}$

64. $\frac{2y - 5}{y - 3}$

66. $t^2 + 4t - 3 - \frac{3}{t - 4}$

67. $2m - 3 + \frac{2}{2m + 7}$

Find each sum. *(Lesson 12-6)*

62. $\frac{3m}{2m + 1} + \frac{3}{2m + 1}$ 63. $\frac{4x}{2x + 3} + \frac{5}{2x + 3}$ 64. $\frac{2y}{y - 3} + \frac{5}{3 - y}$

Find each quotient. *(Lesson 12-5)*

65. $\frac{b^2 + 8b - 20}{b - 2}$ **$b + 10$** 66. $\frac{t^3 - 19t + 9}{t - 4}$ 67. $\frac{4m^2 + 8m - 19}{2m + 7}$

Factor each trinomial, if possible. If the trinomial cannot be factored using integers, write *prime*. *(Lesson 9-4)*

68. $2x^2 + 10x + 8$ **$2(x + 4)(x + 1)$** 69. $5r^2 + 7r - 6$ **$(5r - 3)(r + 2)$** 70. $16p^2 - 4pq - 30q^2$ **$2(2p - 3q)(4p + 5q)$**

71. **BUDGETING** JoAnne Paulsen's take-home pay is $1782 per month. She spends $525 on rent, $120 on groceries, and $40 on gas. She allows herself 5% of the remaining amount for entertainment. How much can she spend on entertainment each month? *(Lesson 3-9)* **$54.85**

Getting Ready for the Next Lesson

76. $\frac{3x}{(x + 2)(x - 1)}$

77. $\frac{x + 4}{x + 6}$

PREREQUISITE SKILL Find each quotient.
*(To review **dividing rational expressions**, see Lesson 12-4.)*

72. $\frac{x}{2} \div \frac{3x}{5}$ **$\frac{5}{6}$** 73. $\frac{a^2}{5b} \div \frac{4a}{10b^2}$ **$\frac{ab}{2}$** 74. $\frac{x + 7}{x} \div \frac{x + 7}{x + 3}$ **$\frac{x + 3}{x}$**

75. $\frac{3n}{2n + 5} \div \frac{12n^2}{2n + 5}$ **$\frac{1}{4n}$** 76. $\frac{3x}{x + 2} \div (x - 1)$ 77. $\frac{x^2 + 7x + 12}{x + 6} \div (x + 3)$

4 Assess

Open-Ended Assessment

Speaking Using a problem from the exercise set, have students work the problem with you, explaining their steps.

Getting Ready for Lesson 12-8

PREREQUISITE SKILL Students will learn about mixed expressions and complex fractions in Lesson 12-8. This will include simplifying rational expressions. Use Exercises 72–77 to determine your students' familiarity with simplifying rational expressions.

Assessment Options

Quiz (Lessons 12-6 and 12-7) is available on p. 774 of the *Chapter 12 Resource Masters.*

Answers

58. Sample answer: This method will always work.

$$\frac{a}{x} + \frac{b}{y} = \frac{a}{x} \cdot \frac{y}{y} + \frac{b}{y} \cdot \frac{x}{x} = \frac{ay}{xy} + \frac{bx}{yx} = \frac{ay + bx}{xy}$$

59. Sample answer: You can use rational expressions and their least common denominators to determine when elections will coincide. Answers should include the following.

- Use each factor of the denominators the greatest number of times it appears.
- 2012

1 Focus

5-Minute Check Transparency 12-8 Use as a quiz or review of Lesson 12-7.

Mathematical Background notes are available for this lesson on p. 640D.

How are rational expressions used in baking?

Ask students:

• Why can't you find the number of cookies that Katelyn can make by just simplifying the given expression? **The units are different. The amount of dough is given in pounds, and the amount of dough per cookie is given in ounces.**

• What is a method that you might be able to use to find out how many cookies Katelyn can make. **You could use dimensional analysis to convert pounds to ounces.**

What You'll Learn

• Simplify mixed expressions.
• Simplify complex fractions.

Vocabulary
• mixed expression
• complex fraction

How are rational expressions used in baking?

Katelyn bought $2\frac{1}{2}$ pounds of chocolate chip cookie dough. If the average cookie requires $1\frac{1}{2}$ ounces of dough, the number of cookies that Katelyn can bake can be found by simplifying the expression $\dfrac{2\frac{1}{2}\text{ pounds}}{1\frac{1}{2}\text{ ounces}}$.

SIMPLIFY MIXED EXPRESSIONS Recall that a number like $2\frac{1}{2}$ is a mixed number because it contains the sum of an integer, 2, and a fraction, $\frac{1}{2}$. An expression like $3 + \dfrac{x+2}{x-3}$ is called a **mixed expression** because it contains the sum of a monomial, 3, and a rational expression, $\dfrac{x+2}{x-3}$. Changing mixed expressions to rational expressions is similar to changing mixed numbers to improper fractions.

Example 1 Mixed Expression to Rational Expression

Simplify $3 + \dfrac{6}{x+3}$.

$$3 + \frac{6}{x+3} = \frac{3(x+3)}{x+3} + \frac{6}{x+3} \qquad \text{The LCD is } x + 3.$$

$$= \frac{3(x+3)+6}{x+3} \qquad \text{Add the numerators.}$$

$$= \frac{3x+9+6}{x+3} \qquad \text{Distributive Property}$$

$$= \frac{3x+15}{x+3} \qquad \text{Simplify.}$$

SIMPLIFY COMPLEX FRACTIONS If a fraction has one or more fractions in the numerator or denominator, it is called a **complex fraction**. You simplify an algebraic complex fraction in the same way that you simplify a numerical complex fraction.

numerical complex fraction

$$\frac{\frac{8}{3}}{\frac{7}{5}} = \frac{8}{3} \div \frac{7}{5}$$

$$= \frac{8}{3} \cdot \frac{5}{7}$$

$$= \frac{40}{21}$$

algebraic complex fraction

$$\frac{\frac{a}{b}}{\frac{c}{d}} = \frac{a}{b} \div \frac{c}{d}$$

$$= \frac{a}{b} \cdot \frac{d}{c}$$

$$= \frac{ad}{bc}$$

Resource Manager

Workbook and Reproducible Masters

Chapter 12 Resource Masters
• Study Guide and Intervention, pp. 747–748
• Skills Practice, p. 749
• Practice, p. 750
• Reading to Learn Mathematics, p. 751
• Enrichment, p. 752

Parent and Student Study Guide Workbook, p. 98
School-to-Career Masters, p. 24

Transparencies
5-Minute Check Transparency 12-8
Answer Key Transparencies

Technology
Interactive Chalkboard

Example 2 *Complex Fraction Involving Numbers*

BAKING Refer to the application at the beginning of the lesson. How many cookies can Katelyn make with $2\frac{1}{2}$ pounds of chocolate chip cookie dough?

To find the total number of cookies, divide the amount of cookie dough by the amount of dough needed for each cookie.

$$\frac{2\frac{1}{2}\ \text{pounds}}{1\frac{1}{2}\ \text{ounces}} = \frac{2\frac{1}{2}\ \cancel{\text{pounds}}}{1\frac{1}{2}\ \text{ounces}} \cdot \frac{16\ \text{ounces}}{1\ \cancel{\text{pound}}}$$ Convert pounds to ounces. Divide by common units.

$$= \frac{16 \cdot 2\frac{1}{2}}{1\frac{1}{2}}$$ Simplify.

$$= \frac{\frac{16}{1} \cdot \frac{5}{2}}{\frac{3}{2}}$$ Express each term as an improper fraction.

$$= \frac{\frac{80}{2}}{\frac{3}{2}}$$ Multiply in the numerator.

$$= \frac{80 \cdot 2}{2 \cdot 3}$$ $\dfrac{\frac{a}{b}}{\frac{c}{d}} = \dfrac{ad}{bc}$

$$= \frac{160}{6} \text{ or } 26\frac{2}{3}$$ Simplify.

Katelyn can make 27 cookies.

Example 3 *Complex Fraction Involving Monomials*

Simplify $\dfrac{\frac{x^2y^2}{a}}{\frac{x^2y}{a^3}}$.

$$\frac{\frac{x^2y^2}{a}}{\frac{x^2y}{a^3}} = \frac{x^2y^2}{a} \div \frac{x^2y}{a^3}$$ Rewrite as a division sentence.

$$= \frac{x^2y^2}{a} \cdot \frac{a^3}{x^2y}$$ Rewrite as multiplication by the reciprocal.

$$= \frac{\overset{1}{\cancel{x^2}}\overset{y}{\cancel{y^2}}}{\cancel{a}} \cdot \frac{\overset{a^2}{\cancel{a^3}}}{\underset{1\ \ 1}{\cancel{x^2y}}}$$ Divide by common factors x^2, y, and a.

$$= a^2y$$ Simplify.

 www.algebra1.com/extra_examples

Lesson 12-8 Mixed Expressions and Complex Fractions   **685**

SIMPLIFY MIXED EXPRESSIONS

> **In-Class Example**   Power Point®

Teaching Tip Point out that since one of the terms of a mixed expression is a monomial, the LCD will be the same as the denominator of the rational expression.

1 Simplify $3 + \dfrac{7}{x-2} \cdot \dfrac{3x+1}{x-2}$.

SIMPLIFY COMPLEX FRACTIONS

> **In-Class Examples**   Power Point®

2 **BAKING** Suppose Katelyn decided to make her cookies with 2 pounds of dough. How many cookies would she be able to make? **21 cookies**

3 Simplify $\dfrac{\frac{a^5b}{c^2}}{\frac{ab^4}{c^4}} \cdot \dfrac{a^4c^2}{b^3}$.

D A I L Y
INTERVENTION   **Differentiated Instruction**

Auditory/Musical Challenge students to come up with a musical mnemonic they can use to remember how to simplify a complex fraction. For example, using the Key Concept box on p. 685, students could replace the variables a, b, c, and d with words such as Apple, Battle, Core, Door and have their tune include a phrase like "Apple and Door over Battle and Core" to represent $\dfrac{ad}{bc}$.

In-Class Example

4 Simplify $\dfrac{b + \dfrac{2}{b + 3}}{b - 4}$.

$\dfrac{(b + 2)(b + 1)}{(b + 3)(b - 4)}$

3 Practice/Apply

Study Notebook

Have students—
• add the definitions/examples of the vocabulary terms to their Vocabulary Builder worksheets for Chapter 12.
• include examples of how to simplify mixed expressions and complex fractions.
• include any other item(s) that they find helpful in mastering the skills in this lesson.

D A I L Y
INTERVENTION **FIND THE ERROR**
Ask students to explain the mistake Lian made. Ask students how many of them have made similar mistakes. Discuss ways students might avoid errors in factoring.

Answers

1. Sample answer: Both mixed numbers and mixed expressions are made up by the sum of an integer or monomial and a fraction or rational expression.

2. Sample answer: $\dfrac{\dfrac{2}{3}}{\dfrac{5}{6}} = \dfrac{2}{3} \div \dfrac{5}{6}$

$= \dfrac{2}{3} \cdot \dfrac{6}{5}$

$= \dfrac{4}{5}$

Example 4 Complex Fraction Involving Polynomials

Simplify $\dfrac{a - \dfrac{15}{a - 2}}{a + 3}$.

The numerator contains a mixed expression. Rewrite it as a rational expression first.

$$\dfrac{a - \dfrac{15}{a - 2}}{a + 3} = \dfrac{\dfrac{a(a - 2)}{a - 2} - \dfrac{15}{a - 2}}{a + 3} \qquad \text{The LCD of the fractions in the numerator is } a - 2.$$

$$= \dfrac{\dfrac{a^2 - 2a - 15}{a - 2}}{a + 3} \qquad \text{Simplify the numerator.}$$

$$= \dfrac{\dfrac{(a + 3)(a - 5)}{a - 2}}{a + 3} \qquad \text{Factor.}$$

$$= \dfrac{(a + 3)(a - 5)}{a - 2} \div (a + 3) \qquad \text{Rewrite as a division sentence.}$$

$$= \dfrac{(a + 3)(a - 5)}{a - 2} \cdot \dfrac{1}{a + 3} \qquad \text{Multiply by the reciprocal of } a + 3.$$

$$= \dfrac{\overset{1}{\cancel{(a + 3)}}(a - 5)}{a - 2} \cdot \dfrac{1}{\underset{1}{\cancel{a + 3}}} \qquad \text{Divide by the GCF, } a + 3.$$

$$= \dfrac{a - 5}{a - 2} \qquad \text{Simplify.}$$

Check for Understanding

Concept Check **1. Describe** the similarities between mixed numbers and mixed rational expressions. **1–2. See margin.**

2. OPEN ENDED Give an example of a complex fraction and show how to simplify it.

3. FIND THE ERROR Bolton and Lian found the LCD of $\dfrac{4}{2x + 1} - \dfrac{5}{x + 1} + \dfrac{2}{x - 1}$.

Bolton	Lian
$\dfrac{4}{2x + 1} - \dfrac{5}{x + 1} + \dfrac{2}{x - 1}$	$\dfrac{4}{2x + 1} - \dfrac{5}{x + 1} + \dfrac{2}{x - 1}$
LCD: $(2x + 1)(x + 1)(x - 1)$	LCD: $2(x + 1)(x - 1)$

Who is correct? Explain your reasoning.
Bolton; Lian omitted the factor $(x + 1)$.

Guided Practice Write each mixed expression as a rational expression.

GUIDED PRACTICE KEY	
Exercises	Examples
4–6	1
7, 10	2
8	3
9	4

4. $3 + \dfrac{4}{x}$ $\dfrac{3x + 4}{x}$

5. $7 + \dfrac{5}{6y}$ $\dfrac{42y + 5}{6y}$

6. $\dfrac{a - 1}{3a} + 2a$ $\dfrac{6a^2 + a - 1}{3a}$

Simplify each expression.

7. $\dfrac{3\frac{1}{2}}{4\frac{3}{4}}$ $\dfrac{14}{19}$

8. $\dfrac{\dfrac{x^3}{y^2}}{\dfrac{y^3}{x}}$ $\dfrac{x^4}{y^5}$

9. $\dfrac{\dfrac{x - y}{a + b}}{\dfrac{x^2 - y^2}{a^2 - b^2}}$ $\dfrac{a - b}{x + y}$

Application 10. **ENTERTAINMENT** The student talent committee is arranging the performances for their holiday pageant. The first-act performances and their lengths are shown in the table. What is the average length of the performances?

$7\frac{29}{100}$ min

Holiday Pageant Line-Up

Performance	Length (min)
A	7
B	$4\frac{1}{2}$
C	$6\frac{1}{2}$
D	$8\frac{1}{4}$
E	$10\frac{1}{5}$

★ indicates increased difficulty

Practice and Apply

Homework Help

For Exercises	See Examples
11–22, 35	1
23–26, 37–40	2
27–32, 36	3
33, 34	4

Extra Practice
See page 848.

Write each mixed expression as a rational expression. 14–22. See margin.

11. $8 + \frac{3}{n}$ $\frac{8n+3}{n}$

12. $4 + \frac{5}{a}$ $\frac{4a+5}{a}$

13. $2x + \frac{x}{y}$ $\frac{2xy+x}{y}$

14. $6z + \frac{2z}{w}$

15. $2m - \frac{4+m}{m}$

16. $3a - \frac{a+1}{2a}$

17. $b^2 + \frac{a-b}{a+b}$

18. $r^2 + \frac{r-4}{r+3}$

19. $5n^2 - \frac{n+3}{n^2-9}$

20. $3s^2 - \frac{s+1}{s^2-1}$

21. $(x-5) + \frac{x+2}{x-3}$

22. $(p+4) + \frac{p+1}{p-4}$

Simplify each expression.

23. $\frac{5\frac{3}{4}}{7\frac{2}{3}}$ $\frac{3}{4}$

24. $\frac{8\frac{2}{7}}{4\frac{4}{5}}$ $\frac{145}{84}$

25. $\frac{\frac{a}{b^3}}{\frac{a^2}{b}}$ $\frac{1}{ab^2}$

26. $\frac{\frac{n^3}{m^2}}{\frac{n^2}{m^2}}$ n

27. $\frac{\frac{x+4}{y-2}}{\frac{x^2}{y^2}}$ $\frac{y^2(x+4)}{x^2(y-2)}$

28. $\frac{\frac{s^3}{t^2}}{\frac{s+t}{s-t}}$ $\frac{s^3(s-t)}{t^2(s+t)}$

29. $\frac{\frac{y^2-1}{y^2+3y-4}}{y+1}$ $\frac{1}{y+4}$

30. $\frac{\frac{a^2-2a-3}{a^2-1}}{a-3}$ $\frac{1}{a-1}$

31. $\frac{\frac{n^2+2n}{n^2+9n+18}}{\frac{n^2-5n}{n^2+n-30}}$ $\frac{n+2}{n+3}$

32. $\frac{\frac{x^2+4x-21}{x^2-9x+18}}{\frac{x^2+3x-28}{x^2-10x+24}}$ 1

33. $\frac{x - \frac{15}{x-2}}{x - \frac{20}{x-1}}$ $\frac{(x+3)(x-1)}{(x-2)(x+4)}$

34. $\frac{n + \frac{35}{n+12}}{n - \frac{63}{n-2}}$

34. $\frac{(n+5)(n-2)}{(n+12)(n-9)}$

★ 35. What is the quotient of $b + \frac{1}{b}$ and $a + \frac{1}{a}$? $\frac{a(b^2+1)}{b(a^2+1)}$

★ 36. What is the product of $\frac{2b^2}{5c}$ and the quotient of $\frac{4b^3}{2c}$ and $\frac{7b^3}{8c^2}$? $\frac{32b^2}{35}$

37. **PARTIES** The student council is planning a party for the school volunteers. There are five 66-ounce bottles of soda left from a recent dance. When poured over ice, $5\frac{1}{2}$ ounces of soda fills a cup. How many servings of soda can they get from the bottles they have? **60**

 www.algebra1.com/self_check_quiz

Lesson 12-8 Mixed Expressions and Complex Fractions   **687**

About the Exercises ...

Organization by Objective
• Simplify Mixed Expressions: 11–22
• Simplify Complex Fractions: 23–34

Odd/Even Assignments
Exercises 11–36 are structured so that students practice the same concepts whether they are assigned odd or even problems.

Assignment Guide
Basic: 11–33 odd, 37–39, 42–68
Average: 11–37 odd, 38, 39, 42–68
Advanced: 12–36 even, 40–62 (optional: 63–68)

Answers

14. $\frac{6wz+2z}{w}$

15. $\frac{2m^2-m-4}{m}$

16. $\frac{6a^2-a-1}{2a}$

17. $\frac{b^3+ab^2+a-b}{a+b}$

18. $\frac{r^3+3r^2+r-4}{r+3}$

19. $\frac{5n^3-15n^2-1}{n-3}$

20. $\frac{3s^3-3s^2-1}{s-1}$

21. $\frac{x^2-7x+17}{x-3}$

22. $\frac{p^2+p-15}{p-4}$

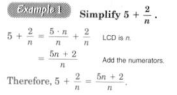

Study Guide and Intervention, p. 747 (shown) and p. 748

Simplify Mixed Expressions Algebraic expressions such as $a + \frac{b}{c}$ and $5 + \frac{x+y}{x+3}$ are called **mixed expressions**. Changing mixed expressions to rational expressions is similar to changing mixed numbers to improper fractions.

Example 1 Simplify $5 + \frac{2}{n}$.

$5 + \frac{2}{n} = \frac{5 \cdot n}{n} + \frac{2}{n}$ LCD is n.

$= \frac{5n+2}{n}$ Add the numerators.

Therefore, $5 + \frac{2}{n} = \frac{5n+2}{n}$.

Example 2 Simplify $2 + \frac{3}{n+3}$.

$2 + \frac{3}{n+3} = \frac{2(n+3)}{n+3} + \frac{3}{n+3}$

$= \frac{2n+6}{n+3} + \frac{3}{n+3}$

$= \frac{2n+6+3}{n+3}$

$= \frac{2n+9}{n+3}$

Therefore, $2 + \frac{3}{n+3} = \frac{2n+9}{n+3}$.

Exercises

Write each mixed expression as a rational expression.

1. $4 + \frac{6}{a}$ $\frac{4a+6}{a}$

2. $\frac{1}{9x} - 3$ $\frac{1-27x}{9x}$

3. $3x - \frac{1}{x^2}$ $\frac{3x^3-1}{x^2}$

4. $\frac{4}{x^2} - 2$ $\frac{4-2x^2}{x^2}$

5. $10 + \frac{60}{x+5}$ $\frac{10x+110}{x+5}$

6. $\frac{h}{h+4} + 2$ $\frac{3h+8}{h+4}$

7. $\frac{y}{y-2} + y^2$ $\frac{y^3-2y^2+y}{y-2}$

8. $4 - \frac{4}{2x+1}$ $\frac{8x}{2x+1}$

9. $1 + \frac{1}{x}$ $\frac{x+1}{x}$

10. $\frac{4}{m-2} - 2m$ $\frac{4-2m^2+4m}{m-2}$

11. $x^2 + \frac{x+2}{x-3}$ $\frac{x^3-3x^2+x+2}{x-3}$

12. $a - 3 + \frac{a-2}{a+3}$ $\frac{a^2+a-11}{a+3}$

13. $4m + \frac{3n}{2t}$ $\frac{8mt+3n}{2t}$

14. $2q^2 + \frac{q}{p+q}$ $\frac{q+2pq^2+2q^3}{p+q}$

15. $\frac{2}{y^2-1} - 4y^2$ $\frac{2-4y^4+4y^2}{y^2-1}$

16. $q^2 + \frac{p+q}{p-q}$ $\frac{pq^2-q^3+p+q}{p-q}$

Skills Practice, p. 749 and Practice, p. 750 (shown)

Write each mixed expression as a rational expression.

1. $14 - \frac{9}{u}$ $\frac{14u-9}{u}$

2. $7d + \frac{4d}{p}$ $\frac{7dp+4d}{p}$

3. $3n + \frac{6-n}{n}$ $\frac{3n^2-n+6}{n}$

4. $5b - \frac{b+3}{2b}$ $\frac{10b^2-b-3}{2b}$

5. $3 + \frac{t+5}{t^2-1}$ $\frac{3t^2+t+2}{t^2-1}$

6. $2s + \frac{s-1}{s+1}$ $\frac{2s^2+3s-1}{s+1}$

7. $2p + \frac{p+1}{p-3}$ $\frac{2p^2-5p+1}{p-3}$

8. $4n^2 + \frac{n-1}{n^2-1}$ $\frac{4n^3+4n^2+1}{n+1}$

9. $(t+1) + \frac{4}{t+5}$ $\frac{t^2+6t+9}{t+5}$

Simplify each expression.

10. $\frac{3\frac{2}{5}}{2\frac{4}{6}}$ $\frac{6}{5}$

11. $\frac{\frac{m^2}{6n}}{\frac{3m}{n^2}}$ $\frac{mn}{18}$

12. $\frac{\frac{x^2-y^2}{x^2}}{\frac{x+y}{3x}}$ $\frac{3(x-y)}{x}$

13. $\frac{\frac{a-4}{a^2}}{\frac{a^2-16}{a}}$ $\frac{1}{a(a+4)}$

14. $\frac{\frac{y^2-7q+12}{q-3}}{q-3}$ $\frac{1}{q+4}$

15. $\frac{\frac{k^2+6k}{k^2+4k-5}}{\frac{k-8}{k^2-9k+8}}$ $\frac{k(k+6)}{k+5}$

16. $\frac{\frac{b^2+b-12}{b^2+3b-4}}{\frac{b-3}{b^2-b}}$ b

17. $\frac{\frac{g-6}{g-9}}{\frac{g-5}{g+4}}$ $\frac{(g+10)(g+4)}{(g+9)(g+5)}$

18. $\frac{\frac{y+\frac{6}{y}-7}{y-\frac{7}{y}+6}}{}$ $\frac{(y-6)(y+6)}{(y-7)(y+7)}$

TRAVEL For Exercises 19 and 20, use the following information.

Ray and Jan are on a $12\frac{1}{2}$-hour drive from Springfield, Missouri, to Chicago, Illinois. They stop for a break every $3\frac{1}{4}$ hours.

19. Write an expression to model this situation. $\frac{12\frac{1}{2}}{3\frac{1}{4}}$

20. How many stops will Ray and Jan make before arriving in Chicago? 3

21. **CARPENTRY** Tai needs several $2\frac{1}{4}$-inch wooden rods to reinforce the frame on a futon. She can cut the rods from a $24\frac{1}{2}$-inch dowel purchased from a hardware store. How many wooden rods can she cut from the dowel? 10

Reading to Learn Mathematics, p. 751   **ELL**

Pre-Activity How are rational expressions used in baking?

Read the introduction to Lesson 12-8 at the top of page 684 in your textbook.

What is another way to write $\frac{2\frac{1}{2}}{1\frac{1}{2}}$? Sample answer: $2\frac{1}{2} \div 1\frac{1}{2}$

Reading the Lesson

1. Tell whether each expression is a mixed expression or complex fraction. Write M for mixed expression and C for complex fraction.

a. $7x + \frac{x+2}{x-5}$ M

b. $\frac{5 + \frac{2}{a-1}}{a^2}$ C

c. $\frac{y+12\frac{1}{4}}{\frac{3}{4}}$ C

d. $(b-6) + \frac{b+3}{b+2}$ M

2. Complete each statement about mixed expressions and complex fractions.

a. A mixed expression is the sum of a monomial and a __rational expression__. To change it to a rational expression, find the __LCD__, rename the monomial as a rational expression using that denominator, and add.

b. A complex fraction is a fraction that has one or more __fractions__ in its numerator or denominator.

3. Complete each statement.

a. One method of simplifying a complex fraction is first to rewrite it as a __division__ expression. Then __multiply__ by the __reciprocal__ of the divisor.

b. Another method is to express a fraction of the form $\frac{\frac{a}{b}}{\frac{c}{d}}$ as $\frac{ad}{bc}$, and then __multiply__.

Helping You Remember

4. Describe an easy way to remember what a mixed expression is.

Sample answer: Think of a mixed expression as being similar to a mixed number. A mixed number can be written as the sum of a whole number and a fraction. A mixed expression is the sum (or difference) of a monomial and a fraction.

ACOUSTICS For Exercises 38 and 39, use the following information.

If a vehicle is moving toward you at v miles per hour and blowing its horn at a frequency of f, then you hear the horn as if it were blowing at a frequency of h.

This can be defined by the equation $h = \frac{f}{1 - \frac{v}{s}}$, where s is the speed of sound, approximately 760 miles per hour.

38. Simplify the complex fraction in the formula. $\frac{fs}{s-v}$

39. Suppose a truck horn blows at 370 cycles per second and is moving toward you at 65 miles per hour. Find the frequency of the horn as you hear it.
404.60 cycles/s

40. **POPULATION** According to the 2000 Census, New Jersey was the most densely populated state, and Alaska was the least densely populated state. The population of New Jersey was 8,414,350, and the population of Alaska was 626,932. The land area of New Jersey is about 7419 square miles, and the land area of Alaska is about 570,374 square miles. How many more people were there per square mile in New Jersey than in Alaska? **about 1133**

★ 41. **BICYCLES** When air is pumped into a bicycle tire, the pressure P required varies inversely as the volume of the air V and is given by the equation $P = \frac{k}{V}$. If the pressure is 30 lb/in^2 when the volume is $1\frac{2}{3}$ cubic feet, find the pressure when the volume is $\frac{3}{4}$ cubic feet. $66\frac{2}{3}$ **lb/in^2**

42. **CRITICAL THINKING** Which expression is equivalent to 0? **a**

a. $\frac{a}{1 - \frac{3}{a}} + \frac{a}{\frac{3}{a} - 1}$

b. $\frac{a - \frac{1}{3}}{b} - \frac{a + \frac{1}{3}}{b}$

c. $\frac{\frac{1}{2} + 2a}{b-1} - \frac{2a + \frac{1}{2}}{1-b}$

43. **WRITING IN MATH** Answer the question that was posed at the beginning of the lesson. **See margin.**

How are rational expressions used in baking?

Include the following in your answer:

• an example of a situation in which you would divide a measurement by a fraction when cooking, and

• an explanation of the process used to simplify a complex fraction.

Standardized Test Practice
Ⓐ Ⓑ Ⓒ Ⓓ

44. The perimeter of hexagon *ABCDEF* is 12. Which expression can be used to represent the measure of $\overline{BC}$? **C**

Ⓐ $\frac{6n-96}{n-8}$

Ⓑ $\frac{9n-96}{n-8}$

Ⓒ $\frac{6n-96}{4n-32}$

Ⓓ $\frac{9n-96}{4n-32}$

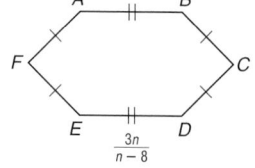

45. Express $\frac{\frac{6mn}{5p}}{\frac{24n^2}{20mp}}$ in simplest form. **C**

Ⓐ $\frac{n}{m^2}$

Ⓑ $\frac{1}{n}$

Ⓒ $\frac{m^2}{n}$

Ⓓ $\frac{36n^3}{25p^2}$

688   **Chapter 12** Rational Expressions and Equations

Enrichment, p. 752

Complex Fractions

Complex fractions are really not complicated. Remember that a fraction can be interpreted as dividing the numerator by the denominator.

$\frac{\frac{2}{5}}{\frac{3}{7}} = \frac{2}{5} \div \frac{3}{7} = \frac{2}{5} \cdot \frac{7}{3} = \frac{2(7)}{3(5)} = \frac{14}{15}$

Let $a, b, c,$ and d be numbers, with $b \neq 0, c \neq 0,$ and $d \neq 0$.

$\frac{\frac{a}{b}}{\frac{c}{d}} = \frac{a}{b} \div \frac{c}{d} = \frac{a}{b} \cdot \frac{d}{c} = \frac{ad}{bc}$ Notice the pattern. numerator of the answer (ad) $\left[\frac{\frac{a}{b}}{\frac{c}{d}}\right]$ denominator of the answer (bc)

Example 1 Simplify $\frac{\frac{5x}{4}}{\frac{x+2}{3}}$.

Example 2 Simplify $\frac{\frac{x}{2}+4}{3x-2}$.

$\frac{\frac{x}{2}+4}{} = \frac{x+8}{2}$

Mixed Review

Find each sum. *(Lesson 12-7)*

46. $\dfrac{12x}{4y^2} + \dfrac{8}{6y}$ $\dfrac{9x + 4y}{3y^2}$

47. $\dfrac{a}{a - b} + \dfrac{b}{2b + 3a}$ $\dfrac{3a^2 + 3ab - b^2}{(a - b)(2b + 3a)}$

48. $\dfrac{7a^2 + 3a - 12}{(3a + 2)(a - 4)^2}$

48. $\dfrac{a + 3}{3a^2 - 10a - 8} + \dfrac{2a}{a^2 - 8a + 16}$

49. $\dfrac{n - 4}{(n - 2)^2} + \dfrac{n - 5}{n^2 + n - 6}$

$\dfrac{2n^2 - 8n - 2}{(n - 2)^2(n + 3)}$

Find each difference. *(Lesson 12-6)*

50. $\dfrac{7}{x^2} - \dfrac{3}{x^2}$ $\dfrac{4}{x^2}$

51. $\dfrac{x}{(x - 3)^2} - \dfrac{3}{(x - 3)^2}$ $\dfrac{1}{x - 3}$

52. $\dfrac{2}{t^2 - t - 2} - \dfrac{t}{t^2 - t - 2}$ $-\dfrac{1}{t + 1}$

53. $\dfrac{2n}{n^2 + 2n - 24} - \dfrac{8}{n^2 + 2n - 24}$ $\dfrac{2}{n + 6}$

54. **BIOLOGY** Ana is working on a biology project for her school's science fair. For her experiment, she needs to have a certain type of bacteria that doubles its population every hour. Right now Ana has 1000 bacteria. If Ana does not interfere with the bacteria, predict how many there will be in ten hours. *(Lesson 10-6)* **1,024,000**

Solve each equation by factoring. Check your solutions. *(Lesson 9-5)*

55. $s^2 = 16$ $\{\pm 4\}$

56. $9p^2 = 64$ $\left\{\pm \dfrac{8}{3}\right\}$

57. $z^3 - 9z = 45 - 5z^2$
$\{-5, -3, 3\}$

FAMILIES For Exercises 58–60, refer to the graph. *(Lesson 8-3)*

58. 1.6014 × 10⁵
5.331 × 10⁴
2.799 × 10⁴
2.298 × 10⁴
1.812 × 10⁴
1.575 × 10⁴
1.119 × 10⁴
1.08 × 10⁴

58. Write each number in the graph using scientific notation.

59. How many times as great is the amount spent on food as the amount spent on clothing? Express your answer in scientific notation. **about 2.59 × 10⁰**

60. What percent of the total amount is spent on housing? **about 33.3%**

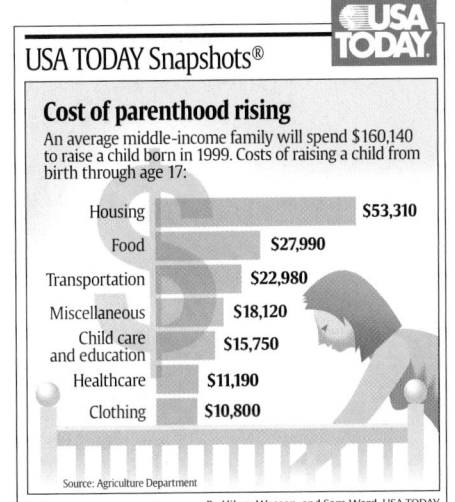

USA TODAY Snapshots®

Cost of parenthood rising

An average middle-income family will spend $160,140 to raise a child born in 1999. Costs of raising a child from birth through age 17:

Housing — $53,310
Food — $27,990
Transportation — $22,980
Miscellaneous — $18,120
Child care and education — $15,750
Healthcare — $11,190
Clothing — $10,800

Source: Agriculture Department

By Hilary Wasson, and Sam Ward, USA TODAY

TELEPHONE RATES For Exercises 61 and 62, use the following information. *(Lesson 5-4)* **61.** $C = 0.16m + 0.99$
A 15-minute call to Mexico costs $3.39. A 24-minute call costs $4.83.

61. Write a linear equation to find the total cost C of an m-minute call.

62. Find the cost of a 9-minute call. **$2.43**

Getting Ready for the Next Lesson

PREREQUISITE SKILL Solve each equation.
(To review solving equations, see Lessons 3-2 through 3-4.)

63. $-12 = \dfrac{x}{4}$ **−48**

64. $1.8 = g - 0.6$ **2.4**

65. $\dfrac{3}{4}n - 3 = 9$ **16**

66. $7x^2 = 28$ **−2, 2**

67. $3.2 = \dfrac{-8 + n}{-7}$ **−14.4**

68. $\dfrac{-3n - (-4)}{-6} = -9$ $-\dfrac{50}{3}$

Open-Ended Assessment

Modeling Have students use fraction bars to prove that the simplification of complex fractions formula is correct. For example, students can model and then use the formula to confirm that $\dfrac{2}{3} \div \dfrac{1}{9} = 6$.

Getting Ready for Lesson 12-9

PREREQUISITE SKILL Students will learn to solve rational equations in Lesson 12-9. In order to solve complicated rational equations, students should first be sure they can solve simpler equations. Use Exercises 63–68 to determine your students' familiarity with solving linear and quadratic equations.

Answer

43. Sample answer: Most measurements used in baking are fractions or mixed numbers, which are examples of rational expressions. Answers should include the following.

- You want to find the number of batches of cookies you can make using the 7 cups of flour you have on hand when a batch requires $1\frac{1}{2}$ cups of flour.

- Divide the expression in the numerator of a complex fraction by the expression in the denominator.

1 Focus

5-Minute Check Transparency 12-9 Use as a quiz or review of Lesson 12-8.

Mathematical Background notes are available for this lesson on p. 640D.

How are rational equations important in the operation of a subway system?

Ask students:

- Why is it important to know where trains are? **Sample answer: so that the trains do not run into each other.**

- If you're given the position of two moving trains, is that sufficient information to determine whether they will collide in the future? **No. You need to know their position, direction of travel, and speed.**

What You'll Learn

- Solve rational equations.
- Eliminate extraneous solutions.

Vocabulary

- rational equations
- work problems
- rate problems
- extraneous solutions

How are rational equations important in the operation of a subway system?

The Washington, D.C., Metrorail is one of the safest subway systems in the world, serving a population of more than 3.5 million. It is vital that a rail system of this size maintain a consistent schedule. Rational equations can be used to determine the exact positions of trains at any given time.

Washington Metropolitan Area Transit Authority

Train	Distance
● Red Line	19.4 mi
● Orange Line	24.14 mi
● Blue Line	19.95 mi
● Green Line	20.59 mi
● Yellow Line	9.46 mi

SOLVE RATIONAL EQUATIONS

Rational equations are equations that contain rational expressions. You can use cross products to solve rational equations, but only when both sides of the equation are single fractions.

Example 1 Use Cross Products

Solve $\dfrac{12}{x+5} = \dfrac{4}{(x+2)}$.

$\dfrac{12}{x+5} = \dfrac{4}{(x+2)}$ Original equation

$12(x+2) = 4(x+5)$ Cross multiply.

$12x + 24 = 4x + 20$ Distributive Property

$8x = -4$ Add $-4x$ and -24 to each side.

$x = -\dfrac{4}{8}$ or $-\dfrac{1}{2}$ Divide each side by 8.

Another method you can use to solve rational equations is to multiply each side of the equation by the LCD to eliminate fractions.

Example 2 Use the LCD

Solve $\dfrac{n-2}{n} - \dfrac{n-3}{n-6} = \dfrac{1}{n}$.

$\dfrac{n-2}{n} - \dfrac{n-3}{n-6} = \dfrac{1}{n}$ Original equation

$n(n-6)\left(\dfrac{n-2}{n} - \dfrac{n-3}{n-6}\right) = n(n-6)\left(\dfrac{1}{n}\right)$ The LCD is $n(n-6)$.

$\left(\dfrac{n(n-6)}{1} \cdot \dfrac{n-2}{n}\right) - \left(\dfrac{n(n-6)}{1} \cdot \dfrac{n-3}{n-6}\right) = \dfrac{n(n-6)}{1} \cdot \dfrac{1}{n}$ Distributive Property

$(n-6)(n-2) - n(n-3) = n-6$ Simplify.

$(n^2 - 8n + 12) - (n^2 - 3n) = n-6$ Multiply.

$n^2 - 8n + 12 - n^2 + 3n = n-6$ Subtract.

$-5n + 12 = n-6$ Simplify.

$-6n = -18$ Subtract 12 and n from each side.

$n = 3$ Divide each side by -6.

Resource Manager

 Workbook and Reproducible Masters

Chapter 12 Resource Masters
- Study Guide and Intervention, pp. 753–754
- Skills Practice, p. 755
- Practice, p. 756
- Reading to Learn Mathematics, p. 757
- Enrichment, p. 758
- Assessment, p. 774

Graphing Calculator and Spreadsheet Masters, p. 45
Parent and Student Study Guide Workbook, p. 99

Transparencies
5-Minute Check Transparency 12-9
Answer Key Transparencies

 Technology
Interactive Chalkboard
Multimedia Applications

A rational equation may have more than one solution.

Example 3 *Multiple Solutions*

Solve $\dfrac{-4}{a+1} + \dfrac{3}{a} = 1$.

$$\dfrac{-4}{a+1} + \dfrac{3}{a} = 1 \qquad \text{Original equation}$$

$$a(a+1)\left(\dfrac{-4}{a+1} + \dfrac{3}{a}\right) = a(a+1)(1) \qquad \text{The LCD is } a(a+1).$$

$$\left(\dfrac{\overset{1}{\cancel{a(a+1)}}}{1} \cdot \dfrac{-4}{\cancel{a+1}}\right) + \left(\dfrac{\overset{1}{\cancel{a(a+1)}}}{1} \cdot \dfrac{3}{\cancel{a}}\right) = a(a+1) \qquad \text{Distributive Property}$$

$$-4a + 3a + 3 = a^2 + a \qquad \text{Simplify.}$$

$$-a + 3 = a^2 + a \qquad \text{Add like terms.}$$

$$0 = a^2 + 2a - 3 \qquad \text{Set equal to 0.}$$

$$0 = (a+3)(a-1) \qquad \text{Factor.}$$

$$a + 3 = 0 \quad \text{or} \quad a - 1 = 0$$

$$a = -3 \qquad\qquad a = 1$$

Study Tip

Look Back
To review **solving quadratic equations by factoring**, see Lessons 9-3 through 9-6.

CHECK   Check by substituting each value in the original equation.

$$\dfrac{-4}{a+1} + \dfrac{3}{a} = 1$$
$$\dfrac{-4}{-3+1} + \dfrac{3}{-3} \overset{?}{=} 1 \quad a = -3$$
$$2 + (-1) \overset{?}{=} 1$$
$$1 = 1$$

$$\dfrac{-4}{a+1} + \dfrac{3}{a} = 1$$
$$\dfrac{-4}{1+1} + \dfrac{3}{1} \overset{?}{=} 1 \quad a = 1$$
$$-2 + 3 \overset{?}{=} 1$$
$$1 = 1$$

The solutions are 1 or −3.

Rational equations can be used to solve **work problems**.

Example 4 *Work Problem*

LAWN CARE   Abbey has a lawn care service. One day she asked her friend Jamal to work with her. Normally, it takes Abbey two hours to mow and trim Mrs. Harris' lawn. When Jamal worked with her, the job took only 1 hour and 20 minutes. How long would it have taken Jamal to do the job himself?

Explore   Since it takes Abbey two hours to do the yard, she can finish $\frac{1}{2}$ the job in one hour. The amount of work Jamal can do in one hour can be represented by $\frac{1}{t}$. To determine how long it takes Jamal to do the job, use the formula Abbey's work + Jamal's work = 1 completed yard.

Study Tip

Work Problems
When solving work problems, remember that each term should represent the portion of a job completed in one unit of time.

Plan   The time that both of them worked was $1\frac{1}{3}$ hours. Each rate multiplied by this time results in the amount of work done by each person.

Solve

$$\underbrace{\dfrac{1}{2}\left(\dfrac{4}{3}\right)}_{\text{Abbey's work}} \; \underbrace{+}_{\text{plus}} \; \underbrace{\dfrac{1}{t}\left(\dfrac{4}{3}\right)}_{\text{Jamal's work}} \; \underbrace{=}_{\text{equals}} \; \underbrace{1}_{\text{total work.}}$$

$$\dfrac{4}{6} + \dfrac{4}{3t} = 1 \qquad \text{Multiply.}$$

(continued on the next page)

---

2 *Teach*

SOLVE RATIONAL EQUATIONS

In-Class Examples   Power Point®

Teaching Tip Remind students to check their solutions by substituting them back into the original equation.

1 Solve $\dfrac{8}{x+3} = \dfrac{2}{x-6}$. **9**

2 Solve $\dfrac{5}{x+1} + \dfrac{1}{x} = \dfrac{2}{x^2+x}$. $\dfrac{1}{6}$

3 Solve $a + \dfrac{a^2-5}{a^2-1} = \dfrac{a^2+a+2}{a+1}$. **3**

4 **TV INSTALLATION** On Saturdays, Lee helps her father install satellite TV systems. The jobs normally take Lee's father about $2\frac{1}{2}$ hours. But when Lee helps, the jobs only take them $1\frac{1}{2}$ hours. If Lee were installing a satellite system herself, how long would the job take? **The job would take Lee $3\frac{3}{4}$ hours by herself.**

5 **TRANSPORTATION** Refer to the application at the beginning of the lesson. Suppose two Red Line trains leave their stations at opposite ends of the line at exactly 2:00 P.M. One train travels between the two stations in 48 minutes and the other train takes 54 minutes. At what time do the two trains pass each other? **The trains pass each other at about 25 minutes after they left their stations, at 2:25 P.M.**

$$6t\left(\frac{4}{6} + \frac{4}{3t}\right) = 6t \cdot 1 \quad \text{The LCD is } 6t.$$

$$\overset{1}{6t}\left(\frac{4}{\underset{1}{6}}\right) + \overset{2}{6t}\left(\frac{4}{\underset{1}{3t}}\right) = 6t \quad \text{Distributive Property}$$

$$4t + 8 = 6t \quad \text{Simplify.}$$

$$8 = 2t \quad \text{Add } -4t \text{ to each side.}$$

$$4 = t \quad \text{Divide each side by 2.}$$

Examine The time that it would take Jamal to do the yard by himself is four hours. This seems reasonable because the combined efforts of the two took longer than half of Abbey's usual time.

Rational equations can also be used to solve **rate problems**.

Example 5 Rate Problem

TRANSPORTATION Refer to the application at the beginning of the lesson. The Yellow Line runs between Huntington and Mt. Vernon Square. Suppose one train leaves Mt. Vernon Square at noon and arrives at Huntington 24 minutes later, and a second train leaves Huntington at noon and arrives at Mt. Vernon Square 28 minutes later. At what time do the two trains pass each other?

Determine the rates of both trains. The total distance is 9.46 miles.

Train 1 $\dfrac{9.46 \text{ mi}}{24 \text{ min}}$ **Train 2** $\dfrac{9.46 \text{ mi}}{28 \text{ min}}$

Study Tip

Rate Problems
You can solve rate problems, also called *uniform motion problems*, more easily if you first make a drawing.

Next, since both trains left at the same time, the time both have traveled when they pass will be the same. And since they started at opposite ends of the route, the sum of their distances is equal to the total route, 9.46 miles.

	r	t	d
Train 1	$\dfrac{9.46 \text{ mi}}{24 \text{ min}}$	t min	$\dfrac{9.46t}{24}$ mi
Train 2	$\dfrac{9.46 \text{ mi}}{28 \text{ min}}$	t min	$\dfrac{9.46t}{28}$ mi

$$\frac{9.46t}{24} + \frac{9.46t}{28} = 9.46 \quad \text{The sum of the distances is 9.46.}$$

$$168\left(\frac{9.46t}{24} + \frac{9.46t}{28}\right) = 168 \cdot 9.46 \quad \text{The LCD is 168.}$$

$$\frac{\overset{7}{168}}{1} \cdot \frac{9.46t}{\underset{1}{24}} + \frac{\overset{6}{168}}{1} \cdot \frac{9.46t}{\underset{1}{28}} = 1589.28 \quad \text{Distributive Property}$$

$$66.22t + 56.76t = 1589.28 \quad \text{Simplify.}$$

$$122.98t = 1589.28 \quad \text{Add.}$$

$$t = 12.92 \quad \text{Divide each side by 122.98.}$$

The trains passed at about 12.92 or about 13 minutes after leaving their stations, which is 12:13 P.M.

DAILY INTERVENTION   **Differentiated Instruction**

Kinesthetic Have students recreate the classic train problem in Example 5 on their own by either walking or riding bikes toward each other over a known distance. Have the two students start at the same time, one traveling at a rate that is faster than the other, and record the time that they meet. Then work out the problem to see if they meet at the expected time.

EXTRANEOUS SOLUTIONS Multiplying each side of an equation by the LCD of two rational expressions can yield results that are not solutions to the original equation. Recall that such solutions are called **extraneous solutions**.

Example 6 No Solution

Solve $\dfrac{3x}{x-1} + \dfrac{6x-9}{x-1} = 6$.

$$\dfrac{3x}{x-1} + \dfrac{6x-9}{x-1} = 6 \qquad \text{Original equation}$$

$$(x-1)\left(\dfrac{3x}{x-1} + \dfrac{6x-9}{x-1}\right) = (x-1)6 \qquad \text{The LCD is } x-1.$$

$$(x-1)\left(\dfrac{3x}{x-1}\right) + (x-1)\left(\dfrac{6x-9}{x-1}\right) = (x-1)6 \qquad \text{Distributive Property}$$

$$3x + 6x - 9 = 6x - 6 \qquad \text{Simplify.}$$

$$9x - 9 = 6x - 6 \qquad \text{Add like terms.}$$

$$3x = 3 \qquad \text{Add 9 to each side.}$$

$$x = 1 \qquad \text{Divide each side by 3.}$$

Since 1 is an excluded value for x, the number 1 is an extraneous solution. Thus, the equation has no solution.

Rational equations can have both valid solutions and extraneous solutions.

Example 7 Extraneous Solution

Solve $\dfrac{2n}{1-n} + \dfrac{n+3}{n^2-1} = 1$.

$$\dfrac{2n}{1-n} + \dfrac{n+3}{n^2-1} = 1$$

$$\dfrac{2n}{1-n} + \dfrac{n+3}{(n-1)(n+1)} = 1$$

$$-\dfrac{2n}{n-1} + \dfrac{n+3}{(n-1)(n+1)} = 1$$

$$(n-1)(n+1)\left(-\dfrac{2n}{n-1} + \dfrac{n+3}{(n-1)(n+1)}\right) = (n-1)(n+1)1$$

$$(n-1)(n+1)\left(-\dfrac{2n}{n-1}\right) + (n-1)(n+1)\left(\dfrac{n+3}{(n-1)(n+1)}\right) = (n-1)(n+1)$$

$$-2n(n+1) + (n+3) = n^2 - 1$$

$$-2n^2 - 2n + n + 3 = n^2 - 1$$

$$-3n^2 - n + 4 = 0$$

$$3n^2 + n - 4 = 0$$

$$(3n+4)(n-1) = 0$$

$3n + 4 = 0 \quad$ or $\quad n - 1 = 0$

$n = -\dfrac{4}{3} \qquad\qquad n = 1$

The number 1 is an extraneous solution, since 1 is an excluded value for n. Thus, $-\dfrac{4}{3}$ is the solution of the equation.

In-Class Examples   Power Point®

6 Solve $\dfrac{3}{x-1} = \dfrac{x+2}{x-1}$.

no solutions

7 Solve $\dfrac{x^2}{x-2} = \dfrac{4}{x-2}$

−2

3 Practice/Apply

Study Notebook

Have students—
• complete the definitions/examples for the remaining terms on their Vocabulary Builder worksheets for Chapter 12.
• include examples of how to solve rational equations.
• include any other item(s) that they find helpful in mastering the skills in this lesson.

DAILY INTERVENTION

Unlocking Misconceptions

Make sure students understand that the equation in Example 6 does have a solution; however, that solution is undefined. Therefore, we say that it has no solutions.

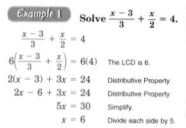

Study Guide and Intervention, p. 753 (shown) and p. 754

Solve Rational Equations Rational equations are equations that contain rational expressions. To solve equations containing rational expressions, multiply each side of the equation by the least common denominator.

Rational equations can be used to solve **work problems** and **rate problems**.

Example 1 Solve $\frac{x-3}{3} + \frac{x}{2} = 4$.

$\frac{x-3}{3} + \frac{x}{2} = 4$

$6\left(\frac{x-3}{3} + \frac{x}{2}\right) = 6(4)$ The LCD is 6.

$2(x-3) + 3x = 24$ Distributive Property

$2x - 6 + 3x = 24$ Distributive Property

$5x = 30$ Simplify.

$x = 6$ Divide each side by 5.

The solution is 6.

Example 2 **WORK PROBLEM** Marla can paint Percy's kitchen in 3 hours. Percy can paint it in 2 hours. Working together, how long will it take Marla and Percy to paint the kitchen?

In t hours, Marla completes $t \cdot \frac{1}{3}$ of the job and Percy completes $t \cdot \frac{1}{2}$ of the job. So an equation for completing the whole job is $\frac{t}{3} + \frac{t}{2} = 1$.

$\frac{t}{3} + \frac{t}{2} = 1$

$2t + 3t = 6$ Multiply each term by 6.

$5t = 6$ Add like terms.

$t = \frac{6}{5}$ Solve.

So it will take Marla and Percy $1\frac{1}{5}$ hours to paint the room if they work together.

Exercises

Solve each equation.

1. $\frac{x-5}{5} + \frac{x}{4} = 8$ **20**

2. $\frac{3}{x} = \frac{6}{x+1}$ **1**

3. $\frac{x-1}{5} = \frac{2x-2}{15}$ **1**

4. $\frac{8}{n-1} = \frac{10}{n+1}$ **9**

5. $s - \frac{4}{s+3} = s$ **-4$\frac{1}{3}$**

6. $\frac{m+4}{m} + \frac{m}{3} = \frac{m}{4}$ **-4**

7. $\frac{q+4}{q-1} + \frac{q}{q+1} = 2$ **-$\frac{3}{2}$**

8. $\frac{5-2x}{2} - \frac{4x+3}{6} = \frac{7x+2}{3}$ **$\frac{10}{17}$**

9. $\frac{m+1}{2} - \frac{m}{1-m} = 1$ **-2**

10. $\frac{x^2-9}{x-3} + x^2 = 9$ **-3 or 2**

11. **GREETING CARDS** It takes Kenesha 45 minutes to prepare 20 greeting cards. It takes Paula 30 minutes to prepare the same number of cards. Working together at this rate, how long will it take to prepare the cards? **18 min**

12. **BOATING** A motorboat went upstream at 15 miles per hour and returned downstream at 20 miles per hour. How far did the boat travel one way if the round trip took 3.5 hours? **30 mi**

Skills Practice, p. 755 and Practice, p. 756 (shown)

Solve each equation. State any extraneous solutions.

1. $\frac{5}{n+2} = \frac{7}{n+6}$ **8**

2. $\frac{x}{x-5} = \frac{x+4}{x-6}$ **4**

3. $\frac{k+5}{k} = \frac{k-1}{k+9}$ **-3**

4. $\frac{2h}{h-1} = \frac{2h+1}{h+2}$ **-$\frac{1}{5}$**

5. $\frac{4y}{3} + \frac{1}{2} = \frac{5y}{6}$ **-1**

6. $\frac{y-2}{4} - \frac{y+2}{5} = -1$ **-2**

7. $\frac{2q-1}{6} - \frac{q}{3} = \frac{q+4}{18}$ **-7**

8. $\frac{5}{p} - \frac{3}{p+2} = 0$ **-$\frac{13}{2}$**

9. $\frac{3t}{t-3} - \frac{1}{9t+3} = 1$ **-$\frac{1}{3}$**

10. $\frac{4x}{2y-1} - \frac{2x}{2x+3} = 1$ **$\frac{3}{2}$**

11. $\frac{d-3}{d} - \frac{d-4}{d-2} = \frac{1}{d}$ **4**

12. $\frac{3y-2}{y-2} + \frac{y^2}{y-2} = -3$ **4; extraneous: 2**

13. $\frac{2}{m+2} - \frac{m+2}{m-2} = \frac{7}{3}$ **-1, $\frac{2}{5}$**

14. $\frac{n+2}{n+3} + \frac{n+5}{n+3} = -\frac{1}{n}$ **-$\frac{9}{2}$, -1**

15. $\frac{1}{z+1} - \frac{6-z}{6z} = 0$ **-3, 2**

16. $\frac{2p}{p-2} - \frac{p+2}{p+4} = -1$ **-3; extraneous: -2**

17. $\frac{5}{x^2-9} - \frac{x}{x+3} = 1$ **-2, 4**

18. $\frac{2}{n-4} - \frac{n+6}{n^2-16} = 1$ **-5, -2**

PUBLISHING For Exercises 19 and 20, use the following information.
Tracey and Alan publish a 10-page independent newspaper once a month. At production, Alan usually spends 6 hours on the layout of the paper. When Tracey helps, layout takes 3 hours and 20 minutes.

19. Write an equation that could be used to determine how long it would take Tracey to do the layout by herself. **Sample answer:** $\frac{1}{6}\left(\frac{10}{3}\right) + \frac{1}{t}\left(\frac{10}{3}\right) = 1$

20. How long would it take Tracey to do the job alone? **7 h 30 min**

TRAVEL For Exercises 21 and 22, use the following information.
Emilio made arrangements to have Lynda pick him up from an auto repair shop after he dropped his car off. He called Lynda to tell her he would start walking and to look for him on the way. Emilio and Lynda live 10 miles from the auto shop. It takes Emilio $2\frac{1}{4}$ hours to walk the distance and Lynda 15 minutes to drive the distance.

21. If Emilio and Lynda leave at the same time, when should Lynda expect to spot Emilio on the road? **in 13$\frac{1}{2}$ min**

22. How far will Emilio have walked when Lynda picks him up? **1 mi**

Reading to Learn Mathematics, p. 757   ELL

Pre-Activity **How are rational equations important in the operation of a subway system?**

Read the introduction to Lesson 12-9 at the top of page 690 in your textbook.

What is some information that would be important in establishing a schedule for a subway system? **Sample answer: the number of trains that operate on each subway line, the speeds at which the trains can travel, the distances between subway stops on each line, the amount of time a train spends stopped to allow passengers to exit and board the train**

Reading the Lesson

1. Is $\frac{\sqrt{x-3}}{4} = 3$ a rational equation? Explain. **No; the expression on the left side of the equation is not a rational expression.**

2. How can you tell by looking at a rational equation whether you can solve it by using cross products? **The equation should have a single fraction on each side.**

3. How does multiplying both sides of a rational equation by the LCD help you solve the equation? **It gets rid of the fractions.**

4. For Example 4 in your textbook, look at the first equation of the Solve stage.
   a. What does the expression $\frac{1}{2}\left(\frac{4}{3}\right)$ represent in this situation? **the part of the total work that Abbey can do in $\frac{4}{3}$ hours**
   b. What does the expression $\frac{1}{4}\left(\frac{4}{3}\right)$ represent? **the part of the total work that Jamal can do in $\frac{4}{3}$ hours**
   c. What does the number 1 on the right side represent? **1 whole job**

5. When you solve a rational equation, in which equation should you substitute to eliminate possible extraneous solutions? **the original equation**

Helping You Remember

6. Think of a word that can help you remember that multiplying by the LCD is one method you can use to solve a rational equation. **Sample answer: Use the word lucid. If your thinking is LuCiD, you will be successful using the LCD.**

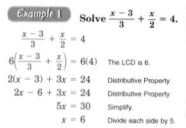

Check for Understanding

Concept Check

GUIDED PRACTICE KEY

Exercises	Examples
4, 5	1
6–8	2
9	7
10	4, 5

1. **OPEN ENDED** Explain why the equation $n + \frac{1}{n-1} = \frac{1}{n-1} + 1$ has no solution. **See margin.**

2. **Write** an expression to represent the amount of work Aminta can do in h hours if it normally takes her 3 hours to change the oil and tune up her car. **$\frac{h}{3} = 1$**

3. **Find a counterexample** for the following statement. *The solution of a rational equation can never be zero.* **Sample answer: $\frac{x}{4} = 0$**

Guided Practice Solve each equation. State any extraneous solutions.

4. $\frac{2}{x} = \frac{3}{x+1}$ **2**

5. $\frac{7}{a-1} = \frac{5}{a+3}$ **-13**

6. $\frac{3x}{5} + \frac{3}{2} = \frac{7x}{10}$ **15**

7. $\frac{x+1}{x} + \frac{x+4}{x} = 6$ **$\frac{5}{4}$**

8. $\frac{5}{k+1} - \frac{7}{k} = \frac{1}{k+1}$ **-$\frac{7}{3}$**

9. $\frac{x+2}{x-2} - \frac{2}{x+2} = \frac{-7}{3}$ **-1, $\frac{2}{5}$**

Application

10. **BASEBALL** Omar has 32 hits in 128 times at bat. He wants his batting average to be .300. His current average is $\frac{32}{128}$ or .250. How many at bats does Omar need to reach his goal if he gets a hit in each of his next b at bats? **10**

★ indicates increased difficulty

Practice and Apply

Solve each equation. State any extraneous solutions.

Homework Help

For Exercises	See Examples
11–14	1
15–19, 21, 23, 26, 27	2
22, 24, 25	3
29–34	4, 5
20, 28	6, 7

Extra Practice
See page 849.

20. no solutions
21. -3
22. 6, -1

11. $\frac{4}{a} = \frac{3}{a-2}$ **8**

12. $\frac{3}{x} = \frac{1}{x-2}$ **3**

13. $\frac{x-3}{x} = \frac{x-3}{x-6}$ **3**

14. $\frac{x}{x+1} = \frac{x-6}{x-1}$ **-$\frac{3}{2}$**

15. $\frac{2n}{3} + \frac{1}{2} = \frac{2n-3}{6}$ **-3**

16. $\frac{5}{4} + \frac{3y}{2} = \frac{7y}{6} - \frac{15}{4}$

17. $\frac{a-1}{a+1} - \frac{2a}{a-1} = -1$ **0**

18. $\frac{7}{x^2-5x} + \frac{3}{5-x} = \frac{4}{x}$ **$\frac{27}{7}$**

19. $\frac{4x}{2x+3} - \frac{2x}{2x-3} = 1$ **1$\frac{1}{2}$**

20. $\frac{5}{5-p} - \frac{p^2}{p-5} = -8$

21. $\frac{a}{3a+6} - \frac{a}{5a+10} = \frac{2}{5}$

22. $\frac{c}{c-4} - \frac{6}{4-c} = c$

23. $\frac{2b-5}{b-2} - 2 = \frac{3}{b+2}$ **1**

24. $\frac{7}{k-3} - \frac{1}{2} = \frac{3}{k-4}$ **5, 10**

25. $\frac{x^2-4}{x-2} + x^2 = 4$ **-2, 1**

26. $\frac{2n}{n-1} + \frac{n-5}{n^2-1} = 1$ **-4; extraneous 1**

★ 27. $\frac{3z}{z^2-5z+4} = \frac{2}{z-4} + \frac{3}{z-1}$ **7**

★ 28. $\frac{4}{m^2-8m+12} = \frac{m}{m-2} + \frac{1}{m-6}$ **-1; extraneous 6**

29. **QUIZZES** Each week, Mandy's algebra teacher gives a 10-point quiz. After 5 weeks, Mandy has earned a total of 36 points for an average of 7.2 points per quiz. She would like to raise her average to 9 points. On how many quizzes must she score 10 points in order to reach her goal? **9**

BOATING For Exercises 30 and 31, use the following information.
Jim and Mateo live across a lake from each other at a distance of about 3 miles. Jim can row his boat to Mateo's house in 1 hour and 20 minutes. Mateo can drive his motorboat the same distance in a half hour.

30. If they leave their houses at the same time and head toward each other, how long will it be before they meet? **about 22 min**

31. How far from the nearest shore will they be when they meet? **about 0.82 mi**

32. **CAR WASH** Ian and Nadya can each wash a car and clean its interior in about 2 hours, but Chris needs 3 hours to do the work. If the three work together, how long will it take to clean seven cars? **5 hr 15 min**

694   Chapter 12   Rational Expressions and Equations

Enrichment, p. 758

Winning Distances

In 1999, Hicham El Guerrouj set a world record for the mile run with a time of 3:43.13 (3 h 43 min 13 s). In 1954, Roger Bannister ran the first mile under 4 minutes at 3:59.4. Had they run those times in the same race, how far in front of Bannister would El Guerrouj have been at the finish?

Use $\frac{d}{t} = r$. Since 3 min 43.13 s = 223.13 s, and 3 min 59.4 s = 239.4 s,

El Guerrouj's rate was $\frac{5280 \text{ ft}}{223.13 \text{ s}}$ and Bannister's rate was $\frac{5280 \text{ ft}}{239.4 \text{ s}}$.

	r	t	d
El Guerrouj	$\frac{5280}{223.13}$	223.13	5280 feet
Bannister	$\frac{5280}{239.4}$	223.13	$\frac{5280}{239.4} \cdot 223.13$ or 4921.2 feet

Therefore, when El Guerrouj hit the tape, he would be 5280 − 4921.2, or 358.8 feet, ahead of Bannister. Let's see whether we can develop a

SWIMMING POOLS For Exercises 33 and 34, use the following information.
The pool in Kara's backyard is cleaned and ready to be filled for the summer. It measures 15 feet long and 10 feet wide with an average depth of 4 feet.

33. What is the volume of the pool? **600 ft³**

34. How many gallons of water will it take to fill the pool? (1 ft³ = 7.5 gal) **4500 gal**

35. **CRITICAL THINKING** Solve $\dfrac{\frac{x+3}{x-2} \cdot \frac{x^2+x-2}{x+5}}{x-1} + 2 = 0$. $-\dfrac{14}{3}$

36. WRITING IN MATH   Answer the question that was posed at the beginning of the lesson. **See margin.**

How are rational equations important in the operation of a subway system?

Include the following in your answer:
- an explanation of how rational equations can be used to approximate the time that trains will pass each other if they leave distant stations and head toward each other.

Standardized Test Practice
Ⓐ Ⓑ Ⓒ Ⓓ

37. What is the value of a in the equation $\dfrac{a-2}{a} - \dfrac{a-3}{a-6} = \dfrac{1}{a}$? **A**

Ⓐ 3   Ⓑ 2   Ⓒ 6   Ⓓ 0

38. Which value is an extraneous solution of $\dfrac{-1}{n+2} = \dfrac{n^2-7n-8}{3n^2+2n-8}$? **D**

Ⓐ 6   Ⓑ 2   Ⓒ −1   Ⓓ −2

Maintain Your Skills

Mixed Review

Simplify each expression. *(Lesson 12-8)*

39. $\dfrac{\frac{x^2+8x+15}{x^2+x-6}}{\frac{x^2+2x-15}{x^2-2x-3}}$ $\dfrac{x+1}{x-2}$

40. $\dfrac{\frac{a^2-6a+5}{a^2+13a+42}}{\frac{a^2-4a+3}{a^2+3a-18}}$ $\dfrac{a-5}{a+7}$

41. $\dfrac{x+2+\frac{2}{x+5}}{x+6+\frac{6}{x+1}}$ $\dfrac{x+1}{x+5}$

Find each difference. *(Lesson 12-7)*

42. $\dfrac{3}{2m-3} - \dfrac{m}{6-4m}$ 42. $\dfrac{6+m}{2(2m-3)}$

43. $\dfrac{y}{y^2-2y+1} - \dfrac{1}{y-1}$ 43. $\dfrac{1}{y^2-2y+1}$

44. $\dfrac{a+2}{a^2-9} - \dfrac{2a}{6a^2-17a-3}$ $\dfrac{4a^2+7a+2}{(6a+1)(a-3)(a+3)}$

Factor each polynomial. *(Lesson 9-2)*

45. $20x - 8y$ **4(5x − 2y)**
46. $14a^2b + 21ab^2$ **7ab(2a + 3b)**
47. $10p^2 - 12p + 25p - 30$ **(2p + 5)(5p − 6)**

48. **CHEMISTRY** One solution is 50% glycol, and another is 30% glycol. How much of each solution should be mixed to make a 100-gallon solution that is 45% glycol? *(Lesson 7-2)* **75 gal of 50%, 25 gal of 30%**

 WebQuest   **Internet Project**

Building the Best Roller Coaster

It is time to complete your project. Use the information and data you have gathered about the building and financing of a roller coaster to prepare a portfolio or Web page. Be sure to include graphs and/or tables in the presentation.

www.algebra1.com/webquest

 www.algebra1.com/self_check_quiz

---

About the Exercises …
Organization by Objective
- **Solve Rational Equations:** 11–19, 21–27
- **Extraneous Solutions:** 20–28

Odd/Even Assignments
Exercises 11–28 are structured so that students practice the same concepts whether they are assigned odd or even problems.

Assignment Guide
Basic: 11–25 odd, 29–31, 35–48
Average: 11–29 odd, 30, 31, 35–48
Advanced: 12–28 even, 32–48

4 Assess

Open-Ended Assessment
Writing Have students create a rate problem and then solve it, showing their work for each step.

Assessment Options
Quiz (Lessons 12-8 and 12-9) is available on p. 774 of the *Chapter 12 Resource Masters.*

Answers

1. Sample answer: When you solve the equation, $n = 1$. But $n \neq 1$, so the equation has no solution.

36. Sample answer: Rational equations are used in solving rate problems, so they can be used to determine traveling times, speeds, and distances related to subways. Answers should include the following.
   - Sample answer: Since both trains leave at the same time, their traveling time is the same. The sum of the distances of both trains is equal to the total distance between the two stations. So, add the two expressions to represent the distance each train travels and solve for time.

Chapter 12 Study Guide and Review

Vocabulary and Concept Check

Vocabulary and Concept Check

- This alphabetical list of vocabulary terms in Chapter 12 includes a page reference where each term was introduced.

- **Assessment** A vocabulary test/review for Chapter 12 is available on p. 772 of the *Chapter 12 Resource Masters*.

Lesson-by-Lesson Review

For each lesson,
- the main ideas are summarized,
- additional examples review concepts, and
- practice exercises are provided.

Vocabulary PuzzleMaker

ELL The Vocabulary PuzzleMaker software improves students' mathematics vocabulary using four puzzle formats—crossword, scramble, word search using a word list, and word search using clues. Students can work on a computer screen or from a printed handout.

MindJogger Videoquizzes

ELL MindJogger Videoquizzes provide an alternative review of concepts presented in this chapter. Students work in teams in a game show format to gain points for correct answers. The questions are presented in three rounds.

Round 1 Concepts (5 questions)
Round 2 Skills (4 questions)
Round 3 Problem Solving (4 questions)

Vocabulary and Concept Check

complex fraction (p. 684)	least common multiple (p. 678)	rate problem (p. 692)
excluded values (p. 648)	least common denominator (p. 679)	rational equation (p. 690)
extraneous solutions (p. 693)	mixed expression (p. 684)	rational expression (p. 648)
inverse variation (p. 642)	product rule (p. 643)	work problem (p. 691)

State whether each sentence is *true* or *false*. If false, replace the underlined expression to make a true sentence.

1. A <u>mixed</u> expression is a fraction whose numerator and denominator are polynomials. **false, rational**

2. The complex fraction $\dfrac{\frac{4}{5}}{\frac{2}{3}}$ can be simplified as $\frac{6}{5}$. **true**

3. The equation $\dfrac{x}{x-1} + \dfrac{2x-3}{x-1} = 2$ has an extraneous solution of <u>1</u>. **true**

4. The mixed expression $6 - \dfrac{a-2}{a+3}$ can be rewritten as $\underline{\dfrac{5a+16}{a+3}}$. **false, $\dfrac{5a+20}{a+3}$**,

5. The least common multiple for $(x^2 - 144)$ and $(x + 12)$ is <u>$x + 12$</u>. **false, $x^2 - 144$**

6. The excluded values for $\dfrac{4x}{x^2 - x - 12}$ are <u>-3 and 4</u>. **true**

Lesson-by-Lesson Review

12-1 Inverse Variation

Concept Summary

- The product rule for inverse variations states that if (x_1, y_1) and (x_2, y_2) are solutions of an inverse variation, then $x_1y_1 = k$ and $x_2y_2 = k$.
- You can use $\dfrac{x_1}{x_2} = \dfrac{y_2}{y_1}$ to solve problems involving inverse variation.

Example If y varies inversely as x and $y = 24$ when $x = 30$, find x when $y = 10$.

$\dfrac{x_1}{x_2} = \dfrac{y_2}{y_1}$ Proportion for inverse variations

$\dfrac{30}{x_2} = \dfrac{10}{24}$ $x_1 = 30$, $y_1 = 24$, and $y_2 = 10$

$720 = 10x_2$ Cross multiply.

$72 = x_2$ Thus, $x = 72$ when $y = 10$.

Exercises Write an inverse variation equation that relates x and y. Assume that y varies inversely as x. Then solve. *See Examples 3 and 4 on page 644.*

7. If $y = 28$ when $x = 42$, find y when $x = 56$. **$xy = 1176$; 21**
8. If $y = 15$ when $x = 5$, find y when $x = 3$. **$xy = 75$; 25**
9. If $y = 18$ when $x = 8$, find x when $y = 3$. **$xy = 144$; 48**
10. If $y = 35$ when $x = 175$, find y when $x = 75$. **$xy = 6125$; 81.67**

 www.algebra1.com/vocabulary_review

FOLDABLES™ Study Organizer

For more information about Foldables, see *Teaching Mathematics with Foldables.*

Have students flip back through their organizers to make sure that they have included information for every lesson page in the organizer. Now is a good time to ask if students have any questions about the concepts that they recorded in their organizers.

Encourage students to refer to their Foldables while completing the Study Guide and Review and use them in preparing for the Chapter Test.

12-2 Rational Expressions

See pages 648–653.

Concept Summary

- Excluded values are values of a variable that result in a denominator of zero.

Example Simplify $\dfrac{x + 4}{x^2 + 12x + 32}$. State the excluded values of x.

$$\frac{x + 4}{x^2 + 12x + 32} = \frac{\overset{1}{\cancel{x + 4}}}{\underset{1}{(\cancel{x + 4})}(x + 8)} \quad \text{Factor.}$$

$$= \frac{1}{x + 8} \quad \text{Simplify.}$$

The expression is undefined when $x = -4$ and $x = -8$.

Exercises Simplify each expression. *See Example 5 on page 650.* **11–14. See margin.**

11. $\dfrac{3x^2y}{12xy^3z}$ 12. $\dfrac{n^2 - 3n}{n - 3}$ 13. $\dfrac{a^2 - 25}{a^2 + 3a - 10}$ 14. $\dfrac{x^2 + 10x + 21}{x^3 + x^2 - 42x}$

12-3 Multiplying Rational Expressions

See pages 655–659.

Concept Summary

- Multiplying rational expressions is similar to multiplying rational numbers.

Example Find $\dfrac{1}{x^2 + x - 12} \cdot \dfrac{x - 3}{x + 5}$.

$$\frac{1}{x^2 + x - 12} \cdot \frac{x - 3}{x + 5} = \frac{1}{(x + 4)\underset{1}{(\cancel{x - 3})}} \cdot \frac{\overset{1}{\cancel{x - 3}}}{x + 5} \quad \text{Factor.}$$

$$= \frac{1}{(x + 4)(x + 5)} \quad \text{Simplify.}$$

Exercises Find each product. *See Examples 1–3 on pages 655 and 656.* **15–20. See margin.**

15. $\dfrac{7b^2}{9} \cdot \dfrac{6a^2}{b}$ 16. $\dfrac{5x^2y}{8ab} \cdot \dfrac{12a^2b}{25x}$ 17. $(3x + 30) \cdot \dfrac{10}{x^2 - 100}$

18. $\dfrac{3a - 6}{a^2 - 9} \cdot \dfrac{a + 3}{a^2 - 2a}$ 19. $\dfrac{x^2 + x - 12}{x + 2} \cdot \dfrac{x + 4}{x^2 - x - 6}$ 20. $\dfrac{b^2 + 19b + 84}{b - 3} \cdot \dfrac{b^2 - 9}{b^2 + 15b + 36}$

12-4 Dividing Rational Expressions

See pages 660–664.

Concept Summary

- Divide rational expressions by multiplying by the reciprocal of the divisor.

Example Find $\dfrac{y^2 - 16}{y^2 - 64} \div \dfrac{y + 4}{y - 8}$.

$$\frac{y^2 - 16}{y^2 - 64} \div \frac{y + 4}{y - 8} = \frac{y^2 - 16}{y^2 - 64} \cdot \frac{y - 8}{y + 4} \quad \text{Multiply by the reciprocal of } \frac{y + 4}{y - 8}.$$

$$= \frac{(y - 4)\overset{1}{(\cancel{y + 4})}}{\underset{1}{(\cancel{y - 8})}(y + 8)} \cdot \frac{\overset{1}{\cancel{y - 8}}}{\underset{1}{\cancel{y + 4}}} \text{ or } \frac{y - 4}{y + 8} \quad \text{Simplify.}$$

Answers

11. $\dfrac{x}{4y^2z}$

12. n

13. $\dfrac{a - 5}{a - 2}$

14. $\dfrac{x + 3}{x(x - 6)}$

15. $\dfrac{14a^2b}{3}$

16. $\dfrac{3axy}{10}$

17. $\dfrac{30}{x - 10}$

18. $\dfrac{3}{a^2 - 3a}$

19. $\dfrac{(x + 4)^2}{(x + 2)^2}$

20. $b + 7$

Answers

25. $2ac^2 - 4a^2c + \dfrac{3c^2}{b}$

26. $x^2 + 4x - 2$

27. $x^2 + 2x - 3$

28. $4b + 1 + \dfrac{8}{12b - 1}$

Exercises Find each quotient. *See Examples 1–4 on pages 660 and 661.*

21. $\dfrac{p^3}{2q} \div \dfrac{p^2}{4q}$ $2p$

22. $\dfrac{y^2}{y + 4} \div \dfrac{3y}{y^2 - 16}$ $\dfrac{y(y - 4)}{3}$

23. $\dfrac{3y - 12}{y + 4} \div (y^2 - 6y + 8)$ $\dfrac{3}{(y + 4)(y - 2)}$

24. $\dfrac{2m^2 + 7m - 15}{m + 5} \div \dfrac{9m^2 - 4}{3m + 2}$ $\dfrac{2m - 3}{3m - 2}$

12-5 Dividing Polynomials

See pages 666–671.

Concept Summary

- To divide a polynomial by a monomial, divide each term of the polynomial by the monomial.
- To divide a polynomial by a binomial, use long division.

Example Find $(x^3 - 2x^2 - 22x + 21) \div (x - 3)$.

$$
\begin{array}{r}
x^2 \;\;\; + x - 19 \\
x - 3 \overline{\smash{)}x^3 - 2x^2 - 22x + 21} \\
\underline{(-)x^3 - 3x^2} \\
x^2 - 22x \\
\underline{(-)x^2 - 3x} \\
-19x + 21 \\
\underline{(-)-19x + 57} \\
-36
\end{array}
$$

Multiply x^2 and $x - 3$.
Subtract.
Multiply x and $x - 3$.
Subtract.
Multiply -19 and $x - 3$.
Subtract.

The quotient is $x^2 + x - 19 - \dfrac{36}{x - 3}$.

Exercises Find each quotient. *See Examples 1–5 on pages 666–668.* **25–28. See margin.**

25. $(4a^2b^2c^2 - 8a^3b^2c + 6abc^2) \div 2ab^2$

26. $(x^3 + 7x^2 + 10x - 6) \div (x + 3)$

27. $\dfrac{x^3 - 7x + 6}{x - 2}$

28. $(48b^2 + 8b + 7) \div (12b - 1)$

12-6 Rational Expressions with Like Denominators

See pages 672–677.

Concept Summary

- Add (or subtract) rational expressions with like denominators by adding (or subtracting) the numerators and writing the sum (or difference) over the denominator.

Example Find $\dfrac{m^2}{m + 4} - \dfrac{16}{m + 4}$.

$$\dfrac{m^2}{m + 4} - \dfrac{16}{m + 4} = \dfrac{m^2 - 16}{m + 4}$$ Subtract the numerators.

$$= \dfrac{(m - 4)\overset{1}{\cancel{(m + 4)}}}{\underset{1}{\cancel{m + 4}}} \text{ or } m - 4$$ Factor.

Exercises Find each sum or difference. *See Examples 1–4 on pages 672 and 673.*

29. $\dfrac{m + 4}{5} + \dfrac{m - 1}{5}$ $\dfrac{2m + 3}{5}$

30. $\dfrac{-5}{2n - 5} + \dfrac{2n}{2n - 5}$ 1

31. $\dfrac{a^2}{a - b} + \dfrac{-b^2}{a - b}$ $a + b$

32. $\dfrac{7a}{b^2} - \dfrac{5a}{b^2}$ $\dfrac{2a}{b^2}$

33. $\dfrac{2x}{x - 3} - \dfrac{6}{x - 3}$ 2

34. $\dfrac{m^2}{m - n} - \dfrac{2mn - n^2}{m - n}$ $m - n$

12-7 Rational Expressions with Unlike Denominators

See pages
678–683.

Concept Summary

- Rewrite rational expressions with unlike denominators using the least common denominator (LCD). Then add or subtract.

Example Find $\dfrac{x}{x+3} + \dfrac{5}{x-2}$.

$$\dfrac{x}{x+3} + \dfrac{5}{x-2} = \dfrac{x-2}{x-2} \cdot \dfrac{x}{x+3} + \dfrac{x+3}{x+3} \cdot \dfrac{5}{x-2} \qquad \text{The LCD is } (x+3)(x-2).$$

$$= \dfrac{x^2 - 2x}{(x+3)(x-2)} + \dfrac{5x+15}{(x+3)(x-2)} \qquad \text{Multiply.}$$

$$= \dfrac{x^2 + 3x + 15}{(x+3)(x-2)} \qquad \text{Add.}$$

Exercises Find each sum or difference. *See Examples 3–5 on pages 679 and 680.*

35. $\dfrac{2c}{3d^2} + \dfrac{3}{2cd} \quad \dfrac{4c^2 + 9d}{6cd^2}$

36. $\dfrac{r^2 + 21r}{r^2 - 9} + \dfrac{3r}{r+3} \quad \dfrac{4r}{r-3}$

37. $\dfrac{3a}{a-2} + \dfrac{5a}{a+1} \quad \dfrac{8a^2 - 7a}{(a-2)(a+1)}$

38. $\dfrac{7n}{3} - \dfrac{9n}{7} \quad \dfrac{22n}{21}$

39. $\dfrac{7}{3a} - \dfrac{3}{6a^2} \quad \dfrac{14a - 3}{6a^2}$

40. $\dfrac{2x}{2x+8} - \dfrac{4}{5x+20} \quad \dfrac{5x-4}{5x+20}$

12-8 Mixed Expressions and Complex Fractions

See pages
684–689.

Concept Summary

- Write mixed expressions as rational expressions in the same way as mixed numbers are changed to improper fractions.
- Simplify complex fractions by writing them as division problems.

Example Simplify $\dfrac{y - \dfrac{40}{y-3}}{y+5}$.

$$\dfrac{y - \dfrac{40}{y-3}}{y+5} = \dfrac{\dfrac{y(y-3)}{(y-3)} - \dfrac{40}{y-3}}{y+5} \qquad \text{The LCD in the numerator is } y-3.$$

$$= \dfrac{\dfrac{y^2 - 3y - 40}{y-3}}{y+5} \qquad \text{Add in the numerator.}$$

$$= \dfrac{y^2 - 3y - 40}{y-3} \div (y+5) \qquad \text{Rewrite as a division sentence.}$$

$$= \dfrac{y^2 - 3y - 40}{y-3} \cdot \dfrac{1}{y+5} \qquad \text{Multiply by the reciprocal of } y+5.$$

$$= \dfrac{(y-8)\overset{1}{\cancel{(y+5)}}}{y-3} \cdot \dfrac{1}{\underset{1}{\cancel{y+5}}} \text{ or } \dfrac{y-8}{y-3} \qquad \text{Factor.}$$

Exercises Write each mixed expression as a rational expression.
See Example 1 on page 684.

41. $4 + \dfrac{x}{x-2} \quad \dfrac{5x-8}{x-2}$

42. $2 - \dfrac{x+2}{x^2-4} \quad \dfrac{2x-5}{x-2}$

43. $3 + \dfrac{x^2+y^2}{x^2-y^2} \quad \dfrac{4x^2-2y^2}{x^2-y^2}$

Study Guide and Review

Chapter 12 **For More ...** • Extra Practice, see pages 846–849.
• Mixed Problem Solving, see page 864.

Simplify each expression. *See Examples 3 and 4 on pages 685 and 686.*

44. $\dfrac{\frac{x^2}{y^3}}{\frac{3x}{9y^2}}$ $\dfrac{3x}{y}$

45. $\dfrac{5 + \frac{4}{a}}{\frac{a}{2} - \frac{3}{4}}$ $\dfrac{20a + 16}{2a^2 - 3a}$

46. $\dfrac{y + 9 - \frac{6}{y+4}}{y + 4 + \frac{2}{y+1}}$ $\dfrac{y^2 + 11y + 10}{y^2 + 6y + 8}$

12-9 Solving Rational Equations

See pages 690–695.

Concept Summary

• Use cross products to solve rational equations with a single fraction on each side of the equal sign.

• Multiply every term of a more complicated rational equation by the LCD to eliminate fractions.

Example Solve $\dfrac{5n}{6} + \dfrac{1}{n-2} = \dfrac{n+1}{3(n-2)}$.

$$\dfrac{5n}{6} + \dfrac{1}{n-2} = \dfrac{n+1}{3(n-2)} \qquad \text{Original equation}$$

$$6(n-2)\left(\dfrac{5n}{6} + \dfrac{1}{n-2}\right) = 6(n-2)\dfrac{n+1}{3(n-2)} \qquad \text{The LCD is } 6(n-2)$$

$$\dfrac{\overset{1}{\cancel{6}}(n-2)(5n)}{\cancel{6}} + \dfrac{\overset{1}{6}(n\cancel{-2})}{\cancel{n-2}} = \dfrac{\overset{2}{6}(n\cancel{-2})(n+1)}{\underset{1}{\cancel{3}}(n\cancel{-2})} \qquad \text{Distributive Property}$$

$$(n-2)(5n) + 6 = 2(n+1) \qquad \text{Simplify.}$$

$$5n^2 - 10n + 6 = 2n + 2 \qquad \text{Multiply.}$$

$$5n^2 - 12n + 4 = 0 \qquad \text{Subtract.}$$

$$(5n - 2)(n - 2) = 0 \qquad \text{Factor.}$$

$$n = \dfrac{2}{5} \text{ or } n = 2$$

CHECK Let $n = \dfrac{2}{5}$.

$$\dfrac{\frac{2}{5} + 1}{3\left(\frac{2}{5} - 2\right)} \overset{?}{=} \dfrac{5\left(\frac{2}{5}\right)}{6} + \dfrac{1}{\frac{2}{5} - 2}$$

$$-\dfrac{7}{24} = -\dfrac{7}{24} \checkmark$$

Let $n = 2$.

$$\dfrac{2 + 1}{3(2 - 2)} \overset{?}{=} \dfrac{5(2)}{6} + \dfrac{1}{2 - 2}$$

$$\dfrac{3}{3(0)} \overset{?}{=} \dfrac{10}{6} + \dfrac{1}{0}$$

When you check the value 2, you get a zero in the denominator. So, 2 is an extraneous solution.

Exercises Solve each equation. State any extraneous solutions.
See Examples 6 and 7 on page 693.

47. $\dfrac{4x}{3} + \dfrac{7}{2} = \dfrac{7x}{12} - \dfrac{1}{4}$ **−5**

48. $\dfrac{11}{2x} - \dfrac{2}{3x} = \dfrac{1}{6}$ **29**

49. $\dfrac{2}{3r} - \dfrac{3r}{r-2} = -3$ **$-\dfrac{1}{4}$**

50. $\dfrac{x-2}{x} - \dfrac{x-3}{x-6} = \dfrac{1}{x}$ **3**

51. $\dfrac{3}{x^2 + 3x} + \dfrac{x+2}{x+3} = \dfrac{1}{x}$ **−1; extraneous 0**

52. $\dfrac{1}{n+4} - \dfrac{1}{n-1} = \dfrac{2}{n^2 + 3n - 4}$ **no solution**

Vocabulary and Concepts

Choose the letter that best matches each algebraic expression.

1. $\dfrac{\frac{a}{b}}{\frac{x}{y}}$ **a**

2. $3 - \dfrac{a+1}{a-1}$ **c**

3. $\dfrac{2}{x^2 + 2x - 4}$ **b**

a. complex fraction
b. rational expression
c. mixed expression

Skills and Applications

Write an inverse variation equation that relates x and y. Assume that y varies inversely as x. Then solve.

4. If $y = 21$ when $x = 40$, find y when $x = 84$. $xy = 840; 10$

5. If $y = 22$ when $x = 4$, find x when $y = 16$. $xy = 88; 5.5$

Simplify each expression. State the excluded values of the variables.

6. $\dfrac{5 - 2m}{6m - 15}$ $-\dfrac{1}{3}; \dfrac{5}{2}$

7. $\dfrac{3 + x}{2x^2 + 5x - 3} \cdot \dfrac{1}{2x - 1}$; $-3, \dfrac{1}{2}$

8. $\dfrac{4c^2 + 12c + 9}{2c^2 - 11c - 21} \cdot \dfrac{2c + 3}{c - 7}$; $-\dfrac{3}{2}, 7$

9. $\dfrac{1 - \frac{9}{t}}{1 - \frac{81}{t^2}}$ $\dfrac{t}{t + 9}$; $-9, 0, 9$

10. $\dfrac{\frac{5}{6} + \frac{u}{t}}{\frac{2u}{t} - 3}$ $\dfrac{6u + 5t}{12u - 18t}$; $n \neq \dfrac{3}{2}t, 0$

11. $\dfrac{x + 4 + \frac{5}{x - 2}}{x + 6 + \frac{15}{x - 2}}$ $\dfrac{x - 1}{x + 1}$; $-3, -1, 2$

Perform the indicated operations.

12. $\dfrac{2x}{x - 7} - \dfrac{14}{x - 7}$ **2**

13. $\dfrac{n + 3}{2n - 8} \cdot \dfrac{6n - 24}{2n + 1}$ $\dfrac{3n + 9}{2n + 1}$

14. $(10m^2 + 9m - 36) \div (2m - 3)$ $5m + 12$

15. $\dfrac{x^2 + 4x - 32}{x + 5} \cdot \dfrac{x - 3}{x^2 - 7x + 12}$ $\dfrac{x + 8}{x + 5}$

16. $\dfrac{z^2 + 2z - 15}{z^2 + 9z + 20} \div (z - 3)$ $\dfrac{1}{z + 4}$

17. $\dfrac{4x^2 + 11x + 6}{x^2 - x - 6} \div \dfrac{x^2 + 8x + 16}{x^2 + x - 12}$ $\dfrac{4x + 3}{x + 4}$

18. $(10z^4 + 5z^3 - z^2) \div 5z^3$ $2z + 1 - \dfrac{1}{5z}$

19. $\dfrac{y}{7y + 14} + \dfrac{6}{6 - 3y}$ $\dfrac{y^2 - 16y - 28}{7(x + 2)(x - 2)}$

20. $\dfrac{x + 5}{x + 2} + 6$ $\dfrac{7x + 17}{x + 2}$

21. $\dfrac{x^2 - 1}{x + 1} - \dfrac{x^2 + 1}{x - 1} - \dfrac{2x}{x - 1}$

Solve each equation. State any extraneous solutions.

22. $\dfrac{2n}{n - 4} - 2 = \dfrac{4}{n + 5}$ -14

23. $\dfrac{3}{x^2 + 5x + 6} - \dfrac{7}{x + 3} = -\dfrac{x - 1}{x + 2}$ 7; extraneous -2

24. **FINANCE** Barrington High School is raising money for Habitat for Humanity by doing lawn work for friends and neighbors. Scott can rake a lawn and bag the leaves in 5 hours, while Kalyn can do it in 3 hours. If Scott and Kalyn work together, how long will it take them to rake a lawn and bag the leaves? $1\dfrac{7}{8}$ h

25. **STANDARDIZED TEST PRACTICE** Which expression can be used to represent the area of the triangle? **B**

Ⓐ $\dfrac{1}{2}(x - y)$

Ⓑ $\dfrac{3}{2}(x - y)$

Ⓒ $\dfrac{1}{4}(x - y)$

Ⓓ $\dfrac{108}{x + y}$

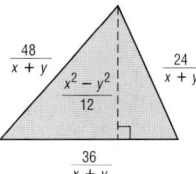

 www.algebra1.com/chapter_test

Chapter 12 Practice Test **701**

Chapter 12 Practice Test

Assessment Options

Vocabulary Test A vocabulary test/review for Chapter 12 can be found on p. 772 of the *Chapter 12 Resource Masters.*

Chapter Tests There are six Chapter 12 Tests and an Open-Ended Assessment task available in the *Chapter 12 Resource Masters.*

Chapter 12 Tests			
Form	Type	Level	Pages
1	MC	basic	759–760
2A	MC	average	761–762
2B	MC	average	763–764
2C	FR	average	765–766
2D	FR	average	767–768
3	FR	advanced	769–770

MC = multiple-choice questions
FR = free-response questions

Open-Ended Assessment Performance tasks for Chapter 12 can be found on p. 771 of the *Chapter 12 Resource Masters.* A sample scoring rubric for these tasks appears on p. A34.

Unit 4 Test A unit test/review can be found on pp. 779–780 of the *Chapter 12 Resource Masters.*

 ExamView® Pro

Use the networkable **ExamView® Pro** to:

- Create **multiple versions** of tests.
- Create **modified** tests for *Inclusion* students.
- **Edit** existing questions and **add** your own questions.
- Use built-in **state curriculum correlations** to create tests aligned with state standards.
- Change **English** tests to **Spanish** and vice versa.

Portfolio Suggestion

Introduction In this chapter, you learned the many different operations used with rational algebraic expressions. Think back to when you first learned about fractions. Fractions are also rational expressions.

Ask Students Pick several of the concepts that you learned in this chapter. Demonstrate them with rational numbers and fractions. How are fractions similar to rational expressions?

Chapter 12 Practice Test **701**

These two pages contain practice questions in the various formats that can be found on the most frequently given standardized tests.

A practice answer sheet for these two pages can be found on p. A1 of the *Chapter 12 Resource Masters*.

Standardized Test Practice
Student Recording Sheet, p. A1

Part 1 Multiple Choice

Select the best answer from the choices given and fill in the corresponding oval.

1. Ⓐ Ⓑ Ⓒ Ⓓ   4. Ⓐ Ⓑ Ⓒ Ⓓ   7. Ⓐ Ⓑ Ⓒ Ⓓ
2. Ⓐ Ⓑ Ⓒ Ⓓ   5. Ⓐ Ⓑ Ⓒ Ⓓ   8. Ⓐ Ⓑ Ⓒ Ⓓ
3. Ⓐ Ⓑ Ⓒ Ⓓ   6. Ⓐ Ⓑ Ⓒ Ⓓ

Part 2 Short Response/Grid In

Solve the problem and write your answer in the blank.

For Questions 9, 11, 13, and 15, also enter your answer by writing each number or symbol in a box. Then fill in the corresponding oval for that number or symbol.

9 _____ (grid in)
10 _____
11 _____ (grid in)
12 _____
13 _____ (grid in)
14 _____
15 _____ (grid in)
16 _____
17 _____
18 _____
19 _____

Part 3 Extended Response

Record your answers for Questions 20–21 on the back of this paper.

Teaching Tip In Question 6, remind students that an ordered pair must satisfy both equations to be a solution.

Additional Practice

See pp. 777–778 in the *Chapter 12 Resource Masters* for additional standardized test practice.

Part 1 Multiple Choice

Record your answers on the answer sheet provided by your teacher or on a sheet of paper.

1. A cylindrical container is 8 inches in height and has a radius of 2.5 inches. What is the volume of the container to the nearest cubic inch? (*Hint:* $V = \pi r^2 h$) (Lesson 3-8) **D**

   Ⓐ 63   Ⓑ 126
   Ⓒ 150   Ⓓ 157

2. Which function includes all of the ordered pairs in the table? (Lesson 4-8) **B**

x	−3	−1	1	3	5
y	10	4	−2	−8	−14

   Ⓐ $y = -2x$ Ⓑ $y = -3x + 1$
   Ⓒ $y = 2x - 4$ Ⓓ $y = 3x + 1$

3. Which equation describes the graph below? (Lesson 5-4) **B**

   Ⓐ $4x - 5y = 40$
   Ⓑ $4x + 5y = -40$
   Ⓒ $4x + 5y = -8$
   Ⓓ $rx - 5y = 10$

   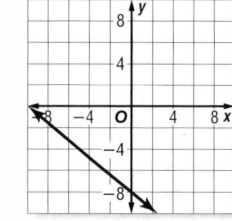

4. Which equation represents the line that passes through $(-12, 5)$ and has a slope of $-\frac{1}{4}$? (Lesson 5-5) **A**

   Ⓐ $x + 4y = 8$ Ⓑ $-x + 4y = 20$
   Ⓒ $-4x + y = 65$ Ⓓ $x + 4y = 5$

   Test-Taking Tip Ⓐ Ⓑ Ⓒ Ⓓ

   Questions 2, 4, 8
   Sometimes sketching the graph of a function can help you to see the relationship between *x* and *y* and answer the question.

5. Which inequality represents the shaded region? (Lesson 6-6) **D**

   Ⓐ $y \le -\frac{1}{2}x - 2$
   Ⓑ $y \ge -\frac{1}{2}x + 2$
   Ⓒ $y \le -2x + 2$
   Ⓓ $y \ge -2x + 2$

   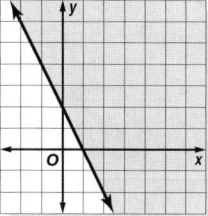

6. Which ordered pair is the solution of the following system of equations? (Lesson 7-4) **B**

   $$3x + y = -2$$
   $$-2x + y = 8$$

   Ⓐ $(-6, 16)$ Ⓑ $(-2, 4)$
   Ⓒ $(-3, 2)$ Ⓓ $(2, -8)$

7. The length of a rectangular door is 2.5 times its width. If the area of the door is 9750 square inches, which equation will determine the width *w* of the door? (Lesson 8-1) **B**

   Ⓐ $w^2 + 2.5w = 9750$
   Ⓑ $2.5w^2 = 9750$
   Ⓒ $2.5w^2 + 9750 = 0$
   Ⓓ $7w = 9750$

8. A scientist monitored a 144-gram sample of a radioactive substance, which decays into a nonradioactive substance. The table shows the amount, in grams, of the radioactive substance remaining at intervals of 20 hours. How many grams of the radioactive substance are likely to remain after 100 hours? (Lessons 10-6 and 10-7) **C**

Time (h)	0	20	40	60	80	100
Mass (g)	144	72	36			

   Ⓐ 1 g   Ⓑ 2.25 g
   Ⓒ 4.5 g   Ⓓ 9 g

ExamView® Pro

Special banks of standardized test questions similar to those on the SAT, ACT, TIMSS 8, NAEP 8, and Algebra 1 End-of-Course tests can be found on this CD-ROM.

Preparing for Standardized Tests
For test-taking strategies and more
practice, see pages 867–884.

Part 2 Short Response/Grid In

Record your answers on the answer sheet
provided by your teacher or on a sheet of
paper.

9. A family drove an average of 350 miles
per day during three days of their trip.
They drove 360 miles on the first day and
270 miles on the second day. How many
miles did they drive on the third day?
(Lesson 3-4) **420**

10. The area of the rectangular playground at
Hillcrest School is 750 square meters. The
length of the playground is 5 meters greater
than its width. What are the length and
width of the playground in meters?
(Lesson 9-5) **$\ell = 30$, $w = 25$**

11. How many roots does the graph of
$y = x^2 + 2x + 3$ have? (Lesson 10-2) **0**

12. Use the Quadratic Formula or factoring
to determine whether the graph of
$y = 16x^2 + 24x + 9$ intersects the x-axis
in zero, one, or two points.   (Lesson 10-4) **one**

13. Find the length of the hypotenuse of a right
triangle if one leg is 6 inches and the other
leg is $\sqrt{10}$ inches. Round to the nearest
tenth of an inch. (Lesson 11-4) **6.8 in.**

14. Simplify $\dfrac{x^2 - 7x + 6}{x^2 + 6x - 7}$. State the excluded
values of x. (Lesson 12-2). $\dfrac{(x-6)}{(x+7)}$; **1, −7**

15. An airplane travels approximately 1030
kilometers per hour. Approximately what
is its speed in meters per second?
(Lesson 12-3) **286**

16. Express $\dfrac{x^2 - 9}{x^3 + x} \cdot \dfrac{3x}{x - 3}$ as a quotient of
two polynomials written in simplest form.
(Lesson 12-3) $\dfrac{3x + 9}{x^2 + 1}$

17. Find $\dfrac{a + 3}{2a + 6} \div \dfrac{6a - 24}{4a + 12}$. (Lesson 12-4) $\dfrac{a + 3}{3(a - 4)}$

18. Express the following quotient in simplest
form.   (Lesson 12-5)
$$\frac{x}{x + 4} \div \frac{4x}{x^2 - 16} \quad \frac{x - 4}{4} \text{ or } \frac{1}{4}x - 1$$

19. Find the
expression for
the perimeter of
the triangle. $\dfrac{9}{t - 10}$
(Lesson 12-6)

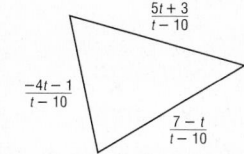

Part 3 Extended Response

Record your answers on a sheet of paper.
Show your work. **20b–c. See margin.**

20. A 12-foot ladder is placed against the
side of a building so that the bottom of
the ladder is 6 feet from the base of the
building.   (Lesson 12-1)

a. Suppose the
bottom of the ladder
is moved closer to
the base of the
building. Does the
height that the ladder
reaches increase or
decrease? **increase**

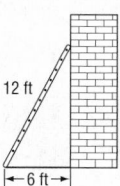

b. What conclusion can you make about the
height the ladder reaches and the
distance between the bottom of the
ladder and the base of the building?

c. Does this relationship form an inverse
variation? Explain your reasoning.

21a. downstream: $\dfrac{30}{8 + c}$, upstream: $\dfrac{18}{8 - c}$

21. The maximum speed of a barge in still water
is 8 miles per hour. At this rate, a 30-mile
trip downstream (with the current) takes as
much time as an 18-mile trip upstream
(against the current).   (Lesson 12-9)

a. Find the rational expressions that
measure the amount of time it takes
for the barge to go downstream and
upstream if c represents the speed of the
current.

b. What is the speed of the current? **2 mph**

Chapters 12   Standardized Test Practice   **703**

Evaluating Extended Response Questions

Extended Response questions
are graded by using a multilevel
rubric that guides you in
assessing a student's knowledge
of a particular concept.

Goal: Students examine a
relationship to see if it is inverse.

Sample Scoring Rubric: The
following rubric is a sample
scoring device. You may wish to
add more detail to this sample to
meet your individual scoring
needs.

Score	Criteria
4	A correct solution that is supported by well-developed, accurate explanations
3	A generally correct solution, but may contain minor flaws in reasoning or computation
2	A partially correct interpretation and/or solution to the problem
1	A correct solution with no supporting evidence or explanation
0	An incorrect solution indicating no mathematical understanding of the concept or task, or no solution is given

Answers

21b. Sample answer: As the distance
between the bottom of the ladder
and the base of the building
decreases, the height that the
ladder reaches increases.

21c. No; sample answer: When the
bottom of the ladder is 6 feet from
the base of the building, it reaches a
height of about 10.4 feet. When the
bottom of the ladder is 4 feet from
the base of the building, it reaches
a height of about 11.3 feet. In order

to form an inverse variation, $6 \cdot 10.4$ must
approximately equal $4 \cdot 11.3$. However,
$6 \cdot 10.4 = 63.6$ and $4 \cdot 11.3 = 45.2$.
Because the products are not equal, this
relationship does not form an inverse
variation.

UNIT 5 Notes

Introduction

In this unit, students will learn how to analyze data using statistical analysis. This includes understanding sampling techniques, histograms, and box-and-whisker plots. Students will then learn how to use probability to predict outcomes.

Assessment Options

Unit 5 Test Pages 881–882 of the *Chapter 14 Resource Masters* may be used as a test or review for Unit 5. This assessment contains both multiple-choice and short answer items.

ExamView® Pro

This CD-ROM can be used to create additional unit tests and review worksheets.

Yearly Progress Pro

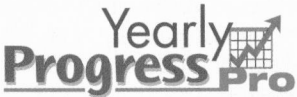

An online, research-based, instructional, assessment, and intervention tool that provides specific feedback on student mastery of state and national standards, instant remediation, and a data management system to track performance. For more information, contact mhdigitallearning.com.

UNIT 5 Data Analysis

Collecting and analyzing data allows you to make decisions and predictions about the future. In this unit, you will learn about statistics and probability.

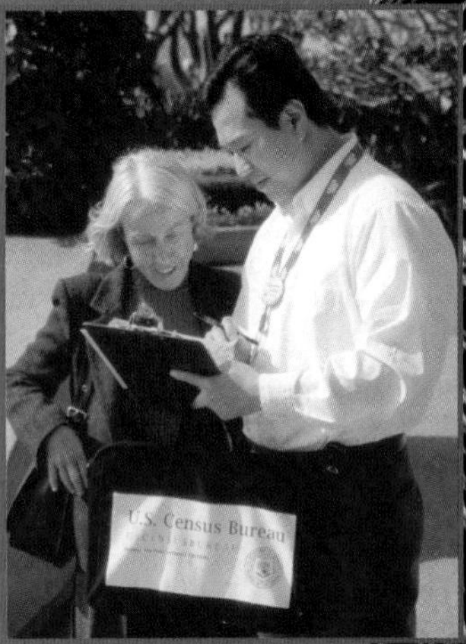

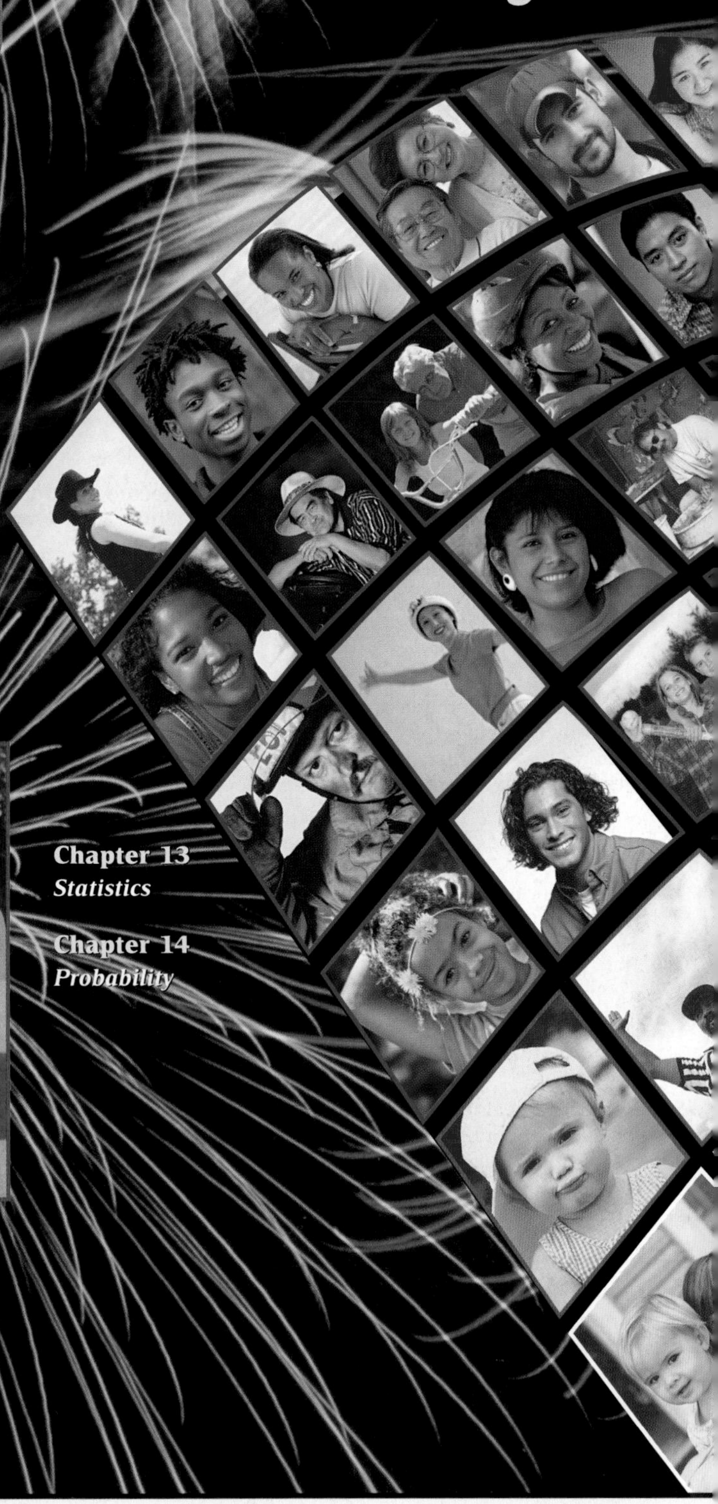

Chapter 13
Statistics

Chapter 14
Probability

What's MATH Got To Do With It?

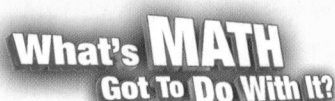

Real-Life Math Videos

What's Math Got to Do With It? Real-Life Math Videos engage students by showing them how math is used in everyday situations. Use Video 4 with this unit.

Have students study the USA TODAY Snapshot.

- Ask students what they can determine from the data in the graph. **The population of the United States grew by 149 million in the 60 years from 1940 to 2000.**

- What might be needed to predict the population of the United States in the year 2050? **Sample answer: More information about the population growth rate and how much it has increased annually.**

Additional USA TODAY Snapshots appearing in Unit 5:

Chapter 13 Cheaper wireless talk (p. 730)

Chapter 14 Women follow football on TV (p. 780)

WebQuest Internet Project

America Counts!

he U.S. government has been counting each erson in the country since its first Census following ndependence was taken in 1790. Befitting the first ensus of the 21st century, the Census Bureau llowed Census 2000 questionnaires to be completed lectronically for the first time. In this project, you ill see how data analysis can be used to compare tatistics about a state of your choice to other states the United States.

Log on to www.algebra1.com/webquest. Begin your WebQuest by reading the Task.

hen continue working
 your WebQuest as
ou study Unit 5.

Lesson	13-5	14-2
Page	742	766

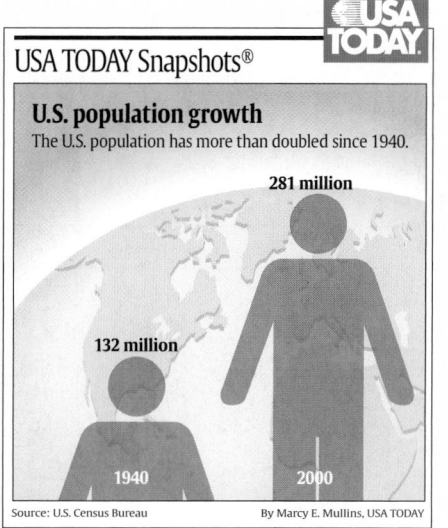

USA TODAY Snapshots®

U.S. population growth
The U.S. population has more than doubled since 1940.

281 million

132 million

1940   2000

Source: U.S. Census Bureau   By Marcy E. Mullins, USA TODAY

WebQuest Internet Project

Problem-Based Learning A WebQuest is an online project in which students do research on the Internet, gather data, and make presentations using word processing, graphing, page-making, or presentation software. In each chapter, students advance to the next step in their WebQuest. At the end of Chapter 14, the project culminates with a presentation of their findings.

Teaching notes and sample answers are available in the *WebQuest and Project Resources*.

Statistics
Chapter Overview and Pacing

Year-long and two-year pacing: pages T20–T21.

LESSON OBJECTIVES	PACING (days)			
	Regular		Block	
	Basic/ Average	Advanced	Basic/ Average	Advanced
13-1 Sampling and Bias *(pp. 708–713)* • Identify various sampling techniques. • Recognize a biased sample.	optional	2	optional	1.5
13-2 Introduction to Matrices *(pp. 715–721)* • Organize data in matrices. • Solve problems by adding or subtracting matrices or by multiplying by a scalar.	optional	2	optional	1
13-3 Histograms *(pp. 722–730)* • Interpret data displayed in histograms. • Display data in histograms. *Follow-Up:* Use a graphing calculator to find an appropriate regression equation.	optional	2	optional	1
13-4 Measures of Variation *(pp. 731–736)* • Find the range of a set of data. • Find the quartiles and interquartile range of a set of data.	optional	2	optional	1
13-5 Box-and-Whisker Plots *(pp. 737–744)* • Organize and use data in box-and-whisker plots. • Organize and use data in parallel box-and-whisker plots. *Follow-Up:* Use tables to determine percentiles.	optional	3	optional	1.5
Study Guide and **Practice Test** *(pp. 745–749)* **Standardized Test Practice** *(pp. 750–751)*	optional	1	optional	0.5
Chapter Assessment	optional	1	optional	0.5
TOTAL		13		7

*An electronic version of this chapter is available on **StudentWorks**™. This backpack solution CD-ROM allows students instant access to the Student Edition, lesson worksheet pages, and web resources.*

Chapter Resource Manager

Timesaving Tools
TeacherWorks™
All-In-One Planner and Resource Center
See pages T5 and T21.

CHAPTER 13 RESOURCE MASTERS

Study Guide and Intervention	Practice (Skills and Average)	Reading to Learn Mathematics	Enrichment	Assessment	Prerequisite Skills Workbook	Applications*	Parent and Student Study Guide Workbook	5-Minute Check Transparencies	Interactive Chalkboard	AlgePASS: Tutorial Plus (lessons)	Materials
781–782	783–784	785	786				101	13-1	13-1		
787–788	789–790	791	792	825		GCS 47	102	13-2	13-2		graphing calculator
793–794	795–796	797	798	825, 827	97–98	GCS 48, SC 25	103	13-3	13-3		graphing calculator, (*Follow-Up:* graphing calculator)
799–800	801–802	803	804	826	1–2, 19–20		104	13-4	13-4		
805–806	807–808	809	810	826		SC 26, SM 103–108	105	13-5	13-5	34	(*Preview:* ruler)
				811–824, 828–830			106				

Key to Abbreviations: GCS = Graphing Calculator and Spreadsheet Masters,
SC = School-to-Career Masters,
SM = Science and Mathematics Lab Manual

ELL Study Guide and Intervention, Skills Practice, Practice, and Parent and Student Study Guide Workbooks are also available in Spanish.

Mathematical Connections and Background

Continuity of Instruction

Prior Knowledge

Students were introduced to analyzing data in tables and graphs, and to determining whether these data are misleading in Chapter 1. In Chapter 2, students learned to add, subtract, and multiply real numbers and how to represent data in line plots and stem-and-leaf plots. They also learned to use the mean, median, and mode of data sets. In Chapter 5, students interpreted scatter plots and found lines of fit.

This Chapter

Students go beyond what they have already learned about statistics by identifying various sampling techniquesand interpreting data. They learn how to organize data in matrices, and manipulate the data by adding and subtracting matrices, or by scalar multiplication. Students then interpret data in histograms, and find the range, quartiles, and interquartile ranges of data sets. Finally students organize and use data in box-and-whisker plots.

Future Connections

Whether on television, in newspapers, or on the Internet, statistics are used to sway public opinion, to inform, or to persuade the public to buy a product. Being able to interpret these statistics is important to being able to make sound decisions. The decisions made based on statistics vary from the trivial, such as what shampoo to buy, to the most important, such as who to vote for in an upcoming election.

13-1 Sampling and Bias

To understand sampling techniques, students must first understand that a sample is a small portion of a larger group called a population. Samples are taken to represent a group because they are smaller and easier to survey. If an entire population is included in a sample, it is a census. Samples are used to find preferences or characteristics of a population.

A sample that is chosen without preference is a random sample. Random samples are chosen in different ways. A simple random sample is exactly as it sounds, with members picked at random from a population without bias. If a population is first segregated into non-overlapping groups, from which random samples are taken, then it is a stratified random sample. An example would be if an algebra teacher randomly chose three people from each of his of her classes. A systematic random sample is picked by following a certain pattern, such as picking every fifth person who walks by.

Samples are biased if they favor one or more parts of a population. Biased samples include convenience samples, in which members of the sample are picked because they are convenient for the person taking the sample. Another example of a biased sample is a voluntary response sample. It is biased because the members of the sample only replied if they wanted to be included.

13-2 Introduction to Matrices

A matrix is a rectangular array of numerical data arranged in regular rows and columns. The dimensions of a matrix are the number of rows and columns in the matrix. Each entry in a matrix is called an element.

If two matrices have the same dimensions, then they can be added or subtracted by adding or subtracting the corresponding elements of the two matrices. If their dimensions are not the same, then they cannot be added or subtracted. Matrices can also be multiplied by a single real number called a scalar. In scalar multiplication, each member of a matrix is multiplied by the same scalar.

13-3 Histograms

Imagine surveying 20 people leaving a shopping mall and finding out that 4 have spent $100 or more, but less than $150. Six have spent $50 or more, but less than $100, and 10 have spent less than $50. These data can be represented in a two-column frequency table. The left column has three intervals, $0–$50, $50–$100, and $100–$150. Then the next column shows the number of people who fit into each category. Each person is counted with a tally mark. The amount represented by the tallies for a category is called the frequency for each category.

Now display the data from the frequency table as a bar graph. The horizontal axis would correspond to the left column of the table, showing three measurement classes; $0–$50, $50–$100, and $100–$150. These must be organized in equal intervals. The vertical axis would correspond to the right column, and would display the frequency for each measurement class. This graph is known as a histogram.

Histograms are used to compare data visually. You can quickly determine form looking at the bars which measurement class has the most, the least, etc.

13-4 Measures of Variation

Knowing how a set of data varies is often very helpful in interpreting the data. Mean, median, and mode, which were studied in Chapter 2, are measures of central tendency. Measures that describe the spread of the values in a set of data are called measures of variation. One such measure is the range, which is the difference between the greatest and least data values. Quartiles are another measure of variation. They are values that separate the data into four equal subsets. The lower quartile separates the lower half of the data into two equal parts. The upper quartile separates the upper half of the data into two equal parts. The interquartile range is the difference between the upper and lower quartiles. An outlier is a value in a set of data that is much less or much greater than the rest of the data.

13-5 Box-and-Whisker Plots

Use a box-and-whisker plot to graphically represent the measures of variation on a number line. The box portion of a box-and-whisker plot extends from the lower quartile to the upper quartile, with the median denoted within the box. The box represents the interquartile range. The whiskers extend from the lower quartile to the least value, and from the upper quartile to the greatest value. If either the greatest or least values are outliers, then the whiskers extend to the least or greatest values that are not outliers. The ends of the whiskers are the extreme values.

Two sets of data can be compared by drawing two box-and-whisker plots above the same number line. This display is called parallel box-and-whisker plots.

Quick Review Math Handbook

Hot Words includes a glossary of terms while Hot Topics consists of explanations of key mathematical concepts with exercises to test comprehension. This valuable resource can be used as a reference in the classroom or for home study.

Lesson	Hot Topics Section	Lesson	Hot Topics Section
GS13	4.4, 5.2	13-3F	4.3
13-1	2.6, 4.1	13-4	4.2, 4.3
13-2	4.2	13-5	4.2
13-3	4.2, 4.4	13-5F	4.2

GS = Getting Started, F = Follow-Up

 Additional mathematical information and teaching notes are available at www.algebra1.com/key_concepts.

DAILY INTERVENTION and Assessment

Key to Abbreviations:
TWE = Teacher Wraparound Edition; CRM = Chapter Resource Masters

Type	Student Edition	Teacher Resources	Technology/Internet
INTERVENTION Ongoing	Prerequisite Skills, pp. 707, 721, 728, 736 Practice Quiz 1, p. 721 Practice Quiz 2, p. 736	5-Minute Check Transparencies *Prerequisite Skills Workbook*, pp. 1–2, 19–20, 97–98 Quizzes, *CRM* pp. 825–826 Mid-Chapter Test, *CRM* p. 827 Study Guide and Intervention, *CRM* pp. 781–782, 787–788, 793–794, 799–800, 805–806	AlgePASS: Tutorial Plus, Lesson 34 www.algebra1.com/self_check_quiz www.algebra1.com/extra_examples
Mixed Review	pp. 713, 721, 728, 736, 742	Cumulative Review, *CRM* p. 828	
Error Analysis	Find the Error, pp. 717, 733	Find the Error, *TWE* pp. 717, 733 Unlocking Misconceptions, *TWE* pp. 725, 732, 738 Tips for New Teachers, *TWE* p. 724	
ASSESSMENT Standardized Test Practice	pp. 713, 720, 723, 724, 726, 728, 736, 742, 749, 750–751	*TWE* pp. 750–751 Standardized Test Practice, *CRM* pp. 829–830	Standardized Test Practice CD-ROM www.algebra1.com/ standardized_test
Open-Ended Assessment	Writing in Math, pp. 713, 720, 728, 736, 742 Open Ended, pp. 710, 717, 725, 733, 739 Standardized Test, p. 751	Modeling: *TWE* p. 728 Speaking: *TWE* pp. 713, 736 Writing: *TWE* pp. 721, 742 Open-Ended Assessment, *CRM* p. 823	
Chapter Assessment	Study Guide, pp. 745–748 Practice Test, p. 749	Multiple-Choice Tests (Forms 1, 2A, 2B), *CRM* pp. 811–816 Free-Response Tests (Forms 2C, 2D, 3), *CRM* pp. 817–822 Vocabulary Test/Review, *CRM* p. 824	ExamView® Pro (see below) MindJogger Videoquizzes www.algebra1.com/ vocabulary_review www.algebra1.com/chapter_test

For more information on Yearly ProgressPro, see p. 704.

Algebra Lesson	Yearly ProgressPro Skill Lesson
13-1	Sampling and Bias
13-2	Introduction to Matrices
13-3	Histograms
13-4	Measures of Variation
13-5	Box-and-Whisker Plots

ExamView® Pro

Use the networkable **ExamView® Pro** to:
- Create **multiple versions** of tests.
- Create **modified** tests for *Inclusion* students.
- **Edit** existing questions and **add** your own questions.
- Use built-in **state curriculum correlations** to create tests aligned with state standards.
- Change **English** tests to **Spanish** and vice versa.

For more information on Intervention and Assessment, see pp. T8–T11.

Reading and Writing in Mathematics

Glencoe Algebra 1 provides numerous opportunities to incorporate reading and writing into the mathematics classroom.

Student Edition

- Foldables Study Organizer, p. 707
- Concept Check questions require students to verbalize and write about what they have learned in the lesson. (pp. 710, 717, 725, 733, 739)
- Reading Mathematics, p. 714
- Writing in Math questions in every lesson, pp. 713, 720, 728, 736, 742
- Reading Study Tip, pp. 732, 737
- WebQuest, p. 742

Teacher Wraparound Edition

- Foldables Study Organizer, pp. 707, 745
- Study Notebook suggestions, pp. 711, 714, 718, 725, 734, 740, 744
- Modeling activities, p. 728
- Speaking activities, pp. 713, 736
- Writing activities, pp. 721, 742
- Differentiated Instruction, (Verbal/Linguistic), p. 720
- **ELL** Resources, pp. 706, 712, 714, 719, 720, 726, 735, 741, 745

Additional Resources

- Vocabulary Builder worksheets require students to define and give examples for key vocabulary terms as they progress through the chapter. (*Chapter 13 Resource Masters*, pp. vii-viii)
- Reading to Learn Mathematics master for each lesson (*Chapter 13 Resource Masters*, pp. 785, 791, 797, 803, 809)
- *Vocabulary PuzzleMaker* software creates crossword, jumble, and word search puzzles using vocabulary lists that you can customize.
- *Teaching Mathematics with Foldables* provides suggestions for promoting cognition and language.
- *Reading and Writing in the Mathematics Classroom*
- *WebQuest and Project Resources*
- *Hot Words/Hot Topics* Sections 2.6, 4.1–4.4, 5.2

For more information on Reading and Writing in Mathematics, see pp. T6–T7.

 **ENGLISH LANGUAGE LEARNERS**

Lesson 13-1
Flexible Groups

Have groups of students create a concept map of all the new vocabulary listed in the lesson. Have students make their map in three columns: one with the term, the next with its definition, and the last with an example.

Lesson 13-3
Higher-Level Thinking

After completing the lesson, have students construct a compare and contrast graphic organizer comparing a bar graph and a histogram. Students should list how the two graphs are alike and how they are different. Have them also note any similarities or differences and when they would use each graph.

Lesson 13-5
Using Applications

Give groups of students the daily high temperatures of a city for the previous month. Have each group analyze the data of their city and construct a box-and-whisker plot. Then, have each group present their findings and a description of the data distribution for their city to the rest of the class.

What You'll Learn

Have students read over the list of objectives and make a list of any words with which they are not familiar.

Why It's Important

Point out to students that this is only one of many reasons why each objective is important. Others are provided in the introduction to each lesson.

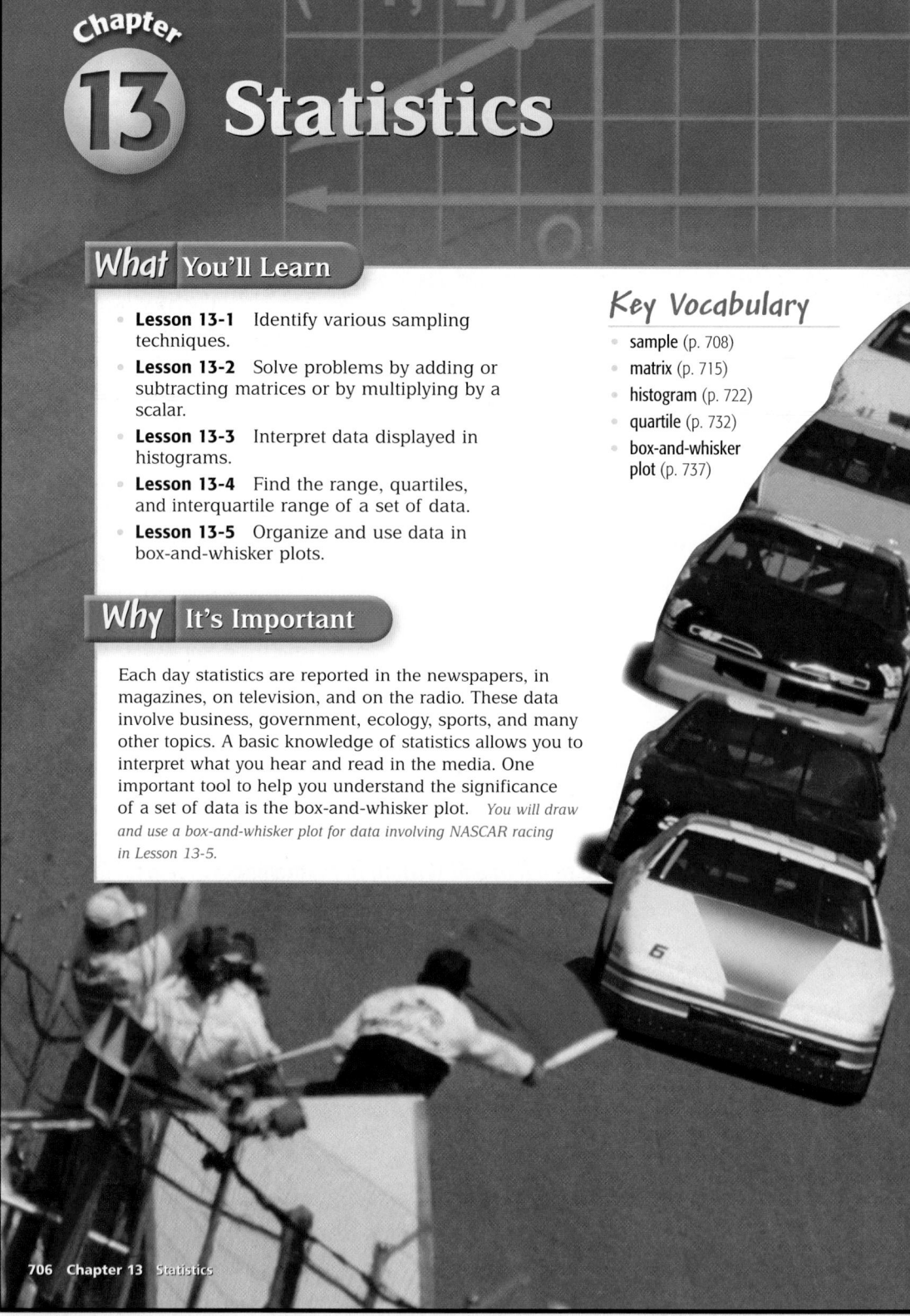

What You'll Learn

- **Lesson 13-1** Identify various sampling techniques.
- **Lesson 13-2** Solve problems by adding or subtracting matrices or by multiplying by a scalar.
- **Lesson 13-3** Interpret data displayed in histograms.
- **Lesson 13-4** Find the range, quartiles, and interquartile range of a set of data.
- **Lesson 13-5** Organize and use data in box-and-whisker plots.

Key Vocabulary

- **sample** (p. 708)
- **matrix** (p. 715)
- **histogram** (p. 722)
- **quartile** (p. 732)
- **box-and-whisker plot** (p. 737)

Why It's Important

Each day statistics are reported in the newspapers, in magazines, on television, and on the radio. These data involve business, government, ecology, sports, and many other topics. A basic knowledge of statistics allows you to interpret what you hear and read in the media. One important tool to help you understand the significance of a set of data is the box-and-whisker plot. *You will draw and use a box-and-whisker plot for data involving NASCAR racing in Lesson 13-5.*

706 Chapter 13 Statistics

Lesson	NCTM Standards	Local Objectives
13-1	1, 5, 6, 8, 9	
13-2	1, 5, 6, 8, 9, 10	
13-3	1, 5, 6, 8, 9, 10	
13-3 Follow-Up	5, 6, 8, 9	
13-4	1, 5, 6, 8, 9, 10	
13-5	1, 5, 6, 8, 9, 10	
13-5 Follow-Up	1, 5, 6, 9, 10	

Key to NCTM Standards:

1=Number & Operations, 2=Algebra, 3=Geometry, 4=Measurement, 5=Data Analysis & Probability, 6=Problem Solving, 7=Reasoning & Proof, 8=Communication, 9=Connections, 10=Representation

Vocabulary Builder   ELL

The Key Vocabulary list introduces students to some of the main vocabulary terms included in this chapter. For a more thorough vocabulary list with pronunciations of new words, give students the Vocabulary Builder worksheets found on pages vii and viii of the *Chapter 13 Resource Masters*. Encourage them to complete the definition of each term as they progress through the chapter. You may suggest that they add these sheets to their study notebooks for future reference when studying for the Chapter 13 test.

Getting Started

▶ **Prerequisite Skills** To be successful in this chapter, you'll need to master these skills and be able to apply them in problem-solving situations. Review these skills before beginning Chapter 13.

For Lesson 13-1   **Use Logical Reasoning**

Find a counterexample for each statement. *(For review, see Lesson 1-7.)*

1. If $a + b = c$, then $a < c$. **Sample answer: If $a = 5$ and $b = -2$, then $c = 3$. However, $5 > 3$.**

2. If a flower is a rose, then it is red. **Sample answer: It could be a yellow rose.**

3. If Tara obeys the speed limit, then she will drive 45 miles per hour or less.

4. If a number is even, then it is divisible by 4. **Sample answer: 6 is even, but not divisible by 4.**

> 3. Sample answer: The speed limit could be 55 mph, and Tara could be driving 50 mph.

For Lesson 13-4   **Find the Median**

Find the median for each set of data. *(For review, see pages 818 and 819.)*

5. 1, 7, 9, 15, 25, 59, 63   **15**

6. 0, 10, 2, 2, 9, 5, 4, 2, 8, 3, 8, 7, 3   **4**

7. 726, 411, 407, 407, 395, 355, 317, 235, 218, 211   **375**

For Lesson 13-5   **Graph Numbers on a Number Line**

Graph each set of numbers on a number line. *(For review, see Lesson 2-1.)*   **8–11. See margin.**

8. {7, 9, 10, 13, 14}
9. {15, 17.5, 19, 20.5, 23}
10. {3.2, 4.8, 5.0, 5.7, 6.1}
11. {2.3, 2.8, 3.1, 3.7, 4.5}

FOLDABLES™ Study Organizer

Statistics Make this Foldable to help you organize your notes. Begin with three sheets of plain $8\frac{1}{2}$" by 11" paper.

Step 1   **Stack Pages**

Stack sheets of paper with edges $\frac{3}{4}$ inch apart.

Step 2   **Fold Up Bottom Edges**

Fold so that all the tabs are the same size.

Step 3   **Crease and Staple**

Staple along the fold.

Step 4   **Turn and Label**

Label the tabs with topics from the chapter.

Reading and Writing As you read and study the chapter, use each page to write notes and examples.

Getting Started

This section provides a review of the basic concepts needed before beginning Chapter 13. Page references are included for additional student help.

Additional review is provided in the *Prerequisite Skills Workbook*, pp. 1–2, 19–20, and 97–98.

Prerequisite Skills in the Getting Ready for the Next Lesson section at the end of each exercise set review a skill needed in the next lesson.

For Lesson	Prerequisite Skill
13-2	Finding Sums and Differences, p. 713
13-3	Interpreting Graphs, p. 721
13-4	Finding the Median, p. 728
13-5	Graphing Numbers on a Number Line, p. 736

Answers

8.
    7 8 9 10 11 12 13 14 15

9.
    15 16 17 18 19 20 21 22 23

10.
    3   4   5   6   7

11.
    1   2   3   4   5

FOLDABLES™ Study Organizer

For more information about Foldables, see *Teaching Mathematics with Foldables*.

Organization of Data and Statistics in Writing Students use their Foldables to take notes, define terms, record concepts, and write examples. On the back of the Foldable, have students record examples of statistics they see in everyday print—newspapers, magazines, and advertisements. Note how writers use statistics to prove or disprove points of view, and discuss the ethical responsibilities writers have when using statistics.

13-1 Sampling and Bias

1 Focus

5-Minute Check Transparency 13-1 Use as a quiz or review of Chapter 12.

Mathematical Background notes are available for this lesson on p. 706C.

Why is sampling important in manufacturing?

Ask students:

- Suppose the manufacturer produces 100 CDs an hour, and takes a sample every hour. How many CDs would be sampled in an 8-hour day? **8**

- What is an example of something you would sample at home? **Sample answer: While cooking, you might sample gravy to check that it tastes good.**

13-1 Sampling and Bias

What You'll Learn

- Identify various sampling techniques.
- Recognize a biased sample.

Vocabulary
- sample
- population
- census
- random sample
- simple random sample
- stratified random sample
- systematic random sample
- biased sample
- convenience sample
- voluntary response sample

Why is sampling important in manufacturing?

Manufacturing music CDs involves burning, or recording, copies from a master. However, not every burn is successful. It is costly and time-consuming to check every CD that is burned. Therefore, in order to monitor production, some CDs are picked at random and checked for defects.

SAMPLING TECHNIQUES When you wish to make an investigation, there are four ways that you can collect data.

- **published data** Use data that are already in a source like a newspaper or book.
- **observational study** Watch naturally occurring events and record the results.
- **experiment** Conduct an experiment and record the results.
- **survey** Ask questions of a group of people and record the results.

When performing an experiment or taking a survey, researchers often choose a sample. A **sample** is some portion of a larger group, called the **population**, selected to represent that group. If all of the units within a population are included, it is called a **census**. Sample data are often used to estimate a characteristic within an entire population, such as voting preferences prior to elections.

Population	Sample
all of the light bulbs manufactured on a production line	24 light bulbs selected from the production line
all of the water in a swimming pool	a test tube of water from the pool
all of the people in the United States	1509 people from throughout the United States

A **random sample** of a population is selected so that it is representative of the entire population. The sample is chosen without any preference. There are several ways to pick a random sample.

Key Concept — *Random Samples*

Type	Definition	Example
Simple Random Sample	A simple random sample is a sample that is as likely to be chosen as any other from the population.	The 26 students in a class are each assigned a different number from 1 to 26. Then three of the 26 numbers are picked at random.
Stratified Random Sample	In a stratified random sample, the population is first divided into similar, nonoverlapping groups. A simple random sample is then selected from each group.	The students in a school are divided into freshman, sophomores, juniors, and seniors. Then two students are randomly selected from each group of students.
Systematic Random Sample	In a systematic random sample, the items are selected according to a specified time or item interval.	Every 2 minutes, an item is pulled off the assembly line. or Every twentieth item is pulled off the assembly line.

Resource Manager

Workbook and Reproducible Masters

Chapter 13 Resource Masters
- Study Guide and Intervention, pp. 781–782
- Skills Practice, p. 783
- Practice, p. 784
- Reading to Learn Mathematics, p. 785
- Enrichment, p. 786

Parent and Student Study Guide Workbook, p. 101

 Transparencies

5-Minute Check Transparency 13-1
Answer Key Transparencies

 Technology

Interactive Chalkboard

Example 1   Classify a Random Sample

Example 1   Classify a Random Sample

ECOLOGY   Ten lakes are selected randomly from a list of all public-access lakes in Minnesota. Then 2 liters of water are drawn from 20 feet deep in each of the ten lakes.

a. Identify the sample and suggest a population from which it was selected.

The sample is ten 2-liter containers of lake water, one from each of 10 lakes. The population is lake water from all of the public-access lakes in Minnesota.

b. Classify the sample as *simple*, *stratified*, or *systematic*.

This is a simple random sample. Each of the ten lakes was equally likely to have been chosen from the list.

BIASED SAMPLE   Random samples are unbiased. In a **biased sample**, one or more parts of a population are favored over others.

Example 2   Identify Sample as Biased or Unbiased

Identify each sample as *biased* or *unbiased*. Explain your reasoning.

a. MANUFACTURING   Every 1000th bolt is pulled from the production line and measured for length.

The sample is chosen using a specified time interval. This is an unbiased sample because it is a systematic random sample.

b. MUSIC   Every tenth customer in line for a certain rock band's concert tickets is asked about his or her favorite rock band.

The sample is a biased sample because customers in line for concert tickets are more likely to name the band giving the concert as a favorite band.

Two popular forms of samples that are often biased include convenience samples and voluntary response samples.

Key Concept		Biased Samples
Type	**Definition**	**Example**
Convenience Sample	A convenience sample includes members of a population that are easily accessed.	To check spoilage, a produce worker selects 10 apples from the top of the bin. The 10 apples are unlikely to represent all of the apples in the bin.
Voluntary Response Sample	A voluntary response sample involves only those who want to participate in the sampling.	A radio call-in show records that 75% of its 40 callers voiced negative opinions about a local football team. Those 40 callers are unlikely to represent the entire local population. Volunteer callers are more likely to have strong opinions and are typically more negative than the entire population.

Example 3   Identify and Classify a Biased Sample

BUSINESS   The travel account records from 4 of the 20 departments in a corporation are to be reviewed. The accountant states that the first 4 departments to voluntarily submit their records will be reviewed.

a. Identify the sample and suggest a population from which it was selected.

The sample is the travel account records from 4 departments in the corporation. The population is the travel account records from all 20 departments in the corporation.

www.algebra1.com/extra_examples

2 Teach

SAMPLING TECHNIQUES

In-Class Example   Power Point®

Teaching Tip Remind students that the sample is what is taken, and the population is the group from which the sample is taken. A population does not have to be a group of people.

1 RETAIL Each day, a department store chain selects one male and one female shopper randomly from each of their 57 stores, and asks them survey questions about their shopping habits.

a. Identify the sample and suggest a population from which it was selected. **The sample is 57 male and 57 female shoppers each day. The population is shoppers in the chain's stores.**

b. Classify the sample as *simple*, *stratified*, or *systematic*. **This is a stratified random sample.**

BIASED SAMPLE

In-Class Example   Power Point®

2 Identify each sample as *biased* or *unbiased*. Explain your reasoning.

a. STUDENT COUNCIL The student council surveys the students in one classroom to decide the theme for the spring dance. **The sample is biased because it includes only the students in one classroom.**

b. SCHOOL The Parent Association surveys the parents of every fifth student on the school roster to decide whether to hold a fundraiser. **The sample is unbiased because the parents are picked using a systematic method.**

Teacher to Teacher

Patricia Taepke   South Hills H.S., West Covina, CA

"I copy pages 708 and 709 for my students to place in their Algebra 1 Study Notebooks. These pages contain a great deal of vocabulary that they may use for future reference. It is arranged in a very concise manner."

3 COMMUNITY The maintenance chairperson of a neighborhood association has been asked by the association to survey the residents of the neighborhood to find out when to hold a neighborhood clean up day. The chairperson decides to ask her immediate neighbors, and the neighbors in the houses directly across the street from her house.

a. Identify the sample, and suggest a population from which it was selected.
The sample is the chairperson's immediate neighbors and the neighbors across the street. The population is the residents of the neighborhood.

b. Classify the sample as a *convenience sample*, or a *voluntary response sample*. **This is a convenience sample because the chairperson asked only her closest neighbors.**

4 SCHOOL The high school Parent Association sent a letter to the parents of all graduating seniors asking them to return the enclosed ballot if they had a preference on where the graduation party was to be held.

a. Identify the sample. **The sample is a group of parents of the graduating seniors.**

b. Suggest a population from which the sample was selected. **The population is all the parents of the graduating seniors.**

c. State whether the sample is *unbiased* (random) or *biased*. If unbiased, classify it as *simple*, *stratified*, or *systematic*. If biased, classify it as *convenience* or *voluntary response*. **The sample is biased. It is a voluntary response sample.**

b. Classify the sample as *convenience* or *voluntary response*.
Since the departments voluntarily submit their records, this is a voluntary response sample.

Example 4 *Identify the Sample*

NEWS REPORTING For an article in the school paper, Rafael needs to determine whether students in his school believe that an arts center should be added to the school. He polls 15 of his friends who sing in the choir. Twelve of them think the school needs an arts center, so Rafael reports that 80% of the students surveyed support the project.

a. Identify the sample.
The sample is a group of students from the choir.

b. Suggest a population from which the sample was selected.
The population for the survey is all of the students in the school.

c. State whether the sample is *unbiased* (random) or *biased*. If unbiased, classify it as *simple*, *stratified*, or *systematic*. If biased, classify it as *convenience* or *voluntary response*.
The sample was not randomly selected from the entire student body. So the reported support is not likey to be representative of the student body. The sample is biased. Since Rafael polled only his friends, it is a convenience sample.

Check for Understanding

Concept Check

GUIDED PRACTICE KEY	
Exercises	Examples
4–7	1–4

4. a group of readers of a newspaper; all readers of the newspaper; biased; voluntary response

Guided Practice

5. work from 4 students; work from all students in the 1st period math class; biased; voluntary response

Study Tip

Reading Math
The data in Exercise 6 could be classified as **univariate**, because there is only one variable, strength. These data could also be classified as **measurement**, because there are different levels of strength measured.

1. Describe how the following three types of sampling techniques are similar and how they are different. **See margin.**
 • simple random sample
 • stratified random sample
 • systematic random sample

2. Explain the difference between a convenience sample and a voluntary response sample. **See margin.**

3. OPEN ENDED Give an example of a biased sample. **Sample answer: Ask the members of the school's football team to name their favorite sport.**

Identify each sample, suggest a population from which it was selected, and state whether it is *unbiased* (random) or *biased*. If unbiased, classify the sample as *simple*, *stratified*, or *systematic*. If biased, classify as *convenience* or *voluntary response*.

4. NEWSPAPERS The local newspaper asks readers to write letters stating their preferred candidate for mayor.

5. SCHOOL A teacher needs a sample of work from 4 students in her first-period math class to display at the school open house. She selects the work of the first 4 students who raise their hands.

6. BUSINESS A hardware store wants to assess the strength of nails it sells. Store personnel select 25 boxes at random from among all of the boxes on the shelves. From each of the 25 boxes, they select one nail at random and subject it to a strength test. **25 nails; all nails on the store shelves; unbiased; stratified**

7. SCHOOL A class advisor hears complaints about an incorrect spelling of the school name on pencils sold at the school store. The advisor goes to the store and asks Namid to gather a sample of pencils and look for spelling errors. Namid grabs the closest box of pencils and counts out 12 pencils from the top of the box. She checks the pencils, returns them to the box, and reports the results to the advisor. **12 pencils; all pencils in the school store; biased; convenience**

DAILY
INTERVENTION   **Differentiated Instruction**

Visual/Spatial Place students in small groups. Give each group a number of different colored beads to serve as a population. Then, have the groups model the different types of random samples with the beads. For example, for stratified random samples, students must first divide the beads into groups by color and then take random beads from each group. Have students describe how they would take a systematic random sample.

★ indicates increased difficulty

Practice and Apply

Homework Help

For Exercises	See Examples
8–28	1–4

Extra Practice
See page 849.

Study Tip

Reading Math
The univariate data in Exercise 9 could be classified as **categorical**, because they reflect two categories, the two brands of cola.

Identify each sample, suggest a population from which it was selected, and state whether it is *unbiased* (random) or *biased*. If unbiased, classify the sample as *simple*, *stratified*, or *systematic*. If biased, classify as *convenience* or *voluntary response*.

8. **SCHOOL**   Pieces of paper with the names of 3 sophomores are drawn from a hat containing identical pieces of paper with all sophomores' names. **3 sophomores; all sophomores in the school; unbiased; simple**

9. **FOOD**   Twenty shoppers outside a fast-food restaurant are asked to name their preferred cola among two choices. **20 shoppers; all shoppers; biased; convenience**

10. **RECYCLING**   An interviewer goes from house to house on weekdays between 9 A.M. and 4 P.M. to determine how many people recycle. **people who are home between 9 A.M. and 4 P.M.; all people in the neighborhood; biased; convenience**

11. **POPULATION**   A state is first divided into its 86 counties and then 10 people from each county are chosen at random. **860 people from a state; all people in the state; unbiased; stratified**

12. **SCOOTERS**   A scooter manufacturer is concerned about quality control. The manufacturer checks the first 5 scooters off the line in the morning and the last 5 off the line in the afternoon for defects. **10 scooters; all scooters manufactured on a particular production line during one day; biased; convenience**

13. **SCHOOL**   To determine who will speak for her class at the school board meeting, Ms. Finchie used the numbers appearing next to her students' names in her grade book. She writes each of the numbers on an identical piece of paper and shuffles the pieces of papers in a box. Without seeing the contents of the box, one student draws 3 pieces of paper from the box. The students whose numbers match the numbers chosen will speak for the class. **3 students; all of the students in Ms. Finchie's class; unbiased; simple**

14. **FARMING**   An 8-ounce jar was filled with corn from a storage silo by dipping the jar into the pile of corn. The corn in the jar was then analyzed for moisture content. **an 8-oz jar of corn; all corn in the storage silo; biased; convenience**

15. **COURT**   The gender makeup of district court judges in the United States is to be estimated from a sample. All judges are grouped geographically by federal reserve districts. Within each of the 11 federal reserve districts, all judges' names are assigned a distinct random number. In each district, the numbers are then listed in order. A number between 1 and 20 inclusive is selected at random, and the judge with that number is selected. Then every 20th name after the first selected number is also included in the sample. **a group of U.S. district court judges; all U.S. district court judges; unbiased; stratified**

16. **TELEVISION**   A television station asks its viewers to share their opinions about a proposed golf course to be built just outside the city limits. Viewers can call one of two 900-numbers. One number represents a "yes" vote, and the other number represents a "no" vote. **a group of people who watch a television station; all people who watch the television station; biased; voluntary response**

17. **GOVERNMENT**   To discuss leadership issues shared by all United States Senators, the President asks 4 of his closest colleagues in the Senate to meet with him. **4 U.S. Senators; all U.S. Senators; biased; convenience**

More About...

Food
Michigan leads the nation in cherry production by growing about 219 million pounds of cherries per year.
Source: *World Book Encyclopedia*

18. **FOOD**   To sample the quality of the Bing cherries throughout the produce department, the produce manager picks up a handful of cherries from the edge of one case and checks to see if these cherries are spoiled. **a handful of Bing cherries; all Bing cherries in the produce department; biased; convenience**

19. **MANUFACTURING**   During the manufacture of high-definition televisions, units are checked for defects. Within the first 10 minutes of a work shift, a television is randomly chosen from the line of completed sets. For the rest of the shift, every 15th television on the line is checked for defects.

19. **a group of high-definition television sets; all high-definition television sets manufactured on one line during one shift; unbiased; systematic**

www.algebra1.com/self_check_quiz

---

3 Practice/Apply

Study Notebook

Have students—
• add the definitions/examples of the vocabulary terms to their Vocabulary Builder worksheets for Chapter 13.
• include explanations on how to identify whether a sample is random, the type of random sample, and whether the sample is biased.
• include any other item(s) that they find helpful in mastering the skills in this lesson.

About the Exercises...

Odd/Even Assignments
Exercises 8–21, 24, 25, 27, and 28 are structured so that students practice the same concepts whether they are assigned odd or even problems.

Assignment Guide

Basic: 9–21 odd, 29–51

Average: 9–21 odd, 22, 23, 29–51

Advanced: 8–20 even, 22–45 (optional: 46–51)

Answers

1. All three are unbiased samples. However, the methods for selecting each type of sample are different. In a simple random sample, a sample is as likely to be chosen as any other from the population. In a stratified random sample, the population is first divided into similar, nonoverlapping groups. Then a simple random sample is selected from each group. In a systematic random sample, the items are selected according to a specified time or item interval.

2. A convenience sample is a biased sample that is determined based on the ease with which it is possible to gather the sample. A voluntary sample is a biased sample composed of voluntary responses.

Identify each sample, suggest a population from which it was selected, and state whether it is *unbiased* (random) or *biased*. If unbiased, classify the sample as *simple, stratified,* or *systematic*. If biased, classify as *convenience* or *voluntary response*.

20. **BUSINESS** To get reactions about a benefits package, a company uses a computer program to randomly pick one person from each of its departments. **a group of employees; all employees of the company; unbiased; stratified**

21. **MOVIES** A magazine is trying to determine the most popular actor of the year. It asks its readers to mail the name of their favorite actor to the magazine's office. **a group of readers of a magazine; all readers of the magazine; biased; voluntary response**

COLLEGE For Exercises 22 and 23, use the following information.
The graph at the right reveals that 56% of survey respondents did not have a formal financial plan for a child's college tuition.

★ 22. **22. We know that the results are from a national survey conducted by Yankelovich Partners for Microsoft Corporation.** Write a statement to describe what you do know about the sample.

★ 23. **23. Additional information needed includes how the survey was conducted, how the survey respondents were selected, and the number of respondents.** What additional information would you like to have about the sample to determine whether the sample is biased?

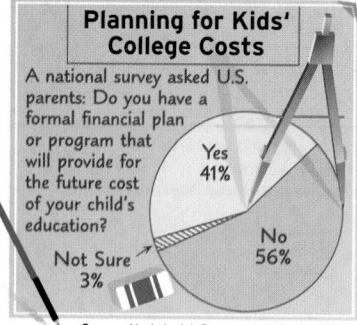

Planning for Kids' College Costs

A national survey asked U.S. parents: Do you have a formal financial plan or program that will provide for the future cost of your child's education?

Yes 41%
No 56%
Not Sure 3%

Source: Yankelovich Partners for Microsoft Corp.

★ 24. **SCHOOL** Suppose you want to sample the opinion of the students in your school about a new dress code. Describe an unbiased way to conduct your survey. **Sample answer: Get a copy of the school's list of students and call every 10th person on the list.**

★ 25. **ELECTIONS** Suppose you are running for mayor of your city and want to know if you are likely to be elected. Describe an unbiased way to poll the voters. **Sample answer: Get a copy of the list of registered voters in the city and call every 100th person.**

★ 26. **FAMILY** Study the graph at the right. Describe the information that is revealed in the graph. What information is there about the type or size of the sample? **See margin.**

Topics at Family Dinners

How the Day Was 73%
Family-Related News 65%
Plans For Tomorrow 49%
Current Events 46%

Source: National Pork Producers Council

★ 27. **27. Sample answer: Randomly pick 5 rows from each field of tomatoes and then pick a tomato every 50 ft along each row.** **FARMING** Suppose you are a farmer and want to know if your tomato crop is ready to harvest. Describe an unbiased way to determine whether the crop is ready to harvest.

★ 28. **MANUFACTURING** Suppose you want to know whether the infant car seats manufactured by your company meet the government standards for safety. Describe an unbiased way to determine whether the seats meet the standards. **Sample answer: Every hour pull one infant seat from the end of the assembly line for testing.**

29. **CRITICAL THINKING** The following is a proposal for surveying a stratified random sample of the student body.

Divide the student body according to those who are on the basketball team, those who are in the band, and those who are in the drama club. Then take a simple random sample from each of the three groups. Conduct the survey using this sample.

Study the proposal. Describe its strengths and weaknesses. Is the sample a stratified random sample? Explain. **See margin.**

712 Chapter 13 Statistics

30. WRITING IN MATH Answer the question that was posed at the beginning of the lesson. **See pp. 751A–751B.**

Why is sampling important in manufacturing?

Include the following in your answer:
- an unbiased way to pick which CDs to check, and
- a biased way to pick which CDs to check.

Standardized Test Practice
Ⓐ Ⓑ Ⓒ Ⓓ

31. To predict the candidate who will win the seat in city council, which method would give the newspaper the most accurate result? **B**
- Ⓐ Ask every 5th person that passes a reporter in the mall.
- Ⓑ Use a list of registered voters and call every 20th person.
- Ⓒ Publish a survey and ask readers to reply.
- Ⓓ Ask reporters at the newspaper.

32. A cookie manufacturer plans to make a new type of cookie and wants to know if people will buy these cookies. For accurate results, which method should they use? **D**
- Ⓐ Ask visitors to their factory to evaluate the cookie.
- Ⓑ Place a sample of the new cookie with their other cookies, and ask people to answer a questionnaire about the cookie.
- Ⓒ Take samples to a school, and ask students to raise their hands if they like the cookie.
- Ⓓ Divide the United States into 6 regions. Then pick 3 cities in each region at random, and conduct a taste test in each of the 18 cities.

Maintain Your Skills

Mixed Review Solve each equation. *(Lesson 12-9)*

33. $\dfrac{10}{3y} - \dfrac{5}{2y} = \dfrac{1}{4}$ $3\dfrac{1}{3}$

34. $\dfrac{3}{r+4} - \dfrac{1}{r} = \dfrac{1}{r}$ **8**

35. $\dfrac{1}{4m} + \dfrac{2m}{m-3} = 2$ $\dfrac{3}{25}$

Simplify. *(Lesson 12-8)*

36. $\dfrac{2 + \dfrac{5}{x}}{\dfrac{x}{3} + \dfrac{5}{6}}$ $\dfrac{6}{x}$

37. $\dfrac{a + \dfrac{35}{a+12}}{a+7}$ $\dfrac{a+5}{a+12}$

38. $\dfrac{\dfrac{t^2-4}{t^2+5t+6}}{t-2}$ $\dfrac{1}{t+3}$

39. GEOMETRY What is the perimeter of $\triangle ABC$? *(Lesson 11-2)* $22\sqrt{6}$ cm

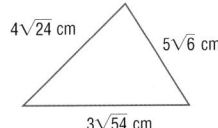

4√24 cm   5√6 cm   3√54 cm

Solve each equation by using the Quadratic Formula. Approximate any irrational roots to the nearest tenth. *(Lesson 10-4)*

40. $x^2 - 6x - 40 = 0$ **−4, 10**

41. $6b^2 + 15 = -19b$ $-1\dfrac{2}{3}, -1\dfrac{1}{2}$

42. $2d^2 = 9d + 3$ **−0.3, 4.8**

Find each product. *(Lesson 8-7)*

43. $(y+5)(y+7)$ $y^2 + 12y + 35$

44. $(c-3)(c-7)$ $c^2 - 10c + 21$

45. $(x+4)(x-8)$ $x^2 - 4x - 32$

Getting Ready for the Next Lesson **BASIC SKILL** Find each sum or difference.

46. $4.5 + 3.8$ **8.3**

47. $16.9 + 7.21$ **24.11**

48. $3.6 + 18.5$ **22.1**

49. $7.6 - 3.8$ **3.8**

50. $18 - 4.7$ **13.3**

51. $13.2 - 0.75$ **12.45**

Lesson 13-1 Sampling and Bias **713**

---

26. The graph shows four phrases with a percent associated with each phrase. We can assume that the percents indicate the percent of respondents who said the indicated topic was discussed during family dinners. Based on the sum of the percents, respondents must have been able to choose or state more than one topic. We do not know how many respondents there were, whether the respondents selected topics from a list of choices or stated their own topics, whether there were any restrictions that may have existed about the topics, and the time period of the family dinners considered in this survey (a night, a week, a month, or more).

---

4 Assess

Open-Ended Assessment

Speaking Pass out newspapers or news magazines and have students scan the articles for the results of opinion polls. When students find such results, have them identify the sample and population for the poll. Then have them describe how the people conducting the poll could make sure the sample was not biased.

Getting Ready for Lesson 13-2

BASIC SKILL Students will learn how to organize data in matrices, and how to add and subtract matrices in Lesson 13-2. It is important that students understand basic addition and subtraction in order to add and subtract matrices. Use Exercises 46–51 to determine your students' familiarity with basic addition and subtraction.

Answer

29. It is a good idea to divide the school population into groups and to take a simple random sample from each group. The problem that prevents this from being a legitimate stratified random sample is the way the three groups are formed. The three groups probably do not represent all students. The students who do not participate in any of these three activities will not be represented in the survey. Other students may be involved in two or three of these activities. These students will be more likely to be chosen for the survey.

Getting Started

Before using this page, ask students if they have ever asked for permission from their parents to do something, and tried to influence the way their parents answered. Have volunteers describe some of the methods they use to influence their parents' decisions.

Teach

Biased Questions Discuss with students why the two questions about sales tax on Internet purchases might have elicited different responses. Explain that the reason for saying "yes" to question two is that the question points out that the tax would have been paid at a store purchase. People are more likely to agree to spending money that they would have otherwise spent elsewhere, so the question is biased.

Assess

Study Notebook

Ask students to summarize what they have learned about asking biased questions in their study notebooks.

ELL English Language Learners may benefit from writing key concepts from this activity in their Study Notebooks in their native language and then in English.

Answers

1a. This question will bias people toward answering "yes" because it gives them a reason to think that recycling will help alleviate a shortage in resources.

Reading Mathematics

Survey Questions

Even though taking a random sample eliminates bias or favoritism in the choice of a sample, questions may be worded to influence people's thoughts in a desired direction. Two different surveys on Internet sales tax had different results.

Question 1
Should there be sales tax on purchases made on the Internet?

Question 2
Do you think people should or should not be required to pay the same sales tax for purchases made over the Internet that they would if they had bought the item in person at a local store?

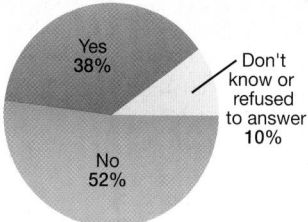

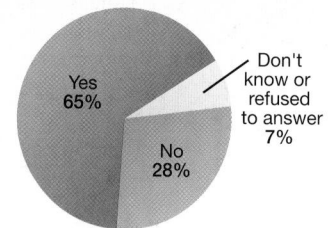

Notice the difference in Questions 1 and 2. Question 2 includes more information. Pointing out that customers pay sales tax for items bought at a local store may give the people answering the survey a reason to answer "yes." Asking the question in that way probably led people to answer the way they did.

Because they are random samples, the results of both of these surveys are accurate. However, the results could be used in a misleading way by someone with an interest in the issue. For example, an Internet retailer would prefer to state the results of Question 1. Be sure to think about survey questions carefully to make sure that you interpret the results correctly.

Reading to Learn

For Exercises 1–2, tell whether each question is likely to bias the results. Explain your reasoning. 1–3. See margin.

1. On a survey on environmental issues:
   a. "Due to diminishing resources, should a law be made to require recycling?"
   b. "Should the government require citizens to participate in recycling efforts?"

2. On a survey on education:
   a. "Should schools fund extracurricular sports programs?"
   b. "The budget of the River Valley School District is short of funds. Should taxes be raised in order for the district to fund extracurricular sports programs?"

3. Suppose you want to determine whether to serve hamburgers or pizza at the class party.
   a. Write a survey question that would likely produce biased results.
   b. Write a survey question that would likely produce unbiased results.

1b. This question will bias people toward answering "no" because most citizens are against the government making laws that require certain behaviors.

2a. This question is not biased. It does not influence a person to answer one way or the other.

2b. This question will bias people toward answering "no" because most people do not want taxes to be raised.

3a. Sample answer: Since we had hamburgers at the last party, would you prefer pizza for the next party?

3b. Sample answer: Would you prefer hamburgers or pizza for the class party?

What You'll Learn

- Organize data in matrices.
- Solve problems by adding or subtracting matrices or by multiplying by a scalar.

Vocabulary
- matrix
- dimensions
- row
- column
- element
- scalar multiplication

How are matrices used to organize data?

To determine the best type of aircraft to use for certain flights, the management of an airline company considers the following aircraft operating statistics.

Aircraft	Number of Seats	Airborne Speed (mph)	Possible Flight Distance (miles)	Fuel per Hour (gallons)	Operating Cost per Hour (dollars)
B747-100	462	512	2297	3517	7224
DC-10-10	297	496	1402	2311	5703
MD-11	259	527	3073	2464	6539
A300-600	228	475	1372	1505	4783

Source: Air Transport Association of America

The table has rows and columns of information. When we concentrate only on the numerical information, we see an array with 4 rows and 5 columns.

$$\begin{bmatrix} 462 & 512 & 2297 & 3517 & 7224 \\ 297 & 496 & 1402 & 2311 & 5703 \\ 259 & 527 & 3073 & 2464 & 6539 \\ 228 & 475 & 1372 & 1505 & 4783 \end{bmatrix}$$

This array of numbers is called a matrix.

Study Tip

Reading Math
A matrix is sometimes called an *ordered array*.

ORGANIZE DATA IN MATRICES If you have ever used a spreadsheet program on the computer, you have worked with matrices. A **matrix** is a rectangular arrangement of numbers in rows and columns. A matrix is usually described by its **dimensions**, or the number of **rows** and **columns**, with the number of rows stated first. Each entry in a matrix is called an **element**.

Example 1 Name Dimensions of Matrices

State the dimensions of each matrix. Then identify the position of the circled element in each matrix.

a. [11 (15) 24]

This matrix has 1 row and 3 columns. Therefore, it is a 1-by-3 matrix.

The circled element is in the first row and the second column.

b. $\begin{bmatrix} -4 & 2 \\ 0 & 1 \\ (3) & -6 \end{bmatrix}$

This matrix has 3 rows and 2 columns. Therefore, it is a 3-by-2 matrix.

The circled element is in the third row and the first column.

1 Focus

5-Minute Check Transparency 13-2 Use as a quiz or review of Lesson 13-1.

Mathematical Background notes are available for this lesson on p. 706C.

Building on Prior Knowledge

In Chapter 2, students learned how to add and subtract rational numbers using a number line. In this lesson, students will use this skill to add and subtract rational numbers in matrices.

How are matrices used to organize data?

Ask students:

- Which lines of numbers are the rows of the matrix? **The rows go from left to right.**
- Which lines of numbers are the columns? **The columns go from top to bottom.**
- In what instances might putting numerical data from a table into a matrix be beneficial? **Sample answer: Putting numerical data into a matrix might make it easier to perform calculations on the data.**

Resource Manager

Workbook and Reproducible Masters

Chapter 13 Resource Masters
- Study Guide and Intervention, pp. 787–788
- Skills Practice, p. 789
- Practice, p. 790
- Reading to Learn Mathematics, p. 791
- Enrichment, p. 792
- Assessment, p. 825

Graphing Calculator and Spreadsheet Masters, p. 47
Parent and Student Study Guide Workbook, p. 102

Transparencies
5-Minute Check Transparency 13-2
Answer Key Transparencies

Technology
Interactive Chalkboard

In-Class Example Power Point®

1 State the dimensions of each matrix. Then identify the position of the circled element in each matrix.

a. $\begin{bmatrix} 12 \\ \textcircled{7} \\ 5 \end{bmatrix}$ 3 by 1; second row, first column

b. $\begin{bmatrix} 2 & 8 & -14 & \textcircled{1} \\ 6 & -3 & -2 & 12 \\ 22 & 15 & 5 & -19 \end{bmatrix}$

3 by 4; first row, fourth column

MATRIX OPERATIONS

In-Class Example Power Point®

2 Find each sum. If the sum does not exist, write *impossible*.

a. $\begin{bmatrix} 2 & 6 \\ -8 & 11 \\ 10 & -5 \end{bmatrix} + \begin{bmatrix} 13 & 7 \\ 9 & 4 \\ -7 & -12 \end{bmatrix}$

$\begin{bmatrix} 15 & 13 \\ 1 & 15 \\ 3 & -17 \end{bmatrix}$

b. $\begin{bmatrix} -14 & 12 \\ 6 & 1 \end{bmatrix} + \begin{bmatrix} 3 & 8 & 1 \\ -6 & -3 & 0 \\ 7 & 20 & 4 \end{bmatrix}$

impossible

More About. . .

College Football

Each year the National Football Foundation awards the MacArthur Bowl to the number one college football team. The bowl is made of about 400 ounces of silver and represents a stadium with rows of seats.

Source: *ESPN Information Please® Sports Almanac*

Two matrices are *equal* only if they have the same dimensions and each element of one matrix is equal to the corresponding element in the other matrix.

$$\begin{bmatrix} 3 & 5 \\ -1 & 4 \end{bmatrix} = \begin{bmatrix} 3 & 5 \\ -1 & 4 \end{bmatrix} \qquad \begin{bmatrix} 2 & 4 \\ 1 & 7 \end{bmatrix} \neq \begin{bmatrix} 2 & 3 \\ 1 & 7 \end{bmatrix} \qquad \begin{bmatrix} 4 & 8 \\ 1 & -3 \end{bmatrix} \neq \begin{bmatrix} 4 & 8 & 0 \\ 1 & -3 & 0 \end{bmatrix}$$

MATRIX OPERATIONS If two matrices have the same dimensions, you can add or subtract them. To do this, add or subtract corresponding elements of the two matrices.

Example 2 Add Matrices

If $A = \begin{bmatrix} 3 & -4 & 7 \\ -1 & 6 & 0 \end{bmatrix}$, $B = \begin{bmatrix} 7 & -4 & -2 \\ 1 & 6 & -3 \end{bmatrix}$, and $C = \begin{bmatrix} 3 & 6 \\ -4 & 5 \end{bmatrix}$, find each sum. **If the sum does not exist, write *impossible*.**

a. $A + B$

$A + B = \begin{bmatrix} 3 & -4 & 7 \\ -1 & 6 & 0 \end{bmatrix} + \begin{bmatrix} 7 & -4 & -2 \\ 1 & 6 & -3 \end{bmatrix}$ Substitution

$ = \begin{bmatrix} 3 + 7 & -4 + (-4) & 7 + (-2) \\ -1 + 1 & 6 + 6 & 0 + (-3) \end{bmatrix}$ Definition of matrix addition

$ = \begin{bmatrix} 10 & -8 & 5 \\ 0 & 12 & -3 \end{bmatrix}$ Simplify.

b. $B + C$

$B + C = \begin{bmatrix} 7 & -4 & -2 \\ 1 & 6 & -3 \end{bmatrix} + \begin{bmatrix} 3 & 6 \\ -4 & 5 \end{bmatrix}$ Substitution

Since B is a 2-by-3 matrix and C is a 2-by-2 matrix, the matrices do not have the same dimensions. Therefore, it is impossible to add these matrices.

Addition and subtraction of matrices can be used to solve real-world problems.

Example 3 Subtract Matrices

COLLEGE FOOTBALL The Division I-A college football teams with the five best records during the 1990s are listed below.

	Overall Record Wins	Losses	Ties		Bowl Record Wins	Losses	Ties
Florida State	109	13	1	Florida State	8	2	0
Nebraska	108	16	1	Nebraska	5	5	0
Marshall	114	25	0	Marshall	2	1	0
Florida	102	22	1	Florida	5	4	0
Tennessee	99	22	2	Tennessee	6	4	0

Use subtraction of matrices to determine the regular season records of these teams during the decade.

$$\begin{bmatrix} 109 & 13 & 1 \\ 108 & 16 & 1 \\ 114 & 25 & 0 \\ 102 & 22 & 1 \\ 99 & 22 & 2 \end{bmatrix} - \begin{bmatrix} 8 & 2 & 0 \\ 5 & 5 & 0 \\ 2 & 1 & 0 \\ 5 & 4 & 0 \\ 6 & 4 & 0 \end{bmatrix} = \begin{bmatrix} 109 - 8 & 13 - 2 & 1 - 0 \\ 108 - 5 & 16 - 5 & 1 - 0 \\ 114 - 2 & 25 - 1 & 0 - 0 \\ 102 - 5 & 22 - 4 & 1 - 0 \\ 99 - 6 & 22 - 4 & 2 - 0 \end{bmatrix}$$

$$= \begin{bmatrix} 101 & 11 & 1 \\ 103 & 11 & 1 \\ 112 & 24 & 0 \\ 97 & 18 & 1 \\ 93 & 18 & 2 \end{bmatrix}$$

Interactive Chalkboard

PowerPoint® Presentations

This CD-ROM is a customizable Microsoft® PowerPoint® presentation that includes:

• Step-by-step, dynamic solutions of each In-Class Example from the Teacher Wraparound Edition
• Additional, Your Turn exercises for each example
• The 5-Minute Check Transparencies
• Hot links to Glencoe Online Study Tools

So, the regular season records of the teams can be described as follows.

Regular Season Record

	Wins	Losses	Ties
Florida State	101	11	1
Nebraska	103	11	1
Marshall	112	24	0
Florida	97	18	1
Tennessee	93	18	2

You can multiply any matrix by a constant called a *scalar*. This is called **scalar multiplication**. When scalar multiplication is performed, each element is multiplied by the scalar and a new matrix is formed.

Key Concept — Scalar Multiplication of a Matrix

$$m\begin{bmatrix} a & b & c \\ d & e & f \end{bmatrix} = \begin{bmatrix} ma & mb & mc \\ md & me & mf \end{bmatrix}$$

Example 4 Perform Scalar Multiplication

If $T = \begin{bmatrix} -4 & 2 \\ 0 & 1 \\ 3 & -6 \end{bmatrix}$, find $3T$.

$3T = 3\begin{bmatrix} -4 & 2 \\ 0 & 1 \\ 3 & -6 \end{bmatrix}$ Substitution

$= \begin{bmatrix} 3(-4) & 3(2) \\ 3(0) & 3(1) \\ 3(3) & 3(-6) \end{bmatrix}$ Definition of scalar multiplication

$= \begin{bmatrix} -12 & 6 \\ 0 & 3 \\ 9 & -18 \end{bmatrix}$ Simplify.

Check for Understanding

Concept Check

1. **Describe** the difference between a 2-by-4 matrix and a 4-by-2 matrix.

1. A 2-by-4 matrix has 2 rows and 4 columns, and a 4-by-2 matrix has 4 rows and 2 columns.

2. **OPEN ENDED** Write two matrices whose sum is $\begin{bmatrix} 0 & 4 & 5 & -3 \\ 1 & -1 & 4 & 9 \end{bmatrix}$. See margin.

3. **FIND THE ERROR** Hiroshi and Estrella are finding $-5\begin{bmatrix} -1 & 3 \\ -2 & 5 \end{bmatrix}$.

Hiroshi

$-5\begin{bmatrix} -1 & 3 \\ -2 & 5 \end{bmatrix} = \begin{bmatrix} 5 & 3 \\ 10 & 5 \end{bmatrix}$

Estrella

$-5\begin{bmatrix} -1 & 3 \\ -2 & 5 \end{bmatrix} = \begin{bmatrix} 5 & -15 \\ 10 & -25 \end{bmatrix}$

Who is correct? Explain your reasoning.   Estrella; Hiroshi did not multiply each element of the matrix by −5.

 www.algebra1.com/extra_examples

Lesson 13-2 Introduction to Matrices 717

Answer

2. Sample answer:

$\begin{bmatrix} 2 & 3 & -1 & 3 \\ 5 & 6 & -2 & -5 \end{bmatrix} + \begin{bmatrix} -2 & 1 & 6 & -6 \\ -4 & -7 & 6 & 14 \end{bmatrix}$

In-Class Examples   Power Point®

Teaching Tip Explain that in this example, the overall record includes the regular season record, plus the bowl (post-season) record.

3 COLLEGE FOOTBALL The Division 1-A current football coaches with the five best overall records as of 2000 are listed below.

Overall Record			
Coach	Won	Lost	Tied
Joe Paterno	322	90	3
Bobby Bowden	315	87	4
Lou Holtz	224	110	7
Jackie Sherrill	172	93	4
Ken Hatfield	147	104	4

Bowl Record			
Coach	Won	Lost	Tied
Joe Paterno	20	9	1
Bobby Bowden	17	6	1
Lou Holtz	11	8	2
Jackie Sherrill	8	6	0
Ken Hatfield	4	6	0

Source: NCAA

Use subtraction of matrices to determine the regular season records of these coaches.

Regular Season Record			
Coach	Won	Lost	Tied
Joe Paterno	302	81	2
Bobby Bowden	298	81	3
Lou Holtz	213	102	5
Jackie Sherrill	164	87	4
Ken Hatfield	143	98	4

4 If $R = \begin{bmatrix} -5 & 8 \\ 12 & -3 \end{bmatrix}$, find $5R$.

$\begin{bmatrix} -25 & 40 \\ 60 & -15 \end{bmatrix}$

DAILY INTERVENTION FIND THE ERROR Have students identify the difference between the two results first, which will help them pinpoint the error.

3 Practice/Apply

Study Notebook

Have students—

- add the definitions/examples of the vocabulary terms to their Vocabulary Builder worksheets for Chapter 13.
- include explanations on how to identify the properties of matrices, and how to perform matrix operations.
- include any other item(s) that they find helpful in mastering the skills in this lesson.

About the Exercises...

Organization by Objective

- **Organize Data in Matrices:** 17–26, 39, 42, 45, 46
- **Matrix Operations:** 27–38, 40, 41, 43, 44, 47, 48

Odd/Even Assignments

Exercises 17–38 are structured so that students practice the same concepts whether they are assigned odd or even problems.

Alert! Exercises 53–57 require students to use graphing calculators.

Assignment Guide

Basic: 17–23 odd, 27–33 odd, 39–41, 49–52, 58–70

Average: 17–37 odd, 39–44, 49–52, 58–70 (optional: 53–57)

Advanced: 18–38 even, 42–68 (optional: 69, 70)

All: Practice Quiz 1 (1–5)

Guided Practice

GUIDED PRACTICE KEY

Exercises	Examples
4–7	1
8–11	2–4
12–16	3

State the dimensions of each matrix. Then, identify the position of the circled element in each matrix.

4. $\begin{bmatrix} 4 & \textcircled{0} & 2 \\ 5 & -1 & -3 \\ 6 & 2 & 7 \end{bmatrix}$ **3 by 3; first row, second column**

5. $\begin{bmatrix} \textcircled{3} & -3 & 1 & 9 \end{bmatrix}$ **1 by 4; first row, first column**

6. $\begin{bmatrix} 5 \\ 2 \\ \textcircled{1} \\ -3 \end{bmatrix}$ **4 by 1; third row, first column**

7. $\begin{bmatrix} 0.6 & \textcircled{4.2} \\ -1.7 & 1.05 \\ 0.625 & -2.1 \end{bmatrix}$ **3 by 2; first row, second column**

If $A = \begin{bmatrix} 20 & -10 \\ 12 & 19 \end{bmatrix}$, $B = \begin{bmatrix} 15 & 14 \\ -10 & 6 \end{bmatrix}$, and $C = \begin{bmatrix} -5 & 7 \end{bmatrix}$, find each sum, difference, or product. If the sum or difference does not exist, write *impossible*.

8. $A + C$ **impossible**
9. $B - A$ **9.** $\begin{bmatrix} -5 & 24 \\ -22 & -13 \end{bmatrix}$
10. $2A$ $\begin{bmatrix} 40 & -20 \\ 24 & 38 \end{bmatrix}$
11. $-4C$ $\begin{bmatrix} 20 & -28 \end{bmatrix}$

Application

Study Tip

Reading Math

The data for Exercises 12–16 could be classified as **bivariate,** because there are two variables, size and thickness of the crust.

PIZZA SALES For Exercises 12–16, use the following tables that list the number of pizzas sold at Sylvia's Pizza one weekend.

FRIDAY	Small	Medium	Large
Thin Crust	12	10	3
Thick Crust	11	8	8
Deep Dish	14	8	10

SATURDAY	Small	Medium	Large
Thin Crust	13	12	11
Thick Crust	1	5	10
Deep Dish	8	11	2

SUNDAY	Small	Medium	Large
Thin Crust	11	8	6
Thick Crust	1	8	11
Deep Dish	10	15	11

12. Create a matrix for each day's data. Name the matrices *F*, *R*, and *N*, respectively.
13. Does *F* equal *R*? Explain. **No; the corresponding elements are not equal.**
14. Create matrix *T* to represent *F* + *R* + *N*.
15. What does *T* represent? **the total sales for the weekend**
16. Which type of pizza had the most sales during the entire weekend?

12. $F = \begin{bmatrix} 12 & 10 & 3 \\ 11 & 8 & 8 \\ 14 & 8 & 10 \end{bmatrix}$ $R = \begin{bmatrix} 13 & 12 & 11 \\ 1 & 5 & 10 \\ 8 & 11 & 2 \end{bmatrix}$ $N = \begin{bmatrix} 11 & 8 & 6 \\ 1 & 8 & 11 \\ 10 & 15 & 11 \end{bmatrix}$

14. $T = \begin{bmatrix} 36 & 30 & 20 \\ 13 & 21 & 29 \\ 32 & 34 & 23 \end{bmatrix}$

16. small, thin crust pizza

★ indicates increased difficulty

Practice and Apply

Homework Help

For Exercises	See Examples
17–26	1
27–38	2–4
39–48	3

Extra Practice
See page 849.

State the dimensions of each matrix. Then, identify the position of the circled element in each matrix. **17–24. See margin.**

17. $\begin{bmatrix} \textcircled{2} & 1 \\ 5 & -8 \end{bmatrix}$

18. $\begin{bmatrix} -36 & 3 \\ \textcircled{25} & -1 \\ 11 & 14 \end{bmatrix}$

19. $\begin{bmatrix} 1 \\ 0 \\ \textcircled{-1} \end{bmatrix}$

20. $\begin{bmatrix} -3 & 56 & -21 \\ 60 & \textcircled{112} & -65 \end{bmatrix}$

21. $\begin{bmatrix} -4 & 0 & -2 \\ 5 & 1 & \textcircled{12} \\ -6 & 3 & -7 \end{bmatrix}$

22. $\begin{bmatrix} 1 & -2 \\ 3 & 4 \\ 1 & 5 \\ \textcircled{-1} & 7 \end{bmatrix}$

23. $\begin{bmatrix} -5 & 3 & 1 \\ 4 & 0 & \textcircled{2} \end{bmatrix}$

24. $\begin{bmatrix} -6 & 3 \\ \textcircled{5} & -4 \end{bmatrix}$

Answers

17. 2 by 2; first row, first column
18. 3 by 2; second row, first column
19. 3 by 1; third row, first column
20. 2 by 3; second row, second column
21. 3 by 3; second row, third column
22. 4 by 2; fourth row, first column
23. 2 by 3; second row, third column
24. 2 by 2; second row, first column

718 Chapter 13 Statistics

25. $\begin{bmatrix} 2 & 1 & 1 \\ 1 & 5 & 1 \end{bmatrix}$

★ 25. Create a 2-by-3 matrix with 2 in the first row and first column and 5 in the second row and second column. The rest of the elements should be ones.

26. $\begin{bmatrix} 0 & 0 \\ 0 & 8 \\ 0 & 4 \end{bmatrix}$

★ 26. Create a 3-by-2 matrix with 8 in the second row and second column and 4 in the third row and second column. The rest of the elements should be zeros.

27. $\begin{bmatrix} -13 & 12 & -7 \\ 5 & 6 & 11 \\ 23 & 18 & 14 \end{bmatrix}$

If $A = \begin{bmatrix} -1 & 5 & 9 \\ 0 & -4 & -2 \\ 3 & 7 & 6 \end{bmatrix}$, $B = \begin{bmatrix} -12 & 7 & -16 \\ 5 & 10 & 13 \\ 20 & 11 & 8 \end{bmatrix}$, $C = \begin{bmatrix} 34 & 91 & 63 \\ 81 & 79 & 60 \end{bmatrix}$, and

28. $\begin{bmatrix} -18 & 100 & 133 \\ 32 & 71 & 105 \end{bmatrix}$

$D = \begin{bmatrix} -52 & 9 & 70 \\ -49 & -8 & 45 \end{bmatrix}$, find each sum, difference, or product. If the sum or difference does not exist, write *impossible*.

29. $\begin{bmatrix} 86 & 82 & -7 \\ 130 & 87 & 15 \end{bmatrix}$

27. $A + B$ 28. $C + D$ 29. $C - D$ 30. $B - A$

30. $\begin{bmatrix} -11 & 2 & -25 \\ 5 & 14 & 15 \\ 17 & 4 & 2 \end{bmatrix}$

31. $5A$ 32. $2C$ 33. $A + C$ 34. $B + D$

★ 35. $2B + A$ 36. $4A - B$ 37. $2C - 3D$ 38. $5D + 2C$

31. $\begin{bmatrix} -5 & 25 & 45 \\ 0 & -20 & -10 \\ 15 & 35 & 30 \end{bmatrix}$

FOOD For Exercises 39–41, use the table that shows the nutritional value of food.

32. $\begin{bmatrix} 68 & 182 & 126 \\ 162 & 158 & 120 \end{bmatrix}$

33. impossible

34. impossible

35. $\begin{bmatrix} -25 & 19 & -23 \\ 10 & 16 & 24 \\ 43 & 29 & 22 \end{bmatrix}$

Food	Calories	Protein (grams)	Fat (grams)	Saturated Fat (grams)
Fish Stick	70	6	3	0.8
Vegetable Soup (1 cup)	70	2	2	0.3
Soft Drink (12 oz)	160	0	0	0
Chocolate-Chip Cookie	185	2	11	3.9

Source: U.S. Department of Agriculture

36. $\begin{bmatrix} 8 & 13 & 52 \\ -5 & -26 & -21 \\ -8 & 17 & 16 \end{bmatrix}$

37. $\begin{bmatrix} 224 & 155 & -84 \\ 309 & 182 & -15 \end{bmatrix}$

39. If $F = [70 \ \ 6 \ \ 3 \ \ 0.8]$ is a matrix representing the nutritional value of a fish stick, create matrices V, S, and C to represent vegetable soup, soft drink, and chocolate chip cookie, respectively.

38. $\begin{bmatrix} -192 & 227 & 476 \\ -83 & 118 & 345 \end{bmatrix}$

40. Suppose Lakeisha has two fish sticks for lunch. Write a matrix representing the nutritional value of the fish sticks. $[140 \ \ 12 \ \ 6 \ \ 1.6]$

39. $V = [70 \ \ 2 \ \ 2 \ \ 0.3]$,
$S = [160 \ \ 0 \ \ 0 \ \ 0]$,
$C = [185 \ \ 2 \ \ 11 \ \ 3.9]$

41. Suppose Lakeisha has two fish sticks, a cup of vegetable soup, a 12-ounce soft drink, and a chocolate chip cookie. Write a matrix representing the nutritional value of her lunch. $[555 \ \ 16 \ \ 19 \ \ 5.8]$

42. $N = \begin{bmatrix} 18 & 28 & 32 & 24 & 21 \\ 24 & 30 & 45 & 47 & 25 \\ 17 & 19 & 26 & 30 & 28 \end{bmatrix}$

FUND-RAISING For Exercises 42–44, use the table that shows the last year's sales of T-shirts for the student council fund-raiser.

Color	XS	S	M	L	XL
Red	18	28	32	24	21
White	24	30	45	47	25
Blue	17	19	26	30	28

44. $\begin{bmatrix} 22 & 34 & 38 & 29 & 25 \\ 29 & 36 & 54 & 56 & 30 \\ 20 & 23 & 31 & 36 & 34 \end{bmatrix}$

42. Create a matrix to show the number of T-shirts sold last year according to size and color. Label this matrix N.

★ 43. The student council anticipates a 20% increase in T-shirt sales this year. What value of the scalar r should be used so that rN results in a matrix that estimates the number of each size and color T-shirts needed this year? 1.20

★ 44. Calculate rN, rounding appropriately, to show estimates for this year's sales.

www.algebra1.com/self_check_quiz

---

45. $A = \begin{bmatrix} 533 & 331 & 4135 & 26 & 15 \\ 515 & 304 & 3840 & 24 & 14 \\ 499 & 325 & 4353 & 41 & 13 \\ 571 & 343 & 4436 & 36 & 15 \end{bmatrix}$

$B = \begin{bmatrix} 571 & 357 & 4413 & 33 & 15 \\ 473 & 284 & 3430 & 28 & 11 \\ 347 & 235 & 3429 & 21 & 18 \\ 533 & 324 & 3730 & 19 & 18 \end{bmatrix}$

47. $T = \begin{bmatrix} 1104 & 688 & 8548 & 59 & 30 \\ 988 & 588 & 7270 & 52 & 25 \\ 846 & 560 & 7782 & 62 & 31 \\ 1104 & 667 & 8166 & 55 & 33 \end{bmatrix}$

50. Matrices can be used to organize data that can be displayed in a rectangular array of numbers. Answers should include the following.

- A table is a rectangular array of numbers with headings to indicate what each row and column represents. A matrix is just the rectangular array of numbers.

- Sample answer: The grades from each of five different tests for each student in a math class can be organized in a matrix.

69. Sample answer: Megan saved steadily from January to June. In July, she withdrew money to go on vacation. She started saving again in September. Then in November, she withdrew money for holiday presents.

FOOTBALL For Exercises 45–48, use the table that shows the passing performance of four National Football League quarterbacks.

1999 Regular Season

Quarterback	Attempts	Completions	Passing Yards	Touchdowns	Interceptions
Peyton Manning	533	331	4135	26	15
Rich Gannon	515	304	3840	24	14
Kurt Warner	499	325	4353	41	13
Steve Beuerlein	571	343	4436	36	15

2000 Regular Season

Quarterback	Attempts	Completions	Passing Yards	Touchdowns	Interceptions
Peyton Manning	571	357	4413	33	15
Rich Gannon	473	284	3430	28	11
Kurt Warner	347	235	3429	21	18
Steve Beuerlein	533	324	3730	19	18

Source: ESPN

45. Create matrix A for the 1999 data and matrix B for the 2000 data. **See margin.**

46. What are the dimensions of each matrix in Exercise 45? **4 by 5, 4 by 5**

47. Calculate $T = A + B$. **See margin.**

48. What does matrix T represent?
the total of the passing statistics for the 1999 and 2000 seasons

49. **CRITICAL THINKING** Suppose M and N are each 3-by-3 matrices. Determine whether each statement is *sometimes*, *always*, or *never* true.
   a. $M = N$ **sometimes**
   b. $M + N = N + M$ **always**
   c. $M - N = N - M$ **sometimes**
   d. $5M = M$ **sometimes**
   e. $M + N = M$ **sometimes**
   f. $5M = N$ **sometimes**

50. **WRITING IN MATH** Answer the question that was posed at the beginning of the lesson. **See margin.**

   How are matrices used to organize data?

   Include the following in your answer:
   - a comparison of a table and a matrix, and
   - description of some real-world data that could be organized in a matrix.

Standardized Test Practice
A B C D

51. Which of the following is equal to $\begin{bmatrix} 3 & 4 & 5 \\ -6 & -1 & 8 \end{bmatrix}$? **C**

   Ⓐ $\begin{bmatrix} -1 & 8 & 3 \\ -4 & 0 & 5 \end{bmatrix} + \begin{bmatrix} 4 & -4 & 2 \\ 2 & -1 & -2 \end{bmatrix}$

   Ⓑ $\begin{bmatrix} 7 & -1 & 2 \\ 3 & 4 & -5 \end{bmatrix} + \begin{bmatrix} -4 & -3 & 3 \\ -3 & -5 & -3 \end{bmatrix}$

   Ⓒ $\begin{bmatrix} 1 & -3 & 5 \\ 7 & -2 & 0 \end{bmatrix} + \begin{bmatrix} 2 & 7 & 0 \\ -13 & 1 & 8 \end{bmatrix}$

   Ⓓ $\begin{bmatrix} 5 & 9 & -2 \\ 3 & 7 & 5 \end{bmatrix} + \begin{bmatrix} -2 & -5 & -3 \\ 3 & -8 & 3 \end{bmatrix}$

52. Suppose M and N are each 2-by-2 matrices. If $M + N = M$, which of the following is true? **B**

   Ⓐ $N = \begin{bmatrix} 1 & 1 \\ 1 & 1 \end{bmatrix}$

   Ⓑ $N = \begin{bmatrix} 0 & 0 \\ 0 & 0 \end{bmatrix}$

   Ⓒ $N = \begin{bmatrix} 1 & 0 \\ 0 & 1 \end{bmatrix}$

   Ⓓ $N = \begin{bmatrix} 0 & 1 \\ 1 & 0 \end{bmatrix}$

DAILY INTERVENTION

Differentiated Instruction   **ELL**

Verbal/Linguistic Write a random matrix on the chalkboard. Call out different elements of the matrix, and have students describe the location of the elements. Or, call out locations within the matrix (first row, second column, etc.) and have students identify the element in those locations.

 **Graphing Calculator**

MATRIX OPERATIONS You can use a graphing calculator to perform matrix operations. Use the EDIT command on the MATRX menu of a TI-83 Plus to enter each of the following matrices.

$$A = \begin{bmatrix} 7.9 & 5.4 & -6.8 \\ -5.9 & 4.4 & -7.7 \end{bmatrix}, B = \begin{bmatrix} -7.2 & -5.8 & 9.1 \\ 4.3 & -8.4 & 5.3 \end{bmatrix}, C = \begin{bmatrix} 9.8 & -1.2 & 5.2 \\ -7.8 & 5.1 & -9.0 \end{bmatrix}$$

Use these stored matrices to find each sum, difference, or product.

53. $A + B$ **54.** $C - B$ **55.** $B + C - A$ **56.** $1.8A$ **57.** $0.4C$

Maintain Your Skills

Mixed Review

53.
$$\begin{bmatrix} 0.7 & -0.4 & 2.3 \\ -1.6 & -4 & -2.4 \end{bmatrix}$$

54.
$$\begin{bmatrix} 17 & 4.6 & -3.9 \\ -12.1 & 13.5 & -14.3 \end{bmatrix}$$

55.
$$\begin{bmatrix} -5.3 & -12.4 & 21.1 \\ 2.4 & -7.7 & 4 \end{bmatrix}$$

56.
$$\begin{bmatrix} 14.22 & 9.72 \\ -10.62 & 7.92 \\ -12.24 \\ -13.86 \end{bmatrix}$$

Getting Ready for the Next Lesson

57.
$$\begin{bmatrix} 3.92 & -0.48 & 2.08 \\ -3.12 & 2.04 & -3.6 \end{bmatrix}$$

PRINTING For Exercises 58 and 59, use the following information.
To determine the quality of calendars printed at a local shop, the last 10 calendars printed each day are examined. *(Lesson 13-1)*

58. Identify the sample. **10 calendars**

59. State whether it is *unbiased* (random) or *biased*. If unbiased, classify the sample as *simple*, *stratified*, or *systematic*. If biased, classify as *convenience* or *voluntary response*. **biased; convenience**

Solve each equation. *(Lesson 12-9)*

60. $\frac{-4}{a+1} + \frac{3}{a} = 1$ **−3, 1**   **61.** $\frac{3}{x} + \frac{4x}{x-3} = 4$ **$\frac{3}{5}$**   **62.** $\frac{d+3}{d+5} + \frac{2}{d-9} = \frac{5}{2d+10}$
1, 5.5

Find the nth term of each geometric sequence. *(Lesson 10-7)*

63. $a_1 = 4, n = 5, r = 3$ **324** **64.** $a_1 = -2, n = 3, r = 7$ **65.** $a_1 = 4, n = 5, r = -2$ **64**
−98

Factor each trinomial, if possible. If the trinomial cannot be factored using integers, write *prime*. *(Lesson 9-3)*

66. $b^2 + 7b + 12$ **67.** $a^2 + 2ab - 3b^2$ **68.** $d^2 + 8d - 15$ **prime**
$(b+3)(b+4)$ **$(a-b)(a+3b)$**

PREREQUISITE SKILL For Exercises 69 and 70, use the graph that shows the amount of money in Megan's savings account. *(To review interpreting graphs, see Lesson 1-9.)*

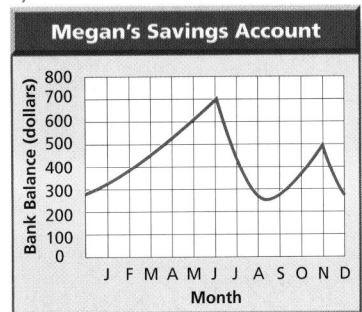

Megan's Savings Account

69. Describe what is happening to Megan's bank balance. Give possible reasons why the graph rises and falls at particular points. **See margin.**

70. Describe the elements in the domain and range. **months of the year; amount of money**

Practice Quiz 1   Lessons 13-1 and 13-2

Identify each sample, suggest a population from which it was selected, and state whether it is *unbiased* (random) or *biased*. If unbiased, classify the sample as *simple*, *stratified*, or *systematic*. If biased, classify as *convenience* or *voluntary response*. *(Lesson 13-1)*

1. Every other household in a neighborhood is surveyed to determine how to improve the neighborhood park.

2. Every other household in a neighborhood is surveyed to determine the favorite candidate for the state's governor. **half of the households in a neighborhood; sample answer: voters in the state; biased; convenience**

Find each sum, difference, or product. *(Lesson 13-2)* **3–5. See margin.**

3. $\begin{bmatrix} -8 & 3 \\ -4 & -9 \end{bmatrix} + \begin{bmatrix} 5 & -7 \\ -1 & 0 \end{bmatrix}$ **4.** $\begin{bmatrix} -9 & 6 & 4 \\ -1 & 3 & 2 \end{bmatrix} - \begin{bmatrix} 7 & -2 & 8 \\ 5 & -3 & 1 \end{bmatrix}$ **5.** $3\begin{bmatrix} 8 & -3 & -4 & 5 \\ 6 & -1 & 2 & 10 \end{bmatrix}$

1. half of the households in a neighborhood; all households in the neighborhood; unbiased; systematic

1 Focus

5-Minute Check Transparency 13-3 Use as a quiz or review of Lesson 13-2.

Mathematical Background notes are available for this lesson on p. 706D.

How are histograms used to display data?

Ask students:

• Compare the frequency table and the graph. From which is it easier to obtain exact data? Explain. **It is easier to get exact data from the table because the exact numerical values are listed.**

• Compare the frequency table and the graph. In which is it easier to compare data? Explain. **It is easier to compare data on the graph because the values are represented visually with bars. It is very easy to compare the height of the bars.**

• Which values from the frequency table are represented on the horizontal axis of the graph? **the score intervals**

• Which values from the frequency table are represented on the vertical axis of the graph? **the number of states in which the score intervals occurred**

What You'll Learn

• Interpret data displayed in histograms.
• Display data in histograms.

Vocabulary
• frequency table
• histogram
• measurement classes
• frequency

How are histograms used to display data?

A **frequency table** shows the frequency of events. The frequency table below shows the number of states with the mean SAT verbal and mathematics scores in each score interval. The data are from the 1999–2000 school year.

SAT Scores		
Score Interval	Verbal Number of States	Mathematics Number of States
$480 \leq s < 500$	11	5
$500 \leq s < 520$	10	18
$520 \leq s < 540$	6	5
$540 \leq s < 560$	8	10
$560 \leq s < 580$	10	5
$580 \leq s < 600$	5	5
$600 \leq s < 620$	0	2

Source: The College Board

The distribution of the mean scores on the SAT verbal exam is displayed in the graph.

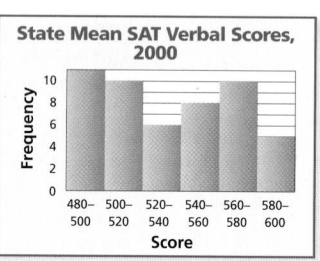

State Mean SAT Verbal Scores, 2000

INTERPRET DATA IN HISTOGRAMS The graph above is called a histogram. A **histogram** is a bar graph in which the data are organized into equal intervals. In the histogram above, the horizontal axis shows the range of data values separated into **measurement classes**, and the vertical axis shows the number of values, or the **frequency**, in each class. Consider the histogram shown below.

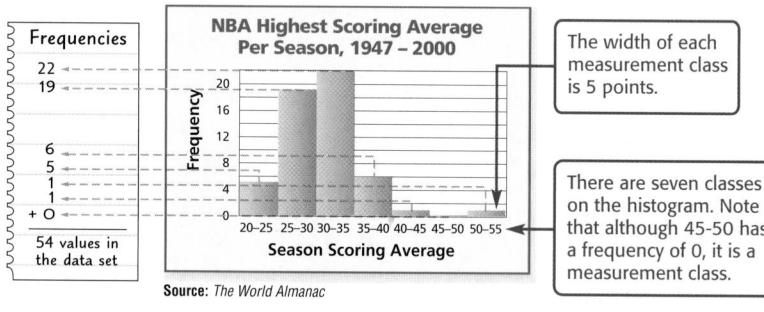

NBA Highest Scoring Average Per Season, 1947 – 2000

 The width of each measurement class is 5 points.

 There are seven classes on the histogram. Note that although 45-50 has a frequency of 0, it is a measurement class.

Source: The World Almanac

722 Chapter 13 Statistics

Resource Manager

📁 **Workbook and Reproducible Masters**

Chapter 13 Resource Masters
• Study Guide and Intervention, pp. 793–794
• Skills Practice, p. 795
• Practice, p. 796
• Reading to Learn Mathematics, p. 797
• Enrichment, p. 798
• Assessment, pp. 825, 827

Graphing Calculator and Spreadsheet Masters, p. 48
Parent and Student Study Guide Workbook, p. 103
Prerequisite Skills Workbook, pp. 97–98
School-to-Career Masters, p. 25

Transparencies
5-Minute Check Transparency 13-3
Answer Key Transparencies

💿 **Technology**
Interactive Chalkboard

A histogram is a visual summary of a frequency table.

Example 1 *Determine Information from a Histogram*

GEOGRAPHY Answer each question about the histogram shown below.

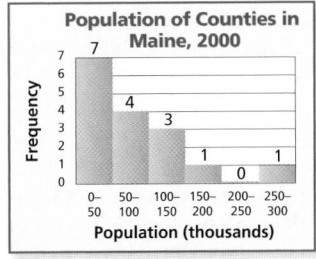

Population of Counties in Maine, 2000

a. In what measurement class does the median occur?

First, add the frequencies to determine the number of counties in Maine.

$7 + 4 + 3 + 1 + 0 + 1 = 16$

There are 16 counties, so the middle data value is between the 8th and 9th data values. Both the 8th and 9th data values are located in the 50–100 thousand measurement class. Therefore, the median occurs in the 50–100 thousand measurement class.

b. Describe the distribution of the data.

- Only two counties have populations above 150 thousand. It is likely that these counties contain the largest cities in Maine.
- There is a gap in the 200–250 thousand measurement class.
- Most of the counties have populations below 150 thousand.
- As population increases, the histogram shows that the number of counties decreases. We say that the distribution is *skewed to the right* or *skewed in the direction of the tail*. The majority of the data values cluster at the lower end of the distribution; the "tail" is to the right.

Study Tip

Look Back
To review **median**, see pages 818 and 819.

You can sometimes use the appearances of histograms to compare data.

Example 2 *Compare Data in Histograms*

Standardized Test Practice
Ⓐ Ⓑ Ⓒ Ⓓ

Multiple-Choice Test Item

Which group of students has a greater median height?

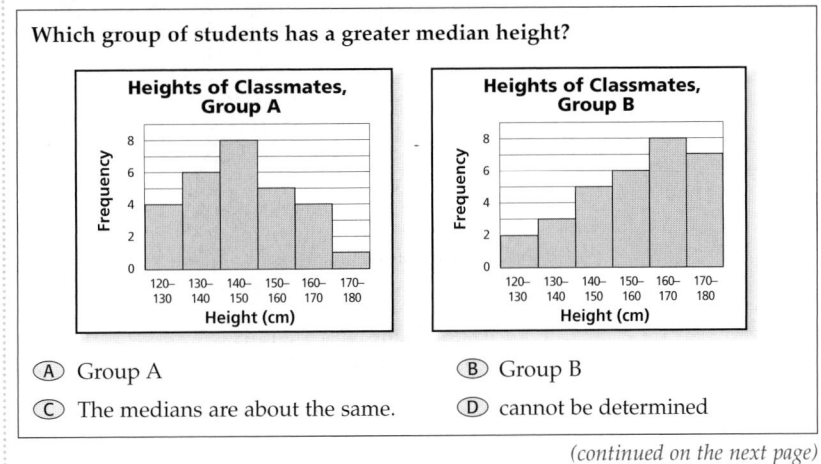

Heights of Classmates, Group A · Heights of Classmates, Group B

Ⓐ Group A

Ⓑ Group B

Ⓒ The medians are about the same.

Ⓓ cannot be determined

(continued on the next page)

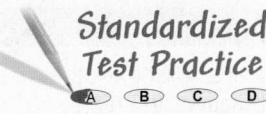
www.algebra1.com/extra_examples

INTERPRET DATA IN HISTOGRAMS

In-Class Examples Power Point®

1 **STUDENT POPULATION** Answer each question about the histogram shown below.

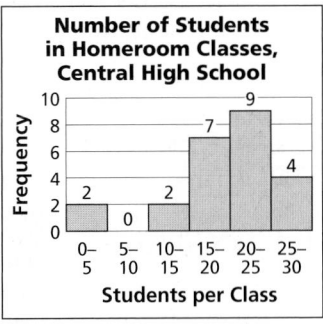

Number of Students in Homeroom Classes, Central High School

a. In what measurement class does the median occur? **in the 20–25 class**

b. Describe the distribution of the data. **Only two homerooms have fewer than 10 students. There is a gap in the 5–10 measurement class. Most homerooms have at least 15 students. The distribution is skewed to the right.**

2 Use the data in the histograms to determine which class has a greater median test score. **C**

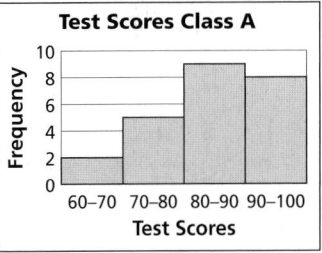

Test Scores Class A

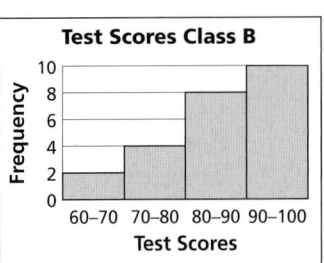

Test Scores Class B

A Class A

B Class B

C The medians are about the same.

D Cannot be determined

Standardized Test Practice
Ⓐ Ⓑ Ⓒ Ⓓ

Explain to students that they should not exclude answer choices C and D because the choices do not seem to answer the question. Just because the question asks which group has the greater height does not mean that the heights cannot be the same, or that you might not have enough data to answer the question.

Technology Consider having students use spreadsheet software to create histograms. A spreadsheet is very useful for organizing data into a frequency table. Then, students can use the spreadsheet's graphing function to turn the frequency table into a histogram.

DISPLAY DATA IN A HISTOGRAM

In-Class Example Power Point®

Teaching Tip Tell students that it is highly advisable to create a frequency table as an intermediate step to creating a histogram. While it might be possible to create a histogram without first creating a frequency table, it is certainly more difficult.

3 FOOTBALL Create a histogram to represent the following scores of top 25 winning college football teams during one week of the 2001 season.

43, 52, 38, 36, 42, 46, 26, 38, 38, 31, 38, 37, 38, 48, 45, 27, 47, 35, 35, 26, 47, 24, 41, 21, 32

Sample answer:

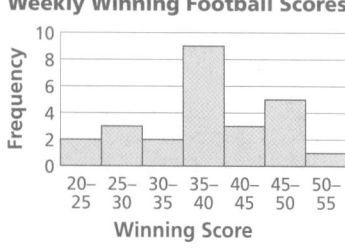

Weekly Winning Football Scores

Answers

1. First identify the greatest and least values in the data set. Use this information to determine appropriate measurement classes. Using these measurement classes, create a frequency table. Then draw the histogram. Always remember to label the axes and give the histogram a title.

Read the Test Item
You have two histograms depicting the heights of two groups of students. You are asked to determine which group of students has a greater median height.

Test-Taking Tip
When answering a test question involving a graph, always read the labels on the graph carefully.

Solve the Test Item
Study the histograms carefully. The measurement classes and the frequency scales are the same for each histogram. The distribution for Group A is somewhat *symmetrical* in shape, while the distribution for Group B is *skewed to the right*. This would indicate that Group B has the greater median height. To check this assumption, locate the measurement class of each median.

Group A
$4 + 6 + 8 + 5 + 4 + 1 = 28$
The median is between the 14th and 15th data values. The median is in the 140–150 measurement class.

Group B
$2 + 3 + 5 + 6 + 8 + 7 = 31$
The median is the 16th data value. The median is in the 150–160 measurement class.

This confirms that Group B has the greater median height. The answer is B.

DISPLAY DATA IN A HISTOGRAM
Data from a list or a frequency table can be used to create a histogram.

Example 3 *Create a Histogram*

SCHOOL Create a histogram to represent the following scores for a 50-point mathematics test.

40, 34, 38, 23, 41, 39, 39, 34, 43, 44, 32, 44, 41, 39, 22, 47, 36, 25, 41, 30, 28, 37, 39, 33, 30, 40, 28

Step 1 Identify the greatest and least values in the data set.
The test scores range from 22 to 47 points.

Step 2 Create measurement classes of equal width.
For these data, use measurement classes from 20 to 50 with a 5-point interval for each class.

Step 3 Create a frequency table using the measurement classes.

Score Intervals	Tally	Frequency
$20 \leq s < 25$	II	2
$25 \leq s < 30$	III	3
$30 \leq s < 35$	ＩＩＩ I	6
$35 \leq s < 40$	ＩＩＩ II	7
$40 \leq s < 45$	ＩＩＩ III	8
$45 \leq s < 50$	I	1

TEACHING TIP
Measurement classes must be unambiguous. Explain to the students that each data value should belong to one and only one measurement class. For data values that fall on a boundary between classes, it is customary to include the data value in the higher of the two classes. Therefore, all values of s such that $20 \leq s < 25$ belong in the 20–25 measurement class.

Step 4 Draw the histogram.
Use the measurement classes to determine the scale for the horizontal axis and the frequency values to determine the scale for the vertical axis. For each measurement class, draw a rectangle as wide as the measurement class and as tall as the frequency for the class. Label the axes and include a descriptive title for the histogram.

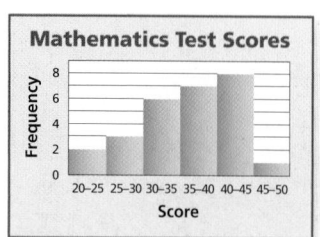

Mathematics Test Scores

Differentiated Instruction

Kinesthetic Give students algebra tiles, beads, beans, or some other small manipulatives. Have students use the manipulatives to create histograms such as the one in Example 3. First, students can use the manipulatives as the tally for the measurement classes in a frequency table. Then students can transfer the manipulatives from the tally column to the actual histogram, using the manipulatives as the columns in the histogram.

Concept Check

3. Sample answer: 1, 1, 2, 4, 5, 5, 8, 9, 10, 11, 12, 13, 22, 24, 41

Guided Practice

GUIDED PRACTICE KEY	
Exercises	Examples
4, 5	1
6, 7, 9	2
8	3

1. **Describe** how to create a histogram. **See margin.**

2. **Write** a compound inequality to represent all of the values v included in a 50–60 measurement class. $50 \le v < 60$

3. **OPEN ENDED** Write a set of data whose histogram would be skewed to the right.

MONEY For Exercises 4 and 5, use the following histogram that shows the amount of money spent by several families during a holiday weekend.

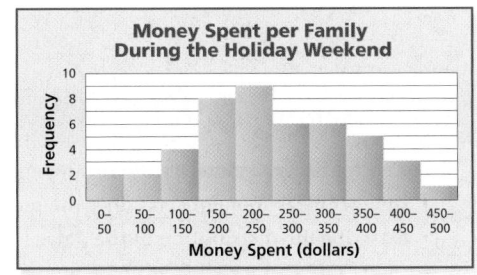

4. In what measurement class does the median occur? **$200–$250**

5. Describe the distribution of the data.

SCHOOL For Exercises 6 and 7, use the following histograms.

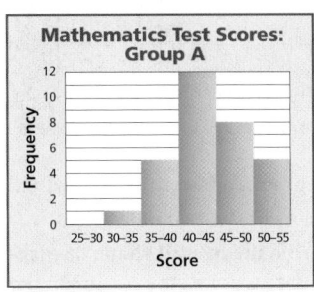 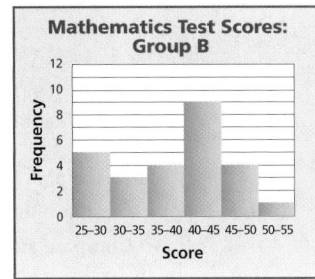

6. Compare the medians of the two data sets.

7. Compare and describe the overall shape of each distribution of data.

8. **AIR TRAVEL** The busiest U.S. airports as determined by the number of passengers arriving and departing are listed below. Create a histogram.

Passenger Traffic at U.S. Airports, 2000			
Airport	Passengers (millions)	Airport	Passengers (millions)
Atlanta (Hartsfield)	80	Minneapolis/St. Paul	37
Chicago (O'Hare)	72	Phoenix (Sky Harbor)	36
Los Angeles	68	Detroit	36
Dallas/Fort Worth	61	Houston (George Bush)	35
San Francisco	41	Newark	34
Denver	39	Miami	34
Las Vegas (McCarran)	37	New York (JFK)	33

Source: Airports Council International

 Online Research **Data Update** What are the current busiest airports? Visit www.algebra1.com/data_update to get statistics on airports.

Lesson 13-3 Histograms **725**

Margin notes:

5. There are no gaps. The data are somewhat symmetrical.

6. Group A: 40–45 points; Group B: 40–45 points

7. The Group A test scores are somewhat more symmetrical in appearance than the Group B test scores. There are 25 of 31 scores in Group A that are 40 or greater, while only 14 of 26 scores of Group B are 40 or greater. Also Group B has 5 scores less than 30. Therefore, we can conclude that Group A performed better overall on the test.

8. See pp. 751A–751B.

Study Notebook

Have students—
- add the definitions/examples of the vocabulary terms to their Vocabulary Builder worksheets for Chapter 13.
- include explanations on how to interpret and create histograms.
- include any other item(s) that they find helpful in mastering the skills in this lesson.

About the Exercises...

Organization by Objective
- **Interpret Data in Histograms:** 10–13
- **Display Data in a Histogram:** 14–22

Odd/Even Assignments

Exercises 10–15 are structured so that students practice the same concepts whether they are assigned odd or even problems.

Alert! Exercise 21 requires students to conduct research on the Internet.

Assignment Guide

Basic: 11, 15–17, 22–25, 30–43

Average: 11–15 odd, 16, 17, 21–25, 30–43 (optional: 26–29)

Advanced: 10–14 even, 18–39 (optional: 40–43)

DAILY INTERVENTION

Unlocking Misconceptions

Measurement Classes Make sure students place data in the correct measurement classes on their histograms. Looking at Example 3, the first measurement class on the histogram is labeled 20–25. This corresponds to the score interval $20 \le s < 25$ in the frequency table. This means that a score of 25 *would not* be included in the first measurement class. Suggest that students label their histogram measurement classes with inequality symbols, like those that are used in the frequency tables.

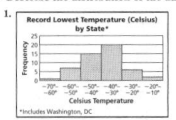
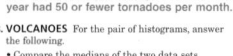
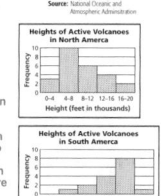
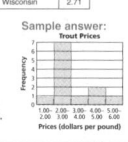
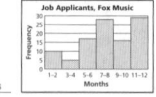

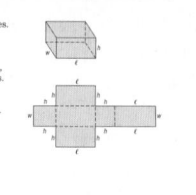

Standardized Test Practice
Ⓐ Ⓑ Ⓒ Ⓓ

9. Which statement about the graph at the right is *not* correct? **B**

Ⓐ The data are skewed to the right.

Ⓑ The median is in the 40–50 thousand measurement class.

Ⓒ There are 32 employees represented by the graph.

Ⓓ The width of each measurement class is $10 thousand.

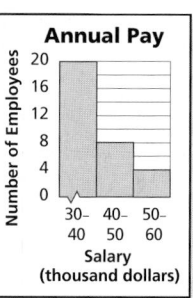

Annual Pay

★ indicates increased difficulty

Practice and Apply

For each histogram, answer the following.
• In what measurement class does the median occur?
• Describe the distribution of the data.

10.
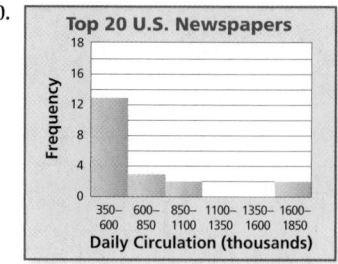

Source: Editor & Publisher International Yearbook

11.
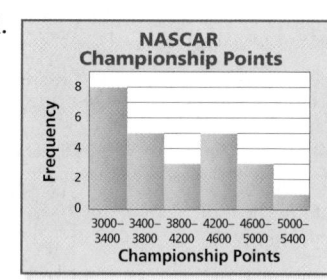

Source: USA TODAY

For each pair of histograms, answer the following.
• Compare the medians of the two data sets.
• Compare and describe the overall shape of each distribution of data.

★ 12.
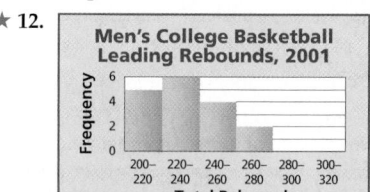

Source: USA TODAY

★ 13.
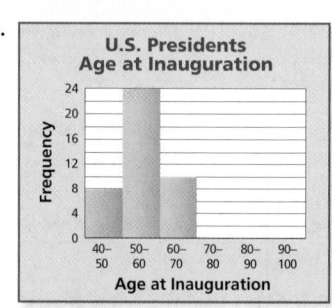

Source: The World Almanac

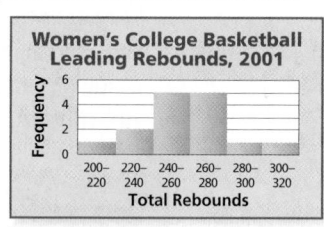

Source: USA TODAY

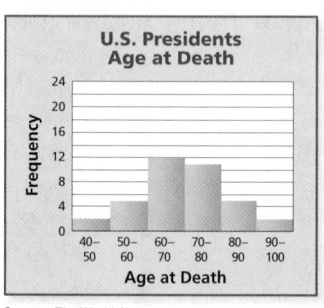

Source: The World Almanac

726   Chapter 13   Statistics

10. 350–600 thousand newspapers; See margin.

11. 3400–3800 points; There are no gaps. The data appear to be skewed to the left.

12. Men: 220–240 rebounds; women: 240–260 rebounds; See margin.

13. Age at inauguration: 50–60 years old; age at death: 60–70 years old; both distributions show a symmetrical shape. The two distributions differ in their spread. The inauguration ages are not spread out as much as the death ages data.

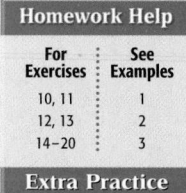
Answer

10. There is a gap between 1100 and 1600 thousand. The histogram is highly skewed to the left, with a vast majority of the data values in the lowest measurement class. Over half of the top 20 newspapers have circulations between 350 and 600 thousand.

Create a histogram to represent each data set. 14–15. See margin.

14. Students' semester averages in a mathematics class: 96.53, 95.96, 94.25, 93.58, 91.91, 90.33, 90.27, 90.11, 89.30, 89.06, 88.33, 88.30, 87.43, 86.67, 86.31, 84.21, 83.53, 82.30, 78.71, 77.51, 73.83

15. Number of raisins found in a snack-size box: 54, 59, 55, 109, 97, 59, 102, 68, 104, 63, 101, 59, 59, 96, 58, 57, 63, 57, 94, 61, 104, 62, 58, 59, 102, 60, 54, 58, 53, 78

BASEBALL For Exercises 16 and 17, use the following table.

Payrolls for Major League Baseball Teams in 2000					
Team	Payroll (millions)	Team	Payroll (millions)	Team	Payroll (millions)
Yankees	$112	Orioles	$59	White Sox	$37
Braves	$94	Tigers	$59	Reds	$36
Red Sox	$91	Rockies	$56	Phillies	$36
Dodgers	$90	Padres	$55	Athletics	$32
Mets	$82	Blue Jays	$54	Pirates	$29
Indians	$77	Giants	$54	Expos	$28
Diamondbacks	$74	Angels	$53	Brewers	$26
Cardinals	$73	Devil Rays	$51	Marlins	$25
Rangers	$62	Astros	$51	Royals	$24
Mariners	$62	Cubs	$50	Twins	$15

Source: *USA TODAY*

16. Create a histogram to represent the payroll data. See pp. 751A–751B.

17. On your histogram, locate and label the median team payroll. $54,000,000

ELECTIONS For Exercises 18–20, use the following table.

Percent of Eligible Voters Who Voted in the 2000 Presidential Election									
State	Percent	State	Percent	State	Percent	State	Percent	State	Percent
MN	68.75	WY	59.70	OH	55.76	MD	51.56	AR	47.79
ME	67.34	CT	58.40	ID	54.46	NJ	51.04	NM	47.40
AK	66.41	SD	58.24	RI	54.29	FL	50.65	SC	46.49
WI	66.07	MI	57.52	LA	54.24	NC	50.28	WV	45.74
VT	63.98	MO	57.49	KS	54.07	AL	49.99	CA	44.09
NH	62.33	WA	56.95	PA	53.66	IN	49.44	GA	43.84
MT	61.52	MA	56.92	IL	52.79	NY	49.42	NV	43.81
IA	60.71	CO	56.78	UT	52.61	TN	49.19	TX	43.15
OR	60.63	NE	56.44	VA	52.05	OK	48.76	AZ	42.26
ND	60.63	DE	56.22	KY	51.59	MS	48.57	HI	40.48

Source: *USA TODAY*

18. Determine the median of the data. 53.865

19. Create a histogram to represent the data. See margin.

20. Write a sentence or two describing the distribution of the data.

21. **RESEARCH** Choose your favorite professional sport. Use the Internet or other reference to find how many games each team in the appropriate league won last season. Use this information to create a histogram. Describe your histogram.

22. **CRITICAL THINKING** Create a histogram with a gap between 20 and 40, one item in the 50–55 measurement class, and the median value in the 50–55 measurement class. See margin.

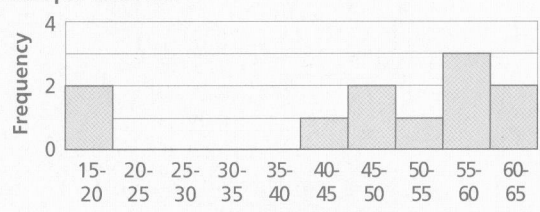

www.algebra1.com/self_check_quiz

More About...

Baseball

The New York Yankees won the 2000 World Series and had the largest payroll of all major league teams that year.

Source: *USA TODAY*

20. Sample answer: There are no gaps. The data are somewhat symmetrical.

21. See students' work.

Answers

12. The men's rebounding data show a vast majority of values are between 200 and 240 rebounds. The women's rebounding data are somewhat symmetrical. The top two women have more rebounds than any of the men.

14. Sample answer:

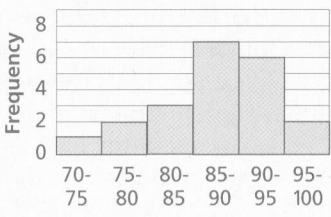

15. Sample answer:

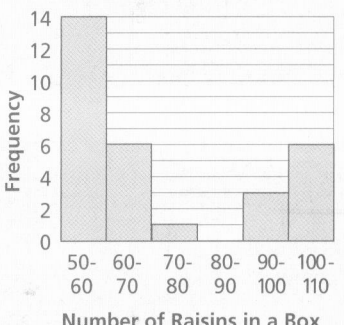

19. Sample answer:

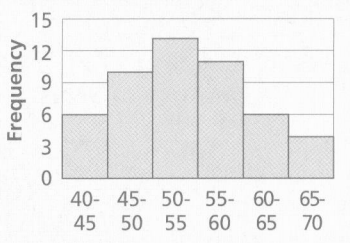

22. Sample answer:

Open-Ended Assessment

Modeling Have students tear strips of paper to make a rough histogram on a subject of their choosing (e.g. ages of people in their neighborhood). Ask students how they chose the length of the strips.

Getting Ready for Lesson 13-4

PREREQUISITE SKILL Students will learn about measures of variation in data in Lesson 13-4. This lesson assumes students are familiar with the concept of median. Use Exercises 40–43 to determine your students' familiarity with finding the median of a set of data.

Assessment Options

Quiz (Lesson 13-3) is available on p. 825 of the *Chapter 13 Resource Masters*.

Mid-Chapter Test (Lessons 13-1 through 13-3) is available on p. 827 of the *Chapter 13 Resource Masters*.

Answers

23. Histograms can be used to show how many states have a median within various intervals. Answers should include the following.

• A histogram is more visual than a frequency table and can show trends easily.

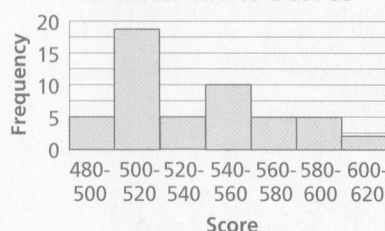

Year 2000 State Mean SAT Mathematics Scores

26. Sample answer:

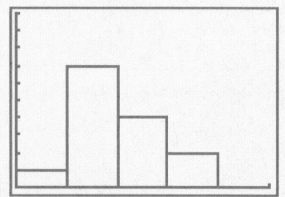

---

23. **WRITING IN MATH** Answer the question that was posed at the beginning of the lesson. **See margin.**

How are histograms used to display data?

Include the following in your answer:
• the advantage of the histogram over the frequency table, and
• a histogram depicting the distribution of the mean scores on the SAT mathematics exam.

Standardized Test Practice
Ⓐ Ⓑ Ⓒ Ⓓ

For Exercises 24 and 25, use the information in the graph.

24. How many employees are represented in the graph? **C**
   Ⓐ 38   Ⓑ 40
   Ⓒ 46   Ⓓ 48

25. In which measurement class is the median of the data located? **B**
   Ⓐ 2–4   Ⓑ 4–6
   Ⓒ 6–8   Ⓓ 8–10

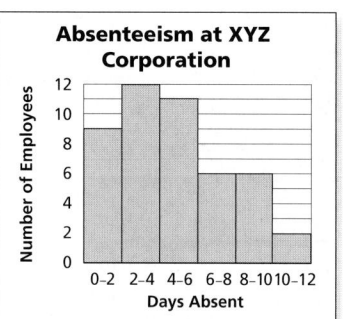

Absenteeism at XYZ Corporation

Graphing Calculator

HISTOGRAMS You can use a graphing calculator to create histograms. On a TI-83 Plus, enter the data in L1. In the STAT PLOT menu, turn on Plot 1 and select the histogram. Define the viewing window and press GRAPH.

Use a graphing calculator to create a histogram for each set of data.

26. 5, 5, 6, 7, 9, 4, 10, 12, 13, 8, 15, 16, 13, 8 **26–29. See margin.**
27. 12, 14, 25, 30, 11, 35, 41, 47, 13, 18, 58, 59, 42, 13, 18
28. 124, 83, 81, 130, 111, 92, 178, 179, 134, 92, 133, 145, 180, 144
29. 2.2, 2.4, 7.5, 9.1, 3.4, 5.1, 6.3, 1.8, 2.8, 3.7, 8.6, 9.5, 3.6, 3.7, 5.0

Maintain Your Skills

Mixed Review

If $A = \begin{bmatrix} -2 & 3 & 7 \\ 0 & -4 & 6 \\ 1 & -5 & 4 \end{bmatrix}$, $B = \begin{bmatrix} -8 & 1 & -1 \\ 2 & 3 & -7 \end{bmatrix}$, and $C = \begin{bmatrix} 7 & -5 & 2 \\ 0 & 0 & 3 \\ -1 & 4 & 6 \end{bmatrix}$, find each sum, difference, or product. If the sum or difference does not exist, write **impossible**. *(Lesson 13-2)*

31. $\begin{bmatrix} 9 & -8 & -5 \\ 0 & 4 & -3 \\ -2 & 9 & 2 \end{bmatrix}$

32. $\begin{bmatrix} -16 & 2 & -2 \\ 4 & 6 & -14 \end{bmatrix}$

33. $\begin{bmatrix} 10 & -15 & -35 \\ 0 & 20 & -30 \\ -5 & 25 & -20 \end{bmatrix}$

30. $A + B$ **impossible**   31. $C - A$ 32. $2B$ 33. $-5A$

34. **MANUFACTURING** Every 15 minutes, a CD player is taken off the assembly line and tested. State whether this sample is *unbiased* (random) or *biased*. If unbiased, classify the sample as *simple*, *stratified*, or *systematic*. If biased, classify as *convenience* or *voluntary response*. *(Lesson 13-1)* **unbiased; systematic**

Find each quotient. Assume that no denominator has a value of 0. *(Lesson 12-4)*

35. $\dfrac{s}{s+7} \div \dfrac{s-5}{s+7}$ $\dfrac{s}{s-5}$

36. $\dfrac{2m^2 + 7m - 15}{m+2} \div \dfrac{2m-3}{m^2 + 5m + 6}$ $(m+5)(m+3)$

Solve each equation. Check your solution. *(Lesson 11-3)*

37. $\sqrt{y+3} + 5 = 9$ **13**   38. $\sqrt{x-2} = x - 4$ **6**   39. $13 = \sqrt{2w-5}$ **87**

Getting Ready for the Next Lesson

PREREQUISITE SKILL Find the median for each set of data.
*(To review **median**, see pages 818 and 819.)*

40. 2, 4, 7, 9, 12, 15 **8**   41. 10, 3, 17, 1, 8, 6, 12, 15 **9**
42. 7, 19, 9, 4, 7, 2 **7**   43. 2.1, 7.4, 13.9, 1.6, 5.21, 3.901 **about 4.56**

---

27. Sample answer:

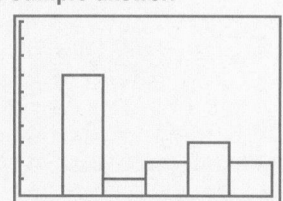

28. Sample answer:

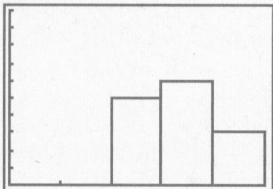

29. Sample answer:

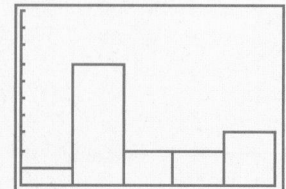

Graphing Calculator Investigation

A Follow-Up of Lesson 13-3

Curve Fitting

If there is a constant increase or decrease in data values, there is a linear trend. If the values are increasing or decreasing more and more rapidly, there may be a quadratic or exponential trend. The curvature of a quadratic trend tends to appear more gradual. Below are three scatter plots, each showing a different trend.

Linear Trend

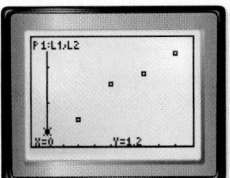

Quadratic Trend

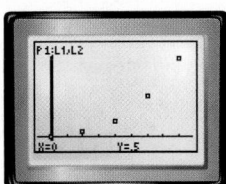

Exponential Trend

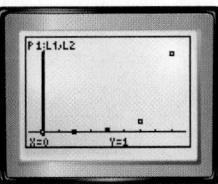

With a TI-83 Plus, you can use the LinReg, QuadReg, and ExpReg functions to find the appropriate regression equation that best fits the data.

FARMING A study is conducted in which groups of 25 corn plants are given a different amount of fertilizer and the gain in height after a certain time is recorded. The table below shows the results.

Fertilizer (mg)	0	20	40	60	80
Gain in Height (in.)	6.48	7.35	8.73	9.00	8.13

Step 1 *Make a scatter plot.*

- Enter the fertilizer in L1 and the height in L2.
  KEYSTROKES: *Review entering a list on page 204.*
- Use STAT PLOT to graph the scatter plot.
  KEYSTROKES: *Review statistical plots on page 204. Use* [ZOOM] 9 *to graph.*

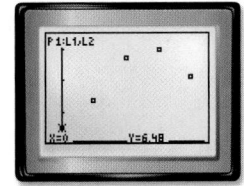

[−8, 88] scl: 5 by [6.0516, 9.4284] scl: 1

The graph appears to be a quadratic regression.

Step 2 *Find the quadratic regression equation.*

- Select QuadReg on the [STAT] CALC menu.
  KEYSTROKES: [STAT] [▶] 5 [ENTER]

The equation is in the form $y = ax^2 + bx + c$.

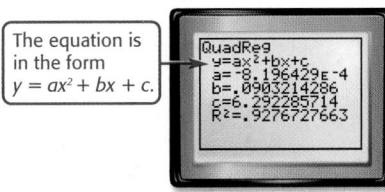

The equation is about $y = -0.0008x^2 + 0.1x + 6.3$.

R^2 is the **coefficient of determination**. The closer R^2 is to 1, the better the model. To choose a quadratic or exponential model, fit both and use the one with the R^2 value closer to 1.

(continued on the next page)

 www.algebra1.com/other_calculator_keystrokes

Graphing Calculator Investigation

A Follow-Up of Lesson 13-3

Getting Started

Know Your Calculator Before entering data for a new problem into a list, press [STAT] 4 [ENTER] to clear any previously entered lists. Also, clear previously entered equations from the Y= list by highlighting each equation and hitting the [CLEAR] key.

Teach

- **Step 1** Make sure students clear previous lists before entering the data. Students should enter the amount of fertilizer in L1 and the gain in height in L2.

- **Step 2** Point out to students that the *a* value, −8.196429E−4, is in *scientific notation*. This value corresponds to -8.196429×10^{-4}, or −0.00082196429.

- **Step 3** Tell students that they must copy the quadratic regression *exactly* to the Y= list in order to get the proper graph.

- **Step 4** To calculate the maximum for the function, press 2nd [CALC] 4. Remind students to set the left and right bounds well away from the vertex, in order to calculate the correct maximum.

Assess

In the example problem, the data suggested that 60 mg of fertilizer produced the greatest gain in height. However, using the quadratic regression equation the calculator came up with a maximum of 55 mg of fertilizer to produce the greatest gain in height. How can you explain this difference? **The quadratic regression equation that is calculated by the graphing calculator is a best fit to data points that do not fall on an actual graphed function. Therefore, there will be slight differences between actual data points, and points that fall on the regression function.**

Answers

1.
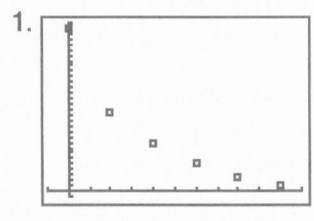

2.
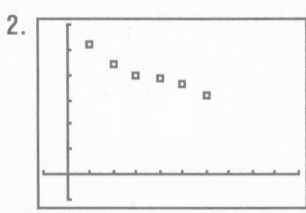

3.
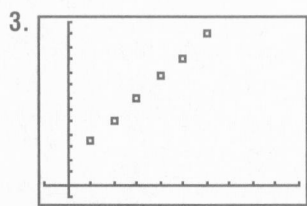

Step 3 *Graph the quadratic regression equation.*

- Copy the equation to the Y= list and graph.

  KEYSTROKES: Y= VARS 5 ▶ ▶ 1
  ZOOM 9

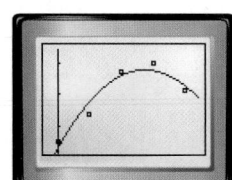

Step 4 *Predict using the equation.*

- Find the amount of fertilizer that produces the maximum gain in height.

On average, about 55 milligrams of the fertilizer produces the maximum gain.

KEYSTROKES:
2nd CALC 4

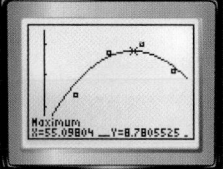

Exercises
1. exponential; 0.9969724389   2. linear; 0.389164209
3. linear; 0.9974802029   4. quadratic; 0.97716799

See margin for graphs.

Plot each set of data points. Determine whether to use a *linear*, *quadratic*, or *exponential* regression equation. State the coefficient of determination.

1.
x	y
0.0	2.98
0.2	1.46
0.4	0.90
0.6	0.51
0.8	0.25
1.0	0.13

2.
x	y
1	25.9
2	22.2
3	20.0
4	19.3
5	18.2
6	15.9

3.
x	y
10	35
20	50
30	70
40	88
50	101
60	120

4.
x	y
1	3.67
3	5.33
5	6.33
7	5.67
9	4.33
11	2.67

TECHNOLOGY The cost of cellular phone use is expected to decrease. For Exercises 5–9, use the graph at the right.

5. Make a scatter plot of the data. **See margin.**

6. Find an appropriate regression equation, and state the coefficient of determination.

7. Use the regression equation to predict the expected cost in 2004. **about 20.5¢**

8. Do you believe that your regression equation is appropriate for a year beyond the range of data, such as 2020? Explain. **No; see margin.**

9. What model may be more appropriate for predicting cost beyond 2003? **a linear model**

6. $y = 0.4107142857x^2 - 1645.696429x + 1,648,561$; 0.9880773362

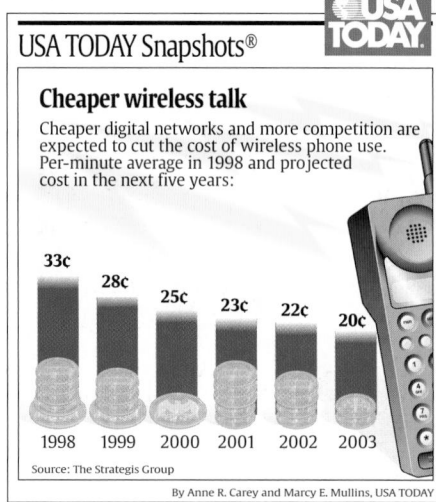

USA TODAY Snapshots®

Cheaper wireless talk

Cheaper digital networks and more competition are expected to cut the cost of wireless phone use. Per-minute average in 1998 and projected cost in the next five years:

33¢ 28¢ 25¢ 23¢ 22¢ 20¢
1998 1999 2000 2001 2002 2003

Source: The Strategis Group

By Anne R. Carey and Marcy E. Mullins, USA TODAY

4.
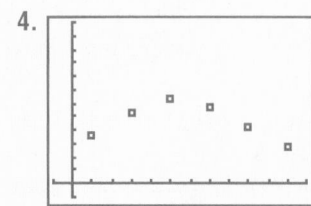

5.
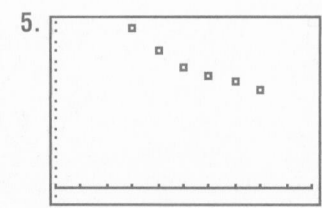

8. **The price will start to increase using the quadratic model.**

Measures of Variation

What You'll Learn

- Find the range of a set of data.
- Find the quartiles and interquartile range of a set of data.

Vocabulary

- range
- measures of variation
- quartiles
- lower quartile
- upper quartile
- interquartile range
- outlier

How is variation used in weather?

The average monthly temperatures for three U.S. cities are given. Which city shows the greatest change in monthly highs?

To answer this question, find the difference between the greatest and least values in each data set.

Buffalo: $80.2 - 30.2 = 50.0$
Honolulu: $88.7 - 80.1 = 8.6$
Tampa: $90.2 - 69.8 = 20.4$

Buffalo shows the greatest change.

Average Monthly High Temperatures (°F)			
Month	Buffalo	Honolulu	Tampa
January	30.2	80.1	69.8
February	31.6	80.5	71.4
March	41.7	81.6	76.6
April	54.2	82.8	81.7
May	66.1	84.7	87.2
June	75.3	86.5	89.5
July	80.2	87.5	90.2
August	77.9	88.7	90.2
September	70.8	88.5	89.0
October	59.4	86.9	84.3
November	47.1	84.1	77.7
December	35.3	81.2	72.1

Source: www.stormfax.com

RANGE The difference between the greatest and the least monthly high temperatures is called the **range** of the temperatures.

Key Concept — Definition of Range

The range of a set of data is the difference between the greatest and the least values of the set.

Study Tip

Look Back
To review **mean, median**, and **mode**, see pages 818 and 819.

The mean, median, and mode describe the central tendency of a set of data. The range of a set of data is a measure of the spread of the data. Measures that describe the spread of the values in a set of data are called **measures of variation**.

Example 1 Find the Range

HOCKEY The number of wins for each team in the Eastern Conference of the NHL for the 1999–2000 season are listed below. Find the range of the data.

Team	Wins	Team	Wins	Team	Wins
Atlanta	14	Montreal	35	Philadelphia	45
Boston	24	New Jersey	45	Pittsburgh	37
Buffalo	35	N.Y. Islanders	24	Tampa Bay	19
Carolina	37	N.Y. Rangers	29	Toronto	45
Florida	43	Ottawa	41	Washington	44

Source: The World Almanac

The greatest number of wins is 45, and the least number of wins is 14. Since $45 - 14 = 31$, the range of the number of wins is 31.

5-Minute Check Transparency 13-4 Use as a quiz or review of Lesson 13-3.

Mathematical Background notes are available for this lesson on p. 706D.

How is variation used in weather?

Ask students:

- How can you tell by looking at the temperature data for Honolulu that its high temperatures vary the least? **The temperatures are all in the 80s, while those of the other cities are not.**

- Describe how a histogram of the Buffalo temperatures would look. **Sample answer: There would be many measurement classes with low frequencies.**

- Describe how a histogram of the Honolulu data would look. **Sample answer: There would probably be only one measurement class, with a high frequency.**

- **Climate** Have students look up climatic data for your city or region and list the average monthly high temperatures. Then ask students to calculate the greatest change in monthly highs. **Answers may vary.**

Resource Manager

Workbook and Reproducible Masters

Chapter 13 Resource Masters
- Study Guide and Intervention, pp. 799–800
- Skills Practice, p. 801
- Practice, p. 802
- Reading to Learn Mathematics, p. 803
- Enrichment, p. 804
- Assessment, p. 826

Parent and Student Study Guide Workbook, p. 104
Prerequisite Skills Workbook, pp. 1–2, 19–20

Transparencies
5-Minute Check Transparency 13-4
Real-World Transparency 13
Answer Key Transparencies

Technology
Interactive Chalkboard

Building on Prior Knowledge

In Lesson 2-5, students learned how to analyze data in stem-and-leaf plots using the measures of central tendency such as mean, median, and mode. In this lesson, students learn more ways to analyze data.

RANGE

In-Class Example Power Point®

1 **COLLEGE FOOTBALL** The teams with the top 15 offensive yardage gains for the 2000 season are listed in the table below. Find the range of the data.

Team	Yardage
Air Force	4971
Boise St.	5459
Clemson	4911
Florida St.	6588
Georgia Tech	4789
Idaho	4985
Indiana	4830
Kentucky	4900
Miami	5069
Michigan	4900
Nebraska	5059
Northwestern	5232
Purdue	5183
Texas	4825
Tulane	4989

The range of yardage gains is 1799.

Answer

3. The range is the difference between the greatest and the least values of the set.

QUARTILES AND INTERQUARTILE RANGE In a set of data, the **quartiles** are values that separate the data into four equal subsets, each containing one fourth of the data. Statisticians often use Q_1, Q_2, and Q_3 to represent the three quartiles. Remember that the median separates the data into two equal parts. Q_2 is the median. Q_1 is the **lower quartile**. It divides the lower half of the data into two equal parts. Likewise Q_3 is the **upper quartile**. It divides the upper half of the data into two equal parts. The difference between the upper and lower quartiles is the **interquartile range** (IQR).

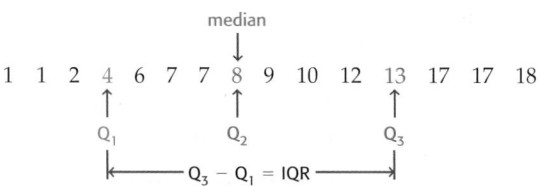

median ↓

1 1 2 4 6 7 7 8 9 10 12 13 17 17 18

↑ Q_1 ↑ Q_2 ↑ Q_3

$Q_3 - Q_1 = IQR$

TEACHING TIP
Point out that the quartiles represent 25%, 50%, and 75% of the data set.

Key Concept — *Definition of Interquartile Range*

The difference between the upper quartile and the lower quartile of a set of data is called the interquartile range. It represents the middle half, or 50%, of the data in the set.

Example 2 *Find the Quartiles and the Interquartile Range*

GEOGRAPHY The areas of the original 13 states are listed in the table. Find the median, the lower quartile, the upper quartile, and the interquartile range of the areas.

Explore You are given a table with the areas of the original 13 states. You are asked to find the median, the lower quartile, the upper quartile, and the interquartile range.

Plan First, list the areas from least to greatest. Then find the median of the data. The median will divide the data into two sets of data. To find the upper and lower quartiles, find the median of each of these sets of data. Finally, subtract the lower quartile from the upper quartile to find the interquartile range.

State	Area (thousand square miles)
Connecticut	6
Delaware	2
Georgia	59
Maryland	12
Massachusetts	11
New Hampshire	9
New Jersey	9
New York	54
North Carolina	54
Pennsylvania	46
Rhode Island	2
South Carolina	32
Virginia	43

Source: www.infoplease.com

Solve

median ↓

2 2 6 9 9 11 **12** 32 43 46 54 54 59

$Q_1 = \dfrac{6 + 9}{2}$ or 7.5 $Q_3 = \dfrac{46 + 54}{2}$ or 50

The median is 12 thousand square miles.

The lower quartile is 7.5 thousand square miles, and the upper quartile is 50 thousand square miles.

The interquartile range is $50 - 7.5$ or 42.5 thousand square miles.

DAILY INTERVENTION — **Unlocking Misconceptions**

Quartiles Point out to students that when they are finding quartiles, the upper and lower half of the data do not include the median. To make sure students have correctly located the quartiles and median, have students look at the set of numbers in a row. There should be an equal number of numbers between each quartile and the median, and between each quartile and the ends.

Examine Check to make sure that the numbers are listed in order. Since 7.5, 12, and 50 divide the data into four equal parts, the lower quartile, median, and upper quartile are correct.

In a set of data, a value that is much less or much greater than the rest of the data is called an **outlier**. An outlier is defined as any element of a set of data that is at least 1.5 interquartile ranges less than the lower quartile or greater than the upper quartile.

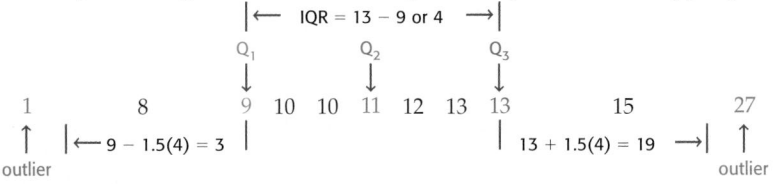

$$\leftarrow \text{IQR} = 13 - 9 \text{ or } 4 \longrightarrow$$

$$Q_1 \qquad Q_2 \qquad Q_3$$

1   8   9   10   10   11   12   13   13   15   27

↑ $\leftarrow 9 - 1.5(4) = 3$ $13 + 1.5(4) = 19 \longrightarrow$ ↑

outlier   outlier

Example 3   Identify Outliers

Identify any outliers in the following set of data.

Stem	Leaf
1	[2 2 7
2	3 [3 3] 4 4 5 6] [6 8 8 9
3	[0 1] 4 6
4	0 6] $1 \mid 2 = 12$

Step 1   **Find the quartiles.**

The brackets group the values in the lower half and the values in the upper half. The boxes are used to find the lower quartile and the upper quartile.

$$Q_1 = \frac{23 + 23}{2} \text{ or } 23 \qquad\qquad Q_3 = \frac{30 + 31}{2} \text{ or } 30.5$$

Step 2   **Find the interquartile range.**

The interquartile range is $30.5 - 23$ or 7.5.

Step 3   **Find the outliers, if any.**

An outlier must be 1.5(7.5) less than the lower quartile, 23, or 1.5(7.5) greater than the upper quartile, 30.5.

$$23 - 1.5(7.5) = 11.75 \qquad\qquad 30.5 + 1.5(7.5) = 41.75$$

There are no values less than 11.75. Since $46 > 41.75$, 46 is the only outlier.

Check for Understanding

Concept Check

1. Sample answer: 1, 4, 5, 6, 7, 8, 15 and 1, 2, 4, 5, 9, 9, 10

2. Outliers may make the mean much greater or much less than the mean of the data excluding the outliers.

1. **OPEN ENDED**   Find a counterexample for the following statement.

   If the range of data set 1 is greater than the range of data set 2, then the interquartile range of data set 1 will be greater than the interquartile range of data set 2.

2. **Describe** how the mean is affected by an outlier.

3. **FIND THE ERROR**   Alonso and Sonia are finding the range of this set of data: 28, 30, 32, 36, 40, 41, 43.

   Alonso
   $43 - 28 = 15$
   The range is 15.

   Sonia
   The range is all numbers between 28 and 43, inclusive.

   Who is correct? Explain your reasoning.   Alonso; see margin.

 www.algebra1.com/extra_examples

Study Notebook

Have students—
- add the definitions/examples of the vocabulary terms to their Vocabulary Builder worksheets for Chapter 13.
- include explanations of how to find the range, median, quartiles, and outliers of a set of data.
- include any other item(s) that they find helpful in mastering the skills in this lesson.

About the Exercises...

Organization by Objective
- **Range:** 19, 24, 29
- **Quartiles and Interquartile Range:** 20–23, 25–28, 30–32

Odd/Even Assignments
Exercises 11–18 are structured so that students practice the same concepts whether they are assigned odd or even problems.

Assignment Guide

Basic: 11–17 odd, 19–23, 34–47

Average: 11–17 odd, 24–28, 34–47

Advanced: 12–18 even, 29–44 (optional: 45–47)

All: Practice Quiz 2 (1–5)

Guided Practice   Find the range, median, lower quartile, upper quartile, and interquartile range of each set of data. Identify any outliers.

GUIDED PRACTICE KEY	
Exercises	Examples
4, 5	1–3
6	1
7–9	2
10	3

4. 85, 77, 58, 69, 62, 73, 25, 82, 67, 77, 59, 75, 69, 76   **60; 71; 62; 77; 15; 25**

5.
Stem	Leaf
7	3 7 8
8	0 0 3 5 7
9	4 6 8
10	0 1 8
11	1 9 7|3 = 7.3

4.6; 9.05; 8.0; 10.05; 2.05; none

Application   **LITTLE LEAGUE   For Exercises 6–10, use the following information.**
The number of runs scored by the winning team in the Little League World Series each year from 1947 to 2000 are given in the line plot below.

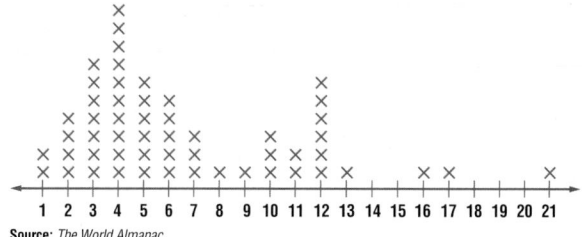

Source: *The World Almanac*

6. What is the range of the data? **20 runs**   7. What is the median of the data? **5 runs**

8. What is the lower quartile and upper quartile of the data? **4 runs; 10 runs**

9. What is the interquartile range of the data? **6 runs**

10. Name any outliers. **21 runs**

★ indicates increased difficulty

Practice and Apply

Homework Help	
For Exercises	**See Examples**
11–18	1–3
19, 24, 29	1
20–22, 25–27, 30, 31	2
23, 28, 32	3

Extra Practice
See page 850.

Find the range, median, lower quartile, upper quartile, and interquartile range of each set of data. Identify any outliers.

11. 85, 77, 58, 69, 62, 73, 55, 82, 67, 77, 59, 92, 75   **37; 73; 60.5; 79.5; 19; none**

12. 28, 42, 37, 31, 34, 29, 44, 28, 38, 40, 39, 42, 30   **16; 37; 29.5; 41; 11.5; none**

13. 30.8, 29.9, 30.0, 31.0, 30.1, 30.5, 30.7, 31.0   **1.1; 30.6; 30.05; 30.9; 0.85; none**

14. 2, 3.4, 5.3, 3, 1, 3.2, 4.9, 2.3   **4.3; 3.1; 2.15; 4.15; 2; none**

15.
Stem	Leaf
5	3 6 8
6	5 8
7	0 3 7 7 9
8	1 4 8 8 9
9	9 5|3 = 53

46; 77; 66.5; 86; 19.5; none

16.
Stem	Leaf
19	3 5 5
20	2 2 5 8
21	5 8 8 9 9 9
22	0 1 7 8 9
23	2 19|3 = 193

39; 218; 202; 221; 19; none

17.
Stem	Leaf
5	0 3 7 9
6	1 3 4 5 5 6
7	1 5 6 6 9
8	1 2 3 5 8
9	2 5 6 9
10	
11	7 5|0 = 5.0

6.7; 7.6; 6.35; 8.65; 2.3; none

18.
Stem	Leaf
0	0 2 3
1	1 7 9
2	2 3 5 6
3	3 4 4 5 9
4	0 7 8 8
5	
6	8 0|2 = 0.2

6.8; 2.95; 1.8; 3.95; 2.15; none

Answer

33. Although the range of the cable-stayed bridges is only somewhat greater than the range of the steel-arch bridges, the interquartile range of the cable-stayed bridges is much greater than the interquartile range of the steel-arch bridges. The outliers of the steel-arch bridges make the ranges of the two types of bridges similar, but in general, the data for steel-arch bridges are more clustered than the data for the cable-stayed bridges.

More About...

National Parks

Yosemite National Park boasts of sparkling lakes, mountain peaks, rushing streams, and beautiful waterfalls. It has about 700 miles of hiking trails.

Source: *World Book Encyclopedia*

• **NATIONAL PARKS** For Exercises 19–23, use the graph at the right.

19. What is the range of the visitors per month?

20. What is the median number of visitors per month?

21. What are the lower quartile and the upper quartile of the data?

22. What is the interquartile range of the data?

23. Name any outliers. **none**

19. 471,561 visitors
20. 293,043.5 visitors
21. 147,066.5 visitors; 470,030 visitors
22. 322,963.5 visitors

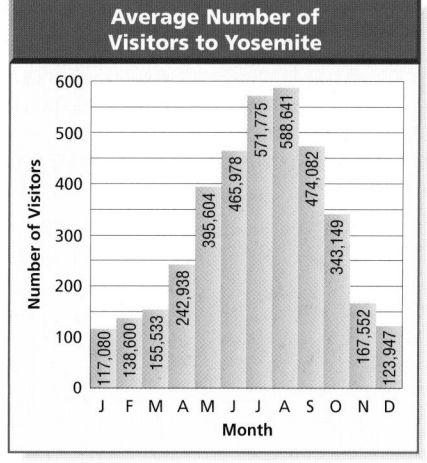

Average Number of Visitors to Yosemite

117,080 / 138,600 / 155,533 / 242,938 / 395,604 / 465,978 / 571,775 / 588,641 / 474,082 / 343,149 / 167,552 / 123,947

Number of Visitors — Month: J F M A M J J A S O N D

Source: *USA TODAY*

NUTRITION For Exercises 24–28, use the following table.

Calories for One Serving of Vegetables					
Vegetable	Calories	Vegetable	Calories	Vegetable	Calories
Asparagus	14	Carrots	28	Lettuce	9
Avocado	304	Cauliflower	10	Onion	60
Bell pepper	20	Celery	17	Potato	89
Broccoli	25	Corn	66	Spinach	9
Brussels sprouts	60	Green beans	30	Tomato	35
Cabbage	17	Jalapeno peppers	13	Zucchini	17

Source: *Vitality*

24. 295 Calories
25. 22.5 Calories

24. What is the range of the data?
25. What is the median of the data?
26. What are the lower quartile and the upper quartile of the data? **14 Calories; 60 Calories**
27. What is the interquartile range of the data? **46 Calories**
28. Identify any outliers. **304 Calories**

BRIDGES For Exercises 29–33, use the following information and the double stem-and-leaf plot at the right.
The main span of cable-stayed bridges and of steel-arch bridges in the United States are given in the stem-and-leaf plot.

★ **29.** Find the ranges for each type of bridge. **1000 ft; 970 ft**

30. 760 ft, 1000 ft, 1280 ft; 820 ft, 980 ft, 1100 ft

★ **30.** Find the quartiles for each type of bridge.

★ **31.** Find the interquartile ranges for each type of bridge. **520 ft; 280 ft**

32. none; 1650 ft and 1700 ft

★ **32.** Identify any outliers.

★ **33.** Compare the ranges and interquartile ranges of the two types of bridges. What can you conclude from these statistics? **See margin.**

Cable-Stayed	Stem	Steel-Arch
6 4 3	6	
9 8 6 5 1 1	7	3 8 8
0	8	0 0 2 3 4
5 2	9	0 1 1 8 8 9
8 2 0 0	10	0 3 8
2	11	0 0
8 2 0	12	0 6
5 2 0	13	
9 0	14	
	15	
3	16	5
	17	0

3 | 6 = 630 feet   7 | 3 = 730 feet

Source: *The World Almanac*

www.algebra1.com/self_check_quiz

Lesson 13-4 Measures of Variation **735**

Study Guide and Intervention, p. 799 (shown) and p. 800

Range A measure of variation called the range describes the spread of numbers in a set of data. The range of a set of data is the difference between the highest and the lowest value.

Example 1 The number of wins for the baseball teams of the American League Central Division are shown at the right. Find the range of the number of wins.

The greatest number of wins is 95 and the least number of wins is 69: 95 − 69 = 26.
The range is 26.

Major League Final Standings, 2000	
Team	Wins
Chicago White Sox	95
Cleveland Indians	90
Detroit Tigers	79
Kansas City Royals	77
Minnesota Twins	69

Source: cbs.sportsline.com

Example 2 Find the range of the student grades below.
58, 95, 72, 85, 84, 88, 91, 92, 93, 45, 80, 81, 92, 93, 50, 79, 84
Since the highest score is 95 and the lowest score is 45, the range is 95 − 45 or 50.

Exercises

Find the range of each set of data.

1.
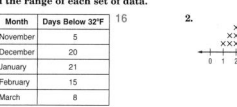

Month	Days Below 32°F
November	5
December	20
January	21
February	15
March	8

16

2. 6

3. 4, 5, 5, 4, 4, 6, 5, 5 2
4. 1, 7, 12, 10 11
5. 3, 0, 4, 9, 6, 4, 0, 1 9
6. 1.5, 0.5, 2, 3, 2.5 2.5

7.

Stem	Leaf
1	2 3 4 6 7 8
2	1 5 5 6 7 8 9
3	0 0 2 3 1|2 = 12

21

8.

Stem	Leaf
18	3 4 6 7
19	0 0 4
20	1 2 2 3 8 8
21	3 4 7 18|3 = 183

34

9. RACING In five pre-race trials, a stock car driver recorded the following speeds in miles per hour: 155, 158, 163, 187, 172. Find the range. **32 mi/h**

10. SWIMMING The swimming times in seconds for the 50-yard butterfly were 36.30, 35.00, 31.60, 34.00, 35.52, 36.39, 38.87, and 41.62. Find the range. **10.02 s**

Skills Practice, p. 801 and Practice, p. 802 (shown)

Find the range, median, lower quartile, upper quartile, and interquartile range of each set of data. Identify any outliers.

1. 73, 39, 58, 42, 71, 84, 27, 23, 36, 57, 70, 52, 35, 51, 29, 38 61; 46.5; 35.5; 64; 28.5; none

2. 42.1, 37.3, 20.0, 45.1, 39.3, 32.0, 38.1, 33.2 25.1; 37.7; 32.6; 40.7; 8.1; 20.0

3.

Stem	Leaf
8	0 1 6
9	3 5
10	0
11	1 5 8 9
12	3 4
13	
14	1 4 7 14|4 = 144

67; 113; 94; 123.5; 29.5; none

4.

Stem	Leaf
0	4 5
1	1 3 7
2	0 7
3	
4	1 4 5 9
5	2 2 3
6	0 1 0|4 = 0.4

5.7; 4.25; 1.5; 5.2; 3.7; none

FARMING For Exercises 5–9, use the table below.

Hired Farm Workers October 8–14, 2000 (thousands)			
Region	Number	Region	Number
Northeast I	50	Lake	71
Northeast II	45	Cornbelt I	56
Appalachian I	40	Cornbelt II	31
Appalachian II	33	Delta	42
Southeast	33	Northern Plains	33
Florida	50	Southern Plains	61

Region	Number
Mountain I	34
Mountain II	24
Mountain III	21
Pacific	78
California	24
Hawaii	8

Source: USDA-NASS Agricultural Statistics

5. What is the range in the number of workers hired? **70 thousand workers**
6. What is the median number of workers hired? **37 thousand workers**
7. What are the lower quartile and the upper quartile of the data? **31 thousand workers; 50 thousand workers**
8. What is the interquartile range of the data? **19 thousand workers**
9. Name any outliers. **none**

ASTRONOMY For Exercises 10–14, use the stem-and-leaf plot that gives the absolute magnitudes of notable comets. Source: NASA

Stem	Leaf
5	5
6	5
7	
8	5
9	0 0 0 0 8
10	6
11	7 9
12	0 0 1 5
13	5 8|5 = 8.5

10. What is the range in magnitudes? **8.0**
11. What is the median magnitude? **10.2**
12. What are the lower quartile and the upper quartile of the data? **9.0; 12.0**
13. What is the interquartile range of the data? **3**
14. Name any outliers. **none**

Reading to Learn Mathematics, p. 803   **ELL**

Pre-Activity How is variation used in weather?

Read the introduction to Lesson 13-4 at the top of page 731 in your textbook.

Which city shows the least change in average monthly high temperatures? **Honolulu**

Reading the Lesson

Complete each sentence or equation.

1. To find the range of a set of data, you need to know the least data value and the ___greatest___ data value.

2. To find the lower quartile of a set of data, you need to find the ___median___ of the lower half of the data set.

3. The upper quartile is the ___median___ of the ___upper___ half of the data set.

4. If Q_1, Q_2, and Q_3 are the three quartiles for a set of data, then you can find the interquartile range by calculating ___Q_3___ − ___Q_1___.

5. Values that are less than Q_1 − 1.5(interquartile range) or greater than Q_3 + 1.5(interquartile range) are called ___outliers___.

6. Use the data diagram below to answer the questions.

7   10 11   14 15 16   18   20 21   38   40
Q_1 / Q_2 / Q_3

a. IQR = ___21___ − ___11___
b. 1.5IQR = ___15___
c. Since Q_3 + 1.5IQR = 36, the data elements ___38___ and ___40___ are outliers.

Helping You Remember

7. Describe an easy way to remember the basic meaning of the term *outlier*. Sample answer: Focus on the first syllable, which is *out-*. Outliers are *out* of the main part of the data set.

Enrichment, p. 804

Standard Deviation

The most commonly used measure of variation is called the **standard deviation**. It shows how far the data are from their mean. You can find the standard deviation using the steps given below.

a. Find the mean of the data.
b. Find the difference between each value and the mean.
c. Square each difference.
d. Find the mean of the squared differences.
e. Find the square root of the mean found in Step **d**. The result is the standard deviation.

Example Calculate the standard deviation of the test scores 82, 71, 63, 78, and 66.

mean of the data $(m) = \dfrac{82 + 71 + 63 + 78 + 66}{5} = \dfrac{360}{5} = 72$

$(x − m)^2$

Open-Ended Assessment

Speaking Give students a set of data on the chalkboard or overhead projector, with the range, quartiles, interquartile range, and so on identified. However, make an intentional mistake in identifying one of the quartiles. Challenge students to find the mistake, explain why it is incorrect, and explain how to correctly find the quartiles.

Getting Ready for Lesson 13-5

PREREQUISITE SKILL Students will learn about box-and-whisker plots in Lesson 13-5. In order to create box-and-whisker plots, students must understand how to graph numbers on number lines. Use Exercises 45–47 to determine your students' familiarity with graphing numbers on a number line.

Assessment Options

Practice Quiz 2 The quiz provides students with a brief review of the concepts and skills in Lessons 13-3 and 13-4. Lesson numbers are given to the right of exercises or instruction lines so students can review concepts not yet mastered.

Quiz (Lesson 13-4) is available on p. 826 of the *Chapter 13 Resource Masters*.

Answers

35. Measures of variation can be used to discuss how much the weather changes during the year. Answers should include the following.
- The range of temperatures is used to discuss the change in temperatures for a certain area during the year and the interquartile range is used to discuss the change in temperature during the moderate 50% of the year.
- The monthly temperatures of the local area listed with the range and interquartile range of the data.

736 Chapter 13 Statistics

---

34. The median, lower quartile, and upper quartile will each decrease by 2 in., since all values will decrease by 2 in. The range and interquartile range will remain the same, since the difference between values will not increase.

Standardized Test Practice
Ⓐ Ⓑ Ⓒ Ⓓ

34. **CRITICAL THINKING** Trey measured the length of each classroom in his school. He then calculated the range, median, lower quartile, upper quartile, and interquartile range of the data. After his calculations, he discovered that the tape measure he had used started at the 2-inch mark instead of at the 0-inch mark. All of his measurements were 2 inches greater than the actual lengths of the rooms. How will the values that Trey calculated change? Explain your reasoning.

35. **WRITING IN MATH** Answer the question that was posed at the beginning of the lesson. **See margin.**

How is variation used in weather?

Include the following in your answer:
- the meaning of the range and interquartile range of temperatures for a city, and
- the average highs for your community with the appropriate measures of variation.

36. What is the range of the following set of data? **B**
53, 57, 62, 48, 45, 65, 40, 42, 55
- Ⓐ 11
- Ⓑ 25
- Ⓒ 53
- Ⓓ 65

37. What is the median of the following set of data? **A**
7, 8, 14, 3, 2, 1, 24, 18, 9, 15
- Ⓐ 8.5
- Ⓑ 10.1
- Ⓒ 11.5
- Ⓓ 23

Maintain Your Skills

Mixed Review

38. Create a histogram to represent the following data. *(Lesson 13-3)* **See margin.**
36, 43, 61, 45, 37, 41, 32, 46, 60, 38, 35, 64, 46, 47, 30, 38, 48, 39

State the dimensions of each matrix. Then identify the position of the circled element in each matrix. *(Lesson 13-2)*

39. $[⑤ \ -3 \ 6]$ **1 by 3; first row, first column**

40. $\begin{bmatrix} 3 & 1 \\ 2 & 9 \\ 4 & ③ \end{bmatrix}$ **3 by 2; third row, second column**

41. $\begin{bmatrix} 4 & 2 & -1 & 3 \\ 5 & ⑨ & 0 & 2 \end{bmatrix}$ **2 by 4; second row, second column**

Simplify each rational expression. State the excluded values of the variables. *(Lesson 12-2)*

42. $\frac{15a}{39a^2}$ $\frac{5}{13a}$; 0

43. $\frac{t-3}{t^2-7t+12}$ $\frac{1}{t-4}$; 3, 4

44. $\frac{m-3}{m^2-9}$ $\frac{1}{m+3}$; -3, 3

Getting Ready for the Next Lesson

PREREQUISITE SKILL Graph each set of numbers on a number line.
(To review number lines, see Lesson 2-1.) **45–47. See margin.**

45. {4, 7, 8, 10, 11}
46. {13, 17, 22, 23, 27}
47. {30, 35, 40, 50, 55}

Practice Quiz 2   Lessons 13-3 and 13-4

For Exercises 1–2, use the histogram at the right. *(Lesson 13-3)*

1. In what measurement class does the median occur? **$10–$20**
2. Describe the distribution of the data. **See pp. 751A–751B.**

For Exercises 3–5, use the following set of data. *(Lesson 13-4)*
1050, 1175, 835, 1075, 1025, 1145, 1100, 1125, 975, 1005, 1125, 1095, 1075, 1055

3. Find the range of the data. **340**
4. Find the median, the lower quartile, the upper quartile, and interquartile range of the data. **1075; 1025; 1125; 100**
5. Identify any outliers of the data. **835**

Monday Book Sales at Brown's Department Store

736 Chapter 13 Statistics

---

38. Sample answer:

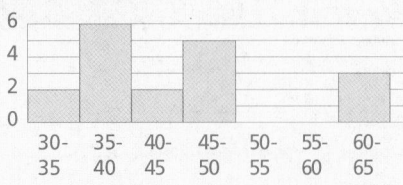

45.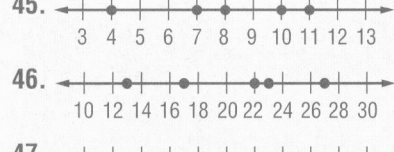

46.

47.

Box-and-Whisker Plots

What You'll Learn

- Organize and use data in box-and-whisker plots.
- Organize and use data in parallel box-and-whisker plots.

Vocabulary
- box-and-whisker plot
- extreme values

How are box-and-whisker plots used to display data?

Everyone should eat a number of calcium-rich foods each day. Selected foods and the amount of calcium in a serving are listed in the table. To create a box-and-whisker plot of the data, you need to find the quartiles of the data.

Calcium-Rich Foods

Food (serving size)	Calcium (milligrams)
Plain Yogurt, Nonfat (8 oz)	452
Plain Yogurt, Low-fat (8 oz)	415
Skim Milk (8 oz)	302
1% Milk (8 oz)	300
Whole Milk (8 oz)	291
Swiss Cheese (1 oz)	272
Tofu (4 oz)	258
Sardines (2 oz)	217
Cheddar Cheese (1 oz)	204
Collards (4 oz)	179
American Cheese (1 oz)	163
Frozen Yogurt with Fruit (4 oz)	154
Salmon (2 oz)	122
Broccoli (4 oz)	89

Source: *Vitality*

89 122 154 163 179 204 217 258 272 291 300 302 415 452

Q_1

$Q_2 = \dfrac{217 + 258}{2}$ or 237.5

Q_3

This information can be displayed on a number line as shown below.

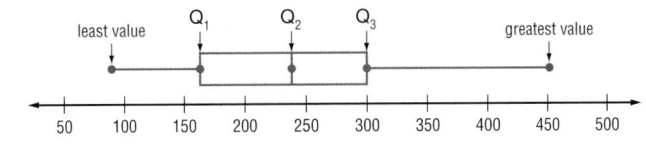

BOX-AND-WHISKER PLOTS Diagrams such as the one above are called **box-and-whisker plots**. The length of the box represents the interquartile range. The line inside the box represents the median. The lines or *whiskers* represent the values in the lower fourth of the data and the upper fourth of the data. The bullets at each end are the **extreme values**. In the box-and-whisker plot above, the least value (LV) is 89, and the greatest value (GV) is 452.

If a set of data has outliers, these data points are represented by bullets. The whisker representing the lower data is drawn from the box to the least value that is not an outlier. The whisker representing the upper data is drawn from the box to the greatest value that is not an outlier.

Study Tip

Reading Math
Box-and-whisker plots are sometimes called *box plots*.

1 Focus

 5-Minute Check Transparency 13-5 Use as a quiz or review of Lesson 13-4.

Mathematical Background notes are available for this lesson on p. 706D.

Building on Prior Knowledge

In Lesson 2-1, students learned how to graph real numbers on a number line. In this lesson, students will apply the skills of graphing numbers on a number line, plus what they learned about measures of variation in Lesson 13-4 to create box-and-whisker plots.

How are box-and-whisker plots used to display data?

Ask students:

- What is the median of the data? **237.5**
- What is the lower quartile? **163**
- What is the upper quartile? **300**
- How does the graph on the number line depict the data? **The graph shows a box that extends from the lower quartile to the upper quartile, with the median marked also. Then it shows lines extending to the least and greatest values.**
- How might a graphical representation of measures of variation be useful? **It gives quick visual cues about the range of data.**

Resource Manager

 **Workbook and Reproducible Masters**

Chapter 13 Resource Masters
- Study Guide and Intervention, pp. 805–806
- Skills Practice, p. 807
- Practice, p. 808
- Reading to Learn Mathematics, p. 809
- Enrichment, p. 810
- Assessment, p. 826

Parent and Student Study Guide Workbook, p. 105
School-to-Career Masters, p. 26
Science and Mathematics Lab Manual, pp. 103–108

Transparencies
5-Minute Check Transparency 13-5
Answer Key Transparencies

Technology
AlgePASS: Tutorial Plus, Lesson 34
Interactive Chalkboard

BOX-AND-WHISKER PLOTS

In-Class Example Power Point®

Teaching Tip Tell students that finding whether outliers exist for the set of data is mandatory in order to create an accurate box-and-whisker plot for a set of data. Without knowing whether outliers exist, the whiskers of the plot may extend to the incorrect point.

1 ECOLOGY The average water level in Lake Travis in central Texas during August is a good indicator of whether the region has had normal rainfall, or is suffering from a drought. The following is a list of the water levels in feet above sea level during August for the years 1990 to 2000.

674, 673, 678, 673, 670, 677, 653, 679, 664, 672, 645

a. Draw a box-and-whisker plot for these data.

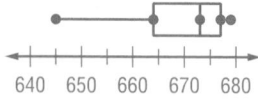

b. What does the box-and-whisker plot tell about the data? **The upper half of the data are less dispersed than the lower half. There are no outliers.**

Answers

4.
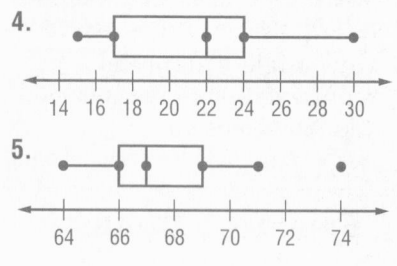

5.

More About . . .

Ecology
The ecosystem of the Everglades in Florida is unique. The Everglades National Park is a subtropical swamp area covering 1,506,499 acres.
Source: *World Book Encyclopedia*

Example 1 *Draw a Box-and-Whisker Plot*

ECOLOGY The amount of rain in Florida from January to May is crucial to its ecosystems. The following is a list of the number of inches of rain in Florida during this crucial period for the years 1990 to 2000.

14.03, 30.11, 16.03, 19.61, 18.15, 16.34, 20.43, 18.46, 22.24, 12.70, 8.25

a. Draw a box-and-whisker plot for these data.

Step 1 Determine the quartiles and any outliers.

Order the data from least to greatest. Use this list to determine the quartiles.

8.25, 12.70, 14.03, 16.03, 16.34, 18.15, 18.46, 19.61, 20.43, 22.24, 30.11

$\qquad\qquad$ ↑ $\qquad\qquad$ ↑ $\qquad\qquad$ ↑

$\qquad\qquad Q_1 \qquad\qquad Q_2 \qquad\qquad Q_3$

Determine the interquartile range.

$IQR = 20.43 - 14.03$ or 6.4

Check to see if there are any outliers.

$14.03 - 1.5(6.4) = 4.43 \qquad 20.43 + 1.5(6.4) = 30.03$

Any numbers less than 4.43 or greater than 30.03 are outliers. The only outlier is 30.11.

Step 2 Draw a number line.

Assign a scale to the number line that includes the extreme values. Above the number line, place bullets to represent the three quartile points, any outliers, the least number that is *not* an outlier, and the greatest number that is *not* an outlier.

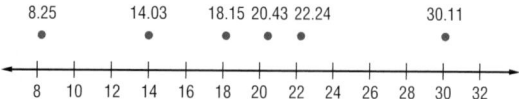

Step 3 Complete the box-and-whisker plot.

Draw a box to designate the data between the upper and lower quartiles. Draw a vertical line through the point representing the median. Draw a line from the lower quartile to the least value that is *not* an outlier. Draw a line from the upper quartile to the greatest value that is *not* an outlier.

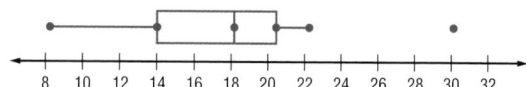

b. What does the box-and-whisker plot tell about the data?

Notice that the whisker and the box for the top half of the data is shorter than the whisker and box for the lower half of the data. Therefore, except for the outlier, the upper half of the data are less spread out than the lower half of the data.

PARALLEL BOX-AND-WHISKER PLOTS Two sets of data can be compared by drawing parallel box-and-whisker plots such as the one shown below.

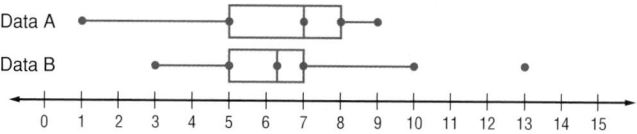

DAILY
INTERVENTION | **Unlocking Misconceptions**

Outliers It is very important for students to understand that the whiskers of a box-and-whisker plot do not necessarily extend to the greatest and least value of a set of data. The upper whisker extends to the greatest value that is *not* an outlier, and the lower whisker extends to the least value that is *not* an outlier.

Example 2 *Draw Parallel Box-and-Whisker Plots*

WEATHER Jalisa Thompson has job offers in Fresno, California, and Brownsville, Texas. Since she likes both job offers, she decides to compare the temperatures of each city.

Average Monthly High Temperatures (°F)											
Month	Jan.	Feb.	March	April	May	June	July	Aug.	Sept.	Oct.	Nov.	Dec.
Fresno	54.1	61.7	66.6	75.1	84.2	92.7	98.6	96.7	90.1	79.7	64.7	53.7
Brownsville	68.9	72.2	78.4	84.0	87.8	91.0	93.3	93.6	90.4	85.3	78.3	71.7

Source: www.stormfax.com

a. Draw a parallel box-and-whisker plot for the data.

Determine the quartiles and outliers for each city.

Fresno

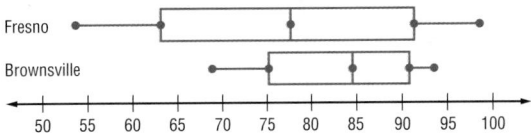

53.7, 54.1, 61.7, 64.7, 66.6, 75.1, 79.7, 84.2, 90.1, 92.7, 96.7, 98.6

$Q_1 = 63.2$ $Q_2 = 77.4$ $Q_3 = 91.4$

Brownsville

68.9, 71.7, 72.2, 78.3, 78.4, 84.0, 85.3, 87.8, 90.4, 91.0, 93.3, 93.6

$Q_1 = 75.25$ $Q_2 = 84.65$ $Q_3 = 90.7$

Neither city has any outliers.

Draw the box-and-whisker plots using the same number line.

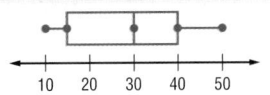

b. Use the parallel box-and-whisker plots to compare the data.

The range of temperatures in Fresno is much greater than in Brownsville. Except for the fourth quartile, Brownville's average temperatures appear to be as high or higher than Fresno's.

Check for Understanding

Concept Check

1. The extreme values are 10 and 50. The quartiles are 15, 30, and 40. There are no outliers.
2. The scale must include the least and greatest values.

1. **Describe** the data represented by the box-and-whisker plot at the right. Include the extreme values, the quartiles, and any outliers.

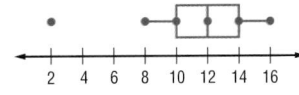

2. **Explain** how to determine the scale of the number line in a box-and-whisker plot.

3. **OPEN ENDED** Write a set of data that could be represented by the box-and-whisker plot at the right. **Sample answer: 2, 8, 10, 11, 11, 12, 13, 13, 14, 15, 16**

Guided Practice Draw a box-and-whisker plot for each set of data. **4–5. See margin.**

4. 30, 28, 24, 24, 22, 22, 21, 17, 16, 15

5. 64, 69, 65, 71, 66, 66, 74, 67, 68, 67

www.algebra1.com/extra_examples

Lesson 13-5 Box-and-Whisker Plots **739**

DAILY INTERVENTION

Differentiated Instruction

Interpersonal Since there are quite a few steps involved in transforming a set of data into a box-and-whisker plot, place students in groups to work on problems involving box-and-whisker plots. Have the group members split up the tasks such as finding the quartiles, the interquartile range, checking for outliers, and graphing the points for the plot.

---

2 CLIMATE Pilar, who grew up on the island of Hawaii, is going to go to college in either Dallas or Nashville. She does not want to live in a place that gets too cold in the winter, so she decided to compare the average monthly low temperatures of each city.

Average Monthly Low Temperatures (°F)		
Month	**Dallas**	**Nashville**
Jan.	32.7	26.5
Feb.	36.9	29.9
Mar.	45.6	39.1
Apr.	54.7	47.5
May	62.6	56.6
June	70	64.7
July	74.1	68.9
Aug.	73.6	67.7
Sept.	66.9	61.1
Oct.	55.8	48.3
Nov.	45.4	39.6
Dec.	36.3	30.9

a. Draw parallel box-and-whisker plots for the data.

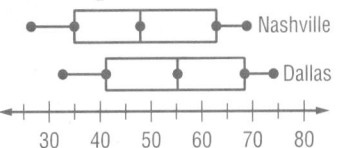

b. Use the parallel box-and-whisker plots to compare the data. **The interquartile range of temperatures for both cities is about the same. However, all quartiles of the Dallas Temperatures are shifted to the right of those of Nashville, meaning Dallas has higher average low temperatures.**

✓ Concept Check

Interquartile Range If the box portion of a box-and-whisker plot is very short, what does this tell you about the data? **The data has a small interquartile range, so there is little variation in the middle part of the data.**

About the Exercises...

Organization by Objective
• **Box-and-Whisker Plots:** 10–19, 28–39
• **Parallel Box-and-Whisker Plots:** 20–27

Odd/Even Assignments
Exercises 10–27 are structured so that students practice the same concepts whether they are assigned odd or even problems.

Assignment Guide

Basic: 11, 15–25 odd, 28–31, 39–57

Average: 11–27 odd, 30–35, 39–57

Advanced: 10–26 even, 32–57

6–7. See margin.

Draw a parallel box-and-whisker plot for each pair of data. Compare the data.

6. A: 22, 18, 22, 17, 32, 24, 31, 26, 28
B: 28, 30, 45, 23, 24, 32, 30, 27, 27

7. A: 8, 15.5, 14, 14, 24, 19, 16.7, 15, 11.4, 16
B: 18, 14, 15.8, 9, 12, 16, 20, 16, 13, 15

Application   **CHARITY**   For Exercises 8 and 9, use the information in the table below.

Top Ten Charities	
Charity	Private Contributions (millions)
Salvation Army	$1397
YMCA of the U.S.A.	$693
American Red Cross	$678
American Cancer Society	$620
Fidelity Investments Charitable Gift Fund	$573
Lutheran Services in America	$559
United Jewish Communities	$524
America's Second Harvest	$472
Habitat for Humanity International	$467
Harvard University	$452

Source: *The Chronicle of Philanthropy*

8. Make a box-and-whisker for the data. **See pp. 751A–751B.**
9. Write a brief description of the data distribution.

★ indicates increased difficulty

9. Most of the data are spread fairly evenly from about $450 million to $700 million. The one outlier ($1397 million) is far removed from the rest of the data.

GUIDED PRACTICE KEY	
Exercises	Examples
4, 5, 8, 9	1
6, 7	2

Practice and Apply

For Exercises 10–13, use the box-and-whisker plot at the right.

10. What is the range of the data? **45**
11. What is the interquartile range of the data? **30**
★ **12.** What fractional part of the data is less than 90? $\frac{1}{4}$
★ **13.** What fractional part of the data is greater than 95? $\frac{1}{2}$

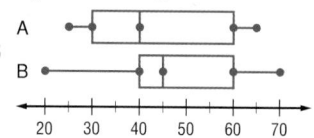

Draw a box-and-whisker plot for each set of data. 14–19. See pp. 751A–751B.

14. 15, 8, 10, 1, 3, 2, 6, 5, 4, 27, 1
15. 20, 2, 12, 5, 4, 16, 17, 7, 6, 16, 5, 0, 5, 30
16. 4, 1, 1, 1, 10, 15, 4, 5, 27, 5, 14, 10, 6, 2, 2, 5, 8
17. 51, 27, 55, 54, 69, 60, 39, 46, 46, 53, 81, 23
18. 15.1, 9.0, 8.5, 5.8, 6.2, 8.5, 10.5, 11.5, 8.8, 7.6
19. 1.3, 1.2, 14, 1.8, 1.6, 5.7, 1.3, 3.7, 3.3, 2, 1.3, 1.3, 7.7, 8.5, 2.2

For Exercises 20–23, use the parallel box-and-whisker plot at the right.

20. Which set of data contains the least value? **B**
21. Which set of data contains the greatest value? **B**
22. Which set of data has the greatest interquartile range? **A**
23. Which set of data has the greatest range? **B**

Draw a parallel box-and-whisker plot for each pair of data. Compare the data.

24. A: 15, 17, 22, 28, 32, 40, 16, 24, 26, 38, 19 **See pp. 751A–751B.**
B: 24, 32, 25, 27, 37, 29, 30, 30, 28, 31, 27

Answers

6.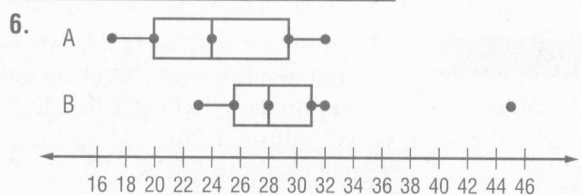

The B data have a greater range than the A data. However, if you exclude the one outlier in the B data, the B data are less diverse than the A data.

7.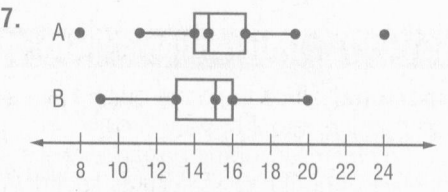

The A data are more diverse than the B data.

25. A: 50, 45, 47, 55, 51, 58, 49, 51, 51, 48, 47   25–27. See pp. 751A–751B.
   B: 40, 41, 48, 39, 41, 41, 38, 37, 35, 37, 45

26. A: 1.5, 3.8, 4.2, 3.5 4.1, 4.4, 4.1, 4.0, 4.0, 3.9
   B: 6.8, 4.2, 7.6, 5.5, 12.2, 6.7, 7.1, 4.8

27. A: 4.4, 4.5, 4.6, 4.5, 4.4, 4.4, 4.1, 4.9, 2.9
   B: 5.1, 4.9, 4.2, 3.9, 4.5, 4.1, 4.3, 4.5, 5.2

PROFESSIONAL SPORTS For
Exercises 28 and 29, use the table
at the right.

28. Draw a box-and-whisker plot
for the data. **See pp. 751A–751B.**

29. What does the box-and-
whisker plot tell about the
data? **The upper half of the
data is very dispersed. The
range of the lower half of
the data is only 1.**

Professional Athletes

Professional Sport	Average Length of Career (years)
Bowling	17
Surfing	10
Hockey	5.5
Baseball	4.5
Basketball	4.5
Tennis	4
Football	3.5
Boxing	3.5

Source: *Men's Health Fitness Special*

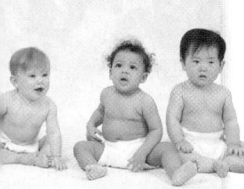
RACING For Exercises 30 and 31, use the following list of earnings in thousands
from the November 2000 NAPA 500 NASCAR Race at the Atlanta Motor
Speedway.

$181, $100, $98, $89, $76, $58, $60; $58; $55, $57, $54, $64, $44, $39, $66, $52, $56, $38,
$56, $51, $49, $38, $50, $48, $48, $40, $36, $36, $39, $36, $47, $36, $47, $38, $35, $46,
$35, $55, $46, $55, $45, $43, $35

Source: *USA TODAY* **30. See pp. 751A–751B; $89,000, $98,000, $100,000, $181,000.**

30. Draw a box-and-whisker plot for the data. Identify any outliers.

31. Determine whether the top half of the data or the bottom half of the data are
more dispersed. Explain. **Top half; the top half of the data goes from $48,000 to
$181,000, while the bottom half goes from $35,000 to $48,000.**

• • • **LIFE EXPECTANCY** For Exercises
32–35, use the box-and-whisker
plot depicting the UNICEF life
expectancy data for 171 countries.

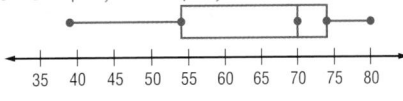

32. Estimate the range and the interquartile range. **41 yr; 20 yr**

33. Determine whether the top half of the data or the bottom half of the data are
more dispersed. Explain.

★ **34.** State three different intervals of ages that contain half the data.

★ **35.** Jamie claims that the number of data values is greater in the interval 54 years
to 70 years than the number of data values in the interval 70 years to 74 years.
Is Jamie correct? Explain.

SOCCER For Exercises 36–38, use the following list of top 50 lifetime scores for
all players in Division 1 soccer leagues in the United States from 1922 to 1999.

253, 223, 193, 189, 152, 150, 138, 137, 135, 131, 131, 129, 128, 126, 124, 119, 118, 108,
107, 102, 101, 100, 96, 92, 87, 83, 82, 81, 80, 78, 78, 76, 74, 74, 73, 73, 72, 71, 69, 68, 67,
65, 64, 63, 63, 62, 61, 61, 61

Source: www.internetsoccer.com

36. Draw a box-and-whisker plot for the data. **See pp. 751A–751B.**

37. Draw a histogram to represent the data. **See pp. 751A–751B.**

★ **38.** Compare and contrast the box-and-whisker plot and the histogram. **See margin.**

**33. Bottom half; the
top half of the data
goes from 70 yr to
80 yr, while the
bottom half goes from
39 yr to 70 yr.**

**34. 39 yr to 70 yr, 54 yr
to 74 yr, 70 yr to 80 yr**

**35. No; although the
interval from 54 yr to
70 yr is wider than the
interval from 70 yr to
74 yr, both intervals
represent 25% of the
data values.**

Answer

**38. Both the box-and-whisker plot and the
histogram give a visual summary of
the data. The box-and-whisker plot
shows the intervals by quartile data,
while the histogram shows the number
of data values for intervals of width 20.**

Open-Ended Assessment

Writing Give students several examples of box-and-whisker plots on the chalkboard or overhead projector. Make sure the example plots have quartiles with different ranges. Some of the plots should have outliers, and others should not have outliers. Have students write several paragraphs about the plots, comparing and contrasting them. Make sure students explain what the plots reveal about the different data sets.

Assessment Options

Quiz (Lesson 13-5) is available on p. 826 of the *Chapter 13 Resource Masters*.

Answer

44. Sample answer:

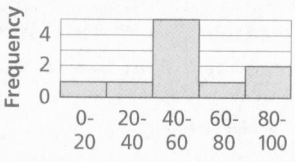

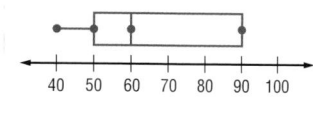

A box-and-whisker plot of population densities will help you compare the states. Visit www.algebra1.com/webquest to continue work on your WebQuest project.

Standardized Test Practice
Ⓐ Ⓑ Ⓒ Ⓓ

---

39. CRITICAL THINKING Write a set of data that could be represented by the box-and-whisker plot at the right. **Sample answer:** 40, 45, 50, 55, 55, 60, 70, 80, 90, 90, 90

40. WRITING IN MATH   Answer the question that was posed at the beginning of the lesson. **See pp. 751A–751B.**

How are box-and-whisker plots used to display data?

Include the following in your answer:
- a sample of a box-and-whisker plot showing what each part of the plot represents, and
- a box-and-whisker plot representing data found in a newspaper or magazine.

For Exercises 41 and 42, use the box-and-whisker plot below.

41. What is the median of the data? **C**
Ⓐ 0   Ⓑ 10
Ⓒ 25   Ⓓ 45

42. Which interval represents 75% of the data? **D**
Ⓐ 0–25   Ⓑ 10–45   Ⓒ 25–50   Ⓓ 0–45

Maintain Your Skills

Mixed Review   For Exercises 43 and 44, use the following data.

13, 32, 45, 45, 54, 55, 58, 67, 82, 93

43. Find the range, median, lower quartile, upper quartile, and interquartile range of the data. Identify any outliers.   *(Lesson 13-4)* **80; 54.5; 45; 67; 22; none**

44. Create a histogram to represent the data.   *(Lesson 13-3)* **See margin.**

Find each sum or difference.   *(Lesson 12-7)*

45. $\dfrac{-y^2 + 6y + 12}{(y-3)(y+4)}$

46. $\dfrac{5r + 5}{(r+3)(r-2)}$

47. $\dfrac{3w-4}{3(5w+2)}$

45. $\dfrac{3}{y-3} - \dfrac{y}{y+4}$ **46.** $\dfrac{2}{r+3} + \dfrac{3}{r-2}$ **47.** $\dfrac{w}{5w+2} - \dfrac{4}{15w+6}$

Find each product. Assume that no denominator has a value of 0.   *(Lesson 12-3)*

48. $\dfrac{7a^2}{5} \cdot \dfrac{15}{14a} \quad \dfrac{3a}{2}$ **49.** $\dfrac{6r+3}{r+6} \cdot \dfrac{r^2+9r+18}{2r+1} \quad 3(r+3)$

Solve each right triangle. State the side length to the nearest tenth and the angle measures to the nearest degree.   *(Lesson 11-7)*

50. $m\angle B = 48°$, $AC \approx 16.3$, $BC \approx 14.7$

51. $m\angle B = 51°$, $AB \approx 15.4$, $BC \approx 9.7$

52. $m\angle A = 44°$, $AB \approx 20.9$, $BC \approx 14.5$

50.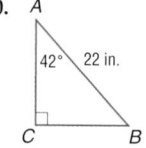

51.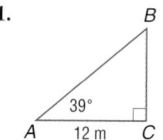

52.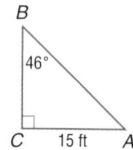

Solve each equation by completing the square. Approximate any irrational roots to the nearest tenth.   *(Lesson 10-3)*

53. $a^2 - 7a + 6 = 0$ **1, 6**   **54.** $x^2 - 6x + 2 = 0$ **55.** $t^2 + 8t - 18 = 0$
0.4, 5.6   **−9.8, 1.8**

Find each sum or difference.   *(Lesson 8-5)*

56. $(7p^2 - p - 7) - (p^2 + 11)$ **57.** $(3a^2 - 8) + (5a^2 + 2a + 7)$
$6p^2 - p - 18$ **$8a^2 + 2a - 1$**

Algebra Activity

A Follow-Up of Lesson 13-5

Investigating Percentiles

When data are arranged in order from least to greatest, you can describe the data using percentiles. A **percentile** is the point below which a given percent of the data lies. For example, 50% of the data falls below the median. So the median is the 50th percentile for the data.

To determine a percentile, a cumulative frequency table can be used. In a **cumulative frequency table**, the frequencies are accumulated for each item.

Collect the Data

A student's score on the SAT is one factor that some colleges consider when selecting applicants. The tables below show the raw scores from a sample math SAT test for 160 juniors in a particular school. For raw scores, the highest possible score is 800 and the lowest is 200.

Table 1: Frequency Table

Math SAT Scores	Number of Students
200–300	2
300–400	19
400–500	44
500–600	55
600–700	32
700–800	8

Table 2: Cumulative Frequency Table

Math SAT Scores	Number of Students	Cumulative Number of Students
200–300	2	2
300–400	19	21
400–500	44	65
500–600	55	120
600–700	32	152
700–800	8	160

The data in each table can be displayed in a histogram.

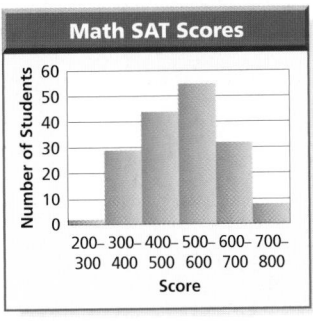

Frequency Histogram

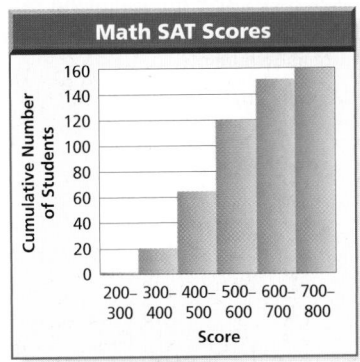

Cumulative Frequency Histogram

Analyze the Data

1. Examine the data in the two tables. Explain how the numbers in Column 3 of Table 2 are determined. **See margin.**

(continued on the next page)

Resource Manager

📁 Teaching Algebra with Manipulatives
- p. 24 (ruler master)
- p. 203 (student recording sheet)

Glencoe Mathematics Classroom Manipulative Kit
- rulers

A Follow-Up of Lesson 13-5

Getting Started

Objective Analyze data using percentiles.

Materials
paper
pencil
ruler

Teach

- Point out to students that the cumulative number of students in the third column of Table 2 shows the number of students who are included in each particular data range, *and* the previous data ranges.

- The histogram for Table 2 is likely to confuse students. At first glance, it looks like 160 students scored in the range of 700–800. Use the table to show students that the number of students who scored in any given range is the difference between that range and the previous range.

Answer

1. To find the number of students in Column 3, add the number from the previous cell to the number of students for the new interval.

Assess

Exercises 4–7 Ask students whether they think adding the percentiles to the *y*-axis of the histogram made the data in the histogram easier to interpret, explaining their answers. **Sample answer: Adding the percentiles to the histogram made it easier to interpret the histogram because without the percentiles, it was easy to mistake that 160 students scored in the 700–800 range, etc.**

Study Notebook

You may wish to have students summarize this activity and what they learned from it.

Answers

2. The horizontal axes of both histograms represent the test score intervals, and the vertical axes of both histograms represent the number of students. The bars for the second histogram are taller than the bars for the first histogram because each bar in the second histogram indicates the cumulative number of students.

3. Sample answer: I prefer the first histogram because you can see the number of students that scored in each interval.

2–3. See margin.

2. Describe the similarities and differences between the two histograms.

3. Which histogram do you prefer for displaying these data? Explain your choice.

Make a Conjecture

Sometimes colleges are not interested in your raw score. They are interested in the percentile. Your percentile indicates what percent of all test-takers scored just as well or lower than you.

4. Use the histogram for Table 2. Place percentile labels on the vertical axis. For example, write 100% next to 160 and 0% next to 0. Now label 25%, 50%, and 75%. What numbers of students correspond to 25%, 50%, and 75%? **40; 80; 120**

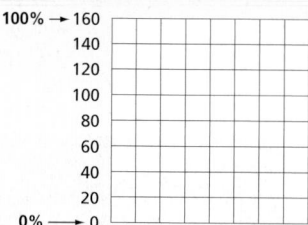

5. Suppose a college is interested in students with scores in the 90th percentile. Using the histogram, move up along the vertical axis to the 90th percentile. Then move right on the horizontal axis to find the score. What is an estimate for the score that represents the 90th percentile? **Sample answer: greater than 600**

6. For a more accurate answer, use a proportion to find 90% of the total number of students. (Recall that the total number of students is 160.) $\frac{s}{160} = \frac{90}{100}$; 144

7. If a student is to be in the 90th percentile, in what interval will the score lie? **600–700**

Extend the Activity

For Exercises 8–10, use the following information.

The weights of 45 babies born at a particular hospital during the month of January are shown below.

9 lb 1 oz	8 lb 2 oz	7 lb 2 oz	10 lb 0 oz	4 lb 4 oz
5 lb 0 oz	7 lb 6 oz	7 lb 8 oz	11 lb 2 oz	6 lb 1 oz
3 lb 8 oz	8 lb 0 oz	7 lb 5 oz	9 lb 15 oz	6 lb 1 oz
7 lb 10 oz	6 lb 9 oz	6 lb 15 oz	7 lb 10 oz	8 lb 0 oz
5 lb 15 oz	8 lb 3 oz	8 lb 1 oz	7 lb 12 oz	7 lb 8 oz
7 lb 7 oz	6 lb 14 oz	7 lb 13 oz	8 lb 0 oz	7 lb 14 oz
5 lb 10 oz	8 lb 5 oz	6 lb 12 oz	8 lb 8 oz	7 lb 11 oz
8 lb 15 oz	9 lb 3 oz	5 lb 14 oz	6 lb 8 oz	8 lb 8 oz
7 lb 4 oz	7 lb 10 oz	8 lb 1 oz	7 lb 8 oz	7 lb 10 oz

8. Make a cumulative frequency table for the data. **8–9. See pp. 751A–751B.**

9. Make a cumulative frequency histogram for the data.

10. Find the weight for a baby in the 80th percentile. **8–9 lb**

Study Guide and Review

Vocabulary and Concept Check

- biased sample (p. 709)
- box-and-whisker plot (p. 737)
- census (p. 708)
- convenience sample (p. 709)
- dimensions (p. 715)
- element (p. 715)
- extreme value (p. 737)
- frequency (p. 722)
- frequency table (p.722)
- histogram (p. 722)
- interquartile range (p. 732)
- lower quartile (p. 732)
- matrix (p. 715)
- measurement classes (p. 722)
- measures of variation (p. 731)
- outlier (p. 733)
- population (p. 708)
- quartiles (p. 732)
- random sample (p. 708)
- range (p. 731)
- sample (p. 708)
- scalar multiplication (p. 717)
- simple random sample (p. 708)
- stratified random sample (p. 708)
- systematic random sample (p. 708)
- upper quartile (p. 732)
- voluntary response sample (p. 709)

1. simple random sample 2. measures of variation 4. systematic random sample

Choose the correct term from the list above that best completes each statement.

1. A(n) ______ is a sample that is as likely to be chosen as any other from the population.
2. Measures that describe the spread of the values in a set of data are called ______.
3. Each ______ separates a data set into four sets with equal number of members.
4. In a(n) ______, the items are selected according to a specified time or item interval.
5. A(n) ______ has a systematic error within it so that certain populations are favored.
6. In a(n) ______, the population is first divided into similar, nonoverlapping groups.
7. The ______ is found by subtracting the lower quartile from the upper quartile.
8. A(n) ______ involves only those who want to participate in the sampling.
9. An extreme value that is much less or greater than the rest of the data is a(n) ______.
10. The ______ is the difference between the greatest and least values of a data set.

5. biased sample 6. stratified random sample 7. interquartile range 8. voluntary response sample

Lesson-by-Lesson Review

13-1 Sampling and Bias

See pages 708–713.

Concept Summary

- Simple random sample, stratified random sample, and systematic random sample are types of unbiased, or random, samples.
- Convenience sample and voluntary response sample are types of biased samples.

Example

GOVERNMENT To determine whether voters support a new trade agreement, 5 people from the list of registered voters in each state and the District of Columbia are selected at random. Identify the sample, suggest a population from which it was selected, and state whether the sample is *unbiased* (random) or *biased*. If unbiased, classify the sample as *simple*, *stratified*, or *systematic*. If biased, classify as *convenience* or *voluntary response*.

Since $5 \times 51 = 255$, the sample is 255 registered voters in the United States. The population is all of the registered voters in the United States.

The sample is unbiased. It is an example of a stratified random sample.

www.algebra1.com/vocabulary_review

Chapter 13 Study Guide and Review

Vocabulary and Concept Check

- This alphabetical list of vocabulary terms in Chapter 13 includes a page reference where each term was introduced.
- **Assessment** A vocabulary test/review for Chapter 13 is available on p. 824 of the *Chapter 13 Resource Masters*.

Lesson-by-Lesson Review

For each lesson,

- the main ideas are summarized,
- additional examples review concepts, and
- practice exercises are provided.

Vocabulary PuzzleMaker

ELL The Vocabulary PuzzleMaker software improves students' mathematics vocabulary using four puzzle formats—crossword, scramble, word search using a word list, and word search using clues. Students can work on a computer screen or from a printed handout.

MindJogger Videoquizzes

ELL MindJogger Videoquizzes provide an alternative review of concepts presented in this chapter. Students work in teams in a game show format to gain points for correct answers. The questions are presented in three rounds.

Round 1 Concepts (5 questions)
Round 2 Skills (4 questions)
Round 3 Problem Solving (4 questions)

FOLDABLES™ Study Organizer

For more information about Foldables, see *Teaching Mathematics with Foldables.*

Have students look through their Foldables to make sure that they have included information for every tab. Now is a good time to ask if students have any questions about the concepts that they recorded in their Foldables.

Encourage students to refer to their Foldables while completing the Study Guide and Review and to use them in preparing for the Chapter Test.

Answers

11. 8 test tubes with results of chemical reactions; the results of all chemical reactions performed; biased; convenience

12. a group of chocolate bars; all chocolate bars made at the candy factory; unbiased; systematic

13. $\begin{bmatrix} 2 & 4 & -4 \\ 4 & 3 & 3 \\ -2 & -3 & 3 \end{bmatrix}$

14. $\begin{bmatrix} 3 & 3 & -9 \\ 6 & 9 & -3 \\ -3 & -6 & 0 \end{bmatrix}$

15. $\begin{bmatrix} -4 & -2 \\ 4 & 0 \end{bmatrix}$

16. $\begin{bmatrix} 1 & -3 \\ 3 & 4 \end{bmatrix}$

17. $\begin{bmatrix} 5 & -1 \\ -1 & 4 \end{bmatrix}$

18. impossible

19. $\begin{bmatrix} 5 & 15 & -5 \\ 10 & 0 & 20 \\ -5 & -5 & 15 \end{bmatrix}$

20. impossible

21. $\begin{bmatrix} 9 & 1 \\ -5 & 4 \end{bmatrix}$

22. $\begin{bmatrix} 1 & 5 & 1 \\ 2 & -3 & 9 \\ -1 & 0 & 6 \end{bmatrix}$

Exercises Identify the sample, suggest a population from which it was selected, and state whether it is *unbiased* (random) or *biased*. If unbiased, classify the sample as *simple, stratified,* or *systematic*. If biased, classify the sample as *convenience* or *voluntary response*. *See Examples 1–3 on pages 709 and 710.*

11. SCIENCE A laboratory technician needs a sample of results of chemical reactions. She selects test tubes from the first 8 experiments performed on Tuesday.

12. CANDY BARS To ensure that all of the chocolate bars are the appropriate weight, every 50th bar on the conveyor belt in the candy factory is removed and weighed.

11–12. See margin.

13-2 Introduction to Matrices

See pages 715–721.

Concept Summary

- A matrix can be used to organize data and make data analysis more convenient.
- Equal matrices must have the same dimensions and corresponding elements are equal.
- Matrices with the same dimensions can be added or subtracted.
- Each element of a matrix can be multiplied by a number called a scalar.

Example If $R = \begin{bmatrix} 2 & 2 \\ -1 & 3 \end{bmatrix}$, $S = \begin{bmatrix} -1 & 3 \\ 0 & 1 \end{bmatrix}$, and $T = \begin{bmatrix} -1 \\ 0 \end{bmatrix}$, find each sum. If it does not exist, write *impossible.*

a. $R + S$

$R + S = \begin{bmatrix} 2 & 2 \\ -1 & 3 \end{bmatrix} + \begin{bmatrix} -1 & 3 \\ 0 & 1 \end{bmatrix}$

$= \begin{bmatrix} 2 + (-1) & 2 + 3 \\ -1 + 0 & 3 + 1 \end{bmatrix}$

$= \begin{bmatrix} 1 & 5 \\ -1 & 4 \end{bmatrix}$

b. $S + T$

$S + T = \begin{bmatrix} -1 & 3 \\ 0 & 1 \end{bmatrix} + \begin{bmatrix} -1 \\ 0 \end{bmatrix}$

Since S is a 2×2 matrix and T is a 2×1 matrix, the matrices do not have the same dimensions. Therefore, it is impossible to add these matrices.

Exercises If $A = \begin{bmatrix} 1 & 3 & -1 \\ 2 & 0 & 4 \\ -1 & -1 & 3 \end{bmatrix}$, $B = \begin{bmatrix} 1 & 1 & -3 \\ 2 & 3 & -1 \\ -1 & -2 & 0 \end{bmatrix}$, $C = \begin{bmatrix} 3 & -2 \\ 1 & 4 \end{bmatrix}$, and $D = \begin{bmatrix} 2 & 1 \\ -2 & 0 \end{bmatrix}$, find each sum, difference, or product. If the sum or difference does not exist, write *impossible.* *See Examples 3 and 4 on pages 716 and 717.* 13–22. See margin.

13. $A + B$	**14.** $3B$	**15.** $-2D$
16. $C - D$	**17.** $C + D$	
18. $B + C$	**19.** $5A$	**20.** $A - D$
21. $C + 3D$	**22.** $2A - B$	

13-3 Histograms

See pages 722–728.

Concept Summary

- A histogram can illustrate the information in a frequency table.
- The distribution of the data can be determined from a histogram.

Example Create a histogram to represent the following high temperatures in twenty states.

118 122 117 105 114 115 122 102 103 110

110 112 106 109 100 103 110 108 111 102

Since the temperatures range from 100 to 122, use measurement classes from 100 to 125 with 5 degree intervals. First create a frequency table and then draw the histogram.

Temperature Intervals	Tally	Frequency
$100 \le d < 105$	IIII I	5
$105 \le d < 110$	IIII	4
$110 \le d < 115$	IIII I	6
$115 \le d < 120$	III	3
$120 \le d < 125$	II	2

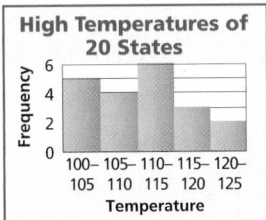

Exercises Create a histogram to represent each data set.   *See Example 3 on page 724.*

23. the number of cellular minutes used last month by employees of a company

122 150 110 290 145 330 300 210 95 101 106 289 219

105 302 29 288 154 235 168 55 84 92 175 180

24. the number of cups of coffee consumed per customer at a snack shop between 6 A.M. and 8 A.M.

0 2 0 2 1 3 2 1 2 3 0 2 2 1 0 2 1 3 0 1 2 2

3 2 1 0 1 2 1 0 2 2 2 1 1 2 1 2 0 3 1 0 0 1

23–24. See margin.

13-4 Measures of Variation

See pages 731–736.

Concept Summary

• The range of the data set is the difference between the greatest and the least values of the set and describes the spread of the data.

• The interquartile range is the difference between the upper and lower quartiles of a set of data. It is the range of the middle half of the data.

• Outliers are values that are much less than or much greater than the rest of the data.

Example Find the range, median, lower quartile, upper quartile, and interquartile range of the set of data below. Identify any outliers.

25, 20, 30, 24, 22, 26, 28, 29, 19

Order the set of data from least to greatest.

19 20 22 24 25 26 28 29 30

   $\uparrow$ $\uparrow$ $\uparrow$

   Q_1 Q_2 Q_3

The range is $30 - 19$ or 11.   The median is the middle number, 25.

The lower quartile is $\frac{20 + 22}{2}$ or 21.   The upper quartile is $\frac{28 + 29}{2}$ or 28.5.

The interquartile range is $28.5 - 21$ or 7.5.

The outliers would be less than $21 - 1.5(7.5)$ or 9.75 and greater than $28.5 + 1.5(7.5)$ or 39.25. There are no outliers.

Chapter 13 Study Guide and Review **747**

Answers

23. Sample answer:

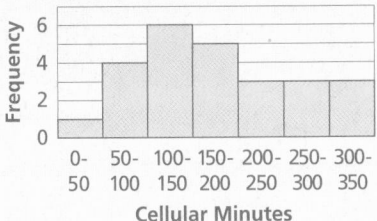

24. Sample answer:

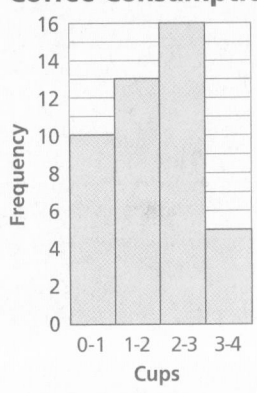

Study Guide and Review

Chapter **13** **For More ...**
- Extra Practice, see pages 849–850.
- Mixed Problem Solving, see page 865.

Answers

29.

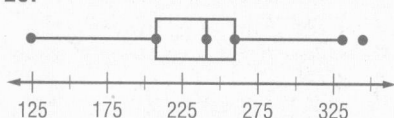

30.

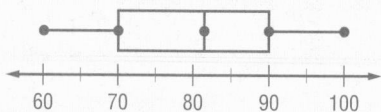

31.

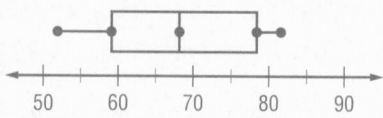

Answers, p. 749

6. 5 dogs; all the dogs in the kennel; biased; convenience

7. set of books from the library; all books checked out of the library on Wednesday; unbiased; stratified

8. $\begin{bmatrix} 6 & 5 & 0 \\ -3 & -2 & -1 \\ 2 & -1 & 2 \end{bmatrix}$

9. $\begin{bmatrix} 0 & -3 & -5 \\ -5 & -1 & 5 \end{bmatrix}$

10. $\begin{bmatrix} 12 & 6 & -3 \\ -6 & -6 & 0 \\ 0 & 3 & 6 \end{bmatrix}$

11. $\begin{bmatrix} -6 & -2 & -12 \\ -8 & 2 & 2 \end{bmatrix}$

12. impossible

13. $\begin{bmatrix} -3 & -4 & -11 \\ -9 & 0 & 6 \end{bmatrix}$

14. Sample answer:

Ages of Men in Billiards Tournament

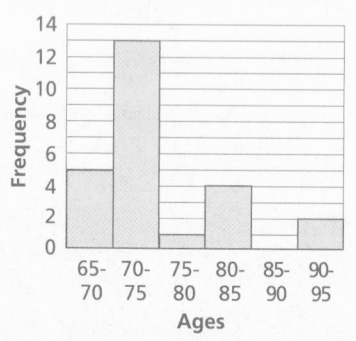

15. Sample answer:

Number of Trading Cards to Share

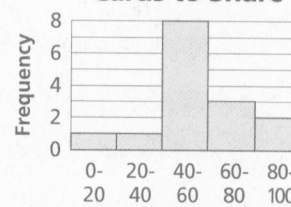

Exercises Find the range, median, lower quartile, upper quartile, and interquartile range of each set of data. Identify any outliers.
See Examples 1–3 on pages 731–733.

25. 30, 90, 40, 70, 50, 100, 80, 60 **70; 65; 45; 85; 40; none**

26. 3, 3.2, 45, 7, 2, 1, 3.4, 4, 5.3, 5, 78, 8, 21, 5 **77; 5; 3.2; 8; 4.8; 21, 45, 78**

27. 85, 77, 58, 69, 62, 73, 55, 82, 67, 77, 59, 92, 75, 69, 76 **37; 73; 62; 77; 15; none**

28. 111.5, 70.7, 59.8, 68.6, 63.8, 254.8, 64.3, 82.3, 91.7, 88.9, 110.5, 77.1
195; 79.7; 66.45; 101.1; 34.65; 254.8

13-5 *Box-and-Whisker Plots*

See pages 737–742.

Concept Summary

- The vertical rule in the box of a box-and-whisker plot represents the median.
- The box of a box-and-whisker plot represents the interquartile range.
- The bullets at each end of a box-and-whisker plot are the extremes.
- Parallel box-and-whisker plots can be used to compare data.

Example The following high temperatures (°F) were recorded during a two-week cold spell in St. Louis. Draw a box-and-whisker plot of the temperatures.

20	2	12	5	4	16	17
7	6	16	5	0	5	30

Order the data from least to greatest.

0 2 4 5 5 5 6 7 12 16 16 17 20 30

Q_1 $\quad Q_2 = \dfrac{6+7}{2}$ or 6.5 $\quad Q_3$

The interquartile range is $16 - 5$ or 11. Check to see if there are any outliers.

$5 - 1.5(11) = -11.5 \qquad 16 + 1.5(11) = 32.5$

There are no outliers.

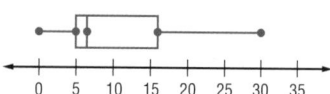

Exercises Draw a box-and-whisker plot for each set of data.
See Example 1 on page 738. **29–31. See margin.**

29. The number of Calories in a serving of French fries at 13 restaurants are 250, 240, 220, 348, 199, 200, 125, 230, 274, 239, 212, 240, and 327.

30. Mrs. Lowery's class has the following scores on their math tests.
60, 70, 70, 75, 80, 85, 85, 90, 95, 100

31. The average daily temperatures on a beach in Florida for each month of one year are 52.4, 55.2, 61.1, 67.0, 73.4, 79.1, 81.6, 81.2, 78.1, 69.8, 61.9, and 55.1.

748 Chapter 13 Statistics

Vocabulary and Concepts

In a matrix, identify each item described.

1. a vertical set of numbers b
2. an entry in a matrix a
3. a horizontal set of numbers c
4. a constant multiplied by each element in the matrix e
5. number of rows and columns d

a. element
b. column
c. row
d. dimensions
e. scalar

Skills and Applications

Identify the sample, suggest a population from which it was selected, and state whether it is *unbiased* (random) or *biased*. If unbiased, classify the sample as *simple*, *stratified*, or *systematic*. If biased, classify as *convenience* or *voluntary response*. 6–7. See margin.

6. **DOGS** A veterinarian needs a sample of dogs in his kennel to be tested for fleas. He selects the first 5 dogs who run from the pen.

7. **LIBRARIES** A librarian wants to sample book titles checked out on Wednesday. He randomly chooses a book for each hour that the library is open.

If $W = \begin{bmatrix} 2 & 3 & 1 \\ -1 & 0 & -1 \\ 2 & -2 & 0 \end{bmatrix}$, $X = \begin{bmatrix} 4 & 2 & -1 \\ -2 & -2 & 0 \\ 0 & 1 & 2 \end{bmatrix}$, $Y = \begin{bmatrix} 3 & -2 & 1 \\ -1 & -2 & 4 \end{bmatrix}$, and $Z = \begin{bmatrix} 3 & 1 & 6 \\ 4 & -1 & -1 \end{bmatrix}$, find each sum, difference, or product. If the sum or difference does not exist, write *impossible*.

8. $W + X$ 9. $Y - Z$ 10. $3X$ 11. $-2Z$ 12. $2W - Z$ 13. $Y - 2Z$

Create a histogram to represent each data set. 8–15. See margin.

14. 68 71 74 90 81 72 71 69 65 92 75 69 71 73 73
    68 74 80 83 70 80 74 74 70 71

15. 10 40 50 52 22 50 60 90 41 51 90 40 75 63 53

Find the range, median, lower quartile, upper quartile, and interquartile range for each set of data. Identify any outliers.

16. 1055, 1075, 1095, 1125, 1005, 975, 1125, 1100, 1145, 1025, 1075 **170; 1075; 1025; 1125; 100; none**
17. 0.4, 0.2, 0.5, 0.9, 0.3, 0.4, 0.5, 1.9, 0.5, 0.7, 0.8, 0.6, 0.2, 0.1, 0.4 **1.8, 0.5, 0.3, 0.7, 0.4; 1.9**

Draw a box-and-whisker plot for each set of data. 18–19. See pp. 751A–751B.

18. 1, 3, 2, 2, 1, 9, 4, 6, 1, 10, 1, 4, 5, 10, 1, 3, 6
19. 14, 18, 9, 9, 12, 22, 16, 12, 14, 16, 15, 13, 9, 10, 11, 12

20. **STANDARDIZED TEST PRACTICE** Which box-and-whisker plot has the greatest interquartile range? B

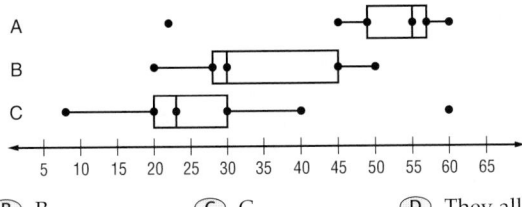

Ⓐ A Ⓑ B Ⓒ C Ⓓ They all have the same interquartile range.

 www.algebra1.com/chapter_test

Chapter 13 Practice Test 749

Portfolio Suggestion

Introduction Maybe you keep track of sports statistics for your favorite team, or perhaps you like to keep track of your grades so you know your average before you get your report card.

Ask Students Pick some statistics in which you are interested and use one of the methods in this chapter to organize or analyze the statistics. You may wish to use a matrix, create histograms, use measures of variation, or create box-and-whisker plots.

Chapter
13 Practice Test

Assessment Options

Vocabulary Test A vocabulary test/review for Chapter 13 can be found on p. 824 of the *Chapter 13 Resource Masters*.

Chapter Tests There are six Chapter 13 Tests and an Open-Ended Assessment task available in the *Chapter 13 Resource Masters*.

Chapter 13 Tests			
Form	Type	Level	Pages
1	MC	basic	811–812
2A	MC	average	813–814
2B	MC	average	815–816
2C	FR	average	817–818
2D	FR	average	819–820
3	FR	advanced	821–822

MC = multiple-choice questions
FR = free-response questions

Open-Ended Assessment
Performance tasks for Chapter 13 can be found on p. 823 of the *Chapter 13 Resource Masters*. A sample scoring rubric for these tasks appears on p. A22.

 ExamView® Pro

Use the networkable **ExamView® Pro** to:

• Create **multiple versions** of tests.
• Create **modified** tests for *Inclusion* students.
• **Edit** existing questions and **add** your own questions.
• Use built-in **state curriculum correlations** to create tests aligned with state standards.
• Change **English** tests to **Spanish** and vice versa.

These two pages contain practice questions in the various formats that can be found on the most frequently given standardized tests.

A practice answer sheet for these two pages can be found on p. A1 of the *Chapter 13 Resource Masters*.

Standardized Test Practice
Student Recording Sheet, p. A1

Part 1 Multiple Choice

Select the best answer from the choices given and fill in the corresponding oval.

1 Ⓐ Ⓑ Ⓒ Ⓓ   4 Ⓐ Ⓑ Ⓒ Ⓓ   7 Ⓐ Ⓑ Ⓒ Ⓓ   9 Ⓐ Ⓑ Ⓒ Ⓓ
2 Ⓐ Ⓑ Ⓒ Ⓓ   5 Ⓐ Ⓑ Ⓒ Ⓓ   8 Ⓐ Ⓑ Ⓒ Ⓓ   10 Ⓐ Ⓑ Ⓒ Ⓓ
3 Ⓐ Ⓑ Ⓒ Ⓓ   6 Ⓐ Ⓑ Ⓒ Ⓓ

Part 2 Short Response/Grid In

Solve the problem and write your answer in the blank.

For Questions 14 and 17, also enter your answer by writing each number or symbol in a box. Then fill in the corresponding oval for that number or symbol.

11 _____   14   17
12 _____
13 _____
14 _____ (grid in)
15 _____
16 _____
17 _____ (grid in)

Part 3 Extended Response

Record your answers for Questions 18–20 on the back of this paper.

Additional Practice

See pp. 829–830 in the *Chapter 13 Resource Masters* for additional standardized test practice.

Part 1 Multiple Choice

Record your answers on the answer sheet provided by your teacher or on a sheet of paper.

1. Which equation represents a line perpendicular to the graph of $y = 4x - 6$? (Lesson 5-6) **B**

Ⓐ $y = \frac{1}{4}x + \frac{1}{6}$ Ⓑ $y = -\frac{1}{4}x + 2$

Ⓒ $y = -4x + 6$ Ⓓ $y = 4x + 6$

2. A certain number is proportional to another number in the ratio 3:5. If 8 is subtracted from the sum of the numbers, the result is 32. What is the greater number? (Lesson 7-2) **B**

Ⓐ 15   Ⓑ 25

Ⓒ 35   Ⓓ 40

3. The expression $(x - 8)^2$ is equivalent to (Lesson 8-8) **B**

Ⓐ $x^2 - 64.$ Ⓑ $x^2 - 16x + 64.$

Ⓒ $x^2 + 16x + 64.$ Ⓓ $x^2 + 64.$

4. What is the least y value of the graph of $y = x^2 - 4$? (Lesson 10-1) **D**

Ⓐ 2   Ⓑ 0

Ⓒ −2   Ⓓ −4

5. The expression $3\sqrt{72} - 3\sqrt{2}$ is equivalent to (Lesson 11-2) **C**

Ⓐ $3\sqrt{70}.$ Ⓑ $3\sqrt{2}.$

Ⓒ $15\sqrt{2}.$ Ⓓ $5\sqrt{2}.$

6. A 12-meter flagpole casts a 9-meter shadow. At the same time, the building next to it casts a 27-meter shadow. How tall is the building? (Lesson 11-6) **B**

Ⓐ 20.25 m   Ⓑ 36 m

Ⓒ 40 m   Ⓓ 84 m

7. Students are conducting a poll at Cedar Grove High School to determine whether to change the school colors. Which would be the best place to find an unbiased sample of students who represent the entire student body? (Lesson 13-1) **D**

Ⓐ a football practice

Ⓑ a freshmen class party

Ⓒ a Spanish class

Ⓓ the cafeteria

8. A Mars year is longer than an Earth year because Mars takes longer to orbit the Sun. The table shows a person's age in both Earth years and Mars years. The data represent which kind of function? (Lesson 13-3) **A**

Earth	10	20	30	40	50
Mars	5.3	10.6	15.9	21.2	26.5

Ⓐ linear function

Ⓑ quadratic function

Ⓒ exponential function

Ⓓ rational function

Use the box-and-whisker plot for Questions 9 and 10.

Miles per Gallon of Four Different Cars

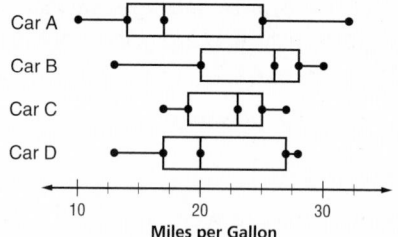

9. Which car shows the least variation in miles per gallon? (Lesson 13-5) **C**

Ⓐ A   Ⓑ B   Ⓒ C   Ⓓ D

10. Which car model has the highest median miles per gallon? (Lesson 13-5) **B**

Ⓐ A   Ⓑ B   Ⓒ C   Ⓓ D

ExamView® Pro

Special banks of standardized test questions similar to those on the SAT, ACT, TIMSS 8, NAEP 8, and Algebra 1 End-of-Course tests can be found on this CD-ROM.

Preparing for Standardized Tests
For test-taking strategies and more
practice, see pages 867–884.

Part 2 | Short Response/Grid In

**Record your answers on the answer sheet
provided by your teacher or on a sheet of
paper.**

11. Factor $x^3 + 8x^2 + 16x$. (Lesson 9-3) $x(x + 4)^2$

12. Solve $6x^2 + x - 2 = 0$ by factoring.
(Lesson 9-4) $-\frac{2}{3}, \frac{1}{2}$

13. Simplify $\sqrt{4\sqrt{9}}$. (Lesson 11-1) $2\sqrt{3}$

14. The map below shows train tracks cutting
across a grid of city streets. Newton Street
is 1.5 miles from Olive Street, Olive Street
is 1.5 miles from Pine Street, and the three
streets are parallel to each other. If the
distance between points A and B is 5 miles,
then what is the distance in miles between
points B and C? (Lesson 11-5) **4**

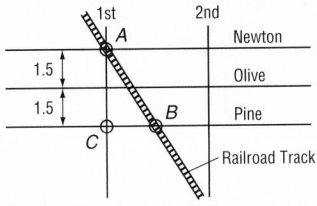

15. Find the difference of $\frac{3a - 2}{2a + 6}$ and $\frac{1 + 5a}{-6 - 2a}$.
(Lesson 12-7) $\frac{8a - 1}{2a + 6}$

16. Simplify $\dfrac{\frac{x - 3}{x^2 - 7x + 12}}{x^2 - 16}$. (Lesson 12-8) $x + 4$

Test-Taking Tip Ⓐ Ⓑ Ⓒ Ⓓ

Question 14
If a problem seems difficult, don't panic. Reread the
question slowly and carefully. Always ask yourself, "What
have I been asked to find?" and, "What information will
help me find the answer?"

www.algebra1.com/standardized_test

17. Maren can do a job in 4 hours. Juliana can
do the same job in 6 hours. Suppose Juliana
works on the job for 2 hours and then is
joined by Maren. Find the number of hours
it will take both working together to finish
the job. (Lesson 12-9) **8/5**

Part 3 | Extended Response

**Record your answers on a sheet of paper.
Show your work.**

18. Let $A = \begin{bmatrix} -1 & 6 & 9 \\ 5 & 0 & -3 \\ 1 & -8 & -7 \end{bmatrix}$ and

$B = \begin{bmatrix} 2 & -4 & 5 \\ -1 & 8 & 8 \\ -5 & 3 & 1 \end{bmatrix}$. Find the following.
(Lesson 13-2)

a. $A + B$ **18a.** $\begin{bmatrix} 1 & 2 & 14 \\ 4 & 8 & 5 \\ -4 & -5 & -6 \end{bmatrix}$

b. $A - B$ **18b.** $\begin{bmatrix} -3 & 10 & 4 \\ 6 & -8 & -8 \\ 6 & -11 & -8 \end{bmatrix}$

c. $-3B$ **18c.** $\begin{bmatrix} -6 & 12 & -15 \\ 3 & -24 & -24 \\ 15 & -9 & -3 \end{bmatrix}$

19. A grocery store ordered the following
number of oranges during the previous
twenty weeks. (Lesson 13-3)

45, 62, 78, 84, 63, 73, 68, 91, 65, 80,
71, 87, 85, 77, 78, 80, 83, 87, 90, 91

a. Construct a histogram. Use intervals of
40–50, 50–60, 60–70, 70–80, 80–90, and
90–100. **See margin.**

b. What percent of the data lies within the
tallest bar? **35%**

c. In what measurement class does the
median occur? **70–80**

20. A recent quiz resulted in the following
scores. (Lesson 13-5)

24, 38, 47, 22, 40, 36, 25, 48, 30, 32, 45,
45, 41, 34, 39, 40, 47, 40, 38, 42, 49

a. Draw a box-and-whisker plot of the data.
See margin.
b. What is the interquartile range? **12**

Evaluating Extended Response Questions

Extended Response questions
are graded by using a multilevel
rubric that guides you in
assessing a student's knowledge
of a particular concept.

Goal: Analyze a data set using the
concepts learned in this chapter.

Sample Scoring Rubric: The following rubric is a sample scoring
device. You may wish to add
more detail to this sample to meet
your individual scoring needs.

Score	Criteria
4	A correct solution that is supported by well-developed, accurate explanations
3	A generally correct solution, but may contain minor flaws in reasoning or computation
2	A partially correct interpretation and/or solution to the problem
1	A correct solution with no supporting evidence or explanation
0	An incorrect solution indicating no mathematical understanding of the concept or task, or no solution is given

Answers

19a.
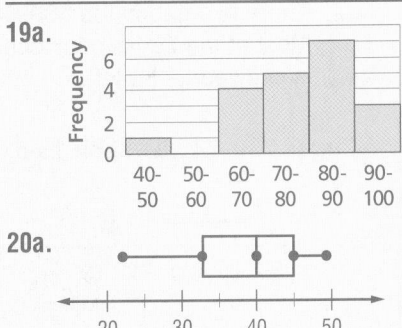

20a.

Pages 710–713, Lesson 13-1

30. Usually it is impossible for a company to test every item coming off its production lines. Therefore, testing a sample of these items is helpful in determining quality control. Answers should include the following.

- Sample answer: An unbiased way to pick the CDs to be checked is to take every 25th CD off the production line.

- Sample answer: A biased way to pick the CDs to be checked is to take the first 5 CDs coming off the production line in the morning.

Pages 725–728, Lesson 13-3

8. Sample answer:

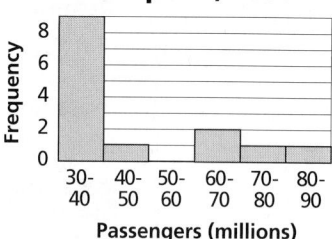

Passenger Traffic at U.S. Airports, 2000

16–17. Sample answer:

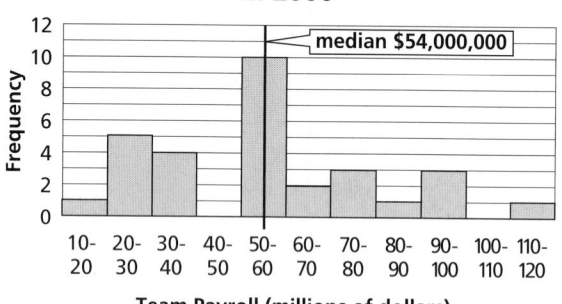

Payrolls for Major League Baseball Teams in 2000

Page 736, Practice Quiz 2

2. There is a gap in the $30-$40 measurement class. Most of the books cost less than $30. The distribution is skewed to the left.

Pages 739–742, Lesson 13-5

8.

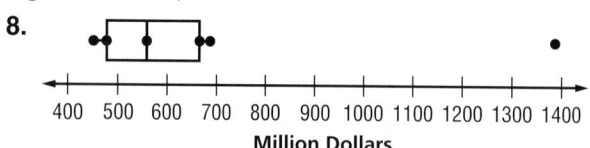

14.

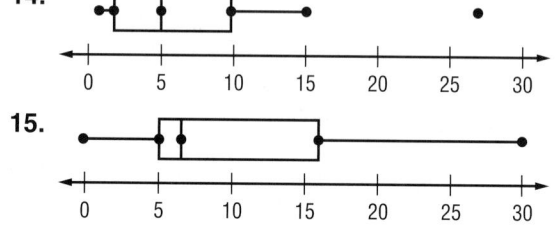

15.

16.

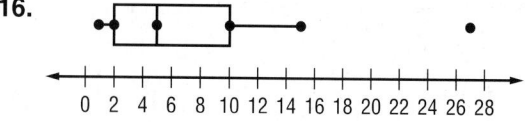

17.

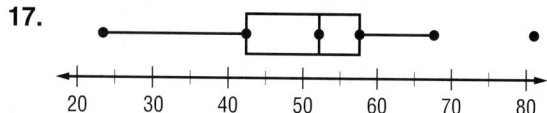

18.

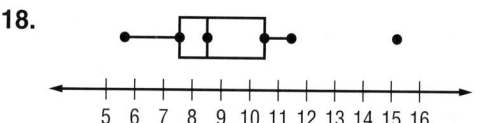

19.

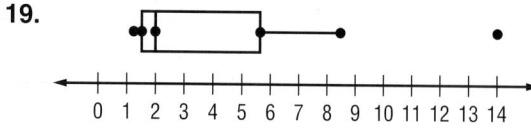

24.

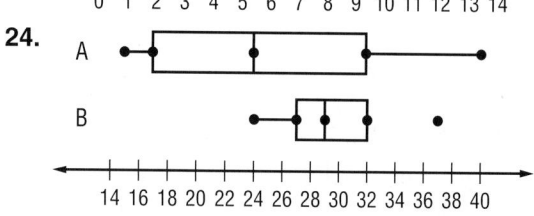

The A data are much more diverse than the B data.

25.

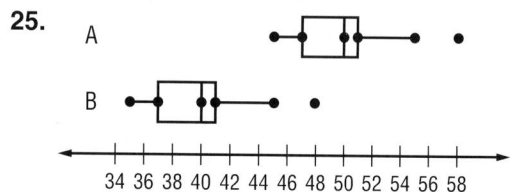

The distribution of both sets of data are similar. In general, the A data are greater than the B data.

26.

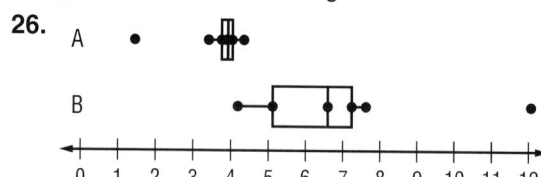

Each set of data has an outlier. In general, the B data are more diverse than the A data.

27.

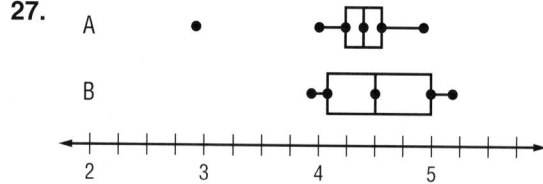

The A data have an outlier. Excluding the outlier, the B data are more diverse than the A data.

28.

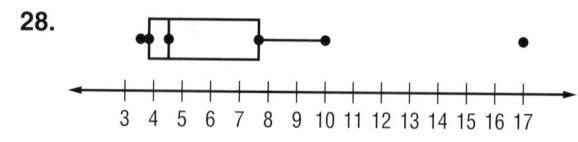

30.

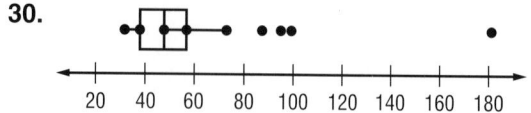

36.

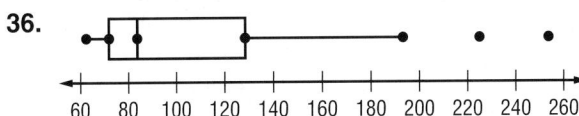

37. Sample answer:

Life-Time Scores for Top 50 U.S. Soccer Players

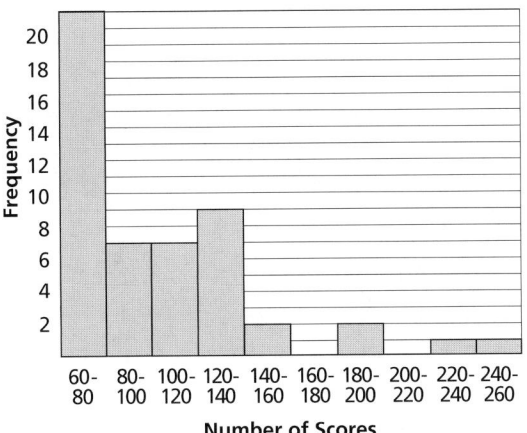

40. Box-and-whisker plots use a number line to show the least value in the data, the greatest value in the data, and the quartiles of the data. They also indicate outliers. Answers should include the following.

-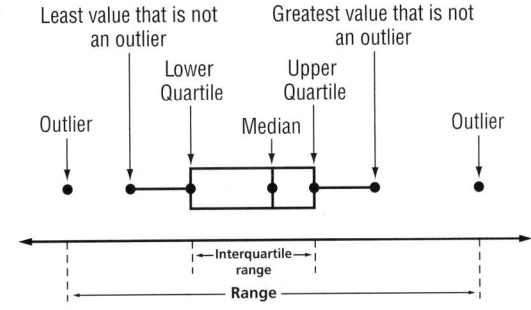

- The students should draw a box-and-whisker representing data they found in a newspaper or magazine.

Pages 743–744, Follow-Up of Lesson 13-5

8. Sample answer:

Weight Interval (pounds)	Number of Babies	Cumulative Number of Babies
3–4	1	1
4–5	1	2
5–6	4	6
6–7	7	13
7–8	16	29
8–9	11	40
9–10	3	43
10–11	1	44
11–12	1	45

9. Sample answer:

Weight of Babies

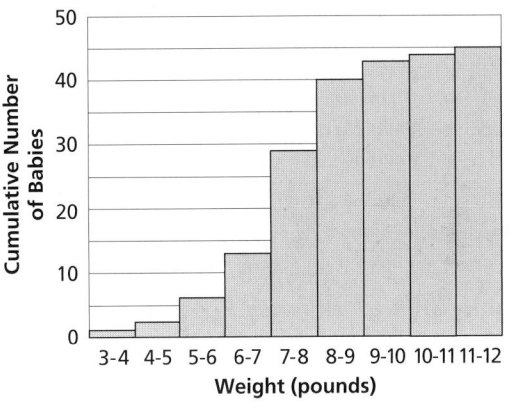

Page 749, Practice Test

18.

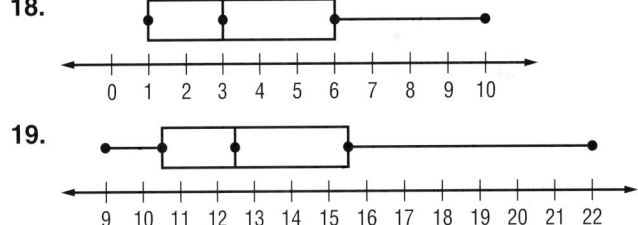

19.

Probability
Chapter Overview and Pacing

Year-long and two-year pacing: pages T20–T21.

LESSON OBJECTIVES

	PACING (days)			
	Regular		**Block**	
	Basic/ Average	Advanced	Basic/ Average	Advanced
14-1 Counting Outcomes *(pp. 754–759)* • Count outcomes using a tree diagram. • Count outcomes using the Fundamental Counting Principle. ***Follow-Up:*** Use finite graphs to determine whether a route is traceable.	optional	1	optional	0.5
14-2 Permutations and Combinations *(pp. 760–767)* • Determine probabilities using permutations. • Determine probabilities using combinations.	optional	2	optional	1
14-3 Probability of Compound Events *(pp. 769–776)* • Find the probability of two independent events or dependent events. • Find the probability of two mutually exclusive or inclusive events.	optional	2	optional	1
14-4 Probability Distributions *(pp. 777–781)* • Use random variables to compute probability. • Use probability distributions to solve real-world problems.	optional	2	optional	1
14-5 Probability Simulations *(pp. 782–788)* • Use theoretical and experimental probability to represent and solve problems involving uncertainty. • Perform probability simulations to model real-world situations involving uncertainty.	optional	2	optional	1
Study Guide and **Practice Test** *(pp. 789–793)* **Standardized Test Practice** *(pp. 794–795)*	optional	1	optional	0.5
Chapter Assessment	optional	1	optional	0.5
TOTAL		11		5.5

An electronic version of this chapter is available on **StudentWorks**™. *This backpack solution CD-ROM allows students instant access to the Student Edition, lesson worksheet pages, and web resources.*

Chapter Resource Manager

Timesaving Tools
TeacherWorks™
All-In-One Planner and Resource Center
See pages T5 and T21.

CHAPTER 14 RESOURCE MASTERS

Study Guide and Intervention	Practice (Skills and Average)	Reading to Learn Mathematics	Enrichment	Assessment	Prerequisite Skills Workbook	Applications*	Parent and Student Study Guide Workbook	5-Minute Check Transparencies	Interactive Chalkboard	AlgePASS: Tutorial Plus (lessons)	Materials
831–832	833–834	835	836				107	14-1	14-1		
837–838	839–840	841	842	875		SC 27	108	14-2	14-2		
843–844	845–846	847	848	875, 877	47–48, 55–56, 67–70, 99–100	SM 109–114	109	14-3	14-3	35	
849–850	851–852	853	854	876		GCS 50	110	14-4	14-4		
855–856	857–858	859	860	876		GCS 49, SC 28	111	14-5	14-5		die, graphing calculator
				861–874, 878–880			112				

Key to Abbreviations: GCS = Graphing Calculator and Spreadsheet Masters,
SC = School-to-Career Masters,
SM = Science and Mathematics Lab Manual

ELL Study Guide and Intervention, Skills Practice, Practice, and Parent and Student Study Guide Workbooks are also available in Spanish.

Mathematical Connections and Background

Continuity of Instruction

Prior Knowledge

In Chapter 2, students were shown how to find the probability and odds of a simple event. While these techniques are great for use with dice, spinners, and board games, situations in the real world produce much more complex probability situations.

This Chapter

In this chapter, students will go beyond simple probability. They will learn to find probabilities using the Fundamental Counting Principle, and by using permutations and combinations. Then students will move on to find probabilities of compound events, and to use probability distributions and simulations.

Future Connections

Understanding probability can be an important decision-making tool. We are often asked to make decisions based on whether we think an event will occur. Using probability can take some of the guesswork out of these decisions.

14-1 Counting Outcomes

Given a choice of three different sandwiches, four different side dishes, and five different soft drinks, how many lunch combinations are there? One can find out by making a tree diagram of all possible outcomes. In the first column, list all of the possibilities for one choice. After each of those possibilities, list all the possibilities of another choice. Repeat for all the possibilities for each choice that is to be made. The list of all possible outcomes is written in the last column. This is the sample space. Each item in the sample space is an event.

Another method of counting outcomes uses the Fundamental Counting Principle. This principle states that given an event M that can occur m ways followed by an event N that occurs n ways, then the event M followed by event N can occur $m \times n$ ways. In other words, *number of choices $\times$ number of choices $\times$ number of choices...*, for each choice that is to be made.

A factorial is the product of a number and all the positive integers between that number and zero. Factorials can be used to determine the number of arrangements or orders for a set of data or events. They are also used to determine permutations and combinations that are studied in the next lesson.

14-2 Permutations and Combinations

A permutation is an arrangement or listing in which order or placement is important. For example, if three students are being picked for class president, vice-president, and secretary, then the order in which they are picked is important. Therefore, this is a permutation. Tree diagrams can be used to show permutations. A symbol for permutations is $_nP_r$, where n is the number of items to choose from and r is the number of items to be chosen. You find the number of permutations by using the formula $\dfrac{n!}{(n-r)!}$.

A combination is an arrangement in which order or placement is not important. For example when picking two pizza toppings from a list of eight, the order in which the toppings are picked is not important. So this is a combination. The symbol for a combination is $_nC_r$. The only way the formula for the number of combinations differs from the formula for the number of permutations is that the denominator is multiplied by $r!$. The formula is $\dfrac{n!}{(n-r)!r!}$.

14-3 Probability of Compound Events

A simple event is a single event. A compound event is two or more simple events. Predicting the probability of rain on two separate days is an example of finding the probability of a compound event. If two events occur separately and the outcome of one does not affect the outcome of the other, then the events are independent. However, if the outcome of one event does affect the outcome of the other event, then the events are dependent.

To find the compound probability of two independent events, find the product of the probabilities of each event: $P(A) \cdot P(B)$. To find the probability of two dependent events, multiply the probability of the first event by the probability of the second event following the first event: $P(A) \cdot P(B$ following $A)$.

Mutually exclusive events are events that cannot occur at the same time. An example is rolling an even number and an odd number on a die. An even and an odd number cannot be rolled at the same time with one die. To find the probability of mutually exclusive events, find the sum of the probabilities of the two events: $P(A) + P(B)$.

Inclusive events can occur at the same time. For example, rolling an odd number or a 5 on a die. Five is an odd number, so both can be rolled at the same time. Use the formula $P(A) + P(B) - P(A$ and $B)$ to find the probability of inclusive events.

14-4 Probability Distributions

A random variable is a variable whose value is the numerical outcome of a random event. The probability of every possible value of the random variable X is called a probability distribution. A probability distribution can be represented in a table or in a probability histogram.

14-5 Probability Simulations

The probabilities studied so far have been theoretical probabilities. These are probabilities that are determined mathematically and describe what should happen. Experimental probability is the probability of an event found by repeated experimentation. The experimentation is called a simulation. What should happen and what actually does happen may differ. Given few trials, experimental probability may differ greatly from the calculated theoretical probability. However, the more trials conducted, the more closely experimental probability will be to theoretical probability. For example, tossing a die 18 times may only result in one outcome of 1. However, theoretical probability predicts a $\frac{1}{6}$ probability. If you toss the die 200 times, however, the experimental probability will probably be very close to $\frac{1}{6}$.

Quick Review Math Handbook

Hot Words includes a glossary of terms while Hot Topics consists of explanations of key mathematical concepts with exercises to test comprehension. This valuable resource can be used as a reference in the classroom or for home study.

Lesson	Hot Topics Section	Lesson	Hot Topics Section
14-1	4.5, 4.6	14-4	2.1, 4.6
14-2	2.3, 2.4, 4.5	14-5	4.6
14-3	2.9, 4.6		

 Additional mathematical information and teaching notes are available at www.algebra1.com/key_concepts.

DAILY INTERVENTION and Assessment

Key to Abbreviations:
TWE = Teacher Wraparound Edition; CRM = Chapter Resource Masters

	Type	Student Edition	Teacher Resources	Technology/Internet
INTERVENTION	Ongoing	Prerequisite Skills, pp. 753, 758, 767, 776, 781 Practice Quiz 1, p. 767 Practice Quiz 2, p. 781	5-Minute Check Transparencies *Prerequisite Skills Workbook*, pp. 47–48, 55–56, 67–70, 99–100 Quizzes, *CRM* pp. 875–876 Mid-Chapter Test, *CRM* p. 877 Study Guide and Intervention, *CRM* pp. 831–832, 837–838, 843–844, 849–850, 855–856	AlgePASS: Tutorial Plus, Lesson 35 www.algebra1.com/self_check_quiz www.algebra1.com/extra_examples
	Mixed Review	pp. 758, 767, 776, 781, 788	Cumulative Review, *CRM* p. 878	
	Error Analysis	Find the Error, pp. 764, 773 Common Misconceptions, p. 760	Find the Error, *TWE* pp. 764, 773 Tips for New Teachers, *TWE* pp. 763, 779	
ASSESSMENT	Standardized Test Practice	pp. 758, 762, 764, 766, 776, 780, 787, 793, 794–795	*TWE* pp. 794–795 Standardized Test Practice, *CRM* pp. 879–880	Standardized Test Practice CD-ROM www.algebra1.com/standardized_test
	Open-Ended Assessment	Writing in Math, pp. 757, 766, 776, 780, 787 Open Ended, pp. 756, 764, 772, 779, 785 Standardized Test, p. 795	Modeling: *TWE* pp. 758, 781, 788 Speaking: *TWE* p. 767 Writing: *TWE* p. 776 Open-Ended Assessment, *CRM* p. 873	
	Chapter Assessment	Study Guide, pp. 789–792 Practice Test, p. 793	Multiple-Choice Tests (Forms 1, 2A, 2B), *CRM* pp. 861–866 Free-Response Tests (Forms 2C, 2D, 3), *CRM* pp. 867–872 Vocabulary Test/Review, *CRM* p. 874	ExamView® Pro (see below) MindJogger Videoquizzes www.algebra1.com/vocabulary_review www.algebra1.com/chapter_test

For more information on Yearly ProgressPro, see p. 704.

Algebra Lesson	Yearly ProgressPro Skill Lesson
14-1	Counting Outcomes
14-2	Permutations and Combinations
14-3	Probability of Compound Events
14-4	Probability Distributions
14-5	Probability Simulations

ExamView® Pro

Use the networkable **ExamView® Pro** to:
- Create **multiple versions** of tests.
- Create **modified** tests for *Inclusion* students.
- **Edit** existing questions and **add** your own questions.
- Use built-in **state curriculum correlations** to create tests aligned with state standards.
- Change **English** tests to **Spanish** and vice versa.

For more information on Intervention and Assessment, see pp. T8–T11.

Reading and Writing in Mathematics

Glencoe Algebra 1 provides numerous opportunities to incorporate reading and writing into the mathematics classroom.

Student Edition

- Foldables Study Organizer, p. 753
- Concept Check questions require students to verbalize and write about what they have learned in the lesson. (pp. 756, 764, 772, 779, 785)
- Reading Mathematics, p. 768
- Writing in Math questions in every lesson, pp. 757, 766, 776, 780, 787
- Reading Study Tip, pp. 771, 777, 783
- WebQuest, pp. 766, 788

Teacher Wraparound Edition

- Foldables Study Organizer, pp. 753, 789
- Study Notebook suggestions, pp. 756, 759, 764, 768, 772, 779, 785
- Modeling activities, pp. 758, 781, 788
- Speaking activities, p. 767
- Writing activities, p. 776
- **ELL** Resources, pp. 752, 757, 766, 768, 774, 780, 787, 789

Additional Resources

- Vocabulary Builder worksheets require students to define and give examples for key vocabulary terms as they progress through the chapter. (*Chapter 14 Resource Masters,* pp. vii-viii)
- Reading to Learn Mathematics master for each lesson (*Chapter 14 Resource Masters,* pp. 835, 841, 847, 853, 859)
- *Vocabulary PuzzleMaker* software creates crossword, jumble, and word search puzzles using vocabulary lists that you can customize.
- *Teaching Mathematics with Foldables* provides suggestions for promoting cognition and language.
- *Reading and Writing in the Mathematics Classroom*
- *WebQuest and Project Resources*
- *Hot Words/Hot Topics* Sections 2.1, 2.3, 2.4, 2.9, 4.5, 4.6

For more information on Reading and Writing in Mathematics, see pp. T6–T7.

PROJECT CRISS℠ Study Skill

Most students already have some knowledge of the topics presented in Chapter 14. Help them build on this knowledge using a **K**now-**W**ant to Learn-**L**earned (KWL) chart like the one at the right. Before starting the chapter, draw the chart on an overhead transparency. Name some topics covered in the chapter, such as permutations and probability of compound events. Have students tell what they already know about the topics as you record their ideas. Next, have them list what they would like to know about the topics. After working through the chapter, again display the chart and have students fill in the last column, describing what they have learned.

Compound Events		
Know	**Want to Learn**	**Learned**
The probability of two independent events A and B occurring is the product of the probability of A and the probability of B.	What is the probability of two events that cannot occur at the same time?	

CReating **I**ndependence **T**hrough **S**tudent-Owned **S**trategies

What You'll Learn

Have students read over the list of objectives and make a list of any words with which they are not familiar.

Why It's Important

Point out to students that this is only one of many reasons why each objective is important. Others are provided in the introduction to each lesson.

Lesson	NCTM Standards	Local Objectives
14-1	1, 5, 6, 8, 9, 10	
14-1 Follow-Up	3, 5, 6, 7, 8, 9, 10	
14-2	1, 5, 6, 8, 9, 10	
14-3	1, 5, 6, 8, 9, 10	
14-4	1, 5, 6, 8, 9, 10	
14-5	1, 5, 6, 8, 9, 10	

Key to NCTM Standards:

1=Number & Operations, 2=Algebra, 3=Geometry, 4=Measurement, 5=Data Analysis & Probability, 6=Problem Solving, 7=Reasoning & Proof, 8=Communication, 9=Connections, 10=Representation

752   Chapter 14   Probability

What You'll Learn

- **Lesson 14-1**   Count outcomes using the Fundamental Counting Principle.
- **Lesson 14-2**   Determine probabilities using permutations and combinations.
- **Lesson 14-3**   Find probabilities of compound events.
- **Lesson 14-4**   Use probability distributions.
- **Lesson 14-5**   Use probability simulations.

Key Vocabulary

- permutation (p. 760)
- combination (p. 762)
- compound event (p. 769)
- theoretical probability (p. 782)
- experimental probability (p. 782)

Why It's Important

The United States Senate forms committees to focus on different issues. These committees are made up of senators from various states and political parties. There are many ways these committees could be formed. *You will learn how to find the number of possible committees in Lesson 14-2.*

Vocabulary Builder

The Key Vocabulary list introduces students to some of the main vocabulary terms included in this chapter. For a more thorough vocabulary list with pronunciations of new words, give students the Vocabulary Builder worksheets found on pages vii and viii of the *Chapter 14 Resource Masters*. Encourage them to complete the definition of each term as they progress through the chapter. You may suggest that they add these sheets to their study notebooks for future reference when studying for the Chapter 14 test.

▶ **Prerequisite Skills** To be successful in this chapter, you'll need to master these skills and be able to apply them in problem-solving situations. Review these skills before beginning Chapter 14.

For Lessons 14-2 through 14-5   **Find Simple Probabilities**

Determine the probability of each event if you randomly select a cube from a bag containing 6 red cubes, 3 blue cubes, 4 yellow cubes, and 1 green cube.
(For review, see Lesson 2-6.)

1. $P(\text{red})$ $\dfrac{3}{7}$ **2.** $P(\text{blue})$ $\dfrac{3}{14}$ **3.** $P(\text{yellow})$ $\dfrac{2}{7}$ **4.** $P(\text{not red})$ $\dfrac{4}{7}$

For Lesson 14-2   **Multiply Fractions**

Find each product.   *(For review, see pages 800 and 801.)*

5. $\dfrac{4}{5} \cdot \dfrac{3}{4}$ $\dfrac{3}{5}$ **6.** $\dfrac{5}{12} \cdot \dfrac{6}{11}$ $\dfrac{5}{22}$ **7.** $\dfrac{7}{20} \cdot \dfrac{4}{19}$ $\dfrac{7}{95}$

8. $\dfrac{4}{32} \cdot \dfrac{7}{32}$ $\dfrac{7}{256}$ **9.** $\dfrac{13}{52} \cdot \dfrac{4}{52}$ $\dfrac{1}{52}$ **10.** $\dfrac{56}{100} \cdot \dfrac{24}{100}$ $\dfrac{84}{625}$

For Lesson 14-4   **Write Decimals as Percents**

Write each decimal as a percent.   *(For review, see pages 804 and 805.)*

11. 0.725 **72.5%**   **12.** 0.148 **14.8%**   **13.** 0.4 **40%**   **14.** 0.0168 **1.68%**

For Lesson 14-5   **Write Fractions as Percents**

Write each fraction as a percent. Round to the nearest tenth.   *(For review, see pages 804 and 805.)*

15. $\dfrac{7}{8}$ **87.5%**   **16.** $\dfrac{33}{80}$ **41.3%**   **17.** $\dfrac{107}{125}$ **85.6%**   **18.** $\dfrac{625}{1024}$ **61%**

Probability Make this Foldable to help you organize your notes. Begin with a sheet of plain $8\frac{1}{2}''$ by $11''$ paper.

Step 1   **Fold in Half**

Fold in half lengthwise.

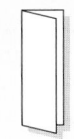

Step 2   **Fold Again in Fourths**

Fold the top to the bottom twice.

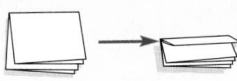

Step 3   **Cut**

Open. Cut along the folds to make four tabs.

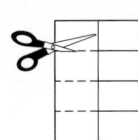

Step 4   **Label**

Label as shown.

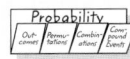

Reading and Writing As you read and study the chapter, write notes and examples for each concept under the tabs.

This section provides a review of the basic concepts needed before beginning Chapter 14. Page references are included for additional student help.

Additional review is provided in the *Prerequisite Skills Workbook*, pp. 47–48, 55–56, 67–70, 99–100.

Prerequisite Skills in the Getting Ready for the Next Lesson section at the end of each exercise set review a skill needed in the next lesson.

For Lesson	Prerequisite Skill
14-2	Simple Probability (p. 758)
14-4	Expressing Fractions as Decimals (p. 776)
14-5	Writing Fractions as Percents (p. 781)

FOLDABLES™
Study Organizer

For more information about Foldables, see *Teaching Mathematics with Foldables.*

Organization of Data with a Concept Map Begin with the central chapter theme of Probability as the title and have students record key words and phrases under the four tabs labeled *outcomes, permutations, combinations,* and *compound events.* Students use their Foldables to take notes, define terms, record concepts, and write examples. Foldable concept maps make great study aids because students view main ideas, recall what they know, and check their responses by looking under the tabs.

1 Focus

5-Minute Check Transparency 14-1 Use as a quiz or review of Chapter 13.

Mathematical Background notes are available for this lesson on p. 752C.

How are possible win-loss records counted in football?

Ask students:

- How many different ways can the team end up with a 3–0 record? **one way**

- Why are there three different ways the team could end up with a 2–1 record? **They could win, win, lose; win, lose, win; or lose, win, win.**

- **Sports** Only in the last few years have college football teams been able to play over-time to break a tie score. Before the overtime rule was established, there were three possible outcomes for a college football game; win, lose, or tie. How many different ways could the teams record be determined in three games if ties were possible outcomes? **27**

What You'll Learn

- Count outcomes using a tree diagram.
- Count outcomes using the Fundamental Counting Principle.

Vocabulary

- tree diagram
- sample space
- event
- Fundamental Counting Principle
- factorial

How are possible win–loss records counted in football?

The championship in the Atlantic Coast Conference is decided by the number of conference wins. If there is a tie in conference wins, then the team with more nonconference wins is champion. If Florida State plays 3 nonconference games, the diagram at the right shows the different records they could have for those games.

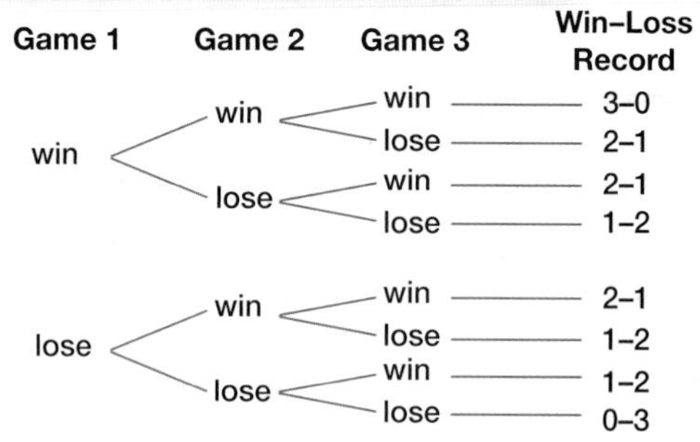

	Game 1	Game 2	Game 3	Win–Loss Record
	win	win	win	3–0
			lose	2–1
		lose	win	2–1
			lose	1–2
	lose	win	win	2–1
			lose	1–2
		lose	win	1–2
			lose	0–3

TREE DIAGRAMS One method used for counting the number of possible outcomes is to draw a **tree diagram**. The last column of a tree diagram shows all of the possible outcomes. The list of all possible outcomes is called the **sample space**, while any collection of one or more outcomes in the sample space is called an **event**.

Example 1 *Tree Diagram*

A football team uses red jerseys for road games, white jerseys for home games, and gray jerseys for practice games. The team uses gray or black pants, and black or white shoes. Use a tree diagram to determine the number of possible uniforms.

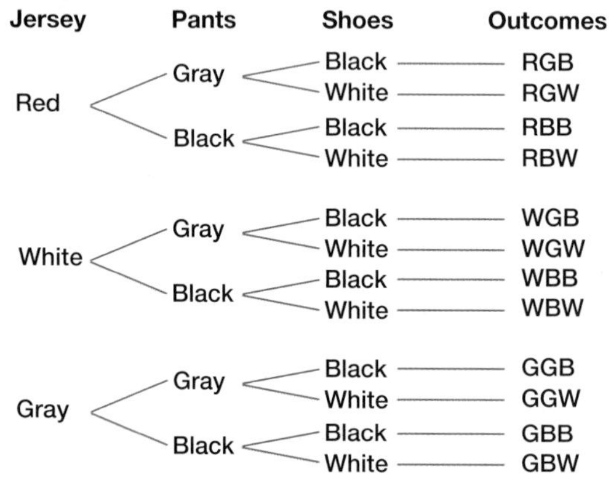

Jersey	Pants	Shoes	Outcomes
Red	Gray	Black	RGB
		White	RGW
	Black	Black	RBB
		White	RBW
White	Gray	Black	WGB
		White	WGW
	Black	Black	WBB
		White	WBW
Gray	Gray	Black	GGB
		White	GGW
	Black	Black	GBB
		White	GBW

The tree diagram shows that there are 12 possible uniforms.

Resource Manager

📂 Workbook and Reproducible Masters

Chapter 14 Resource Masters
- Study Guide and Intervention, pp. 831–832
- Skills Practice, p. 833
- Practice, p. 834
- Reading to Learn Mathematics, p. 835
- Enrichment, p. 836

Parent and Student Study Guide Workbook, p. 107

Transparencies

5-Minute Check Transparency 14-1
Answer Key Transparencies

Technology

Interactive Chalkboard

THE FUNDAMENTAL COUNTING PRINCIPLE The number of possible uniforms in Example 1 can also be found by multiplying the number of choices for each item. If the team can choose from 3 different colored jerseys, 2 different colored pants, and 2 different colored pairs of shoes, there are $3 \cdot 2 \cdot 2$ or 12 possible uniforms. This example illustrates the **Fundamental Counting Principle**.

Key Concept — Fundamental Counting Principle

If an event M can occur in m ways and is followed by an event N that can occur in n ways, then the event M followed by event N can occur in $m \cdot n$ ways.

Example 2 — Fundamental Counting Principle

The Uptown Deli offers a lunch special in which you can choose a sandwich, a side dish, and a beverage. If there are 10 different sandwiches, 12 different side dishes, and 7 different beverages from which to choose, how many different lunch specials can you order?

Multiply to find the number of lunch specials.

sandwich choices		side dish choices		beverage choices		number of specials
10	$\cdot$	12	$\cdot$	7	$=$	840

The number of different lunch specials is 840.

Example 3 — Counting Arrangements

Mackenzie is setting up a display of the ten most popular video games from the previous week. If she places the games side-by-side on a shelf, in how many different ways can she arrange them?

The number of ways to arrange the games can be found by multiplying the number of choices for each position.

- Mackenzie has ten games from which to choose for the first position.
- After choosing a game for the first position, there are nine games left from which to choose for the second position.
- There are now eight choices for the third position.
- This process continues until there is only one choice left for the last position.

Let n represent the number of arrangements.

$n = 10 \cdot 9 \cdot 8 \cdot 7 \cdot 6 \cdot 5 \cdot 4 \cdot 3 \cdot 2 \cdot 1$ or 3,628,800

There are 3,628,800 different ways to arrange the video games.

The expression $n = 10 \cdot 9 \cdot 8 \cdot 7 \cdot 6 \cdot 5 \cdot 4 \cdot 3 \cdot 2 \cdot 1$ used in Example 3 can be written as 10! using a **factorial**.

Key Concept — Factorial

- **Words** The expression $n!$, read n factorial, where n is greater than zero, is the product of all positive integers beginning with n and counting backward to 1.
- **Symbols** $n! = n \cdot (n-1) \cdot (n-2) \cdot \ldots \cdot 3 \cdot 2 \cdot 1$
- **Example** $5! = 5 \cdot 4 \cdot 3 \cdot 2 \cdot 1$ or 120

By definition, $0! = 1$.

www.algebra1.com/extra_examples

TREE DIAGRAMS

In-Class Example Power Point®

1. At football games, a student concession stand sells sandwiches on either wheat or rye bread. The sandwiches come with salami, turkey, or ham; and either chips, a brownie, or fruit. Use a tree diagram to determine the number of possible sandwich combinations.
18 possible combinations

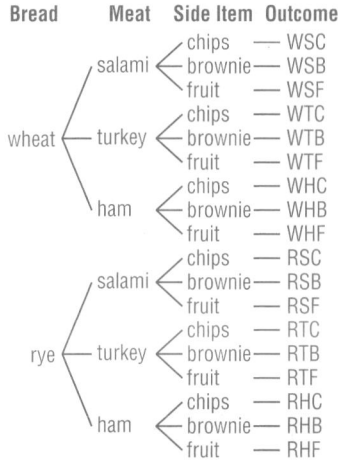

THE FUNDAMENTAL COUNTING PRINCIPLE

In-Class Examples Power Point®

2. The Too Cheap computer company sells custom made personal computers. Customers have a choice of 11 different hard drives, 6 different keyboards, 4 different mice, and 4 different monitors. How many different custom computers can you order?
$11 \cdot 6 \cdot 4 \cdot 4 = 1056$ different custom computers

3. There are 8 students in the Algebra Club at Central High School. The students want to stand in a line for their yearbook picture. How many different ways could the 8 students stand for their picture?
$8 \cdot 7 \cdot 6 \cdot 5 \cdot 4 \cdot 3 \cdot 2 \cdot 1 = 40{,}320$ ways they could stand

---

DAILY INTERVENTION — Differentiated Instruction

Logical Students may wonder why 0! is defined as being equal to 1. Show them that $3! = \dfrac{4!}{4}$, $2! = \dfrac{3!}{3}$, and $1! = \dfrac{2!}{2}$, so that the next logical conclusion is that $0! = \dfrac{1!}{1}$.

4 Find the value of 9!.
9! = 9 · 8 · 7 · 6 · 5 · 4 · 3 · 2 · 1 = 362,880

Teaching Tip Explain to students that in Part b of Example 5, even though Zach and Kurt only get to ride 8 of the roller coasters, there are still 12 to choose from when they ride the first one, 11 for the second one, 10 for the third one, and so on.

5 **OUTDOORS** Jill and Miranda are going to a National Park for their vacation. Near the campground where they are staying, there are 8 hiking trails.

a. How many different ways can they hike all the trails if they hike each trail only once? **40,320**

b. If they only have time to hike on 5 of the trails, how many ways can they do this? **6720**

More About . . .

Roller Coasters · · · · ·

In 2000, there were 646 roller coasters in the United States.

Type	Number
Wood	118
Steel	445
Inverted	35
Stand Up	10
Suspended	11
Wild Mouse	27

Source: Roller Coaster Database

Example 4 Factorial

Find the value of each expression.

a. 6!
  6! = 6 · 5 · 4 · 3 · 2 · 1   Definition of factorial
    = 720   Simplify.

b. 10!
  10! = 10 · 9 · 8 · 7 · 6 · 5 · 4 · 3 · 2 · 1   Definition of factorial
    = 3,628,800   Simplify.

Example 5 Use Factorials to Solve a Problem

· · **ROLLER COASTERS** Zach and Kurt are going to an amusement park. They cannot decide in which order to ride the 12 roller coasters in the park.

a. **How many different orders can they ride all of the roller coasters if they ride each once?**

Use a factorial.

12! = 12 · 11 · 10 · 9 · 8 · 7 · 6 · 5 · 4 · 3 · 2 · 1   Definition of factorial
    = 479,001,600   Simplify.

There are 479,001,600 ways in which Zach and Kurt can ride all 12 roller coasters.

b. **If they only have time to ride 8 of the roller coasters, how many ways can they do this?**

Use the Fundamental Counting Principle to find the sample space.

s = 12 · 11 · 10 · 9 · 8 · 7 · 6 · 5   Fundamental Counting Principle
    = 19,958,400   Simplify.

There are 19,958,400 ways for Zach and Kurt to ride 8 of the roller coasters.

3 Practice/Apply

Study Notebook

Have students—
• add the definitions/examples of the vocabulary terms to their Vocabulary Builder worksheets for Chapter 14.
• include any other item(s) that they find helpful in mastering the skills in this lesson.

Check for Understanding

Concept Check

1. **OPEN ENDED** Give an example of an event that has 7 · 6 or 42 outcomes. **Sample answer: choosing 2 books from 7 books on a shelf**

2. See margin.

2. **Draw** a tree diagram to represent the outcomes of tossing a coin three times.

3. **Explain** what the notation 5! means. **5! = 5 • 4 • 3 • 2 • 1**

Guided Practice

For Exercises 4–6, suppose the spinner at the right is spun three times.

4. Draw a tree diagram to show the sample space. **See pp. 795A–795B.**

5. How many outcomes are possible? **64**

6. How many outcomes involve both green and blue? **18**

7. Find the value of 8!. **40,320**

GUIDED PRACTICE KEY	
Exercises	Examples
4–6	1–3
7	4
8	5

Application

8. **SCHOOL** In a science class, each student must choose a lab project from a list of 15, write a paper on one of 6 topics, and give a presentation about one of 8 subjects. How many different ways can students choose to do their assignments? **720**

Answers

2.

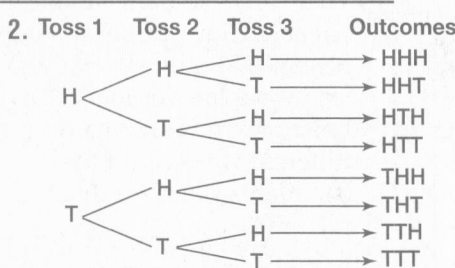

19.

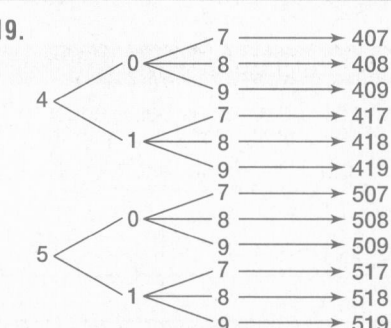

20. **Columbus in three games : C-C-C;**
Columbus in four games: C-C-D-C, C-D-C-C,
D-C-C-C; Columbus in five games: C-C-D-D-C,
C-D-C-D-C, C-D-D-C-C, D-C-C-D-C,
D-C-D-C-C, D-D-C-C-C; D.C. in three games:
D-D-D; D.C. in four games: C-D-D-D,
D-C-D-D, D-D-C-D; D.C. in five games:
C-C-D-D-D, C-D-C-D-D, C-D-D-C-D,
D-C-C-D-D, D-C-D-C-D, D-D-C-C-D

Practice and Apply

Homework Help

For Exercises	See Examples
9, 10, 19	1
11–14	4
15–18, 20–22	2, 3, 5

Extra Practice
See page 851.

Draw a tree diagram to show the sample space for each event. Determine the number of possible outcomes. 9–10. See pp. 795A–795B for diagrams.

9. earning an A, B, or C in English, Math, and Science classes **27**

10. buying a computer with a choice of a CD-ROM, a CD recorder, or a DVD drive, one of 2 monitors, and either a printer or a scanner **12**

Find the value of each expression.

11. 4! **24** 12. 7! **5040** 13. 11! **39,916,800** 14. 13! **6,227,020,800**

15. Three dice, one red, one white, and one blue are rolled. How many outcomes are possible? **216**

16. How many outfits are possible if you choose one each of 5 shirts, 3 pairs of pants, 3 pairs of shoes, and 4 jackets? **180**

17. **TRAVEL** Suppose four different airlines fly from Seattle to Denver. Those same four airlines and two others fly from Denver to St. Louis. If there are no direct flights from Seattle to St. Louis, in how many ways can a traveler book a flight from Seattle to St. Louis? **24**

★ **COMMUNICATIONS** For Exercises 18 and 19, use the following information.
A new 3-digit area code is needed in a certain area to accommodate new telephone numbers.

18. If the first digit must be odd, the second digit must be a 0 or a 1, and the third digit can be anything, how many area codes are possible? **100**

19. Draw a tree diagram to show the different area codes using 4 or 5 for the first digit, 0 or 1 for the second digit, and 7, 8, or 9 for the third digit. **See margin.**

★ **SOCCER** For Exercises 20–22, use the following information.
The Columbus Crew are playing the D.C. United in a best three-out-of-five championship soccer series.

20. What are the possible outcomes of the series? **See margin.**

21. How many outcomes require exactly four games to determine the champion? **6**

22. How many ways can D.C. United win the championship? **10**

23. **CRITICAL THINKING** To get to and from school, Tucker can walk, ride his bike, or get a ride with a friend. Suppose that one week he walked 60% of the time, rode his bike 20% of the time, and rode with his friend 20% of the time. How many outcomes represent this situation? Assume that he returns home the same way that he went to school. **20**

24. **WRITING IN MATH** Answer the question that was posed at the beginning of the lesson. **See margin.**

How are possible win–loss records counted in football?

Include the following in your answer:
- a few sentences describing how a tree diagram can be used to count the wins and losses of a football team, and
- a demonstration of how to find the number of possible outcomes for a team that plays 4 home games.

 www.algebra1.com/self_check_quiz

24. Sample answer: You can make a chart showing all possible outcomes to help determine a football team's record. Answers should include the following.
- a tree diagram or calculations to show 16 possible outcomes

Enrichment, p. 836

Pascal's Triangle

Pascal's Triangle is a pattern of numbers used at many levels of mathematics. It is named for Blaise Pascal, a seventeenth-century French mathematician who discovered several applications of the pattern. However, records of the triangle have been traced as far back as twelfth-century China and Persia. In the year 1303, the Chinese mathematician Zhū-Shìjié wrote *The Precious Mirror of the Four Elements,* in which he described how the triangle could be used to solve polynomial equations. The figure at the right is adapted from the original Chinese manuscript. In the figure, some circles are empty while others contain Chinese symbols.

At the right a portion of Pascal's Triangle is Arabic nur...

Study Guide and Intervention, p. 831 (shown) and p. 832

Tree Diagrams One method used for counting the number of possible outcomes of an event is to draw a **tree diagram**. The last column of the tree diagram shows all of the possible outcomes. The list of all possible outcomes is called the **sample space**, and a specific outcome is called an **event**.

Example 1 Suppose you can set up a stereo system with a choice of video, DVD, or laser disk players, a choice of cassette or graphic equalizer audio components, and a choice of single or dual speakers. Draw a tree diagram to show the sample space.

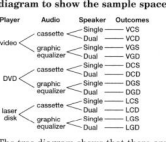

The tree diagram shows that there are 12 ways to set up the stereo system.

Example 2 A food stand offers ice cream cones in vanilla or chocolate flavors. It also offers fudge or caramel toppings, and it uses sugar or cake cones. Use a tree diagram to determine the number of possible ice cream cones.

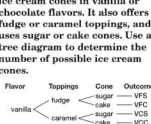

The tree diagram shows that there are 8 possible ice cream cones.

Exercises

The spinner at the right is spun twice.

1. Draw a tree diagram to show the sample space.

2. How many outcomes are possible? 16

A pizza can be ordered with a choice of sausage, pepperoni, or mushrooms for toppings, a choice of thin or pan for the crust, and a choice of medium or large for the size.

3. Draw a tree diagram to show the sample space.

4. How many pizzas are possible? 12

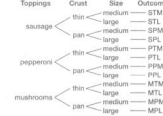

Skills Practice, p. 833 and Practice, p. 834 (shown)

Draw a tree diagram to show the sample space for each event. Determine the number of possible outcomes.

1. dining at an Italian, Mexican, or French restaurant, for lunch, early bird (early dinner special), or dinner, and with or without dessert 18

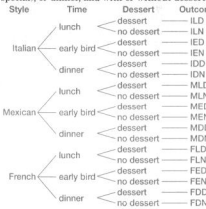

There are 18 possible outcomes.

Find the value of each expression.

2. 5! 120 3. 8! 40,320 4. 10! 3,628,800 5. 12! 479,001,600

6. How many different vacation plans are possible when choosing one each of 12 destinations, 3 lengths of stay, 5 travel options, and 4 types of accommodations? 720

7. How many different ways can you arrange your work if you can choose from 7 weekly schedules, 6 daily schedules, and one of 3 types of duties? 126

8. How many different ways can you treat a minor cut if you can choose from 3 methods of cleansing the cut, 5 antibiotic creams, 2 antibacterial sprays, and 6 types of bandages? 180

9. **TESTING** A teacher gives a quick quiz that has 4 true/false questions and 2 multiple choice questions, each of which has 5 answer choices. In how many ways can the quiz be answered if one answer is given for each question? 400

CLASS RINGS Students at Pacific High can choose class rings in one each of 8 styles, 5 metals, 2 finishes, 14 stones, 7 cuts of stone, 4 tops, 3 printing styles, and 30 inscriptions.

10. How many different choices are there for a class ring? 2,822,400

11. If a student narrows the choice to 2 styles, 3 metals, 4 cuts of stone, and 5 inscriptions (and has already made the remaining decisions), how many different choices for a ring remain? 120

Reading to Learn Mathematics, p. 835 **ELL**

Pre-Activity How are possible win/loss football records counted?

Read the introduction to Lesson 14-1 at the top of page 754 in your textbook. Then complete the diagram.

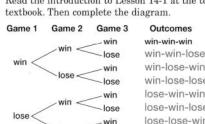

Game 1	Game 2	Game 3	Outcomes
win	win	win	win-win-win
		lose	win-win-lose
	lose	win	win-lose-win
		lose	win-lose-lose
lose	win	win	lose-win-win
		lose	lose-win-lose
	lose	win	lose-lose-win
		lose	lose-lose-lose

Reading the Lesson

Use the tree diagram above for Exercises 1–4.

1. What is the sample space?
win-win-win, win-win-lose, win-lose-win, win-lose-lose, lose-win-win, lose-win-lose, lose-lose-win, lose-lose-lose

2. Name two different outcomes.
Sample answer: win-win-lose, win-lose-win

3. Three different outcomes result in a win/loss record of 2-1. What are they?
win-win-lose, win-lose-win, lose-win-win

4. Use the Fundamental Counting Principle to complete the chart.

	Game 1		Game 2		Game 3		Number of Outcomes
Number of Choices	2	·	2	·	2	=	8

Helping You Remember

5. Suppose you are training the new disc jockey for a school radio station. He has chosen 10 selections to play from a new CD. How could you use factorials to explain to him the number of different ways the selections could be played?
Multiply the number of possible choices for each slot in the playlist. There are 10 choices for the first song, nine choices for the second song, and so on. So the selections can be played in 10 · 9 · 8 · 7 · 6 · 5 · 4 · 3 · 2 · 1 = 3,628,800 ways.

About the Exercises...

Organization by Objective
- **Tree Diagrams:** 9–10, 19
- **The Fundamental Counting Principle:** 15–17, 20–22

Odd/Even Assignments
Exercises 9–16 are structured so that students practice the same concepts whether they are assigned odd or even problems.

Assignment Guide

Basic: 9–17 odd, 23–51

Average: 9–17 odd, 18, 19, 23–51

Advanced: 10–16 even, 20–45 (optional: 46–51)

4 Assess

Open-Ended Assessment

Modeling Have students use construction paper to model sandwich ingredients, such as different types of bread, meat, and vegetables. Have students first calculate how many different sandwiches they could make. Then have them make the sandwiches to confirm their calculations.

Getting Ready for Lesson 14-2

PREREQUISITE SKILL Students will learn about permutations and combinations in Lesson 14-2 and use them to determine the probability of a given event. Use Exercises 46–51 to determine your students' familiarity with simple probability.

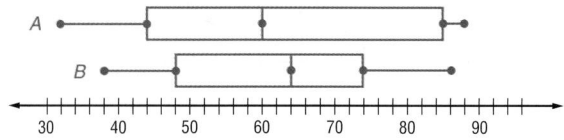
Standardized Test Practice

25. Evaluate 9!. **A**
(A) 362,880   (B) 40,320   (C) 36   (D) 8

26. A car manufacturer offers a sports car in 4 different models with 6 different option packages. Each model is available in 12 different colors. How many different possibilities are available for this car? **C**
(A) 96   (B) 144   (C) 288   (D) 384

Maintain Your Skills

Mixed Review For Exercises 27–30, use box-and-whisker plots A and B. *(Lesson 13-5)*

27. Determine the least value, greatest value, lower quartile, upper quartile, and median for each plot. **A: 32, 88, 44, 85, 60; B: 38, 86, 48, 74, 64**

28. Which set of data contains the least value? **A**

29. Which plot has the smaller interquartile range? **B**

30. Which plot has the greater range? **A**

For Exercises 31–34, use the stem-and-leaf plot.
(Lesson 13-4)

Stem	Leaf
3	0 1 4 5
4	4 4 8
5	6 9
6	6 8
7	1 6
8	0 1
9	
10	9

$3 \mid 0 = 30$

31. Find the range of the data. **79**

32. What is the median? **57.5**

33. Determine the upper quartile, lower quartile, and interquartile range of the data. **73.5; 39.5; 34.0**

34. Identify any outliers. **none**

Find each sum or difference. *(Lesson 12-7)*

35. $\dfrac{2x+1}{3x-1} + \dfrac{x+4}{x-2} \quad \dfrac{5x^2+8x-6}{(3x-1)(x-2)}$

36. $\dfrac{4n}{2n+6} + \dfrac{3}{n+3} \quad \dfrac{2n+3}{n+3}$

37. $\dfrac{3z+2}{3z-6} - \dfrac{z+2}{z^2-4} \quad \dfrac{3z-1}{3z-6}$

38. $\dfrac{m-n}{m+n} - \dfrac{1}{m^2-n^2} \quad \dfrac{m^2-2mn+n^2-1}{m^2-n^2}$

Solve each equation. *(Lesson 11-3)*

39. $5\sqrt{2n^2-28} = 20 \quad \pm\sqrt{22}$

40. $\sqrt{5x^2-7} = 2x \quad \sqrt{7}$

41. $\sqrt{x+2} = x-4 \quad 7$

Solve each equation by completing the square. Round to the nearest tenth if necessary. *(Lesson 10-3)*

42. $b^2 - 6b + 4 = 0 \quad \mathbf{0.8, 5.2}$

43. $n^2 + 8n - 5 = 0 \quad \mathbf{-8.6, 0.6}$

44. $x^2 - 11x - 17 = 0 \quad \mathbf{-1.4, 12.4}$

45. $2p^2 + 10p + 3 = 0 \quad \mathbf{-4.7, -0.3}$

Getting Ready for the Next Lesson

PREREQUISITE SKILL One card is drawn at random from a standard deck of cards. Find each probability. *(To review simple probability, see Lesson 2-6.)*

46. $P(10) \quad \dfrac{1}{13}$

47. $P(\text{ace}) \quad \dfrac{1}{13}$

48. $P(\text{red } 5) \quad \dfrac{1}{26}$

49. $P(\text{queen of clubs}) \quad \dfrac{1}{52}$

50. $P(\text{even number}) \quad \dfrac{5}{13}$

51. $P(3 \text{ or king}) \quad \dfrac{2}{13}$

Study Tip

Deck of Cards
In this text, a *standard deck of cards* always means a deck of 52 playing cards. There are 4 suits—clubs (black), diamonds (red), hearts (red), and spades (black)—with 13 cards in each suit.

Answers (page 759)

1. yes; sample answer: Front St., Main St., Second Ave., State St., Elm St., First Ave., Town St.

4. Yes; all nodes can be connected without retracing an edge.

5. No; all nodes cannot be connected without retracing an edge.

6. Yes; all nodes can be connected without retracing an edge.

7a.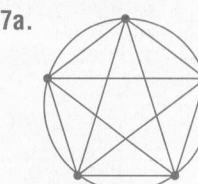

8. Sample answer: If you follow the edges of a graph, you should cover each edge only once.

Algebra Activity

A Follow-Up of Lesson 14-1

Finite Graphs

The City Bus Company provides daily bus service between City College and Southland Mall, City College and downtown, downtown and Southland Mall, downtown and City Park, and City Park and the zoo. The daily routes can be represented using a **finite graph** like the one at the right.

The graph is called a **network**, and each point on the graph is called a **node**. The paths connecting the nodes are called **edges**. A network is said to be **traceable** if all of the nodes can be connected, and each edge can be covered exactly once when the graph is used.

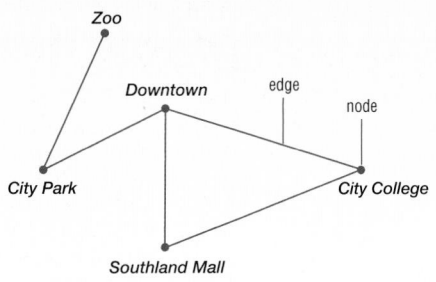

Collect the Data

The graph represents the streets on Alek's newspaper route. To get his route completed as quickly as possible, Alek would like to ride his bike down each street only once.

- Copy the graph onto your paper.
- Beginning at Alek's home, trace over his route without lifting your pencil. Remember to trace each edge only once.
- Compare your graph with those of your classmates.

Analyze the Data

1. Is Alek's route traceable? If so, describe his route. **See margin.**

2. Is there more than one traceable route that begins at Alek's house? If so, how many? **yes; 4**

3. Suppose it does not matter where Alek starts his route. How many traceable routes are possible now? **8**

Determine whether each graph is traceable. Explain your reasoning. **4–6. See margin.**

4.

5.

6.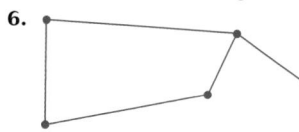

7. The campus for Centerburgh High School has five buildings built around the edge of a circular courtyard. There is a sidewalk between each pair of buildings.

   a. Draw a graph of the campus. **See margin.**

   b. Is the graph traceable? **yes**

   c. Suppose that there is not a sidewalk between the pairs of adjacent buildings. Is it possible to reach all five buildings without walking down any sidewalk more than once? **yes**

8. **Make a conjecture** for a rule to determine whether a graph is traceable. **See margin.**

Algebra Activity Finite Graphs **759**

Resource Manager

Teaching Algebra with Manipulatives
- p. 206 (student recording sheet)

Algebra Activity

A Follow-Up of Lesson 14-1

Getting Started

Objective Determine whether finite graphs are traceable.

Materials
paper
pencil

Teach

- If blank transparencies are available, have students use the transparencies to trace the graphs.

- It is important for students to compare their tracings of Alek's route with those of their classmates to see that there is more than one possible route.

- When students answer question 3, they will find that there are only two possible starting points on this graph; Alek's house and the other end of State Street.

- Help students make the connection between finding possible routes on traceable graphs and counting outcomes. When students find that there are two possible starting points, each with four possible routes, they can use the Fundamental Counting Principle to determine that there are eight total routes.

Assess

Work with students to formulate a conjecture about when a graph is traceable and when it is not.

Study Notebook

You may wish to have students summarize this activity and what they learned from it.

Algebra Activity Finite Graphs **759**

1 Focus

5-Minute Check Transparency 14-2 Use as a quiz or review of Lesson 14-1.

Mathematical Background notes are available for this lesson on p. 752C.

How can combinations be used to form committees?

Ask students:

- Suppose Senators Kennedy, Jeffords, and Collins are three of the members of the committee. Explain why the order in which they are selected does not matter. **No matter how the three senators are selected, all three are still on the committee.**

- If there were more Democrats in the Senate than Republicans, would the number of ways the committee members could be selected be affected? Explain. **No. There will still be 18 committee members, which does not change the ways in which they could be selected.**

Vocabulary
- permutation
- combination

Study Tip

Common Misconception
When arranging two objects *A* and *B* using a permutation, the arrangement *AB* is different from the arrangement *BA*.

What You'll Learn

- Determine probabilities using permutations.
- Determine probabilities using combinations.

How can combinations be used to form committees?

The United States Senate forms various committees by selecting senators from both political parties. The Senate Health, Education, Labor, and Pensions Committee of the 106th Congress was made up of 10 Republican senators and 8 Democratic senators. How many different ways could the committee have been selected? The members of the committee were selected in no particular order. This is an example of a combination.

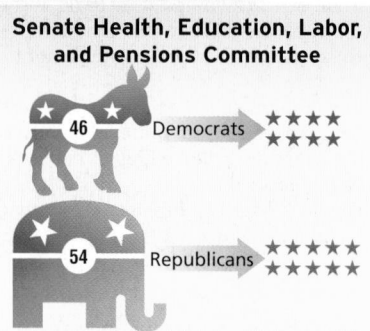

Senate Health, Education, Labor, and Pensions Committee

46 Democrats ★★★★ ★★★★

54 Republicans ★★★★★ ★★★★★

PERMUTATIONS An arrangement or listing in which order or placement is important is called a **permutation**.

Example 1 Tree Diagram Permutation

EMPLOYMENT The manager of a coffee shop needs to hire two employees, one to work at the counter and one to work at the drive-through window. Katie, Bob, Alicia, and Jeremiah all applied for a job. How many possible ways are there for the manager to place the applicants?

Use a tree diagram to show the possible arrangements.

Counter	Drive-Through	Outcomes
Katie (K)	Bob	KB
	Alicia	KA
	Jeremiah	KJ
Bob (B)	Katie	BK
	Alicia	BA
	Jeremiah	BJ
Alicia (A)	Jeremiah	AJ
	Katie	AK
	Bob	AB
Jeremiah (J)	Katie	JK
	Bob	JB
	Alicia	JA

There are 12 different ways for the 4 applicants to hold the 2 positions.

Resource Manager

 Workbook and Reproducible Masters

Chapter 14 Resource Masters
- Study Guide and Intervention, pp. 837–838
- Skills Practice, p. 839
- Practice, p. 840
- Reading to Learn Mathematics, p. 841
- Enrichment, p. 842
- Assessment, p. 875

Parent and Student Study Guide Workbook, p. 108
School-to-Career Masters, p. 27

Transparencies

5-Minute Check Transparency 14-2
Answer Key Transparencies

Technology

Interactive Chalkboard

In Example 1, the positions are in a specific order, so each arrangement is unique. The symbol $_4P_2$ denotes the number of permutations when arranging 4 applicants in 2 positions. You can also use the Fundamental Counting Principle to determine the number of permutations.

$$
\begin{array}{cc}
\overbrace{\text{ways to choose}}^{\text{first employee}} & \overbrace{\text{ways to choose}}^{\text{second employee}}
\end{array}
$$

$$
_4P_2 = 4 \cdot 3
$$

$$
= 4 \cdot 3 \cdot \frac{2 \cdot 1}{2 \cdot 1} \qquad \frac{2 \cdot 1}{2 \cdot 1} = 1
$$

$$
= \frac{4 \cdot 3 \cdot 2 \cdot 1}{2 \cdot 1} \qquad \text{Multiply.}
$$

$$
= \frac{4!}{2!} \qquad 4 \cdot 3 \cdot 2 \cdot 1 = 4!, \; 2 \cdot 1 = 2!
$$

In general, $_nP_r$ is used to denote the number of permutations of n objects taken r at a time.

Key Concept — Permutation

- **Words** The number of permutations of n objects taken r at a time is the quotient of $n!$ and $(n-r)!$.
- **Symbols** $_nP_r = \dfrac{n!}{(n-r)!}$

Example 2 Permutation

Find $_{10}P_6$.

$$
_nP_r = \frac{n!}{(n-r)!} \qquad \text{Definition of } _nP_r
$$

$$
_{10}P_6 = \frac{10!}{(10-6)!} \qquad n = 10, r = 6.
$$

$$
_{10}P_6 = \frac{10!}{4!} \qquad \text{Subtract.}
$$

$$
_{10}P_6 = \frac{10 \cdot 9 \cdot 8 \cdot 7 \cdot 6 \cdot 5 \cdot \overset{1}{\cancel{4 \cdot 3 \cdot 2 \cdot 1}}}{\underset{1}{\cancel{4 \cdot 3 \cdot 2 \cdot 1}}} \qquad \text{Definition of factorial}
$$

$$
_{10}P_6 = 10 \cdot 9 \cdot 8 \cdot 7 \cdot 6 \cdot 5 \text{ or } 151{,}200 \qquad \text{Simplify.}
$$

There are 151,200 permutations of 10 objects taken 6 at a time.

Permutations are often used to find the probability of events occurring.

Example 3 Permutation and Probability

A word processing program requires a user to enter a 7-digit registration code made up of the digits 1, 2, 4, 5, 6, 7, and 9. Each number has to be used, and no number can be used more than once.

a. How many different registration codes are possible?

Since the order of the numbers in the code is important, this situation is a permutation of 7 digits taken 7 at a time.

$$
_nP_r = \frac{n!}{(n-r)!} \qquad \text{Definition of permutation}
$$

$$
_7P_7 = \frac{7!}{(7-7)!} \qquad n = 7, r = 7; \text{ recall that } 0! = 1.
$$

$$
_7P_7 = \frac{7 \cdot 6 \cdot 5 \cdot 4 \cdot 3 \cdot 2 \cdot 1}{1} \text{ or } 5040 \qquad \text{Definition of factorial}
$$

There are 5040 possible codes with the digits 1, 2, 4, 5, 6, 7, and 9.

 www.algebra1.com/extra_examples

Lesson 14-2 Permutations and Combinations **761**

---

2 Teach

PERMUTATIONS

In-Class Examples Power Point®

Reading Tip Permutations of n objects taken r at a time can also be written as $P(n, r)$.

1 Ms. Baraza asks pairs of students to go in front of her Spanish class to read statements in Spanish, and then to translate the statement into English. One student is the Spanish speaker and one is the English speaker. If Ms. Baraza has to choose between Jeff, Kathy, Guillermo, Ana, and Patrice, how many different ways can Ms. Baraza pair the students? **20 ways**

2 Find $_8P_4$.
There are 1680 permutations of 8 objects taken 4 at a time.

Teaching Tip Point out to students that the numbers 0, 3, and 8 are not possible choices.

3 Shaquille has a 5-digit pass code to access his e-mail account. The code is made up of the even digits 2, 4, 6, 8, and 0. Each digit can be used only once.

a. How many different pass codes could Shaquille have?
120

b. What is the probability that the first two digits of his code are both greater than 5?
$\dfrac{1}{10}$ or 10%

DAILY INTERVENTION

Differentiated Instruction

Visual/Spatial Have students write the digits 1, 2, 4, 5, 6, 7, and 9 on index cards. Have them rearrange the cards in different ways to help them visualize how the permutation formula relates to the cards. Compare their results with the calculations in Example 3.

COMBINATIONS

In-Class Example Power Point®

Reading Tip Combinations of *n* objects taken *r* at a time can also be written $C(n, r)$.

4 **TEST ITEM** Customers at Tony's Pizzeria can choose 4 out of 12 toppings for each pizza for no extra charge. How many different combinations of pizza toppings can be chosen? **A**

A 495
B 792
C 11,880
D 95,040

Teaching Tip After students learn how to calculate combinations and have worked Example 4, discuss the difference between combinations and permutations. In Example 4, the order in which the students are chosen does not matter because the positions for which they are being chosen are the same. They are all four going to be members of the student council, with the same duties. However, if the homeroom was choosing 4 out of 7 students to be president, vice president, secretary, and treasurer of the student council, then the order in which they are chosen does matter.

---

b. **What is the probability that the first three digits of the code are even numbers?**

Use the Fundamental Counting Principle to determine the number of ways for the first three digits to be even.

- There are 3 even digits and 4 odd digits.
- The number of choices for the first three digits, if they are even, is $3 \cdot 2 \cdot 1$.
- The number of choices for the remaining odd digits is $4 \cdot 3 \cdot 2 \cdot 1$.
- The number of favorable outcomes is $3 \cdot 2 \cdot 1 \cdot 4 \cdot 3 \cdot 2 \cdot 1$ or 144. There are 144 ways for this event to occur out of the 5040 possible permutations.

$P(\text{first 3 digits even}) = \dfrac{144}{5040}$ ← number of favorable outcomes
← number of possible outcomes

$= \dfrac{1}{35}$ Simplify.

The probability that the first three digits of the code are even is $\dfrac{1}{35}$ or about 3%.

COMBINATIONS

An arrangement or listing in which order is not important is called a **combination**. For example, if you are choosing 2 salad ingredients from a list of 10, the order in which you choose the ingredients does not matter.

Key Concept   *Combination*

- **Words**   The number of combinations of *n* objects taken *r* at a time is the quotient of $n!$ and $(n - r)!r!$.

- **Symbols** $\displaystyle {}_nC_r = \frac{n!}{(n - r)!r!}$

 *Standardized Test Practice* Ⓐ Ⓑ Ⓒ Ⓓ

Example **4** *Combination*

Multiple-Choice Test Item

> The students of Mr. DeLuca's homeroom had to choose 4 out of the 7 people who were nominated to serve on the Student Council. How many different groups of students could be selected?
>
> Ⓐ 840   Ⓑ 210
> Ⓒ 35   Ⓓ 24

Read the Test Item

The order in which the students are chosen does not matter, so this situation represents a combination of 7 people taken 4 at a time.

Test-Taking Tip

Read each question carefully to determine whether the situation involves a permutation or a combination. Often, the answer choices include examples of both.

Solve the Test Item

$\displaystyle {}_nC_r = \frac{n!}{(n - r)!r!}$ Definition of combination

$\displaystyle {}_7C_4 = \frac{7!}{(7 - 4)!4!}$ $n = 7, r = 4$

$\displaystyle = \frac{7 \cdot 6 \cdot 5 \cdot \cancel{4 \cdot 3 \cdot 2 \cdot 1}}{3 \cdot 2 \cdot 1 \cdot \cancel{4 \cdot 3 \cdot 2 \cdot 1}}$ Definition of factorial

$\displaystyle = \frac{7 \cdot 6 \cdot 5}{3 \cdot 2 \cdot 1}$ or 35   Simplify.

There are 35 different groups of students that could be selected. Choice C is correct.

 *Standardized Test Practice* Ⓐ Ⓑ Ⓒ Ⓓ

Example 4 Tell students to pay close attention to the order in which the information is given in word problems. Because 4 is listed before 7 in the problem, students might mistakenly think that $n = 4$ and $r = 7$. Choice A is the correct number of permutations for ${}_7P_4$. However this problem involves combinations.

Combinations and the products of combinations can be used to determine probabilities.

Example 5 Use Combinations

SCHOOL A science teacher at Sunnydale High School needs to choose 12 students out of 16 to serve as peer tutors. A group of 7 seniors, 5 juniors, and 4 sophomores have volunteered to be tutors.

a. How many different ways can the teacher choose 12 students?

The order in which the students are chosen does not matter, so we must find the number of combinations of 16 students taken 12 at a time.

$$_nC_r = \frac{n!}{(n-r)!r!}$$ Definition of combination

$$_{16}C_{12} = \frac{16!}{(16-12)!12!}$$ $n = 16, r = 12$

$$= \frac{16!}{4!12!}$$ $16 - 12 = 4$

$$= \frac{16 \cdot 15 \cdot 14 \cdot 13 \cdot \overset{1}{12!}}{4! \cdot \underset{1}{12!}}$$ Divide by the GCF, 12!.

$$= \frac{43{,}680}{24} \text{ or } 1820$$ Simplify.

There are 1820 ways to choose 12 students out of 16.

b. If the students are chosen randomly, what is the probability that 4 seniors, 4 juniors, and 4 sophomores will be selected?

There are three questions to consider.
- How many ways can 4 seniors be chosen from 7?
- How many ways can 4 juniors be chosen from 5?
- How many ways can 4 sophomores be chosen from 4?

Using the Fundamental Counting Principle, the answer can be determined with the product of the three combinations.

ways to choose 4 seniors out of 7 $(_7C_4)$ · ways to choose 4 juniors out of 5 $(_5C_4)$ · ways to choose 4 sophomores out of 4 $(_4C_4)$

$$(_7C_4)(_5C_4)(_4C_4) = \frac{7!}{(7-4)!4!} \cdot \frac{5!}{(5-4)!4!} \cdot \frac{4!}{(4-4)!4!}$$ Definition of combination

$$= \frac{7!}{3!4!} \cdot \frac{5!}{1!4!} \cdot \frac{4!}{0!4!}$$ Simplify.

$$= \frac{7 \cdot 6 \cdot 5}{3!} \cdot \frac{5}{1}$$ Divide by the GCF, 4!.

$$= 175$$ Simplify.

There are 175 ways to choose this particular combination out of 1820 possible combinations.

$$P(\text{4 seniors, 4 juniors, 4 sophomores}) = \frac{175}{1820}$$ ← number of favorable outcomes\n← number of possible outcomes

$$= \frac{5}{52}$$ Simplify.

The probability that the science teacher will randomly select 4 seniors, 4 juniors, and 4 sophomores is $\frac{5}{52}$ or about 10%.

Combinations
The number of combinations of n objects taken n at a time is 1.
$$_nC_n = 1$$

Teaching Tip Multi-part problems such as Example 5 often contain more information than is necessary to solve the first part of the problem. For example, to solve part a, it is not necessary to know that the group of students includes 7 seniors, 5 juniors, and 4 sophomores. The only necessary information is that 12 students are to be chosen out of a group of 16.

5 **MONEY** Diane has a bag full of coins. There are 10 pennies, 6 nickels, 4 dimes, and 2 quarters in the bag.

a. How many different ways can Diane pull four coins out of the bag? **There are 7315 ways to pull 4 coins out of a bag of 22.**

b. What is the probability that she will pull two pennies and two nickels out of the bag? **The probability that Diane will select two pennies and two nickels is $\frac{675}{7315}$, or about 9%.**

 **Concept Check**

Combinations Explain why you would expect the number of combinations of n items taken r at a time to be less than the number of permutations of n items taken r at a time. **Sample answer: The number of combinations is less because order does not matter. For example, in a permutation, AB is different from BA because order matters. In a combination, AB and BA are the same.**

Tips for New Teachers

The details in Example 5 might be confusing for some students. Consider representing the problem information on an overhead transparency. Assign three different colors to represent seniors, juniors, and sophomores. Then draw groups of colored dots to represent the 16 students. In part **b** of Example 5, show students how to focus on one group of students at a time by examining only one color of dot.

Study Notebook

Have students—

• add the definitions/examples of the vocabulary terms to their Vocabulary Builder worksheets for Chapter 14.

• include an example of how to find the number of permutations and number of combinations of n items taken r at a time.

• include any other item(s) that they find helpful in mastering the skills in this lesson.

DAILY
INTERVENTION **FIND THE ERROR**

First, students must determine whether Eric and Alisa need to find the number of permutations or combinations. Since the order in which the bus visits the sites does not matter, they need to find the number of combinations. Next, students must examine whether Eric or Alisa used the correct procedure to find the number of combinations.

Answers

1. Sample answer: Order is important in a permutation but not in a combination.

   Permutation: the finishing order of a race

   Combination: toppings on a pizza

2. $_nC_n = \dfrac{n!}{(n-n)!n!} = \dfrac{n!}{0!n!}$ or 1, since $0! = 1$.

   $_nP_n = \dfrac{n!}{(n-n)!} = \dfrac{n!}{0!}$ or $n!$, since $0! = 1$.

3. Alisa; both are correct in that the situation is a combination, but Alisa's method correctly computes the combination. Eric's calculations find the number of permutations.

Check for Understanding

Concept Check
1–3. See margin.

1. **OPEN ENDED** Describe the difference between a permutation and a combination. Then give an example of each.

2. **Demonstrate** and explain why $_nC_r = 1$ whenever $n = r$. What does $_nP_r$ always equal when $n = r$?

3. **FIND THE ERROR** Eric and Alisa are taking a trip to Washington, D.C. Their tour bus stops at the Lincoln Memorial, the Jefferson Memorial, the Washington Monument, the White House, the Capitol Building, the Supreme Court, and the Pentagon. Both are finding the number of ways they can choose to visit 5 of these 7 sites.

Eric	Alisa
$_7C_5 = \dfrac{7!}{2!}$ or 2520	$_7C_5 = \dfrac{7!}{2!\,5!}$ or 21

   Who is correct? Explain your reasoning.

Guided Practice

Determine whether each situation involves a *permutation* or *combination*. Explain your reasoning. **4. Combination; order is not important.**

GUIDED PRACTICE KEY	
Exercises	Examples
4, 5, 10, 13	1, 4
6–9, 11, 12	2, 3, 5

4. choosing 6 books from a selection of 12 for summer reading

5. choosing digits for a personal identification number
Permutation; order is important.

Evaluate each expression.

6. $_8P_5$ 6720   7. $_7C_5$ 21   8. $(_{10}P_5)(_3P_2)$
   181,440
9. $(_6C_2)(_4C_3)$ 60

For Exercises 10–12, use the following information.
The digits 0 through 9 are written on index cards. Three of the cards are randomly selected to form a 3-digit code.

10. Permutation; the order of the digits is important.

10. Does this situation represent a permutation or a combination? Explain.

11. How many different codes are possible? 720

12. What is the probability that all 3 digits will be odd? $\dfrac{1}{12}$

Standardized Test Practice
Ⓐ Ⓑ Ⓒ Ⓓ

13. A diner offers a choice of two side items from the list with each entrée. How many ways can two items be selected? **B**

    Ⓐ 15   Ⓑ 28
    Ⓒ 30   Ⓓ 56

Side Items	
French fries	mixed vegetables
baked potato	rice pilaf
cole slaw	baked beans
small salad	applesauce

Practice and Apply

Determine whether each situation involves a *permutation* or *combination*. Explain your reasoning.

14. team captains for the soccer team **Combination; order is not important.**

15. three mannequins in a display window **Permutation; order is important.**

16. a hand of 10 cards from a selection of 52 **Combination; order is not important.**

17. the batting order of the New York Yankees **Permutation; order is important.**

18. Permutation; order is important.

20. Combination; order is not important.

More About. . .

Softball

The game of softball was developed in 1888 as an indoor sport for practicing baseball during the winter months.

Source: www.encyclopedia.com

18. first place and runner-up winners for the table tennis tournament

19. a selection of 5 DVDs from a group of eight **Combination; order is not important.**

20. selection of 2 candy bars from six equally-sized bars

21. the selection of 2 trombones, 3 clarinets, and 2 trumpets for a jazz combo
Combination; order is not important.

Evaluate each expression.

22. $_{12}P_3$ **1320**

23. $_4P_1$ **4**

24. $_6C_6$ **1**

25. $_7C_3$ **35**

26. $_{15}C_3$ **455**

27. $_{20}C_8$ **125,970**

28. $_{15}P_3$ **2730**

29. $_{16}P_5$ **524,160**

30. $(_7P_7)(_7P_1)$ **35,280**

31. $(_{20}P_2)(_{16}P_4)$ **16,598,400**

32. $(_3C_2)(_7C_4)$ **105**

33. $(_8C_5)(_5P_5)$ **6720**

SOFTBALL For Exercises 34 and 35, use the following information.
The manager of a softball team needs to prepare a batting lineup using her nine starting players.

34. Does this situation involve a permutation or a combination? **permutation**

35. How many different lineups can she make? **362,880**

SCHOOL For Exercises 36–39, use the following information.
Mrs. Moyer's class has to choose 4 out of 12 people to serve on an activity committee.

36. Does the selection of the students involve a permutation or a combination? Explain. **Combination; order does not matter.**

37. How many different groups of students could be selected? **495**

38. Suppose the students are selected for the positions of chairperson, activities planner, activity leader, and treasurer. How many different groups of students could be selected? **11,880**

39. What is the probability that any one of the students is chosen to be the chairperson? $\frac{1}{12}$

GAMES For Exercises 40–42, use the following information.
In your turn of a certain game, you roll five different-colored dice.

40. Do the outcomes of rolling the five dice represent a permutation or a combination? Explain. **Permutation; order matters.**

41. How many outcomes are possible? **7776**

42. What is the probability that all five dice show the same number on one roll? $\frac{1}{1296}$

BUSINESS For Exercises 43 and 44, use the following information.
There are six positions available in the research department of a software company. Of the applicants, 15 are men and 10 are women.

43. In how many ways could 4 men and 2 women be chosen if each were equally qualified? **61,425**

44. What is the probability that five women are selected if the positions are randomly filled? $\frac{27}{1265}$

TRACK For Exercises 45 and 46, use the following information.
Central High School is competing against West High School at a track meet. Each team entered 4 girls to run the 1600-meter event. The top three finishers are awarded medals.

45. How many different ways can the runners place first, second, and third? **336**

46. If all eight runners have an equal chance of placing, what is the probability that the first and second place finishers are from West and the third place finisher is from Central? $\frac{1}{7} \approx 14\%$

Study Guide and Intervention, p. 837 (shown) and p. 838

Permutations An arrangement or listing in which order or placement is important is called a **permutation**. For example the arrangement AB of choices A and B is different from the arrangement BA of these same two choices.

Permutations	$_nP_r = \dfrac{n!}{(n-r)!}$

Example 1 Find $_6P_2$.

$_nP_r = \dfrac{n!}{(n-r)!}$ Definition of $_nP_r$

$_6P_2 = \dfrac{6!}{(6-2)!}$ $n = 6, r = 2$

$= \dfrac{6!}{4!}$ Simplify

$= \dfrac{6 \cdot 5 \cdot 4 \cdot 3 \cdot 2 \cdot 1}{4 \cdot 3 \cdot 2 \cdot 1}$ Definition of factorial

$= 6 \cdot 5$ or 30 Simplify

There are 30 permutations of 6 objects taken 2 at a time.

Example 2 A specific program requires the user to enter a 5-digit password. The digits cannot repeat and can be any five of the digits 1, 2, 3, 4, 7, 8, and 9.

a. How many different passwords are possible?

$_nP_r = \dfrac{n!}{(n-r)!}$

$_7P_5 = \dfrac{7!}{(7-5)!}$

$= \dfrac{7 \cdot 6 \cdot 5 \cdot 4 \cdot 3 \cdot 2 \cdot 1}{2 \cdot 1}$

$= 7 \cdot 6 \cdot 5 \cdot 4 \cdot 3$ or 2520

There are 2520 ways to create a password.

b. What is the probability that the first two digits are odd numbers with the other digits any of the remaining numbers?

$P(\text{first two digits odd}) = \dfrac{\text{number of favorable outcomes}}{\text{number of possible outcomes}}$

Since there are 4 odd digits, the number of choices for the first digit is 4, and the number of choices for the second digit is 3. Then there are 5 choices left for the third digit, 4 for the fourth, and 3 for the fifth, so the number of favorable outcomes is $4 \cdot 3 \cdot 5 \cdot 4 \cdot 3$, or 720.

The probability is $\dfrac{720}{2520} \approx 28.6\%$.

Exercises

Evaluate of each expression.

1. $_7P_4$ 840
2. $_{12}P_7$ 3,991,680
3. $(_9P_5)(_{10}P_2)$ 87,091,200

4. A club with ten members wants to choose a president, vice-president, secretary, and treasurer. Six of the members are women, and four are men.
 a. How many different sets of officers are possible? 5040
 b. What is the probability that all officers will be women. 7.1%

Skills Practice, p. 839 and Practice, p. 840 (shown)

Determine whether each situation involves a *permutation* or *combination*. Explain your reasoning. Sample explanations are given.

1. choosing two dogs from a litter of two males and three females Combination; The order is not important in the choice of the two dogs.

2. a simple melody formed by playing the notes on 8 different piano keys Permutation; The sound of the melody depends on the order in which the notes are played.

3. a selection of nine muffins from a shelf of twenty-three Combination; The order does not matter in the selection of the muffins.

4. the selection of a four-letter acronym (word formed from the initial letters of other words) in which two of the letters cannot be C or P Permutation; The letters of the acronym must be arranged in a certain order.

5. choosing an alphanumeric password to access a website Permutation; The choice of letters and numbers must be in an exact order for the password to work.

Evaluate each expression.

6. $_{11}P_3$ 990
7. $_6P_3$ 120
8. $_{15}P_3$ 2730
9. $_{11}C_9$ 10
10. $_{12}C_9$ 220
11. $_7C_3$ 35
12. $_7C_4$ 35
13. $_{12}C_4$ 495
14. $_{13}P_3$ 1716
15. $(_8C_4)(_9C_6)$ 3920
16. $(_{17}C_2)(_8C_6)$ 3808
17. $(_{16}C_{15})(_{16}C_1)$ 256
18. $(_8P_3)(_8P_2)$ 18,816
19. $(_5P_4)(_6P_5)$ 86,400
20. $(_{13}P_1)(_{15}P_1)$ 195
21. $(_{10}C_3)(_{10}P_3)$ 86,400
22. $(_{15}P_4)(_4C_3)$ 131,040
23. $(_{14}C_7)(_{12}C_3)$ 9,369,360

24. SPORT In how many orders can the top five finishers in a race finish? 120

JUDICIAL PROCEDURE The court system in a community needs to assign 3 out of 8 judges to a docket of criminal cases. Five of the judges are male and three are female.

25. Does the selection of judges involve a permutation or a combination? combination

26. In how many ways could three judges be chosen? 56

27. If the judges are chosen randomly, what is the probability that all 3 judges are male? $\frac{5}{28}$, or about 18%

Reading to Learn Mathematics, p. 841   ELL

Pre-Activity How can combinations be used to form committees?

Read the introduction to Lesson 14-2 at the top of page 760 in your textbook.

What is meant by the term *combination*?

A group of objects not arranged in any particular order

Reading the Lesson

Complete the chart.

	Situation	Permutation or Combination?	Explain Your Choice
1.	3 of 7 students are chosen to go to a job fair	combination	See students' work.
2.	arrangement of student work for the school art show	permutation	See students' work.
3.	4-digit student I.D. numbers	permutation	See students' work.
4.	choosing 4 out of 12 possible pizza toppings	combination	See students' work.

Helping You Remember

5. To help you remember how the terms *permutation* and *combination* are different, think of everyday words that start with the letters P and C and that illustrate the meaning of each word. Explain how the words illustrate the two terms.

Sample answer: P for *phone number*, since the order of the digits in a phone number is important; C for *club*, since who is in a club is the important thing, not the order in which the names of the club members are listed

---

DINING   For Exercises 47–49, use the following information.

For lunch in the school cafeteria, you can select one item from each category to get the daily combo.

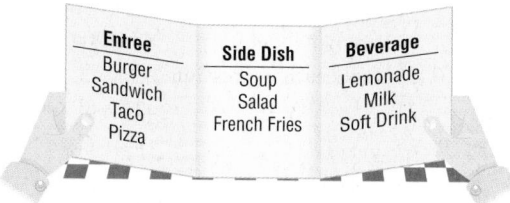

Entree	Side Dish	Beverage
Burger	Soup	Lemonade
Sandwich	Salad	Milk
Taco	French Fries	Soft Drink
Pizza		

47. Find the number of possible meal combinations. **36**

48. If a side dish is chosen at random, what is the probability that a student will choose soup? $\frac{1}{3}$ **or about 33%**

49. What is the probability that a student will randomly choose a sandwich and soup? $\frac{1}{12}$ **or about 8%**

CRITICAL THINKING   For Exercises 50 and 51, use the following information.

Larisa is trying to solve a word puzzle. She needs to arrange the letters H, P, S, T, A, E, and O into a two-word arrangement.

50. How many different arrangements of the letters can she make? **30,240**

51. Assuming that each arrangement has an equal chance of occurring, what is the probability that she will form the words *tap shoe* on her first try? $\dfrac{1}{30,240}$

SWIMMING   For Exercises 52–54, use the following information.

A swimming coach plans to pick four swimmers out of a group of 6 to form the 400-meter freestyle relay team.

52. How many different teams can he form? **15**

53. The coach must decide in which order the four swimmers should swim. He timed the swimmers in each possible order and chose the best time. How many relays did the four swimmers have to swim so that the coach could collect all of the data necessary? **24**

54. If Tomás is chosen to be on the team, what is the probability that he will swim in the third leg? $\frac{1}{4} = 25\%$

55. **WRITING IN MATH**   Answer the question that was posed at the beginning of the lesson. **See margin.**

How can combinations be used to form committees?

Include the following in your answer:

- a few sentences explaining why forming a Senate committee is a combination, and
- an explanation of how to find the number of ways to select the committee if committee positions are based upon seniority.

56. There are 12 songs on a CD. If 10 songs are played randomly and each song is played once, how many arrangements are there? **B**

   (A) 479,001,600   (B) 239,500,800   (C) 66   (D) 1

57. Julie remembered that the 4 digits of her locker combination were 4, 9, 15, and 22, but not their order. What is the maximum number of attempts Julie has to make to find the correct combination? **C**

   (A) 4   (B) 16   (C) 24   (D) 256

766   **Chapter 14**   Probability

WebQuest

You can use permutations and combinations to analyze data on U.S. schools. Visit www.algebra1.com/webquest to continue work on your WebQuest project.

Standardized Test Practice
(A) (B) (C) (D)

Enrichment, p. 842

Latin Squares

In designing a statistical experiment, it is important to try to randomize the variables. For example, suppose 4 different motor oils are being compared to see which give the best gasoline mileage. An experimenter might then choose 4 different drivers and four different cars. To test-drive all the possible combinations, the experimenter would need 64 test-drives.

To reduce the number of test drives, a statistician might use an arrangement called a **Latin Square**.

For this example, the four motor oils are labeled A, B, C, and D and are arranged as shown. Each oil must appear exactly one time in each row and column of the square.

The drivers are labeled D_1, D_2, D_3, and D_4; the cars are labeled C_1, C_2, C_3, and C_4.

	D_1	D_2	D_3	D_4
C_1	A	B	C	D
C_2	B	A	D	C
C_3	C	D	A	B
C_4	D	C	B	A

Now, the number of test-drives is just 16, one for each cell of the ...

Mixed Review

58. The Sanchez family acts as a host family for a foreign exchange student during each school year. It is equally likely that they will host a girl or a boy. How many different ways can they host boys and girls over the next four years? *(Lesson 14-1)*
16

STATISTICS For Exercises **59–62, use the table at the right.**
(Lesson 13-5)

Highest Paying Occupations in America	
Occupation	**Median Salary**
Physician	$148,000
Dentist	$93,000
Lobbyist	$91,300
Management Consultant	$61,900
Lawyer	$60,500
Electrical Engineer	$59,100
School Principal	$57,300
Aeronautical Engineer	$56,700
Airline Pilot	$56,500
Civil Engineer	$55,800

Source: U.S. Bureau of Labor Statistics

59. Make a box-and-whisker plot of the data. **See margin.**

60. What is the range of the data? **$92,200**

61. Identify the lower and upper quartiles. **$56,700, $91,300**

62. Name any outliers. **$148,000**

 Online Research **Data Update** For current data on the highest-paying occupations, visit: www.algebra1.com/data_update

Simplify each expression. *(Lesson 12-2)*

63. $\dfrac{x+3}{x^2+6x+9} \cdot \dfrac{1}{x+3}$

64. $\dfrac{x^2-49}{x^2-2x-35} \cdot \dfrac{x+7}{x+5}$

65. $\dfrac{n^2-n-20}{n^2+9n+20} \cdot \dfrac{n-5}{n+5}$

Find the distance between each pair of points whose coordinates are given. Express answers in simplest radical form and as decimal approximations rounded to the nearest hundredth if necessary. *(Lesson 11-5)*

66. (12, 20), (16, 34) $2\sqrt{53}$, 14.56
67. (−18, 7), (2, 15) $4\sqrt{29}$, 21.54
68. (−2, 5), $\left(-\frac{1}{2}, 3\right)$ $2\frac{1}{2}$, 2.5

Solve each equation by using the Quadratic Formula. Approximate irrational roots to the nearest hundredth. *(Lesson 10-4)*

69. $m^2+4m+2=0$ −0.59, −3.41
70. $2s^2+s-15=0$ $\frac{5}{2}$, −3
71. $2n^2-n=4$ 1.69, −1.19

Getting Ready for the Next Lesson

PREREQUISITE SKILL Find each sum or difference.
(To review fractions, see pages 798 and 799.)

72. $\dfrac{8}{52}+\dfrac{4}{52}$ $\frac{3}{13}$
73. $\dfrac{7}{32}+\dfrac{5}{8}$ $\frac{27}{32}$
74. $\dfrac{5}{15}+\dfrac{6}{15}-\dfrac{2}{15}$ $\frac{3}{5}$

75. $\dfrac{15}{24}+\dfrac{11}{24}-\dfrac{3}{4}$ $\frac{1}{3}$
76. $\dfrac{2}{3}+\dfrac{15}{36}-\dfrac{1}{4}$ $\frac{5}{6}$
77. $\dfrac{16}{25}+\dfrac{3}{10}-\dfrac{1}{4}$ $\frac{69}{100}$

Practice Quiz 1

Lessons 14-1 and 14-2

Find the number of outcomes for each event. *(Lesson 14-1)*

1. A die is rolled and two coins are tossed. **24**

2. A certain model of mountain bike comes in 5 sizes, 4 colors, with regular or off-road tires, and with a choice of 1 of 5 accessories. **200**

Find each value. *(Lesson 14-2)*

3. $_{13}C_8$ **1287**

4. $_9P_6$ **60,480**

5. A flower bouquet has 5 carnations, 6 roses, and 3 lilies. If four flowers are selected at random, what is the probability of selecting two roses and two lilies? *(Lesson 14-2)* $\frac{45}{1001}$

Answers

55. Sample answer: Combinations can be used to find how many different ways a committee can be formed by various members. Answers should include the following.
- Order of selection is not important.
- Order is important due to seniority, so you need to find the number of permutations.

59.

50 60 70 80 90 100 110 120 130 140 150

Open Ended Assessment

Speaking Divide the class into two groups. Have one group explain what a permutation is while the other group explains what a combination is. The groups should use their own members as examples. For instance, the group explaining permutations might show why order does matter when assigning 4 different tasks to volunteers from a group. The group explaining combinations can explain why order does not matter when choosing 4 out of 6 group members to help carry a heavy box.

Getting Ready for Lesson 14-3

BASIC SKILL Students will learn about finding the probability of compound events in Lesson 14-3. In calculating these probabilities, students will be required to multiply and add probabilities, which are usually expressed as fractions. Use Exercises 72–77 to determine your students' familiarity with adding and subtracting fractions.

Assessment Options

Practice Quiz 1 The quiz provides students with a brief review of the concepts and skills in Lessons 14-1 and 14-2. Lesson numbers are given to the right of the exercises or instruction lines so students can review concepts not yet mastered.

Quiz (Lessons 14-1 and 14-2) is available on p. 875 of the *Chapter 14 Resource Masters*.

Reading Mathematics

Getting Started

Before you discuss the meanings of the mathematical words in this activity, ask students for examples of words that are easy to understand because of their roots. Examples include *premature* and *postgraduate*. Ask students to explain these words based on the meanings of their roots.

Teach

Connecting to Vocabulary Ask students for other definitions of the words *combine*, *binary*, *mutation*, and *commute*. Use students' answers to explain the mathematical meanings of combination and permutation.

Students who are not from farming communities may not be familiar with the definition of combine that is given. Have students define in their own words the *verb* combine.

If students answer no for Exercise 1, invite volunteers to suggest mnemonics to help remember the mathematical meanings of the words *combination* and *permutation*.

Assess

Study Notebook

Ask students to suggest what they have learned about mathematical words and their related words.

ELL English Language Learners may benefit from writing key concepts from this activity in their Study Notebooks in their native language and then in English.

768 Chapter 14 Probability

Mathematical Words and Related Words

You may have noticed that many words used in mathematics contain roots of other words and are closely related to other English words. You can use the more familiar meanings of these related words to better understand mathematical meanings.

The table shows two mathematical terms along with related words and their meanings as well as additional notes.

Mathematical Term and Meaning	Related Words and Meanings	Notes
combination A combination is a selection of distinct objects from a group of objects, where the order in which they were selected does not matter.	*combine* (n): a harvesting machine that performs many functions *binary*: a base-two numerical system	*Combine* originally meant to put just two things together; it now means to put any number of things together.
permutation A permutation is an arrangement of distinct objects from a group of objects, where the arrangement is in a certain order.	*mutation*: a change in genes or other characteristics *commute*: to change places; for example, $2 + 5 = 5 + 2$	

Notice how the meanings of the related words can give an insight to the meanings of the mathematical terms.

Reading to Learn 1–4. See pp. 795A–795B.

1. Do the related words of combination and permutation help you to remember their mathematical meanings? Explain.

2. What is a similarity and a difference between the mathematical meanings of combination and permutation?

3. **RESEARCH** Use the Internet or other reference to find the mathematical meaning of the word *factorial* and meanings of at least two related words. How are these meanings connected?

4. **RESEARCH** Use the Internet or other reference to find the meanings of the word *probability* and its Latin origins *probus* and *probare*. Compare the three.

Probability of Compound Events

- Find the probability of two independent events or dependent events.
- Find the probability of two mutually exclusive or inclusive events.

Vocabulary
- simple event
- compound event
- independent events
- dependent events
- complements
- mutually exclusive
- inclusive

How are probabilities used by meteorologists?

The weather forecast for the weekend calls for rain. By using the probabilities for both days, we can find other probabilities for the weekend. What is the probability that it will rain on both days? only on Saturday? Saturday or Sunday?

Weekend Forecast: Rain Likely

Saturday 40%

Sunday 80%

INDEPENDENT AND DEPENDENT EVENTS A single event, like rain on Saturday, is called a **simple event**. Suppose you wanted to determine the probability that it will rain both Saturday and Sunday. This is an example of a **compound event**, which is made up of two or more simple events. The weather on Saturday does not affect the weather on Sunday. These two events are called **independent events** because the outcome of one event does not affect the outcome of the other.

> **Key Concept**   *Probability of Independent Events*
>
> - **Words**   If two events, A and B, are independent, then the probability of both events occurring is the product of the probability of A and the probability of B.
>
> - **Symbols** $P(A \text{ and } B) = P(A) \cdot P(B)$
>
> - **Model**
>
>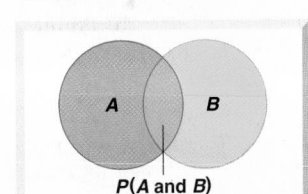
>
> $P(A \text{ and } B)$

Example 1 *Independent Events*

Refer to the application above. Find the probability that it will rain on Saturday and Sunday.

$$P(A \text{ and } B) = P(A) \cdot P(B) \qquad \text{Definition of independent events}$$

$$P(\text{Saturday and Sunday}) = \underline{P(\text{Saturday})} \cdot \underline{P(\text{Sunday})}$$

$$= \quad 0.4 \quad \cdot \quad 0.8 \qquad 40\% = 0.4 \text{ and } 80\% = 0.8$$

$$= 0.32 \qquad \text{Multiply.}$$

The probability that it will rain on Saturday and Sunday is 32%.

---

1 Focus

 5-Minute Check Transparency 14-3 Use as a quiz or review of Lesson 14-2.

Mathematical Background notes are available for this lesson on p. 752D.

How are probabilities used by meteorologists?

Ask students:

- Suppose it does not rain on Saturday. Does this affect whether it will rain on Sunday? **No**

- Think about the word independent. What does independent mean? **free or unrelated**

- Could the word independent be used to describe the weather on Saturday as related to the weather on Sunday? Explain. **Yes. Because the weather on Saturday does not affect the weather on Sunday, these events are independent of each other.**

- **Meteorology** If the weather on one day does not affect the weather on the next day, is there anything that does affect the weather on any given day of the year? Explain. **The season affects the weather. For example, the probability of having snow in July in most parts of the country is very low because the weather in July is too warm for snow.**

Resource Manager

 Transparencies

5-Minute Check Transparency 14-3
Real-World Transparency 14
Answer Key Transparencies

Technology

AlgePASS: Tutorial Plus, Lesson 35
Interactive Chalkboard

Workbook and Reproducible Masters

Chapter 14 Resource Masters
- Study Guide and Intervention, pp. 843–844
- Skills Practice, p. 845
- Practice, p. 846
- Reading to Learn Mathematics, p. 847
- Enrichment, p. 848
- Assessment, pp. 875, 877

Parent and Student Study Guide Workbook, p. 109
Prerequisite Skills Workbook,
   pp. 47–48, 55–56, 67–70, 99–100
Science and Mathematics Lab Manual,
   pp. 109–114

2 Teach

INDEPENDENT AND DEPENDENT EVENTS

In-Class Examples Power Point®

1 **TRAVEL** Roberta is flying from Birmingham to Chicago to visit her grandmother. She has to fly from Birmingham to Houston on the first leg of her trip. In Houston she changes planes and heads on to Chicago. The airline reports that the flight from Birmingham to Houston has a 90% on time record, and the flight from Houston to Chicago has a 50% on time record. What is the probability that both flights will be on time? **45%**

2 At the school carnival, winners in the ring-toss game are randomly given a prize from a bag that contains 4 sunglasses, 6 hairbrushes, and 5 key chains. Three prizes are randomly drawn from the bag and not replaced. Find each probability.

a. P(sunglasses, hairbrush, key chain) $\frac{4}{91}$

b. P(hairbrush, hairbrush, key chain) $\frac{5}{91}$

c. P(sunglasses, hairbrush, not key chain) $\frac{32}{455}$

When the outcome of one event affects the outcome of another event, the events are **dependent events**. For example, drawing a card from a deck, not returning it, then drawing a second card are dependent events because the drawing of the second card is dependent on the drawing of the first card.

Key Concept | *Probability of Dependent Events*

- **Words** If two events, A and B, are dependent, then the probability of both events occurring is the product of the probability of A and the probability of B after A occurs.
- **Symbols** $P(A \text{ and } B) = P(A) \cdot P(B \text{ following } A)$

Example 2 | Dependent Events

A bag contains 8 red marbles, 12 blue marbles, 9 yellow marbles, and 11 green marbles. Three marbles are randomly drawn from the bag and not replaced. Find each probability if the marbles are drawn in the order indicated.

a. P(red, blue, green)

The selection of the first marble affects the selection of the next marble since there is one less marble from which to choose. So, the events are dependent.

First marble: $P(\text{red}) = \frac{8}{40} \text{ or } \frac{1}{5}$ ← number of red marbles
  ← total number of marbles

Second marble: $P(\text{blue}) = \frac{12}{39} \text{ or } \frac{4}{13}$ ← number of blue marbles
  ← number of marbles remaining

Third marble: $P(\text{green}) = \frac{11}{38}$ ← number of green marbles
  ← number of marbles remaining

$P(\text{red, blue, green}) = P(\text{red}) \cdot P(\text{blue}) \cdot P(\text{green})$

$= \frac{1}{5} \cdot \frac{4}{13} \cdot \frac{11}{38}$ Substitution

$= \frac{44}{2470} \text{ or } \frac{22}{1235}$ Multiply.

The probability of drawing red, blue, and green marbles is $\frac{22}{1235}$.

b. P(blue, yellow, yellow)

Notice that after selecting a yellow marble, not only is there one fewer marble from which to choose, there is also one fewer yellow marble.

$P(\text{blue, yellow, yellow}) = P(\text{blue}) \cdot P(\text{yellow}) \cdot P(\text{yellow})$

$= \frac{12}{40} \cdot \frac{9}{39} \cdot \frac{8}{38}$ Substitution

$= \frac{864}{59,280} \text{ or } \frac{18}{1235}$ Multiply.

The probability of drawing a blue and then two yellow marbles is $\frac{18}{1235}$.

c. P(red, yellow, *not* green)

Since the marble that is not green is selected after the first two marbles, there are $29 - 2$ or 27 marbles that are not green.

$P(\text{red, yellow, } not \text{ green}) = P(\text{red}) \cdot P(\text{yellow}) \cdot P(\text{not green})$

$= \frac{8}{40} \cdot \frac{9}{39} \cdot \frac{27}{38}$

$= \frac{1944}{59,280} \text{ or } \frac{81}{2470}$

The probability of drawing a red, a yellow, and *not* a green marble is $\frac{81}{2470}$.

> **Study Tip**
>
> **More Than Two Dependent Events**
> Notice that the formula for the probability of dependent events can be applied to more than two events.

770   Chapter 14   Probability

DAILY
INTERVENTION   **Differentiated Instruction**

Naturalist Bring a packet of raw sunflower seeds or other fast-sprouting seeds to class. Ensure you have slightly more seeds than you do students. Explain that each student will take a seed and plant it either on school grounds or in a small plant pot. As students take a seed from the packet, lead them to understand that the number of seeds from which they can choose is a dependent event for all but the first student.

In part **c** of Example 2, the events for drawing a marble that is green and for drawing a marble that is *not* green are called **complements**. Consider the probabilities for drawing the third marble.

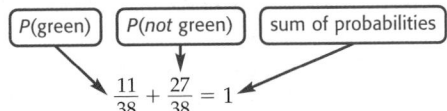

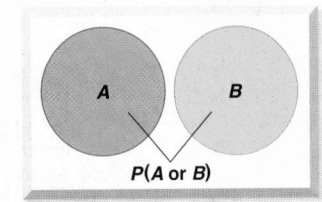

$$\frac{11}{38} + \frac{27}{38} = 1$$

This is always true for any two complementary events.

Study Tip

Reading Math
A complement is one of two parts that make up a whole.

MUTUALLY EXCLUSIVE AND INCLUSIVE EVENTS
Events that cannot occur at the same time are called **mutually exclusive**. Suppose you want to find the probability of rolling a 2 *or* a 4 on a die. Since a die cannot show both a 2 and a 4 at the same time, the events are mutually exclusive.

Key Concept — Mutually Exclusive Events

- **Words** If two events, *A* and *B*, are mutually exclusive, then the probability that either *A* or *B* occurs is the sum of their probabilities.

- **Symbols** $P(A \text{ or } B) = P(A) + P(B)$

- **Model**

A   B

$P(A \text{ or } B)$

Example 3 *Mutually Exclusive Events*

During a magic trick, a magician randomly draws one card from a standard deck of cards. What is the probability that the card drawn is a heart or a diamond?

Since a card cannot be both a heart and a diamond, the events are mutually exclusive.

$P(\text{heart}) = \frac{13}{52} \text{ or } \frac{1}{4}$ ← number of hearts / total number of cards

$P(\text{diamond}) = \frac{13}{52} \text{ or } \frac{1}{4}$ ← number of diamonds / total number of cards

$P(\text{heart or diamond}) = P(\text{heart}) + P(\text{diamond})$ Definition of mutually exclusive events

$= \frac{1}{4} + \frac{1}{4}$ Substitution

$= \frac{2}{4} \text{ or } \frac{1}{2}$ Add.

The probability of drawing a heart or a diamond is $\frac{1}{2}$.

Suppose you wanted to find the probability of randomly selecting an ace or a spade from a standard deck of cards. Since it is possible to draw a card that is both an ace and a spade, these events are not mutually exclusive. They are called **inclusive** events.

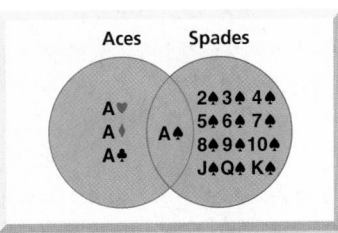

Aces   Spades

A♥
A♦   A♠   2♠ 3♠ 4♠
A♠   5♠ 6♠ 7♠
             8♠ 9♠ 10♠
             J♠ Q♠ K♠

Teaching Tip Explain to students that there are four suits or types of cards in a standard card deck: spades, hearts, diamonds, and clubs. There are 13 cards in each suit, for a total of 52 cards. The cards in each suit are; ace, 2, 3, 4, 5, 6, 7, 8, 9, 10, jack, queen, and king. If possible, bring a deck of cards to school for students to examine.

3 Alfred is going to the Lakeshore Animal Shelter to pick a new pet. Today, the shelter has 8 dogs, 7 cats, and 5 rabbits available for adoption. If Alfred randomly picks an animal to adopt, what is the probability that the animal would be a cat or a dog? **The probability of randomly picking a cat or a dog is $\frac{3}{4}$.**

4 A dog has just given birth to a litter of 9 puppies. There are 3 brown females, 2 brown males, 1 mixed-color female, and 3 mixed-color males. If you choose a puppy at random from the litter, what is the probability that the puppy will be male or mixed-color? **The probability of a puppy picked at random being male or mixed-color is $\frac{2}{3}$ or about 67%.**

Teaching Tip If students are having trouble understanding why they must subtract the probability of *A* and *B* both occurring when finding the probability of inclusive events, the additional example above should clarify the issue. For example, if you add the probability of picking a puppy that is male $\left(\frac{5}{9}\right)$ to the probability of picking a puppy that is mixed-color $\left(\frac{4}{9}\right)$, the sum is $\frac{9}{9}$, or 100%. This is obviously incorrect because not all the puppies are male, nor are they all mixed-color. However, when you subtract the probability of picking a puppy that is male and mixed-color $\left(\frac{3}{9}\right)$, you get the correct probability of $\frac{2}{3}$.

3 Practice/Apply

Study Notebook

Have students—
• add the definitions/examples of the vocabulary terms to their Vocabulary Builder worksheets for Chapter 14.
• include any other item(s) that they find helpful in mastering the skills in this lesson.

If the formula for the probability of mutually exclusive events is used, the probability of drawing an ace of spades is counted twice, once for an ace and once for a spade. To correct this, you must subtract the probability of drawing the ace of spades from the sum of the individual probabilities.

Key Concept — Probability of Inclusive Events

• **Words** If two events, *A* and *B*, are inclusive, then the probability that either *A* or *B* occurs is the sum of their probabilities decreased by the probability of both occurring.

• **Model**

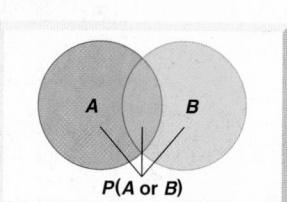

P(*A* or *B*)

• **Symbols** $P(A \text{ or } B) = P(A) + P(B) - P(A \text{ and } B)$

Example 4 Inclusive Events

GAMES In the game of bingo, balls or tiles are numbered 1 through 75. These numbers correspond to columns on a bingo card. The numbers 1 through 15 can appear in the B column, 16 through 30 in the I column, 31 through 45 in the N column, 46 through 60 in the G column, and 61 through 75 in the O column. A number is selected at random. What is the probability that it is a multiple of 4 or is in the O column?

Since the numbers 64, 68, and 72 are multiples of 4 and they can be in the O column, these events are inclusive.

$P(A \text{ or } B) = P(A) + P(B) - P(A \text{ and } B)$ Definition of inclusive events

$P(\text{multiple of 4 or O column})$

$= \underbrace{P(\text{multiple of 4})} + \underbrace{P(\text{O column})} - \underbrace{P(\text{multiple of 4 and O column})}$

$= \dfrac{18}{75} + \dfrac{15}{75} - \dfrac{3}{75}$ Substitution

$= \dfrac{18 + 15 - 3}{75}$ LCD is 75.

$= \dfrac{30}{75} \text{ or } \dfrac{2}{5}$ Simplify.

The probability of a number being a multiple of 4 or in the O column is $\frac{2}{5}$ or 40%.

Check for Understanding

Concept Check 1–3. See margin.

1. **Explain** the difference between a simple event and a compound event.

2. **Find a counterexample** for the following statement.
   If two events are independent, then the probability of both events occurring is less than 1.

3. **OPEN ENDED** Explain how dependent events are different than independent events. Give specific examples in your explanation.

Answers

1. A simple event is a single event, while a compound event involves two or more simple events.

2. Sample answer: The probability of rolling a number less than or equal to six on a number cube and tossing heads or tails on a coin.

3. Sample answer: With dependent events, a first object is selected and not replaced. With independent events, a first object is selected and replaced.

4. FIND THE ERROR On the school debate team, 6 of the 14 girls are seniors, and 9 of the 20 boys are seniors. Chloe and Amber are both seniors on the team. Each girl calculated the probability that either a girl or a senior would randomly be selected to argue a position at a state debate. **See margin.**

Chloe	Amber
P(girl or senior)	P(girl or senior)
$= \frac{14}{34} + \frac{15}{34} - \frac{6}{34}$	$= \frac{6}{34} + \frac{15}{34} - \frac{14}{34}$
$= \frac{23}{34}$	$= \frac{7}{34}$

Who is correct? Explain your reasoning.

Guided Practice

GUIDED PRACTICE KEY

Exercises	Examples
5, 7, 13–15	1
6, 8	2
9, 11	3
10, 12	4

A bin contains 8 blue chips, 5 red chips, 6 green chips, and 2 yellow chips. Find each probability.

5. drawing a red chip, replacing it, then drawing a green chip $\frac{10}{147}$

6. selecting two yellow chips without replacement $\frac{1}{210}$

7. choosing green, then blue, then red, replacing each chip after it is drawn $\frac{80}{3087}$

8. choosing green, then blue, then red without replacing each chip $\frac{4}{133}$

A student is selected at random from a group of 12 male and 12 female students. There are 3 male students and 3 female students from each of the 9th, 10th, 11th, and 12th grades. Find each probability.

9. P(9th or 12th grader) $\frac{1}{2}$

10. P(10th grader or female) $\frac{5}{8}$

11. P(male or female) 1

12. P(male or not 11th grader) $\frac{7}{8}$

Application **BUSINESS** For Exercises 13–15, use the following information.
Mr. Salyer is a buyer for an electronics store. He received a shipment of 5 DVD players in which one is defective. He randomly chose 3 of the DVD players to test.

13. Determine whether choosing one DVD player after another indicates independent or dependent events. **independent**

14. What is the probability that he selected the defective player? $\frac{3}{5}$

15. Suppose the defective player is one of the three that Mr. Salyer tested. What is the probability that the last one tested was the defective one? $\frac{1}{3}$

★ indicates increased difficulty

Practice and Apply

Homework Help

For Exercises	See Examples
16–19, 24, 25, 28–31	2
20–23, 32–34	1
26, 27, 41, 44, 45	4
36–40, 42, 43, 46, 47	3

Extra Practice
See page 851.

A bag contains 2 red, 6 blue, 7 yellow, and 3 orange marbles. Once a marble is selected, it is not replaced. Find each probability.

16. P(2 orange) $\frac{1}{51}$

17. P(blue, then red) $\frac{2}{51}$

18. P(2 yellows in a row then orange) $\frac{7}{272}$

19. P(blue, then yellow, then red) $\frac{7}{408}$

A die is rolled and a spinner like the one at the right is spun. Find each probability.

20. P(3 and D) $\frac{1}{30}$

21. P(an odd number and a vowel) $\frac{1}{5}$

22. P(a prime number and A) $\frac{1}{10}$

23. P(2 and A, B, or C) $\frac{1}{10}$

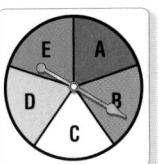

DAILY
INTERVENTION **FIND THE ERROR**
Both Chloe and Amber are using the correct procedure for finding the probability of mutually inclusive events. However, one of the girls is not adding and subtracting the correct probabilities. Suggest that students decide for themselves which probabilities to add, and which one to subtract, and then compare their solutions to those of Amber and Chloe.

About the Exercises...
Organization by Objective
• **Independent and Dependent Events:** 16–23, 28–34, 36–40
• **Mutually Exclusive and Inclusive Events:** 24–27, 41–47

Odd/Even Assignments
Exercises 16–27 are structured so that students practice the same concepts whether they are assigned odd or even problems.

Assignment Guide
Basic: 17–27 odd, 28–35, 48–75
Average: 17–27 odd, 35–40, 48–75
Advanced: 16–26 even, 38–66 (optional: 67–75)

Answer

4. Chloe; Sample answer: Since it is possible for the person chosen to be a girl and a senior, the events are inclusive. So, add the probability that a girl is chosen, $\frac{14}{34}$, and the probability that a senior is chosen, $\frac{15}{34}$, then subtract the probability that a senior girl is chosen, $\frac{6}{34}$.

Raffle tickets numbered 1 through 30 are placed in a box. Tickets for a second raffle numbered 21 to 48 are placed in another box. One ticket is randomly drawn from each box. Find each probability.

24. Both tickets are even. $\frac{1}{4}$

25. Both tickets are greater than 20 and less than 30. $\frac{27}{280}$

26. The first ticket is greater than 10, and the second ticket is less than 40 or odd. $\frac{23}{42}$

27. The first ticket is greater than 12 or prime, and the second ticket is a multiple of 6 or a multiple of 4. $\frac{69}{280}$

SAFETY For Exercises 28–31, use the following information.

A carbon monoxide detector system uses two sensors, A and B. If carbon monoxide is present, there is a 96% chance that sensor A will detect it, a 92% chance that sensor B will detect it, and a 90% chance that both sensors will detect it.

28. Draw a Venn diagram that illustrates this situation. **See margin.**

29. If carbon monoxide is present, what is the probability that it will be detected? **98% or 0.98**

30. What is the probability that carbon monoxide would go undetected? **2% or 0.02**

31. Do sensors A and B operate independently of each other? Explain. **no;** $P(A \text{ and } B) \neq P(A) \cdot P(B)$

BIOLOGY For Exercises 32–34, use the table and following information.

Each person carries two types of genes for eye color. The gene for brown eyes (B) is dominant over the gene for blue eyes (b). That is, if a person has one gene for brown eyes and the other for blue, that person will have brown eyes. The Punnett square at the right shows the genes for two parents.

	B	b
B	BB	Bb
b	Bb	bb

32. What is the probability that any child will have blue eyes? $\frac{1}{4}$

33. What is the probability that the couple's two children both have brown eyes? $\frac{9}{16}$

34. Find the probability that the first or the second child has blue eyes. $\frac{7}{16}$

35. **RESEARCH** Use the Internet or other reference to investigate various blood types. Use this information to determine the probability of a child having blood type O if the father has blood type A(Ai) and the mother has blood type B(Bi). $\frac{1}{4}$

TRANSPORTATION For Exercises 36 and 37, use the graph and the following information.

The U.S. Census Bureau conducted an American Community Survey in Lake County, Illinois. The circle graph at the right shows the survey results of how people commute to work.

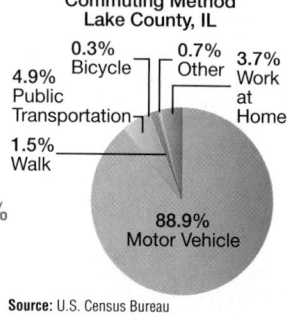

Commuting Method Lake County, IL
- 0.3% Bicycle
- 0.7% Other
- 3.7% Work at Home
- 4.9% Public Transportation
- 1.5% Walk
- 88.9% Motor Vehicle

Source: U.S. Census Bureau

36. If a person from Lake County was chosen at random, what is the probability that he or she uses public transportation or walks to work? **6.4%**

37. If offices are being built in Lake County to accommodate 400 employees, what is the minimum number of parking spaces an architect should plan for the parking lot? **356**

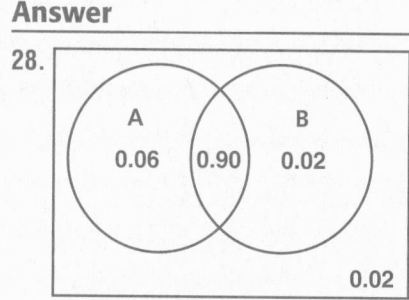

Safety

In the U.S., 60% of carbon monoxide emissions come from transportation sources. The largest contributor is highway motor vehicles. In urban areas, motor vehicles can contribute more than 90%.

Source: U.S. Environmental Protection Agency

Answer

28.

A Venn diagram with two overlapping circles labeled A and B: A only 0.06, overlap 0.90, B only 0.02, outside 0.02

ECONOMICS For Exercises 38–40, use the table below that compares the total number of hourly workers who earned the minimum wage of $5.15 with those making less than minimum wage.

Number of Hourly Workers (thousands)			
Age (years)	Total	At $5.15	Below $5.15
16–24	15,793	1145	2080
25+	55,287	970	2043

Source: U.S. Bureau of Labor Statistics

38. If an hourly worker was chosen at random, what is the probability that he or she earned minimum wage? less than minimum wage? ≈ 0.03; ≈ 0.06

39. What is the probability that a randomly-chosen hourly worker earned less than or equal to minimum wage? ≈ 0.09

40. If you randomly chose an hourly worker from each age group, which would you expect to have earned no more than minimum wage? Explain.
A worker in the 16–24 age group; the probability is greater for that age group.

GEOMETRY For Exercises 41–43, use the figure and the following information.
Two of the six non-straight angles in the figure are chosen at random.

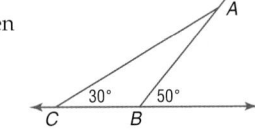

★ 41. What is the probability of choosing an angle inside $\triangle ABC$ or an obtuse angle? **1**

★ 42. What is the probability of selecting a straight angle or a right angle inside $\triangle ABC$? **0**

★ 43. Find the probability of picking a 20° angle or a 130° angle. $\dfrac{3}{5}$

A dart is thrown at a dartboard like the one at the right. If the dart can land anywhere on the board, find the probability that it lands in each of the following.

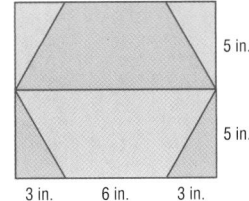

5 in.

5 in.

3 in.   6 in.   3 in.

★ 44. a triangle or a red region $\dfrac{5}{8}$

★ 45. a trapezoid or a blue region $\dfrac{7}{8}$

★ 46. a blue triangle or a red triangle $\dfrac{1}{4}$

★ 47. a square or a hexagon $\dfrac{3}{4}$

CRITICAL THINKING For Exercises 48–51, use the following information.
A sample of high school students were asked if they:
  A) drive a car to school,
  B) are involved in after-school activities, or
  C) have a part-time job.
The results of the survey are shown in the Venn diagram.

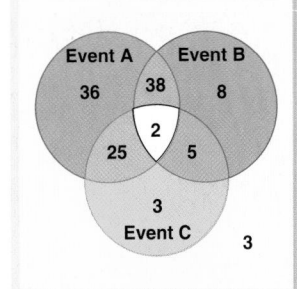

48. How many students were surveyed? **120**

49. How many students said that they drive a car to school? **101**

50. If a high school student is chosen at random, what is the probability that he or she does all three? $\dfrac{1}{60}$

51. What is the probability that a randomly-chosen student drives a car to school or is involved in after-school activities or has a part-time job? $\dfrac{39}{40}$

Open-Ended Assessment

Writing Have students write an example of how they could use a probability calculation in their daily lives. The example should include both a description of how the probability calculation could be used, and a sample calculation with sample data.

Getting Ready for Lesson 14-4

PREREQUISITE SKILL Students will learn about probability distributions in Lesson 14-4. In probability distributions, the probabilities are most often expressed as decimals instead of fractions. Use Exercises 67–75 to determine your students' familiarity with expressing fractions as decimals.

Assessment Options

Quiz (Lesson 14-3) is available on p. 875 of the *Chapter 14 Resource Masters*.

Mid-Chapter Test (Lessons 14-1 through 14-3) is available on p. 877 of the *Chapter 14 Resource Masters*.

Answer

52. Sample answer: Meteorologists use probabilities to forecast the weather. Answers should include the following.
- You can use compound probabilities to forecast the weather over an extended period of time.
- 80%

---

52. **WRITING IN MATH** Answer the question that was posed at the beginning of the lesson. **See margin.**

How are probabilities used by meteorologists?

Include the following in your answer:
- a few sentences about how compound probabilities can be used to predict the weather, and
- assuming that the events are independent, the probability that it will rain either Saturday or Sunday if there is a 30% chance of rain on Saturday and a 50% chance of rain Sunday. **80%**

Standardized Test Practice
Ⓐ Ⓑ Ⓒ Ⓓ

53. A bag contains 8 red marbles, 5 blue marbles, 4 green marbles, and 7 yellow marbles. Five marbles are randomly drawn from the bag and not replaced. What is the probability that the first three marbles drawn are red? **C**

Ⓐ $\frac{1}{27}$ Ⓑ $\frac{28}{1771}$ Ⓒ $\frac{7}{253}$ Ⓓ $\frac{7}{288}$

54. Yolanda usually makes 80% of her free throws. What is the probability that she will make at least one free throw in her next three attempts? **A**

Ⓐ 99.2% Ⓑ 51.2% Ⓒ 38.4% Ⓓ 9.6%

Maintain Your Skills

Mixed Review **CIVICS** For Exercises 55 and 56, use the following information.
The Stratford town council wants to form a 3-person parks committee. Five people have applied to be on the committee. *(Lesson 14-2)*

55. How many committees are possible? **10**

56. What is the probability of any one person being selected if each has an equal chance? $\frac{3}{5}$

57. **BUSINESS** A real estate developer built a strip mall with seven different-sized stores. Ten small businesses have shown interest in renting space in the mall. The developer must decide which business would be best suited for each store. How many different arrangements are possible? *(Lesson 14-1)* **604,800**

Find each sum or difference. *(Lesson 13-2)*

58. $\begin{bmatrix} 3 & -6 \\ -1 & 2 \end{bmatrix} + \begin{bmatrix} -2 & 4 \\ 1 & 5 \end{bmatrix} \begin{bmatrix} 1 & -2 \\ 0 & 7 \end{bmatrix}$ 59. $\begin{bmatrix} -4 & -5 \\ 8 & 8 \end{bmatrix} - \begin{bmatrix} -9 & -7 \\ 4 & 9 \end{bmatrix} \begin{bmatrix} 5 & 2 \\ 4 & -1 \end{bmatrix}$

60. Find the quotient of $\frac{2m^2 + 7m - 15}{m + 5}$ and $\frac{9m^2 - 4}{3m + 2}$. *(Lesson 12-4)* $\frac{2m - 3}{3m - 2}$

Simplify. *(Lesson 11-1)*

61. $\sqrt{45}$ $3\sqrt{5}$ 62. $\sqrt{128}$ $8\sqrt{2}$ 63. $\sqrt{40b^4}$ $2b^2\sqrt{10}$

64. $\sqrt{120a^3b}$ $2|a|\sqrt{30ab}$ 65. $3\sqrt{7} \cdot 6\sqrt{2}$ $18\sqrt{14}$ 66. $\sqrt{3}(\sqrt{3} + \sqrt{6})$ $3 + 3\sqrt{2}$

Getting Ready for the Next Lesson **PREREQUISITE SKILL** Express each fraction as a decimal. Round to the nearest thousandth. *(To review expressing fractions as decimals, see pages 804 and 805.)*

67. $\frac{9}{24}$ 0.375   68. $\frac{2}{15}$ 0.133   69. $\frac{63}{128}$ 0.492

70. $\frac{5}{52}$ 0.096   71. $\frac{8}{36}$ 0.222   72. $\frac{11}{38}$ 0.289

73. $\frac{81}{2470}$ 0.033   74. $\frac{18}{1235}$ 0.015   75. $\frac{128}{3570}$ 0.036

14-4 Probability Distributions

What You'll Learn

- Use random variables to compute probability.
- Use probability distributions to solve real-world problems.

Vocabulary
- random variable
- probability distribution
- probability histogram

How can a pet store owner use a probability distribution?

The owner of a pet store asked customers how many pets they owned. The results of this survey are shown in the table.

Number of Pets	Number of Customers
0	3
1	37
2	33
3	18
4	9

RANDOM VARIABLES AND PROBABILITY A **random variable** is a variable whose value is the numerical outcome of a random event. In the situation above, we can let the random variable X represent the number of pets owned. Thus, X can equal 0, 1, 2, 3, or 4.

Example 1 Random Variable

Refer to the application above.

a. Find the probability that a randomly-chosen customer has 2 pets.

There is only one outcome in which there are 2 pets owned, and there are 100 survey results.

$$P(X = 2) = \frac{2 \text{ pets owned}}{\text{customers surveyed}}$$

$$= \frac{33}{100}$$

The probability that a randomly-chosen customer has 2 pets is $\frac{33}{100}$ or 33%.

b. Find the probability that a randomly-chosen customer has at least 3 pets.

There are 18 + 9 or 27 outcomes in which a customer owns at least 3 pets.

$$P(X \geq 3) = \frac{27}{100}$$

The probability that a randomly-chosen customer owns at least 3 pets is $\frac{27}{100}$ or 27%.

Study Tip

Reading Math
The notation $P(X = 2)$ means the same as $P(2 \text{ pets})$, the probability of a customer having 2 pets.

PROBABILITY DISTRIBUTIONS The probability of every possible value of the random variable X is called a **probability distribution**.

Key Concept — Properties of Probability Distributions

1. The probability of each value of X is greater than or equal to 0 and less than or equal to 1.
2. The probabilities of all of the values of X add up to 1.

 www.algebra1.com/extra_examples

Workbook and Reproducible Masters

Chapter 14 Resource Masters
- Study Guide and Intervention, pp. 849–850
- Skills Practice, p. 851
- Practice, p. 852
- Reading to Learn Mathematics, p. 853
- Enrichment, p. 854
- Assessment, p. 876

Graphing Calculator and Spreadsheet Masters, p. 50
Parent and Student Study Guide Workbook, p. 110

---

1 Focus

5-Minute Check Transparency 14-4 Use as a quiz or review of Lesson 14-3.

Mathematical Background notes are available for this lesson on p. 752D.

How can a pet store owner use a probability distribution?

Ask students:

- How many customers were surveyed? **100**

- The pet owners surveyed own how many pets total? **They own 193 pets.**

- **Pets** Use a table similar to the one shown on this page to survey the students in your classroom to find out how many pets each student owns. What is the greatest number of pets owned by a student in your class? Are there students who have no pets? **Answers depend on student responses to the survey.**

Resource Manager

 Transparencies
5-Minute Check Transparency 14-4
Answer Key Transparencies

 Technology
Interactive Chalkboard

RANDOM VARIABLES AND PROBABILITY

In-Class Example Power Point®

1 Use the data from Example 1 in the Student Edition to solve the following problems.

a. Find the probability that a randomly chosen customer has at most 2 pets.

$P(X \le 2) = \frac{73}{100}$ or 73%

b. Find the probability that a randomly chosen customer has 2 or 3 pets.

$P(2 \le X \le 3) = \frac{51}{100}$ or about 51%

PROBABILITY DISTRIBUTIONS

In-Class Example Power Point®

2 The table below shows the probability distribution of the number of students in each grade at Sunnybrook High School.

X = Grade	P(X)
9	0.29
10	0.26
11	0.25
12	0.2

a. If a student is chosen at random, what is the probability that he or she is in grade 11 or above?

$P(X = 11) + P(X = 12) = 0.45$

b. Make a probability histogram of the data.

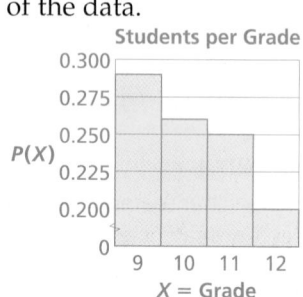

Students per Grade — X = Grade (vertical axis P(X))

The probability distribution for a random variable can be given in a table or in a **probability histogram**. The probability distribution and a probability histogram for the application at the beginning of the lesson are shown below.

Probability Distribution Table

X = Number of Pets	P(X)
0	0.03
1	0.37
2	0.33
3	0.18
4	0.09

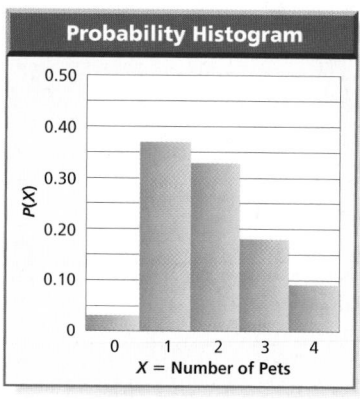

Probability Histogram — X = Number of Pets (vertical axis P(X))

Example 2 *Probability Distribution*

CARS The table shows the probability distribution of the number of vehicles per household for the Columbus, Ohio, area.

Vehicles per Household Columbus, OH

X = Number of Vehicles	Probability
0	0.10
1	0.42
2	0.36
3+	0.12

Source: U.S. Census Bureau

a. Show that the distribution is valid.

Check to see that each property holds.

1. For each value of X, the probability is greater than or equal to 0 and less than or equal to 1.
2. $0.10 + 0.42 + 0.36 + 0.12 = 1$, so the probabilities add up to 1.

b. What is the probability that a household has fewer than 2 vehicles?

Recall that the probability of a compound event is the sum of the probabilities of each individual event.

The probability of a household having fewer than 2 vehicles is the sum of the probability of 0 vehicles and the probability of 1 vehicle.

$P(X < 2) = P(X = 0) + P(X = 1)$ Sum of individual probabilities

$\qquad\quad = 0.10 + 0.42$ or 0.52 $P(X = 0) = 0.10, P(X = 1) = 0.42$

c. Make a probability histogram of the data.

Draw and label the vertical and horizontal axes. Remember to use equal intervals on each axis. Include a title.

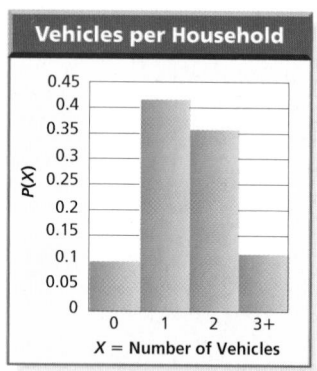

Vehicles per Household — X = Number of Vehicles (vertical axis P(X))

More About. . .

Cars •

In 1900, there were 8000 registered cars in the United States. By 2000, there were over 133 million registered cars. This is an increase of more than 1,662,400%.

Source: *The World Almanac*

DAILY
INTERVENTION   **Differentiated Instruction**

Interpersonal Place students in small groups and have the groups collect data for probability distribution tables and histograms. Students could collect data such as the number of siblings of their classmates, the number of desks in the classrooms in your hallway, and so on. Have groups share their distribution tables and histograms once they have gathered their data.

Check for Understanding

Concept Check

1–3. See margin.

1. **List** the conditions that must be satisfied to have a valid probability distribution.

2. **Explain** why the probability of tossing a coin three times and getting 1 head and 2 tails is the same as the probability of getting 1 tail and 2 heads.

3. **OPEN ENDED** Describe a situation that could be displayed in a probability histogram.

Guided Practice

GUIDED PRACTICE KEY	
Exercises	Examples
4–6	1
7–9	2

5. $P(X = 4) = \dfrac{1}{12}$,

$P(X = 5) = \dfrac{1}{9}$,

$P(X = 6) = \dfrac{5}{36}$

For Exercises 4–6, use the table that shows the possible sums when rolling two dice and the number of ways each sum can be found.

Sum of Two Dice	2	3	4	5	6	7	8	9	10	11	12
Ways to Achieve Sum	1	2	3	4	5	6	5	4	3	2	1

4. Draw a table to show the sample space of all possible outcomes. See pp. 795A–795B.

5. Find the probabilities for $X = 4$, $X = 5$, and $X = 6$.

6. What is the probability that the sum of two dice is greater than 6 on each of three separate rolls? $\dfrac{343}{1728}$

Application

GRADES For Exercises 7–9, use the table that shows a class's grade distribution, where A = 4.0, B = 3.0, C = 2.0, D = 1.0, and F = 0.

X = Grade	0	1.0	2.0	3.0	4.0
Probability	0.05	0.10	0.40	0.40	0.05

7. 0.05 + 0.10 + 0.40 + 0.40 + 0.05 = 1

7. Show that the probability distribution is valid.

8. What is the probability that a student passes the course? 0.95

9. What is the probability that a student chosen at random from the class receives a grade of B or better? 0.45

Practice and Apply

Homework Help

For Exercises	See Examples
10, 11, 14, 18	1
12, 13, 15–17, 19–22	2

Extra Practice
See page 852.

10–13. See pp. 795A–795B.

14. Let X = number of CDs; X = 100, 200, 300, 400, 500.

15. 0.10 + 0.15 + 0.40 + 0.25 + 0.10 = 1

For Exercises 10–13, the spinner shown is spun three times.

10. Write the sample space with all possible outcomes.

11. Find the probability distribution X, where X represents the number of times the spinner lands on blue for $X = 0$, $X = 1$, $X = 2$, and $X = 3$.

12. Make a probability histogram.

13. Do all possible outcomes have an equal chance of occurring? Explain.

SALES For Exercises 14–17, use the following information.
A music store manager takes an inventory of the top 10 CDs sold each week. After several weeks, the manager has enough information to estimate sales and make a probability distribution table.

Number of Top 10 CDs Sold Each Week	0–100	101–200	201–300	301–400	401–500
Probability	0.10	0.15	0.40	0.25	0.10

14. Define a random variable and list its values.

15. Show that this is a valid probability distribution.

16. In a given week, what is the probability that no more than 400 CDs sell? 0.90

17. In a given week, what is the probability that more than 200 CDs sell? 0.75

www.algebra1.com/self_check_quiz

3 Practice/Apply

Study Notebook

Have students—
- add the definitions/examples of the vocabulary terms to their Vocabulary Builder worksheets for Chapter 14.
- include any other item(s) that they find helpful in mastering the skills in this lesson.

About the Exercises...

Organization by Objective
- **Random Variables and Probability:** 10–15
- **Probability Distributions:** 16–22

Odd/Even Assignments
Exercises 10–17 are structured so that students practice the same concepts whether they are assigned odd or even problems.

Assignment Guide

Basic: 10–17, 23–48

Average: 10–17, 23–48

Advanced: 18–42 (optional: 43–48)

All: Practice Quiz 2 (1–5)

Answers

1. The probability of each event is between 0 and 1 inclusive. The probabilities for each value of the random variable add up to 1.

2. Sample answer: The probability of tossing a coin and getting a head versus getting a tail is the same. No matter what is tossed, the same probability is multiplied three times.

3. Sample answer: the number of possible correct answers on a 5-question multiple choice quiz, and the probability of each

Random Variables and Probability Distributions A random variable X is a variable whose value is the numerical outcome of a random event.

Example A teacher asked her students how many siblings they have. The results are shown in the table at the right.

Number of Siblings	Number of Students
0	1
1	15
2	8
3	2
4	1

a. Find the probability that a randomly selected student has 2 siblings.

The random variable X can equal 0, 1, 2, 3, or 4. In the table, the value $X = 2$ is paired with 8 outcomes, and there are 27 students surveyed.

$P(X = 2) = \dfrac{2 \text{ siblings}}{27 \text{ students surveyed}}$

$= \dfrac{8}{27}$

The probability that a randomly selected student has 2 siblings is $\frac{8}{27}$, or 29.6%.

b. Find the probability that a randomly selected student has at least three siblings.

$P(X \geq 3) = \dfrac{2 + 1}{27}$

The probability that a randomly selected student has at least 3 siblings is $\frac{1}{9}$, or 11.1%.

Exercises

For Exercises 1–3, use the grade distribution shown at the right. A grade of A = 5, B = 4, C = 3, D = 2, F = 1.

X = Grade	5	4	3	2	1
Number of Students	6	9	5	4	1

1. Find the probability that a randomly selected student in this class received a grade of C. $\frac{1}{5}$

2. Find the probability that a randomly selected student in this class received a grade lower than a C. $\frac{1}{5}$

3. What is the probability that a randomly selected student in this class passes the course, that is, gets at least a D? $\frac{24}{25}$

4. The table shows the results of tossing 3 coins 50 times. What is the probability of getting 2 or 3 heads? 48%

X = Number of Heads	0	1	2	3
Number of Times	6	20	19	5

For Exercises 1–3, the spinner shown is spun two times.

1. Write the sample space with all possible outcomes.
BB, BW, BR, BY, BG, WB, WW, WR, WY, WG, RB, RW, RR, RY, RG, YB, YW, YR, YY, YG, GB, GW, GR, GY, GG

2. Find the probability distribution X, where X represents the number of times the spinner lands on blue for $X = 0$, $X = 1$, and $X = 2$. $P(X = 0) = 0.64$, $P(X = 1) = 0.32$, $P(X = 2) = 0.04$

3. Make a probability histogram.
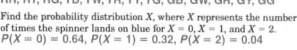
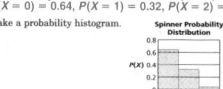

TELECOMMUNICATIONS For Exercises 4–6, use the table that shows the probability distribution of the number of telephones per student's household at Wilson High.

X = Number of Telephones	1	2	3	4	5+
Probability	0.01	0.16	0.34	0.39	0.10

4. Show that this is a valid probability distribution. $0.01 + 0.16 + 0.34 + 0.39 + 0.10 = 1$

5. If a student is chosen at random, what is the probability that there are more than 3 telephones at the student's home? 0.49

6. Make a probability histogram.

LANDSCAPING For Exercises 7–9, use the table that shows the probability distribution of the number of shrubs (rounded to the nearest 50) ordered by corporate clients of a landscaping company over the past five years.

Number of Shrubs	50	100	150	200	250
Probability	0.11	0.24	0.45	0.16	0.04

7. Define a random variable and list its values. Let X = the number of shrubs ordered; X = 50, 100, 150, 200, 250

8. Show that this is a valid probability distribution. $0.11 + 0.24 + 0.45 + 0.16 + 0.04 = 1$

9. What is the probability that a client's (rounded) order was at least 150 shrubs? 0.65

Pre-Activity How can a pet store owner use a probability distribution?

Read the introduction to Lesson 14-4 at the top of page 777 in your textbook.

• How many customers did the store owner survey? 80 customers

• Based on the survey, it is most likely that a customer would have ___1___ pet(s) and least likely that they would have ___4___ pet(s).

Reading the Lesson

The table below shows the probability of various family sizes in the United States.

X = Size of Family	Probability
2	0.42
3	0.23
4	0.21
5	0.10
6	0.03
7	0.01

1. For each value of X, is the probability greater than or equal to 0 and less than or equal to 1? yes

2. What is the sum of the probabilities? 1

3. Is the probability distribution valid? yes

4. Complete the probability histogram of the data.
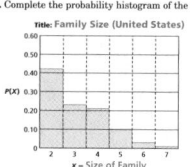

Helping You Remember

5. Use the outcomes of tossing a coin to describe how the probabilities of the possible outcomes add up to 1. $P(\text{heads}) = 0.5$; $P(\text{tails}) = 0.5$; $0.5 + 0.5 = 1$

EDUCATION For Exercises 18–20, use the table that shows the education level of persons aged 25 and older in the United States. 19–20. See pp. 795A–795B.

X = Level of Education	Probability
Some High School	0.167
High School Graduate	0.333
Some College	0.173
Associate's Degree	0.075
Bachelor's Degree	0.170
Advanced Degree	0.082

Source: U.S. Census Bureau

18. If a person was randomly selected, what is the probability that he or she completed at most some college? 0.673

19. Make a probability histogram of the data.

20. Explain how you can find the probability that a randomly selected person has earned at least a bachelor's degree.

SPORTS For Exercises 21 and 22, use the graph that shows the sports most watched by women on TV.

21. Determine whether this is a valid probability distribution. Justify your answer. See pp. 795A–795B.

22. Based on the graph, in a group of 35 women how many would you expect to say they watch figure skating? 2

23. **CRITICAL THINKING** Suppose a married couple has children until they have a girl. Let the random variable X represent the number of children in their family. a–b. See pp. 795A–795B.

a. Calculate the probabilities for $X = 1, 2, 3,$ and 4.

b. Find the probability that the couple will have more than 4 children.

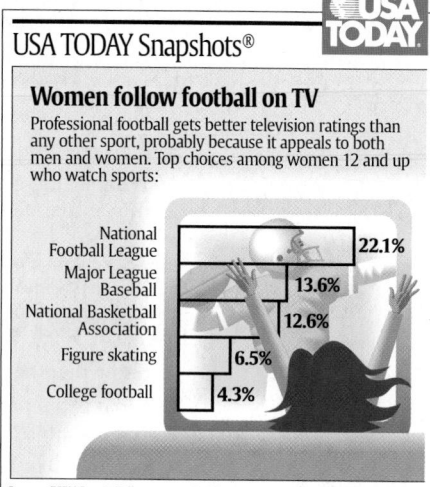

USA TODAY Snapshots®

Women follow football on TV

Professional football gets better television ratings than any other sport, probably because it appeals to both men and women. Top choices among women 12 and up who watch sports:

National Football League 22.1%
Major League Baseball 13.6%
National Basketball Association 12.6%
Figure skating 6.5%
College football 4.3%

Source: ESPN Sports Poll   By Ellen J. Horrow and Sam Ward, USA TODAY

24. **WRITING IN MATH** Answer the question that was posed at the beginning of the lesson. See pp. 795A–795B.

How can a pet store owner use a probability distribution?

Include the following in your answer:

• a sentence or two describing how to create a probability distribution, and

• an explanation of how the store owner could use a probability distribution to establish a frequent buyer program.

Standardized Test Practice
Ⓐ Ⓑ Ⓒ Ⓓ

25. The table shows the probability distribution for the number of heads when four coins are tossed. What is the probability that there are no more than two heads showing on a random toss? A

X = Number of Heads	0	1	2	3	4
Probability $P(X)$	0.0625	0.25	0.375	0.25	0.0625

Ⓐ 0.6875   Ⓑ 0.375   Ⓒ 0.875   Ⓓ 0.3125

26. On a random roll of two dice, what is the probability that the sum of the numbers showing is less than 5? B

Ⓐ 0.08   Ⓑ 0.17   Ⓒ 0.11   Ⓓ 0.28

Golden Rectangles

A **golden rectangle** has the property that its sides satisfy the following proportion.

$$\frac{a + b}{a} = \frac{a}{b}$$

Two quadratic equations can be written from the proportion. These are sometimes called **golden quadratic** equations.

1. In the proportion, let $a = 1$. Use cross-multiplication to write a quadratic equation. $b^2 + b - 1 = 0$

2. Solve the equation in Exercise 1 for b. $b = \dfrac{-1 + \sqrt{5}}{2}$

3. In the proportion, let $b = 1$. Write a quadratic equation in a. $a^2 - a - 1 = 0$

4. Solve the equation in Exercise 3 for a. $a = \dfrac{1 + \sqrt{5}}{2}$

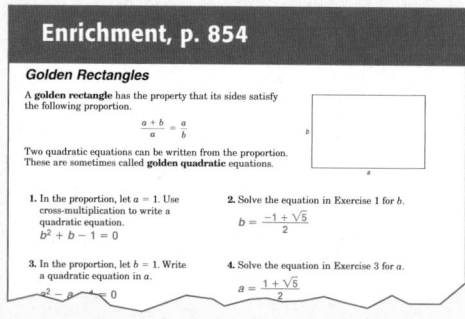

Mixed Review **A card is drawn from a standard deck of 52 cards. Find each probability.**
(Lesson 14-3)

27. P(ace or 10) $\dfrac{2}{13}$ 28. P(3 or diamond) $\dfrac{4}{13}$ 29. P(odd number or spade) $\dfrac{25}{52}$

Evaluate. *(Lesson 14-2)*

30. $_{10}C_7$ **120**   31. $_{12}C_5$ **792**   32. $(_6P_3)(_5P_3)$ **7200**

Let $A = \begin{bmatrix} 1 & 4 \\ 5 & 7 \end{bmatrix}$ and $B = \begin{bmatrix} -3 & 0 \\ -2 & 5 \end{bmatrix}$. *(Lesson 13-2)*

33. Find $A + B$. $\begin{bmatrix} -2 & 4 \\ 3 & 12 \end{bmatrix}$ 34. Find $B - A$. $\begin{bmatrix} -4 & -4 \\ -7 & -2 \end{bmatrix}$

Write an inverse variation equation that relates x and y. Assume that y varies inversely as x. Then solve. *(Lesson 12-1)*

35. If $y = -2.4$ when $x = -0.6$, find y when $x = 1.8$. $xy = 1.44; 0.8$

36. If $y = 4$ when $x = -1$, find x when $y = -3$. $xy = -4; \dfrac{4}{3}$

Simplify each expression. *(Lesson 11-2)*

37. $3\sqrt{8} + 7\sqrt{2}$ $13\sqrt{2}$ 38. $2\sqrt{3} + \sqrt{12}$ $4\sqrt{3}$ 39. $3\sqrt{7} - 2\sqrt{28}$ $-\sqrt{7}$

SAVINGS For Exercises 40–42, use the following information.
Selena is investing her $900 tax refund in a certificate of deposit that matures in 4 years. The interest rate is 8.25% compounded quarterly. *(Lesson 10-6)*

40. Determine the balance in the account after 4 years. **$1247.68**

41. Her friend Monique invests the same amount of money at the same interest rate, but her bank compounds interest monthly. Determine how much she will have after 4 years. **$1250.46**

42. Which type of compounding appears more profitable? Explain.
Sample answer: Monthly; the interest earned is higher than quarterly.

Getting Ready for the Next Lesson **PREREQUISITE SKILL** Write each fraction as a percent rounded to the nearest whole number. *(To review writing fractions as percents, see pages 804 and 805.)*

43. $\dfrac{16}{80}$ **20%**   44. $\dfrac{20}{52}$ **38%**   45. $\dfrac{30}{114}$ **26%**

46. $\dfrac{57}{120}$ **48%**   47. $\dfrac{72}{340}$ **21%**   48. $\dfrac{54}{162}$ **33%**

Practice Quiz 2 *Lessons 14-3 and 14-4*

For Exercises 1–3, use the probability distribution for the number of people in a household. *(Lesson 14-4)*

1. Show that the probability distribution is valid.

2. If a household is chosen at random, what is the probability that 4 or more people live in it? **0.25 or 25%**

3. Make a histogram of the data. **See margin.**
1. 0.25 + 0.32 + 0.18 + 0.15 + 0.07 + 0.02 + 0.01 = 1

A ten-sided die, numbered 1 through 10, is rolled. Find each probability.

4. P(odd or greater than 4) $\dfrac{4}{5}$

5. P(less than 3 or greater than 7) $\dfrac{1}{2}$

American Households	
X = Number of People	Probability
1	0.25
2	0.32
3	0.18
4	0.15
5	0.07
6	0.02
7+	0.01

Source: U.S. Census Bureau

---

4 Assess

Open Ended Assessment
Modeling Ask student volunteers to go to the chalkboard or overhead projector. Give the students sets of data to put into probability distribution tables and histograms. Have students model how to determine whether the given data fits the properties of probability distributions.

Getting Ready for Lesson 14-5

PREREQUISITE SKILL Students will learn about probability simulations in Lesson 14-5. When calculating probability from a simulation, the initial fraction may have a numerator and denominator that are very large numbers. Students may then simplify those fractions or change them to a percent. Use Exercises 43–48 to determine your students' familiarity with changing fractions to percents.

Assessment Options

Practice Quiz 2 The quiz provides students with a brief review of the concepts and skills in Lesson 14-3 and 14-4. Lesson numbers are given to the right of the exercises or instruction lines so students can review concepts not yet mastered.

Quiz (Lesson 14-4) is available on p. 876 of the *Chapter 14 Resource Masters*.

Answer

3.
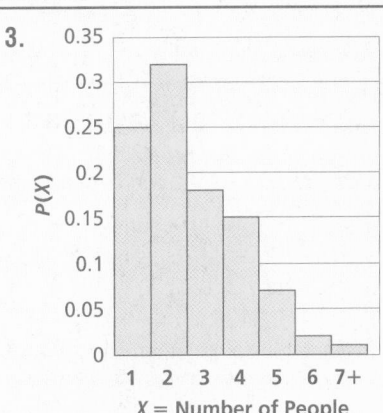

---

1 Focus

5-Minute Check Transparency 14-5 Use as a quiz or review of Lesson 14-4.

Mathematical Background notes are available for this lesson on p. 752D.

Building on Prior Knowledge

In Lesson 2-6, students learned to find the probability of simple events. In this lesson, students will learn that the probabilities they calculated in Lesson 2-6 were theoretical probabilities.

How can probability simulations be used in health care?

Ask students:

- If researchers think the probability of success of their new drug will be 70%, how many patients out of 100 should see an improvement in their condition? **70**

- How did the expected success rate compare to the number of people who actually saw their condition improve in the three studies? **Fewer than 70 improved in the first study, more than 70 improved in the second study, and fewer than 70 improved in the third study.**

Career Choices

Medical Researcher

Many medical researchers conduct research to advance knowledge of living organisms, including viruses and bacteria.

📖 *Online Research*
For information about a career as a medical researcher, visit: www.algebra1.com/careers

---

14-5 Probability Simulations

What You'll Learn

- Use theoretical and experimental probability to represent and solve problems involving uncertainty.
- Perform probability simulations to model real-world situations involving uncertainty.

Vocabulary
- theoretical probability
- experimental probability
- relative frequency
- empirical study
- simulation

How can probability simulations be used in health care?

A pharmaceutical company is developing a new medication to treat a certain heart condition. Based on similar drugs, researchers at the company expect the new drug to work successfully in 70% of patients.

To test the drug's effectiveness, the company performs three clinical studies. Each study involves 100 volunteers who use the drug for six months. The results of the studies are shown in the table.

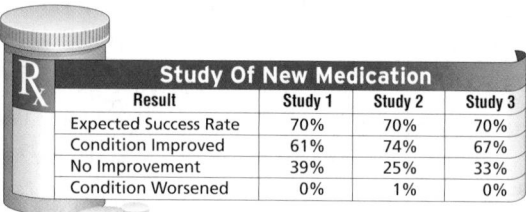

Study Of New Medication			
Result	Study 1	Study 2	Study 3
Expected Success Rate	70%	70%	70%
Condition Improved	61%	74%	67%
No Improvement	39%	25%	33%
Condition Worsened	0%	1%	0%

THEORETICAL AND EXPERIMENTAL PROBABILITY The probability we have used to describe events in previous lessons is theoretical probability. **Theoretical probabilities** are determined mathematically and describe what should happen. In the situation above, the expected success rate of 70% is a theoretical probability.

A second type of probability we can use is **experimental probability**, which is determined using data from tests or experiments. Experimental probability is the ratio of the number of times an outcome occurred to the total number of events or trials. This ratio is also known as the **relative frequency**.

$$\text{experimental probability} = \frac{\text{frequency of an outcome}}{\text{total number of trials}}$$

Example 1 *Experimental Probability*

MEDICAL RESEARCH Refer to the application at the beginning of the lesson. What is the experimental probability that the drug was successful for a patient in Study 1?

In Study 1, the drug worked successfully in 61 of the 100 patients.

$$\text{experimental probability} = \frac{61}{100} \quad \begin{array}{l} \leftarrow \text{frequency of successes} \\ \leftarrow \text{total number of patients} \end{array}$$

The experimental probability of Study 1 is $\frac{61}{100}$ or 61%.

Resource Manager

📁 **Workbook and Reproducible Masters**

Chapter 14 Resource Masters
- Study Guide and Intervention, pp. 855–856
- Skills Practice, p. 857
- Practice, p. 858
- Reading to Learn Mathematics, p. 859
- Enrichment, p. 860
- Assessment, p. 876

Graphing Calculator and Spreadsheet Masters, p. 49
Parent and Student Study Guide Workbook, p. 111
School-to-Career Masters, p. 28
Teaching Algebra With Manipulatives Masters, pp. 22, 209

 Transparencies

5-Minute Check Transparency 14-5
Answer Key Transparencies

 Technology

Interactive Chalkboard

It is often useful to perform an experiment repeatedly, collect and combine the data, and analyze the results. This is known as an **empirical study**.

Example 2 Empirical Study

Refer to the application at the beginning of the lesson. What is the experimental probability that the drug was successful for all three studies?

The number of successful outcomes of the three studies was $61 + 74 + 67$ or 202 out of the 300 total patients.

$$\text{experimental probability} = \frac{202}{300} \text{ or } \frac{101}{150}$$

The experimental probability of the three studies was $\frac{101}{150}$ or about 67%.

PERFORMING SIMULATIONS A method that is often used to find experimental probability is a simulation. A **simulation** allows you to use objects to act out an event that would be difficult or impractical to perform.

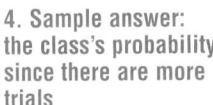

Algebra Activity

Simulations

Collect the Data

- Roll a die 20 times. Record the value on the die after each roll.
- Determine the experimental probability distribution for X, the value on the die.
- Combine your results with the rest of the class to find the experimental probability distribution for X given the new number of trials.
  (20 · the number of students in your class)

Analyze the Data

1. Find the theoretical probability of rolling a 2. $\frac{1}{6}$
2. Find the theoretical probability of rolling a 1 or a 6. $\frac{1}{3}$
3. Find the theoretical probability of rolling a value less than 4. $\frac{1}{2}$
4. Compare the experimental and theoretical probabilities. Which pair of probabilities was closer to each other: your individual probabilities or your class's probabilities?
5. Suppose each person rolls the die 50 times. Explain how this would affect the experimental probabilities for the class.

Make a Conjecture

6. What can you conclude about the relationship between the number of experiments in a simulation and the experimental probability?

You can conduct simulations of the outcomes for many problems by using one or more objects such as dice, coins, marbles, or spinners. The objects you choose should have the same number of outcomes as the number of possible outcomes of the problem, and all outcomes should be equally likely.

 www.algebra1.com/extra_examples

---

4. Sample answer: the class's probability since there are more trials

5. Sample answer: The class's probability should be closer to the theoretical probability.

6. Sample answer: The more times an experiment is performed, the experimental probability is closer to the theoretical probability.

Study Tip

Reading Math
The *Law of Large Numbers* states that as the number of trials increases, the experimental probability gets closer to the theoretical probability.

---

2 Teach

THEORETICAL AND EXPERIMENTAL PROBABILITY

In-Class Examples

1 Miguel shot 50 free throws in the gym and found that his experimental probability of making a free throw was 40%. How many free throws did Miguel make? **Miguel made 20 free throws.**

2 Refer to the application at the beginning of the lesson. What is the experimental probability that the drug would cause a patient to show no improvement for all three studies? $\frac{97}{300}$ or about 32%

Algebra Activity

Materials dice

- Have students create a probability distribution table to record the number of times each number comes up.
- Suggest that students repeat the die tosses 100 times for experimental results that will more closely resemble the theoretical probability.

3 In the last 30 school days, Bobbie's older brother has given her a ride to school 5 times.

a. What could be used to simulate whether Bobbie's brother will give her a ride to school? **Bobbie got a ride to school on $\frac{5}{30}$ or $\frac{1}{6}$ days. You could use one side of a die to represent a ride to school.**

b. Describe a way to simulate whether Bobbie's brother will give her a ride to school in the next 20 school days. **Let the 1-side of the die equal a ride to school. Toss the die 20 times and record each result.**

Teaching Tip Point out to students that this simulation is only valid if Ali's dog gives birth to 4 puppies as expected.

4 Use the data in Example 4 to answer the following questions.

a. What is an alternative to using 4 coins that could model the possible combinations of the puppies? **Sample answer: A spinner with 16 equal divisions.**

b. Find the theoretical probability that there will be 4 female puppies in a litter. **The theoretical probability is $\frac{1}{16}$.**

c. How does the theoretical probability that there will be 4 females compare with Ali's results? **The theoretical probability is a little more than 6% and the experimental probability is 6% so they are very close.**

Example 3 Simulation

In one season, Malcolm made 75% of the field goals he attempted.

a. What could be used to simulate his kicking a field goal? Explain.

You could use a spinner like the one at the right, where 75% of the spinner represents making a field goal.

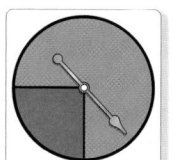

b. Describe a way to simulate his next 8 attempts.

Spin the spinner once to simulate a kick. Record the result, then repeat this 7 more times.

Example 4 Theoretical and Experimental Probability

DOGS Ali raises purebred dogs. One of her dogs is expecting a litter of four puppies, and Ali would like to figure out the most likely mix of male and female puppies. Assume that $P(\text{male}) = P(\text{female}) = \frac{1}{2}$.

a. What objects can be used to model the possible outcomes of the puppies?

Each puppy can be male or female, so there are $2 \cdot 2 \cdot 2 \cdot 2$ or 16 possible outcomes for the litter. Use a simulation that also has 2 outcomes for each of 4 events. One possible simulation would be to toss four coins, one for each puppy, with heads representing female and tails representing male.

b. Find the theoretical probability that there will be two female and two male puppies.

There are 16 possible outcomes, and the number of combinations that have two female and two male puppies is $_4C_2$ or 6. So the theoretical probability is $\frac{6}{16}$ or $\frac{3}{8}$.

c. The results of a simulation Ali performed are shown in the table below. What is the experimental probability that there will be three male puppies?

Outcomes	Frequency
4 female, 0 male	3
3 female, 1 male	13
2 female, 2 male	18
1 female, 3 male	12
0 female, 4 male	4

Ali performed 50 trials and 12 of those resulted in three males. So, the experimental probability is $\frac{12}{50}$ or 24%.

d. How does the experimental probability compare to the theoretical probability of a litter with three males?

Theoretical probability

$$P(3 \text{ males}) = \frac{_4C_3}{16} \qquad \leftarrow \frac{\text{combinations with 3 male puppies}}{\text{possible outcomes}}$$

$$= \frac{4}{16} \text{ or } 25\% \quad \text{Simplify.}$$

The experimental probability, 24%, is very close to the theoretical probability.

Study Tip

Alternative Simulation
You could also create a spinner with two even parts and spin it 4 times to simulate the outcomes of the puppies.

DAILY
INTERVENTION | **Differentiated Instruction**

Kinesthetic Allow students to design their own experiments to find experimental probability, such as finding the probability of tossing a wad of paper in a wastebasket, the probability of a student being able to do more than 10 jumping jacks in 10 seconds, and so on.

Check for Understanding

Concept Check

1–3. See margin.

1. **Explain** why it is useful to carry out an empirical study when calculating experimental probabilities.

2. **Analyze** the relationship between the theoretical and experimental probability of an event as the number of trials in a simulation increases.

3. **OPEN ENDED** Describe a situation that could be represented by a simulation. What objects would you use for this experiment?

4. **Tell** whether the theoretical probability and the experimental probability of an event are *sometimes*, *always*, or *never* the same. **sometimes**

Guided Practice

GUIDED PRACTICE KEY	
Exercises	Examples
5–7	3
8–12	4

5. So far this season, Rita has made 60% of her free throws. Describe a simulation that could be used to predict the outcome of her next 25 free throws. **See margin.**

6–8. See students' work.

For Exercises 6–8, roll a die 25 times and record your results.

6. Based on your results, what is the probability of rolling a 3?

7. Based on your results, what is the probability of rolling a 5 or an odd number?

8. Compare your results to the theoretical probabilities.

Application

9. See margin.

ASTRONOMY For Exercises 9–12, use the following information.
Enrique is writing a report about meteorites and wants to determine the probability that a meteor reaching Earth's surface hits land. He knows that 70% of Earth's surface is covered by water. He places 7 blue marbles and 3 brown marbles in a bag to represent hitting water $\left(\frac{7}{10}\right)$ and hitting land $\left(\frac{3}{10}\right)$. He draws a marble from the bag, records the color, and then replaces the marble. The table shows the results of his experiment.

Blue	Brown
56	19

9. Did Enrique choose an appropriate simulation for his research? Explain.

10. What is the theoretical probability that a meteorite reaching Earth's surface hits land? **30%**

11. Based on his results, what is the probability that a meteorite hits land? **about 0.25 or 25%**

12. Using the experimental probability, how many of the next 500 meteorites that strike Earth would you expect to hit land? **125**

Practice and Apply

Homework Help	
For Exercises	See Examples
13–16	3
17–21, 25–31	4
22–24	1, 2

Extra Practice
See page 852.

13. What could you use to simulate the outcome of guessing on 15 true-false questions? **Sample answer: a coin tossed 15 times**

14. There are 12 cans of cola, 8 cans of diet cola, and 4 cans of root beer in a cooler. What could be used for a simulation determining the probability of randomly picking any one type of soft drink? **See margin.**

For Exercises 15 and 16, use the following information.
Central City Mall is randomly giving each shopper one of 12 different gifts during the holidays. **15–16. See margin.**

15. What could be used to perform a simulation of this situation? Explain your choice.

16. How could you use this simulation to model the next 100 gifts handed out?

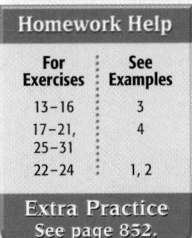 www.algebra1.com/self_check_quiz

3 Practice/Apply

Study Notebook

Have students—
- complete the definitions/examples for the remaining terms on their Vocabulary Builder worksheets for Chapter 14.
- include any other item(s) that they find helpful in mastering the skills in this lesson.

Answers

1. An empirical study uses more data than a single study, and provides better calculations of probability.

2. As the number of trials increases, the experimental probabilities tend toward the theoretical probabilities.

3. Sample answer: a survey of 100 people voting in a two-person election where 50% of the people favor each candidate; 100 coin tosses

5. Sample answer: 5 marbles of two colors where three of the marbles are one color to represent making a free throw, and the other two are a different color to represent missing a free throw. Randomly pick one marble to simulate a free throw 25 times.

9. Yes; 70% of the marbles in the bag represent water and 30% represent land.

14. Sample answer: a spinner divided into 3 sections where $\frac{1}{2}$ represents cola, $\frac{1}{3}$ represents diet cola, and $\frac{1}{6}$ represents root beer

15. Sample answer: a coin and a die since there are 12 possible outcomes

16. Sample answer: toss a coin and roll a die 100 times each

 **Teacher to Teacher**

Ruth Casey   Anderson County H.S., Lawrenceburg, KY

"I like to do an activity similar to the one done in Exercises 9–12. I have my students toss an inflated globe around the room. Students record whether the person catching the ball does so with his or her right thumb on land or on water."

Answers

22. P(Preschool) = 0.060
P(Kindergarten) = 0.058
P(Elementary) = 0.480
P(High School) = 0.255
P(College) = 0.146

28. MMMMM, MMMMF, MMMFM, MMMFF, MMFMM, MMFMF, MMFFM, MMFFF, MFMMM, MFMMF, MFMFM, MFMFF, MFFMM, MFFMF, MFFFM, MFFFF, FMMMM, FMMMF, FMMFM, FMMFF, FMFMM, FMFMF, FMFFM, FMFFF, FFMMM, FFMMF, FFMFM, FFMFF, FFFMM, FFFMF, FFFFM, FFFFF

32. No; there were 181 heads out of the 300 tosses. The experimental probability of heads is about 60%.

33. Sample answer: Probability can be used to determine the likelihood that a medication or treatment will be successful. Answers should include the following.

- Experimental probability is determining probability based on trials or studies.

- To have the experimental more closely resemble the theoretical probability the researches should perform more trials.

For Exercises 17 and 18, toss 3 coins, one at a time, 25 times and record your results.

17. Based on your results, what is the probability that any two coins will show heads? **See students' work.**

18. Based on your results, what is the probability that the first and third coins show tails? **See students' work.**

19–20. See students' work.

For Exercises 19–21, roll two dice 50 times and record the sums.

19. Based on your results, what is the probability that the sum is 8?

20. Based on your results, what is the probability that the sum is 7, or the sum is greater than 5?

21. If you roll the dice 25 more times, which sum would you expect to see about 10% of the time? **4 or 9**

CITY PLANNING For Exercises 22–24, use the following information.
The Lewiston City Council sent surveys to randomly selected households to determine current and future enrollment for the local school district. The results of the survey are shown in the table.

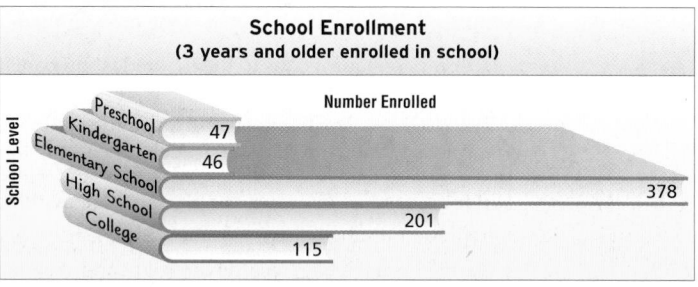

School Enrollment
(3 years and older enrolled in school)

22. Find the experimental probability distribution for the number of people enrolled at each level. **See margin.**

23. Based on the survey, what is the probability that a student chosen at random is in elementary school or high school? **≈ 0.74 or 74%**

24. Suppose the school district is expecting school enrollment to increase by 1800 over the next 5 years due to new buildings in the area. Of the new enrollment, how many will most likely be in kindergarten? **105**

RESTAURANTS For Exercises 25–27, use the following information.
A family restaurant gives children a free toy with each children's meal. There are eight different toys that are randomly given. There is an equally likely chance of getting each toy each time. **25. Sample answer: 3 coins   26. See students' work.**

25. What objects could be used to perform a simulation of this situation?

26. Conduct a simulation until you have one of each toy. Record your results.

27. Based on your results, how many meals must be purchased so that you get all 8 toys? **See students' work.**

29–31. See students' work.

ANIMALS For Exercises 28–31, use the following information.
Refer to Example 4 on page 784. Suppose Ali's dog is expecting a litter of 5 puppies.

28. List the possible outcomes of the genders of the puppies. **See margin.**

29. Perform a simulation and list your results in a table.

30. Based on your results, what is the probability that there will be 3 females and two males in the litter?

31. What is the experimental probability of the litter having at least three male puppies?

More About...

Animals •⋯⋯⋯⋯⋯
Labrador retrievers are the most popular breed of dog in the United States.
Source: American Kennel Club

32. CRITICAL THINKING The captain of a football team believes that the coin the referee uses for the opening coin toss gives an advantage to one team. The referee has players toss the coin 50 times each and record their results. Based on the results, do you think the coin is fair? Explain your reasoning. **See margin.**

Player	1	2	3	4	5	6
Heads	38	31	29	27	26	30
Tails	12	19	21	23	24	20

33. WRITING IN MATH Answer the question that was posed at the beginning of the lesson. **See margin.**

How can probability simulations be used in health care?

Include the following in your answer:
- a few sentences explaining experimental probability, and
- an explanation of why an experimental probability of 75% found in 400 trials is more reliable than an experimental probability of 75% found in 50 trials.

Standardized Test Practice
Ⓐ Ⓑ Ⓒ Ⓓ

34. Ramón tossed two coins and rolled a die. What is the probability that he tossed two tails and rolled a 3? **D**

Ⓐ $\frac{1}{4}$ Ⓑ $\frac{1}{6}$ Ⓒ $\frac{5}{12}$ Ⓓ $\frac{1}{24}$

35. If a coin is tossed three times, what is the probability that the results will be heads exactly one time? **B**

Ⓐ $\frac{2}{3}$ Ⓑ $\frac{3}{8}$ Ⓒ $\frac{1}{5}$ Ⓓ $\frac{1}{8}$

Graphing Calculator

SIMULATION For Exercises 36–38, use the following information.

When you are performing an experiment that involves a large number of trials that cannot be simulated using an object like a coin or a spinner, you can use the random number generator function on a graphing calculator. The TI-83 Plus program at the right will perform T trials by generating random numbers between 1 and P, the number of possible outcomes.

36–38. See students' work.

36. Run the program to simulate 50 trials of an event that has 15 outcomes. Record your results.

37. What is the experimental probability of displaying the number 10?

38. Repeat the experiment several times. Find the experimental probability of displaying the number 10. Has the probability changed from the probability found in Exercise 37? Explain why or why not.

```
PROGRAM: SIMULATE
:Disp "ENTER THE NUMBER"
:Disp "OF POSSIBLE"
:Disp "OUTCOMES"
:Input P
:Disp "ENTER THE NUMBER"
:Disp "OF TRIALS"
:Input T
:For(N, 1, T)
:randInt(1, P)→S
:Disp S
:Pause
:End
```

ENTERTAINMENT For Exercises 39–41, use the following information and the graphing calculator program above.

A CD changer contains 5 CDs with 14 songs each. When "Random" is selected, each CD is equally likely to be chosen as each song. **39–41. See students' work.**

39. Use the program **SIMULATE** to perform a simulation of randomly playing 40 songs from the 5 CDs. (*Hint:* Number the songs sequentially from 1, CD 1 track 1, to 70, CD 5 track 14.)

40. Do the experimental probabilities for your simulation support the statement that each CD is equally likely to be chosen? Explain.

41. Based on your results, what is the probability that the first three songs played are on the third disc?

Lesson 14-5 Probability Simulations **787**

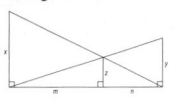
Lesson 14-5 Probability Simulations **787**

Open-Ended Assessment

Modeling Place students in groups and have them brainstorm ways to simulate 8 possible outcomes in a probability experiment. After brainstorming, have students select a method and build the actual simulator.

Assessment Options

Quiz (Lesson 14-5) is available on p. 876 of the *Chapter 14 Resource Masters*.

Mixed Review

42. $0.579 + 0.276 + 0.107 + 0.038 = 1$

For Exercises 42–44, use the probability distribution for the random variable X, the number of computers per household. *(Lesson 14-4)*

Computers per Household	
X = Number of Computers	$P(X)$
0	0.579
1	0.276
2	0.107
3+	0.038

Source: U.S. Dept. of Commerce

42. Show that the probability distribution is valid.

43. If a household is chosen at random, what is the probability that it has at least 2 computers? **0.145**

44. Determine the probability of randomly selecting a household with no more than one computer. **0.855**

For Exercises 45–47, use the following information.
A jar contains 18 nickels, 25 dimes, and 12 quarters. Three coins are randomly selected. Find each probability. *(Lesson 14-3)*

45. picking three dimes, replacing each after it is drawn $\dfrac{125}{1331}$

46. a nickel, then a quarter, then a dime without replacing the coins $\dfrac{20}{583}$

47. 2 dimes and a quarter, without replacing the coins, if order does not matter $\dfrac{80}{583}$

Solve each equation. *(Lesson 12-9)*

48. $\dfrac{2a-3}{a-3} - 2 = \dfrac{12}{a+3}$ **5**   **49.** $\dfrac{r^2}{r-7} + \dfrac{50}{7-r} = 14$ **6, 8** **50.** $\dfrac{x-2}{x} - \dfrac{x-3}{x-6} = \dfrac{1}{x}$ **3**

51. $\dfrac{2x-3}{7} - \dfrac{x}{2} = \dfrac{x+3}{14} - \dfrac{9}{4}$ **52.** $\dfrac{5n}{n+1} + \dfrac{1}{n} = 5\dfrac{1}{4}$ **53.** $\dfrac{a+2}{a-2} - \dfrac{2}{a+2} = \dfrac{-7}{3}$ $-1, \dfrac{2}{5}$

54. CONSTRUCTION To paint his house, Lonnie needs to purchase an extension ladder that reaches at least 24 feet off the ground. Ladder manufacturers recommend the angle formed by the ladder and the ground be no more than 75°. What is the shortest ladder he could buy to reach 24 feet safely? *(Lesson 11-7)* **at least 25 feet long**

Determine whether the following side measures would form a right triangle. *(Lesson 11-4)*

55. $5, 7, 9$ **no**   **56.** $3\sqrt{34}, 9, 15$ **yes**   **57.** $36, 86.4, 93.6$ **yes**

Solve each equation. Check your solutions. *(Lesson 9-6)*

58. $(x-6)^2 = 4$ **4, 8**   **59.** $x^2 + 121 = 22x$ **11**   **60.** $4x^2 + 12x + 9 = 0$ $-\dfrac{3}{2}$

61. $25x^2 + 20x = -4$ $-\dfrac{2}{5}$ **62.** $49x^2 - 84x + 36 = 0$ $\dfrac{6}{7}$ **63.** $180x - 100 = 81x^2$ $\dfrac{10}{9}$

 **Internet Project**

America Counts!

It is time to complete your project. Use the information and data you have gathered about populations to prepare a brochure or Web page. Be sure to identify the state you have chosen for this project. Include graphs, tables, and/or calculations in the presentation.

 www.algebra1.com/webquest

Study Guide and Review

Vocabulary and Concept Check

combination (p. 762)	experimental probability (p. 782)	mutually exclusive (p. 771)	relative frequency (p. 782)
complements (p. 771)	factorial (p. 755)	network (p. 759)	sample space (p. 754)
compound event (p. 769)	finite graph (p. 759)	node (p. 759)	simple event (p. 769)
dependent events (p. 770)	Fundamental Counting Principle (p. 755)	permutation (p. 760)	simulation (p. 783)
edge (p. 759)		probability distribution (p. 777)	theoretical probability (p. 782)
empirical study (p. 783)	inclusive (p. 771)	probability histogram (p. 778)	traceable (p. 759)
event (p. 754)	independent events (p. 769)	random variable (p. 777)	tree diagram (p. 754)

Choose the word or term that best completes each sentence.

1. The arrangement or listing in which order is important is called a (*combination*, *permutation*).
2. The notation 10! refers to a (*prime factor*, *factorial*).
3. Rolling one die and then another die are (*dependent*, *independent*) events.
4. The sum of probabilities of complements equals (*0*, *1*).
5. Randomly drawing a coin from a bag and then drawing another coin are dependent events if the coins (*are*, *are not*) replaced.
6. Events that cannot occur at the same time are (*inclusive*, *mutually exclusive*).
7. The sum of the probabilities in a probability distribution equals (*0*, *1*).
8. (*Experimental*, *Theoretical*) probabilities are precise and predictable.

Lesson-by-Lesson Review

14-1 *Counting Outcomes*

See pages 754–758.

Concept Summary
- Use a tree diagram to make a list of possible outcomes.
- If an event M can occur m ways and is followed by an event N that can occur n ways, the event M followed by event N can occur $m \cdot n$ ways.

Example

When Jerri packs her lunch, she can choose to make a turkey or roast beef sandwich on French or sourdough bread. She also can pack an apple or an orange. Draw a tree diagram to show the number of different ways Jerri can select these items.

Meat	Bread	Fruit	Possible Lunches
Turkey	French	Apple	TFA
		Orange	TFO
	Sourdough	Apple	TSA
		Orange	TSO
Roast Beef	French	Apple	RFA
		Orange	RFO
	Sourdough	Apple	RSA
		Orange	RSO

There are 8 different ways for Jerri to select these items.

Vocabulary and Concept Check

- This alphabetical list of vocabulary terms in Chapter 14 includes a page reference where each term was introduced.
- **Assessment** A vocabulary test/review for Chapter 14 is available on p. 874 of the *Chapter 14 Resource Masters*.

Lesson-by-Lesson Review

For each lesson,
- the main ideas are summarized,
- additional examples review concepts, and
- practice exercises are provided.

Vocabulary PuzzleMaker

ELL The Vocabulary PuzzleMaker software improves students' mathematics vocabulary using four puzzle formats—crossword, scramble, word search using a word list, and word search using clues. Students can work on a computer screen or from a printed handout.

MindJogger Videoquizzes

ELL MindJogger Videoquizzes provide an alternative review of concepts presented in this chapter. Students work in teams in a game show format to gain points for correct answers. The questions are presented in three rounds.

Round 1 Concepts (5 questions)
Round 2 Skills (4 questions)
Round 3 Problem Solving (4 questions)

FOLDABLES™ Study Organizer

For more information about Foldables, see *Teaching Mathematics with Foldables.*

Have students look through the chapter to make sure they have included examples in their Foldables to illustrate outcomes, permutations, combinations, and compound events.

Encourage students to refer to their Foldables while completing the Study Guide and Review and to use them in preparing for the Chapter Test.

Exercises Determine the number of outcomes for each event.
See Examples 1–3 on pages 754 and 755.

9. Samantha wants to watch 3 videos one rainy afternoon. She has a choice of 3 comedies, 4 dramas, and 3 musicals. **720**

10. Marquis buys 4 books, one from each category. He can choose from 12 mystery, 8 science fiction, 10 classics, and 5 biographies. **4800**

11. The Jackson Jackals and the Westfield Tigers are going to play a best three-out-of-five games baseball tournament. **20**

14-2 Permutations and Combinations

See pages 760–767.

Concept Summary

- In a permutation, the order of objects is important. $_nP_r = \dfrac{n!}{(n-r)!}$
- In a combination, the order of objects is not important. $_nC_r = \dfrac{n!}{(n-r)!\,r!}$

Examples

1 Find $_{12}C_8$.

$$_{12}C_8 = \frac{12!}{(12-8)!8!}$$

$$= \frac{12!}{4!8!}$$

$$= \frac{12 \cdot 11 \cdot 10 \cdot 9}{4!}$$

$$= 495$$

2 Find $_9P_4$.

$$_9P_4 = \frac{9!}{(9-4)!}$$

$$= \frac{9!}{5!}$$

$$= \frac{9 \cdot 8 \cdot 7 \cdot 6 \cdot 5 \cdot 4 \cdot 3 \cdot 2 \cdot 1}{5 \cdot 4 \cdot 3 \cdot 2 \cdot 1}$$

$$= 3024$$

Exercises Evaluate each expression. *See Examples 1, 2, and 4 on pages 760–762.*

12. $_4P_2$ **12**

13. $_8C_3$ **56**

14. $_4C_4$ **1**

15. $(_7C_1)(_6C_3)$ **140**

16. $(_7P_3)(_7P_2)$ **8820**

17. $(_3C_2)(_4P_1)$ **12**

14-3 Probability of Compound Events

See pages 769–776.

Concept Summary

- For independent events, use $P(A \text{ and } B) = P(A) \cdot P(B)$.
- For dependent events, use $P(A \text{ and } B) = P(A) \cdot P(B \text{ following } A)$.
- For mutually exclusive events, use $P(A \text{ or } B) = P(A) + P(B)$.
- For inclusive events, use $P(A \text{ or } B) = P(A) + P(B) - P(A \text{ and } B)$.

Example A box contains 8 red chips, 6 blue chips, and 12 white chips. Three chips are randomly drawn from the box and not replaced. Find *P*(red, white, blue).

First chip: $P(\text{red}) = \dfrac{8}{26}$ ← number of red chips / total number of chips

Second chip: $P(\text{white}) = \dfrac{12}{25}$ ← number of white chips / number of chips remaining

Third chip: $P(\text{blue}) = \dfrac{6}{24}$ ← number of blue chips / number of chips remaining

$P(\text{red, white, blue}) = \underline{P(\text{red})} \cdot \underline{P(\text{white})} \cdot \underline{P(\text{blue})}$

$$= \frac{8}{26} \cdot \frac{12}{25} \cdot \frac{6}{24}$$

$$= \frac{576}{15,600} \text{ or } \frac{12}{325}$$

Exercises   A bag of colored paper clips contains 30 red clips, 22 blue clips, and 22 green clips. Find each probability if three clips are drawn randomly from the bag and are not replaced.   *See Example 2 on page 770.*

18. $P(\text{blue, red, green})$ **19.** $P(\text{red, red, blue})$ **20.** $P(\text{red, green, not blue})$

One card is randomly drawn from a standard deck of 52 cards. Find each probability.   *See Examples 3 and 4 on pages 771 and 772.*

21. $P(\text{diamond or club})$ $\frac{1}{2}$ **22.** $P(\text{heart or red})$ $\frac{1}{2}$ **23.** $P(10 \text{ or spade})$ $\frac{4}{13}$

18. $\dfrac{605}{16,206}$

19. $\dfrac{1595}{32,412}$

20. $\dfrac{1375}{16,206}$

14-4 Probability Distributions

See pages 777–781.

Concept Summary

Probability distributions have the following properties.

- For each value of X, $0 \leq P(X) \leq 1$.
- The sum of the probabilities of each value of X is 1.

Example   A local cable provider asked its subscribers how many televisions they had in their homes. The results of their survey are shown in the probability distribution.

a. Show that the probability distribution is valid.

For each value of X, the probability is greater than or equal to 0 and less than or equal to 1.

$0.18 + 0.36 + 0.34 + 0.08 + 0.04 = 1$, so the probabilities add up to 1.

b. If a household is selected at random, what is the probability that it has fewer than 4 televisions?

$P(X < 4) = P(X = 1) + P(X = 2) + P(X = 3)$
$\qquad\quad = 0.18 + 0.36 + 0.34$
$\qquad\quad = 0.88$

Televisions per Household	
X = Number of Televisions	Probability
1	0.18
2	0.36
3	0.34
4	0.08
5+	0.04

24. $0.04 + 0.12 + 0.37 + 0.30 + 0.17 = 1$

Exercises   The table shows the probability distribution for the number of extracurricular activities in which students at Boardwalk High School participate.   *See Example 2 on page 778.*

24. Show that the probability distribution is valid.

25. If a student is chosen at random, what is the probability that the student participates in 1 to 3 activities? **0.79 or 79%**

26. Make a probability histogram of the data. **See margin.**

Extracurricular Activities	
X = Number of Activities	Probability
0	0.04
1	0.12
2	0.37
3	0.30
4+	0.17

Answer

26. Extracurricular Activities

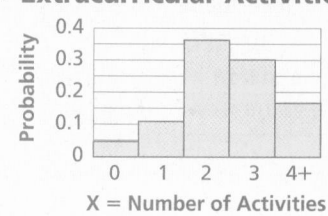

For More ... • Extra Practice, see pages 851–852.
• Mixed Problem Solving, see page 866.

Answer (page 793)

21.

Four Coins Tossed

x = Number of Heads	Probability
0	0.0625
1	0.25
2	0.375
3	0.25
4	0.0625

14-5 Probability Simulations

See pages 782–788.

Concept Summary

- Theoretical probability describes expected outcomes, while experimental probabilities describe tested outcomes.
- Simulations are used to perform experiments that would be difficult or impossible to perform in real life.

Example A group of 3 coins are tossed.

a. Find the theoretical probability that there will be 2 heads and 1 tail.

Each coin toss can be heads or tails, so there are $2 \cdot 2 \cdot 2$ or 8 possible outcomes. There are 3 possible combinations of 2 heads and one tail, HHT, HTH, or THH. So, the theoretical probability is $\frac{3}{8}$.

b. The results of a simulation in which three coins are tossed ten times are shown in the table. What is the experimental probability that there will be 1 head and 2 tails?

Of the 10 trials, 3 resulted in 1 head and 2 tails, so the experimental probability is $\frac{3}{10}$ or 30%.

Outcomes	Frequency
3 heads, 0 tails	1
2 heads, 1 tail	4
1 head, 2 tails	3
0 heads, 3 tails	2

c. Compare the theoretical probability of 2 heads and 1 tail and the experimental probability of 2 heads and 1 tail.

The theoretical probability is $\frac{3}{8}$ or 37.5%, while the experimental probability is $\frac{3}{10}$ or 30%. The probabilities are close.

Exercises While studying flower colors in biology class, students are given the Punnett square at the right. The Punnett square shows that red parent plant flowers (Rr) produce red flowers (RR and Rr) and pink flowers (rr).
See Examples 1, 3, and 4 on pages 782 and 784.

	R	r
R	RR	Rr
r	Rr	rr

27. If 5 flowers are produced, find the theoretical probability that there will be 4 red flowers and 1 pink flower. **39.6%**

28. Describe items that the students could use to simulate the colors of 5 flowers.

29. The results of a simulation of flowers are shown in the table. What is the experimental probability that there will be 3 red flowers and 2 pink flowers? **28.8%**

Outcomes	Frequency
5 red, 0 pink	15
4 red, 1 pink	30
3 red, 2 pink	23
2 red, 3 pink	7
1 red, 4 pink	4
0 red, 5 pink	1

28. Sample answer: There are 6 possible outcomes. So, you could use a die.

Vocabulary and Concepts

1. Seven students lining up to buy tickets for a school play is an example of a (*permutation*, *combination*).

2. Rolling a die and recording the result 25 times would be used to find (*theoretical*, *experimental*) probability.

3. A (*random variable*, *probability distribution*) is the numerical outcome of an event.

Skills and Applications

There are two roads from Ashville to Bakersville, four roads from Bakersville to Clifton, and two roads from Clifton to Derry.

4. Draw a tree diagram showing the possible routes from Ashville to Derry. See pp. 795A–795B.

5. How many different routes are there from Ashville to Derry? **16**

Determine whether each situation involves a *permutation* or a *combination*. Then determine the number of possible arrangements.

6. Six students in a class meet in a room that has nine chairs. **combination; 84**

7. The top four finishers in a race with ten participants. **permutation; 5040**

8. A class has 15 girls and 19 boys. A committee is formed with two girls and two boys, each with a separate responsibility. **permutation; 71,820**

A bag contains 4 red, 6 blue, 4 yellow, and 2 green marbles. Once a marble is selected, it is not replaced. Find each probability.

9. $P(\text{blue, green})$ $\frac{1}{20}$

10. $P(\text{yellow, yellow})$ $\frac{1}{20}$

11. $P(\text{red, blue, yellow})$ $\frac{1}{35}$

12. $P(\text{blue, red, not green})$ $\frac{3}{35}$

The spinner is spun, and a die is rolled. Find each probability.

13. $P(\text{yellow, 4})$ $\frac{1}{48}$

14. $P(\text{red, even})$ $\frac{1}{8}$

15. $P(\text{purple or white, not prime})$ $\frac{1}{8}$

16. $P(\text{green, even or less than 5})$ $\frac{5}{48}$

During a magic trick, a magician randomly selects a card from a standard deck of 52 cards. Without replacing it, the magician has a member of the audience randomly select a card. Find each probability.

17. $P(\text{club, heart})$ $\frac{13}{204}$

18. $P(\text{black 7, diamond})$ $\frac{1}{102}$

19. $P(\text{queen or red, jack of spades})$ $\frac{7}{663}$

20. $P(\text{black 10, ace or heart})$ $\frac{8}{663}$

The table shows the number of ways four coins can land heads up when they are tossed at the same time.

Four Coins Tossed	
Number of Heads	Possible Outcomes
0	1
1	4
2	6
3	4
4	1

21. Set up a probability distribution of the possible outcomes. **See margin.**

22. Find the probability that there will be no heads. **6.25%**

23. Find the probability that there will be at least two heads. **68.75%**

24. Find the probability that there will be two tails. **37.5%**

25. **STANDARDIZED TEST PRACTICE** Two numbers *a* and *b* can be arranged in two different orders, *a, b* and *b, a*. In how many ways can three numbers be arranged? **D**

Ⓐ 3 Ⓑ 4 Ⓒ 5 Ⓓ 6

  www.algebra1.com/chapter_test

Assessment Options

Vocabulary Test A vocabulary test/review for Chapter 14 can be found on p. 874 of the *Chapter 14 Resource Masters*.

Chapter Tests There are six Chapter 14 Tests and an Open-Ended Assessment task available in the *Chapter 14 Resource Masters*.

Chapter 14 Tests			
Form	Type	Level	Pages
1	MC	basic	861–862
2A	MC	average	863–864
2B	MC	average	865–866
2C	FR	average	867–868
2D	FR	average	869–870
3	FR	advanced	871–872

MC = multiple-choice questions
FR = free-response questions

Open-Ended Assessment Performance tasks for Chapter 14 can be found on p. 873 of the *Chapter 14 Resource Masters*. A sample scoring rubric for these tasks appears on p. A22.

Unit 5 Test A unit test/review can be found on pp. 881–882 of the *Chapter 14 Resource Masters*.

End-of-Year Tests A Second Semester Test for Chapters 7–14 and a Final Test for Chapters 1–14 can be found on pp. 883–892 of the *Chapter 14 Resource Masters*.

 ExamView® Pro
Use the networkable **ExamView® Pro** to:

• Create **multiple versions** of tests.
• Create **modified** tests for *Inclusion* students.
• **Edit** existing questions and **add** your own questions.
• Use built-in **state curriculum correlations** to create tests aligned with state standards.
• Change **English** tests to **Spanish** and vice versa.

Portfolio Suggestion

Introduction There are countless applications for probabilities outside the classroom. Some that have been discussed in this chapter include predicting the weather, predicting the sex of puppies, and so on.

Ask Students Find an example of a way that probabilities are used outside the classroom. Describe how the probability is calculated, and what it is used to predict. Place your descriptions in your portfolio.

These two pages contain practice questions in the various formats that can be found on the most frequently given standardized tests.

A practice answer sheet for these two pages can be found on p. A1 of the *Chapter 14 Resource Masters*.

Standardized Test Practice
Student Recording Sheet, p. A1

Part 1 *Multiple Choice*

Select the best answer from the choices given and fill in the corresponding oval.

1 Ⓐ Ⓑ Ⓒ Ⓓ   4 Ⓐ Ⓑ Ⓒ Ⓓ   7 Ⓐ Ⓑ Ⓒ Ⓓ
2 Ⓐ Ⓑ Ⓒ Ⓓ   5 Ⓐ Ⓑ Ⓒ Ⓓ   8 Ⓐ Ⓑ Ⓒ Ⓓ
3 Ⓐ Ⓑ Ⓒ Ⓓ   6 Ⓐ Ⓑ Ⓒ Ⓓ   9 Ⓐ Ⓑ Ⓒ Ⓓ

Part 2 *Short Response/Grid In*

Solve the problem and write your answer in the blank.

For Questions 13–15, also enter your answer by writing each number or symbol in a box. Then fill in the corresponding oval for that number or symbol.

10 _____   13   14   15
11 _____
12 _____
13 _____ (grid in)
14 _____ (grid in)
15 _____ (grid in)

Part 3 *Extended Response*

Record your answers for Questions 16–17 on the back of this paper.

Additional Practice

See pp. 879–880 in the *Chapter 14 Resource Masters* for additional standardized test practice.

Part 1 | Multiple Choice

Record your answers on the answer sheet provided by your teacher or on a sheet of paper.

1. If the average of a and b is 20, and the average of a, b, and c is 25, then what is the value of c? (Prerequisite Skill) **D**

   Ⓐ 10   Ⓑ 15
   Ⓒ 25   Ⓓ 35

2. The volume of a cube is 27 cubic inches. Its total surface area, in square inches, is (Lesson 3-8) **D**

   Ⓐ 9.   Ⓑ $6\sqrt{3}$.
   Ⓒ $18\sqrt{3}$.   Ⓓ 54.

3. A truck travels 50 miles from Oakton to Newton in exactly 1 hour. When the truck is halfway between Oakton and Newton, a car leaves Oakton and travels at 60 miles per hour. How many miles has the car traveled when the truck reaches Newton? (Lesson 3-8) **B**

   Ⓐ 25   Ⓑ 30
   Ⓒ 50   Ⓓ 60

4. Which equation would best represent the graphed data? (Lesson 5-7) **A**

   Table-Tennis Ball Bounce

   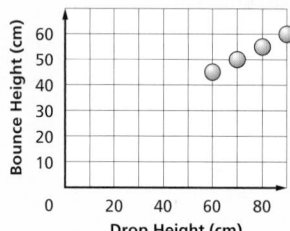

   Ⓐ $y = \frac{1}{2}x + 15$ Ⓑ $y = 2x + 15$
   Ⓒ $y = 2x$ Ⓓ $y = \frac{1}{2}x$

5. If a child is equally likely to be born a boy or a girl, what is the probability that a family of 3 children will contain exactly one boy? (Lesson 7-5) **C**

   Ⓐ $\frac{1}{8}$ Ⓑ $\frac{1}{4}$
   Ⓒ $\frac{3}{8}$ Ⓓ $\frac{1}{2}$

6. What is the value of 5^{-2}? (Lesson 8-2) **C**

   Ⓐ -25 Ⓑ $-\frac{1}{25}$
   Ⓒ $\frac{1}{25}$ Ⓓ $-\sqrt{5}$

7. What are the solutions of $x^2 + x = 20$? (Lesson 9-4) **D**

   Ⓐ $-4, 5$ Ⓑ $-2, 10$
   Ⓒ $2, 10$ Ⓓ $4, -5$

8. Two airplanes are flying at the same altitude. One plane is two miles west and two miles north of an airport. The other plane is seven miles west and eight miles north of the same airport. How many miles apart are the airplanes? (Lesson 11-4) **B**

   Ⓐ 2.8   Ⓑ 7.8
   Ⓒ 10.6   Ⓓ 11.0

9. A certain password consists of three characters, and each character is a letter of the alphabet. Each letter can be used more than once. How many different passwords are possible? (Lesson 14-1) **D**

   Ⓐ 78   Ⓑ 2600
   Ⓒ 15,600   Ⓓ 17,576

Test-Taking Tip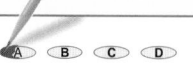

If you are allowed to write in your test booklet, underline key words, do calculations, sketch diagrams, cross out answer choices as you eliminate them, and mark any questions that you skip. But do not make any marks on the *answer sheet* except your answers.

ExamView® Pro

Special banks of standardized test questions similar to those on the SAT, ACT, TIMSS 8, NAEP 8, and Algebra 1 End-of-Course tests can be found on this CD-ROM.

Preparing for Standardized Tests
For test-taking strategies and more
practice, see pages 867–884.

Part 2 | Short Response/Grid In

Record your answers on the answer sheet
provided by your teacher or on a sheet of
paper.

10. What are the coordinates of the point of
    intersection of the lines represented by the
    equations $x + 4y = 0$ and $2x - 3y = 11$?
    (Lesson 7-2) **(4, −1)**

11. Is $4\left(x - \frac{1}{2}\right)^2 - 1 = 4x^2 - 4x$ true for *all* values
    of *x*, *some* values of *x*, or *no* values of *x*?
    (Lesson 8-8) **all**

12. Triangle *ABC* has sides of length $a = 5$,
    $b = 7$, and $c = \sqrt{74}$. What is the measure,
    in degrees, of the angle opposite side *c*?
    (Lesson 11-4) **90°**

13. All seven-digit telephone numbers in a town
    begin with the same three digits. Of the last
    four digits in any given phone number,
    neither the first nor the last digit can be 0.
    How many telephone numbers are available
    in this town?   (Lesson 14-2) **8100**

14. In the board game shown below, you move
    your game piece along the arrows from
    square to square. To determine which
    direction to move your game piece, you roll a
    number cube with sides numbered 1, 2, 3, 4,
    5, and 6. If you roll 1 or 2, you move your
    game piece one space to the left. If you roll 3,
    4, 5, or 6, you move your game piece one
    square to the right. What is the probability
    that you will reach the goal within two turns?
    (Lesson 14-3) **4/9**

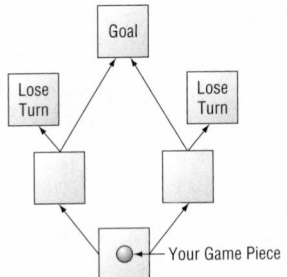

15. An eight-sided die numbered 1–8 is rolled
    50 times during the span of a board game. If
    a 7 is rolled twelve times, what is the
    theoretical probability of rolling a number
    other than 7?   (Lesson 14-5) **7/8**

Part 3 | Extended Response

Record your answers on a sheet of paper.
Show your work.

16. The histogram shows the number of sales
    DVD World has made during one weekend
    of business.   (Lesson 13-3)

Sales at DVD World

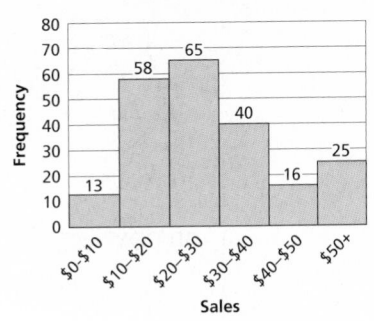

a. What was the total number of sales
   during the weekend? **217**

b. In what measurement class does the
   median occur? **$20-$30**

c. Describe the distribution of the data.
   See margin.

17. At WackyWorld Pizza, the Random Special
    is a random selection of two different
    toppings on a large cheese pizza. The
    available toppings are pepperoni, sausage,
    onion, mushrooms, and green peppers.
    (Lessons 14-2 and 14-3)

a. How many different Random Specials
   are possible? Show how you found your
   answer. **See margin.**

b. If you order the Random Special, what
   is the probability that it will have
   mushrooms? $\frac{2}{5}$

c. If you order the Random Special, what is
   the probabililty that it will have neither
   onion nor green peppers? $\frac{3}{10}$

Chapter 14 Standardized Test Practice **795**

Evaluating Extended Response Questions

Extended Response questions
are graded by using a multilevel
rubric that guides you in
assessing a student's knowledge
of a particular concept.

Goal: Count outcomes and find
a probability.

Sample Scoring Rubric: The
following rubric is a sample
scoring device. You may wish to
add more detail to this sample to
meet your individual scoring
needs.

Score	Criteria
4	A correct solution that is supported by well-developed, accurate explanations
3	A generally correct solution, but may contain minor flaws in reasoning or computation
2	A partially correct interpretation and/or solution to the problem
1	A correct solution with no supporting evidence or explanation
0	An incorrect solution indicating no mathematical understanding of the concept or task, or no solution is given

Answer

17a. **10 Random Specials are
     possible.**

     You can list all of the combina-
     tions, using letters for each
     topping.

     PS   PO   PM   PG
          SO   SM   SG
               OM   OG
                    MG

     There are 10 possible
     combinations.

Answers

16c. Sample answer: Sales at DVD World were mostly between $10 and $40 with the majority
     coming in the $20–$30 range. The data are somewhat symmetrical with a spike in the
     $50+ range and there are no gaps.

Pages 756–758, Lesson 14-1

4.

Spin 1	Spin 2	Spin 3	Outcomes

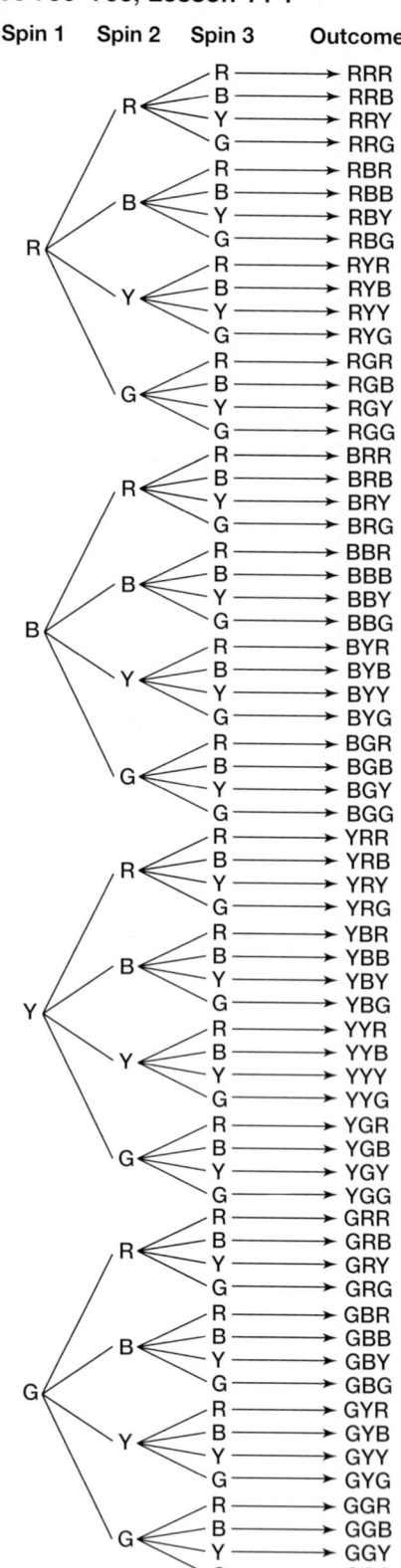

9.

English	Math	Science	Outcomes

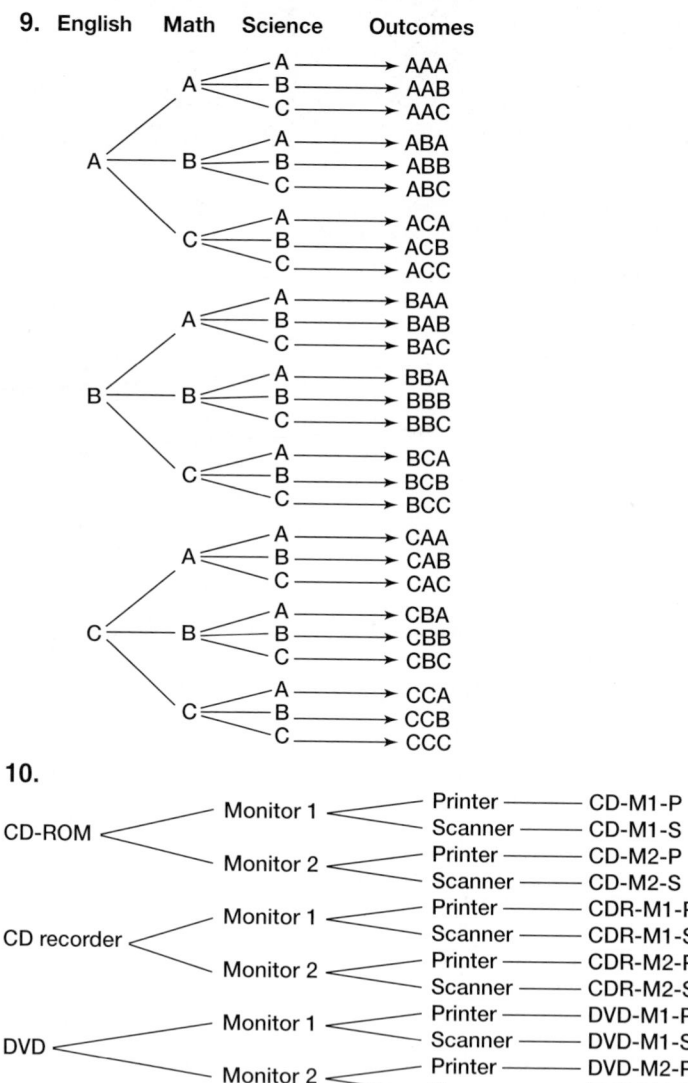

10.

CD-ROM	Monitor 1	Printer	CD-M1-P
		Scanner	CD-M1-S
	Monitor 2	Printer	CD-M2-P
		Scanner	CD-M2-S
CD recorder	Monitor 1	Printer	CDR-M1-P
		Scanner	CDR-M1-S
	Monitor 2	Printer	CDR-M2-P
		Scanner	CDR-M2-S
DVD	Monitor 1	Printer	DVD-M1-P
		Scanner	DVD-M1-S
	Monitor 2	Printer	DVD-M2-P
		Scanner	DVD-M2-S

Page 768, Reading Mathematics

1. Sample answer: Yes; Combine can mean placing many things together, as you do in a combination. A mutation is a change in genes and the order in which they appear as in a permutation.

2. Sample answer: Both permutations and combinations involve selecting items. However, a permutation considers the order of the selected items.

3. Sample answer:

factorial—the product of all the positive integers from 1 to *n*—symbol *n*!

factor—any of the numbers or symbols in mathematics that when multiplied together form a product

factorization—the operation of resolving a quantity into factors

The meanings all involve products.

4. probability—the quality or state of being probable; something (as an event or circumstance) that is probable

probus—upright, liberal, generous

probare—to test, approve, prove

Sample answer: The words all involve something being true or approved.

Pages 779–781, Lesson 14-4

4.

	1	2	3	4	5	6
1	2	3	4	5	6	7
2	3	4	5	6	7	8
3	4	5	6	7	8	9
4	5	6	7	8	9	10
5	6	7	8	9	10	11
6	7	8	9	10	11	12

10. RRR, RRB, RBR, RBB, BRR, BRB, BBR, BBB

11. $P(X = 0) = \frac{1}{64}$, $P(X = 1) = \frac{9}{64}$, $P(X = 2) = \frac{27}{64}$,

$P(X = 3) = \frac{27}{64}$

12.

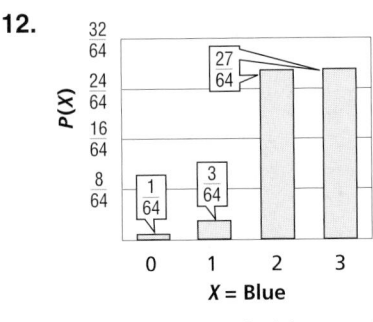

13. No; it is more probable to spin blue than red.

19.

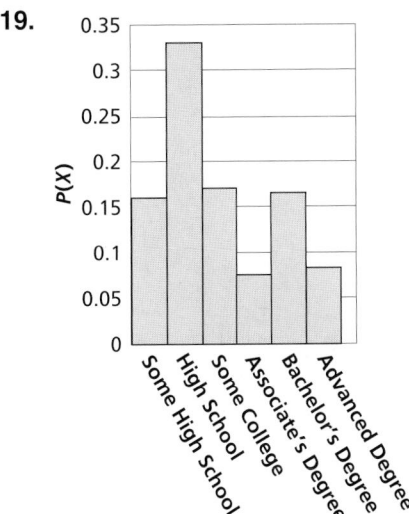

20. Sample answer: Add the values for the bars representing bachelor's and advanced degrees.

21. No; 0.221 + 0.043 + 0.136 + 0.126 + 0.065 = 0.591. The sum of the probabilities does not equal 1.

23a. $P(X = 1) = \frac{1}{2}$, $P(X = 2) = \frac{1}{4}$, $P(X = 3) = \frac{1}{8}$,

$P(X = 4) = \frac{1}{16}$

23b. $\frac{1}{16}$

24. Sample answer: A pet store owner could use probability distributions to plan sales and special events. Answers should include the following.

- Determine the probability of each outcome of an event and list them in a table.

- The owner could look at the probability of a customer owning more than one pet and create special discounts for larger purchases.

Page 793, Practice Test

4.

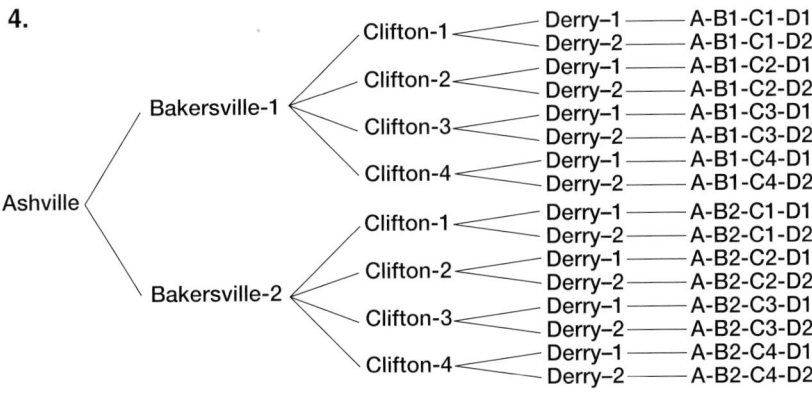

Student Handbook

Prerequisite Skills

❶ Operations with Fractions: Adding and Subtracting

- To add or subtract fractions with the same denominator, add or subtract the numerators and write the sum or difference over the denominator.

Example 1 Find each sum or difference.

a. $\frac{3}{5} + \frac{1}{5}$

$$\frac{3}{5} + \frac{1}{5} = \frac{3+1}{5} \quad \text{The denominators are the same.} \\ \text{Add the numerators.}$$

$$= \frac{4}{5} \quad \text{Simplify.}$$

b. $\frac{5}{9} - \frac{4}{9}$

$$\frac{5}{9} - \frac{4}{9} = \frac{5-4}{9} \quad \text{The denominators are the same.} \\ \text{Subtract the numerators.}$$

$$= \frac{1}{9} \quad \text{Simplify.}$$

- To write a fraction in simplest form, divide both the numerator and the denominator by their greatest common factor (GCF).

Example 2 Write each fraction in simplest form.

a. $\frac{4}{16}$

$$\frac{4}{16} = \frac{4 \div 4}{16 \div 4} \quad \text{Divide 4 and 16 by their GCF, 4.}$$

$$= \frac{1}{4} \quad \text{Simplify.}$$

b. $\frac{24}{36}$

$$\frac{24}{36} = \frac{24 \div 12}{36 \div 12} \quad \text{Divide 24 and 36 by their GCF, 12.}$$

$$= \frac{2}{3} \quad \text{Simplify.}$$

Example 3 Find each sum or difference. Write in simplest form.

a. $\frac{7}{16} - \frac{1}{16}$

$$\frac{7}{16} - \frac{1}{16} = \frac{6}{16} \quad \text{The denominators are the same.} \\ \text{Subtract the numerators.}$$

$$= \frac{3}{8} \quad \text{Simplify.}$$

b. $\frac{5}{8} + \frac{7}{8}$

$$\frac{5}{8} + \frac{7}{8} = \frac{12}{8} \quad \text{The denominators are the same.} \\ \text{Add the numerators.}$$

$$= 1\frac{4}{8} \text{ or } 1\frac{1}{2} \quad \text{Rename } \frac{12}{8} \text{ as a mixed number in simplest form.}$$

- To add or subtract fractions with unlike denominators, first find the least common denominator (LCD). Rename each fraction with the LCD, and then add or subtract. Simplify if necessary.

Example 4 Find each sum or difference. Write in simplest form.

a. $\frac{2}{9} + \frac{1}{3}$

$\frac{2}{9} + \frac{1}{3} = \frac{2}{9} + \frac{3}{9}$ The LCD for 9 and 3 is 9. Rename $\frac{1}{3}$ as $\frac{3}{9}$.

$= \frac{5}{9}$ Add the numerators.

b. $\frac{1}{2} + \frac{2}{3}$

$\frac{1}{2} + \frac{2}{3} = \frac{3}{6} + \frac{4}{6}$ The LCD for 2 and 3 is 6. Rename $\frac{1}{2}$ as $\frac{3}{6}$ and $\frac{2}{3}$ as $\frac{4}{6}$.

$= \frac{7}{6}$ or $1\frac{1}{6}$ Simplify.

c. $\frac{3}{8} - \frac{1}{3}$

$\frac{3}{8} - \frac{1}{3} = \frac{9}{24} - \frac{8}{24}$ The LCD for 8 and 3 is 24. Rename $\frac{3}{8}$ as $\frac{9}{24}$ and $\frac{1}{3}$ as $\frac{8}{24}$.

$= \frac{1}{24}$ Simplify.

d. $\frac{7}{10} - \frac{2}{15}$

$\frac{7}{10} - \frac{2}{15} = \frac{21}{30} - \frac{4}{30}$ The LCD for 10 and 15 is 30. Rename $\frac{7}{10}$ as $\frac{21}{30}$ and $\frac{2}{15}$ as $\frac{4}{30}$.

$= \frac{17}{30}$ Simplify.

Exercises   Find each sum or difference.

1. $\frac{2}{5} + \frac{1}{5}$ $\frac{3}{5}$

2. $\frac{2}{7} - \frac{1}{7}$ $\frac{1}{7}$

3. $\frac{4}{3} + \frac{4}{3}$ $\frac{8}{3}$ or $2\frac{2}{3}$

4. $\frac{3}{9} + \frac{4}{9}$ $\frac{7}{9}$

5. $\frac{5}{16} - \frac{4}{16}$ $\frac{1}{16}$

6. $\frac{7}{2} - \frac{4}{2}$ $\frac{3}{2}$ or $1\frac{1}{2}$

Simplify.

7. $\frac{6}{9}$ $\frac{2}{3}$

8. $\frac{7}{14}$ $\frac{1}{2}$

9. $\frac{28}{40}$ $\frac{7}{10}$

10. $\frac{16}{100}$ $\frac{4}{25}$

11. $\frac{27}{99}$ $\frac{3}{11}$

12. $\frac{24}{180}$ $\frac{2}{15}$

Find each sum or difference. Write in simplest form.

13. $\frac{2}{9} + \frac{1}{9}$ $\frac{1}{3}$

14. $\frac{2}{15} + \frac{7}{15}$ $\frac{3}{5}$

15. $\frac{2}{3} + \frac{1}{3}$ 1

16. $\frac{7}{8} - \frac{3}{8}$ $\frac{1}{2}$

17. $\frac{4}{9} - \frac{1}{9}$ $\frac{1}{3}$

18. $\frac{5}{4} - \frac{3}{4}$ $\frac{1}{2}$

19. $\frac{1}{2} + \frac{1}{4}$ $\frac{3}{4}$

20. $\frac{1}{2} - \frac{1}{3}$ $\frac{1}{6}$

21. $\frac{4}{3} + \frac{5}{9}$ $1\frac{8}{9}$

22. $1\frac{1}{2} - \frac{3}{2}$ 0

23. $\frac{1}{4} + \frac{1}{5}$ $\frac{9}{20}$

24. $\frac{2}{3} + \frac{1}{4}$ $\frac{11}{12}$

25. $\frac{3}{2} + \frac{1}{2}$ 2

26. $\frac{8}{9} - \frac{2}{3}$ $\frac{2}{9}$

27. $\frac{3}{7} + \frac{5}{14}$ $\frac{11}{14}$

28. $\frac{13}{20} - \frac{2}{5}$ $\frac{1}{4}$

29. $1 - \frac{1}{19}$ $\frac{18}{19}$

30. $\frac{9}{10} - \frac{3}{5}$ $\frac{3}{10}$

31. $\frac{3}{4} - \frac{2}{3}$ $\frac{1}{12}$

32. $\frac{4}{15} + \frac{3}{4}$ $1\frac{1}{60}$

33. $\frac{11}{12} - \frac{4}{15}$ $\frac{13}{20}$

34. $\frac{3}{11} + \frac{1}{8}$ $\frac{35}{88}$

35. $\frac{94}{100} - \frac{11}{25}$ $\frac{1}{2}$

36. $\frac{3}{25} + \frac{5}{6}$ $\frac{143}{150}$

❷ Operations with Fractions: Multiplying and Dividing

- To multiply fractions, multiply the numerators and multiply the denominators.

Example 1 Find each product.

a. $\dfrac{2}{5} \cdot \dfrac{1}{3}$

$$\dfrac{2}{5} \cdot \dfrac{1}{3} = \dfrac{2 \cdot 1}{5 \cdot 3}$$ Multiply the numerators.
Multiply the denominators.

$$= \dfrac{2}{15}$$ Simplify.

b. $\dfrac{7}{3} \cdot \dfrac{1}{11}$

$$\dfrac{7}{3} \cdot \dfrac{1}{11} = \dfrac{7 \cdot 1}{3 \cdot 11}$$ Multiply the numerators.
Multiply the denominators.

$$= \dfrac{7}{33}$$ Simplify.

- If the fractions have common factors in the numerators and denominators, you can simplify before you multiply by canceling.

Example 2 Find each product. Simplify before multiplying.

a. $\dfrac{3}{4} \cdot \dfrac{4}{7}$

$$\dfrac{3}{4} \cdot \dfrac{4}{7} = \dfrac{3}{\overset{}{\cancel{4}}} \cdot \dfrac{\overset{1}{\cancel{4}}}{7}$$ Divide by the GCF, 4.

$$= \dfrac{3}{7}$$ Simplify.

b. $\dfrac{4}{9} \cdot \dfrac{45}{49}$

$$\dfrac{4}{9} \cdot \dfrac{45}{49} = \dfrac{4}{\underset{1}{\cancel{9}}} \cdot \dfrac{\overset{5}{\cancel{45}}}{49}$$ Divide by the GCF, 9.

$$= \dfrac{20}{49}$$ Multiply the numerators and denominators.

- Two numbers whose product is 1 are called **multiplicative inverses** or **reciprocals**.

Example 3 Name the reciprocal of each number.

a. $\dfrac{3}{8}$

$$\dfrac{3}{8} \cdot \dfrac{8}{3} = 1$$ The product is 1.

The reciprocal of $\dfrac{3}{8}$ is $\dfrac{8}{3}$.

b. $\dfrac{1}{6}$

$$\dfrac{1}{6} \cdot \dfrac{6}{1} = 1$$ The product is 1.

The reciprocal of $\dfrac{1}{6}$ is 6.

c. $2\dfrac{4}{5}$

$$2\dfrac{4}{5} = \dfrac{14}{5}$$ Write $2\dfrac{4}{5}$ as an improper fraction.

$$\dfrac{14}{5} \cdot \dfrac{5}{14} = 1$$ The product is 1.

The reciprocal of $2\dfrac{4}{5}$ is $\dfrac{5}{14}$.

- To divide one fraction by another fraction, multiply the dividend by the multiplicative inverse of the divisor.

Example 4 Find each quotient.

a. $\frac{1}{3} \div \frac{1}{2}$

$$\frac{1}{3} \div \frac{1}{2} = \frac{1}{3} \cdot \frac{2}{1} \qquad \text{Multiply } \frac{1}{3} \text{ by } \frac{2}{1}, \text{ the reciprocal of } \frac{1}{2}.$$
$$= \frac{2}{3} \qquad \text{Simplify.}$$

b. $\frac{3}{8} \div \frac{2}{3}$

$$\frac{3}{8} \div \frac{2}{3} = \frac{3}{8} \cdot \frac{3}{2} \qquad \text{Multiply } \frac{3}{8} \text{ by } \frac{3}{2}, \text{ the reciprocal of } \frac{2}{3}.$$
$$= \frac{9}{16} \qquad \text{Simplify.}$$

c. $4 \div \frac{5}{6}$

$$4 \div \frac{5}{6} = \frac{4}{1} \cdot \frac{6}{5} \qquad \text{Multiply } 4 \text{ by } \frac{6}{5}, \text{ the reciprocal of } \frac{5}{6}.$$
$$= \frac{24}{5} \text{ or } 4\frac{4}{5} \qquad \text{Simplify.}$$

d. $\frac{3}{4} \div 2\frac{1}{2}$

$$\frac{3}{4} \div 2\frac{1}{2} = \frac{3}{4} \cdot \frac{2}{5} \qquad \text{Multiply } \frac{3}{4} \text{ by } \frac{2}{5}, \text{ the reciprocal of } 2\frac{1}{2}.$$
$$= \frac{6}{20} \text{ or } \frac{3}{10} \qquad \text{Simplify.}$$

Exercises Find each product.

1. $\frac{3}{4} \cdot \frac{1}{5}$ $\frac{3}{20}$

2. $\frac{2}{7} \cdot \frac{1}{3}$ $\frac{2}{21}$

3. $\frac{1}{5} \cdot \frac{3}{20}$ $\frac{3}{100}$

4. $\frac{2}{5} \cdot \frac{3}{7}$ $\frac{6}{35}$

5. $\frac{5}{2} \cdot \frac{1}{4}$ $\frac{5}{8}$

6. $\frac{7}{2} \cdot \frac{3}{2}$ $\frac{21}{4}$ or $5\frac{1}{4}$

7. $\frac{1}{3} \cdot \frac{2}{5}$ $\frac{2}{15}$

8. $\frac{2}{3} \cdot \frac{1}{11}$ $\frac{2}{33}$

Find each product. Simplify before multiplying if possible.

9. $\frac{2}{9} \cdot \frac{1}{2}$ $\frac{1}{9}$

10. $\frac{15}{2} \cdot \frac{7}{15}$ $\frac{7}{2}$ or $3\frac{1}{2}$

11. $\frac{3}{2} \cdot \frac{1}{3}$ $\frac{1}{2}$

12. $\frac{1}{3} \cdot \frac{6}{5}$ $\frac{2}{5}$

13. $\frac{9}{4} \cdot \frac{1}{18}$ $\frac{1}{8}$

14. $\frac{11}{3} \cdot \frac{9}{44}$ $\frac{3}{4}$

15. $\frac{2}{7} \cdot \frac{14}{3}$ $\frac{4}{3}$ or $1\frac{1}{3}$

16. $\frac{2}{11} \cdot \frac{110}{17}$ $\frac{20}{17}$ or $1\frac{3}{17}$

17. $\frac{1}{3} \cdot \frac{12}{19}$ $\frac{4}{19}$

18. $\frac{1}{3} \cdot \frac{15}{2}$ $\frac{5}{2}$ or $2\frac{1}{2}$

19. $\frac{30}{11} \cdot \frac{1}{3}$ $\frac{10}{11}$

20. $\frac{6}{5} \cdot \frac{10}{12}$ 1

Name the reciprocal of each number.

21. $\frac{6}{7}$ $\frac{7}{6}$ or $1\frac{1}{6}$

22. $\frac{3}{2}$ $\frac{2}{3}$

23. $\frac{1}{22}$ 22

24. $\frac{14}{23}$ $\frac{23}{14}$ or $1\frac{9}{14}$

25. $2\frac{3}{4}$ $\frac{4}{11}$

26. $5\frac{1}{3}$ $\frac{3}{16}$

Find each quotient.

27. $\frac{2}{3} \div \frac{1}{3}$ 2

28. $\frac{16}{9} \div \frac{4}{9}$ 4

29. $\frac{3}{2} \div \frac{1}{2}$ 3

30. $\frac{3}{7} \div \frac{1}{5}$ $\frac{15}{7}$ or $2\frac{1}{7}$

31. $\frac{9}{10} \div \frac{3}{7}$ $\frac{21}{10}$ or $2\frac{1}{10}$

32. $\frac{1}{2} \div \frac{3}{5}$ $\frac{5}{6}$

33. $2\frac{1}{4} \div \frac{1}{2}$ $\frac{9}{2}$ or $4\frac{1}{2}$

34. $1\frac{1}{3} \div \frac{2}{3}$ 2

35. $\frac{11}{12} \div 1\frac{2}{3}$ $\frac{11}{20}$

36. $\frac{3}{8} \div \frac{1}{4}$ $\frac{3}{2}$ or $1\frac{1}{2}$

37. $\frac{1}{3} \div 1\frac{1}{5}$ $\frac{5}{18}$

38. $\frac{3}{25} \div \frac{2}{15}$ $\frac{9}{10}$

❸ The Percent Proportion

- A **percent** is a ratio that compares a number to 100. To write a percent as a fraction, express the ratio as a fraction with a denominator of 100. Fractions should be stated in simplest form.

Example 1   Express each percent as a fraction.

     a. 25%

$$25\% = \frac{25}{100} \text{ or } \frac{1}{4} \qquad \text{Definition of percent}$$

     b. 107%

$$107\% = \frac{107}{100} \text{ or } 1\frac{7}{100} \qquad \text{Definition of percent}$$

     c. 0.5%

$$0.5\% = \frac{0.5}{100} \qquad\qquad \text{Definition of percent}$$
$$= \frac{5}{1000} \text{ or } \frac{1}{200} \qquad \text{Simplify.}$$

- In the **percent proportion**, the ratio of a part of something (part) to the whole (base) is equal to the percent written as a fraction.

$$\begin{array}{l} \text{part} \rightarrow \\ \text{base} \rightarrow \end{array} \frac{a}{b} = \frac{p}{100} \leftarrow \text{percent} \qquad\qquad \text{Example:} \;\; \overbrace{10}^{\text{part}} \;\; \text{is} \;\; \overbrace{25\%}^{\text{percent}} \;\; \text{of} \;\; \overbrace{40.}^{\text{base}}$$

Example 2   **40% of 30 is what number?**

The percent is 40, and the base is 30. Let a represent the part.

$$\frac{a}{b} = \frac{p}{100} \qquad \text{Use the percent proportion}$$
$$\frac{a}{30} = \frac{40}{100} \qquad \text{Replace } b \text{ with 30 and } p \text{ with 40.}$$
$$100a = 30(40) \qquad \text{Find the cross products.}$$
$$100a = 1200 \qquad \text{Simplify.}$$
$$\frac{100a}{100} = \frac{1200}{100} \qquad \text{Divide each side by 100.}$$
$$a = 12 \qquad \text{Simplify.}$$

The part is 12. So, 40% of 30 is 12.

Example 3   **Kelsey took a survey of some of the students in her lunch period. 42 out of the 70 students Kelsey surveyed said their family had a pet. What percent of the students had pets?**

You know the part, 42, and the base, 70.
Let p represent the percent.

$$\frac{a}{b} = \frac{p}{100} \qquad \text{Use the percent proportion.}$$
$$\frac{42}{70} = \frac{p}{100} \qquad \text{Replace } a \text{ with 42 and } b \text{ with 70.}$$
$$4200 = 70p \qquad \text{Find the cross products.}$$
$$\frac{4200}{70} = \frac{70p}{70} \qquad \text{Divide each side by 70.}$$
$$60 = p \qquad \text{Simplify.}$$

The percent is 60, so $\frac{60}{100}$ or 60% of the students had pets.

Example 4

67.5 is 75% of what number?

You know the percent, 75, and the part, 67.5.
Let b represent the base.

$\dfrac{a}{b} = \dfrac{p}{100}$ Use the percent proportion.

$\dfrac{67.5}{b} = \dfrac{75}{100}$ $75\% = \dfrac{75}{100}$, so $p = 75$.
Replace a with 67.5 and p with 75.

$6750 = 75b$ Find the cross products.

$\dfrac{6750}{75} = \dfrac{75b}{75}$ Divide each side by 75.

$90 = b$ Simplify.

The base is 90, so 67.5 is 75% of 90.

Exercises   **Express each percent as a fraction.**   3. $\dfrac{11}{100}$ 4. $\dfrac{120}{100}$ or $\dfrac{6}{5}$ 5. $\dfrac{78}{100}$ or $\dfrac{39}{50}$

1. 5% $\dfrac{5}{100}$ or $\dfrac{1}{20}$

2. 60% $\dfrac{60}{100}$ or $\dfrac{3}{5}$

3. 11% $\dfrac{11}{100}$

4. 120%

5. 78%

6. 2.5% $\dfrac{2.5}{100}$ or $\dfrac{1}{40}$

7. 0.9% $\dfrac{9}{1000}$

8. 0.4% $\dfrac{4}{1000}$ or $\dfrac{1}{250}$

9. 1400% **14**

Use the percent proportion to find each number.

10. 25 is what percent of 125? **20**

11. 16 is what percent of 40? **40**

12. 14 is 20% of what number? **70**

13. 50% of what number is 80? **160**

14. What number is 25% of 18? **4.5**

15. Find 10% of 95. **9.5**

16. What percent of 48 is 30? **62.5**

17. What number is 150% of 32? **48**

18. 5% of what number is 3.5? **70**

19. 1 is what percent of 400? **0.25**

20. Find 0.5% of 250. **1.25**

21. 49 is 200% of what number? **24.5**

22. 15 is what percent of 12? **125**

23. 48 is what percent of 32? **150**

24. Madeline usually makes 85% of her shots in basketball. If she shoots 20 shots, how many will she likely make? **17**

25. Brian answered 36 items correctly on a 40-item test. What percent did he answer correctly? **90%**

26. José told his dad that he won 80% of the solitaire games he played yesterday. If he won 4 games, how many games did he play? **5**

27. A glucose solution is prepared by dissolving 6 milliliters of glucose in 120 milliliters of solution. What is the percent of glucose in the solution? **5%**

HEALTH   **For Exercises 28–30, use the following information.**
The U.S. Food and Drug Administration requires food manufacturers to label their products with a nutritional label. The sample label shown at the right shows a portion of the information from a package of macaroni and cheese.

28. The label states that a seving contains 3 grams of saturated fat, which is 15% of the daily value recommended for a 2000-Calorie diet. How many grams of saturated fat are recommended for a 2000-Calorie diet. **20 grams**

29. The 470 milligrams of sodium (salt) in the macaroni and cheese is 20% of the recommended daily value. What is the recommended daily value of sodium? **2350 mg or 2.375 g**

30. For a healthy diet, the National Research Council recommends that no more than 30 percent of total Calories come from fat. What percent of the Calories in a serving of this macaroni and cheese come from fat? **44%**

Nutrition Facts		
Serving Size 1 cup (228g)		
Servings per container 2		
Amount per serving		
Calories 250 Calories from Fat 110		
		%Daily value*
Total Fat 12g		18%
Saturated Fat 3g		15%
Cholesterol 30mg		10%
Sodium 470mg		20%
Total Carbohydrate 31g		10%
Dietary Fiber 0g		0%
Sugars 5g		
Protein 5g		
Vitamin A 4%	•	Vitamin C 2%
Calcium 20%	•	Iron 4%

❹ Expressing Fractions as Decimals and Percents

- To write a fraction as a decimal, divide the numerator by the denominator.
  To write a decimal as a fraction, write the decimal as a fraction with denominator of 10, 100, 1000, … . Then simplify if possible.

Example 1 Write each fraction as a decimal.

a. $\frac{5}{8}$

$\frac{5}{8} = 5 \div 8$

$= 0.625$

b. $\frac{3}{5}$

$\frac{3}{5} = 3 \div 5$

$= 0.6$

c. $\frac{1}{3}$

$\frac{1}{3} = 1 \div 3$

$= 0.333\ldots$

Example 2 Write each decimal as a fraction.

a. 0.4

$0.4 = \frac{4}{10}$ or $\frac{2}{5}$

b. 0.005

$0.005 = \frac{5}{1000}$ or $\frac{1}{200}$

c. 0.98

$0.98 = \frac{98}{100}$ or $\frac{49}{50}$

- To write a fraction for a repeating decimal, use the method in Example 3 below.

Example 3 Write each decimal as a fraction.

a. $0.\overline{3}$

Let $N = 0.\overline{3}$ or 0.333…

Then $10N = 3.\overline{3}$ or 3.333…

$\begin{array}{l} 10N = 3.333\ldots \\ -1N = 0.333\ldots \\ \hline 9N = 3 \end{array}$ Subtract 1*N* from 10*N*.

$N = \frac{3}{9}$ or $\frac{1}{3}$

So, $0.\overline{3} = \frac{1}{3}$.

b. $0.\overline{72}$

Let $N = 0.\overline{72}$ or 0.7272…

Then $100N = 72.7272\ldots$

$\begin{array}{l} 100N = 72.7272 \\ -1N = 00.7272 \\ \hline 99N = 72 \end{array}$ Subtract 1*N* from 100*N*.

$N = \frac{72}{99}$ or $\frac{8}{11}$

So, $0.\overline{72} = \frac{8}{11}$.

- To write a decimal as a percent, multiply by 100 and add the % symbol. Recall that to multiply by 100, you can move the decimal point two places to the right.

- To write a percent as a decimal, divide by 100 and remove the % symbol. Recall that to divide by 100, you can move the decimal point two places to the left.

Example 4 Write each decimal as a percent.

Multiply by 100 and add the % symbol.

a. 0.35

$0.35 = 0.35$

$= 35\%$

b. 0.06

$0.06 = 0.06$

$= 6\%$

c. 0.008

$0.008 = 0.008$

$= 0.8\%$

Example 5 Write each percent as a decimal.

Divide by 100 and remove the % symbol.

a. 36%

$36\% = 36\%$

$= 0.36$

b. 9%

$9\% = 09\%$

$= 0.09$

c. 120%

$120\% = 120\%$

$= 1.2$

- To write a fraction as a percent, express the fraction as a decimal. Then express the decimal as a percent.

Example 6 Write each fraction as a percent. Round to the nearest tenth of a percent, if necessary.

a. $\frac{1}{8}$

$\frac{1}{8} = 0.125$

$= 12.5\%$

b. $\frac{2}{3}$

$\frac{2}{3} = 0.6666\ldots$

$= 66.7\%$

c. $\frac{3}{600}$

$\frac{3}{600} = 0.005$

$= 0.5\%$

- To write a percent as a fraction, express the percent as a decimal. Then express the decimal as a fraction. Simplify if possible.

Example 7 Write each percent as a fraction.

a. 30%

$30\% = 0.30$

$= \frac{30}{100}$ or $\frac{3}{10}$

b. 140%

$140\% = 1.4$

$= \frac{14}{10}$ or $1\frac{2}{5}$

c. 0.2%

$00.2\% = 0.002$

$= \frac{2}{1000}$ or $\frac{1}{500}$

Exercises Write each fraction as a decimal.

1. $\frac{3}{8}$ **0.375**
2. $\frac{2}{5}$ **0.4**
3. $\frac{2}{3}$ **$0.\overline{6}$**
4. $\frac{3}{4}$ **0.75**
5. $\frac{1}{2}$ **0.5**
6. $\frac{5}{9}$ **$0.\overline{5}$**
7. $\frac{3}{10}$ **0.3**
8. $\frac{5}{6}$ **$0.8\overline{3}$**

Write each decimal as a fraction.

9. 0.9 **$\frac{9}{10}$**
10. 0.25 **$\frac{1}{4}$**
11. 5.24 **$\frac{131}{25}$**
12. $0.\overline{45}$ **$\frac{5}{11}$**
13. $0.\overline{6}$ **$\frac{2}{3}$**
14. 0.0034 **$\frac{17}{5000}$**
15. 2.08 **$\frac{52}{25}$**
16. 0.004 **$\frac{1}{250}$**

Write each decimal as a percent.

17. 0.4 **40%**
18. 0.08 **8%**
19. 2.5 **250%**
20. 0.33 **33%**
21. 0.065 **6.5%**
22. 5 **500%**
23. 0.005 **0.5%**
24. $0.\overline{3}$ **$33.\overline{3}\%$**

Write each percent as a decimal.

25. 45% **0.45**
26. 3% **0.03**
27. 68% **0.68**
28. 115% **1.15**
29. 200% **2**
30. 0.1% **0.001**
31. 5.2% **0.052**
32. 10.5% **0.105**

Write each fraction as a percent. Round to the nearest tenth of a percent, if necessary.

33. $\frac{3}{4}$ **75%**
34. $\frac{9}{20}$ **45%**
35. $\frac{1}{2}$ **50%**
36. $\frac{1}{6}$ **16.7%**
37. $\frac{1}{3}$ **33.3%**
38. $\frac{7}{8}$ **87.5%**
39. $\frac{6}{5}$ **120%**
40. $\frac{19}{25}$ **76%**

Write each percent as a fraction.

41. 70% **$\frac{7}{10}$**
42. 3% **$\frac{3}{100}$**
43. 52% **$\frac{13}{25}$**
44. 25% **$\frac{1}{4}$**
45. 6% **$\frac{3}{50}$**
46. 135% **$1\frac{7}{20}$**
47. 0.1% **$\frac{1}{1000}$**
48. 0.5% **$\frac{1}{200}$**

⑤ Making Bar and Line Graphs

- One way to organize data is by using a frequency table. In a **frequency table**, you use **tally marks** to record and display the frequency of events.

Example 1 Make a frequency table to organize the temperature data in the chart at the right.

Noon Temperature (°F)					
52	48	60	39	55	56
60	63	70	58	59	54
63	65	66	73	76	51
54	60	52	48	47	54

Step 1 Make a table with three columns: Temperature, Tally, and Frequency. Add a title.

Step 2 Use intervals to organize the temperatures. In this case, we are using intervals of 10.

Step 3 Use tally marks to record the temperatures in each interval.

Step 4 Count the tally marks in each row and record in the Frequency column.

Noon Temperature (°F)		
Temperature	**Tally**	**Frequency**
30–39	I	1
40–49	III	3
50–59	IIII IIII	10
60–69	IIII II	7
70–79	III	3

- A **bar graph** compares different categories of data by showing each as a bar whose length is related to the frequency.

Example 2 The table below shows the results of a survey of students' favorite snacks. Make a bar graph to display the data.

Product	Number of Students
Bagel Chips	10
Fruit	18
Popcorn	15
Potato Chips	20
Pretzels	16
Snack Nuts	9
Tortilla Chips	17

Step 1 Draw a horizontal axis and a vertical axis. Label the axes as shown. Add a title.

Step 2 Draw a bar to represent each category. The vertical scale is the number of students who chose each snack. The horizontal scale identifies the snack chosen.

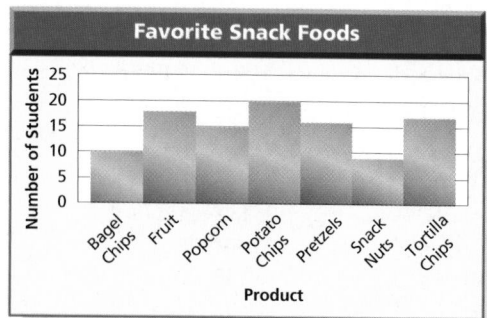

- Another way to represent data is by using a **line graph**. A line graph usually shows how data changes over a period of time.

Example 3

Sales at the Marshall High School Store are shown in the table below. Make a line graph of the data.

School Store Sales Amounts			
September	$670	February	$388
October	$229	March	$412
November	$300	April	$309
December	$168	May	$198
January	$290		

Step 1 Draw a horizontal axis and a vertical axis and label them as shown. Include a title.

Step 2 Plot the points to represent the data.

Step 3 Draw a line connecting each pair of consecutive points.

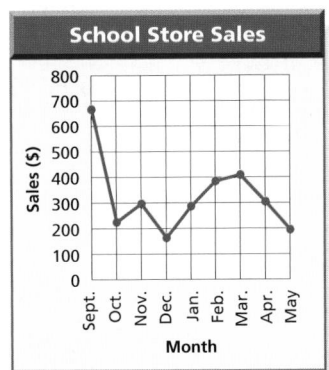

Exercises   Determine whether a bar graph or a line graph is the better choice to display the data.

1. the growth of a plant   line graph

2. comparison of the populations in Idaho, Montana, and Texas   bar graph

3. the number of students in each of the classes at your school   bar graph

4. your height over the past eight years   line graph

5. the numbers of your friends that shower in the morning versus the number that shower at night   bar graph

6. Alana surveyed several students to find the number of hours of sleep they typically get each night. The results are shown at the right. Make a bar graph of the data. **See margin.**

Hours of Sleep					
Alana	8	Kwam	7.5	Tomás	7.75
Nick	8.25	Kate	7.25	Sharla	8.5

7. Marcus started a lawn care service. The chart shows how much money he made over the 15 weeks of summer break. Make a line graph of the data. **See margin.**

Lawn Care Profits ($)								
Week	1	2	3	4	5	6	7	8
Profit	25	40	45	50	75	85	95	95
Week	9	10	11	12	13	14	15	
Profit	125	140	135	150	165	165	175	

8. The frequency table at the right shows the ages of people attending a high school play. Make a bar graph to display the data. **See margin.**

Age	Tally	Frequency
under 20	IIII IIII IIII IIII IIII IIII IIII IIII IIII II	47
20–39	IIII IIII IIII IIII IIII IIII IIII IIII IIII III	43
40–59	IIII IIII IIII IIII IIII IIII I	31
60 and over	IIII III	8

6.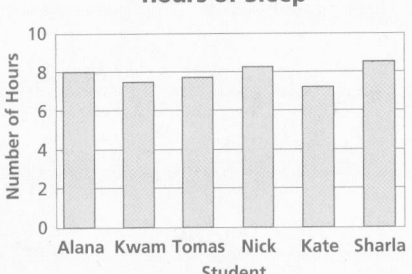

7.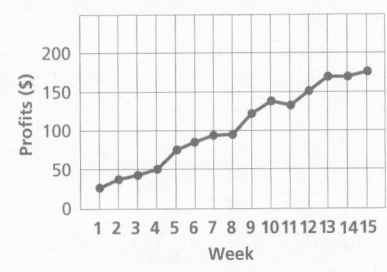

8.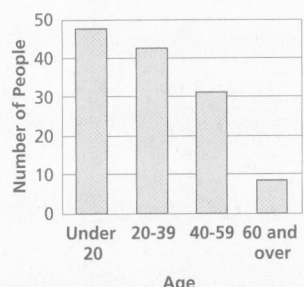

⑥ Making Circle Graphs

A **circle graph** is a graph that shows the relationship between parts of the data and the whole. The circle represents the total data. Individual data are represented by parts of the circle. The examples show how to construct a circle graph.

Example 1 The table shows the percent of her income that Ms. Garcia spends in each category. Make a circle graph to represent the data.

How Ms. Garcia Spends Her Money	
Category	Amount Spent
Savings	10%
Car Payment/Insurance	20%
Food	20%
Clothing	10%
Rent	30%
Other	10%

Step 1 Find the number of degrees for each category. Since there are 360° in a circle, multiply each percent by 360 to find the number of degrees for each section of the graph.

Savings, Clothing, Other

$$10\% \text{ of } 360° = 0.1 \cdot 360°$$
$$= 36°$$

The sections for Savings, Clothing, and Other are each 36°.

Car Payment, Food

$$20\% \text{ of } 360° = 0.2 \cdot 360°$$
$$= 72°$$

The sections for Car Payment and Food are each 72°.

Rent

$$30\% \text{ of } 360° = 0.3 \cdot 360°$$
$$= 108°$$

The section for Rent is 108°.

Step 2 Use a compass to draw a circle. Then draw a radius.

Step 3 Use a protractor to draw a 36° angle to make the section representing Savings. (You can start with any angle.)

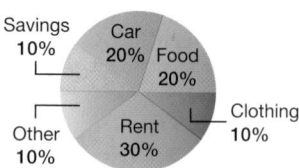

Step 4 Repeat for the remaining sections.

Step 5 Label each section of the graph with the category and percent. Give the graph a title.

How Ms. Garcia Spends her Money

Savings 10% · Car 20% · Food 20% · Clothing 10% · Other 10% · Rent 30%

Example 2

The table shows how Jessie uses her time on a typical Saturday. Make a circle graph of the data.

First find the ratio that compares each number of hours to the total number of hours in a day, 24.

Activity	Hours
Jogging	1
Reading	2
Sleeping	9
Eating	2
Talking on the Phone	1
Time with Friends and Family	4
Studying	5

Jogging: $\frac{1}{24}$ Reading: $\frac{2}{24}$ Sleeping: $\frac{9}{24}$ Eating: $\frac{2}{24}$

Phone: $\frac{1}{24}$ Friends: $\frac{4}{24}$ Studying: $\frac{5}{24}$

Then multiply each ratio by 360 to find the number of degrees for each section of the graph.

Jogging, Phone: $\frac{1}{24} \cdot 360° = 15°$

Reading, Eating: $\frac{2}{24} \cdot 360° = 30°$

Sleeping: $\frac{9}{24} \cdot 360° = 135°$

Friends: $\frac{4}{24} \cdot 360° = 60°$

Studying: $\frac{5}{24} \cdot 360° = 75°$

Make the circle graph.

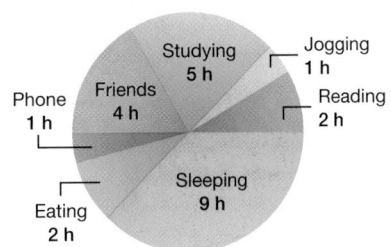

Saturday Time Use

Studying 5 h · Jogging 1 h · Reading 2 h · Sleeping 9 h · Eating 2 h · Phone 1 h · Friends 4 h

Exercises

1. The table at the right shows the percent of the world's population living in each continent or region. Make a circle graph of the data. **See margin.**

World Population, 2000	
Continent or Region	**Percent of World Total, 2000**
North America	7.9%
South America	5.7%
Europe	12.0%
Asia	60.7%
Africa	13.2%
Australia	0.5%
Antarctica	0%

Source: U.S. Census Bureau

2. The number of bones in each part of the human body is shown in the table at the right. Make a circle graph of the data. **See margin.**

Types of Human Bones	Number
Skull	29
Spine	26
Ribs and Breastbone	25
Shoulders, Arms, and Hands	64
Pelvis, Legs, and Feet	62

1. World Population, 2000

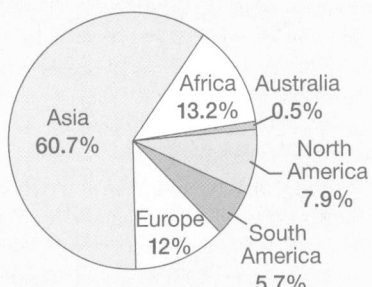

Asia 60.7% · Africa 13.2% · Australia 0.5% · North America 7.9% · South America 5.7% · Europe 12%

2. Bones in the Human Body

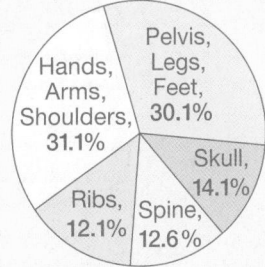

Hands, Arms, Shoulders, 31.1% · Pelvis, Legs, Feet, 30.1% · Skull, 14.1% · Spine, 12.6% · Ribs, 12.1%

❼ *Identifying Two-Dimensional Figures*

- Two-dimensional figures can be classified by the number of sides.

Number of Sides	Figure
3	**Tri**angle
4	**Quadri**lateral
5	**Pent**agon
6	**Hex**agon
8	**Oct**agon

← The prefixes tell the number of sides.

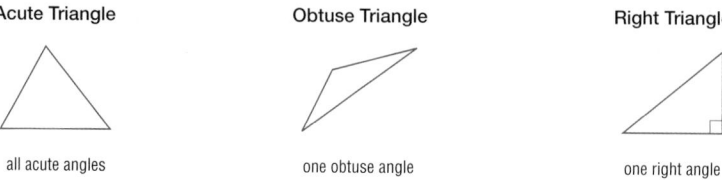

Triangle   Quadrilateral   Pentagon   Hexagon   Octagon

- Triangles can be classified by their angles. An **acute** angle measures less than 90°. An **obtuse** angle measures more than 90°. A **right** angle measures exactly 90°.

Acute Triangle

all acute angles

Obtuse Triangle

one obtuse angle

Right Triangle

one right angle

- Triangles can also be classified by their sides. Recall that **congruent** means having the same measure. Matching marks are used to show congruent parts.

Scalene Triangle

no sides congruent

Isosceles Triangle

at least two sides congruent

Equilateral Triangle

all sides congruent

Example

Classify each triangle using all names that apply.

a.

b.

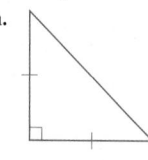

The triangle has one right angle and two congruent sides. It is a right isosceles triangle.

The triangle has one obtuse angle and no congruent sides. It is an obtuse scalene triangle.

- The diagram below shows how quadrilaterals are classified. Notice that the diagram goes from most general to most specific.

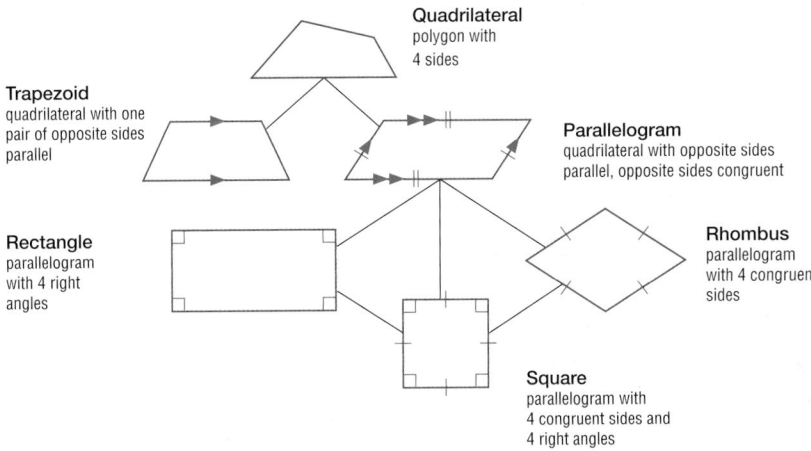

Quadrilateral
polygon with 4 sides

Trapezoid
quadrilateral with one pair of opposite sides parallel

Parallelogram
quadrilateral with opposite sides parallel, opposite sides congruent

Rectangle
parallelogram with 4 right angles

Rhombus
parallelogram with 4 congruent sides

Square
parallelogram with 4 congruent sides and 4 right angles

Exercises **Classify each figure using all names that apply.**

1. 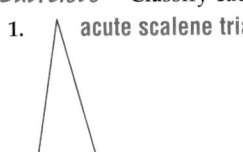 acute scalene triangle

2. 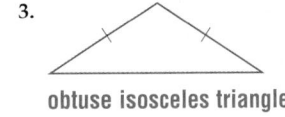 acute equilateral triangle

3. 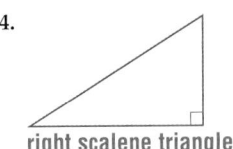 obtuse isosceles triangle

4. 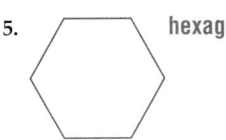 right scalene triangle

5. hexagon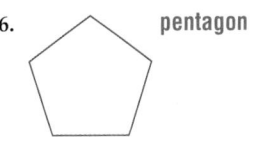

6. pentagon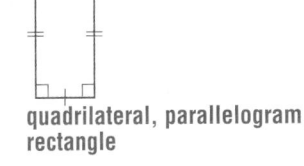

7. 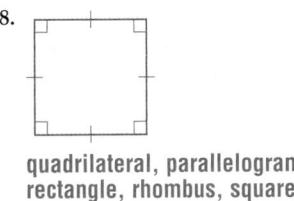 quadrilateral, parallelogram, rectangle

8. 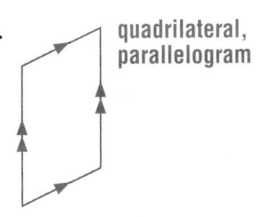 quadrilateral, parallelogram, rectangle, rhombus, square

9. 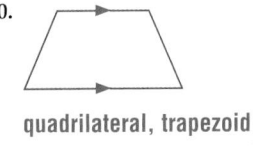 quadrilateral, parallelogram

10. 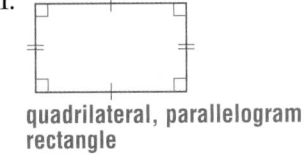 quadrilateral, trapezoid

11.  quadrilateral, parallelogram, rectangle

12. 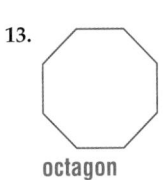 quadrilateral, parallelogram, rhombus

13. 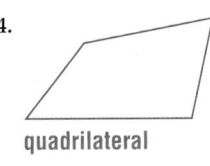 octagon

14. 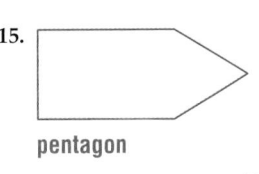 quadrilateral

15. pentagon

❽ Identifying Three-Dimensional Figures

Prisms and pyramids are two types of three-dimensional figures. A **prism** has two parallel, congruent faces called **bases**. A **pyramid** has one base that is a polygon and faces that are triangles.

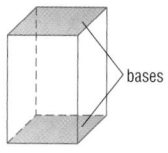
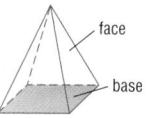

Prism   Pyramid

Prisms and pyramids are named by the shape of their bases.

Name	triangular prism	rectangular prism	triangular pyramid	rectangular pyramid
Number of Bases	2	2	1	1
Polygon Base	triangle	rectangle	triangle	rectangle
Figure	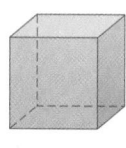			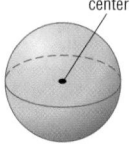

A **cube** is a rectangular prism in which all of the faces are squares.

A **cone** is a shape in space that has a circular base and one **vertex**.

A **sphere** is the set of all points a given distance from a given point called the center.

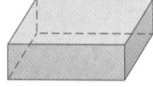

Cube

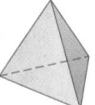

Cone

center

Sphere

Exercises   Classify each solid figure using the name that *best* describes it.

1.

rectangular prism

2.

triangular pyramid

3.

sphere

4.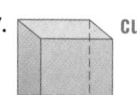

triangular prism

5.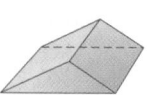

rectangular pyramid

6.  cone

7. 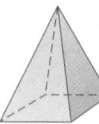 cube

8. triangular prism

9. rectangular pyramid

⑨ Perimeter and Area of Squares and Rectangles

Perimeter is the distance around a geometric figure. Perimeter is measured in linear units.

- To find the perimeter of a rectangle, multiply two times the sum of the length and width, or $2(\ell + w)$.

- To find the perimeter of a square, multiply four times the length of a side, or $4s$.

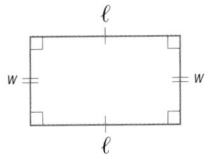
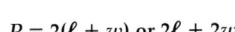
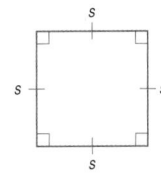

$$P = 2(\ell + w) \text{ or } 2\ell + 2w \qquad\qquad P = 4s$$

Area is the number of square units needed to cover a surface. Area is measured in square units.

- To find the area of a rectangle, multiply the length times the width, or $\ell \cdot w$.

- To find the area of a square, find the square of the length of a side, or s^2.

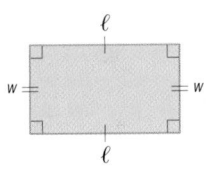
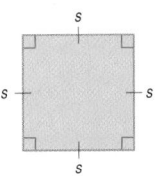

$$A = \ell w \qquad\qquad\qquad A = s^2$$

Example 1   **Find the perimeter and area of each rectangle.**

a. A rectangle has a length of 3 units and a width of 5 units.

$$
\begin{aligned}
P &= 2(\ell + w) && \text{Perimeter formula} \\
&= 2(3 + 5) && \text{Replace } \ell \text{ with 3 and } w \text{ with 5.} \\
&= 2(8) && \text{Add.} \\
&= 16 && \text{Multiply.}
\end{aligned}
$$

$$
\begin{aligned}
A &= \ell \cdot w && \text{Area formula} \\
&= 3 \cdot 5 && \text{Replace } \ell \text{ with 3 and } w \text{ with 5.} \\
&= 15 && \text{Simplify.}
\end{aligned}
$$

The perimeter is 16 units, and the area is 15 square units.

b. A rectangle has a length of 1 inch and a width of 10 inches.

$$
\begin{aligned}
P &= 2(\ell + w) && \text{Perimeter formula} \\
&= 2(1 + 10) && \text{Replace } \ell \text{ with 1 and } w \text{ with 10.} \\
&= 2(11) && \text{Add.} \\
&= 22 && \text{Multiply.}
\end{aligned}
$$

$$
\begin{aligned}
A &= \ell \cdot w && \text{Area formula} \\
&= 1 \cdot 10 && \text{Replace } \ell \text{ with 1 and } w \text{ with 10.} \\
&= 10 && \text{Simplify.}
\end{aligned}
$$

The perimeter is 22 inches, and the area is 10 square inches.

Example 2 Find the perimeter and area of each square.

a. A square has a side of length 8 feet.

$P = 4s$ Perimeter formula

    $= 4(8)$ $s = 8$

    $= 32$ Multiply.

$A = s^2$ Area formula

    $= 8^2$ $s = 8$

    $= 64$ Multiply.

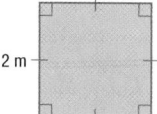
8 ft

The perimeter is 32 feet, and the area is 64 square feet.

b. A square has a side of length 2 meters.

$P = 4s$ Perimeter formula

    $= 4(2)$ $s = 2$

    $= 8$ Multiply.

$A = s^2$ Area formula

    $= 2^2$ $s = 2$

    $= 4$ Multiply.

2 m

The perimeter is 8 meters, and the area is 4 square meters.

Exercises **Find the perimeter and area of each figure.**

1. 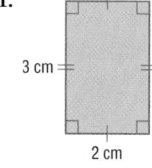 $P = 10$ cm; $A = 6$ cm^2

3 cm

2 cm

2. 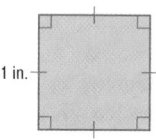 $P = 4$ in.; $A = 1$ in^2

1 in.

3.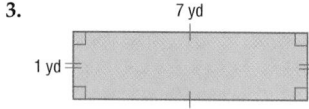

7 yd

1 yd

$P = 16$ yd; $A = 7$ yd^2

4. 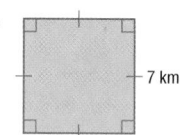 $P = 28$ km; $A = 49$ km^2

7 km

5. a rectangle with length 6 feet and width 4 feet $P = 20$ ft; $A = 24$ ft^2

6. a rectangle with length 12 centimeters and width 9 centimeters $P = 42$ cm; $A = 108$ cm^2

7. a square with length 3 meters $P = 12$ m; $A = 9$ m^2

8. a square with length 15 inches $P = 60$ in.; $A = 225$ in^2

9. a rectangle with width $8\frac{1}{2}$ inches and length 11 inches $P = 39$ in.; $A = 93\frac{1}{2}$ in^2

10. a rectangular room with width $12\frac{1}{4}$ feet and length $14\frac{1}{2}$ feet $P = 53\frac{1}{2}$ ft; $A = 177\frac{5}{8}$ ft^2

11. a square with length 2.4 centimeters $P = 9.6$ cm; $A = 5.76$ cm^2

12. a square garden with length 5.8 meters $P = 23.2$ m; $A = 33.64$ m^2

13. RECREATION The Granville Parks and Recreation Department uses an empty city lot for a community vegetable garden. Each participant is allotted a space of 18 feet by 90 feet for a garden. What is the perimeter and area of each plot?   216 ft; 1620 ft^2

⑩ Area and Circumference of Circles

A **circle** is the set of all points in a plane that are the same distance from a given point.

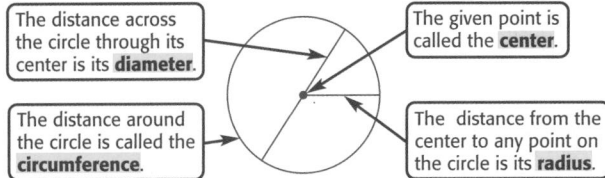

The distance across the circle through its center is its **diameter**.

The given point is called the **center**.

The distance around the circle is called the **circumference**.

The distance from the center to any point on the circle is its **radius**.

- The formula for the circumference of a circle is $C = \pi d$ or $C = 2\pi r$.

Example 1 Find the circumference of each circle.

a. The radius is 3 feet.

Use the formula $C = 2\pi r$.

$$C = 2\pi r \quad \text{Write the formula.}$$
$$= 2\pi(3) \quad \text{Replace } r \text{ with 3.}$$
$$= 6\pi \quad \text{Simplify.}$$

The exact circumference is 6π feet.

6 [π] [ENTER]   18.84955592

To the nearest tenth, the circumference is 18.8 feet.

b. The diameter is 24 centimeters.

Use the formula $C = \pi d$.

$$C = \pi d \quad \text{Write the formula.}$$
$$= \pi(24) \quad \text{Replace } d \text{ with 24.}$$
$$= 24\pi \quad \text{Simplify.}$$
$$\approx 75.4 \quad \text{Use a calculator to evaluate } 24\pi.$$

The circumference is about 75.4 centimeters.

- The formula for the area of a circle is $A = \pi r^2$.

Example 2 Find the area of each circle to the nearest tenth.

a. The radius is 4 inches.

$$A = \pi r^2 \quad \text{Write the formula.}$$
$$= \pi(4)^2 \quad \text{Replace } r \text{ with 4.}$$
$$= 16\pi \quad \text{Simplify.}$$
$$\approx 50.3 \quad \text{Use a calculator to evaluate } 16\pi.$$

The area of the circle is about 50.3 square inches.

b. The diameter is 20 centimeters.

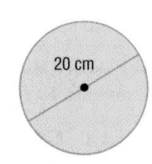

The radius is one-half times the diameter, or 10 centimeters.

$$A = \pi r^2 \quad \text{Write the formula.}$$
$$= \pi(10)^2 \quad \text{Replace } r \text{ with 10.}$$
$$= 100\pi \quad \text{Simplify.}$$
$$\approx 314.2 \quad \text{Use a calculator to evaluate } 100\pi.$$

The area of the circle is about 314.2 square centimeters.

Example 3 **HISTORY** Stonehenge is an ancient monument in Wiltshire, England. Historians are not sure who erected Stonehenge or why. It may have been used as a calendar. The giant stones of Stonehenge are arranged in a circle 30 meters in diameter. Find the circumference and the area of the circle.

$C = \pi d$ Write the formula.

$= \pi(30)$ Replace d with 30.

$= 30\pi$ Simplify.

≈ 94.2 Use a calculator to evaluate 30π.

Find the radius to evaluate the formula for the area. The radius is one-half times the diameter, or 15 meters.

$A = \pi r^2$ Write the formula.

$= \pi(15)^2$ Replace r with 15.

$= 225\pi$ Simplify.

≈ 706.9 Use a calculator to evaluate 225π.

The circumference of Stonehenge is about 94.2 meters, and the area is about 706.9 square meters.

Exercises   **Find the circumference of each circle. Round to the nearest tenth.**

1.   **18.8 m**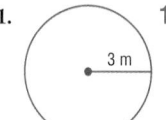

2.   **31.4 in.**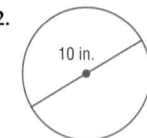

3.   **75.4 cm**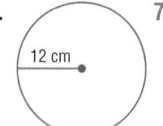

4. The radius is 1.5 kilometers. **9.4 km**

5. The diameter is 1 yard. **3.1 yd**

6. The diameter is $5\frac{1}{4}$ feet. **16.5 ft**

7. The radius is $24\frac{1}{2}$ inches. **153.9 in.**

Find the area of each circle. Round to the nearest tenth.

8.   **78.5 in²**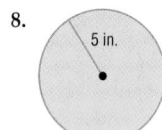

9.   **12.6 ft²**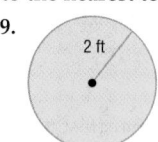

10.   **3.1 km²**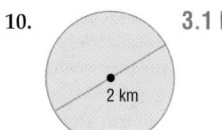

11. The diameter is 4 yards. **12.6 yd²**

12. The radius is 1 meter. **3.1 m²**

13. The radius is 1.5 feet. **7.1 ft²**

14. The diameter is 15 centimeters. **176.7 cm²**

15. **GEOGRAPHY** Earth's circumference is approximately 25,000 miles. If you could dig a tunnel to the center of the Earth, how long would the tunnel be? **about 3979 mi**

16. **CYCLING** The tire for a 10-speed bicycle has a diameter of 27 inches. Find the distance the bicycle will travel in 10 rotations of the tire. **about 848.2 in.**

17. **PUBLIC SAFETY** The Belleville City Council is considering installing a new tornado warning system. The sound emitted from the siren would be heard for a 2-mile radius. Find the area of the region that will benefit from the system. **about 13 mi²**

18. **CITY PLANNING** The circular region inside the streets at DuPont Circle in Washington, D.C., is 250 feet across. How much area do the grass and sidewalk cover? **about 49,087.4 ft²**

⑪ Volume

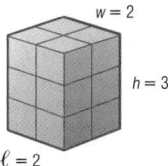

Volume is the measure of space occupied by a solid. Volume is measured in cubic units. The prism at the right has a volume of 12 cubic units.

- To find the volume of a rectangular prism, use the formula $V = \ell \cdot w \cdot h$. Stated in words, volume equals length times width times height.

Example

Find the volume of the rectangular prism.

A rectangular prism has a height of 3 feet, width of 4 feet, and length of 2 feet.

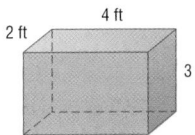

$V = \ell \cdot w \cdot h$ Write the formula.

$V = 2 \cdot 4 \cdot 3$ Replace ℓ with 2, w with 4, and h with 3.

$V = 24$ Simplify.

The volume is 24 cubic feet.

Exercises   **Find the volume of each rectangular prism given the length, width, and height.**

1. $\ell = 2$ in., $w = 5$ in., $h = \frac{1}{2}$ in. **5 in³**

2. $\ell = 12$ cm, $w = 3$ cm, $h = 2$ cm **72 cm³**

3. $\ell = 6$ yd, $w = 2$ yd, $h = 1$ yd **12 yd³**

4. $\ell = 100$ m, $w = 1$ m, $h = 10$ m **1000 m³**

Find the volume of each rectangular prism.

5. **20 m³**

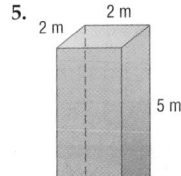

6. **144 in³**

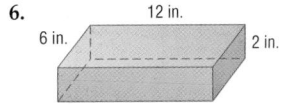

7. **AQUARIUMS**   An aquarium is 8 feet long, 5 feet wide, and 5.5 feet deep. What is the volume of the tank? **220 ft³**

8. **COOKING**   What is the volume of a microwave oven that is 18 inches wide by 10 inches long with a depth of $11\frac{1}{2}$ inches? **2070 in³**

9. **GEOMETRY**   A cube measures 2 meters on a side. What is its volume? **8 m³**

FIREWOOD   For Exercises 10–12, use the following.
Firewood is usually sold by a measure known as a cord. A full cord may be a stack $8 \times 4 \times 4$ feet or a stack $8 \times 8 \times 2$ feet.

10. What is the volume of a full cord of firewood? **128 ft³**

11. A "short cord" or "face cord" of wood is $8 \times 4 \times$ the length of the logs. What is the volume of a short cord of $2\frac{1}{2}$-foot logs? **80 ft³**

12. If you have an area that is 12 feet long and 2 feet wide in which to store your firewood, how high will the stack be if it is a full cord of wood? **5 ft 4 in.**

⑫ Mean, Median, and Mode

Measures of central tendency are numbers used to represent a set of data. Three types of measures of central tendency are mean, median, and mode.

- The **mean** is the sum of the numbers in a set of data divided by the number of items.

Example 1 Katherine is running a lemonade stand. She made $3.50 on Tuesday, $4.00 on Wednesday, $5.00 on Thursday, and $4.50 on Friday. What was her mean daily profit?

$$\text{mean} = \frac{\text{sum of daily profits}}{\text{number of days}}$$

$$= \frac{\$3.50 + \$4.00 + \$5.00 + \$4.50}{4}$$

$$= \frac{\$17.00}{4} \text{ or } \$4.25$$

Katherine's mean daily profit was $4.25.

- The **median** is the middle number in a set of data when the data are arranged in numerical order. If there are an even number of data, the median is the mean of the two middle numbers.

- The **mode** is the number or numbers that appear most often in a set of data. If no item appears most often, the set has no mode.

Example 2 The table shows the number of hits Marcus made for his team. Find the median of the data.

To find the median, order the numbers from least to greatest. The median is in the middle.

2, 3, 3, 5, 6, 7

$$\frac{3+5}{2} = 4$$

There is an even number of items. Find the mean of the middle two.

The median number of hits is 4.

Team Played	Number of Hits by Marcus
Badgers	3
Hornets	6
Bulldogs	5
Vikings	2
Rangers	3
Panthers	7

Example 3 The table shows the heights of the members of the 2001–2002 University of Kentucky Men's Basketball team. What is the mode of the heights?

The mode is the number that occurs most frequently. 74 occurs three times, 81 occurs twice, and all the other heights occur once. The mode height is 74.

Player	Height (in.)
Blevins	74
Bogans	77
Camara	83
Daniels	79
Estill	81
Fitch	75
Hawkins	73
Heissenbuttel	76
Parker	80
Prince	81
Sears	78
Smith	74
Stone	82
Tackett	74

Source: ESPN

- You can use measures of central tendency to solve problems.

Example 4

On her first five history tests, Yoko received the following scores: 82, 96, 92, 83, and 91. What test score must Yoko earn on the sixth test so that her average (mean) for all six tests will be 90%?

$$\text{mean} = \frac{\text{sum of the first five scores} + \text{sixth score}}{6}$$ Write an equation.

$$90 = \frac{82 + 96 + 92 + 83 + 91 + x}{6}$$ Use x to represent the sixth score.

$$90 = \frac{444 + x}{6}$$ Simplify.

$$540 = 444 + x$$ Multiply each side by 6.

$$96 = x$$ Subtract 444 from each side.

To have an average score of 90, Yoko must earn a 96 on the sixth test.

Exercises Find the mean, median, and mode for each set of data. **6. 200; 200; 201, and 199**

1. {1, 2, 3, 5, 5, 6, 13} **5; 5; 5**
2. {3, 5, 8, 1, 4, 11, 3} **5; 4; 3**
3. {52, 53, 53, 53, 55, 55, 57} **54; 53; 53**
4. {8, 7, 5, 19} **9.75; 7.5; no mode**
5. {3, 11, 26, 4, 1} **9; 4; no mode**
6. {201, 201, 200, 199, 199}
7. {4, 5, 6, 7, 8} **6; 6; no mode**
8. {3, 7, 21, 23, 63, 27, 29, 95, 23} **$32\frac{1}{3}$; 23, 23**

9. **SCHOOL** The table shows the cost of some school supplies. Find the mean, median, and mode costs.
mean: $2.50, median: $2.25, mode: $2.00

Cost of School Supplies	
Supply	**Cost**
Pencils	$0.50
Pens	$2.00
Paper	$2.00
Pocket Folder	$1.25
Calculator	$5.25
Notebook	$3.00
Erasers	$2.50
Markers	$3.50

10. **NUTRITION** The table shows the number of servings of fruits and vegetables that Cole eats one week. Find the mean, median, and mode.
mean: 5, median: 5, mode: 3 and 5

Cole's Fruits and Vegetable Servings	
Day	**Number of Servings**
Monday	5
Tuesday	7
Wednesday	5
Thursday	4
Friday	3
Saturday	3
Sunday	8

11. **TELEVISION RATINGS** The ratings for the top television programs during one week are shown in the table at the right. Find the mean, median, and mode of the ratings. Round to the nearest hundredth. **13.45; 13.2; 11.4**

12. **EDUCATION** Bill's scores on his first four science tests are 86, 90, 84, and 91. What test score must Bill earn on the fifth test so that his average (mean) will be exactly 88? **89**

13. **BOWLING** Sue's average for 9 games of bowling is 108. What is the lowest score she can receive for the tenth game to have an average of 110? **128**

14. **EDUCATION** Olivia has an average score of 92 on five French tests. If she earns a score of 96 on the sixth test, what will her new average score be? **92.7**

Network Primetime Television Ratings	
Program	**Rating**
1	17.6
2	16.0
3	14.1
4	13.7
5	13.5
6	12.9
7	12.3
8	11.6
9	11.4
10	11.4

Source: Nielsen Media Research

Extra Practice

Lesson 1-1

(pages 6–9)

Write an algebraic expression for each verbal expression.

1. the sum of b and 21 $b + 21$
2. the product of x and 7 $7x$
3. a number t increased by 6 $t + 6$
4. the sum of 4 and 6 times a number z $4 + 6z$
5. -10 increased by 4 times a number a $-10 + 4a$
6. the sum of 8 and -2 times n $8 + (-2n)$
7. one-half the cube of a number x $\frac{1}{2}x^3$
8. four-fifths the square of m $\frac{4}{5}m^2$

Evaluate each expression.

9. 2^4 **16**
10. 10^2 **100**
11. 7^3 **343**
12. 20^3 **8000**
13. 3^6 **729**
14. 4^5 **1024**

15–23. Sample answers given.

Write a verbal expression for each algebraic expression. 19. five times n squared minus 6

15. $2n$ 2 times n
16. 10^7 ten to the seventh power
17. m^5 m to the fifth power
18. xy the product of x and y
19. $5n^2 - 6$
20. $9a^3 + 1$ nine times a cubed plus 1
21. $x^3 \cdot y^2$ x cubed times y squared
22. $c^4 \cdot d^6$ c to the fourth power times d to the sixth power
23. $3e + 2e^2$ 3 times e plus 2 times e squared

Lesson 1-2

(pages 11–15)

Evaluate each expression.

1. $3 + 8 \div 2 - 5$ **2**
2. $4 + 7 \cdot 2 + 8$ **26**
3. $5(9 + 3) - 3 \cdot 4$ **48**
4. $9 - 3^2$ **0**
5. $(8 - 1) \cdot 3$ **21**
6. $4(5 - 3)^2$ **16**
7. $3(12 + 3) - 5 \cdot 9$ **0**
8. $5^3 + 6^3 - 5^2$ **316**
9. $16 \div 2 \cdot 5 \cdot 3 \div 6$ **20**
10. $7(5^3 + 3^2)$ **938**
11. $\frac{9 \cdot 4 + 2 \cdot 6}{6 \cdot 4}$ **2**
12. $25 - \frac{1}{3}(18 + 9)$ **16**

Evaluate each expression if $a = 2$, $b = 5$, $x = 4$, and $n = 10$.

13. $8a + b$ **21**
14. $48 + ab$ **58**
15. $a(6 - 3n)$ **−48**
16. $bx + an$ **40**
17. $x^2 - 4n$ **−24**
18. $3b + 16a - 9n$ **−43**
19. $n^2 + 3(a + 4)$ **118'**
20. $(2x)^2 + an - 5b$ **59**
21. $[a + 8(b - 2)]^2 \div 4$ **169**

Lesson 1-3

(pages 16–20)

Find the solution of each equation if the replacement sets are $x = \{0, 2, 4, 6, 8\}$ and $y = \{1, 3, 5, 7, 9\}$.

1. $x - 4 = 4$ **8**
2. $25 - y = 18$ **7**
3. $3x + 1 = 25$ **8**
4. $5y - 4 = 11$ **3**
5. $14 = \frac{96}{x} + 2$ **8**
6. $0 = \frac{y}{3} - 3$ **9**

Solve each equation.

7. $x = \frac{27 + 9}{2}$ **18**
8. $\frac{18 - 7}{13 - 2} = y$ **1**
9. $n = \frac{6(5) + 3}{2(4) + 3}$ **3**
10. $\frac{5(4) - 6}{2^2 + 3} = z$ **2**
11. $\frac{7^2 + 9(2 + 1)}{2(10) - 1} = t$ **4**
12. $a = \frac{3^3 + 5^2}{2(3 - 1)}$ **13**

Find the solution set for each inequality if the replacement sets are $x = \{4, 5, 6, 7, 8\}$ and $y = \{10, 12, 14, 16\}$.

13. $x + 2 > 7$ **{6, 7, 8}**
14. $x - 1 < 8$ **{4, 5, 6, 7, 8}**
15. $2x \leq 15$ **{4, 5, 6, 7}**
16. $3y \geq 36$ **{12, 14, 16}**
17. $\frac{x}{3} < 2$ **{4, 5}**
18. $\frac{5y}{4} \geq 20$ **{16}**

Lesson 1-4

Name the property used in each equation. Then find the value of n.

1. $4 \cdot 3 = 4 \cdot n$ **Reflexive Prop.; 3**

2. $\frac{5}{4} = n + 0$ **Additive Identity; $\frac{5}{4}$**

3. $15 = 15 \cdot n$ **Multiplicative Identity; 1**

4. $\frac{2}{3}n = 1$ **Multiplicative Inverse; $\frac{3}{2}$**

5. $2.7 + 1.3 = 2.7 + n$ **Reflexive Prop.; 1.3**

6. $n\left(6^2 \cdot \frac{1}{36}\right) = 4$ **Multiplicative Identity and Multiplicative Inverse; 4**

7. $8n = 0$ **Multiplicative Prop. of 0; 0**

8. $n = \frac{1}{9} \cdot 9$ **Multiplicative Inverse; 1**

9. $5 + 7 = 5 + n$ **Reflexive Prop.; 7**

10. $(13 - 4)(2) = 9n$ **Substitution; 2**

Evaluate each expression. Name the property used in each step. **11–13. See margin.**

11. $\frac{2}{3}[15 \div (12 - 2)]$

12. $\frac{7}{4}\left[4 \cdot \left(\frac{1}{8} \cdot 8\right)\right]$

13. $[(18 \div 3) \cdot 0] \cdot 10$

Lesson 1-5 1–9. See margin for expressions.

Rewrite each expression using the Distributive Property. Then simplify.

1. $5(2 + 9)$ **55**
2. $8(10 + 20)$ **240**
3. $20(8 - 3)$ **100**
4. $3(5 + w)$ **$15 + 3w$**
5. $(h - 8)7$ **$7h - 56$**
6. $6(y + 4)$ **$6y + 24$**
7. $9(3n + 5)$ **$27n + 45$**
8. $32\left(x - \frac{1}{8}\right)$ **$32x - 4$**
9. $c(7 - d)$ **$7c - cd$**

Use the Distributive Property to find each product.

10. $6 \cdot 55$ **330**
11. $15(108)$ **1620**
12. $1689 \cdot 5$ **8445**
13. 7×314 **2198**
14. $36\left(5\frac{1}{4}\right)$ **189**
15. $\left(4\frac{1}{18}\right) \cdot 18$ **73**

Simplify each expression. If not possible, write *simplified*.

16. $13a + 5a$ **$18a$**
17. $21x - 10x$ **$11x$**
18. $8(3x + 7)$ **$24x + 56$**
19. $4m - 4n$ **simplified**
20. $3(5am - 4)$ **$15am - 12$**
21. $15x^2 + 7x^2$ **$22x^2$**
22. $9y^2 + 13y^2 + 3$ **$22y^2 + 3$**
23. $11a^2 - 11a^2 + 12a^2$ **$12a^2$**
24. $6a + 7a + 12b + 8b$ **$13a + 20b$**

Lesson 1-6

Evaluate each expression.

1. $23 + 8 + 37 + 12$ **80**
2. $19 + 46 + 81 + 54$ **200**
3. $10.25 + 2.5 + 3.75$ **16.5**
4. $22.5 + 17.6 + 44.5$ **84.6**
5. $2\frac{1}{3} + 6 + 3\frac{2}{3} + 4$ **16**
6. $5\frac{6}{7} + 15 + 4\frac{1}{7} + 25$ **50**
7. $6 \cdot 8 \cdot 5 \cdot 3$ **720**
8. $18 \cdot 5 \cdot 2 \cdot 5$ **900**
9. $0.25 \cdot 7 \cdot 8$ **14**
10. $90 \cdot 12 \cdot 0.5$ **540**
11. $5\frac{1}{3} \cdot 4 \cdot 6$ **128**
12. $4\frac{5}{6} \cdot 10 \cdot 12$ **580**

Simplify each expression. **15. $3a + 13b + 2c$** **22. $-11 + 3uv + u$** **24. $11.8a + 8.8b$**

13. $5a + 6b + 7a$ **$12a + 6b$**
14. $8x + 4y + 9x$ **$17x + 4y$**
15. $3a + 5b + 2c + 8b$
16. $\frac{2}{3}x^2 + 5x + x^2$ **$\frac{5}{3}x^2 + 5x$**
17. $(4p - 7q) + (5q - 8p)$ **$-4p - 2q$**
18. $8q + 5r - 7q - 6r$ **$q - r$**
19. $4(2x + y) + 5x$ **$13x + 4y$**
20. $9r^5 + 2r^2 + r^5$ **$10r^5 + 2r^2$**
21. $12b^3 + 12 + 12b^3$ **$24b^3 + 12$**
22. $7 + 3(uv - 6) + u$
23. $3(x + 2y) + 4(3x + y)$ **$15x + 10y$**
24. $6.2(a + b) + 2.6(a + b) + 3a$
25. $3 + 8(st + 3w) + 3st$ **$3 + 11st + 24w$**
26. $5.4(s - 3t) + 3.6(s - 4)$ **$9s - 16.2t - 14.4$**
27. $3[4 + 5(2x + 3y)]$ **$12 + 30x + 45y$**

Lesson 1-4

11. $\frac{2}{3}[15 \div (10)]$, Substitution; $\frac{2}{3}\left(\frac{3}{2}\right)$, Substitution; 1, Multiplicative Inverse

12. $\frac{7}{4}[4 \cdot 1]$, Multiplicative Inverse; $\frac{7}{4}(4)$, Multiplicative Identity; 7, Substitution

13. $[(6) \cdot 0] \cdot 10$, Substitution; $(0) \cdot 10$, Multiplicative Prop. of 0; 0, Multiplicative Prop. of 0

Lesson 1-7

1. hypothesis: an animal is a dog; conclusion: it barks

2. hypothesis: a figure is a pentagon; conclusion: it has five sides

3. hypothesis: $3x - 1 = 8$; conclusion: $x = 3$

4. hypothesis: 0.5 is the reciprocal of 2; conclusion: $0.5 \cdot 2 = 1$

5. hypothesis: a figure is a square; conclusion: it has four congruent sides; If a figure is a square, then it has four congruent sides.

6. hypothesis: $a = 4$; conclusion: $6a + 10 = 34$; If $a = 4$, then $6a + 10 = 34$.

7. hypothesis: it is night; conclusion: the video store is open; If it is night, then the video store is open.

8. hypothesis: it is Thursday; conclusion: the band does not have practice; If it is Thursday, then the band does not have practice.

9. It can snow in May in some locations.

10. You may live in Portland, Maine.

11. If $y = 3$, then $2y + 4 = 10$, is true, but $y < 3$ is false.

12. Sample answer: $a = -1$

Lesson 1-8

1. Sample answer: The temperatures increase from January through the summer and then begin to decrease again.

2. Sample answer: The roller coaster goes down a small hill, coasts at about the same speed, increases in speed on the way down the hill, decreases again on the way up the hill, increases down another hill, and then slows down for the end of the ride.

3. Sample answer: The jogger increases in speed, runs about the same speed, increases again, runs at a faster pace for a while, decreases, maintains a speed, and finally slows down at the finish of the run.

4. Sample answer: The hiker walks away from the camp, stops for a rest, hikes a little further, and then returns to camp.

Lesson 1-7

(pages 37–42)

Identify the hypothesis and conclusion of each statement. 1–4. See margin.

1. If an animal is a dog, then it barks.

2. If a figure is a pentagon, then it has five sides.

3. If $3x - 1 = 8$, then $x = 3$.

4. If 0.5 is the reciprocal of 2, then $0.5 \cdot 2 = 1$.

Identify the hypotheses and conclusion of each statement. Then write the statement in if-then form. 5–8. See margin.

5. A square has four congruent sides.

6. $6a + 10 = 34$ when $a = 4$.

7. The video store is open every night.

8. The band does not have practice on Thursday.

Find a counterexample for each statement. 9–12. See margin.

9. If the season is spring, then it does not snow.

10. If you live in Portland, then you live in Oregon.

11. If $2y + 4 = 10$, then $y < 3$.

12. If $a^2 > 0$, then $a > 0$.

Lesson 1-8

(pages 43–48)

Describe what is happening in each graph. 1–4. See margin.

1. The graph shows the average monthly high temperatures for a city over a one-year period.

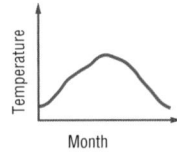

2. The graph shows the speed of a roller coaster car during a two-minute ride.

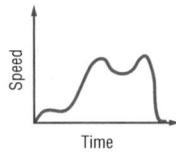

3. The graph shows the speed of a jogger over time.

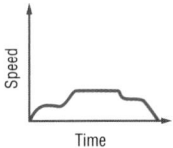

4. The graph shows the distance from camp traveled by a hiker over time.

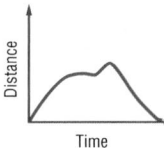

Lesson 1-9

(pages 50–55)

For Exercises 1–4, use the graph, which shows the five states that were the birthplace of the most U.S. presidents. 1–4. See margin.

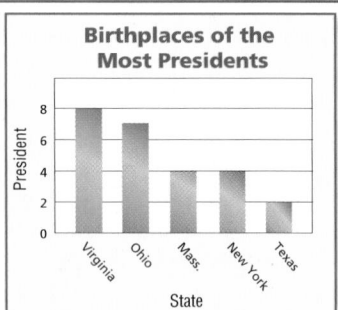

Birthplaces of the Most Presidents

1. How many times more presidents were born in Virginia than Texas?

2. Did any states have the same number of presidents? If so, which states?

3. Would it be appropriate to display this data in a circle graph? Explain.

4. By the year 2001, there had been forty-three different presidents. What percent of U.S. presidents at that time had been born in Ohio?

Lesson 1-9

1. 4 times

2. yes; Massachusetts and New York

3. No; you need to have the birthplaces of all presidents to compare parts to the whole in a circle graph.

4. about 16%

Lesson 2-1 (pages 68–72)

Name the coordinates of the points graphed on each number line. 1–6. See margin.

1.
```
+——+——+——+——+——+——+——+——+——+
-4  -3  -2  -1   0   1   2   3   4
```

2.
```
+——+——+——+——+——+——+——+——+——+——+
  -3  -2  -1   0   1   2   3   4   5   6
```

3.
```
+——+——+——+——+——+——+——+——+——+
-4  -3  -2  -1   0   1   2   3   4
```

4.
```
+——+——+——+——+——+——+——+——+——+——+
  5   6   7   8   9  10  11  12  13  14  15
```

5.
```
+——+——+——+——+——+——+——+——+——+——+
-9  -8  -7  -6  -5  -4  -3  -2  -1   0
```

6.
```
+——+——+——+——+——+——+——+——+——+——+——+
  -3  -2  -1   0   1   2   3   4   5   6   7
```

Graph each set of numbers. 7–10. See margin.

7. $\{-2, -4, -6\}$

8. $\{\ldots, -3, -2, -1, 0\}$

9. {integers greater than -1}

10. {integers less than -5 and greater than -10}

Find each absolute value.

11. $|22|$ **22**

12. $|-2.5|$ **2.5**

13. $\left|\dfrac{2}{3}\right|$ $\dfrac{2}{3}$

14. $\left|-\dfrac{7}{8}\right|$ $\dfrac{7}{8}$

Lesson 2-2 (pages 73–78)

Find each sum.

1. $3 + 16$ **19**

2. $-27 + 19$ **−8**

3. $8 + (-13)$ **−5**

4. $-14 + (-9)$ **−23**

5. $-25 + 47$ **22**

6. $97 + (-79)$ **18**

7. $-4.8 + 3.2$ **−1.6**

8. $-1.7 + (-3.4)$ **−5.1**

9. $-0.009 + 0.06$ **0.051**

10. $-\dfrac{11}{9} + \left(-\dfrac{7}{9}\right)$ **−2**

11. $-\dfrac{3}{5} + \dfrac{5}{6}$ $\dfrac{7}{30}$

12. $\dfrac{3}{8} + \left(-\dfrac{7}{12}\right)$ $-\dfrac{5}{24}$

Find each difference.

13. $27 - 14$ **13**

14. $8 - 17$ **−9**

15. $12 - (-15)$ **27**

16. $-35 - (-12)$ **−23**

17. $-2 - (-1.3)$ **−0.7**

18. $1.9 - (-7)$ **8.9**

19. $-4.5 - 8.6$ **−13.1**

20. $89.3 - (-14.2)$ **103.5**

21. $-18 - (-1.3)$ **−16.7**

22. $\dfrac{5}{11} - \dfrac{6}{11}$ $-\dfrac{1}{11}$

23. $\dfrac{2}{7} - \dfrac{3}{14}$ $\dfrac{1}{14}$

24. $-\dfrac{7}{15} - \left(-\dfrac{5}{12}\right)$ $-\dfrac{1}{20}$

Lesson 2-3 (pages 79–83)

Find each product.

1. $5(12)$ **60**

2. $(-6)(11)$ **−66**

3. $(-7)(-5)$ **35**

4. $(-6)(4)(-3)$ **72**

5. $\left(-\dfrac{7}{8}\right)\left(-\dfrac{1}{3}\right)$ $\dfrac{7}{24}$

6. $(5)\left(-\dfrac{2}{5}\right)$ **−2**

7. $\left(-4\dfrac{1}{2}\right)\left(2\dfrac{1}{3}\right)$ $-10\dfrac{1}{2}$

8. $\left(-1\dfrac{2}{7}\right)\left(-3\dfrac{5}{9}\right)$ $4\dfrac{4}{7}$

9. $(-5.34)(3.2)$ **−17.088**

10. $(-6.8)(-5.415)$ **36.822**

11. $(4.2)(-5.1)(3.6)$ **−77.112**

12. $(-3.9)(1.6)(8.4)$ **−52.416**

Simplify each expression.

13. $5(-3a) - 6a$ **−21a**

14. $-8(-x) - 3x$ **5x**

15. $2(6y - 2y)$ **8y**

16. $(c + 7c)(-3)$ **−24c**

17. $-3n(4b) + 2a(3b)$ **−12bn + 6ab**

18. $-7(2m - 3n)$ **−14m + 21n**

Lesson 2-1

1. $\{-3, -2, -1, 0, 1, 2, 3, 4\}$

2. $\{-2, 0, 2, 3, 6\}$

3. $\{2, 3, 4\}$

4. $\{7, 8, 9, 10, 11, 12, 13\}$

5. $\{-6, -4, -2, 0\}$

6. $\{-2, -1, 0, 1, 2, 3, 4\}$

7.
```
+——+——+——+——+——+——+——+
-6  -5  -4  -3  -2  -1   0   1
```

8.
```
+——+——+——+——+——+——+——+——+
-6  -5  -4  -3  -2  -1   0   1   2   3
```

9.
```
+——+——+——+——+——+——+——+
-2  -1   0   1   2   3   4
```

10.

```
+——+——+——+——+——+——+——+——+——+——+
-10 -9  -8  -7  -6  -5  -4  -3  -2  -1   0   1
```

Lesson 2-4

(pages 84–87)

Find each quotient.

1. $-49 \div (-7)$ **7**
2. $52 \div (-4)$ **−13**
3. $-66 \div (0.5)$ **−132**
4. $25.8 \div (-2)$ **−12.9**
5. $-55.25 \div (-0.25)$ **221**
6. $-82.1 \div (16.42)$ **−5**
7. $-\frac{2}{5} \div 5$ **$-\frac{2}{25}$**
8. $\frac{7}{8} \div (-4)$ **$-\frac{7}{32}$**
9. $-4 \div \left(-\frac{7}{10}\right)$ **$5\frac{5}{7}$**
10. $\frac{3}{2} \div \left(-\frac{1}{2}\right)$ **−3**
11. $-\frac{8}{5} \div \left(-\frac{5}{8}\right)$ **$\frac{64}{25}$**
12. $-\frac{13}{15} \div \frac{3}{25}$ **$-7\frac{2}{9}$**

Simplify each expression.

13. $\frac{32a}{4}$ **$8a$**
14. $\frac{12x}{-2}$ **$-6x$**
15. $\frac{5n + 15}{-5}$ **$-n - 3$**
16. $\frac{-2b - 10}{-2}$ **$b + 5$**
17. $\frac{65x - 15y}{5}$ **$13x - 3y$**
18. $\frac{2a - 10b}{-2}$ **$-a + 5b$**
19. $\frac{-27c + (-99b)}{9}$ **$-3c - 11b$**
20. $\frac{-3n + (-3m)}{-3}$ **$n + m$**

Lesson 2-5

(pages 88–94)

Use each set of data to make a line plot. 1–4. See margin.

1. 134, 147, 137, 138, 156, 140, 134, 145, 139, 152, 139, 155, 144, 135, 144
2. 19, 12, 11, 11, 7, 7, 8, 13, 12, 12, 9, 9, 8, 15, 11, 4, 12, 7, 7, 6
3. 66, 74, 72, 78, 68, 75, 80, 69, 62, 65, 63, 78, 71, 78, 76, 75, 80, 69, 62, 71, 76, 79, 70, 64, 62, 74, 74, 75, 70
4. 131, 133, 146, 141, 131, 138, 154, 156, 158, 160, 152, 150, 154, 160

Use each set of data to make a stem-and-leaf plot. 5–7. See margin.

5. 22 17 35 19 45 23 35 18 22 47 39 23 17 44 35 19 18 40 10
6. 1.2 1.3 5.6 4.1 1.1 2.0 1.9 3.0 4.5 2.1 4.1 1.2 1.8 1.0 3.2 2.2 2.5
7. 123 134 111 105 108 121 133 135 109 101 130 101 139 129 137 104

Lesson 2-6

(pages 96–101)

Find the probability of each event.

1. A coin will land tails up. $\frac{1}{2}$
2. You eat this month. **1**
3. A baby will be a girl. $\frac{1}{2}$
4. You will see a blue elephant. **0**
5. This is an algebra book. **1**
6. Today is Wednesday. $\frac{1}{7}$

A computer randomly picks a letter in the word *success*. Find each probability.

7. the letter e $\frac{1}{7}$
8. P(not c) $\frac{5}{7}$
9. the letter s $\frac{3}{7}$
10. the letter b **0**
11. P(vowel) $\frac{2}{7}$
12. the letters u or c $\frac{3}{7}$

One die is rolled. Find the odds of each outcome.

13. a 4 **1:5**
14. a number greater than 3 **1:1**
15. a multiple of 3 **1:2**
16. a number less than 5 **2:1**
17. an odd number **1:1**
18. not a 6 **5:1**

Lesson 2-5

1–4. See below.

5.
Stem	Leaf
1	0 7 7 8 8 9 9
2	2 2 3 3
3	5 5 5 9
4	0 4 5 7

$1|0 = 10$

6.
Stem	Leaf
1	0 1 2 2 3 8 9
2	0 1 2 5
3	0 2
4	1 1 5
5	6

$1|0 = 1.0$

7.
Stem	Leaf
10	1 1 4 5 8 9
11	1
12	1 3 9
13	0 3 4 5 7 9

$10|1 = 101$

1.
2.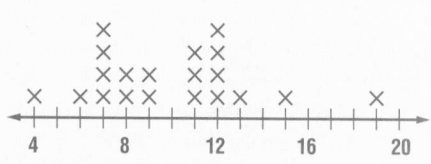
3.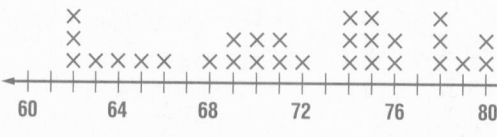
4.

Lesson 2-7

(pages 103–109)

Find each square root. If necessary, round to the nearest hundredth.

1. $\sqrt{121}$ **11**
2. $-\sqrt{36}$ **−6**
3. $\sqrt{2.89}$ **1.7**
4. $-\sqrt{125}$ **−11.18**
5. $\sqrt{\frac{81}{100}}$ **$\frac{9}{10}$**
6. $-\sqrt{\frac{36}{196}}$ **$-\frac{3}{7}$**
7. $\pm\sqrt{9.61}$ **±3.1**
8. $\pm\sqrt{\frac{7}{8}}$ **±0.94**

Name the set or sets of numbers to which each real number belongs.

9. $-\sqrt{149}$ **irrationals**
10. $\frac{5}{6}$ **rationals**
11. $\sqrt{\frac{8}{2}}$
12. $-\frac{66}{55}$ **rationals**
13. $\sqrt{225}$
14. $-\sqrt{\frac{3}{4}}$ **irrationals**
15. $\frac{-1}{7}$ **rationals**
16. $\sqrt{0.0016}$ **rationals**

Replace each ● with <, >, or = to make each sentence true.

17. $6.\overline{16}$ ● 6 **>**
18. 3.88 ● $\sqrt{15}$ **>**
19. $-\sqrt{529}$ ● -20 **<**
20. $-\sqrt{0.25}$ ● $-0.\overline{5}$ **>**
21. $\frac{1}{3}$ ● $\frac{\sqrt{3}}{3}$ **<**
22. $\frac{1}{\sqrt{3}}$ ● $\frac{\sqrt{3}}{3}$ **=**
23. $-\sqrt{\frac{1}{4}}$ ● $-\frac{1}{4}$ **<**
24. $-\frac{1}{6}$ ● $-\frac{1}{\sqrt{6}}$ **>**

11. rationals, integers, whole numbers, natural numbers
13. rationals, integers, whole numbers, natural numbers

Lesson 3-1

(pages 120–126)

Translate each sentence into an equation or formula.

1. A number z times 2 minus 6 is the same as m divided by 3. **$2z - 6 = m \div 3$**
2. The cube of a decreased by the square of b is equal to c. **$a^3 - b^2 = c$**
3. Twenty-nine decreased by the product of x and y is the same as z. **$29 - xy = z$**
4. The perimeter P of an isosceles triangle is the sum of twice the length of leg a and the length of the base b. **$P = 2a + b$**
5. Thirty increased by the quotient of s and t is equal to v. **$30 + (s \div t) = v$**
6. The area A of a rhombus is half the product of lengths of the diagonals a and b. **$A = 0.5ab$**

Translate each equation into a verbal sentence. 7–12. See margin for sample answers.

7. $0.5x + 3 = -10$
8. $\frac{n}{-6} = 2n + 1$
9. $18 - 5h = 13h$
10. $n^2 = 16$
11. $2x^2 + 3 = 21$
12. $\frac{m}{n} + 4 = 12$

Lesson 3-2

(pages 128–134)

Solve each equation. Then check your solution.

1. $-2 + g = 7$ **9**
2. $9 + s = -5$ **−14**
3. $-4 + y = -9$ **−5**
4. $m + 6 = 2$ **−4**
5. $t + (-4) = 10$ **14**
6. $v - 7 = -4$ **3**
7. $a - (-6) = -5$ **−11**
8. $-2 - x = -8$ **6**
9. $d + (-44) = -61$ **−17**
10. $e - (-26) = 41$ **15**
11. $p - 47 = 22$ **69**
12. $-63 - f = -82$ **19**
13. $c + 5.4 = -11.33$ **−16.73**
14. $-6.11 + b = 14.321$ **20.431**
15. $-5 = y - 22.7$ **17.7**
16. $-5 - q = 1.19$ **−6.19**
17. $n + (-4.361) = 59.78$ **64.141**
18. $t - (-46.1) = -3.673$ **−49.773**
19. $\frac{7}{10} - a = \frac{1}{2}$ **$\frac{1}{5}$**
20. $f - \left(-\frac{1}{8}\right) = \frac{3}{10}$ **$\frac{7}{40}$**
21. $-4\frac{5}{12} = t - \left(-10\frac{1}{36}\right)$ **$-14\frac{4}{9}$**
22. $x + \frac{3}{8} = \frac{1}{4}$ **$-\frac{1}{8}$**
23. $1\frac{7}{16} + s = \frac{9}{8}$ **$-\frac{5}{16}$**
24. $17\frac{8}{9} = d + \left(-2\frac{5}{6}\right)$ **$20\frac{13}{18}$**

Extra Practice

Lesson 3-1

7. **Sample answer:** The sum of five-tenths times x and three is equal to negative ten.
8. **Sample answer:** The quotient of n and negative six is the same as the sum of two times n and one.
9. **Sample answer:** Eighteen decreased by five times h is the same as thirteen times h.
10. **Sample answer:** The square of n is equal to sixteen.
11. **Sample answer:** The sum of 3 and twice x squared is equal to twenty-one.
12. **Sample answer:** The sum of 4 and the quotient of m and n is equal to twelve.

Extra Practice

Lesson 3-3

(pages 135–140)

Solve each equation. Then check your solution.

1. $7p = 35$ **5**
2. $-3x = -24$ **8**
3. $2y = -3$ **−1.5**
4. $62y = -2356$ **−38**
5. $\frac{a}{-6} = -2$ **12**
6. $\frac{c}{-59} = -7$ **413**
7. $\frac{f}{14} = -63$ **−882**
8. $84 = \frac{x}{97}$ **8148**
9. $\frac{w}{5} = 3$ **15**
10. $\frac{q}{9} = -3$ **−27**
11. $\frac{2}{5}x = \frac{4}{7}$ **$\frac{10}{7}$**
12. $\frac{z}{6} = -\frac{5}{12}$ **$-\frac{5}{2}$**
13. $-\frac{5}{9}r = 7\frac{1}{2}$ **$-13\frac{1}{2}$**
14. $2\frac{1}{6}j = 5\frac{1}{5}$ **$2\frac{2}{5}$**
15. $3 = 1\frac{7}{11}q$ **$1\frac{5}{6}$**
16. $-1\frac{3}{4}p = -\frac{5}{8}$ **$\frac{5}{14}$**
17. $57k = 0.1824$ **0.0032**
18. $0.0022b = 0.1958$ **89**
19. $5j = -32.15$ **−6.43**
20. $\frac{w}{-2} = -2.48$ **4.96**
21. $\frac{z}{2.8} = -6.2$ **−17.36**
22. $\frac{x}{-0.063} = 0.015$ **−0.000945**
23. $15\frac{3}{8} = -5p$ **$-3\frac{3}{40}$**
24. $-18\frac{1}{4} = 2.5x$ **−7.3**

Lesson 3-4

(pages 142–148)

Solve each equation. Then check your solution.

1. $2x - 5 = 3$ **4**
2. $4t + 5 = 37$ **8**
3. $7a + 6 = -36$ **−6**
4. $47 = -8g + 7$ **−5**
5. $-3c - 9 = -24$ **5**
6. $5k - 7 = -52$ **−9**
7. $5s + 4s = -72$ **−8**
8. $3x - 7 = 2$ **3**
9. $8 + 3x = 5$ **−1**
10. $-3y + 7.569 = 24.069$ **−5.5**
11. $7 - 9.1f = 137.585$ **−14.35**
12. $6.5 = 2.4m - 4.9$ **4.75**
13. $\frac{e}{5} + 6 = -2$ **−40**
14. $\frac{d}{4} - 8 = -5$ **12**
15. $-\frac{4}{13}y - 7 = 6$ **$-42\frac{1}{4}$**
16. $\frac{p + 3}{10} = 4$ **37**
17. $\frac{h - 7}{6} = 1$ **13**
18. $\frac{5f + 1}{8} = -3$ **−5**
19. $\frac{4n - 8}{-2} = 12$ **−4**
20. $\frac{-3t - 4}{2} = 8$ **$-6\frac{2}{3}$**
21. $4.8a - 3 + 1.2a = 9$ **2**

Lesson 3-5

(pages 149–154)

Solve each equation. Then check your solution.

1. $5x + 1 = 3x - 3$ **−2**
2. $6 - 8n = 5n + 19$ **−1**
3. $-3z + 5 = 2z + 5$ **0**
4. $\frac{2}{3}h + 5 = -4 - \frac{1}{3}h$ **−9**
5. $\frac{1}{2}a - 4 = 3 - \frac{1}{4}a$ **$9\frac{1}{3}$**
6. $6(y - 5) = 18 - 2y$ **6**
7. $-28 + p = 7(p - 10)$ **7**
8. $\frac{1}{3}(b - 9) = b + 9$ **−18**
9. $-4x + 6 = 0.5(x + 30)$ **−2**
10. $4(2y - 1) = -8(0.5 - y)$ **all real numbers**
11. $1.9s + 6 = 3.1 - s$ **−1**
12. $2.85y - 7 = 12.85y - 2$ **−0.5**
13. $2.9m + 1.7 = 3.5 + 2.3m$ **3**
14. $3(x + 1) - 5 = 3x - 2$ **all real numbers**
15. $\frac{x}{2} - \frac{1}{3} = \frac{x}{3} - \frac{1}{2}$ **−1**
16. $\frac{6v - 9}{3} = v$ **3**
17. $\frac{3t + 1}{4} = \frac{3}{4}t - 5$ **no solution**
18. $0.4(x - 12) = 1.2(x - 4)$ **0**
19. $3y - \frac{4}{5} = \frac{1}{3}y$ **$\frac{3}{10}$**
20. $\frac{3}{4}x - 4 = 7 + \frac{1}{2}x$ **44**
21. $-0.2(1 - x) = 2(4 + 0.1x)$ **no solution**

Solve each proportion.

1. $\frac{4}{5} = \frac{x}{20}$ **16**

2. $\frac{b}{63} = \frac{3}{7}$ **27**

3. $\frac{y}{5} = \frac{3}{4}$ **3.75**

4. $\frac{7}{4} = \frac{3}{a}$ **$\frac{12}{7}$**

5. $\frac{t-5}{4} = \frac{3}{2}$ **11**

6. $\frac{x}{9} = \frac{0.24}{3}$ **0.72**

7. $\frac{n}{3} = \frac{n+4}{7}$ **3**

8. $\frac{12q}{-7} = \frac{30}{14}$ **$-\frac{5}{4}$**

9. $\frac{1}{y-3} = \frac{3}{y-5}$ **2**

10. $\frac{x}{8.71} = \frac{4}{17.42}$ **2**

11. $\frac{a-3}{8} = \frac{3}{4}$ **9**

12. $\frac{6p-2}{7} = \frac{5p+7}{8}$ **5**

13. $\frac{2}{9} = \frac{k+3}{2}$ **$-\frac{23}{9}$ or $-2.\overline{5}$**

14. $\frac{5m-3}{4} = \frac{5m+3}{6}$ **3**

15. $\frac{w-5}{4} = \frac{w+3}{3}$ **-27**

16. $\frac{96.8}{t} = \frac{12.1}{7}$ **56**

17. $\frac{r-1}{r+1} = \frac{3}{5}$ **4**

18. $\frac{4n+5}{5} = \frac{2n+7}{7}$ **0**

State whether each percent of change is a percent of increase or a percent of decrease. Then find each percent of change. Round to the nearest whole percent.

1. original: $100
   new: $67 **decrease; 33%**

2. original: 62 acres
   new: 98 acres **increase, 58%**

3. original: 322 people
   new: 289 people **decrease, 10%**

4. original: 78 pennies
   new: 36 pennies **decrease, 54%**

5. original: $212
   new: $230 **increase, 8%**

6. original: 35 mph
   new: 65 mph **increase, 86%**

Find the final price of each item.

7. television: $299
   discount: 20% **$239.20**

8. book: $15.95
   sales tax: 7% **$17.07**

9. software: $36.90
   sales tax: 6.25% **$39.21**

10. boots: $49.99
    discount: 15%
    sales tax: 3.5% **$43.98**

11. jacket: $65
    discount: 30%
    sales tax: 4% **$47.32**

12. backpack: $28.95
    discount: 10%
    sales tax: 5% **$27.36**

Solve each equation or formula for x.

1. $x + r = q$ **$q - r$**

2. $ax + 4 = 7$ **$\frac{3}{a}$**

3. $2bx - b = -5$ **$\frac{-5 + b}{2b}$**

4. $\frac{x-c}{c+a} = a$ **$a^2 + ac + c$**

5. $\frac{x+y}{c} = d$ **$cd - y$**

6. $\frac{ax+1}{2} = b$ **$\frac{2b-1}{a}$**

7. $d(x - 3) = 5$ **$\frac{3d+5}{d}$**

8. $nx - a = bx + d$ **$\frac{a+d}{n-b}$**

9. $3x - r = r(-3 + x)$ **$\frac{-2r}{3-r}$**

10. $y = \frac{5}{9}(x - 32)$ **$\frac{9}{5}y + 32$**

11. $A = \frac{1}{2}h(x + y)$ **$\frac{2A}{h} - y$**

12. $A = 2\pi r^2 + 2\pi rx$ **$\frac{A}{2\pi r} - r$**

Lesson 4-1

10–18.

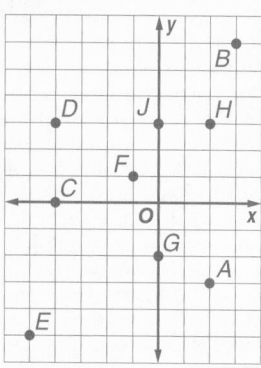

Lesson 4-2

4.

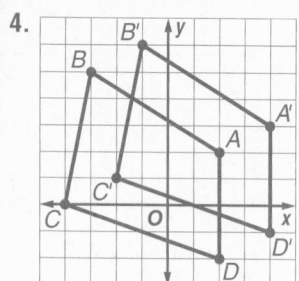

5.

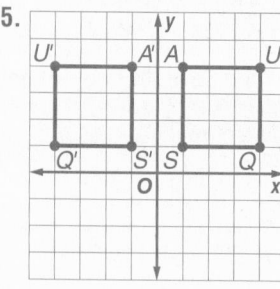

6.

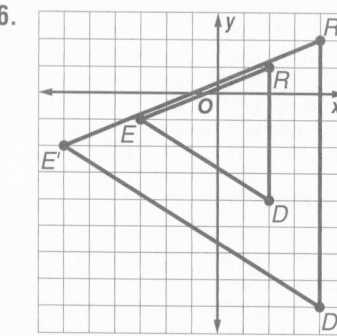

7.

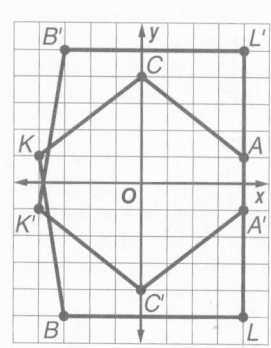

Lesson 3-9

(pages 171–177)

1. **ADVERTISING** An advertisement for grape drink claims that the drink contains 10% grape juice. How much pure grape juice would have to be added to 5 quarts of the drink to obtain a mixture containing 40% grape juice? **2.5 qt**

2. **GRADES** In Ms. Pham's social studies class, a test is worth four times as much as homework. If a student has an average of 85% on tests and 95% on homework, what is the student's average? **87%**

3. **ENTERTAINMENT** At the Golden Oldies Theater, tickets for adults cost $5.50 and tickets for children cost $3.50. How many of each kind of ticket were purchased if 21 tickets were bought for $83.50? **5 adults, 16 children**

4. **FOOD** Wes is mixing peanuts and chocolate pieces. Peanuts sell for $4.50 a pound and the chocolate sells for $6.50 a pound. How many pounds of chocolate mixes with 5 pounds of peanuts to obtain a mixture that sells for $5.25 a pound? **3 lb**

5. **TRAVEL** Missoula and Bozeman are 210 miles apart. Sheila leaves Missoula for Bozeman and averages 55 miles per hour. At the same time, Casey leaves Bozeman and averages 65 miles per hour as he drives to Missoula. When will they meet? How far will they be from Bozeman? **1.75 h; 113.75 mi**

Lesson 4-1

(pages 192–196)

Write the ordered pair for each point shown at the right. Name the quadrant in which the point is located.

1. B (1, 2); I
2. T (−5, 0); none
3. P (6, −2); IV
4. Q (0, 6); none
5. A (−2, −2); III
6. K (4, 5); I
7. J (2, −5); IV
8. L (4, 0); none
9. S (−3, 5); II

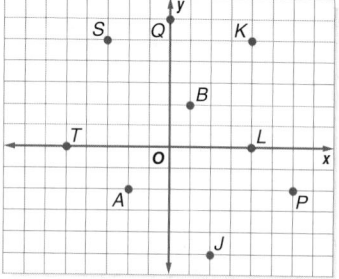

Plot each point on a coordinate plane. **10–18. See margin.**

10. $A(2, -3)$
11. $B(3, 6)$
12. $C(-4, 0)$
13. $D(-4, 3)$
14. $E(-5, -5)$
15. $F(-1, 1)$
16. $G(0, -2)$
17. $H(2, 3)$
18. $J(0, 3)$

Lesson 4-2

(pages 197–203)

Determine whether each transformation is a *reflection, translation, dilation,* or *rotation.*

1. reflection
2. translation
3. dilation

For Exercises 4–9, complete parts a and b.

a. Find the coordinates of the vertices of each figure after the given transformation is performed.

b. Graph the preimage and its image. **4–9. See margin for graphs.**

4. quadrilateral $ABCD$ with $A(2, 2)$, $B(-3, 5)$, $C(-4, 0)$, and $D(2, -2)$ translated 1 unit up and 2 units right **$A'(4, 3)$, $B'(-1, 6)$, $C'(-2, 1)$, $D'(4, -1)$**

5. square $SQUA$ with $S(1, 1)$, $Q(4, 1)$, $U(4, 4)$, and $A(1, 4)$ reflected over the y-axis

6. $\triangle RED$ with $R(2, 1)$, $E(-3, -1)$, and $D(2, -4)$ dilated by a scale factor of 2

7. pentagon $BLACK$ with $B(-3, -5)$, $L(4, -5)$, $A(4, 1)$, $C(0, 4)$, and $K(-4, 1)$ reflected over the x-axis **$B'(-3, 5)$, $L'(4, 5)$, $A'(4, -1)$, $C'(0, -4)$, $K'(-4, -1)$**

8. $\triangle ANG$ with $A(2, 1)$, $N(4, 1)$, and $G(3, 4)$ rotated 90° counterclockwise about the origin

9. parallelogram $GRAM$ with $G(-3, -2)$, $R(4, -2)$, $A(6, 4)$, and $M(-1, 4)$ translated 2 units down and 1 unit left **$G'(-4, -4)$, $R'(3, -4)$, $A'(5, 2)$, $M'(-2, 2)$**

5. $S'(-1, 1)$, $Q'(-4, 1)$, $U'(-4, 4)$, $A'(-1, 4)$

6. $R'(4, 2)$, $E'(-6, -2)$, $D'(4, -8)$

8. $A'(-1, 2)$, $N'(-1, 4)$, $G'(-4, 3)$

8.

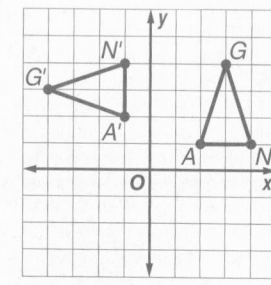

9.

Lesson 4-3

(pages 205–211)

Express each relation as a table, a graph, and a mapping. Then determine the domain and range. **1–4. See pp. 852A–852H.**

1. {(5, 2), (0, 0), (−9, −1)}

2. {(−4, 2), (−2, 0), (0, 2), (2, 4)}

3. {(7, 5), (−2, −3), (4, 0), (5, −7), (−9, 2)}

4. {(3.1, −1), (−4.7, 3.9), (2.4, −3.6), (−9, 12.12)}

Express the relation shown in each table, mapping, or graph as a set of ordered pairs. Then write the inverse of the relation. **5–10. See margin.**

5.

x	y
1	3
2	4
3	5
4	6
5	7

6.

x	y
−4	1
−2	3
0	1
2	3
4	1

7.

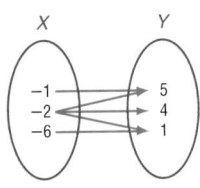

8.

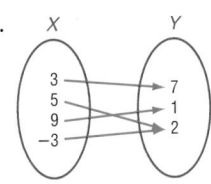

9.

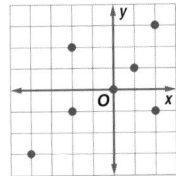

10.

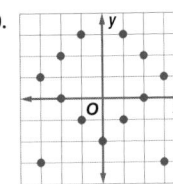

Lesson 4-4

(pages 212–217)

Find the solution set for each equation, given the replacement set. **1.** {(0, −1), (2, 5)}

1. $y = 3x - 1$; {(0, −1), (4, 2), (2, 4), (2, 5)}

2. $3y = x + 7$; {(1, 8), (0, 7), (2, 3), (5, 4)}{(2, 3), (5, 4)}

3. $4x = 8 - 2y$; {(2, 0), (0, 4), (0, 2), (−4, 12)} {(2, 0), (0, 4), (−4, 12)}

4. $3x = 10 - 4y$; {(3, 0.25), (−10, 5), (2, 1), (5, 5)} {(2, 1), (3, 0.25)}

Solve each equation if the domain is {−2, −1, 0, 1, 2}. **5–13. See margin.**

5. $x + y = 3$

6. $y = x$

7. $y = 5x + 1$

8. $4x + 3y = 13$

9. $5y = 8 - 4x$

10. $2x + y = 4$

11. $y = 4 + x$

12. $2x + 3y = 10$

13. $2y = 3x + 1$

Solve each equation for the given domain. Graph the solution set. **14–21. See margin.**

14. $x = y + 1$ for $x = \{-2, -1, 0, 1, 2\}$

15. $y = x + 1$ for $x = \{-3, -1, 0, 1, 3\}$

16. $x + 4y = 2$ for $x = \{-8, -4, 0, 4, 8\}$

17. $y - 3 = x$ for $x = \{-5, -1, 3, 7, 9\}$

18. $x + y = -2$ for $x = \{-4, -3, 0, 1, 3\}$

19. $2x - 3y = -5$ for $x = \{-5, -3, 0, 5, 6\}$

20. $3y = \frac{2}{3}x - 4$ for $x = \{-6, -3, 0, 1, 3\}$

21. $-2y = 8 - \frac{3}{2}x$ for $x = \{-4, 0, 4, 6, 8\}$

Lesson 4-5

(pages 218–223)

Determine whether each equation is a linear equation. If so, write the equation in standard form. **1–6. See pp. 852A–852H.**

1. $3x = 2y$

2. $2x - 3 = y^2$

3. $4x = 2y + 8$

4. $5x - 7y = 2x - 7$

5. $2x + 5x = 7y + 2$

6. $\frac{1}{x} + \frac{5}{y} = -4$

Graph each equation. **7–18. See pp. 852A–852H.**

7. $3x + y = 4$

8. $y = 3x + 1$

9. $3x - 2y = 12$

10. $2x - y = 6$

11. $2x - 3y = 8$

12. $y = -2$

13. $y = 5x - 7$

14. $x = 4$

15. $x + \frac{1}{3}y = 2$

16. $5x - 2y = 8$

17. $4.5x + 2.5y = 9$

18. $\frac{1}{2}x + 3y = 12$

Lesson 4-4

5. {(−2, 5), (−1, 4), (0, 3), (1, 2), (2, 1)}

6. {(−2, −2), (−1, −1), (0, 0), (1, 1), (2, 2)}

7. {(−2, −9), (−1, −4), (0, 1), (1, 6), (2, 11)}

8. $\left\{(-2, 7), \left(-1, \frac{17}{3}\right), \left(0, \frac{13}{3}\right), (1, 3), \left(2, \frac{5}{3}\right)\right\}$

9. $\left\{\left(-2, \frac{16}{5}\right), \left(-1, \frac{12}{5}\right), \left(0, \frac{8}{5}\right), \left(1, \frac{4}{5}\right), (2, 0)\right\}$

10. {(−2, 8), (−1, 6), (0, 4), (1, 2), (2, 0)}

11. {(−2, 2), (−1, 3), (0, 4), (1, 5), (2, 6)}

12. $\left\{\left(-2, \frac{14}{3}\right), (-1, 4), \left(0, \frac{10}{3}\right), \left(1, \frac{8}{3}\right), (2, 2)\right\}$

13. $\left\{\left(-2, -\frac{5}{2}\right), (-1, -1), \left(0, \frac{1}{2}\right), (1, 2), \left(2, \frac{7}{2}\right)\right\}$

14. {(−2, −3), (−1, −2), (0, −1), (1, 0), (2, 1)}

15. {(−3, −2), (−1, 0), (0, 1), (1, 2), (3, 4)}

Answers continued on page 852A.

Lesson 4-3

5. {(1, 3), (2, 4), (3, 5), (4, 6), (5, 7)}; {(3, 1), (4, 2), (5, 3), (6, 4), (7, 5)}

6. {(−4, 1), (−2, 3), (0, 1), (2, 3), (4, 1)}; {(1, −4), (3, −2), (1, 0), (3, 2), (1, 4)}

7. {(−1, 5), (−2, 5), (−2, 4), (−2, 1), (−6, 1)}; {(5, −1), (5, −2), (4, −2), (1, −2), (1, −6)}

8. {(3, 7), (5, 2), (9, 1), (−3, 2)}; {(7, 3), (2, 5), (1, 9), (2, −3)}

9. {(−4, −3), (−2, 2), (−2, −1), (0, 0), (1, 1), (2, 3), (2, −1)}; {(−3, −4), (2, −2), (−1, −2), (0, 0), (1, 1), (3, 2), (−1, 2)}

10. {(−3, 1), (−3, −3), (−2, 2), (−2, 0), (−1, 3), (−1, −1), (0, −2), (1, −1), (1, 3), (2, 0), (2, 2), (3, 1), (3, −3)}; {(1, −3), (−3, −3), (2, −2), (0, −2), (3, −1), (−1, −1), (−2, 0), (−1, 1), (3, 1), (0, 2), (2, 2), (1, 3), (−3, 3)}

Lesson 4-7

19.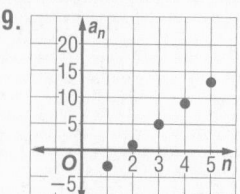

20.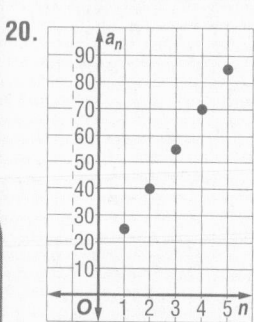

21.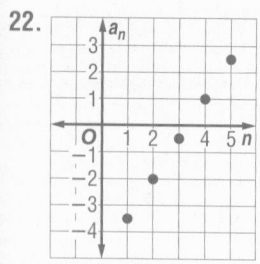

22.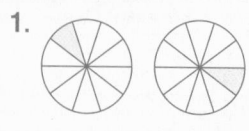

Lesson 4-8

1.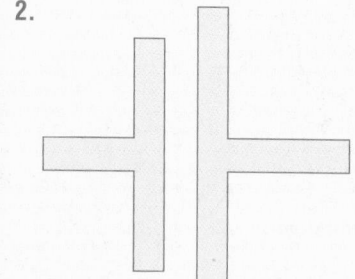

2.

3. 56, 67, 78

4. 15, 9, 3

5. 10.8, 12.0, 13.2

6. 68, 63.5, 59

7. 64, 128, 256

8. 5, 1, 0.2

Lesson 4-6
(pages 226–231)

Determine whether each relation is a function.

1. 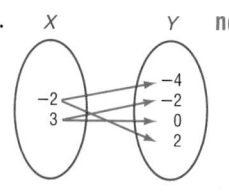 no

x	y
1	3
2	5
1	−7
2	9

2. no

3. yes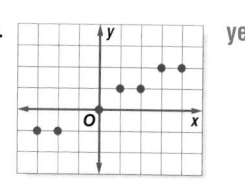

4. {(−2, 4), (1, 3), (5, 2), (1, 4)} no   **5.** {(5, 4), (−6, 5), (4, 5), (0, 4)} yes   **6.** {(3, 1), (5, 1), (7, 1)} yes

7. {(3, −2), (4, 7), (−2, 7), (4, 5)} no   **8.** $y = 2$ yes   **9.** $x^2 + y = 11$ yes

If $f(x) = 2x + 5$ and $g(x) = 3x^2 − 1$, find each value.

10. $f(−4)$ −3   **11.** $g(2)$ 11   **12.** $f(3) − 5$ 6   **13.** $g(−2) + 4$ 15

14. $f(b^2)$ $2b^2 + 5$ **15.** $g(a + 1)$ $3a^2 + 6a + 2$ **16.** $f(0) + g(3)$ 31   **17.** $f(n) + g(n)$ $3n^2 + 2n + 4$

Lesson 4-7
(pages 233–238)

Determine whether each sequence is an arithmetic sequence. If it is, state the common difference.

1. −2, −1, 0, 1, ... yes; 1   **2.** 3, 5, 8, 12, ... no   **3.** 2, 4, 8, 16, ... no

4. −21, −16, −11, −6, ... yes; 5   **5.** 0, 0.25, 0.5, 0.75, ... yes; 0.25   **6.** $\frac{1}{3}, \frac{1}{9}, \frac{1}{27}, \frac{1}{81}, ...$ no

Find the next three terms of each arithmetic sequence.   **8.** −12, −14, −16   **9.** 0.4, 1.0, 1.6

7. 3, 13, 23, 33, ... 43, 53, 63   **8.** −4, −6, −8, −10, ...

10. 5, 13, 21, 29, ... 37, 45, 53   **11.** $\frac{3}{4}, \frac{7}{8}, 1, \frac{9}{8}, ...$ $\frac{5}{4}, \frac{11}{8}, \frac{3}{2}$ **9.** −2, −1.4, −0.8, −0.2, ...

12. $−\frac{1}{3}, −\frac{5}{6}, −\frac{4}{3}, −\frac{11}{6}, ...$ $−\frac{7}{3}, −\frac{17}{6}, −\frac{10}{3}$

Find the nth term of each arithmetic sequence described.

13. $a_1 = 3, d = 6, n = 12$ 69   **14.** $a_1 = −2, d = 4, n = 8$ 26   **15.** $a_1 = −1, d = −3, n = 10$ −28

16. $a_1 = 2.2, d = 1.4, n = 5$ 7.8   **17.** −2, −7, −12, ... for $n = 12$ −57   **18.** $2\frac{1}{2}, 2\frac{1}{8}, 1\frac{3}{4}, 1\frac{3}{8}, ...$ for $n = 10$ $−\frac{7}{8}$

Write an equation for the nth term of the arithmetic sequence. Then graph the first five terms in the sequence. 19–22. See margin for graphs.

19. −3, 1, 5, 9, ...
$a_n = −7 + 4n$

20. 25, 40, 55, 70, ...
$a_n = 10 + 15n$

21. −9, −3, 3, 9, ...
$a_n = −15 + 6n$

22. −3.5, −2, −0.5, 1, ...
$a_n = −5 + 1.5n$

Lesson 4-8
(pages 240–245)

Find the next two items for each pattern. 1–2. See margin.

1.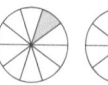

2.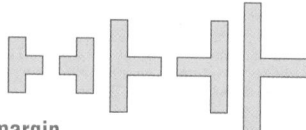

Find the next three terms in each sequence. 3–11. See margin.

3. 12, 23, 34, 45, ...   **4.** 39, 33, 27, 21, ...   **5.** 6.0, 7.2, 8.4, 9.6, ...

6. 86, 81.5, 77, 72.5, ...   **7.** 4, 8, 16, 32, ...   **8.** 3125, 625, 125, 25, ...

9. 15, 16, 18, 21, 25, 30, ...   **10.** $w − 2, w − 4, w − 6, w − 8, ...$ **11.** 13, 10, 11, 8, 9, 6, ...

Write an equation in function notation for each relation. 12–15. See margin.

12. 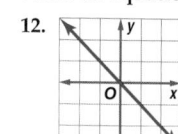   **13.** 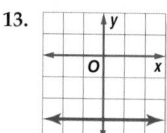   **14.** 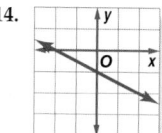   **15.**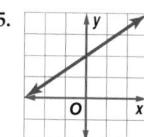

---

9. 36, 43, 51

10. $w − 10, w − 12, w − 14$

11. 7, 4, 5

12. $f(x) = −x$

13. $f(x) = −3$

14. $f(x) = −\frac{1}{2}x − 1$

15. $f(x) = \frac{2}{3}x + 2$

Lesson 5-1

(pages 256–262)

Find the slope of the line that passes through each pair of points.

1. 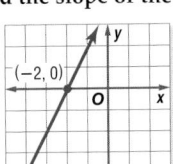 2

2. 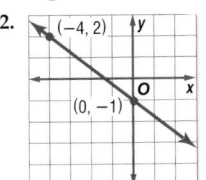 $-\dfrac{3}{4}$

3. $(-2, 2), (3, -3)$ **−1**

4. $(-2, -8), (1, 4)$ **4**

5. $(3, 4), (4, 6)$ **2**

6. $(-5, 4), (-1, 11)$ $\dfrac{7}{4}$

7. $(18, -4), (6, -10)$ $\dfrac{1}{2}$

8. $(-4, -6), (-4, -8)$ **undefined**

9. $(0, 0), (-1, 3)$ **−3**

10. $(-8, 1), (2, 1)$ **0**

Find the value of r so the line that passes through each pair of points has the given slope.

11. $(-1, r), (1, -4), m = -5$ **6**

12. $(r, -2), (-7, -1), m = -\dfrac{1}{4}$ **−3**

13. $(-3, 2), (7, r), m = \dfrac{2}{3}$ $\dfrac{26}{3}$

Lesson 5-2

(pages 264–270)

Name the constant of variation for each equation. Then determine the slope of the line that passes through each pair of points.

1. 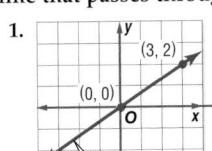 $\dfrac{2}{3}; \dfrac{2}{3}$

2. 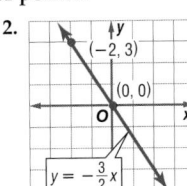 $-\dfrac{3}{2}; -\dfrac{3}{2}$

3. 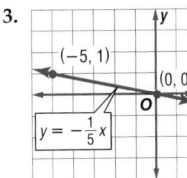 $-\dfrac{1}{5}; -\dfrac{1}{5}$

Graph each equation. **4–6. See margin.**

4. $y = 5x$

5. $y = -6x$

6. $y = -\dfrac{4}{3}x$

Write a direct variation equation that relates x and y. Assume that y varies directly as x. Then solve. **7–10. See margin for equations.**

7. If $y = 45$ when $x = 9$, find y when $x = 7$. **35**

8. If $y = -7$ when $x = -1$, find x when $y = -84$. **−12**

9. If $y = 450$ when $x = -6$, find y when $x = 10$. **−750**

10. If $y = 6$ when $x = 48$, find y when $x = 20$. **2.5**

Lesson 5-3

(pages 272–277)

Write an equation of the line with the given slope and y-intercept. **1–6. See margin.**

1. slope: 5, y-intercept: -15

2. slope: -6, y-intercept: 3

3. slope: 0.3, y-intercept: -2.6

4. slope: $-\dfrac{4}{3}$, y-intercept: $\dfrac{5}{3}$

5. slope: $-\dfrac{2}{5}$, y-intercept: 2

6. slope: $\dfrac{7}{4}$, y-intercept: -2

Write an equation of the line shown in each graph.

7. 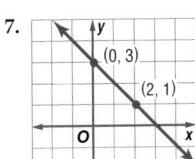 $y = -x + 3$

8. 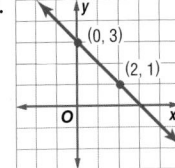 $y = -\dfrac{1}{2}x - 3$

9. 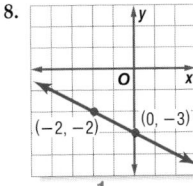 $y = \dfrac{1}{3}x + 2$

Graph each equation. **10–12. See margin.**

10. $y = 5x - 1$

11. $y = -2x + 3$

12. $3x - y = 6$

Lesson 5-2

4.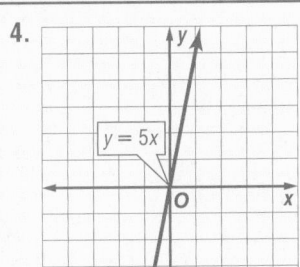

5.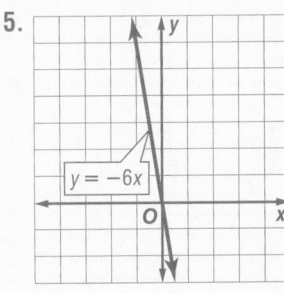

6.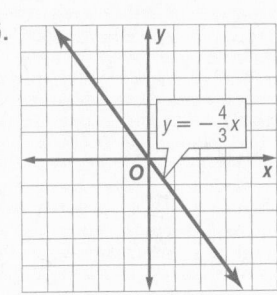

7. $y = 5x$

8. $y = 7x$

9. $y = -75x$

10. $y = -x$

Lesson 5-3

1. $y = 5x - 15$

2. $y = -6x + 3$

3. $y = 0.3x - 2.6$

4. $y = -\dfrac{4}{3}x + \dfrac{5}{3}$

5. $y = -\dfrac{2}{5}x + 2$

6. $y = \dfrac{7}{4}x - 2$

10.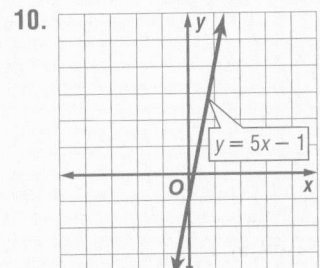

11.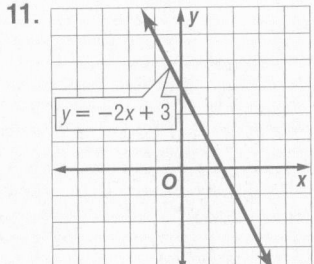

12.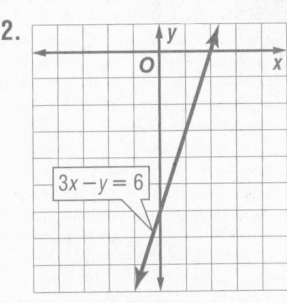

Lesson 5-5

7. $2x - y = 11$

8. $x + 2y = -12$

9. $2x + 3y = 22$

10. $4x - 3y = 30$

11. $3x - 2y = -11$

12. $19x + 5y = 8$

13. $y = -2x - 9$

14. $y = 4x - 7$

15. $y = -4x + 14$

16. $y = \frac{4}{5}x + 3$

17. $y = -\frac{3}{4}x + \frac{7}{2}$

18. $y = \frac{2}{3}x + \frac{1}{12}$

Lesson 5-6

1. $y = 4x + 2$

2. $y = 2x - 2$

3. $y = \frac{2}{3}x + 2$

4. $y = -3x + 13$

5. $y = -\frac{3}{8}x + 4$

6. $y = \frac{1}{5}x + \frac{13}{5}$

7. $y = \frac{5}{3}x - 1$

8. $y = \frac{1}{6}x + \frac{10}{3}$

9. $y = -\frac{4}{3}x$

10. $y = -\frac{3}{4}x + 3$

11. $y = -\frac{5}{3}x + 17$

12. $y = \frac{1}{2}x - \frac{7}{2}$

Lesson 5-4
(pages 280–285)

Write an equation of the line that passes through each point with the given slope.

1. $(0, 0)$; $m = -2$ $y = -2x$

2. $(-3, 2)$; $m = 4$ $y = 4x + 14$

3. $(0, 5)$; $m = -1$ $y = -x + 5$

4. $(-2, 3)$; $m = -\frac{1}{4}$ $y = -\frac{1}{4}x + \frac{5}{2}$

5. $(1, -5)$; $m = \frac{2}{3}$ $y = \frac{2}{3}x - \frac{17}{3}$

6. $\left(\frac{1}{2}, \frac{1}{4}\right)$; $m = 8$ $y = 8x - \frac{15}{4}$

Write an equation of the line that passes through each pair of points.

7. $(-1, 7)$, $(8, -2)$ $y = -x + 6$

8. $(4, 0)$, $(0, 5)$ $y = -\frac{5}{4}x + 5$

9. $(8, -1)$, $(7, -1)$ $y = -1$

10. $(1, 0)$, $(0, 1)$ $y = -x + 1$

11. $(5, 7)$, $(-1, 3)$ $y = \frac{2}{3}x + \frac{11}{3}$

12. $(-3, -5)$, $(3, -15)$ $y = -\frac{5}{3}x - 10$

13. $(-2, 3)$, $(1, 3)$ $y = 3$

14. $(0, 0)$, $(-4, 3)$ $y = -\frac{3}{4}x$

15. $\left(-\frac{1}{2}, \frac{1}{2}\right)$, $\left(\frac{1}{4}, \frac{3}{4}\right)$ $y = \frac{1}{3}x + \frac{2}{3}$

Write an equation of the line that has each pair of intercepts. 16–21. See margin.

16. x-intercept: 2, y-intercept: 1 $y = -\frac{1}{2}x + 1$

17. x-intercept: 1, y-intercept: -4 $y = 4x - 4$

18. x-intercept: 5, y-intercept: 5 $y = -x + 5$

19. x-intercept: -1, y-intercept: 3 $y = 3x + 3$

20. x-intercept: -4, y-intercept: -1 $y = -\frac{1}{4}x - 1$

21. x-intercept: 3, y-intercept: -3 $y = x - 3$

Lesson 5-5
(pages 286–291)

Write the point-slope form of an equation for a line that passes through each point with the given slope. 2. $y - 4 = -5(x - 5)$

1. $(5, -2)$, $m = 3$ $y + 2 = 3(x - 5)$

2. $(5, 4)$, $m = -5$

3. $(0, 6)$, $m = -2$ $y - 6 = -2x$

4. $(-3, 1)$, $m = 0$ $y - 1 = 0$

5. $(-1, 0)$, $m = \frac{2}{3}$ $y = \frac{2}{3}(x + 1)$

6. $(-2, -4)$, $m = \frac{3}{4}$

$y + 4 = \frac{3}{4}(x + 2)$

Write each equation in standard form. 7–12. See margin.

7. $y + 3 = 2(x - 4)$

8. $y + 3 = -\frac{1}{2}(x + 6)$

9. $y - 4 = -\frac{2}{3}(x - 5)$

10. $y + 2 = \frac{4}{3}(x - 6)$

11. $y - 1 = 1.5(x + 3)$

12. $y + 6 = -3.8(x - 2)$

Write each equation in slope-intercept form. 13–18. See margin.

13. $y - 1 = -2(x + 5)$

14. $y + 3 = 4(x - 1)$

15. $y - 6 = -4(x - 2)$

16. $y + 1 = \frac{4}{5}(x + 5)$

17. $y - 2 = -\frac{3}{4}(x - 2)$

18. $y + \frac{1}{4} = \frac{2}{3}\left(x + \frac{1}{2}\right)$

Lesson 5-6
(pages 292–297)

Write the slope-intercept form of an equation of the line that passes through the given point and is parallel to the graph of each equation. 1–6. See margin.

1. $(1, 6)$, $y = 4x - 2$

2. $(4, 6)$, $y = 2x - 7$

3. $(-3, 0)$, $y = \frac{2}{3}x + 1$

4. $(5, -2)$, $y = -3x - 7$

5. $(0, 4)$, $3x + 8y = 4$

6. $(2, 3)$, $x - 5y = 7$

Write the slope-intercept form of an equation that passes through the given point and is perpendicular to the graph of each equation. 7–12. See margin.

7. $(0, -1)$, $y = -\frac{3}{5}x + 4$

8. $(-2, 3)$, $6x + y = 4$

9. $(0, 0)$, $y = \frac{3}{4}x - 1$

10. $(4, 0)$, $4x - 3y = 2$

11. $(6, 7)$, $3x - 5y = 1$

12. $(5, -1)$, $8x + 4y = 15$

Lesson 5-7

(pages 298–305)

Determine whether each graph shows a *positive correlation*, a *negative correlation*, or *no correlation*. If there is a positive or negative correlation, describe its meaning in the situation. **1–3. See margin.**

1.

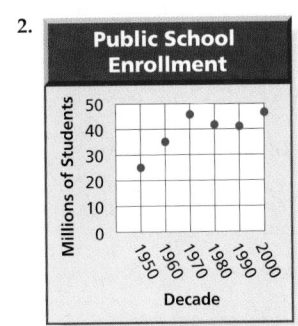

2.

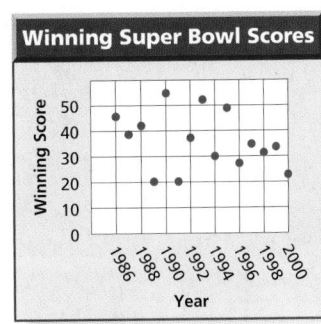

3.

Winning Super Bowl Scores

Source: *ESPN Almanac*

5. $y = \frac{7}{2}x - 6955$ **6.** 62.5 million metric tons of fish

For Exercises 4–6, use the scatter plot that shows the year and the amount of fish caught in China in millions of metric tons.

4. Describe the relationship that exists in the data. **positive correlation**

5. Use the points (1994, 24) and (1998, 38) to write the slope-intercept form of an equation for the line of fit shown in the scatter plot.

6. Predict the amount of fish that will be caught in China in 2005.

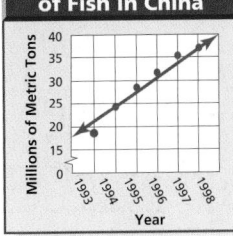

Source: *The World Almanac*

Lesson 6-1 1–16. See margin for graphs.   2, 5, 8–12. See margin.

(pages 318–323)

Solve each inequality. Then check your solution and graph it on a number line. 4. $\{h \mid h > -9\}$

1. $c + 9 \le 3$ $\{c \mid c \le -6\}$ 2. $d - (-3) < 13$ 3. $z - 4 > 20$ $\{z \mid z > 24\}$ 4. $h - (-7) > -2$

5. $-11 > d - 4$ 6. $2x > x - 3$ $\{x \mid x > -3\}$ 7. $2x - 3 \ge x$ $\{x \mid x \ge 3\}$ 8. $16 + w < -20$

9. $14p > 5 + 13p$ 10. $-7 < 16 - z$ 11. $1.1v - 1 > 2.1v - 3$ 12. $\frac{1}{2}t + \frac{1}{4} \ge \frac{3}{2}t - \frac{2}{3}$

13. $9x < 8x - 2$ 14. $-2 + 9n \le 10n$ 15. $a - 2.3 \ge -7.8$ 16. $5z - 6 > 4z$ $\{z \mid z > 6\}$
   $\{x \mid x < -2\}$ $\{n \mid n \ge -2\}$ $\{a \mid a \ge -5.5\}$

Define a variable, write an inequality, and solve each problem. 17–18. See margin for sample answers: Let $n =$ the number.

17. The sum of a number and negative six is greater than 9.

18. Negative five times a number is less than the sum of negative six times the number and 12.

Lesson 6-2 3. $\{w \mid w > -36\}$ 8. $\{x \mid x > 0.6\}$ 11. $\{m \mid m \ge -33\}$

(pages 325–331)

Solve each inequality. Then check your solution. 12. $\{a \mid a > 500\}$

1. $7b \ge -49$ $\{b \mid b \ge -7\}$ 2. $-5j < -60$ $\{j \mid j > 12\}$ 3. $\frac{w}{3} > -12$ 4. $\frac{p}{5} < 8$ $\{p \mid p < 40\}$

5. $-8f < 48$ $\{f \mid f > -6\}$ 6. $-0.25t \ge -10$ $\{t \mid t \le 40\}$ 7. $\frac{g}{-8} < 4$ $\{g \mid g > -32\}$ 8. $-4.3x < -2.58$

9. $4c \ge -6$ $\{c \mid c \ge -1.5\}$ 10. $6 \le 0.8n$ $\{n \mid n \ge 7.5\}$ 11. $\frac{2}{3}m \ge -22$ 12. $-25 > -0.05a$

13. $-15a < -28$ 14. $-\frac{7}{9}x < 42$ $\{x \mid x > -54\}$ 15. $0.375y \le 32$ 16. $-7y \ge 91$
   $\{y \mid y \le -13\}$

Define a variable, write an inequality, and solve each problem. 17–19. Let $n =$ the number.

17. Negative one times a number is greater than -7. $-n > -7$; $\{n \mid n < 7\}$

18. Three fifths of a number is at least negative 10. $\frac{3}{5}n \ge -10$; $\{n \mid n \ge -\frac{50}{3}\}$

19. Seventy-five percent of a number is at most 100. $0.75n \le 100$; $\{n \mid n \le 133.\overline{3}\}$

13. $\{a \mid a > \frac{28}{15}\}$

15. $\{y \mid y \le \frac{256}{3}\}$

1.

2. $\{d \mid d < 10\}$

3.

4.

5. $\{d \mid d < -7\}$

6.

7.

8. $\{w \mid w < -36\}$

9. $\{p \mid p > 5\}$

10. $\{z \mid z < 23\}$

11. $\{v \mid v < 2\}$

12. $\{t \mid t \le \frac{11}{12}\}$

13.

14.

15.

16.

17. Sample answer if $n =$ the number: $n + (-6) > 9$; $\{n \mid n > 15\}$

18. Sample answer if $n =$ the number: $-5n < -6n + 12$; $\{n \mid n < 12\}$

Lesson 5-7

1. **Negative; the value of a car decreases as it ages.**

2. **Positive; the number of students enrolled has been increasing.**

3. **no correlation**

1.
   $-8 \quad -6 \quad -4 \quad -2 \quad 0 \quad 2 \quad 4$

2.
   $-3 \quad -2 \quad -1 \quad 0 \quad 1 \quad 2 \quad 3$

3.
   $-4 \quad -2 \quad 0 \quad 2 \quad 4 \quad 6$

4.
   $-2 \quad 0 \quad 2 \quad 4 \quad 6$

5.
   $-6 \quad -4 \quad -2 \quad 0 \quad 2 \quad 4 \quad 6$

6.
   $-8 \quad -6 \quad -4 \quad -2 \quad 0 \quad 2$

7.
   $-4 \quad -2 \quad 0 \quad 2 \quad 4$

8.
   $-3 \quad -2 \quad -1 \quad 0 \quad 1 \quad 2 \quad 3$

9.
   $-2 \quad -1 \quad 0 \quad 1 \quad 2 \quad 3$

10.
    $-2 \quad -1 \quad 0 \quad 1 \quad 2$

11.
    $-3 \quad -2 \quad -1 \quad 0 \quad 1 \quad 2 \quad 3$

12.
    $0 \quad 4 \quad 8 \quad 12 \quad 16 \quad 20$

13.
    $-16 \quad -12 \quad -8 \quad -4 \quad 0 \quad 4 \quad 8$

14.
    $-3 \quad -2 \quad -1 \quad 0 \quad 1 \quad 2 \quad 3$

15.
    $-8 \quad -4 \quad 0 \quad 4 \quad 8$

16.
    $0 \quad 4 \quad 8 \quad 12 \quad 16$

Lesson 6-3   *(pages 332–337)*

Solve each inequality. Then check your solution.

1. $3y - 4 > -37$ $\{y \mid y > -11\}$
2. $7s - 12 < 13$
3. $-5e + 9 > 24$ $\{e \mid e < -3\}$
4. $-6v - 3 \geq -33$ $\{v \mid v \leq 5\}$
5. $-2k + 12 < 30$ $\{k \mid k > -9\}$
6. $-2x + 1 < 16 - x$ $\{x \mid x > -15\}$
7. $15t - 4 > 11t - 16$ $\{t \mid t > -3\}$
8. $13 - y \leq 29 + 2y$
9. $5q + 7 \leq 3(q + 1)$ $\{q \mid q \leq -2\}$
10. $2(w + 4) \geq 7(w - 1)$ $\{w \mid w \leq 3\}$
11. $-4t - 5 > 2t + 13$ $\{t \mid t < -3\}$
12. $\frac{2t + 5}{3} < -9$ $\{t \mid t < -16\}$
13. $\frac{z}{4} + 7 \geq -5$ $\{z \mid z \geq -48\}$
14. $13r - 11 > 7r + 37$ $\{r \mid r > 8\}$
15. $8c - (c - 5) > c + 17$ $\{c \mid c > 2\}$
16. $-5(k + 4) \geq 3(k - 4)$ $\{k \mid k \leq -1\}$
17. $9m + 7 < 2(4m - 1)$ $\{m \mid m < -9\}$
18. $3(3y + 1) < 13y - 8$
19. $5x \leq 10(3x + 4)$ $\left\{x \mid x \geq -\frac{8}{5}\right\}$
20. $3\left(a + \frac{2}{3}\right) \geq a - 1$ $\left\{a \mid a \geq -\frac{3}{2}\right\}$

2. $\left\{s \mid s < \frac{25}{7}\right\}$ 8. $\left\{y \mid y \geq -\frac{16}{3}\right\}$ 18. $\left\{y \mid y > \frac{11}{4}\right\}$

Lesson 6-4   *(pages 339–344)*

Solve each compound inequality. Then graph the solution set. 1–16. See margin for graphs.

1. $2 + x < -5$ or $2 + x > 5$ $\{x \mid x < -7 \text{ or } x > 3\}$
2. $-4 + t > -5$ or $-4 + t < 7$ $\{t \mid t \text{ is a real number.}\}$
3. $3 \leq 2g + 7$ and $2g + 7 \leq 15$ $\{g \mid -2 \leq g \leq 4\}$
4. $2v - 2 \leq 3v$ and $4v - 1 \geq 3v$ $\{v \mid v \geq 1\}$
5. $3b - 4 \leq 7b + 12$ and $8b - 7 \leq 25$ $\{b \mid -4 \leq b \leq 4\}$
6. $-9 < 2z + 7 < 10$ $\{z \mid -8 < z < 1.5\}$
7. $5m - 8 \geq 10 - m$ or $5m + 11 < -9$
8. $12c - 4 \leq 5c + 10$ or $-4c - 1 \leq c + 24$
9. $2h - 2 \leq 3h \leq 4h - 1$ $\{h \mid h \geq 1\}$
10. $3p + 6 < 8 - p$ and $5p + 8 \geq p + 6$
11. $2r + 8 > 16 - 2r$ and $7r + 21 < r - 9$ $\varnothing$
12. $-4j + 3 < j + 22$ and $j - 3 < 2j - 15$ $\{j \mid j > 12\}$
13. $2(q - 4) \leq 3(q + 2)$ or $q - 8 \leq 4 - q$
14. $\frac{1}{2}w + 5 \geq w + 2 \geq \frac{1}{2}w + 9$ $\varnothing$
15. $n - (6 - n) > 10$ or $-3n - 1 > 20$
16. $-(2x + 5) \leq x + 5 \leq 2x - 9$ $\{x \mid x \geq 14\}$

7. $\{m \mid m < -4 \text{ or } m \geq 3\}$ 8. $\{c \mid c \text{ is a real number.}\}$ 10. $\left\{p \mid -\frac{1}{2} \leq p < \frac{1}{2}\right\}$ 13. $\{q \mid -14 \leq q \leq 6\}$
15. $\{n \mid n < -7 \text{ or } n > 8\}$

Lesson 6-5   *(pages 345–351)*

Solve each open sentence. Then graph the solution set. 1–20. See pp. 852A–852H for graphs.

1. $|y - 9| < 19$ $\{y \mid -10 < y < 28\}$
2. $|g + 6| > 8$ $\{g \mid g < -14 \text{ or } g > 2\}$
3. $|t - 5| \leq 3$ $\{t \mid 2 \leq t \leq 8\}$
4. $|a + 5| \geq 0$ $\{a \mid a \text{ is a real number.}\}$
5. $|14 - 2z| = 16$ $\{-1, 15\}$
6. $|a - 5| = -3$ $\varnothing$
7. $|2m - 5| > 13$ $\{m \mid m < -4 \text{ or } m > 9\}$
8. $|14 - w| \geq 20$ $\{w \mid w \leq -6 \text{ or } w \geq 34\}$
9. $|13 - 5y| = 8$
10. $|3p + 5| \leq 23$ $\left\{p \mid -\frac{28}{3} \leq p \leq 6\right\}$
11. $|6b - 12| \leq 36$ $\{b \mid -4 \leq b \leq 8\}$
12. $|25 - 3x| < 5$
13. $|7 + 8x| > 39$ $\{x \mid x < -5.75 \text{ or } x > 4\}$
14. $|4c + 5| \geq 25$ $\{c \mid c \leq -7.5 \text{ or } c \geq 5\}$
15. $|4 - 5s| > 46$ $\{s \mid s < -8.4 \text{ or } s > 10\}$
16. $|4 - (1 - x)| \geq 10$ $\{x \mid x \leq -13 \text{ or } x \geq 7\}$
17. $\left|\frac{2n - 1}{3}\right| = 10$ $\{-14.5, 15.5\}$
18. $\left|\frac{7 - 2b}{2}\right| \leq 3$ $\{b \mid 0.5 \leq b \leq 6.5\}$
19. $|-2 + (x - 3)| \leq 7$ $\{x \mid -2 \leq x \leq 12\}$
20. $|-3 - (2b - 6)| \geq 10$ $\{b \mid b \leq -3.5 \text{ or } b \geq 6.5\}$

9. $\left\{-1, \frac{21}{5}\right\}$ 12. $\left\{x \mid 6\frac{2}{3} < x < 10\right\}$

Lesson 6-6

(pages 352–357)

Determine which ordered pairs are part of the solution set for each inequality.

1. $x + y \geq 0$, $\{(0, 0), (1, -3), (2, 2), (3, -3)\}$ **{(0, 0), (2, 2), (3, −3)}**
2. $2x + y \leq 8$, $\{(0, 0), (-1, -1), (3, -2), (8, 0)\}$ **{(0, 0), (−1, −1), (3, −2)}**
3. $y > x$, $\{(0, 0), (2, 0), (-3, 4), (2, -1)\}$ **{(−3, 4)}**
4. $3x - 2y < 1$, $\{(0, 0), (3, 2), (-4, -5), (0, 6)\}$ **{(0, 0), (−4, −5), (0, 6)}**

Graph each inequality. 5–19. See margin.

5. $y \leq -2$
6. $x < 4$
7. $x + y < -2$
8. $x + y \geq -4$
9. $y > 4x - 1$
10. $3x + y > 1$
11. $3y - 2x \leq 2$
12. $x < y$
13. $3x + y \leq 4$
14. $5x - y < 5$
15. $-2x + 6y \geq 12$
16. $-x + 3y \leq 9$
17. $y > -3x + 7$
18. $3x + 8y \leq 4$
19. $5x - 2y \geq 6$

Lesson 7-1

(pages 369–374)

Graph each system of equations. Then determine whether the system has *no* solution, *one* solution, or *infinitely many* solutions. If the system has one solution, name it. 1–15. See pp. 852A–852H for graphs.

1. $y = 3x$
   $4x + 2y = 30$ **(3, 9)**
2. $x = -2y$
   $x + y = 1$ **(2, −1)**
3. $y = x + 4$
   $3x + 2y = 18$ **(2, 6)**
4. $x + y = 6$
   $x - y = 2$ **(4, 2)**
5. $x + y = 6$
   $3x + 3y = 3$ **no solution**
6. $y = -3x$
   $4x + y = 2$ **(2, −6)**
7. $2x + y = 8$
   $x - y = 4$ **(4, 0)**
8. $\frac{1}{5}x - y = \frac{12}{5}$
   $3x - 5y = 6$ **(−3, −3)**
9. $x + 2y = 0$
   $y + 3 = -x$ **(−6, 3)**
10. $x + 2y = -9$
    $x - y = 6$ **(1, −5)**
11. $x + \frac{1}{2}y = 3$
    $y = 3x - 4$ **(2, 2)**
12. $\frac{2}{3}x + \frac{1}{2}y = 2$
    $4x + 3y = 12$ **infinitely many**
13. $y = x - 4$
    $x + \frac{1}{2}y = \frac{5}{2}$ **(3, −1)**
14. $2x + y = 3$
    $4x + 2y = 6$ **infinitely many**
15. $12x - y = -21$
    $\frac{1}{2}x + \frac{2}{3}y = -3$ **(−2, −3)**

Lesson 7-2

(pages 376–381)

Use substitution to solve each system of equations. If the system does *not* have exactly one solution, state whether it has *no* solutions or *infinitely many* solutions.

1. $y = x$
   $5x = 12y$ **(0, 0)**
2. $y = 7 - x$
   $2x - y = 8$ **(5, 2)**
3. $x = 5 - y$
   $3y = 3x + 1$ $\left(\frac{7}{3}, \frac{8}{3}\right)$
4. $3x + y = 6$
   $y + 2 = x$ **(2, 0)**
5. $x - 3y = 3$
   $2x + 9y = 11$ $\left(4, \frac{1}{3}\right)$
6. $3x = -18 + 2y$
   $x + 3y = 4$ $\left(-\frac{46}{11}, \frac{30}{11}\right)$
7. $x + 2y = 10$
   $-x + y = 2$ **(2, 4)**
8. $2x = 3 - y$
   $2y = 12 - x$ **(−2, 7)**
9. $6y - x = -36$
   $y = -3x$ $\left(\frac{36}{19}, -\frac{108}{19}\right)$
10. $\frac{3}{4}x + \frac{1}{3}y = 1$
    $x - y = 10$ **(4, −6)**
11. $x + 6y = 1$
    $3x - 10y = 31$ **(7, −1)**
12. $3x - 2y = 12$
    $\frac{3}{2}x - y = 3$ **no solution**
13. $2x + 3y = 5$
    $4x - 9y = 9$ $\left(\frac{12}{5}, \frac{1}{15}\right)$
14. $x = 4 - 8y$
    $3x + 24y = 12$ **infinitely many**
15. $3x - 2y = -3$
    $25x + 10y = 215$ **(5, 9)**

Lesson 6-6

5.
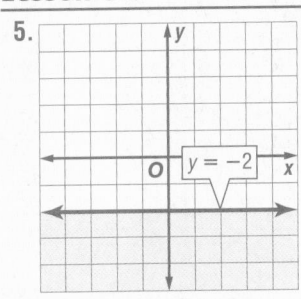

6.
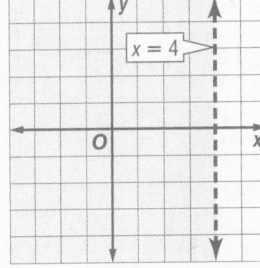

7.
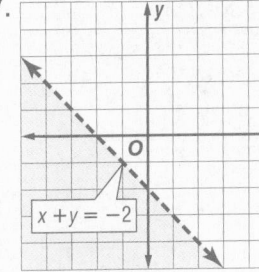

8.
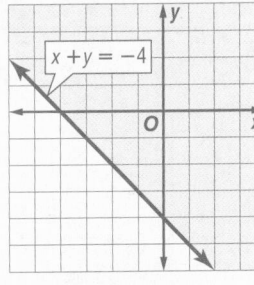

9.
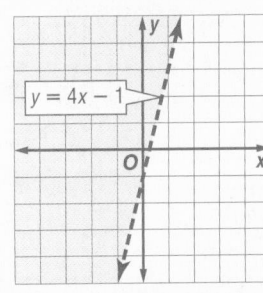

10.
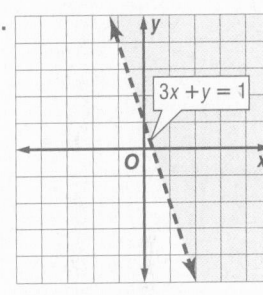

11.
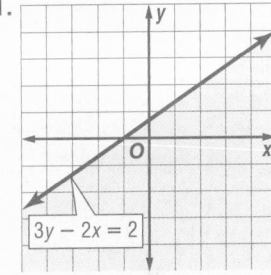

12.
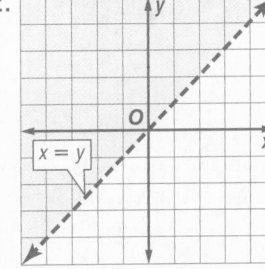

13.
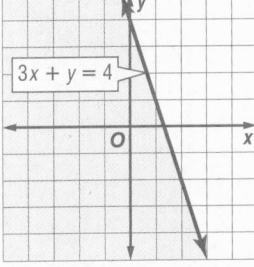

Answers continued on page 852C.

Lesson 7-5

1.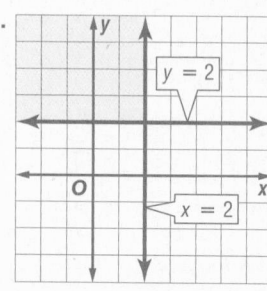

2.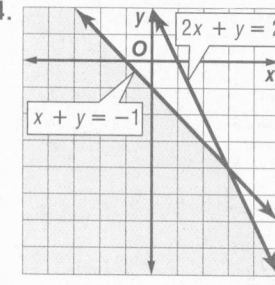

3.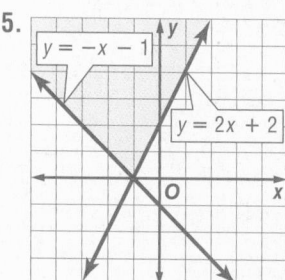

4.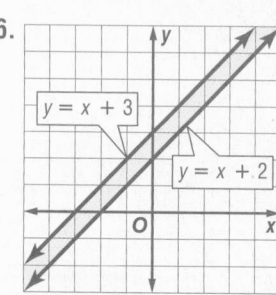

5.

6.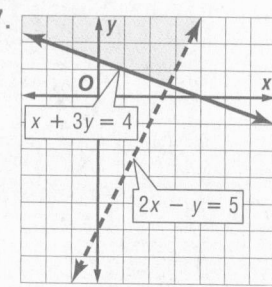

Answers continued on page 852D.

Lesson 7-3

(pages 382–386)

Use elimination to solve each system of equations.

1. $x + y = 7$
$x - y = 9$ **(8, −1)**

2. $2x - y = 32$
$2x + y = 60$ **(23, 14)**

3. $-y + x = 6$
$y + x = 5$ $\left(\dfrac{11}{2}, -\dfrac{1}{2}\right)$

4. $s + 2t = 6$
$3s - 2t = 2$ **(2, 2)**

5. $x = y - 7$
$2x - 5y = -2$ **(−11, −4)**

6. $3x + 5y = -16$
$3x - 2y = -2$ **(−2, −2)**

7. $x - y = 3$
$x + y = 3$ **(3, 0)**

8. $x + y = 8$
$2x - y = 6$ $\left(\dfrac{14}{3}, \dfrac{10}{3}\right)$

9. $2s - 3t = -4$
$s = 7 - 3t$ **(1, 2)**

10. $-6x + 16y = -8$
$6x - 42 = 16y$ **no solution**

11. $3x + 0.2y = 7$
$3x = 0.4y + 4$ **(2, 5)**

12. $9x + 2y = 26$
$1.5x - 2y = 13$ $\left(\dfrac{26}{7}, -\dfrac{26}{7}\right)$

13. $x = y$
$x + y = 7$ **(3.5, 3.5)**

14. $4x - \dfrac{1}{3}y = 8$
$5x + \dfrac{1}{3}y = 6$ $\left(\dfrac{14}{9}, -\dfrac{16}{3}\right)$

15. $2x - y = 3$
$\dfrac{2}{3}x - y = -1$ **(3, 3)**

Lesson 7-4

(pages 387–392)

Use elimination to solve each system of equations.

1. $-3x + 2y = 10$
$-2x - y = -5$ **(0, 5)**

2. $2x + 5y = 13$
$4x - 3y = -13$ **(−1, 3)**

3. $5x + 3y = 4$
$-4x + 5y = -18$ **(2, −2)**

4. $\dfrac{1}{3}x - y = -1$
$\dfrac{1}{5}x - \dfrac{2}{5}y = -1$ **(−9, −2)**

5. $3x - 5y = 8$
$4x - 7y = 10$ **(6, 2)**

6. $x - 0.5y = 1$
$0.4x + y = -2$ **(0, −2)**

7. $x + 8y = 3$
$4x - 2y = 7$ $\left(\dfrac{31}{17}, \dfrac{5}{34}\right)$

8. $4x - y = 4$
$x + 2y = 3$ $\left(\dfrac{11}{9}, \dfrac{8}{9}\right)$

9. $3y - 8x = 9$
$y - x = 2$ $\left(-\dfrac{3}{5}, \dfrac{7}{5}\right)$

10. $x + 4y = 30$
$2x - y = -6$ $\left(\dfrac{2}{3}, \dfrac{22}{3}\right)$

11. $3x - 2y = 0$
$4x + 4y = 5$ $\left(\dfrac{1}{2}, \dfrac{3}{4}\right)$

12. $9x - 3y = 5$
$x + y = 1$ $\left(\dfrac{2}{3}, \dfrac{1}{3}\right)$

13. $2x - 7y = 9$
$-3x + 4y = 6$ **(−6, −3)**

14. $2x - 6y = -16$
$5x + 7y = -18$ **(−5, 1)**

15. $6x - 3y = -9$
$-8x + 2y = 4$ $\left(\dfrac{1}{2}, 4\right)$

Lesson 7-5

(pages 394–398)

Solve each system of inequalities by graphing. **1–15. See margin.**

1. $x > 3$
$y < 6$

2. $y > 2$
$y > -x + 2$

3. $x \le 2$
$y + 3 \ge 5$

4. $x + y \le -1$
$2x + y \le 2$

5. $y \ge 2x + 2$
$y \ge -x - 1$

6. $y \le x + 3$
$y \ge x + 2$

7. $x + 3y \ge 4$
$2x - y < 5$

8. $y - x > 1$
$y + 2x \le 10$

9. $5x - 2y > 15$
$2x - 3y < 6$

10. $4x + 3y > 4$
$2x - y < 0$

11. $4x + 5y \ge 20$
$y \ge x + 1$

12. $-4x + 10y \le 5$
$-2x + 5y < -1$

13. $y - x \ge 0$
$y \le 3$
$x \ge 0$

14. $y > 2x$
$x > -3$
$y < 4$

15. $y \le x$
$x + y < 4$
$y \ge -3$

7.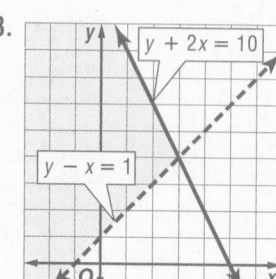

8.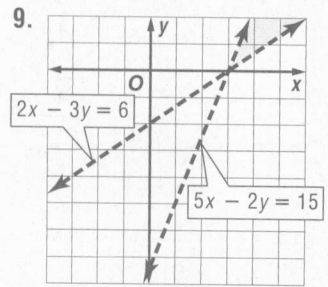

9.

Lesson 8-1

(pages 410–415)

Determine whether each expression is a monomial. Write *yes* or *no*. Explain your reasoning. 1–4. See margin for explanations.

1. $n^2 - 3$ **no**
2. 53 **yes**
3. $9a^2b^3$ **yes**
4. $15 - x^2y$ **no**

Simplify.

5. $a^5(a)(a^7)$ a^{13}
6. $(r^3t^4)(r^4t^4)$ r^7t^8
7. $(x^3y^4)(xy^3)$ x^4y^7
8. $(bc^3)(b^4c^3)$ b^5c^6
9. $(-3mn^2)(5m^3n^2)$ $-15m^4n^4$
10. $[(3^3)^2]^2$ 531,441
11. $(3s^3t^2)(-4s^3t^2)$ $-12s^6t^4$
12. $x^3(x^4y^3)$ x^7y^3
13. $(1.1g^2h^4)^3$ $1.331g^6h^{12}$
14. $-\frac{3}{4}a(a^2b^3c^4)$ $-\frac{3}{4}a^3b^3c^4$
15. $\left(\frac{1}{2}w^3\right)^2(w^4)^2$ $\frac{1}{4}w^{14}$
16. $[(-2^3)^3]^2$ 262,144
17. $\left(\frac{2}{3}y^3\right)(3y^2)^3$ $18y^9$
18. $(10s^3t)(-2s^2t^2)^3$ $-80s^9t^7$
19. $(-0.2u^3w^4)^3$ $-0.008u^9w^{12}$

Lesson 8-2

(pages 417–423)

Simplify. Assume that no denominator is equal to zero.

1. $\frac{6^{10}}{6^7}$ 6^3 or 216
2. $\frac{b^6c^5}{b^3c^2}$ b^3c^3
3. $\frac{(-a)^4b^8}{a^4b^7}$ b
4. $\frac{(-x)^3y^3}{x^3y^6}$ $-\frac{1}{y^3}$
5. $\frac{12ab^5}{4a^4b^3}$ $\frac{3b^2}{a^3}$
6. $\frac{24x^5}{-8x^2}$ $-3x^3$
7. $\frac{-9h^2k^4}{18h^5j^3k^4}$ $-\frac{1}{2h^3j^3}$
8. $\left(\frac{2a^2b^4}{3a^3b}\right)^2$ $\frac{4b^6}{9a^2}$
9. $\frac{9a^2b^7c^3}{2a^5b^4c^5}$ $\frac{9b^3}{2a^3c^2}$
10. $\frac{-15xy^{-5}z^7}{-10x^{-4}y^6z^{-4}}$ $\frac{3x^5z^{11}}{2y^{11}}$
11. 3^{-4} $\frac{1}{81}$
12. $\left(\frac{5}{6}\right)^{-2}$ $\frac{36}{25}$
13. $a^5b^0a^{-7}$ $\frac{1}{a^2}$
14. $\frac{(-u^{-3}v^3)^2}{(u^3v)^{-3}}$ u^3v^9
15. $\left(\frac{a^3}{b^2}\right)^{-3}$ $\frac{b^6}{a^9}$
16. $\left(\frac{2x}{y^{-3}}\right)^{-2}$ $\frac{1}{4x^2y^6}$
17. $\frac{(-r)s^5}{r^{-3}s^{-4}}$ $-r^4s^9$
18. $\frac{28a^{-4}b^0}{14a^3b^{-1}}$ $\frac{2b}{a^7}$
19. $\frac{(j^2k^3m)^4}{(jk^4)^{-1}}$ $j^9k^{16}m^4$
20. $\left(\frac{-2x^4y}{4y^2}\right)^0$ 1
21. $\frac{-18x^0a^{-3}}{-6x^{-2}a^{-3}}$ $3x^2$
22. $\left(\frac{2a^3b^{-2}}{2^{-1}a^{-5}b^3}\right)^{-1}$ $\frac{b^5}{4a^8}$
23. $\left(\frac{5n^{-1}m^2}{2nm^{-2}}\right)^0$ 1
24. $\frac{(3ab^2c)^{-3}}{(2a^2bc^2)^2}$ $\frac{1}{108a^7b^8c^7}$

Lesson 8-3

(pages 425–430)

Express each number in standard notation.

1. 2.6×10^5 **260,000**
2. 4×10^{-3} **0.004**
3. 6.72×10^3 **6720**
4. 4.93×10^{-4} **0.000493**
5. 1.654×10^{-6} **0.000001654**
6. 7.348×10^7 **73,480,000**

Express each number in scientific notation. 13. 1.21212×10^{-1}

7. 6500 6.5×10^3
8. 953.56 9.5356×10^2
9. 0.697 6.97×10^{-1}
10. 843.5 8.435×10^2
11. 568,000 5.68×10^5
12. 0.0000269 2.69×10^{-5}
13. 0.121212
14. 543×10^4 5.43×10^6
15. 739.9×10^{-5}
    7.399×10^{-3}
16. 6480×10^{-2}
    6.48×10^1
17. 0.366×10^{-7}
    3.66×10^{-8}
18. 167×10^3 1.67×10^5

Evaluate. Express each result in scientific and standard notation. 19–27. See margin.

19. $(2 \times 10^5)(3 \times 10^{-8})$
20. $\frac{4.8 \times 10^3}{1.6 \times 10^1}$
21. $(4 \times 10^2)(1.5 \times 10^6)$
22. $\frac{8.1 \times 10^2}{2.7 \times 10^{-3}}$
23. $\frac{7.8 \times 10^{-5}}{1.3 \times 10^{-7}}$
24. $(2.2 \times 10^{-2})(3.2 \times 10^5)$
25. $(3.1 \times 10^4)(4.2 \times 10^{-5})$
26. $(78 \times 10^6)(0.01 \times 10^5)$
27. $\frac{2.31 \times 10^{-2}}{3.3 \times 10^{-3}}$

Extra Practice **837**

Extra Practice

Lesson 8-1

1. It shows subtraction, not multiplication of variables.
2. It is a real number and therefore a monomial.
3. It is a product of a number and two variables.
4. It shows subtraction, not multiplication of variables.

Lesson 8-3

19. 6×10^{-3}; 0.006
20. 3.0×10^2; 300
21. 6.0×10^8; 600,000,000
22. 3.0×10^5; 300,000
23. 6.0×10^2; 600
24. 7.04×10^3; 7040
25. 1.302×10^0; 1.302
26. 7.8×10^{10}; 78,000,000,000
27. 7.0×10^0; 7

Extra Practice

Lesson 8-4

13. $-3x + 2x^2 + 4x^3 - x^5$

14. $-1 + x - x^2 + x^3$

15. $2a - 4ax + 3ax^2$

16. $-b^3 - 2bx + 4x^2 - 5bx^3$

17. $1 + 2x^2 - x^6 + x^8$

18. $d^3 - c^2d^2x + cdx^2$

19. $-3x^3 + 5x^2 + 2x + 7$

20. $x^5 + 4x^3 - 6x - 20$

21. $b^3x^2 + \frac{2}{3}bx + 5b$

22. $3px^3 + 21p^2x + p^4$

23. $-6a^2x^3 + 3ax^2 - 8x + 7a^3$

24. $4x^4 + \frac{1}{3}s^2x^3 - \frac{2}{5}s^4x^2 + \frac{1}{4}x$

Lesson 8-5

5. $-12t^2 - 8ts - 3s^2$

6. $4a^2 - 12ab - 10b^2$

7. $-a^2 - 10b^2 + 9c^2 + 2b$

8. $-3z^2 + 13z - 3$

9. $7d - 7e - 3f - 6$

10. $6g + 5h - 9 - 6k$

11. $8x^2 + 5xy - 15y^2$

12. $11m + 4mn - 7n$

13. $-3x^2 - 8y^2 + 11z^2 + 12$

14. $13z^4 - 2z^3 - 5z^2$

Lesson 8-6

7. $-3ab^3 - 4a^2b^2 + 6a^3b$

8. $36m^4n + 4m^3n - 20m^2n^2$

9. $-16s^3t^5 + 28s^6t^2 - 12s^2t^5$

10. $-3x^3 - \frac{1}{3}x^2 + \frac{5}{3}x$

11. $-16m^3n + 6m^2n^2 - 2mn^3$

12. $-\frac{1}{4}ab^4 + \frac{1}{3}ab^3 - \frac{3}{4}ab^2$

13. $-6a^2 + 41a$

14. $72b^2 - 33b - 14$

15. $2x^2 - 6x$

16. $2n^2 + 55n - 33$

17. $-2x^2 - 3x + 9$

18. $4mn - 4m - 5n^2 - 5n$

19. $-3x$

20. $-2c^2 - 6c + 15a$

21. $-5n + 13n^2$

Lesson 8-4

(pages 432–436)

State whether each expression is a polynomial. If the expression is a polynomial, identify it as a *monomial*, a *binomial*, or a *trinomial*.

1. $5x^2y + 3xy - 7$ **yes; trinomial**

2. 0 **yes; monomial**

3. $\frac{5}{k} - k^2y$ **no**

4. $3a^2x - 5a$ **yes; binomial**

Find the degree of each polynomial.

5. $a + 5c$ **1**

6. $14abcd - 6d^3$ **4**

7. $\frac{a^3}{4}$ **3**

8. 10 **0**

9. $-4h^5$ **5**

10. $\frac{x^2}{3} - \frac{x}{2} + \frac{1}{5}$ **2**

11. -6 **0**

12. $a^2b^3 - a^3b^2$ **5**

Arrange the terms of each polynomial so that the powers of x are in ascending order. **13–18. See margin.**

13. $2x^2 - 3x + 4x^3 - x^5$

14. $x^3 - x^2 + x - 1$

15. $2a + 3ax^2 - 4ax$

16. $-5bx^3 - 2bx + 4x^2 - b^3$

17. $x^8 + 2x^2 - x^6 + 1$

18. $cdx^2 - c^2d^2x + d^3$

Arrange the terms of each polynomial so that the powers of x are in descending order. **19–24. See margin.**

19. $5x^2 - 3x^3 + 7 + 2x$

20. $-6x + x^5 + 4x^3 - 20$

21. $5b + b^3x^2 + \frac{2}{3}bx$

22. $21p^2x + 3px^3 + p^4$

23. $3ax^2 - 6a^2x^3 + 7a^3 - 8x$

24. $\frac{1}{3}s^2x^3 + 4x^4 - \frac{2}{5}s^4x^2 + \frac{1}{4}x$

Lesson 8-5

(pages 439–443)

Find each sum or difference. **5–14. See margin.**

1. $(3a^2 + 5) + (4a^2 - 1)$ **$7a^2 + 4$**

2. $(5x - 3) + (-2x + 1)$ **$3x - 2$**

3. $(6z + 2) - (9z + 3)$ **$-3z - 1$**

4. $(-4n + 7) - (-7n - 8)$ **$3n + 15$**

5. $(-7t^2 + 4ts - 6s^2) + (-5t^2 - 12ts + 3s^2)$

6. $(6a^2 - 7ab - 4b^2) - (2a^2 + 5ab + 6b^2)$

7. $(4a^2 - 10b^2 + 7c^2) + (-5a^2 + 2c^2 + 2b)$

8. $(z^2 + 6z - 8) - (4z^2 - 7z - 5)$

9. $(4d + 3e - 8f) - (-3d + 10e - 5f + 6)$

10. $(7g + 8h - 9) + (-g - 3h - 6k)$

11. $(9x^2 - 11xy - 3y^2) - (x^2 - 16xy + 12y^2)$

12. $(-3m + 9mn - 5n) + (14m - 5mn - 2n)$

13. $(4x^2 - 8y^2 - 3z^2) - (7x^2 - 14z^2 - 12)$

14. $(17z^4 - 5z^2 + 3z) - (4z^4 + 2z^3 + 3z)$

15. $(6 - 7y + 3y^2) + (3 - 5y - 2y^2) + (-12 - 8y + y^2)$ **$2y^2 - 20y - 3$**

16. $(-7c^2 - 2c - 5) + (9c - 6) + (16c^2 + 3) + (-9c^2 - 7c + 7)$ **-1**

Lesson 8-6

(pages 444–449)

Find each product. **7–12. See margin.**

1. $-3(8x + 5)$ **$-24x - 15$**

2. $3b(5b + 8)$ **$15b^2 + 24b$**

3. $1.1a(2a + 7)$ **$2.2a^2 + 7.7a$**

4. $\frac{1}{2}x(8x - 6)$ **$4x^2 - 3x$**

5. $7xy(5x^2 - y^2)$ **$35x^3y - 7xy^3$**

6. $5y(y^2 - 3y + 6)$ **$5y^3 - 15y^2 + 30y$**

7. $-ab(3b^2 + 4ab - 6a^2)$

8. $4m^2(9m^2n + mn - 5n^2)$

9. $4st^2(-4s^2t^3 + 7s^5 - 3st^3)$

10. $-\frac{1}{3}x(9x^2 + x - 5)$

11. $-2mn(8m^2 - 3mn + n^2)$

12. $-\frac{3}{4}ab^2\left(\frac{1}{3}b^2 - \frac{4}{9}b + 1\right)$

Simplify. **13–21. See margin.**

13. $-3a(2a - 12) + 5a$

14. $6(12b^2 - 2b) + 7(-2 - 3b)$

15. $x(x - 6) + x(x - 2) + 2x$

16. $11(n - 3) + 2(n^2 + 22n)$

17. $-2x(x + 3) + 3(x + 3)$

18. $4m(n - 1) - 5n(n + 1)$

19. $-7xy + x(7y - 3)$

20. $5(-c + 3a) - c(2c + 1)$

21. $-9n(1 - n) + 4(n^2 + n)$

Solve each equation.

22. $-6(11 - 2x) = 7(-2 - 2x)$ **2**

23. $11(n - 3) + 5 = 2n + 44$ **8**

24. $a(a - 6) + 2a = 3 + a(a - 2)$ **-1.5**

25. $q(2q + 3) + 20 = 2q(q - 3)$ **$-\frac{20}{9}$**

26. $w(w + 12) = w(w + 14) + 12$ **-6**

27. $x(x - 3) + 4x - 3 = 8x + x(3 + x)$ **$-\frac{3}{10}$**

28. $-3(x + 5) + x(x - 1) = x(x + 2) - 3$ **-2**

29. $n(n - 5) + n(n + 2) = 2n(n - 1) + 1.5$ **-1.5**

Lesson 8-7

(pages 452–457)

Find each product. 12, 15, 16, 20–22, 25–27, 30. See margin.

1. $(d + 2)(d + 5)$ $d^2 + 7d + 10$
2. $(z + 7)(z - 4)$ $z^2 + 3z - 28$
3. $(m - 8)(m - 5)$ $m^2 - 13m + 40$
4. $(a + 2)(a - 19)$ $a^2 - 17a - 38$
5. $(c + 15)(c - 3)$ $c^2 + 12c - 45$
6. $(x + y)(x - 2y)$ $x^2 - xy - 2y^2$
7. $(2x - 5)(x + 6)$ $2x^2 + 7x - 30$
8. $(7a - 4)(2a - 5)$ $14a^2 - 43a + 20$
9. $(4x + y)(2x - 3y)$ $8x^2 - 10xy - 3y^2$
10. $(7v + 3)(v + 4)$ $7v^2 + 31v + 12$
11. $(7s - 8)(3s - 2)$ $21s^2 - 38s + 16$
12. $(4g + 3h)(2g - 5h)$
13. $(4a + 3)(2a - 1)$ $8a^2 + 2a - 3$
14. $(7y - 1)(2y - 3)$ $14y^2 - 23y + 3$
15. $(2x + 3y)(4x + 2y)$
16. $(12r - 4s)(5r + 8s)$
17. $(-a + 1)(-3a - 2)$ $3a^2 - a - 2$
18. $(2n - 4)(-3n - 2)$ $-6n^2 + 8n + 8$
19. $(x - 2)(x^2 + 2x + 4)$ $x^3 - 8$
20. $(3x + 5)(2x^2 - 5x + 11)$
21. $(4s + 5)(3s^2 + 8s - 9)$
22. $(3a + 5)(-8a^2 + 2a + 3)$
23. $(a - b)(a^2 + ab + b^2)$ $a^3 - b^3$
24. $(c + d)(c^2 - cd + d^2)$ $c^3 + d^3$
25. $(5x - 2)(-5x^2 + 2x + 7)$
26. $(-n + 2)(-2n^2 + n - 1)$
27. $(x^2 - 7x + 4)(2x^2 - 3x - 6)$
28. $(x^2 + x + 1)(x^2 - x - 1)$ $x^4 - x^2 - 2x - 1$
29. $(a^2 + 2a + 5)(a^2 - 3a - 7)$ $a^4 - a^3 - 8a^2 - 29a - 35$
30. $(5x^4 - 2x^2 + 1)(x^2 - 5x + 3)$

Lesson 8-8

(pages 458–463)

Find each product. 4. $100x^2 - 121y^2$ 17. $25a^2 - 120ab + 144b^2$ 27–30. See margin.

1. $(t + 7)^2$ $t^2 + 14t + 49$
2. $(w - 12)(w + 12)$ $w^2 - 144$
3. $(q - 4h)^2$ $q^2 - 8qh + 16h^2$
4. $(10x + 11y)(10x - 11y)$
5. $(4e + 3)^2$ $16e^2 + 24e + 9$
6. $(2b - 4d)(2b + 4d)$ $4b^2 - 16d^2$
7. $(a + 2b)^2$ $a^2 + 4ab + 4b^2$
8. $(3x + y)^2$ $9x^2 + 6xy + y^2$
9. $(6m + 2n)^2$ $36m^2 + 24mn + 4n^2$
10. $(3m - 7d)^2$ $9m^2 - 42md + 49d^2$
11. $(5b - 6)(5b + 6)$ $25b^2 - 36$
12. $(1 + x)^2$ $1 + 2x + x^2$
13. $(5x - 9y)^2$ $25x^2 - 90xy + 81y^2$
14. $(8a - 2b)(8a + 2b)$ $64a^2 - 4b^2$
15. $\left(\frac{1}{4}x + 4\right)^2$ $\frac{1}{16}x^2 + 2x + 16$
16. $(c - 3d)^2$ $c^2 - 6d + 9d^2$
17. $(5a - 12b)^2$
18. $\left(\frac{1}{2}x + y\right)^2$ $\frac{1}{4}x^2 + xy + y^2$
19. $(n^2 + 1)^2$ $n^4 + 2n^2 + 1$
20. $(k^2 - 3j)^2$ $k^4 - 6k^2j + 9j^2$
21. $(a^2 - 5)(a^2 + 5)$ $a^4 - 25$
22. $(2x^3 - 7)(2x^3 + 7)$ $4x^6 - 49$
23. $(3x^3 - 9y)(3x^3 + 9y)$ $9x^6 - 81y^2$
24. $(7a^2 - b)(7a^2 + b)$ $49a^4 - b^2$
25. $\left(\frac{1}{2}x - 10\right)\left(\frac{1}{2}x + 10\right)$ $\frac{1}{4}x^2 - 100$
26. $\left(\frac{1}{3}n - m\right)\left(\frac{1}{3}n + m\right)$ $\frac{1}{9}n^2 - m^2$
27. $(a - 1)(a - 1)(a - 1)$
28. $(x + 2)(x - 2)(2x + 5)$
29. $(4x - 1)(4x + 1)(x - 4)$
30. $(x - 5)(x + 5)(x + 4)(x - 4)$
31. $(a + 1)(a + 1)(a - 1)(a - 1)$ $a^4 - 2a^2 + 1$
32. $(n - 1)(n + 1)(n - 1)$ $n^3 - n^2 - n + 1$
33. $(2c + 3)(2c + 3)(2c - 3)(2c - 3)$ $16c^4 - 72c^2 + 81$
34. $(4d + 5e)(4d + 5e)(4d - 5e)(4d - 5e)$ $256d^4 - 800e^2d^2 + 625e^4$

Lesson 9-1

(pages 474–479)

Find the factors of each number. Then classify each number as *prime* or *composite*.

1. 23 1, 23; prime
2. 21 1, 3, 7, 21; composite
3. 81 1, 3, 9, 27, 81; composite
4. 24 1, 2, 3, 4, 6, 8, 12, 24; composite
5. 18 1, 2, 3, 6, 9, 18; composite
6. 22 1, 2, 11, 22; composite

Find the prime factorization of each integer.

7. 42 $2 \cdot 3 \cdot 7$
8. 267 $3 \cdot 89$
9. -72 $-1 \cdot 2^3 \cdot 3^2$
10. 164 $2^2 \cdot 41$
11. -57 $-1 \cdot 3 \cdot 19$
12. -60 $-1 \cdot 2^2 \cdot 3 \cdot 5$

Factor each monomial completely. 13–18. See margin.

13. $240mn$
14. $-64a^3b$
15. $-26xy^2$
16. $-231xy^2z$
17. $44rs^2t^3$
18. $-756m^2n^2$

Find the GCF of each set of monomials.

19. 16, 60 4
20. 15, 50 5
21. 45, 80 5
22. 29, 58 29
23. 55, 305 5
24. 126, 252 126
25. 128, 245 1
26. $7y^2$, $14y^2$ $7y^2$
27. $4xy$, $-6x$ $2x$
28. $35t^2$, $7t$ $7t$
29. $16pq^2$, $12p^2q$, $4pq$ $4pq$
30. 5, 15, 10 5
31. $12mn$, $10mn$, $15mn$ mn
32. $14xy$, $12y$, $20x$ 2
33. $26jk^4$, $16jk^3$, $8j^2$ $2j$

Lesson 8-7

12. $8g^2 - 14gh - 15h^2$
15. $8x^2 + 16xy + 6y^2$
16. $60r^2 + 76rs - 32s^2$
20. $6x^3 - 5x^2 + 8x + 55$
21. $12s^3 + 47s^2 + 4s - 45$
22. $-24a^3 - 34a^2 + 19a + 15$
25. $-25x^3 + 20x^2 + 31x - 14$
26. $2n^3 - 5n^2 + 3n - 2$
27. $2x^4 - 17x^3 + 23x^2 + 30x - 24$
30. $5x^6 - 25x^5 + 13x^4 + 10x^3 - 5x^2 - 5x + 3$

Lesson 8-8

27. $a^3 - 3a^2 + 3a - 1$
28. $2x^3 + 5x^2 - 8x - 20$
29. $16x^3 - 64x^2 - x + 4$
30. $x^4 - 41x^2 + 400$

Lesson 9-1

13. $2 \cdot 2 \cdot 2 \cdot 2 \cdot 3 \cdot 5 \cdot m \cdot n$
14. $-1 \cdot 2 \cdot 2 \cdot 2 \cdot 2 \cdot 2 \cdot 2 \cdot a \cdot a \cdot a \cdot b$
15. $-1 \cdot 2 \cdot 13 \cdot x \cdot y \cdot y$
16. $-1 \cdot 3 \cdot 7 \cdot 11 \cdot x \cdot y \cdot y \cdot z$
17. $2 \cdot 2 \cdot 11 \cdot r \cdot s \cdot s \cdot t \cdot t \cdot t$
18. $-1 \cdot 2 \cdot 2 \cdot 3 \cdot 3 \cdot 3 \cdot 7 \cdot m \cdot m \cdot n \cdot n$

8. $2mn(m^2n - 8n + 4)$

9. $(2x + b)(a + 3c)$

10. $(2m + r)(3x - 2)$

11. $(3x - 4)(a - 2b)$

12. $(a + 1)(a - 2b)$

13. $(2a + b)(4c - d)$

14. $2(e^2 + f)(g + 2h)$

15. $(x - y)(x - y)$

Lesson 9-2
(pages 481–486)

Factor each polynomial. 8–15. See margin.

1. $10a^2 + 40a$ $10a(a + 4)$
2. $15wx - 35wx^2$ $5wx(3 - 7x)$
3. $27a^2b + 9b^3$ $9b(3a^2 + b^2)$
4. $11x + 44x^2y$ $11x(1 + 4xy)$
5. $16y^2 + 8y$ $8y(2y + 1)$
6. $14mn^2 + 2mn$ $2mn(7n + 1)$
7. $25a^2b^2 + 30ab^3$ $5ab^2(5a + 6b)$
8. $2m^3n^2 - 16mn^2 + 8mn$
9. $2ax + 6xc + ba + 3bc$
10. $6mx - 4m + 3rx - 2r$
11. $3ax - 6bx + 8b - 4a$
12. $a^2 - 2ab + a - 2b$
13. $8ac - 2ad + 4bc - bd$
14. $2e^2g + 2fg + 4e^2h + 4fh$
15. $x^2 - xy - xy + y^2$

Solve each equation. Check your solutions.

16. $a(a - 9) = 0$ $\{0, 9\}$
17. $d(d + 11) = 0$ $\{-11, 0\}$
18. $z(z - 2.5) = 0$ $\{0, 2.5\}$
19. $(2y + 6)(y - 1) = 0$ $\{-3, 1\}$
20. $(4n - 7)(3n + 2) = 0$ $\left\{-\frac{2}{3}, \frac{7}{4}\right\}$
21. $(a - 1)(a + 1) = 0$ $\{-1, 1\}$
22. $10x^2 - 20x = 0$ $\{0, 2\}$
23. $8b^2 - 12b = 0$ $\{0, 1.5\}$
24. $14d^2 + 49d = 0$ $\{0, -3.5\}$
25. $15a^2 = 60a$ $\{0, 4\}$
26. $33x^2 = -22x$ $\left\{-\frac{2}{3}, 0\right\}$
27. $32x^2 = 16x$ $\left\{0, \frac{1}{2}\right\}$

Lesson 9-3
(pages 489–494)

Factor each trinomial.

1. $x^2 - 9x + 14$ $(x - 7)(x - 2)$
2. $a^2 - 9a - 36$ $(a - 12)(a + 3)$
3. $x^2 + 2x - 15$ $(x + 5)(x - 3)$
4. $n^2 - 8n + 15$ $(n - 5)(n - 3)$
5. $b^2 + 22b + 21$ $(b + 21)(b + 1)$
6. $c^2 + 2c - 3$ $(c + 3)(c - 1)$
7. $x^2 - 5x - 24$ $(x - 8)(x + 3)$
8. $n^2 - 8n + 7$ $(n - 7)(n - 1)$
9. $m^2 - 10m - 39$ $(m - 13)(m + 3)$
10. $z^2 + 15z + 36$ $(z + 12)(z + 3)$
11. $s^2 - 13st - 30t^2$ $(s - 15t)(s + 2t)$
12. $y^2 + 2y - 35$ $(y + 7)(y - 5)$
13. $r^2 + 3r - 40$ $(r + 8)(r - 5)$
14. $x^2 + 5x - 6$ $(x + 6)(x - 1)$
15. $x^2 - 4xy - 5y^2$ $(x - 5y)(x + y)$
16. $r^2 + 16r + 63$ $(r + 9)(r + 7)$
17. $v^2 + 24v - 52$ $(v + 26)(v - 2)$
18. $k^2 - 27kj - 90j^2$ $(k - 30j)(k + 3j)$

Solve each equation. Check your solutions.

19. $a^2 + 3a - 4 = 0$ $\{-4, 1\}$
20. $x^2 - 8x - 20 = 0$ $\{-2, 10\}$
21. $b^2 + 11b + 24 = 0$ $\{-8, -3\}$
22. $y^2 + y - 42 = 0$ $\{-7, 6\}$
23. $k^2 + 2k - 24 = 0$ $\{-6, 4\}$
24. $r^2 - 13r - 48 = 0$ $\{-3, 16\}$
25. $n^2 - 9n = -18$ $\{3, 6\}$
26. $2z + z^2 = 35$ $\{-7, 5\}$
27. $-20x + 19 = -x^2$ $\{1, 19\}$
28. $10 + a^2 = -7a$ $\{-5, -2\}$
29. $z^2 - 57 = 16z$ $\{-3, 19\}$
30. $x^2 = -14x - 33$ $\{-11, -3\}$
31. $22x - x^2 = 96$ $\{6, 16\}$
32. $-144 = q^2 - 26q$ $\{8, 18\}$
33. $x^2 + 84 = 20x$ $\{6, 14\}$

Lesson 9-4
(pages 495–500)

Factor each trinomial, if possible. If the trinomial cannot be factored using integers, write *prime*. 10. $(2m - 3)(4m + 1)$ 17. $(3c + d)(4c - 5d)$ 18. $(5n - m)(6n + m)$

1. $4a^2 + 4a - 63$ $(2a - 7)(2a + 9)$
2. $3x^2 - 7x - 6$ $(3x + 2)(x - 3)$
3. $4r^2 - 25r + 6$ $(4r - 1)(r - 6)$
4. $2z^2 - 11z + 15$ $(2z - 5)(z - 3)$
5. $3a^2 - 2a - 21$ $(3a + 7)(a - 3)$
6. $4y^2 + 11y + 6$ $(4y + 3)(y + 2)$
7. $6n^2 + 7n - 3$ $(2n + 3)(3n - 1)$
8. $5x^2 - 17x + 14$ $(5x - 7)(x - 2)$
9. $2n^2 - 11n + 13$ **prime**
10. $8m^2 - 10m - 3$
11. $6y^2 + 2y - 2$ $2(3y^2 + y - 1)$
12. $2r^2 + 3r - 14$ $(2r + 7)(r - 2)$
13. $5a^2 - 3a + 15$ **prime**
14. $18v^2 + 24v + 12$ $6(3v^2 + 4v + 2)$
15. $4k^2 + 2k - 12$ $2(2k - 3)(k + 2)$
16. $10x^2 - 20xy + 10y^2$ $10(x - y)(x - y)$
17. $12c^2 - 11cd - 5d^2$
18. $30n^2 - mn - m^2$

Solve each equation. Check your solutions. 24. $\left\{-\frac{1}{6}, \frac{3}{2}\right\}$ 28. $\left\{-2, \frac{3}{2}\right\}$ 29. $\left\{-2, \frac{5}{13}\right\}$ 30. $\left\{-\frac{2}{7}, 2\right\}$

19. $8t^2 + 32t + 24 = 0$ $\{-3, -1\}$
20. $6y^2 + 72y + 192 = 0$ $\{-8, -4\}$
21. $5x^2 + 3x - 2 = 0$ $\left\{-1, \frac{2}{5}\right\}$
22. $9x^2 + 18x - 27 = 0$ $\{-3, 1\}$
23. $4x^2 - 4x - 4 = 4$ $\{-1, 2\}$
24. $12n^2 - 16n - 3 = 0$
25. $12x^2 - x - 35 = 0$ $\left\{-\frac{5}{3}, \frac{7}{4}\right\}$
26. $18x^2 + 36x - 14 = 0$ $\left\{-\frac{7}{3}, \frac{1}{3}\right\}$
27. $15a^2 + a - 2 = 0$ $\left\{-\frac{2}{5}, \frac{1}{3}\right\}$
28. $14b^2 + 7b - 42 = 0$
29. $13r^2 + 21r - 10 = 0$
30. $35y^2 - 60y - 20 = 0$
31. $16x^2 - 4x - 6 = 0$ $\left\{-\frac{1}{2}, \frac{3}{4}\right\}$
32. $28d^2 + 5d - 3 = 0$ $\left\{-\frac{3}{7}, \frac{1}{4}\right\}$
33. $30x^2 - 9x - 3 = 0$ $\left\{-\frac{1}{5}, \frac{1}{2}\right\}$

Lesson 9-5

(pages 501–506)

Factor each polynomial, if possible. If the polynomial cannot be factored, write prime. **13.** $(3x - 10y)(3x + 10y)$

1. $x^2 - 9$ $(x - 3)(x + 3)$
2. $a^2 - 64$ $(a - 8)(a + 8)$
3. $4x^2 - 9y^2$ $(2x - 3y)(2x + 3y)$
4. $1 - 9z^2$ $(1 - 3z)(1 + 3z)$
5. $16a^2 - 9b^2$ $(4a - 3b)(4a + 3b)$
6. $8x^2 - 12y^2$ $4(2x^2 - 3y^2)$
7. $a^2 - 4b^2$ $(a - 2b)(a + 2b)$
8. $x^2 - y^2$ $(x - y)(x + y)$
9. $75r^2 - 48$ $3(5r - 4)(5r + 4)$
10. $x^2 - 36y^2$ $(x - 6y)(x + 6y)$
11. $3a^2 - 16$ prime
12. $12t^2 - 75$ $3(2t - 5)(2t + 5)$
13. $9x^2 - 100y^2$
14. $49 - a^2b^2$ $(7 - ab)(7 + ab)$
15. $5a^2 - 48$ prime
16. $169 - 16t^2$ $(13 - 4t)(13 + 4t)$
17. $8r^2 - 4$ $4(2r^2 - 1)$
18. $-45m^2 + 5$
$-5(3m - 1)(3m + 1)$

Solve each equation by factoring. Check your solutions.

19. $4x^2 = 16$ $\{\pm 2\}$
20. $2x^2 = 50$ $\{\pm 5\}$
21. $9n^2 - 4 = 0$ $\left\{\pm\frac{2}{3}\right\}$
22. $a^2 - \frac{25}{36} = 0$ $\left\{\pm\frac{5}{6}\right\}$
23. $\frac{16}{9} - b^2 = 0$ $\left\{\pm\frac{4}{3}\right\}$
24. $18 - \frac{1}{2}x^2 = 0$ $\{\pm 6\}$
25. $20 - 5g^2 = 0$ $\{\pm 2\}$
26. $16 - \frac{1}{4}p^2 = 0$ $\{\pm 8\}$
27. $\frac{1}{4}c^2 - \frac{4}{9} = 0$ $\left\{\pm\frac{4}{3}\right\}$
28. $3z^2 - 48 = 0$ $\{\pm 4\}$
29. $72 - 2z^2 = 0$ $\{\pm 6\}$
30. $25a^2 = 1$ $\left\{\pm\frac{1}{5}\right\}$
31. $2q^3 - 2q = 0$ $\{-1, 0, 1\}$
32. $3r^3 = 48r$ $\{-4, 0, 4\}$
33. $100d - 4d^3 = 0$ $\{-5, 0, 5\}$

Lesson 9-6

(pages 508–514)

Determine whether each trinomial is a perfect square trinomial. If so, factor it.

1. $x^2 + 12x + 36$ yes; $(x + 6)^2$
2. $n^2 - 13n + 36$ no
3. $a^2 + 4a + 4$ yes; $(a + 2)^2$
4. $x^2 - 10x - 100$ no
5. $2n^2 + 17n + 21$ no
6. $4a^2 - 20a + 25$ yes; $(2a - 5)^2$

Factor each polynomial, if possible. If the polynomial cannot be factored, write prime.

7. $3x^2 - 75$ $3(x - 5)(x + 5)$
8. $n^2 - 8n + 16$ $(n - 4)^2$
9. $4p^2 + 12pr + 9r^2$ $(2p + 3r)^2$
10. $6a^2 + 72$ $6(a^2 + 12)$
11. $s^2 + 30s + 225$ $(s + 15)^2$
12. $24x^2 + 24x + 9$ $3(8x^2 + 8x + 3)$
13. $1 - 10z + 25z^2$ $(1 - 5z)^2$
14. $28 - 63b^2$ $7(2 - 3b)(2 + 3b)$
15. $4c^2 + 2c - 7$ prime

Solve each equation. Check your solutions.

16. $x^2 + 22x + 121 = 0$ $\{-11\}$
17. $343d^2 = 7$ $\left\{\pm\frac{1}{7}\right\}$
18. $(a - 7)^2 = 5$ $7 \pm \sqrt{5}$
19. $c^2 + 10c + 36 = 11$ $\{-5\}$
20. $16s^2 + 81 = 72s$ $\left\{\frac{9}{4}\right\}$
21. $9p^2 - 42p + 20 = -29$ $\left\{\frac{7}{3}\right\}$

Lesson 10-1

(pages 524–530)

Use a table of values to graph each function. **1–6. See margin.**

1. $y = x^2 + 6x + 8$
2. $y = -x^2 + 3x$
3. $y = -x^2$
4. $y = x^2 + x + 3$
5. $y = x^2 + 1$
6. $y = 3x^2 + 6x + 16$

Write the equation of the axis of symmetry, and find the coordinates of the vertex of the graph of each equation. Identify the vertex as a maximum or minimum. Then graph the equation. **7–24. See margin.**

7. $y = -x^2 + 2x - 3$
8. $y = 3x^2 + 24x + 80$
9. $y = x^2 - 4x - 4$
10. $y = 5x^2 - 20x + 37$
11. $y = 3x^2 + 6x + 3$
12. $y = 2x^2 + 12x$
13. $y = x^2 - 6x + 5$
14. $y = x^2 + 6x + 9$
15. $y = -x^2 + 16x - 15$
16. $y = 4x^2 - 1$
17. $y = -2x^2 - 2x + 4$
18. $y = 6x^2 - 12x - 4$
19. $y = -x^2 - 1$
20. $y = -x^2 + x + 1$
21. $y = -5x^2 - 3x + 2$
22. $y = -x^2 + x + 20$
23. $y = 2x^2 + 5x - 2$
24. $y = -3x^2 - 18x - 15$

4.

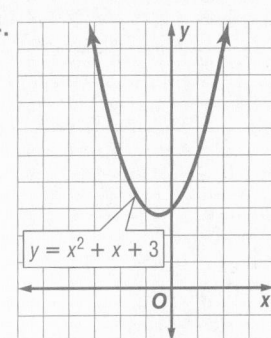

5.

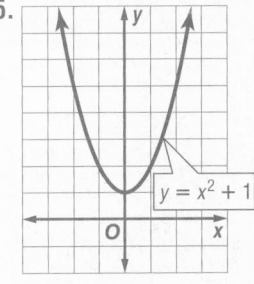

6.

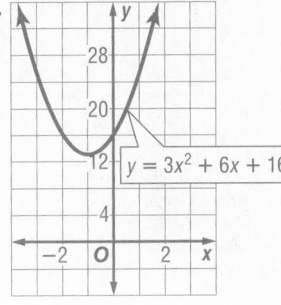

7. $x = 1$; $(1, -2)$; maximum

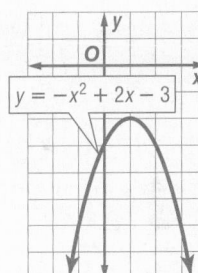

8. $x = -4$; $(-4, 32)$; minimum

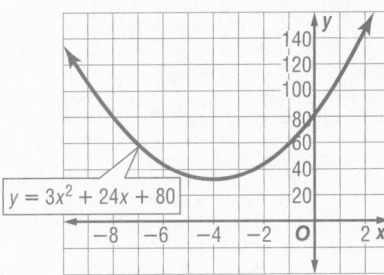

Answers continued on page 852D.

Lesson 10-1

1.

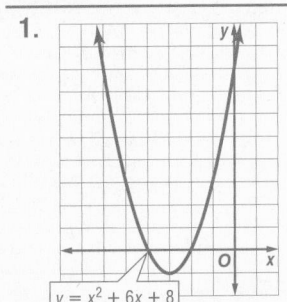

2.

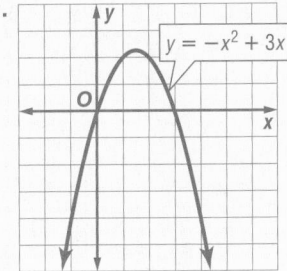

3.

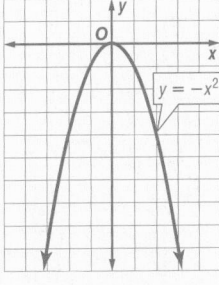

Lesson 10-2

1.
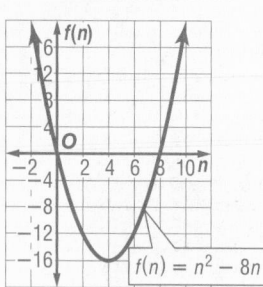
$f(a) = a^2 - 25$

2.
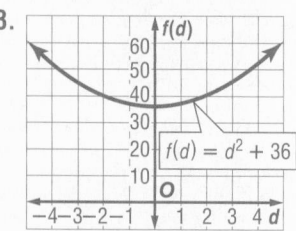
$f(n) = n^2 - 8n$

3.
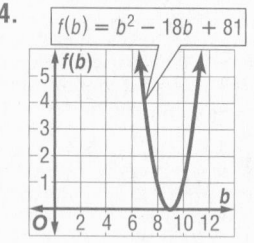
$f(d) = d^2 + 36$

4.
$f(b) = b^2 - 18b + 81$
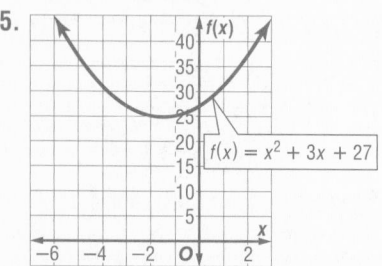

5.
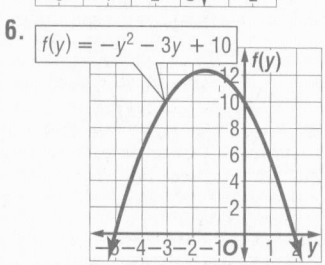
$f(x) = x^2 + 3x + 27$

6.
$f(y) = -y^2 - 3y + 10$
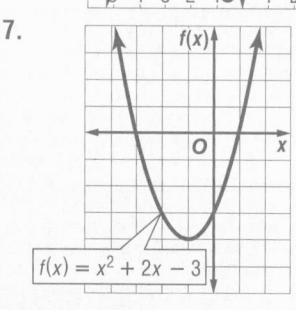

7.
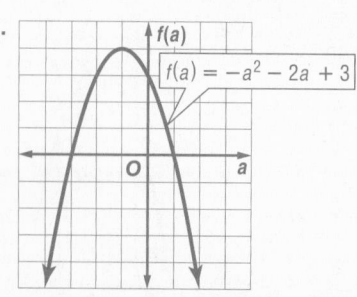
$f(x) = x^2 + 2x - 3$

Lesson 10-2
(pages 533–538)

Solve each equation by graphing. 1–6. See margin for graphs.

1. $a^2 - 25 = 0$ **−5, 5**
2. $n^2 - 8n = 0$ **0, 8**
3. $d^2 + 36 = 0$ **∅**
4. $b^2 - 18b + 81 = 0$ **9**
5. $x^2 + 3x + 27 = 0$ **∅**
6. $-y^2 - 3y + 10 = 0$ **−5, 2**

Solve each equation by graphing. If integral roots cannot be found, estimate the roots by stating the consecutive integers between which the roots lie. 7–24. See margin for graphs.

7. $x^2 + 2x - 3 = 0$ **−3, 1**
8. $-x^2 + 6x - 5 = 0$ **1, 5**
9. $-a^2 - 2a + 3 = 0$ **−3, 1**
10. $2r^2 - 8r + 5 = 0$ **$0 < r < 1$,**
11. $-3x^2 + 6x - 9 = 0$ **∅**
12. $c^2 + c = 0$ **−1, 0**
13. $3t^2 + 2 = 0$ **∅** **$3 < r < 4$**
14. $-b^2 + 5b + 2 = 0$ **$-1 < b < 0$,**
15. $3x^2 + 7x = 1$
16. $x^2 + 5x - 24 = 0$ **−8, 3**
17. $8 - n^2 = 0$ **$5 < b < 6$**
18. $x^2 - 7x = 18$ **−2, 9**
19. $a^2 + 12a + 36 = 0$ **−6**
20. $64 - x^2 = 0$ **−8, 8**
21. $-4x^2 + 2x = -1$ **$-1 < x < 0$,**
22. $5z^2 + 8z = 1$
23. $p = 27 - p^2$
24. $6w = -15 - 3w^2$ **$0 < x < 1$**
    $-2 < z < -1, 0 < z < 1$
    $-6 < p < -5, 4 < p < 5$
    ∅

15. **$-3 < x < -2, 0 < x < 1$**   17. **$-3 < n < -2, 2 < n < 3$**

Lesson 10-3
(pages 539–544)

Solve each equation. Round to the nearest tenth, if necessary.

1. $x^2 - 4x + 4 = 9$ **−1, 5**
2. $t^2 - 6t + 9 = 16$ **−1, 7**
3. $b^2 + 10b + 25 = 11$ **−8.3, −1.7**
4. $a^2 - 22a + 121 = 3$ **9.3, 12.7**
5. $x^2 + 2x + 1 = 81$ **−10, 8**
6. $t^2 - 36t + 324 = 85$ **8.8, 27.2**

Find the value of c that makes each trinomial a perfect square.

7. $a^2 + 20a + c$ **100**
8. $x^2 + 10x + c$ **25**
9. $t^2 + 12t + c$ **36**
10. $y^2 - 9y + c$ **$\frac{81}{4}$**
11. $p^2 - 14p + c$ **49**
12. $b^2 + 13b + c$ **$\frac{169}{4}$**

Solve each equation by completing the square. Round to the nearest tenth, if necessary.

13. $a^2 - 8a - 84 = 0$ **−6, 14**
14. $c^2 + 6 = -5c$ **−3, −2**
15. $p^2 - 8p + 5 = 0$ **0.7, 7.3**
16. $2y^2 + 7y - 4 = 0$ **−4, $\frac{1}{2}$**
17. $t^2 + 3t = 40$ **5, −8**
18. $x^2 + 8x - 9 = 0$ **−9, 1**
19. $y^2 + 5y - 84 = 0$ **−12, 7**
20. $t^2 + 12t + 32 = 0$ **−4, −8**
21. $2x - 3x^2 = -8$ **2, $-\frac{4}{3}$**
22. $2y^2 - y - 9 = 0$ **−1.9, 2.4**
23. $2z^2 - 5z - 4 = 0$ **−0.6, 3.1**
24. $8t^2 - 12t - 1 = 0$ **−0.1, 1.6**

Lesson 10-4
(pages 546–552)

Solve each equation by using the Quadratic Formula. Round to the nearest tenth, if necessary.

1. $x^2 - 8x - 4 = 0$ **−0.5, 8.5**
2. $x^2 + 7x - 8 = 0$ **−8, 1**
3. $x^2 - 5x + 6 = 0$ **2, 3**
4. $y^2 - 7y - 8 = 0$ **−1, 8**
5. $m^2 - 2m = 35$ **−5, 7**
6. $4n^2 - 20n = 0$ **0, 5**
7. $m^2 + 4m + 2 = 0$ **−0.6, −3.4**
8. $2t^2 - t - 15 = 0$ **−2.5, 3**
9. $5t^2 = 125$ **−5, 5**
10. $t^2 + 16 = 0$ **∅**
11. $-4x^2 + 8x = -3$ **−0.3, 2.3**
12. $3k^2 + 2 = -8k$ **−2.4, −0.3**
13. $8t^2 + 10t + 3 = 0$ **$-\frac{3}{4}, -\frac{1}{2}$**
14. $3x^2 - \frac{5}{4}x - \frac{1}{2} = 0$ **$\frac{2}{3}, -\frac{1}{4}$**
15. $-5b^2 + 3b - 1 = 0$ **∅**
16. $s^2 + 8s + 7 = 0$ **−7, −1**
17. $d^2 - 14d + 24 = 0$ **2, 12**
18. $3k^2 + 11k = 4$ **−4, $\frac{1}{3}$**
19. $n^2 - 3n + 1 = 0$ **2.6, 0.4**
20. $2z^2 + 5z - 1 = 0$ **0.2, −2.7**
21. $3h^2 = 27$ **3, −3**

State the value of the discriminant for each equation. Then determine the number of real roots of the equation.

22. $3f^2 + 2f = 6$ **76; 2 real roots**
23. $2x^2 = 0.7x + 0.3$ **2.89; 2 real roots**
24. $3w^2 - 2w + 8 = 0$ **−92; no real roots**
25. $4r^2 - 12r + 9 = 0$ **0; 1 real root**
26. $x^2 - 5x = -9$ **−11; no real roots**
27. $25t^2 + 30t = -9$ **0; 1 real root**

8.
$f(x) = -x^2 + 6x - 5$

9.
$f(a) = -a^2 - 2a + 3$

Answers continued on page 852E.

Lesson 10-5

(pages 554–560)

Graph each function. State the *y*-intercept. Then use the graph to determine the approximate value of the given expression. Use a calculator to confirm the value.   **1–3. See margin for graphs.**

1. $y = 7^x$; $7^{1.5}$ **1; 18.5**

2. $\left(\frac{1}{3}\right)^x$; $\left(\frac{1}{3}\right)^{5.6}$ **1; 0.002**

3. $y = \left(\frac{3}{5}\right)^x$; $\left(\frac{3}{5}\right)^{-4.2}$ **1; 8.5**

Graph each function. State the *y*-intercept. **4–15. See margin for graphs.**

4. $y = 3^x + 1$ **2**

5. $y = 2^x - 5$ **−4**

6. $y = 2^x + 3$ **8**

7. $y = 3^{x+1}$ **3**

8. $y = \left(\frac{2}{3}\right)^x$ **1**

9. $y = 5\left(\frac{2}{5}\right)^x$ **5**

10. $y = 5(3^x)$ **5**

11. $y = 4(5)^x$ **4**

12. $y = 2(5)^x + 1$ **3**

13. $y = \left(\frac{1}{2}\right)^{x+1}$ $\frac{1}{2}$

14. $y = \left(\frac{1}{8}\right)^x$ **1**

15. $y = \left(\frac{3}{4}\right)^x - 2$ **−1**

Determine whether the data in each table display exponential behavior. Explain why or why not. **16–17. See margin.**

16.

x	−1	0	1	2
y	−5	−1	3	7

17.

x	1	2	3	4
y	25	125	625	3125

Lesson 10-6

1a. $M = 8500\left(1 + \frac{0.0725}{12}\right)^{12(4)}$

(pages 561–565)

1. EDUCATION   Marco is saving for tuition costs at a state university. He deposited $8500 in a 4-year certificate of deposit earning 7.25% compounded monthly.

a. Write an equation for the amount of money Marco will have at the end of four years.

b. Find the amount of money he will have for his tuition at the end of the four years. **$11,349.73**

2. TRANSPORTATION   Elise is buying a new car selling for $21,500. The rate of depreciation on this type of car is 8% per year.

a. Write an equation for the value of the car in 5 years. $V = 21,500(1 - 0.08)^5$

b. Find the value of the car in 5 years. **$14,170.25**

3. POPULATION   In 1990, the town of Belgrade, Montana, had a population of 3422. For each of the next 8 years, the population increased by 4.9% per year.

a. Write an equation for the population of Belgrade in 1998. $P = 3422(1 + 0.049)^8$

b. Find the population of Belgrade in 1998. **5017**

Lesson 10-7

(pages 567–572)

Determine whether each sequence is geometric.

1. 12, 23, 34, 45, … **no**

2. 6, 7.2, 8.64, 10.368, … **yes**

3. 39, 33, 27, 21, … **no**

4. 86, 68.8, 55.04, 44.032, … **yes**

5. 4, 8, 16, 32, … **yes**

6. 13, 10, 11, 8, 9, 6, … **no**

Find the next three terms in each geometric sequence. **7–12. See margin.**

7. 3125, 625, 125, 25, …

8. 15, −45, 135, −405, …

9. 243, 81, 27, 9, …

10. 15, −7.5, 3.75, −1.875, …

11. −25, −15, −9, −5.4, …

12. $\frac{1}{4}, \frac{1}{10}, \frac{1}{25}, \frac{2}{125}, …$

Find the *n*th term of each geometric sequence. **13–21. See margin.**

13. $a_1 = 1, n = 10, r = 6$

14. $a_1 = -1, n = 7, r = -4$

15. $a_1 = -6, n = 4, r = 0.4$

16. $a_1 = 100, n = 10, r = 0.1$

17. $a_1 = -750, n = 5, r = -1.5$

18. $a_1 = 64, n = 5, r = 8$

19. $a_1 = 0.5, n = 9, r = -10$

20. $a_1 = -20, n = 6, r = 2.5$

21. $a_1 = 350, n = 4, r = -0.9$

Find the geometric means in each sequence.

22. 1, ____ , 81 **±9**

23. −81, ____ , −9 **±27**

24. 504, ____ , 14 **±84**

25. 0.5, ____ , 162 **±9**

26. −1, ____ , −4 **±2**

27. 0.25, ____ , 0.36 **±0.3**

28. $\frac{1}{2}$, ____ , $\frac{1}{8}$ $\pm\frac{1}{4}$

29. $-\frac{2}{3}$, ____ , $-\frac{32}{27}$ $\pm\frac{8}{9}$

30. 6.25, ____ , 2.25 **±3.75**

Lesson 10-7

7. 5, 1, 0.2

8. 1215, −3645, 10,935

9. 3, 1, $\frac{1}{3}$

10. 0.9375, −0.46875, 0.234375

11. −3.24, −1.944, −1.1664

12. $\frac{4}{625}, \frac{8}{3125}, \frac{16}{15,625}$

13. 10,077,696

14. −4096

15. −0.384

16. 0.0000001

17. −3796.875

18. 262,144

19. 50,000,000

20. −1953.125

21. −255.15

1.

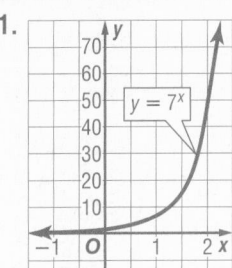

2.

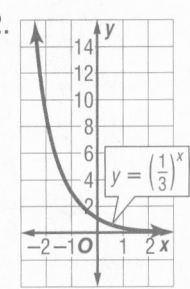

3.

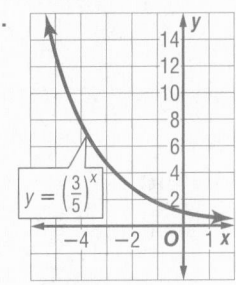

4.

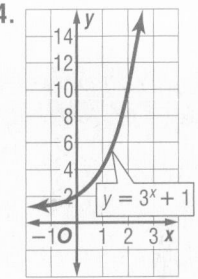

5.

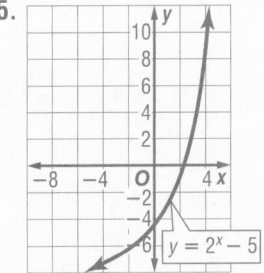

6.

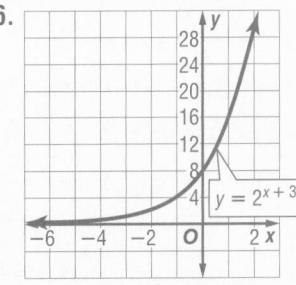

Answers continued on page 852F.

Lesson 11-1

(pages 587–593)

Simplify.

1. $\sqrt{50}$ $5\sqrt{2}$
2. $\sqrt{200}$ $10\sqrt{2}$
3. $\sqrt{162}$ $9\sqrt{2}$
4. $\sqrt{700}$ $10\sqrt{7}$

5. $\dfrac{\sqrt{3}}{\sqrt{5}}$ $\dfrac{\sqrt{15}}{5}$
6. $\dfrac{\sqrt{72}}{\sqrt{6}}$ $2\sqrt{3}$
7. $\sqrt{\dfrac{8}{7}}$ $\dfrac{2\sqrt{14}}{7}$
8. $\sqrt{\dfrac{7}{32}}$ $\dfrac{\sqrt{14}}{8}$

9. $\sqrt{\dfrac{5}{8}} \cdot \sqrt{\dfrac{2}{6}}$ $\dfrac{\sqrt{30}}{12}$
10. $\sqrt{\dfrac{2}{3}} \cdot \sqrt{\dfrac{3}{2}}$ 1
11. $\sqrt{\dfrac{2x}{30}}$ $\dfrac{\sqrt{15x}}{15}$
12. $\sqrt{\dfrac{50}{z^2}}$ $\dfrac{5\sqrt{2}}{|z|}$

13. $\sqrt{10} \cdot \sqrt{20}$ $10\sqrt{2}$
14. $\sqrt{7} \cdot \sqrt{3}$ $\sqrt{21}$
15. $6\sqrt{2} \cdot \sqrt{3}$ $6\sqrt{6}$
16. $5\sqrt{6} \cdot 2\sqrt{3}$ $30\sqrt{2}$

17. $\sqrt{4x^4y^3}$ $2x^2|y|\sqrt{y}$
18. $\sqrt{200m^2y^3}$ $10|my|\sqrt{2y}$
19. $\sqrt{12ts^3}$ $2|s|\sqrt{3st}$
20. $\sqrt{175a^4b^6}$ $5a^2|b^3|\sqrt{7}$

21. $\sqrt{\dfrac{54}{g^2}}$ $\dfrac{3\sqrt{6}}{|g|}$
22. $\sqrt{99x^3y^7}$ $3|xy^3|\sqrt{11xy}$
23. $\sqrt{\dfrac{32c^5}{9d^2}}$ $\dfrac{4c^2\sqrt{2c}}{3|d|}$
24. $\sqrt{\dfrac{27p^4}{3p^2}}$ $3|p|$

25. $\dfrac{1}{3+\sqrt{5}}$ $\dfrac{3-\sqrt{5}}{4}$
26. $\dfrac{2}{\sqrt{3}-5}$ $\dfrac{\sqrt{3}+5}{-11}$
27. $\dfrac{\sqrt{3}}{\sqrt{3}-5}$ $\dfrac{3+5\sqrt{3}}{-22}$
28. $\dfrac{\sqrt{6}}{7-2\sqrt{3}}$ $\dfrac{7\sqrt{6}+6\sqrt{2}}{37}$

Lesson 11-2

(pages 594–598)

Simplify each expression. 4. $14\sqrt{7} - \sqrt{2}$ 10. $-6\sqrt{7} + 24\sqrt{5}$ 15. $69\sqrt{2} - 10\sqrt{3}$

1. $3\sqrt{11} + 6\sqrt{11} - 2\sqrt{11}$ $7\sqrt{11}$
2. $6\sqrt{13} + 7\sqrt{13}$ $13\sqrt{13}$
3. $2\sqrt{12} + 5\sqrt{3}$ $9\sqrt{3}$

4. $9\sqrt{7} - 4\sqrt{2} + 3\sqrt{2} + 5\sqrt{7}$
5. $3\sqrt{5} - 5\sqrt{3}$ in simplest form
6. $4\sqrt{8} - 3\sqrt{5}$ $8\sqrt{2} - 3\sqrt{5}$

7. $2\sqrt{27} - 4\sqrt{12}$ $-2\sqrt{3}$
8. $8\sqrt{32} + 4\sqrt{50}$ $52\sqrt{2}$
9. $\sqrt{45} + 6\sqrt{20}$ $15\sqrt{5}$

10. $2\sqrt{63} - 6\sqrt{28} + 8\sqrt{45}$
11. $14\sqrt{3t} + 8\sqrt{3t}$ $22\sqrt{3t}$
12. $7\sqrt{6x} - 12\sqrt{6x}$ $-5\sqrt{6x}$

13. $5\sqrt{7} - 3\sqrt{28}$ $-\sqrt{7}$
14. $7\sqrt{8} - \sqrt{18}$ $11\sqrt{2}$
15. $7\sqrt{98} + 5\sqrt{32} - 2\sqrt{75}$

16. $4\sqrt{6} + 3\sqrt{2} - 2\sqrt{5}$
17. $-3\sqrt{20} + 2\sqrt{45} - \sqrt{7}$ $-\sqrt{7}$
18. $4\sqrt{75} + 6\sqrt{27}$ $38\sqrt{3}$

19. $10\sqrt{\dfrac{1}{5}} - \sqrt{45} - 12\sqrt{\dfrac{5}{9}}$ $-5\sqrt{5}$
20. $\sqrt{15} - \sqrt{\dfrac{3}{5}}$ $\dfrac{4\sqrt{15}}{5}$
21. $3\sqrt{\dfrac{1}{3}} - 9\sqrt{\dfrac{1}{12}} + \sqrt{243}$ $\dfrac{17\sqrt{3}}{2}$

16. in simplest form

Find each product. 27. $4\sqrt{21} - 12\sqrt{35} + \sqrt{6} - 3\sqrt{10}$

22. $\sqrt{3}(\sqrt{5} + 2)$ $\sqrt{15} + 2\sqrt{3}$
23. $\sqrt{2}(\sqrt{2} + 3\sqrt{5})$ $2 + 3\sqrt{10}$
24. $(\sqrt{2} + 5)^2$ $27 + 10\sqrt{2}$

25. $(3 - \sqrt{7})(3 + \sqrt{7})$ 2
26. $(\sqrt{2} + \sqrt{3})(\sqrt{3} + \sqrt{2})$
27. $(4\sqrt{7} + \sqrt{2})(\sqrt{3} - 3\sqrt{5})$

$2\sqrt{6} + 5$

Lesson 11-3

(pages 599–604)

Solve each equation. Check your solution.

1. $\sqrt{5x} = 5$ 5
2. $4\sqrt{7} = \sqrt{-m}$ -112
3. $\sqrt{t} - 5 = 0$ 25

4. $\sqrt{3b} + 2 = 0$ no solution
5. $\sqrt{x-3} = 6$ 39
6. $5 - \sqrt{3x} = 1$ $\dfrac{16}{3}$

7. $2 + 3\sqrt{y} = 13$ $\dfrac{121}{9}$
8. $\sqrt{3g} = 6$ 12
9. $\sqrt{a} - 2 = 0$ 4

10. $\sqrt{2j} - 4 = 8$ 72
11. $5 + \sqrt{x} = 9$ 16
12. $\sqrt{5y+4} = 7$ 9

13. $7 + \sqrt{5c} = 9$ $\dfrac{4}{5}$
14. $2\sqrt{5t} = 10$ 5
15. $\sqrt{44} = 2\sqrt{p}$ 11

16. $4\sqrt{x-5} = 15$ $\dfrac{305}{16}$
17. $4 - \sqrt{x-3} = 9$ no solution
18. $\sqrt{10x^2 - 5} = 3x$ $\sqrt{5}$

19. $\sqrt{2a^2 - 144} = a$ 12
20. $\sqrt{3y+1} = y - 3$ 8
21. $\sqrt{2x^2 - 12} = x$ $2\sqrt{3}$

22. $\sqrt{b^2 + 16} + 2b = 5b$ $\sqrt{2}$
23. $\sqrt{m+2} + m = 4$ 2
24. $\sqrt{3 - 2c} + 3 = 2c$ $\dfrac{3}{2}$

Lesson 11-4
 *(pages 606–611)*

If c is the measure of the hypotenuse of a right triangle, find each missing measure. If necessary, round to the nearest hundredth.

1. $b = 20, c = 29, a = ?$ **21**
2. $a = 7, b = 24, c = ?$ **25**
3. $a = 2, b = 6, c = ?$ **6.32**
4. $b = 10, c = \sqrt{200}, a = ?$ **10**
5. $a = 3, c = 3\sqrt{2}, b = ?$ **3**
6. $a = 6, c = 14, b = ?$ **12.65**
7. $a = \sqrt{11}, c = \sqrt{47}, b = ?$ **6**
8. $a = \sqrt{13}, b = 6, c = ?$ **7**
9. $a = \sqrt{6}, b = 3, c = ?$ **3.87**
10. $b = \sqrt{75}, c = 10, a = ?$ **5**
11. $b = 9, c = \sqrt{130}, a = ?$ **7**
12. $a = 9, c = 15, b = ?$ **12**
13. $b = 5, c = 11, a = ?$ **9.80**
14. $a = \sqrt{33}, b = 4, c = ?$ **7**
15. $a = 5, c = \sqrt{34}, b = ?$ **3**

Determine whether the following side measures form right triangles.

16. 14, 48, 50 **yes**
17. 20, 30, 40 **no**
18. 21, 72, 75 **yes**
19. $5, 12, \sqrt{119}$ **yes**
20. 15, 39, 36 **yes**
21. $\sqrt{5}, 12, 13$ **no**
22. $10, 12, \sqrt{22}$ **no**
23. 2, 3, 4 **no**
24. $\sqrt{7}, 8, \sqrt{71}$ **yes**

Lesson 11-5
(pages 612–616)

Find the distance between each pair of points whose coordinates are given. Express answers in simplest radical form and as decimal approximations rounded to the nearest hundredth if necessary.

1. $(4, 2), (-2, 10)$ **10**
2. $(-5, 1), (7, 6)$ **13**
3. $(4, -2), (1, 2)$ **5**
4. $(-2, 4), (4, -2)$ **$6\sqrt{2}$ or 8.49**
5. $(3, 1), (-2, -1)$ **$\sqrt{29}$ or 5.39**
6. $(-2, 4), (7, -8)$ **15**
7. $(-5, 0), (-9, 6)$ **$2\sqrt{13}$ or 7.21**
8. $(5, -1), (5, 13)$ **14**
9. $(2, -3), (10, 8)$ **$\sqrt{185}$ or 13.60**
10. $(-7, 5), (2, -7)$ **15**
11. $(-6, -2), (-5, 4)$ **$\sqrt{37}$ or 6.08**
12. $(8, -10), (3, 2)$ **13**
13. $(4, -3), (7, -9)$ **$3\sqrt{5}$ or 6.71**
14. $(6, 3), (9, 7)$ **5**
15. $(10, 0), (9, 7)$ **$5\sqrt{2}$ or 7.07**
16. $(2, -1), (-3, 3)$ **$\sqrt{41}$ or 6.40**
17. $(-5, 4), (3, -2)$ **10**
18. $(0, -9), (0, 7)$ **16**
19. $(-1, 7), (8, 4)$ **$3\sqrt{10}$ or 9.49**
20. $(-9, 2), (3, -3)$ **13**
21. $(3\sqrt{2}, 7), (5\sqrt{2}, 9)$ **$2\sqrt{3}$ or 3.46**
22. $(6, 3), (10, 0)$ **5**
23. $(3, 6), (5, -5)$ **$5\sqrt{5}$ or 11.18**
24. $(-4, 2), (5, 4)$ **$\sqrt{85}$ or 9.22**

Find the possible values of a if the points with the given coordinates are the indicated distance apart.

25. $(0, 0), (a, 3); d = 5$ **−4 or 4**
26. $(2, -1), (-6, a); d = 10$ **−7 or 5**
27. $(1, 0), (a, 6); d = \sqrt{61}$ **−4 or 6**
28. $(-2, a), (5, 10); d = \sqrt{85}$ **4 or 16**
29. $(15, a), (0, 4); d = \sqrt{274}$ **−3 or 11**
30. $(3, 3), (a, 9); d = \sqrt{136}$ **−7 or 13**

Lesson 11-6
(pages 617–622)

Determine whether each pair of triangles is similar. Justify your answer. **1–3. See margin.**

1.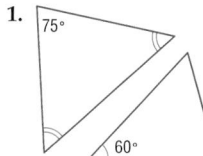

2.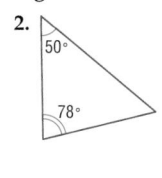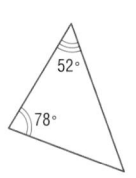

3.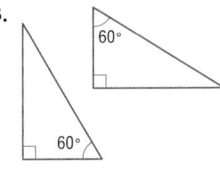

For each set of measures given, find the measures of the missing sides if $\triangle ABC \sim \triangle DEF$.

4. $a = 5, d = 10, b = 8, c = 7$ **$e = 16, f = 14$**
5. $a = 2, b = 3, c = 4, d = 3$ **$e = 4.5, f = 6$**
6. $a = 6, d = 4.5, e = 7, f = 7.5$ **$b = 9\frac{1}{3}, c = 10$**
7. $a = 15, c = 20, b = 18, f = 10$ **$d = 7.5, e = 9$**
8. $f = 17.5, d = 8.5, e = 11, a = 1.7$ **$b = 2.2, c = 3.5$**
9. $b = 5.6, e = 7, a = 4, c = 7.2$ **$d = 5, f = 9$**
10. $e = 125, a = 80, d = 100, f = 218.75$ **$b = 100, c = 175$**

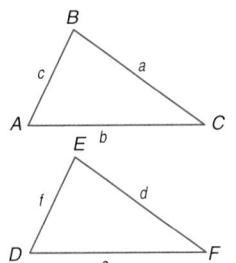

Lesson 11-6

1. No; corresponding angles do not have equal measures.

2. Yes; corresponding angles have equal measures.

3. Yes; corresponding angles have equal measures.

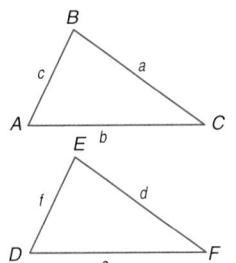

Lesson 11-7

16. $\angle A = 30°$, $BC \approx 8.7$, $AB \approx 17.3$

17. $\angle Z = 35°$, $XY \approx 14.7$, $XZ \approx 25.6$

18. $\angle M \approx 63°$, $\angle L \approx 27°$, $LM \approx 17.9$

Lesson 12-1

1. $y = \dfrac{75}{x}$

2. $y = \dfrac{-15}{x}$

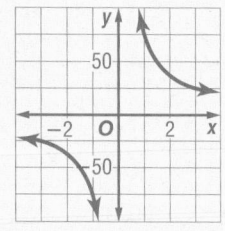

3. $y = \dfrac{12}{x}$

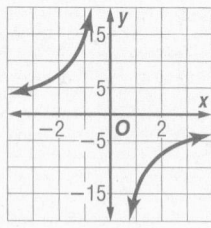

4. $y = \dfrac{-0.5}{x}$

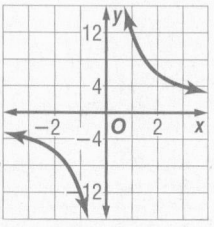

5. $y = \dfrac{-7.5}{x}$

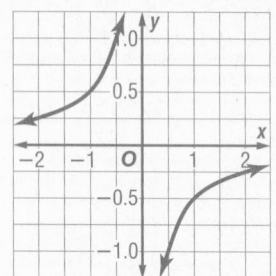

6. $y = \dfrac{2}{x}$

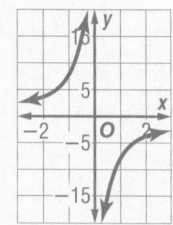

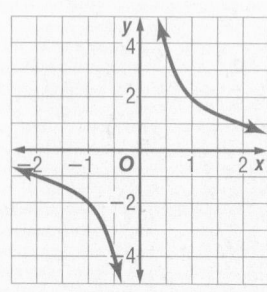

Lesson 11-7   *(pages 624–631)*

For each triangle, find sin N, cos N, and tan N to the nearest ten thousandth.

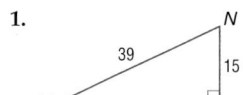

1.

sin $N = 0.9231$,
cos $N = 0.3846$,
tan $N = 2.4$

2.

sin $N = 0.28$,
cos $N = 0.96$,
tan $N = 0.2917$

3.

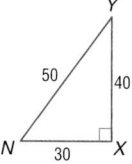

sin $N = 0.8$, cos $N = 0.6$,
tan $N = 1.3333$

Use a calculator to find the value of each trigonometric ratio to the nearest ten thousandth.

4. cos 25° **0.9063**

5. tan 31° **0.6009**

6. sin 71° **0.9455**

7. cos 64° **0.4384**

8. tan 9° **0.1584**

9. sin 2° **0.0349**

Use a calculator to find the measure of each angle to the nearest degree.

10. tan $B = 0.5427$ **28°**

11. cos $A = 0.8480$ **32°**

12. sin $J = 0.9654$ **75°**

13. cos $Q = 0.3645$ **69°**

14. sin $R = 0.2104$ **12°**

15. tan $V = 11.4301$ **85°**

Solve each right triangle. State the side lengths to the nearest tenth and the angle measures to the nearest degree. **16–18. See margin.**

16.

17.

18.

Lesson 12-1   *(pages 642–647)*

Graph each variation if y varies inversely as x. **1–6. See margin.**

1. $y = 10$ when $x = 7.5$

2. $y = -5$ when $x = 3$

3. $y = -6$ when $x = -2$

4. $y = 1$ when $x = -0.5$

5. $y = -2.5$ when $x = 3$

6. $y = -2$ when $x = -1$

Write an inverse variation equation that relates x and y. Assume that y varies inversely as x. Then solve. **7–16. See margin.**

7. If $y = 54$ when $x = 4$, find x when $y = 27$.

8. If $y = 18$ when $x = 6$, find x when $y = 12$.

9. If $y = 12$ when $x = 24$, find x when $y = 9$.

10. If $y = 8$ when $x = -8$, find y when $x = -16$.

11. If $y = 3$ when $x = -8$, find y when $x = 4$.

12. If $y = 27$ when $x = \frac{1}{3}$, find y when $x = \frac{3}{4}$.

13. If $y = -3$ when $x = -8$, find y when $x = 2$.

14. If $y = -3$ when $x = -3$, find x when $y = 4$.

15. If $y = -7.5$ when $x = 2.5$, find y when $x = -2.5$.

16. If $y = -0.4$ when $x = -3.2$, find x when $y = -0.2$.

Lesson 12-2   *(pages 648–653)*

State the excluded values for each rational expression.

1. $\dfrac{x}{x+1}$ **−1**

2. $\dfrac{m}{n}$ $n \neq 0$

3. $\dfrac{c-2}{c^2-4}$ **−2, 2**

4. $\dfrac{b^2-5b+6}{b^2-8b+15}$ **3, 5**

Simplify each expression. State the excluded values of the variables. **9, 10, 12, 15, 16. See margin.**

5. $\dfrac{13a}{39a^2}$ $\dfrac{1}{3a}$; $a \neq 0$

6. $\dfrac{38x^2}{42xy}$ $\dfrac{19x}{21y}$; $x, y \neq 0$

7. $\dfrac{p+5}{2(p+5)}$ $\dfrac{1}{2}$; $p \neq 5$

8. $\dfrac{a+b}{a^2-b^2}$ $\dfrac{1}{a-b}$; $a \neq \pm b$

9. $\dfrac{y+4}{y^2-16}$

10. $\dfrac{c^2-4}{c^2+4c+4}$

11. $\dfrac{a^2-a}{a-1}$ a; $a \neq 1$

12. $\dfrac{x^2+4}{x^4-16}$

13. $\dfrac{r^3-r^2}{r-1}$ r^2; $r \neq 1$

14. $\dfrac{4t^2-8}{4t-4}$ $\dfrac{t^2-2}{t-1}$; $t \neq 1$

15. $\dfrac{6y^3-12y^2}{12y^2-18}$

16. $\dfrac{5x^2+10x+5}{3x^2+6x+3}$

---

7. $y = \dfrac{216}{x}$; **8**

8. $y = \dfrac{108}{x}$; **9**

9. $y = \dfrac{288}{x}$; **32**

10. $y = \dfrac{-64}{x}$; **4**

11. $y = \dfrac{-24}{x}$; **−6**

12. $y = \dfrac{9}{x}$; **12**

13. $y = \dfrac{24}{x}$; **12**

14. $y = \dfrac{9}{x}$; **2.25**

15. $y = \dfrac{-18.75}{x}$; **7.5**

16. $y = \dfrac{1.28}{x}$; **−6.4**

Lesson 12-2

9. $\dfrac{1}{y-4}$; $y \neq -4, 4$

10. $\dfrac{c-2}{c+2}$; $c \neq -2$

12. $\dfrac{1}{x^2-4}$; $x \neq \pm 2$

15. $\dfrac{y^2(y-2)}{2y^2-3}$; $y \neq \pm\dfrac{\sqrt{6}}{2}$

16. $\dfrac{5}{3}$; $x \neq -1$

Lesson 12-3
(pages 655–659)

Find each product.

1. $\frac{a^2b}{b^2c} \cdot \frac{c}{d}$ $\frac{a^2}{bd}$

2. $\frac{6a^2n}{8n^2} \cdot \frac{12n}{9a}$ a

3. $\frac{2a^2d}{3bc} \cdot \frac{9b^2c}{16ad^2}$ $\frac{3ab}{8d}$

4. $\frac{10n^3}{6x^3} \cdot \frac{12n^2x^4}{25n^2x^2}$ $\frac{4n^3}{5x}$

5. $\frac{6m^3n}{10a^2} \cdot \frac{4a^2m}{9n^3}$ $\frac{4m^4}{15n^2}$

6. $\frac{(a-5)(a+1)}{(a+1)(a+7)} \cdot \frac{(a+7)(a-6)}{(a+8)(a-5)}$

7. $\frac{x-1}{(x+2)(x-3)} \cdot \frac{x+2}{(x-3)(x-1)}$

8. $\frac{5n-5}{3} \cdot \frac{9}{n-1}$ 15

9. $\frac{a^2}{a-b} \cdot \frac{3a-3b}{a}$ $3a$

10. $\frac{2a+4b}{5} \cdot \frac{25}{6a+8b}$ $\frac{5a+10b}{3a+4b}$

11. $\frac{3}{x-y} \cdot \frac{(x-y)^2}{6}$ $\frac{x-y}{2}$

12. $\frac{x+5}{3x} \cdot \frac{12x^2}{x^2+7x+10}$

13. $\frac{a^2-b^2}{4} \cdot \frac{16}{a+b}$ $4a-4b$

14. $\frac{4a+8}{a^2-25} \cdot \frac{a-5}{5a+10}$ $\frac{4}{5a+25}$

15. $\frac{r^2}{r-s} \cdot \frac{r^2-s^2}{s^2}$

16. $\frac{a^2-b^2}{a-b} \cdot \frac{7}{a+b}$ 7

17. $\frac{x^2+10x+9}{x^2+11x+18} \cdot \frac{x^2+3x+2}{x^2+7x+6}$

18. $\frac{x^2-6x+5}{x^2+7x+12} \cdot \frac{x^2+14x+40}{x^2+5x-50}$

6. $\frac{a-6}{a+8}$ 7. $\frac{1}{(x-3)^2}$ 12. $\frac{4x}{x+2}$ 15. $\frac{r^3+r^2s}{s^2}$ 17. $\frac{x+1}{x+6}$ 18. $\frac{x-1}{x+3}$

Lesson 12-4
(pages 660–664)

Find each quotient.

1. $\frac{5m^2n}{12a^2} \div \frac{30m^4}{18an}$ $\frac{n^2}{4am^2}$

2. $\frac{25g^7h}{28t^3} \div \frac{5g^5h^2}{42s^2t^3}$ $\frac{15g^2s^2}{2h}$

3. $\frac{6a+4b}{36} \div \frac{3a+2b}{45}$ $\frac{5}{2}$

4. $\frac{x^2y}{18z} \div \frac{2yz}{3x^2}$ $\frac{x^4}{12z^2}$

5. $\frac{p^2}{14qr^3} \div \frac{2r^2p}{7q}$ $\frac{p}{4r^5}$

6. $\frac{5e-f}{5e+f} \div (25e^2-f^2)$ $\frac{1}{(5e+f)^2}$

7. $\frac{t^2-2t-15}{t-5} \div \frac{t+3}{t+5}$ $t+5$

8. $\frac{5x+10}{x+2} \div (x+2)$ $\frac{5}{x+2}$

9. $\frac{3d}{2d^2-3d} \div \frac{9}{2d-3}$ $\frac{1}{3}$

10. $\frac{3v^2-27}{15v} \div \frac{v+3}{v^2}$ $\frac{v(v-3)}{5}$

11. $\frac{3g^2+15g}{4} \div \frac{g+5}{g^2}$ $\frac{3g^3}{4}$

12. $\frac{b^2-9}{4b} \div (b-3)$ $\frac{b+3}{4b}$

13. $\frac{p^2}{y^2-4} \div \frac{p}{2-y}$ $\frac{-p}{y+2}$

14. $\frac{k^2-81}{k^2-36} \div \frac{k-9}{k+6}$ $\frac{k+9}{k-6}$

15. $\frac{2a^3}{a+1} \div \frac{a^2}{a+1}$ $2a$

16. $\frac{x^2-16}{16-x^2} \div \frac{7}{x}$ $-\frac{x}{7}$

17. $\frac{y}{5} \div \frac{y^2-25}{5-y}$ $\frac{-y}{5y+25}$

18. $\frac{3m}{m+1} \div (m-2)$ $\frac{3m}{m^2-m-2}$

19. $\frac{2m+16}{m-2} \div \frac{m^2+6m-16}{m^2+m-6}$ $\frac{2m+6}{m-2}$

20. $\frac{a^2+3a-10}{a^2+3a+2} \div \frac{a^2+3a-10}{a^2-2a-3}$ $\frac{a-3}{a+2}$

21. $\frac{x^2-x-2}{x^2+4x+3} \div \frac{x^2-6x+8}{x^2-x-12}$ 1

Lesson 12-5
(pages 666–671)

Find each quotient.

1. $(2x^2-11x-20) \div (2x+3)$ $x-7+\frac{1}{2x+3}$

2. $(a^2+10a+21) \div (a+3)$ $a+7$

3. $(m^2+4m-5) \div (m+5)$ $m-1$

4. $(x^2-2x-35) \div (x-7)$ $x+5$

5. $(c^2+6c-27) \div (c+9)$ $c-3$

6. $(y^2-6y-25) \div (y+7)$ $y-13+\frac{66}{y+7}$

7. $(3t^2-14t-24) \div (3t+4)$ $t-6$

8. $(2r^2-3r-35) \div (2r+7)$ $r-5$

9. $\frac{12n^2+36n+15}{6n+3}$ $2n+5$

10. $\frac{10x^2+29x+21}{5x+7}$ $2x+3$

11. $\frac{4t^3+17t^2-1}{4t+1}$ t^2+4t-1

12. $\frac{2a^3+9a^2+5a-12}{a+3}$ $2a^2+3a-4$

13. $\frac{4m^2+4m-15}{2m-3}$ $2m+5$

14. $\frac{6t^3+5t^2+12}{2t+3}$ $3t^2-2t+3+\frac{3}{2t+3}$

15. $\frac{27c^2-24c+8}{9c-2}$ $3c-2+\frac{4}{9c-2}$

16. $\frac{4b^3+7b^2-2b+4}{b+2}$ $4b^2-b+\frac{4}{b+2}$

17. $\frac{t^3-19t+9}{t-4}$ $t^2+4t-3-\frac{3}{t-4}$

18. $\frac{9x^3+2x-10}{3x-2}$ $3x^2+2x+2-\frac{6}{3x-2}$

Lesson 12-6

(pages 672–677)

Find each sum.

1. $\dfrac{4}{z} + \dfrac{3}{z}$ $\dfrac{7}{z}$

2. $\dfrac{a}{12} + \dfrac{2a}{12}$ $\dfrac{a}{4}$

3. $\dfrac{5}{2t} + \dfrac{-7}{2t}$ $-\dfrac{1}{t}$

4. $\dfrac{y}{2} + \dfrac{y}{2}$ y

5. $\dfrac{b}{x} + \dfrac{2}{x}$ $\dfrac{b+2}{x}$

6. $\dfrac{y}{2} + \dfrac{y-6}{2}$ $y-3$

7. $\dfrac{x}{x+1} + \dfrac{1}{x+1}$ 1

8. $\dfrac{2n}{2n-5} + \dfrac{5}{5-2n}$ 1

9. $\dfrac{x-y}{2-y} + \dfrac{x+y}{y-2}$ $\dfrac{2y}{y-2}$

10. $\dfrac{r^2}{r-s} + \dfrac{s^2}{r-s}$ $\dfrac{r^2+s^2}{r-s}$

11. $\dfrac{12n}{3n+2} + \dfrac{8}{3n+2}$ 4

12. $\dfrac{6x}{x+y} + \dfrac{6y}{x+y}$ 6

Find each difference.

13. $\dfrac{5x}{24} - \dfrac{3x}{24}$ $\dfrac{x}{12}$

14. $\dfrac{7p}{3} - \dfrac{8p}{3}$ $\dfrac{-p}{3}$

15. $\dfrac{8k}{5m} - \dfrac{3k}{5m}$ $\dfrac{k}{m}$

16. $\dfrac{8}{m-2} - \dfrac{6}{m-2}$ $\dfrac{2}{m-2}$

17. $\dfrac{y}{b+6} - \dfrac{2y}{b+6}$ $\dfrac{-y}{b+6}$

18. $\dfrac{a+2}{6} - \dfrac{a+3}{6}$ $-\dfrac{1}{6}$

19. $\dfrac{2a}{2a+5} - \dfrac{5}{2a+5}$ $\dfrac{2a-5}{2a+5}$

20. $\dfrac{1}{4z+1} - \dfrac{(-4z)}{4z+1}$ 1

21. $\dfrac{3a}{a-2} - \dfrac{3a}{a-2}$ 0

22. $\dfrac{n}{n-1} - \dfrac{1}{1-n}$ $\dfrac{n+1}{n-1}$

23. $\dfrac{a}{a-7} - \dfrac{(-7)}{7-a}$ 1

24. $\dfrac{2a}{6a-3} - \dfrac{(-1)}{3-6a}$ $\dfrac{1}{3}$

Lesson 12-7

(pages 678–683)

Find the LCM for each pair of expressions.

1. $27a^2bc,\ 36ab^2c^2$ $108\,a^2b^2c^2$

2. $3m-1,\ 6m-2$ $6m-2$

3. $x^2+2x+1,\ x^2-2x-3$
  $(x+1)^2(x-3)$

Find each sum.

4. $\dfrac{s}{3} + \dfrac{2s}{7}$ $\dfrac{13s}{21}$

5. $\dfrac{5}{2a} + \dfrac{-3}{6a}$ $\dfrac{2}{a}$

6. $\dfrac{6}{5x} + \dfrac{7}{10x^2}$ $\dfrac{12x+7}{10x^2}$

7. $\dfrac{5}{xy} + \dfrac{6}{yz}$ $\dfrac{5z+6x}{xyz}$

8. $\dfrac{2}{t} + \dfrac{t+3}{s}$ $\dfrac{2s+t^2+3t}{st}$

9. $\dfrac{a}{a-b} + \dfrac{b}{2b+3a}$ $\dfrac{3a^2+3ab-b^2}{3a^2-ab-2b^2}$

10. $\dfrac{4a}{2a+6} + \dfrac{3}{a+3}$ $\dfrac{2a+3}{a+3}$

11. $\dfrac{3t+2}{3t-2} + \dfrac{t+2}{t^2-4}$ $\dfrac{3t^2-t-6}{3t^2-8t+4}$

12. $\dfrac{-3}{a-5} + \dfrac{-6}{a^2-5a}$ $\dfrac{-3a-6}{a^2-5a}$

Find each difference.

13. $\dfrac{2n}{5} - \dfrac{3m}{4}$ $\dfrac{8n-15m}{20}$

14. $\dfrac{3z}{7w^2} - \dfrac{2z}{w}$ $\dfrac{3z-14wz}{7w^2}$

15. $\dfrac{s}{t^2} - \dfrac{r}{3t}$ $\dfrac{3s-rt}{3t^2}$

16. $\dfrac{a}{a^2-4} - \dfrac{4}{a+2}$ $\dfrac{-3a+8}{a^2-4}$

17. $\dfrac{m}{m-n} - \dfrac{5}{m}$ $\dfrac{m^2-5m+5n}{m(m-n)}$

18. $\dfrac{y+5}{y-5} - \dfrac{2y}{y^2-25}$ $\dfrac{y^2+8y+25}{y^2-25}$

19. $\dfrac{t+10}{t^2-100} - \dfrac{1}{10-t}$ $\dfrac{2}{t-10}$

20. $\dfrac{2a-6}{a^2-3a-10} - \dfrac{3a+5}{a^2-4a-12}$ $\dfrac{-a^2-8a+61}{(a+2)(a-5)(a-6)}$

Lesson 12-8

(pages 684–689)

Write each mixed expression as a rational expression.

1. $4 + \dfrac{2}{x}$ $\dfrac{4x+2}{x}$

2. $8 + \dfrac{5}{3t}$ $\dfrac{24t+5}{3t}$

3. $\dfrac{b+1}{2b} + 3b$ $\dfrac{6b^2+b+1}{2b}$

4. $3z + \dfrac{z+2}{z}$ $\dfrac{3z^2+z+2}{z}$

5. $\dfrac{2}{a-2} + a^2$ $\dfrac{a^3-2a^2+2}{a-2}$

6. $3r^2 + \dfrac{4}{2r+1}$ $\dfrac{6r^3+3r^2+4}{2r+1}$

Simplify each expression.   14. $\dfrac{(a-2)(a^2+a+2)}{(a+1)(a^2-2a-3)}$

7. $\dfrac{3\frac{1}{2}}{4\frac{3}{4}}$ $\dfrac{14}{19}$

8. $\dfrac{\frac{x^2}{y}}{\frac{y}{x^3}}$ $\dfrac{x^5}{y^2}$

9. $\dfrac{\frac{t^4}{u}}{\frac{t^3}{u^2}}$ tu

10. $\dfrac{\frac{x-3}{x+1}}{\frac{x^2}{y^2}}$ $\dfrac{y^2(x-3)}{x^2(x+1)}$

11. $\dfrac{\frac{y}{3}+\frac{5}{6}}{2+\frac{5}{y}}$ $\dfrac{y}{6}$

12. $\dfrac{\frac{1}{x}+\frac{1}{y}}{\frac{1}{y}-\frac{1}{x}}$ $\dfrac{x+y}{x-y}$

13. $\dfrac{\frac{t-2}{t^2-4}}{t^2+5t+6}$ $t+3$

14. $\dfrac{a+\frac{2}{a+1}}{a-\frac{3}{a-2}}$

Lesson 12-9
(pages 690–695)

Solve each equation. State any extraneous solutions.

1. $\dfrac{k}{6} + \dfrac{2k}{3} = -\dfrac{5}{2}$ **−3**

2. $\dfrac{2x}{7} + \dfrac{27}{10} = \dfrac{4x}{5}$ **5.25**

3. $\dfrac{18}{b} = \dfrac{3}{b} + 3$ **5**

4. $\dfrac{3}{5x} + \dfrac{7}{2x} = 1$ **$\dfrac{41}{10}$**

5. $\dfrac{2a-3}{6} = \dfrac{2a}{3} + \dfrac{1}{2}$ **−3**

6. $\dfrac{3x+2}{x} + \dfrac{x+3}{x} = 5$ **5**

7. $\dfrac{2b-3}{7} - \dfrac{b}{2} = \dfrac{b+3}{14}$ **$-\dfrac{9}{4}$**

8. $\dfrac{2y}{y-4} - \dfrac{3}{5} = 3$ **9**

9. $\dfrac{2t}{t+3} + \dfrac{3}{t} = 2$ **3**

10. $\dfrac{5x}{x+1} + \dfrac{1}{x} = 5$ **$\dfrac{1}{4}$**

11. $\dfrac{r-2}{r+2} - \dfrac{2r}{r+9} = 6$ **−6, −3**

12. $\dfrac{m}{m+1} + \dfrac{5}{m-1} = 1$ **$-\dfrac{3}{2}$**

13. $\dfrac{2x}{x-3} - \dfrac{4x}{3-x} = 12$ **6**

14. $\dfrac{14}{b-6} = \dfrac{1}{2} + \dfrac{6}{b-8}$ **10, 20**

15. $\dfrac{a}{4a+15} - 3 = -2$ **−5**

16. $\dfrac{5x}{3x+10} + \dfrac{2x}{x+5} = 2$ **−4, 5**

17. $\dfrac{2a-3}{a-3} - 2 = \dfrac{12}{a+2}$ **$\dfrac{14}{3}$**

18. $\dfrac{z+3}{z-1} + \dfrac{z+1}{z-3} = 2$ **2**

Lesson 13-1
(pages 708–713)

Identify each sample, suggest a population from which it was selected, and state if it is unbiased (random) or biased. If unbiased, classify the sample as *simple*, *stratified*, or *systematic*. If biased, classify as *convenience* or *voluntary response*. 1–8. See margin.

1. The sheriff has heard that many dogs in the county do not have licenses. He drives from his office and checks the licenses of the first ten dogs he encounters.

2. The school administration wants to check on the incidence of students leaving campus without permission at lunch. An announcement is placed in the school bulletin for 25 students to volunteer to answer questions about leaving campus.

3. The store manager of an ice cream store wants to see whether employees are making ice cream cones within the weight guidelines he provided. During each of three shifts, he selects every tenth cone to weigh.

4. Every fifth car is selected from the assembly line. The cars are also identified by the day of the week during which they were produced.

5. A table is set up outside of a large department store. All people entering the store are given a survey about their preference of brand for blue jeans. As people leave the store, they can return the survey.

6. A community is considering building a new swimming pool. Every twentieth person on a list of residents is contacted in person for their opinion on the new pool.

7. A state wildlife department is concerned about a report that malformed frogs are increasing in the state's lakes. Residents are asked to write in to the state department if they see a malformed frog.

8. The manager at a grocery store has been told that many cartons of strawberries are spoiled. She asks one of her employees to bring in the top 10 cartons on the shelf.

Lesson 13-2
(pages 715–721)

State the dimensions of each matrix.

1. $[1 \quad 0 \quad -2 \quad 5]$ **1 by 4**

2. $\begin{bmatrix} 1 & 0 \\ 0 & 1 \end{bmatrix}$ **2 by 2**

3. $\begin{bmatrix} 1 & -1 & 1 \\ -1 & 1 & -1 \\ 1 & -1 & 1 \end{bmatrix}$ **3 by 3**

4. $[10]$ **1 by 1**

If $A = \begin{bmatrix} 2 & -4 \\ -3 & 5 \end{bmatrix}$, $B = \begin{bmatrix} 1 & -1 & 4 \\ 0 & 3 & -2 \end{bmatrix}$, $C = \begin{bmatrix} 1 & 0 \\ 0 & 1 \end{bmatrix}$, and $D = \begin{bmatrix} -5 & 1 & -4 \\ -3 & 0 & 2 \end{bmatrix}$, find each sum, difference, or product. If the sum or difference does not exist, write *impossible*. 5–16. See margin.

5. $A + B$
6. $A + C$
7. $B + D$
8. $D - B$
9. $2B$
10. $3C$
11. $A - C$
12. $-5C$
13. $2A + C$
14. $3D - B$
15. $5B + C$
16. $2C + 3A$

Lesson 13-1

1. 10 dogs from a county; all dogs in the county; biased; convenience

2. 25 students; all students at the school; biased; voluntary response

3. ice cream cones made during three shifts; all ice cream cones made during three shifts; unbiased; systematic random sample

4. a group of automobiles manufactured at a particular plant; all automobiles manufactured at the plant; unbiased; stratified random sample

5. a group of people shopping at a department store; all people shopping at the department store; biased; voluntary response

6. a group of community residents; all residents of the community; unbiased; systematic random sample

7. a group of malformed frogs; all frogs in a state's lakes; biased; voluntary response

8. 10 cartons of strawberries; all cartons of strawberries in a store; biased; convenience

Lesson 13-2

5. impossible

6. $\begin{bmatrix} 3 & -4 \\ -3 & 6 \end{bmatrix}$

7. $\begin{bmatrix} -4 & 0 & 0 \\ -3 & 3 & 0 \end{bmatrix}$

8. $\begin{bmatrix} -6 & 2 & -8 \\ -3 & -3 & 4 \end{bmatrix}$

9. $\begin{bmatrix} 2 & -2 & 8 \\ 0 & 6 & -4 \end{bmatrix}$

10. $\begin{bmatrix} 3 & 0 \\ 0 & 3 \end{bmatrix}$

11. $\begin{bmatrix} 1 & -4 \\ -3 & 4 \end{bmatrix}$

12. $\begin{bmatrix} -5 & 0 \\ 0 & -5 \end{bmatrix}$

13. $\begin{bmatrix} 5 & -8 \\ -6 & 11 \end{bmatrix}$

14. $\begin{bmatrix} -16 & 4 & -16 \\ -9 & -3 & 8 \end{bmatrix}$

15. impossible

16. $\begin{bmatrix} 8 & -12 \\ -9 & 17 \end{bmatrix}$

Lesson 13-3

1. 1000–1500 miles; The data appear to be skewed to the left.

2. 70–75 percent; About half of the data lie in the 70–80 percent range.

Lesson 13-4

1. 46; 43; 33.5; 47.5; 14; 10

2. 34; 81; 68; 95; 27; none

3. 70; 65; 45; 85; 40; none

4. 8; 4; 2.4; 7.1; 4.7; none

5. 73; 31; 13; 56; 43; none

6. 663; 400; 251; 587.5; 336.5; none

Lesson 13-5

1.
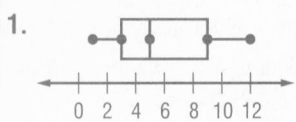

2.
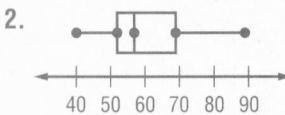

3.
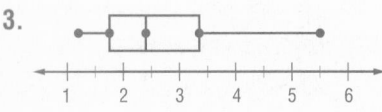

4.
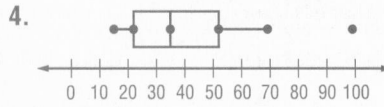

5.
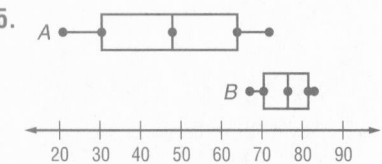

The A data are much more diverse than the B data. In general, the B data are greater than the A data.

6.
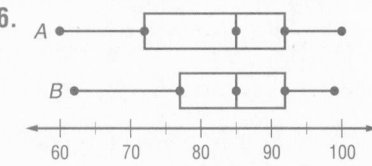

The two data sets have about the same range, but the middle 50% of the data are greater for set A.

Lesson 13-3

(pages 722–728)

For each histogram, answer the following.

• In what measurement class does the median occur?

• Describe the distribution of the data. 1–2. See margin.

1.
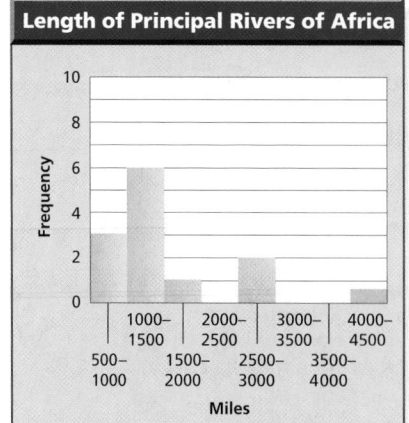

2.
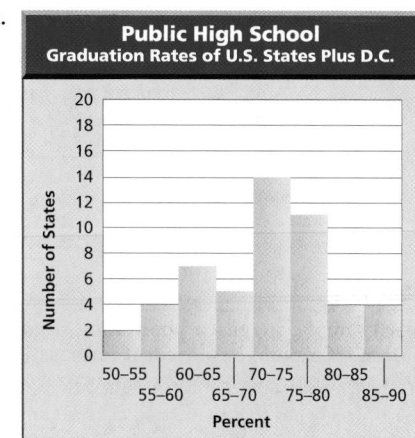

Create a histogram to represent each data set. 3–5. See pp. 852A–852H.

3. Sale prices of notebooks at various department stores, in cents: 13, 69, 89, 25, 55, 20, 99, 75, 42, 18, 66, 88, 89, 79, 75, 65, 25, 99, 66, 78

4. Number of fish in tanks at a pet store: 1, 25, 7, 4, 54, 15, 12, 6, 2, 1, 25, 17, 20, 5, 6, 15, 24, 2, 17, 1, 5, 7, 20, 12, 12, 3

5. Number of defective light bulbs found on the assembly line during each of 20 shifts: 5, 1, 7, 6, 4, 3, 2, 1, 10, 12, 1, 2, 0, 7, 6, 2, 8, 4, 2, 0

Lesson 13-4

(pages 731–736)

Find the range, median, lower quartile, upper quartile, and interquartile range of each set of data. Identify any outliers. 1–6. See margin.

1. 56, 45, 37, 43, 10, 34, 33, 45, 50

2. 77, 78, 68, 96, 99, 84, 65, 95, 65, 84

3. 30, 90, 40, 70, 50, 100, 80, 60

4. 4, 5.2, 1, 3, 2.4, 6, 3.7, 8, 1.3, 7.1, 9

5. 25°, 56°, 13°, 44°, 0°, 31°, 73°, 66°, 4°, 29°, 37°

6. 234, 648, 369, 112, 527, 775, 406, 268, 400

Lesson 13-5

(pages 737–742)

Draw a box-and-whisker plot for each set of data. 1–4. See margin.

1. 3, 2, 1, 5, 7, 9, 2, 11, 3, 4, 8, 8, 10, 12, 4

2. 59, 63, 69, 69, 49, 40, 55, 69, 55, 89, 45, 55

3. 1.8, 2.2, 1.2, 3.5, 5.5, 3.2, 1.2, 4.2, 3.0, 2.6, 1.7, 1.8

4. 15, 18, 25, 37, 52, 69, 22, 35, 50, 65, 15, 99, 35, 25

Draw a parallel box-and-whisker plot for each set of data. Compare the data. 5–8. See margin.

5. A: 21, 24, 34, 46, 58, 67, 72, 70, 61, 50, 40, 27
   B: 67, 69, 72, 75, 79, 81, 83, 83, 82, 78, 74, 69

6. A: 100, 85, 65, 72, 83, 92, 92, 60, 99, 88, 75, 76, 92, 91, 70
   B: 98, 82, 85, 62, 77, 85, 91, 95, 77, 65, 99, 73, 81, 92, 88

7. A: 3.6, 2.2, 2.2, 1.5, 1.1, 0.5, 0.8, 0.4, 0.8, 2.3, 3.0, 3.8
   B: 5.4, 4.0, 3.8, 2.5, 1.8, 1.6, 0.9, 1.2, 1.9, 3.3, 5.7, 6.0

8. A: 4.75, 6.25, 7.95, 2.65, 5.25, 6.50, 8.25, 3.25, 4.25
   B: 9.50, 8.65, 3.25, 5.25, 4.50, 5.75, 6.95, 5.50, 4.25

7.
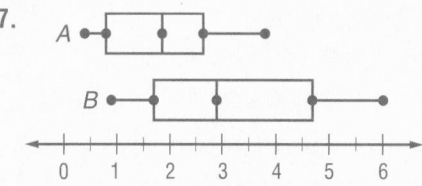

The B data are more diverse than the A data. In general, the B data are greater than the A data.

8.
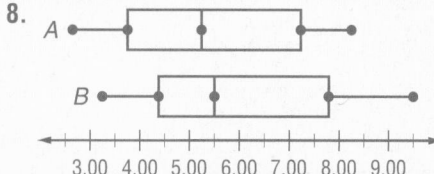

The distribution of both sets are similar. The values for B are somewhat greater than the values for A.

Lesson 14-1

(pages 754–758)

Draw a tree diagram to show the sample space for each event. Determine the number of possible outcomes. 1–4. See pp. 852A–852H for diagrams.

1. choosing a dinner special at a restaurant offering the choice of lettuce salad or coleslaw; chicken, beef, or fish; and ice cream, pudding, or cookies **18**

2. tossing a coin four times **16**

3. spinning a spinner with five equal-sized sections, one each of white, yellow, blue, red, and green, two times **25**

4. selecting a sundae with choice of vanilla or butter pecan ice cream; chocolate, strawberry, or marshmallow topping; and walnuts or peanuts **12**

Determine the number of possible outcomes for each situation.

5. A state offers special graphic license plates. Each license plate features two digits followed by two letters. Any digit and any letter can be used in the appropriate space. **67,600**

6. A lounge chair can be ordered with a choice of rocking or non-rocking, swivel or non-swivel, cotton, leather, or plush cover, and in green, blue, maroon, or black. **48**

7. At the Big Mountain Ski Resort, you can choose from three types of boots, four types of skis, and five types of poles. **60**

8. A game is played by rolling three four-sided dice, one red, one blue, and one white. **64**

Find the value of each expression.

9. $8!$ **40,320**   10. $1!$ **1**   11. $0!$ **1**   12. $5!$ **120**

13. $2!$ **2**   14. $9!$ **362,880**   15. $3!$ **6**   16. $14!$ **87,178,291,200**

Lesson 14-2

(pages 760–767)

Determine whether each situation involves a *permutation* or *combination*. Explain your reasoning. 1–7. See margin for explanations.

1. three topping flavors for a sundae from ten topping choices **combination**

2. selection and placement of four runners on a relay team from 8 runners **permutation**

3. five rides to ride at an amusement park with twelve rides **combination**

4. first, second, and third place winners for a 10K race **permutation**

5. a three-letter arrangement from eight different letters **permutation**

6. selection of five digits from ten digits for a combination lock **permutation**

7. selecting six items from twelve possible items to include in a custom gift basket **combination**

Evaluate each expression.

8. $_5P_2$ **20**   9. $_7P_7$ **5040**   10. $_{10}C_2$ **45**   11. $_6C_5$ **6**

12. $_8P_2$ **56**   13. $_{18}C_{10}$ **43,758**   14. $_{13}C_{13}$ **1**   15. $_9P_6$ **60,480**

16. $(_7P_3)(_4P_2)$ **2520**   17. $(_8C_6)(_7C_5)$ **588**   18. $(_3C_2)(_{10}P_{10})$ **10,886,400**   19. $(_3P_2)(_{10}C_{10})$ **6**

Lesson 14-3

(pages 769–776)

A red die and a blue die are rolled. Find each probability.

1. $P(\text{red 1, blue 1})$ $\frac{1}{36}$ 2. $P(\text{red even, blue even})$ $\frac{1}{4}$ 3. $P(\text{red prime number, blue even})$ $\frac{1}{4}$

4. $P(\text{red 6, blue greater than 4})$ $\frac{1}{18}$ 5. $P(\text{red greater than 2, blue greater than 3})$ $\frac{1}{3}$

At a carnival game, toy ducks are selected from a pond to win prizes. Once a duck is selected, it is not replaced. The pond contains 8 red, 2 yellow, 1 gold, 4 blue, and 40 black ducks. Find each probability. 11. $\frac{4}{78,705}$

6. $P(\text{red, then gold})$ $\frac{4}{1485}$ 7. $P(\text{2 black})$ $\frac{52}{99}$ 8. $P(\text{2 yellow})$ $\frac{1}{1485}$

9. $P(\text{black, then gold})$ $\frac{4}{297}$ 10. $P(\text{3 blacks, then red})$ $\frac{304}{5247}$ 11. $P(\text{yellow, then blue, then gold})$

12. $P(\text{2 gold})$ **0**   13. $P(\text{4 blue})$ $\frac{1}{341,055}$ 14. $P(\text{4 blue, then gold})$ $\frac{1}{17,393,805}$

Lesson 14-2

1. Order is not important.

2. Order of runners can make a difference.

3. Order is not important.

4. Order of winning is important.

5. Order is important with letters.

6. Order is important with a lock.

7. Order is not important.

Lesson 14-4

(pages 777–781)

For Exercises 1–3, use the table that shows the possible products when rolling two dice and the number of ways each product can be found. **1–2. See margin.**

Product	Ways	Product	Ways	Product	Ways
1	1	8	2	18	2
2	2	9	1	20	2
3	2	10	2	24	2
4	3	12	4	25	1
5	2	15	2	30	2
6	4	16	1	36	1

1. Draw a table to show the sample space of all possible outcomes.
2. Find the probability for $X = 9$, $X = 12$, and $X = 24$.
3. What is the probability that the product of two dice is greater than 15 on two separate rolls? $\dfrac{121}{1296}$

For Exercises 4–7, use the table that shows a probability distribution for the number of customers that enter a particular store during a business day. **4. See margin.**

Number of Customers	0–500	501–1000	1001–1500	1501–2000	2000–2500
Probability	0.05	0.25	0.35	0.30	0.05

4. Define a random variable and list its values.
5. Show that this is a valid probability distribution. $0.05 + 0.25 + 0.35 + 0.30 + 0.05 = 1$
6. During a business day, what is the probability that fewer than 1001 customers enter? **0.30**
7. During a business day, what is the probability that more than 500 customers enter? **0.95**

Lesson 14-5

(pages 782–788)

For Exercises 1–3, toss 4 coins, one at a time, 50 times and record your results. **1–2. See students' work.**

1. Based on your results, what is the probability that any two coins will show tails?
2. Based on your results, what is the probability that the first and fourth coins show heads?
3. What is the theoretical probability that all four coins show heads? $\dfrac{1}{16}$

For Exercises 4–6, roll two dice 50 times and record the products.

4. Based on your results, what is the probability that the product is 15? **See students' work.**
5. If you roll the dice 50 more times, which product would you expect to see about 10% of the time? **6 or 12**
6. What is the theoretical probability that the product of the dice will be 2? $\dfrac{1}{18}$

For Exercises 7–9, use the following information.
A survey was sent to randomly selected households asking the number of people living in each of the households. The results of the survey are shown in the table.

7. Find the experimental probability distribution for the number of households of each size. **See margin.**
8. Based on the survey, what is the probability that a person chosen at random lives in a household with five or more people? **about 0.11 or 11%**
9. Based on the survey, what is the probability that a person chosen at random lives in a household with 1 or 2 people? **about 0.34 or 34%**

Number of People Per Household Surveyed	
Number in Household	Number of Households
1	172
2	293
3	482
4	256
5 or more	148

Lesson 14-4

1.

×	1	2	3	4	5	6
1	1	2	3	4	5	6
2	2	4	6	8	10	12
3	3	6	9	12	15	18
4	4	8	12	16	20	24
5	5	10	15	20	25	30
6	6	12	18	24	30	36

2. $P(X = 9) = \dfrac{1}{36}$; $P(X = 12) = \dfrac{1}{9}$;

$P(X = 24) = \dfrac{1}{18}$

4. Let X = number of customers; x = 500, 1000, 1500, 2000, 2500

Lesson 14-5

7. $P(1) \approx 12.7\%$; $P(2) \approx 21.7\%$; $P(3) \approx 35.7\%$; $P(4) \approx 18.9\%$; $P(5 \text{ or more}) \approx 11.0\%$

Page 829, Lesson 4-3

1. D = {−9, 0, 5}; R = {−1, 0, 2}

x	y
5	2
0	0
−9	−1

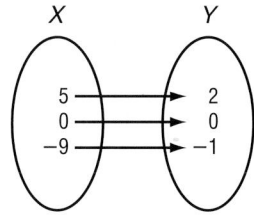

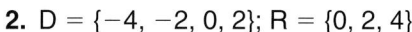

2. D = {−4, −2, 0, 2}; R = {0, 2, 4}

x	y
−4	2
−2	0
0	2
2	4

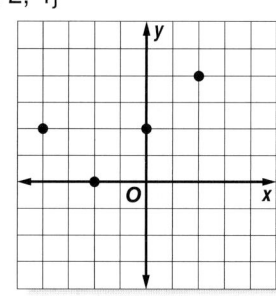

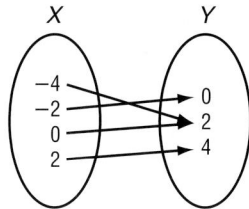

3. D = {−9, −2, 4, 5, 7}; R = {−7, −3, 0, 2, 5}

x	y
7	5
−2	−3
4	0
5	−7
−9	2

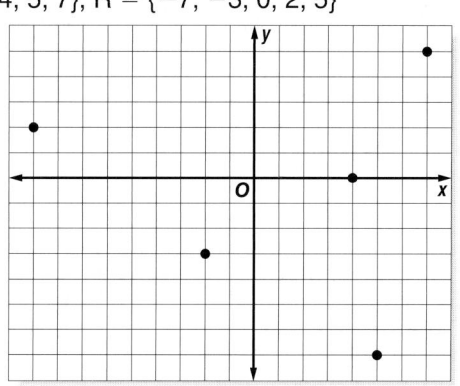

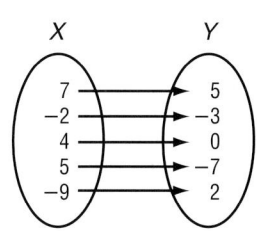

4. D = {−9, −4.7, 2.4, 3.1}; R = {−3.6, −1, 3.9, 12.12}

x	y
3.1	−1
−4.7	3.9
2.4	−3.6
−9	12.12

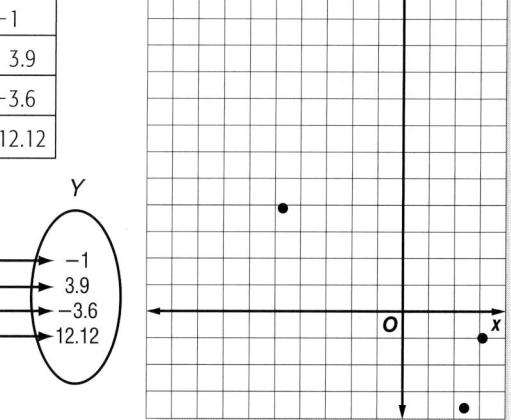

Page 829, Lesson 4-4

16. {(−8, 2.5), (−4, 1.5), (0, 0.5), (4, −0.5), (8, −1.5)}

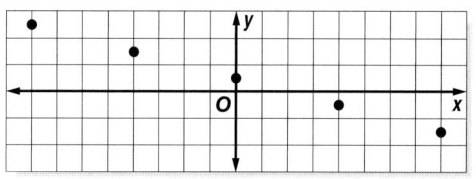

17. {(−5, −2), (−1, 2), (3, 6), (7, 10), (9, 12)}

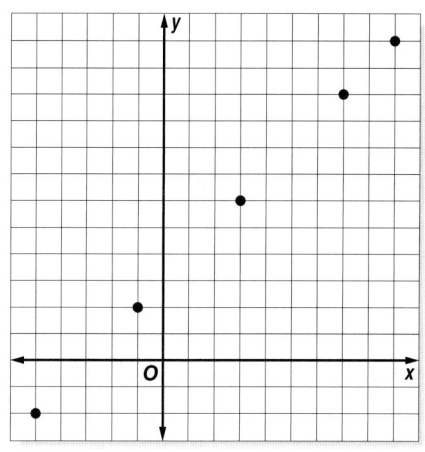

18. {(−4, 2), (−3, 1), (0, −2), (1, −3), (3, −5)}

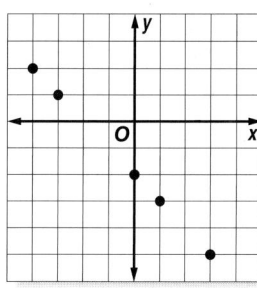

19. $\left\{\left(-5, -\dfrac{5}{3}\right), \left(-3, -\dfrac{1}{3}\right), \left(0, \dfrac{5}{3}\right), (5, 5), \left(6, \dfrac{17}{3}\right)\right\}$

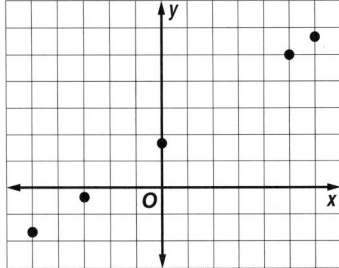

20. $\left\{\left(-6, -\dfrac{8}{3}\right), (-3, -2), \left(0, -\dfrac{4}{3}\right), \left(1, -\dfrac{10}{9}\right), \left(3, -\dfrac{2}{3}\right)\right\}$

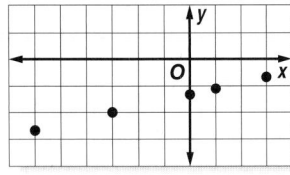

21. $\{(-4, -7), (0, -4), (4, -1), (6, 0.5), (8, 2)\}$

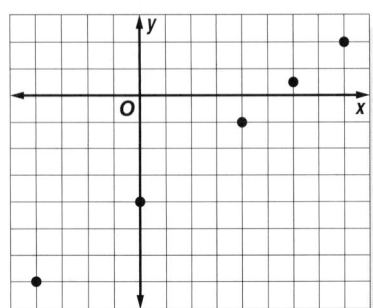

Page 829, Lesson 4-5

1. yes; $3x - 2y = 0$ **2.** no

3. yes; $4x - 2y = 8$ **4.** yes; $3x - 7y = -7$

5. yes; $7x - 7y = 2$ **6.** no

7. 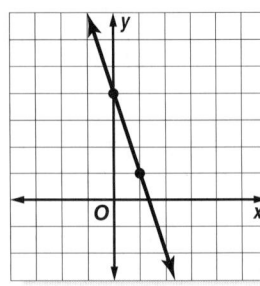   **8.**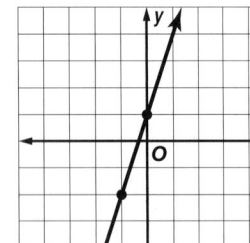

9. 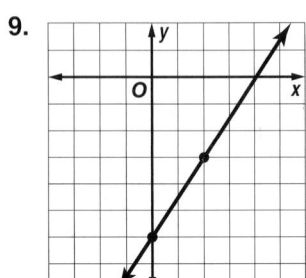   **10.**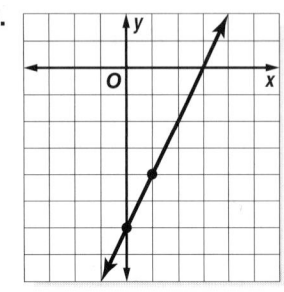

11. 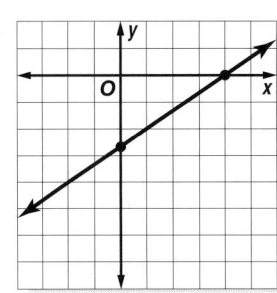   **12.**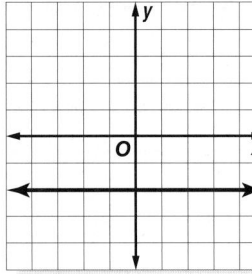

13. 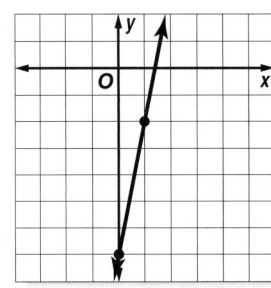   **14.**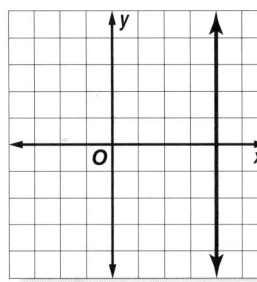

15. 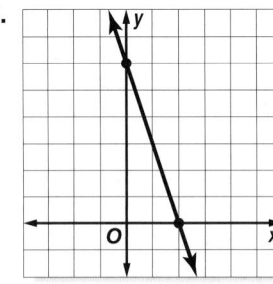   **16.**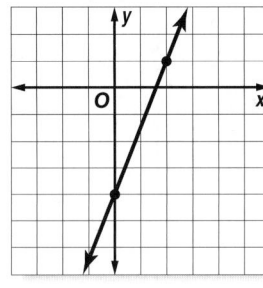

17. 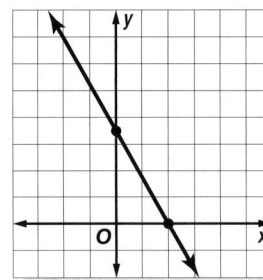   **18.**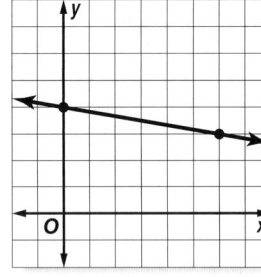

Page 834, Lesson 6-5

1.

2.

3.

4.

5.

6.

7.

8.

9.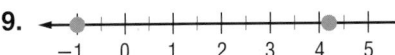
(number line from −1 to 5; closed dot at −1, closed dot at 4)

10.
(number line from −10 to 6; closed dot at −9, closed dot at 6, shaded between)

11.
(number line from −6 to 8; closed dot at −4, closed dot at 6, shaded between)

12.
(number line from 0 to 12; open dot at 7, open dot at 10, shaded between)

13.
(number line from −6 to 6; open dot at −5, open dot at 5, shaded between)

14.
(number line from −8 to 6; closed dot at −7, closed dot at 4)

15.
(number line from −8 to 10; open dot at −7, open dot at 9)

16.
(number line from −16 to 8; closed dot at −14, closed dot at 8)

17.
(number line from −16 to 16; closed dot at −14, closed dot at 15)

18.
(number line from 0 to 6; closed dot at 1, closed dot at 6, shaded between)

19.
(number line from −2 to 12; closed dot at −1, closed dot at 11, shaded between)

20.
(number line from −6 to 8; closed dot at −4, closed dot at 7)

Page 835, Lesson 6-6

14.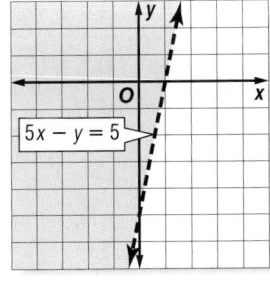
$5x - y = 5$

15.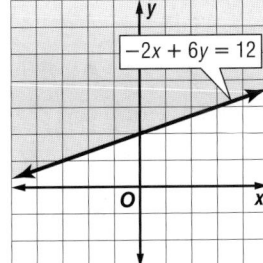
$-2x + 6y = 12$

16.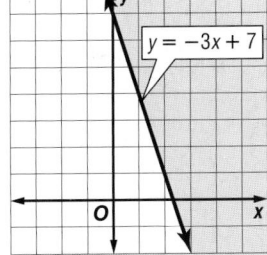
$-x + 3y = 9$

17.
$y = -3x + 7$

18.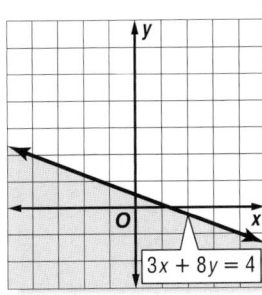
$3x + 8y = 4$

19.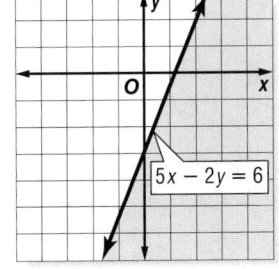
$5x - 2y = 6$

Page 835, Lesson 7-1

1.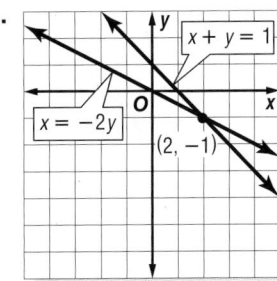
$4x + 2y = 30$, $(3, 9)$, $y = 3x$

2.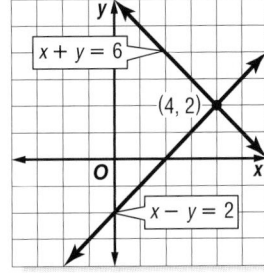
$x + y = 1$, $x = -2y$, $(2, -1)$

3.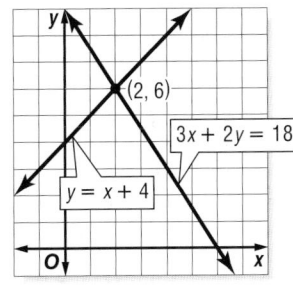
$(2, 6)$, $3x + 2y = 18$, $y = x + 4$

4.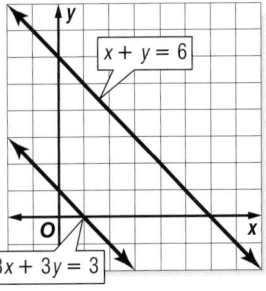
$x + y = 6$, $(4, 2)$, $x - y = 2$

5.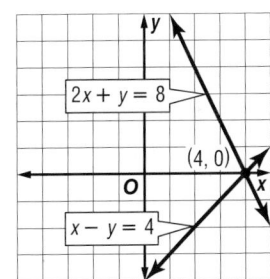
$x + y = 6$, $3x + 3y = 3$

6.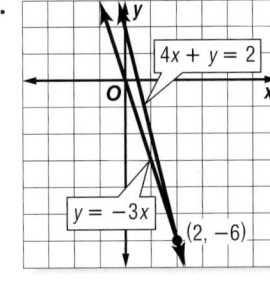
$4x + y = 2$, $y = -3x$, $(2, -6)$

7.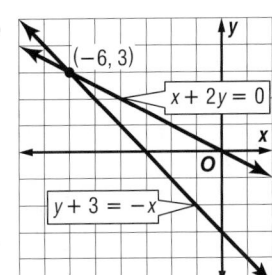
$2x + y = 8$, $(4, 0)$, $x - y = 4$

8.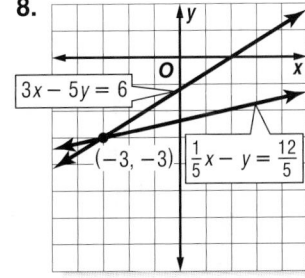
$3x - 5y = 6$, $(-3, -3)$, $\frac{1}{5}x - y = \frac{12}{5}$

9.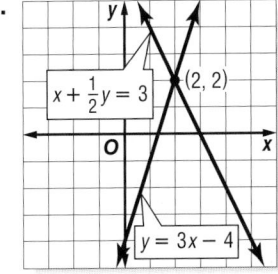
$(-6, 3)$, $x + 2y = 0$, $y + 3 = -x$

10.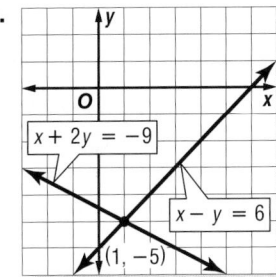
$x + 2y = -9$, $x - y = 6$, $(1, -5)$

11.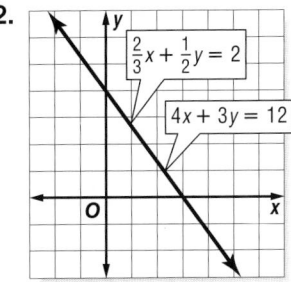
$x + \frac{1}{2}y = 3$, $(2, 2)$, $y = 3x - 4$

12.
$\frac{2}{3}x + \frac{1}{2}y = 2$, $4x + 3y = 12$

13.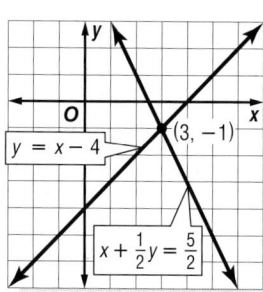

14.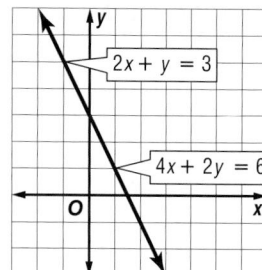

15.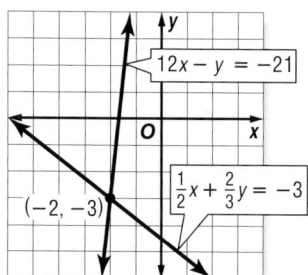

Page 836, Lesson 7-5

10.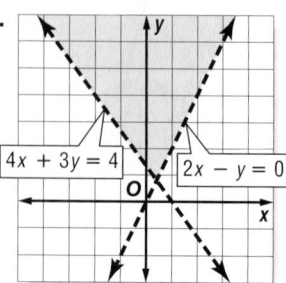

11.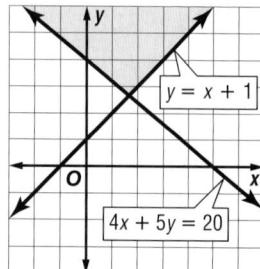

12.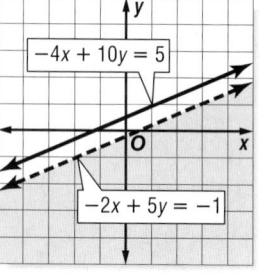

13.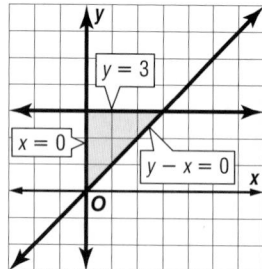

14.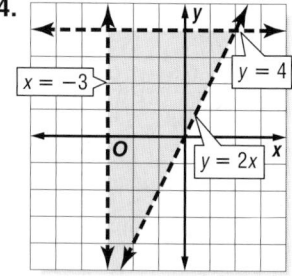

15.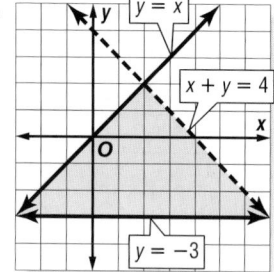

Page 841, Lesson 10-1

9. $x = 2$; $(2, -8)$; minimum

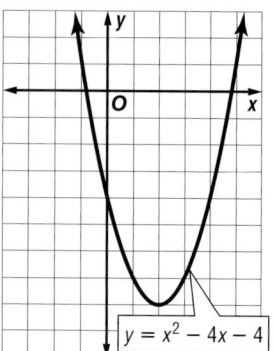

10. $x = 2$; $(2, 17)$; minimum

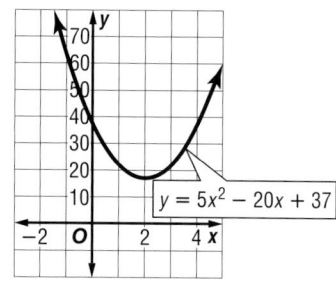

11. $x = -1$; $(-1, 0)$; minimum

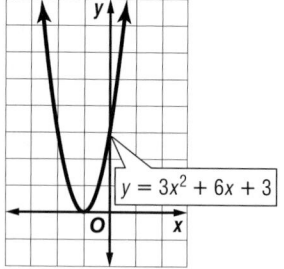

12. $x = -3$; $(-3, -18)$; minimum

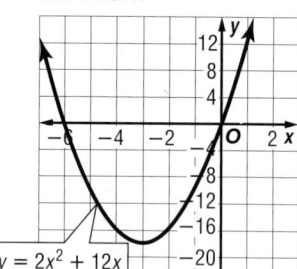

13. $x = 3$; $(3, -4)$; minimum

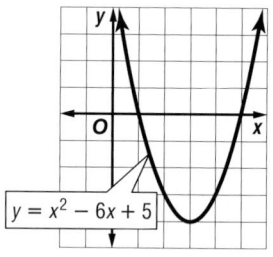

14. $x = -3$; $(-3, 0)$; minimum

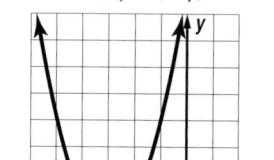

15. $x = 8$; $(8, 49)$; maximum

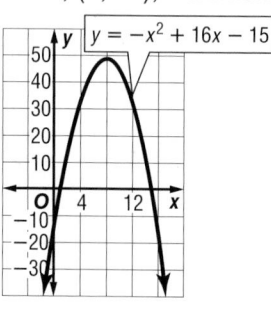

16. $x = 0$; $(0, -1)$; minimum

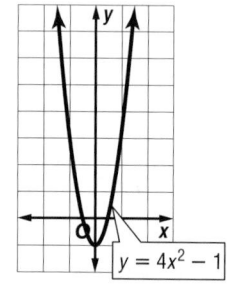

17. $x = -\frac{1}{2}$; $\left(-\frac{1}{2}, 4\frac{1}{2}\right)$; maximum

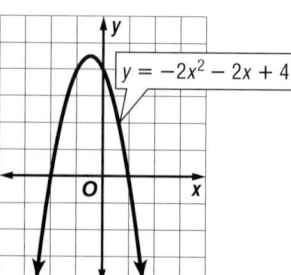

18. $x = 1$; $(1, -10)$; minimum

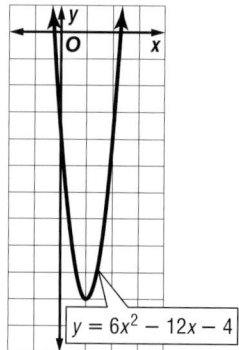

19. $x = 0$; $(0, -1)$; maximum **20.** $x = \frac{1}{2}$; $\left(\frac{1}{2}, 1\frac{1}{4}\right)$; maximum

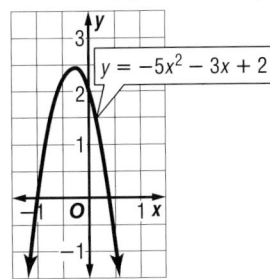

21. $x = -0.3$; $(-0.3, 2.45)$; maximum

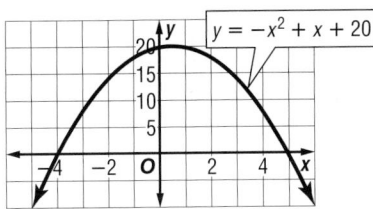

22. $x = \frac{1}{2}$; $\left(\frac{1}{2}, 20\frac{1}{4}\right)$; maximum

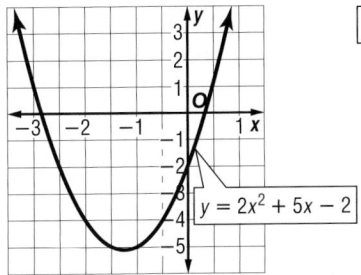

23. $x = -1.25$; $(-1.25, -5.125)$; minimum **24.** $x = -3$; $(-3, 12)$; maximum

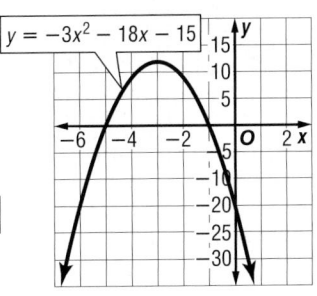

Page 842, Lesson 10-2

10.

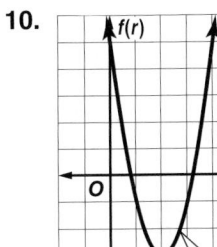

11.

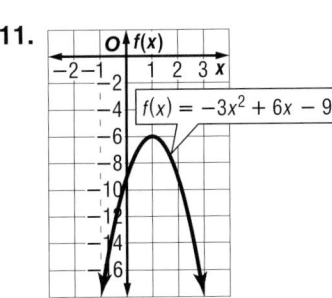

12.

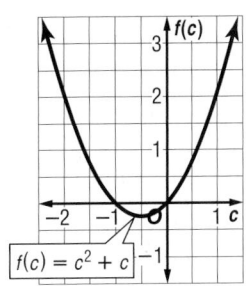

13.

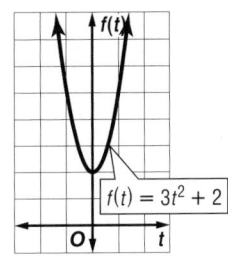

14.

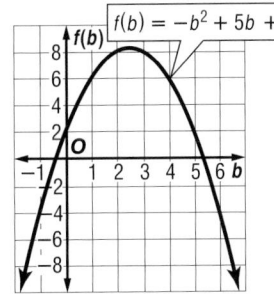

15.

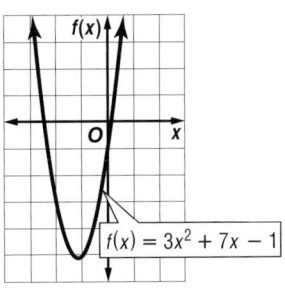

16.

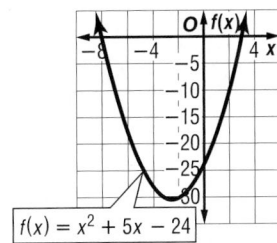

17.

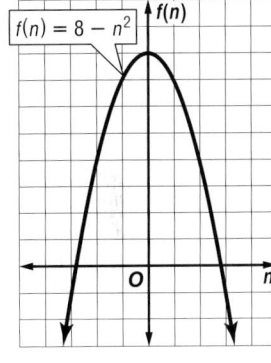

18.

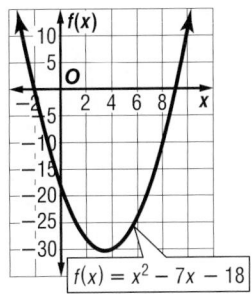

19.

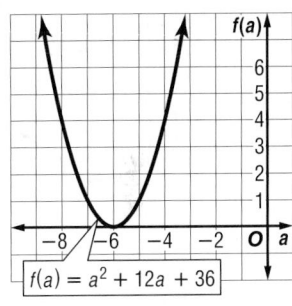

20.

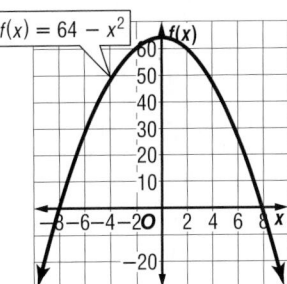

21.

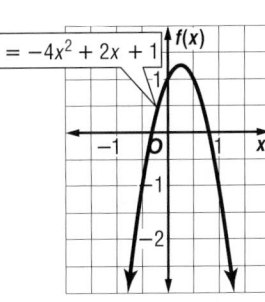

22.

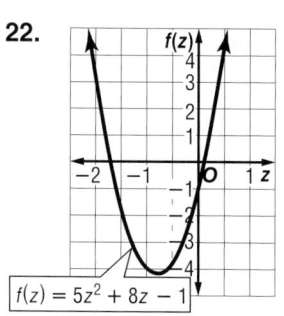

$f(z) = 5z^2 + 8z - 1$

23.

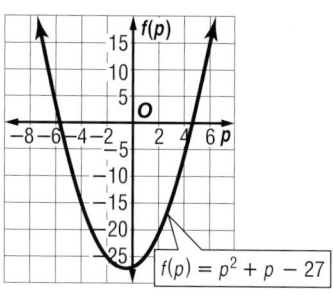

$f(p) = p^2 + p - 27$

24.

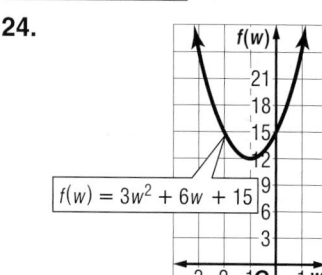

$f(w) = 3w^2 + 6w + 15$

Page 843, Lesson 10-5

7.

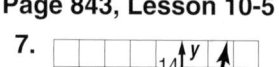

$y = 3^{x+1}$

8.

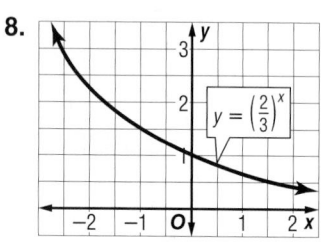

$y = \left(\frac{2}{3}\right)^x$

9.

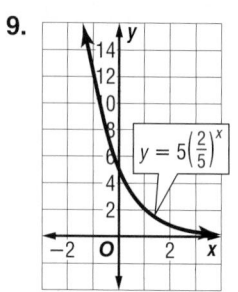

$y = 5\left(\frac{2}{5}\right)^x$

10.

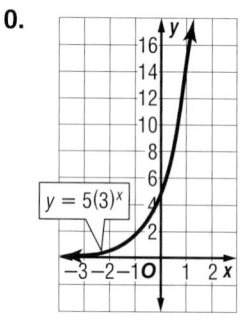

$y = 5(3)^x$

11.

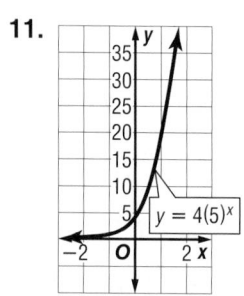

$y = 4(5)^x$

12.

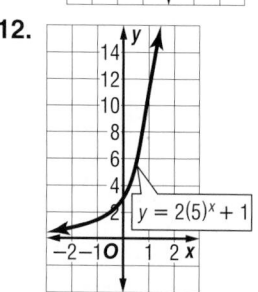

$y = 2(5)^x + 1$

13.

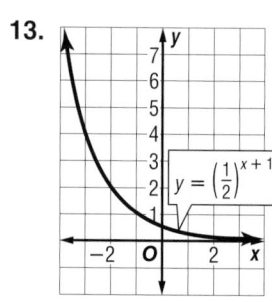

$y = \left(\frac{1}{2}\right)^{x+1}$

14.

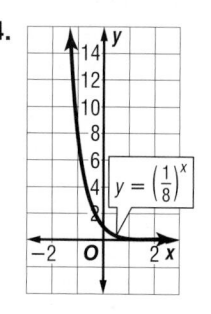

$y = \left(\frac{1}{8}\right)^x$

15.

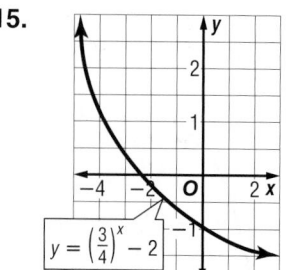

$y = \left(\frac{3}{4}\right)^x - 2$

16. No; the domain values are at regular intervals and the range values have a common difference of 4.

17. Yes; the domain values are at regular intervals and the range values have a common factor of 5.

Page 850, Lesson 13-3

3. Sample answer:

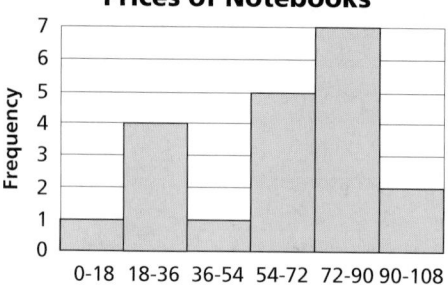

Prices of Notebooks

4. Sample answer:

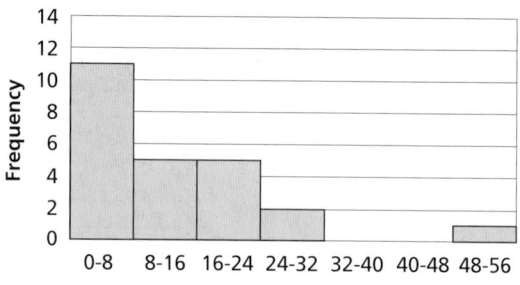

Number of Fish Per Tank

5. Sample answer:

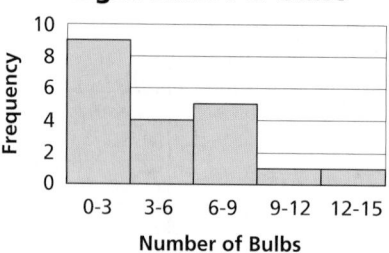

Number of Defective Light Bulbs Per Shift

1.

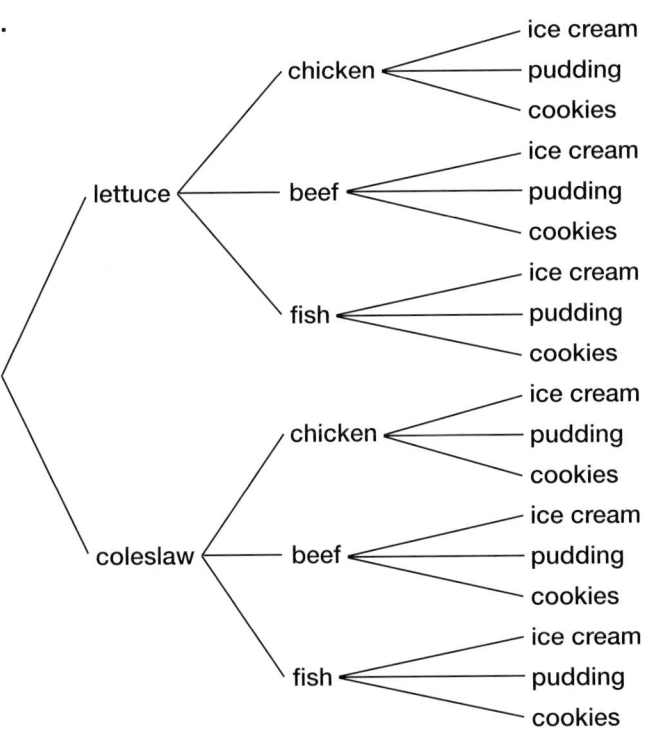

2.

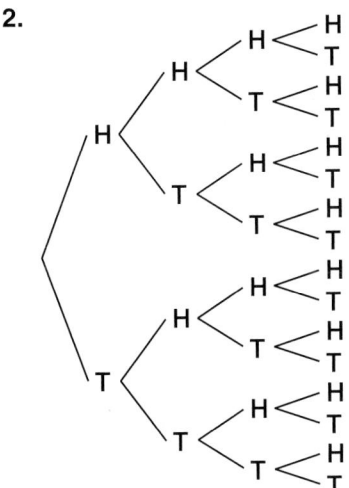

3.

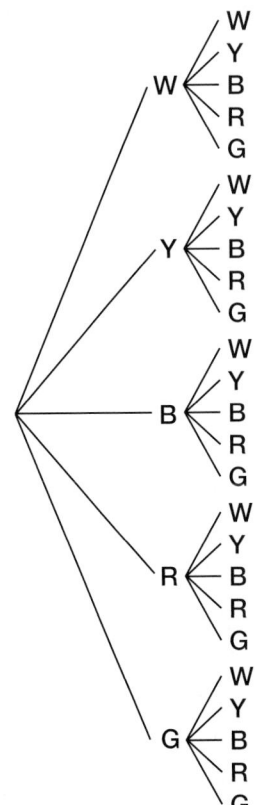

4.

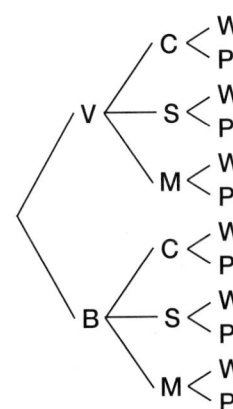

Notes

Mixed Problem Solving

Chapter 1   The Language of Algebra
(pages 4–65)

GEOMETRY   For Exercises 1 and 2, use the following information.
The surface area of a cone is the sum of the product of π and the radius r squared, and the product of π, the radius r, and the slant height ℓ. *(Lesson 1-1)*

1. Write an expression that represents the surface area of the cone. $\pi r^2 + \pi r \ell$

2. Suppose the radius and the slant height of a cone have the same measure r. Write an expression that represents the surface area of this cone. $2\pi r^2$

SALES   For Exercises 3 and 4, use the following information.
At the Farmer's Market, merchants can rent a small table for $5.00 and a large table for $8.50. For the first market, 25 small and 10 large tables were rented. For the second market, 35 small and 12 large were rented. *(Lesson 1-2)*

3. Write an expression to show how much money was collected for table rentals during the two markets. $25(5) + 10(8.5) + 35(5) + 12(8.5)$

4. Evaluate the expression to determine how much was collected at the two markets. **$487**

ENTERTAINMENT   For Exercises 5–7, use the following information.
The Morrows are planning to go to a water park. The table shows the ticket prices. The family has 2 adults, 2 children, and a grandparent who wants to observe. They want to spend no more than $55. *(Lesson 1-3)*

Admission Prices ($)		
Ticket	Full Day	Half Day
Adult	16.95	10.95
Child (6–18)	12.95	8.95
Observer	4.95	3.95

5. Write an inequality to show the cost for the family to go to the water park. **See margin.**

6. How much would it cost the Morrows to go for a full day? a half day? **$64.75; $43.75**

7. Can the family go to the water park for a full day and stay within their budget? **no**

RETAIL   For Exercises 8–10, use the following information.
A department store is having a sale of children's clothing. The table shows the prices. *(Lesson 1-4)*

Shorts	T-Shirts	Tank Tops
$7.99	$8.99	$6.99
$5.99	$4.99	$2.99

8. Write three different expressions that represent 8 pairs of shorts and 8 tops. **See margin.**

9. Evaluate the three expressions in Exercise 8 to find the costs of the 16 items. What do you notice about all the total costs? **See margin.**

10. On the final sale day, if you buy 8 shorts and 8 tops, you receive a discount of 15% on the entire purchase. Find the greatest and least amount of money you can spend on the 16 items at the sale. **$115.46; $61.06**

11. **CRAFTS**   Mandy makes baby blankets and stuffed rabbits to sell at craft fairs. She sells blankets for $28 and rabbits for $18. Write and evaluate an expression to find her total amount of sales if she sells 25 blankets and 25 rabbits. *(Lesson 1-5)*
$25(28 + 18) = \$1150$

12. **BASEBALL**   Tickets to a baseball game cost $18.95, $12.95, or $9.95. A hot dog and soda combo costs $5.50. Members of the Madison family are having a reunion. They buy 10 tickets in each price category and plan to buy 30 combos. What is the total cost for the tickets and meals? *(Lesson 1-6)* **$583.50**

13. **GEOMETRY**   Two perpendicular lines meet to form four right angles. Write two different if-then statements for this definition. *(Lesson 1-7)* **See margin.**

14. **JOBS**   Laurie mows lawns to earn extra money. She knows that she can mow at most 30 lawns in one week. She determines that she profits $15 on each lawn she mows. Identify a reasonable domain and range for this situation and draw a graph. *(Lesson 1-8)* **See margin.**

15. **STATISTICS**   Draw two graphs of the data. One graph should accurately display the data and the other should be misleading. Explain why it is misleading. *(Lesson 1-9)* **See margin.**

Population Density of Montana (people per square mile)	
Year	Density
1920	3.8
1960	4.6
1980	5.4
1990	5.5
2000	6.2

Source: *The World Almanac*

---

5. Let a represent adult price, c represent child price, and g represent observer price. Then $2a + 2c + g \le 55$.

8. Sample answer: $8(7.99) + 4(4.99) + 4(6.99); 8(5.99) + 4(8.99) + 4(2.99); 4(7.99) + 4(5.99) + 4(4.99) + 4(2.99)$

9. Sample answer: $111.84; $95.84; $87.84; All totals end in $0.84.

13. If two lines are perpendicular, then they meet to form four right angles. If two lines meet to form four right angles, then they are perpendicular.

14. A reasonable domain is 0 through 30 and a reasonable range is 0 through 450.

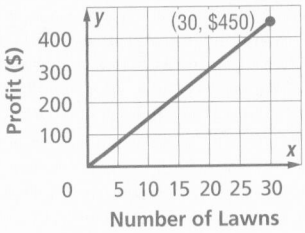

15. Sample answer: The second graph is misleading because the intervals for the years are not equal and the intervals for the y-axis are not equal.

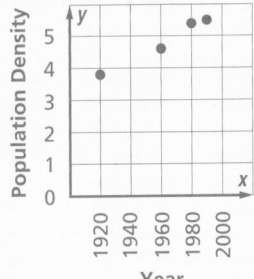

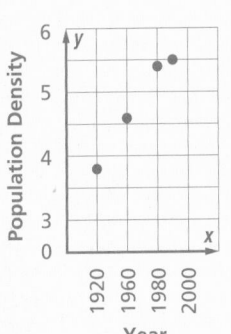

Chapter 2

8.

Stem	Leaf
7	1 7
8	1 6 9
9	0 1 1 6
10	2 4 5
11	0 9
12	5 8 7|1 = 7.1

10. mean: about 9.8; median: 9.35; mode: 9.1

11. Sample answer: Yes, many of the data values are around 9.1.

WEATHER   For Exercises 1–3, use the following information.

The following values are the monthly normal temperatures for Barrow, Alaska. *(Lesson 2-1)*

1. −18, −15, −13, −11, −2, −2, 14, 19, 31, 34, 38, 39

−13	−2	19	39	−15	38
31	−11	−2	14	−18	34

Source: *The World Almanac*

2. 18, 15, 13, 11, 2, 2, 14, 19, 31, 34, 38, 39

1. Order the temperatures from least to greatest.

2. Write the absolute values of the twelve temperatures.

3. Do you think the temperatures are in order from January through December in the table? Why or why not? **No; the lowest temperatures should be at the beginning and end of the table for Jan. and Dec.**

4. GEOGRAPHY The highest point in Asia is Mount Everest at 29,035 feet above sea level and the lowest point is the Dead Sea at 1312 feet below sea level. What is the difference between these two elevations? **Source:** *The World Almanac* *(Lesson 2-2)* **30,347 ft**

PHYSICAL SCIENCE   For Exercises 5 and 6, use the following information.

As you ascend in the Earth's atmosphere, the temperature drops about 3.6°F for every increase of 1000 feet in altitude. **Source:** www.infoplease.com *(Lesson 2-3)*

5. If you ascend 10,000 feet, what is the change in temperature? **−36°F**

6. If the temperature drops from 70°F at sea level to −38°F, what is the altitude you have reached? **30,000 ft**

7. NUMBER THEORY If a two-digit whole number is divided by the sum of its digits a certain value is obtained. For example, $\frac{71}{7+1} = 8.875$, $\frac{42}{4+2} = 7$, $\frac{10}{1+0} = 10$. Find the two-digit number that gives the least result. *(Lesson 2-4)* **19, 1.9**

WEATHER   For Exercises 8–11, use the following information.

The table shows the average wind speeds for sixteen windy U.S. cities. *(Lesson 2-5)*

8, 10, 11. See margin.

8.9	7.1	9.1	9.0	10.2	12.5	11.9	11.0
12.8	10.4	10.5	8.6	7.7	9.6	9.1	8.1

Source: *The World Almanac*

8. Make a stem-and-leaf plot of the data.

9. What is the difference between the least and greatest values? **5.7**

10. Find the mean, median, and mode of the data.

11. Does the mode represent the data well? Explain.

POPULATION   For Exercises 12–14, use the following information.

The table shows the predicted number, in millions, of people in the U.S. in each age category for 2010. Population is rounded to the nearest million. *(Lesson 2-6)* **12.** $\frac{20}{299} \approx 7\%$ **14.** $\frac{256}{299} \approx 86\%$

U.S. Population				
Age	**People (millions)**	**Age**	**People (millions)**
under 5	20	35–44	39
5–14	39	45–54	44
15–24	43	55–64	35
25–34	39	65 & over	40

Source: *The World Almanac*

12. What is the probability that a person in the U.S. picked at random will be under age 5?

13. What are the odds that a randomly selected person will be 65 or over? **40:259**

14. What is the probability that a person picked at random will not be 15–24 years old?

GARDENING   For Exercises 15 and 16, use the following information.

A garden is to be created in the shape of a right triangle. The sides forming the right angle, called the legs, have lengths of 20 feet and 45 feet. The Pythagorean Theorem states that the length of the longest side, or hypotenuse, of a right triangle is the square root of the sum of the squares of the legs. *(Lesson 2-7)*

15. Find the length of the hypotenuse of the garden to the nearest foot. **49 ft**

16. Suppose that the gardener wants the length of the hypotenuse of the garden to be changed to 55 feet while one leg remains 45 feet. What should be the length of the other leg of the garden to the nearest foot? **32 ft**

SWIMMING   For Exercises 17–19, use the following information.

In the 2000 summer Olympic games, the winning time for the men's 400-meter run was approximately 44 seconds. The winning time for the men's 400-meter freestyle swimming event was about 3 minutes 41 seconds. Round your answers for Exercises 17 and 18 to the nearest meter. **Source:** *The World Almanac* *(Lesson 2-4)*

17. What was the speed in meters per second for the 400-meter run? **9 m/s**

18. What was the speed in meters per second for the 400-meter freestyle? **2 m/s**

19. How do the speeds for the two events compare? **The running speed is 4.5 times faster than the swimming speed.**

GEOMETRY For Exercises 1–4, use the following information.
The lateral surface area L of a cylinder is two times π times the product of the radius r and the height h. (Lesson 3-1) **1. $L = 2\pi rh$ 2. 197.8 in²**

1. Write a formula for the lateral area of a cylinder.

2. Find the lateral area of a cylinder with a radius of 4.5 inches and a height of 7 inches. Use 3.14 for π and round the answer to the nearest tenth.

3. The total surface area T of a cylinder includes the area of the two bases of the cylinder, which are circles. The formula for the area of one circle is πr^2. Write a formula for the total surface area T of a cylinder. $T = 2\pi rh + 2\pi r^2$

4. Find the total surface area of the cylinder in Exercise 2. Round to the nearest tenth. **325.0 in²**

RIVERS For Exercises 5 and 6, use the following information.
The Congo River in Africa is 2900 miles long. That is 310 miles longer than the Niger River, which is also in Africa. **Source:** The World Almanac (Lesson 3-2)

5. Write an equation you could use to find the length of the Niger River. $n + 310 = 2900$

6. What is the length of the Niger River? **2590 mi**

ANIMALS For Exercises 7 and 8, use the following information.
The average length of a yellow-banded angelfish is 12 inches. This is 4.8 times as long as an average common goldfish. **Source:** Scholastic Records (Lesson 3-3)

7. Write an equation you could use to find the length of the common goldfish. $4.8g = 12$

8. What is the length of an average common goldfish? **2.5 in.**

9. **PETS** In 1999, there were 9860 Great Danes registered with the American Kennel Club. The number of registered Labrador Retrievers was 6997 more than fifteen times the number of registered Great Danes. How many registered Labrador Retrievers were there? **Source:** The World Almanac (Lesson 3-4) **154,897 retrievers**

10. **ENTERTAINMENT** Four families went to a baseball game. A vendor selling bags of popcorn came by. The Wilson family bought half of the bags of popcorn plus one. The Martinez family bought half of the remaining bags of popcorn plus one. The Brightfeather family bought half of the remaining bags of popcorn plus one. The Wimberly family bought half of the remaining bags of popcorn plus one, leaving the vendor with no bags of popcorn. If the Wimberlys bought 2 bags of popcorn, how many bags did each of the four families buy? (Lesson 3-4)
Wilson, 16 bags; Martinez, 8 bags; Brightfeather, 4 bags; Wimberly, 2 bags

11. **NUMBER THEORY** Five times the greatest of three consecutive even integers is equal to twice the sum of the other two integers plus 42. What are the three integers? (Lesson 3-5) **26, 28, 30**

12. **GEOMETRY** One angle of a triangle measures 10° more than the second. The measure of the third angle is twice the sum of the measures of the first two angles. Find the measure of each angle. (Lesson 3-5) **25°, 35°, 120°**

13. **POOLS** Tyler needs to add 1.5 pounds of a chemical to the water in his pool for each 5000 gallons of water. The pool holds 12,500 gallons. How much chemical should he add to the water? (Lesson 3-6) **3.75 pounds**

14. **COMPUTERS** A computer manufacturer dropped the selling price of a large-screen monitor from $2999 to $1999. What was the percent of decrease in the selling price of the monitor? (Lesson 3-7) **about 33%**

SKIING For Exercises 15 and 16, use the following information.
Michael is registering for a ski camp in British Columbia, Canada. The cost of the camp is $1254, but the Canadian government imposes a general sales tax of 7%. (Lesson 3-7) **15. $1341.78**

15. What is the total cost of the camp including tax?

16. As a U.S. citizen, Michael can apply for a refund of one-half of the tax. What is the amount of the refund he can receive? **$43.89**

FINANCE For Exercises 17 and 18, use the following information.
Allison is using a spreadsheet to solve a problem about investing. She is using the formula $I = Prt$, where I is the amount of interest earned, P is the amount of money invested, r is the rate of interest as a decimal, and t is the period of time the money is invested in years. (Lesson 3-8)

17. Allison needs to find the amount of money invested P for given amounts of interest, given rates, and given time. The formula needs to be solved for P to use in the spreadsheet. Solve the formula for P. $P = I \div (rt)$

18. Allison uses these values in the formula in Exercise 17: $I = 1848.75, $r = 7.25\%$, $t = 6$ years. Find P. **$4250**

19. **CHEMISTRY** Isaac had 40 gallons of a 15% iodine solution. How many gallons of a 40% iodine solution must he add to make a 20% iodine solution? (Lesson 3-9) **10 gal**

Chapter 4

3. pentagon

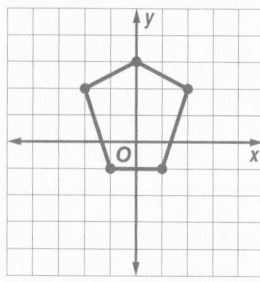

4. (0.75, −0.75), (1.5, 1.5), (0, 2.25), (−1.5, 1.5), and (−0.75, −0.75)

6. See below right.

7. No; for each 2 unit increase in height, the increase in weight is not constant.

8. Sample answer: 171 lb; from 72 to 74 in., there is an increase of 8 in., so 8 · 2 = 16 and added to 155 is 171.

9. Mercury: 0.387 AU; Mars: 1.523 AU; Jupiter: 5.202 AU; Pluto: 39.223 AU

10. If the number of AU is less than 1, the planet is closer than Earth. If the number of AU is greater than 1, the planet is further than Earth.

11. 25,110,000,000,000 miles

12.

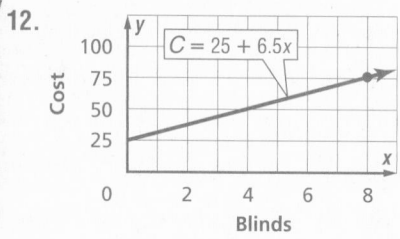

Blinds

14.

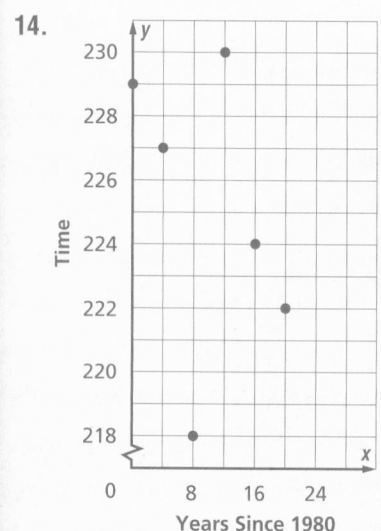

Years Since 1980

RECREATION   For Exercises 1 and 2, use the following information.
A community has a recreational building and a pool. Consider the coordinates of the building to be (0, 0) and each block to be one unit. *(Lesson 4-1)*

1. If the pool lies one block south and 2 blocks east of the building, what are its coordinates? **(2, −1)**

2. If the entrance to the community lies 5 blocks north and 3 blocks west of the building, what are its coordinates? **(−3, 5)**

DESIGN   For Exercises 3–5, use the following information. 5. 11 units², 6.2 units²
A T-shirt design has vertices at (1, −1), (2, 2), (0, 3), (−2, 2), and (−1, −1). *(Lesson 4-2)*

3. Draw the polygon on a coordinate plane. What polygon is represented by the design? **See margin.**

4. The designer wants to make smaller T-shirts using a dilation of the design by a factor of 0.75. What are the coordinates of the dilation? **See margin.**

5. Estimate the area of each design.

HEALTH   For Exercises 6–8, use the following information.
The table shows suggested weights for adults for various heights in inches. *(Lesson 4-3)*
6–8. See margin.

Height	Weight	Height	Weight
60	102	68	131
62	109	70	139
64	116	72	147
66	124	74	155

Source: *The World Almanac*

6. Graph the relation.

7. Do the data lie on a straight line? Explain.

8. Estimate a suggested weight for a person who is 78 inches tall. Explain your method.

PLANETS   For Exercises 9–11, use the following information. 9–11. See margin.
An astronomical unit (AU) is used to express great distances in space. It is based upon the distance from Earth to the Sun. A formula for converting any distance d in miles to AU is $AU = \dfrac{d}{93,000,000}$. The table shows the average distances from the Sun of four planets in miles. *(Lesson 4-4)*

Planet	Distance from Sun
Mercury	36,000,000
Mars	141,650,000
Jupiter	483,750,000
Pluto	3,647,720,000

Source: *The World Almanac*

9. Find the number of AU for each planet rounded to the nearest thousandth.

10. How can you determine which planets are further from the Sun than Earth?

11. Alpha Centauri is 270,000 AU from the Sun. How far is that in miles?

HOME DECOR   For Exercises 12 and 13, use the following information.
Pam is having blinds installed at her home. The cost for installation for any number of blinds can be described by $c = 25 + 6.5x$. *(Lesson 4-5)*

12. Graph the equation. **See margin.**

13. If Pam has 8 blinds installed, what is the cost? **$77**

SPORTS   For Exercises 14–16, use the following information.
The table shows the winning times of the Olympic mens' 50-km walk for various years. The times are rounded to the nearest minute. *(Lesson 4-6)*
14–16. See margin.

Year	Years Since 1980	Time
1980	0	229
1984	4	227
1988	8	218
1992	12	230
1996	16	224
2000	20	222

Source: ESPN

14. Graph the relation using columns 2 and 3.

15. Is the relation a function? Explain.

16. Predict a winning time for the 2008 games.

JEWELRY   For Exercises 17 and 18, use the following information. 17. $a_n = 5n − 4$
A necklace is made with beads placed in a circular pattern. The rows have the following numbers of beads: 1, 6, 11, 16, 21, 26, and 31. *(Lesson 4-7)*

17. Write a formula for the beads in each row.

18. If a larger necklace is made with 20 rows, find the number of beads in row 20. **96**

GEOMETRY

19. The table below shows the area of squares with sides of various lengths. *(Lesson 4-8)* **See margin.**

Side	Area	Side	Area
1	1	4	
2	4	5	
3	9	6	

Write the first 10 numbers that would appear in the area column. Describe the pattern.

15. Yes; each value of x is paired with only one value of y.

16. Sample answer: 218 min

19. 1, 4, 9, 16, 25, 36, 49, 64, 81, 100; The values for area are the squares of consecutive integers.

6.

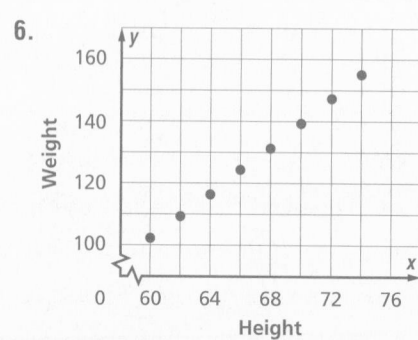

Height

Mixed Problem Solving

FARMING For Exercises 1–3, use the following information.

The graph shows wheat prices per bushel from 1940 through 1999. *(Lesson 5-1)*

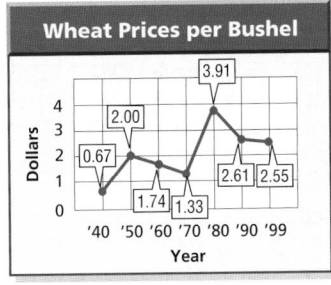

Wheat Prices per Bushel

Source: *The World Almanac*

1. For which time period was the rate of change the greatest? the least? **1970–1980; 1990–1999**

2. Find the rate of change from 1940 to 1950. **$0.133**

3. Explain the meaning of the slope from 1980 to 1990. **a drop in price**

SOUND For Exercises 4 and 5, use the following information.

The table shows the distance traveled by sound in water for various times in seconds. *(Lesson 5-2)*

Time (seconds) x	Distance (feet) y
0	0
1	4820
2	9640
3	14,460
4	19,280

Source: *New York Public Library*

4. Write an equation that relates distance traveled to time. **$y = 4820x$**

5. Find the time for a distance of 72,300 feet. **15 s**

POPULATION For Exercises 6–8, use the following information.

In 1990, the population of Wyoming was 453,589. Over the next decade, it increased by about 2890 per year. **Source:** *The World Almanac (Lesson 5-3)*

6. Assume the rate of change remains the same. Write a linear equation to find the population y of Wyoming at any time. Let x represent the number of years since 1990. **$y = 453,589 + 2890x$**

7. Graph the equation. **See margin.**

8. Estimate the population in 2005. **496,939**

HEALTH For Exercises 9 and 10, use the following information.

A chart shows ideal heights and weights for adults with a medium build. A person with height of 60 inches should have a weight of 112 pounds and a person with height of 66 inches should have a weight of 136 pounds. **Source:** *The World Almanac (Lesson 5-4)*

9. Write a linear equation to estimate the weight of a person of any height. **$y = 4x - 128$**

10. Estimate the weight of a person who is 72 inches tall. **160 lb**

TRAVEL For Exercises 11–13, use the following information.

Between 1990 and 2000, the number of people taking cruises increased by about 300,000 each year. In 1990, about 3.6 million people took a cruise. **Source:** *USA TODAY (Lesson 5-5)* 12. **$y = 300,000x - 593,400,000$**

11. Write the point-slope form of an equation to find the total number of people taking a cruise y for any year x. **$y - 3,600,000 = 300,000(x - 1990)$**

12. Write the equation in slope-intercept form.

13. Estimate the number of people who will take a cruise in 2010. **9,600,000 people**

GEOMETRY For Exercises 14 and 15, use the following information.

A quadrilateral has sides with equations $y = -2x$, $2x + y = 6$, $y = \frac{1}{2}x + 6$, and $x - 2y = 9$.

Graph the four equations to form the quadrilateral.

14. Determine whether the figure is a rectangle. **yes**

15. Explain your reasoning. *(Lesson 5-6)* **See margin.**

ADOPTION For Exercises 16–18, use the following information. **16–17. See margin.**

The table shows the number of children from Russia adopted by U.S. citizens from 1992–1999. The x values are shown as Years Since 1992. *(Lesson 5-7)*

Years Since 1992 x	Number of Children y
0	324
1	746
2	1530
3	1896
4	2454
5	3816
6	4491
7	4348

Source: *The World Almanac*

16. Draw a scatter plot and a line of fit for the data.

17. Write the slope-intercept form of the equation for the line of fit.

18. Predict the number of children who will be adopted in 2005. **8163 children**

7. See below.

15. Opposite sides have the same slopes, so they are parallel. Consecutive sides have slopes that are opposite reciprocals, so they are perpendicular.

16. Sample answer:

Adopted Russian Children

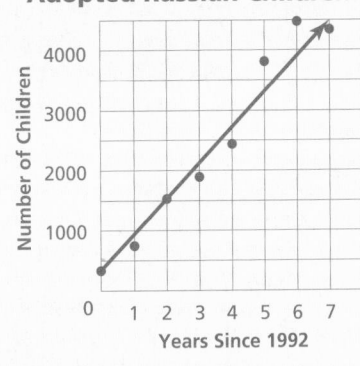

17. Sample answer using (0, 324) and (2, 1530): $y = 603x + 324$

Mixed Problem Solving

7.
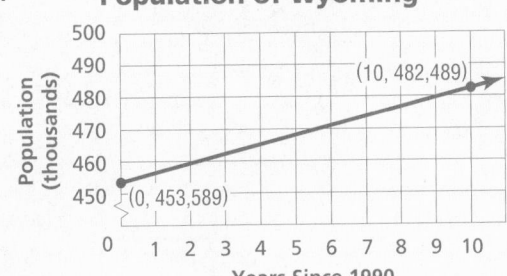

Population of Wyoming

17.

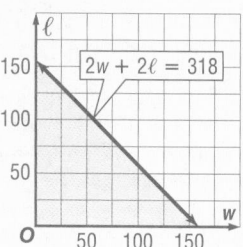

$2w + 2\ell = 318$

MONEY   For Exercises 1 and 2, use the following information.

Scott's allowance for July is $50. He wants to attend a concert that costs $26. *(Lesson 6–1)*

1. Write and solve an inequality that shows how much money he can spend in July after buying a concert ticket. $a + 26 \leq 50; \ a \leq 24$

2. He spends $2.99 for lunch with his friends and $12.49 for a CD. Write and solve an inequality that shows how much money he can spend after these purchases and the concert ticket. $a + 26 + 2.99 + 12.49 \leq 50; \ a \leq 8.52$

ANIMALS   For Exercises 3–5, use the following information.

The world's heaviest flying bird is the great bustard. A male bustard can be up to 4 feet long and weigh up to 40 pounds. *(Scholastic Book of World Records) (Lesson 6–2)*

3. Write an inequality that describes the range of lengths of male bustards. $0 < \ell \leq 4$

4. Write an inequality that describes the range of weights of male bustards. $0 < w \leq 40$

5. Male bustards are usually about four times heavier than females. Write and solve an inequality that describes the range of weights of female bustards. $0 < 4w \leq 40; \ 0 < w \leq 10$

FOOD   For Exercises 6–8, use the following information. $6. \ 1.5a - 0.3a \geq 75$

Jennie wants to make at least $75 selling caramel-coated apples at the County Fair. She plans to sell each apple for $1.50. *(Lesson 6-3)*

6. Let a be the number of apples she makes and sells. Write an inequality to find the number of apples she needs to sell to reach her goal if each apple costs her $0.30 to make.

7. Solve the inequality. $a \geq 62.5$

8. Interpret the meaning of the solution to the inequality. **Jennie must make and sell 63 or more apples to make $75 or more.**

RETAIL   For Exercises 9–11, use the following information.

A sporting goods store is printing coupons that allow the customer to save $15 on any pair of shoes in the store. *(Lesson 6-4)*

9. The most expensive pair of shoes is $149.95 and the least expensive pair of shoes is $24.95. What is the range of prices for the shoes for customers who have the coupons? $9.95 \leq p \leq 134.95$

10. You decide to buy a pair of shoes with a regular price of $109.95. You have a choice of using the coupon or having a 15% discount on the price. Which option should you choose? **15% discount**

11. For what price of shoe is a 15% discount the same as $15 off the regular price? **$100**

WEATHER   For Exercises 12–15, use the following information.

The table shows the average normal temperatures for Honolulu, Hawaii, for each month in degrees Fahrenheit. *(Lesson 6-5)*

January	73	July	81
February	73	August	81
March	74	September	81
April	76	October	80
May	78	November	77
June	79	December	74

Source: *The World Almanac*

12. What is the mean of the temperatures to the nearest whole degree? **77°**

13. By how many degrees does the lowest temperature vary from the mean? **4°**

14. By how many degrees does the highest temperature vary from the mean? **4°**

15. Write an inequality to show the normal range of temperatures for Honolulu during the year. $|t - 77| \leq 4$

QUILTING   For Exercises 16–18, use the following information. 18. 79.5 in. by 79.5 in.; 6320.25 in²

Ingrid is making a quilt in the shape of a rectangle. She wants the perimeter of the quilt to be no more than 318 inches. *(Lesson 6-6)* 16. $2w + 2\ell \leq 318$

16. Write an inequality that represents this situation.

17. Graph the inequality and name two different dimensions for the quilt.

18. What are the dimensions and area of the largest possible quilt Ingrid can make with a perimeter of no more than 318 inches? 17. See margin for graph; 70 in. by 75 in.; 72 in. by 72 in.

GEOGRAPHY   For Exercises 19–21, use the following information.

The table shows the area of land in square miles and in acres of the largest and smallest U.S. states. *(Lesson 6-4)*

State	Square Miles	Acres
Alaska	570,473	365,481,600
Rhode Island	1045	677,120

Source: *The World Almanac and U.S.A. Almanac*

19. Write an inequality that shows the range of square miles for U.S. states. $1045 \leq m \leq 570{,}473$

20. Write an inequality that shows the range of acres for U.S. states. $677{,}120 \leq m \leq 365{,}481{,}600$

21. **RESEARCH** About how many acres are in a square mile? Do the figures in the table agree with that fact? **640 acres; Alaska is very close but Rhode Island is a little off.**

WORKING   For Exercises 1–3, use the following information.

The table shows the percent of men and women 65 years and older that were working in the U.S. in the given years. *(Lesson 7-1)* **1.** $y = -0.17x + 19.3$

U.S. Workers over 65		
Year	Percent of Men	Percent of Women
1980	19.3	8.2
1990	17.6	8.4

Source: *The World Almanac*

1. Let the year 1980 be 0. Assume that the rate of change remains the same for years after 1990. Write an equation to represent the percent of working elderly men y in any year x.

2. Write an equation to represent the percent of working elderly women. $y = 0.02x + 8.2$

3. Assume the rate of increase or decrease in working men and women remains the same for years after 1990. Estimate when the percent of working men and women will be the same. **in about 58 years from 1980 or in 2038**

SPORTS   For Exercises 4–7, use the following information.

The table shows the winning times for the men's and women's Triathlon World Championship for 1995 and 2000. *(Lesson 7-2)*
4. men: 108, 112; women: 125, 115

Year	Men's	Women's
1995	1:48:29	2:04:58
2000	1:51:41	1:54:43

Source: *ESPN Sports Almanac*

4. The times in the table are in hours, minutes, and seconds. Rewrite the times in minutes rounded to the nearest minute.

5. Let the year 1995 be 0. Assume that the rate of change remains the same for years after 1995. Write an equation to represent the men's winning times y in any year x. $y = 0.8x + 108$

6. Write an equation to represent the women's winning times in any year. $y = -2x + 125$

7. If the trend continues, when would you expect the men's and women's winning times to be the same? **in about 6 years from 1995 or in 2001**

8. **TRAVEL**   While driving to Fullerton, Mrs. Sumner travels at an average speed of 40 mph. On the return trip, she travels at an average speed of 56 mph and saves two hours of travel time. How far does Mrs. Sumner live from Fullerton? *(Lesson 7-2)* **280 miles**

MONEY   For Exercises 9–11, use the following information.

In 1998, the sum of the number of $2 bills in circulation and the number of $50 bills in circulation was 1,500,888,647. The number of $50 bills was 366,593,903 more than the number of $2 bills. *(Lesson 7-3)* **Source:** *The World Almanac for Kids*

9. Write a system of equations to represent this situation.

10. Find the number of each type of bill in circulation.

11. Find the amount of money that was in circulation in $2 and $50 bills. **$47,821,358,494**

9. $t + f = 1{,}500{,}888{,}647$; $f = t + 366{,}593{,}903$
10. $2: 567,147,372; $50: 933,741,275

SPORTS   For Exercises 12–15, use the following information.

In the 2000 Summer Olympic Games, the total number of gold and silver medals won by the U.S. was 64. Gold medals are worth 3 points and silver medals are worth 2 points. The total points scored for gold and silver medals was 168. *(Lesson 7-4)* **Source:** *ESPN Almanac* **12.** $g + s = 64$ **13.** $3g + 2s = 168$

12. Write an equation for the sum of the number of gold and silver medals won by the U.S.

13. Write an equation for the sum of the points earned by the U.S. for gold and silver medals.

14. How many gold and silver medals did the U.S. win? **40 gold, 24 silver**

15. The total points scored by the U.S. was 201. Bronze medals are worth 1 point. How many bronze medals were won? **33**

RADIO   For Exercises 16–20, use the following information.

KSKY radio station is giving away tickets to an amusement park as part of a summer promotion. Each child ticket costs $15 and each adult ticket costs $20. The station wants to spend no more than $800 on tickets. They also want the number of child tickets to be greater than twice the number of adult tickets. *(Lesson 7-5)* **17.** $c > 2a$

16. Write an inequality for the total cost of c child tickets and a adult tickets. $15c + 20a \leq 800$

17. Write an inequality to represent the relationship between the number of child and adult tickets.

18. Write two inequalities that would assure you that the number of adult and the number of child tickets would not be negative. $a \geq 0$; $c \geq 0$

19. Graph the system of four inequalities to show possible numbers of tickets that the station can buy. **See margin.**

20. Give three possible combinations of child and adult tickets for the station to buy. **Sample answer: (adult, child) = (5, 40), (10, 30), (12, 32)**

19.

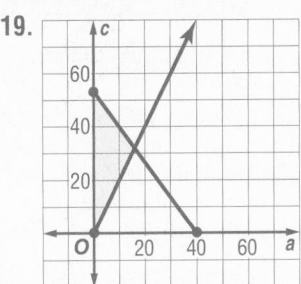

Mixed Problem Solving

Chapter 8

1. Yes; each is the product of variables and/or a real number.

2. 27 ft³; 54 ft²

3. 6 units

5. 300,000,000; 300,000,000; 229,000,000; 204,000,000; 197,000,000; 195,000,000

10. 17.3 people/square mile; Since 2010 is 90 years after 1920, substitute 90 into the polynomial and simplify.

15. You add one more each time to the previous number. For example, $0 + 2 = 2, 2 + 3 = 5, 5 + 4 = 9$, and so on.

18. 4000 is the amount of the investment, 1 will add the amount of the investment to the interest, 0.05 is the interest rate as a decimal, and 2 is the number of years of the investment.

GEOMETRY   For Exercises 1–4, use the following information.

If the side length of a cube is s, then the volume is presented by s^3 and the surface area is represented by $6s^2$. *(Lesson 8-1)* **1–3. See margin.**

1. Are the expressions for volume and surface area monomials? Explain.

2. If the side of a cube measures 3 feet, find the volume and surface area.

3. Find a side length s such that the volume and surface area have the same numerical value.

4. The volume of a cylinder can be found by multiplying the radius squared times the height times π, or $V = \pi r^2 h$. Suppose you have two cylinders. Each measure of the second is twice the measure of the first, so $V = \pi(2r)^2(2h)$. What is the ratio of the volume of the first cylinder to the second cylinder? *(Lesson 8-2)* **1:8**

LIGHT   For Exercises 5–7, use the table that shows the speed of light in various materials. *(Lesson 8-3)* **5. See margin.   6. 1.54 times**

Material	Speed m/s
vacuum	3.00×10^8
air	3.00×10^8
ice	2.29×10^8
glycerine	2.04×10^8
crown glass	1.97×10^8
rock salt	1.95×10^8

Source: *Glencoe Physics*

5. Express each speed in standard notation.

6. To the nearest hundredth, how many times as fast does light travel in a vacuum as in rock salt?

7. Through which material does light travel about 1.17 times as fast as through rock salt? **ice**

POPULATION   For Exercises 8–10, use the following information.

The table shows the population density for the state of Nevada for various years. *(Lesson 8-4)*

Year	Years Since 1920	People/Square Mile
1920	0	0.7
1960	40	2.6
1980	60	7.3
1990	70	10.9

Source: *The World Almanac*

8. The population density d of Nevada from 1920 to 1990 can be modeled by $d = 0.003y^2 - 0.086y + 0.708$, where y represents the number of years since 1920. Identify the type of polynomial for $0.003y^2 - 0.086y + 0.708$. **trinomial**

9. What is the degree of this polynomial? **2**

10. Predict the population density of Nevada for the year 2010. Explain your method. **See margin.**

RADIO   For Exercises 11 and 12, use the following information.

From 1997 to 2000, the number of radio stations presenting primarily news and talk N and the total number of radio stations of all types R in the U.S. could be modeled by the following equations, where x is the number of years since 1997. *(Lesson 8-5)*
Source: *The World Almanac* **11. $O = 95.6x + 8962.6$**

$$N = 37.9x + 1315.9$$
$$R = 133.5x + 10{,}278.5$$

11. Find an equation that models the number of radio stations O that are *not* primarily news and talk in the U.S. for this time period.

12. If this trend continues, how many radio stations that are not news and talk will there be in the year 2015? **about 10,683 stations**

GEOMETRY   For Exercises 13–15, use the following information.

The number of diagonals of a polygon can be found by using the formula $d = 0.5n(n - 3)$, where d is the number of diagonals and n is the number of sides of the polygon. *(Lesson 8-6)*

13. Use the Distributive Property to write the expression as a polynomial. **$0.5n^2 - 1.5n$**

14. Find the number of diagonals for polygons with 3 through 10 sides. **0, 2, 5, 9, 14, 20, 27, 35**

15. Describe any patterns you see in the numbers you wrote in Exercise 14. **See margin.**

GEOMETRY   For Exercises 16 and 17, use the following information.

A rectangular prism has dimensions of x, $x + 3$, and $2x + 5$. *(Lesson 8-7)* **16. $2x^3 + 11x^2 + 15x$**

16. Find the volume of the prism in terms of x.

17. Choose two values for x. How do the volumes compare? **See students' work.**

MONEY   For Exercises 18–20, use the following information.

Money invested in a certificate of deposit or CD collects interest once per year. Suppose you invest $4000 in a 2-year CD. *(Lesson 8-8)* **18. See margin.**

18. If the interest rate is 5% per year, the expression $4000(1 + 0.05)^2$ can be evaluated to find the total amount of money you will have at the end of two years. Explain the numbers in this expression.

19. Find the amount of money at the end of two years. **$4410**

20. Suppose you invest $10,000 in a CD for 4 years at a rate of 6.25%. What is the total amount of money you will have at the end of 4 years? **about $12,744**

FLOORING For Exercises 1 and 2, use the following information.

Eric is refinishing his dining room floor. The floor measures 10 feet by 12 feet. Flooring World offers a wood-like flooring in 1-foot by 1-foot squares, 2-foot by 2-foot squares, 3-foot by 3-foot squares, and 2-foot by 3-foot rectangular pieces. *(Lesson 9-1)*

1. Without cutting the pieces, which of the four types of flooring can Eric use in the dining room? Explain. **See margin.**

2. The price per piece of each type of flooring is shown in the table. If Eric wants to spend the least money, which should he choose? What will be the total cost of his choice? **2 by 3; $420**

Size	1 × 1	2 × 2	3 × 3	2 × 3
Price	$3.75	$15.00	$32.00	$21.00

FIREWORKS For Exercises 3–5, use the following information.

At a Fourth of July celebration, a rocket is launched with an initial velocity of 125 feet per second. The height h of the rocket in feet above sea level is modeled by the formula $h = 125t - 16t^2$, where t is the time in seconds after the rocket is launched. *(Lesson 9-2)*

3. What is the height of the rocket when it returns to the ground? **0 ft**

4. Let $h = 0$ in the equation $h = 125t - 16t^2$ and solve for t. **{0, 7.8125}**

5. How many seconds will it take for the rocket to return to the ground? **about 7.8 s**

FOOTBALL For Exercises 6–8, use the following information.

Some small high schools play six-man football as a team sport. The dimensions of the field are less then the dimensions of a standard football field. Including the end zones, the length of the field, in feet, is 60 feet more than twice the width. *(Lesson 9-3)*

6. Write an expression for the area of the six-man football field. **$w(2w + 60)$**

7. If the area of the field is 36,000 square feet, what are the dimensions of the field? (*Hint:* Factor a 2 out of the equation before factoring.) **120 ft by 300 ft**

8. What are the dimensions of the field in yards? **40 yd by 100 yd**

PHYSICAL SCIENCE For Exercises 9 and 10, use the following information.

Teril throws a ball upward while standing on the top of a 500-foot tall apartment building. Its height h, in feet, after t seconds is given by the equation $h = -16t^2 + 48t + 506$. *(Lesson 9-4)*

9. What do the values 48 and 506 in the equation represent? **See margin.**

10. The ball falls on a balcony that is 218 feet above the ground. How many seconds was the ball in the air? **6 s**

DECKS For Exercises 11 and 12, use the following information.

Zelda is building a deck in her back yard. The plans for the deck show that it is to be 24 feet by 24 feet. Zelda wants to reduce one dimension by a number of feet and increase the other dimension by the same number of feet. *(Lesson 9-5)*

11. If the area of the reduced deck is 512 square feet, what are the dimensions of the deck? **16 ft by 32 ft**

12. Suppose Zelda wants to reduce the deck to one-half the area of the deck in the plans. Can she reduce each dimension by the same length and use dimensions that are whole numbers? Explain. **See margin.**

BUILDINGS For Exercises 13–15, use the following information.

The Petronas Towers I and II in Kuala Lumpur, Malaysia, are both 1483 feet tall. A model for the height h in feet of a dropped object is $h = -16t^2$, where t is the time in seconds after the object is dropped. *(Lesson 9-6)* **Source:** *The World Almanac*

13. To the nearest tenth of a second, how long will it take for an object dropped from the top of one of the towers to hit the ground? **9.6 s**

14. In 1900, the tallest building in the world was the Park Row Building in New York City with a height of 386 feet. How much longer will it take an object to reach the ground from the Petronas Tower I than from the Park Row Building? **about 4.7 s**

15. If a new building is built such that an object takes 12 seconds to reach the ground when dropped from the top, how tall is the building? **2304 ft**

POOLS For Exercises 16–19, use the following information.

Susan wants to buy an aboveground swimming pool for her yard. Model A is 42 inches deep and holds 1750 cubic feet of water. The length of the pool is 5 feet more than the width. *(Lesson 9-6)*

16. What is the area of water that is exposed to the air? **500 ft²**

17. What are the dimensions of the pool? **20 ft by 25 ft**

18. A Model B pool holds twice as much water as Model A. What are some possible dimensions for this pool? **See margin.**

19. Model C has length and width that are both twice as long as Model A, but the height is the same. What is the ratio of the volume of Model A to Model C? **1:4**

Chapter 9

1. 1 by 1, 2 by 2, and 2 by 3; The 3-foot squares will not cover the 10-foot dimension without cutting.

9. 48 is the initial velocity of the ball and 506 is the height from which the ball is thrown which is 500 feet plus 6 feet, Teril's height.

12. No; the equation is not factorable, so there are no whole number solutions.

18. Sample answer: 20 ft by 50 ft by 42 in.

Chapter 10

6.
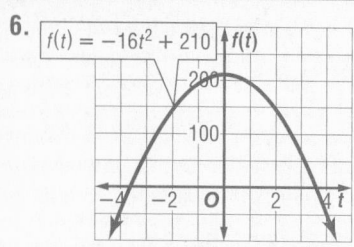
$f(t) = -16t^2 + 210$

11. 3.8, 41.2; The values mean that 3.8 years and 41.2 years after 1977, 30% of households had cable TV.

12. No; the parabola only reaches a maximum height of about 68, meaning that no more than 68% of homes will ever have cable, which is not realistic.

13.
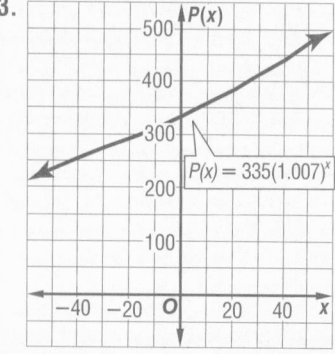
$P(x) = 335(1.007)^x$

15. about 5,455,480,760 people

18. Sample answer: Aaron could reinvest the money he does not need each year and earn additional interest during the time he is attending college.

19. $\dfrac{1}{8}, \dfrac{3}{16}, \dfrac{9}{32}, \dfrac{27}{64}, \dfrac{81}{128}, \dfrac{243}{256}, \dfrac{729}{512},$ $\dfrac{2187}{1024}, \dfrac{6561}{2048}, \dfrac{19{,}683}{4096}$

20. $a_n = \dfrac{1}{8}\left(\dfrac{3}{2}\right)^{n-1}$

PHYSICAL SCIENCE   For Exercises 1–4, use the following information.
A ball is released 6 feet above the ground and thrown vertically into the air. The equation $h = -16t^2 + 112t + 6$ gives the height of the ball if the initial velocity is 112 feet per second. *(Lesson 10-1)*

1. Write the equation of the axis of symmetry and find the coordinates of the vertex of the graph of the equation. $x = 3.5$; (3.5, 202)

2. What is the maximum height above the ground that the ball reaches? **202 ft**

3. How many seconds after release does the ball reach its maximum height? **3.5 s**

4. How many seconds is the ball in the air? **about 7 s**

RIDES   For Exercises 5–7, use the following information.
At an amusement park in Minnesota a popular ride whisks riders to the top of a 250-foot tower and drops them at speeds exceeding 50 miles per hour. A function for the path of a rider is $h = -16t^2 + 250$, where h is the height and t is the time in seconds. *(Lesson 10-3)*

5. The ride stops the descent of the rider 40 feet above the ground. Write an equation that models the drop of the rider. $40 = -16t^2 + 250$

6. Solve the equation by graphing the related function. How many roots does the equation have? **2; See margin for graph.**

7. About how many seconds does it take to complete the ride? **about 3.6 s**

PROJECTS   For Exercises 8–10, use the following information.   **8.** $(22 - 2x)(27 - 5x) = 396$
Jude is making a poster for his science project. The poster board is 22 inches wide by 27 inches tall. He wants to cover two thirds of the area with text or pictures and leave a top margin 3 times as wide as the side margins and a bottom margin twice as wide as the side margins. *(Lesson 10-3)*

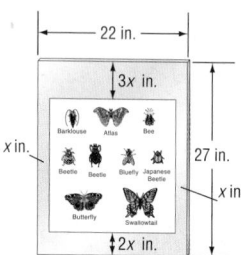

8. Write an equation that represents this situation.

9. Solve your equation for x by completing the square. Round to the nearest tenth. **15.1, 1.3**

10. What should be the widths of the margins? **about 1.3 in. on the sides, 3.9 in. on the top, and 2.6 in. on the bottom**

TELEVISION   For Exercises 11 and 12, use the following information.   **11–12. See margin.**
The number of U.S. households with cable television has been on the rise. The percent of households with cable y can be approximated by the quadratic function $y = -0.11x^2 + 4.95x + 12.69$, where x stands for the number of years after 1977. *(Lesson 10-4)*

11. Use the Quadratic Formula to solve for x when $y = 30$. What do these values represent?

12. Do you think a quadratic function is a good model for this data? Why or why not?

POPULATION   For Exercises 13–15, use the following information.
The population of Asia from 1650 to 2000 can be estimated by the function $P(x) = 335(1.007)^x$, where x is the number of years since 1650 and the population is in millions of people. *(Lesson 10-5)*   **13. 335**

13. Graph the function and name the y-intercept.

14. What does the y-intercept represent in this problem? **335,000,000 people in 1650**

15. Use the function to approximate the number of people in Asia in 2050. **See margin.**

MONEY   For Exercises 16–18, use the following information.
In 1999, Aaron placed $10,000 he received as an inheritance in a 4-year certificate of deposit at an interest rate of 7.45% compounded yearly. *(Lesson 10-6)*   **16. $13,329.86   17. $14,221.35**

16. Aaron plans to take all the money out of his investment at the end of 4 years. Find the amount of money Aaron will have at the end of 4 years.

17. He plans to use the money for college tuition. From 1999 on, it is predicted that tuition will rise 6% per year from the 1999 cost of $2575. Aaron intends to begin college in 2003 and attend for 4 years. What will be his total tuition cost?

18. What recommendations would you make to Aaron for paying for the total cost of his tuition? **See margin.**

TRAINING   For Exercises 19–22, use the following information.   **20. See margin.   21. 9th**
Laurie wants to run a 5K race but has never run before. A 5K race is about 3 miles so she wants to work up slowly to running 3 miles. *(Lesson 10-7)*

19. Laurie's trainer advises her to run every other day and to begin by running one eighth of a mile. Each running session she is to run one and a half times her previous distance. Write the first 10 terms of this sequence. **See margin.**

20. Write a formula for the nth term of this sequence.

21. During which session will Laurie exceed 3 miles?

22. Will Laurie be ready for a 5K race in two weeks from the start of her training program? **no**

(pages 584–639)

SATELLITES   **For Exercises 1–3, use the following information.**
A satellite is launched into orbit 200 kilometers above Earth. The orbital velocity of a satellite is given by the formula $v = \sqrt{\dfrac{Gm_E}{r}}$, where v is velocity in meters per second, G is a given constant, m_E is the mass of Earth, and r is the radius of the satellite's orbit. *(Lesson 11-1)* **2. 7779 m/s**

1. The radius of Earth is 6,380,000 meters. What is the radius of the satellite's orbit in meters? **6,580,000 m**

2. The mass of Earth is 5.97×10^{24} kilogram and the constant G is 6.67×10^{-11} N · m²/kg² where N is in Newtons. Use the formula to find the orbital velocity of the satellite in meters per second.

3. The orbital period of the satellite can be found by using the formula $T = \dfrac{2\pi r}{v}$, where r is the radius of the orbit and v is the orbital velocity of the satellite in meters per second. Find the orbital period of the satellite in hours. **about 1.5 h**

RIDES   **For Exercises 4–6, use the following information.**
The designer of a roller coaster must consider the height of the hill and the velocity of the coaster as it travels over the hill. Certain hills give riders a feeling of weightlessness. The formula $d = \sqrt{\dfrac{2hv^2}{g}}$ allows designers to find the correct distance from the center of the hill that the coaster should begin its drop for maximum fun. *(Lesson 11-2)*

4. In the formula above, d is the distance from the center of the hill, h is the height of the hill, v is the velocity of the coaster at the top of the hill in meters per second, and g is a gravity constant of 9.8 meters per second squared. If a hill is 10 meters high and the velocity of the coaster is 10 m/s, find d. **14.29 m**

5. Find d if the height of the hill is 10 meters but the velocity is 20 m/s. How does d compare to the value in Exercise 4? **28.57 m; twice as great**

6. Suppose you find the same formula in another book written as $d = 1.4\sqrt{\dfrac{hv^2}{g}}$. Will this produce the same value of d? Explain. **Yes; because $\sqrt{2} \approx 1.4$**

7. **PACKAGING**   A cylindrical container of chocolate drink mix has a volume of about 162 in³. The formula for volume of a cylinder is $V = \pi r^2 h$, where r is the radius and h is the height. The radius of the container can be found by using the formula $r = \sqrt{\dfrac{V}{\pi h}}$. If the height is 8.25 inches, find the radius of the container. *(Lesson 11-3)* **about 2.5 in.**

TOWN SQUARES   **For Exercises 8 and 9, use the following information.**
Tiananmen Square in Beijing, China, is the largest town square in the world, covering 98 acres.
Source: *The Guinness Book of Records*   *(Lesson 11-4)*

8. One square mile is 640 acres. Assuming that Tiananmen Square is a square, how many feet long is a side to the nearest foot? **2066 ft**

9. To the nearest foot, what is the diagonal distance across Tiananmen Square? **2922 ft**

PIZZA DELIVERY   **For Exercises 10 and 11, use the following information.**
The Pizza Place delivers pizza to any location within a radius of 5 miles from the store for free. Tyrone drives 32 blocks north and then 45 blocks east to deliver a pizza. In this city, there are about 6 blocks per half mile. *(Lesson 11-5)* **10–11. See margin.**

10. Should there be a charge for the delivery? Explain.

11. Describe two delivery situations that would result in about 5 miles.

GEOMETRY   **For Exercises 12–14, use the following information.**
A triangle on the coordinate plane has vertices $(1, 1)$, $(-3, 2)$, and $(-7, -5)$. *(Lesson 11-6)*

12. What is the perimeter of the triangle? Express the answer in simplest radical form and as a decimal approximation rounded to the nearest hundredth.

13. Suppose a new triangle is formed by multiplying each coordinate by 2. What is the perimeter of the new triangle in simplest radical form and as a decimal rounded to the nearest hundredth?

14. Are the two triangles similar? Explain your reasoning. **See margin.**

12. $10 + \sqrt{17} + \sqrt{65}$; 22.19
13. $20 + 2\sqrt{17} + 2\sqrt{65}$; 44.37

ESCALATORS   **For Exercises 15 and 16, use the following information.**
The longest escalator is located in Hong Kong, China. The escalator has a length of 745 feet and rises 377 feet vertically from start to finish. **Source:** *The Guinness Book of Records*   *(Lesson 11-7)*

15. Draw a diagram of the escalator. **See margin.**

16. To the nearest degree, what is the angle of elevation of the escalator? **30°**

Chapter 11

10. No; the distance is about 55 blocks or about 4.6 mi.

11. Sample answer: 40 blocks south and 45 blocks west; 38 blocks north and 47 blocks west

14. Yes; the ratio of each pair of corresponding sides is 1:2.

15.

745 ft   377 ft

Mixed Problem Solving

Chapter 12

1.

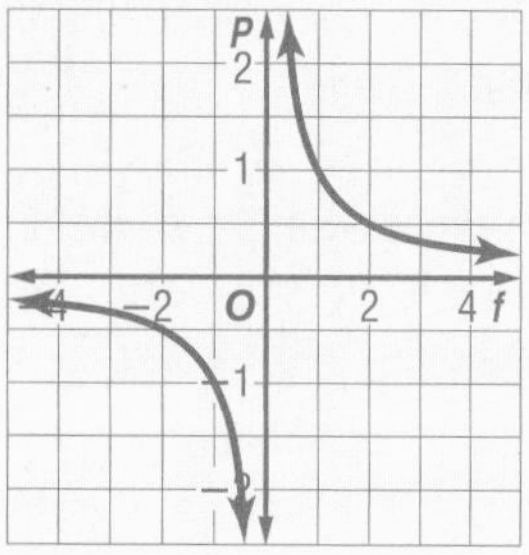

4. **Sample answer: One value is negative and the other is positive.**

5.

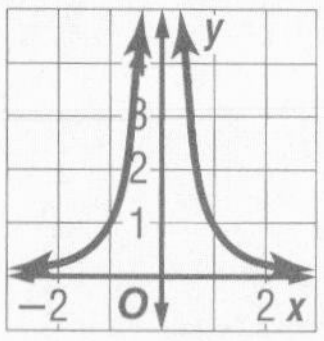

The graph looks like an inverse variation graph except it lies in Quadrants I and II, consecutive quadrants, not opposite quadrants.

6. **The values of x must be positive since x represents distance.**

11. **Mercury: about 5188 min; Venus: about 9677 min; Earth: 13,405 min; Mars: 20,430 min; Jupiter: about 69,713 min; Saturn: about 128,136 min; Uranus: about 257,168 min; Pluto: about 403,226 min**

15. **No; they need $2\frac{3}{8}$ yd for one of each type. Then $30 \div 2\frac{3}{8}$ yd is not a whole number so they cannot use the entire bolt by making an equal number of each type.**

Mixed Problem Solving

OPTOMETRY For Exercises 1–4, use the following information.
When a person does not have clear vision either at a distance or close up, an optometrist can prescribe lenses to correct the condition. The power P of a lens, in a unit called diopters, is equal to 1 divided by the focal length f, in meters, of the lens. The formula is $P = \frac{1}{f}$. *(Lesson 12-1)*

1. Graph the inverse variation $P = \frac{1}{f}$. **See margin.**
2. Find the power of a lens with focal length +20 centimeters. (*Hint*: Change 20 centimeters to meters.) **5 diopters**
3. Find the power of a lens with focal length −40 centimeters. (*Hint*: Change 40 centimeters to meters.) **−2.5 diopters**
4. What do you notice about the powers in Exercises 2 and 3? **See margin.**

PHYSICS For Exercises 5 and 6, use the following information.
Some principles in physics, such as gravitational force between two objects, depend upon a relationship known as the inverse square law. The inverse square law means that two variables are related by the relationship $y = \frac{1}{x^2}$, where x is distance. *(Lesson 12-2)*

5. Make a table of values and graph $y = \frac{1}{x^2}$. Describe the shape of the graph.
6. If x represents distance, how does this affect the domain of the graph? **5–6. See margin.**

FERRIS WHEELS For Exercises 7–9, use the following information.
George Ferris built the first Ferris wheel for the World's Columbian Exposition in Chicago in 1892. It had a diameter of 250 feet. *(Lesson 12-3)*

7. To find the speed traveled by a car located on the circumference of the wheel, you can find the circumference of a circle and divide by the time it takes for one rotation of the wheel. (Recall that $C = \pi d$.) Write a rational expression for the speed of a car rotating in time t. $\frac{\pi d}{t}$
8. Suppose the first Ferris wheel rotated once every 5 minutes. What was the speed of a car on the circumference in feet per minute? **157 ft/min**
9. Use dimensional analysis to find the speed of a car in miles per hour. **1.8 mi/h**
10. **MOTOR VEHICLES** In 1999, the U.S. produced 13,063,000 motor vehicles. This was 23.2% of the total motor vehicle production for the whole world. How many motor vehicles were produced worldwide in 1999? **Source:** *The World Almanac* *(Lesson 12-4)* **56,306,034 vehicles**
11. **LIGHT** The speed of light is approximately 1.86×10^5 miles per second. The table shows the distances, in miles, of the planets from the Sun. Find the amount of time in minutes that it takes for light from the Sun to reach each planet. *(Lesson 12-5)* **See margin.**

Planet	Miles	Planet	Miles
Mercury	5.79×10^{10}	Jupiter	7.78×10^{11}
Venus	1.08×10^{11}	Saturn	1.43×10^{12}
Earth	1.496×10^{11}	Uranus	2.87×10^{12}
Mars	2.28×10^{11}	Pluto	4.50×10^{12}

12. **GEOGRAPHY** The land areas of all the continents, in thousands of square miles, are given in the table. Use this information to write the fraction of the land area of the world that is part of North and South America. *(Lesson 12-6)* $\frac{163}{579}$

Continent	Area
North America	9400
South America	6900
Europe	3800
Asia	17,400
Africa	11,700
Oceania	3300
Antarctica	5400

Source: *The World Almanac*

13. **GARDENING** Celeste builds decorative gardens in her landscaping business. She uses either 35, 50, or 75 bricks for one garden depending upon the design. What is the least number of bricks she should order that would allow her to build a whole number of each type of garden? *(Lesson 12-7)* **1050**

CRAFTS For Exercises 14 and 15, use the following information. 15. See margin.
Jordan and her aunt Jennie make tablecloths to sell at craft fairs. A small one takes one-half yard of fabric, a medium takes five-eighths yard, and a large takes one and one-quarter yard. *(Lesson 12-8)*

14. How many yards of fabric do they need to make one of each type of tablecloth? $2\frac{3}{8}$ **yd**
15. A particular bolt of fabric contains 30 yards of fabric. Can they use the entire bolt by making an equal number of each type of tablecloth? Explain.
16. **CONSTRUCTION** Rick has a crew of workers that can side a particular size house in 6 days. Phil's crew can side the same house in 4 days. If the two crews work together, how long will it take to side the house? *(Lesson 12-9)* **2.4 days**

Mixed Problem Solving

864 Mixed Problem Solving

CAREERS For Exercises 1 and 2, use the following information.

The graph below shows the results of a survey of students asking their preferences for a future career. *(Lesson 13-1)* **1–2. See margin.**

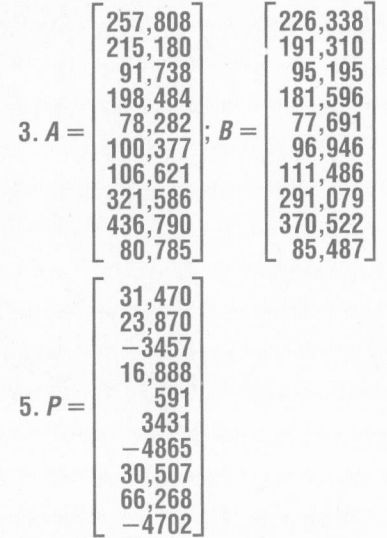

Looking into the Future
Top career choices of students age 14–18

Male
Engineering — 11%
Business — 7%
Computer software Development — 6%
Computer hardware Development — 6%

Female
Teaching — 12%
Medical doctor — 10%
Law — 7%
Nursing — 7%

Source: *USA TODAY*

1. Write a statement to describe what you do know about the sample.

2. What additional information would you like to have about the sample to determine whether the sample is biased?

POPULATIONS For Exercises 3–7, use the following information.

The table shows the populations for ten U.S. cities in 1990 and 1999. *(Lesson 13-2)*

City	1990	1999
Anchorage, AK	226,338	257,808
Asheville, NC	191,310	215,180
Elmira, NY	95,195	91,738
Gainesville, FL	181,596	198,484
Great Falls, MT	77,691	78,282
Kokomo, IN	96,946	100,377
Lawton, OK	111,486	106,621
Macon, GA	291,079	321,586
Modesto, CA	370,522	436,790
Pine Bluff, AR	85,487	80,785

Source: U.S. Census Bureau

3. Create matrix A for the 1999 data and matrix B for the 1990 data. **See margin.**

4. What are the dimensions of each matrix in Exercise 3? **10×1**

5. Calculate $P = A - B$. **See margin.**

6. What does matrix P represent? **See margin.**

7. Which city had the greatest percent decrease in population from 1990 to 1999? **Pine Bluff, AR**

WEATHER For Exercises 8–11, use the table that shows the highest and lowest (H/L) temperature ever recorded in each U.S. state.

State	H/L (°F)	State	H/L (°F)	State	H/L (°F)
AL	112/−27	LA	114/−16	OH	113/−39
AK	100/−80	ME	105/−48	OK	120/−27
AZ	128/−29	MD	109/−40	OR	119/−54
AR	120/−29	MA	107/−35	PA	111/−42
CA	134/−45	MI	112/−51	RI	104/−25
CO	118/−61	MN	114/−60	SC	111/−19
CT	106/−32	MS	115/−19	SD	120/−58
DE	110/−17	MO	118/−40	TN	113/−32
FL	108/−2	MT	117/−70	TX	120/−23
GA	112/−17	NE	118/−47	UT	117/−69
HI	100/12	NV	125/−50	VT	105/−50
ID	118/−60	NH	106/−46	VA	110/−30
IL	117/−36	NJ	110/−34	WA	118/−48
IN	116/−36	NM	122/−50	WV	112/−37
IA	118/−47	NY	108/−52	WI	114/−54
KS	121/−40	NC	110/−34	WY	114/−66
KY	114/−37	ND	121/−60		

Source: *The World Almanac* **8b–d. See margin.**

8. Consider the high temperature data. *(Lesson 13-3)*
   a. Determine the median of the data. **114**
   b. Create a histogram to represent the data. Use at least four measurement classes.
   c. Write a sentence or two describing the distribution of the data.
   d. Does finding the median of the set of data help you to make a histogram for the data? Explain.

9. Consider the low temperature data. *(Lesson 13-4)*
   a. What is the range of the temperature data? **92**
   b. What is the lower quartile and the upper quartile of the data? **−51, −29**
   c. What is the interquartile range of the data? **22**
   d. Name any outliers. **12**

10. Draw a parallel box-and-whisker plot for the high and low temperatures. *(Lesson 13-5)*
    a. Compare the data in the two plots.
    b. How does the range of the high temperature data compare to the range of the low temperature data? **10a–b. See margin.**

11. Make a table that shows the differences between the highest and lowest temperatures for each state. *(Lesson 13-5)* **11a. See students' work.**
    a. Create any graph of your choice that shows the difference between the high and low temperature for each state.
    b. Describe the data in your graph in part **a**. **See margin.**

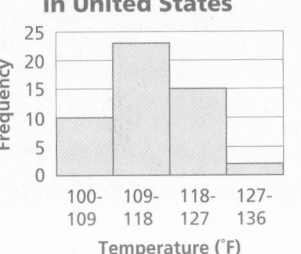

3. $A = \begin{bmatrix} 257,808 \\ 215,180 \\ 91,738 \\ 198,484 \\ 78,282 \\ 100,377 \\ 106,621 \\ 321,586 \\ 436,790 \\ 80,785 \end{bmatrix}$; $B = \begin{bmatrix} 226,338 \\ 191,310 \\ 95,195 \\ 181,596 \\ 77,691 \\ 96,946 \\ 111,486 \\ 291,079 \\ 370,522 \\ 85,487 \end{bmatrix}$

5. $P = \begin{bmatrix} 31,470 \\ 23,870 \\ -3457 \\ 16,888 \\ 591 \\ 3431 \\ -4865 \\ 30,507 \\ 66,268 \\ -4702 \end{bmatrix}$

6. Matrix P is the increase or decrease in population of the selected cities from 1990 to 1999.

8b. Sample answer:

Record High Temperatures in United States

(histogram: Frequency vs Temperature (°F), classes 100-109, 109-118, 118-127, 127-136)

8c. Sample answer: More than half of the states had high temperatures of less than 118 °F. Only two states had temperatures over 126°F.

8d. Yes; to find the median, you must order the data from least to greatest. Now it is easier to place the values into measurement classes.

10a. See below for graph.

   The range of the low temperatures is much greater than the range for the high temperatures. Both data sets have one outlier at the high end of the data.

10b. The range of the low temperatures is almost 3 times greater than the range for the high temperatures.

11b. Sample answer: More than half of the states had temperature differences between 129 and 170°F.

Chapter 13

1. Sample answer: The sample contained students ages 14–18.

2. Sample answers: How were the students sampled? Was it random or were they volunteers? Were the students given only certain careers as choices? How many students responded?

10a.

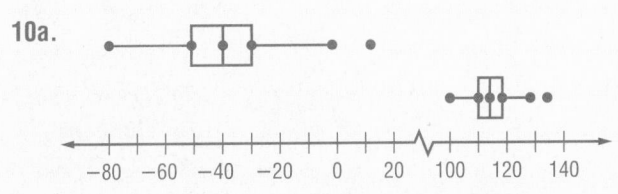

FLOWERS   For Exercises 1–3, use the following information.

A flower shop is making special floral arrangements for a holiday. The table shows the options available and the costs of each option. *(Lesson 14-1)*

Vase	Deluxe	Standard	Economy
Cost	$12.00	$8.00	$5.00

Ribbon	Velvet	Satin
Cost	$3.00	$2.00

Flowers	Orchids	Roses	Daisies
Cost	$35.00	$20.00	$12.00

Card	Large	Small
Cost	$2.50	$1.75

1. How many floral arrangements are possible? Each arrangement has one vase, one ribbon, one type of flowers, and one card. **36**

2. What is the cost of the most expensive arrangement? the least expensive? **$52.50; $20.75**

3. What is the cost of each of the four most expensive arrangements? **$52.50; $51.75; $51.50; $50.75**

GAMES   For Exercises 4–6, use the following information.

Melissa is playing a board game that requires you to make words to score points. There are 12 letters left in the box and she must choose 4. She cannot see the letters that can be chosen. *(Lesson 14-2)*

4. Suppose that the 12 letters are all different. In how many ways can she choose 4 of the 12 letters? **495**

5. She chooses the four letters A, T, R, and E. How many different arrangements of three letters can she make from her letters? **24**

6. How many of the three-letter arrangements are words? List the words you find. **See margin.**

BASEBALL   For Exercises 7–10, use the following information.

During the 2000 baseball season, these Houston Astros players had the following number of times at bat and hits. You can consider the probability that a player gets a hit as the number of hits compared to the number of times at bat. Round each probability to the nearest hundredth for Exercises 7–10. *(Lesson 14-3)*
7–10. See margin.

Name	Times at Bat	Hits
Alou	454	161
Ward	264	68
Cedeno	259	73
Hidalgo	558	175

Source: *ESPN*

7. On his next at bat, what is the probability that Hidalgo will get a hit? $\frac{175}{558} \approx 0.314$

8. Which player has the greatest chance to get a hit on his next at bat? **Alou**

9. Suppose Ward and then Cedeno are to be the first players at bat in a new inning. What is the probability that both get a hit? **0.073**

10. If the manager wants the greatest probability that two of these four players will get consecutive hits, which two should he choose? What is the probability of these two players both getting a hit? **Alou, Hidalgo; 0.111**

DRIVING   For Exercises 11–13, use the following information.

The table shows a probability distribution for various age categories of licensed drivers in the U.S. for the year 1998. *(Lesson 14-4)*

X = Age Category	Probability
under 20	0.053
20–34	0.284
35–49	0.323
50–64	0.198
65 and over	0.142

Source: *The World Almanac*

11. Determine whether this is a valid probability distribution. Justify your answer. **See margin.**

12. If a driver in the U.S. is randomly selected, what is the probability that the person is under 20 years old? **0.053**

13. If a driver in the U.S. is randomly selected, what is the probability the person is 50 years old or over? **0.34**

14. 7776 numbers; Find 6 · 6 · 6 · 6 · 6 since there are 6 possibilities for each digit.

LOTTERIES   For Exercises 14–16, use the following information.

A state sells lottery tickets, each with a five-digit number such that each digit can be 1–6. When you purchase a ticket, you select a number that you think will win and it is printed on your ticket. Then, once per week, a random 5-digit number is generated as the winning number. *(Lesson 14-5)*

14. How many five-digit numbers are possible? Explain how you calculated the number of possible outcomes.

15. Perform a simulation for winning the lottery. Describe the objects you used to perform the simulation. **See margin.**

16. According to your experiment, if you buy one ticket, what is the experimental probability of winning the lottery?
See students' work. The theoretical probability is about 0.00013.

Chapter 14

6. 9; ART, ATE, ARE, TAR, TEA, RAT, EAT, EAR, ERA

7. $\frac{175}{558} \approx 0.314$

11. yes; 0.053 + 0.284 + 0.323 + 0.198 + 0.142 = 1

15. Sample answer: Roll five dice and record the results each time. Each roll represents one person picking a winning number.

Becoming a Better Test-Taker

At some time in your life, you will probably have to take a standardized test. Sometimes this test may determine if you go on to the next grade or course, or even if you will graduate from high school. This section of your textbook is dedicated to making you a better test-taker.

TYPES OF TEST QUESTIONS   In the following pages, you will see examples of four types of questions commonly seen on standardized tests. A description of each type of question is shown in the table below.

Type of Question	Description	See Pages
multiple choice	4 or 5 possible answer choices are given from which you choose the best answer.	868–871
gridded response	You solve the problem. Then you enter the answer in a special grid and shade in the corresponding circles.	872–875
short response	You solve the problem, showing your work and/or explaining your reasoning.	876–879
extended response	You solve a multi-part problem, showing your work and/or explaining your reasoning.	880–884

PRACTICE   After being introduced to each type of question, you can practice that type of question. Each set of practice questions is divided into five sections that represent the concepts most commonly assessed on standardized tests.

- Number and Operations
- Algebra
- Geometry
- Measurement
- Data Analysis and Probability

USING A CALCULATOR   On some tests, you are permitted to use a calculator. You should check with your teacher to determine if calculator use is permitted on the test you will be taking, and if so, what type of calculator can be used.

TEST-TAKING TIPS   In addition to Test-Taking Tips like the one shown at the right, here are some additional thoughts that might help you.

- Get a good night's rest before the test. Cramming the night before does not improve your results.

- Budget your time when taking a test. Don't dwell on problems that you cannot solve. Just make sure to leave that question blank on your answer sheet.

- Watch for key words like NOT and EXCEPT. Also look for order words like LEAST, GREATEST, FIRST, and LAST.

> **Test-Taking Tip**
> If you are allowed to use a calculator, make sure you are familiar with how it works so that you won't waste time trying to figure out the calculator when taking the test.

Multiple-Choice Questions

Multiple-choice questions are the most common type of questions on standardized tests. These questions are sometimes called *selected-response questions*. You are asked to choose the best answer from four or five possible answers.

To record a multiple-choice answer, you may be asked to shade in a bubble that is a circle or an oval, or to just write the letter of your choice. Always make sure that your shading is dark enough and completely covers the bubble.

The answer to a multiple-choice question is usually not immediately obvious from the choices, but you may be able to eliminate some of the possibilities by using your knowledge of mathematics. Another answer choice might be that the correct answer is not given.

Incomplete Shading
Ⓐ Ⓑ Ⓒ⃝ Ⓓ
Too light shading
Ⓐ Ⓑ Ⓒ Ⓓ
Correct shading
Ⓐ Ⓑ ⬤ Ⓓ

Example 1

A storm signal flag is used to warn small craft of wind speeds that are greater than 38 miles per hour. The length of the square flag is always three times the length of the side of the black square. If y is the area of the black square and x is the length of the side of the flag, which equation describes the relationship between x and y?

Ⓐ $y = \frac{1}{3}x^2$

Ⓑ $y = \frac{1}{9}x^2$

Ⓒ $y = x^2 - 1$

Ⓓ $y = 3x$

Ⓔ $y = 9x$

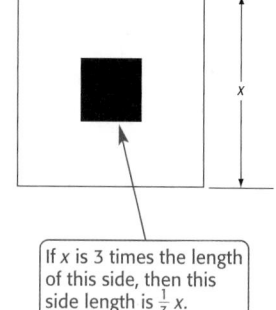

If x is 3 times the length of this side, then this side length is $\frac{1}{3}x$.

Strategy

Elimination
You can eliminate any obvious wrong answers.

For the area of a square, $A = s^2$. So, $A = x \cdot x$ or x^2.

The area of the black square is part of the area of the flag, which is x^2. Eliminate choices D and E because they do not include x^2.

$A = \left(\frac{1}{3}x\right)^2$ or $\frac{1}{9}x^2$ square units

So, $y = \frac{1}{9}x^2$. This is choice B.

Use some random numbers to check your choice.

Multiples of 3 make calculations easier.

Length of Flag (x)	Length of Black Square	Area of Black Square	Area $= \frac{1}{9}x^2$
12	4	16	$16 \stackrel{?}{=} \frac{1}{9}(12^2)$ ✓
27	9	81	$81 \stackrel{?}{=} \frac{1}{9}(27^2)$ ✓
60	20	400	$400 \stackrel{?}{=} \frac{1}{9}(60^2)$ ✓

Many multiple-choice questions are actually two- or three-step problems. If you do not read the question carefully, you may select a choice that is an intermediate step instead of the correct final answer.

Example 2

Barrington can skateboard down a hill five times as fast as he can walk up the hill. If it takes 9 minutes to walk up the hill and skateboard back down, how many minutes does it take him to walk up the hill?

Strategy

Reread the Problem
Read the problem carefully to find what the question is asking.

     Ⓕ 1.5 min   Ⓖ 4.5 min   Ⓗ 7.2 min   Ⓙ 7.5 min

Before involving any algebra, let's think about the problem using random numbers.

Skating is five times as fast as walking, so walking time equals 5 times the skate time. Use a table to find a pattern

Skate Time	Skate Time × 5 = Walk Time
6 min	$6 \cdot 5 = 30$ min
3 min	$3 \cdot 5 = 15$ min
2 min	$2 \cdot 5 = 10$ min
x min	$x \cdot 5 = 5x$ min

Use the pattern to find a general expression for walk time given any skate time.

The problem states that the walk time and the skate time total 9 minutes.

Use the expression to write an equation for the problem.

$$x + 5x = 9 \qquad \text{skate time + walk time = 9 minutes}$$
$$6x = 9 \qquad \text{Add like terms.}$$
$$x = 1.5 \qquad \text{Divide each side by 6.}$$

Looking at the choices, you might think that choice F is the correct answer. But what does x represent, and what is the problem asking?

The problem asks for the time it takes to walk up the hill, but the value of x is the time it takes to skateboard. So, the actual answer is found using $5x$ or $5(1.5)$, which is 7.5 minutes.

The correct choice is J.

Example 3

The Band Boosters are making ice cream to sell at an Open House. Each batch of ice cream calls for 5 cups of milk. They plan to make 20 batches. How many gallons of milk do they need?

Strategy

Units of Measure
Make certain your answer reflects the correct unit of measure.

     Ⓐ 800   Ⓑ 100   Ⓒ 25   Ⓓ 12.5   Ⓔ 6.25

The Band Boosters need 5×20 or 100 cups of milk. However, choice B is not the correct answer. The question asks for *gallons* of milk.

4 cups = 1 quart and 4 quarts = 1 gallon, so 1 gallon = 4×4 or 16 cups.

$100 \text{ cups} \times \dfrac{1 \text{ gallon}}{16 \text{ cups}} = 6.25$ gallons, which is choice E.

Multiple Choice Practice

Choose the best answer.

Number and Operations

1. One mile on land is 5280 feet, while one nautical mile is 6076 feet. What is the ratio of the length of a nautical mile to the length of a land mile as a decimal rounded to the nearest hundredth? **C**

(A) 0.87 (B) 1.01 (C) 1.15 (D) 5.68

2. The star Proxima Centauri is 24,792,500 million miles from Earth. The star Epsilon Eridani is 6.345×10^{13} miles from Earth. In scientific notation, how much farther from Earth is Epsilon Eridani than Proxima Centauri? **B**

(A) 0.697×10^{14} mi   (B) 3.866×10^{13} mi

(C) 6.097×10^{13} mi   (D) 38.658×10^{12} mi

3. In 1976, the cost per gallon for regular unleaded gasoline was 61 cents. In 2002, the cost was $1.29 per gallon. To the nearest percent, what was the percent of increase in the cost per gallon of gas from 1976 to 2002? **D**

(A) 1%   (B) 53%   (C) 95%   (D) 111%

4. The serial numbers on a particular model of personal data assistant (PDA) consist of two letters followed by five digits. How many serial numbers are possible if any letter of the alphabet and any digit 0–9 can be used in any position in the serial number? **B**

(A) 676,000,000   (B) 67,600,000

(C) 6,760,000   (D) 676,000

Algebra

5. The graph shows the approximate relationship between the latitude of a location in the Northern Hemisphere and its distance in miles from the equator. If y represents the distance of a location from the equator and x represents the measure of latitude, which equation describes the relationship between x and y? **C**

(graph: Miles from Equator vs. Latitude of Location, points at (10, 690), (20, 1380), (30, 2070), (40, 2760))

(A) $y = x + 69$ (B) $y = x + 690$

(C) $y = 69x$ (D) $y = 10x$

6. A particular prepaid phone card can be used from a pay phone. The charge is 30 cents to connect and then 4.5 cents per minute. If y is the total cost of a call in cents where x is the number of minutes, which equation describes the relation between x and y? **A**

(A) $y = 4.5x + 30$ (B) $y = 30x + 4.5$

(C) $y = 0.45x + 0.30$ (D) $y = 0.30x + 0.45$

7. Katie drove to the lake for a weekend outing. The lake is 100 miles from her home. On the trip back, she drove for an hour, stopped for lunch for an hour, and then finished the trip home. Which graph best represents her trip home and the distance from her home at various times? **B**

(A)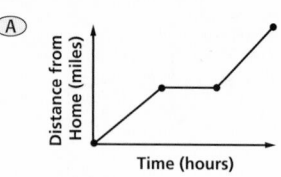

(B)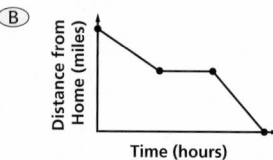

(C)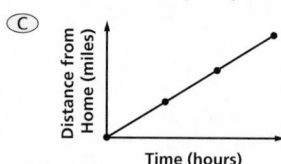

(D)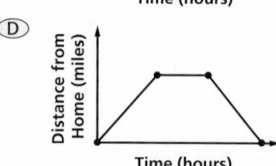

8. Temperature can be given in degrees Fahrenheit or degrees Celsius. The formula $F = \frac{9}{5}C + 32$ can be used to change any temperature given in degrees Celsius to degrees Fahrenheit. Solve the formula for C. **A**

(A) $C = \frac{5}{9}(F - 32)$ (B) $C = F + 32 - \frac{9}{5}$

(C) $C = \frac{5}{9}F - 32$ (D) $C = \frac{9}{5}(F - 32)$

Geometry

9. Which of the following statements are true about the 4-inch quilt square? **E**

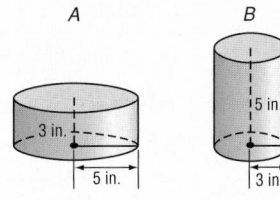

Ⓐ *VSWT* is a square.

Ⓑ *UVTX* ≅ *VSWT*

Ⓒ Four right angles are formed at *V*.

Ⓓ Only A and B are true.

Ⓔ A, B, and C are true.

10. At the Daniels County Fair, the carnival rides are positioned as shown. What is the value of *x*? **A**

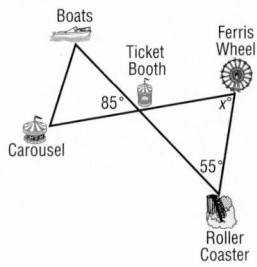

Ⓐ 40

Ⓑ 47.5

Ⓒ 55

Ⓓ 70

Ⓔ 85

11. The diagram shows a map of the Clearwater Wilderness hiking area. To the nearest tenth of a mile, what is the distance from the Parking Lot to Bear Ridge using the most direct route? **A**

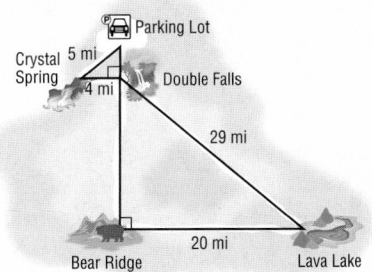

Ⓐ 24 mi

Ⓑ 25.5 mi

Ⓒ 26 mi

Ⓓ 30.4 mi

Measurement

12. Laura expects about 60 people to attend a party. She estimates that she will need one quart of punch for every two people. How many gallons of punch should she prepare? **A**

Ⓐ 7.5

Ⓑ 15

Ⓒ 30

Ⓓ 34

13. Stone Mountain Manufacturers are designing two sizes of cylindrical cans below. What is the ratio of the volume of can A to the volume of can B? **D**

Ⓐ 9 to 25

Ⓑ 25 to 3

Ⓒ 3 to 5

Ⓓ 5 to 3

Data Analysis and Probability

14. The 2000 populations of the five least-populated U.S. states are shown in the table. Which statement is true about this set of data? **E**

State	Population
Alaska	626,932
North Dakota	642,200
South Dakota	754,844
Vermont	608,827
Wyoming	493,782

Source: U.S. Census Bureau

Ⓐ The mode of the data set is 642,200.

Ⓑ The median of the data set is 626,932.

Ⓒ The mean of the data set is 625,317.

Ⓓ A and C are true.

Ⓔ B and C are true.

Gridded-Response Questions

Gridded-response questions are other types of questions on standardized tests. These questions are sometimes called *student-produced responses* or *grid-ins*, because you must create the answer yourself, not just choose from four or five possible answers.

For gridded response, you must mark your answer on a grid printed on an answer sheet. The grid contains a row of four or five boxes at the top, two rows of ovals or circles with decimal and fraction symbols, and four or five columns of ovals, numbered 0–9. Since there is no negative symbol on the grid, answers are never negative. At the right is an example of a grid from an answer sheet.

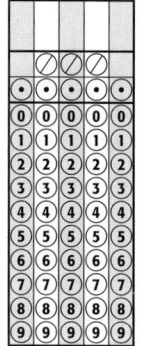

How do you correctly fill in the grid?

Example 1 Diego drove 174 miles to his grandmother's house. He made the drive in 3 hours without any stops. At this rate, how far in miles can Diego drive in 5 hours?

What value do you need to find?

You need to find the number of miles Diego can drive in 5 hours.

Write a proportion for the problem. Let m represent the number of miles.

$$\text{miles} \longrightarrow \frac{174}{3} = \frac{m}{5} \longleftarrow \text{miles}$$
$$\text{hours} \longrightarrow \qquad\qquad \longleftarrow \text{hours}$$

Solve the proportion.

$\dfrac{174}{3} = \dfrac{m}{5}$ Original proportion

$870 = 3m$ Find the cross products.

$290 = m$ Divide each side by 3.

How do you fill in the grid for the answer?

- Write your answer in the answer boxes.

- Write only one digit or symbol in each answer box.

- Do not write any digits or symbols outside the answer boxes.

- You may write your answer with the first digit in the left answer box, or with the last digit in the right answer box. You may leave blank any boxes you do not need on the right or the left side of your answer.

- Fill in only one bubble for every answer box that you have written in. Be sure not to fill in a bubble under a blank answer box.

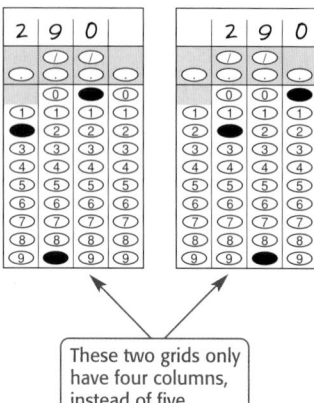

These two grids only have four columns, instead of five.

Many gridded response questions result in an answer that is a fraction or a decimal. These values can also be filled in on the grid.

How do you grid decimals and fractions?

Example 2   **What is the slope of the line that passes through (−2, 3) and (2, 4)?**

Let $(-2, 3) = (x_1, y_1)$ and $(2, 4) = (x_2, y_2)$.

$m = \dfrac{y_2 - y_1}{x_2 - x_1}$ Slope formula

$= \dfrac{4 - 3}{2 - (-2)}$ or $\dfrac{1}{4}$ Substitute and simplify.

How do you grid the answer?

You can either grid the fraction $\dfrac{1}{4}$, or rewrite it as 0.25 and grid the decimal. Be sure to write the decimal point or fraction bar in the answer box. The following are acceptable answer responses that represent $\dfrac{1}{4}$ and 0.25.

Strategy

Decimals and Fractions
Fill in the grid with decimal and fraction answers.

> Fractions do not have to be written in lowest terms. Any equivalent fraction that fits the grid will be counted as correct.

Some problems may result in an answer that is a mixed number. Before filling in the grid, change the mixed number to an equivalent improper fraction or decimal. For example, if the answer is $1\dfrac{1}{2}$, do not enter 1 1/2 as this will be interpreted as $\dfrac{11}{2}$. Instead, either enter 3/2 or 1.5.

How do you grid mixed numbers?

Example 3   **Amber's cookie recipe calls for $1\dfrac{1}{3}$ cups of coconut. If Amber plans to make 4 batches of cookies, how much coconut does she need?**

Find the amount of coconut needed using a proportion.

coconut ⟶ $\dfrac{1\frac{1}{3}}{1} = \dfrac{x}{4}$ ⟵ batches

$4\left(1\dfrac{1}{3}\right) = 1x$

$4\left(\dfrac{4}{3}\right) = x$

$\dfrac{16}{3} = x$

Leave the answer as the improper fraction $\dfrac{16}{3}$, as you cannot correctly grid $5\dfrac{1}{3}$.

Gridded-Response Practice

Solve each problem. Then copy and complete a grid like the one shown on page 873.

Number and Operations

1. China has the most days of school per year for children with 251 days. If there are 365 days in a year, what percent of the days of the year do Chinese students spend in school? Round to the nearest tenth of a percent. **68.8**

2. Charles is building a deck and wants to buy some long boards that he can cut into various lengths without wasting any lumber. He would like to cut any board into all lengths of 24 inches, 48 inches, or 60 inches. In feet, what is the shortest length of boards that he can buy? **20**

3. At a sale, an item was discounted 20%. After several weeks, the sale price was discounted an additional 25%. What was the total percent discount from the original price of the item? **40**

4. The Andromeda Spiral galaxy is 2.2×10^6 light-years from Earth. The Ursa Minor dwarf is 2.5×10^5 light-years from Earth. How many times as far is the Andromeda Spiral as Ursa Minor dwarf from Earth? **8.8**

5. Twenty students want to attend the World Language Convention. The school budget will only allow for four students to attend. In how many ways can four students be chosen from the twenty students to attend the convention? **4845**

Algebra

6. Find the y-intercept of the graph of the equation $3x + 4y - 5 = 0$. **5/4 or 1.25**

7. Name the x-coordinate of the solution of the system of equations $2x - y = 7$ and $3x + 2y = 7$. **3**

8. Solve $2b - 2(3b - 5) = 8(b - 7)$ for b. **11/2 or 5.5**

9. Kersi read 36 pages of a novel in 2 hours. Find the number of hours it will take him to read the remaining 135 pages if he reads them at the same rate? **15/2 or 7.5**

10. If $f(x) = x + 3$ and $g(x) = x^2 - 2x + 5$, find $6[f(g(1))]$. **42**

11. The Donaldsons have a fish pond in their yard that measures 8 feet by 15 feet. They want to put a walkway around the pond that measures the same width on all sides of the pond, as shown in the diagram. They want the total area of the pond and walkway to be 294 square feet. What will be the width of the walkway in feet? **3**

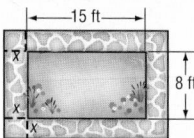

Geometry

12. $\triangle MNP$ is reflected over the x-axis. What is the x-coordinate of the image of point N? **2**

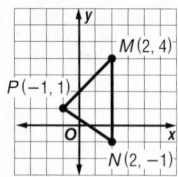

13. The pattern for the square tile shown in the diagram is to be enlarged so that it will measure 15 inches on a side. By what scale factor must the pattern be enlarged? **24**

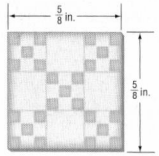

14. Find the measure of $\angle A$ to the nearest degree. **56**

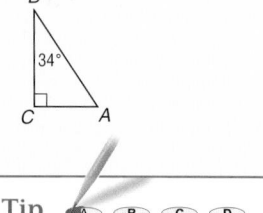

Test-Taking Tip ⒶⒷⒸⒹ

Question 14
Remember that the hypotenuse of a right triangle is always opposite the right angle.

15. Use the diagram for △ABO and △XBY. Find the length of $\overline{BX}$. **9**

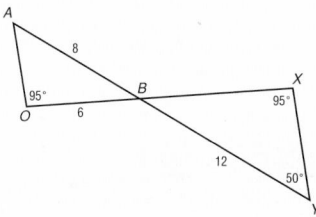

16. A triangle has a perimeter of 96 centimeters. The ratio of measures of its three sides is 6:8:10. Find the length of the longest side in centimeters. **40**

17. The scale on a map of Texas is 0.75 inch = 5 miles. The distance on the map from San Antonio to Dallas is 8.25 inches. What is the actual distance from San Antonio to Dallas in miles? **275**

Measurement

18. Pluto is the farthest planet from the Sun in this solar system at 2756 million miles. If light travels at 186,000 miles per second, how many minutes does it take for a particular ray of light to reach Pluto from the Sun? Round to the nearest minute. **247**

19. Noah drove 342 miles and used 12 gallons of gas. At this same rate, how many gallons of gas will he use on his entire trip of 1140 miles? **40**

20. The jumping surface of a trampoline is shaped like a circle with a diameter of 14 feet. Find the area of the jumping surface. Use 3.14 for π and round to the nearest square foot. **154**

21. A cone is drilled out of a cylinder of wood. If the cone and cylinder have the same base and height, find the volume of the remaining wood. Use 3.14 for π and round to the nearest cubic inch. **1055**

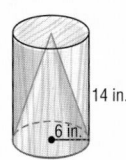
14 in.
6 in.

22. The front of a storage building is shaped like a trapezoid as shown. Find the area in square feet of the front of the storage building. **176**

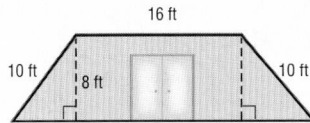
16 ft
10 ft   8 ft   10 ft

Data Analysis and Probability

23. The table shows the average size in acres of farms in the six states with the largest farms. Find the median of the farm data in acres. **2600**

Average Size of Farms for 2001	
State	Acres per Farm
Alaska	1586
Arizona	3644
Montana	2124
Nevada	2267
New Mexico	2933
Wyoming	3761

24. The Lindley Park Pavilion is available to rent for parties. There is a fee to rent the pavilion and then a charge per hour. The graph shows the total amount you would pay to rent the pavilion for various numbers of hours. If a function is written to model the charge to rent the pavilion, where x is the number of hours and y is the total charge, what is the rate of change of the function? **10**

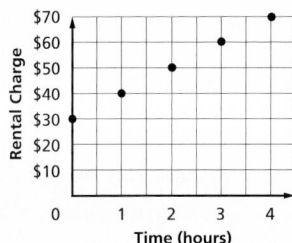

25. A particular game is played by rolling three tetrahedral (4-sided) dice. The faces of each die are numbered with the digits 1–4. How many outcomes are in the sample space for the event of rolling the three dice once? **64**

26. In a carnival game, the blindfolded contestant draws two toy ducks from a pond without replacement. The pond contains 2 yellow ducks, 10 black ducks, 22 white ducks, and 8 red ducks. The best prize is won by drawing two yellow ducks. What is the probability of drawing two yellow ducks? Write your answer as a percent rounded to the nearest tenth of a percent. **0.1**

Short-Response Questions

Short-response questions require you to provide a solution to the problem, as well as any method, explanation, and/or justification you used to arrive at the solution. These are sometimes called *constructed-response, open-response, open-ended, free-response,* or *student-produced questions.* The following is a sample rubric, or scoring guide, for scoring short-response questions.

Credit	Score	Criteria
Full	2	Full credit: The answer is correct and a full explanation is provided that shows each step in arriving at the final answer.
Partial	1	Partial credit: There are two different ways to receive partial credit. • The answer is correct, but the explanation provided is incomplete or incorrect. • The answer is incorrect, but the explanation and method of solving the problem is correct.
None	0	No credit: Either an answer is not provided or the answer does not make sense.

> On some standardized tests, no credit is given for a correct answer if your work is not shown.

Example

Susana is painting two large rooms at her art studio. She has calculated that each room has 4000 square feet to be painted. It says on the can of paint that one gallon covers 300 square feet of smooth surface for one coat and that two coats should be applied for best results. What is the minimum number of 5-gallon cans of paint Susana needs to buy to apply two coats in the two rooms of her studio?

Full Credit Solution

First find the total number of square feet to be painted.
$$4000 \times 2 = 8000 \text{ ft}^2$$

Since 1 gallon covers 300 ft², multiply 8000 ft² by the unit rate $\dfrac{1 \text{ gal}}{300 \text{ ft}^2}$.

$$8000 \text{ ft}^2 \times \frac{1 \text{ gal}}{300 \text{ ft}^2} = \frac{8000}{300} \text{ gal}$$
$$= 26\frac{2}{3} \text{ gal.}$$

> The steps, calculations, and reasoning are clearly stated.

Each can of paint contains 5 gallons, so divide $26\frac{2}{3}$ gallons by 5 gallons

$$26\frac{2}{3} \div 5 = \frac{80}{3} \div 5 = \frac{\overset{16}{\cancel{80}}}{3} \times \frac{1}{\underset{1}{\cancel{5}}} = \frac{16}{3} = 5\frac{1}{3}$$

> The solution of the problem is clearly stated.

Since Susana cannot buy a fraction of a can of paint, she needs to buy 6 cans of paint.

Partial Credit Solution

In this sample solution, the answer is correct; however there is no justification for any of the calculations.

> **There is no explanation of how $26\frac{2}{3}$ was obtained.**

$$26\frac{2}{3} \div 5 = \frac{80}{3} \div 5$$

$$= \frac{\overset{16}{\cancel{80}}}{3} \times \frac{1}{\underset{1}{\cancel{5}}}$$

$$= \frac{16}{3}$$

$$= 5\frac{1}{3}$$

Susana will need to buy 6 cans of paint.

Partial Credit Solution

In this sample solution, the answer is incorrect. However, after the first statement, all of the calculations and reasoning are correct.

There are 4000 ft² to be painted and one gallon of paint covers 300 ft².

$$4000 \text{ft}^2 \times \frac{1 \text{ gal}}{300 \text{ ft}^2} = \frac{4000}{300} \text{ gal}$$

$$= 13\frac{1}{3} \text{ gal}$$

> **The first step of doubling the square footage for painting the second room was left out.**

Each can of paint contains five gallons. So 2 cans would contain 10 gallons, which is not enough. Three cans of paint would contain 15 gallons which is enough.

Therefore, Susana will need to buy 3 cans of paint.

No Credit Solution

> **The wrong operations are used, so the answer is incorrect. Also, there are no units of measure given with any of the calculations.**

$300 \times 2 = 600$

$600 \div 5 = 120$

$4000 \div 120 = 33\frac{1}{3}$

Susana will need 34 cans of paint.

Short-Response Practice

Solve each problem. Show all your work.

Number and Operations

1. The world's slowest fish is the sea horse. The average speed of a sea horse is 0.001 mile per hour. What is the rate of speed of a sea horse in feet per minute? **0.088 ft/min**

2. Two buses arrive at the Central Avenue bus stop at 8 A.M. The route for the City Loop bus takes 35 minutes, while the route for the By-Pass bus takes 20 minutes. What is the next time that the two buses will both be at the Central Avenue bus stop? **10:20 A.M.**

3. Toya's Clothing World purchased some denim jackets for $35. The jackets are marked up 40%. Later in the season, the jackets are discounted 25%. How much does the store lose or gain on the sale of one jacket at the discounted price? **gain of $1.75**

4. A femtosecond is 10^{-15} second, and a millisecond is 10^{-3} second. How many times faster is a millisecond than a femtosecond? **10^{12} times greater**

5. Find the next three terms in the sequence.

$1, 3, 9, 27, \ldots$ **81, 243, 729**

Algebra

6. Find the slope of the graph of $5x - 2y + 1 = 0$. **$\dfrac{5}{2}$ or 2.5**

7. Simplify $5 + x(1 - x) + 3x$. Write the result in the form $ax^2 + bx + c$. **$-x^2 + 4x + 5$**

8. Solve $17 - 3x \geq 23$. **$x \leq -2$**

9. The table shows what Gerardo charges in dollars for his consulting services for various numbers of hours. Write an equation that can be used to find the charge for any amount of time, where y is the total charge in dollars and x is the number of hours. **$y = 25 + 15x$**

Hours	Charge	Hours	Charge
0	$25	2	$55
1	$40	3	$70

10. The population of Clark County, Nevada, was 1,375,765 in 2000 and 1,464,653 in 2001. Let x represent the years since 2000 and y represent the total population of Clark County. Suppose the county continues to increase at the same rate. Write an equation that represents the population of the county for any year after 2000. **$y = 88{,}888x + 1{,}375{,}765$**

Geometry

11. $\triangle ABC$ is dilated with scale factor 2.5. Find the coordinates of dilated $\triangle A'B'C'$. **$A'(2.5, 2.5)$, $B'(5, -5)$, $C'(-5, -2.5)$**

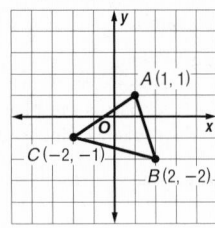

12. At a particular time in its flight, a plane is 10,000 feet above a lake. The distance from the lake to the airport is 5 miles. Find the distance in feet from the plane to the airport. **about 28,230 ft**

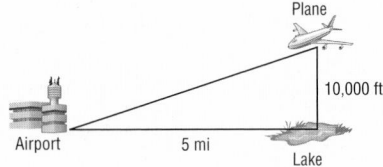

13. Refer to the diagram of the two similar triangles below. Find the value of a. **61.5**

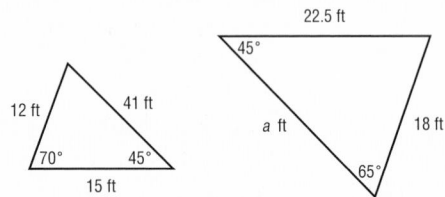

14. The vertices of two triangles are $P(3, 3)$, $Q(7, 3)$, $R(3, 10)$, and $S(-1, 4)$, $T(3, 4)$, $U(-1, 11)$. Which transformation moves $\triangle PQR$ to $\triangle STU$? **translation $(x - 4)$, $(y + 1)$**

15. Aaron has a square garden in his front yard. The length of a side of the garden is 9 feet. Casey wants to plant 6 flowering bushes evenly spaced out along the diagonal. Approximately how many inches apart should he plant the bushes?

30.5 in. apart

Measurement

16. One inch is equivalent to approximately 2.54 centimeters. Nikki is 61 inches tall. What is her height in centimeters? **154.94 cm**

17. During the holidays, Evan works at Cheese Haus. He packages gift baskets containing a variety of cheeses and sausages. During one four-hour shift, he packaged 20 baskets. At this rate, how many baskets will he package if he works 26 hours in one week? **130 baskets**

18. Ms. Ortega built a box for her garden and placed a round barrel inside to be used for a fountain in the center of the box. The barrel touches the box at its sides as shown. She wants to put potting soil in the shaded corners of the box at a depth of 6 inches. How many cubic feet of soil will she need? Use 3.14 for π and round to the nearest tenth of a cubic foot.

1.7 ft³

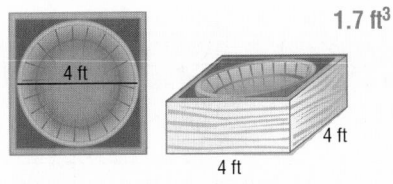

19. A line segment has its midpoint located at (1, −5) and one endpoint at (−2, −7). Find the length of the line to the nearest tenth. **7.2**

Test-Taking Tip Ⓐ Ⓑ Ⓒ Ⓓ

Question 20
Most standardized tests will include any commonly used formulas at the front of the test booklet. Quickly review the list before you begin so that you know what formulas are available.

---

20. A child's portable swimming pool is 6 feet across and is filled to a depth of 8 inches. One gallon of water is 231 cubic inches. What is the volume of water in the pool in gallons? Use 3.14 as an approximation for π and round to the nearest gallon. **141 gal**

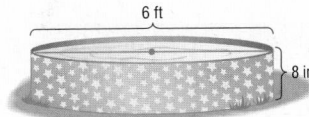

Data Analysis and Probability

21. The table shows the five lowest recorded temperatures on Earth. Find the mean of the temperatures. **−108.16°F**

Location	Temperature (°F)
Vostok, Antarctica	−138.6
Plateau Station, Antarctica	−129.2
Oymyakon, Russia	−96.0
Verkhoyansk, Russia	−90.0
Northice, Greenland	−87.0

Source: *The World Almanac*

22. Two six-sided dice are rolled. The sum of the numbers of dots on the faces of the two dice is recorded. What is the probability that the sum is 10? $\frac{1}{12}$

23. The table shows the amount of a particular chemical that is needed to treat various sizes of swimming pools. Write the equation for a line to model the data. Let x represent the capacity of the pool in gallons and y represent the amount of the chemical in ounces. $y = 0.003x$

Pool Capacity (gal)	Amount of Chemical (oz)
5000	15
10,000	30
15,000	45
20,000	60
25,000	75

24. Fifty balls are placed in a bin. They are labeled from 1 through 50. Two balls are drawn without replacement. What is the probability that both balls show an even number? $\frac{12}{49}$

Extended-Response Questions

Extended-response questions are often called *open-ended* or *constructed-response questions*. Most extended-response questions have multiple parts. You must answer all parts correctly to receive full credit.

Extended-response questions are similar to short-response questions in that you must show all of your work in solving the problem, and a rubric is used to determine whether you receive full, partial, or no credit. The following is a sample rubric for scoring extended-response questions.

Credit	Score	Criteria
Full	4	A correct solution is given that is supported by well-developed, accurate explanations
Partial	3, 2, 1	A generally correct solution is given that may contain minor flaws in reasoning or computation or an incomplete solution. The more correct the solution, the greater the score.
None	0	An incorrect solution is given indicating no mathematical understanding of the concept, or no solution is given.

On some standardized tests, no credit is given for a correct answer if your work is not shown.

Make sure that when the problem says to *Show your work,* show every aspect of your solution including figures, sketches of graphing calculator screens, or reasoning behind computations.

Example

The table shows the population density in the United States on April 1 in each decade of the 20th century.

a. Make a scatter plot of the data.

b. Alaska and Hawaii became states in the same year. Between what two census dates do you think this happened. Why did you choose those years?

c. Use the data and your graph to predict the population density in 2010. Explain your reasoning.

U.S. Population Density	
Year	People Per Square Mile
1910	31.0
1920	35.6
1930	41.2
1940	44.2
1950	50.7
1960	50.6
1970	57.4
1980	64.0
1990	70.3
2000	79.6

Source: U.S. Census Bureau

Full Credit Solution

Part a A complete scatter plot includes a title for the graph, appropriate scales and labels for the axes, and correctly graphed points.

- The student should determine that the year data should go on the x-axis while the people per square mile data should go on the y-axis.

- On the x-axis, each square should represent 10 years.

- The y-axis could start at 0, or it could show data starting at 30 with a broken line to indicate that some of the scale is missing.

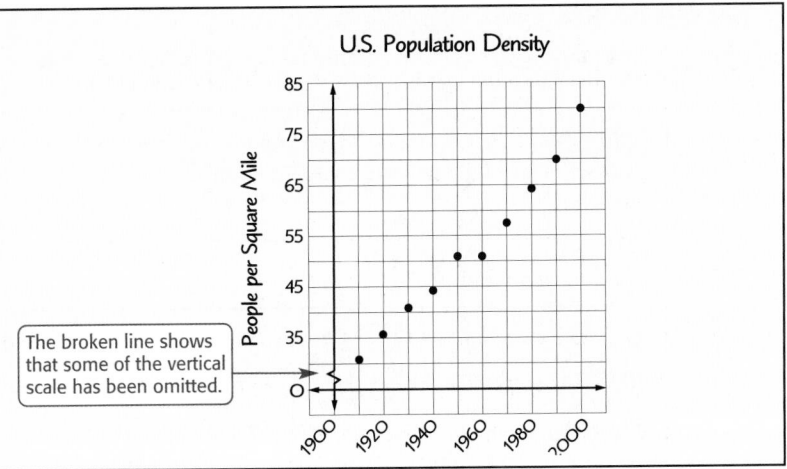

U.S. Population Density

People per Square Mile

The broken line shows that some of the vertical scale has been omitted.

You might know when Alaska became a state. So, another acceptable reason is that both Alaska and Hawaii became states in 1959.

Part b

1950–1960 because when Alaska became a state it added little population but a lot of land, which made the people per square mile ratio less.

Part c

About 85.0, because the population per square mile would probably get larger so I connected the first point and the last point. The rate of change for each year was $\frac{79.6 - 31.0}{2000 - 1910}$ or about 0.54. I added 10 × 0.54, or 5.4 to 79.6 to get the next 10-year point.

Actually, any estimate from 84 to 86 might be acceptable. You could also use different points to find the equation for a line of best fit for the data, and then find the corresponding *y* value for *x* = 2010.

Partial Credit Solution

Part a This sample answer includes no labels for the graph or the axes and one of the points is not graphed correctly.

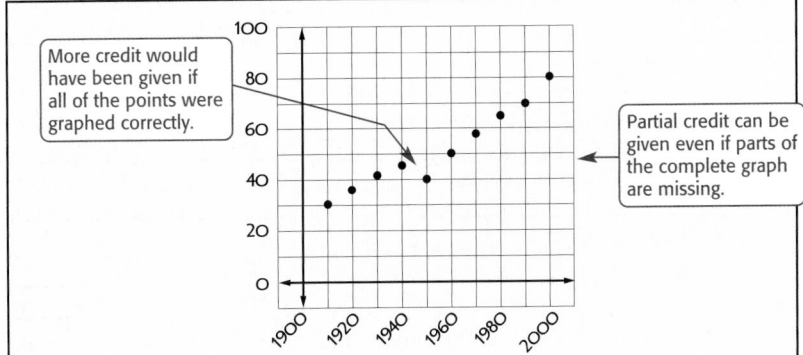

More credit would have been given if all of the points were graphed correctly.

Partial credit can be given even if parts of the complete graph are missing.

Part b Partial credit is given because the reasoning is correct, but the reasoning was based on the incorrect graph in Part a.

> 1940–1950, because when Alaska became a state it added little population but a lot of land, which made the people per square mile ratio less.

Part c Full credit is given for Part c.

> Suppose I draw a line of best fit through points (1910, 31.0) and (1990, 70.3). The slope would be $\frac{70.3 - 31.0}{1990 - 1910}$ or about 0.49. Now use the slope and one of the points to find the y-intercept.
>
> $y = mx + b$ So an equation of my
> $70.3 = 0.49(1990) + b$ line of best fit is
> $-904.8 = b$ $y = 0.49x - 904.8$.
>
> If $x = 2010$, then $y = 0.49(2010) - 904.8$ or about 80.1 people per square mile in the year 2010.

This sample answer might have received a score of 2 or 1. Had the student graphed all points correctly and gotten Part B correct, the score would probably have been a 3.

No Credit Solution

Part a

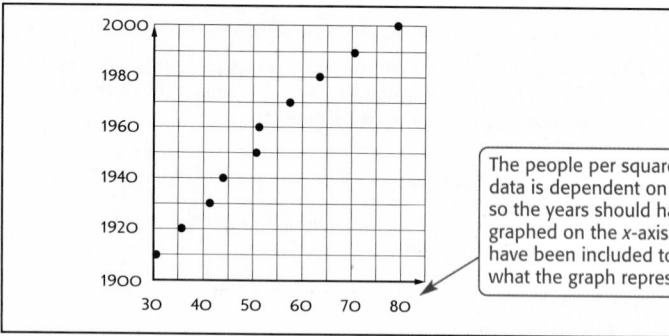

The people per square mile data is dependent on the year, so the years should have been graphed on the x-axis. No labels have been included to identify what the graph represents.

Part b

> I have no idea.

Part c

> 85, because it is the next grid line.

In this sample answer, the student does not understand how to represent data on a graph or how to interpret the data after the points are graphed.

Extended Response Practice

Solve each problem. Show all your work.

Number and Operations

1. The table shows what one dollar in U.S. money was worth in five countries in 1970 and in 2001. **a–c. See margin.**

Money Equivalent to One U.S. Dollar		
Country	1970 Value	2001 Value
France	5.5 francs	7 francs
Germany	3.6 marks	2 marks
Great Britain	0.4 pounds	0.67 pounds
Italy	623 lire	2040 lire
Japan	358 yen	117 yen

   a. For which country was the percent of increase or decrease in the number of units of currency that was equivalent to \$1 the greatest from 1970 to 2001?

   b. Suppose a U.S. citizen traveled to Germany in 1970 and in 2001. In which year would the traveler receive a better value for their money? Explain.

   c. In 2001, what was the value of one franc in yen?

2. The table shows some data about the planets and the Sun. The radius is given in miles and the volume, mass, and gravity quantities are related to the volume and mass of Earth, which has a value of 1. **a–c. See margin.**

	Volume	Mass	Density	Radius	Gravity
Sun	1,304,000	332,950	0.26	434,474	28
Mercury	0.056	0.0553	0.98	1516	0.38
Venus	0.857	0.815	0.95	3760	0.91
Moon	0.0203	0.0123	0.61	1079	0.17
Mars	0.151	0.107	0.71	2106	0.38
Jupiter	1321	317.83	0.24	43,441	2.36
Saturn	764	95.16	0.12	36,184	0.92
Uranus	63	14.54	0.23	15,759	0.89
Neptune	58	17.15	0.30	15,301	1.12
Pluto	0.007	0.0021	0.32	743	0.06

   a. Make and test a conjecture relating volume, mass, and density.

   b. Describe the relationship between radius and gravity.

   c. Can you be sure that the relationship in part b holds true for all planets? Explain.

Algebra

3. The graph shows the altitude of a glider during various times of his flight after being released from a tow plane. **a–e. See margin.**

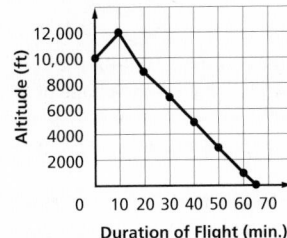

   a. What point on the graph represents the moment the glider was released from the tow plane? Explain the meaning of this point in terms of altitude.

   b. During which time period did the greatest rate of descent of the glider take place? Explain your reasoning.

   c. How long did it take the glider to reach an altitude of 0 feet? Where is this point on the graph?

   d. What is the equation of a line that represents the glider's altitude y as the time increased from 20 to 60 minutes?

   e. Explain what the slope of the line in part d represents?

4. John has just received his learner's permit which allows him to practice driving with a licensed driver. His mother has agreed to take him driving every day for two weeks. On the first day, John will drive for 20 minutes. Each day after that, John's mother has agreed he can drive 15 minutes more than the day before. **a–c. See margin.**

   a. Write a formula for the nth term of the sequence. Explain how you found the formula.

   b. For how many minutes will John drive on the last day? Show how you found the number of minutes.

   c. John's driver's education teacher requires that each student drive for 30 hours with an adult outside of class. Will John fulfill this requirement? Explain.

1a. Italy had a 227% increase.

1b. 1970; you could get more marks for every U.S. dollar and buy more merchandise.

1c. There were about 16.7 yen for 1 franc.

2a. Sample answer: In each case, mass ÷ volume is approximately equal to the density.

2b. Sample answer: The greater the radius, the greater the gravity. However, the relationship does not look like it is strictly linear.

2c. Sample answer: No, you would need to examine the similar statistics for all the planets.

3a. The glider was released when $x = 0$. The altitude of 10,000 feet is the altitude of the glider upon release.

3b. During 10 to 20 minutes after release, the rate of descent was greatest as the slope of the line is greatest and the line is steepest.

3c. It appears to have taken about 65 minutes. It is the x-intercept, where the altitude y is 0.

3d. $y = -200x + 13,000$

3e. The slope is the rate of descent of the glider, which is 200 feet per minute.

4a. $a_n = 5 + 15n$; If x represents the days and y represents the number of minutes, Anna will drive 20 minutes on the first day (1, 20) and 35 minutes on the second day (2, 35). Using these points, I found the point-slope form of the equation to be $y = 15x + 5$. Then, I changed the equation into the formula with variables a_n and n.

4b. $a_{14} = 5 + 15(14)$ or 215 minutes; sample answer: I substituted $n = 14$ days into the formula.

4c. No; the total of all the minutes for 14 days is only 1645 minutes while 30 hours is 1800 minutes. He will be short 155 minutes.

5a. $Q'(-2, 3)$, $U'(-2, -2)$, $A'(4, -3)$, $D'(1, 2)$; sample answer: Since the reflection occurred over the y-axis, I found the opposite of the x-coordinate for each point.

5b. $(-a, b)$

5c. A reflection over the x-axis will make the polygon look "upside down." The coordinates of the vertices will be $Q'(2, -3)$, $U'(2, 2)$, $A'(-4, 3)$, $D'(-1, -2)$.

6a. The ratio is 4 to 3.

6b. The ratio is 1 to 1.

6c. Sample answer: $r = a$; $h = 4a$

7a. The distance is 105 kilometers. Sample answer: I set up the proportion $\frac{2\text{ cm}}{30\text{ km}} = \frac{7\text{ cm}}{x\text{ km}}$, $x = 105$.

7b. The distance is 74.4 miles.

7c. She will need about 20 gallons. Sample answer: I found 54 cm = 810 km = 502.2 mi. Then I divided 25 mi/gal into 502.2 mi to get 20.088 gal.

8a. The area of region 6 is about 12.4 in^2.

8b. The area of region 1 is about 2.4 in^2.

8c. $\frac{\pi}{25}$; Sample answer: The area of region 5 is $\frac{1}{4}\pi 2^2$, or π in^2. The area of the square is 5^2 or 25. So, the ratio is π to 25 or $\frac{\pi}{25}$.

9a.

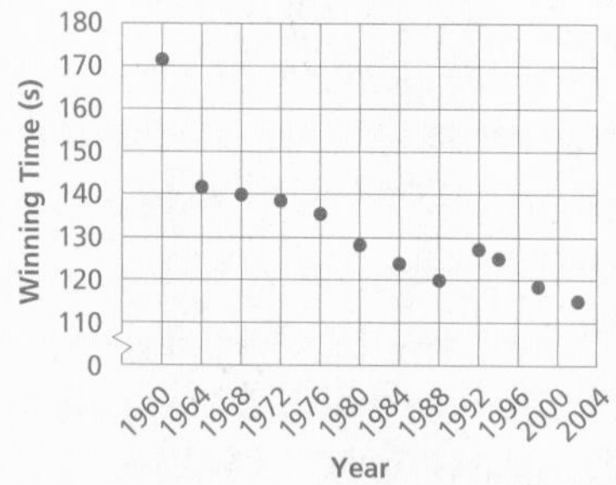

9b. Sample answer: In recent years, the times have decreased by 4 seconds every 4 years. Since 2010 is 8 years from 2002, the winning time in 2010 will be about 114 − 2(4) or 106 seconds.

Geometry

5. Polygon *QUAD* is shown on a coordinate plane. **a–c. See margin.**

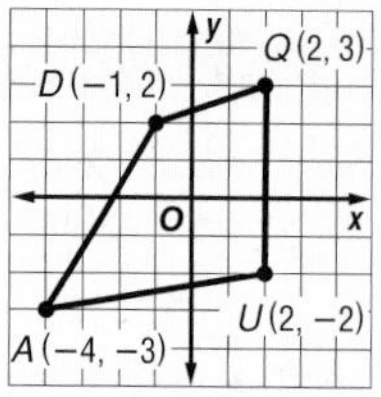

a. Find the coordinates of the vertices of $Q'U'A'D'$, which is the image of *QUAD* after a reflection over the y-axis. Explain.

b. Suppose point $M(a, b)$ is reflected over the y-axis. What will be the coordinates of the image M'?

c. Describe a reflection that will make *QUAD* look "upside down." What will be the coordinates of the vertices of the image?

6. The diagram shows a sphere with a radius of a and a cylinder with a radius and a height of a. **a–c. See margin.**

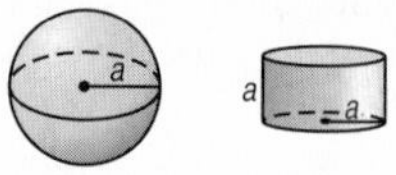

a. What is the ratio of the volume of the sphere to the volume of the cylinder?

b. What is the ratio of the surface area of the sphere to the surface area of the cylinder?

c. The ratio of the volume of another cylinder is 3 times the volume of the sphere shown. Give one possible set of measures for the radius and height of the cylinder in terms of a.

Measurement

7. Alexis is using a map of the province of Saskatchewan in Canada. The scale for the map shows that 2 centimeters on the map is 30 kilometers in actual distance. **a–c. See margin.**

a. The distance on the map between two cities measures 7 centimeters. What is the actual distance between the two cities in kilometers? Show how you found the distance.

b. Alexis is more familiar with distances in miles. The distance between two other cities is 8 centimeters. If one kilometer is about 0.62 mile, what is the distance in miles?

c. Alexis' entire trip measures 54 centimeters. If her car averages 25 miles per gallon of gasoline, how many gallons will she need to complete the trip? Round to the nearest gallon. Explain.

Test-Taking Tip (A) (B) (C) (D)

Question 5

In a reflection over the x-axis, the x-coordinate remains the same, and the y-coordinate changes its sign. In a reflection over the y-axis, the y-coordinate remains the same, and the x-coordinate changes its sign.

8. The diagram shows a pattern for a quilt square called Colorful Fan. **a–c. See margin.**

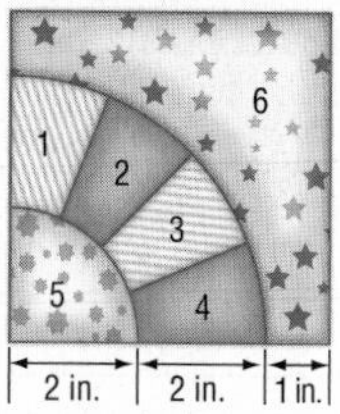

a. What is the area of region 6? Explain.

b. What is the area of region 1? Explain.

c. What is the ratio of the area of region 5 to the area of the entire square? Show how you found the ratio. Leave the ratio in terms of π.

Data Analysis and Probability

9. The table shows the Olympics winning times in the women's 1500-meter speed skating event. The times are to the nearest second.

Year	Time (s)	Year	Time (s)
1960	172	1984	124
1964	143	1988	121
1968	142	1992	126
1972	141	1994	122
1976	137	1998	118
1980	131	2002	114

a. Make a scatter plot of the data. **a–b. See margin.**

b. Use the data and your graph to predict the winning time in 2010.

10. There are 1320 ways for three students to win first, second, and third place during a debate. **a–c. See margin.**

a. How many students are on the debate team?

b. What is the probability that a student will come in one of the first three places if each student has an equal chance of succeeding?

c. If the teacher announces the third place winner, what is the probability that one particular other student will win first or second place?

10a. There are 12 students on the debate team because there are 12 · 11 · 10 or 1320 ways for three students to win the top three places during the debate.

10b. $\frac{\text{ways to come in the first 3 places}}{\text{number of students}} = \frac{3}{20}$ or 15%

10c. $\frac{2}{19}$ or about 10.5%

Glossary/Glosario

Cómo usar el glosario en español:
1. Busca el término en inglés que desees encontrar.
2. El término en español, junto con la definición, se encuentran en la columna de la derecha.

English   *Español*

A

absolute value (p. 69) The absolute value of a number n is its distance from zero on a number line and is represented by $|n|$.

valor absoluto El valor absoluto de un número n es la distancia que n dista de cero en una recta numérica. Se denota con $|n|$.

additive identity (p. 21) For any number a, $a + 0 = 0 + a = a$.

identidad de la adición Para cualquier número a, $a + 0 = 0 + a = a$.

additive inverses (p. 75) A number and its opposite are additive inverses of each other. The sum of a number and its additive inverse is 0.

inversos aditivos Un número y su opuesto son inversos aditivos mutuos. La suma de un número y su inverso aditivo es 0.

algebraic expression (p. 6) An expression consisting of one or more numbers and variables along with one or more arithmetic operations.

expresión algebraica Una expresión que consiste en uno o más números y variables, junto con una o más operaciones aritméticas.

angle of depression (p. 626) The angle formed by a horizontal line of sight and a line of sight below it.

ángulo de depresión Ángulo formado por una línea visual horizontal y otra línea visual debajo de ella.

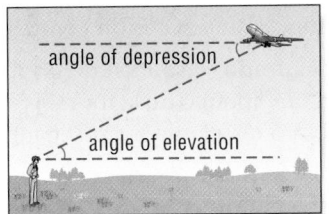

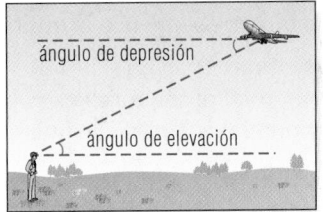

angle of elevation (p. 626) The angle formed by a horizontal line of sight and a line of sight above it.

ángulo de elevación Ángulo formado por una línea visual horizontal y otra línea visual sobre ella.

arithmetic sequence (p. 233) A numerical pattern that increases or decreases at a constant rate or value. The difference between successive terms of the sequence is constant.

sucesión aritmética Un patrón numérico que aumenta o disminuye a una tasa o valor constante. La diferencia entre términos consecutivos de la sucesión es siempre la misma.

axis of symmetry (p. 525) The vertical line containing the vertex of a parabola.

eje de simetría La recta vertical que pasa por el vértice de una parábola.

B

back-to-back stem-and-leaf plot (p. 89) Used to compare two related sets of data.

diagrama de tallo y hojas consecutivo Se usa para comparar dos conjuntos relacionados de datos.

bar graph (p. 50) A graph that compares different categories of data by showing each category as a bar whose length is related to the frequency.

gráfica de barras Gráfica que compara categorías distintas de datos al exhibir cada categoría con una barra cuya longitud está relacionada con la frecuencia.

base (p. 7) In an expression of the form x^n, the base is x.

base En una expresión de la forma x^n, la base es x.

best-fit line (p. 300) The line that most closely approximates the data in a scatter plot.

recta de ajuste óptimo La recta que mejor aproxima los datos de una gráfica de dispersión.

biased sample (p. 709) A sample in which one or more parts of the population are favored over others.

muestra sesgada Muestra en que se favorece una o más partes de una población en vez de otras partes.

binomial (p. 422)   The sum of two monomials.

boundary (p. 353)   A line or curve that separates the coordinate plane into regions.

box-and-whisker plot (p. 737)   A diagram that divides a set of data into four parts using the median and quartiles.

binomio   La suma de dos monomios.

frontera   Recta o curva que divide el plano de coordenadas en regiones.

diagrama de caja y patillas   Diagrama que divide un conjunto de datos en cuatro partes usando la mediana y los cuartiles.

C

census (p. 708)   A sample in which all of the units within a population are included.

circle graph (p. 51)   A graph that compares parts of a set of data as a percent of the whole set.

coefficient (p. 29)   The numerical factor of a term.

combination (p. 762)   An arrangement or listing in which order is not important.

common difference (p. 233)   The difference between the terms in a sequence.

common ratio (p. 567)   The number by which each term in a geometric sequence is multiplied.

completing the square (p. 539)   To add a constant term to a binomial of the form $x^2 + bx$ so that the resulting trinomial is a perfect square.

complex fraction (p. 684)   A fraction that has one or more fractions in the numerator or denominator.

composite numbers (p. 474)   A whole number, greater than 1, that has more than two factors.

compound event (p. 769)   Two or more simple events.

compound inequality (p. 339)   Two or more inequalities that are connected by the words *and* or *or*.

conclusion (p. 37)   The part of a conditional statement immediately following the word *then*.

conditional statements (p. 37)   Statements written in the form *If A, then B*.

conjugates (p. 590)   Binomials of the form $a\sqrt{b} + c\sqrt{d}$ and $a\sqrt{b} - c\sqrt{d}$.

consecutive integers (p. 144)   Integers in counting order.

consistent (p. 369)   A system of equations that has at least one ordered pair that satisfies both equations.

constant (p. 410)   A monomial that is a real number.

constant of variation (p. 264)   The number k in equations of the form $y = kx$.

convenience sample (p. 709)   A sample that includes members of a population that are easily accessed.

coordinate (p. 69)   The number that corresponds to a point on a number line.

censo   Muestra en que se incluyen todas las unidades de una población.

gráfica circular   Gráfica que compara partes de un conjunto de datos como porcentajes del conjunto entero.

coeficiente   Factor numérico de un término.

combinación   Arreglo o lista en que el orden no es importante.

diferencia común   Diferencia entre términos consecutivos de una sucesión.

razón común   El número por el que se multiplica cada término de una sucesión geométrica.

completar el cuadrado   Adición de un término constante a un binomio de la forma $x^2 + bx$, para que el trinomio resultante sea un cuadrado perfecto.

fracción compleja   Fracción con una o más fracciones en el numerador o denominador.

números compuestos   Número entero mayor que 1 que posee más de dos factores.

evento compuesto   Dos o más eventos simples.

desigualdad compuesta   Dos o más desigualdades que están unidas por las palabras *y* u *o*.

conclusión   Parte de un enunciado condicional que sigue inmediatamente a la palabra *entonces*.

enunciados condicionales   Enunciados de la forma *Si A, entonces B*.

conjugados   Binomios de la forma $a\sqrt{b} + c\sqrt{d}$ y $a\sqrt{b} - c\sqrt{d}$.

enteros consecutivos   Enteros en el orden de contar.

consistente   Sistema de ecuaciones para el cual existe al menos un par ordenado que satisface ambas ecuaciones.

constante   Monomio que es un número real.

constante de variación   El número k en ecuaciones de la forma $y = kx$.

muestra de conveniencia   Muestra que incluye miembros de una población fácilmente accesibles.

coordenada   Número que corresponde a un punto en una recta numérica.

coordinate plane (pp. 43, 192)   The plane containing the *x*- and *y*-axes.

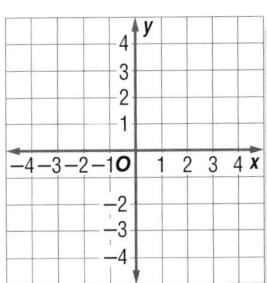

plano de coordenadas   Plano que contiene los ejes *x* y *y*.

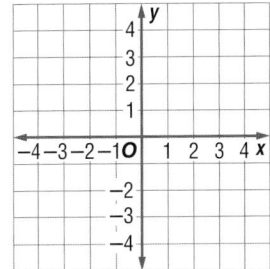

coordinate system (p. 43)   The grid formed by the intersection of two number lines, the horizontal axis and the vertical axis.

corollary (p. 608)   A statement that can be easily proved using a theorem.

cosine (p. 624)   In a right triangle with acute angle *A*, the cosine of

$$\angle A = \frac{\text{the measure of the leg adjacent to } \angle A}{\text{the measure of the hypotenuse}}$$

counterexample (p. 38)   A specific case in which a statement is false.

cumulative frequency histogram (p. 743)   A histogram organized using a cumulative frequency table.

cumulative frequency table (p. 743)   A table in which the frequencies are accumulated for each item.

sistema de coordenadas   Cuadriculado formado por la intersección de dos rectas numéricas: los ejes *x* y *y*.

corolario   Enunciado que puede probarse fácilmente mediante el uso de un teorema.

coseno   En un triángulo rectángulo con ángulo agudo *A*, el coseno del

$$\angle A = \frac{\text{la medida del cateto adyacente al } \angle A}{\text{la medida de la hipotenusa}}$$

contraejemplo   Ejemplo específico de la falsedad de un enunciado.

histograma de frecuencia cumulativa   Un histograma organizado a partir de una tabla de frecuencia cumulativa.

tabla de frecuencia cumulativa   Una tabla en que se acumulan las frecuencias para cada elemento.

D

data (p. 50)   Numerical information gathered for statistical purposes.

deductive reasoning (p. 38)   The process of using facts, rules, definitions, or properties to reach a valid conclusion.

defining a variable (p. 121)   Choosing a variable to represent one of the unspecified numbers in a problem and using it to write expressions for the other unspecified numbers in the problem.

degree of a monomial (p. 433)   The sum of the exponents of all its variables.

degree of a polynomial (p. 433)   The greatest degree of any term in the polynomial.

dependent (p. 369)   A system of equations that has an infinite number of solutions.

dependent events (p. 770)   Two or more events in which the outcome of one event affects the outcome of the other events.

dependent variable (p. 44)   The variable in a relation whose value depends on the value of the independent variable.

datos   Información numérica que se recopila con propósitos estadísticos.

razonamiento deductivo   Proceso de usar hechos, reglas, definiciones o propiedades para sacar conclusiones válidas.

definir una variable   Consiste en escoger una variable para representar uno de los números desconocidos en un problema y luego usarla para escribir expresiones para otros números desconocidos en el problema.

grado de un monomio   Suma de los exponentes de todas sus variables.

grado de un polinomio   El grado mayor de cualquier término del polinomio.

dependiente   Sistema de ecuaciones que posee un número infinito de soluciones.

eventos dependientes   Dos o más eventos en que el resultado de un evento afecta el resultado de los otros eventos.

variable dependiente   La variable de una relación cuyo valor depende del valor de la variable independiente.

difference of squares (pp. 460, 502)   Two perfect squares separated by a subtraction sign.
$a^2 - b^2 = (a + b)(a - b)$ or
$a^2 - b^2 = (a - b)(a + b)$.

dilation (p. 197)   A transformation in which a figure is enlarged or reduced.

dimensional analysis (p. 167)   The process of carrying units throughout a computation.

direct variation (p. 264)   An equation of the form $y = kx$, where $k \neq 0$.

discriminant (p. 548)   In the Quadratic Formula, the expression under the radical sign, $b^2 - 4ac$.

Distance Formula (p. 612)   The distance d between any two points with coordinates (x_1, y_1) and (x_2, y_2) is given by the formula
$d = \sqrt{(x_2 - x_1)^2 + (y_2 - y_1)^2}$.

domain (p. 45)   The set of the first numbers of the ordered pairs in a relation.

diferencia de cuadrados   Dos cuadrados perfectos separados por el signo de sustracción.
$a^2 - b^2 = (a + b)(a - b)$ o
$a^2 - b^2 = (a - b)(a + b)$.

dilatación   Una transformación en la cual se amplía o se reduce una figura.

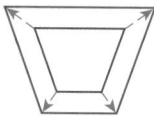

análisis dimensional   Proceso de tomar en cuenta las unidades de medida al hacer cálculos.

variación directa   Una ecuación de la forma $y = kx$, donde $k \neq 0$.

discriminante   En la fórmula cuadrática, la expresión debajo del signo radical, $b^2 - 4ac$.

Fórmula de la distancia   La distancia d entre cualquier par de puntos con coordenadas (x_1, y_1) y (x_2, y_2) viene dada por la fórmula
$d = \sqrt{(x_2 - y_1)^2 + (y_2 - y_1)^2}$.

dominio   Conjunto de los primeros números de los pares ordenados de una relación.

E

element   **1.** (p. 16)   Each object or number in a set. **2.** (p. 715)   Each entry in a matrix.

elimination (p. 382)   The use of addition or subtraction to eliminate one variable and solve a system of equations.

empirical study (p. 782)   Performing an experiment repeatedly, collecting and combining data, and analyzing the results.

equally likely (p. 97)   Outcomes for which the probability of each occurring is equal.

equation (p. 16)   A mathematical sentence that contains an equals sign, =.

equation in two variables (p. 212)   An equation that contains two unknown values.

equivalent equations (p. 128)   Equivalent equations have the same solution.

equivalent expressions (p. 29)   Expressions that denote the same number.

evaluate (p. 7)   To find the value of an expression.

event (p. 754)   Any collection of one or more outcomes in the sample space.

excluded values (p. 648)   Any values of a variable that result in a denominator of 0 must be excluded from the domain of that variable.

experimental probability (p. 782)   What actually occurs when conducting a probability experiment, or the ratio of relative frequency to the total number of events or trials.

elemento   **1.** Cada número u objeto de un conjunto. **2.** Cada entrada de una matriz.

eliminación   El uso de la adición o la sustracción para eliminar una variable y resolver así un sistema de ecuaciones.

estudio empírico   Ejecución repetida de un experimento, recopilación y combinación de datos y análisis de resultados.

equiprobable   Resultados que tienen la misma probabilidad de ocurrir.

ecuación   Enunciado matemático que contiene el signo de igualdad, =.

ecuación en dos variables   Una ecuación que tiene dos incógnitas.

ecuaciones equivalentes   Ecuaciones equivalentes poseen la misma solución.

expresiones equivalentes   Expresiones que denotan el mismo número.

evaluar   Calcular el valor de una expresión.

evento   Cualquier colección de uno o más resultados de un espacio muestral.

valores excluidos   Cualquier valor de una variable cuyo resultado sea un denominador igual a cero, debe excluirse del dominio de dicha variable.

probabilidad experimental   Lo que realmente sucede cuando se realiza un experimento probabilístico o la razón de la frecuencia relativa al número total de eventos o pruebas.

exponent (p. 7)   In an expression of the form x^n, the exponent is n. It indicates the number of times x is used as a factor.

exponential function (p. 554)   A function that can be described by an equation of the form $y = a^x$, where $a > 0$ and $a \neq 1$.

extraneous solutions (p. 601, 693)   Results that are not solutions to the original equation.

extremes (p. 156)   In the ratio $\frac{a}{b} = \frac{c}{d}$, a and d are the extremes.

exponente   En una expresión de la forma x^n, el exponente es n. Éste indica cuántas veces se usa x como factor.

función exponencial   Función que puede describirse mediante una ecuación de la forma $y = a^x$, donde $a > 0$ y $a \neq 1$.

soluciones extrañas   Resultados que no son soluciones de la ecuación original.

extremos   En la razón $\frac{a}{b} = \frac{c}{d}$, a y d son los extremos.

F

factored form (p. 475)   A monomial expressed as a product of prime numbers and variables and no variable has an exponent greater than 1.

factorial (p. 755)   The expression $n!$, read n factorial, where n is greater than zero, is the product of all positive integers beginning with n and counting backward to 1.

factoring (p. 481)   To express a polynomial as the product of monomials and polynomials.

factoring by grouping (p. 482)   The use of the Distributive Property to factor some polynomials having four or more terms.

factors (p. 6)   In an algebraic expression, the quantities being multiplied are called factors.

family of graphs (pp. 265, 531)   Graphs and equations of graphs that have at least one characteristic in common.

FOIL method (p. 453)   To multiply two binomials, find the sum of the products of the First terms, the Outer terms, the Inner terms, and the Last terms.

formula (p. 122)   An equation that states a rule for the relationship between certain quantities.

four-step problem-solving plan (p. 121)
Step 1   Explore the problem.
Step 2   Plan the solution.
Step 3   Solve the problem.
Step 4   Examine the solution.

frequency (pp. 88, 722)   How often a piece of data occurs.

frequency table (p. 722)   A table of tally marks used to record and display how often events occur.

function (pp. 43, 226)   A relation in which each element of the domain is paired with exactly one element of the range.

function notation (p. 227)   A way to name a function that is defined by an equation. In function notation, the equation $y = 3x - 8$ is written as $f(x) = 3x - 8$.

forma reducida   Monomio escrito como el producto de números primos y variables y en el que ninguna variable tiene un exponente mayor que 1.

factorial   La expresión $n!$, que se lee n factorial, donde n que es mayor que cero, es el producto de todos los números naturales, comenzando con n y contando hacia atrás hasta llegar al 1.

factorización   La escritura de un polinomio como producto de monomios y polinomios.

factorización por agrupamiento   Uso de la Propiedad distributiva para factorizar polinomios que poseen cuatro o más términos.

factores   En una expresión algebraica, los factores son las cantidades que se multiplican.

familia de gráficas   Gráficas y ecuaciones de gráficas que tienen al menos una característica común.

método FOIL   Para multiplicar dos binomios, busca la suma de los productos de los primeros (First) términos, los términos exteriores (Outer), los términos interiores (Inner) y los últimos términos (Last).

fórmula   Ecuación que establece una relación entre ciertas cantidades.

plan de cuatro pasos para resolver problemas
Paso 1   Explora el problema.
Paso 2   Planifica la solución.
Paso 3   Resuelve el problema.
Paso 4   Examina la solución.

frecuencia   Las veces que aparece un dato.

tabla de frecuencia   Una tabla de cuentas que se usa para anotar y exhibir la frecuencia de eventos.

función   Una relación en que a cada elemento del dominio le corresponde un único elemento del rango.

notación funcional   Una manera de nombrar una función definida por una ecuación. En notación funcional, la ecuación $y = 3x - 8$ se escribe $f(x) = 3x - 8$.

Fundamental Counting Principle (p. 755)   If an
event M can occur in m ways and is followed by
an event N that can occur in n ways, then the
event M followed by the event N can occur in
$m \times n$ ways.

Principio fundamental de contar   Si un evento M
puede ocurrir de m maneras y lo sigue un evento
N que puede ocurrir de n maneras, entonces el
evento M seguido del evento N puede ocurrir de
$m \times n$ maneras.

general equation for exponential decay (p. 562)
$y = C(1 - r)^t$, where y is the final amount, C is
the initial amount, r is the rate of decay expressed
as a decimal, and t is time.

ecuación general de desintegración exponencial
$y = C(1 - r)^t$, donde y es la cantidad final, C es la
cantidad inicial, r es la tasa de desintegración
escrita como decimal y t es el tiempo.

general equation for exponential growth (p. 561)
$y = C(1 + r)^t$, where y is the final amount, C is
the initial amount, r is the rate of change
expressed as a decimal, and t is time.

ecuación general de crecimiento exponencial
$y = C(1 + r)^t$, donde y es la cantidad final, C es
la cantidad inicial, r es la tasa de cambio del
crecimiento escrita como decimal y t es el tiempo.

geometric means (p. 570)   Missing terms between
two nonconsecutive terms in a geometric
sequence.

medios geométricos   Términos que faltan entre dos
términos no consecutivos de una sucesión
geométrica.

geometric sequence (p. 567)   A sequence in which
each term after the nonzero first term is found by
multiplying the previous term by a constant
called the common ratio r, where $r \neq 0$ or 1.

sucesión geométrica   Sucesión en que cada término
no nulo, después del primer término se calcula
multiplicando el término anterior por una
constante r llamada razón común, con $r \neq 0$ ó 1.

graph (pp. 69, 193) To draw, or plot, the points named
by certain numbers or ordered pairs on a number
line or coordinate plane.

graficar   Marcar los puntos que denotan ciertos
números en una recta numérica o ciertos pares
ordenados en un plano de coordenadas.

greatest common factor (GCF) (p. 476)   The product of
the prime factors common to two or more integers.

máximo común divisor (MCD)   El producto de
los factores primos comunes a dos o más enteros.

half-plane (p. 353)   The region of the graph of an
inequality on one side of a boundary.

semiplano   Región de la gráfica de una desigualdad
en un lado de la frontera.

histogram (p. 722)   A bar graph in which the data
are organized into equal intervals.

histograma   Una gráfica de barras en que los datos
aparecen organizados en intervalos iguales.

hypotenuse (p. 606)   The side
opposite the right angle in a
right triangle.

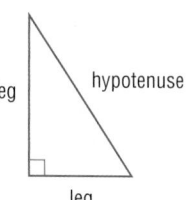

hipotenusa   Lado opuesto
al ángulo recto en un
triángulo rectángulo.

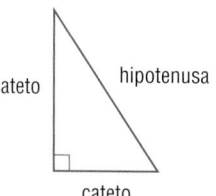

hypothesis (p. 37)   The part of a conditional
statement immediately following the word *if*.

hipótesis   Parte de un enunciado condicional que
sigue inmediatamente a la palabra *si*.

identity (p. 150)   An equation that is true for every
value of the variable.

identidad   Ecuación que es verdadera para cada
valor de la variable.

if-then statements (p. 37)   Conditional statements in
the form *If A, then B.*

enunciados si-entonces   Enunciados condicionales
de la forma *Si A, entonces B.*

image (p. 197)   The position of a figure after a
transformation.

imagen   Posición de una figura después de una
transformación.

inclusive (p. 771)   Two events that can occur at the
same time.

inclusivos   Dos eventos que pueden ocurrir
simultáneamente.

inconsistent (p. 369)   A system of equations with no
ordered pair that satisfy both equations.

inconsistente   Un sistema de ecuaciones para el cual
no existe par ordenado alguno que satisfaga
ambas ecuaciones.

independent (p. 369)   A system of equations with exactly one solution.

independent events (p. 769)   Two or more events in which the outcome of one event does not affect the outcome of the other events.

independent variable (p. 44)   The variable in a function whose value is subject to choice.

inductive reasoning (p. 240)   A conclusion based on a pattern of examples.

inequality (p. 17)   An open sentence that contains the symbol $<$, $\leq$, $>$, or $\geq$.

infinity (p. 68)   Lines and sets that never end continue to infinity.

integers (p. 68)   The set $\{\ldots, -2, -1, 0, 1, 2, \ldots\}$.

interquartile range (p. 732)   The difference between the Upper and Lower quartiles; represents the middle half of the data in the set.

intersection (p. 339)   The graph of a compound inequality containing *and*; the solution is the set of elements common to both inequalities.

inverse (p. 206)   The inverse of any relation is obtained by switching the coordinates in each ordered pair.

inverse variation (p. 642)   An equation of the form $xy = k$, where $k \neq 0$.

irrational numbers (p. 104)   Numbers that cannot be expressed as terminating or repeating decimals.

independiente   Un sistema de ecuaciones que posee una única solución.

eventos independientes   El resultado de un evento no afecta el resultado del otro evento.

variable independiente   La variable de una función sujeta a elección.

razonamiento inductivo   Conclusión basada en un patrón de ejemplos.

desigualdad   Enunciado abierto que contiene uno o más de los símbolos $<$, $\leq$, $>$ o $\geq$.

indefinidamente   Rectas y conjuntos interminables continúan indefinidamente.

enteros   El conjunto $\{\ldots, -2, -1, 0, 1, 2, \ldots\}$.

amplitud intercuartílica   Diferencia entre el cuartil superior y el inferior; representa la mitad central de los datos del conjunto.

intersección   Gráfica de una desigualdad compuesta que contiene la palabra *y*; la solución es el conjunto de soluciones de ambas desigualdades.

inversa   La inversa de una relación se halla intercambiando las coordenadas de cada par ordenado.

variación inversa   Ecuación de la forma $xy = k$, donde $k \neq 0$.

números irracionales   Números que no pueden escribirse como decimales terminales o periódicos.

L

least common denominator (LCD) (p. 678)   The least common multiple of the denominators of two or more fractions.

least common multiple (LCM) (p. 678)   The least number that is a common multiple of two or more numbers.

legs (p. 606)   The sides of a right triangle that form the right angle.

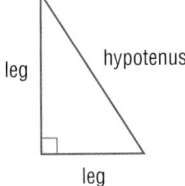

like terms (p. 28)   Terms that contain the same variables, with corresponding variables having the same exponent.

linear equation (p. 218)   An equation in the form $Ax + By = C$, whose graph is a straight line.

linear extrapolation (p. 283)   The use of a linear equation to predict values that are outside the range of data.

linear interpolation (p. 301)   The use of a linear equation to predict values that are inside of the data range.

mínimo denominador común (mcd)   El mínimo común múltiplo de los denominadores de dos o más fracciones.

mínimo común múltiplo (mcm)   El número menor que es múltiplo común de dos o más números.

catetos   Lados de un triángulo rectángulo que forman el ángulo recto del mismo.

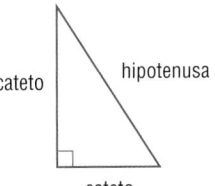

términos semejantes   Expresiones que tienen las mismas variables, con las variables correspondientes elevadas a los mismos exponentes.

ecuación lineal   Ecuación de la forma $Ax + By = C$, cuya gráfica es una recta.

extrapolación lineal   Uso de una ecuación lineal para predecir valores fuera de la amplitud de los datos.

interpolación lineal   Uso de una ecuación lineal para predecir valores dentro de la amplitud de los datos.

line graph (p. 51)   Numerical data displayed to show trends or changes over time.

line of fit (p. 304)   A line that describes the trend of the data in a scatter plot.

line plot (p. 88)   A number line labeled with a scale to include all the data with an × placed above a data point each time it occurs.

lower quartile (p. 732)   Divides the lower half of the data into two equal parts.

gráfica lineal   Datos numéricos exhibidos para mostrar tendencias o cambios con el tiempo.

recta de ajuste   Recta que describe la tendencia de los datos en una gráfica de dispersión.

esquema lineal   Recta numérica marcada con una escala que incluye todos los datos, colocando × sobre cada uno de ellos para indicar su frecuencia.

cuartil inferior   Éste divide en dos partes iguales la mitad inferior de un conjunto de datos.

M

mapping (p. 205)   Illustrates how each element of the domain is paired with an element in the range.

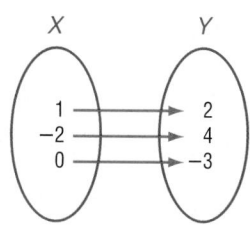

aplicaciones   Ilustra la correspondencia entre cada elemento del dominio con un elemento del rango.

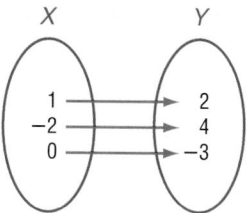

matrix (p. 715)   A rectangular arrangement of numbers in rows and columns.

maximum (p. 525)   The highest point on the graph of a curve.

measures of central tendency (p. 90)   Numbers or pieces of data that can represent the whole set of data.

measures of variation (p. 731)   Measures that describe the spread of the values in a set of data.

minimum (p. 524)   The lowest point on the graph of a curve.

mixed expression (p. 684)   An expression that contains the sum of a monomial and a rational expression.

mixture problems (p. 171)   Problems in which two or more parts are combined into a whole.

monomial (p. 410)   A number, a variable, or a product of a number and one or more variables.

multiplicative identity (p. 22)   For any number $a, a \cdot 1 = 1 \cdot a = a$.

multiplicative inverses (p. 22)   Two numbers whose product is 1.

multi-step equations (p. 143)   Equations with more than one operation.

mutually exclusive (p. 771)   Events that cannot occur at the same time.

matriz   Un arreglo rectangular de números en filas y columnas.

máximo   El punto más alto en la gráfica de una curva.

medidas de tendencia central   Números o datos que pueden representar todo el conjunto de datos.

medidas de variación   Medidas que describen la dispersión de los valores de un conjunto de datos.

mínimo   El punto más bajo en la gráfica de una curva.

expresión mixta   Expresión que contiene la suma de un monomio y una expresión racional.

problemas de mezclas   Problemas en que dos o más partes se combinan en un todo.

monomio   Número, variable o producto de un número por una o más variables.

identidad de la multiplicación   Para cualquier número $a, a \cdot 1 = 1 \cdot a = a$.

inversos multiplicativos   Dos números cuyo producto es igual a 1.

ecuaciones de varios pasos   Ecuaciones con más de una operación.

mutuamente exclusivos   Eventos que no pueden ocurrir simultáneamente.

N

natural numbers (p. 68)   The set $\{1, 2, 3, \ldots\}$.

negative correlation (p. 298)   In a scatter plot, as x increases, y decreases.

negative exponent (p. 419)   For any nonzero number a and any integer n, $a^{-n} = \frac{1}{a^n}$ and $\frac{1}{a^{-n}} = a^n$.

números naturales   El conjunto $\{1, 2, 3, \ldots\}$.

correlación negativa   En una gráfica de dispersión, a medida que x aumenta, y disminuye.

exponente negativo   Para cualquier número no nulo a y cualquier entero n, $a^{-n} = \frac{1}{a^n}$ y $\frac{1}{a^{-n}} = a^n$.

negative number (p. 68)   Any value less than zero.

number theory (p. 144)   The study of numbers and the relationships between them.

número negativo   Cualquier valor menor que cero.

teoría de números   El estudio de números y de las relaciones entre ellos.

O

odds (p. 97)   The ratio that compares the number of ways an event can occur (successes) to the number of ways the event cannot occur (failures).

open sentence (p. 16)   A mathematical statement with one or more variables.

opposites (p. 74)   Every positive rational number and its negative pair.

ordered pair (p. 43)   A set of numbers or coordinates used to locate any point on a coordinate plane, written in the form (x, y).

order of operations (p. 11)
1. Evaluate expressions inside grouping symbols.
2. Evaluate all powers.
3. Do all multiplications and/or divisions from left to right.
4. Do all additions and/or subtractions from left to right.

origin (p. 43)   The point where the two axes intersect at their zero points.

outlier (p. 733)   Any element of a set of data that is at least 1.5 interquartile ranges less than the lower quartile or greater than the upper quartile.

posibilidades   Razón que compara el número de maneras en que puede ocurrir un evento (éxitos) al número de maneras en que no puede ocurrir (fracasos).

enunciado abierto   Un enunciado matemático que contiene una o más variables.

opuestos   Cada número racional positivo y su opuesto negativo.

par ordenado   Un par de números que se usa para ubicar cualquier punto de un plano de coordenadas y que se escribe en la forma (x, y).

orden de las operaciones
1. Evalúa las expresiones dentro de los símbolos de agrupamiento.
2. Evalúa todas las potencias.
3. Multiplica o divide de izquierda a derecha.
4. Suma o resta de izquierda a derecha.

origen   Punto donde se intersecan los dos ejes en sus puntos cero.

valor atípico   Cualquier dato que está por lo menos a 1.5 amplitudes intercuartílicas debajo del cuartil inferior o por encima del cuartil superior.

P

parabola (p. 524)   The graph of a quadratic function.

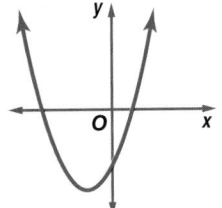

parábola   La gráfica de una función cuadrática.

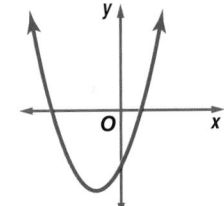

parallel lines (p. 292)   Lines in the same plane that never intersect and have the same slope.

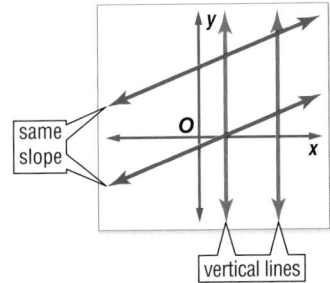

rectas paralelas   Rectas en el mismo plano que no se intersecan jamás y que tienen pendientes iguales.

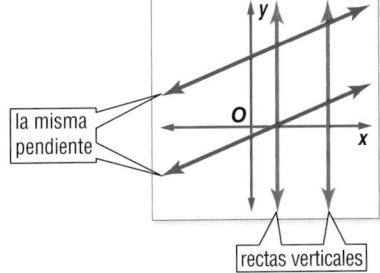

parent graph (p. 265)   The simplest of the graphs in a family of graphs.

percent of change (p. 160)   When an increase or decrease is expressed as a percent.

gráfica madre   La gráfica más sencilla en una familia de gráficas.

porcentaje de cambio   Cuando un aumento o disminución se escribe como un tanto por ciento.

percent of decrease (p. 160)   The ratio of an amount of decrease to the previous amount, expressed as a percent.

percent of increase (p. 160)   The ratio of an amount of increase to the previous amount, expressed as a percent.

percentile (p. 743)   The point below which a given percent of the data lies.

perfect square (p. 103)   A number whose square root is a rational number.

perfect square trinomial (p. 508)   Trinomials that are the square of a binomial. $(a + b)^2 = (a + b)(a + b) = a^2 + 2ab + b^2$ or $(a - b)^2 = (a - b)(a - b) = a^2 - 2ab - b^2$

permutation (p. 760)   An arrangement or listing in which order is important.

perpendicular lines (p. 293)   Lines that meet to form right angles.

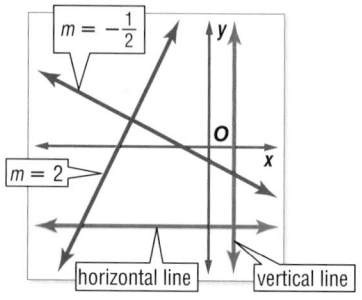

point-slope form (p. 286)   An equation of the form $y - y_1 = m(x - x_1)$, where m is the slope and (x_1, y_1) is a given point on a nonvertical line.

polynomial (p. 432)   A monomial or sum of monomials.

population (p. 708)   A large group of data usually represented by a sample.

positive correlation (p. 298)   In a scatter plot, as x increases, y increases.

positive number (p. 68)   Any value that is greater than zero.

power (p. 7)   An expression of the form x^n, read x to the nth power.

power of a quotient (p. 418)   For any integer m and real numbers a and b, $b \neq 0$, $\left(\dfrac{a}{b}\right)^m = \dfrac{a^m}{b^m}$.

preimage (p. 197)   The position of a figure before a transformation.

prime factorization (p. 475)   A whole number expressed as a product of factors that are all prime numbers.

prime number (p. 474)   A whole number, greater than 1, whose only factors are 1 and itself.

prime polynomial (p. 497)   A polynomial that cannot be written as a product of two polynomials with integral coefficients.

porcentaje de disminución   Razón de la cantidad de disminución a la cantidad original, escrita como un tanto por ciento.

porcentaje de aumento   Razón de la cantidad de aumento a la cantidad original, escrita como un tanto por ciento.

percentil   Punto bajo el cual yace un tanto por ciento de los datos.

cuadrado perfecto   Número cuya raíz cuadrada es un número racional.

trinomio cuadrado perfecto   Trinomios que son el cuadrado de un binomio. $(a + b)^2 = (a + b)(a + b) = a^2 + 2ab + b^2$ o $(a - b)^2 = (a - b)(a - b) = a^2 - 2ab - b^2$

permutación   Arreglo o lista en que el orden es importante.

rectas perpendiculares   Rectas que se intersecan formando un ángulo recto.

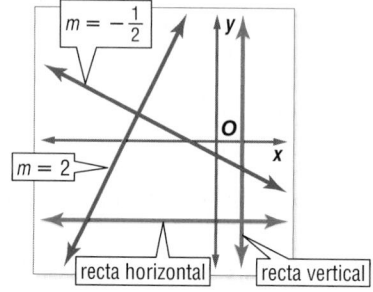

forma punto-pendiente   Ecuación de la forma $y - y_1 = m(x - x_1)$, donde m es la pendiente y (x_1, y_1) es un punto dado de una recta no vertical.

polinomio   Un monomio o la suma de monomios.

población   Grupo grande de datos, representado por lo general por una muestra.

correlación positiva   En una gráfica de dispersión, a medida que x aumenta, y aumenta.

número positivos   Cualquier valor mayor que cero.

potencia   Una expresión de la forma x^n, se lee x a la *enésima potencia*.

potencia de un cociente   Para cualquier entero m y números reales a y b, $b \neq 0$, $\left(\dfrac{a}{b}\right)^m = \dfrac{a^m}{b^m}$.

preimagen   Posición de una figura antes de una transformación.

factorización prima   Número entero escrito como producto de factores primos.

número primo   Número entero mayor que 1 cuyos únicos factores son 1 y sí mismo.

polinomio primo   Polinomio que no puede escribirse como producto de dos polinomios con coeficientes enteros.

principal square root (p. 103)   The nonnegative square root of a number.

probability (p. 96)   The ratio of the number of favorable outcomes for an event to the number of possible outcomes of the event.

$$P(a) = \frac{\text{number of favorable outcomes}}{\text{total number of possible outcomes}}.$$

probability distribution (p. 777)   The probability of every possible value of the random variable x.

probability histogram (p. 778)   A way to give the probability distribution for a random variable and obtain other data.

product (p. 6)   In an algebraic expression, the result of quantities being multiplied is called the product.

proportion (p. 155)   An equation of the form $\frac{a}{b} = \frac{c}{d}$ stating that two ratios are equivalent.

Pythagorean Theorem (p. 606)   If a and b are the measures of the legs of a right triangle and c is the measure of the hypotenuse, then $c^2 = a^2 + b^2$.

Pythagorean triple (p. 607)   Whole numbers that satisfy the Pythagorean Theorem.

raíz cuadrada principal   La raíz cuadrada no negativa de un número.

probabilidad   Razón del número de resultados favorables de un evento al número de resultados posibles.

$$P(a) = \frac{\text{número de resultados favorables}}{\text{número total de resultados posibles}}.$$

distribución de probabilidad   Probabilidad de cada valor posible de una variable aleatoria x.

histograma probabilístico   Una manera de exhibir la distribución de probabilidad de una variable aleatoria y obtener otros datos.

producto   En una expresión algebraica, se llama producto al resultado de las cantidades que se multiplican.

proporción   Ecuación de la forma $\frac{a}{b} = \frac{c}{d}$ que afirma la equivalencia de dos razones.

Teorema de Pitágoras   Si a y b son las longitudes de los catetos de un triángulo rectángulo y si c es la longitud de la hipotenusa, entonces $c^2 = a^2 + b^2$.

Triple pitagórico   Números enteros que satisfacen el Teorema de Pitágoras.

Q

quadrants (p. 193)   The four regions into which the x- and y-axes separate the coordinate plane.

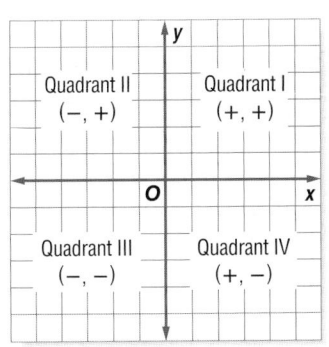

cuadrantes   Las cuatro regiones en las que los ejes x y y dividen el plano de coordenadas.

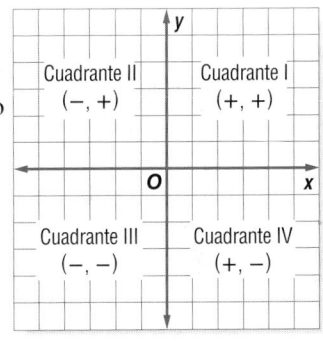

quadratic equation (p. 533)   An equation of the form $ax^2 + bx + c = 0$, where $a \neq 0$.

Quadratic Formula (p. 546)   The solutions of a quadratic equation in the form $ax^2 + bx + c = 0$, where $a \neq 0$, are given by the formula
$$x = \frac{-b \pm \sqrt{b^2 - 4ac}}{2a}.$$

quadratic function (p. 524)   An equation of the form $y = ax^2 + bx + c$, where $a \neq 0$.

quartiles (p. 732)   Values that divide the data into four equal parts.

ecuación cuadrática   Ecuación de la forma $ax^2 + bx + c = 0$, donde $a \neq 0$.

Fórmula cuadrática   Las soluciones de una ecuación cuadrática de la forma $ax^2 + bx + c = 0$, donde $a \neq 0$, vienen dadas por la fórmula
$$x = \frac{-b \pm \sqrt{b^2 - 4ac}}{2a}.$$

función cuadrática   Función de la forma $y = ax^2 + bx + c$, donde $a \neq 0$.

cuartiles   Valores que dividen un conjunto de datos en cuatro partes iguales.

R

radical equations (p. 600)   Equations that contain radicals with variables in the radicand.

radical sign (p. 103)   The symbol $\sqrt{\ }$, used to indicate a nonnegative square root.

ecuaciones radicales   Ecuaciones que contienen radicales con variables en el radicando.

signo radical   El símbolo $\sqrt{\ }$, que se usa para indicar la raíz cuadrada no negativa.

radicand (p. 587)   The expression that is under the radical sign.

random sample (p. 708)   A sample that is chosen without any preference, representative of the entire population.

random variable (p. 777)   A variable whose value is the numerical outcome of a random event.

range (p. 45)   The set of second numbers of the ordered pairs in a relation.

range (p. 731)   The difference between the greatest and the least values of a set of data.

rate (p. 157)   The ratio of two measurements having different units of measure.

rate of change (p. 258)   How a quantity is changing over time.

ratio (p. 155)   A comparison of two numbers by division.

rational approximation (p. 105)   A rational number that is close to, but not equal to, the value of an irrational number.

rational equations (p. 690)   Equations that contain rational expressions.

rational expression (p. 648)   An algebraic fraction whose numerator and denominator are polynomials.

rationalizing the denominator (p. 589)   A method used to eliminate radicals from the denominator of a fraction.

rational numbers (p. 68)   The set of numbers expressed in the form of a fraction $\frac{a}{b}$, where a and b are integers and $b \neq 0$.

real numbers (p. 104)   The set of rational numbers and the set of irrational numbers together.

reciprocal (p. 21)   The multiplicative inverse of a number.

reflection (p. 197)   A type of transformation in which a figure is flipped over a line.

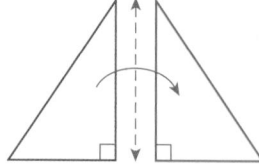

relation (p. 45)   A set of ordered pairs.

relative frequency (p. 782)   The number of times an outcome occurred in a probability experiment.

replacement set (p. 16)   A set of numbers from which replacements for a variable may be chosen.

roots (p. 533)   The solutions of a quadratic equation.

radicando   La expresión debajo del signo radical.

muestra aleatoria   Muestra tomada sin preferencia alguna y que es representativa de toda la población.

variable aleatoria   Una variable cuyos valores son los resultados numéricos de un evento aleatorio.

rango   Conjunto de los segundos números de los pares ordenados de una relación.

amplitud   Diferencia entre los valores máximo y mínimo de un conjunto de datos.

tasa   Razón de dos medidas que tienen distintas unidades de medida.

tasa de cambio   Cómo cambia una cantidad con el tiempo.

razón   Comparación de dos números mediante división.

aproximación racional   Número racional que está cercano, pero que no es igual, al valor de un número irracional.

ecuaciones racionales   Ecuaciones que contienen expresiones racionales.

expresión racional   Fracción algebraica cuyo numerador y denominador son polinomios.

racionalizar el denominador   Método que se usa para eliminar radicales del denominador de una fracción.

números racionales   Conjunto de los números que pueden escribirse en forma de fracción $\frac{a}{b}$, donde a y b son enteros y $b \neq 0$.

números reales   El conjunto de los números racionales junto con el conjunto de los números irracionales.

recíproco   Inverso multiplicativo de un número.

reflexión   Tipo de transformación en que una figura se voltea a través de una recta.

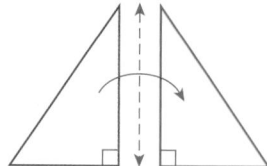

relación   Conjunto de pares ordenados.

frecuencia relativa   Número de veces que aparece un resultado en un experimento probabilístico.

conjunto de sustitución   Conjunto de números del cual se pueden escoger sustituciones para una variable.

raíces   Las soluciones de una ecuación cuadrática.

rotation (p. 197)   A type of transformation in which a figure is turned around a point.

rotación   Tipo de transformación en que una figura se hace girar alrededor de un punto fijo.

S

sample (p. 708)   Some portion of a larger group selected to represent that group.

muestra   Porción de un grupo más grande que se escoge para representarlo.

sample space (pp. 96, 754)   The list of all possible outcomes.

espacio muestral   Lista de todos los resultados posibles.

scalar multiplication (p. 717)   Each element is multiplied by the scalar, or constant, and a new matrix is formed.
$$m = \begin{bmatrix} a & b & c \\ d & e & f \end{bmatrix} = \begin{bmatrix} ma & mb & mc \\ md & me & mf \end{bmatrix}$$

multiplicación escalar   Cada elemento se multiplica por el escalar o constante, formándose así una nueva matriz.
$$m = \begin{bmatrix} a & b & c \\ d & e & f \end{bmatrix} = \begin{bmatrix} ma & mb & mc \\ md & me & mf \end{bmatrix}$$

scale (p. 157)   A ratio or rate used when making a model of something that is too large or too small to be conveniently shown at actual size.

escala   Razón o tasa que se usa al construir un modelo de algo que es demasiado grande o pequeño como para mostrarlo de tamaño natural.

scatter plot (p. 298)   Two sets of data plotted as ordered pairs in a coordinate plane.

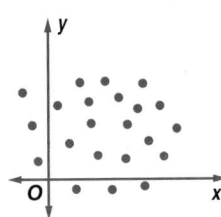

gráfica de dispersión   Dos conjuntos de datos graficados como pares ordenados en un plano de coordenadas.

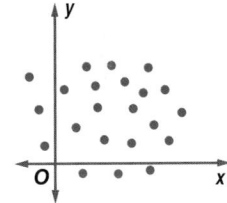

scientific notation (p. 425)   A number of the form $a \times 10^n$, where $1 \le a < 10$ and n is an integer.

notación científica   Número de la forma $a \times 10^n$, donde $1 \le a < 10$ y n es un entero.

sequence (p. 233)   A set of numbers in a specific order.

sucesión   Conjunto de números en un orden específico.

set (p. 16)   A collection of objects or numbers, often shown using braces { } and usually named by a capital letter.

conjunto   Colección de objetos o números, que a menudo se exhiben usando paréntesis de corchete { } y que se identifican por lo general mediante una letra mayúscula .

set-builder notation (p. 319)   A concise way of writing a solution set. For example, $\{t \mid t < 17\}$ represents the set of all numbers t such that t is less than 17.

notación de construcción de conjuntos   Manera concisa de escribir un conjunto solución. Por ejemplo, $\{t \mid t < 17\}$ representa el conjunto de todos los números t que son menores o iguales que 17.

similar (p. 617)   Having the same shape but not necessarily the same size.

semejantes   Que tienen la misma forma, pero no necesariamente el mismo tamaño.

simple event (pp. 96, 769)   A single event.

evento simple   Un sólo evento.

simple random sample (p. 708)   A sample that is as likely to be chosen as any other from the population.

muestra aleatoria simple   Muestra de una población que tiene la misma probabilidad de escogerse que cualquier otra.

simplest form (p. 29)   An expression is in simplest form when it is replaced by an equivalent expression having no like terms or parentheses.

forma reducida   Una expresión está reducida cuando se puede sustituir por una expresión equivalente que no tiene ni términos semejantes ni paréntesis.

simulation (p. 783)   Using an object to act out an event that would be difficult or impractical to perform.

simulación   Uso de un objeto para representar un evento que pudiera ser difícil o poco práctico de ejecutar.

sine (p. 624)   In a right triangle with acute angle A, the sine of $\angle A = \dfrac{\text{measure of leg opposite } \angle A}{\text{measure of hypotenuse}}$.

seno   En un triángulo rectángulo con ángulo agudo A, el seno del $\angle A = \dfrac{\text{medida del cateto opuesto a } \angle A}{\text{medida de la hipotenusa}}$.

slope (p. 256)   The ratio of the change in the y-coordinates (rise) to the corresponding change in the x-coordinates (run) as you move from one point to another along a line.

pendiente   Razón del cambio en la coordenada y (elevación) al cambio correspondiente en la coordenada x (desplazamiento) a medida que uno se mueve de un punto a otro en una recta.

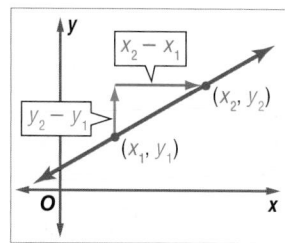

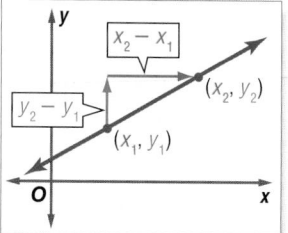

slope-intercept form (p. 272)   An equation of the form $y = mx + b$, where m is the slope and b is the y-intercept.

forma pendiente-intersección   Ecuación de la forma $y = mx + b$, donde m es la pendiente y b es la intersección y.

solution (pp. 16, 212)   A replacement value for the variable in an open sentence.

solución   Valor de sustitución de la variable en un enunciado abierto.

solution set (p. 16)   The set of elements from the replacement set that make an open sentence true.

conjunto solución   Conjunto de elementos del conjunto de sustitución que hacen verdadero un enunciado abierto.

solve an equation (p. 129)   The process of finding all values of the variable that make the equation a true statement.

resolver una ecuación   Proceso en que se hallan todos los valores de la variable que hacen verdadera la ecuación.

solving an open sentence (p. 16)   Finding a replacement value for the variable that results in a true sentence or an ordered pair that results in a true statement when substituted into the equation.

resolver un enunciado abierto   Hallar un valor de sustitución de la variable que resulte en un enunciado verdadero o un par ordenado que resulte en una proposición verdadera cuando se lo sustituye en la ecuación.

solving a triangle (p. 626)   Finding all of the measures of the sides and the angles in a right triangle.

resolver un triángulo   Hallar las medidas de todos los lados y ángulos de un triángulo rectángulo.

square root (p. 103)   One of two equal factors of a number.

raíz cuadrada   Uno de dos factores iguales de un número.

standard form (p. 218)   The standard form of a linear equation is $Ax + By = C$, where $A \geq 0$, and A and B are not both zero, and A, B, and C are integers whose greatest common factor is 1.

forma estándar   La forma estándar de una ecuación lineal es $Ax + By = C$, donde $A \geq 0$ y ni A ni B son ambos cero y A, B, y C son enteros cuyo máximo común divisor es 1.

stem-and-leaf plot (p. 89)   A system used to separate data into two numbers that are used to form a stem and a leaf.

diagrama de tallo y hojas   Sistema que se usa para separar datos en dos números que se usan para formar un tallo y una hoja.

stratified random sample (p. 708)   A sample in which the population is first divided into similar, nonoverlapping groups; a simple random sample is then selected from each group.

muestra aleatoria estratificada   Muestra en que la población se divide en grupos similares que no se sobreponen; luego se selecciona una muestra aleatoria simple, de cada grupo.

symmetry (p. 525)   A geometric property of figures that can be folded and each half matches the other exactly.

simetría   Propiedad geométrica de figuras que pueden plegarse de modo que cada mitad corresponde exactamente a la otra.

system of equations (p. 369)   A set of equations with the same variables.

sistema de ecuaciones   Conjunto de ecuaciones con las mismas variables.

system of inequalities (p. 394)   A set of two or more inequalities with the same variables.

sistema de desigualdades   Conjunto de dos o más desigualdades con las mismas variables.

systematic random sample (p. 708) A sample in which the items in the sample are selected according to a specified time or item interval.

muestra aleatoria sistemática Muestra en que los elementos de la muestra se escogen según un intervalo de tiempo o elemento específico.

T

tangent (p. 624) In a right triangle with acute angle A, the tangent cosine of

$$\angle A = \frac{\text{measure of leg opposite } \angle A}{\text{measure of leg adjacent to } \angle A}.$$

tangente En un triángulo rectángulo con ángulo agudo A, el coseno tangente de

$$\angle A = \frac{\text{medida del cateto opuesto a } \angle A}{\text{medida del cateto adyacente a } \angle A}.$$

term (p. 28) A number, a variable, or a product or quotient of numbers and variables.

término Número, variable o producto, o cociente de números y variables.

terms (p. 233) The numbers in a sequence.

términos Los números de una sucesión.

theoretical probability (p. 782) What should happen in a probability experiment.

probabilidad teórica Lo que debería ocurrir en un experimento probabilístico.

transformation (p. 197) Movements of geometric figures.

transformación Desplazamiento de figuras geométricas.

translation (p. 197)
A transformation in which a figure is slid in any direction.

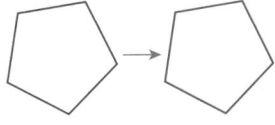

translación
Transformación en que una figura se desliza en cualquier dirección.

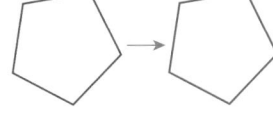

tree diagram (p. 754) A diagram used to show the total number of possible outcomes.

diagrama de árbol Diagrama que se usa para mostrar el número total de resultados posibles.

trigonometric ratios (p. 624) The ratios of the measures of two sides of a right triangle.

razones trigonométricas Razones de las longitudes de dos lados de un triángulo rectángulo.

trinomials (p. 432) The sum of three monomials.

trinomios Suma de tres monomios.

U

uniform motion problems (p. 172) Problems in which an object moves at a certain speed, or rate.

problemas de movimiento uniforme Problemas en que el cuerpo se mueve a cierta velocidad o tasa.

union (p. 340) The graph of a compound inequality containing *or*; the solution is a solution of either inequality, not necessarily both.

unión Gráfica de una desigualdad compuesta que contiene la palabra *o*; la solución es el conjunto de soluciones de por lo menos una de las desigualdades, no necesariamente ambas.

upper quartile (p. 732) The median of the upper half of a set of numbers.

cuartil superior La mediana de la mitad superior de un conjunto de datos.

V

variable (p. 6) Symbols used to represent unspecified numbers or values.

variable Símbolos que se usan para representar números o valores no especificados.

vertex (p. 525) The maximum or minimum point of a parabola.

vértice Punto máximo o mínimo de una parábola.

vertical line test (p. 227) If any vertical line passes through no more than one point of the graph of a relation, then the relation is a function.

prueba de la recta vertical Si cualquier recta vertical pasa por un sólo punto de la gráfica de una relación, entonces la relación es una función.

voluntary response sample (p. 709) A sample that involves only those who want to participate.

muestra de respuesta voluntaria Muestra que involucra sólo aquellos que quieren participar.

W

weighted average (p. 171) The sum of the product of the number of units and the value per unit divided by the sum of the number of units, represented by M.

promedio ponderado Suma del producto del número de unidades por el valor unitario dividida entre la suma del número de unidades y la cual se denota por M.

whole numbers (p. 68)   The set {0, 1, 2, 3, …}.

números enteros   El conjunto {0, 1, 2, 3, …}.

X

x-axis (p. 43)
   The horizontal
   number line on a
   coordinate plane.

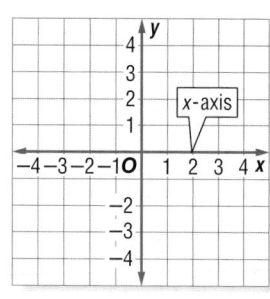

eje x   Recta numérica
   horizontal que forma
   parte de un plano de
   coordenadas.

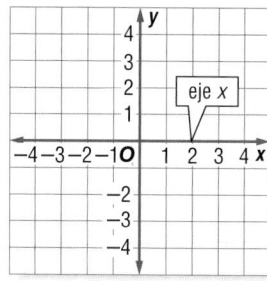

x-coordinate (p. 43)   The first number in an ordered pair.

coordenada x   El primer número de un par ordenado.

x-intercept (p. 220)   The coordinate at which a graph intersects the x-axis.

intersección x   Punto o puntos en los que una gráfica interseca el eje x.

Y

y-axis (p. 43)
   The vertical
   number line on a
   coordinate plane.

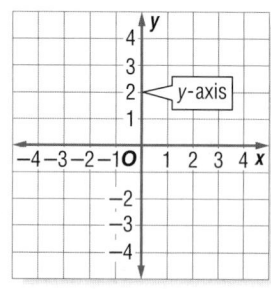

eje y   Recta numérica
   vertical que forma
   parte de un plano de
   coordenadas.

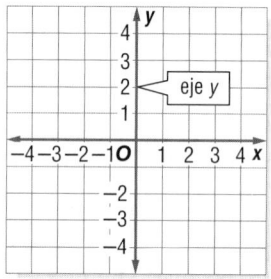

y-coordinate (p. 43)   The second number in an ordered pair.

coordenada y   El segundo número de un par ordenado.

y-intercept (p. 220)   The coordinate at which a graph intersects the y-axis.

intersección y   Punto o puntos en los que una gráfica interseca el eje y.

Z

zero exponent (p. 419)   For any nonzero number a, $a^0 = 1$.

exponente cero   Para cualquier número no nulo a, $a^0 = 1$.

zeros (p. 533)   The roots, or x-intercepts, of a quadratic function.

ceros   Las raíces o intersecciones x de una función cuadrática.

Selected Answers

Chapter 1   The Language of Algebra

Page 5   Chapter 1   Getting Started
1. 64   **3.** 162   **5.** 19   **7.** 24   **9.** 16.6 m   **11.** $5\frac{1}{2}$ ft   **13.** 7.2
15. 1.8   **17.** 9   **19.** $\frac{5}{12}$

Pages 8–9   Lesson 1-1
1. Algebraic expressions include variables and numbers, while verbal expressions contain words.   **3.** Sample answer: a^5 **5.** Sample answer: $3x - 24$ **7.** 256   **9.** one half of n cubed   **11.** $35 + z$ **13.** $16p$ **15.** $49 + 2x$ **17.** $\frac{2}{3}x^2$
19. $s + 12d$ **21.** 36   **23.** 81   **25.** 243   **27.** 1,000,000
29. $8.5b + 3.99d$ **31.** 7 times p **33.** three cubed   **35.** three times x squared plus four   **37.** a to the fourth power times b squared   **39.** Sample answer: one-fifth 12 times z squared
41. 3 times x squared minus 2 times x **43.** $x + \frac{1}{11}x$ **45.** $3.5m$
47. You can use the expression $4s$ to find the perimeter of a baseball diamond. Answers should include the following.

- four times the length of the sides and the sum of the four sides
- $s + s + s + s$

49. B   **51.** 6.76   **53.** 3.2   **55.** $\frac{7}{12}$ **57.** $\frac{7}{6}$ or $1\frac{1}{6}$

Pages 13–15   Lesson 1-2
1. Sample answer: First add the numbers in parentheses, $(2 + 5)$. Next square 6. Then multiply 7 by 3. Subtract inside the brackets. Multiply that by 8. Divide, then add 3.
3. Chase; Laurie raised the incorrect quantity to the second power.   **5.** 26   **7.** 51   **9.** $\frac{11}{100}$ **11.** 160   **13.** $20.00 + 2 \times 9.95$
15. 12   **17.** 21   **19.** 0   **21.** 4   **23.** 8   **25.** 6   **27.** $\frac{87}{2}$
or $43\frac{1}{2}$ **29.** 44 cm^2 **31.** $1625   **33.** 1763   **35.** 24   **37.** 253
39. $\frac{37}{8}$ or $4\frac{5}{8}$ **41.** the sum of salary, commission, and

4 bonuses   **43.** $54,900   **45.** Use the order of operations to determine how many extra hours were used then how much the extra hours cost. Then find the total cost. Answers should include the following.

- $6[4.95 + 0.99(n)] - 25.00$
- You can use an expression to calculate a specific value without calculating all possible values.

47. B   **49.** 2.074377092   **51.** $a^3 \cdot b^4$ **53.** $a + b + \frac{b}{a}$
55. $3(55 - w^3)$ **57.** 12   **59.** 256   **61.** 12 less than q squared
63. x cubed divided by nine   **65.** 7.212   **67.** 14.7775
69. $3\frac{11}{35}$ **71.** 36

Pages 18–20   Lesson 1-3
1. Sample answer: An open sentence contains an equals sign or inequality sign.   **3.** Sample answer: An open sentence has at least one variable because it is neither true nor false until specific values are used for the variable.
5. 15   **7.** 1.6   **9.** 3   **11.** {2, 2.5, 3}   **13.** 1000 Calories   **15.** 12
17. 3   **19.** 18   **21.** $1\frac{1}{2}$ **23.** 1.4   **25.** 5.3   **27.** $22.50
29. 11.05   **31.** 5   **33.** 9   **35.** 36   **37.** {6, 7}   **39.** {10, 15, 20,
25}   **41.** {3.4, 3.6, 3.8, 4}   **43.** $\left\{0, \frac{1}{3}, \frac{2}{3}, 1, 1\frac{1}{3}\right\}$ **45.** $g = 15,579$
$+ 6220 + 18,995$ **47.** $39n + 10.95 \le 102.50$

49. The solution set includes all numbers less than or equal to $\frac{1}{3}$.   **51.** B   **53.** $r^2 + 3s$; 19   **55.** $(r + s)t^2$; $\frac{7}{4}$ **57.** 173
59. 50,628   **61.** $\frac{4}{21}$ **63.** $\frac{2}{7}$ **65.** $\frac{16}{63}$ **67.** $\frac{16}{75}$

Page 21   Practice Quiz 1
1. twenty less than x **3.** a cubed   **5.** 28   **7.** 29   **9.** 8

Pages 23–25   Lesson 1-4
1. no; $3 + 1 \ne 3$ **3.** Sample answer: You cannot divide by zero.   **5.** Additive Identity; 17
7. $6(12 - 48 \div 4)$
$= 6(12 - 12)$ Substitution
$= 6(0)$ Substitution
$= 0$ Multiplicative Property of Zero
9. $4(20) + 7$ **11.** 87 yr   **13.** Multiplicative Identity; 5
15. Reflexive; 0.25   **17.** Additive Identity; $\frac{1}{3}$
19. Multiplicative Inverse; 1   **21.** Substitution; 3
23. Multiplicative Identity; 2
25. $\frac{2}{3}[3 \div (2 \cdot 1)]$

$= \frac{2}{3}(3 \div 2)$ Multiplicative Identity

$= \frac{2}{3} \cdot \frac{3}{2}$ Substitution

$= 1$ Multiplicative Inverse
27. $6 \cdot \frac{1}{6} + 5(12 \div 4 - 3)$

$= 6 \cdot \frac{1}{6} + 5(3 - 3)$ Substitution

$= 6 \cdot \frac{1}{6} + 5(0)$ Substitution

$= 6 \cdot \frac{1}{6} + 0$ Mult. Property of Zero

$= 1 + 0$ Multiplicative Inverse
$= 1$ Additive Identity
29. $7 - 8(9 - 3^2)$
$= 7 - 8(9 - 9)$ Substitution
$= 7 - 8(0)$ Substitution
$= 7 - 0$ Mult. Property of Zero
$= 7$ Additive Identity
31. $25(5 - 3) + 80(2.5 - 1) + 40(10 - 6)$
$= 25(2) + 80(2.5 - 1) + 40(10 - 6)$ Substitution
$= 25(2) + 80(1.5) + 40(10 - 6)$ Substitution
$= 25(2) + 80(1.5) + 40(4)$ Substitution
$= 50 + 120 + 160$ Substitution
$= 330$ Substitution
33. $1653y = 1653$, where $y = 1$ **35.** $8(100,000 + 50,000 + 400,000) + 3(50,000 + 50,000 + 400,000) + 4(50,000 + 50,000 + 400,000)$ **37.** Sometimes; Sample answer: true: $x = 2, y = 1, z = 4, w = 3; 2 \cdot 4 > 1 \cdot 3$; false: $x = 1, y = -1, z = -2, w = -3; 1(-2) < (-1)(-3)$ **39.** A   **41.** False; $4 - 5 = -1$, which is not a whole number.   **43.** False; $1 \div 2 = \frac{1}{2}$, which is not a whole number.   **45.** {11, 12, 13}
47. {3, 3.25, 3.5, 3.75, 4}   **49.** $\left\{1\frac{1}{4}\right\}$ **51.** 20   **53.** 31   **55.** 29
57. 80   **59.** 28   **61.** 10

Pages 29–31   Lesson 1-5
1. Sample answer: The numbers inside the parentheses are each multiplied by the number outside the parentheses then the products are added.   **3.** Courtney; Ben forgot that w^4 is really $1 \cdot w^4$.   **5.** $8 + 2t$ **7.** 1632   **9.** $14m$

11. simplified   **13.** 12(19.95 + 2)   **15.** 96   **17.** 48
19. $6x + 18$ **21.** $8 + 2x$ **23.** $28y - 4$ **25.** $ab - 6a$
27. $2a - 6b + 4c$ **29.** 4(110,000 + 17,500)   **31.** 485   **33.** 102
35. 38   **37.** 12(5 + 12 + 18)   **39.** 6(78 + 20 + 12)
41. $1956   **43.** $9b$ **45.** $17a^2$ **47.** $45x - 75$ **49.** $7y^3 + y^4$
51. $30m + 5n$ **53.** $\frac{8}{5}a$ **55.** You can use the Distributive
Property to calculate quickly by expressing any number as
a sum or difference of more convenient numbers. Answers
should include the following.
- Both methods result in the correct method. In one
  method you multiply then add, and in the other you add
  then multiply.
57. C   **59.** Substitution   **61.** Multiplicative Inverse
63. Reflexive   **65.** 2258 ft   **67.** 11   **69.** 35   **71.** 168 cm²

Pages 34–36   Lesson 1-6
1. Sample answer: The Associative Property says that
the way you group numbers together when adding or
multiplying does not change the result. **3.** Sample answer:
$1 + 5 + 8 = 8 + 1 + 5; (1 \cdot 5)8 = 1(5 \cdot 8)$ **5.** 10   **7.** 130
9. $7a + 10b$ **11.** $14x + 6$ **13.** $15x + 10y$ **15.** 46.8 cm²
17. 53   **19.** 20.5   **21.** $9\frac{3}{4}$ **23.** 540   **25.** 32   **27.** 420   **29.** $291
31. $77.38   **33.** $2x + 10y$ **35.** $7a^3 + 14a$ **37.** $17n + 36$
39. $9.5x + 5.5y$ **41.** $2.9f + 1.2g$ **43.** $\frac{2}{3} + \frac{23}{10}p + \frac{6}{5}q$
45. $5(xy) + 3xy$
$\quad = 5(xy) + 3(xy)$ *Associative Property* (×)
$\quad = xy(5 + 3)$ *Distributive Property*
$\quad = xy(8)$ *Substitution*
$\quad = 8xy$ *Commutative Property* (×)
47. $6(x + y^2) - 3\left(x + \frac{1}{2}y^2\right)$
$\quad = 6x + 6y^2 - 3x - 3\left(\frac{1}{2}y^2\right)$ *Distributive Property*
$\quad = 6x - 3x + 6y^2 - \frac{3}{2}y^2$ *Commutative Property* (+)
$\quad = x(6 - 3) + y^2\left(6 - \frac{3}{2}\right)$ *Distributive Property*
$\quad = x(3) + y^2\left(4\frac{1}{2}\right)$ *Substitution*
$\quad = 3x + 4\frac{1}{2}y^2$ *Commutative Property* (×)
49. You can use the Commutative and Associative
Properties to rearrange and group numbers for easier
calculations. Answers should include the following.
- $d = (0.4 + 1.1) + (1.5 + 1.5) + (1.9 + 1.8 + 0.8)$
51. B   **53.** $15 + 6p$ **55.** $13m + 6n$ **57.** $3t^2 + 4t$ **59.** 36
61. 18   **63.** 60   **65.** 13

Page 36   Practice Quiz 2
1. j   **3.** i   **5.** g   **7.** b   **9.** h

Pages 39–42   Lesson 1-7
1. Sample answer: If it rains, then you get wet. H: it rains;
C: you get wet   **3.** Sample answer: You can use deductive
reasoning to determine whether a hypothesis and its
conclusion are both true or whether one or both are false.
5. H: you play tennis; C: you run fast   **7.** H: Lance does not
have homework; C: he watches television; If Lance does not
have homework, then he watches television.
9. H: a quadrilateral with four right angles; C: it is a rectangle;
If a quadrilateral has four right angles, then it is a rectangle.
11. No valid conclusion; the last digit could be any even
number.   **13.** Anna could have a schedule without science
class.   **15.** $x = 1$ **17.** A   **19.** H: you are in Hawaii; C: you
are in the tropics   **21.** H: $4(b + 9) \le 68$; C: $b \le 8$
23. H: $a = b$ and $b = c$; C: $a = c$ **25.** H: it is after school; C:
Greg will call; If it is after school, then Greg will call.

27. H: a number is divisible by 9; C: the sum of its digits is a
multiple of 9; If a number is divisible by 9, then the sum of
its digits is a multiple of 9.   **29.** H: $s > 9$; C: $4s + 6 > 42$;
If $s > 9$, then $4s + 6 > 42$ **31.** Ian will buy a VCR.
33. No valid conclusion; the hypothesis does not say Ian
won't buy a VCR if it costs $150 or more.   **35.** No valid
conclusion; the conditional does not mention Ian buying 2
VCRs.   **37.** There is a professional team in Canada.
39. Left-handed people can have right-handed parents.
41. $2(8.5) = 17$ **43.** $\frac{6}{3} \cdot \frac{1}{2} = 1$
45. Sample answer:

[number line with points R, P, Q]

47. Numbers that end in 0, 2, 4, 6, or 8 are in the "divisible by
2" circle. Numbers whose digits have a sum divisible by 3 are
in the "divisible by 3" circle. Numbers that end in 0 or 5 are in
the "divisible by 5" circle.   **49.** no counterexamples   **51.** You
can use if-then statements to help determine when food is
finished cooking. Answers should include the following.
- Hypothesis: you have small, underpopped kernels
  Conclusion: you have not used enough oil in your pan
- If the gelatin is firm and rubbery, then it is ready to eat.
  If the water is boiling, lower the temperature.
53. C   **55.** $a + 15b$ **57.** $23mn + 24$ **59.** $12x^2 + 12x$
61. Multiplicative Identity; 64   **63.** Substitution; 5
65. Additive Identity; 0   **67.** 41   **69.** 2   **71.** $3n - 10$
73. 36   **75.** 171   **77.** 225.5

Pages 46–48   Lesson 1-8
1. The numbers represent different values. The first number
represents the number on the horizontal axis and the second
represents the number on the vertical axis.   **5.** Graph B
7. (0, 500), (0.2, 480), (0.4, 422), (0.6, 324), (0.8, 186), (1, 10)
9.

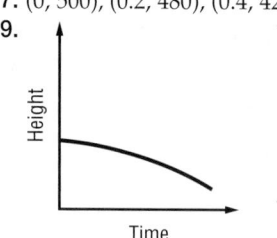

Time / Height

11. Rashaad's account is
increasing as he makes
deposits and earns interest.
Then he pays some bills. He
then makes some deposits
and earns interest and so on.
13. Graph B

15.

[graph with Cost vs Time axes; Cost axis 5–45, Time axis 0–36]

17. The independent variable is the number of sides and
the dependent variable is the sum of the angle measures.
19. 1080, 1260, 1440   **21.**

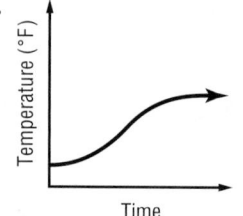

Temperature (°F) / Time

23. Real-world data can be recorded and visualized in a graph and by expressing an event as a function of another event. Answers should include the following.
- A graph gives you a visual representation of the situation which is easier to analyze and evaluate.
- During the first 24 hours, blood flow to the brain decreases to 50% at the moment of the injury and gradually increases to about 60%.
- Significant improvement occurs during the first two days.
25. A **27.** H: a shopper has 9 or fewer items; C: the shopper can use the express lane **29.** Substitution; 3
31. Multiplicative Identity; 1

Pages 53–55 Lesson 1-9
1. Compare parts to the whole; compare different categories of data; show changes in data over time. **3.** Sample answer: The percentages of the data do not total 100.
5. tennis **7.** 14,900 **9.** Bar graph; a bar graph is used to compare similar data in the same category. **11.** The vertical axis needs to begin at 0. **13.** Sample answer: about 250 time as great **15.** Sample answer: about 2250 **17.** Yes, the graph is misleading because the sum of the percentages is not 100. To fix the graph, each section must be drawn accurately and another section that represents "other" toppings should be added. **19.** Tables and graphs provide an organized and quick way to examine data. Answers should include the following.
- Examine the existing pattern and use it to continue a graph to the future.
- Make sure the scale begins at zero and is consistent. Circle graphs should have all percents total 100%. The right kind of graph should be used for the given data.
21. C **23.** Sample answer: $x = 12$ **25.** $6 + 6 + 2 + 2 = 16$
27. $6x^2 + 10x$

Pages 57–62 Chapter 1 Study Guide and Review
1. a **3.** g **5.** h **7.** i **9.** b **11.** x^5 **13.** $x + 21$ **15.** 27
17. 625 **19.** the product of three and a number m to the fifth power **21.** 11 **23.** 9 **25.** 0 **27.** 20 **29.** 26 **31.** 96
33. 23 **35.** 16 **37.** 13 **39.** 2 **41.** 4 **43.** 9 **45.** {6, 7, 8}
47. {5, 6, 7, 8}
49. $\frac{1}{2} \cdot 2 + 2[2 \cdot 3 - 1]$
$= \frac{1}{2} \cdot 2 + 2[6 - 1]$ *Substitution*
$= \frac{1}{2} \cdot 2 + 2 \cdot 5$ *Substitution*
$= 1 + 2 \cdot 5$ *Multiplicative Inverse*
$= 1 + 10$ *Substitution*
$= 11$ *Substitution*
51. $1.2 - 0.05 + 2^3$
$= 1.2 - 0.05 + 8$ *Substitution*
$= 1.15 + 8$ *Substitution*
$= 9.15$ *Substitution*
53. $3(4 \div 4)^2 - \frac{1}{4}(8)$
$= 3(1)^2 - \frac{1}{4}(8)$ *Substitution*
$= 3 \cdot 1 - \frac{1}{4}(8)$ *Substitution*
$= 3 - \frac{1}{4}(8)$ *Multiplicative Identity*
$= 3 - 2$ *Substitution*
$= 1$ *Substitution*
55. 72 **57.** $1 - 3p$ **59.** $24x - 56y$ **61.** simplified
63. $8m + 8n$ **65.** $12y - 5x$ **67.** $9w^2 + w$ **69.** $6a + 13b + 2c$
71. $17n - 24$

73. $2pq + pq$
$= (2 + 1)pq$ *Distributive Property*
$= 3pq$ *Substitution*
75. $3x^2 + (x^2 + 7x)$
$= (3x^2 + x^2) + 7x$ *Associative Property*
$= 4x^2 + 7x$ *Substitution*
77. H: a figure is a triangle, C: it has three sides; If a figure is a triangle, then it has three sides. **79.** $a = 15, b = 1, c = 12$ **81.**

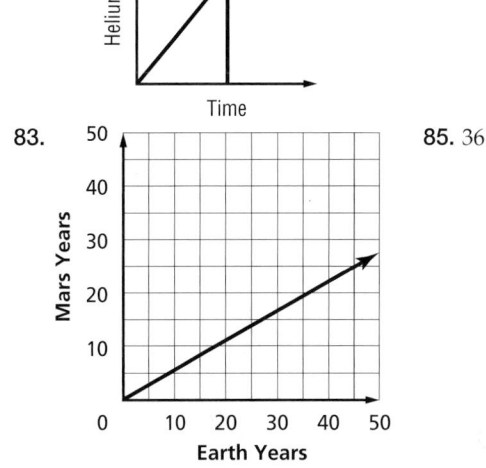

83.

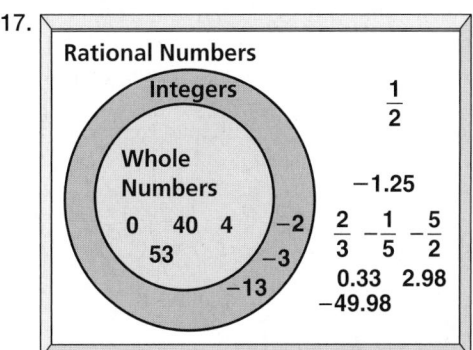

85. 36

Chapter 2   Real Numbers

Page 67 Getting Started
1. 2.36 **3.** 56.32 **5.** $\frac{11}{12}$ **7.** $\frac{3}{8}$ **9.** 4 **11.** 21.6 **13.** $1\frac{1}{2}$
15. 2.1 **17.** $8\frac{1}{6}$; 8; none **19.** 8; 7; 7 **21.** 0.81 **23.** $\frac{16}{25}$

Pages 70–72 Lesson 2-1
1. always **3.** Sample answer: Describing directions such as north versus south, or left versus right.
5. $\left\{..., -\frac{11}{2}, -\frac{9}{2}, -\frac{7}{2}, -\frac{5}{2}, -\frac{3}{2}\right\}$
7.

-4 -3 -2 -1 0 1 2 3 4

9.

-9 -8 -7 -6 -5 -4 -3 -2 -1 0 1

11. 18 **13.** $\frac{5}{6}$ **15.** 36

17.

Rational Numbers
Integers
Whole Numbers
0 40 4
53
$\frac{1}{2}$
-1.25
-2
-3
-13
$\frac{2}{3}$ $-\frac{1}{5}$ $-\frac{5}{2}$
0.33 2.98
-49.98

19. {-7, -6, -5, -3, -2} **21.** {..., 0, 0.2, 0.4, 0.6, 0.8}
23. $\left\{\frac{1}{5}, \frac{4}{5}, \frac{7}{5}, \frac{8}{5}, 2\right\}$
25.

-1 0 1 2 3 4 5 6 7 8 9 10

27.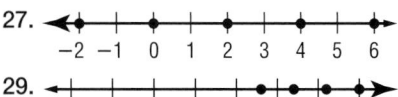
number line from −2 to 6 with dots at −1, 1, 3, 5

29.
number line from −7 to 0 with dots at −2, −1, 0

31.
number line from −4 to 3 with dots at −3, −2, −1, 1

33.
number line from −6 to 10 with dots filled from −4 to 8

35. 10 **37.** 61 **39.** 6.8 **41.** $\frac{35}{80}$ **43.** Philadelphia, PA; Sample answer: It had the greatest absolute value. **45.** 55

47. 34 **49.** 14 **51.** 1.3 **53.** $\frac{1}{4}$ **55.** $\frac{13}{20}$ **57.** 0

59. Bismark, ND 11; Caribou, ME 5; Chicago, IL 4; Fairbanks, AK 9; International Falls, MN 13; Kansas City, MO 7; Sacramento, CA 34; Shreveport, LA 33 **61.** D

63. December **65.** February, July, October **67.** $9x + 2y$

69. $4 + 80x + 32y$ **71.** $\frac{1}{3}$ **73.** $\frac{25}{24}$ or $1\frac{1}{24}$ **75.** $\frac{5}{12}$ **77.** $\frac{7}{18}$

Pages 76–78 Lesson 2-2

1. Sample answer: $\frac{1}{5} - \frac{3}{5}$ **3.** Gabriella; subtracting $-\frac{6}{9}$ is the same as adding $\frac{6}{9}$. **5.** −69 **7.** −17.43 **9.** $\frac{7}{60}$ **11.** 31.1

13. 10.25 **15.** $\frac{13}{60}$ **17.** 5 **19.** −22 **21.** −123 **23.** −5.4

25. −14.7 **27.** −14.7 **29.** $\frac{32}{21}$ or $1\frac{11}{21}$ **31.** $\frac{13}{55}$ **33.** $-\frac{199}{240}$

35. $2\frac{5}{8}$ **37.** 400 points **39.** −27 **41.** 33 **43.** −19 **45.** −16

47. 1.798 **49.** 105.3 **51.** $-\frac{5}{6}$ **53.** $-\frac{11}{16}$ **55.** $-\frac{49}{12}$ or $-4\frac{1}{12}$

57. −2, −6, −4, −4 **59.** Under; yes, it is better than par 72. **61.** week 7 **63.** Sometimes; the equation is false for positive values of x, but true for all other values of x. **65.** C **67.** 15.4 **69.** 15.9

71.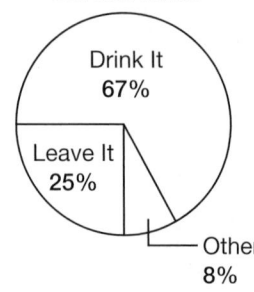

Cereal Milk
Drink It 67%
Leave It 25%
Other 8%

73. {5, 6}
75. $q^2 - 8$ **77.** $\frac{1}{3}$
79. $\frac{5}{8}$ **81.** 5

Pages 81–83 Lesson 2-3

1. ab will be negative if one factor is negative and the other factor is positive. Let $a = -2$ and $b = 3$: $-2(3) = -6$. Let $a = 2$ and $b = -3$: $2(-3) = -6$. **3.** Since multiplication is repeated addition, multiplying a negative number by another negative number is the same as adding repeatedly in the opposite, or positive direction. **5.** −40 **7.** 90.48 **9.** $-\frac{28}{135}$

11. $-57xy$ **13.** $-\frac{15}{8}$ or $-1\frac{7}{8}$ **15.** $56\frac{1}{4}$ t **17.** 176 **19.** −192

21. 3888 **23.** $\frac{5}{27}$ **25.** $-\frac{12}{35}$ **27.** $4\frac{1}{2}$ **29.** 0.845 **31.** −0.48

33. 8 **35.** $-45n$ **37.** $-28d$ **39.** $-21mn -12st$
41. −$134.50 **43.** −30.42 **45.** 4.5 **47.** −13.53
49. −208.377 **51.** $1205.35 **53.** 60 million **55.** Positive; the product of two negative numbers is positive and all even numbers can be divided into groups of two. **57.** B
59. −12.1 **61.** 56

63.
number line from −4 to 6 with dots at −3, −1, 1, 3, 5

65.
number line from −1 to 2 with dots at $-\frac{1}{3}$, $\frac{2}{3}$, 1

67. Sample answer: $x = 5$ **69.** $\frac{5}{16}$ **71.** $6\frac{2}{3}$ **73.** $1\frac{1}{3}$ **75.** $\frac{2}{3}$

Page 83 Practice Quiz 1

1. {−4, −1, 1, 6} **3.** −8 **5.** −8.15 **7.** 108 **9.** $16xy - 3yz$

Pages 86–87 Lesson 2-4

1. Sample answer: Dividing and multiplying numbers with the same signs both result in a positive answer while dividing or multiplying numbers with different signs results in a negative answer. However, when you divide rational numbers in fractional form, you must multiply by a reciprocal. **3.** To divide by a rational number, multiply by its reciprocal. **5.** −9 **7.** 25.76 **9.** $-\frac{5}{6}$ **11.** $-65a$ **13.** 1.2

15. 1.67 **17.** 8 **19.** 60 **21.** −7.05 **23.** −2.28 **25.** 12.9

27. $-\frac{1}{12}$ **29.** $-\frac{35}{3}$ or $-11\frac{2}{3}$ **31.** $\frac{10}{9}$ or $1\frac{1}{9}$ **33.** $-\frac{175}{192}$

35. $\frac{222}{5}$ or $44\frac{2}{5}$ **37.** $9c$ **39.** $-r -3$ **41.** $20a - 25b$
43. $-f -2g$ **45.** 2 **47.** −16.25 **49.** 2.08 **51.** −1.21
53. 1.76 **55.** $1998.75 **57.** 16-karat gold **59.** Sample answer: You use division to find the mean of a set of data. Answers should include the following.

- You could track the mean number of turtles stranded each year and note if the value increases or decreases.
- Weather or pollution could affect the turtles.

61. B **63.** 3 **65.** 0.48 **67.** −6 **69.** $-\frac{11}{24}$ **71.** $20b + 24$

73. $3x + 4y$ **75.** 6.25; 5.5; 3 **77.** 79.25; 79.5; 84

Pages 91–94 Lesson 2-5

1. They describe the data as a whole. **3.** Sample answer: 13, 14, 14, 28
5.
line plot with X marks from 0 to 14

7. The mean and the median both represent the data accurately as they are fairly central. **9.** 3.6

11.

Stem	Leaf
5	4 5 5 6
6	0 1 4 9
7	0 3 5 7 8
8	0 0 3 5 8 8 8
9	0
10	0 2 5
11	0

$5|4 = 54$

13. The mode is not the best measure as it is higher than most of the values.

15.
line plot with X marks from −2 to 3

17. 23 **19.** Sample answer: Median; most of the data are near 2.

21.

Stem	Leaf
1	8 8
2	2 3 6 6 6 8 9
3	0 1 1 2 3 4
4	7

$1|8 = 18$

23. 118 **27.** Mean or median; both are centrally located and the mode is too high. **29.** 7
31. Sample answer: Yes; most of the data are near the median. **33.** 22

35.

Stem	Leaf
3	0 4 7
4	
5	2 9
6	2 7
7	7
8	4 5 3|0 = 30

37. no mode   **39.** High school: $10,123; College: $11,464; Bachelor's Degree: $18,454; Doctoral Degree: $21,608

41. Sample answer: Because the range in salaries is often very great with extreme values on both the high end and low end.   **43.** C   **45.** -4 **47.** -13.5 **49.** $-17x$ **51.** $-3t$ **53.** 1   **55.** 9   **57.** $\frac{2}{3}$ **59.** $\frac{7}{10}$ **61.** $\frac{1}{2}$ **63.** $\frac{4}{9}$

Pages 98–101   Lesson 2-6

1. Sample answers: impossible event: a number greater than 6; certain event: a number from 1 to 6; equally likely event: even number   **3.** Doug; Mark determined the odds in favor of picking a red card.   **5.** $\frac{1}{26}$ **7.** $\frac{1}{26}$ **9.** 3:7   **11.** 6:4

13. $\frac{3}{10}$ **15.** $\frac{1}{3} \approx 33\%$ **17.** $\frac{1}{2} = 50\%$ **19.** $\frac{13}{30} \approx 43\%$

21. $1 = 100\%$ **23.** $\frac{7}{12} \approx 58\%$ **25.** $1 = 100\%$ **27.** $\frac{25}{36} \approx 69\%$

29. $\frac{1}{6} \approx 17\%$ **31.** $\frac{2}{3} \approx 67\%$ **33.** $\frac{1}{2} = 50\%$ **35.** $\frac{15}{31} \approx 48\%$

37. 4:20 or 1:5   **39.** 13:11   **41.** 9:15 or 3:5   **43.** 12:20 or 3:5

45. 15:17   **47.** 13:19   **49.** 1:2   **51.** $\frac{19}{40} = 47.5\%$ **53.** 7:13   **x**

55. 42:4 or 21:2   **57.** $\frac{1}{1,000,001}$ **59.** $\frac{6}{7} \approx 86\%$ **61.** B

63.

Stem	Leaf
5	8.3
6	4.3 5.1 5.5 6.7 7.0 8.7 9.3
7	0.0 2.8 3.2 5.8 7.4 7.4 5|8.3 = 58.3

65. $-\frac{5}{3}$ or $-1\frac{2}{3}$ **67.** -3.9 **69.** $-\frac{5}{8}$ **71.** 4.25   **73.** $\frac{2}{3}$ **75.** 36

77. 64   **79.** 2.56   **81.** $\frac{16}{81}$

Page 101   Practice Quiz 2

1. 17   **3.** -11.7 **5.** $x + 8$ **7.** Sample answer: scale 0–5.0

9. $\frac{13}{18}$

Pages 107–109   Lesson 2-7

1. Sometimes; the square root of a number can be negative, such as $\sqrt{16} = 4$ and $-\sqrt{16} = -4$.   **3.** There is no real number that can be multiplied by itself to result in a negative product.   **5.** 1.2   **7.** 5.66   **9.** rationals
11. naturals, wholes, integers, rationals
13.

15. $=$ **17.** $-15, \frac{1}{8}, 0.\overline{15}, \sqrt{\frac{1}{8}}$ **19.** C   **21.** 9   **23.** 2.5

25. -9.70 **27.** $\pm\frac{5}{7}$ **29.** 0.77   **31.** ±22.65 **33.** naturals, wholes, integers, rationals   **35.** rationals   **37.** irrationals
39. rationals   **41.** rationals   **43.** rationals   **45.** rationals
47. irrationals   **49.** irrational   **51.** No; Jerome was traveling at about 32.4 mph.

53.

55.

57.

59. $<$ **61.** $<$ **63.** $>$ **65.** $0.\overline{24}, \sqrt{0.06}, \frac{\sqrt{9}}{12}$ **67.** $-4.\overline{83}, -\frac{3}{8}, 0.4, \sqrt{8}$ **69.** $7\frac{4}{9}, \sqrt{122}, \sqrt{200}$ **71.** about 3.4 mi
73. They are true if q and r are positive and $q > r$.
75. The length of the side is the square root of the area.
77. Sample answer: By using the formula Surface Area = $\sqrt{\dfrac{\text{height} \times \text{weight}}{3600}}$, you need to use square roots to calculate the quantity. Answers should include the following.
- You must multiply height by weight first. Divide that product by 3600. Then determine the square root of that result.
- Sample answers: exposure to radiation or chemicals; heat loss; scuba suits
- Sample answers: determining height, distance

79. B   **81.** 5:8   **83.** 12:1   **85.** -61 **87.** $5.1x - 7.6y$

Pages 110–114   Chapter 2   Study Guide and Review

1. true   **3.** true   **5.** true   **7.** false; sample answer: $0.\overline{6}$ or $0.666\ldots$

9.

11.

13. 5   **15.** 14   **17.** -5 **19.** -1.4 **21.** $\frac{1}{2}$ **23.** 16   **25.** -2.5
27. $\frac{13}{24}$ **29.** -36 **31.** 8.64   **33.** $\frac{3}{10}$ **35.** n **37.** -9
39. -10.9 **41.** -20 **43.** $-2 + 4x$ **45.** $-x + 6y$ **47.** -3.2
49.

Stem	Leaf
1	2 2 2 3 4 4 5 5 5 5 6 6 7
	7 7 7 8 8 9 9 9 9 9
2	0 1 1 1 2 6 6 8
3	0 1|2 = 12

51. Sample answer; Median; it is closest in value to most of the data   **53.** $\frac{1}{4}$ **55.** $\frac{1}{4}$ **57.** 18:31   **59.** 25:24   **61.** ±1.1
63. $\pm\frac{2}{15}$ **65.** naturals, wholes, integers, rationals   **67.** $<$
69. $>$

Chapter 3   Solving Linear Equations

Page 119   Chapter 3   Getting Started

1. $\frac{1}{2}t + 5$ **3.** $3a + b^2$ **5.** $95 - 9y$ **7.** 15   **9.** 16   **11.** 7
13. 5   **15.** 25%   **17.** 300%   **19.** 160%

Pages 123–126   Lesson 3-1

1. Explore the problem, plan the solution, solve the problem, and examine the solution.   **3.** Sample answer: After sixteen people joined the drama club, there were 30 members. How many members did the club have before the new members?   **5.** $5(m + n) = 7n$ **7.** $C = 2\pi r$ **9.** $\frac{1}{3}$ of b minus $\frac{3}{4}$ equals 2 times a.   **11.** $155 + g = 160$
13. $200 - 3x = 9$ **15.** $\frac{1}{3}q + 25 = 2q$ **17.** $2(v + w) = 2z$
19. $g \div h = 2(g + h) + 7$ **21.** $0.46E = P$ **23.** $A = bh$

25. $P = 2(a + b)$ **27.** $c^2 = a^2 + b^2$ **29.** d minus 14 equals 5.
31. k squared plus 17 equals 53 minus j.   **33.** $\frac{3}{4}$ of p plus $\frac{1}{2}$
equals p.   **35.** 7 times the sum of m and n equals 10 times n
plus 17.   **37.** The area A of a trapezoid equals one-half
times the product of the height h and the sum of the bases,
a and b.   **39.** Sample answer: Lindsey is 7 inches taller than
Yolanda. If 2 times Yolanda's height plus Lindsey's height
equals 193 inches, find Yolanda's height.   **41.** $V = \frac{1}{3}\pi r^2 h$
43. $V = \frac{4}{3}\pi r^3$ **45.** $1912 + y$ **47.** 16 yr   **49.** $a + (4a + 15) = 60$
53. Equations can be used to describe the relationships of the
heights of various parts of a structure. Answers should
include the following.

• The equation representing the Sears Tower is
  $1454 + a = 1707$.

55. D   **57.** $-\frac{5}{6}$ **59.** -7.42 **61.** $\frac{1}{2}$ **63.** $8d + 3$ **65.** $8a + 6b$
67. 408   **69.** 9.37   **71.** 1.88   **73.** $\frac{13}{15}$ **75.** $\frac{1}{9}$

Pages 131–134   Lesson 3-2

1. Sample answers: $n = 13$, $n + 16 = 29$, $n + 12 = 25$
3. (1) Add -94 to each side. (2) Subtract 94 from each side.
5. -13 **7.** 171   **9.** $\frac{5}{6}$ **11.** $n + (-37) = -91$; -54 **13.** 16.8 h
15. 23   **17.** 28   **19.** 38   **21.** 43   **23.** -96 **25.** 73   **27.** 3.45
29. -2.58 **31.** 15.65   **33.** $1\frac{7}{12}$ **35.** $1\frac{1}{8}$ **37.** $-\frac{2}{15}$ **39.** 19
41. $x + 55 = 78$; 23   **43.** $n - 18 = 31$; 49   **45.** $n + (-16) =$
-21; -5 **47.** $n - \frac{1}{2} = -\frac{3}{4}$; $-\frac{1}{4}$ **49.** Sometimes, if $x = 0$,
$x + x = x$ is true.   **51.** $\ell + 10 = 34$ **53.** 37 mi   **55.** Sample
answer: 29 mi; 29 is the average of 24 (for the 8-cylinder
engine) and 34 (for the 4-cylinder engine).   **57.** 31 ft
59. $11.4 + x = 13.6$; 2.2 million volumes   **61.** $24.0 + 13.6 +$
$11.4 = x$; 49.0 million volumes   **63.** $1379 + 679 + 1707 + x =$
$1286 + 634 + 3714$; 1869   **65.** $a = b$, $x = 0$ **67.** C
69. $A = \pi r^2$ **71.** $<$ **73.** $=$ **75.**

Stem	Leaf
0	5 8
1	1 2 4 7
2	3 6 8 9
3	
4	1 5 $0|5 = 0.5$

77. H: it is Friday; C: there will be a science quiz
79. $(2^5 - 5^2) + (4^2 - 2^4)$

$= (32 - 25) + (16 - 16)$ *Substitution*
$= 7 + 0$ *Substitution*
$= 7$ *Additive Identity*

81. $\{1, 3, 5\}$ **83.** 10.545   **85.** 0.22   **87.** $\frac{1}{6}$ **89.** $3\frac{1}{3}$

Pages 138–140   Lesson 3-3

1. Sample answer: $4x = -12$ **3.** Juanita; to find an
equivalent equation with $1n$ on one side of the equation,
you must divide each side by 8 or multiply each side by $\frac{1}{8}$.
5. -35 **7.** $1\frac{1}{9}$ **9.** $\frac{10}{13}$ **11.** $\frac{2}{5}n = -24$; -60 **13.** -11
15. 35   **17.** -77 **19.** 21   **21.** 10   **23.** -6.2 **25.** -3.5
27. $8\frac{6}{13}$ **29.** $\frac{11}{15}$ **31.** 30   **33.** $7n = -84$; -12 **35.** $\frac{1}{5}n =$
12; 60   **37.** $2\frac{1}{2}n = 1\frac{1}{5}$; $\frac{12}{25}$ **39.** $\ell = \frac{1}{7}p$ **41.** 455 people
43. 0.48 s   **45.** about 0.02 s   **47.** $x + 8x = 477$ **49.** 424 g
51. You can use the distance formula and the speed of light
to find the time it takes light from the stars to reach Earth.
Answers should include the following.

• Solve the equation by dividing each side of the equation
  by 5,870,000,000,000. The answer is 53 years.
• The equation $5{,}870{,}000{,}000{,}000t = 821{,}800{,}000{,}000{,}000$
  describes the situation for the star in the Big Dipper
  farthest from Earth.

53. A   **55.** 13   **57.** $10a = 5(b + c)$ **59.** 0.00879
61.

$$\begin{array}{c}\bullet \quad \bullet \quad \bullet \quad \bullet \\ -4 \; -3 \; -2 \; -1 \;\; 0 \;\; 1 \;\; 2 \;\; 3 \;\; 4\end{array}$$

63.

$$\begin{array}{c}\longleftarrow \bullet \quad \bullet \\ -7 \; -6 \; -5 \; -4 \; -3 \; -2 \; -1 \;\; 0 \;\; 1\end{array}$$

65. Commutative Property of Addition   **67.** 25   **69.** 9

Page 140   Practice Quiz 1

1. $S = 4\pi r^2$ **3.** -45 **5.** -24 **7.** 27   **9.** -9

Pages 145–148   Lesson 3-4

1. Sample answers: $2x + 3 = -1$, $3x - 1 = -7$ **3.** $n - 2$
5. 6   **7.** -1 **9.** $12\frac{2}{3}$ **11.** 28   **13.** $12 - 2n = -34$; 23
15. 12 letters   **17.** 24   **19.** 80 lb   **21.** \$60   **23.** -6 **25.** -7
27. -15 **29.** -56 **31.** -125 **33.** $25\frac{1}{3}$ **35.** -42.72
37. -12.6 **39.** 7   **41.** 2   **43.** $29 = 13 + 4n$; 4   **45.** $n +$
$(n + 2) + (n + 4) = -30$; $-12, -10, -8$ **47.** $n + (n + 2) +$
$(n + 4) + (n + 6) = 8$; $-1, 1, 3, 5$ **49.** 16 cm, 18 cm, 20 cm
51. 10 in.   **53.** \$75,000   **55.** never   **57.** B   **59.** -3
61. -126 **63.** 5   **65.** -13 **67.** $2\frac{1}{4}$ **69.** 29 models
71. 1:1   **73.** $-\frac{2}{7}$ **75.** $-\frac{3}{4}a + 4$ **77.** 153   **79.** 20   **81.** $5m + \frac{n}{2}$
83. $3a + b^2$ **85.** $6m$ **87.** $-8g$ **89.** $-10m$

Pages 151–154   Lesson 3-5

1a. Incorrect; the 2 must be distributed over both g and 5; 6.
1b. correct   **1c.** Incorrect; to eliminate $-6z$ on the left side
of the equal sign, $6z$ must be added to each side of the
equation; 1.   **3.** Sample answer: $2x - 5 = 2x + 5$ **5.** 4
7. 3   **9.** 2.6   **11.** all numbers   **13.** D   **15a.** Subtract v from
each side.   **15b.** Simplify.   **15c.** Subtract 9 from each side.
15d. Simplify.   **15e.** Divide each side by 6.   **15f.** Simplify.
17. 4   **19.** -3 **21.** $-1\frac{1}{2}$ **23.** 4   **25.** 8   **27.** no solution
29. 2   **31.** 10   **33.** -4 **35.** 4   **37.** 0.925   **39.** all numbers
41. -36 **43.** 26, 28, 30   **45.** 8-penny   **47.** 2.5 by 0.5 and
1.5 by 1.5   **49.** Sample answer: $3(x + 1) = x - 1$ **51.** D
53. 90   **55.** -2 **57.** $33\frac{1}{3}$ min
59.

$$\begin{array}{c}
\quad\quad\quad\quad\quad\quad\times \\
\quad\quad\quad\quad\quad\quad\times \\
\quad\quad\quad\quad\times\;\times\quad\quad\times\;\times \\
\quad\quad\times\quad\quad\times\;\times\quad\times\;\times\quad\quad\quad\times \\
\hline
18 \quad 20 \quad 22 \quad 24 \quad 26 \quad 28
\end{array}$$

61. -4 **63.** Sample answer: $1 + 3 = 4$ **65.** 5   **67.** 0
69. $\frac{4}{7}$ **71.** $\frac{1}{15}$ **73.** $\frac{2}{3}$ **75.** $\frac{1}{3}$

Page 158–159   Lesson 3-6

3. Find the cross products and divide by the value with the
variable.   **5.** no   **7.** 8   **9.** 4.62   **11.** yes   **13.** no   **15.** no
17. USA: $\frac{871}{2116}$; USSR/Russia: $\frac{498}{1278}$; Germany: $\frac{374}{1182}$; GB: $\frac{180}{638}$;
France: $\frac{188}{598}$; Italy: $\frac{179}{479}$; Sweden: $\frac{136}{469}$ **19.** 20   **21.** 18   **23.** $9\frac{1}{3}$
25. 2.28   **27.** 1.23   **29.** $19\frac{1}{3}$ **31.** 14 days   **33.** 3 in.   **35.** 18
37. Sample answer: Ratios are used to determine how much
of each ingredient to use for a given number of servings.
Answers should include the following.

- To determine how much honey is needed if you use 3 eggs, write and solve the proportion $2:\frac{3}{4} = 3:h$, where h is the amount of honey.
- To alter the recipe to get 5 servings, multiply each amount by $1\frac{1}{4}$.

39. C **41.** no solution **43.** -2 **45.** -8 **47.** -1
49. 0.4125 **51.** 77 **53.** 0.85 **55.** 30% **57.** 40%

Page 162–164 Lesson 3-7

1. Percent of increase and percent of decrease are both percents of change. If the new number is greater than the original number, the percent of change is a percent of increase. If the new number is less than the original number, the percent of change is a percent of decrease.
3. Laura; Cory used the new number as the base instead of the original number. **5.** increase; 11% **7.** decrease; 20%
9. $16.91 **11.** $13.37 **13.** about 77% **15.** decrease; 28%
17. increase; 162% **19.** decrease; 27% **21.** increase; 6%
23. increase; 23% **25.** decrease; 14% **27.** 30% **29.** 8 g
31. $14.77 **33.** $7.93 **35.** $42.69 **37.** $27.00 **39.** $24.41
41. $96.77 **43.** $101.76 **45.** $46.33 **47.** India
49. always; $x\%$ of $y \rightarrow \frac{x}{100} = \frac{P}{y}$ or $P = \frac{xy}{100}$; $y\%$ of $x \rightarrow \frac{y}{100} = \frac{P}{x}$ or $P = \frac{xy}{100}$ **51.** B **53.** 9 **55.** 18 **57.** -6 **59.** $\frac{1}{10}$
61. $\frac{4}{27}$ **63.** false **65.** true **67.** -3 **69.** -11 **71.** 3

Page 164 Practice Quiz 2

1. $-8\frac{1}{3}$ **3.** 1.5 **5.** all numbers **7.** 5 **9.** 5

Pages 168–170 Lesson 3-8

1. (1) Subtract az from each side. (2) Add y to each side. (3) Use the Distributive Property to write $ax - az$ as $a(x - z)$. (4) Divide each side by $x - z$. **3.** Sample answer for a triangle: $A = \frac{1}{2}bh$; $b = \frac{2A}{h}$ **5.** $a = \frac{54 + y}{5}$ **7.** $y = 3c - a$
9. $w = \frac{5 + t}{m - 2}$ **11.** $h = \frac{2A}{b}$ **13.** $g = -\frac{h}{4}$ **15.** $m = \frac{y - b}{x}$
17. $y = \frac{am - z}{7}$ **19.** $m = \frac{6y - 5x}{k}$ **21.** $x = \frac{n - 20}{3a}$
23. $y = \frac{3c - 2}{b}$ **25.** $y = \frac{4}{3}(c - b)$ **27.** $A = \frac{2S - nt}{n}$
29. $a = \frac{c + b}{r - t}$ **31.** $t - 5 = r + 6$; $t = r + 11$ **33.** $\frac{5}{8}x = \frac{1}{2}y + 3$; $y = \frac{5}{4}x - 6$ **35.** 6 m **37.** 3 errors **39.** 225 lb

41. about 17.4 cm
43. Equations from physics can be used to determine the height needed to produce the desired results. Answers should include the following.
- Use the following steps to solve for h. (1) Use the Distributive Property to write the equation in the form $195g - hg = \frac{1}{2}mv^2$. (2) Subtract $195g$ from each side. (3) Divide each side by $-g$.
- The second hill should be 157 ft.
45. C **47.** $9.75 **49.** 22.5 **51.** 5 **53.** $\frac{2}{3}$, 1.1, $\sqrt{5}$, 3
55. $\frac{1}{4}$ **57.** Multiplicative Identity Property **59.** Reflexive Property **61.** $12 - 6t$ **63.** $-21a - 7b$ **65.** $-9 + 3t$

Pages 174–177 Lesson 3-9

1. Sample answer: grade point average
3.

	Number of Coins	Value of Each Coin	Total Value
Dimes	d	$0.10	$0.10d$
Quarters	$d - 8$	$0.25	$0.25(d - 8)$

5. $0.10(6 - p) + 1.00p = 0.40(6)$ **7.** 4 qt **9.** about 3.56
11.

	Number of Dozens	Price per Dozen	Total Price
Peanut Butter	p	$6.50	$6.50p$
Chocolate Chip	$p - 85$	$9.00	$9.00(p - 85)$

13. 311 doz
15.

	Number of Ounces	Price per Ounce	Value
Gold	g	$270	$270g$
Silver	$15 - g$	$5	$5(15 - g)$
Alloy	15	$164	$164(15)$

17. 9 oz
19.

	r	t	$d = rt$
Eastbound Train	40	t	$40t$
Westbound Train	30	t	$30t$

21. $3\frac{1}{2}$ h **23.** 15 lb **25.** 200 g of 25% alloy, 800 g of 50% alloy
27. 120 mL of 25% solution, 20 mL of 60% solution **29.** 87
31. 15 s **33.** 3.2 qt **35.** about 98.0
37. A weighted average is used to determine a skater's average. Answers should include the following.
- The score of the short program is added to twice the score of the long program. The sum is divided by 3.
- $\frac{4.9(1) + 5.2(2)}{1 + 2} = 5.1$
39. C **41.** $b = 4a + 25$ **43.** increase; 20% **45.** 2:1
47. $3xy$ **49.** $\{..., -2, -1, 0, 1, 2, 3\}$

Pages 179–184 Chapter 3 Study Guide and Review

1. Addition **3.** different **5.** identity **7.** increase
9. weighted average **11.** $3n - 21 = 57$ **13.** $a^2 + b^3 = 16$
15. -16 **17.** 21 **19.** -8.5 **21.** -7 **23.** 40 **25.** -10
27. 3 **29.** -153 **31.** 11 **33.** 2 **35.** 1 **37.** -3 **39.** 18
41. 9 **43.** 1 **45.** decrease; 20% **47.** increase; 6%
49. $10.39 **51.** $y = \frac{b + c}{a}$ **53.** $y = \frac{7a + 9b}{8}$ **55.** 450 mph, 530 mph

Chapter 4 Graphing Relations and Functions

Page 191 Chapter 4 Getting Started

1.

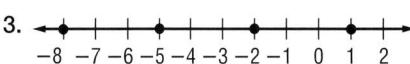

3.

5. $21 - 3t$ **7.** $-15b + 10$ **9.** $y = 1 - 2x$ **11.** $y = 2x - 4$
13. $y = 18 - 8x$ **15.** 6 **17.** 0 **19.** 3

Pages 194–196 Lesson 4-1

1.

3. Sample answer: I(3, 3), II(-3, 3), III(-3, -3), IV(3, -3) **5.** (-1, 1); II **7.** (-4, -2); III

8–11.

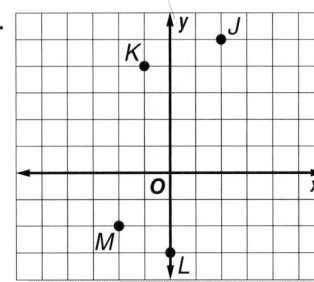

13. (−4, 5); II
15. (−1, −3); III
17. (−3, 3); II
19. (2, −1); IV
21. (0, 4); none
23. (7, −12)

25–36.

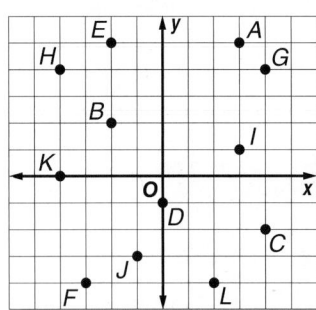

37. Sample answer: Louisville and Richmond **39.** coins, (3, 5); plate, (7, 2); goblet, (8, 4); vase, (5, 9) **41.** C4
43. B5, C2, D4, E1

45. Archaeologists used coordinate systems as a mapping guide and as a system to record locations of artifacts. Answers should include the following.
- The grid gives archaeologists a point of reference so they can identify and explain to others the location of artifacts in a site they are excavating. You can divide the space so more people can work at the same time in different areas.
- Knowing the exact location of artifacts helps archaeologists reconstruct historical events.

47. B **49.** (7, −5) **51.** 320 mph **53.** $d = c$ **55.** $t = \frac{3a}{11}$
57. 7.94 **59.** −16 **61.** 51 **63.** 30 **65.** 48 **67.** $-x - 3$
69. $-6x + 15$ **71.** $\frac{5}{4}x - \frac{1}{2}y$

Pages 200–203 Lesson 4-2

1.

Transformation	Size	Shape	Orientation
Reflection	same	same	changes
Rotation	same	same	changes
Translation	same	same	same
Dilation	changes	same	same

3. translation

5. $P'(1, -2), Q'(4, -4), R'(2, 3)$

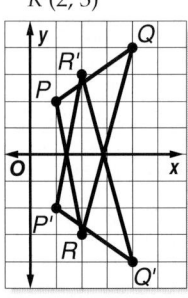

7. $E'(-2, 8), F'(10, -2), G'(4, -8), H'(-8, 2)$

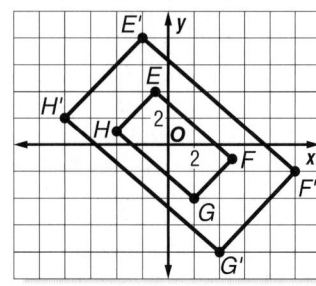

9.

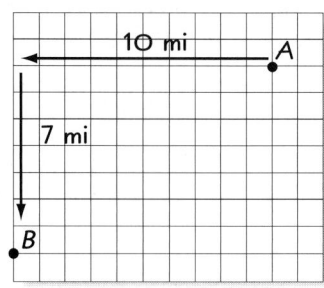

11. translation
13. reflection
15. reflection

17. $R'(-2, 0), S'(2, -3), T'(2, 3)$

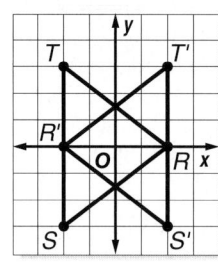

19. $R'(2, 3), S'(4, 2), T'(7, 5), U'(5, 7)$

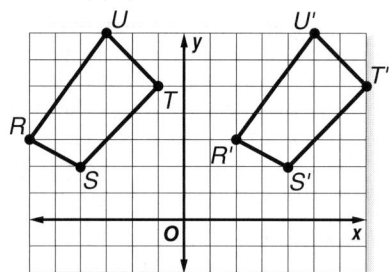

21. $J'(-2, 1), K'(-1, 2), L'(2, 2), M'(-2, -2)$

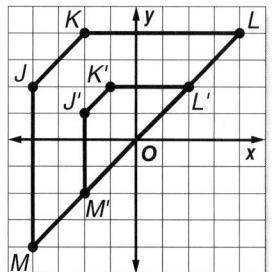

23. $F'(3, -2), G'(-2, -5), H'(-6, -3)$

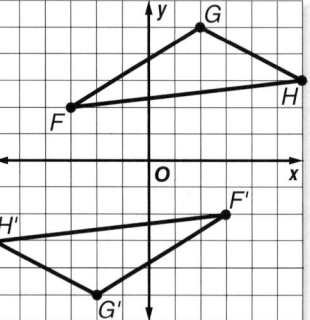

25. $W'(-1, -2), X'(3, -2), Y'(0, 4), Z'(-4, 4)$

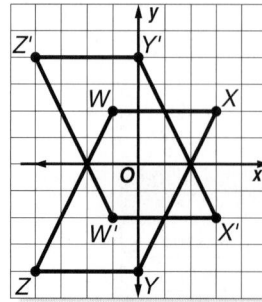

27. $A(-5, -1), B(-3, -3), C(-5, -5), D(-5, -4), E(-8, -4), F(-8, -2), G(-5, -2)$

29.

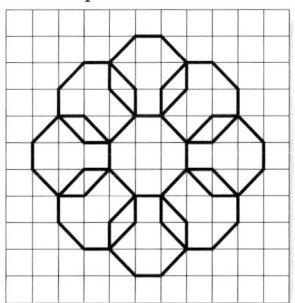

31. $\frac{1}{2}$

33. 90° counterclockwise rotation

35. (0, 0), (1800, 0), (1800, 1600), (0, 1600)

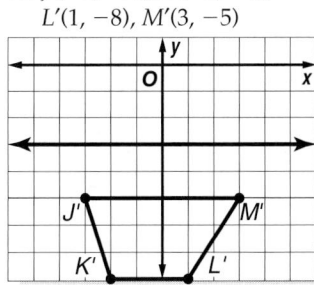

37. The pattern resembles a snowflake.

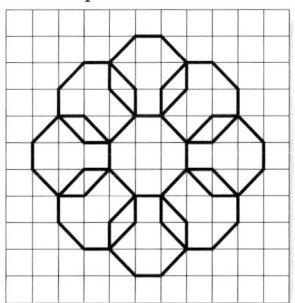

39. (y, −x)   **41.** Artists use computer graphics to simulate movement, change the size of objects, and create designs. Answers should include the following.

• Objects can appear to move by using a series of translations. Moving forward can be simulated by enlarging objects using dilations so they appear to be getting closer.

• Computer graphics are used in special effects in movies, animated cartoons, and web design.

43. C

45. J′(−3, −5), K′(−2, −8),   **47–52.**
L′(1, −8), M′(3, −5)

53. 10 mL   **55.** $\frac{1}{12} \approx 8\%$ **57.** $\frac{5}{6} \approx 83\%$ **59.** {(0, 100), (5, 90) (10, 81), (15, 73), (20, 66), (25, 60), (30, 55)}

Pages 208–211   Lesson 4-3

1. A relation can be represented as a set of ordered pairs, a table, a graph, or a mapping.   **3.** The domain of a relation is the range of the inverse, and the range of a relation is the domain of the inverse.

5. D = {−1, 3, 5, 6}; R = {−3, 4, 9}

x	y
6	4
3	−3
−1	9
5	−3

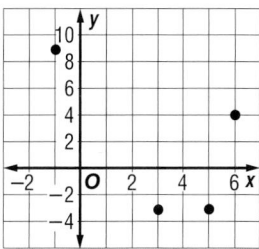
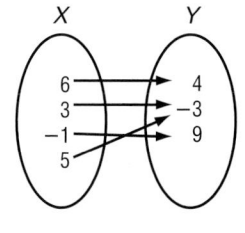

7. D = {−4, −1, 6}; R = {7, 8, 9}

x	y
−4	8
−1	9
−4	7
6	9

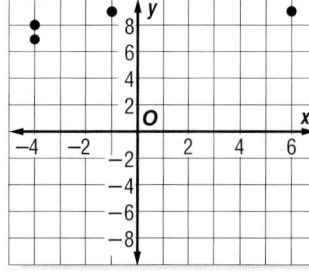
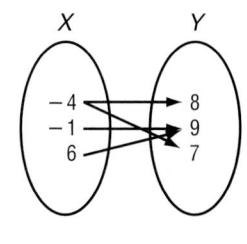

9. {(−4, 9), (2, 5), (−2, −2), (11, 12)}; {(9, −4), (5, 2), (−2, −2), (12, 11)}   **11.** {(2, 8), (3, 7), (4, 6), (5, 7)}; {(8, 2), (7, 3), (6, 4), (7, 5)}   **13.** {(−4, −4), (−3, 0), (0, −3), (2, 1), (2, −1)}; {(−4, −4), (0, −3), (−3, 0), (1, 2), (−1, 2)}   **15.** {1989, 1990, 1991, 1992, 1993, 1994, 1995, 1996, 1997, 1998, 1999}

17. There are fewer students per computer in more recent years. So the number of computers in schools has increased.

19. D = {−5, 2, 5, 6}; R = {0, 2, 4, 7}

x	y
5	2
−5	0
6	4
2	7

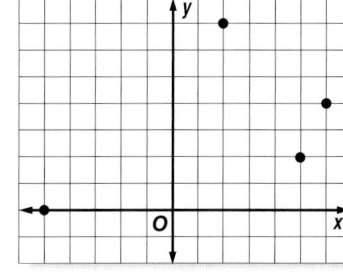

21. D = {1, 2, 3}; R = {−9, 7, 8}

x	y
3	8
3	7
2	−9
1	−9

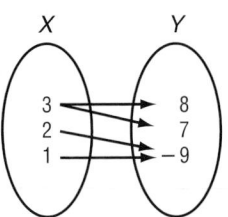

23. D = {−5, −1, 0}; R = {1, 2, 6, 9}

x	y
0	2
−5	1
0	6
−1	9

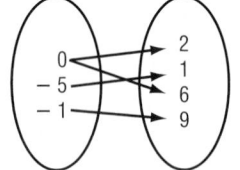

25. D = {−3, −2, 3, 4, 7}; R = {2, 4, 5, 6}

x	y
7	6
3	4
4	5
−2	6
−3	2

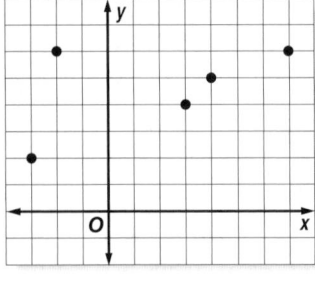
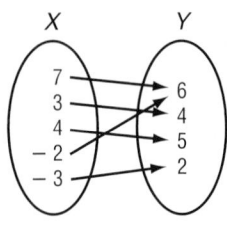

27. {(0, 3), (−5, 2), (4, 7), (−3, 2)}; {(3, 0), (2, −5), (7, 4), (2, −3)}   **29.** {(−8, 4), (−1, 1), (0, 6), (5, 4)}; {(4, −8), (1, −1), (6, 0), (4, 5)}   **31.** {(−3, 3), (1, 3), (4, 2), (−1, −5)}; {(3, −3), (3, 1), (2, 4), (−5, −1)}   **33.** {(1, 16.50), (1.75, 28.30), (2.5, 49.10), (3.25, 87.60), (4, 103.40)}; {(16.50, 1), (28.30, 1.75), (49.10, 2.5), (87.60, 3.25), (103.40, 4)}   **35.** {(2, 0), (2, 4), (3, 7), (5, 0), (5, 8), (−7, 7)}; {(0, 2), (4, 2), (7, 3), (0, 5), (8, 5), (7, −7)}
37. {(−3, −1), (−3, −3), (−3, −5), (0, 3), (2, 3), (4, 3)}; {(−1, −3), (−3, −3), (−5, −3), (3, 0), (3, 2), (3, 4)}
39. {(212.0, 0), (210.2, 1000), (208.4, 2000), (206.5, 3000), (201.9, 5000), (193.7, 10,000)}   **41.** D = {1991, 1992, 1993, 1994, 1995, 1996, 1997, 1998, 1999, 2000}; R = {6.3, 7.5, 9.2, 9.5, 9.8, 10, 10.4}   **43.** The production seems to go up and down every other year, however from 1995 through 1998, farmers have produced more corn each year.   **45.** D = {100, 105, 110, 115, 120, 125, 130}; R = {40, 42, 44, 46, 48, 50, 52}   **47.** D = {40, 42, 44, 46, 48, 50, 52}; R = {100, 105, 110, 115, 120, 125, 130}
49. Sample answer: F = {(−1, 1), (−2, 2), (−3, 3)}, G = {(1, −2), (2, −3), (3, −1)}; The elements in the domain and range of F should be paired differently in G.   **51.** B

53a.
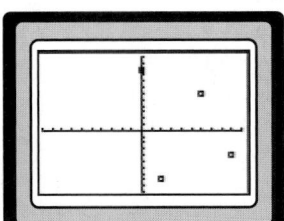

53b. [−10, 10] scl: 1 by [−10, 12] scl: 1

53c. {(10, 0), (−8, 2), (6, 6), (−4, 9)}

53d. (0, 10), none; (10, 0), none; (2, −8), IV; (−8, 2), II; (6, 6), I; (6, 6), I; (9, −4), IV; (−4, 9), II

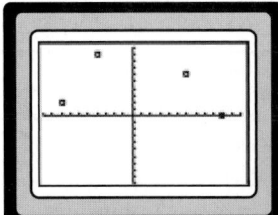

55a.
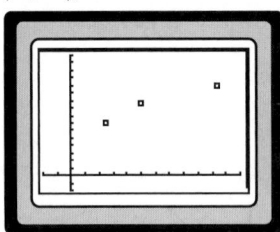

55b. [−10, 80] scl: 5 by [−10, 60] scl: 5

55c. {(12, 35), (25, 48), (52, 60)}

55d. (35, 12), (48, 25), and (60, 52) are all in I. (12, 35), (25, 48), and (52, 60) are all in I.   **57.** rotation
59. translation   **61.** (3, 2); I
63. (1, −1); IV   **65.** (−4, −2); III   **67.** (−2, 5); II   **69.** 8
71. 9   **73.** 9n + 13   **75.** {5}
77. {3}   **79.** {6}

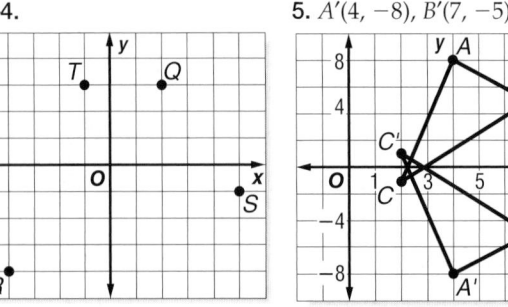

Page 211   Practice Quiz 1
1–4.

5. A′(4, −8), B′(7, −5), C′(2, 1)

7. D = {1, 2, 4}; R = {3, 5, 6}; I = {(3, 1), (6, 4), (3, 2), (5, 1)}
9. D = {−8, 11, 15}; R = {3, 5, 22, 31}; I = {(5, 11), (3, 15), (22, −8), (31, 11)}

Pages 214–217   Lesson 4-4
1. Substitute the values for *x* and solve for *x*.   **3.** Bryan; *x* represents the domain and *y* represents the range. So, replace *x* with 5 and *y* with 1.   **5.** {(−7, −3), (−2, −1)}
7. {(−3, 7), (−1, 5), (0, 4), (2, 2)}   **9.** {(−3, 11), (−1, 8), (0, 6.5), (2, 3.5)}

11. $\{(-4, -1), (-2, 0), (0, 1), (2, 2), (4, 3)\}$

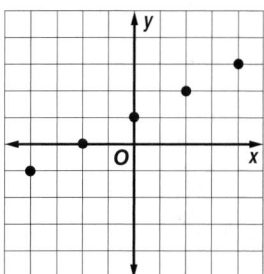

13. 12 karats **15.** $\{(4, -4), (2, 2)\}$ **17.** $\{(3, 0), (2, 1), (4, -1)\}$ **19.** $\{(0.25, 3.5), (1, 2)\}$ **21.** $\{(-2, -1), (-1, 1), (1, 5), (3, 9), (4, 11)\}$ **23.** $\{(-2, 9), (-1, 8), (1, 6), (3, 4), (4, 3)\}$ **25.** $\{(-2, -9), (-1, -3), (1, 9), (3, 21), (4, 27)\}$

27. $\{(-2, -2), (-1, -1), (1, 1), (3, 3), (4, 4)\}$ **29.** $\{(-2, 10), (-1, 8.5), (1, 5.5), (3, 2.5), (4, 1)\}$ **31.** $\{(-2, -24), (-1, -18), (1, -6), (3, 6), (4, 12)\}$

33. $\{(-5, -16), (-2, -7), (1, 2), (3, 8), (4, 11)\}$

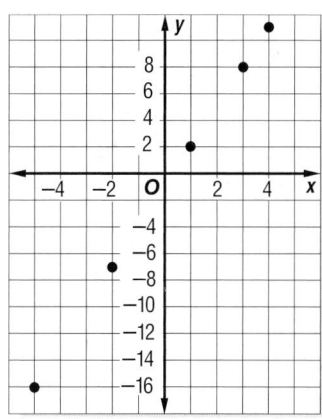

35. $\{(-4, 7), (-1, 3.25), (0, 2), (2, -0.5), (4, -3), (6, -5.5)\}$

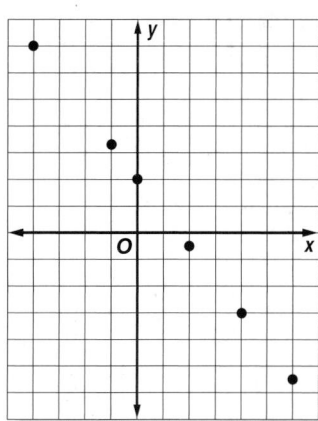

37. $\{(-4, -4), (-2, -3.5), (0, -3), (2, -2.5), (4, -2), (6, -1.5)\}$

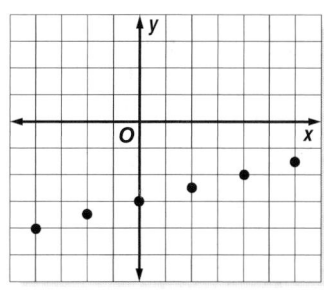

39. $\{-14, -12, -4, 6, 8\}$ **41.** New York: 1.1°C, Chicago: −5°C, San Francisco: 12.8°C, Miami: 22.2°C, Washington, D.C.: 4.4°C **43.** w is independent; ℓ is dependent.

45.

Male		
Length of Tibia (cm)	Height (cm)	(T, H)
30.5	154.9	(30.5, 154.9)
34.8	165.2	(34.8, 165.2)
36.3	168.8	(36.3, 168.8)
37.9	172.7	(37.9, 172.7)

Female		
Length of Tibia (cm)	Height (cm)	(T, H)
30.5	148.9	(30.5, 148.9)
34.8	159.6	(34.8, 159.6)
36.3	163.4	(36.3, 163.4)
37.9	167.4	(37.9, 167.4)

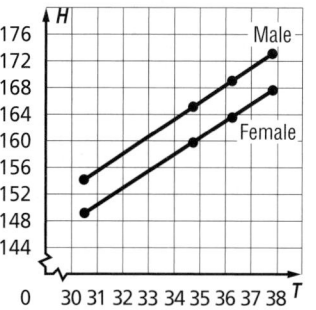

47a. $\{-6, -4, 0, 4, 6\}$ **47b.** $\{-13, -8, -4, 4, 8, 13\}$
47c. $\{-5, 0, 4, 8, 13\}$ **49.** When traveling to other countries, currency and measurement systems are often different. You need to convert these systems to the system with which you are familiar. Answers should include the following.

• At the current exchange rate, 15 pounds is roughly 10 dollars and 10 pounds is roughly 7 dollars. Keeping track of every 15 pounds you spend would be relatively easy.

• If the exchange rate is 0.90 compared to the dollar, then items will cost less in dollars. For example, an item that is 10 in local currency is equivalent to $9.00. If the exchange rate is 1.04, then items will cost more in dollars. For example, an item that costs 10 in local currency is equivalent to $10.40.

51. C **53.** $\{(-8, 94), (-5, 74.5), (0, 42), (3, 22.5), (7, -3.5), (12, -36)\}$ **55.** $\{(-2.5, -4.26), (-1.75, -3.21), (0, -0.76), (1.25, 0.99), (3.33, 3.90)\}$ **57.** $\{(2, 7), (6, -4), (6, -1), (11, 8)\}$; $\{(7, 2), (-4, 6), (-1, 6), (8, 11)\}$
59. $X'(6, 4), Y'(5, 0), Z'(-3, 3)$

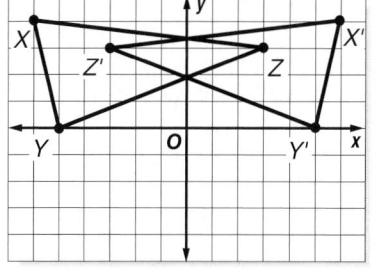

61. yes **63.** yes **65.** no **67.** H: it is hot; C: we will go swimming **69.** H: $3n - 7 = 17$; C: $n = 8$ **71.** 5 **73.** −2 **75.** 12

Pages 221–223 Lesson 4-5
1. The former will be a graph of four points, and the latter will be a graph of a line. **3.** Determine the point at which the graph intersects the x-axis by letting $y = 0$ and solving for x. Likewise, determine the point at which the graph intersects the y-axis by letting $x = 0$ and solving for y.

Draw a line through the two points. **5.** yes; $3y = -2$ **7.** no

9.

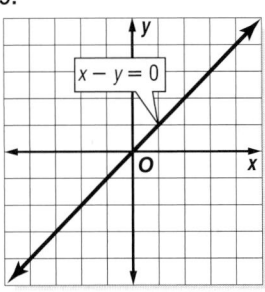

$x - y = 0$

11.

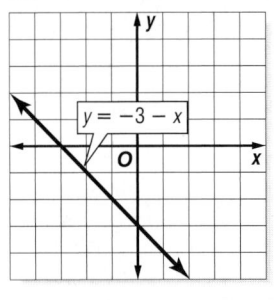

$y = -3 - x$

39.

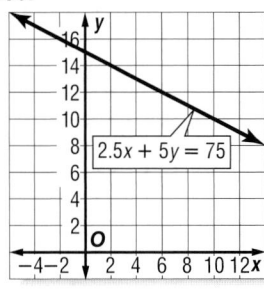

$2.5x + 5y = 75$

41.

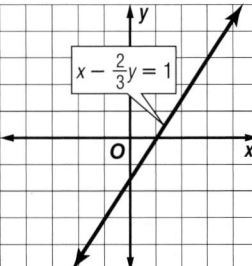

$x - \frac{2}{3}y = 1$

13.

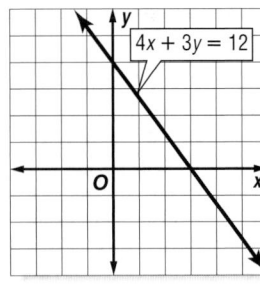

$4x + 3y = 12$

15. $15.75
17. yes; $2x + y = 6$
19. yes; $y = -5$ **21.** no
23. yes; $3x - 4y = 60$
25. yes; $3a = 2$

43.

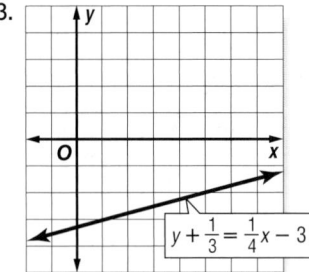

$y + \frac{1}{3} = \frac{1}{4}x - 3$

45. $5x + 3y = 15$
47. 7.5, 15

27.

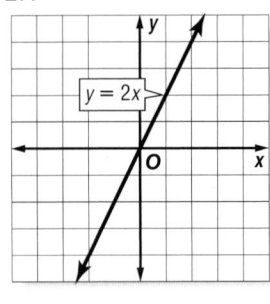

$y = 2x$

29.

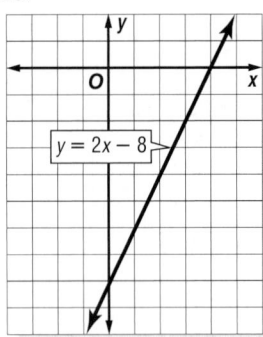

$y = 2x - 8$

31.

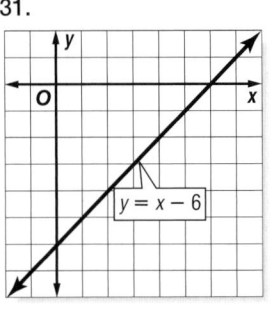

$y = x - 6$

33.

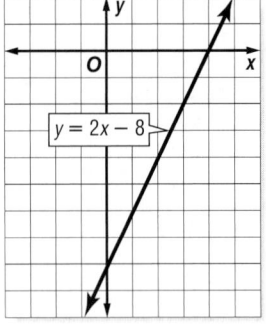

$x = 4y - 6$

49.

t	d
0	0
2	0.42
4	0.84
6	1.26
8	1.68
10	2.1
12	2.52
14	2.94
16	3.36

51. about 14 s **53.** about 171 lb
55. 186.7 psi **57.** Substitute
the values for x and y into the
equation $2x - y = 8$. If the value
of $2x - y$ is less than 8, then the
point lies *above* the line. If the
value of $2x - y$ is greater than 8,
then the point lies *below* the line.
If the value of $2x - y$ equals 8,
then the point lies *on* the line.
Sample answers: (1, 5) lies above
the line, (5, 1) lies below the line,
(6, 4) lies on the line. **59.** A **61.** {(−3, −8), (−1, −6),
(2, −3), (5, 0), (8, 3)} **63.** {(−3, 21), (−1, 15), (2, 6), (5, −3),
(8, −12)} **65.** {(−3, −30), (−1, −18), (2, 0), (5, 18), (8, 36)}
67. D = {−4, −3, 3}; R = {−1, 1, 2, 5}

x	y
3	5
−4	−1
−3	2
3	1

35.

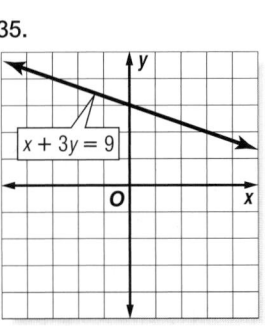

$x + 3y = 9$

37.

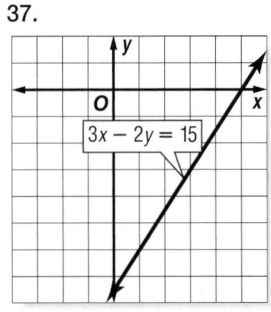

$3x - 2y = 15$

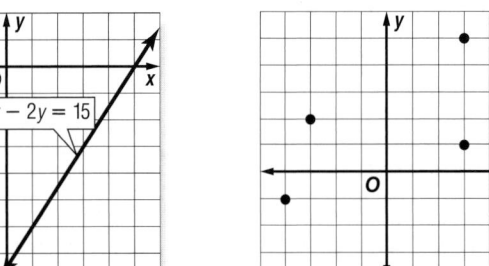

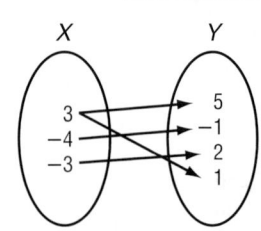

Selected Answers

69. D = {−1, 1, 3}; R = {−1, 0, 4, 5}

x	y
1	4
3	0
−1	−1
3	5

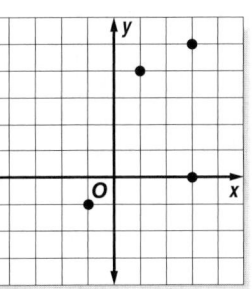

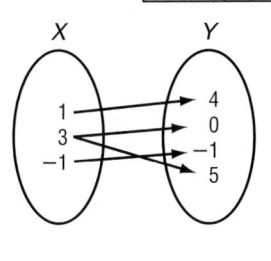

- As barometric pressure decreases, temperature increases. As barometric pressure increases, temperature decreases.
- The relation is not a function since there is more than one temperature for a given barometric pressure. However, there is still a pattern in the data and the two variables are related.

55. A

57.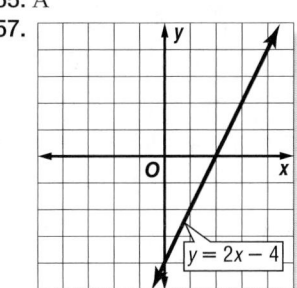

59. {(3, 12), (−1, −8)}
61. approximately 3 h 9 min **63.** Reflexive; 3.5
65. −4 **67.** 20 **69.** $\frac{5}{8}$

y = 2x − 4

71. 3 **73.** 4

75.

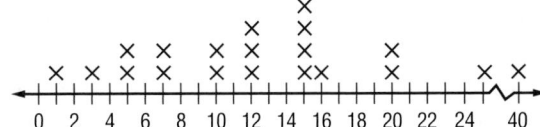

77. 15 yr **79.** 39 **81.** 48 **83.** 408

Pages 228–231 Lesson 4-6

1. y is not a function of x since 3 in the domain is paired with 2 and −3 in the range. x is not a function of y since −3 in the domain of the inverse is paired with 4 and 3 in the range. **3.** $x = c$, where c is any constant **5.** no **7.** yes
9. yes **11.** 2 **13.** $t^2 − 3$ **15.** $4x + 15$ **17.** no **19.** yes
21. yes **23.** yes **25.** yes **27.** yes **29.** no **31.** yes
33. 1 **35.** 0 **37.** 26 **39.** $3a^2 + 7$ **41.** $6m − 8$
43. $6x^2 + 4$ **45.** $f(h) = 77 − 0.005h$
47.

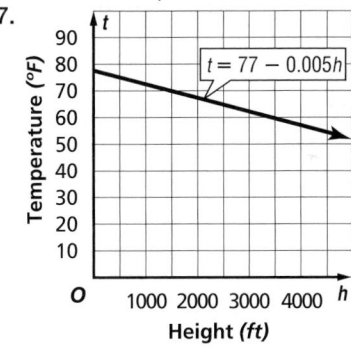

49.

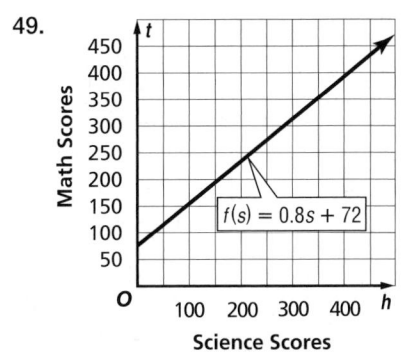

51. Krista's math score is above the average because the point at (260, 320) lies above the graph of the line for $f(s)$.
53. Functions can be used in meteorology to determine if there is a relationship between certain weather conditions. This can help to predict future weather patterns. Answers should include the following.

Page 231 Practice Quiz 2

1. {(−3, 2), (−1, 4), (0, 5), (2, 7), (4, 9)} **3.** {(−3, 5.5), (−1, 4.5), (0, 4), (2, 3), (4, 2)}
5.

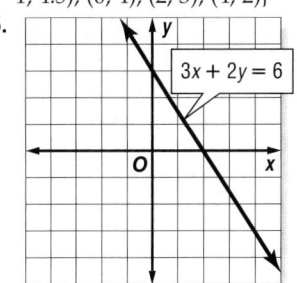

3x + 2y = 6

7. no **9.** $6a + 5$

Pages 236–238 Lesson 4-7

1. Sample answer: 2, −8, −18, −28, … **3.** Marisela; to find the common difference, subtract the first term from the second term. **5.** no **7.** 14, 9, 4 **9.** −90 **11.** 101
13. $a_n = 5n + 7$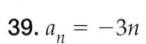

15. yes; −1 **17.** no
19. yes; 0.5 **21.** 16, 19, 22
23. −82, −86, −90
25. $3\frac{2}{3}$, 4, $4\frac{1}{3}$ **27.** 125
29. 1264 **31.** $3\frac{1}{4}$ **33.** 25
35. 25 **37.** 17

39. $a_n = −3n$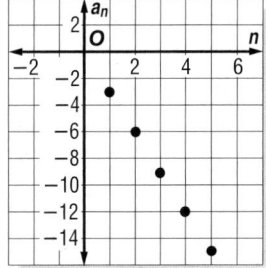

41. $a_n = 6n − 4$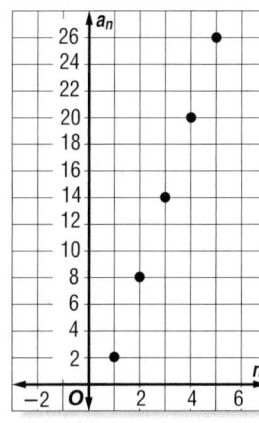

43. 4 **45.** $P(n) = 3n + 2$ **47.** $a_n = 8n + 20$ **49.** Yes, the section was oversold by 4 seats. **51.** $a_n = 4n + 5$

53.

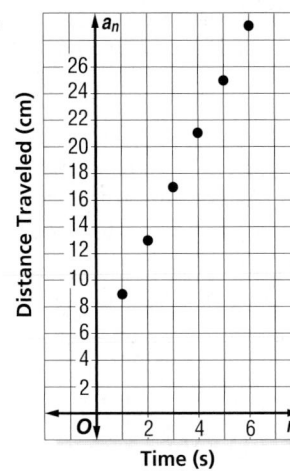

55. $92,500
57. 45 **59.** C
61. 10 **63.** 32
65. yes; $x + y = 18$
67. $200 - 3x = 9$
69. -21 **71.** 12
73. $-\dfrac{5}{14}$
75. $(-2, 2)$
77. $(-4, -2)$
79. $(3, 5)$

Pages 243–245 Lesson 4-8

1. Once you recognize a pattern, you can find a general rule that can be written as an algebraic expression. **3.** Test the values of the domain in the equation. If the resulting values match the range, the equation is correct. **5.** 16, 22, 29
7. $f(x) = x$
9.

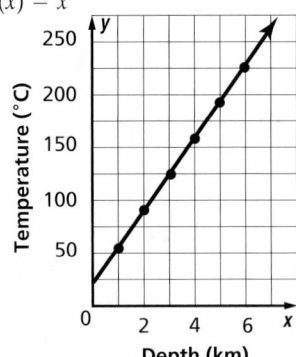

11. 370°

13.

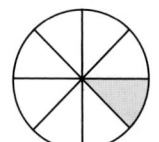 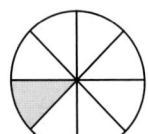 ;

15. 10, 13, 11 **17.** 27, 35, 44 **19.** $4x + 1, 5x + 1, 6x + 1$
21. $f(x) = \dfrac{1}{2}x$ **23.** $f(x) = 6 - x$ **25.** $f(x) = 12 - 3x$
27. 1, 1, 2, 3, 5, 8, 13, 21, 34, 55, 89, 144 **29.** $f(a) = -0.9a + 193$
31. 5, 8, 11, 14 cm **33.** 74 cm **35.** B **37.** 13, 16, 19
39. $-1, 5, 11$ **41.** no

Pages 246–250 Chapter 4 Study Guide and Review
1. e **3.** d **5.** k **7.** c **9.** b
11–16.

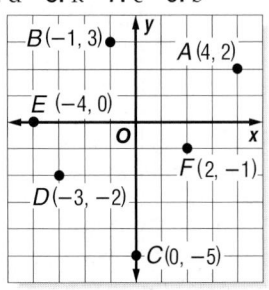

17. $A'(3, -3), B'(5, -4),$
$C'(4, 3)$

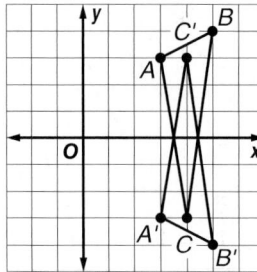

19. $G'(1, 1), H'(3, 0), I'(3, 1),$
$J'(1, 2)$

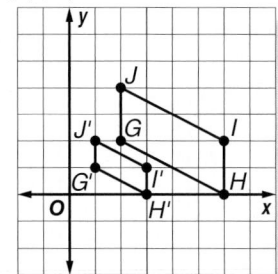

21. D = $\{-2, 3, 4\}$, R = $\{-2, 0, 6\}$

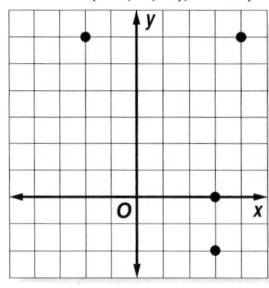

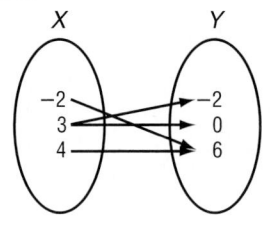

23. D = $\{-3, 3, 5, 9\}$, R = $\{3, 8\}$

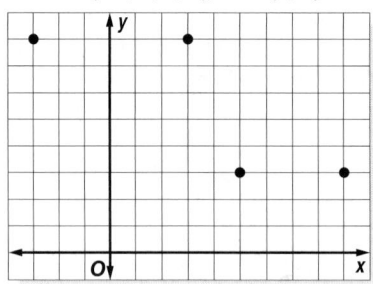

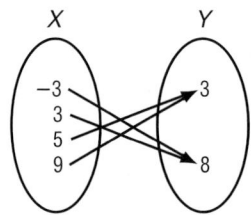

25. $\{(-4, -13), (-2, -11),$
$(0, -9), (2, -7), (4, -5)\}$

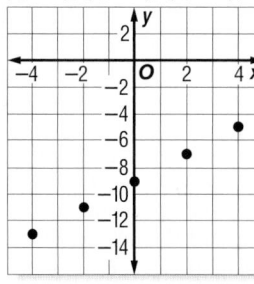

27. $\{(-4, -11), (-2, -3),$
$(0, 5), (2, 13), (4, 21)\}$

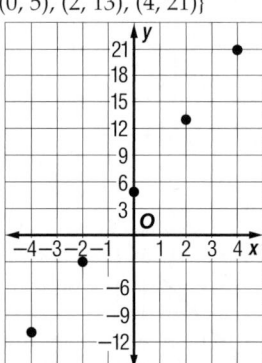

29. $\left\{\left(-4, 10\frac{1}{2}\right), \left(-2, 7\frac{1}{2}\right),\right.$ $\left.\left(0, 4\frac{1}{2}\right), \left(2, 1\frac{1}{2}\right), \left(4, -1\frac{1}{2}\right)\right\}$

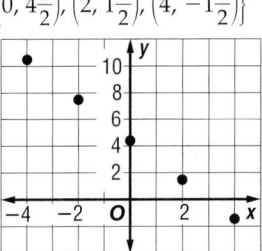

31.

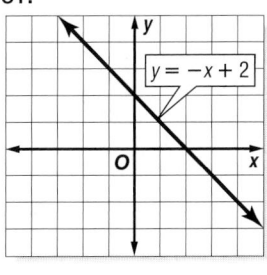

33.

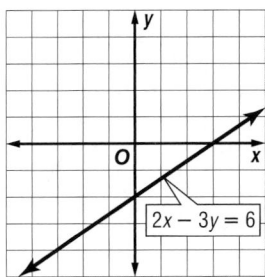

35.

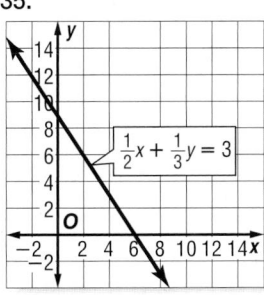

37. yes **39.** yes **41.** 3 **43.** 18 **45.** $4a^2 + 2a + 1$
47. 26, 31, 36 **49.** 6, 4, 2 **51.** −11, −5, 1 **53.** $f(x) = -x - 1$

Chapter 5 Analyzing Linear Equations

Page 255 Chapter 5 Getting Started
1. $\frac{1}{5}$ **3.** $-\frac{1}{4}$ **5.** $\frac{1}{3}$ **7.** 3 **9.** $\frac{1}{4}$ **11.** $-\frac{3}{4}$ **13.** 0 **15.** (1, 2)
17. (2, −3) **19.** (−2, 2)

Pages 259–262 Lesson 5-1
1. Sample answer: Use (−1, −3) as (x_1, y_1) and (3, −5) as (x_2, y_2) in the slope formula. **3.** The difference in the x values is always the 0, and division by 0 is undefined.
5. $\frac{3}{2}$ **7.** −4 **9.** 0 **11.** 5 **13.** 1.5 million subscribers per year
15. $\frac{3}{4}$ **17.** −2 **19.** undefined **21.** $\frac{10}{7}$ **23.** $\frac{3}{8}$
25. undefined **27.** 0 **29.** $-\frac{1}{2}$ **31.** $\frac{15}{4}$ **33.** $-\frac{2}{3}$
35. Sample answer: $\frac{8}{11}$ **37.** $\frac{s}{r}$, if $r \neq 0$ **39.** 4 **41.** −1 **43.** 1
45. $\frac{1}{4}$ **47.** 7 **49.** (−4, −5) is in Quadrant III and (4, 5) is in

Quadrant I. The segment connecting them goes from lower left to upper right, which is a positive slope. **51.** 12–14; steepest part of the graph **53.** '90–'95; '80–'85 **55.** a

decline in enrollment **57.** 13 ft 9 in. **59.** D **61.** $\frac{1}{3}$; The

slope is the same regardless of points chosen. **63.** $f(x) = 5x$
65. yes **67.** no

69.

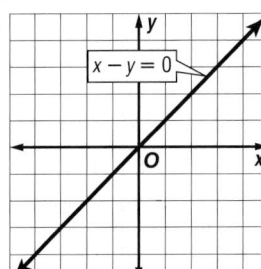

71. −21 **73.** −36
75. $-\frac{7}{24}$ **77.** 9
79. $26\frac{2}{3}$ **81.** $4\frac{1}{2}$
83. $20\frac{4}{7}$ **85.** $10\frac{2}{3}$

Pages 267–270 Lesson 5-2
1. $y = kx$ **3.** They are equal. **5.** 1; 1
7.

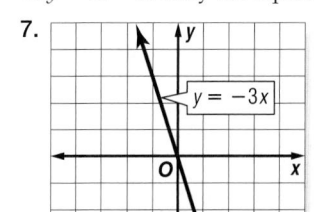

9. $y = \frac{9}{2}x$; 10
11. $y = \frac{1}{2}x$; 10

13.

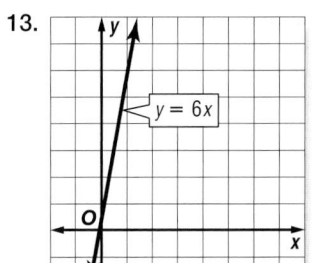

15. 2; 2
17. $-\frac{1}{2}$; $-\frac{1}{2}$
19. $\frac{3}{2}$; $\frac{3}{2}$

21.

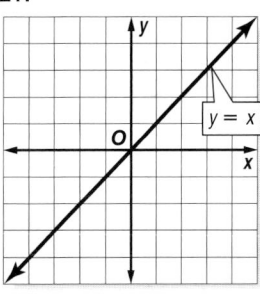

23.

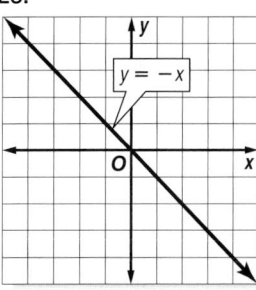

25.

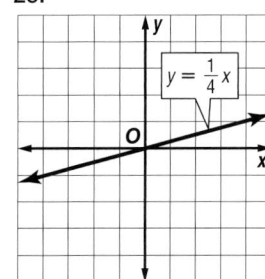

27.

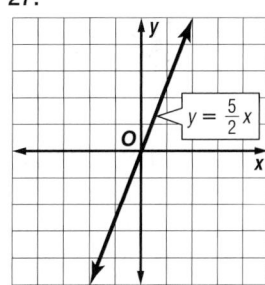

29.

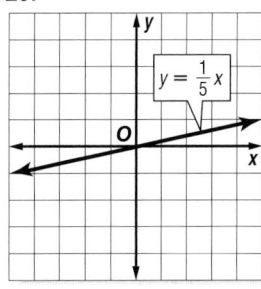

31.

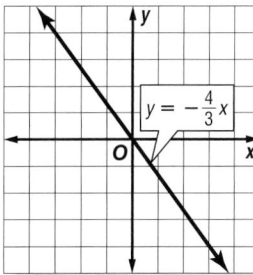

33. $y = 2x$; 10 **35.** $y = -4x$; −5 **37.** $y = \frac{1}{3}x$; −8
39. $y = 5x$; 100 **41.** $y = \frac{32}{3}x$; 12

43. $C = 3.14d$

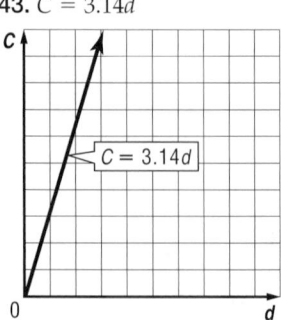

45. $C = 0.99n$

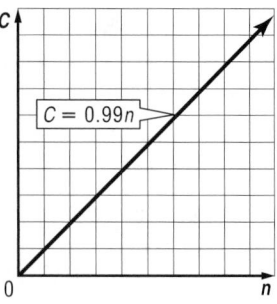

47. It also doubles. If $\frac{y}{x} = k$, and x is multiplied by 2, y must also be multiplied by 2 to maintain the value of k.
49. 2   **51.** 3   **53.** 23 lb   **55.** 5 yrs 4 mos   **57.** D
59.

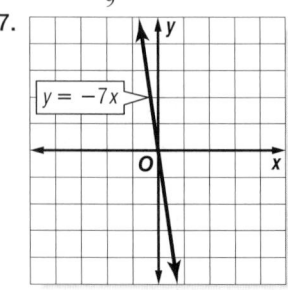

61. Sample answer: $y = -5x$ **63.** -3
65. 2

67.

x	0	1	2	3	4	5
y	1	5	9	13	17	21

69. 3   **71.** -15 **73.** $y = 3x + 8$ **75.** $y = 4x - 3$
77. $y = -3x + 4$

Page 270   Practice Quiz 1
1. -2 **3.** $\frac{1}{9}$ **5.** 4
7.

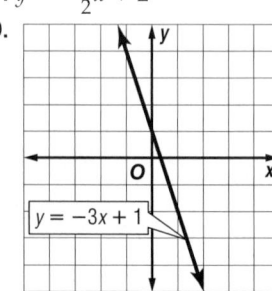

9. $y = 3x;\ -9$

Pages 275–277   Lesson 5-3
1. Sample answer: $y = 7x + 2$ **3.** slope   **5.** $y = 4x - 2$
7. $y = -\frac{3}{2}x + 2$
9.

11. $T = 50 + 5w$ **13.** \$85
15. $y = 3x - 5$
17. $y = -\frac{3}{5}x$
19. $y = 0.5x + 7.5$
21. $y = \frac{3}{2}x - 4$
23. $y = -\frac{2}{3}x + 1$
25. $y = 2$ **27.** $y = 3x$

29.

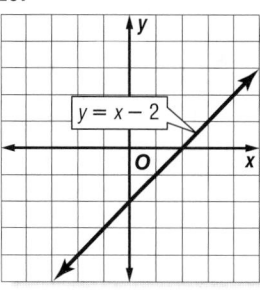

31.

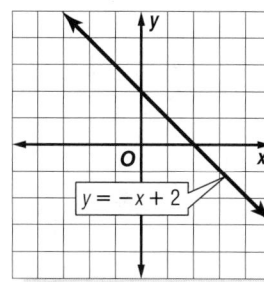

33.

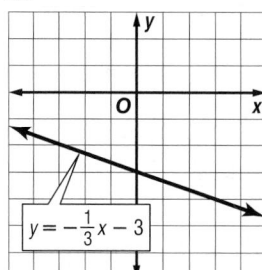

35.

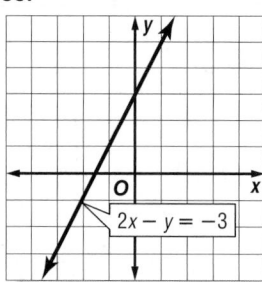

37.

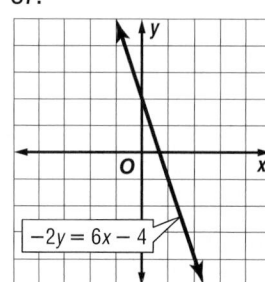

39.

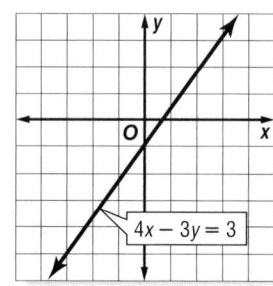

41. $C = 50 + 25h$ **43.** $T = 15 - 2h$ **45.** $S = 16 + t$
47. $R = 5.5 - 0.12t$ **49.** 1.54   **51.** D   **53.** $y = -\frac{A}{B}x + \frac{C}{B}$,
where $B \neq 0$ **55a.** $m = -2, b = -4$ **55b.** $m = -\frac{3}{4}, b = 3$
55c. $m = \frac{2}{3}, b = -3$ **57.** $y = \frac{15}{4}x, 37\frac{1}{2}$ **59.** undefined
61. $-0.5, \frac{3}{4}, \frac{7}{8}, 2.5$ **63.** 23   **65.** -2 **67.** $-\frac{4}{3}$

Pages 283–285   Lesson 5-4
1. When you have the slope and one point, you can substitute these values in for x, y, and m to find b. When you are given two points, you must first find the slope and then use the first procedure.   **3.** Sometimes; if the x- and y-intercepts are both zero, you cannot write the equation of the graph.   **5.** $y = -3x + 16$ **7.** $y = -x + 6$ **9.** $y = \frac{1}{2}x - \frac{1}{2}$
11. $y = 3x - 1$ **13.** $y = 3x - 17$ **15.** $y = -2x + 6$
17. $y = -\frac{2}{3}x - 3$ **19.** $y = x - 3$ **21.** $y = x - 2$ **23.** $y = -2x + 1$ **25.** $y = -2$ **27.** $y = \frac{1}{2}x + \frac{1}{2}$ **29.** $y = -\frac{1}{4}x + \frac{11}{16}$
31. $y = -\frac{4}{3}x + 4$ **33.** $y = x - 2$ **35.** about 27.6 years
37. about 26.05 years   **39.** 205,000   **41.** $y = \frac{2}{7}x - 2$
43. $(7, 0); (0, -2)$
45. Answers should include the following.
- Linear extrapolation is when you use a linear equation to predict values that are outside of the given points on the graph.
- You can use the slope-intercept form of the equation to find the y-value for any requested x-value.
47. B

49.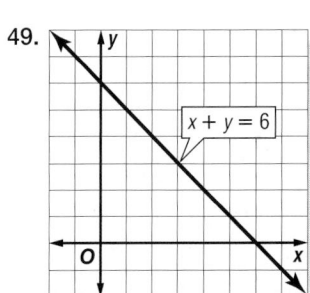

51. $V = 2.5b$
53. $\{-2, 0, 5\}$ **55.** $<$
57. -3 **59.** 5 **61.** -15

47. If two equations have the same slope, then the lines are parallel. Answers should include the following.
- Sample answer: $y = -5x + 1$; The graphs have the same slope.
- Sample answer: $y = \frac{1}{5}x$; The slopes are negative reciprocals of each other.

49. C   **51.** $y - 7 = 5(x + 4)$ **53.** $C = 0.22m + 0.99$
55. $y = -\frac{1}{2}x + \frac{3}{2}$ **57.** $y = -5x + 11$ **59.** $y = 9$

Pages 289–291   Lesson 5-5

1. They are the coordinates of any point on the graph of the equation.   **3.** Sample answer: $y - 2 = 4(x + 1); y = 4x + 6$
5. $y + 2 = 3(x + 1)$ **7.** $4x - y = -13$ **9.** $5x - 2y = 11$
11. $y = -\frac{2}{3}x + 1$ **13.** $y - 3 = 2(x + 1)$ or $y + 1 = 2(x + 3)$
15. $y - 8 = 2(x - 3)$ **17.** $y - 4 = -3(x + 2)$ **19.** $y - 6 = 0$
21. $y + 3 = \frac{3}{4}(x - 8)$ **23.** $y + 3 = -\frac{5}{8}(x - 1)$
25. $y - 8 = \frac{7}{2}(x + 4)$ **27.** $y + 9 = 0$ **29.** $4x - y = -5$
31. $2x + y = -7$ **33.** $x - 2y = 12$ **35.** $2x + 5y = 26$
37. $5x - 3y = -24$ **39.** $13x - 10y = -151$ **41.** $y = 3x - 1$
43. $y = -2x + 8$ **45.** $y = \frac{1}{2}x - 1$ **47.** $y = -\frac{1}{4}x - \frac{7}{2}$
49. $y = x - 1$ **51.** $y = -3x - \frac{7}{4}$ **53.** $y + 3 = 10(x - 5);$
$y = 10x - 53; 10x - y = 53$ **55.** $y - 210 = 5(x - 12)$
57. $150   **59.** $y = 1500x - 2,964,310$ **61.** $\overline{RQ}: y + 3 = \frac{1}{2}(x + 1)$ or $y + 1 = \frac{1}{2}(x - 3); \overline{QP}: y + 1 = -2(x - 3)$ or $y - 3 = -2(x - 1); \overline{PS}: y - 3 = \frac{1}{2}(x - 1)$ or $y - 1 = \frac{1}{2}(x + 3);$
$\overline{RS}: y + 3 = -2(x + 1)$ or $y - 1 = -2(x + 3)$ **63.** $\overline{RQ}: x - 2y = 5; \overline{QP}: 2x + y = 5; \overline{PS}: x - 2y = -5; \overline{RS}: 2x + y = -5$
65. Answers should include the following.
- Write the definition of the slope using (x, y) as one point and (x_1, y_1) as the other. Then solve the equation so that the ys are on one side and the slope and xs are on the other.

67. $y = mx - 2m - 5$ **69.** All of the equations are the same.   **71.** Regardless of which two points on a line you select, the slope-intercept form of the equation will always be the same.   **73.** $y = 3x + 10$ **75.** $y = -1$ **77.** -6 **79.** 7
81. $\frac{1}{10}$ **83.** -1 **85.** -9 **87.** $-\frac{3}{2}$

Pages 295–297   Lesson 5-6

1. The slope is $\frac{3}{2}$, so the slope of a line perpendicular to the given line is $-\frac{2}{3}$.   **3.** Parallel lines lie in the same plane and never intersect. Perpendicular lines intersect at right angles.

5. $y = x + 1$ **7.** $y = 3x + 8$ **9.** $y = -3x - 8$ **11.** $y = \frac{1}{2}x - 3$
13. $y = x - 9$ **15.** $y = x + 5$ **17.** $y = \frac{1}{2}x - \frac{3}{2}$
19. $y = -\frac{1}{3}x - \frac{13}{3}$ **21.** $y = \frac{1}{2}x + \frac{3}{2}$ **23.** $y = -6x - 9$
25. The lines for $x = 3$ and $x = -1$ are parallel because all vertical lines are parallel. The lines for $y = \frac{2}{3}x + 2$ and $y = \frac{2}{3}x - 3$ are parallel because they have the same slope. Thus, both pairs of opposite sides are parallel and the figure is a parallelogram.   **27.** $y = \frac{1}{3}x - 6$ **29.** $y = -\frac{1}{4}x + \frac{5}{4}$
31. $y = \frac{1}{8}x + 5$ **33.** $y = -\frac{3}{2}x + 13$ **35.** $y = -\frac{5}{2}x + 2$
37. $y = -\frac{1}{5}x - 1$ **39.** $y = -3$ **41.** $y = -\frac{1}{2}x + 2$
43. parallel   **45.** They are perpendicular, because the slopes are 3 and $-\frac{1}{3}$.

Page 297   Practice Quiz 2

1. $y = 4x - 3$ **3.** $y = \frac{5}{2}x + \frac{1}{2}$ **5.** $x - 2y = -11,$
$y = \frac{1}{2}x + \frac{11}{2}$

Pages 301–305   Lesson 5-7

1. If the data points form a linear pattern such that y increases as x increases, there is a positive correlation. If the linear pattern shows that y decreases as x increases, there is a negative correlation.   **3.** Linear extrapolation predicts values outside the range of the data set. Linear interpolation predicts values inside the range of the data.
5. Negative; the more TV you watch, the less you exercise.
7. positive correlation

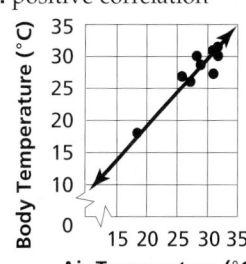

9. 40.1°C
11. no correlation
13. Positive; the higher the sugar content, the more Calories.
15. 18.85 million
17. $3600

19.

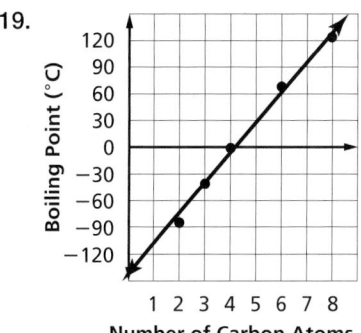

21. Sample answer: -116°C   **23.** Sample answer: 7
25.

27. Sample answer: about $17.3 billion

29.

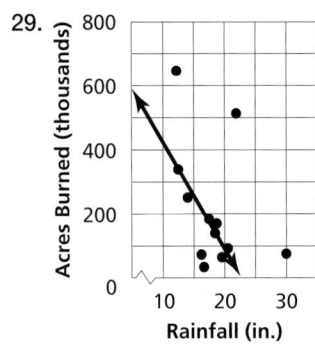

31. using (12.7, 340) and (17.5, 194) and rounding, $y = -30.4x + 726.3$ **33.** The data point lies beyond the main grouping of data points. It can be ignored as an extreme value.
37. You can visualize a line to determine whether the data has a positive or negative correlation. Answers should include the following.

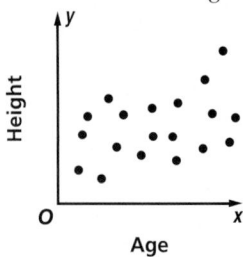

• Write a linear equation for the line of fit. Then substitute the person's height and solve for the corresponding age.
39. B   **45.** $y = -4x - 3$ **47.** $y - 3 = -2(x + 2)$ **49.** $y + 3 = x + 3$ **51.** 4, -1.6 **53.** -5 **55.** 3

31.

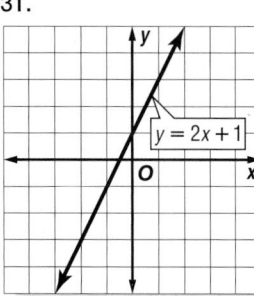

33.

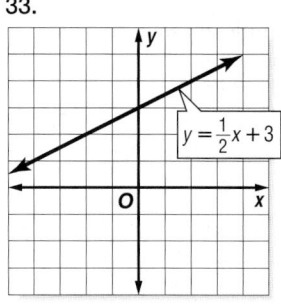

35.

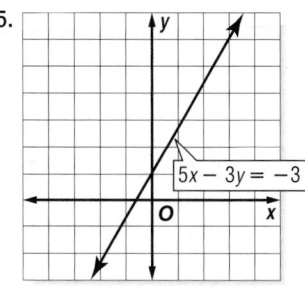

37. $y = x + 6$
39. $y = \frac{1}{2}x + \frac{11}{2}$
41. $y = 2x + 10$
43. $y = -1$
45. $y - 6 = 5(x - 4)$
47. $y + 3 = \frac{1}{2}(x - 5)$
49. $y + 2 = 3\left(x - \frac{1}{4}\right)$
51. $2x - y = -3$
53. $3x - 2y = 20$

55. $y = -2x + 6$ **57.** $y = \frac{5}{12}x + 4$ **59.** $y = -\frac{1}{3}x + 1$

61. $y = \frac{1}{2}x - 3$ **63.** $y = -\frac{7}{2}x - 14$ **65.** $y = 5x - 15$

67.

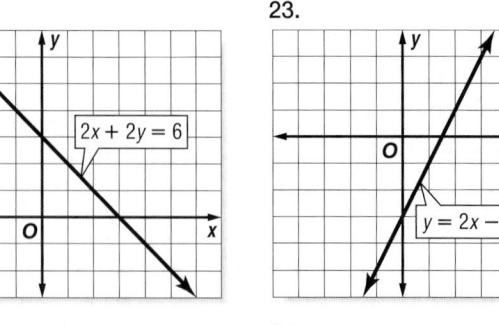

69. $38\frac{1}{3}$ long tons

Pages 308–312   Chapter 5   Study Guide and Review
1. direct variation   **3.** parallel   **5.** slope-intercept   **7.** 3
9. undefined   **11.** 1.5
13.

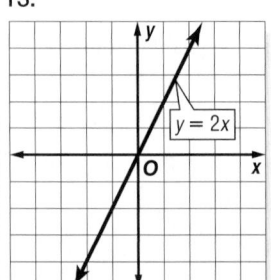

15.

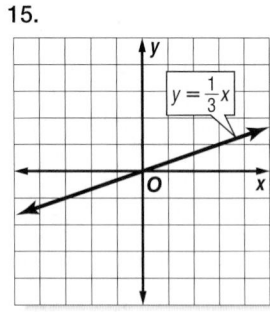

17.

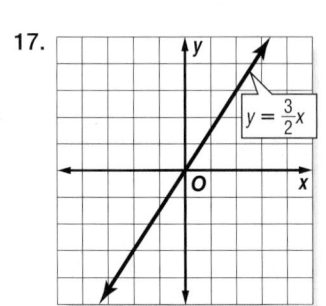

19. $y = -\frac{2}{3}x$
21. $y = -x$
23. $y = -2x$
25. $y = 3x + 2$
27. $y = 4$
29. $y = 0.5x - 0.3$

Chapter 6   Solving Linear Inequalities

Page 317   Chapter 6   Getting Started
1. 53   **3.** -9 **5.** -45 **7.** 4   **9.** 22   **11.** 4   **13.** 8   **15.** 30
17. 7   **19.** 1
21.

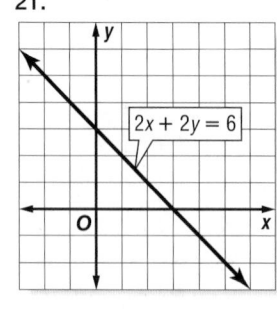

23.

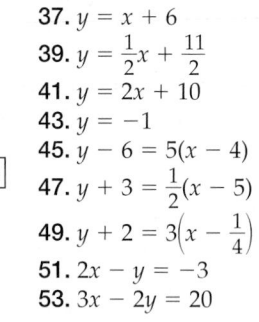

25.

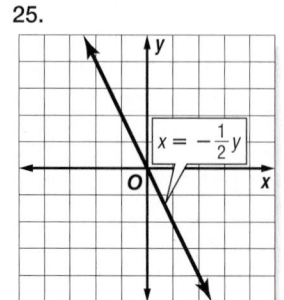

27.

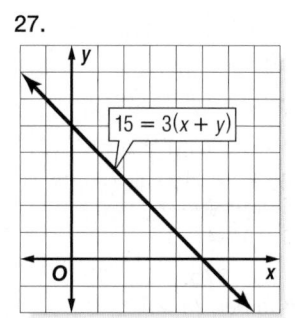

Pages 321–323 Lesson 6-1

1. Sample answers: $y + 1 < -2$, $y - 1 < -4$, $y + 3 < 0$
3. The set of all numbers b such that b is greater than or equal to -5.
5. $\{a \mid a < -2\}$

7. $\{t \mid t \geq 12\}$

9. $\{r \mid r \leq 6.7\}$

11. Sample answer: Let $n =$ the number; $n - 8 \leq 14$; $\{n \mid n \leq 22\}$. **13.** no more than 33 g **15.** f **17.** c **19.** b
21. $\{d \mid d \leq 2\}$ **23.** $\{s \mid s > 4\}$

25. $\{r \mid r < -4\}$ **27.** $\{m \mid m \geq 3\}$

29. $\{f \mid f < -3\}$ **31.** $\{w \mid w \geq 1\}$

33. $\{a \mid a \leq -5\}$ **35.** $\{x \mid x \geq 0.6\}$

37. $\left\{p \mid p \leq 1\frac{1}{9}\right\}$

39a. 12 **39b.** 7 **39c.** 16 **41.** Sample answer: Let $n =$ the number; $n - 5 < 33$; $\{n \mid n < 38\}$. **43.** Sample answer: Let $n =$ the number; $2n > n + 14$; $\{n \mid n > 14\}$. **45.** Sample answer: Let $n =$ the number; $4n \leq 3n + (-2)$; $\{n \mid n \leq -2\}$.
47. at least 199,999,998,900 stars **49.** at least \$3747 **51.** no more than \$33 **53a.** always **53b.** never **53c.** sometimes
55. $\{p \mid p > 25\}$ **57.** C **59.** no **61.** $y = -x + 4$ **63.** 31, 37 **65.** 48, 96 **67.** $\{(-1, 8), (3, 4), (5, 2)\}$ **69.** 7 **71.** 21
73. 49 **75.** 24.5

Pages 328–331 Lesson 6-2

1. You could solve the inequality by multiplying each side by $-\frac{1}{7}$ or by dividing each side by -7. In either case, you must reverse the direction of the inequality symbol.
3. Ilonia; when you divide each side of an inequality by a negative number, you must reverse the direction of the inequality symbol. **5.** c **7.** $\{t \mid t < -108\}$
9. $\{f \mid f \geq 0.36\}$ **11.** Sample answer: Let $n =$ the number; $\frac{1}{2}n \geq 26$; $\{n \mid n \geq 52\}$. **13.** d **15.** e **17.** b **19.** $\{g \mid g \leq 24\}$
21. $\{d \mid d \leq -6\}$ **23.** $\{m \mid m \geq 35\}$ **25.** $\{r \mid r > 49\}$
27. $\{y \mid y \geq -24\}$ **29.** $\{q \mid q \geq 44\}$ **31.** $\{w \mid w > -2.72\}$
33. $\left\{c \mid c < -\frac{1}{10}\right\}$
35. $\{y \mid y < -4\}$

37a. 3.5 **37b.** -14 **37c.** -6 **39.** Sample answer: Let $n =$ the number; $7n > 28$; $\{n \mid n > 4\}$. **41.** Sample answer: Let $n =$

the number; $24 \leq \frac{1}{3}n$; $\{n \mid n \geq 72\}$. **43.** Sample answer: Let $n =$ the number; $0.25n \geq 90$; $\{n \mid n \geq 360\}$. **45.** less than $4\frac{1}{4}$ ft
47. no more than 27 min **49.** up to about 6 ft **51.** at least 3 times **53.** at least 175 spaces
55. Inequalities can be used to compare the heights of walls. Answers should include the following.
• If x represents the number of bricks and the wall must be no higher than 4 ft or 48 in., then $3x \leq 48$.
• To solve this inequality, divide each side by 3 and do not change the direction of the inequality. The wall must be 16 bricks high or fewer.
57. C
59. $\{g \mid g \leq -7\}$

61. Sample answer:

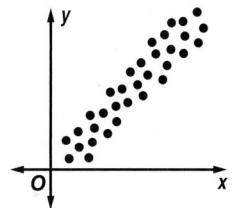

63. $y = -2$ **65.** -10 **67.** $3w + 2$ **69.** 6 **71.** 5 **73.** 7
75. 12 **77.** -8

Page 331 Practice Quiz 1

1. $\{h \mid h > 3\}$

3. $\{p \mid p \leq -5\}$

5. $\{g \mid g \leq -1\}$

7. $\{v \mid v < 35\}$ **9.** $\{r \mid r > -13\}$

Pages 334–337 Lesson 6-3

1. To solve both the equation and the inequality, you first subtract 6 from each side and then divide each side by -5. In the equation, the equal sign does not change. In the inequality, the inequality sign is reversed because you divided by a negative number. **3a.** Distributive Property
3b. Add 12 to each side. **3c.** Divide each side by 3.
5. $\{r \mid r \geq -18\}$ **7.** $\{g \mid g < -1\}$ **9.** Sample answer: Let $n =$ the number; $7 - 2n < 3n + 32$; $\{n \mid n > -5\}$. **11a.** Subtract 7 from each side. **11b.** Multiply each side by $\frac{5}{2}$.
13.

$4(t - 7) \leq 2(t + 9)$	Original inequality
$4t - 28 \leq 2t + 18$	Distributive Property
$4t - 28 - 2t \leq 2t + 18 - 2t$	Subtract $2t$ from each side.
$2t - 28 \leq 18$	Simplify.
$2t - 28 + 28 \leq 18 + 28$	Add 28 to each side.
$2t \leq 46$	Simplify.
$\dfrac{2t}{2} \leq \dfrac{46}{2}$	Divide each side by 2.
$t \leq 23$	Simplify.

$\{t \mid t \leq 23\}$

15. $\{t \mid t \geq 3\}$ **17.** $\{d \mid d > -125\}$ **19.** $\left\{q \mid q \leq 3\frac{1}{3}\right\}$
21. $\{r \mid r \geq -9\}$ **23.** $\{v \mid v \geq 19\}$ **25.** $\{w \mid w \leq 1\}$

27. $\{t \mid t \geq -1\}$ **29.** $\varnothing$ **31.** $\{v \mid v \geq 4.5\}$
33. $\{y \mid y \leq 11\}$

35. Sample answer: Let $n =$ the number; $\frac{1}{8}n - 5 \geq 30$;
$\{n \mid n \geq 280\}$.   **37.** Sample answer: Let $n =$ the number;

$-4n + 9 \leq n - 21; \{n \mid n \geq 6\}$.   **39.** $3a - 15 < 90$

41. $\dfrac{91 + 95 + 88 + s}{4} \geq 92$ **43.** $\dfrac{5(F - 32)}{9} < -38$ **45.** more

than $12\frac{1}{2}$ weeks   **47.** 3 or fewer toppings   **49.** no change

51. 7, 9; 5, 7; 3, 5; 1, 3
53. Inequalities can be used to describe the temperatures
for which an element is a gas or a solid. Answers should
include the following.
- The inequality for temperatures in degrees Celsius for
  which bromine is a gas is $\frac{9}{5}C + 32 > 138$.
- Sample answer: Scientists may use inequalities to
  describe the temperatures for which an element is a solid.

55. C   **57.** $\{x \mid x \leq 8\}$ **59.** up to 416 mi
61. $\{t \mid t < 8\}$

63. $y + 3 = 2(x - 1)$ **65.** $y - 6 = 0$ **67.** $\dfrac{7}{3}$
69. yes; $4x - 2y = 7$ **71.** yes; $x + 0y = 12$ **73.** 2.5
75.

77.

79.

81.

Pages 341–344   Lesson 6-4
1. A compound inequality containing *and* is true if and only
if both inequalities are true. A compound inequality
containing *or* is true if and only if at least one of the
inequalities is true.   **3.** Sample answer: $x < -2$ and $x > 3$
5.

7. $x \leq -1$ or $x \geq 5$
9. $\{n \mid n \leq 2$ or $n \geq 8\}$

11. $\{x \mid -4 < x \leq 1\}$

13. about $4.44 \leq x \leq 6.67$
15.

17.

19.

21. $-7 < x < -3$ **23.** $x \leq -7$ or $x \geq -6$ **25.** $x = 2$ or
$x > 5$ **27.** $t \leq 18$ or $t \geq 22$
29. $\{f \mid -13 \leq f \leq -5\}$

31. $\{h \mid h < -1\}$

33. $\{y \mid 3 < y < 6\}$

35. $\{q \mid -1 < q < 6\}$

37. $\{n \mid n \leq 4\}$

39. $\varnothing$

41. $\{b \mid b < -12$ or $b > -12\}$

43. Sample answer: Let $n =$ the number; $-8 < 3n + 4 < 10$;
$\{n \mid -4 < n < 2\}$.   **45.** Sample answer: Let $n =$ the number;
$0 < \frac{1}{2}n \leq 1; \{n \mid 0 < n \leq 2\}$.   **47.** between \$145 and \$230
inclusive   **49a.** $x \geq 5$ and $x \leq 8$ **49b.** $x > 6$ or $x < 1$
51. $\{h \mid 15 \leq h \leq 50{,}000\}$; $\{h \mid 20 \leq h \leq 20{,}000\}$ **53.** Sample
answer: troposphere: $a \leq 10$; stratosphere: $10 < a \leq 30$;
mesosphere: $30 < a \leq 50$; thermosphere: $50 < a \leq 400$;
exosphere: $a > 400$ **55.** A   **57a.** $\{x \mid x < -6$ or $x > -1\}$
57b. $\{x \mid -2 \leq x \leq 8\}$ **59.** $\{d \mid d \geq 5\}$ **61.** $\{t \mid t < 169\}$
63. 2.25   **65.** $\{(6, 0), (-3, 5), (2, -2), (-3, 3)\}$; $\{-3, 2, 6\}$;
$\{-2, 0, 3, 5\}$; $\{(0, 6), (5, -3), (-2, 2), (3, -3)\}$ **67.** $\{(3, 4),$
$(3, 2), (2, 9), (5, 4), (5, 8), (-7, 2)\}$; $\{-7, 2, 3, 5\}$; $\{2, 4, 8, 9\}$;
$\{(4, 3), (2, 3), (9, 2), (4, 5), (8, 5), (2, -7)\}$ **69.** 5:1   **71.** -470
73. 7   **75.** 1   **77.** 6   **79.** 1

Page 344   Practice Quiz 2
1. $\{b \mid b < 7\}$ **3.** $\{t \mid t < -3\}$ **5.** $\{m \mid m \geq 3\}$
7. $\{x \mid 3 < x < 9\}$

9. $\{m \mid m > 3$ or $m < -1\}$

Pages 348–351   Lesson 6-5
1. The solution of $|x - 2| > 6$ includes all values that are
less than -4 or greater than 8. The solution of $|x - 2| < 6$
includes all values that are greater than -4 and less than 8.
3. Leslie; you need to consider the case when the value
inside the absolute value symbols is positive and the case
when the value inside the absolute value symbols is
negative. So $x + 3 = 2$ or $x + 3 = -2$.   **5.** c
7. $\{-13, 7\}$

9. $\{w \mid w < -5$ or $w > 25\}$

11. $|x - 1| = 3$ **13.** $\{d \mid 1.499 \leq d \leq 1.501\}$ **15.** f   **17.** b
19. d   **21.** $|t - 38| \leq 1.5$ **23.** $|s - 55| \leq 3$

25. $\{-11, -7\}$

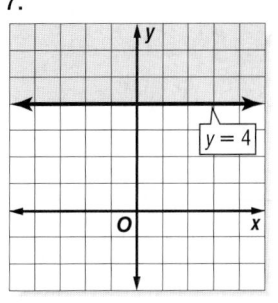 (number line)

27. $\{-0.8, 4\}$

29. $\{t \mid -10 < t < -6\}$

31. $\{w \mid w \leq 3 \text{ or } w \geq 9\}$

33. $\left\{k \mid k \leq -4 \text{ or } k \geq 1\frac{1}{3}\right\}$

35. $\varnothing$

37. $\{w \mid 0 \leq w \leq 18\}$

39. $\left\{x \mid x \leq -2\frac{2}{3} \text{ or } x \geq 4\right\}$

41. $|x - 3| = 5$ **43.** $|x + 3| < 4$ **45.** $|x + 10| \geq 2$
47. $\{d \mid 266 \leq d \leq 294\}$ **49.** $\{t \mid 65 \leq t \leq 71\}$ **51.** $\{p \mid 28 \leq p \leq 32\}$ **53.** $\{a \mid 2.5 \leq a \leq 3.5\}$ **55a.** 1.8, 4.2 **55b.** $|x - 3| = 1.2$ **57.** B **59.** between 114 and 152 beats per min
61. $\left\{x \mid x \leq -1\frac{1}{3}\right\}$ **63.** $-2; 4$ **65.** $-\frac{2}{3}; 0$ **67.** $x = \dfrac{3z + 2y}{e}$
69. -5 **71.** 4.2 **73.** Substitution Property

75.

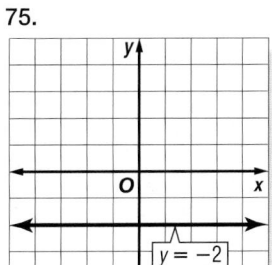

77.

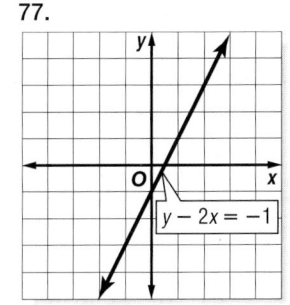

79.

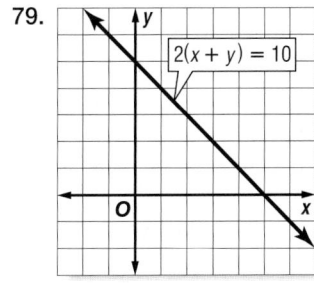

---

1. The graph of $y = x + 2$ is a line. The graph of $y < x + 2$ does not include the boundary $y = x + 2$, and it includes all ordered pairs in the half-plane that contains the origin.
3. If the test point results in a true statement, shade the half-plane that contains the point. If the test point results in a false statement, shade the other half-plane. **5.** $\{(2, 6)\}$

7.

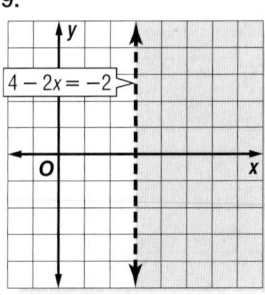

9.

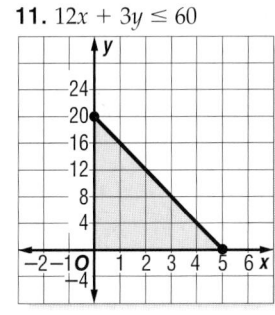

11. $12x + 3y \leq 60$

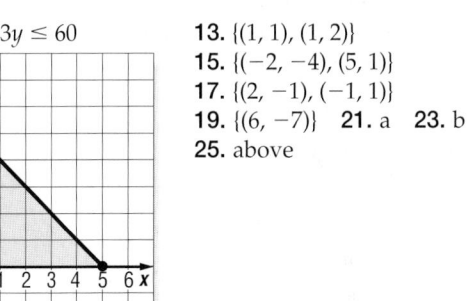

13. $\{(1, 1), (1, 2)\}$
15. $\{(-2, -4), (5, 1)\}$
17. $\{(2, -1), (-1, 1)\}$
19. $\{(6, -7)\}$ **21.** a **23.** b
25. above

27.

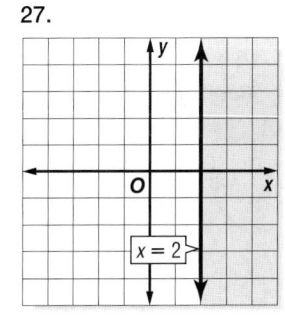

29.

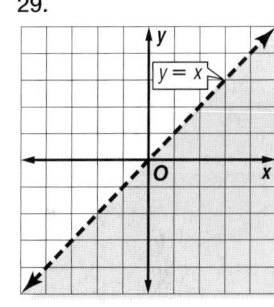

31.

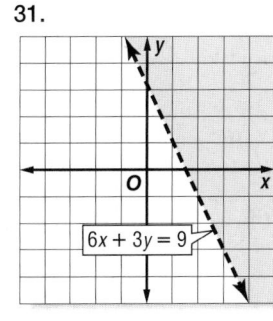

33.

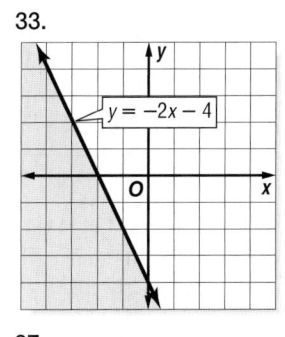

35.

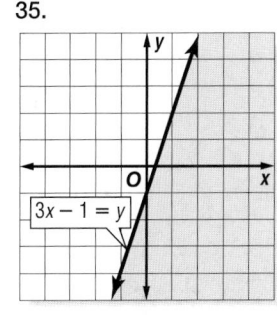

37.

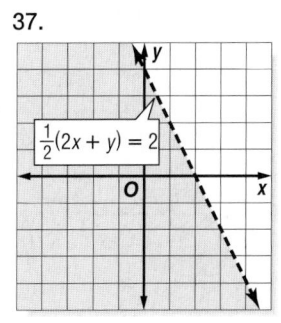

39. The solution set is limited to pairs of positive numbers.

41. No, the weight will be greater than 4000 pounds.

43.

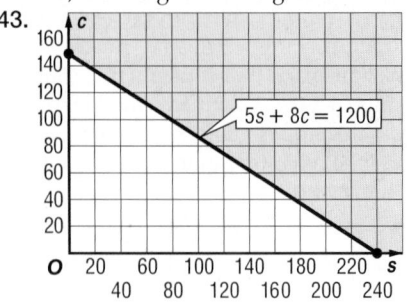
5s + 8c = 1200

45.

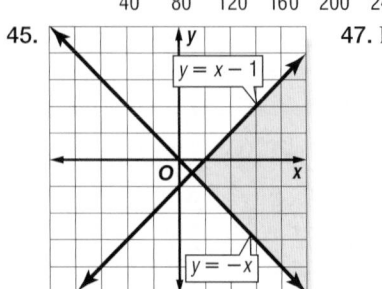
y = x − 1
y = −x

47. D

49. {−7, 4}

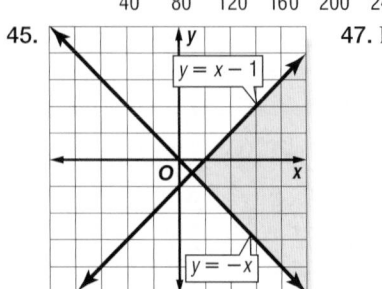
−10 −8 −6 −4 −2 0 2 4 6 8 10

51. {y | y ≤ −4 or y ≥ −1}

−8 −7 −6 −5 −4 −3 −2 −1 0 1 2

53. {m | m < −2 or m > 3}

−5 −4 −3 −2 −1 0 1 2 3 4 5

55. increase; 42%   **57.** 23   **59.** 3.25   **61.** −3c   **63.** 6y − 3

Pages 359–362   Chapter 6   Study Guide and Review

1. f   **3.** d   **5.** c   **7.** h

9. {c | c > −19}

−25   −23   −21   −19   −17   −15

11. {w | w ≤ 37}

35 36 37 38 39 40 41 42 43 44 45

13. {n | n ≤ −0.15}

−2   −1   0   1   2

15. {h | h ≤ −1}

−5 −4 −3 −2 −1 0 1 2 3 4 5

17. Sample answer: Let n = the number; 21 ≥ n + (−2); {n | n ≤ 23}.   **19.** {r | r ≤ 6}   **21.** {m | m > −11}   **23.** {d | d < 65}

25. {p | p ≤ −25}   **27.** {h | h < −2}   **29.** {x | x > −2}

31. {q | q > −7}   **33.** {x | x ≥ 4}   **35.** Sample answer:
Let n = the number; $\frac{2}{3}n − 27 ≥ 9$; {n | n ≥ 54}.

37. {k | −1 < k < 3}

−5 −4 −3 −2 −1 0 1 2 3 4 5

39. {a | a ≤ 11 or a ≥ 16}

9 10 11 12 13 14 15 16 17 18 19

41. {y | y < −1}

−5 −4 −3 −2 −1 0 1 2 3 4 5

43. {−7, −3}

−9 −8 −7 −6 −5 −4 −3 −2 −1 0 1

45. {w | w ≤ −9 or w ≥ −7}

−10 −9 −8 −7 −6 −5 −4 −3 −2 −1 0

47. {t | −7 ≤ t ≤ −1}

−9 −8 −7 −6 −5 −4 −3 −2 −1 0 1

49. $\left\{ d \mid −4 < d < 1\frac{1}{3} \right\}$

−6 −5 −4 −3 −2 −1 0 1 2 3 4

51. {(2, −5), (−1, 6)}   **53.** {(5, 10), (3, 6)}

55.

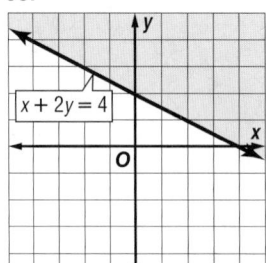
x + 2y = 4

57.

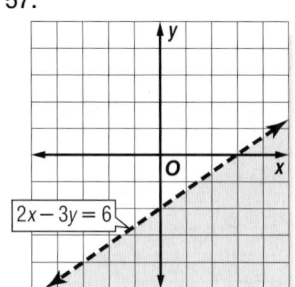
2x − 3y = 6

Chapter 7   Solving Systems of Linear Equations and Inequalities

Page 367   Chapter 7   Getting Started

1.

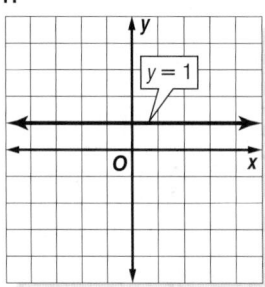
y = 1

3.

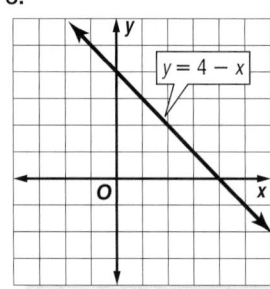
y = 4 − x

5.

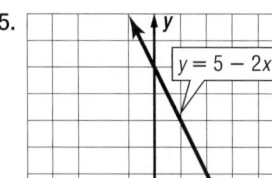
y = 5 − 2x

7. $x = \frac{a}{2}$ **9.** $b = \frac{120 + d}{7c}$

11. x   **13.** 27x   **15.** 13y

17. 5x   **19.** 7x

Page 371–374   Lesson 7-1

1. Sample answer:

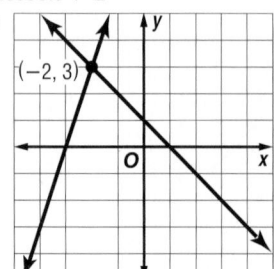
(−2, 3)

3. Sample answer: The graphs of the equations $x + y = 3$ and $2x + 2y = 6$ have a slope of -1. Since the graphs of the equations coincide, there are infinitely many solutions.
5. no solution   **7.** one

9.

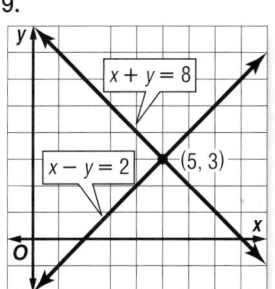

one; (5, 3)

11.

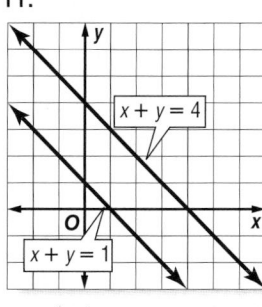

no solution

13.

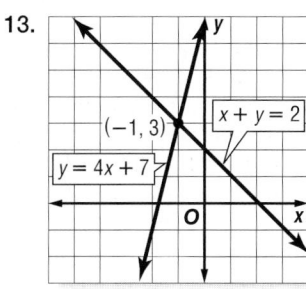

one; $(-1, 3)$
15. one **17.** infinitely many **19.** one **21.** one

23.

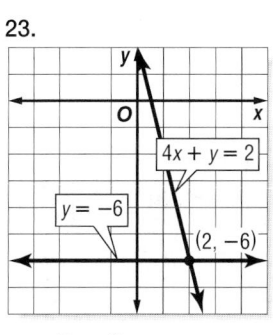

one; $(2, -6)$

25.

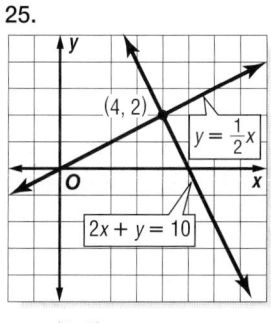

one; $(4, 2)$

27.

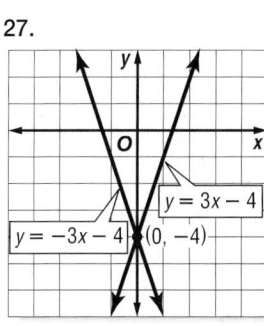

one; $(0, -4)$

29.

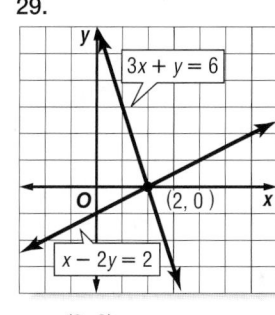

one; $(2, 0)$

31.

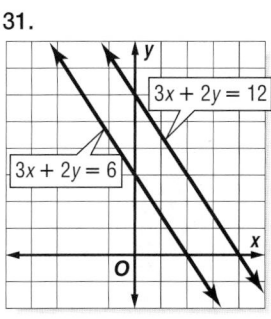

no solution

33.

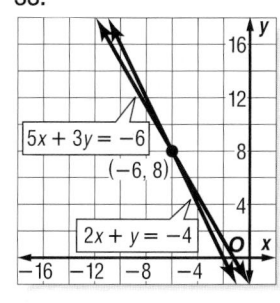

one; $(-6, 8)$

35.

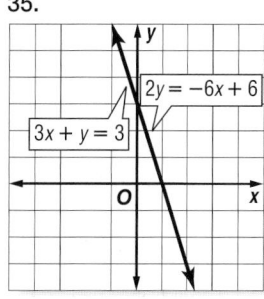

infinitely many

37.

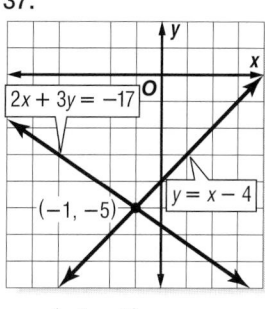

one; $(-1, -5)$

39.

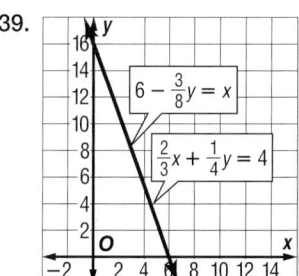

infinitely many
41. 13 m by 7 m
43. 21 units^2 **45.** 70 m
47. \$40 **49.** neither
51. $p = 60 + 0.4t$

53.

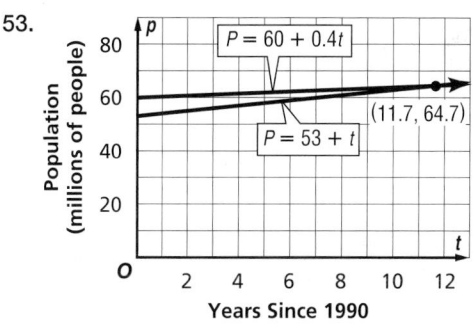

55. $A = 4$, $B = -4$ **57.** B **59.** $\{(5, -6)\}$ **61.** $\{n \mid 1.95 < n < 2.05\}$ **63.** $x - 3y = 3$ **65.** $y = 2x$ **67.** $q = \dfrac{7m - n}{10}$

Pages 379–381 Lesson 7-2
1. Substitution may result in a more accurate solution.
3. Sample answer: $y = x + 3$ and $2y = 2x + 6$ **5.** (3, 1)
7. infinitely many **9.** no solution **11.** (2, 10) **13.** $(-23, -7)$
15. (6, 7) **17.** no solution **19.** (7, 2) **21.** (2, 0) **23.** $\left(4\frac{1}{2}, \frac{3}{4}\right)$
25. (5, 2) **27.** $\left(2\frac{2}{3}, 4\frac{1}{3}\right)$ **29.** 14 in., 14 in., 18 in. **31.** 320 gal of 25% acid, 180 gal of 50% acid **33.** Yankees: 26, Reds: 5
35. The second offer is better if she sells less than \$80,000. The first offer is better if she sells more than \$80,000.
37. during the year 2023 **39.** $(-1, 5, -4)$ **41.** B

43.

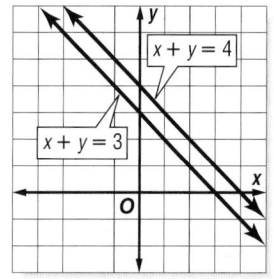

no solution

45.

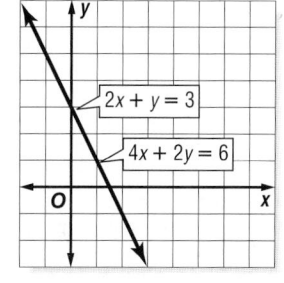

infinitely many

47.

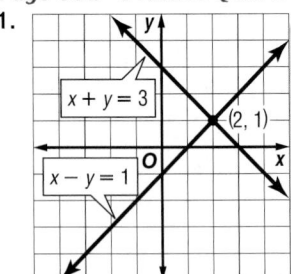

$x = 4$

49. 50 lb **51.** 12t
53. 5$d - b$

47.

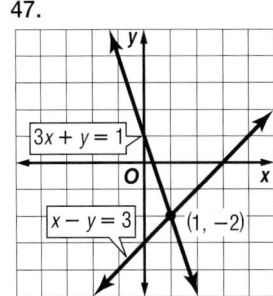

$3x + y = 1$

$x - y = 3$ (1, −2)

49.

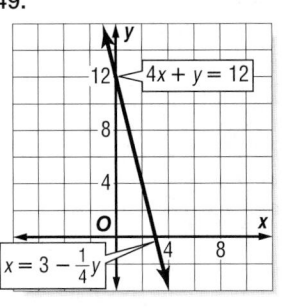

12 $4x + y = 12$
8
4

$x = 3 - \frac{1}{4}y$ 4 8

one; (1, −2)

infinitely many

51. $6x + 8y$ **53.** $6m - 9n$

Page 381   Practice Quiz 1

1.

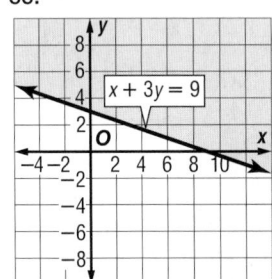

$x + y = 3$
(2, 1)
O
$x - y = 1$

one; (2, 1)

3. (−4, 4)   **5.** infinitely many

Pages 384–386   Lesson 7-3

1. Sample answer: $2a + b = 5, a - b = 4$ **3.** Michael; in order to eliminate the s terms, you must add the two equations.   **5.** (−1, 3)   **7.** (0, −5)   **9.** $\left(-2\frac{1}{2}, -2\right)$ **11.** D
13. (3, −1)   **15.** (−1, 2)   **17.** (7, 4)   **19.** (−2, 3)   **21.** (1, −1)
23. $\left(2, -1\frac{1}{2}\right)$ **25.** $\left(\frac{3}{16}, -\frac{1}{2}\right)$ **27.** (15.8, 3.4)   **29.** (24, 4)
31. 32, 19   **33.** 5, 9   **35.** adult: \$16, student: \$9
37. $y = 0.0048x + 1.28$ **39.** 2048; 1.51 billion

41. Elimination can be used to solve problems about meteorology if the coefficients of one variable are the same or are additive inverses. Answers should include the following.
- The two equations in the system of equations are added or subtracted so that one of the variables is eliminated. You then solve for the remaining variable. This number is substituted into one of the original equations, and that equation is solved for the other variable.
-
  $\begin{array}{ll} n + d = 24 & \textit{Write the equations in column} \\ \underline{(+)\, n - d = 12} & \textit{form and add.} \\ & \textit{Notice that the d variable} \\ 2n = 36 & \textit{is eliminated.} \\ \dfrac{2n}{2} = \dfrac{36}{2} & \textit{Divide each side by 2.} \\ n = 18 & \textit{Simplify.} \\ n + d = 24 & \textit{First equation} \\ 18 + d = 24 & \textit{n = 18} \\ 18 + d - 18 = 24 - 18 & \textit{Subtract 18 from each side.} \\ d = 6 & \textit{Simplify.} \end{array}$

On the winter solstice, Seward, Alaska, has 18 hours of nighttime and 6 hours of daylight.

43. C   **45.** (1, −1)

Pages 390–392   Lesson 7-4

1. If one of the variables cannot be eliminated by adding or subtracting the equations, you must multiply one or both of the equations by numbers so that a variable will be eliminated when the equations are added or subtracted.
3. Sample answer: (1) You could solve the first equation for a and substitute the resulting expression for a in the second equation. Then find the value of b. Use this value for b and one of the original equations to find the value of a. (2) You could multiply the first equation by 3 and add this new equation to the second equation. This will eliminate the b term. Find the value of a. Use this value for a and one of the original equations to find the value of b.   **5.** (−1, 1)   **7.** (1.25, 2.75)   **9.** elimination (+); (2, 0)   **11.** elimination (−); (7, 11.5)   **13.** (−9, −13)   **15.** (2, 1)   **17.** (−1, 5)
19. (−1, −2)   **21.** (10, 12)   **23.** (2, −8)   **25.** 2, −5
27. elimination (×);(−2, 1)   **29.** substitution; (2, 6)
31. elimination (+); $\left(8, \frac{4}{3}\right)$ **33.** elimination (×) or substitution; (3, 1)   **35.** elimination (−); no solution
37. elimination (−); (24, 4)   **39.** 640 2-point field goals, 61 3-point field goals   **41.** 95   **43.** 475 mph   **45.** A   **47.** (6, 2)
49. (11, 7)**51.** (−4, 4)   **53.** more than \$325,000
55.

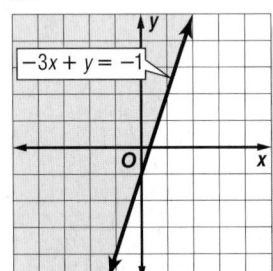

8
6
4 $x + 3y = 9$
2
O
$-4 -2$ $2\ 4\ 6\ 8\ 10$
-2
-4
-6
-8

57.

$-3x + y = -1$
O

Page 392   Practice Quiz 2

1. (2, −2)   **3.** (5, 3)   **5.** \$0.45; \$0.15

Pages 396–398   Lesson 7-5

1. Sample answer:

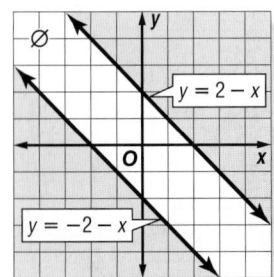

$\varnothing$
$y = 2 - x$
O
$y = -2 - x$

3. Kayla; the graph of $x + 2y \geq -2$ is the region representing $x + 2y = -2$ and the half-plane above it.

5.

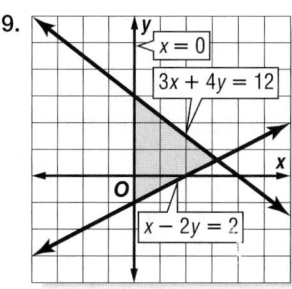

7.

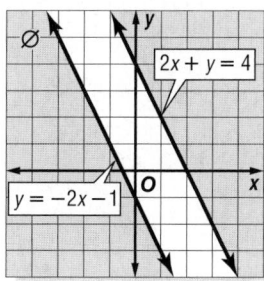

$2x + y = 4$

$y = -2x - 1$

9.

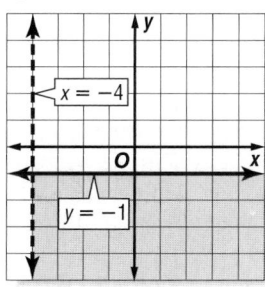

$x = 0$

$3x + 4y = 12$

$x - 2y = 2$

11. Sample answers: walk: 15 min, jog: 15 min; walk: 10 min, jog: 20 min; walk: 5 min, jog: 25 min

13.

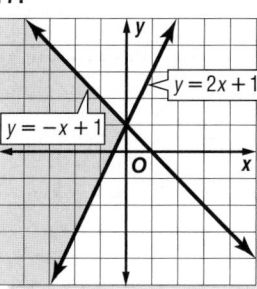

$x = -4$

$y = -1$

15.

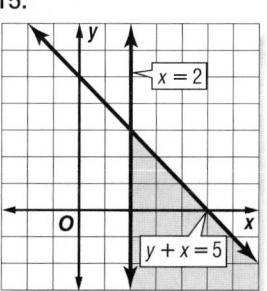

$x = 2$

$y + x = 5$

17.

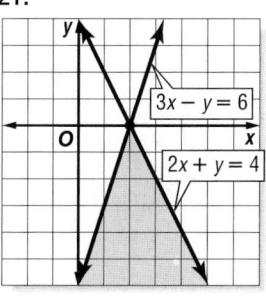

$y = 2x + 1$

$y = -x + 1$

19.

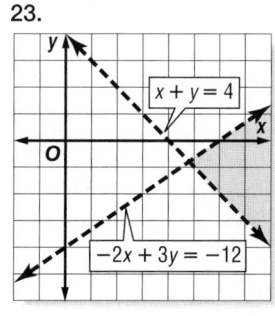

$y - x = 3$

$y - x = 1$

21.

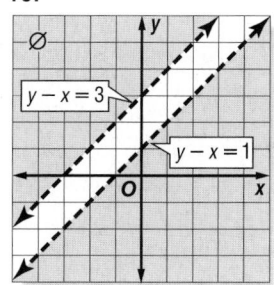

$3x - y = 6$

$2x + y = 4$

23.

$x + y = 4$

$-2x + 3y = -12$

25.

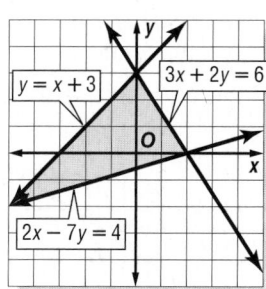

$y = x + 3$

$3x + 2y = 6$

$2x - 7y = 4$

27. $y \leq x, y > x - 3$

29.

Green Paint

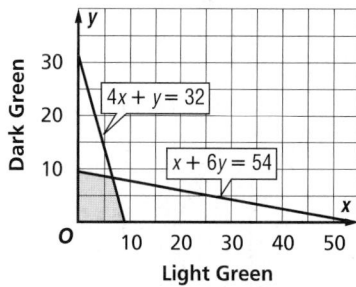

$4x + y = 32$

$x + 6y = 54$

Dark Green (y-axis)

Light Green (x-axis)

31.

Appropriate Cholesterol Levels

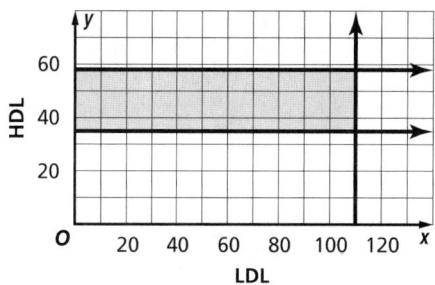

HDL (y-axis)

LDL (x-axis)

33.

Furniture Manufacturing

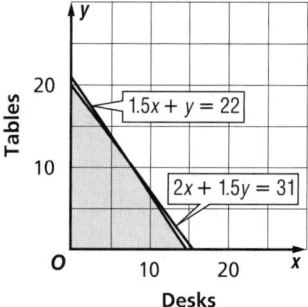

$1.5x + y = 22$

$2x + 1.5y = 31$

Tables (y-axis)

Desks (x-axis)

35. By graphing a system of equations, you can see the appropriate range of Calories and fat intake. Answers should include the following.

- Two sample appropriate Calorie and fat intakes are 2200 Calories and 60 g of fat and 2300 Calories and 65 g of fat.
- The graph represents $2000 \leq c \leq 2400$ and $60 \leq f \leq 75$.

37.

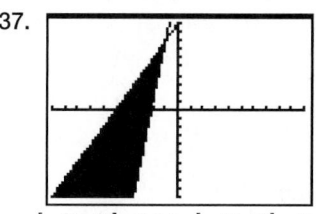

$[-10, 10]$ scl: 1 by $[-10, 10]$ scl: 1

39. D   **41.** $(2, -1)$
43. $(-2, 3)$ **45.** $(-1, 3)$
47. $y = 2x - 9$
49. $y = \frac{1}{3}x - \frac{11}{3}$

1. independent   **3.** dependent   **5.** infinitely many
7.   **9.**

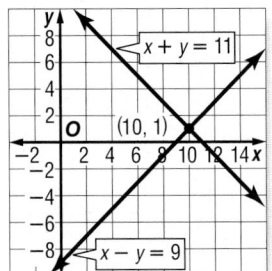   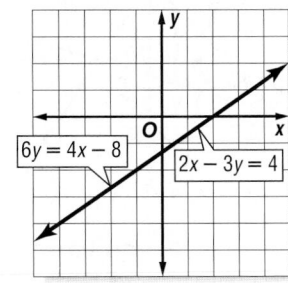

one; (10, 1)   infinitely many
11. (3, −5)   **13.** $\left(\frac{1}{2}, \frac{1}{2}\right)$ **15.** (2, 2)   **17.** (4, 1)   **19.** (5, 1)
21. $\left(2\frac{4}{5}, \frac{4}{5}\right)$ **23.** substitution; $\left(1\frac{3}{5}, 3\frac{1}{5}\right)$ **25.** substitution; (0, 0)
27.   **29.**

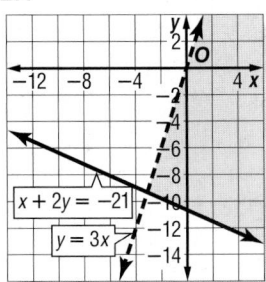   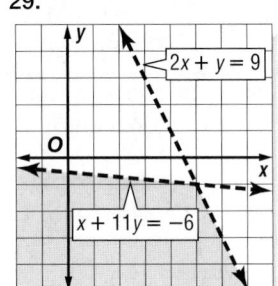

Chapter 8   Polynomials

Page 409   Chapter 8   Getting Started
1. 2^5 **3.** 5^2 **5.** a^6 **7.** $\left(\frac{1}{2}\right)^5$ **9.** 9   **11.** 25   **13.** 36   **15.** $\frac{16}{81}$
17. 63 yd^2 **19.** 84 ft^3

Pages 413–415   Lesson 8-1
1a. Sample answer: $n^2(n^5) = n^7$ **1b.** Sample answer: $(n^2)^5 = n^{10}$ **1c.** Sample answer: $(nm^2)^5 = n^5 n^{10}$
3. Poloma; when finding the product of powers with the same base, keep the same base and add the exponents. Do not multiply the bases.   **5.** No; $\frac{4a}{3b}$ shows division as well as multiplication.   **7.** x^{11} **9.** 2^{18} or 262,144
11. $-48m^3n^3$ **13.** $5n^5$ **15.** Yes; 12 is a real number and therefore a monomial.   **17.** No; $a - 2b$ shows subtraction, not multiplication of variables.   **19.** No; $\frac{x}{y^2}$ shows division, not multiplication of variables.   **21.** a^2b^6 **23.** $-28c^4d^7$
25. $30a^5b^7c^6$ **27.** $81p^2q^{14}$ **29.** 3^{16} or 43,046,721   **31.** $0.25x^6$
33. $-\frac{27}{64}c^3$ **35.** $-432c^2d^8$ **37.** $144a^8g^{14}$ **39.** $-9x^3y^9$
41. $40b^{12}$ **43.** $15f^5g^5$ **45.** $(49x^8)\pi$ **47.** x^3y^5 **49.** 10^{12} or 1 trillion   **51.** 2; 8; 32   **53.** 2^{22} or 4,194,304 ways
55. False. If $a = 4$, then $(-4)^2 = 16$ and $-4^2 = -16$.
57. False. Let $a = 3$, $b = 4$, and $n = 2$. Then $(a + b)^n = (3 + 4)^2$ or 49 and $a^n + b^n = 3^2 + 4^2$ or 25.   **59.** D

61.   **63.**

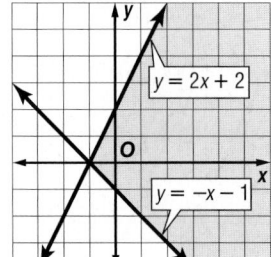   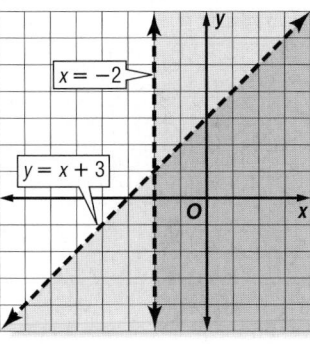

65. (−3, −4)   **67.** $\{h \mid h \le -7 \text{ or } h \ge 1\}$

69. $\varnothing$

71. dilation   **73.** reflection   **75.** $\frac{1}{3}$ **77.** 2   **79.** $\frac{7}{18}$ **81.** $\frac{11}{8}$

Pages 421–423   Lesson 8-2
1. Sample answer: $9xy$ and $6xy^2$ **3.** Jamal; a factor is moved from the numerator of a fraction to the denominator or vice versa only if the *exponent* of the factor is negative; $-4 \ne \frac{1}{4}$.   **5.** x^6y^5 **7.** $\frac{1}{y^4}$ **9.** $\frac{g^8}{d^3c^5}$ **11.** $c^{11}d^{12}$ **13.** C
15. 3^6 or 729   **17.** y^2z^7 **19.** $\frac{81m^{28}}{256x^{20}y^{12}}$ **21.** $\frac{1}{3b^4}$ **23.** $\frac{1}{n^3p^4}$
25. $\frac{1}{125}$ **27.** $\frac{8}{27}$ **29.** $\frac{6k^{17}}{h^3}$ **31.** $\frac{19}{3z^{12}}$ **33.** $\frac{p}{q}$ **35.** 1
37. $\frac{27a^9c^3}{8b^9}$ **39.** $10ab$ units   **41.** jet plane   **43.** $\left(\frac{1}{2}\right)^n$
45. $\frac{1}{10^5}$ to $\frac{1}{10^4}$ cm; $\frac{1}{100,000}$ to $\frac{1}{10,000}$ cm   **47.** a^{n+3} **49.** c^{11}

51. You can compare pH levels by finding the ratio of one pH level to another written in terms of the concentration c of hydrogen ions, $c = \left(\frac{1}{10}\right)^{pH}$. Answers should include the following.
• Sample answer: To compare a pH of 8 with a pH of 9 requires simplifying the quotient of powers.

$$\frac{\left(\frac{1}{10}\right)^8}{\left(\frac{1}{10}\right)^9} \cdot \frac{\left(\frac{1}{10}\right)^8}{\left(\frac{1}{10}\right)^9} = \left(\frac{1}{10}\right)^{8-9}$$

$$= \left(\frac{1}{10}\right)^{-1}$$

$$= \frac{1}{\left(\frac{1}{10}\right)^1} \quad \textit{Negative Exponent Property}$$

$$= 10$$

Thus, a pH of 8 is ten times more acidic than a pH of 9.
53. Since each number is obtained by dividing the previous number by 3, $3^1 = 3$ and $3^0 = 1$.   **55.** $12x^8y^4$ **57.** $9c^2d^{10}$
59. $-108a^3b^9$ **61.** Sample answers: 3 oz of mozzarella, 4 oz of Swiss; 4 oz of mozzarella, 3 oz of Swiss; 5 oz of mozzarella, 3 oz of Swiss   **63.** $y = -2x + 3$ **65.** $y = \frac{3}{2}x + 2$

67.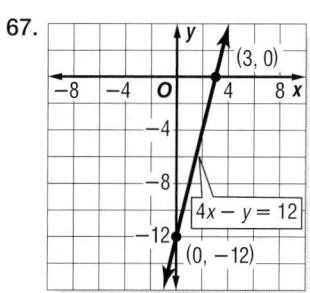

69. ± 11 **71.** -7.21
73. 10^{-13} **75.** 10^7
77. 10^{-11}

Pages 428–430   Lesson 8-3

1. When numbers between 0 and 1 are written in scientific notation, the exponent is negative. If the number is not between 0 and 1, use a positive exponent **3.** Sample answer: 6.5 million; 6,500,000; 6.5×10^6 **5.** 4590
7. 0.000036 **9.** 5.67×10^{-3} **11.** 3.002×10^{15} **13.** 1.88×10^{-7}; 0.000000188 **15.** 5×10^9; 5,000,000,000 **17.** \$933.33
19. 0.0000000061 **21.** 80,000,000 **23.** 0.299 **25.** 6.89
27. 238,900 **29.** 0.00000000000000000000000000000091095
31. 3.4402×10^7 **33.** 9.0465×10^{-4} **35.** 3.807×10^2
37. 8.73×10^{12} **39.** 8.1×10^{-6} **41.** 1×10^9
43. $6.02214299 \times 10^{23}$ **45.** 1.71×10^9; 1,710,000,000
47. 1.44×10^{-8}; 0.0000000144 **49.** 2.548×10^5; 254,800
51. 4×10^{-4}; 0.0004 **53.** 2.3×10^{-6}; 0.0000023 **55.** 9.3×10^{-7}; 0.00000093 **57.** about \$20,236 **59.** about 1.4×10^{14} or 140 trillion tons

61. Astronomers work with very large numbers such as the masses of planets. Scientific notation allows them to more easily perform calculations with these numbers. Answers should include the following.

Planet	Mass (kg)
Mercury	330,000,000,000,000,000,000,000
Venus	4,870,000,000,000,000,000,000,000
Earth	5,970,000,000,000,000,000,000,000
Mars	642,000,000,000,000,000,000,000
Jupiter	1,900,000,000,000,000,000,000,000,000
Saturn	569,000,000,000,000,000,000,000,000
Uranus	86,800,000,000,000,000,000,000,000
Neptune	102,000,000,000,000,000,000,000,000
Pluto	12,700,000,000,000,000,000,000

- Scientific notation allows you to fit numbers such as these into a smaller table. It allows you to compare large values quickly by comparing the powers of 10 instead of counting zeros to find place value. For computation, scientific notation allows you work with fewer place values and to express your answers in a compact form.

63. 6.75×10^{18} **65.** 8.52×10^{-6} **67.** 1.09×10^3 **69.** $-\dfrac{4n^5}{p^5}$
71. no **73.** yes

75. $\{d \mid d > 18\}$

77. 20 **79.** 37 **81.** 10

Page 430   Practice Quiz 1

1. n^8 **3.** $-128w^{11}z^{18}$ **5.** $\dfrac{36k^6}{49n^2p^8}$ **7.** 4.48×10^6; 4,480,000
9. 4×10^{-2}; 0.04

Pages 434–436   Lesson 8-4

1. Sample answer: -8 **3a.** true; **3b.** false; $3x + 5$
3c. true **5.** yes; monomial **7.** 0 **9.** 5 **11.** $2a + 4x^2 -$

$7a^2x^3 - 2ax^5$ **13.** $x^3 + 3x^2y + 3xy^2 + y^3$ **15.** yes; monomial **17.** yes; binomial **19.** yes; trinomial
21. $0.5bh$ **23.** $0.5xy - \pi r^2$ **25.** 3 **27.** 2 **29.** 4 **31.** 2
33. 3 **35.** 7 **37.** $-1 + 2x + 3x^2$ **39.** $8c - c^3x^2 + c^2x^3$
41. $4 - 5a^7 + 2ax^2 + 3ax^5$ **43.** $6y + 3xy^2 + x^2y - 4x^3$
45. $x^5 + 3x^3 + 5$ **47.** $2a^2x^3 + 4a^3x^2 - 5a$ **49.** $cx^3 - 5c^3x^2 + 11x + c^2$ **51.** $-2x^4 - 9x^2y + 8x + 7y^2$ **53.** $0.25q + 0.10d + 0.05n$ **55.** $\pi r^2h + \dfrac{2}{3}\pi r^3$ **57.** True; for the degree of a binomial to be zero, the highest degree of both terms would need to be zero. Then the terms would be like terms. With these like terms combined, the expression is not a binomial, but a monomial. Therefore, the degree of a binomial can never be zero. Only a monomial can have a degree of zero.

59. B **61.** 1.23×10^7 **63.** 1.2×10^7 **65.** $\dfrac{1}{b^2c}$ **67.** $\dfrac{16x^6y^4}{9z^2}$
69. no **71.** $\dfrac{1}{2}$ **73.** $7a^2 + 3a$ **75.** $a - 2b$

Page 441–443   Lesson 8-5

1. The powers of x and y are not the same. **3.** Kendra; Esteban added the additive inverses of both polynomials when he should have added the opposite of the polynomial being subtracted. **5.** $9y^2 - 3y - 1$ **7.** $11a^2 + 6a + 1$
9. $3ax^2 - 9x - 9a + 8a^2x$ **11.** about 297,692,000 **13.** $13z - 10z^2$ **15.** $-2n^2 + 7n + 5$ **17.** $5b^3 - 8b^2 - 4b$ **19.** $2g^3 - 9g$
21. $-2x - 3xy$ **23.** $3ab^2 + 11ab - 4$ **25.** $3x^2 - 12x + 5ax + 3a^2$
27. $8x^2 - 6x + 15$ **29.** $11x^3 - 7x^2 - 9$ **31.** $6x^2 - 15x + 12$
33. 260 outdoor screens **35.** Original number $= 10x + y$; show that the new number will always be represented by $10y + x$.

new number $= 9(y - x) + (10x + y)$
$= 9y - 9x + 10x + y$
$= 10y + x$

37. $40 - 2x$ **39.** $140 - 4x \le 108$; 8 in.
41. $x + 1$ **43.** 4 **45.** A **47.** 5 **49.** 3 **51.** 8,000,000
53. 0.0005
55.

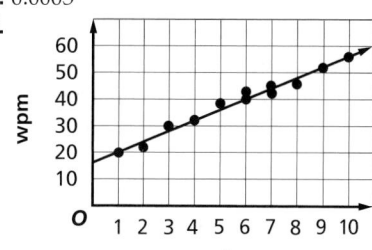

57. Sample answer: $y = 4x + 17$ **59.** No; there's a limit as to how fast one can keyboard. **61.** $D = \{-4, -1, 5\}$; $R = \{2, -3, 0, 1\}$ **63.** $18x - 48$ **65.** $35p - 28q$
67. $8x^2 + 24x - 32$

Page 446–449   Lesson 8-6

1. Distributive Property; Product of Powers Property
3. Sample answer: $4x$ and $x^2 + 2x + 3$; $4x^3 + 8x^2 + 12x$
5. $18b^5 - 27b^4 + 9b^3 - 72b^2$ **7.** $-20x^3y + 48x^2y^2 - 28xy^3$
9. $20n^4 + 30n^3 - 14n^2 - 13n$ **11.** $\dfrac{5}{3}$ **13.** $T = 10,700 - 0.03x$
15. $5r^2 + r^3$ **17.** $-32x - 12x^2$ **19.** $7ag^4 + 14a^2g^2$
21. $-6b^4 + 8b^3 - 18b^2$ **23.** $40x^3y + 16x^2y^3 - 24x^2y$
25. $-15hk^4 - \dfrac{15}{4}h^2k^2 + 6hk^2$ **27.** $-10a^3b^2 - 25a^4b^2 + 5a^3b^3 - 5a^6b$ **29.** $-2d^2 + 19d$ **31.** $20w^2 - 18w + 10$ **33.** $46m^3 + 14m^2 - 32m + 20$ **35.** $6c^3 - 23c^2 + 20c - 8$ **37.** $6x^2 + 8x$
39. -2 **41.** $-\dfrac{1}{3}$ **43.** 0 **45.** $\dfrac{7}{4}$ **47.** -5 **49.** $T = -0.03x + 6360$ **51.** $20x^2 + 48x$ **53.** $x + 2$ **55.** Let x and y be integers.

Then $2x$ and $2y$ are even numbers, and $(2x)(2y) = 4xy$. $4xy$ is divisible by 2 since one of its factors, 4, is divisible by 2. Therefore, $4xy$ is an even number.

57. Let x and y be integers. Then $2x$ is an even number and $2y + 1$ is an odd number. Their product, $2x(2y + 1)$, is always even since one of its factors is 2.   **59.** $2.20

61. $126

63. Answers should include the following.
- The product of a monomial and a polynomial can be modeled using an area model. The area of the figure shown at the beginning of the lesson is the product of its length $2x$ and width $(x + 3)$. This product is $2x(x + 3)$, which when the Distributive Property is applied becomes $2x(x) + 2x(3)$ or $2x^2 + 6x$. This is the same result obtained when the areas of the algebra tiles are added together.
- Sample answer: $(3x)(2x + 1)$
$$(3x)(2x + 1) = (3x)(2x) + (3x)(1)$$
$$= 6x^2 + 3x$$

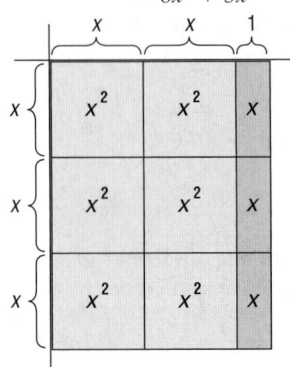

65. A   **67.** $-4y^2 + 5y + 3$ **69.** $7p^3 - 3p^2 - 2p - 7$
71. yes; binomial   **73.** yes; monomial   **75.** $9n + 4 \geq 7 - 13n$; $\left\{ n \mid n \geq \frac{3}{22} \right\}$ **77.** $y = -2x - 3$ **79.** $50

81.

Stem	Leaf
1	0 4 5 8 8 8
2	0 0 1 1 2
3	0 4
4	3 4 $3 \mid 4 = 34$

83. $6x^3$
85. $12y^2 - 24y$
87. $18p^4 - 24p^3 + 36p^2$

Page 449   Practice Quiz 2
1. 4   **3.** 3   **5.** $-12 + 9x + 4x^2 + 5x^3$ **7.** $10n^2 - 4n + 2$
9. $15a^5b - 10a^4b^2 + 30a^3b^3$

Pages 455–457   Lesson 8-7
1.

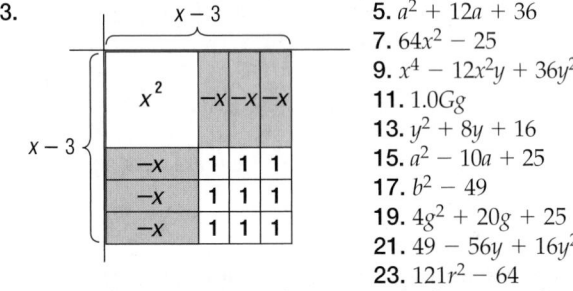

5. $x^2 + 4x - 12$
7. $4h^2 + 33h + 35$
9. $10g^2 + 19g - 56$
11. $6k^3 + 2k^2 - 29k + 15$
13. $b^2 + 10b + 16$
15. $x^2 - 13x + 36$
17. $y^2 - 4y - 32$
19. $2w^2 + 9w - 35$
21. $40d^2 + 31d + 6$
23. $35x^2 - 27x + 4$
25. $4n^2 + 12n + 9$

27. $100r^2 - 16$ **29.** $40x^2 - 22xy - 8y^2$ **31.** $p^3 + 6p^2 + p - 28$
33. $6x^3 - 23x^2 + 22x - 5$ **35.** $n^4 + 2n^3 - 17n^2 + 22n - 8$
37. $8a^4 + 2a^3 + 15a^2 + 31a - 56$ **39.** $2x^2 + 3x - 20$ units^2
41. $\frac{15}{2}x^2 + 3x - 24$ units^2 **43.** $2a^3 + 10a^2 - 2a - 10$ units^3

---

45. $a^3 + 3a^2 + 2a$ **47.** Sample answer: 6; the result is the same as the product in Exercise 46.   **49.** $x - 2, x + 4$
51. bigger; 10 ft^2 **53.** 20 ft by 24 ft
55. Multiplying binomials and two-digit numbers each involve the use of the Distributive Property twice. Each procedure involves four multiplications and the addition of like terms. Answers should include the following.
- $24 \times 36 = (4 + 20)(6 + 30)$
$$= (4 + 20)6 + (4 + 20)30$$
$$= (24 + 120) + (120 + 600)$$
$$= 144 + 720$$
$$= 864$$
- The like terms in vertical two-digit multiplication are digits with the same place value.

57. B   **59.** $-28y^3 + 16y^2 - 12y$ **61.** $36x^2 - 42$
63. $(181 - 7x)°$ **65.** one; $(-6, 3)$ **67.** 5   **69.** $t = \frac{v}{a}$
71. $y = -\frac{4}{3}x + \frac{7}{3}$ **73.** $49x^2$ **75.** $16y^4$ **77.** $9g^8$

Pages 461–463   Lesson 8-8
1. The patterns are the same except for their middle terms. The middle terms have different signs.
3.

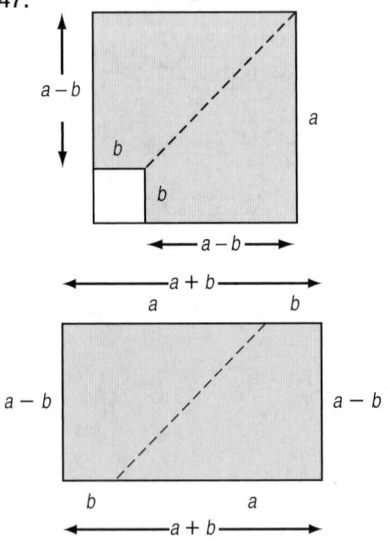

5. $a^2 + 12a + 36$
7. $64x^2 - 25$
9. $x^4 - 12x^2y + 36y^2$
11. $1.0Gg$
13. $y^2 + 8y + 16$
15. $a^2 - 10a + 25$
17. $b^2 - 49$
19. $4g^2 + 20g + 25$
21. $49 - 56y + 16y^2$
23. $121r^2 - 64$

25. $a^2 + 10ab + 25b^2$ **27.** $4x^2 - 36xy + 81y^2$ **29.** $25w^2 - 196$
31. $x^6 + 8x^3y + 16y^2$ **33.** $64a^4 - 81b^6$ **35.** $\frac{4}{9}x^2 - 8x + 36$
37. $4n^3 + 20n^2 - n - 5$ **39.** $0.5Bb + 0.5bb$ **41.** Sample answer: 2; yes   **43.** $(a + 1)^2$ **45.** $s + 2, s + 3$

47.

Area of rectangle $= (a - b)(a + b)$
OR

Area of a trapezoid = $\frac{1}{2}$(height)(base 1 + base 2)

$A_1 = \frac{1}{2}(a - b)(a + b)$ $A_2 = \frac{1}{2}(a - b)(a + b)$

Total area of shaded region

$= \left[\frac{1}{2}(a - b)(a + b)\right] + \left[\frac{1}{2}(a - b)(a + b)\right]$

$= (a - b)(a + b)$

49. C **51a.** $a^3 + 3a^2b + 3ab^2 + b^3$ **51b.** $x^3 + 6x^2 + 12x + 8$
51c. $(a + b)^3$

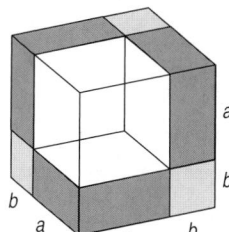

53. $c^2 - 6c - 27$ **55.** $24n^2 - 25n - 25$ **57.** $4k^3 - 6k^2 - 26k + 35$ **59.** $\frac{4}{3}$ **61.** $\frac{1}{2}$
63. $(3, -4)$ **65.** $y = x + 5$
67. $y = \frac{1}{5}x + 6$ **69.** 61

Pages 464–468 Chapter 8 Study Guide and Review

1. negative exponent **3.** Quotient of Powers **5.** trinomial
7. polynomial **9.** binomial **11.** y^7 **13.** $20a^5x^5$ **15.** $576x^5y^2$
17. $-\frac{1}{2}m^4n^8$ **19.** 531,441 **21.** $\frac{27b^3c^6}{64d^3}$ **23.** $\frac{27b}{14}$ **25.** $\frac{bx^3}{3ay^2}$

27. $\frac{1}{64a^6}$ **29.** 240,000 **31.** 4,880,000,000 **33.** 7.96×10^5

35. 6×10^{11}; 600,000,000,000 **37.** 1.68×10^{-5}; 0.0000168
39. 4 **41.** 6 **43.** 7 **45.** $-4x^4 + 5x^3y^2 - 2x^2y^3 + xy - 27$
47. $4x^2 - 5xy + 6y^2$ **49.** $21m^4 - 10m - 1$ **51.** $-7p^2 - 2p + 25$ **53.** $10x^2 - 19x + 63$ **55.** $2x^2 - 17xy^2 + 10x + 10y^2$
57. $1\frac{1}{7}$ **59.** $4a^2 + 13a - 12$ **61.** $20r^2 - 13rs - 21s^2$
63. $12p^3 - 13p^2 + 11p - 6$ **65.** $16x^2 + 56x + 49$
67. $25x^2 - 9y^2$ **69.** $9m^2 + 24mn + 16n^2$

Chapter 9 Factoring

Page 473 Chapter 9 Getting Started

1. $12 - 3x$ **3.** $-7n^2 + 21n - 7$ **5.** $x^2 + 11x + 28$
7. $54a^2 - 12ab - 2b^2$ **9.** $y^2 + 18y + 81$ **11.** $n^2 - 25$
13. 11 **15.** $\frac{5}{6}$

Pages 477–479 Lesson 9-1

1. false; 2 **3.** Sample answer: $5x^2$ and $10x^3$
5. 1, 17; prime **7.** $3^2 \cdot 5$ **9.** $-1 \cdot 2 \cdot 3 \cdot 5^2$ **11.** $3 \cdot 13 \cdot b \cdot b \cdot b \cdot c \cdot c$ **13.** 5 **15.** 9 **17.** $6a^2b$ **19.** 5 rows of 24 plants,
6 rows of 20 plants, 8 rows of 15 plants, 10 rows of 12 plants,
12 rows of 10 plants, 15 rows of 8 plants, 20 rows of 6 plants,
or 24 rows of 5 plants **21.** 1, 5, 25; composite **23.** 1, 61;
prime **25.** 1, 7, 17, 119; composite **27.** 1, 2, 4, 8, 16, 19, 38,
76, 152, 304; composite **29.** 194 mm; the factors of 96
whose sum when doubled is the greatest are 1 and 96.
31. 3 packages in the box of 18 cookies and 4 packages in
the box of 24 cookies **33.** $-1 \cdot 2 \cdot 7^2$ **35.** $2 \cdot 3 \cdot 17$
37. $2^2 \cdot 3^2 \cdot 5$ **39.** $-1 \cdot 2 \cdot 3 \cdot 7 \cdot 11$ **41.** $5 \cdot 17 \cdot x \cdot x \cdot y \cdot y$
43. $2 \cdot 5 \cdot 5 \cdot g \cdot h$ **45.** $3 \cdot 3 \cdot 3 \cdot 3 \cdot 3 \cdot n \cdot n \cdot n \cdot m$
47. $-1 \cdot 13 \cdot 13 \cdot a \cdot a \cdot b \cdot c \cdot c$ **49.** 1 **51.** 14 **53.** 21
55. $6d$ **57.** 1 **59.** 7 **61.** $16a^2b$ **63.** 15 **65.** 7, 31
67. base: 1 cm, height 40 cm; base 2 cm; height 20 cm; base
4 cm, height 10 cm; base 5 cm, height 8 cm, base 8 cm, height
5 cm, base 10 cm, height 4 cm; base 20 cm, height 2 cm; base
40 cm, height 1 cm
69. Scientists listening to radio signals would suspect that a
modulated signal beginning with prime numbers would
indicate a message from an extraterrestrial. Answers should
include the following.
• 2, 3, 5, 7, 11, 13, 17, 19, 23, 29, 31, 37, 41, 43, 47, 53, 59, 61,
67, 71, 79, 83, 89, 97, 101, 103, 107, 109, 113

• Sample answer: It is unlikely that any natural
phenomenon would produce such an artificial and
specifically mathematical pattern.
71. A **73.** $9a^2 - 25$ **75.** $12r^2 - 16r - 35$ **77.** $b^3 + 7b^2 - 6b - 72$ **79.** 0 **81.** $10x + 40$ **83.** $6g^2 - 8g$ **85.** $7(b + c)$

Pages 484–486 Lesson 9-2

1. $4(x^2 + 3x)$, $x(4x + 12)$, or $4x(x + 3)$; $4x(x + 3)$; $4x$ is the
GCF of $4x^2$ and $12x$. **3.** The division would eliminate 2 as
a solution. **5.** $8xz(2 - 5z)$ **7.** $2ab(a^2b + 4 + 8ab^2)$
9. $(5c + 2d)(1 - 2c)$ **11.** $\{-2, 4\}$ **13.** 0 ft **15.** 6.25 s; The
answer 0 is not reasonable since it represents the time when
the flare is launched. **17.** $4(4a + b)$ **19.** $x(x^2y^2 + 1)$
21. $2h(7g - 9)$ **23.** $8bc(c + 3)$ **25.** $6abc^2(3a - 8c)$
27. $x(15xy^2 + 25y + 1)$ **29.** $3pq(p^2 - 3q + 12)$ **31.** $(x + 7)$
$(x + 5)$ **33.** $(3y + 2)(4y + 3)$ **35.** $(6x - 1)(3x - 5)$
37. $(m + x)(2y + 7)$ **39.** $(2x - 3)(5x - 7y)$ **41.** 35
43. 63 games **45.** $2r^2(4 - \pi)$ **47.** $81a^2 - 72ab + 16b^2$ cm²
49. $\{-16, 0\}$ **51.** $\{-3, 7\}$ **53.** $\left\{-\frac{5}{4}, \frac{7}{3}\right\}$ **55.** $\{0, 5\}$
57. $\left\{0, \frac{6}{7}\right\}$ **59.** $\left\{-\frac{3}{4}, 0\right\}$ **61.** about 2.8 s
63. Answers should include the following.
• Let $h = 0$ in the equation $h = 151t - 16t^2$. To solve $0 = 151t - 16t^2$, factor the right-hand side as $t(151 - 16t)$.
Then, since $t(151 - 16t) = 0$, either $t = 0$ or $151 - 16t = 0$.
solving each equation for t, we find that $t = 0$ or $t \approx 9.44$.
• The solution $t = 0$ represents the point at which the ball
was initially thrown into the air. The solution $t \approx 9.44$
represents how long it took after the ball was thrown for
it to return to the same height at which it was thrown.
65. C **67.** 1, 2, 3, 4, 5, 6, 10, 12, 15, 20, 25, 30, 50, 60, 75,
100, 150, 300; composite **69.** $16s^6 + 24s^3 + 9$
71. $9k^2 + 48k + 64$ **73.** $\frac{3x}{2y^5}$ **75.** 37 shares
77. $x^2 - 9x + 20$ **79.** $18a^2 - 6a - 4$ **81.** $8y^2 - 14y - 15$

Page 486 Practice Quiz 1

1. 1, 3, 5, 9, 15, 25, 45, 75, 225; composite **3.** $2 \cdot 3 \cdot 13 \cdot a \cdot a \cdot b \cdot c \cdot c \cdot c$ **5.** $xy(4y - 1)$ **7.** $(2p - 5)(3y + 8)$ **9.** $\{0, 3\}$

Pages 492–494 Lesson 9-3

1. In this trinomial, $b = 6$ and $c = 9$. This means that $m + n$
is positive and mn is positive. Only two positive numbers
have both a positive sum and product. Therefore, negative
factors of 9 need not be considered. **3.** Aleta; to use the
Zero Product Property, one side of the equation must equal
zero. **5.** $(c - 1)(c - 2)$ **7.** $(p + 5)(p - 7)$ **9.** $(x - 3y)$
$(x - y)$ **11.** $\{-9, 4\}$ **13.** $\{-9, -1\}$ **15.** $\{-7, 10\}$
17. $(a + 3)(a + 5)$ **19.** $(c + 5)(c + 7)$ **21.** $(m - 1)(m - 21)$
23. $(p - 8)(p - 9)$ **25.** $(x - 1)(x + 7)$ **27.** $(h - 5)(h + 8)$
29. $(y - 7)(y + 6)$ **31.** $(w + 12)(w - 6)$ **33.** $(a + b)(a + 4b)$
35. $4x + 48$ **37.** $\{-14, -2\}$ **39.** $\{-6, 2\}$ **41.** $\{-4, 7\}$
43. $\{3, 16\}$ **45.** $\{2, -9\}$ **47.** $\{4, 6\}$ **49.** $\{-25, 2\}$
51. $\{-17, 3\}$ **53.** $\{4, 14\}$ **55.** -14 and -12 or 12 and 14
57. $-18, 18$ **59.** 7, 12, 15, 16 **61.** $w(w + 52)$ m²
63. Answers should include the following.
• You would use a guess-and-check process, listing the
factors of 54, checking to see which pairs added to 15.
• To factor a trinomial of the form $x^2 + ax + c$, you also
use a guess-and-check process, list the factors of c, and
check to see which ones add to a.
65. 15 **67.** yes **69.** no; $(x - 10)(x + 21)$ **71.** $\left\{0, \frac{4}{7}\right\}$
73. 12 **75.** $5x^2y^4$ **77.** $1(1.54) + 17.31(1.54) = (1 + 17.31)$
(1.54) or $18.31(1.54)$ **79.** $(a + 4)(3a + 2)$ **81.** $(2p + 7)(p - 3)$
83. $(2g - 3)(2g - 1)$

Pages 498–500 Lesson 9-4

1. m and n are the factors of ac that add to b.   **3.** Craig; when factoring a trinomial of the form $ax^2 + bx + c$, where $a \neq 1$, you must find the factors of ac not of c.   **5.** prime
7. $(x + 4)(2x + 5)$ **9.** $(2n + 5)(2n - 7)$ **11.** $\left\{\dfrac{1}{2}, \dfrac{7}{5}\right\}$
13. 1 s   **15.** $(3x + 2)(x + 1)$ **17.** $(5d - 4)(d + 2)$
19. $(3g - 2)(3g - 2)$ **21.** $(x - 4)(2x + 5)$ **23.** prime
25. $(5n + 2)(2n - 3)$ **27.** $(2x + 3)(7x - 4)$ **29.** $5(3x + 2)$ $(2x - 3)$ **31.** $(12a - 5b)(3a + 2b)$ **33.** $\pm31, \pm17, \pm13, \pm11$
35. $\left\{-5, -\dfrac{2}{5}\right\}$ **37.** $\left\{-\dfrac{1}{6}, \dfrac{3}{4}\right\}$ **39.** $\left\{-\dfrac{5}{7}, \dfrac{5}{2}\right\}$ **41.** $\left\{-\dfrac{2}{3}, 3\right\}$
43. $\left\{\dfrac{1}{2}, \dfrac{2}{3}\right\}$ **45.** $\{-4, 12\}$ **47.** $\left\{-4, \dfrac{2}{3}\right\}$ **49.** 1 in.   **51.** 2.5 s
53. Answers should include the following.
- $2x + 3$ by $x + 2$
- With algebra tiles, you can try various ways to make a rectangle with the necessary tiles. Once you make the rectangle, however, the dimensions of the rectangle are the factors of the polynomial. In a way, you have to go through the guess-and-check process whether you are factoring algebraically or geometrically (using algebra tiles).

x^2	x	x	x
x^2	x	x	x
x	1	1	1
	1	1	1

x^2	x	x
x^2	x	x
x	1	1
x	1	1
x	1	1

Guess $(2x + 1)(x + 3)$ incorrect because 8 x tiles are needed to complete the rectangle.
55. B   **57.** prime   **59.** $\left\{-\dfrac{7}{5}, 4\right\}$ **61.** $\{0, 12\}$ **63.** 4   **65.** 6
67. 10   **69.** 13

Page 500 Practice Quiz 2

1. $(x + 4)(x - 18)$ **3.** $(4a - 1)(4a - 5)$ **5.** $2(3c + 1)(4c + 9)$
7. $\{-16, 2\}$ **9.** $\left\{-\dfrac{3}{4}, \dfrac{4}{3}\right\}$

Pages 504–506 Lesson 9-5

1. The binomial is the difference of two terms, each of which is a perfect square.   **3.** Yes; $3n^2 - 48 = 3(n^2 - 16) = 3(n + 4)(n - 4)$.   **5.** $(n + 9)(n - 9)$ **7.** $2x^3(x + 7)(x - 7)$
9. prime   **11.** $\left\{-\dfrac{5}{2}, \dfrac{5}{2}\right\}$ **13.** $\left\{-\dfrac{1}{6}, \dfrac{1}{6}\right\}$ **15.** 12 in. by 12 in.
17. $(n + 6)(n - 6)$ **19.** $(5 + 2p)(5 - 2p)$ **21.** $(11 + 3r)$ $(11 - 3r)$ **23.** prime   **25.** $(13y + 6z)(13y - 6z)$
27. $3(x - 5)(x + 5)$ **29.** $2(2g^2 - 25)$ **31.** $5x(2x - 3y)$ $(2x + 3y)$ **33.** $(a + b + c)(a + b - c)$ **35.** $\left\{\pm\dfrac{8}{3}\right\}$ **37.** $\left\{\pm\dfrac{5}{2}\right\}$
39. $\left\{\pm\dfrac{9}{10}\right\}$ **41.** $\{\pm10\}$ **43.** $\left\{-\dfrac{5}{3}, 0, \dfrac{5}{3}\right\}$ **45.** $\left\{-\dfrac{3}{2}, 0, \dfrac{3}{2}, 4\right\}$
47. 2 in.   **49.** 36 mph   **51.** The flaw is in line 5. Since $a = b$, $a - b = 0$. Therefore dividing by $a - b$ is dividing by zero, which is undefined.   **53.** A   **55.** prime
57. $(3p + 5)(7p - 2)$ **59.** $\{3, 5\}$ **61.** between 83 and 99, inclusive   **63.** $r > \dfrac{7}{10}$

$$\xleftarrow{\quad} \; \overset{4/10 \quad 6/10 \quad 8/10 \quad 1 \quad 12/10 \quad 14/10}{\longrightarrow}$$

65. $x^2 + 2x + 1$ **67.** $x^2 + 16x + 64$ **69.** $25x^2 - 20x + 4$

Pages 512–514 Lesson 9-6

1. Determine if the first term is a perfect square. Then determine if the last term is a perfect square. Finally, check to see if the middle term is equal to twice the product of the square roots of the first and last terms.
3. Sample answer: $x^3 + 5x^2 - 4x - 20$ **5.** no
7. $(c - 3)(c - 2)$ **9.** $(2x - 7)(4x + 5)$ **11.** $(m - 2)(m + 2)$ $(3m + 2n)$ **13.** $\{\pm4\}$ **15.** $\left\{5 \pm \sqrt{13}\right\}$ **17.** no   **19.** yes; $(2y - 11)^2$ **21.** yes; $(3n + 7)^2$ **23.** $8x + 20$ **25.** $4(k + 5)$ $(k - 5)$ **27.** prime   **29.** $3t(3t - 2)(t + 8)$ **31.** $2(5n + 1)$ $(2n + 3)$ **33.** $3x(4x - 3)(2x - 5)$ **35.** $-3(3g - 5)^2$
37. $(a^2 + 2)(4a + 3b^2)$ **39.** $(y^2 + z^2)(x + 1)(x - 1)$
41. $x - 3y$ m, $x + 3y$ m, $xy + 7$ m   **43.** $\{-4\}$ **45.** $\left\{\dfrac{4}{7}\right\}$
47. $\left\{\dfrac{1}{3}\right\}$ **49.** $\{-5, 3\}$ **51.** $\left\{8 \pm \sqrt{7}\right\}$ **53.** $\left\{-1 \pm \sqrt{6}\right\}$
55. $B = \dfrac{L}{16}(D - 4)^2$ **57.** 144 ft   **59.** yes; 2 s   **61.** 4, -4
63. 16   **65.** 100   **67.** C   **69.** ±5 **71.** $\pm\dfrac{9}{7}$ **73.** $-\dfrac{5}{3}; -\dfrac{1}{4}$
75. $y = -\dfrac{1}{2}x + \dfrac{9}{2}$ **77.** 2030 ft   **79.** $-3, -2.5, -2$

Pages 515–518 Chapter 9 Study Guide and Review

1. false, composite   **3.** false, sample answer: 64   **5.** false, $2^4 \cdot 3$ **7.** true   **9.** true   **11.** $2^2 \cdot 7$ **13.** $2 \cdot 3 \cdot 5^2$
15. $-1 \cdot 83$ **17.** 5   **19.** $4ab$ **21.** $5n$ **23.** $13(x + 2y)$
25. $2a(13b + 9c + 16a)$ **27.** $2(r + 3p)(2s + m)$ **29.** $\left\{0, \dfrac{5}{2}\right\}$
31. $\left\{0, -\dfrac{7}{4}\right\}$ **33.** $(x - 12)(x + 3)$ **35.** $(r - 3)(r - 6)$
37. $(m + 4n)(m - 8n)$ **39.** $\{-6, 11\}$ **41.** prime
43. $(5r + 2)(5r + 2)$ **45.** $(4b + 3)(3b + 2)$ **47.** $\left\{4, -\dfrac{5}{2}\right\}$
49. $\left\{\dfrac{3}{4}, -\dfrac{4}{5}\right\}$ **51.** prime   **53.** $\{-4, 4\}$ **55.** $\left\{-\dfrac{9}{4}, \dfrac{9}{4}\right\}$
57. $(3k - 2)^2$ **59.** $2(4n - 5)^2$ **61.** $\left\{\dfrac{9}{7}\right\}$ **63.** $\left\{\pm\dfrac{1}{2}\right\}$

Chapter 10 Quadratic and Exponential Functions

Page 523 Chapter 10 Getting Started

1. Sample answer:

x	y
-6	-1
-4	1
-2	3
0	5
2	7

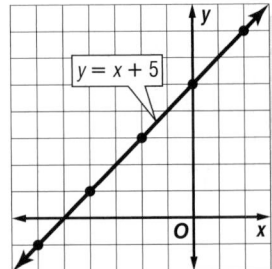
$y = x + 5$

3. Sample answer:

x	y
-4	-1
-2	0
0	1
2	2
4	3

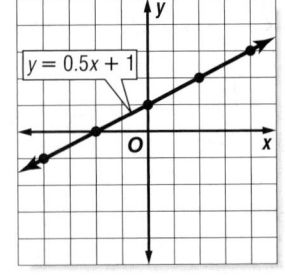
$y = 0.5x + 1$

5. Sample answer:

x	y
0	−4
3	−2
6	0

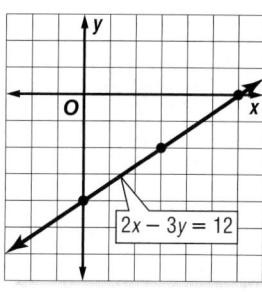

7. Sample answer:

x	y
−6	0
−4	−1
−2	−2
0	−3
2	−4

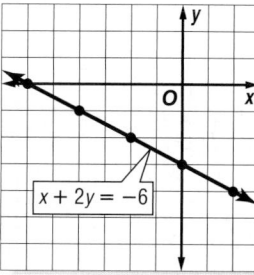

9. yes; $(t + 6)^2$ **11.** no **13.** yes; $(3b − 1)^2$ **15.** yes; $(2p + 3)^2$
17. 21, 25, 29 **19.** 8, 11, 14 **21.** −21, −26, −31 **23.** 8.1,
8.8, 9.5

Pages 528–530 Lesson 10-1
1. Both types of parabolas are U shaped. A parabola with
a maximum opens downward, and its corresponding
equation has a negative coefficient for the x^2 term.
A parabola with a minimum opens upward, and its
corresponding equation has a positive coefficient for the
x^2 term. **3.** If you locate several points of the graph on one
side of the axis of symmetry, you can locate corresponding
points on the other side of the axis of symmetry to help
graph the equation.

5.

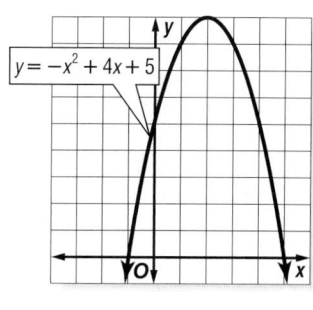

7. $x = 2.5$; (2.5, 12.25);
maximum

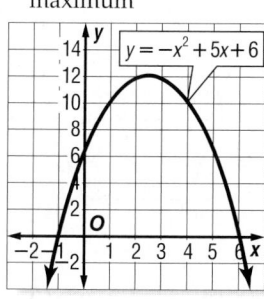

9. B
11.

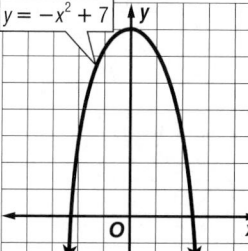

13.

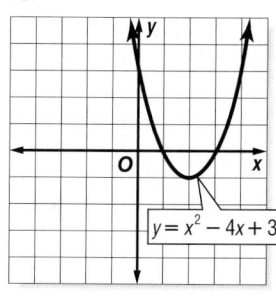

15.

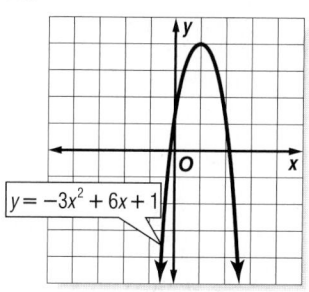

17. $x = \dfrac{5}{8}$

19. $x = 0$; (0, 0); maximum

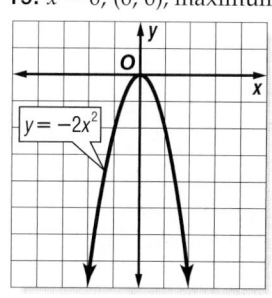

21. $x = 0$; (0, 5); maximum

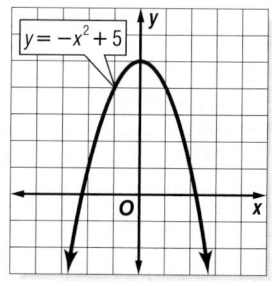

23. $x = −3$; (−3, 24);
maximum

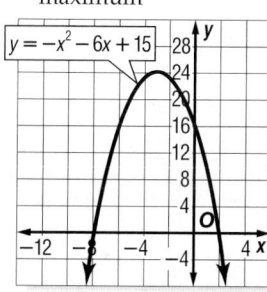

25. $x = −1$; (−1, 17);
minimum

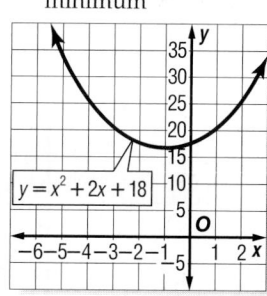

27. $x = 1$; (1, 1); minimum

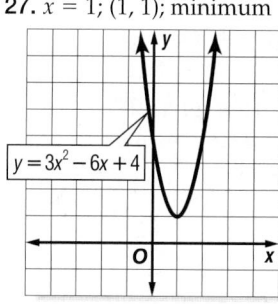

29. $x = 2$; (2, 1); minimum

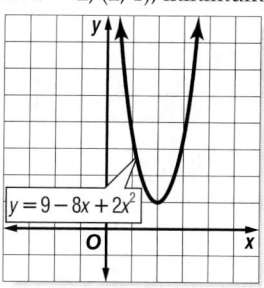

31. $x = 4$; (4, −3); maximum

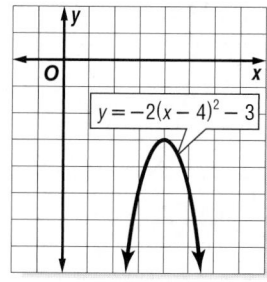

33. $x = −2$; (−2, −1); minimum

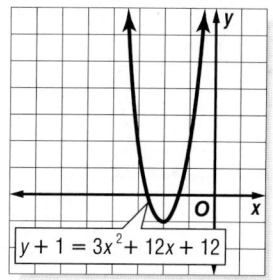

35. $x = -1; (-1, -1);$ minimum

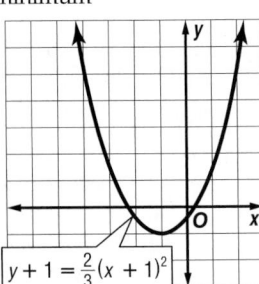

$y + 1 = \frac{2}{3}(x + 1)^2$

37. $x = -1$ **39.** 19 ft
41. $A = x(20 - x)$ or
$A = -x^2 + 20x$ **43.** 100 m²
45. 630 ft **47.** 1959

49.

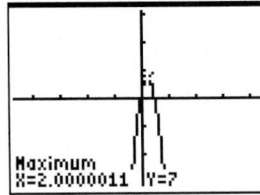

Minimum
X=19.166676 Y=20.197917

51. In order to coordinate a firework with recorded music, you must know when and how high it will explode. Answers should include the following.
- The rocket will explode when the rocket reaches the vertex or when $t = -\frac{39.2}{2(-4.9)}$ which is 4 seconds.
- The height of the rocket when it explodes is the height when $t = 4$. Therefore, $h = -4.9(4^2) + 39.2(4) + 1.6$ or 80 meters.

53. D

55.

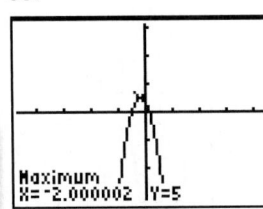

Maximum
X=2.0000011 Y=7

maximum; (2, 7)

57.

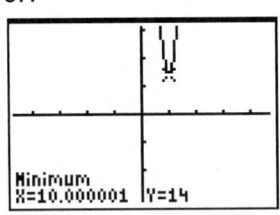

Minimum
X=10.000001 Y=14

minimum; (10, 14)

59.

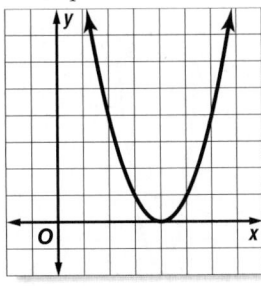

Maximum
X=-2.000002 Y=5

maximum; (−2, 5)

61. $(a + 11)^2$
63. $(2q - 3)(2q + 3)$
65. $(1 - 4g)(1 + 4g)$
67. $6p^2 - p - 18$
69. $\{b \mid b > -12\}$ **71.** $\{r \mid r \leq \frac{8}{9}\}$
73. $y = -7$ **75.** 8 **77.** −3.5
79. −2.5

Pages 535–538 Lesson 10-2

1. −3, −1
3. Sample answer:

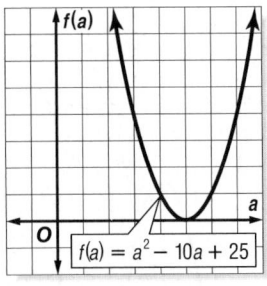

5.

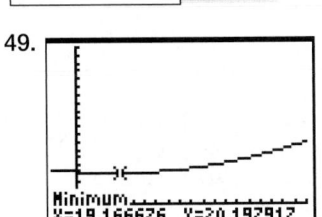

$f(a) = a^2 - 10a + 25$

5

7.

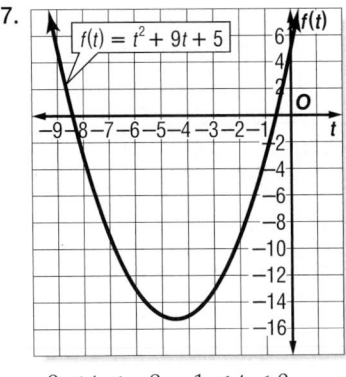

$f(t) = t^2 + 9t + 5$

$-9 < t < -8, -1 < t < 0$

9.

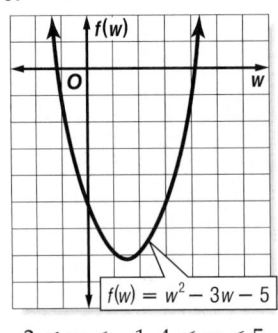

$f(w) = w^2 - 3w - 5$

$-2 < w < -1, 4 < w < 5$

11.

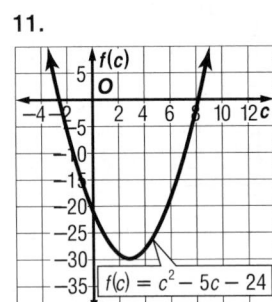

$f(c) = c^2 - 5c - 24$

$-3, 8$

13.

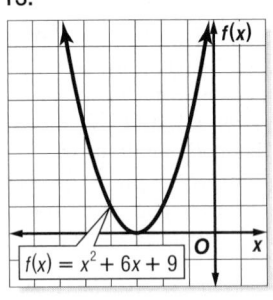

$f(x) = x^2 + 6x + 9$

-3

15.

$f(x) = x^2 + 2x + 5$

$\varnothing$

17.

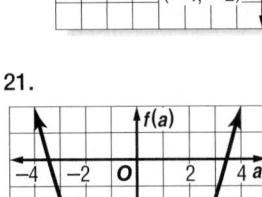

$(-6, 0)$ $(-2, 0)$
$(-4, -2)$

19. 4, 5

21.

$f(a) = a^2 - 12$

$-4 < a < -3, 3 < a < 4$

23.

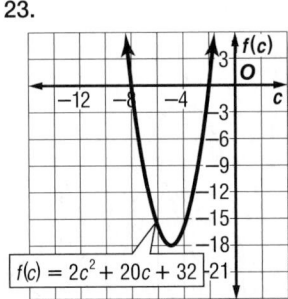

$f(c) = 2c^2 + 20c + 32$

$-8, -2$

25.

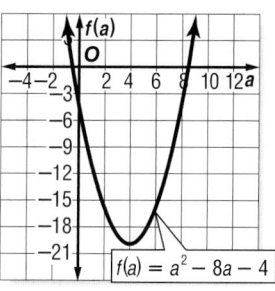

$f(x) = x^2 + 6x + 6$

$-5 < x < -4, -2 < x < -1$

27.

$f(a) = a^2 - 8a - 4$

$-1 < a < 0, 8 < a < 9$

29.

$f(m) = m^2 - 10m + 21$

$3, 7$

31.

$f(n) = 12n^2 - 26n - 30$

$-1 < n < 0, 3$

33. Sample answer:

$(-1, 6)$

35.

$f(x) = -x^2 - 4x + 12$

$-6, 2$

37. 16 ft **39.** \$297
41. about 9 s
43. 100,000 ft^2
45. about 65 ft
47. $-3, 0, 1$ **49.** C
51. $-2, 1, 2$

53. $x = -3$; $(-3, 0)$; minimum

$y = x^2 + 6x + 9$

55. $x = 6$; $(6, -13)$; minimum

$y = 0.5x^2 - 6x + 5$

57. {5} **59.** $\dfrac{m^3}{3}$ **61.** $-\dfrac{m^5 y^4}{3}$ **63.** yes; $(a + 7)^2$ **65.** no
67. no

Pages 542–544   Lesson 10-3
1. Sample answer:

x	1	1
x	1	1
x^2	x	x

$x^2 + 4x + 4$

3. Divide each side by 5.
5. $-11.5, -2.5$ **7.** $\dfrac{25}{4}$ **9.** $-4, -3$
11. $-0.4, 4.4$ **13.** $0.2, 2.3$ **15.** $-2, 6$
17. $2.6, 5.4$ **19.** $-12.2, -3.8$ **21.** 64
23. 121 **25.** $\dfrac{49}{4}$ **27.** $-18, 18$
29. $-2, 6$ **31.** $-3, 22$ **33.** $1, 4$

35. $-3, -1$ **37.** $-1.9, 11.9$ **39.** $2\frac{1}{3}$ **41.** $-1, \frac{2}{3}$ **43.** $-2.5, 0.5$
45. $-1\frac{1}{2}, 4$ **47.** $-2 \pm \sqrt{4 - c}$ **49.** 1.5 m **51.** There are no real solutions since completing the square results in $(x + 2)^2 = -8$ and the square of a number cannot be negative.
53. Al-Khwarizmi used squares to geometrically represent quadratic equations. Answers should include the following.
• Al-Khwarizmi represented x^2 by a square whose sides were each x units long. To this square, he added 4 rectangles with length x units long and width $\dfrac{8}{4}$ or 2 units long. This area represents 35. To make this a square, four 4×4 squares must by added.
• To solve $x^2 + 8x = 35$ by completing the square, use the following steps.

$x^2 + 8x = 35$ *Original equation*
$x^2 + 8x + 16 = 35 + 16$ *Since $\left(\frac{8}{2}\right)^2 = 16$, add 16 to each side.*
$(x + 4)^2 = 51$ *Factor $x^2 + 8x + 16$.*
$x + 4 = \pm\sqrt{51}$ *Take the square root of each side.*
$x + 4 - 4 = \pm\sqrt{51} - 4$ *Subtract 4 from each side.*
$x = -4 \pm\sqrt{51}$ *Simplify.*
$x = -4 - \sqrt{51}$ or $x = -4 + \sqrt{51}$
$x \approx -11.14$ $x \approx 3.14$
The solution set is {−11.14, 3.14}.

55. A

57.

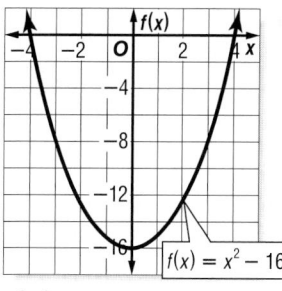

$f(x) = x^2 - 16$

$-4, 4$

59.

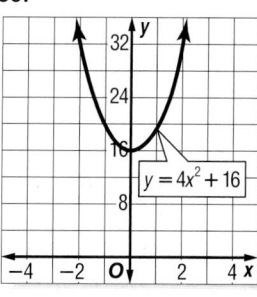

$y = 4x^2 + 16$

61.

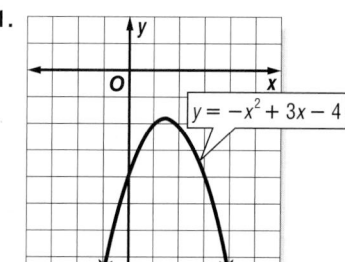

$y = -x^2 + 3x - 4$

63. $8m^2 n$ **65.** $(4, 1)$
67. $-3 < x < 1$
69. $y = -\dfrac{3}{5}x + \dfrac{14}{5}$
71. $y = -2x$ **73.** 5
75. 9.4

Page 544 Practice Quiz 1

1. $x = 0.5$; $(0.5, -6.25)$; **3.** $x = -1$; $(-1, 8)$; maximum
minimum

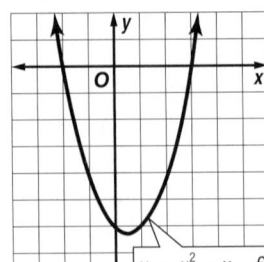

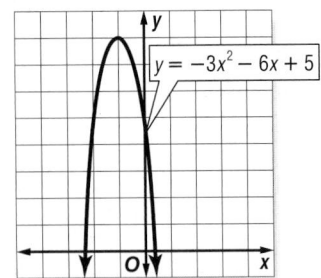

$y = -3x^2 - 6x + 5$

$y = x^2 - x - 6$

5.

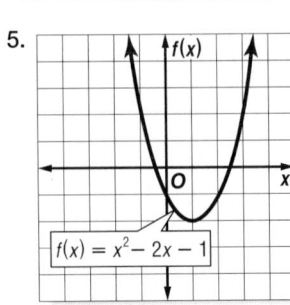

$f(x) = x^2 - 2x - 1$

7. $-5, -3$ **9.** $4.8, 9.2$

$-1 < x < 0, 2 < x < 3$

Pages 550–552 Lesson 10-4

1. Sample answer: (1) Factor $x^2 - 2x - 15$ as $(x + 3)(x - 5)$.
Then according to the Zero Product Property, either $x + 3 = 0$
or $x - 5 = 0$. Solving these equations, $x = -3$ or $x = 5$.
(2) Rewrite the equation as $x^2 - 2x = 15$. Then add 1 to
each side of the equation to complete the square on the left
side. Then $(x - 1)^2 = 16$. Taking the square root of each
side, $x - 1 = \pm 4$. Therefore, $x = 1 \pm 4$ and $x = -3$ or $x = 5$.
(3) Use the Quadratic Formula. Therefore,

$x = \dfrac{-2 \pm \sqrt{(-2)^2 - 4(1)(-15)}}{2(1)}$ or $x = \dfrac{2 \pm \sqrt{64}}{2}$. Simplifying

the expression, $x = -3$ or $x = 5$. **3.** Juanita; you must first
write the equation in the form $ax^2 + bx + c = 0$ to
determine the values of a, b, and c. Therefore, the value of
c is -2, not 2. **5.** $-12, 1$ **7.** $\varnothing$ **9.** $\dfrac{1}{5}, \dfrac{2}{5}$ **11.** 0; 1 real root

13. about 18.8 cm by 18.8 cm **15.** $-10, -2$ **17.** $-\dfrac{4}{5}, 1$

19. $\varnothing$ **21.** 5 **23.** $-0.4, 3.9$ **25.** $-0.5, 0.6$ **27.** $-\dfrac{3}{4}, \dfrac{5}{6}$

29. $-0.3, 0.6$ **31.** $-0.6, 2.6$ **33.** 5 cm by 16 cm **35.** -9
and -7 or 7 and 9 **37.** about -0.2 and 1.4 **39.** 5; 2 real roots
41. -20; no real roots **43.** 0; 1 real root **45.** 0 **47.** about
2.3 s **49.** about 29.4 ft/s **51.** about 41 yr **53.** 2049;
Sample answer: No; the death rate from cancer will
never be 0 unless a cure is found. If and when a cure
will be found cannot be predicted. **55.** A **57.** 1, 7
59. $-0.4, 12.4$

61.

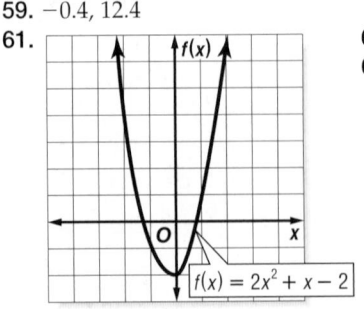

$f(x) = 2x^2 + x - 2$

$-2 < x < -1, 0 < x < 1$

63. $y^3(15x + y)$
65. 1.672×10^{-21}

67.

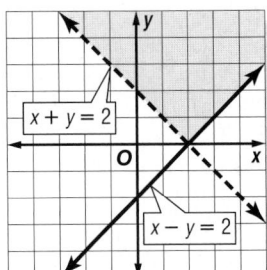

$x + y = 2$

$x - y = 2$

69. $\{m \mid m > 5\}$
71. $\{k \mid k \le -4\}$ **73.** 147

Pages 557–560 Lesson 10-5

1. never **3.** Kiski; the graph of $y = \left(\dfrac{1}{3}\right)^x$ decreases as x
increases.

5.

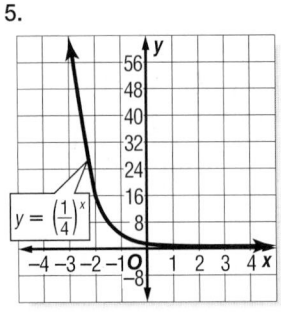

$y = \left(\dfrac{1}{4}\right)^x$

$1; 0.1$

7.

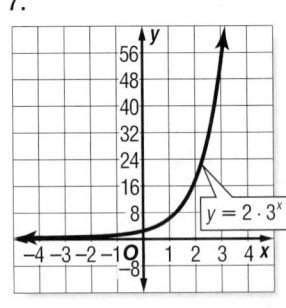

$y = 2 \cdot 3^x$

2

9. Yes; the domain values are at regular intervals and the
range values have a common factor 6.
11. about 1.84×10^{19} grains

13.

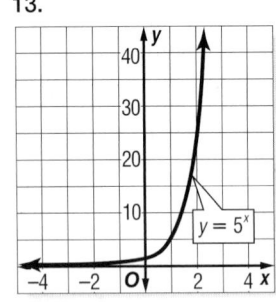

$y = 5^x$

$1; 5.9$

15.

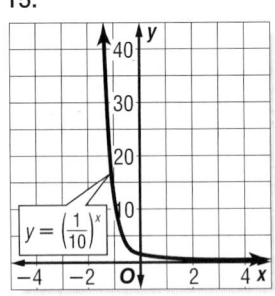

$y = \left(\dfrac{1}{10}\right)^x$

$1; 20.0$

17.

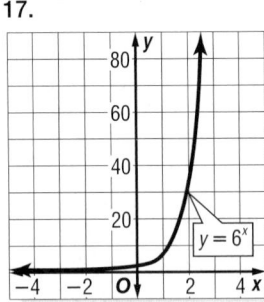

$y = 6^x$

$1; 1.7$

19.

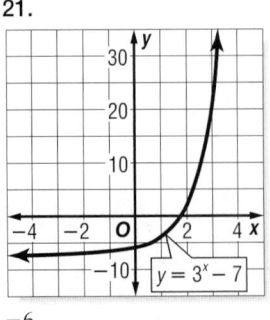

$y = 5(2^x)$

5

21.

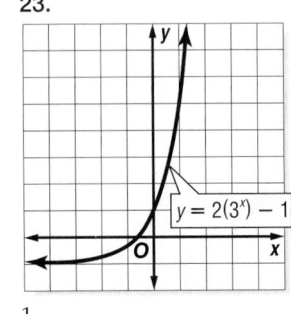

$y = 3^x - 7$

-6

23.

$y = 2(3^x) - 1$

1

R50 Selected Answers

Selected Answers

25.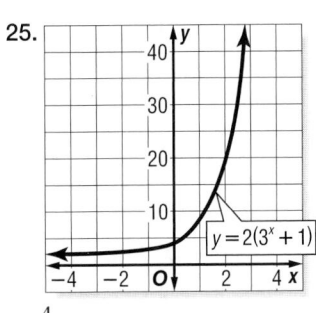

27. No; the domain values are at regular intervals and the range values have a common difference 3. **29.** Yes; the domain values are at regular intervals and the range values have a common factor 0.75.

31. No; the domain values are at regular intervals, but the range values do not change. **33.** about \$37.27 million; about \$41.74 million; about \$46.75 million **35.** \$12 million sales in 1995 **37.** $y = 729\left(\frac{1}{3}\right)^x$ **39.** 6 rounds **41.** 10th week **43.** a translation 2 units up **45.** If the number of items on each level of a piece of art is a given number times the number of items on the previous level, an exponential function can be used to describe the situation. Answers should include the following.

- For the carving of the pliers, $y = 2^x$.
- For this situation, x is an integer between 0 and 8 inclusive. The values of y are 1, 2, 4, 8, 16, 32, 64, 128, and 256.
-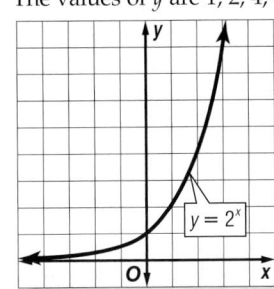

47. A **49.** -1.8, 0.3 **51.** 2, 5 **53.** -5.4, -0.6 **55.** prime **57.** 6, 9 **59.** $\{x \mid x \leq 2\}$ **61.** 11.25 **63.** 144

Page 560   Practice Quiz 2
1. -7, 5 **3.** -0.2, 2.2
5. 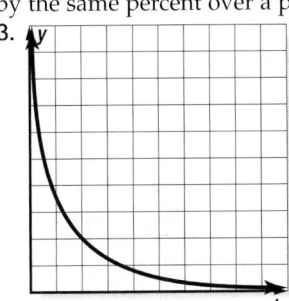 -3

Pages 563–565   Lesson 10-6
1. Exponential growth is an increase by the same percent over a period of time, while exponential decay is a decrease by the same percent over a period of time.

3.

5. about \$43,041
7. about 1,767,128 people
9. $C = 18.9(1.19)^t$
11. $W = 43.2(1.06)^t$
13. about 122,848,204 people
15. about \$14,607.78
17. about \$135,849,289
19. about \$10,761.68
21. about 15.98%
23. growth; 2.6% increase

25. 128 g **27.** about 76.36 g **31.** C

33. 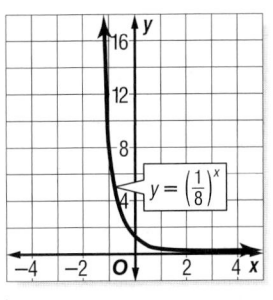 1

35. 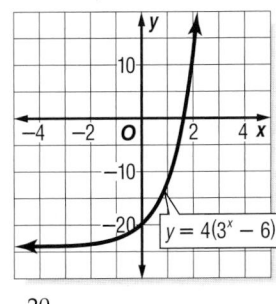 -20

37. -0.6, 2.6 **39.** $m^{10}b^2$ **41.** $0.09x^6y^4$ **43.** $\{1\}$ **45.** yes **47.** -5, -8, -11

Pages 570–572   Lesson 10-7
1. Both arithmetic sequences and geometric sequences are lists of related numbers. In an arithmetic sequence, each term is found by adding the previous term to a constant called the common difference. In a geometric sequence, each term is found by multiplying the previous term by a constant called the common ratio. **3.** Sample answer: 1, 4, 9, 16, 25, 36, ... **5.** yes **7.** 1280, 5120, 20,480 **9.** -40.5, 60.75, -91.125 **11.** -32 **13.** ± 14 **15.** ± 20 **17.** yes **19.** no **21.** no **23.** yes **25.** 256, -1024, 4096 **27.** 64, 32, 16 **29.** -0.3125, 0.078125, -0.01953125 **31.** $\frac{8}{81}$, $\frac{16}{243}$, $\frac{32}{729}$ **33.** 48 in², 24 in², 12 in², 6 in², 3 in² **35.** 320 **37.** 250 **39.** -288 **41.** 0.5859375 **43.** ± 10 **45.** ± 45 **47.** ± 32 **49.** ± 14 **51.** ± 3.5 **53.** $\pm\frac{3}{10}$ **55.** 6 m, 3.6 m, 2.16 m **57.** 18 questions **59.** in 16 days **61.** always

63. Since the distance of each bounce is $\frac{3}{4}$ times the distance of the last bounce, the list of the distances from the stopping place is a geometric sequence. Answers should include the following.
- To find the 10th term, multiply the first term 80 by $\frac{3}{4}$ to the 9th power.
- The 17th bounce will be the first bounce less than 1 ft from the resting place.

65. $1/7$ **67.** 0 **69.** about \$1822.01 **71.** Yes; the domain values are at regular intervals and the range values have a common factor 3. **73.** $(2x + 3)(x - 4)$

Pages 574–578   Chapter 10   Study Guide and Review
1. d **3.** i **5.** c **7.** b **9.** f
11. $x = -1$; $(-1, -1)$; minimum
13. $x = 1\frac{1}{2}$; $\left(1\frac{1}{2}, -6\frac{1}{4}\right)$; minimum

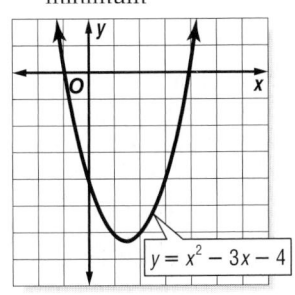

15. $x = 0$; $(0, 1)$; maximum   **17.**

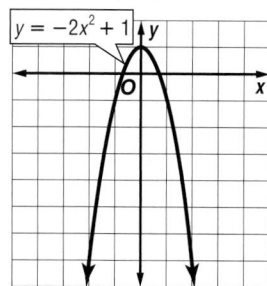

$-3, 4$

19.

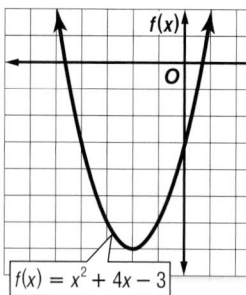

$-5 < x < -4, 0 < x < 1$

21.

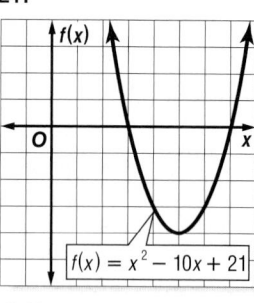

$3, 7$

23. $-1.2, 1.2$ **25.** $-0.7, 7.7$ **27.** $-4.4, 0.4$ **29.** $-2, 10$
31. $-2.5, 1.5$ **33.** $-4, 0$

35.

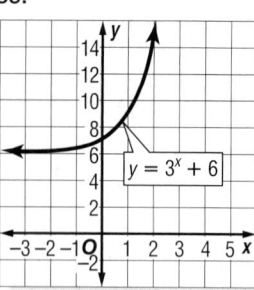

7

37.

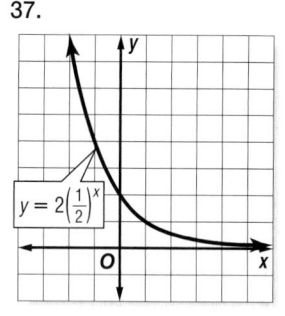

2

39. \$12,067.68   **41.** \$24,688.36   **43.** $\frac{56}{27}$ **45.** ± 10 **47.** $\pm\frac{1}{2}$

Chapter 11   Radical Expressions and Triangles

Page 585   Chapter 11   Getting Started
1. 5   **3.** 7.48   **5.** $a + 7b$ **7.** $16c$ **9.** $\{0, 5\}$ **11.** $\{-3, 9\}$
13. yes   **15.** no

Pages 589–592   Lesson 11-1
1. Both x^4 and x^2 are positive even if x is a negative number.
3. Sample answer: $2\sqrt{2} + 3\sqrt{3}$ and $2\sqrt{2} - 3\sqrt{3}$;
-19 **5.** 4   **7.** $3|ab|\sqrt{6}$ **9.** $\frac{2\sqrt{6}}{3}$ **11.** $\frac{8(3 + \sqrt{2})}{7}$ **13.** 28 ft²
15. $3\sqrt{2}$ **17.** $4\sqrt{5}$ **19.** $\sqrt{30}$ **21.** $84\sqrt{5}$ **23.** $2a^2\sqrt{10}$
25. $7|x^3y^3|\sqrt{3y}$ **27.** $\frac{\sqrt{6}}{3}$ **29.** $\frac{\sqrt{2t}}{4}$ **31.** $\frac{c^2\sqrt{5cd}}{2|d^3|}$
33. $\frac{54 + 9\sqrt{2}}{17}$ **35.** $2\sqrt{7} - 2\sqrt{2}$ **37.** $\frac{-16 - 12\sqrt{3}}{11}$
39. $60\sqrt{2}$ or about 84.9 cm²   **41.** $s = \sqrt{A}$; $6\sqrt{2}$ in.
43. $6\sqrt{5}$ or about 13.4 m/s   **45.** $3\sqrt{2d}$ **47.** about 44.5 mph,
about 51.4 mph   **49.** $20\sqrt{3}$ or about 34.6 ft²   **51.** A lot of
formulas and calculations that are used in space exploration
contain radical expressions. Answers should include the
following.
• To determine the escape velocity of a planet, you would
  need to know its mass and the radius. It would be very

important to know the escape velocity of a planet before
you landed on it so you would know if you had enough
fuel and velocity to launch from it to get back into space.
• The astronomical body with the smaller radius would
  have a greater escape velocity. As the radius decreases,
  the escape velocity increases.
53. B   **55.** 6°F   **57.** x^2 **59.** $a^{-\frac{5}{6}}$ or $\frac{\sqrt[6]{a}}{a}$ **61.** $s^{18}t^6\sqrt{s}$

63. $16, -32, 64$ **65.** $144, 864, 5184$ **67.** $0.08, 0.016, 0.0032$
69. 84.9°C   **71.** $(5x - 4)(7x - 3)$ **73.** $3(x - 7)(x + 5)$
75. $(4x - 3)(2x - 1)$ **77.** $\{(2, 0), (1, 2.5)\}$ **79.** $\left\{\left(4, -\frac{1}{2}\right), (2, 1)\right\}$
81. 6   **83.** -1885 **85.** $a^2 + 7a + 10$ **87.** $4x^2 + x - 3$
89. $12a^2 + 13ab - 14b^2$

Pages 595–597   Lesson 11-2
1. to determine if there are any like radicands   **3.** Sample
answer: $\left(\sqrt{2} + \sqrt{3}\right)^2 = 2 + 2\sqrt{6} + 3$ or $5 + 2\sqrt{6}$
5. $-5\sqrt{6}$ **7.** $4\sqrt{3}$ **9.** $9\sqrt{3} + 3$ **11.** $17 + 7\sqrt{5}$
13. $10\sqrt{110} - 5\sqrt{330} \approx 14.05$ volts   **15.** $13\sqrt{6}$ **17.** 0
19. $10\sqrt{5b}$ **21.** $4\sqrt{6} - 6\sqrt{2} + 5\sqrt{17}$ **23.** $\sqrt{6} + 4\sqrt{3}$
25. $-2\sqrt{2}$ **27.** $\frac{4\sqrt{10}}{5}$ **29.** $\frac{53\sqrt{7}}{7}$ **31.** $10\sqrt{2} + 3\sqrt{10}$
33. $59 - 14\sqrt{10}$ **35.** $3\sqrt{7}$ **37.** $15\sqrt{2} + 11\sqrt{5}$
39. $\sqrt{3} + 2$ cm   **41.** $5\sqrt{87} - 25\sqrt{3} \approx 3.34$ mi   **43.** 6 in.
45. 40 ft/s; 80 ft/s   **47.** The velocity should be $\sqrt{9}$ or 3
times the velocity of an object falling 25 feet; $3 \cdot 40 =$
120 ft/s, $\sqrt{2(32)(225)} = 120$ ft/s.   **49.** Sample answer:
$a = 4, b = 9$; $\sqrt{4 + 9} \neq \sqrt{4} + \sqrt{9}$ **51.** The distance a
person can see is related to the height of the person using
$d = \sqrt{\frac{3h}{2}}$. Answers should include the following.
• You can find how far each lifeguard can see from the
  height of the lifeguard tower. Each tower should have
  some overlap to cover the entire beach area.
• On early ships, a lookout position (Crow's nest) was
  situated high on the foremast. Sailors could see farther
  from this position than from the ship's deck.
53. D   **55.** $8\sqrt{2}$ **57.** $\frac{5}{2}$ **59.** $\frac{3\sqrt{14}}{16|ab|}$ **61.** -5103
63. $\left\{\pm\frac{9}{7}\right\}$ **65.** $\left\{-\frac{5}{4}, 0, \frac{5}{4}\right\}$ **67.** $n \geq \frac{5}{8}$ **69.** $k > \frac{3}{5}$
71. $x^2 - 4x + 4$ **73.** $x^2 + 12x + 36$ **75.** $4x^2 - 12x + 9$

Pages 600–603   Lesson 11-3
1. Isolate the radical on one side of the equation. Square
each side of the equation and simplify. Then check for
extraneous solutions.   **3.** Sample answer: $\sqrt{x + 1} = 8$; 63
5. 25   **7.** 7   **9.** 2   **11.** 3   **13.** 6   **15.** about 5994 m   **17.** 100
19. 50   **21.** 4   **23.** no solution   **25.** 5   **27.** 2   **29.** 180
31. 2   **33.** 57   **35.** 2   **37.** 2, 3   **39.** 3   **41.** 6   **43.** 2   **45.** 11
47. sometimes   **49.** about 0.0619   **51.** $4\sqrt{6}$ or about 9.8 m
53. It increases by a factor of $\sqrt{2}$.   **55.** about 2.43 ft
57. about 43.84°C   **59.** $V < 330.45$ m/s   **61.** You can
determine the time it takes an object to fall from a given height
using a radical equation. Answers should include the following.
• It would take a skydiver approximately 42 seconds to fall
  10,000 feet. Using the equation, it would take 25 seconds.
  The time is different in the two calculations because air
  resistance slows the skydiver.
• A skydiver can increase the speed of his fall by lowering
  air resistance. This can be done by pulling his arms and
  legs close to his body. A skydiver can decrease his speed

by holding his arms and legs out, which increases the air resistance.
63. C **65.** 11 **67.** 15.08 **69.** no solution **71.** $20\sqrt{3}$
73. $8\sqrt{3}$ **75.** $3\left(\sqrt{10} - \sqrt{3}\right)$ **77.** yes; $(2n - 7)^2$
79. $r^2 - r - 12$ **81.** $6p^3 + 7p^2 - 2p + 45$ **83.** $14x - 7y = -3$
85. $15x - 2y = 49$ **87.** 25 **89.** $4\sqrt{13}$

Page 603   Practice Quiz 1
1. $4\sqrt{3}$ **3.** $\dfrac{-2 + \sqrt{10}}{2}$ **5.** $20\sqrt{3}$ **7.** $11 + 4\sqrt{7}$ or about
21.6 cm^2 **9.** 4

Pages 607–610   Lesson 11-4
1.
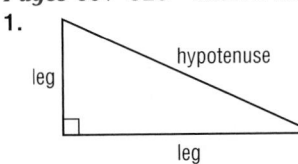
3. $d = \sqrt{2s^2}$ or $d = s\sqrt{2}$
5. 9 **7.** 60 **9.** $\sqrt{65} \approx 8.06$
11. Yes; $16^2 + 30^2 = 34^2$.
13. 14.14 **15.** 53
17. 42.13 **19.** 65 **21.** 11
23. $\sqrt{115} \approx 10.72$ **25.** $\sqrt{67} \approx 8.19$ **27.** $\sqrt{253} \approx 15.91$
29. $17x$ **31.** Yes; $30^2 + 40^2 = 50^2$. **33.** No; $24^2 + 30^2 \neq 36^2$.
35. Yes; $15^2 + \left(\sqrt{31}\right)^2 = 16^2$. **37.** 18 ft **39.** $4\sqrt{3}$ in. or
about 6.93 in. **41.** about 415.8 ft **43.** The roller coaster makes a total horizontal advance of 404 feet, reaches a vertical height of 208 feet, and travels a total track length of about 628.3 feet. **45.** about 116.6 ft **47.** 900 ft^2
49. about 1081.7 ft, 324.5 ft **51.** C **53.** 144 **55.** 12
57. $-3\sqrt{z}$ **59.** 5^5 or 3125 **61.** $\dfrac{2a^2b^3}{c^8}$ **63.** 5 **65.** $\sqrt{53}$
67. $\sqrt{130}$

Pages 612–615   Lesson 11-5
1. The values that are subtracted are squared before being added and the square of a negative number is always positive. The sum of two positive numbers is positive, so the distance will never be negative. **3.** There are exactly two points that lie on the line $y = -3$ that are 10 units from the point (7, 5). **5.** 13 **7.** $\sqrt{10} \approx 3.16$ **9.** 2 or -14
11. about 25.5 yd, 25 yd **13.** 20 **15.** 5 **17.** $4\sqrt{5} \approx 8.94$
19. $\sqrt{41} \approx 6.40$ **21.** $\dfrac{10}{3} \approx 3.33$ **23.** $\dfrac{13}{10}$ or 1.30
25. $2\sqrt{14} \approx 7.48$ **27.** 1 or 7 **29.** -2 or 4 **31.** -10 or 4
33. two; $AB = BC = 10$ **35.** 3 **37.** 109 mi **39.** Yes; it will take her about 10.6 minutes to walk between the two buildings. **41.** Minneapolis-St. Cloud, 53 mi; St. Paul-Rochester, 64 mi, Minneapolis-Eau Claire, 79 mi; Duluth-St. Cloud, 118 mi **43.** Compare the slopes of the two potential legs to determine whether the slopes are negative reciprocals of each other. You can also compute the lengths of the three sides and determine whether the square of the longest side length is equal to the sum of the squares of the other two side lengths. Neither test holds true in this case because the triangle is not a right triangle. **45.** B **47.** 25
49. 3 **51.** 11 **53.** {2, 10} **55.** Asia, 1.113×10^{12}; Europe, 1.016×10^{12}; U.S./Canada, 8.84×10^{11}; Latin America, 2.41×10^{11}; Middle East, 1.012×10^{11}; Africa, 5.61×10^{10}.
57. $\{m \mid m \geq 9\}$
59. $\{x \mid x \leq -3\}$

61. $\{r \mid r \geq 9.1\}$
63. 6 **65.** 12 **67.** 1

Pages 618–621   Lesson 11-6
1. If the measures of the angles of one triangle equal the measures of the corresponding angles of another triangle, and the lengths of the sides are proportional, then the two triangles are similar. **3.** Consuela; the arcs indicate which angles correspond. The vertices of the triangles are written in order to show the corresponding parts. **5.** Yes; the angle measures are equal. **7.** $b = 15, d = 12$ **9.** $d = 10.2, e = 9$
11. Yes; the angle measures are equal. **13.** No; the angle measures are not equal. **15.** No; the angle measures are not equal. **17.** $\ell = 12, m = 6$ **19.** $k = \dfrac{55}{6}, \ell = \dfrac{22}{3}$
21. $k = 3, o = 8$ **23.** $k = 2.8, m = 3.6$ **25.** always **27.** $3\frac{1}{3}$ in.
29. 8 **31.** about 53 ft **33.** Yes; all circles are similar because they have the same shape. **35.** 4:1; The area of the first is πr^2 and the area of the other is $\pi(2r)^2 = 4\pi r^2$. **37.** D
39. 5 **41.** $\sqrt{26} \approx 5.1$ **43.** Yes; $25^2 + 60^2 = 65^2$. **45.** Yes; $49^2 + 168^2 = 175^2$. **47.** $3x^2 - 7x + 1$ **49.** $-3x^2 + 6x + 3$
51. $(3, -2)$ **53.** $(1.5, 0)$ **55.** about -0.044 **57.** $-\dfrac{5}{6}$ or $-0.8\overline{3}$
59. $\dfrac{9}{5}$ or 1.8 **61.** $-\dfrac{1}{3}$ or $-0.\overline{3}$

Page 621   Practice Quiz 2
1. 50 **3.** $2\sqrt{5} \approx 4.47$ **5.** $\sqrt{306} \approx 17.49$ **7.** $2\sqrt{2} \approx 2.83$
9. $a = 20, c = 15$

Pages 627–630   Lesson 11-7
1. If you know the measure of the hypotenuse, use sine or cosine, depending on whether you know the measure of the adjacent side or the opposite side. If you know the measures of the two legs, use tangent. **3.** They are equal.
5. sin $Y = 0.3846$, cos $Y = 0.9231$, tan $Y = 0.4167$ **7.** 0.2588
9. 80° **11.** 18° **13.** 22° **15.** $\angle A = 60°, AC = 21$ in., $BC \approx 36.4$ in. **17.** $\angle B = 35°, BC = 5.7$ in., $AB = 7.0$ in.
19. sin $R = 0.6$, cos $R = 0.8$, tan $R = 0.75$ **21.** sin $R = 0.7241$, cos $R = 0.6897$, tan $R = 1.05$ **23.** sin $R = 0.5369$, cos $R = 0.8437$, tan $R = 0.6364$ **25.** 0.5 **27.** 0.7071
29. 0.6249 **31.** 2.3559 **33.** 0.9781 **35.** 40° **37.** 62°
39. 33° **41.** 12° **43.** 39° **45.** 51° **47.** 36° **49.** 37°
51. 56° **53.** $\angle A = 63°, AC \approx 9.1$ in., $BC \approx 17.8$ in.
55. $\angle B = 50°, AC \approx 12.3$ ft, $BC \approx 10.3$ ft **57.** $\angle B = 52°$, $AC \approx 30.7$ in., $AB \approx 39$ in. **59.** $\angle A \approx 23°, \angle B \approx 67°$, $AB = 13$ ft **61.** about 8.1° **63.** about 20.6° **65.** about 2.74 m to 0.7 m **67.** If you know the distance between two points and the angles from these two points to a third point, you can determine the distance to the third point by forming a triangle and using trigonometric ratios. Answers should include the following.
• If you measure your distance from the mountain and the angle of elevation to the peak of the mountain from two different points, you can write an equation using trigonometric ratios to determine its height, similar to Example 5.
• You need to know the altitude of the two points you are measuring.
69. D **71.** $k = 8, o = 13.5$ **73.** -5 or 3 **75.** $4s^3 - 9s^2 + 12s$
77. $(11, 3)$ **79.** $(-2, 1)$

1. false, $-3 - \sqrt{7}$ **3.** true **5.** false, $3x + 19 = x^2 + 6x + 9$

7. false, $\dfrac{x\sqrt{2xy}}{y}$ **9.** $\dfrac{2\sqrt{15}}{|y|}$ **11.** $57 - 24\sqrt{3}$

13. $\dfrac{5\sqrt{21} - 3\sqrt{35}}{15}$ **15.** $5\sqrt{3} + 5\sqrt{5}$ **17.** $36\sqrt{3}$

19. $-6\sqrt{2} - 12\sqrt{7}$ **21.** $3\sqrt{2} + 3\sqrt{6}$ **23.** $\sqrt{6} - 1$

25. no solution **27.** $\dfrac{26}{7}$ **29.** 12 **31.** 34 **33.** $\sqrt{115} \approx 10.72$

35. 24 **37.** no **39.** yes **41.** 17 **43.** $\sqrt{205} \approx 14.32$

45. $\sqrt{137} \approx 11.70$ **47.** 5 or -1 **49.** 10 or -14

51. $d = \dfrac{45}{8}$, $e = \dfrac{27}{4}$ **53.** $b = \dfrac{44}{3}$, $d = 6$ **55.** 0.5283

57. 0.8491 **59.** 1.6071 **61.** 39° **63.** 12° **65.** 27°

Chapter 12 Rational Expressions and Equations

Page 641 Chapter 12 Getting Started

1. $-\dfrac{63}{16}$ **3.** 5 **5.** 4.62 **7.** 10.8 **9.** 6 **11.** $4m^2n$

13. $3c^2d(1 - 2d)$ **15.** $(x + 3)(x + 8)$ **17.** $(2x + 7)(x - 3)$

19. -1 **21.** $-\dfrac{149}{6}$ **23.** $\dfrac{31}{7}$ **25.** $8, -7$

1. Sample answer: $xy = 8$ **3.** b; Sample answer: As the price increases, the number purchased decreases.

5. $xy = 12$ **7.** $xy = 24; 4$

9. $xy = 8; \dfrac{1}{4}$

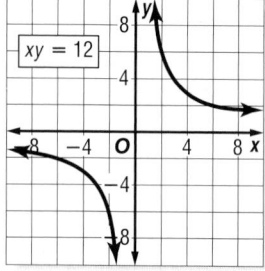

11. $xy = -192$ **13.** $xy = 75$

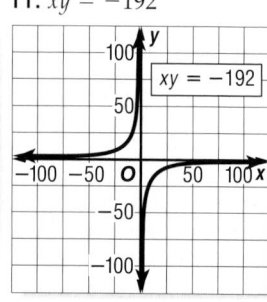

15. $xy = 72$

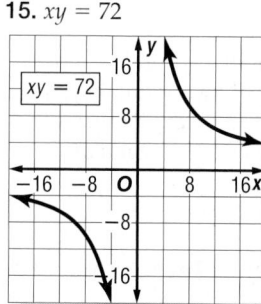

17. $xy = 60; 20$
19. $xy = -8.5; 8.5$
21. $xy = 28.16; 8.8$
23. $xy = 16; \dfrac{16}{7}$ **25.** $xy = \dfrac{14}{3}; \dfrac{2}{3}$
27. $xy = 26.84; 8.3875$ **29.** 8 in.

31. 7.2 h **33.** about 37 min
35. 20 m^3 **37.** 24 kg **39.** It is one third of what it was.
41. B **43.** 41° **45.** 73°
47. $a = 6, f = 14$ **49.** -9

51.

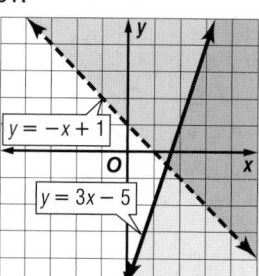

53.

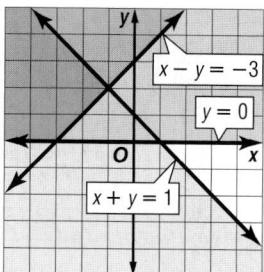

55. 3 **57.** 30 **59.** $6xy^2$

1. Sample answer: Factor the denominator, set each factor equal to 0, and solve for x. **3.** Sample answer: You need to determine excluded values before simplifying. One or more factors may have been canceled in the denominator. **5.** -3

7. $\dfrac{4}{5xy}$; $0, 0$ **9.** $\dfrac{1}{x + 4}$; -4 **11.** $\dfrac{a + 6}{a + 4}$; $-4, 2$ **13.** $\dfrac{b + 1}{b - 9}$; $4, 9$

15. $\dfrac{4}{9 + 2g}$ **17.** -5 **19.** $-5, 5$ **21.** $-5, 3$ **23.** $-7, -5$

25. $\dfrac{a^2}{3b}$; $0, 0$ **27.** $\dfrac{3x}{8z}$; $0, 0, 0$ **29.** $\dfrac{mn}{12n - 4m}$; $m \neq 3n, 0, 0$

31. $z + 8$; -2 **33.** $\dfrac{2}{y + 5}$; $-5, 2$ **35.** $\dfrac{a + 3}{a + 9}$; $-9, 3$

37. $\dfrac{(b + 4)(b - 2)}{(b - 4)(b - 16)}$; $4, 16$ **39.** $\dfrac{n - 2}{n(n - 6)}$; $0, 6$ **41.** $\dfrac{3}{4}$; $-2, -1$

43. about 29 min **45.** The times are not doubled; the difference is 12 minutes. **47.** 42.75 **49.** $450 + 4n$ **51.** 41

53. $\dfrac{\pi x^2}{4x^2}$ or $\dfrac{\pi}{4}$ **55a.** Sample answer: The graphs appear to be identical because the second equation is the simplified form of the first equation. **55b.** Sample answer: The first graph has a hole at $x = 4$ because it is an excluded value of the equation. **57.** C **59.** $xy = 60; -5$ **61.** $xy = -7.5; 0.9375$

63. 71° **65.** 45° **67.** 7 **69.** 6 **71.** 1536, 6144, 24,576

73. $\dfrac{81}{64}, \dfrac{243}{256}, \dfrac{729}{1024}$ **75.** 7 **77.** 15,300 **79.** 72

1. Sample answer: $\dfrac{2}{1}, \dfrac{1}{x}$ **3.** Amiri; sample answer: Amiri correctly divided by the GCF. **5.** $\dfrac{2t}{s}$ **7.** $2(x + 2)$ **9.** $\dfrac{x + 3}{5}$

11. $1\dfrac{2}{3}$ days **13.** $\dfrac{2}{n}$ **15.** $\dfrac{12ag}{5b}$ **17.** $\dfrac{n - 4}{n + 4}$ **19.** $\dfrac{(x - 1)(x + 7)}{(x - 7)(x + 1)}$

21. $\dfrac{y - 2}{y - 1}$ **23.** $\dfrac{x - 6}{(x + 8)(x + 2)}$ **25.** $\dfrac{2}{n(n + 3)}$ **27.** $\dfrac{(a - 3)(a + 3)}{(a - 4)(a + 2)}$

29. about 16.67 m/s **31.** 20 yd^3 **33.** about $16.02

35. 3 lanes $\cdot \dfrac{13 \text{ miles}}{1 \text{ lane}} \cdot \dfrac{5280 \text{ feet}}{1 \text{ mile}} \cdot \dfrac{1 \text{ vehicle}}{30 \text{ feet}}$ **37.** 5.72 h

39. Sample answer: Multiply rational expressions to perform dimensional analysis. Answers should include the following.

• 25 lights $\cdot\ h$ hours $\cdot \dfrac{60 \text{ watts}}{\text{light}} \cdot \dfrac{1 \text{ kilowatt}}{1000 \text{ watts}} \cdot \dfrac{15 \text{ cents}}{1 \text{ kilowatt hour}} \cdot \dfrac{1 \text{ dollar}}{100 \text{ cents}}$

• Sample answer: converting units of measure

41. A **43.** $-5, 2$ **45.** $xy = 72; 12$ **47.** $xy = -192; -48$

49. -7^3 or -343 **51.** $\dfrac{4b^4c^5}{a^3}$ **53.** $\{r \mid r \geq 2.1\}$ **55.** 11 days

57. $(n + 8)(n - 8)$ **59.** $(a + 7)(a - 5)$ **61.** $3x(x - 2)(x - 6)$

Page 659 Practice Quiz 1

1. $xy = 196$

(graph showing curve labeled $xy = 196$ with y-axis marked 160, 120, 80, 40 and -80, -120, -160; x-axis marked -8 -6 -4 -2 O 2 4 6 8 x)

3. $\dfrac{4a}{7b}$ 5. $\dfrac{b+1}{b-9}$ 7. $3m^2$

9. $\dfrac{4}{5(n+5)}$

Pages 662–664 Lesson 12-4

1. Sample answer: $\dfrac{15z}{4y^2} \div \dfrac{3x}{4y}$ 3. Sample answer: Divide the density by the given volume, then perform dimensional analysis. 5. $\dfrac{2a}{a+7}$ 7. $\dfrac{2}{x+5}$ 9. $\dfrac{2(x-2)(x+3)}{(x+1)(x+9)}$

11. $\dfrac{2}{9}$ lb/in^2 13. ab 15. $\dfrac{x}{2y^2}$ 17. $\dfrac{sy^2}{z^2}$ 19. $\dfrac{b+3}{4b}$

21. $\dfrac{3k}{(k+1)(k-2)}$ 23. $\dfrac{3(x+4)}{4(2x-9)}$ 25. 648 27. 225

29. $x+3$ 31. $\dfrac{(x+1)(x-1)}{2}$ 33. $\dfrac{3(a+4)}{2(a-3)}$ 35. $\dfrac{x+4}{x+3}$

37. about 9.2 mph 39. $n = 20{,}000$ yd$^3 \div$

$\left[\dfrac{5 \text{ ft}(18 \text{ ft} + 15 \text{ ft})}{2} \cdot 9 \text{ ft} \cdot \dfrac{1 \text{ yd}^3}{27 \text{ ft}^3}\right]$; $727.\overline{27}$

41. 63.5 mph 43. $\left(x - \dfrac{1}{2}\right)\left(x - \dfrac{3}{4}\right)(x)$

45. Sample answer: Divide the number of cans recycled by $\dfrac{5}{8}$ to find the total number of cans produced. Answers should include the following.

• $x = 63{,}900{,}000$ cans $\div \dfrac{5}{8} \cdot \dfrac{1 \text{ pound}}{33 \text{ cans}}$

47. C 49. $\dfrac{x-2}{x+2}$ 51. $\dfrac{7(x+2y)(x+5)}{x+y}$ 53. $-\dfrac{x+5}{x+6}$

55. $\dfrac{n+4}{n-4}$ 57. $\left\{\dfrac{4}{3}\right\}$ 59. $\left\{-6 \pm \sqrt{14}\right\}$ 61. 3 63. $\{g \mid g \geq 7.5\}$

65. $\{x \mid x \geq -0.7\}$ 67. $\left\{r \mid r < -\dfrac{1}{20}\right\}$ 69. 39,000 covers

71. $\dfrac{m^3}{5}$ 73. $\dfrac{b^3}{c^3}$ 75. $\dfrac{7x^4}{z}$

Pages 669–671 Lesson 12-5

1. b and c 3. Sample answer: $x^3 + 2x^2 + 8$; $x^3 + 2x^2 + 0x + 8$ 5. $2 + \dfrac{5}{a} + \dfrac{2}{7b^2}$ 7. $r + 3 + \dfrac{9}{r+9}$ 9. $b + 2 - \dfrac{3}{2b-1}$

11. $\dfrac{x}{3} + 3 - \dfrac{7}{3x}$ 13. $3s - \dfrac{5}{t} + \dfrac{8t}{s^2}$ 15. $x + 4$ 17. $n - 7$

19. $z - 9 + \dfrac{33}{z+7}$ 21. $2r + 7$ 23. $t + 6$ 25. $3x^2 + 2x - 3$

$- \dfrac{1}{x+2}$ 27. $3x^2 + \dfrac{6}{2x-3}$ 29. $3n^2 - 2n + 3 + \dfrac{3}{2n+3}$

31. $\dfrac{150(60-x)}{x}$ 33. 3 rolls 35. 5/$1.02, 10/$0.93, 16/$0.82; 18-inch

37.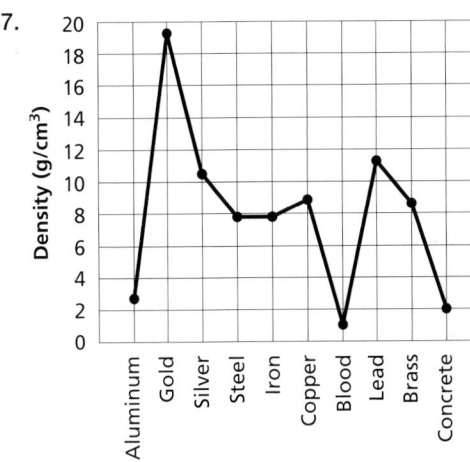

39. $2w + 4$ 41. 12 43. Sample answer: Division can be used to find the number of pieces of fabric available when you divide a large piece of fabric into smaller pieces. Answers should include the following.

• The two expressions are equivalent. If you use the Distributive Property, you can separate the numerator into two expressions with the same denominator.

• When you simplify the right side of the equation, the numerator is $a - b$ and the denominator is c. This is the same as the expression on the left.

45. B 47. $\dfrac{m+4}{m+1}$ 49. $\dfrac{1}{z+6}$ 51. $10\sqrt{2}$ 53. $(d+5)(d-8)$

55. prime 57. $4m^3 + 6n^2 - n$ 59. $-2a^3 - 2a^2b + b^2 - 3b^3$

Pages 674–677 Lesson 12-6

1. Sample answer: $\dfrac{x+6}{x+2} + \dfrac{x-4}{x+2} = 1$ 3. Sample answer: Two rational expressions whose sum is 0 are additive inverses, while two rational expressions whose difference is 0 are equivalent expressions. 5. $\dfrac{a}{2}$ 7. $\dfrac{3-n}{n-1}$ 9. $-\dfrac{a}{6}$

11. $\dfrac{3m+6}{m-2}$ 13. $\dfrac{1}{10}$ 15. z 17. $n-1$ 19. 3 21. $\dfrac{n-3}{n+3}$

23. $\dfrac{3a+1}{a-4}$ 25. $\dfrac{14b+7}{2b+6}$ 27. $\dfrac{22x+7}{2x+5}$ 29. $\dfrac{2n}{3}$ 31. $\dfrac{1}{3}$

33. $\dfrac{10}{z-2}$ 35. $\dfrac{4-7m}{7m-2}$ 37. $\dfrac{10y}{y-3}$ 39. 3 41. $\dfrac{4b-23}{2b+12}$

43. $\dfrac{60}{n}$ 45. $\dfrac{1}{7.48}$ ft^3 47. $\dfrac{x}{16}; \dfrac{x}{18}; \dfrac{x}{24}$ 49. c 51. A

53. $x^2 + 2x - 3$ 55. $\dfrac{b+3}{4b}$ 57. $(a+7)(a+2)$

59. $(y-4z)(y-7z)$ 61. $7x^2 - 3x + 22$ 63. 36 65. 24

67. 30 69. 400 71. 144

Page 677 Practice Quiz 2

1. $\dfrac{a}{a+11}$ 3. $\dfrac{x-1}{x+5}$ 5. $x - 5 - \dfrac{1}{2x+3}$ 7. $\dfrac{7}{x+7}$ 9. $\dfrac{3x}{3x+2}$

Pages 681–683 Lesson 12-7

1. Sample answer: To find the LCD, determine the least common multiple of all of the factors of the denominators.

3. Sample answer: $\dfrac{x}{2x+6}, \dfrac{5}{x+3}$ 5. $6(x-2)$ 7. $\dfrac{12x+7}{10x^2}$

9. $\dfrac{y^2 + 12y + 25}{(y-5)(y+5)}$ 11. $\dfrac{2z-wz}{4w^2}$ 13. $\dfrac{4}{(b-4)(b+4)}$ 15. C

17. $21x^2y$ 19. $(2n-5)(n+2)$ 21. $(p+1)(p-6)$

23. $\dfrac{2+7a}{a^3}$ 25. $\dfrac{15m+28}{35m^2}$ 27. $\dfrac{n^2+12}{(n+4)(n-3)}$

29. $\dfrac{7x^2+3x}{(x-3)(x+1)}$ 31. $\dfrac{1}{3}$ 33. $\dfrac{7y+39}{(y+3)(y-3)}$

35. $\dfrac{3x^2 + 6x + 6}{(x+4)(x-1)^2}$ **37.** $\dfrac{a^3 - a^2b + a^2 + ab}{(a+b)(a-b)^2}$ **39.** $\dfrac{4 - 25x}{15x^2}$

41. $\dfrac{5ax - a}{7x^2}$ **43.** $\dfrac{k^2 - 6k - 15}{(k+5)(k-3)}$ **45.** $\dfrac{2m^2 - m - 9}{(m+1)(2m+5)}$

47. $\dfrac{-3a + 6}{a(a-6)}$ **49.** $\dfrac{3a + 5}{-3(a-2)}$ **51.** $\dfrac{4a^2 + 2a + 4}{(a+4)(a+1)(a-1)}$

53. $\dfrac{-m^3 - 11m^2 - 56m - 48}{(m-4)(m+4)^2}$ **55.** 12 mi; \$30 **57.** 66,000 mi

59. Sample answer: You can use rational expressions and their least common denominators to determine when elections will coincide. Answers should include the following.
- Use each factor of the denominators the greatest number of times it appears.
- 2012

61. C **63.** $\dfrac{4x + 5}{2x + 3}$ **65.** $b + 10$ **67.** $2m - 3 + \dfrac{2}{2m + 7}$

69. $(5r - 3)(r + 2)$ **71.** \$54.85 **73.** $\dfrac{ab}{2}$ **75.** $\dfrac{1}{4n}$ **77.** $\dfrac{x + 4}{x + 6}$

Pages 686–689 Lesson 12-8

1. Sample answer: Both mixed numbers and mixed expressions are made up by the sum of an integer or monomial and a fraction or rational expression. **3.** Bolton; Lian omitted the factor $(x + 1)$. **5.** $\dfrac{42y + 5}{6y}$ **7.** $\dfrac{14}{19}$

9. $\dfrac{a - b}{x + y}$ **11.** $\dfrac{8n + 3}{n}$ **13.** $\dfrac{2xy + x}{y}$ **15.** $\dfrac{2m^2 - m - 4}{m}$

17. $\dfrac{b^3 + ab^2 + a - b}{a + b}$ **19.** $\dfrac{5n^3 - 15n^2 - 1}{n - 3}$ **21.** $\dfrac{x^2 - 7x + 17}{x - 3}$

23. $\dfrac{3}{4}$ **25.** $\dfrac{1}{ab^2}$ **27.** $\dfrac{y^2(x + 4)}{x^2(y - 2)}$ **29.** $\dfrac{1}{y + 4}$ **31.** $\dfrac{n + 2}{n + 3}$

33. $\dfrac{(x + 3)(x - 1)}{(x - 2)(x + 4)}$ **35.** $\dfrac{a(b^2 + 1)}{b(a^2 + 1)}$ **37.** 60 **39.** 404.60 cycles/s

41. $66\dfrac{2}{3}$ lb/in^2

43. Sample answer: Most measurements used in baking are fractions or mixed numbers, which are examples of rational expressions. Answers should include the following.
- You want to find the number of batches of cookies you can make using the 7 cups of flour you have on hand when a batch requires $1\dfrac{1}{2}$ cups of flour.
- Divide the expression in the numerator of a complex fraction by the expression in the denominator.

45. C **47.** $\dfrac{3a^2 + 3ab - b^2}{(a - b)(2b + 3a)}$ **49.** $\dfrac{2n^2 - 8n - 2}{(n - 2)^2(n + 3)}$ **51.** $\dfrac{1}{x - 3}$

53. $\dfrac{2}{n + 6}$ **55.** $\{\pm 4\}$ **57.** $\{-5, -3, 3\}$ **59.** about 2.59×10^0

61. $C = 0.16m + 0.99$ **63.** -48 **65.** 16 **67.** -14.4

Pages 693–695 Lesson 12-9

1. Sample answer: When you solve the equation, $n = 1$. But $n < 1$, so the equation has no solution. **3.** Sample answer: $\dfrac{x}{4} = 0$ **5.** -13 **7.** $\dfrac{5}{4}$ **9.** $-1, \dfrac{2}{5}$ **11.** 8 **13.** 3 **15.** -3

17. 0 **19.** $\dfrac{1}{2}$ **21.** -3 **23.** 1 **25.** $-2, 1$ **27.** 7 **29.** 9

31. about 0.82 mi **33.** 600 ft^3 **35.** $-\dfrac{14}{3}$ **37.** A **39.** $\dfrac{x + 1}{x - 2}$

41. $\dfrac{x + 1}{x + 5}$ **43.** $\dfrac{1}{y^2 - 2y + 1}$ **45.** $4(5x - 2y)$

47. $(2p + 5)(5p - 6)$

Pages 696–700 Chapter 12 Study Guide and Review

1. false, rational **3.** true **5.** false, $x^2 - 144$ **7.** $xy = 1176$; 21

9. $xy = 144$; 48 **11.** $\dfrac{x}{4y^2z}$ **13.** $\dfrac{a - 5}{a - 2}$ **15.** $\dfrac{14a^2b}{3}$ **17.** $\dfrac{30}{x - 10}$

19. $\dfrac{(x + 4)^2}{(x + 2)^2}$ **21.** $2p$ **23.** $\dfrac{3}{(y + 4)(y - 2)}$ **25.** $2ac^2 - 4a^2c + \dfrac{3c^2}{b}$

27. $x^2 + 2x - 3$ **29.** $\dfrac{2m + 3}{5}$ **31.** $a + b$ **33.** 2 **35.** $\dfrac{4c^2 + 9d}{6cd^2}$

37. $\dfrac{8d^2 - 7a}{(a - 2)(a + 1)}$ **39.** $\dfrac{14a - 3}{6a^2}$ **41.** $\dfrac{5x - 8}{x - 2}$ **43.** $\dfrac{4x^2 - 2y^2}{x^2 - y^2}$

45. $\dfrac{20a + 16}{2a^2 - 3a}$ **47.** -5 **49.** $-\dfrac{1}{4}$ **51.** -1; extraneous 0

Chapter 13 Statistics

Page 707 Chapter 13 Getting Started

1. Sample answer: If $a = 5$ and $b = -2$, then $c = 3$. However, $5 > 3$. **3.** Sample answer: The speed limit could be 55 mph, and Tara could be driving 50 mph. **5.** 15

7. 375

9.

15 16 17 18 19 20 21 22 23

11.

1 2 3 4 5

Pages 710–713 Lesson 13-1

1. All three are unbiased samples. However, the methods for selecting each type of sample are different. In a simple random sample, a sample is as likely to be chosen as any other from the population. In a stratified random sample, the population is first divided into similar, nonoverlapping groups. Then a simple random sample is selected from each group. In a systematic random sample, the items are selected according to a specified time or item interval.

3. Sample answer: Ask the members of the school's football team to name their favorite sport. **5.** work from 4 students; work from all students in the 1st period math class; biased; voluntary response **7.** 12 pencils; all pencils in the school store; biased; convenience **9.** 20 shoppers; all shoppers; biased; convenience **11.** 860 people from a state; all people in the state; unbiased; stratified **13.** 3 students; all of the students in Ms. Finchie's class; unbiased; simple **15.** a group of U.S. district court judges; all U.S. district court judges; unbiased; stratified **17.** 4 U.S. Senators; all U.S. Senators; biased; convenience **19.** a group of high-definition television sets; all high-definition television sets manufactured on one line during one shift; unbiased; systematic **21.** a group of readers of a magazine; all readers of the magazine; biased; voluntary response

23. Additional information needed includes how the survey was conducted, how the survey respondents were selected, and the number of respondents. **25.** Sample answer: Get a copy of the list of registered voters in the city and call every 100th person. **27.** Sample answer: Randomly pick 5 rows from each field of tomatoes and then pick a tomato every 50 ft along each row. **29.** It is a good idea to divide the school population into groups and to take a simple random sample from each group. The problem that prevents this from being a legitimate stratified random sample is the way the three groups are formed. The three groups probably do not represent all students. The students who do not participate in any of these three activities will not be represented in the survey. Other students may be involved in two or three of these activities. These students will be more likely to be chosen for the survey. **31.** B **33.** $3\dfrac{1}{3}$ **35.** $\dfrac{3}{25}$ **37.** $\dfrac{a + 5}{a + 12}$ **39.** $22\sqrt{6}$ cm

41. $-1\dfrac{2}{3}, -1\dfrac{1}{2}$ **43.** $y^2 + 12y + 35$ **45.** $x^2 - 4x - 32$

47. 24.11 **49.** 3.8 **51.** 12.45

Pages 717–721 Lesson 13-2

1. A 2-by-4 matrix has 2 rows and 4 columns, and a 4-by-2 matrix has 4 rows and 2 columns. **3.** Estrella; Hiroshi did

not multiply each element of the matrix by −5.   **5.** 1 by 4; first row, first column   **7.** 3 by 2; first row, second column

9. $\begin{bmatrix} -5 & 24 \\ -22 & -13 \end{bmatrix}$ **11.** [20 −28]   **13.** No; the corresponding elements are not equal.   **15.** the total sales for the weekend   **17.** 2 by 2; first row, first column

19. 3 by 1; third row, first column   **21.** 3 by 3; second row, third column   **23.** 2 by 3; second row, third column

25. $\begin{bmatrix} 2 & 1 & 1 \\ 1 & 5 & 1 \end{bmatrix}$ **27.** $\begin{bmatrix} -13 & 12 & -7 \\ 5 & 6 & 11 \\ 23 & 18 & 14 \end{bmatrix}$

29. $\begin{bmatrix} 86 & 82 & -7 \\ 130 & 87 & 15 \end{bmatrix}$ **31.** $\begin{bmatrix} -5 & 25 & 45 \\ 0 & -20 & -10 \\ 15 & 35 & 30 \end{bmatrix}$

33. impossible   **35.** $\begin{bmatrix} -25 & 19 & -23 \\ 10 & 16 & 24 \\ 43 & 29 & 22 \end{bmatrix}$

37. $\begin{bmatrix} 224 & 155 & -84 \\ 309 & 182 & -15 \end{bmatrix}$ **39.** $V = [70 \ \ 2 \ \ 2 \ \ 0.3]$,

$S = [160\,0 \ \ 0 \ \ 0]$, $C = [185 \ \ 2 \ \ 11 \ \ 3.9]$

41. [555 16 19 5.8]   **43.** 1.20

45. $A = \begin{bmatrix} 533 & 331 & 4135 & 26 & 15 \\ 515 & 304 & 3840 & 24 & 14 \\ 499 & 325 & 4353 & 41 & 13 \\ 571 & 343 & 4436 & 36 & 15 \end{bmatrix}$,

$B = \begin{bmatrix} 571 & 357 & 4413 & 33 & 15 \\ 473 & 284 & 3430 & 28 & 11 \\ 347 & 235 & 3429 & 21 & 18 \\ 533 & 324 & 3730 & 19 & 18 \end{bmatrix}$

47. $T = \begin{bmatrix} 1104 & 688 & 8548 & 59 & 30 \\ 988 & 588 & 7270 & 52 & 25 \\ 846 & 560 & 7782 & 62 & 31 \\ 1104 & 667 & 8166 & 55 & 33 \end{bmatrix}$

49a. sometimes   **49b.** always   **49c.** sometimes
49d. sometimes   **49e.** sometimes   **49f.** sometimes   **51.** C

53. $\begin{bmatrix} 0.7 & -0.4 & 2.3 \\ -1.6 & -4 & -2.4 \end{bmatrix}$ **55.** $\begin{bmatrix} -5.3 & -12.4 & 21.1 \\ 2.4 & -7.7 & 4 \end{bmatrix}$

57. $\begin{bmatrix} 3.92 & -0.48 & 2.08 \\ -3.12 & 2.04 & -3.6 \end{bmatrix}$ **59.** biased; convenience

61. $\frac{3}{5}$ **63.** 324   **65.** 64   **67.** $(a - b)(a + 3b)$ **69.** Sample answer: Megan saved steadily from January to June. In July, she withdrew money to go on vacation. She started saving again in September. Then in November, she withdrew money for holiday presents.

Page 721   Practice Quiz 1
1. half of the households in a neighborhood; all households in the neighborhood; unbiased; systematic   **3.** $\begin{bmatrix} -3 & -4 \\ -5 & -9 \end{bmatrix}$

5. $\begin{bmatrix} 24 & -9 & -12 & 15 \\ 18 & -3 & 6 & 30 \end{bmatrix}$

Pages 725–728   Lesson 13-3
1. First identify the greatest and least values in the data set. Use this information to determine appropriate measurement classes. Using these measurement classes, create a frequency table. Then draw the histogram. Always remember to label the axes and give the histogram a title.   **3.** Sample answer:

1, 1, 2, 4, 5, 5, 8, 9, 10, 11, 12, 13, 22, 24, 41   **5.** There are no gaps. The data are somewhat symmetrical.   **7.** The Group A test scores are somewhat more symmetrical in appearance than the Group B test scores. There are 25 of 31 scores in Group A that are 40 or greater, while only 14 of 26 scores in Group B are 40 or greater. Also, Group B has 5 scores less than 30. Therefore, we can conclude that Group A performed better overall on the test.   **9.** B
11. 3400–3800 points; There are no gaps. The data appear to be skewed to the right.   **13.** Age at inauguration: 50–60 years old; age at death: 60–70 years old; both distributions show a symmetrical shape. The two distributions differ in their spread. The inauguration ages are not spread out as much as the death ages data.
15. Sample answer:

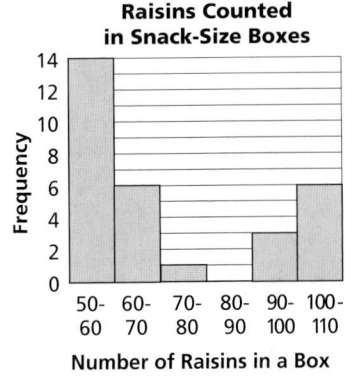

Raisins Counted in Snack-Size Boxes

17. Sample answer:

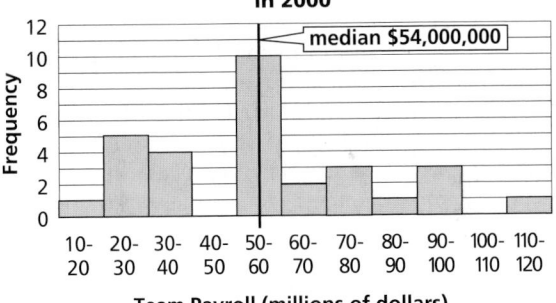

Payrolls for Major League Baseball Teams in 2000

19. Sample answer:

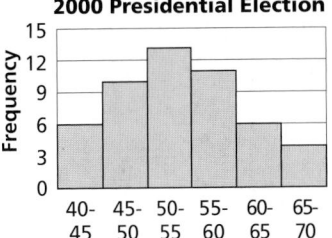

Percent of Eligible Voters Who Voted in the 2000 Presidential Election

23. Histograms can be used to show how many states have a median within various intervals. Answers should include the following.
• A histogram is more visual than a frequency table and can show trends easily.

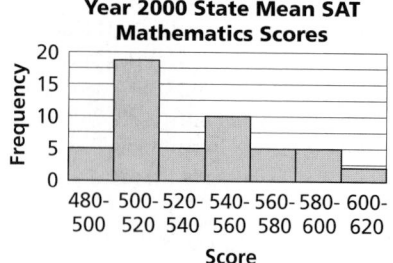

Year 2000 State Mean SAT Mathematics Scores

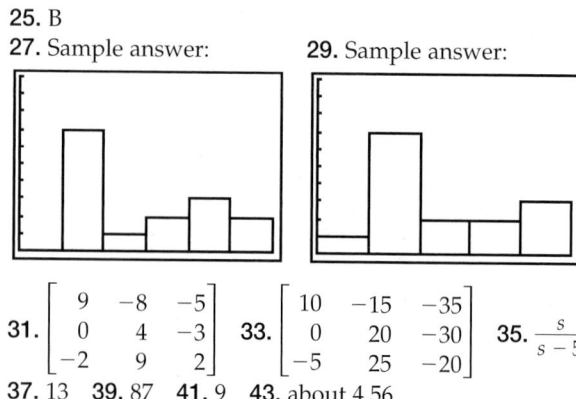

25. B

27. Sample answer:

29. Sample answer:

31. $\begin{bmatrix} 9 & -8 & -5 \\ 0 & 4 & -3 \\ -2 & 9 & 2 \end{bmatrix}$ **33.** $\begin{bmatrix} 10 & -15 & -35 \\ 0 & 20 & -30 \\ -5 & 25 & -20 \end{bmatrix}$ **35.** $\frac{s}{s-5}$

37. 13 **39.** 87 **41.** 9 **43.** about 4.56

Pages 733–736 Lesson 13-4

1. Sample answer: 1, 4, 5, 6, 7, 8, 15 and 1, 2, 4, 5, 9, 9, 10
3. Alonso; the range is the difference between the greatest and the least values of the set. **5.** 4.6; 9.05; 8.0; 10.05; 2.05; none **7.** 5 runs **9.** 6 runs **11.** 37; 73; 60.5; 79.5; 19; none **13.** 1.1; 30.6; 30.05; 30.9; 0.85; none **15.** 46; 77; 66.5; 86; 19.5; none **17.** 6.7; 7.6; 6.35; 8.65; 2.3; none **19.** 471,561 visitors **21.** 147,066.5 visitors; 470,030 visitors **23.** none **25.** 22.5 Calories **27.** 46 Calories **29.** 1000 ft; 970 ft **31.** 520 ft; 280 ft **33.** Although the range of the cable-stayed bridges is only somewhat greater than the range of the steel-arch bridges, the interquartile range of the cable-stayed bridges is much greater than the interquartile range of the steel-arch bridges. The outliers of the steel-arch bridges make the ranges of the two types of bridges similar, but in general, the data for steel-arch bridges are more clustered than the data for the cable-stayed bridges.
35. Measures of variation can be used to discuss how much the weather changes during the year. Answers should include the following.

- The range of temperatures is used to discuss the change in temperatures for a certain area during the year and the interquartile range is used to discuss the change in temperature during the moderate 50% of the year.
- The monthly temperatures of the local area listed with the range and interquartile range of the data.

37. A **39.** 1 by 3; first row, first column **41.** 2 by 4; second row, second column **43.** $\frac{1}{t-4}$; 3, 4

45.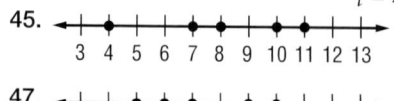

47.

Page 736 Practice Quiz 2
1. $10–$20 **3.** 340 **5.** 835

1. The extreme values are 10 and 50. The quartiles are 15, 30, and 40. There are no outliers. **3.** Sample answer: 2, 8, 10, 11, 11, 12, 13, 13, 14, 15, 16

5.
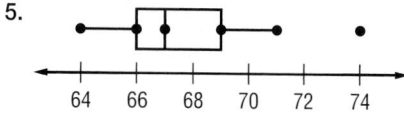

7.
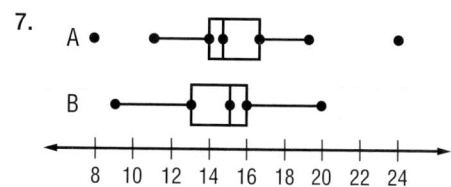

The A data are more diverse than the B data.
9. Most of the data are spread fairly evenly from about $450 million to $700 million. The one outlier ($1397 million) is far removed from the rest of the data. **11.** 30 **13.** $\frac{1}{2}$

15.
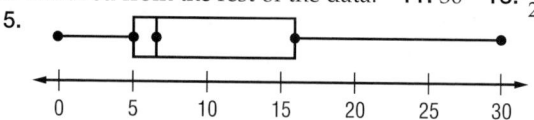

17.
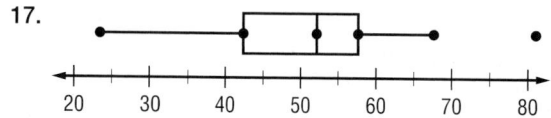

19.
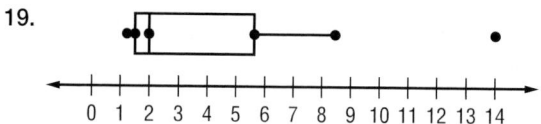

21. B **23.** B

25.
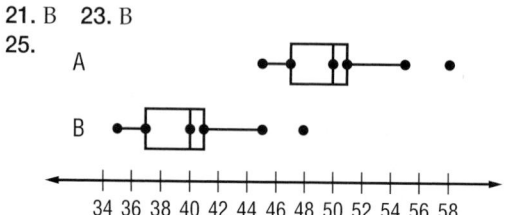

The distribution of both sets of data are similar. In general, the A data are greater than the B data.

27.
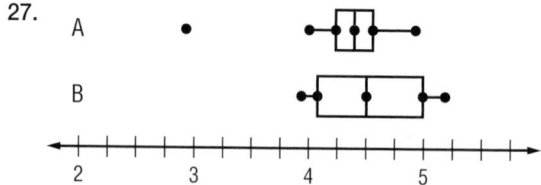

The A data have an outlier. Excluding the outlier, the B data are more diverse than the A data. **29.** The upper half of the data is very dispersed. The range of the lower half of the data is only 1. **31.** Top half; the top half of the data goes from $48,000 to $181,000, while the bottom half goes from $35,000 to $48,000. **33.** Bottom half; the top half of the data goes from 70 yr to 80 yr, while the bottom half goes from 39 yr to 70 yr. **35.** No; although the interval from 54 yr to 70 yr is wider than the interval from 70 yr to 74 yr, both intervals represent 25% of the data values.

37. Sample answer:

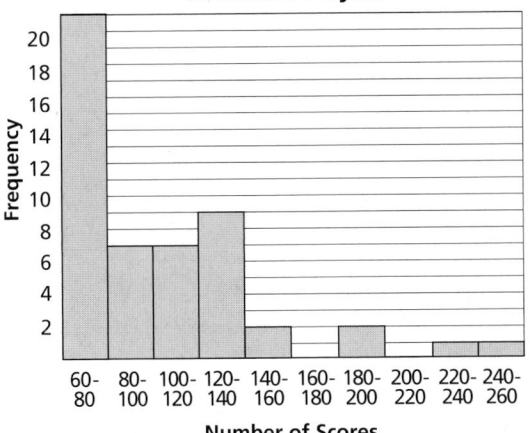

Life-Time Scores for Top 50 U.S. Soccer Players

39. Sample answer: 40, 45, 50, 55, 55, 60, 70, 80, 90, 90, 90

41. C **43.** 80; 54.5; 45; 67; 22; none **45.** $\dfrac{-y^2 + 6y + 12}{(y-3)(y+4)}$

47. $\dfrac{3w-4}{3(5w+2)}$ **49.** $3(r+3)$ **51.** $m\angle B = 51°$, $AB \approx 15.4$,
$BC \approx 9.7$ **53.** 1, 6 **55.** $-9.8, 1.8$ **57.** $8a^2 + 2a - 1$

Pages 745–748 Chapter 13 Study Guide and Review
1. simple random sample **3.** quartile **5.** biased sample
7. interquartile range **9.** outlier **11.** 8 test tubes with
results of chemical reactions; the results of all chemical
reactions performed; biased; convenience

13. $\begin{bmatrix} 2 & 4 & -4 \\ 4 & 3 & 3 \\ -2 & -3 & 3 \end{bmatrix}$ **15.** $\begin{bmatrix} -4 & -2 \\ 4 & 0 \end{bmatrix}$ **17.** $\begin{bmatrix} 5 & -1 \\ -1 & 4 \end{bmatrix}$

19. $\begin{bmatrix} 5 & 15 & -5 \\ 10 & 0 & 20 \\ -5 & -5 & 15 \end{bmatrix}$ **21.** $\begin{bmatrix} 9 & 1 \\ -5 & 4 \end{bmatrix}$

23. Sample answer:

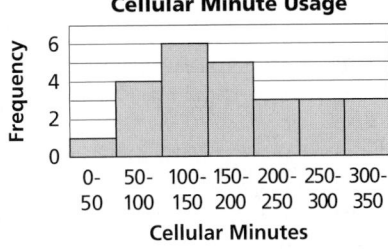

Cellular Minute Usage

25. 70; 65; 45; 85; 40; none **27.** 37; 73; 62; 77; 15; none
29.

31.

Chapter 14 Probability

Page 753 Chapter 14 Getting Started
1. $\dfrac{3}{7}$ **3.** $\dfrac{2}{7}$ **5.** $\dfrac{3}{5}$ **7.** $\dfrac{7}{95}$ **9.** $\dfrac{1}{52}$ **11.** 72.5% **13.** 40%
15. 87.5% **17.** 85.6%

Pages 756–758 Lesson 14-1
1. Sample answer: choosing 2 books from 7 books on a
shelf **3.** $5! = 5 \cdot 4 \cdot 3 \cdot 2 \cdot 1$ **5.** 64 **7.** 40,320
9. 27

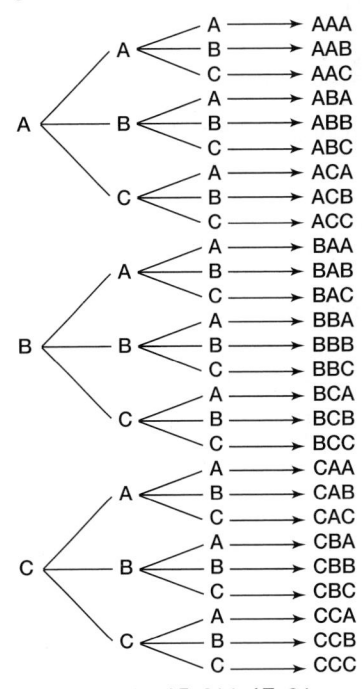

11. 24 **13.** 39,916,800 **15.** 216 **17.** 24
19.

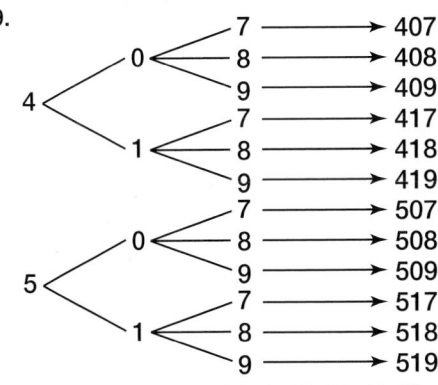

21. 6 **23.** 20 **25.** A **27.** A: 32, 88, 44, 85, 60; B: 38, 86, 48, 74, 64 **29.** B **31.** 79 **33.** 73.5; 39.5; 34.0

35. $\dfrac{5x^2 + 8x - 6}{(3x-1)(x-2)}$ **37.** $\dfrac{3z-1}{3z-6}$ **39.** $\pm\sqrt{22}$ **41.** 7

43. $-8.6, 0.6$ **45.** $-4.7, -0.3$ **47.** $\dfrac{1}{13}$ **49.** $\dfrac{1}{52}$ **51.** $\dfrac{2}{13}$

Pages 764–767 Lesson 14-2
1. Sample answer: Order is important in a permutation but not
in a combination. Permutation: the finishing order of a race
Combination: toppings on a pizza **3.** Alisa; both are correct in
that the situation is a combination, but Alisa's method correctly
computes the combination. Eric's calculations find the number
of permutations. **5.** Permutation; order is important. **7.** 21
9. 60 **11.** 720 **13.** B **15.** Permutation; order is important.
17. Permutation; order is important. **19.** Combination;
order is not important. **21.** Combination; order is not
important. **23.** 4 **25.** 35 **27.** 125,970 **29.** 524,160
31. 16,598,400 **33.** 6720 **35.** 362,880 **37.** 495 **39.** $\dfrac{1}{12}$

41. 7776 **43.** 61,425 **45.** 336 **47.** 36 **49.** $\dfrac{1}{12}$ or about 8%

51. $\dfrac{1}{30,240}$ **53.** 24 **55.** Sample answer: Combinations
can be used to show how many different ways a committee

can be formed by various members. Answers should include the following.
- Order of selection is not important.
- Order is important due to seniority, so you need to find the number of permutations.

57. C   **59.**

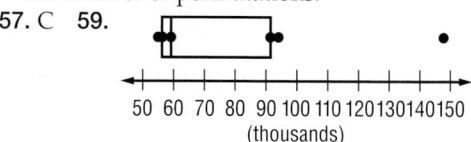

50 60 70 80 90 100 110 120 130 140 150
(thousands)

61. $56,700, $91,300   **63.** $\dfrac{1}{x+3}$ **65.** $\dfrac{n-5}{n+5}$ **67.** $4\sqrt{29}$, 21.54

69. -0.59, -3.41 **71.** 1.69, -1.19 **73.** $\dfrac{27}{32}$ **75.** $\dfrac{1}{3}$ **77.** $\dfrac{69}{100}$

Page 767   Practice Quiz 1
1. 24   **3.** 1287   **5.** $\dfrac{45}{1001}$

Pages 772–776   Lesson 14-3
1. A simple event is a single event, while a compound event involves two or more simple events.   **3.** Sample answer: With dependent events, a first object is selected and not replaced. With independent events, a first object is selected and replaced.   **5.** $\dfrac{10}{147}$ **7.** $\dfrac{80}{3087}$ **9.** $\dfrac{1}{2}$ **11.** 1   **13.** independent

15. $\dfrac{1}{3}$ **17.** $\dfrac{2}{51}$ **19.** $\dfrac{7}{408}$ **21.** $\dfrac{1}{5}$ **23.** $\dfrac{1}{10}$ **25.** $\dfrac{27}{280}$ **27.** $\dfrac{69}{280}$

29. 98% or 0.98   **31.** no; $P(A \text{ and } B) \neq P(A) \cdot P(B)$ **33.** $\dfrac{9}{16}$

35. $\dfrac{1}{4}$ **37.** 356   **39.** ≈ 0.09 **41.** 1   **43.** $\dfrac{3}{5}$ **45.** $\dfrac{7}{8}$ **47.** $\dfrac{3}{4}$

49. 101   **51.** $\dfrac{39}{40}$ **53.** C   **55.** 10   **57.** 604,800   **59.** $\begin{bmatrix} 5 & 2 \\ 4 & -1 \end{bmatrix}$

61. $3\sqrt{5}$ **63.** $2b^2\sqrt{10}$ **65.** $18\sqrt{14}$ **67.** 0.375   **69.** 0.492

71. 0.222   **73.** 0.033   **75.** 0.036

Pages 779–781   Lesson 14-4
1. The probability of each event is between 0 and 1 inclusive. The probabilities for each value of the random variable add up to 1.   **3.** Sample answer: the number of possible correct answers on a 5-question multiple-choice quiz, and the probability of each   **5.** $P(X = 4) = \dfrac{1}{12}$, $P(X = 5) = \dfrac{1}{9}$, $P(X = 6) = \dfrac{5}{36}$ **7.** $0.05 + 0.10 + 0.40 + 0.40 + 0.05 = 1$ **9.** 0.45   **11.** $P(X = 0) = \dfrac{1}{64}$, $P(X = 1) = \dfrac{3}{64}$, $P(X = 2) = \dfrac{9}{64}$, $P(X = 3) = \dfrac{27}{64}$ **13.** No; it is more probable to spin blue than red.   **15.** $0.10 + 0.15 + 0.40 + 0.25 + 0.10 = 1$ **17.** 0.75
19.

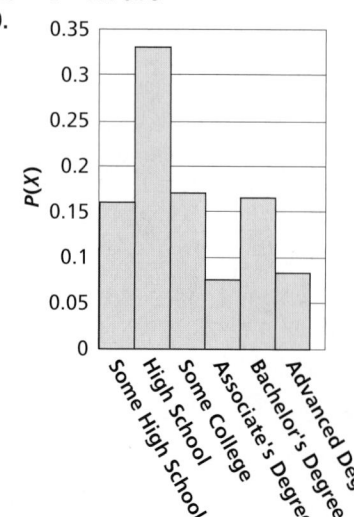

21. No; $0.221 + 0.136 + 0.126 + 0.065 + 0.043 = 0.591$. The sum of the probabilities does not equal 1.   **23a.** $P(X = 1) = \dfrac{1}{2}$, $P(X = 2) = \dfrac{1}{4}$, $P(X = 3) = \dfrac{1}{8}$, $P(X = 4) = \dfrac{1}{16}$ **23b.** $\dfrac{1}{16}$

25. A   **27.** $\dfrac{2}{13}$ **29.** $\dfrac{25}{52}$ **31.** 792   **33.** $\begin{bmatrix} -2 & 4 \\ 3 & 12 \end{bmatrix}$

35. $xy = 1.44$; 0.8   **37.** $13\sqrt{2}$ **39.** $-\sqrt{7}$ **41.** $1250.46
43. 20%   **45.** 26%   **47.** 21%

Page 781   Practice Quiz 2
1. $0.25 + 0.32 + 0.18 + 0.15 + 0.07 + 0.02 + 0.01 = 1$
3.

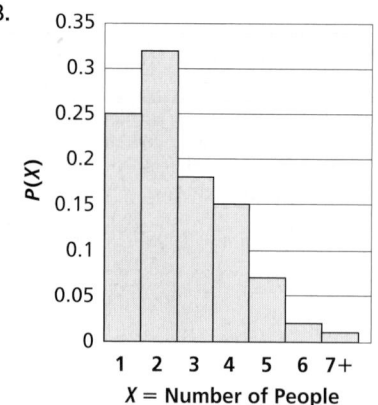

5. $\dfrac{1}{2}$

Pages 785–788   Lesson 14-5
1. An empirical study uses more data than a single study, and provides better calculations of probability.   **3.** Sample answer: a survey of 100 people voting in a two-person election where 50% of the people favor each candidate; 100 coin tosses   **5.** Sample answer: 5 marbles of two colors where three of the marbles are one color to represent making a free throw, and the other two are a different color to represent missing a free throw. Randomly pick one marble to simulate a free throw 25 times.   **9.** Yes; 70% of the marbles in the bag represent water and 30% represent land.   **11.** about 0.25 or 25%   **13.** Sample answer: a coin tossed 15 times   **15.** Sample answer: a coin and a number cube since there are 12 possible outcomes   **21.** 4 or 9
23. ≈ 0.74 or 74%   **25.** Sample answer: 3 coins
33. Sample answer: Probability can be used to determine the likelihood that a medication or treatment will be successful. Answers should include the following.
- Experimental probability is determining probability based on trials or studies.
- To have the experimental more closely resemble the theoretical probability the researchers should perform more trials.

35. B   **43.** 0.145   **45.** $\dfrac{125}{1331}$ **47.** $\dfrac{80}{583}$ **49.** 6, 8   **51.** $-\dfrac{9}{4}$
53. $-1, \dfrac{2}{5}$ **55.** no   **57.** yes   **59.** 11   **61.** $-\dfrac{2}{5}$ **63.** $\dfrac{10}{9}$

Pages 789–792   Chapter 14   Study Guide and Review
1. permutation   **3.** independent   **5.** are not   **7.** 1   **9.** 720
11. 20   **13.** 56   **15.** 140   **17.** 12   **19.** $\dfrac{1595}{32,412}$ **21.** $\dfrac{1}{2}$

23. $\dfrac{4}{13}$ **25.** 0.79 or 79%   **27.** 39.6%   **29.** 28.8%

Photo Credits

About the Cover: Named after the 15-century explorer, the 11-mile Vasco da Gama Bridge in Lisbon, Portugal, is one of the longest bridges in the world. The main span of the bridge is a cable-stayed bridge. In this type of bridge, cables are attached to towers, which bear the weight of the roadway. In a *radial* pattern, the cables extend from several points on the road to a single point at the top of the tower. In a *parallel* pattern, the cables are attached to the tower at different heights, forming parallel lines.

Index

Red type denotes items only in the Teacher's Wraparound Edition.

Formulas and Measures

Formulas

Slope	$m = \dfrac{y_2 - y_1}{x_2 - x_1}$		
Distance on a coordinate plane	$d = \sqrt{(x_2 - x_1)^2 + (y_2 - y_1)^2}$		
Midpoint on a coordinate plane	$M = \left(\dfrac{x_1 + x_2}{2}, \dfrac{y_1 + y_2}{2}\right)$		
Pythagorean Theorem	$a^2 + b^2 = c^2$		
Quadratic Formula	$x = \dfrac{-b \pm \sqrt{b^2 - 4ac}}{2a}$		
Perimeter of a rectangle	$P = 2\ell + 2w$ or $P = 2(\ell + w)$		
Circumference of a circle	$C = 2\pi r$ or $C = \pi d$		
Area	rectangle	$A = \ell w$	
	parallelogram	$A = bh$	
	triangle	$A = \dfrac{1}{2}bh$	
	trapezoid	$A = \dfrac{1}{2}h(b_1 + b_2)$	
	circle	$A = \pi r^2$	
Surface Area	cube	$S = 6s^2$	
	prism	$S = Ph + 2B$	
	cylinder	$S = 2\pi rh + 2\pi r^2$	
	regular pyramid	$S = \dfrac{1}{2}P\ell + B$	
	cone	$S = \pi r\ell + \pi r^2$	
Volume	cube	$V = s^3$	
	prism	$V = Bh$	
	cylinder	$V = \pi r^2 h$	
	regular pyramid	$V = \dfrac{1}{3}Bh$	
	cone	$V = \dfrac{1}{3}\pi r^2 h$	

Measures

Measure	Metric	Customary
Length	kilometer (km) = 1000 meters (m) 1 meter = 100 centimeters (cm) 1 centimeter = 10 millimeters (mm)	1 mile (mi) = 1760 yards (yd) 1 mile = 5280 feet (ft) 1 yard = 3 feet 1 foot = 12 inches (in.) 1 yard = 36 inches
Volume and Capacity	1 liter (L) = 1000 milliliters (mL) 1 kiloliter (kL) = 1000 liters	1 gallon (gal) = 4 quarts (qt) 1 gallon = 128 fluid ounces (fl oz) 1 quart = 2 pints (pt) 1 pint = 2 cups (c) 1 cup = 8 fluid ounces
Weight and Mass	1 kilogram (kg) = 1000 grams (g) 1 gram = 1000 milligrams (mg) 1 metric ton (t) = 1000 kilograms	1 ton (T) = 2000 pounds (lb) 1 pound = 16 ounces (oz)